THESAURUS OF THE ARTS

THESAURUS OF THE ARTS

DRAMA · MUSIC · RADIO · PAINTING

SCREEN · TELEVISION · LITERATURE

SCULPTURE · ARCHITECTURE · BALLET

BY ALBERT E. WIER

G. P. PUTNAM'S SONS, NEW YORK

MANUFACTURED IN THE UNITED STATES OF AMERICA

FOREWORD

THIS VOLUME was conceived with a definite objective—to furnish concise, non-technical information regarding the personalities, subjects, and terms connected with literature, music, painting, sculpture, ballet, drama, motion pictures, and television. If it succeeds in increasing the reader's knowledge and consequently his enjoyment of these arts, the author will feel amply recompensed for the years of research required in its preparation.

A. E. W.

NOTE. Cross references in the text of this volume are indicated by small capitals. For example: in the first reference, $\mathbf{A}$, on the opposite page, small capitals on OBOE, ORGAN, and PIANO indicate cross references on these subjects.

A

A in music the name of the sixth tone of the natural scale of C-major. Sounded by the OBOE, ORGAN, PIANO or any fixed-tone instrument, it is used to give the PITCH for the other instruments in an orchestra. The number of vibrations of the tone, usually referred to as *Standard A,* and adopted in 1859 in Europe, is 435.4 per second at a temperature of 59° Fahrenheit; in the United States it is generally 440 per second.

Aakjaer, Jeppe (1866-1930), Danish novelist and poet whose works reflect a life spent chiefly on a farm in Jutland; one of his novels, *Children of Wrath,* brought him considerable fame, but his poetical works are regarded as more enduring.

Aarestrup, Emil (1800-1856), Danish poet who was unappreciated before his death, but now classed with Christian WINTHER, one of Denmark's finest lyric poets; his collected poems were published in 1877.

Abacus, in architecture the polygonal block forming the top of the CAPITAL of a COLUMN or a PILLAR.

Abadie, Paul (1812-1884), French architect who restored many of the famous medieval buildings in France; he succeeded Eugène VIOLLET-LE-DUC in the work of restoring the Cathedral of NOTRE DAME in Paris.

Aba-Novak, Vilmos (1894-), Hungarian painter who studied at the School for Drawing Instructors in Budapest, and became a teacher at the Polytechnic School there after serving in World War I. He exhibited several pictures in 1922, and won a scholarship for study in Rome in 1929, later showing in many European cities and at the Carnegie Internationals of 1931 and 1935. Deeply influenced by both Italian and French art, as well as by the work of his countryman, Karoly FERENCZY, he became especially skilful in the use of TEMPERA, painting many colorful scenes of Magyar peasant life. A series of frescoes in a Hungarian church depicts episodes in the life of Christ and His apostles.

Abarbanell, Lina (1880-), German singer and actress who appeared first at the Irving Place Theatre, New York, in 1905 under the management of Heinrich CONRIED, later making her debut as Gretel in HANSEL AND GRETEL at the Metropolitan Opera House. After mastering English, she created the part of Ilsa in The STUDENT PRINCE, and also appeared in *Madame Sherry,* and in The MERRY WIDOW. She has been featured since in many other musical comedies and plays.

Abbate or **Dell'Abbato, Niccolo** (1512-1571), celebrated Italian fresco painter of the Bolognese school who accompanied PRIMATICCIO to France in 1552 to assist in the decoration of the royal palace at FONTAINEBLEAU where he was known as "Messer Niccolino," and remained until his death. One of his pictures in the Dresden Gallery, *The martyrdom of St. Peter and St. Paul,* reveals an unusual degree of imagination in drawing and coloring.

Abbey, Edwin Austin (1852-1911), American painter and illustrator who studied at the Pennsylvania School of Fine Arts, and later joined the art department of Harper Brothers, New York, in company with Howard PYLE, Joseph PENNELL and several other noted illustrators. After being sent to England in 1877 to make illustrations in Shakespeare's domain for the poems of Robert HERRICK, he returned to the United States to prepare the murals for the Boston Public Library depicting the *Quest for the Holy Grail,* spending twelve years at the task. In 1902 he painted the official pictures of the coronation of King Edward VII of England, comprising an elaborately grouped series of portraits. His last important work was some murals for the State Capitol of Harrisburg, Pennsylvania, left unfinished at his death. The influence of MILLAIS and ROSSETTI is to be seen in Abbey's *King Lear* at the Metropolitan Museum of Art, New York; many critics regard a series of pen drawings illustrating the works of Shakespeare as his finest achievement.

Abbey, Henry Eugene (1846-1896), American opera impresario, previously in the jewelry and theatrical business, who leased the newly constructed METROPOLITAN OPERA HOUSE, New York, for the initial season, 1883-84, and opened with a performance of Gounod's *Faust.* His stars included NILSSON, SCALCHI, CAMPANINI, PUENTE, and SEMBRICH; he lost more than $500,000, due partly to an unsuccessful road tour. In 1891-92 and from 1893 to 1897, Abbey, in partnership with John B. Schoeffel and Maurice GRAU, resumed direction of the Metropolitan, but in spite of the fact that his singers included among others Jean and Édouard DE RESZKE, NORDICA, Lilli LEHMANN, ALBANI, MELBA, MAUREL, and PLANCON, the enormous expenses exceeded the receipts.

Abbey, in architecture a group of buildings surrounding a church, occupied by a monastic or conventual organization under the direction of either an abbot or an abbess. In the Middle Ages, most abbeys were under the jurisdiction of Benedictine, Cistercian or Carthusian monks, and a systematic plan was carried out in the arrangement of the church, the cells for the monks and the REFECTORY, all of which were usually sheltered within a wall stout enough to resist marauders. The ROMANESQUE style of architecture was used in the 11th century, followed by GOTHIC in the 13th and RENAISSANCE in the 15th century. Covered walks connecting the buildings were known as CLOISTERS.

Abbey Theatre, a theatre opened in Dublin in 1904 by Miss A. E. F. HORNIMAN of the Irish National Theatre Society, the members of which included W. B. YEATS, Sean O'CASEY, Lady GREGORY and J. M. SYNGE whose plays, *Riders to the Sea* and *The Playboy of the Western World* were first performed there. Many fine actors, among them Dudley DIGGES, Sara ALLGOOD, and Arthur Sinclair, were members of the company either in Dublin or on its several American tours in 1911, 1932, 1934 and 1937. Lady Gregory has given much interesting information regarding the theatre in her book, *Our Irish Theatre.*

Abbott, Eleanor Hallowell (1872-), American author educated at Radcliffe College, Cambridge, Mass.: among her best works are *Molly Make-Believe* (1910); *Sick-a-Bed Lady and Other Stories; White Linen Nurse; Little Eve Edgerton; The Indiscreet Letter; Old Dad; Love and the Ladies; Being Little in Cambridge When Everybody Else Was Big,* the last-named an autobiography.

Abbott, Emma (1850-1891), American operatic soprano who sang in New York churches for several years, studied in Europe with Sangiovanni, Delle Sedie, Wartel and Mathilde MARCHESI, making her debut at Covent Garden, London, in 1876 in *The Daughter of the Regiment.* She returned to the United States in 1877, making her first appearance in the same opera, and later forming her own company. Her repertory included standard Italian works and English operettas: for some years she rivaled Clara Louise KELLOGG in popular favor.

Abbott, George (1889-), American playwright, actor, stage, and motion picture director; graduate of the University of Rochester and student of English under Professor George Pierce BAKER at Harvard University where his first play, *Head of the Family,* was produced by the Harvard Dramatic Club. After acting in David Belasco's "Daddies" and several other plays, he produced *Chicago, Boy Meets Girl,* and *Room Service.* His successful plays include *The Fall Guy,* written with James Gleason (1925); *Broadway,* with Philip Dunning; *Three Men on a Horse,* with John C. Holm. He has also directed or collaborated on the stories or dialogue of *All Quiet on the Western Front, Manslaughter* and other motion pictures.

Abbott, Jacob (1803-1879), American author of juvenile books including *The Rollo Books* (28 vols.); *The Franconia Stories* (10 vols.); *The Marco Paul Series* (6 vols.): his works comprise more than 200 titles.

Abbott, Keene (1876-), American novelist and writer of short stories in which the scenes are laid in the great plains of the Southwest: he displays a rare degree of sympathetic understanding in his novels, *A Melody in Silver* (1911) and *Wine o' the Winds.* Mabel Avery Abbott, his wife, has written excellent short stories, and a novel, *Captain Martha Mary.*

Abbott, William (1798-1843), English actor who appeared with William MACREADY at the COVENT GARDEN THEATRE in 1816. He organized a company in 1827 headed by Henrietta SMITHSON and Macready, that presented Shakespeare in Paris, resulting in the mad infatuation for Miss Smithson on the part of the French composer, Hector BERLIOZ, which ended in an unhappy marriage.

Abdullah, Achmed (1881-), English novelist and playwright educated at ETON and the University of Paris; he served for many years in the British army, seeing active service in India, Africa and South Africa. His works include many novels: also the plays, *Toto,* with Leo Ditrichstein; *The Grand Duke,* with Lionel Atwill, and the films, *The Thief of Bagdad* and *The Lives of a Bengal Lancer.*

à Beckett, Gilbert Abbott (1811-1856), English humorist, one of the founders of PUNCH, and author of the *Comic Blackstone,* a *Comic History of England,* and of more than fifty popular plays. His eldest son, **Gilbert Arthur à Beckett** (1837-1891), was also a playwright, and a librettist of light operas.

Abel, Walter (1898-), American stage and screen actor, graduate of the American Academy of Dramatic Arts. He first appeared in *Forbidden* at the Manhattan Opera House, New York, in 1919; since then he has portrayed important roles in *Back to Methuselah, Desire Under the Elms, The Sea-Gull, Mourning Becomes Electra,* and numerous other plays. His motion-picture appearances include *The Three Musketeers; Fury; The Lady Consents; The Witness Chair; Men With Wings; Holiday Inn.*

Abelard, Pierre (1079-1142), French philosopher and theologian many of whose disciples became famous; his tragic love for HÉLOISE, related in his *Story of My Misfortunes* (Historia Calamitatum) and in their correspondence, has become a favorite theme for poets.

Abenezra or **Abraham ben Meir Ibn Ezra** (1092?-1167), Jewish poet and man of letters; born in Spain, and an indefatigable traveler in Africa, Italy, France and England. His poems were of exceptional beauty, and he was also a learned commentator on the Hebrew Bible.

Abercrombie, Lascelles (1881-1938), English literary critic and poet: author of many long poems in blank verse distinguished by extraordinary imagination, particularly those based on scriptural subjects. His works include *Thomas Hardy, a critical study;* a drama, *Deborah; Interludes and Poems* and *Emblems of Love.*

Abington, Frances Barton (1737-1815), English actress who rose to great heights in her profession: she appeared first at the Haymarket Theatre, London, in Mrs. CENTLIVRE's comedy, *The Busybody,* in 1755. After achieving success in a Dublin theatre, she became leading lady for David GARRICK at the DRURY LANE THEATRE, London, for eighteen years, creating many important roles such as Lady Teazle in *The School for Scandal,* and also gaining a high reputation as Portia,

Desdemona, Ophelia and other Shakespearean heroines. Her portrait was painted by Sir Joshua REYNOLDS.

Ablesimoff, Alexander Anisimovitch (1742-1783), Russian playwright who was the first to introduce peasant folksongs and folklore into his dramas. He wrote what may be considered the first Russian SINGSPIEL, *Melnik,* in 1779; it was given more than fifty performances during a single season at Moscow.

Aborn Opera Company, an American opera company organized in 1902 by Milton Aborn (1864-1933) and his brother, Sargent Aborn (1866-), to present opera in English at low prices. The enterprise was a success for more than twenty years; several singers who later became important members of the Metropolitan Opera Company received their first practical stage experience in its ranks. The Aborn brothers also managed the CENTURY OPERA COMPANY at the Century Theatre, New York, for the seasons 1913-14 and 1914-15.

About, Edmond François Valentin (1828-1885), French novelist and journalist, a contemporary of Hippolyte Adolphe TAINE. After teaching for a short time in the French School at Athens, he devoted himself to writing novels including *Vittoria Savelli; Tolla; Madelon; L'Infâme;* and a trilogy *Veille Roche.* His best works are those of a farcical character such as *Le Roi des montagnes* and *L'Homme à l'oreille cassée* in which his natural wit and vivacity were given full play.

Abracadabra, a magical formula or cabalistic word used by the philosophers of the early Christian era to invoke the aid of friendly spirits to avert pestilence and other ills; the word was usually written in triangular form, and is now used for any jargon of nonsensical words.

Abramovich, Solomon Jacob (1836-1917), Russian-Jewish literary critic who wrote in both Yiddish and Hebrew: his books have made such a strong appeal to the working class that he is generally regarded as the father of modern Yiddish literature. He also excelled in the field of literary criticism.

Abravanel, Maurice de (1903-), Greek orchestral conductor who studied at Lausanne University, and with Kurt WEILL; he conducted in many German cities beside directing ballet in Paris and London. In 1936-38 he conducted at the Metropolitan Opera House, New York, and in 1940-41 at the Chicago Opera House.

Absolute Music, pure or abstract music composed without reference to subject matter of any kind such as a poem or text, and entirely dependent for enjoyment or understanding on its own form and themes. Such music is in direct contrast to PROGRAM MUSIC which seeks its inspiration in poetry, drama or nature, and endeavors to depict or imitate its chosen subject.

Absolute Pitch, the exact position of a musical tone in its particular scale, correctly determined by the number of vibrations per second. A sense of absolute pitch is said to be possessed by those who can identify by name any given tone when sounded alone, or can hum or sing any tone on request. Only trained musicians are presumed to possess the ability to distinguish tones; on the other hand untrained musicians, especially children, are often able to do so.

Abt, Franz (1819-1885), German composer of more than two thousand songs in both solo and part form; many of them, such as *When the Swallows Homeward Fly* and *Over the Stars There is Rest,* have become an integral part of the folk music of Germany although their musical content is of too light a character to class them with the art songs of Franz SCHUBERT and other composers.

Abulfaraj or **Abu-l-Faraj** (897-967), Arabian scholar and poet, famous for his *Book of Songs* containing valuable information regarding the songs of Arabia, with the life stories of the composers and the bards who sang them.

Abutment, in architecture a structure of stone or brick built inside an ARCH, STRUT or VAULT to resist lateral pressure. If built outside a wall, it is called a BUTTRESS.

Academic Festival, an overture written by Johannes BRAHMS in appreciation of the degree of Doctor of Music conferred on him by Breslau University. The opening theme is reminiscent of the RAKOCZY MARCH; the second is a folk song *We have built a stately house,* a favorite of the German Students Association, and the finale utilizes a college song with Latin words, *Gaudeamus Igitur,* well-known to American as well as German students. The first performance was given at Breslau on January 4, 1881; there is a Columbia recording by the New York Philharmonic Orchestra under John Barbirolli, and a Victor recording by the Vienna Philharmonic Orchestra with Bruno Walter.

Académie de Musique (Paris), an institution founded in Paris on June 28, 1669, for presenting operas and dramas with music in French; it has undergone many changes, but is still the leading opera house in France, known today to the music world simply as *L'Opéra.* The Académie was formally opened on March 19, 1671, with a pastoral opera, *Pomone* by Robert CAMBERT, which ran for nearly eight months. Jean Baptiste LULLY became the director in 1672, and produced more than twenty of his own operas until his death in 1687; Jean Phillipe RAMEAU assumed the directorship from 1737 to 1760, writing twenty-four operas. In 1774 GLUCK's *Iphigenia in Aulis* was produced, and from 1804 on a continuous flow of fine dramatic works was forthcoming from SPONTINI, KREUTZER, CHERUBINI, LESUEUR, HALÉVY and AUBER, followed by French adaptations of operas by WEBER, ROSSINI and MEYERBEER. The present opera house, a most imposing and luxurious building, was opened on January 5, 1875, with the première of HALÉVY's *La Juive:* since that time the operas of BERLIOZ, MASSENET, SAINT-SAËNS and many other famous French composers have been presented, making a grand total of more than one thousand operas and ballets from 1671 to 1942.

Académie française, L', see French Academy, The.

Academy, in literature a word derived, according to some authorities, from *Academus,* a Greek legendary hero to whom a grove near Athens was consecrated. The society formed by PLATO and his students about 387 B.C. was given the name "Academy": this was called the *Old Academy* after about 175 B.C. when Arcesilaus formed the *Middle Academy,* and was succeeded by the *New Academy* founded by Carneades. Many institutions throughout the world were later given this name, one of the most important being the ACADEMIE FRANCAISE (Paris). In the 18th and 19th centuries it was used as the designation of intermediate schools.

Academy of Fine Arts (Florence, Italy), founded in the 14th century, this institution fell upon evil times during the occupany of Italy by the French, but was partially restored in 1783. It contains halls of marble and plaster figures for the use of sculptors; also several of Michelangelo's sculptures, including the celebrated statue of DAVID. An assembly of 13th and 17th century Tuscan paintings for study purposes is on display in the Galleria dell' Accademia, and the Conservatory of Music connected with the Academy has an interesting collection of antique musical instruments.

Academy of Music (New York), an opera house opened on Oct. 2, 1854, on East 14th Street at Irving Place, succeeding the ASTOR PLACE OPERA HOUSE as the home of opera. Destroyed by fire in 1866, it was rebuilt in 1867, and continued to be used until about 1900, although the Metropolitan Opera House superseded it in 1883 as a Mecca for opera-goers. The concerts of the NEW YORK PHILHARMONIC-SYMPHONY SOCIETY were given there from 1879 to 1886; it also housed all of Colonel MAPLESON's New York opera seasons. Adelina PATTI made her operatic debut on its stage, and the American premières of Verdi's OTELLO, AIDA, *Il* TROVATORE, *La* TRAVIATA, and RIGOLETTO took place there.

A Cappella or **alla Cappella** (It.), in music singing by a church CHOIR or vocal CHORUS without ORGAN or other instrumental accompaniment.

Accelerando (It.), in music, "accelerating," or gradually growing livelier or faster.

Accent, in music the correct, natural emphasis or stress recurring at regular periods on certain notes; the simplest example is the customary emphasis on the first note of each measure.

Accidental, in music a sign, such as a SHARP, double sharp, FLAT or double flat, indicating that a NOTE is to be raised a half or a whole TONE. The natural sign is employed to restore a note to its original status.

Accius, Lucius, a Roman tragic poet and dramatist who flourished about 170 B.C.; he selected his themes from Greek history and mythology except in his tragedy, *Brutus,* in which he utilized scenes from Roman history. Only fragments of his works have been discovered.

Accolti, Bernardo (1465-1536), Italian poet, son of the distinguished historian, Benedetto Accolti (c.1415-1466). He achieved a great reputation as an impromptu versifier, gaining the nickname, *"l'Unico Aretino,"* his ability in this respect being attested by Cardinal Bembo. His works, published at Florence in 1513 with the titles *Comedia, Virginia, Capitoli e Strambotti,* etc., have been reprinted several times.

Accompaniment, in music the part in a composition which underlies and supports the solo voice or instrument. If essential to the effectiveness of the solo part, it is called an OBBLIGATO; if it can be dispensed with, it is designated as AD LIBITUM.

Accordion, a portable free-reed instrument invented by Damian of Vienna in 1829; it consists of two keyboards joined together by a bellows. The ordinary model has a DIATONIC or incomplete CHROMATIC scale in the right hand, and from two to ten keys for harmonic bass chords in the left hand. The modernized form, called the *Piano Accordion,* and generally used in dance orchestras, has a series of chromatic keys like those of the piano for the right hand, and a wide range of bass chords for the left hand. These instruments cost from $75.00 to $1,000, and are of far more musical significance than the original Viennese instrument which could be played in only one key.

Achard, Louis Amédée Eugéne (1814-1875), French novelist and political writer; his best work is *Belle Rose,* and most of his novels depict conflict in family life and society.

Achates, the companion of AENEAS in Virgil's *Aeneid,* so loyal to Aeneas that the expression "fidus Achates" has become proverbial for a devoted faithful friend.

Achenbach, Andreas (1815-1910), German landscape painter who studied under Friedrich Wilhelm SCHADOW-GODENHAUS in Dusseldorf, and became the founder of the German realistic school. He was a master of technique, but his pictures lack personality in some respects. His finest works are displayed at the Berlin National Gallery, the Pinakothek in Munich, and in Dresden, Cologne, and Hamburg galleries. His brother, **Oswald Achenbach** (1827-1905) was trained by Andreas; his landscapes, many of which are to be found in German galleries, abound in vivid, colorful effects.

Acheron, in Greek mythology a son of the goddess CERES. For assuaging the thirst of the Titans during their struggle with Zeus, he was transformed into a river in Hades over which CHARON ferried the souls of the dead. Later the name "Acheron" was used to designate the entire underworld.

Achilles, the hero of Homer's ILIAD; his mother, Thetis, is said to have dipped his naked body, when first born, in the river STYX, thereby rendering him invulnerable except in that part of the heel by which she held him. After Achilles had fought valiantly for nine years in the TROJAN WAR, he was slain by PARIS, whose arrow was guided to the vulnerable part of his heel by the god APOLLO.

4

Achron, Joseph (1886-), Russian-American violinist and composer who studied the violin with Leopold AUER, and harmony with Anatol LIADOFF. After giving more than a thousand recitals in all parts of the world he came to the United States; his compositions include works for orchestra; violin sonatas; violin concertos, and incidental music for both stage and screen.

Achsharumov, Nicholas Dmitrivitch (1819-?), Russian novelist and literary critic who attracted attention by his essays on TOLSTOY, TURGENEV and other Russian writers; his successful novels include *The Double* (1850), *The Gambler, An Unusual Case* and *The Model*.

Achurch, Janet (1864-1916), English actress and producer, real name Janet Achurch Sharp. She made her stage debut in 1883, and after appearing for a few years with Sir Herbert Beerbohm Tree's company, she produced IBSEN'S *A Doll's House* in English at the Novelty Theatre, London, playing the role of Nora herself. She appeared later in Shakespeare and in plays by George Bernard SHAW.

Ackermann, Louise Victorine Choquet (1813-1890), French poet: author of *Poésies, premières poésies, poésies philosophiques* (1874), verses of sombre, powerful character expressing passionate, surging revolt against the sufferings of humanity. Italian critics praised the verses highly, but voicing disapproval of what they elected to term "their desperate impiety."

Acoustics, in music the science of musical tones as distinguished from mere noises. A TONE of sustained pitch is generated by regular, constant vibrations of air actuated by similar vibrations in the instrument producing the tones. According to HELMHOLTZ, "the sensation caused by a musical tone is produced by *periodic movements,* and the sensation caused by a noise is generated by *imperiodic movements.*" Sound is deflected from smooth surfaces; it becomes clearer by adding furniture and draperies to absorb stray tones.

Acrolith, in Greek sculpture a statue in which the TORSO was made of wood, and the head, hands, and feet of marble. The wooden trunk was concealed by the use of gilt or draperies, and only the marble parts were exposed. A Greek writer of the 2nd century, PAUSANIAS, mentions acroliths frequently in his works, the most famous specimen being the ATHENA AREIA at Platae, an ancient city near Athens.

Acropolis (Athens), the fortified hill, about 260 feet in height, with an ovular flat top 500 feet wide and more than 1000 feet long, where PERICLES and other Athenian rulers placed some of the finest Greek temples and sculptures. It was surrounded by a wall of masonry, parts of which are still in existence and was reached by a winding path ending at the PROPYLAEUM, the entrance to the group of buildings. A passage known as the SACRED WAY revealed a colossal statue in bronze of Pallas Athena, the goddess of wisdom; other buildings included the PARTHENON, the ERECHTHEUM, the temple of NIKE Apteros and the theatre of DIONYSUS.

Acropolis Museum (Athens), a museum built in 1878 to house the sculptured remains left on the ACROPOLIS up to that time, and also any further accumulations from more recent excavations. The various rooms are named after their particular contents: *I Room of the Bull; II Room of the Triple-bodied Monster; III Room of the Images; IV Room of the Marbles; V Room of the Calf-Bearer; VI Archaic Room; VII Room of the Ephebos; VIII Parthenon Room; IX Nike Room.*

Act, (*a*) in drama the natural division of a play, sometimes separated into two or more scenes. In Greek plays the action was continuous from beginning to end; if the principal actor or actors left the stage, the chorus remained to enact an integral part of the drama. (*b*) In music the individual sections of an opera or operetta, generally separated by orchestral entr'actes. The length of an opera determines the number of acts; the most striking example of a one-act work of this character is Mascagni's CAVALLERIA RUSTICANA, where a lapse of time in the action is indicated by an orchestral interlude instead of lowering the curtain.

Actaeon, in Greek mythology a famous Theban hunter who accidentally saw the goddess DIANA nude while bathing; he was changed into a stag as punishment, and killed by his own dogs. Greek dramatists, poets and sculptors made much use of the legend; a marble group, discovered in Greece and now in the BRITISH MUSEUM, portrays the story.

Acting, Origin of, actors first achieved prominence when the religious dances of the Greeks gradually became dramatic in character, and individuals were selected for parts requiring special ability. In Greece actors were highly regarded, but in Rome they were held in disrepute; in England during the Elizabethan period actors were classed with beggars and vagabonds, and in France, even in MOLIÈRE's time, they ranked with peddlers and rat-catchers. In the opinion of Brooks ATKINSON, writing in the New York Times on Sept. 10, 1939, "the prestige of Henry IRVING changed the conception of the actor . . . actors now are culturally acceptable although, like artists in general, they are still somewhat suspect by middle-class moralists."

Action, (*a*) in drama the term used to differentiate the physical movements or gestures, required by the plot of a play, from the mental reactions called for by its psychological aspects. (*b*) In music the term employed for the mechanism in any instrument such as the piano, organ, harp etc., which enables the player to achieve his technical and tonal effects.

Actor Families, the list of families in which members of more than one generation have adopted the stage as a profession is extremely lengthy; a list follows which covers most of the prominent names: the Barretts, Barrymores, Trees, Boucicaults, Cohans, Coopers, Davenports, Drews, Du Mauriers, Forbes-Robertsons, Grossmiths, Irvings, Jeffersons, Kembles, Lupinos, Macreadys, Maudes, Rathbones, Sotherns, Terrys, Wallacks, and Wyndhams. This volume contains information regarding the most distinguished members of all these families.

Actors Equity Association, a theatrical union founded in 1912, and affiliated with the American Federation of Labor. Charles D. Coburn, Frank Gillmore, Milton Sills and Grant Stewart were members of the first committee. With rare exceptions, no actor is permitted to appear professionally without becoming a member of the association, and all arrangements with managers and producers are effected through its offices. A similar association operates in the interest of actors in Great Britain.

Actors, Types of, in stage parlance there are many kinds and types of actors; among them is the *character actor* who portrays elderly people, lawyers, doctors or dialect roles; the *heavy* who specializes in villainy of various kinds; the *juvenile* who plays adolescent parts; the *leading man* who appears opposite the *star;* the *ingenue* who assumes parts with secondary love or comedy interest. In addition there is the *walkon* who rarely speaks, and the *extras* or *supers* employed in mob or race-track scenes; these are readily recruited from the ranks of amateurs aspiring to professional standing.

Actress, a female actor. Actresses were unknown in ancient drama; according to historians they appeared first during the 16th century in Italian, French, and German theatres, and almost a century elapsed before they appeared in England. Among the first to be favorably received were Isabella ANDREINI; Madeleine and Armande BEJART who appeared in the plays of MOLIERE; Nell GWYN; Carolina NEUBER who became manager as well as actress, and many others whose names will be found in this volume.

Acuña, Manuel (1849-1873), Mexican poet and dramatist; one of a group of younger writers who registered their dissatisfaction with political and religious conditions in Mexico by writing satirical plays and verses. Acuña wrote a highly successful play, *The Past* (*El Pasado*), but ended his own life through brooding over conditions he regarded as unbearable in Mexico.

Acuña de Figueroa, Francisco de (1790-1862), Uruguayan poet who wrote odes, satires, and heroic poems in classic forms, assembled in the collection, *Poetic Mosaic.* While his style is flawless, Acuña has been criticized as wanting in poetic ardor; this cannot be said of his verses for the Uruguayan national anthem.

Adagio, (a) in music a term indicating a very slow tempo; the word is also used as the title of the slow movement in a SONATA or SYMPHONY. (b) In BALLET, *Adagio* signifies the climax where the BALLERINA, either alone or assisted by her partner, displays virtuosity in the same manner as an opera singer demonstrates vocal powers in an aria.

Adam, Adolphe Charles (1803-1856), French operatic composer who studied with BOIELDIEU at the Paris Conservatory, and was extremely successful in the field of OPÉRA-COMIQUE; one of his 39 operas, *Le Postillon de Longjumeau,* is still popular in France, and has been filmed. Adam also wrote fourteen ballets, one of which, GISELLE, is in the repertory of contemporary ballet companies.

Adam, Albrecht (1786-1862), German historical painter and engraver, famous for his military pictures such as *Napoleon and His Staff.* Four of his sons, *Benno Adam* (1812-1892), *Franz Adam* (1815-1886), *Eugen Adam* (1817-1880), *Julius Adam* (1826-1874), and a grandson, *Julius Adam* (1852-1913), were also distinguished painters of military, landscape and animal pictures.

Adam, François Gaspard Balthasar (1710-1761), French sculptor, brother of Lambert Sigisbert ADAM and of Nicolas Sebastien ADAM. Frederick the Great chose him as director of the School of Sculpture in Berlin where he spent the greater part of his life supervising the students, and executing works for the palaces and parks at Sans Souci and Potsdam.

Adam, Lambert Sigisbert (1700-1759), French sculptor, known as Adam L'aîné, who exhibited first in 1737 at the Salon after being elected to the Academy through the influence of Cardinal Polignac. His important works include the restoration of twelve statues found in the Villa of Marina; a colossal group in stone, *The Seine and the Marne,* for the park at St. Cloud; two groups, *Hunting* and *Fishing,* in Berlin for Frederick the Great, and a statue of St. Jerome.

Adam, Nicolas Sebastien (1705-1778), French sculptor, brother of Lambert Sigisbert ADAM with whom he worked for a time. His masterpieces include a marble statue, *Prometheus Chained,* and mausoleums for Cardinal de Fleury and Queen Catherine Opalinska of Poland.

Adam, Robert (1728-1792), Scottish architect who was assisted in his most important works by his brother James (1730-94), also an architect. After spending four years in Italy studying the remains of Roman architecture, he held the post of architect to the King of England from 1762 to 1768, resigning to erect the extraordinary block of buildings, known as the *Adelphi,* with the assistance of James and two other brothers, John and William. The houses faced the Thames River, and were erected on an imposing terrace beneath which were massive arches and vaults suggestive of the ruins of Diocletian's palace at Spalato, an ancient city on the Adriatic Sea, of which Adam had made a study while in Italy. These stately mansions were greatly in demand as homes for artists and literary men. For more than thirty years, Adam designed and superintended the erection of public and private buildings: among them the University of Edinburgh and many city and country homes for the nobility. He also left an enduring mark on English furniture, superseding carved work with painted furniture decorated with exquisite foreign inlays, and ornamented with wreaths, PATERAE and the fan-shaped design so often associated with his work.

Adam (Miracle Play), first performed in the 12th century, and regarded as the earliest dramatic work in medieval French. It was performed on temporary stages erected in front of churches, and achieved great popularity in its day. The simple action unfolded the tale of Adam and Eve, and the murder of Abel by Cain, ending with the customary assurance of man's final salvation.

Adam de la Halle (c.1220-1287), French poet and musician; author of *Le Congé,* a poem of farewell to his wife, and *Le Jeu de Robin et Marion* (The Play of Robin and Marion) which is considered the first example of OPERA-COMIQUE.

Adamic, Louis (1899-), American author born in Austria who came to the United States in 1915; his works include *Dynamite: the Story of Class Violence in America* (1931); *Laughing in the Jungle,* an autobiography; *The Native's Return; Grandsons; Cradle of Life; The House of Antigua: A Restoration; My America; From Many Lands.*

Adams, Charles (1834-1900), American dramatic tenor, pupil of Barbieri in Vienna, and one of the first American singers to appear at the Royal Opera, Berlin, the Imperial Opera, Vienna, La SCALA, Milan, and COVENT GARDEN, London. In 1878 Adams created the title role in the première of Wagner's RIENZI at the Academy of Music, New York, achieving distinction for his acting as well as singing; he finally settled in Boston as a teacher.

Adams, Franklin Pierce (1881-), American journalist, editor and author; he joined the staff of the Chicago *Journal* in 1903, and after working on the New York *Evening Mail, Tribune* and *World,* he placed his column, "The Conning Tower" with the New York *Herald-Tribune* in 1931. His Saturday review of current affairs mimics the style of the *Diary* by Samuel PEPYS, and it is said to have created a new interest in the 17th century writer. Adams is a prominent figure in the radio "quiz" hour, known as INFORMATION PLEASE; his most recent literary work is an anthology of light verse, *Innocent Merriment.*

Adams, Herbert (1858-), American sculptor, pupil of Antonin MERCIÉ in Paris. He experimented with both polychrome and tinted marbles, excellent results being obtained in *The Rabbi's Daughter,* and in a bust of the actress, Julia MARLOWE. He also finished the bronze doors begun by Olin WARNER for the Congressional Library, Washington, and created the Vanderbilt memorial bronze doors for St. Bartholomew's Church, New York.

Adams, Maude, née **Kiskadden** (1872-), American actress: at sixteen she appeared with E. H. Sothern's company in an ingenue role, later joining Charles Frohman's stock company when her acting began to excite unusual interest. She became a star in BARRIE's *Little Minister,* achieved great success in *Romeo and Juliet,* ROSTAND's *Chantecler* and *L'Aiglon,* but rose to her greatest heights in Barrie's *Peter Pan, Quality Street, What Every Woman Knows,* and *A Kiss for Cinderella.* Miss Adams retired in 1918 for thirteen

years, returning in 1931 as Portia in *The Merchant of Venice,* and appearing in 1934 in *Twelfth Night.*

Adams, Oscar Fay (1855-1919), American editor and compiler of *Through the Years with the Poets* (12 vols. 1886); *A Brief Handbook of English Authors* (1884); *Dear Old Story Tellers* (1889); *Dictionary of American Authors* (1897).

Adams, Samuel Hopkins (1871-), American novelist who achieved a considerable degree of success with the novels *Revelry, The Gorgeous Hussy,* and *The President's Mystery Story.*

Adams, Sarah Flower (1805-1848), English poet and hymn writer; her finest works are a dramatic poem, *Vivia Perpetua* (1841), and the immortal verses for the hymn *Nearer, My God to Thee,* set to music by Lowell MASON.

Adams, Suzanne (1872-), American operatic soprano who studied with Bouhy in Paris, and made her debut in 1894 at L'Opera, Paris, in Gounod's ROMEO AND JULIET after being coached by the composer. Her debut at the METROPOLITAN OPERA HOUSE, New York in 1899 was made in the same opera with Jean de RESZKE as Romeo. She achieved international fame as an opera and oratorio singer.

Adams, Wayman (1883-), American painter who studied with William Merritt CHASE in Italy, and also in Spain under Robert HENRI. He has had remarkable success in portraits generally completed in one sitting; they include likenesses of Joseph PENNELL, Booth TARKINGTON and James Whitcomb RILEY: all are painted exactly as the artist saw his subjects. Adams won a number of medals for his portraiture, but has attempted little in other fields of painting

Adams, William Taylor (1822-1897), American journalist and author of juvenile stories written under the pen name, *Oliver Optic.* He wrote *The Riverdale Series* (6 vols. 1862), and edited *Oliver Optic's Magazine;* his juvenile novels number one hundred twenty-five, and his newspaper stories more than a thousand.

Adamsen, Amandus Heinrich (1855-), Estonian sculptor who evinced such remarkable ability in wood carving as a youth that he was admitted to the St. Petersburg Academy of Arts and Sciences. A portrait in relief of *Tsar Alexander III* was highly praised, and his productions have ranged from wooden statuettes, such as *Waiting* in the Tallinn Museum, to statues of heroic proportions including *Genius Freed* and *Victory of Truth* shown at the Nizhni Novgorod Exhibition in 1895.

Adaptation, in drama, the rearrangement of a play, or, in the case of a dramatized novel or poem, alteration of the form, language or less important details, thereby reconstructing and perhaps rewording the original.

Addams, Clifford Isaac (1876-1942), American painter who studied at the Drexler Institute, Philadelphia, and at the WHISTLER Academy in Paris, later becoming Whistler's assistant. Among his best known works are *Decoration* and *Portrait of the Artist's Wife* in the Pennsylvania Academy of Fine Arts. He also executed fine murals for the City Hall, Asheville, N. C., and received many prizes and awards.

Addison, Joseph (1672-1719), English poet, dramatist and essayist educated at OXFORD UNIVERSITY where he was famed for his Latin verse. His first important poem, *The Campaign,* celebrating the Duke of Marlborough's victory at Blenheim over the French and Bavarians, was written in 1704. From 1710 to 1714 he contributed more than 270 essays to Richard Steele's magazine, the *Tatler* and the *Spectator:* the portrait of Sir Roger de Coverly was developed in the latter periodical. Addison's only play, *Cato,* produced in 1713, was a brilliant success, even though it was weak from the dramatic standpoint, because both political parties—Whigs and Tories—chose to regard it as favorable to their causes.

Ade, George (1866-), American dramatist, librettist and humorist. He was a newspaper writer for several years, and his earlier books were elaborations of successful journalistic sketches such as *Stories of the Streets and the Town:* the most successful was *Fables in Slang* (1899). Ade wrote the librettos for three popular comic operas: *The Sultan of Sulu, The Sho-gun,* and *Peggy from Paris;* also several very successful plays including *The College Widow, Father and the Boys,* and *The County Chairman.* He has written a number of film scenarios.

Adeler, Max, see **Clark, Charles Heber.**

Adler, Denkmar (1844-1900), American architect, born in Germany, who came to the United States when he was ten years old; served in the Civil War and played an important part in the rebuilding of Chicago after the great fire in 1871. In 1880 he entered into partnership with Louis SULLIVAN; their buildings in St. Louis and Chicago from 1890 to 1900 are among the first important examples of skyscraper design in the United States.

Adler, Luther (1903-), American actor, member of a family group reputed to be the largest in the contemporary American theatre. The founder was the famous Jewish tragedian, Jacob P. Adler (1855-1926), known as the "Jewish Henry Irving": of the seventeen members the most distinguished are his son, Luther, and his daughter, Stella. Luther Adler made his first appearance as a child actor at the Thalia Theatre, New York, in 1908, and his formal debut in 1921 with the Provincetown Players. Later he toured with Margaret Anglin in *Iphigenia* and has appeared in leading roles for both the Theatre Guild and Group Theatre. In 1938 he made his London debut in *Golden Boy.*

Ad libitum or **Ad lib.,** (*a*) in drama, to extemporize by introducing impromptu, original remarks between the prepared speeches of a play, either because of a memory lapse or to interpolate matter of local interest; (*b*) in music, a direction indicating that the performer may vary the tempo or expression.

Admirable Crichton, see **Crichton, James.**

Adobe, in architecture a Spanish American term for sun-dried clay brick made by American Indians in the Southwest for home-building purposes; it was used in Latin America, and taken by the Spaniards to Spain from Mexico and Peru. Small bricks are called *adobes* and larger ones, from one to three yards in length, are named *adobines.* The advantages appear to be that houses built of adobe are warm in winter and cool in summer; the material is fireproof and procurable at little cost.

Adonis, in mythology a youth of extraordinary beauty, unnatural son of King Theias by his daughter Smyrna (Myrrha). APHRODITE saved his life when he was born, and entrusted him to PERSEPHONE who favored the youth so greatly that she refused to give him up. ZEUS, when appealed to in the matter, decided that Adonis should spend a third of the year with each of the goddesses, and have the balance of the time for himself. Adonis was finally killed by a boar sent by DIANA.

Adoration of the Magi, a favorite subject for painters of all nationalities and periods as may be judged from the following partial list: ALLORI, BELLINI, BOTTICELLI, CRANACH, DÜRER, GAROFALO, GENTILE DA FABRIANO, FRA ANGELICO, GHIRLANDAIO, LIPPI, POUSSIN, RAPHAEL, REMBRANDT, RUBENS, SODOMA, STEFANO, TINTORETTO, TITIAN, VELASQUEZ, VERONESE, DA VINCI, VIVARINI.

Adventures in a Perambulator, an orchestral suite by John Alden CARPENTER first performed by the CHICAGO SYMPHONY ORCHESTRA under the direction of Frederick STOCK in 1915, and described by the composer as an exploration into infant psychology. Critics are agreed that the suite is replete with humor and rare invention both in themes and rhythms: there is a Victor recording by the Minneapolis Symphony Orchestra directed by Eugene Ormandy.

Ady, Endre (1877-1919), Hungarian author and poet who spent a considerable part of his life in Paris absorbing modernistic influences which are manifest in his verses. He may be listed among the finest Magyar poets in respect to patriotic fervor, erotic fancy and rich imagination. Several volumes of his prose works have been published.

Aeginetan Marbles, a series of ancient Greek sculptures, probably dating from 500 B.C. and found on the island of Aegina in 1811. They were reconstructed by the Danish sculptor, Bertel THORVALDSEN, but the method of restoration has been severely criticized. The marbles evidently constituted the decorative parts of the pediments of a temple, and represented scenes in the TROJAN WAR, the figures being painted although the colors are almost effaced. The sculptures, now in the Glyptothek, Munich, are regarded as among the most valuable specimens of ancient Greek art.

Aegis or **Egis,** in Greek mythology the shield or defensive armor carried by ZEUS, ATHENA and APOLLO; Athena's aegis bore the head of MEDUSA. The word has now taken on the meaning of protection or support; therefore, to appear "under the aegis" of a prominent person means that their financial or moral support has been secured.

Aeneas, in Greek and Roman mythology a famous Trojan hero, the son of Anchises and APH-RODITE. In Homer's ILIAD he was second only to HECTOR in the gallant defense of Troy, and a favorite of the gods. After the fall of Troy, according to the story of Aeneas continued by VIR-GIL in the *Aeneid;* he traveled in company with his father and little son through Thrace, Delos, Crete and Italy, finally being wrecked on the African coast at CARTHAGE. He refused to remain with DIDO, queen of Carthage, who ended her life in despair. After seven years of wandering, Aeneas landed at the kingdom of Latium, where he married Lavinia, daughter of the king, and founded the city of Lavinium in her honor. An opera, DIDO AND AENEAS, by Henry PURCELL, is founded on the refusal of Aeneas to marry the Carthaginian queen.

Aeolian Hall (New York), a concert and recital hall in great favor during the early part of the 20th century, located on 42nd St. between Fifth and Sixth Avenues, and directly opposite Bryant Park. It seated 1400 persons, and recitals were given there by all great European and American artists. After the building was torn down, recitals were transferred to TOWN HALL. On Feb. 12, 1924, Paul WHITEMAN introduced modern jazz to concert hall audiences by a performance of the RHAPSODY IN BLUE by George GERSHWIN.

Aeolian Harp, a musical instrument, also called a LYRE, named after the Greek god, AEOLUS. It consists of a narrow, oblong box of wood with gut strings stretched across bridges at either end. When placed at an open window in the path of a current of air, the wind, passing obliquely over the strings, creates pleasingly ethereal sounds.

Aeolus, in Greek mythology the god of the winds, and king of the island of Aeolia. In Homer's ODYSSEY, Aeolus entertains ODYSSEUS, and presents him with a favorable wind to facilitate his journey; also with a bag in which unfavorable breezes are confined. The companions of Odysseus open the bag, hoping to find gold or jewels in it; the unfavorable breezes escape and drive the travelers back to the island, but they are expelled by the angry Aeolus.

Aertsen, Pieter (c.1505-1573), Dutch painter of still life and figures, nicknamed "Long Peter" (Lange Pier) because of his unusual height. His paintings of rustic life in somewhat spicy vein, such as *People Flirting, The Beer Shop, Dance of the Eggs* and *The Kitchen,* are extraordinarily natural in both subjects and detail.

Aeschylus (525-456 B.C.), Athenian poet, actor and dramatist generally regarded as the founder of Greek drama, and the first of three distinguished tragedians—the others being SOPHOCLES and EURIPIDES—many of whose plays have survived in their entirety. His career as a dramatist began in 499 B.C. at Athens, and ended with the production of the *Oresteia* in 458 B.C. During this period he was victorious in the dramatic contests at least twenty times, and wrote more than eighty plays. Seven of these—*Supplices, Persae, Septem contra Thebas, Prometheus Bound, Agamemnon, Choephoroe* and *Eumenides*—are in complete form, and there are fragments of more than seventy others. Aeschylus may be said to have originated tragedy as a dramatic art-form by adding an actor (known as the "answerer") to reply to the "leader," thereby adding dialogue to recitation. He also greatly increased the range of subjects for dramatic treatment, and raised the general level of drama from both the intellectual and artistic standpoints. *Agamemnon* is generally regarded as the finest and most dramatic of Greek tragedies, comparable only to the *Oedipus Rex* of Sophocles.

Aesop (c.620-560 B.C.), noted Greek fabulist, supposed to have been a slave who finally received his freedom from Iadmon of Samos. The Athenians are said to have erected a statue by the famous sculptor, LYSIPPUS, in his honor, and his fables were collected by a 14th century monk, Maximus Planudes. The versions known today are taken from the Latin of Valerius BABRIUS, a Roman author or scholar who apparently lived during the 8th century in Syria.

Aesopus, Clodius, distinguished Roman tragedian of the first century B.C. whose birth and death dates are unknown; CICERO was well acquainted with him, and also with the comedian, QUINTUS ROSCIUS. Aesopus made his last appearance in 55 B.C. at the dedication of a theatre erected by POMPEY, a famous Roman general and rival of Julius CAESAR.

Aesthetics, the study of the beautiful in its various aspects, especially in reference to the fine arts. Beauty manifests itself through the medium of the eye in painting, sculpture, architecture and literature; through the ear in instrumental and vocal music, and through both the ear and the eye in drama, opera and ballet. The eleventh edition of the *Encyclopedia Britannica* contains an illuminating essay on this subject.

Afanasyev, Alexander Nikolaievitch (1826-1871), Russian author and collector of Slav folk tales; he published an interesting study of the poetical attitude of the ancient Slavs in respect to nature and its wonders.

Afranius, Lucius, Roman author of humorous poetry who came into favor about 94 B.C. His comedies, for which, according to his own admission, he borrowed extensively from MENANDER, were concerned with the affairs of the middle-class Roman, and they were extremely popular for that reason.

Africaine, L', grand opera in five acts, music by Giacomo MEYERBEER; libretto by Eugène SCRIBE; first produced at L'Opéra, Paris, in 1865, and at the Academy of Music, New York, during the same year. The plot is based on the love of the Princess Inez, daughter of the King of Portugal, for the explorer, Vasco da Gama.

Afternoon of a Faun, or correctly *Prelude to the Afternoon of a Faun,* a symphonic poem com-

9

posed by Claude DEBUSSY in 1892, and played for the first time at Paris in 1894. The work was inspired by a poem from the pen of Stephané MALLARME, and somewhat obscure in its meaning; as interpreted by Edmund GOSSE its substance is as follows: "A faun—a simple sensuous, passionate being—wakens in the forest, and tries to recall the events of the previous afternoon. He cannot remember; his impressions grow more vague, and as the sun grows warmer, he curls up and goes to sleep again." The work was received at its première with mixed sentiments, but it is now one of the most popular symphonic poems. There is a Victor recording by the Philadelphia Orchestra under Leopold Stokowski, and a Columbia recording by the London Philharmonic Orchestra with Sir Thomas Beecham.

Afternoon of a Faun, The (*L'Après-midi d'un faune*), a ballet in one act, libretto and choreography by Vaslav NIJINSKY; music by Claude DEBUSSY; first produced at Paris in 1912 with Nijinsky in the role of the faun. Leonide MASSINE danced the part at the METROPOLITAN OPERA HOUSE première.

Afzelius, Arvid August (1785-1871), Swedish poet, clergyman and mythologist. He collaborated with the eminent historian, Erik Gustaf Geijer, in a monumental collection of Swedish folk songs, and also published translations of Scandinavian SAGA.

Agamemnon, in Greek mythology, king of Mycenae and leader of the expedition against the Trojans after the abduction by PARIS of HELEN, wife of his brother, MENELAUS. Agamemnon, murdered by his wife, CLYTEMNESTRA and her lover, Aegisthus, was avenged by his son, ORESTES who killed his mother. Many dramatists have used the adventures of Agamemnon as a subject; among them AESCHYLUS in the ORESTEIA.

Agasias, the name of two Greek sculptors both of whom were disciples of the Ephesian school about 100 B.C. One, the son of Dositheus, created a remarkable statue, known as the BORGHESE WARRIOR and now in the LOUVRE; the other, son of Menophilus, carved an equally striking statue of a warrior or gladiator, which is in the Art Museum at Athens.

Agate, (*a*) the name given a variegated waxlike quartz in which the colors are usually in bands or layers; these bands can be artificially colored to produce more vivid shades. Agate is found in South America, in the United States and in India: the commercial adapting of the quartz for use in jewelry has always been done in Germany. (*b*) the name given to a 5½ point face of printer's type: it is one of the three smallest type faces in use.

Agatharchus, Athenian painter of the 5th century B.C.; erroneously credited with having introduced the three-dimensional background into the theatre, whereas he merely painted a background picturing a palace or temple on the wooden front of a stage building.

Agathon (c.448-c.400 B.C.), Greek tragic poet: an intimate of EURIPIDES and PLATO. All his works are lost, but he is mentioned by ARISTOPHANES, and by Plato in his *Symposium* as having given a banquet to celebrate receiving a prize for a tragedy in 416 B.C.

Age, in classical mythology one of the divisions into which various periods of history are separated in respect to cultural, moral or geological aspects. The Greek poet, HESIOD in his epic, *Works and Days,* names the ages as follows: I *The Golden Age,* of perfect happiness; II *The Silver Age,* less happy but more luxurious; III *The Bronze Age,* warlike and cruel; IV *The Heroic Age* in which chivalry flourished in the TROJAN WAR; V *The Iron Age,* a licentious period from which justice and piety are absent. OVID in his METAMORPHOSES follows Hesiod closely, but omits the Heroic Age.

Ageladas, Greek sculptor of the Argive school who worked in the latter part of the 6th, and the first part of the 5th century B.C. He carved many statues of victors at the Olympian contests, and was said, without corroborative evidence, to have been the teacher of MYRON, POLYCLITUS and PHIDIAS.

Agesander, Greek sculptor of the 1st century, B.C.: born in Rhodes, and said by PLINY to have been associated with Polydorus and Athenodorus in the making of a Greek statue, THE LAOCOÖN from 42 B.C. to 21 B.C.

Agitato, in music a direction indicating that the passage is to be played in an agitated, restless or stirring manner.

Agora, in ancient Greece an assembly of the people called by the king: later the word was used to designate the place of meeting. The agora finally became the mart for the sale of merchandise as well as for public festivals: the one at Athens was surrounded by public buildings and adorned with trees.

Agoracritus, Greek sculptor of the 5th century B.C., said to have been the favorite pupil of PHIDIAS. Part of the head of his colossal statue, *Nemesis,* at Rhamnus is now in the BRITISH MUSEUM, and fragments of its pedestal are in the Art Museum at Athens; some authorities pronounce it the work of Phidias.

Agostino, Veneziano (c.1490-c.1540), Italian engraver, a pupil of Marc Antonio RAIMONDI; his plates, copies of RAPHAEL, MICHELANGELO and many other masters, are extremely rare, and consequently highly prized.

Agostino and **Agnola da Siena,** Italian architects and sculptors who, because they worked together at times during the first part of the 14th century, have been erroneously called brothers. They both studied under Giovanni PISANO, and created many fine buildings in Siena: their finest work was the tomb of Bishop Guido Tarlati in the cathedral at Arezzo.

Agostino d'Antonio di Duccio (c.1418-c.1498), Italian sculptor and architect who created four exquisite small reliefs on the façade of the Cathedral at Modena in 1442, and executed his greatest artistic achievement, the façade of the Church of Saint Bernardino at Perugia in 1461.

Agoult, Marie Catherine Sophie de Flavigny, *Comtesse d'* (1805-1876), French author who used the pseudonym "Daniel Stern." She was the daughter of a French officer and married Count Charles d'Agoult in 1827, entertaining at her salon such celebrities as DE VIGNY, CHOPIN and MEYERBEER. After separating from her husband, she became the mistress of Franz LISZT; one of her children by the latter was Cosima WAGNER who married Richard WAGNER after divorcing the German composer's intimate friend and intrepid champion, Hans VON BÜLOW. Mme. Agoult's separation from Liszt is related in thinly disguised form in her novel *Nélida* (1845). A stirring drama, *Jeanne d'Arc,* was staged in 1857 at Turin with brilliant success, but her historical and political essays are regarded as more important contributions to French literature.

Aguilera, Ventura Ruiz (1820-1881), Spanish poet and journalist who achieved considerable fame with two volumes of poems, *Ecos nacionales* in 1849, and *Elegias y Armonias* in 1863; later works reveal declining powers, but the Christian spirit pervading his verses give evidence of sincere devotion, and an engaging personality.

Aherne, Brian (1902-), English stage and screen actor, educated at Malvern College; debut in 1913 at the Garrick Theatre, London, in *Where the Rainbow Ends.* He toured Australia with Dion Boucicault, and later appeared in London in *White Cargo, The Silver Cord* and *Craig's Wife.* He made his American stage debut in *The Barretts of Wimpole Street* in 1931, also appearing in *Romeo and Juliet* with Katharine Cornell in 1935. His film appearances include *Beloved Enemy, The Great Garrick, Juarez, Captain Fury,* and *Smilin' Through.*

Ahlers, Anny (1906-1933), German actress who first appeared as a child dancer in 1913, and continued as a danseuse until 1922. After studying singing, she made her debut at Hamburg in 1924 with great success in OFFENBACH'S operetta, ORPHEUS IN THE UNDERWORLD; later she was starred with Richard TAUBER in *The Song of Love.* Her appearance in 1932 at His Majesty's Theatre, London, in the title role of *The Dubarry* was a signal success, cut short by her tragic death in 1933.

Aicard, Jean François Victor (1848-1921), French poet, dramatist, and novelist; his most highly praised volume of poems was *Poèmes de Provence. Le Père Lebonnard* was his most successful play, and *Le Roi de Camargue* achieved considerable popularity as a novel. Aicard also wrote *La Venus de Milo,* an account of the discovery of the statue based on newly found documents.

Aichenwald, Yuli Isayevich (1872-1928), Russian literary critic of the Impressionist School who left Russia after the Revolution in 1917. One of his books, *Silhouettes of Russian Authors,* a series of essays revealing genuine understanding of the writers' aims, achieved considerable success.

Aïda, a grand opera in five acts, libretto by Antonio GHISLANZONI, music by Giuseppe VERDI, produced at Cairo, Egypt, in 1871; the American première took place at the Academy of Music, New York, in 1873. The story is: Amneris, daughter of the king of Egypt, loves Rhadames, captain of the guard, but he desires Aïda, daughter of Amonasro, king of Ethiopia. After Rhadames returns victorious from a war against the Ethiopians, Amneris discovers that Aïda, who is her slave as a hostage, returns Rhadames' love, and plans her downfall. Amonasro compels Aïda to procure military information from the unsuspecting Rhadames; he is condemned to be buried alive, but as the tomb is being sealed, Aïda appears to share his fate. There are complete recordings by both Victor and Columbia.

Aiken, Conrad Potter (1889-), American poet, novelist and anthologist who has an enthusiastic following among those who are intellectually capable of understanding his subtly rhythmic verses, replete with metaphysical, philosophical and introspective thought. They include *Earth Triumphant, Nocturne of Remembered Spring,* and *Selected Poems.* Aiken has edited two anthologies, *Modern American Poets* and *American Poetry, 1671-1928;* he has also written two novels, and two volumes of short stories.

Aiken, George L. (1830-1876), American actor and dramatist noted for his skill in adapting novels and short stories for the stage. He dramatized Harriet Beecher STOWE'S novel, UNCLE TOM'S CABIN; it was first produced at Troy, N. Y., followed by a run, unprecedented at the time in the theatre history, of more than 300 nights in New York.

Aimard, Gustave (1818-1883), the pen name used by Olivier Gloux, a French novelist who wrote a series of adventure stories so clearly in the style of James Fenimore COOPER that he was known as "the French Cooper." Among the best are *The Arkansas Trappers, Mexican Nights* and *The Virgin Forest:* many of his novels have been translated into English.

Ainsworth, William Harrison (1805-1882), English novelist whose first work, *Sir John Chiverton,* was praised by Sir Walter SCOTT, encouraging him to publish *Rookwood* (1834) which was so successful that he devoted his life to writing historical romances such as *Jack Sheppard, The Tower of London, Guy Fawkes, Windsor Castle* and many others received with great favor. He also edited *Bentley's Miscellany* and founded *Ainsworth's Magazine.*

Air, in music a term meaning "melody" or "tune": also used (*a*) in Elizabethan music as the name of a vocal work in several parts; (*b*) as the title of a movement in orchestral suites by Bach, Handel and others; (*c*) as the name for any single aria in an opera.

Air for the G String, the title given by August WILHELMJ to the second movement of Johann

Sebastian BACH's third orchestral suite when he arranged it as a solo for the G string of the violin, transposing it from D major to C major. It is now frequently played in C major by the string sections of symphony orchestras with the 1st and 2nd violins playing the melody in unison. There are Columbia and Victor recordings in this form.

Aisle, in architecture the term applied to the lateral divisions of a cathedral, church, theatre or any public building containing seats in regular formation. The original church of ST. PETER'S at Rome had double aisles on each side of the central area; English cathedrals usually have only one aisle on each side of the NAVE, but most European cathedrals have two aisles. COLONNADES or ARCADES generally divide the aisles from the nave.

Aitken, Robert Ingersoll (1878-), American sculptor and designer of the gold coin in the denomination of fifty dollars issued by the United States; he also created the monuments to William McKinley at Berkeley, St. Helena and San Francisco, Calif.; and the Dewey memorial in the latter city, and *The Four Elements* at the Panama-Pacific International Exposition.

Ajax, a Greek hero, son of Telamon, described in Homer's ILIAD as of colossal size, and equalled only by ACHILLES in strength and bravery. After the death of Achilles, whose body he rescued from the Trojans, he entered into a competition with ODYSSEUS for the armor of the slain hero; he was so enraged when AGAMEMNON declared Odysseus the victor that he killed himself with a sword presented to him by HECTOR.

Akeley, Carl Ethan (1864-1926), American animal sculptor and naturalist who developed a method of mounting animal groups calling for the knowledge of ANATOMY and modeling which forms an important part of a sculptor's training. Among his works are several bronze groups of wild life in Africa; an elephant group, *The Wounded Comrade,* and *The Chrysalis,* a bronze statue symbolic of evolution.

Akenside, Mark (1721-1770), English poet and physician to the queen under George III; his verses are dignified and musical, but a certain cold quality pervades them. His finest work, a didactic poem, *The Pleasures of Imagination* (1744), was accepted by the publisher, Dodsley, only after Alexander POPE, whose style it imitates in certain respects, assured him that the price asked, about $100, was not exorbitant. Akenside revised and republished it in 1757 with the title *The Pleasure of the Imagination.*

Akers, Benjamin Paul (1825-1861), American sculptor, known as "St. Paul" Akers because of his religious spirit; his finest creation is *The Pearl Diver* in the Public Library at Portland, Maine.

Akins, Zoë (1886-), American dramatist, journalist and screen writer; her successful plays include *Declassée* (1919) in which Ethel Barrymore was starred; *The Greeks Had a Word For It* (1930) and *The Old Maid* (1935), a dramatiza-

tion of Edith WHARTON's novel and winner of the Pulitzer Prize. She has written many film scenarios including those for the two last-mentioned plays.

Aksakov, Sergei Timofeievich (1791-1859), Russian author whose chief work was *The Family Chronicle* (1856), a masterly description of his own childhood, picturing life on a Russian gentleman's estate and distinguished by rare charm of diction and warmth of feeling. In 1858 he published a sequel, *The Childhood of Bragoff, the Grandson.*

Alabaster, in ancient architecture the name of a mineral used by the Egyptians and Romans for the linings of tombs, ceilings of temples, and also for perfume ointment vases. A SARCOPHAGUS sculptured from a single block of translucent alabaster, discovered near Thebes in 1817, is now in the Soane Museum, London.

Aladdin, the hero of the tale, *Aladdin and the Wonderful Lamp* in the ARABIAN NIGHTS. Aladdin, the lamp, and the genie it could summon have been the inspiration for a multitude of operas, operettas, plays, ballets and spectacles for more than two hundred years.

Alamanni, Luigi (1495-1556), Italian poet: he was at first in favor with Cardinal Giuliano de' Medici, but conspired against him, and fled to France. His principal work is a didactic poem, *The Cultivation of the Fields,* in imitation of VIRGIL'S *Georgics.*

Alarçon, Juan Ruiz de (1581-1639), Spanish dramatist, born in Mexico, and sent to Spain in 1600 for a legal education. He was a hunchback, but, while embittered by his deformity, his talents enabled him to achieve extraordinary success with plays such as *La verdad sospechosa* and *El Tejedor de Segovia,* the latter containing a mixture of national sentiment and expression which combine to make of it a masterpiece in the fullest sense of the word.

Alarçon y Mendoza, Pedro Antonio de (1833-1891), Spanish author, dramatist and journalist; his first novel, *El Final de Norma* (1855), was well received: a play, *El Hijo prodigo,* was hissed off the boards, but his resetting of ancient tale, *El Somberos de tres picos* (1874), became as popular throughout Europe as in Spain. Unfortunately Alarçon's imagination gradually waned through failing health, and his later works are of much less importance.

Alard, Jean Delphin (1815-1888), French violinist, composer and teacher, pupil of Habeneck at the Paris Conservatory, and professor of violin at the same institution from 1843 to 1875. He was a fine instructor, numbering Pablo de SARASATE among his pupils; he also wrote a violin method which became standard; composed many charmingly melodious solos for his instrument, and edited forty classic violin works in a series known as *Les maitres classiques du violon.*

Alarums and Excursions, an expression, found in the plays of Shakespeare and other Elizabethan dramatists, indicating the sounding of alarms and the movements of armies in battle scenes.

Albanese, Licia (1913-   ), Italian lyric soprano who studied the piano before deciding on an operatic career; her debut was made in 1935 at Parma in MADAME BUTTERFLY. She has since sung at the principal opera houses in Naples, Rome, Paris, Monte Carlo, and in London at COVENT GARDEN for the Coronation Festival. She made her debut in 1940 at the METROPOLITAN OPERA HOUSE, New York, in Madame Butterfly, and has appeared there in several leading roles including that of Violetta in La TRAVIATA.

Albani, Emma, stage name of **Marie Louise Cecilia Emma Lajeunesse** (1852-1930), Canadian dramatic soprano. She sang first at the Roman Catholic Cathedral, Albany, N. Y.; studied in Europe under LAMPERTI, and made her debut at Messina, Italy, during 1870 in La Sonnambula. In 1874, after singing in Russia and the United States, she joined the Covent Garden Opera, London, remaining there until 1896, when she sang Isolde in German to the Tristan of Jean de Reszke. Albani retired in 1906, after she had achieved equal success as an oratorio singer. Her memoirs, Emma Albani, Forty Years of Song, were published in 1911.

Albani, Francesco (1578-1660), Italian painter of the Bolognese school, pupil of Denis CALVAERT at the same time as Guido RENI, both later seeking instruction from Lodovico CARRACCI. His competition with Guido Reni spurred both to their finest creations; Albani's frescoes on mythological subjects, such as the Adventures of Aeneas for the Fava Palace are his finest work. Later he went to Rome, and worked with Annibale Carracci and with DOMENICHINO, architect of the VATICAN, creating a Fall of Phaeton as a decoration for the palace of Bassano di Sutri. His best sacred works are a Saint Sebastian and an Assumption of the Virgin in the church of St. Sebastian at Rome.

Albani, Mathias (c.1620-c.1712), Italian violin maker, a pupil of Jacobus STAINER. His instruments were classed with those of AMATI and STRADIVARIUS; the woods carefully selected, the varnish brownish-red and the tone of excellent quality. The prices today in the United States of Albani's violins range from $750.00 to $3000.00; his son, **Johann Michael Albani** (c.1677-1730), also made fine instruments which command equally high prices.

Albatross, an aquatic bird resembling the petrel, the largest variety of which is found in the Pacific Ocean. It has extraordinary powers of endurance, due to the length of its wings which, when extended, average 12 feet and in extreme cases 17 feet. An albatross has been known to accompany a ship for several days without being seen to alight on the water. Sailors regard it as a bird of good omen, and the evil which befalls anyone who kills an albatross is familiar to those who have read COLERIDGE's The ANCIENT MARINER.

Albeniz, Isaac (1860-1909), Spanish pianist and composer, who gave evidence of such talent that at the age of six he became a piano pupil of MARMONTEL, and later of Brassin and LISZT, with Dupont, GEVAERT and Jadassohn as his teachers in composition. Albeniz wrote several operas, but his piano compositions, such as the suites Iberia and Catalonia, are the principal source of his fame; some of his works show the influence of the French impressionistic school.

Alberich, a dwarf, one of the two Nibelungs (inhabitants of the underworld), in Wagner's cycle of music dramas, The Ring of the Nibelungs. He steals the glittering mass known as the Rhinegold from the Rhine daughters, and forges from it a ring which gives him power over the entire world; he also forces his brother, MIME, to fashion him a magic helmet, the Tarnhelm, to make him invisible, or to change his form whenever it suits his evil purposes.

d'Albert, Eugène Francis Charles (1864-1932), Scottish pianist and composer, pupil of STAINER, PROUT and SULLIVAN in harmony and composition, and of Ernst Pauer and Franz LISZT in piano: the latter called him "the young Tausig" because of his dazzling technique. He concertized extensively many years, and toured the United States with the violinist, Pablo de SARASATE, in 1889, and alone in 1892 and 1904. Two of his 16 operas, Tiefland and Die Toten Augen (The Dead Eyes), were performed several times in the United States; he also composed two piano concertos, a violoncello concerto, and some chamber music. He edited the Well-Tempered Clavichord and was one of the editors of the complete edition of Bach published by Breitkopf and Härtel.

Albert, full name **Ferdinand Albert Decombe,** (1789-1865), French dancer and choreographer whose desire to succed in his art was kindled by seeing Madame VESTRIS dance at Bordeaux. He attained the rank of premier danseur at L'Opera in Paris in 1817, and was appointed ballet master in 1829. Among Albert's most successful ballets were Le Seductor au Village, Cendrillon, and La Jolie Fille de Gand. He also produced many works by other choreographers at the principal European theatres for more than thirty years.

Albert Hall (London), see **Royal Albert Hall (London).**

Alberti, Leone Battista (1404-1472), Italian architect, painter, poet, musician, author and philosopher; he drew the plans for the Rucellai Palace, the Saint Andrea and Saint Sebastien churches at Mantua, and the church of San Francesco at Rimini, leaving their actual execution to others. His treatises include Della statua on sculpture, De pictura on painting and De re aedificatoria on architecture; the latter work has been translated into Italian, French, Spanish and English, and was influential in shaping the ideas for the RENAISSANCE, and in creating enthusiasm for the revival of ancient Roman architecture.

Albertina (Vienna), formerly the palace of the Archduke Frederick of Austria built by Montoyer in 1801-04, and now housing the Albertina Graphic

Collection comprising prints, drawings and architectural plans, the most complete of its kind in the world; also the musical and papyri sections of the National Library. The Albertina collection, which has been state property since 1919, was founded in 1795 by Duke Albert of Sachsen-Teschen; in 1920 the assembly of engravings in the National Library was added.

Albertinelli, Mariotto (1474-1515), Italian painter of the Florentine school and of noble descent; a pupil of Piero di Cosimo and also of Fra Bartolommeo with whom he worked on a *Last Judgment,* originally in the church of Santa Maria Nuova and now in the Uffizi Gallery, Florence. His original works include a *Visitation* and a *Holy Family,* both in the Uffizi; also a *Virgin Enthroned* and a *Crucifixion* in the Certosa di Galuzzo.

Alboni, Marietta (1823-1894), Italian operatic contralto who had the honor of being coached by Gioacchino Rossini. She made her debut in 1843 at La Scala, Milan, in Donizetti's Lucrezia Borgia; toured Europe and appeared as a rival to Jenny Lind at Covent Garden, London. In 1853 she made a triumphal tour of both North and South America.

Albrechtsberger, Johann Georg (1736-1809), Austrian theoretical writer, composer, and teacher of many distinguished pupils including Ludwig van Beethoven. His greatest technical work is *Gründliche Anweisung zur Komposition* (1790); his 250 compositions have little interest at the present time, with the exception of a fine *Te Deum.*

Albright Art Gallery, a subsidiary of the Buffalo Fine Arts Academy, Buffalo, N. Y. Among the painters and sculptors who are represented are Cezanne, Renoir, Gauguin, Picasso, Brancusi, Lehmbruck, Monet, Bellows, Childe Hassam, Ingres, Winslow Homer, Ryder, Tamayo, Lorrain and Credi. There are also many interesting sculptures including a famous life-size wood carving of St. Gorgon represented as a French courtier of the 15th century, and a life-size statue of a Roman poet, perhaps Ennius, of the 2nd century, B.C.

Alcaeus, Greek lyric poet who lived about 600 B.C., and was a contemporary of Sappho. He was of noble birth, and in the center of political feuds to such an extent that for a time he was forced to remain in exile. His verses include martial songs, hymns to the gods and a few love songs, all of sufficient excellence to merit his position as second among the nine lyric poets of the Alexandrine school. The Roman poet, Quintus Horatius Horace, thought well enough of his verses to use them as models.

Alcamenes (c.440-402 B.C.), a Greek sculptor said by Pliny to have been a pupil of Phidias. His works were executed in gold, ivory, marble and bronze; they include a *Hecate* placed near the Temple of Athena Nike at Athens; a *Dionysus* in an Athenian theatre, and a statue called *Aphrodite of the Gardens* at Athens. Some authorities contend that the Discobolus at the

Vatican is a copy of a bronze statue by Alcamenes.

Alcantara, Bridge of, a magnificent bridge built in Western Spain for the Roman emperor Trajan by the architect Julius Caius Lacer about 105 A.D. It spanned the Tagus River for a distance of 620 feet, and was 190 feet high at the center piers; these were surmounted by a fortified gateway, and the entire construction was of granite blocks without cement. Emperor Charles V partially restored the bridge in 1543; three hundred years later Queen Isabella II also had reconstruction work done on it.

Alcazar, the palace of the Moorish kings at Seville, later occupied by Spanish royalty. The edifice resembles the Alhambra in its architectural design: it was extremely beautiful in the days of the Moors, but the coloring of the restored parts are somewhat garish. From the time of Pedro the Cruel, additions were made under Christian rule, and elaborate gardens were laid out by Charles V of Spain. Another palace at Segovia has the same name; it was occupied by Castilian monarchs from the 14th century.

Alceste, grand opera in two acts: libretto by Raniero Calsabigi and music by Christoph Willibald von Gluck; produced at Vienna in 1767. The story is: Queen Alceste prays to Apollo for the recovery of King Admetus of Pherae; Apollo demands that someone die in his place, and Alceste willingly offers herself. Hercules rushes to Alceste's aid, whereupon Apollo relents and permits Alceste to return to the arms of her husband. The opera was so badly received by the Viennese that Gluck produced his next work, *Iphigenia in Aulis,* at L'Opéra in Paris under the patronage of Marie Antoinette.

Alcestis, in Greek mythology the wife of Admetus, king of Pherae in Thessaly. She is the heroine of plays by Euripides and Sophocles, of a poem by Robert Browning and of an opera Alceste by Gluck.

Alcman, Greek poet of the 6th century, B.C.; only a few short fragments remain of his work, but these have assigned him a high place among Greek lyric poets. He was regarded as the inventor of the love song form: one fragment was paraphrased by Goethe with the title *Über allen Gipfeln ist Ruh.*

Alcoforado, Marianna (1640-1723), Portuguese author who became a nun at sixteen, and was betrayed and deserted in her twenty-fifth year by Noel Bouton, later the Marquis de Chamilly. The five letters written by Marianna to her lover were published anonymously at Paris in 1669 with the title *Letters of a Portuguese Nun;* they were designed to expostulate with her errant lover. According to the *Encyclopedia Britannica* they "reveal a passion which in the course of two centuries has lost nothing of its heat. Perhaps their dominant note is reality, and, sad reading as they are from the moral standpoint, their absolute candor, exquisite tenderness and entire self-abandonment have excited the wonder and admiration of great men and women of all ages, from Madame de Sevigné to William E. Gladstone."

Alcott, Louisa May (1832-1888), American novelist who started on a literary career in order to assist in the support of her family. After writing some rather lurid melodramas, among them *The Bandits' Bride*, her first book, *Flower Fables*, was published in 1854: her masterpiece—*Little Women or Meg, Jo, Beth and Amy*—did not appear until 1868. This was followed by her autobiography, equally human and convincing; both books had enormous sales, and were translated into several languages. The books which came later, *An Old-fashioned Girl, Aunt Jo's Scrap Bag* (6 volumes), and several others were fashioned along the same lines; their spontaneous freshness attracted millions of loyal readers.

Alcove, in architecture the term for a recess or niche in a room, usually screened off by the use of pillars, a balustrade, or draperies.

Alda, Frances, stage name of **Frances Davis** (1883-), Australian operatic soprano who made her debut at L'OPÉRA-COMIQUE, Paris, in 1904 in the title role of MASSENET'S MANON. After singing in European and South American opera houses, she appeared in RIGOLETTO at the Metropolitan Opera House, New York, in 1908, remaining there until 1929, and creating the chief soprano roles in Charpentier's LOUISE, Borodin's PRINCE IGOR and other operas. She was married to Giulio Gatti-Casazza, director of the Metropolitan for a time; her autobiography, *Men, Women and Tenors,* was published in 1937.

Aldanov, M. A. (1888-), pen name of **Mark Aleksandrovich Landau-Aldanov,** Russian essayist and novelist who has lived in Paris since 1919. The following works have been translated into English: *Lenin* (1922); *Saint Helena: Little Island; The Ninth Thermidor; The Devil's Bridge; The Key.*

Aldegrever, Heinrich (1502-c.1558), German painter and engraver whose real name was Heinrich Trippenmeker: he is famous chiefly because of his fine engravings which class him as one of the most accomplished of the so-called "Little Masters." Among his best works are *Christ Crowned with Thorns; Portrait of Philip von Waldeck; Portrait of Engelbert Therlaen; Anabaptist David Joris.* He appears to have been influenced by Albrecht DÜRER although there is no evidence that he was the latter's pupil.

Alden, John (c.1599-1687), one of the Pilgrim Fathers, and said to have been the first to step on Plymouth Rock, a distinction also claimed for Mary Chilton. In 1621 he married Priscilla Mullens; LONGFELLOW used his courtship as the theme of *The Courtship of Miles Standish.* Alden was a magistrate for more than fifty years; he outlived all the other signers of the Mayflower compact.

Aldine Press, a printing establishment, founded by an Italian scholar, Aldo Manutina (1450-1515), near the end of the 15th century in Venice, and famous not only for its improvements in typography such as the introduction of italics, but also for exquisite editions of the classics, including works of Musaeus, Aristotle, Thucydides, Herodotus, SOPHOCLES, XENOPHON, EURIPIDES and Demosthenes as well as the masterpieces of Latin and Italian literature. Aldo's son, Paolo (1512-1574) and his grandson, Aldo Manutina, Jr. (1547-1597), were also renowned scholars who continued the founder's work after his death.

Aldington, Richard (1892-), English poet and novelist; his volumes of verse include *Images Old and New, A Fool i' the Forest* and *Collected Poems.* His novels comprise *Death of a Hero* and *The Colonel's Daughter.* In 1913 he married the poet, Hilda DOOLITTLE.

Aldis, Dorothy (1897-), American novelist and poet: her works include *Everything and Anything* (1926); *Murder in a Haystack; Any Spring; Time at Her Heels; Before Things Happen.*

Aldrich, Bess Streeter (1881-), American novelist educated at the Iowa State Teachers' College: her works include *Mother Mason* (1924); *The Rim of the Prairie; The Cutters; A Lantern in Her Hand; A White Bird Flying; Miss Bishop; Spring Came on Forever; The Man Who Caught the Weather; Song of Years; The Drum Goes Dead.*

Aldrich, Richard (1863-1937), American music critic, educated in music under John K. PAINE at Harvard College. He was critic of the Providence *Journal,* the Washington *Evening Star,* the New York *Tribune* as assistant to Henry E. KREHBIEL, and finally critic of the New York *Times* from 1902 to 1924. He wrote *A Guide to Parsifal, A Guide to the Ring of the Nibelung,* and *A History of the Philharmonic Society* (with H. E. Krehbiel): he also contributed to the second and third editions of GROVE'S *Dictionary of Music and Musicians* and COBBETT'S *Encyclopedic Survey of Chamber Music.*

Aldrich, Thomas Bailey (1836-1907), American editor, poet and novelist whose first successful work, *The Story of a Bad Boy,* was published in 1870. His novels, *Prudence Palfrey* and *The Stillwater Tragedy* were well received, but a book of short stories, *Marjorie Daw and Other People,* as well as several volumes of collected poetry established his reputation not only as an imaginative writer, but as a poet of unusual skill. Aldrich was editor of the *Atlantic Monthly* from 1881 to 1890.

Aldrich, William Truman (1880-), American architect, graduate of the Massachusetts Institute of Technology, Boston, Mass., and the ECOLE DES BEAUX ARTS, Paris. His works include the Worcester (Mass.) Art Museum, The Boston (Mass.) Museum of Fine Arts, and the Benedict Monument to Music, Providence, R. I.

Alecsandri, Vasily (1821-1890), Rumanian poet who studied in Paris, and later became director of the French Theatre at Jassy (Rumania) for which he wrote several comedies. He excelled in descriptions of natural scenery: his war poems are highly regarded, and his collections of Rumanian folk songs are invaluable.

Alegria, Ciro (1909-), Peruvian novelist who won the Latin-American prize novel contest in 1941 with his book, *El Mundo es ancho e ajeno* (The World is Broad and Alien). Another novel, *La Serpiente de oro* (The Gold Serpent), was a best seller in South America; Alegria has been an exile in Chile after being imprisoned in his native country for political activities.

Alemān, Mateo (1547-c.1610), Spanish physician and author of a satirical novel, *The Life and Deeds of the Picaroon Guzman de Alfarache,* an outstanding example of the picaresque novel originated by Diego Mendoza. It was translated into every European language: James Mabbe's English version is entitled *The Rogue, or the Life of Guzman de Alfarache.*

Aleotti, Giambattista (1546-1636), Italian architect, also known as "L'Argenta" from the name of his native town near Ferrara. His principal work was the celebrated Farnese Theatre at Parma, built in 1618-19 and considered an extraordinary adaptation of the classical theatre to the requirements of Italian drama. The Farnese had two tiers of boxes like those planned for the Olympic Theatre at Vicenza by Andrea Palladio.

Alessi, Galeazzo (1512-1572), Italian architect; a pupil of G. B. Caporali and Giulio Dante; the cities of Perugia, Genoa, Milan and Bologna are indebted to him for magnificent churches, hospitals, universities and palaces which came into being as if by magic under his skillful planning and personal direction. Among them were the Doria Palace in Genoa and the Marino Palace at Milan.

Alexander, Francis (1800-1881), American portrait painter who taught himself the use of color on a Connecticut farm, and after studying with Alexander Robertson in New York spent two winters in Rome (1831-32), and finally settled in Boston for nearly ten years. Among his best portraits are those of Charles DICKENS, Daniel WEBSTER, and Mrs. Fletcher Webster.

Alexander, Sir George (1858-1918), English actor and theatrical producer: in 1880 he became a member of Sir Henry IRVING's company for eight years. After assuming the direction of the Avenue Theatre, London, in 1890, he leased the St. James Theatre in 1892, and produced plays there with unique success for more than twenty-five years; among them Oscar WILDE's *Lady Windermere's Fan,* PINERO's *The Second Mrs. Tanqueray,* Haddon CHAMBERS' *The Idler,* H. A. JONES' *The Masquerader* and Anthony HOPE's' *Prisoner of Zenda* and *Rupert of Hentzau.* The part of Rudolph Rassendyll in the last two mentioned was his most successful role.

Alexander, Hartley Burr (1873-1939), American philosopher and poet: his volumes of poems include *The Mid Earth Life* (1907); *Odes on the Generations of Man; Odes and Lyrics; Manito Masks; God's Drum.* Part of Alexander's poetical inspiration is derived from American Indian lore.

Alexander, John White (1856-1915), American mural and portrait painter who was first an illustrator on *Harper's Magazine,* studied in Munich, Venice, and Paris (1890-1900), and attracted favorable attention with two portraits of girls entitled *Gris* and *Noir.* His finest murals are *The Evolution of the Book* in the Congressional Library, Washington, D. C., and a series depicting the iron industry at the Carnegie Institute, Pittsburgh, Pa. Among his finest portraits are those of Walt WHITMAN (in the Metropolitan Museum of Art), Robert Louis STEVENSON, Joseph JEFFERSON, Oliver Wendell HOLMES and John BURROUGHS.

Alexander the Great (356-323 B.C.), a king of Macedon and son of Philip II: he was a pupil of Aristotle, and succeeded his father in 336 B.C. After conquering Thrace, Illyria, Thebes and other opposition in Greece, he subjugated Egypt in 332 B.C., founding ALEXANDRIA and also invading Persia and India. He became the subject of one of the most famous medieval romances said to have been written in Alexandria about the middle of the 3rd century.

Alexandria, a city in Egypt and now its chief seaport. Founded by ALEXANDER THE GREAT in 332 B.C. it became the center of Greek and Hebrew culture; it was used by CLEOPATRA as a capital, and occupied at various times by Julius CAESAR, Marc ANTONY, OCTAVIAN, NAPOLEON I, and finally by the British. Its enormous library of more than 600,000 rolls of PAPYRUS in every ancient language, and the Museum (Greek University) made it a powerful rival of Rome itself for the study of astronomy, literature, and geography as well as all other arts and sciences.

Alexandrine Verse, a heroic verse of six iambic feet, much used in French epic poetry; it comprises a line of from twelve to thirteen syllables containing a final unstressed syllable if there are thirteen syllables. It is used in dramas by RACINE and CORNEILLE, and was probably derived from a series of romances, collected in the 12th century, in which ALEXANDER THE GREAT was hailed as the pride of chivalry. It was revived by Pierre de RONSARD, a French diplomat called the "Prince of Poets," in an effort to lead the poetic forms of his time back to classic models.

Alexis, Wilibald, see **Häring, Georg Wilhelm Heinrich.**

Alfani, Domenico (c.1480-c.1553), Italian painter and contemporary of RAPHAEL who worked with him in the studio of PERUGINO; the influence of both masters is shown in Alfani's pictures such as the *Madonna* and *Holy Family* in Perugia. Later in life, Alfani was influenced by painters of the Florentine school; the change can be seen in several works including *The Adoration of the Magi* and *The Virgin between St. John and a Saint.*

Alfani, Orazio di Paris (1510-1583), Italian painter who studied and worked with his father, Domenico ALFANI. He was the first president of the Academy at Perugia, and it is difficult to distinguish his work from that of his father, particularly in the *Holy Family* in the Uffizi Gallery, and *The Mystic Marriage of St. Catherine* in the

16

Louvre. On the other hand, some of his paintings have been adjudged early works of RAPHAEL.

Alfano, Franco (1876-), Italian composer of symphonic, chamber and operatic works; his one success in the United States was an opera, *Resurrection,* first produced at Turin in 1904, and at Chicago in 1925 with Mary GARDEN as the heroine. Another work, *Madonna Imperia,* was a failure at the Metropolitan Opera House, New York, in 1928.

Alfieri, Vittorio, Count (1749-1803), Italian tragic poet and dramatist who led an adventurous and exceedingly stormy life, due largely to what he describes in his memoirs as "an irritable, impetuous and almost ungovernable temper." In 1775 a drama, *Cleopatra,* achieved a degree of success which led to his writing nineteen tragedies from 1776 to 1786, thereby founding an entirely new school in Italian drama, and being looked upon by his successors as having originated a bold style which adds immeasurably to the realism of tragedy. The strongest of these dramas was *Saul;* none of their plots, with perhaps a single exception, *Rosamund,* were of Alfieri's invention, but were based on characters or incidents in mythology or literature. He also wrote six comedies of political significance, five odes on American independence inspired by the Revolution of 1776, and some prose works which can in no sense be compared with his dramas.

Alfred the Great (c.849-c.899), King of England, and also one of the most romantic and greatly loved heroes of history. His interest in literature led him to assemble a group of scholars from all sections of his kingdom to further the cause of education. He translated Gregory the Great's *Pastoral Care,* Bede's *Ecclesiastical History,* Boethius' *Consolation of Philosophy,* and the *Epitome of Universal History* by Paulus Orosius, making interesting and significant interpolations and comments.

Algardi, Alessandro (1602-1654), Italian sculptor and architect of the Bolognese school, and a pupil of Lodovici CARRACCI. He worked chiefly in Rome, creating the statue of *St. Magdalene* for the Church of San Silvestro and the immense bas-relief, *Attila's Retreat from Rome,* in which the principal figures are ten feet high, for the altar of Saint Leo in St. Peter's. His architectural masterpieces included the Villa Pamfili Doria for Prince Pamfili, and the superb façade of the Church of St. Ignatius.

Alger, Horatio (1834-1899), American clergyman: author of juvenile fiction who came to New York in 1864 to assist in managing the Newsboy's Lodging House. He wrote more than one hundred novels: among them *Tom the Bootblack* or *The Road to Success, Ralph Raymond's Heir,* and *Frank Fowler, the Cash Boy,* designed to prove to American youth, especially those exposed through poverty to temptation, that virtue is its own reward. Most of the royalties received from the books were spent on the newsboys.

Alhambra, The, an ancient citadel and palace, enclosed within a fortified wall; built by the Moorish kings of Granada between 1248 and 1354, and occupied until their expulsion in 1492. The name "Alhambra," which signifies "the red" in Arabic, was probably derived from the color of the bricks of which the outer wall was built. Architecturally the buildings are regarded as the finest product of Moorish art: they comprise the citadel, the palace, and the living quarters for the retainers. Among the interesting sections are the Gate of Pomegranates, the Gate of Judgment, the Palace of the Cisterns, the Wine Tower, the Court of the Myrtles, the Hall of the Ambassadors, the Court of Lions, the Hall of the Abencerrages, the Hall of the Two Sisters, and the Hall of Justice. Some idea of the magnificent furnishings may be obtained from the famous vase of the Alhambra, dated about 1320: it stands more than four feet high, enameled in blue and gold against a white background. A picturesque account of the Alhambra may be found in *The Alhambra* by Washington IRVING, written during his stay in Spain from 1826 to 1832 as attaché to the American embassy at Madrid.

Alhambra Theatre Ballet, a form of ballet produced at the Alhambra Theatre, London, from 1871 to 1914 in which one or more ballets were presented in connection with vaudeville. The theatre had its permanent *corps de ballet;* the music for more than 100 ballets was composed by Georges Jacoby, a German ballet and light opera composer. The choreographers included A. Bertrand, Carlo Coppi and Alfredo Curti, and the long list of principal dancers contains the names of Palladino, Legnani, Mossetti, Vicenti and Cormani.

Ali Baba, the hero of one of the most popular tales in THE ARABIAN NIGHTS, an Arabic collection of folk legends and tales, many of which are of East Indian origin. Investigation has proved, however, that the story, *Ali Baba and the Forty Thieves,* was not in the earliest editions of the collection.

Alkan, Charles Henri Valentin Morhange (1813-1888), French pianist and composer, admitted to the Paris Conservatory at the age of six, and later becoming a distinguished teacher for more than fifty years. He composed a series of piano preludes in emulation of CHOPIN, but only one of his works, an etude called *Le Vent* (The Wind), is in the concert repertory today.

Allan, David (1774-1796), Scottish historical painter who spent thirteen years in Rome copying works of the old masters, later creating an original work, *The Origin of Portraiture.* In 1780 he succeeded Alexander Runciman as director of the Academy of Arts at Edinburgh, and painted the works through which he became known as the "Scottish Hogarth" because of their humorous aspects: these include *Scotch Wedding, Highland Dance* and *Repentance Stool.*

Allan, Maud, Canadian classical dancer who studied at Berlin and Vienna, and made her debut at Vienna in 1903. Her appearance in London in 1908 in *The Vision of Salome,* the music from the score of Richard STRAUSS' opera, caused a sensation, and her dance founded on GRIEG'S PEER GYNT music was characterized by critics as "a beautiful art of transposition." She has toured Europe, the Far East and the United States with great success; like Isadora DUNCAN, she usually dances barefoot, and clad in loose Greek robes.

Allan, Sir William (1782-1850), Scottish painter who spent some years in Russia drawing vivid sketches of which he made good use in his pictures *The Circassian Captives, Bashkirs Conducting Convicts to Siberia, Siberian Exiles,* and *Haslan Gheray Crossing the Kuban River.* The last two mentioned were purchased by the Grand Duke Nicholas while on a visit to Edinburgh. He painted many pictures of Scottish history; a portrait of Lord Byron; two companion pictures of *The Battle of Waterloo,* and another, *Peter the Great Teaching his Subjects the Art of Shipbuilding,* for the Czar of Russia.

Allan-Despreaux, Louise Rosalie (1810-1856), French actress who first appeared as a child with TALMA at Brussels in 1820, and later at the Comédie Française in children's and ingenue roles. After playing at the French Theatre in St. Petersburg, she returned to the Théâtre Française in a comedy by Alfred de Musset in 1847, thereby laying the foundations of his fame as a dramatist, and becoming herself a rival of the hitherto incomparable RACHAEL.

Allard, Mademoiselle, 18th century dramatic ballerina who succeeded to the fame and adulation accorded Mlle. CAMARGO; her dancing partners included VESTRIS, DAUBERVAL and GARDEL. Balletomanes declared that she surpassed all other ballerinas in fiery spirit, agility and expressive postures. She acted as *prima ballerina* in many ballets by MOZART and ROSSINI.

Allegory, a Greek word meaning literally "one thing said for another," applied in literature as a figure of rhetoric, but understandable through the eyes as embodied in painting, sculpture or dramatic art. There are allegories in OVID's *Metamorphoses,* SPENSER's *Faerie Queen* and BUNYAN's *Pilgrim's Progress.* An allegory differs from a *metaphor* in being of greater length, and from an *analogy* in appealing to the imagination rather than to the reasoning powers.

Allegretto (It.), in music a term indicating a moderately fast tempo slower than *Allegro* and faster than *Andante.*

Allegri, Gregorio (c.1585-1652), an Italian composer of sacred and instrumental music; his most famous work is a *Miserere* for two choirs, still performed annually at the SISTINE CHAPEL, ROME. It remained uncopied and used only by the SISTINE CHOIR for many years, but MOZART heard it in 1769, and wrote it out from memory. Dr. Charles BURNEY published it in 1771.

Allegro (It.), in music a term indicating a brisk, lively tempo, slower than *Presto* and faster than *Allegretto.*

Allemand (Ger.), (*a*) the name of a German dance either in 3-4 or 2-4 time resembling the LANDLER, and of distinctly national character. (*b*) The name of one of the movements in suites written by BACH, HANDEL and other classic composers.

Allen, Fred (1894-), American screen and radio actor, real name John F. Sullivan. His career started as a vaudeville actor under the name of Fred James; after serving in World War I, he made his debut on the New York stage in Arthur HAMMERSTEIN's *Polly,* followed by appearances in various musical productions including the *Greenwich Village Follies.* In 1935 he made his screen debut in *Thanks a Million,* also appearing in *Sally, Irene and Mary* and *Love Thy Neighbor* (with Jack BENNY).

Allen, Hervey (1889-), American poet and novelist educated at the University of Pittsburgh; his works include *Ballads of the Border* (1916); *Wampum and Old Gold; Carolina Chansons,* in collaboration with Du Bose Heyward; *Israfel,* the Life and Times of Edgar Allan Poe; *New Legends,* a volume of poems; *Anthony Adverse,* one of the "best sellers" in American literature; *Action at Aquila; The Forest and the Fort.*

Allen, James Lane (1849-1925), American novelist who taught Latin, English and modern languages at several colleges before he embarked on a literary career. He was thoroughly conversant with the impoverished condition of the South after the Civil War, and his successful contributions to periodicals led to the publication of several well-received books including *The Blue Grass Region; John Gray; A Kentucky Cardinal; Aftermath; Choir Invisible; A Cathedral Singer.*

Allen, Paul Hastings (1883-), American pianist and composer who studied and concertized in Europe for twenty years, finally returning to Boston, Mass., where he teaches composition. His compositions include two symphonies, one of which was awarded the PADEREWSKI prize in 1910; seven grand operas, four of which were performed in Italy; chamber music and choral works.

Allen, Viola (1869-), American actress who made her debut at the Madison Square Theatre, New York, on July 4, 1886, replacing Annie RUSSEL in the title role of *Esmeralda.* Among the famous actors with whom she appeared were John McCULLOUGH, Tomasso SALVINI and Joseph JEFFERSON; from 1893 to 1898 she was a member of the Charles FROHMAN Stock Company at the Empire Theatre, New York. Her career as a star started in 1898 in *The Christian,* followed by *The White Sister, The Daughter of Heaven, Macbeth, The Merry Wives of Windsor* and many other important productions.

Alleyn, Edward (1566-1626), English actor of the Elizabethan era who became a formidable rival of Richard BURBAGE, the great Shakespearean actor, and was also associated with Philip HENSLOWE in the building and operation of several theatres. He appeared in MARLOWE's *Tamburlaine* and *The Jew of Malta;* founded Dulwich College in 1613, and left a considerable fortune from which money was donated for the erection of ten almshouses.

Allgood, Sara (1883-), Irish actress who made her debut on the stage in Dublin as a member of the Irish National Theatre Society in 1904 and has appeared in many of the plays produced at the ABBEY THEATRE by the Society. She has also played with Mrs. Patrick CAMPBELL; with Miss HORNIMAN's repertory company in SHAKESPEARE; in THE BEGGAR'S OPERA and in THE CHOCOLATE SOLDIER. Since 1936 she has played important roles in several films including *The Passing of the Third Floor Back* and *Storm in a Tea Cup; That Hamilton Woman; How Green Was My Valley; This Above All.*

Allibone, Samuel Austin (1816-1889), American author and librarian, originally engaged in business, but who acquired such a profound knowledge of American and English litreature that his *Critical Dictionary of English Literature and British and American Authors* (3 volumes, 1858-71), containing nearly 47,000 entries, is a reference work still highly regarded, two additional volumes having been added in 1891. He compiled two volumes of poetical quotations, and was librarian of the Lenox Library, New York, from 1879 to 1888.

Alliteration, in rhetoric the beginning of two or more consecutive words with the same sound; the following Shakespearean line is an excellent example: *Full fathom five thy father lies.* Its use was not unusual with classic writers such as CICERO and LUCRETIUS; examples are to be found in POPE, GRAY, COLERIDGE and others.

Allori, Agnola di Cosima, see **Bronzino, Il**

Allori, Alessandro (1535-1607), Italian painter of the Florentine school, also known as Alessandro Bronzino, due to the fact that Il BRONZINO was his foster father and teacher. Allori was a great admirer of MICHELANGELO, copying and often exaggerating the master's style. He painted portraits of many Florentine notables; also pictures and murals for churches and public buildings.

Allori, Cristofani (1577-1621), Italian painter, son of Alessandro ALLORI; he became dissatisfied with his father's instruction, and enrolled himself as a pupil of Gregorio PAGANI, a great Florentine who taught him to unite accurate drawing with rich coloring, the result being that he became one of the greatest artists of his period. Allori's finest works are *Judith and Holofernes, Saint Julian* and *The Sacrifice of Isaac.*

Allston, Washington (1779-1843), American painter and poet, a pupil of Edward Green MALBONE and Charles FRASER in America, and of Benjamin WEST in London. Later he studied in Paris, Florence and Rome where he became a lifelong friend of Samuel Taylor COLERIDGE, the distinguished English poet. Allston evinced such consummate skill in color and the distribution of light and shade that he has been called the "American Titian." Among his best pictures, many of which are on Biblical subjects, are *Dead Man Revived, St. Peter Liberated by the Angel, Saul and the Witch of Endor;* also the vast *Belshazzar's Feast,* left unfinished. His volume of poetry, *The Sylphs of the Seasons and other Poems,* affords evidence of true communion with nature and humanity.

Allward, Walter Seymour (1875-), Canadian sculptor whose remarkable creations are to be seen in England as well as America; they include *Peace* a symbolic figure on the Northwest Rebellion Monument at Queen's Park, Toronto; the great Vimy Ridge memorial in London, and an obelisk at Toronto, seventy feet in height, to honor Canadian soldiers who were killed in the Boer War.

Almanac, a publication, ranging in size from a pamphlet to a book, and originally containing a calendar of the days, weeks and months as well as information regarding the movements of the heavenly bodies. The derivation of the word is uncertain; it was first used by Roger Bacon in 1292, and later by RABELAIS and NOSTRADAMUS, the latter adding political prophecies finally forbidden by French law. Among famous English almanacs were Moore's (1657-1715) and *Poor Robin* (1663-1828): in the United States *Bradford's Almanac* (c.1685) and *Poor Richard's Almanac,* published by Benjamin FRANKLIN (1732-57) and *The Old Farmer's Almanac,* all of which enjoyed enormous sales in their day. The almanacs popular today in the United States are *The World Almanac* (New York), *The Daily News Almanac* (Chicago), and *The Texas Almanac* (Dallas).

Alma-Tadema, Sir Laurence (1836-1912), English painter, born at Donrijp, a Frisian village in The Netherlands, and a pupil of Gustav WAPPERS and Hendrik LEYS. He became a naturalized British subject in 1873, and was knighted by Queen Victoria in 1899. After the success of his first picture, *The Education of the Children of Clovis,* at the Antwerp Exhibition in 1861, he painted a series of pictures, among them *The Death of the Firstborn,* portraying life in ancient Egypt, followed by a similar group picturing scenes and personalities in ancient Greece and Rome of which *Tarquinius Superbus* and *The Wine Shop* are excellent examples. Both series reveal a profound knowledge of archaeology. Alma-Tadema's skill in painting flowers, textile, metals, marbles, and pottery has been highly praised: his wife, Laura Epps, achieved a high reputation as an artist.

Almaviva, Count, the name of the Spanish grandee in BEAUMARCHAIS' comedy and ROSSINI's opera, THE BARBER OF SEVILLE, who succeeds in marrying the lovely Rosina by tricking her guardian, Doctor Bartolo. The role has been essayed by most great Italian and French tenors, but not always with success because of the necessity for a keen sense of humor in portraying it.

Almeida-Garrett, João Baptista de (1799-1854), Portuguese poet, dramatist and statesman. His earliest plays were three classic tragedies: *Lucrecia, Merope,* and *Cato.* These were followed by his finest poem, *Dona Branca,* and new settings of old folk-poems, *Adozinda and Bernal-Francez.* His next step was to revive Portuguese drama with the plays *Auto de Gil Vicente, Alfageme de Santarem,* and *Frei Luiz de Sousa.* His lyrics have been adjudged sincere yet melancholy, and his plays boldly realistic and eloquent from the dramatic point of view.

19

Almeiis, The, a class of Egyptian dancers still existent in Egypt, the Arabian desert, Tunis, Algiers, Tripoli, and Morocco. Their style was the exact opposite of that of the HAWASI DANCERS; the latter strove to express sensual passion whereas the Almeiis dancers attempted classical dances. Lucien Petipa composed a brilliant ballet, based on the dances of the Almeiis, entitled *The Daughter of the Pharaoh.*

Almonry, the name of the chamber where alms are given to the poor at cathedrals, churches and abbeys; the latter usually had separate buildings near the outer gate so that the establishment itself would not be disturbed.

Almquist, Karl Jonas Ludwig (1793-1886), Swedish author who first headed a body of colonists to Wermland, a wild section of Sweden, but became famous through the publication from 1832 to 1835 of a series of novels called *The Book of the Thorn-Rose.* After writing a long succession of poetic, philosophical and educational works which led to his being considered foremost among Swedish authors, he was suddenly accused of murder, and convicted of forgery: he fled to America and his career remains obscure until his return to Germany in 1865.

Alpenhorn, a curved horn, from three to eight feet long and made of wood: used by herdsmen in the Alps to call their cattle with the traditional melody, the *Ranz des vaches.*

Alphabet, in literature the letters that form the elements of written language in order as determined by usage. A series of characters representing syllables is called a *syllabary.* The English alphabet, like most of the alphabets of Europe, is derived from the Latin; the origin of the Latin alphabet is not certain, but it resembles those used in sections of Africa and Southern Asia.

Alsop, Richard (1761-1815), American author and wit; his best-known work is *The Echo* (1807), written in collaboration with Theodore Dwight. He also published a volume of poetry, *American Poems,* in 1793.

Also Sprach Zarathustra, see **Thus Spake Zarathustra.**

Altar, in architecture the platform, consisting of base and pedestal, used in ancient temples to supplicate or sacrifice to the gods, and in Christian churches to offer prayers and celebrate the Holy Communion. Altars have been found in Mesopotamia, Egypt, Palestine, Greece, Rome, and in both North and South America, but the earliest Christian churches were without them until the period of pagan persecution ended. After the 6th century, the presence of two or more altars became a general practice when more than one martyr was buried in a church. Among the finest examples are the altars in the churches of St. Ambrogio (Milan), St. Cecilia (Rome), and in ST. PAUL'S CATHEDRAL, London.

Altarpiece, in painting the name given to the picture placed behind the altar in churches and cathedrals. Very few are found before the Ro-

manesque period; the pictures are painted on stone, ivory, silver or silver gilt, and are usually scenes from the life of Christ and the Virgin. The most remarkable example is the enameled altarpiece of Klosterneuborg, made in 1811 by Nicholas de Verdun, and picturing the life of Christ in fifty-one panels.

Altdorfer, Albrecht (1480-1538), German painter and architect, known as the "Giorgione of the North," and designer of the city of Ratisbon. His works *The Holy Family at the Fountain* and *The Battle of Arbell,* are remarkable for their minute detail and careful attention to the backgrounds. Altdorfer was also a fine engraver on wood and copper, ranking with Albrecht DÜRER.

Althouse, Paul Shearer (1889-), American dramatic tenor, pupil in New York of Percy Rector Stephens and Oscar SAENGER. He made his debut at the Metropolitan Opera House, New York in 1913, creating the role of Dmitri in BORIS GODUNOFF, and appearing there in all the leading tenor roles of Wagerian operas. Althouse was also a member of the Chicago and San Francisco opera companies, and has concertized in the United States, Europe and Australia besides making many radio appearances.

Altichiero da Zevio (c.1330-c.1395), Italian painter, founder of the VERONESE school, and strongly influenced by GIOTTO. Examples of his frescoes are to be found in several churches at Padua and Verona; he was a great lover of detail and brilliant coloring, in these respects becoming a forerunner of Jacopo BELLINI and Vittore CARPACCIO.

Altman, Benjamin (1840-1913), American merchant and art collector who assembled the greatest number of REMBRANDT'S works ever brought together in a private collection which also contained fine works by VELASQUEZ, VAN DYCK, CUYP, RUYSDAEL, Fra ANGELICO, BOTTICELLI, MANTEGNA, VERMEER and DÜRER; it was bequeathed to the Metropolitan Museum of Art, New York.

Alto, in music (*a*) the name of the deeper of the two principal divisions of boys' or women's voices, also called *contralto;* (*b*) a name for the VIOLA.

Alto-relievo, in architecture the term applied to sculpture in high relief, projecting more than one-half the outline of the principal figures from the plane to which it is attached: the antithesis of BASSO-RELIEVO.

Altschuler, Modest (1873-), Russian violoncellist and conductor; pupil of Fitzenhagen in violoncello and Arensky in composition. After coming to New York, he organized the Russian Symphony Orchestra in 1904 for the purpose of introducing the works of IPPOLITOW-IWANOW, LIADOFF, RACHMANINOFF, SCRIABIN and other Russian composers. The regular seasons continued until 1919, and the orchestra made several transcontinental tours with great success. Many of the finest Russian works were given first performances in the United States under Altschuler's leadership.

Alvarez, stage name of **Albert Raymond Gourron** (1861-1933), dramatic tenor who studied in Paris under Albert de Martini and made his debut at L'Opéra, Paris, in GOUNOD'S ROMEO AND JULIET in 1892: seven years later he made his debut in the same opera at the METROPOLITAN OPERA HOUSE, New York, remaining for several seasons beside appearing at the MANHATTAN OPERA HOUSE, and at COVENT GARDEN, London.

Alvarez, José (1768-1827), Spanish sculptor, pupil of the French sculptor, Verdiguier, at Cordova; a statue, GANYMEDE, executed in Paris while studying there under a grant from Charles IV of Spain, and now in the Prada at Madrid, placed him in the foremost rank of Spanish sculptors. His greatest work was a group, *Antilochus and Memnon* commissioned by Ferdinand VII. Alvarez' son, known as **Don José Alvarez y Bougel** (1805-1829), also a fine sculptor and painter, died before his powers had the opportunity to mature.

Alvarez-Quintero, Serafin (1871-) and **Joaquin** (1873), Spanish dramatists and brothers who, since the production in 1890 of a jointly written farce, *Fencing and Love,* have collaborated in many successful comedies of witty and brilliant character, the result being that they were admitted to the Spanish Academy in 1922. Several of their plays, which in some respects resemble those of Sir James BARRIE, have been translated and produced in both England and the United States; among them *Women Have Their Way, The Lady from Alfaqueque, A Hundred Years Old,* and *Fortunato.*

Alvary, Max (1858-1898), German dramatic tenor who was a son of Andreas ACHENBACH, a famous painter. After studying with Julius Stockhausen and Francesco LAMPERTI he made his debut at Weimar; after singing at Munich he appeared in TRISTAN AND ISOLDE at BAYREUTH in 1891, and in SIEGFRIED at COVENT GARDEN, London, in 1892. His debut at the METROPOLITAN OPERA HOUSE, New York, took place in 1885 as Don José in a German version of CARMEN with Lilli LEHMANN as Carmen; he sang Wagnerian roles there until 1896.

Alverdes, Paul (1897-), German novelist educated at Jena and Munich Universities; his novels, *The Whistlers' Room* (1929), *Reinhold: or The Transformed,* and *Changed Man* are published in English.

Amadeo, Giovanni Antonio (c.1447-1522), Italian architect and sculptor who was appointed chief architect of the Certosa at Pavia in 1490, and made a new design for the façade which was carried out by his successors. He also built the cupola of the Milan Cathedral, and is considered the finest of the Lombard sculptors.

Amadis of Gaul, a celebrated romance of chivalry claimed by both Spanish and Portuguese authorities, and probably written in the 14th century. Its popularity after being translated into French continued for more than one hundred years until the appearance of CERVANTES' DON QUIXOTE. Jean Baptiste LULLY and Johann Christian BACH composed operas with librettos based on the romance, both of which achieved signal success because the French and Italian people regarded the hero, Amadis, as a model of chivalric devotion to his beloved.

Amalie, Marie Frederike Auguste (1794-1870), German dramatist who wrote under the pen name "Amalie Heiter." She was Duchess of Saxony, and sister of King John of Saxony. Among her comedies, which are simple in conception, but well adapted for the theatre, are *The Uncle, The Prince's Fiancée,* and *The Young Lady From the Country.*

Amaryllis, (*a*) in literature the name of a country maiden, and much used in ancient pastoral poetry: (*b*) in music the title of an air supposed to have been written by Louis XIII of France, and arranged by Henri Ghys.

Amateis, Louis (1855-1913), Italian sculptor and architect who studied at the Royal Academy, Turin, and won a commission for the decoration of the Palace of Fine Arts in that city. He came to the United States in 1884, became an American citizen, and designed the brass doors for the Capitol at Washington, D.C. He also founded the School of Architecture and Fine Arts at Columbia University; executed the Alamo monument in Austin, Texas; *El Caney,* a group for the Pan-American Exposition, and several memorials of World War I in American cities.

Amati, a renowned family of violin, viola and violoncello makers founded by **Andrea Amati** (c.1535-c.1581). His violins are golden brown in color and sell today for from $3000.00 to $5000.00. His sons, **Antonio Amati** (c.1555-c.1630) and **Girolamo Amati** (1556-1630) worked together, introducing violins of a larger model which bring from $4000.00 to $7500.00 in the present market. Girolamo's son, **Nicoló Amati** (1596-1684), is considered the greatest member of the family; his violins are fashioned in both the small and large models, and are valued at from $3000.00 to $7500.00.

Amato, Pasquale (1878-1942), Italian operatic baritone who made his debut in 1900 at Naples in LA TRAVIATA, and after singing in Europe and Great Britain, made his first American appearance in 1908 at the METROPOLITAN OPERA HOUSE, New York, in the same opera. He remained there until 1921, retiring in order to devote himself to teaching, coaching and appearing in radio broadcasting of standard operas. Amato was a distinct asset to opera at the Metropolitan, creating many important roles such as Jack Rance in THE GIRL OF THE GOLDEN WEST and PRINCE IGOR in Borodin's opera of the same title.

Amaya, Carmen, contemporary Spanish flamenco dancer who appeared at the Barcelona Exposition at seven, and danced with Raquel Meller when she was eight years old. After touring Europe and appearing at the Folies Bergére, Paris, she emigrated to Buenos Aires, Argentina, in 1936, and appeared there with such great success that the Amaya Theatre was built for her, and her artistry was the subject of favorable comment by Arturo TOSCANINI and Leopold STOKOWSKI. Her debut in New York in 1941 was extraordinarily successful, the dance critics calling her "the human Vesuvius." Her dancing partner, Antonio Triana, is also a distinguished virtuoso highly praised by Manuel de FALLA for his dancing in the latter's ballet, EL AMOR BRUJO.

Amazons, in Greek mythology a nation of female warriors who lived in Pontus, a region in Asia Minor; no men were allowed in their domains, and their leader, Penthesilea, was killed by ACHILLES at TROY when the Amazons fought against the Greeks. Bohemia is said to have had a band of Amazons who warred against the reigning Duke in the 8th century, and Orellana, a Spanish explorer, claimed that he was obliged to fight a band of women in South America. The name is used to describe any woman displaying masculine or belligerent characteristics.

Amber, a substance of vegetable origin washed up by the ocean in several parts of the world, but found in large quantities in the Baltic Sea. A varnish is made from it which was successfully used by Jan Van EYCK and many of the early Flemish painters; it is still employed for the same purpose. The term is also applied to a certain warm tone, ranging from a pale yellow to a light carmine, found in paintings.

Ambrogio Stefani da Fossano, see **Borgognone, Ambrogio.**

Ambulatory, see **Cloister.**

Ameche, Don, contemporary American stage, screen and radio actor who first won distinction in a program known as *Empire Builders;* he has appeared in many notable films such as *In Old Chicago; Alexander's Ragtime Band; The Three Musketeers; The Story of Alexander Graham Bell; Swanee River; Lillian Russell; Four Sons; The Magnificent Dope.*

America, a patriotic hymn of the United States, beginning with the lines "My Country, 'tis of Thee." The verses were written in 1832 by Samuel Francis Smith after looking through a book of German songs for a suitable melody. The tune he selected was one already used by Germany and Switzerland for a patriotic song; also by the British for "God Save the King." Henry CAREY, an English composer, claimed credit for the air, but his contention has been often disputed.

American Academy of Arts and Letters, a branch of the National Institute of Arts and Letters, founded in 1904 and limited to fifty members. Its purpose is to administrate the Evangeline Wilbour Blackfield Foundation, established "to assist the Academy to determine its duty regarding both the preservation of the English language in its beauty and integrity, and its cautious enrichment by such terms as grow out of modern conditions." Among its representative members, both living and dead, may be mentioned Nicholas Murray Butler, William Dean HOWELLS, Booth TARKINGTON, Eugene O'NEILL, Deems TAYLOR and George Pierce BAKER.

American Ballet, School of, see **Kirstein, Lincoln Edward.**

American Copyright, see **Copyright.**

American Laboratory Theatre, an experimental group headed by Richard BOLESLAWSKI, Polish stage and screen director, and Maria OUSPENSKAYA, distinguished stage and screen actress; its productions include plays by SHAKESPEARE, Thornton WILDER, Jules ROMAINS, Miriam STOCKTON, Lynn RIGGS, Knut HAMSUN, Arthur SCHNITZLER and Amelie Rives TROUBETZKY.

American Library Association. An organization founded at Chicago, Ill., in 1876 as a result of the Centennial Exhibition in Philadelphia; among its publications are a Monthly Bulletin, a Handbook, and The American Library Association Catalog which was issued first in 1893. A revised edition appeared in 1926, and supplements are issued regularly which add to the annotated basic list of 10,000 books. Catalogs are also published in special fields, and the organization is affiliated with many other educational enterprises.

American Opera Company, an organization formed in 1885 by Mrs. Jeannette THURBER to present grand opera in English with American singers at the ACADEMY OF MUSIC, NEW YORK. The first of 66 performances was given on Jan. 4, 1886, with Theodore THOMAS as artistic director, and an orchestra recruited from the NEW YORK PHILHARMONIC-SYMPHONY ORCHESTRA. The financial backing proved inadequate, and the organization was succeeded by the NATIONAL OPERA COMPANY. Another company with this name functioned under the direction of Vladimir ROSING in 1927-29, sponsored by the American Society for Opera in English; its roster of singers was drawn largely from graduate students of the EASTMAN SCHOOL OF MUSIC, Rochester, N. Y.

"American" Quartet, Op. 96 (Antonin Dvořák), a string quartet composed by Antonin DVORAK in 1893 during his vacation in Spillville, Ia., where he was very much at home in a Bohemian colony. The composer denied emphatically that the themes for this work were founded directly on traditional American negro tunes, and declared that he merely embodied the idioms of such songs in his own themes. Recordings are available by the BUDAPEST QUARTET (Victor) and the ROTH QUARTET (Columbia).

American Society of Ancient Instruments, The, a chamber music ensemble founded at Philadelphia in 1927 by Ben Stad, a Dutch violinist, to present 17th and 18th century ensemble music using the instruments for which it was actually composed. The instruments used as the QUINTON (a viol with five strings), the VIOLA DA GAMBA, the bass VIOL and the HARPSICHORD. Many Victor recordings have been made by the Society of works by PURCELL, SACCHINI, BYRD, HANDEL and Karl Philipp Emanuel BACH: the ensemble has also given many recitals in the United States.

American Society of Composers, Authors and Publishers (usually referred to as ASCAP), a non-profit association of composers, authors and publishers, with a membership of 1500 in the United States, and 50,000 in twenty similar foreign organizations affiliated with it. Founded with Victor

HERBERT as the leading spirit in 1914, its purpose is to reform copyright laws in respect to musical and literary property at home as well as abroad, to arbitrate disputes, to prosecute infringements and to collect phonograph and radio royalties.

Ames, Ezra (1768-1836), American portrait painter whose likeness of George Washington in the capitol at Albany, N. Y., received high praise; he also painted Governor George Clinton and many other New York state legislators.

Ames, Joseph Alexander (1816-1872), American portrait painter who studied with Washington ALLSTON, and made excellent likenesses of Ralph Waldo EMERSON, Pope Pius IX, William H. Prescott (the historian), Rufus Choate and Daniel WEBSTER: his *Death of Webster* is regarded as his finest work.

Ames, Winthrop (1871-1937), American theatrical producer, first interested in art, particularly architecture. After directing the Castle Square Theatre, Boston, for several years, he assumed the management in 1908 of the New Theatre, New York, a commendable enterprise that failed because the size of the auditorium failed to establish the proper degree of intimacy between actors and audience. Nevertheless excellent productions were made of several of SHAKESPEARE's plays and numerous modern American and English dramas. Ames also managed the Little Theatre where sumptuous productions of an intimate character were made of Gilbert and Sullivan's IOLANTHE, The PIRATES OF PENZANCE and The MIKADO from 1925 to 1927.

Amfitheatroff, Daniele (1901-), Russian conductor and composer, pupil of Scherbatcheff and Wihtol at Petrograd. He became a naturalized Italian, and assistant conductor to Bernardo MOLINARI with the Augusteo Symphony Orchestra at Rome from 1924-29; in 1938 he became conductor of the MINNEAPOLIS SYMPHONY ORCHESTRA. He has written an *American Panorama* for orchestra, embodying characteristic American and Hawaiian rhythms as well as other symphonic and chamber music works.

Amfortas, the son of Titurel, ruler of the Kingdom of the GRAIL in Richard Wagner's sacred festival drama, PARSIFAL; he succumbs to the wiles of KUNDRY, and is wounded with the sacred spear by the sorcerer, Klingsor.

Amicis, Edmondo de (1846-1908), Italian novelist, traveler and soldier who abandoned military life for a literary career. His works include several brilliant volumes of travel in Spain, England, Turkey and Africa which have been translated into several languages, and the novels *The College Friends, The Paternal Home,* and *Cuore* (Heart): the latter was published in English with the title, "The Heart of a Schoolboy."

Amiel, Henri Frederic (1821-1881), Swiss critic, philosopher and poet; a student in German universities and professor of philosophy at the Geneva Academy. His fame rests on the *Journal Intime* (1883), in which he displays remarkable

powers of self-examination; Matthew ARNOLD was one of his most enthusiastic admirers.

Ammanati, Bartolommeo (1511-1592), Italian architect and sculptor, pupil of Bartolommeo Bandinelli at Florence, Jacopo SANSOVINO at Padua and a follower of MICHELANGELO. He built many residences and palaces in Florence, including the Vitali, Pucci and Guigni Palaces, and the court façade for the Pitti Palace; a colossal statue of HERCULES at Padua; the magnificent Santa Trinita bridge over the Arno, and several fountains at Florence.

Ammers-Kuller, Jo van (1884-), Dutch author and dramatist; her novels include *The House of Joy* (1922) and *The Rebel Generation,* the latter enormously successful both as a book and as a play in Holland. A visit to the United States resulted in *Tantalus;* another novel, *No Surrender,* concerns itself with the suffragette movement in England. All the above are available in English translations.

Ammon or **Amon,** one of the ancient Egyptian gods, represented in various forms as a man, a ram or a man with a ram's head. He is identified with the Greek ZEUS and the Roman JUPITER; his principal temple was on an oasis in the Libyan desert at a considerable distance from Memphis, and for a time the high priest exerted political powers exceeding that of the PHARAOH.

Amneris, daughter of the king of Egypt and rival of Aïda, the daughter of the Ethiopian king, Amonasro, for the love of Rhadames, captain of the guard, in Giuseppe VERDI's opera AÏDA.

Amor brujo, El, a ballet in one act by G. Martinez Sierra, music by Manuel de FALLA, first produced in 1915 at Madrid. The plot concerns itself with the scheming of a young lover, Carmelo, to induce his sweetheart, Candelas, to cease her grieving for her dead fiance, and accept his devotion.

Amore dei tre re, L', see **Love of Three Kings, The.**

Amos and Andy, a team of radio and screen comedians composed of Freeman F. Gosden (Amos) and Charles J. Correll (Andy). Both had some amateur stage experience before combining their exceptional abilities as blackface comedians in a radio dialogue act called "Sam 'n' Henry" in 1926. In 1928 the name of the act was changed to "Amos and Andy"; it was broadcast continuously until February, 1943. The team has also appeared on the screen in *Check and Double Check* and *The Big Broadcast of 1936.*

Amour des trois oranges, L', see **Love for Three Oranges, The.**

Amphion, in Greek mythology, a son of ZEUS and Antiope who became a great singer and performer on the lyre. With his twin brother, Zethus, he fortified the city of THEBES with a wall of huge stone blocks which fell into place of themselves at the sound of his lyre. Amphion killed himself after the death of his wife, NIOBE.

Amphitheatre, the name used in ancient Greece and Rome to designate a large building, with seats on all sides, in which gladiatorial contests were held. The earliest building of the kind still standing was built at POMPEII about 80 B.C., and the first at Rome in 59 B.C.; these were completely outshadowed by the Amphitheatrum Flavium, built at Rome in A.D. 80 and referred to since the 8th century as the COLISEUM. Later amphitheatres became numerous in both Greece, Italy and even in France.

Amphitryon, in Greek mythology king of THEBES, and husband of Alcmene; she became the mother of HERCULES by JUPITER who deceived her by assuming the form of Amphitryon. The Roman dramatist, PLAUTUS, and the French playwright, MOLIÉRE, wrote comedies based on this story.

Amphora, a terra-cotta vase, utilized undecorated by the Greeks and Romans for storing wine and grain, and when decorated with the figures of gods and scenes of various kinds, used as prizes in athletic and musical contests. Much information regarding the everyday life of the ancients has been gleaned from vases of this character.

Amsler, Samuel (1791-1849), Swiss engraver, pupil of Karl Ernst Hess and Johan Heinrich Lips, succeeding the former as professor of copper engraving at the Munich Academy. He was a great admirer of RAPHAEL, reproducing many of his works with remarkable fidelity. He spent six years on reproducing Johann Friedrich Overbeck's *Union Between Religion and the Arts.*

Amyot, Jacques (1513-1593), French scholar noted for his translations of Greek authors, including Heliodorus, Longinus and PLUTARCH. His style was so elegantly fluent and full of color that the translations are regarded as classics in themselves. Pierre CORNEILLE used his rendering of *Plutarch's Lives* as the source of his tragedies; SHAKESPEARE also consulted the English translation by Sir Thomas North.

Anabasis, a Greek word meaning "march up country," used by Xenophon as the title to his account of one of the most brilliant military exploits of history: the masterly retreat of the Ten Thousand, a Greek mercenary band, after the battle of Cunaxa. Their path led them up the Tigris through Armenia, and on through the mountains, in the freezing cold of December, down to the sea at Trapezus (Trebizond) and from there back to their homeland, a distance of more than 2000 miles. The Anabasis has furnished subject matter, through its vivid descriptions, for painters and sculptors of all ages.

Anachronism, any representation of an event or object in painting, sculpture, literature or drama, either pictorially or in words, in which the order of time is altered. In medieval paintings of scenes from the BIBLE, the architecture, clothing and other details were often pictured as of the artist's period rather than of the events themselves.

Anacreon (c.560 B.C.-c.478 B.C.), Greek lyric poet about whom little is known except that, on

his own admission, he fled from Teos, an Ionian city in Asia Minor, when Cyrus the Great was besieging Greek cities, and finally settled in Samos. He was then brought to Athens by Hipparchus; there he met the poet SIMONIDES and other brilliant literary men, and finally returned to Teos where he died. Anacreon wrote graceful and elegant verses extolling the virtues of love and wine; imitations at a later date by the English poets COWLEY, PHILLIPS and MOORE were known as *Anacreontics.* Only fragments remain of Anacreon's other poems; a marble statue, found in 1835 and now in the Villa Borghese, is said to be a likeness.

Anacreon, an opera-ballet by Luigi CHERUBINI in two acts, libretto by Mendouze; first performed at L'Opéra, Paris, in 1803, but only partially successful because of its inane libretto. The overture only has survived; it is frequently heard on concert programs, the composer making excellent use of the French horn.

Anacreontic Society, an aristocratic musical club founded at London, England, by wealthy amateurs in 1766; meetings were held at the Crown and Anchor Tavern in the Strand where Joseph HAYDN was an occasional visitor. The official song of the club, *To Anacreon in Heaven,* is interesting because the music, written by John Stafford SMITH, is that used for the American national hymn, *The Star Spangled Banner,* for which the words were written by Francis Scott KEY.

Anacreontics, see **Anacreon.**

Analysis, in music the process of reducing a musical composition into its individual parts or elements in respect to form, thematic content and harmonic structure.

Analytical Notes, Musical, see **Program Notes, Musical.**

Anapest, in poetry (*1*) a metrical foot consisting of three syllables, the first two short and the third long; (*2*) a verse made up either entirely or mainly of such measures.

Anatomy, the study of human organisms, certain branches of which are vitally important to painters and sculptors desiring to portray the human body; they comprise the study of bones, and the study of muscles.

Anatomy of Melancholy, see **Burton, Robert.**

Ancelot, Jacques Arsène François (1794-1854), French dramatist, poet and novelist whose five-act tragedy, Louis IX, was produced in 1819 at the Theatre Français in Paris with such great success that it brought him a pension of 2000 francs from Louis XVIII. Several more plays, *Frisque, Olga, Elizabeth d'Angleterre* and *Maria Padilla* were well received; also a poem, *Marie de Brabant,* and a four-volume novel, *L'Homme du mond,* also dramatized with success.

Ancient Mariner, The, a poem by Samuel Taylor COLERIDGE, the result of his friendship with William WORDSWORTH. A joint book of poetry was projected for which Wordsworth was to create verses on commonplace subjects, and Coleridge to handle the supernatural. The volume was published in 1798, and *The Ancient Mariner* was included; the shooting of the ALBATROSS originated with Wordsworth who got the idea from George Shelvocke's *Voyage,* published in 1726.

Ancona, Alessandro d' (1835-1914), Italian critic and man of letters whose greatest contribution to the world's literature was *Manuale della letteratura,* a comprehensive anthology of Italian literature with illuminating critical notes on the authors.

Andante, in music a tempo mark indicating a moderately slow, or faster than ADAGIO and slower than ALLEGRETTO; the qualifying words SOSTENUTO or CANTABILE are frequently used, the first indicating "tranquilly" and the second "smoothly flowing."

Andersen, Hans Christian (1805-1875), Danish novelist, poet and writer of fairy stories; his imaginative talents first displayed themselves when, as a lad of ten, he built a toy theatre with puppet actors to produce plays by Ludwig HOLBERG and SHAKESPEARE. His first successful novel was published in 1835; also the initial volume of the immortal *Fairy Tales* which, as often happens with literary masterpieces, sold slowly at first, but have long since passed the multi-million mark after being translated into at least twenty languages. Several more volumes of fairy tales appeared between 1836 and 1872; also books of poetry and travel.

Anderson, Alexander (1775-1870), American engraver known as the father of wood engraving in the United States; his works included hundreds of book illustrations in addition to plates for Bell's *Anatomy,* WEBSTER'S *Elementary Spelling Book,* and HOLBEIN'S *Dance of Death* issued with the title "Emblem's of Mortality."

Anderson, John Hargis (1896-1943), American dramatic critic, dramatist and author; graduate of the University of Virginia, critic of the New York *Evening Post* from 1924 to 1928, and of the New York *Journal* (now the New York *Journal-American*) from 1928 to 1937. He is the author of *Box Office* (1929) and *The American Theatre,* and has adapted two plays, *The Inspector General* and *The Fatal Alibi.*

Anderson, John Murray (1886-), Canadian stage and screen director; producer of the first Greenwich Follies in 1919 and several succeeding versions. He has directed important productions at the London Hippodrome and Alhambra, the New York Hippodrome, Winter Garden and RADIO CITY MUSIC HALL. He has also directed many important films including Paul WHITEMAN'S *King of Jazz,* also staging the pageants for the Fort Worth (Texas) Centennial and the Cleveland (Ohio) Aquacade.

Anderson, Judith (1898-), Australian-American actress who made her first appearance in *A Royal Divorce* at Sydney, Australia, in 1915, and her New York debut with a stock company in 1918. She has played stellar roles in *Dear Brutus, Cobra, Strange Interlude, Mourning Becomes Electra, The Three Sisters,* and *The Old Maid,* also appearing in several motion pictures.

Anderson, Marian (1908-), American negro contralto, pupil of Giuseppe Boghetti; in 1925 she made her debut with the New York Philharmonic-Symphony Orchestra at the LEWISOHN STADIUM, New York, after winning a competition against 300 competitors. After giving a recital at Town Hall, New York, she studied in Europe, and later toured Germany, Scandinavia, France, Belgium, Holland, Italy, Russia and South America, making her formal debut in recital at CARNEGIE HALL, New York, in 1935. Since then she has toured the United States with great success, also making recordings and radio appearances.

Anderson, Mary Antoinette (1859-1940), American actress who studied for the stage when encouraged by Charlotte CUSHMAN, and made her debut in *Romeo and Juliet* at Louisville, Ky., in 1875. This was followed by two years of touring with a stock company, and by a formal debut in 1877 at the Fifth Avenue Theatre, New York in *The Lady of Lyons.* She appeared at the Lyceum Theatre, London, in 1883, and as Rosalind in *As You Like It* at the opening of the Shakespeare Memorial Theatre at STRATFORD-ON-AVON. Her beauty as well as her histrionic ability accounted for her success. Miss Anderson retired in 1896 after her marriage to Antonio de Navarro; she published an autobiography, *A Few Memories,* and collaborated with Robert HICHENS in the dramatization of his novel, *The Garden of Allah.*

Anderson, Maxwell (1888-), American dramatist, a graduate of the University of North Dakota and Stanford University, Calif. After several years in journalism, his first great success was *What Price Glory* (1924) written in collaboration with Laurence STALLINGS, followed by *Saturday's Children; Elizabeth the Queen; Both Your Houses,* a Pulitzer Prize play; *Mary of Scotland; Winterset; High Tor; Knickerbocker Holiday; Eve of St. Mark.* Anderson has also prepared the screen versions of several of his plays, and also of "All Quiet on the Western Front," "Rain," and "Death Takes a Holiday."

Anderson, Sherwood (1876-1941), American novelist and dramatist who, after serving in the Spanish American War and engaging in business, published his first novel, *Windy McPherson's Son,* in 1916, followed by *Marching Men; Mid-American Chants; Winesburg, Ohio; Dark Laughter; Beyond Desire; Triumph of the Egg:* also dramatizations of the last-named and of *Winesburg, Ohio.* He edited two weekly newspapers, one Republican and the other Democratic, in Marion, Va.

Andrea Chenier, grand opera in four acts: libretto by Luigi Illica and music by Umberto GIORDANO; first produced at Milan in 1896, and at the ACADEMY OF MUSIC, NEW YORK, during the same year. The opera dramatizes the career of André Marie CHENIER, a French poet guillotined as a royalist sympathizer in 1794. The story in brief is: Chenier has written a poem denouncing the treatment of the poor by the rich, but because his beloved, Madeleine de Coignay, is one of the aristocracy, he is led to the guillotine voluntarily accompanied by Madeleine, parallelling the supreme sacrifice of the heroine in Verdi's AIDA.

Andreani, Andrea (1540-1623), Italian engraver on wood in CHIAROSCURO; his engravings are chiefly copies of RAPHAEL, TITIAN, DURER, and MANTEGNA, and are extremely scarce. The treatment of light and shade surpass the effects created by any of his contemporaries or predecessors.

Andreini, Francesco (1548-1624), Italian actor and writer of the scenarios from which strolling actors in the 16th and 17th centuries improvised their lines. He joined the GELOSI, (Zealous Players) a celebrated Italian troupe, and appeared in dashing military roles with great success, even being summoned to Paris by Henry IV of France to entertain his bride, Marie de' MEDICI.

Andreini, Isabel (1562-1604), Italian actress, poet, and wife of Francesco ANDREINI. She was distinguished not only by her acting, but for her irreproachable character, and regarded as the first notable actress on the stage in Europe. She wrote a volume of sonnets and a pastoral, *Myrtila*. Her son, **Giambattista** or **Giovanni Andreini** (1578-1650), was a popular comedian. He founded a troupe called the *Fidele*, and wrote several fantastic plays; one of them, *L'Adamo* (Adam) according to the Italian belief, was the basis of MILTON'S "PARADISE LOST," the English poet having seen the play while traveling in Italy.

Andrews, Mary Raymond Shipman (1865?-1936), American novelist and short story writer; her works include *The Perfect Tribute* (1906); *The Enchanted Forest; The Lifted Bondage; The Eternal Masculine; The Eternal Feminine; A Lost Commander; Florence Nightingale.*

Andreyanova, Elena (1819-1857), Russian ballerina, pupil of Carlo BLASIS, and one of the first Russian dancers of international reputation. She was in a ballet troupe with Marie TAGLIONI in 1839, and performed the title role in GISELLE at St. Petersburg in 1842. After three years of success in that city she appeared in the principal cities of Europe, dancing with Fanny ELSSLER and Carlotta GRISI, receiving the highest praise for her abilities as a character dancer and mime.

Andreyev, Leonid Nikolaievitch (1870-1919), Russian novelist, short story writer and dramatist. Born in poverty and imbued with a hopeless attitude toward life, he attempted suicide three times, but after the success of his first short story, *They Lived* (1889), he achieved considerable popularity. He was intensely patriotic during World War I, and anti-Bolshevist in 1918; his last work *S.O.S.*, published in Finland, was directed against the Red Terror. His finest plays are *He Who Gets Slapped*, produced by the THEATRE GUILD in New York and also filmed; *Anathema; The Waltz of the Dogs; Samson in Chains.*

Andrieux, François Guillaume Jean Stanislas (1759-1833), French poet and dramatist; his plays

in verse, chiefly comedies of intrigue and ranking next to those of BEAUMARCHAIS, include *Les Étourdis; Le Trésor; Molière avec ses amis; La Comédienne.* He also wrote a tragedy, *Lucius Junius Brutus,* and some excellent fables.

Androclus or **Androcles,** in Roman legend a runaway slave who extracted a thorn from a lion's paw; years later, when doomed to die in the arena, the same lion, chosen to destroy him, recognized his benefactor, and by fawning upon instead of rending him, procured his freedom from the wonder-struck Roman emperor. George Bernard SHAW wrote a play, *Androcles and the Lion,* based on the legend.

Andromache, in Greek mythology the wife of HECTOR, a hero of the siege of TROY who was slain by ACHILLES. She was given as a prize to Hector's son, Pyrrhus; when he was slain at Delphi, she returned to Asia Minor with her youngest son, Pergamus, who founded the city bearing his name. Andromache, according to HOMER, was distinguished for her affectionate nature, and the fortitude with which she endured her misfortunes.

Andromeda, in Greek mythology the daughter of Cassiopeia, Queen of the Ethiopians, who declared her beauty equal to that of the NEREIDS, thereby offending POSEIDON who sent a sea monster to destroy both man and beast throughout the land. The oracle of AMMON decreed that Andromeda, the queen's daughter, must be chained to a rock as a sacrifice to the monster. She was rescued by PERSEUS who married her, and founded the family of the Perseidae.

Androuet du Cerceau, a 16th and 17th century family of French architects founded by **Jacques Androuet** (c.1510-c.1580) who was architect to the king of France; two volumes of his engravings contain valuable information regarding buildings, palaces and chateaux at PARIS and ROME. His sons, **Baptiste Androuet** (1544-1590), who built the Pont Neuf at Paris, and **Jacques II Androuet** (?-1614), who worked on the TUILERIES, labored together at the LOUVRE. **Jean Androuet** (?-1650), a grandson, built the Hotel de Sully and part of the Pont du Change at Paris; there were several more distinguished architects in the family before the close of the 17th century.

Angel, Heather (1909-), English stage and screen actress who made her first appearance at the Old Vic, London, in 1926, later appearing in Shakespearean plays, melodramas and comedies. She began her screen career in 1930, and is well-known to American audiences by her work in *Berkeley Square, Springtime for Henry, The Three Musketeers, That Hamilton Woman;* also in several *Bull-dog Drummond* and *Charlie Chan* detective films.

Angel, John (1881-), Anglo-American sculptor, graduate of the Albert Memorial and the Lambeth Art Schools, London. After working and studying in Athens and Rome, he exhibited at the Royal Academy in 1927; among his works are memorials of World War I in England; statuary on the Cathedral of St. John the Divine,

New York; statuary in St. Patrick's Cathedral, New York; statues of Alexander Hamilton and William M. Rice as well as many groups on religious subjects in American churches.

Angelico, Fra Giovanni da Fiesole, also known as **Guido di Pietro da Mugello** (1387-1455), Italian fresco, panel and miniature painter of whom little is known until he became a Dominican friar. His first works, a *Madonna and the Saints* and an *Annunciation,* were painted at Cortona in 1408; some of his finest frescoes and altarpieces were created in churches and convents at Fiesole in 1418 and the ensuing years before the monks removed to the Cloister of San Marco at Florence in 1436. Here he painted *Christ as a Pilgrim* and a magnificent *Crucifixion,* picturing the Virgin Mary on one side and the several founders of monastic orders on the other. These were for the Church of San Marco; on an upper floor he painted more than forty frescoes portraying scenes from the life of Christ. Ten years later Angelico went to Rome for the decoration of the Chapel of the Sacrament which has since been razed; in 1448 he painted a series of frescoes depicting incidents in the lives of Saint Stephen and Saint Lawrence, regarded as his masterpiece. Angelico is considered one of the greatest painters of religious subjects: his paintings are deftly treated as to color, and the figures are idealistically if not realistically impressive. More than two hundred works have been preserved: most of them are to be seen in Florence.

Angels, in theology an order of spiritual beings endowed with immortal life and attendant upon the Deity. In art the conventional representation is in the form of youthful, human figures with wings, the bodies generally draped in white. They have been pictured by artists from the earliest period of painting: their attributes are trumpets and other musical instruments, swords, sceptres, and censers.

Angelus, a daily devotion in the Roman Catholic Church to be said by the laity three times a day: at six in the morning, at noon, and at six in the evening. In some English and European churches the custom still survives of ringing a bell three times at each period. J. F. MILLET's painting, *The Angelus,* is well-known in the art world; Jules MASSENET's "Angelus," one of the movements in his orchestral suite, *Scenes Pittoresques,* is greatly admired in the world of music.

Angerstein, John Julius (1735-1823), English philanthropist and art collector: his collection of fifty paintings by the great masters became the property of the British Government in 1824, and became the nucleus of the NATIONAL GALLERY, LONDON.

Angiolini, Gaspare, 18th century dancer, choreographer, composer, and ballet master. In 1761 he acted as choreographer for GLUCK's ballet, *Don Juan,* produced at the Burgtheater, Vienna: in 1768 he became ballet director at the opera house in Moscow, producing a nationalistic ballet of which he was the composer as well as the choreographer.

Anglin, Margaret (1876-), Canadian-American actress, graduate of the Empire Dramatic School, New York, operated in connection with the EMPIRE THEATRE managed by Charles FROHMAN. Her debut was in *Shenandoah* in 1894: after playing in the companies of James O'NEILL and E. H. SOTHERN, she had her first great success in 1898 with Richard MANSFIELD in *Cyrano de Bergerac.* From 1900 to 1903 she was leading lady with Charles Frohman's Empire Theatre Stock Company in *Mrs. Dane's Defence* and other contemporary plays; co-starred with Henry MILLER in *Camille,* and played the feminine lead in William Vaughan MOODY's *The Great Divide.* One of the most sincere and versatile actresses of the American stage, Miss Anglin appeared up to 1938 in more than 100 plays, including classic Greek drama.

Anguier, Francois (c.1604-1669), French sculptor, pupil of Simon Guillain; his chief works are the monument in Paris to Cardinal de Berulle, founder of the Carmelite order, and the tomb of Henry II of France at Moulins. His brother, **Michel Anguier** (c.1612-1686), also a sculptor, created a marble group, *The Nativity,* at the Church of Val-de-Grace in Paris in addition to decorating the apartment of Anne of Austria in the old. LOUVRE at Paris.

Anguissola, Sofonisba (1528-1625), Italian painter who studied with Bernardino Campi, and later instructed her five sisters, Elena, Minerva, Lucia, Europa and Anna-Maria in the art. Signora Anguissola was an exceedingly attractive woman judged by her self-portrait in the Museum of Naples: she was famous for her portraiture, so much so that she was called to the court of Spain to paint several portraits, but later returned to Italy.

Animato or **Animando** (It.) in music a direction calling for increased animation or liveliness in tempo.

Anisfeld, Boris (1879-), Russian-American artist and scenic designer who studied at the Petrograd Academy of Fine Arts. He came to the United States in 1918, and was naturalized in 1924. His stage works include scenery for the Maryinsky Theatre, Petrograd; the DIAGHILEFF Opera Russe and Ballet Russe, Paris; the METROPOLITAN OPERA COMPANY, New York, and the CHICAGO OPERA COMPANY. Since 1928 he has been professor of painting at the Chicago Art Institute, and has exhibited in large cities: his pictures are in the Brooklyn Museum, N. Y., and many other art galleries throughout the United States.

Anker Larsen, Johannes (1874-), Danish novelist and dramatist who studied theology at the University of Copenhagen, later becoming an actor and finally producer of plays at Copenhagen theatres. His novels, *The Philosopher's Stone* (1924), *Martha and Mary, A Stranger in Paradise,* and *With the Door Open* have been published in English.

Annabella, French stage and screen actress who first played in a stock company at Joinville, France; she appeared in the French films, *Le*

Million and *Fourteenth of July* directed by Rene CLAIR; also in many others produced at Berlin, London, Vienna, and Budapest. She is the wife of Tyrone POWER, and has played in *Suez* and several other American films with him.

Annensky, Innocente Feodorovitch (1855-1890), Russian poet and translator; his works include two volumes of impressionistic verse, *Quiet Songs* (1904) and *The Cypress Chest;* he also made a complete translation of the 19 plays of EURIPIDES which have survived in their entirety.

Annunzio, Gabriele d' (1863-1938), Italian poet, novelist and dramatist; his first work, a volume of poetry, *First Spring,* was published in 1879, and his first novel, *Pleasure,* ten years later. His literary works include the novels, *The Child of Pleasure* and *The Flame of Life,* the latter being the story of his romance with the Italian actress, Eleonora DUSE. Among the best of his plays, which are characterized by the same sensuously romantic sentiment as his novels and poems, are *La Gioconda, The Dead City, Francesca da Rimini, The Martyrdom of St. Sebastian,* and *Fedra.*

Anschütz, Karl (1815-1870), German orchestral and operatic conductor who came to New York in 1857 as director of the Strakosch-Ullmann Opera Company. He formed a company in 1862 to present German opera at Wallack's Theatre, New York: the venture was undeservedly a failure, probably because he had no featured artists but merely fully competent singers. He also conducted the Arion Singing Society in New York for several years.

Ansdell, Richard (1815-1885), English painter of genre pictures, and a follower of LANDSEER: his paintings of animals were extremely popular; among them were *Stag at Bay, The Combat, Battle for the Standard* and *Hunting the Boar.*

Ansky, S. A. (1863-1920), the pen name of Solomon Rappaport, Jewish playwright: his drama *The Dybbuk,* translated by Henry G. Alsberg and Winifred Katzin, was produced with great success at New York in 1926.

Anspacher, Louis Kaufman (1878-), American dramatist and lecturer: graduate of the College of the City of New York and Columbia University, New York. He has lectured extensively for nearly forty years: among his plays may be mentioned a poetical drama, *Tristan and Isolde* (1904); *The Glass House; The Rape of Belgium* (with Max MARCIN); *All the King's Horses; The Achievement of Happiness; They Saw the Light; The Unchastened Woman.*

Antenor, a Greek sculptor of the 6th century B.C.; he was the son of a Greek painter, Eumares, and has the distinction of being the only sculptor of the era of whom an authentic work has been discovered. A votive statue of a woman, inscribed with his name, is now in the ACROPOLIS MUSEUM. Antenor's most important work, a bronze group called *The Tyrannicides,* was removed from ATHENS during the Persian wars by XERXES, but later returned by ALEXANDER THE GREAT: it finally disappeared.

Antheil, George (1900-), American composer of Polish parentage, and a pupil of Constantine von Sternberg and Ernest Bloch. He won a Guggenheim fellowship for study in Europe where his orchestral works were performed and also his opera, *Transatlantique.* An opera, *Helen Retires,* was produced in New York, and American orchestras have played his *Symphony in F* and *Capriccio.* Antheil has also composed chamber music and incidental music for films such as Noel COWARD'S *The Scoundrel* and Cecil de Mille's THE PLAINSMAN.

Anthem, in music a sacred vocal work, founded on words or verses from the BIBLE, sung by a choir with or without ORGAN or other instrumental accompaniment. It originated in the service of the Church of England, and is analogous to the MOTET sung in Roman Catholic and Lutheran services. Many of the great English composers of the 16th to the 18th century, such as TALLIS, BYRD, GIBBONS, and PURCELL, composed anthems, and thousands have been written by modern English and American composers.

Anthology, in literature a collection of poetry, essays or short stories covering either an entire or a certain period. The first great collection of this character was the *Greek Anthology,* started by Meleager of Gadara, a Greek poet, about 60 B.C., and continued by Philippus of Thessalonica. A *Latin Anthology* was compiled by Joseph Scaliger in 1573, and there are many modern anthologies of English poetry by Francis Palgrave (*The Golden Treasury of English Songs and Lyrics*) and Arthur QUILLER-COUCH (*The Oxford Book of English Verse*). There are several anthologies of American poetry such as *Modern American Poetry* (1919), edited by Louis UNTERMEYER.

Anthony, Andrew Varick Stout (1835-1906), American engraver and illustrator of the works of John Greenleaf WHITTIER, Henry W. LONGFELLOW and Nathaniel HAWTHORNE; for many years he wrote a column, *Scraps from an Artist's Note Book,* for Harper's Magazine.

Antigone, in Greek mythology the daughter of OEDIPUS: she accompanied her father into exile after his disgrace and abdication from the throne of Thebes. When her brothers Eteocles and Polynices were killed in the war against Thebes, Antigone was forbidden by Creon, regent of Thebes, to bury Polynices; when she disobeyed his command, she was buried alive. SOPHOCLES' drama, *Antigone,* relates the story.

Antin, Mary (1881-), American author, born in Russia; she came to the United States in 1894 and studied at Columbia University, New York. She is greatly interested in the problem of immigration: her most successful book, *The Promised Land* (1899), and two other volumes, *From Polotzk to Boston* and *They Who Knock at Our Gates,* are on this subject.

Antioch, a city in Syria, founded about 300 B.C., and eventually rivaling even ROME in the splendor of its temples, public buildings, baths and statues. Antioch became the MECCA for the early followers of Jesus who were called "Christians" for the first time there. At its zenith, the city had a population of at least 300,000; at the present time it is about 30,000, and nothing remains of the original architecture except parts of the walls and water system.

Antiphanes (c.408-334 B.C.), Greek dramatist, apparently a foreigner who settled in Athens; he began writing about 387 B.C., and more than two hundred comedies are known by the titles. The fragments preserved in the Athens Museum afford ample evidence of his ability to pen striking sentiments in pithy verse.

Antiphilus, a Greek painter of the 4th century B.C. whose patrons were Philip of Macedon and Ptolemy I. of Egypt. He was a contemporary of APELLES; invented a grotesque figure called *grylli*, a figure part animal, bird, and man, and is said to have been skilled in portraying light and shade.

Antiphony, in music a responsive method of singing, first by two choirs or a divided choir in Roman Catholic church services, and later by both choir and congregation in churches of all denominations.

Antique, in art a term originally restricted to remains of ancient Greek and Roman art such as sculptures, paintings, gems, medals, etc. Pluralized, it now embraces not only objects of art, but furniture, rugs, silver and gold ware, and many other articles connected with home decoration. The United States Treasury Department, in estimating duties, collects a tariff on all articles manufactured after 1700: only those made before that year are classified as antiques. Interesting examples of American antiques may be seen at the Metropolitan Museum of Art, New York and Henry Ford's Museum in Detroit.

Antoine, André (1858-), French actor and theatrical producer; originally an amateur actor, but finally founding the Théâtre Libre at Paris in order to present his original ideas for interpreting dramas dealing with the problems of life. Assisted by noted dramatists such as ZOLA, BRIEUX, CUREL and PORTO-RICHE, his productions attracted such interest that similar theatres were established in Berlin and London. Antoine gave up the direction of the Théâtre Libre in 1894, and associated himself with the Gymnase and Odéon in Paris.

Antoine, Jacques Denis (1733-1801), French architect chosen as a young unknown in competition with established architects to build the Paris Mint (La Monnaie) in 1768. His work was so well received that he was awarded a commission to restore the Palais de Justice which had been damaged by fire; many fine buildings were designed and executed by him including the Chapel of St. Nicholas, the Hotel Jancort and the Hotel de la rue d'Enfer, later occupied by Madame de Chateaubriand.

Antoinette, Marie (1755-1793), queen of France, wife of Louis XVI and distinguished in music by her championship of Christoph Willibald von GLUCK in his memorable struggle for supremacy in French opera with Nicola PICCINNI,

the Italian composer imported by Madame DU BARRY. Gluck's dramatic operas, *Iphigenia in Aulis, Armide* and *Iphigenia in Tauris* finally won a decisive victory over Piccinni's antiquated lyric operas; even Piccinni is said to have admitted their superiority.

Antokolski, Markus (1843-1902), Russian sculptor who became popular through his statues and busts of national heroes, gaining fame in the same manner as the French historical painter, PAUL DELAROCHE. His statue, *Ivan the Terrible*, brought him fame, a life pension and a seat in the Academy: other works include *Jermak, Nestor, Socrates, The Miser, Peter the Great, Spinoza* and *Mephistopheles.* Some authorities pronounce his art academic and without originality; others declare it daringly independent in conception.

Antonella da Messina (c.1430-1493), Italian painter, born in Messina, Sicily; his real name was Antonella di Giovanni degli Antoni. He became interested in painting in oil by the Flemish artist, Jan Van Eyck, and spent some time acquiring the art in The Netherlands. On his return to Italy he introduced the new art, and several painters such as BARTOLOMMEO and Giovanni BELLINI followed his example. Antonella combined the Flemish passion for detail with Italian simplicity and vivid coloring, thereby exercising a powerful and beneficial influence over the artists of his time. There are twenty authenticated pictures by him in existence, the finest of which is the portrait of a nameless man in the Berlin Museum.

Antony, Marc (c.83 B.C.-30 B.C.), Roman consul and general, of interest in this volume because of his eloquent oration at Julius CAESAR's funeral, his hatred and eventual share in the death of CICERO; his infatuation for CLEOPATRA, Queen of Egypt, and tragic suicide. His career in relation to Caesar and Cleopatra has been the source of inspiration for plays by SHAKESPEARE and DRYDEN; operas and ballets by CIMAROSA and many other Italian composers; paintings, sculptures and mural decorations by artists of many nationalities.

Antwerp Cathedral, one of the finest cathedrals in Europe; begun 1352 and finished in 1518. Its tower, 400 feet in height, can be seen from many miles around; the choir was added in 1550, but a second tower, shown in the original plans, has never been added. Three of RUBENS' finest works —*The Descent from the Cross, The Elevation of the Cross* and *The Assumption*—were hung in this cathedral.

Antwerp Museum, also known as the Royal Museum of Fine Arts and located at Antwerp, Belgium. It was erected in 1879 under the direction of the architects, J. J. Winders and Franz van Dyck, and comprises a sculpture gallery; a RUBENS collection of more than 2000 original pictures, engravings, etchings, reproductions and photographs, a VAN DYCK assembly of the same character as the Rubens, and a gallery comprising 800 paintings by the old masters, and 550 paintings by modern and contemporary artists.

Anwari, Auhad-uddin Ali, Persian poet of the 12th century, a favorite of the Sultan Sinjar; it is said that during the siege of the castle of Hazarasp by the Sultan, Anwari carried on a poetical contest with Rashidi, his rival, by means of verses fastened to arrows exchanged by the combatants. His poems both long and short are found in the Diwan, and his chief work, *Tears of Khorassan* has been translated into English by Captain Kirkpatrick of the British army.

Anzengruber, Ludwig (1839-1889), Austrian dramatist, novelist and actor whose first stage success was a drama directed against the clergy, *Der Pfarrer von Kirchfeld* (1870). His plays, in which he displayed a fertile imagination, deal chiefly with Austrian peasant life, and he is considered the only important dramatist of his period. A novel, *Der Schandfleck,* published in 1876 and revised in 1884, was well received, as were also his tales of Austrian country folk entitled *Wolken und Sunn'-schein.*

Apelles, Greek painter of the 4th century, considered the greatest artist of antiquity and probably born at Colophon in 370 B.C. He studied under Ephorus at EPHESUS, with Pamphilus at Sicyon, and became the life-long friend of ALEXANDER THE GREAT whose portrait he painted holding a thunderbolt of Zeus so realistically that the monarch decreed that no other artist should picture him. Among his finest creations were *Alexander on Horseback, Procession of the High Priest of Artemis, Calumny, Heracles* and *Aphrodite Rising from the Waves.* His chief merits were simplicity in design, charm and dignity of expression as well as beauty of line.

Apellicon, famous Athenian book collector of the 1st century B.C. who not only expended large sums on his library, but also purloined important original documents from the archives of Athens and other cities. He owned a remarkable copy of HOMER'S ILIAD, and acquired manuscripts of the works of Aristotle and Theophrastus, including their personal libraries. Apellicon died about 84 B.C., and the Roman dictator, Sulla, removed the library to Rome where the grammarian, Tyrannion, copied the Aristotelian manuscripts from which the philosopher, Andronicus of Rhodes, prepared a new edition.

Aphorism, in literature a word, derived from the Greek, used to describe any general truth conveyed in a short, pithy sentence, and in such a manner that it may readily become unforgettable. The title was first used by Hippocrates, a Greek physician called the "Father of Medicine," in his *Aphorisms* containing terse truths regarding medical matters: the first aphorism reads in part as follows: "Life is short, art is long, opportunity fleeting, experimenting dangerous, reasoning difficult."

Aphrodite, in Greek mythology the goddess of love, beauty, fruitfulness and war; she is said to have been born of the foam of the sea, and is identified with the Semitic goddess ASTARTE and the Roman VENUS. Ancient art portrayed Aphrodite as a goddess in dignified poses, but later artists painted her as a charming woman with languishing eyes and laughing mouth. APELLES pictured her rising from the waves, and there were

several statues; one by PRAXITELES which has disappeared, and four which are extant: the *Venus de Milo* at the Louvre, the *Capitoline Venus* at Rome, the *Medicean Venus* at Florence and the *Venus at the Bath*.in the Vatican at Rome.

Apis, the sacred bull of MEMPHIS, and the most important of all the animals worshiped in Egypt. Each bull was supposed to have been conceived by a ray of light from the celestial sphere, and accordingly provided with elaborate living quarters, mourned at death and buried at great expense. Excavations at Memphis have brought to light the tombs of sixty bulls, each separate from the other, and with its own chapel.

Apocalypse, the name of the last book of the BIBLE, known in English as the *Book of Revelation; the Four Horsemen of the Apocalypse* are the allegorical characters in Revelation VI:1-8. In the Douay version of the Bible, the white horse is ridden by Christ, the red horse by war, the black horse by famine, and the pale horse by pestilence. A novel by the Spanish author, Vicente Blasco IBANEZ entitled "The Four Horsemen of the Apocalypse" was a best seller in many languages.

Apollinaire, Guillaume (1880-1918), French poet, novelist, and essayist who published a mimeographed volume of war poems while serving as an aviator in the French army during World War I. His most popular novel, *The Poet Assassinated,* was published in English in 1923, and some of his poems are included in *The European Caravan* (1931) edited by Samuel Putnam.

Apollo, in Greek mythology the god of manly beauty, youth, music, prophecy, and later identified with *Helios,* the god of light. He was one of the most important of the Olympian divinities, also figuring as the guardian of groves, the protector of cattle and as a god of war in Homer's *Iliad.* He is usually portrayed with the lyre or bow; many animals were sacred to him, and there were no less than seven festivals in his honor. Among the famous statues were the APOLLO BELVEDERE now in the Vatican: *Apollo Musagetes* (Vatican), the *Apollo Sauroctonus* (Villa Albani, Rome) and the *Colossus of Rhodes,* a gigantic statue of him as Helios, the sun-god.

Apollo, Temple of, see **Temple of Apollo (Delphi).**

Apollo Belvedere, famous statue of the Greek god, APOLLO, discovered in the 15th century on the estate of Cardinal Giuliano della Rovere who, when he became Pope Julius II, removed it to the Vatican. The sculptor Montorsoli, pupil of MICHELANGELO, repaired the hands, and the statue is a marble copy of a bronze original, representing Apollo as a naked youth with a garment draped over the right arm, and a shield in his left hand.

Apollodorus, a Greek painter of the Athenian school about 615 B.C., said to have improved the art of perspective, and to have developed CHIAROSCURO. Pliny places three of his pictures: *Odysseus, Priest at His Devotions,* and *Ajax Struck by Lightning* in the Pergamum at Athens.

Apollodorus of Damascus, a distinguished Greek architect who worked in the 2nd century B.C.; in A.D. 104 he built a stone bridge over the Danube and many other public works for the emperor Trajan, including his monument in the centre of the Roman Forum. He was banished and later executed by the Emperor Hadrian for ridiculing the latter's pretensions as an architect.

Apologue, an allegory or fable, usually short, used to inculcate a moral or useful lesson; among the distinguished writers of apologues were AESOP, HORACE, LIVY, LA FONTAINE, GAY, LESSING and LA MOTTE; Jean Jacques ROUSSEAU challenged its usefulness both from the educational and moral viewpoint.

Apology for Poetry, written in 1594 by Sir Philip SIDNEY, and first published separately; in 1598 it appeared in the Countess of Pembroke's *Arcadia* in which its title was "The Defence of Poesie." The word "poetry" is considered in its broadest sense as applicable to any imaginative literary conception, and, while the subject matter has great interest, the work appeals most because of simple, almost musical prose style in which it is conceived.

Appiani, Andrea (1754-1817), Italian fresco and oil painter, considered the best of his period. He chose CORREGGIO as his model, and painted fine frescoes in the Church of Santa Maria and the royal palace at Milan in addition to a portrait of NAPOLEON I, who granted him a pension which was revoked after the latter's abdication. Three oil paintings—*Rinaldo in the Garden of Armida, Olympus,* and *Venus and Love,* are highly regarded. Appiani was known as "the elder" to distinguish him from his grand-nephew, the historical painter, Andrea Appiani (1817-1865).

Appian Way (Via Appia), the most celebrated of the ancient Roman highways, and the first public work of the kind; it was started at Rome in 312 B.C. by Appius Claudius Caecus, and carried to Capua, but did not reach Brundisium (now Brindisi) until 224 B.C. It forms one of the most notable memorials of antiquity for some distance after leaving Rome because of the ruins of fine buildings, temples and tombs; its width of only fifteen feet, according to long, perfectly preserved stretches still in existence, is a little disappointing to the imagination in comparison with the broad highways of modern times.

Apple of discord, in Greek mythology brought by ERIS, the goddess of discord, to the marriage feast of Thetis and Peleus. An inscription on the apple read "for the fairest," and a dispute arose as to whether it should be awarded to APHRODITE, ATHENA or HERA. The Trojan prince, PARIS, being chosen judge, awarded it to Aphrodite; in return she aided him in abducting HELEN, wife of Menelaus, King of Sparta, and the Trojan War was the result.

Appliqué, a general term for ornaments set into or fixed on objects of art such as bronze ornaments on a wood panel, or the ornament affixed to the vertical surface of a wall to which a candelabra or electric light fixture is fastened.

Appoggiatura, see **Grace note.**

Apron, in ancient theatre construction that part of the stage which projects in front of the curtain; it was eliminated first at the Haymarket Theatre, London, and later transformed into the orchestra.

Apse, in architecture the end of a church behind the CHOIR, or the TRANSEPT; usually semicircular or polygonal in contour. It was used in ancient Roman temples, in early Christian churches, and in Greek religious edifices. A smaller or secondary apse is known as an *apsidiole.*

Apthorp, William Foster (1848-1913), American music critic and author, graduate of Harvard University and pupil of John Knowles PAINE. He taught the piano and theoretical subjects at the NEW ENGLAND CONSERVATORY OF MUSIC; acted as critic for the *Atlantic Monthly* and the Boston *Evening Transcript,* and prepared the program notes for the BOSTON SYMPHONY ORCHESTRA concerts from 1892 to 1901. His works include a life of BERLIOZ, a volume of essays, *Musicians and Music Lovers,* and *The Opera, Past and Present.*

Apuleius, Lucius, Latin author of satires and fiction: born in Northern Africa during the 2nd century A.D., and endowed with ample means, he traveled to CARTHAGE and ATHENS to study philosophy. His principal work was a romance, *The Golden Ass* or *Metamorphoses,* which was widely read in his own day, and has since been imitated or borrowed from by BOCCACCIO, FIELDING, SMOLLETT, CERVANTES, and other modern writers. He also wrote an amusing satirical *Apology* as a defense when accused of sorcery by relatives of his wife.

Aquamarine, in jewelry a transparent variety of the *beryl,* either blue-green or green in color, and mined in Russia and Ceylon: in the finest stones the color is said to be that of clear sea water.

Aquarelle, in painting, a work executed with thin water color or ink.

Aquatint, in painting an ETCHING in which the spaces are bitten into the metal with an acid, thereby producing an effect similar to that of a drawing in water colors or INDIA INK.

Aqueduct, in architecture an artificial channel, constructed underground, on the surface or elevated on walls which are either solid or pierced with arches, the purpose being to convey water usually by gravitation. Aqueducts were used in Egypt, Babylonia, Assyria, Palestine, Greece and in different parts of the Roman Empire: among famous ones are these built by Eupalinus at Samos which included a tunnel 4200 feet long; the Aqua Claudia at Rome; the Pont du Gard at Nimes built by the Romans; the Segovia aqueduct, also of Roman construction. Excellent examples in the United States are the Croton and Catskill aqueducts which supply water for New York City, and the 240-mile aqueduct furnishing Los Angeles with water.

Arabesque, a term, meaning simply "Arabian," and applied: (*a*) to certain forms of decorative design, consisting of gracefully interlaced curved lines against a background, in architecture, painting and sculpture; curiously enough the word is not applied to any designs derived from Arabian or Moorish art. (b) In music the word is used as a title for instrumental pieces such as Robert Schumann's Arabesque, Op. 18. (c) In ballet, the term designating a dance posture in which the arm is extended with the opposite leg backward.

Arabian Nights, The, correctly called **The Book of 1001 Nights,** a series of fantastic Eastern tales joined together by the tale of Scheherezade who kept her husband, the Sultan Shariah, from killing her by telling the stories for 1001 consecutive nights until his blood lust disappeared. The first European edition was in French by Antoine Galland (1704), and there are two remarkable English translations: an expurgated edition by E. W. LANE (1840), and an unexpurgated by Sir Richard BURTON (1885). The Russian composer, Peter Ilich TSCHAIKOWSKY, composed an orchestral suite, SCHERERAZADE, inspired by the tales.

Arachne, in Greek mythology a maiden, the daughter of a dyer in Lydia, who dared to surpass the goddess, ATHENA, in the art of weaving. When Athena destroyed Arachne's masterpiece because she could find no flaw in it, Arachne tried to hang herself; the goddess relented; changed the rope into a cobweb, and Arachne into a spider.

Aragon, Louis (1879-   ), French poet and novelist who was one of the leaders in the Surrealist School of artistic endeavor in painting, sculpture, and literature. His works include a poem, *Red Front* (1933); *The Bells of Basel; Residential Quarter; The Century Was Young;* all of the above have been translated into English.

Aram, Eugene (1704-1759), English philologist who murdered his intimate friend, Daniel Clark, in 1745, but did not pay the supreme penalty for his crime until 1759 after the skeleton was discovered in a cave. Aram defended himself unsuccessfully, was convicted and finally confessed before his execution. Robert HOOD wrote a ballad, *The Dream of Eugene Aram,* and Bulwar LYTTON a novel, *Eugene Aram;* a motion picture has also utilized the dramatic highlights of the trial.

Arany, János (1817-1882), Hungarian poet, considered the greatest after Alexander PETŐFI: his first successful work was a satirical poem, *The Lost Constitution* (1845), which won a prize from the Kisfaludy Society, Hungary's famous literary association. In 1846 he began his great poetic trilogy, *Toldi, Toldi's Evening,* and *Toldi's Love;* the last-named was completed in 1879. This was followed by a series of Magyar ballads regarded as among the most beautiful in the language: he also edited a Hungarian translation of SHAKESPEARE, and in many respects elevated Magyar literature.

Araujo Porto-Alegre, Manoel de (1806-1879), Brazilian poet who studied at the Academy of Arts in Rio de Janeiro and also at Paris and Rome. His principal works are an epic poem, *Colombo,* celebrating the discovery of America,

and a lyric cycle, *Brasilianos,* replete with exquisite descriptions of natural scenery.

Arblay, Madame d' (1752-1840), English novelist who was the daughter of Charles Burney, a distinguished music historian, and an intimate friend of Dr. Samuel Johnson. Her works include *Evelina* (1778); *Cecilia; Camilla; The Wanderer;* she also wrote memoirs of her father.

Arbos, Enrique Fernandez (1863-1939), Spanish violinist and composer, pupil of MONASTERIO, VIEUXTEMPS and JOACHIM in violin, and of Gevaert in composition. He was concertmaster of the Berlin Philharmonic Orchestra, violinist to the Queen of Spain, professor of violin at the Madrid Conservatory and concertmaster of the Madrid Symphony Orchestra. Arbos composed many violin pieces, orchestrated ALBENIZ'S suite, *Iberia,* and edited the violin works of Henri Vieuxtemps.

Arbuthnot, John (1667-1735), Scotch humorist and physician to Queen Anne; his claim to fame is justly based on the satirical *The History of John Bull* (1712), first attributed to Jonathan SWIFT, and also said to have created ideas for "Gulliver's Travels" in Swift's mind.

Arc, Jeanne d', see **Joan of Arc.**

Arcade, in architecture a series of ARCHES supported by either COLUMNS or PIERS; often open for use as an entrance or to admit light, and as frequently closed at the back. The earliest examples known are those in the COLOSSEUM at ROME; also in DIOCLETIAN's palace at Spalata. The term is also applied to covered passages serving as thoroughfares between streets such as the Burlington Arcade in London. The city of Bologna, Italy, has continuous arcades over the sidewalks to serve as protection from the sun.

Arcadia, in literature the name given a mythical region or scene typical of simple pleasures, rustic innocence or peaceful quiet; the term is derived from Arcadia, a picturesque district of Greece surrounded by the Peloponnesian mountains, and famed as the abode of unsophisticated people living in perfect harmony. Artists, poets and composers have drawn inspiration from the word.

Arc de Triomphe de l'Étoile, a majestic triumphal arch on the Champs Elysées in Paris where the Place de l'Étoile (a star-shaped area) forms an intersection from which twelve avenues radiate. It was begun by the architect, Jean François CHALGRIN, in 1806 for NAPOLEON I in commemoration of his victories, and the construction carried on after Chalgrin's death by several famous architects until its completion in 1836. The dimensions are 160 feet high, 150 feet wide, and 72 feet deep; the arch is surrounded by symbolic groups. After World War I the body of an unknown French soldier was interred there; a perpetual flame was installed, and the Arch became a national shrine until the German invasion in World War II.

Arch, in architecture a structural arrangement of bricks or stone used for spanning the opening in a wall, and assembled in an upward curve in such a manner that stability is achieved by mutual pressure. A series of continuous arches constitute a *barrel vault;* the arch has been used since ancient times, and is constructed in numerous forms including the pointed, semicircular, horseshoe, ogee and flat styles. In modern steel construction, the term is used for the masonry filling the space between steel beams, thereby becoming a support for the floors.

Archaism, in literature the use of an obsolete word, expression, idiom, form of speech or literary style belonging to another period; for example the writing of a poem in the style of SPENSER's *Faerie Queene* or CHAUCER's *Canterbury Tales.*

"Archduke" Trio, Op. 97 (Beethoven), a trio for PIANO, VIOLIN and VIOLONCELLO, regarded as the composer's greatest work in this form. It was sketched in 1810, completed in 1811 and first performed the same year with Beethoven at the piano: unfortunately his playing was marred by deafness, but no other chamber work from his pen displays so much originality, technical skill and sensitive musicianship. The grandeur of the first movement, the vivacity of the *Scherzo,* the divinely beautiful theme of the *Adagio* with its exquisite variations, and the exuberant gayety of the *Finale* combine in creating a genuine masterpiece. There is a Victor recording by CORTOT, THIBAUD and CASALS, and a Columbia recording by MURDOCH, SAMMONS and SQUIRE.

Archer, William (1856-1924), English author, dramatic critic, translator and playwright, educated at the University of Edinburgh, and from 1879 dramatic critic of *Figaro, The World, The Tribune* and *The Star.* He translated many of IBSEN's plays and edited the Norwegian dramatist's *Prose Dramas.* His original works include *The Theatrical World; God and Mr. Wells; A National Theatre* (with GRANVILLE-BARKER), and *The Old Drama and the New.* Archer also wrote a very successful melodrama, *The Green Goddess* (1921), in which George ARLISS was starred; it was equally popular as a motion picture.

Archilochus, Greek lyric poet and writer of satires who flourished about 650 B.C. He is said to be the inventor of iambic poetry, especially as used in satirical poems; according to critics his verses teem with inherent strength, nervous vigor, impetuous vehemence and extraordinary energy. His contemporaries thought so highly of him that, according to the ENCYCLOPEDIA BRITANNICA, statues of HOMER and Archilochus were dedicated on the same day.

Archipenko, Alexander (1887-), Russian sculptor and painter born in the Ukraine; his style is distinctly modern, and he specializes in female nudes.

Architectural Magazines. Several magazines which cover subjects of interest to the professional architect, the student, and the lover of architecture are published in the United States; they include the *Architect and Engineer; Architectural Design; Architectural Digest; Architectural Forum; Architectural Record.*

Architectural Painter, the name applied to a painter who executes only paintings in which the subjects are architectural in character; Jan Van der Heyden, Emanuel De Witte, and CANALETTO may be placed in this classification.

Architecture, the art of constructing buildings in such a manner as to not only make them practically useful, but also attractive from the standpoints of beauty and harmony. The architect must be endowed with both imagination and technical skill; he must also possess at least a working knowledge of engineering. The first buildings which are worthy of being designated as architecture are those of the Egyptians about 4000 B.C.: the Assyrians also displayed imagination in construction, but the Greeks developed the simplest and purest forms of architecture which reached its highest point in the marble temples such as the PARTHENON in the 5th century, B.C. Roman architecture copied largely from Greek and Asiatic forms; its main contribution was the invention of CONCRETE as well as the erection of an enormous number of buildings and bridges in every country over which the Roman Empire held sway. In Byzantine architecture entirely new methods were employed, particularly in the use of abutments and the principles involved therein. Romanesque architecture in the 11th century adapted or improved on Byzantine construction; Gothic architecture in the 13th century carried the masonry form of construction to higher levels, and developed vaulted forms. Renaissance architecture in the 15th century may be said to have borrowed from every previous style; it was followed by the Baroque Period during the 17th century in which excessive ornamentation was the predominating feature. The 18th century gave birth to both Georgian and Colonial styles, and the first part of the 19th century witnessed the revival of the classic (Greek and Roman) as well as the Gothic styles. Architects from 1850 up to the present time now concentrate mainly on steel and reinforced concrete construction, combining original designs with the best architectural forms of all periods. In Greek and Roman architecture, the various types are designated as Doric, Ionic, Corinthian, Tuscan and Composite; definite information regarding rules of construction were laid down in books by Andrea PALLADIO and Jacopo VIGNOLA, both distinguished Italian architects of the 16th century.

Architrave, in architecture the chief beam which rests directly on the COLUMNS, and supports the superstructive. It is the lowest of the three divisions of the ENTABLATURE: the other two are the FRIEZE and the CORNICE. The word is also applied to the MOULDING around a doorway or window frame, but the more precise term is ARCHIVOLT.

Archivolt, in architecture a band of concentric mouldings employed as ornamentation for the arch of a façade: the band may be made up of a single or many rows with or without embellishment.

Arden, Forest of, an English forest which extended through Warwickshire and other counties of England in medieval times. It is apparently the woodland in Shakespeare's "As You Like It" judging by the references to Robin Hood and other bits of description in the play; Malone and other Shakespearean editors, however, contend that Shakespeare had in mind the forest of Ardennes in French Flanders.

Arditi, Luigi (1822-1903), Italian conductor and composer who studied violin, piano and composition at the Milan Conservatory, wrote an opera, *I Briganti* in 1840, and toured the United States with the famous double-bass player, Giovanni BOTTESINI, in 1847. He was a successful opera conductor in Europe, England and the United States, but is remembered chiefly through his coloratura waltz songs, *Il Bacio* and *Parla*.

Arena, a word meaning "sand" in Latin, and applied to the central part of an amphitheatre where gladiatorial contests took place in ancient times. The word is now used for any open area on which displays or contests take place, and is also used interchangeably with AMPHITHEATRE.

Arena Goldoni, an open-air theatre in Florence, Italy, built in 1818, and named in honor of the Italian dramatist, Carlo GOLDONI. Its operation was in accordance with the best traditions; Gordon CRAIG, a distinguished English dramatic writer and director, took over its direction in 1908, and produced many Italian, French, German, English and American plays there for many years with great success.

Arensky, Anton Stepanovitch (1861-1906), Russian composer and pianist; pupil in composition of Nicholas RIMSKY-KORSAKOW, professor of composition at the Moscow Conservatory and conductor of the Imperial Court Choir at Petrograd. His works include three operas; several symphonies and other orchestral works; pieces for piano and for violin; also several suites for two pianos—four hands which are still in vogue. Arensky's talents ran along lyric rather than dramatic lines.

Ares, in Greek mythology the god of war, son of Zeus and Hera and husband (or lover) of Aphrodite. He was pictured as a warrior in the full panoply of war, and usually carrying a torch. The Roman name was Mars.

Arethusa, in Greek mythology one of the NEREIDS who was changed into a fountain when she was pursued by Alpheus, a mighty hunter; the latter changed his form to a river, and made his way beneath the sea to unite himself with the fountain.

Aretinian syllables, the syllables *ut, re, mi, fa, sol, la,* employed by GUIDO D'AREZZO to designate the notes of the hexachord, a series of six tones, used by him in the 11th century and derived from the initial syllables of the first phrases on a hymn to St. John. The syllable *ut* was changed to *do* in the 17th century, and the syllable *si* added for the seventh syllable in order to name the complete scale.

Aretino, Pietro (1492-1556), Italian poet and dramatist who led an adventurous life, and achieved considerable notoriety for the *Sonnetti Lussuriosi,* satirical verses in which he attacked many prominent men of his day. He was supported largely in his later years by contributions from those who feared the lash of his verses: on the other hand he was an intimate friend of TITIAN who painted his portrait. Aretino's five comedies are regarded as his best work.

Arezzo, Guido d', see **Guido d'Arezzo.**

Argensola, Lupercio Leonardo (1559-1613), Spanish poet and dramatist; his tragedies, *Phyllis, Isabella,* and *Alexandra* brought him fame as a young man, and were praised by CERVANTES. His ballads and sonnets are exceptionally rich in pictorial fancy and singularly pure diction.

Argentina, La (1888-1936), Spanish dancer whose real name was Antonia Mercé. She was born in Buenos Aires of Spanish parents on a dancing tour of South America; her father was premier danseur of the Opera in Madrid, and her mother première danseuse, a position she assumed herself at the age of eleven. She appeared first in 1918 without marked success in New York; in 1927 her first great triumph was scored at a solo concert in Paris, a success repeated at TOWN HALL, New York, in 1928, when John MARTIN said of her: "To rank her as second to Anna PAVLOWA is to make an invidious comparison for she is second to none in her own individual way!" She toured America in 1929, and returned every season, with the exception of one, until her death.

Argentinita, contemporary Spanish dancer born in Buenos Aires, Argentine Republic, who was taught the traditional dances of old Spain by her father who later had her trained in a classic ballet school at Madrid. At ten she appeared with famous dancers, and a few years later she was the ranking classic dancer in Spain, and gave many recitals, also gaining the necessary knowledge of acting, singing and mime by joining Martinez Sierra's dramatic company. She learned all the native popular dances by visiting the Spanish provinces, and in 1929 presented a company of gypsies trained to perform classic ballet as well as their native dances at Madrid; later the organization toured Europe, South America, Cuba and Mexico. Her debut in 1930 with Leslie's "International Revue" was unfortunate in that it was not the right medium for the display of her talent, but she quickly gained recognition through four solo recitals. She returned to Spain to reorganize the Madrid Ballet, leaving again, when civil war broke out, to tour Europe and England. In 1940 Argentinita returned to New York, and her performance with Leonide MASSINE in "Capriccio Espagnol" established her position as one of the great Spanish dancers of all time.

Argonauts, The, in Greek mythology the band of heroes who joined in the quest for the golden fleece. The expedition sailed from Iolcus in a ship called the *Argo* to Colchis, where its leader, Jason, demanded the fleece from king Aeetes. Medea, daughter of Aeetes, quieted the dragon who guarded the fleece with a drug so that Jason was able to seize it; she accompanied Jason on his return voyage to Iolcus.

Argus, in Greek mythology (*a*) an earth-born hero who was called *Panoptes* (all-seeing) because he had eyes all over his body. He was killed by HERMES, but HERA transferred his eyes to the peacock's tail; (b) according to Homer, the name of ODYSSEUS' faithful dog who recognized his master on his return to Ithaca after many years of wandering.

Argyle, Pearl, contemporary English ballerina, the first of her countrymen to make a name in ballet. She studied with Marie RAMBERT, and made her debut at the Ballet Club, London, later appearing at the Camargo Society and at the SADLER'S WELLS BALLET. Her name is especially associated with CHABRIER's ballet, *The Bar at the Folies-Bergère,* in which she made a great impression as the barmaid. Miss Argyle has also appeared in *The Lady of Shalott,* a ballet with music by Jean SIBELIUS, and in Ernest BLOCH's *The Descent of Hebe,* besides giving instruction in ballet dancing.

Aria (It.), in music literally an "air" or "melody": the name given a song for a solo voice, with or without instrumental or vocal accompaniment, in opera or oratorio. The aria was developed in the 17th century from a plain-song melody to the *aria da capo* of the 18th century: this comprised two parts with the first part repeated. A vocal or instrumental piece of less pretentious character is called an *arietta.*

Ariadne, in Greek mythology the daughter of MINOS, King of Crete. She gave her lover, THESEUS, a spool of thread so that he found his way out of the labyrinth after he killed the Minotaur, a monster created half man and half bull. After Theseus deserted her on the island of Naxos, she was rescued and wedded to DIONYSUS; ZEUS immortalized her, and her bridal tiara was placed among the stars.

Ariel, a spirit in Jewish and medieval legend used as a character in SHAKESPEARE's *The Tempest,* and also in Alexander POPE's *The Rape of the Lock.*

Arion of Methyma, a semi-legendary Greek poet and musician, born at Lesbos, who flourished about 625 B.C. He is said to have invented, or at least to have improved the DITHYRAMB, and also to have been such a skilful performer on the lyre that, when cast into the sea by some sailors who had stolen his possessions, he was carried safely to shore on the back of a dolphin who was captivated by his singing and playing.

Ariosto, Ludovico (1474-1533), Italian poet of noble birth and regarded as one of his country's greatest bards in both lyric and epic verse. He finished his masterpiece, *Orlando Furioso,* in 1532, while in the employ of Cardinal d'Este, but received little recognition from the prelate. He also wrote excellent satirical poems in defense of liberty, and several comedies among them *The Pretenders* and *The Sorcerer* of which he superintended the production at a theatre in Ferrara.

Aristides, Greek painter of the 4th century B.C., born at Thebes, and said to have been related to the famous painter, NICOMACHUS, with whom he studied. He excelled in vivid and realistic expres-

sion; a painting, *Storming of a City,* greatly intrigued ALEXANDER THE GREAT, another, *Dionysos and Ariadne,* was retained by the Roman general, Lucius Mummius, even when he was offered 200 talents (about $200,000) for it.

Aristophanes (c.448-c.385 B.C.), Greek dramatist, regarded as the greatest classical writer of comedies. He was a mere youth when his first comedy, *The Banqueters,* was produced in 427 B.C. All three of his sons, Philippus, Araros and Nicostratus, were comic poets. The number of comedies written by Aristophanes is said to have been fifty-four; of these eleven are extant: *Plutus, The Knights, The Clouds, The Wasps, The Frogs, The Birds, The Acharnians, Peace, Lysistrata, The Priestesses of Demeter* and *Women in Politics.* The charm of his plays lies in his satirical skill combined with ability to write exquisitely in the lyric form.

Arlen, Michael (1895-), Bulgarian novelist and dramatist, real name Dikran Kuyumjian, educated at English colleges, who became a naturalized British subject in 1922. His career began as a free-lance journalist in 1913, and his plays include *Dear Father; The Green Hat* which was very successful in New York; *The Zoo* (with Winchell Smith); *Good Losers* (with Walter Hackett): also several novels such as *The London Venture, The Romantic Lady, Piracy, Men Dislike Women, Crooked Coronet* and *The Flying Dutchman.*

"Arlésienne" Suites, L', two orchestral suites arranged from incidental music composed by Georges BIZET for Alphonse DAUDET's play, *L'Arlésienne,* produced at the Théâtre du Vaudeville, Paris, on Oct. 1, 1872. The original music was scored for small orchestra; Bizet himself reorchestrated the numbers used for the first suite, making excellent use of the saxophone; the second suite was arranged by Ernest Guiraud after Bizet's death. There are four movements in each suite; there are Victor recordings of Suite No. 1 by the Philadelphia Orchestra with Leopold Stokowski, and of Suite No. 2 by the Boston "Pops" Orchestra conducted by Arthur Fiedler.

Arliss, George (1868-), English stage and screen actor, especially noted for his characterizations. He made his first appearance on the English stage in 1886, toured the English colonies from 1887 to 1901, and came to the United States during the same year with Mrs. Patrick CAMPBELL in *The Second Mrs. Tanqueray.* In 1902 he appeared in David BELASCO's *Darling of the Gods,* later becoming leading man with Minnie Maddern FISKE in repertory, and starring in *Disraeli, The Green Goddess* and *The Merchant of Venice.* His film career started in 1920: among his pictures are *Disraeli, The Green Goddess, Old English, Alexander Hamilton, The House of Rothschild, Voltaire* and *The Iron Duke.*

Armería (Madrid), a museum containing the finest collection of ARMOR in the world, formerly located in the Royal Palace, but now in a building of its own. The display is almost bewildering in its extent and magnificence; it may best be described as a veritable army of warlike effigies on foot and on horseback, clad in the finest suits of armor fashioned in the 12th to the 17th century. The walls are covered with battle-axes, lances, swords, and muskets; there are swords which belonged to Cortez and Pizarro, flashing blades made in Toledo, the armor worn by Columbus, the sword carried by King Ferdinand in his battles with the Moors, and many more weapons capable of dealing out death as swiftly, although not as effectively from the standpoint of wholesale slaughter, as the deadly implements of modern warfare.

Armida, a character in Torquato TASSO's sublime epic poem, portraying a beautiful woman used by Satan to beguile the Christian crusaders. The hero, Rinaldo, after first yielding to her wiles, finally converts and marries her. The poem was the source of the librettos for operas by LULLY, CHERUBINI, ROSSINI, and of Gluck's *Rinaldo* from which the air "Lascia ch'io Pianga" is still heard in vocal recitals.

Armitage, Edward (1817-1896), English painter, pupil of Paul DELAROCHE at the ECOLE DES BEAUX ARTS, Paris. He also studied in Rome; exhibited two pictures, *Henry VIII and Katherine Parr* and *Trafalgar, 1805,* at the Royal Academy, London, in 1845, and painted several fine battle scenes after visiting Russia during the Crimean War. Later in life he turned his attention to religious subjects; among the best is *The Remorse of Judas* in the NATIONAL GALLERY, LONDON.

Armitage, Merle (1893-), American opera impresario, concert manager, author and book designer. He directed the tours of many famous singers, and of the famous ballerina, Anna PAVLOWA; he also managed the Scotti Grand Opera Company, the Russian Grand Opera, the Beggar's Opera Company and the DIAGHILEFF Ballet. In 1924 he founded the Los Angeles Grand Opera Association, and has written studies of Arnold SCHÖNBERG, George GERSHWIN and Igor STRAVINSKY in addition to many books on the fine arts.

Armor, the term for defensive equipment worn, from about the 12th century, by knight and soldier alike, as protection against such weapons as the lance and crossbow. It was usually made of metal, but cheaper substitutes such as hardened leather, quilted cloth and horn were used by the ordinary soldiery. The various kinds of armor included *chain mail armor* in the 12th and 13th centuries; *mixed mail and chain armor* in the 14th and 15th centuries; *complete mail armor* in the 17th century. The introduction of gunpowder relegated armor from the battlefield to the tournament, where it became known as *decorative armor:* officers and mounted men used partial armor up to the beginning of the 18th century, but the cuirass (breastplate) and helmet were still used by cavalry. The eleventh edition of the ENCYCLOPEDIA BRITANNICA contains a comprehensive, illustrated article on armor; the finest collection of armor is in the ARMERIA, a museum in Madrid.

Arms, John Taylor (1887-), American architect, etcher and author educated at Princeton University and the Massachusetts Institute of Tech-

nology. After service in World War I, he devoted himself entirely to etching; among his most representative plates are *Cavendish Common* (1938); *In Memoriam, Chartres Cathedral; Venetian Mirror; Sunlight on Stone, Caudebec-en-Caux; Shadows of Venice; Gothic Glory; Lace in Stone, Rouen Cathedral; Arch of the Conca, Perugia; From the Ponte Vecchio; Stockholm; Aspiration; Study in Stone, Cathedral of Orense;* he has also published a *Handbook of Print Making and Print Makers* (1934).

Armstead, Henry Hugh (1828-1905), English sculptor, first trained in the art of silversmith, but finally becoming one of the greatest sculptors of his day. He worked in both bronze and marble; among his finest creations are sculptures for the Albert Memorial, Kings College (Cambridge), and *St. Paul, David and Moses* in WESTMINSTER ABBEY.

Armstrong, Anthony (1897-), English dramatist and author; his successful plays include *Ten Minute Alibi* produced at New York in 1933, and *Mile Away Murder* (London, 1936). He has also written fifteen detective and humorous novels, several of which have been published in the United States, and many plays.

Armstrong, Helen Maitland (1869-), American artist, born in Italy. She studied with William Merritt CHASE, and has designed and executed many stained glass windows, mosaics, mural decorations, etc. for churches and buildings in the United States.

Armstrong, Paul (1869-1915), American journalist and playwright who used the pen name "Right Cross." His plays include *The Heir to the Hoorah* (1905); *Ann Lamont; St. Ann: In a Blaze of Glory; For a Woman; Alias Jimmy Valentine:* the latter was a signal success both on the stage and the screen.

Arnaud, Leopold (1895-), American architect, graduate of Columbia University, New York, and the ECOLE DES BEAUX ARTS, Paris. He has acted as chief designer for several prominent American architectural firms, and has been connected with Columbia University as lecturer, instructor, and professor of architecture since 1929.

Arnault, Antoine (1766-1834), French dramatist and fabulist whose first play, *Marius à Minturus* (1791), won him fame, and was followed by a tragedy, *Lucréce* (1792). He was a faithful adherent of NAPOLEON I; after the latter's fall he exiled himself until 1819. Another play, *Germanicus,* was almost the cause of a serious political disturbance. Arnault is better known today through his *Fables,* couched in gracefully flowing verse; his son, **Emile Lucien Arnault** (1787-1863), wrote several dramas for François Joseph TALMA, the distinguished French tragedian.

Arne, Thomas Augustine (1710-1778), a distinguished English composer who wrote musical settings for ADDISON's *Rosamond* and Field's *Tragedy of Tragedies,* Dalton's *Comus* and the MASQUE, *Alfred* in which was included the famous *Rule Britannia.* He composed two oratorios, *Abel* and

Judith, and was the first English composer to make use of women's voices in sacred choruses.

Arnim, Elizabeth or **Bettina von** (1785-1859), German writer, sister of Clemens BRENTANO: she was said to have been a friend of Beethoven, and of Goethe with whom she quarreled because of her insolent behavior to his wife. In 1835 she published a volume entitled *Goethe's Correspondence With a Child,* based on letters written to her by the great poet. Although treated with the greatest license from the poetic point of view, it is one of the finest examples of romanticism.

Arno, Peter (1904-), American illustrator whose humorous cartoons have appeared for some years in *The New Yorker.* He has also published several collections including *Peter Arno's Circus* (1931); *Peter Arno's Favorites; Whoops Dearie!*

Arnold, Edward (1890-), American stage and screen actor, who made his first stage appearance at New York in 1919, and later played in *The Jazz Singer, The Storm, Miracle at Verdun* and many other successes. He entered the films in 1936, and has appeared in many notable pictures including *Diamond Jim Brady, Cardinal Richelieu, Crime and Punishment, Come and Get It, Idiot's Delight, Mr. Smith Goes to Washington, Meet John Doe, The Devil and Daniel Webster* and *The War Against Mrs. Hadley.*

Arnold, Sir Edwin (1832-1904), English poet and journalist on the staff of the London *Daily Telegraph* for more than forty years: he made the arrangements whereby his newspaper co-operated with the *New York Herald* in financing Sir Henry M. Stanley's African expedition to discover the source of the Congo River. His works include two epic poems: *The Light of Asia* (1879) and *The Light of the World* (1891); the success of both was increased rather than diminished by pedantic criticism. Arnold also wrote two volumes of poetry and several picturesque books of travel. His third wife was a Japanese lady who probably inspired his drama, *Adzuma, or The Japanese Wife.*

Arnold, Matthew (1822-1888), English poet and literary critic who won his first laurels at Rugby in 1840 with his poem, *Alaric at Home.* He was appointed an inspector of elementary schools, and wrote several treatises on educational matters. His poems, such as *The Strayed Reveler and Other Poems, Poems, Second Series, New Poems* and a tragedy, *Merope,* were published between 1849 and 1867. They were followed by a long series of works in the field of literary criticism: among them are *On Translating Homer, Essays in Criticism, Culture and Anarchy, and Friendship's Garland.*

Arnold, Maurice (1865-1937), American violinist and composer, student at the Cincinnati College of Music, and later at Breslau of Max BRUCH in composition. His *American Plantation Dances* interested Antonin DVORAK in 1894, when he was director of the National Conservatory of Music in New York, and Arnold was given the post of instructor in composition there. His compositions include a symphony and other orchestral works,

a violin sonata, many piano pieces and a comic opera, *The Merry Benedicts.*

Arnolfo di Cambio (c.1232-c.1310), Italian architect of the Florentine school regarding whom little is known; some authorities claim that he is identical with *Arnolfo di Firenze,* a sculptor of note during the same period, but there is no concrete proof available. He was granted freedom from taxation by the Signorie of Florence for outstanding achievements in church building; among them St. Croce, the Duomo, St. Maria Maggiore, and St. Trinita.

Arnould, Madeleine Sophie (1744-1802), French dramatic soprano whom David GARRICK pronounced the greatest actress on the French stage. She sang at l'Opéra, Paris, from 1757 to 1778, creating many important roles including Iphigenia in GLUCK's *Iphigenia in Aulis,* and Eurydice in the same master's *Orpheus and Eurydice.* She was also noted for her witty sayings, and her portrait was painted by Jean-Baptiste GREUZE.

Arnould-Plessy, Jean Sylvanie (1819-1897), French actress who made her debut at the Comédie-Française, Paris in Alexandre Duval's *La Fille d'honneur* with great success in 1834, being favorably compared with Mlle. MARS. She appeared for eleven years at the Comédie-Française, leaving there for the French Theatre in St. Petersburg for an engagement lasting nine years, and finally returning to the Comédie in 1855 for an eight-year period during which she rose to even greater heights when she succeeded Mlle. Mars.

Arouet, François Marie de, see **Voltaire, François Marie Arouet de.**

Arpeggio (It.), in music the notes of a CHORD played in rapid, even succession, producing a harp-like effect: when it is intended that chords composed of three or more notes are to be performed in this manner, the instruction *arpeggiando* or *quasi arpa* is placed over them.

Arrangement, in music the adaptation of a composition for performance on an instrument or combination of instruments for which it was not originally composed. As an example, many songs are arranged so that they may be played on the PIANO, VIOLIN, VIOLONCELLO, etc.; and many instrumental pieces are arranged for solo or choral singing.

Arrau, Claudio (1904-), Chilean pianist who studied with Martin Krause in Berlin and won the Grand International Prize for Pianists at Geneva in 1927. He has since appeared in recital and with the major orchestras of Europe, England and the United States: he is characterized by critics as the possessor of a masterly technique and a remarkable tonal command of the piano.

Arrom, Cecilia, see **Caballero, Fernan.**

Arrotino, L' (The Knife-grinder), a famous ancient statue, now in the UFFIZI GALLERY, Florence, which in all probability was originally a part of a pictorial group such as Greek sculptors of the Alexandrian period were inclined to create; it represents a slave in a crouching position sharpening a knife. It has been greatly admired for the fidelity with which the muscles of the slave are carved, and is often used by artists as a model.

Arrow System of Score Reading, in music, a method simplifying the reading, i.e., following with the eye, scores of orchestral or chamber music. The system, invented by Albert E. Wier, employs an arrow which moves from staff to staff as the melodic line shifts from one instrument to another, enabling anyone who can read ordinary instrumental or vocal music to follow a score. The system is used in collective volumes of symphonies and symphonic poems published by Harcourt, Brace & Co.; also several volumes of chamber music issued by Longmans, Green & Co.

Arsène Arnaud, see **Claretie, Jules.**

Artagnan, Charles de Baatz d' (1611-1673), a Gascon gentleman who held the post of captain of the musketeers for Louis XIV; his memoirs, written and published by Courtils de Sandras in 1701, were the historical basis for the character of the same name in Alexandre Dumas' romance, *The Three Musketeers,* and its sequels, *Twenty Years Later, The Vicomte de Bragelonne,* and *The Man in the Iron Mask.*

Artemis, in Roman mythology the Greek goddess identified with Diana.

Artemus Ward, see **Ward, Artemus.**

Arthur, Jean née **Gladys Green** (1908-), American motion-picture actress who began her screen career in 1923, and made her first stage appearance in *Foreign Affairs* on April 13, 1932. Among the notable films in which she has appeared are *The Mysterious Dr. Fu Manchu, The Return of Dr. Fu Manchu, The Defense Rests, Mr. Deeds Goes to Town, You Can't Take It With You, Mr. Smith Goes to Washington* and *The Talk of the Town.*

Arthur, Julia (1869-), Canadian actress, real name Ida Lewis, who appeared in amateur theatricals before making her professional debut in 1883 with the Bandmann Stock Company, playing Shakespearean heroines, and touring the entire United States before she was twenty years old. Her New York debut was made in *The Black Masque* in 1892, followed by Oscar Wilde's *Lady Windermere's Fan* and Thomas Bailey Aldrich's *Mercedes.* In 1895 she made her London debut in Shakespeare with Sir Henry Irving's Lyceum Company, also accompanying it to New York. Among the plays in which Miss Arthur has appeared with success are *King Arthur, A Lady of Quality, Pygmalion and Galatea, The Eternal Magdalene, Liberty Aflame* and *Out There.*

Arthur, King, a British king who, according to Geoffrey Monmouth's *Historia Britonum* (c.1136), ruled over Britain in the 5th and 6th centuries, and waged many successful campaigns in Europe which brought him to the very gates of Rome. He is the hero of a series of romantic tales known as the *Matière de Bretagne* (Master of Britain). There is no positive evidence that King Arthur

ever existed: he is presumably a semi-legendary rather than an historic personality, and the tales may be drawn from the mythology and folk lore of not only Wales, but of Scandinavia, France and other European countries. Lord Alfred Tennyson, in his *Idylls of a King,* has painted a glowing picture of King Arthur surrounded by his gallant knights.

Arthur, Timothy Shay (1809-1885), American novelist and editor of *Arthur's Home Magazine* from 1852 to 1885. He wrote more than one hundred moral and temperance tracts, and a novel, *Ten Nights in a Bar-room* which attained immense popularity as a play, and as a melodrama performed by innumerable stock companies.

Art Magazines. Several periodicals of interest to those interested in painting, sculpture and allied arts are published in the United States: among them are *American Artist; Art Digest; Art in America; Art News; Art Quarterly; California Arts and Architecture; Magazine of Art; School Arts Magazine.* All of these magazines can be purchased through local bookstores or dealers in periodicals.

Art of Fugue, The, a work written in 1749 by Johann Sebastian Bach to provide practical examples of counterpoint. It comprises fourteen fugues for one clavier, two fugues for two claviers, and four canons, and was first published in 1752. One subject is used for the entire work which has since been arranged for two pianos—four hands by Erich Schwebsch, for orchestra by Wolfgang Graeser and for string quartet by Roy Harris.

Art of Musical Russia Inc., The, an organization founded in 1933 to present Russian operas with native artists who came to the United States after World War I. The company appeared in 1934 first at the Casino Theatre, New York, in Boris Godunoff with Eugene Plotnikoff as conductor; it has also played at the Metropolitan Opera House and Mecca Temple, New York, in addition to making extensive tours presenting Shostakovich's Lady Macbeth of Mzensk, Tcherepnin's *Ol-Ol,* Tschaikowsky's Eugene Onegin, Borodin's Prince Igor and many other Russian operas.

Artôt, Alexandre-Joseph (1815-1845), French violinist and composer, pupil of Rodolphe Kreutzer at the Paris Conservatory of Music. He was one of the greatest virtuosos of his day, and toured Europe and Great Britain with tremendous success, appearing in the United States in 1843. His works include a concerto and many solo pieces for violin.

Art Song, a form of solo vocal composition distinguished from the folk song by its more elaborate structure, broader conception from the literary and musical standpoints, and higher degree of subtlety in nuance; one of the finest examples is Franz Schubert's *Erl King.* Other European composers who have written many outstanding art songs are Schumann, Mendelssohn, Loewe, Franz, Brahms, Wolf, Richard Wagner, Tosti, Massenet, Franck, Faure, Debussy,

LISZT, BORODIN, MOUSSORGSKY, DVORAK, SIBELIUS, ELGAR, DELIUS and several Americans inluding CHADWICK, MACDOWELL and NEVIN.

Art Students League, The, an organization founded at New York in 1875, and incorporated three years later. For some years it occupied cramped and generally inadequate quarters in a building formerly used as a piano factory in East Twenty-third Street: in 1891 about nine hundred students suffered inconveniences which were entirely eliminated when the League moved into the American Fine Arts Building on West Fifty-seventh Street during October 1893. Here more than 11,000 square feet of completely appointed, lighted, and ventilated studio space was provided in a building designed by Henry J. HARDENBERGH, architect of the old Waldorf-Astoria Hotel and of the Plaza Hotel. In February, 1943, an exhibition of paintings and sculpture was opened in celebration of the fiftieth anniversary of the League's residence in Fifty-seventh Street; the 227 canvases on display included works by William Merritt CHASE, Frank DUVENECK, Thomas EAKINS, George McINNESS, John LA FORGE, Augustus SAINT-GAUDENS; Joseph PENNELL, George BELLOWS, Robert HENRI, and many other artists who were either students or instructors at the school.

Artsybashev, Mikhail Petrovich (1878-1927), Russian novelist and dramatist who gave up the career of a caricaturist when he gained more fame as a short story writer. His first novel, *Sanine* (1907), opposing Bolshevism, was a tremendous success, but it was suppressed in Russia and many other countries: after the Revolution in 1917 he was forced to leave, and went to Poland where he devoted himself to anti-Bolshevik journalism. His novels, of which many are available in English, include *Ivan Lande, The Millionaire,* and *The Breaking Point:* his plays include *Jealousy* (1913), *Enemies, The Law of the Savage,* and *War.*

Asbjornsen, Peter Christian (1812-1885), Swedish author and naturalist; in 1841 he published *Norwegian Folk Stories* (4 volumes) with his friend, Jörgen Moe; they are regarded as an invaluable contribution to folk literature. In 1845 he added a volume, *Norwegian Fairy Stories and Folk Legends* which was translated into English by Sir George W. Dasent with the title *Popular Tales from the Norse* in 1858.

ASCAP, see **American Society of Composers, Authors and Publishers.**

Asch, Sholem (1880-), Jewish novelist, short story writer, and dramatist who was born in Poland, and lived in Russia for many years. He came to the United States first in 1909, and has made his permanent home there since 1938. His greatest drama, *God of Vengeance,* was presented on many European stages, but suppressed in New York: his notable works include *Three Cities; The Nazarene; The Apostle; Mottke the Thief; Salvation; Children of Abraham.*

Ashton, Frederick (1903-), English dancer and choreographer who was inspired by the desire for a career in ballet by seeing Anna PAVLOWA

perform. He studied with Leonide MASSINE and Marie RAMBERT, and spent a year with Ida RUBINSTEIN's company, his debut was made at the Lyric Theatre, London, in 1926 in the ballet *Riverside Nights,* followed by engagements with Ida Rubinstein, Marie Rambert, the CAMARGO Society and other ballet companies. His ability as a choreographer was proved in *The Lady of Shalott, Façade, Les Rendez-vous, Nocturnes* and *Apparitions.* In 1933 Ashton came to the United States to act as choreographer and producer of *Four Saints in Three Acts,* an opera-ballet by Gertrude STEIN and Virgil THOMSON.

Ashton, Winifred, see **Dane, Clemence.**

Aside, in drama, an antique device, best-known as used by Richard Brinsley SHERIDAN in *The School for Scandal,* which allows an actor to speak directly to his audience for the purpose of imparting information or critical observation; it has been employed in modern plays by Eugene O'NEILL in *Strange Interlude,* and by James JOYCE in ULYSSES.

Aspasia, a Greek courtesan of the 5th century, B.C., who held court at Athens, and became the mistress of PERICLES, Athenian statesman who made her son his heir. She was famous for her beauty and learning, and was surrounded at her banquets by many of the most distinguished men of letters; a bust inscribed with her name is in the Pio Clementino Museum in the VATICAN.

Asper, Hans (1499-1571), Swiss painter famous for his drawings of flowers, animals and birds used as illustrations for Gessner's *History of Animals,* and for his fine portraits such as those of Ulrich Zwingli and his daughter, Regula Gwalter. The contention that Asper imitated Hans HOLBEIN is refuted by close comparison of their work.

Assumption of the Virgin, a favorite religious subject for many of the greater and lesser lights among the painters of the world; the finest examples are those by BARTOLOMMEO, BOTTICELLI, CARRACCI, CORREGGIO, GUERCINO, MANTEGNA, MURILLO, PERUGINO, POUSSIN, RUBENS, SARTO, TINTORETTO, TITIAN, and VERONESE.

Astaire, Adele (1898-), American actress and dancer who first appeared in American vaudeville and reviews in 1912; for a period of twenty years she was featured in notable productions including *Apple Blossoms; For Goodness' Sake* with her brother, Fred ASTAIRE; *Lady Be Good,* the musical play by George GERSHWIN.

Astaire, Fred (1900-), American actor and dancer who made his debut in American vaudeville with his sister, Adele ASTAIRE in 1916, and later appeared with her in several productions including *For Goodness' Sake* and *Lady Be Good:* he also played in *The Gay Divorcée* in both New York and London. Astaire is also a favorite screen actor; his films include an adaptation of *The Gay Divorcée:* also *Roberta; Top Hat; Shall We Dance; The Story of Vernon and Irene Castle,* and *Holiday Inn* with Bing CROSBY.

Astarte, a Semitic goddess known in the Bible as Ashtoreth; in many respects her attributes identify her with the Greek goddess, *Aphrodite,* or the Roman *Venus.*

Asther, Nils (1901-), Swedish dramatic and motion picture actor, educated at Lunel University and graduate of the Royal Dramatic School, obtaining stage experience in the Royal Dramatic Theatre. He has appeared in many notable films produced in Europe and the United States including *Sorrell and Son, Adrienne Lecouvreur, Wild Orchids, Candlelight, Storm at Daybreak,* and *The Bitter Tea of General Yen* in which he co-starred with Barbara STANWYCK.

Astley's Amphitheatre, an enormous and beautifully decorated theatre designed and built by Philip Astley at London in 1804: it was twice burned down, rebuilt and razed in 1895. Many grand spectacles were produced on its immense stage, 146 feet wide and equipped with the latest mechanical stage devices of its time; battle scenes and equestrian shows were a special feature.

Aston, Anthony (c.1690-1731), English actor and dramatist who made his first appearance on the London stage early in the 18th century; his play, *Love in a Hurry,* was performed at Dublin in 1709. After touring the English provinces in plays of his own making, he came to Charleston, Va., and has the distinction of being the first professional actor to appear on the American stage.

Astor, Mary (1906-), American motion picture actress who has appeared in numerous silent and talking films including *Beau Brummel; Dodsworth; The Prisoner of Zenda; The Hurricane; Brigham Young: Frontiersman; The Maltese Falcon; Across the Pacific.*

Astor Place Opera House, erected in 1847 at Astor Place, New York, under a guarantee of one hundred and fifty of the city's social and financial elite to maintain Italian opera there for five years: the seating capacity was 1800, and arranged, according to Max MARETZEK, so that everybody could not only see, but also be seen. The opening opera was VERDI's *Ernani,* but the management was inefficient and the performances mediocre, the result being financial disaster: in 1850 the building was converted into a mercantile library.

Atalanta, in Greek mythology, a famous huntress who agreed to marry any suitor who could outrun her, the contestant to die if he failed. Hippomenes won the race by dropping, one by one, three golden apples given him by APHRODITE; Atalanta stopped to pick them up and fell behind. Both were so happy at the result that they forgot to thank Aphrodite, and were transformed into lions.

Atchison, Joseph Anthony (1895-), American sculptor and painter, pupil of Paul Wayland BARTLETT and George Julian ZOLNAY: his works include the *World Flight Memorial* at the Smithsonian Institution, Washington, D. C.; allegorical and industrial panels at the Cleveland (Ohio) Public Auditorium; the Roosevelt Inaugural Medal (1937); the bronze fountain figure, *I*

Found a Turtle; also many privately owned paintings.

Ate, in Greek mythology the goddess of crime, hatred and retribution; she was so wicked that she induced her father, ZEUS, to make a false oath. For this she was cast out of OLYMPUS, and came to earth where she continued to work evil, always followed by the *Litae* who strove to atone for her wicked deeds.

Athena, in Greek mythology the goddess of wisdom, also called *Athenai, Pallas* or *Pallas Athene:* with ZEUS and APOLLO she formed a trinity embodying all the powers of divinity. She was also the goddess of war, the guardian of Greek cities and the patron of arts and industries peculiar to women. A great statue of Athena, thirty feet high and made of ivory and gold, stood in the PARTHENON on the ACROPOLIS at ATHENS; she was represented standing and helmeted, with a shield and spear at her left, and a figure of NIKE, the goddess of victory in her right hand.

Athenaeum, the name given in ancient Greece to buildings dedicated to ATHENA, especially a temple at ATHENS where poets and learned men gathered to read their works aloud. The emperor Hadrian built an academy for educational purposes at ROME to which he gave this name; since that time the name has frequently been applied to similar institutions of learning, to literary clubs, and as a title for magazines devoted to BELLES-LETTRES.

Athena Parthenos, see **Athena.**

Athens, a city in ancient Greece celebrated for its architectural wonders the majority of which were erected on the ACROPOLIS during the reign of PERICLES when Greek painting, sculpture, literature and philosophy were at their zenith; among the notable buildings were the PARTHENON, the ODEUM, the ERECTHEUM, the THESEUM and the THEATRE OF DIONYSUS. The dramatic works of AESCHYLUS, SOPHOCLES, EURIPIDES and ARISTOPHANES were first produced in Athens, and ZENOPHON, PLATO, Demosthenes, Aristotle and SOCRATES were among her many great prose writers, orators, philosophers and thinkers.

Athens, Theatre of, see **Theatre.**

Atherton, Gertrude Franklin (1857-), American novelist and poet educated at several private schools; author of many novels including *The Doomswoman* (1892); *The Californians; The Aristocrats; The Conqueror; Tower of Ivory; The Avalanche; Sleeping Fires; The Immortal Marriage; The Sophisticates; The House of Lee.* She also wrote *California: An Intimate History,* and an autobiography, *The Adventures of a Novelist.*

Atkinson, Brooks (1894-), American dramatic critic, educated at Harvard University. Starting as assistant dramatic critic of the *Boston Transcript* in 1918, he came to New York in 1922 as literary editor of the *New York Times,* becoming dramatic critic in 1926. Mr. Atkinson also writes on American theatrical matters for the London *Daily Telegraph*, and is the author of *Skyline Promenader, Henry Thoreau, East of the Hudson* and the *Cingalese Prince*.

Atlantis, in Grecian legend an island in the Atlantic Ocean, first chronicled by *Plato*, and presumably located somewhere west of Gibraltar, then known as the PILLARS OF HERCULES. It was said to have been a powerful nation nine thousand years before the time of SOLON (c.600 B.C.), but was finally inundated by the sea, disappearing beneath the waves forever. Francis Bacon left an allegorical fragment, *The New Atlantis*, in which he represents himself as being wrecked on a similar island, and discovering an ideal community there.

Atlas, in Greek mythology the son of a TITAN, and brother of PROMETHEUS. HOMER describes him in the ODYSSEY as "one who knows the depth of the entire sea, and supports the tall pillars which hold heaven and earth apart." The plural of Atlas, *Atlantes* was the classical term in architecture for sculptured, life-size figures of men used to support the superstructures of temples and baths: in the 18th century, half figures of powerfully muscled men utilized for similar support were known as CARYATIDES.

Atonality, in music the term applied to music in a constant state of MODULATION over the twelve-tone CHROMATIC scale, thereby dispensing with a central keynote. Arnold SCHÖNBERG has composed music of this type; he takes exception to the term "atonality," asserting that his works are written "by means of twelve notes between which no relationship exists other than their relationship to one another." Alban BERG, Schönberg's most ardent disciple and composer of an opera, WOZZECK, written in atonal style, gave a radio talk on the subject which may be found in Nicholas SLONIMSKY's *Music Since 1900*.

Atrium, in classic Roman architecture the name given the central room of a dwelling in which the hearth was placed; later the hearth was removed, and the room became what is now known as the "living room" in modern houses and apartments. The center of the roof over the atrium was open to admit light and air; rain water was collected by gutters and discharged into a marble basin or cistern. It was at the residence of the censor, called the *Atrium Libertatis*, that Asinius Pollio founded the first public library in Rome.

Attacca (It.), in music, a direction placed at the end of a movement in a composition to indicate that the ensuing movement is to be played without pausing.

Attack, in music, the method or style employed by a performer in beginning a PHRASE, PASSAGE or entire piece; it applies equally to instrumental or vocal music.

Atterbohm, Per Daniel Amadeus (1790-1855), Swedish poet, critic and dramatist, greatly influenced by the philosophy of Schelling and Hegel, and considered foremost among the romantic Swedish poets. His works include a cycle of lyric poems, *The Flowers;* a critical volume, *Swedish Seers and Poets;* also the plays, *The Isle of Blessedness* and *The Blue Bird*.

Atterburg, Kurt (1887-), Swedish composer, conductor and critic who first studied radio engineering, pupil of Max SCHILLINGS. His sixth symphony won the SCHUBERT contest in 1928 resulting in the award of a prize of $10,000 by the Columbia Phonograph Co. Later, after the symphony was performed, Atterburg wrote a pamphlet, *How I Fooled the World*, claiming he copied Schubert's style without serious intent. He has written six symphonies, an orchestral rhapsody, various concertos and chamber music; he is regarded as one of the leading composers of Sweden.

Atterbury, Grosvenor (1869-), American architect, graduate of Yale University, the Architectural School at Columbia University, and the ECOLE DES BEAUX ARTS, PARIS. His works include Forest Hills Garden, L. I., for the Russell Sage Foundation; the restoration of the City Hall, New York; the American Wing of the METROPOLITAN MUSEUM OF ART, New York, the Russell Sage Foundation Building and School of Social Work; the Medical Library at Yale University.

Attitude, in ballet, a dance pose in which one arm is raised overhead, and the opposite leg extended backward; *attitude à deux bras* is the same pose with both arms raised.

Atwell, Roy (1878-), American comedian and singer who appeared in operettas and revues almost continuously from 1900 to 1931. His farce comedy, *Here Comes the Bride*, was produced by Max MARCIN at New York, and a sketch, *The Christmas Letter*, won a prize from the LAMBS CLUB. Atwell excelled in the delivery of topical songs such as "A Little Bug Will Get You" with which he provoked much merriment in Franz Lehar's *Alone at Last*.

Atwill, Lionel (1885-), English stage and screen actor, who made his debut in 1905 at the Garrick Theatre, London, and appeared in many notable plays including *The Pillars of Society, A Fool's Paradise, The Bondman, Richelieu, The Little Minister, The Walls of Jericho, The Lodger, Hedda Gabler, A Doll's House* and *The Grand Duke*. He also produced several plays, and appeared in many films such as *Last Train from Madrid, The Great Garrick, The Great Waltz,* and *The Hound of the Baskervilles*.

Aubade, in music the title for short instrumental or orchestral pieces in lyric style; the word is also used to describe morning music in contrast to evening music, or SERENADE.

Aubé, Jean Paul (1837-1916), French sculptor and painter, a student at the ECOLE DES BEAUX ARTS, PARIS: his works include a bust of Prosper Mérimée in the Paris Institute and the monument to Leon Gambetta, French statesman and orator. One of his pictures, *Interior of a Studio*, was exhibited at the Paris Salon in 1910.

Auber, Daniel François Esprit (1782-1871), French operatic composer whose first work, *Julie,* was produced by amateurs. His talent was recognized by Luigi CHERUBINI, and more than forty operas were composed between 1813 and 1869, the outstanding successes being *Masaniello, Fra Diavolo* and *The Crown of Diamonds.* The first-named is ranked with the masterpieces of MEYER-BEER and ROSSINI: the second was one of the most popular comic operas ever produced. Auber's last opera was written at 87.

Aubert, Louis (1877-), French composer, pupil of FAURE, LAVIGNAC and D'INDY at the PARIS CONSERVATORY; in 1938 he was a member of the faculty of that institution. His opera, *La Forêt bleue,* was produced at Boston, Mass., in 1913; he has also written three ballets, several orchestral works, instrumental solo pieces, song cycles with orchestral accompaniment, and a treatise on harmony.

Aubert de Gaspe, Philippe (1786-1871), French-Canadian author; his novel, *The Canadians of Old,* was translated into English in 1864. It is considered a classic because of the picturesque fidelity with which it describes life in Quebec at the close of the 18th century, and there is much of historical importance in his *Memoirs,* published in 1866.

Aubignac, François Hedelin (1604-1676), French abbé, dramatist, and dramatic theorist who played a prominent part in the literary controversies of his day. His four tragedies, *La Cyminde, La Pucelle d'Orléans, Zénobie* and *Le Martyre de Sainte Catherine* were justly pronounced mediocre by Pierre CORNEILLE, the eminent French dramatist, but his treatise, *Pratique du théâtre,* commissioned by Cardinal RICHELIEU in 1640 and published in 1657, established a practical code of laws in regard to dramatic construction and methods.

Aubrey, Octave (1881-), French historian and novelist educated at the University of Paris; the novels which have made him world-famous are those in which, like Dumas, he has combined historical knowledge with his unquestioned abilities as a writer of fiction. Among the fictional and biographical works which are available in English are *The Empress Might-Have-Been* (1927); *On the King's Couch; The Lost King; The Emperor Falls in Love; The Phantom Emperor; Gaspard Hauser: The Orphan of Europe; Eugenie: Empress of the French; Napoleon: Soldier and Emperor.*

Auden, Wystan Hugh (1907-), English poet, a graduate of Christ Church, Oxford, and collaborator with Christopher Isherwood in three verse plays; *The Dog Beneath the Skin, The Ascent of F6,* and *On the Frontier.* He has recorded his experiences in China in *Journey to a War,* and has published two volumes of poems: *Selected Poems* and *Double Man.*

Audoux, Marguerite (?-1937), French author who wrote an autobiographical novel, while employed at needle-work, entitled *Marie Claire,* which achieved great success in France and in an English translation. The sequel, *L'Atelier de Marie Claire* (Marie Claire's Workshop) was not as successful.

Audran, Edmond (1842-1901), French light opera composer whose first operetta was produced at Paris in 1862; it was followed by more than forty productions in Parisian theatres. Three of these—*Olivette, The Mascot,* and *Miss Helyett* were tremendous successes in Europe, Great Britain, and the United States.

Audubon, John James (1785-1851), American ornithologist, painter, and author born in Haiti, and educated in France. After painting portraits and teaching drawing for a time, he went to London where he succeeded in finding a publisher for his great work, *Birds of America,* published in parts between 1827 and 1838. The accompanying text, *Ornithological Biography* in five volumes, appeared between 1831 and 1839. His other great work, *Viviparous Quadrupeds of North America,* was completed by his sons, J. J. and J. W. Audubon: the plates were published between 1842 and 1845, and the accompanying text between 1846 and 1854. In 1932 his home in New York was purchased as a shrine: there is a national association of Audubon societies for the study and preservation of wild life.

Auer, Leopold (1845-1930), distinguished Hungarian violinist, conductor, teacher and writer; student at the Pest and Vienna Conservatories, receiving instruction from Kohnel, Dont and JOACHIM. He became soloist to the Tsar of Russia, professor of violin at the Petrograd Conservatory and conductor of the concerts given by the Imperial Russian Musical Society. In 1918 he came to the United States, concertizing and teaching there for twelve years. Auer's pupils included Jascha HEIFETZ, Mischa ELMAN, Efrem ZIMBALIST and many other present-day virtuosos; his books include *Violin Playing as I Teach It, My Long Life in Music,* and *Violin Master Works and Their Interpretation.*

Auer, Mischa (1905-), Russian stage and screen actor who first appeared in 1928 in the film, *Something Always Happens.* Since that time he has played eccentric roles suited to his dialectic talents and bizarre sense of humor in more than fifty pictures.

Auerbach, Berthold (1812-1882), German novelist of Jewish parentage whose first successful work was a romantic biography of Spinoza, the eminent Dutch philosopher, also of Jewish extraction. He is famous, however, for the *Schwarzwalder Dorfgeschichten,* stories of peasant life in the Black Forest, published in 1841, and imitated by many writers.

Augean Stables, in Greek mythology the stables of King Augeas of Elis in which an enormous number of oxen were kept without their quarters being cleansed for many years. HERCULES cleansed it by diverting the waters of the rivers Peneus and Alpheus so that they passed through: the expression in time came to mean anything exceedingly filthy and corrupt, particularly in politics.

Augier, Guillaume Victor Émile (1820-1889), French dramatist whose first play, *La Ciguë,* was refused in 1844 at the Théâtre Français, but performed with success at the Odéon. The result

42

was a series of realistic plays, sometimes written with collaborators, which achieved their dual purpose of exposing social foibles and improving the morals of the audiences: the themes were conjugal fidelity and honesty in business and politics. Among the notable plays were *Les Fils de Giboyer, Les Effrontés, Le Gendre de M. Poirer, L'Aventurière* and *Madame Caverlet.*

Auguste, see **Clesinger, Jean Baptiste.**

Aulin, Tor (1866-1914), Swedish violinist, conductor and composer, pupil of Emile SAURET in violin and Philipp SCHARWENKA in composition. He founded a string quartet which toured Europe successfully, concertized as the greatest Scandinavian violinist since Ole BULL, and conducted the Stockholm Philharmonic Society. His compositions comprise an orchestral suite, three violin concertos and many pleasing violin pieces.

Aulos, the name of the FLUTE, the most important instrument in ancient Greece, employed in the Olympic games to quicken the energies of the contestants, and in the Pythian games as a solo instrument. The aulos was made with either one or two tubes, but with only one mouthpiece: elaborately constructed instruments sold for more than a thousand dollars, and skilled performers such as Lamia and Nichomachus were accorded the highest honors. The aulos was also used in ancient Rome where it was known as the *tibia.*

Aumer, Jean Pierre (1776-1833), French dancer, ballet-master and choreographer, trained by DAUBERVAL under whose direction he made his debut at Bordeaux. In 1798 he appeared at L'Opéra, Paris, and produced his first ballet, *Jenny, or the Secret Marriage,* at the Théâtre de la Porte Saint-Martin, Paris in 1806. After twenty-four years of success as balletmaster and choreographer at Lyon, Cassel and Vienna, he returned to L'Opéra, Paris, remaining there until his death. Aumer's best ballets were *Les Deux Creoles, Les Amours d'Antoine et de Cléopâtre, Les Pages du Duc de Vendôme,* and *La Somnambule.*

Aureole or **Aureola,** in painting, the radiant, luminous cloud which surrounds the entire figure in sacred paintings, confined in early Christian art to the Holy Trinity, but later including the Virgin Mary and certain saints. When the halo is only round the head, it is called a *nimbus;* if both aureola and nimbus are used on the same figure, the combination is called a *glory.*

Aurora, in Roman mythology, the goddess of the dawn, called *Eos* in Greek legend. In painting or sculpture Aurora is pictured as a young woman rising from the sea in a chariot drawn by winged horses, or as a maiden strewing flowers before the chariot of HELIOS, the sun god.

Aus der Ohe, Adele (1864-1937), German pianist and composer, pupil of Theodor KULLAK and of Franz LISZT. After touring Europe with phenomenal success, she came to the United States in 1887, and concertized for seventeen years with the major orchestras and in recital. She became an invalid, and was pensioned by the Bagby Music Lovers Foundation of New York. Her compositions for the piano are melodious and well conceived; many of them were published.

Auslander, Joseph (1897-), American author and poet, educated at Harvard University and at the Sorbonne, Paris; he taught at Harvard from 1919-23 and has lectured on poetry at Columbia University, New York, since 1929. His poetical works include *Cyclops Eye; Hell in Harness; No Traveler Returns; Riders at the Gate.* He has also translated the fables of Jean de LA FONTAINE in addition to becoming editor of poetry for *The North American Review,* and consultant in English poetry for the LIBRARY OF CONGRESS.

Aus Meinem Leben, the subtitle of a string quartet by Bedrich (Friedrich) SMETANA: translated the title means *From My Life,* and the composer has left a detailed description of the import of the four movements. The first portrays his early love of art, romantic tendencies, and unsatisfied yearnings; the second recalls the happy days of his youth; the third pictures the bliss of his courtship and marriage; the fourth the joy of discovering how to treat national material in music. The quartet is recorded by the Primrose String Quartet for Victor, and by the Curtis String Quartet for Columbia.

Austen, Jane (1775-1817), English novelist, daughter of a clergyman and one of a large family. Four of her novels, *Sense and Sensibility, Mansfield Park, Pride and Prejudice,* and *Emma* were published during her lifetime, but her own name did not appear on the title pages, and she received little public recognition. The novel, *Pride and Prejudice,* was dramatized by Helen Jerome, and was also a highly successful motion picture.

Austin, Alfred (1835-1913), English poet-laureate, educated at London University, and a practising barrister for a short time. His satire, *The Season,* was well received in 1861, but a book criticizing the poetry of TENNYSON, BROWNING, MATTHEW ARNOLD and SWINBURNE was a failure. He had better success with a tragedy in verse, *Savonarola.* His prose works, *The Garden That I Love* and *In Veronica's Garden* indicate a deep love of England.

Austin, Jane Goodwin (1831-1894), American author of novels and short stories descriptive of life in colonial New England; intimate with HAWTHORNE, EMERSON and Louisa ALCOTT. Her best work was the series known as the "Pilgrim Books" of which *Standish of Standish* and *Betty Alden* are representative.

Austin, Mary (1868-1934), American author and dramatist whose stories of Indian life in the southwestern part of the United States were favorably received: among them are *The Basket Woman, Starry Adventure,* and *The Land of Little Rain.* She also wrote essays on aboriginal literature, a study of American poetry, an autobiography, and two plays: *The Arrow Maker* and *Fire,* both of which were staged.

Auto-da-fé, the name of the public ceremony during which the decrees of the Spanish INQUISI-

TION were pronounced and carried out. The procedure included a procession of church dignitaries and accused persons, after which a solemn mass was celebrated and sentences imposed. Many painters have portrayed both the scene of the judgment, and the burning of the condemned.

Autran, Joseph (1813-1877), French poet and dramatist who when a youth addressed an ode to Alphonse LAMARTINE who obtained parental consent to his desire for a literary career. His best works are *La Mer*, which may have been the inspiration for Debussy's orchestral work of the same title; *Ludibria ventis; Vie rurale; Laboureurs et soldats;* and a tragedy *The Daughter of Aeschylus,* produced in 1848 with considerable success at the Odéon, Paris.

Autry, Gene (1907-), American actor, singer and song writer who has appeared on the screen since 1928 with great success in Western melodramas of which he is the focal figure as the singing hero; he is also a favorite radio performer, and his recordings have sold in the millions.

Autumn Leaves, a ballet with music by Frédéric CHOPIN; libretto and choreography by Anna PAVLOWA; first produced at Rio de Janeiro, Brazil, in 1918 with Mlle. Pavlowa as the *Chrysanthemum* and Alexander Volinine as *The Poet.* The story concerns itself with a boisterous *Autumn Wind* which destroys the chrysanthemum despite the efforts of the poet to protect her. Pavlowa was greatly attached to this ballet, her only essay in choreography.

Ave Maria, a prayer to the Virgin, used in the Roman Catholic Church and founded on the salutation, "Hail, Mary," of the angel Gabriel to the Virgin at the Annunciation. The prayer has been a favorite source of inspiration for composers since the 7th century; the settings by Franz SCHUBERT and Charles GOUNOD are both equally popular.

Avernus, a lake at Campania, Italy, originally a volcanic crater, but filled with water since the days of ancient Rome. It is the subject of many legends, one of which describes it as the entrance through which ODYSSEUS and AENEAS descended to HADES.

Ayrer, Jakob (? -1605), German dramatist regarding whom little is known although he was the most important playwright of his day in Germany. He spent most of his life in Nuremberg, where a collection of his dramas was published under the title *Opus Theatricum* in 1618. Ayrer is recognized as the successor of Hans SACHS; he is also said to have been influenced by Elizabethan plays presented by troupes of English actors in Germany, and the plots of his comedies, *Von der schönen Phoenicia* and *Von der Schönen Sidea,* are self-evidently drawn from the same sources as Shakespeare's *Much Ado About Nothing* and *The Tempest.*

Ayres, Lew (1908-), American motion-picture actor, graduate of the University of Arizona and a skilled musician who played with well-known orchestras until he assumed the role of the young lover in *The Kiss* with Greta GARBO. He has appeared in many notable films including *All Quiet on the Western Front, State Fair, Last Train from Madrid,* and in several films centered around the engaging character of *Dr. Kildare.*

Aytoun, William Edmondstoune (1813-1865), Scottish humorist and poet, a graduate of the University of Edinburgh and admitted to the bar in 1850, although, as he expressed it "I followed the law, but never could overtake it." After joining the editorial staff of *Blackwood's Magazine,* where he remained until his death, he wrote with Sir Theodore Martin a series of humorous articles on the fads and follies of his day which were published in 1855 with great success as the *Bon Gaultier Ballads.* His reputation as a poet rests on *The Lays of the Scottish Cavaliers* (1848): he also wrote a novel, *Norman Sinclair,* said to be based on his personal experiences.

Azucena, the Spanish gypsy in Verdi's opera, IL TROVATORE, who burned her own child at the stake when she had intended to destroy the infant Manrico, brother of the Count di Luna in revenge for his execution of her mother. She is avenged when the Count executes Manrico after the latter has won the love of the Countess Leonora.

B

Baal, in ancient mythology the name given to several Semitic gods in Assyria, Arabia, Phoenicia, Abyssinia, and other countries in Asia and Africa; they were usually deities of nature, or more specifically of the sun, rivers, and springs. The most important of these gods appears to have been the *Baal* worshiped at Tyre by the Phoenicians; an idol known as the Golden CALF was associated with this cult.

Babbitt, Irving (1865-1933), American essayist educated at Harvard University, and for more than twenty years professor at that institution: he also lectured at many American colleges, and edited the works of Racine, Voltaire, Taine and Renan. Among his works are *Literature and the American College* (1908); *The New Laokoön; Rousseau and Romanticism; On Being Creative and Other Essays.*

Babel, Isaac (1894-), Russian novelist ranked among the best of the Soviet authors. Among his novels is *Red Cavalry;* this has been translated into English, and contains a series of tales of the Cossacks similar to those related by Nicolai GOGOL in "Taras Bulba." Another novel, written in the somewhat involved dialect of the Russian Jew and entitled *Tales of Odessa,* exploits the adventures of a Jewish bandit; a third, *Benia Krik* has also been translated.

Babin, Victor, see **Vronsky and Babin.**

Babo, Josef Marius (1756-1822), German dramatist who wrote a cycle of plays of chivalry in imitation of GOETHE's "Götz von Berlichingen";

one of them, *Otto von Wittelsbach* (1781), was a great success as were also two comedies, *Homely Happiness* and *The Pulse*.

Babrius, a fabulist of the 1st century, B.C., whose tales were written in Greek verse: little information about him is available except that he was probably a Roman. The manuscript of his work, containing 123 fables, was found in a convent on Mount Athor, and is now in the BRITISH MUSEUM. The verses are excellent, and the authenticity of the collection is generally admitted; an excellent English version by James Davies appeared about 1860.

Baccaloni, Salvatore (1904-   ), Italian operatic bass who was first trained as an architect, his abilities as a singer being developed purely as an avocation until a famous teacher suggested intensive training with an operatic career as its goal. His debut was made at Rome in 1921: in the United States his first appearance was with the Chicago Opera Company in 1930. Ten years later he made his debut with the Metropolitan Opera Company, New York, and he is now (1943), an outstanding member of the organization appearing in the basso buffo roles of *The Marriage of Figaro; The Barber of Seville, Don Pasquale, L'Elisir d'Amore,* and *The Daughter of the Regiment.*

Bacchae, see **Bacchantes.**

Bacchanale, a ballet in one act: libretto by Salvador Dali, choreography by Leonide MASSINE; music adapted from the Venusberg Music (Bacchanale) composed by Richard WAGNER for the première of TANNHAUSER at L'Opéra, Paris, where a ballet was required regardless of its being apropos. The plot is of psycho-analytic character, revolving around Ludwig II of Bavaria and his paranoic dreams of Venusberg as he listens to the music created by Wagner.

Bacchanale (Samson and Delilah), the ballet in the opera *Samson and Delilah,* libretto by Ferdinand Lemaire, music by Camille SAINT-SAENS; first performed at the Hoftheater, Weimar, in 1877, and in the United States at the French Opera House, New Orleans, in 1893. The ballet takes place during Act III in the Temple of Dagon just before Samson, his vision and strength miraculously restored, tears down the marble pillars of the temple, and finds death in the ruins together with his enemies. There is a Victor recording by the Boston "Pops" Orchestra under Arthur FIEDLER.

Bacchanalia, the name in Latin for the mystic festivals in honor of BACCHUS, the Roman god of wine. Originally sacred in character, they degenerated into drunken orgies at which all manner of crimes and political conspiracies were planned, the result being that they were finally forbidden by law.

Bacchantes, in Greek and Roman religious rites the name of women worshipers of Dionysus; they were also called *Bacchae.* One of Euripides' tragedies, *Bacchae,* is said to have pictured the wild frenzy of these women at a Dionysian festival.

Bacchus, see **Dionysus.**

Bacchylides, Greek lyric poet who was born about 480 B.C.; a nephew of Simonides and listed by Plutarch among the poets who became successful after being exiled from Greece. His poems are distinguished by simplicity, clarity and picturesque detail; his *Odes of Victory* are excellent examples of his talent.

Baccio d'Agnola (c.1460-1543), Florentine sculptor and architect who was first an excellent woodcarver who created beautiful figures and designs at the Palazzo Vecchio in FLORENCE. He studied architecture at Rome, and later planned the Villa Borghese and the Palazzo Bartolini: he was the first architect to use frontispieces for doors and windows in residences, construction previously confined to churches. His studio is said to have been a gathering place for MICHELANGELO, SANSOVINO, RAPHAEL and many other famous artists.

Baccio della Porta, see **Bartolommeo di Paghola del Fattorino, Fra.**

Bach, Johann Christian (1735-1782), German organist, pianist and composer; the youngest surviving son of Johann Sebastian BACH, and pupil of his brother, Karl Philipp Emanuel BACH, and of Padre MARTINI. After spending two years in Italy, he went to England in 1762 where he succeeded George Frederick HANDEL as music master, and remained there until his death. His works include fifteen operas; an oratorio; chamber music; also many concertos and other compositions for the piano which greatly influenced Wolfgang Amadeus MOZART. He was nicknamed the *English Bach.*

Bach, Johann Christoph Friedrich (1732-1795), German composer; ninth son of Johann Sebastian BACH, and chamber musician to Count von Lippe at Bückeburg. His compositions, which include cantatas, an oratorio, chamber music, and piano sonatas, are less brilliant than those of his brothers, Johann Christian BACH and Karl Philipp Emanuel BACH, but they are music of the finest calibre. He was nicknamed the *Bückeburg Bach.*

Bach, Johann Sebastian (1685-1750), German organist, clavichordist, and composer who studied the violin with his father, Johann Ambrosius Bach; the clavichord with his brother, Johann Christoph Bach, and the organ with George Böhm. After occupying posts as organist at various small churches, he became organist at Arnstadt in 1704: in 1705 he secured a leave of absence, and walked to Lübeck and back, a distance of 225 miles, to hear the organ and choir music of Dietrich BUXTEHUDE which so impressed him that he greatly overstayed his leave. In 1723 he succeeded Johann KUHNAU as cantor at the Thomasschule, Leipzig, also becoming organist and director of music at the Thomaskirche and the Nicolaikirche, the two principal churches. He remained at these posts for the rest of his life, making occasional visits to Dresden and Potsdam: at the latter city he was the guest of FREDERICK THE GREAT of Prussia for whom he improvised on the newly-made pianos of Gottfried SILBERMANN. His compositions, greatly neglected for more than one hundred years after his death, but now regarded as the finest of the pre-classical period, include five sets of sacred works for every Sunday and feast day of the year; almost two hundred cantatas; the PASSIONS of *St. John* and *St. Matthew; the Christmas, Easter,* and *Ascension* oratorios; several secular cantatas, the *Mass in B Minor;* organ preludes, fugues, toccatas, and fantasias; many suites, inventions, toccatas, and pieces for clavichord and harpsichord including the 24 preludes and fugues in all keys entitled The WELL-TEMPERED CLAVICHORD; the MUSIKALISCHE OPFER; The ART OF FUGUE; six suites for solo violoncello; three sonatas and three partitas for solo violin; four suites for orchestra; concertos for harpsichord, violin, oboe, and flute.

Bach, Karl Philipp Emanuel (1714-1788), German clavichordist, pianist and composer who studied with his father, Johann Sebastian BACH, and became chamber-musician to FREDERICK THE GREAT in 1740. He remained at this post until 1767 when he succeeded Georg TELEMANN as music director of the Johanneum, and of the five principal churches at Hamburg. He was regarded as the greatest CLAVIER virtuoso of his day, and his compositions, while not as intricately intellectual as those of his father, were written during a period of transition in musical composition: he is regarded as the originator of the SONATA FORM with its emphasis on melody and ornamentation, and Joseph HAYDN was greatly influenced by him. His compositions include fifty-two concertos and more than two hundred solo pieces for clavier; eighteen symphonies, chamber music, oratorios, Passions and cantatas. He was nicknamed the *Berlin* or *Hamburg Bach.*

Bach, Wilhelm Friedemann (1710-1784), German organist and composer who studied with his father, Johann Sebastian BACH, and with Johann Gottlieb Graun. He became an outstanding organist at Dresden and Halle, and is regarded today as the most gifted of Johann Sebastian Bach's sons: a tendency toward dissipation wrecked what apparently might have been a distinguished career. His compositions include cantatas, organ works, chamber music, piano concertos, and piano pieces. He was nicknamed the *Dresden* or *Halle Bach.*

Bach Choir, Bethlehem, see **Bethlehem Bach Choir.**

Bach Circle, an organization founded in 1937 by Yella PESSL, one of the foremost contemporary exponents of the harpsichord, the keyboard instrument of the 17th and 18th centuries. Its purpose has been to present rarely heard chamber music works by Johann Sebastian BACH, his sons, his predecessors, and his contemporaries including HANDEL, PURCELL, COUPERIN and SCARLETTI; the spirit of the music to be preserved by performing it in the form in which it was originally written. Among the works which have been presented are J. S. Bach's MUSIKALISCHE OPFER by a string and woodwind ensemble; a sonata for viola and harpsichord by Wilhelm Friedemann Bach; Johann Sebastian Bach's *Wedding Cantata* for soprano, oboe, strings and harpsichord; Handel's Sonata in G minor for oboe, viola de gamba, and harpsi-

chord; and Couperin's *Les Fastes de la grande et ancienne Menestrandise* for harpsichord.

Bachaus, Wilhelm (1884-), German pianist, pupil of Alois Reckendorf and Eugene D'ALBERT: from 1900 he taught and concertized, winning the Anton RUBINSTEIN prize of 5000 francs in 1905. From 1912 to the present time he has toured the entire world several times, making use of his superb technique entirely in the interest of supremely artistic ideals: he is highly regarded in American musical circles, and has made many fine recordings.

Bacheller, Irving (1859-), American novelist, a graduate of St. Lawrence University and a journalist for several years. Three of his novels, *Eben Holden* (1900), *Silas Strong,* and *D'ri and I* were very successful; also his autobiography, *Coming Up the Road: the Story of a North Country Boyhood.*

Bacher, Otto Henry (1856-1909), American artist who was an illustrator for both the *Century Magazine* and *Harper's Magazine,* and was recognized as one of the foremost pen-and-ink artists of his day: his etchings included the distinguished *Danube Series.*

Baciccio, Il, see **Gaulli, Giovanni Battista.**

Backhuysen, Ludolf (1631-1708), Dutch painter, pupil of Allart van EVERDINGEN, and later becoming famous for his sea-pieces, particularly those picturing the ocean in its wildest moods of wind and waves: he is said to have acted as instructor in drawing to PETER THE GREAT of Russia.

Baclanova, Olga (1899-), Russian actress and singer who was educated at the Cherniavsky Institute in Moscow, and appeared at the Moscow Art Theatre at sixteen. Among the notable productions in which she has been featured are *The Daughter of Madame Angot, Carmencita* and the *Soldier, The Miracle, Grand Hotel, The Cat and the Fiddle* and *Idiot's Delight:* she has also acted in many important films.

Bacon, Francis, Baron Verulam (1561-1626), English statesman, philosopher, and essayist who was a favorite of both Queen ELIZABETH and James I: his reputation and honor are somewhat tarnished by his having worked against his friend and patron, the Earl of ESSEX, resulting in the latter being executed. His works include *Essays* (1597), regarded as immortal because of their perfect style and their rich knowledge of human relations; *The New Atlantis* (1627), one of the world's greatest Utopian speculations from the scientific point of view.

Bacon, Frank (1864-1922), American actor and dramatist: after playing in stock companies with his wife, he wrote the phenomenal stage success, *Lightnin',* with Winchell Smith in 1918, and played the stellar role in it until his death. A motion-picture version featured Will ROGERS in the role created by Bacon in the stage play.

Bacon, Henry (1866-1924), American architect who studied at the University of Illinois, and was connected with the firm of McKim, Mead and White from 1888 to 1897, after which he worked independently. His greatest work was the Lincoln Memorial at Washington, D. C., erected at a cost of $2,500,000; other creations included the Lafayette Monument, Brooklyn, N. Y.; the Longfellow Monument, Cambridge, Mass.; the Centennial Monument, Chicago, Ill.; also many public and private business buildings. In 1923 he was presented with the gold medal of the American Institute of Architects.

Bacon, Josephine Dodge Daskam (1876-), American poet, novelist, and writer of juvenile stories educated at Smith College. Her works include *Smith College Stories* (1900); *Middle-Aged Love Stories; Poems; The Domestic Adventurers; In the Border Country; The Inheritance; Medusa's Head; Luck of Lowry; Kathy; The Root and the Flower; Down in the Closet; The World in His Heart.*

Bacon, Katherine (1896-), English pianist, student at the PEABODY CONSERVATORY, Baltimore, Md., and the INSTUTE OF MUSICAL ART, New York. Her debut was made at AEOLIAN HALL, New York, in 1921; since then she has concertized and taught with great success, her specialty being recitals covering Beethoven's thirty-two piano sonatas, and Schubert's entire piano works.

Bacon, Leonard (1887-), American poet and critic educated at Yale University, and later professor of English at the University of California. His works include *Ulug Beg* (1923); *Animula Vagula; Guinea-Fowl and Other Poultry; The Legend of the Quincibald; The Furioso; The Voyage of Autoleon; Bullinger Bound, and Other Poems; Sunderland Capture and Other Poems.*

Bacon, Peggy (1895-), American artist, illustrator, and writer who studied at the ART STUDENTS' LEAGUE and the School of Fine and Applied Arts, New York, and was awarded a Guggenheim fellowship in 1934. She has contributed verses, stories, and drawings to many American magazines: among her drawings with text are *Light-hearted Kitten; Mercy and the Mouse; Animosities; Ballad of Tangle Street.*

Badajoz, Juan de, 16th century Spanish architect who superintended the construction of the Cathedral of Leon, and was consulted during the erection of the cathedrals at Seville and Salamanca. His plans for the cloister of the Benedictine Monastery of St. Zoil at Carrion de los Condes was so exquisitely laid out in sculptures that it was regarded as a marvel of execution in the Spanish mode.

Badger, Joseph (1708-1785), American portrait painter; originally a commercial sign maker and entirely self-educated; his portraits of John Adams, the second president of the United States, and other distinguished men in public life compare favorably with those painted by the most distinguished artists of his day.

Badinage (Fr.), a word meaning playful raillery or banter: in music it is frequently used as the title of an orchestral or instrumental composition of light or gay character; for example, *Badinage* by Victor Herbert.

Baedeker, Karl (1801-1859), German publisher who instituted a series of guide books for travelers in all parts of the world: the volumes were modeled on the series published by John Murray, and prepared with such meticulous accuracy that they became the standard literature of this nature. English translations were available in the United States, but the volumes have become almost entirely unprocurable since World War II.

Baer, William Jacob (1860-1941), American miniature painter who studied at the Munich Academy for several years. He exercised considerable influence in reviving the art of miniature painting in the United States, becoming first president of the Society of Painters in Miniature, New York. Among his best miniatures are *The Golden Hour; Daphne; In Arcadia; Nymph; Phoebe; Madonna with the Auburn Hair.*

Baermann, Heinrich Joseph (1784-1847), German clarinettist; one of the greatest virtuosos of all time on his instrument. He became first clarinettist of the court orchestra at Munich, and was intimate with Felix MENDELSSOHN who wrote two duos for clarinet and basset-horn for him; also with Carl Maria von WEBER who composed a concerto and a quintet for clarinet and strings in his honor.

Bagatelle (Fr.), a word meaning a "trifling thing": in music it is often used as the title of a fanciful orchestral or instrumental piece such as *Bagatelle* (Für Elise) for piano solo by Ludwig van BEETHOVEN.

Bagdad or **Baghdad,** the capital city of Iraq: in the 9th century it was one of the greatest cities in the world with a population of almost 2,000,000. In literature and art it vied with the Spanish city, Cordova, and is still called "the glorious city" in Turkish official papers. HARUN AL-RASHID was the greatest of its caliphs, and its magnificence is the subject of much comment throughout *The* ARABIAN NIGHTS.

Baggesen, Jens Immanuel (1764-1826), Danish poet, author of *Comic Tales* (1785), a volume of poetry which made him a favorite bard at twenty-one. His finest work was *The Labyrinth,* later entitled *Wanderings of a Poet,* and a narrative of his incessant wanderings throughout Europe. Danish literature was greatly enriched by Baggesen's firm and polished style; he might have reached even greater heights if his egotism and passion could have been restrained.

Bagnacavallo (1484-1542), Italian painter who had the distinction of being among those chosen by RAPHAEL to assist him in the tremendous task of decorating the VATICAN; his real name was Bartolommeo Ramenghi, but he preferred to use the name of the Italian town (Bagnacavallo) in which he was born. Among his best works are *Madonna in Glory and Saints; Circumcision; Holy Family and Saints.* His son, Giovanni Battista Bagnacavallo, worked at Rome with VASARI, and assisted PRIMATICCIO at FONTAINEBLEAU.

Bagnold, Enid, contemporary English poet and novelist presumed to be the author of *Serena Blandish,* an outstanding success in 1925 as a novel, and in 1928 as a play in a dramatic version by S. N. BEHRMAN. Her works include *A Diary Without Dates* (1917); *Sailing Ships* (poems); *The Happy Foreigner; National Velvet; The Door of Life.*

Bagpipe, an ancient wind instrument known in Oriental countries, Greece and Rome: it was a favorite instrument in many sections of Europe in the Middle Ages, and is still used in Ireland and Scotland. It consists of a leather bag kept supplied with air by a small bellows worked by the player's arm; the pipes are usually four in number, one of them, the *chanter,* playing the melody and the others playing a *drone,* a monotonous reiteration of certain low-pitched musical tones.

Bahr, Hermann (1863-1934), Austrian critic, journalist, theatre manager, and dramatist educated at the University of Vienna. He settled in Vienna as a social and literary critic; edited several papers and managed the Deutsches Theater. He voiced his firm stand against French modernism in three volumes of essays: *A Critique of Modernism, The Overthrow of Naturalism,* and *Studies in Modern Criticism.* As a dramatist, Bahr is often compared with Arthur SCHNITZLER; one of his numerous plays, *The Concert* (1909), was produced in New York, and his novel, *The Master,* has been translated.

Baif, Jean Antoine (1532-1589), French poet: one of the literary league known as the "Pleiade," and an advocate of changing French poetry to the rhyme-free metres of Latin verse. He made fine translations of Greek and Roman dramas: his original works, *The Mimes, Precepts and Proverbs,* are also noteworthy.

Bailey, Philip James (1816-1902), English poet, educated in Glasgow and admitted to the bar in 1840. His principal work is *Festus* (1839), a dramatic poem based on the legend of *Faust:* it was extremely long and considered incoherent in many respects, but achieved remarkable success, running through eleven editions in fifty years. Bailey's other works, among them *The Angel World* and *The Universal Hymn* which he added to *Festus,* did not enhance his reputation.

Bailey, Temple, contemporary American novelist and short story writer: her numerous works include *Judy* (1907); *Glory of Youth; Mistress Anne; Peacock Feathers; Enchanted Ground; The Radiant Tree; Fair as the Moon; The Blue Cloak.*

Baillie, Joanna (1762-1851), Scottish poet and dramatist: the first volume of her *Plays on the Passions,* was published in 1798, and one of them, *The Family Legend,* was performed with some success at Edinburgh under the patronage of Sir Walter Scott. Her shorter poems are her best work, and she had many distinguished intimates including Sir Walter SCOTT, Lord Francis Jeffrey, and Sarah Kemble SIDDONS, the famous actress.

Baillot, Pierre-Marie-François, de Sales (1771-1842), French violinist who studied under various Italian and French teachers: after many vicissitudes he became professor of violin at the Paris Conservatory and solo violinist in the royal orchestra. He wrote an excellent text-book, *L'Art du Violon,* and a violin method, in collaboration with Pierre RODE and Rodolphe KREUTZER, which has been republished in several languages. Baillot's pupils included Jacques Mazas and Charles DANCLA; his numerous chamber music works and violin solos are no longer played.

Bailly, Joseph Alexis (1825-1883), American sculptor of French parentage: among his works are statues of Benjamin FRANKLIN and George WASHINGTON. He also made an equestrian statue of President Blanco of Venezuela, and taught art for some years at the PENNSYLVANIA ACADEMY OF FINE ARTS, Philadelphia.

Bailly, Louis (1882-), French violinist: a graduate of the Paris Conservatory, and for many years a member of the Capet, FLONZALEY, Elman and Curtis String Quartets. He has appeared as soloist with many of the major symphony orchestras, and is now the head of the viola and chamber-music departments of the CURTIS INSTITUTE OF MUSIC, Philadelphia.

Baily, Edward Hodges (1788-1867), English sculptor; his father was a famous carver of figureheads for ships. Two of his studies of HOMER came to the notice of John FLAXMAN, the result being that he became a pupil of the famous sculptor. In 1811 he won the Academy gold medal for his *Hercules Restoring Alcestis to Admetus;* in 1821 he was admitted to the Royal Academy. Among his finest works are the statue of Admiral Nelson in Trafalgar Square, London, and busts of Samuel JOHNSON, Earl Grey, Lord Mansfield, and Sir Isaac Newton.

Baini, Giuseppe (1775-1844), Italian priest, music critic, author, and composer; pupil of Giuseppe Jannaconi, one of the last of the composers in the style of Palestrina. His compositions are severely ecclesiastical in style; his *Miserere for Ten Voices* (1821) is still used during Holy Week at the Sistine Chapel in the Vatican, Rome. Baini is most famous, however, for his *Life of Palestrina* in which he used the phrase, "Il Principe della Musica" (The Prince of Music), which remains firmly associated with the name of PALESTRINA.

Bainter, Fay (1892-), American stage and screen actress who made her first appearance on the boards with the Belasco Stock Company at Los Angeles, and her New York debut in 1912 at Daly's Theatre in *The Rose of Panama.* Her greatest stage role was that of Ming Toy in *East is West* (1922); in 1934 she played the part of Fran Dodsworth in Sinclair Lewis's *Dodsworth* with Walter HUSTON. Miss Bainter has also appeared in many motion pictures including *Jezebel, Quality Street, The Arkansas Traveler, The Shining Hour, Daughters Courageous,* and *The War against Mrs. Hadley.*

Baker, Elizabeth (1879-), English magazine writer and dramatist who achieved success with a

48

play, *Chains* (1909), which was regarded as unique because it escaped the customarily stereotyped conventions of stage drama, particularly the "eternal triangle." Among her plays are *Partnership, Miss Robinson,* and *Penelope Forgives.*

Baker, George Pierce (1866-1935), American educator and author and founder in 1905 of the famous 47 WORKSHOP, a school for drama at Harvard University, Cambridge, Mass., where he taught in the Department of English from 1888 to 1924. Many of those who are important figures in the theatre of today—dramatists, directors and producers—found the Workshop a source of inspiration as well as education in dramatic technique. Among his many pupils were Eugene O'NEILL, Philip BARRY, George ABBOTT and S. N. BEHRMAN. In 1925 Baker went to Yale University, New Haven, Conn., where he became professor of drama, and chairman of the Department of Drama, School of Fine Arts and director of the University Theatre until his retirement in 1933. Among his published works are *The Development of Shakespeare as a Dramatist* (1907), *Dramatic Technique,* and *Some Unpublished Correspondence of David Garrick.* He also edited four series of *Plays of the 47 Workshop; Yale One Act Plays* and *Yale Long Plays.*

Baker, Ray Stannard (1870-), American journalist and author; graduate of the University of Michigan: he joined the staff of *McClure's Magazine* in 1907, and later became one of the editors of the *American Magazine.* Under the pen-name "David Grayson" he published several volumes of essays including *Adventures in Contentment* (1907), *Adventures in Understanding, The Friendly Road, Adventures in Solitude, The Countryman's Year,* and an autobiography, *Native American: The Book of My Youth.* His biography of Woodrow Wilson won the Pulitzer Prize in 1940.

Baker, Theodore (1851-1934), German-American translator, compiler, and author of two important musical works; *Baker's Biographical Dictionary of Musicians* (1900; 4th revised edition 1940); *Dictionary of Musical Terms* (1895). Dr. Baker made known the findings of a serious study of North American Indian Music in a thesis written in 1882.

Bakhuisen, Ludolf, see **Backhuysen, Ludolf.**

Bakst, Leon (1866-1924), Russian painter and scenic artist: in 1900 he began painting scenery for plays, especially Greek tragedies produced at St. Petersburg. His individualistic style attracted much favorable comment, and his reputation was greatly enhanced by the scenery and costumes created in 1909 for the DIAGHILEFF Russian Ballet in Paris, especially for the ballets *Scheherazade* and *Cleopatra.* His paintings are in the METROPOLITAN MUSEUM, New York, and the VICTORIA AND ALBERT MUSEUM, London: many of the finest were shown in the United States in 1913-14.

Bal, Le, a modern ballet in one act and two scenes: libretto by George Balanchine and music by Vittorio Rieti; first produced at Monte Carlo in 1929. The fantastic plot concerns itself with the trials and tribulations of a young man at a ball who is confronted with not only a double of his sweetheart, but also a stand-in of himself. The latter finally departs with the lady, leaving the frustrated lover alone and completely bewildered as the curtain descends.

Balaieff, Nikita, see **Chauve Souris.**

Balakirev, Mily Alexeivitch (1837-1910), Russian pianist, composer, and founder, along with CUI, MOUSSORGSKY, RIMSKY-KORSAKOW and BORODIN, of the national Russian music school. As an orchestral conductor he introduced the works not only of young Slav composers, but also of European composers including BERLIOZ and LISZT to Russian audiences. His works include two symphonic poems, *Russia* and *Tamara;* incidental music to *King Lear;* several overtures; an Oriental fantasy for piano, *Islamey,* also arranged for orchestra; many pieces and arrangements for the piano.

Balalaika, a stringed instrument extremely popular in Russia, especially in the Ukraine: it consists of a triangular soundboard, glued to a vaulted back and forming a body with a triangular base so that it can stand in an upright position. The fretted fingerboard has from two to four strings, usually tuned to produce a minor chord: the strings are plucked with the fingers, and pleasing glissando effects can be produced. In many respects the balalaika resembles the GUITAR and is made in so many sizes, from the small soprano to the large bass, that a miniature string orchestra is frequently formed of the combination.

Balanchine, George (1904-), Russian ballet dancer and choreographer; real name George Melitonovich Balanchivadze. He studied at the Imperial School of Ballet at St. Petersburg, and became a member of the ballet at the Maryinsky Theatre in 1921, also studying music at the Imperial Conservatory. From 1925 to 1928 he danced with the DIAGHILEFF Russian ballet; was appointed choreographer, and wrote nine ballets. He also directed ballet at Monte Carlo; formed his own company in 1933, and founded the American Ballet Company, with Lincoln KIRSTEIN and Edward M. M. Warburg, which was so successful at the Adelphi Theatre, New York, in 1935 that he was made ballet master at the Metropolitan Opera House, New York, where he remained until 1938. In 1940 Balanchine acted as choreographer for *Balustrade,* a ballet based on Igor Stravinsky's violin concerto; he also designed the choreography for *Babes in Arms* and *I Married an Angel.* Among his important ballets are *The Nightingale, Barabau, La Pastorale, The Triumph of Neptune, La Chatte, Mozartiana, The Prodigal Son, Les Sept Péchés Capitaux, Cotillon, Alma Mater, Orpheus,* and *The Card Party.* He has also staged many dances for the films such as *The Goldwyn Follies* (1937).

Balassa, Bálint, Baron of Kekko and Gymart (1551-1594), Hungarian lyric poet whose works of widely varying character include religious hymns, patriotic songs, love sonnets and translations of Latin and German poets. He was a man of violent passions in his amours and in his military career, finally dying of wounds received during the war between Hungary and Turkey in 1594.

Balassa was the inventor of a STROPHE still bearing his name, and consisting of nine lines or three rhyming pairs alternating with rhyming third, sixth and ninth lines.

Balcony, in architecture a type of platform projecting from the wall of a building, and supported by columns or brackets. In theatres the term was first applied to a stage box, but now designates the gallery over the dress circle.

Baldachin, in architecture a structure in the form of a canopy supported by columns, and either suspended from the roof of or projecting from the wall of a church: usually over the altar as in St. Peter's at Rome where the baldachin is about 95 feet high.

Balderston, John Lloyd (1889-), American newspaper correspondent, author and dramatist: he worked as correspondent of the *Philadelphia Record*, as editor of *The Outlook*, London, and as correspondent of the *New York World*. His plays include *Tongo; Berkeley Square* (with J. C. Squire); *Dracula* (with Hamilton Deane); *Frankenstein* (with Peggy Webling); also *The Genius of the Marne* which was originally published in book form.

Baldovinetti, Alessio (1425-1499), Italian painter of murals, chests, shields, banners, and designs in glass; also a worker in mosaic. He is given credit for having experimented with new methods of paint mixing, and to have employed oil paints before Antonella da MESSINA. The UFFIZI Gallery, FLORENCE, has three of his Madonnas and there is a profile portrait of a lady in the NATIONAL GALLERY, London. Baldovinetti's chief pupil was Domenico GHIRLANDAIO.

Baldridge, C. Le Roy (1889-), American artist who acted as illustrator for "The Stars and Stripes," the official newspaper of the American Expeditionary Force during World War I. He also illustrated *I Was There,* containing drawings of World War I; Caroline Singer's *White Africans and Black; Boomba Lives in Africa; Half the World is Isfahan* and many other books.

Baldung, Hans (1480-1545), German painter: pupil of Albrecht DÜRER, and surnamed *Grün* because of his frequent use of the color green in his pictures. His best-known work is the high altar of the Cathedral of Freiburg, in the center of which is a portrayal of the *Coronation of the Virgin* with the *Annunciation*, the *Visitation*, the *Nativity*, and the *Flight into Egypt* on the wings. Baldung learned the art of strange, dazzling light effects from Mathias GRUNWALD with whom he was intimate, but his work lacks the mellowness of the latter's work in this respect.

Baldwin, Faith (1893-), American novelist educated in Brooklyn, New York: her works include *Mavis of Green Hill* (1921); *Laurel of Stony Stream; Three Women; Make Believe; District Nurse; American Family; Blue Horizons.*

Balen, Hendrik van (1575-1632), Flemish painter, a collaborator with Jan BREUGHEL: he painted charmingly artistic figures into the latter's landscapes. Balen specialized in mythological pictures such as the *Rape of Europa* (in which the landscape and flowers were painted in by Breughel), *Diana at the Chase,* and *Banquet of the Gods.*

Balestier, Charles Wolcott (1861-1891), American publisher and novelist who collaborated with his brother-in-law, Rudyard KIPLING on *The Naulahka.* His works include *A Potent Philtre* (1884); *A Fair Device; A Victorious Defeat; The Average Woman; Benefits Forgot.*

Balestrieri, Tommaso (c.1735-c.1790), Italian violin maker influenced by GUANERIUS and STRADIVARIUS. His violins are along large and broad lines: they are distinguished by fine tone and workmanship with the varnish ranging from yellow to rich orange-red, and are sold today for from $2500.00 to $8000.00.

Balfe, Michael William (1808-1870), Irish singer and composer of operas in English: his first success was *The Siege of Rochelle* at the DRURY LANE THEATRE in London (1835). In 1843 *The Bohemian Girl* achieved enormous popularity in London, Paris and other European cities as well as in the United States. No one of the twenty operas which followed had anything more than ephemeral success.

Balinese Music, an unusual kind of music practised by natives of the island of Bali in the Malay Archipelago near the island of Java; it is used in their social and religious life, and the *gamelans,* or orchestras, are in every village. The instruments include large and small DRUMS, XYLOPHONES with metal bars, and GONGS of many types and in several sizes. The leader uses either a rebab (two-stringed violin) or a drum: there are also instruments resembling the FLUTE, CLARINET and PSALTERY. The music is in RONDO form, and the musical drama or opera, known as *Ardja,* usually begins at midnight and lasts until dawn. An interesting account of the rites and festivals in which music plays an important part is to be found in *Island of Bali* by Miguel Covarrubias.

Ball, Thomas (1819-1911), American painter and sculptor who studied in Europe, but developed a style, unmistakably American, which had a distinct influence on the monumental art in the United States. Originally a portrait painter, he turned to sculpture; his first success in 1851 was a bust of Jenny LIND. Among his works is the equestrian statue of Washington in the Boston Public Gardens; Daniel Webster in Central Park, New York; the Lincoln Emancipation group at Washington, D. C., and a statue of Edwin Booth as "Coriolanus" in the Actors' Home, Philadelphia. Ball published his autobiography, *My Three Score Years and Ten,* in 1891.

Ballad, in literature, according to Webster's Dictionary, "a romantic poem characterized by simplicity of structure and impersonality of authorship, usually founded upon ancient folk legend or tradition." It may be added that the ballad is almost always objective, written in direct (non-poetic) and conventional language interspersed with set phrases, and frequently with a refrain either inane or meaningless. The literatures of all peoples are replete with ballads: there are several hundred Scotch, English, Irish and Welsh ballads, and an uncounted number of American ballads among the negroes, cowboys and mountaineers. The structure of the verses varies according to the literacy of the country at the period when the ballad was transcribed.

Ballade (It. and Ger.), in music originally the name of a song with dance accompaniment, called in Italy a *balletta:* in medieval England, France and Germany a long narrative poem sung around the campfire, or at banquets and song festivals. In modern music the term *ballade* is associated with songs having dramatic text such as Schubert's ERL-KING. In piano music, CHOPIN and BRAHMS are prominent among those who used the word for compositions of indefinite form conveying romantic or dramatic ideas.

Ballad Opera, a form of dramatic entertainment employing music which became popular in England from 1728 when John Gay's *The Beggar's Opera* was produced with the music assembled from folk tunes by Dr. PEPUSCH with such success that HANDEL was forced to close the theatre where he was presenting Italian opera. In 1762 ballad opera was revived in England with Ben Jonson's *The Village Opera:* in Germany a ballad opera *The Devil is Loose* had tremendous success in 1743. Mozart's immortal work in this form, *The Abduction from the Seraglio,* delighted the Viennese in 1782. In France, Rousseau wrote a ballad opera, *The Village Soothsayer,* that remained popular for fifty years.

Ballantyne, Robert Michael (1825-1894), Scottish author for years in the employ of the Hudson's Bay Company, the result being his first book, *Hudson's Bay; or, Life in the Wilds of North America* (1848). In 1856 he began writing a series of nearly 100 books of adventure for juveniles including *The Young Fur Traders; The World of Ice; Erling the Bold,* etc.; all imbued with personal knowledge of the scenes and people described, graphic in literary style, and thoroughly healthy in moral tone.

Ballerina (It.), in ballet a female dancer; the *prima ballerina* is the principal female dancer in a ballet company. The term was originally applied to a dancer in the COMMEDIA DELL'ARTE.

Ballet, the term for a series of dances of aesthetic character executed by a solo dancer or an ensemble, and presented as part of an opera, or as a complete theatrical performance with a story interpreted through dance and pantomime. Ballet began in Italy during the 15th century, and in France with the founding of the National Academy of the Dance in 1661: its development can be traced through an unbroken line of dancers and teachers down to the present day. Many of the great instructors, dancers, choreographers and composers who brought the ballet to its eminent position in the art world are discussed in this volume.

Ballet blanc (Fr.), in ballet the term for a ballet in the classic style, called "white ballet"

because the ballerinas wear the traditional white skirt.

Ballet Mécanique, a modern ballet in one act; libretto and choreography by Adolf BOLM; music by Alexander Mossolov; first performed in August, 1932, at the Hollywood Bowl, Los Angeles, Calif. The scene is laid in a factory lighted by the glow of blast furnaces, and the movements of the machines are simulated by dancers clad in white, black, and silver. The music was written by Mossolov for the film, *The Mad Genius* in 1931; it was transferred to the ballet which has become very popular. Bolm obtained his idea for the choreography through visits to American factories.

Ballet Russe de Monte Carlo, see **De Basil, Colonel Wassily.**

Ballet Theatre, The, an organization founded in 1939; its management was assumed in 1941 by S. Hurok, whose reputation was already established as impresario for Anna PAVLOWA, Feodor CHALIAPIN, Isadore DUNCAN and other great artists. The company was recruited from various Russian ballet companies which had previously appeared in America; among the outstanding choreographers, ballerinas, and male dancers engaged were Leonide MASSINE, Irina BARONOVA, Alice MARKOVA, and Anton DOLIN. To these were added the finest American talent in the original Ballet Theatre: in 1942-43 the organization consisted of forty-two Americans, four Russians, four English, two Canadians, one French, one Jugoslav, and one Pole among the principals and *corps du ballet.* Karen CONRAD, Nora Kaye, Annabelle Lyon, Lucia CHASE, Ian GIBSON, Jerome Robbins and George Skibine were also members of the company. The outstanding classic and modern ballets which are always favorites have been retained in the repertory, and many new or unfamiliar ballets, have been added including BLUE-BEARD; RUSSIAN SOLDIER; PILLAR OF FIRE; Aleko; PAS DE QUATRE; LILAC GARDEN; Don Domingo; PETER AND THE WOLF; Chopin Concerto; Rodeo; Romantic Age; GALA PERFORMANCE; Dark Elegies.

Balletomane, in ballet the term applied to a ballet enthusiast: in Russia, where it originated, it referred specifically to persons who rarely missed a "first-night" at the ballet, and always occupied certain seats.

Ballets, Soviet, see **Soviet Ballets.**

Ballon (It.), in ballet the method or action of the dancer's feet in stepping, similar to the smooth, bouncing movement of a ball. The term *balloné* is applied to describe the dancing of Maria TAG-LIONI or any other 19th century ballerina who danced largely off the floor.

Balmont, Constantin (1867-   ), Russian poet of the symbolist school who left Russia to reside in Paris after the Revolution in 1917. He translated many works by Walt WHITMAN, Edgar Allan POE, Hendrik IBSEN, CALDERON, and others. The finest of his own works were published from 1894 to 1904; among them *Under the Northern Sky* (1894), *Silence,* and *Only Love* reflect the influence of his extensive travels in South America, Africa and Europe. Such poetical works as the *Liturgy of Beauty* and *The Bird of Flame* establish him among the finest Russian lyric poets.

Balsamo, Joseph, see **Cagliostro, Count Alessandro.**

Baltard, Louis Pierre (1765-1846), French architect and engraver, originally a landscape painter: travel in Italy induced him to study architecture, but his greatest fame is as an engraver in such works as the two-volume *Paris and Her Monuments* (1803), the illustrations of Napoleon's wars, and a magnificent series called *The Grand Prize of Architecture*. His son, **Victor Baltard** (1805-1874), was an architect of note who introduced fresco decorations by modern artists in Paris churches, and also built the great Central Market in Paris.

Baltazarini, see **Beaujoyeulx, Balthasard de.**

Balustrade, in architecture the front of a gallery usually built of iron, wood or stone; the latter is generally employed for public buildings, and the amount of ornamentation varies in accordance with the style of architecture.

Balzac, Honoré de (1799-1850), French novelist whose first success was *Le Dernier Chouan* (1829), followed by *Le Peau de Chagrin*. He worked for twenty years at a feverish pace, sleeping only for a few hours in the early part of the evening, on a series of novels to which he gave the general title *La Comédie Humaine*, (The Human Comedy), in which are included the sub-series: I *Scenes of Private Life;* II *Scenes of Paris Life;* III *Scenes of Political Life;* IV *Scenes of Military Life,* etc. The best novels in the *Comedy* are *Eugénie Grandet, Le Pére Goriot, César Birotteau, Cousin Betty,* and *Cousin Pons.* Unfortunately Balzac lacked literary style, and leaned towards bathos in melodramatic moments: only his vivid imagination and powers of observation have saved him from oblivion. Over-production— nearly one hundred novels according to Larousse's Dictionary—almost proved his undoing. His *Droll Tales* were probably undertaken because of the constant need of funds which hung like a dark shadow over his entire career.

Balzac, Jean de (1597-1654), French essayist, royal councillor under Cardinal Richelieu, historiographer of France, and one of the most influential founders of the Académie Française. He was considered as great an uplifting influence on French prose as François de MALHERBE on poetry; the euphony and elegant symmetry of his phraseology were models for a long period. His greatest work was the famous *Lettres* (1624); somewhat affected in style, but introducing a new degree of clarity into French prose.

Bambi, see **Salten, Felix.**

Bambochade (It.), in painting the term used to describe a picture portraying a gay or humorous scene of family life. Paintings of this kind were first made by Pieter van Laer, nicknamed *Il Bamboccio* because he was a cripple: his imitators were known as *bambocciate,* hence the term *bambochade.*

Bamboschek, Giuseppe (1891-   ), Italian pianist, organist, and conductor who studied at the Trieste Conservatory: he held a post as organist at thirteen, and at eighteen conducted the orchestral concerts in his native city. In 1913 he became one of the conductors at the Metropolitan Opera House, and remained there until 1929. He has also conducted at the Lewisohn Stadium, New York; the Philadelphia Opera Company; the St. Louis Municipal Opera; the Hippodrome Opera, New York.

Bampton, Rose (1909-   ), American operatic soprano who studied singing at the CURTIS INSTITUTE OF MUSIC, Philadelphia. She first appeared in 1932 at the Metropolitan Opera House as a mezzo-soprano in *La Gioconda;* after retraining her voice and touring Europe, she reappeared in 1937 at the Metropolitan in the soprano role of Leonore in *Il Trovatore.* She is married to Wilfred PELLETIER, one of the conductors at the Metropolitan, and has made many appearances with the major symphony orchestras and on radio broadcasts.

Bancroft, Marie Effie Wilton, Lady (1839-1921), English actress who appeared in juvenile parts in 1846, and made her debut at the Lyceum Theatre, London, in 1856. In 1865 she undertook the management of the Prince of Wales Theatre with Henry J. Byron, producing and appearing in *Caste* and *Society* by Thomas W. ROBERTSON which established her reputation as a comedian; in 1867 she married **Sir Squire Bancroft** (1841-1926), her leading man, and presented many light comedy successes at the Haymarket Theatre, of which they assumed the management in 1880. Lady Bancroft collaborated with her husband in two books on the drama: *On and Off the Stage* and *Recollections of Sixty Years.*

Band, in music a group of musicians playing wood-wind and brass instruments without the stringed instruments (violin, viola, violoncello, doublebass, etc.) used in an orchestra. The tone quality of a band is less delicate and more monotonous in quality than that of an orchestra. A band employing only brass instruments is called a *brass band;* when wood-wind instruments are added it is known as a *military band.* In modern jazz parlance, the unusual ensemble in which brass and wood-wind instruments predominate over the strings, is usually referred to as a "band."

Bandel, Joseph Ernst von (1800-1876), German sculptor whose chief work was the monument at Detmold to Arminius, a German national hero who defeated the legions of Rome in A.D. 9. He also made many busts and statues of distinguished Germans.

Bandello, Matteo (c.1480-1562), Italian priest and novelist who, after leading a roving life, was made Bishop of Agen by Henry II in 1550. His principal work is a collection of over two hundred tales, *Novelle,* in the style of Decameron; some of these are from old French and others from Eastern sources. It is said that the tales were sources for Shakespeare's *Romeo and Juliet* and several more of his plays.

Bandinelli, Baccio (c.1490-1560), Italian sculptor and painter; an earnest imitator of MICHELANGELO without the divine genius of his predecessor. One of his earlier sculptures was a colossal *Hercules* regarding which Benvenuto CELLINI penned a disparaging sonnet; another important work was the group, *Hercules and Cacus*, ordered by the MEDICI as a companion to Michelangelo's *David* on the Piazza dell Signoria, Florence, which still attracts attention at the present time. His best painting is *The Murder of the Innocents*.

Bang, Herman Joachim (1857-1912), Danish novelist educated at the Academy of Sorö; his novels were much admired by Henrik IBSEN and Jonas LIE. Two of his works have been translated into English: *Denied a Country* and *Ida Brandt*. Two others, *Families Without Hope* and *Faedra* were also very popular in Denmark. He died at Ogden, Utah, while on a lecture tour of the United States.

Bangs, John Kendrick (1862-1922), American humorist, novelist, poet, and dramatist for many years connected with *Harper's Magazine* and *Puck*. His works, more than thirty in number, include *New Waggings of Old Tales* (with F. D. Sherman, 1887); *A Houseboat on the Styx, The Pursuit of the Houseboat*, and *Coffee and Repartee*. He also wrote a musical version of *The School For Scandal* for Lillian RUSSELL.

Banim, John (1798-1842), Irish novelist, poet and dramatist: his best work is *Tales of the O'Hara Family* in collaboration with his brother, **Michael Banim** (1796-1874). Other works include the tragedy, *Damon and Pythias*, produced at London in 1821; the novels *The Nowlans and The Boylans*, a poem *"The Celt's Paradise"* and a volume of essays, *Revelations of the Dead-Alive*.

Banjo, an instrument of the guitar type: its body consists of a circular hoop over one side of which a parchment or sheepskin is held tautly in place by a metal ring. The fingerboard is fretted, and equipped with from five to nine strings plucked with a plectrum. It is supposed to have originated in Africa, and was the favorite instrument of the negro slaves in the South: it also plays an important part in the modern dance orchestra.

Bankhead, Tallulah (1902-), American actress, daughter of William Brockman Bankhead, former Speaker of the House of Representatives, Washington. She made her debut in 1918 at the Bijou Theatre, New York, and in 1923 appeared in London with Sir Gerald DuMaurier in *The Dancers*. Among the successful plays in which she has appeared are *The Green Hat; The Gold Diggers; Let Us Be Gay; Dark Victory; Rain; Antony and Cleopatra; The Circle; The Little Foxes*. Her appearances on the screen include *Tarnished Lady; The Cheat; His House in Order*.

Banks, Thomas (1735-1805), English sculptor who spent two years in St. Petersburg in the service of the Empress Catherine who purchased his *Cupid Tormenting a Butterfly*. Among his important works are *Achilles and Briseis*, which brought about his admission to the Royal Academy, London, and *Shakespeare Attended by Painting and Poetry*, now at Stratford-on-Avon: he also created some fine busts and monuments.

Banner, Peter (c.1794-1828), Anglo-American architect who worked in Boston from 1794: his finest creation was the Park Street Church in Boston built in 1809. It is a remarkable edifice, original in conception and having an attractive tower suggesting the type used by Sir Christopher WREN, architect of St. Paul's Cathedral, London.

Banning, Margaret Culkin (1891-), American novelist educated at Vassar College: her works include *This Marrying* (1920); *Half Loaves; Spellbinders; Money of Her Own; The First Woman; The Iron Will; Enough to Live On; A Week in New York*.

Bantock, Sir Granville (1868-), English conductor, editor and composer, graduate of the Royal Academy of Music, London. He founded and edited the *New Quarterly Musical Review* in 1893. Among his notable works are the operas *The Seal Woman, The Great God Pan*, and *Pierrot of the Minute;* the symphonies *Hebridean, Atalanta in Calydon* and *Vanity of Vanities;* many orchestral overtures, suites and variations; chamber music, choral songs and piano pieces.

Banville, Théodore Faullain de (1823-1891), French poet and dramatist: his first poetical works, *Les Cariatides* (1842) and *Les Stalactites* (1846), secured him the support of Alfred de VIGNY. Several of his comedies in verse were produced at the Théâtre Français; these were followed by *Camées parisiennes, Contes bourgeois, Contes héroiques*, and a stream of prose and poetical literature until his death. He was intimate with most of the distinguished literary men of his time, and, while lacking genius, is regarded as a charming writer exercising a good influence on his art.

Baptistery, in architecture a small church or chapel, used for baptism, and usually erected near a large church. The form of the edifice was usually circular: excellent examples are found at Florence, Rome and Padua as well as at Poitiers and Aix-la-Chapelle, France.

Baratynski, Eugene Abramovitch (1800-1844), Russian poet who wrote his first work, *Eda*, while serving in the Russian army in Finland. Influence at court secured him leave from the army in 1827; he settled in Moscow where his greatest poem, *The Gipsy*, was written. Baratynski's style resembled that of Alexander PUSHKIN; a collected edition in Russian appeared in 1844.

Barbauld, Anna Letitia (1743-1825), English poet whose *Hymns in Prose* (1781) and *Early Lessons*, written for children, became extremely popular, and were translated into several languages. Her greatest work was the editing of *British Novelists*, an impressive series of fifty volumes, carefully annotated and provided with pithy biographies.

Barber, Margaret Fairless (1869-1901), English author who used the pen name "Michael Fairless." At one time she was a nurse known as the "Fighting Sister" in London's worst slums: her works include *The Gathering of Brother Hilarius* (1901); *The Roadmender; The Grey Brethren.* A complete edition of her works was published in 1932.

Barber, Samuel (1910-   ), American composer, nephew of Louise HOMER and graduate of the CURTIS INSTITUTE OF MUSIC, Philadelphia: he won the Prix de Rome in 1935 and a *Symphony in One Movement* was conducted by Bernardo MOLINARI at Rome in 1936, the first American work to be played at the SALZBURG FESTIVALS. His works include an overture, *School for Scandal; Essay for Orchestra; Music for a Scene from Shelley,* chamber music and songs.

Barber of Seville, The, (*1*) in drama a play by the French dramatist, Pierre BEAUMARCHAIS, which was prohibited for two years, and a complete failure at its première in 1775. The author remodeled and shortened it in time for the second performance, resulting in a success which still holds its place on the French stage. (*2*) A grand opera in two acts, libretto by Cesare Sterbini after Beaumarchais; music by ROSSINI. It was first produced at Rome in 1816, and was a complete failure because the opera-going public at first refused to accept any work, regardless of its merits, designed to take the place of an opera based on the same play by Giovanni PAISIELLO which had been a favorite since its first production in 1776. Rossini, believing that his opera was a better work, took its failure with good grace, and eventually his faith was justified by its enormous success all over the world. It was first produced in English at the Park Theatre in New York in 1819, and in Italian with Manuel GARCIA in 1825. The plot, like the play mentioned above, concerns itself with the various stratagems employed by a certain Count Almaviva to court and wed Rosina, the lovely ward of the elderly Doctor Bartolo whom the latter plans to marry for her fortune. There is a complete Columbia recording of the opera in Italian by the artists and orchestra of La SCALA, Milan, and an abridged Victor recording, prepared by Ronald Wise and Giuseppe Bamboschek. The overture is extremely popular as a concert work; there is a Victor recording by the New York Philharmonic Symphony Orchestra under Arturo TOSCANINI, and a Columbia recording by the Columbia Broadcasting Orchestra conducted by Howard BARLOW.

Barber Shop Music, in music an expression which originated during the 17th century in English tonsorial shops where customers, awaiting their turn for the barber's chair, were accustomed to strumming on some simple instrument to while away the time. In the United States it has been applied to the impromptu harmonization of popular tunes by an amateur male quartet, usually at a convivial assembly of some description.

Barbey d'Aurevilly, Jules (1808-1889), French litterateur who wrote several novels: among them *Une Vieille Maitresse* (1851), *Le Chevalier Destouches,* and a collection of extraordinary stories, *Les Diaboliques.* Paul Bourget describes him as a dreamer with an exquisite sense of vision; Jules Lemaître classes his writings as exaggerated Byronism.

Barbier, Paul Jules (1825-1901), French dramatist, poet, and librettist; his first successful drama in verse was *A Poet* (1847), followed by *The Shades of Molière, André Chenier,* and a comedy, *Willy Nilly.* He collaborated with Michel Carré in a series of dramas, vaudevilles and librettos for grand and comic operas by MEYERBEER, GOUNOD and AMBROISE THOMAS. After the Franco-Prussian War he published several collections of patriotic poems and plays in verse.

Barbieri, Giovanni Francesco, see **Guercino.**

Barbirolli, John B. (1899-   ), English violoncellist and conductor educated at Trinity College and the Royal Academy of Music, London. He was a member of the International String Quartet (1920-24), organizing and conducting his own orchestra in 1925. He has conducted the Scottish Orchestra (Glasgow), the Leeds Music Festivals, the British Broadcasting Orchestra, the London Philharmonic Orchestra, the Covent Garden Opera, and has also appeared as guest conductor of Continental orchestras. In 1937 he began a three-year engagement as permanent conductor of the New York Philharmonic-Symphony Orchestra, and during 1941-42 has appeared as one of a number of distinguished conductors engaged for the celebration of the orchestra's centennial. In 1943 he became permanent conductor of the HALLE ORCHESTRA, Birmingham, England.

Barbizon School, in painting the name given a group of painters who met from 1830 to 1870 at Barbizon (or Barbison) in the forest of Fontainebleau, where the famous French painter, Jean François MILLET had his home, and formed a school of naturalistic painting opposed to the traditions of the Academy. They found their inspiration in the landscape, animals and peasants: in the group were DAUBIGNY, DUPRE, DIAZ, MILLET, COROT (for a time), Théodore ROUSSEAU and several others. Examples of this school are to be found in the METROPOLITAN ART MUSEUM, New York, and at the LOUVRE in Paris.

Barbour, John (c.1316-1395), Scottish poet, educated at Oxford and author of a lengthy poem, *Brus (The Bruce),* a narrative work in twenty books comprising more than 13,500 lines, its purpose being partly historical and partly patriotic. He is also credited by several writers of the Middle Ages with the authorship of several more long poems such as *The Siege of Troy* and *Legends of the Saints* which make him one of the most prolific of Scottish poets.

Barbour, Ralph Henry (1870-   ), American novelist: his works include *The Land of Joy* (1903); *The Lilac Girl; The Turner Twins; Phyllis in Bohemia,* the last named written with L. H.

Bickford, using the pen name "Richard Stillman Powell."

Barbusse, Henri (1873-1935), French novelist and litterateur educated at the Collège Rollin, and editor of the magazine, *Je Sais Tout* (I Know All). His novels include *Les Suppliants* (1903), *L'Enfer,* and a starkly brutal and realistic story of World War I entitled, *Le Feu* (1916), which won the Prix Goncourt in 1917, and is a unique portrayal of the horrors of modern war.

Barcarolle (It.), in music the name applied to the songs sung by Venetian gondoliers. CHOPIN and RUBINSTEIN both used it as the title for piano compositions in which the accompaniment part in the left hand suggests the rippling motion of waves.

Barclay, John (1582-1621), Scottish poet, born in France and educated in a Jesuit College, who found great favor with James I. He wrote a romance in Latin, *Argenis,* greatly admired by Cardinal RICHELIEU and Samuel COLERIDGE: it became the basis for FENELON's famous poem *Telemachus.*

Bard, a poet and minstrel in ancient Celtic countries comprising Wales, Ireland, Cornwall, the Isle of Man in Great Britain, and also Brittany in France. The bard had a variety of names in the various countries; among them TROUVERE, skald, gleeman, TROUBADOR and MINNESINGER; he composed verses, often extemporaneous, celebrating heroic achievements and usually accompanying himself on the harp. Bards were granted the privileges of nobility by a Welsh king, Howel Dha, even to the extent of making their prerogatives hereditary: Edward I of England reduced them to the status of professional minstrels dependent on the generosity of the populace. The Welsh EISTEDDFOD was an assembly of bards held in Wales: after the bards disappeared, the assembly became a festival for singing societies held not only in Wales, but in many other countries where there were Welsh communities. In Ireland at the banquet hall of the palace at Tara (the ancient capital of Erin), the bards were highly honored, but in Scotland the term was applied to vagabond minstrels.

Bardi, Giovanni, Count of Vernio (1534-1612), a distinguished Florentine nobleman at whose home litterateurs and musicians assembled to discuss musical and literary problems. He had considerable influence in reviving the classic Greek dramatico-musical forms from which modern opera evolved during the 16th to the 18th centuries. His coterie included CACCINI, Strozzi, Corsi, PERI and RINUCCINI, all of whom played an important part in the development of opera.

Barefoot Dancing, in ballet a style of dancing introduced by Isadora DUNCAN who expressed her opinion that it was essential to be barefoot in order to express the grace and nobility of the human body. Another dancer, Maude ALLAN, usually danced barefoot, and the great dancer and choreographer, Michel FOKINE, was bitterly condemned by balletomanes when he became an advocate of discarding the ballet shoe, hitherto the sacred symbol of the art.

Bargello Museum (Florence), the Royal National Museum housed in a 13th century palace formerly the home of the Podestà, the city official, but later used as a prison. It contains collections of armor; frescoes by GIOTTO, works of MICHELANGELO including his *David;* masterpieces by Benvenuto CELLINI, Giovanni da Bologna, DONATELLO, Jacopo SANSOVINA, Antonio POLLAJUOLO and one of the most important collections in the world of Florentine Renaissance sculptures.

Barham, Richard Harris (1788-1845), English clergyman, poet and novelist educated at St. Paul's and Oxford. Using the pen-name "Thomas Ingoldsby," he wrote the *Ingoldsby Legends* in prose and verse (1840-47) which are now classics in humorous literature. He also wrote *My Cousin Nicholas,* a novel.

Bar-Hebraeus, see Abulfaraj.

Barilli, Milena Pavlovitch (1911-), Yugoslavian painter who studied at the ECOLE DES BEAUX ARTS in Belgrade, and in Munich with Franz von Stück. She exhibited first at Belgrade in 1929, and later in Paris, Rome, Florence, London and New York. Her works include portraits of King Peter II of Jugoslavia, Prince Karl of Sweden, Archduke Franz Joseph of Austria, Queen Marie of Rumania; among her finest canvases is the imaginative *St. Joan.* Mlle. Barilli is a cousin of King Peter II of Jugoslavia.

Baring, Maurice (1874-), English poet and novelist educated at Eton College and in Germany and Italy: for some years he was in the British diplomatic service. His novels include *A Triangle* (1923); *Cat's Cradle; Daphne Adeane; Tinker's Leave; The Coat Without Seam; Roger Peckham; The Lonely Lady of Dulwich; Darby and Joan; Collected Poems.*

Baring-Gould, Sabine (1834-1924), English clergyman, poet and novelist: author of *Mehalah, a Story of the Salt Marshes* (1880), *John Herring; Red Spider.* He wrote the verses for the hymn, *Onward, Christian Soldiers,* music by Sir Arthur Sullivan, and also several volumes of folklore including *The Book of Werewolves* and *Curious Myths of the Middle Ages.*

Baritone, in music (*1*) the male voice intermediate in compass between the bass and tenor. If the quality of the voice resembles that of a bass, it is called a *bass baritone:* (*2*) a brass wind instrument used in military bands; its compass is an octave below the TRUMPET or CORNET, and about the same as the trombone in B♭. The *euphonium* is practically the same as the baritone except that it is more flexible as a solo instrument because of its smaller bore.

Barker, Harley Granville, see Granville-Barker, Harley.

Barker, James Nelson (1784-1858), American dramatist appointed Comptroller of the Treasury under President Van Buren. Of his ten plays only five have survived: one of them, *Superstition,* was extraordinarily powerful, and is regarded by critics as the best drama of the American stage up to its period. Barker also made an adaptation of Sir Walter SCOTT's *Marmion* which has been reprinted in A. H. Quinn's *Representative American Plays* (1917).

Barker, Thomas (1769-1847), English painter, lithographer, and one of the most distinguished artists of his day: many of his rural scenes were used as textile and ceramic designs. His lithographs of landscapes and bucolic scenes are exceptionally fine. His son, **Thomas Jones Barker** (1815-82), who studied with his father, and also with Horace VERNET in Paris, painted *The Bride of Death* for Louis Philippe of France which won him the Cross of the Legion of Honor. His military paintings, particularly *The Meeting of Wellington and Blücher after Waterloo* and *Balaklava —One of the Six Hundred,* are his chief claim to fame.

Barlach, Ernest Heinrich (1870-), German sculptor influenced in his art by DAUMIER and RODIN; a worker in wood, porcelain, terra cotta, and bronze. He was particularly inspired by Russian wood carvings; his own subjects are taken from the daily life of peasants whose expressions of joy or sorrow reflect the emotions of the common people in all countries. Barlach has made many fine portrait busts and numerous drawings and woodcuts for books. His sculptures include the War Memorial in Güstrow Cathedral, and examples of his work are in museums at Berlin, Dresden, Munich, and Vienna.

Barlow, Howard (1892-), American orchestral conductor educated at the University of Colorado and Columbia University, New York. He studied music with Cornelius RYBNER and Daniel Gregory MASON, making his debut as conductor at the MacDowell Colony Festival, Peterboro, N.H., in 1919. Since that time he has conducted the American-National Orchestra, New York, the Neighborhood Playhouse Orchestra, New York, the Baltimore Symphony Orchestra, and the Columbia Broadcasting Symphony Orchestra (1927-42). In 1942 he was one of the guest conductors of the New York Philharmonic Orchestra.

Barlow, Jane (1857-1917), Irish poet, critic, and author of stories of life among the Irish peasantry; her works include *Bogland Studies* (1892); *Irish Idylls; Kerrigan's Quality; Maureen's Fairing; Strangers at Lisconnel; Ghost Bereft; By Beach and Bog Land.*

Barlow, Joel (1754-1812), American statesman and poet: author of a long epic poem, originally published in 1787 as *The Vision of Columbus,* but revised and re-issued in 1807 as *The Columbiad.* His works include *The Conspiracy of Kings* and the famous poem, *Hasty Pudding.* In 1811, President Madison sent him on a special mission to NAPOLEON I at Wilna, Russia, but he died of exposure at Cracow, Poland, during the French retreat from Moscow.

Barlow, Samuel L. M. (1892-), American composer who studied at Harvard University and at the INSTITUTE OF MUSICAL ART, New York; also with Ottorino RESPIGHI and Isidor PHILIPP in Europe. His opera, *Mon ami Pierrot,* was the first work of the kind to be presented at the Opéra-Comique in Paris. Barlow's compositions include a ballet; incidental music for plays; a tone poem; *Alba,* for orchestra; a piano concerto; a *Vocalise* for orchestra; a concerto for magiclantern and orchestra; chamber music; piano pieces and songs.

Barnabee, Henry Clay (1833-1917), American actor and singer who made his debut at the Music Hall in Boston assisted by Annie Louise CARY. In 1879 he became a member of the Boston Ideal Opera Company; in 1887 he organized, with Tom KARL and W. H. MacDonald, the BOSTONIANS, a company which presented light opera with unprecedented success for twenty-five years. Among their popular productions were Victor HERBERT's *The Serenade* and Reginald DE KOVEN's *Robin Hood,* in which Barnabee scored a personal triumph in the role of the Sheriff of Nottingham. His autobiography, *My Wanderings,* was published in 1913.

Barnard, George Grey (1863-1938), American sculptor who learned taxidermy in his youth in order to preserve his specimens for models, later studying at the Art Institute in Chicago, and at the ECOLE DES BEAUX ARTS, Paris, where he learned to work directly in stone. His principal works include *Brotherly Love* or *Two Friends* (1887); the allegorical *Two Natures* in the Metropolitan Museum of Art, New York; *The Great God Pan* at Columbia University, New York; *The Hewer* in Cairo, Ill.; the *Rose Maiden* at Muscatine, Ia.; the symbolic entrance group, *The Apotheosis,* at the Pennsylvania State Capitol at Harrisburg; the great bronze statue, *Lincoln* in Cincinnati. Through the generosity of John D. Rockefeller his collection of several hundred examples of medieval art of all kinds, formerly in the Metropolitan Museum of Art, New York, has been removed to a building and grounds at Fort Tryon Park, opposite the Palisades, which is known as The CLOISTERS.

Barnard, Lady Anne (1750-1825), Scottish poet who wrote a remarkable series of letters, *South Africa a Century Ago,* from 1797 to 1802 to Henry Dundas, British secretary of war. She is best-known today by the ballad *Auld Robin Gray,* music by the Reverend William Graves; it was published anonymously in 1783, but Lady Barnard admitted its authorship in 1823 in a letter to Sir Walter SCOTT.

Barnby, Sir Joseph (1838-1896), English composer and choir director educated at the Royal Academy of Music, London. He conducted the Barnby Choir and the Albert Hall Choral Society (succeeding Charles GOUNOD) until his death. His compositions include an oratorio, *Rebekah;* many services and anthems; about 150 hymn tunes collected in one volume in 1917; numerous part songs including the immortal *Sweet and Low.* Barnby was a pioneer in introducing the sacred music of Charles Gounod in Great Britain.

Barnes, Barnabe (c.1569-1609), English poet and dramatist; educated at Oxford and companion to the Earl of Essex in France. He wrote two tragedies, *The Devil's Charter* and *The Battle of Evesham*, but his best literary work was included in *Parthenophil and Parthenope* (1593), a volume of sonnets and odes.

Barnes, Margaret Ayer (1886-), American novelist educated at Bryn Mawr College: her works include *Prevailing Winds* (1928); *Years of Grace* which won the 1930 Pulitzer Prize; *Westward Passage; Within This Present; Edna, His Wife; Wisdom's Gate.* One of her plays, *Dishonored Lady* (1930), was written in collaboration with Edward SHELDON.

Barnfield, Richard (1574-1627), English poet educated at Oxford who published his first work, *The Affectionate Shepherd,* anonymously in 1594: it was followed by *Cynthia, with Certain Sonnets,* a eulogy on Queen Elizabeth, written in the style of SPENSER's FAERIE QUEENE. He also wrote a poem in praise of money, *The Encomion of Lady Pecunia,* and two sonnets, *If Music and Sweet Poetry Agree* and *As it Fell Upon a Day* for which Shakespeare received credit.

Barnum, Phineas Taylor (1810-1891), American showman and circus owner who brought the famous Swedish soprano, Jenny Lind, to the United States in 1850, and managed her concert tours for nearly two years, with the result that lovers of fine singing were more than satisfied with her magnificent vocalizing, and the singer earned more than $100,000, a prodigious amount for an artist to be paid at this period in American music.

Barocchio, or **Barozzi, Jacopo** (1507-1573), Italian architect, also called *Da Vignola* after the city in which he was born. After working at Bologna, Perugia, and several other cities, he became architect for Pope Julius III, succeeding MICHELANGELO at St. Peters, and building a villa for the Pope, and the famous *Castle of Caprarola* for Alexander Farnese, his nephew. He wrote two excellent, technical architectural works: *The Five Orders of Architecture* (1561) and *Practical Perspective* (1583). He was a staunch advocate of the classic tradition in architecture when the style known as "baroque" was corrupting new edifices; it is unfortunate and ironically unjust that Barocchio's name was connected with the new style because of its somewhat similar sound.

Baroccio or **Barocci, Federigo** (1528-1612), Italian painter greatly inspired in his ambitions while on a visit to Rome by MICHELANGELO. He lived in his native city, Urbino, for the greater part of his life; many of his paintings for churches there, including a *St. Sebastian* in the Cathedral, are still in existence. Among the frescoes made while he was in Rome are a *Visitation;* a *Last Supper; Burning of Troy,* the latter at the Borghese Palace. Baroccio's efforts to accentuate light and shade sometimes produced an artificial effect, but his fresh and cheerful colors were often combined to create softly harmonious tints. He was also known as Fiori da Urbino.

Baroja y Nessi, Pio (1872-), Spanish novelist who first practiced medicine before devoting himself to a literary career: he barely escaped being executed in the Spanish revolution of 1936, but finally succeeded in reaching Paris. Among his works published in English are *The City of the Discreet* (1917); *Caesar or Nothing; Red Dawn; The Lord of Labraz; The Tree of Knowledge; Paradox King.*

Baron, Michel (1653-1729), French actor and dramatist, son of a distinguished actor and a talented actress bearing the family name of Boyron. He delighted MOLIERE with his talent for acting at twelve, later becoming a member of the great dramatist's company and remaining with it until Molière's death. He then joined the Hôtel de Bourgogne Company, playing the principal roles in RACINE's tragedies, and in his own comedies, *The Man of Good Fortune* and *The Coquette.* In 1720 he appeared at the Palais Royal in many parts: his son, Etienne Michel Baron (1676-1711), was a fine actor as were also his grandson and two granddaughters.

Baronova, Irina (1919-), Russian ballerina who studied with Olga Preobrajenska in Paris, and made her first appearance in 1932 at the Théâtre Mogador, Paris, in George BALANCHINE's ballet based on *Orpheus in the Underworld* by OFFENBACH. She appeared from 1933 to 1939 with Colonel de BASIL's Ballet Russe, the Covent Garden Russian Ballet and Educational Ballets, Ltd. In 1940 she was a guest star of the Ballet Russe de Monte Carlo, and also appeared in the Metro-Goldwyn-Mayer film, *Florian.* Her greatest successes include *Les Sylphides, Jeux d'Enfants, Le Beau Danube, Union Pacific, Le Coq d'Or,* and *Paganini.*

Baroque, in architecture a term specifically applied to certain forms of architecture, painting, sculpture, furniture, and household decoration. It applies to the extravagant designs developed in Italy and France during the first part of the 18th century; MICHELANGELO is held responsible by some authorities for the spread of the baroque style because he was the first great artist to break away from the severe classic styles of BAROCCHIO and PALLADIO. Unfortunately many of the artists who attempted to break the classic bonds were not able to do so with moderation, the result being heaviness, broken contours, and senseless as well as meaningless exaggerations. It is only fair to state that a reaction has taken place which seeks to demonstrate that baroque has its advantages as well as its disadvantages.

Barozzi, Jacopo, see **Barocchio, Jacopo.**

Barr, Amelia Edith (1831-1919), Anglo-American novelist who came to America in 1854, publishing her first book, *Romance and Reality* in 1872. Her 75 novels include *Jan Vedder's Wife; A Daughter of Fife; A Bow of Orange Ribbon; Remember the Alamo; Friend Oliva; Joan; Master of His Fate; An Orkney Maid; Measure of a Man; The Winning of Lucia.* Her autobiography, *All the Days of My Life,* was published in 1913.

Barr, Robert (1850-1912), Scottish journalist and novelist who came with his parents to Canada in 1854; he joined the editorial staff of the Detroit (Mich.) *Free Press* in 1876, writing under the penname of "Luke Sharp." He founded a magazine, the *Idler*, with Jerome K. JEROME in 1892, and published the novels, *In the Midst of Alarms* (1894); *The Mutable Many; Countess Tekla; The Sword Maker; The Tempestuous Petticoat.*

Barre, in ballet the name of a rod extending around the walls of a dance studio, used by the students to steady them during preliminary exercising, and taking the place of the partner's hand.

Barrel Organ, a mechanical wind instrument invented in the 18th century; its mechanism consists of a revolving cylinder fitted with pegs which open valves admitting air to a set of pipes producing the tones necessary to play a melody with its accompaniment. The familiar organ seen on the public streets, on which a crank is turned by hand, is called a hurdy-gurdy: this is technically incorrect as the latter instrument is of entirely different construction, and is obsolete.

Barrère, Georges (1876-), French flute virtuoso who studied at the Paris Conservatory. He was solo flutist at the Colonne Concerts and the Opèra from 1897 to 1905: in the latter year he founded the Society of Modern Wind Instruments. From 1905 to 1928 he was solo flutist of the NEW YORK SYMPHONY ORCHESTRA under Walter Damrosch. He has founded or been a member of the Barrère Ensemble; the Trio de Lutèce, the Barrère Little Symphony; the Barrère-Britt Concertino. He has composed and arranged many works for flute, and is an officer of the French Academy and a Chevalier of the Legion of Honor.

Barrès, Maurice (1862-1923), French publicist and novelist who attracted attention with his study of egoism, *Le Culte*, published in three volumes: I *Under the Eye of the Barbarians;* II *A Free Man;* III *The Garden of Berenice* (1888-91). The volumes reveal the artificialities of an over-refined and decadent culture; the world was divided into two divisions; *moi* (Barrès) and *barbares,* all those not in sympathy with him. Another trilogy, *Le Roman de l'énergie nationale,* purports to be a plea for local patriotism in the French provinces.

Barrett, Lawrence (1838-1891), American actor; family name Brannigan. His stage debut was made at Detroit in 1853 in the role of Murad in *The French Spy:* a year later he appeared at the Chambers Street Theatre, New York, in *The Hunchback.* After ably supporting Edwin BOOTH and E. L. DAVENPORT, he acquitted himself creditably in the Civil War. A partnership with John B. McCULLOUGH in San Francisco retrieved losses sustained in a theatre venture at New Orleans, and he again joined Edwin Booth in 1875, playing with him in Shakespeare, except while Booth was in England, until his death in 1891. It is said that there was never a more ideal combination than Booth as Brutus and Barrett as Cassius in *Julius Caesar.* His versatility becomes evident in the following list of roles: Hamlet, Lear, Macbeth, Shylock, Richard III, Othello, Lanciottio in George Henry Boker's *Francesca da Rimini,* and the title role in Bulwer Lytton's drama, *Richelieu.* He wrote a life of Edwin Forrest and a sketch of

Edwin Booth: his granddaughter, Edith Barrett, is a well-known contemporary actress.

Barrett, Wilson (1846-1904), English actor, manager and dramatist. After theatrical experience in touring the British provinces with his wife in *East Lynne,* he leased the Old Court Theatre, London, in 1879 to introduce Helena MODJESKA, famous Polish actress in *Adrienne Lecouvreur.* In 1881 he took over the Princess Theatre, playing the stellar role in *The Silver King,* a melodrama by Henry Arthur JONES which ran for three hundred nights. He toured the United States several times, and when melodrama no longer attracted, he dramatized his own novel, *The Sign of the Cross,* and appeared in it with signal success. Barrett's interpretations of Shakespearean roles were highly regarded.

Barretto, Larry (1890-), American novelist who won the French Croix de Guerre in World War I: his works include *A Conqueror Passes* (1924); *To Babylon; Old Enchantment; The Indiscreet Years; Three Roads from Paradise; Bright Mexico; Tomorrow Will Be Different; Journey Through Time.*

Barrias, Felix Joseph (1822-1907), French painter of historical scenes and portraits who first made a showing at the Paris Salon in 1840, and continued to do so for over sixty-five years. His works include *The Death of Chopin; The Triumph of Venus; The Jubilee of 1300 at Rome; The Death of Socrates; Dante; Titian Painting a Venus; Allegory of Music; Michelangelo in the Sistine Chapel.* He was a brother of Louis Ernest BARRIAS.

Barrias, Louis Ernest (1841-1905), French sculptor, brother of Felix Joseph Barrias, a distinguished painter. After working at the studios of Cavelier and Jouffroy in Paris, and spending some time in Rome, he exhibited *The Oath of Spartacus* at the Paris Salon with great success in 1872. A large group, *The First Funeral,* showing the body of Abel carried by Adam and Eve, exhibited in 1876, brought him even greater acclamation from brother artists who presented him with a medal. Among other works are the *Victor Hugo Memorial,* Paris; a polychrome marble statue, *Nature Disrobing;* a statue of Joan of Arc, and many fine busts.

Barrie, Sir James Matthew (1860-1937), English novelist and playwright, educated at Edinburgh University. After some journalistic work in London papers his first success, *A Window in Thrums,* was published in 1889, followed by *My Lady Nicotine* and *The Little Minister,* the latter establishing his reputation as a novelist of the first rank. This was followed by *Margaret Ogilvy, Sentimental Tommy, Tommy and Grizel,* and *The Little White Bird.* From 1902 Barrie devoted himself almost entirely to play writing: the long list includes such important plays as *The Professor's Love Story; The Little Minister; Quality Street; The Admirable Crichton; Peter Pan; Alice Sit-by-the-Fire; Pantaloon; What Every Woman Knows; The Twelve-Pound Look; Rosalind; A Kiss for Cinderella; Dear Brutus; The Old Lady Shows Her Medals; Mary Rose.*

Barrie, Wendy (1913-), English stage and screen actress, born in Hong Kong. She had some stage experience, but has appeared principally in films including *The Private Life of Henry VIII; Dead End; Five Came Back; The Hound of the Baskervilles;* also in several of the "Saint" films with George SANDERS in the role of Leslie CHARTERIS' engaging adventurer.

Barrientos, Maria (1884-), Spanish coloratura soprano; a graduate in piano, violin and composition of the Barcelona Conservatory at the age of twelve. Her singing ability was discovered after a severe illness, and she made her operatic debut in 1899 (at the astonishing age of fourteen) at Barcelona as Selika in Meyerbeer's *L'Africaine*. She toured Europe for fifteen years, appearing in more than 20 operas with great success: after three years retirement she made her debut in *Lucia di Lammermoor* at the Metropolitan Opera House, New York, in 1916, remaining there for many seasons, and retiring in 1939.

Barrington, E., see **Beck, Lily Adams.**

Barrison, Mabel (c.1880-), Anglo-Viennese dancer, of the school created by Isadora DUNCAN, who won recognition in Vienna, Munich and other German cities. Critics declared her dancing more adept and natural than that of the Weisenthal Sisters because she treated her art with greater freedom and loftier purpose.

Barry, Sir Charles (1795-1860), English architect who traveled in Greece, Asia Minor, France, Italy, and Egypt before building several churches in England. Among his finest works in London are the Traveler's Club and the Reform Club; Bridgewater House; the reconstruction of the Treasury Buildings, Whitehall; The Houses of Parliament at Westminster (1840-1860). Barry was also a fine landscape architect; one of his sons, **Edward Middleton Barry** (1830-1880), assisted his father at the Houses of Parliament, and designed the Covent Garden Theatre, and the new building for the National Art Gallery.

Barry, Elizabeth (1658-1713), English actress, said to have been a failure until coached by the Earl of Rochester who laid a wager that he could make her a success. After her first appearance in 1673 on the London stage under the direction of Sir William D'Avenant she became, as one critic stated, "mistress of all the passions of the mind" in Shakespeare's *Macbeth,* Tates *King Lear,* Southerne's *The Fatal Marriage,* Otway's *Venice Preserved,* Boyle's *Mustapha* and more than a hundred other tragic roles. In recognition of her services to the stage, James II ordered the benefits reserved for authors extended to distinguished actors. She retired from the stage in 1709.

Barry, James (1741-1806), Irish painter whose talent as a youth attracted the attention of Edmund Burke who sent him to Rome for five years' study. He was for a time a member and professor of painting at the Royal Academy, London, but was expelled because of his demands for special equipment for the students, and his contemptuous attitude toward what he termed "amateur methods" on the part of other teachers. Among his works are *Adam and Eve; Venus Rising from the Sea; Death of General Wolfe; Jupiter and Juno on Mount Ida; Lear and Cordelia,* the last-named painted for BOYDELL's Shakespeare.

Barry, Jeanne Bécu du see **Du Barry, Marie Jeanne Bécu.**

Barry, Philip (1896-), American dramatist educated at Yale, and student of playwriting under George Pierce BAKER at Harvard University, where his play, *You and I* (1923), won a prize and was successfully produced in New York. He has written two types of plays; drawing-room comedies and serious, symbolical dramas: the former have gained commercial success, but the latter have failed to gain popular approval. Among his plays are *In a Garden; White Wings; Paris Bound; Holiday; Animal Kingdom; Here Come the Clowns; Philadelphia Story* and *Without Love,* the last two written for Katherine Hepburn.

Barry, Spranger (1719-1777), Irish actor who appeared at Dublin in 1744, and at London in 1746 at the Drury Lane Theatre as alternate in the roles of Hamlet and Macbeth with David GARRICK. Jealousy developed on the part of Garrick, and in 1750 Barry and his leading lady, Mrs. CIBBER, established themselves at the Covent Garden Theatre in Shakespearean repertory. He was an extremely handsome man, excelling in the roles of Romeo and Othello: his second wife, **Ann Street Barry** (1734-1801), was a noted tragic actress whose portrayal of Desdemona was considered equal if not superior to that of Mrs. SIDDONS.

Barrymore, Maurice (1848-1905), Anglo-American actor who was educated at Cambridge University, England, and appeared first on the stage in the British provinces with a stock company presenting Dion BOUCICAULT's play, *London Assurance.* He came to the United States in the same year to play at Daly's Theatre, New York, in *Under the Gaslight,* later becoming leading man for Helena MODJESKA, Olga NETHERSOLE, Lily LANGTRY, Minnie Maddern FISKE and many other famous actresses. In 1876 he married Georgiana DREW (1856-1893) an American actress trained by her mother, Louisa Lane, an accomplished actress and wife of John Drew, Sr. (1825-62). Georgiana appeared with her husband, Maurice Barrymore, and also with Edwin BOOTH and Lawrence BARRETT in Shakespeare's dramas. She was the mother of **Lionel Barrymore** (1878-), born in London while his parents were playing there; his first appearance on the New York stage in 1893 was with his grandmother, Mrs. John Drew, Sr. (already mentioned above) in *The Road to Ruin.* In the ensuing fifty years he has appeared in many fine plays such as *The Mummy and the Hummingbird, Arizona, Sag Harbor, The Second in Command, Pantaloon, Peter Ibbetson, The Jest, The Copperhead, Macbeth,* and *Laugh, Clown, Laugh!* His film career began in 1907 with the Biograph Company: since then he has been in numerous films among the more recent of which are *The Voice of Bugle Ann, The Road to Glory, Camille, Captains Courageous, You Can't Take It With You, Tennessee Johnson,* and the classic *Doctor Kildare* series. Lionel Barrymore has made many radio appearances: his sister **Ethel Barrymore** (1879-), also made her stage debut sponsored by her grandmother, Mrs. John Drew, Sr., in *The Rivals* at the EMPIRE THEATRE, New York, in 1894. After appearing at London with Sir Henry IRVING in *The Bells* and *Peter the Great* (1897), she starred in Clyde FITCH's *Captain Jinks of the Horse Marines* under the management of Charles FROHMAN, later establishing herself as one of America's finest actresses in such plays as *Alice Sit-by-the-Fire; The Second Mrs. Tanqueray; The Twelve Pound Look; Declassée; The Constant Wife; Whiteoaks; The Kingdom of God; The School for Scandal*, and *The Corn Was Green*. Her brother, **John Barrymore** (1882-1942) made his first professional appearance on the stage in 1903 at the Cleveland Theatre, Chicago, in *Magda*, rapidly building a reputation comparable to that of his sister, Ethel Barrymore, as a dramatic actor in such plays as *The Dictator, Alice Sit-by-the-Fire, Pantaloon, The Fortune Hunter, The Affairs of Anatol, The Yellow Ticket, Peter Ibbetson, The Jest, Richard III, Hamlet* (1924), and *My Dear Children* (1939) after fourteen years absence from the stage. He began his film career in 1912 with *The Dictator*, and appeared during the last few years in *Romeo and Juliet; Maytime;* the *Bulldog Drummond* series; *Marie Antoinette; The Great Profile*. He also did much broadcasting, sometimes with his daughter, Diana Barrymore, who has made her entry recently into motion pictures.

Bartered Bride, The (Die Verkaufte Braut), a grand opera in nationalistic style with music by Friedrich SMETANA, and libretto by Karel Sabina: first produced at Prague in 1866; in Czech at Chicago, Ill., in 1893, and in German at the Metropolitan Opera House with Gustave Mahler conducting in 1909. It was a great success in Bohemia, and has been produced, usually in German with the names of the characters altered, in many Continental opera houses, and in Great Britain. The plot is a simple story of Bohemian peasant life: Hans, a young peasant, loves Marie, daughter of a wealthy farmer, Micha, but an obstacle presents itself in the person of Ketsal, a marriage broker, who holds out the prospect of further riches to the maiden's father if she marries Wenzel, the half-witted son of Micha. Naturally Marie objects strenuously, but Hans, when offered three hundred gulden to surrender Marie, agrees to do so provided the contract stipulates that Marie is to marry *the true son of Micha*. After the money is paid, Hans reveals himself as the long-lost, first-born son of Micha, and the only one who is entitled to be called Micha's true son according to Bohemian laws. There is a complete Victor recording in Czech by the National Opera Company, Prague: the overture, which is a popular concert and radio work, is recorded by the Boston "Pops" Orchestra under Max FIEDLER, and by the New York Philharmonic Orchestra directed by Arturo TOSCANINI.

Bartet, Jeanne Julia (1854-), French actress trained at the Paris Conservatory: her successful debut at the Vaudeville Theatre in 1872 led to an engagement in 1880 for many years at the Comédie Française where she played the chief roles in both tragedy and comedy with consummate skill. She appeared in 1908 at London where her extraordinary abilities were displayed in a large repertory.

Barthelemy, Auguste Marseille (1796-1867), French poet who collaborated with his intimate friend, J. P. A. Méry, in a series of satiric, political epics for one of which he was imprisoned and fined. His outstanding works were the historical epic, *Napoleon in Egypt* (1828) describing the romantic side of the campaign, and a biographical history of the forty members of the French Academy.

Barthelmess, Richard (1897-), American screen actor who first attracted attention in *Tol'able David* and as the leading man in *War Brides*. Among the many pictures in which he has played important roles are *Broken Blossoms; Shore Leave; The Amateur Gentleman; Ransom's Folly; The Patent Leather Kid; The Little Shepherd of Kingdom Come* and *Only Angels Have Wings*. In 1939 he appeared on the New York stage in *The Postman Always Rings Twice*.

Bartholdi, Frédéric-Auguste (1834-1904), French sculptor who also studied architecture and painting. His inspiration ran along grandiose lines: among his works are several monumental fountains; *The Lion of Belfort,* a colossal figure 78 feet long and 52 feet high in front of the castle at Belfort, France; the *Statue of Liberty* in New York harbor, and a statue of Lafayette in New York City.

Bartholomé, Paul Albert (1848-1928), French sculptor and painter: failing to achieve success in the latter art after studying with Barthélemy Menns in Geneva, and with Jean Léon Gérôme in Paris, he devoted himself to sculpture. In 1895 he completed a group known as *Monument to the Dead* which was purchased by the city of Paris, and placed in the cemetery of Pére-Lachaise in 1899. Two figures, *Little Girl Weeping* and *Bust of Madame X,* are in the LUXEMBOURG: a statue depicting the heroism of Paris during World War I is in the courtyard of the Carrousel.

Bartholomew, Edward Sheffield (1822-1858), American sculptor whose promising career was cut short by his untimely death: his works include *Eve Repentant; Ganymede; Hagar and Ishmael; Sappho; Genius of Connecticut*.

Bartholomew, Freddie (1924-), English motion-picture actor who recited and acted juvenile parts at three years of age: he came to America with his aunt in 1935, and played the role of David in the adaptation of Dickens' *David Copperfield*. Other pictures in which he has appeared include *Little Lord Fauntleroy; Anna Karenina; Lloyd's of London; Lord Jeff; Captains Courageous; Kidnapped; Tom Brown's School Days; Swiss Family Robinson*.

Bartik, Otakar (1868-1936), Czech balletmaster and choreographer; pupil of Franz ONDRICEK in violin and Anton DVORAK in composition. After directing ballet in Prague and Germany, he was engaged at the Metropolitan Opera House, New York, in 1908, remaining there for twenty-five ears, and producing the ballets in *The Bartered Bride; Pique Dame; Prince Igor; Shanewis*. He wrote the choreography for Borodin's *Polovetsian Dances*, and also his own ballet, *Omitake San* with music by Rudolf FRIML.

Bartlett, Ethel (1902-), English pianist who studied with Tobias MATTHAY and Artur SCHNABEL, making her debut as a pianist in London, with John Barbirolli conducting, in 1916. She formed the piano duo, **Bartlett and Robinson,** in 1927 with her husband, Rae Robertson: they have appeared with great success in Great Britain, the United States, Canada, South America and Europe.

Bartlett, Homer Newton (1845-1920), American pianist, organist, composer, pupil of Sebastian Bach MILLS, and organist for more than fifty years at various New York churches. His compositions include chamber music; an opera, *La Valière;* a violin concerto; sacred and secular choral music; many songs and piano pieces of which the *Grande Polka de Concert* was a favorite toward the end of the 19th century.

Bartlett, John (1820-1905), American publisher and compiler of literary reference works: he was proprietor of the University Bookstore at Cambridge, Mass., until 1863 when he became a member of Little, Brown & Company, and senior partner in 1871. His most important work was *Familiar Quotations* (1855), which has passed through many editions, and is still the standard work of its kind. Bartlett also compiled a *Shakespeare Concordance* and a *Shakespeare Phrase Book*.

Bartlett, John Russell (1805-1886), American historian who was appointed a member of the commission delegated to the task of surveying the boundary between the United States and Mexico in 1853; his *Personal Narrative* (1854) remains an invaluable record of his work in this connection. He also prepared a *Dictionary of Americanisms,* a widely-used reference work during his period.

Bartlett, Michael (1901-), American singer and actor, educated at Princeton University, and trained in singing at Milan where he made his debut in *Lucia di Lammermoor* in 1928. He appeared with the Philadelphia Opera Company in 1929, and made his stage debut in 1932 at the Manhattan Theatre, New York, in *Through the Years*. Among the plays in which he has been featured are *The Cat and the Fiddle; School for Husbands; Three Waltzes*. After 1935 he appeared in several films including *Love Me Forever* and *The Lilac Domino*.

Bartlett, Paul Wayland (1865-1925), American sculptor, son of Truman Howe Bartlett, critic, sculptor, and teacher of modeling at the Massachusetts Institute of Technology. The younger Bartlett studied at the Ecole des Beaux Arts, Paris, under Cavelier and FREMIET, specializing in animal figures. In 1888 his *Bohemian Bear Trainer* won a gold medal at the Paris Salon, and in 1895 he was made Chevalier of the Legion of Honor. Among his works are the *Ghost Dancer* at the Columbian Exposition; *The Dying Lion,*

statues of *Columbus, Michelangelo* and *Law* at the Congressional Library, Washington; figures for the façade of the New York Public Library; a fountain, *Genius,* at the Pan-American Exposition; an equestrian statue of *Lafayette* in the courtyard of the LOUVRE. Bartlett's work is comparable to that of Auguste RODIN in the use of figures boldly grouped in unified masses as well as dignified and heroic figures treated individually.

Bartlett and Robinson, see **Bartlett, Ethel.**

Bartók, Béla (1881-), Hungarian pianist, collector of folk music, writer and composer: graduate of the Royal Academy in Budapest where he became professor of piano in 1907. In 1919 he headed the Music Commission of the Hungarian Government with Ernest DOHNANYI and Zoltan KODALY. He has toured Europe and the United States as pianist playing his own works. His opera, *Duke Bluebeard's Castle,* and a pantomime-opera, *The Wooden Prince* have been successfully produced: he has composed orchestral and chamber music, songs and piano pieces. His folksong collections, in 12 volumes, comprise 2700 Hungarian, 3500 Magyar-Rumanian, and several hundred Arabian songs.

Bartoli, Adolfo (1833-1894), Italian historian of literature, and a recognized arbiter of matters connected with his country's literature. He was the author of *The First Two Centuries of Italian Literature* (1870), and *History of Italian Literature* (1878), both invaluable reference volumes.

Bartolini, Lorenzo (c.1777-1850), Italian sculptor, pupil in Paris of Lemot. His fame was established by a bas-relief, *Cleobis and Biton,* but his great patron was Napoleon I of whom he made a large bust, and who sent him to Carrera to establish a school for sculptors. His best works are *Charity, Hercules and Lichas,* and *Faith in God;* Italian critics class him with Antonio CANOVA and Bertel THORWALDSEN.

Bartolommeo di Pagholo del Fattorino, Fra (1475?-1517), Italian painter, also called **Fra Bartolommeo** after he became a Dominican friar, and *Baccio della Porta* because his home was near a gate *(Porta)* in Florence. He was friendly with RAPHAEL, and influenced in his art by both Giovanni BELLINI and GIORGIONE. His paintings, which give evidence of transition in style from the 15th to the 16th century, include a striking profile of Girolamo SAVONAROLA, of whom Bartolommeo was a fervant disciple; an *Apparition of the Virgin* now in the Academy at Florence; a *Madonna with Six Saints; The Last Judgment* (with ALBERTINELLI), and *St. Mark,* a masterpiece in fresco.

Bartolommeo Veneto (c.1480-1555), Italian painter, pupil of Gentile BELLINI, and famous for the fine drawing and brilliant coloring in his portraits, *Massimiliano Sforza* and *Lucrezia Borgia:* the former is now in the United States, and the latter in Frankfurt, Germany. Several of his Madonnas are highly regarded: also the *Portrait of a Man,* and a *Salome*.

Bartolozzi, Francesco (1725-1813), Italian engraver, son of a goldsmith: he displayed so much skill at designing that he studied painting and engraving, and, after considerable success in Venice, went to London where he lived for forty years, becoming one of the original members of the Royal Academy. He created many fine engravings, among them plates for BOYDELL's *Shakespeare Gallery*. In 1802 he became director of the National Academy at Lisbon, remaining there until his death. His son, **Gaetano Stephane Bartolozzi** (1757-1821), was an excellent engraver, but famous chiefly as the father of Lucia Elizabeth VESTRIS, a distinguished actress.

Barton, Bernard (1784-1849), English poet educated at a Quaker school in Ipswich, and known as the "Quaker poet." He was an intimate friend of Charles LAMB, and published many volumes of verse, such as *Household Verses*, which are worthy of more attention than they receive today.

Barton, Fanny, see **Abington, Frances Barton.**

Barton, James (1890-), American actor, son of James Barton of the Primrose and West Minstrels. He first appeared in vaudeville in 1894; toured as Topsy in *Uncle Tom's Cabin*, and appeared in stock companies for several years before his debut at New York in 1919 in *The Passing Show of 1919*, and subsequently in *The Last Waltz, Rose of Stamboul*, several Ziegfeld productions, and *Burlesque*. He finally succeeded Henry Hull as Jeeter Lester in *Tobacco Road* in 1934, playing the part continuously for five years. He has also appeared in films such as *Captain Hurricane; His Family Tree; The Shepherd of the Hills.*

Bartsch, Johann Adam Bernhard (1757-1821), Austrian engraver of works by Albrecht DURER and Hans BURGKMAIR, although he made a few originals. He executed more than 500 plates, and wrote a remarkable work in 21 volumes, *Le Peinter-Graveur,* replete with technical criticisms and iconographical studies.

Barye, Antoine Louis (1796-1875), French sculptor of wild animals who was first a goldsmith, later studying sculpture with François BOSIO and painting with Antoine GROS. While earning his living from 1823 to 1828 in the shop of the goldsmith, Fauconnier, he made sixty small miniatures of animals, one of which was *Stork Perched on a Tortoise*, and studied the daily life of the wild beasts in the Jardin des Plantes. Among his greatest creations are *Tiger Devouring a Crocodile; Lion Crushing a Serpent* which was bought by the French Government; the *Dead Gazelle; Stag Surprised by a Lynx; Lion in Repose; The Centaur and Lapith; Theseus and the Minotaur* and *Minerva.* More than one hundred of his bronzes are in the Corcoran Gallery, Washington, D. C.

Barytone, see **Baritone.**

Barzin, Leon (1900-), Belgian-American violinist and conductor who came to the United States with his father in 1902. He studied the violin with Eugéne YSAYE, and composition with Abraham Lilienthal; became a violinist with the National Symphony and New York Philharmonic Orchestras, and in 1930 conductor and director of the American Orchestral Society, an organization training young musicians in the art of orchestra playing. He has been guest conductor of many American orchestras.

Base, in architecture the lowest member of a COLUMN; in Egyptian and early Greek architecture it consisted of a raised slab in either stone or cement on which the wooden column was placed to keep it dry. At a later date, the base was of stone or marble elaborately carved: during the 15th century it was sometimes constructed in two stages, the lower one known as the base course.

Bashkirtseff, Maria Constantinova (1860-1884), Russian writer, singer, and painter who acquired a superior education in the classics and modern languages, and studied painting at Tony ROBERT FLEURY's studio in Paris. Due to her premature death at twenty-four her talent for painting was hardly developed in such pictures as *Jean and Jacques, Meeting,* and a portrait of her cousin for which she received honorable mention at the Paris Salon. Her diary, published posthumously, proved a thoroughly human journal, and was reprinted in several languages. She also executed some charming pastel portraits.

Basilica, in Roman architecture the name of a public hall, with aisles and COLONNADES, for the administration of justice, the transaction of business, or for serious discussions. In the early days of Christianity, such buildings were often converted into churches; among the most famous were those of Aemilia, Constantine, and Julia in the Roman forum.

Baskerville, John (1706-1775), distinguished English printer and type-founder whose name is still used on certain type faces employed in bookmaking both in England and the United States. He was elected printer to the University of Cambridge in 1758; among his productions were fine editions of VERGIL, MILTON, HORACE, JUVENAL and of the BIBLE.

Bass, in music (*1*) the lowest tone in a chord; (*2*) the lowest voice or part in a musical composition; (*3*) the lowest male voice in pitch; (*4*) when prefixed to the name of an instrument such as the CLARINET or DRUM (i.e. bass clarinet or bass drum) it places the instrument as the lowest in pitch of its type. In special cases such as the BASSOON, TUBA and other instruments where an even lower-pitched instrument is made, the prefix *contra* is added.

Bass Clarinet, see **Clarinet.**

Bass Drum, see **Drum.**

Bassano, Jacopo da Ponte (1510-1592), Italian painter of the Venetian school: his real name was *Jacopo* (or *Giacomo*) *da Ponte,* and he was a pupil of his father, Francesco da Ponte, called *Bassano* after the name of the town in which he was born. He was attracted and probably influenced by the works of TITIAN in the portrayal of his favorite subjects: peasants, cattle and rural landscapes. He painted only a few great pictures among which are an altarpiece, *The Nativity* at Bassano; *The Good Samaritan* and *Christ and the Money Changers*. Two of Bassano's four sons, Leandro and Francesco, worked with him; in his vigorously dramatic moments, some critics see in him the forerunner of REMBRANDT and VELASQUEZ.

Basset-Horn, in music a wood-wind instrument misnamed (in exactly the same way as the ENG-LISH HORN) because it is not a horn, but the tenor member of the CLARINET family. In appearance it is the same as the ordinary clarinet except that the body of the instrument is bent near the mouthpiece, and the bell is wider and made of metal. The pitch is a fifth below that of the clarinet in C, and it is a transposing instrument in the orchestra, with a rich, reedy tone most appreciated by MOZART, BEETHOVEN and MENDELSSOHN, and also used by other composers of the classic and romantic periods. The basset-horn is no longer used in orchestral scores except in rare instances.

Basshe, Emjo (1900-1939), Russian-American dramatist who came to the United States as a boy of twelve; he worked as a reporter, and also backstage at the PROVINCETOWN THEATRE in Provincetown and New York. His works include *Adam Solitaire* (1925); *Earth; Centuries; Portrait of a Tenement House; Doomsday Circus*. The variety and virility of his ideas indicate the possibilities of even greater accomplishment if he had lived longer.

Bassoon, a wood-wind instrument of the OBOE family, serving as the bass for the WOOD-WIND. The wooden tube doubles back on itself, forming two parallel air chambers, and the long curved metal mouthpiece uses a double REED. Its resemblance to a bundle of wooden sticks accounts for the name, *fagotto*, in Italian. All the great masters except HANDEL made good use of its possibilities for tragic or humorous orchestral effects; MOZART and WEBER wrote concertos for it, and modern composers include the bassoon and contrabassoon in their scores.

Basso-relievo (It.) or **Bas-relief,** in architecture the term applied to a form of sculpture in which the design projects only slightly from the plane of the background; it has also been called "sculpture painting." Egyptian reliefs actually sink below the plane surface of the background, and, in the Panathenaic procession of the PARTHENON, the bas-relief is practically flat. When the bas-relief projects more than half, it is known as ALTO-RELIEVO.

Bastien-Lepage, Jules (1848-1884), French painter who studied at the Ecole des Beaux Arts in Paris under Alexander CABANEL. In 1874 his *Song of Spring,* a picture of a young girl sitting on a knoll looking down on a village, attracted favorable attention, and gradually his reputation was established, although the judges at the Salon awarded him few prizes. Among his finest works are portraits of Sarah BERNHARDT and the Prince of Wales; *Annunciation to the Shepherds; Priam at the feet of Achilles; The First Communion;* *Joan of Arc Listening to the Voices; The Potato Gatherers* and *Pére Jacques.*

Bastille, a fortified building in Paris the erection of which was started in 1369; it was enlarged and used both as a fortress and a prison for political offenders. Among the famous personages who were incarcerated there may be mentioned the MAN IN THE IRON MASK, VOLTAIRE, MIRABEAU and the Cardinal de Rohan; many were arrested on a LETTRE DE CACHET, an arbitrary order of imprisonment in which the name was left blank: in divers instances the incarceration was kept a secret. The real outbreak of the FRENCH REVOLUTION is said to have been initiated with the destruction of the Bastille on July 14, 1789, as the first victory gained by the French people over a despotic government existing over many centuries: July 14 has been a national holiday in France ever since.

Bat, The, see **Fledermaus, Die.**

Bataille, Henri (1872-1922), French poet and dramatist: his works include two volumes of poetry; *The White Chamber* (1895) and *The Beautiful Voyage.* His numerous stage successes began with *Maman Colibri* in 1904: among the others, many of which concern themselves with abnormal matters, are *The Fair Leper; The Masque; The Foolish Virgin; The Amazon; Possession; Human Flesh.* Bataille published a volume of war poems, *The Divine Tragedy* in 1916.

Bateman, the name of a family of actors, dramatists and theatrical managers who left their mark on American and English drama during the period from 1855 to 1885. The first member was **Hezekiah Linthicum Bateman** (1812-1875), born in Baltimore, Md., who played with Mrs. Charles Kean and managed a theatre in St. Louis in 1855. In 1871 he leased the Lyceum Theatre, London, and presented Sir Henry IRVING in the first performance of *The Bells.* His wife, **Sidney Frances Bateman,** was the daughter of an English comedian, Joseph Cowell, who settled in the United States and wrote interesting reminiscences of the early American theatre. She appeared on the stage at fourteen in New Orleans, and after her marriage wrote a successful play, *Self,* in which she and her husband played the stellar roles. Her other plays were *Fanchette; Geraldine; The Golden Calf,* and a dramatization of Wilkie Collins' novel, *The Dead Secret.* Four of Mrs. Bateman's daughters also appeared successfully on the stage: **Kate Josephine** (1843-1917) was a favorite *Juliet* and *Lady Macbeth* in the days of the Civil War; appeared opposite Sir Henry Irving in London about 1880, and founded a school of acting there in 1892: her daughter Sidney also became an accomplished actress. **Virginia Bateman,** younger sister of Kate Josephine, was born in 1854, appeared in her mother's play, *Fanchette,* in London, and also played important parts at the Lyceum; another sister, **Isabel Bateman,** was a well-known actress on the London stage.

Bates, Arlo (1850-1918), American essayist, poet and novelist; his works include *The Pagans* (1884); *A Wheel of Fire; Berries in the Brier* (Poems); *Sonnets in Shadow; The Philistines;*

The Puritans; Under the Beech Tree (Poems); *Love in a Cloud; The Diary of a Saint.*

Bates, Blanche (1873-), American actress who made her New York debut in 1897 under the management of Augustin Daly in *The Taming of the Shrew.* Among the numerous plays in which she played important roles or starred may be mentioned *The Great Ruby; The Three Musketeers; Madame Butterfly; Under Two Flags; Darling of the Gods; Hedda Gabler; The Girl of the Golden West; Diplomacy; Molière; The Famous Mrs. Fair; Candida; Dangerous Corner.*

Bates, Harry (1850-1899), English sculptor, a student at the Lambeth School of Art, and pupil of Auguste RODIN after he won a scholarship with his relief, *Socrates Teaching the People in the Agora.* His masterpiece is an allegorical presentation of *Love and Life,* a winged male figure in bronze crowning a female figure in ivory: other fine works include a colossal equestrian statue of Lord Roberts at Calcutta; a statue of Queen Victoria; *Hounds in Leash* and *Pandora.* His early death left unfulfilled many of Bates' fine ideas for future works.

Bates, Katharine Lee (1859-1929), American editor and poet; educated at Wellesley College where she became a teacher in 1885, and professor of English literature from 1891 to 1925. Her poems, especially verses designed for children, are charmingly conceived, but she is best remembered as author of the hymn, *America the Beautiful,* which has taken on special significance since the beginning of World War II.

Bathos, in literature a descent from the sublime to the ridiculous in literature or speech, usually described as anticlimax. Alexander POPE wrote a satire on bathos, the title being a burlesque of an essay, *The Sublime,* by Dionysius Cassius Longinus, a Greek philosopher of Plato's school.

Baths, special structures erected in ancient Greece and Rome, as well as in Oriental countries, for public and private bathing: the ruins of several elaborate buildings of this character have been excavated by archaeologists. The Roman emperors vied in constructing enormous public baths, known as *thermae,* containing not only quarters for ablution, but also gymnasiums, libraries, stadiums and theatres. There were rooms for disrobing, anointing, and cold, tepid or hot bathing; the means contrived for the latter were particularly complicated. The exteriors of the buildings were rarely ornamental, but the interiors made use of every decorative device, such as mosaics, marble, and metals to create an atmosphere of luxury, particularly in the private baths. The Romans often placed their baths adjacent to natural springs and stufae, thereby saving the expense of heating equipment. The baths of Diocletian, Titus and Caracella were equipped with thousands of marble seats for bathers: open colonnades and seats for men of letters were provided where new works were read, or the latest news debated. Baths are described at great length in Greek and Roman literature; novels on classic themes frequently contain scenes laid in them.

Baton, in music the stick used by an orchestral conductor to beat time; its use may be traced to the SISTINE CHOIR at Rome. In 1738 the conductor directed while playing the HARPSICHORD, and striking the baton intermittently against the desk of the instrument. MENDELSSOHN was one of the first conductors to direct from the podium rather than at the piano. The baton used today measures from 14 to 28 inches in length, and is of a light color so as to be more readily seen by the players. It is often provided with means for illumination when used in theatres or motion picture houses.

Batoni, Pompeo Girolamo (1708-1787), Italian painter, regarded by many authorities as an artist who accomplished much in rescuing 18th century painting from the harmful mannerisms inherited from the 17th century. He was an excellent portrait painter, and created a great many pictures of which the masterpiece is the group, *Peace and War.*

Battement (Fr.), in ballet the name of a dance movement in which the leg is raised off the ground; *grand battement* is a movement when the leg is raised high; *petit battement* is the same movement when the leg is barely raised; *battement tendu* is a movement where one leg is extended in the front, side or back until the tip of the stretched limb barely rests on the floor.

Batterie (Fr.), in ballet a dance movement in which the dancer beats his feet together while in the air; in the *grand batterie* the feet are widely separated; in the *petite batterie* the radius of the movement is small.

Battery, in music the name of the group of percussion instruments, comprising the SIDE DRUM, BASS DRUM, TIMPANI, TRIANGLE, etc., in the orchestra; the French term is *batterie.*

Battle Hymn of the Republic, an American patriotic song of the Civil War, the words written by Julia Ward Howe and sung to the tune used previously for the song *John Brown's Body Lies a-Mould'ring in the Grave.* The melody itself is ascribed to William Steffe, a composer of hymns and Sunday School songs, but doubts have been expressed regarding his claim. The poem was first published in the *Atlantic Monthly* in 1862.

Battlement, in military architecture the term designating the parapet of a wall in which sections have been removed at intervals to permit the discharge of arrows or other weapons of war. The cut-out spaces are called *crenels,* and the intervening wall spaces are designated *merlons.* Traces of battlements have been found in Egypt, Syria, Greece, Pompeii and Turkey: in some cases they were elaborately decorated.

Baucis and Philemon, in Greek mythology two mortals who gave food and shelter to the gods, ZEUS and HERMES, when they visited the earth in the guise of men, and were refused assistance by cruel neighbors. The gods sent a flood to destroy the wicked ones, and changed their hosts' poor home into a temple. When Baucis and Philemon died at the same time, they were changed into evergreen trees.

Baudelaire, Charles Pierre (1821-1867), French poet who made fine translations of Edgar Allan Poe's works, and wrote a famous volume of poems, *Flowers of Evil* (1857), in which he created exquisite lyrics which were unfortunately wasted on questionable subjects; the result being that the volume was banned until the offensive topics were removed.

Baudry, Paul Jacques Aimé (1828-1886), French painter who studied at the Ecole des Beaux Arts, Paris. In 1850 he won the Grand Prix de Rome with his picture, *Zenobia Found on the Banks of the Araxes:* his murals for the foyer of the Paris Opera House, and at the chateau of Chantilly are among his finest creations, but his ceiling fresco, *The Glorification of the Law,* in the Palais de Justice, Paris, is considered his masterpiece. His brother, an architect, and two of Baudry's fellow painters, Dubois and Mercie, erected a monument in 1890 to him in Paris, and a statue by Gerome is to be seen at La Roche-sur-Yonne.

Bauer, Harold (1873-), American pianist who first studied the violin with his father and Adolf Pollitzer. After touring as a violinist for several years, he studied the piano with Ignaz Paderewski for a year; the only instruction he ever had on the instrument. After touring Europe, Great Britain and Australia, he made his debut in the United States in 1900 with the Boston Symphony Orchestra. He has appeared with all the major American orchestras, and has given many recitals, and chamber music concerts with noted artists. He founded the Beethoven Association in 1919, and dissolved it in 1940. He has edited many classical and modern works for piano.

Bauer, Marion Eugenie (1887-), American composer and writer; educated at Whitman College, Walla Walla, Wash., and a student of music with Walter Rothwell and Henry Holden Huss in America and André Gedalge, Nadia Boulanger and Louis Campbell-Tipton in Paris. She is now (1943) assistant professor of music at New York University, and has lectured for many years on musical subjects both in America and England. Her compositions include incidental music for Aeschylus' *Prometheus Bound,* pieces for orchestra, chamber music, choral works, songs, piano, and violin pieces. Among her books may be mentioned *How Music Grew,* (1925), with Ethel Peyser; *Music Through the Ages; Twentieth Century Music; Musical Questions and Quizzes.*

Bauernfeld, Eduard von (1802-1890), Austrian lawyer, poet and dramatist educated at the University of Vienna: his comedies are among the best of those written by German playwrights of the 19th century. Among them are *Das Liebes-Protokoll; Die Ewige Liebe; Moderne Jugund* and *Der Landfrieden.* Among music lovers Bauernfeld is distinguished by his long friendship with Franz Schubert; in his reminiscences, *Alt Wien,* he goes into much detail regarding the intimacy of the "happy three"; Schubert, Bauernfeld and Moritz von Schwind, one of Germany's greatest painters.

Baum, Lyman Frank (1856-1919), American author who wrote a popular juvenile book, *Father Goose,* in 1899, followed by a series of fourteen stories the first of which was *The Wonderful Wizard of Oz,* from which a musical play was made for Fred Stone and David Montgomery, music by Paul Tietjens. Some of his stories for girls and boys were published with the pen names "Edith Van Dyne" and "Floyd Akers."

Baum, Vicki (1888-), Austrian novelist and dramatist: her reputation was established through the novel, *Grand Hotel,* which was translated into English, dramatized, and screened with remarkable success. She came to America in 1931, and has been acting as a screen writer in Hollywood. Among her plays are *The Divine Drudge, Summer Night* and *Grand Hotel;* she published a novel, *Marion Alive,* in 1942.

Baur, Harry (?-1943), French stage and screen actor who studied music at the Marseilles Conservatory of Music, and made his debut on the amateur stage. After serving in the French army during World War I, he returned to the stage for a time, but finally became a screen star. He appeared as a character actor in many films including *Les Miserables; The Life and Loves of Beethoven; The Golem; Dark Eyes; A Man and His Wife; The Polish Jew; Rasputin; The Mad Emperor; Moscow Nights; Crime and Punishment.* In 1936 he published his memoirs in *Pour Vous,* a French periodical.

Bax, Sir Arnold E. Trevor (1883-), English composer; graduate of the Royal Academy of Music, London, under Tobias Matthay in piano and Frederick Corder in composition. His works include six symphonies; several symphonic poems; concertos for violoncello and for violin; two ballets; chamber music; choral works; piano pieces; violin pieces; songs and arrangements of folk songs. While at heart a romanticist, Bax's works are modern in spirit and development: he has not connected himself with any institutions of music, appeared as a conductor of his orchestral works, or in recitals of his many piano compositions.

Baxter, Warner (1893-), American stage and screen actor who entered the films in 1922; among the pictures in which he has appeared may be mentioned *Miss Brewster's Millions; The Squaw Man; The Cisco Kid; Grand Canary; The Prisoner of Shark Island; Slave Ship; To Mary— With Love; Barricade; Earth Bound; Adam Had Four Sons.*

Bayer, Karl Robert Emmerich (1835-1902), German novelist who wrote under the pen name "Robert Byr." His many novels have had a large sale: they include *The Struggle for Life; A Secret Dispatch; The Road to Fortune; The Ironworm.*

Baylis, Lillian, see **Sadler's Wells Ballet.**

Bayly, Thomas Haynes (1797-1839), English writer of song lyrics, novelist, and dramatist; he was educated at Oxford with the view of becoming a clergyman, but abandoned the idea when his ability for versifying proved itself in songs such as *We Met—'Twas in a Crowd, Gaily the*

65

Troubadour and *Long, Long Ago*. He wrote two novels; *The Aylmers* and *A Legend of Killarney:* one of his plays, *Perfection*, produced by Madame VESTRIS, was highly praised by Lord Chesterfield.

Bayne, Beverly (1895-), American screen actress who appeared in more than five hundred films; she was the wife of Francis X. BUSHMAN, and one of the most capable and admired actresses of the silent screen.

Bayreuth, a city in Bavaria, Germany, where Richard WAGNER built the Festspielhaus, a theatre of his own designing for the performance of the NIBELUNGEN RING, and his other music dramas and operas. The necessary funds were raised by Wagner Societies in all parts of the world, and the building was opened in 1876 with a performance of the "Ring." Wagner's villa, Wahnfried, was erected in the suburbs, and both Wagner, his wife, Cosima Wagner, and his friend, Franz LISZT are buried there. The Wagner Memorial Museum, comprising 23 rooms of interesting relics, is also located at Bayreuth.

Bayreuth Festivals, the name given a series of yearly performances of Richard WAGNER's music dramas presented at the theatre erected at BAYREUTH, and known as the Festspielhaus. The first festival was given in 1876; it included three presentations of the "Ring" (The RHINEGOLD; The VALKYRIE; SIEGFRIED; The DUSK OF THE GODS); the conductors being Hans RICHTER, Anton SEIDL, and Felix MOTTL; the singers included Lilli LEHMANN, Albert NIEMANN, and Amalia MATERNA. The theatre remained closed until 1882 when the festivals were resumed: twenty more were given up to 1914 when they were interrupted by World War I. They were resumed in 1924, and twelve more festivals were given up to 1938 when they were again interrupted by World War II: among the famous conductors were Arturo TOSCANINI, Karl MUCK and Wilhelm FURTWANGLER.

Bazin, René (1853-1922), French litterateur and novelist who became professor of law at the Catholic University in Paris. He wrote an interesting book of travel, *The Italians of Today*, and several novels delineating characters and scenes in French provincial life: among them are *Un Tache d'encre* (1888); *Les Oberlé*, which was successfully dramatized; *Le Blé qui léve* and *La Terre qui meurt*, a story of La Vendée.

Bazzi, Giovanni Antonio, see **Sodoma, Il.**

Bazzini, Antonio (1818-1897), Italian composer and violinist; a prolific writer of church music at seventeen. PAGANINI recognized his abilities, and suggested that he tour Europe, the result being triumphal appearances in Italy, France, Germany, Denmark, Poland and England. His compositions include an opera, orchestral works, sacred music, chamber music, and many fine violin solos.

Beach, Mrs. H. H. A. (1867-), American composer; maiden-name Amy Marcy Cheney. After studying piano with Ernest Perabo and Karl Baermann, and harmony with Junius W. Hill, she made her debut in 1883 as a pianist in Boston, appearing in recital, and also with the Boston Symphony and Chicago Symphony orchestras. After her marriage to Dr. Beach, she devoted herself entirely to composition: her more than 200 works include the *Gaelic Symphony,* a piano concerto, chamber music for various combinations, pieces for piano solo and two pianos, violin pieces, and many delightful songs.

Beach, Rex (1877-), American novelist educated at Rollins College, Fla., and trained for the bar. His successful novels include *The Spoilers* (1906), which has been dramatized and screened; *The Barrier; Going Some; The Auction Block; The Silver Horde; The Ne'er-do-Well* and *Rainbow's End; The Goose Woman; Jungle Gold.*

Beaconsfield, Benjamin Disraeli, Earl of, see **Disraeli, Benjamin, Lord Beaconsfield.**

Beal, Gifford Reynolds (1879-), American painter; pupil of William Merritt CHASE and at the ART STUDENTS' LEAGUE. He was first recognized as a marine painter, but his scenes at garden parties and views of circus life are also well-balanced works in vivid colors. Beal's pictures, *The Albany Boat, Freight Yards,* and *Across the Valley* are typical of his art: he has received several medals and honorariums, and is well represented in American art museums.

Beard, Daniel Carter (1850-1941), American artist and founder of the Boy Scout Organization in the United States, of which he became the national leader. Mr. Beard also taught woodcraft at a school initiated by him called the Dan Beard Outdoor School. He wrote many articles on subjects relating to nature; also several books for boys including *The American Boy's Book of Wild Animals* and *Field and Forest Handy Books.*

Beard, James Henry (c.1814-1893), American painter whose portraits of Henry Clay, John Quincy Adams, Zachary Taylor and William H. Harrison are well-known: he devoted himself to painting animals in his later years. His brother, William Holbrook Beard, was a portrait painter who also worked on satirical and humorous subjects, and his son, **Thomas Francis Beard** (1842-1905), known as "Frank" Beard, was an illustrator for Harper's Magazine during the Civil War, and equally famous for his political and temperance cartoons.

Beardsley, Aubrey Vincent (1872-1898), English illustrator in black and white who engaged in art as a profession when Sir Edward BURNE-JONES and PUVIS DE CHAVANNES advised him to do so after seeing his sketches. His fantastic ideas at first resulted in violent criticism, chiefly because he ignored both perspective and proportion, but his work was later recognized as that of a genius-innovator, especially the frontispiece to *Volpone,* and his designs for Oscar WILDE's *Salome,* POPE's *Rape of the Lock* and the *Lysistrata* of ARISTOPHANES.

Beat, in music the movement of a conductor's arm indicating the time of a vocal or instrumental composition to a body of singers or players. The *down-beat,* or heavy accent, is indicated by a downward motion of the arm; the *up-beat,* or light beat, is indicated by either an upward or a side-wise motion.

Beatrice Portinari (1266-1290), an Italian lady, resident in FLORENCE, who was presumed to be the Beatrice of DANTE's *Divine Comedy* and *Vita Nuova:* her identity in this connection has been a matter of controversy for many years.

Beattie, James (1735-1803), Scottish writer on philosophy and poet, educated at Marischal College, Aberdeen, and a violent opponent of David Hume's philosophical theories. His best work is a poem in Spenserian style, *The Minstrel,* notable for its fine descriptions of natural scenery; his portrait was painted by Sir Joshua REYNOLDS.

Beau Brummel, the nickname given **George Brummel** (1778-1840), an English gentleman famous as a leader of fashionable society in London. He was an intimate friend of the Prince of Wales (later King George IV), who was said to have been greatly upset when told that Brummel did not care for the cut of his coat. Beau himself was in no sense extravagant in his dress, but rather studiously correct in attire and manners. His one failing was an unconquerable propensity for gambling: he was imprisoned for debt in 1835, and his misfortunes affected him to such an extent that he died insane. The American dramatist, Clyde FITCH, wrote a play, *Beau Brummel,* which proved a great success for Richard MANSFIELD.

Beauchamp, 17th century director of the Academy of Dancing, choreographer and balletmaster of the Paris Opéra during the reign of Louis XIV, who probably instructed the French king in twenty-seven grand ballets in which the royal dancer appeared at court. All of Beauchamp's ballets were on allegorical subjects, and required complex mechanical contrivances for their performance.

Beau Danube, Le, a romantic ballet in one act: libretto and choreography by Leonide MASSINE; music by Johann STRAUSS arranged by Roger Desormière; first performed at Monte Carlo in 1933. The story of the ballet revolves around a flirtatious hussar, an innocent young girl and a street dancer; introduces the *Blue Danube Waltz* as the piece de resistance, and ends with innocence triumphant. Alexandra DANILOVA has always been associated with the role of the street dancer, performing opposite Leonide MASSINE as the hussar.

Beaujoyeulx, Balthasard de (? -c.1587), Italian violinist who came to France about 1555, changing his name to the above from "Baltazarini." He was in the service of CATHERINE DE' MEDICI, and shared in the composition of the *Ballet comique de la Reine,* produced in 1581, regarded as one of the forerunners of French opera.

Beaumarchais, Pierre Augustin Caron de (1732-1799), French dramatist: as a young man he invented a new type of escapement for watches, and made a watch for Mme. de POMPADOUR. A visit to Spain resulted in an incident on which he drew to a considerable extent in his first drama, *Eugénie* (1767), followed in two years by

another, *Les Deux Amis:* neither one had much success. After acting as secret agent for Louis XV for the recovery of certain papers, the result being his imprisonment for a time by the Austrian government, he induced the French authorities to give secret aid to the American colonies during the Revolutionary War to the extent of forty ships carrying arms and ammunition. In 1775 *The* BARBER OF SEVILLE, his famous comedy, was produced: it was a failure at the première, but a complete success at the second performance, after being shortened and the action speeded up. ROSSINI composed an opera, still a great favorite, based on this comedy. In 1784, in spite of opposition on the part of Louis XVI, another successful comedy, THE MARRIAGE OF FIGARO was produced: MOZART composed an opera using its plot which is now in the repertoire of every grand opera company. Beaumarchais left a substantial legacy to drama in his *Essay on the Nature of Serious Drama:* his famous *Memoirs* have never been surpassed for satirical humor and vivacity of style; even VOLTAIRE was an admirer of them.

Beaumont, Cyril W., contemporary English teacher of stage dancing, and author of several important works on the art of the ballet: they include *The Complete Book of the Ballet* (1938); *Supplement to the Complete Book of the Ballet; The History of Harlequin; A Manual of the Theory and Practice of Classical Theatrical Dancing; A History of Ballet in Russia.*

Beaumont, Francis (1584-1616), English poet and dramatist, educated at Oxford, who published his first poem, *Salmacis and Hermaphroditus* in 1602. He wrote several original plays including *The Woman Hater* and *The Knight of the Burning Pestle,* and collaborated with John FLETCHER (1579-1625), also a poet and dramatist, in the plays *Cupid's Revenge; The Captain; The Scornful Lady; The Beggar's Bush; The Coxcomb; The Maid's Tragedy; Philaster, or Love Lies a-Bleeding* and *Four Plays in One.* Both men were intimates of Ben JONSON and other celebrities who gathered at the MERMAID TAVERN, for literary discussion and conviviality.

Beaux, Cecilia (1863-1942), American painter; pupil of ROBERT-FLEURY, BOUGUEREAU and DAGNAN-BOUVERET. In 1890 she exhibited at the Paris Exposition, and in 1893 at the Philadelphia Art Club where she was awarded a gold medal. Her paintings, to be seen in most of the famous galleries in Europe and America, include *The Last Days of Infancy; A New England Woman; The Dancing Lesson; Girl With Cat.* She published her autobiography, *Background with Figures* in 1930.

Beccafumi, Domenico di Pace (1486-1551), Italian painter and sculptor, also known as *Il Mecherino* or *Mecarino.* He painted the frescoes in the City Hall at Siena, and labored from 1517 to 1544 on the pavement of the Siena Cathedral, improving the technical processes employed in doing the work, and designing innumerable Bible scenes from the Old Testament. He invented a colossal mechanical horse used in the procession of the emperor Charles V when he entered Siena.

Bechstein, Karl (1826-1900), German piano manufacturer who worked as an artisan in German factories, and established himself at Berlin in 1856 with branches later in France, Russia and England. For many years the Bechstein was one of the finest pianos made in Europe, ranking with the instruments made by STEINWAY of Germany, BROADWOOD of England and ERARD of France. After World War I the German factory was taken over by Swiss interests: the London branch was operated by Carl Bechstein, a grandson of the founder, until his death in 1931 when it became an independent British firm.

Beck, Lily Adams (?-1931), English author who wrote novels and interesting studies of Oriental life such as *The Splendor of Asia* under her own name; she became better known for romantic biographies of Lord BYRON, Ann Boleyn, NAPOLEON I and others under the pen name "E. Barrington," and a historic work, *The Glory of Egypt* with the pseudonym "Louis Moresby."

Beck, Martin (1868-), German-American theatrical manager and impresario. He became the managing director of the Radio-Keith-Orpheum vaudeville houses all over the United States, and built several fine theatres in New York and Chicago. In 1934 he brought the famous D'OYLY CARTE Opera Company to the United States for their first engagement in Gilbert and Sullivan operettas; its success was so great that the company played return engagements for many years.

Becker, May Lamberton (1873-), American editor, lecturer, and critic: her works include *Adventures in Reading* (1927); *Books and Windows; Under Twenty; First Adventures in Reading; Choosing Books for Children; Introducing Charles Dickens; Growing Up With America; The Home Book of Christmas.*

Beckford, William (1760-1844), English author and litterateur: a man of great wealth who collected art treasures during his travels, and displayed them in a costly residence, Fonthill Abbey, in Wiltshire. His works include an Oriental romance, revealing extraordinary powers of imagination, entitled *Vathek* (1782), originally written in French and translated by the Reverend Samuel Henley; *Biographical Memoirs of Extraordinary Painters* conceived in a satiric vein; a series of letters based on his travels entitled *Portuguese Letters.*

Beckwith, James Carroll (1852-1917), American portrait painter; student at the National Academy of Design, New York, and of Carolus DURAN in Paris. His portraits include many of the notables of his day including Mark TWAIN, T. A. Janvier, General Schofield and William Walton. His painting, *The Blacksmith* hangs in the National Museum, Washington, D.C.; he was one of the professors at the ART STUDENTS' LEAGUE, New York, for many years.

Becque, Henri François (1837-1899), French dramatist who became one of the leading exponents of naturalistic drama in France. In 1867 he wrote the libretto of an opera, *Sardanapalus*, for the composer, Victorin JONCIÈRES: this was followed by the plays *Michel Pauper; The Vultures; La Parisienne* (his most successful play); *Virtuous Women; A Four-Handed Game* and many others. His comedies were mainly distinguished for their bitingly, satirical comments on the society of his time; he has been widely imitated by his successors.

Becquer, Gustavo Adolfo (1836-1870), Spanish poet and author of romantic tales who earned a precarious living by translating foreign books into Spanish. His style in the prose tales, *El Rayo de Luna* and *La Mujer de piedra*, is comparable to that of Ernst HOFFMANN and Edgar Allan POE: his poetry, which gives evidence of sincerity and exquisite sweetness, bears some resemblance to the work of Heinrich HEINE.

Beddoes, Thomas Lovell (1803-1849), English poet and dramatist; his mother was a sister of the English novelist, Maria EDGEWORTH. He led a wandering life as a doctor and politician in Germany and Switzerland, with occasional visits to England. His works include *The Improvisatore* (1820), which was suppressed; a drama, *The Bride's Tragedy*, and a fantastic, incoherent drama, *Death's Jest Book or The Fool's Tragedy*, on which he worked for twenty years: it was published after his death.

Bedel, Maurice (1884-), French poet and novelist who was educated at the College of Sainte-Croix, and studied painting at the Académie Julien: he served in World War I and his finest works, *Jerome, or The Latitude of Love* (1928), *Molinoff, or The Count in the Kitchen*, and *The New Arcadia* have been published in English.

Bedford-Jones, Henry James O'Brien (1887-), American author born in Canada and now an American citizen: one of the most prolific and successful writers for American and English magazines. He has published nearly seventy books on widely varying subjects: they include *The Cross and the Hammer* (1912); *Son of Cincinnati; This Fiction Business; Cyrano; D'Artgnan's Letter; Drums of Dambala; King's Pardon; The Mission and the Man.*

Beecham, Sir Thomas (1879-), English orchestral conductor who studied music at Oxford University. After conducting the Queen's Hall Orchestra in 1905, he established and directed the New Symphony Orchestra from 1906 to 1908, after which he founded the Beecham Symphony Orchestra. Early in 1910 he gave a season of grand opera in London, followed by two months of *opéra-comique* in the spring, and another series of grand opera in the fall of the same year. The company continued from 1913 to 1916, after which Sir Thomas became artistic director of the Royal Philharmonic Orchestra; conductor of opera at Covent Garden; guest conductor of opera in European houses, and guest conductor of the New York Philharmonic-Symphony Orchestra, the Philadelphia Orchestra, and many other major orchestras in the United States. He has conducted the Seattle Symphony Orchestra since 1941; also the Brooklyn (N. Y.) Symphony Orchestra, and at the Metropolitan Opera House. His autobiography, *A Mingled Chime,* appeared in 1943: he has also directed many recordings of symphonic works.

Beechey, Sir William (1753-1839), English portrait painter; student at the Royal Academy, and in 1793 appointed court painter to Queen Charlotte. In 1798 he executed an equestrian painting of George III which caused a sensation, and resulted in his being knighted. He painted many of the nobility and distinguished persons of his time: his likeness of the sculptor, *Joseph Nollekens,* and a portrait study, *Brother and Sister,* now in the Louvre, Paris, are placed among his best works.

Beer, Thomas (1889-1940), American author who wrote *The Mauve Decade* (1926), a humorous study of "the American way" during the final years of the 19th century: also biographies of the American novelist, Stephen Crane, and of the American capitalist and politician, Mark Hanna, who dominated the Republican party from 1880 until his death in 1904.

Beerbohm, Max (1872-), English dramatic critic, author, and caricaturist educated at Oxford. He succeeded George Bernard SHAW as dramatic critic of the London *Saturday Review:* his works include *The Works of Max Beerbohm* (1896); *The Happy Hypocrite; Zuleika Dobson; Seven Men; The Dreadful Dragon of Hay Hill.* His work as a caricaturist is highly regarded; his books of drawings include *Caricatures of Twenty-five Gentlemen* (1896); *The Poet's Corner; Fifty Caricatures; Rossetti and His Circle* and *Observations.* He also edited and made contributions to the biography of Sir Herbert Beerbohm TREE published in 1920.

Beers, Henry Augustin (1847-1926), American author; educated at Yale University and professor of literature there from 1880 to 1916. He was the author of *A Century of American Literature* (1878); *From Chaucer to Tennyson; Initial Studies in American Letters; The Ways of Yale; The History of English Romanticism* and *A Suburban Pastoral and Other Tales.*

Beery, Noah (1884-), American stage and screen actor; among the many pictures in which he has played important roles are *Four Feathers; Out of Singapore; David Harum; Sweet Adeline; Bad Man of Brimstone; The Tulsa Kid.* His son, **Noah Beery, Jr.** (1915-), is also a well-known actor who gained his stage experience in a stock company with his father, and appeared first in the silent film, *The Mark of Zorro,* with Douglas Fairbanks, Sr.; he has played in numerous pictures of Western life.

Beery, Wallace (1889-), American stage and screen actor, brother of Noah BEERY. He appeared first in 1913 in Essanay pictures, and later formed a company to make films in Japan. Among the pictures in which he has appeared during the last ten years may be mentioned *The Champ; Hell Divers; Grand Hotel; Dinner at Eight; Viva Villa; Treasure Island; The Mighty Barnum; Ah, Wilderness; China Seas; Old Hutch; The Good Old Soak; The Bad Man; The Bugle Sounds.*

Beethoven, Ludwig van (1770-1827), German composer who was first trained by his father, and played the organ as a child of twelve in the Ducal Chapel at Bonn. In 1792 he went to Vienna to study, and remained there the rest of his life, becoming a pupil of Josef HAYDN, and Johann Georg ALBRECHTSBERGER, and possibly of Antonio SALIERI in dramatic composition; the latter a highly successful composer of Italian opera, and director of music at the Austrian court. Beethoven brought many manuscripts with him, and, after appearing as pianist at the houses of several noble patrons of music, he was able to get most of them published on excellent terms in comparison to those secured by MOZART and SCHUBERT. Among these patrons were Prince Lichnowsky, Count Waldstein, Prince Lobkowitz, and the Archduke Rudolph, all of whom treated him generously in spite of his notorious arrogance. Domestic troubles in Beethoven's brother's family, especially with his nephew, Karl, for whom he had an unusual amount of affection, caused him a great deal of worry and sorrow. Deafness came upon him in 1800, and in 1819 he was totally deaf, the result being that he never heard the performances of some of his greatest works: his faithful friend through this period was Anton SCHINDLER. Beethoven is generally regarded as the greatest instrumental composer of all time: his works include 9 symphonies; incidental music to *Prometheus, Egmont,* and *The Ruins of Athens;* 5 piano concertos; a violin concerto; a triple concerto for violin, violoncello, and piano with orchestra; the opera, *Fidelio;* 38 piano concertos; 21 sets of piano variations; 10 violin sonatas; 5 violoncello sonatas; 16 string quartets, and many other chamber works for string and wind instruments. A complete edition of his works was published (1864-67) by Breitkopf and Härtel, Leipzig: there are many biographies including those by Emil LUDWIG, Romain ROLLAND, Robert Haven SCHAUFFLER, and Alexander W. THAYER.

Beethoven Association, an organization founded in 1919 by a group of artists headed by Harold BAUER with the purpose of giving a yearly series of concerts in a spirit of artistic fraternity. Its original aim was to present rarely heard chamber works by Ludwig van Beethoven, but the scope of the programs was gradually widened: in the 1933-34 season an extra concert was given by an orchestra of twenty-seven musicians from the New York Philharmonic Symphony Orchestra under the baton of Arturo TOSCANINI. It was also responsible for the publication of Alexander Wheelock Thayer's monumental life of Beethoven, and possessed many mementos of the master, among them his piano. The association was dissolved in 1940.

Beets, Nicolas (1814-1903), Dutch poet, critic and novelist: his early poetry was influenced by, and in the vein of Lord BYRON, but his original talent matured in *Ada of Holland* (1840), and the lyric cycles *Cornflowers* and *The Children of the Sea.* His finest work was a series of tales and sketches of Dutch life, *Camera Obscura,* published with the pen-name "Hildebrand."

Begarelli, Antonio (c.1498-1565), Italian sculptor in terra cotta. He specialized in complete pictures in which the figures were life-size: they were placed in niches and gave the illusion of living persons. His most important works were the *Descent from the Cross* and *The Lamentation,* both in churches at Modena.

Begas, Karl Joseph (1794-1854), German painter who early displayed a remarkable talent for drawing, and studied with Antoine Jean GROS. His copy of the *Madonna della Sedia* attracted the attention of the king of Prussia who became his patron, and commissioned the painting of several large pictures of Biblical scenes and historical events which were hung at churches in Berlin, and at the royal residence in Potsdam. He was also a fine portrait painter of German artists and men of letters. His son, **Oskar Begas** (1828-83), was also a portrait painter and professor of painting in Berlin: another son **Reinhold Begas** (1831-1911), was a sculptor of the naturalistic school, creating a colossal statue, *Borussia* for the Hall of Glory, Berlin, the statue of Bismarck in front of the Reichstag building, and the sarcophagus of the Empress Frederick. The youngest son, **Karl Begas, Jr.** (1845-1916), was also a noted sculptor and pupil of his brother: his works include *Sister and Brother* in the National Gallery and the *Boar Hunt* in the Tiergarten.

Beggar's Opera, a ballad opera: libretto by John GAY, music arranged from folk melodies by Dr. Christopher PEPUSCH; first produced at London in 1728. It was probably first performed in the United States at New York in 1750, and presented again at the Greenwich Village Theatre in 1920. The work was a satire on Italian opera, and also on polite society: the plot concerns itself with a handsome ruffian, Macheath, leader of a band of highwaymen whose secret wife, Polly Peachum really loves him in spite of his frequent amorous adventures. He is captured through the treachery of his wife's father, and condemned to the gallows. When finally reprieved, he decides to remain faithful to Polly.

Beggar Student, The, a comic opera in three acts: libretto by Zell and GENEE; music by Karl MILLOCKER. It was first produced at Vienna in 1881, and at New York in 1885: the story revolves around an amorous nobleman, General Ollendorf, who, when slapped in the face by Laura, daughter of the Countess Palmatica, releases Symon, a poor student from jail, and forces him to pose as a wealthy nobleman, and to court Laura successfully. His plot to disgrace the haughty Laura by disclosing Symon is foiled when the King of Poland is restored to his throne; Symon is ennobled and the lovers are reunited.

Beham, Hans Sebald (1500-1550), German painter and engraver; one of the "Little Masters of Engraving" who excelled in miniatures. His works include a table-top, with scenes from the life of David, at the LOUVRE, Paris, and exquisite miniatures for the missal of the Archbishop Albrecht of Brandenburg, Prussia. He was an industrious and able engraver, making more than a thousand woodcuts, and several hundred copper plates. His brother, **Barthel Beham,** (1502-1540), a pupil of Albrecht DURER, spent a large part of his life in Italy; his paintings include *Apollo and Daphne, Lucretia, Cleopatra, Virgin at the Window,* and a fine portrait of Charles V.

Behn, Aphra (1640-1689), English poet, dramatist and novelist; said to be the first woman playwright who wrote for the English stage. The early part of her life was spent in Dutch Guiana where she gathered the material for her first novel, *Oroonoko,* a romance about a native prince of this name whom she met there. Her life was a turbulent one as a diplomatic spy, amply evidenced by her many novels and plays which are packed with coarse wit and amorous intrigue. DRYDEN and OTWAY admired her plays which include *The Forc'd Marriage; The Amorous Prince; Abdelazar; The Rover; The Younger Brother and The Town Fop.* She was buried in the Poets Corner of WESTMINSTER ABBEY.

Behrens, Peter (1868-), German architect who was a pioneer in the use of steel, concrete and glass for business buildings and apartment houses during the latter part of the 19th and the first part of the 20th century. Among his creations are the German Embassy in Leningrad, the Turbine Factory in Berlin, and the Abbey of St. Peter at Salzburg. LE CORBUSIER, a famous Swiss architect, and Walter GROPIUS were among his pupils.

Behrman, Samuel Nathaniel (1893-), American dramatist who was graduated from Harvard University and Yale University, studying the art of play writing under Professor George Pierce Baker at Harvard. His plays include *The Second Man* (1927); *Serena Blandish; Meteor; Brief Moment; Biography; Amphitryon* (adapted from a play by Jean Giraudoux); *Wine of Choice* and *No Time for Comedy.* Although his plays do not seem, or perhaps aim, to offer a solution for some of the intricate problems of life with which they concern themselves, Behrman is greatly admired for his skill in writing brilliant dialogue.

Beith, John Hay, see Hay, Ian.

Béjart, Madeleine (1618-1672), a French actress, member of a poor family in which there were eleven children, several of whom were connected with the French stage around the time of Molière. She joined MOLIERE at the l'Illustre Théâtre, Paris, in 1643 and remained there until her death: she was an excellent actress in soubrette parts. Her brother, **Joseph Béjart** (1617-1659), was also a member of Molière's company, creating parts in several of the latter's plays: also **Louis Béjart** (c.1630-1678), an actor of great ability who played the role of Dubois in *The Misanthrope* and Alacantor in *The Forc'd Marriage.* **Armande Béjart** (1645-1700), a sister of Madeleine, was trained by Molière and became his wife: their son was sponsored at his baptism by Louis XIV and Queen Henrietta of England. She excelled in Molière's *The Misanthrope, The Imaginary Illness,* and *Tartuffe.* The marriage proved to be an unfortunate one because of her indifference and lack of gratitude: they separated in 1665, but were reconciled in 1672. After Molière's death in 1673, Mme. Molière continued to act successfully until her retirement in 1694.

Bekker, Elizabeth (1738-1804), Dutch novelist who wrote in collaboration with Agatha Deken: it is difficult to determine the parts written by each one in the novels, *The History of Sara Burgerhart* (1782), *The History of William Leevend,* and *Cornelia Wildschut.*

Belasco, David (1859-1931), American actor, producer, and dramatist who first appeared on the stage at San Francisco in 1871, and is said to have played at least two hundred roles in melodramas and plays of every description. He was taught much about playwriting by Dion BOUCICAULT, and acted with Edwin BOOTH, John McCULLOUGH, Lawrence BARRETT and the elder SOTHERN. His first play, *Hearts of Oak,* was produced at Chicago in 1879 with James A. HERNE as his partner. In 1880 he became stage manager of the Madison Square Theatre, New York, and in 1886 an associate of Daniel FROHMAN at the Lyceum: from that time on he was one of the greatest producers and playwrights in the annals of the American stage. Belasco opened the Belasco Theatre, New York, in 1902, and built the Stuyvesant (now the Belasco) in 1907. His plays include *Lord Chumley; Men and Women; The Heart of Maryland; DuBarry; The Darling of the Gods; The Girl of the Golden West; The Return of Peter Grimm; The Auctioneer,* and *Zaza.* Among the actors and actresses whom he directed, or for whom he wrote plays were Mrs. Leslie CARTER, E. H. SOTHERN, David WARFIELD, Frances STARR, Leo DITRICHSTEIN, Ina CLAIRE, Mary PICKFORD and Leonore ULRICH. His reminiscences, *The Theatre Through the Stage Door,* were published in 1919: his collection of press-books, programs, and photographs is now in the New York Public Library.

Belfry, (a) in ancient warfare a movable wooden tower, built in several stages and protected with metal or rawhide, used for attack purposes; (b) a watch tower equipped with an alarm bell or gong; (c) in architecture specifically a detached tower or campanile containing bells, and in a broader sense the loft in the tower of a church.

Bell, Acton, see **Brontë, Anne.**

Bell, Clive (1881-), English writer and critic of art and literature; among his books are *Art* (1914); *Since Cezanne; An Account of French Painting; Enjoying Pictures.*

Bell, Currer, see **Brontë, Charlotte.**

Bell, Digby Valentine (1851-1917), American actor and baritone who studied in Italy, and made his debut at Malta in *La Sonnambula.* After appearing in grand opera for several years, he decided to devote himself to comic opera, appearing with the Lillian Russell Opera Company in *Giroflé-Girofla, The Grand Duchess* and other operettas. He was also a distinguished legitimate actor, starring in HOYT's *A Midnight Bell;* Augustus THOMAS' *Hoosier Doctor* and *The Education of Mr. Pipp;* also in James A. HERNE's *Shore Acres.*

Bell, Ellis, see **Brontë, Emily Jane.**

Bell, John (1811-1895), American sculptor, creator of the Wellington Monument in London, and the American group on the Albert Memorial, also in London: a replica in terra cotta is to be seen in Washington, D. C.

Bell, in music a hollow metallic instrument in the PERCUSSION class, vibrated by a swinging clapper on the inside, or by a hammer on the outside. This is the form of bell used in churches and homes; another entirely different type, known as the GLOCKENSPIEL or ORCHESTRA BELLS, is used by orchestras.

Bellamann, Henry (1882-), American musician, poet and novelist educated at Westminster College and the University of Denver: he also studied music with Charles M. WIDOR and Isidor PHILIPP in Paris. His works include *A Music Teacher's Note Book* (1920); *Cups of Illusion* (Poems); *Petenera's Daughter; The Upward Pass; Crescendo; The Richest Woman in Town; The Gray Man Walks; Kings Row,* successful both as a novel and a motion picture; *Floods of Spring.*

Bellamy, Edward (1850-1898), American author: his first novels, *Dr. Heidenhoff's Process* (1880), and *Mrs. Ludington's Sister* were overshadowed by the enormous success of *Looking Backward* (1888), a socialistic romance setting forth ideas of co-operative life in American communities. The book's sale exceeded a million copies: it was translated into several languages, and many "Bellamy Clubs" were organized. He published a sequel, *Equality,* in 1898 which failed to excite anything approaching the same interest.

Bellamy, Mrs. George Ann (c.1731-1788), Irish actress, illegitimate daughter of Lord Tryawley, who had her educated in a French convent. While in London, she met Mrs. (Peg) WOFFINGTON and David GARRICK. Her personal charm and histrionic ability raised her to fame in a short time; she appeared all over the United Kingdom in the most important tragic roles, playing Juliet to Garrick's Romeo in 1750. In 1785 she wrote an elaborate *Apology* in six volumes; actually a history of her notoriously licentious professional and private life.

Bellamy, Jacobus (1757-1786), Dutch poet: author of *Anacreontic Songs* (1782); *Patriotic Songs;* also a romance in verse, *Roosje,* which is unequalled in Dutch literature for its touching simplicity.

Bellamy, Ralph (1905-), American stage and screen actor: after some stage experience in *Holiday* and *Coquette,* he has appeared in numerous films including *The Magnificent Lie; Rebecca of Sunnybrook Farm; The Awful Truth; Boy Meets Girl; His Girl Friday; Brother Orchid:* also in several "Ellery Queen" films.

Bellange, Hippolyte (1800-1866), French painter of historical and battle scenes, pupil of Antoine GROS and of the ECOLE DES BEAUX ARTS. Many of his pictures have been engraved: they include *Napoleon's Return from Elba; Battle of Wagram; Emperor of Russia; Soldier's Farewell; Soldier's Return; The Guard Dies,* his last work. His pictures are to be found in the LOUVRE and many other French art galleries.

Bellay, Joachim du (1524-1560), French writer and poet: a pupil of RONSARD, and one of the most important members of the PLEIADE. His education was limited, his knowledge being gained by studying classic and French poets. Among his works, *Les Antiquités de Rome,* translated into English verse by Edmund SPENSER (1591), and *Regrets* are impressions in sonnet form of ancient and modern Rome, written in a vein of exquisite melancholy.

Belleau, Rémy (1528-1577), French poet and dramatist; a member of the PLEIADE, and ranked with BELLAY and RONSARD. His style is less affected than that of many of his contemporaries, and his verse graceful and melodious, especially in his translation of *The Odes of Anacreon* (1576), and in *Bergerie,* an unusual combination of verse containing many passages of consummate beauty such as "April." He wrote a comedy, *La Reconnue,* which gained some recognition.

Belle Fatma, La, a dancer who appeared at Paris in 1900, claiming to be a descendant of the ALMEIIS, dancers for the PHARAOHS in 5000 B.C. She gave performances portraying Egyptian wedding scenes, and a *Dance of the Glasses,* the success of which was due to her personal beauty, and her power of suggesting erotic emotion, the result being that she contributed nothing of importance to the art of dancing.

Bellerophon, in Greek mythology a mortal who killed the CHIMAERA, a she-monster vomiting flames from a lion's head, while mounted on the back of the winged horse, PEGASUS. When he tried to ride Pegasus up to heaven, he fell and wandered about blind until he died.

Belles-Lettres, in literature a term used to designate the more imaginative forms of literary composition such as poetry, essays, drama, orations or fiction characterized by emotional qualities. It is said that Jonathan SWIFT first used the term in 1710.

Bellew, Kyrle (1855-1911), English actor who first appeared in 1874 on the stage in Australia: he came to London and played with Sir Henry IRVING at the Lyceum Theatre from 1878 to 1800. In 1888 he toured the world with Mrs. James BROWNE-POTTER (Cora Urquhart), one of the first American society women to choose a stage career. He was one of the handsomest men on the stage, and scored a tremendous success in the role of *Raffles,* that most engaging and well-dressed of all fiction rogues. Bellew appeared in New York and toured the United States in various society plays suited to his abilities from 1900 until his death in Salt Lake City, Utah.

Bellini, Gentile (c.1426-1507), Italian painter of the Venetian school; eldest son and pupil of Jacopo BELLINI for many years. He worked with his brother, Giovanni BELLINI for many years. In 1479, Mohammed II of Turkey, a strange man who was deeply interested in the study of religions, philosophy, and art, asked the Republic of Venice for a painter, and Gentile was sent there: his picture of the monarch, now in the National Gallery, is extremely interesting, and he was given the title of Bey by Mohammed. On his return to Venice, he did a great deal of restoration work on old pictures for the State: among his extant paintings, which are extremely few, may be mentioned *Adoration of the Magi* and *St. Mark Preaching at Alexandria.*

Bellini, Giovanni (c.1430-1516), Italian painter of the Venetian school, and one of the great artists who created the richly colored style of painting in Venice. He was the son and pupil of Jacopo BELLINI with whom he studied, becoming later a pupil of MANTEGNA. His life was spent chiefly in Venice, and his early works included many pictures of the *Madonna* in which Mantegna's influence is apparent. Among his finest pictures are *Agony in the Garden* at the National Gallery, London, and a *Crucifixion* at the Correo Museum, Venice. Bellini's altar pieces, done in oil, are highly regarded, especially the one at the church of St. Zaccaria in Venice. Many great painters, among them Giorgione and Titian, were his pupils.

Bellini, Jacopo (c.1400-1464), Italian painter of the Venetian school, pupil of Gentile da FABRIANO with whom he went to Rome where he was known as Jacopo di Venetia. He was also influenced by PISANELLO, and by painters of the Florentine school. He was an excellent draftsman, but without profound knowledge of anatomy although his heads are well proportioned: one of his sketch books is in the BRITISH MUSEUM, London. Among his most important works are an enormous *Crucifixion* in the cathedral at Verona, destroyed by fire in 1759; an *Annunciation* in Brescia, and three different portrayals of the *Madonna* now in the Uffizi Gallery, Florence, the Academy of Fine Arts, Florence, and the Louvre, Paris.

Bellini, Vincenzo (1801-1835), Italian opera composer whose teacher was the famous dramatic composer, Nicola Antonio ZINGARELLI, but he is said to have learned most from self-study of scores by HAYDN, MOZART, JOMMELLI, PAISELLO and PERGOLESI. His first opera, *Adelson e Salvini* (1825) was presented by students of the Naples Conservatory. Encouraged by its success, the following operas were produced: *Il Pirata; La Straniera; I Puritani; I Capuletti e Montecchi; Norma;* the latter was his greatest success, although a failure at its first performance even with Giuditta PASTA in the title role. Bellini composed tender and fervent melodies, but his monotonous harmonies and poor orchestrations, due to his lack of technical training, constituted themselves serious deterrents to his rivaling Gioachino ROSSINI.

Bellman, Karl Michael (1740-1795), Swedish poet who was also a gifted improviser and composer of music for his lyrics. As a chronicler in verse of the rollicking life of his native city, Stockholm, he has never been surpassed: Gustavus III was his patron. His works, *Fredmans* *epistlar* (1790) and *Fredmans sanger,* include ballads, drinking songs, pastorals and bacchanales: a superb bronze bust by John Niklas BYSTROM was placed in the Zoological Garden at Stockholm in 1829, and a festival in his honor there became a yearly event.

Belloc, Hilaire (1870-), English man of letters born in France of an English mother and French father. He was educated at Baliol College, Oxford, and soon became known as a versatile writer and speaker. Naturalized in 1902, he sat in the House of Commons from 1906 to 1910; among his works, which include poetry, juvenile books, essays, biography and fiction, may be mentioned *The Bad Child's Book of Beasts* (1896); *Danton; Robespierre; Marie Antoinette; Wolsey; The Path to Rome; Joan of Arc.* His sister, **Marie Adelaide Belloc-Lowndes** (1868-), is a writer of short stories and novels: two of the latter, *The Chink in the Armour* (1912) and *The Lodger* (1913) were dramatized by H. A. Vachell, and successfully produced. She also wrote a juvenile history of World War I entitled *Told in Gallant Deeds.*

Bellona, in Roman mythology the goddess of war corresponding to the Greek deity, *Enyo.* Her temple at Rome was erected in the Campus Martius near the Flaminian Circus, and her worship was encouraged by the family of the Claudii.

Bellows, Albert Fitch (1829-1883), American painter who first studied architecture, and later painting at Antwerp and Paris. He did much of his work in England: his earlier pictures were in oil, but he used water colors almost exclusively in landscapes such as *Afternoon in Surrey; Sunday in Devonshire; New England Village School; The Parsonage* and *A Village Scene.*

Bellows, George Wesley (1882-1925), American painter and engraver; graduate of Ohio State University and pupil of Robert HENRI, Kenneth Hays Miller and H. G. Marratta. He began showing his pictures at American exhibitions in 1904, and was elected an associate member of the National Academy of Design at twenty-seven. His pictures reveal a great variety of subjects including family scenes, sporting events, circus spectacles and crowds at the seashore: his portraits reveal a real insight into the characteristics of his subjects. Among his best pictures are *Edith Cavell; Up the River; Men of the Docks; Stag at Sharkey's; North River:* many of them are in American art galleries. His works were frequently exhibited with success in European salons, and he won many prizes.

Bellows, a contrivance for accumulating and propelling the wind supplying the pipes or reeds of the ORGAN, HARMONIUM, ACCORDION, CONCERTINA, BAGPIPE and other instruments of similar character. When larger organs came into being in the 15th century, and no automatic mechanical contrivances such as are used today for supplying air had been invented, it was found that the bellows worked by hand were not sufficiently powerful. A series of ten or more bellows were constructed with a single wooden shoe on each one; the men who worked them held on to a transverse bar, and placed their feet in the shoes of two bellows at a time, raising one as he lowered the other.

Belot, Adolphe (1829-1890), French novelist and dramatist who achieved success with a comedy, *The Testament of Cesar Girodot,* in 1859; his other plays were not so well received, and he turned to writing novels including *The Venus of Gordes* (with Ernest DAUDET); *The Drama of the Rue de la Paix,* and *Article 47.* All three were dramatic successes on the French and English stages.

Belvedere, in architecture (*a*) a structure built in the upper part of a building so as to command a view of the surroundings; there are several forms such as the turret, cupola, loggia or open gallery; (*b*) the term is also applied to any small building open to the air, of which a summerhouse is the best example.

Belvedere Gallery, a gallery and court of the VATICAN, Rome, erected in 1490 for Pope Innocent VIII from designs originating with Antonio POLLAIUOLO. Some of the most perfectly preserved and rarest specimens of Greek and Roman art are on exhibition in this gallery; among them the LAOCOON, the APOLLO BELVEDERE and the TORSO OF HERCULES.

Belvedere Museum (Vienna), an art collection housed in the Belvedere Palace; built in 1714 by Johann Lukas von Hildebrandt for Prince Eugene of Savoy, and considered one of the better examples of BAROQUE. When the prince died in 1736, the palace was dismantled, and the building acquired in 1752 by the Austrian Government. The historical and art collection of the Austrian Gallery was placed there: the art section comprises the *Baroque Museum,* comprising a small but select assembly of Austrian paintings and sculpture of the 18th century; the *Nineteenth Century Gallery,* containing nearly 500 paintings and sculptures by Austrian masters; the *Modern Gallery* of paintings and sculptures dated from 1890.

Belviso, Thomas H. (1898-), American violinist, conductor and composer who studied at Yale University and the Institute of Musical Art with Horatio PARKER, Franz KNEISEL, Louis SVECENSKI and Percy GOETSCHIUS. Among his varied activities may be mentioned the formation of "The Thomas H. Belviso Orchestras," one of the largest organizations of its kind in the United States, for which he made special orchestrations; the musical direction of the Paramount-Publix chain of motion picture theatres; the composing and scoring of music for films; the general supervision of the musical content of all programs for the National Broadcasting Company since 1930. In this capacity he has composed and directed the music for Shakespearean and Radio Guild productions; also an outstanding series of "mood music" for use in electric transcription by radio stations as incidental music in dramatic broadcasts.

Belyi, Andrei (1880-1934), pen name of **Nicolaievitch Bugayev,** Russian author of literature of the Symbolist School. His works, in a style which may be described as "rhythmic prose," include *Northern Symphony, Dramatic Symphony, The*

Return, and *The Cup of Snowstorms.* He has written some novels: among them *The Crime of Nicholas Letaev* and *The Silver Dove.*

Bemelmans, Ludwig (1898-), Hungarian painter and author: his works include *Hansi* (1934); *Golden Basket; Quito Express; Life Class; Madeline.*

Ben-Ami, Jacob (1890-), Jewish actor who first appeared at the Jewish Art Theatre, New York, in 1918, making a deep impression on his audience. After mastering English, he made his debut in 1920 at the Greenwich Village Theatre, New York, in *Samson and Delilah:* since that time he has appeared in many plays including *The Idle Inn; The Failures; Man and the Masses; John; The Sea Gull; Siegfried; Camille; The Cherry Orchard; Payment Deferred.*

Benavente y Martinez, Jacinto (1866-), Spanish critic, poet and dramatist: his first poems appeared in 1886; a critical work, *Letters of Women* in 1893, and his first play, *El Nido Ajeno,* in 1894. His successful plays include *Saturday Night; Vested Interests; La Malquerida* (The Passion Flower); *Mistress of the House; Fabricated Truth* and *Bread Eaten From the Hand.* His comedies were at first criticized as being merely brilliant, satirical dialogue without dramatic action, but he was finally recognized as the superior of José ECHEGARAY, who had practically monopolized the Spanish theatre. Benevente was awarded the Nobel Prize in 1922.

Ben Bolt, a ballad popular in the United States since 1850: the words were written by Thomas Dunn ENGLISH, an American physician; the music was adapted from a German folk song by Nelson Kneass, who sang it in a play called *The Battle of Buena Vista.* Its waning popularity was revived when used as the "theme song" in the play, *Trilby,* by Gerald DU MAURIER.

Benchley, Robert Charles (1889-), American dramatic critic, humorist, and actor educated at Harvard University. He became editor of the *New York Tribune Sunday Magazine* in 1916, and has been dramatic editor of *Life* magazine (1920-29) and the *New Yorker* magazine. He is the author of several humorous books, and has appeared in several screen comedies and amusing movie "shorts."

Bendemann, Eduard Julius Friedrich (1811-1889), German historical and portrait painter, pupil of Johann Gottfried SCHADOW. His painting, *Jews in Exile* (1832), established his reputation, and was awarded the great gold medal at Paris in 1836. While professor of painting at the Dresden Academy, he created some large frescoes at the Royal Palace. His works include *Boaz and Ruth; Servian Princesses; Shepherd and Shepherdess:* also fine portraits of Prince Anton von Hohenzollern and Joseph JOACHIM, the celebrated Hungarian violinist.

Bendix, Max (1866-), American violinist, composer and conductor, educated in Cincinnati, New York and Berlin. He was concertmaster of the Metropolitan Opera Company, the Theodore Thomas Orchestra, the Manhattan Opera Company, and conducted the Savage English Opera Company, the Gallo English Opera Company and the St. Louis Municipal Opera, also directing the music at the Chicago World's Fair in 1933. His compositions include incidental music for *Experience* and *Romeo and Juliet;* ballet music; orchestra pieces; violin solos and many songs.

Benédette, Le, see **Castiglione, Giovanni.**

Benelli, Sem (c.1875-), Italian poet and dramatist: his finest work, *The Jest* (La Cena della Beffe), was produced with great success at New York in 1919 with Lionel and John BARRYMORE in the principal roles. It was also set to music by Umberto GIORDANO; first produced at LA SCALA, Milan, in 1924, and the Metropolitan Opera House, New York, in 1926. Another play, *The Love of Three Kings,* was scored as an opera by Italo MONTEMEZZI; produced at La Scala, Milan, in 1913, and at the Metropolitan Opera House in 1914.

Benét, Stephen Vincent (1898-1943), American poet and novelist; brother of William Rose BENÉT. Two volumes of his poems, *Five Men and Pompey* and *Young Adventure* appeared in 1915 and 1918 before he was graduated from Yale University. His works include *John Brown's Body,* an epic poem of the Civil War; two novels, *The Beginnings of Wisdom* and *Spanish Bayonet;* several volumes of poems, one of which was awarded the Pulitzer Prize in 1928. His poem, *Western Star,* an epic of the American spirit of progress, was published posthumously in 1943.

Benét, William Rose (1886-), American editor, novelist, and poet, a graduate of Yale University who has been associated over the years with many prominent periodicals and newspapers including *The Saturday Evening Post, The Century Magazine, The Saturday Review of Literature,* and the *New York Evening Post.* His works include two novels, *The First Person Singular* (1922) and *Rip Tide,* a novel in verse; *Merchants from Cathay; The Great White Wall; Moons of Grandeur; Man Possessed.* He is a brother of Stephen Vincent BENÉT.

Bennett, Arnold (1867-1931), English editor, novelist, and dramatist educated at London University. After studying law, he began to write, editing a magazine, *Woman,* and securing acceptance of short stories by *Tit-Bits* and *The Yellow Book.* In 1900 he devoted himself entirely to writing: equipped with an intensive knowledge of the pottery manufacturing region where he was born, he published *The Old Wives' Tale* (1908), followed by *Clayhanger; Hilda Lessways; These Twain; Riceyman Steps; Lord Raingo.* He had two dramatic successes; *Milestones* with Edward KNOBLOCK and *The Great Adventure,* based on his novel "Buried Alive." His *Journal,* a chronicle of ceaseless activities, was published posthumously.

Bennett, Constance (1905-), American screen actress; daughter of Richard BENNETT and educated in New York and Paris. Her first appearance was in *Cytharea,* followed by *The Goose Woman; Sally, Irene and Mary; This Thing*

Called Love; Three Faces East; Common Clay; Lady With a Past; Affairs of Cellini; Topper; Topper Takes a Trip; Tailspin; Escape to Glory; Two-Faced Woman.

Bennett, Joan (1910-), American stage and screen actress; daughter of Richard BENNETT and educated in Waterbury, Conn., and Paris. Her first stage appearance was with her father in *Jarnegan,* and her film debut in *Bulldog Drummond* with Ronald COLMAN. Other films include *Three Live Ghosts; Disraeli; Moby Dick; Little Women; Trade Winds; The Man in the Iron Mask; The Housekeeper's Daughter; I Married a Nazi; Twin Beds; The Wife Takes a Flyer.*

Bennett, John (1865-), American illustrator and author: his works include *Master Skylark* (1897); *Barnaby Lee; Treasure of Peyre Gaillard; Madame Margot; The Pigtail of Ah Lee Ben Loo.*

Bennett, Richard (1872-), American actor who studied engineering before making his stage debut at Chicago in *The Limited Mail:* his first appearance in New York was at the New Amsterdam Theatre in *The Round of Pleasure.* Later he became a member of Charles Frohman's company: among the plays in which he appeared were *The White Heather; The Royal Family; Jim Bludso; The Lion and the Mouse; Strongheart; Divorçons; The Hypocrites.* His film career began in 1913, resulting in more than fifty screen appearances. The film stars, Constance BENNETT and Joan BENNETT are his daughters.

Bennett, Robert Russell (1894-), American composer who studied with Carl BUSCH in Kansas City, and won a Guggenheim Fellowship for study in Paris under Nadia BOULANGER. He has orchestrated many musical comedies for production in New York, and since 1930 has acted as composer, orchestrator, and conductor of music for films in Hollywood. His *Abraham Lincoln Symphony* has had numerous performances, and an opera *Maria Malibran* was presented by the Juilliard Opera Company. His compositions include orchestral works, choral works, chamber music, operas, a ballet, and music for films.

Bennett, Sir William Sterndale (1816-1875), English pianist and composer who studied at the Royal Academy of Music, London, and at Leipzig. His first piano concerto was written at sixteen, and his *Naiades Overture* played by the Gewandhaus Orchestra when he was twenty-one. He directed chamber music concerts from 1843, established the Bach Society in 1848, and conducted the Philharmonic Society from 1856 to 1866, at the same time becoming professor of music at Cambridge University. Bennett was also a fine concert pianist: his works include a symphony, several overtures, four piano concertos, an oratorio, and many fine piano pieces.

Benny, Jack, contemporary American screen and radio comedian; he has appeared in many musical reviews on the screen; also in film adaptations of stage successes such as *Charley's Aunt* and *George Washington Slept Here.* He was co-starred in a comedy *Love Thy Neighbor* with the radio comedian, Fred ALLEN.

Benois, Alexander Nicolaievitch (1870-), Russian litterateur; a man of encyclopedic knowledge in every branch of art and literature, and the descendant of a long line of architects and painters. He edited a magazine, *The World of Art,* with Serge DIAGHILEFF, the ballet impresario, and created the scenery for several ballets; among them *Le Pavillon d'Armide* by Alexander Tcherepnin, and *Petrouchka* by Igor Stravinsky.

Benoit de Sainte-Maure, 12th century French trouvère born in Touraine: he wrote no less than 42,000 lines in a *Chronicle of the Dukes of Normandy* (1135), and 30,000 lines in a *Romance of Troy,* founded on ancient records and later translated into several languages. BOCCACCIO, CHAUCER and SHAKESPEARE appear to be in his debt for the tale of *Troilus and Cressida.*

Benson, Sir Francis Robert (1858-1939), English actor educated at Oxford where he managed an amateur performance of *Agamemnon* by AESCHYLUS. He appeared in 1882 under Sir Henry IRVING as Paris in *Romeo and Juliet,* and later organized his own company in which he toured the provinces, and played leading roles opposite Gertrude Constance Cockburn, his wife. He gained his reputation while on tour, but brought his company to London several times with great success. From 1888 he managed the Shakespearean Festival at STRATFORD-ON-AVON. As an actor his romantic and intellectual powers were exceptional: he excelled as Hamlet, Lear, Petrucchio, Coriolanus and Richard II.

Benson, Frank Weston (1862-), American painter and etcher who studied at the Art School of the Boston Museum of Fine Arts, and at the Académie Julien with Gustave BOULANGER and Jules LEFEBVRE. He exerted considerable influence on American painting in the post of instructor at the Boston Museum of Fine Arts, and was particularly successful in securing charming effects of sunshine in his pictures. His etchings of wild geese and ducks have been greatly praised for their natural character; also his murals, *Graces* and the *Seasons* at the Library of Congress, Washington, D. C.

Benson, Stella (1892-1933), English short story writer and novelist: some of her books such as *Goodbye Stranger* (1926), *The Far-Away Bride,* and the story of an automobile tour of the United States entitled *The Little World* had a large sale in America and Canada.

Bentley, John F. (1839-1902), English architect who designed many fine ecclesiastical monuments and churches: his masterpiece is the Roman Catholic *Cathedral of Westminster,* London. This is an immense edifice, based upon the Cathedral at Angoulême, France, designed by Perigord, and a combination of Byzantine and Romanesque architecture.

Benton, Thomas Hart (1889-), American painter, student at the Art Institute, Chicago, and in Paris, where he remained for five years. When he returned to the United States, he painted scenery for screen productions, and did much work in camouflage for the United States Navy during

World War I. Travel throughout America, during which he made numerous sketches, resulted in regional decorations for the New School for Social Research, New York; the *Arts of Life in America* for the Whitney Museum of American Art, New York; the *History of Indiana* in the Indiana Building at the Chicago Exposition in 1933: this was later removed to the War Memorial at Indianapolis. Benton has executed many single paintings and has taught at the ART STUDENTS' LEAGUE, New York.

Bentonelli, Joseph (1902-), American tenor; real name Joseph Benton: a pupil of Jean de RESZKE at Paris where he made his debut with the De Reszke Ensemble in 1925. After appearing in various European opera houses he became a member of the Chicago Opera Company in 1934, and made his debut at the Metropolitan Opera House as des Grieux in *Manon* in 1936. His repertory includes all important tenor roles in Italian, and he has created the leading parts in several modern Italian operas.

Beowulf, the hero in a celebrated Anglo-Saxon epic poem in two parts: the first describes Beowulf's destruction of the man-eating sea monster, Grendel and his ferocious mother; the second his slaying of a fiery dragon, and his death from its poisonous bite. The poem is written in alliterative verse, and the scenes are laid in Scandinavia: it is regarded by some authorities as the oldest work of its kind.

Béranger, Pierre Jean de (1780-1857), French poet and writer of song lyrics. After quarreling with his father, he lived in the garret made famous by his own verses: he was assisted by Lucien Bonaparte who secured him a clerical position in the Imperial University, and later some of the most distinguished men of the day were his intimates. His first two song collections were published in 1815, and he became the idol of the working classes. The second series of two volumes, *Chansons Nouvelles,* led to his imprisonment because of their Republican views. Béranger's songs are full of wit and light-hearted musical grace: his autobiography was issued in 1840.

Berceuse, in music the name of a cradle-song or lullaby; also of any instrumental piece of the same character. The outstanding example in piano music is the *Berceuse* by Frédéric CHOPIN.

Berchem (or **Berghem**) **Nicolaes Pietersz** (1620-1683), Dutch painter who studied with his father, Pieter Claasz van Haarlem, and other fine artists in Holland: it has never been ascertained why he changed his name. His numerous paintings, especially his landscapes such as *Rest,* exquisitely executed in respect to atmospheric effects, are in great demand, as are also his etchings and drawings: examples are in the Metropolitan Museum of Art, New York, the Amsterdam Museum, and the Hermitage, St. Petersburg.

Bercher, Jean, see **Dauberval.**

Bercovici, Konrad (1882-), Rumanian-American musician and novelist who spent much of his youth among the gypsies of his native land. He was educated in private schools, and studied music in Paris: his first position when he came to the United States in 1916 was that of organist at Grace Episcopal Church in New York. His works include *Crimes of Charity* (1917); *Dust of New York; Ghitza and Other Romances of Gypsy Blood; The Marriage Guest; Volga Boatman; The Story of the Gypsies; The Crusades; The Incredible Balkans; It's the Gypsy in Me.*

Berekhiah Naqdan, Jewish fabulist the date of whose birth is a subject of dispute; some authorities place him in the 12th and others in the 13th century. His principal known work is a collection in rimed verse, *Fox Fables:* he was also a grammarian famous for his punctuation of Biblical texts.

Berenson, Bernhard (1865-), American critic and author of important works on the historical aspects and aesthetics of art; a graduate of Harvard University who has spent many years among the art treasures and in art centers of Europe. His works include *Venetian Painters of the Renaissance; Florentine Painters of the Renaissance; Medieval Art; Sienese Paintings; North Italian Painters of the Renaissance.* He has contributed many reviews of paintings and articles on art subjects to American and European periodicals.

Berezowsky, Nicolai T. (1900-), Russian violinist, conductor and composer who came to the United States in 1922; joined the New York Philharmonic Orchestra, and continued his studies with Paul KOCHANSKI and Rubin GOLDMARK at the Juilliard Graduate School. He has received several awards for his orchestral works, many of which have been played by major American orchestras. Berezowsky's works include 3 symphonies; *Hebrew Suite;* a violin concerto; chamber music for various ensembles. He has acted as guest conductor of several important orchestras, and is a member of the Coolidge String Quartet.

Berg, Alban (1885-1935), Austrian composer who was a pupil and intimate friend of Arnold SCHONBERG. While he accepted the theories of his teacher and adopted the twelve-tone scale, Alban's individualty is apparent in all his works which include the operas, *Wozzeck* and *Lulu;* a lyric suite for string quartet which is an excellent example of twelve-tone music; a violin concerto; a piano forte sonata; four pieces for clarinet and piano. Berg wrote thematic analyses and explanatory guides to Schönberg's works, and gave a radio lecture on the meaning and purpose of ATONALITY.

Bergamask, in music and ballet an Italian dance originating in Bergamo, Italy: it has assumed somewhat of a clownish character, especially in imitative dances such as the *Bergomask* in MENDELSSOHN'S incidental music to Shakespeare's "Midsummer Night's Dream."

Bergamasco, Il, see **Castello, Giovanni Battista.**

Berge, Edward (1876-1924), American sculptor whose creations are to be found in many foreign countries: his genius expressed itself in fountain designs utilizing fanciful figures and other decorative features. Among his finest works are the *Piéta* in St. Patrick's Church, Washington, D. C., the *Soldiers' and Sailors' Memorial* at Prince George, Maryland, and the *Gist Memorial* at Charleston, South Carolina.

Bergen, Edgar (1903-), American actor and ventriloquist educated at Northwestern University, Chicago. After playing in a vaudeville sketch, *The Operation*, in American and European theatres, he appeared in a series of film "shorts," in 1935 becoming a featured attraction (with his dummy, "Charlie McCarthy") on Rudy Vallee's radio broadcasts, and since 1938 on a commercial radio broadcast. Bergen has been featured with his dummy in a number of comedy films.

Bergerac, Savinien Cyrano de (1619-1655), French soldier, novelist, and dramatist who fought an incredible number of duels brought about by comments on the unusual size of his nose. His works include a tragedy, *Agrippina*, a source of inspiration to Pierre Corneille; a comedy, *The Pedant Laughing-stock*, which intrigued Molière; a *Comic History of the Sun* are said to have furnished ideas for "Gulliver's Travels" by Jonathan SWIFT. He is the hero of the play, *Cyrano de Bergerac* by Edmond ROSTAND; of an opera by Walter DAMROSCH, and an operetta by Victor HERBERT.

Bergerat, Auguste Emile (1845-1923), French journalist, novelist and dramatist: he was a son-in-law of the painter, Theophile GAUTIER, and wrote witty articles under the pen name "Caliban" for the Paris *Figaro*, later published collectively as *The Life and Adventures of Sieur Caliban* (1886), with two sequels. His novels include *Faublas in Spite of Himself* and *The Rape:* his plays, *The Bergomask Night, Captain Fracasse,* and *The Fountain of Joy* were successful because of their wit and imagination.

Bergman, Ingrid (1917-), Swedish stage and screen actress trained at the "Lyceum for Flicker," a department of the Royal Dramatic School at Stockholm. She has appeared in several American films including *Intermezzo, a Love Story; Adam Had Four Sons; Rage in Heaven; Dr. Jekyll and Mr. Hyde; Casablanca.*

Bergner, Elizabeth (1900-), Austrian actress who studied for the stage in Vienna from 1915 to 1919, and made her debut at Zurich, Switzerland, in 1919. Her international success was made in *St. Joan* in 1924: she also appeared in Shakespeare's plays, and in modern dramas including *The Last of Mrs. Cheyney, The Constant Nymph, Strange Interlude, The Circle of Chalk, Amphitryon 38.* Her first appearance at London was in 1933 as Gemma in *Escape Me Never:* this was followed by Barrie's last play, *The Boy David,* written especially for her. She has appeared in many foreign films, and in English pictures including *Catherine the Great, Escape Me Never, As You Like It, Dreaming Lips* and *Stolen Life.*

Bergonzi, Carlo (1683-1747), Italian violin maker, a contemporary of STRADIVARIUS and GUANERIUS: he is supposed to have continued the business of Antonio Stradivarius after the death of the latter's

sons. His violins, distinguished by their reddish-brown and orange-red varnishes, have increased substantially in value during recent years: they are now priced at from $6,000 to $12,000. The violins made by his son, Michel Angelo, and his grandson, Nicola, are not so much in demand.

Bergsöe, Jorgen Vilhelm (1835-1911), Danish naturalist, poet, and novelist who wrote the first of his cycle of novels, *From the Piazza del Popolo* (1866), a sensational success, while suffering partial blindness through the excessive use of the microscope in his important biological research at Messina. His works include a volume of poems, *Now and Then;* a novel, *Who Was He?;* a natural history, *From Meadow and Woodland* and a historical study, *Rome under Pius IX.*

Bergstrom, Hjalmar (1868-1914), Danish dramatist who attempted to write plays at thirteen: he taught in a Copenhagen high school while experimenting in writing short stories and novels, but was recognized immediately as genuinely talented when his first play, *Ida's Wedding,* was produced in 1902. His plays include *Mint Street; Lynggard & Co.; Karen Borneman; The Birthday Party,* and many others. At the time of his death, Bergstrom was regarded as giving promise of conceiving even greater dramatic creations.

Bériot, Charles-Auguste de (1802-1870), French violinist and composer; pupil of Jean Baptiste VIOTTI and Pierre BAILLOT. He made his debut at Paris in 1821; became violinist to the King of France, and made many concert tours of Europe and Great Britain with his wife, Mme. Garcia-MALIBRAN, a famous singer. He was professor of the violin at the Brussels Conservatory for seven years: his compositions comprise 7 violin concertos, 11 sets of variations, and a fine method for the violin.

Berlage, Hendrik Petrus (1856-), Dutch architect trained at Amsterdam where he designed the Bourse. He was one of the first to break away from the GOTHIC and RENAISSANCE styles which he had followed in his studies, and through him a new form was developed in Holland combining simplicity and dignity through the use of brick: the Christian Science Church in The Hague (1914) is a good example. For some years Berlage acted as architectural adviser to the municipalities of The Hague, Amsterdam, and Rotterdam.

Berlin, Irving (1888-), American composer and publisher: his first song, *Marie from Sunny Italy* was published in 1907. It was followed by *Alexander's Ragtime Band,* and many other pseudo-Southern negro songs in addition to the ballads, *You Forgot to Remember, Say It With Flowers.* The long list of revues and musical plays for which he has written the music includes *Watch Your Step* (1914); *The Century Girl* (with Victor Herbert); several Ziegfeld Follies: among his screen play successes are *Top Hat; Follow the Fleet; Alexander's Ragtime Band* and *Holiday Inn.*

Berliner, Emile (1851-1929), American inventor, German born, who came to the United States in

1870. He deserves honorable mention in this volume for the invention of the modern radio microphone which is a development of the telephone transmitter invented by him in 1877; also for the invention of the first practical disc phonograph record, and the machinery required for economical, commercial manufacture. These two inventions brought the phonograph and the radio into the homes of millions of Americans, thereby enhancing the enjoyment of the leisure hour—a substantial contribution to artistic culture.

Berlioz, Hector (1803-1869), French composer who forsook the medical profession for music, studying at the Paris Conservatory with Anton Reicha. He chafed under classical rules, and joined the romanticist movement whole-heartedly, evidenced by the *Fantastic Symphony* which appeared in 1828. Despite the opposition of Luigi CHERUBINI he won the Grand Prix de Rome with a cantata, *Sardanapale*, and his works began to receive respectful hearings: they included the operas *Benvenuto Cellini, Béatrice et Bénédict,* and a trilogy, *Les Troyens, La Prise de Troie,* and *Les Troyens à Carthage,* none of which were accorded favor. Another work, an "operatic cantata," *La Damnation de Faust,* in which Berlioz indulged his passion for unusual orchestral combinations and tonal effects, was received with both praise and condemnation; the same may be said of the sacred trilogy, *L'Enfance du Christ;* the *Carnaval Romain* Overture; the symphonies, *Harold in Italy* and *Romeo and Juliet;* the *Requiem,* the *Grande Symphonie funèbre* for full military band with strings and chorus. Berlioz' greatest service to the musical art was not his operas or symphonies because of the lack of inspiration in his themes, and the absence of coherent construction due to his limited technical knowledge: it was in his perfecting the science of orchestration, the principles of which are to be found in his *Treatise on Instrumentation* which has been translated into English. A complete edition of his works, with the exception of the operas, *Benvenuto Cellini* and *Les Troyens,* has been published by Breitkopf and Härtel. His memoirs record his travels, and afford an interesting study of his personality.

Bernard, Sam (1863-1927), American dialect comedian born in England who came to the United States in 1867 with his parents. After many years of touring in vaudeville and with burlesque companies, he became the German dialect comedian with the WEBER AND FIELDS Broadway Music Hall Company in New York; he also appeared as the principal comedian in *The Girl From Kay's* and *The Rich Mr. Hoggenheimer.*

Bernardes, Diego (c.1540-1596), Portuguese poet, called the "Sweet singer of the Lima," a river flowing through his native village, Ponte de Lima. He was attached to the Portuguese troubadour, Sa de Miranda: in his company he penned exquisite elegies, sonnets, odes, and songs full of tender thoughts gracefully expressed.

Bernhard, Karl (1798-1865), pen-name of **Nicolai de Saint Aubain,** Danish novelist who was sponsored by his celebrated kinswoman, Countess GYLLEMBOURG-EHRENSVARD, herself a distinguished novelist. Bernhard was also a nephew of the poet,

Peter Andreas Heiberg, but completely overshadowed the latter's fame with his many excellent novels including *The Favorite of Fortune, For and Against,* and *The Two Friends,* all founded on historical events or personal experiences of the author.

Bernhardt, Sarah (1844-1923), French actress; real name Rosine Bernard. Her parents were French and Dutch of Jewish descent, but she was baptized at twelve, and educated in a convent. She studied dramatic art at the Paris Conservatory, made her debut at the Comédie Française in 1862, but achieved no real success until 1867 when, she appeared in Shakespeare's *King Lear* at the Odéon. After the Franco-Prussian War, she returned to the Comédie Française and by 1879 had become the greatest actress of her day in many dramas including *Phèdre; Adrienne Lecouvreur, Camille, Frou-Frou, Hernani, Fedora, La Tosca, Hamlet, L'Aiglon, Theodora, Cleopatra,* and *Jeanne d'Arc.* She appeared in all the capitals of Europe, England, Australia, Egypt, Denmark, Russia and the Americas, making her debut at New York in 1880, and returning in 1886, 1889, 1896 and 1910. In 1912 she played the title role in the film, *Queen Elizabeth.* A festival in her honor at Paris in 1896 emphasized her position at the head of her profession: she had appeared in one hundred twelve roles of which she created forty. In 1915 her leg was amputated, but she continued to give performances for the French soldiers at the front in World War I.

Berni (or Bernia), Francesco (1497-1536), Italian poet who joined a circle of brilliant litterateurs in Rome, and became its most distinguished associate through his witty, sparkling verses, known as *Poesie bernesca* and widely imitated. His greatest work was the editing of BOIARDO's *Orlando Innamorato,* a sequel to ARIOSTO's *Orlando Furioso:* he revised almost every line into graceful, polished words, and added a few stanzas of his own, in the style of Ariosto, to each canto.

Bernini, Giovanni Lorenzo (1598-1680), Italian architect, sculptor, and painter trained in Rome where he created most of his finest works. At the age of fifteen he made four statues for the Casino of Cardinal Scipio Borghese: his later works include the great COLONNADE for the piazza in front of St. Peter's; the *St. Theresa* at the Church of Santa Maria Della Vittoria, the bronze BALDACHIN (canopy), about 95 feet high, over the high altar at St. Peter's; the royal staircase in the VATICAN; and the magnificent fountains in the Piazza Navone. He painted more than two hundred pictures and left a fortune amounting to five hundred thousand dollars.

Bernstein, Aline (1882-), American designer of stage costumes and settings educated in the public schools of New York City. Her career started in 1924 with designs for *The Little Clay Cart;* she has designed settings or costumes for many plays including *The Dybbuk; Caprice; Reunion in Vienna; Animal Kingdom; The Cherry Orchard; The Sea Gull; Peter Pan; Alison's House; Liliom; Grand Hotel; The Little Foxes.* She aided in the installing of the MUSEUM OF COS-

TUME ART in Rockefeller Center, and has published *Three Blue Suits* and *The Journey Down.*

Bernstein, Henry Léon Gustave Charles (1876-), French dramatist; born in Paris of Jewish parents. He belongs to the naturalistic school of French playwrights: his first play, *Le Marche*, was produced in 1900, and followed by many successes including *La Detour; La Rafale; Le Secret; Israel; Samson and Le Voleur.* All the above were produced in English in the United States.

Berruguete, Alonzo (c.1480-1561), Spanish sculptor, painter, and architect; son and pupil of Pedro Berruguete, painter to Philip I of Spain, and ranked with PERUGINO. After the death of his father, he went to Rome where he studied and worked with MICHELANGELO in the VATICAN; also with Donato Bramante for whom he made copies of the LAOCOON, discovered in 1506. He was the leading exponent of the Renaissance in Spain as court scupltor to Charles V; his finest works include the wood carvings and alabaster sculptures for the choir stalls and bishop's throne in the Cathedral of Toledo; also the tomb of Cardinal D. Juan de Tavera in the same cathedral.

Bertini, Henri (1798-1876), French pianist and composer who made a tour through the Netherlands and Germany, as a prodigy at twelve. After further study, he resided in Paris for nearly forty years, making many concert tours. He was a pianist of fine attainments and lofty ideals: his compositions include almost 200 piano pieces, and many valuable technical studies.

Bertoletti, see **Gasparo da Salo.**

Beryl, a mineral much prized as a gem by ancient Greek and Roman jewelers; its crystallized, hexagonal form made it ideal for ear pendants. It was also a prized gem during the Renaissance, but has lost its popularity today. Other varieties of the mineral include the EMERALD and the AQUAMARINE, both of which are in high favor.

Besant, Sir Walter (1836-1901), English novelist educated at Christ's College, Cambridge. His first novels, *Ready-Money Mortiboy* (1872), *The Golden Butterfly,* and several others were written in collaboration with James Rice (1845-1892). Besant's first novel written alone, *All Sorts and Conditions of Men* (1882), was a powerful story of life in London's East End; this book and another, *The Children of Gibeon,* had much influence in alleviating social evils and the sweat-shop system in the British metropolis. Among other popular novels were *Dorothy Forster; Armorel of Lyonesse* and *Beyond the Dreams of Avarice;* also critical essays, biographical works, three books on London, and an unfinished volume, *A Survey of London.*

Besier, Rudolf (1878-1942), English dramatist, born in Java of Dutch parentage, and educated in England and at Heidelberg. After some years as a journalist, his first play, *The Virgin Goddess* was produced in 1906, followed by *Oliver Latimer's Husband, Lady Patricia, Kipps* (with H. G. Wells), *Kultur at Home, Secrets* (with May Edginton) and *The Barretts of Wimpole Street:* the latter proved a tremendously successful drama in 1931 for Katharine CORNELL in the role of Elizabeth Barrett, and was equally popular as a motion picture.

Beskow, Baron Bernhard von (1796-1868), Swedish historian, poet and dramatist: son of a wealthy merchant and from 1834 to his death perpetual secretary of the Swedish Academy. His poetry has little interest, but his historical plays, while grandiose in style, had considerable influence on the Swedish stage: they include *Erik XIV,* and four *Dramatic Studies,* one of which, *Thorkel Knutsson,* has acquired considerable fame.

Besnard, Paul Albert (1849-1934), French painter, student at the ECOLE DES BEAUX ARTS, Paris, and winner of the Prix de Rome in 1874. His father had been a pupil of Jean Auguste INGRES, and his mother, a painter of miniatures, gave him his first instruction. After several years of study in Rome, he went to London to paint some important portraits, including that of General Wolseley. Mural paintings at the School of Pharmacy, Paris, increased his reputation, and his sketches of travel in Spain, Algiers and India were well received. After following academic tradition for years, he devoted himself to the study of light and color from the impressionist point of view: his portrait of Madame REJANE, and *Woman Warming Herself* are examples of his unconventional work.

Best, Edna (1900-), English stage and screen actress who appeared in several stage successes, and in the silent films with Herbert Marshall. Since 1930 she has appeared in many talking films including *Loose Ends, Sleeping Partners, The Calendar, Michael and Mary* (with Herbert MARSHALL), *South Riding* (with Ralph RICHARDSON) and *Intermezzo, a Love Story* (with Leslie HOWARD).

Bethlehem, a town in Palestine located about six miles from Jerusalem: it was the birthplace of David and of Christ, and one of the most sacred edifices in the world, the *Convent of the Nativity,* is located there. It comprises a series of structures, erected by both the Latin and Greek creeds, surrounding the church built by the Empress Helena and the Emperor Constantine. The church measures 86 by 136 feet: there are four long sections of Corinthian columns 19 feet in height, and the CHOIR is richly ornamented. Beneath the church are the tortuous chambers known as the *Grotto of the Nativity.*

Bethlehem Bach Choir, an organization in Bethlehem, Pa., which was preceded by the Bethlehem Choral Union, founded in 1882, and succeeded in 1900 by the Bethlehem Bach Choir. The new ensemble functioned until 1905, and after suspending for seven years, resumed in 1912 under the sponsorship of Charles M. Schwab. Dr. J. Fred Wolle conducted until his death in 1933, and was succeeded by Dr. Bruce Carey until 1938 when Ifor Jones assumed the baton. The annual festival is usually held in June, and the number of singers has increased from about one hundred to almost three hundred in 1938. Thirty-one annual festivals have been held since 1900, and the

B Minor Mass by Johann Sebastian Bach has been sung thirty times.

Betterton, Thomas (c. 1635-1710), English actor who appeared first in 1660 at the Cockpit in Drury Lane, and in 1661 at the opening of the new theatre at Lincoln's Inn Fields under the management of Sir William DAVENANT in his play, *The Siege of Rhodes*. He soon became a national favorite; in 1665 he went to France to look into scenic improvements at Paris theatres, and brought back the idea of shifting scenes instead of using tapestries. After an unfortunate business speculation, and the failure of the New Playhouse in 1695, he retired in 1710: he was buried in WESTMINSTER ABBEY. His repertory included many Shakespearean roles: he was not only an actor of great histrionic ability, but also a man conspicuous for his unblemished character in a profession noted for its loose morals. His wife, **Mary Saunders Betterton** (c.1642-1712) was a distinguished actress who co-starred with him until she retired in 1693.

Betti, Adolfo (1875-), Italian violinist who studied with César THOMPSON from 1892 to 1896, and after four years in Vienna succeeded Thomson at the Conservatory in Brussels. In 1903 he became leader of the Flonzaley Quartet, retaining this position for 26 years: during this period the quartet gave 2500 concerts in America, Europe, and Great Britain. Betti was awarded the Coolidge Medal in 1933 for distinguished service in the field of chamber music: he also edited the string quartets of Franz Schubert, and directed the Flonzaley Quartet in many Victor recordings.

Betty, William Henry West (1791-1874), English actor nicknamed "the young Roscius" because of his remarkable histrionic ability as a boy. He appeared first at Belfast, Ireland, in an English version of VOLTAIRE's *Zaire* at the age of twelve, later touring Ireland and Scotland where he was favorably compared with the greatest actors of the day. He arrived at London in 1804, and was such an astounding success at the DRURY LANE THEATRE that on one occasion William Pitt adjourned the House of Commons to permit the members to see him in *Hamlet*. He failed to retain his popularity after his juvenile career ended, but lived comfortably on the fortune he amassed. His son, **Henry Betty** (1819-1897) also adopted the stage as his profession.

Bewick, Thomas (1753-1828), English engraver on wood who demonstrated his talent at an early age, but had no instruction except that which he derived from studying natural objects His first great work, the designs for *Select Fables* by John GAY, appeared in 1784, and his finest achievement, the two-volume *History of British Birds* from 1797 to 1804. His engravings for *The Deserted Village* by Oliver GOLDSMITH were also highly praised.

Beyle, Marie Henri, see **Stendhal.**

Bhavabhuti, Indian dramatic poet whose fame is only second to that of KALIDASA: he was the author of two plays: *The Life of Rama* and *The Later Life of Rama;* each one is in seven acts, and together constitute a dramatization of the life of the famous Hindu hero. His third play, *The*

Secret Marriage, relates the trials of Madhava and Malate, sweethearts from childhood whose happiness is threatened by the whims of a king.

Bianco, Bartolommeo (?-1656), Italian architect of the Genoese school, and a pupil of Galeazzo ALESSI. His designs were less grandiose, but in many respects more impressive than those of his teacher, an opinion expressed by many authorities who have inspected the fine buildings of the University of Genoa, and the monumental VESTIBULE of the Palazza Durazzo-Pallavicino.

Bibesco, Marthe Lucie, Princesse (1887-), Rumanian essayist and novelist who was educated in France, and married her cousin, Prince George Bibesco, grandson of the Prince of Wallachia (now Rumania). Many of her works are published in English; they include *Catherine-Paris* (1928); *The Green Parrot; Balloons; Worlds Apart; Katia; The Eight Paradises; Isvor: The Country of Willows; Royal Portraits; Egyptian Day; Some Royalties and a Prime Minister; Crusade for the Anemone: Alexander of Asia; A Daughter of Napoleon.*

Bible, The, the sacred book of Christianity, composed of the writings accepted as inspired by divine authority, and including the New Testament and the Old Testament either as a whole or in part. The Hebrew version of the Old Testament dates from the 9th century, A.D., and the Greek version of the New Testament from the 4th century A.D. The division into chapters is said to have been done by Stephen Langton, later Archbishop of Canterbury, and the numbering of the verses by Robert Stephen. The Bible was first translated in its entirety into English by John Wycliffe in about 1382: Martin Luther's Bible was completed in 1535. Another version, made up of writings accepted by the Jews, is known as the *Rabbinical Bible;* other versions include the *Matthews Bible* (1537); *Great Bible* (1539); *Cranmer's Bible* (1540); *Geneva Bible* (1560); *King James Bible* (1582); *Douay Bible* (1610, revised 1881-85); *American Bible* (1901). There are also many other Bibles with special names because of peculiarities in translation or errors in printing.

Bibliography, in literature a word with a triple meaning: (*a*) the description and history of books; (*b*) a list of books by an individual author; (*c*) a list of books on a particular subject. There are several words derived from the term which have interesting meanings: *biblioclasm* is the mutilation or destruction of books; a *biblioclast* is a person who mutilates or destroys books; *bibliogenesis* is the creation of books; *bibliolatry* is the worship of books; a *bibliophile* is a person who loves books, and a *bibliomaniac* is a person with a passion for collecting books. The above list makes no pretense of being complete as the reader will realize if he consults *Webster's Unabridged Dictionary.* Curiously enough the term was used in post-classical Greek to describe the writing of books; in 1761 an English dictionary defined a *bibliographer* as "one who writes or copies books."

Biches, Les, a ballet in one act; choreography by Bronislava Nijinska and music by François POULENC; first performed in 1924 at Monte Carlo.

The ballet, which has no libretto, may be regarded as a satire portraying a house party held at the home of one of the "Four-Hundred" with constantly changing partners in the dances. The flirtatious hostess was created at the première by Bronislava NIJINSKA who designed the choreography.

Bickerstaffe, Isaac (c.1735-c.1812), English dramatist at one time Lord Lieutenant of Ireland. He was the author of many farces and burlesques with songs such as *Maid of the Mill* (founded on "Pamela" by Samuel RICHARDSON); *Love in a Village; The Captive*. His career was abruptly ended in 1772 when he fled to Europe after being accused of a felony.

Biedermeier, in furniture the name given a style prevalent in Germany in the early part of the 19th century. The name itself was taken from a humorous character, *Papa Biedermeier,* featured in verse in the magazine "Fliegende Blätter." The designs were adapted from many sources; French Empire, Directoire and even the English Sheraton and Hepplewhite. The pieces were distinguished by curves and decorations of thin gilt metals: domestic woods were used instead of imported stock. Many of the original pieces are collector's items.

Bierce, Ambrose (1842-c.1914), American journalist and author who had the reputation of being a caustic wit. After serving with distinction in the Civil War, he contributed to and edited the *Argonaut* and the *News Letter:* while in England during 1872, his vitriolic sketches, *The Fiend's Delight* and *Cobwebs from an Empty Skull* brought him prominently before readers. On returning to San Francisco his column, *Prattle,* in the "Examiner" did much to increase his reputation. The short stories, *Tales of Soldiers and Civilians* and *Can Such Things Be?* were his best work. The exact date of his death is not known as he disappeared during a visit to Mexico.

Bierstadt, Alberto (1830-1902), American painter born in Germany, and brought to this country as an infant. He returned to Germany in 1853 to study with Andreas ACHENBACH and Karl LESSING; he also visited Rome but finally returned to the United States. After making a cross-country trip with a surveying expedition, he devoted himself to pictures of the Rocky Mountains and the Yosemite Valley; these include *Estes Park, Colorado; Sierra Nevadas; The Valley of the Yosemite; The Rocky Mountains; Shoshone Village.* He painted two fine historical pictures: *The Discovery of the Hudson River* and *The Settlement of California.*

Biggers, Earl Derr (1884-1933), American novelist and writer of detective stories educated at Harvard University: his first successful novel was *Seven Keys to Baldpate* (1913) which developed into a sensational stage hit as dramatized by George M. COHAN. In 1925 he invented the character, *Charlie Chan,* a Chinese detective so ably depicted on the screen by Warner OLAND. Biggers' works include six Charlie Chan stories, and the novels, *Love Insurance; The Agony Column,* and *Fifty Candles.*

Bigordi, Domenico, see **Ghirlandaio.**

Bihārī-Lāl, Hindu author of the 17th century: little is known of him except that his patron was the Raja of Amber, and that he was probably a Brahman by caste. His principal work is the *Sab-sai,* comprising seven hundred couplets, each complete in itself and concerned with the amorous passages between Radha, the queen of the maidens of Braj, and her divine lover, the son of Vasudeva. He is said to have received a gold piece worth $5.00 (16 rupees) for each couplet.

Billboard, The, a unique publication in the theatrical world which is the oldest and most widely circulated amusement periodical in the world. Founded in 1893, it interests itself in the personalities and happenings on the legitimate stage, vaudeville, night clubs, dance bands, circus carnivals and radio. It inaugurated a mail-forwarding service for people in the show business which is used regularly by performers whose only permanent address is "c/o *The Billboard.*"

Billing, in theatrical parlance the publicity given an actor in the form of bills and posters placed in the lobby of a theatre, and on billboards throughout the city in which performances are being given.

Billings, Josh, pen name of Henry Wheeler Shaw (1818-1885), American farmer, auctioneer and humorist who contributed droll sketches in farmers' dialect to the *New York Weekly* for twenty years, and later published them in collected form: *Josh Billings on Ice; Josh Billings Spice Box,* etc. His lectures, which were along the same lines as his writings, invariably drew large audiences.

Billingsgate, in literature a term applied to foul, abusive language: the word was originally the name of a fish market near London Bridge notorious for the coarse language used by the hucksters.

Billington, Elizabeth (c.1768-1818), English opera singer born in London of German parents: she had a voice of extraordinary compass and a remarkably attractive personality but her acting was extremely poor. After her debut in 1784 at Dublin in Gluck's *Orpheus and Eurydice,* she appeared in a ballad opera *Love in a Village,* at Covent Garden in 1786 with such success that her appearances alternately at Drury Lane and Covent Garden earned her more than $50,000 in a single season.

Billy the Kid, American folk ballet in one act: libretto by Lincoln Kirstein; music by Aaron COPLAND. It was first produced at the Civic Opera House, Chicago, in 1938. The action revolves around a notorious Western desperado, Billy the Kid, a murderer who pursues his gory career until killed by his own bosom friend.

Bingham, Amelia (1869-1927), American actress educated at Ohio Wesleyan University: her first important appearance in New York was under the management of Charles FROHMAN in *The White Heather.* In 1901 she organized her own stock company, and produced a play by Clyde FITCH, entitled *The Climbers,* which proved a great success. She also appeared in *A Modern Magdalen, The Frisky Mrs. Johnson* and *A Modern Lady Godiva.*

Bingham, George Caleb (1811-1879), American painter; student at the Pennsylvania Academy of Fine Arts and in Germany. He occupied the chair of Professor of Art at the University of Missouri, and painted many fine portraits and genre works including *The Emigration of Daniel Boone, The Jolly Flatboat Men,* and *Stump Speaking.*

Binyon, Laurence (1869-1943), English poet and dramatist: after graduating from Oxford University he became curator in 1895 of the Department of Prints and Drawings at the BRITISH MUSEUM, London; his *Catalogue of English Drawings in the British Museum* was issued in 1898. He published many poetical works from 1894 to 1906; also two poetical dramas, *Paris and Oenone* and *Attila* in 1907. A critical volume, *Court Painters of the Grand Mogul,* and a volume of collected war poems, *The Four Years,* as well as a finely edited *Golden Treasury of Modern Lyrics* added greatly to his reputation: a drama, *Sakuntala,* was produced at London in 1920.

Biography, in literature the term applied to the history of an individual in the form of facts regarding his personal life, or his deeds in relation to the times in which he lived. In classical literature, the *Memoir of Socrates* by ZENOPHON and *Lives of the Twelve Cæsars* by SUETONIUS are excellent examples; the *Life of Dr. Samuel Johnson* by James BOSWELL is regarded by many authorities as the most interesting work of its kind in any language. The first biographical dictionary, the *Bibliotheca Universalis* compiled by Konrad von Gesner, was published at Zurich, Switzerland, in Greek, Latin, and Hebrew from 1516 to 1565; the Swedish Dictionary of National Biography was completed between 1835 and 1837, and followed by similar works published in Austria, Holland, Belgium, Germany and England. The British *Dictionary of National Biography,* by Sir Leslie Stephen and Sidney Lee, is issued in 66 volumes; its counterpart in the United States is the *Dictionary of American Biography.* For ordinary reference use, interesting non-critical information regarding notable living personalities in public life as well as in the arts and professions are to be found in the *Who's Who* volumes published in America and Europe.

Birch, Reginald Bathhurst (1856-1943), American illustrator born in London, England. Among his notable works are the illustrations for Frances Hodgson Burnett's *Little Lord Fauntleroy* and *Sara Crewe;* John Bennett's *Master Skylark;* Louisa May Alcott's *Little Men.* In 1939 Elisabeth B. Hamilton published *Reginald Birch—His Book,* assembling the illustrations drawn from 1886 to 1938.

Birch, Thomas (1779-1851), English painter: little is known of him except that he came to America in 1793, and while on a visit to the Delaware capes, turned his attention to painting navy battles including *Engagement between the "Constitu-*

tion" and the "Guerriere" and *Engagement between the "Wasp" and the "Frolic,"* now in the Harrison Collection, Philadelphia.

Bishop, Sir Henry Rowley (1786-1855), English composer and pupil of Francesco Bianchi. His first opera, *The Circassian Bride,* was a success at Drury Lane in 1809, and he occupied a prominent place in English music as a conductor, musical director, teacher, and composer of more than one hundred operas and musical pieces. He is best remembered as the composer of the music for the ballad, "Home, Sweet Home," written by John Howard PAYNE for the opera *Clari, the Maid of Milan,* produced at Covent Garden, London, and in New York in 1823. The original manuscript of this song is in the possession of the University of Rochester, N. Y.

Bishop, John Peale (1892-   ), American poet and novelist; his works include a volume of poems, *Green Fruit* (1917); *The Undertaker's Garland,* in collaboration with Edmund Wilson, Jr.; *Many Thousands Gone; Act of Darkness; Selected Poems.*

Bishop, Morris (1893-   ), American humorous poet connected with the Department of Romance Languages at Cornell University since 1921. His works include *A Gallery of Eccentrics* (1928); *Paramount Poems; Love Rimes of Petrarch; The Odyssey of Cabeza de Vaca; Pascal: The Life of Genius; Ronsard: Prince of Poets; Spilt Milk.*

Bispham, David (1857-1921), American dramatic and concert baritone who studied in Europe with Liuigi Vannuccini and Francesco LAMPERTI; also in London with William Shakespeare and Alberto Randegger. His debut in opera was made at London in the light opera *Basoche* by André MESSAGER in 1891, and in 1892 at Drury Lane in *Tristan and Isolde:* in 1896 he appeared at the METROPOLITAN OPERA HOUSE in *Die Meistersinger,* and from then until 1909 sang each season in both houses. Bispham was distinguished not only as a concert singer, but as a reciter of Tennyson's *Enoch Arden* with music by Richard Strauss, and Shakespeare's *Midsummer Night's Dream* with Mendelssohn's music. The Bispham Memorial Medal Award established in 1921 has been won by Henry HADLEY, Deems TAYLOR, Howard HANSEN, Walter DAMROSCH, Charles Wakefield CADMAN and many other American composers. Bispham's autobiography, *A Quaker Singer's Recollections,* was published in 1920.

Bissel, George Edwin (1839-1920), American sculptor who served in the Civil War, and studied his art in Europe. He lived for some years in Paris: among his finest creations are the *Soldiers' and Sailors' Monument* at Waterbury, Conn., *President Arthur* in Madison Square, New York; *Abraham Lincoln* at Edinburgh; *Robert Burns* and *Highland Mary,* the Scotch poet's great love, at Ayr, Scotland.

Bissen, Hermann Wilhelm (1798-1868), Danish sculptor; a pupil of Bertel Thorwaldsen who thought so highly of his ability that he was requested to complete some unfinished works in Thorwaldsen's will. Bissen became director of the Academy of Arts, Copenhagen, in 1850, and created many outstanding original works.

Bitter, Karl Theodore Francis (1867-1915), American sculptor; born in Vienna where he studied his art, migrating to the United States in 1889, and later becoming a naturalized American citizen. His works include the *Astor Memorial Gates* at Trinity Church, New York; a group for the *Admiral Dewey Arch,* New York; the *Louisiana Purchase Memorial* at St. Louis; the *Carl Schurz Memorial,* New York, and the large relief, *Triumph of Civilization,* in the Broad Street Station of the Philadelphia Railroad at Philadelphia.

Bitterman, Peter (1898-1942), American architect who studied at the Columbia University School of Architecture, and acted as coordinator in charge of the interior of the United States Building at the New York World's Fair in 1939. He was the designer of a *cosmosarium* or glass house in which people may look at the earth from the objective view of a philosopher: a model was exhibited in 1936 at the Hayden Planetarium of the American Museum of Natural History, New York.

Bitzius, Albrecht (1797-1854), Swiss novelist who used the pseudonymn "Jeremias Gotthelf." This pen name was adopted because his story, *The Peasant's Mirror* (1837), a realistic description of peasant life, had an imaginary character, Jeremias Gotthelf, as its narrator, and the great success of the book made the name a good omen. Several other novels along the same lines including *The Joys and Sorrows of a Schoolmaster* and *Uli, the Servant* were partially successful although hampered by the echo of local political controversies in which Bitzius was involved.

Bixby's Hotel, a hotel in New York City opened at Broadway and Park Place in the early part of the 19th century by Daniel Bixby, formerly proprietor of a bookstore in Lowell, Mass. Shortly after its opening, it became a rendezvous for some of the most prominent authors and publishers including James Fenimore COOPER, Nathaniel HAWTHORNE, Oliver Wendell HOLMES, Ralph Waldo EMERSON, Bayard TAYLOR and both Phoebe and Alice CARY.

Bizet, Georges (1838-1875), French composer who began his studies at nine with Antoine MARMONTEL in piano, and Jacques HALEVY in composition at the PARIS CONSERVATORY. In 1857 he won the Grand Prix de Rome, and an award offered by Jacques OFFENBACH for his setting of a comic opera, *The Miracle Doctor.* His operas *The Pearl Fishers* (1863) and *The Fair Maid of Perth* (1867), were both failures from the standpoint of popular success; another opera, *Djamileh* met with the same fate. The tide was turned by his incidental music for *L'Arlésienne,* a play by Alphonse DAUDET, later rearranged into two orchestral suites. Bizet's masterpiece, the opera *Carmen,* when produced at the Opéra-Comique in 1875, was almost a complete failure at its première, but before 1878 it was heard in Vienna, Brussels, St. Petersburg, Florence, and in many other Continental cities as well as London and New York. Parisian opera lovers called for it 37 times during 1875, but unfortunately Bizet did not live to enjoy his final success. Other works include 3 symphonies, one of which has recently been given many performances; a *Petite Suite* for orchestra; another suite entitled *Jeux d'Enfants;* also many songs and piano pieces.

Bjoerling, Jussi (1911-), Swedish tenor; graduate of the Royal Opera School, Stockholm, where he made his debut in 1930 as Don Ottavio in *Don Giovanni* by Wolfgang Amadeus MOZART. He came first to the United States with the Bjoerling Quartet composed of his father, his brothers and himself: in 1937 he made his debut with the Chicago Civic Opera Company in *La Bohéme,* and in 1938 became a member of the Metropolitan Opera Company. Bjoerling has more than fifty roles in his repertory.

Björnson, Björnstjerne (1832-1910), Norwegian poet, novelist and dramatist who was graduated at the University of Christiana in 1852. In 1857 his first novel, *Synnove Solbakken* was published, and his first play, *Between the Battles,* was produced. Several more novels, including *The Fishermaiden* and *In the Paths of God,* followed, and many plays, among which may be mentioned *Lame Hulda; Sigurd Slembe; Sigurd Jorsalfar,* with incidental music by Edvard GRIEG; *The Bankrupt,* and *When the New Wine Blooms.* He was successful also as director of the Ole BULL Theatre in Bergen and the theatre at Oslo; won the Nobel Prize for literature in 1903; wrote the words of the Norwegian national anthem, and played a prominent part in the separation of Norway from Sweden in 1905. He visited the United States in 1881 and lived in Paris from 1882 to 1887; his son, **Björn Björnson** (1859-), also a dramatist, became director of the National Theatre at Christiania in 1898.

Black, Frank (1896-), American pianist, composer and conductor; pupil of Rafael JOSEFFY in piano and Charles Maskell in composition. He conducted at the Fox Theatre, Philadelphia; directed recording for the Brunswick Corporation; coached the Revelers Quartet and became general musical director of the National Broadcasting Company in 1933, organizing and conducting the NBC String Symphony broadcasts. His compositions include incidental music for *The White Cliffs of Dover* by Alice Duer MILLER and radio plays by Arch OBOLER; he has also arranged many standard piano and chamber music works for string orchestra including several piano sonatas by BEETHOVEN and MOZART; choral preludes by Johann Sebastian BACH; string quartets by MENDELSSOHN and DEBUSSY.

Black, William (1841-1898), Scottish novelist who was a distinguished journalist and war correspondent before the publication of his first successful novel, *A Daughter of Heth* (1871), which was followed by several more including *The Strange Adventures of a Phaeton; A Princess of Thule; Shandon Bells; White Wings; White Heather* and *Wild Eelin,* all of which were popular favorites. Black's characters were interesting, and his descriptions of Scotch scenery picturesque.

Blackburn, Joseph (c.1700-c.1765), American painter who specialized in portraits in his studio at Boston, Mass., from about 1750 to 1765. He was patronized by early New England families such as the Apthorps, Lowells, Saltonstalls, Winthrops, Winslows and Bullfinches, and many of his portraits are in private collections as well as in the gallery of the Massachusetts Historical Society. Some of his unsigned works were credited to John Singleton COPLEY, who was his pupil.

Blackfriars Theatre, a playhouse erected in 1576 by the English actor and producer, James BURBAGE, near an ancient Dominican friary: it became the center of dramatic development in England. It was also used as a winter playhouse for Shakespearean productions by Richard BURBAGE because the Globe Theatre, which was used for summer productions, had no roof. In 1600 Burbage made it the home of a troupe of child actors, and it was used as the theatre for the King's Men who succeeded the Chamberlain's Men.

Blackmer, Sidney (1898-), American stage and screen actor; graduate of the University of North Carolina. He made his first appearance in 1917 on the New York stage in *The Morris Dance,* and toured with Ben GREET's Company. After playing in *The Thirteenth Chair,* he served in France during World War I, and upon his return appeared in numerous stage productions including *39 East, The Robbery, The Rivals* and *Scaramouche.* His screen appearances since 1929 include *The Count of Monte Cristo; The Little Colonel; The President's Mystery; Heidi; In Old Chicago; Suez; Trade Winds;* also an interesting "short," *Theodore Roosevelt,* in which he enacted the title role.

Blackmore, Richard Doddridge (1825-1900), English novelist; a graduate of Oxford. When his health failed, he bought a farm and settled down as a market-gardener and writer. His first two novels, *Clara Vaughan* and *Cradock Nowell,* were well received, but his third, *Lorna Doone* (1869) was an immediate and enormous success which he was unable to repeat although several more excellent novels, among them *Maid of Sker, Springhaven,* and *Dariel,* appeared during the ensuing twenty years.

Blackwood, Algernon (1869-), English novelist who was at one time connected in a journalistic capacity with the New York *Sun* and *Times.* A collection of ghost stories in 1906 was so well received that he continued his career with several novels in which uncanny and weird happenings are featured: they include *John Silence, The Lost Valley, The Centaur,* and *The Garden of Survival.*

Blake, William (1757-1827), English painter, poet and engraver: at fourteen he was apprenticed to an engraver with whom he remained for several years, finally going into business for himself in 1782, assisted by his wife, Catherine Boucher. His works include illustrations for the complete works of William COWPER, the plates for his own books of poems including *Songs of Innocence* and *Songs of Experience;* YOUNG's

Night Thoughts; DANTE's *Divine Comedy* and GRAY's *Poems.* He engraved both the text and drawings for his poems with the latter tinted by hand: an extensive collection of his paintings and engravings are to be seen at the NATIONAL GALLERY, London.

Blakelock, Ralph Albert (1847-1919), American painter who studied for a time at Cooper Union Institute in New York, but was chiefly self-taught. His works are largely landscapes: a trip to the West brought him in close touch with American Indians for whom he developed a great interest and respect. Among his finest creations are *Sunset; Moonlight; Indian Encampment; October Sunshine* and *The Capture.*

Blanchard, Jacques (1600-1638), French painter who spent several years in intensive study of the old masters at Rome and Venice, and developed powers as a colorist that led to his being called "the French Titian." Several of his finest works were destroyed when the Hotel Perault and the Hotel Bullion in Paris were razed: among those still in existence are *St. Paul; The Holy Family; The Virgin and St. Anne; Charity;* all in the Louvre, Paris.

Blanche, Jacques Emile (1861-), French painter; pupil of Henri GERVEX and Ferdinand Humbert. He paints in a style which suggests the great 18th century English artists except that his coloring is more vivid, and his drawing fuller of nervous animation. His works, chiefly portraits, constitute a gallery of the intellectual and artistic personalities of his day, including *The Thaulow Family,* DEBUSSY, RODIN, *Jose Maria Sert, Portrait of a Lady* and *Girl With a Straw Hat.*

Bland, James A., 19th century American composer of mixed blood educated at Howard University, Washington, D. C.: he was a member of the Haverly Minstrel Company and toured the United States for many years. Of his many songs, *Carry Me Back to Old Virginny, Oh, Dem Golden Slippers,* and *In the Evening by the Moonlight* have retained their popularity over a period of nearly sixty years: it is said that more than 200,000 of the recordings made by Alma GLUCK of *Carry Me Back to Old Virginny* were sold, and more than a million copies of the sheet music.

Blank verse, in literature the term for a style of poetry employing unrhymed lines, usually in iambic pentameter, and used by CHAUCER about 1370. Italian poets and dramatists, headed by Gian Trissino, made use of it in the 15th century; a tragedy by SACKVILLE and NORTON, *Gorboduc,* was written in blank verse in 1562; Christopher MARLOWE made excellent use of it in his *Tragical History of Dr. Faustus,* but SHAKESPEARE carried it to greatest perfection in respect to variety and flexibility. Although blank verse has been subjected to constant minor revision by poets including WORDSWORTH, SHELLEY, TENNYSON and BROWNING, no radical changes or improvements have been made.

Blasco Ibáñez, Vicente, see **Ibáñez, Vicente Blasco.**

Blashfield, Edwin Howland (1848-1936), American mural painter; pupil of Léon Bonnat, Henri Chapu and Jean Gérôme at Paris from 1867 to 1870. He then spent some time in Florence and Brussels, returning to Paris, and finally to the United States in 1881. His creations include murals for the Manufacturers and Liberal Arts Building at the Columbian Exposition, Chicago; the dome of the Library of Congress, Washington, D. C.; the Court House in Baltimore, Md., the state capitols of Minnesota, Iowa and Wisconsin; the Assembly Hall of the College of the City of New York. Blashfield also edited VASARI's *Lives of the Painters* and wrote *Mural Painting in America*.

Blasis, Carlo (1803-1878), Italian dancer and choreographer trained under Salvatore VIGANO. He made his first appearance at twelve, and, after further study with DAUBERVEL in addition to dancing at L'Opera, Paris, in 1817, became *premier danseur* at LA SCALA, Milan, where he produced his first ballet, *Il Finto Feudatorio* in 1819. He then became solo dancer and choreographer at the King's Theatre, London: an injury in 1837 ended his stage career, and he was made director of the Royal Academy of Dancing at La Scala, Milan. His famous pupils included Fanny CERITO and Carlotta GRISI. Blasis also wrote an important text book on ballet, *The Code of Terpsichore*.

Blauvelt, Lillian Evans (1874-), American concert and dramatic soprano; pupil of J. Bouhy in New York and Paris. After concertizing in Europe, she made her operatic debut in GOUNOD's *Mireille* in 1893 at Brussels. Upon returning to the United States she appeared with the major symphony orchestras under Anton SEIDL, Walter DAMROSCH and Theodore THOMAS. In 1899 she appeared before Queen Victoria, and sang a variety of roles for several seasons at Covent Garden, London.

Blech, Leo (1871-), German composer conductor who studied at the Hoch-schule für Musik, Berlin: while conducting at the Municipal Theatre at Aachen he received further instruction from Engelbert HUMPERDINCK. From 1913 to 1923 he acted as general music director at the Berlin Opera: after two years' absence he returned and continued as director until 1936. In 1939 he was conducting in Riga. He has composed several operas, three symphonic poems, and various instrumental pieces and songs. Blech's conducting of recordings sold with the Victor label is extremely popular with lovers of orchestra music.

Blechen, Karl Edouard (1798-1840), German painter; trained at the Berlin Academy: in 1827 he went to Italy and painted many landscapes including *Camp Near Lake Muggel; Villa Este; View near Narni; Villa Borghese; View at Tivoli; View at Naples*. The National Gallery at Berlin owns many of his works.

Bledsoe, Jules (1902-1943), American negro composer and baritone, educated at several colleges in the South, at Columbia University, New York, and at the Chicago Musical College. He studied voice in Rome and Paris; made his concert debut in 1924 at New York; appeared with the Boston Symphony orchestra, and created the leading roles for baritone or bass in *Deep River, The Show Boat,* and *The Voodoo King*. He also appeared in grand opera from 1932 to 1934 and has been concertizing since that time in the United States and Europe. His compositions include an *African Suite* for violin with orchestra accompaniment, and numerous songs.

Blessington, Marguerite (1789-1849), Irish novelist and writer who, after being forced into marriage at fifteen with a drunken army officer who died in a debtor's prison, married Charles John Gardner, Earl of Blessington. After her husband's death in 1829, his estate was encumbered with debt through her reckless extravagance tinged with generosity, and she embarked on a literary career to increase her income. Her home in Kensington was the center of a coterie of men and women distinguished in literature, art, and fashion: she edited two popular magazines, and her books, *Idler in Italy* and *Idler in France*, were widely read because of the wealth of anecdote and personal gossip.

Blicher, Steen Steenson (1782-1848), Danish poet and novelist who made a fine translation of OSSIAN (1807-09), and published a volume of poems in 1814 which created little interest; in 1842 his masterpiece, *The Knitting-Room,* a collection of short stories in Jutland dialect, caused a sensation in Danish literary circles.

Blinn, Holbrook (1872-1928), American actor educated at Stanford University: among the successful plays in which he starred were *The New South; The Cat and the Cherub; The Great Silence; The Battle of the Strong; To Have and To Hold; Sweet and Twenty; Scrooge* (in London); *The Duchess of Dantzic; Salomy Jane; The Man of the Hour*.

Bliss, Arthur (1891-), English composer who studied with Charles Wood, Charles Villiers STANFORD, Ralph Vaughan WILLIAMS and Gustav HOLST. Among his compositions are a ballet; several orchestral works including a "Color Symphony," a concerto for two pianos, choral works, and chamber music.

Blitzstein, Marc (1905-), American composer, student at the University of Pennsylvania, and later in Europe with Nadia BOULANGER and Arnold SCHONBERG. His compositions include several operas, ballets, orchestral works and chamber music. His play with music, *The Cradle Will Rock,* was produced at the Venice Theatre, New York, in 1937 without scenery, with the actors in the audience and the composer at the piano due to difficulties with the Federal Theatre Project. It ran successfully for ten days, and was revived during 1937. Another opera, *No For an Answer,* was produced in 1941.

Bloch, Ernest (1880-), Jewish composer, born in Switzerland, and a pupil of JAQUES-DALCROZE, Eugene YSAYE, Ivan Knorr, and Ludwig Thuille. He lectured at the Geneva Conservatory, conducted concerts at Lausanne, became professor of composition at the Lausanne Conservatory, toured the United States with the dancer, Maud ALLEN, and settled in New York as a teacher of composition. He has conducted his own compositions with many of the major American orchestras, and won the *Musical America Prize* of $3000 with his symphonic poem, *America*. His numerous compositions include two operas; songs for solo voice and for chorus with orchestra; several symphonic poems; a symphony, *Israel;* a Hebrew rhapsody, *Schelomo,* for violoncello and orchestra; chamber music for many combinations, a sacred service, and many miscellaneous pieces for various instruments.

Bloemaert, Abraham (1564-1651), Dutch painter and engraver; a pupil of Gerritt Splinter and Joos de Beer. He was distinguished as a colorist, painting and etching animals, landscapes and flowers. All four of his sons achieved a reputation in their father's profession; Gerard HONTHORST and Jacob G. Cuyp were also his pupils.

Blomfield, Sir Reginald (1856-1942), English architect educated at Oxford and the Royal Academy School of Architecture. He designed many fine country houses and buildings in London including the United University Club; the Goldsmiths' College; the Imperial War Cross; also buildings at Oxford and Bath. During World War I he was in charge of trench work, and at its conclusion principal architect of the Imperial War Graves Commission. His *History of Renaissance Architecture in England* and *History of French Architecture* are standard text books.

Blondel, François (1618-1686), French architect who was first trained for a career in science: a tour of Europe which included Rome inspired the desire to become an architect. His works include the *Porte St. Denis,* Paris, and the Arsenal at Rochefort: he was the first director of the Academy of Architecture, and wrote several important treatises including *The Course of Architecture* (1675). His nephew, **Jacques François Blondell** (1705-74), was architect to Louis XV: his designs in rococo style conform more to the fashion of the day than to artistic ideals, but his work, *French Architecture,* is an invaluable collection containing drawings of many famous buildings long out of existence.

Blondel de Nesle, twelfth-century French trouvère, and friend of RICHARD COEUR DE LION whom he accompanied on the crusade of 1192. Tradition has it that Blondel discovered the presence of Richard, when the latter was captured and imprisoned in 1193 by Duke Leopold of Austria in the castle of Durrenstein, by singing a song which they had composed under the tower where he was confined: this incident was used in 1874 by Andre Grétry in his opera, *Richard Coeur de Lion.* More than twenty of Blondel's songs are in existence.

Bloodstone, a semi-precious stone of green jasper containing red spots: it was highly regarded during the Middle Ages because it was supposed to be the stone upon which the blood

of Christ dropped while he was nailed to the cross.

Bloomfield, Robert (1766-1823), English poet: a farmer's boy who was apprenticed later to a shoemaker. The poem which made him famous, *The Farmer's Boy,* published in 1800 with wood engravings by Thomas BEWICK, reached a sale of more than 25,000 copies in two years. Four other volumes, *Rural Tales, News from the Farm, Wild Flowers,* and *The Banks of the Wye,* also enjoyed a considerable degree of popular favor.

Bloomfield-Zeisler, Fannie, see **Zeisler, Fannie Bloomfield.**

Blossom Time, a musical play: music by Sigmund ROMBERG and book by Dorothy Donnelly; first produced at New York in 1921. Romberg's music was chiefly arrangements of Franz SCHUBERT's songs and a theme from the "Unfinished" Symphony which is utilized in the song, *This is My Song of Love.* The plot revolves around Franz Schubert, portrayed as even more ingenuous and awkward than he was in real life, aiding the urbane Baron Franz Schober in wooing his (Schubert's) sweetheart.

Blouet, Guillaume Abel (1795-1853), French architect who won the Grand Prix de Rome in 1821 with his design for a "Palais de Justice." In 1848 he was named architect of the château at FONTAINEBLEAU, vacant since NAPOLEON I signed his abdication there in 1814, and executed important restoration work.

Blouet, Paul (1848-1903), French cavalry officer and author: in 1872 he went to England as correspondent for several French newspapers, and also taught French in St. Paul's School, London, until the success of his first book, *John Bull and His Island,* published in 1883 under the pen name "Max O'Rell," induced him to embark on a literary career. He made several successful tours of the United States as a fluently humorous speaker: his books include *John Bull and his Daughters, Jonathan and His Continent,* and *A Frenchman in America.*

Bluebeard, in French folklore, as related by Charles PERRAULT, a man who married a beautiful young girl, Fatima, and gave her the keys of his castle with strict instructions not to open one particular door. Fatima could not resist the temptation to disobey his orders, and discovered the bodies of several murdered wives. An indelible stain on the key betrayed her, and she was about to be slain also when rescued by her friends. It is said that the original of Bluebeard was Giles de Retz, a Marshal of France notorious for his cruelty and licentiousness. Many plays, operettas and a grand opera, *Ariadne and Bluebeard,* libretto by Maurice MAETERLINCK and music by Paul DUKAS, have utilized this story.

Bluebeard, a humorous ballet in four acts based on the opera, *Barbe Bleue* (1866), by Henry Meilhac and Ludovic Halévy. The book and choreography for the ballet are by Michel FOKINE with music adapted from Jacques OFFENBACH; first produced at Mexico City in 1941.

The ballet takes place in the mythical domain of King Bobiche at the beginning of the 16th century: it concerns the sad experiences of the monarch who, having exiled his infant daughter, grows into an unhappy old man, infuriated by the infidelities of his queen, Clementine, and plagued by the philanderings of Baron Bluebeard, his impetuous vassal.

Blue Boy, The, see **Gainsborough, Thomas.**

Blues, in music a term applied to certain American Negro songs of sadness or lamentation, distinctive in their harmonic and rhythmical structure: their invention is credited to William G. HANDY in his song, *The St. Louis Blues*. In modern jazz bands the exponents of these songs are known as "blue" or "torch" singers, and their composition is not confined to Negro writers.

Blum, Robert Frederick (1857-1903), American painter and illustrator who was practically self-taught except for some instruction at art schools in Cincinnati and Philadelphia. His first published sketches *Japanese Jugglers,* appeared in *St. Nicholas,* and he also wrote articles with illustrations for *Scribner's Magazine* and the *Century Magazine.* He illustrated Sir Edwin ARNOLD's *Japonica:* his Venetian pictures such as *A Bright Day at Venice, The Amaya,* and *The Lace-Makers* are highly regarded, but his masterpiece was the mural, *Music and the Dance* (1895) for MENDELSSOHN HALL, New York.

Blüthner, Julius (1824-1910), German piano manufacturer who started in Leipzig with three workmen in 1853, and finally employed five hundred skilled artisans who made more than 60,000 instruments in fifty years. In 1873 he patented the *Aliquot Grand Piano* in which an additional unused string, tuned an octave higher, was stretched over each unison string.

Boards, in theatrical parlance the stage of a theatre: to "go upon the boards" means to become an actor.

Bocage, Manuel Maria Barbosa de (1765-1805), Portuguese poet who lead an adventurous and profligate existence during which he was arrested several times. He was an adept at improvising rhymed poems sung with the guitar, and writing imitations of Brazilian *modinhas.* William BECKFORD, author of *Vathek,* describes him as a "pale, limber odd-looking man, the queerest but probably the most original of God's poetical creatures, possessing the true wand of enchantment." His collected poems were published fifty years after his death.

Boccaccio, Giovanni (1313-1375), Italian poet and novelist who lived at Naples, where he became an intimate friend of PETRARCH, and he acted as ambassador several times for the Florentine State. His greatest work is the *Decameron* (1348-58), a collection of prose tales which assumed a prominent place in Italian literature. Other works include an authoritative biography of DANTE; the novels *Filocopo, L'Amorosa Fiammetta,* and *Filostrata,* an epic on the subject of TROILUS AND CRESSIDA.

Boccador, Il (? -c.1549), Italian architect, real name *Domenico di Cortona,* who was employed by Louis XII and Francis I of France, and worked on the Chateau de Chambord before he undertook the designs and construction of the Hôtel de Ville in Paris in 1533. The latter is regarded as his chef-d'oeuvre: it was the predecessor of the present structure which was built in 1871.

Boccherini, Luigi (1743-1805), Italian violoncellist and composer: his first string quartets (1768) established his reputation as a chamber music composer, and he became chamber virtuoso to the King of Spain, chamber composer to Friedrich Wilhelm II of Prussia, and a protegé of Lucien Bonaparte. All of these honors, however, brought him little income, and he died in poverty. Boccherini was a prolific composer of symphonies and chamber music: a minuet from one of his string quintets has been popular more than a hundred years, but his works are rarely heard in their entirety.

Bodanzky, Artur (1877-1939), Austrian violinist and conductor whose career in the latter capacity began in operetta. He acted as assistant to Gustav MAHLER at the Vienna Opera, and as conductor at the Theater-an-der Wien, Vienna. After conducting at Berlin, Prague, and Mannheim, where he arranged a Mahler festival in 1912 lasting three days, he produced the first *Parsifal* at Covent Garden, London, and succeeded Alfred HERTZ as conductor of German opera at the Metropolitan Opera House, New York, in 1915. He also directed the Society of the FRIENDS OF MUSIC in New York from 1916 to 1931, introducing many works as yet unheard in the United States. He revised and produced a new edition of WEBER's *Oberon* at the Metropolitan Opera House; also revisions of Weber's *Der Freischütz,* MOZART's *Don Giovanni,* PURCELL's *Dido and Aeneas* and BEETHOVEN's *Fidelio.*

Bodenheim, Maxwell (1893-), American poet and novelist entirely self-educated: his poetical works include *Minna and Myself* (1918); *Advice; Introducing Irony; The Sardonic Arm; The King of Spain; Against This Age; Returning to Emotion.* His novels include *Blackguard; Crazy Man; Replenishing Jessica; Ninth Avenue; Georgie May; Sixty Seconds; A Virtuous Girl; Duke Herring; Run, Sheep, Run; New York Madness; Slow Vision; Lights in the Valley.*

Bodenstedt, Friedrich Martin von (1819-1892), German author and poet who acted as tutor of the family of Prince Gallitzin in Moscow, and was appointed head of a public school at Tiflis in Transcaucasia. His proximity to Persia led to his interest in Oriental literature and life: a volume of original poetry in Oriental style, *The Songs of Mirza Schaffy* (English edition, 1880), had a success comparable with Edward FITZGERALD's translation of the RUBAIYAT by OMAR KHAYYAM. He also published two important books: *The People of the Caucasus and Their Struggle for Freedom against the Russians* and *A Thousand and One Days in the Orient.*

Bodleian Library, a library at Oxford University, Oxford, England: the original library, established in 1445 and destroyed during the reign of Edward VI (1537-1553), was largely replaced early in the 17th century through the untiring efforts of Sir Thomas Bodley (1514-1613), an English scholar and diplomatic envoy of Queen Elizabeth who spent seventeen years in working on it, contributing many books and manuscripts, and leaving a fund for its maintenance. There are more than 40,000 Biblical, rabbinical and Oriental manuscripts in the library exclusive of books: it also receives a copy of every book published in the British Empire.

Bodley, George Frederick (1827-1907), English architect, pupil of Sir George Gilbert Scott under whom he became an enthusiastic advocate of the Gothic revival in church architecture. He built many of the finest modern churches in England such as All Saints at Cambridge, and the Cathedral of St. Peter and St. Paul in Washington, D. C., in this instance working with his pupil, James Vaughan. Bodley was also a poet, skilled draftsman, designer of wall-papers and chintzes, and a rare connoisseur of art in general.

Bodmer, Johann Jakob (1698-1783), Swiss author and professor of Helvetian history at the University of Zurich. He made a prose translation in German of Milton's *Paradise Lost* (1732), and aided greatly in the dissemination of knowledge regarding English literature in Germany. He also made a valuable contribution to German literature with his editions of the songs of the minnesingers and the *Nibelunglied*.

Bodoni, Giambattista (1740-1813), Italian printer who published fine editions of Homer, Vergil, and other classic authors; also a magnificent *Manual of Typography* containing examples of the vast collections of types which he originated. Unfortunately Bodoni, whose name is used to designate certain modern type faces, paid more attention to the appearance of his books in respect to title-pages and margins than to editing and proofreading, the result being that they have been sharply criticized by William Morris and other authorities.

Body, in music (*a*) the resonance box of a stringed instrument such as the VIOLIN or GUITAR; (*b*) the tube of an ORGAN pipe above its mouth (tone opening); (*c*) the name applied to a musical TONE which, when sounded, is full and sonorous. In architecture the term is applied to the NAVE or central portion of a church.

Boecklin, Arnold (1827-1901), Swiss landscape, mural and historical painter; a student at Düsseldorf, Paris, Brussels and Rome. His first important creations were three frescoes in Basel; later he worked at Munich, Florence and Zurich. He was strongly influenced by Botticelli's *Primavera*, and the triptich of Hugo van der Goes at Florence. Among his finest works are *Ride of Death; Pilgrims of Emmaus; The Furies; The Murderer; Villa by the Sea; Island of the Dead; A Roman Landscape.* He also modeled busts of contemporaries in a satirical vein which made him many enemies.

Boehm, Sir Joseph Edgar (1834-1890), English sculptor of Hungarian parentage: after studying in Paris, Italy and England, he became a sculptor of busts and statues. His works include the colossal statue of Queen Victoria at Windsor Castle; the monument of the Duke of Kent in St. Georges Chapel; the statue of Carlyle on the Thames embankment at Chelsea, the sarcophagus in Westminster of Dean Stanley; the equestrian statue of the Duke of Wellington at Hyde Park; also busts of Gladstone, Lord Wolsey and Herbert Spencer, and a fine group, *Herdsman and Bull.*

Boehm, Theobald, see **Böhm, Theobald.**

Böellmann, Léon (1862-1897), French organist and composer; student at the Niedermeyer School, Paris, under Eugene Gigout. His works, all of importance in French music, include *Variations symphoniques* for violoncello and orchestra; *Fantaisie dialoguée* for orchestra with organ; *Suite gothique* for organ; several chamber works and a collection of one hundred pieces for organ, *Heures mystiques* (Mystic Hours). Böellman's premature demise cut short a career of great promise.

Boethus, Greek sculptor who flourished during the early part of the 12th century, B.C. He was distinguished for his treatment of children: a copy of his *Boy Struggling with a Goose* is in the Louvre, Paris, and copies of *Boy Extracting a Thorn from His Foot* are in several museums. Pliny and Pausanias both mention his works in their writings.

Boex, Joseph Henri, see **Rosny, J. H.**

Boex, Seraphine Justin Francis, see **Rosny, J.H.**

Bogan, Louise (1897-), American poet educated at the Girls' Latin School and Boston University, Boston, Mass. Her works include *Body of This Death* (1923); *Dark Summer; The Sleeping Fury; Poems and New Poems.*

Bogart, Humphrey (1899-), American stage and screen actor, educated at Trinity School, New York, and Andover Academy, Andover, Mass. He served in the navy during World War I, and appeared first on the stage in 1920 with Grace George. Among the plays in which he appeared were *Meet the Wife; Cradle Snatchers; Saturday's Children; Invitation to Murder; The Petrified Forest; Ceiling Zero; Rain.* He entered the films in 1936; among his pictures are *The Petrified Forest; China Clipper; The Great O'Malley; Kid Galahad; Dead End; The Amazing Dr. Clitterhouse; Across the Pacific; Casablanca.*

Bogatyri (Russian Heroes), a ballet in a prologue and three scenes: libretto and choreography by Leonide Massine; music by Alexander Borodin; first performed at the Metropolitan Opera House, New York, in 1938. The Bogatyri were semi-legendary heroes who supported the first Christian monarch of Russia, Prince Vladimir, the tales of their prowess resembling the Nibelungen legends. The music, selected from the works of Alexander Borodin, includes the *Nocturne* from the String Quartet No. 2; the Symphony No. 2; and the "Unfinished" Symphony.

Bogdanova, Nadeshda Constantinova (1836- ?), Russian ballerina: her father was a dancer and teacher at the Moscow Imperial Ballet. She studied with Arthur SAINT-LEON in Paris, and danced there in 1855, but left because of anti-Russian sentiment after the Crimean War. After appearing at Berlin and Warsaw, she achieved real success at St. Petersburg in 1856, remaining there until 1864 when her abilities began to decline.

Bogdanovich, Hippolitus (1744-1803), Russian poet whose early attempts at poetry earned him a college education. His finest work is a lyric poem, *Dushenka,* a charming elaboration of *The Lover of Cupid and Psyche,* by the French poet, Jean de LA FONTAINE.

Boggs, Frank Myers (1855-1926), American painter; pupil of Jean GEROME in Paris: his pictures include *French Coast; Old Canal at Dordrecht; A Rough Day at Honfleur* (awarded a prize of $2500 by the American Art Gallery); *Place de la Bastille; On the Thames.* The last-named painting is in the METROPOLITAN MUSEUM OF ART, New York.

Bohème, La, grand opera in four acts: libretto by Giuseppe Giacosa and Luigi Illica based on the novel, *The Life of Bohemia* by Henri Murger; music by Giacomo Puccini; first produced at the Teatro Regio, Turin, in 1896, and at the METRO-POLITAN OPERA HOUSE, New York, in 1900. The story is: The time is Christmas Eve and the four Bohemians, Rudolph, a poet, Schaunard, a musician, Marcel, a painter, and Colline, a philosopher, are living in Paris as best they can. Rudolph and Marcel are in their attic room, suffering with hunger and cold; in the midst of their attempt to start a fire burning with pages torn from Rudolph's play, Colline enters to enjoy the warmth followed shortly after by Schaunard, who has made some money, and brings food and drink. All but Rudolph go out to have a good time: he promises to join them later in the evening. There is a knock at the door, and Mimi, whose candle has blown out, appears. Rudolph attempts to light it again; then both candles are snuffed out by a draught. She loses the key to her room; when they both search for it, Rudolph finds it, but fails to say so. In the moonlight they tell each other of their struggles, and finally depart to join the others at the Cafe Momus. Seated at a table, they all make merry; later, Musetta, Marcel's old sweetheart, after sending her rich old companion, Alcindoro, on an errand, becomes one of the party, and has their bill added to Alcindoro's. Mimi parts from Rudolph because of his jealousy; Marcel and Musetta, after being reunited on Christmas Eve, separate again after a quarrel. Time passes: Mimi becomes ill, and Musetta brings her back to Rudolph, who vows they will never part again. Mimi whispers her love, and dies in his arms while their grief-stricken friends stand at her bedside. There is a complete Victor recording, with Beniamino Gigli as Rudolph, and a Columbia recording made by the soloists, chorus and orchestra of LA SCALA, Milan. There is a wide selection of recordings by famous singers of *Che gelida manina, Mi chiamano Mimi,* and all other important arias, duos, trios and quartets.

Bohemia, in literature, music, drama, painting, and sculpture the name of a community where artists, actors, and literary people live an unconventional life. According to the Stanford Dictionary, the term was introduced from the French who associated Bohemia (La Bohème) with gypsies, by William Makepeace THACKERAY. A novel, *La Vie de Bohème* (The Life of Bohemia) by Henri Murger was not only a great success in 1848, but an instantaneous stage hit as a play in 1849: in 1898 it became the basis of the grand opera, *La Bohème,* by Giacomo Puccini.

Bohemian Girl, The, a grand opera: libretto in English by Alfred Bunn, music by Michael William BALFE; first performed at London in 1843, and at New York in 1844. The story is: Arline, daughter of Count Arnheim, is abducted by Devilshoof, leader of a band of gypsies, and is betrothed to Thaddeus, a Polish exile who has joined the gypsies. Arline is accused of theft at a fair: she is recognized through a scar when brought before her own father for trial, and restored to her proper sphere. She renews her pledge to Thaddeus, who proves to be of noble descent, and when the gypsy queen orders one of the tribesmen to kill Thaddeus, Devilshoof deflects the bullet so that it lodges in the heart of the queen, and disappears as the curtain falls. There is a Victor recording of the overture, and numerous recordings of the ballads, *I Dreamt I Dwelt in Marble Halls* and *Then You'll Remember Me.*

Bohl de Faber, see **Caballero, Fernan.**

Bohm, Max (1868-1923), American painter who studied at the Art School in Cleveland, Ohio, and at Paris. He exhibited successfully at the Paris Salon, lecturing and painting in both London and Paris for several years. His finest works include the group portrait, *The Family; Crossing the Bar; On the Sea* (En Mer); *Nature,* and *The Evening Meal,* the last two in the METROPOLITAN MUSEUM OF ART, New York. Bohm is well represented in many American galleries and museums.

Böhm, Theobald (1794-1881), German flutist and inventor of a system of construction which resulted in a marked improvement in WOODWIND instruments such as the FLUTE, PICCOLO, OBOE, BASSOON and CLARINET, the latter through the aid of Friedrich Klose. As these improvements are of a technical nature, and therefore of interest only to players of the instruments mentioned, they do not require elucidation here: they improved not only the tone but the fingering of the instruments so that musical passages, difficult and in some instances impossible to execute by the old system, can be readily performed.

Bohnen, Michael (1888-), Russian operatic basso who studied at the Conservatory in Keulen, and made his debut in *Der Freischütz* in 1911 at Wiesbaden; sang at Bayreuth and many other European opera houses, and appeared at the Metropolitan Opera House, New York, in *Mona Lisa* in 1923. He created the chief role in *Jonny spielt auf,* a jazz opera by Ernst Krěnek in 1929. Bohnen combines acting ability with a fine voice, and has made many concert tours.

Boiardo, Count Matteo Maria (1434-1494), Italian soldier, diplomat and poet; his great epic, *Orlando Inamorato* (c.1478) was composed for the edification of Duke Hercules and his courtiers: it is one of the most important romantic poems in Italian literature.

Boieldieu, François Adrien (1775-1834), French composer whose only real instruction emanated from Luigi CHERUBINI and Henri MEHUL. From 1803 to 1811 he conducted the Imperial opera at Petrograd, and after his return to Paris taught piano and composition at the PARIS CONSERVATORY. He was one of the foremost composers of opéra-comique: in some respects his melodic ability and dramatic instinct rank him with Carl Maria von WEBER, and in others he is comparable with Daniel AUBER and Adolphe Adam. His numerous operas include *La Dame Blanche,* the overture of which is a standard concert piece; *Jean de Paris* and *Le petit chaperon rouge.*

Boileau-Despreaux, Nicolas (1636-1711), French literary critic and poet who first studied theology and later law, finally devoting himself to writing. His abilities were first recognized when a satire embodying the farewell of a poet to the city of Paris appeared in 1660: a second satire was written in honor of Molière with equal success. His masterpieces, *L'Art poetique* and *Le Lutrin,* appeared in 1674: later several other satires were published, but they were so biting and so conspicuously directed at various prominent people that he was admitted to the French Academy in 1864 only at the insistence of the king.

Boilly, Louis Leopold (1761-1845), French painter and lithographer; son and pupil of Arnould Boilly, a sculptor in wood. He painted some large pictures of the French Revolution and the Empire, but found his greatest inspiration in watching sights on the boulevards, interiors of restaurants, and the entrances to little theatres, and painting soldiers, chess players, street urchins, rag men, and barkers. Among these works are *Distribution of Food in the Champs-Elysées* and *The Arrival of Coaches in the Courtyard.* Boilly's pictures are valuable for their details in respect to the fashions, types, and manners of his time.

Boito, Arrigo (1842-1918), Italian poet, librettist, and composer who studied at the Milan Conservatory: two cantatas composed when he was eighteen won him a gold medal, and two years of travel in foreign countries. His first opera, *Mefistofele,* produced at LA SCALA, Milan, in 1868, for which he wrote both the libretto and music, was a failure because its unusual style offended the opponents of Richard WAGNER: it was remodeled, and has been performed more than five thousand times in opera houses all over the world. An unfinished opera, *Nero,* was completed after his death by Arturo TOSCANINI and produced at La Scala, Milan, in 1924. Boito also wrote the librettos for *La Gioconda* by Amilcare PONCHIELLI, and for *Otello* and *Falstaff* by Giuseppe VERDI.

Bojer, Johan (1872-), Norwegian novelist and dramatist whose first success was the novel, *The Power of a Lie* (1903), later adapted into a popular play. Among other works are *The Great Hun-ger; The New Temple; God and the Woman; The Last of the Vikings; The Emigrants; The Everlasting Struggle.*

Bok, Edward William (1863-1930), American author and editor, born in Holland, and brought to the United States when he was seven. He edited the *Ladies Home Journal* from 1889 to 1919, originating many features of interest to women that combined to make the magazine supreme in its field. His book, *The Americanization of Edward Bok* (an autobiography), won the Pulitzer Prize in 1920: he was greatly interested in peace movements to which he made liberal contributions.

Bok, Marie Louise Curtis (1876-), American patron of music and wife of Edward William Bok. In 1924 she founded and endowed the CURTIS INSTITUTE OF MUSIC, Philadelphia, Pa.: its director for many years was the distinguished pianist, Josef HOFMANN. The Institute provides free instruction under famous teachers for highly talented students. She purchased the Burrell collection of Wagneriana, and brought it to the United States, and has received many honorary degrees, decorations and medals for her services in behalf of music in America.

Boker, George Henry (1823-1890), American poet and dramatist; a graduate of Princeton University. His first play, *Calaynos,* was produced at London (England) in 1849, and the following year at Philadelphia, Pa. His plays include *Leonor de Guzman; Francesca da Rimini; Anne Boleyn; All the World's a Mask:* his poems are also highly regarded.

Bol, Ferdinand (1616-1680), Dutch painter and etcher; said to be one of the favorite pupils of REMBRANDT: his painting of sacred subjects and of portraits compares favorably with that of his famous master. Examples of Bol's work are to be found in nearly all European galleries: among the best are *Joseph Presenting Jacob to Pharaoh,* and his chef-d'oeuvre, *Regents of the Leprosy Hospital.*

Boland, Mary (1885-), American stage and screen actress who made her first appearance at Detroit in *A Social Highwayman.* After considerable experience she appeared at the Savoy Theatre, New York, with Robert Edeson in *Strongheart:* among the many plays in which she had important roles were *The Dictator; Lord Chumley; The Ranger; When Knights Were Bold* (with Francis WILSON); *The Perplexed Husband* (with John DREW); *Alias Jimmy Valentine; The Cradle Snatchers; The Vinegar Tree.* She has appeared in motion pictures since 1932 in comedy roles.

Boldini, Giovanni (1842-1931), Italian painter, pupil of his father, Antonio Boldini, and at the Florence Academy. After traveling extensively, he met Sir Cornwallis West who induced him to settle in London: his success in portrait painting was immediate, and it became the fashion to have one's portrait made by Boldini. Later he lived in Paris, when his work showed the influence of WATTEAU and FRAGONARD: he painted several actresses, among them Eleanora DUSE, in their favorite roles. Among his best portraits are those of

James McNeill WHISTLER, Lina CAVALIERI and the Duchess of Marlborough.

Boldrewood, Rolf, see **Browne, Thomas Alexander.**

Bolero, a Spanish national dance, in lively tempo and ¾ time, in which the dancer accompanies his movement with CASTANETS. It was introduced into Spain during the 18th century, and, like the fandango of which it was a development probably originated in Morocco. Frederic CHOPIN's *Bolero, Op. 19* is an interesting original work, but the most popular dance in this form at the present time was written by Maurice RAVEL.

Bolero (Ravel), an orchestral dance-poem by Maurice RAVEL: it was written for and first produced by the dancer, Ida RUBINSTEIN, as a ballet divertissement of Paris in 1928. It is said that the hypnotic power of the insistent rhythm and the extraordinary performance of Ida Rubinstein roused the audience to a frenzy which resulted in a furore. Ravel was practically unknown as a composer in the United States until the *Bolero* was introduced by Arturo TOSCANINI at a concert of the New York Philharmonic-Symphony Orchestra in 1929. Its première was received with so much enthusiasm that there was good reason to fear that it would be "played out" by constant repetition, but this has not proved true because the exciting rhythm, the colorful orchestration, and the tremendous climax never fail to hold the interest of the audience. There are Victor recordings by the Boston "Pops" Orchestra, and by the Boston Symphony Orchestra conducted by Serge KOUSSEVITZKY; there is also a Columbia recording by the All American Youth Orchestra with Leopold STOKOWSKI.

Boleslawski, Richard (1889-1937), Polish actor, stage director, and producer, born in Warsaw. From 1906 to 1915 he acted in the company at the Moscow Art Theatre, and came to the United States in 1920 after serving in World War I. Among his fine productions were *Revue Russe* (1922); *The Vagabond King; White Eagle; Ballyhoo; Judas:* also many productions for the American Laboratory Theatre. He was also director for several films including *The Woman Pursued; Men in White; Clive of India.*

Bolitho, Hector (1898-), New Zealand novelist and biographer who had some experience in journalism before publishing his first book, *The Island of Wonder,* in 1920. His novels include *Solemn Boy; Judith Silver; The House in Half Moon Street.* He is also considered a more or less accredited biographer of the British royal family: his numerous works of this character include studies of Queen Victoria, the Prince Consort, Edward VIII, and George VI.

Bolm, Adolph (1884-), Russian dancer and choreographer: after graduating from the Russian Imperial School, he organized a tour for Anna PAVLOWA out of Russia, and later joined the DIAGHILEFF Ballet as premier danseur and ballet master, preparing the company for its first appearance in the United States. He appeared at the Metropolitan Opera House, New York, in *Le Coq*

d'Or and *Petroushka;* toured with the Barrère Little Symphony; joined the Chicago Opera Company as premier danseur and ballet master, producing many American modern ballets. In 1940 he created the choreography for PROKOFIEFF'S *Peter and the Wolf* for the BALLET THEATRE.

Bologna, Giovanni da (1524-1608), Flemish sculptor who went to Italy and settled at Florence in 1553. His real name was Jean Bologne or Boullongne: he was also known as *Il Fiammingo* (the Fleming). Among his finest works are a bronze figure of MERCURY in the BARGELLO MUSEUM, Florence; a marble group, *The Rape of the Sabines;* a magnificent fountain at Bologna; an equestrian statue in bronze of Cosimo de Medici, and a finely decorated door at the Cathedral of Pisa.

Bolton, Charles Webber (1855-1942), American architect educated at Lafayette College: he designed more than five hundred churches in the United States including the Central Park Methodist Church in Buffalo; First Methodist in Tulsa, Okla.; Richardson Memorial Presbyterian Church, Bala-Cynwyd Methodist Church, and the West Side Presbyterian Church, all in Philadelphia, and St. Paul's Lutheran Church of Ardmore, Pa. Other buildings for which he drew plans are Brainerd Hall and Gayley Hall at Lafayette College.

Boltraffio, Giovanni Antonio (1467-1516), Italian painter: after studying with LEONARDO DA VINCI, he turned his attention to portraiture, and many of his paintings are to be seen in Italian galleries. He painted several Madonnas including *Madonna and Child; Madonna Casio; Madonna with a Vase of Flowers.*

Bonaparte, see **Napoleon I.**

Bonci, Alessandro (1870-1940), Italian lyric tenor: after studying at the Liceo Rossini, Pesaro, he made his debut in 1896 at Parma in VERDI's *Falstaff* and later at LA SCALA, Milan, in BELLINI's *I Puritani.* His success was immediate, and after singing for ten years in Europe, South America and Australia, he made his debut in 1906 at the MANHATTAN OPERA HOUSE, New York, in Bellini's *I Puritani,* and in 1908 at the Metropolitan Opera House. Bonci had a remarkably beautiful voice which he handled exquisitely: he was one of the few Italian tenors to be recognized as an interpreter of art songs.

Bond, Carrie Jacobs (1862-), American composer of about 175 sentimental songs some of which bid fair to become as permanently popular as those of Stephen FOSTER. She began as an amateur composer, but was so successful that one of her songs, *A Perfect Day,* reached a sale of more than a million copies. Two other songs, *Just a-Wearyin' for You* and *I Love You Truly,* have also enjoyed large sales.

Bond, Jessie (1853-1942), English actress and vocalist who studied with Manuel GARCIA at the Royal Academy of Music, London, and made her debut in GILBERT and SULLIVAN's *H.M.S. Pinafore* in 1878 at the Opéra-Comique, London. In 1879 she appeared in the first production of *The Pirates* *of Penzance* at the Fifth Avenue Theatre, New York: she remained with the Savoy Opera Company until 1899 when she retired. At the time of her death in 1942, she was one of the two remaining members of the original Savoy Opera Company.

Bone, Henry (1755-1834), English painter who specialized in enamel, establishing his reputation by exhibiting a portrait of his wife in 1780 at the Royal Academy, London. His work on china and pottery was so remarkable that in 1800 he was appointed enamel painter to the English court.

Bone, Muirhead (1876-), Scottish painter and etcher: after studying architecture at the Glasgow School of Art, he decided that a painter's career held more interest for him. After studying etchings by MERYON and WHISTLER, he settled in London, giving his first exhibition in 1902, and finally developing into one of the finest draftsmen and etchers of his time. In 1915 he became official artist of the British army during World War I, making remarkably accurate drawings of regions before and after devastation. He also made some fine drawings of scenes in various sections of Spain.

Bonelli, Richard (1894-), American baritone educated at Syracuse University, and a student of dramatic singing with Jean de RESZKE. He made his debut in *Faust* at the Academy of Music, Brooklyn, N. Y., in 1915, and after singing in Europe, became a member of the CHICAGO OPERA COMPANY from 1925 to 1931, and joined the METROPOLITAN OPERA COMPANY in 1932. Bonelli has made many concert appearances with major orchestras, and his repertory includes all the leading baritone roles.

Bones, a device of the PERCUSSION type consisting of two pairs of clappers made of bone, wood or ivory. They are used to mark the rhythm of a dance or song, and performers on them in minstrel shows were extraordinarily expert.

Bonfigli, Benedetto (c.1440-1496), Italian painter; one of a group of artists including PERUGINO who advanced the Umbrian school of painting into the foremost rank. Among his works are frescoes in the Capella dei Priori at Perugia which he began in 1454 and left unfinished in 1496. Many of his signed works are to be seen in Perugia.

Bonheur, Rosa (1822-1899), French painter of Jewish extraction; the eldest of four children all of whom were artists of lesser note than their distinguished sister. Her father was her first teacher, and she also had lessons from Léon COGNIET. She exhibited at the Paris Salon from 1840 to 1855: like her contemporary, Jacques Raymond BRASCASSAT (1804-67), the anatomy of her animals is faultless, and her execution vigorous and firm. Among the finest of her works are *Ploughing in the Nivernais; The Horse Fair; Hay Harvest in Auvergne; Sheep in Repose.*

Bonifazio, Veronese de Pitati (1487-1553), Italian painter of the Venetian school; a pupil of Palma Vecchio and one of the most brilliant painters of his day, portraying scenes (presumed to be sacred in character) embellished with pages, ladies and cavaliers all gayly dressed in rich colors. His works include *The Massacre of the Innocents; Judgment of Solon; Christ Enthroned and Surrounded by Saints.*

Bonington, Richard Parkes (1801-1828), English painter who went to Paris at fifteen, and studied at the ECOLE DES BEAUX-ARTS, and at the atelier of Antoine GROS where all students with revolutionary ideas gathered. He exhibited his first landscapes in 1824 at the Paris Salon, and in 1827 showed several pictures at the Royal Academy, London. His career was ended a year later by his death from consumption. Among his best works are *Grand Canal in Venice; Sea Coast; Coast Scene, Normandy; Henry III, King of France:* some of these show the influence of John CONSTABLE.

Bonnard, Pierre (1867-), French painter who studied at the Académie Julien in Paris with BOUGUEREAU and ROBERT-FLEURY. After working with posters and stage settings, he devoted himself exclusively to painting scenes which reveal the influence of DEGAS, RENOIR, and even of Japanese print-makers especially in the brilliant coloring. He has done much book illustrating for the works of VERLAINE, MIRABEAU and others. His pictures are to be found in many French galleries, and also in American private collections.

Bonnat, Léon Joseph Florentin (1833-1922), French painter; pupil of Federico de Madiazo at Madrid and of Leon COGNIET in Paris, later becoming professor of painting at the ECOLE DES BEAUX-ARTS where he succeeded Paul DUBOIS as director. His portraits are most characteristic of his work, especially those of Victor HUGO, Louis Pasteur and Alexandre DUMAS, but paintings such as *The Martyrdom of St. Denis, Christ Crucified,* and *Roman Girl at a Fountain* are equally distinguished.

Bonnet, Joseph (1884-), French organist and composer; pupil of his father and of Alexander GUILMANT at the PARIS CONSERVATORY. In 1906 he entered and won the competition for the post of organist at Saint-Eustache, a position he has retained for more than thirty-three years. In 1917 his debut in New York was attended with such great success that he toured the United States twice, presenting a series of historical recitals illustrating the development of organ music. His compositions include sacred vocal music, and concert works for the organ.

Bonnie Blue Flag, The, the title of a song popular in the South during the Civil War; the words were written by Harry McCarthy to the tune of an Irish folksong, "The Irish Jaunting Car." The song was first offered at a New Orleans theatre in 1861, causing the greatest excitement with its stirring first line, "We are a band of brothers, and native to the soil."

Bonnivard, François de, see **Prisoner of Chillon, The.**

Bonstelle, Jessie (1870-1932), American actress, theatre manager, and director: after touring with road company in *Bertha, the Beautiful Sewing Machine Girl* and other melodramas, she appeared in theatres managed by Augustin DALY and the SHUBERTS, after which she directed a stock company at the Garrick Theatre, Detroit, for fourteen years. In 1923 she tested new plays for Broadway producers at the Harlem Opera House, New York, and gave the benefit of her experience to many prominent actors including William POWELL, Katharine CORNELL, Melvyn DOUGLAS and Frank MORGAN.

Bonvin, François (1817-1887), French painter distinguished for his small pictures of familiar, home-like scenes such as the living rooms, dining rooms, and kitchens of apartments and houses, depicting housewives busy at household tasks; excellent examples of his work include *A Cook at her Stove; Servant at the Fountain; The Workroom; Men Drinking at an Inn.*

Book, (*a*) in literature the name of any literary work, presumably complete in itself and forming a volume, or if separated into more than one volume, a single co-ordinated literary undertaking. The predecessors of the printed book were PAPYRUS rolls in Egypt as early as 4000 B.C., and clay tablets in Babylonia about 2400 B.C. The first printed book was probably made by the Chinese printer, Wang Chieh, in A.D. 868: it is generally agreed that type for printing originated in China and Korea. The German printer, Johann GUTENBERG is credited with being the inventor of movable type in Europe, and the first book printed from movable type was the Mazarin Bible issued at Mainz, Germany, in 1455. The term "book" is also applied to the various sections of a comprehensive work; the smaller divisions are called chapters. (*b*) In drama the term used for the manuscript of a play: (*c*) in music the term used instead of "libretto" for the texts of operettas, ballets, and musical plays originally written in English.

Bookplate, (*a*) a label, also known as *ex-libris,* placed either in or upon a book to indicate its ownership, or its proper position in a library; (*b*) the engraved plate for printing the label itself. The earliest movable bookplates were on books dated 1480 in Germany where they appear to have originated: the engraving was often the work of such great masters as Albrecht DÜRER, Lucas CRANACH and Hans HOLBEIN. The METROPOLITAN MUSEUM OF ART has a collection of 25,000 bookplates: another series of 4000 is to be seen in the Harvard University Library.

Booth, Barton (1681-1733), English actor: his success in a Latin play while in college induced him to join a theatrical troupe at Dublin in 1698. With the assistance of Thomas BETTERTON he appeared from 1705 to 1708 at the Haymarket Theatre in many tragic roles with uniform success and played at the DRURY LANE THEATRE for twenty years. His greatest parts were the title roles in *King Lear, Antony and Cleopatra, Othello, Julius Caesar,* and in ADDISON's drama, *Cato.*

Booth, Edwin Thomas (1833-1893), American actor, son of Junius Brutus BOOTH; he first appeared in Colley CIBBER's *Richard III* with his father in 1849 at the Boston Museum. After his father's death in 1852, he began to build a high position for himself in the theatre, gaining vast experience by touring California, Australia, England and Germany. He was pronounced superior to Edwin FORREST, and several Shakespearean productions at the Winter Garden Theatre, New York, from 1863-67 were enormously successful. In 1868 he built a magnificent theatre bearing his name in New York: a fine stock company in Shakespearean repertory drew great crowds, but his management was not prudent, and it was taken away in 1874. From that time until 1891, he toured America to rehabilitate his finances. Booth was the founder of the PLAYERS' CLUB, giving up his fine residence in Gramercy Park for its quarters. Among his finest roles were Macbeth, Othello, Shylock, Richard III, Petruchio, Richelieu and Brutus. Otis Skinner's biography, *The Last Tragedian* (1939), offers much new information on his career.

Booth, John Wilkes (1839-1865), American actor, son of Junius Brutus BOOTH, and brother of Edwin BOOTH, with both of whom he appeared in Shakespeare's *Julius Caesar* in 1864, about six months before he assassinated President Lincoln on April 14, 1865, at Ford's Theatre, Washington, D. C., while the president was attending a performance of *Our American Cousin* with Laura KEANE. Twelve days later he was killed while trying to effect his escape from a barn in which he had been hiding.

Booth, Junius Brutus (1796-1852), English actor who was a lawyer, printer, painter, and sculptor before he appeared for the first time on the stage at Deptford in 1813. After touring in the provinces, he was successful in being engaged to play Iago to the Othello of Edmund KEAN at Drury Lane in 1817. In 1821 he came to Richmond, Virginia, appearing in *Richard III*: from that time on he toured the United States until his death. Booth was an eccentric man who also drank to excess, making it difficult to ascertain the exact reasons for his whims. He excelled in such roles as Richard III, Hamlet, King Lear and Shylock: Edwin BOOTH and John Wilkes BOOTH, the latter assassinator of Abraham LINCOLN, were his sons.

Boothby, Guy Newell (1867-1905), Australian novelist who spent much of his life traveling in Asia, Africa, China, Japan, and also in his native country. His novels, chiefly tales of adventure based on his experiences, include *The Beautiful White Devil* (1896) and *Doctor Nikola.*

Boothe, Clare (1903-), American editor and dramatist for many years on the editorial staff of *Vanity Fair.* After writing several plays including *Entirely Irregular* (with Paul Gallico); *O Pyramids* and *Abide With Me,* her greatest success, a satire on society, *The Women,* was produced in 1936. This was followed by *Kiss the Boys Goodbye* in 1938, and *Margin for Error,* the latter arousing the ire of the Nazi government. Her married name is Clare Boothe Luce; in 1942 she was elected a member of Congress.

Bordone, Paris (1495-1570), Italian painter who was a pupil of TITIAN and a disciple of GIORGIONE: he imitated Titian so closely that even today some of Bordone's pictures pass for those of his teacher. There is a *Holy Family* and an *Adoration of the Shepherds* at Venice, but his most admired picture, *Fisherman Returning the Ring to the Doge,* is at the Academy of Venice. Bordone was also a fine portrait painter.

Bordoni, Faustina (1693-1781), Italian dramatic soprano, who was trained by Michelangelo Gasparini who developed her beautiful voice to such a degree that George Frederick HANDEL, after hearing her in Vienna, engaged her for his opera company in London. In 1730 she married the German operatic composer, Johann Adolf HASSE, and shared his successful career at Dresden and Vienna.

Borenius, Tancred (1885-), Finnish teacher and historian of art who became professor of the history of art at University College, London, in 1922. Among his treatises are *English Medieval Painting; Florentine Frescoes; Four Early Italian Engravers; The English Primitives.*

Borghese Gallery (Rome), an art collection housed in the Villa Borghese, designed by a Dutch architect, Jan van Zans (known as Vansanzio), for Cardinal Scipio Borghese. The cardinal had already assembled a fine art collection when the State acquired the building and its art objects in 1901. Many of the masterpieces of Italian art are in the collection such as CORREGGIO's *Danae Overcome By the Prayers of Cupid,* and TITIAN's *Sacred and Profane Love.*

Borghese Warrior, a statue, now in the LOUVRE, Paris; it is presumed to be the creation of AGASIAS, son of Dositheus of Ephesus. The statue is also known as the *Borghese Gladiator,* and is dated about the 1st century B.C.: it is a nude figure in an attitude of rapid advance, the left arm raised above the head, and the right arm (restored) grasping a sword extended downward and backward in the line of the body.

Borgia, Cesare (1476-1507), Italian cardinal and the natural son of Pope Alexander VI who created him Cardinal in 1492: he resigned the Cardinalate in 1497, and married the daughter of the King of Navarre. After engaging in several political conspiracies, he was imprisoned after the death of Alexander VI by both Pope Julius II and the King of Aragon, but finally escaped, and was killed in the service of the King of Navarre. He was a handsome man both educated and eloquent, but an adept in the cruel and perfidious political scheming of his day. His sister, **Lucrezia Borgia** (1480-1519), was married to Giovanni Sforza, lord of Pesaro, but her father, Pope Alexander VI, annulled the marriage and made a more suitable match for her with the natural son of Alfonso II of Naples, Alfonso of Bisceghi, who was murdered by Cesare Borgia in 1500. During the following year she was wedded to the Duke of Ferrara. She was a woman of great beauty, and a patron of the arts. History has completely absolved her of all the shocking crimes, attributed to her by vicious calumniators, which were dramatized by Victor HUGO, and made the subject of an opera by Gaetano DONIZETTI.

Borglum, John Gutzon de la Mothe (1867-1941), American sculptor who studied at the San Francisco Art Association under Virgil Williams, in Paris at the Académie Julien and the ECOLE DES BEAUX-ARTS. After executing some murals he returned to New York in 1902, his work showing evidence of RODIN's influence in his *Mares of Diomedes* and other studies of horses. Among his works are the *Sheridan Monument* and a colossal head of Lincoln in the rotunda of the Capitol, Washington, D. C., figures of apostles in the Cathedral of St. John the Divine, New York; the Lincoln Monument in Newark, N. J. Two gigantic works are the memorial to the leaders of the Southern Confederacy on Stone Mountain, Georgia (planned but only partly executed by him), and the portraits of Washington, Jefferson, Lincoln and Theodore Roosevelt on the side of Mount Rushmore, South Dakota.

Borglum, Solon Hannibal (1868-1922), American sculptor, brother of John Gutzon BORGLUM; he specialized in subjects taken from the daily life of cowboys, Indians, horses and cattle, representing them with extraordinary finesse. Among his creations are *Lassoing Wild Horses; Burial on the Plains; On the Border of White Man's Land; The Last Round-up.*

Borgognone, Ambrogio (c.1450-c.1524), Italian painter and architect whose real name was Ambrogio Stefani da Fossano; the name "Borgognone" had something to do with his affiliation to the Burgundian school of painting. He was a pupil of Vincenzo FOPPA, and his greatest work was accomplished at the Certosa of the Carthusians at Pavia where his painting, *Way to Golgotha,* is to be seen. Other creations include a *Life of Mary* in four panels, a *Coronation of the Virgin,* and an *Assumption* now in the BRERA MUSEUM.

Borgognone, Il, see **Courtois, Jacques.**

Bori, Lucrezia (1888-), Spanish dramatic soprano who studied with Melchior Vidal, and made her European debut as Micaela in *Carmen* at Rome in 1908, and her American debut in *Manon Lescaut* at the Metropolitan Opera House, New York, in 1912. She remained there until 1915, achieving great success in 1914 as Fiora in MONTEMEZZI's *Love of Three Kings.* After an absence of several years as the result of a vocal affliction, she returned to the Metropolitan in 1921, and remained there until her retirement in 1936. She was particularly successful in the principal roles of DEBUSSY's *Pelléas et Mélisande;* Deems TAYLOR's *Peter Ibbetson;* LEONI's *L'Oracolo;* CHARPENTIER's *Louise* and RIMSKY-KORSAKOW's *Snow-Maiden.*

Boris, Ruthanna (1918-), American dancer who studied at the Metropolitan Opera Ballet School, and also with George BALANCHINE. She appeared first as a child of ten in the Metropolitan ballet: in 1934 she performed the solo dances in Balanchine's choreography for *Carmen* at the opera house. At the present time (1943) she is *prima ballerina* at the Metropolitan Opera House: she has also appeared with the American Ballet

Caravan and as guest dancer at the Radio City Music Hall.

Boris Godunoff, (*a*) in drama a historical drama by Alexander PUSHKIN, written in 1826; (*b*) in music an opera founded on Pushkin's drama, the libretto and music by Modeste MOUSSORGSKY; first performed in Russian at St. Petersburg in 1875, and in Italian at the Metropolitan Opera House, New York, in 1913. The revision and re-orchestration of the work by Nicholas RIMSKY-KORSAKOW was used, and Arturo TOSCANINI conducted. In 1921 the role of Boris was sung for the first time by Feodor CHALIAPIN in Russian while the rest of the cast sang in Italian. The story is: Boris Godounoff, regent for the Czarevitch Dimitri, murders him and is crowned Czar amid the acclamations of the people. Gregory, a young monk, determines to avenge the Czarevitch by impersonating him, and leads a Polish army in Russia. The boyars assemble to condemn the pretender, but Godounoff, tortured by remorse, dies after bequeathing his crown in a dramatic speech to his young son. No recordings have been made of the work in its entirety, but, there are Victor recordings of the *Coronation Scene; Varlaam's song, In the Town of Kazan;* the *Monologue,* and the *Death of Boris* by Feodor Chaliapin; also a Columbia recording of the *Revolutionary Scene.*

Borlin, Jean (1893-1931), Swedish dancer and choreographer: at twelve he was a member of the corps de ballet at the Theatre Royal, Stockholm. In 1911, Michel FOKINE came to Stockholm to produce several ballets: Borlin's grace and agility made a favorable impression, and he became his pupil. In 1920 he made his first appearance at Paris in a dance recital, and the successful seasons of the Swedish troupe which he trained began there the same year. He was an exponent of modern ballet, and in reality ahead of his time: among his greatest creations were *Nuit de Saint Jean; Les Vierges Folles; El Greco; L'Homme et son Desir; Skating Rink; The Creation of the World; La Jarre; Relâche.* In most of these he acted as premier danseur.

Bornier, Vicomte Henri de (1825-1901), French poet and dramatist; his first volume of verse, *Les Premières Feuilles,* was well received in 1845, and the Comédie Française accepted his first play, *Luther's Wedding,* during the same year. He held a position for thirty years in the library of the Arsenal: his works include a heroic drama, *The Daughter of Roland,* the libretto of JONCIERE's opera, *Dmitri,* and several novels.

Borodin, Alexander Porfirievitch (1833-1887), Russian chemist and composer: he had very little technical training in music, but learned much from his association with Franz LISZT, and with several distinguished Russian composers including BALAKIREV, MOUSSORGSKY and CUI. His most famous work is the posthumous opera, PRINCE IGOR, completed and orchestrated by Nicholas Rimsky-Korsakow. It was first performed at Moscow in 1890, and at the Metropolitan Opera House, New York, in 1915. Other works include two symphonies (one completed by Alexander GLAZOUNOFF); a symphonic poem, *On the Steppes of Central Russia;* chamber music; songs and piano pieces.

Borowski, Felix (1872-), Anglo-American violinist, composer and music critic who studied at the Cologne Conservatory. In 1897 he became director of the departments of musical history and composition at the Chicago Musical College, and its president from 1916 to 1925. He has lectured at Northwestern University, Ill., acted as music critic for Chicago newspapers and as annotator of the programs of the Chicago Symphony. His works include operas, ballets, orchestral works, chamber music and pieces for piano and violin including the popular *Adoration.*

Borromini, Francesco (1599-1667), Italian architect; one of the chief exponents of BAROQUE architecture of which Jacopo BAROCCHIO was a bitter opponent. Borromini's bold exaggerations, marking a fearless and reckless departure from the traditions of RENAISSANCE, appears to have given him a wide influence, but his works give evidence of both originality and skill, and carry out the principal aim of baroque which is to combine architecture with painting and sculpture. Among his designs in baroque are the Church of St. Agnes in Piazzo Navona, and the church of La Sapienza in Rome.

Boscan Almogaver, Juan (c.1495-1542), Spanish poet of noble birth, and for some years an officer in the army of Spain. His works include a poem in blank verse, *Hero y Leander,* and another poem, *Octava Rima,* which is written in skillful imitation of PETRARCH. His poems were published by his wife in 1543 after his death: he has the distinction of having introduced Italian poetical metres into Spanish literature, thereby founding a new school.

Bosch, Jerome (c.1450-1516), Dutch painter; real name Jerome van Aken, possibly derived from Aix-la-Chapelle where his family originally lived; the name "Bosch" is the Dutch equivalent for Bois-le-Duc where he was born. His career began with designing stained glass and tapestries: one of his first pictures was *The Last Judgment,* followed by *The Walk to Calvary; Adoration of the Magi; The Temptation of St. Anthony; Martyrdom of St. Julia.* Bosch was realistic in his depicting of gloomy souls surrounded by fearful monsters, toads with men's faces, and insects in fantastic shapes and movements.

Bosio, Baron François Joseph (1768-1846), French sculptor; a pupil of PAJOU and rival of Chaudet. After being commissioned by NAPOLEON I to design twenty bas-reliefs for the VENDOME COLUMN, he made busts of Empress Josephine and other members of the royal family. Among his works are an equestrian statue of Louis XIV; a marble group, *The Death of Louis XVI; Love Seducing Innocence; Hercules Fighting Achelous.*

Bosse, Abraham (1602-1676), French painter and engraver; teacher at the Academy of Painting, Paris, and author of important treatises on various phases of art. He engraved more than a thousand scenes of French life in the 17th century: one of his paintings, *The Foolish Virgins,* is to be seen in the CLUNY MUSEUM, Paris.

95

Bossi, Enrico (1861-1925), Italian pianist, organist, conductor and composer; student at the Liceo Rossini, Bologna, and at Milan under several masters including the opera composer, Amilcare PONCHIELLI. He occupied positions as choirmaster and organist, professor of composition and organ, succeeding Giuseppe MARTUCCI as director of the Liceo Musicale at Bologna. He conducted the Benedetto Marcello Society Concerts in Venice, and toured Europe, England, the United States as pianist and organist. His works include operas, orchestral works, sacred vocal works, chamber music; also a method for the modern organ in collaboration with Giovanni Tebaldini.

Bossi, Giuseppe (1777-1816), Italian painter and writer on art subjects: student at the Brera Academy in Milan and later at Rome with CANOVA. His best works include a copy of the *Last Judgment* of MICHELANGELO; the pictures, *Aurora by Night* and *Oedipus and Creon;* a copy of LEONARDO DA VINCI'S *Last Supper;* a series of monochrome drawings depicting scenes in the life of da Vinci, and also two monographs on the latter's life.

Bostonians, The, a light opera company organized in 1887 by Henry Clay BARNABEE, Tom KARL, and William H. Macdonald who were previously connected with the Boston Ideal Opera Company, founded in 1879 to produce Gilbert and Sullivan's *H.M.S. Pinafore.* The Bostonians survived for twenty-five years: among its successful productions by American composers were *Robin Hood, The Fencing Master* and *The Knickerbockers* by Reginald DE KOVEN; *Prince Ananias* and *The Serenade* by Victor HERBERT. Among the singers were Alice NIELSEN, Grace van Studdiford, Jessie Bartlett Davis, Joseph Sheehan, George B. Frothingham and the three founders of the company.

Boston Museum of Fine Arts, an institution on Huntington Avenue, Boston, Mass., which houses remarkable collections of Asiatic, Chinese and Japanese sculpture and painting; also one of the largest and most important collections of prints in the United States. The gallery of Western painting includes representative works by VELASQUEZ, EL GRECO, REMBRANDT, LORENZETTI, CANALETTO, GAUGIN, RUBENS, RENOIR, Van der WEYDEN, CRANACH, INGRES, MILLET, Van GOGH, BLAKE, COPLEY, STUART, Winslow HOMER and Robert HENRI.

Boston Opera Company, an organization founded at Boston, Mass., in 1909 on the lines of the METROPOLITAN OPERA COMPANY, New York. A modern opera house was erected, and the first performance under the direction of Henry RUSSELL took place on Nov. 8, 1909 with Lillian NORDICA, Louise HOMER and Florencio CONSTANTINO in the cast of *La Gioconda.* The company continued until 1914; Henry Russell took it to Paris in the spring of that year for a two-month's season at the Théâtre des Champs-Elysées.

Boston Symphony Orchestra, a symphony orchestra founded by Henry Lee Higginson, banker, in 1881. Sir George HENSCHEL was the first conductor (1881-1884); he was followed by Wilhelm GERICKE, Artur NIKISCH, Emil PAUR, Karl MUCK, Max FIEDLER, Henri RABAUD, Pierre MONTEUX and

in 1924 by Serge KOUSSEVITZKY who still holds the conductor's baton. There have been many distinguished guest conductors including Henry HADLEY, Alfredo CASELLA, Ottorino RESPIGHI, Sir Thomas BEECHAM, E. Fernandez ARBOS, Arthur HONEGGER, Alexander GLAZOUNOFF, Sir Henry WOOD, Sir Adrian BOULT, Dimitri MITROPOULOS, Serge PROKOFIEFF and Nadia BOULANGER. A supplementary season of popular concerts is presented every summer under the baton of Arthur FIEDLER.

Boswell, James (1740-1795), Scottish lawyer who was admitted to the English bar in 1786. In 1766 he visited Corsica where he was entertained by General Pasquale Paoli, the Corsican patriot: Boswell's book, *An Account of Corsica,* appeared in 1786. He made friends with Dr. Samuel JOHNSON in 1763, and accompanied him on a journey to the Hebrides ten years later. An account of this trip appeared in 1786, and his famous *Life of Samuel Johnson* in 1791. Although this biography was decried by Thomas MACAULAY, it is regarded today as one of the finest works of its kind.

Bottesini, Giovanni (1821-1889), Italian composer, conductor, and double-bass virtuoso who studied at the Milan Conservatory. He made his first appearance as a virtuoso in 1840 with tremendous success, and concertized for more than 40 years. He also conducted at Palermo, Barcelona, London and Paris; founded the Quartet Society at Florence, and conducted the première of *Aïda* at Cairo, Egypt, at the request of Giuseppe VERDI. His works include operas; orchestral music; an oratorio; chamber music; a method and solo pieces for double-bass; also several songs.

Botticelli, Sandro (1444-1510), Italian painter; pupil of Fra Filippo LIPPI. His earliest works, *Fortitude* and *Virtues* reveal that, like Lippi, he strove for lineal and lyric beauty rather than plastic strength and direct statement of the subject. In 1477 he painted an *Adoration of the Magi* and portraits of several members of the Medici family: these were followed by the fresco of *St. Augustin* and frescoes of the *Life of Moses* in the Sistine Chapel, Rome. Then came the *Madonna between St. John the Baptist and St. John the Evangelist;* the famous *Spring; The Birth of Venus;* portrait of *Lorenzo Lorenzano; The Coronation of the Virgin* and *Madonna Adoring the Child* in the National Gallery, London.

Bottome, Phyllis (1884-), English novelist whose father was an American clergyman: she lived from 1893 to 1900 in the United States, but has resided abroad since. Her works include *Raw Material* (1905); *Broken Music; The Dark Tower; The Crystal Heart; Old Wine; Belated Reckoning; Plain Case; Windlestraws; Tatter'd Loving; Wind in His Fists; Devil's Due; The Advances of Harriet; Private Worlds; Innocence and Experience; Level Crossing; The Mortal Storm; Murder in the Bud; The Heart of a Child; Masks and Faces; The Mansion House of Liberty; London Pride.*

Bottomley, Gordon (1874-), English poet who had little classical education because of ill-health, but has devoted his life to writing verse. His poems include *The Mickle Drede* (1896); *Poems* *at White-Nights; The Gate of Smaragdus; Chambers of Imagery* (2 series); *A Vision of Giorgione; Poems of Thirty Years; Festival Preludes.* He has also written many dramas and comedies in verse.

Bouchard, Henry (1875-), French sculptor specializing in groups and statues of laborers in many walks of life such as his *Blacksmith in Repose, The Dockhand, The Iron-workers,* and *The Fishermen.* He also created some fine statues of historical figures including a bronze statuette, *Charles the Bold.* One of his finest inspirations is the group, *Girl with a Gazelle,* in bronze, to be seen at the METROPOLITAN MUSEUM OF ART, New York.

Bouchardon, Edme (1698-1762), French sculptor; son of the architect and sculptor, Jean Baptiste Bouchardon, with whom he studied, later continuing his work with Guillaume COUSTOU in Paris. In 1722 he won the first prize at L'Académie Royale for his *Gideon Choosing His Soldiers by Observing the Way They Drank.* Later he acquired a passion for antique art objects, copying many busts and statues. In Rome his works included *Hercules, Sleeping Fawn, Fawn With a Kid, Flute Player* and several busts. In Paris he created a fine equestrian statue of Louis XIV, part of the Fountain of Neptune at Versailles, and the enormous fountain in the Rue de Grenelle on which he worked six years, and earned not only the amount promised him, but also a liberal pension. His marble statuette, *Christ Bearing the Cross,* made him a member of the Académie Royale; this was followed by another fine work, *Cupid Making a Bow from Hercules' Club,* and a fine equestrian statue of Louis XV which stood for nearly thirty years in the Place de la Concorde. Bouchardon selected Jean PIGALLE to finish this work because of ill-health: he died before it was erected.

Boucher, François (1703-1770), French painter regarded as a true son of Paris because he played on its streets as a child, and roamed them as a youth. He was a pupil of François LE MOYNE whose influence as well as that of WATTEAU, is plainly discernible in his works. He finally became a director of the French Academy, after his fortunes were looked after by Mme. de POMPADOUR. His works cover the entire gamut of painting from portraits to landscapes: among the best are *Voluptuary; Birth and Triumph of Venus; Peace and War; Winter Scene; Venus at Her Toilet.* He was also a director of the Gobelin tapestry works, and the weavers profited by his seemingly inexhaustible ability to supply charming scenes for reproduction.

Bouchor, Joseph Felix (1853-), French historical painter, commissioned by the French Government in 1914 to make official paintings of the scenes where the principal battles were fought, and also a series of portraits of the leaders among the Allies in World War I: they are now government property.

Bouchor, Maurice (1855-1929), French dramatist and poet who published a volume of poems, *Merry Songs,* at nineteen; and later several more including *Poems of Love and the Sea; The Mod-*

ern Faust; Stories of Paris in Rhyme. Three odd plays, *Tobie, Noël,* and *Saint-Cécile,* in the form of mysteries without the reverential spirit, were produced at the Marionette Theatre at Paris (1890-92): the actors were lay figures of life size made by his brother, the sculptor, Joseph Felix BOUCHOR. The author with his friends spoke the lines of the plays from behind the wings.

Boucicault, Dion (1822-1890), Irish actor and dramatist: his first play, *London Assurance* (1841) was produced with great success at Covent Garden, but he did not appear as an actor himself until 1852 in his own play, *The Vampire.* On November 10 of the same year, he made his debut at New York in his own play, *Used Up,* followed by the great successes, *The Colleen Bawn, The Octoroon* (an anti-slavery melodrama), and *The Shaughran.* He had much to do with the passing of the first copyright law in 1856, and collaborated with Joseph JEFFERSON in the stage adaptation of *Rip Van Winkle,* produced in 1865 at London, England, with extraordinary success. He either wrote or adapted more than 150 plays in many of which he appeared with his wife, Agnes Robertson: their three children, Dion, Nina and Aubrey all adopted the stage as a profession. Bouicault settled in the United States in 1876, and lived in New York until his death: he wrote an essay *The Art of Acting,* a copy of which may be had in the Columbia University Dramatic Publications.

Boudin, Eugene (1824-1898), French painter who studied at the ECOLE DES BEAUX-ARTS, Paris. His first picture, *The Pardon of St. Anne* (1859) was followed by many landscapes made in Brittany, Normandy and Holland, painted chiefly in foggy weather, and using only grays and blacks. They include *The Beach near Trouville; Low-Tide; The In-coming Tide; Road to Brest; The Pilot-boat; Russian Corvette.* Boudin's canvases are highly valued by connoisseurs, and are to be found in many private collections.

Boughton, George Henry (c.1834-1905), Anglo-American painter who came to the United States as a child: he studied later in Paris, and lived for some time in London, where he was influenced by Frederick WALKER. The delicate grace of his pictures soon assured his reputation: among them are *Return of the Mayflower; The Scarlet Letter; Puritans Going to Church; A Puritan Girl.* He also designed fine illustrations for several books including *Rip van Winkle* by Washington IRVING.

Boughton, Rutland (1878-), English composer and opera impresario; student at the Royal Academy of Music, London, and later conductor of the New Choral Society at Birmingham. He became an advocate of Wagnerian music drama theories, and established an English "Bayreuth" with the aid of Reginald Buckley at Glastonbury for the production of music dramas based on legends of King Arthur. In 1914 the Glastonbury Festival Players produced *The Birth of Arthur* and *The Immortal Hour:* further performances were deferred until after World War I. Boughton's works include *Snow White,* a ballet; *Bethlehem,* a choral drama; *The Round Table,* a music drama; *Alkestis,* a music drama; *The Queen of Cornwall,* a music drama founded on Hardy's play; also orchestral pieces, choral works, chamber music and several treatises on music drama and kindred subjects.

Bouguereau, Adolphe William (1825-1905), French painter whose fame was established by important frescoes such as his *Apollo and the Muses* in the foyer of the Great Theatre at Bordeaux. He was also distinguished as a painter of religious scenes such as *Virgin as a Consoler; Jesus and John the Baptist; The Holy Women at the Sepulchre; Prayer; Invocation.* Among his secular works are *The Return from the Fields; Return of Spring,* destroyed by a fanatic because of its nudity; *The Little Beggar Girls; Sappho; Love Victorious; Love in a Shower.*

Bouilhet, Louis Hyacinthe (1822-1869), French dramatist and poet; a school friend of Gustave FLAUBERT to whom his first poem, *Meloenis,* a story of Rome, was dedicated. His poem, *Fossiles,* attracted interest because it utilized a scientific subject as poetical material: several of his plays were successful including *Madame de Montarcy, Helene Peyron,* and *L'Oncle Million.*

Boulanger, Gustave Rodolphe Clarence (1824-1888), French historical painter; pupil of Paul DELAROCHE. He won the Prix de Rome in 1849, and traveled in Africa. Among his many fine paintings are *Caesar at the Rubicon; Arabian Herdsmen; Hercules at the Feet of Omphale; Horsemen of the Sahara; Caesar at the Head of the Tenth Legion; Arabian Story-Teller; Summer Bath at Pompeii:* he also painted the frescoes for the Foyer de la Danse in the Paris Opera House.

Boulanger, Nadia (1887-), French organist, teacher and conductor; a graduate of the Paris Conservatory. She has taught harmony, counterpoint and history of music at the École normale, Paris; also at the American Conservatory, Fontainebleau. She has visited the United States several times to lecture at Harvard, Radcliffe, Wellesley and other colleges; to conduct the Boston Symphony Orchestra, and to give organ recitals. Among her pupils are Aaron COPLAND, Roy HARRIS, Walter PISTON and Jean FRANCAIX.

Boulle or **Buhl, André Charles** (1642-1732), a French cabinetmaker who originated a fashion of furniture inlay which is now known by his name. At thirty he was among the artisans lodging in the galleries of the LOUVRE, selected by Henry IV to do artistic work for the crown. He was employed for many years at VERSAILLES creating the mirrored walls, the floors in mosaics of wood, and the panelings now regarded as his greatest work. He was an inveterate collector of paintings, engravings and art objects; so much so that he left his three sons a heavily-involved business. Superb examples of his cabinets, commodes, bureaus and tables, resplendent in MARQUETERIE and his own particular style of inlay, are to be seen at VERSAILLES, FONTAINEBLEAU and the LOUVRE.

Boullongne or **Boulogne,** a family of French painters, several of whom achieved fame including **Louis Boullongne** (1609-1674), a painter of historical and religious scenes who studied with Jacques BLANCHARD and at Rome: his works in-

clude paintings for NOTRE DAME, Paris, and decorative work on public buildings. His daughters, Genevieve (1645-1708), and Madeleine (1646-1710) were both painters. His son, **Bon Boullongne** (1649-1717), was his pupil, and studied for five years at Rome under the patronage of Louis XIV: he painted the grand staircase at VERSAILLES under the direction of Charles LE BRUN, decorated several Paris churches, and painted *Juno and Flora* and *The Toilet of Venus* for the TRIANON at Versailles. His brother, **Louis Boullongne** (1654-1733), won the French Academy Prize at eighteen, and studied in Rome where he made full-size copies of RAPHAEL's Vatican frescoes for the GOBELIN tapestry manufactory. He painted the *Purification* and *Flight into Egypt* for NOTRE DAME, Paris, and decorative works at FONTAINEBLEAU, becoming director of the French Academy in 1722 and painter to Louis XIV in 1725.

Boult, Sir Adrian Cedric (1889-), English conductor who studied at Westminster School, Christ Church, Oxford, and the Leipzig Conservatory. He has conducted at the Covent Garden Opera, London; the Birmingham Orchestra; Royal Philharmonic Society, London; the Diaghileff Ballet, London; the London Philharmonic Orchestra; the Birmingham Festival Choral Society; also orchestras at Barcelona, Munich, Prague and Vienna. In 1930 he became musical director and first conductor of the British Broadcasting Company, touring Europe with the orchestra in 1935-36. He is the author of *A Handbook on the Technique of Conducting* (1921).

Bourchier, Arthur (1864-1927), English actor, dramatist, manager, and producer educated at Oxford where he founded the Oxford University Amateur Dramatic Company. He appeared first with Mrs. Lily LANGTRY in 1889; also with Charles WYNDHAM and in New York and London at the theatres controlled by Augustin DALY. In 1894 he married Violet VANBRUGH (sister of Irene VANBRUGH), appearing with her in *The Chili Widow* in a run of 300 nights at the Royalty Theatre, London. He ranked highly as a comedian and tragedian, and appeared for many years with his wife in modern plays at the Garrick Theatre, London, which he managed with Sir Charles WYNDHAM as his partner.

Bourdelle, Emile-Antoine (1861-1929), French sculptor who studied at the École des Beaux-Arts in Toulouse, and the École Nationale des Beaux-Arts in Paris. He also learned much from Jean FALGUIERE and Auguste RODIN, but finally opened his own studio where he could work out his ideas on sculpture, drawing inspiration from ancient Greek and Gothic figures. His works include statues of heroic size such as *Hercules and The Dying Centaur;* reliefs and mural panels for the Théâtre des Champs-Elysées; a frieze for the opera house at Marseilles; an equestrian statue of General Alvear with four symbolic figures surrounding it, at Buenos Aires; memorials to the soldier dead in World War I at Montauban, and to the American soldier dead at Pointe Grave. Bourdelle also illustrated several books, and made fine busts of BEETHOVEN, RODIN and Anatole FRANCE; he was the last of the classic French sculptors.

Bourdet, Edouard (1887-), French dramatist, appointed director of the Comédie Française in 1936. His plays include *The Rubicon; The Open Cage; The Shepherd's Hour; La Prisonnière,* produced at New York as *The Captive,* and permitted to run for several months before being closed by the police. In a duel with Henri BERNSTEIN over the delay in producing the latter's play, *Judith,* Bourdet received a slight wound.

Bourdon, Sebastien (1616-1671), French painter who was first a soldier, and later studied in Rome. His works include an enormous canvas, *Downfall of Simon the Magician* at the Montpelier Cathedral; *The Martyrdom of Saint Peter* at Notre Dame, Paris; portraits of Queen Christina of Sweden and her courtiers; decorations at the Tuileries commissioned by Louis XIV which were completed by Nicholas Lovi, his pupil and rival. In many respects Bourdon was largely an imitator, especially of Claude LORRAIN and Nicholas POUSSIN: his portraits, resembling those of CARAVAGGIO, have more individuality, particularly the likeness of Nicholas Fouquet at VERSAILLES.

Bourgeois Gentilhomme, Le, a humorous ballet in two scenes; libretto founded on Molière's play with the same title; music by Richard STRAUSS; choreography by George BALANCHINE. The plot revolves around the efforts of Cleonte, in love with Lucile, to win permission from Monsieur Jourdain, her socially ambitious father, to marry his lady-love by pretending he is a Turkish prince. As usual, all ends happily after some amusing situations: only a semblance of Molière's play is to be found in the libretto.

Bourget, Paul Charles Joseph (1852-1935), French critic, poet and novelist: his first works were a volume of poems, *Restless Life* (1875), and a volume entitled *Essays on Contemporary Psychology.* These were followed by a long series of psycho-analytical novels beginning with *A Cruel Enigma* (1885); *A Crime of Love; Lies; The Disciple,* considered by many critics his best work. Two of his novels, *The Barricade* and *The Tribune* were successfully dramatized. Many of his books have been translated into English; one entitled *Outre-Mer,* is a volume on America and Americans.

Bourguignon, Le, see **Courtois, Jacques.**

Bourke-White, Margaret (1906-), American photographer and author; her works include *Eyes on Russia* (1931); *U. S. S. R.; North of the Danube,* in collaboration with Erskine Caldwell.

Bourrée, (*1*) in music a movement in the orchestral and instrumental suites of Johann Sebastian BACH, George Frederick HANDEL and other pre-classic composers. (*2*) In the early ballet a dance of French or Spanish origin in rapid 2-4 or 4-4 time.

Boursault, Edmé (1638-1701), French poet and dramatist, who produced his first play at Paris when he was fourteen. He was involved in a long quarrel with Molière whom he rivaled by producing several successful plays including *Le Mercure galant,* the title later changed to *La Comédie sans titre* (1683); *Germanicus; Esope à la ville; Esope à la cour.* His plays were imitated later by Sir John VANBRUGH.

Boursse, Esaias or **Esias** (1630-1673), Dutch painter and disciple of Pieter de HOOCH: his paintings are extremely rare, many of them are marked with the names of Pieter de Hooch or Jan VERMEER. Two signed by Pieter de Hooch at the Rijks Museum in Amsterdam are now known to be the work of Boursse. He specialized in pictures of interiors with figures such as *Woman with a Child in Cradle; Boy Blowing Soap Bubbles; Woman Spinning; Woman Cooking.*

Boutet de Monvel, Bernard (1881-), French painter; son and pupil of Louis Maurice BOUTET DE MONVEL, also of Luc-Olivier MERSON. He served with distinction in World War I, and then spent some time in Morocco, resulting in an exhibition at Paris in 1925 of paintings depicting Arab types and scenes with serene coloring and brilliant lighting contrasts. He has made many portrait-studies of famous persons, and also some exquisite decorative panels.

Boutet de Monvel, Louis Maurice (1851-1913), French painter; pupil of CABANEL, Jules LEFEBVRE and CAROLUS-DURAN. His paintings include *Marguerite and Martha at Church; The Good Samaritan; Lesson Before the Sabbath; Sun Effect in Algeria;* panels illustrating the life of Jeanne d'Arc in the Church at Domremy. He was equally gifted as an illustrator, especially in depicting children for books such as *Songs for Children; Songs of France; Our Children.*

Boutique Fantasque, a humorous ballet in one act: libretto based on an old German ballet; music arranged by Ottorino RESPIGHI from some pieces by Gioacchino ROSSINI discovered by Serge DIAGHILEFF in an album inscribed *Les Riens;* choreography by Leonide MASSINE; first produced at the Alhambra Theatre, London, in 1919. There are nearly thirty characters required for the plot which revolves around a toy shop. The ballet is very old: it was produced with the title, *The Fairy Doll* at St. Petersburg in 1888 with music by Josef Bayer, and revived by Anna PAVLOWA with the same title in New York about 1915. Only the original idea in the old ballet was utilized in the Diaghileff-Massine production.

Bouts, Dierik or **Dirk** or **Thierry** (c.1410-1475), Flemish painter, known not only under the three Christian names given above, but also as **van Haarlem, Stuerbout,** and **Dierik de Louvain.** Little is known of his career except that he was born in Haarlem, spent two years at The Hague, and finally settled in Louvain. His earliest known work is *Portrait of a Man,* dated 1462: others include *Martyrdom of St. Erasmus; The Last Supper; Christ in the House of the Pharisee; The Unjust Sentence of the Emperor Otho; Em-*

peror Otho Repairing His Injustice; Adoration of the Kings. Bouts was an able and sincere painter, but his faces, even in the most dramatic scenes, are invariably placid and serene.

Bouvet, Marie Marguerite (1865-1915), American writer and novelist of French parentage: her first work was a book of quotations from the French. Later she wrote many novelettes for children which became popular: they include *Sweet William; Prince Tip-Top; Pierette; Little Marjorie's Love Story; A Child of Tuscany; Clotilde.*

Bow, Clara (1905-), American screen actress who won fame originally in a beauty contest: one of her first pictures was *Down to the Sea in Ships* in which her characterization of a lovable stowaway led to her being signed to play opposite Glenn Hunter in *Grit.* This was followed by *Black Oxen; Maytime; Poisoned Paradise; Helen's Babies; The Adorable Scofflaw,* and many others of slight but sufficiently entertaining content for the average screen fan. It is said that the pronouncement of Elinor GLYN, author of the most sensational novel of its day, *Three Weeks,* that Miss Bow possessed a certain indefinable quality, known as "it," had much to do with her success.

Bow, a contrivance used on stringed instruments, such as the VIOLIN, VIOLA, VIOLONCELLO, etc., to produce musical sounds. The ancient bows curved outward, but modern bows curve slightly inward: the stick is an elastic wooden rod, and the horse-hairs, numbering from 175 to 250, are attached to the upper part of the stick, called the point or head, and at the opposite end to a mechanism, called the nut, which slides up and down on a screw so that the hairs can be held at any desired degree of tension. The hair is rubbed with rosin so that, as the bow is drawn across the strings, they are set in vibration, and their fundamentally weak tone strengthened by passing through the resonance box, or body of the instrument.

Bowery, The, a street in the lower part of New York, extending from Chatham Square to Cooper Square. It was originally lined on both sides by the farms and estates of Dutch burghers: one of them, the home of the Dutch governor, Peter Stuyvesant, was called *The Bouwerie,* from which the street got its Anglicized name. After the Dutch lost control of New York, and the street became part of the mail-carrier's route to Boston, it gradually degenerated into a highway lined with taverns, and finally with low saloons and dives of every possible description. Nevertheless the Bowery has interest in this volume not only because the famous Episcopal Church, *St. Mark's-in-the-Bouwerie* and other landmarks are still there, but also because some of the city's most important theatrical and musical events took place between 1825 and 1900 in buildings either erected on or near it. Among the buildings may be mentioned the ASTOR PLACE OPERA HOUSE; the Bowery Theatre (burned and rebuilt several times); the Chatham Garden Theatre; the Chatham Theatre; the Cooper Union (Institute); the London Theatre; the National Theatre; the

People's Theatre; the Stadt Theatre; the Thalia Theatre; the Windsor Theatre. Some of the greatest actors including Edwin BOOTH, Junius Brutus BOOTH, Edmund KEAN, James WALLACK, Edwin FORREST, William MACREADY, Charles and Fanny KEMBLE, Tyrone POWER, Ellen TREE, and Charlotte CUSHMAN appeared in these theatres. Many actors of today and yesterday, including Eddie CANTOR, George M. COHAN, Sam BERNARD, De Wolf HOPPER, WEBER AND FIELDS, McINTYRE AND HEATH, Pat ROONEY, Al JOLSON and Francis WILSON, got their first experience in vaudeville or burlesque there. America's greatest composer of ballads, Stephen FOSTER, died on the Bowery. Readers who would know more of its history can find much of interest in *Old Bowery Days* by Alvin F. Harlow.

Bowes, Major Edward, contemporary American theatrical producer, motion-picture theatre manager, and radio director. He was first associated with Archibald SELWYN in producing stage plays; later vice-president of Goldwyn Pictures and managing director of the Capitol Theatre where he instituted the Capitol Family Hour, a popular radio hour from 1925 to 1941. In 1935 he originated the Major Bowes Amateur Hour, one of radio's most successful and apparently permanent features. He published a collection of his favorite poems in 1939 with the title, *Verses I Like.*

Bowker, Richard Rogers (1848-1933), American editor, publisher, and author who edited the important book trade weekly periodical, *Publishers' Weekly,* from 1884 to 1918, and was one of the founders of *The Library Journal* in 1876. His works include *Copyright: Its Law and Its Literature* (1886) and *Copyright: Its History and Its Law* (1912).

Bowman, Patricia, contemporary ballet dancer who made her first appearance at Washington, D. C., at thirteen. Later she danced as *prima ballerina* at the Roxy Theatre, New York, with Leonide MASSINE, and at the RADIO CITY MUSIC HALL; she has appeared as leading dancer with the Mordkin Ballet and the BALLET THEATRE. Michel FOKINE created the ballets, *Persian Angel* and *Tennis,* for her.

Boyd, Belle (1843-1900), American actress, author, and Confederate spy during the Civil War. She was active in the interests of the Southern Confederacy from 1861 to 1863, securing information for General Stonewall Jackson. After being caught and imprisoned twice, she escaped to England where she appeared on the stage in London. When hostilities ceased, she returned to the United States to appear with various stock companies touring the Midwest. Her memoirs, *Belle Boyd in Camp and Prison,* are the chief source of information regarding her accomplishments as a spy.

Boyd, Ernest Augustus (1887-), Irish-American critic and author educated in Switzerland and Germany: his works include *Contemporary Drama of Ireland* (1917); *Ireland's Literary Renaissance; Studies in Ten Literatures; The Pretty Lady.*

Boyd, James (1888-), American novelist educated at Princeton University and Trinity College, Cambridge, England. His novels, all of which cover different periods of American history, are factual and realistic; they include *Drums* (1925); *Marching On; Long Hunt; Roll River; Bitter Creek.*

Boyd, Thomas (1898-1935), American novelist and biographer who enlisted in the Marine Corps during World War I: his works include *Through the Wheat* (1923); *The Dark Cloud; Samuel Drummond; Shadow of the Long Knives; Simon Girty, The White Savage; Mad Anthony Wayne; Light Horse Harry Lee; In Time of Peace; Poor John Fitch, Inventor of the Steamboat.*

Boydell, John (1719-1804), English publisher of prints and engravings: by employing the finest artists his name became a synonym for artistry in engraving. He created a Shakespeare gallery where the finest works of eminent painters were exhibited to the public: a volume of the engravings of these paintings formed a companion work to his illustrated edition of Shakespeare's works.

Boyer, Charles (1899-), French stage and screen actor, trained at the Paris Conservatory. He made his debut in 1920 at Paris in *Les Jardins de Murcie*, later appearing in several other plays, and in his first talking film, *Barcarole*, in 1930. After assuming roles in several French versions of American films at Hollywood, he has appeared in numerous English pictures including *Caravan; Private Worlds; Shanghai; Garden of Allah; History is Made at Night; Mayerling; Conquest; Algiers; Love Affair; All This and Heaven Too; Back Street; Hold Back the Dawn.*

Boyesen, Hjalmar Hjorth (1848-1895), American writer and novelist, born in Norway and graduate of the University of Christiania, who came to the United States in 1869. In 1874 he taught German at Cornell and in 1881 Germanic languages and literature at Columbia University, remaining at the latter institution until his death. His works include *Gunnar* (1874); *Falconberg; The Mammon of Unrighteousness; Tales from Two Hemispheres; A Daughter of the Philistines; Vagabond Tales; Norseland Tales.* He also wrote four volumes of critical studies; a history of Norway; a book of poems, *Idyls of Norway;* four books for boys on life in Norway. One of his short stories, *Ilka on the Hilltop,* was successfully dramatized in 1884.

Boyle, John J. (1851-1917), American sculptor; student at the PENNSYLVANIA ACADEMY OF FINE ARTS, Philadelphia, Pa., and at the ECOLE DES BEAUX-ARTS, Paris. He exhibited at the Paris Salon in 1879; his works include *Stone Age*, Fairmount Park, Philadelphia; *The Alarm*, Lincoln Park, Chicago; *The Savage Age* at the Pan-American Exposition (1901); a statue of *Benjamin Franklin*, Philadelphia, statues of *Plato* and *Bacon* at the Congressional Library, Washington, D. C.

Boyle, Kay (1903-), American novelist and poet who was educated in the United States, and lived abroad from 1922 to 1941 when she returned to America. Her works include *Wedding Day and Other Stories* (1929); *Plagued by the Nightingale; Year Before Last; The First Lover; Gentlemen, I Address You Privately; My Next Bride; The White Horses of Vienna; Death of a Man; Monday Night; Glad Day* (Poems); *The Crazy Hunter; Armistice Diary.*

Boyron, Michel, see **Baron, Michel.**

Boz, see **Dickens, Charles.**

Bracegirdle, Anne (c.1674-1748), English actress: protegé of Thomas BETTERTON, who made her debut on the stage in a juvenile role at six. After appearing in various parts for several years, she played the roles of Araminta in William CONGREVE's *The Old Bachelor* in 1693 and of Angelica in *Love for Love* in 1695, the latter bringing her great acclaim. She was also applauded for her acting in Shakespeare's *Measure for Measure, King Lear* and *The Merchant of Venice*, but left the stage in 1707 because the public preferred Anne OLDFIELD to her in the role of Mrs. Brittle in Betterton's comedy, *The Amorous Widow.* Both Nicholas ROWE and William Congreve were her admirers.

Brackenridge, Hugh Henry (1748-1816), American jurist, novelist, and dramatist: born in Scotland and a judge of the Pennsylvania Supreme Court from 1799 until his death. His works include a novel, *Modern Chivalry, or The Adventures of Captain Farrago and Teague O'Regan, his Servant,* published in four volumes (1792-97): it was a satire on American politics and reprinted several times. He also wrote several plays dealing with the American Revolution, and a volume of patriotic verse.

Bracquemond, Felix (1833-1914), French painter, etcher and porcelain decorator who worked as a lithographer's assistant before he studied painting with a pupil of Jean INGRES. A portrait of his grandmother, painted when he was nineteen, attracted the attention of the novelist, Theophile GAUTIER. Bracquemond finally devoted himself exclusively to engraving and etching: his more than 800 works, which include landscapes, portraits and reproductions of paintings by MEISSONIER, MOREAU and COROT, brought about a revival of the art of etching in France. He was also connected with the SEVRES porcelain and Haviland china factories, and intimate with WHISTLER and other proponents of impressionism.

Brada, Ede (1879-), Austrian dancer and choreographer who was *premier danseur* at the Royal Opera at Vienna and at the Royal Hungarian Opera House at Budapest. He became balletmaster and choreographer at the latter theatre in 1921, retiring to act as dancing instructor at the Franz Joseph Institute at Budapest. He created more than fifty ballets at Budapest; among them *Princess Malve, Prince Argyl,* and *Carnival at Pest.*

Brada, Rezsö (1906-), Hungarian dancer and choreographer; son of Ede BRADA, balletmaster and choreographer for many years of the Royal

Hungarian Opera House, Budapest. He studied with his father, and in the United States with Chester HALE and Albertina RASCH. He became a member of the Royal Opera Ballet in 1921, and was made balletmaster fourteen years later. He has also toured Europe and America as a *premier danseur*, and produced or created the choreography for many ballets including *The Holy Torch, Lysistrata; Hunyadi Laszlo; La Vida Breve,* and *Rip van Winkle.*

Braddon, Mary Elizabeth (1837-), English novelist who wrote verses and short stories at an early age, and published several novels including *Lady Audley's Secret* (1862), *Aurora Floyd, The Legacy, John Marchmont's Legacy,* and many other stories with sensational, melodramatic plots revealing remarkable inventive skill.

Bradford, Roark (1896-), American novelist who worked first on newspapers in Atlanta and New Orleans: his first success came when he won the O. Henry Memorial Award in 1927 for a short story. His Bible stories, *Ol' Man Adam and His Chillun,* published in 1928, were the inspiration for the play, *Green Pastures,* which won the Pulitzer prize for Marc CONNELLY in 1930. Bradford has contributed many stories to national magazines: among his published books are *This Side of Jordan; Ol' King David and the Philistine Boys; How Come Christmas; John Henry and Kingdom Coming.*

Bradford, William (1823-1892), American painter largely self-taught: after painting many scenes on the North Atlantic coast, he accompanied Dr. Hayes on two expeditions to the North Pole, and was the first painter in America to depict scenes in the Arctic Circle. Among these were *The Steamer "Panther" in Medford Bay under the Light of the Midnight Sun; Arctic Whales Homeward Bound; Tracking a Whale in Baffin's Bay; Crushed by Icebergs; Arctic Scene.*

Bradstreet, Anne Dudley (1612-1672), Anglo-American poet, born in England and daughter of Thomas Dudley, four-time governor of Massachusetts in colonial days, and one of the members of the first board of overseers for Harvard College. She came to New England with her husband, Simon Bradstreet, in 1630: a volume of her poems entitled *The Tenth Muse Lately Sprung Up in America* was published in London in 1650, and a second volume, *Several Poems,* was issued at Boston in 1678. The latter contains her finest poems with the title "Contemplations": her verse, while artificial according to modern standards, was well received, and she is regarded as the first woman who sought a literary career for herself in early New England.

Brady, Alice (1892-1939), American stage and screen actress who was the daughter of William A. Brady, a prominent theatrical manager. She first studied for a career in grand opera, but turned to the stage, appearing in Robert MANTELL's production of *As You Like It* in 1909. After playing in Gilbert and Sullivan operettas, and with De Wolf HOPPER in musical plays, she appeared in *Little Women; Sinners; Zander the Great; A Most Immoral Lady; Ladies of the Jury; Mourning Becomes Electra.* She first appeared in the silent films in 1914, and later in many important talking pictures including *When Ladies Meet; Gay Divorcée; In Old Chicago.* Miss Brady's versatility in creating tragic or comedy roles was unique.

Brady, William A. (1863-), American theatrical producer and manager, father of Alice BRADY, distinguished American actress by his first wife, Marie René, and later married to Grace George. He acted himself from 1882 to 1928, and either built or managed the Manhattan Theatre, the Playhouse, and the Forty-eighth Street Theatre (now the Windsor). His productions included *Way Down East; Uncle Tom's Cabin; The Two Orphans; Trilby; The Pit; Bought and Paid For; The White Feather; Alibi; Street Scene; A Church Mouse; Alice Sit-by-the-Fire.* Many famous actresses including Grace GEORGE, Alice BRADY, Helen GAHAGAN, Douglas FAIRBANKS, Mary NASH and Helen HAYES were under his management.

Braekeleer, Henri Jean Augustin de (1840-1888), Belgian painter trained by his father and his uncle, Baron Henri LEYS. He exhibited his pictures, *The Laundry* and *The Coppersmith's Workshop* at Antwerp in 1861, and received medals at Brussels in 1872 for *The Geographer* and *The Lesson;* also at Vienna in 1873 for *The Painter's Studio* and *Grandmother's Birthday.* He was fond of painting interiors with laborers working or drinkers seated around the table: *The Tavern* and *A Man Sitting* are considered his masterpieces.

Braga, Gaetano (1829-1907), Italian violoncellist, trained at the Naples Conservatory: he toured Europe successfully as a virtuoso for many years, finally settling in Paris and in London where he wrote several operas, one of which, *La Reginella* (1871), was a genuine success. He is remembered today as the composer of *The Angel's Serenade,* a song with violin or violoncello obbligato.

Braga Téofilo (1843-1924), Portuguese scholar and poet who studied at the University of Coimbra, and published a series of volumes containing popular romances, songs and fairy tales. His poetical works include *Green Leaves,* a youthful work; *The Vision of Time,* a series of pictures of world evolution written in the Victor HUGO manner; *Undine Lake,* the last-named considered his best creation. In 1870 to 1876, he published a twenty-volume history of Portuguese literature.

Braham, John (c.1774-1856), English operatic tenor of Jewish parentage, the family name being Abraham. His voice failed him after his debut in 1787: after a few years it developed exceptionally fine quality, and in 1796 he appeared at Drury Lane with such success that after he was featured in 1797 at the Italian Theatre, London, in GRETRY's *Azor et Zemire.* He sang for sixty years in European and English houses with undisputed supremacy in opera, oratorio and recital. In 1824 he sang the role of Max in the English version of WEBER's *Der Freischutz,* and created the part of Sir Huön in the same composer's *Oberon*.

Brahma, the name in Hindu religion of the first member of the *Trimurti* or Hindu trinity; Brahma is conceived as the creator of the world which presumably endures for more than two billion years, and then is recreated by him. He is opposed to Vishnu the preserver and Siva the destroyer: his consort, Brahmi or Sarasvati, is the goddess of speech. Images of Brahma represent him in red with four heads.

Brahms, Johannes (1833-1897), German pianist and composer who first studied with his father and later with Eduard Marxsen. In 1853 he toured Europe as accompanist to the Hungarian violinist, Eduard REMENYI: the violinist, Joseph JOACHIM, became interested in his abilities as a pianist and composer, and the result was a lifelong friendship. Joachim introduced him to Franz LISZT and Robert SCHUMANN: Brahms' piano compositions and chamber music works interested Schumann to such an extent that he wrote an article in the *Neue Zeitschrift* (Oct. 8, 1853), declaring that the young Brahms was the great composer of the future. In December, 1853, Brahms gave a concert at Leipzig which resulted in two publishers undertaking to print his compositions, and from that time on he devoted himself to composition, although he assumed the directorship of Singakademie at Vienna for a short time and made occasional concert tours with Joachim. In 1878 he selected Vienna as his permanent home, and remained there until his death. His compositions include the *German Requiem* and many other sacred and secular vocal works such as the *Liebeslieder;* four symphonies; two serenades; two piano concertos; a violin concerto; a concerto for violin and violoncello; two overtures; orchestral variations on a theme by Haydn; many chamber works including string quartets, sextets, piano trios; many sonatas for piano, violin, violoncello and clarinet; numerous piano pieces; nearly three hundred songs; five piano studies and a book of piano exercises. In addition he arranged four volumes of Hungarian dances for piano duet: these brought him a degree of fame which he deprecated because of his feeling that they obscured his original work as a composer. The consensus of opinion appears to be that he was the last of the great classic masters.

Braille, Louis (c.1809-1852), French inventor of a method of printing for the blind. Afflicted with blindness through an unfortunate accident when he was ten years of age, he was admitted to the National Institution for the Young Blind at Paris: later he became a professor there, and not only made his method available for those who desired to read books, but also for those who wished to read music. This was possible because he was a thorough musician, at one time playing the organ in a church at Paris. At the present time many libraries in the United States, Europe and Great Britain have Braille sections for both literature and music. It appears somewhat ironic that his system, the first practical one, was not adopted until some years after his death even in the institution where he had personally proved its efficiency.

Brailowsky, Alexander (1896-), Russian pianist; pupil of Theodor LESCHETIZKY at Vienna in 1911, making his debut at Paris after World War I. Later he toured Europe, South America, Australia, the Orient and Mexico: during 1924 he presented a complete Chopin cycle at Paris and many other cities. He made his American debut in 1924, and toured the entire United States in 1936, presenting all of Chopin's piano works (except those with orchestra) in six recitals at New York in 1937 and 1943. He has also made many fine recordings.

Braithwaite, William Stanley Beaumont (1878-), American Negro poet and anthologist mainly self-educated: he has been given honorary degrees by two Southern colleges for his accomplishments in the field of poetry. His works include *Lyrics of Life and Love* (1916); *Our Essayists and Critics of Today;* Şandy *Star* (Poems); *Frost on the Green Leaf,* short stories. He has also compiled anthologies of magazine verse, British poets, American poets, Massachusetts poets, and *A Contemporary Anthology of Verse by Catholic Sisters.*

Bramante (c.1444-1514), Italian architect and painter whose real name was Donato d'Agnolo; also incorrectly called Lazzari. He was a pupil of Fra BARTOLOMMEO, and also studied architecture with Scirro Scirri; after traveling and working in various towns, he reached Milan in 1476, remaining there for nearly twenty-five years, and then proceeding to Rome. Here he was consulted on almost all important architectural operations, the greatest of which was the rebuilding of ST. PETERS for Pope Julius II. He accomplished a large part of the work which was completed, and considerably altered from the original designs, by MICHELANGELO and Giovanni BERNINI. He also built the long corridor at the Vatican connecting the BELVEDERE with the older palace; his work on the court of the Loggia was completed by RAPHAEL who also painted the mural decorations.

Bramantino (c.1450-c.1535), Italian painter and architect; his real name was Bartolommeo Suardi, his nickname arising from the fact that he was a pupil and imitator of BRAMANTE. His best works include *The Crucifixion; Madonna and the Angels; Flight into Egypt; Piéta.*

Branch, Anna Hempstead (1875-1937), American poet and dramatist educated at Smith College and the Academy of Dramatic Art. She is recognized as a conservative poet with serious purpose as well as passion and imagination, and at her best in verses dealing with home life in her books, *The Heart of the Road* and *The Shoes That Danced.* In 1908 her play, *Rose of the World,* was produced in New York.

Brancusi, Constantin (1876-), Rumanian sculptor: student at the Bucharest Academy of Arts, and pupil of Mercié at the ECOLE DES BEAUX-ARTS, Paris, and at RODIN's studio. His first work of importance was *The Kiss,* an abstract study representing two primitive figures. This work and *The Sleeping Muse* reveal the influence of Rodin, but his creations since 1915, such as *The New Born,* have the polished, egg-shaped characteristics of all his designs. The best examples are his *Bird in Space, Leda,* and *Mlle. Pogany.* Many American museums have his sculptures on exhibition.

Brand, Max, pseudonym of **Frederick Faust** (1892-), author of Western stories, and of the several novels which form the basis of the *Dr. Kildare Series* of motion pictures in which Lionel BARRYMORE has appeared for several years. He is said to have written almost a hundred books under the pen name "Max Brand": the dictated wordage aggregates many millions, and the price paid the highest in the history of the so-called "pulp" magazines. His books have been translated into several languages, and the sales of his engrossingly interesting stories of international spies during World War I were almost as large in England as in the United States.

Brandenburg Concertos, The, a series of six concerti grossi composed by Johann Sebastian BACH in 1721 for the private orchestra of the Margrave of Brandenburg, a German noble greatly interested in music. The Margrave died in 1734, and the six manuscripts were sold with some other music for a ridiculously low price, but fortunately they were preserved. Bach termed them "concertos with several instruments in which two or more play solo parts supported by the rest of the ensemble." There are Columbia recordings of all six concerti by the Busch Ensemble, and Victor recordings by the École Normale Chamber Orchestra at Paris.

Brandes, Carl Edvard Cohen (1847-1927), Danish dramatic critic and novelist: born in Copenhagen of Jewish parentage and educated at Copenhagen University. He first wrote critical works on Danish and European drama, followed by several plays including *A Visit,* translated by William Archer and produced in London about 1890; *A Betrothal; Under a Vow; Under the Rule.* His novel, *Young Blood,* was suppressed, and his plays, said to be the foundation of modern Danish drama, are practically unknown in the United States.

Brandes, Georg Morris Cohen (1842-1927), Danish man of letters, considered the greatest critic in Denmark. He traveled extensively in England, France and Germany, and after becoming acquainted with many distinguished figures in the literary world, wrote numerous works on contemporary literature in the various countries which won him world-wide recognition. Included among these are *Main Currents of Nineteenth Century Literature* (6 volumes, 1871-1890); *French Aesthetics in Our Day; Esaias Tegner; Benjamin Disraeli; Shakespeare; Jesus, a Myth; Creative Spirits of the Nineteenth Century.*

Brandon-Thomas, Jevan (1898-), English actor, producer, and dramatist who made his first appearance in 1919 on the English stage in *Charley's Aunt.* He has appeared since in many plays including *The Yellow Jacket; The Secret Agent;* Shakespearean repertory with the Ben GREET Company; *The Great Adventure; Peg o' My Heart.* He presented his own repertory company at Edinburgh and Glasgow in 1934: his plays

include *The Glory of the Sun* (1925); *Passing Brompton Road; Big Fleas ——,* and several one-act plays.

Brangane, in Richard Wagner's TRISTAN AND ISOLDE the faithful attendant of ISOLDE: when ordered by Isolde to prepare a poison for the wine which she and Tristan are about to take, she pours a love instead of a death potion into the goblet.

Brangwyn, Frank (1867-), Belgian painter born at Bruges of English and Welsh ancestry. He came to London with his father in 1875, and after working with William MORRIS on tapestry designs, began sketching on the English seacoast: his first painting was accepted by the Royal Academy in 1885. Later he traveled and made many sketches in Asia Minor, Constantinople, Russia and South Africa. His works include murals in Skinners' Hall, London, decorative panels in Rockefeller Center, New York City; historical murals for the new Court House, Cleveland, Ohio: also the paintings *Trade on the Beach, Sweetheart Seller,* and *Burial at Sea.* Brangwyn's etchings reveal a remarkable degree of technical skill combined with balanced composition.

Branscombe, Gena (1881-), Canadian pianist and composer who studied at the Chicago Musical College, the INSTITUTE OF MUSICAL ART, and Columbia University, New York; also with Engelbert HUMPERDINCK, and Rudolf GANZ. She has occupied responsible positions as a teacher and conductor: her compositions include a symphonic suite, *Quebec;* works for mixed and male chorus; more than 100 songs; piano pieces; violin pieces.

Bransom, Paul (1885-), American painter and illustrator who specializes in canvases and illustrations picturing animals and forest scenes. Among the books he has illustrated are Jack London's *Call of the Wild;* Charles Robert's *Hoof and Claw;* Kenneth Grahame's *The Wind in the Willows.*

Brant or **Brandt, Sebastian** (1457-1521), German satirical poet; author of *The Ship of Fools* (1494), a satire replete with jovial humor on the follies and vices of his day. It was cleverly illustrated, and translated into English by Henry Watson under the title, *The Grete Shyppe of Fooles of the Worlde* (1508).

Brantôme, Pierre de Bourdeille (c.1540-1614), French traveler, soldier, and author who accompanied Mary STUART to Scotland, and the Knights of St. John in their crusades. After being wounded, he retired to his estates, and occupied twenty years writing his memoirs, consisting of sections entitled *Lives of Illustrious Men; Great Captains of Foreign Countries; Illustrious Men of France; Courteous Ladies.* All the above are merely spicy and vivid accounts, written in charmingly piquant style, of the foibles and frailties of his time.

Branzell, Karin Maria (1891-), Swedish contralto and opera singer; a pupil of Hofer, Bachner and Rosati. She made her debut at Stockholm in 1911, and after singing at the Stockholm and Berlin Opera houses, she appeared as Fricka in *Die*

Walküre at the METROPOLITAN OPERA HOUSE, New York, in 1924. She has made extensive concert tours and has also sung leading soprano roles in opera: her repertory includes principal contralto parts in *Carmen, Aïda, Il Trovatore, Lohengrin, Tristan and Isolde,* and many other operas.

Braque, Georges (1881-), French painter, considered one of the first exponents of FAUVISM, and also one of the founders of CUBISM. His method was to compose pictures of simple architectural forms divided into smaller parts at will and each one treated as a separate unit: most of his pictures are of still life, but there are also some landscapes. He has also added fragments of paper and fabric to his pictures which are to be found in many European and American art galleries.

Bras, in French a word meaning either "arm" or "arms" in reference to the human body. In ballet the term, *bras au repos,* means that the arms are to be at rest: the term, *bras bas,* signifies that the arms are to be held low.

Brascassat, Jacques Raymond (1804-1867), French painter who studied at Paris, and won the Prix de Rome with his painting, *Meleager Hunting.* After creating many landscapes in Italy, he revived the painting of animals in his pictures such as *Landscape with Animals; Study of a Dog; Death of the Boar of Calydon; Bulls Fighting Cow Attacked by Wolves.* He was highly regarded as a draftsman.

Brasher, Rex (1869-), American ornithologist whose superb, life-size paintings of birds in their exact, natural colors have been the subject of favorable comment in artistic circles all over the world. Publication of his monumental work, *Birds and Trees of North America,* in which the plates are hand-colored, was started in 1929.

Braslau, Sophie (1892-1935), American pianist and contralto: pupil of Alexander LAMBERT and of Buzzi Peccia. Her debut was made in *Boris Godunoff* at the Metropolitan Opera House in 1913, where she remained until 1921, appearing in *Carmen, Aïda, Rigoletto,* and *Il Trovatore.* She also appeared in special concerts with Sergei RACHMANINOFF and frequently in radio broadcasts.

Brass-band, an organization in which there are no reed instruments such as CLARINETS, OBOES, BASSOONS or SAXOPHONES: the name differentiates it from the *military band* in which reed instruments are employed.

Bravura, con (It.), in music an expression signifying that a musical passage is to be played boldly and spiritedly.

Bray, Sir Reginald (? -1503), English statesman and architect, created a knight of the Garter by Henry VII, and invested by that monarch with several high offices. He designed the Chapel for Henry VII at Westminster Abbey, and St. George's Chapel at Windsor.

Brecht, Bertolt (1898-), German poet, dramatist, and novelist educated at the universities of Munich and Berlin. His first great dramatic success, *Trommeln in der Nacht,* was produced in 1922: his other plays include *Im Dickicht des Stadt; Baal; Edward II; Mann ist Mann.* He also adapted Jaroslov Hasek's novel, *The Good Soldier,* and prepared a version of John GAY's *Beggar's Opera* with music by Kurt WEILL which ran for more than a year in Berlin, and was also presented on the New York stage. After the Nazi regime was established in Germany, Brecht was exiled and is now living in the United States. His novels include *A Penny for the Poor* which has also been published in English.

Breck, George William (1863-1920), American painter of murals: among his best works are a reproduction of RAPHAEL's *School of Athens* at the University of Virginia; historic murals at the Flower Memorial Library, Watertown, N. Y.; mosaics in St. Paul's Protestant Episcopal Church, Rome, Italy. Breck's paintings are highly regarded both for their fine draftmanship and their vivid coloring.

Brederoo, Gerbrand Adriaanszoon (1585-1618), Dutch poet and dramatist; considered the greatest humorous dramatist of Holland. His poetical works include *The Meditative Song-Book* and *The Great Fountain of Love:* his dramatic masterpieces include *Jerolimo* (Spaansche Brabander Jerolimo), based on a play by Inigo Lopez de MENDOZA, and *Moortje,* an adaptation of a play by TERENCE.

Bree, Mattheus Ignatius van (1773-1839), Flemish painter of historical pictures; student at the Antwerp Academy and at Paris where he won the Prix de Rome in 1797. His pictures include *The Entry of Bonaparte into Antwerp; Death of Egmont; Death of Rubens; Patriotism of Burgomaster van der Werfft.* He became professor at the Antwerp Academy, and later its director.

Breese, Edmund (1871-1936), American actor who made his first stage appearance in a Western stock company. In 1898 he supported James O'NEILL in *The Count of Monte Cristo, Virginius,* and other dramas. In 1906 he made his greatest success in *The Lion and the Mouse.*

Breil, Joseph Carl (1870-1926), American operatic tenor, conductor, and composer who studied at Milan and Leipzig. He sang with the Emma JUCH Opera Company and conducted theatre orchestras: his opera, *The Legend,* was produced at the Metropolitan Opera House in 1919, and he was one of the pioneer composers in the motion-picture field.

Bremer, Fredrika (1801-1865), Swedish novelist born in Finland and educated at Stockholm. Her first success, *The H Family,* was published in 1830: several others including *The Diary, The President's Family, The Home,* and *The Neighbors* were so widely read and translated into German and English that her income permitted her to travel in Europe and America. She recorded her experiences and impressions in *Homes of the New World,* published in 1853 in Sweden, England and the United States. She championed women's rights in the novels *Hertha* and *Father and Daughter*.

Brennan, Alfred Laurens (1853-1921), American pen-and-ink artist who is ranked with the finest illustrators of his day including Edwin Austin ABBEY, Joseph PENNELL and Robert Frederick BLUM. He made more than seven thousand drawings during his long and honored career; a contemporary, Joseph PENNELL, in his book, *Pen Drawings and Pen Draughtsmen*, calls him the finest technician in America.

Brent, George (1904-   ), Irish-American screen actor; graduate of the University of Dublin. He has appeared in many popular films including *So Big; Miss Pinkerton; 42nd Street; Lily Turner; Stamboul Quest; The Right to Live; Special Agent; The Case Against Mrs. Ames; Jezebel; The Old Maid; The Rains Came; The Great Lie; International Lady; Twin Beds*.

Brentano, Clemens (1778-1842), German poet and novelist, and brother of Elizabeth von Arnim. He wrote a life of the Virgin Mary based on alleged revelations, and two excellent volumes of poetry, *The Merry Musicians* and *The Foundling of Prague* which resemble the verses of Heinrich HEINE. His novels include *The Good Kasper* and *Fair Annie;* also a collection of folk tales, *The Boy's Magic Horn,* written in collaboration with his brother-in-law, and published after his death.

Brentano, Elizabeth, see **Arnim, Elizabeth von.**

Brera Museum (Milan), an art collection in the Palazzo di Brera, Naples; originally built as a Jesuit college in 1651, but turned over to the Academy of Fine Arts in 1776. There is a library of about 300,000 volumes, a collection of 60,000 coins, and an excellent observatory in addition to the picture gallery. This was formed in 1806; among its treasures are RAPHAEL's *Sposalizio;* frescoes by BRAMANTINO; pictures by MANTEGNA, CRIVELLI, CIMA, TITIAN, LOTTO, LUINI, REMBRANDT and VAN DYCK.

Breton, Jules Adolphe Aimé Louis (1827-1906), French painter, pupil of Martin Drolling. He was one of the best French painters of village and country life: among his finest works are *The Gleaner; Blessing the Fields; Peasant Girl Knitting; End of the Day; Blessing the Harvest; Vintage at Chateau Lagrange*.

Bretón de los Herreros, Manuel (1796-1873), Spanish dramatist educated at Madrid, and author of more than 350 original plays, the first of which, *A la vejez viruelas* (1824), proved him worthy of being ranked with the leading dramatists of his day in humorous delineation of character, and clever dexterity in metre. His plays, *Marcela; Muérete; y verás!,* and *La Escuela del Matrimonio* (The School for Matrimony) will probably always remain on the Spanish stage.

Breughel, Jan (1568-1625), Flemish painter, elder son of Pieter BREUGHEL, called "Velvet" Breughel for some as yet unknown reason. He specialized at first in painting flowers and fruits, but devoted himself finally to landscapes in two

of which, *Terrestrial Paradise* and *Vertumnus and Pomona,* RUBENS painted the figures. Among his finest works are *Daniel in the Lion's Den; The Five Senses; The Fish Market; Earthly Paradise; Christ Stilling the Tempest; Venus and Cupid in an Armory*.

Breughel, Peter (c.1525-1569), Flemish painter, known also as "Peasant Breughel" and "Breughel the Droll." He was a pupil of Pieter Koeck van Aelst, and also under the influence of Hieronymus Bosch. He spent some of his life in France and Italy, but returned to Antwerp where he was elected to the Academy in 1551. He painted chiefly scenes from peasant life and scriptural subjects including *Triumph of Death; Village Dance; Job on his Dunghill; Peasants' Brawl; Peasants' Frolic; Christ on Lake Genesareth; Children's Frolic; Village Wedding; Return of the Herds*. His son, **Pieter Breughel** (1564-1637), was called "Peter the Younger" to distinguish him from his father, and also "Hell-fire Breughel" because of his partiality for ghostly, diabolical subjects: his pictures are inferior to those of his father in coloring and imagination.

Bréval, Lucienne (1869-1935), operatic soprano who was trained first as a pianist, and later studied voice at the Paris Conservatory. She made her debut in 1892 at the Paris Opera House in MEYERBEER's *L'Africaine*, and remained there as principal soprano for many years, creating the chief roles in many operas by modern French composers, and in first performances of WAGNER's music dramas. In 1900 she made her debut at the Metropolitan Opera House, New York, in MASSENET's *Le Cid*, and in 1901 she sang the role of Brünnhilde in German at Boston, Mass.: her repertory comprised more than fifty important roles.

Breve, in musical notation a note equivalent to two whole notes, the latter called semibreves. The breve is the longest note employed in modern music; it is written in a special way, and rarely met with in ordinary music.

Brevoort, James Renwick (1832-1918), American painter, pupil of Thomas Seir Cummings. During seven years of sketching and painting in Italy, Holland and England he conceived ideas for many fine works including *May Morning on Lake Como; Scene in Holland; Storm on an English Moor; Heidelberg Castle at Sunset; Morning in Early Winter*. He paid particular attention to perspective and color effects in his canvases.

Brian, Donald (1877-   ), Canadian actor and singer who made his first appearance on the New York stage in 1899: since that time he has appeared with great success in numerous musical plays including *Floradora; The Silver Slipper; Little Johnny Jones; Forty-five Minutes from Broadway; The Merry Widow; The Dollar Princess; The Chocolate Soldier; No, No, Nanette*. He has been received with equal favor in plays such as *The Marriage Market; The Courtesan; Becky Sharp; Candle Light; Private Lives; Reunion in Vienna; Accent on Youth; Petticoat Fever*.

Brianza, Carlotta, Italian ballerina; pupil of Carlo BLASIUS, and one of the greatest dancers on the European stage in the latter part of the 19th and the early part of the 20th century. In 1890 she created the role of *The Sleeping Princess* at the Imperial Theatre, St. Petersburg: among those who witnessed her performance was Anna PAVLOWA, then eight years old. Brianza inspired the child to such an extent that she declared her intention to become a great ballerina, a resolution she lived to fulfill in the fullest sense of the word. In 1938, Brianza was known to be teaching the art of dancing in Paris.

Brice, Fanny (1891-), American stage, screen, and radio actress whose real name is Fanny Borach. She studied for the stage under James O'Neill, and after experience in stock companies and vaudeville, appeared in the 1910 edition of Florenz ZIEGFELD's "Follies" with such success that she reappeared every year until 1923 with the exception of two seasons. In 1926 she was starred in the play, *Fanny*, written for her by David BELASCO, and appeared later in several musical productions, revues and films. She has achieved great popularity on a radio program in the role of a troublesome child known as "Baby Snooks."

Brick Architecture, a constructional form first used in Chaldea where the absence of stone rendered it necessary to use sun-dried bricks for the erection of immense monuments. Because of its primary characteristics, brick cannot be employed in architectural construction requiring the use of the COLUMN or ENTABLATURE, therefore the vault form of construction is used for the roof, and either ornamentation or contrasted brick and stone substituted for sculptural decoration. Classic architects regarded brick as ignoble material, but there are fine examples of this type of construction in the Cathedral at Albi, Italy, the Alhambra at Granada, Spain, and on the Place des Vosges, Paris, France.

Brico, Antonia (1902-), American pianist, orchestral conductor: graduate of the University of California, pupil of Karl MUCK in conducting at the State Academy, Berlin, and piano-pupil of Sigismund STOJOWSKI. Her European debut as a conductor was made with the Berlin Philharmonic Orchestra in 1920, and her American debut with the Los Angeles Philharmonic Orchestra in 1930. Since that time she has been guest conductor with many orchestras in the United States and Europe.

Bridge, Ann, the pseudonym under which a contemporary English novelist, whose identity is carefully concealed, has written several successful works among which are *Peking Picnic* which won the *Atlantic Monthly* Prize in 1932; *Ginger Griffin, Illyrian Spring; The Song in the House and Other Short Stories; Enchanter's Nightshade; Four-Part Setting.*

Bridge, Frank (1879-), English violinist, violist, conductor and composer; pupil of Charles Villiers STANFORD, and violist with the JOACHIM QUARTET and the English Quartet. He has also conducted grand opera at Covent Garden, symphony concerts with the Queen's Hall and Royal Philharmonic orchestras, and has been guest conductor of his own compositions with many American orchestras. His numerous orchestral and chamber music works are highly regarded in Europe, Great Britain and the United States.

Bridge, Sir John Frederick (1844-1924), English organist and composer; pupil of John Goss, and organist at Windsor Castle, Manchester Cathedral and WESTMINSTER ABBEY. He taught at the Royal Academy of Music, London; conducted the Royal Choral and the Madrigal Society, and played the organ at Queen Victoria's Jubilee in 1887, and at the coronation of King Edward VII in 1902. His compositions include four oratorios; an overture for orchestra; anthems and other church music; also several important textbooks in harmony and counterpoint.

Bridge, a thin, arched piece of wood, placed in an upright position on the belly (top) of a stringed instrument, on which the strings are placed so that the bow can pass over them, and create musical tones.

Bridge of Sighs, The, a bridge in Venice which spans the Rio della Paglia connecting the Ducal Palace with the Carceri, or prisons. It dates from about 1500, and is located 32 feet above the water; enclosed on the sides with an arched roof overhead. It was divided into two passages through one of which prisoners passed for judgment, and were led to their fate through the other. For many years the bridge of the prison in New York City, known as the "Tombs" and connecting the prison with the trial courts, was also known as the "Bridge of Sighs."

Bridges, Robert Seymour (1844-1930), English poet and dramatist educated at Eton and Oxford who practiced medicine until 1882: his principal works are an essay, *Milton's Prosody* (1893), another on *John Keats*; several dramas including *Nero; Achilles in Scyros; Palicio; The Return of Ulysses; The Christian Captives.* In 1916 he compiled an anthology, *The Spirit of Man:* the last of his poetical works, *Testament of Beauty,* published in 1929, is regarded as his most inspired verse although *The Growth of Love,* a series of sixty-nine sonnets written fifty years earlier, are also highly prized.

Bridgman, Frederick Arthur (1847-1927), American painter who began as a draftsman for the American Bank Note Company, studied art at the Brooklyn Art School and at the National Academy of Design, finally becoming a pupil of Jean Leon GEROME in Paris. After a trip to Egypt, his pictures of the Orient brought him fame: one of them, *Funeral Procession of a Mummy on the Nile,* brought him the cross of the Legion of Honor, and was bought by James Gordon Bennett. His pictures include *An American Circus in Normandy; Procession of the Bull Apis; Rumanian Lady; Nubian Story Teller; Family Bath at Cairo.*

Bridie, James (1888-), Scottish dramatist who began his career as a doctor, and served in the Medical Corps of the English army during World War I. His first play, *The Sunlight Sonata,* was produced in 1928: since then he has written several witty and mentally exhilarating comedies including *What It Is To Be Young; Tobias and* the Angel; The Anatomist; Jonah and the Whale; The Sleeping Clergyman; Marriage Is No Joke.

Brieux, Eugéne (1858-1932), French dramatist who began his playwriting career with a farce comedy, *Bernard Palissy* (1879) in collaboration with Gaston Salandri. Thirteen years later another play, *La Blanchette* was a success: it was followed by many others including *Cogwheels; The Benefactors; The Red Robe; Damaged Goods*, which created a sensation in the United States; *Maternity; False Gods; Because I Love You*. Brieux is regarded by authoritative critics as a reformer intent on discovering practical remedies for specific evils.

Brigg Fair (Delius), an English rhapsody for orchestra by Frederick DELIUS inspired by an old English folk song discovered by Percy GRAINGER to whom the work is dedicated. The construction of the composition is similar in many respects to that of the *Afternoon of a Faun* by Claude DEBUSSY because it makes similar use of reed instruments, muted strings and harp. Delius is a composer who has many staunch admirers, and as many equally sincere detractors: there is a Columbia recording by the Royal Philharmonic Orchestra directed by Sir Thomas BEECHAM.

Briggs, Clare (1875-1930), American cartoonist connected for many years with prominent newspapers in St. Louis, New York, and Chicago. His cartoons such as *When a Feller Needs a Friend, Mr. and Mrs., Ain't It a Grand and Glorious Feeling?*, and *Skin-nay* proved an unfailing source of amusement to American newspaper readers.

Brighouse, Harold (1882-), English dramatist: his first plays, *The Doorway* and *Dealing in Futures*, were produced in 1909, followed by many more written for Miss Horniman's Repertory Company at the Gaiety Theatre, Manchester. His best-known plays are *Hobson's Choice* and *What's Bred in the Bone.*

Brill, Paul (1554-1626), Flemish painter who studied in Rome with his brother, Mattys Brill (1550-1584), and assisted him in painting landscape frescoes at the VATICAN. He remained a true Fleming in the essential sincerity of his execution, thereby influencing even such great artists as RUBENS and CARRACCI. Among his best creations are *Christ Casting Out a Devil* and *Mountain Landscape.* Many of his fine landscapes, some large paintings, and others in miniature, are to be seen at the Ambrosiana, Milan.

Brindisi (It.), in music a drinking song: excellent examples are to be found in operas such as Verdi's *La Traviata*, Donizetti's *Lucrezia Borgia* and Mascagni's *Cavalleria Rusticana.*

Brinsmead, John (1814-1908), English piano manufacturer who founded his own business at London in 1836, and patented an improved action in 1868. His sons, Thomas and Edgar, became partners in the business in 1863; the latter wrote a comprehensive *History of the Pianoforte.*

Brinton, Christian (1870-), American art critic connected for many years with *The Critic* and *Art in America:* his works include *Modern Artists* (1908); *Masterpieces of American Painting; Impressions of Art at the Panama-Pacific Exposition; Introduction to the History of Scandinavian Art.*

Brion, Gustave (1824-1877), French painter; pupil of Gabriel GUERIN, and famous for his pictures of Alsatian peasants such as *Wood Cutters of the Black Forest; Alsatian Wedding; Pilgrims of St. Odile; Wolfhunting in Spain; Brittany Peasants at Prayer.* He also created superb illustrations for "Les Miserables" by Victor HUGO.

Brisé (Fr.), a word meaning "broken," and used in ballet with some other word as *Pas brisé*, a step in which the movement or step is broken; *Brisé volé*, a step in which the dancer crosses the feet in the air, and lands on one foot with the other still raised.

Brisson, Carl (1895-), Danish stage and screen actor, dancer and singer: real name Carl Pedersen. His first stage appearance was made in 1916 as a dancer with his sister: after playing in Sweden in his own musical revues, he appeared at London in *The Merry Widow, The Dollar Princess,* and other musical productions. His screen career began in 1928: among the films in which he has starred are *The Manxman;* Elinor Glyn's *Knowing Men; Two Hearts in Waltz Time; Murder at the Vanities; All The King's Horses.*

Bristol, John Bunyan (1826-1909), American painter, pupil of Henry Ary at Hudson, N. Y. His landscapes first brought him favorable attention: they include *View of Lake Champlain* (1878); *Lake Placid; Valley of the Connecticut; Afternoon in Haying Time; Monument Mountains.* His work is characterized by scrupulous attention to details, and an atmosphere of charm in sentiment and coloring.

Bristol Board, in art a fine quality of calendered cardboard of smooth and satiny texture used to mount drawings in pencil, crayon or water color. Board of extra quality, and pure white in color, is employed for pen and ink drawings designed for reproduction by photo-engraving.

Bristow, George Frederick (1825-1898), American violinist, conductor, and composer who played the violin at the Olympic Theatre, and taught in the public schools of New York City. His opera, *Rip van Winkle,* was produced at Niblo's Garden, New York, in 1855: it was the second opera by an American composer, and enjoyed a run of four weeks. The libretto took quite some liberties with Washington Irving's story: the music was said by critics to be melodious and agreeable, but its orchestration was condemned as "inanimate and lifeless." Bristow also wrote several symphonies, two strings quartets, two oratorios, two cantatas, and numerous pieces for organ, piano, and violin.

British Museum, an English institution in which all the State's treasured possessions in literature, art, and science are assembled. The nucleus of the vast collection, the largest of its kind in the world, is the *Cotton Libraries,* comprising state papers, Biblical and other manuscripts, given to the nation in 1702. The Harleian Library and Sir Hans Sloane art and natural history collections were added by purchase in 1753, and the institution opened to the public in 1759 under its present name in the building known as Montague House. Larger quarters for the rapidly expanding collection were secured by erecting a new building on the same site in 1823, with further additions in 1854, 1873 and 1913. Some slight idea of the immensity of the art treasures it contains may be gathered from the following outline. The library section comprises over 4,000,000 books to which are added by law a copy of every book or literary publication of any description copyrighted in the United Kingdom: there are manuscripts and printed books in all languages. The art sections comprise prints and drawings; Egyptian and Assyrian antiquities including the famous Rosetta Stone; Greek and Roman antiquities; medieval antiquities of Great Britain and Europe; ceramics and objects relating to ethnology; coins and medals. Among the collections that have been added since 1759 are the libraries of George II, George III, and George IV; the antiques assembled by Sir William Hamilton; a collection of Egyptian antiquities; the Elgin marbles; the Sir Henry Layard collection of Assyrian antiquities; the art objects excavated at Halicarnassus by Sir Charles Newton and at Ephesus by J. J. Wood. The great circular reading room with its lofty dome, is located in the quadrangle surrounded by the main building.

Brittain, Vera (1896?-), English poet, essayist and novelist, educated at Somerville College, Oxford, who served as a nurse in army hospitals during World War I. Her works include *The Dark Tide* (1923); *Not Without Honour; Women's Work in Modern England; Halcyon; Testament of Youth; Poems of the War and After; Honourable Estate; Thrice a Stranger; Testament of Friendship.*

Britten, Benjamin (1913-), English pianist composer; pupil of Frank BRIDGE, John IRELAND and Harold SAMUEL. He has written music for the films and for theatrical productions: many of his works have been performed at the festivals held by the *International Society for Contemporary Music* at London, Florence, Barcelona, and Salzburg. Britten's compositions include orchestral pieces, choral works, chamber music, songs and piano pieces.

Brizeux, Julien (1803-1858), French poet and dramatist of Irish ancestry who was educated for the law. In 1827 he collaborated with Philippe Busoni in a one-act comedy in verse, *Racine:* this was followed by a complete translation of *The Divine Comedy;* a set of poems, *Les Ternaires;* a rustic idyl, *Marie; Histories poetiques.* He is regarded as a disciple of Alphonse LAMARTINE, and was a zealous student of Breton philology and archaeology.

Broadhurst, George Howells (1866-1937), Anglo-American journalist and dramatist who came to the United States in 1886: for several years he managed theatres in San Francisco, Milwaukee and Baltimore, and also acted as editor for small newspapers, finally becoming manager of the

Broadhurst Theatre, New York, where many of his plays were produced including *The Coward; What Happened to Jones; Why Smith Left Home; The House That Jack Built; The Crimson Alibi; The Red Falcon* and *Bought and Paid For,* declared by Arnold BENNETT to be the finest commercial play he had ever seen.

Broadwood and Sons, the oldest manufactory still in business of musical instruments with keyboards: it was founded about 1728 by Burkhard Shudi (or Tschudi), a skilled maker of harpsichords, and the business carried on by his son-in-law, John Broadwood, who patented an improved square piano in 1783 and 1788. Later his sons continued the manufacture of square pianos until a grandson, Henry John Tschudi, designed and patented a grand piano which established a fine reputation for the house which is still managed by members of the Broadway family.

Brobdingnag (incorrectly **Brobdignag**), in literature the imaginary country in *Gulliver's Travels,* by Jonathan SWIFT, where everything animate and inanimate is on an enormous scale: its inhabitants are "as tall as an ordinary spire steeple." The word is now used to describe a giant or any object of unusual size such as a "Brobdingnagian" hat.

Broch, Hermann (1886-), German novelist educated in Austria, who was director of a textile manufacturing company when his outstanding symbolistic novel in the form of a trilogy, *The Sleepwalkers,* was published in 1931: it was published in English a year later. In 1934 a second novel of humanitarian character, *The Unknown Quantity* appeared: this was issued in translation a year later. Broch has lived in the United States for some years, and was awarded a Guggenheim fellowship in 1941.

Brock, Sir Thomas (1847-1922), English sculptor; a pupil of John Henry FOLEY at the Royal Academy, London, and influenced to a considerable extent by the romantic tendencies of his day. His works include *The Moment of Peril, The Genius of Poetry;* a bust of Queen Victoria; a bust of Henry W. Longfellow; the memorial statue of Queen Victoria at Buckingham Palace; portrait of Thomas Gainsborough; the colossal equestrian statue of *Edward, the Black Prince,* at Leeds.

Brockway, Howard A. (1870-), American pianist and composer who studied in Berlin with Hans Barth and Otis B. Boise. After concertizing and teaching in New York, he joined the faculty of the Peabody Institute, Baltimore, for several years, and returned to New York to teach piano, composition and musical history at the David Mannes School and the INSTITUTE OF MUSICAL ART. His compositions include a symphony; a sonata and solo pieces for violin with orchestra; chamber music, choral music and piano pieces. He has also edited two volumes of folk songs from the highlands of Kentucky in collaboration with Lorraine Wyman.

Brod, Max (1884-), German poet, essayist, novelist, and dramatist of Jewish extraction educated at the Prague University. He is now living in Palestine where he is director of the Habima Theatre at Tel Aviv. Among his works are a biography of Franz KAFKA and another of Heinrich HEINE: he is also the author of several volumes of poems, essays and plays. Among his works published in English are *The Redemption of Tycho Brahe* (1928); *Reubeni: Prince of the Jews; Three Loves; The Kingdom of Love.*

Brodsky, Adolf (1851-1929), Russian violinist; pupil of Josef HELLMESBERGER and Ferdinand LAUB. He was a member of the Hellmesberger Quartet; professor of violin at the Moscow Conservatory and the Leipzig Conservatory; founder of the Brodsky Quartet; concertmaster of the New York Symphony Orchestra (1891-94); leader of the Hallé Orchestra and successor of Sir Charles Hallé as director of the Royal College of Music at Birmingham, England. Brodsky was intimate with GRIEG, BRAHMS and TSCHAIKOWSKY: he introduced the Tschaikowsky violin concerto at a concert of the Philharmonic Society in 1882 at Vienna.

Brodsky, Vera (1909-   ), American pianist who studied with Alexander LAMBERT and Josef LHEVINNE. After concertizing in Europe and America, she formed a duo-piano ensemble with Harold Triggs in 1932 which appeared successfully in concerts and broadcasts. She also taught duo-piano playing at the CURTIS INSTITUTE OF MUSIC, Philadelphia, and the INSTITUTE OF MUSICAL ART, New York. Since 1941 she has appeared in three series of piano recitals presented by the Columbia Broadcasting Company; the first (1941) presented the principal piano works of Johannes BRAHMS; the second (1942) a series of piano compositions by living American and English composers; the third (1943) offered the rarely heard works of classic and modern Spanish composers. She has also played several concertos with the Columbia Broadcasting Company Symphony Orchestra.

Brome, Richard (?-1652), English dramatist who started his career while acting as a servant to Ben JONSON, a connection which developed into a friendship so firm that knowledge of his personality comes chiefly from Jonson's introductory lines to *The Northern Lasse* (1632), the play that made Brome famous. He wrote fifteen plays among which are *Court Beggar; The English Moor; City Wit; The Love-Sick Court; A Jovial Crew;* all the above titles have an explanatory subtitle in accordance with the custom of the period.

Bromfield, Louis (1896-   ), American novelist and dramatist; in 1926 his novel, *Early Autumn,* won the Pulitzer Prize. Among his successful novels are *Possession; Twenty-four Hours; The Rains Came,* a popular film in 1939; *The Green Bay Tree,* dramatized as *The House of Women* in 1927; *Mrs. Parkington.* His plays include *Times Have Changed* and *De Luxe.*

Brontë, Anne (1820-1849), English poet and novelist who used the pen name "Acton Bell." She published poems with her sister and the novels *Agnes Grey* (1847), and *The Tenant of Wildfell Hall.* She was the sister of Charlotte BRONTE and Emily BRONTE.

Brontë, Charlotte (1816-1855), English poet and novelist who used the pen name "Currer Bell." Her novels, some of which embody personal experiences, include *Jane Eyre* (1847); *Shirley; Villette; The Professor;* and *Emma,* the last-named unfinished. She was the sister of Anne BRONTE and Emily BRONTE: her novel, *Jane Eyre,* added much-needed vitality to novels of the Victorian period, and it was the discovery that her sisters were writing verse that led to the publication in 1846 of a volume of poetry under their pseudonyms.

Brontë, Emily Jane (1818-1848), English poet and novelist who used the pen name "Ellis Bell." Her novel, *Wuthering Heights,* published in 1847, gives evidence of an extraordinarily powerful imagination verging on the fantastic; it was also an immensely popular motion-picture. She was the sister of Anne BRONTE and Charlotte BRONTE.

Bronze, in metallurgy an alloy of copper, tin, and zinc: it is particularly adapted for the casting of statues, statuettes and vases. The Japanese and Chinese were the first to perfect the art of casting in bronze, followed by the ancient Greeks and Romans, and by the Florentine masters including CELLINI, DONATELLO and GHIBERTI. Enormous bronze vases were cast for the gardens in VERSAILLES, and the casting of bronze equestrian statues was carried to the pinnacle of perfection during the 18th and 19th centuries.

Bronzino, Alessandro, see **Allori, Alessandro.**

Bronzino, Il, Italian painter whose real name was Agnolo di Cosimo Allori. He studied with Jacopo da PONTORMO, and, while his frescoes at the Palazzo Vecchio are regarded as artificial and forced, his portraits of Cosimo de' MEDICI, Lucrezia Pucci Panciatichi, DANTE, BOCCACCIO and PETRARCH are highly regarded: some authorities compare him to HOLBEIN the Younger. His largest work, *The Descent of Christ into Limbo* is in the Uffizi Gallery, Florence, and several of his paintings are in London and the United States.

Brook, Alexander (1898-   ), American painter and writer on art trained at the ART STUDENTS LEAGUE, New York City, under John C. Johansen and Kenneth Hayes Miller. After being associated with the Whitney Studio Club and teaching at the Art Students' League, he won several prizes at American exhibitions, and a Guggenheim Fellowship in 1931. His style is characterized by a certain mysticism secured in a peculiarly individual manner by emphasizing dull tones by contrasting brilliant patches of color. He is represented in the Albright Gallery, Buffalo, the Whitney Museum of Modern Art, New York, and several other American galleries.

Brook, Clive (1891-   ), English stage and screen actor: after serving in World War I, he made his first appearance at London in 1920 in *Just Like Judy.* Since that time he has played in many screen successes including *Three Faces East; The Four Feathers; The Return of Sherlock Holmes; The Tarnished Lady; Shanghai Express; Where Sinners Meet; Cavalcade; Gallant Lady; Action* *for Slander; The Ware Case; Return to Yester-day; Convoy.*

Brook, Frances (1724-1789), English dramatist and novelist; several of her romances including *The History of Lady Julia Mandeville* (1763), *Emily Montague,* and *The Excursion* were popular in their day: her stage pieces were inconsequential, and are now entirely forgotten.

Brooke, Henry (c.1703-1783), Irish novelist and dramatist educated at Trinity College, Dublin, and a friend of Alexander POPE. His play, *Gustavus Vasa* (1739) was rehearsed but never performed at the Drury Lane Theatre, London, because it had too strong an element of Irish patriotism, but it was produced in Ireland with great success with the title, *The Patriot.* His most successful novel was *The Fool of Quality,* published in five parts from 1765 to 1770.

Brooke, Rupert (1887-1915), English poet educated at Rugby and Cambridge University. He traveled extensively in Europe, the United States, and the South Seas, and served at the beginning of World War I in the Royal Navy, dying of blood poisoning while a member of the Dardanelles Expedition. His works include *Poems* (1911); *Other Poems:* among the best poems in these volumes are "The Great Lover," "The Old Vicarage," "The Soldier," and "The Dead."

Brooklyn Institute of Arts and Sciences, The, an institution in Brooklyn, N. Y., founded in 1824 for the culture of the arts and sciences, embracing twenty-six departments of which the fine arts division has more than a thousand members. It includes a museum of the arts and sciences, a museum for children, and a botanical garden. The main museum contains an excellent art collection including the James Joseph TISSOT water-color drawings depicting the life of Christ, water colors by John Singer SARGENT, and many sculptures by Antoine Louis BARYE.

Brooks, Charles Shirley (1816-1874), English novelist and dramatist: his successful novels include *Aspen Court* (1855), *The Gordian Knot, The Silver Cord,* and *Sooner or Later;* the last-named illustrated by George DU MAURIER. His plays, principally of the burlesque type, included *Anything For a Change* and *The Daughter of the Stars.* Brooks was a real humorist and wit who numbered William Makepeace THACKERAY among his intimate friends.

Brooks, Maria Gowen (1795-1845), American poet who used the pen name "Maria del Occidente" after her first collection of poems, *Judith, Esther and Other Poems* (1820) was lauded by Robert SOUTHEY. A tragedy, *Zophiel,* was written while she was living in Cuba; her *Idomen* is an autobiography.

Brooks, Richard Edwin (1865-1919), American sculptor and medalist whose *Song of the Wave,* now in the METROPOLITAN MUSEUM OF ART, was recognized by the Paris Salon in 1895; several of his portrait busts are in Statuary Hall, Washington, D. C., and in galleries in other American cities.

Brooks, Van Wyck (1886-), American critic and author of several important volumes of criticism including *The Wine of the Puritans* (1909); *America's Coming-of-Age; The Pilgrimage of Henry James; The Ordeal of Mark Twain; The Life of Emerson; The Flowering of New England; New England: Indian Summer.*

Broome, William (1689-1745), English clergyman and poet educated at Cambridge. He assisted Alexander POPE in translating the ILIAD and ODYSSEY of HOMER, translated some of the odes of ANACREON, and published a volume of verse, *Poems on Several Occasions,* in 1727.

Broschi, Carlo, see **Farinelli.**

Brosse, Salomon de (1565-1626), French architect who built the Palace of the Luxembourg in Paris between 1615 and 1624 for Marie de Médicis, and a hunting lodge for Louis XIII at VERSAILLES which later developed into the magnificent palace sponsored by Louis XIV: also the Parliament House in Rennes, now the Palace of Justice.

Broughton, Rhoda (1840-1920), English novelist, daughter of a clergyman. Her first novel, *Cometh Up as a Flower* (1867), followed by *Not Wisely but too Well* and *Red as a Rose is She,* were regarded as daring experiments to be kept away from young women, but when mid-Victorian ideas of propriety grew more liberal, her abilities were soon recognized. She published about twenty novels: the last one, *A Fool in Her Folly,* appeared posthumously.

Broun, Heywood Campbell (1888-1939), American journalist, essayist, and novelist whose syndicated column appeared in the Scripps-Howard newspapers from 1928 until his death in 1939. His works include *Seeing Things at Night* (1921); *Pieces of Hate; The Boy Grew Older; The Sun Field;* successfully dramatized by Milton Lazarus; *Sitting on the World; Gandle Follows His Nose; Anthony Comstock: Roundsman of the Lord,* with Margaret Leech; *It Seems to Me,* 1925-35. A collected edition of his works was published in 1941.

Brouwer, Adriaen (1605-1638), Flemish painter, said to have been a pupil of Frans HALS, although this has been a matter of dispute. In company with his friend, the painter Joost van Craesbecke, Brouwer sought his inspiration in taverns, police stations and gambling houses: his colorings are excellent and the figures natural and full of spirit. Among his best pictures are *The Drinker; The Smoker; The Village Inn; Spanish Soldiers at Dice; Fiddler in the Tavern; Peasant's Brawl; Surgical Operation; Old Woman at Her Toilet; Peasant Asleep in a Tavern.* The Pinakothek at Munich has many of his pictures which are highly prized by collectors.

Browers, Henry John Isaac (1792-1834), American sculptor who made excellent busts in plaster of John Adams, James Madison, Dolly Madison, Thomas JEFFERSON, DeWitt Clinton and many others distinguished Americans: unfortunately his plans to create a gallery of celebrities in bronze were never realized.

Brown, Alice (1857-), American essayist, novelist and dramatist who was on the editorial staff of *The Youth's Companion* for many years: her works include *Fools of Nature* (1887); *Meadow Grass;* biographies of *Robert Louis Stevenson* and *Mercy Otis Warren; The Prisoner; The Marriage Feast; Tiverton Tales* and *Country Neighbors,* stories of life in New England.

Brown, Bolton (1864-1936), American etcher, lithographer, and painter who studied at the Syracuse University Art School, and later taught drawing and painting at Cornell and Leland Stanford Universities. He gave lectures on a new method of lithography of his invention, and his work was exhibited at many museums and libraries including the LIBRARY OF CONGRESS and the BRITISH MUSEUM. An excellent example of his art, *The Bathers,* may be seen at the National Arts Club, New York.

Brown, Charles Brockden (1771-1810), American novelist many of whose novels attained a considerable vogue in England, France and Germany: he was regarded as the most distinguished American writer of fiction previous to James Fenimore COOPER. His novels include *Wieland,* a story of ventriloquism; *Ormond; Arthur Mervyn,* a tale of the yellow-fever plague of 1793 in Philadelphia; *Edgar Huntley,* a story of somnambulism. His attempts at writing psychological novels were realized later in Edgar Allan POE's tales.

Brown, Eddy (1895-), American violinist and composer who studied with Jenö HUBAY and Leopold AUER, and made a concert tour of Europe at fourteen. He made his American debut at the Metropolitan Opera House, New York in 1916; toured the United States and founded the Eddy Brown String Quartet. In 1930 he started many fine broadcasts on the radio, and founded the Chamber of Music Society of America in 1932. He became musical director of Radio Station WQXR in New York, instituting many outstanding musical programs. He has composed violin pieces and lectured on the history of the violin.

Brown, Ford Madox (1821-1893), English painter, born in Calais, France; he studied at Ghent, with Baron WAPPERS at the Antwerp Academy and with Baron LEYS at the Belgian Academy, where he learned the art of combining historical accuracy with picturesque charm. His pictures are inspired by historical, religious or legendary events: they include *The Dream of Sardanapalus; Cromwell at St. Ives; Romeo and Juliet; Christ Washing Peter's Feet; Chaucer at the Court of Edward III; The Last of England* in which he depicted the emotions of people leaving England to begin life anew in a foreign land.

Brown, Henry Kirke (1814-1886), American sculptor who first attempted to imitate the work of an itinerant silhouette-cutter. He studied painting with Chester HARDING, but eventually turned to sculpture, and studied for four years in Italy. In 1846 he opened a studio at New York and became a successful sculptor of portrait busts and studies of the American Indian. His works include a bust of William Cullen Bryant; an equestrian statue of George Washington, in which he

was assisted by his pupil, John Quincy Adams WARD; another of General Winfield Scott; statues of Lincoln and others for Statuary Hall in the Capitol at Washington, D. C.

Brown, John (1800-1859), American anti-slavery leader in the stirring outbreaks in Kansas previous to the Civil War. On Oct. 16, 1859, he seized the arsenal at Harper's Ferry, Virginia, with the purpose of securing weapons with which to arm the negroes for a general insurrection. He was captured two days later, tried, and executed by the commonwealth of Virginia on Dec. 2, 1859. His death was commemorated in the song, *John Brown's Body Lies a'Mouldering in the Grave,* the tune used being the same as that for *The Battle Hymn of the Republic.*

Brown, John (1810-1882), Scottish physician and essayist on homely subjects such as old-fashioned people, children, and dogs: his writings are tinged with an inimitable degree of pathos and humor, and two of his works, *Rab and His Friends* and *Marjorie,* will live forever in English literature.

Brown, John Carter (1797-1874), American philanthropist who assembled a remarkable collection of books relating to America and published before 1800. It included more than 5500 titles catalogued in four volumes by John Russell Bartlett between 1865 and 1871. Brown himself acquired several thousand additional books before his death, and bequeathed the collection to Brown University, Providence, R. I., together with a fireproof building to house it. The books accumulated by his son, John Nicholas Brown, were later added to the original collection, now known as the John Carter Brown Library.

Brown, John George (1831-1913), American painter, born in England, who studied at the Edinburgh Academy, and at the National Academy of Design, New York, after he came to the United States in 1853. His works, dealing chiefly with child life on the streets, include *Passing Show; Street Boys at Play; Curling in Central Park; His First Cigar; Meditation; Longshoreman's Noon; The Music Lesson:* the last three are to be seen at the METROPOLITAN MUSEUM OF ART, New York.

Brown, John Mason (1900-), American dramatic critic and author; a graduate of Harvard University, and dramatic critic for the *Theatre Arts Monthly* (1924-28); lecturer at the AMERICAN LABORATORY THEATRE (1925-31); dramatic critic of the New York *Evening Post* from 1929, and lecturer at several American colleges on dramatic art. His books include *The Modern Theatre in Revolt* (1929); *Upstage: The American Theatre in Performance; Letters from Greenroom Ghosts; The Art of Playgoing; Two on the Aisle; Broadway in Review; Accustomed As I Am.*

Brown, Mather (1761-1831), American painter of portraits and historical scenes who worked in England. His pictures, many of which are in the National Portrait Gallery, London, include a life-size portrait of George IV at Buckingham Palace; Lord Cornwallis; John Adams; Thomas Jefferson.

His most distinguished historical painting is *Marquis Cornwallis Receiving the Sons of Tippo Sahib as Hostages,* portraying the scene at Arikera in 1791 when Cornwallis defeated the Sultan of Mysore.

Brown, Oliver Madox (1855-1874), English author and painter; son of Ford Madox Brown, from whom he inherited his artistic talent in water-color painting. Although he died young, the stories and poems such as *"The Black Swan"* in his *Literary Remains* (1876), are valued for their imaginative power; Dante Gabriel ROSSETTI wrote a sonnet to his memory.

Brown, Thomas Edward (1830-1897), English physician and poet who made a special study of the manners and people in the Isle of Man: his poems, written in Manx dialect, include *Betsey Lee; Fo'c'sle Yarns; The Manx Witch; The Doctor and Other Poems.* His poem, *My Garden,* has been frequently quoted and set to music.

Brown-Potter, Mrs. James, see **Potter, Cora Urquhart.**

Browne, Charles Farrar, see **Ward, Artemus.**

Browne, Hablot Knight (1815-1882), English artist and illustrator whose only education in his chosen field was obtained as an apprentice to an engraver on steel. In 1833 his drawing, *John Gilpin,* won a prize from the Society of Arts, London, and he had definitely decided on a career as a painter when he met Charles DICKENS in 1836. His illustrations for Dickens' *Pickwick Papers, David Copperfield, Dombey and Son, Bleak House,* and *Martin Chuzzlewit* made him famous: he also made the illustrations for twenty novels by Charles LEVER, and for several of Harrison AINSWORTH's stories.

Browne, Maurice (1881-), English actor, dramatist, and theatre director who came to the United States in 1912 as director of the Little Theatre, Chicago, remaining there until 1918. Among his later productions are *The Trial of Joan of Arc; Iphigenia in Aulis* with Margaret ANGLIN; *Candida; Journey's End; Othello* with Paul ROBESON; *Hamlet* with John GIELGUD; *Street Scene; The Improper Duchess, The Unknown Warrior,* in which he acted himself with a notable success. One of his plays, *Wings Over Europe* (1932), was a distinct contribution to the English drama.

Browne, Thomas Alexander (1826-1915), Australian novelist born in England, and son of Captain Sylvester J. Browne, one of the founders of Melbourne, Australia. His books, which were written with the pen-name "Rolf Boldrewood," include *Ups and Downs; Robbery under Arms; Life and Adventures in the Bush; A Squatter's Dream Story; A Modern Buccaneer.* His experience as a magistrate and commissioner in the Australian goldfields assisted in giving his tales an atmosphere of reality and credibility.

Brownell, William Crary (1851-1928), American critic and essayist who was literary adviser for Charles Scribner's Sons for forty years. His works include *French Traits* (1889); *French Art; Victorian Prose Masters; American Prose Masters; Criticism; Standards; The Genius of Style.* An anthology of his works was prepared by his wife, Gertrude Hall Brownell, herself a poet, novelist and translator of the works of Edmond ROSTAND.

Brownie, in Scottish and Cornish folk tales a goblin who watches over the homes of country people, often doing the household "chores" in the middle of the night when the "folks" are asleep. The well-known author and illustrator, Palmer Cox, embodied his own conception of a "brownie" in a series of popular children's stories.

Browning, Elizabeth Barrett (1806-1861), English poet who was an invalid for many years through the bursting of a blood vessel in her lungs. In 1846 she was secretly married to Robert Browning in spite of the objections advanced by her tyrannical father: the house on Wimpole Street in which she lived previous to her marriage was made the scene of Rudolf Besier's play, *The Barretts of Wimpole Street,* later successfully filmed. Her works include *The Seraphim* (1838); *Sonnets from the Portuguese; Casa Guidi Windows; Aurora Leigh; Isobel's Child; Rhyme of the Duchess May; Romaunt of Margaret.*

Browning, Robert (1812-1889), English poet, dramatist, and husband of Elizabeth Barrett BROWNING. His first dramatic poem, *Pauline,* was published anonymously in 1833; among the works which followed were *Paracelsus; Strafford,* a tragedy produced by William C. MACREADY without success; *Bells and Pomegranates; Men and Women; The Ring and the Book,* dramatized in 1926 by Arthur Goodrich with the title *Caponsacchi,* and enjoying a run of more than six months in New York. It was also used as the basis of an opera produced at Freiburg, Germany, in 1932, the libretto adapted from Goodrich's play, and the music by Richard HAGEMAN. Browning wrote several tragedies, but only one of them, *King Victor and King Charles,* was received favorably when produced in 1842.

Brownlee, John (1901-), Australian baritone educated at Geelong College: Nellie MELBA, a famous operatic soprano also an Australian by birth, encouraged him to study in London with Dinh Gilly, and his debut was made in 1926 at Covent Garden, London, at Melba's farewell appearance in *La Bohème.* After appearing at the Grand Opera, Paris, and touring Europe and South America, he joined the Metropolitan Opera Company, New York, in 1937.

Bruce, Nigel (1895-), English stage and screen actor born in San Diego, Calif., while his parents were touring the United States. He made his debut in 1920 on the London stage in *The Creaking Chair,* followed by appearances in many other plays in London and New York before entering the films in 1931. Among the pictures in which he has had important roles are *Escape; Springtime for Henry; Treasure Island; The Scarlet Pimpernel; Becky Sharp; Under Two Flags; Charge of the Light Brigade; Kidnapped; Suez; The Hound of the Baskervilles; Adventures of Sherlock Holmes; The Rains Came; The Bluebird; Hudson's Bay; Rebecca; Susan and God; Suspicion; Roxie Hart; This Above All.*

Bruce-Joy, Albert (1842-1924), Irish sculptor whose works include portrait busts of Matthew ARNOLD, Mary ANDERSON, King Edward VII and Chauncey Depew. He also modeled colossal statues of William Ewart Gladstone and Arthur Balfour: he possessed an unusual ability to incorporate into each of his portraits the facial expression peculiar to the subject.

Bruch, Max (1838-1920), German pianist and composer who was trained first by his mother, and later by Ferdinand Hiller and Carl REINECKE at the Mozart Foundation, Frankfort. His first symphony was played at Cologne when he was fourteen, and a dramatic work, based on Goethe's SINGSPIEL, *Scherz, List und Rache,* was performed in 1858. After visiting various German cities, he produced his first opera *Loreley* at Mannheim in 1863. The famous G minor violin concerto appeared in 1865, and his opera, *Hermione,* based on Shakespeare's "Winter's Tale," in 1872. Bruce made a visit to the United States in 1883, directing his cantata, *Arminius,* at Boston, Mass.: it was in his epic cantatas, also known as secular oratorios, that he excelled as a composer. His arrangement for violoncello and orchestra of a Hebrew melody, *Kol Nidrei,* is highly regarded. Bruce held many responsible positions as teacher, choral director and orchestral conductor: he was also elected a member of several academies and honored with degrees.

Bruckner, Anton (1824-1896), Austrian organist, teacher and composer: he was chiefly self-taught, but studied so intelligently that he finally secured the position of organist at the Cathedral in Linz-on-Danube in competition with several well-schooled rivals. He studied counterpoint later with Simon Sechter, and succeeded him as court organist and professor at the Conservatory in Vienna. Recitals in France and England established him as one of the greatest organists of his time. His compositions include nine symphonies, a requiem, four masses, several choral works, and a string quintet. Bruckner's greatest accomplishment, according to many authorities, was the transference of Richard Wagner's music-drama technique in instrumentation to the symphony, and in erecting an entirely new structural form in symphonic composition.

Brüll, Ignaz (1846-1907), Moravian composer who studied at the Vienna Conservatory. He made several tours as a concert pianist, playing twenty recitals in London during 1878, and finally settled in Vienna. His first opera, *The Beggar of Samarkand* (1864) was hardly a success, but the second, *The Golden Cross,* produced at Berlin in 1875, was a signal success in all European opera houses; none of his other works in this form attained the same degree of popularity. Brüll's works also include a ballet; several orchestra pieces; two piano concertos, a violin concerto; a piano trio, songs and piano pieces.

Brulov, Karl Pavlovich (1799-1853), Russian painter who studied at the St. Petersburg Academy and in Rome; on his return to Russia he became court painter and professor at the same academy. His finest creations include *Last Day at Pompeii* (1833); *Murder of Inez de Castro;*

The Ascension; also many landscapes as a result of his travels in Greece, Asia Minor and Palestine.

Bruneau, Alfred (1857-1934), French violoncellist and composer: pupil at the Paris Conservatory of FRANCHOMME and MASSENET. He won the Prix de Rome in 1881 with his cantata, *Sainte-Geneviève;* became music critic for several Paris papers; conducted at the Opéra-Comique, and succeeded Ernest REYER as inspector of musical instruction in France. He composed many operas among which *The Attack on the Mill, Messidor, L'Ouragan, La Rêve,* and *Le Roi Candaule* were oustanding successes. He also wrote orchestral works, songs, and ensemble pieces for various combinations of wood and stringed instruments: his critical writings are also of genuine importance.

Brunelleschi, Filippo (1377-1446), Italian architect who first became a skilled goldsmith, designed houses in FLORENCE, and went to ROME for further study. He was one of the first architects to apply the scientific principles of perspective to his plans. Among his important works in Florence are the Pazzi Chapel; the great dome of the Cathedral church of Santa Maria de Fiore which exceeds that of ST. PETER'S, Rome, in some measurements; the Pitti Palace; the churches of San Lorenzo and Santo Spirito.

Brunet, Jacques Charles (1780-1867), French bibliographer, son of a bookseller in Paris; his greatest work was a comprehensive biographical dictionary, regarded as the pioneer book of its kind in European literature, entitled *Manuel du libraire et de l'amateur de livres*. It was published in 1810, and Brunet brought out several revised and enlarged editions.

Brunetière, Ferdinand (1849-1906), French literary and dramatic critic; editor of the *Revue des Deux Mondes* and professor of literature at the École Normale, Paris. He was a critic of the idealist as opposed to the naturalist school: his works include *Epochs in the French Theatre; The Evolution of French Poetry to the 19th Century; The Naturalist Romance; History and Literature.*

Brunner, Arnold William (1857-1925), American architect, graduate of the Institute of Technology, Boston, Mass.; among the important buildings or groups designed by him are the Temple Bethel, New York; the Pennsylvania Capitol, Harrisburg; the Civic Center in Cleveland, Ohio; the buildings at Denison University, Granville, Ohio.

Brünnhilde, the heroine of the cycle of music dramas, *The Ring of the Nibelungs,* written and composed by Richard WAGNER. In The VALKYRIE, the god Wotan deprives her of immortality because she aids the lovers, Sieglinde and Siegmund, and condemns her to slumber on a high mountain, surrounded by fire, until some mortal hero rescues her. In SIEGFRIED, she is rescued by Siegfried, and in The DUSK OF THE GODS, she rides her horse upon Siegfried's funeral pyre, and perishes as Valhalla, the castle of the gods, burns on the distant heights.

Brünnhilde's Immolation, the final scene in Richard WAGNER's The DUSK OF THE GODS; Siegfried has been murdered by HAGEN, and Brünnhilde orders his funeral pyre erected. She gazes long at his prostrate body after he has been laid on the pyre, and sets the fire which is to consume it: then she mounts her winged charger, GRANE, and drives him into the flames. The RHINE MAIDENS draw HAGEN to his death in the deep waters of the RHINE, and the castle of Valhalla, abode of the gods, is aflame. There is a Victor recording of this magnificent scene with Kirsten FLAGSTAD.

Bruno, Paul (1874-), German painter and architect who studied at the School of Applied Arts, Dresden, and the Academy at Munich. His drawings for *Simplizissimus* first attracted favorable attention, and designs for the Fine Arts Industry were also regarded as outstanding: in 1900 he received the Grand Prix in Paris as well as many other medals and honors. After being appointed director of instruction at the Berlin State Museum of Applied Arts, he wrote a treatise, *The Education of Artists at State Schools,* which is considered the finest of its kind.

Brush, George de Forest (1855-1941), American painter who studied at the National Academy of Design, New York, and at the ECOLE DES BEAUX-ARTS under Jean Léon GEROME in Paris. His paintings of North American Indians including *Moose Hunt, Aztec King,* and *Mourning her Brave,* attracted attention from 1883. Many of his works, both pictures and portraits, reveal the influence of Dutch, German, and Flemish masters: these include *Mother and Child; In the Garden; Mother and Children; The Young Violinist; Family Group.* All of these are in American galleries: Brush pictured his wife and children in many of his works.

Brush, Katharine (1902-), American short story writer and novelist who has written film scenarios: her works include *Glitter* (1926); *Night Club* (short stories); *Young Man of Manhattan; Red Headed Woman; Other Women; Don't Ever Leave Me; This is On Me,* an autobiography; *You Go Your Way; The Boy From Maine.*

Brut, in literature a poetical version of the legendary history of Britain by Layamon or Laweman, an English priest who lived about 1200. The work comprises about 64,000 lines, and is a paraphrase of a poetical tale, *Roman de Brut,* by Wace, an Anglo-Norman poet. The manuscript is the property of the BRITISH MUSEUM, London.

Brutus, full name **Marcus Junius Brutus** (85 B.C.-42 B.C.), Roman politician and scholar; at first a friend of Julius Caesar, but later one of the group who assassinated him on March 15, 42 B.C. He joined Cassius in the struggle against Marc ANTONY; when the former was defeated, Brutus committed suicide. The murder of Caesar is the main theme of SHAKESPEARE's *Julius Caesar.*

Bruyn, Bartholomeus (1493-1556), German painter who worked at first in Flemish and German styles, but later in the manner of RAPHAEL and MICHELANGELO. His important works include *The Woman with the Necklace; The Adoration of the Magi; Saint Ursula; Burgomaster Arnold von Brauweiler; St. Catherine; Young Noble and Wife.*

Bryant, William Cullen (1794-1878), American poet and journalist educated at Williams College, and admitted to the bar in 1815. He published his first success, *Thanatopsis,* in 1817; a volume of poetry in 1821, and later joined the staff of the *New York Evening Post,* becoming its editor and part owner in 1829. His works include translations of the ILIAD and the ODYSSEY; complete editions of his poetical works were published in 1883, and of his prose writings in 1884. The latter included *Letters of Travel* originally published in the *Evening Post* and his orations.

Bryaxis, Greek sculptor who lived during the 4th century, B.C., and worked with SCOPAS, LEOCHARES and TIMOTHEUS on the Mausoleum at Halicarnassus about 350 B.C. His work on this memorial cannot be distinguished from his companions, but he is said to have made a great statue of APOLLO at Antioch, and another of SERAPIS at Sinope.

Bryusov, Valery Yakovlevich (1873-1924), Russian short story writer, poet, and novelist who was an admirer, and to a certain extent an imitator of Nicholas PUSHKIN. His works include historical novels, verse and essays on Russian poets: a volume of short stories, *The Republic of the Southern Cross and Other Stories* was published in English (1918).

Buccina, a brass wind-instrument used in the ancient Roman army: it consisted of a narrow brass tube, from eleven to twelve feet in length, bent into the shape of a large C, and played through a cup-shaped mouthpiece. The instrument encircled the player's head like the modern HELICON, and was used for signal purposes, and to sound the night watches, the player being called the *buccinator.* The buccina may be considered the progenitor of the TRUMPET and TROMBONE: three instruments found in the ruins of POMPEII are in the National Museum at Naples.

Buchan, John, 1st Baron Tweedsmuir (1875-1940), Scottish statesman and author educated at Glasgow University and Oxford, and admitted to the bar in 1901. After diplomatic service in South Africa, he became a partner in Thomas Nelson and Sons, Edinburgh; served in World War I on the British Headquarters Staff and as Director of Information under the Prime Minister; represented the Scottish universities in Parliament, and became Governor-General of Canada in 1935. His works include a *History of the Great War* (World War I) published in 1922; biographies of Sir Walter SCOTT, Sir Walter RALEIGH and Julius CAESAR. He also edited several volumes of the *Nations of Today* Series, and wrote many popular novels including *John Burnet of Barns; Prester John; The Thirty-Nine Steps,* later adapted into a very successful film; *Green Mantle; Hunting Tower; Midwinter; John Macnab.*

Buchanan, Robert Williams (1841-1901), Scottish poet, author, and dramatist educated at Glasgow University: his works comprise several volumes of poetry including *London Poems; Napoleon Fallen; The City of Dreams; The Wandering Jew.* He also wrote several plays, and the novels, *The Shadow of the Sword* and *A Child of Nature.* He once attacked Dante Gabriel ROSSETTI who wrote him a letter, now famous, in reply.

Büchner, Georg (1813-1837), German dramatist, also a student of medicine, who is said to have shown the greatest dramatic talent of his period; in the few years of his creative career he wrote a powerful drama of the French Revolution, *Danton's Death* (1835), which was presented by Max REINHARDT, and staged at New York by Orson WELLES in 1938. His tragedy, WOZZECK, was the basis of an opera by Alban BERG.

Buck, Dudley (1839-1909), American organist, conductor and composer who studied with Ignaz MOSCHELES and other masters at the Leipzig Conservatory. He occupied important posts as organist, choral director, and orchestral conductor in the United States, and was one of the first American composers to receive international recognition for his sacred and secular cantatas. His works comprise operas, orchestral pieces; organ sonatas, solo pieces; and transcriptions; organ studies and a treatise on choir-accompaniment. His son, **Dudley Buck, Jr.** (1869-1941), was an opera and concert tenor who studied with Jean de RESZKE in Paris, and made his debut at Sheffield, England, in *Cavalleria Rusticana.* He concertized, taught singing in New York for many years, and in 1939 became permanently connected with the Columbia School of Music in Chicago, Ill.

Buck, Pearl Sydenstricker (1892-   ), American novelist educated at Randolph-Macon College, Virginia. She became a missionary to China where many years of her life were spent with her first husband, John Lossing Buck. Her novels include *East Wind, West Wind* (1930); *The Good Earth,* which was awarded the Pulitzer Prize, staged by the New York Theatre Guild and filmed with Luise Rainer and Paul Muni. Her later novels include *Sons* and *The Mother.*

Buckingham, George Villiers, Duke of (1592-1628), English nobleman and favorite of James I who rescued him several times from the serious consequences of his ill-advised political acts. He was also very close to Charles I, executed in 1649. Alexandre DUMAS, PERE, idealized him in *The Three Musketeers,* using his flirtation with Anne of Austria, and his death at the hands of James FELTON as dramatic incidents.

Bucolics, in literature a term applied to pastoral poetry, and first used in the 14th century to describe the *Eclogues* of VERGIL; Pierre RONSARD also used the word as the general title of his eclogues. The most famous collection of bucolics in ancient literature is that of THEOCRITUS.

Budapest String Quartet, an organization founded at Budapest in 1921, and for more than twenty years one of the foremost chamber ensembles in the world. It has given more than a thousand concerts in Europe, Great Britain, Australia and the United States where it is now permanently located. The quartet appears regularly in concerts and on the radio: it has made many fine recordings.

Buddha (c.562-482 B.C.), the title of *Siddartha* or *Gautama,* the founder of Buddhism, and the son of Suddhodana, a wealthy landowner. His youth was passed in opulence, but at twenty-nine he left his wife and family to become a recluse, emerging from his hermit life with the belief that he was possessed of perfect truth, and calling himself Buddha, "the enlightened." His doctrines were fourfold: (*1*) existence is suffering; (*2*) the cause of pain is desire; (*3*) pain ceases with desire suppressed; (*4*) the way to perfect life is the law of Buddha. The doctrines of Buddha have undergone many changes in two thousand years, but there are 400,000,000 people in Ceylon, Tibet, China, and Japan who are firm believers in them.

Buddhist Art, an art originating in India where BUDDHA was born, although his doctrines no longer hold sway there. The sculpture, however, is more Hellenic in character, and its development can be followed in Tibet, China, Korea, Japan, and other countries where Buddhism is the main religion. Buddha is represented sitting upon a lotus flower with his eyes lowered in the ecstasy which emanates from renunciation of the world and its pleasures. The idea of repose dominates all manifestations of Buddhist art.

Bugle, a wind-instrument, made of brass with a cupped mouth-piece similar to that of the TRUMPET. Here the resemblance ceases: the bugle has a shorter, more conical tube, and is not equipped with keys or valves in the model used for giving military signals. The compass of the instrument is eight notes, but only five are required for the regulation calls in the American army and navy.

Buhl, André Charles, see **Boulle, André Charles.**

Bulfinch, Charles (1763-1844), American architect educated at Harvard. After several years of travel and study in Europe, he settled in 1787 at Boston: among his important works were the Massachusetts State House (1795); the completion of the National Capitol at Washington, D. C.; University Hall, Cambridge; Massachusetts General Hospital; Massachusetts State Prison; also a series of sixteen residences, called "Franklin Crescent" and inspired by the Adelphi buildings erected in London by Robert ADAM in 1762. Bullfinch's work was marked by a happy union of elegance, simplicity, sincerity, and refinement which had a lasting influence on the development of architectural design in the United States.

Bulfinch, Thomas (1796-1867), American author who was graduated from Harvard University in 1814. He was primarily engaged in business enterprises, but found the time to write three books: *The Age of Fable, The Age of Chivalry,* and *Legends of Charlemagne* which are standard in their field.

Bull, John (c.1562-1628), English organist, harpsichordist, and composer; organist at Hereford Cathedral, and successor in 1591 of William Blitheman at the Chapel Royal. He also officiated as organist for the Archduke of Brussels, and at the Cathedral of Notre Dame at Antwerp: he was friendly with Jan SWEELINCK, and exerted great influence on the development of harpsichord and piano music. Bull wrote more than 200 works for the harpsichord and the organ.

Bull, Ole Bornemann (1810-1880), Norwegian violinist and composer: he had some local instruction, but was rebuffed by Ludwig SPOHR, and encouraged only to seek an artistic career when he heard Nicoló PAGANINI play in Paris. His debut was made, with the assistance of Frédéric CHOPIN and Henri ERNST, at Paris in 1832: from that time on his life was a series of brilliant and profitable concert tours in England, Italy, and the United States. His biography was written in 1883 by his second wife, an American lady, Sara Chapman Thorp. His compositions include two violin concertos, and several solo pieces.

Bullen, Frank Thomas (1857-1915), English novelist whose education ended at nine: for some years he traveled to all parts of the world as a sailor. His first successful book, *The Cruise of the Cachelot*, was published in 1906: it was followed by *Call of the Deep* and *A Compleat Sea Cook*. Bullen also wrote many magazine articles and essays on various subjects.

Bülow, Hans Guido von (1830-1894), German pianist, composer, conductor and critic; pupil of Friedrich WIECK and Moritz HAUPTMANN. He manifested genuine sympathy with the radical ideas of Richard WAGNER, and after touring successfully as a pianist, and succeeding Theodor KULLAK as professor of piano at the Stern Conservatory, Berlin, he married Cosima Liszt, and joined Wagner at Munich. After separating from Cosima Liszt, who later married Wagner, he made many concert tours, including 139 concerts in the United States (1875-6); he also developed into one of the greatest conductors of orchestral music.

Bulwer, William Henry Lytton Earle, Baron Dalling and Bulwer (1801-1872), English diplomat and author; elder brother of Edward BULWER-LYTTON, and ambassador to the United States (1849-52). His literary works include *An Autumn in Greece; France, Social, Literary and Political; Historical Characters; Life of Byron.*

Bulwer-Lytton, Edward George Earle Lytton, first Baron Lytton (1803-1873), English poet, dramatist, and novelist: his novels display great versatility, skill in treating psychological and social problems, and variety of incident and portraiture. They include *Falkland* (1827); *Devereux; Paul Clifford; Eugene Aram; Godolphin; Last Days of Pompeii; Rienzi; Ernest Maltravers; The Last of the Barons; The Caxtons; Kenelm Chillingly.* Three of his dramas, *The Lady of Lyons, Richelieu,* and *Money,* in which Charles MACREADY and Sir Henry IRVING appeared, are still in the stock repertory.

Bulwer-Lytton, Edward Robert, first Earl of Lytton (1831-1891), English statesman, poet, novelist, and son of Edward BULWER-LYTTON. He had a brilliant diplomatic career in Europe, and as viceroy of India (1875-80), being made an earl in recognition of his services in the Afghan wars. His works, written under his pseudonym, "Owen Meredith," include *Clytemnestra and Other Poems* (1855), *The Wanderer; Lucile,* a novel in verse; *Orval; Fables in Song; Glenaveril,* or *The Metamorphosis; After Paradise; King Poppy.*

Bunce, Oliver Bell (1828-1890), American author and dramatist: among his works are *Romance of the Revolution* (1852); *A Bachelor's Story; My House: an Ideal; Adventures of Timias Terrystone; Dont: a Manual of Mistakes and Improprieties.* One of his dramatic works, *Love in '76,* was produced by Laura KEANE at New York in 1857, and considered one of the finest plays ever written on the subject of the American Revolution.

Bunce, William Gedney (1840-1916), American painter who studied with William HART in New York, Andreas ACHENBACH in Dusseldorf, and Jean Paul CLAYS in Antwerp. His works include *Venice at Night; Morning at Venice; Twilight in Holland; Sunset in Venice; Watch Hill-Rhode Island; Venetian Boats:* his paintings were poetically conceived, finely drawn, and harmoniously colored.

Bunin, Ivan Alexeievich (1870-), Russian novelist and poet whose first poems, published in 1889, were awarded the Pushkin Prize, the highest literary honor in Russia. He translated *Hiawatha* by Henry W. LONGFELLOW, *Manfred* by Lord BYRON and *Lady Godiva* by Alfred TENNYSON. His greatest novels are *Sukhodel; The Village; An Evening in the Spring; The Gentleman from San Francisco; Mitya's Love;* also a volume of short stories entitled *The Dreams of Chang.* The Nobel Prize was awarded him in 1933 at Paris where he is living in exile.

Bunner, Henry Cuyler (1855-1896), American poet, journalist, short story writer, and editor of *Puck* from 1887 until his death. His works include *A Woman of Honor* (1883); *Airs from Arcady and Elsewhere; The Story of a New York House.* He excelled as a writer of short stories in collected form such as *Zadoc Pine; The Midge;* two series of *Short Sixes; Love in Old Clothes.*

Bunny, John (1863-1915), American screen actor who appeared first as "end-man" for a minstrel show in 1883, entered the films in 1910, and for five years occupied a unique position as the most popular screen comedian with his pictures shown all over the world. He appeared in more than one hundred fifty one-reel comedies.

Bunyan, John (1628-1688), English nonconformist preacher and author arrested in 1660 under the laws against nonconformists, and imprisoned until 1672 when Charles II suspended the statutes. During his incarceration he wrote part of *Pilgrim's Progress,* probably the best known allegory in the English language, completing it in 1684: a dramatic version was prepared by James MacArthur in 1907. His other works include *The Holy War* and *Life and Death of Mr. Badman,* both in allegorical form.

Burbage, James (? -1597), English actor, reputed to have been born near Stratford-on-Avon, who first appeared with the Earl of Leicester's players in 1574. He erected the first building specially intended for plays, and called "The Theatre," in 1576: he also built another theatre called "The Curtain," and converted a large house at Blackfriars into a theatre with the same name. He was the father of Richard Burbage.

Burbage, Richard (c.1567-1619), English actor and principal member of the Lord Chamberlain's Men, Shakespeare's company. He inherited the Blackfriar's Theatre from his father, James Burbage, and is said to have built the Globe Theatre where Shakespeare played from 1599. He is credited with having been the original creator of Hamlet, King Lear, Richard III and Othello. Shakespeare left him a signet ring in his will, and the Felton portrait of Shakespeare is attributed to Burbage by some authorities.

Burch, Gladys (1899-), American author of books relating to music; graduate of the University of Michigan, and since 1933 manager of the music literature department of G. Schirmer, Inc., New York City. Her published books include *Modern Composers for Boys and Girls* and *Richard Wagner Who Followed a Star:* she is also co-author of *The Music Quiz; A Child's Book of Famous Composers; The Junior Quiz; Famous Pianists for Boys and Girls.*

Burchfield, Charles E. (1893-), American painter who studied with Henry G. Keller at the Cleveland School of Art. He developed a penchant for strongly-lined and weird subjects, but after a period of army training during World War I, his viewpoint became more normal and realistic in scenes portraying relics of Victorian architecture, although he still retains a somewhat gloomy atmosphere in such pictures as *November Evening* and *Over the Dam.* His works are chiefly in water-color; they are to be seen in many American museums.

Burgess, Gelett (1866-), American illustrator, designer, and humorist educated at the Massachusetts Institute of Technology, Boston, Mass. After demonstrating his ability as a magazine illustrator, he has written many books including *The Purple Cow; Goops and How To Be Them; Are You a Bromide?; The Maxims of Methusaleh; Why Men Hate Women.* His works in serious vein include *War the Creator.*

Burgess, Neil (1846-1910), American actor who made his first appearance on the stage with Spalding's Bell Ringers in 1865: required on one occasion to assume a female part, he achieved so much success that he continued as a delineator of women's roles. His greatest success was as Abigail Prue in *The County Fair.*

Burgkmair, Hans (1473-1531), German engraver and painter; pupil of his father and of Albrecht Durer. He is credited with the making of more than 700 woodcuts, the most important of which are 135 large-size prints, executed in chiaroscuro and picturing the genealogy and brilliant exploits of Maximilian I. He also painted in fresco and in distemper: his *Holy Family* at the Berlin Gallery is an excellent example of his talent.

Burin, a tool used for cutting by an engraver on metal or on wood: also known as a *graver.* It is made of tempered steel, one end being ground off obliquely to a sharp point, and the handle is flattened on one side so that the burin can be held close to the plate.

Burke, Billie (1885-), American stage and screen actress who made her debut on the London stage at the Prince of Wales Theatre in 1903; she has appeared in many plays including *The Duchess of Dantzic; The Blue Moon; The Belle of Mayfair; My Wife* (with John Drew); *Love Watches; The Amazons; A Marriage of Convenience; The Marquise; The Truth Game; The Vinegar Tree.* She has also appeared in many films including *Craig's Wife; Bill of Divorcement; Dinner at Eight; Becky Sharp; Topper; Topper Takes a Trip; Wizard of Oz; Eternally Yours.*

Burke, Thomas (1886-), English author of short stories, essayist, and novelist: his works include several volumes of short stories including *Limehouse Nights* (1916); *Twinkletoes; More Limehouse Nights; East of Mansion House; A Tea-Shop in Limehouse; Night Pieces.* His novels include *The Wind and the Rain* (1926); *Abduction: A Story of Limehouse;* also many volumes of poetry and essays.

Burleigh, Cecil (1885-), American violinist and composer; pupil of Emile Sauret, Hugo Heerman and Felix Borowski. After several years of concertizing, he has taught the violin at many American musical institutions including the Western Institute of Music in Denver, Colo., and the University of Wisconsin. His compositions include orchestral pieces; violin concertos; violin sonatas; a violin suite, many characteristic violin solos, and pieces for the piano.

Burleigh, Henry Thacker (1866-), American Negro composer and baritone who studied at the National Conservatory, New York, where he later taught singing. He has been baritone soloist at St. George's Episcopal Church since 1894, and sang at Temple Emanu-El for nearly forty years. He has written several excellent songs, and has arranged many negro spirituals.

Burlesque (a), in music an extravaganza or travesty, of some serious drama or subject, in which music plays a more or less important part: the Italian term *burla,* meaning "fun" or "joke," was used by Johann Sebastian Bach as the title of a movement in his *Partita in A minor* for piano, and Richard STRAUSS composed a *Burlesca* for piano and orchestra. (*b*) In literature and drama the term is applied to a literary or dramatic travesty revealing a ludicrous, extravagant incongruity between the chosen subject and its treatment. In literature, the *Batrachomachia* (Battle of the Frogs and Mice), attributed to HOMER, is an excellent example of burlesque; also the *Opere Burlesche* (Burlesque Operas) of Francesco Berni (1497-1535); the travesties of *Vergil* by Paul SCARRON (1610-1660); CHAUCER'S *Rime of Sir Thopas; The Beggar's Opera* by John GAY; the play, *The Critic* (1779) by Richard Brinsley SHERIDAN; *Don Quixote* by Miguel de CERVANTES. (*c*) a term applied in the last part of the 19th century to a type of theatrical entertainment characterized chiefly by broad humor, slap-stick comedy, and abbreviated costumes for the female players: it consisted mainly of a travesty interspersed with comedy acts, ballet dancing, acrobatic feats, and song acts. Many legitimate comedians of the modern stage, including Leon Errol, Bert Lahr, Bobby CLARKE, Fanny BRICE, W. C. FIELDS and Jack Pearl served their apprenticeship in shows of this character.

Burlingame, Roger (1889-), American writer and novelist; son of Edward Livermore Burlingame, at one time editor of *Scribner's Magazine,* and educated at Harvard University. His works include *You Too* (1924); *Susan Shane; High Thursday; The Heir; Peace Veterans; Cartwheels; Three Bags Full; March of the Iron Men; Engines of Democracy; Whittling Boy,* a biography of Eli Whitney, inventor of the cotton gin.

Burman, Ben Lucien (1895-), American novelist who served in World War I, and completed his education at Harvard University which was interrupted by his enlistment in the army; after considerable experience in the journalistic field he devoted himself exclusively to writing several successful novels including *Mississippi* (1929); *Steamboat 'Round the Bend; Blow for a Landing; Big River to Cross.*

Burmester, Willy (1869-1933), German violin virtuoso who studied with Joseph JOACHIM at the Berlin Hochschule, and made many concert tours of Europe, England and the United States. As a younger artist his technical mastery of the violin appeared to be his principal virtue, but later he became a virtuoso of real distinction. He composed a serenade for string quartet and doublebass, and a few virtuoso pieces: his autobiography, *Fifty Years in the Life of an Artist* was published in 1926.

Burnand, Sir Francis Cowley (1836-1917), English writer, librettist, and dramatist; educated at Cambridge University. In 1880 he succeeded Tom Taylor as editor of *Punch,* retaining the office for twenty-six years, and republishing his many contributions in several volumes. He wrote two successful plays, *Ixion* and a burlesque of *Black-eyed Susan* by Douglas JERROLD. He also wrote the librettos for *Cox and Box* and *The Contrabandista* for which the musical scores were written by Sir Arthur SULLIVAN.

Burne-Jones, Sir Edward Coley (1833-1898), English painter educated at Oxford; while a theological student there he made the acquaintance of Dante Gabriel ROSSETTI who was painting some frescoes, and showed the great master some sketches so powerfully and poetically conceived that Rosetti permitted him to paint the fresco, *Death of Merlin,* in the Debating Hall of the University. He visited Italy in 1859 and 1862: his first paintings exhibited at the Royal Academy, including *The Merciful Night, Pyramus and Thisbe, The Evening Star,* and *Phyllis and Demophoon,* attracted little attention. When the GROSVENOR GALLERY opened in 1877, the paintings *Mirror of Venus, Beguiling of Merlin,* and *Days of Creation* did much to establish his reputation. Among his finest works are *Cophetua and the Beggar; Song of the Nibelung; St. George and the Dragon; Chaucer's Dream; The Wheel of Fortune; Pygmalion and the Statue; Depths of the Sea; The Star of Bethlehem.* Burne-Jones was also a master of the stained-glass, tapestry and mosaic arts, and equally gifted as a book illustrator: his works in all these fields reveal a mixture of mysticism and idealism.

Burnett, Frances Hodgson (1849-1924), American novelist, born in England, who came to the United States with her parents in 1865. She began as a writer of short stories for magazines: a novel, *That Lass of Lowrie's,* established her as a novelist in 1877, and many others followed, including *Through One Administration, A Lady of Quality,* and *Little Lord Fauntleroy,* a story of child life which also had great success as a play, and as a film.

Burney, Charles (1726-1814), English music historian and composer: pupil of Dr. Thomas ARNE in London, and harpsichordist of the concerts at the King's Arms, Cornhill, until 1760 when he resigned to write his *General History of Music.* He visited France, Switzerland, Italy, Germany, Holland, and Austria to obtain information for his work, making the acquaintance of many musicians and scholars including HASSE, GLUCK, METASTASIO and VOLTAIRE. The complete work appeared in four volumes from 1776 to 1789, at about the same time as the "General History of the Science and Practice of Music" by Sir John HAWKINS, his rival. A new edition of Burney's work with critical notes was published in 1935.

Burney, Frances, see **Arblay, Madame d'.**

Burnham, Daniel Hudson (1846-1912), American architect who was elected president of the American Institute of Architects in 1894. He designed the buildings for the World's Fair at Chicago, and also many private buildings here including the Masonic Temple, the Great Northern Hotel, and the Railway Exchange: also the Wanamaker store in New York, the Union Station in Washington, and the Pennsylvania Railroad Station in Pittsburgh. He was commissioned by the United States Government to design plans for the beautifying of Manila in the Philippine Islands, and was chairman of the national committee for the improvement of Washington, D. C.

Burns, Robert (1759-1796), Scottish poet whose education was slight: his first volume of poems,

Poems, chiefly in Scottish dialect appeared in 1786, his name spelt as above instead of the original family name, *Burnes* or *Burness.* Several more volumes appeared from 1787, and he spent two years in Edinburgh where he met many celebrities, and was lionized until the novelty of his poems waned. Unfortunately he contracted the habit of excessive drinking which led to his premature death. Among his most famous poems are *Duncan Gray; O Wert Thou in the Cauld Blast; Tam O'Shanter; The Jolly Beggars; The Cotter's Saturday Night; Highland Mary; Halloween; To a Mountain Daisy.*

Burroughs, Edgar Rice (1875-), American novelist who created the character "Tarzan" in his first novel, *Tarzan of the Apes,* published in 1914. More than twenty novels have been issued in the series, reaching a sale of 25,000,000 copies in more than fifty languages in addition to being screened, broadcast and transformed into comic strips.

Burroughs, John (1837-1921), American naturalist and essayist who settled on a farm at Esopus, New York, and devoted himself to fruit-culture and writing. His first book, *Walt Whitman, Poet and Person* (1867), made him well-known: it was followed by many volumes containing essays descriptive of nature including *Wake-Robin; Winter Sunshine; Birds and Poets; Locusts and Wild Honey; Fresh Fields; The Light of Day.* He was called "The Sage of Slabsides," and numbered Theodore Roosevelt, Thomas Alva Edison, and Henry Ford among his intimate friends.

Burt, Maxwell Struthers (1882-), American poet and novelist who was educated at Princeton University. His works include *In the High Hills* (1914); *John O'May and Other Stories; Songs and Portraits* (Poems); *Chance Encounters; The Interpreter's House; The Diary of a Dude Wrangler,* an autobiography; *When I Grew Up to Middle Age* (Poems); *The Delectable Mountains; They Could Not Sleep; The Other Side; Festival; Entertaining the Islanders; Escape from America; Powder River; Along these Streets.*

Burton, Sir Frederick William (1816-1900), Irish painter and art connoisseur educated in Dublin. He spent twenty years in Europe studying the works of the old masters, and was appointed director of the British National Gallery in 1874. During the twenty years that he held this post, he purchased more than 500 pictures, among the most important being *Virgin of the Rocks* by LEONARDO DA VINCI; the *Ansidei Madonna* of RAPHAEL; *The Ambassadors* by Hans HOLBEIN; the equestrian portrait of *Charles I* by Anthony VAN DYCK.

Burton, Richard (1861-1940), American poet and critic educated at Trinity College, Hartford, Ct., and Johns Hopkins University, Baltimore, Md. His works include *Dumb in June* (Poems) 1895; *Memorial Day and Other Poems; Ballad of the Unsuccessful; John Greenleaf Whittier; Literary Leaders of America; Masters of the English Novel; The New American Drama; Bernard Shaw; The Man and the Mask; Charles Dickens; Masters of the English Novel.*

Burton, Sir Richard Francis (1821-1890), English Orientalist and translator for many years in the service of the East India Company. During this period he learned the languages and customs of the Indians, Persians, Afghans, Hindustani, and Arabians, and finally made a pilgrimage to Mecca in the guise of a Mohammedan devotee. He wrote many books of travel, and made a literal translation of the ARABIAN NIGHTS with the title *The Thousand Nights and One Night,* published in 16 volumes from 1885 to 1888.

Burton, Robert (1577-1640), English clergyman and author; his one work of importance is *The Anatomy of Melancholy,* published about 1621 under the pseudonym "Democritus Junior," and since frequently republished, often in abridged form. The work is a vast storehouse of shrewd comment, learned quotations, humor and erudition from which John MILTON, Laurence STERNE and many other writers did not scruple to borrow liberally. The discussion of melancholy is divided into three parts: (*1*) the causes and symptoms of melancholy; (*2*) the cure of melancholy; (*3*) erotic and religious melancholy.

Busch, Adolf (1891-), German violinist who studied at the Cologne Conservatory with Willy HESS. He was a friend of Max REGER; became concertmaster of the Vienna Konzertverein, and succeeded Henri MARTEAU as professor of violin at the Berlin Hochschule. He is the leader of the Busch Quartet, and of the Busch Trio in which Rudolf SERKIN is the pianist.

Busch, Carl (1862-), Danish-American violinist, conductor and composer; pupil of Tofte, Hartmann and GADE at the Royal Conservatory of Music in Copenhagen. He settled in Kansas City, Mo., in 1887: since that time he has been active as conductor of the Kansas City Symphony Orchestra (1912-18), and guest conductor of many American orchestras. He made a valuable collection of old and rare musical instruments, and has written orchestral pieces, cantatas, violin pieces, and songs based on American Indian themes.

Busch, Fritz (1890-), German conductor; brother of Adolf BUSCH, and pupil of Fritz STEINBACH in conducting at the Cologne Conservatory. He has held many responsible positions as conductor of concerts and opera at Riga, Gotha, Aixla-Chapelle, Dresden and Buenos Aires.

Bushman, Francis X. (1885-), American screen actor, educated at Ammondale College, Maryland. He entered the silent films in 1911, appearing in many pictures produced by Essanay, Vitagraph, Metro-Goldwyn-Mayer and Universal. Among them may be mentioned *Ben Hur; Lady in Ermine; The Grip of the Yukon; Thirteenth Juror; Marriage Clause; Charge of the Gauchos.* In 1937 he assumed the leading role in a screen serial, *Dick Tracy,* and has also appeared in radio dramas.

Busley, Jessie (1869-), American actress who made her first appearance with Robert B. MANTELL's company, and her first success in *The Bells of Haslemere* at New York in 1894. Among the notable plays in which she has appeared are *The*

Sporting Duchess; Mice and Men; The Admirable Crichton; In the Bishop's Carriage; Beverley of Graustark; Old Heidelberg; Pollyanna; The Pillars of Society; Peter Ibbetson; Alien Corn; The Great Waltz; The Women. She has also played roles in many films.

Buson, Yosa (1716-1783), Japanese painter who worked along the lines laid down by Sakaki Hyakusen, and was influenced to a considerable degree by late MING artists. About 1775 he developed an individual technique in a series of poetic sketches: he was the teacher of GOSHUN.

Busoni, Ferruccio Benvenuto (1866-1924), Italian pianist and composer who studied with his mother, and made his debut at Vienna when eight years old. After further study under W. A. Remy, he began regular tours in 1881 throughout Europe, and came to the United States in 1891, teaching at the NEW ENGLAND CONSERVATORY OF MUSIC until 1893. After touring for some years, he taught in Berlin and Vienna, and again toured the United States in 1909 and 1911; he was made a member of the Legion d'Honneur in 1913, a distinction previously bestowed on only two Italian composers, Gioacchino ROSSINI and Giuseppe VERDI. His compositions included operas; orchestral works; concertos for piano; concertos for violin; chamber music. He also transcribed many of Johann Sebastian BACH's organ works for the piano; edited the piano works in Breitkopf and Härtel's complete edition of LISZT's works, and edited Bach's "Well-Tempered Clavichord," adding special studies and critical notes.

Butler, Lady Elizabeth Southerden Thompson (1844-1933), English painter born at Lausanne, Switzerland, and a pupil of Giuseppe Bellucci. Among her best pictures are *The Dawn of Waterloo; Quatre Bras; Balaclava; Rorke's Drift; The Camel Corps* and *Roll Call:* the last-named was purchased for Windsor Castle by Queen Victoria.

Butler, Ellis Parker (1869-1937), American humorist whose short story, *Pigs is Pigs,* brought him fame: a novel, *Jack-Knife Man,* was published in 1913. The rest of his writings were chiefly in the form of hilarious humor.

Butler, Samuel (1612-1680), English poet; student for a short period at Cambridge, and in the service as a clerk of Sir Samuel Luke who is supposed to be the original of Butler's heroic-comic poem, *Hudibras,* aimed at Puritanism, of which Sir Luke was the incarnation. The poem is regarded as the greatest single production of wit in its time: many of its lines have become mottos.

Butler, Samuel (1835-1902), English author and musician: his works include a novel, *The Way of All Flesh,* which was published after his death, and a romantic tale, *Erewhon, or Over the Range,* which was a satire on both the Darwinian theory and sanctimonious religion. He was also the composer of a secular oratorio, *Narcissus,* which he declared to be written in the "style of Handel."

Butt, Dame Clara (1873-1936), English contralto singer who studied at the Royal College of Music, and with Jacques Bouhy and Etelka GER-

STER. Her debut, made in *The Golden Legend* by Sir Arthur Sullivan in 1892, was followed by concert tours of Great Britain: in 1913-14 she made a world tour with R. Kennerly Rumford, her husband and a noted baritone. Several composers wrote works especially designed for her use such as *Sea Pictures* by Sir Edward Elgar.

Butterworth, Hezekiah (1839-1905), American poet and author; for many years editor of the *Youth's Companion.* His works include three volumes of poetry, and many stories and travel books for children including *Zig-Zag Journeys; The Wampum Belt; The Boyhood of Lincoln; The Patriot Schoolmaster.*

Buttress, in architecture a projecting structure of masonry or wood for supporting the wall of a building, and resisting lateral pressure or strain. A *flying buttress* carries the thrust of a vault horizontally across a space.

Buxtehude, Dietrich (1637-1707), Swedish organist and composer who held many fine positions as organist, including the Marienkirche at Lubeck, from 1668 until his death. In 1673 he established musical services, called "Evening Music," and held each year on the five Sundays before Christmas: Johann Sebastian BACH walked 225 miles in 1705 from his home at Arnstadt to attend them. His compositions, published in two great volumes, exercised a strong influence on Bach, who was only twenty-two years old when Buxtehude died.

Byington, Spring, contemporary screen actress who has appeared in many important films including *Little Women; Way Down East; Mutiny on the Bounty; Ah, Wilderness; The Voice of Bugle Ann; Charge of the Light Brigade; Dodsworth; Jezebel; You Can't Take It With You; The Story of Alexander Graham Bell; Blue Bird.*

Bylina (plural **Bylini**), in Russian literature the name given a folk tale of epic or balladic character: the word corresponds to the Scandinavian term, SAGA, and epics of this character originated in the 11th century.

Bynner, Witter (1881-), American critic and poet educated at Harvard College: his works include *Grenstone Poems* (1917); *The Beloved Stranger;* a satirical literary hoax, *Spectra,* written under the pseudonym, "Emanuel Morgan" with Arthur Davison; *Caravan; Indian Earth; The Jade Mountain,* written with Kiang Kang Hu. His critical works include *The Pamphlet Poets* and *The Persistence of Poetry.*

Byr, Robert, see **Bayer, Karl Robert Emmerich.**

Byrd, William (c.1542-1623), English organist and composer, presumably a pupil of Thomas TALLIS, who held important posts as organist at Lincoln Cathedral and the Chapel Royal. In 1575 Tallis and Byrd were granted the exclusive right to print and sell music and music paper by Queen Elizabeth, and when the license did not yield them a living, the worthy queen gave them an annuity. After the death of Tallis in 1585, Byrd composed sonnets, madrigals, many pieces for the virginials, services, anthems, psalms, masses and motets: he surpassed all English composers of his period in versatility and fecundity in the creation of vocal music, chamber and keyboard music.

Byrne, Donn (1889-1928), American short-story writer and novelist; full name Brian Oswald Donn-Byrne. He was educated at University College, Dublin, although born in New York City: his novels include *Stories Without Women* (1915); *Messer Marco Polo; Blind Raftery; Hangman's House; Destiny Bay; The Changelings.*

Byron, Arthur (1872-1943), American stage and screen actor; son of Oliver Doud BYRON, and a nephew of Ada REHAN. He appeared first in 1889 with his father's company, and made his debut in 1890 in New York at the People's Theatre in *The Plunger.* After a year with Sol Smith RUSSELL, he played for several seasons with John DREW, and starred in *Major André* by Clyde FITCH in 1903; also in *Petticoats and Bayonets* and *The Stubborness of Geraldine.* In subsequent years he acted as leading man for Maxine ELLIOTT, Maude ADAMS, Ethel BARRYMORE, and Katharine CORNELL in *St. Joan.* Byron has appeared in many important films including *The House of Rothschild; Oil for the Lamps of China; The Prisoner of Shark Island.*

Byron, George Gordon Byron, 6th **Baron** (1788-1824), English poet and dramatist born with a malformation of both feet: his family traced its origin back to the Norman conquest. In 1798, on the death of his granduncle, William, fifth Lord Byron, he inherited the title and estate including Newstead Abbey. Byron was educated at Cambridge University, traveled extensively in Portugal, Spain, Turkey and Greece, and lived a life full of amorous incident and adventure: he died about a year after joining the Greek Liberals in an attempt to revolutionize the government. The most important in the long list of his works are *Hours of Idleness* (1807); *The Giaour; The Corsair; The Prisoner of Chillon; Childe Harold; Manfred; Mazeppa; Marino Faliero; The Two Foscari; Sardanapalus; Don Juan:* the latter is considered his masterpiece.

Byron, Henry James (1834-1884), English actor, novelist, and dramatist who gave up the study of law for the stage: his plays include *Cyril's Success* (1868); *Our Boys,* a farce which ran for four years in London; *Lost at Sea* (with Dion BOUCICAULT); *Forty Thieves* with Francis Cowley BURNAND and William S. GILBERT.

Byron, Oliver Doud (1842-1920), American actor who made his first appearance with Joseph JEFFERSON in a dramatization of *Nicholas Nickleby* by Charles DICKENS at Baltimore in 1856. He supported Edwin BOOTH, James Henry HACKETT, and starred in Shakespeare at twenty-one. Among the most successful plays in which he appeared were *Across the Continent; The Plunger; The Man on the Box; The Lion and the Mouse; General John Reagan.* His son, Arthur BYRON, is his worthy successor on the stage.

Bystrom, John Niklas (1783-1848), Swedish sculptor who studied under John Tobias SERGEL at Stockholm, and also spent some time at Rome, modeling a half life-size work, *The Reclining Bacchante* which immediately placed him among the greatest Swedish sculptors. His works include *Hebe; Pandora; Juno Suckling Hercules; Girl Entering the Bath:* he also made colossal statues of the kings of Sweden.

C

Caballero, Fernan (1796-1877), Spanish novelist whose real name was Cecilia Francisca Josefa Böhl de Faber. In 1840 she published an anonymous romance, *Sola:* her greatest success, *The Sea Gull,* appeared in 1849, and was followed by *The Family of Alvaredo, Clemencia,* several volumes of short stories and a collection of Spanish fairy tales.

Cabanel, Alexandre (1823-1889), French painter who studied with François Edouard Picot, and won the Prix de Rome in 1845. His finest works are *The Birth of Venus* and *The Death of Francesca da Rimini and Paolo:* he was also a very successful portrait painter, but his likenesses, while elegant and well colored, do not reflect individuality in the features of his sitters. Cabanel also had many pupils at his studio.

Cabat, Louis (1812-1893), French painter who became director of the French Academy at Rome after studying with Camille Flers, and became leader of the movement for naturalistic landscape painting in France. His finest works include *Festival of Virgin on the Water; Pond at Ville d'Avray; Forest of Fontainebleau; Autumn Evening; Woods of Chanteloube.*

Cabell, James Branch (1879-), American novelist educated at William and Mary College: his works include *The Eagle's Shadow* (1904); *Jurgen; Figures of Earth; The Cream of the Jest; The Silver Chest; Gallantry; The Line of Love; Chivalry; Dommei,* originally called "The Soul of Millicent"; *Beyond Life; The High Place; Straws and Prayer Books; Some of Us.* An attempt to have his novel, *Jurgen,* suppressed was unsuccessful.

Cabinet, a furniture piece originating in the Orient and frequently mentioned in the ARABIAN NIGHTS: it first appeared during the 17th century in Italy, Spain, France, and England in the form of a small coffer designed to hold jewelry and other valuables of similar character. The addition of inner compartments, drawers, and pigeon holes resulted in larger cabinets made of walnut, ebony, and other fine woods; the ornamentation became elaborate by the use of gilt, ebony, gold, silver, mother-of-pearl, and fine paintings by famous artists. Among the many furniture makers who produced superb cabinets, the name of André Charles BOULLE (or Buhl) occupies first place.

Cable, George Washington (1844-1925), American novelist who was a Confederate soldier in the Civil War, after which he began to contribute sketches and short stories to newspapers and magazines. His novels, dealing chiefly with life in the South, include *Old Creole Days* (1879); *The Grandissimes; Madame Delphine; Dr. Sevier; The Silent South; John March, Southerner; Bonaventure; Strong Hearts; The Cavalier; Bylow Hill; Gideon's Band; The Flower of the Chapdelaines.*

Cabriole, in ballet a step in which the dancer keeps one foot on the floor while raising the other, and then beats the calves of the legs together with a scissors-like motion.

Caccini, Giulio (c.1546-1618), Italian singer and composer; nicknamed "Romano" because he was born at Rome. He studied singing and lute playing with Scipione della Palla, first composing madrigals, and later vocal pieces in recitative form which he sang to his own accompaniment on the THEORBO. In 1600 his opera, *Il rapimento di Cefalo,* was the first work of the kind to be performed in a public theatre. Another opera, *Eurydice,* was composed after Jacopo PERI had previously written an opera on the same subject, but both works were first performed during the same year.

Cachucha, a Spanish dance in triple time similar to the BOLERO: Sir Arthur SULLIVAN composed an excellent example of this dance for his operetta, *The Gondoliers.*

Cacophony, in music a term applied to harsh or discordant music caused by false harmonies, noisy combinations of sound, or false intonation. When the orchestral tone poems of Richard STRAUSS were first performed, the term "cacophonous" was often applied to them by conservative critics whose ears were offended by the unusual combinations of musical sounds.

Cadalso, José de (1741-1782), Spanish soldier, poet, and dramatist killed at the siege of Gibraltar in 1782. His satire on superficial knowledge, *The Sages of the Violet,* was a success; also a tragedy in verse, *Don Sancho Garcia,* and a prose work, *Moroccan Letters.*

Cadence, (a) in music the close or fall of a melodic strain, or a chord sequence, to a harmonic point of rest: the ordinary forms are the *perfect cadence,* the *imperfect cadence,* the *plagal cadence,* and the *deceptive cadence.* (b) A form of versification sometimes used in free verse in which the metrical unit is a verse or STROPHE which returns at regular intervals with rhythms comparable to those of speech.

Cadenza, in music (a) a brilliant passage in a vocal solo which has the effect of being extemporaneous, but is usually written by the composer. (b) An elaborate passage introduced into an instrumental CONCERTO near the conclusion of any one or all of the customary three movements: the musical material is usually taken from the themes of the work, and is prepared either by the composer, or some virtuoso on the instrument for which the concerto is written.

Cadman, Charles Wakefield (1881-), American organist, pianist, and composer who studied with Emil PAUR, Leo Oehmler, and Luigi von Kunits. He made a study of American Indian music, lecturing and appearing in recitals in the United States and Europe. His several operas include *Shanewis* and *A Witch of Salem;* the former produced in 1918 at the Metropolitan Opera House, New York, and the latter in 1926 at the Chicago Civic Opera: he has also written seven school operettas; orchestral works; chamber music; cantatas and almost two hundred songs. Many of the latter, such as *At Dawning* and *From the Land of the Sky-blue Water,* have achieved worldwide popularity.

Cadmus, in Greek mythology the son of a Phoenician king, the founder of the city of THEBES, and inventor of the alphabet. He was regarded as a wise king who married Harmonia, the daughter of ARES and APHRODITE; after death they were changed into snakes that watched over their tomb while their souls were led to the ELYSIAN FIELDS.

Caduceus, in Greek mythology the staff used by HERMES (Mercury), a messenger of the gods who conducted the souls of the dead to the underworld. The staff consisted of a rod with prongs twisted into the form of two serpents, and a pair of wings to signify that its bearer was a swift messenger of the gods.

Caedmon, an Anglo-Saxon poet supposed to have lived, according to Bede's *Ecclesiastical History,* as an ignorant man until he was commanded in a dream to "sing the beginning of created things," the result being metrical translations of parts of the Old Testament. Linguistic experts have undertaken to prove that these translations, as published in 1564 by Franciscus Junius, a Dutch scholar, could not have been made by Caedmon.

Caerlon, a town in Monmouthshire, England, near Newport: it was important in the days of the Roman occupation, and is also famous for its connection with the legends of King Arthur retold by Alfred TENNYSON in his IDYLLS OF THE KING.

Caesar, Caius Julius (c.100 B.C.-44 B.C.), Roman general, statesman, and author: the *Commentaries* are his only literary work extant. It comprises a history of the Gallic Wars in which he was the leader. His political career, ending in his assassination in the Roman Senate House on March 15, 44 B.C., has been dramatized by SHAKESPEARE and other playwrights; operas in which he was the hero were written by Reinhard Keiser and George Frederick HANDEL. His likeness and scenes from his career have been subjects for painters and sculptors ever since the close of the classic and the beginning of the Christian era.

Caesura, in poetry a break in a verse caused by the ending of a word within a foot, and applied specifically to breaks which occur at certain places near the middle of the verse.

Café Society, a ballet in one act: choreography by Catherine Littlefield and music by Ferde GROFE; first produced at the Civic Opera House, Chicago, in 1938. The scene of this strictly modernistic ballet is a night club where the debutantes, collegians and playboys assemble to greet the guests of honor including the screen star, literary lion, local columnist, pugilistic champion, and the usual pair of Newlyweds: the action, pantomime, and dancing are naturally in accordance with the surroundings.

Caffarelli, real name, **Gaetano Majorano** (1703-1783), Italian male soprano; a peasant boy whose beautiful voice was discovered by a local musician who sent him to Nicola PORPORA at Naples with whom he studied for five years. His debut in a female role at Rome in 1724 was a sensational event: he sang with tremendous success all over Europe for many years, amassing a fortune and retiring after purchasing the estate and assuming the title of the Duke of Santo-Dorato.

Caffieri, the name of a remarkable family of Italian artists who settled in France during the 17th century. **Philippe Caffieri** (1634-1716), was a ship sculptor for Louis XIV, and an associate of the architect Charles Le BRUN. **Jacques Caffieri** (1678-1755), worked with his father, Philippe, on the adornment of Versailles, and made the bronzes for the Passemant clock in the Château. **Philippe Caffieri** (1714-1777), was the fifth son of Jacques who made bronze substitutes for the silver crosses and chandeliers melted down by Louis XIV to pay the expenses of his armies. **Jean Jacques Caffieri** (1725-1792), was the most celebrated of Jacques' sons: he studied with J. B. Lemoyne, won the Grand Prize for sculpture, and studied in Rome for five years. His finest works include several busts of French musicians and playwrights including LULLY, CORNEILLE, QUINAULT, ROUSSEAU, and MOLIERE; his masterpiece was the *Rotrou* at the Comédie Française.

Caffin, Charles Henry (1854-1918), Anglo-American art critic born in England and educated at Oxford. After coming to the United States in 1892, he was employed in the decoration department at the World's Fair, Chicago, in 1893, and later became art critic for several newspapers and magazines. His books include *American Masters of Painting* (1902); *Story of American Painting; How to Study Old Masters; How to Study Architecture;* also histories of Dutch and Spanish painting.

Cagliari, Paolo, see **Veronese, Paul.**

Cagliostro, Count Alessandro, assumed name of **Joseph Balsamo** (1743-1795), an Italian adventurer, notorious for his impostures in Russia, Paris, Greece, and the Far East. He pretended to be a doctor, a mesmerist, and an alchemist possessing the secret of the philosophers' stone, and, because of his personal magnetism and bold-faced daring, made a great reputation and vast wealth for himself at the court of Louis XVI of France. He was imprisoned in the Bastille for complicity in the diamond necklace conspiracy, and is said to have finally died in the Fortress of San Leone at Rome where he was condemned to life imprisonment by the Inquisition. His sensational career inspired a biography by Thomas CARLYLE; a play, *The Grand Cophto*, by GOETHE; a novel, *Memoirs of a Physician*, by Alexandre DUMAS, PERE; comic operas by Adolphe ADAM and Johann STRAUSS, JR.

Cagney, James (1904-), American stage and screen actor educated at Columbia University. He made his first appearance on the New York stage in 1920: after playing in vaudeville and legitimate productions for several years, he entered the films in 1930. Among the numerous films in which he has appeared are *The Crowd Roars; Devil Dogs of the Air; A Midsummer Night's Dream; Boy Meets Girl; Angels with Dirty Faces; Roaring Twenties; The Fighting 69th; Yankee Doodle Dandy.*

Cagnola, Luigi, Marchese (1762-1833), Italian architect educated at the Clementine College in Rome, and at the University of Pavia. In 1806 he built a triumphal arch of wood at Milan, for the marriage of Eugène Beauharnais to the princess of Bavaria, so strikingly beautiful that it was carried out in marble as the *Arch of Peace.* He also built the Porta di Marengo and the Chapel of St. Marcellina at Milan.

Cahill, Marie (1870-1933), American actress and singer who appeared in many of the musical comedies produced by Charles K. HOYT, Augustin DALY and George W. Lederer. She made her debut in 1889 on the New York stage in *C. O. D.:* among the productions in which she played leading roles were *Morocco Bound; Sporting Life; Sally in Our Alley; Nancy Brown; The Opera Ball; Just Around the Corner.*

Caine, Georgia, contemporary American stage and screen actress educated at the College of Notre Dame, San Francisco. She appeared on the stage as a child in her father's company, playing many ingenue parts at fifteen. Later she appeared in many musical comedies including *The Messenger Boy; Foxy Quiller; Miss Hook of Holland; The Geisha; The Merry Widow.* She has also had important roles in many films including *The Cradle Song; The Count of Monte Cristo; Time Out for Romance; Remember the Night; The Affairs of Cappy Ricks.*

Caine, Sir Thomas Henry Hall (1853-1931), English novelist and dramatist who first studied architecture, and did some journalistic work before publishing his first novel, *Shadow of a Crime* in 1885. This was followed by many successful books including *The Son of Hagar; The Deemster; The Bondman; The Manxman; The Christian; The Eternal City; The Prodigal Son; The Woman Thou Gavest Me; The Master of Man.* Several of these novels were dramatized and filmed with the hearty approval of the public, and his autobiography, *My Story*, was also well received.

Cairo Museum (Egypt), a national repository of objects of art, utensils, clothing, and weapons found in the various excavation projects. It was founded by Mehemet Ali in 1835, but little real progress was made until 1858 when Auguste Mariette assumed charge of the museum for Ismail Pasha. In 1881, after Mariette's death, Professor Maspero assumed the directorship and in 1902 the collection was housed in a special fire and floodproof building: it is a genuine treasure-house of Egyptian antiques.

Calabrese, II (1613-1699), Italian painter who studied with Giovanni LANFRANCO at Rome and with GUERCINO at Cento. After a study of the great masters' works in many Italian cities, he went to Malta to paint frescoes of the life of St. John the Baptist in the cathedral. His finest creations are the *History of Pope Celestine V; Return of the Prodigal Son; Christ Blessing the Children; History of St. Catherine.* Calabrese usually selected gloomy subjects, but he treated them effectively.

Calamatta, Luigi (1802-1869), Italian engraver; professor at the École des Beaux-Arts, Brussels and at the Brera Academy, Milan: he engraved the death mask of Napoleon I made at St. Helena; the *Madonna di Foligno* of Raphael; also a portrait of his master, Jean INGRES and the latter's likeness of Nicoló PAGANINI.

Calame, Alexandre (1810-1864), Swiss painter and head of the Geneva Art School whose forte was portraying the scenic beauties of the Alps in such fine works as *Lake of the Four Cantons; Mont Blanc; Jungfrau; Lake Lucerne; Waterfall near Meyringen.* Another great work was his painting, *The Ruins of Paestum.*

Calamis, Greek sculptor who lived during the first half of the 5th century, B.C. His many and varied works include a bronze chariot for Hieron of Syracuse, an Olympian victor; a statue of APHRODITE at the entrance to the ACROPOLIS, ATHENS; a statue of APOLLO at OLYMPIA; a statue of HERMIONE at Delphi; a colossal statue of APOLLO taken to Rome by Lucullus. He worked in both marble and bronze, and ancient critics praised his sculptures for their graceful delicacy rather than their vigor.

Calamity Jane (c.1852-1903), the nick-name given by Western settlers to **Martha Jane Burke.** Her parents moved from Missouri in 1864 to Virginia City, Montana, where the girl imbibed the atmosphere of mining camps, wearing men's clothes, and learning to shoot and ride: the inference of her nick-name was that any man who trifled with her invited trouble. Her biography, *Calamity Jane,* by D. Aikman, was published in 1927, and she was one of the characters in a recent Western film of the historical type.

Calcar, Jan von, see **Kalkar, Hans von.**

Caldara, Polidoro, see **Caravaggio, Polidoro Caldara da.**

Calder, Alexander Stirling (1870-), American sculptor: his works include a group, *The Triumph of Energy,* at the Panama Pacific Exposition; *The Man Cub* at the Metropolitan Museum of Art, New York; the Depew Fountain at Indianapolis; the Lee Memorial at Laurel Cemetery and the Shakespeare memorial, *Tragedy and Comedy* in Philadelphia.

Calderon, Philip Hermogenes (1833-1898), English painter; pupil of J. M. Leigh at London and of François Edouard Picot in Paris; his finest pictures include *Broken Vows; Young Lord Hamlet; Her Most High, Noble and Puissant Grace;*

Moonlight Serenade; Captives of His Bow; The Renunciation of St. Elizabeth; Toujours Fidéle (Always Faithful).

Calderon de la Barca, Pedro (1600-1681), Spanish poet and dramatist of noble birth: educated at Salamanca and by the Jesuits for the priesthood, he turned to secular play writing, but also wrote 72 "Sacramental Acts" or out-door plays, for Corpus-Christi Day, the best of which is *The Divine Orpheus.* He became a priest in 1651, but continued to write both religious and secular plays: one of the former, *The Wonder-Working Magician,* was translated by Percy Bysshe SHELLEY and beautifully paraphrased by Edward Fitzgerald. Among his secular dramas are *The Alcade of Zalamea; The Woman Ghost; No Magic Like Love; The Physician of His Honor; The Constant Prince; Love After Death.*

Caldwell, Erskine (1903-), American novelist educated at Erskine College, the University of Virginia, and the University of Pennsylvania. His novels include *Tobacco Road* (1932) which had the longest run (eight years) in dramatized form of any play in the history of the American theatre; *God's Little Acre, Trouble in July.*

Calf, The Golden, an image made of gold by the Israelites after Moses ascended the Mount Yahweh, and failed to return when expected. They proceeded to worship the image, and were saved from destruction only by the return of Moses. In the opera, *Faust,* by Charles GOUNOD, Mephistopheles sings a satirical aria entitled *Le veau d'or* (The Golden Calf).

Calhern, Louis (1895-), American stage and screen actor who made his debut at New York in 1914 with the Cecil Spooner Stock Company: he was also a member of Margaret ANGLIN's company, and played leading roles in many important productions including *The White Peacock; The Song and Dance Man; The Rhapsody; Dinner at Eight; Golden Boy.* He has also been featured in many films including *The Gorgeous Hussy; The Life of Émile Zola; The Count of Monte Cristo; The Affairs of Cappy Ricks; Remember the Night; The Wife Takes a Flyer.*

Caliban, in literature the name of a deformed, repulsive slave in *The Tempest* by William SHAKESPEARE; he is the servant of Prospero, the rightful Duke of Milan, a benevolent magician living in exile on an island with his daughter, Miranda.

California Palace of the Legion of Honor, an art museum presented to the city of San Francisco by Adolph B. Spreckels as a memorial to the three thousand Californians who were killed in World War I. Two galleries are devoted to a collection of one hundred sculptures by Auguste RODIN; another contains tapestries representing the life of Jeanne d'Arc, bronzes by Arthur PUTNAM, the animal sculptor, and many fine paintings by European masters from the 16th to the 19th century.

Callaghan, Morley (1903-), Canadian novelist educated at the University of Toronto: his works include *Strange Fugitive* (1928); *It's Never Over; Broken Journey; They Shall Inherit the Earth; More Joy in Heaven.*

Callcott, Sir Augustus Wall (1779-1844), English painter who first studied for a musical career, singing for some years in the choir of WESTMINSTER ABBEY. In 1799 he exhibited his first painting at the Royal Academy, London, and was elected a member in 1810. His figure paintings, *Raphael and La Fornarina* and *Milton Dictating to his Daughters* are excellent, but his landscapes such as *The Mouth of the Tyne* and *Old Jetty at Southampton* are more distinguished in respect to refined taste and serene beauty.

Callicrates, Greek architect who worked in ATHENS during the 5th century, B.C. He is credited with having built the PARTHENON between 450-440 B.C. with the assistance of Ictinus, and also to have erected the Temple of the Wingless Victory.

Callimachus, Greek sculptor who worked at ATHENS near the end of the 5th century B.C. He was a pupil of CALAMIS, and made the gold lamp which burned night and day in the ERECTHEUM. He is credited with originating the Corinthian column, and using a running drill to sink deep lines into the drapery folds of marble sculptures.

Callimachus, Greek grammarian and poet who lived about 250 B.C., and founded a school in ALEXANDRIA attended by many famous grammarians and poets. He was a profound scholar, but the few examples extant of his hymns and an epic poem, *Hecate*, reveal a labored style unrelieved by poetic genius.

Callinus of Ephesus, Greek poet of the 7th century, B.C.; numbered among the earliest elegiac poets. There are very few of his works extant: the longest is a portion of a patriotic poem in which he endeavors to rouse his countrymen, the Ionians, to fight more valiantly in their struggle with the Magnesians.

Calliope (*a*) in Greek mythology the muse who presides over epic poetry and eloquence: she was the last of the nine sisters, according to HESIOD, but regarded as the greatest, and was also the mother of ORPHEUS, his father being the god, APOLLO. (*b*) In music the name used for a species of pipe ORGAN in which harsh and piercing tones are produced by steam under pressure instead of wind: its use is almost entirely confined to circuses and carnivals.

Callisto, in Greek mythology an Arcadian nymph; daughter of Lycaon and a companion of ARTEMIS. She was transformed into a bear for having born a son, Arcas, to ZEUS. Her son would have shot her while hunting in the forest, but Zeus used a swift wind to carry them both up to the skies where Callisto became the constellation Ursa Major, and Arcas the constellation Arcturus.

Callot, Jacques (1592-1635), French engraver who studied with Antonio Tempesta and also with Philippe Thomassin at Rome. His plates number more than 1600: he had a remarkable talent for grouping many figures in small space, and both variety and verve characterized his work. Some of his best works are *Miseries of War; Temptation of St. Anthony; Conversion of St. Paul; Martyrdom of St. Sebastian,* and many views of buildings and bridges in Paris.

Calore, con (It.), in music a term indicating that a passage is to be played with fire or passion.

Calpurnius, Roman bucolic poet, surnamed Titus Calpurnius Siculus, who probably lived during the reign of NERO in the first century of the Christian era because the seven *Eclogues* accredited to him appear to describe Nero and the games held in an amphitheatre erected by the emperor in A.D. 57. Many authorities regard him as an imitator of VERGIL.

Calvaert, Denis (1540-1619), Flemish painter who studied the anatomy of the human form so thoroughly at Bologna that his paintings appear to have been created by an Italian. Later he copied the works of RAPHAEL for a time, and returned to Bologna where he founded a school at which Guido RENI and DOMENICHINO were students. His works include *St. Francis and St. Domenic; Danae; Souls in Purgatory; Virgin and St. Apollonia.*

Calvé, Emma (1858-1942), French operatic soprano whose real name was Emma Roquer. After studying at Paris she made her debut in 1882 as Marguerite in *Faust* at La Monnaie in Brussels. She then coached with Mme. MARCHESI, and entered the Opéra-Comique, remaining with the company three years, and also singing at La SCALA, Milan, and at COVENT GARDEN, London. Her debut at the METROPOLITAN OPERA HOUSE in 1893 as Santuzza in CAVALLERIA RUSTICANA was fairly successful, but her performance in the title role of CARMEN three weeks later caused a veritable sensation, and her reappearance in the same role at Hammerstein's Manhattan Opera House in 1908 was attended with even more acclaim. After 1910 Mme. Calvé appeared only in concert; her autobiography, *My Life,* was published in 1922. Her repertory included the leading soprano roles in MEFISTOFELE, *Herodiade* and *Les Pêcheurs de perles.*

Calverley, Charles Stuart (1831-1884), English poet and humorist educated at Oxford and Cambridge. He was a brilliant scholar, and his ability as a humorist became evident in his *Verses and Translations* (1862), and several similar collections published before his death: a complete edition appeared in 1901.

Calvocoressi, Michel D. (1877-   ), French critic and writer on music, born of Greek parents in Marseilles. He has been a tireless worker in the interests of Russian music in France and England: his works include *Russian Music;* biographies of LISZT, GLINKA, SCHUMANN, and MOUSSORGSKY; a French translation of RIMSKY-KORSAKOW'S *Treatise on Instrumentation; The Principles and Methods of Musical Criticism; Musical Taste and How to Form It.*

Calydonian Boar, in Greek mythology a savage boar sent by ARTEMIS to punish king Aeneus of

Calydon for failing to offer her the proper sacrifices. The boar was killed by Meleager and ATALANTA, a famous huntress who inflicted the first wound.

Calypso, in Greek mythology a daughter of ATLAS, and queen of the island of Ogygia, who entertained ODYSSEUS when he was shipwrecked there: she induced him to remain for seven years, but he longed to return home nothwithstanding her promise of eternal youth. ZEUS sent HERMES to effect his release, and Calypso died of grief.

Camargo, stage name of **Marie Anne de Cupis** (1710-1770), a famous ballerina born in Brussels of Spanish parents. She was the pupil of her father, a teacher of dancing to the Belgian aristocracy, and of Françoise de Prévost, première danseuse at the Paris Opéra. In 1726 she made her debut there in a divertissement, *The Character of the Dance,* originally written for Mlle. Prévost: her success aroused the jealousy of the older dancer, but Camargo became the rage of Paris. Her portrait was painted by LA TOUR and LANCRET, and she had many devoted admirers for one of whom, the Comte de Clermont, third son of Louis XIII, she retired from the stage in 1735, but returned in 1741 to even greater triumphs until her final retirement in 1751. Camargo was evidently a very great dancer, and withal an equally charming personality: the Camargo ballet shoe was used long after her demise; a society dance was named after her; Charles Lecocq wrote an opera entitled *Camargo,* and in 1930 the CAMARGO SOCIETY produced artistic ballets for four years in London in a repertory comprising not only old favorites such as *Giselle* and *Coppelia,* but also new ones by Darius MILHAUD, Vaughan WILLIAMS, and William WALTON.

Camargo Society, The, an organization formed at London, England, in 1930 in order to revive the art of ballet after the death of Serge DIAGHILEFF, and to offer substantial aid to English dancers, choreographers, and composers in the production of new ballets. Performances were presented at the Cambridge Theatre on Sunday evenings: the roster of dancers included KARSAVINA, LOPOKOVA, MARKOVA, and DOLIN: among the ballets given were VAUGHAN WILLIAMS' *Job,* and WALTON's *Façade.* After the establishment of the Vic-Wells Ballet, Marie RAMBERT's Ballet Club, and the revival of the Ballet Russe, the Society was dissolved.

Cambert, Robert (1628-1677), French opera composer, pupil of Jacques Chambonnières and music director to Anne of Austria. His first work, *La Pastorale,* was produced at the Chateau d'Issy in 1659, followed by *Ariane, Adonis,* and *Pomone* produced at the Paris Opéra in 1671. He is credited with being the first French composer of opera, but his career was ended with the coming of Jean Baptiste LULLY: he went to London and became Master of the Music to Charles II.

Cambiaso, Luca (1527-1585), Italian painter, son and pupil of Giovanni Cambiaso, and also known as *Luchetto da Genova.* He painted important pictures at fifteen, and worked so rapidly that he was said to have two right hands. He

studied the works of the great masters in Florence and Rome, and painted several *Madonnas* of calm, serious, and noble mien. His best works include the *Presentation at the Temple; The Entombment; The Rape of the Sabines,* and the colossal, much-admired *Paradise* at the ESCORIAL, Madrid.

Cambré, in ballet a term meaning "arched," describing the position of a dancer's body when bent from the waist backward, or to either side.

Cambridge, Ada, see **Cross, Mrs. George Frederick.**

Cambridge, (*a*) in England a town in Cambridgeshire of significance as being the location of Cambridge University, the fount of learning for many literati, authors, poets, dramatists, musicians, painters, sculptors and architects. (*b*) A city with a population exceeding 100,000 in Middlesex County, Massachusetts, and as famous as an intellectual center as Cambridge in England. The first printing press in America was used there: three important colleges—Harvard, Radcliffe (for women) and the Massachusetts Institute of Technology, removed from Boston in 1915—are within the city limits. Henry Wadsworth LONGFELLOW and James Russell LOWELL lived there, and George Washington assumed command of the Continental Army in 1775 at Craigie House.

Cameo, a miniature carving in relief on precious or semi-precious stones such as the agate, onyx, sardonyx, and chalcedony. The colors created by the different layers of quartz are used to shade the various parts of the work. The ancient Greeks and Romans were adepts in the art of carving cameos not only for decorative purposes, but also for use in personal adornment: Rome still originates the finest creations of this character. Cameos are also carved on shell, but the results are not as artistic.

Camera obscura, a form of camera used by artists for viewing scenes and objects in making drawings. It consists of a darkened chamber having an aperture provided with a lens through which the image is formed on the opposite surface which is usually a piece of ground glass. Double reflection corrects the inversion of the first image.

Cameron, Sir David Young (1865-), Scottish painter and etcher; a pupil at the Glasgow Art School and Edinburgh School of Art. His paintings include many fine landscapes made in Scotland, and he has illustrated many books including Maxwell's *Story of the Tweed* and Walton's *The Compleat Angler.* He has published several delightful collections of etchings.

Cammaerts, Emile (1878-), Belgian poet, author, and dramatist who translated the works of John RUSKIN into French, produced two successful plays, and wrote several volumes of poetry on themes suggested by World War I: they include *Belgian Poems; New Belgian Poems, Through the Iron Bars,* and *Messines.* English translations have found a wide and well-satisfied audience. He has also written critical and historical works on Belgium and England.

Camoens, Luis Vaz de (1524-1580), Portuguese courtier, soldier and poet of noble birth: his masterpiece was *The Lusiad*, an epic poem describing the adventures of Vasco di Gama. It is regarded as the national epic of Portugal, teeming with religious enthusiasm, love of country, chivalrous spirit, and imaginative descriptive passages in correct and noble style. Fine English translations by Sir Richard BURTON and J. J. Aubertin are available.

Camouflage, a French word used in World War I to denominate the method of concealing gun emplacements and other defensive or offensive weapons of war, the desired results being achieved by the use of certain colors such as gray, green and brown, in special tones accentuated or reduced by painted outlines or cast shadows. The method, which artists have done much to improve, is still in use in World War II.

Campagna, Girolamo (c.1550-c.1623), Italian sculptor who studied with Jacopo SANSOVINO; his works include a *Piéta* at the Church of San Giuliano at Venice; a *St. Sebastian;* a *Virgin;* two colossal ATLANTES, and several portrait statues.

Campagnola, Domenico (c.1490-c.1564), Italian painter and engraver who studied with Giulio Campagnola (a relative but not, as has been erroneously stated, his father), and with TITIAN. His works in oil and fresco are to be found chiefly in churches at Padua. His frescoes in the Scuola del Santo at Padua rival those of Titian in the same building, and his engravings, woodcuts, and drawings are also greatly admired.

Campagnola, Giulio (c.1480-c.1513), Italian painter and engraver who studied with Girolamo Campagnola, a pupil of Francesco SQUARCIONE. He was an excellent miniature painter, but is best-known by his fine engravings of works by Giovanni BELLINI and GIORGIONE.

Campagnoli, Bartolomeo (1751-1827), Italian violinist who studied at Bologna and later of Pietro Nardini at Florence. He toured Europe for many years, and occupied several important posts as concertmaster and director: his works include chamber music; flute concertos; seven famous studies (Divertissements) for violin; studies for viola and a violin method.

Campana, Pedro, see **Kempener, Pieter de.**

Campanari, Giuseppe (1859-1937), Italian operatic baritone who was first a violoncellist at La SCALA, Milan, and with the BOSTON SYMPHONY ORCHESTRA. After studying voice, he made his debut in 1893 with the Hinrich Opera Company at New York, and created the role of Tonio in PAGLIACCI at the American première in the same year. In 1895 he joined the METROPOLITAN OPERA COMPANY, singing the role of Ford in the first performance of VERDI'S FALSTAFF, and considered one of the finest interpreters of the title role in *The Barber of Seville*. He remained with the company until 1898, after which he devoted himself to concertizing and teaching.

Campanari, Leandro (1857-1939), Italian violinist and conductor who toured Italy as a prodigy at twelve, and later studied at the Milan Conservatory. He made his debut with the BOSTON SYMPHONY ORCHESTRA in 1881; organized the Campanari String Quartet and became the first violin professor at the NEW ENGLAND CONSERVATORY OF MUSIC, Boston. After returning to Europe for several years, he headed the violin department of the CINCINNATI CONSERVATORY OF MUSIC; conducted orchestral concerts at La SCALA, Milan; opera at the MANHATTAN OPERA HOUSE, New York, finally settling in San Francisco as a teacher of violin and voice.

Campanile, in architecture the Italian form of a bell tower, usually built separately and adjacent to a church or public building. The earliest examples date from the 6th century, and were circular in shape, but square towers came into prominence in the 8th century. Some of the finest examples are at St. Mark's, Venice; St. Georgia di Velabro, Rome; Giotto's Campanile, Florence, and the campanile of the Palazzo del Signore, Verona.

Campanini, Cleofonte (1860-1919), Italian conductor and opera impresario; brother of Italo CAMPANINI. He studied at the Parma Conservatory, and in 1883 became assistant conductor at the METROPOLITAN OPERA HOUSE, New York, returning in 1887 to direct the American première of Verdi's *Otello*. After conducting in various European opera houses, he became chief conductor in 1906 at HAMMERSTEIN'S MANHATTAN OPERA HOUSE, remaining until 1909, and joining the CHICAGO OPERA COMPANY in 1910, and becoming its musical director from 1913 until his death. Campanini was in the front rank of operatic conductors; during his career in the United States he introduced Massenet's THAIS and JONGLEUR DE NOTRE DAME; Debussy's PELLEAS ET MELISANDE; Charpentier's LOUISE; Wolf-Ferrari's JEWELS OF THE MADONNA, and Herbert's NATOMA.

Campanini, Italo (1846-1896), Italian operatic tenor; brother of Cleofonte CAMPANINI. After studying at Parma, he made his debut in 1869 as Manrico in Verdi's Il TROVATORE at Odessa, Russia, without much success; after coaching by LAMPERTI, he made his second debut at Florence in Wagner's LOHENGRIN to tumultuous applause. He toured the United States first in 1873; again in 1879 with Christine NILSSON, and in 1892 with Adelina PATTI. From 1883 to his death he lived in New York.

Campanology, the science of bells, especially in regard to the art of ringing, known in England as *change ringing* which means continuous production without repetition of changes, i.e., the order in which a set of bells is struck. The statement that campanology is an extremely difficult art may seem exaggerated to the uninitiated, but such is the case: it requires a considerable period of study and practice for a bell-ringer to master his art.

Campbell, Mrs. Patrick (1865-1940), English stage and screen actress who created the title role in *The Second Mrs. Tanqueray* by Arthur PINERO at the St. James Theatre, London, in 1893; she was also outstanding in *Macbeth, Romeo and Juliet, Hamlet,* SUDERMANN's *Magda,* IBSEN's *Ghosts* and SHAW's *Pygmalion,* being favorably compared with BERNHARDT and DUSE. She visited the United States several times, and appeared in several films including *Rip Tide* and *Crime and Punishment.*

Campbell, Roy (1902-), English poet who was born in South Africa and educated at Oxford: his works include *The Flaming Terrapin* (1924); *Wayzgoose, Flowering Reeds; Flowering Rifle.*

Campbell, Thomas (1777-1844), Scottish poet whose first volume of verse, *The Pleasures of Hope* (1799); reached its fourth edition inside of a year from the day of its publication: other works include *Gertrude; The Exile of Erin; Hohenlinden; Ye Mariners of England* and *Battle of the Baltic,* three stimulating war poems. The sayings, "Distance lends enchantment to the view" and "Coming events cast their shadows before" are extracted from his verses.

Camphausen, Wilhelm (1818-1885), German painter; pupil of Frederick von SCHADOW and professor of his art at Düsseldorf Academy. His finest pictures include *Cromwell's Cavalry; Frederick the Great at Potsdam; Prince Eugene at the Battle of Belgrade;* also colossal equestrian paintings of FREDERICK THE GREAT and Emperor Wilhelm.

Camphuysen, Dirk Rafelsz (1586-1627), Dutch painter, theologian and poet; pupil of Abraham Govaerts. He produced some exquisite landscapes, small in size but of great beauty in sunset and snow effects. His translation of the *Psalms* is regarded as remarkable for its poetic feeling. His son, Govaert Camphuysen (1624-1674), and his nephew, Raphael Camphuysen (1598-1657) were both painters; the latter is said to have been a disciple of Pieter POTTER.

Campi, Giulio (1500-1572), Italian painter who studied with his father, Galeazzo Campi (1475-1536); with Giulio ROMANO, and later made an intensive study of the master works of RAPHAEL, TITIAN and CORREGGIO. Most of his works are in the church of St. Margaret at Cremona, his native town. He founded a school of painting followed by his brothers, Vincenzo and Antonio; he also had a pupil Bernardino Campi (1522-1592) whose work was often mistaken for that of Titian.

Campin, Robert, see **Flemalle, Master of.**

Campoamor Y Campoosorio, Don Ramon de (1817-1901), Spanish statesman, dramatist and poet; one of the most prolific and at the same time popular Spanish authors. His plays and miscellaneous writings are of no importance today, but his poems, *Dolores* (Sorrows), and his stories in verse such as *The Good and Wise* and *Juana's Lover* are considered masterpieces.

Camuccini, Vincenzo (c.1773-1844), Italian painter who belonged to the school of Louis DAVID: he was director of the Neapolitan Academy at Rome, and curator of the paintings at the VATICAN. His works include *The Assassination of Caesar; Death of Virginius; Devotion of the Roman Women; Presentation of Christ in the Temple.* His valuable collection of paintings, including RAPHAEL's *Madonna with the Pink,* became the property of the Duke of Northumberland.

Canada, National Gallery of, see **National Gallery of Canada.**

Canaletto (1697-1768), Italian painter; real name Antonio Canale. He spent several years in Rome, and upon returning to Venice painted many scenes in that city which established his reputation including *View on the Grand Canal; Regatta on the Grand Canal; The Imperial Ambassador at the Doge's Palace; The Piazzetta.* His nephew and pupil Bernardo Bellotto (1724-1780), also known as Canaletto, painted works greatly resembling those of his uncle.

Canby, Henry Seidel (1878-), American editor and critic; educated at Yale University where he has taught since 1900. Among his works are *The Short Story* (1902); *Classic Americans; Designed for Reading* (with others); *The Age of Confidence (Life in the Nineties); Seven Years' Harvest; Thoreau.* He was also one of the founders of the *Saturday Review of Literature.*

Canfield, Dorothy, see **Fisher, Dorothy Canfield.**

Canio, the principal character in I PAGLIACCI, an opera by Ruggiero LEONCAVALLO; he is an actor in an itinerant troupe who kills his wife's lover, Silvio, during the action of a play, and, letting fall his bloody knife, cries "The comedy is finished."

Cannan, Gilbert (1884-), English novelist, critic, and dramatist educated at Cambridge University, London, who founded the Manchester Repertory Theatre with John DRINKWATER. His works include a translation of Romain ROLLAND's *Jean Christophe;* the novels, *Peter Homonculus* (1909); *Round the Corner; Mendel; Sembal,* and *The House of Prophecy:* also several plays.

Cano, Alonso (1601-1667), Spanish painter, architect and sculptor; also known as *El Racionero.* He was a pupil of Don Juan MONTANES, of Don Francesco PACHEO, and an intimate friend of VELASQUEZ. As chief architect and painter for Philip IV of Spain, his greatest work was the Granada Cathedral: his statues and busts include *Virgin and Child; Crucifixion; Immaculate Conception; Virgin with a Rosary; St. John the Baptist; St. Francis of Assisi.* His paintings include *Christ Blessing the Children, Ass of Balaam,* and many others which did not achieve the greatness of his scultpures.

Canon, in music the strictest form of musical imitation in which two or more voices or parts take up exactly the same theme in succession. The first voice or part is called the *antecedent* or *leader;* the second is called the *consequent* or *answer.* If the theme is reproduced exactly, the canon is known as *strict;* if the theme is altered, the canon is known as *free.* One of the best-known canons is the old English round, *Sumer Is Icumen In* (Summer Is Coming In): the form was used effectively by BACH, HANDEL, MOZART, BEETHOVEN and SCHUBERT.

Canonicus (c.1560-1647), American Indian sachem who was chief of the Narragansett tribe in New England when the Pilgrim Fathers landed at Plymouth, Mass., in 1620. He gave Roger Williams the land on which the town of Providence was founded in 1636, and acknowledged the sovereignty of Great Britain in 1644. He has become a personality in many short stories and novels dealing with colonial life in New England.

Canopy, in architecture an ornamental structure resembling a roof which projects from a wall or rests on pillars, and is placed over a door, window, throne, shrine, niche, or statue.

Canova, Antonio (1757-1822), Italian sculptor who devoted himself to the study of classic masters such as RAPHAEL, and is regarded as the leader of the classical revival in Italian sculpture. His works include *Theseus and the Minotaur; Cupid and Psyche; Pauline Borghese; Perseus with the Head of Medusa; Hercules and Lichas; Three Graces.* He executed commissions for NAPOLEON I, and was once called to London to pass on the artistic value of the ELGIN MARBLES.

Cantabile (It.), in music a term indicating that a passage or entire composition is to be played in a singing manner: it is often used in the form *Andante cantabile.*

Cantarini, Simone (1612-1648), Italian painter and etcher known at *Il Pesarese* and *Simone da Pesaro.* He was a pupil of Guido RENI, and a friend of DOMENCHINO: some of his works have been attributed to his master. Among his paintings are *St. Anthony; Magdalene; Transfiguration; Portrait of Guido:* his finest etching is *Jupiter, Neptune,* and *Plato Honoring the Arms of Cardinal Borghese.*

Cantata, in music (*a*) a term originally distinguishing a vocal composition from an instrumental: (*b*) the term used since the 17th century for a sacred or secular vocal work comprising arias, recitatives, ensembles and choruses for use in churches or concert halls. CARISSIMI was the first composer to write a church cantata, a form also used by Johann Sebastian BACH for more than two hundred works. The cantata is still a favorite form of musical composition by modern composers.

Cantemir (or Kantemir), Prince Antiochus Dmitrievitch (1708-1744), Russian diplomat and poet. He is considered the father of secular writing in Russia; his *Satires,* written in verse, were his most important work, invaluable in their descriptions of Russian life and manners. Many of the verses have become proverbs with the Russian people.

Canterbury Tales, a work by Geoffrey CHAUCER (c.1340-1400), consisting of a prologue and a series of tales in verse and prose supposed to be related by the members of a band of pilgrims who meet at the Tabard Inn in Southwark on their way to the shrine of Thomas à Becket at Canterbury. The work comprised about 17,000 lines, and almost fifty different manuscripts exist in the possession of the Chaucer Society which has printed six of the best in parallel columns.

Cantilena, in music (*a*) a ballad or light song of popular character: (*b*) in instrumental music a melodious phrase or melody resembling a song.

Cantilever, in architecture a bracket of stone, iron or wood, greater in length than breadth and used to support a balcony or cornice: it is also employed in the construction of bridges.

Canto, (*a*) in literature one of the divisions of a long poem, as in Dante's *Divine Comedy* which contains one hundred cantos: (*b*) in music the name given to the highest vocal part in a concerted piece: in ancient music this part was the tenor, but in modern music it is usually the soprano. The *cantus firmus* in ancient music is that part of the music which remains true to the original motive.

Cantor, Eddie (1893-   ), American stage, screen and radio comedian who made his debut in vaudeville in 1907: his appearances on the stage include *Canary Cottage* (1915), *Kid Boots, Whoopee,* and *Banjo Eyes.* Among the films in which he has been featured are *Kid Boots; Whoopee; Palmy Days: The Kid from Spain; Roman Scandals; Ali Baba Goes to Town; Forty Little Mothers.*

Cantor, in sacred music the name of the singer in charge of the musical part of the service. In Jewish synagogues the title is applied to the solo singer who intones the chants: in Christian churches it is applied to the choirmaster, also called the precentor.

Cantoria, in architecture the gallery or balcony used by the singers in a church. The finest example is the one made for the cathedral at Florence about 1440 by Luca della ROBBIA: it is decorated with ten magnificent panels of singing angels and dancing boys.

Cantù, Cesare (1804-1895), Italian author who, while imprisoned for a political offense, wrote a historical romance, *Margherita Pusterla* (1838) which became a "best-seller": it gave a graphic picture of prison life, and was actually written on rags with a tooth-pick blackened by candle smoke. His *Storia universale* (Universal History), a vast work in seventy-two volumes, passed through many editions, and was translated into several languages, but his political bias often influenced his accuracy.

Canvas, in painting the cloth used by the artist on which to record his impressions: it differs from the ordinary commercial variety because it is made in a single warp of cream or bleached flax of the best quality, and is given a special sizing to prepare the surface for the paint.

Capek, Karel (1890-1938), Czechoslovakian dramatist, poet, novelist, and essayist. His first play, *The Robbers,* was produced in 1920: in 1923 a play satirizing the machine age entitled *R.U.R.* (Rossom's Universal Robots), made him a celebrity in Europe and the United States, where it was produced at New York by the THEATRE GUILD, although a revival in 1942 failed to please present-day audiences. His plays include *The Makropoulos Affair* and *Loupeznik;* he also wrote novels and a series of travel sketches. His brother, **Josef Capek** (1887-1927) was an excellent painter who illustrated some of his brother's books, and collaborated with him in two plays: *The Life of Insects* (1921), produced by William A. BRADY as *The World We Live In,* and *Adam the Creator.*

Capell, Edward (1713-1781), English Shakespearean critic for many years deputy inspector of plays: in 1768 he published his monumental ten-volume edition of SHAKESPEARE which corrected all the errors which he found in Sir Thomas Hanmer's edition. From 1774 to 1783 he completed a commentary entitled *Notes and Various Readings of Shakespeare.*

Capital, in architecture the upper part of a COLUMN which includes the whole of the ornamentation between the SHAFT and the ARCHITRAVE. The oldest examples are found in Egypt and other parts of the Far East including Assyria, Phoenicia, and Persia, but the Greeks carved the most perfect capitals of all time. There are also many types of Romanesque and Gothic capitals: the Renaissance reverted to the classic type, the only changes made being in the character and amount of decoration.

Capitano, in drama the stock character in a COMMEDIA DELL'ARTE, the early form of drama in Italy. The character was popular because it was a grotesque and therefore an arresting personality: boastful but cowardly, terrifying in appearance, but laughable because of its arrant cowardice. The long-nosed mask and fierce mustache were the chief features of the make-up.

Capitol, the name of one of the hills in ancient Rome, known as the *Mons Capitolinus* (Capitoline Hill). Several of the most important buildings of ancient Rome were located there including the Temple of Jupiter Capitolinus, dedicated in 509 B.C. to JUPITER, JUNO and MINERVA. It was damaged several times, but always rebuilt so that it remained the most important Roman temple until the advent of Christianity. During the first fifteen hundred years of the Christian era the temple was gradually completely razed so that only the foundation remained: in the 16th century a part of the hill was utilized for a group of buildings designed by MICHELANGELO for the Roman municipality, including the rectangle, surrounded by several structures, known today as the Campidoglio (Square of the Capitol). The Capitol also was the location of the *Tarpeian Rock* from which criminals condemned by the state were thrown to their death.

Capitol (Washington D.C.), one of the finest buildings from the architectural standpoint in the United States, occupying an area of three and one-half acres. Its length and width approximate 750 by 350 feet, and its height from the base line to the top of the *Statue of Freedom* is 267 feet; the latter was modeled by Thomas CRAWFORD, father of Francis Marion CRAWFORD, the novelist, and weighs seven and one half tons. The cornerstone was laid in 1793 by George Washington; the designs were made by Dr. William Thornton, and the construction supervised by Stephen H. Hallet, James Hoban, George Hadfield and B. H. Latrobe, all distinguished architects. Charles BULFINCH, Thomas U. Walter, and Edward Clark superintended the construction of the central portion and extensions from 1818 to 1857; since that time separate buildings for various purposes have been added. The historical paintings of John TRUMBULL, John G. CHAPMAN, John Vanderlyn, Robert W. Weir, Howard Chandler CHRISTY, William H. Powell, Emanuel Leutze, James Walker, and Francis Bicknell Carpenter are to be seen in various parts of the main building and wings.

Capitoline Museum (Rome), one of the principal repositories of the antiquities of Rome founded in 1471 by Pope Sixtus IV who presented the papal collections to the Italian people: the collection was greatly enriched by Popes Clement XII and Benedict XIV. The objects of art include statuary, vases, bronzes and mosaics; among them, the colossal statue of MARS, the DYING GAUL, the Satyr by PRAXITELES, the Capitoline Venus. It also contains a long double line of statues and busts of Roman emperors and their wives.

Cappadocia Frescoes, an extensive series of ancient frescoes discovered in burial chapels and underground churches in Cappadocia, a province in Asia Minor. Several hundred frescoes are in well-preserved condition at the churches of Gueureine and Soghanli: some of them belong to the 8th century, and are painted on the bare surface of the rocks; others of later date are painted on a coat of plaster, and represent episodes in the life of the Virgin, the life of Christ, and the feasts of the church. The colors are pleasing and the faces Oriental in character.

Capriccio, in music (*a*) the title given to instrumental compositions in free form, and usually distinguished by original melodic, harmonic, and rhythmic characteristics. The title has been used by BRAHMS for piano compositions, and by many modern composers for orchestral works. (*b*) The direction *a capriccio* or *capriccioso* over a passage of music indicates that it is to be played "at pleasure," "capriciously" or "fantastically."

Capriccio Espagnol, an orchestral work by Nicholas RIMSKY-KORSAKOW composed and first played at a concert of the Russian Symphony Society on October 31, 1887. The composer writes about it as follows: "I composed the *Capriccio* from the sketches of my projected virtuoso violin fantasy on Spanish themes. The work went without difficulties; it was played with a perfection and enthusiasm the like of which it never possessed later even when directed by NIKISCH himself." Peter TSCHAIKOWSKY was one of its greatest admirers; he wrote Rimsky-Korsakow "Your *Capriccio Espagnol* is a colossal piece of instrumentation, and you may regard yourself as the greatest master of the present day." There is a Victor recording by the Boston "Pops" Orchestra directed by Arthur Fiedler, and a Columbia recording by the New York Philharmonic-Symphony Orchestra under John Barbirolli.

Capriccio Espagnol, a Spanish folk ballet in one act: libretto by Leonide MASSINE; choreography by Leonide Massine and ARGENTINITA; music from RIMSKY-KORSAKOW's *Capriccio Espagnol;* first produced at Monte Carlo in 1939. The scene is a Spanish town on the day of a fair or festival, and the dances follow exactly the indications on the original score of Rimsky-Korsakow's orchestral fantasy as follows: I *Alborada;* II *Variation, Seguidilla;* III *Alborada;* IV *Gipsy Scene and Dance;* V *Austrian Fandango.*

Capuana, Luigi (1839-1915), Italian poet, novelist, journalist, and dramatic critic. His works include the novels *Giacinta* (1879) and *The Marchesa of Roccaverdina;* several volumes of short stories such as *Profiles of Women* and *Homo;* two collections of fairy tales; a volume of rhythmical prose entitled *Semi-Rhythms.*

Capulets and Montagues, the names of the two noble families at Verona who war with each other in SHAKESPEARE's *Romeo and Juliet.* The heroine, Juliet, is a daughter of the Capulets, and the hero, Romeo, is a son of the Montagues.

Capus, Alfred (1858-1922), French journalist, author, and dramatist whose first play, *La Mari malgré lui,* was produced in 1879. He was successful as editor of *Figaro;* wrote several fine novels such as *False Departure* and *Years of Adventure:* also many plays of which the principal characteristics are ironic realism and philosophic fatalism; among them are *Brignol and His Daughter; The Husbands of Leontine; The Chatelaine; The Adventurer; The Beauty Institute.*

Caragiali, Ioan (1852-1912), Rumanian short-story writer, novelist, and dramatist; his novels, *Faclia de paste, Noptea furtunosa* (Stormy Night), and *Scrissaren perduta* (The Lost Letter) are highly regarded, as well as the tragedy, *Napasta* (Contempt), as well as several comedies satirizing the effects of veneering old customs, has placed him in the front rank of Rumanian playwrights.

Caran d'Ache, pen-name of **Emmanuel Poire** (1858-1909), French artist, caricaturist and illustrator who was born and educated at Moscow; his pen-name means "lead pencil." He was famous for his gift of pictorial anecdote; i.e., illustrating a story at its different stages. His work appeared in several magazines including *La Vie parisienne* and *Le Figaro illustré;* he has also published several volumes of sketches, and illustrated many books.

Caravaggio, Michelangelo Amerighi da (1569-1609), Italian painter who started his career as apprentice to a mason, and led a life crowded with extraordinary episodes such as duels, hasty flights, arrests, and finally death from exposure.

In the absence of teachers he studied the paintings of VERONESE, TITIAN, and MICHELANGELO, but developed a naturalistic art which was reflected in the works of his successors. Among his finest works are *Flight into Egypt; Death of the Virgin; The Entombment of Christ; Martyrdom of St. Sebastian; The Card Players.* He was extremely successful in creating new lighting effects by the use of lamps in unusual places, thereby obtaining sharp contrasts and intense, gloomy effects.

Caravaggio, Polidoro Caldara da (c.1492-1543), Italian painter, real name *Polidoro Caldara:* his talent attracted the attention of RAPHAEL who permitted him to paint several frescoes in the galleries of the VATICAN. Most of his paintings are known only through engravings, but two works, *Crucifixion* and *Christ Bearing the Cross* are in the NAPLES MUSEUM.

Carco, Francis (1886-), French poet and novelist who served in World War I, and wrote many successful tales dealing with the underworld; the works that are published in English include *The Hounded Man* (1924); *The Romance of François Villon; The Last Bohemia; Perversity.*

Cards, Playing. Sets of cards used in playing games first appeared during the 14th century in Europe; the earliest sets were painted by hand and were very costly. The designs in use today are copies of 16th century cards; they are of much significance because it is believed that they had considerable influence in developing the art of wood engraving.

Carducci (Carducho), Bartolommeo (1560-1608), Italian painter, sculptor, and architect who studied architecture and sculpture under AMMANATI, and painting with Federigo ZUCCARO with whom he went to Madrid to paint the ceiling and some of the frescoes in the ESCORIAL. His greatest painting was *The Descent from the Cross,* and he was a favorite of Philip III who gave him the task of decorating the gallery of the PRADO. He left this work unfinished; his brother, **Vincenzo Carducci** (1568-1638), completed it, and also executed several fine paintings for Philip IV; among them *Scenes from the Life of the Virgin.* He also wrote a valuable treatise on painting, *De las Excelencias de la Pintura* (1633).

Carducci, Giosue (1836-1907), Italian poet, professor of Italian literature at the University of Bologna, and founder of a school which exerted a profound influence on Italian poetry and prose. His works include essays on the history of literature, and many poetical works including *Rimes* (1857); the much-discussed *Hymn to Satan; The Decennials; Serious Trifles; Poems of Entrio Romano,* the name being a pseudonymn; *Iambics and Epodes; New Rimes.*

Carducho, Bartolommeo, see **Carducci, Bartolommeo.**

Carew, Thomas (c.1598-c.1639), English poet; an intimate friend of CHARLES I and Ben JONSON, and one of a group known as the CAVALIER POETS. His poems, in the forms of songs or odes, are graceful and elegant, but sometimes licentious, as in the case of *Rapture:* he also wrote a masque, *Coelum Britanicum,* performed at Whitehall in 1633 with Charles I and his courtiers in the cast.

Carey, Henry (c.1685-1743), English musician and dramatic writer, chiefly self-taught, but a pupil of GEMINIANI for a time. His works include nine ballad operas and more than 90 ballads including the still popular *Sally in Our Alley.* He also claimed authorship of *God Save the King,* but this has been hotly disputed.

Caricature, a term derived from the Italian word, *caricatura,* and applied to a picture or a written description marked by exaggeration or distortion. The word was used first by Sir Thomas Browne in the middle of the 17th century; then in the London *Spectator,* and in 1757 by Ben JONSON in his dictionary. Caricature in painting was practiced by the Romans, and in literature by ARISTOPHANES and other Greek dramatists: in England it was used by Jonathan SWIFT and Henry FIELDING in their writings, and by HOGARTH and CRUIKSHANK in their illustrations: in the United States by Thomas NAST who baited Tammany Hall with his symbolic drawings of the now familiar tiger and donkey. Caricature was also the chief feature of popular magazines such as *Puck* and *Judge,* and in many vaudeville and radio acts.

Carillon (Fr.), a set of bells differing from a chime in being fixed in position and assembled in greater number. A carillon is played either by hand by means of a keyboard, or by machinery utilizing the principle of the cylinder, set with pegs or studs, used in a barrel organ. The keyboard consists of either one or two rows of keys, and the same number of foot pedals operating levers which strike the bells. There are many carillons in European and English cities: in the United States the Riverside Church in New York has a carillon of 72 bells which is probably the largest in the world.

Carissimi, Giacomo (c.1604-1674), Italian organist and composer; he is distinguished for having broken away from the contrapuntal tradition established by PALESTRINA, and devoting himself to the development of the monodic style in which the melody is confined to a single voice accompanied by one or more instruments. He also developed RECITATIVE in his five oratorios including *Jeptha, The Judgment of Solomon, Balthazar, Jonas,* and *Jonah.*

Carle, Richard (1871-), American stage and screen actor who appeared for many years on the American and English stage in plays and musical comedies including *The Lady Slavey; The Greek Slave; Ma'm'selle 'Awkins,* his own play; *The Casino Girl; The Spring Chicken,* adapted by him; *The Girl from Montmartre; Words and Music.* He was also a veteran of the silent film, and has appeared since 1934 in many talking pictures.

Carlen, Emilia Flygare (1807-1892), Swedish novelist whose first story, *Waldemar Klein* (1838), was followed by many successful novels including *Gustav Lindorm; The Professor; Chamberlain Lassmann; A Warehouse on the Cliffs,* the last-named considered her finest work. Another interesting volume is her *Reminiscences of Swedish Literary Life.*

Carleton, Will (1845-1912), American lecturer and author of a famous poem, *Over the Hills to the Poorhouse;* also many popular ballads of American home life including *Poems* (1871); *Farm Legends; City Ballads; City Legends; Rhymes of Our Planet.* His lecture tours in the United States and Europe did much to increase his circle of readers.

Carleton, William (1794-1869), Irish novelist whose intimate knowledge of the twists of Irish peasant character, and keen sense of humor accounted for the success of his first book, *Traits and Stories of Irish Peasantry.* Several of his tales including *Willy Reilly, The Fair of Emyvale, Fardorougha the Miser,* and *The Black Prophet* reveal great dramatic power, and a vein of realistic humor.

Carlisle, James Reynold (1886-), American violin maker who produced his first instrument in 1910, and has made about 1500 instruments in thirty years. His violins are modeled after STRADIVARIUS and GUANERIUS, and his varnish is a special preparation requiring the aid of strong sunlight in its preparation. The prices range from $100.00 to $300.00, making them well within the reach of serious students and orchestral players.

Carl Rosa Opera Company, an organization founded in 1875 by Carlo Rosa (1842-1889), formerly an operatic impresario in the United States and husband of PAREPA-ROSA, for the production of opera in English. The company toured the English provinces, and also appeared occasionally in London: its repertory included most of the standard operas, and also many works by English composers. Augustus HARRIS managed the company from 1889 to 1923 when he was succeeded by H. N. Phillips: the organization has played an important part in British musical affairs.

Carlsen, Emil (1853-1932), American painter born in Copenhagen, Denmark: he came to the United States at nineteen, and developed into a fine painter of landscapes and marine views, winning many awards. His works include *Summer Clouds; Moonlight on the Kattegat; Open Sea; Still Life; The South Strand; Moonlight on a Calm Sea.*

Carlyle, Thomas (1795-1881), Scotch essayist educated at Edinburgh University, and author of several works which come within the scope of this volume including *Life of Schiller* (1824); *Sartor Resartus,* a spiritual autobiography; *The French Revolution;* a history lacking factual form, but dramatically impressive; *Heroes, Hero Worship and the Heroic in History; Life and Letters of Oliver Cromwell* in which he evinces distrust of democracy; *Frederick the Great.* His style was one of the most effective, if unusual, in all English literature.

Carmagnole (Fr.), a dance, accompanied by a song, which gained great popularity with the French people during the French Revolution in the period known as the "Reign of Terror". The words began with the phrase "Madame Veto has promised"; Madame Veto was the revolutionary nickname for Marie ANTOINETTE.

Carman, Bliss (1861-1929), Canadian journalist and poet educated at the Universities of New Brunswick, Edinburgh and Harvard. His works include *Low Tide on Grand Pré* (1893); *Songs from Vagabondia*, with Richard Hovey; *Behind the Arras, a Book of the Unseen; Pipes of Pan*, a series; *Ballads and Lyrics; Far Horizons*. He is regarded as Canada's most distinguished poet.

Carmen, a grand opera in four acts: libretto by Henri Meilhac and Ludovic Halévy; music by Georges Bizet; first produced at the Opéra-Comique, Paris, in 1875, and at the Academy of Music, New York, in 1878 with Minnie HAUK creating the title role. The story is: Don José, a corporal in the Spanish army, becomes infatuated with Carmen, a girl from a cigarette factory who flirts with him. She is arrested in a stabbing affray, and is permitted to escape while in the charge of Don José, who is jailed for his delinquency. He goes in search of Carmen, and finds her flirting with the toreador, Escamillo: the wily girl persuades him to desert the army, and join the smugglers at their camp in the mountains, but soon tires of her soldier lover. Escamillo appears at the camp: a quarrel results between Escamillo and Don José, but they are parted by Carmen and the gypsies, and Escamillo invites them all, especially Carmen, to attend the bullfight at Seville. Micaela, Don Jose's affianced sweetheart, whom he has neglected for Carmen, comes to tell him that his mother is dying, and he leaves, warning Carmen to be true. She meets Don José by chance at the entrance to the arena; he begs her to return to him, and when she refuses, stabs her just as the audience is leaving after the bullfight. There are complete recordings by Victor and Columbia; also separate records of the *Toreador Song, Flower Song* and all other important arias and ensembles.

Carmen, Sylva, see **Elizabeth, Pauline Elisabeth Ottilie Louise.**

Carmer, Carl Lamson (1893-   ), American essayist and poet educated at Hamilton College and the Harvard Graduate School. His works include *Frenchtown* (1927); *Deep South; Stars Fell on Alabama; Listen for a Lonesome Drum; The Hudson;* also a novel, *Genesee River.*

Carnaval (Schumann), a series of twenty-one short compositions for the piano; written by Robert Schumann, and published with the subtitle, *Petite sketches on four notes.* The three odd musical figures known as *Sphinxes* which occur in the work are played either as single notes or in octaves; there are complete Victor recordings by Sergei RACHMANINOFF and Myra HESS. The work was arranged for orchestra by RIMSKY-KORSAKOW, GLAZOUNOFF, LIADOFF and TCHERPNIN; there is a Victor recording by the London Philharmonic Orchestra under Eugène GOOSSENS. This orchestration was used in connection with the *Carnaval Ballet* produced at Paris in 1910 with Michel FOKINE as librettist and choreographer, and Leon BAKST as designer of the scenery and costumes.

Carnaval des Animaux, see **Carnival of Animals.**

Carnaval Romain (Overture), an orchestral work by Hector BERLIOZ; originally the prelude to Act II of his opera, *Benvenuto Cellini,* but altered into a concert overture and first performed at Paris in 1844, under the direction of the composer, with such great success that it had to be immediately repeated. As a prelude in the opera, it had ill-success, as directed by François Habeneck, conductor at the Paris Opéra; Berlioz blamed its failure on Habeneck's slow tempo in the final *Saltarello.* There is a Columbia recording by the London Philharmonic Orchestra with Sir Thomas Beecham, and a Victor recording by the Boston "Pops" Orchestra under Arthur Fiedler.

Carnavalet Museum (Paris), a building erected in the 16th century by Jean Bullant and Jean Goujon for François de Kernevenoy: the present name may be a gradual corruption of the former owner's name. It is now the home of the Paris Municipal Museum containing valuable relics and records of every description pertaining to the French Revolution.

Carnegie, Andrew (1835-1919), American capitalist, steel magnate, writer, and philanthropist. Among his benefactions were the *Carnegie Libraries* founded in the United States, Great Britain and other English-speaking countries, the buildings being built and equipped wherever the local authorities provided sites and maintenance, thereby insuring local interest and a feeling of responsibility for the success of the project: more than $60,000,000 was expended. Carnegie contributed several articles to periodicals, and also wrote *An American Four-in-Hand in Britain* (1883); *Round the World; Triumphant Democracy.*

Carnegie Hall (New York), a building erected in 1891 at the corner of Seventh Avenue and Fifty-seventh Street, New York, by Andrew Carnegie in accordance with a suggestion of Dr. Walter DAMROSCH that a concert hall be provided for the ORATORIO SOCIETY OF NEW YORK, of which he was the conductor, and Carnegie the president. The cost of the building, which comprises a main hall with a seating capacity of 3000, a recital hall seating 1200 and three smaller auditoriums each with a seating capacity of 500 persons, was $2,000,000: Carnegie paid 90% of this amount, but placed the building on a self-supporting basis. The main hall, originally known as the *New York Music Hall*, was opened by a concert of the SYMPHONY SOCIETY OF NEW YORK with Peter TSCHAIKOWSKY conducting his *March Solennelle:* a few days later Ignace PADEREWSKI made his New York debut there. In 1895 the name of the building was changed to Carnegie Hall, and in 1896 additions were made including ten stories of studios which have been continuously used for forty-six years by teachers of music, dramatic art, painting and sculpture. The musical history of this great institution has been recorded in the book, *The House That Music Built*, by Ethel Peyser. The concerts of the New York Philharmonic Symphony Orchestra have been held at Carnegie Hall regularly since 1892, and all other American orchestras as well as European organizations, choral societies, and virtuosos have selected it for their concerts and debuts.

Carnegie Institute (Pittsburgh), an institution founded by Andrew Carnegie in 1896, and maintained by his endowment. The departments of interest to lovers of the arts are the **Carnegie Library** which contains a total of more than 700,000 volumes in which is included a comprehensive collection of books relating to the arts: the **Department of Fine Arts** comprising collections of architecture, sculptures, and paintings; the **Music Hall** which fosters the musical needs of the community with a series of seventy-five recitals each season. The *Hall of Architecture* contains many choice examples of Egyptian, Greek, Roman, Gothic, Renaissance, Romanesque, and late Renaissance architecture in the form of cast reproductions of doorways, columns, and monuments arranged in chronological order. *The Gallery of Paintings* contains canvases by artists of all nationalities, and may be said to be contemporary as the majority have been created during the last forty years: they include works by DAGNAN-BOUVERET, ORPEN, ZULOAGA, WHISTLER, HOMER, BELLOWS, BLANCHE, CASSATT, DERAIN, DUVENECK, HENRI, INNESS, PISSARO, SARGENT, STUART, BROOK, and many other distinguished American and foreign artists. In the *Hall of Sculpture* are to be found examples of Egyptian, Assyrian, Persian, Greek, and Roman sculptures either in the original, or in the form of casts: there are also figures, busts, and groups by many distinguished sculptors including BARNARD, BARYE, BITTER, HOUDON, HUNTINGTON, MACMONNIES, MACNEIL, MANSHIP, RODIN, SAINT-GAUDENS, VONNOH, and WEINMAN.

Carnelian, a variety of chalcedony, usually reddish in color and used to a considerable extent as a stone for seals. Its older name was *cornelian,* and some varieties are brown, yellow or white in color. It can be distinguished from SARD by the fact that carnelian is a brilliant shade of red, and sard is brown in color.

Carneval Overture (Dvořák), an orchestral work by Antonin Dvořák; the second in a cycle of three overtures originally entitled "Nature, Life and Love," written in 1891 and first performed in 1892. Dvořák left the following clue to its meaning: "Imagine a lonely wanderer reaching a great city as night comes on, and a carnival is in full swing. On every side the sounds of musical instruments are heard; a pair of straying lovers pledge mutual devotion and joyous cries are heard as the people give vent to their feelings in folk songs and dances." There is a Victor recording by the Boston "Pops" Orchestra under Arthur Fiedler, and a Columbia recording by the Columbia Broadcasting Symphony Orchestra with Howard Barlow.

Carnival of Animals (Carnaval des Animaux), an orchestral suite, for an unusual combination of instruments, composed by Camille SAINT-SAENS, and written as a musical joke for a festive occasion. Saint-Saëns forbade its further performance or publication until after his death: it was performed in 1922 at Chicago under the direction of Louis HASSELMANS. The titles of some of the

movements afford a clue to its humor: *Royal March of the Lions; Hens and Cocks; Tortoises; The Elephant; Kangaroos; Aquarium; Donkeys; Pianists; Le Cygne (The Swan).* The last-named is arranged in the suite for violoncello: Saint-Saëns permitted this to be published, and it is without doubt the composition by which he is best known to the average music lover. There is a Victor recording of the complete work by the Philadelphia Orchestra under Leopold Stokowski, and records of "The Swan" by CASALS, PIATIGORSKY and ELMAN.

Caro, Annibale (1507-1566), Italian poet and translator who for many years was confidential secretary to the Duke of Parma, and a friend of Benvenuto CELLINI. He made an excellent translation of VIRGIL's *Aeneid* and wrote some beautiful sonnets.

Caro, Miguel Antonio (1843-1909), Spanish-American author and poet born in Colombia, and president of his country from 1894 to 1898. His poetical works include *Hours of Love,* and a fine translation of VIRGIL's complete works into Spanish verse. His prose writings cover a variety of subjects including literature and history. Caro's father, **José Eusebio Caro** (1817-1853), was also a poet, but as he was a reformer with stern principles, his verse reflects his unyielding and somewhat gloomy attitude toward life except in an exquisite set of verses addressed to his son.

Carol, a song of joyous character with words that indicate its association with Christmas. French carols are called *noëls,* and English are known as *nowells.* The first carols were written by a curious group of nomads called "Gipsy Scholars," composed of men educated as priests who forsook their calling to live by their wits. Folk songs were used as tunes for early carols, and the first carol printed completely as to both words and music was the *Coventry Carol* in 1521.

Carolus-Duran (1837-1917), French painter whose real name was Charles Auguste Émile Durand. He studied at the Academy in Lille, and left home at fifteen to study at the Swiss Academy, at the Louvre, and in Spain where he was greatly influenced by VELASQUEZ. His first work, *Evening Prayer,* exhibited at the Paris salon in 1865, started him on the road to success; it was followed by *The Assassinated; Lady With the Glove; Madame Feydeau; Seaside; The Glory of Marie de Medicis; Old Lithograph; Triumph of Bacchus; Spanish Sponge Merchant.* His portrait studio was well patronized by distinguished sitters including Louis Pasteur, Gustave DORE, Charles GOUNOD and many others: John Singer SARGENT was one of his pupils.

Caron, Pierre Augustin, see **Beaumarchais.**

Caroto, Giovanni Francesco (c.1480-1546), Italian painter who was a pupil of MANTEGNA, and so greatly influenced by Leonardo da VINCI and RAPHAEL that he was called the "Proteus of painters." Nevertheless he developed an intensively original style in rich color effects, plainly visible in his *Virgin in Glory; St. Ursula; Virgin with St. Anne and the Saints; History of Tobias.* He worked with his brother, **Giovanni Caroto** (c.1488-c.1550), also a painter, with whom he has often been confused.

Carpaccio, Vittore or **Vittorio Scarpaza** (c.1465-c.1522), Italian painter; member of an old Venetian family. He was a pupil of Lazzaro Bastiani, and greatly influenced by Giovanni BELLINI. He was one of the greatest of the early Venetian historical and religious painters: his finest works include a portrait of Pope Alexander III; a series of nine paintings. *The Life of St. Ursula; St. Jerome and the Lion; Christ in the Garden of Olives; The Storming of St. Stephen; Christ with the Instruments of the Passion; Presentation in the Temple.*

Carpeaux, Jean Baptiste (1827-1875), French sculptor and painter who studied at the ECOLE DES BEAUX-ARTS, Paris, and won the Prix de Rome with his statue, *Hector with His Son Astyanax.* He was influenced by both DONATELLO and MICHELANGELO, and his finest works include the dramatic group, *Ugolino and His Sons; Girl With a Shell;* another group, *The Dance* for the Paris Opera House; *The Four Quarters of the World,* a fountain symbolizing Europe, Asia, Africa and America. He was one of the great sculptors of the naturalistic school.

Carpenter, John Alden (1876-), American composer who studied with John K. PAINE at Harvard and Sir Edward ELGAR. His works include the ballets *Krazy Kat* and SKYSCRAPERS; an orchestral suite, ADVENTURES IN A PERAMBULATOR; a concerto for piano and orchestra; a symphony; two symphonic poems; a violin concerto; several chamber music works; songs and piano pieces. He possesses a fund of melodic invention combined with harmonic ingenuity, and a keen sense of what may be termed "musical humor."

Carracci, Agostino (c.1557-c.1607), Italian painter and engraver; a pupil of Domenico TIBALDI and Cornelius Cort, and a relative of Lodovico CARRACCI, with whom he founded the Eclectic School in Bologna. He assisted Annibale CARRACCI in painting the *Triumph of Galatea* and *Cephalus and Aurora* in the Farnese Palace, Rome: among his best works are *Last Communion of St. Jerome; Adulteress before Christ; Infant Hercules; Celestial, Terrestrial and Venal Love; Hercules and Atlas; The Assumption.*

Carracci, Annibale (1560-1609), Italian painter; pupil of his uncle, Lodovico CARRACCI, and brother of Agostino CARRACCI. He taught at the Eclectic School founded by his uncle in Bologna; and made several paintings for the Farnese Palace, Rome; among them *Juno before Jupiter* and *The Triumph of Bacchus.* His finest works are *St. Roch Giving Alms; Madonna of the Cherries; Birth of the Virgin; Temptation of St. Anthony; The Entombment of Christ.*

Carracci, Ludovico (1555-1619), Italian painter who was advised to give up painting by his teachers, Prospero Fontana and TINTORETTO: he persisted in his ambition, and founded one of the most important institutions in Italy, the Eclectic School at Bologna at which both DOMENICHINO

and Guido RENI were pupils. Among his best works are *Christ Crowned With Thorns; Transfiguration; Preaching of John the Baptist; Conversion of St. Paul.*

Carradine, John (1906-), American stage and screen actor who appeared in Shakespearean plays before he entered the films in 1936: he has had important roles in many pictures including *Les Miserables; The Prisoner of Shark Island; Under Two Flags; Mary of Scotland; Daniel Boone; Winterset; Garden of Allah; Captains Courageous; Hound of the Baskervilles; Captain Fury; Grapes of Wrath; Chad Hanna; Western Union.*

Carrara, a town in Tuscany, Italy, where the Romans quarried the fine, white marble until the fall of the Roman Empire, and from which marble has been steadily removed to erect impressive buildings and carve noble sculptures since the 12th century. The quarries employed five thousand workmen, and shipments worth more than a million dollars were made yearly. The town has a museum of antiquities which contains some Roman relics found in the ancient quarries when they were reopened.

Carreño, Teresa (1853-1917), Venezuelan singer, composer, and pianist who made her debut, and gave five recitals at the ACADEMY OF MUSIC, New York, as a child of nine. Later she studied with Louis GOTTSCHALK and Anton RUBINSTEIN, and also appeared with great success as an operatic singer in England, the United States, and South America. In 1882 she devoted her entire energies to the piano, and by 1890 was recognized both in America and Europe as one of the world's greatest pianists. She composed concert piano pieces, and was the teacher of Edward MACDOWELL, as well as a powerful factor in securing appreciation of his abilities as a composer.

Carreño de Miranda, Juan (1614-1685), Spanish painter said to have been influenced by TITIAN, VAN DYCK and VELASQUEZ: he succeeded the last-named as court painter to Charles II of Spain. His works, numerous and complicated, include *St. Sebastian; St. Anthony Feeding the Fishes; Baptism of Christ;* frescoes in the cupola of the Church of St. Antonio of the Portuguese at Madrid; portraits of Charles II and of Queen Marianna, mother of Charles II.

Carrère, John Merven (1858-1911), American architect, born in Rio de Janeiro, Brazil, of French and Scotch parentage. He studied in Switzerland at the Institute Breitenstein at Grenchen, and at the ECOLE DES BEAUX-ARTS in Paris. In 1886 he entered into partnership with Thomas HASTINGS, a fellow student in Paris. Among the many fine works which resulted were the New York Public Library, the office buildings for the House and the Senate at Washington, D. C.; the architectural approaches to the Manhattan Bridge, New York City; the Carnegie Institute, Washington, D. C.; many great hotels throughout the United States including the Ponce de Leon and Alcazar Hotels, St. Augustine, Florida.

Carriera, Rosalba (1675-1757), Italian painter who first worked at lace making before she began to study under FRA DIAMANTINI, and became famous at twenty-four for her miniatures and crayon portraits. She visited Paris in 1720; painted Louis XV and other members of the royal family, and was elected to the French Academy. She was the most famous portrait painter of her time: more than 140 of her portraits are in the Dresden Gallery.

Carrier-Belleuse, Pierre (1851-1933), French painter who collaborated with several other artists after World War I in a vast panorama, *The Pantheon of the War,* in which the likenesses of the statesmen, generals, and military heroes of the war were grouped together. It was exhibited in 1927 at New York, and, after being sold to the citizens of Washington, D. C., was shown at the Bicentennial Exposition.

Carrière, Eugene (1849-1906), French painter attracted to his art by seeing the pastels of Georges de LA TOUR in a museum at Saint-Quentin. He studied at the ECOLE DES BEAUX-ARTS, and with Alexandre CABANEL. While a prisoner in Dresden during the Franco-Prussian War, he had the opportunity to study the great masters, and later at the Louvre in Paris. Among his finest works are *Young Mother Nursing Her Child; Two Friends; Sick Child; Woman at Her Toilet; Maternity; The Family;* he also painted some large works at the Hôtel de Ville and the Sorbonne in Paris.

Carrillo, Leo, American stage and screen actor who first appeared on the vaudeville stage in 1913, and later in numerous successful plays including *Twin Beds; Lombardi, Ltd.; They Knew What They Wanted.* He has also played important roles in the talking films; among them *History is Made at Night; 52nd Street; The Barrier; Girl of the Golden West; Blockade; Fisherman's Wharf; Chicken Wagon Family.*

Carroll, John (1892-), American painter who studied at the University of California, and with Frank DUVENECK, giving his first public exhibition in 1922. He went to Europe in 1925, later teaching at the ART STUDENTS' LEAGUE, New York, and again going to Europe on a GUGGENHEIM FELLOWSHIP. In 1930 he became head of the department of painting of the Society of Arts and Crafts in Detroit: among his creations are a mural in the Detroit Institute of Arts, and the canvas, *White Lace.*

Carroll, Lewis (1832-1897), English author educated at Oxford where he was a lecturer on mathematics for some years; his real name was Charles Lutwidge Dodgson. His reputation was made by his stories for children, only fully appreciated for their wit and imagination by adults: they include *Alice's Adventures in Wonderland* (1865); *Through the Looking-Glass and What Alice Found There.* He also wrote a collection of humorous verse, *Phantasmagoria;* a facetious poem, *The Hunting of the Snark,* and several works on mathematics and logic.

Carroll, Madeleine (1906-), English stage and screen actress educated at Birmingham University. After making her first stage appearance at New Brighton in 1927, she appeared in many important plays including *Beau Geste; French Leave; Enchantment; The Toy Cart; Veronica.* Among the films in which she has played the feminine lead are *Escape; School for Scandal; Thirty-nine Steps; Secret Agent; The Case Against Mrs. Ames; The Prisoner of Zenda; Blockade; Safari; Honeymoon in Bali; My Son, My Son; Virginia; One Night in Lisbon; Bahama Passage; My Favorite Blonde.*

Carroll, Paul Vincent (1900-), Irish dramatist who, after early instruction from his father, went to Dublin and became interested in the ABBEY THEATRE movement while studying to be a school teacher, a profession he followed for a few years. His first play, *The Watched Pot,* was produced in 1931; the following year *Things That Are Caesar's,* written in collaboration with Teresa Deevy, was awarded the Abbey Theatre prize. Since then he has written *Shadow and Substance* and *The White Steed.*

Carrucci, Jacopo, see **Pontormo, Jacopo Da.**

Carryl, Charles Edward (1841-1920), American author: his works include *Davy and the Goblin* (1885); *The Admiral's Caravan; The River Syndicate and Other Stories.*

Carryl, Guy Wetmore (1873-1904), American novelist and humorist: among his best-known works are *Fables for the Frivolous* (1898); *Mother Goose for Grown-Ups; The Lieutenant-Governor; The Garden of Years and Other Poems.*

Carstens, Asmus Jacob (1754-1798), German portrait and historical painter, said to have been influenced by Giulio ROMANO. His works include *Death of Aeschylus; Battle of Rossbach; Fall of the Rebel Angels; Socrates Saving the Life of Alcibiades; Ganymede and the Eagle.* A great exhibition of his paintings was made at Rome in 1795: he had many distinguished pupils including Peter CORNELIUS, and was considered the founder of the new German school of historical painting.

Carte, Richard D'Oyly (1844-1901), English grand opera and light opera impresario. In 1870 he opened a concert and theatre agency in London, presenting Charles GOUNOD, Adelina PATTI, MARIO and many other noted musicians. In 1875 he produced TRIAL BY JURY, the first operetta by Sir Arthur SULLIVAN and Sir William S. GILBERT, and later all the other operettas written by these collaborators. The SAVOY THEATRE was erected especially for their productions. He also attempted to establish a permanent home in 1887 for grand opera written by British composers, but the venture failed for lack of suitable new operas. His wife continued to manage the Savoy Theatre until her death in 1913; she was succeeded by his youngest son, **Rupert D'Oyly Carte** (1876-), who also managed the D'Oyly Carte Opera Company on its American tours beginning in 1934.

Carter, Elizabeth (1717-1806), English poet, translator, and friend of Samuel JOHNSON, Edmund Burke, Samuel RICHARDSON, and other famous men of her day. Her works include an excellent translation of Epictetus, and a volume of poems in which an *Ode to Wisdom* is greatly admired.

Carter, Mrs. Leslie (1862-1937), American actress who appeared in 1890 on the New York stage in *The Ugly Duckling,* after being coached by David BELASCO. In 1895 she made the greatest success of her career in Belasco's play, *The Heart of Maryland,* followed by *Zaza* and *Dubarry.* After terminating her contract with Belasco, she toured the United States in the above-mentioned plays, and also in *La Tosca; The Circle* with John Drew; *Stella Dallas; The Shanghai Gesture.* She also appeared in a talking film, *The Vanishing Pioneer,* when she was more than seventy years of age.

Carter, Nick, a fictional character who appeared in many dime novels published in the latter part of the nineteenth century. It was used by many writers including George Charles Jenks, Eugene Taylor Sawyer, John Russell Coryell and Frederick William Davis: the pen name "Nick Carter" was substituted for the real names of the authors.

Carthage, a historically famous city in North Africa, said to have been founded by the Phoenicians in the middle of the 9th century, B.C., and located near the present city of Tunis. It had a population of more than 700,000 in 300 B.C., and became a powerful rival of Syracuse and Rome, but was finally overthrown in the Punic Wars lasting from 264 B.C. to 146 B.C. The famous Carthaginian general, HANNIBAL, and the mythical Queen DIDO who was said to have founded CARTHAGE and to have committed suicide because of her love for AENEAS, have been favorite subjects in drama, literature, painting, and sculpture.

Carton, Richard Claude (1856-1928), English dramatist, whose real name was Richard Claude Critchett. His plays were chiefly farcical comedies, many of which were written for his wife, Katherine Compton, an excellent actress known on the stage as "Miss Compton," and much admired for her burlesques of aristocratic ladies. His most successful plays were *Lord and Lady Algy* and *Lady Huntworth's Experiment.*

Cartoon, a term used in the graphic arts in two senses: (*a*) The drawing for a larger fresco, oil painting, tapestry, or sculptured group: the finest classical examples are seven cartoons by RAPHAEL now in the VICTORIA AND ALBERT MUSEUM, London, originally designed for tapestries to decorate the SISTINE CHAPEL at the VATICAN, Rome. (*b*) A political drawing used in newspapers and magazines to satirize persons or events of interest to the general public: the cartoons of Thomas NAST on the Tweed ring are an excellent example. The animated cartoon, originated by Walt DISNEY, has been a source of delight to screen audiences all over the world.

Caruso, Enrico (1873-1921), Italian operatic tenor trained under Guglielmo Vergine; he appeared first in 1895 at Caserta, a town near Naples in *Faust,* and the following year at Naples in *La Traviata, La Favorita,* and *La Gioconda.* After singing with tremendous success in South America, Europe and England, he made his debut in 1903 at the Metropolitan Opera House, New York, in *Rigoletto,* appearing each season thereafter, and

making a total of 600 appearances before his death. In 1907 he won equal success in Germany and Austria, and his repertoire included at least 50 operas in Italian and French. He made many records of operatic arias which had an enormous world-wide sale, and was the highest paid singer of all time. His voice was that of an ideal dramatic tenor, its sweetness and power regulated by perfect breath control.

Carving, the art of cutting designs in wood, minerals of various kinds, ivory or metal, with tools and drills specially designed for the purpose: an artist who carves in stone or marble is generally called a *sculptor,* while an artisan who produces the less important decorative parts of architecture by cutting in wood is usually referred to as a *carver.*

Cary, Alice (1820-1871), American poet who published a volume of poetry with her sister, **Phoebe Cary** (1824-1871), entitled *Poems of Alice and Phoebe Cary* (1850). Alice Cary also wrote prose works including *Clovernook; Hagar; Married: not Mated; Snowberries.* Phoebe Cary published *Poems of Faith, Hope, and Love,* and wrote the hymn, *One Sweetly Solemn Thought.*

Cary, Annie Louise (1841-1921), American operatic contralto who studied in Milan and made her debut in 1867 at Copenhagen, Denmark, as Azucena in *Il Trovatore.* After further study with Pauline VIARDOT-GARCIA, she appeared in 1870 at Covent Garden, London, in *Lucrezia Borgia,* and made her operatic debut at the ACADEMY OF MUSIC, New York, in 1873 as Amneris in the first American performance of *Aida,* although she had sung there in 1870 with the Strakosch Concert Company. She was the first American woman to sing Wagnerian roles in the United States. Miss Cary retired in 1880 because of a throat affection: she bequeathed $50,000 to the People's Symphony Concerts, New York.

Caryatid, in architecture the sculptured figure of a woman usually employed as an ornamental support to a building in place of a column or pilaster. It was used during the RENAISSANCE, and again in the classical revival of the 19th century not only in architecture, but for home and garden furniture. The finest classical examples are those of the ERECHTHEUM, a temple on the ACROPOLIS at ATHENS.

Caryll, Ivan (1861-1921), Belgian composer who studied at the Liége Conservatory: his training and genius for conceiving piquant melodies resulted in his composing the music for some of the most delightful operettas and musical comedies produced in London and New York during the latter part of the 19th and the early part of the 20th century including *The Duchess of Danzig, The Earl and the Girl, Our Miss Gibbs,* and *The Pink Lady.*

Casadesus, Robert (1899-   ), French pianist and composer trained at the PARIS CONSERVATORY under Louis Diémer and Xavier Leroux: he has toured Europe, South America and the United States since 1922, appearing as soloist with the major symphony orchestras. He has taught at the American Conservatory at FONTAINEBLEAU, and has written a piano concerto; a violin concerto; a concerto for two pianos; chamber music; six sonatas and twenty-four preludes for piano; pieces for two pianos; many piano pieces.

Casals, Pablo (1876-), Spanish violoncellist, composer, and conductor who studied with his father, and with Tomás Breton in Barcelona under royal patronage. He made his debut in 1898 at the Concerts Lamoureux in Paris, became solo 'cellist at the Paris Grand Opera, and later professor of the violoncello at the Barcelona Conservatory. From 1895 he toured Europe, the United States, and South America with tremendous success, being recognized as the greatest virtuoso of the period. In 1919 he organized the Pablo Casals Orchestra in Barcelona, and conducted it for twenty years: he was also a member of the Cortot-Thibaud-Casals Trio, renowned for its chamber music concerts and recordings.

Casella, Alfredo (1883-), Italian pianist, conductor, writer, and composer who studied with his mother, and with Louis Diémer and Gabriel FAURE at the PARIS CONSERVATORY. He toured Europe successfully as a piano virtuoso; acted as guest conductor of many symphony orchestras; taught advanced piano classes at the Paris Conservatory; conducted many American orchestras, and won the Musical Fund Society (Philadelphia) and the Coolidge prizes for composition. His compositions include several operas and ballets; symphonies and orchestral works; chamber music; concertos for various instruments, and many piano pieces including two series written in the style of ten modern composers. He also re-orchestrated works by BALAKIREV and ALBENIZ, and wrote a history of music and a biography of Igor STRAVINSKY.

Casement, in architecture a frame constructed of wood or metal in such a manner as to hold window glass, and hung by hinges placed at the sides, top or bottom.

Casgrain, Abbé Henri Raymond (1831-1904), French-Canadian priest and author whose *Canadian Legends* (1861) established his reputation: later his *Pilgrimage to the Land of Evangeline* was honored by the French Academy. He also wrote historical works dealing with the pioneer days in Canada.

Casilear, John William (1811-1893), American painter and engraver who studied in Europe: his pictures include *Swiss Lake; September Afternoon; Catskill Twilight; Trout Brook; Scene in New Hampshire.* One of his line engravings, *Sibyl,* affords ample evidence of his skill, also reflected in the details of his landscapes.

Casorati, Felice (1886-), Italian painter influenced by the works of Peter BREUGHEL and TITIAN: he also became interested in cubism, attempting to depict solid forms in correct perspective blocked out in color. He also experimented in light effects, and individualized portraits such as his *Gualino* and *Silvana Cenni.* Casorati has also made stage settings for SPONTINI's *La Vestale* and Monteverdi's *Orfeo:* many European museums have examples of his work.

Cassandra, in Greek mythology a Trojan princess, daughter of PRIAM and HECUBA. The god APOLLO taught her the art of prophecy in exchange for her promise that he would become her lover; when she broke her promise, Apollo cursed her so that when she predicted the fall of TROY no one would believe her. After Troy was taken, she became the slave of AGAMEMNON, and was finally murdered by CLYTEMNESTRA.

Cassatt, Mary (1845-1926), American painter and engraver who spent her girlhood in France, and upon returning to the United States studied at the PENNSYLVANIA ACADEMY OF FINE ARTS, Philadelphia. In 1868 she returned to France, and made her home near Paris, with the exception of a few short visits to the United States. She was influenced in her work by CORREGGIO, VELASQUEZ and RUBENS, and joined the Impressionist group, being intimate with DEGAS, MANET, RENOIR and CEZANNE. Her favorite subject was that of a mother and a child in their daily intimate relationship; among her finest works are *The Young Mother;* a portrait of her own mother; *Mother and Child.* She also painted a mural, *Modern Women,* for the Women's Building at the Chicago Exposition.

Casse-Noisette, see **Nutcracker Suite.**

Casse-Noisette (Ballet), see **"Nutcracker" Ballet.**

Castagna, Bruna (1908-), Italian dramatic contralto who was a fine pianist at fourteen: she made her operatic debut in 1925 at Mantua in *Boris Godunoff* with Ezio PINZA in the title role; sang at opera houses in Europe, South America, Spain and Australia; made her American debut in 1934 at the New York Hippodrome in *Carmen,* and her debut in *Aïda* at the Metropolitan Opera House in 1936. She excels in the roles of Carmen, Amneris, Norma, Azucena, Delilah and Eurydice.

Castagno, Andrea del (c.1390-1457), Italian painter, also known as Andrea di Bartolommeo di Simone. He was a disciple of MASACCIO, and therefore of the naturalistic school; among his best works are *Last Supper; The Nine Worthies,* a group portrait of Boccaccio, Petrarch, Dante and other celebrities; *The Entombment of Christ; Resurrection; Dead Christ With Angels.*

Castaigne, André (1861-), French painter and illustrator: his reputation in the latter capacity was based on his drawings for *Century Magazine* and *Scribner's Magazine* while on a visit to the United States in 1890. He specialized in scenes of life on the West Coast such as his *Fortyniner's Ball.* He directed an art school in Baltimore, Md.; his paintings, *The Deluge, Dante and Beatrice,* and *After the Battle* are in the Peabody Gallery there.

Castanets, in music a percussion instrument consisting of a pair of small, concave pieces of hardwood or ivory, fastened together by a cord long enough to pass over the player's thumb while he clicks the pieces between his palms and middle fingers. They produce a clicking sound rather than a musical tone, and are usually used to accompany Spanish music.

139

Castelli, Ignaz Franz (1781-1862), Austrian poet and dramatist educated at the University of Vienna. During Napoleon's invasion of Austria, he wrote a *War Song* for the Austrian Army which became so popular that he was obliged to escape the ire of the French by leaving the country. He wrote more than 200 plays; also the libretto for an opera, *The Swiss Family*, music by Joseph Weigl, which was performed in every German opera house for more than a century. He assembled a remarkable collection of pictures, art objects, and a library of several thousand plays.

Castello, Giovanni Battista (c.1500-1569), Italian painter, sculptor and architect known as *Il Bergamasco* because his birthplace was near Bergamo. He held the position of architect to Philip II of Spain, and his best-known paintings include *The Martyrdom of St. Sebastian* and *Christ Judging the World*.

Castello, Valerio (1625-1669), Italian painter noted for his fine historical scenes and a pupil of Giovanni de' Ferrari and Il Sarzana. His style in his greatest work, *The Rape of the Sabines*, is compared favorably with that of TINTORETTO, CORREGGIO and VERONESE.

Castello Branco, Camillo (1826-1890), Portuguese novelist and poet regarded as one of Portugal's finest romancists: his more than 100 novels include *Mysteries of Lisbon* (1854); *Love of Perdition; The Marquis of Torres Novas; Brilliants from Brazil,* and a fine volume of verse with the unique title, *A Book.*

Castelnuovo-Tedesco, Mario (1895-   ), Italian pianist, conductor, and composer; student of composition in the Royal Institute Cherubini, Florence, with Ildebrando PIZZETTI. He toured the United States as a pianist and guest conductor of major symphony orchestras: his works include several operas of which *La Mandragola* is the most notable; many orchestral works; a violin concerto based on Italian folk-songs; a piano concerto; chamber music; choral works; many songs including thirty-three settings of Shakespeare.

Casti, Giovanni Battista (1721-1803), Italian courtier and poet whose fame sprang from his *Gay Stories in Ottava Rima,* and a witty satirical poem, *Talking Animals,* published in English as "The Court and Parliament of Beasts." He also wrote the librettos of two comic operas, and a poetic satire on court life in the reign of Catherine II of Russia as he saw it while attached to the Italian Embassy at St. Petersburg.

Castiglione, Count Baldassare (1478-1529), Italian statesman, author, and poet. His verses in Latin and Italian are characterized by grace and finesse, but his principal claim to fame is a prose work *Il Cortegiano,* also called *Il Libro d'oro,* and translated into English as *The Book of the Courtier.* It is in the form of a debate between distinguished people on the question of what constitutes a perfect courtier, and occupies a unique place in literature.

Castiglione, Giovanni Benedetto (1616-1670), Italian painter and etcher called *Il Grechetto* in Italy and *Le Benédette* in France. He excelled in painting fairs, markets and country scenes with animals, rivaling Jacopo BASSANO in the last-named. Among his finest works are *The Nativity of Jesus; Noah Entering the Ark; Expulsion from the Temple; Birds and Animals.* His brother Salvatore, and his son Francesco both excelled in the same subjects, the result being confusion as to the authorship of some paintings.

Casting, Plaster, see **Plaster Casting.**

Castle, Egerton (1858-1920), English novelist educated at King's College, London, and Trinity College, Cambridge. After his marriage to an Irish lady, Agnes Sweetman, several romantic novels were published signed "By Agnes and Egerton Castle." They include *The Pride of Jennico* (1898); *The Sacred Orchard; The Incomparable Bellairs; The Bath Comedy; Pamela Pounce:* all of them proved to be best sellers, and were also successfully dramatized.

Castle, in architecture a large fortified building or group of buildings first erected in the Middle Ages. The medieval castle originally consisted of a TOWER (also known as a KEEP), with smaller buildings surrounded by a high wall, and encircled by a moat with a drawbridge. This form was very much elaborated by the inclusion of a courtyard, an assembly hall, a chapel and living quarters for retainers. Among the famous buildings of this character were the original LOUVRE at Paris and the TOWER OF LONDON.

Castle Garden Theatre, a building near the Battery, New York City, placed on the former site of Fort Clinton, the latter built in 1807. It opened as a theatre in 1845, and Jenny LIND made her American debut there. In 1858 it became a reception depot for immigrants, and in 1890 the Municipal Aquarium: it was torn down in 1942.

Castlemon, Harry, see **Fosdick, Charles Austin.**

Castor and Pollux, in Greek and Roman mythology the twin sons of Leda by ZEUS; also called the *Dioscuri.* They took part in the Calydonian Hunt, the adventures of the Argonauts, and were changed, after Castor's death, into the twin stars called the *Gemini.* They were the patrons of sailors, public games, and hospitality.

Castrati (singular **Castrato**), Italian male singers whose youthful voices have been made permanent by the surgical operation of castration; also called *evirati.* Artificial male soprano, mezzo-soprano and alto singers were common in the 17th and 18th centuries in both church and operatic singing: two notable artists were CAFFARELLI and CRESCENTINI who earned enormous sums in opera.

Castro y Bellvis, Guillen de (1569-1631), Spanish dramatist and friend of Lope de Vega whose style he imitated in several comedies. The two dramas which made him famous are *The Youthful Adventures of the Cid* (1599) and *The Achievements of the Cid* from the first of which the French dramatist, Pierre CORNEILLE, obtained the material for his tragedy on the same subject.

Catacombs, in architecture a subterranean cemetery consisting of passages or galleries lined with recesses on both sides for tombs; also used by the early Christians as refuges from persecution and secret places of worship. The term (in the singular) was originally applied to the catacomb under the Church of St. Sebastian, Rome: the most famous are those used by the early Christians on the APPIAN WAY near Rome. The catacombs of Paris were abandoned stone quarries used for the bones of the dead. The beginnings of the art of painting in Italy can be studied from crude frescoes on the walls of some of the catacombs.

Catafalque, a word of which the origin is uncertain although it is found in several European languages; it refers to a scaffold or platform, constructed of wood and usually beautifully decorated, used at funeral ceremonies to receive either the coffin or an effigy of the deceased: the word is also used for an open funeral car or hearse.

Catch, in music an unaccompanied round sung by three or more voices written as a continuous melody: it was necessary for each singer to "catch" or pick up his part at the proper time; hence the name. An excellent example is the nursery rhyme, *Three Blind Mice.*

Catena, Vincenzo di Biagio (c.1465-1531), Italian painter strongly influenced by Giovanni BELLINI: he was ranked with GIORGIONE and TITIAN, and his works include *Madonna and Saints; Knight Adoring the Christ Child; Christ Giving the Keys to St. Peter; The Martyrdom of St. Christina.*

Cathedral, in architecture a church which contains the bishop's throne or chair, known as the *cathedra,* and accordingly the principal religious edifice in a diocese. Among the great cathedrals of the world are St. Sophia at Constantinople; St. Marks at Venice; the Cathedral at Seville; St. Peter's at Rome; Notre Dame at Paris; St. Patrick's at New York; St. John the Divine at New York; the Cathedral at Antwerp; St. Paul's Cathedral, London. It was in cathedral construction that Gothic architecture reached its noblest expression.

Cather, Willa Sibert (1876-　), American poet and novelist educated at the University of Virginia. After experience in journalism, and on the editorial staff of *McClure's Magazine,* she published a book of verse, *April Twilights* (1903): her first great success was a novel, *O Pioneers* (1913), followed by *The Song of the Lark; My Antonia; A Lost Lady; Death Comes for the Archbishop; One of Ours,* which won the Pulitzer Prize in 1923; *The Professor's House; Shadows on the Rock; Lucy Gayheart; Sapphira and the Slave Girl.* She has also written interesting short stories, *Youth and the Bright Medusa* and *Obscure Destinies,* and a book of essays, *Not Under Forty.*

Catherine de Medici (1519-1589), Italian lady; daughter of Lorenzo de Medici, duke of Urbino: she married Henry II of France in 1533, by whom she became the mother of three French kings: Frances II, Charles IX, and Henry III. She acted as regent, and is said to have deliberately encouraged all three of her sons in dissipation so that she could hold the reins of political power: she persuaded Charles IX to give the order for the bloody massacre of St. Bartholomew in 1572. Her career has been the subject of many romances and dramas, and several incidents have been pictured by famous artists: her one redeeming characteristic appears to have been a love for the arts.

Catherine the Great (1729-1796), one of the most famous empresses of Russia who brought about the deposition of her husband, Peter III, in 1762, and ruled with an iron hand until her death. She extended the boundaries of Russia by vast conquests, introduced a new code of laws, and did so much to encourage the arts that she was called the "Semiramis of the North." She has been introduced as a personality into drama and literature: portraits and busts were made of her by many great artists.

Catherwood, Mary Hartwell (1847-1902), American author of historical romances, particularly of life in French Canada, and pioneer life in the Middle West: her works include *Craque-o' Doom; The Romance of Dollard; A Woman in Armor; The Lady of Fort St. John; Old Kaskaskia; The White Islander;* also a history, *The Days of Jeanne D'Arc.*

Catlin, George (1796-1872), American author and artist who traveled and lived among American Indians of whom he painted hundreds of portraits. He published a two-volume work, *Manners, Customs, and Condition of the North American Indian* with about three hundred illustrations: nearly 500 portraits and scenes of Indian tribal life are in the Catlin Gallery of the National Museum, Washington, D. C., and several hundred sketches are in the American Museum of Natural History, New York.

Cat's eye, the name given to a gem which exhibits opalescent reflection from within which resemble the eye of a cat, the effect being called *chatoyancy.* The stones are usually green in color, and the more costly variety is made from chrysoberyl, mined in Ceylon.

Cattermole, George (1800-1868), English painter and illustrator; one of the first water-colorists in England. His works include *A Terrible Secret; The Murder of the Bishop of Liége, Armourer Relating the Story of the Sword.* He also illustrated many books including the series of WAVERLEY NOVELS by Sir Walter SCOTT.

Catullus, Caius Valerius (c. B.C. 84-c. B.C. 54), Roman poet; a friend of CICERO and CAESAR, and famed for the fecundity of his genius and the felicity of his expression. About 116 of his lyric, elegiac and epigrammatic works have been preserved including his *Lyrics to Lesbia;* a legend, *Attis;* and an EPITHALAMIUM (ode), *Thetis and Peleus.*

Caucasian Sketches, an orchestral suite by Michael IPPOLITOW-IWANOW; a favorite work on American concert and radio programs. A synopsis of the four movements follows: I *In the Mountain Pass,* a picture of the shimmering waterfalls and deep gorges of the Caucasian Mountains; II *In the Village*, depicting the strange customs of the natives; III *In the Mosque*, reflecting the simple faith of the Georgians in Mohammed as the prophet of Allah; IV *Procession of the Sardar*, picturing the Sardar, or chief magistrate, passing through the village. There is a Victor recording of the complete work by the Boston "Pops" Orchestra under Arthur Fiedler.

Cavalcante, Guido (c.1240-1300), Italian philosopher, poet, and friend of Dante: his *Songs of Love* and verses in praise of Dante were very popular in his day, and have been frequently reprinted.

Cavalcaselle, Giovanni Battista (1820-1897), Italian art critic and writer; while in England he collaborated with Joseph A. Crowe in two important works on art; *Early Flemish Painters* (1857-72) and *History of Painting in Italy*, the latter recently revised. He also wrote biographies of TITIAN and RAPHAEL.

Cavalier, a word ordinarily meaning "an armed horseman": in the English Civil Wars it was applied to adherents of Charles I to distinguish them from the Roundheads, or supporters of Parliament.

Cavalier Poets, in literature the name given to a group of English poets associated with the court of Charles I; it included Robert HERRICK, Thomas CAREW, Richard LOVELACE, and Sir John SUCKLING.

Cavalieri, Emilio (c.1550-1602), Italian composer associated with the Tuscan court at FLORENCE, and one of the experimenters in the monodic style of composition i.e., melodies set to accompaniment by one or more instruments as opposed to the polyphonic compositions of PALESTRINA and others. His most famous work was *La Rappresentazione di Anima e di Corpo*, a morality play with music, formerly incorrectly regarded as the first oratorio.

Cavalieri, Lina (1874-), Italian dramatic soprano who studied at Paris, and made her debut at Lisbon, Portugal, in 1900. She sang in many European opera houses before appearing in 1906 at the Metropolitan Opera House in *Fedora*, remaining there until 1908 when she joined Oscar HAMMERSTEIN's Company at the MANHATTAN OPERA HOUSE, New York. In 1915-16 she sang with the CHICAGO OPERA COMPANY: her personal beauty and fiery temperament aided greatly in portrayals of the title roles in MASSENET's *Thaïs* and *Manon*.

Cavalieri d'Arpino Il, see Cesari, Giuseppe.

Cavalleria Rusticana (Rustic Chivalry), a grand opera in one act; libretto by Giovanni Targioni-Tarzetti and Guido Menasci based on a novel by Giovanni VERGA; music by Pietro MASCAGNI; first produced at Rome on May 17, 1890, and in the United States at the Grand Opera House, Philadelphia, on Sept. 9, 1891. The story is: Turiddu, a young Sicilian soldier, returning from the war, finds that his former sweetheart, Lola, has married the carter, Alfio. He consoles himself with Santuzza, a peasant girl, but soon tires of her and flirts with Lola who readily encourages him. Santuzza pleads with Turiddu outside the church on Easter morning to break with Lola: he refuses and reviles her. Santuzza takes her revenge by informing Alfio of Lola's infidelity: Alfio challenges Turiddu and the latter, after imploring his mother to care for Santuzza, is killed in the duel. There are complete recordings by both Columbia and Victor; also individual records of the principal arias and duets.

Cavalli, Francesco (1602-1676), Italian organist and composer whose real name was Pier Francesco Caletti-Bruni, but who assumed the name of his protector, Federigo Cavalli, a Venetian nobleman. He was a pupil of Claudio MONTEVERDI, and the composer of more than thirty operas which were a distinct advance over those written by his teacher: the outstanding ones were *Il Giasone* (1649), *Serse*, *L'Erismena*, and *Ercole Amante*.

Cavallini, Pietro (c.1250-c.1330), Italian painter and mosaicist; a pupil of GIOTTO whom he assisted in mosaic work at St. Peter's, Rome. He was equally skillful as a painter, mosaicist, sculptor and architect, and was said to have executed the mosaics and sculptures for the tomb of Edward the Confessor in WESTMINSTER ABBEY, although authorities disagree on this particular work.

Cavatina, (*a*) in vocal music a short song of any description. The term was occasionally used for an instrumental composition: BEETHOVEN gave it to the second movement of his string quartet in B♭ Op. 130. (*b*) In opera a melodious air of simple character which avoids all the coloratura effects achieved in the usual operatic ARIA.

Cave paintings, rude pictures of human beings and animals painted, carved or cut into the walls of caves in Spain, France, Italy, and India. They are believed to have been in existence since the Stone Age or even the Glacial Period: paintings of animals were made in ochre and black. The most remarkable painting of this character, that of a group of bulls, was discovered in 1879 at the Cave of Altamira in Cantabria, Spain.

Cawein, Madison Julius (1865-1914), American poet and dramatist whose works include *Blooms of the Berry* (1887); *The Triumph of Music; Lyrics and Idyls; Days and Dreams; Kentucky Poems; Poems of Nature and Love; Accolon of Gaul; Undertones; The Shadow Garden and Other Plays; The Republic*. His pictures in verse of Kentucky scenes and people were outstanding.

Cawthorn, Joseph (1867-), American stage and screen actor who appeared for many years as the principal comedian in operettas and musical comedies including *The Singing Girl; The Fortune Teller; The Hoyden; Little Nemo; The Slim Princess; The Sunshine Girl; The Half-Moon; The Girl from Utah; Sunny*. He has also assumed character roles in several films such as *The Great Ziegfeld, One Rainy Afternoon*, and *Harmony Lane*.

Caxton, William (c.1422-1491), the first English printer: he was originally in the business of selling cloth, but after translating into English a volume entitled *Recueil des Histoires de Troye,* he learned the art of printing, and produced the above-mentioned book in either Cologne or Bruges. In 1476 he left the latter city, and set up his press at Westminster: for the rest of his life he was constantly engaged in printing books with the aid of several assistants among whom was Wynkyn de Worde, who succeeded him in the business.

Caylus, Marie Marguerite de Villette, Marquise de (1673-1729), French writer; niece of the Marquise de Maintenon and famous at the court of Louis XIV for her charm and beauty. She left her memoirs, *Souvenirs de Madame de Caylus,* later edited by Voltaire, in which a valuable insight into the life of Louis XIV is afforded through the medium of a naive and beautiful style.

Cazin, Jean Charles (1841-1901), French painter; pupil of Lecocq de Boisbaudran, and famous for his landscapes and historical paintings. He spent some time in London where he allied himself with the Pre-Raphaelites: among his best works are *The Flight into Egypt; Hagar and Ishmael; Souvenir de fête; Journée faite.* He is regarded as one of the greatest modern painters, giving equal importance to figures and details in his landscapes. His wife, Marie Cazin, was his pupil, and distinguished herself in both sculpture and painting.

Cean-Bermudez, Juan Agustin (1749-1829), Spanish painter and founder of an academy of fine arts at Seville. His reputation rests on his historical works on Spanish art and artists: they include a historical dictionary of the great artists in Spain, a dialogue on the art of painting, and a treatise on Spanish architecture and architects.

Cecchetti, Enrico (1850-1928), Italian dancer and teacher of his art who first appeared among the children in Giuseppe Rota's ballet, *Il Jocatore,* and after years of study with Giovanni Lepri made his debut at La SCALA, Milan, in 1870. He toured Europe, and in 1874 visited Russia, remaining there for several years. He returned to La Scala, Milan, but 1887 saw his return to St. Petersburg where he remained until 1902 when he became director of the Imperial Ballet at Warsaw. In 1910 he accepted the post of instructor to DIAGHILEFF's Russian Ballet; among his pupils were NIJINSKY, KARSAVINA, LOPOKOVA, IDZIKOWSKY, WOIZIKOWSKY, MASSINE, LIFAR and PAVLOWA. Cecchetti's ballet school was opened in London in 1919, and he taught there until his death: he was without question one of the greatest ballet dancers and teachers of all time.

Cech, Svatopluk (1846-1908), Czech journalist, author and poet: after winning fame as a writer of short stories and poems, he published several long epic poems including *Dreams* (1872); *The Adamites; The Storm; Keys of Heaven; Songs of a Slave.* His novels include *The Candidate for Immortality* and *Stories, Arabesques and Humoresques.*

Cecilia, Saint, a Roman lady who suffered martyrdom with her husband either about A.D. 230 at Rome under the emperor Alexander Severus, or in Sicily about A.D. 180. She is supposed to be the patron saint of music and of the organ, an idea derived from the fact that the ancient legend declared that she praised God by instrumental as well as vocal music. Her imaginary likeness has been painted by innumerable artists including RAPHAEL, RUBENS, VERONESE, DOMENICHINO, GUERCINO and Sir Joshua REYNOLDS. DRYDEN paid tribute to her in his *Ode for St. Cecilia's Day,* and CHAUCER tells her story in his CANTERBURY TALES.

Ceiling, in architecture the overhead covering of a church or building of any description. In early buildings such as cathedrals, the ceilings were of boards, leaving the carved or moulded beams showing, and often richly painted or gilded. The use of plaster began in the 16th century with the beams still showing, and with interlaced ornamentation and pendants: some architects employed stucco, glass mosaic, and fresco painting. Plaster ceilings with PANEL work were banished when Robert ADAM originated ceilings in which panels were barely suggested, substituting rings of leaves and arabesque work found on the ceilings of ancient Roman tombs and Pompeian baths: a modification of this style is still popular.

Celakovsky, Frantisek Ladislav (1799-1852), Czech poet and philologist: in 1822 he published a collection, *Slav Folksongs,* followed by several more of the same character, which wielded considerable influence upon Czech literature at his period and for many years to come. He also translated the works of Sir Walter SCOTT; Johann GOETHE and others into Czech with excellent results.

Celesta, a keyboard instrument of the percussion type, invented by Auguste MUSTEL in 1886. Steel plates, suspended over wood resonators, are struck by hammers when the keys are pressed down, producing tones of ethereal character and exquisite purity. Peter TSCHAIKOWSKY used the celesta with extraordinary success in his *"Nutcracker" Suite,* and many other modern composers have taken advantage of its highly individual tonal color.

Céleste or **Céleste-Elliott** (c.1814-1882), French dancer and actress who made her debut at the Bowery Theatre, New York, in 1815. She returned as a romantic actress in 1834 to create an hitherto unheard-of sensation: President Andrew Jackson introduced her to his cabinet as an adopted citizen of the Union. When she went back to London in 1837, she had amassed a fortune of $200,000, but was seen in New York in 1851-2 and 1865-68, electrifying her audiences as the Hebrew mother, Miriam, in *The Woman in Red.* Her favorite role was that of Miami in John Baldwin Buckstone's drama, *Green Bushes.*

Celestina, La, a Spanish prose tragedy in twenty-one acts or scenes: its original title was *The Tragicomedy of Calisto and Melibea.* It was probably the work of Fernando de Rojas, a Spanish Jew living in Toledo: the date is set as about 1497, and its publication in Spain was followed by acceptance of its importance throughout Europe. It was copied by at least a score of Spanish authors and dramatists, and translated into English by James Mabbe in 1631. The plot revolves around the love of a master for a certain lady whose maid is being courted by his servant: it remains an extraordinary exposition of human frailty.

Cella, in architecture the ancient Roman name for the sanctuary of a temple, corresponding to the *naos* in a Greek temple. The cella was enclosed within walls, and contained the statue of the god or goddess to whom the temple was dedicated. If more than one deity was worshiped, a separate cella was built for each one.

Cellier, Alfred (1844-1891), English orchestral conductor and light opera composer: he directed symphony concerts in Belfast, Manchester, and other English cities, and wrote two comic operas, *Dorothy* (1886) and *The Mountebanks* which achieved great success.

Cellini, Benvenuto (1500-1571), Italian sculptor, goldsmith and author who studied with Michelangelo Bandinelli, father of the sculptor, Baccio BANDINELLI, and with the famous goldsmith, Marcone. After being banished from Florence for dueling, he placed himself under the patronage of Pope Clement VII at Rome, and achieved a reputation as the greatest artisan of his day in the fabrication of jewel settings, candlesticks, medals, silver and gold plate, and in fact of everything classed as an object of art. In 1538, after fighting in defense of Rome against the Constable de Bourbon, he was falsely accused of treason and imprisoned: he escaped in 1539, and worked at the court of Francis I in Paris where he made his first attempt at sculpture, the subject chosen being the *Nymph of Fontainebleau.* He returned to Florence in 1545, and served Cosimo I and his family until his death. Most of his metal productions are lost, but there remain a gold and enamel saltcellar made for Francis I of France and two exquisite gold cups which are the property of the Metropolitan Museum of Art, New York. Among his sculptures are the great bronze bust of Cosimo I; a life-size *Crucifixion; Perseus with the Head of Medusa.* Cellini wrote his autobiography which was circulated in manuscript until published in 1730: it is entertaining as a record of his escapades, but unreliable in many respects as a chronicle of political events because of its obvious bias.

'Cello, see **Violoncello.**

Cembalo, in music the name originally applied to a DULCIMER, and later used as the general name for various instruments having wire strings struck by hammers. In 1721 Gottfried SILBERMANN invented a variety of the clavichord called the *cembalo d'amore:* its strings were twice as long as the ordinary instrument, and produced twice the tone volume because they were stretched over two bridges and struck in the middle.

Cenci, Beatrice (1577-1599), Roman lady, daughter of Francesco Cenci, a dissolute and vicious noble: his cruelty to his second wife, Lucrezia Petroni, and to Beatrice, led to his murder for which she and others were hanged on Sept. 11,

1599. She has been made the subject of SHELLEY's tragedy, *The Cenci,* and Guerazzi's novel, *Beatrice Cenci;* the Italian painter, Guido RENI, made a likeness of her to be seen in the Barberini Palace, Rome.

Cennini, Cennino di Drea (c.1365-1440), Italian painter whose frescoes, *Scenes in the Life of Christ* are in the Church of the Compagnia della Croce di Giorno at Volterra: he is best-known as the author of the oldest modern work on the technical processes of painting, *Trattato della pittura* which has been translated into English (1899).

Censorship. The ancient function of censorship, according to Webster's Dictionary, was the inspection, and consequently the supervision of the morals and conduct of the Roman people by magistrates known as censors. Censorship of literature was legal in Greece and Rome: the church of the Middle Ages and of the Reformation censored literature and drama. In modern days its legal powers have been exercised in connection with the drama and various forms of art including photography and motion pictures: it has functioned to some extent in respect to dress, speech, literature and the press. To clarify the above statements, it is necessary to add that there is no censorship of the drama or motion pictures (except for political reasons in connection with World War I or World War II) in foreign countries except England, where there has been strict supervision of the theatre since 1545, legalized in 1737. In the United States there is Federal and state censorship of motion pictures, but the stage is left to make its own decisions except in respect to obscenity. Opinions differ widely as to the extent to which censorship benefits or impedes the development of the arts.

Centaur, in Greek mythology a member of a race descended from Ixion, a wicked king of Thessaly who was punished in the infernal regions by being bound to a perpetually revolving fiery wheel. Centaurs were wild, coarse people with bodies half man and half horse.

Centlivre, Susannah (c.1667-1723), English actress and playwright whose real name was Susannah Freeman. After her second husband was killed in a duel, she wrote a successful play, *The Perjured Husband* (1700); this was followed by several farces including *The Gamester; A Bold Stroke for a Wife; The Busy Body; The Basset Table,* and *The Wonder! A Woman Keeps a Secret* in which David GARRICK found a congenial role. Her marriage to Joseph Centlivre, chef to Queen Anne's household did not interfere with her acting and writing: she was on friendly terms with Nicholas Rowe, George FARQUHAR and Sir Richard STEELE.

Century Opera Company, The, an organization formed at New York in 1913 to present opera in English with American singers at low admission prices. The New Theatre was leased and re-named the Century Theatre, and Milton ABORN, with his brother, Sargent Aborn, were managers for the first season, opening Sept. 15, 1913, and closing in April, 1914. The opera in English policy was not strictly carried out: several works were given in the original languages, and during the following year the plan had to be abandoned.

Cephisodotus, the name of two Greek sculptors who worked in the 4th century B.C.: the elder Cephisodotus is presumed to have been the father of PRAXITELES. A copy of his *Irene and Plutus* (Peace Carrying Wealth), is in the Munich Museum. The younger Cephisodotus is supposed to have been the son of Praxiteles, and to have made portraits of MENANDER and Lycurgus.

Ceramics, the art of making all kinds of objects such as common pottery, bricks, tiles, faïences, and terra cotta from a plastic material with a clay base: the process including shaping, baking, decorating, and glazing. Enameled and glazed pottery was known to the Egyptians and Chaldeans, but the Greeks made pottery only of soft clay. Dutch and Delft pottery came into fashion in the 18th century at about the same time that WEDGWOOD enjoyed a vogue in England: china was unknown to the ancients, and appeared in China about the 9th century A.D. SEVRES and Danish porcelains were brought to the highest degree of perfection in the 19th century.

Cerberus, in Greek mythology the three-headed dog who guarded the entrance to HADES; he permitted anyone to enter, but none to escape. One of HERCULES' tasks was to capture him and bring him to the upperworld, a feat often pictured in Greek vase paintings, representing Cerberus with a lion's mane and a tail of writhing snakes.

Ceres, in Roman mythology the goddess of grain, and of the harvest, identified with the Greek deity, Demeter. An ancient statue of her is in the GLYPTOTHEK at Munich: the head, arms, and feet are of white marble, and the draperies of polished black marble.

Cerezo, Mateo (1635-1685), Spanish painter, pupil of his father and of Juan CARRENO in Madrid. He was a brilliant and delicate worker inspired by Van DYCK; among his fine creations are a *Crucifixion;* a *Magdalene; Christ in Agony; John the Baptist; Christ at Emmaus;* the last known only through an etching by José de Castillo.

Cerito, Fanny (1821-1899), Italian ballerina and choreographer who made her debut at Naples in 1835, and danced with great success in Vienna and London where she appeared in *Le Lac des Feés* and *La Sylphide,* and danced in Lutz's famous *Pas de Quatre* with GRAHN, GRISI and TAGLIONI. She made her debut at the Paris Opera in 1847 in the ballet, *La Fille de Marbre* arranged by her husband, Arthur ST. LEON, also a distinguished dancer and choreographer. Her original ballets included *Rosida* and *Gemma,* a ballet based on hypnotism.

Cerography, the art of writing on a wax plate or tablet known to the Romans who used a stylus for inscribing. When painting is done on wax surfaces, the process is known as ENCAUSTIC PAINTING.

Cervantes Saavedra, Miguel de (1547-1616), Spanish author and dramatist; a soldier of fortune who was captured by corsairs and held five years in captivity. Later he spent some time in Constantinople, and after returning to Madrid, wrote a pastoral romance, *Galatea* in 1584, and his first drama, *Numancia,* in 1586. The first part of *Don Quixote,* the novel which made him world-famous because of its humor and quaint philosophy, was published in 1605: the second part did not appear until ten years later when he was spurred on to complete it through the appearance of a spurious sequel.

Cesari, Giuseppe (c.1570-1640), Italian painter also known as *Il Cavaliere d'Arpino* and *Il Giuseppino.* He was a fine painter of men's heads and of horses, but that his knowledge of human anatomy was slight is revealed in his frescoes in the Capitol at Rome on which he worked at various intervals for forty years. Other works of importance include *Adam and Eve Expelled from Paradise* and *Perseus and Andromeda.*

Céspedes, Pablo de (1538-1608), Spanish poet, painter, architect, and sculptor; a pupil of Federigo ZUCCARO, and also greatly influenced by the works of MICHELANGELO and RAPHAEL. Excellent examples of his work are to be found in Seville, Madrid, and at the cathedral in Cordova where his masterpiece, *The Last Supper,* is to be seen. He is said to have introduced the use of CHIAROSCURO in Spanish art: his poem, *The Art of Painting,* of which a few hundred lines have been preserved, is written in the finest Spanish didactic verse, and contains an enthusiastic eulogy of Michelangelo.

Cézanne, Paul (1839-1906), French painter who originally studied for the bar, and was an intimate friend of Émile Zola. After being refused admission to the Ecole des Beaux-Arts in Paris, he studied the works of the old masters at the LOUVRE, and finally joined the group of impressionist painters. His exhibits at the Paris Salon provoked so much ridicule that he retired to his birthplace, Aix, in Provence, and isolated himself for twenty years, painting assiduously but remaining absolutely unknown until 1895 when fifty of his works were exhibited, including still lifes of fruit, landscapes, strange nudes and strong portraits which at first frightened people. Finally recognition came from Maurice DENIS and Paul GAUGUIN: the importance of his individual style and leadership among modern French painters was fully established after another exhibition of his works in 1904. Any attempt to analyze Cézanne's works, according to Edward Alden JEWELL, is to arrive at the inevitable conclusion that, in such works as *Garçon au Gilet Rouge, L'Estaque, L'Homme a la Blouse Bleue,* and *Mont Ste. Victoire,* "Cezanne is Cezanne." His works are to be seen at the Luxembourg, Paris, at the National Gallery, Berlin, and at the Metropolitan Museum of Art, New York.

Chabas, Paul Emile (1869-1937), French painter whose pictures have received many medals and awards: they include *The First Bath* and *September Morn,* a painting in the nude which caused a sensation in Europe and the United States when first exhibited.

Chabrier, Alexis Emmanuel (1841-1894), French composer who first studied law, and worked in the French Ministry of the Interior: he was chiefly self-taught except for some instruction in harmony, and in piano under Edouard Wolf at the Lycée St. Louis, Paris. His first works were successful operettas, followed by two favorably received operas: *Gwendoline* and *Le Roi malgré lui.* In 1883 his orchestral rhapsody on Spanish themes, *España*, achieved tremendous success, and is one of the popular concert numbers today: another favorite work for orchestra is the *Joyeuse Marche*, and the *Bourrée Fantasque* for piano is a well-known recital piece.

Chaconne, in music the title of a dance in slow tempo resembling the PASSACAGLIA; said to have originated in Spain, and often used as one of the movements in the dance suites and sonatas of the 17th century. It usually consists of a series of variations in 3-4 time on a GROUND BASS, the accent placed on the second beat of each measure. Among the composers who have used this form are HANDEL, GLUCK, BEETHOVEN and BRAHMS, but the outstanding example is the *Chaconne* by Johann Sebastian BACH in his fourth violin sonata. It has been arranged for orchestra by Joachim RAFF, Ottorino RESPIGHI and Alfredo CASELLA: MENDELSSOHN and SCHUMANN both wrote a piano accompaniment for the violin solo part, but virtuosos prefer to play it in the original form. There is a Victor recording by Yehudi Menuhin, and a Columbia recording by Nathan Milstein.

Chadwick, an American painter, Christian name unknown, who worked in California from 1849 during the gold rush. His picture, *Placer Mining,* dated 1854, affords an excellent idea of the process known as "placer" mining: the miners extracted gold from sand and gravel deposits on the banks of rivers by washing away the deposits so that the gold nuggets remained in the pans or troughs.

Chadwick, George Whitefield (1854-1931), American organist and composer; pupil of Eugene Thayer in organ, and of REINECKE, JADASSOHN, and RHEINBERGER in harmony and composition. He succeeded Carl FAELTEN as director of the NEW ENGLAND CONSERVATORY OF MUSIC, Boston, Mass., in 1897, retiring in 1931; he also conducted the Worcester Music Festival for several seasons. His works include five operas; several operettas; numerous orchestral works including three symphonies and the overtures, *Rip van Winkle* and *Melpomene;* chamber music; choral music, nearly 100 songs; organ studies and pieces; treatises in harmony. His comic opera, *Tabasco,* was a genuine success.

Chair, in furniture the name of a seat for one person, usually movable, equipped with four legs or rockers, a back, and in some cases with arms. Chairs were used in ancient Egypt, Greece and Rome by the nobility and the wealthy, while the common people sat on stools and benches: in Rome the X-type of folding chair appears to have been reserved for magistrates and rulers. Among the various types of chairs may be mentioned the traveling chair of the Middle Ages in folding form capped with a canopy; the Gothic wainscoted chair with a solid back; the Italian Renaissance chair to which upholstery was added; the Louis XV fauteuil, a comfortable armchair with upholstered seat; the Jacobean chairs combining Gothic and Renaissance styles; the Baroque chair with its imposing elaborate carving and turned legs; the Queen Anne chair which was Baroque in style with an English touch added. CHIPPENDALE, HEPPLEWHITE, and SHERATON in England developed chairs with designs borrowed from classical periods. In the United States, Duncan PHYFE originated a graceful form of chair: the Morris chair, and the rocking chair were also of American design. The bent metaltubing chair designed by Marcel Breuer is the only radically new type of chair.

Chalcedony, a general term for a variety of quartz, denominated as cryptocrystalline because its structure is so fine that the crystals can be seen only under a microscope. The luster is waxy, and many ornamental stones, among them the AGATE, BLOODSTONE, CARNELIAN, ONYX, and SARD, are cut from chalcedony in a great variety of colors including white, gray, blue, yellow, and brown.

Chalet, in architecture a type of dwelling originating in Switzerland, and also to be found in other countries bordering on the Alps. Its unique feature from the earliest days was a single roof covering not only the living quarters, but also attached stables and storehouses for food or fuel. The upper floor usually projects, and is supported by substantial brackets. The amount of carving both on the outside and interior depends entirely on the ability of the owners to pay for the decoration of the posts, brackets and floor beams, all of which are exposed. The chalet is almost always copied in miniature for Swiss clocks used in the home.

Chalgrin, Jean François (1739-1811), French architect who won the grand prize of the Academy of Architecture including a three-year stay in Italy, and later became architect to the king. Among his notable works were the meeting halls of the Directoire and of the Senate; a grand staircase in the Luxembourg; the hall of the Odéon; the ARC DE TRIOMPHE DE L'ETOILE for Napoleon I: he died before the latter was completed.

Chaliapin, Feodor Ivanovitch (1873-1938), Russian operatic bass who had practically no training in singing before joining a traveling opera company in 1890, and successfully assuming leading roles because of the extraordinary quality of his voice. His formal debut was made in 1896 at a private opera house in Moscow where he caused a sensation which was repeated when he appeared in the title role of BOITO's *Mefistofele* at La SCALA, Milan. When he made his American debut in 1907 at the Metropolitan Opera House, New York, in the same opera, his singing was greatly admired, but the robust character of his acting was received with mixed feelings.

After singing with immense success at Covent Garden, London, for several years, he returned to the Metropolitan in 1921 to be received with open arms, and to remain for eight seasons. He also appeared with the Chicago Opera Company; toured the United States with his own company, and concertized extensively. Chaliapin was the greatest dramatic singer of his time: his finest roles were Boris Godunoff; King Philip in Verdi's *Don Carlos;* Don Quixote in Massenet's *Don Quixote* of which he made a magnificent screen version.

Challener, Frederick Sproston (1869-), Canadian painter who studied in England, Italy, and the Far East, and was elected to the Royal Canadian Academy in 1899. He has painted many murals in Canadian theatres and hotels, and a picture for the Canadian War Memorials entitled *Departure of Convoy, 1st Contingent C.E.F. from Gaspe Bay in 1914.* Among other notable paintings are *Workers of the Fields; Song at Twilight; Fathers of the Confederation; When Lights Are Low.*

Chamberlain, John Rensselaer (1903-), American author educated at Yale who has also been successful in the journalistic and editorial fields. His works include *Farewell to Reform* (1932); *After the Genteel Tradition; Books That Changed Our Minds; The American Stakes.*

Chamber Music, in music the general title applied to instrumental or vocal works better suited for performance in a room or small hall than in a concert auditorium. The term is usually applied to works for a string quartet, consisting of 1st and 2nd violins, viola and violoncello. All the great classic, romantic and modern masters including HAYDN, MOZART, BEETHOVEN, SCHUBERT, SCHUMANN, MENDELSSOHN, and BRAHMS composed chamber music for stringed instruments, or in combination with wind instruments, the piano and the harp.

Chambers, Charles Haddon (1860-1921), Australian dramatist who was engaged in propaganda work for the British Foreign Office during World War I; his plays include *Captain Swift; The Idler; The Tyranny of Tears* which proved a great success for Sir Charles WYNDHAM in 1891; *The Saving Grace; Passers-by.*

Chambers, George (1803-1840), English painter who was a sailor for several years, and did a great deal of sketching while at sea. He took some lessons of a drawing master, and succeeded in selling some paintings of ships: later he worked with Thomas Horner on a great panorama of the city of London for the Colosseum, an exhibition building demolished in 1860. His finest works are two historical paintings: *The Bombardment of Algiers in 1816* and *The Capture of Porto Bello* in the Greenwich Hospital, London.

Chambers, Robert William (1865-1933); American painter and novelist who was a fellow student of Charles Dana GIBSON at the ART STUDENTS' LEAGUE, New York, and also studied at the ECOLE DES BEAUX-ARTS, Paris: his canvases were accepted at the Salon when he was only twenty-four. Among his most popular novels were *In the Quarter* (1893); *Cardigan; The Fighting Chance; The Firing Line; Ailsa Page; The Common Law; The Tracer of Lost Persons,* on which a favorite radio hour is based; *The Danger Mark; The Hidden Children.* Chambers also wrote a play, *The Witch of Ellangowan,* for Ada REHAN.

Chambers, Sir William (1726-1796), English architect and author; born at Stockholm, Sweden, and brought to England in 1728. At sixteen he made a sea voyage to Canton, China, and executed many drawings of Chinese architecture and furniture. In 1744 he spent several years in Italy and Paris studying architecture, and on his return to England in 1755, made his reputation by the buildings erected at Kew for Augusta, princess dowager of Wales; he also taught architectural drawing to the Prince of Wales, later George III. His volume, *Designs for Chinese Buildings,* illustrated with the sketches made as a youth, appeared in 1757: in later years a *Treatise on Civil Architecture,* and a volume entitled *Dissertation on Oriental Gardening* were published. He was appointed architect of Somerset House, his greatest creation, in 1775, and also designed many city and country houses for the nobility. Among his unusual commissions were the state coach for George III, and a combination bureau, dressing case, jewel cabinet, and pipe organ for Charles IV, King of Spain. Among his friends were Samuel JOHNSON, Oliver GOLDSMITH, Sir. Joshua REYNOLDS, Dr. Charles BURNEY and David GARRICK.

Chambord, the most famous château on the Loire River in France, located at Loir-et-cher on the left bank. Its plan is simple, the special feature being a double staircase in which the spirals overlap in such a way that a person ascending does not meet another descending. From this staircase as a center, four great halls, each abutting a lofty tower, stretch out in the form of a Greek cross. The skylight over the staircase has a bewildering array of chimneys, turrets and windows. Francis I began work on the château in 1519 with Pierre Nepveu and others executing the plans of Domenico di Cortona, known as Boccador.

Chaminade, Cécile (1857-), French pianist and composer; a pupil of Le Couppey and GODARD. She composed at eight, and after her debut as a pianist in 1875 made successful tours for many years. Her compositions include a popular *Ballet-Symphonie* (1888); a comic opera, *La Sevilláne;* several orchestral works; a *Concertstück* for piano and orchestra; more than two hundred piano pieces and many songs.

Champaigne, Philippe de (1602-1674), Belgian painter who worked on the decoration of the Luxembourg with Nicholas POUSSIN at Paris in 1621. He succeeded DUCHESNE as painter to the Queen of France, and became director of the Paris Academy. His numerous works include the *Crucifixion* in the Carmelite Church at Paris; several portraits of Cardinal Richelieu; the *Dead Christ* and *Last Supper* at the LOUVRE. Champaigne painted with stern reality, lacking both the charm and warmth of brilliant color, but his work reveals piety and humanity strictly in accordance with his grave and dignified life.

Champenoise School of Sculpture, a school started at Troyes, France, near the end of the 15th century, and continuing through part of the 16th century. Its development paralleled the passing of the Gothic to the Renaissance styles of which the statue of St. Martha in the church of St. Urbain at Troyes is an excellent example: most of the artists' works indicating the changes are unfortunately anonymous.

Champmeslé, Marie (1642-1698), French actress who married Charles Chevillet, an actor, and appeared in 1669 at the Théâtre du Marais in Paris, and the following year in Racine's *Andromaque* in which she achieved instantaneous fame at the Hôtel de Bourgogne. RACINE became her friend and patron, writing several of his finest dramas for her including *Phèdre,* her greatest role, and the one in which she first appeared at the Comédie Française. She remained there as leading tragedienne for more than twenty years: among her friends were Jean de LA FONTAINE and Nicolas BOILEAU-DESPREAUX.

Champney, Benjamin (1817-1907), American painter who studied in Paris and Italy. He did a great deal of sketching in both countries, particularly at FONTAINEBLEAU and its environs: one of his most remarkable works was a vast panorama of the RHINE which was destroyed at New York by a fire. Some of his landscapes of Swiss and White Mountains (New Hampshire) scenery are greatly inspired. He was also founder and first president of the Boston Art Society where many of his pictures are on exhibition.

Champney, James Wells (1843-), American painter who studied at the Antwerp Academy, and made sketches in England, Europe, Africa, South America, Canada and the Southern part of the United States; he also lectured on anatomy at the National Academy, New York. Among his notable pictures are *Sere Leaf; He Loves Me; When the Two Paths Meet; Autumn Revery; Hide and Seek; Your Good Health, Sir.*

Chamson, André (1900-), French essayist and novelist educated at the Lycée at Montpellier and at the Sorbonne. Among his novels published in English are *The Road* (1929); *Roux the Bandit; The Crime of the Just; The Mountain Tavern; Barren Harvest.*

Chan, Charlie, a character in detective stories written by Earl Derr BIGGERS; a Chinese detective connected with Police Headquarters at Honolulu, Hawaii, and ably portrayed on the screen by Warner OLAND.

Chancel, in architecture that part of the church which is closest to the altar, and occupied by the deacons and others assisting the officiating clergyman. In the earliest churches it was separated from the nave by an open railing, and was known in Roman Catholic churches as the SANCTUARY. When space was needed for the choir, the railing was moved farther back; a richly decorated screen substituted in many English cathedrals, and the word "choir" used interchangeably with chancel.

Chand Bardai, Hindu poet who lived about 1200 at the court of Prithwi Raja, last Hindu ruler of Delhi. His principal work, written in ballad form and at least 100,000 stanzas in length, is entitled *Prithiraj Rasau,* and is invaluable as a chronicle of political events and of the daily life and customs of that part of India during his period.

Chaney, Lon, Sr. (1883-1930), American stage and screen actor who made his dramatic debut at 17 in *The Little Tycoon.* He became interested in motion pictures, and made his first real success in *Hell Morgan's Girl:* this was followed by *The Miracle Man; The Hunchback of Notre Dame; The Blackbird; The Unholy Three,* his first talking picture; *The Phantom of the Opera; Big City; While the City Sleeps; Laugh, Clown, Laugh; He Who Gets Slapped.* His fame rested largely on his skill in make-up, and power to distort his face and body. His son, Lon Chaney, Jr., is also a well-known screen actor.

Changement, in ballet a term signifying a change of feet, i.e., that the working foot at the end of a step (or series of steps) is in an opposite position to where it was at the beginning; also called *changement des pieds.*

Channing, William Ellery (1818-1901), American author, poet and friend of Ralph Waldo EMERSON, Nathaniel HAWTHORNE and Henry Thoreau: he wrote a biography of the latter, *Thoreau, the Poet-Naturalist,* and published several volumes of verse including *The Woodman; Near Home; The Wanderer; John Brown; Conversation in Rome.*

Chanova, Ruth (1918-1943), American ballet dancer who studied at the Pavley-Oukrainsky Ballet School in Los Angeles, and made her debut in the corps de ballet of the Los Angeles Opera Company. In 1934 she appeared at Monte Carlo with Colonel DE BASIL's company, creating the title role in Mme. NIJINSKA's ballet, *Ophelia;* in 1935 she joined the company formed by Leon WOIZIKOWSKI, touring Germany, France and Spain, and became première danseuse of the Metropolitan Opera Company, New York.

Chanson, in music a solo song with improvised instrumental accompaniment developed by TROUVERES, the medieval poets and singers of ancient France. The lyric was made up of equal stanzas known as COUPLETS, each generally ending with a refrain, the latter sometimes made a separate member of the chanson. Later polyphonic chansons were composed by Johannes OKEGHEM and Josquin DES PRES; in the 16th century they reached their highest point in the songs of Clement Jannequin, but the decadent poems of Pierre de RONSARD brought about the decay of the form.

Chanson de Geste, in literature the name given to any French epic poem of the 12th century or later relating exploits of French history either factual or legendary: the verses were of the assonant type containing ten to twelve syllables, and the most famous example is the *Chanson de Roland*. The poems varied in length from less than a thousand to 20,000 lines, and were usually written by TROUVERES.

Chanson de Roland, a French epic poem, or CHANSON DE GESTE, said to have been written by Theroulde (or Turoldur), an 11th century TROU-VERE. It comprises 4,000 lines, and is the tale of Roland's death at Roncevaux (or Roncesvalles), and Charlemagne's subsequent vengeance. It was first published in complete form by M. F. Michel in 1837.

Chant, (*a*) in church music a sacred song without metre, known as a Gregorian melody: the several verses of a prose text, usually taken from the Bible, are intoned on each note. Sometimes the verses are sung alternately by the officiating clergyman and the congregation, or by the choir and the congregation. (*b*) The term is also applied to the songs of the Incas, North American Indians, Hindus and African Negroes: there is also evidence that songs of this character were used by the Assyrians, Egyptians, and Jews.

Chantey, or **shanty,** a sailor's song, usually sung while working at duties on board ship such as reefing or hauling: three excellent examples are *Blow the Man Down; Haul on the Bowlin'*, and *Were You Ever in Rio Grand?* The work songs of other laborers are also sometimes called chanteys.

Chantrey, Sir Francis Legatt (1781-1842), English painter and sculptor who first showed evidence of his talent in wood carving, and later in painting, bust sculpture, and clay modeling. His first successful work was an imaginative bust of *Satan,* followed by colossal busts of Nelson and other British admirals. His works include a statue of Washington in the State House at Boston, Mass.; of George III in the Guildhall, London; an equestrian statue of the Duke of Wellington in front of the London Exchange. He was equally distinguished as a delineator of children, and left a fund of more than $1,000,000 for the purchase by the Royal Academy of paintings and sculptures executed by British or foreign artists within the shores of Great Britain.

Chao Meng-Fu (1254-1322), a Chinese government official and painter who worked during the Yuan dynasty: he was especially famous for his fine delineation of horses, and his paintings became so treasured after his death that he received the posthumous title of *Duke of Chou.*

Chapbook, the name given to pamphlets sold in Great Britain and the United States during the latter part of the 18th century and the first half of the 19th century, the average price ranging from one to three cents. The contents included simple versions of popular stories, travels, biographies and religious treatises. They were sold by itinerant dealers known as chapmen, and are said to have first appeared in the 15th century; Samuel PEPYS made a collection of the earlier types.

Chapel, in architecture a religious edifice of small dimensions, either directly joined to or erected in proximity to a church. The term is also applied to a church, regardless of its size, which is connected with a university, college or institution of any kind. The most striking example is perhaps the SISTINE CHAPEL which belongs to the VATICAN near Rome; MICHELANGELO'S famous painting of *The Last Judgment* is to be seen there, and it is also famous for its choir. The chapels attached to the colleges at Oxford and at Cambridge University in England are as large as the average church, and exquisitely architectured.

Chapelain, Jean (1595-1674), French critic and poet who worked on an epic poem, *La Pucelle,* for twenty years, and published the first twelve cantos in 1656: the remaining twelve cantos were not issued until 1882 because the first part was damned by the scathing satire of BOILEAU regardless of the fact that it ran through six editions in eighteen months. He was one of the first members of the French Academy, planning its *Grammar* and *Dictionary:* he also had much to do with the practical establishment of the Abbe D'AUBIGNAC'S dramatic theories in the French theatre.

Chaplin, Charles Spencer (1889-), Anglo-American screen actor and producer who appeared on the stage as a boy of seven in a music-hall troupe. In 1905 he played the role of Billy the page boy in William Gillette's drama, *The Painful Predicament of Sherlock Holmes,* resuming his music-hall career with Fred Karno's Comedians with whom he came to the United States in 1910 to create a sensation as the leading comedian in a sketch entitled *A Night in an English Music Hall.* He entered the silent pictures in 1913, appearing in Keystone comedies, and founding his own studio in 1918. His notable screen comedies include *The Rink; Tillie's Punctured Romance; The Immigrant; The Tramp; A Dog's Life; The Kid; The Idle Class; The Gold Rush; The Circus; City Lights; Shoulder Arms; Modern Times; The Great Dictator.* He also produced a drama, *A Woman of Paris,* in which he did not appear, and in 1942 a new version of *The Gold Rush* appeared in which he acted as narrator. Chaplin has probably made more people laugh to their heart's content with his impersonation of a pathetic little tramp than any other comedian on stage or screen: his films have been a delight in every country of the world where there are motion-picture theatres.

Chaplin, Charles Joshua (1825-1891), French painter and etcher who studied at the ECOLE DES BEAUX-ARTS, Paris, and was employed in 1860 to redecorate the TUILERIES and several other public and private buildings. Among his notable works are *Evening on the Moors; Muleteer of Lozère; Soap Bubbles; Devotion; Love's Messenger.* He etched many of his own works, and also those of RUBENS and other great masters.

Chapman, George (c.1559-1634), English poet and dramatist who was intimate with SHAKE-SPEARE, JONSON and DEKKER: his greatest claim to immortality are his translations of the ILIAD and ODYSSEY of HOMER which have been praised by KEATS, COLERIDGE and LAMB. His first play The *Blinde Beggar of Alexandria* (1596) was followed by many others including *The Shadow of Night; Caesar and Pompey; The Gentleman Usher; Eastward Hoe; All Fooles*. His plays are among the best of his time excluding those of Shakespeare, but the translations of Homer are far more important as literature.

Chapman, John Gadsby (1808-1889), American painter, etcher and wood-engraver who illustrated many books: he studied in Italy, and finally located his studio at Rome for many years. Among his finest creations were *Etruscan Girl; The Last Arrow; Valley of Mexico; Sunset on the Campagna; Baptism of Pocahontas*, the latter in the rotunda of the CAPITOL at Washington, D. C.

Chappell, George Shepard (1878-), American architect and author who uses the pen name, "Walter E. Traprock." His works include *Rollo in Society* (1921); *The Cruise of the Kawa; Dr. Traprock's Memory Book*.

Chapu, Henri (1833-1891), French sculptor of the realistic school who also contrived to infuse into his works the perfection of form, serenity, and repose of the classic masters. He created many fine portrait busts; a remarkable figure, *Youth,* on his monument to Henri Regnault, and a *St. Joan Listening to the Voices* now in the LUXEMBOURG, Paris.

Characteristic piece, in music a composition of distinct character seeking to convey a definite mood, impression, scene or event. Excellent examples are to be found in MASSENET's *Angelus,* GRIEG's *Morning* in the "Peer Gynt" Suite, and DEBUSSY's *Clair de Lune.*

Charade, a riddle, said to have been invented in France during the 18th century, which is usually acted out on a stage or platform: the players go through gestures or dialogue indicating the syllables in their exact order, and the audience is required to guess each syllable, and to combine their meanings into one word. Franz SCHUBERT, the Austrian composer, was very fond of watching or taking part in charades. THACKERAY gives a brilliant, detailed description of an acted charade in *Vanity Fair.*

Chardin, Jean Baptiste Simeon (1699-1779), French painter who studied with Pierre Cazes and Noël COYPEL, acquiring considerable fame as a painter of interiors in middle-class French homes: among his notable creations are *The Cook; Le Bénédicité; The Skate; The Buffet; Supplies for Lunch; Young Woman Knitting*. Portraits of himself and his wife in pastel are in the Louvre, Paris.

Chares of Lindus, see **Colossus of Rhodes.**

Chariot, the first vehicle in antiquity, and the original model of the modern carriage. Chariots drawn by asses were used in Babylon before horses were introduced by Aryan invaders through whom both horses and chariots were brought to Assyria and Egypt. Greek chariots had two wheels, and from two to four horses: the wheels were of wood with from four to eight spokes, and tires of bronze or iron. The body was of wood, resting directly without springs on the axle and open in the back. The Assyrians and Persians attached sharp irons resembling scythes to the wheels for destructive use in battle, but the Greeks and Romans used chariots only for races in public games, or for triumphal processions.

Charioteer of Delphi, a bronze statue discovered at the excavations in DELPHI, an ancient town in Greece famous for its oracle of APOLLO. It was a part of an elaborate group originally consisting of a chariot to which are harnessed four horses, a charioteer standing by the side of his master, and either one or two attendants on each side. There is evidence pointing to the 5th century B.C. as the period of its construction: CALAMIS, PYTHAGORAS and ONATAS are among those who may have been its creator.

Charlemagne (c.742-814), King of the Franks and emperor of the Romans: the event in his career which has interest in this volume is his expedition in 778 against the Arabs in Spain, ending in the destruction of the Frankish rear-guard under Roland at Roncevaux, the result being the latter's death, and the writing of the famous CHANSON DE ROLAND. Charlemagne resided chiefly at Aix-la-Chapelle where his patronage of letters attracted many famous men to his court; among them Alcuin who wrote a biography entitled *Life of Charlemagne.*

Charles I of England (1600-1649), King of England, second son of James I, who reigned from March 27, 1625, until he surrendered to the Scottish army on May 5, 1846: he was tried for treason and executed on January 30, 1649. He has been glorified in the D'ARTAGNAN romances written by Alexandre DUMAS, PERE: one volume of the series contains an exciting account of an attempt on the part of D'Artagnan and his associates, Athos, Porthos and Aramis, to rescue the king at the scaffold.

Charlet, Nicolas Toussaint (1792-1845), French painter and lithographer; a pupil of Baron GROS who first distinguished himself by his lithographs of incidents in the Napoleonic Wars such as his *Grenadier of Waterloo* printed in 1817. He produced more than 2000 lithographs in addition to many water colors and oil paintings including *Episode in the Russian Campaign; Passage of the Rhine by Moreau; Wounded Soldiers at Rest in a Ravine; The Retreat from Russia.*

Charnwood, Godfrey Rathbone Benson, 1st Baron (1864-), English biographer and novelist educated at Oxford, and prominent in English politics. His works include a detective novel, *Tracks in the Snow,* written under the pen name, "Godfrey Benson" (1906); a biography of Abraham Lincoln, highly regarded for its understanding of Lincoln as a man; a biography of Theodore Roosevelt, also considered outstanding.

Charon, in Greek mythology the son of EREBUS and Nox (or Nyx), the goddess of night. He ferried the souls over the river STYX, and was rewarded by a gold coin placed in the mouth of the deceased. He was supposed to be a grim, morose, old man clad in black, and was finally regarded as the symbol of death and the underworld.

Charpentier, Gustave (1860-), French composer who studied at the PARIS CONSERVATORY, won the Grand Prix de Rome in 1887 with a cantata, and succeeded Jules MASSENET as a member of the French Institute. His works include the world-famous grand opera, *Louise* (1900) and its less successful sequel, *Julien* (1913). He also wrote a fine orchestral suite, *Impressions of Italy*, and a symphonic drama, *The Life of a Poet*, played at the Grand Opera, Paris, in 1892.

Charteris, Leslie (1907-), English writer of detective and adventure stories born in Singapore, and educated at Cambridge University. He created the character of the "Saint," who has been described as a modern RAFFLES, in *Enter the Saint* published in 1930: the novel became a best seller, and many more have been published with almost unvarying success. The screen adaptations, with George SANDERS in the role of the "Saint," have also been received with great enthusiasm.

Chartier, Alain (c.1390-c.1430), French poet; graduate of the University of Paris and author of a poem, *The Book of Four Ladies*, written after the battle of Agincourt in which the English defeated the French. He rendered a real service to France in his *Quadrilogue-invectif* by urging that the various factions lay aside their differences in the hour of defeat, and work for the common cause. One of his patriotic poems, *Ballad of Fougières*, is said to have had considerable influence.

Chartron, en, in ballet a term signifying a grouping of dancers in the form of a horseshoe.

Charybdis, see **Scylla.**

Chase, Lucia, contemporary American ballet dancer who studied at the THEATRE GUILD School and with Mikhail MORDKIN. In 1937 she became one of the leading ballerinas with the Mordkin Ballet Company; in 1939 she joined the BALLET THEATRE as soloist and ballerina. She excels in the leading roles in the ballets, *La Fille Mal Gardée, Les Sylphides, Giselle, The Great American Goof, Judgment of Paris,* and *Carnaval.*

Chase, Mary Ellen (1887-), American author educated at the University of Maine and now (1943) professor of literature at Smith College. In 1931 her short story, *Salesmanship,* won a prize of $2500 from the *Pictorial Review;* her outstanding novels include *Mary Peters* (1934); *Silas Crockett; Mary Christmas; Windswept.*

Chase, William Merritt (1849-1916), American painter who studied at the Munich Academy under Karl von PILOTY, and in Venice where he was greatly influenced by TINTORETTO. In 1877 he returned to the United States to teach at the ART STUDENTS' LEAGUE and the Brooklyn Art School, spending his summers sketching in France, Spain, Italy, and Holland: on one of these trips he painted the portrait of James McNeill Whistler.

He also gave lessons at his summer home at Shinnecock Hills, Long Island, N. Y.; opened the Chase School of Art, and for many years headed the Society of American Artists. Among his notable works are *Ready for the Ride; The Apprentice; Court Jester; Carmencita; Lady in Black; Alice in Her Grandmother's Gown; Fishmarket in Venice; A Broken Jug;* also portraits of the American painter, Frank DUVENECK, and of the philanthropist, Peter Cooper.

Chasing, in art a method of producing ornamental designs or patterns, either indented or raised, on metal surfaces by the use of steel cutters or punches. It came into use first in ancient Greece for the decoration of armor, and for indicating ornamentation in drapery on bronze statues. Imitation chasing is produced on plated ware by means of steel dies.

Chasins, Abram (1903-), American pianist and composer; student at the Ethical Culture School, Juilliard Foundation, and Columbia University, New York, under Ernest HUTCHESON and Rubin GOLDMARK. He also studied the piano with Josef HOFMANN. He has toured Europe and the United States as a concert pianist, and has written more than eighty compositions for either one or two pianos including two concertos, 24 preludes, *Three Chinese Pieces,* and *Parade.*

Chassé, in ballet a term signifying a step in which one foot follows or replaces the other in position; also called *pas chassé.*

Chassériau, Théodore (1819-1856), French painter at Samana in the Antilles; a pupil of Jean INGRES and Paul DELAROCHE. He exhibited at the Salon of 1836, and continued to do so for several years until recognition came for such notable creations as *Venus; Susanna; Tepidarium at Pompeii; Mary Stuart Defending Rizzio; Andromeda Bound to the Rock; Women of Troy Weeping by the Sea; Christ in the Garden of Olives; Two Sisters; A Bather Asleep Near a Spring; The Arabian Challenge;* also many etchings for Shakespeare's "Othello" and "Hamlet." His decorations in the Palais d'Orsay, Paris, considered by some critics his greatest work, have been destroyed.

Château, in architecture a form of residence in France developed from the medieval castle, and planned more for convenient living than defense although fortifications were provided in the shape of walls and moats, and a tower with thick walls where the inmates of the château took refuge when attacked or besieged. Among the most famous were the châteaux of Coucy, Gaillard, Vincennes, Chambord, Blois, Chaumont, Louvre and Fontainebleau: many of the defensive parts such as the turrets disappeared in châteaux of the 17th century, Italian decorative features replacing them.

Chateaubriand, Francois René Auguste (1768-1848), French statesman, essayist, and author who visited the United States in 1791 while on a voyage in search of the Northwest Passage. He lived for some time among American Indians, writing three novels entitled *Atala* (1801), *René* and *The Natchez* in charming literary style, and with interesting descriptions of life remote from civilization which won immediate recognition. He also wrote a five-volume work defending the Catholic faith; a three-volume *Journey from Paris to Jerusalem;* an exquisitely melancholy romance, *The Adventures of the Last of the Abencerages,* and an autobiography, *Mémoires d'outre-tombe.*

Chatrian, Alexandre, see **Erckmann-Chatrian.**

Chatterton, Ruth (1893-), American stage and screen actress who made her debut in 1909 at the Columbia Theatre, Washington, D. C., in *Merely Mary Ann;* since then she has appeared in many notable plays including *The Prince Chap; Cousin Kate; Charley's Aunt; Daddy Long-Legs; Frederic Lemaitre; A Marriage of Convenience; The Green Hat; The Affairs of Anatol.* She has also played important roles in numerous films including *Madame X; The Sins of the Fathers; The Magnificent Lie; Once a Lady; Lily Turner; Dodsworth; A Royal Divorce; The Rat.*

Chatterton, Thomas (1752-1770), English poet who wrote several poems at twelve years of age which he called the *Rowley Poems,* claiming that they were copies of 15th century manuscripts. In 1769 he tried to secure Horace Walpole as a patron: after being repulsed, he committed suicide a few months later. There is no doubt that Chatterton possessed abilities which under different circumstances would have made him a great poet rather than a precocious fakir; the intrinsic beauties of the *Bristowe Tragedie, Aella,* and *An Excellente Balade of Charitie* afford ample evidence of his genius.

Chaucer, Geoffrey (c.1340-1400), English poet regarded as one of the fathers of English poetry, and the greatest figure in English literature before SHAKESPEARE. He lead a life full of adventure both as a soldier, diplomat, and civic official: his literary career began with a translation into English of the French ROMANCE OF THE ROSE, of which only part has been preserved, and a poem, *The Book of the Duchesse.* The works which followed included the poem, *Troilus and Crisyede;* a collection of stories entitled *The Legende of Good Women;* another collection, *Canterbury Tales,* considered his greatest work. These tales were supposed to be related by the members of a band of pilgrims bound for Canterbury to visit the shrine of Thomas à Becket, the murdered Archbishop of Canterbury. They were begun in 1387; left unfinished at Chaucer's death, and regarded as the greatest word-picture ever painted of English life in the Middle Ages.

Chausson, Ernest (1855-1899), French composer who studied at the PARIS CONSERVATORY with Jules MASSENET and César FRANCK, and was appointed secretary of the National Society of Music in Paris. His works include a lyric drama, *King Arthur;* a symphony; a piano concerto; a violin concerto; a *Poème* for violin and orchestra; chamber music; choral music and songs.

Chautauqua Institution, a system of adult education founded in 1874 primarily for the purpose of disseminating religious instruction, but also taking note of the fact that such education should be rounded out by knowledge of the best in litera-

ture, art, and science. Two of these developments are of interest in this volume; (*1*) the *Chautauqua Library and Scientific Circle* designed to furnish a continuous home reading program; (*2*) the Chautauqua series of musical events in the summer of which the orchestral concerts with soloists are broadcast to millions of listeners.

Chauve Souris, La (The Bat of Moscow), a form of dramatic entertainment originated by Nikita Balieff, a member of the company at the Moscow Art Theatre. In form it may be classed as vaudeville of the higher order, and was first presented in a cellar by Balieff and a group of his associates to an audience of friends. The program consisted of a series of disconnected episodes such as a parody on Verdi's *La Traviata:* a ballad of GLINKA; a series of Russian dances; a tableau, *Copenhagen Porcelain;* dramatic sketches or satires by GOGOL and GORKY; a fantasy, *The Musical Snuff Box,* and the amusing *Parade of the Wooden Soldiers.* The show was taken to Paris in 1920, and brought to New York in 1922: it created a sensation, and returned regularly for several years with a wealth of new features.

Chauvin, Nicholas, a veteran soldier of the Napoleonic wars who had such a passionately blind admiration for Napoleon I that the term *chauvinism* was coined from his name to describe unreasoning, blind, exaggerated love of country; the equivalent in English is *jingoism.*

Chavez, Carlos (1899-), Mexican orchestral conductor and composer who studied in New York, Berlin, and Paris, becoming director of the Fine Arts Department of the Mexican Government in 1933. He made many appearances as guest conductor of the BOSTON SYMPHONY ORCHESTRA and several other American orchestras, and organized the Symphony Orchestra of Mexico City in 1928. His compositions include orchestral works; chamber music; a concerto for harp and orchestra; a piano sonata and many piano pieces.

Cheatham, Kitty, contemporary American singer and diseuse who began her stage career in 1887 as prima donna with the McCaull Opera Company, and later became a member of the Augustin DALY Stock Company. For many years she has given recitals of children's songs and literature, her repertory including more than a thousand songs in several languages; she has also pioneered in the fields of community singing and children's orchestral concerts. She is the author of *Kitty Cheatham-Her Book* which affords an excellent picture of many years of useful activity.

Checkmate, a ballet in one act; libretto and music by Arthur Bliss; choreography by Ninette de Valois; first produced at the Théâtre des Champs-Elysées, Paris, in 1937. The plot revolves around a gigantic chessboard, and the action unfolds along the lines of an actual game of chess, the dancers clothed as red and black pawns, black castles, queens, kings and bishops: also two chess players—Love and Death—clad in armor.

Chekhov, Anton Pavlovich (1860-1904), Russian author of short stories and dramatist who first studied medicine. He published his first volume of short stories in 1886, and his first play, *On the High Road,* was produced in 1884. His stories are all of people pathetic in their isolation and failure to understand each other: his plays, according to John Mason BROWN, are not only realistic but the quintessence of truth. Among the greatest of the latter are *The Sea Gull; Uncle Vanya; The Cherry Orchard,* considered his masterpiece; *The Three Sisters;* recently (1943) revived by Katherine Cornell. All of the plays mentioned above were produced at the Moscow Art Theatre, and presented in English in New York.

Chemet, Renée, contemporary French violinist who studied with Henri Berthelier at the Paris Conservatory, and developed a style which has resulted in her being named the "female Kreisler." She has toured Europe, Great Britain and the United States with great success, and has also made many broadcasts and recordings.

Cheney, John (1801-1885), American engraver and illustrator who studied in Paris while doing engraving work for American publishing houses. He ranked highly as an illustrator of books designed for sale as gifts or holiday presents, and his brother, **Seth Wells Cheney** (1810-1856) was also an engraver and crayon portraitist who received instruction from Eugène ISABEY and Paul DELAROCHE; among his sitters for a crayon portrait were William Cullen BRYANT and James Russell LOWELL.

Cheney, John Vance (1848-1922), American essayist and poet, for many years librarian of the San Francisco Public Library and the Newberry Library at Chicago. His works include *The Old Doctor* (1885); a volume of poems, *Thistle Drift;* several volumes of essays such as *That Dome in Air* and *The Golden Guess.*

Cheney, Sheldon (1886-), American art critic educated at various art schools, and at the University of California. He first became well-known as a designer of book plates: in 1916 he founded the *Theatre Arts Magazine* (now *Theatre Arts Monthly*). Among his important works are *The New Movement in the Theatre* (1914); *The Open Air Theatre; Modern Art and the Theatre; The Art Theatre; The Theatre: 3000 Years of Drama, Acting and Stagecraft; A World History of Art.*

Cheng, a Chinese instrument consisting of a gourd with from 12 to 24 graduated pipes fitted with finger-holes and free reeds: sounds are produced by the performer's breath passing through a short mouthpiece. It is supposed to be the ancestor of the accordion, concertina, and other free reed instruments.

Ch'eng Yen-ch'iu, contemporary Chinese actor, regarded by many critics as the peer of MEI LAN-FANG in female roles. He is equally magnetic as an actor with his melancholy, expressive gestures, and as a singer with a smoothly flowing technique: his lengthy tours in Europe have unquestionably had their effect on his attitude toward musical, scenic, and acting problems.

Chenier, André Marie de (1762-1794), French poet born at Constantinople of a Greek mother while his father was consul-general there. He wrote the appeal to the people for Louis XVI after the latter was sentenced to death; penned a eulogy of Charlotte CORDAY after she killed Jean Paul Marat, and was guillotined in 1794 only two days before the end of the reign of terror. Among his poems are *"L'Aveugle," "Le Jeune Captive,"* and *"Le Jeune Malade,"* considered the finest creations of 18th century French poets. The Italian composer, Umberto GIORDANO, wrote an opera, *Andrea Chenier,* based on his career. His younger brother, **Marie Joseph de Chenier** (1764-1811) wrote several plays which succeeded only because of their revolutionary sentiments; one of his patriotic songs, *Chant du Depart* (Parting Song), was almost as popular as the "Marseillaise." An important work for Napoleon I was the preparation in 1808 of a *Historical Picture of the Progress of French Literature from 1789 to 1808* which is marred by his violent prejudices.

Ch'en Jung, Chinese painter who worked in the 13th century, and achieved world-wide fame with his remarkable paintings of dragons: a strikingly original example of his art is to be seen at the Museum of Fine Arts in Boston.

Cherbuliez, Victor (1829-1899), French novelist who studied at the Universities of Geneva, Paris, Bonn, and Berlin, becoming editor of the *Revue des Deux Mondes* in 1864. His series of novels, written under the pen name "G. Valbert," began with *Count Kostia* in 1863, followed by *Paul Mere; Romance of a Respectable Woman; The Vocation of Count Ghislain; Ladislas Bolski's Adventure; Samuel Brohl & Co.:* the last-named was honored by the French Academy to which he was elected. He also wrote essays on politics, literature and art, and many of his novels were translated into English.

Chernyshevsky, Nikolai Gavrilovich (1828-1889), Russian political writer and author who directed his energies to the task of bettering the condition of emancipated serfs by contributing salient articles in Russian newspapers and magazines. In 1862 he was imprisoned for his political views: during his incarceration he wrote a novel, *What to Do?* which became a best seller with the younger element in Russia, and was followed by several other works of similar character which led to his being exiled to Siberia in 1864, and not allowed to return until almost twenty years later. He was a voluminous writer: one of his greatest contributions to Russian literature was a translation of Weber's "Universal History."

Chersiphron, a Greek architect who was the builder, with the assistance of his son Metagenes, of the great Ionic temple of ARTEMIS at EPHESUS in the 6th century, B.C. The temple was twice destroyed by fire, and was rebuilt with such magnificence that it was considered one of the seven wonders of the world: some of its sculptures are now in the BRITISH MUSEUM.

Cherubini, Luigi (1760-1842), Italian composer who first studied with his father and later with Sarti at Milan, with whom he perfected himself in counterpoint. His composition began at thirteen with a mass and a stage piece: in 1780 his opera, *Quinto Fabio,* was the first of a long series of dramatic works in Italian style of which *Armida* and *Alessandro nelle Indie* were outstanding. In 1786 he went to Paris to produce a number of operas the first of which, *Demofoonte,* was a failure, but several others including *Lodoiska, Les Deux Journées, Anacreon,* and *Faniska* achieved the highest possible degree of success. From 1821 until his retirement in 1841 he was director of the PARIS CONSERVATORY, and stands out as one of the most distinguished composers of the first half of the 19th century.

Chest, in furniture a large box of wood or metal with a hinged lid utilized for storage of clothing and valuables of various kinds. It was also used as a seat in ancient times when chairs were a luxury: the nobility used the chest as a carrier of treasured possessions of an intimate character when traveling from one residence to another. Chests were covered with leather embossed with insignia, and it was only after furniture became more plentiful that legs were added, and permanent places assigned them. Among the styles of chests prized by collectors are the Italian *cassone* or marriage chests which were ornately carved and painted; BOULLE (or Buhl) chests by the famous French cabinet maker; JACOBEAN chests; the "tulip" chests made by the Dutch settlers in the United States, so called because tulips were painted on the covers.

Chester, George Randolph (1869-1924), American short story writer who created the characters of "Get-Rich-Quick Wallingford" and "Blackie Daw" in his first book, *Get-Rich-Quick Wallingford* published in 1909: it was not only a best seller, but an outstanding stage success as dramatized by George M. COHAN, and an exceedingly popular screen play.

Chesterton, Gilbert Keith (1874-1936), English essayist, journalist, poet, and novelist educated at St. Paul's School, London: he first contemplated studying art, but decided on a literary career which he pursued along distinctly original if somewhat unconventional paths. His works include critical essays on DICKENS, BROWNING, SHAW and STEVENSON; a series of detective stories known as the *Father Brown Series; A Short History of England;* a play, *The Judgment of Dr. Johnson; The Ballad of the White Horse; What I Saw in America.* He contributed to the *Illustrated London News* for many years, and edited a magazine, *G. K. C's Weekly.* His autobiography was published after his death.

Chevalier, Albert (1861-1923), English actor, singer, dramatist, and composer, who appeared on the stage as a child, and made his first stage appearance at London in 1877, playing legitimate parts until 1891 when he created a sensation at the Pavilion Music Hall with his original coster songs, sung in dialect and including *Mrs. 'Enry 'Awkins, My Old Dutch, The Little Nipper,* and *Knocked 'Em in the Old Kent Road.* He appeared for many years with unvarying success in both Great Britain and the United States: in 1898 one of his plays, *Tommy Dodd,* was produced in London, and his reminiscences, *Before I Forget,* contain an interesting and amusing account of his American tours.

Chevalier, Maurice (1889-), French actor and novelist who first appeared in revues at the Folies-Bergère, Paris, in 1909, remaining there until 1913 as dancing partner of MISTINGUETTE. After serving in World War I he reappeared at the Folies-Bergère, and made his London debut at the Palace Theatre. In 1929 he made his first New York appearance at Ziegfeld's New Amsterdam Roof Garden: since that time he has appeared chiefly in French and English theatres. His numerous films include *The Love Parade; The Playboy of Paris; The Smiling Lieutenant; The Merry Widow; The Man From the Folies-Bergère; The Beloved Vagabond.* In 1938 he was made a Chevalier of the Legion of Honor for "signal services to French propaganda in all countries."

Chevreuse, Marie de Rohan, Duchess of (1600-1679), French political intriguer; daughter of the Duke of Montbazon, and wife of the Duke of Chevreuse. She was one of the most powerful enemies of Cardinal RICHELIEU who finally succeeded in banishing her in 1633. After the death of Louis XIII she returned, but was coldly received by Anne of Austria, and when uncovered in a conspiracy against Cardinal MAZARIN, was again banished. Her beauty and genius for intrigue are pictured in the historical works of Alexandre DUMAS, PERE.

Chevy Chase, an old English ballad recounting the incidents of the battle of Otterburn, an encounter between the Percy and Douglas families on the border between England and Scotland. A painting by Sir Edwin LANDSEER called *Earl Percy of Northumberland Hunting on the Property of the Scottish Earl of Douglas,* was exhibited at the Royal Academy, London, in 1826.

Chiaroscuro, in painting an Italian term for a method of painting by using deep shadows to emphasize the modeling of the figures or objects, thereby creating and accentuating the pictorial design in addition to adding three-dimensional effects. The Dutch painters including REMBRANDT were the acknowledged pioneers in this method, but both Leonardo DA VINCI and CORREGGIO excelled in its use.

Chicago Art Institute, an institution in Chicago, Ill., embracing an art school with an enrollment of more than 4,000 students: the art gallery contains a wide variety of fine paintings by VERONESE, VAN DER WEYDEN, MASSYS, CRANACH, MONET, RENOIR, DEGAS, TOULOUSE-LAUTREC, SEURAT and PICASSO. There is also the Goodman Memorial Theatre connected with the dramatic department, and the Burnham Library of Architecture.

Chicago Musical College, an institution founded in 1867 at Chicago, Ill., by Dr. Florenz Ziegfeld, father of the theatrical producer Florenz Ziegfeld, who obtained the finest teachers in Europe and America for its faculty, and remained its director for almost fifty years. After 1905 Felix BOROWSKI and Carl D. Kinsey were associated with the college: the latter acted as manager until 1933 when Rudolph GANZ became president. The institution offers training in all branches of music and allied arts: a summer school of eleven weeks is held annually.

Chicago Opera Company, see **Chicago-Philadelphia Opera Company.**

Chicago-Philadelphia Opera Company, an organization founded in Chicago in 1910: its roster of singers was recruited from the members of Oscar Hammerstein's MANHATTAN OPERA COMPANY after it disbanded. Andreas DIPPEL was the first manager, and Cleofonte CAMPANINI the principal conductor; in 1913 Campanini became the artistic director until his death in 1919. Mary GARDEN became its director from 1921 to 1922: the company was renamed the Chicago Civic Opera Company in 1921, and the Chicago Civic Opera Association in 1928 when it moved from the Auditorium to the newly built Civic Opera House. Among the singers were Mary Garden, Claudio MUZIO, Rosa RAISA, Charles HACKETT, René MAISON, Richard BONELLI, John Charles THOMAS, Lotte LEHMANN, and Paul ALTHOUSE. The opera season lasted thirteen weeks each year with an eight-week tour of the South, West, New York, Philadelphia, and Boston.

Chicago Symphony Orchestra, an organization founded at Chicago by Marshall Field and others in 1891 as the Chicago Orchestra; in 1906 the name was changed to the *Theodore Thomas Orchestra,* and to the *Chicago Symphony Orchestra* in 1912. The orchestra has had only two permanent conductors: Theodore Thomas from 1891 to 1905, and Frederick Stock from 1905 to 1942. Eric DeLamarter assisted Frederick Stock from 1918 to 1936, and Hans Lange became associate conductor in 1936, and acting conductor in 1942 after Stock's death. The orchestra is self-sustaining and owns its own auditorium, Orchestra Hall; popular Saturday night concerts began in 1914, and Young People's concerts in 1919. In 1943 Desiré Defauw was appointed conductor of the orchestra.

Chickering, Jonas (1798-1853), American piano manufacturer who was one of the pioneers in the development of the upright piano, and invented the full metal plate for both square and grand pianos. His son, **Thomas E. Chickering** (1824-1871) was awarded the first prize for grand pianos in 1867 at the Paris Exposition, and made a Chevalier of the Legion of Honor. The business was continued until 1908 by his sons and grandsons, and finally became a subsidiary of the Aeolian American Corporation.

Ch'ien Hsuan (1235-1290), Chinese painter of the Yuan dynasty who followed the style of the academic school of Sung. He excelled in hand scrolls with life-like figures of birds, insects and flowers: a fine example of his work is in the Detroit Institute of Arts.

Chikamatsu Monzayemon (1653-1724), Japanese priest and dramatist who left the priesthood to write plays for the Kabuki Shibai, a theatre to which those not permitted to see the aristocratic *Nō* and *Kyogen* dramas were admitted. He also wrote *Joruri* (Puppet) plays, bringing this form of entertainment to such perfection that they continued for more than two hundred years. He is called the Japanese Shakespeare; his works include more than fifty plays in from three to five acts such as *The Battles of Kokusinya and Chishingura.*

Child, Richard Washburn (1881-1935), American diplomat and novelist whose works include *Jim Hands* (1910); *The Vanishing Men; A Diplomat Looks at Europe.*

Children in the Theatre. The presence of children in dramatic presentations has been common since the 16th century in England, particularly during the reign of Queen ELIZABETH (1558-1603). Among the most renowned were the *Children of the Chapel* at Blackfriars in 1597 followed by the *Children of Revels to the Queen* at Blackfriars in 1604, succeeded by the *Children to the Queen* at Whitefriars in 1610. One of the most precocious child actors was William Henry West BETTY, known as the "Young Roscius" who appeared at thirteen as Hamlet and Romeo with adult actors about 1804; another was John Howard PAYNE, author of the words of "Home, Sweet Home," who appeared at sixteen on the American stage, and at theatres in Ireland with Eliza O'Neill, the most famous tragic actress in the early part of the 19th century. Another interesting development in the theatrical world near the end of the 19th century was the appearance in England and the United States of children's companies in Gilbert & Sullivan operettas; Julia MARLOWE made her debut at twelve in "H.M.S. Pinafore" as a sailor, and shortly after appeared as Sir Joseph Porter. The screen can also take the credit for having introduced many child actors including Shirley TEMPLE, Freddie BARTHOLOMEW, Lillian GISH, Dorothy GISH, Jackie COOGAN and Jackie COOPER.

Children's Corner (Debussy), a suite for piano by Claude DEBUSSY, dedicated "to my dear little Chouchou with her father's apologies for what follows." The suite comprises six numbers: I *Doctor Gradus ad Parnassum;* II *Jumbo's Lullaby;* III *Doll's Serenade; IV The Snow is Dancing;* V *The Little Shepherd;* VI *Golliwogg's Cakewalk:* the last-named is extremely popular as a recital piece. There is a Columbia recording by Walter Gieseking, and a Victor recording for orchestra, arranged by André Caplet and played by the Paris Conservatory Orchestra directed by Piero Coppola.

Chillon, see **Prisoner of Chillon, The.**

Chimaera, in Greek mythology a female monster breathing fire, and resembling in appearance a lion, goat and dragon combined, which devastated part of Greece before being destroyed by BELLEREPHON. The word is used at the present time to characterize any fantastic idea or product of the imagination.

Chimes, (a) a set of tuned bells which produce a sequence of musical sounds, or a tune when played by hand or mechanically. The number and size of the bells vary from the miniature ones used in clocks to those employed in church towers. Elaborate installations with keyboards are called CARILLONS. (b) In orchestral music the effect of chimes is secured by employing a series of tuned metal tubes freely suspended from a wooden or metal stand, and struck by a mallet held in the hand. They are used to imitate bells in musical works such as the *1812 Overture* by TSCHAIKOW-

SKY, and in *Parsifal*, Richard WAGNER's sacred drama.

Chimes of Normandy, The, a comic opera in three acts: libretto by Clairville and Babet; music by Robert PLANQUETTE; first produced at Paris in 1877. The story is: Henri, Marquis de Villeroi, returns to his childhood home, the village of Corneville, just as the annual country fair is in progress. He learns from Serpolette, a scheming village maiden, that the old miser, Gaspard, is planning to marry his niece, Germaine, to the local sheriff, but she is in love with Jean Grenicheux, a young fisherman. Henri, aided by Serpolette, Germaine and Grenicheux, discover that the miser has hidden his gold in the Villeroi Castle: when the castle bells are run, Gaspard loses his mind, and the scheming Seropletti claims to be the lost heiress and marchioness. Unfortunately for her, Gaspard regains his reason and the true marchioness proves to be Germaine; she marries Henri as the bells of the castle ring out.

Chinese Music, regarded by some authorities as the oldest in existence; it employs a chromatic scale of pitchpipes, or lus, which divides the octave into twelve intervals, and a five-tone or pentatonic scale, similar to the five black notes on the piano, which has existed from earliest times. The twelve lus are divided into six yang or masculine tones related to the sun, and six yin or feminine tones related to the moon. In the same manner, the five tones of the pentatonic scale are interconnected with the five planets, colors and senses. No staff is used for the musical characters which are written in vertical columns succeeding each other from right to left; the music itself is limited to melodies founded on the five notes of the pentatonic scale.

Chintreuil, Antoine (1816-1873), French painter; a pupil of COROT whose influence is reflected in his paintings, especially in the skillful treatment of foreground and sunlight. Among his notable works are *After the Rain; Sunset with Ruins; Thicket with Deer; Rain and Sunlight; Vapors of Evening; Country in Autumn.*

Chippendale, Thomas (1718-1779), English cabinet maker and furniture designer: his father was a craftsman of considerable reputation in the same line, and opened a shop with him at London in 1727. Later the factory was removed to St. Martin's Lane where he worked with his partners, James Rannie and Thomas Haig, until his death. From 1750 he was the most fashionable designer in England of furniture in every form including chairs, cabinets, desks, bookcases, sideboards, tables, mirrors and chests: he worked chiefly with dark mahogany, and his designs were copied by many English and American furniture makers. The business was continued until 1822 by his son, Thomas Chippendale, Jr.

Chirico, Giorgio de (1888-   ), Italian painter born in Greece of Italian parents. He studied at an art school in Athens, and later at the Munich Academy from which he went to Italy to study the old masters. In 1911 he came under the influence in Paris of the cubist painters, PICASSO and Reynal; from 1915 to 1924 he worked at Rome,

returning to Paris in 1924 to become one of the founders of the Surrealist movement in which the form and color values of paintings are subordinated to their literary significance; the meaning of his pictures is far from clear to the average lover of paintings in the accepted sense of the word. Chirico has also made some striking scenic designs for modern ballets.

Chiron, in Greek mythology one of the centaurs who was celebrated for his knowledge of the art of healing, and the teacher of Aesculapius. JASON, HERCULES and ACHILLES; a wall painting discovered at Pompeii shows him teaching Achilles to play the lyre. When a poisoned arrow from the bow of Hercules accidentally struck him, he renounced his immortality in favor of PROMETHEUS.

Chiton, the garment worn next to the body in ancient Greece by both men and women. The Dorian chiton was made of wool, folded over at the top to form a double covering above the waist, and fastened by a girdle and *fibulae*, the Greek equivalent of safety pins. The Ionian chiton was a loosely flowing, sleeved gown made of wool, and sewed rather than pinned. Chitons for men were usually shorter in length.

Chivers, Thomas Holley (1809-1858), American poet and friend of Edgar Allan POE; at one time he was accused of plagiarism because his style of writing resembled that of Poe. Among his poetical works were *The Lost Pleiad* (1842); *Virginalia, or Songs of My Summer Nights; Atalanta.*

Chloë, see **Daphnis and Chloë.**

Cho-Cho-San, the name of the Japanese geisha in Giacomo PUCCINI's grand opera, *Madame Butterfly,* who marries Lieutenant Pinkerton; she remains faithful when he deserts her, and commits suicide when he returns to claim her child.

Chocolate Soldier, The, comic opera in three acts: book based on George Bernard SHAW's play, *Arms and the Man;* music by Oscar STRAUS; first produced at Vienna in 1908, and at New York in 1909 where it had a run of almost three hundred performances, and was successfully revived in 1921 and 1930 in addition to many radio broadcasts The "chocolate soldier" was the nickname given Lieutenant Bumerli because of his love for candy and the great song success was the soprano aria *My Hero.*

Cho Densu or **Min Cho** (1352-1431), Japanese painter who worked along the lines of the Takuma school, but was also influenced by artists of the Yuan period. His works, such as *The Hundred Rakan,* reveal bold brush strokes and vivid coloring, also making use of shading in order to give the suggestion of depth along contour lines.

Chodowiecki, Daniel Nicolas (1726-1801), Polish painter and engraver who studied oil painting at Berlin, and became one of the most prolific and popular engravers of his time after his miniatures such as *The Life of Christ,* and a painting, *The Departure of Jean Calas,* proclaimed him a master of his art. He engraved more than 3000 subjects including illustrations for DON QUIXOTE, *The Vicar* *of Wakefield, Clarissa Harlowe,* and for Shakespeare's works. He became director of the Berlin Academy in 1797.

Choerilus of Athens, Greek dramatist and poet who is said to have competed with AESCHYLUS and SOPHOCLES about 500 B.C.: none of his more than one hundred plays has survived, but he is credited with having introduced improvements in masks and costumes for the theatre.

Choir, (*a*) in architecture that part of a church occupied by and reserved for the clergy and the singers; it is also referred to as the CHANCEL. (*b*) An organized group of singers who perform the musical portion of a church service. It may be composed of men and boys, women and girls, or of both men and women: in the latter case it is called a *mixed choir.* (*c*) That part of an organ, usually the lowest bank of keys, which controls the softer stops used for accompanying singers.

Choki, Japanese painter and color printer who worked between 1785 and 1805: he was a pupil of KIYONAGA, and influenced by UTAMORO, his fellow pupil. Some of his plates such as *The Hunt with Fireflies, Sunset,* and *Woman Rowing on the Sumida* have never been surpassed in Japanese art. His name is sometimes erroneously read as Nagayoshi.

Chopin, Frédéric Francois (1810-1849), Polish pianist and composer, born of a Polish mother and a French father. He studied the piano with Albert Zwyny and composition with Joseph Elsner at the Warsaw School of Music, appearing first as a pianist at nine. In 1825 his first works, a *Rondo* and a set of variations on an Italian air, *La ci darem la mano,* were published. After concertizing in Berlin, Dresden, Leipzig, Prague, Vienna, and Munich, he appeared in Paris with such success that he made his permanent home there until his death. His friends included many noted musicians including LISZT, CHERUBINI, BELLINI, BERLIOZ, MEYERBEER and PLEYEL; also literary geniuses such as BALZAC and HEINE. In 1836 he was introduced to George SAND (Madame Dudevant) by Franz Liszt, an unfortunate meeting for Chopin because of his inability through the sensitivity of his nature to understand a woman so much of the world, and their intimacy ceased in 1844. Financial worries induced Chopin, already a consumptive, to fulfill concert engagements at London in 1848 and 1849: he returned to Paris during the latter year only to die. His piano compositions include concertos, sonatas, scherzos, ballades, rondos, impromptus, polonaises, nocturnes, mazurkas and waltzes which take precedence over all other works of similar character.

Chopsticks, in music a waltz tune played on one piano by two persons for purposes of musical burlesque. Five great composers, BORODIN, CUI, LIADOFF, RIMSKY-KORSAKOW, and LISZT, wrote a suite of compositions based on the tune; it comprises twenty-four variations to which are added fourteen little pieces published with the title *Paraphrases.*

Choragus, (*a*) the title of the leader of the chorus in ancient Greek drama: he was chosen not only to instruct the chorus at the Dionysian festivals in ATHENS, but also to pay the expenses, therefore he apparently shouldered the responsibilities of the "backer" or "angel" in modern stage parlance. (*b*) The title of the assistant to the professor of music at Oxford University whose duties consist of conducting the vocal and instrumental rehearsals twice a week, and in assisting the professor in conducting examinations for degrees in music.

Choral or **Chorale,** in music a metrical hymn used in the services of the German Lutheran Church, set to a simple tune of devotional character, and sung usually in unison. Martin LUTHER (1483-1546) used many folk songs and familiar hymn tunes for his chorales: one of the most famous was *Ein' feste Burg ist unser Gott.* From the 16th to the 18th century many fine four-part settings were made of these chorals; Johann Sebastian BACH set more than four hundred. The organ accompaniments added greatly to the dignity and musical significance of the chorals.

Choral Symphony (Beethoven), see **Symphony No. 9, Op. 123 (Beethoven).**

Chord, in music the simultaneous combination of three or more musical tones of different pitch in thirds, or in any inverted form reducible to thirds. A three-toned chord is called a *triad;* a five-toned chord a *chord of the seventh;* a seventoned a *chord of the ninth.* The study of harmony explains the functions of the various kinds of chords.

Choreartium, a symphonic ballet in four parts: choreography by Leonide MASSINE; music by Johannes BRAHMS; first performed at the Alhambra Theatre, London, in 1933. This ballet has neither libretto nor cast of characters, relying entirely on stage composition and groupings of the dancers suggesting various famous works in sculpture and painting. The music is the fourth symphony of Johannes Brahms used in its entirety.

Choreography, in dancing a word used in three senses: (*a*) the art of representing dancing by signs or motions in the same way as music is represented by notes. (*b*) The art of dancing for the stage. (*c*) The art of arranging dances and the steps used in them for a ballet performance.

Choron, Alexander Étienne (1772-1834), French litterateur who became interested in music to such an extent that he devoted his entire life to the publication of classical musical works and theoretical treatises. In 1817 he founded the Institution of Classic and Religious Music, and published a *Historical Dictionary of Musicians* in collaboration with François Fayolle in 1810. He also left the sketches and notes from which Juste Adrien Lafage prepared a six-volume musical encyclopedia which was published in 1836-39.

Chorus, (*a*) in music the name given a body of singers who perform choral numbers in concerts, oratorios or operas. Small church groups are called choirs, and large choirs are called choruses. (*b*) In ancient Greek tragedies and comedies the word "chorus" referred not only to the singers, but also to the dancers and actors. Opera and oratorio choruses number from fifty to three hundred voices: among the fine organizations of this kind in the United States are the chorus of the METROPOLITAN OPERA HOUSE, New York; the HANDEL AND HAYDN SOCIETY at Boston, Mass.; the ORATORIO SOCIETY OF NEW YORK; the BETHLEHEM BACH CHOIR of Bethlehem, Pa.

Chotzinoff, Samuel (1889-), American pianist and music critic, born in Russia who came to the United States at an early age. He studied with Daniel Gregory MASON at Columbia University; acted as accompanist for Jascha HEIFETZ, Efrem ZIMBALIST and Alma GLUCK, and became music critic for the New York *World*, and the New York *Post*. In 1937 he was influential in securing the services of Arturo TOSCANINI as conductor of the NBC Symphony Orchestra: he is now (1943) manager of the Music Division of the National Broadcasting Company.

Chrétien or **Chréstien de Troyes,** a French poet of the 12th century who wrote several epics on King ARTHUR and his court including *Irec and Enid; Cliges; The Knight of La Charette; Perceval the Welshman* in which the legend of the Holy GRAIL and that of King ARTHUR are joined. He was a master of invention, and his works were used as models for two centuries by TROUVERES and Arthurian poets.

Christians, Mady (1900-), German stage and screen actress who came to the United States with her parents to appear in juvenile parts at the Irving Place Theatre, New York. She went to Vienna in 1917 to study with Max REINHARDT, appearing there in Shakespearean roles as well as in *The Guardsman* and *Cyrano de Bergerac.* Returning to the United States in 1931, she played in *The Divine Drudge, Heartbreak House,* and in several Shakespearean productions with Maurice Evans; her appearances on the screen include *Seventh Heaven, Heidi, Come and Get It,* and *Ship Café.*

Christ in Art, the life of the Messiah as recorded in the Bible has inspired painters, engravers, sculptors, and workers in mosaic, ivory, gold and silver from the beginning of the Christian era. The following list offers some of the incidents chosen for portrayal together with the names of the painters: *The Nativity* (Carracci, Correggio, Rembrandt, Titian); *The Holy Family* (Michelangelo, Andrea del Sarto, Sodoma); *Adoration of the Magi* (Botticelli, Dürer, Mantegna); *Adoration of the Shepherds* (Correggio, Murillo, Rembrandt, Velasquez); *Baptism* (Reni, Rubens, Tintoretto, Veronese); *Flight into Egypt* (Bramantino, Correggio, Dosso Dossi); *Christ Among the Doctors* (Borgognone, Caravaggio, Spagnoletto, Veronese); *Christ in the Carpenter Shop* (Millais); *Christ and Magdalen* (Albertinelli, Rembrandt); *Christ in the Garden of Gethsemane* (El Greco, Perugino, Overbeck, Raphael); *The Last Supper* (Leonardo da Vinci); *Betrayal of Christ* (Giotto, Hebert, Fra Angelico); *Christ at Calvary* (Breughel, Mignard, Munkacsy, Titian, Rubens, Veronese); *The Crucifixion* (Fra Angelico, Pisano, Rubens, Velasquez); *Crowning With Thorns* (Michelangelo, Van Dyck, Caravag-

gio, Guercino); *Descent from the Cross* (Giotto, Van der Weyden, Fra Angelico); *Entombment* (Raphael, Titian); *Ascension* (Perugino, Giotto, Rubens).

Christie, Mrs. Agatha (189?-), English writer of detective fiction who created the character of "Hercule Poirot," a French detective who rivals "Sherlock Holmes" in the affection of the mystery-reading public. Mrs. Christie's success since the publication of her first novel, *The Mysterious Affair at Styles,* in 1920, has been little short of phenomenal: almost all of her more than thirty stories have been "best sellers."

Christie's, one of the most important institutions in the world for the sale at auction of art objects of every description; founded by James Christie in 1766, and first located in the old Royal Academy rooms, Pall Mall, London. In 1823 it removed to 8 King Street, St. James, where it has continued for more than one hundred twenty years.

Christina, Queen of Sweden (1626-1689), daughter of King Gustavus Adolphus, succeeding him in 1632 under a regency consisting of five officers of the crown, and becoming actually queen in 1644. She was a patron of the arts and sciences to such a liberal degree that one-half the crown lands were given away when she named her cousin, Charles Augustus (Charles X) as her successor in 1654, and settled in Rome, again patronizing men of letters and collecting a library which was purchased by Pope Alexander VIII after her death. She tried twice to regain the Swedish throne, but was denied because she had become a Roman Catholic: her fortune was dissipated and she finally died penniless at Rome. The consensus of opinion on the part of historians appears to be that her brilliant qualities were overshadowed by inordinate pride, egotism, and a prodigality which gave no consideration to the financial necessities of her country. The Swedish screen actress, Greta GARBO appeared in the title role of a film, *Queen Christina,* in 1935 with John GILBERT.

Christus, Petrus (c.1410-1473), Flemish painter who was probably a pupil of Hubert van EYCK: he obtained the right of citizenship at Bruges in 1444, and lived there the rest of his life. Among his notable pictures are *Portrait of a Man; St. Eloi Receiving a Betrothed Couple; The Last Judgment; Madonna with a Carthusian Monk; The Goldsmith's Shop; Madonna with Saints.*

Christy, Edwin P. (1815-1862), American singer and director of minstrel shows who first appeared on the stage at Albany, N. Y., in 1844, and made his New York debut at Palma's Opera House in 1845 with the Virginia Minstrels. The company gave more than 2500 performances with Christy as principal singer and interlocutor. His fame is intermixed with that of Stephen FOSTER because he was not only the first to sing *The Old Folks at Home,* but also had his name for several years (by arrangement with Foster) as its composer. In 1850 Christy took his company to England, and achieved as much success in Great Britain as in the United States.

Christy, Howard Chandler (1873-   ), American portrait painter and illustrator; student at the National Academy of Design, and of William Merritt CHASE at the ART STUDENTS' LEAGUE, New York. His letters and illustrations while with Roosevelt's "Rough Riders" in the Spanish American War were published in *Scribner's Magazine*; *Harper's Magazine*, and *Collier's Weekly*. He illustrated the works of James Whitcomb RILEY, and received many medals and awards. Among his portraits of distinguished Americans are those of Calvin Coolidge, Charles E. Hughes, Eddie Rickenbacker, Amelia Earhart, Will ROGERS, and Colonel Theodore Roosevelt. He also painted the *Signing the Constitution* in the Capitol, Washington, D. C.

Chromatic, in music (*a*) a note that is foreign to the scale indicated in the signature of the music; it is indicated by an accidental, i.e., a sharp, flat or natural, referred to as a *chromatic sign;* (*b*) a *chromatic scale* is a scale containing all the tones employed in ordinary music; (*c*) a *chromatic instrument* is any instrument capable of producing all the tones of the chromatic scale; (*d*) *chromatic signs* are the characters used in raising or lowering the pitch of notes such as the sharp, double-sharp, flat, and double-flat.

Chryselephantine, in sculpture a term applied to statues made in ancient Greece, and executed in ivory, gold and other precious metals. PHIDIAS, one of the greatest Greek sculptors, created many figures of this character which were of colossal size, and adorned temples on the PARTHENON.

Church, Frederick Edwin (1826-1900), American painter who specialized in landscapes, and was one of the prominent members of the HUDSON RIVER SCHOOL. He used the wonders of nature for his subjects after traveling extensively in North and South America. Among his notable works, which sold for high prices in their time, were *Great Fall of Niagara; Heart of the Andes; Jerusalem; The Parthenon; Twilight; Morning in the Tropics.*

Church, Frederick Stuart (1842-1924), American painter and illustrator who studied at the Chicago Academy of Design and the New York National Academy of Design. His specialty was painting animals in water color, and drawing in black and white. Among his best pictures are *Mad as March Hares; Peacocks in the Snow; Moonrise; Sea Serpent; The Phantom; St. Cecilia.*

Churchill, Berton (1876-1940), Canadian stage and screen actor who made his New York debut in 1908 with William FAVERSHAM in *The World and His Wife,* and appeared later in numerous plays including *The Trail of the Lonesome Pine; The Cinderella Man; Alias the Deacon; Carnival; Five Star Final.* His film career began in 1929: among the pictures in which he played important roles were *Parnell; In Old Chicago; Sweethearts; Stage Coach; Daughters Courageous.*

Churchill, Charles (1731-1764), English poet; author of a satire upon the stage of his time, *The Rosciad* (1761), in which only GARRICK and a few other popular actors and actresses were praised.

Among his other works of the same character were *The Ghost;* a satire upon Dr. Samuel JOHNSON, *The Author; The Farewell; The Conference.*

Churchill, Winston (1871-   ), American novelist who was graduated from the United States Naval Academy in 1894; his successful works include *Richard Carvel* (1899); *The Crisis* (1901), dramatized successfully in 1927; *The Crossing; Coniston; The Inside of the Cup.*

Churchill, Winston Leonard Spencer (1874-   ), English statesman, soldier, and author educated at Harrow School and the Royal Military College, Sandhurst. He was captured by the Boers while acting as correspondent for the London *Morning Post* during the South African War; became a member of Parliament in 1900, and First Lord of the Admiralty in 1911, serving his country through World War I as minister of munitions and as secretary for war. After the resignation of Neville Chamberlain in 1940, he became Prime Minister, and has directed the operations of Great Britain during World War II since that time. His literary works include biographies of *Lord Randolph Churchill* (1906); *Marlborough: His Life and Times; Great Contemporaries:* also *My African Journey; A Roving Commission,* the story of his early life; two collections of speeches, *While England Slept* (1938), and *Blood, Sweat and Tears* (1941).

Churriguera, José (1650-1725), Spanish sculptor and architect who established his reputation at Madrid in 1689 with a catafalque designed for the funeral rites of Queen Maria Louisa. His various sculptures and architectural works, executed with the aid of his sons, were of the BAROQUE type in which dignity and restraint were sacrificed for theatrical effect to such an extent that the opprobrious term, *churrigueresque,* was coined to describe the extravagances of architectural design in Spain and its colonies in America and Mexico during the latter part of the 18th and the early part of the 19th century.

Cibber (Cibert), Caius Gabriel (1630-1700), Danish sculptor; son of the king of Denmark's cabinet maker. He studied as a youth in Rome, and went to England during the first years of the Restoration. His statues, *Melancholy* and *Raving Madness,* are now at South Kensington, London. In 1688 he fought for William of Orange, and was appointed carver to the king: he built the Danish church in London, and his son by a second wife was the English actor and dramatist, Colley CIBBER.

Cibber, Colley (1671-1757), English actor and dramatist who first appeared at the Theatre Royal, London, in 1690. His first play, *Love's Last Shift,* was produced in 1696: in 1704 he appeared with Anne OLDFIELD in his play, *The Careless Husband,* highly praised by Horace WALPOLE, but ridiculed by Alexander POPE and Dr. Samuel JOHNSON. He was made Poet Laureate by George I in 1730, and published his autobiography in 1740 with the title *An Apology for the Life of Colley Cibber, Comedian . . . with an Historical View of the Stage during his Own Time.* His wife was a tragic actress of distinction, and the sister of the composer, Thomas Augustin ARNE;

his son, Theophilus Cibber, was also an actor and theatre manager.

Cicero, Marcus Tullius (106 B.C.-43 B.C.), Roman statesman, orator, and writer on philosophy: he held many important offices as questor, aedile, consul, and proconsul, and was killed after he pronounced the *Philippics* against Marc Antony who in revenge secured Octavian's permission to place Cicero's name on the proscribed list of the Second Triumvirate. Of his orations, fifty-seven are extant in complete form with fragments of twenty more: he also wrote several treatises on oratory of which he was the greatest master in ancient times; many essays on philosophy, religion; more than 850 letters to his friends of which those addressed to his brother, Quintus, to his most intimate friend, Titus Pomponius Atticus, and to Decimus Junius Brutus at about the time of Caesar's assassination are the most interesting.

Cid, The (c.1040-1099), the principal national hero of Spain, famous for his exploits in the war against the Moors. His real name was Rodrigo Diaz de Bivar, and he was, according to authoritative chronicles, a soldier of fortune who allied himself with Spain, or the infidels who harassed her, as seemed most expedient for his own fortunes. The *Poem of the Cid*, written in the latter half of the 12th century, exists only in a fragment of about 3700 lines praising the Cid as a national hero; plays lionizing him were written by Guillen de Castro and Pierre Corneille; also operas by Sacchini, Cornelius and Massenet.

Cienfuegos, Nicasio Alvarez de (1764-1809), Spanish poet and dramatist; an alumnus of the School of Poets at Salamanca. His works include a tragedy, *Pitaco*, a masterpiece which won him admission to the Spanish Academy: also a comedy, *The Magnanimous Sisters*; many sonnets, odes and elegies.

Cignani, Carlo, Count (1628-1719), Italian painter of the Bolognese school who was a pupil of Francesco Albani, and also studied the works of Correggio and Annibale Carracci. He spent twenty years of his life painting the *Assumption of the Virgin* for the dome of the Cathedral at Forli: other notable works include two frescoes for Cardinal Farnese in the Public Palace at Bologna; a *Mater Dolorosa; Achilles and Ulysses; Death of Cleopatra; Adam and Eve.*

Cignaroli, Giovanni (1706-1770), Italian painter of the Venetian school who studied the works of Veronese and Correggio, and became one of the founders and in 1769 director of the Academy of Fine Arts at Verona. His notable works include *Death of Rachael; Flight Into Egypt; Madonna with Saints; Triumph of Pomponius.*

Cigoli, Lodovici Cardi da (1559-1613), Italian painter of the Florentine school who was a pupil of Alessandro Allori, and also studied and imitated the works of Correggio so closely that he was sometimes referred to as the "Correggio of Tuscany." His painting for St. Peter's in Rome, *Lame Man Healed by Peter*, was highly praised for its drawing and pleasing effects of light and shade.

Cima, Giovanni Battista or **Cima da Conegliano** (c.1459-c.1517), Venetian painter who is said to have studied with Giovanni Bellini; his works also reveal the influence of Giorgione. Among his works are many fine Madonnas with or without saints; a *Baptism of Christ;* The *Glorification of St. Peter; David and Jonathan; Tobias with the Saints.*

Cimabue, Giovanni (c.1240-c.1302), Italian painter, also known as *Cenni di Pepo,* and said by Dante to be the greatest painter of his period. There is little documentary evidence to support the contention that he created such works as the frescoes of the *Madonna With Angels; St. Francis;* five scenes from the life of the Virgin and other masterpieces in the Church of St. Francis at Assisi; also the mosaic, *Christ in Glory,* in the Cathedral of Pisa. On the basis of such evidence as exists, some authorities consider Cimabue the father of modern painting.

Cimarosa, Domenico (1749-1801), Italian dramatic composer whose talent at an early age earned him a scholarship at the Conservatory of Saint Maria of Loreto in Naples where he was a pupil of Sacchini and Piccinni. He produced an oratorio and an opera in 1770 and 1772 with little success, but his next opera, *La finta parigina,* was so favorably received that he embarked on a career of producing nearly 80 operas with scarcely any actual failures. In 1792 he saw his greatest success, *The Secret Marriage,* produced at Vienna: it has been performed thousands of times in opera houses all over the world, and is the only one of his operas which is in the modern repertory.

Cimarosiana, a ballet in one act without libretto: the music taken from the works of Domenico Cimarosa; choreography by Leonide Massine; first produced in 1920 at Covent Garden, London. The action revolves around a series of whimsical, ludicrous characters who perform a series of varied dances ending in a spectacular finale.

Cimon of Cleonae, a Greek painter who worked during the 9th century, B.C., and is said by Pliny to have introduced improvements in drawing by representing figures in positions other than erect, faces looking back, up, or down, and folds in garments more distinctly. These improvements have been discovered in the paintings on Greek vases of his period.

Cincinnati Conservatory of Music, an institution founded by Clara Baur in 1867: its direction was assumed after her death by a niece, Bertha Baur, who presented the conservatory in 1930 to the Cincinnati Institute of Fine Arts. It is now affiliated with the University of Cincinnati, and is not run for profit. Instruction is given in all branches of music, and courses offered leading to Bachelor of Music and higher degrees.

Cincinnati Symphony Orchestra, an organization founded in 1895, and conducted during its first season by Frank Van der Stucken, Anton Seidl and Henry Schradieck. Van der Stucken became permanent conductor from 1896 to 1907, and Leopold Stokowski from 1909 to 1912. Since then many prominent musicians have acted as permanent or guest conductors; among them Victor HERBERT, Henry HADLEY, Ossip GABRILOWITSCH, Eugene YSAYE, Eugène GOOSSENS, Alfredo CASELLA, Richard STRAUSS, Ottorino RESPIGHI, Igor STRAVINSKY, Walter DAMROSCH and Eugene ORMANDY.

Cinderella, a ballet in one act: libretto founded on the familiar story of Cinderella in the fairy tale by Charles PERRAULT; music by Frederic d'Erlanger; choreography by Michel FOKINE; first produced at the Royal Opera, Covent Garden, London, in 1938. The comedy element is introduced by having the roles of the two ugly sisters played by male dancers.

Cino da Pistoia (1270-1336), Italian jurist and poet whose real name was Guittoncino de Sinabaldi: he is said to have carried on the tradition of DANTE during the interval between the latter and PETRARCH, with both of whom he was intimate. His greatest legal work was a commentary on the Justinian Code: his sonnet *Rimes*, first published in 1559, in memory of his lady, Maria Selvaggia, is full of tender passion eloquently phrased.

Cinq Mars, Henri Coeffier, Marquis de (1620-1642), French courtier who was a favorite of Louis XIII. During a conspiracy against Cardinal RICHELIEU he had treasonable communication with Spain for which he was tried and beheaded in 1642. Alfred de VIGNY wrote a popular historical novel with Cinq Mars as the principal character in 1826; Charles GOUNOD's opera on the same subject was produced at the Paris Opéra-Comique in 1877.

Cipriani, Giovanni Battista (1727-1785), Italian painter, illustrator, and engraver who was associated in London with the English architect and sculptor, Joseph Wilton, for whom he executed frescoes, paintings and decorative drawings for Buckingham Palace and Somerset House. He also made many pen and ink drawings for publishers; most of them were engraved by Francesco BARTOLOZZI. His drawings of children were excellent; among his works were the allegorical paintings for the state coach of George III, and exquisite designs for satin-wood furniture made by Robert ADAM.

Circe, in Greek mythology a sorceress who murdered her husband, the Prince of Colchis, and was placed on the desert island of Aenea where, according to HOMER, ODYSSEUS was wrecked on the way home from the siege of Troy. With her magic power she changed his companions into swine, but Odysseus, protected by a magic herb, forced her to restore them to human form, and to aid him on his homeward journey through the land of shades.

Circus, (a) the building used by the ancient Romans for chariot races, games and gladiatorial contests. The oldest and greatest building of this character was the Circus Maximus, first built about 650 B.C., rebuilt by Julius CAESAR, NERO, Domitian, and Trajan so that in its final form it accommodated more than 350,000 spectators.

There were many other great buildings of the same character in Italy including the COLISEUM; also in France and at Constantinople, the latter built by the Roman emperor, Septimius Severus. (b) The name given to an outdoor exhibition of wild animals, living freaks of nature, clowns and acrobats which may be said to have begun in 1768 when Philip Astley wandered through the English provinces giving trick riding performances on horses. The first famous aggregation of this character in the United States was John Robinson's circus about 1824; Adam Forepaugh's Circus began its tours in 1861, and P. T. BARNUM's Circus the most pretentious of all, in 1871; the latter became the Barnum and Bailey Circus in 1887. In 1907 it was purchased by Ringling Brothers who finally merged their own show with the Barnum and Bailey organization to produce what is actually "the greatest show on earth." Similar circuses were also organized in England and Germany, but never on the same grand scale.

Cire Perdue Process, in sculpture a method of casting described by Benvenuto CELLINI in his treatise on sculpture. The statue to be cast was modeled in clay slightly smaller than the size of the completed bronze; this was covered by a coating of wax. Soft clay was used to strengthen the mold and iron hoops held it together: it was then placed in a hot oven and the wax allowed to run off, leaving a hollow between the core and the mold over which melted bronze was poured. After cooling the outer mold was broken away, and the figure was ready for rubbing down and polishing.

Ciseaux, in ballet a term indicating a "scissors step" in which the dancer spreads his feet widely either in the air or on the toes. The same direction is conveyed by *pas de ciseaux* or *pas de sissone.*

Cisneros, Eleonora de (1878-1934), American dramatic mezzo-soprano, family name Broadfoot, who studied with Jean de RESZKE in Paris: she made her American debut in 1900 at a Sunday concert at the Metropolitan Opera Company, and her first operatic appearance in AIDA at the Philadelphia Academy of Music in 1901. After successful engagements at sixteen foreign opera houses including Turin, Milan, Rio de Janeiro, London, and Vienna, she appeared from 1907 to 1909 at the MANHATTAN OPERA HOUSE. She excelled in the mezzo-soprano roles of AIDA, CARMEN, La GIOCONDA, Il TROVATORE, LOHENGRIN, and TSCHAIKOWSKY's *Pique Dame.*

Citadel, in ancient and medieval architecture a fortified stronghold that commands a city either for defense in time of war, or for control of the populace in riots, insurrections or revolutions.

Cithara, an ancient musical instrument known as far back as 1700 B.C. in Egypt, Assyria, Greece, and Rome. It consisted of a sound chest, hollowed out from a solid block of wood, out of which two arms of unequal length extend to be joined together at the top. Thus a frame was formed over which from 4 to 20 strings were stretched and plucked by the fingers, or with a PLECTRUM. Examples are to be seen in musical instrument collections at Berlin, London and Rome.

Civic Repertory Theatre, a theatrical organization founded in 1926 by Eva LE GALLIENNE at the Fourteenth Street Theatre in New York. From 1926 to 1933 the works of the best dramatists, including SHAKESPEARE, GOLDONI, CHEKHOV, and IBSEN, were offered at rates not exceeding $1.50 for the choicest orchestra seats; Miss Le Gallienne appeared regularly herself in company with many distinguished actors including NAZIMOVA, Jacob BEN-AMI and Burgess MEREDITH.

Civic Theatre, a name for municipal theatres coined by Percy MACKAYE: his book, *The Playhouse and the Play,* is a masterly exposition of his ideas on the subject of theatres operated by municipalities or communities.

Clair, René, contemporary French film director who began writing and directing his own stories for the silent screen in 1926: among his notable contributions to the talking films are *Roof Tops of Paris; The Million; Liberty for Us; Fourteenth of July; The Last Millionaire; The Ghost Goes West; Flame of New Orleans.*

Claire, Ina (1892-), American stage and screen actress; real name Ina Fagan. She made her debut on the New York stage at the American Music Hall in 1909 as an impersonator of Sir Harry LAUDER. After playing all the important vaudeville circuits, she appeared in many musical plays and dramas including *The Quaker Girl; The Girl from Utah; The Gold Diggers; Bluebeard's Eighth Wife; The Awful Truth; The Last of Mrs. Cheyney; Reunion in Vienna; Biography; Our Betters; Barchester Towers.* Miss Claire has also appeared in several films including *The Awful Truth; The Royal Family of Broadway; The Greeks Had a Word For Them; Rebound; Ninotchka.*

Claire, Marion, contemporary American soprano who studied with Pompilio Malatesta at Milan, making her debut there in 1926 in La BOHEME, and also appearing at the Berlin State Opera. Her debut with the Chicago Civic Opera Association in La Bohème took place in 1929: since then she has appeared in concert, and as leading soprano in grand and light opera broadcasts.

Clairon, Mlle. or **La** (1723-1803), French actress whose real name was Claire Josephe Hippolyte Leris: after touring the French provinces she appeared in Paris in 1743 in RACINE's *Phèdre* despite violent opposition because of irregularities in her private life. She scored a real triumph, and appeared there for twenty-two years sharing public favor with Mlle. Dumesnil in tragedies by VOLTAIRE, MARMONTEL and others. Oliver GOLDSMITH praised her beauty and figure; David GARRICK said that she possessed "everything that art and a good understanding with great natural spirit can give her."

Clare, John (1793-1864), English poet who wrote poems of rural life although said to be absolutely uneducated: among them were *Poems Descriptive of Rural Life and Scenery* (1820); *The Village Minstrel; Shepherd's Calendar; The Rural Muse.*

Claretie, Jules, pseudonym of **Arsène Arnaud** (1840-1913), French litterateur, dramatist and theatre manager; director from 1885 to 1913 of the Comédie-Française, and a member of the French Academy. His works include a five-volume history of the French Revolution; a history of French literature; many plays including *Les Muscadins, Les Mirabeau,* and *Le Regiment de champagne;* several novels including *The Assassin, Puyjoli, The Accuser* and *La Cigarette:* the last named was the basis of the opera, *La Navarraise,* by Jules MASSENET.

Clarina, a musical instrument belonging to the wood-winds invented by Wilhelm Heckel, and used since 1891 at BAYREUTH in *Tristan and Isolde* for playing the shepherd's music instead of the holztrompete, or wooden trumpet contrived by Richard WAGNER. It is a hybrid instrument with the characteristics of both the OBOE and CLARINET.

Clarinet, a single-reed wind instrument developed by J. C. Denner in 1690 from the chalumeau, a primitive instrument with a range of only a comparatively few notes, to an instrument with a range of more than two octaves. It was again improved by Hyacinthe KLOSE in 1843 when he adapted the BOEHM key system for the flute to the clarinet so that it could play in all keys. Its rich mellowness in the lower registers, and penetrating acuteness in the higher ranges adapts itself perfectly to both orchestral and band music: MOZART was the first composer to make use of it in symphonic works, and WAGNER created extraordinarily dramatic effects with the bass clarinet in the RING OF THE NIBELUNGS.

Clark, Barrett H. (1890-), American author and dramatic editor educated at the University of Chicago and the University of Paris. He acted and directed for Minnie Maddern FISKE, taught dramatic art at Chautauqua; edited plays for Samuel French, Ltd., read plays for the THEATRE GUILD and edited *Drama Magazine.* He has written many important books on theatrical subjects including *The Continental Drama of Today* (1914); *British and American Drama of Today; Contemporary French Dramatists; A Study of the Modern Drama;* a biography of Eugene O'NEILL. He has edited *The World's Best Plays* (58 volumes), and has translated many foreign plays.

Clark, Bobby (1888-), American stage and screen comedian, full name Robert Edward Clark, who formed the team of Clark and McCullough with Paul McCullough in 1905, and appeared in vaudeville, musical plays, and revues until McCullough's death in 1936. He has acted since in the *Ziegfeld Follies of 1936,* and in *The Streets of Paris:* in 1942 he made a highly successful appearance as Bob Acres in a revival of *The Rivals.*

Clark, Charles Heber (1847-1915), American journalist and author of the humorous *Out of the Hurly Burly* (1874); also *Random Shots; Captain Bluitt; The Quakeress,* and two books of short stories. He wrote under the pen name "Max Adeler."

Clark, Lewis Gaylord (1808-1873), American editor and poet for many years connected with the *Knickerbocker Magazine:* his works include a volume of poems (1848); *Knick-Knacks from an Editor's Table; The Knickerbocker Sketch-Book.* His brother, **Willis Gaylord Clark** (1808-1841), was editor of the *New York Mirror,* and of the *Philadelphia Gazette.* His contributions in the form of humorous verse were published with the title, *Ollapodiana,* after his death.

Clarke, Thomas Shields (1860-1920), American painter and sculptor; student at the ART STUDENTS' LEAGUE, New York. He also studied painting with GEROME and DAGNAN-BOUVERET, and sculpture with Henri CHAPU. His sculptures include *The Cider Press;* four Caryatides, *The Seasons,* for the Appellate Court House, New York; an *Alma Mater* for Princeton University where he was graduated. His paintings include *Night Market in Morocco* and *A Fool's Fool.*

Classic, in music the term applied to musical works of any kind that have stood the test of time through their intrinsic merits such as the symphonies of BEETHOVEN or the waltzes of STRAUSS: it is also used to describe new works that are modeled to a greater or lesser degree after older masterpieces. The term is also applied to literary works, plays, paintings, sculptures, and architectural creations of any period that give evidence of possessing the same degree of intrinsic merit and permanency as the musical compositions previously mentioned.

Classical Symphony (Prokofieff), a symphony composed during 1916-17 by the Russian composer, Serge PROKOFIEFF; it was first played at Petrograd in April, 1918, and in New York at a Russian symphony concert in December of the same year. Boris Asafieff, the Russian music critic to whom it was dedicated, has this to say: "The composer's idea in writing this work was to catch the spirit of MOZART, and to put down that which, if he were living now, Mozart might put into his scores." The charming thematic content of this work and the absolute perfection of its form are among its most engaging features. There is a Victor recording by the Boston Symphony Orchestra with Serge Koussevitzky, and a Columbia recording by the Minneapolis Orchestra under the baton of Dimitri Mitropoulos.

Classicism, a term denoting, according to WEBSTER'S DICTIONARY, "the principles and characteristics of Greek and Roman literature and art; considered as embodying formal elegance, simplicity, dignity and correctness of style, and just and lucid conception and order." Any tendency on the part of architects, dramatists, authors, painters or sculptors to seek inspiration in the culture of Greece and Rome is usually referred to as a "return to classicism."

Classic Revival, in architecture and the arts the name applied to the renewed interest in classic Greek and Roman design which influenced the arts at the end of the 18th and during the first half of the 19th century in Europe, England, and the United States. The chief cause of the movement was the publication in 1762 of a volume, *Antiquities of Athens,* written by James Stuart and Nicholas Revett who spent three years in research at ATHENS before publishing their monumental work. The chief evidence of the revival was manifested in such buildings as Thomas JEFFERSON's design for the Virginia State Capitol in 1785; the Bank of the United States, Philadelphia, in 1819 by Benjamin H. LATROBE; also the dome and wings of the CAPITOL at Washington built during the revival period which was succeeded about 1865 by the VICTORIAN PERIOD of romanticism.

Claudel, Paul (1868-   ), French diplomat, poet and dramatist who came to the United States in 1926 as ambassador for his country. His style as a poet places him among the symbolists, and is not easy of comprehension for the uninitiated. His plays are also symbolistic: they include *L'Otage* (1911); *The Tidings Brought to Mary,* produced by the New York THEATRE GUILD in 1922; *Le Pain dur; Le Père humilié; The Satin Slipper; Ways and Crossways; Tête d'Or.* Other works include *The Book of Christopher Columbus,* and a dramatic poem, *Letters to a Doubter.*

Claude Lorrain (1600-1682), French painter whose real name was Claude Gellée or Gelée. His works, chiefly landscapes, became extremely popular after he settled in Rome under the patronage of Pope Urban VIII, the king of Spain and many other nobles. In 1634 he began a series of 200 tinted drawings of his pictures in six volumes, which was completed in 1675: they reveal the fact that he was one of the finest landscape painters of his time, and that he exercised a beneficial influence on the art.

Claude Michel, see **Clodion.**

Claudian (Claudius Claudianus), Latin poet who lived about 365 A.D., and is considered the last of the Latin epic poets. He is believed to have been born in ALEXANDRIA of Roman parentage, and was famed for his command of the Latin language as displayed in *Rufinus* and *The Rape of Proserpine.*

Clausen, Sir George (1852-   ), English painter; pupil of Edwin Long, BOUGUEREAU and Robert FLEURY, and author of *Lectures on Painting* and *Aims and Ideals in Art.* He was a fine painter of landscapes and country life: among his important works are *Girl at the Gate; The Gleaners Returning; End of a Winter's Day; Ploughman's Breakfast.*

Claussen, Julia (1879-   ), Swedish dramatic mezzo-soprano who studied at the Royal Academy of Music, Stockholm, making her debut in 1903 at the Royal Opera in that city, and becoming a member of the company until 1912. She made her American debut with the CHICAGO OPERA COMPANY in 1913, and at the METROPOLITAN OPERA HOUSE, New York, in 1917 in SAINT-SAENS' *Samson and Delilah,* remaining there until 1932, and also appearing as soloist with the leading symphony orchestras.

Clavichord, an instrument which may be considered one of the precursors of the PIANO; it was invented about 1400, and differed in its action from the piano in having upright metal wedges instead of hammers for striking the strings. The tone was delicate, but without volume; it was a favorite with Johann Sebastian BACH who wrote The WELL TEMPERED CLAVICHORD for it.

Clavier (Fr.) or **Klavier** (Ger.), the general name in French and German for all keyboard instruments except the organ; in classical days for the CLAVICHORD, and at the present time for the piano.

Clays, Paul Jean (1819-1900), Belgian painter who studied with Théodore GUDIN. He made a specialty of marine painting: among his notable pictures are *Boats in a Dutch Port; Calm on the Scheldt; The Open North Sea; Bay of Ostend; Arrival of Queen Victoria at Ostend.* He is regarded as one of the great Belgian artists, and was the recipient of many honors.

Cleef or **Cleve Josse** (c.1518-c.1550), Flemish painter, nicknamed "The Fool," and one of the best portraitists in the style of HOLBEIN: among his finest works are a portrait of himself and his wife; a *Last Judgment; Saint Cosmo and Saint Damian.*

Clef, in music the symbol placed at the beginning of every staff to indicate the exact pitch of the notes. In piano music the *treble clef,* also called the *G clef,* and the *bass clef* are used: in violin music the *treble clef;* in viola the *treble* and *alto clefs;* in violoncello and double-bass the *bass clef.* For woodwind and brass instruments the several clefs mentioned above are used in such a manner that the notation is conveniently placed for technical performance.

Clemens, Samuel Langhorne, see **Twain, Mark.**

Clément, Edmond (1867-1928), French dramatic tenor who studied at the PARIS CONSERVATORY, and made his debut in 1889 at the Opéra-Comique in GOUNOD's *Mireille.* His success was so pronounced that he remained there as principal tenor for 20 years; in 1909 he appeared at the Century Theatre, New York, in MASSENET's *Werther,* and later with the Metropolitan Opera Company and the Boston Opera Company, besides making an extended concert tour of the United States. Clément possessed a light tenor voice gracefully handled: he excelled in Massenet's *Manon* and also created the tenor roles in many French operas including BRUNEAU's *The Attack on the Mill.*

Clementi, Muzio (1752-1832), Italian pianist and composer who made such progress in the study of the piano and organ as a child that he won a position as church organist at the age of nine. In 1770 he created a furore in England by his virtuosity as a pianist, and toured Europe with equal success. After a friendly competition with MOZART at Vienna, he changed his bravura style to that of a serious artist. Clementi also established a piano manufactory, a music publishing house, and taught many famous pianists including John FIELD, Johann CRAMER, Ignaz MOSCHÉLES and Frederick KALKBRENNER. His compositions for the piano include many sonatas and the famous *Gradus ad Parnassum,* a series of piano exercises.

Cleopatra, the last queen of Egypt; co-ruler with her brother, Ptolemy, from 51 to 59 A.D. The latter expelled her, and she was reinstated by Julius CAESAR, with whom she went to Rome and had one son, Caeserion, later put to death by Octavianus. After her return to Egypt, she obtained complete ascendancy over Marc ANTONY to whom she bore three children: when their combined fleet was defeated by Octavianus she committed suicide. Besides possessing great beauty she had a brilliant mind: SHAKESPEARE, DRYDEN, and SHAW made her the heroine of plays; MASSENET of the opera, *Cleopatra* (1915). In 1934 Claudette COLBERT appeared in the title role of the film, *Cleopatra.*

Cleopatra, ballet in one act: libretto and choreography by Michel FOKINE; music by Anton ARENSKY and other Russian composers; first produced at Paris in 1909. The original musical score by Arensky was augmented by numbers taken from RIMSKY-KORSAKOW's *Mlada,* GLINKA's *Russlan and Ludmilla,* GLAZOUNOFF's *The Seasons,* and MOUSSORGSKY's *Khovanchina.* The story revolves around the infatuation of Amoun, an Egyptian youth, for his royal mistress. In the first production Ida RUBINSTEIN mimed the part of Cleopatra with Fokine as Amoun, and Anna PAVLOWA as an Egyptian maiden who loves him.

Cleopatra's Needles, a pair of Egyptian obelisks of pink granite which were removed from Heliopolis to ALEXANDRIA by Caesar Augustus of Rome about 14 B.C. They were given to England and the United States in 1878 and 1880 by Ismail Pasha: one was set up on the Thames embankment, and the other in Central Park, New York. The latter is 69½ feet high, and stands on a massive cube of granite supported by four giant bronze crabs; its sides are incised with hieroglyphs containing the names of Thothmes III, Rameses II, and Seti II, rulers of Egypt from the 16th to the 14th centuries B.C.

Clerestory, in architecture the upper story of the NAVE of a church, the walls extending above the aisles permitting the addition of windows for additional lighting. The same method of construction was used in Egyptian temples, and in Roman baths, basilicas, and palaces.

Clésinger, Jean-Baptiste, called **Auguste** (1814-1883), French sculptor whose first success was a marble figure, *Woman Bitten by a Serpent,* at the French salon in 1847. Among his best works are a bust of *George Sand; Reclining Bacchante;* a large bust, *Liberty;* a colossal statue, *Fraternity;* a monument to Frédéric Chopin; a *Piéta;* a *Last Supper;* a group, *Cornelius and His Children;* a group, *Fight Between Two Bulls.*

Cleveland, John (1613-1658), English poet whose poems were more highly regarded than those of John MILTON by his contemporaries; he expressed his indignation at the surrender of Charles I of England to the Scotch army in his satirical poem, *The Rebel;* other satires included *Fuscara* or *The Bee Errant,* distinguished by bitter invective.

Cleveland Museum of Art, an institution opened at Cleveland, Ohio, in 1916, and housing one of the finest medieval art collections in the United States: also choice assemblies of arms, armor, textiles, tapestries, pottery, drawings, prints, and examples of the goldsmith's art. The gallery of paintings contains outstanding works by LIPPI, COPLEY, FEKE, FRENCH, EL GRECO, SARTO, TINTORETTO, POUSSIN, RUBENS, RENOIR, TOULOUSE-LAUTREC, BELLOWS, RYDER, STROZZI, TURNER, WATTEAU, DELACROIX, PUVIS DE CHAVANNES, CEZANNE, REDON, REMBRANDT, REYNOLDS, DROUAIS, VAN DYCK, and HOBBEMA. Among the sculptors whose works are to be seen are RODIN, Luca Della ROBBIA, ROSSELLINO, CLODION, HASELTINE, Malvina HOFFMAN and Janet SCUDDER. The Garden Court has installed in it a pipe organ on which some of the world's greatest organists have given recitals: through the Department of Musical Arts, a regular schedule of musical events brings outstanding soloists, vocal and instrumental groups to the Museum.

Cleveland Orchestra, an organization founded in 1918 by the Cleveland (Ohio) Musical Arts Association with Nikolai SOKOLOFF as its conductor from 1918 to 1933. Artur RODZINSKI succeeded him, remaining until 1943 when he resigned to direct the New York Philharmonic-Symphony Society. Arthur SHEPHERD was assistant to Sokoloff from 1920 to 1928: in 1931 the orchestra gave its first concert in Severance Hall, an auditorium presented to it by Mr. and Mrs. J. L. Severance of Cleveland. Children's concerts have been given by the orchestra every season since it was organized. Eric LEINSDORF became conductor in 1943.

Clevenger, Shobal Vail (1812-1843), American sculptor who first worked for a stone carver, and later studied in Rome where he executed a figure, *North American Indian,* said by critics to be the first distinctive example of American sculpture. His portrait busts of *Daniel Webster* and *Henry Clay* are regarded as extraordinarily lifelike.

Cliff dwellings, in archaeology the term for the homes of primitive races made by utilizing natural recesses or openings in high cliffs. Many such dwellings are to be found among the canyons of Arizona, New Mexico, Utah and Colorado: some of these are still used by the descendants of the Pueblo Indians who constructed them. More than three hundred homes of this character are to be seen at the Mesa Verde National Park in Colorado.

Clifton, Chalmers (1889-), American composer and conductor who studied at the Cincinnati Conservatory, Harvard University, and with Gédalge and d'Indy in Paris. He has conducted the Musical Art and Cecilia Societies in Boston; the San Carlo Opera Company; the American Orchestral Society; many festival orchestras, and has acted as guest conductor of several major orchestras in the United States. His compositions include a violin sonata, piano sonatas, and a suite for trumpet and orchestra; he has also orchestrated twenty of Edward MACDOWELL's piano pieces.

Clinedinst, Benjamin West (1860-1931), American painter and illustrator who studied at the

ECOLE DES BEAUX-ARTS, Paris, and with CABANEL and BONNAT. He illustrated the works of HAWTHORNE, STEVENSON, Mark TWAIN and Bret HARTE; he also painted portraits of Theodore Roosevelt, Admiral Robert Peary and many other distinguished Americans.

Clio, in Greek mythology the name of the muse of history.

Clive, Catherine (1711-1785), Irish actress who first appeared in 1728 at the DRURY LANE THEATRE, London, and later established her reputation as an actress and singer in Charles Coffey's *The Devil to Pay* in 1731. She sang at the Drury Lane for more than twenty years, also taking part in several of HANDEL's oratorios: her acting was praised by David GARRICK, Oliver GOLDSMITH and Ben JONSON.

"Clock" Symphony (Haydn), one of the twelve symphonies composed by Joseph HAYDN during 1791 and 1794 when he visited London to write six symphonies during each of the two seasons for Johann Peter SALOMON, director of the Salomon Concerts. This symphony, the tenth in the two series, was first performed at the Haymarket Theatre on May 4, 1795. The reason for the nickname, "The Clock," lies in the measured slow rhythm with which the second movement begins, and which it maintains throughout. The rhythm is identified by staccato notes in the bassoons and pizzicato passages in all the strings except the first violins which play an engagingly, delicately simple melody. There are occasional contrasting passages more robust in character for purposes of variety, but the "tick" of a clock persists throughout even when the characteristic figure and melody are transferred to different instrumental groups. There is a Victor recording by the New York Philharmonic-Symphony Orchestra under Arturo Toscanini, and a Columbia recording by the Columbia Broadcasting Symphony Orchestra directed by Howard Barlow.

Clodion or **Claude Michel** (1738-1814), French sculptor who worked largely in terra cotta: he won the Grand Prix de Rome in 1759 after studying with his uncle, Lambert Sigisbert ADAM, and spent many years in Italy. His works include *Triumph of Galatea; Saint Cecilia;* many decorative groups, friezes and statuettes of children, satyrs, nymphs and fauns; a life-size group, *Deluge Scene.*

Cloisonné, a method of decorating metal objects by means of designs outlined with bent wire fillets secured to the surface: the spaces between the wires are covered by colored enamels in paste form, and heat applied to fuse the enamel with the surface. French, Chinese and Japanese artisans have developed the art of decorating vases, cigarette cases, jewel boxes, and atomizers for perfume to such an extent that objects embellished in this manner are highly prized.

Cloister or **Ambulatory,** in architecture a covered passage one side of which is walled, and the other an open arcade or colonnade connecting buildings used for religious purposes. It was first found in European monasteries about the 11th century: an excellent example may be seen at WESTMINSTER ABBEY, London.

Cloisters, The, a museum of medieval art in New York City located in Fort Tryon Park opposite the Palisades, and in full view of the Hudson River. The modern structure is not far from the modest brick building in which George Grey BARNARD first assembled the antiques purchased by John D. Rockefeller, Jr., in 1925, and presented to the METROPOLITAN MUSEUM OF ART, which form the nucleus of the collection opened to the public in 1938 as a branch of the main institution. Among the architectural units are four cloisters reconstructed with parts from old monasteries, a Romanesque chapel rebuilt with sections from a ruined Romanesque church, and a complete chapter house of the XII century. The magnificent Gothic tapestries, *The Hunt of the Unicorn* are among the world's greatest treasures. Sculptured doorways, frescoed walls, polychromed statues, and stained glass windows find themselves at home in this setting. The Cloisters offers to visitors something more than a record of man's artistic achievement from the 12th through the 15th century: with its medieval gardens and rampart walks, it recreates for the twentieth-century American something of the mind and the spirit of medieval Europe.

Close Harmony, in music the term applied to four-part harmony when the chords are so arranged that the three highest tones are within the compass of an octave.

Closson, William Baxter (1848-1926), American painter and engraver on wood who did much fine work for American book and art publishers: his copies of masterpieces by European painters and original book designs won him many awards. His pastels and oil paintings, largely in a delicately refined style resembling WATTEAU, were also the subject of much praise.

Clotho, in Greek mythology one of the three FATES: she is portrayed in art with a distaff spinning the thread of life with her associates, Atropos and Lachesis.

Clouet, François (c.1510-c.1572), French painter who studied with his father, **Jean Clouet** (c.1485-c.1541) who was court painter for Louis XII and Francis I of France. Their paintings are difficult to distinguish because of confused markings, but it would appear that both were excellent painters of portraits and historical scenes; François succeeded his father as painter to Francis I, also holding the same position with Henry II, Francis II, and Charles IX.

Clovio, Giorgio (1498-1578), Italian priest and painter said to have studied at Rome with Giulio ROMANO: his works include a book of twenty-six pictures, portraying the procession of *Corpus Domini* in Rome, on which he spent nine years; twelve miniatures of the exploits in battle of Charles V of France; a beautifully illustrated biography of Frederick, duke of Urbino.

Clown, see **Pantomime.**

Clubs, Theatrical, see **Theatrical Clubs.**

Cluny Museum (Paris), a collection of medieval art objects in the Maison Cluny acquired by A. du Sommerard as a repository, and purchased by the city of Paris in 1842, later being transferred to the state. The building is in Gothic style, and distinguished for the exquisite carving of the doors and dormer windows: while the collection supplements exhibitions of the same kind in the LOUVRE, the lighting sometimes interferes with close examination or study of its treasures.

Clytemnestra, in Greek mythology the sister of HELEN of TROY, wife of AGAMEMNON, and mother of his three children, ELECTRA, ORESTES and IPHIGENIA. With the aid of her lover, Aegisthus, she murdered her husband on his return from Troy; Orestes killed both her and her lover to avenge his father's death.

Coates, Albert (1882-), English composer and conductor born in Russia who studied at the Leipzig Conservatory with Artur NIKISCH, and made his debut as conductor of the Elberfeld Opera in 1906, directing later at Dresden, Mannheim, St. Petersburg, and at Covent Garden, London. He has acted as guest conductor of the NEW YORK PHILHARMONIC-SYMPHONY SOCIETY, and at the EASTMAN School of Music, Rochester, N. Y. His compositions include the operas, *Sardanapalus, Samuel Pepys,* and *The Pickwicks;* also the symphonic poems *Lancelot* and *The Eagle.*

Coatsworth, Elizabeth Jane (1893-), American novelist, poet, and writer of stories for children: she has written a novel, *Here I Stay* (1938); several volumes of poetry including *Fox Footprints* and *Compass Rose;* many juvenile stories such as *The Cat Who Went to Heaven; The Golden Horseshoe,* and *The Littlest House.*

Cobb, Irvin (1876-), American humorist and dramatist who joined the staff of the New York *World* in 1905, and acted as correspondent for the *Saturday Evening Post* during World War I. His works include *Back Home* (1912); *Old Judge Priest; The Life of the Party; Speaking of Operations; Ladies and Gentlemen; Exit Laughing; Judge Priest Turns Detective.*

Cobbett, Walter Willson (1847-1937), English capitalist and amateur musician who was greatly interested in chamber music; he established the *Cobbett Award* for creative work in this field which has been won by several English composers. He also founded the London Chamber Music Society, and edited a comprehensive *Cyclopedic Survey of Chamber Music* in 1930.

Coburn, Charles Douville (1877-), American stage and screen actor and producer who managed a theatre in Savannah, Ga., at seventeen, and organized the Coburn Shakespearean Players in 1905 with his wife, Ivah Wills Coburn (1882-1937), playing the leading roles. Later he appeared in many important dramas at New York; produced *The Yellow Jacket* in 1916; played Old Bill in *The Better 'Ole;* organized the *Mohawk Drama Festival* in 1934 at Union College, Schenectady, New York. He has also played important roles in many films including *Of Human Hearts; Yellow Jacket; Idiot's Delight; Stanley and Livingstone; Bachelor Mother; Florian; Edison the Man; The Devil and Miss Jones; H. M. Pulham, Esq.; King's Row; In This Our Life.*

Cochran, Charles B. (1873-), English actor, producer and manager who first appeared in 1892 at NIBLO'S GARDENS, New York, in a dramatization of Jules VERNE's *Around the World in Eighty Days.* Among his more than a hundred important productions in New York and London may be mentioned *The Better 'Ole; The Man Who Came Back; Anna Christie; Porgy; Paris Bound; Bitter Sweet; Grand Hotel; Conversation Piece:* he also introduced the CHAUVE SOURIS, Sacha GUITRY and Eleonora DUSE to the London theatre. His reminiscences have appeared in two books entitled *Secrets of a Showman* and *I Had Almost Forgotten.*

Cockerell, Charles Robert (1788-1863), English architect who studied the architectural ruins of ancient Greece and Italy, conducting excavation operations resulting in the BRITISH MUSEUM securing many interesting fragments. He also superintended the alterations made on the Bank of England in 1837, erected the University Galleries at Oxford and many important public buildings.

Cocteau, Jean (1891-), French poet, novelist, and essayist: his works include *Discours du Grand Sommeil; Poesies; Plain-Chant; Le Secret Professional; Vocabulaire.* His poetry is that of a modernist, and much of it has been translated; he has also written the librettos of several modern ballets.

Cocx, Gonzales, see **Coques, Gonzalez.**

Coda, in music a passage in a sonata or symphony which finishes a movement, and begins where the repetition of the first theme ends. In pre-classical music the coda was merely a few chords followed by a cadence to bring the movement to a close: in the classical period MOZART and BEETHOVEN developed the coda to the point that it became a second development.

Coello, Alonzo Sanchez (1515-1590), Spanish painter who studied in Italy, and returned to Madrid in 1541 to execute many religious works which were later destroyed by fire: among those extant is a *St. Sebastian.* His daughter, Isabella Sanchez, was a fine portraitist.

Coello, Claudio (c.1625-1693), Spanish painter whose father was a famous sculptor in bronze: he studied with Francisco Rizi, and worked with CARREÑO DE MIRANDA who permitted him to copy master works by TITIAN, RUBENS and VAN DYCK. He studied fresco painting with Ximinez Donoso, and finally became court painter at Madrid. His greatest work was executed in the ESCORIAL; it is an immense altarpiece representing Charles II of Spain and his courtiers adoring the Host. There are more than fifty portraits in the group so finely painted that Coello is now recognized as the foremost painter of his day, and the last important artist of the Madrid school.

Coffin, Robert Peter Tristram (1892-), American biographer, essayist, and poet; his works include a volume of poems, *Christchurch* (1924); *Book of Crowns and Cottages; Duke of Buckingham; Lost Paradise,* an autobiography; *Strange Holiness* which won the Pulitzer Prize for poetry in 1936; *Maine Ballads; Collected Poems.*

Coffin, William Anderson (1855-1925), American art critic and painter who studied at the Yale School of Fine Arts and with Léon BONNAT in Paris. He acted as art critic for several newspapers and magazines: his works, which are on exhibition at many American art museums, include *Evening; Dawn; October Frost; End of the Storm.*

Coghlan, Charles (1841-1899), Irish actor who made his debut at the Haymarket Theatre, London, in 1860, and came to the United States in 1876, playing with Augustin DALY's Company and the Union Square Stock Company at New York in many important plays including *A Celebrated Case; The Royal Box; Citizen Pierre,* and *Tess of the d'Urbervilles* with Mrs. FISKE. His sister, **Rose Coghlan** (1850-1932) made her American debut in 1872 with Edward Askew SOTHERN: she also played with Barry Sullivan, and with Joseph JEFFERSON in *Rip Van Winkle.* Her finest roles were in *School for Scandal; Diplomacy; London Assurance; Debureau:* she appeared in the last-named when seventy years old.

Cogniet, Léon (1794-1880), French painter who studied with Pierre Narcisse GUERIN, and later founded one of the best art schools in Paris: his notable works include *Marius at Carthage; Massacre of the Innocents; Rape of Rebecca; Tintoretto Painting His Dead Daughter; Napoleon in Egypt; Numa in the Grotto of Egeria.*

Cohan, George Michael (1878-1942), American actor, dramatist, and producer who first appeared at nine in *Daniel Boone* at Haverstraw, Rhode Island, and in 1901 in vaudeville with his sketch, *The Governor's Son,* with his father, mother, and Ethel Levey, his first wife. His first successful musical play, *Little Johnny Jones,* was produced in 1904; it was followed by many others including *Get Rich Quick Wallingford; Forty-five Minutes from Broadway; Broadway Jones; The Miracle Man; Seven Keys to Baldpate.* Later plays included *The Tavern,* with Cora D. Gaunt; *The Song and Dance Man; American Born; Pigeons and People; The Honeymooners,* the last-named a revised version of the vaudeville sketch, *Running for Office.* His performance of the role of the father in Eugene O'NEILL's play, *Ah, Wilderness,* was his crowning achievement as an actor. Cohan's autobiography was published with the title, *Twenty Years on Broadway and the Years It Took to Get There:* he also produced many successful plays other than his own in association with Sam H. Harris, and appeared in the film, *The Phantom President,* in 1932. In 1941 he was the recipient of a Congressional Medal for his services to the morale of the nation in writing the songs *Over There* and *You're a Grand Old Flag.*

Cohen, Frederic (1904-), German composer and conductor who was educated at the Universities of Leipzig, Berlin and Cologne, and studied music at the Leipzig and Berlin Conservatories. After conducting opera in various German cities, he collaborated with Kurt Jooss in founding the Jooss Ballet in 1928, and toured the United States with the company from 1932 to 1942. He has composed the music for numerous ballets including *The Green Table, The Prodigal Son, The Seven Heroes,* and *The Mirror.*

Cohen, Octavus Roy (1891-   ), American novelist and author of short stories and detective fiction educated at Clemson College. His short stories of Southern negro life, in which he created the characters "Florian Slappey" and "Epic Peters," have been published for many years in the *Saturday Evening Post;* other works include *Polished Ebony* (1919); *Assorted Chocolates; Carbon Copies; East of Broadway; Florian Slappey; Romance in Crimson; Strange Honeymoon; Lady in Armor.*

Colbert, Claudette (1905-   ), Franco-American stage and screen actress educated in Paris and at the Washington Irving High School, New York. She made her debut in 1923 on the New York stage in *The Marionette Man,* and later assumed star roles in many important plays including *The Ghost Train; The Barker; Within the Law; A Kiss in a Taxi; The Mulberry Bush; Dynamo.* Her screen appearances from 1932 include *The Sign of the Cross; Three-Cornered Moon; It Happened One Night; Cleopatra; Imitation of Life; Private Worlds; Under Two Flags; Tovarich; Zaza; Drums Along the Mohawk; Boom Town; Arise, My Love; Skylark; Remember the Day.*

Cole, Rossetter Gleason (1866-   ), American composer who studied at the Music Department of the University of Michigan and at the Meisterschule in Berlin with Max BRUCH. He has held many responsible positions as professor of musical theory in American conservatories and colleges including the University of Wisconsin, Columbia University and the Cosmopolitan School of Music, Chicago. His compositions include operas, orchestral works, organ works, a fine violin sonata, piano pieces and songs.

Cole, Thomas (1801-1848), American painter, born in England, who came to the United States in 1819. He studied at the PENNSYLVANIA ACADEMY OF FINE ARTS in 1823: two years later he settled in New York to achieve success through the aid of a kindly patron. His earlier works were of the Hudson School, but after travel in Europe he revealed the romantic influence in the series of pictures called *The Course of Empire;* also in *The Voyage of Life* and *Departure and Return.*

Cole, Timothy (1852-1931), American wood engraver born in London, England, who came to the United States when a boy of six. In 1883 he went to Europe to engrave the masterpieces of Italian, Dutch, Flemish and English painters which were published in book form with his own critical notes. He also wrote essays on art for *Scribner's Magazine* and *Century Magazine,* and two treatises: *Wood Engraving* (1916) and *The Magic Line* (1917).

Coleman, Glenn O. (1887-1932), American painter who studied first in Indianapolis, and later in New York with William Merritt CHASE. He painted many pictures of the Brooklyn Bridge and Chinatown sections of lower New York in which realism, human interest, humor, and melancholy are the dominating motives. Some of his earlier works lack certainty of form and color, but later these faults were corrected. Examples of his work are in the Detroit Institute of Arts and the Phillips Memorial Gallery at Washington, D. C.

Coleridge, Samuel Taylor (1772-1834), English philosopher and poet educated at Oxford and Cambridge where he was on a friendly footing with Charles LAMB, Samuel BUTLER, Robert SOUTHEY and many other distinguished English authors. His most famous work was *The Ancient Mariner* (1798): other works include *Poems on Various Subjects; The Destiny of Nations; Ode to the Departing Year; Fears in Solitude; Wallenstein; Remorse,* a tragedy; *Christabel; Kubla Khan; Pains of Sleep.* His plays lack the vitality which is necessary to project them from the stage to the audience. His daughter **Sara Coleridge** (1802-1852), reveals some of her father's genius in her fairy ballad, *Phantasmion.*

Coleridge-Taylor, Samuel (1875-1912), English composer born of an English mother and a Negro father who was a physician at Sierra Leone. He studied composition at the ROYAL ACADEMY OF MUSIC, London, under Charles Villiers STANFORD; taught at various institutions; founded amateur string orchestra, and made three concert tours of the United States conducting his own compositions. His works include operas, symphonies, chamber music, violin pieces, piano pieces and songs: world-wide recognition has been accorded his trilogy for solo voices, chorus and orchestra, *The Song of Hiawatha.*

Colet, Louise Revoil (1810-1876), French poet and novelist whose verses were crowned four times by the French Academy between 1839 and 1855: the one entitled *The Woman's Poem* is considered her masterpiece. Among her many novels the most successful was *Bruised Hearts:* she also wrote several interesting travel books.

Colette, Gabrielle Claudine (1873-   ), French novelist who wrote under the pen name "Colette." Her first success was a series of novels, published from 1900 to 1903, including *Claudine at School* and *Claudine in Paris:* her first husband, Henri Gauthier-Villars, collaborated with her under the pen name "Willy." Later she published a collection of animal stories, and in 1910 began a series of psychological studies of women with the novel, *Renée, the Vagabond of Love:* her success with these even exceeded that of the Claudine series. In 1910 she married the French statesman, Henri de Jouvenel, author of a biography of Mirabeau.

Coliseum or Colosseum, an amphitheatre in Rome located on the Via Sacra (Sacred Way): its construction was started by Vespasian in 72 A.D. and completed by Titus in 80 A.D. It was 617 feet long, 512 feet deep, and four stories high: the arena measured 282 by 150 feet. The exterior was of stone and the interior faced with marble: 80,000 spectators could be seated and the shows comprised gladiatorial combats, athletic games, and the wholesale destruction of Christians by wild beasts. In the 8th century earthquakes partially destroyed it, and from the 15th to the 17th century architects used it as a quarry for removing stone to be used in new buildings, although a substantial part remains standing.

College of Music of Cincinnati, an endowed institution founded in 1878, and affiliated with the University of Cincinnati. Theodore THOMAS was the first director: he was succeeded by Frank Van der STUCKEN, Adolph HAHN, and other able musicians. The College has maintained close relations with the Cincinnati May Festival Association, and courses in all branches of music, musical education, and drama leading to diplomas and degrees are offered. Among the distinguished graduates of the College are Max BENDIX, Theodore Spiering, Clarence Adler, and Ernest LA PRADE, director of musical research for the National Broadcasting Company. The orchestra was conducted by Thomas, Van der Stucken, and during the Golden Jubilee in 1928 by Frederick STOCK of the Chicago Symphony Orchestra.

Colles, Henry Cope (1879-1943), English musicologist and critic who studied at the Royal College of Music, London, and at Oxford University. He was music critic of the London *Times* from 1906 to 1919, and guest critic of the New York *Times*. His works include *Brahms* (1909); *The Growth of Music; The Chamber Music of Brahms; English Church Music:* he also added chapters to Parry's "Evolution of the Art of Music"; edited the third and fourth revised editions of Grove's "Dictionary of Music and Musicians," and wrote Volume 7 (Symphony and Drama) of the "Oxford History of Music."

Collett, Jakobine Camilla (1813-1895), Norwegian author whose novels are regarded as forerunners of the social dramas emanating from the pens of Hendrik IBSEN and other Scandinavian playwrights. Among them were *The Daughters of the Country Magistrate* (1853-55); *In the Long Nights; Last Leaves; Against the Stream.* After her death a memorial statue was dedicated at Oslo, and her interesting letters were included in a biography by Alfred Collett.

Collier, Constance (1878-), English actress who first appeared on the stage at three years of age as the fairy Peaseblossom in Shakespeare's *Midsummer Night's Dream,* and in 1884 as the child, Sissy, in *The Silver King* with Wilson BARRETT. Since then she has played in many important productions including *The Sign of the Cross; Sweet Nell of Old Drury; The Ghetto; The School for Scandal; Ulysses; Oliver Twist; Ben Hur; Nero; Trilby; Colonel Newcome; Antony and Cleopatra; Peter Ibbetson.* She has also appeared on the screen in *Shadow of a Doubt; Peter Ibbetson; Little Lord Fauntleroy; Stage Door; Zaza; Susan and God.*

Collier, John Payne (1789-1883), English critic and author whose works include a *Poetical Decameron* (1820); *History of English Poetry to the*

Time of Shakespeare; Annals of the Stage to the Restoration; also a complete edition of Shakespeare's works.

Collier, Sr., William (1866-), American actor whose father and mother were both on the stage: his first appearance was made in a juvenile opera company playing H.M.S. PINAFORE. He also played with the Augustin DALY Stock Company in New York, and in many successful comedies including *The City Directory; Little Christopher; The Rivals; The Man from Mexico; On the Quiet; A Fool and His Money; The Dictator.* He also played comedy parts in films produced by Mack Sennett and Thomas Ince, and in many talking films. He was under contract at various times to WEBER AND FIELDS, Charles FROHMAN, George White and Florenz ZIEGFELD.

Collin, Heinrich Joseph (1771-1811), Austrian poet and dramatist: his best tragedy is one of a series on classic subjects entitled *Regulus.* His poems on martial subjects such as *Songs for the Militia,* and a historical ballad, *Kaiser Max on the Walls of St. Martin's,* were highly regarded in Austria.

Collinge, Patricia (1894-), Irish actress who made her debut at ten years of age as Ching-a-Ling in *Little Black Sambo* at the Garrick Theatre, London: since then she has appeared in many successful plays including *The Blue Bird; Everywoman; The New Henrietta; The Show-Shop; Pollyanna; The Rivals; Merton of the Movies; The Dark Angel; The Importance of Being Earnest; Becky Sharp; Hedda Gabler; The Little Foxes.* She has also played important roles in numerous films including *The Little Foxes* and *The Shadow of a Doubt.*

Collins, Dale (1897-), Australian novelist and author of travel books: his works include *Sea-Tracks of the Speejacks Around the World* (1923); *Ordeal,* a thrilling tale of the sea which he dramatized in 1924; *The Sentimentalists; The Mutiny of Madame Yes; The Love Watch.*

Collins, Sewell (1876-1934), American dramatist, critic and producer. His first play, *Miss Patsy,* was produced at New York in 1910, followed by *Shepherd's Pie* and *Anne One Hundred;* he also acted as producer of *Outward Bound* (New York, 1923); *The Wreckers* (London, 1927); *The Left Bank* (London, 1932).

Collins, William (1721-1759), an English poet whose melancholy temperament as a youth resulted in his comparatively early demise in an insane asylum. Among his finest works are *The Passions; Ode to Evening; Dirge to Cymbeline;* also the odes *To Evening,* and *To Simplicity.*

Collins, Wilkie (1824-1889), English novelist, son of a well-known landscape painter, William Collins. His most popular books were *The Woman in White* (1860); *The Moonstone; The New Magdalene; No Name.* He was a master of plot construction, and exerted a considerable degree of influence on English fiction, especially the type dealing with criminal deduction.

Colman, George, the Elder (1732-1794), English dramatist and manager of the COVENT GARDEN and HAYMARKET theatres. His brilliantly humorous plays included *The Jealous Wife* (1761); *The Clandestine Marriage*, with David GARRICK; *The Deuce in Him; New Brooms; The Separate Maintenance*. He also edited the plays of BEAUMONT and FLETCHER, and translated the comedies of TERENCE.

Colman, George, the Younger (1762-1836), English dramatist, poet and manager of the HAYMARKET THEATRE, London, succeeding his father, George Colman, the Elder. His plays included *John Bull; The Iron Chest; The Heir-at-Law:* he also wrote the humorous poems *Broad Grins* and *Poetic Vagaries* in addition to an autobiography, *Random Recollections*.

Colman, Ronald (1891-), English actor who played first in amateur theatricals: after service in World War I he appeared successfully in several stage productions including *The Misleading Lady, Damaged Goods, East is West*, and *The Green Goddess..* His greatest success has been in the films: his popularity began in 1923 in *The White Sister* with Lillian Gish; since then he has appeared in *Romola; The Eternal City; Kiki; Stella Dallas; Lady Windermere's Fan; Beau Geste; Raffles; Arrowsmith; Cynara; Clive of India; A Tale of Two Cities; Under Two Flags; Lost Horizon; If I Were King; Prisoner of Zenda; Random Harvest*.

Colman, Samuel (1832-1920), American painter who studied in Spain, Italy, France, and England: he was the first president of the American Water Color Society in 1866. His notable pictures include *Ships of the Western Plains; Spanish Peaks; Colorado; Bay of Gibraltar; Market Day in Brittany; Emigrant Train*.

Colomb or **Columb**, **Michel** (c.1430-1512), French sculptor who settled in Tours in 1460: his most important work was the tomb for Francis II of France and his wife. It was begun in 1502, completed in five years, and is now in the cathedral at Nantes. Colomb is considered the first great sculptor of the French Renaissance.

Colonna, Vittoria (1490-1547), Italian poet who lived in retirement after the death of her husband, the Marquis of Pescara. He was the inspiration for many of her love sonnets and elegiac poems published at Parma in 1538: her religious poems, *Rime Spirituali*, were issued later at Florence. She was an intimate friend of MICHELANGELO who made drawings for her, and dedicated some of his finest sonnets to her.

Colonnade, in architecture a succession of columns in a straight or curved row: if extended to enclose a building it is known as a PERISTYLE. Colonnades were used to line the streets of Rome and many cities in Syria and Asia Minor. Their use was revived in the United States during the early part of the 19th century for residences, and also play a conspicuous part in the architecture of government buildings at Washington, D. C.

Colonne, Édouard (1838-1910), French violinist and conductor; pupil at the Paris Conservatory of Sauzay in violin and Ambroise THOMAS in composition. In 1873 he established a series of concerts first known as the "Concert National," later famous as the "Concerts du Châtelet," and now as the "Concerts Colonne." He brought out most of the major works of Hector BERLIOZ, and many other orchestral creations by European composers. He also directed at L'Opéra, Paris, and conducted the New York Philharmonic-Symphony Orchestra in 1905.

Colophon, in literature the name given to a final paragraph in early manuscripts and printed books; placed at the end, and containing information about the author and other pertinent data. The latter was finally transferred to the title-page, and the term is now applied also to any special mark or device identifying the publisher.

Coloratura (It.), in vocal music passages ornamented with runs and trills enhancing the brilliancy of a song, and affording ample opportunity for the display of skill on the part of the singer. The English form of the word is *coloratura* when used as an adjective.

Colors, the term for the hues of the rainbow, or of the spectrum; also the tints produced from the blending of these hues. White is characterized as the complete presence of color, produced by irregular reflection of all the rays of the spectrum; black is said to be the complete absence of color. Colors are divided into two classifications: the three *primary colors* are red, yellow and blue which in combination give white; the three *secondary colors* are orange, green and violet.

Color Television, see **Television**.

Colosseum, see **Coliseum**.

Colossus of Rhodes, The, a bronze statue of the sun god, HELIOS, erected at RHODES during the latter part of the 3rd century, B.C.; the sculptor was Chares of Lindus, a pupil of LYSIPPUS. Its height was approximately 100 feet, and Chares spent twelve years on the construction. About 224 B.C. it was destroyed by an earthquake, and huge pieces lay around. A legend originated in the 16th century that ships could pass between the legs of the statue.

Colum, Padraic (1881-), Irish poet and dramatist. He was one of the founders of the Irish National Theatre, and came to the United States in 1914. His works include *Wild Earth* (1907); *My Irish Year; The King of Ireland's Son; The Boy Who Knew What the Bird Said; The Golden Fleece; The Fountain of Youth; The Legend of St. Columba; The Story of Lowry Maen*. He also edited an *Anthology of Irish Verse*.

Columbarium, a Latin word meaning "pigeonhole" applied in ancient times to a building containing small niches in which persons unable to bear the expense of a tomb placed urns containing the ashes of the dead in small niches arranged in tiers. Livia Drusilla, wife of the Roman emperor Augustus, built a columbarium for her slaves with 3,000 niches for urns.

Columbia Broadcasting Company, a radio broadcasting organization which transmits over its extensive network a varied series of features in connection with music, literature, drama, painting, and sculpture: (a) in *music* the COLUMBIA BROADCASTING SYMPHONY ORCHESTRA is presented on Sunday afternoons during the late spring, summer and early fall, and the Columbia Concert Orchestra throughout the entire year. It also broadcasts the Sunday afternoon concerts of the NEW YORK PHILHARMONIC-SYMPHONY SOCIETY; its Young People's Concerts and many of its summer concerts at the Lewisohn Stadium. The PHILADELPHIA ORCHESTRA, the CLEVELAND ORCHESTRA, and the INDIANAPOLIS SYMPHONY ORCHESTRA also have been presented, in addition to series of concerts by the Cincinnati Conservatory of Music, the EASTMAN SCHOOL OF MUSIC, the CURTIS INSTITUTE OF MUSIC, and the Mannes Music School, New York. Orchestral concerts by the League of Composers and the NATIONAL FEDERATION OF MUSIC CLUBS have been broadcast: also chamber music concerts sponsored by the Elizabeth Sprague COOLIDGE Foundation, and individual recitals by Wanda LANDOWSKA, Vera BRODSKY, Lotte LEHMANN, Joseph SZIGETI, Nino MARTINI, Egon PETRI, and William PRIMROSE. (b) In *literature* an interesting half-hour is provided weekly by INVITATION TO LEARNING, a series of discussions by litterateurs of the world's greatest books with Mark VAN DOREN presiding; "Poet's Gold" in which extracts from standard and contemporary poetry are read; "Of Men and Books" during which John T. FREDERICK criticizes contemporary literature and interviews prominent authors; "Radio Reader" in which entire books are read by Mark van Doren, Margaret Webster, and Madeleine CARROLL. (c) In the field of *visual arts* there are programs such as "What's Art to Me?" discussing various phases of painting and sculpture not only from the standpoint of their merits, but also in the relation to daily life. The broadcasting of drama is discussed in a separate article, RADIO DRAMA.

Columbia Broadcasting Symphony Orchestra, an organization inaugurated by the COLUMBIA BROADCASTING COMPANY as an important part of its contribution to music culture in America, in 1927; its conductor then as now was Howard BARLOW. During the fifteen years of its existence the orchestra has presented not only the finest works of classic, romantic and modern European composers, but has played many works by American composers. In 1937 and 1938 it gave the world première of twelve specially commissioned compositions by American composers including Aaron COPLAND, Howard HANSON, Walter PISTON and Roy HARRIS comprising symphonic works and short operas. The orchestra has also given first performances of Bernard HERMANN's *First Symphony*; Randall THOMPSON's one-act opera, *Solomon and Balkis;* Johnny Green's *Music for Elizabeth,* among many other works. The orchestra has also given the first American performance of MIASKOVSKY's 21st Symphony, the American radio premières of DELIUS' violin and piano concertos, and the first performance of Stanley Bate's *Concertino* for piano and orchestra. In the early days of radio Barlow and the orchestra did a great amount of pioneering work, presenting such weekly series as "Understanding Music,"

"Understanding Opera," and "Everybody's Music": also an opera series which included excerpts from *Boris Godounov* and *Die Meistersinger* with soloists and chorus. In 1942 the orchestra presented a notable "Music of Free Nations" series, featuring works currently forbidden performance in conquered countries. Among the musicians who have appeared as guest conductors with the Columbia Broadcasting Symphony are Sir Thomas BEECHAM, Erich LEINSDORF, Howard HANSON, Darius MILHAUD, Nicolai MALKO, and Bernard HERRMANN.

Columbine, one of the principal characters in the Italian commedia dell'arte of the 15th century: she was the daughter of Pantalone (Pantaloon), and the object of Harlequin's adoration, as in LEONCAVALLO's opera, I PAGLIACCI. Later the character became a stock one in English pantomime, and the probable antecedent of the SOUBRETTE.

Column, in architecture a cylindrical, vertical support usually constructed in three parts: the BASE, the SHAFT or cylinder, and the CAPITAL. The earliest examples, dating back to 2600 B.C., are found in Egypt: others have been discovered in Assyria, Persia, Greece and Rome. The principal types of columns are the *Corinthian, Doric, Gothic, Ionic, Romanesque* and *Renaissance.* Columns are said to be clustered when several are placed in juxtaposition in Gothic architecture: they are said to be coupled when placed two and two or side by side.

Colvin, Sir Sidney (1845-1927), English critic, professor of arts at Cambridge, and curator of prints at the BRITISH MUSEUM. His works include biographies of LANDOR, KEATS, and DURER; *Children in Italian and English design; A Florentine Picture Chronicle*: he also edited the works of Robert Louis STEVENSON of whom he was an intimate friend.

Coman, Charlotte Buell (1833-1924), American painter who studied at Paris with Émile Vernier, and spent several years in France and Holland: her notable works include *Sunset at the Seaside; Near Fontainebleau; Cottage in Picardy; Old Windmills in Holland; Clearing Off; Poppy Field in Normandy.*

Comédie-Française, the official name of the Théâtre Français, a state institution now located on the Rue de Richelieu, Paris. It had its beginning in the Theatre de l'Hotel Bourgogne in 1552, succeeded by the Théâtre du Marais in 1600. In 1680, after the death of Molière, his company at the Hôtel Guenegaud and that of the Hôtel Bourgogne were merged by order of Louis XIV: it was called the Comédie-Française, and a new theatre building provided. It was suppressed during the Revolution, reopened by Napoleon I in 1803 and has continued ever since. The policy is to produce standard French plays by CORNEILLE, MOLIERE, RACINE and others; there are no stars in the company. The original theatre was destroyed in 1900: the art objects and records were saved, and a new building erected.

Comédie Humaine, a collection of novels by Honoré de BALZAC, arranged and connected by classification to form what he termed "a complete society" with the same characters appearing and reappearing. The books he selected are generally regarded as his masterpieces, and portray vividly the society of his period.

Comedy, in drama the term applied to a type of theatrical production whose chief purpose is to amuse. It is distinguished from TRAGEDY by having a happy ending, amusing situations and light dialogue: it is differentiated from FARCE and BURLESQUE by the absence of crude or boisterous jests, but there is a subtle meaning to this demarcation which is not readily defined. The supreme writer of Greek comedies was ARISTOPHANES; of English comedies SHAKESPEARE, and of French comedies MOLIERE.

Comic Opera, see **Opera.**

Commedia dell'arte, in drama a style of theatrical performance in Italy which was popular from the 16th to the 18th centuries. It was presented by professional actors, and also known as *commedia all improviso* because the lines and action were improvised. Its invention was credited to Francesco Cherea, a favorite actor of Leo X (Giovanni de' Medici). The skeleton, or what would now be termed the scenario of the play, was written in advance, and the dialogue improvised by the actors who played stock characters such as HARLEQUIN, CAPITANO, PANTALONE, COLUMBINE, and many others.

Commentator, in theatrical parlance the name sometimes given to a character known in olden times as the master of ceremonies, jester or harlequin, first functioning at the Dionysian festivals in ancient Greece, the Commedia dell'arte in Italy, and the French, German and English carnival plays. Today the commentator is both seen and heard in the revival of vaudeville, and unseen but heard in radio entertainment; famous commentators of an earlier period on the stage include Raymond HITCHCOCK, Ed WYNN, Will ROGERS and Nikita BALIEFF of the famous CHAUVE SOURIS. Dramatists have introduced commentators in plays from Elizabethan times down to the present day.

Community Theatres, see **Little Theatres.**

Compass, in music the range of an instrument or of a human voice, referring to the series of tones it can produce or vocalize from the lowest to the highest.

Comus, in Greek mythology the name of the god of laughter or mirth, usually pictured as a youth with wings bearing a drinking cup and a torch. Ben JONSON introduces Comus in his masque, *Pleasure Reconciled by Virtue*: the masque, *Comus*, by MILTON, introduces a character which, in the poet's own words, "never yet was heard in tale or song."

Conant, Alban Jasper (1821-1915), American painter who specialized in portraiture: among his sitters were Abraham Lincoln, General William Tecumseh Sherman, Bishop Potter, and many cabinet members and justices of the Supreme Court of the United States. He was also deeply interested in archaeology.

Concert, in music the name applied to a public performance by an instrumental organization or a vocal ensemble either with or without soloists: when a public performance of musical works is given by an individual artist, it is called a *recital*. Concerts first came into being in England about the middle of the 17th century: they were initiated by John Banister, leader of the King's Band, from 1672 to 1678, and rose to great heights in 1791 with the HAYDN and SALOMON concerts in London. At the beginning of the 18th century, the Collegia Musica in Germany, Sweden and Switzerland began giving concerts; the Concerts Spirituel was founded at Paris in 1725, and the Gewandhaus concerts at Leipzig in 1781. The first advertised concert in the United States was given at the "Great Room in the house of Dr. Noyes" near the Sun Tavern, Boston, in December, 1731. The development of symphonic music has aided considerably in increasing the interest in concerts: at the present time radio increases the audience from that of the concert hall to millions of listeners all over the world.

Concertina, a musical instrument similar in principle to the ACCORDION although differing to some extent in its external appearance. It was invented by Sir Charles Wheatstone in 1829, and produces the same tone whether the bellows are drawn in or out. There are four sizes; soprano, tenor, bass and contrabass: the instrument is capable of great expression, and the tone quality can be varied to a considerable degree.

Concertmaster, the title given to the leader of the violins in an orchestra: his duties are to assist the conductor in drilling the players, and to take his place in an emergency. In the major orchestras, concertmasters are appointed for the first violins and the second violins.

Concerto, in music the name given to an instrumental composition designed to demonstrate the technical and musical skill of a performer on any instrument: it is also applied to works written for two or more performers on the same or different instruments. Although there is much argument on the matter, some authorities believe that Giuseppe Torelli, who published a *concerto da camera* for two violins and bass in 1686, was the first to use the title. The form was developed by VIVALDI, CORELLI, BACH, and MOZART, but perfected by BEETHOVEN and BRAHMS who gave more prominence and musical beauty to the orchestral accompaniment. The innovations of ultra-modern composers will probably not be permanently adopted.

Concerto Grosso, in music a term used during the latter part of the 17th and the early part of the 18th century to describe a work for either a string or a full orchestra in which two or more of the players have solo parts. The six BRANDENBURG CONCERTOS by Johann Sebastian BACH are excellent examples of this form as composed in the classical period.

Concertos, for descriptive notes on concertos, for various instruments, see DOUBLE CONCERTOS,

PIANO CONCERTOS, VIOLIN CONCERTOS, VIOLONCELLO CONCERTOS.

Concrete, in architecture a material for building made by mixing broken stone or gravel with sand and cement combined with water, and allowed to harden. It was well-known to the ancients, but first used for large buildings by the Romans who used lime for the binding agent. It is now the principal construction material for large buildings of all kinds, the advantage being ease of transportation and general stability, especially when reinforced with steel rods or wire mesh.

Condell, Henry (?-1627), English actor who edited the first folio of SHAKESPEARE'S plays in 1623 in collaboration with John Heming: he also acted in Shakespeare's company, and was part owner with Richard BURBAGE and John HEMING of the Globe and the BLACKFRIARS theatres. He was one of Shakespeare's intimate friends remembered in his will.

Conductor, in music the title of the person directing a simultaneous performance of a composition by a group of musicians: in the case of a symphony orchestra the title "conductor" is considered correct, but the musician directing a dance orchestra or jazz band is usually called the "leader." A conductor's duties are to control the tempo as well as the quality and quantity of tone produced by the players: he must understand the correct motions made with the baton to indicate the tempo. In addition he must have a thorough understanding of the form, instrumentation, rhythms, themes, and musical significance of every composition he undertakes to conduct.

Conegliano, see **Cima, Giovanni Battista.**

Confucius (550 B.C.-478 B.C.), Chinese philosopher, descendant of a noble but impoverished family who became a teacher in his twenty-second year, and chief magistrate in the city of Chung-tu. He retired from public office when he was fifty-six years old, and devoted himself to writing and teaching. His *Analects* is an exposition of his philosophical doctrines; he also compiled a collection of 300 ancient poems, and his last work, *Annals of Lee* or *Spring and Autumn,* may be regarded as an ethical manual from which many of his wise sayings are often quoted.

Congreve, William (1670-1729), English novelist and dramatist educated at Kilkenny and Trinity College in Dublin where he became intimate with Jonathan SWIFT. In 1692 he published under the pen name "Cleophil" a novel, *Incognita,* or *Love and Duty Reconciled:* his first play, *The Old Bachelor,* was a tremendous success in 1693 although it was as immoral as witty. This was followed by *The Double Dealer, Love for Love* and *The Mourning Bride,* all of which were received with enthusiasm. His masterpiece, *The Way of the World,* was a failure because public taste had turned in another direction when it was produced. Many of his plays have been successfully revived on the modern stage.

Connelly, Marc (1891-), American dramatist whose first play, *The Amber Princess,* was produced in 1916. In 1921 he began his collaboration with George KAUFMAN in several successful plays including *Dulcy; To The Ladies; Merton of the Movies; Helen of Troy; Beggar on Horseback.* His greatest success was his Negro fantasy based on Roark BRADFORD'S book, "Ol' Man Adam an' His Chillun," and entitled *Green Pastures* which received the Pulitzer Prize, and ran for nearly two years on the New York stage. He has also written or collaborated on several screen scenarios.

Connolly, James Brendan (1868-), American athlete and novelist who acted as naval correspondent for *Collier's Magazine* during World War I: his novels, most of which are stories of the sea, include *Out of Gloucester* (1902); *The Seiners; Crested Seas; The Trawler; Steel Decks; Port of Gloucester; Canton Captain.*

Connolly, Walter (1887-1940), American actor educated at St. Xavier College and the College of Music, Cincinnati; also at the University of Dublin. His professional debut was made in 1911 when he joined the SOTHERN-MARLOWE Shakespearean players; later he appeared in many successful plays including *The Woman of Bronze; The Springboard; Possession; Uncle Vanya; Six Characters in Search of an Author; The Late Christopher Bean; The Good Fairy.* He was one of the most distinguished screen actors, assuming important roles in numerous films including *The Bitter Tea of General Yen; A Man's Castle; It Happened One Night; The Good Earth; Huckleberry Finn; The Great Victor Herbert.*

Conrad, Joseph (1857-1924), English novelist born in Poland; real name Joseph Conrad Korzeniowski. He was the son of a Polish exile, and entered the French and the English merchant marine service: after being advanced to the position of mate he became a British subject. After retiring from the service, he wrote several highly successful novels including *Almayer's Folly* (1895); *An Outcast of the Islands; The Nigger of the Narcissus; Lord Jim; Youth; Typhoon; The Arrow of Gold; The Rescue; The Rover;* the last-named was left unfinished, and published with the title, *Suspense,* in 1925.

Conrad, Karen, contemporary American ballet dancer who studied with Catherine LITTLEFIELD and Alexis DOLINOFF. She began her career as a member of the Philadelphia Ballet, appearing with the company in the United States and Europe, and later joining the MORDKIN Ballet. In 1939 she was one of the first ballerinas with the BALLET THEATRE, and has remained with the company since it was taken over by S. Hurok.

Conrad, Robert T. (1810-1858), American journalist, poet, and dramatist whose first play, *Conrad of Naples,* was produced in 1832 at the Arch Street Theatre, Philadelphia. He was the publisher of the *Daily Commercial Intelligencer* which later became the Philadelphia *Gazette,* and also wrote a tragedy, *Aylmere,* in which Edwin FORREST played the role of Jack Cade.

Conried, Heinrich (1848-1909), Austrian actor, theatrical manager and operatic impresario: in 1878 he came to the United States to manage the

Germania Theatre in New York, and later the Irving Place Theatre. From 1903 to 1908 he was managing director of the Metropolitan Opera House, presenting Enrico Caruso, and giving the first American production of *Parsifal*. He also produced *Salome* by Richard Strauss in the face of indignant protest, and resigned in 1908 because of ill-health.

Conscience, Hendrik (1812-1883), Flemish novelist regarded as one of the re-creators of Flemish literature. His first work, *In the Wonder Year 1566* (1837), a series of scenes in the War for Dutch Independence, received much praise; it was followed by *The Lion of Flanders; What a Mother Can Suffer; The Conscript; Blind Rosa; The Decayed Gentleman; The Miser*. He also wrote a musical drama, *The Poet and his Dream*, and possessed extraordinary ability as a chronicler of Flemish people and their customs.

Conservatoire de Musique (Paris), see **Paris Conservatory of Music.**

Console, in architecture a projecting base supporting cornices or balconies which project still further. It is usually ornamented with VOLUTES at both ends, the curves extending in different directions. In furniture the console is a table, supported by curved feet, which usually occupies a fixed place before a mirror or a window: the finest examples are of the period of Louis XIV.

Consonance, in music the pleasing effect on the organ of hearing when certain combinations of two or more musical tones are sounded simultaneously. In the study of musical theory certain intervals, specifically fourths, fifths and octaves, are called *perfect consonances*: major and minor thirds and sixths are called *imperfect consonances*. The opposite of consonance is DISSONANCE.

Constable, John (1776-1837), English painter who studied at the Royal Academy, London, and also with Joseph Farington and R. R. Reinagle. He exhibited his first picture in 1802, but was not elected to the Royal Academy until 1829, and never enjoyed the esteem in his lifetime that he deserved in his own country. Nevertheless he had few equals as a landscape painter; among his notable paintings are *Cornfield; Farm in the Valley; Water Meadows near Salisbury; Rainbow; Leaping Horse; Dedham Mill*. The Diploma Gallery in Burlington House has about five hundred examples in the form of oil paintings, sketches, water-colors, and pencil drawings presented by Constable's daughter.

Constant, Jean Joseph Benjamin (1845-1902), French painter who studied at the ECOLE DES BEAUX-ARTS, Paris, and with CABANEL. He gained immediate recognition with his first picture, *Hamlet and the King,* exhibited at the Salon in 1869: his travels in Morocco resulted in several pictures including *Justice in the Harem* and *Moroccan Prisoners* which added further to his reputation as one of the great French masters. Constant painted many fine portraits including those of Queen Victoria and Queen Alexandra: among his notable works are *Samson and Delilah; Terrace at Evening; Caliph's Recreations; Last Rebels; Christ in the Tomb.*

Constantine, Arch of, a triumphal arch built by the Emperor Constantine in 312 A.D.; the largest and best preserved of the Roman triumphal arches. It is in reality composed of three arches, and the inscription dedicating it to "the divinity" probably refers to Christ. The quality of many of the sculptures is not of the finest character; they do not compare with the bas-reliefs and medallions taken from the triumphal arch of Marcus Aurelius, and from other buildings in Rome.

Constantino, Florencio (1869-1919), Spanish operatic tenor who made his debut at Montevideo, Uruguay, and after singing with great success in Europe, appeared with Henry Russell's San Carlo Company in 1906. He was principal tenor with the Boston Opera Company in 1909: he also appeared at the Metropolitan and the Manhattan Opera Houses, New York, and as principal tenor with the Los Angeles Grand Opera Company in 1915. His repertoire included the leading tenor roles in the standard Italian and French operas.

Contes Russes, a Russian folk ballet in one act: libretto based on Russian fairy tales; choreography by Leonide Massine; music by Anatol Liadoff; first produced at the Coliseum, London, in 1919. As presented in its original form by the Diaghileff Company in San Sebastian, Spain, the ballet had only one tale; later two more tales, two comedy interludes, and a finale were added. The play is supposed to be performed by village actors: Russian folk dancing and icon paintings are drawn on largely by Massine for his choreographic ideas.

Contralto, the lowest-pitched female voice: the term is now used interchangeably with ALTO, and usually means a low alto as opposed to a high alto voice.

Contredanse (Fr.), an English dance which became popular during the 18th century in France: it is performed by couples facing each other rather than in marching order. Each phrase is eight measures long in 2-4 or 6-8 time, and is usually repeated; Mozart wrote frequently in this form, but the finest example is a set of twelve composed by Beethoven.

Contucci, Andrea, see **Sansovino, Andrea.**

Converse, Frederick Shepherd (1871-1940), American composer; a graduate of Harvard University, and pupil of Carl Baermann in piano, and of George W. Chadwick and Josef Rheinberger in composition. He taught for many years at the New England Conservatory and Harvard College. His works include *The Pipe of Desire,* the first American opera to be presented at the Metropolitan Opera House (1910); several symphonies; symphonic poems; a fantasy; the ultra-modern tone poem, *Flivver Ten Million;* chamber music; choral music; piano pieces and songs.

Coogan, Jackie (1914-   ), American screen actor who made his debut as a child of four with Charles Chaplin in the silent film *The Kid;* this was followed by appearances in *Peck's Bad Boy; Oliver Twist; Circus Days; A Boy of Flanders; Old Clothes.* After several years in school, he returned to the talking screen in *Tom Sawyer; Huckleberry Finn,* and other pictures of lignter character.

Cook, George Cram (1873-1924), American novelist and dramatist. He was one of the founders and directors of the Provincetown Players: his works include *In Hampton Roads* (1899); *Suppressed Desires* with Susan GLASPELL; *The Spring; Greek Coins,* the last-named a volume of poems written in Greece where he spent the latter part of his life among the Greek country people.

Cook, Madge Carr (1856-1933), English-American actress who made her debut as a child of three as Fleance in *Macbeth:* she came to America in 1887, making her debut in *The Beautiful Star* at NIBLO's GARDENS, but her greatest success was in the title role of *Mrs. Wiggs of the Cabbage Patch* in which she appeared in both the United States and England. The distinguished American actress, Eleanor ROBSON, is her daughter.

Cooke, George Frederick (1756-1811), English actor who played with strolling companies in the provinces until 1778 when he appeared at the HAYMARKET, London; in 1801 he became the rival of John KEMBLE in SHAKESPEARE's plays, later playing with the latter and Mrs. SIDDONS. He came to the United States in 1810 to be hailed as one of the greatest English tragedians: intemperance brought about his death in New York, and Edmund KEAN erected a monument to his memory in St. Paul's churchyard

Cooke, John Esten (1830-1886), American biographer and novelist who served in the Civil War, and wrote biographies of Stonewall Jackson and General Robert E. Lee. His novels include *Leather Stocking and Silk* (1854); *Virginia Comedians; Henry St. John, Gentleman; My Lady Pokahontas.* He also wrote *Virginia; a History of the People.*

Cooke, Rose Terry (1827-1892), American poet, novelist, and writer of short stories. Her complete poems, including *The Gentian* and *The Two Villages,* were published in 1888, and her stories of New England rural life such as *Happy Dodd, Rootbound,* and *Huckleberries* were well received. A novel, *Steadfast,* appeared in 1889, a few years before her death, and many of her poems and short stories were published in the *Atlantic Monthly.*

Coolbrith, Ina Donna (1842-1928), American librarian and poet. She was taken to California as a child in a covered wagon; became librarian at Oakland in 1874; worked with Bret HARTE, and was made poet laureate of California in 1915 by an act of legislature. Her works include *A Perfect Day and Other Poems* (1884); *The Singer of the Sea; Songs from the Golden Gate; Wings of Sunset.*

Coolidge, Elizabeth Sprague (1864-), American music patron, pianist, and composer; in 1918 she founded the Berkshire Chamber Music Festivals at Pittsfield, Mass., later removed to Washington, D. C. She also sponsored the Coolidge Foundation in the Library of Congress under the supervision of the Music Division of the Library: concerts and musical festivals are conducted and prizes have been awarded to American and foreign musicians who have written works for performance there. Her other benefactions include the Coolidge Medal for distinguished services to chamber music and sponsorship of appearances by artists and ensembles in the United States and abroad. She has received many honorary degrees from American colleges as well as foreign decorations for her services to music.

Coolus, Romain, pseudonym of **René Weil** (1868-), French dramatist whose first successful play, *The Lovers of Sazy,* was produced in 1901. He has written and produced many plays of which the distinctive features are satirical characterizations and an unconventional attitude toward love. In 1923 Avery HOPWOOD adapted his play, *The Alarm Clock,* for production in New York.

Cooper, Gary (1901-), American screen actor, educated at Iowa College, Grinnell, Iowa. He has appeared in numerous films including *The Winning of Barbara Worth; A Farewell to Arms; Today We Live; Design for Living; Alice in Wonderland; Lives of a Bengal Lancer; Peter Ibbetson; Desire; The General Died at Dawn; The Adventures of Marco Polo; The Cowboy and the Lady; Beau Geste; The Westerner; Meet John Doe; Sergeant York; Pride of the Yankees.*

Cooper, Jackie (1923-), American juvenile actor who appeared as a child of six in *Our Gang* comedies and later in *Skippy; Donovan's Kid; The Champ* (with Wallace BEERY); *When a Feller Needs a Friend; Lone Cowboy; The Bowery; Treasure Island; Peck's Bad Boy; The Spirit of Culver,* and other films of similar character.

Cooper, James Fenimore (1789-1851), American novelist who studied at Yale College: he joined the American navy in 1806, and resigned in 1811 to settle in Westchester, New York. His first novel, *Precaution,* published anonymously in 1821, attracted some attention, but another issued in the same year, *The Spy,* was an instantaneous and unprecedented success. These were followed by *The Pioneers; The Pilot; The Last of the Mohicans; The Prairie; The Red Rover; The Pathfinder; The Deerslayer.* All of the last-named were enormously popular, but several more written later in life were poorly received: his *History of the Navy of the United States* was published in 1839.

Cooper, Thomas Sidney (1803-1902), English painter who studied at the Royal Academy, London, and with VERBOECKHOVEN at Brussels. Among his notable paintings are *Mountains in Cumberland; Waterloo; Children of the Mist; God's Acre; Milking Time in the Meadows.* In 1882 he presented the city in which he was born, Canterbury, with an art gallery.

Cooper, Violet Kemble (1889-), English actress who made her debut in 1905 on the London stage in *Charley's Aunt,* and in 1912 on the New York stage in *The Indiscretion of Truth.* Among the plays in which she has appeared are *Peg o' My Heart; Dear Brutus; The School for Scandal;*

The Servant in the House; Lysistrata; The Shining Hour; Peter Ibbetson; Mary of Scotland. She has also been seen in many films including *Our Betters; The Fountain; David Copperfield; Vanessa, Her Love Story; The Invisible Ray; Romeo and Juliet.*

Cope, Charles West (1811-1890), English painter, pupil of his father, Charles Cope: he also studied at the Royal Academy, London, and in Venice, Florence, Rome, and Naples. Among his notable works are eight frescoes in the Houses of Parliament of which two: *The Embarkation of the Pilgrim Fathers* and *The Black Prince Receiving the Order of the Garter,* are regarded as the finest examples of his art. His illustrations for GRAY's *Elegy* and GOLDSMITH's *Poems* were greatly admired.

Copeland, George, contemporary American pianist who studied with Carlo Buonamici, and concertized in both Europe and America. His repertoire consists of modern French and Spanish works; among them his own transcription of DE-BUSSY's *Afternoon of a Faun.*

Coping, in architecture the capping or covering of a wall, constructed of stone, brick, tile, slate, metal, or wood, and usually rendered waterproof by some approved method.

Copland, Aaron (1900-), American pianist and composer who studied composition with Rubin GOLDMARK and Nadia BOULANGER, and piano with Clarence Adler and Victor Wittgenstein. He has lectured on modern music, and appeared as soloist in his piano concerto with major symphony orchestras. His compositions include symphonies and other orchestral works, chamber music, and piano pieces: he is also the author of *What to Listen for in Music* and *Our New Music.*

Copley, John Singleton (1738-1815), American painter largely self-educated. He began his career as a portrait painter: after studying at Rome he went to England in 1775, and was admitted to the Royal Academy in 1783 after his most famous picture, *The Death of Lord Chatham* became popular. Among his most famous paintings are *The Death of Major Pierson; The Siege of Gibraltar; Youth Rescued from a Shark; The Red-Cross Knight; Offer of the Crown to Lady Jane Grey.* His portraits include those of John Hancock, Samuel Adams, John Quincy Adams, the Copley Family, and Lord Cornwallis. Although he lived chiefly in England, Copley is regarded as of the American school because his most characteristic works were painted in this country.

Coppard, Alfred Edgar (1878-), English poet and prose writer chiefly self-educated, and regarded by critics as one of the first authors to express in prose the peculiarly distinctive attributes of English lyric poetry. His prose works include *Adam and Eve* and *Pinch Me* (1921); *The Black Dog; Fishmonger's Fiddle; The Field of Mustard; Silver Circus; Nixey's Harlequin; Polly Oliver:* also a volume, *Collected Poems.*

Coppée, François Edouard Joachim (1842-1908), French poet, novelist and dramatist: his first collected verses, *Le Reliquaire,* were published in 1866, followed by *Les Intimités* and *Poèmes Modernes.* All the above are concerned with life, labors, and loves of the poor and obscure. A play, *Le Passant,* was successfully produced at the Odéon, Paris, in 1869: others favorably received included *Les Bijoux de la délivrence; Severo Torelli; Madame de Maintenon; Les Jacobites; Pour la couronne.* His most successful novels were *Le Coupable,* a study in criminal psychology, and *La Bonne Souffrance.* Coppée is regarded as one of the finest French poets.

Coppelia, a ballet in two acts: libretto adapted from E. T. A. HOFFMANN's tale, *The Sandman,* by Nuitter and Saint-Léon; choreography by Louis Merante; music by Léo DELIBES; first produced at Paris in 1870. The subtitle is "The Girl with the Enamel Eyes," and the plot revolves around a mechanical doll, Coppelia who is also the chief character in Hoffmann's tale. The score is one of Delibes' finest inspirations, and the ballet is still in the repertory of European, English, and American companies.

Coppet, Edward J. de, see **Flonzaley Quartet.**

Coppola, Piero (1888-), French composer and conductor who studied at the Milan Conservatory: he has conducted at La SCALA, Milan, Brussels, London, Scandinavia, and Paris where he has also made many fine recordings of orchestral works. His compositions include two operas, several orchestral works, and violin pieces.

Copyright, the privilege granted by law whereby authors and artists are given the exclusive right to publish and otherwise dispose of their works. In the United States this protection is enforced by the Copyright Act of 1909 and its various amendments: application blanks for copyright in the United States and its possessions can be secured from the Register of Copyrights, Library of Congress, Washington, D. C. Two complete copies of the work, containing the notice of copyright as prescribed by law, must accompany each application: the fee is $2.00 for a published work, and $1.00 if it is unpublished. The copyright remains in force for 28 years from the date of publication, and a renewal period of 28 years is granted if applied for by the original owner or his heirs. No further renewal is granted; the work then becomes public property, and may be republished or used by any person without fee. All the above regulations apply to copyright granted for the United States and its possessions; copyright protection may be also secured in foreign countries that have entered into reciprocal agreements with the United States. At the beginning of World War II the list of countries in which copyright protection for American works could be obtained included Argentina, Belgium, Bolivia, Brazil, Chile, China, Costa Rica, Cuba, Czechoslovakia, Danzig (Free City), Denmark, Dominican Republic, Ecuador, Finland, France, Germany, Great Britain and possessions, Greece, Guatemala, Haiti, Honduras, Hungary, Irish Free State, Italy, Japan, Korea, Luxemburg, Mexico, the Netherlands and its possessions, New Zealand, Nicaragua, Norway, Palestine, Panama, Paraguay, Peru, Poland, Portugal, Rumania, Salvador, Siam, Spain,

Switzerland, Sweden, Tunis, Uruguay. The list of works that can be copyrighted includes books, pamphlets, lectures, addresses, sermons, feature articles, musical compositions, dramatic works, periodicals, photographs, paintings, and sculptures.

Coq d'Or, Le (The Golden Cockerel), an opera by Nicholas RIMSKY-KORSAKOW first produced in its original operatic form at Moscow in 1909, and as an "opera-ballet" at L'Opéra, Paris, in 1914. It was first performed in the latter form at the Metropolitan Opera House, New York, in 1918, with Maria BARRIENTOS, Adamo Didur, Sophie BRASLAU and Rafaelo Diaz as the singers, and Rosina Galli, Adolph Bohm, Queenie Smith and Giuseppe Bonfiglio as the dancers. The story is: King Dodon, an old and senile king, is presented by an astrologer with a golden cock possessing the power to forecast future events. After the king retires, the golden cock sounds the war alarm: King Dodon sends his sons to battle, but when he arrives, they have been slain and his army routed. When dawn comes, a beautiful woman, Queen Shemaka, appears: she lures Dodon into a dance, and he finally falls down exhausted. The lovely lady agrees to become his bride, but the astrologer appears, and claims her as his reward. Dodon kills the astrologer, and is in turn slain by the golden cock. Darkness descends upon the stage: when light returns, the astrologer announces that the story was only a fairy tale. The symphonic suite arranged from the opera is available in a Victor recording by the London Symphony Orchestra under Eugène Goossens; there are also Victor recordings of the celebrated *Hymn to the Sun* by Lily PONS and by Fritz Kreisler.

Coquelin, Benoît Constant (1841-1909), French actor, known as *Coquelin Aîné,* who studied dramatic art with Henri REGNIER at the Paris Conservatory, and achieved his first great success in BEAUMARCHAIS' *Marriage of Figaro* in 1861. During the next twenty-two years he created the leading roles in forty-four plays: among his greatest successes were DUMAS' (FILS) *The Stranger,* ROSTAND's *Cyrano de Bergerac,* and *L'Aiglon.* He toured the United States in 1900 with Sarah BERNHARDT, and wrote several books on the history of the stage and the art of acting: among them, *Art and the Comedian* (1880), and *The Art of the Comedian* (1894). His son, Jean Coquelin (1865-), is also a well-known actor who made his debut at the Théâtre-Français, and later created the role of Raigone in Rostand's *Cyrano de Bergerac.*

Coquelin, Ernest Alexandre Honoré (1848-1909), French actor, younger brother of Benoît Constant Coquelin, and known as *Coquelin cadet.* He studied at the PARIS CONSERVATORY, and after winning first prize for a comedy, made his debut at the Odéon in 1867. He appeared in several plays with his brother, and created roles in many modern comedies: he also wrote and recited monologues presented in Paris salons, and published them under the pen name "Pirouette."

Coques or **Cocx, Gonzales** (c.1614-1684), Flemish painter who studied with Pieter BREUGHEL, son of "Hell Fire" Breughel: he was greatly influenced by VAN DYCK and copied him so faithfully in style that he was known as "the little Van Dyck." One of his canvases at The Hague pictures him at a table with his wife and two children, and surrounded by the signed masterpieces of several contemporaries. His notable works include *The Verhelst Family; Prince of Orange and his Family; David Teniers; Archduke Leopold; Luc Faydherbe.*

Coralli, Jean (1779-1854), French choreographer who studied at the School of Ballet at the Paris Opéra. His first ballets were produced at Vienna in 1800: from 1815 to 1822 he brought out many more at Milan, Lisbon, and Marseilles. His style of composition was characterized as refined, delicate and full of poetic feeling; among his best ballets are *Le Diable Boiteux; La Tarentule; Giselle ou les Wilis; La Peri; Ozai.*

Cor anglais, see **English horn.**

Corbels, in architecture projecting pieces of stone or wood employed to support a cornice, an arch, or the projecting part of a gallery. They were first used in the 11th century, but disappeared from cornices in the 13th century, and were used only to support balustrades.

Corbett, Elizabeth Frances (1887-), American novelist educated at the University of Wisconsin: her works include *Cecily and the Wide World* (1916); *The Young Mrs. Meigs; The Graper Girls; The Constant Sex; Mrs. Meigs and Mr. Cunningham; The Queen's Holiday; Mr. and Mrs. Meigs; Excuse Me, Mrs. Meigs.*

Corbett, Harvey Wiley (1873-), American architect who studied at the University of California and the ECOLE DES BEAUX-ARTS, Paris. Among his important works are the Bush Terminal Building, Brooklyn, N. Y.; Bush House, London; the Roerich Building, New York; the Washington National Memorial, Alexandria, Va.; buildings in Radio City, New York. He has also acted as consulting architect for public-works' commissions, and is a member of the American Institute of Architects and the Royal Institute of British architects.

Corbino, Jon (1905-), American painter born in Italy who was brought to the United States as a child of eight. He studied at the ART STUDENTS' LEAGUE, New York, and at the summer school of the Pennsylvania Academy, giving his first showing at eighteen and granted a GUGGENHEIM FELLOWSHIP in 1936 and 1937. Among his typical works, which are to be seen in several American museums and galleries, is *Flood Refugees,* painted in Rockport, Mass.

Corcoran Gallery of Art (Washington), an institution at Washington, D. C., founded and endowed by William Wilson Corcoran (1798-1888), American art collector, and taken over by Act of Congress in 1870. The Gallery presents a representative collection of the work of American painters and sculptors, offering a chronological survey of the development of American art. It begins with the late 18th and early 19th century portraits by COPLEY, STUART, MALBONE, and others; the HUDSON RIVER SCHOOL is represented by the works of COLE, DURAND, KENSETT, INNESS, and WYANT. The genre painting of the mid-nineteenth century is seen in the works of WYLIE, and Boham; the individualists of the latter part of the 19th century include HOMER, RYDER, EAKINS, DUVENECK, CHASE, ROBINSON, HASSAM, METCALF, CASSATT, SARGENT, THAYER, and FULLER. Twentieth century artists include MELCHERS, DAVIES, PRENDERGAST, BENSON, TARBELL, SPEICHER, BROOK, JOHANSEN, CARLSEN, LIE, KARFIOL, PHILIPP, and WATKINS. In the gallery of sculptures are representative works by POWERS, MILLS, RINEHART, HART, REMINGTON, SAINT-GAUDENS, SARGENT, FRENCH, GREGORY, HOFFMAN, KONTI, McNEIL, MANSHIP, and PROCTOR. There is also a fine section of drawings and etchings, and more than 100 original bronzes executed by the French animal sculptor, Antoine Louis BARYE.

Corday, Charlotte (1768-1793), a French lady educated in a convent at Caen: influenced by the writings of Voltaire, she was at first in sympathy with the principles of the French Revolution, but finally decided that Jean Paul Marat, the most bloodthirsty of the Terrorists, should be exterminated because of his persecution of the Girondists. She proceeded to gain an audience with Marat while he was in his bath, and stabbed him; was tried by the Revolutionary Tribunal and guillotined. Three tragedies were written of which she was the heroine, but only one, by J. B. Salles, was of real dramatic worth. Lamartine referred to her as "the angel assassinated."

Corder, Frederick (1852-1932), English composer, conductor, theorist and teacher of musical composition who studied at the Royal Academy of Music, London, and with Ferdinand Hiller at Cologne. He founded the Society of British Composers in 1905, and numbered many later distinguished composers among his pupils. He composed in all forms, and wrote theoretical treatises on harmony, composition, and musical history. In collaboration with his wife he made the first English translation of Wagner's *Ring of the Nibelungs, Die Meistersinger,* and *Parsifal.*

Corelli, Arcangelo (1653-1713), Italian violinist and composer who was practically self-taught: he never rose to virtuoso heights because of his innate modesty and timidity, but he laid the foundation for the systematizing of bowing and shifting, and also introduced double-stopping. Among his pupils were Anet, GEMINIANI, and LOCATELLI: his compositions, now regarded as classics comparable with those of Johann Sebastian BACH, include several concerti grossi and works in sonata form for one or two violins with bass.

Corelli, Marie (1864-1924), English novelist; daughter of an Italian father and a Scottish mother. Her first romantic novel, *A Romance of Two Worlds* (1886), was an immediate success: it was followed by *Vendetta, Barabbas, Thelma, Ardath, The Soul of Lilith, The Sorrows of Satan, The Mighty Atom, The Master Christian, Temporal Power.* All of these enjoyed a large sale although many critics damned them as purely sensational and poorly written.

Corinth, Lovis (1858-1925), German painter whose work formed a transition between impressionism and expressionism: his works include numerous charming landscapes, pictures of still life, and five portraits of Max LIEBERMANN and other contemporaries. He also wrote an interesting volume entitled *Tales of an Artist's Life.*

Coriolanus (Beethoven), an overture composed by Ludwig van BEETHOVEN, and inspired by a tragedy written by an Austrian government official and dramatist, Heinrich Joseph von Collin, and not, as many have believed by SHAKESPEARE's drama with the same title. There are two widely differing interpretations of the scenes depicted by Beethoven in the overture: Richard WAGNER was of the opinion that the work portrayed the meeting between Coriolanus and his wife at the gates of his native city; the composer, J. F. Reichardt believed that the composition was a portrait of Beethoven himself, and consequently a better picture of the composer than of Coriolanus. There is a Victor recording by the London Symphony Orchestra with Bruno Walter, and a Columbia recording by the Minneapolis Symphony Orchestra under Dmitri Mitroupoulos.

Cormon, Fernand (1845-1924), French painter who studied with CABANEL and FROMENTIN, finally becoming one of the greatest historical painters of modern France. His art bordered on the sensational with scenes depicting bloodshed such as *Murder in the Seraglio; Death of Ravara; Queen of Lanka; Cain Flying Before Jehovah's Curse:* he also painted several canvases picturing the Stone Age, and many portraits.

Corneille, Pierre (1606-1684), French poet and dramatist who first practiced law for several years until the favorable reception accorded his first play, *Mélite* (1629) at Rouen induced him to embark on a career as a dramatist. Between 1634 and 1636 five of his comedies, a tragi-comedy and a tragedy, *Medée,* were produced: during the latter year his first great success, *Le Cid,* elicited the greatest praise and also resulted in a controversy, fomented by Cardinal RICHELIEU, which only served to increase his reputation. This was followed by many more dramas and comedies of which the most important are *Horace; Cinna; Polyeucte; Nicomède; Le Menteur.* He is regarded as the first of the great French dramatists to free the French stage from strictures due to Greek and Latin influences.

Corneille, Thomas (1625-1709), French dramatist; brother of Pierre CORNEILLE, and author of more than forty plays including *Ariane* (1672); *Le festin de Pierre; Le Mort d'Annibal; Le Comte d'Essex,* in which RACHAEL attained great success: *Timocrate* which had the longest run (80 nights) of any play produced at Paris during the 17th century. He also made a fine translation of Ovid's *Metamorphoses.*

Cornelisz, Cornelis (1562-1638), Dutch painter; pupil of Pieter AERTSEN, and founder with Karl van Mander of the Haarlem Academy. His group portraits influenced even Frans HALS; among his notable canvases are *Adam and Eve; Archers' Banquet;* an *Auto-da-fé; Christ Blessing the Children; Venus and Adonis; Bathsheba.*

Cornelius, Peter (1824-1874), German composer a relative of the famous painter Peter CORNELIUS, who studied composition with Wilhelm Dehn at Berlin, and taught at the Royal Music School. His first opera, *The Barber of Bagdad*, was produced by Franz LISZT at Weimar in 1858; the second, *Le Cid*, at Weimar in 1865. His operas both held the stage in Germany until recently, but he is chiefly famous for his efforts to promote the music dramas of Richard WAGNER.

Cornelius, Peter (1783-1867), German painter who studied at the Academy in Düsseldorf of which his father was president. He first joined the group of painters known as the NAZARENES, but after studying the works of RAPHAEL and MICHELANGELO, he gave new life to the art of fresco painting; became director of the Academy at Düsseldorf, and the leading spirit in a new school of German art in company with Friedrich OVERBECK and Friedrich SCHADOW-GODENHAUS. Among his notable works are drawings for Goethe's *Faust; The Nibelungenlied; Holy Family; Flight into Egypt; Last Judgment.*

Cornell, Katharine (1898-), American actress born in Germany of American parents: her American debut was made in 1916 with the Washington Square Players at New York in *Bushida* and her London debut in 1919 in *Little Women.* Her first great success in America came in *A Bill of Divorcement* in 1921, and she has since appeared, under the management of her husband, Guthrie McCLINTIC, in many fine plays including *The Outsider; Candida; The Green Hat; The Letter; The Doctor's Dilemma; The Age of Innocence; Alien Corn; The Barretts of Wimpole Street; Romeo and Juliet, Saint Joan; No Time for Comedy.* In 1942 she presented and appeared in Anton CHEKHOV's dramatic classic, *The Three Sisters.*

Cornet, a musical instrument belonging to the horn family constructed of brass with three pistons. It has the most flexible technique of all brass instruments, but the tone is much coarser than the TRUMPET: the latter has replaced it in symphony orchestras except in scores where both cornets and trumpets are required for special effects. Two of the great cornet virtuosos were an American, Paris W. Chambers, and an Englishman, Jules LEVY, soloist with Gilmore's Band.

Cornice, in architecture the molding projection at the top of a wall, employed to effect the throwing off the rain water from the roof so that it does not strike the face of the building. The term is also applied to any construction of similar character over doors or windows.

Cornwall, Barry, see **Procter, Bryan Waller.**

Coronation Concerto (Mozart), a concerto for the Harpsichord (Köchel 537), composed by Wolfgang Amadeus MOZART in 1788, a year in which he had reached the final stages of poverty and dejection: in spite of this he conceived not only this exquisite work, but also his three greatest symphonies. The name "Coronation" is derived from its having been first performed during the

coronation festivities of King Leopold II at Prague: there is a Victor recording by Wanda LANDOWSKA with a chamber orchestra.

Coronation of Poppea, The, an opera with music by Claudio MONTEVERDI and libretto by Busenello; first produced at Venice in 1642, and in the United States at Smith College, Northampton, Mass., in 1926. The story is: Otho, a Roman noble returning from a journey, finds his mistress, Poppea, entertaining the Emperor Nero, and plans revenge. Nero is planning to marry Poppea, after divorcing his wife, Octavia: the latter persuades Otho, disguised as Drusilla, to kill Poppea, but her life is saved by Amor, the god of love. Drusilla, really innocent, is accused and about to be put to death when Otho confesses his guilt, and implicates Octavia. Both are banished, but Drusilla is permitted to accompany Otho. There is a Columbia recording of the lullaby in Act II, *May Sweet Oblivion Lull Thee* by Doris Owens with harpsichord accompaniment: also a Victor recording by Ezio Pinza with piano.

Corot, Jean Baptiste Camille (1796-1875), French painter who studied with Victor Bertin and Achille Michallon, and by intensive study of nature learned to couple breadth of treatment with careful attention to detail. His works were chiefly landscapes, figures and historical scenes; they include *Dance of the Nymphs; Roman Forum; Fire of Sodom; Bacchante Detaining Love; Little Shepherd; Christ in the Garden of Olives; Souvenir of the Ville d'Avray; Arras Road; Wounded Eurydice; Bacchante with a Panther; Young Girl with a Mandolin; Shepherd's Star.* Corot received large sums for his paintings during the latter part of his life, and they are among the costly collector's items today; he was a painter gifted with highly poetic and tender feeling.

Corps de ballet, in ballet the name given the group of dancers in a ballet company excluding the principal male and female dancers.

Correggio, Antonio Allegri (c.1494-1534), Italian painter; real name Antonio Allegri. His first real teacher was Francesco Bianchi after he had studied anatomy with Dr. Lombardi, and the first stages of the art of painting with his uncle, Lorenzo Allegri. Among his finest works are *Rest in Flight; Mystic Marriage of St. Catherine; Christ in Glory; St. John the Evangelist; The Madonna of St. Francis; Virgin and Child with Angels; Assumption of the Virgin; Danae; Antiope; The Nativity; Rape of Ganymede; Madonna of St. Jerome; Madonna with the Rabbit.* In mastery of the art of foreshortening, and in distributing light and shade over vast frescoes with many figures, Correggio was unsurpassed.

Corrente, see **Courante.**

Corrigan, Emmett (1868-), American actor; real name Anthony P. Zilles: he first appeared at Baltimore, Md., later joining the Charles FROHMAN Stock Company in New York, and the Dearborn Stock Company in Chicago. He assumed the leading role in the dramatization of

Ben Hur by General Lew Wallace, and also appeared on the stage in the adaptation of the latter's *The Prince of India.*

Cortese, Giacomo, see **Courtois, Jacques.**

Cortissoz, Royal (1869-), American lecturer and writer on art; critic on the New York *Herald Tribune* since 1891. His books include a critical biography of *Saint-Gaudens* (1907) and a memoir of *John La Farge; American Artists; Personalities in Art; The Painter's Craft.* He has also lectured at the Metropolitan Museum of Art, New York, and at many other museums throughout the United States.

Cortona, Domenico di, see **Boccador, Il.**

Cortona, Pietro da (1596-1669), Italian painter; real name Pietro Berrettini. He studied with Andrea Commodi at Florence, and with Baccio Ciarpi at Rome; his notable works include frescoes for the Palazzo Barberini at Rome, and historical paintings for the Palazzo Pitti at Florence; also many sacred canvases such as *Daniel in the Lion's Den; Holy Family; The Nativity.*

Cortot, Alfred (1877-), French pianist and conductor born in Switzerland of a French father and Swiss mother: he studied at the PARIS CONSERVATORY, and made his debut in 1896 at a Colonne concert. In 1902 he conducted the première of Wagner's *Götterdämmerung* in Paris, and founded a series of concerts to promote the German master's music. After touring Europe and the United States with great success as a virtuoso pianist, he formed a pianoforte trio with Jacques THIBAUD and Pablo CASALS which toured successfully and made many fine records. In 1919 he became one of the founders and the director of the Normal School of Music at Paris, and has written several critical works on French piano music and its composers.

Coryphée, in ballet a leading member of the corps de ballet; not to be confused with the *prima ballerina* or principal dancer.

Così fan tutte, a grand opera in two acts: music by Wolfgang Amadeus MOZART; libretto by Lorenzo DA PONTE: produced at Vienna in 1790 at the command of Emperor Josef II of Austria. The inanity of the libretto has banished the opera from the opera house, but there is a complete Victor recording (20 records) by the Glyndebourne Festival Company and a Victor recording of the overture by the British Broadcasting Company Symphony Orchestra under Sir Adrian BOULT.

Cossa, Francesco del (c.1435-c.1477), Italian painter who worked with his father, and was strongly influenced by Piero della FRANCESCA. His works include a *Piéta; Madonna with the Saints; Allegory of Autumn; Annunciation;* also many altarpieces and frescoes.

Costa, Lorenzo di Ottavio (1460-1535), Italian painter who connected himself with the Bolognese school: in 1483 he painted a fine fresco, *Madonna*

and *Child with the Bentivoglio Family,* followed by *Triumphs of Death and Fame* in the church of San Jacinto, Bologna. Other notable works include several Madonnas in various churches, and the *Adoration of the Magi,* predella to FRANCIA's Nativity altar in the Bologna Pinacoteca.

Costello, Dolores (1905-), American screen actress, daughter of Maurice COSTELLO. Since 1924 she has appeared in many pictures including *The College Widow; Heart of Maryland; Little Lord Fauntleroy; King of the Turf; The Magnificent Ambersons.*

Costello, Maurice (1877-), American stage and screen actor born of Irish and Spanish parentage. His stage debut was made in 1897: in 1909 he appeared for the Vitagraph Company in the first motion-picture stock company ever formed, playing opposite Florence TURNER. Among his notable pictures for the silent screen were *A Tale of Two Cities; The Man Who Couldn't Beat God; For the Honor of the Family; Conceit; The Law and the Lady; Camille; The Wagon Show.* His daughter, Dolores COSTELLO, is a distinguished screen actress.

Coster, Samuel (1579-1662), Dutch dramatist: one of the founders of the Dutch Academy, and distinguished for his comedies, *The Play of Tüsken van der Schelden* and *The Play of the Rich Man;* also for the tragedies *Iphigenia, Polyxena,* and *Isabella.*

Cotes, Sarah Jeannette, see **Duncan, Sara Jeannette.**

Cotillon, a romantic ballet; libretto by Boris Kochno; music by Emmanuel CHABRIER; choreography by George BALANCHINE; first produced at Monte Carlo in 1932. The plot is extremely tenuous, revolving around the daughter of the house at what is presumably her social debut, the scene being a ballroom. The music is selected from various Chabrier compositions including *Menuet Pompeux; Tourbillon; Scherzo Valse; Danse Rustique:* there is a Columbia recording by the London Philharmonic Orchestra.

Cotman, John Sell (1782-1842), English painter and etcher; one of the group of distinguished artists who formed the Norwich School. His ability as a painter in both water-color and oil became apparent in such works as *Wherries on Breydon* and *Gale at Sea:* he also made fine etchings of Norman and Gothic architecture.

Cottet, Charles (1863-1925), French painter who studied at the ECOLE DES BEAUX-ARTS, Paris, and under Puvis de CHAVANNES and Alfred ROLL. His reputation was made by three gloomy but impressive landscapes made in Brittany called *The Country of the Sea, Church in Brittany,* and *Burial in Brittany.*

Counterpoint, in music the art of combining melodies so that, when played simultaneously, each melody remains to a certain extent independent even while merging itself with the others to create correct and pleasing harmony. Special forms of counterpoint are called CANON and FUGUE. Composers employing counterpoint in their works are called contrapuntists; they began with Johann OKEGHEM in the 15th century, succeeded by Orlando di LASSUS, Adrian WILLAERT, Guillaume DUFAY; Josquin DES PREZ, PALESTRINA and Johann Sebastian BACH, the acknowledged supreme master of the art in the 18th century.

Country-dance, a popular dance in England from the earliest times: the name does not signify any particular set of dance steps or figures, and the music has been written in a variety of rhythms. John Playford compiled a collection of about one hundred of these dances in 1651 which ran through many editions, and finally was increased in size to several volumes. The dances written by Edward GERMAN for Sir Henry Irving's production of Shakespeare's *Henry VIII* are excellent modern imitations.

Couperin, François, surnamed **le Grand** (1668-1733), French organist, harpsichordist, and composer who received his surname because of his superiority in organ playing, although his genius as a composer for the harpsichord overshadowed all his other abilities. He occupied the posts of organist of the Royal Chapel, music master to the family of Louis XIV, and director of the Royal Concerts held on Sunday afternoons in the royal apartments. His daughters, Marie Madelaine and Marguerite Antoinette, were accomplished musicians: the latter frequently acted as substitute for her father at court. Couperin's compositions include organ pieces, trio sonatas and more than 250 pieces for the harpsichord.

Couperus, Louis Marie Anne (1863-1923), Dutch poet and novelist of Scottish ancestry. His first novel, *Eline Vere* (1889) was followed by *Footsteps of Fate; Ecstasy;* a series of four novels known as "books of the small souls"; *Old People and the Things that Pass.* He also wrote two volumes of poetry; two historical romances and two mythological fantasies, *Dionysius* and *Hercules.*

Couplet, (*a*) in poetry two separate metrical lines united by an identity of rhyme: in French poetry the term is not confined to two lines, but usually employed for a stanza. VOLTAIRE, LE SAGE and other French writers often wrote witty couplets designed to catch popular fancy. (*b*) The term applied to rhymed verses of gay and graceful character in French comic operas or vaudevilles.

Courante, a lively French dance that became extremely popular during the 17th century, and was later made a movement in the dance suites written by the pre-classic composers. It followed the ALLEMANDE which was in slow time, thereby effecting a sharp contrast. The Italian *corrente* is entirely different: its chief feature is swift passages composed of notes of equal time value.

Courbet, Gustave (1819-1877), French painter who studied the masterpieces of Italian, Flemish and French masters at the LOUVRE in order to prepare himself for his chosen career. His earlier pictures were refused at the Paris Salon, but in

1849 *After Dinner at Ornans* at least brought him notice because it was both abused and praised, as was *Funeral at Ornans.* During the Commune he gave the order for the destruction of the Vêndome Column for which he was jailed, and finally died in exile. Among other pictures representative of his art are *Village Maidens; The Bathers; Bonjour, Monsieur Courbet, Siesta during the Haymaking; Sleeping Lace-maker; Woman With a Parrot.*

Courboin, Charles Marie (1886-), Belgian composer and organist who studied at the University and the Conservatory at Brussels under Jan Blockx and Alphonse Mailly. He has toured France, England, Germany, and America as a virtuoso, and held many important posts as church organist since he came to the United States in 1904. He is also the designer of more than 140 important organs, and has composed organ works and masses.

Courtleigh, William (1869-1930), Canadian actor, educated in the United States, who first attracted attention as an amateur actor. After writing and playing in an original melodrama, he appeared in Fanny DAVENPORT's company in New York; among the plays in which he had leading roles were *Blue Jeans; In Old Kentucky; District Attorney; Northern Lights,* the first of the Indian plays; *Sporting Life; Trelawney of the Wells; A Rich Man's Son; Alice of Old Vincennes; The Redemption of David Corson.*

Courtois, Jacques (1621-1676), French painter who studied with his father; he was also known as Le Bourguignon, Giacomo Cortese, and Il Borgognone. Later he became a pupil of Francesco ALBANI and Guido RENI, painting many remarkable battle scenes. His brother, **Guillaume Courtois** (1628-1679), was also a painter of genuine ability: his notable works include *Battle of Joshua; Crucifixion of St. Andrew; Christ Admonishing Martha.*

Cousin, Jean (c.1500-c.1590), French painter who first painted on glass: his windows in the Sainte Chapelle at Vincennes are considered among the finest in France. The only authentic picture in existence from his brush is a *Last Judgment* in the LOUVRE at Paris. He wrote a treatise on perspective, and another on portraiture.

Coustou, Nicolas (1658-1733), French sculptor who studied with his father, Francois Coustou, and with Antoine COYSEVOX: he won the Colbert prize which gave him four years study at Rome, and later became Chancellor of the Academy of Fine Arts, Paris. His notable works include *The Seine and the Marne, La Saone,* and *Berger Chasseur* in the gardens of the TUILERIES. His brother, **Guillaume Coustou** (1677-1746) was an even greater sculptor, and a pupil of Pierre LEGROS. He worked alone and with his brother for Louis XV at VERSAILLES and Marly: among his finest sculptures are the famous group *The Horses of Marly; Meeting of the Ocean and the Mediterranean; Daphne; Louis XIII Offering His Sceptre and Crown to the Virgin.* His son, **Guillaume Coustou II** (1716-1777), studied in Rome and worked with his father on the *Horses of Marly.*

His outstanding individual work is the tomb of the Dauphin Louis, and of the Dauphine Maria Josephe de Saxe at the Sens Cathedral.

Couture, Thomas (1815-1879), French painter who studied with Baron A. J. GROS and Paul DELAROCHE, and completed his studies in Rome. His notable paintings include *Prodigal Son; Thirst for Gold; Wandering Minstrel; Day Dreams; The Falconer; Romans of the Decadence:* the last-named was an enormous canvas once greatly admired, but now judged more severely as lacking in character and commonplace in execution.

Covent Garden, an open space north of the Strand in London which was first the garden of the Abbey of St. Peter, Westminster. In the early part of the 17th century the site of the garden was transformed into a square by Inigo JONES, and occupied by the main flower, fruit and vegetable market in London. In 1732 the **Covent Garden Theatre** opened with William CONGREVE's play, *The Way of the World:* many famous actors including David GARRICK, Mrs. Cibber, Peg WOFFINGTON, and John Philip KEMBLE appeared there. The operas of George Frederick HANDEL were also produced, and in 1810, after the first house which had been destroyed by fire in 1809, the new theatre, one of the largest in Europe, was the scene of a series of fifty musical productions of every description directed by Sir Henry Rowley BISHOP, composer of "Home, Sweet Home." Weber's *Der Freischutz* and *Oberon* were also produced. In 1846 the theatre was turned into an opera house as the "Royal Italian Opera." GRISI, MARIO, ALBONI, PATTI, FAURE, NILSSON, and ALBANI sang there. In 1858 a new house was built, and since that time most of the great singers from all parts of the world have appeared there including, NORDICA, HAUK, de LUSSAN, MELBA, SCALCHI, EAMES, CALVE, CARUSO, the de RESZKES, MAUREL, PLANCON, BISPHAM, TAMAGNO, ALVAREZ, MELCHIOR, FLAGSTAD, SCHORR, and Lotte LEHMANN.

Coward, Noel (1899-), English actor, dramatist, composer and producer who made his professional debut in 1911 with Sir Charles HAWTREY, and appeared in various plays until 1917 when he served in World War I. His career as a dramatist and composer began with *I'll Leave It To You* in 1920: among the successes which followed are *The Vortex; The Rat Trap; Hay Fever; Easy Virtue; This Year of Grace; Bitter Sweet; Private Lives; Cavalcade; Words and Music; Design for Living; Conversation Piece* (nine one-act plays); *Tonight at 8:30; Blithe Spirit.* He appeared in David Wark Griffith's film, *Hearts of the World* (1917); the McArthur-Hecht film, *The Scoundrel* (1934), and in 1942 wrote, produced and played the principal role in the film, *In Which We Serve,* an epic of World War II.

Cowell, Henry Dixon (1897-), American composer who studied at the University of California, the New York Institute of Applied Music, and with Richard Buhlig. He toured Europe and the United States as a concert pianist; invented an electrical instrument, the Rhythmicon in collaboration with Leon THEREMIN; taught at several American universities; composed over five hundred orchestral, chamber and piano works, and organized the Pan American Composers Association and the New Music Society.

Cowen, Sir Frederic Hymen (1852-1935), English conductor and composer who studied with Sir Julius Benedict, Ignaz MOSCHELES, Carl REINECKE, and Hans RICHTER. He conducted the London Philharmonic Orchestra, the Liverpool Philharmonic Orchestra and the Hallé Orchestra at Manchester: his compositions include operas, oratorios, cantatas, symphonies, and other orchestral works; chamber music and more than 250 songs.

Cowl, Jane (1890-), American actress who studied at Columbia University, New York. Her debut was made in 1903 at the Belasco Theatre, New York, in *Sweet Kitty Bellairs:* since then she has played leading roles in *The Music Master; Rose of the Rancho; A Grand Army Man; The Easiest Way; Within the Law; Common Clay; Lilac Time; Information Please; Smilin' Through; Romeo and Juliet; Pelléas and Mélisande; The Road to Rome; Paolo and Francesca; Twelfth Night; Camille; The Shining Hour; Rain from Heaven; First Lady.* She has also acted as collaborator on several plays.

Cowles, Eugene (1860-), American bass singer and composer born in Canada and naturalized in 1879. He joined the BOSTONIANS in 1888, creating the role of Will Scarlett in Reginald De Koven's *Robin Hood:* in 1898 he became leading bass in the Alice Nielsen Opera Company, and also appeared in Gilbert and Sullivan operettas. His compositions include two well-known songs: *Forgotten* and *Crossing the Bar.*

Cowley, Abraham (1618-1667), English poet who published a volume of verse, *Poetical Blossoms,* in 1633, four years before he entered Cambridge University. His works include a scriptural epic on King David, *Davideis;* a poetic drama, *The Guardian;* a collection of love poems, *The Mistress.*

Cowley, Hannah (1743-1809), English dramatist whose first play, *The Runaways,* was a success for David GARRICK in 1776: it was followed by *The Belle's Stratagem, A Bold Stroke for a Husband, More Ways Than One,* and *A School for Greybeards,* all of which were produced at Drury Lane or Covent Garden.

Cowper, William (1731-1800), English poet who was admitted to the bar, but never practiced because of his innate timidity and neurotic temperament which finally led to insanity. His works include a volume of satirical poems (1782); *The Task;* translations of HOMER's "Iliad" and "Odyssey"; *John Gilpin.* He displayed an innate love of humanity in his verse which blossomed later in the poetry of BURNS, SHELLEY, and WORDSWORTH.

Cox, Kenyon (1856-1919), American painter who studied at Paris under CAROLUS-DURAN and J. L. GEROME, and later taught with much success at the ART STUDENTS' LEAGUE, New York. His murals include *Art and Science* at the Congressional Library, Washington, D. C.; the frieze for the court room of the Appellate Court, New

York; *The Marriage of the Atlantic and the Pacific* at the State Capitol, St. Paul, Minn. Among his best canvases are *The Harp Player; Moonrise; The Hunting Nymph; Portrait of Augustus Saint-Gaudens.* His wife and pupil, **Louise Howland King,** is also a painter famous for her portraits of children.

Cox, Palmer (1840-1924), American illustrator and writer of books for young people; born in Quebec but resident in the United States from 1875. His *Brownie Books* were very popular with young people; also *Hans von Petter's Trip to Gotham* and *How Columbus Discovered America.*

Coypel, the name of a distinguished French family of painters beginning with **Noel Coypel** (1628-1707), also known as Coypel le Poussin because his art was so much influenced by Nicolas POUSSIN. His works include *Solon Maintaining Justice; Malediction of Cain; Apollo Crowned with Victory.* His son and pupil, **Antoine Coypel** (1661-1722) became a member of the French Academy when he was twenty years old: his notable canvases include *Athalia Driven from the Temple; Christ Healing the Blind; Young Girl Caressing a Dog.* His stepbrother, **Noel Nicolas Coypel** (1692-1734), was a famous painter in pastel of allegorical works including *Venus, Bacchus, and Cupid; The Triumph of Amphitrite; Venus with Sea Nymphs.* **Charles Antoine Coypel** (1694-1752), son and pupil of Antoine Coypel, became court painter and director of the French Academy: his notable paintings include *Perseus and Andromeda; Medea Pursued by Jason;* and a series of pictures inspired by Cervantes' "Don Quixote."

Coysevox, Antoine (1640-1720), French sculptor who studied with Louis Lerambert, and at twenty-six made a bust of the painter, Charles LE BRUN which won him admission to the Royal Academy. He created many works at Marly, Versailles, and the Louvre under the patronage of Louis XIV; among them *Winged Horses; Mercury and Fame; Neptune and Amphitrite; Justice and Force:* also statues considered remarkably lifelike of Louis XIV; Louis XV, Colbert, Mazarin, Maria Theresa of Austria and many other notable persons.

Cozens, John Robert (1752-1797), English painter; pupil of his father, Alexander Cozens, a Russian artist who died in 1786. His landscapes in water color, and of the impressionistic school, were greatly admired by John CONSTABLE, who declared that he was "all poetry."

Cozzens, James Gould (1903-), American novelist who was educated at Harvard, but left in his sophomore year to devote himself to writing: his works include *Confusion* (1924); *Michael Scarlett; The Son of Perdition; S. S. San Pedro; The Last Adam; Ask Me Tomorrow.*

Crabbe, George (1754-1832), English clergyman poet whose works deal chiefly with the lives and sorrows of the poor. The poem, *The Village* (1781), made him famous: it was followed by *The Parish Register; The Borough; Tales in Verse; Tales of the Hall.* His verses are said to have solaced the last hours of Sir Walter SCOTT, and Thomas HARDY freely admitted having learned much of the art of realistic writing from Crabbe.

Crabtree, Lotta (1847-1924), American actress who was taught dancing by Lola MONTEZ, and became a popular actress in juvenile parts in the mining camps of California. She achieved her first success in New York as Little Nell in Dickens' *Old Curiosity Shop* in 1867; visited London in 1883, and appeared on the American stage in numerous melodramas and comedies until 1891 when she retired after having amassed a considerable fortune.

Cracovienne, see **Krakoviak.**

Craddock, Charles Egbert, see **Murfree, Mary Noailles.**

Cradle of Liberty, see **Faneuil Hall.**

Craig, Edward Gordon (1872-), English actor; son of Ellen TERRY and educated at Bradfield College and Heidelberg University. He made his debut in 1889 under Sir Henry IRVING at the Lyceum Theatre, London, in *The Dead Heart,* and appeared until 1897 in Shakespearean repertory and other standard plays. In 1900 he began a series of productions with his own scenic ideas; they included Purcell's opera *Dido and Aeneas;* Purcell's *Mask of Love; Much Ado About Nothing; Venice Preserved;* Ibsen's *Rosmersholm;* Shakespeare's *Macbeth.* His ideas as to the simplification of scenery were used by Max REINHARDT in the German version of *Venice Preserved* at Berlin; by Eleonora DUSE for production of *Electra* in Italy, and by the Moscow Art Theatre for *Hamlet.* In 1913 Craig founded a School for the Art of the Theatre at the ARENA GOLDONI, Florence, where he also produced many plays. His many works on dramatic theory include *The Art of the Theatre* (1905) published in English, French, German, Russian, and Japanese; *The Theatre Advancing; Books and Theatres.* He published biographies of Sir Henry Irving and Ellen Terry: also a theatrical magazine, *The Mask,* from 1908 to 1923.

Craigie, Pearl (1867-1906), Anglo-American novelist and dramatist born in the United States, but taken to London in 1868, and educated there and in Paris. She used the pen name "John Oliver Hobbes," and her first brilliant, epigrammatic book, *Some Emotions and a Moral,* was published successfully in 1891: it was followed by *The Sinner's Comedy; A Study in Temptations; The Serious Wooing; Love and the Soul Hunters; The Vineyard.* Ellen Terry presented her first play, *Journeys End in Lovers' Meetings,* in 1895: she also wrote *The Ambassador; A Repentance; Wisdom of the Wise; The Flute of Pan,* and collaborated on *The Bishop's Move.*

Craik, Dinah Maria Muloch, see **Mulock, Dinah Maria.**

Cram, Ralph Adams (1863-), American architect who learned the rudiments of his art in an architect's office, and acted as art critic for the Boston *Transcript* for two years. In 1889 he formed the firm of Cram and Wentworth which finally became, after several changes, Cram and Ferguson. In his search for an architecture more suited to modern American conditions than the Romanesque, he decided upon the English Gothic style which has worked out admirably in St. Thomas' Church, and the Cathedral of St. John the Divine, New York; buildings at the United States Military Academy, West Point; the Graduate College at Princeton University, Princeton, N. J. He has written several books on architectural subjects.

Cramer, Johann Baptist (1771-1858), German pianist, publisher, and composer who studied with Muzio CLEMENTI. He concertized as a virtuoso pianist in Europe and England, wrote many compositions, exercises and an instruction method for the piano, and founded the music publishing house of Cramer & Company.

Cranach, Lucas (1472-1553), German painter who studied with his father. He was court painter for Frederick the Wise of Wittenberg and several Saxon electors, and also a friend of LUTHER, painting portraits of both him and his family. Among his best works are portraits of Charles V and the emperor Maximilian; *Crucifixion; Repose in Egypt; Marriage of St. Catharine; Family of the Virgin; Christ Blessing the Children; The Adulterous Woman; The Judgment of Paris.*

Cranch, Christopher Pearce (1813-1892), American artist and poet; his works include *Poems* (1844); *The Last of the Huggermuggers;* a translation in verse of Virgil's "Aeneid"; *Ariel and Caliban, with Other Poems.*

Crane, Hart (1899-1932), American poet who worked as a copy writer in an advertising house in New York: the architectural grandeur of the city inspired his first volume of poems, *White Buildings* (1926); this was followed by *The Bridge,* a study in verse of Brooklyn Bridge. He was a great admirer and disciple of Walt WHITMAN.

Crane, Walter (1871-1900), American novelist educated at Lafayette College and Syracuse University. His finest work, *The Red Badge of Courage* (1896), was a vivid picture of the Civil War: two volumes of short stories; *The Open Boat and Other Tales* and *Whilomville Stories* were also greatly admired.

Crane, William Henry (1845-1928), American actor who appeared in 1863 with the Harriet Holman Company in operettas: his first success was achieved in Bronson HOWARD's comedy, *The Henrietta,* with Stuart ROBSON in 1887: it was revived twenty-six years later with Mr. Crane in the same part. Among the plays of American life in which he appeared were *The Senator; On Probation; A Fool of Fortune; The Head of the Family; David Harum; The Spenders; The American Lord; Father and the Boys.*

Cratinus (c.520-422 B.C.), Athenian dramatist whose comedies were distinguished by their vigorous political satire: he even attacked PERICLES at the pinnacle of his power in Athens. Only fragments remain of twenty-one comedies of which

nine won prizes: one of them, *The Bottle,* was awarded the honors over "The Clouds" of ARISTOPHANES.

Craven, Frank (1880-), American stage and screen actor and dramatist who made his debut as a child in *The Silver King,* and his mature debut in *Artie* at the Garrick Theatre, New York, in 1907. He has since appeared in many successful plays including *The Writing on the Wall; Bought and Paid For; Under Fire; That's Gratitude; Our Town.* He has played in his own comedies, *Too Many Cooks* and *Money from Home,* and has appeared in many films: among them *State Fair; Our Town; That's Gratitude; Barbary Coast; Penrod and Sam; Blossoms on Broadway.*

Craven, Thomas (1889-), American author of books on art, educated at the University of Kansas and Kansas Wesleyan University: his works include *Men of Art* (1931); *Modern Art:* he has also edited *A Treasury of American Prints* and *A Treasury of Art Masterpieces.*

Crawford, Francis Marion (1854-1909), American novelist, son of Thomas CRAWFORD, a well-known sculptor, and educated at Trinity College, Cambridge, and Heidelberg. His first novel, *Mr. Isaacs* (1882), is considered his masterpiece; the others which followed included *Dr. Claudius; A Roman Singer; An American Politician; Zoroaster; Saracinesca; Paul Patoff; Sant' Ilario; Greifenstein; A Cigarette Maker's Romance,* successfully dramatized. He also wrote a play, *Francesca da Rimini,* in which Sarah BERNHARDT appeared in Paris. From 1883 he made his home in Italy.

Crawford, Joan, contemporary screen actress who danced in several revues under the name, Lucille Le Sueur, before appearing in many films including *Sally, Irene and Mary; Spring Fever; Adrienne Lecouvreur; Rain; No More Ladies; The Gorgeous Hussy; The Last of Mrs. Cheyney; The Shining Hour; The Woman; Strange Cargo; Susan and God; A Woman's Face; When Ladies Meet; Reunion in France.*

Crawford, Ralston (1906-), American painter born in Canada who came to the United States as a child, studying at the Otis Art Institute and working in the Walt DISNEY Studio at Los Angeles, also attending the PENNSYLVANIA ACADEMY and spending three years in Paris. He began to exhibit his paintings of grain elevators, mills, and highways in 1938: he believes that pictures of this kind are in accordance with the age of machines. His painting, *Overseas Highway,* picturing a section of the Florida-Key West Highway, is typical of his art.

Crawford, Thomas (1813-1857), American sculptor who studied with Albert THORWALDSEN in Rome where he worked most of his life. His works include *Orpheus Entering Hades in Search of Eurydice; Babes in the Wood; Sappho; The Dancers; The Hunter;* busts of Henry Clay, Josiah Quincy and Ludwig van Beethoven; the equestrian statue of Washington at Richmond, Va. He executed the colossal figures, *Armed Liberty* in bronze surmounting the dome of the Capitol at Washington, D. C., and the bronze doors of the

Senate portico contrasting the terrors of war with the blessings of peace. The novelist, Francis Marion CRAWFORD, was his son.

Crayer, Gaspard de (1582-1669), Flemish painter who studied at Brussels with Raphael Coxcie, and was intimate with VAN DYCK and RUBENS: he imitated the latter's bold drawing and coloring, and painted principally religious subjects including *The Miraculous Draught of Fishes; Judgment of Solomon; Madonna with Saints; St. Theresa Receiving a Necklace from the Madonna.*

Crayon, in painting a pencil made of artificially prepared substances such as clay, chalk, or graphite; the required tints are secured by adding coloring in the correct proportions. Crayons are used by artists to effect groupings of colors in landscapes, portraits or still-life drawings. The term is also used for a drawing of this kind.

Creatore, Giuseppe (1871-), Italian band conductor; graduate of the Naples Conservatory of Music in 1887. After conducting bands in Italy he came to the United States in 1900, organized a band and toured for six years. In 1906 he returned to Italy to form another band with which he toured Italy, England and America. In 1917 he organized an opera company with an Italian, German, and French repertory with which he toured until 1921. Since then he has continued to engage in band and opera activities up to 1939, and has been guest conductor of several American major orchestras. His band concerts at Atlantic City were enjoyed by several hundred thousand people.

Crébillon, Prosper Jolyot de (1674-1762), French poet and dramatist: his first successful works were the tragedies *Idomenée* (1705); *Atrée et Thyeste; Electra; Rhadamiste et Zénobie,* the latter regarded as his masterpiece. After eighteen years in retirement, his dramas *Pyrrhus* and *Catiline* were equally successful under the patronage of Mme. de POMPADOUR. Crébillon's dramas were marked by scenes of unnatural horror and generally pervaded by gloom. His son, **Claude Prosper Jolyot de Crébillon** (1707-1777) was a novelist, appointed censor of public morals by Mme. de Pompadour; a somewhat peculiar office for an author who wrote *Le Sopha* and several other highly immoral romances.

Credi, Lorenzo di (1459-1537), Italian painter who studied with his father, and with Andrea VERROCCHIO, PERUGINO, and LEONARDO DA VINCI with whom he also worked, imitating their masterpieces with such skill that it was said to be difficult to distinguish the originals from the copies. He executed several fine altar-pieces including *Madonna and St. John the Baptist; Holy Family; The Nativity; Madonna Adoring the Infant Christ.*

Cregar, Allan (1916-), American stage and screen actor, educated in England, who has appeared in several films including *Hudson's Bay; Blood and Sand; Charley's Aunt; I Wake Up Screaming; This Gun For Hire.*

Cremer, Jacobus Jan (1827-1880), Dutch novelist and poet who was first a painter, and later adopted a literary career. His series, *Stories of Betuwe,* are distinguished by their faithful portraiture and unsophisticated humor: he was at his best in describing rural scenes and people. He also published a volume of poetry.

Cremona, a city in Italy near Milan founded by the Romans in 218 B.C.; it is famous as the home of the Cremonese school of painting in the 16th and 17th centuries, and also as the city in which the workshops of the great violin makers, AMATI, STRADIVARIUS and GUANERIUS were located.

Crescendo, in music a term indicating an increase in the volume of tone expressed by the full word, or its abbreviations, *cres.* or *cresc.;* also by a sign in the form of an acute angle, the vertex indicating the note at which the increase in sound should begin.

Crescentini, Girolamo (1762-1846), Italian artificial mezzo-soprano (CASTRATO) who made his debut at Rome in 1783: he was so popular there and in other Italian, French and English cities that he was nicknamed "the Italian Orpheus." Francois FETIS, the music historian, declared that no one could surpass him in beautiful tones, forceful expression, and exquisite phrasing. He retired in 1816 to become professor of singing at the Naples Royal Conservatory of Music.

Crespi, Giuseppe Maria (1665-1747), Italian painter also known as "Lo Spagnuolo" because of his penchant for fine clothes. He copied the works of CORREGGIO, BAROCCIO, TITIAN, and VERONESE, and later in life those of GUERCINO and Pietro da CORTONA. His works include *Massacre of the Innocents;* a series of paintings depicting the *Seven Sacraments, Ecce Homo; Chiron Teaching Achilles to Shoot.*

Cressent, Charles (1685-1768), French cabinet maker and sculptor; son of Francois Cressent, a sculptor, and pupil of André Charles BOULLE. He became famous at first as a sculptor and worker in bronze, and his female figures in bronze placed at the corners of tables were especially admired. His furniture is described in three catalogs written by him for sales purposes: it was characterized by subtly curving lines and lavish adornments such as scrolls, shells, and dragons.

Creswick, Thomas (1811-1869), English painter who studied with J. V. Barker at Birmingham, and spent considerable time sketching in Ireland, Wales, and England: among his notable canvases are *Pathway to the Village Church; Pleasant Way Home; Passing Showers; Old Trees; Wind on Shore;* he also illustrated GRAY's "Elegy," MILTON's "L'Allegro" and GOLDSMITH's "Deserted Village."

Crews, Laura Hope (1880-1942), American stage and screen actress who appeared first as a child of four at Woodward's Garden, San Francisco, and made her debut in New York with the Donnelly Stock Company in 1900. Among the plays in which she appeared were *Brown of Harvard; The Great Divide; Ransom's Folly; The Faith Healer; What Happened to Jones; The Havoc; Peter Ibbetson; Hay Fever; The Silver Cord;*

Mr. Pim Passes By; Jubilee; Arsenic and Old Lace. She also played important roles in many films including *The Silver Cord; Camille; The Sisters; Idiot's Delight; Gone With the Wind; The Rains Came; The Flame of New Orleans; The Man Who Came to Dinner.*

Crichton, James (1560-1582), Scottish scholar and adventurer who became so famous for his extraordinary accomplishments, and attainments in the languages, sciences and arts that he was called "the admirable Crichton." At seventeen he was the master of twelve languages, and bested the professors of the University at Padua in an argument over the correct interpretation of Aristotle: he is said to have been treacherously murdered by the Duke of Mantua.

Crisp, Donald, contemporary English actor, educated at Oxford University, who came to the United States in 1906. He acted as assistant to David Wark GRIFFITH, and directed films for the American Biograph Company and Douglas Fairbanks, Sr., for many years. Among the numerous pictures in which he appeared are *The Pagan; Svengali; The Crime Doctor; The Little Minister; What Every Woman Knows; Mutiny on the Bounty; Oil for the Lamps of China; Charge of the Light Brigade; Mary of Scotland; Parnell; Jezebel; The Sisters; Wuthering Heights; The Sea Hawk; Dr. Jekyll and Mr. Hyde; How Green Was My Valley.*

Crist, Bainbridge (1883-), American singing teacher and composer who first practiced law for several years with music as an avocation; later he studied composition with Paul JUON and voice with William SHAKESPEARE. His compositions include choreographic dramas, ballets, orchestral works, solo and choral works with orchestra, piano pieces and songs.

Cristofori, Bartolommeo (1655-1731), Italian maker of harpsichords who is credited with having made the first practical pianoforte, differing from the harpsichord by having its strings struck by hammers instead of being plucked by quills to produce the sounds. A pianoforte made by Cristofori is in the collection of musical instruments at the METROPOLITAN MUSEUM OF ART, New York; there has been much argument pro and con as to the justness of his claim to priority.

Critchett, Richard Claude, see **Carton, Richard Claude.**

Crivelli, Carlo (c.1432-1495), Italian painter who spent most of his maturity as an itinerant painter in The Marches, a province in Italy. He painted in tempera, and his works include *Virgin and Child; Piéta with St. Jerome and a Martyr; Macerata Madonna; St. George on Horseback; Coronation of the Virgin; Madonna with Saints.*

Crockett, Samuel Rutherford (1860-1914), Scottish minister and novelist who was educated at the University of Edinburgh. His works include *The Stickit Minister* (1893); *The Raiders; Mad Sir Uchtred; The Lilac Sunbonnet; Sweetheart Travelers; Cleg Kelly; Arab of the City; The Grey Man of Auchendrayne;* he also published a volume of poems.

Croesus, a Lydian king, last of his line, who was so famous for his wealth that "rich as Croesus" became a popular saying. One of the visitors to his court about 550 B.C., was Solon, a famous Athenian law-maker numbered among the seven wise men of Greece.

Crome, John (1768-1821), English painter, called "Old Crome," who first worked as a coach painter, and educated himself by studying nature and masterpieces of the Dutch school. After being aided in his studies by Sir William BEECHEY, he specialized in landscapes and marine scenes including *Mousehold Heath; The Old Oak; Clump of Tree on Hautbois Common; Bruges on the Ostend River; Fishmarket at Boulogne..* He founded the Norwich School of Arts in 1805.

Cronin, Archibald Joseph (1896-), Scottish physician and novelist; his first novel, *Hatter's Castle,* was so successful that it was translated into several languages, resulting in his devoting himself exclusively to writing. Later novels include *Three Loves; Grand Canary; The Stars Look Down; The Citadel;* adapted for the screen; *The Keys of the Kingdom.*

Cronus, in Greek mythology the youngest of the TITANS, and the son of Uranus, god of the skies, and GAEA, goddess of the earth. He was the father of ZEUS and POSEIDON. He overthrew Uranus with the aid of his brothers, the Titans, but was later defeated by the Olympian gods led by Zeus. He finally ruled over the ISLANDS OF THE BLEST on earth so well that his reign was known as the Golden Age.

Crooks, Richard (1900-), American concert and opera tenor who studied with Frank LA FORGE and sang in New York churches as a boy soprano and tenor. He concertized in Europe, and made his operatic debut in 1927 at Hamburg in *Tosca;* in 1930 he appeared for the first time in America with the Philadelphia Opera Company in *Tosca,* and in 1933 with the Metropolitan Opera Company in *Manon.* He has concertized successfully for many years, and appears at regular intervals in broadcasts.

Cropper, Roy (1898-), American actor and singer who appeared first as a boy of twelve with William FAVERSHAM in *Herod,* and made his debut in 1921 at New York in *Chu-Chin-Chow.* Among the musical plays in which he appeared are *Blossom Time; The Student Prince; Naughty Marietta; The Fortune Teller; The Prince of Pilsen; The Chocolate Soldier; The Geisha; The Firefly;* also in Gilbert and Sullivan operettas.

Crosby, Bing (1904-), American screen and radio actor and singer who appeared in a vocal trio with Paul WHITEMAN for three years before entering the fields of motion pictures and radio. Since 1933 he has appeared as both actor and singer in numerous films including *College Humor; Here is My Heart; Pennies from Heaven; Doctor Rhythm; The Road to Singapore; The Road to Zanzibar; Holiday Inn; The Road to Morocco;* also appearing in regular commercial broadcasts.

Crosby, Fanny (1820-1915), American song and hymn writer who was blind from childhood: she was educated at the New York Institute for the Blind, and was employed as a teacher there for many years. She wrote the verse for George F. Root's songs, *The Hazel Dell* and *There's Music in the Air*: also the words for many hymns published in *Gospel Hymns*. Her autobiography was published with the title, *Memories of Eighty Years*.

Crosman, Henrietta (1865-), American actress who made her debut in 1883 at New York in *The White Slave*, later appearing with the Lyceum Stock Company under Daniel FROHMAN. Among the many plays in which she has had important roles are *The Charity Ball; The Rajah; Burmah; Mistress Nell; Nance Oldfield; Sweet Kitty Bellairs; The Almighty Dollar; Madeline; The Christian Pilgrim; Erstwhile Susan*. She has also appeared in several films including *The Moon's Our Home; Girl of the Ozarks; Follow Your Heart, and The Man in Possession*.

Cross, Mrs. George Frederick, 19th century Australian novelist who wrote under the pen name "Ada Cambridge"; among her successful stories are *A Marked Man; My Guardian; Not All in Vain; The Three Miss Kings*.

Cross, in Christian painting and sculpture the cross is the symbol of the Passion of Jesus Christ; in the *Latin cross* the lower limb is longer than the other three: in the *Maltese cross* the four equal limbs widen from the center outwards. The cross used in processionals has an extra-long lower limb with or without the figure of Christ upon it, and is often made of precious metals studded with gems.

Crothers, Rachel (1878-), American actress and dramatist who produced several short plays while a student at the Stanhope-Wheatcroft School of Acting, and made her stage debut in the Felix Morris Company. Among her successful plays, chiefly social comedies conceived from the viewpoint of a modern woman, are *Nora* (1903); *A Man's World; The Three of Us; The Coming of Mrs. Patrick; Old Lady 31; Mother Carey's Chickens*, with Kate Douglas WIGGIN; *Nice People; Expressing Willie; Let Us Be Gay; When Ladies Meet; Susan and God*: she prepared the screen scenario of the two last named.

Crouth or **Crowd,** an ancient stringed instrument played with a bow, presumed to be of Welsh, Irish, or French origin, and found among peasants of these countries as late as the 19th century. Efforts have been made by some authorities, in face of much opposition, to prove it the direct ancestor of the VIOLIN.

Crowe, Sir Joseph Archer (1828-1896), English art critic who studied for a time with Paul DELAROCHE; while on a visit to Italy in 1847 he became intimate with the distinguished Italian art critic, Giovanni Battista CAVALCASELLE (1820-1897), and collaborated with him on several historically important works on art including *Early Flemish Painters* (1857), and *A New History of Painting in Italy from the Second to the Sixteenth Cen-* tury; the latter a five-volume work published in 1864-1871.

Crowninshield, Frederic (1845-1918), American painter and decorative artist who studied with Alexander CABANEL and Thomas COUTURE; also at the ECOLE DES BEAUX-ARTS. He was director of the American Academy at Rome, and later opened a studio in Boston, Mass. His canvases include *Perugia; Taormina; Capri Cliff*: he also executed many fine murals and stained glass windows, and wrote several critical works on art subjects.

Cruikshank, George (1792-1878), English painter, illustrator, and caricaturist whose father, Isaac Cruikshank, was also a painter and caricaturist. Before he was twenty years old, George was a successful and popular artist: among the books he illustrated were *Oliver Twist; Jack Sheppard; Guy Fawkes; The Ingoldsby Legends; Rookwood; The Tower of London;* Grimm's *Popular German stories.* His versatility, imagination, and keen sense of satirical humor were displayed in hundreds of caricatures for magazines of various kinds: the subjects were foreign wars, enemies of England, the foibles of the great and the wealthy, and the humors of the common people. He was an advocate of teetotalism, and produced many illustrations showing the dire effects of intemperance such as *The Bottle* (8 plates) and *The Drunkard's Children* (8 plates). His greatest painting, *The Worship of Bacchus,* is in the National Gallery, London.

Crusenstolphe, Magnus Jakob (1795-1865), Swedish novelist and politician: his imprisonment for opposing the authorities in 1838 caused a series of riots in Stockholm which made him a public hero. His political writings lack the interest of his historical tales, *Little Stories.* A novel, *Two Marriages,* was a decided success because of its realism.

Cruz, Ramon de la (1731-1794), Spanish poet, translator and dramatist who wrote more than 300 dramatic works including dramas, comedies and musical plays. He is said to have rescued the native stage from an inundation of French plays, and also translated the comedies of Shakespeare.

Crypt, in architecture a vault or subterranean chamber usually constructed under churches and cathedrals: in ancient times it was the name of any vaulted structure entirely or partially under the ground. Crypts were authorized in sacred edifices by decree of the Council of Mainz in 813 A.D.: they were developed into elaborate sanctuaries for the distinguished dead in the 11th and 12th centuries. In many churches crypts containing the bones of a saint, or the remains of a martyr were placed beneath the high altar.

Csiky, Gregor (1842-1891), Hungarian novelist and dramatist; his works include the successful comedies *The Oracle* and *Suspicion;* the tragedies *Janus, Spartacus, The Magician, The Iron Man,* and *The Irresistible One.* He also wrote several excellent novels, and translated the plays of SOPHOCLES, EURIPIDES, PLAUTUS, and MOLIERE. He was without question the greatest Hungarian dramatist of the last half of the 19th century.

Csok, Istvan or **Stephen** (1865-), Hungarian painter who studied with SZEKELY, BOUGUEREAU and Robert FLEURY. His canvases such as *Communion* and *Orpheus* reveal the technique of impressionism as does the historical *Elizabeth Bathory*: another fine work which demonstrates his ability to re-create Hungarian rural atmosphere is *Godfather at Breakfast*.

Cubism, a movement in art begun in 1910 in rebellion against the art of the Impressionist School: its purpose was to convey ideas through abstract forms derived from architecture and geometry. Among the leaders in the movement were Georges BRAQUE, Fernand Leger, Pablo PICASSO, and Paul CEZANNE.

Cueva, Juan de la (1550-1607), Spanish poet and dramatist regarded as a pioneer in advocating national subjects as dramatic themes, as a forerunner of Lope DE VEGA, and as one of the founders of Spanish national drama. His book, *Works* (1582), contained a series of sonnets, lyric poems and elegies: it was followed by *Phoebean Chorus of Historical Romances*, and a epic poem, *The Conquest of Retica*. His tragedies include *The Death of Virginia* and *The Sack of Rome*: the best of his ten comedies is *The Aged Lover*.

Cui, César Antonovitch (1835-1918), Russian composer who studied with Stanislaw MONIUSZKO and Mily BALAKIREW; he was also professor of military fortification at the St. Petersburg Engineering Academy. He acted as music critic for the St. Petersburg *Gazette*, and wrote a series of musical essays on Russian music for the Paris *Revue et Gazette Musicale*. His compositions include nine operas; orchestral works; concert and solo pieces for piano and for violin; choral works; chamber music; suites for two pianos and more than two hundred songs.

Cullen, Countée (1903-), American Negro poet who studied at New York University: his first volume of verse in classical metres was published in 1925: other works include *Caroling Dusk and Copper Sun; The Ballad of the Brown Girl; The Black Christ;* also a novel entitled *One Way to Heaven.*

Cumberland, Richard (1732-1811), English dramatist, novelist, essayist, and poet. His comedies include *The Fashionable Lover; The Wheel of Fortune; The Brothers; The West Indian* produced by David GARRICK in 1771. He also wrote a volume of essays entitled, *The Observer;* several novels of little importance; *Anecdotes of Eminent Painters in Spain,* and a volume of memoirs.

Cummings, Edward Estlin (1894-), American author, painter and poet educated at Harvard University: his works include *The Enormous Room* (1922), a narrative in prose of imprisonment in France during World War I; a play entitled *him* which was produced by the Provincetown Players; several volumes of poetry including *Tulips* and *Chimneys.*

Cummins, Maria Susann (1827-1866), American novelist whose first book, *The Lamplighter,* had enormous success because of its idyllic charm and tenderness, and was translated into several languages: it was followed by *Mabel Vaughan* and *Haunted Hearts.*

Cuneiform, a form of writing used by the Babylonians and Assyrians: the name is derived from the Latin *cuneus,* meaning a wedge, and was first used in 1700 by Thomas Hyde, professor of Hebrew at Oxford. Each character is composed of one or more signs in the form of a wedge, therefore the name is really appropriate, and is to be found in the vocabulary of most modern languages except German. An interesting explanation of cuneiform can be found in the 11th edition of the *Encyclopedia Britannica.*

Cunningham, Allan (1784-1842), Scottish poet who wrote a dramatic poem, *Sir Marmaduke Maxwell,* while a reporter on a London newspaper: also two interesting novels, *Lord Roldan* and *Paul Jones.* He also published *The Songs of Scotland Ancient and Modern* in which he included his famous nautical ballad "A Wet Sheet and a Flowing Sea"; also a *Critical History of the Literature of the Last Fifty Years* and *Lives of the Most Eminent British Painters, Sculptors and Architects.*

Cupid, in ancient Roman mythology the Latin name for the god of love, known in Greek as *Eros* and in Latin also as *Amor.* Poets and artists of the ALEXANDRINE SCHOOL are responsible for the delineation of Cupid as a mischievous infant or youth with human characteristics: he is usually depicted with a bow and arrow, and is associated with PSYCHE.

Cupola, in architecture a spherical or nearly spherical roof for a building, or any section thereof; the term is also applied to any small structure erected over the roof.

Curel, François de, Vicomte (1854-1928), French novelist and dramatist educated for the profession of civil engineer: his first literary efforts were two novels: *L'Eté du fruits secs* (1885) and *Le Sauvetage du grand duc.* In 1891 three of his plays were produced in Paris: they were followed by many others including *The Other Side of a Saint; The Fossils; The Dancer; The Wild Girl; The Comedy of a Genius; The Quick and the Dead; The Inhuman Land;* the two last named were concerned with World War I.

Curious Women, The, see **Donne Curiose, Le.**

Curran, Charles C. (1861-1942), American painter who studied at the Cincinnati School of Design, the New York ART STUDENT'S LEAGUE and the Académie Julien, Paris. He painted many landscapes in Ohio which are conspicuous for their refinement and delicate technique as the result of his study with French masters. He won the Altman Prize of $1,000 in 1932 in addition to many other awards and medals: his portrait of Mayor George B. McClellan hangs in the City Hall, New York.

Currier Gallery of Art, an institution at Manchester, N. H., in which the gallery of paintings includes works by COPLEY, SARGENT, RAEBURN,

STUART, CLAYS, ISABEY, BONHEUR, BOUGEREAU, INNES, SCHREYER, WYANT, CAZIN, HENRI, INMAN, Winslow HOMER, Childe HASSAM, and many other famous European and American artists.

Currier and Ives, an American firm of lithographers founded in 1835 at New York by Nathaniel Currier; in 1850 J. Merritt Ives, a well-known artist, entered into a partnership with him, and from 1857 their prints were marked with the firm name. Their numerous prints depicted scenes of every phase of American life during the last half of the 19th century; among them many horseracing and other sporting events. They have become exceedingly rare, and are now collectors' items.

Curry, John Steuart (1897-   ), American painter who studied at the Art Institutes at Kansas City, Mo., and Chicago, Ill.; also in Paris. His works include: *Baptism in Kansas; Line Storm; Tornado over Kansas; Circus Elephants;* murals for the Department of Justice and Department of Interior, Washington, D. C.; murals for the Kansas state capitol at Topeka. He has taught at the ART STUDENTS' LEAGUE, New York, and at the University of Wisconsin: his paintings are in several American art museums.

Curtain, in the theatre a word having several meanings; (*a*) a movable ornamental screen for concealing the stage between scenes or acts; (*b*) a fireproof screen, usually made of asbestos, for preventing the spread of fire from or to the stage; (*c*) the descent of the curtain after a scene or act; (*d*) the final situation or line in a play. The term was first used near the end of the 17th century. One of the most elaborate curtains in American theatres is the one in use at the MUSIC HALL, RADIO CITY, New York.

Curtis, Cyrus Hermann Kotzschmar (1850-1933), American publisher and philanthropist who worked on various newspapers, and finally started a periodical in Philadelphia, the *Tribune and Farmer* out of which the *Ladies Home Journal* developed. After it became a successful women's magazine, he founded the Curtis Publishing Company in 1890, purchasing *The Saturday Evening Post* in 1897, and later the *Country Gentleman.* He also acquired several newspapers including the Philadelphia *Public Ledger,* the Philadelphia *Press,* the New York *Evening Post,* and the Philadelphia *Inquirer:* he also endowed the CURTIS INSTITUTE OF MUSIC in Philadelphia, and contributed liberally to many educational and charitable institutions.

Curtis, George William (1824-1892), American essayist who was largely self-educated, and received his first impressions of literary life from contact with Ralph Waldo EMERSON and other leaders of the Transcendental School. He traveled in Europe and the East as correspondent for the New York *Tribune,* and later became editor of *Harper's Weekly,* and a contributor to *Harper's Magazine.* His works include *Nile Notes of a Howadji* (1851); *Lotus Eating; Potiphar Papers; Prue and I:* the latter is considered his finest work.

Curtis Institute of Music, a conservatory of music founded and endowed by Cyrus H. K. CURTIS in 1924. In 1926 Josef HOFMANN became the director, and tuition fees were abolished, students being accepted on the basis of their artistic ability. Among the noted musicians who have been members of the faculty are Efrem ZIMBALIST, Carl FLESCH, Leopold AUER, Louis BAILLY, Moriz ROSENTHAL, and Marcella SEMBRICH. The Institute Orchestra has been conducted by Leopold STOKOWSKI, Artur RODZINSKI, and Fritz REINER. Josef Hofmann resigned as director in 1938: he was succeeded by Randall THOMPSON and later by Efrem ZIMBALIST.

Curwood, James Oliver (1878-1927), American journalist and novelist who spent a great deal of his leisure time in the wilds of Canada: the knowledge gained of hunting, trapping and fishing forms a realistic background for his numerous novels including *God's Country and the Woman; Nomads of the North; The Valley of Silent Men; Kazan; The Plains of Abraham,* and *The Black Hunter.* All of the above enjoyed a large sale with readers who enjoy exciting stories with vivid descriptions of outdoor life.

Cushing, Otho (1871-1942), American artist and cartoonist who studied at the Boston School of Fine Arts and the Acadèmie Julien in Paris. He taught drawing for many years at the Massachusetts Institute of Technology, Boston, Mass., before joining the art department of *Life Magazine* in which he drew humorous drawings of people in ancient Greek costumes, and a series of cartoons on the activities of President Theodore Roosevelt. During World War I he supervised the camouflaging of air fields on the western front.

Cushman, Charlotte (1816-1876), American actress who made her first appearance on the operatic stage in 1835 as a contralto in MOZART'S *The Marriage of Figaro* at the Tremont Theatre, Boston, Mass. After her singing voice failed, she made her dramatic debut in 1836 at New York in Shakespeare's *Macbeth.* After considerable experience with stock companies, she toured the United States with William MACREADY in 1845, and made a successful debut in classic repertory at London in 1854. Her best roles were Lady Macbeth, and Meg Merrilies in a dramatization of SCOTT'S *Guy Mannering:* her commanding figure and low voice enabled her to play male parts such as Shylock, Romeo and Cardinal Wolsey.

Custis, George Washington Parke (1781-1857), American dramatist; a grandson of Martha Washington who was adopted by George Washington after his father, John Parke Custis, was killed in the Revolutionary War. Several of his plays including *The Indian Prophecy, Pocohontas,* and *The Railroad* were produced in American theatres: he also wrote a book entitled *Recollections of Washington,* and his daughter, Mary Custis, became the wife of the Confederate general, Robert E. Lee.

Cuvilliès, François de (1698-1767), French architect, engraver, and decorator who introduced the ROCOCO style of French decoration in Germany as architect to Emperor Charles VII. He designed the Residenz-Theater, the Archbishop's Palace, and the Amalienburg, a pavilion in the park of Nymphenburg at Munich, and wrote several treatises on architectural decoration which were edited by his son, **François Cuvilliès the Younger** (1734-1805), who succeeded him at the court of Munich.

Cuyp, Aelbert (1620-1691), Dutch painter who studied with his father, Jacob Gerritsz Cuyp (1594-c.1650), and painted large canvases with solidly painted figures standing boldly in relief against backgrounds of golden light, the subjects usually being country life or gay cavaliers. Among his finest paintings are: *Promenade; Moonlight on the Sea; Dapple Grey Horses; Cock and Hen; Mussel-Eater; View of Dordrecht; The Storm.*

Cuypers, Petrus Josephus Hubertus (1827-1921), Dutch architect who studied with Eugène Violet-le-Duc, and was instrumental in stimulating the interest of the Dutch in architecture. He selected Gothic and 16th century Netherland designs as models in designing the Rijks Museum at Amsterdam, and in restoring many churches and municipal buildings in Holland.

Cyclops, in Greek mythology a one-eyed giant, member of a group known as *Cyclopes* descended from Uranus, the god of the skies, and Gaea, goddess of the earth. One of the Cyclopes, Polyphemus, imprisoned Ulysses in a cave, but he escaped after succeeding in blinding his captor.

Cyclorama, (*a*) in stage scenery a device used in outdoor settings to represent the sky in the form of a curved, light-blue drop or a plaster dome. (*b*) In painting a vast circular canvas on which is pictured a scenic panorama or historical event which constitutes an evening's entertainment in itself; among the notable American paintings of this character may be mentioned *The Battle of Vicksburg; The Battle of the Monitor and the Merrimac; The Battle of Gettysburg.* Cycloramas are usually illuminated by a trough running around the base in which lights are installed.

Cygnaus, Fredrik (1807-1881), Finnish poet educated at the University of Abo where he later occupied the post of professor of literature for several years: he also lectured on modern literature at the University of Helsingfors. His poetical works, published in six volumes, were entitled *Skaldestycken.*

Cymbals, in the orchestra a pair of brass or bronze concave plates with broad, flat rims from 10 to 16 inches in diameter. Holes are bored near the center of each plate for the insertion of the strap by which it is held. Cymbals are usually played in pairs, and held one in each hand: they are struck together with a sliding motion, produce a sound of indeterminate pitch, and are employed to create weird or thrilling effects. In small orchestras one cymbal is attached to the bass drum so that a single performer can operate both instruments.

Cyrano de Bergerac, see **Bergerac, Savinien Cyrano de.**

Czajkowski, Michal (1808-1886), Polish novelist who was one of the insurgents in the Polish Revolution of 1831: he went to Paris and later to Constantinople where he embraced the Mohammedan religion, and called himself Sadyk Pasha. He was pardoned by the Russians in 1873, but committed suicide when told that his Polish countrymen considered him a traitor. His works included many exciting tales of Cossack life: several of them, including *The Moslem and the Christian* and *The Black Pilgrim,* have been translated into English.

Czárdás, the favorite national dance of Hungary: the name is that of an inn, Czárda, where it was first danced. The dance is in two parts: *lassu,* or slow movement, and *fris,* or fast movement: they are usually played alternately, and the music itself is of intensely passionate character.

Czermak or **Cermak, Jaroslav** (1831-1878), Bohemian painter who studied at Prague, Antwerp, and Brussels; he also visited Holland and traveled in Normandy before completing his artistic training with Nicolas Robert-Fleury in Paris. Among his most notable paintings are *Dalibo in Prison; Marius at the Ruins of Carthage; Slovakian Emigrants; Poet Lomnicky as a Beggar on the Bridge at Prague; Defense of a Pass by the Taborites.* His vigorous conception and execution combined with rich coloring won him unstinted praise and many awards.

Czerny, Carl (1791-1857), Austrian pianist, teacher, and composer who studied with Beethoven, and was intimate with Muzio Clementi and Johann Hummel. He concertized for a time, but finally devoted himself to composing and teaching: among his distinguished pupils were Liszt, Döhler, and Thalberg. His compositions numbered more than a thousand works of every character, but his piano studies, still invaluable, are the only ones that have survived.

Czuczor, Gergely (1800-1866), Hungarian monk and poet whose first epic poem, *The Battle of Augsburg* (1824) brought him immediate fame: it was followed by another successful epic ballad, *The Diet of Arad.* The erotic character of his first volume of poems resulted in severe discipline from his superiors, and an impassioned plea for national patriotism published in 1848, entitled *Reveil,* earned him a prison sentence.

D

Dabo, Leon (1868-), American painter who specialized in landscapes and murals: the former include many scenes along the Hudson River, New York, such as *The Hudson in Winter* and *Dawn Beyond the Hudson.* His murals *Ascension* and *The Life of Christ* are to be seen in the Church of St. John the Baptist in Brooklyn, N. Y.: he also executed the friezes for the Flower Memorial Library, Watertown, N. Y.

Dactyl, in poetry a three-syllable measure consisting of one long or accented syllable followed by two short or unaccented syllables.

Dadaism, in painting an art movement said to have started more or less as a joke or hoax during World War I at a tavern in Zurich, Switzerland, by the artist, Tristan Tzara. The avowed purpose at a meeting in Paris during 1920 was the overthrow of all traditional art forms and methods of procedure, but the movement apparently died of its own inanity.

Dado, in architecture a cube of stone forming the main part of a pedestal. The term is also applied to a plain, flat surface at the base of a wall in a room: it is usually decorated in a different color, or with a design different from that of the upper part of the wall.

Daedalus, in Greek mythology a sculptor and architect who built the labyrinth for King MINOS: when the latter imprisoned him, he fashioned wings of wax so that he and his son, ICARUS, could fly away. Icarus flew too close to the sun, and fell into the sea when the heat melted the wax, but Daedalus arrived safely in Sicily.

Dafydd ab Gwilym (c.1340-c.1400), Welsh poet regarded as the greatest of the medieval bards, and as a reformer who accomplished much in raising the artistic level of Welsh poetry. He was a student of the works of HOMER, VIRGIL, OVID, HORACE, and the early Italian masters of versifying: the poems, *The Lark, The Wind,* and *The Mist* are considered the finest examples of a poet who chose nature rather than war for his theme.

Dagnan-Bouveret, Pascal Adolphe Jean (1852-1929), French painter who studied with J. L. Gérôme, and exhibited a canvas, *Wedding Party at a Photographer's,* in 1879 which attracted considerable attention. His notable works include *An Accident; Lover's Quarrel; The Conscripts; Hamlet and the Grave Diggers; Apollo and the Muses; Madonna of the Roses; Horses at a Watering Trough.*

Daguerre, Louis Jacques Mandé (1789-1851), French painter and inventor with Joseph Niepce of the daguerreotype, an early variety of photograph, first used in 1839, and produced on a silver plate, or a copper plate covered with silver. The plate was sensitized with iodine, and after exposure the image was developed with vapor of mercury. He also devoted himself to scene painting, and in 1822 opened the *Diorama* in Paris where partly translucent paintings were displayed through an opening: remarkable panoramic, scenic effects were secured through skilful lighting and other devices.

Daguerreotype, see **Daguerre, Louis Jacques Mandé.**

Dahl, Johann Kristen Clausen (1778-1857), Norwegian painter who was chiefly self-taught: he settled in Dresden in 1818, and was made a member of the Dresden Academy and professor of painting there. Among his best canvases are *Outbreak of Vesuvius; Winter at Munich; Dresden by Moonlight; Harbor of Copenhagen; Storm at Sea; Kronberg Castle by Moonlight.* He is regarded as an artist of the Munich school.

Dahl, Michael (1656-1742), Swedish painter who attained a high position as a portraitist. He lived in London, Paris, and Rome: in the last named city he painted the portrait of Queen CHRISTINA of Sweden. In 1688 he returned to London where he was patronized by Queen Anne and the English aristocracy, and became for some years a formidable rival of Sir Godfrey KNELLER.

Dahl, Vladimir Ivanovich (1802-1872), Russian philologist and author educated at the Institution for Naval Cadets at St. Petersburg. He wrote, under the pen name of "Kossack Lugansky," the stories of Russian life *The Dream and the Waking; A Story of Misery; Happiness; The Door Keeper; The Officer's Valet.* His greatest contribution to Russian literature is *A Dictionary of the Russian Tongue* (4 volumes, 1861-1866), drawn from investigations including 4,000 folk tales and 30,000 proverbs.

Dahn, Julius Sophus (1834-1912), German historian, poet, dramatist, and novelist: his historical masterpiece was *The Kings of the Germans* (6 volumes, 1861-1871). His epic poem, *Harald and Theano,* and his *Ballads and Songs* are distinguished by their forceful thoughts and rich verbiage; among his novels *The Struggle for Rome* is foremost for its poetic fancy. His dramas, *German Fidelity* and *King Roderick,* exhibit a profound knowledge of dramatic verse.

Daingerfield, Elliott (1859-1932), American painter who studied at the ART STUDENTS' LEAGUE, New York. His landscapes such as *Slumbering Fog, Midnight Moon,* and *Trees at the Grand Canyon* are regarded as vivid reproductions of the poetic in nature. He also executed fine murals including *Christ Stilling the Tempest* at the Metropolitan Museum of Art, New York, and *The Child of Mary* at the National Gallery, Washington, D.C.

Dais, in architecture the name in medieval days for a part of the floor in a hall, raised a step above the rest of the floor, and used as the dining place for the nobility or the master of a mansion. In ordinary use today the term means any raised platform.

Dalcroze, Émile Jaques, see **Jaques-Dalcroze, Émile.**

Dalgleish, Alice (1893-   ), American editor and author of books for juveniles; her works include *First Experiences with Literature* (1932); *The Smiths and Rusty; Wings for the Smiths; America Begins; America Builds Homes; The Young Aunts; Wooden Shoes in America; A Book for Jennifer; St. George and the Dragon.*

Dali, Salvador (1904-   ), Spanish painter who studied for a time at the Academy of Fine Arts in Madrid, but was asked to leave because of his unusual ideas regarding art and the teaching of art. His present style is said by contemporary critics to have developed through stages of naturalism, impressionism, futurism, and cubism: all of his experiences in art are related in his autobiography, *The Secret Life of Salvador Dali* (1942). He has also collaborated with Luis Bunuel in surrealist films, and lectured on his own paintings, which he describes as paranoic dreams, at the Whitney Museum of Modern Art, New York.

Dalin, Olof von (1708-1763), Swedish poet and dramatist whose efforts to infuse a sense of the joy of living into the poetry of his native land earned him the title of "father of modern Swedish literature." He also enriched the Swedish language by introducing elements of foreign speech and expression. His works include an epic poem, *Sweden's Liberties*, a drama, *Brynhilda*, and a comedy, *The Jealous Man:* he also wrote many songs and ballads which reveal a genuine sense of humor.

Dallin, Cyrus Edwin (1861-), American sculptor who studied at the ECOLE DES BEAUX-ARTS, and the Académie Julien at Paris: also with Henri CHAPU. He specialized, through knowledge gained during his early life in the West, in portrayals of the American Indian; his works include *The Medicine Man* (Fairmount Park, Philadelphia); *Signal of Peace*, (Lincoln Park, Chicago); *Pioneer Monument*, (Salt Lake City); *The Appeal to the Great Spirit*, (Museum of Fine Arts, Boston).

Dall' Ongaro, Francesco (1808-1873), Italian priest, poet, and dramatist who was unfrocked because of his activities as an ardent patriot, and later exiled. His works include two volumes of poetry; several dramas in one of which, *Bianca Capello*, Adelaide RISTORI appeared: also several comedies, and numerous popular ballads, songs, and hymns.

Dalmores, Charles (1871-1939), French operatic tenor who first studied the French horn and played in the Colonne and Lamoureux Orchestras at Paris: after studying with Dauphin he made his debut at Rouen in 1899 with such success that he was engaged at all the great opera houses in Europe. He appeared as Julien in Charpentier's LOUISE in 1908 with Hammerstein's MANHATTAN OPERA COMPANY, and appeared later with the Philadelphia-Chicago Opera Company and the Philadelphia Opera Company. His repertory included not only leading roles in French operas, but also in Wagner's music dramas.

Dalou, Aimé Jules (1838-1902), French sculptor who studied with CARPEAUX and Duret, and settled permanently in England when the riots of the Commune started at Paris in 1871, becoming professor of sculpture in the SOUTH KENSINGTON MUSEUM, London. His works include *The Embroiderer; The Peasant Woman; The Shepherdess; Fraternity; Mirabeau Answering M. de Dreux-Baeze; Triumph of the Republic; The Procession of Silenus*. His portraiture in statues or busts is remarkable: he laid the foundation for the vast improvement in British sculpture which followed.

Daly, Arnold (1875-1927), American actor and producer who made his New York debut in 1899 in *Puddin'head Wilson*, and appeared later with Julia MARLOWE in *Barbara Frietchie*. He produced and appeared in many of George Bernard SHAW's plays including *Candida; Mrs. Warren's Profession; You Never Can Tell; How He Lied to Her Husband; The Man of Destiny; John Bull's Other Island; Arms and the Man.*

Daly, Augustin (1838-1899), American dramatist and theatrical manager, considered one of the greatest American managers. After some years as a dramatic critic for New York newspapers he made his debut as manager in 1867 with the English melodrama, *Under the Gaslight,* and in 1869 became manager of the Fifth Avenue Theatre, New York, where he produced Shakespearean and standard repertory plays with E. L. DAVENPORT, Fanny DAVENPORT, Clara MORRIS and other stars. In 1879 he opened Daly's Theatre, New York, and in 1893 Daly's Theatre in London: his stock company in which John DREW and Ada REHAN were the stars played in both theatres. Among the American actors who owed their training and first success to Daly were Clara Morris, John Drew, Fanny Davenport, Maude ADAMS, and Mrs. GILBERT.

Damnation of Faust, The, a dramatic cantata or opera by Hector BERLIOZ; book based on GOETHE's drama "Faust"; first performed at the Opéra-Comique, Paris, in 1846, and at the Metropolitan Opera House, New York, in 1906. Three excerpts from this work are standard orchestral concert pieces: *Hungarian March, Dance of the Sylphs,* and *Minuet of the Will o' the Wisps.* All of these numbers are available in Columbia and Victor recordings.

Damocles, a courtier of the elder Dionysius of Syracuse (430 B.C.-367 B.C.), a ruler of Syracuse who ruled wisely, and was also a dramatist. According to CICERO and HORACE, when Damocles envied the happiness and security of his sovereign, Dionysius invited him to a banquet at which he found himself seated under a naked sword suspended by a single hair. The moral of this tale, whether it be true or false, is obvious.

Damon and Pythias, the heroes of a Greek legend which runs as follows: Pythias (or correctly Phintias), on being condemned to death by the tyrant, Dionysius the Elder of Syracuse, pleaded for his liberty for a short time to put his affairs in order. Damon pledged his life for the return of his friend, and Pythias came back before the appointed hour. Dionysius was so struck by this manifestation of fidelity that he released both of them.

Damophon, Greek sculptor who worked during the 2nd century B.C.: fragments of colossal heads representing DEMETER, PERSEPHONE and ARTEMIS are preserved where they were found in Arcadia, and also at the Athens Museum. There has been much controversy as to the exact period in which Damophon executed statues for the people of Messene and other Peloponnesian cities.

Damrosch, Frank Heino (1859-1937), American organist, conductor and composer, elder brother of Walter DAMROSCH, who came to the United States with his father, Leopold DAMROSCH in 1871. He was educated at the College of the City of New York and Yale University, and studied music with

Anton BRUCKNER and Moritz MOSZKOWSKI. He conducted many musical societies and choruses in New York and Philadelphia; supervised music in New York Public Schools (1897-1905), and directed the INSTITUTE OF MUSICAL ART, New York, from 1905 to 1933.

Damrosch, Leopold (1832-1885), German violinist and conductor who was educated at Berlin University, and studied music with Franz RIES and Siegfried Dehn. He became solo violinist in the Grand Ducal Orchestra at Weimar, and was an intimate friend of Franz LISZT. After conducting in orchestras in Germany he came to the United States in 1871 to conduct the Arion Society, also founding the ORATORIO SOCIETY in 1873 and the SYMPHONY SOCIETY in 1878. In 1884-85 he organized a German opera company which he conducted with Anton SEIDL at the Metropolitan Opera House, presenting Wagner's "Ring" cycle, *Tristan and Isolde*, and *Die Meistersinger* for the first time in the United States. He was the father of Frank DAMROSCH and Walter DAMROSCH.

Damrosch, Walter Johannes (1862-   ), American composer and conductor, younger brother of Frank DAMROSCH, who came to the United States with his father, Leopold DAMROSCH, in 1871. He studied composition with Felix Draeseke and composition with his father whom he succeeded as conductor of the ORATORIO SOCIETY and the SYMPHONY SOCIETY. After acting as assistant conductor of German opera at the Metropolitan Opera House, New York, from 1885 to 1891, he organized the Damrosch Opera Company (1894-1899). He also conducted Wagner's works at the Metropolitan Opera House (1900-1902) and the Symphony Society from 1885 to 1927 through various reorganizations. His compositions include four grand operas; a comic opera; incidental music; a sonata for violin and piano; numerous songs including the world-famous *Danny Deever*. Since 1928 he has conducted the NATIONAL BROADCASTING COMPANY SYMPHONY ORCHESTRA in weekly music appreciation broadcasts to public schools and colleges in the United States and Canada.

Dana, Richard Henry, the Elder (1787-1879), American essayist and poet whose lectures on Shakespeare's characters aroused public interest in the works of the famous dramatist. His poems include *The Change of Home* (1824), *The Dying Raven*, and *The Buccaneers:* the latter contains realistic descriptions of ocean scenery. His son, **Richard Henry Dana,** the Younger (1815-1882), was obliged to suspend his college studies because of an eye affliction, and shipped as a seaman on a whaling vessel for a two year voyage: he published his experiences in a masterly narrative, *Two Years Before the Mast* (1837). Among the volumes published later were *The Seaman's Friend,* and *To Cuba and Back.*

Danaids, in Greek mythology the fifty daughters of Danaus, king of Argos: they were condemned, all except one, to pour water through sieves in Hades as punishment for murdering their husbands, the fifty sons of Aegyptus, on their wedding night.

Danby, Francis (1793-1861), English painter who was chiefly self-taught: his canvases include *The Upas Tree; The Delivery of the Israelites; Disappointed Love; The Golden Age; The Evening Gun; Fisherman's Home.* Both his sons, James Francis and Thomas, were painters of excellent reputation.

Dance, George, the Elder (1700-1768), English architect who was appointed architect to the city of London: he designed many fine churches and the famous Mansion House. His eldest son, **James Dance** (1722-1744) was educated at Oxford, changed his name to James Love, and became an actor at the Drury Lane Theatre. His brother, **Sir Nathaniel Dance-Holland** (1735-1811), third son of George Dance, the Elder, became a portrait painter of considerable note, and painted George III, his queen, and David GARRICK as Richard III. Another brother, **George Dance,** the Younger (1741-1825), the youngest son of George Dance the Elder, succeeded his father as architect to the city of London; distinguished himself with designs for Blackfriars Bridge, and rebuilt NEWGATE PRISON in 1770. He was one of the founders of the Royal Academy, and also drew seventy-two chalk portraits of his friends which were published in 1808-1814. His son, **Charles Dance** (1794-1863), was one of the first of the burlesque writers: many of his farces were produced by Madame VESTRIS at the Olympic Theatre, London.

Dance, a series of rhythmical steps, with or without varying movements of the body, generally accompanied and timed by music, or in the case of primitive peoples by drums. Dancing is believed to be the most ancient of the arts: it was used in the religious rites of the ancient Egyptians, Hebrews, Chinese, East Indians, and Greeks. The Indians of both North and South America, also employed dancing in their religious ceremonies. After the advent of Christianity, dancing became a favorite amusement of the people, and much of the world's loveliest music was written for folk dancing. The development of ballet also resulted in the creation of musical works which have become immortal, and the same may be said of the dance music written by Johann STRAUSS and others for the ballroom. The acrobatic character of dances since the start of the 20th century, beginning with the cakewalk and ending with the rhumba of the present day, have not proved sources of inspiration to the better class of composers; therefore little music of permanent character has been produced in this field.

Dance of Death (Dance macabre), the theme of an allegorical morality play originating in the 14th century in Germany, and designed to remind the living of the inevitability of death. It became extraordinarily popular, and was treated in tapestry, bas reliefs, and paintings: an excellent example is a series of 53 drawings by Hans HOLBEIN the Younger called *Imagines Mortis,* although they do not represent a dance. The dramatists, STRINDBERG and WEDEKIND, made use of the idea; also Camille SAINT-SAENS in his symphonic poem, DANSE MACABRE.

Dance of the Russian Sailors, see **Red Poppy, The.**

Dance of the Seven Veils (Strauss). an orchestral excerpt from the opera, SALOME, by Richard

STRAUSS, the plot of which follows closely that of the play by Oscar WILDE. Salome, sister of Herod, begs that John the Baptist, who has refused her amorous advances, be slain: she executes the "Dance of the Seven Veils," casting them aside one by one, and finally demands the head of the prophet on a silver platter. Her wish is granted, but Herod has her crushed between the brazen shield of his guards. There is a Columbia recording by the Cleveland Orchestra with Artur Rodzinski, and a Victor recording by the Philadelphia Orchestra under Leopold Stowkowski.

Dancla, Charles (1818-1907), French violinist, teacher, and composer who studied at the Paris Conservatory under Pierre BAILLOT and Jacques HALEVY: after extensive concertizing he became professor of violin at the PARIS CONSERVATORY, and leader of a fine string quartet. His compositions include symphonies, chamber music, and many solo pieces and études for the violin.

Dancourt, Florent Carton (1661-1725), English actor and dramatist who was a great favorite of Louis XIV for his impersonations in the plays of MOLIERE. Among his successful plays were *Le Chevalier à la mode; Les Bourgeoises de qualité; Le galant Jardinier; Les Trois Cousines.*

Dane, Clemence, pseudonymn of **Winifred Ashton,** contemporary English novelist, actress, and dramatist. Among her successful novels are *Regiment of Women; First the Blade; Wandering Stars; Broome Stages.* Her plays include *A Bill of Divorcement; Will Shakespeare; The Way Things Happen; Naboth's Vineyard; Wild December; Moonlight is Silver.* She has also collaborated on several plays with Helen Simpson, and prepared the film scenarios for *Anna Karenina; Fire Over England; Farewell Again; Sidewalks of London; A Bill of Divorcement.*

Danforth, William (1867-1941), American actor and singer who first appeared in juvenile Gilbert and Sullivan companies, and made his formal debut in 1899 on the New York stage in Victor HERBERT's *The Ameer.* He appeared in many successful operettas and musical plays including *The Wizard of the Nile; Miss Hook of Holland; The Yankee Consul; Wang; Happyland; Robin Hood,* and Gilbert and Sullivan operettas.

D'Angelo, Louis (1888-), Italian bass-baritone who came to the United States as a boy, and first sang in church before studying voice in New York. He made his debut in 1912 with the ABORN Opera Company in AIDA, and appeared later with the SAVAGE OPERA COMPANY, the SAN FRANCISCO OPERA ASSOCIATION, and the RAVINIA OPERA COMPANY in Chicago. In 1918 he became a member of the METROPOLITAN OPERA COMPANY: since then he has appeared in 35 Italian, French and German operas. In 1943 he celebrated his twenty-fifth year with the company in a gala performance of ROSSINI's BARBER OF SEVILLE.

Danican, Francois André, see **Philidor.**

Daniel, Arnaud or **Arnaut,** a 12th century troubadour who attached himself to the court of RICHARD COEUR DE LION; he was greatly praised by PETRARCH and DANTE, both of whom used the SESTINA, a form of verse invented by him.

Daniell, Thomas (1749-1840), English painter and etcher famous for his Oriental paintings and engravings published in *Oriental Scenery,* a large six-volume work in which he was assisted by his nephew, **William Daniell** (1769-1837), whose drawings were also published in book form including *A Voyage Around Great Britain.* He also painted a picture of the Hindu method of taming wild elephants. William's brother, Samuel Daniell, published drawings of African and Ceylonese scenery.

Daniels, Bebe (1901-), American stage and screen actress who appeared at four as a child actor in Richard III, and started her screen career at seven as the child lead in the silent film, *A Common Enemy.* At thirteen she was leading woman in Harold LLOYD comedies; among the notable American and British film productions in which she has appeared are *Rio Rita; Reaching for the Moon; Honor of the Family; 42nd Street; Counsellor-at-Law; Registered Nurse; Return of Carol Deane.*

Daniels, Frank (1860-1935), American actor and singer who studied at the NEW ENGLAND CONSERVATORY OF MUSIC, and made his debut in The Chimes of Normandy at Chelsea, Mass., in 1879. Among the operettas and musical plays in which he appeared were The *Beggar Student; A Rag Baby; Princess Bonnie; The Wizard of the Nile; The Idol's Eye; The Ameer; Sergeant Brue; The Tattooed Man.*

Daniel Stern, see **Agoult, Marie Catherine.**

Danilova, Alexandra (1907-), Russian ballerina who studied at the school of the Russian Imperial Ballet, and made her debut at St. Petersburg. In 1924 she appeared with George BALANCHINE's company at the Empire Theatre, London; joined the Serge DIAGHILEFF Company in 1925, and remained until Diaghileff's death in 1929. Her greatest successes include The FIRE-BIRD, The SLEEPING PRINCESS, PETROUCHKA; Le BEAU DANUBE, Carnaval, and La BOUTIQUE FANTASQUE.

Dannat, William T. (1853-1929), American painter who studied at the Munich Academy and with Paul MUNKACSY in Paris. He attracted attention first with pictures made in Spain: his canvases include *La Robe Rouge; The Quartette; Cafe Chantant; Sacristy in Arragon:* he also became a very successful portrait painter.

Dannay, Frederic, see **Queen, Ellery.**

Dannecker, Johann Heinrich von (1759-1841), German sculptor who studied with Augustin PAJOU in Paris, and with Antonio CANOVA in Rome where he met GOETHE with whom he developed a life-long intimacy. Later he became professor of sculpture and finally director at the Academy of Stuttgart. Among his notable works are statues of *Ceres* and *Bacchus; Girl Lamenting Her Dead Bird; Sappho; Psyche; Ariadne on a Panther;* a statue of Christ, statues of SCHILLER and Count Metternich.

Dannreuther, Edward George (1844-1905), Alsatian pianist and musicographer who studied at the Leipzig Conservatory with Hans RICHTER and Ignaz MOSCHELES. He settled in England in 1861, presenting for the first time the piano concertos of CHOPIN, GRIEG and TSCHAIKOWSKY, and conducting the music dramas of Richard WAGNER and works of modern composers. His works include contributions to "Groves' Dictionary of Music," a two-volume treatise, *Musical Ornamentation,* and *The Romantic Period,* the sixth volume of the "Oxford History of Music." He lectured on music several times in the United States.

D'Annunzio, Gabriele, see **Annunzio, Gabriele d'.**

Danse Macabre (Saint-Saëns), a symphonic poem inspired by verses written by Dr. Henry Cazalis (Jean Labor), and first performed in 1784 at Paris. The synopsis is as follows: "Death beats a measure, drums on a tomb, plays a dance at night on his old violin. Skeletons come out of their hiding to dance in their shrouds, and listen to the rattling of bones: in a twinkling the dance is over for the cock has crowed." The XYLOPHONE is introduced to simulate the rattling of bones. There is a Columbia recording by the Chicago Orchestra with Frederick Stock, and a Victor recording by the Philadelphia Orchestra with Leopold Stokowski.

Danses Slaves et Tziganes, a Russian folk ballet; choreography by Bronislava Nijinsky; music by Alexander DARGOMYZHSKY; first produced at the Metropolitan Opera House, New York, in 1936. The ballet has no plot; the music for the Russian and gypsy folk dances are taken from Dargomyzhsky's opera, *Roussalka.*

Danseur, in ballet the French name for a male dancer: the principal male dancer is called *premier danseur.* A female dancer is known as a *danseuse;* the principal female dancer as a *première danseuse.* In Italian a female dancer is known as a *ballerina,* and the principal female dancer as a *prima ballerina.*

Dantan, Joseph Édouard (1848-1897), French painter, son of Jean Pierre Dantan (1800-1869), a well-known sculptor. He studied with Isadore PILS, and executed many historical paintings including *Destruction of Pompeii; Hercules at the Feet of Omphale; Monk Carving a Crucifix; Corner of a Studio; Christ Calling Peter and Andrew; Burial of a Child; Entr'acte during a First Night at the Theatre.* He also made illustrations for books by Émile ZOLA and Victor HUGO.

Dante (originally **Durante**) **Alighieri** (1265-1321), Italian poet and philosopher: his parents belonged to an ancient Roman family, and his birthplace is supposed to have been Florence although Ravenna is given by some authorities. He met BEATRICE PORTINARI when she was a child of eight: she aroused feelings in him of what has been variously described as romantic passion or impersonal, platonic love. His *La Vita nuova* (The New Love), written in 1292, relates the story of his affection for her, yet her marriage in 1287 to Simone de'Bardi did not disturb him greatly,

and he married Gemma Donati shortly after she died. From 1290 to 1303 Dante was involved in political struggles from which he emerged a disappointed man who passed the rest of his life wandering in Italy watching the trend of events from various retreats. His works beside "La Vita nuova" already mentioned include *The Divine Comedy; Convito* (Banquet), an allegorical poem; lyrics, epistles, eclogues, and various treatises.

Daphne, in Greek mythology, the daughter of the Arcadian river god, Ladon: when she was pursued by the amorous Apollo, her mother, Gaea, changed her into a laurel tree sacred to the god.

Daphnis and Chloë, in literature a Greek pastoral romance attributed to Longus, the great sophist of the 4th or 5th century, although the manuscript found at Mount Cassin does not name the author. The tale of bucolic life and love has had many imitators since the first version appeared in 1559; the finest is Bernardin de Saint Pierre's *Paul and Virginia.*

Daphnis and Chloë, a ballet in one act; libretto and choreography by Michel FOKINE; music by Maurice RAVEL; first produced in 1912 at Paris. The plot revolves around the love of Daphnis, a shepherd, for Chloë, a village maiden, and is taken from a romance written by Longus, a Greek sophist of the 5th century A.D. Greek sculpture is the source of the dances, and Ravel's music is regarded as one of the finest accomplishments in modern French music. There are recordings by both Columbia and Victor of the two orchestral suites arranged by the composer from the music of the ballet.

Da Ponte, Lorenzo (1749-1838), Italian poet who wrote the librettos for several of MOZART's operas including DON GIOVANNI, *Così fan tutte,* and The MARRIAGE OF FIGARO. He came to the United States in 1805, and remained there until his death. Among his various unsuccessful enterprises was the Italian Opera House at New York built in 1833. For some years he taught Italian at Columbia University: his memoirs were published in four volumes (1823-1827).

D'Arblay, Madame, see **Arblay, Madame d'.**

Dargomyzhsky, Alexander (1813-1869), Russian composer whose first opera, *Esmeralda,* was a great success in 1847: it was followed in 1856 by ROUSSALKA, his best work, and in 1867 by an opera-ballet, *The Triumph of Bacchus.* His posthumous opera, *The Stone Guest,* was orchestrated by Nicholas RIMSKY-KORSAKOW, and produced at St. Petersburg in 1872. He also composed many instrumental pieces and songs.

Dario, Felix Ruben (1867-1916), Spanish-American poet, born in Nicaragua: his first volume of verse and prose, *Azul* (Blue), appeared in 1888, and was followed by *Profanas and Other Poems; Songs of Life and Hope; Wandering Song.* His autobiography appeared in 1918 in the collected edition of his works.

Darley, Felix Octavius Carr (1822-1888), American painter and illustrator famous for his drawings illustrating the works of James Fenimore COOPER, Washington IRVING, Henry W. LONGFELLOW, Charles DICKENS, Nathaniel HAWTHORNE, and many other famous authors. He was also the author of *Sketches Abroad with Pen and Pencil* (1868) which was a best seller in its field.

Darrieux, Danielle (1917-   ), French screen actress and singer educated at Lycée LaTour and the PARIS CONSERVATORY OF MUSIC. Her appearances in the films include *The Crisis is Ended; Nero; Mayerling; Women's Club; The Rage of Paris; Counsel for Romance; Mademoiselle My Mother; Katia.*

D'Artagnan, see **Artagnan, Charles de Baatz d'.**

D'Arville, Camille (1863-1932), Dutch light opera prima donna who appeared first at London, England, at the Strand Theatre in operettas, and later with the Carl Rosa Company. Among the light operas in which she appeared in the United States from 1888 were *The Grand Duchess; The Daughter of Madame Angot;* ROBIN HOOD; *The Knickerbockers; Madeleine, or The Magic Kiss.*

Daskam, Josephine Dodge, see **Bacon, Josephine Dodge Daskam.**

Dass, Petter (1647-1708), Norwegian poet considered the father of modern Norwegian poetry although few of his works were published during his lifetime: they include *The Trumpet of Nordland* (1739), a rhymed description of Nordland from which the inhabitants of that province can repeat long extracts; *The Norwegian Song of the Valley; Spiritual Pastime.* His works are full of curious mental reactions, homely fancies, and genuine humor.

Dauberval or **D'Auberval** (1742-1806), French ballet dancer and choreographer who studied with Jean NOVERRE, and made his debut as premier danseur at L'Opéra, Paris, in 1763. He left the opera house in 1783, and produced several ballets from 1785 to 1791 at Bordeaux including *La Fille Mal Gardée,* his best work; *Le Deserteur; L'Epreuve Villageoise, Télémaque.* He did much toward advancing Noverre's theories, and is regarded as the inventor of the comedy element in ballet.

Daubigny, Charles François (1817-1878), French painter who studied with his father and in Italy, finally becoming allied with the BARBIZON SCHOOL. He was already established as a landscape painter when he was twenty years old: later he made several visits to England and Holland. His notable paintings and etchings include *Stormy Weather; The Little Cavaliers; Moonrise in the Valley of Andilly; Springtime; Return of the Flock—Moonlight; Windmills at Dordrecht; The Banks of the Oise; Moonlight.* For his river scenes he built himself a kind of cabin on a barge in which he floated on the Seine or Oise Rivers: the washerwomen on the shores nicknamed the boat "Le Botin" (the little box).

Daudet, Alphonse (1840-1897), French poet, novelist, and dramatist whose first published poems were a failure. Greater success came with two

plays, *The Last Idol* (1862) and *The White Daisy* (1865), but his true field, that of a novelist, was discovered in the charming stories, *The Little Thing* and *Story of a Child.* His novel, *Fromont Jr. and Risler Sr.* was translated into all European languages, and not less famous were *The Nabob, Kings in Exile,* and *Sappho.* A novel and happy vein was struck in the *Tartarin de Tarascon* series of novels; he also wrote interesting reminiscences entitled *Thirty Years of Paris.* His wife, Julia Allard Daudet, collaborated with him and also penned some interesting volumes of impressions and recollections of her distinguished husband. Daudet's son, **Leon Daudet** (1868-   ), was also a novelist: he wrote a biography of his father, and several realistic novels such as *Germe et Poussière* and *L'Astre noir.* **Louis Marie Ernest Daudet** (1837-1921), brother of Alphonse Daudet, wrote historical studies and several novels including *The Venus of Gordes; The Bloom of Sin; Martha:* he also published an autobiography entitled *My Brother and Myself.*

Daughter of the Regiment, The, comic opera in two acts: libretto by Saint-Georges and Bayard; music by Gaetano Donizetti; first produced at Paris in 1840, and at New York in 1843. The story is slight; that of a young and pretty vivandière in the French army, Marie, who becomes ennobled, but finally marries her sweetheart, Tonio, a mountain lad who has risen to the rank of an officer. The opera was revived recently at the Metropolitan Opera House, New York, for Lily PONS who has made Victor recordings of the three popular arias.

Daumet, Pierre Jerome Honoré (1826-1911), French architect who studied at the ECOLE DES BEAUX-ARTS, Paris, and was awarded the Prix de Rome in 1855. He is famous for his restorations of old French buildings including the castle at Chantilly and the Palace of Justice at Paris: in 1889 his designs exhibited at the Paris Exposition won a gold medal.

Daumier, Honoré Victorin (1808-1879), French painter and caricaturist who mastered the lithographic art at an early age, and made plates for music publishers, advertisers and book publishers. His cartoon, *Gargantua,* a caricature of Louis-Philippe, led to his imprisonment in 1832: upon his release he continued his war on the corruption of the government and the foibles of bourgeois society with *Parisian Emotions, The Bohemians of Paris,* and *Ancient History.* Among his fine paintings are *Christ and His Apostles; The Good Samaritan; Third-class Carriage; Don Quixote and Sancho Panza.*

D'Avenant, Sir William (1606-1668), English poet, dramatist, and producer: some authorities contend that he was a son of William Shakespeare. His first play, *Albovine,* was produced in 1629: he was appointed poet laureate in 1638 and in 1639 became manager of the Cockpit, the first theatre on Drury Lane, London. During the Civil Wars he adhered to the Crown and was knighted in 1643: in 1651 he was accused of treason, and was saved from death by the poet John MILTON. His numerous dramatic works include a comedy, *The Wits,* and the first English opera, *The Siege* *of Rhodes.* He also is said to have been the first to introduce scene shifting, and to have women playing in his productions.

Davenport, Edward Loomis (1816-1877), American actor who played minor parts in 1836 with Junius Brutus Booth, and later appeared as leading man for Cora Mowatt, accompanying her to London where he played with William Macready. He was outstanding as Hamlet, Brutus, and in other Shakespearean roles, but equally at home in character parts such as Bill Sykes and Sir Giles Overreach. He was the father of Fanny Davenport; his son, **Harry Davenport** (1866-) born in New York, is a stage and screen actor who appeared as a child with Joseph Jefferson, in *Rip Van Winkle,* and with John McCullough in Richard III. His formal stage debut was made in Monte Cristo, and he has appeared in many plays including *La Tosca; Sweet Lavender; Money; the Burgomaster; The Goddess; The Naked Truth; Lightnin'; The Music Master; Hay Fever; Topaz; Three Men on a Horse.* He has played important roles in numerous films including *The Life of Zola; You Can't Take It With You; The Story of Alexander Graham Bell; Gone With the Wind; All This and Heaven Too; For- eign Correspondent.*

Davenport, Fanny Lily Gipsy (1850-1898), American actress, born in England: her father was the distinguished actor, Edward Loomis Davenport, and she played juvenile parts in 1858 in New York in his company. She learned much from Mrs. John Drew at the Arch Street Theatre, Philadelphia, and also from Augustin Daly as a member of his stock company from 1869 to 1877. She toured the United States successfully for many years with her own company, appearing in *Hamlet, Falstaff,* and other Shakespearean plays: she also achieved fame in Sardou's *La Tosca, Fedora,* and *Cleopatra.*

Davenport, Homer (1867-1912), American cartoonist who was self-taught, and for many years on the staff of the Hearst newspapers. His cartoons played an important part in the Spanish-American War, and in Theodore Roosevelt's campaign of 1904. Among his well-remembered drawings may be mentioned the kindly representation of *Uncle Sam,* the arrogant figure, *Trust,* and the caricature of Mark Hanna with the dollar-marked suit.

Davenport, Marcia (1903-), American writer on music educated at Wellesley College and at the University of Grenoble, France: her books include *Mozart* (1932), *Of Lena Geyer,* and *The Valley of Decision.* She has also acted as music critic for *The Stage,* and as a radio commentator on operas for the Metropolitan, San Francisco, and Salzburg opera companies.

David, Félicien (1810-1876), French composer who studied at the Paris Conservatory under Henri Reber and Joseph Fetis. In 1844 a symphonic ode, *Le Désert,* was received with the greatest enthusiasm: it was followed in 1851 by an opera, *The Pearl of Brazil,* which was also a brilliant success. One of the coloratura arias in the latter work, "Charmant oiseau," is still considered among the finest of its kind.

David, Ferdinand (1810-1873), German violinist, teacher and composer who studied with Louis Spohr and Moritz Hauptmann. In 1836 Felix Mendelssohn secured his appointment as concertmaster of the Gewandhaus Orchestra, Leipzig, and in 1843 professor of violin at the Leipzig Conservatory where August Wilhelmj and Joseph Joachim were among his many distinguished pupils. His greatest works were a violin method and the *High School of Violin Playing:* he also composed symphonies, chamber music, and many concertos and concert pieces for the violin in addition to editing practically all the great violin works of the classic masters.

David, Gerard (c.1450-1523), Flemish painter regarded as the last great artist of the Bruges school, and said to have been influenced by Van Eyck, Van der Weyden, Memling, and Matsys. His notable works include *Birth of Christ; Adoration of the Shepherds; Piéta; Judgment of Cambyses; Christ Taking Leave of His Mother; Last Judgment; Rest on the Flight into Egypt; Descent from the Cross; The Crucifixion; Marriage of St. Catharine; Madonna with Angels and Saints.*

David, Jacques Louis (1748-1825), French painter who studied with François Boucher and J. M. Vien, winning the Prix de Rome in 1775 with his canvas, *Loves of Antiochus and Stratonice.* His most important paintings include *Blind Belisarius Asking Alms; The Grief of Andromache; The Oath of the Horatii; Love of Paris and Helen; Brutus; Coronation of Napoleon I; Marat Assassinated; Rape of the Sabines; Distribution of the Eagles; Napoleon on Horseback; The Sabines; Death of the Sabines.* He also painted many portraits including that of Mme. Récamier which was left unfinished.

David, Pierre Jean (1789-1856), French sculptor who studied at the Ecole des Beaux-Arts in Paris, and after winning the Prix de Rome with the painting *Epaminondas,* spent five years in Rome where he conceived a great admiration for Antonio Canova's works. When he returned to Paris, he received many commissions for monuments among which was the memorial to the Greek liberator, *Bozzaris:* it consists of a young female figure called *Reviving Greece* of which Victor Hugo said: "It is difficult to see anything more beautiful in the world." His notable works include *Philopoemen; The Great Condé;* Thomas Jefferson and Lafayette; the last two are in Washington, D. C. The Musée David at Angers has an almost complete collection of his sculptures.

David, Statue of, a colossal figure of the Biblical character, *David,* executed by Michelangelo out of an enormous block of marble on which another sculptor, Agostino d'Antonio di Duccio, had worked unsuccessfully nearly a half century before. Michelangelo paid little attention to previous treatment of the subject, but executed his own conception in the form of a youthful, frowning giant tensely bent on destroying his enemy, *Goliath.* It was set up on the terrace of the Palace of the Signory at Florence in 1504, and removed in 1882 to a hall in the Academy of Fine Arts in the same city.

Davidson, Donald (1893-), American poet and essayist educated at Vanderbilt University: his poetical works include *An Outland Piper* (1924); *The Tall Men; Lee in the Mountains and Other Poems*. He also edited *British Poetry of the Eighteen-Nineties*.

Davidson, Jo (1883-), American sculptor of Russian extraction who studied at the ART STUDENTS' LEAGUE, New York, and the Yale School of Fine Arts: also under the direction of George de Forest Brush and Hermon A. MacNeil, and at the ECOLE DES BEAUX-ARTS, Paris. He proved himself a master of portrait sculpture: after World War I he was authorized to make bronze busts of Woodrow Wilson, General Pershing, Colonel House, Field-Marshal Haig, Marshal Joffre and Marshal Foch. He has also made a head of Franklin D. Roosevelt much praised for its fidelity.

Davidson, John (1857-1900), Scotch novelist and poet whose volumes of verses include *Fleet Street Eclogues; A Random Itinerary; Ballads and Songs; Earl Lavender*. He also wrote two novels entitled *Perfervid* and *Baptist Lake*.

Davies, Arthur Bowen (1862-1928), American painter who studied at the Art Institute of Chicago, the ART STUDENTS' LEAGUE, New York, and in Italy with the financial aid of Benjamin ALTMAN. His earlier paintings reflect something comparable to WATTEAU, but he finally developed a symbolic, abstract style which gave unmistakable evidence of his imaginative ability. Among his best canvases are *The Girdle of Aries; Dream; Maya, Mirror of Illusions; Spring in a Valley; Night Overture; Children of Yesterday; After-Thoughts of Earth*.

Davies, Ben (1858-), Welsh operatic, oratorio, and concert tenor who studied at the Royal Academy of Music, and made his debut in The Bohemian Girl with the Carl Rosa Opera Company in 1881. His success later as an oratorio singer led him to devote himself almost exclusively to concert work except to assume the title role in Sir Arthur Sullivan's grand opera, *Ivanhoe*, in 1891. He toured the United States and Germany several times.

Davies, David Thomas Ffrangcon, see **Ffrangcon-Davies, David Thomas.**

Davies, Marion (1900-), American screen actress who has appeared in many silent and talking films including *When Knighthood Was in Flower* (1918); *Little Old New York; Beverly of Graustark; Quality Street; The Floradora Girl; Polly of the Circus; Page Miss Glory; Cain and Mabel.*

Da Vignola, see **Barocchio, Jacopo.**

Da Vinci, Leonardo, see **Leonardo da Vinci.**

Davis, Alexander Jackson (1803-1892), American architect who designed many important buildings for Federal and State governments including the Custom House, New York, the Patent Office, Washington, D. C., and several state capitols. He

was one of the greatest architects of his period, and a founder of the American Institute of Architects.

Davis, Bette (1908-), American screen actress who entered the films in 1930 after some stage experience; among the numerous films in which she appeared are *The Crowd Roars; Three on a Match; Of Human Bondage; Special Agent; Dangerous; Petrified Forest; Jezebel; The Sisters; The Old Maid; All This and Heaven Too; The Man Who Came to Dinner; The Little Foxes; In This Our Life; Now Voyager.*

Davis, Charles Harold (1856-1933), American painter whose works are to be seen in many American museums and galleries: his realistic style is plainly evident in such canvases as *An Evening in Winter; Evening after the Storm; Late Afternoon; The Brook; Valley in the Evening; Twilight.*

Davis, Elmer Holmes (1890-), American essayist, novelist, journalist, and radio commentator educated at Franklin College and Queens College. His works include *History of the New York Times* (1921); *Times Have Changed*, a novel; *I'll Show You the Town*, a novel; *Strange Women*, a novel; *Show Window*, a volume of essays; *White Pants Willie*, a novel; *Love Among the Ruins*, a volume of short stories; *Not To Mention the War*, a book of essays. Mr. Davis was named director in 1942 of a new Office of War Information for the dissemination of news and propaganda concerning World War II.

Davis, Frederick William (1858-1933), American author of dime novels in the "Nick Carter" series under the pen names "Nicholas Carter" and "Scott Campbell."

Davis, Owen (1874-), American dramatist educated at the University of Tennessee and Harvard University: his first play *Through the Breakers*, was produced in 1898 and was followed by several more sensational melodramas. He has written or adapted more than three hundred plays of which the following are outstanding: *Alibi* (1919); *Detour; The Nervous Wreck; Icebound*, winner of the Pulitzer Prize in 1923; *The Great Gatsby; The Good Earth; Jezebel; Etham Frome; Mr. and Mrs. North*. He has also prepared screen and radio scenarios for some of his plays.

Davis, Rebecca Harding (1831-1910), American short-story writer and novelist who contributed to the *Atlantic Monthly* and other magazines: her works include *Life in the Iron Mills* (1861); *Margaret Howth; A Law Unto Herself; Berrytown; Waiting for the Verdict; Dallas Galbraith; Kent Hampden; Natasqua; Frances Walstrup; Doctor Warrick's Daughters*. She was the mother of Richard Harding DAVIS.

Davis, Richard Harding (1864-1916), American journalist, novelist, and playwright; son of Rebecca Harding DAVIS, distinguished novelist. His success as a journalist started with his report on the Johnstown Flood in 1889, and as an author with the publication of *Gallagher and Other Stories* in 1891. Among his successful stories and novels are *Stories for Boys; Van Bibber and Others; Our English Cousins; Princess Aline; Soldiers of Fortune; In the Fog; Ransom's Folly; The Bar Sinister.* His most successful plays were *The Dictator* and *Miss Civilization;* also a musical comedy, *The Girl from Home.*

Davison, Edward Lewis (1898-), American poet born in Glasgow, Scotland: his works include *Poems* (1920); *Harvest of Youth; The Heart's Unreason; The Ninth Witch and Other Critical Essays.* He also edited *Cambridge Poets, 1914-1920.*

Dawson, Coningsby William (1883-), Anglo-American novelist and poet who was graduated from Merton College, Oxford, in 1905, and came to the United States with his family during the same year. He served with the Canadian Expeditionary Force during World War I: in 1920-21 he traveled through Central and Eastern Europe in the interests of American relief for starving children. His works include *The Worker and Other Poems* (1906); *The House of the Weeping Woman; Murder Point; Road to Avalon; The Kingdom Round the Corner; The Unknown Soldier; The Auctioning of Mary Angel; Inspiration Valley; Tell Us of the Night.*

Day, Clarence Shepard (1874-1935), American illustrator and author educated at Yale University: his grandfather, Benjamin H. Day, founded the New York *Sun,* and his uncle was the inventor of the Ben Day process of engraving. His works include *This Simian World* (1920); *The Crow's Nest,* revised as *After All; Thoughts Without Words; God and My Father; Life With Father; Life With Mother.*

Day, Holman Francis (1865-1935), American novelist and poet educated at Colby College: his works include *Up in Maine* (1900); *Squire Phin; King Spruce; The Ramrodders; The Red Lane; The Rider of the King Log; The Loving are the Daring; Leadbetter's Luck; Starwagons; Ships of Joy.*

Dazey, Charles Turner (1855-1938), American dramatist: his plays include *In Old Kentucky* (1893); *The War of Wealth; Home Folks; The Suburbans; The American Lord* with George Broadhurst; *The Stranger; A Night Out* with May Robson.

De Angelis, Jefferson (1859-1933), American singer, comedian, and manager of his own opera company which toured the world from 1880 to 1884. He sang in more than one hundred light operas with Colonel McCaull's company (1887-1890), and was principal comedian in a series of musical comedies at the Casino Theatre, New York, from 1891 to 1895. In 1897-8 he appeared with Lillian Russell and Della Fox in *The Wedding Day*: his greatest success was achieved in *Fantana* at the Lyric Theatre, New York, in 1905.

Dearth, Henry Golden (1864-1918), American painter who studied at the Ecole des Beaux-Arts, Paris: his paintings of forest scenes and sand dunes in the bluish-grey of twilight are highly regarded. Among his finest canvases are *Old Church at Montreuil; In the Gloaming; Cornelia; Sunset in Normandy; Dreamland.*

Death and the Maiden (Schubert), the name given to the *String Quartet in D minor* by Franz Schubert because the second movement introduces his song, "Death and the Maiden," embellished with five superb variations. Despite the fact that Schubert, because of his early death, was not supposed to have had sufficiently great experience in chamber music composition, the quartet is the peer of the finest works of either Mozart or Beethoven: there is a Victor recording by the Busch Quartet, and a Columbia recording by the Roth Quartet.

Death and Transfiguration (Strauss), an orchestral tone poem composed by Richard Strauss in 1888-89, and first performed under the direction of the composer at Eisenach in 1890. The musical synopsis is as follows: a sick man fights for his life with Death, and in his delirium recalls his childhood, youth and manhood. When Death finally strikes, deliverance—Transfiguration—is granted him in Heaven. There is a Victor recording by the Philadelphia Orchestra with Leopold Stokowski.

De Basil, Colonel Wassily, contemporary Russian impresario, director-general of the Ballet Russe de Monte Carlo. After a distinguished military career, he became manager for the pianist, Vladimir Horowitz and took the Russian Opera Company, of which Feodor Chaliapin was a member, on tour through Europe. In 1931 he gave a few evenings of ballet in connection with an opera company organized as *L'Opéra Russe à Paris;* they were so successful that he organized the Ballet Russe de Monte Carlo, creating a new worldwide interest in the art by employing the finest choreographers such as Massine, Fokine, Balanchine, Bronisla Nijinska, and the greatest dancers including Lichine, Woizikovsky, Danilova, Verchinina, Baranova, Lifar and Markova. The ballet master was Leonide Massine, and the company was a feature at Covent Garden from 1934 to 1937: it has also toured the United States for several seasons since 1933.

De Beck, William Morgan (1890-1942), American painter and cartoonist, known to his legion of admirers as "Billy de Beck": he studied at the Academy of Fine Arts, Chicago, and for a time was distinguished for his imitations of the drawings of Charles Dana Gibson. His most famous cartoon, *Barney Google and Spark Plug* originated in 1919, and has appeared continuously ever since: it became such a favorite with the comic-strip readers that a popular song by Billy Rose and Con Conrad with the title "Barney Google" enjoyed an enormous sale. Some of the expressions he originated, such as "heebie-jeebies," "horse-feathers," and "time's a'wastin'," have become slang classics.

De Brosse, Jehan (c.1562-1626), French architect considered the greatest designer of the first half of the 17th century: in 1614 he became architect to Henry IV of France, and built the Palais du Luxembourg (known at the time as the Palais Medicis for the queen-mother, Marie de Medicis.

In order to bring water to the elaborate fountain in the palace, he built the aqueduct of Arcueil. His son, **Paul de Brosse,** was also an architect who worked on the cathedral at Troyes.

Deburau, Gaspard (1796-1846), French actor who charmed audiences and created an entirely new role for himself in the ancient character of Pierrot. According to Sheldon Cheney "it was Deburau who fixed Pierrot in the mold we all visualize now at the mention of the name; sad, powdery, languishing, poetic." His son, **Charles Deburau** (1829-1873) carried on in the same tradition, but never equaled his father's ability as a mime.

Debussy, Claude Achille (1862-1918), French composer who was admitted to the Paris Conservatory at eleven: he studied piano with Francois Marmontel, composition with Ernest Guiraud, and won the Grand Prix de Rome in 1884 with his cantata, *L'Enfant Prodigue.* He was the acknowledged leader of the modern impressionistic school as a brilliant colorist in the field of orchestra music, and as the originator of an entirely new type of piano music in both the technical and the musical sense. His principal works include an opera, *Pelléas et Mélisande;* the orchestral tone poem, *Afternoon of a Faun; La Mer; Images;* three *Nocturnes* for orchestra and women's chorus; a string quartet; *Fantasie* for piano and orchestra; *Rhapsodie* for saxophone and orchestra; three ballets; suites, preludes and other solo pieces for piano; many songs.

Decameron, The, a collection of one hundred tales by Giovanni Boccaccio; ten of these are represented as told each day for ten days during the plague in 1348 at Florence. They were written between 1344 and 1350, and are preceded by a splendid description of the plague. The stories range from the pathetic to the licentious, but there are few works which have as much influence on literature: they are regarded by some critics as the foundation on which the modern short story rests.

De Camp, Joseph Rodefer (1858-1923), American painter who studied with Frank Duveneck and at the Royal Academy in Munich; later he taught at the Pennsylvania Academy of Fine Arts, Philadelphia, and the Boston Museum of Fine Arts. His notable works include *The New Gown; Woman Drying Her Hair; Little Hotel;* also several fine portraits.

Decamps, Alexandre Gabriel (1803-1860), French painter who studied with his father, and later with Abel de Pujol, Louis David, and Jean Ingres. His notable paintings include *Lapwing Shooting; Turkish Patrol; Ronde de Nuit; Children at a Fountain; Samson; The Good Samaritan; Joseph Sold by His Brethren; The Watering Place; The Monkey Connoisseurs,* a satire on the jury of the French Academy of Painting. He was one of the founders of the French Romantic School with Ingres, Delacroix, and others.

De Cordoba, Pedro (1881-), American actor who made his debut in 1902 at Utica, N. Y., in *If I Were King* with E. H. Sothern. He made his first appearance in 1903 at New York in *The Proud Prince,* and from 1904 to 1907 played Shakespearean parts with the Sothern-Marlowe Company. Among the plays in which he has appeared are *Don Caesar de Bazan; Merely Mary Ann; The Master of the House; Joseph and His Brethren; Lady Windermere's Fan; the Wanderer; Tiger Rose; Nemesis; Laucelot and Elaine; The Servant in the House; Woman of Bronze;* also many of Shakespeare's plays. He has appeared in many silent films.

De Coster, Charles Theodore Henri (1827-1879), Belgian poet and dramatist: his works include a poem, *The Owl's Mirror;* a volume entitled *Flemish Legends; Stories of Brabant;* a comedy, *Jenny.* His master work was *The Legend and the Heroic Adventures, Joyous and Glorious, of Till Eulenspiegel,* written in antiquated style and derived largely from the famous medieval allegory, "Renard the Fox."

Decourcelle, Pierre (1856-), French novelist and dramatist whose first play, *The Ace of Clubs,* was a tremendous success for Sarah Bernhardt, followed by a long series of dramas, comedies, and musical plays including *The Amazon; The Abbé Constantin,* founded on Ludovic Halévy's novel; *The Man with the Broken Ear,* based on Edmond About's story. He also scored sensational success with his novels, *The Gray Hat* and *Fan Fan.*

Deeping, George Warwick (1877-), English novelist educated at Cambridge University: his works include *Uther and Igraine* (1903); *The Bridge of Desire; The House of Adventure; The Captive Wife; Sorrell and Son; Ten Commandments; Seven Men Came Back; The Woman at the Door; The Malice of Men; The Dark House.*

Defauw, Desiré (1885-), Belgian orchestral conductor who studied the violin with Johan Smit. In 1914 he founded the Defauw String Quartet, later becoming professor of violin at the Antwerp Conservatory, and conductor of the Defauw Concerts at Brussels. In 1938 and 1940 he acted as guest conductor of the National Broadcasting Company Symphony Orchestra in New York, and also conducted the Symphony Orchestra in Montreal, Canada: in 1943 he succeeded Frederick Stock as conductor of the Chicago Symphony Orchestra.

Defoe, Daniel (c.1660-1731), English essayist and novelist who first became famous through his various political, economic, and social tracts: one of these, *The Shortest Way with the Dissenters* (1703) resulted in his imprisonment. He was also a prolific writer of fiction including *Robinson Crusoe* (1719) his most famous work; *Further Adventures of Robinson Crusoe; King of Pirates; Memoirs of a Cavalier; Captain Singleton; Moll Flanders,* an extraordinary novel; *Roxana; Journal of the Plague Year.* The last-named is an account of an event which took place before Defoe was born, yet so true to the actual facts and vividly written that it would seem to be penned by someone who actually passed through the awful visitation of death.

Defregger, Franz von (1835-1921), Austrian painter who studied at the Munich Academy, in

Paris, and with Ferdinand PILOTY at Munich. His notable canvases include *The Forester's Last Return; The Beggar Singers; The Zither Player; Andreas Hofer's Last Walk; The Fashionable Tyrolese; The Dance;* the last named picture brought 48,000 francs at an auction sale in 1883. The humor and characterization in his painting often surpass the drawing and coloring.

Degas, Edgar Hilaire Germain (1834-1917), French painter who studied at the ECOLE DES BEAUX-ARTS, Paris, and spent some time studying the Italian masters' works at Rome. He belonged to the impressionist school, and never wearied of painting contemporary life in oil, tempera or pastel. His notable paintings include *The Star Dancer; "Robert Le Diable" Ballet; Dancer Fastening her Sandal; Dancers Practicing at the Bar; Woman at her Toilet; The Rehearsal; Woman with Chrysanthemums.*

Degree, in music one of the eight consecutive tones in a major or minor diatonic scale: the method of counting is from the lowest note (keynote) upwards. The word *step* is also used in the same connection.

De Greef, Arthur (1862-), Belgian composer and pianist who studied the piano with Louis Brassin and Franz LISZT, toured Europe and England playing many of his friend, Edvard GRIEG's works, and taught at the Brussels Conservatory, also making many fine recordings. His compositions include a concerto and a fantasy for piano; orchestral works; a sonata for two pianos; many piano pieces.

De Haas, Maurice Frederick Hendrick (1832-1895), American painter, born in Holland, who studied at the Rotterdam Academy and with some of the English water-colorists in London. He settled in New York in 1859, and gained a considerable reputation for his water colors including *Rapids above Niagara; Farragut Passing the Forts at the Battle of New Orleans; Tropical Sunset at Sea.* His brother, **William Frederick De Haas** (1830-1880) was also a painter of marine scenes; he lived in the United States from 1854.

De Havilland, Olivia (1916-), American screen actress who has appeared since 1935 in many films including *Midsummer Night's Dream; Captain Blood; Anthony Adverse; Charge of the Light Brigade; The Great Garrick; Dodge City; Gone With the Wind; Raffles; The Male Animal.*

Dehodencq, Edme Alexis Alfred (1822-1882), French painter who studied with Leon COGNIET: that he spent considerable time in Spain and North Africa is evident in the stirringly glowing coloring of his pictures such as *Bull Fight in Spain, Morocco Story Teller,* and *Jewish Festival in Tangiers.* His masterpiece is probably the painting in the Louvre depicting the arrest of Charlotte Corday.

Deineka (or Deyneka), Alexander (1899-), Russian painter and engraver who studied at the Kharkov Art School in 1915, and at the State Higher Art and Technical School at Moscow in 1921. He illustrated the book, *In the Fire,* by

Henri Barbusse; also a number of children's books. His poster designs were widely exhibited in Russia, Western Europe and the United States. In paintings such as *The Russian Riviera* he pictures the modern type of Russian factory worker in his original way, painting in oil, watercolor and inks with equal facility.

Déjazet, Pauline (1798-1875), French actress who became so successful in soubrette or ingenue parts at the Gymnaze, Paris, from 1820 to 1827 that roles of this character became known as *Déjazets:* at her own Thêatre Déjazet she played youthful parts in SARDOU's plays marvelously when she was sixty-five years of age.

Dekker, Edward Douwes (1820-1887), Dutch dramatist and novelist who used the pseudonym "Multatule." He spent several years in government service in the Dutch East Indies, and wrote a novel, *Max Havelaar,* in which he directly accused the Dutch Government of shocking maladministration of its colonies. He also wrote an admirable volume, *Parables;* also a novel, *The Blessed Virgin.*

Dekker, Thomas (c.1570-1641), English dramatist about whom little is known before 1600 when his plays began to be produced with considerable success. Among them were *Shoemaker's Holiday; Old Fortunatus; The Honest Whore* with Thomas MIDDLETON; *Westward, Ho!* with John WEBSTER; *The Roaring Girl* with Thomas Middleton; *The Virgin Martyr* with Philip MASSINGER. When Ben JONSON ridiculed him in a play, *The Poetaster,* Dekker retaliated with his comedy, *Satiromastex,* and apparently got the best of the argument.

De Koven, Reginald (1859-1920), American composer, critic and conductor who was educated at Oxford, and trained in piano, singing and harmony in Germany and Italy; also by Richard GENEE and Léo DELIBES in operatic composition. In 1887 his operetta, *The Begum,* was produced in Philadelphia with great success: it was followed by many other popular light operas among which were ROBIN HOOD, *The Fencing Master, Rob Roy, The Highwayman* and *Red Feather.* His grand opera, *The Canterbury Pilgrims,* was produced in 1917 at the Metropolitan Opera House, New York, and another, *Rip van Winkle,* at the Chicago Civic Opera in 1919. De Koven founded the Philharmonic Orchestra at Washington, D. C., in 1902: he also acted as music critic for several newspapers and magazines.

Delaborde, Henri, Count (1811-1899), French painter and art critic who studied with Eugène DELACROIX and Paul DELAROCHE. His notable paintings include *Hagar in the Desert; Conversion of St. Augustine; Conquest of Damietta; Knights of St. John of Jerusalem.* He contributed magazine critical articles to periodicals and wrote a critical biography of Jean Ingres, and a history of the Académie des Beaux-Arts.

Delacroix, Ferdinand Victor Eugène (1798-1863), French painter who studied with Baron Guerin at Paris; his first picture, *Dante and Virgil,* shown at the Salon in 1822, was a success although it displeased Guerin, and departed radically from the classic lines laid down by Louis David. Among his notable works, most of which were the target of bitter invective from academicians, are *Massacre of Chios; Marino Faliero Decapitated; Sardanapalus; Triumph of Apollo; Abduction of Rebecca; Christ on Lake Gennesaret; Christ on the Cross; Jewish Wedding in Morocco.* He executed more than 800 oil paintings, and almost twice as many water colors, crayons and etchings.

Delafield, E. M. (1890-), the pen name of the English novelist and short-story writer, Mrs. Edmée Elizabeth Monica de la Pasture Dashwood; her mother was also a novelist of excellent reputation. Her works include *Zella Sees Herself* (1917); *The War Workers; The Diary of a Provincial Lady; The Provincial Lady Goes Further; The Provincial Lady in America; Straw Without Bricks; The Provincial Lady in War Time.*

De la Mare, Walter John (1873-), British poet who first worked in the clerical department of a commercial house: after his *Songs of Childhood* appeared in 1901, and a novel, *Henry Brocken,* in 1904, a government pension enabled him to devote himself entirely to a literary career. His works include *The Listeners and Other Poems; Peacock Pie! Motley and Other Poems;* a fairy play, *Crossings; The Veil;* a novel, *Memoirs of a Midget; The Riddle; Broomsticks; Down-adown Derry; Poems for Children; Fleeting and Other Poems.*

De Lamarter, Eric (1880-), American organist, choirmaster, conductor, and composer who studied the organ with Alexandre Guilmant and Charles Widor in Paris. He was organist and choirmaster of important churches in Chicago; assistant conductor of the Chicago Symphony Orchestra for eighteen years; conductor of the Chicago Civic Orchestra for nearly twenty years, and music critic of several Chicago newspapers. His compositions include ballets, orchestral works, chamber music, organ concertos and solo pieces; church music and part songs.

Deland, Margaret Wade (1857-), American poet, short story writer, and novelist who first achieved success in 1888 with a novel, *John Ward, Preacher.* She has also published *The Story of a Child; Mr. Tommy Dove and Other Stories; Philip and his Wife; Dr. Lavender's People; Old Chester Tales; The Awakening of Helena Ritchie; The Iron Woman; Old Chester Secret; The Kays: Captain Archer's Daughter; Old Chester Days.*

Delaroche, Hippolyte, called **Paul** (1797-1856), French painter who studied with Louis Watelet and Baron Gros, and exhibited his first picture, *Josabeth Saving Joas,* in 1822. Its success brought on a lifelong intimacy with Jean-Louis Gericault and Ferdinand Delacroix, the three forming the center of a distinguished group of historical painters. His notable pictures include *The Death of Queen Elizabeth; The Princes in the Tower of London; Execution of Lady Jane Grey; Assassination of the Duc de Guise; Napoleon at Fontainebleau; The Field of Battle; Cromwell Surveying the Remains of Charles I.* In 1837 Delaroche undertook his greatest commission, a picture more than one hundred feet long in the semicircular lecture theatre of the Ecole des Beaux-Arts, Paris: it portrays seventy-five of the distinguished artists of modern times standing on both sides of a series of white marble steps on the topmost of which are three thrones occupied by the architects and sculptors of the Parthenon. It was completed in 1841 and damaged by fire in 1855: Delaroche undertook to repair it, but died before he completed the work, and Nicolas Robert-Fleury finished the repairs.

De la Roche, Mazo (1885-), Canadian novelist who won the *Atlantic Monthly* prize of $10,000 in 1927 for her novel, *Jalna:* several more novels in the Jalna series have been issued including *Young Renny; Whiteoak Heritage; Whiteoaks of Jalna; Finch's Fortune; The Master of Jalna; Whiteoak Harvest; Wakefield's Course.* Ethel Barrymore appeared in a dramatization called *Whiteoaks* in 1936. The series is extremely popular, overshadowing all her other literary efforts.

Delaunay, Jules Elie (1828-1891), French painter who studied with Jean Flandrin at the Ecole des Beaux-Arts, Paris, and in Italy after he won the Prix de Rome. He executed three fine panels at the Paris Opera House, and twelve paintings for the grand hall of the state council in the Palais Royal: also a series of scenes from the life of Saint Genevieve (left unfinished) for the Pantheon. Other canvases include *Plague in Rome;* a nude *Diana,* and *Lesson on the Flute.*

Delavigne, Jean François Casimir (1793-1843), French lyric poet and dramatist who sounded a patriotic note in his satirical poems, *Messenian Odes* (1818) directed against the monarchy of the Restoration. His historical dramas include *The Sicilian Vespers; Marino Faliero; Don John of Austria; The Children of Edward; The Daughter of the Cid; Louis XI.* He was one of the first dramatists to write for the French stage when the classical tradition was being affected by the growing romantic and realistic movement.

Deledda, Grazia (1875-), Italian novelist who was awarded the Nobel Prize in 1926. Her works include *Elias Portolu* (1903); *The Doves and the Hawks; Reeds in the Wind; After the Divorce; The Mother;* the last two were translated into English.

Delibes, Léo (1836-1891), French dramatic composer who studied with Adolphe Adam and André Benoist at the Paris Conservatory. He composed several successful ballets including *La Source,* later called *Naila; Coppelia,* and his greatest success, *Sylvia.* All three of these ballets are still performed on the stage, and as concert music for orchestra. He also wrote an opera, Lakme, which is in the modern operatic repertory.

Delius, Frederick (1862-1934), English composer of German parentage: at first he was practically self-taught because of his parents' opposition to a musical career, but finally received instruction from Carl Reinecke, Hans Sitt and Salomon Jadassohn at the Leipzig Conservatory. He was an intimate friend of Edvard Grieg, and lived most of his life in Paris. His compositions include several operas; orchestral works; concertos and solo pieces for violin and violoncello with orchestra; chamber music and choral works.

Dell, Floyd (1887-   ), American journalist and novelist: his works include *Moon Calf* (1920); *The Briary Bush; Janet March; Runaway; An Old Man's Folly; An Unmarried Father; Outline of Marriage; Love Without Money; Diana Stair.* He has also written several plays.

Della Chiesa, Vivian (1915-   ), American soprano of Italian parentage who studied at the Chicago Musical College, and won a radio broadcast contest for unknown singers in 1936: in the same year she made a successful appearance as Mimi in La BOHEME with the Chicago Opera Company. She has since appeared in recital, and is one of the most successful singers in the field of broadcasting.

Della Porta, Giacomo (1541-1604), Italian architect of the early baroque period: he designed the façade of the *Gesù* and the Universita della Sapienza, Rome. His most important work was reconstructing the dome made by MICHELANGELO for St. Peter's, Rome: in order to secure greater stability he increased its height.

Della Robbia, the name of a distinguished family of Florentine architects, sculptors and workers in glazed terra cotta. The founder of the Della Robbia workshop was **Luca della Robbia** (1400-1482), who was first a goldsmith: among his notable works are the cantoria (balcony for the singers) in the cathedral at Florence; a tomb for Bishop Federighi, and a *Madonna of the Roses* in the Bargello, Florence. He also discovered a method of enameling terra cotta with a glaze composed of white and blue; among the finest examples of this process are the *Resurrection* and the *Ascension* in the Duomo of Florence. Luca's nephew, **Andrea della Robbia** (1435-1525), was his pupil and coworker, also employing glazed terra cotta: among his best creations are the decoration of the Loggia dei Innocenti at Florence; a Madonna in the Bargello, Florence; *Adoration of the Magi; Coronation of the Virgin.* Andrea had several sons who worked in terra cotta in Tuscany, the Marches, Umbria, Naples and Sicily. The most distinguished was **Giovanni della Robbia** (1469-1529), who created a beautiful fountain at the Church of Santa Maria Novello; also *Bearing of the Cross* now in the National Museum, Florence. His work was more ornamental, but inferior in modeling and coloring. A grandnephew of Luca, **Girolamo della Robbia** (1488-1566), was a distinguished architect and sculptor who designed the Château de Madrid in Paris, and modeled a figure of Catherine de Medicis which is now in the ECOLE DES BEAUX-ARTS, Paris.

Della Robbia Ware, in architecture the term applied to pieces of terra cotta, faïence, or majolica formed into friezes, and panels by the DELLA ROBBIA family in the 15th century, and used for the decoration of churches and public buildings in Florence and many other Italian cities. Examples are to be seen in Italian, English, and American museums.

Delorme or **De L'orme, Philibert** (c.1510-1570), French architect who studied with his father and in Italy where he learned much from the Roman works of antiquity. He was chief architect for Francis I and Henry II of France; among his finest works were the château at Anet for Diane de Poitiers, the ballroom at Fontainebleau, and the new Palace of the Tuileries.

Delphi, a town in ancient Greece near Mount Parnassus; it was the seat of the world-renowned **Delphian Oracle,** founded in prehistoric days and consulted until it was silenced by Theodosius I, Emperor of Rome. The founder, according to Greek mythology, was Gaea, the earth goddess: Apollo wrested it from her by killing the serpent who guarded the oracle. The oracle was located in the Temple of Apollo, and those who sought information regarding the future brought rich gifts, and were given prophecies in verse by priests representing Pythia, the prophetess.

Delsarte, François Alexandre Nicolas Cheri (1811-1871), French tenor who developed a method in which he co-ordinated the teaching of singing, declamation, gymnastics, and dancing which the well-known dramatist, Steele MACKAYE promoted for years in the United States. He also invented an apparatus to facilitate the work of the piano tuner.

Demeter, see **Ceres.**

Demeter of Cnidus, a Greek statue discovered at Cnidus and now in the BRITISH MUSEUM. The seated woman appears to be mourning for her daughter, PERSEPHONE; it has been compared with the familiar figure, *Mater dolorosa,* so often painted and sculptured by artists of later periods. It may have been the work of SCOPAS, and probably belongs to the 4th century, B.C.

DeMille, Cecil Blount (1881-   ), American actor, playwright, stage and film producer who studied at the American Academy of Dramatic Arts, New York, and made his stage debut in 1900 in *Hearts are Trumps* at the Garden Theatre, New York. After acting in several plays, and becoming co-author of *The Northwest Mounted* and *The Return of Peter Grimm,* he devoted his attention from 1913 exclusively to producing more than sixty films including *The Squaw Man* (1913); *The Ten Commandments; The King of Kings; The Sign of the Cross; Cleopatra; The Crusader; The Plainsman; The Buccaneer; Union Pacific; Land of Liberty; Northwest Mounted Police; Reap the Wild Wind; The Story of Dr. Wassell.*

De Mille, William (1878-   ), American dramatist and film director educated at Columbia University and the Academy of Dramatic Arts, New York; brother of Cecil DE MILLE. Among his numerous plays are *Strongheart* (1905); *Classmates; The Warrens of Virginia; The Royal Mounted; The Woman.* Among his film productions are *The Heir to the Hoorah; The Prince Chap; What Every Woman Knows; Bought and Paid For; Grumpy; Craig's Wife.*

Deming, Edwin Willard (1860-1942), American painter and sculptor who was born on the prairies of the Southwest, and grew up with Indians as his playmates. After being in business until 1880, he studied in Paris, and executed some of the finest paintings and sculptures ever made of the American Indian. His works are to be found in the American Museum of Natural History, New York; the Brooklyn Museum of Arts and Sciences, Brooklyn; the Black Hawk Museum in Wisconsin.

De Morgan, William Freud (1839-1917), English artist and author; designer of stained glass, tiles and pottery which made him internationally famous. In 1905 he published a novel, *Joseph Vance,* which achieved immediate popularity; it was followed by several more including *Alice-for-Short; Somehow Good; It Can Never Happen Again;* all his novels show the influence of Charles DICKENS.

Demuth, Charles (1883-1935), American painter who studied with William Merritt CHASE at the PENNSYLVANIA ACADEMY OF FINE ARTS and in Paris. He illustrated several books including Émile ZOLA's *Nana,* Henry JAMES' *The Beast in the Jungle,* and made some color drawings of famous actors and actresses which were probably inspired by Ignace FANTIN-LATOUR. His works include studies of flowers in water color, and odd scenes in great cities in oil and tempera somewhat influenced by cubism. His pictures are to be seen at the Metropolitan Museum of Art, New York, and the Phillips Memorial Gallery in Washington, D. C.

Denis, Maurice (1870-), French painter and writer on art: his murals on sacred subjects are to be seen in many French churches, and he has published *The Symbolism of Gauguin* (1912), and *New Theories on Modern Art and Religious Art* (1914-1921).

Denishawn School, see **St. Denis, Ruth.**

Dennery (or **D'Ennery**), **Adolphe** (1811-1899), French dramatist whose real surname was Philippe: his first play, *Émile,* produced in 1831, was followed by more than two hundred written alone or in collaboration. His most famous work, *Les Deux Orphelines,* written in collaboration with Eugène Cormon, became a favorite on the English and American stages as *The Two Orphans.* He also wrote librettos for operas by Charles GOUNOD and Daniel AUBER.

Denon, Dominique Vivant (1747-1825), French dramatist, author and artist who accompanied Napoleon I on his expeditions to Egypt, and made sketches of ancient monuments of art, resulting in the publication of a two-volume work, *Travels in Lower and Upper Egypt,* illustrated with 141 plates, and establishing his reputation as an artist. He also accompanied Napoleon I on his expeditions to Austria, Spain, and Poland, acting as adviser in the selection of art treasures to be removed. He left an unfinished history of ancient and modern art which was published posthumously, and wrote a successful novel, *Point de lendemain.*

Dent, Edward Joseph (1876-), English musicologist educated at Cambridge under Charles Villiers STANFORD: in 1922 he was one of the organizers of the INTERNATIONAL SOCIETY OF CONTEMPORARY MUSIC, and active in founding the British Musical Society. In addition to his contributions to the Encyclopedia Britannica, Grove's Dictionary, Cobbett's Encyclopedia of Chamber Music, and the Oxford History of Music, he is the author of *Alessandro Scarlatti, His Life and Works* (1905); *Mozart's Operas, a Critical Study; Terpander, or Music and the Future; Foundations of English Opera; Ferruccio Busoni; Music of the Renaissance in Italy; Handel.*

Denza, Luigi (1846-1922), Italian composer who studied with Giuseppe Mercadante; he was a prolific composer of songs many of which have achieved great popularity: the one best-known in the United States is *Funiculi-Funicula.*

De Quincey, Thomas (1785-1859), English author and essayist who was educated at Oxford; in 1820 Charles Lamb aided him in becoming a contributor to the *London Magazine* in which his most famous work, *Confessions of an English Opium Eater,* appeared in 1821. His works include *Autobiographic Sketches,* and numerous essays on historical, literary and miscellaneous subjects.

Derain, André (1880-), French painter who studied at the Acadèmie Julien and with Eugène CARRIERE, later coming in contact with Henri MATISSE, Vincent van GOGH, Eugène GAUGUIN, and Paul CEZANNE; during World War I he was influenced by Auguste RENOIR. Among his notable canvases are *Olive Trees in the Midi; The Mandolin Player; A Forest Road; Dancers in Repose; The Guitar Player.* He has also illustrated books by Maurice de Vlaminck, G. Gabory and V. Muselli.

De Reszke, Édouard (1853-1917), Polish dramatic bass who made his operatic debut in 1876 at Paris in VERDI's AIDA: after singing in Italian opera houses, Paris, and London, he added Wagner roles to his repertory. He made his American debut at Chicago in *Lohengrin* during the visit of the Metropolitan Opera Company to that city in 1891: during the same year he appeared with his brother, Jean de RESZKE, at the Metropolitan Opera House, New York, in GOUNOD's *Romeo et Juliette.* His repertory was extensive, and included Wagnerian roles in German; critics admired him equally as Plunkett in MARTHA, or as Mephistopheles in FAUST. He was the principal basso at the Metropolitan until the close of the season 1902-1903.

De Reszke, Jean (1850-1925), Polish dramatic tenor who made his first appearance in opera as a baritone at Venice in 1874: five years later he made his debut as a tenor in MEYERBEER's *Robert le Diable* at Madrid, and in 1885 he scored a triumph at the Grand Opera, Paris, in MASSENET's *Le Cid.* His American debut took place in 1891 at the Metropolitan Opera House in Gounod's *Romeo et Juliette,* and he remained there as chief tenor for ten years with the exception of the season 1899-1900. In 1895 he created a sensation by appearing for the first time in TRISTAN AND ISOLDE, singing in German. He retired from the stage in 1902, and taught singing in Paris for many years.

Derzhavin, Gavril Romanovich (1743-1816), Russian poet who won the patronage of Catherine

II with an ode, FELIZA, and held several responsible positions at court. Originality in conception, splendid imagery and mastery of the Russian language are displayed in other odes including *God, Waterfall,* and *The Nobleman.*

Desaugiers, Marc Antoine Madeleine (1772-1827), French dramatist and song writer who became famous as a writer of numerous successful comedies, operas, and vaudevilles produced in Paris after 1797: among them *Monsieur Vautour* and *The Reign of a Term and the Term of a Reign,* the latter a satire on Napoleon I. His convivial and satirical lyrics can be favorably compared with those of Pierre BERANGER with whom he was intimate. His father, **Marc Antoine Desaugiers** (1742-1793), was a composer of light operas, and wrote a cantata, *Hiérodrame,* in celebration of the fall of the Bastille in 1789.

Desbrosses, Jean Alfred (1835-1906), French painter who studied with Ary SCHEFFER and Antoine Chintreuil: his works include *In the Mountains; Lake of Chambon; Ascent of the Little St. Bernard; Valley of Salanches.*

Descamps, Jean Baptiste (1706-1791), French painter who studied with his uncle, Louis COYPEL, and Nicolas de LARGILLIERE: his works include several paintings of the coronation of Louis XV; five episodes in the history of Dunkirk; *A Mother in Her Kitchen with Two Children* (his masterpiece). He founded an art school at Rouen and published a four-volume work on the lives of famous Flemish, German and Dutch painters.

Deschamps, Eustace (c.1346-c.1406), French poet, also called Morel, who studied at the University of Orleans, and later occupied several important posts at the French court under Charles V. His works include *A Mirror of Marriage* which is a satire against women, several fine historical ballades and patriotic poems, and a volume, *The Poetic Art,* in which he lays down rules for versifying. He is regarded as one of the first French poets to deviate from the formless narrative tales of the French trouvères.

Deschamps, Louis Henri (1846-1902), French painter who studied with Alexandre CABANEL; his works include *Poor Little Girl; Little Winnower Defending His Grain; Woman Dreaming; The Girl Mother; Resignation.*

Desdemona, the heroine of Shakespeare's drama, *Othello,* in which she becomes the innocent victim of Othello's jealousy fomented by Iago; it is said that the role of Desdemona is the first in which a woman appeared on the English stage. She is also the leading feminine character in VERDI's grand opera, *Otello,* based upon Shakespeare's play.

Desgoffe, Alexandre (1805-1882), French painter who studied with Jean INGRES: his works include *View near Arbonne; Hercules and the Nemean Lion; Narcissus at the Fountain; Joseph Sold by his Brethren;* also several fine landscapes painted at Rome and Naples.

Des Grieux, Chevalier, the hero of an 18th century romance, *The Story of Manon Lescaut,* by the Abbé PREVOST (1679-1763): also the principal tenor role in MASSENET's opera, *Manon,* first produced at Paris in 1883, and in PUCCINI's opera, *Manon Lescaut,* first performed at Turin in 1893.

Desiderio da Settignano (1428-1464), French sculptor said to have been either a pupil of DONATELLO, or to have been profoundly influenced by the latter's works. He was one of the second generation of Renaissance sculptors at Florence, and the exquisite character of his carving in marble and wood is to be seen at many churches. *A Laughing Child* created by him is in a Vienna museum; also a fine marble chimney piece at the Victoria and Albert Museum, London.

Design, (1) in painting and sculpture the preliminary sketch of a picture or monument, usually consisting of lines which form the basis and indicate the more important points of the completed work. (2) In architecture the plans prepared by the architect for a building.

Desmarets de Saint Sorlin, Jean (1595-1676), French poet who was a favorite of Cardinal Richeliu: his works include a character comedy, *The Visionaries* (1637); the epic poems, *Clovis* and *Mary Magdalene;* also many religious poems.

Desnoyers, August Gaspard, Baron (1779-1857), French engraver who studied with Alexander TARDIEU, and was appointed engraver to the French court in 1825. His outstanding plates include reproductions of works by RAPHAEL and Leonardo da VINCI.

Despiau, Charles (1874-), French sculptor who studied at the École des Arts Decoratifs under Louvrier de Lajolais, and with Hector Lemaire who had studied with Jean CARPEAUX; he also had instruction at the ECOLE DES BEAUX-ARTS from Louis BARRIAS. He acted as assistant for a time to Auguste RODIN, learning much about the proper interpretation of the human figure. Among his works are portrait busts, figures in modern dress, and studies of the nude such as *Eve* in the Luxembourg Museum, Paris. Examples of his work are to be seen in the Buffalo Fine Arts Academy and the Detroit Institute of Arts.

Desportes, Alexander François (1661-1743), French painter who studied with Nicasius Bernaert, a Flemish animal painter. He acquired a great reputation in Poland at the court of King Sobieski: his works include *Wolf Hunt; Boar Hunt; Game Guarded by Dogs; Dog and Partridges.* Animal and hunting pictures were his specialty although he painted some fine portraits at the Polish court.

Desportes, Philippe (1546-1606), French poet whose works are remarkable for their purity in style: they include more than 450 sonnets and elegies in exquisite metrical form.

Despreaux, Jean Étienne (1748-1820), French composer, poet, and ballet master who entered the corps de ballet of L'Opera, Paris, in 1764, but suffered an injury to his foot which ended his career as a dancer. He married the danseuse, Madeleine Guimard, in 1789, and amused guests in his home by putting diminutive white stockings and shoes on his fingers, and imitating the styles of contemporary ballerinas with such skill in a tiny model theatre that their identity was readily revealed.

Des Pres, Josquin (c.1450-1521), Dutch composer whose real name has been spelled in many different ways; the one given here is that generally accepted. Little is known of his life beyond the fact that he was probably a pupil of Johannes OKEGHEM, and court musician to Lorenzo de' Medici and Louis XII of France. His works were chiefly masses and motets: they were universally sung and admired, and both contrapuntal and homophonic in construction as the result of Italian influence.

Dessoff, Margarethe (1874-   ), Austrian vocal teacher and choral conductor who studied at the Frankfort Conservatory. After founding and conducting several choirs and choruses in Germany, she came to New York in 1922 to conduct the Madrigal Chorus at the INSTITUTE OF MUSICAL ART: she also founded and conducted the Dessoff Choirs, the A Cappella Singers, and the Vecchi Singers. She has written sacred music for women's choruses.

Destinn, Emmy (1878-1930), Bohemian dramatic soprano whose real name was Emmy Kittl: she selected her stage name in appreciation of the voice training received from Mme. Marie Loewe-Destinn. She made her European debut in 1898 at the Royal Opera, Berlin, in MASCAGNI'S CAVALLERIA RUSTICANA, and her American debut in 1908 at the Metropolitan Opera House in *Aïda*. She created the role of Minnie in Puccini's *Girl of the Golden West*, and scored another great success as Marie in SMETANA'S BARTERED BRIDE.

Destouches, Philippe Nericault (1680-1754), French dramatist who is regarded as the originator of sentimental comedy on the French stage: among his seventeen comedies are *Le Philosophe Marie* (1727), considered his finest work; *Le Glorieux*; *Le Dissipateur*; *La Fausse Agnes*.

Detaille, Jean Baptiste Édouard (1848-1912), French painter who studied with Jean MEISSONIER, and specialized in historical paintings, particularly of battles. His works include *The Conquerors; The Retreat; Bonaparte in Egypt; Defense of Champigny; Napoleon and His Generals at Austerlitz; The Cossacks of the Ataman; Halt of the Infantry; Vincendon Brigade.*

Detective Fiction, one of the most entertaining fields of literature when considered from the standpoint of the millions of people in England, France and America who beguile at least some of their leisure with crime detection stories and novels. An exhaustive ten-volume anthology, *The World's Best Detective Stories*, compiled by Eugene Thwing, was published in 1929, and there are many other less comprehensive one-volume collections available. The principal American, English, and French detective fiction writers of today and yesterday include George Barton, Mrs. BELLOC-LOWNDES, Earl Derr BIGGERS, Charles Gordon Booth, John Dixon Carr, Leslie CHARTERIS, G. B. CHESTERTON, Wilson Collison, Agatha CHRISTIE,

Will Cuppy, Carroll John Daly, Sir Arthur Conan DOYLE, George Dyer, Mignon EBERHART, J. S. Fletcher, Leslie Ford, Emile GABORIAU, Fortune Boisgobey, Erle Stanley GARDNER, Anna Katherine GREENE, Dashiell HAMMETT, Julian HAWTHORNE, Arthur Hornblow, Maurice Le Blanc, F. Van Wyck Mason, E. Phillips OPPENHEIM, Fulton Oursler, Frank L. Packard, Allan Pinkerton, Edgar Allan POE, Ellery QUEEN, Arthur B. REEVE, Mary Roberts RINEHART, Mabel Seeley, Georges SIMENON, Vincent Starrett, Rex STOUT, Phoebe Atwood Taylor, S. S. VAN DINE, Edgar WALLACE, Carolyn Wells, and Martyn Wyndham.

Detroit Symphony Orchestra, an organization founded at Detroit, Michigan, in 1914 with Weston Gales as conductor until 1918; he was succeeded by Ossip GABRILOWITSCH who re-organized the ensemble, and directed it until his death in 1936. After two seasons of guest conductors including MOLINARI, REINER, ITURBI, and ENESCO, the orchestra reverted to the two-conductor policy with Franco Ghione and Victor KOLAR. The orchestra presents its concerts in Orchestra Hall, one of the finest concert halls in America from the architectural and acoustic standpoints.

Dett, Robert Nathaniel (1882-   ), American Negro composer and writer, born in Canada and educated at the Oberlin Conservatory of Music, Columbia and Harvard Universities, and the EASTMAN School of Music: he has received many musical degrees and awards, and occupied several important posts as instructor. His compositions include two oratorios, many choruses, and suites for piano; one of these, *In the Bottoms*, contains the world famous JUBA *Dance*. He has also published a collection of Negro spirituals.

Deucalion and Pyrrha, in Greek mythology Deucalion was the son of PROMETHEUS; when he and his wife, Pyrrha, became the sole survivors of a flood, they were bidden by an oracle to cast stones behind them which were turned into men. Hellen, son of the pair, is supposed to be the progenitor of the Hellenic race.

Deus, Joao de (1830-1896), Portuguese poet regarded as one of the greatest his country produced, and as a pioneer of a new era in Portuguese poetry. His poems such as *Field Flowers* and *A Branch of Blooms* reveal an abundance of national spirit, original ideas, and deep sensibility.

Deutsch, Babette (1895-   ), American poet and novelist educated at the Ethical Culture School and Barnard University, New York. In addition to her poetical work she has translated many Russian and German books in collaboration with her husband, Avrahm Yarmolinsky, head of the Slavonic Division of the New York Public Library. Her poetical works include *Banners* (1919); *Honey Out of the Rock; Fire For the Night; One Part Love.* Her novels include *A Brittle Heaven; In Such a Night; Mask of Silenus.*

Development, in music the term applied to the elaboration of a musical theme by means of rhythmic, melodic or harmonic changes or variations: it is usually used in connection with a formal composition such as a FUGUE, SONATA or SYMPHONY.

Developpé, in ballet a term designating a slow movement in which the leg is extended gradually into some previously determined position: the complete expression is *temps developpé.*

De Vere, Sir Aubrey (1788-1846), Irish poet whose works include *Julian the Apostate* (1822); the historical dramas, *The Duke of Mercia and Mary Tudor; The Lamentations of Ireland.* His son, **Sir Aubrey Thomas De Vere** (1814-1902), was also a poet whose verses were said by William Wordsworth to be "the most perfect of the age"; they include *Poems* (1834), *Irish Odes,* and *Alexander the Great.*

Devéria, Eugène François Marie Joseph (1805-1865), French painter who studied with GIRODET-TRIOSON: his paintings include the famous *Birth of Henry IV; Death of Joan of Arc; The Four Henrys; Reception of Columbus by Ferdinand and Isabella.* His brother, **Achille Devéria** (1810- ?) was also a pupil of Girodet-Trioson: he executed many portraits of contemporary singers and actors; also several religious pictures including *Charity, Faith, Love, and Hope; Descent from the Cross; Annunciation.*

Devil's Trill, in music the title given to a violin sonata composed by Giuseppe Tartini in 1713. He records the circumstances under which he conceived this work as follows: "One night I dreamed that I had made a compact with the devil, who promised to be at my service on all occasions. At last I thought I would offer my violin to the devil: to my great astonishment I heard him play a solo so singularly beautiful that it surpassed all the music I had ever heard or conceived in the whole course of my life. The violence of the sensation awoke me: instantly I seized my violin in the hopes of remembering some portion of what I had heard, but in vain! The work which this dream suggested is doubtless the best of all my compositions." There is a Columbia recording of this sonata by Nathan MILSTEIN, and a Victor recording by Yehudi MENUHIN.

De Vinne, Theodore Low (1828-1914), American printer who established a business which from 1877 did much to raise the level of the art in the United States. He founded the De Vinne Press, and printed *St. Nicholas Magazine,* the *Century Magazine,* the *Century Dictionary,* and many fine editions issued by the Grolier Club. He also was the author of *The Invention of Printing* (1876), and *The Practice of Typography,* an exhaustive treatise in four volumes.

De Voto, Bernard Augustine (1897-), American novelist educated at the University of Utah and Harvard University: his works include *The Crooked Mile* (1924); *The Chariot of Fire; Mark Twain's America; We Accept With Pleasure; Mark Twain in Eruption; Essays on Mark Twain; The Year of Decision: 1846.*

Devrient, Ludwig (1784-1832), German actor who made his debut in 1804 at Gera in SCHILLER'S *Bride of Messina:* later he appeared in the latter's drama, *The Robbers,* and attained such success in Shakespearean plays that he became the rival of August Iffland, and succeeded him as the popular

idol in Berlin. His nephew, **Karl August Devrient** (1797-1872), was also a fine actor who married Wilhelmine Schroder, a famous German soprano known as SCHRODER-DEVRIENT; another nephew, **Philipp Eduard Devrient** (1801-1877), was a distinguished theatre director and author of a monumental history of the German stage. Still another nephew, **Gustav Emil Devrient** (1803-1872), became one of the finest tragedians in the German theatre: when he appeared in London, his characterization of Hamlet was considered superior to that of either John Philip KEMBLE or Edmund KEAN.

Dewey, Charles Melville (1849-), American painter who studied with CAROLUS-DURAN in Paris: his works include *Sunshine and Shadow; Edge of the Forest; The Sun Shower; Harvest Moon; The Close of Day; Ebb Tide; After the Rain; Water Lily; Study by the Sea.*

Dewing, Thomas Wilmer (1851-), American painter who studied with Gustave BOULANGER and Jules LEFEBVRE; his works, distinguished for their delicacy and finish, include *The Days; The Lady in Green and Gray; Summer; Lady With a Mask.* His wife, **Maria Richards Oakey Dewing** (1845-1927), was also a painter who studied with John La Farge and Thomas COUTURE: her paintings of flowers and figures, considered exceptional, include *Mother and Child* and *Child with Doll.*

De Wint, Peter (1784-1849), English painter who studied with J. R. Smith and at the Royal Academy, London. His works which are chiefly in water color include landscapes painted in England and Normandy; among them *A Cornfield* and *Woody Landscape with Water.*

Diabelli, Anton (1781-1858), Austrian pianist, composer and music publisher who was encouraged in his music study by Michael HAYDN, brother of Joseph HAYDN who later also took an interest in him. In 1824 he founded the publishing house of Diabelli and Company, issuing the works of Franz SCHUBERT, but paying him almost nothing and complaining about his productiveness. BEETHOVEN did him the honor of writing thirty-three variation (Op. 120) based on a trivial waltz theme of his (Diabelli's) composition.

Diaghileff, Sergei Pavlovich (1872-1929), Russian ballet master, and founder of the Russian magazine, *Mir Isskustva* (The World of Art) which had a profound influence, and may even be said to have revolutionized all forms of art in Russia. He first organized exhibitions of Russian painting, music, and opera in Paris: in 1909 he brought, after conquering innumerable difficulties, a Russian ballet company to Paris which achieved such success that it revolutionized the history of ballet in Western Europe and later in America. His organization was known as the *Ballet Russe* with Leon BAKST as the scenic designer and Michael FOKINE as the choreographer. Among the many modern composers who collaborated with him were Igor STRAVINSKY in THE FIREBIRD, PETROUCHKA and SACRE DU PRINTEMPS; Claude DEBUSSY in AFTERNOON OF A FAUN; RAVEL in DAPHNIS AND CHLOE. The list of dancers, equally brilliant, includes Anna PAVLOWA, Vaslav NIJINSKY, Leonide MASSINE, Michael MORDKIN and Serge LIFAR. Diaghileff's seasons at Monte Carlo, Paris, London, and in the United States were invariably sensational successes.

Diagoras of Melos, Greek sophist and poet of the 5th century, B.C.; he was surnamed "the Atheist" because he became an agnostic when the gods failed to avenge the defeat of the citizens of Melos by the Athenians. After first writing hymns, he attacked the divinities in a work on the mysteries, and was condemned to death at Athens.

Dialogue, (a) in literature a conversation between two people, set down in writing and said to have originated in ancient Greece. Among the famous classic writers in this form were PLATO, Lucien of Samosata, and Torquato TASSO. It was also used by FONTENELLE, FENELON, Berkeley, LANDOR, WIELAND, and VALDES; among the modern writers are Henri Lavedan, Anstey Guthrie and Oliver Wendell HOLMES. (b) In drama the principal means of conveying to the audience information about the characters or incidents in a play which it is necessary for them to know in advance of the appearance of characters, or of the occurrence of incidents.

Diamante, Juan Bautista (c.1640-c.1684), Spanish soldier and dramatist who is said to have introduced French theatrical methods into Spain: his forty-five plays are founded on Spanish history; one of them, *Who Honors His Father,* bears such a strong resemblance in its wording to COR-NEILLE'S *Le Cid* that some critics incline to credit him as the real author.

Diamond, the most prized gem of both early and modern times because it is the most brilliant in lustre and the least subject to decomposition of all precious stones. It is also the hardest of all minerals, thereby becoming of great value in the industrial arts for grinding, polishing, and drilling. The real brilliancy of a diamond does not reveal itself until it has been faceted by a diamond cutter, an art which was perfected only about 1750. Diamonds were first mined in India and Borneo: later they were discovered in Brazil, and in 1867 in South Africa, now the main source of supply. Many stones of large size have been mined; among them the Great Mogul, the Orloff, the Victoria, the Kohinoor, the Excelsior, the Cullinan, the Hope, and the Tiffany. The history of such gems is clothed in romance, and not infrequently stained with blood.

Diana, in Roman mythology a goddess now identified with the Greek goddess, ARTEMIS: she was the divinity of the moon and of light, forest, chase, and war. A great temple, requiring one hundred years to construct, and placed among the SEVEN WONDERS OF THE WORLD, was begun at Ephesus about 356 B.C.; excavations from 1869 to 1874 resulted in the unearthing of sculptures by PHIDIAS and POLYCLETUS, and a portrait of Alexander the Great by APELLES. Her most important temple in Rome was on the Aventine, one of the seven hills of ancient Rome.

Diary, in literature a daily record of the personal experiences or observations published because of its interest to the world in part or in general. A diary differs from a memoir in that the latter is in the form of reminiscences instead of chronological order. Some of the famous diarists are John EVELYN, Samuel PEPYS, Jonathan SWIFT, Philip Doddridge, Madame d'ARBLAY (Fanny Burney), Jules and Edmond de Goncourt, Edmond Barbier, the Marquis de Dangeau, and the Duc de Saint-Simon; the last-named is a brilliant record of the reign of Louis XIV of France.

Dias, Antonio Gonçalves (1823-1866), Brazilian poet whose verses give evidence of originality, humor, and tenderness: they include three volumes of lyric poems.

Diatonic, in music the term applied to the standard major or minor scale, comprising the tones to which the letters A B C D E F G have been assigned. The term is also applied to intervals or chords formed of the same notes, or to a melody composed of only these notes.

Diaz de la Pena, Narcisse Virgile (1808-1876), French painter of Spanish parentage: he first learned his art in a porcelain factory at Paris, but was mainly self-taught except for advice from Sigalon and Souchon. Among his finest works are *Hunter and Dogs; Forest of Fontainebleau; The Road; Bohemians on Holiday; Two Rivals; The Spell; Love Disarmed.*

Dibdin, Charles (1745-1814), English actor, lyric poet, novelist, and dramatist who opened his own miniature theatre, the *Sans Souci,* in London where he produced many original plays in which he acted, and for which he wrote the music. He also produced an operetta, *The Shepherd's Artifice,* at the Covent Garden Theatre, and another, *The Quaker,* at the Drury Lane Theatre, London. He composed many popular songs including the immortal *Tom Bowling;* also several novels. Both of his sons, Charles and Thomas John Dibdin, were also popular dramatists.

Dickens, Charles John Huffam (1812-1870), English novelist who received an elementary education in private schools: he learned shorthand in 1829, and after working in a lawyer's office, became a reporter for the London *Morning Chronicle* in 1835. His story, "A Dinner at Poplar Walk" (1833) was the beginning of a series printed as *Sketches by Boz* in 1836; the publication of *Pickwick Papers* in 1836-37 established his reputation. He visited the United States in 1842 and 1867, and some of his experiences were recorded in his *American Notes.* His works include *Oliver Twist; Nicholas Nickleby; The Old Curiosity Shop; Barnaby Rudge; A Christmas Carol; Martin Chuzzlewit; The Cricket on the Hearth; Dombey and Son; David Copperfield; Bleak House; Hard Times; Little Dorrit; A Tale of Two Cities; The Uncommercial Traveler; Great Expectations; Our Mutual Friend; The Mystery of Edwin Drood,* the last-named left unfinished. His eldest son **Charles Dickens** (1837-1896), was educated at King's College; became assistant to his father, and also editor of a *Dictionary of London.*

Dickinson, Emily (1830-1886), American poet whose works were published after her death with the exception of some verses printed in magazines: they include *Poems,* in three series issued from 1890 to 1896; *The Single Hound: Poems of a Lifetime; Complete Poems.* Martha Dickinson Bianchi and MacGregor Jenkins wrote biographies of Miss Dickinson.

Dickinson, Preston (1891-1930), American painter who was trained at the ART STUDENTS' LEAGUE, New York, and at the LOUVRE, Paris, where he studied the works of the old masters. He was influenced to some extent by Paul CEZANNE, and by Japanese prints. His style in painting mirrored the innate restlessness of his nature: it was technically almost flawless but somewhat lacking in substance. His pictures are to be seen in many American art galleries and museums.

Dickinson, Thomas (1877-), American author of books relating to the theatre who served in the Spanish-American War, and finished his education at Columbia University and the University of Wisconsin. His works include *The Case of American Drama* (1915); *The Contemporary Drama of England; The Insurgent Theatre; Playwrights of the New American Theatre; An Outline of Contemporary Drama; The Theatre in a Changing Europe* (in collaboration).

Dicksee, Sir Francis Bernard (1853-1928), English painter who studied with his father and at the Royal Academy, London, exhibited his first painting *Elijah Confronting Ahab* in 1876: it received the gold medal, and his next picture, *Harmony,* was purchased by the Academy. His works include *Evangeline; Romeo and Juliet; Mountain of the Winds; The Ideal; Chivalry; Dawn.* He also painted many fine portraits; his sister, **Margaret Isabel Dicksee** (1858-1903), was also a painter of genuine ability.

Didelot, Charles Louis (1767-1836), French dancer, ballet master, and choreographer, born at Stockholm, Sweden, who studied with DAUBERVAL, NOVERRE, and Auguste VESTRIS, and appeared first at the Paris L'Opéra in 1790: later he acted as dancer and ballet master at St. Petersburg and London. His first successful ballet, *Flore et Zephire,* was produced at London in 1796: it was followed by *Apollo and Daphnis; Theseus and Ariadne; The Caliph of Bagdad; Alceste; Roland and Morgana; Dido; The Prisoner of the Caucasus,* and many others which attracted lovers of the ballet because of their picturesque beauty and novel stage effects.

Diderot, Denis (1713-1784), French critic of art and literature, considered the greatest intellectual force of his time, and also distinguished as an encyclopedist, novelist, and dramatist. His greatest work was a monumental encyclopedia compiled in collaboration with Jean le Rond d'Alembert. An important contribution to dramatic criticism, entitled *La Paradoxe sur le comédien,* advances some original theories on the correct reactions of the actor in regard to his audience. His plays include *The Natural Son* and *The Father of the Family.*

Dido, in Roman mythology a Tyrian princess who fled to Africa after her husband, Acerbas, was killed by her brother, and founded the city of CARTHAGE. According to VIRGIL, Dido fell in love with AENEAS when he visited Carthage, and committed suicide when he abandoned her to return to his native land: another version attributes her suicide to unwillingness to marry Iarbas, an African monarch who sold her the land on which Carthage was erected.

Dido and Aeneas, a grand opera in three acts: libretto by Nahum Tate and music by Henry PURCELL; first produced with amateur singers at Josias Priest's Boarding School at Chelsea, England about 1689. It was revived at the Royal College of Music, London, in 1895 on the bicentenary of Purcell's death, and has been presented at several colleges in the United States. The plot unfolds the love of Queen DIDO of Carthage for the Trojan hero, AENEAS: when Aeneas leaves her to return to his native land, she dies of a broken heart. Her song, *When I am Laid in Earth,* is one of the most poignant utterances of grief in all opera.

Dielman, Frederick (1847-1935), American painter, born in Germany who came to the United States as a child, and later studied at the Royal Academy in Munich. His works include mural panels, *Law and History,* for the Congressional Library, Washington, and mosaic panels, *Thrift,* at the Albany, N. Y., Savings Bank. He was president of the National Academy of Design and The Fine Arts Federation of New York: also art director of several institutions including the College of the City of New York and Cooper Union, New York.

Dies Irae, a hymn of the Roman Catholic church which now forms the second division of the requiem: the literal meaning of the Latin words is "Day of wrath." The hymn, attributed to Thomas of Celano, comprises seventeen stanzas of three trochaic lines, and six irregular final lines. Hector BERLIOZ introduces the chanting of the Dies Irae into the last movement of his *Symphonie Fantastique* (Fantastic Symphony).

Dietrich, Marlene (1904-), German stage and screen actress who first appeared in a German version of *Broadway* after dramatic training with Max Reinhardt. Among the films in which she appeared are *Blue Angel; Morocco; Dishonored; Shanghai Express; The Devil is a Woman; Song of Songs; Scarlet Empress; Desire; Garden of Allah; Knight Without Armour; Destry Rides Again; The Flame of New Orleans; The Spoilers; Pittsburgh.*

Dietrichson, Lorenz Henrik Segelcke (1834-1917), Norwegian poet and critic of literature and art who became professor of the history of art at the Academy of Arts at Stockholm, and at the University of Oslo. His works include the poems *Olaf Lilijekraus* (1857); *Kivleflätten;* several fine critical works on art, and an outstanding volume of reminiscences.

Dietz, John (1911-), American radio engineer and director educated at Marietta College, Ohio: after experience as chief radio operator for an air line, he worked with Orson WELLES as sound engineer for dramatic productions at the Columbia Broadcasting Company. In 1939 he assumed the direction of children's shows at the Transamerican Broadcasting Company, rejoining CBS in 1942 as director of *Commandos,* a dramatic feature concerning World War II, and of *Our Secret Weapon,* a propaganda series of broadcasts with Rex Stout as commentator.

Dieux Mendiants, Les, see **Gods Go A-Begging, The.**

Digges, Dudley (1880-   ), Irish stage and screen actor and producer who appeared first with the Abbey Players at Dublin, and made his American debut in 1904 with Minnie Maddern Fiske at the Manhattan Theatre, New York. In 1911 he became stage manager for George Arliss, and from 1919 to 1930 appeared in many Theatre Guild productions including *Heartbreak House, Liliom, Mr. Pim Passes By, Hedda Gabler,* and *Outward Bound.* He also produced *Candida, Pygmalion,* and *Becky Sharp* for the Guild, appearing more than three thousand times in twenty-four plays. He has also played leading roles in many film productions including *Outward Bound, The Maltese Falcon, Alexander Hamilton, Emperor Jones, Mutiny on the Bounty, The Voice of Bugle Ann, The General Died at Dawn, The Light That Failed; Raffles.*

Dilke, Emilia Frances Strong, Lady (1840-1904), English art critic and collector: her works include *The Renaissance of Art in France* (1879); *Art in the Modern State;* also volumes on French architects, sculptors, engravers and draughtsmen.

Dilling, Mildred, contemporary American harpist who studied with Henriette Renie in Paris: she has appeared in Europe with Yvette Guilbert, Edouard de Reszke and Jean de Reszke, and in the United States with Alma Gluck and Frances Alda, also giving recitals, teaching in prominent conservatories, and publishing two volumes of harp transcriptions.

Dillingham, Charles B. (1868-1934), American theatrical producer who had considerable experience as a journalist, and a dramatic critic of the New York *Sun* before producing *Mlle. Modiste; Chin-Chin; Watch Your Step; Blossom Time; A Bill of Divorcement; Bulldog Drummond; Stepping Stones.* He also produced all the musical plays in which Fred Stone and David Montgomery appeared including *The Wizard of Oz,* and acted as manager for Margaret Anglin, Fritzi Scheff, Maxine Elliott, and several other distinguished actors.

Dillon, George (1906-   ), American poet educated at the University of Chicago: his works include *The Boy in the Wind* (1927); *The Flowering Stone,* which won the Pulitzer prize in 1932; *Flowers of Evil,* in collaboration with Edna St. Vincent Millay.

Dime Novels, the "pulp publications" of America from the years 1850 to 1900 which came into being through the success of the "Penny Dreadfuls" in Great Britain. The name "dime novels" is hardly accurate because many of the thrillers sold for the paltry sum of five cents, and were excellent value at that if the amount of blood-curdling adventure furnished for a nickel is considered.

Dimnet, Ernest, Abbé (1866-   ), French priest and author educated at the Cathedral School at Cambrai, and later taught at the Catholic University of Lille and the College Stanislas in Paris. After World War I he lectured in the United States, and raised $100,000 for the restoration of Lille University: he is now (1943) Canon of the Cathedral at Cambrai. Among his works published in English are *Paul Bourget* (1913); *France Herself Again; From a Paris Balcony; The Brontë Sisters; My Old World; My New World.*

D'Indy, Vincent, see **d'Indy, Vincent.**

Dine, S. S. van, see **Wright, Willard Huntington.**

Dinehart, Alan (1889-   ), American stage and screen actor educated at the University of Montana; he made his stage debut in 1912 at the Bush Temple of Music, Chicago, and in New York at the Palace Theatre in a sketch entitled "The Meanest Man in the World" of which he was co-author. He has since appeared in New York and on tour in many successful plays. During his film career, started in 1932, he has played important roles in more than fifty motion pictures.

Dingelstedt, Franz von, Baron (1814-1881), German poet, novelist, and dramatist: his first success, *Songs of a Cosmopolitan Night Watchman* (1841), shocked government officials. His works include a society novel, *The Amazons;* a splendid tragedy, *The House of the Barneveldts:* he also adapted many of Shakespeare's plays for the German stage, and became director of the Royal Theatre in Munich and the Granducal Theatre in Weimar.

Diniz da Cruz e Silva, Antonio (1731-1799), Portuguese lawyer and poet born in Lisbon who became counsel to the Supreme Court in Rio de Janeiro, Brazil, and was one of the founders of the distinguished literary society known as the *Lisbon Arcadia.* His works include more than 300 sonnets; an epic poem, *Brazil's Metamorphoses,* and a heroic-comic epic, *Hyssop,* which was translated into French prose, and republished several times.

Dinocrates, Greek architect of the 3rd century, B.C., who designed the new city of Alexandria for Alexander the Great, and arranged broad streets on a regular plan to replace the tortuously winding narrow ones of the older city. He also constructed the vast funeral pyre of Hephaestus, the Roman god of fire and metallurgy.

Diocletian (245-313), Roman emperor of humble birth who distinguished himself as a soldier, and was proclaimed emperor by the army in 284 A.D. He erected many fine buildings in Rome, especially the baths, parts of which are still standing. He also built a magnificent palace at Spalato, a city on the Adriatic Sea: the ruins were studied by Robert Adam, a famous English architect who utilized some of his findings in the *Adelphi,* a block of buildings erected in London.

Diomede or **Diomedes,** in Greek mythology one of the bravest heroes of the TROJAN WAR: he was a favorite of ATHENA who aided him not only in overcoming mortals, but in attacking the gods themselves. He aided in the capture of Troy by carrying off the PALLADIUM, an image of PALLAS ATHENA which had rendered the besieged city impregnable.

Dionysus, in Greek mythology the god of nature and vegetation, especially of wine, and therefore usually referred to as the god of wine; the name *Bacchus* was also used in Greece from the 5th century, and the god was regarded as the patron of poetry and music. Great festivals called the *Dionysia* were held in his honor: they lasted for six days, celebrating the departure of winter and the advent of summer. Authorities regard these festivals as the original source of Greek drama and therefore of all drama.

Dionysus, Theatre of, a theatre in ATHENS, Greece, located beneath the south side of the ACROPOLIS. Plays were probably first given at the beginning of the 5th century B.C.: it was excavated in 1864, and all the sixty-seven seats around the orchestra, made of Pentelic marble, were found perfectly preserved with the names inscribed of the priests and high personages who occupied them. The plays of EURIPIDES, SOPHOCLES, AESCHYLUS, and ARISTOPHANES were performed there.

Diorama, see **Daguerre, Louis Jacques Mandé.**

Dioscuri, see **Castor and Pollux.**

Dippel, Andreas (1866-1932), German operatic tenor and impresario who studied dramatic singing while employed by a banking house, and made his European debut in 1887 at the Stadt Theater in Bremen, and his American debut in 1890 at the Metropolitan Opera House, New York, in FRANCHETTI'S *Asrael*. He sang at the Vienna Court Opera from 1893 to 1898, and at the Metropolitan Opera House from 1898 to 1908; also at Covent Garden, London, the Royal Opera in Munich and at the BAYREUTH Festivals. His repertory included 150 leading roles in German, French, and Italian operas. In 1908 he became administrative manager of the Metropolitan Opera Company, and from 1910 to 1913 manager of the Philadelphia-Chicago Opera Company: in the latter year he organized a company to produce comic operas of the better class.

Diptych, the Roman name for a tablet in two parts joined by a hinge: the inner surfaces were covered with wax and written on with a stylus, and the outer sides were usually decorated with sculptures in wood, ivory, gold, or silver. During the Middle Ages, pictures of the Madonna, the Saints, or scenes from the Passion were substituted for writing, and the diptych used as a portable altar. A tablet with three panels was called a *triptych,* and a tablet with four or more panels a *polytych.*

Direction, in drama the task of co-ordinating the functional elements of the theatre with the essential parts of the drama, usually undertaken by both the director of the play and its producer.

In addition to supervising the casting of the parts, the diction, and the gestures of the actors, the scenery, lighting, and costumes must also be placed in harmonious, reciprocal relation so that the audience understands perfectly the message conveyed by the play through the medium of spoken words, gestures, scenic effects, and a subtly created atmosphere of reality.

Directoire Style, in furniture the style favored during the period of the French Directorate (1795-1799) in chairs, tables, desks, mirrors, beds, sofas, writing cabinets, consoles, etc. It may be regarded as transitional in that it departed from the splendor of the Louis XVI period, substituting waxed woods for marquetry, chintzes for rich damasks, and wall papers for tapestries: its keynote may be said to have been simplicity.

Dirge, in music a vocal or instrumental composition to be sung either at a funeral, or at a service in commemoration of the dead. The term is also applicable to some orchestral works: the second movement of BEETHOVEN'S *"Eroica" Symphony* may be considered a dirge although its title is actually *Marche funèbre,* and the same may be said of the *Marche funèbre* in CHOPIN'S Piano Sonata, Op. 35.

Discobolus, a statue by MYRON, a Greek sculptor of the 5th century: it pictures the throwing of the discus, a popular sport at the ancient Greek games. The original is lost, and the figure, which shows the athlete ready to throw the discus, is only to be seen in copies at the VATICAN, Rome, the BRITISH MUSEUM, London, and in a restoration by Professor Fürtwangler at the Munich Museum.

Discus, a flat circular stone from 8 to 12 inches in diameter and weighing from 4 to 5 pounds; it was used by the ancient Greeks for throwing as an exercise in gymnastics. The sport is often mentioned in the works of HOMER, and was one of the contests in the ancient Olympic Games. Discus throwing was introduced at the revival of the Olympic Games in 1896, and has since become a popular sport in Europe, Great Britain and the United States.

Diseuse, in drama a feminine dramatic monologist; the rarely used masculine form is *diseur:* among the actresses who have distinguished themselves in this field are Mlle. Yvette GUILBERT, Ruth DRAPER, and Cornelia Otis SKINNER.

Disney, Walter (1901-   ), American artist and producer of film cartoons who first engaged in commercial art; in 1919 he produced a series of pictorial cartoons followed by the *Alice Comedies* which combined live actors and cartoons, and the *Oswald Cartoons.* The production of *Mickey Mouse* cartoons began in 1928, followed by many others including the *Silly Symphony* cartoons; *Snow White and the Seven Dwarfs; Ferdinand the Bull; The Ugly Duckling; Pinocchio; Fantasia; The Reluctant Dragon; Dumbo; Bambi; Saludos Amigos:* the last-named takes "Mickey Mouse" on a goodwill tour of South America. Mr. Disney has received several awards from the motion picture industry, and degrees from American colleges in recognition of the originality of his ideas and the artistic qualities of his cartoons.

Disraeli, Benjamin, Lord Beaconsfield (1804-1881), English statesman and novelist, son of Isaac Disraeli (1766-1848), author of several critical works on literary subjects. Benjamin Disraeli became prime minister in 1868, resigning during the same year, but again holding the office under Queen Victoria from 1874 to 1880. His works include *Vivian Grey* (1826-27); *The Young Duke; Contarini Fleming; Venetia; Coningsby; Sybil; Tancred; Lothair; Endymion.*

Dissonance, in musical theory the sounding simultaneously of tones in such remote relationship that their combination produces beats. The most exact definition appears to be that in the *Encyclopedia* of the Paris Conservatory of Music: "the effect produced by two tones which seem to repulse each other, and to give the impression of two separate sounds even though struck together."

Distemper, in painting a process in which the pigments are combined with a size in which glue is the base instead of white of egg. The resulting mixture is used for scene painting or the decoration of walls and ceilings.

Distich, in poetry another name for the COUPLET.

Dithyramb, an ode or hymn in honor of DIONYSUS out of which it would appear that ancient Greek tragedy was developed. Under the guidance of ARION OF METHYMA it became a choral ode sung by many singers interspersed with spoken verses: this was the nucleus from which Greek drama rose to great heights centuries later.

Ditrichstein, Leo James (1865-1928), Hungarian actor and dramatist who made his stage debut at Berlin, and came to the United States in 1890 to appear in *Honor* by Hermann SUDERMANN. After quickly mastering English, he appeared in the original production of *Trilby:* also in his own plays including *Gossip, A Superfluous Husband,* and *The Head of the Family,* all three written in collaboration with Clyde FITCH; he also wrote and played in *The Song of the Sword, The Last Appeal,* and *The Ambitious Mrs. Alcott.*

Dittersdorf, Karl Ditters von (1739-1799), Austrian violinist and composer who became a favorite of the nobility: he accompanied Christoph Willibald von GLUCK on his journey to Italy in 1761, and succeeded Michael HAYDN as concertmaster to the Bishop of Gross-Wardein in Hungary. His works include a successful opera, *The Apothecary and the Doctor;* several oratorios; many symphonies; a concerto grosso; chamber music including many fine string quartets. In his operatic works Dittersdorf may be regarded as the precursor of Wolfgang Amadeus MOZART although he lacked the latter's consummate dramatic genius.

Ditzen, Rudolph (1893-), German novelist who uses the pen name "Hans Fallada": his works published in English include *Little Man, What Now?* (1933); *The World Outside; Once We Had a Child; An Old Heart Goes A-Journeying; Sparrow Farm; Wolf Among Wolves.*

Divertissement, in ballet the French term for a dance complete in itself, executed alone or as part of a ballet: a single scene in a ballet, such as a rustic festival in which dancers take part is also called a *divertissement.*

Divine Comedy (Divina Commedia), an epic poem by the Italian poet, DANTE Alghieri (1265-1321), called a comedy by Dante because the poem has a happy ending: the epithet "divine," was added by admirers. It is divided into three parts; *Inferno, Purgatory,* and *Paradise:* Dante is conducted on his journey through the first two by VIRGIL, and through Paradise by BEATRICE PORTINARI for whom the poem was written as a memorial after her death in 1290. English translations have been made by Henry W. Carey, Charles Eliot Norton, and Henry Wadsworth LONGFELLOW.

Dix, Beulah Marie (1876-), American playwright; her works include *Soldier Rigdale* (1899); *The Fair Maid of Graystones; The Road to Yesterday; The Lilac Room; Fighting Blade; Moloch; Across the Border; Pity of God.*

Dix, Otto (1891-), German painter who studied at the School of Arts and Crafts and the Academy at Dresden, later becoming professor at the Düsseldorf Academy and a member of the Prussian Academy. He was influenced by DURER, HOLBEIN, BALDUNG, and GOYA in his realistic paintings of the German peasantry, and the satiric realism of his figure studies, nudes, and portraits. The MUSEUM OF MODERN ART owns his *Child With Doll,* a typical work.

Dix, Richard (1895-), American stage and screen actor who received his dramatic training in the Northwestern School of Dramatics, later appearing with William FAVERSHAM and with stock companies. He has appeared in many films including *The Christian; Seven Keys to Baldpate; Cimarron; Public Defender; Secret Service; Stingaree; Special Investigator; Man of Conquest; Badlands of Dakota; Tombstone.*

Dixey, Henry E. (1859-1943), American actor who made his debut on the stage at the age of ten in *Under the Gaslight* at the Howard Athenaeum, Boston: after appearing in many plays and comic operas, he scored a sensational success in *Adonis* at the Bijou Theatre, New York, with an uninterrupted run of 619 performances. Among other plays in which he appeared were *Oliver Goldsmith; The Burgomaster; A Modern Magdalen; The Man on the Box; Bought and Paid For; The Rivals; Tarnish; The Merry Malones.*

Dixie, a song written in 1859 by Daniel Decatur EMMETT (1815-1904), while he was a member of Bryant's Minstrels; it created a sensation, and all the numerous minstrel companies touring the United States featured it as a song and dance. When the Civil War broke out, the Confederate troops sang it while camping and marching: the words seemed to fit the Southern cause, and several attempts to write a lyric favoring the North failed lamentably. *Dixie* today is a ditty of both the North and the South as the song is inherently American because of its care-free and generally cheerful character.

Dixon, Thomas (1864-), American novelist educated at Wake Forest College and Johns Hopkins University, and admitted to the bar in 1886. His novels include *The Leopard's Spots* (1902); *The One Woman; The Clansman* a best-seller glorifying the Ku Klux Klan, from which David Wark GRIFFITH made one of the most moving incidents of his silent film, "The Birth of a Nation." Dixon wrote many more novels of melodramatic character: one of them, *The Flaming Sword* (1939) pictured the collapse of American democracy through Communistic plotting with the Southern Negro.

Djanel, Lily (1909-), French dramatic soprano who studied at the Paris Conservatory, and with Louis Bachner, making her debut in Carmen at the Théâtre Royal, Liége, in 1930. After singing at the Paris Opéra, the Opéra-Comique, and at Monte Carlo, she appeared in 1941 at the Teatro Colon in Buenos Aires, and made her debut in 1942 at the METROPOLITAN OPERA HOUSE in *Carmen*, appearing later in STRAUSS' *Salome*. Among her highly praised roles are Tosca, Thaïs, Louise, and Melisande.

Djinn, see **Jinni.**

Dmitriev, Ivan Ivanovich (1760-1837), Russian poet and from 1810 to 1814 minister of justice for Alexander II of Russia: he was so greatly encouraged by Nicholas KARAMZIN's praise of his first poem, *The Dove*, that he devoted himself to writing after 1814. His works, modeled on the French poets, include a translation of Jean de LA FONTAINE's *Fables*: also songs, odes, and an epico-dramatic poem, *Jermak, Conqueror of Siberia*.

Dobell, Sydney Thompson (1824-1874), English poet whose first important work, *The Roman,* was inspired by interest in the cause of Italian freedom. His other works include a poem, *Balder,* and a volume of verses, *England in Time of War*: many of the verses from the latter have been included in anthologies.

Dobie, Charles Caldwell (1881-), American novelist and short story writer who published his first story when he was thirty years old: his works include *The Blood Red Dawn* (1920); *Less Than Kin; San Francisco Tales; San Francisco's Chinatown; San Francisco Adventure; The Crystal Ball,* a volume of short stories.

Dobie, James Frank (1888-), American editor and author: his works include *A Vaquero of the Brush Country* (1929); *Coronado's Children; On the Open Range; Tales of the Mustang; The Longhorns.*

Döblin, Alfred (1878-), German novelist, poet, and dramatist educated for the practice of medicine: his works published in English include *Alexanderplatz* (1931); *Men Without Mercy; The Living Thoughts of Confucius.* His novel of Chinese life, *The Three Springs of Wang-lun,* and another with its scenes laid in the Thirty Years War, *Wallenstein,* have not been translated into English although they were successful in Germany.

Döbrentei, Gabor (1786-1851), Hungarian poet who founded a magazine, the *Transylvanian Museum,* which exerted a powerful influence in developing Magyar literature. As director of the new Hungarian theatre he introduced the plays of SCHILLER and SHAKESPEARE to Hungarian audiences: his works include songs, odes, and elegies many of which, such as the *Alpine Violet* and *Hussar Songs* have been translated.

Dobrowen, Issay Alexandrovitch (1893-), Russian pianist, composer, and conductor who studied composition with Serge TANEIEV at the Moscow Conservatory, and piano with Leopold GODOWSKY in Vienna, later becoming professor of the piano and conductor at Moscow, and conducting opera and symphonic concerts in Dresden, Berlin, Sofia, Oslo, and Frankfort. He has been guest conductor of the New York Philharmonic, San Francisco, and Minneapolis Symphony Orchestras. His compositions include a Russian fairy play; concertos for piano and for violin; pieces for violin and many fine piano works.

Dobson, Henry Austin (1840-1921), English poet and biographer educated as a civil engineer: his works, considered inimitable in respect to fanciful ideas and artistic finish, include *Vignettes in Rhyme* (1873); *Proverbs in Porcelain; Old World Idyls; At the Sign of the Lyre.* He also wrote biographies of William HOGARTH, Henry FIELDING and Oliver GOLDSMITH besides contributing to the British "Dictionary of National Biography."

Dobson, William (1610-1646), English painter who studied with Sir Robert Peake, and copied the works of Anthony VAN DYCK so accurately that he succeeded the latter as court painter to Charles I of England. His works include *The Beheading of John the Baptist* and many portraits of the English nobility of his time.

Dodd, John Kew (1752-1839), English bow maker regarded in England as the equal of François TOURTE in France. His bows are finely made and perfectly balanced although some of them were fashioned a little short. He was extremely jealous of his reputation, cutting all his own sticks, and refusing thousands of dollars for a copy of the pattern. His bows command prices at the present time ranging from $85.00 to $250.00.

Dodd, Lee Wilson (1879-1933), American novelist, poet, and dramatist: his works include *A Modern Alchemist and Other Poems* (1906); *The Return of Eve; Speed; The Middle Miles and Other Poems; Pals First; The Book of Susan; Lilia Chenoworth; The Girl Next Door; The Changelings; The Great Enlightenment.*

Dodge, Mary Abigail (1833-1896), American essayist and poet who used the pen name "Gail Hamilton": her works include *Country Living and Country Thinking* (1862); *Gala Days; Summer Rest; A Battle of the Books; First Love is Best; Our Young Folks.*

Dodge, Mary Elizabeth Mapes (1831-1905), American editor, poet, and author: her works include *The Irvington Stories* (1865); *Hans Brinker; Rhymes and Jingles; Along the Way* republished as *Poems and Verses; Donald and Dorothy; The*

Land of Pluck; The Golden Gate. She was editor of *St. Nicholas Magazine* from 1873 to 1905.

Dodgson, Charles Lutwidge, see **Carroll, Lewis.**

Dodsley, Robert (1703-1764), English poet, dramatist, bookseller, and publisher, who was friendly with Alexander POPE, Samuel JOHNSON, and Oliver GOLDSMITH. His works include a volume of verse; a satiric drama, *The Toy Shop,* produced at Covent Garden, and two comedies, *The King and the Miller of Mansfield,* and *Sir John Cockle at Court.*

Doge, the official title of the high magistrates in the medieval republics of VENICE and Genoa. The first doge of Venice was elected by the people in 697: the tenure of office was for life, and the power of the doge was practically absolute. Later the duties of the doge became perfunctory, and the office was abolished in 1805.

Doges' Palace (Venice), a building at Venice begun by Marino FALIERO in 1354 in which the different sections and the decorations are among the finest of the period: they include the allegorical and Biblical sculptures of the capitals; the great entrance; the courtyard; the *Giants' Staircase* with its colossal figures of MARS and NEPTUNE. The halls throughout the palace are covered with masterpieces by TINTORETTO, TITIAN, VERONESE, and many other famous Venetian painters.

Dohnányi, Ernst von (1877-), Hungarian pianist, conductor, and composer who studied with Eugène D'ALBERT, and toured Europe, Great Britain, and the United States with phenomenal success. He taught the piano at the Hochschule in Berlin, and directed the Royal Music School at Budapest in addition to conducting the Philharmonic Orchestra in the latter city, and becoming music director of the Hungarian Broadcasting Company. His early compositions were greatly praised by Johannes BRAHMS, and his mature works have fully justified the great German master's predictions: they include two operas and a ballet; two symphonies; concertos for violoncello and for violin; *Variations on a Nursery Rhyme* for piano and orchestra; piano pieces and songs.

Dolce, in music a term indicating that the music is to be played sweetly or softly: the superlative, *dolcissimo,* implies that the greatest possible degree of softness or sweetness is to be attained.

Dolci, Carlo (1616-1686), Italian painter who studied with Jacopo Vignali, and actually executed a figure of St. John at eleven years of age which was greatly praised: among his finest works are *Magdalen; Ecce Homo; St. Sebastian; Four Evangelists; Adoration of the Magi; St. Andrew Praying before his Crucifixion;* the latter is considered his finest creation.

Dole, Nathan Haskell (1852-1935), American novelist, historian, and poet educated at Harvard University: his works include *Young Folks' History of Russia* (1881); *A Score of Famous Composers; On the Point,* a novel; *The Hawthorne Tree,* poems; *Omar the Tentmaker; The Building of the Organ,* poems; *Life of Count Tolstoy.* He also translated works by TOLSTOY and DAUDET in addition to editing juvenile books, and volumes of the Greek and Latin poets.

Dolin, Anton (1904-), English ballet dancer and choreographer whose real name is Patrick Healey-Kay; he studied with Bronislava NIJINSKA, and made his debut with the DIAGHILEFF Ballet in 1924. In 1938 he appeared with the Covent Garden Ballet Russe, and in 1939 became principal classic dancer and choreographer of the BALLET THEATRE in New York. His choreographic productions include new settings of *Gisella, Pas de Quatre, Capriccioso, Swan Lake,* and *The Sleeping Beauty.*

Dolinoff, Alexis, contemporary Russian ballet and character dancer who studied with CECCHETTI, PAVLOWA, PREOBRAJENSKA, and NIJINSKA, appearing first with the Wolkowsky Dance Group at the Crystal Palace Circus, London. He has been solo dancer with the Anna Pavlowa Ballet, the Ida RUBINSTEIN Ballet, the CHAUVE SOURIS, the Philadelphia Grand Opera Company, and several other leading organizations. He has also distinguished himself as a ballet-master, choreographer, and teacher.

Dolmen, in archaeology the name applied to a circle of monoliths usually enclosing a sepulchral monument known as a barrow or cairn: it consists of a large, flat stone laid as a roof across two or more upright stones. The Welsh name is *cromlech;* dolmens are also found in England, France, Spain, North Africa, and the Far East.

Dolmetsch, Arnold (1858-1940), French pianist and violinist who studied the latter instrument with Henri VIEUXTEMPS: later he mastered the art of playing the viola d'amore and studied the ancient methods of making and repairing virginals, spinets, and harpsichords, becoming an authority on the subject. He also established the Dolmetsch Trio devoted to the performance of preclassic music on the original instruments, and founded the annual chamber music festivals at Haslemere in Surrey for the same purpose.

Dome, in architecture a term applied to a spherical or spheroidal vault of which a circle is the horizontal plane. It may surmount either a circular wall, a square, or a polygonal area, and was one of the earliest forms of covering a building. It was much used in ancient Roman and early Italian architecture; the Pantheon and St. Peter's at Rome; also St. Mark's at Venice are excellent examples. It is also found on Egyptian and Indian mosques. Other outstanding examples are the domes on St. Paul's, London; the Invalides at Paris, and the Cathedral at Granada in Spain.

Domenichino, Il (1581-1641), the name used by Domenico Zampieri, an Italian painter who studied with Denis CALVAERT, and worked with Annibale CARRACCI at Rome, for whom he painted two murals picturing the *Legend of Perseus* in eight scenes. His works include *Martyrdom of St. Andrew; Communion of St. Jerome; Deliverance of St. Peter; Venus Finding the Body of Adonis; Guardian Angel; St. Cecilia; The Hunt.*

Domenichino, Veneziano (c.1400-1461), Italian painter whose influence on later painters including his pupil, Piero della FRANCESCHI was profound. Only a few of his authenticated works are in existence: they include an altarpiece in the Uffizi Museum; *Adoration of the Magi;* a fresco fragment representing the *Madonna Enthroned;* a fresco of *St. Francis and St. John the Baptist.*

Domestic Symphony, see **Sinfonia Domestica.**

Donalda, Pauline (1882-), Canadian dramatic soprano who studied at the Royal Victoria College, Montreal, and with E. Duvernoy in Paris, making her debut in 1904 at Nice in Massenet's *Manon,* and at Hammerstein's Opera House, New York, in 1906 in Gounod's *Faust.* After appearing at the Opéra-Comique, Paris, and at Covent Garden, London, for many years, she taught singing in Paris from 1923 to 1937, returning to Montreal in 1937 to establish a vocal studio.

Donald Duck, a character in Walt DISNEY's animated film cartoons said to have come into being through Disney's hearing an imitator of birds and animals mimic a scared little girl recite "Mary Had a Little Lamb." The first picture in which the now world-famous duck had the stellar part was *Modern Inventions* (1937): since that time he has appeared in many films seen in every part of the world, and is actually in receipt of regular fan mail.

Donat, Robert (1905-), English stage and screen actor who made his debut in 1921 at London as Lucius in *Julius Caesar:* he has since appeared in other Shakespearean plays, and in *Iphigenia in Tauris; The Rivals; Mary Rose; Precious Bane.* He has also played stellar roles in many films including *The Count of Monte Cristo; Thirty-Nine Steps; The Ghost Goes West; Knight Without Armour; The Citadel; Goodbye, Mr. Chips; The Young Mr. Pitt.*

Donatello (c.1386-1466), Italian sculptor whose name is the diminutive of Donato di Betto Bardi: it is not known with whom he studied, but he became one of the greatest sculptors of all time. His masterpieces include the figures of *St. George* and *David* now in the BARGELLO MUSEUM; the equestrian statue, *Gattamalata,* in Padua; *Il Zuccone* for the Campanile in Florence; *The Annunciation; Madonna and Child* at the Church of San Antonio, Padua; *Dancing Children* at the Museum of the Duomo, Florence.

Donato d'Agnolo, see **Bramante.**

Don Cossack Russian Male Choir, an organization of Russian singers formed after World War I, and composed of White Russian emigrants. The leader is Serge Jaroff (1896-) who studied at the Academy for Choral Singing in Moscow: none of the other members were musicians before, but were selected and trained by Jaroff. The choir made its first American tour in 1929, and in 1936 its 3000th performance at Carnegie Hall, New York; it has also toured Europe, Great Britain, Canada, and Australia. The vocal range of the choir extends from the famous Russian *basso profundo* low notes to falsetto notes in the soprano

range. There are Columbia recordings available of many works sung by the choir.

Don Giovanni, a grand opera in two acts; text by Lorenzo DA PONTE; music by Wolfgang Amadeus MOZART; first produced at the National Theatre, Prague, in 1787, and at the Park Theatre, New York, in 1826. The librettist, Da Ponte, who was living in New York, was present. The story is: Don Giovanni, a dissolute Spanish nobleman, kills the Governor of Seville, Donna Anna's father, while attempting to seduce her: he escapes unrecognized but her fiance, Don Ottavio, swears vengeance; Donna Elvira, whom Don Giovanni has betrayed, also seeks his downfall. After an attempt to disrupt the wedding of a country maiden, Zerlino, Don Giovanni visits the graveyard where the Governor is buried: he invites the statue on the grave to dine with him, and the invitation is accepted. While Don Giovanni is eating, Donna Elvira comes and begs him to change his way of living, but he scorns her. Then the ghostly statue arrives and calls upon the rake to repent or be damned: Don Giovanni laughs at the warning. After the statue has departed, darkness settles upon the hall; devils appear and drag the Don into the abyss. There is a complete Victor recording in Italian by the Glyndebourne Opera Company; also many Victor and Columbia recordings of individual arias and concerted numbers.

Don Giovanni (Overture), the overture to the opera of the same name by Wolfgang Amadeus MOZART, and one of the most popular orchestral works in concert, on the radio, and in recorded form. Otto JAHN, Mozart's biographer, makes the following comment on the speed with which Mozart could compose: "The day of performance approached, and on the previous evening the overture was still unwritten. We have already told how he parted late from the merry company, and sat down to write with a glass of punch before him, and his wife telling him stories; how sleep overcame him, and he was obliged to lie down for several hours before completing his task; how the copyist was sent for at seven o'clock in the morning, and the overture was ready at the appointed time." There is a Columbia recording by the London Philharmonic orchestra conducted by Sir Thomas Beecham.

Doni, Giovanni Battista (1594-1647), Italian nobleman, scholar, and patron of the arts: he became greatly interested in music, and invented an instrument called the amphicord—a kind of double lyre—which he dedicated to Pope Urban VIII. His valuable critical discussions of the earliest operas were published in 1903 by Angelo Solerti in his volume, *The Origin of Melodrama.*

Donizetti, Gaetano (1797-1848), Italian composer who studied at the Bergamo School of Music and the Bologna Liceo Filarmonico with Gioacchino ROSSINI and Vincenzo BELLINI: he constitutes the trio of composers who produced outstanding operatic works during the first half of the 19th century. His first opera, *Enrico di Borgogna,* was successfully produced in 1818: during the following twenty-six years he composed more than sixty operas of which several are still in the operatic repertory today including *Anne Boleyn; Elixir of Love; Lucrezia Borgia; Marino Faliero; Lucia di Lammermoor; Daughter of the Regiment; La Favorita; Linda da Chamounix; Don Pasquale.*

Don José, the principal male character in the opera, CARMEN, by Georges BIZET. He is a Spanish soldier who falls in love with Carmen, a cigarette girl; deserts the army to be near her, and finally kills her when she jilts him for the toreador, ESCAMILLO.

Don Juan, a tragi-comic ballet in one act: libretto by Eric Allatini and Michel FOKINE; music by Christoph Willibald von GLUCK; choreography by Michel Fokine; first produced at London, England, in 1936. The libretto follows closely the original story which Gluck used in the ballet produced in 1761, and the plot approximates that of MOZART's DON GIOVANNI. The *Dance of the Furies* in the final scene was also used in Gluck's opera, *Orfeo.*

Don Juan (Strauss), a tone composed by Richard STRAUSS in 1887-88, and first played by the Court Orchestra at Weimar in 1889: Artur NIKISCH conducted it with the BOSTON SYMPHONY ORCHESTRA in 1891. The work had its inspiration from a poem written by Nicholas LENAU in 1844; the poet's conception of Don Juan is not a hot-blooded, conscienceless libertine, but a man seeking but failing to find the ideal woman; he permits himself to be killed. There is a Victor recording by the London Philharmonic Orchestra under Fritz Busch, and a Columbia recording by the Pittsburgh Symphony Orchestra conducted by Fritz Reiner.

Donlevy, Brian (1903-), American stage and screen actor who was trained at the United States Naval Academy, and served in the French Aviation Force during World War I. He made his stage debut in 1924 at New York in *What Price Glory?*: after appearing in numerous successful plays he started his film career in the talking films in 1935. Among the many pictures in which he has been featured are *Barbary Coast; In Old Chicago; Jesse James; Union Pacific; Beau Geste; Destry Rides Again; The Great McGinty; Brigham Young; The Remarkable Andrew; Two Yanks in Trinidad; Wake Island.*

Donnay, Charles Maurice (1859-), French dramatist who made his debut as a playwright in 1891 with *Phryné*, a series of Greek scenes; in 1894 Mme. Réjane appeared in the title role of *Lysistrata*, a four act comedy. He is classed as a satiric realist, and his numerous successful plays include *The Family Boarding House; The Emancipated Woman; The Torrent; The Rise of Virginia.*

Donne, John (1573-1631), English clergyman and poet described by Izaak Walton as an eloquent speaker from the pulpit: his most important poetical works are his *Satires; An Anatomy of the World; The Progress of the Soul; Holy Sonnets.* The dawn of the 20th century witnessed a considerable revival of interest in Donne's poetical works.

Donne Curiose, Le, (The Curious Women), a comic opera in three acts: libretto by Luigi Sugana based on a comedy by Carlo GOLDONI; music by Ermanno WOLF-FERRARI; first produced at Munich in 1903, and at the Metropolitan Opera House, New York, in 1912. The plot is a slender one: the wives of some business men in Venice are curious as to what goes on in a club to which they are not admitted. They use various stratagems to break in, and, finding their husbands merely enjoying an excellent dinner, join them and all ends well.

Donnelly, Ignatius (1831-1901), American reformer and author: his works include *Atlantis* (1882); *Ragnarok; The Age of Fire and Gravel; The Great Cryptogram*, in which he undertook to prove that Francis BACON wrote the plays of Shakespeare; *Caesar's Column*, his most popular novel.

Donoghue, John (c.1852-1903), American sculptor who studied at the Academy of Design, New York, and also in Paris: his works include *Sophocles Leading the Chorus after the Battle of Salamis*, exhibited in 1885; *Saint Paul*, a figure now in the Library of Congress, Washington, D. C.

Don Quixote, the title of a satirical novel of adventure by Miguel de CERVANTES Saavedra; its hero, Don Quixote de la Mancha, goes forth with his squire, Sancho Panza, in search of adventure with extremely amusing results. The book became a universal favorite in Spain, and was translated into English and every European language including Turkish. Cervantes claimed that his purpose in writing the book was to "render abhorred of men the false and absurd stories contained in books on chivalry." An opera based on the episodes in the book was composed by Jules MASSENET in 1910, and an orchestral tone poem by Richard Strauss in 1897; more than a dozen other composers have written operas around the adventures of the doughty knight and his squire.

Don Quixote (Strauss), a tone poem composed by Richard STRAUSS in 1897, and performed for the first time at Cologne in 1898. Its subtitle is "Fantastic Variations on a Theme of Knightly Character": the theme for Don Quixote is assigned to the violoncello, and for Sancho Panza, his squire, to the viola. The ten variations seek to depict in music the assault upon the windmill, the battle with sheep, the unfortunate attack upon the pilgrims whom the worthy knight mistakes for robbers, the vision of his lady love, Dulcinea, and several other ludicrous adventures. There is a Victor recording by the Philharmonic Orchestra under Eugene Ormandy, and a Columbia recording by The New York Philharmonic Orchestra with Sir Thomas Beecham.

Doolittle, Hilda (1886-), American poet who writes under the pen name "H.D.," and is recognized as one of the leading Imagist poets who seek to convey their messages to readers through the direct medium of words. Her works include *Sea Garden* (1916); *Hymen; Heliodora and Other Poems; Palimpsest*, a novel; *Hedylus*, a novel; *Collected Poems.*

Door, in architecture an opening used for the purpose of entrance or exit. The most primitive form was a piece of hide or cloth utilized to keep out cold or heat: this was succeeded by a wooden or marble slab held in place by wooden pivots or other devices. The doors for King Solomon's temple, according to the BIBLE, were made of olive wood inlaid with gold: those described in HOMER were cased or inlaid with silver or brass. Roman doors were built in single, double or triple form by the use of hinges, and many doors in churches were made of cast bronze, or covered with heavy bronze plates on which great sculptors from the 10th to the 18th century carved exquisite figures and designs.

Doré, Gustave (1833-1882), French painter, sculptor, and illustrator who first contributed to the *Journal pour Rire,* and other magazines: among the books he illustrated were RABELAIS' works; BALZAC'S *Droll Tales;* the Bible; LA FONTAINE'S *Fables;* DANTE'S *Divine Comedy;* Cervantes' *Don Quixote;* POE'S *The Raven.* His pictures are marred by poor drawing and coloring, but his sculptures, such as the monument to Alexandre DUMAS, PERE, and the colossal *Vintage Vase* at the Golden Gate Park, San Francisco, are of the highest order.

Dorigny, Sir Nicholas (c.1656-1746), French engraver who studied with his father, Michel Dorigny, and became famous for his engravings of RAPHAEL, RENI, CARRACCI, DOMENICHINO, and other masters. He was knighted by Queen Anne of England in 1720 after he engraved the cartoons of Raphael at Hampton Court.

Dormer, in architecture a window projecting from the slope of a roof. Windows of this character were used as decoration for façades in the 15th century: they were frequently made of carved stone with balustrades.

Dorset, Charles Sackville, 6th **Earl of** (1638-1706), English poet, courtier, and patron of John DRYDEN, Samuel BUTLER, and William WYCHERLY: he wrote only a few poems of which one, *To all You Ladies Now at Hand,* written on the eve of a British naval victory in 1665, shows a sea-fighting spirit which has awarded it a place in many anthologies.

Dos Passos, John (1896-), American poet, essayist, novelist, who was educated at Harvard, and served as an ambulance driver in the French Army during World War I. His works include *One Man's Initiation* (1917); *Three Soldiers; A Pushcart at the Curb,* a book of verse; *Streets of Night; Manhattan Transfer; The 42nd Parallel; Journeys between Wars; Adventures of a Young Man; The Ground We Stand On; Number One.*

Dosso Dossi, Giovanni (1479-1542), Italian painter whose real name was Giovanni di Lutero: he was influenced by the great Venetian painters, and may have been a pupil of Lorenzo COSTA. His landscapes and many fine frescoes may have been inspired by GIORGIONE and TITIAN, and he was the intimate friend of the Italian poet, ARIOSTO, who praised him in his "Orlando Furioso." Among his finest creations are *St. George and St. Sebastian; Circe; The Three Ages of Man.*

Dostoievsky, Feodor Miklailovich (1821-1881), Russian short story writer and novelist: his first novel, *Poor Folk* (1844-45), was a decided success. In 1849 he was arrested and imprisoned for political activities: after his release his popular works included *The House of the Dead; Memoirs from Underground; Crime and Punishment; The Gambler; The Idiot; The Brothers Karamazov.* Critics unite in pronouncing Dostoievsky the one Russian author who may be regarded as the equal of Leo TOLSTOY.

Dou, Gerard (1613-1675), Dutch painter who was a pupil of REMBRANDT from 1628-1631: his works include *The Dropsical Woman; The Young Mother; The Young Man; The Poulterer's Shop; A Lady at Her Toilet.* There are several spellings of his name; among them *Dow* and *Douw.* Gabriel METSU and Franz von MIERIS were among his numerous pupils.

Double-bass or **Contrabass,** the largest and lowest-toned of the instruments in the violin family with the exception of the double contrabass and the octobass: the latter are rarely if ever used in modern orchestras. Double-basses have either three or four strings: the notes are written on the staff an octave higher than they actually sound. The great virtuosos on this instrument include Giovanni BOTTESINI, Domenico DRAGONETTI, and Serge KOUSSEVITZKY; the latter is now (1943) conductor of the Boston Symphony Orchestra.

Double Concerto, in music a concerto composed for two instruments of the same or different kinds, usually with orchestral accompaniment. Among the most interesting examples are the *Concerto for Two Violins in D minor* by Johann Sebastian BACH; the *Concerto for Violin and Violoncello* by Johannes BRAHMS; the *Concerto for Flute and Harp* and the *Sinfonie Concertante for Violin and Viola* by Wolfgang Amadeus MOZART; also concertos for two pianos-four hands with orchestra accompaniment by Johann Sebastian Bach, Wolfgang Amadeus Mozart, Arnold BAX, Arthur BLISS, and Francis POULENC.

Doucet, Henri Lucien (1856-1895), French painter who studied with Jules LEFEBVRE and Gustave BOULANGER; his works include *Adam and Eve; Hagar;* a portrait of Mme. Galli-Marie as Carmen; *A Spanish Woman; After the Ball*: his paintings are regarded as realistic, and characterized by daring and verve.

Dougherty, Paul (1877-), American painter who first took his degree in law, and then spent five years in Europe studying painting and exhibiting his first picture at the Paris Salon in 1901. He has since won many honors, medals, and prizes: his works include *October Seas; The Road to Cayey; Lake Louise; The Land and the Sea; Flood Tide; Moonlight Cove; A Freshening Gale; Sun and Storm.*

Doughty, Thomas (1793-1856), American painter, practically self-taught, who was one of the pioneers of the HUDSON RIVER SCHOOL, and received recognition at home and abroad for his fine landscapes. His works include *Scene on the Susquehanna; Delaware Water Gap; View on the*

Hudson; Departure of Columbus from Palos; Peep at the Catskills.

Douglas, Gavin (c.1474-1522), Scottish clergyman and poet: his original works include the allegory, *The Palice of Honor* (c.1501), and another allegory, *King Hart.* He also translated VIRGIL'S AENEID, thereby making the first English version of a great classic poet: his work reveals the influence of Geoffrey CHAUCER.

Douglas, Lloyd Cassel (1877-), American novelist educated for the ministry, and for many years a prominent congregational clergyman: his works include *Magnificent Obsession* (1929); *Precious Jeopardy; Green Light; White Banners; Home for Christmas; Disputed Passage; Invitation to Live; The Robe.*

Douglas, Melvyn (1901-), American stage and screen actor who made his stage debut with Jessie BONSTELLE'S stock company in Chicago, and later appeared in numerous plays before beginning his film career in the capacity of a director in 1931. Since 1936 he has played leading roles in many motion pictures including *Tonight or Never; Counsellor-at-Law; The Gorgeous Hussy; Theodora Goes Wild; Captains Courageous; Arsene Lupin Returns; The Toy Wife; The Shining Hour; Ninotchka; The Amazing Mr. Williams; The Two-Faced Woman.*

Douglas, Norman (1868-), English novelist educated in Germany; his first successful work, *South Wind,* was published in 1917: other books include *Together; Fountain in the Sand; Three of Them; Looking Back,* an autobiography.

Doumic, René (1860-1937), French critic of literature and drama; member of the French Academy and editor of the Revue des Deux Mondes. His works include *A History of French Literature,* and critical essays on George SAND and Alphonse LAMARTINE.

Dowdey, Clifford (1904-), American novelist educated at Columbia University: his works include *Bugles Blow No More; Gamble's Hundred; Sing for a Penny.* His novels concern themselves with the disruptive power of war on the people of Virginia, particularly in Richmond where he was born.

Dowling, Eddie (1895-), American actor, dramatist, and producer who made his stage debut in *Quo Vadis* at Providence, R. I., in 1909, and his first New York appearance in *The Velvet Lady* in 1917. He played the leading role in *Sally, Irene and Mary,* of which he was co-author, in 1922; also in *The Fall Guy* and *Honeymoon Lane.* His important productions include *Thumbs Up; Agatha Calling; Richard II; Shadow and Substance; The White Steed; The Time of Your Life; Here Come the Clowns;* his performance in the two last-named plays established him as a serious actor of rare ability.

Downes, Olin (1886-), American music critic and writer who studied the piano with Carl Baermann: he was music critic of the Boston *Post* from 1906 to 1924, and since that time for the New York *Times.* His books include *The Lure of Music* (1918); *Symphonic Broadcasts; Symphonic Masterpieces;* he also edited *Songs of Russia,* and has contributed critical articles to musical periodicals.

Doxology, in music a psalm or hymn in praise of God. The term is particularly applied to the *Gloria in Excelcis,* and the *Gloria Patri*: the latter is used at the end of the psalms, or at the close of the service in Christian churches of several denominations.

Doyle, Sir Arthur Conan (1859-1930), English author educated for the practice of medicine: after serving as a doctor in the Boer War, his pamphlets in defense of the British cause, *The Great Boer War* and *The Cause and the Conflict of the War,* won him his knighthood. His works include several historical novels and romances as well as a play, *The Story of Waterloo,* in which Sir Henry IRVING appeared with success, but his immortality is assured by the creation of one of the most popular characters in literature—*Sherlock Holmes*—said to have been inspired by the master detectives in the stories of Emile GABORIAU and Edgar Allan POE. The books in which Sherlock Holmes appears include *A Study in Scarlet* (1887); *The Sign of the Four; The Adventures of Sherlock Holmes; The Hound of the Baskervilles; The Return of Sherlock Holmes; The Valley of Fear; His Last Bow; The Case-Book of Sherlock Holmes.* Conan Doyle also became deeply interested in spiritualism, and wrote several books on the subject.

Doyle, Richard (1824-1883), English painter and caricaturist who studied with his father, John Doyle (1797-1868), also a caricaturist whose "Political Sketches" were famous. Richard Doyle was a fine water-colorist whose paintings were exhibited at the GROSVENOR GALLERY, but he became famous through his cover for *Punch,* and his illustrations for Charles DICKENS' *Christmas Stories,* and THACKERAY'S *The Newcomes.*

D'Oyly Carte Opera Company, see **Carte, Richard D'Oyly.**

Drachmann, Holger (1846-1908), Danish poet, novelist, and dramatist who first aspired to be a painter, but finally devoted himself to literature. His first book of poems, *Digte,* appeared in 1872; it was followed by another, *Muffled Melodies,* which assured his recognition. His works include *Young Blood; Paul and Virginia; East of the Sun and Moon*: also the plays, *Once Upon a Time, Wayland the Smith,* and *Brave Karl* which made him the most popular Danish dramatist.

Dractonius, Blossius Aemilius, Carthaginian poet of Spanish parentage who lived in the latter part of the 5th century A.D. He is said to be the author of a poem of about 1000 hexameters called *The Tragedy of Orestes*: he also wrote three books of sacred verse in praise of Christianity.

Dragonette, Jessica, contemporary American concert, screen, and radio singer who studied with Estelle LIEBLING and Frank LA FORGE: she has appeared for many years in recital on tours of the

United States, and on radio broadcasts. She acted as the singing voice of the Princess Glory in the screen version of Jonathan Swift's *Gulliver's Travels*.

Dragonetti, Domenico (1763-1846), Italian virtuoso on the double-bass, nicknamed "the Paganini of the double-bass"; chiefly self-taught, and a friend of both Haydn and Beethoven. He played at the "Antient Concerts" and with the London (England) Philharmonic Orchestra for more than fifty years, leaving his collection of scores, engravings, and instruments to the British Museum except a violoncello made by Gasparo da Salo which he willed to Saint Mark's in Venice, the city in which he was born.

Drake, Friedrich (1805-1882), German sculptor who studied with Christian Daniel Rauch: his works include a statue of Rauch; an equestrian statue of Emperor William I; *The Eight Provinces of Prussia* for the Royal Palace at Berlin, and a statue of Karl Friedrich Schinkel.

Drake, Joseph Rodman (1795-1820), American poet who wrote a series of short political lyrics with Fitz-Greene Halleck, signed "The Croakers," which appeared in the New York *Evening Post* in 1819. His works include *The Culprit Fay* (1819); *The American Flag; Abelard to Heloïse; Niagara; Bronx*.

Drama, the title of a literary composition in either prose or verse intended to portray life, or to tell a story when presented by one or more actors. In its most primitive form, religious ceremonials with dances, drama may be said to have originated about 2000 B.C. in the Orient in several countries such as Egypt where the god Osiris was the central figure in a passion play; in Palestine with the *Book of Job* and the *Songs of Solomon* from the Bible; in China where ceremonial rites and dancing were dedicated to the gods of harvest and famine; in Japan where it was brought by Korean scholars from China; in India where it is believed that the Hindus possessed a perfected form of drama before the Greeks; also in Persia, Polynesia, and Java. In Greece drama developed from the ceremonial music and dancing in connection with the Dionysian festivals, finally maturing during the 5th century B.C. in the presentation of tragedies by the first great dramatists, Aeschylus, Sophocles and Euripides, and of comedies by the earliest distinguished comic playwright, Aristophanes. In Rome imitation of Greek drama developed a dramatic school which failed to equal its model in quality although the tragedies of Seneca and the comedies of Terence and Plautus were of a high order. In the Middle Ages the Roman Catholic church revived the drama, which had all but expired with the passing of the Greek and Roman golden age, by presenting miracle or passion plays including six comedies on religious themes by Hrotswitha, a Benedictine nun. These were followed by mystery and morality plays also founded on the Bible. In Italy, the commedia dell'arte of the 15th and 16th century offered plays for which the dialogue was improvised from scenarios intrinsically on the level of the low comedy found in American 19th century burlesque. There was considerable improvement

effected by the plays of Goldoni and Gozzi in the 18th century, and by the dramas and comedies of Manzoni and Ferrari in the 19th century: Vega, Praga, and D'Annunzio produced some fine dramas in the 20th century, but Pirandello may be said to dominate the Italian stage at the present time. In France during the 16th and 17th centuries, the stage was in the hands of Alexandre Hardy, Corneille, Moliere, and Racine: Crebillon, Voltaire, and Chenier carried on in the 18th century, and Alexandre Dumas pere, Vigny, Hugo, Scribe, Augier, Alexandre Dumas fils, Sardou, and Rostand were the leading figures in the 19th century. During the first forty years of the 20th century the leading dramatists include Becque, Brieux, Bourget, Bernstein, Pagnol, Rolland, Maeterlinck, and Guitry. In Spain the first great dramatists were Encina, Lope de Vega, Calderon de la Barca, Gabriel Tellez, and Ruiz de Alarcon from the 15th to the 17th centuries. They were followed by the Alvarez-Quinteros in the 18th century and scarcely anyone of note in the 19th century: the leading lights in the 20th century are Benavente, Echegaray, and Perez Galdos. In Germany the first important figure was Hans Sachs in the 16th century who produced more than two hundred plays; the crude melodramas and comic sketches of the 17th and 18th centuries were thrust aside by the dramas of Lessing, Goethe, Schiller, von Kotzebue, and von Klinger. In the 19th century the dominant figures were von Schlegel, Tieck, and von Kleist, and in the first four decades of the 20th century Gerhart Hauptmann dominated the stage with Wedekind, Strindberg, and George Kaiser also rendering excellent service to the dramatic art. In Austria, a country which may be said to be a conglomerate nation in which it is more difficult to build a national theatre, the outstanding dramatists were Grillparzer, Schnitzler, and Hofmannsthal: Viennese comedy was its outstanding contribution to the gaiety of an otherwise sombre world. In Hungary Ferenc Molnar is the commanding figure with Melchior Lengyel looming up beside him; in Poland Alexander Fredro and Stanislas Wyzpianski were the outstanding dramatists before World War I, and Stephen Zeromski has made a strong appeal with his social views. In Czechoslovakia the plays of Karel Capek mark him as the greatest playwright of his country, but in Yugoslavia, Bulgaria, and Rumania the work of native dramatists has little international significance because of the lack of either performance or translation. In Russia the theatre had little importance historically until the third decade of the 19th century when Pushkin, Gogol, Turgenev, Ostrovsky, Pisemsky, Alexis Tolstoy, Chekhov, Gorky, Leo Tolstoy, Andreyev, and Evreinov became the dominating figures up to the Russian Revolution: in Soviet Russia drama has been employed with excellent results as propaganda by many playwrights under the direction of the government. In Finland and Denmark drama has progressed on nationalistic lines with little of interest to the rest of the world: in Sweden one really great dramatist, August Strindberg, a creator of naturalistic plays, stands out as an international figure, and in Norway the outstanding playwrights are Bjornson and Ibsen. In Great Britain mystery and morality plays were the only forms of drama from the 10th to the

15th century when SHAKESPEARE, KYD, MARLOWE, GREENE, NASH, JONSON, CHAPMAN, BEAUMONT and FLETCHER, DEKKER, WEBSTER, MARSTON, GOLDSMITH, MASSINGER, and FORD were the outstanding dramatists until the latter part of the 17th century, followed by CONGREVE, ETHEREGE, WYCHERLEY, SHERIDAN, CIBBER, STEELE, DRYDEN, and FIELDING. In the 19th century KNOWLES, LYTTON, BOUCICAULT, PINERO, JONES, BARRIE, WILDE, SHAW, GRANVILLE-BARKER, GALSWORTHY, ERVINE, MASEFIELD, MAUGHAM, COWARD, SHERRIFF, SYNGE, DUNSANY, and many other distinguished playwrights complete the history of drama up to the present time. In **America** the native dramatist was entirely missing until 1690 when Benjamin Colman produced a play at Harvard College, followed during the 18th century by George FARQUHAR, Robert Hunter, Thomas Godfrey, Jr., Henry BRACKINRIDGE, Philip Freneau, Charlotte LENNOX, and Royall TYLER. The 19th century heralded the appearance of Mrs. MOWATT, Augustin DALY, Augustus THOMAS, George AIKEN, and Steele MACKAYE: in the 20th century William Vaughan MOODY, Charles KLEIN, George H. BROADHURST, Eugene WALTER, George M. COHAN, Edward SHELDON, Ben HECHT, Charles MACARTHUR, George ABBOTT, Philip DUNNING, Maxwell ANDERSON, Laurence STALLINGS, Elmer RICE, Eugene O'NEILL, S. N. BEHRMANN and many others have contributed to dramatic history along constructive lines.

Drama, Radio, see **Radio Drama.**

Dramatic Collections, see **Theatre Collections.**

Dramatic Copyright, see **Copyright.**

Dramatic Libraries, see **Theatrical Libraries.**

Dramatic Schools. The path of those who aspire to become successful playwrights has been made less difficult by the many educational institutions in the United States where those interested in the technique of dramatic composition including the actual writing of plays may study the theory of playwriting, and also have worthwhile original works produced. Several hundred universities and colleges including Yale, Dartmouth, Leland Stanford, Princeton, and the Universities of Texas, Iowa, North Carolina, and California have special departments, and there are private schools in New York, Chicago, Cleveland, Seattle, Pasadena, and Hollywood.

Draper, Paul, contemporary American choreographic tap dancer who appeared first at RADIO CITY MUSIC HALL, New York: his father, Paul Draper, was a distinguished concert singer, and he is a nephew of the famous diseuse, Ruth DRAPER. He has appeared with the BOSTON SYMPHONY ORCHESTRA; according to critical opinion: "by regarding it as a form of artistic expression, he has given tap dancing incomparable scope: the skill, accuracy, fluidity, and imagery of his style and ideas are thoroughly engrossing."

Draper, Ruth (1889-), American diseuse and monologist who made her debut in 1915, and has toured the United States, Europe, Great Britain, and South Africa. She is the author of the many miniature plays which she presents: they include *Opening a Bazaar; In County Kerry; Three Generations; In a Church in Italy; In a Railway Station on the Western Plains; Vive la France; Three Women and Mr. Clifford; A Class in Soul Culture; A Board of Managers Meeting.* A few stage properties, occasional changes of costume, and a remarkable ability to vary the intonation of her voice are the means of introducing several imaginary characters.

Drapery, in painting and sculpture the art of arranging clothing or material in such a manner as to hang gracefully in folds. In ancient sculpture a part of the figure was usually left uncovered, and the drapery arranged in loose folds over the rest. In medieval sculpture and painting draperies were hung in almost straight lines: in the 15th century it followed the lines of the body more closely, and in the 17th and 18th centuries it was employed as a medium for creating artistic effects.

Drawing, in art the act of representing an object by means of lines, or the product of such representation which may be accomplished with a pencil, any other kind of pointed instrument, or a brush. Drawings are called *pencil, ink, charcoal, crayon, water-color,* etc., in reference to the medium employed to produce them: they are also classified as *free-hand, working, finished, architectural, mechanical,* etc., in accordance with the purposes for which they are executed.

Drayton, Michael (1563-1631), English poet and dramatist whose first volume of spiritual poems, *The Harmony of the Church* (1591) was destroyed by order of the Archbishop of Canterbury: his works include *The Shepherd's Garland; Ballad of Agincourt;* a drama, *Sir John Oldcastle; Poly-Olbion,* a gazeteer of Great Britain in verse.

Drdla, Franz (1868-), Austrian violinist and composer who studied at the Vienna Conservatory under Georg HELLMESBERGER, toured Europe and the United States as a virtuoso, and later settled in Prague. His works for the violin include the world-famous *Souvenir* and the *Serenade in A* popularized by Jan KUBELIK; he also wrote operettas, piano pieces, songs, and many fine violin solos.

Dreiser, Theodore (1871-), American author and dramatist who edited several magazines before devoting himself exclusively to writing: his works include *Sister Carrie* (1900); *Jennie Gerhardt; The Financier; The Genius; The Hand of the Potter,* dramatized in 1921; *An American Tragedy,* his most successful novel which was dramatized and screened; *Chains;* also numerous essays and short stories. He was the brother of Paul DRESSER, a successful popular song writer who changed the spelling of his name.

Dresden Art Gallery, a picture gallery in Dresden, Germany, founded by Augustus I, and constantly augmented from time to time by his successors: there are more than 2500 paintings of which the most notable is Raphael's *Sistine Madonna;* Holbein's *Madonna;* Correggio's *The Night* and Mary *Magdalene;* Titian's *Venus* and *Tribute Money;* Veronese's *The Adoration* and

Marriage in Cana; Rembrandt's *Portrait of Himself and Wife;* Van Dyck's *Charles I;* Rubens' *The Judgment of Paris* and *Boar Hunt.* The works of many modern painters including DEFREGGER, Vautier, MAKART, MUNKACSY, BOCKLIN, THOMA, DELAROCHE, SARGENT, ACHENBACH, SCHNEIDER, and CANALETTO are also on display; also an outstanding collection of engravings.

Dresser, Paul (1857-1911), American composer of popular songs whose name was originally Dreiser: his compositions include *The Blue and the Gray* which was popular during the Spanish-American War, and *On the Banks of the Wabash Far Away* which has become a folk song in the same sense as Stephen Foster's "Old Folks at Home." He was a brother of Theodore DREISER, an American novelist who wrote the chorus of the "Wabash" ballad.

Dressler, Marie (1869-1934), American actress born in Canada who made her debut in 1885 as Cigarette in *Under Two Flags,* and her first success with Camille D'ARVILLE in *Madeleine, or The Magic Kiss.* She also appeared in *"1492";* My *Lady Nicotine* with Lillian RUSSELL; *The Lady Slavey; Tillie's Nightmare,* and as a star with WEBER AND FIELDS. From 1916 she was featured in many silent and talking films including *Tillie's Punctured Romance* with Charles CHAPLIN; *Ann Christie; Min and Bill* with Wallace BEERY; *Tugboat Annie; Dinner at Eight; The Late Christopher Bean.* Her autobiography, *The Life Story of an Ugly Duckling,* was published in 1924.

Drew, John (1827-1862), American stage actor and manager born in Ireland who made his debut at the Bowery Theatre, New York, played light comedy parts on tour, and organized a famous stock company at the Arch Street Theatre, Philadelphia, in which he played until his death. He co-starred with his wife, **Louisa Lane Drew** (1820-1897) who was the daughter of an English actor, and came to the United States when she was seven years old. She appeared as leading lady for Junius Brutus BOOTH and Edwin FORREST; married John Drew in 1850 and after his death in 1862 assumed the management of the Arch Street Theatre Stock Company, maintaining the high standards established by her husband, and becoming famous for her characterizations of Lady Teazle, Peg Woffington, and Mrs. Malaprop. Her *Autobiographical Sketch* was published in 1899. Her eldest son, **John Drew** (1853-1927), was trained by his mother, and made his debut with the Arch Street Theatre Stock Company in 1873: he joined the Augustin DALY Stock Company at New York in 1875, and became leading man for Fanny DAVENPORT, and for Ada REHAN in *The School for Scandal, The Taming of the Shrew, Twelfth Night* and other Shakespearean plays. He also appeared in many modern comedies including *The Masked Ball* by Clyde Fitch; *The Butterflies* with Maude Adams; *The Circle* by Somerset Maugham. His last appearance was in a revival in 1927 of *Trelawney of the Wells:* his autobiography, *My Years on the Stage,* was published in 1922. His sister, **Georgiana Drew** (1856-1893) was the wife of Maurice BARRYMORE, appearing with him and other distinguished actors in Shakespearean plays.

Drinkwater, John (1882-1937), English poet, actor, biographer, and dramatist who published a volume of poems in 1903, and was one of the founders in 1907 of the Pilgrim Players which later developed into the Birmingham Repertory Theatre. He published numerous volumes of poetry including *Cromwell and Other Poems; Loyalties; Seeds of Time; Summer Harvest; American Vignettes; Christmas Poems.* While manager of the Birmingham Theatre he wrote several plays including *Abraham Lincoln* (1918); *Mary Stuart; Oliver Cromwell; Robert E. Lee; Robert Burns; A Man's House; Garibaldi:* he appeared himself as Abraham Lincoln, and in other roles of his plays. His biographical works include *Lincoln: The World Emancipator* (1920); *The Pilgrim of Eternity—Byron; Mr. Charles: King of England.*

Drossinis, George (1859-), Greek poet born in Athens; his verses, distinguished by unsophisticated sentiment and charming simplicity of language, include *Spiders' Webs* (1880); *Stalactites; Idylls; Straw Flowers; Amaranths.*

Droste-Hülshoff, Annette Elisabeth von, Baroness (1797-1848), German poet and novelist highly educated in the sciences, and intimate with the famous savants of her time. She is regarded as the most distinguished poetess of her country: her works include a volume of poems (1838); *Walther; The Hospital of St. Bernard; The Battle in Loener Brucht.*

Drouais, François Hubert (1727-1775), French painter who was the son and pupil of a distinguished painter of miniatures, **Hubert Drouais** (1699-1767). He also studied with BOUCHER, and painted the portraits of *Mme. de Pompadour, Comte d'Artois, Madame Dubarry, Madame Favart,* and the *Emperor Joseph II* of Austria. His son, **Jean Germain Drouais** (1763-1788), was a favorite pupil of Louis DAVID, and also greatly influenced by the works of RAPHAEL; his works include *The Wounded Gladiator; Christ and the Canaanite Woman; Philoctetes on the Island of Lemnos; Departure of Tiberius Gracchus.*

Droz, Gustave (1832-1895), French writer of humorous short stories who was the son of a sculptor, Jules Droz (1807-1872), and educated as an artist: his works include a book of sketches entitled *Monsieur, Madame and Baby* (1866) which was an immediate success; *Between Us! Sadnesses and Smiles; A Bunch of Letters.*

Drum, an instrument of percussion: the body of wood or metal is hollow and usually cylindrical with both ends covered with a membrane, called the head, stretched by means of a hoop tightened at will by an endless cord with leather braces, or by an arrangement of rods and screws. The various types of drums used in orchestras and bands include the *bass drum,* a large drum played with a ball-end stick; the *kettle drum* or *timpano;* the *snare* or *side drum;* the *tenor drum* used for military purposes.

Drummond, William (1585-1649), Scottish poet, known as *William of Hawthornden,* who was one of the last of the poets who wrote in the Elizabethan style: his works include *Tears on the*

Death of Moeliades (Prince Henry); *Sonnets, Songs and Madrigals; River of Forth Feasting; Flowers of Zion; Cypresse Grove.* He also wrote a *History of Scotland during the Five Jameses,* a work better as literature than as a chronicle.

Drury Lane Theatre, opened in 1663 at London, England, with the name "Theatre Royal in Drury Lane"; burned down in 1672 and rebuilt with Sir Christopher WREN as architect in 1674. David GARRICK appeared there in 1742, and Mrs. SIDDONS in 1775; the theatre was demolished in 1791, and after being rebuilt was opened for the performance of plays. On Feb. 23, 1809, Sir Henry Bishop's opera, *The Circassian Bride,* was produced there: on the same day the theatre was again destroyed by fire, but again rebuilt, and used for mutilated versions of Italian operas. In 1833 Alfred Bunn gave the premières of BALFE's *Bohemian Girl* and WALLACE's *Maritana* there, and Marie MALIBRAN appeared in Italian opera. After the burning in 1867 of Her Majesty's Theatre, Henry MAPLESON presented his annual season of grand opera at the Drury Lane until 1877, and in 1880 *The Flying Dutchman,* the first of Wagner's operas to be heard in England, was produced there. Among the noted singers who made their debuts in the Drury Lane Theatre were the de RESZKE brothers and Feodor CHALIAPIN.

Dryden, John (1631-1700), English critic, poet, and dramatist who was educated at Westminster School and Trinity College, Cambridge. He first achieved success in 1659 with verses on Oliver Cromwell's death entitled *Heroick Stanzas:* his poetical works include *Astrea Reduc; Annus Mirabilis; Absalom and Achitophel; Pindaric Odes* including the famous "Alexander's Feast." He also wrote a critical essay, *Dramatick Poesie,* and several plays including *The Indian Queen,* with Sir Robert Howard; *Marriage à la Mode; The Conquest of Granada; Don Sebastian.*

Dry Point, in art an engraving made with a sharp steel needle instead of the *burin,* the tool customarily used by an engraver.

Duban, Jacques Felix (1797-1870), French architect who was one of the pioneers in the revival of the use of varied colors in architecture; he was occupied for many years in restoration work on the ECOLE DES BEAUX-ARTS and the LOUVRE in Paris, applying the classic forms to modern alterations.

Du Barry, Marie Jeanne Bécu, Countess of (1743-1793), French adventuress who was the illegitimate daughter of poor parents: she was first the mistress of the Comte du Barry who introduced her to Louis XV in 1768, and married her to his brother, Guillaume du Barry, in order that she could be presented at court in 1769. She became the king's favorite, and was influential in both politics and court festivities. She retired at the accession of Louis XVI: in 1793 she was tried by the Revolutionary Tribunal and guillotined after conviction for having conspired against the republic. Her ready wit, gracious manners, and great beauty have made her a subject in drama, literature, painting, and music. In 1932, Grace MOORE scored a triumph in an English version of Karl

MILLOCKER's operetta, *Madame Du Barry,* originally produced with great success in 1882.

Dubensky, Arcady (1890-), Russian violinist and composer educated at the Moscow Conservatory of Music; he came to the United States in 1921 and joined the New York Symphony Orchestra and later the New York Philharmonic-Symphony Society. Among his composition are several operas; numerous orchestral works including a symphony, an overture, *Tom Sawyer,* a *Fantasy on a Negro Theme* for tuba and orchestra, and a *Fuge for Eighteen Violins;* chamber music for various combinations of instruments.

Du Bois, Guy Pène (1884-), American painter and art critic who studied at the William Merritt CHASE School, New York, and in Europe. His paintings include scenes in night clubs, restaurants, and satirical pieces such as the famous *Waiter!;* his portraits include *Jeanne Eagels as Sadie Thompson in "Rain"* and *Robert W. Chandler.* He has occupied posts as art critic on New York newspapers, and as editor of the magazine *Arts and Decoration:* he has also written an autobiography, *Artists Say Such Funny Things* (1940).

Dubois, Paul (1829-1905), French sculptor and painter who studied with Toussaint at the ECOLE DES BEAUX-ARTS, and in Italy where he was greatly impressed by the art of the Florentine masters. His finest works include *Narcissus; St. John; The Florentine Singer;* a nude, *Eve; Jeanne d'Arc;* the equestrian statue of the Constable of Montmorency; the tomb of General Lamoricière for which he made statues representing *Military Courage, Charity, Faith,* and *Civil Courage.* He also painted portraits which lack the power and breadth of his sculptures.

Dubois, Théodore (1837-1924), French organist and composer who studied with Marmontel, Benoist, and Ambroise THOMAS at the Paris Conservatory, succeeding the last-named as director there in 1896, and retiring in 1905. His compositions include several grand and light operas; a ballet; many oratorios and cantatas; a symphony and two symphonic poems; two piano concertos; a violin concerto; many pieces for organ.

Dubufe, Édouard Louis (1818-1883), French painter who studied with his father, **Claude Marie Dubufe** (1790-1864), who was a pupil of Louis DAVID, and as popular with the public as he was abused by the critics. Édouard also studied with Paul DELAROCHE: his works include many religious paintings including *Miracle of Roses, Bathsheba,* and *Morning Prayer:* also numerous finely executed portraits such as those of Rosa Bonheur, Empress Eugénie, Charles Gounod, and Alexandre Dumas, fils.

Ducal Palace (Venice), see **Doges' Palace (Venice).**

Duccio di Buoninsegna (c.1260-c.1320), early Italian painter who is first mentioned as decorating twelve chests at Sienna where he exerted great influence in the development of the Sienese school. The only authenticated work is the large *Maestà,* or double altar, dated 1311: the predella belonging to it, now in various museums, includes *Nativity with Two Prophets; Annunciation; Christ Healing the Blind; Transfiguration; Christ Calling the Children of Zebedee; Temptation of Christ; Christ and the Samaritan Woman; The Raising of Lazarus.*

Ducis, Jean François (1733-1816), French poet and dramatist who was successful as an adapter for the French stage of Shakespeare's plays, but not so fortunate with his original works. His first original tragedy, *Amélise,* produced in 1768, was a failure, but his adaptations of Shakespeare's *Hamlet, Romeo and Juliet, King Lear, Macbeth,* and *Othello* were all received with enthusiasm. It must be borne in mind that his adaptations altered the original plays in plot, characters, and scenic arrangement.

Duclos, Charles (1704-1772), French author who wrote two romances, *The Baroness of Luz* (1741), and *The Confessions of the Count de****** (1747) which brought him favorable notice. The work which places him among the most famous memoirists is his *Secret Memoirs of the Reign of Louis XIV, the Regency, and the Reign of Louis XV,* for which he used the suppressed memoirs of the Duke de SAINT-SIMON: they afford a graphic picture of court life in respect to its vices and intrigues.

Ducornet, Louis César Joseph (1806-1856), French painter, born without arms, who studied with Baron Gérard. He painted with his feet, achieving remarkable results in conception, composition, and coloring: the drawing is the only drawback. His paintings include *Slave Merchant; Death of Mary Magdalen; Parting of Hector and Andromache; Christ in the Sepulchre; Repose in Egypt.*

Ducreux, Joseph (1737-1802), French painter who was a pupil of De Latour, and an intimate friend of Jean Baptiste GREUZE. In 1793 he painted the portrait of Marie ANTOINETTE in Vienna: when she became Queen of France she conferred the title of Painter to the Queen on him. He painted many figures prominent in the French Revolution including ROBESPIERRE and Louis XVI during his captivity; also self-portraits in comic attitudes.

Dudevant, Madame Amantine, see **Sand, George.**

Dudley, Bide (1877-), American dramatic critic and playwright: his plays include *Odds and Ends,* with John Godfrey, (1917); *The Little Whopper; Sue Dear; The Matinée Girl; Bye Bye Bonnie,* with Louis Simon; *Come Along All; Oh, Henry; Borrowed Love.*

Duez, Ernest Ange (1843-1896), French painter who studied with CAROLUS-DURAN: his works include *Honeymoon; Splendor and Misery of Courtesans; Whitsuntide Roses; Around the Lamp; Evening in Villerville; St. Cuthbert.*

Dufay, Guillaume (c.1400-1474), French composer of church music who was a choir boy at the Cathedral of Cambrai and entered the Papal Choir at Rome in 1428: he served as chorister and chapelmaster at several courts, and finally became canon of the cathedral in which he was formerly a chorister. His works include chansons in three voices, masses, motets, and other church music.

Duff, Mary Ann Dyke (1794-1857), English actress who married an Irish actor, John Duff: she came to the United States with him, and made her debut in Boston. She was highly regarded in Shakespearean roles such as Ophelia, Desdemona, Lady Macbeth: she also acted as leading lady for Junius Brutus BOOTH and Edmund KEAN.

Duff-Gordon, Lucie, Lady (1821-1869), English author who became friends as a child with Heinrich HEINE, the distinguished German poet. Her London salon, after her marriage to Sir Alexander Duff-Gordon, was filled for many years with men and women of letters. She translated several works from the German, and wrote a series of letters from Egypt in 1865 which attracted much favorable attention when they were published.

Dufresnoy, Charles Alphonse, see **Fresnoy, Charles Alphonse du.**

Dufresnoy, Charles de la Rivière (1654-1724), French poet and dramatist who was a favorite of Louis XIV: he wrote a volume of poems, and several plays including *The Double Widowhood; The Village Flirt; The Match Made and Unmade.*

Dugazon, Jean Henri Gourgaud (1746-1809), French actor who made his debut at the COMEDIE-FRANCAISE in 1770, and rose to great heights with the company. He became an ardent Revolutionist, and followed François Joseph TALMA to the Republican Theatre, but in 1799 returned to the restored Comédie-Française. His first wife, Louise Rose Lefèvre, from whom he was divorced, was an accomplished actress and singer at the Comédie-Italienne for more than twenty years.

Dughet, Gaspard (1613-1675), French painter also known as *Le Guaspre* and as *Gaspard Poussin:* he studied with Nicolas POUSSIN, his brother-in-law, and also spent three years in Rome. He is especially renowned for his landscapes including *View of Damascus; Landscape with Fishermen; Cascades of Tivoli; Mountain Landscape;* he also painted the walls of the Borghese Palace in Rome, and several friezes in the Colonna Palace.

Duhamel, Georges (1884-), French novelist, playwright, poet, and essayist who performed more than two thousand operations as a volunteer surgeon during World War I: among his works that have been translated are the novels *The New Book of Martyrs; Civilization; Papa Pasquier; Caged Beasts; In Sight of the Promised Land; The Fortunes of the Pasquiers; Confession at Midnight; Salavin's Journal; The Lyonnais Club; End of Illusion;* also several plays and volumes of essays.

Duiffoprugcar, correctly **Tieffenbrucker, Gaspar** (c.1514-1571), Bavarian instrument maker said to have been the first maker of violins. There is much difference of opinion in regard to the truth of this statement: Louis VIDAL, French author of *The Instruments With a Bow* (1876), claims that Vuillaume made the violins in 1827 from the pattern of a VIOLA DA GAMBA fashioned by Duiffoprugcar.

Dujardin, Karel (c.1625-1678), Dutch painter who studied with Nicolaes BERCHEM, and probably with Paul POTTER: his landscapes were particularly fine. His paintings include *Italian Charlatans; Landscape with Cattle; Sheep and Goats; Horseman Before Inn; Cascade in Italy; David After Slaying Goliath; Diogenes and Boy.*

Dukas, Paul (1865-1935), French composer who studied with Théodore DUBOIS at the Paris Conservatory, and won the second Prix de Rome with a cantata. He became professor of composition at the Conservatory; taught at the École Normale de Musique, and assisted in editing the complete works of Jean Philippe RAMEAU. His compositions include three overtures; a symphony; an orchestral scherzo, *The* SORCERER'S APPRENTICE; an opera, *Bluebeard;* a ballet, *La Peri;* several works for the piano.

Dukelsky, Vladimir (1903-), Russian composer of both classical and popular music, writing the latter under the pen name **Vernon Duke.** He studied composition under Richard GLIERE, and came to the United States about 1920; later he lived in Paris and London, finally settling in New York in 1929. His works include a ballet, *Zephyr and Flora,* produced by DIAGHILEFF; a ballade for piano and orchestra, an oratorio; chamber music. He has also written an operetta and many songs for musical productions.

Dukes, Ashley (1885-), English dramatist, critic, and editor of the English edition of *Theatre Arts.* His plays include *The Man With a Load of Mischief* (1924); *One More River; The Dumb Wife of Cheapside; Matchmaker's Arms;* he has also made several adaptations.

Dulcimer, an ancient stringed instrument constructed in various forms: the general appearance is that of a square or oblong box strung with wire strings played by being struck with small mallets or hammers. The heads of the hammers are soft on one end and hard on the other, producing varying tonal effects. In some respects the dulcimer may be considered a precursor of the PIANO.

Dumanoir, Philippe (1806-1865), French dramatist who wrote more than two hundred vaudevilles either alone or in collaboration: the famous actress, Pauline Déjazet, appeared with great success in many of his pieces.

Dumas, Alexandre, known as **Dumas pére** (1802-1870), French novelist and dramatist: his tremendous series of historical romances and plays were made possible by using collaborators and assistants among whom was Auguste Maquet. Much of the enormous sums earned by Dumas was dissipated for the benefit of a group of people who lived as his home which he called "Monte Cristo." His most popular romances include the *Three Musketeers* Series; *The Corsican Brothers;* the *Queen Margot* Series; the *Dame de Monsoreau* Series; *The Count of Monte Cristo.* He also wrote several plays, one of which, *Henry III and His Court,* was produced at the COMEDIE-FRANCAISE in 1829: it was such a complete departure from the already decadent French drama that its success was overwhelming, winning Dumas' reputation as a dramatist, and the friendship of Victor HUGO. Several of the successful romances mentioned above were dramatized and screened in France, England, and the United States.

Dumas, Alexandre, known as **Dumas fils** (1824-1895), French author and dramatist, son of Alexandre DUMAS, PERE. His first play, *La Dame aux camélias (Camille),* produced in 1852, was an adaptation of his novel published in 1848: it has held the stage all over the world for more than sixty years. In 1853 Verdi's opera, La TRAVIATA, was produced in Venice; the libretto was based on "Camille." Other successful plays included *The Clemenceau Affair; The Outer Edge of Society; Ideas of Madame Aubray; Denise; Francillon; The Stranger:* he also wrote many essays on social subjects.

Du Maurier, George Louis Palmella Busson (1834-1896), English artist and novelist born in Paris, and son of a Frenchman who became a British subject. He did many social satires for *Punch;* became a well-known water-colorist in addition to writing two popular novels: *Peter Ibbetson* (1891) and *Trilby* (1894). Both books were successful when adapted for the stage and screen; in 1931 *Peter Ibbetson* was presented as an opera by Deems TAYLOR at the METROPOLITAN OPERA HOUSE, New York. His son, **Sir Gerald Du Maurier** (1873-1934), was a distinguished actor and producer: among the plays in which he appeared were the dramatization of his father's novel, *Trilby; Brewster's Millions; Hamlet; The Daring Girl; Interference.* Sir Gerald's daughter, **Daphne du Maurier** (1907-), has written a study of her father entitled *Gerald: A Portrait;* an historical picture of the family called *The Du Mauriers;* also *Jamaica Inn; Rebecca,* successful both as a novel and on the screen; *Frenchmen's Creek.*

Dumka (Czech), in music a composition in slow tempo indicating sadness or grief: Antonin DVORAK used it effectively in the **Dumky Trio,** Op. 90 in which three examples of the *dumka* are linked together: there is a Columbia recording of this work.

Dumont, the name of a distinguished family of French sculptors and painters including **François Dumont** (1688-1726), a sculptor who executed fine work at the church of Saint-Sulpice, Paris; **Jacques Dumont** (1701-1781), painter of allegorical pictures and brother of François Dumont, who was also known as "Le Romain." Other famous members of the family who became sculptors were **Edmé Dumont** (1720-1775), **Jacques Edmé Dumont** (1761-1844), and **Augustin Alexander Dumont** (1801-1884): the latter executed the colossal *Napoleon I* on the VENDOME COLUMN, and *The Genius of Liberty* on the July Column in Paris.

Dumont, François (1751-1831), French miniature painter who studied with Jean Girardet, and also in Rome: he painted portraits of Louis XVI, Marie ANTOINETTE, Louis XVIII, and many other notable of his day. His younger brother, **Tony Dumont,** was also a fine miniaturist: due to the fact that both signed their works with their surnames only, there has been some difficulty experienced in assigning authorship.

Duna, Steffi, contemporary Hungarian ballerina and actress who made her debut as a child dancer at the Budapest Opera, and later toured Europe. Her stage appearances include *Wonder Bar* with Francis LEDERER in Berlin; Noel COWARD's *Words and Music;* in London; *The Beggar's Opera* in New York. She has also had leading roles in many films including *La Cucaracha; Anthony Adverse; Pagliacci; The Magnificent Fraud; Waterloo Bridge.*

Dunbar, Paul Laurence (1872-1906), American Negro poet: his works include *Lyrics of Lowly Life* (1896), considered one of the best volumes of poetry written by a Negro. His complete poetical works were published in 1913, and he also wrote short stories and several novels including *The Sport of the Gods.*

Dunbar, William (c.1460-c.1522), Scottish poet and priest who was frequently employed by James IV in affairs of state: his works include *The Thistle and the Rose; Dance of the Seven Deadly Sins Through Hell; The Two Married Women; The Golden Targe;* the autobiographical *Visitation of St. Francis.* He has been favorably compared with SPENSER, CHAUCER, and COWPER.

Duncan I (1034-c.1040), king of Scotland who was murdered by MACBETH, one of his generals, who succeeded him as king from about 1040 to 1057. The event is the nucleus of the plot of Shakespeare's play, *Macbeth,* first performed about 1610: a grand opera based on the play, with music by Giuseppe VERDI, was produced in 1847 at FLORENCE.

Duncan, Isadora (1878-1927), American classical dancer who made her debut at Chicago in 1899 with little success. She attempted to introduce a new system of dancing based on Greek classical forms, and had much greater success in Europe, eventually establishing dance studios in the United States, Paris, Berlin, and Moscow. She wrote a book containing her theories entitled *The Art of the Dance,* and also an autobiography, *My Life.*

Duncan, Sara Jeannette (c.1861-1922), Canadian novelist who published her first novel, *A Social Departure,* in 1890. Much of her life was spent in India where she wrote *The Simple Adventures of a Mem Sahib; The Story of Sonny Sahib; His Honour and a Lady; The Burnt Offering; His Royal Happiness,* and several other interesting novels.

Duncan, Thomas (1807-1845), Scottish painter trained at the Perth Academy, and under Sir William Allen: his finest paintings include *Prince Charles Edward and the Highlanders; Prince Charles Edward Asleep after the Battle of Culloden; Cupid; Martyrdom of John Brown of Priesthill.* He became an important influence in the development of art in Scotland.

Dunlap, William (1766-1839), American painter and dramatist; he painted a portrait of George Washington, and worked under Benjamin WEST for several years in London. His plays include *The Father* (1789); *André; Leicester:* he also wrote a *History of the American Theatre* and *History of the Rise and Progress of the Art of Design in the United States.* He was also one of the founders of the National Academy of Design.

Dunn, Emma (1875-), English actress who made her first appearance in 1907 at New York as Ase in *Peer Gynt* with Richard MANSFIELD. Among the plays in which she assumed leading roles are *The Warrens of Virginia; The Easiest Way; Mother; The Governor's Lady; Sinners; Old Lady 31; Sonny.* She has appeared since 1919 in many films including *Mr. Deeds Goes to Town; Seven Keys to Baldpate; The Emperor's Candlesticks; Madame X; The Cowboy and the Lady;* several "Dr. Kildare" films; *The Great Dictator; Ladies in Retirement.*

Dunne, Finley Peter (1867-1936), American humorist who was also an able journalist, and at various times editor of the New York *Morning Telegraph,* the *American Magazine* and *Collier's Weekly.* He created the humorous, philosophical character, "Mr. Dooley," and his works include *Mr. Dooley in Peace and War* (1898); *Mr. Dooley in the Hearts of His Countrymen; Mr. Dooley's Philosophy; Mr. Dooley's Opinions; Observations by Mr. Dooley.* He is regarded as the greatest humorist after Mark TWAIN.

Dunne, Irene (1904-), American stage and screen actress and singer educated at a convent, and trained at the Chicago College of Music. Her stage appearances include *Irene* and *Show Boat:* she has also appeared in many films including *Cimarron; Ann Vickers; Stingaree; The Age of Innocence; Sweet Adeline; Roberta; The Magnificent Obsession; Show Boat; Theodora Goes Wild; High, Wide and Handsome; The Awful Truth; Love Affair; Invitation to Happiness; Penny Serenade.*

Dunning, Philip (1890-), American actor and dramatist who made his New York debut in 1911 at Wallack's Theatre, New York, in *Pomander Walk:* he also appeared in *Ruggles of Red Gap; Object—Matrimony; The Dancer; The Wonderful Thing.* He collaborated with George ABBOTT in *Broadway* and *Lily Turner;* with Joseph Schrank in *Page Miss Glory;* with Jack Donohue in *The Understudy.* In 1931 he joined the United Artists Corporation as author and director of motion pictures.

Dunsany, Edward John Moreton Drax Plunkett, Lord (1878-), Irish dramatist and author who is a leader in the Celtic movement, and writes his plays in English. His works are fanciful in character: they include *The Glittering Gate* (1909); *The Gods of the Mountain; A Night at an Inn; The Lost Silk Hat; The Laughter of the Gods.* His volumes of stories include *The Gods of Pegana; Dreamer's Tales:* he has written an autobiography, *Patches of Sunlight.*

Dunstable, John (c.1370-1453), English composer who was also an astrologer and mathematician: very few of his works were printed, and his importance as a 15th century English composer whose genius fully equaled that of Guillaume Dufay was not revealed until six of his manuscripts were discovered by F. X. Haberl in 1884. He composed both secular and sacred music: some of his double motets are of remarkable excellence.

Dupré, Jules (1811-1889), French painter who was the son of a well-known manufacturer of China; he was influenced by the Barbizon School, and after his first three pictures at the Paris Salon in 1831 attracted some attention, proved his ability with the painting, *Sunset*, in 1832. Among his best works are *Morning; Environs of Southampton; The Old Oak; The Hay Wagon; Sunset on the Coast.*

Dupré, Marcel (1886-), French organist and composer who studied the organ with his father at the Paris Conservatory, and also with Alexandre Guilmant and Charles Widor, succeding the latter as organist at St. Sulpice, Paris. He toured the United States first in 1922, presenting remarkable programs of Bach's organ works and improvisations. His compositions include a concerto for organ and orchestra, many organ pieces, church music, and an organ method.

Duquesnoy, François (1594-c.1642), Flemish sculptor also known as François Flamand and Il Fiammingo; he was among the first sculptors to picture correctly the anatomical peculiarities of children in terra cotta, bronze and marble. His works include statues of *St. Susanna and St. Andrew*, and *Pope Innocent X:* also groups of children on the altar of St. Peter's in Rome.

Durán, Agustin (1769-1862), Spanish poet and dramatic critic whose first work, *On the Decadence of the Spanish Theatre* (1828), led to its liberation from French traditions. His greatest poetical work was a poem of chivalry, *Three Citrons in the Garden of Love.*

Durand, Alice Marie Céleste, see **Greville, Henry.**

Durand, Asher Brown (1796-1886), American painter and engraver who was chiefly self-taught although he was a pupil and partner of Peter Maverick. His engravings of landscapes, historical, and literary notabilities places him among the finest American engravers; they include *Signing of the Declaration of Independence* by John Trumbull; *Ariadne* by John Vanderlyn; *The Wrath of Peter Stuyvesant;* also engravings for many literary annuals.

Durand, Charles August Émile, see **Carolus-Duran.**

Durante, Francesco (1864-1755), Italian composer who was the founder of the Neapolitan school of composition, and a distinguished teacher who numbered Nicola Jomelli, Giovanni Pergolesi, and Giovanni Paisiello among his pupils. His compositions included masses, psalms, motets, and sonatas for the harpsichord.

Duranty, Walter (1884-), English journalist and novelist educated at Eton and Cambridge: he represented the New York *Times* in Paris, and acted as its correspondent during World War I with the French army and in Moscow. His fictional works include *The Curious Lottery and Other Tales of Russian Justice* (1929); *One Life, One Kopeck; The Gold Train.* He also wrote an autobiography, *I Write as I Please.*

Durbin, Deanna (1922-), American screen actress born in Canada: she has appeared on the screen in *Three Smart Girls; One Hundred Men and a Girl* (with Leopold Stokowski); *Mad About Music; Three Smart Girls Grow Up; First Love;* also in a memorial to Will Rogers.

Dürer, Albrecht (1471-1528), German painter and engraver; the facts regarding his career are available from his own books entitled *The Family Chronicle, Letters from Venice,* and *Journal of a Visit to the Low Countries.* He studied with Michael Wolgemut, and worked with Martin Schongauer: his innumerable engravings and paintings include *Men and Women Bathing; Apocalypse according to St. John; The Large Hercules; Nemises; Adam and Eve; Feast of the Rosary; Martyrdom of Ten Thousand; Large Passion; Small Passion; Portrait of an Unknown Man; The Four Apostles,* his last work.

Duse, Eleonora (1859-1924), Italian actress whose father and grandfather were distinguished actors; she appeared first as a child of four in Victor Hugo's *Les Miserables,* and achieved her first success in 1878 as the leading lady in Guillaume Augier's *Les Fourchambault.* After touring Italy in such plays as *Théodora, Divorçons,* and *Fedora,* she electrified Europe, South America, England, and the United States in *Camille* and *Magda:* George Bernard Shaw pronounced her superior to Sarah Bernhardt. She assured Gabriele D'Annunzio's reputation as a dramatist by her acting in *La Gioconda* and *Francesca da Rimini,* and was amazingly successful as Paula in *The Second Mrs. Tanqueray.*

Dushkin, Samuel (1897-), Polish violinist and composer who studied with Leopold Auer and Fritz Kreisler, making his debut at Paris in 1918, and his first American appearance in 1924. He has been soloist with leading American and European orchestras, giving first performances of works by Ravel, Pierne, and Stravinsky. He has also edited classic and modern violin works for various publishers.

Dusk of the Gods, see **Ring of the Nibelungs.**

Dussek, Johann Ladislaus (1760-1812), Bohemian pianist, organist, teacher, and composer who studied with Karl Philipp Emanuel Bach at Hamburg, and toured Europe as a pianist, appearing before Marie Antoinette in 1786 at Paris. He shares the invention of what is known as the "singing touch" in piano playing with Muzio Clementi: he wrote nearly one hundred concertos, sonatas, fantasias, variations, waltzes, and a method for the piano.

Dutch Treat Club, an organization in New York functioning as a weekly luncheon club: it was founded in 1905 with a membership including authors, critics, musicians, actors, painters, and others who have contributed to American culture. The annual party has as its feature the publication of a book written and designed by members: dramatic and musical short plays are also presented for which the scripts and music are written by members.

Dutt, Michael (1824-1873), Indian poet and dramatist who was educated at the Hindu College of Calcutta, and later became a Christian, writing verses in English. He finally decided to write only in his native language: his works include three classic dramas, and an epic poem, *Meghanad-Badha*, adapted from the ancient Sanskrit epic, *Rayamana*, which established him as the greatest of native poets.

Duun, Olav (1876-1939), Norwegian novelist who published a volume of short stories in 1907. His finest work, a series of six novels called *The People of Juvik*, was begun in 1918: it presents the social and economic problems of four generations of peasant land owners, and several of the volumes have been translated.

Duveneck, Frank (1848-1919), American painter, sculptor, and engraver who studied at the Munich Academy, winning many prizes: in 1878 he opened an art studio in Cincinnati, O., where he taught many students who later became famous including William Merritt CHASE, John TWACHTMAN, and John W. ALEXANDER. His outstanding paintings include *Whistling Boy; The Circassian; Young Man with a Ruff; The Blacksmith.* Among his etchings are *The Grand Canal* and *The Rialto;* his notable sculptures include a bronze memorial to his wife; a bust of Charles W. ELIOT, and a statue of Ralph Waldo EMERSON. He taught at the Art School of the Cincinnati Museum for the last twenty-five years of his life, also presenting the institution with a fine collection of his paintings.

Duyckinck, George (1823-1863), American author and editor, educated at Columbia University: his works of interest in this volume include a *Cyclopedia of American Literature* (1855) with his brother, Evert Augustus Duyckinck (1816-1878): also an edition of SHAKESPEARE's works in collaboration with William Cullen BRYANT.

Duyse, Prudens van (1804-1859), Flemish poet whose patriotic verse and poems are of interest today only because they reawakened a love of the Flemish tongue, thereby bringing about a revival of native literature. He also wrote several plays, and a history of Flanders.

Dvořák, Antonin (1841-1904), Bohemian organist, violinist, and composer who studied at the Prague Organ School, and earned his living by playing the violin in the National Theatre. In 1873 a *Hymn* for mixed chorus and orchestra brought him favorable notice, and his *Symphony in Eb*, performed at Prague with Frederich SMETANA conducting, established his reputation as a composer. His new works were praised and promoted by Franz LISZT, Johannes BRAHMS, and Hans von BÜLOW, and great encouragement was given him in 1884 when he visited England. In 1892 he became director of the National Conservatory in New York: upon his return to Bohemia he was connected with the Prague Conservatory as professor of composition and artistic director until his death. His numerous compositions include several operas, nine symphonies; five symphonic poems; three overtures; concertos for piano, violin and violoncello; choral music; piano pieces. His most popular compositions are the *"New World" Symphony,* the *"American" String Quartet,* the *Slavonic Dances,* the *Humoresque* for piano, and the song, *Songs My Mother Taught Me.*

Dwight, John Sullivan (1813-1893), American music critic who was educated at Harvard and first became a clergyman. In 1848 he turned to music as a profession, and founded a musical periodical, *Dwight's Journal of Music* in 1852, remaining its editor until 1881. The magazine championed the works of Robert SCHUMANN, Richard WAGNER, and Johannes BRAHMS in face of much opposition from prejudiced musicians: he also published historical essays on music by Alexander W. THAYER, the biographer of BEETHOVEN.

Dyce, William (1806-1864), Scottish painter who studied at the Royal Scottish Academy in Edinburgh, and the Royal Academy at London; in 1825 he spent a year in Rome, later becoming professor of fine arts at King's College, London, and a member of the Royal Academy. His works include the frescoes of *King Arthur* in the Houses of Parliament; *The Infant Hercules Strangling the Serpents; The Descent of Venus; Baptism of Ethelbert; King Joash Shooting the Arrow of Deliverance.*

Dying Gaul, a Greek statue of the school of Pergamum, incorrectly called the "Dying Gladiator." It pictures a Gaul attempting to struggle to his feet after being wounded, and the restraint with which it is treated only enhances its reality. The figure is now in the CAPITOLINE MUSEUM, Rome.

Dying Swan, The, a short ballet created by Michel FOKINE in 1905 for Anna PAVLOWA: it is called a choreographic tragedy, and is based on a composition for violoncello entitled *Le Cygne* (The Swan) by Camille SAINT-SAENS. Fokine was so inspired by the haunting melody that the simple steps and movements created by him, and so exquisitely interpreted by Pavlowa, give it a unique position in ballet. She danced in it to tumultuous applause all over the world.

Dyk, Viktor (1877-1931), Czechoslovakian poet, satirist, and dramatist whose sincere patriotism imparts a fervent charm to his simple, concise, and pointed diction. Among his works are the dramas in verse, *The Life Force* (1898), and *Ninth Night*: also a volume, evidently recalling a period of incarceration for a political offense, and entitled *Windows.*

Dynamics, in music the department of musical science that seeks to elucidate the relative intensity in loudness or softness of musical terms: the marks placed upon music indicating such varying degrees are called *dynamic marks.*

E

Eagels, Jeanne (1894-1929), American actress who first appeared at seven as Puck in Shakespeare's *Midsummer Night's Dream,* and made her formal debut in 1911 on the New York stage in *Jumping Jupiter.* She achieved her greatest success as Sadie Thompson in *Rain,* also appearing in *The Outcast; The Great Pursuit; The Professor's Love Story; Daddies; The Night Watch.*

Eakins, Thomas (1844-1916), American painter and sculptor who studied at the PENNSYLVANIA ACADEMY OF FINE ARTS, supplementing its instruction with a course in anatomy. He also worked with Jean GEROME and Léon BONNAT in Paris, later becoming professor of painting at the Pennsylvania Academy, and now ranked with Winslow Homer as one of America's finest realistic painters. His works include *The Surgical Clinic of Professor Gross; The Concert; The Crucifixion; The Violoncello Player;* among his finest sculptures are the horses on the Soldiers and Sailors Monument near Prospect Park, Brooklyn, N. Y.

Eames, Emma (1865-), American soprano, born in China of American parents, who studied with Mme. MARCHESI in Paris, and made her debut in 1889 in GOUNOD'S *Romeo and Juliet* at the L'Opéra. After singing there for two years she appeared at Covent Garden, London, and made her American debut in 1891 at the Metropolitan Opera House, New York, in *Faust* with Édouard and Jean de RESZKE, appearing regularly until 1909. Her repertory included many of the leading soprano roles in French, Italian, and German opera, and her distinguished career in opera was signalized by decorations from Queen Victoria and the French Academy.

Earle, Ralph (1751-1801), American painter who was largely self-taught, and traveled as an itinerant artist for many years. He made sketches at the battlefields of Lexington and Concord from which he painted four scenes that are regarded as the first historical paintings by an American artist. His works include a large picture of Niagara Falls, and portraits of many political notabilities.

Earle, Virginia (1875-1937), American actress and singer who made her first appearance on the stage in 1887 as Nanki-Poo in *The Mikado* as presented by a juvenile opera company. Among the musical productions in which she appeared during her long and successful career on the stage were *Evangeline; Wang; The Lady Slavey; The Geisha; The Circus Girl; A Runaway Girl; The Casino Girl; Belle of Bohemia; Floradora; Sergeant Kitty; Milk White Flag.* She also appeared with Ada REHAN in Shakespeare's plays, being favorably noticed as Ariel in *The Tempest.*

East, Alfred (1849-1913), English painter and etcher who studied at the Glasgow School of Art and at the ECOLE DES BEAUX-ARTS, Paris, with ROBERT-FLEURY and Bouguereau. His notable works include *The Silent Somme; A Haunt of Ancient Peace; Returning from Church; Morning Moon; The Golden Valley.* He also published *The Art of Landscape Painting in Oil Color.*

Eastlake, Sir Charles Lock (1793-1865), English painter and art critic who studied at the Royal Academy School, and exhibited his first picture, *Christ Restoring Life to the Daughter of Jairus,* in 1813. While painting at Plymouth he sketched Napoleon I as a prisoner on *H.M.S. Bellerophon,* and painted a life-sized portrait of him. His works include *Pilgrims Arriving in Sight of Rome; Byron's Dream; Christ Blessing Little Children; Comus; Hagar and Ishmael.* He also wrote treatises on painting, and translated German works on the same subject.

Eastman, George (1854-1932), American inventor and philanthropist who devised the flexible, transparent film in 1888 which changed amateur photography from an expensive pastime to an inexpensive and accordingly universal hobby: it is also the basic element through which the motion picture became possible. Eastman became one of the world's greatest patrons of music by founding and endowing the **Eastman School of Music** in connection with the University of Rochester.

Eastman, Max Forrester (1883-), American author and literary critic educated at Williams College and Columbia University: his works include *The Enjoyment of Poetry* (1913); *The Literary Mind; Art and the Life of Action; Enjoyment of Laughter.* He also compiled an *Anthology for the Enjoyment of Poetry.*

Easton-Maclennan, Florence (1884-), English dramatic soprano who studied at the Royal Academy of Music, London, and made her debut in 1903 with the MOODY-MANNERS OPERA Co. in *Madame Butterfly* at Covent Garden, London. She appeared in the United States from 1904 to 1907 with the SAVAGE English Opera Company in *Parsifal* and *Madame Butterfly:* in 1915 she joined the CHICAGO OPERA COMPANY, and from 1917 to 1928, and also from 1936 to 1938 was a valued member of the METROPOLITAN OPERA COMPANY, New York.

Eaton, Walter Prichard (1878-), American author and dramatic critic educated at Harvard University who became dramatic critic for the New York *Tribune,* the New York *Sun,* and the *American Magazine* between 1902 and 1918: in 1933 he assumed the post of associate professor of play writing at Yale University. His dramatic works include *The American Stage of Today* (1908); *At the New Theatre and Others; Plays and Players; Queen Victoria,* a play with David Carb; *The Actor's Heritage; The Theatre Guild; The First Ten Years; The Drama in English.* He has written many Boy Scout books, and volumes describing the New England countryside.

Eaton, Wyatt (1849-1896), American painter born in Canada who studied at the ECOLE DES BEAUX-ARTS, Paris, with Jean Louis GEROME. He was friendly with J. B. MILLET and Jules BASTIEN-LEPAGE at Barbizon, and one of the founders of the Society of American Artists in New York.

His works include portraits of William Cullen BRYANT and many other American poets: also of Bishop Potter and President Garfield.

Eberhart, Mignon Good (1899-   ), American writer of detective fiction who has achieved remarkable success in this field: in 1930 her novel, *While the Patient Slept*, won the Scotland Yard Prize of $5000. She has her own particular method of building up suspense in such stories as *The Patient in Room 18* (1929); *Murder by an Aristocrat; The Glass Slipper*, and *The Hangman's Whip*.

Eberle, Abastenia St. Leger (1878-   ), American sculptor who studied with Kenyon Cox and George Grey BARNARD: among her notable works are *Victory; Girl on Roller Skates; Hurdy Gurdy; Little Mother; Stray Cat; Windy Doorstep;* also numerous portraits.

Eberlein, Gustav (1847-1926), German sculptor who executed monuments for several German monarchs and for Bismarck; the frieze of fifty life-size figures on the façade of the Ministry of Public Instruction, Berlin; also many mythological figures and groups including *Cupid With His Bow; Greek Flute Player; Bathing Nymph; Bacchantes; Venus Binding Cupid.*

Ebers, Georg Moritz (1837-1898), German Egyptologist and novelist: his novels, written with the idea of interesting readers in Egyptian lore, include *An Egyptian Princess* (1864); *Uarda; Homo Sum; The Sisters; The Emperor; Serapis; The Bride of the Nile.* They were all well received, and have been translated into English.

Eça de Queiroz, José Maria (1845-1900), Portuguese novelist who created a style in prose writing that revivified his country's literature: his works include a sensational novel, *The Mystery of Cintra Road* (1870), written in collaboration with Ramalho Ortigão; a series of satirical sketches, *The Farpas; The Crime of Father Amaro; Cousin Basil; The Maias; The Relic.*

Echegaray, José (1832-1916), Spanish dramatist who was also a distinguished mathematician, engineer, and statesman: his plays, which introduced tragic scenes from ordinary life, include *Madness or Sanctity* (1882); *Mariana; The Son of Don Juan; The World and His Wife.* From 1874 to 1905 Echegaray's plays were favorites in Spain, and also produced in foreign countries including the United States.

Eckersberg, Cristoffer-Vilhelm (1783-1853), Danish painter who studied with Nikolai Abilgaard, and with Jacques Louis DAVID for several years. He was a friend of THORVALDSEN, painting a portrait of him which hangs in the Academy of Fine Arts at Copenhagen. His notable works include many fine landscapes and seascapes: also *The Spartan Boy; Danish Ship; Bacchus and Ariadne; Ulysses.* He is regarded as the founder of the modern Danish school of painting, casting aside conventional tone colors for the unclouded atmosphere and natural outlines of Danish scenery.

Eclectic School, in painting an Italian school of painting founded by AGOSTINO, Annibale, and Ludovico CARRACCI about 1585, together with DOMENICHINO, Guido RENI, and GUERCINO at a later date. The purpose was to combine the excellent points of the great masters such as RAPHAEL's skill in design, MICHELANGELO's art in drawing, TITIAN's taste in color, and CORREGGIO's proficiency in chiaroscuro. Another school with the same name was founded by Hippolyte DELAROCHE in the early part of the 19th century: its purpose was to combine the drawing of the classic with the color of the romantic school.

Eclogue, in literature a short, pastoral dialogue in verse: the name has been applied to works by the Latin poets including VIRGIL and CALPURNIUS, but is now used as a general term for pastoral poetry. French and Spanish poets used the title; those of Segrais and Garcilasso de la Vega are excellent examples.

École des Beaux-Arts (Paris), a national school for the study of the fine arts founded in 1648: its original name was École Académique, changed in 1793 to the present title. Painting and other graphic arts, sculpture, and architecture are taught free of charge to those who can pass the required examination. All students are allowed to compete for the grand prize, known as the PRIX DE ROME, which permits the winners to study at the Academy of France in Rome. Teachers are selected from the finest French artists: while French students predominate, foreigners including Americans are welcomed.

Edda, in literature the title of two remarkable collections of Icelandic saga: The *Elder,* or *Poetic Edda,* also known as the *Edda of Saemund the Wise,* a collection of heroic and mythological songs probably written between the 10th and 14th centuries: the *Younger,* or *Prose Edda,* also known as the *Edda of Snorri Sturleson;* a prose work on Norse mythology and the methods of the poets or skalds, supposed to have been written by the historian and poet, Snorri STURLESON (1178-1241).

Eddy, Clarence (1851-1937), American organist and composer who studied with Dudley BUCK, and also in Berlin. He toured extensively in Germany, Austria, Switzerland, and Holland before settling in Chicago, Ill.: from there he made many tours of the United States, also playing at most of the great expositions between 1876 and 1915 at Philadelphia, Chicago, Buffalo, St. Louis, and San Francisco. His compositions include works for the organ, church music, and songs.

Eddy, Nelson (1901-   ), American actor and singer who studied under David BISPHAM, making his stage debut in 1922, and later appearing in Gilbert and Sullivan operettas. He sang with the Philadelphia Civic Opera Company for several years, making his New York debut in 1931 at the Metropolitan Opera House in Alban BERG's opera WOZZECK. He has appeared in many motion pictures including *Naughty Marietta; Rose Marie; Maytime; Rosalie; The Girl of the Golden West; Sweethearts; Let Freedom Ring; Balalaika; New Moon; Bitter Sweet; Chocolate Soldier; I Married an Angel; The Phantom of the Opera.*

Edelinck, Gérard (c.1640-1707), Flemish engraver who studied at Antwerp with Cornelisz Galle, and also at Paris under de Poilly: his work was highly appreciated by Louis XIV of France who appointed him teacher at an academy established for the training of tapestry workers. His notable works include *Holy Family,* after RAPHAEL; *Combat of Four Knights,* after LEONARDO DA VINCI; he also made many fine engravings of portraits including those of Louis XIV, John DRYDEN, LA FONTAINE, and Descartes.

Edgeworth, Maria (1767-1849), Irish novelist who was assisted in her first attempts at literary composition by her father: her successful novels include *Castle Rackrent* (1800); *Belinda; The Absentee; Ormond;* she also wrote some charming tales for children. Her books are regarded as character studies rather than absorbing narratives because the plots of her stories lack vitality.

Edgren, Anna Carlotta Leffler (1849-1892), Swedish novelist and dramatist: her first three works, a volume of short stories, *By Chance,* the dramas, *The Actress* and *The Curate* were successes anonymously in 1873: later she put her name on *From Life, How Men Do Good,* and *Domestic Happiness.* Her later dramas of note include *Ideal Women* and *A Rescuing Angel.*

Edison, Thomas Alva (1847-1931), American inventor whose creation of the carbon telephone transmitter had much to do with the invention of the phonograph. He also patented a kinetoscope in 1887 which started others working on a motion picture projector which was finally perfected with his assistance: the final invention of talking films was based on the results of his previous experiments in synchronizing his phonograph and motion picture devices.

Edmonds, Walter (1903-), American novelist who was educated at Harvard University: one of his stories was accepted by *Scribner's Magazine* while he was still in college. His works include *Rome Haul* (1929); which was dramatized by Marc Connelly, and screened as "The Farmer Takes a Wife"; *Drums Along the Mohawk,* also adapted for the films; *Chad Hanna,* another success on the screen; *The Matchlock Gun; Young Ames.*

Edwards, George Wharton (1859-), American painter and author who studied in Europe, and is distinguished also as an illustrator and author. His works include *Thumbnail Sketches* (1886); *Brittany and the Bretons; The Forest of Arden; Vanished Halls and Cathedrals of France; Belgium Old and New.* His travel books on European cities and countries have also achieved success.

Edwards, Gus (1881-), American stage, screen, and radio actor, song writer, producer, and publisher who made his debut with the Newsboy Quintet in the Gaiety Theatre, Brooklyn, N. Y. After writing the hit song, *School Days,* he founded a publishing business, issuing several of his successes including *By the Light of the Silvery Moon, In My Merry Oldsmobile,* and *Tammany.* He also produced a revue, *School Days,* in vaudeville:

among his talent discoveries were Earl Carroll, Eddie CANTOR, Groucho MARX, Mae Murray, George Jessel, and Helen MENKEN. A motion picture produced in 1939, *The Star Maker,* featured the most interesting incidents of his career.

Edwards, Julian (1855-1910), English composer who studied with Sir George Macfarren, and after conducting English opera at Covent Garden, London, came to the United States in 1888. Several of his light operas achieved a high degree of success; they include *Madeleine, or the Magic Kiss* (1902); *Brian Boru; Dolly Varden; The Patriot.*

Eeckhout, Gerbrand van den (1621-1674), Dutch painter and engraver who studied with REMBRANDT, copying his style so perfectly that it is difficult to distinguish some of his works from those of the great master. His works include *Anna Consecrating Her Son to the Lord; The Continence of Scipio; Children in a Park; Woman Taken in Adultery; Destruction of Sodom and Gomorrah; Resting Huntsman.*

Egge, Peter (1869-), Norwegian novelist and dramatist who published his first novel, *Common People,* when he was twenty-two years old, and has since become one of the most prolific authors in Norway. His novels, *The Heart* and *Hansine Solstad,* have achieved great success: the latter has been translated into English and several other languages. His comedy, *Love and Friendship,* and a drama, *Defect,* have been successfully produced in Norway and other European countries; Egge appears to rank in popularity with Knut HAMSUN and Sigrid UNDSET.

Eggerth, Marta, contemporary Hungarian screen actress; she has appeared in many important European films including *Grand Hotel; A Song, A Kiss, A Maiden; Dream of Schönbrunn; The Tsarevitch; Casta Diva; The Unfinished Symphony; My Heart is Calling; The Czardas Duchess; The Charm of La Bohéme.*

Eggleston, Edward (1837-1902), American clergyman and novelist who wrote several successful novels dealing with life in the Hoosier State (Indiana): they include *The Hoosier Schoolmaster* (1871); *The Circuit Rider; The Hoosier Schoolboy; The Graysons; The Faith Doctor.* His stories picture the pioneer customs and employ the dialect used in the Middle West. His brother, **George Cary Eggleston** (1839-1911), was literary editor of the New York *Evening Post* for many years, also writing a *History of the Confederate War,* and many stirring stories for boys.

Egmont, Lamoral, Count of (1522-1568), Flemish general and statesman who was Governor of Flanders under Philip II of Spain, and later co-operated with William of Orange. The Duke of Alba succeeded in bringing about his arrest and execution, and the tragic incidents of his career form the basis of a drama by GOETHE with incidental music by Ludwig van BEETHOVEN. The overture is a standard orchestral work: there is a Victor recording by the National Broadcasting Company Orchestra with Arturo Toscanini and a Columbia recording by the Vienna Philharmonic Orchestra directed by Felix Weingartner.

Ehrenbourg, Ilya (1891-), Russian novelist, journalist, and poet who led an adventurous life in Russia before the Revolution, and in France during World War I: since 1941 he acted as correspondent in the Russo-German War for Overseas News Service. Among his works published in English are *The Love of Jeanne Ney; The Extraordinary Adventures of Julio Jurenito and His Disciples; A Street in Moscow; Out of Chaos.*

Eichberg, Julius (1824-1893), German violinist and composer who studied at the Brussels Conservatory, and came to the United States in 1857; settling in Boston in 1859 and founding the Boston Conservatory of Music. He directed the concerts at the Boston Museum for many years, and produced two very successful comic operettas entitled *The Doctor of Alcantara* and *The Two Cadis.*

Eichheim, Henry (1870-1942), American violinist and composer who studied at the Chicago College of Music, and played in the THOMAS ORCHESTRA and the BOSTON SYMPHONY Orchestra. He collected musical material and unusual instruments in the Orient, and composed several works designed to introduce Oriental music to Western concert audiences: they include three ballets in Chinese and Burmese style; *Oriental Impressions* for orchestra; *Burma,* an orchestral suite; *Bali; Japanese Nocturne.* There are Victor recordings of the last two works by the Philadelphia Orchestra under Leopold STOKOWSKI.

Eichholtz, Jacob (1776-1842), American painter who studied with Gilbert STUART, but learned his art chiefly through self-study. He painted portraits of Chief Justices John Marshall and John Bannister Gibson: also many other notabilities of political, business, and social importance.

Eiffel, Alexandre Gustav (1832-1923), French engineer who conducted important researches in structural steel design which resulted in the increased use of steel in architecture. He also designed the **Eiffel Tower** erected at the Paris Exposition in 1889: it was nearly a thousand feet high, and the surrounding country could be seen for more than eighty miles from the platform at the top of the tower. The French wireless, telegraphic service operated from the Eiffel Tower.

"1812"—Solemn Overture (Tschaikowsky), an orchestral overture written by Peter Ilich TSCHAIKOWSKY in 1880 for performance at the consecration ceremonies for the Temple of Christ in Moscow: the overture was to be played in the public square before the cathedral, and the battery of big guns replaced by artillery salvos, but there is no accurate account of the actual ceremonies. The themes used besides the original ones written by the composer, are the Russian chorale, "God Preserve Thy People"; the Russian National Hymn, and the French "Marseillaise." There is a Victor recording by the Boston "Pops" Orchestra under Arthur Fiedler, and a Columbia recording by the Cleveland Orchestra with Artur Rodzinski.

Eilshemius, Louis Michel (1864-), American painter and author: his works include *Songs of Spring* (1895); *Lady Vere and Other Narratives; Sweetbrier; Songs of Southern Scenes; Fragments and Flashes of Thought; Nannie.*

Eine Kleine Nachtmusik (Mozart), a serenade written in the form of a quintet for two violins, viola, violoncello, and double-bass by Wolfgang Amadeus MOZART, and without doubt his best-known composition in the field of chamber music. The instrumental serenade, consisting of a few short movements in varying style and tempo, was extremely popular in Mozart's day, and it was he who perfected the form. There is a Victor recording by the Berlin Philharmonic Orchestra under Bruno Walter, and a Columbia recording by the London Symphony Orchestra with Felix Weingartner.

Einstein, Alfred (1880-), German musicologist and writer who studied at Munich under Adolf Sandberger and Anton Beer-Walbrunn. In 1919 he edited a new German edition of *Riemann's Music Lexicorn,* and in 1937 a revision of Köchel's *Catalogue of Mozart's Works* in German, correcting many errors and adding many important facts. He also wrote a *Short History of Music* in English, and a *Life of Gluck* in the "Master Musician" Series.

Eisteddfod, a festival held annually in Wales at which prizes are awarded for poetical and musical works, and also vocal and instrumental performances. The rules governing the festival were established by Gruffydd ap Cynan, a Welsh prince of the 12th century, and they were continued until the end of the 17th century, and re-established in the 19th century.

Ekhof, Konrad (1720-1778), German actor and dramatist considered the originator of genuine German drama, and the founder of the realistic school of acting. He headed the Schönemann company at Hamburg in 1757; headed the Ackermann group of players in 1764, and in 1775 became associate director of the Court Theatre at Gotha. He was considered the greatest tragic actor of his time, and founded the Academy of Actors, the first permanent institution of its kind in Germany.

Elche, Bust of, a piece of sculpture found at Elche, formerly known as Ilice, an ancient city in Spain. There has been much speculation as to whether the bust is a part of a full-length statue, and its polychrome is still intact: there is also no authentic evidence as to the identity of the sculptor, but many authorities are agreed that it was the creation of a Greek artist.

El Dorado, the legendary country sought by Italian, Spanish and Portuguese explorers in South America: it was believed that a land existed where gold was as plentiful as non-precious ores in other countries, and its location was actually placed on some 15th and 16th century maps. The words are now used figuratively to designate any country where there is wealth, or the fulfillment of one's desires.

Electra, in Greek mythology the daughter of CLYTEMNESTRA and AGAMEMNON: when the latter was murdered by her mother's paramour, Aegisthus, Electra aided her brother Orestes to avenge the crime. She was the heroine of plays by AESCHYLUS, SOPHOCLES, and EURIPIDES, as well as dramas by several French playwrights. Richard

STRAUSS composed the music for an opera, *Electra;* the libretto was written by Hugo von HOFMANN- STHAL based on the play by Sophocles. It was produced at Dresden in 1909; at the Manhattan Opera House, New York, in 1910, and at the Metropolitan Opera House in 1932.

Elegiac Melodies Op. 34 (Grieg), two delight- ful songs from Op. 38 transcribed by Edvard GRIEG himself for string orchestra: No. 1 is en- titled *Heart Wounds* and No. 2 *Last Spring.* There is a Columbia recording by the Minneapolis Symphony Orchestra under the direction of Dim- tri Mitropoulos, and a Victor recording by the London Philharmonic Orchestra under Eugene Goossens.

Elegy, (*a*) in literature a poem written in elegiac verse, usually dignified and sorrowful in character. The Roman poets including OVID and CATULLUS excelled in the form: immortal elegies were also written by SPENSER, MILTON, SHAKESPEARE, POPE, COWPER, GRAY, SHELLEY, ARNOLD, SWINBURNE, STEVENSON, BRYANT, Walt WHITMAN, TENNYSON, and LAMARTINE. (*b*) In music a composition of mournful character either vocal or instrumental; also called a dirge.

Elegy (Gray), an elegiac poem written by Thomas GRAY which was first published in 1751: eleven editions were printed in a short time, and it had the dubious distinction of being imitated, parodied, and pirated. It was also translated into most European languages including Russian, and also into Hebrew, Greek, and Latin.

Eleusinian Mysteries, the most famous of the religious mysteries of the ancient world, origi- nating at Eleusis, a city in Attica, and carried on by the Athenians after the conquest of Eleusis. The *Lesser Mysteries* were celebrated in the early spring, and symbolized the coming to life of vege- tables and fruits; the *Greater Mysteries* marked their yearly passing: on the 19th and 20th days occurred the solemn procession to the sea known as *Iacchus* because the marchers carried an image of this god who was identical with Bacchus or Di- onysus.

Elevation, in ballet a term meaning "lightness"; consequently the ability of a dancer to leap high in the air. The height attained is not as impor- tant as the ability to land gently, thereby preserv- ing the illusion of flying.

Elgar, Sir Edward (1857-1934), English com- poser who received some training from his father, and a few violin lessons from Adolf Pollitzer at the Royal Academy of Music in London. For some years he played the organ and conducted an amateur orchestra, but devoted himself exclusively to composition after 1899 when his *Enigma Varia- tions* for orchestra were splendidly received at the Norwich Music Festival. His numerous works cover the entire field of musical composition: out- standing are the oratorios *The Dream of Gerontius* and *Caractacus;* the concert overture *Cockaigne;* the marches *Pomp and Circumstance; Sea Pieces* for alto voice and orchestra; the *Severn Suite* for orchestra; the violin solo, *La Capricieuse;* ENIGMA VARIATIONS; *Salut d'Amour.*

Elgin Marbles, a series of ancient sculptures re- moved at a cost of $250,000 from Athens, Greece, to England in 1806, by the Earl of Elgin who received permission from the Turkish Government while envoy extraordinary at Constantinople. They included a large part of the frieze of the PARTHENON executed by PHIDIAS, a caryatid, and a column from the ERECHTHEUM. They were purchased by the British Museum in 1816, and replicas are on exhibition at the Metropolitan Museum of Art, New York.

Eliot, Charles William (1834-1926), American educator and editor who studied at Harvard Uni- versity, and later became its president for a period of forty years. His greatest contribution to the advancement of learning is *The Harvard Classics,* also known as the "Five-Foot Shelf of Books," and comprising fifty volumes containing 418 lit- erary masterpieces by more than three hundred classical and modern authors of poetry, fiction, drama, essays, biography, travelogues, and reli- gious works in addition to approved editions of legendary tales and epic poems. The set is pro- vided with a reader's guide and a chronological index.

Eliot, George, pen name of **Mary Ann** (or **Marian) Evans** (1819-1880), English novelist who was reared in an atmosphere of strict religious training against which she rebelled successfully, supplementing the narrowness of her early school- ing by reading and the study of languages. She also became intimate with several distinguished authors including Herbert SPENCER, Thomas CAR- LYLE, Harriet Martineau, and James Mill. Her first successful book was *Scenes of Clerical Life* (1875), published under her pen name: this was followed by *Adam Bede; The Mill on the Floss; Silas Marner; Romola,* which appeared later in a de luxe edition illustrated by Sir Frederick LEIGH- TON; *The Spanish Gypsy,* a dramatic poem; *Mid- dlemarch; Daniel Deronda.* A biography, *The Life of George Eliot,* was published in 1874 by her second husband, J. W. Cross.

Eliot, Thomas Stearns (1888-), American poet, dramatist, and essayist educated at Harvard, the Sorbonne, and Oxford: he became a British subject in 1927. His poetical works include *Pruf- rock* (1917); *The Waste Land; Ash Wednesday; East Coker; Burnt Norton; The Dry Salvages.* He has written essays such as *Sacred Wood, Dante,* and *Dryden:* his plays include *The Rock; Murder in the Cathedral,* and *Family Reunion.*

Elixir of Love, The (Elisir d'Amore, L'), a comic opera in two acts: libretto by Felice Ro- mani; music by Gaetano Donizetti: first produced at Milan in 1832; at the French Opera House in New Orleans in 1842, and at the Metropolitan Opera House, New York, in 1904. The story is simple: a country lad, Nemorino, buys a bottle of an "Elixir of Love" from the quack, Doctor Dul- camara: the elixir, which is merely a heady wine, makes Nemorino act coldly toward his beloved, but after some complications, he finally wins her. The aria, *Una furtiva lagrima,* has been a favorite with tenors for more than a hundred years: it was the aria sung by Enrico CARUSO on Dec. 11, 1920, when the malady that proved fatal to him mani- fested itself.

Elizabeth, the principal female character in Richard Wagner's opera, Tannhäuser: she loves Tannhäuser, but becomes so grief-stricken when he declares his love for Venus that she dies before his return from a penitential pilgrimage to Rome.

Elizabeth, Pauline Ottilie Luise (1843-1916), queen of Rumania, born in Germany and married to Prince Charles of Rumania in 1869. She became queen in 1881, and queen dowager in 1914. Her pen name as an author was "Carmen Sylva": her works, written in German, include *Rumanic Poems* (1880); the novels, *Astra* and *From Two Worlds;* the tragedies *Anne Boleyn* and *Master Manole.* Many of her works have been translated into English.

Elizabeth, Queen of England (1533-1603), queen of England from 1558 to 1603, and included in this volume because of her interest in literature, music, and other arts. Among the great poets, dramatists, and authors who flourished during her reign were Edmund SPENSER, Sir Philip SIDNEY, Michael DRAYTON, Christopher MARLOWE, SHAKESPEARE, and Francis BACON. The musicians of note included John DOWLAND, Robert Jones, Thomas Campion, and William BYRD.

Elizabethan Style, a mode in architecture and the decorative arts developed during the reign of Queen Elizabeth of England (1558-1603) which revealed itself in the designing of residences, particularly country homes: Renaissance ideas were partly retained, but a much broader interpretation made of ornamentation. The design of the large assembly hall of the older manors was still prominent, but a broad staircase, and a second floor gallery were added. Paneling in oak and ceilings in decorative plaster removed the sombre character of medieval design.

Elliott, Charles Loring (1812-1868), American painter who studied at the American Academy, New York, for a time with John TRUMBULL, and traveled widely as an itinerant painter. He returned to New York in 1845, and was highly successful as a portrait painter: among his sitters were John Ericsson, Matthew Vassar, James Fenimore COOPER, F. E. Church, and Asher Brown DURAND. One of his portraits was exhibited at the Paris Exposition in 1866 as a typical example of American art of the period.

Elliott, Gertrude (1874-), American actress; sister of Maxine ELLIOTT and wife of Sir Johnston FORBES-ROBERTSON. She made her first appearance on the stage in 1894 with Rose COGHLAN in *A Woman of No Importance:* among the plays in which she enacted leading roles were *London Assurance; Diplomacy; The Rivals; A Gilded Fool; An American Citizen; A Royal Family; Hamlet; Mice and Men; Othello; The Light That Failed; Mrs. Grundy; The Passing of the Third Floor Back; Caesar and Cleopatra.*

Elliott, John (1858-1925), American painter who was born in England and studied in Paris and Rome. His paintings include likenesses of King Humbert of Italy, Julia Ward Howe, and a study of Dante. He also painted sixteen portraits of young Americans who lost their lives in World War I: his murals include *Vintage; The Triumph of Time;* a decoration for a ceiling in the Boston Public Library; *Diana of the Tides* for the New National Museum at Washington, D. C.

Elliott, Maxine (1871-), American actress and sister of Gertrude ELLIOTT; her debut on the stage was made in 1890 at New York in *The Middleman* with E. S. WILLARD. She appeared with the Augustin DALY Company in both New York and London, and starred under Charles B. DILLINGHAM in *Her Own Way, The Chaperon, The Inferior Sex,* and *Lord and Lady Algy.* She was also featured in two silent films: *The Eternal Magdalen* and *Fighting Odds.*

Ellora, a village in India famous for its monuments and temples cut in rock along a mile-long stretch of country. There are twenty Buddhist and Brahmin temples in monolithic form: one of the caverns encloses a famous image of BUDDHA. Another great structure is the Kailasa temple cut out of a single block of stone; the courtyard is almost 300 feet long and more than 150 feet wide, and the columned halls, obelisks, and towers of the temple occupy the center. Colossal statues of the gods and bas-reliefs representing scenes from the RAMAYANA are to be found throughout the temple.

Elman, Mischa (1892-), Russian violinist who studied with Leopold AUER at the Imperial Conservatory at St. Petersburg, and made his debut there in 1904. After touring Germany and England, he made his New York debut in 1908, later appearing with all the important symphony orchestras, and giving many recitals. He has published many arrangements of classic and modern music for the violin, and has made numerous recordings.

Elmes, Harvey Lonsdale (1813-1847), English architect who studied with his father who was also a distinguished architect. His plans for St. George's Hall, Liverpool, accepted in a country-wide competition, were based on the tepidarium of the Baths of Caracalla; the building, begun in 1841 and completed by C. R. Cockerell after the designer's death, was regarded as the finest example of classic revival in Great Britain.

Elsheimer, Adam (1578-c.1620), German painter also known as Adam Tedesco; he studied with a pupil of Mathias GRUNEWALD in Frankfort, and later in Rome. He was the teacher of Peter LASTMAN who in turn became the instructor of REMBRANDT. His notable works include *Flight into Egypt; The Good Samaritan; Philemon and Baucis:* critics regard him as one of the founders of modern landscape painting.

Elson, Louis Charles (1848-1920), American musicographer, critic, and professor of musical theory and lecturer on musical subjects at the NEW ENGLAND CONSERVATORY OF MUSIC, Boston, Mass., from 1881 until his death; also lecturer for the city of Boston on music, and music critic of the Boston *Advertiser.* His notable books include *Curiosities of Music* (1880); *The National Music of America; A History of American Music; Shakespeare in Music; Women in Music; Children in*

Music; he also edited the *University Encyclopedia of Music.*

Elssler, Fanny (1810-1884), Austrian dancer, trained for the ballet as a child with her sister, Therese, who made her first appearance in 1817 at the Kartner-Thor Theatre in Vienna. After dancing in Naples, she achieved a signal triumph at Berlin in 1830, and until her retirement in 1851, captivated audiences in the opera houses of Europe, England, and the United States where she appeared for two years. She was the successful rival of TAGLIONI at L'Opéra, Paris, and shone particularly in her interpretation of the Spanish CACHUCA.

Eltinge, Julian (1883-1941), American actor and female impersonator who made his debut as an actor in *Mr. Wix of Wickham,* and scored his first success in vaudeville as a female impersonator in 1906. After touring the United States and England he appeared in the dual character of Mrs. Monte and Hal Blake in *The Fascinating Widow* in 1911; also in *The Crinoline Girl; Her Grace The Vampire; Countess Charming.* He was featured as a female impersonator in several motion pictures.

Elwell, Frank Edwin (1858-1922), American sculptor who occupied the post of curator at the METROPOLITAN MUSEUM OF ART, New York, from 1903 to 1905. His works include *Diana and the Lion; Death of Strength; Egypt Awaking; Charles Dickens and Little Nell; Water Boy of Pompeii; Kronos,* a fountain on exhibition at the Pan-American Exposition; *Greece and Rome.*

Élysée, Palace of the, a residence in Paris built in 1718 for the Count of Evreux, and later purchased for Mme. de POMPADOUR: it was also occupied by NAPOLEON I and Napoleon III, and was later enlarged and altered before becoming the official residence of the presidents of France.

Elysian Fields (Elysium), in Greek mythology the land of the righteous after their removal from the earth: heroes beloved of the gods were transported to Elysium, without the pain of dying, to live in happiness and serenity in a country where the atmosphere was tempered by zephyrs from the nearby ocean.

Emerald, a brilliant green variety of beryl, highly prized as a gem in ancient and modern times. The emerald was obtained in Upper Egypt, and it was also cleverly imitated by the Egyptians. It is found in South America, Peru, Colombia, Russia, Austria, Norway, Wales, and occasionally in the United States. The blue variety is known as AQUAMARINE, and the Brazilian variety as TOURMALINE.

Emerson, John (1874-   ), American actor and dramatist who made his stage debut in 1904, and was associated with the repertory company formed by Minnie Maddern FISKE. He also acted as stage director for Charles FROHMAN: his plays, written in collaboration with his wife, Anita Loos, include *Gentlemen Prefer Blondes* and *The Social Register.*

Emerson, Ralph Waldo (1803-1882), American poet, essayist, and lecturer educated at Harvard University, and at the Divinity School in Cambridge, Mass. He lectured for nearly forty years on human culture and philosophy: his works include *Nature* (1836); *Representative Men; English Traits; The Conduct of Life; Society and Solitude; Letters and Social Aims;* two volumes of poems. He also edited a volume of poems, *Parnassus,* selected from the entire range of English literature. His son, **Edward Waldo Emerson** (1844-1930), was educated at Harvard College, and practiced medicine: his works include *Emerson in Concord,* the editing of his father's correspondence, and the *Journals* in ten volumes from 1909 to 1914.

Eminescu, Michael (1849-1889), Rumanian poet and journalist whom political strife affected so strongly that he died insane. His fame as Rumania's great lyric poet is founded on his first volume of poems in which the elevation of thought and beauty of versification reached the highest pinnacle: Carmen Sylva, Queen of Rumania, translated some of his poems into German.

Emmett, Daniel Decatur (1815-1904), American minstrel singer and comedian who was one of the founders of the Virginia Minstrels, the first blackface troupe to tour the United States during the last half of the 19th century. He was the author of *Ole Dan Tucker, Dixie,* and many other songs popular in minstrel entertainment.

Emperor Jones, The, a grand opera in two acts, prologue, and interlude: libretto based on Eugene O'NEILL's play of the same name, and music by Louis GRUENBERG: first produced in 1933 at the Metropolitan Opera House, New York. The plot revolves around the Negro murderer, Jones, who escapes from a chain-gang in America, and hides in Africa where he dominates the Negroes who believe that he is invulnerable except for one silver bullet in his own revolver. A trader, Henry Smithers, tells Jones the natives are about to revolt: he escapes through the jungle, but his conscience frightens him, and when some natives approach, he kills himself with the one silver bullet.

"Emperor" Quartet (Haydn), a quartet for two violins, viola, and violoncello composed by Joseph HAYDN: it is the third of six quartets in Op. 76, and is called the "Emperor" or "Kaiser" quartet because the slow movement consists of a series of variations founded on the *Austrian National Hymn* which he had composed in 1797. There is a Columbia recording by the Lener Quartet, and a Victor recording by the Pro Arte Quartet.

"Emperor" Waltzes (Strauss), a set of waltzes, also known as the *Kaiser Waltzes,* composed by Johann STRAUSS, Jr. in honor of Emperor Franz Josef. A Frenchman, Wilhelm Ritter, wrote a study of the waltzes composed by Strauss in the last period of his creative periods: he compares them with works by Beethoven and Wagner, and pronounces the "Emperor" Waltzes as "the most beautiful flower that the fantastic tree of Strauss music had borne for seventy-five years." There is a Victor recording by the Boston "Pops" Orchestra under Arthur Fiedler, and by the Vienna Philharmonic Orchestra with Bruno Walter.

Empire Style, a mode in furniture and interior decoration which may be described as the embodiment of the CLASSIC REVIVAL in France during the early part of the 19th century, eventually exerting its influence in other European countries and the United States. The style is identified more or less with the reign of NAPOLEON I, and is accordingly clothed in the regal atmosphere with which the conqueror of Europe invested his court. Interior architectural fittings and furniture were made of costly woods such as rosewood and mahogany, and decorated with gilt or bronze mountings: the general effect, however, was overpowering, and in the middle of the 19th century was replaced by a simpler, less costly style.

Empire Theatre (New York), a theatre in New York which opened in 1893 with a performance of David BELASCO's drama of Indian and army life, *The Girl I Left Behind Me,* in which Edna Wallace HOPPER was the star. The Charles FROHMAN Stock Company, with Maude ADAMS as the leading woman, and Ethel BARRYMORE the ingenue, appeared there for several years. Other famous players connected with its history include Julia MARLOWE, John DREW, Otis SKINNER, Dennis KING, William GILLETTE, Hilda SPONG, Billie BURKE, Effie SHANNON, Helen HAYES, Judith ANDERSON, George ABBOTT, Jeanne EAGELS, Pauline LORD, Helen MENKEN, Ruth GORDON, Katherine CORNELL, and Violet HEMING. Many of the actors mentioned were present at the celebration of the fiftieth anniversary on Jan. 25, 1943; by a curious coincidence, a performance of the most successful play ever staged in the theatre, *Life with Father,* preceded the ceremonies.

Empire Theatre Ballets (London), a series of ballet performances inaugurated at the Empire Theatre, London, in 1884; Katti Lanner, daughter of Joseph LANNER, rival of Johann STRAUSS, Jr., in the field of dance music, became the ballet mistress in 1887. Many classic and modern ballets were produced and Mlle. Adeline GENÉE made her London debut in 1897, retiring ten years later. Adolf BOLM and Lydia KYASHT also appeared in many of the ballets which were patriotic, historical, or topical in character: the last-named were more in the nature of revues.

Enamel, in art the name given to a hard vitreous compound obtained by fusing mineral materials colored with metallic oxides. The product is used in the composition of small pictures and designs: it originated in the Orient where Byzantine artisans produced exquisite works in the 10th and 11th centuries. In the Occident enamel has been chiefly associated with jewelry: the workshops at Limoges, France, produced beautiful designs in the 16th century. Leonard LIMOSIN was the most famous enamelist during this period, recreating paintings of the FONTAINEBLEAU School, and portraits in the style of CLOUET. Other famous enamelists of the earlier period include Jean Penicaud and Pierre Raymond: among those who have revived it in modern times are Claudius Popelin, Paul Grandhomme, Fernand Thesmar, Alexander Fischer, and Lucien Falize.

Encaustic Painting, a process invented and developed by the ancient Egyptians, Greeks, and Romans: the medium was a mixture of resin, wax, and color formed into small cylinders, and spread on with a SPATULA. It was probably used in the decoration of residences at HERCULANEUM and POMPEII: the wax method is more difficult than the use of oil, but less so than the employment of TEMPERA.

Enchainement, in ballet a term describing the sequence of steps in a dance.

Enchanted Lake (Liadoff), a symphonic poem composed by Anatol Liadoff, a pupil of Nicholas RIMSKY-KORSAKOW and his equal as a brilliant orchestrator. In this work he portrays a lake reflecting the trees of a great forest in the mirrored surface, and sheltering beneath its deep waters the lovely water-nymphs which play an important part in Russian folk lore. There is a Victor recording by the Boston Symphony Orchestra directed by Serge Koussevitzky.

Encina or **Enzina, Juan del** (1469-c.1533), Spanish poet and dramatist educated at the University of Salamanca; his works include *Cancionero* (Song Book), published in 1492, and prefaced by a dissertation on Castilian poesy; fourteen dramas, one of which *Placido y Victoriano,* was banned by the Spanish Inquisition; *Tribagia,* a description of his pilgrimage to Jerusalem in 1518 after becoming a priest. He is considered the founder of Spanish drama.

Endymion, in Greek mythology a young shepherd beloved of Selene, goddess of the moon: he was granted immortality by the deity in order that she might enjoy his society undisturbed.

Enesco, Georges (1881-), Rumanian composer who studied the violin with Joseph HELLMESBERGER and Martin MARSICK; his instructors in musical theory and composition were Robert Fuchs, Gabriel FAURE, and Jules MASSENET. In 1897 he presented a successful concert of his own works in Paris; in 1898 his RUMANIAN RHAPSODY No. 1, a favorite concert, radio, and record work, was performed by the Colonne Orchestra. He was appointed court violinist to ELIZABETH, QUEEN OF RUMANIA, and while conducting master violin classes at the École Normale de Musique, Paris, taught Yehudi MENUHIN for several years. He toured the United States several times as violinist, conductor, and composer, and also directed a series of concerts of the New York Philharmonic-Symphony Orchestra in 1938 and 1939. His compositions include two Rumanian Rhapsodies; three symphonies; three orchestral suites; three violin sonatas; an octet for four violins; chamber music for various instruments; two suites and many solo pieces for piano: *Chansons de Clement Marot* and other songs.

Engel, Carl (1883-), American musicographer born in France; educated at the Universities of Strasbourg and Munich, and a pupil of Ludwig Thuille. He came to the United States in 1905, assuming various editorial posts before succeeding Oscar G. SONNECK as head of the Music Division of the Congressional Library in 1922. He has edited the *Musical Quarterly* since 1929, and has written essays on musical subjects in addition to composing chamber music, piano pieces and songs.

Englander, Ludwig (1859-1914), Austrian composer of comic operas who came to the United States in 1882 to conduct the light opera company at the Thalia Theatre, New York, where his first operetta, *The Prince Consort,* was produced. His successful works include *The Little Corporal; The Casino Girl; The Rounders; The Strollers; The Madcap Princess; The Jewel of Asia; The Gay White Way.*

Engleheart, George (1752-1829), English painter who studied with George Barrett and Sir Joshua REYNOLDS, and became a famous miniaturist. He made twenty-five portraits of George III, and many copies in miniature of paintings by Reynolds: in forty years he created nearly five thousand miniatures, and earned an average of $6000 each year. His nephew, **John Cox Dillman Engleheart** (1784-1862) studied with him, and also became a distinguished miniaturist although ill-health brought his activities to an end in 1828.

English, Thomas Dunn (1819-1902), American novelist, dramatist, and poet; his works include *Walter Woolfe* (1847); *The Mormons,* a play produced in 1858; *Jacob Schuyler's Millions;* a poem, *Ben Bolt* (1843) which became popular as a song at the time of the Civil War, and was introduced into the novel *Trilby* by George DU MAURIER.

English Horn, a musical instrument known in German as *Englisch Horn,* and in French as *cor anglais:* it is not a horn but an alto OBOE larger than the standard instrument, and a fifth lower in pitch. The tone is richer than that of the oboe, and Christoph Willibald von GLUCK was the first composer to appreciate its merits in the orchestra. Other composers who have used it effectively are ROSSINI, MEYERBEER, and DVORAK: the latter used it to great advantage in the "New World" symphony.

Engraving, in art a form of painting by printing, usually done in black ink. The picture is cut either in wood, where the drawing or design is in relief, or in copper where the hollows when filled with ink retrace the design when printed on paper. Engraving on wood is known as *relief engraving;* on copper or steel it is called *intaglio engraving.* Other methods are designated as *aquatint, crayon, color, mechanical,* or *electro-chemical.* Engraving in the styles mentioned above is a comparatively modern invention: the first wood engravings appeared in the 14th century. In Italy decided preference for copper manifested itself at an early date: among the famous artists who were either painters and engravers as well, or who devoted themselves exclusively to engraving, were BOTTICELLI, POLLAIUOLO, LIPPI, MANTEGNA, RAIMONDI, the CARRACCIS, DURER, BEHAM, VAN LEYDEN, RUBENS, VAN DYCK, REMBRANDT, REYNOLDS, TIEPOLO, GOYA, and TOULOUSE-LAUTREC.

Enharmonic, in Greek music a form of scale in which the quarter tone is used, thereby distinguishing it from the diatonic and chromatic scales. In modern music enharmonic tones are those derived from different degrees, but practically the same in pitch: for example G♯ and A♭. An enharmonic change is produced in the harmonic relations of a chord by regarding it as identical with a chord of different notation.

"Enigma" Variations (Elgar), a series of variations for orchestra by Edward Elgar, the theme given the title "Enigma" by the composer. There are fourteen variations, and the score is dedicated to fourteen of his friends. Each variation has the initials of the friend to whom it is dedicated: it is presumed to describe their idiosyncracies, and judging by the serious character of the music they were all of the refined and intellectual type. They were first played at London in 1899: there is a Victor recording by the British Broadcasting Symphony Orchestra directed by Sir Adrian Boult.

Enlèvement, in ballet the lifting of a ballerina in the air by a male dancer.

Ennius, Quintus (239-169 B.C.), Roman poet who was intimate with Cato the elder and Scipio Africanus. His works include narrative epics, tragedies, and comedies: only fragments have been preserved, but they afford evidence that he made great improvements in Latin verse; he was frequently imitated by VIRGIL and LUCRETIUS.

En Saga (Sibelius), a symphonic poem by Jean Sibelius composed in 1892: it seems to relate no specific story, but is epic in character with a slow and a fast movement having two especially virile themes. The work is remarkable for its division of the strings into many parts; Franz LISZT and Richard WAGNER had already developed the idea, but Sibelius carries it still farther. There is a Victor recording by the London Philharmonic Orchestra with Sir Thomas Beecham.

Ensemble, in music a term describing the tonal effect produced by a combination of instruments, of singers, or of both: for example, an orchestra alone, a chorus of voices alone, or a combination of both. The term is usually employed in connection with a small group of instrumentalists rendering chamber music.

Ensor, James, Baron (1860-1942), Belgian painter, musician, and poet who studied at the Brussels Academy for three years, and became famous as a painter of mystical, macabre subjects. Many of his works were sold at sums exceeding $5000, and were exhibited at Paris, Berlin, Rome, and other European cities: he was knighted by King Albert of Belgium. His notable works include *The Tribulation of St. Anthony,* formerly in the Cologne Museum, but banned by the Nazi Government, and now in the Museum of Modern Art, New York City.

Entablature, in architecture the term for the superstructure supported by COLUMNS or PILASTERS in ancient Greek, Roman, and Renaissance architecture. The parts consist of the ARCHITRAVE, the ABACUS, the FRIEZE, and the CORNICE.

Entasis, in architecture a slight convex curve given to the vertical outline of a column in order to correct the optical illusion of hollowness in an extended straight line.

Enters, Angna, contemporary dance mime, author, and artist who made her debut in 1926 at New York: after appearing in Paris and making a transcontinental tour, she was awarded a GUG-

GENHEIM FELLOWSHIP in 1934 and 1935. She has exhibited more than nine hundred water colors and drawings in American galleries, and is the author of *First Person Plural,* and a play, *Love Possessed Juana.*

Entrechat, in ballet a step in which the dancer leaps in the air and crosses the feet in a scissor-like movement four to eight times, each crossing being counted as two movements. Vaslav NI-JINSKY was the first dancer to achieve ten crossings.

Entry of the Gods into Valhalla, the music which ends *The Rhinegold,* the first of the dramas of THE RING OF THE NIBELUNGS, a tetralogy composed by Richard Wagner. It was first produced at Bayreuth in 1876, and at the Metropolitan Opera House in 1889 with Anton SEIDL conducting. As the music is played, the gods, headed by WOTAN and FRICKA cross a bridge made of a rainbow to VALHALLA, the castle built by the giants, FAFNER and Fasolt, who received the Rhinegold as their reward. Suddenly the Rhine daughters' song is heard in a plea for the return of the gold: the orchestra, in a tremendous *fortissimo* burst, combines the motives of the rainbow and of Valhalla. There is a Victor recording by a symphony orchestra under Albert Coates, and a Columbia recording by the Bayreuth Festival Orchestra conducted by Franz von Hoesslin.

Eos, see **Aurora.**

Ephesus, a city in ancient Asia Minor famous for its Temple of Artemis and as the residence of Christ's disciple, Paul. A great theatre, mentioned in the Bible, was erected there: the orchestra was 110 feet in diameter, and the proscenium was 22 feet wide. There was also an ODEUM and a STADIUM constructed on a large scale.

Epic, in literature a lengthy narrative poem originating in ancient Greece, and first used to chronicle achievements in battle and conquest. The great epics of the world's literature include the Greek ILIAD and ODYSSEY of HOMER; the Roman AENEID of VIRGIL, and *Thebaid* of Statius; the French CHANSON DE ROLAND; the German BEOWULF; the Icelandic *Atlamal;* the Finnish *Kalevala;* the Italian *Jerusalem Delivered* by TASSO; the Spanish Le CID; the Portuguese *Lusiads;* the East-Indian RAMAYANA. More modern examples are *The Faerie Queen* of Spenser, and the PARADISE LOST of MILTON.

Epicharmus (c.540-450 B.C.), Greek comic poet who lived at Megara in Sicily and at Syracuse. His works include about 35 comedies of which only a few fragments have survived: they are replete with rough, satirical humor, but, unlike the comedies of ARISTOPHANES, they lack all jibes at political leaders which were permitted by the Athenian authorities, but forbidden in Syracuse.

Epicurus (341-270 B.C.), Greek philosopher who established a school at Athens about 305 B.C.: his teaching was that the supreme good of life is found in pleasure; not the fleeting pleasures of food and drink, but in the delight resulting from the practice of virtue. Unfortunately Epicurean doctrines have been deliberately or unintentionally misinterpreted so that Epicureanism has become a synonym of refined self-indulgence.

Epigram, in literature a word which applies in the correct sense to anything written; its meaning today has been narrowed down to designate a pithy or antithetical saying. Among the most distinguished authors of epigrams are CATULLUS, SANNAZARO, SPENSER, DRYDEN, SWIFT, ADDISON, JOHNSON, GOLDSMITH, ROUSSEAU, VOLTAIRE, LESSING, and LANDOR.

Epilogue, in literature and drama a supplement to the usual ending similar in some respects to the peroration of a speech. It was used by SHAKESPEARE, BEAUMONT, FLETCHER, Ben JONSON, and DRYDEN: the latter published a treatise, *Defence of the Epilogue,* championing its use. It is seldom used in modern literature or drama.

Epimenides, Greek poet and prophet who may have lived in the 6th century B.C., although his existence is questioned by some historical authorities. He was said to have possessed the gift of prophecy, and to have written a book of oracles and an epic poem on the ARGONAUTS.

Epitaph, in literature an inscription on a tomb, or anything written in praise or censure of a dead person whether or not actually inscribed on his tomb. Epitaphs were written on Egyptian sarcophagi, and many tender or stirring verses were placed on ancient Greek tombs. Roman epitaphs rarely recorded more than bare facts of birth and death. John MILTON wrote a now famous epitaph on SHAKESPEARE, and Alexander POPE and Samuel JOHNSON composed many fine inscriptions of this character. French epitaphs reveal grace, wit, and occasional tenderness; Étienne PASQUIER wrote several which can be so classified.

Epithalamium, in ancient Greece a song in praise of bride and bridegroom, usually sung by a chorus of young people outside the door of the nuptial chamber: it was also used in Rome. SAPPHO, ANACREON, PINDAR, CATULLUS, and CLAUDIAN were among the poets who wrote verses of this character; later writers include BUCHANAN, RONSARD, MALHERBE, METASTASIO, SPENSER, JONSON, DONNE, and TENNYSON.

Epode, in ancient Greek literature the third part of an ode: it followed the strophe and the antistrophe, thereby completing the composition.

Epreuve d'Amour, L' (The Proof of Love), a humorous ballet in one act; libretto by André Derain and Michel FOKINE; choreography by Michel Fokine; music by Wolfgang Amadeus MOZART; first performance in 1936 at Monte Carlo. The plot revolves around the attempts of an avaricious Chinese mandarin to marry Chung-Yang, a beautiful Oriental maiden, to a wealthy ambassador, but his infamous schemes are foiled. The music of Mozart is an hitherto unknown score written in Oriental vein, and the role of Chung-Yang was created by Vera NEMCHINOVA.

Epstein, Jacob (1880-), American sculptor of Russo-Polish parentage who studied at the ART

STUDENTS' LEAGUE, New York, and at the ECOLE DES BEAUX-ARTS, Paris. He spent much of his time studying Egyptian sculpture in the LOUVRE, and also the works of Auguste RODIN. In 1905 he settled in London: his notable works include eighteen large figures for the British Medical Association Building; The *Oscar Wilde Memorial* in Paris; a marble *Venus;* a standing figure of Christ in bronze; the groups, *Day* and *Night* on the Underground Railways Building, London; the *American Soldier* in bronze at the Metropolitan Museum of Art, New York. No modern sculptor's work has been more highly praised or bitterly criticized.

Equal Temperament, a method of tuning instruments that is a compromise between the theory of acoustics, and the practical art of tuning. It aims to make all semitones equal so that an octave shall comprise twelve equal half-tones: in this way each scale is approximately correct, and modulation to any other scale is equally correct.

Érard, Sébastien (1752-1831), French maker of harps and pianos whose invention of a mechanical harpsichord in 1776 led the Duchess of Villeroy to establish a workshop for him in her villa where he produced in 1777 the first piano made in France. He founded an instrument factory in Paris with his brother, Jean Baptiste Érard, and perfected the double-mechanism for the harp which vastly increased its usefulness both as a solo and as an orchestral instrument. His greatest accomplishment was the invention in 1809 of a repetitive action for the grand piano.

Ercilla y Zúñiga, Alonso de (1533-1595), Spanish poet and soldier who served in the war against the Araucanian natives of Chile. His epic poem, *The Araucanian Woman* is a narrative of his experiences: it was highly praised by CERVANTES and VOLTAIRE.

Erckmann-Chatrian, in French drama the name placed on historical novels and plays written in collaboration by **Émile Erckmann** (1822-1899) and **Alexandre Chatrian** (1826-1890) for a period of more than forty years. Their joint works include *The Illustrious Dr. Mathews* (1859); *Friend Fritz; The Polish Jew,* adapted for Sir Henry IRVING and produced as "The Bells"; *Les Rantzau.* The last-named was adapted as an opera for which the music was composed by Pietro MASCAGNI.

Erdélyi, János (1814-1868), Hungarian poet, critic, and folklorist: his works include a volume of poems (1844), and a collection of 300 national songs, twenty folk tales and almost 7400 proverbs.

Erebus, in Greek mythology the place of darkness through which souls passed to HADES.

Erechtheum, a temple on the ACROPOLIS at Athens: it contained the ancient image of Athena Polias, and altars to POSEIDON, ERECHTHEUS, Butes and HEPHAESTUS. It also contained the gold lamp, designed by CALLIMACHUS, which burned for a year without filling. During the reign of Justinian it was used as a church: when Athens was captured by the Turks it became a harem. One of its columns and a caryatid is now in the ELGIN MARBLES collection at the British Museum.

Erechtheus, a king of Athens who, when the city was attacked by Eumolpus, leader of the Thracians, sacrificed one of his daughters as ordered by the oracle: Eumolpus was slain and the Thracians defeated, but Poseiden, father of Eumolpus, killed Erechtheus. The Erechtheum was built in his honor.

Erinna, Greek poet who lived about 350 B.C., and was a friend of SAPPHO: her poems were among the finest of her time although she died when she was nineteen. Ancient critical authorities ranked her poem, *The Distaff,* of which only four lines are extant, with those of HOMER.

Erinyes, in Greek mythology the three avenging deities also known as the Furies: they were said to be the goddesses of the curse placed on criminals whom they pursued on earth and tormented in the underworld. There are many forms of representation in Greek art: the most common is as three winged maidens with bloodshot eyes, claw-like nails, and writhing snakes in their hair.

Eris, in Greek mythology the goddess of discord, and the sister of ARES, the god of war. She caused strife at the wedding feast of Peleus and Thetis by casting an apple on which was written "to the fairest": HERA, APHRODITE, and ATHENA claimed it, and PARIS awarded it to Aphrodite.

Erkel, Franz (1810-1893), Hungarian pianist and composer who studied with his father, and was appointed director of the National Theatre at Pest in 1837. He founded and directed the Philharmonic Orchestra and taught the piano and composition at the National Musical Academy. His compositions include nine operas of which *Hunyady Laszlo* (1844) is still the favorite Hungarian work of this character. He also wrote the Hungarian national hymn, and is regarded as the founder of the Hungarian national opera. The overture to *Hunyadi Laszlo* is available in a Gramaphone (English Victor) recording by the Budapest Chamber Orchestra.

Erlach, Johann Bernard Fischer von (1658-1723), Austrian architect whose best known buildings in Vienna, such as the Palace of Prince Eugène and the Church of St. Carlo Borromeo, are a combination of the baroque and classical styles which prove him a designer of the first rank in addition to being an innovator.

Erlanger, Abraham L. (1860-1930), American theatrical manager and producer who controlled with his associate, Marc Klaw, the finest theatres in the principal cities of the United States during the first part of the 20th century. He also worked in collaboration with Charles B. DILLINGHAM and Florenz ZIEGFELD; the trio produced hundreds of plays such as *The Wandering Jew, The Perfect Fool,* and *Honeymoon Lane.*

Erlking, in German legend a character pictured as a gigantic, bearded horseman who snatches children from their parents, and carries them away to his hidden retreat. GOETHE used the legend as the basis of one of his ballads, later set to music by Franz SCHUBERT: there are Victor and Columbia recordings of *The Erlking* by several singers of distinction.

Erminie, a comic operetta in two acts: libretto by Claxson Bellamy and Harry Paulton; music by Edward JAKOBOWSKI; first produced in 1885 at London, England, and later at every theatre in Europe and the Americas where comic-opera lovers congregate. The plot revolves around two enterprising thieves who rob a young man on the way to his betrothal with Erminie, a lady he has never seen: one of them passes himself off as the prospective bridegroom, but is finally discovered, and all ends happily. The outstanding hit-song, *Lullaby,* is available in American recordings.

Ernani, a grand opera in four acts founded on "Hernani," a play by Victor HUGO: libretto by Francesco Piave and music by Guiseppe VERDI; first produced in 1844 at Venice, and at the Park Theatre, New York, in 1847. It did not reach the Metropolitan Opera House, New York, until 1902 when the roles of Elvira and Don Ruy Gomez de Silva were created by Marcella SEMBRICH and Édouard de RESZKE.

Ernst, Wilhelm (1814-1865), German violinist who studied with Joseph Böhm and Joseph Mayseder. He developed a great admiration for Nicoló PAGANINI, following him on his tours to observe his style and technique, and finally becoming a formidable rival of the great Italian master. His compositions are extremely difficult from the technical standpoint; they include an *Elegie; a Concerto in F♯ minor; Otello Fantasie; Variations on the "Carnival of Venice."*

"Eroica" Symphony (Beethoven), the third of the symphonies composed by Ludwig van BEETHOVEN: it was completed in 1804, and first performed in 1805 at Vienna with Beethoven conducting. It was originally dedicated to NAPOLEON I while he was First Consul of France, but the inscription crossed out when Napoleon declared himself Emperor, and re-dedicated to Prince Maximilian Lobkowitz. In view of the universal admiration for the symphony today, it is interesting to read that the critic of the *Allgemeine Musikalische Zeitung* declared it "a daring wild fantasia of inordinate length." There is a Victor recording by the National Broadcasting Symphony Orchestra under Arturo Toscanini, and a Columbia recording by the New York Philharmonic-Symphony Orchestra with Bruno Walter.

Eros, see **Cupid.**

Erskine, John (1879-), American author and musician who was educated at Columbia University, and studied the piano and musical composition with Ernest HUTCHESON and Edward MACDOWELL. He occupied the post of professor of English at Columbia University for many years, and was also connected with the JUILLIARD School of Music. His numerous publications include *The Private Life of Helen of Troy; The Cambridge History of American Literature* in collaboration with several others: also several volumes of essays and poems.

Ertz, Susan, contemporary Anglo-American novelist: her works include *Madame Claire* (1922); *Nina; After Noon; Now East, Now West; The Galaxy; The Story of Julian; The Proselyte; No Hearts To Break; Black, White and Caroline; One Fight More.*

Ervine, St. John Greer (1883-), Irish dramatist, critic, and novelist educated in Belfast: his early plays, *Mixed Marriage* and *The Magnanimous Lover,* were produced at the ABBEY THEATRE in Dublin. His plays include *Jane Clegg; John Ferguson; The Wonderful Visit* in collaboration with H. G. Wells; *The First Mrs. Fraser; The Christies; Boyd's Daughter.* His novels include *Mrs. Martin's Man; Alice and a Family; Changing Winds; The Foolish Lovers; The Wayward Man.*

Escamillo, in opera the name of the toreador in BIZET'S *Carmen:* he becomes enamored of Carmen, the cigarette maker, and an invitation to watch his triumph at the amphitheatre in Seville leads to her murder by the discarded lover, Don José.

Escorial or **Escurial** (Madrid), a group of buildings in Spain located in a hamlet named Escorial about thirty miles from Madrid. They comprise a monastery, church, mausoleum, and palace built for royal occupancy by Philip II: the plans were prepared and the erection supervised by Bautista de Toledo, and after his death by Juan Herrera. The artistic treasures included frescoes by Tibaldi, Carbajol, Carducci, and Giordano; there were also paintings by TITIAN, TINTORETTO, VELASQUEZ, and many other famous artists which, where movable, were later taken to Madrid.

España Rhapsody (Chabrier), a symphonic poem by Emmanuel CHABRIER originally composed from musical sketches made during 1883 in Spain for two pianos—four hands. Most of the themes are of Spanish origin: only one, the energetic motive assigned to the trombones, is original with Chabrier. It was first performed by the Lamoureux Orchestra in 1883: there is a Columbia recording by the London Philharmonic Orchestra under Sir Thomas Beecham, and a Victor recording by the Boston "Pops" Orchestra with Arthur Fiedler.

Espiña, Concha (1880-), Spanish poet and novelist who had some verses accepted for publication by a magazine when she was twelve years old: her works published in English include *Mariflor* (1924); *The Red Beacon; Woman and the Sea.*

Espinel, Vicente (1551-1634), Spanish musician, novelist, and poet: his works include a volume, *Various Verses* (1591), which proves his skill as a wit. His picaresque novel, *Life of the Esquire Marcos de Obregon,* is presumed to be an autobiography in fictional style; LE SAGE did not hesitate to borrow some of its incidents and characters for "Gil Blas." Espinel was also an accomplished musician who added a fifth string to the regular model of the guitar.

Espinosa, Édouard (1872-), French dancer who studied with his father, and made his debut in 1889 at London. He appeared with Sir Henry IRVING for several years, and also under the management of Charles FROHMAN in New York: since 1896 he has been ballet master at Covent Garden, the Hippodrome, and other London theatres preparing the dances for more than three hundred productions such as *Chu-Chin-Chow* and *The Last*

Waltz. He also arranged the dances for many notable films, established the British Ballet Company, edited *The Dancer,* and published several books on ballet technique.

Espronceda, José de (1810-1842), Spanish poet and revolutionist who was often exiled for his political activities: he was an admirer of Lord BYRON whom he imitated to the point of exaggeration in *The Pirate; The Beggar; The Headsman; The Student of Salamanca,* a weird tale; *The Clean Demon,* left incomplete, but considered his greatest work.

Essay, in literature a composition of moderate length on some special subject or topic: it is usually written in prose and both shorter and less complete than a treatise. The French author, Michel MONTAIGNE, used and perhaps originated the word in its now accepted meaning in his *Essais* (1850): among the famous essayists may be mentioned BACON, ADDISON, LAMB, COWLEY, STEELE, DE QUINCEY, CARLISLE, BRANDES, SCHOPENHAUER, CHESTERTON, IRVING, THOREAU, and EMERSON.

Essex, Robert Devereux, second Earl of (1567-1601), the favorite of Queen Elizabeth of England over whom he quarreled with Sir Walter RALEIGH. He was a man of violent temper, and the cause of much anxiety to the queen not only through his political ambitions, but because of his amorous relations with ladies of the court. In 1600 he became involved in a plot against Elizabeth with James VI of Scotland, and his quondam friend, Lord Francis BACON, was chiefly instrumental in securing the queen's consent to his execution. Incidents of his stormy career have been used as the basis for an American motion picture, *The Private Lives of Elizabeth and Essex,* and a play, *Elizabeth the Queen,* by Maxwell ANDERSON.

Essipoff, Annette (1851-1914), Russian pianist who studied with Theodor LESCHETIZKY to whom she was married from 1880 to 1892. She made her debut at St. Petersburg in 1874, and later made extensive tours of Europe, appearing in 1876 in the United States. Later she became professor of piano at the St. Petersburg Conservatory; Serge PROKOFIEFF and Isador ACHRON were her pupils.

Este, an ancient noble house of Italy which was prominent in the political history of that country from about the 2nd to the 16th century, reaching its pinnacle of power about 1520. Certain members of the family were patrons of literature and other arts: they include **Lionello Este** (1407-1450) who promoted literature, surrounding himself with learned men and establishing a printing press. The next member was his brother, **Ercole Este** (1431-1505) who gathered men eminent in literature and art around him; among them BOIARDO and ARIOSTO. His daughter, **Beatrice d'Este** (1475-1497), surrounded herself before her premature death at twenty-two with distinguished artists including CORREGGIO, CASTIGLIONE, BRAMANTE, and LEONARDO DA VINCI. Her sister, **Isabella d'Este** (1474-1539) was not only a diplomat in her relations with Cesare BORGIA, but also the patroness of RAPHAEL, MANTEGNA, and ROMANO.

Esterházy von Galantha, a distinguished noble Hungarian family of interest in this volume because of its patronage of arts, particularly the art of music. Prince **Paul von Esterházy** (1635-1713) wrote sacred vocal works that are excellent examples of Hungarian composition during his period; Prince **Paul Anton Esterházy** (? -1762), was the first of the family to employ Joseph HAYDN as director of his private orchestra; Prince **Nicholas Joseph Esterházy** (1714-1790), brother of Paul Anton, built the magnificent Schloss Esterházy which rivaled Versailles in splendor. It housed a private theatre and concert hall where Joseph Haydn continued to direct the concerts and presentations of opera for thirty years; Prince **Nicholas Esterházy** (1765-1833), who expended so much on his estate and its maintenance that he was obliged to dispense with Haydn and his orchestra, but dismissed him with a pension; Prince **Nicholas Esterházy** (1839-1897), who also maintained a private theatre, and employed a staff of composers, authors, and performers.

Estrella, Arnaldo, a contemporary Brazilian pianist who began the study of the piano as a child: he was trained at the National Conservatory of Music in Rio de Janeiro, and made his debut with the Municipal Orchestra there. After winning the Columbia Concerts Award, he made his American debut with the New York Philharmonic-Symphony Orchestra in 1943, the concert also being broadcast over the WABC network.

Etching, in art a process of engraving in which the furrows are produced by acid eating into the metal rather than by the use of the burin which actually cuts the furrows. The copper or zinc plate is covered with a ground of wax or other substance: this is smoked black so that the lines drawn with the steel etching needle can be readily seen. After the drawing is completed the plate is placed in an acid bath until the lines are sufficiently eroded in respect to its more delicate lines: the latter are then stopped out, and the heavier sections treated separately until the desired depth is reached. The completed plate is then printed on the etcher's hand press.

Étex, Antoine (1808-1888), French sculptor, painter, and architect; his works as a sculptor include *Death of Hyacinthus* and the groups, *Peace and War* on each side of the ARC DE TRIOMPHE. His paintings include *Eurydice, Martyrdom of St. Sebastian,* and *Glory of the United States* in the City Hall, New York. As an architect his outstanding work is the tomb of NAPOLEON I.

Etherege, Sir George (c.1635-1691), English dramatist of whom little is known of his early life except that he was said to have been educated at Oxford. His first comedy, *The Comical Revenge, or Love in a Tub* (1664) was a success as were several others of the same licentious character which, on the other hand reveal extraordinary ability as a wit, and as a delineator of fops and rakes.

Étienne, Charles Guillaume (1778-1845), French dramatist and opera librettist: his first work, an opera, *Le Rêve* (1799), written with Antoine Frédéric Gresnick, was a success. It was followed by several plays including *The Two Sons-in-Law* which also scored success although his claim to original authorship was disputed. Two more operas, *Cinderella* and *Joconde*, delighted Parisians: he also wrote a *History of the French Theatre* in collaboration with Alphonse Martainville.

Eton College, the most famous and largest of the public schools in England, located about twenty miles from London, and adjacent to Windsor. The low school buildings are genuinely picturesque with their battlements and towers: they enclose two large courts, and were erected by order of Henry VI although the principal annual celebration on June 4th is in honor of George III who was the most generous patron of the college. Countless distinguished British men of letters and artists attended the school before going to Oxford or Cambridge: it is usually chosen as the school attended by the younger generation in fiction and plays.

Etty, William (1787-1849), English painter who studied with Sir Thomas LAWRENCE: after many rejections his painting, *Telemachus Rescuing Antiope*, was exhibited at the Royal Academy in 1811. In 1828-29 his *Coral Finders* and *Cleopatra's Arrival in Celicia* were recognized as the work of genius, and he was admitted to the Academy. His notable works include *The Lute Player; Cupid and Psyche; Bathing Woman; Joan of Arc; Combat; David's Chief Captain.*

Étude, in music a study designed to aid in the mastery of technical difficulties, and differing from the *exercise* in being composed on a more elevated plane. Etudes that are so inspired musically as to be enjoyed by recital audiences are called *concert études;* typical examples are the piano études by Frédéric CHOPIN and Franz LISZT, as well as the *Caprices* for violin solo by Nicolo PAGANINI.

Études (Chopin), two groups of piano studies comprising twelve in Op. 10 and twelve in Op. 25 composed not only for the perfecting of technique, but as studies in melody, rhythm, harmony, and emotional expression. Franz LISZT once said of them: "Compositions which are thus modestly named are none the less types of perfection in a mode which he himself erected and stamped, as he did all his other works, with the deep impress of his poetic genius." There are Victor recordings of both Op. 10 and Op. 25 by Wilhelm Bachaus: also recordings of the most popular études such as the "Black Keys," the "Revolutionary," the "Aeolian Harp," and the "Butterfly" played by distinguished pianists.

Eugene Onegin, a grand opera in three acts: libretto based on the romance in verse by Alexander PUSHKIN; music by Peter TSCHAIKOWSKY; first produced at Moscow in 1879, and at the METROPOLITAN OPERA HOUSE, New York, in 1920. The story is: Onegin, the somewhat Byronic hero with whom most of the young women he meets fall in love, flirts with a country girl of gentle birth, Tatiana: when the affair grows too serious, he tells Tatiana he does not reciprocate her love, and is challenged by her sister's suitor, Lenski, whom he kills in a duel. Years later he meets Tatiana who has married Prince Gremin: this time it is he who falls desperately in love, and is rejected by the woman he had callously discarded years before. There are Victor recordings of the *Waltz*

and of the *Polonaise* by the Boston "Pops" Orchestra under Arthur FIEDLER.

Eulenspiegel, Till, a character in German folklore pictured as a wily vagabond of peasant origin who played his tricks on tradesmen, innkeepers, priests, and members of the nobility. He was brutal, coarse, and obscene: nevertheless the tales were translated into almost all European languages, the English equivalent being "Howleglas." A symphonic poem, TILL EULENSPIEGEL'S MERRY PRANKS, by Richard STRAUSS, is based on the legend.

Euphonium, see **Baritone.**

Euphranor, Greek painter and sculptor who lived during the 4th century B.C., and is said to have rivaled LYSIPPUS in his delineation of the human form. The Roman author, PLINY, lists a number of paintings and sculptures of which the originals or copies have never been found: they include *Theseus with Democracy and Demos; A Cavalry Charge;* also statues of PARIS, and ALEXANDER THE GREAT.

Euphronios, Greek potter and painter who worked from about 500 to 460 B.C. in his own studio producing vases of extraordinary perfection. One of his finest works is a cup representing the exploits of THESEUS, one scene picturing him receiving the lost ring of King MINOS from the sea goddess Amphitrite while his patroness, ATHENA, looks on.

Euphrosyne, see **Graces, The Three.**

Eupolis, Greek poet and dramatist who was said by HORACE to rank with CRATINUS and ARISTOPHANES; he defeated the latter in several Olympic contests. Only fragments of his seventeen known plays are in existence; they contain violent attacks on wealthy patrons of learning, on Alcibiades, and on ARISTOPHANES.

Eupompus, Greek painter who worked during the 4th century B.C., and is said to have been the teacher of LYSIPPUS and PAMPHILUS: he founded a school at Sicyon, and there is a record of one of his paintings, *Victor in the Olympic Games.*

Eurhythmics, a system of harmonious movements of the human body developed by Émile JAQUES-DALCROZE, teacher of musical theory at the Conservatory of Music in Geneva, Switzerland. The method was first used in connection with musical education, but has since been successfully applied to the training of children. The system correlates physical movements of the body with the rhythms of music.

Euridice, (*1*) a musical work by Jacopo Peri, said to be the second "opera" or drama set to music with vocal solos supported by instruments: it was composed for performance at the marriage festivities of Henry IV of France and Maria de' Medici in 1600, and was received with the greatest enthusiasm as a new art form. There is a Victor recording by Ralph Crane of two baritone arias, *Funesta piagge* and *Non piango e non sospiro.*

Euripides (480-406 B.C.), Greek poet and dramatist considered, with AESCHYLUS and SOPHOCLES, one of the three great masters of Greek tragedy. His first work, *The Daughters of Pelias,* was produced at ATHENS in 455 B.C.: he wrote between seventy-five and ninety plays of which eighteen are extant. Only five received the first prize in the dramatic contests probably because his dramas were not on as grand or noble plan as those of Sophocles and Aeschylus. The list of extant plays includes *Alcestis; Medea; Hippolytus; Hecuba; Andromache; Ion; The Suppliants; Heracleidae; The Mad Heracles; Iphigenia Among the Tauri; The Trojan Women; Helen; The Phoenician Maid; Electra; Orestes; Iphigenia at Aulis; Bacchae; Cyclops.*

Europa, in Greek mythology a princess with whom ZEUS became enamored: he assumed the form of a white bull, and carried her away from her home in Phoenicia to Crete. She became the mother of Minos, king of Crete and owner of the MINOTAUR. TITIAN painted a picture of Europa's abduction.

Eurydice, in Greek mythology the wife of OR- PHEUS: she died after being bitten by a serpent. Orpheus begged the gods to return her from HADES, and his wish was granted provided he refrained from looking back at her when they were led out of Hades. He failed to fulfill the condition, and Eurydice was lost to him forever.

Euryanthe, grand opera in three acts: libretto by Helmine von Chezy; music by Carl Maria von WEBER; first produced at Vienna in 1823, and at the Metropolitan Opera House, New York, in 1887. The libretto, described by Pitts SANBORN as "a mixture of Shakespeare's 'Cymbeline' and Wagner's 'Lohengrin,'" was theatrically impossible, resulting in the failure of the work, but the *Overture* is a standard concert number: there is a Victor recording by the British Broadcasting Symphony Orchestra, and a Columbia recording by the Chicago Symphony Orchestra.

Euterpe, in Greek mythology one of the nine Muses; the goddess of pleasure, lyric poetry, and music. She is said to have invented the FLUTE, and was also the patron of the wild simple music of the people rather than of the classical art. She is usually pictured with a flute in her hand, or with musical instruments around her.

Eutychides, Greek sculptor who worked in the latter part of the 4th century B.C.; he was a pupil of LYSIPPUS, and his greatest work, *Fortune,* was designed at Antioch. The goddess was seated on a rock with the water of the river Orontes at her feet. A marble copy is in the Vatican at Rome.

Eva, in drama a character in *Uncle Tom's Cabin,* a play dramatized from the novel by Harriet Beecher STOWE which exerted a powerful influence at the time of the Civil War. Eva was the child friend of Uncle Tom: her death is the most famous scene in the play, and the role has been essayed by hundreds of actresses of high and low degree.

Evangeline, a Tale of Acadie, an idyllic poem written by Henry W. Longfellow, and published in 1847. Its story is based on the forcible removal of a body of French settlers from the village of Grand Pré in Acadie, now known as Nova Scotia. Evangeline and her lover Gabriel are separated: they seek and actually pass one another several times unseen until they meet many years later in a hospital where he is dying.

Evans, Caradoc (1883-), Welsh short story writer and novelist who had great difficulty in learning the English language before he decided on a literary career; his works include *My People; Stories of the Peasantry of West Wales; Stories of the London Welsh; Nothing to Pay; This Way to Heaven; Wasps.*

Evans, Maurice (1901-), English actor and producer who made his professional debut at the Festival Theatre, Cambridge, England, in 1926 in *The Oresteia* of AESCHYLUS, and his first American appearance in 1935 with Katherine CORNELL in *Romeo and Juliet.* In 1937 his production and appearance in the title role of Shakespeare's *Richard II* resulted in a six month's run in New York, and an extended tour of the United States. He achieved equal success in *Saint Joan; St. Helena; Henry IV* (Part I); *Hamlet* in the original uncut version, and has also appeared in several English and American films.

Evans, Rudulph (1878-), American sculptor one of whose sculptures, *The Golden Hour,* was purchased for the Luxembourg, Paris: there is a replica in the Metropolitan Museum of Art, New York. His notable works include *Venus; Dawn; Boy and Panther; Venus Aphrodite.*

Evelyn, John (1620-1706), English author who wrote on many subjects including the sciences, gardening, art and numismatics: his notable accomplishment from the literary and historical standpoints is a *Diary,* first published in 1818-19, in which he paints an interesting picture of life in England under the Stuarts.

Everdingen, Allart van (1621-1675), Dutch painter who is said to have studied under Roland Savery at Utrecht: he is credited with having introduced Scandinavian scenery into Dutch painting, and to have inspired Jacob van RUISDAEL to execute his pictures of rocks and waterfalls. His works include *Rocky Landscape; Norwegian Waterfall; Storm at Sea; Stag Hunt; Snowstorm on the Zuyder Zee.*

Everyman, in drama the title of a morality play said to have originated in Holland: it was first performed during the 15th century, and published in 1529. The chief character, *Everyman,* is summoned by Death to the Judgment Seat: when he calls upon his friends Strength, Beauty, Knowledge, Fellowship and Good Deeds to accompany him, all desert him except Good Deeds. In 1902 Edith Wynne MATTHISON created the title role in an English revival of the play.

Evirati, see **Castrati.**

Ewald, Johannes (1743-1781), Danish clergyman, dramatist, and poet: his works include the plays *Balder's Death* and *The Fishers:* the latter contains the lyric, "King Christian Stood by the Lofty Mast," which is now the Danish national hymn. He also wrote a Biblical drama, *Adam and Eve,* and *Elegies on the Death of Frederick V.*

Ewen, David (1907-   ), American author of books on musical subjects who was born in Poland and came to the United States as a child. He was educated at Columbia University; in addition to articles in American and European musical periodicals, his works include *Pioneers of Music; Living Musicians; Music Comes to America; The Book of Modern Composers; Dictators of the Baton; Rhapsody in Jazz: a Life of George Gershwin.*

Ewing, Juliana Horatia (1841-1885), English writer and poet who first wrote little plays for numerous brothers and sisters: her brother, Alfred Scott Gatty, provided music to accompany them. Her works for children include *A Flatiron for a Farthing* (1873); *Dandelion Clocks and Other Tales; Jackanapes; Jan of the Windmill; The Story of a Short Life; A Sweet Little Deer; Blue-Red.*

Excalibur, in Arthurian legend the sword which King Arthur received from the Lady of the Lake: he who wore its sheath could never be wounded. One legend claims that the sword was embedded in stone, and only the knight who could draw it out could be king. Hundreds of knights tried and failed, but King Arthur drew it forth with ease.

Exercices à la barre, in ballet the training exercises for dancing performed on a bar fixed horizontally against the wall of a room for ballet practice: when the exercises are performed without the aid of the bar they are known as *exercices au milieu.*

Expression, in music the employment by an orchestral conductor, a choral director, or an instrumental or vocal soloist of personally conceived NUANCES not indicated on the musical score, thereby creating an individualistic interpretation. Excessive liberties taken with the tempo or dynamic marks originally placed on the work by the composer are usually undesirable because they create an impression of eccentricity rather than of legitimate self-expression.

Eyck, Hubert or **Huybrecht van** (c.1366-1426), Flemish painter of whom there are no authentic records until 1424 when he was a distinguished painter in Ghent: he is said to have perfected the art of oil painting aided by his brother, Jan van EYCK, by applying a colorless varnish which facilitated the drying of the oil. His works include *Crucifixion; Last Judgment; St. Cecilia and the Angels; The Vision of St. Francis of Assisi; The Three Marys at the Sepulchre.*

Eyck, Jan or **John van** (c.1380-c.1440), Flemish painter who studied with his brother, Hubert van EYCK, and became court painter to Philip the Good, Duke of Burgundy. His works include the completion of the altarpiece at the Church of St. Bavon, Ghent, left unfinished by his brother; *Madonna with Saints; Man With a Turban; The*

Scholar; Consecration of Thomas à Becket; Triumph of the Church; Madonna and Child; Giovanni Arnolfini and Wife, his finest portrait.

Ezekiel, Moses Jacob (1844-1917), American sculptor who studied in Berlin, and after 1874 lived in Rome: his works include a marble group, *Religious Liberty,* in Fairmont Park, Philadelphia; the Jefferson monument at Louisville, Ky.; also statues of *Eve, Pan, Amor,* and *Mercury* which reveal the influence of Italian sculptors.

F

Fable, in literature a story of marvelous happenings of legendary or mythical character intended to emphasize a precept in which animals or inanimate objects act and speak like humans. The form is of East Indian and Chinese origin, and the list of classical and modern famous fabulists includes AESOP, BABRIUS, LA FONTAINE, and LESSING.

Fabre, Ferdinand (1830-1898), French novelist who wrote a remarkable novel, *L'Abbé Tigrane* (1873) which is a vivid picture of the life of a priest in France; his works include *The Courbezans; Julien Savignac; Lucifer; My Uncle Célestin; Abbé Roitelet.*

Fabre d'Eglantine, Philippe François Nazaire (1750-1794), French poet, actor, and dramatist: his one successful play, *Philinte* (1790), was supposed to be a continuation of "Le Misanthrope" by MOLIÈRE; he also prepared part of the new Revolutionary calendar, but in spite of his loyalty to the cause, was guillotined in company with Danton and Desmoulins.

Fabriano, Gentile da (c.1370-c.1427), Italian painter said to have been the pupil of Allegretto Nuzzi, and probably of Fra ANGELICO; his notable works include *The Adoration of the Magi;* a fresco of the *Madonna; Coronation of the Virgin with Saints; Virgin Adoring the Infant Christ; Madonna in Glory; Presentation in the Temple.*

Fabricius, Johan Wigmore (1899-   ), Dutch novelist who first studied art at Amsterdam, and acted as war correspondent at the Austro-Italian front in World War I; his works published in English include *The Love of Mario Ferraro; Java Ho!,* a tale of the 17th century for boys; *The Girl in the Blue Hat; The Son of Marietta; A Castle in Carinthia.*

Fabritius, Carel or **Karel** (c.1620-1654), Dutch painter who studied and worked in REMBRANDT'S studio: his works which are not numerous, but characterized by cultured originality and impeccable technique, include *Portrait of a Man; The Sentinel; Family Group; The Goldfinch; Portrait of a Soldier.*

Fabulist, a writer of fables; also applied in an ironical sense to anyone who is inclined to exaggerate.

Façade, in architecture the front of a building; applied specifically to the principal entrance with its pretensions to architectural design because the term is used generally for the four or more sides of any structure.

Façade, a ballet in one act: choreography by Frederick ASHTON; music from a suite of dances by William WALTON; created for and produced by the Camargo Society in 1931. It was first an entertainment for voice and six instruments presented at London in 1923: later the composer elaborated several of the numbers into an orchestral suite which was used for the music of the ballet. The music itself burlesques the various dances such as the polka, fox-trot, tango, etc.: there is a Victor recording by the London Philharmonic Orchestra directed by the composer.

Fackeltanz (Ger.), the title of music for a torch-light procession on the occasion of a royal wedding: the music, usually played by a military band, consisted of a polonaise or minuet in three parts, two of which were played loudly, and the middle section softly. The best example is to be found in MEYERBEER'S *Fackeltanz No. 1,* recorded by the Victor Brass Ensemble.

Fadiman, Clifton (1904-), American literary critic educated at Columbia University: his works include *I Believe: The Personal Philosophies of Certain Eminent Men and Women of Our Time.* He has edited the book column in *The New Yorker* since 1933, and has acted as master of ceremonies on the radio program, *Information, Please,* since 1938.

Fadrusz, John (1858-1903), Hungarian sculptor who became a skilled wood carver as a boy, and later studied with Viktor TILGNER in Vienna: his works include *Christ on the Cross;* equestrian statues of Empress Maria Theresa and King Mathias I; the Mozart monument in Vienna; a fountain at the Pressburg Theatre; portrait busts and statues of Hungarian and Austrian statesmen. He was considered one of the most forcefully expressive sculptors of the 19th century.

Faed, Thomas (1826-1900), Scottish painter who studied with his brother, **John Faed** (1819-1912), a successful miniaturist and landscapist. His pictures of Scottish life are highly regarded; they include *Rustic Toilet; The Highland Mother; Faults on Both Sides; Last of the Clan; Burns and Highland Mary; Sir Walter Scott and His Friends.*

Faelten, Carl (1846-1925), German pianist who was chiefly self-taught, but profited greatly by several years of friendship with Joachim RAFF. He taught the piano at the NEW ENGLAND CONSERVATORY OF MUSIC, Boston, Mass., from 1885 to 1890: from that year until 1897 he acted as director. In 1897 he founded the Faelten Pianoforte School with his brother, Reinhold Faelten with whom he compiled a *Fundamental Training Course for Pianoforte,* and wrote several books of études and studies.

Faenza, a town in Italy about thirty miles from Bologna famous since the 15th century for the manufacture of faïence: a museum of ceramics, containing examples of the potter's art from all over the world, is located there.

Faerie Queene, The, an allegorical poem on the subject of chivalry by Edmund SPENSER (1552-1599): the original plan called for twelve books of which the first three were published in 1590 and the second three in 1596. Parts of the books left uncompleted at his death were issued in 1611. George SAINTSBURY, in his "History of Elizabethan Literature," makes the following comment: "The existing poem, comprising between thirty and forty thousand lines, exhibits so many and such varied excellences that it is difficult to believe that the poet could have done anything new in kind."

Fafner, the giant in Wagner's music drama, *The Rhinegold,* who builds VALHALLA, the castle of the gods, for WOTAN; he is aided by his brother, Fasolt. When Wotan gives them the Rhinegold in payment for their work, Fafner kills his brother, and changes himself into a fiery dragon to guard the gold. He is finally slain by SIEGFRIED who forges a magic sword with which to overcome him.

Fagan, James Bernard (1873-1933), English actor and dramatist who appeared with Sir Herbert Beebohm TREE, and also produced several plays in London and New York: they include *The Rebel* (1899); *Under Which King; The Earth; And So to Bed; The Greater Love; The Improper Duchess.*

Faguet, Emile (1847-1916), French literary critic and historian who became professor of poetry at the Sorbonne, Paris: his works include *Literary History of France; French Tragedy of the Sixteenth Century;* also individual studies of ROUSSEAU, CORNEILLE, BALZAC, LA FONTAINE, and others in a volume entitled *The Great Masters of the Seventeenth Century.*

Faïence, the general name for a kind of pottery made of glazed or enameled earth at FAENZA, Italy. The secret of making it was known to the Persians, Assyrians, Arabians, and Chinese: there are specimens of brilliantly decorated faïence in the form of tiles, vases, jugs, and bowls in the museum at SEVRES. It was also used for tombs.

Fair at Sorotchinsk, The, a humorous opera by Modest MOUSSORGSKY which he left unfinished at his death. A version completed by Cesar CUI was produced at Petrograd in 1917; another by Nicholas TCHEREPNIN was performed at Monte Carlo in 1923, and in Italian at the Metropolitan Opera House, New York, in 1930. The outstanding instrumental number is the *Hopak* or *Gopak,* a lively Russian dance of which there is a Victor recording by the London Symphony directed by Albert Coates: also a Victor recording for piano, played by Sergei Rachmaninoff, which is his own transcription.

Fairbank, Janet Ayer (1875-), American novelist, sister of the novelist, Margaret Ayer BARNES, who dedicated her novel "Westward Passage" to her. She was educated at the University of Chicago: her works include *Home* (1910); *The Cort-*

landts of Washington Square; The Smiths; The Lion's Den; The Bright Land; Rich Man-Poor Man.

Fairbanks, Avard Tennyson (1897-), American sculptor who studied in New York and Paris: his works include *Hawaiian Motherhood; Doughboy of Idaho,* a memorial of World War I; *Old Oregon Trail; Pioneer Mothers; Three Witnesses.* He is also well-known as a teacher of his art.

Fairbanks, Douglas, Jr. (1909-), American stage and screen actor; son of Douglas FAIRBANKS (1883-1939). After making his stage debut in *Young Woodley* and *Saturday's Children* in 1929, he has appeared almost exclusively in talking films including *Catherine the Great; The Amateur Gentleman; Mimi; The Accused; The Prisoner of Zenda; Gunga Din; Until I Die; Joy of Living; The Sun Never Sets; The Rage of Paris; Safari; The Corsican Brothers.*

Fairbanks, Douglas, Sr. (1883-1939), American stage and screen actor who made his debut in 1902 at New York, and achieved his greatest success in 1908 on the legitimate stage in *A Gentleman from Mississippi.* In 1914 he began his career in the films with David Wark GRIFFITH, appearing in *The Americano, The Half Breed,* and *Manhattan Madness.* Among his greatest screen successes were *The Three Musketeers; Robin Hood; The Mark of Zorro; The Thief of Bagdad; The Gaucho; The Iron Mask; The Taming of the Shrew.* In 1920 he was one of the founders of United Artists, Inc., with Mary PICKFORD, and Charles CHAPLIN.

Fairchild, Blair (1877-1933), American pianist and composer who studied with Walter Spalding at Harvard University, and with Giuseppe Buonomici and Charles WIDOR in Europe. His compositions include three ballets; three symphonic poems; *Étude Symphonique* for violin and orchestra; chamber works for various combinations; choral music; piano pieces and songs.

Falcone, Aniello (1600-1665), Italian painter, also known as L'Oracolo delle Battaglie: he studied with SPAGNOLETTO, and became famous as a painter of battle scenes including *Fight Between Turks and Cavalry,* and a series of pictures in the Naples Museum relating to the revolt of MASANIELLO, and the plague of 1656. He was the teacher of Salvator ROSA, and Louis XIV was one of his patrons.

Falconer, William (1732-1769), Scottish poet who was shipwrecked in the Mediterranean as a youth of eighteen: his poem, *The Shipwreck* (1762) was the result of this experience, and was well received. He was made a naval officer through the influence of the Duke of York, and was never heard from after his ship, the "Aurora," foundered off the Cape of Good Hope.

Falconet, Etienne Maurice (1716-1791), French sculptor who studied with Jean Baptiste LEMOYNE: his notable works include a colossal equestrian statue of Peter the Great in bronze, *Nymph Entering the Bath,* and *Pygmalion and the Statue.* He also created models for the manufacture of

SÈVRES china; one of them is the *Clock of the Three Graces* in marble at the LOUVRE which is reproduced in china. Many of his works such as the *Assumption* at St. Roche were destroyed during the French Revolution.

Falguière, Jean Alexandre Joseph (1831-1900), French sculptor and painter who studied at the ECOLE DES BEAUX-ARTS in Paris, and won the Prix de Rome in 1859. His sculptures include *The Winner of the Cock Fight; The Little Martyr; St. Vincent de Paul; Christian Martyr; Corneille; Lamartine;* a monument to Lafayette at Washington, D. C.; also a series of nudes including *Diana, Juno,* and *Woman With a Peacock.* His pictures such as *The Wrestlers* reveal ability, but lack of proper technical training.

Faliero or **Falier, Marino** (c.1274-1355), a doge of Venice who was appointed to office in 1354: he conspired with the populace against the patricians, and was executed for treason in 1355, and his place among the portraits of the doges in the Hall of the Grand Council of Venice was replaced by a painting of the ducal throne with a pall laid over it. BYRON and DELAVIGNE wrote tragedies based on his life, and E. T. A. HOFFMANN, a novel entitled *Doge and Dogaressa.* An opera, *Marino Falieri,* by Donizetti was produced in 1835.

Falkland, Samuel, see **Heijermans, Hermann.**

Fall, Leo (1873-1925), Austrian operetta composer who studied with his father, a bandmaster, and at the Vienna Conservatory with Robert Fuchs: his successful works include *Frau Denise* (1902); *Irrlicht; Der Liebe Augustin; The Dollar Princess,* which was popular in the United States; *The Rose of Stamboul; Madame Pompadour.*

Falla, Manuel de (1876-), Spanish composer who studied composition with Felipe PEDRELL and Jose Trago: in 1907 he taught music in Paris, becoming intimate with RAVEL, DUKAS, and DEBUSSY, and returning in 1914 to Spain where he finally settled at Granada. Among his pupils are Ernesto Halffter and Joaquin Nin-Culmell. Among his notable works are the opera *La Vida breve;* the ballets El AMOR BRUJO, and the THREE-CORNERED HAT; *Nights in the Gardens of Spain* for piano and orchestra; a concerto for piano or harpsichord; piano pieces and songs.

Fallada, Hans, see **Ditzen, Rudolph.**

Falsetto, in music the method used by male singers, generally tenors, to produce high-pitched tones similar to those of the female voice. The effect is ordinarily not as pleasing as that of the natural voice, but it is occasionally found useful to produce a high note without straining.

Falstaff, Sir John, a character in SHAKESPEARE'S *King Henry IV,* and also in *The Merry Wives of Windsor:* the name was first Sir John Oldcastle, but was changed because it was originally the name of an English gentleman who died as a Christian martyr. In the play Falstaff is an obese, good-tempered, and witty old knight who is also a confirmed liar, drunkard, and swindler.

Falstaff, a lyric comedy in three acts: libretto by Arrigo BOITO founded on Shakespeare's play, *The Merry Wives of Windsor;* music by Giuseppe VERDI; first produced at Milan in 1893, and at the METROPOLITAN OPERA HOUSE, New York, in 1895, with Victor MAUREL creating the title role at both performances. The plot follows closely that of the play; Falstaff's efforts to trifle with the affections of two comely housewives results first in his having to hide in a clothes basket, and finally in being soundly thrashed. There is a Columbia recording of the entire opera sung in Italian.

Fanciulla del West, La, see **Girl of the Golden West, The.**

Fandango, a lively dance popular in Spain since the 16th century. It is in triple time, and usually accompanied by castanets, or by a tambourine when danced by a man. Authorities are divided in opinion as to whether it is of Moorish or South American origin; dancing festivals in the southwestern section of America are referred to as *fandangos.* The concluding section of the CAPRICCIO ESPAGNOL by RIMSKY-KORSAKOW is an example of the dance.

Faneuil Hall, a public market containing a hall for town meetings in Boston, Mass. It was built by Peter Faneuil (1700-1743); burned in 1761, rebuilt in 1763, and enlarged under the direction of Charles BULFINCH in 1806. It was the principal meeting place for American patriots during the Revolutionary War, and called the "Cradle of Liberty": scenes in many historical novels and plays concerned with the American Revolution are laid there.

Fantasia, in music an instrumental composition originating in the 17th and 18th centuries with composers such as Dietrich BUXTEHUDE and Johann Sebastian BACH who wrote organ works containing a fantasia used as a prelude in *free* form to a fugue in *strict* form. MOZART, BEETHOVEN, SCHUBERT, SCHUMANN, and LISZT developed the fantasia for the harpsichord and piano; modern composers such as Vaughan WILLIAMS have composed in this form for orchestra.

Fantastic Symphony (Berlioz), see **Symphonie Fantastique** (Berlioz).

Fantin-Latour, Ignace Henri Jean Théodore (1836-1904), French painter and lithographer who studied with his father, and with Thomas COUTURE; he was an intimate of INGRES, COROT, COURBET, and DELACROIX. His works include *Toast to Truth; Tannhäuser; The Damnation of Faust; A Studio at Batignolles; Homage to Delacroix; Around the Piano; The Corner of the Table;* the last four mentioned were group portraits of famous contemporary artists, musicians, and authors. He also painted exquisite pictures of flowers: his lithographs included portraits and fanciful interpretations of music by great masters.

Fan Vault, in architecture a method of masonry vaulting in which the ribs are all of one curve, equally spaced and diverging in such a manner as to suggest an open fan.

Farandole, a Provençal dance resembling the GIGUE, and usually performed by a large number of people holding each other by the hand. One of the finest modern dances in this form is to be found in the incidental music written for Alphonse DAUDET's play, *L'Arlésienne,* by Georges BIZET.

Farce, in drama a comedy the purpose of which is to provoke laughter through ridiculous incidents and situations in which the art of the actor is not paramount. Some authorities consider *The Barber of Seville* by BEAUMARCHAIS an extended farce rather than a comedy: an excellent American example is *Charley's Aunt,* which is a farcical play replete with impossible but highly amusing situations. A *farce-comedy* is a play in which the elements of both dramatic forms are combined as in the plays of George M. COHAN.

"Farewell" Symphony (Haydn), a work written by Joseph HAYDN in 1772 for Prince Nicholas ESTERHAZY's orchestra of which he was the conductor for many years. Shortly before composing the symphony, he had asked the prince for an extended leave of absence which the latter was loath to grant at the moment. Haydn orchestrated the last movement of the work so that one by one the players stopped and left the room so that at its conclusion only two players were left to play the last few measures; whether the hint produced the desired result is not known. There is a Columbia recording by the London Symphony with Sir Henry Wood.

Farid ud-Dīn Attār (1119-1229), Persian poet who lived to the extreme age of 110 years. He was said to have written more than one hundred thousand couplets: his most famous work, *Mantik uttair* or *Language of Birds,* is a long allegorical poem in which a feathered tribe decide that they no longer wish for a republican government, but desire a king. Their subsequent adventures in search of a monarch and its ultimate failure is supposed to picture the search of the human soul for the divine.

Farina, Salvatore (1846-1918), Italian novelist who first studied law; he has been compared with Charles DICKENS because of his humorously sentimental style, and his sympathy for lowly life. His works include *Two Amours* (1869); *A Secret; Forbidden Fruit; Il Signor,* a delightful delineation of an egoist; *Living for Love; For Life and Death.*

Farinato, Paolo (1525-1606), Italian painter and architect influenced by Veronese, Titian, Romano, and Giorgione. His works in the churches and palaces of Verona, Mantua, and Padua include *The Miracle of the Loaves and Fishes; St. Michael Expelling Lucifer; Massacre of the Innocents; Abraham and Hagar; Marriage of St. Catherine; Presentation in the Temple.*

Farinelli (1705-1782), Italian artificial soprano, real name Carlo Broschi, who studied with his father and with Niccolo PORPORA. His debut was made in 1722 at Naples in Porpora's opera, *Eumene:* through natural ability combined with arduous study he became the greatest CASTRATO of his time, appearing in Italy, England, Austria, and Spain with extraordinary success, and earning tremendous sums of money. He was a special favorite of King Philip V of Spain who was cured of melancholy by his singing.

Farjeon, Benjamin Leopold (1838-1903), Anglo-Australian novelist born in England who went to Australia as a young man, and lived there until 1869 when he returned to London to devote himself to a literary career. His first novel, *Grif* (1870), made his reputation; it was followed by several others including *Joshua Marvel; The Sacred Nugget; Toilers of Babylon; The King of No Land.*

Farjeon, Eleanor (1881-), English author of children's stories who is a grandchild of the American actor, Joseph JEFFERSON. Her works include *Martin Pippin in the Apple Orchard* (1922), and many more charming stories for children. Her brother, **Joseph Jefferson Farjeon** (1883-), has written numerous mystery stories including *The Master Criminal* (1924), and a successful play, *No. 17,* later published as a novel.

Farnese Bacchus, an ancient Greek torso dated about the 4th century B.C.: its lines are simple, but amply expressive of the sensuous character of the god. Several other figures, busts, and statues found in Greek and Roman cities are known under the name "Farnese": they include *(1)* the **Farnese Bull,** a large group representing Dirce being bound to the horns of a bull by her stepsons because of her treatment of their mother, Antiope; it was discovered at the Baths of Caracalla. *(2)* **Farnese Flora,** a statue nearly twelve feet high of the goddess holding her tunic in her right hand as she steps forward. *(3)* **Farnese Hercules,** a statue representing Hercules nude and leaning on his club. *(4)* **Farnese Homer,** a bust of the Greek poet admirable for the intellectuality of its expression. *(5)* **Farnese Juno,** a large bust of HERA in which the countenance is calmly expressive. *(6)* **Farnese Minerva,** a statue in which the figure is helmeted with two figures of PEGASUS and an AEGIS on its breast.

Farnese Palace, a building in Rome which is regarded as one of the finest examples of Renaissance architecture; it was designed by Antonio SANGALLO for Cardinal Alessandro Farnese. After Sangallo's death, MICHELANGELO continued the work which was finally completed by Giacomo della Porta. The palace was decorated with frescoes by Annibale CARRACCI, and after the passing of the Farnese family it was inherited by the king of Naples. The magnificent collection of sculptures was dispersed, most of it going to the National Museum in Naples.

Farnese Villa, a museum in Rome which was formerly a residence of the Farnese family. It contains many famous frescoes and paintings by RAPHAEL, Giulio ROMANO, Sebastiano del PIOMBO, PERUZZI, and other distinguished artists.

Farnham, Sally James (?-1943), American sculptor who was self-taught although she was encouraged in her career by Frederick REMINGTON: her notable works include the equestrian statue of Simon Bolivar presented to the city of New York by the Brazilian Government; a bronze statue of Will ROGERS on his pony; several memorials of World War I in American cities; portrait busts executed from life of Marshal Foch, and of Presidents Theodore Roosevelt, and Herbert Hoover.

Farnol, Jeffery (1878-), English novelist whose first successful story, *The Broad Highway* (1910), was written while he was living in New York. Three years later, another best-seller, *The Amateur Gentleman,* appeared: among his numerous romantic tales are *Beltane the Smith; The Geste of Duke Jocelyn; The Loring Mystery; The Jade of Destiny; The Lonely Road; Adam Penfeather.*

Farnum, Dustin (1876-1929), American actor who made his amateur stage debut with his brother, William FARNUM, while they were both still in school. After appearing with various stock companies, he achieved his first success as Lieutenant Denton in *Arizona* by Augustus THOMAS. This was followed by his greatest role, that of the Virginian in the dramatization of Owen Wister's novel of that name. He also appeared in *The Squaw Man* and *Cameo Kirby,* making his debut in the silent films in 1913 as the hero in *Soldiers of Fortune* by Richard Harding Davis.

Farnum, William (1876-), American stage and screen actor and brother of Dustin FARNUM; his debut was made in 1890 at Richmond, Va., in *Julius Caesar.* After playing with Margaret MATHER and Olga NETHERSOLE, he scored his first success in *Ben Hur,* and also in the *Prince of India,* later appearing in *The Shepherd King, Ingomar,* and *The Littlest Rebel.* He has appeared since 1925 in many films including *Dubarry; If I Were King; The Painted Desert; The Scarlet Letter; Custer's Last Stand; Maid of Salem; The Spoilers.*

Farquhar, George (1678-1707), Irish actor and dramatist educated at Trinity College, Dublin; his first play, *Love and a Bottle,* was produced in 1699: it was followed by *The Constant Couple; Sir Harry Wildair; Love and Business; The Inconstant; The Twin Rivals; The Stagecoach; The Beaux Stratagem.* His characters "Lady Bountiful" implying generosity, and "Boniface" as a general term for an innkeeper, have become standard expressions in English.

Farrar, Geraldine (1882-), American dramatic soprano who studied with Emma THURSBY and Lilli LEHMANN, making her debut in 1901 at the Royal Opera, Berlin, in GOUNOD's *Faust.* In 1906 she made her first appearance at the Metropolitan Opera House in Gounod's *Romeo et Juliette,* continuing as one of the leading sopranos until 1922, and from that time making concert appearances in Europe and the United States. Her repertory included all the important modern German, French, and Italian operatic roles; she also appeared in a silent screen version of CARMEN.

Farrell, Eileen (1920-), American concert and radio soprano who studied with Merle Alcock: in 1941 she was so successful in a radio audition that she was engaged for a series of "Songs of the Centuries" programs on the Columbia Broadcasting System. She has since appeared regularly in short recitals with the Columbia Concert Orchestra, presenting programs of standard songs of lyric character.

Farren, Elizabeth (c.1759-1829), Irish actress who achieved her first success in 1777 as Kate Hardcastle in *She Stoops to Conquer:* in 1782 she replaced Frances ABINGTON as leading lady at the DRURY LANE THEATRE, London. She was regarded as equally able in either tragic or comedy roles.

Farrer, Henry (1843-1903), American painter and etcher born in England: he was chiefly self-taught and settled in New York when he was twenty years old. His notable works include *A Quiet Pool; Winter; Sweet Restful Eve; A Windy Day; Now Came Still Evening On.* His etchings are also highly regarded.

Farwell, Arthur (1872-), American composer who studied with Engelbert HUMPERDINCK in Berlin and Alexander GUILMANT in Paris: he held many posts as director and as teacher of musical theory in American institutions, and founded the Wa-Wan Press at Newton Center, Mass., to publish works by American composers, especially those based on American Indian melodies and folk lore. He has composed numerous works for orchestra, piano, and chamber music combinations; many of them based on American Indian tunes.

Fates, The, in Greek mythology three sisters known in Roman legend as *Parcae,* and in Germanic as *Norns.* They were the daughters of ZEUS: Clotho spun the web of life, Lachesis determined its length, and Atropos severed the web. In this way they were supposed to regulate the lives of men and women.

"Father of ——," the title given many distinguished persons in various fields of art; for example the *Father of Comedy* is ARISTOPHANES; the *Father of English Poetry* is CHAUCER; the *Father of Epic Poetry* is HOMER; the *Father of Greek Tragedy* is AESCHYLUS; the *Father of Ridicule* is RABELAIS; the *Father of the Symphony* is HAYDN; the *Father of German Literature* is LESSING.

Fatima, in Arabian legend the seventh and last wife of BLUEBEARD; regarded as the personification of female curiosity.

Faucit, Helen (1817-1898), English actress who made her debut in 1936 at London in *The Hunchback,* and later achieved great success in Shakespearean roles, and in plays by Alexandre DUMAS, FILS, Bulwer LYTTON, and BROWNING. She retired in 1871, but reappeared at the opening of the Memorial Theatre at Stratford-on-Avon: she also wrote a work entitled *On Some of the Female Characters of Shakespeare.*

Faulkner or **Falkner, William** (1897-), American poet and novelist who studied at the University of Mississippi and at Oxford: his works include *The Marble Faun,* a volume of poems (1924); *Soldier's Pay,* containing a description of his experiences in the Canadian Air Force during

World War I; *The Sound and the Fury; Sanctuary; Light in August; A Green Bough,* a volume of poems; also two volumes of short stories entitled *These Thirteen* and *Go Down, Moses.*

Faun, in Roman mythology a deity represented as having human shape with pointed ears and horns, or as half man and half goat. PRAXITELES, a Greek sculptor, created a statue of a faun: a copy in the CAPITOLINE MUSEUM at Rome was the inspiration for HAWTHORNE'S *The Marble Faun.* Claude DEBUSSY composed a symphonic poem, *The Afternoon of a Faun,* inspired by a poem of Stephané MALLARME.

Faure, Élie (1873-), French art critic and historian who was trained as a surgeon, but became such a devoted student and admirer of the arts that he was appointed as critic of *L'Aurore* through the influence of Emile ZOLA and Anatole FRANCE. His works published in English include *History of Art* (1921-1930), published in four volumes; *Art of Cineplastics; The Italian Renaissance.*

Fauré, Gabriel (1845-1924), French organist and composer who studied with Camille SAINT-SAENS: he occupied several important posts as organist, and succeeded Jules MASSENET as professor of composition and Theodore DUBOIS as director of the PARIS CONSERVATORY OF MUSIC. Among his famous pupils were Aubert, Nadia BOULANGER, ENESCO, Laparra, RAVEL, ROGER-DUCASSE, and Florent SCHMITT. His compositions include several operas; a ballet; a violin concerto; a *Ballade* for piano and orchestra; incidental music for several plays; chamber music; piano pieces; violin pieces; also many fine song cycles and individual songs.

Faure, Jean-Baptiste (1830-1914), French dramatic baritone who studied at the Paris Conservatory of Music, and made his operatic debut in Massé's *Galathée* at the Opéra-Comique, Paris, in 1852, remaining there as principal baritone for eight years. From 1861 to 1876 he was first baritone at L'Opéra, Paris, and also taught for a time at the Conservatory. He was the composer of *The Palms (Les Rameaux),* popular for all time as a sacred song on Palm Sunday.

Fauset, Jessie Redmon (c.1884-), American Negro poet and novelist educated at Cornell University, the University of Pennsylvania, and at the Sorbonne, Paris, later teaching at schools in Washington, D. C., and in New York City. Her works include *There is Confusion* (1924); *Plum Bun; The Chinaberry Tree; Comedy, American Style.*

Faussett, Hugh l'Anson (1895-), English poet, biographer, and literary critic educated at Cambridge where he won the Chancellor's Medal for English poetry: his works include *The Lady Alcuin and Other New Poems; Keats: A Study in Development; Tennyson; John Donne; Samuel Taylor Coleridge; The Proving of Psyche; Poet of Democracy; Walt Whitman.*

Faust, Doctor Johann (?-c.1538), in German folk lore a magician and astrologer who led a licentious life, and was finally carried away to hell by the devil who lived with him in the form of a black dog. MARLOWE's play, *Dr. Faustus* (1593), was based on a version of Faust's life published by John Spiess in 1587: GOETHE, KLINGER, HEINE, and LENAU were among the many German authors who wrote plays or novels on the subject. There are operas by Charles GOUNOD, Louis SPOHR, and Ferruccio BUSONI; a dramatic legend by Hector BERLIOZ, and a symphony by Franz LISZT.

Faust, Frederick, see **Brand, Max.**

Faust, grand opera in five acts: libretto by Jules Barbier and Michel Carré; music by Charles GOUNOD; first produced at Paris in 1859, and at Philadelphia, Pa., in 1863. The story is: Faust, an aged philosopher, wearies of fame, and sells his soul to Mephistopheles in return for being restored to youth. He meets, loves and betrays Marguerite, whose brother, Valentine, has left her in the care of Dame Martha while he is away at war. Upon his return, Valentine challenges Faust, but is killed through the intervention of Mephistopheles. Marguerite loses her reason, kills her new-born child, and is condemned to death. She refuses to accept the aid of either Faust or Mephistopheles, and finally dies with angels chanting her pardon while Faust is led to the lower regions to keep his compact with Satan. There are complete recordings by both Victor and Columbia: also many records of the principal arias, duets, trios, quartets, and choruses.

Fauvists, a term derived from the French *fauve,* the original meaning of which is a deer: about 1900 it was applied, in the sense of "wild beasts" (Fauvists) to a group of impressionistic painters in France; among them MATISSE, DERAIN, Dufy, VLAMINCK, and BRAQUE. The general characteristics of their works were broad patterns of color in large areas joined by heavy outlines.

Favart, Charles Simon (1710-1792), French dramatist and theatrical producer: his first vaudeville, *Les Deux Jumelles* (1734), was so successful that he continued to write in the same vein, and became a director of the Opèra-Comique. His comedies and operettas, more than 150 in number, were so popular with his wife, Marie Duronceray, in the principal feminine roles that, while performing for the army of Marshal Saxe at the front during the war with Flanders, hostilities were temporarily stopped so that the enemy could see the performance.

Faversham, William (1868-1940), English actor who made his debut in 1885 at London, and his first New York appearance in 1887 on the New York stage in *Pen and Ink* at the Union Square Theatre. He played with Mrs. FISKE for two seasons, and with the FROHMAN Empire Theatre Company for several years. Among the notable plays in which he starred were *A Royal Rival; The World and His Wife; Herod; The Prince and the Pauper; Lord and Lady Algy; The Squaw Man; Julius Caesar; Othello.* He also appeared in several motion pictures.

Fawcett, Edgar (1847-1904), American poet, novelist, and dramatist educated at Columbia University: his novels include *Purple and Fine Linen; A Gentleman of Leisure; Miriam Balestier; Rutherford; Women Must Weep; A New York Family; Outrageous Fortune.* His poetical works include *Short Poems for Short People* and *Romance and Revery.*

Fay, Andreas (1786-1864), Hungarian poet and novelist who was prominent in politics until Louis Kossuth became the leader at Pest: his works include *New Garland* (1818), a volume of poems; *Fables,* a volume of prose; *The Two Báthorys,* a tragedy; *The House of the Betekys,* a two-volume socialistic novel which gained him a place among the great masters of Hungarian prose.

Faye, Alice (1915-), American screen actress and singer who first achieved success with the Rudy Vallee Company in Hollywood: among the films in which she has appeared are *In Old Chicago; Sally, Irene, and Mary; Rose of Washington Square; Barricade; Little Old New York; Lillian Russell.*

Fayum Portraits, a series of portraits painted by classic Greek artists, and found in mummy cases at Fayum, a province in Egypt. The portraits of dead people were painted on wood, and held in place on the cases by wrappings. Archaeologists place them as executed between 200 and 500 A.D.: while the painting is conventional, it affords an excellent idea of the quality of work done by mediocre artists of the period.

Fechter, Charles Albert (1824-1879), French actor said to have been born in London, and first a successful sculptor, winning the grand medal of the ECOLE DES BEAUX-ARTS at Paris in 1844. He made his debut at the COMEDIE-FRANCAISE during the same year, and scored a triumph when he created the role of Armand Duval in Dumas' *La Dame aux camélias* in 1852. Among the plays in which he appeared were *Ruy Blas; The Corsican Brothers; Don César de Bazan; Hamlet; Othello* (playing either the Moor or Iago); *The Lady of Lyons; Monte Cristo.* He came to the United States in 1870, appearing with great success, and remaining until his death.

Federal Theatre Project, a project inaugurated in 1935 by the Works Progress Administration of the United States of America to subsidize the American theatre, and aid in solving unemployment. The producing centers were New York, Boston, Philadelphia, Atlanta, New Orleans, Chicago, Denver, Seattle, San Francisco and Los Angeles: among the important productions were *Macbeth* with a Negro company; a *Swing Mikado;* George Bernard SHAW's *Androcles and the Lion; Horse Eats Hat; Doctor Faustus; Pinocchio; Murder in the Cathedral.* Many well-known American dramatists were associated with the project which ended in July, 1939.

Feith, Rhijnvis (1753-1824), Dutch poet, short story writer, and dramatist educated at the University of Leiden: his works include a novel, *Julia* (1783-); *Odes and Poems;* a tragedy, *Lady Jane*

Grey; also a novel, *Ferdinand and Constance,* which shows the influence of GOETHE.

Feke, Robert (c.1706-c.1750), American portrait painter probably born on Long Island, and said to have studied in Spain. He worked in New York, Newport, and Philadelphia, and one of his portraits, that of Lady Mary Wanton, is in the Redwood Library, Newport, R. I.

Félibien, André (1619-1695), French architect who became friendly with Nicholas POUSSIN, and was appointed historiographer to the king of France by Colbert. He was also secretary of the Academy of Architecture, and found time to write important works such as *The Lives and Works of Famous Ancient and Modern Painters,* issued in several volumes (1666-88); *Origin of Painting; Principles of Architecture, Sculpture and Painting.* His son, **Jean François Felibien** (c.1658-1733), was also a distinguished architect who wrote a number of treatises on his art.

Fellows, Sir Charles (1799-1860), English traveler and archaeologist who discovered in 1838 the ruins of the ancient city of Xanthus, capital of Lycia in Asia Minor, and in 1841 the ruins of thirteen more cities. More than twenty-five cases of historically valuable marbles were sent to the British Museam in 1844, and he was knighted for his services in contributing at his own expense to the enrichment of the antique art section of that institution.

Felton, John (c.1595-1628), English assassin who killed the Duke of BUCKINGHAM on August 23, 1628, and was executed on November 28, 1628. The reason for his deed was the refusal of the duke to grant him a captaincy, but Alexandre DUMAS, PERE, in 'one of the "Three Musketeers" novels, has made him the tool of Milady, an adventuress seeking Buckingham's death.

Felu, Charles (1820-?), Belgian painter born without arms: he learned to draw with his right foot, and executed extraordinarily fine sketches which gained him admittance to the Antwerp Academy in 1859. There he studied painting: his works include many excellent copies of the great masters, and also some fine portraits.

Femmes de Bonne Humeur, Les (The Good-Humored Ladies), a choreographic comedy in one act: choreography by Leonide MASSINE; music arranged from Domenico SCARLATTI by Vincenzo Tommasini; first produced at Rome in 1917. It was based on a play by Carlo GOLDONI, and was unique in that the pantomime was as important as the dancing.

Fencing, the art of using edged or pointed weapons, such as the rapier, saber, or foil for attack or defense. It was first practised and developed as an art by the Italians in the 16th century, and attained great popularity later in France, England, and the United States. It is frequently portrayed in painting and sculpture: actors on both the stage and screen find it necessary to have a thorough knowledge of the art in connection with the presentation of many dramas.

Fenton, Lavinia (1708-1760), English actress who made her debut in OTWAY's *Orphans* in 1726, and achieved her greatest success as Polly in John GAY's *Beggar's Opera.* She was the most talked-of person in London: HOGARTH caricatured her with the Duke of Bolton, whom she eventually married, seated in a box.

Ferber, Edna (1887-), American author and dramatist who worked as a reporter before embarking on a literary career: her first successful novel, *Dawn O'Hara* (1911), was followed by several more before the "best sellers," *So Big* (1924), *Show Boat* (1926), and *Cimarron* (1929) appeared. Her successful plays include *Show Boat,* with Oscar Hammerstein II; *The Royal Family; Dinner at Eight; Stage Door;* the last three in collaboration with George S. Kaufman. Her autobiography, *A Peculiar Treasure,* was published in 1939.

Ferdinand the Bull, see **Leaf, Munro.**

Ferenczy, Karely (1862-1917), Hungarian painter, born in Vienna, who studied at Naples, Paris, and Munich. His naturalistic style, combined with poetic feeling, was acquired while at the Académie Julien in Paris where he was strongly influenced by BASTIEN-LEPAGE. His notable paintings include *Joseph Sold by His Brothers* and *A Woman Pressing:* he also illustrated several books.

Ferguson, Elsie (1883-), American actress who made her debut at New York in 1900 as a member of the chorus in *The Belle of New York:* the musical plays and dramas in which she has appeared include *The Girl from Kay's; The Earl of Pawtucket; The Bondman; Such a Little Queen; Caste; Dolly Madison; Rosedale; Outcast; The Merchant of Venice* with Sir Herbert TREE; *Sacred and Profane Love; She Stoops to Conquer.* She has also appeared in notable films on both the silent and the talking screen.

Fergusson, Harvey (1890-), American novelist who was educated at Washington and Lee University and later worked in the United States Forestry Service. His works include *The Blood of the Conquerors* (1921); *Women and Wives; Wolf Song; Footloose McGarnigal; The Life of Riley:* he also edited *The Last Rustler: The Autobiography of Lee Sage.*

Fergusson, James (1808-1886), Scottish writer on architectural subjects: his important works include *The History of Architecture* (1865) and *The True Principles of Beauty in Art.* The first-named work stands without peer in English literature because of its comprehensiveness and critically analytical presentation of the subject.

Fernald, Chester Bailey (1869-), American writer and dramatist: his plays include *The Cat and the Cherub* (1897); *Always Afternoon; Tomorrow.* In 1924 his translation of *The Mask and the Face* was produced in London with great success.

Ferrari, Gaudenzio (c.1481-1546), Italian painter who studied with PERUGINO, and was influenced by RAPHAEL and Leonardo da VINCI. He worked with Raphael at Rome, and was also associated with Giulio ROMANO. His important works include an altarpiece, *Marriage of St. Catherine,* at San Gaudenzio, Varallo; *Choir of Singing Angels; Marriage of the Virgin* in the Como Cathedral; *St. George and St. Anthony; The Annunciation; The Crucifixion.*

Ferreira, Antonio (1528-1569), Portuguese poet and dramatist who held a professorship at the University of Coimbra, and later became a judge of the supreme court at Lisbon. His works include sonnets and odes which brought him the title of the "Portuguese Horace" and a tragedy, *Inez de Castro,* modeled on the classic Greek drama.

Ferri, Ciro (1634-1689), Italian painter who studied with Pietro da CORTONA: his works include *Repose in Egypt; Christ Appearing to Magdalene; Rape of Helen; David and Saul; Christ on the Cross; St. Ambrose Healing a Sick Man.* He was also a fine architect and an excellent etcher of illustrations and frontispieces for books.

Ferrier, Susan Edmonstone (1782-1854), Scottish novelist to whom Sir Walter SCOTT gave high praise: her works include *Marriage* (1818); *The Inheritance; Destiny.* She is distinguished for her delineation of Scotch character as well as for her unfailing sense of humor.

Fescennine Verses, one of the earliest forms of Italian verse: it originated at harvest and vintage festivals, and consists of doggerel lines recited in dialogue form developed later in Roman comic drama. At first containing only harmless banter, the verses developed into scurrilous raillery finally banned by Roman law.

Fessenden, Thomas Green (1771-1837), American author who was educated at Dartmouth College, and used the pen name "Christopher Caustic." His works include *Jonathan's Courtship,* a ballad; a satirical poem, *Terrible Tractoration,* published anonymously while on a visit to London; *The Ladies' Monitor; The American Clerk's Companion.*

Festoon, in architecture an arrangement of flowers, leaves or fruit tied together and suspended by ribbons. It was used by the Greek and Romans for the decoration of altars, friezes, and panels: during the Renaissance it was employed by architects with excellent pictorial effect.

Fête Dieu à Seville (Albeniz), the third movement in the suite, IBERIA, by Isaac ALBENIZ, regarded as the outstanding work in Spanish piano music. It depicts a famous Spanish religious festival day, Corpus Christi, with the procession carrying the Sacred Host through the narrow streets, and the throngs of people raising their voices in a song of lamentation. There is a Columbia recording by the Madrid Symphony Orchestra directed by Fernandez Arbos, and a Victor recording by the Philadelphia Orchestra with Leopold Stokowski.

Fétis, François-Joseph (1784-1871), Belgian musical historian, theorist, composer, and critic who studied with François BOIELDIEU at the Paris Conservatory. Among his notable accomplishments were a revision of the musical ritual of the Roman Catholic Church; *Treatise on Counterpoint and Fugue* (1824); *Universal Biography of Musicians and General Catalogue of Music* in eight volumes, issued from 1833 to 1844; biographies of Paganini and Stradivarius; *General History of Music to the Fifteenth Century.* His compositions include operas, orchestral works, chamber works, piano pieces, and sacred music.

Feuchtwanger, Lion (1884-), German novelist and dramatist educated at the Universities of Munich and Berlin. His works include *Power* (1926); *The Ugly Duchess; Success; Josephus; The Oppermanns; The Jew of Rome; Moscow 1937; The Pretender; The Devil in France; Josephus and the Emperor.* Among his successful plays are *Warren Hastings; Prisoners of War; Peace,* a translation of a work by Aristophanes.

Feuerbach, Anselm (1829-1880), German painter who studied at the art schools in Düsseldorf and Munich, and with COUTURE in Paris: his notable works include *Hafiz at the Fountain; The Fall of the Titans; Iphigenia; Medea; Dante at Ravenna; The Battle of the Amazons; The Concert; Orpheus and Eurydice; Plato's Symposium; The Judgment of Paris.*

Feuermann, Emanuel (1902-1942), Austrian violoncellist who studied with A. Walter in Vienna and with Paul Klengel in Leipzig. He became solo violoncellist with the Gurzenich Orchestra and professor of violoncello at the Cologne Conservatory in 1918, touring Europe and the United States from 1923 to 1930. He appeared with all the major American orchestras, and made many solo recordings; also records of important chamber works with Jascha HEIFETZ and Artur RUBINSTEIN.

Feuillet, Octave (1821-1890), French novelist and dramatist educated at the Lycée Louis-le-Grand in Paris, and for a time assistant to Alexandre DUMAS, PERE. His works include *Bellah* (1852); *La Petite Comtesse; Dalila; Sibylle; Julia de Trécoeur; The Romance of a Poor Young Man,* which was also a success as a drama. His plays include *The Sphinx* and *Led Astray:* the latter was adapted for the English stage by Dion BOUCICAULT.

Féval, Paul (1860-), French poet and novelist whose first work of note was *The Son of D'Artagnan* (1914), in which he borrowed the famous character created by Alexandre DUMAS, PERE. After service on the French Maritime Board during World War I, he made use of the character D'Artagnan in *Years Between* (in collaboration with M. Lassez), and also of Cyrano de Bergerac in *Comrades at Arms* and *Salute to Cyrano.* He founded the Society of French novelists, and has written several scenarios for the French cinema.

Féval, Paul Henri Corentin (1817-1887), French novelist who was first trained for the legal profession: his works, some of which, written under the pen name "Sir Francis Trolopp," include *The Seals Club* (1841); *The Mysteries of London,* a series of eleven volumes similar to Eugene Sue's

"Mysteries of Paris," which were dramatized and translated into English. One of his novels, *The Hunchback*, was adapted for the stage in collaboration with Victorien SARDOU. His son, Paul FEVAL, was also a novelist and dramatist of some distinction.

Feydeau, Ernest Aimé (1821-1873), French poet, novelist, and dramatist: his works include *Les Nationales* (1844), a volume of poetry; *Fanny*, a novel of corrupt Paris; the novels, *Daniel*, *A Debut at the Opera*, and *The Countess de Chalis*. He also produced several plays with little success, and attempted to refute the charge of indecency in his novels by an elaborate apology entitled *On the Luxury of Women*.

Feydeau, Georges (1862-1921), French dramatist whose most successful play, *Le Dame de chez Maxim* (1899), became a favorite on the London stage as *The Lady from Maxim's:* his other farces include *Tailor for Ladies; The Free Exchange Hotel; The Duchess of the Fôlies-Bergère.*

Ffrangcon-Davies, David Thomas (1856-1918), Welsh baritone educated at Oxford, and ordained a priest in 1884. He studied singing with William SHAKESPEARE and Alberto RANDEGGER, making his debut in 1890 with the Carl Rosa Opera Company at London. From 1896 he sang chiefly in concert and oratorio, achieving great success in Great Britain, the United States, Germany, and Switzerland. He created the role of Cedric in Sir Arthur SULLIVAN's *Ivanhoe* in 1891, and wrote a treatise, *The Singing of the Future*, in 1906.

Fibich, Zdenko (1850-1900), Bohemian composer who studied at the Prague and Leipzig Conservatories, and later became dramatic director at the Bohemian National Theatre in Prague. His works include several successful operas; incidental music to Vrchlicky's dramatic trilogy, *Hippodameia*; symphonic poems; overtures; chamber music; more than three hundred short piano pieces one of which, *Poéme*, has become a world-wide favorite since it was first played as a violin solo by Jan KUBELIK in 1900.

Ficke, Arthur Davison (1883-), American essayist and poet who was educated at Harvard University, and served in World War I. His works include *From the Isles* (1907); *The Happy Princess; Twelve Japanese Painters; Sonnets of a Portrait Painter; Chats on Japanese Prints; Out of Silence; Mountain Against Mountain; The Blue Jade Sceptre; Tumultuous Shore and Other Poems.*

Fiction, in literature the term applied to all imaginative works in narrative forms such as the romance, novel, short story, and fable. References to the majority of the distinguished authors in this field will be found in this volume.

Fidelio, a grand opera in three (later two) acts: libretto by Joseph Sonnleithner and Georg Treitschke; music by Ludwig van BEETHOVEN; first produced in three acts at Vienna in 1805, in two acts in 1806, and in its final form also at Vienna in 1814. It was produced in the United States in English at the Park Theatre, New York, in 1839;

at the Broadway Theatre, New York, in German in 1856, and was not performed at the Metropolitan Opera House, New York, in German, until 1884. There are Columbia and Victor recordings of the four FIDELIO OVERTURES composed for the various versions of the opera; also recordings of the various arias and ensemble numbers.

Fidelio (Overtures), a series of four overtures composed by Ludwig van BEETHOVEN for his grand opera, *Fidelio:* only one of these bears the title, "Fidelio"; the other three are known as "Leonore" Overtures Nos. 1, 2, and 3. The chronological sequence of the overtures, as generally accepted, is as follows: *Leonore No. 2* in C major, composed in 1805 for the first production of the opera "Leonore" (later re-named "Fidelio"); *Leonore No. 3* in C major, composed for a revival of the opera in 1806; *Leonore No. 1* in C major, Op. 138, written for a projected performance of the opera at Prague in 1807; "Fidelio" in E major, written for the final revision of the opera in 1814. There are Columbia and Victor recordings of all four overtures.

Fiedler, Arthur (1894-), American violinist and conductor who studied with his father, Emanuel Fiedler, a member of the BOSTON SYMPHONY ORCHESTRA, and also at the Royal Academy of Music, Berlin. He became a member of the Boston Symphony Orchestra in 1915; organized the Boston Sinfonietta in 1925, and has conducted the Boston Symphony "Pops" Concerts since 1930 besides directing the Cecilia Society, the Boston Male Choir, and the MacDowell Club Orchestra. He has also conducted many admirable Victor recordings by the Boston Symphony "Pops" Orchestra.

Fiedler, Max (1859-1939), German pianist and conductor who studied at the Leipzig Conservatory, and later became director of the Hamburg Conservatory and conductor of the Hamburg Philharmonic Society. He was guest conductor of the NEW YORK PHILHARMONIC-SYMPHONY ORCHESTRA in the season of 1905-06, and regular conductor of the BOSTON SYMPHONY ORCHESTRA from 1908 to 1912.

Field, Eugene (1850-1895), American poet and journalist who won universal recognition for his poetry and stories, particularly his poems for children admirable in their understanding of the child's world of thought. His works include *Love Songs of Childhood; A Little Book of Western Verse; A Second Book of Verse; The Holy Cross and Other Tales; The Love Affairs of a Biblomaniac.*

Field, John (1782-1837), Irish composer and pianist who was apprenticed to Muzio CLEMENTI with whom he studied the piano, and also demonstrated the pianos made by his teacher. After appearing successfully as a virtuoso in Paris, he settled at St. Petersburg, Russia, in 1804 as a highly appreciated pianist and teacher. His compositions for the piano are transitional between those of Clementi and CHOPIN: his nocturnes were original in name and conception. In addition to the latter he wrote many concertos, fantasias, and miscellaneous pieces for the piano.

Field, Nathan (1587-1633), English actor and dramatist who first appeared as a child actor in the company at Queen Elizabeth's chapel in 1600, and joined the King's Players about 1619. In 1623 he appeared with Shakespeare's Players, and also acted in plays by Ben JONSON and Francis BEAUMONT. He wrote the plays *A Woman is a Weathercock* and *Amends for Ladies*, and also collaborated with Philip MASSINGER and John FLETCHER.

Field, Rachel (1894-1942), American poet, novelist, dramatist, and writer of children's fiction who was educated at Radcliffe College, and studied dramatic art in Professor George Pierce BAKER's 47 WORKSHOP at Harvard. Her works include *The Pointed People* (1924); *Polly Patchwork; Hitty: Her First Hundred Years; A Circus Garland* (Poems); *Calico Bush; Hepatica Hawks; All This, and Heaven Too; And Now Tomorrow.*

Fielding, Henry (1707-1754), English novelist and dramatist who first studied law, and had little success as the author of some light stage pieces: his notable novels include *Joseph Andrews* (1743); *Tom Jones,* considered his masterpiece and one of the greatest novels in the English language; *Amelia; The History of Jonathan Wild,* an ironic story directed against the upholders of conventional morality.

Fields, Gracie (1898-), English actress and singer who first appeared with a juvenile company in 1912. In 1918 she played the role of Sally Perkins in *Mr. Tower of London* which established a record in seven years of 4000 performances: in 1925 she appeared in *By Request* which enjoyed a run of three years. She has sung in all the major English and American music halls, and has also appeared in many motion pictures and radio broadcasts.

Fields, Lew, see **Weber and Fields.**

Fields, W. C. (1880-), American stage and screen actor, real name Dukenfield, who appeared first in vaudeville for several years, and also in musical productions such as the *Ziegfeld Follies.* He has played humorous roles in numerous films including *That Royle Girl; Tillie's Punctured Romance; Alice in Wonderland; Mrs. Wiggs of the Cabbage Patch; David Copperfield* in which he was outstanding as Mr. Micawber.

Fiesole, Mino da, see **Mino da Fiesole.**

Fife, an extremely small and shrill-toned instrument belonging to the FLUTE family: in the original form it differed from the PICCOLO in having six finger-holes without keys, but the modern instrument now has from four to six keys. The fife is used almost entirely for military music with drums.

Figaro, in drama a character introduced by BEAUMARCHAIS into his comedies, *The Barber of Seville* and *The Marriage of Figaro.* In the former play he is a barber and in the latter a valet: he is gay, shrewd, lively, and witty by nature, and his schemes are original and daring. The character of Figaro is also to be found in PASIELLO's and ROSSINI's comic operas, both entitled THE BARBER OF SEVILLE, and in MOZART's comic opera, THE MARRIAGE OF FIGARO: all three are adapted from Beaumarchais' comedies.

Figueroa, Francisco de (c.1540-c.1620), Spanish poet called by his contemporaries "the Divine Figueroa," and winner of the poets' crown at Rome. He wrote with equal facility in Castilian and Italian: about sixty of his eclogues in blank verse were saved by his friends who had copies when he burned all his verses just before his death; they were later published in collected form.

Figure, (*a*) in painting or sculpture the representation of a human being or animal; (*b*) in literature an expression in the form of a metaphor; (*c*) in ballet a fixed set of steps; (*d*) in music a short succession of notes which, when repeated or varied, constitute a phrase.

Figured bass, in music a system of figures placed over or under an instrumental bass part to indicate the chord for each note: it may be regarded as a system of musical shorthand. In Italy it was known as *basso continuo,* and in England as *thoroughbass:* some of the earlier opera composers such as PERI and MONTEVERDI were the first to use it.

Figurine, in sculpture a small carved or molded figure or statuette, usually made in TERRA COTTA and decorated by painting or gilding. They have been found in tombs, especially at Tanagra, a city in ancient Greece.

Fildes, Sir Luke (1844-1927), English painter trained at the South Kensington and Royal Academy Schools: he was first a successful illustrator, but later achieved high rank with notable paintings including *The Village Wedding; An Al-fresco Toilette; The Doctor; The Casual Ward; Return of the Penitent;* portraits of King George, Edward VII, and Queen Alexandra.

Filigree, in the art of the goldsmith the intertwining of fine gold or silver wire into a design joined with solder by the use of a blow torch. It was an art well understood by the Egyptians, Chinese, and Greeks, and also employed from the 11th to the 13th century in making reliquaries, the boxes in which relics were kept. The Moorish artisans were also skilled in fashioning designs filigreed in silver: examples are to be seen in all the great European, English, and American art museums.

Finck, Henry Theophilus (1854-1926), American author and music critic who was educated at Harvard, and studied the theory of music with John K. PAINE. He acted as music critic of *The Nation* and the New York *Evening Post:* his notable books include *Chopin and Other Musical Essays* (1889); *Wagner and His Works; Paderewski and His Art; Songs and Song Writers; Grieg and His Music; Richard Strauss; My Adventures in the Golden Age of Music.* He also edited volumes of SCHUBERT and of GRIEG songs.

Finden, William (1787-1852), English line-engraver who first gained distinction with his plates for Smirke's illustrations of CERVANTES' *Don*

Quixote. Edward Finden, his younger brother, worked with him: the largest plate they produced was a portrait of George IV made from a painting by Sir Thomas LAWRENCE at a cost of $10,000. He made fine plates of illustrations for the works of BYRON, but lost the fortune he had accumulated through a set of plates entitled *Gallery of British Art.*

Fine Arts, The, according to *Webster's Dictionary* the fine arts are those "concerned with the creation of objects of the imagination and taste for their own sake, and without relation to the utility of the object produced." The major arts referred to are architecture, sculpture, painting, music, poetry, and the minor arts of dancing and drama.

Fingal's Cave (Overture), an orchestral work by Felix MENDELSSOHN also known as the "Hebrides" Overture and the "Solitary Island" Overture. It was inspired by a visit to Fingal's Cave on Staffa, one of the Inner Hebrides islands off the coast of Scotland, and when first performed by the LONDON PHILHARMONIC SOCIETY at COVENT GARDEN in 1832 created a great sensation. There is a Victor recording by the British Broadcasting Orchestra with Sir Adrian Boult, and a Columbia recording by the London Philharmonic Orchestra directed by Sir Thomas Beecham.

Finger, Charles Joseph (1869-1941), Anglo-American author of adventure and travel books who was born in England, and became an American citizen in 1896. His numerous works include *Highwaymen* (1923); *Bushrangers; David Livingstone; Magic Tower; Adventures under Sapphire Skies; Frontier Ballads,* with David Guion. His story for boys, *Courageous Companions,* won the prize awarded by Longmans, Green and Co., for the best juvenile story of the year: an autobiography, *Seven Horizons,* was published in 1930.

Fingerboard, a strip of wood, usually ebony, glued on the neck of stringed instruments, such as the violin, viola, violoncello, double-bass, guitar, banjo, and mandolin: the strings are stretched over it, and when the fingers of the left hand press down upon it, sounds are produced differing from those produced by the open string.

Fingering, in music (*a*) the method of applying the fingers to the strings or keys of a musical instrument in order to produce various combinations of notes. (*b*) The numerals placed under or over the notes of a musical composition indicating the fingers to be used on the strings or keys.

Finial, in architecture the term for a knot, cluster of foliage or flowers, or any other form of ornament employed to top a pinnacle, gable, or canopy.

Finiguerra, Maso or **Tommaso** (1426-1464), Italian goldsmith and engraver erroneously credited with the invention of the art of copper-plate engraving whereas the actual fact is that he raised the level of the art by the superior quality of his prints. Benvenuto CELLINI claims that he was the greatest master of NIELLO engraving during his

period: the only authentic works by him still in existence are the cartoons for some figures made for the cathedral in Florence.

Finlandia (Sibelius), a symphonic poem composed by Jean SIBELIUS in 1894 during the period when Russia dominated Finland: it aroused such patriotic enthusiasm that its performance was forbidden. Contrary to rumor it is not a fantasia on folk tunes: the themes are all original with Sibelius, and is a successful attempt on his part to impart in music a stirring impression of the national spirit and life. There is a Columbia recording by the Cleveland Orchestra with Artur Rodzinski, and a Victor recording by the Philadelphia Orchestra conducted by Eugene Ormandy.

Finley, Martha (1828-1909), American novelist who wrote under the pen name of "Martha Farquharson": her most notable accomplishment was the series of books for girls which began with *Elsie Dinsmore* in 1868, and continued in a series of more than twenty simple, well-narrated stories. Aside from these she wrote *Wanted—A Pedigree* and *The Thorn in the Nest.*

Finney, Charles Grandiose (1905-), American novelist who was educated at the University of Missouri, and joined the American Army in 1927, serving three years with the 15th Infantry at Tientsin, China: his novels include *The Circus of Dr. Lao* (1935); *The Unholy City; Past the End of the Pavement.*

Fiorenzo di Lorenzo (c.1440-1522), Italian painter regarding whom little authentic information is available: he is credited with having studied with at least twelve masters; among them are PISANELLO, BONFIGLI, and MANTEGNA. Forty-five of his pictures are in the Pinacoteca at Perugia: they include *The Nativity; Adoration of the Magi; Adoration of the Shepherds; Madonna Enthroned in the Clouds.* He is said to have been the master of PERUGINO and PINTURICCHIO.

Fiori da Urbino, see **Baroccio** or **Barocci, Federigo.**

Fiorillo, Federigo (1753-c.1823), Italian violinist and composer regarding whose musical activities little is known except that he lived in Paris from 1785 to 1788, and played the viola in Johann SALOMON's Quartet at London. He composed concertos for the violin, and also the immortal *Thirty-six Caprices,* as important to the violinist today as they were more than one hundred years ago.

Fiorillo, Johann Dominicus (1748-1821), German painter of historical subjects, and author of important works on his art including a *History of the Pictorial Arts* (1798-1808), and a *History of the Pictorial Arts in Germany and the Netherlands* (1815-1820), valued because of their information on art in the later middle ages. His only painting of note is *The Surrender of Briseis.*

Firdausi or **Firdusi** (c.935-c.1020), Persian poet of wealthy parentage who was highly educated, and considered the greatest of his country's epic poets. His greatest work was *The Book of Kings,* an epic poem in nearly 60,000 verses which narrates the heroic deeds of Persia's monarchs: thirty-five years was consumed in its composition.

Firebird, The (L'Oiseau de Feu), a spectacular ballet in one act: libretto and choreography by Michel FOKINE; music by Igor STRAVINSKY; first produced at Paris in 1910. The story is: The young prince, Ivan Tsarevitch, finds himself in an orchard where a gorgeous golden bird is plucking golden apples from a silver tree. Ivan seizes the bird, but, touched by her entreaties, releases her; in gratitude she leaves him one of her magic feathers. When day breaks, Ivan discovers that he is in the park of an old castle, the home of the wicked ogre, Kastchei. Presently twelve maidens, followed by a thirteenth, emerge from the hall and dance and play among the trees. The prince, attracted by the thirteenth maiden, remains with the princesses, although they warn him that Kastchei may arrive at any moment and turn him to stone. At length they depart, and the prince, made bold by love, flings open the castle gates. Out swarm Kastchei's prisoners, a motley and grotesque group, followed by the ogre himself; his attempt to petrify Ivan is foiled by the Firebird's feather. At this critical moment the Firebird herself appears, and causes the monster and his subjects to dance until they are exhausted. Then she divulges the secret of Kastchei's power; an egg in a casket, which, if broken, would mean the ogre's death. Ivan loses no time in dashing the egg to pieces and Kastchei expires. The petrified prisoners come to life, and join in the general merrymaking while Ivan and the beautiful princess gaze expectantly into each other's eyes. Stravinsky has arranged a symphonic suite from the music which is a favorite concert and radio work: there is a Columbia recording conducted by Igor Stravinsky, and a Victor recording by the Philadelphia Orchestra with Leopold Stokowski.

Firefly, The, a comic opera in three acts; book by Otto HARBACH; music by Rudolf FRIML: first produced at New York in 1912 with Emma TRENTINI and Roy ATWELL. The plot concerns a street singer, Nina, who after becoming a stowaway on a boat to Bermuda, and suspected of theft as a notorious pickpocket, finally wins her hero, Jack Travers. There are many engaging songs of which there are Victor recordings in album form.

Fireworks (Stravinsky), a tone poem composed by Igor STRAVINSKY in 1908, and sent to Nicholas RIMSKY-KORSAKOW in commemoration of the marriage of the latter's daughter: it was returned undelivered because of Rimsky-Korsakow's death. Critics consider it the first concrete indication of "radical" tendencies on Stravinsky's part in attempting to picture the colors and brilliance of fireworks. There is no American-made recording at the present time, but there is a foreign record by the Colonne Orchestra conducted by Gabriel Pierné.

Firkins, Oscar W. (1864-1932), American literary and dramatic critic educated at the University of Minnesota and later Professor of Comparative Literature there: his notable works include *Ralph Waldo Emerson* (1915); *Jane Austen; William Deans Howells; Selected Essays.* He also wrote

several plays, and acted as dramatic critic for the New York *Weekly Review* from 1915 to 1918.

Fischer von Erlach, Johann Bernhard (c.1656-1723), Austrian architect for many years architectural designer to the court: among his creations were many churches and palaces for the nobility including the castle of Schönbrunn, the summer residence of the emperor of Austria.

Fisher, Dorothy Canfield (1879-), American novelist educated at Ohio State University, Columbia University, and the Sorbonne, Paris. Her notable works include *Gunhild* (1907); *The Squirrel Cage; Hillsboro People; The Bent Twig; The Brimming Cup; Her Son's Wife; Seasoned Timber.* She also translated Guido PAPINI's *Christ,* and wrote a treatise on the Montessori system of education.

Fisher, Harrison (1875-1934), American illustrator who worked first in the newspaper field, and later created the "American Girl" or "Fisher Girl" type of cover for magazines. He also illustrated many books: among the collections of his pictures are *The Harrison Fisher Book* (1907); *A Dream of Fair Woman; Bachelor Belles; American Beauties; Pictures in Color.*

Fisher, Suzanne, contemporary American soprano who studied at the CINCINNATI CONSERVATORY OF MUSIC, the JUILLIARD Graduate School, and at Fontainebleau, making her debut in 1931 at the Berlin State Opera in Richard STRAUSS' *Egyptian Helen,* and her first appearance in 1935 at the Metropolitan Opera House, New York, in PUCCINI's *Madame Butterfly.* She has given many recitals which reveal her superior attainments as a lyric as well as a dramatic soprano.

Fisher, Vardis (1895-), American poet, essayist, and novelist educated at the University of Utah and the University of Chicago: his works include *Sonnets to an Imaginary Madonna* (1927); *Toilers of the Hills; In Tragic Life; The Neurotic Nightingale,* a volume of essays; *Children of God; The City of Illusion.*

Fisher, William Arms (1861-), American composer and editor who studied with William SHAKESPEARE, Horatio W. PARKER, and Antonin DVORAK. In 1897 he became editor for the Oliver Ditson Company, Boston, the monumental "Musician's Library" appearing under his direction. He is the author of the words to the song, *Going Home,* for which the music was adapted from the *Largo* of Dvořák's "New World Symphony," and has also composed many fine songs.

Fisher, William Mark (1841-1923), American painter who studied with George INNESS, and later at Paris: he opened a studio in Boston, but meeting with little success went to London. His works include *Scotch Hillside; Normandy Orchard; Road to Menil; A Kerry Pastoral; Weaned Calves; The Last of Autumn; Feeding the Fowls.*

Fisk Jubilee Singers, an organization of American Negro singers formed in 1871 at Fisk University, Nashville, Tenn.: its success may be judged by the fact that $150,000 was raised for the institution. The group sang at Patrick S. GILMORE's Jubilee at Boston in 1872, and carried their renditions of Negro spirituals and folk songs all over Europe, appearing by command before many royal personages.

Fiske, Harrison Grey (1861-1942), American journalist, theatre manager, and dramatist who was for many years editor and proprietor of the New York *Dramatic Mirror*. He was the husband of Minnie Maddern FISKE and the author of numerous plays including *Fontenelle*, with Mrs. Fiske; *Hester Crewe; The Queen of Liars*, later known as *Marie Deloche; The District Attorney*, with Charles KLEIN; also English versions of *Divorçons* and *Ghosts*. He also acted as manager for Mrs. Fiske, and produced many plays.

Fiske, Minnie Maddern (1865-1932), American actress whose family name was Mary Augusta Davey. She appeared at the age of three as the little Duke of York in *Richard III* at Little Rock, Arkansas: in 1870 she played with Laura KEENE, and appeared later in juvenile and ingenue parts with John McCULLOUGH, Junius Brutus BOOTH, J. K. Emmett, Oliver Doud BYRON, E. L. DAVENPORT, becoming a star at sixteen. Among the many plays in which she appeared as a star were *A Doll's House; Divorçons; Frou-Frou; A Light from St. Agnes; Tess of the D'Urbervilles; Becky Sharp; Hedda Gabler; Leah Kleschna; Rosermersholm; Ghosts; Pillars of Society*. She married Harrison Grey FISKE in 1888, and appeared at the Manhattan Theatre, New York, in several of his plays and in many of her own productions.

Fitch, William Clyde (1865-1909), American dramatist who was graduated from Amherst College in 1886: three years later he wrote a highly successful play, *Beau Brummel*, for Richard MANSFIELD. It was followed by many more dramas and plays of American society life including *The Moth and the Flame; Nathan Hale; Barbara Frietchie; The Cowboy and the Lady*, adapted for the films by S. N. BEHRMANN in 1938; *The Climbers; Captain Jinks of the Horse Marines; The Stubbornness of Geraldine*. Many of his plays were produced in London and in Continental theatres.

Fitelberg, Gregor (1879-), Polish composer and conductor who studied the violin with Stanislaus Barcewicz and composition with Sigismund Noskowski. In 1905 he founded a group of composers known as "Young Poland," among whom were Karol SZYMANOWSKI and Ludomir ROZYCKI: he has conducted the Warsaw Philharmonic Orchestra, the Vienna Opera, and many other European organizations as well as the NATIONAL BROADCASTING COMPANY SYMPHONY ORCHESTRA in New York. His works include a symphony, a *Polish Rhapsody*, a symphonic poem, and chamber music.

Fitzgerald, Edward (1809-1883), English poet whose works were chiefly remodeled translations of foreign works: they include *Six Dramas of Calderno* (1853), the *Agamemnon* of Aeschylus, the *Oedipus* of Sophocles, and his masterpiece, the *Rubáiyát of Omar Khayyám* which was utterly neglected until Gabriel ROSSETTI chanted its praises so loudly that it has since placed Fitzgerald among the immortals.

Fitzgerald, Francis Scott Key (1896-1940), American novelist who was educated at Princeton University and served in World War I: his first novel, *This Side of Paradise*, was published in 1920, followed by *The Beautiful and the Damned; The Great Gatsby; Tender is the Night; The Last Tycoon*.

Fitzwilliam Museum (Cambridge, England), a massive building in the classical style containing the collection of paintings, engravings, illuminated manuscripts, and books bequeathed to Cambridge University by Richard, Viscount Fitzwilliam in 1816, the building itself was begun in 1837. Many works by great masters including RUBENS, HOGARTH, TITIAN, REMBRANDT, and HOLBEIN are in the museum which also has an archaeological annex founded in 1884.

Five Positions, in ballet the five fundamental positions of the feet upon which the entire technique of classical dancing is based; established by Pierre Beauchamps at the Academy of the Dance founded by LOUIS XIV in 1661.

Flageolet, a primitive FLUTE resembling the ordinary tin whistle: its body is either cylindrical or conical and has from six to eight finger holes. It is also known as "recorder," "English flute," "flute à bec," and "beak flute": it was used in the scores of Johann Sebastian BACH and HANDEL, but is not found in those of HAYDN.

Flagg, Ernest (1857-), American architect trained at the ECOLE DES BEAUX-ARTS, Paris. In 1891 he began practising as an architect at New York: his works include St. Luke's Hospital and the Singer Building in New York; the Corcoran Art Gallery, Washington, D. C.; buildings for the United States Naval Academy, Annapolis, Md. His book *Small Houses: Their Economic Design and Construction*, makes valuable suggestions regarding economies in construction.

Flagg, George Whiting (1816-1897), American painter who studied with his uncle, Washington ALLSTON, and in Europe. His notable paintings include *Jacob and Rachel at the Well; The Good Samaritan; Murder of the Princes in the Tower; Landing of the Pilgrims; The Scarlet Letter; The Match Girl*.

Flagg, James Montgomery (1877-), American painter, illustrator, and author who studied in New York, London, and Paris. He contributed illustrations and cover designs to many American national magazines, and made stirring posters for the State of New York during World War I. His published works include *Yankee Girls Abroad* (1900); *All in the Same Boat; The Adventures of Kitty Cobb; Boulevard All the Way—Maybe*.

Flagstad, Kirsten (1895-), Norwegian dramatic soprano who studied with her mother, and made her debut in 1913 at the National Theatre, Oslo, in D'ALBERT's *Tiefland*. She appeared at the BAYREUTH FESTIVALS in 1933 and 1934, and made her American debut in 1935 at the Metropolitan

Opera House as Sieglinde in WAGNER's *The Valkyrie*. She has since toured the United States, Honolulu, and Australia. Her repertory includes all the principal Wagnerian roles for soprano, and many French and Italian operas which she sings in Norwegian or Swedish.

Flamand, François, see **Duquesnoy, François.**

Flamboyant Style, in architecture the term applied to the late Gothic style of architecture in France during the 15th and 16th centuries, corresponding to the perpendicular style in England: it is characterized by curves resembling flames in their contours employed for the decoration of balustrades and other projecting parts.

Flanagan, Hallie (1890-), American educator in the dramatic field who became director of the Experimental Theatre at Grinnell College in 1922, and in 1923 production assistant of George Pierce BAKER at the Harvard 47 Workshop. She founded the Experimental Theatre at Vassar College in 1925 and was granted a GUGGENHEIM FELLOWSHIP for study of playwriting and production in foreign countries. In 1935 she became director of the FEDERAL THEATRE PROJECT, returning to Vassar after the project was abandoned in 1939: she was granted leave of absence to become Dean of Smith College. Her works include *Shifting Scenes of the Modern European Theatre* and *Dynamo* (1943): the latter is her report on the Experimental Theatre at Vassar.

Flandrau, Charles Macomb (1871-1938), American essayist and novelist educated at Harvard University: his works include *Harvard Episodes* (1897); *The Diary of a Freshman; Viva Mexico!,* considered an outstanding travel volume; *Prejudices; Loquacities; Sophomores Abroad.*

Flandrin, Jean Hippolyte (1809-1864), French painter who studied with his brother, Paul, at the studio of Jean INGRES in Paris. His works are chiefly religious or historical: they include *St. Clair Healing the Blind; Jesus and the Little Children; Dante and Virgil; Euripides Writing His Tragedies; Christ Entering Jerusalem; Study of a Young Girl; Portrait of Napoleon III.*

Flannagan, John B. (1895-1942), American sculptor who studied in the United States, Paris, and Ireland. He was accustomed to working in common stone and granite, which was one of his favorite mediums: among his interesting works are a *Snake* executed in limestone, a *Dragon* which suggests a laughing crocodile; *Triumph of the Egg.*

Flat, in music a character which lowers the pitch of the note before which it is placed by a semitone: when placed in the signature of a composition it indicates that all notes occurring on the same line or space are lowered without the use of the character before each note. A double-flat lowers the pitch of the note before which it is placed by two semitones; i.e., a whole tone.

Flaubert, Gustave (1821-1880), French novelist who achieved great success in 1857 with a novel entitled *Madame Bovary:* it remains his master-

piece. His other works included *Salammbô,* a romance of Carthage which was used as the libretto for an opera by Ernest REYER in 1890; *The History of a Young Man; The Temptation of St. Anthony.*

Flavin, Martin (1883-), American dramatist educated at the University of Chicago, and engaged for twenty years in the business of manufacturing. His plays include *Children of the Moon* (1923); *The Criminal Code; Broken Dishes; Cross Roads; Achilles Had a Heel; Tapestry in Gray; Around the Corner.*

Flaxman, John (1755-1826), English sculptor and illustrator who exhibited TERRA COTTA figures at twelve, and became a student at the Royal Academy, London, after having produced a *Death of Caesar.* He made pottery designs for Josiah WEDGWOOD and illustrated HOMER's *Iliad, Odyssey,* and DANTE's *Divine Comedy:* his notable sculptures include *Pompey; Hercules in the Garment of Nessus; Death of Caesar; Mercury and Pandora; Resignation; Maternal Love; Cupid and Psyche; Raphael; Michelangelo;* the Nelson Memorial at Westminster; also the famous *Shield of Achilles.*

Flèche, in architecture the French term for a slender spire, especially one of timber covered with lead erected over the intersection of the nave and transepts of a church. An excellent example is the flèche of NOTRE DAME, Paris, which rises to the height of nearly 100 feet.

Flecker, James Elroy (1884-1915), English poet and dramatist educated at Oxford, and for five years in the British consular service. His works include *The Bridge of Fire* (1908); *The King of Alsander,* a novel; two plays, *Hassan* and *Don Juan;* also several volumes of poems.

Fledermaus, Die (The Bat), a comic opera in three acts: libretto by Richard GENEE and Karl Hoffner adapted from a French story by Henri MEILHAC and Ludovic HALEVY; music by Johann STRAUSS, Jr.; first produced at Vienna in 1874 and in New York at the Casino Theatre in 1885 under the direction of Heinrich CONRIED with De Wolfe HOPPER in the cast. The next New York production was in 1912 with the title, *The Merry Countess,* and Maurice Farkoa was the star comedian: in 1929 another presentation offered it as *A Wonderful Night,* and in 1933 it masqueraded as *Champagne Sec* with Peggy WOOD, Helen Ford, and Kitty Carlisle caroling and dancing to the original tuneful strains by the waltz king. The latest offering in 1942 was the Max REINHARDT version with the title, *Rosalinda,* which held the boards until 1943. The overture is a favorite concert, radio, and phonograph work: there is a Victor recording by the Minneapolis Symphony Orchestra under Eugene Ormandy, and a Columbia recording in which Bruno Walter directs the Berlin State Opera Orchestra.

Fleischer, Editha (1898-), German lyric soprano who studied with Lilli LEHMANN, and made her debut at the Berlin Opera in 1919. She appeared at the SALZBURG FESTIVALS, and was a member of the Wagnerian Opera Company which toured the United States in 1922-24. In 1926 she made her debut with the METROPOLITAN OPERA COMPANY of which she was a member for ten years. Her repertory includes the leading lyric soprano roles in WAGNER, MOZART, and PUCCINI operas.

Fleischer, Max (1889-), Austro-American artist and cartoonist educated at the ART STUDENTS' LEAGUE and Cooper Union Institute, New York. During World War I he was engaged by the general staff of the United States Army to produce technical motion pictures for the rapid training of soldiers. He also produced scientific motion pictures including Darwin's *Theory of Evolution* and Einstein's *Theory of Relativity*. The film-going public heartily enjoyed his *Out of the Inkwell* cartoons, and his production of *Gulliver's Travels* in 1939.

Flémal, Flemael, or **Flémall, Bartholet** (1614-1675), Flemish painter who studied with his father, and with Hans Jordaens: after spending several years in Rome and Florence he decorated several churches in Paris and Liege. His notable works include *Flight of Aeneas from Troy; Raising of the Cross; Mysteries of the Old and New Testaments; Alexander Leaving for Asia; Chastisement of Heliodorus; Death of Lucretia.*

Flémalle, Master of, one of the names under which **Robert Campin** (1375-1444) was known: he was also called "Master of the Mouse-Trap," and "Master of Mérode." Little is known of his life except that he was the teacher of Rogier Van der WEYDEN and Jacques Daret. His notable works include a triptych, *The Annunciation; Virgin and Child; The Good Thief; Descent from the Cross; Virgin in Glory.*

Fleming, Peter (1907-), English traveler and novelist educated at Oxford who spent a long period in Russia, China, Japan, and Brazil as special correspondent for the London *Times:* his works include *Brazilian Adventure* (1933); *Variety; One's Company; News from Tartary; Flying Visit; A Story To Tell and Other Tales.*

Flesch, Karl (1873-), Hungarian violinist who studied with Jakob Grün and Martin MARSICK, and is equally famous as a virtuoso and teacher. He has toured all the countries of Europe, and also the United States in addition to becoming professor of the violin at the Hochschule, Berlin, and at the CURTIS INSTITUTE OF MUSIC, Philadelphia. He has written *The Art of Violin Playing,* and has also edited the violin compositions and studies of classic and modern masters.

Fletcher, Alice C. (1838-1923), American ethnologist who devoted her life to the study of the North American Indian, spending many years of her life in direct contact with various tribes. Her works include *Indian Story and Song from North America; A Study of Omaha Indian Music; Indian Games and Dances.*

Fletcher, John (1579-1625), English dramatist who studied at Cambridge University: his friendship and collaboration with Francis BEAUMONT in dramatic writing is characterized by Algernon

SWINBURNE as "the most perfect union in genius and friendship." He produced many plays: exactly which were original, and which were in collaboration with MIDDLETON, MASSINGER, ROWLEY, and Shirley is a much-discussed question. The following are some of the plays said by some authorities to have been his own: *The Faithful Shepherdess; Bonduca; The Wild Goose Chase; Monsieur Thomas; Valentinian; Wit Without Money; The Chances.*

Fletcher, John Gould (1886-), American writer and poet educated at Harvard College; his works include *The Dominant City* (1913); *Fire and Wine; Irradiations; Sand and Spray; Goblins and Pagodas; Japanese Prints; Paul Gauguin: His Life and Art; Branches of Adam; The Epic of Arkansas; Elegies; The Two Frontiers; Life is My Song,* an autobiography. His *Selected Poems* won the Pulitzer Prize for poetry in 1939.

Fletcher, Joseph Smith (1863-1935), English antiquarian, poet, and author of detective fiction; his novels of this kind include *Adventures of Archer Dawe* (1909); *The Middle Temple Murder,* said to have been greatly praised by Woodrow Wilson; *The Charing Cross Mystery; Murder at Wride's Park; The Missing Chancellor; Murder in the Squire's Pew.* He also wrote *A Picturesque History of Yorkshire,* and published a volume of poems.

Fleury, see **Robert-Fleury, Joseph Nicolas.**

Flight of the Bumble Bee (Rimsky-Korsakow), an orchestral scherzo in Act III of Nicholas RIMSKY-KORSAKOW's opera, *The Tale of Tsar Saltan,* produced in 1900: the libretto based on a story by Alexander PUSHKIN. The music depicts the movements of a bumble bee which flies across the sea to an enchanted island where it buzzes around a swan which is really a princess. There is a Victor recording by the Chicago Symphony Orchestra under Frederick Stock, and a Columbia recording by the All-American Orchestra directed by Leopold Stokowski: also a Victor recording by Jascha Heifetz.

Flinck, Govaert (1615-1660), Dutch painter who studied with REMBRANDT, and is said to have approached the latter closest in style with the exception of Gerbrand van den EECKHOUT. His notable pictures include *Solomon Praying for Wisdom; The Archers; The Expulsion of Hagar; Portrait of an Old Man; Solomon and the Queen of Sheba; Bathsheba's Appeal to David.*

Floating Theatre, see **Show boat.**

Flonzaley Quartet, an organization founded by Edward J. de Coppet, a wealthy man accustomed to engaging artists for private quartet performances. In 1903 he commissioned the violinist, Alfred POCHON, to engage three other artists willing to devote their time exclusively to quartet playing: as first formed, the members were Adolfo BETTI, Alfred Pochon, Ugo Ara, and Ivan d'Archambeau. The quartet, with several changes in membership, appeared regularly in public from 1905 to 1927, giving 2500 concerts in the United States and 500 in Europe. It introduced many new American and foreign works in addition to making numerous recordings.

Flora, in Roman mythology the goddess of spring and of flowers; in 170 B.C. a festival was held in her honor which lasted six days during which there were theatrical spectacles and animal hunts, the entire proceedings characterized by licentiousness and debauchery.

Floradora, a musical play: book by Owen Hall and music by Leslie STUART; first produced in 1899 at London where it ran for five hundred performances, and in 1900 at the Casino Theatre, New York, where it broke all records, and toured the United States for eight years. A slang expression, "Are there any more at home like you?" developed from the famous Sextette "Oh, Tell Me, Pretty Maiden," which was the hit song of the production.

Florence, William Jermyn (1831-1891), American actor, real name Bernard Conlin: he appeared in a number of plays on Irish and Yankee subjects, but achieved his greatest success in Benjamin Woolf's *The Mighty Dollar* which was presented more than 2500 times with his wife, **Malvina Pray Littel Florence** (1830-1906) who was the first American actress to appear on the London stage. Among Florence's best roles were Bob Brierly in *Ticket-of-Leave Man,* Sir Lucius O'Trigger in *The Rivals,* and Ezekiel Homespun in *Heir-at-Law* with Joseph JEFFERSON.

Florence (Italy), a city in Italy founded about 180 B.C., and famous for its intimate association from the historical standpoint with the arts including painting, sculpture, architecture, literature, and music. It contains many fine churches including the Duomo (St. Maria del Fiore), the Badia, Santo Spirito, and Santa Maria Novello. The art museums include the UFFIZI, the PITTI, the Accademia, the BARGELLO, the Opera del Duomo; the Michelangelo and the Etruscan and Egyptian Museums, all of these are filled with paintings, sculptures, and art objects of every description. Among the great artists and literary men who lived in or are associated with Florence are DANTE, BOCCACCIO, LULLY, CELLINI, CHERUBINI, CIMABUE, GIOTTO, BRUNELLESCHI, della ROBBIA, GHIBERTI, DONATELLO, LIPPI, GHIRLANDAIO, Fra ANGELICO, RAPHAEL, Leonardo da VINCI, and MICHELANGELO. Its celebrated personages included the members of the Medici family, SAVONAROLA, MACHIAVELLI, and Vespucci. The city is also famous for its libraries, academies, and universities of learning, conservatories of music and art schools.

Florian, Jean Pierre Claris de (1755-1794), French poet, novelist, and dramatist who was greatly admired by VOLTAIRE for his wit: his works include several sparkling comedies; the pastoral romances *Galatea* and *Estelle;* the metrical romances *Numa Pompilius* and *Gonsalvo of Cordova:* he also made a popular abridgment of CERVANTES' "Don Quixote."

Floris, Frans (c.1520-1570), Flemish painter whose real name was Frans de Vriendt: he visited Florence and Rome to study the works of the great masters such as MICHELANGELO and RAPHAEL, and finally settled in Antwerp. There he opened a studio in which more than a hundred students were trained, and painted many pictures on a grand scale for William of Orange and the nobility. His notable works include *Mars and Venus Ensnared by Vulcan; The Last Judgment; The Fall of the Rebellious Angels; Adam and Eve Under the Tree; The Nine Muses; Christ and the Little Children.*

Flotow, Friedrich von (1812-1883), German composer who studied with Anton Reicha. His works include about thirty dramatic pieces of which two have survived the test of time: *Stradella,* the overture to which is a popular concert piece today, and *Martha,* a romantic grand opera still presented in opera houses all over the world. There are Columbia and Victor recordings of both overtures, and of the most important arias.

Flute, a wind instrument made of either wood or metal: with its counterpart in half size, the PICCOLO, the two instruments assume the highest-pitched parts in orchestral and band music. The flute was greatly improved in 1832 by Theobald BOEHM who replaced the six to eight open holes with his famous key system. It was first used in orchestras about 1565: two flutes were called for by most classical composers until Josef HAYDN added another. Three flutes were used by WAGNER and VERDI, and most modern scores require the latter number.

Flygare-Carlén, Emilie Smith (1807-1892), Swedish novelist who published her first book, *Waldemar Klein,* in 1838: in 1841 she married the poet, Johan Gabriel Carlen, and her home at Stockholm became the Mecca for Swedish men of letters. Her notable novels include *The Rose of Tistelon; The Hermit; The Merchant's House on the Cliffs.* She wrote an autobiography, *Reminiscences of Swedish Literary Life,* and her daughter, **Rosa Carlén** (1836-1883), was also a successful novelist.

Flying Buttress, in architecture a prop or pier standing at some distance from a wall surmounted by an arch, thereby counteracting the outward thrust. It was used in Roman architecture, and in the early Romanesque period: in the 15th century it was decorated.

Flying Dutchman, The, (*a*) in legends of the sea a spectre ship which haunted the sea near the Cape of Good Hope, a promontory off the coast of South Africa: its captain was said to be condemned, because of his blasphemy, to sail the ocean forever without making a port. (*b*) A grand opera in three acts: libretto and music by Richard WAGNER; first produced at Dresden in 1843, and in the United States at Philadelphia in 1876. The *Overture* is a popular concert, radio, and phonograph work: there is a Columbia recording by the London Philharmonic Orchestra under Sir Thomas Beecham, and a Victor recording by the Berlin State Orchestra conducted by Leo Blech.

Fock, Dirk (1886-), Dutch composer and conductor born in the Dutch East Indies: he studied in Holland and Germany, and after conducting for some years in Europe, directed the Concertgebouw Orchestra in Amsterdam, the NEW YORK PHILHARMONIC-SYMPHONY ORCHESTRA, the American Orchestral Society, and the Vienna Konzertverein. His compositions include *Ein hohes Lied,* a recitation with orchestra, and a musical pageant, *From Aeon to Aeon,* written in the form of an ancient mystery play.

Fogazzaro, Antonio (1842-1911), Italian poet and novelist considered the logical successor of Alessandro MANZONI as a romancer: his works available in translation include *The Patriot* (1907); *The Sinner; The Saint; The Woman; The Politician; Leila.* His style in writing is characterized by simplicity and pathos; a strong contrast to the fiery impetuosity of D'ANNUNZIO.

Fogelberg, Benedict or **Bengt Erland** (1786-1854), Swedish sculptor who studied with Johann SERGELL: also in Paris under Pierre GUERIN, and in Rome where he carefully analyzed the works of the masters. His notable creations include *Cupid and Psyche; Venus Entering the Bath; Venus and Cupid; Odin; Thor; Balder;* he also made figures and busts of Gustavus Adolphus, Charles XII, and Charles XIII of Sweden.

Fokine, Michel (1880-1942), Russian dancer, choreographer, and one of the founders of the modern Russian ballet. He studied dancing as a child at the Maryinsky Theatre, St. Petersburg, under Platon Karsavin, later acting as an instructor in dancing and finally becoming the first choreographic director of Serge DIAGHILEFF's Russian Ballet in 1900. He appeared with the company at the Châtelet, Paris, in 1909, and also in Berlin, Brussels, Rome, Monte Carlo, and at Covent Garden in 1911. His ballet creations, more than seventy in number, include *Acis and Galathea, The Dying Swan* for Anna PAVLOWA, PRINCE IGOR, SCHEHERAZADE, CLEOPATRA, CARNAVAL, LES SYLPHIDES, DAPHNIS AND CHLOE, THAMAR, LES PRELUDES, THE FIREBIRD, PAPILLONS, PETROUCHKA, Midas, LE COQ D'OR, LE REVE DE LA MARQUISE, *La Spectre de la Rose, Paganini, Bluebeard, La Belle Helene.* Fokine founded his own *American Ballet* in 1925, dancing with his wife, Vera Fokina: he directed the René Blum Ballet de Monte Carlo in 1926, the Ballet Russe in 1937, the Education Ballet in 1939, and the Ballet Teatro in 1940.

Foldes, Jolan (1903-), Hungarian novelist who studied at the Sorbonne in Paris, and acted as secretary of the Hungarian Embassy in Egypt. Among her works available in translation are *The Street of the Fishing Cat; I'm Getting Married; Prelude to Love; Egyptian Interlude; Marrons Glaces; Rudi Finds a Way.*

Foley, John Henry (1818-1847), Irish sculptor who studied at the school of the Royal Dublin Society and the Royal Academy, London: his works include *Lear and Cordelia; Prospero and Miranda; Youth at a Stream; The Muse of Painting; Caractacus;* the symbolical group, *Asia,* and the statue of *Prince Albert* for the Albert Memorial, London; *Stonewall Jackson* at Richmond, Va.; *Goldsmith* and *Burke* at Trinity College,

Dublin. His statue, *Sir James Outram,* is considered his masterpiece.

Folia, La or **Folies d'Espagne,** a sonata for violin by Arcangelo CORELLI which not only is an outstanding composition from the musical standpoint, but also possesses a historic interest. The theme is that of an ancient Spanish dance performed by men dressed in women's clothes, and gyrating so madly to the tambourine that it became known as "La Folia" or dance of folly. There are two Columbia recordings; one for violin with harpsichord, and another by Joseph Szigeti with piano accompaniment.

Folk Dances, a term used to designate the national dances of many nations: it includes the country dances of the peasantry danced to melodies the composers of which are usually unknown. Among the conspicuous examples are the English MORRIS DANCE; the Scotch HIGHLAND FLING, the Irish JIG and REEL, the German LANDLER, the Spanish FANDANGO, the Bohemian POLKA, the Hungarian CZARDAS, the Italian TARENTELLA or SALTARELLO, the Russian TREPAK, the Norwegian cross dance, and the American SQUARE DANCES.

Folk Song, in music a song of the people, based either on a legendary event or on an ordinary happening in life, usually simple in lyric, melody, and accompaniment: it is differentiated from the art song by the lack of studied character and skilled technique which characterizes the latter form. Folk-songs show distinct racial characteristics: in Northern Europe, for example, they are usually melancholy in lyric and minor in melody; in Southern Europe they are lively in text and vivacious in melody. They probably originated in the songs of the MINNESINGER, TROUBADOUR, and TROUVERE in the 10th to the 13th centuries.

Fonda, Henry (1905-), American stage and screen actor who gained his first experience at the Community Playhouse, Omaha, Nebraska, and made his first success in *The Farmer Takes a Wife* at New York in 1934. He has appeared in many motion pictures including *The Farmer Takes a Wife; Way Down East; Blockade; Jezebel; The Story of Alexander Graham Bell; Young Mr. Lincoln; Drums Along the Mohawk; Grapes of Wrath; Lillian Russell; Chad Hanna; The Lady Eve; The Male Animal; The Magnificent Dope.*

Fontaine, Joan (1917-), American screen actress born of American parentage in Tokyo, Japan: she entered the films in 1937, and has appeared in *The Man Who Found Himself; Quality Street; Gunga Din; Man of Conquest; The Women; Rebecca; Suspicion; This Above All; The Constant Nymph.*

Fontaine, Pierre François Léonard (1762-1853), French architect and member of a family distinguished in his art: he was first successful in designing furniture with his friend, Charles PERCIER. After the establishment of the consulate he was employed with Percier by NAPOLEON I, then First Consul, to restore the palaces of St. Cloud and MALMAISON, the TUILERIES, and the LOUVRE. They also worked together on the Arc de Triomphe du Carrousel, and Fontaine wrote a number of historical, architectural works.

Fontainebleau, Château of, a palace begun in 1528 by Francis I of France although there is documentary proof that a château occupied by the kings of France was located there in 1169. The architect for the new château was Gilles Le Breton who designed the façade of the White Horse Court, the gallery of Francis I, the gallery of Henry II, the new Chapel St. Saturnin, and the peristyle of the Oval Court: the other buildings were completed by Pierre Chambiges and Pierre Girard. The entrance is by a monumental flight of steps, and the apartments, some decorated by Benvenuto CELLINI and PRIMATICCIO are of great historic and artistic interest: the gardens, park, and forest are equally famous. The latter, comprising more than 40,000 acres, was a favorite meeting place for painters, especially those of the original BARBIZON SCHOOL. Pope Pius VII signed his abdication of temporal power at Fontainebleau in 1813, and NAPOLEON I also signed his abdication there.

Fontainebleau School, see **Barbizon School.**

Fontana, Domenico (1543-1607), Italian architect who studied architecture with his brother at Rome, and was under the protection of Cardinal Montalto who, after he became Pope Sixtus V, made him pontifical architect. His works include the setting up of a great obelisk brought from Egypt by Caligula; the library of the Vatican; he also completed the dome and lantern of ST. PETER'S with Giacomo della Porta, and built a palace at Naples for the King of the Two Sicilies.

Fontana, Prospero (1512-1597), Italian painter who studied with Innocenza da IMOLA, and worked with Giorgio VASARI: he became so distinguished as a portraitist that MICHELANGELO introduced him to Pope Julius III, the result being that he remained in his and succeeding popes' employ for many years. He was the teacher of both Ludovico and Agostino CARRACCI, and his daughter, **Lavinia Fontana** (1552-1614) was a distinguished artist who painted the portraits of illustrious personages in Bologna, and also several religious works including *Virgin Lifting a Veil from the Sleeping Infant Christ,* and *Queen of Sheba Visiting Solomon.*

Fontane, Theodor (1819-1898), German poet and novelist who acted as a war correspondent in the Franco-Prussian War, and fell into the hands of the French. He published his first volume of poems, *Men and Heroes,* in 1850, and another, *Collected Ballads,* in 1892. His novels of German life include *Count Petöfy; Under the Pear Tree; Mrs. Jenny Treibel; Effie Priest; Before the Storm.*

Fontanes, Louis, Marquess de (1757-1821), French poet who was proscribed by the Revolutionary Tribunal for editing papers opposed to the Terror and fled to England where he became friendly with CHATEAUBRIAND. He returned later to act as a mediator between NAPOLEON I and the litterateurs. He was the author of several graceful poems including *The Forest of Navarre,* the

Carthusian Nun, and *All-Souls* which was an imitation of Gray's famous "Elegy."

Fontanne, Lynn (1882-   ), Anglo-American actress who made her debut with Ellen TERRY in BARRIE's *Alice-Sit-by-the-Fire,* later acting in pantomime at the DRURY LANE. In 1923 she appeared in *Sweet Nell of Old Drury* with Alfred LUNT to whom she was married in 1924, and joined the THEATRE GUILD, New York, during the same year. The plays in which she has acted with her husband include *The Guardsman; Arms and the Man; The Goat Song; Pygmalion; The Brothers Karamazov; The Doctor's Dilemma; Caprice; Elizabeth the Queen; Reunion in Vienna; Design for Living; The Taming of the Shrew; Idiot's Delight; Amphitryon; The Sea Gull; The Pirate.*

Fonteyn, Margot, contemporary English ballerina who started her dancing career in Shanghai, and later studied at the SADLER's WELLS Ballet School, London, making her debut at that theatre, and inheriting many of MARKOVA's· roles. Her repertory is exceedingly varied: it includes *Swan Lake, Les Sylphides,* and *Giselle* in addition to many of the modernistic ballets.

Fon-Vizin, or **Von-Visin, Denis Ivanovich** (1744-1792), Russian satirist and dramatist often called "the Russian Molière": his two comedies, *The Brigadier* and *The Minor, or Mother's Favorite Son,* which ridiculed certain inherent peculiarities of Russian character, made him famous.

Foot, in poetry a series of words marked off as constituting a metrical unit, similar to a measure in music, and thereby becoming one of the regularly recurring fundamental divisions of a verse.

Foote, Arthur (1853-1937), American pianist, organist, and composer who studied with B. J. Lang, Stephen Emery, and John K. PAINE at Harvard University. He appeared in chamber music concerts with the KNEISEL QUARTET, and was one of the founders of the American Guild of Organists. His compositions include several works for orchestra; a violin concerto; chamber music; many piano pieces; more than 100 songs; organ music, a technical treatise on harmony with W. R. Spalding.

Foote, Mary Hallock (1847-1938), American illustrator and novelist: in 1876 she married a mining engineer, Arthur De Wint Foote, and lived mainly in the Rocky Mountain section of the United States. Her works include *The Led Horse Claim; John Bodewin's Testimony; In Exile and Other Stories; Coeur d'Alene; The Valley Road; The Ground Swell.*

Foote, Samuel (1720-1777), English actor and dramatist who studied without success at Oxford, and was also a failure for a time on the stage. His fame came chiefly from a form of entertainment originated by him, called *Diversions of the Morning,* which consisted of imitations of actors and prominent people of the hour. His plays include *The Knights* (1748); *The Englishman in Paris; The Orators; The Lame Lover; The Maid of Bath; The Nabob; The Capuchin,* a second version of *The Trip to Calais* forbidden by the censor.

Foppa, Vincenzo (c.1427-c.1515), Italian painter who settled in Pavia about 1456, and remained as the head of the Lombard School until he was succeeded by LEONARDO DA VINCI. His works include *Crucifixion; St. Jerome; Madonna with the Baptist and Evangelist; Martyrdom of St. Sebastian.* He was patronized by Francesca and Galeazzo Sforza while residing in Milan; many of his frescoes made later in Genoa were destroyed.

Forain, Jean Louis (1852-1931), French painter and caricaturist who worked along the lines of Honoré DAUMIER in deriding the foibles of the French bourgeoisie: his style is that of MANET or DEGAS with a seemingly inherent caustic, bitter tone added. He contributed to FIGARO, and published *Comédie Parisienne,* a series of two hundred and fifty sketches in book form.

Forbes, Edwin (1839-1895), American painter, illustrator, and etcher whose remarkable drawings, made on the battle-field as special correspondent and illustrator for Frank *Leslie's Illustrated Magazine,* thrilled American readers during the Civil War. The War Office in Washington, D. C., has a series of Forbes' etchings in copper known as *Life Studies of the Great Army.*

Forbes, Esther (c.1894-), American short story writer and novelist educated at the University of Wisconsin, and engaged for a time in editorial work for Houghton, Mifflin and Company, Boston, Mass. Her works include *O Genteel Lady!* (1926); *A Mirror for Witches; Miss Marvel; Paradise; The General's Lady; Paul Revere and the World He Lived In* which won the 1943 Pulitzer Prize for history.

Forbes, James (1871-1938), American dramatist born in Canada: his plays include *The Chorus Lady* (1906); *The Traveling Salesman; A Rich Man's Son; The Show Shop; The Famous Mrs. Fair.*

Forbes, Ralph (1905-), English actor who made his debut in 1924 at London in *The Flame,* and his first American appearance during the same year at New York in *Havoc.* He has played leading roles in many talking films including *Beau Geste; The Green Goddess; The Barretts of Wimpole Street; The Three Musketeers; Romeo and Juliet; Mary of Scotland; Daniel Boone; The Last of Mrs. Cheyney; Kidnapped; If I Were King; The Hound of the Baskervilles; Private Lives of Elizabeth and Essex; Tower of London; Curtain Call.*

Forbes-Robertson, Sir Johnston (1853-1937), English actor who was the eldest son of John Forbes-Robertson, an art critic and journalist. He made his debut at the Princess Theatre, London, in *Mary Queen of Scots,* and later appeared with Marie BANCROFT, Sir Henry IRVING, Wilson BARRETT, Mary ANDERSON, and John HARE. Among the plays in which he appeared with his wife, Gertrude ELLIOTT, sister of Maxine ELLIOTT, were KIPLING's *The Light That Failed;* SHAW's *Caesar and Cleopatra; Mice and Men; Hamlet; The Passing of the Third Floor Back.* In 1925 his autobiography, *Player under Three Reigns,* was published.

Force, Peter (1790-1868), American journalist whose life work was an invaluable collection of 22,000 books and 40,000 pamphlets entitled *American Archives:* it was purchased in 1867 by the Federal Government, and placed in the Library of Congress.

Ford, Edward Onslow (1852-1901), English sculptor who received some instruction in Munich, but was chiefly self-taught. His notable portraits and statues include Sir Henry IRVING as *Hamlet;* Queen Victoria; the Maharajah of Mysore; ALMA-TADEMA: he also created some smaller pieces including *Peace; Folly; Echo; Egyptian Singer; Applause; Snow Drift.*

Ford, Ford Madox (1873-1939), English poet and novelist, son of Dr. Francis Hueffer, and grandson of Ford Madox BROWN, an English painter. He collaborated with Joseph CONRAD in the novels, *The Inheritors* (1901) and *Romance* (1903): his original novels include *The Fifth Queen* (1906); *The Half Moon; The Fifth Queen Crowned; Mr. Apollo; The Portrait; Ladies Whose Bright Eyes; The Panel; The Young Lovell; Privy Seal; Some Do Not; No More Parades; A Man Could Stand Up; The Last Post.* The four last-named were a series of novels regarding World War I. Ford also founded the *English Review* in 1908 which had a remarkable number of distinguished contributors, and a magazine called the *Transatlantic Review* at Paris after World War I.

Ford, John (1586-1639), English poet and dramatist who was admitted to the bar although there is no evidence that he ever practiced law. He wrote several successful plays including *The Broken Heart* and *Perkin Warbeck:* he also collaborated with Thomas DEKKER and William ROWLEY in *The Witch of Edmonton.*

Ford, Paul Leicester (1865-1902), American biographer and novelist: his works include *The Honorable Peter Sterling* (1894); *The Great H. & A. Train Robbery; The True George Washington; The Many-Sided Franklin; Janice Meredith,* a popular novel which was equally successful as a play.

Foreign Legion (Legion etrangère), an infantry regiment in the French army recruited chiefly of foreigners who, for reasons best known to themselves, wish to bury their identities or to begin a new career. Louis Philippe is said to have formed this particular legion in 1831 although Francis I also had a similar regiment: before World War I the Foreign Legion had its headquarters in Algeria, and permitted men born in Alsace-Lorraine under German rule to enlist. Interesting stories of the regiment have been written by George SURDEZ.

Forester, Cecil Scott (1899-), English newspaper correspondent and novelist born in Cairo, Egypt, and educated at Dulwich College, London: his works include *Payment Deferred* (1926); *Love Lies Dreaming; The Shadow of the Hawk; Two-and-Twenty; The General; Beat to Quarters; Flying Colors; A Ship of the Line; Captain Hornblower, R.N., The Captain from Connecticut.*

Forester, Frank, see **Herbert, Henry William.**

Forest Murmurs (Siegfried), an orchestral interlude in Richard WAGNER'S music drama, *Siegfried,* the third of the dramas in the RING OF THE NIBELUNGS. Siegfried has killed the dragon, Fafner, and having tasted its blood, suddenly discovers that the forest murmurs and birds' songs (as played by the orchestra) become intelligible, and can tell him of the future. There is a Victor recording by the New York Philharmonic-Symphony Orchestra under Willem Mengelberg, and a Columbia recording by the Pittsburgh Symphony Orchestra conducted by Fritz Reiner.

Form, in music the element or combination of elements underlying a musical composition; an essential arrangement in order to prevent a musical work becoming incoherent. A *figure* is a group of notes expressing a musical idea within a measure; a *phrase* is a four-measure, complete musical thought: two phrases form a *period* and sixteen measures form a *double-period.* The *three-part song form* is the commonest type of musical form, and the *sonata form* is used in sonatas, concertos, symphonies, and concerted music.

Forrest, Edwin (1806-1872), American actor who made his first appearance in 1820 at the Walnut Theatre, Philadelphia, in Home's *Douglas,* and his New York debut in 1826 at the Bowery Theatre in *Othello.* In 1836 he appeared with great success in London as Spartacus in *The Gladiator,* and engaged in a rivalry with William MACREADY which is supposed to have caused the Astor Place Riot in 1849. He was pre-eminent in Shakespearean roles, and left much of the fortune he amassed on the stage for the founding of a home for aged actors.

Forster, Edward Morgan (1879-), English novelist and short story writer educated at King's College, Cambridge: his works include *Where Angels Fear to Tread* (1905); *The Longest Journey; The Room With a View; Howard's End; A Passage to India; Aspects of the Novel; The Celestial Omnibus; England's Pleasant Land.*

Förster, Ernst Joachim (1800-1885), German painter and art critic who studied at Berlin with Reinhard Zimmerman and Wilhelm SCHADOW. His notable works include frescoes at the University of Bonn and the Royal Palace at Munich. In 1837 he discovered and restored some of ALTICHIERI'S murals in Padua; he also wrote histories of German and of Italian art.

Forster, John W. L. (1853-1938), Canadian painter considered the dean of the Dominion's portrait artists. His pictures were exhibited in Paris when he was thirty years of age: among his portraits are those of five Canadian prime ministers and three governors general. While on a visit to Japan he painted the portrait of the former Emperor Mitsohito and his empress. Among his other works are *Hiawatha's Vision, Lundy's Lane,* and *The Departure of Canada's First Contingent in World War I.*

Forsyth, Cecil (1870-), English composer, conductor, and writer who studied with Sir Charles Villiers STANFORD and Sir Charles Hubert Hastings PARRY at the College of Music, London. His compositions include operas, orchestral works, a viola concerto, chamber works and songs. Among his theoretical works are *Music and Nationalism; Orchestration; A History of Music,* with Charles Villiers Stanford.

Forte (It.), in music an expression indicating that a passage is to be played loudly or strongly: if extreme loudness is required, the superlative form, *fortissimo,* is used.

Fortune Teller, The, a comic opera in three acts: libretto by Harry B. SMITH; music by Victor HERBERT; first produced at Wallack's Theatre, New York, in 1898. The *Gypsy Love Song* has been a popular favorite for more than forty years: there are Victor and Columbia recordings of this song, and of the famous *Czardas.*

Fortuny y Carbo, Mariano (c.1838-1874), Spanish painter who first modeled wax figures, and later studied at the Barcelona Academy, and in Rome. His works include *La Vicaria; Choosing a Model; The Snake Charmer; Moors Playing With a Vulture; The Rehearsal; A Spanish Lady.* His instinctive love of detail, and his ability to correlate brilliant hues gave his pictures considerable charm.

Forty-niners, the colloquial name given to the many thousands of adventurous spirits from all parts of the United States who made the weary trek in wagon trains across the Rocky Mountains in the famous gold rush of 1849. Some traveled by boat around Cape Horn, and others crossed the narrower neck of the continent at Central America, but all endured privations whether they went by land or sea. Stephen FOSTER'S minstrel ditty, *Oh, Susannah,* was said to have been the favorite song for raising the spirits of these intrepid travelers through Indian infested sections: for many years melodramas based on their actual or imaginary experiences were popular throughout the United States.

47 Workshop, see **Baker, George Pierce.**

Forum, Roman, the center of the life of ancient Rome from the time of the first kings, occupying the hollow between the Capitol and the Palatine. It was used for public assemblies, the funeral ceremonies of patricians, and the triumphs of victorious generals. During the period from the 6th century B.C. to the 7th century A.D. magnificent buildings were erected which were later transformed into churches, or razed and the materials used for the construction of palaces and fortresses for the nobles who established themselves on the Palatine. Among these edifices, which were located on each side of the Sacred Way, were the Temple of Saturn; the Temple of Castor and Pollux; the Temple of Concord; the Temple of Vesta; the Triumphal Arch of Septimus Severus; the Column of Phocas; the Atrium (Palace) of Vesta; the Rostra from which Caesar and Cicero spoke. Excavations were begun in the 16th century and continued in the 19th century: the Forum has been pictured in paintings by many famous artists, and has also been made the scene of numerous plays by Shakespeare, Corneille, Racine, and other dramatists.

Forza del Destino, La, a grand opera in four acts: libretto by Francesco Maria Piave; music by Giuseppe Verdi; first produced at St. Petersburg in 1862, and at the Academy of Music, New York, in 1865. The plot is a melodrama of the most sanguinary character, but there are several outstanding soprano and tenor arias in addition to the favorite tenor and baritone duet, *Solenne in quest' ora* (In this solemn hour), of which there are both Columbia and Victor recordings.

Foscari, Francesco (1373-1457), a doge of Venice from 1423 to 1457: he was elected to office without the custom usually employed of asking the approval of the people. The last years of his reign were saddened by the charges brought against Jacopo Foscari, his son, through the efforts of his rival, Giacopo Loredano, of complicity in the assassination of a member of the Council of Ten. He was forced to witness the torture on the rack of his son: the incident is portrayed in a painting by Eugene Delacroix. The father and son are the subjects of a tragedy by Lord Byron, and also of an opera with the same title by Giuseppe Verdi.

Foscolo, Ugo (1778-1827), Italian patriot and poet whose first work, a tragedy entitled *Thyeste,* was received with great acclaim at Venice in 1797. His works include the dramas *Ajax* and *Ricciarda;* also two fine epic poems, *Italy* and *The Graves.*

Fosdick, Charles Austin (1842-1915), American author of books for boys who wrote under the pen name "Harry Castlemon." Among his most popular works were the *Gunboat Series* (1864-68); the *Rocky Mountain Series;* The *Rod and Gun Series.*

Fosdick, James William (1858-), American painter who specialized in murals, and was one of the pioneers in the art of pyrography, a process of producing a design on wood, leather, etc., by the use of fire. His paintings of note include *Adoration of St. Joan of Arc* and *Louis XIV.*

Foster, Myles Birket (1825-1899), English painter and illustrator on wood and copper of many works by English and American poets. His notable paintings in water-color include *Feeding the Ducks; Sailing the Boat; Arundel Mill; The Primrose Gatherers.*

Foster, Stephen Collins (1826-1864), American composer who was almost entirely self-taught: his first song, *Open Thy Lattice, Love,* was written when he was sixteen although he had previously composed a waltz for four flutes. From 1842 to 1864 he wrote many songs which became popular favorites although the name of the minstrel, Edwin P. Christy, appeared on some of them as the composer: they include *Louisiana Belle; Uncle Ned; Oh! Susannah; My Old Kentucky Home; Old Dog Tray; Massa's in de Cold Ground; Gentle Annie; Old Black Joe; Camptown Races; Nelly Was a Lady; Ellen Bayne; Hard Times Come Again No More; Jeanie With the Light Brown Hair; Nelly Bly; Oh, Boys,* *Carry Me 'Long; Beautiful Dreamer,* his last song. Foster wrote more than two hundred songs for many of which he accepted fifty copies in lieu of royalty: those on royalty never yielded him returns commensurate with the claims of the publishers in regard to their unquestionably enormous sales. The latter part of his life was marred by excessive drinking, resulting in his premature death in a Bowery lodging house at the age of thirty-eight. A collection of Fosteriana owned by Josiah Kirby Lilly was installed in the Stephen Foster Memorial on the campus of the University of Pittsburgh in 1937.

Foucquet, Jean, see **Fouquet, Jean.**

Fouetté, in ballet a step in which one leg is turned while the other accompanies it with a whipping motion. A skilled dancer can execute as many as thirty consecutive turns in this manner without lowering the working leg.

Fountain, in architecture and sculpture the term applied to an assemblage of jets through which water flows naturally or by artificial means. Greek shrines were built over springs, and the Romans fed their numerous fountains by means of aqueducts. In the Gothic period fountains resembled small pyramidal buildings, and during the Renaissance they were often constructed in the form of several flat basins surmounting each other. Italy and France have produced the finest fountains: Rome, Naples, Genoa, Florence, and Paris are replete with masterpieces of this character.

Fountain of Youth, a mythical spring said in the Indian legend of Central America to have the power of healing the sick and of restoring youth through its water. Several Spanish explorers, including Ponce de Leon and De Soto, conducted extensive expeditions in search of it during the 16th century.

Fountains of Rome (Resphigi), a symphonic poem by Ottorino Resphigi composed in 1916; first performed at Rome in 1918 under the direction of Arturo Toscanini, and at New York by the Philharmonic-Symphony Orchestra under Josef Stransky in 1919. The four sections are described as follows: I *The Fountain of Valle Giulia at Dawn* depicts a pastoral landscape and passing cattle; II *The Triton Fountain at Morn,* a call summoning troops of naiads and tritons who dance between the jets of water; III *The Fountain of Trevi at Mid-Day,* triumphal passage of Neptune's chariot across the water's surface; IV *The Villa Medici Fountain at Sunset,* the nostalgic sunset air is full of tolling bells, birds twittering, leaves rustling which peacefully die into the silence of night. There is a Victor recording by the New York Philharmonic-Symphony Orchestra directed by John Barbirolli.

Fouqué, Baron Friedrich de la Motte (1777-1843), German romantic poet and novelist highly regarded during his period: his works include *Romances from the Vale of Roncesval; The Story of the Noble Knight Galmy and a Fair Duchess of Brittany; Alwin;* a hero drama, *Sigurd the Snake-Killer; Undine; Sintram and His Companions.* He was highly versed in Scandinavian mythology, and the legendary tales of medieval France on which he based many of his romances.

Fouquet, Jean or **Jehan** (c.1416-1485), French painter who traveled in Italy, and painted a portrait of Pope Eugenius IV in 1445: he is regarded as one of the most distinguished representatives of early French art combined with that of the Flemings. He was court painter to Louis XI, and his illustrations, portraits, and altarpieces make evident his importance: among them is a diptych representing Agnes Sorel as the Virgin, and forty miniatures from a *Book of Hours.*

Fouquet or **Foucquet, Nicolas** (1615-1680), French nobleman, known as the Marquis de Belle-Isle, who acted as superintendent of finance from 1652 to 1661 for Louis XIV: he was accused of peculation in 1661, and after a trial lasting three years, was first sentenced to banishment, and finally to life imprisonment. He was an inveterate collector of works of art, and the generous patron of MOLIERE, LA FONTAINE, SCARRON, and many other men of letters. Alexandre DUMAS, PERE has made him a martyr in the historical romance, *The Man in the Iron Mask.*

Four Horsemen of the Apocalypse, see **Apocalypse.**

Four Saints in Three Acts, a unique work in operatic form: libretto by Gertrude STEIN, and music by Virgil THOMSON; produced at New York in 1934. Some of the odd features are the lack of plot, the arrangement in four instead of three acts, and the appearance of not four, but fifteen saints. The comment of Burns MANTLE, dramatic critic of the New York *Daily News,* is well worth quoting: "A colored cast against a cellophane setting representing visionary Spain: libretto incomprehensible. It prevails by virtue of its music . . . a suave and charming score."

Four Stars, in drama a method of indicating the highest degree of praise for a play by a critic. It was first used by the New York *Daily News* with fewer and sometimes fractional stars indicating lesser degrees of praise: critics of the films have also made use of the idea.

Fowler, Frank (1852-1910), American painter who studied with Edwin White at Florence, and with CAROLUS-DURAN in Paris whom he assisted in painting the fresco, *The Apotheosis of Marie de Medici,* in the Luxembourg Museum. His paintings include *Young Bacchus; Fatima;* also portraits of Governors Tilden and Flower at the State Capitol, Albany, N. Y. He also published textbooks on oil, portrait and figure painting.

Fowler, Gene (1890-), American biographer and novelist who has had a wide experience in the sports department of journalism: his works include *Trumpet in the Dust* (1930); *Shoe the Wild Mare; The Great Magoo,* a play in collaboration with Ben HECHT; *Timber Line; Father Goose; The Mighty Barnum; The Story of Mack Sennett; Salute to Yesterday; Illusion in Java.*

Fox, Della (1872-1913), American actress and singer who appeared first in a juvenile Gilbert and Sullivan company: among the productions in which she was featured are *Castles in the Air, Wang* and *Panjandrum* with De Wolf HOPPER; *The Wedding Day* with Lillian RUSSELL and Jefferson DE ANGELIS; *Fleur de Lis; The Little Trooper; The Little Host.*

Fox, Fontaine (1884-), American cartoonist who originated the "Toonerville Trolley" cartoon which appears in the New York SUN and affiliated newspapers. His books include *Fontaine Fox's Funny Folk* (1917), and *Toonerville Trolley and Other Cartoons.*

Fox, John, Jr. (1863-1919), American novelist educated at Transylvania and Harvard University, and war correspondent in the Spanish-American and Russo-Japanese wars. His works include *The Kentuckians* (1899); *The Little Shepherd of Kingdom Come; A Knight of the Cumberland; The Trail of the Lonesome Pine; The Heart of the Hills; Erskine: Pioneer.* He also wrote several volumes of short stories.

Foy, Eddie (1857-1928), American stage comedian, real name Edward Fitzgerald, who first appeared in vaudeville and minstrel shows: among the productions in which he was starred are *Cinderella* or *The Crystal Slipper; Bluebeard; Sinbad the Sailor; Ali Baba; Topsy Turvey; The Strollers; The Earl and the Girl.* His son, **Eddie Foy, Jr.,** is a successful screen actor.

Foyatier, Denis (1793-1863), French sculptor whose place in the Hall of Fame is assured by his magnificent equestrian statue of JOAN OF ARC at Orléans in France. In time of peace a day rarely passes when provincial visitors to the city fail to place bouquets of garden flowers at the foot of the statue.

Fra Angelico, see **Angelico, Fra Giovanni da Fiesole.**

Fra Bartolommeo, see **Bartolommeo di Pagholo del Fattorino, Fra.**

Fra Diamante (c.1430-c.1492), Italian painter who was a pupil of Fra Filippo LIPPI with whom he worked on frescoes in churches at Prato and Spoleto. He imitated his master to such an extent that it is impossible to separate his work from that of Lippi even in the frescoes at Spoleto which he completed after Lippi's death.

Fragonard, Jean Honoré (1732-1806), French painter who studied with Jean CHARDIN, François BOUCHER, Pietro CORTONA, and Giovanni TIEPOLO: later he became court painter for Louis XV. His notable works include *Coresus Sacrificing Himself to Save Callirhoe; The Visit; The Fountain of Love; Bathing Women;* a series of five paintings called *The Progress of Love in the Hearts of Young Girls; The Jealousy of Childhood; Gardens of Fontainebleau; Happy Motherhood; The Music Lesson; The Sleeping Bacchante.*

Frampton, Sir George James (1860-1928), English sculptor of the idealistic school who frequently used color on his statues: the most notable are *Peter Pan* and the *Edith Cavell Memorial.*

Françaix, Jean (1912-   ), French composer who studied with Isidor PHILIPP and Nadia BOULANGER at the Paris Conservatory: his works, which have been successfully performed at the international music festivals and in the United States, include several ballets; a symphony; a concertino and a concerto for piano; chamber music and piano pieces.

France, Anatole (1844-1924), French novelist and critic whose real name was Jacques Anatole François Thibault. His first literary success was a novel, *The Crime of Sylvester Bonnard* (1881); it gained a prize from the French Academy, but was later described by its author as "insipid and tedious." A long series of successful novels and other works followed; those available in English include *Mother of Pearl; Thaïs; The Life of Joan of Arc; Penguin Island; At the Sign of the Reine Pedauque; The Revolt of the Angels; The Man Who Married a Dumb Wife; The Human Tragedy; The Seven Wives of Bluebeard; The Bloom of Life.*

Francesca da Rimini, Italian noblewoman of the 13th century: she was the daughter of Guido da Polenta, who married her by proxy to Giovanni Malatesta, Lord of Rimini and nicknamed "The Lame" because of a deformity. Dante immortalized her in the "Inferno," an episode in the *Divine Comedy:* Francesca tells him of her love for Paolo, younger brother of Giovanni, who killed them both when he discovered their guilt. Tragedies on the subject were written by Silvio Pellico and George BOKER; poems by Gabriel D'ANNUNZIO and Leigh HUNT; operas by Ambroise THOMAS, Serge RACHMANINOFF, and Francesco Leoni; a symphonic poem by Peter Ilich TSCHAIKOWSKY; paintings by INGRES, CABANEL, WATTS, and SCHEFFER.

Francesca da Rimini (Ballet), (a) a ballet produced at the Maryinsky Theatre at St. Petersburg in 1915: libretto and choreography by Michel FOKINE: music adapted from Peter Ilich TSCHAIKOWSKY's symphonic fantasia with the same title. (b) a ballet produced at the Royal Opera House, Covent Garden, London, in 1937: libretto by David LICHINE and Henry Clifford; choreography by David Lichine; music also adapted from the Tschaikowsky fantasia. The plot follows along the lines of DANTE'S tale, and also reflects the atmosphere of the painting by Jean INGRES.

Francesca da Rimini (Symphonic Fantasia), composed by Peter Ilich TSCHAIKOWSKY in 1876: it was first played at Moscow in 1877. The score bears a preface in which the composer quotes a passage from the fifth canto of Dante's "Inferno" which reads as follows: "Dante, coming into the second circle of Hell, sees the punishment of carnal sinners. . . . Among these he meets with Francesca da Rimini, who relates her story." There is a Victor recording by the New York Philharmonic-Symphony Orchestra with John Barbirolli, and a Columbia recording by the London Symphony Orchestra under Sir Thomas Beecham.

Francescatti, Zino (1905-   ), French violinist who studied with his father who was a pupil of Camillo SIVORI, the latter being the only pupil of Niccoló PAGANINI. He scored a success in the BEETHOVEN violin concerto at ten, and made a formal debut with the Paris Conservatory Orchestra in 1927, followed by tours through Europe and South America. Since 1939 he has appeared with the New York Philharmonic-Symphony Orchestra, the Chicago Symphony Orchestra, and several other major orchestras: he was one of the four violinists selected to appear during the centennial season (1941-42) of the New York Philharmonic-Symphony Orchestra.

Franceschi, Piero de (c.1418-1492), Italian painter also known as Piero della Francesca: he studied and worked with Domenico VENEZIANO, assisting him in painting the chapel of St. Egidio in the church of St. Maria Novello at Florence. His works include *History of the Cross at Arezzo; Resurrection; Nativity; Baptism of Christ; Hercules; Triumph of Chivalry;* also a treatise on perspective.

Franceschini, Baldassare (1611-1689), Italian painter who studied with Cosimo Daddi and Matteo Rosselli: his notable works include the oil painting, *St. John the Evangelist;* and a fresco, *Coronation of the Virgin,* in the cupola of the Annuziata at Florence.

Franceschini, Marcantonio (1648-1729), Italian painter who studied with Carlo CIGNANI and also worked with him. His notable creations include a history of the Republic of Genoa in pictures at the Hall of Public Counsel; *Birth of Adonis; Venus and Cupid; Joseph and Potiphar's Wife;* also many frescoes in churches and palaces at Genoa and Bologna. He developed an entirely original style bearing little resemblance to that of Cignani.

Franchetti, Alberto (1860-   ), French dramatic composer who studied with Felix Draeseke and at the Munich Conservatory, later becoming director of the Cherubini Conservatory in Florence. His compositions include a dramatic legend, *Asrael,* and the operas *Christopher Columbus* and *Germania:* also orchestral works and a set of variations for string quartet.

Franchomme, Auguste Joseph (1808-1884), French violoncellist who studied at the PARIS CONSERVATORY, and founded a series of classical concerts with Delphin ALARD and Charles HALLE. He taught at the Paris Conservatory, and was intimate with both Felix MENDELSSOHN and Frédéric CHOPIN. In 1819 he purchased the Stradivarius violoncello,. formerly belonging to Jean Duport, for $5000: he composed a concerto and solo pieces for his instrument.

Francia or **Francesco Raibolini** (1450-1517), Italian painter who was apprenticed to a goldsmith, becoming expert in this art as well as that of engraving dies for medals. After making friends with Andrea MANTEGNA, he turned to painting: among his notable works are *Virgin Enthroned with St. Augustine; Judith and Holophernes; Crucifixion; Child and St. Anna; Virgin Adoring the Infant Jesus.* He is credited with having more than two hundred pupils, among whom was the famous engraver, Marcantonio RAIMONDI.

Franciabigio, Mercantonio (1482-1525), Italian painter who studied with Mariotto ALBERTINELLI and Piero di COSIMO. His works of note include *Marriage of the Virgin* in collaboration with Andrea del SARTO: he mutilated this painting because the friars uncovered the canvas before it was completed; *Meeting of the Baptist with Jesus; The Triumph of Cicero; Young Man With a Letter; Calumny of Apelles; Bathsheba Bathing.*

Francis, Kay (1905-), American screen actress educated in private schools: she has played leading roles in many important films including *Raffles; For the Defense; One Way Passage; Cynara; Storm at Daybreak; Mandalay; Wonder Bar; British Agent; I Found Stella Parish; The Man Who Lost Himself; Charley's Aunt; Always in My Heart.*

Franck, César Auguste (1822-1890), Belgian composer, born in Liége, who toured Belgium as a piano virtuoso at eleven. He studied at the PARIS CONSERVATORY from 1837 to 1842 under Pierre Zimmerman and François Benoist, succeeding the latter in 1872 as professor of organ at the Paris Conservatory, and as organist at the Church of Saint Clotilde. He remained at this post until his death: his pupils at the Paris Conservatory included Vincent d'INDY, Ernest CHAUSSON; Guy ROPARTZ, Gabriel PIERNE and many others who later became distinguished composers. He developed a style of composition in which individuality and lofty ideas are expressed in classic form, and is justly regarded as the leading composer of the French school in and after his time. His works include several operas; four oratorios; a symphony and three symphonic poems; *Variations Symphoniques* for piano and orchestra; a quintet for piano and strings, a violin sonata; church music; organ pieces; *Prelude, Chorale and Fugue* and other pieces for piano.

Francken or **Franck,** a family of Flemish painters who worked at Antwerp during the 16th and 17th centuries. Of the eldest member of the family, **Nicholas of Herenthals** (c.1520-1680), nothing is known except that he was a painter. His eldest son, **Hieronymus Francken** (c.1540-1610), was a pupil of Frans FLORIS and was employed in the decoration of Fontainebleau: among his works is *Beheading of John the Baptist.* His brother, **Frans Francken I** (c.1542-1616), also studied under Frans Floris, and one of his paintings, *Christ on the Road to Golgotha,* is in the Dresden Museum. Another brother, **Ambrose Francken** (1544-1618), also worked at Fontainebleau, and created several fine works including *The Miracle of the Loaves and Fishes* and *The Martyrdom of St. Crispin.* Frans Francken I had three sons, one of whom, **Hieronymus Francken II** (1578-1623), painted an ambitious work entitled *Horatius Cocles Defending the Sublician Bridge.* Another of his sons, **Frans Francken II** (1581-1642), was the creator of several works which place him as the most distinguished painter in the family: they include *Adoration of the Virgin; Seven Works of Charity; The Prodigal Son; Woman Taken in Adultery.*

Francucci, Innocenzo da, see **Imola, Innocenzo da.**

Frank, Bruno (1887-), German novelist educated at Munich, Leipzig, and Strassburg and other German universities: in 1937 the THEATRE GUILD produced his plays, *Storm Over Patsy* and *Young Madame Conte.* Among his works published in English are *The Days of the King; Trenck; Twelve Thousand,* a play; *The Persians are Coming; A Man Called Cervantes; Lost Heritage.*

Frank, Leonhard (1882-), German novelist whose first success was a novel, *The Robber Band* (1914): his works include *Carl and Anna,* a short story successfully dramatized; *Brother and Sister; The Singers; In the Last Coach and Other Stories; The Cause of the Crime; Three of the Three Million.*

Frank, Waldo (1889-), American novelist and essayist educated at Yale University: his works include *The Unwelcome Man* (1917); *Our America; City Block; Virgin Spain; The Re-Discovery of America; The Death and Birth of David Markand; The Bridegroom Cometh.*

Franken, Rose (1895-), American novelist and dramatist: her works include *Pattern* (1925); *Another Language,* a play; *Mr. Dooley, Jr.,* a juvenile play; *Twice Born; Claudia; Claudia and David; The Book of Claudia; Another Claudia.* Her play, *Claudia,* was a great success, and adapted to the screen.

Frankenstein, the principal character in a romance published by Mrs. Mary Shelley in 1818: a young medical student creates a live monster from materials gathered from bodies out of graves and the dissecting room. The creature murders the student's friend and his wife, and finally comes to an end in the ocean. Horror motion pictures on the subject have achieved a considerable degree of success in the United States with Bela LUGOSI and Boris KARLOFF enacting horror roles.

Frankie and Johnnie, the title of the most popular ballad ever sung in the United States: it has been attributed to various sources, the story it relates assigned to many different localities. More than three hundred variations in verse and tune were sung during the second half of the 19th century.

Frankl, Ludwig August (1810-1894), Austrian poet whose works include *A Lay of Hapsburg* (1832); an epic poem, *Christopher Columbus;* a Biblical poem, *Rachael;* a heroic poem, *John of Austria.* His poem, *The University,* was the first work not subjected to government censorship in Austria.

Franklin, Benjamin (1706-1790), American statesman, diplomat, printer, editor, and author: among his activities of interest in this volume are the publication of *Poor Richard's Almanac* from 1732 to 1757, and an *Autobiography* edited by John Bigelow in 1868. John Brougham wrote a play, *Franklin,* in 1846, and there are biographies by W. Cabell Bruce (1918), Bernard Faÿ (1929), V. W. Crane (1936), and Carl Van Doren (1938).

Franklin, Frederick (1915-), English ballet dancer who studied with Nicholas LEGAT after appearing with MISTINGUETTE. He was a member of the Markova-Dolin Company, and joined the Ballet Russe in 1938.

Franko, Nahan (1861-1930), American violinist and conductor, brother of Sam FRANKO, who studied the violin as a child in Berlin, and toured America in 1869 with Carlotta PATTI. In 1870 he returned to Europe for further study with August WILHELMJ and Joseph JOACHIM. After playing in the THEODORE THOMAS ORCHESTRA and other similar organizations, he became concertmaster at the METROPOLITAN OPERA HOUSE in 1883, and was the first American to conduct opera there. He remained at the Metropolitan until 1907, after which he organized his own orchestra for playing in concert halls and at private functions.

Franko, Sam (1857-1937), American violinist and conductor, brother of Nahan FRANKO, who studied the violin in Europe with Joseph JOACHIM, Henri VIEUXTEMPS, and Hubert LEONARD, and toured France and Germany for several years. He was a member of the Mendelssohn Quintette Club, Boston, in 1880, and concertmaster of the THEODORE THOMAS ORCHESTRA in 1884. In 1900 he organized a series of "Concerts of Old Music," presenting chamber music of the 17th and 18th centuries, and introduced Arnold DOLMETSCH and his family, playing viols and recorders. From 1910 to 1915 he was head of the violin department of the Stern Conservatory in Berlin, finally returning to New York, where he taught until his death. He made numerous transcriptions for the violin, and wrote an autobiography, *Chords and Discords,* published in 1938.

Franz, Robert (1815-1892), German song composer whose family name was Knauth, changed in 1847 by official permission. He studied at Dessau under Franz Schneider from 1835-37, and then devoted six years to the study of BACH, BEETHOVEN, HANDEL, and SCHUBERT works. His first series of twelve songs were praised by SCHUMANN and LISZT: his works include 350 songs distinguished for their purity and dignity although they do not rank with those of BRAHMS, SCHUMANN, SCHUBERT, or Hugo WOLF.

Franzen, Frans Michael (1772-1847), Swedish poet, born in Finland, who held the post of professor of literature and ethics at the University of Abo: when Russia annexed Finland, he returned to Sweden and published several volumes of poetry (1824-1836), in simple, idyllic style in striking contrast to the customary didactic style of Swedish verse.

Franzos, Karl Emil (1848-1904), Austrian novelist who became a newspaper correspondent, and traveled extensively in Europe and Asia. His first work, *Semi-Asia* (1876), sketches of life in southern Russia and Rumania, was enormously popular and translated into several languages: his novels include *A Struggle for the Right, The Old Doctor's God,* and *The Truth-Seeker.*

Fraser, Charles (1782-1860), American painter who first practised law for several years, but after 1818 devoted himself to art: he painted more than 300 miniatures and 140 historical pictures and landscapes exhibited at Charleston, S. C., in 1857.

Fraser, James Earle (1876-), American sculptor whose notable works include *The End of the Trail;* the tomb of *Bishop Potter* in the Cathedral of St. John the Divine, New York; *Alexander Hamilton; Lewis and Clark;* the monument to *Thomas Jefferson* at Jefferson City, Mo.; also portrait busts of Theodore Roosevelt and Augustus SAINT-GAUDENS. He also designed the Indian and buffalo heads on the American five-cent coin: his wife, **Laura Gardin Fraser,** is also a distinguished sculptor.

Frauenlob, see **Meissen, Heinrich von.**

Fraunces' Tavern, a restaurant in New York City at the corner of Broad and Pearl Streets: the building was originally the residence of Étienne De Lancey, a French Huguenot refugee. It was built in 1700, and purchased by Samuel Fraunces in 1762. His daughter foiled a plot by some Tory innkeepers to poison General Washington when he first took command in New York. The tavern served only the finest food and wines: it became the haunt of American patriots before the Revolution, and of British officers during the occupation. After the war ended, Washington took leave of his officers there. The tavern still continues to serve its customers, and many historically interesting objects are to be seen there.

Frazee, John (1790-1852), American sculptor who was entirely self-taught: his notable works include busts of *Daniel Webster, John Marshall,* and *John Wells.* He worked in New Jersey and New York although many of his finest creations are in the Boston Athenaeum.

Fréchette, Louis Honoré (1839-1908), Canadian poet and journalist who was associate editor of the *Journal de Québec;* his works include *My Leisure Hours* (1863); *Voice of an Exile;* an epic poem, *The Legend of a People; Birds of Snow.* He translated several Shakespearean plays for the Théâtre Français, Paris, and his poem, *Northern Blooms,* was crowned by the French Academy.

Frederic, Harold (1856-1898), American journalist who lived in London for some years as correspondent for the New York *Times:* his novels include *In the Valley* (1890); *The Copperhead,* a story of the Civil War; *March Hares; The Market Place; The Damnation of Theron Ware,* a character study considered his finest work.

Frederick, John Towner (1893-), American editor and novelist educated at Iowa State University: in 1915 he founded a magazine, *The Midland,* originally conceived as a regional periodical, but soon becoming national in reputation because of its discoveries of new authors including Paul Engle, Marquis Childs, and Albert Halper. Frederick's novels include *Druida* (1923) and *Green Bush:* since 1938 he has conducted a radio program, "Of Men and Books," for the discussion of new books on the Columbia Broadcasting Company network.

Frederick the Great (1712-1786), a king of Prussia, correct title, Frederick II: he has a place in this volume because of his interest in literature and music. He wrote and spoke in French, despising German as the "language of boors" according to his own statement, although he prophesied a great future for it in an essay written in French on German literature. Among his literary works are *Memoires pour server à l'histoire de Brandebourg,* valuable because of light thrown on the motivation of some of his acts. He was also an admirer of RACINE and VOLTAIRE who visited him at Potsdam, and with whom he had frequent violent arguments. Frederick was also a composer and a performer on the flute which he studied with Johann QUANTZ. He erected a new opera house at Berlin in 1742, ordered regular singing in German schools, interested himself in the newly-invented pianos made by SILBERMANN, and wrote more than one hundred compositions for the flute in addition to an opera.

Fredro, Alexander (1793-1876), Polish dramatist whose comedies were so popular in his native country that he was called "the Molière of Poland": they include *Mr. Moneybags* (1821); *Ladies and Hussars; Man and Wife; Revenge.* He was the first of the Polish dramatists to write original plays instead of seeking material in French farces.

Freeman, Douglas Southall (1886-), American editor and author educated at Richmond College and Johns Hopkins University: his works include a four-volume biography of General Robert E. Lee (1934-35) which received the Pulitzer Prize for an American biography in 1935.

Freeman, Harold Weber (1899-), English novelist who was educated at Oxford and served in World War I: his works include *Joseph and His Brothers* (1928); *Down in the Valley; Fathers of Their People; Pond Hall's Progress; Hester and Her Family; Andrew to the Lions; His Own Place.*

Freeman, Mary Eleanor Wilkins (1852-1930), American short story writer and novelist partly educated at Mount Holyoke Seminary: her tales of the rigidly circumspect social life of rural New England have a niche of their own in American literature: the choicest of her short stories are included in *A Humble Romance and Other Stories* (1887) and *A New England Nun and Other Stories* (1911). In 1927 another selection of her stories was published under the editorship of Henry W. Lanier.

Freeman, Richard Austin (1862-), English writer of scientific detective fiction who was a surgeon by profession, and served in this capacity during World War I. Christopher Morley has expressed the opinion that Freeman's detective character, Dr. John Thorndyke, is "the most carefully established crime savant since Sherlock Holmes." The "Thorndyke Cases" began with the publication of *John Thorndyke's Cases* in 1909: he has written many sequels, and several other scientific detective stories on different themes.

Freer Gallery of Art (Washington, D. C.), a collection of paintings and art objects donated by Charles Lang Freer (1856-1919), American capitalist and connoisseur of art, to the Smithsonian Institution with an additional gift of $1,000,000 for a building designed in accordance with his ideas. The collection comprises many paintings and etchings by James WHISTLER and other American artists; also Chinese and Japanese paintings and prints, and an unequaled collection of antique glazed pottery from the Orient.

Free Verse (Vers libre), in poetry the term for rhythmical verse as distinguished from metrical verse: the form is used by European, English, and American poets desiring freedom from the conventional restrictions of metre.

Freischütz, Der, grand opera in three acts: libretto by Johann Friedrich Kind; music by Carl Maria von WEBER; first produced at Berlin in 1821, and in New York in 1825 at the Park Theatre in English. The story is: Max, a young hunter who is in love with Agatha, cannot shoot sufficiently well to win her hand in a contest started by her father. Caspar: another suitor for Agatha's hand, has sold himself to the fiend, Zamiel; in exchange for magic bullets that never miss. He persuades Max to cast magic bullets for himself; Max is successful, but his seventh bullet he believes kills Agatha, who has appeared to him in the form of a dove. The fiend, Zamiel, however, has caused the bullet to pierce the heart of Caspar; he claims the latter as his victim and Agatha becomes the bride of Max. The overture to the opera is a favorite with concert, radio, and record music lovers: there is a Victor recording by the Boston "Pops" Orchestra under Arthur Fiedler, and a Columbia recording by the London Symphony Orchestra with Sir Thomas Beecham.

Frémiet, Emmanuel (1824-1910), French sculptor who studied with François RUDE, and specialized in sculptures of animals and figures in armor: his works include *Gazelle; Wounded Bear; Wounded Dog; Roman Horseman; Chief of the Gauls; Faun Playing with Bear Cub; Gorilla Carrying Off a Woman; Sea Horses and Dolphins; Stone Age Man.* He also executed equestrian statues of Napoleon I, Louis d'Orleans, and Joan of Arc.

Fremstad, Olive (1870-), Swedish dramatic soprano who came to the United States as a child of twelve. She first studied the piano, and later started cultivating her voice: in 1893 she trained under Lilli LEHMANN at Berlin, and made her debut in 1895 at Cologne in *Il Trovatore.* After singing at Bayreuth and for several years at Cologne, Munich, Vienna, and London opera houses, she made an extraordinarily successful debut in 1903 at the METROPOLITAN OPERA HOUSE, New York, as Sieglinde in *The Valkyrie,* remaining with the company for eleven years in leading soprano and alto roles; the latter rendered possible because of the remarkable range of her voice. She was particularly successful in the roles of Isolde and Brunnhilde.

French, Alice (1850-1934), American short story writer and novelist who used the pen name "Octave Thanet": her works, which were chiefly of Midwestern life, include: *Knitters in the Sun*

(1887); *Expiation; A Book of True Lovers; Missionary Sheriff; The Man of the Hour; The Lion's Share; A Step on the Stair.*

French, Daniel Chester (1850-1931), American sculptor who studied with John Quincy Adams WARD, and under Thomas BALL in Florence. His numerous and varied works include *The Minute Man,* unveiled on the centenary of the battle of Concord; *Death Staying the Hand of the Sculptor; John Harvard; Ralph Waldo Emerson;* the great *Lincoln* of the Lincoln Memorial, Washington, D. C.; *Alma Mater* at Columbia University, New York; also equestrian statues of General Grant, General Washington, and General Joseph Hooker.

French Academy, The (L'Académie française), an institution for the preservation and purification of the French language established by the order of the king in 1635; the number of members, originally eight, was finally increased to forty, and any vacancy resulting from death was filled through an election held by the members themselves. The Academy went out of existence during the French Revolution in 1793, but was restored in 1795 although the reorganization bore little resemblance to the original. At the present time the language and literature classes are the most important; the members are known as "The Immortals," but as many great French authors and scholars—for example, Alphonse DAUDET— were never elected, its influence on literature has been seriously questioned.

French Horn, a brass wind instrument of conical bore played with a funnel-shaped mouthpiece: it is an improved form of the medieval hunting horn, and is said to have been introduced into the orchestra by Jean Baptiste LULLY in 1664. Johann Sebastian BACH employed two horns in the BRANDENBURG CONCERTOS in 1721: two horns became standard in orchestras until BEETHOVEN added the 3rd and 4th horn. Richard WAGNER used eight horns in some of his music dramas.

French Revolution, The, the name given to the internal conflict in France which began in 1789 and ended, according to some authorities, in 1795 at the close of the Convention, or according to other historians in 1804 at the abandonment of the Consulate. Painters, poets, writers of historical fiction and composers have found an inexhaustible source of inspiration for artistic endeavor in the events and personalities directly connected with the Revolution.

Freneau, Philip (1752-1832), American poet educated at Princeton University who was a schoolmate of James Madison, and on friendly terms with Thomas JEFFERSON: he owned and captained the privateer "Aurora" in 1780, and after his capture and release by the British wrote the poem *The British Prison Ship.* His poems include *The American Village* (1772); *The Home of Night; Eutaw Springs; The Indian Student; The Wild Honeysuckle.*

Frenssen, Gustav (1863-), German clergyman and novelist who first became famous as a preacher: in 1901 his novel, *Jorn Uhl,* became a best-seller in Germany, enjoying a sale of more than 200,000 copies in its first year, and eventually over 400,000 copies. His works published in English include *Holyland; The Three Comrades; The Pastor of Poggsee; Peter Moor's Journey to Southwest Africa.*

Frére, Charles Théodore (1815-1888), French painter who studied with Léon COGNIET in Paris, and traveled with the Empress Eugénie on her trip to Egypt. His notable paintings include *Caravan at a Ford; Cairo; Bazaar in Beyrout; Ruins of Karnac at Thebes; Jerusalem from the Valley of Jehoshaphat; The Pyramids of Gizeh.* His brother, **Pierre Édouard Frére** (1819-1886), was also a painter who studied at the ECOLE DES BEAUX-ARTS and with Paul DELAROCHE. His numerous works include *Preparing for Church; Going to School; The Flute Lesson; Storm in a Tub; Women Spinning; The Reading Lesson.*

Fresco, in painting a mural executed in water color on the fresh, damp plaster of a wall: the colors are applied to small areas which are kept damp, and frequently gone over two or three times to insure their brilliancy and permanency. The additional coats must be added on the same day as the first coat is applied. Before the 13th century frescoes were more or less primitive: later painters including CIMABUE, GIOTTO, TIEPOLO, MASSACCIO, GHIRLANDAIO, RAPHAEL, MICHELANGELO, and TITIAN brought the mural art to its highest degree of perfection in the churches and cathedrals of Italy.

Frescobaldi, Girolamo (1583-1643), Italian organist and composer who studied with Luzzaschi at Ferrara, and became organist at St. Peter's at Rome in 1608, remaining there, except for six years at Florence, until his death. His compositions include a great variety of church music and works for organ: they are distinguished by innovations in harmony, new developments in form, and improvements in notation.

Fresnoy, Charles Alphonse Du (1611-1668), French poet and painter whose fame rests not on his paintings, but on his poem in Latin entitled *De Arte Graphica* (Of Graphic Arts). It contains his observations and deductions on the art of painting, and was written during a long period of study in Italy: it may be regarded as a critical treatise of great value to students. John DRYDEN made an English prose translation.

Fret, in musical instruments, such as the mandolin, guitar, and zither, a narrow piece of wood, metal, or ivory which crosses the fingerboard: by pressing the finger against a string the length of the string is shortened, and the pitch raised.

Fret work, in architecture a design in flat or semicircular molding applied to a flat surface, and varied by interlacing. It was perhaps first used in Greek temples although something similar has been discovered on the ceilings of tombs in Egypt.

Freytag, Gustav (1816-1895), German poet, novelist, and dramatist: his plays include *The Bridal Tour* (1844); *The Savant; The Valentine; The Journalists,* the latter his greatest success. He also wrote two very popular novels entitled *Debit and Credit* and *The Lost Manuscript;* also a cycle of six stories, portraying the progress of German civilization, and called *The Ancestors.*

Friars, The, an association of theatrical press agents founded in 1904 by Charles Emerson Cook, Channing POLLOCK and others, which is officially known as the Press Agents Association. The clubhouse is known as the "monastery"; the chief officer as the "abbot," and the occasional public and private performances as "frolics."

Frick Museum (New York), a collection of 14th to 19th century paintings and art objects assembled by **Henry Clay Frick** (1849-1919), capitalist and art collector, and donated to the public, along with an endowment of $15,000,000, for display not in the conventional museum, but as the furnishings and decoration of his early twentieth-century home on Fifth Avenue, New York City. The principal part of the collection consists of 14th to 19th century paintings by Italian, French, Spanish, English, and Dutch masters. There are also bronzes and portrait busts; Chinese and French porcelains; English, French, and Italian period furniture, and rare Persian rugs.

Fricka, a character in Richard Wagner's THE RING OF THE NIBELUNGS: she is the wife of WOTAN and the goddess of marriage who objects violently to the union of Siegmund and Sieglinde, and forces her husband to permit Hunding to kill Siegmund.

Friedberg, Carl (1872-), German pianist who studied with Clara SCHUMANN and Engelbert HUMPERDINCK. He made his debut at Vienna in 1892, and toured the United States in 1914 with great success, becoming professor of piano in 1916 at the INSTITUTE OF MUSICAL ART, New York, and numbering among his pupils Percy GRAINGER, Ethel LEGINSKA, Germaine Schnitzer, and Elly NEY. He is also distinguished as a chamber music artist.

Friedheim, Arthur (1859-1932), German pianist and composer born in St. Petersburg, who studied with Franz LISZT and Anton RUBINSTEIN. He toured the United States in 1891 and subsequent years, also teaching at the Chicago College of Music in 1897, the Canadian Academy of Music at Toronto in 1921, and finally settling in New York where he remained until his death. His works include an opera, a concerto, and numerous pieces for piano.

Friedlander, Leo (1889-), American sculptor trained in New York, Paris, Brussels, and at the American Academy in Rome: his numerous works include sculptures for the Washington Memorial Arch at Valley Forge, Pa.; heads of BEETHOVEN and BACH at the Eastman School of Music, Rochester, N. Y.; colossal figures at the Masonic Temple, Detroit; the central pediment for the Museum of the City of New York; the equestrian groups, *Lewis and Clark* and *The Covered Wagon* for the Oregon State Capitol.

Friedman, Ignaz (1882-), Polish pianist and composer who studied with Theodor LESCHETIZKY

in Vienna. After concertizing in Europe and South America, he toured the United States in 1920 with great success, and is now residing in the United States. He has edited the works of SCHUMANN, LISZT, and CHOPIN, of whom he is a noted interpreter, and has composed many fine works for the piano.

Friends of Music, The Society of, an organization founded by Mrs. Harriet Lanier for the purpose of presenting rare and unknown musical works in the orchestral, chamber music, and operatic fields. Its first concert, conducted by Franz KNEISEL with the Metropolitan Opera House Orchestra, was given in 1913: among the works presented before the society was discontinued in 1931 were *Chamber Symphony* by Arnold Schönberg; Gustave MAHLER's *Eighth Symphony* and *Song of the Earth;* works by Ernest BLOCH; Arthur HONEGGER's *King David;* PURCELL's *Dido and Aeneas;* also many BACH cantatas.

Fries, Wulf (1825-1902), German violoncellist who was chiefly self-taught: he came to Boston, Mass., in 1847, and joined the Mendelssohn Quintette Club of which he was 'cellist for twenty-three years. He was a member of several other musical organizations, and exercised considerable influence in Boston as a musician of high attainments.

Frieze, in architecture the part of the entablature between the ARCHITRAVE and the CORNICE: the term is also applied to any oblong, horizontal feature used for decorative purposes. One of the most striking classic examples was the frieze on the wall of the PARTHENON which measured over three feet in height and about five hundred feet in length: a large piece of this is to be seen in the BRITISH MUSEUM.

Friml, Rudolf (1881-), Bohemian pianist and composer who studied at the Prague Conservatory, and toured Europe and the United States in 1900 as accompanist for the violinist, Jan KUBELIK. After his second visit with Kubelik in 1906 he remained in the United States, becoming a distinguished piano virtuoso, and composing many successful light operettas including *The Firefly* (1912); *High Jinks; Katinka; Rose Marie; The Vagabond King.* He has also written many charming piano pieces, and is now (1943) in Hollywood composing music for films.

Frishmuth, Harriet Whitney (1880-), American sculptor who studied with BORGLUM and RODIN, winning the SAINT-GAUDEN's Prize: her works include *Play Days; The Vine; Joy of the Waters; Slav Dancer.* Critics praise the knowledge of anatomy displayed in her nude creations.

Frith, William Powell (1819-1909), English painter who studied with Henry Sass and at the Royal Academy School. His notable works include *The Derby Day; Ramsgate Sands; The Railway Station; Marriage of the Prince of Wales* (the future King Edward VII) commissioned by Queen Victoria; *The Race for Wealth; The Road to Ruin.* His paintings present an accurate, absorbing picture of life in Mid-Victorian England.

Froberger, Johann Jacob (c.1605-1667), German organist and composer who entered the Imperial Choir at Vienna, becoming court organist in 1637, and later studying with FRESCOBALDI at Rome. He made many successful concert tours to Paris and London, and composed toccatas, fantasias, fugues, and partitas for the organ. He was the creator of the suite form comprising the ALLEMANDE, COURANTE, SARABANDE, and GIGUE.

Frohman, Charles (1860-1915), American theatrical manager who entered the business with his brother, Daniel FROHMAN, in 1877 at the Madison Square Theatre, New York, and organized the Charles Frohman Stock Company in 1890, after his first success with Bronson HOWARD's *Shenandoah* in 1899. He opened the Empire Theatre, New York, in 1893, and was also connected with the Criterion, Garrick, Knickerbocker, Lyceum, and Savoy Theatres at various times. Among the stars who appeared under his management were Maude ADAMS, Ethel BARRYMORE, Otis SKINNER, May ROBSON, Margaret ANGLIN, Blanche BATES, Billie BURKE, William GILLETTE, Julia MARLOWE, E. H. SOTHERN, John DREW, Effie SHANNON. In 1897 he produced many of BARRIE's plays at the Duke of York Theatre, London; he also presented Julia MARLOWE and E. H. Sothern in Shakespeare's plays, and in 1910 established a repertory theatre for the production of plays by Barrie, SHAW, GALSWORTHY, and GRANVILLE-BARKER. He was among the victims in the sinking of the Cunard liner, "Lusitania" in 1915.

Frohman, Daniel (1853-1940), American theatrical manager who directed the Madison Square Theatre, New York, with his brother, Charles FROHMAN, in 1877, and founded the Daniel Frohman Stock Company at the Lyceum Theatre in 1887 with David BELASCO as stage manager and Henry MILLER, William FAVERSHAM, Effie SHANNON, Henrietta CROSMAN, May ROBSON, and James K. HACKETT as members of the company. He was associated with his brother in many theatrical enterprises, and for more than fifty years director of the Actor's Fund of America.

Froissart, Jean (c.1337-c.1410), French historian and poet who was a favorite of Queen Philippa in England, and traveled with the Black Prince in 1366. His history of Western Europe, entitled *Chronicles,* is actually a picture of chivalry in the 15th century: he also added verses of his own to a collection by Wenceslaus of Brabant, and gave them the title *Meliador, or The Knight of the Golden Sun.*

Fromentin, Eugène (1820-1876), French painter and author who studied with Louis CABAT, and went to Algiers for inspiration for his paintings. Among his pictures are *The Quarry; Thirst; Gorges of the Chiffa; Moorish Burial; Arab Bivouac; The Nile; The Falcon Hunt.* His literary works include *Masters of Yesterday,* considered one of the finest critiques of art written in the 19th century, and a novel, *Dominique,* dedicated to George SAND, and distinguished for its delicately emotional earnestness.

Frost, Arthur Burdet (1851-1928), American illustrator and humorist who studied with Thomas EAKINS at the Academy of Fine Arts, Philadelphia. He illustrated books by Thomas Nelson PAGE, Mark TWAIN, Joel Chandler HARRIS, and John Kendrick BANGS, and wrote *Stuff and Nonsense* (1884); *The Bull Calf and Other Stories; Carlo.* His drawings for Chandler's "Uncle Remus" stories are world-famous, and he also made illustrations for *Harper's Magazine, Collier's,* and *Scribner's Magazine.*

Frost, Robert (1875-), American poet educated at Dartmouth College and Harvard University: his works include *A Boy's Will* (1913); *North of Boston; New Hampshire,* which received the Pulitzer prize for poetry in 1924; *Collected Poems,* a Pulitzer prize winner in 1931; *A Further Range,* a Pulitzer prize winner in 1937. From 1916 to 1938 he was professor of English at Amherst College; in 1943 another of his works, *A Witness Tree,* again won the Pulitzer prize, making a total of four awards in twenty years.

Fry, William Henry (1813-1864), American journalist and composer who acted as critic for the New York *Tribune* in 1852-53, and worked zealously through his writings and lectures toward greater recognition of American composers. In 1845, his opera, *Leonora,* produced in Philadelphia, was the first work of its kind by an American composer to receive public performance. In 1864 another opera, *Notre Dame de Paris,* was produced in Philadelphia, and later in New York: he also wrote four symphonies with program titles and several cantatas.

Fuchs, Emil (1866-1929), Austrian sculptor, medalist, and painter who executed many commissions for royalty in Europe and England before settling at New York in 1905, and becoming an American citizen. His most famous work is the group in marble labeled *Mother Love:* he also executed portrait busts of *Paderewski, Cecil Rhodes,* and many other famous persons. An autobiography, *With Pencil, Brush and Chisel,* presents interesting memoirs of his career.

Fuertes, Louis Agassiz (1874-1927), American naturalist and artist who created several murals and groups of bird life at the Museum of Natural History, New York: his naturalistic paintings of birds have been a feature of important works on ornithology published in the United States since 1900.

Fugue (It.), in music a term derived from the Latin "fugare," meaning "to pursue." It is applied to the most highly developed form of instrumental or vocal composition in which a theme begun in one part or voice is taken successively by as many parts or voices as are called for in the score. Each part, as it follows or "pursues" the part which precedes it, becomes prominent. A *double fugue* is one in which two or more melodies interweave while acting as accompaniments: in Italian musical nomenclature there are fifty or more terms descriptive of various varieties of fugue.

Führich, Joseph von (1800-1876), Austrian painter and engraver, born in Bohemia, who has been described as a NAZARENE because his pictures were chiefly of a religious character. He studied at the Prague Academy, spending his life in Prague and in Vienna where he became a teacher in the Academy of Art. His works include pictures in the church of St. Nepomuk, and the great series of paintings at the Lerchenfeld church in Vienna. He also illustrated Tieck's *Genofeva*, and several religious books by Thomas à Kempis.

Fulda, Ludwig (1862-   ), German poet and dramatist: he translated plays by MOLIERE, ROSTAND, and IBSEN, and wrote a play, *The Talisman* (1893), which became one of the most popular comedies of the latter part of the 19th century. His plays include *The Wild Chase; The Lost Paradise; The Blockhead; The Shadow of the Ass; The Enchanted Princess.*

Fuleihan, Anis (1900-   ), Cyprian composer and pianist, born in Cyprus, who came to the United States in 1915, continued his study of the piano with Alberto JONAS, and made his debut at AEOLIAN HALL, New York, in 1919. He concertized in America and the Near East, and was awarded a GUGGENHEIM FELLOWSHIP in 1939. His compositions include several orchestral works; a suite for chamber orchestra; two concertos for piano; a concerto for two pianos; a violin concerto; *Symphonie Concertante* for string quartet and orchestra.

Fuller, George (1822-1884), American painter who studied with Henry KIRKE BROWN, worked at the Boston Artists' Association for a time, and in 1857 became a member of the National Academy of Design in New York. He met with so little success that he turned to raising tobacco in Connecticut for many years: it was only in 1876 that recognition was accorded his delicately conceived canvases including *The Turkey Pasture; Romany Girl; She Was a Witch; Nydia; The Quadroon; Winifred Dysart:* the last-named is considered his masterpiece.

Fuller, Loie (1862-1928), American dancer who gave lectures on temperance when a child of six, and toured for some years with stock dramatic companies. She originated the use of a voluminous white skirt which caught the colors of calcium lights as she danced, thereby achieving entirely new effects, becoming a feature attraction not only in the United States, but also in Berlin, Paris, London, and other cities in Europe.

Fuller, Margaret (1810-1850), American author who was prematurely educated by her father at an early age to such an extent that she was studying Latin at six, and was reading the works of SHAKESPEARE, MOLIERE, GOETHE, SCHILLER, and CERVANTES at eight. She was intimate with Ralph Waldo EMERSON, Nathaniel HAWTHORNE, and many other eminent men and women of her day: in 1844-46 she acted as literary critic of the New York *Tribune* at the call of Horace Greeley, and in 1847 she married the Marquis Giovanni Angelo Ossoli while on a visit to Rome, Italy, and did hospital service during the Roman revolution of 1848-49. A life teeming with activity was terminated when she as well as her infant child and husband were drowned when the ship on which

they were coming to the United States foundered off Fire Island Beach. Her works include *Summer on the Lakes* (1843); *Woman in the Nineteenth Century; Literature and Art; At Home and Abroad; Life Without and Life Within; Love Letters:* her memoirs were edited by Ralph Waldo Emerson, William H. Channing, and James F. Clarke in 1852.

Fuller, Thomas (1608-1661), English clergyman, poet, and historian: his one work of real interest today is entitled *The Worthies of England*, which affords an immense amount of biographical data accompanied by acute observations on famous English personages. He also wrote a history of the Crusades entitled *The Holy Warre*.

Fuller-Maitland, John Alexander (1856-1936), English pianist, harpsichordist, and music critic of the London *Times* from 1889 to 1911: he contributed to the first edition of *Grove's Dictionary*, and was chief editor of the second edition (1904-1910). His works include *Schumann* (1884); *Masters of German Music; English Music in the 19th Century; The Age of Bach and Handel*, the 4th volume of the *Oxford History of Music; Joseph Joachim; Brahms; The Spell of Music; Bach's Brandenburg Concertos; The Music of Parry and Stanford.*

Fullerton, Lady Georgiana Charlotte (1812-1885), English novelist whose first story, *Ellen Middleton* (1844), was followed by *Grantley Manor*. In 1846 she became a Catholic convert, and her novels such as *Lady Bird, Too Strange Not to be True*, and *A Will and a Way* were tales intended to be mildly religious as well as entertaining.

Furiant (Furie), in music a rapid Bohemian dance in which the rhythms alternate and the music is sharply accented. Excellent examples are to be found in the works of Friedrich SMETANA and Antonin DVORAK.

Furies, see **Erinyes.**

Furness, Horace Howard (1833-1912), American scholar and editor who was educated at Harvard University, and admitted to the bar in 1859. He edited the first fifteen volumes of the *New Variorum Shakespeare* (1871-1912): after his death, his son, *Horace Howard Furness* (1865-1930), edited the remaining four volumes. The Horace Howard Furness Library of Shakespeareana is now in the library of the University of Pennsylvania.

Furniss, Harry (1854-1925), Irish caricaturist educated in Dublin who as a boy edited a *Schoolboy's Punch* in imitation of the original, and later made caricatures for the *Illustrated London News* and *Punch*: in the latter his cartoons for Lucy's "Diary of Toby, M.P." earned him a national reputation. He also illustrated the collected works of THACKERAY and DICKENS: his published works include *America in a Hurry* (1900) and *Confessions of a Caricaturist.*

Furniture, the collective term for cabinets, desks, chairs, tables, beds, used today to include articles more correctly called furnishings. The ancient Egyptians developed most of the types in use at the present day including chairs, armchairs, folding chairs, dining tables, occasional tables, chest of drawers: these were so substantially constructed that the pieces found in excavated tombs are in a remarkable state of preservation. The ancient Greeks had most of the types mentioned above, and the Romans were influenced largely in designing and construction by Greek art. Oriental furniture, largely made of teak and ebony, was either richly carved or exquisitely inlaid. In the 15th century, Western Europe and Russia developed a type of furniture with designs drawn from GOTHIC architecture, but the style was highly distinctive in every country including France, Germany, Norway, Denmark, The Netherlands, Holland, and also England. The periods that followed include the RENAISSANCE (divided into Early, High, and Late), the BAROQUE, the Rococo, and finally a return to the classic designs of Greece and Rome. Styles in France were known as LOUIS XIV, Louis XV, Louis XVI, and EMPIRE; the latter arriving with the accession of Napoleon I to the French throne. In England styles were first copies from Europe: the GEORGIAN period (1735-1805) had the advantage of the artistry of CHIPPENDALE, Robert ADAM, HEPPLEWHITE, and SHERATON. In America colonial furniture developed largely as required by the needs of the settlers from a practical standpoint. Several hitherto unknown pieces were created or developed including the highboy, the low-boy, dressing table, the Windsor chair, the four post bed, the Morris chair, the rocking chair, and the child's crib with rockers. The trend in the United States today is toward furniture in which metal plays an important part, and the newest designs may be regarded as a combination of all previous periods with the special thought in mind of space limitation in modern apartments.

Fursch-Madi, Emmy (1847-1894), French dramatic soprano who studied at the PARIS CONSERVATORY, and made her operatic debut in that city in GOUNOD's *Faust*. She created the title role of *Aïda* in Brussels at VERDI's request, and sang with the French Opera Company at New Orleans, La., in 1874, later returning to appear in 1884 at the Metropolitan Opera House, N. Y., in PONCHIELLI's *La Gioconda*. Her last appearance at the Metropolitan was as Ortrud in WAGNER's *Lohengrin* during 1894.

Furst, William Wallace (1852-1917), American composer educated at Rock Hill College, Baltimore. He became orchestra leader at the Empire Theatre, New York, and wrote several successful operettas including *The Isle of Champagne* in which Thomas Q. SEABROOKE was starred.

Furtwangler, Wilhelm (1886-), German conductor and composer who studied with Max SCHILLINGS, Josef RHEINBERGER, and Felix MOTTL. He succeeded Artur BODANZKY as conductor at Mannheim in 1915; Richard STRAUSS at the Symphonic Concerts of the Berlin Opera in 1920; Artur NIKISCH at the Philharmonic Concerts in Berlin in 1922; conducted the NEW YORK PHILHARMONIC-SYMPHONY ORCHESTRA in 1926-27 and at the BAYREUTH FESTIVALS since 1931. His compositions include a symphony, a string quartet, a sonata for violin, and a piano concerto.

Fuseli, Henry (1741-1825), English painter of Swiss parentage whose father, John Caspar Fuseli, was a landscape painter of ability, and author of a history of painting in Switzerland. He exhibited a painting, *Nightmare*, at the Royal Academy, London, in 1782: he became professor of painting there in 1799, and his most distinguished pupil was William BLAKE. His notable works include *Titania and Bottom* from Shakespeare's "Midsummer Night's Dream"; *The Dream of Queen Katherine; Joseph Interpreting the Dreams of the Baker and Butler; Hamlet Breaking Away from His Attendants to Follow the Ghost*.

Futrelle, Jacques (1875-1912), American journalist and writer of detective fiction who created the character of "The Thinking Machine": he was one of the "Titanic" victims in 1912. Among his novels are *The Chase of the Golden Plate* (1906); *The Thinking Machine*, later re-issued as *The Problem of Cell 13; The Thinking Machine on the Case; The Simple Case of Susan; The Diamond Master; My Lady's Garter*.

Futurism, a radical movement in the fields of poetry, painting, sculpture, drama, and other artists which originated in Italy at the start of the 20th century with Filippo Tommasso Marinetti as the prime mover. It promoted the idea of rejecting all traditions and conventions in favor of untrammeled, personal expression, and affected painting and drama to a considerable extent for a time.

Fux, Johann Joseph (1660-1741), Austrian composer about whose musical training little is known: he was appointed master of music at the Austrian court at Vienna in 1715, holding the post under three successive emperors until his death in 1741. He composed nearly 400 works, and wrote a treatise on counterpoint, *Gradus ad Parnassum*, which was studied by HADYN and MOZART although it was based on the obsolete church modes.

Fyt, Jan (1611-1661), Flemish painter who studied with Franz SNYDERS, and was greatly influenced by REMBRANDT: he became amazingly proficient in portraying animal and bird life, and worked frequently with RUBENS and Jacob JORDAENS. His works include *Hunted Roe Deer with Dogs in Water; Page and Parrot; Dead Birds; Diana and Her Nymph; Bear Hunt; Silenus Among Fruit and Flowers; Cat With a Hare and Birds*.

G

Gabin, Jean (1904-), French screen actor who appeared with MISTINGUETTE and Elsie JANIS in Paris. He has played leading roles in numerous French films including *Pepe le Moko; La Grande Illusion; La Bête Humaine; Escape from Yesterday; Moontide*, the latter an American production. In 1939 he joined a regiment of marines at the beginning of World War II.

Gable, Clark (1901-), American stage and screen actor who made his first appearance in stock companies touring the United States, and from 1928 to 1930 in several plays at New York and San Francisco theatres. Since entering the films in 1930 he has had leading roles in numerous pictures including *Hell Divers; Polly of the Circus; Susan Lenox; The Easiest Way; The White Sister; Strange Interlude; Men in White; China Seas; Mutiny on the Bounty; It Happened One Night; Parnell; Idiot's Delight; Gone With the Wind; Boomtown; Comrade X; They Met in Bombay; Honky Tonk.*

Gable, in architecture the upper part or vertical end of wall from the CORNICE or eaves to the ridge of the roof: it is usually triangular, and high in proportion to its width. A *gable roof* is one in which gables are formed at either or at several ends. The gable was frequently used in Gothic and Romanesque architecture: gables in old Belgian and Scotch houses were sometimes built in a series of projections resembling steps, called corbie steps, instead of the conventional straight lines.

Gaboriau, Émile (1835-1873), French author of detective fiction who published a few novels with little success until he discovered his real field of endeavor in a mystery story, *The Lerouge Affair* (1866). This was followed by a long series of novels dealing with police affairs including *The Crime of Orcival; File No. 113; Monsieur Lecocq; The Infernal Life; The Fall; The Rope Around the Neck; The Slaves of Paris.*

Gabriel, Jacques Ange (1690-1782), French architect who was trained by his father, Jacques Gabriel, and succeeded him in 1742 as architect to the king, and Inspector General of Buildings. He worked for more than thirty years on restorations, alterations, and additions to the Louvre and Versailles, also designing and decorating the Place Louis XV, now known as the Place de la Concorde. Gabriel was successful in imparting a new atmosphere of dignity, purity, and restraint to French architecture: one of his finest creations was the Petit Trianon at Versailles, a miniature residence presented by Louis XV to Madame DU BARRY.

Gabrilowitsch, Ossip (1878-1936), Russian pianist and conductor who studied with Anton RUBINSTEIN and Alexander GLAZUNOFF at the St. Petersburg Conservatory, and with Theodor LESCHETIZKY at Vienna. He toured Europe and Great Britain with extraordinary success which was repeated when he made his New York debut in 1900. After continuing his pianistic career for seventeen years he became conductor of the DETROIT SYMPHONY ORCHESTRA in 1918, and from 1928 until shortly before his death also directed the PHILADELPHIA ORCHESTRA, sharing the baton with Leopold STOKOWSKI. He married the singer, Clara Clemens, daughter of Mark TWAIN, in 1909, and appeared frequently in recitals with her.

Gaddi, Taddeo (c.1300-c.1366), Italian painter who studied with GIOTTO, working with him for twenty-four years. He painted the frescoes *The Legend of the Virgin* at the Church of Saint Croce in Florence: other notable works include a *Madonna; Life of Christ; Life of St. Francis; Virgin and Child; St. John the Evangelist.* His son,

Agnola Gaddhi (c.1340-1396), studied with him: his works including *The Raising of Lazarus; The Legend of the Virgin and Her Girdle; The Legend of the True Cross; Madonna, Angels, and Saints.*

Gade, Niels Wilhelm (1817-1890), Danish violinist and composer who was intimate with Felix MENDELSSOHN and Robert SCHUMANN: he frequently conducted the GEWANDHAUS ORCHESTRA in Leipzig when Mendelssohn was absent, and succeeded him as director in 1847. His compositions include eight symphonies and many other orchestral works; three violin sonatas; chamber music; violin concertos, piano pieces, and songs. He exerted a strong influence on music in Scandinavia.

Gadski, Johanna (1872-1932), German dramatic soprano who studied with Frau Schroeder-Chaloupka at Stettin, and made her debut in 1889 at Berlin in Lortzing's *Undine,* and her first appearance in the United States in 1895 with the Damrosch Opera Company in *Lohengrin.* She joined the METROPOLITAN OPERA COMPANY in 1898-1904, and became famous for her interpretations of Wagnerian roles, also singing at the BAYREUTH FESTIVALS, COVENT GARDEN, and again with the Metropolitan Opera Company from 1907 to 1917. She also established a reputation as a singer of lieder; her operatic repertory included forty roles.

Gaea, in Greek mythology the goddess who personifies the earth. According to HOMER she was the mother of ERECHTHEUS, and was worshipped by the Romans as *Tellus.*

Gág, Wanda (1893-), American artist and writer of stories for children: her works include *Millions of Cats* (1928); *The Funny Thing; Snippy and Snappy; The A B C Bunny; Gone is Gone; Tales from Grimm; Snow White and the Seven Dwarfs; Growing Pains,* an autobiography; *Nothing at All.*

Gagliano, Alexander (c.1160-1725), Italian violin maker who is said to have studied with Antonio STRADIVARIUS. His first instruments appeared in 1695: they are made of handsomely figured wood, and varnished from dark red to orange. The market price today ranges from $1000.00 to $3000.00. His eldest son, **Nicolo Gagliano** (c.1695-c.1790), was also a violin maker whose instruments are of distinctly higher quality, and modeled after those of Stradivarius. Their prices today range from $2000.00 to $4000.00: some of his violoncellos have been sold for $8000.00.

Gahagan, Helen (1900-), American actress and singer who was educated at Barnard College, and made her New York debut in 1922 at the Playhouse in *Manhattan:* she has played leading roles in *Dreams For Sale; Chains; Leah Kleschna; The Enchanted Cottage; Young Woodley; Diplomacy; To-night or Never; The Cat and the Fiddle; Mary of Scotland; Mother Lode; The Merry Widow.* She studied singing in Europe from 1928 to 1930, and sang at the SALZBURG FESTIVAL in 1937.

Gaige, Crosby (1882-), American theatrical producer educated at Columbia University. He acted as director of productions for Edgar and

Archibald SELWYN from 1905 to 1923, and started as an independent producer in 1926. Among his successful productions are *Within the Law; The Butter and Egg Man; The Road to Happiness; The Shannons of Broadway; The House Beautiful; Accent on Youth.*

Gail Hamilton, see **Dodge, Mary Abigail.**

Gainsborough, Thomas (1727-1788), English painter who studied drawing and engraving in London at the age of fourteen, and finally settled at Ipswich, and later at Bath. He painted portraits of the aristocracy and the English stage, exhibiting regularly at the Royal Academy. Among his sitters were Laurence STERNE, Samuel RICHARDSON, Mrs. SIDDONS, The Duchess of Devonshire, William Pitt, Dr. JOHNSON, and Master Buttall, who sat for the painting known as *The Blue Boy* in which he sought to disprove Sir Joshua REYNOLDS' contention that the blue could not be used as the dominating color in a portrait. His paintings of note include *The Cottage Door; The Market Cart; The Horse Pond; Forest Landscape at Sunset; The Hay Wagon; The Return from Harvest; Woodman and His Dog in a Storm; Wagon and Horses Passing a Brook.* Gainsborough was a lover of music and of the theatre: he painted the portraits without charge of many actors, and was lavish in giving away sketches and pictures of his creation.

Gaité Parisienne, a comedy ballet in one act: libretto by Count Etienne de Beaumont; choreography by Leonid MASSINE; music adapted from the music of Jacques OFFENBACH; first produced in 1938 at Monte Carlo. The fragile plot concerns itself with the attentions of the guests in a French café to the flower girl and the glove seller, introducing the famous Can-Can girls with their black-stockinged legs; the entire interest of the ballet is in the scintillating score arranged from Offenbach's music.

Galahad, in the legends of King Arthur, a famous knight of the Round Table who was the son of LANCELOT: he was called "the chaste," and achieved the quest of the Holy GRAIL.

Gala Performance, a ballet in one act: book and choreography by Antony TUDOR; music by Serge PROKOFIEFF; first produced at London by the London Ballet in 1938, and in New York by the BALLET THEATRE in 1940. The purpose is to present a ballet performance as it progresses behind the scenes, and from the stage as seen by the audience: glimpses are given of the *corps de ballet* practicing, the whims of the ballerinas, the anxieties of the conductor; the attempts of rival ballerinas to "steal the curtain."

Galatea, see **Pygmalion.**

Galdós, see **Pérez Galdós, Benito.**

Gale, Zona (1874-1938), American novelist, poet, and dramatist who was educated at the University of Wisconsin, and had considerable experience in journalism before embarking on a literary career. Her works include *Romance Island* (1906); *Friendship Village; Heart's Kindred; A Daughter of Tomorrow; Miss Lulu Bett,* dramatized and awarded the Pulitzer Prize in 1920; *Birth,* also dramatized as *Mr. Pitt; Faint Perfume; Preface to a Life; Borgia; Papa la Fleur; Light Woman.*

Gallait, Louis (1810-1887), Belgian painter who studied with Philippe Hennequin at the Tournay Academy and settled in Paris: his paintings include *The Beggars; Death of Palestrina; Montaigne Visiting Tasso in Prison; Christ Healing the Blind; Conquest of Antioch; Samson and Delilah; Plague at Tournay; The Minstrel Boy; Prayer after Vintage; Death of Egmont.* He also painted fifteen historical portraits of great warriors, legislators and patrons of art.

Gallegos, Romulo (1884-), Venezuelan journalist and novelist whose romance, *Dona Barbara,* was a "best seller" in South America, and was later translated into English. Another colorful novel is entitled *The Climbing Plant* (La Trepadora).

Gallery, in architecture, a covered passage outside a main wall; used as a veranda if located on a ground floor, or as a BALCONY if on an upper floor. The term is used in GOTHIC ARCHITECTURE to denote the division into stories of the interior or exterior façades of a church. In olden times pictures were frequently used to decorate galleries: hence the use of the term for any private or public room utilized for the display of paintings.

Galley, (*a*) a large, low, single-decked vessel propelled by both oars and sails; used in the Middle Ages for war, commercial, and pleasure purposes. The galley was found principally in the Mediterranean, and measured from one hundred to two hundred feet in length: there were often as many as twenty oars on each side manned by side rowers who were usually slaves, prisoners of war, or convicts. (*b*) the term for the kitchen of a vessel. (*c*) in typesetting the name of a metal tray used to hold a section of type after it has been set; also used as the name of the rough proof taken of the type in the galley.

Gallico, Paolo (1868-), Italian pianist, teacher, and composer who studied with Julius Epstein at the Vienna Conservatory: after touring Europe as a virtuoso he settled at New York in 1892, appearing with the principal orchestras, in recital, and teaching advanced classes. His compositions include a dramatic oratorio, *Apocalypse;* an opera, *Harlekin; Symphonic Episode;* a sextet; piano pieces and songs. In 1943 he appeared in a recital at Town Hall, New York, to mark the fiftieth anniversary of his first appearance in recital.

Galli-Curci, Amelita (1889-), Italian coloratura soprano who first studied the piano at the Milan Conservatory, but was chiefly self-taught as a singer. Her operatic debut was made as Gilda in *Rigoletto* at Rome in 1909: after singing in Europe and South America she appeared in 1916 with great success in *Rigoletto* with the CHICAGO OPERA COMPANY. In 1920 she made her debut at the METROPOLITAN OPERA HOUSE in La *Traviata,* remaining there until 1930: later she toured practically the entire world as a concert singer. Her repertory includes the coloratura roles in all standard Italian and French operas.

Gallo, Fortune (1878-), American band and operatic impresario born in Italy who came to the United States when he was seventeen years old. After directing the tours of several famous bands, he founded the SAN CARLO OPERA COMPANY which he still directs, and in 1920 managed the tour of the Ballet Russe with Anna PAVLOWA in the United States. He also managed the tour of Eleanora DUSE in 1925; produced a film version of Leoncavallo's *Pagliacci* in 1928, and presented grand opera and light opera performances at Jones's Beach, Long Island, and the Randall's Island Stadium, New York.

Galsworthy, John (1867-1933), English novelist and dramatist, educated at Oxford, who was encouraged to embark on a literary career by Joseph CONRAD, and reached the age of forty before he gained recognition. His novels include *From the Four Winds* (1897); *The Forsyte Saga* which comprised *The Man of Property, Indian Summer, In Chancery, Awakening,* and *To Let; The White Monkey; The Silver Spoon; Maid in Waiting; Flowering Wilderness.* Among his notable plays are *The Silver Box; Strife; Justice; The Pigeon; The Mob; The Skin Game; Loyalties; Escape; The Roof.* His understanding of the social order of his day, and his brilliant dialogue in both novels and plays assure him of a high position in English literature.

Gambarelli, Maria, contemporary ballet dancer, born in Italy of Italian-American parentage, who came to the United States as a child, and studied dancing at the Metropolitan School of Ballet. She appeared for several years as *première danseuse* at the Capitol Theatre, New York, and organized a production school to train dance units for American theatres. She has appeared in several films, and is now (1943) *première danseuse* at the Metropolitan Opera House, New York.

Games, see **Olympic Games.**

Gammer Gurton's Needle, an English comedy acted at Christ's College, Cambridge, in 1566, and published in 1575. It was the second work of its kind in England, the first being *Ralph Roister Doister.* The story is a simple one: Gammer Gurton loses her needle, and is involved in quarrels of various kinds before she finds it where she left it—in the breeches of her husband. The author, long said to be Bishop John Still, was probably William Stevenson.

Ganso, Emil (1895-), American painter, born in Germany, who came to the United States in 1912, working as a baker and studying at the National Academy of Design, New York, and with Jules Pascin. In 1933 he won a GUGGENHEIM FELLOWSHIP, and has become well known for his paintings such as *Bearsville Meadow* (Woodstock County, New York), and also for his etchings, lithographs, and aquatints. His works are to be seen in the METROPOLITAN MUSEUM OF ART, New York, and in many other museums and galleries in the United States.

Ganymede, in Greek mythology the cupbearer of the gods on OLYMPUS, said to have been a Trojan youth, famed for his beauty, who was brought to Olympus by ZEUS himself in the form of an eagle: he succeeded HEBE in her duties as cupbearer.

Ganz, Rudolf (1877-), Swiss pianist, composer, and conductor who made his debut in 1899 with the Berlin Philharmonic Orchestra; in 1900 he became the head of the piano department at the CHICAGO MUSICAL COLLEGE, and later toured the world as a virtuoso. From 1921 to 1927 he conducted the ST. LOUIS SYMPHONY ORCHESTRA, and from 1938 the Young People's Concerts of the NEW YORK PHILHARMONIC-SYMPHONY ORCHESTRA. In 1940 he became director of the Chicago Musical College. His compositions include a symphony and several other orchestral works; a *Concert Piece* for piano and orchestra; *Variations on a Theme by Brahms* for piano; numerous piano pieces and about two hundred songs.

Garay, János (1812-1853), Hungarian dramatist and poet educated at the University of Pest: his works include several historical dramas such as *Arbocz; The Skirmisher and Other Poems,* and a historical poem, entitled *St. Ladislaus,* in twelve cantos. He held the post of professor of Hungarian literature and language at the University of Pest for a year, but was obliged to relinquish it through illness.

Garbo, Greta (1906-), Swedish screen actress who began her career as a dancer, and achieved remarkable success in *Goesta Berling.* Among the American film productions in which she has appeared since 1926 are *The Torrent; The Temptress; The Flesh and the Devil; Anna Karenina; Susan Lenox; Wild Orchids; Mata Hari; Grand Hotel; Queen Christina; Camille; Conquest; Ninotchka; Two-Faced Woman.*

García, Manuel del Popola Vicente (1775-1832), Spanish dramatic tenor, composer, and singing teacher who was successful as an operatic singer at the age of seventeen: he became famous on the operatic stage in Spain, France, Italy, England, and the United States, visiting the last-named country in 1825-26 with his family and a distinguished company to give 79 performances. He was also a successful teacher, and his daughters, Marie MALIBRAN and Pauline VIARDOT-GARCIA were both great singers. His son, **Manuel Patricio García** (1805-1906), was a famous teacher who taught at the PARIS CONSERVATORY OF MUSIC and at the ROYAL ACADEMY OF MUSIC, London. Jenny LIND was one of his pupils, and he also invented the laryngoscope.

García-Gutiérrez, Antonio (c.1812-1884), Spanish dramatist who first studied medicine, and had little success in the theatre until his play, *El Trovador* (The Troubador), produced in 1826, made him famous: Giuseppe VERDI's opera, *Il Trovatore,* was based on it. Another tragedy, *Simon Boccanegra,* was also a great success in 1843: again Verdi wrote an opera with the same title using Gutiérrez' play as its basis.

García Lorca, Federico (1899-1936), Spanish poet and dramatist educated at the University of

Granada: he wrote several successful plays including *Mariana Pineda* and *Amor de Don Perlimplín con Belisa en su Jardini;* the latter was produced at New York in 1935 with the title *Bitter Oleander.* García visited the United States in 1929, and South America in 1933: he was murdered during the Spanish Civil War, and his works are banned in Spain: *Bitter Oleander* and some of his poetical works have been translated.

Gardel, Pierre (1758-1840), French violinist, dancer, and choreographer who appeared at L'Opéra, Paris, in 1771, and became *premier danseur* in 1775. He was obliged to stop dancing in 1791 because of an accident, and became a member of the advisory board at L'Opéra. His ballets include *The Judgment of Paris; La Dansomanie* in which he introduced the waltz; *Paul and Virginia; La Marseillaise* in which he dramatized the famous French national hymn during the Revolution. He acted as choreographer for more than forty years, and was one of the first dancers to dispense with the mask usually worn while performing.

Garden, Mary (1877-), American dramatic soprano born in Scotland who came to the United States as a child: after studying singing in Paris with several famous teachers she made her debut in 1900 at the OPERA-COMIQUE, Paris, in CHARPENTIER'S *Louise.* She created the role of Mélisande in DEBUSSY'S *Pelléas et Mélisande* in 1902, and also achieved great success in MASSENET'S *Thaïs* at her New York debut in 1907 at the MANHATTAN OPERA HOUSE. From 1910 to 1931 she was a member of the CHICAGO OPERA COMPANY, acting as its director for a year after the death of Cleofonte CAMPANINI in 1919. Her extraordinary success was largely due to her ability as an actress in such operas as LOUISE, PELLEAS ET MELISANDE, THAIS, SALOME, and CARMEN.

Gardner, Erle Stanley (1889-), American author of detective fiction who was admitted to the California bar at twenty-one, and practiced there as a trial lawyer for more than twenty years. He has created three distinct characters for his various series of detective stories: the first is "Perry Mason," a brilliant defense lawyer who knows all the legal tricks, but uses them only in righteous causes; the second, Douglas Selby, a hard-hitting district attorney; the third, Terry Clane, a resourceful detective. His stories number in excess of twenty-five beginning with *The Case of the Velvet Claws* in 1932: he has also contributed to detective-fiction magazines.

Gardner, Samuel (1891-), American violinist and composer, born in Russia, who came to the United States as a child: he studied the violin with Felix Winternitz and Franz KNEISEL, and composition with Percy GOETSCHIUS and Charles Martin LOEFFLER. His compositions include a piano quintet; a violin concerto; a fantasy, *Broadway,* for orchestra; several interesting violin pieces, and a method of class teaching for the violin.

Gargantua, the shortened title of a satirical romance in prose and verse by RABELAIS: the correct title is. *The Life of Gargantua and Panta-*

gruel. Gargantua is pictured as a gigantic king with an insatiable appetite, but with remarkably humanistic ideas. The term *gargantuan* is now used to describe anyone with an extraordinary appetite: in recent years an unusually large specimen of the ape family exhibited in the United States was named Gargantua.

Gargoyle, in architecture a carved termination to a waterspout projecting from the roof gutter at the upper part of a building: it was first employed by Gothic architects who permitted sculptors to give rein to their imagination in the most fantastic forms such as CHIMAERAS, SIRENS, and all forms of mythical animals. Gargoyles in the forms of lions' heads were used in Greek temples, and various forms are also found in Egypt.

Garland, Hamlin (1860-1940), American novelist and poet: his works include *Main Traveled Roads* (1890); *Prairie Folks; Prairie Songs,* a book of poems; *A Son of the Middle Border,* an autobiography; *A Daughter of the Middle Border,* winning the Pulitzer Prize for American biography in 1922; *Afternoon Neighbors.* His books reflect chiefly life on the farms of the Middle West.

Garland, Robert (1895-), American journalist and dramatist who has filled posts as dramatic critic and columnist on the *Baltimore Daily Post,* the *New York World-Telegram,* and the *New York American:* his plays include *The Double Miracle; The Importance of Being a Rough Neck; Calling All Men,* in collaboration with Leonard Sillman.

Garnet, the term applied to a group of closely related minerals many of which are used as gem stones, and consist mainly of aluminum silicates in which various metallic oxides are present. As a gem stone it has little value because of its abundance, and is of little use to the engraver because of its tendency to splinter. The Egyptians used the garnet for beads, and polished slabs, inlaid with mosaic work, have been found in Anglo-Saxon jewelry.

Garnett, David (1892-), English novelist whose early work, *Lady Into Fox* (1923) won two literary prizes: it was followed by *A Man in the Zoo; The Sailor's Return; Go She Must!; The Grasshoppers Come; A Rabbit in the Air; Pocahontas; War in the Air.*

Garnier, Jean Louis Charles (1825-1898), French architect who studied at the ECOLE DES BEAUX-ARTS, Paris, and worked in Greece where he made a restoration of a temple devoted to JUPITER at Aegina. He built the Opera House in Paris (1860-75); the Casino at Monte Carlo; the tombs of Jacques OFFENBACH and Georges BIZET in Paris, and the Astronomical Observatory at Nice.

Garnier, Robert (1534-1690), French poet and dramatist who wrote several classical tragedies modeled on SENECA and EURIPIDES: the most successful were *Bradamente* and *Les Juives.* In the opinion of some authorities Garnier was the greatest French tragic poet of the 16th century: he laid the foundation in his poetic and dramatic technique for the greater achievements of the 17th century.

Garofalo, Il (1481-1559), Italian painter whose real name was Benvenuto Tisi: he was a pupil and friend of Dosso Dossi, and worked at Ferrara and Rome. His notable works include *Massacre of the Innocents; Adoration of the Magi; Raising of Lazarus; Neptune and Pallas; Sacrifice to Ceres; Triumph of Bacchus.* He was a friend and imitator of RAPHAEL.

Garrett, João Baptista Almeida de, see **Almeida-Garrett, João Baptista de.**

Garrick, David (1717-1779), English actor who studied at a school opened in Edial by Samuel JOHNSON: when the school closed he went to London, and engaged in the wine business with his brother. He made his first success on the stage in 1741, appearing in *Richard III.* From 1742 to 1745 he played at the DRURY LANE THEATRE, London: after a season with Richard Brinsley SHERIDAN and Margaret (Peg) WOFFINGTON in Dublin he leased the Drury Lane Theatre in 1747, remaining there for nearly thirty years. He produced many new plays and at least twenty-four of Shakespeare's works, initiating improvements in scenic effects and lighting, and abolishing the custom of seating privileged persons on the stage. His charm as an actor was due in part to his natural method of speaking in contrast to the customary ranting: Charles CHURCHILL once remarked that "to be pleased with nature is to be pleased with Garrick."

Garrison, Mabel (1886-), American coloratura soprano who studied at the Peabody Conservatory of Music; and also with Oscar Saenger and Herbert WITHERSPOON. Her debut was made in *Mignon* with the Aborn Opera Company at Boston in 1912, and she appeared with the Metropolitan Opera Company from 1914 to 1922, one of her best roles being that of Queen Shemaka in Rimsky-Korsakow's *Le Coq d'Or.* After appearing in opera and concerts in Europe, the Orient, and the United States, she became professor of singing at Smith College.

Garson, Greer, contemporary Irish stage and screen actress educated at London University: she made her stage debut at Birmingham, England, in *Street Scene,* and appeared in numerous plays before entering the films in 1938. She has played leading roles in several films including *Goodbye, Mr. Chips; Remember?; Pride and Prejudice; Blossoms in the Dust; When Ladies Meet; Mrs. Miniver; Random Harvest.*

Gaskell, Elizabeth Cleghorn (1810-1865), English novelist who was the wife of a Unitarian minister and mother of several children before she became successful as an author with *Cranford* (1853), a series of stories of village life which has become a classic. Among her works were *Sylvia,* a tale of the press-gang, and a biography of her intimate friend, Charlotte BRONTE; the latter was bitterly assailed by members of the Brontë family.

Gasparo da Salo (c.1542-1609), Italian maker of viols, viole de gamba, and contrabass viols: he is said to have modernized the form of the violin in respect to the shape of the f-holes and the curve of the scroll. The celebrated violin maker, Giovanni Pablo MAGGINI, was his pupil.

Gatti, Bernardo (c.1490-1575), Italian painter known as *Il Sojaro* (The Cooper) because of his father's trade. He was a pupil of CORREGGIO: among his notable works are *Miracle of the Loaves and Fishes; Assumption of the Virgin; St. George and the Dragon,* a fresco; *Ecce Homo; Crucifixion;* he also completed Giovanni PORDENONE's fresco, *The Life of the Madonna.*

Gatti-Casazza, Giulio (1869-1940), Italian opera impresario educated at the Universities of Ferrara and Bologna: in 1893 he became director of the Municipal Theatre at Ferrara, and in 1898 assumed the directorship of LA SCALA in Milan where he introduced WAGNER's music dramas in Italian, a policy which resulted in their genuine appreciation. In 1908 he succeeded Heinrich CONRIED as director of the METROPOLITAN OPERA HOUSE, New York, remaining until 1935. Among his innovations and achievements were the offering of a $10,000 prize for operas by American composers which was won by Horatio W. PARKER in 1912 with *Mona;* the presentation of American operas and ballets by Frederick S. CONVERSE, Walter DAMROSCH, Reginald DE KOVEN, Victor HERBERT, Charles Wakefield CADMAN, Joseph C. BREIL, John Adam HUGO, Henry HADLEY, John Alden CARPENTER, Deems TAYLOR, Howard HANSON, and Louis GRUENBERG; the world premières of foreign operas by HUMPERDINCK, PUCCINI, GRANADOS, and GIORDANO: the building of a reserve fund of $1,500,000 which was depleted only through the depression of 1929; the featuring of younger American singers including Sophie BRASLAU, Reinald WERRENRATH, Clarence WHITEHILL, Paul ALTHOUSE, Herbert WITHERSPOON, Riccardo MARTIN, Orville HARROLD, Richard CROOKS, Frederick JAGEL and many others.

Gaubert, Philippe (1879-), French flutist, composer, and conductor who studied the flute with Claude Taffanel at the PARIS CONSERVATORY OF MUSIC. He conducted the concerts at the Conservatory from 1919 to 1938, and also directed at the Paris Opéra from 1920 in addition to becoming professor of flute at the Conservatory. His compositions include two operas; a symphony and other orchestral works; chamber music and pieces for flute: he also conducted many fine recordings.

Gaudier-Brzeska, Henri (1891-1915), French sculptor who won a scholarship as a boy of fourteen for study in English art schools: he also studied and worked in Germany and Holland, and was killed in one of the first engagements in World War I. He created many animal figures and groups: among his works are *The Dancer, The Singer,* and *The Lovers,* fashioned in accordance with the principles of VORTICISM, a movement in art developed in England in the period preceding World War I.

Gauguin, Paul (1848-1903), French painter who served in the French navy, and started to study painting as an avocation while working in a French banking house. In 1891 he went to Tahiti where he remained until his death. He created a number of pictures of life in Tahiti which caused a sensation when they were exhibited in Paris: among them are *Two Maori Women; The Old Spirit; Alone; Lovely Days*, and *The Flight*. His autobiography, *Noa Noa*, describes his life on the islands of the South Pacific which he regarded as an earthly paradise.

Gaul, Gilbert William (1855-1919), American painter who specialized in pictures portraying incidents in the Civil War: many were used to illustrate works on the conflict; among them *Charging the Battery, Guerillas Returning From a Raid; Battery H in Action; News From Home; On the Lookout; Cold Comfort in the Outpost.*

Gaulli, Giovanni Battista (1639-1709), Italian painter also known as Il Baciccio: by self-study of the great masters he formed an individual style which brought him a considerable reputation. His works include a fresco in the vault of the Church of The Christ, Rome, representing St. Xavier being taken into Heaven: he also made portraits of several popes and distinguished personages of his day.

Gautier, Louise Judith (1850-1917), French poet and novelist who acquired a knowledge of Chinese from a mandarin who was a guest of her father, and became greatly interested in Oriental languages and literature. Her works include *The Book of Jade* (1867); *The Imperial Dragon*, a Chinese romance; *The Usurper*, a Japanese romance; *Potiphar's Wife*, a tale of Persia; *Poems of the Dragon Fly.*

Gautier, Théophile (1811-1872), French poet, dramatic critic, and novelist educated at the Collège Charlemagne in Paris, and for many years critic of drama and art for LA PRESS and other periodicals in Paris. His poems include *Albertus, The Comedy of Death*, and *Espana:* his novels *Mademoiselle de Maupin, French France*, and *Captain Fracasse:* his best critical work is *The History of the Dramatic Art in France.*

Gavotte, an old French dance in common time and in two parts: as it begins on the third beat of the measure, each section ends on a half bar. It is one of the movements in the suites composed by BACH, HANDEL, RAMEAU, GOSSEC, and LULLY: sometimes a second gavotte serves as a "trio" before the repetition of the first. One of the most popular works in this form, composd by Christoph Willibald von GLUCK, was arranged for piano solo by Johannes BRAHMS.

Gay, Edward (1837-1928), American painter, born in Dublin, who studied with James HART in Albany, N. Y., and with Karl Lessing in Düsseldorf. His works, distinguished by their exquisite sunlight effects, include *Mohawk Valley Home; Broad Acres; Harvest Time; Spring Morning; Waving Grain; A Fjord in Norway; Haymaking.*

Gay, John (1685-1732), English poet and playwright who wrote the libretto for a ballad opera, *The Beggar's Opera*, which was produced in 1728, and held the stage for more than a century because of its pungent wit, and the popularity of the English and Irish folk tunes employed by Dr. John Christopher PEPUSCH in setting the lyrics. The opera made Gay a rich man: its sequel, *Polly*, was banned for a time because of its political references.

Gay, Maria (1879-1943), Spanish dramatic singer who mastered the violin and the art of sculpture before she taught herself to sing. After singing with Raoul PUGNO and Eugene YSAYE, she created a sensation at her debut in *Carmen* at Brussels in 1902. In 1908, she appeared at the Metropolitan Opera House, New York, in *Carmen* with Arturo TOSCANINI conducting: she also sang with the BOSTON OPERA COMPANY and the CHICAGO OPERA COMPANY, and finally settled in New York as a vocal teacher.

Gay, Walter (1856-1937), American painter who studied with Leon BONNAT and Benjamin CONSTANT in Paris: his notable works include *Fall Flowers; Unsuccessful Musician; The Armorer; The Cigarette Makers; The Spinners; November; Bénédicité*. He was the recipient of many medals and awards in foreign cities.

Gebhardt, Eduard von (1838-1925), German painter who studied at the St. Petersburg Academy under Karl LESSING, and at the Düsseldorf Academy: his works include *Christ's Entry into Jerusalem; Raising of the Daughter of Jairus; The Brothers Van Eyck; Reformer at Work; The Ascension; Jacob and the Angel; Christ Walking on the Sea*. His art was based on that of the old Flemish masters to which he added a touch of modern realism.

Geddes, Norman Bel (1893-), American scenic designer and painter whose first production in New York was the setting for Charles Wakefield CADMAN's opera, *Shanewis*, at the Metropolitan Opera House in 1918: among the settings he has made are *The Miracle; The Eternal Road; Divine Comedy; The Rivals; The School for Scandal; Jeanne d'Arc; Arabesque; Ziegfeld Follies* (1925); *Lysistrata; Hamlet; Dead End*; the films, *Feet of Clay* and *The Sorrows of Satan*; a futurama, *Highways and Horizons* at the New York World's Fair in 1939.

Geefs, Willem or **Guillaume** (1805-1883), Belgian sculptor who was one of a family in which six brothers became sculptors. His most realistic work is a portrait statue of Count Belliard in the Rue Royale at Brussels; he also made a statue of King Leopold I of Belgium.

Geertgen van Haarlem (c.1464-1493), Dutch painter who studied with Albert van Outwater; he was also known as Gerrit van Haarlem. He lived with the Knights of St. John at Haarlem, and was sometimes called Geertgen van Sint Jans although he did not belong to the Order. His works include an altarpiece on one wing of which was painted the *Legend of the Bones of St. John the Baptist*, and on the other a *Pietá; View of Haarlem Cathedral; Crucifixion; Adoration of the Magi; Raising of Lazarus; Christ in the Tomb.*

Geijerstam, Gösta af (1888-), Swedish novelist who was first educated as a painter. His works deal largely with those who find it difficult to find a place for themselves in the world: those available in English include *Northern Summer* (1940); *Storevik; Iva; Northern Winter.*

Geisha, the Japanese term for a person of pleasing accomplishments, and used as the name of a professional singing and dancing girl in Japan: training for the profession begins at an extremely early age. In Japanese drama the role of a geisha when required in a play is assumed by a female impersonator. Sidney JONES' opera, *The Geisha,* first produced in 1896 at London, is said to have had more success in translation for the Continental stage than *The Mikado* of Gilbert and Sullivan.

Gellée or **Gelée,** see **Claude Lorrain.**

Gellhorn, Martha Ellis (1908-), American journalist and novelist whose works include *What Mad Pursuit* (1934), a study of three neurotic young women in college; *The Trouble I've Seen,* a novel of living conditions in the industrial centers of the United States; *A Stricken Field,* dealing with conditions in Czechoslovakia after its seizure by Germany; *The Heart of Another,* a series of short stories laid in foreign cities.

Gelosi, in drama a celebrated troupe of Italian professional players who performed in Italy during the 16th century. The members were famous for their skill in improvising their lines from a scenario: Francesco ANDREINI played at one time with the company.

Gem, the name given to a jewel of any kind which has beauty and intrinsic value regardless of its setting; it is also applied to cut and polished semi-precious stones, and to carved or engraved precious stones. The list of gems includes the DIAMOND, RUBY, EMERALD, SAPPHIRE, OPAL, BLOODSTONE, JASPER, PEARL, AQUAMARINE, BERYL, TOPAZ, GARNET, MOONSTONE, ROSE QUARTZ, TOURMALINE, CARNELIAN, SARDONYX, ZIRCON, CAT'S EYE, AMETHYST, ONYX, TURQUOISE, JADE.

Geminiani, Francesco (1687-1762), Italian violinist and composer who studied with Alessandro SCARLATTI and Arcangelo CORELLI: he concertized and taught at various times in Italy, London, and Dublin, and wrote the first known method for the violin, *The Art of Playing on the Violin* (1730). He also wrote many sonatas for the violin with FIGURED BASS, six concerti grossi, and many works for various instrumental combinations.

Gemito, Vincenzo (1852-1929), Italian sculptor who worked for silversmiths, studied drawings, and taught himself by studying the sculptures in museums. He received some instruction from Mariano FORTUNY and MEISSONIER. Among his works, which are confined chiefly to bronze statues of small size, are *The Water Carrier, Verdi,* and *The Young Fisherman.* His output was extremely limited because worry over a commission unfilled through conditions beyond his control, unbalanced his mind for twenty-two years.

Gemünder, August Martin Ludwig (1814-1895), German violin maker who came to the United States in 1846, and later opened a shop in New York with his brother, **George Gemünder** (1816-1899): they made fine violins which were awarded medals in both America and Europe, and were sold at from $150.00 to $500.00. The business was continued by August M., Oscar A., and Rudolph Gemünder: more than a thousand fine violins were made by the various members of the family.

Genée, Adeline (1878-), Danish ballerina who made her first appearance on the stage as a child of eight, and became principal dancer at the Opera House, Copenhagen, in 1895. After appearing at opera houses in Berlin and Munich, she made her London debut at the Empire Theatre in 1897, remaining there for ten years. In 1907 she made her American debut at the New York Theatre in *The Soul Kiss,* and after appearing at the METROPOLITAN OPERA HOUSE and touring Australia, she retired in 1916. She received the Order of "Ingenii et Arti" from the King of Denmark in 1937.

Genée, Richard (1823-1895), Austrian opera composer who occupied many important positions as musical director in European theatres, and wrote light opera librettos for Johann STRAUSS, Jr., Franz von SUPPE, and Carl MILLOCKER. His operas include the highly successful *Nanon* (1877), and *The Last of the Mohicans,* an operetta founded on the novel by James Fenimore COOPER.

Genelli, Bonaventura (1798-1868), German painter and illustrator who studied at the Berlin Academy, and in Rome with OVERBECK. His works include *The Triumph of Bacchus and Ariadne; Hercules Playing the Lyre; Aesop Telling His Fables; Rebecca at the Well.* He is best known as an illustrator of the works of DANTE and HOMER.

Genghis Khan, see **Jenghiz Khan.**

Genie, see **Jinni.**

Genoa, a city in Italy associated with the arts of painting, sculpture, architecture, and music. Many of its fine marble palaces such as the Ducal Palace and the Municipal Palace, were built by the famous architect, Galeazzo ALESSI: the Palazzo Bianco contains a fine collection of pictures by distinguished Genoese painters, and the Municipal Museum contains the Guanerius violin bequeathed by its most famous son, the violinist, Nicoló PAGANINI.

Genre, the term applied to painting or sculpture in which the subjects are taken from real or fanciful life as contrasted with historical and religious scenes. The first painters of distinction in this field were Dutch and Flemish, but in the 18th and 19th centuries French and English artists became its exponents. In sculpture the subjects are more limited because marble and bronze do not lend themselves to treatment of this nature.

Genth, Lillian Mathilde (1876-), American painter who studied with Elliott DAINGERFIELD, James WHISTLER, and at the Colorossi Atelier. Her works have received both American and foreign awards, and are to be seen in art museums at Pittsburgh, Philadelphia, New York, Brooklyn,

Los Angeles, Paris, and London: she specializes in nude figures with appropriate backgrounds.

Gentile da Fabriano, see **Fabriano, Gentile da.**

Gentileschi, Orazio (1562-1647), Italian painter whose real name was Orazio Lomi: he mastered his art by self-study at Rome, and was employed on important works by Popes Clement VIII and Paul V. His finest creations include *Saint Cecilia and Saint Valerian; David After the Death of Goliath; The Annunciation; Moses Saved from the Waters.* He was included by VAN DYCK in his portraits of a hundred distinguished men.

George, Gladys (1904-), American stage and screen actress who made a first appearance as a child of three, and her New York debut in 1918 at the Shubert Theatre. After ten years' experience in stock companies she appeared in *Why Men Leave Home,* and achieved great success in *Personal Appearance.* She has also played leading roles in numerous films including *Valiant is the Word for Carrie; They Gave Him a Gun; Madame X; Marie Antoinette; A Child is Born; The Way of All Flesh; The Maltese Falcon.*

George, Grace (1879-), American actress who was trained at the American Academy of Dramatic Art, New York, and made her formal debut in 1898 at the Manhattan Theatre, New York, in *The Turtle.* Among the important plays in which she has appeared are *Frou-frou; Pretty Peggy; The Two Orphans; The Marriage of William Ashe; Clothes; A Woman's Way; The School for Scandal; Much Ado About Nothing; Carnival; Divorçons; The Liars; Major Barbara; Marie Antoinette; The First Mrs. Fraser; The Circle; Matrimony Preferred.*

George, Stefan (1868-1933), German poet educated at the Universities of Berlin, Munich and Paris: very few of his works are available in English, and many of his poems were printed only for private circulation, but such works as *Hymns* (1890), *The Year of the Soul,* and *The Tapestry of Life* place him among the greatest German poets, although it is quite evident that he was influenced by French, Italian, and English lyricists.

Georgian Style, a mode of architecture popular in England from about 1700 to 1800 during the reigns of the four Georges, and also in the United States during the same period. Its basis was Italian: a copy of the styles instituted by Andrea PALLADIO who is regarded as the founder of modern architecture by many authorities. The American name for the style, which manifested itself chiefly in residences, was "Colonial": many public buildings were also designed in the new mode.

Gérard, François Pascal Simon, Baron (1770-1837), French painter who studied with Augustin PAJOU and Louis DAVID: his works include *Joseph and His Brethren; Entry of Henry IV into Paris; Belisarius; Daphnis and Chloë; The Three Ages; Signing of the Concordat; Battle of Austerlitz; Psyche and Love.* His fame comes chiefly from more than three hundred portraits including those of NAPOLEON I, Murat, Empress Josephine, Madame RECAMIER, and Madame PASTA.

Gérard, Jean Ignace (1803-1847), French caricaturist and illustrator who settled at Paris in 1824, and built a great reputation for his drawings and caricatures in magazines: among his collected works are *The Metamorphoses of the Day,* picturing human beings with animal heads; *The Tribulations of Propriety.* He also illustrated LAFONTAINE's *Fables,* and signed some of his work "Grandville."

Gérardy, Jean (1877-1929), Belgian violoncellist who studied with Robert Bellmann and also at the Liége Conservatory, making his debut in 1890 with great success in London. After further study with F. Grützmacher he toured Europe and the United States in 1899, also appearing in chamber music concerts with Eugene YSAYE; Raoul PUGNO, Fritz KREISLER, Henri MARTEAU, and Leopold GODOWSKY. Gérardy was one of the great violoncellists of all time, ranking with Pablo CASALS.

Gerhardt, Elena (1883-), German coloratura soprano who studied at the Leipzig Conservatory, and made her debut in a recital with Artur NIKISCH at the piano in 1903. She has devoted herself to concert, oratorio, and recital singing, touring Europe, Great Britain, and America with great success as a singer of lieder, especially those of BRAHMS and SCHUBERT.

Géricault, Jean Louis André Théodore (1791-1824), French painter who studied with Horace VERNET and Pierre GUERIN: his notable works include *Cavalry Officer on Horseback; Wounded Cuirassier; Raft of the Medusa; The Derby at Epsom; Child Feeding a Horse; Wreck of the Medusa.* He was the leader of the realist movement in France, and a master of the painting of horses.

Gericke, Wilhelm (1845-1925), Austrian orchestral conductor who studied with Felix Dessoff at the Vienna Conservatory. From 1884 to 1889 he was conductor of the BOSTON SYMPHONY ORCHESTRA, returning to Vienna to conduct the Gesellschaft Concerts, and succeeding Emil PAUR from 1898 to 1906 as conductor again of the Boston Symphony Orchestra. He was especially famous as an expert in perfecting the technical virtuosity of an orchestra.

German, Sir Edward (1862-1936), English composer who studied at the Royal Academy of Music, London. In 1888 he composed the incidental music for Sir Henry IRVING's production of *Richard III*: this was so successful that he wrote the score for *Henry VIII, As You Like It, Much Ado About Nothing,* and *Nell Gwyn.* His successful light operas include *Merrie England; A Princess of Kensington; Tom Jones.* He also complete the operetta, *The Emerald Isle,* left unfinished by Sir Arthur SULLIVAN, and composed orchestral works.

Gérôme, Jean Léon (1824-1904), French painter and sculptor who studied with Paul DELAROCHE: his notable works include *The Cockfight; Anacreon with Bacchus and Cupid; Age of Augustus; Gladiators Saluting Caesar; Death of Caesar; Night in the Desert; Pygmalion and Galatea; Christian Martyrs; Great Bath at Brusa.* His sculptures, which are pronounced superior to his paintings by some critics, include equestrian statues of NAPOLEON I and FREDERICK THE GREAT.

Gershwin, George (1898-1937), American composer who studied with Ernest HUTCHESON, Edward Kilenyi, and Rubin GOLDMARK. Among his successful musical plays were *Lady Be Good* (1924); *Oh Kay!*; *Funny Face*; *Girl Crazy*; *Of Thee I Sing*. His best known work outside of the field of popular music is the *Rhapsody in Blue* (1924), the outstanding feature of which was the orchestration by Ferdinand GROFE; other compositions include a *Second Rhapsody*; a piano concerto; an orchestral suite, *An American in Paris*; also the "folk opera," *Porgy and Bess* (1935), a work uniting grand opera and musical comedy which was successfully revived in 1942.

Gerster, Etelka (1855-1920), Hungarian dramatic soprano who studied with Mathilde MARCHESI, and made her debut in 1876 at Venice in *Rigoletto*. After singing with great success at European opera houses, she appeared in the United States in 1878 under the management of Colonel Henry MAPLESON at the Academy of Music, New York, returning in 1883 and 1887. From 1897 to 1917 she conducted a singing school at Berlin, publishing a *Singing Guide* in 1906.

Gervex, Henri (1852-1929), French painter who studied with Alexandre CABANEL and Eugène FROMENTIN: his works include *Satyr Playing With a Bacchante*; *Rolla*; *Diana and Endymion*; *Autopsy in a Hospital* (Dr. Péan at the Saltpétrière); *The History of the Century*, a panorama; *Nana*; *Maternity*; *Coronation of Nicholas II*. He also was commissioned by the French Government for the decoration of several public buildings.

Gessner, Salomon or **Solomon** (1730-1788), Swiss poet and painter who trained himself in the latter art: among his works are *Arcadian Well*; *Dreamer*; *The Fisherman*; *The Well in the Woods*. His most successful poetical work was *Der Tod Abels* (The Death of Abel), a mock-heroic pastoral which was translated into many languages.

Gesso (It.), in painting or sculpture the term for prepared plaster (plaster of Paris) mixed with a binding material, and used as a background for paintings or reliefs.

Gest, Morris (1861-1942), American theatrical producer and manager born in Russia who came to the United States as a youth, and was educated in Boston public schools where he began his career as a producer in 1900. From 1905-1928 he combined with F. Ray Comstock in many successful productions including *Chu-Chin-Chow*; *The Rose of China*; *Polly Preferred*; *Lysistrata*; *The Whip*; *Stolen Orders*. During this period they leased the Manhattan Opera House and the Century Theatre; introduced Russian Ballet, the CHAUVE-SOURIS, and the Moscow ART THEATRE COMPANY in New York, in addition to presenting Max REINHARDT's *The Miracle*, and the Freiburg Passion Play. In 1936 Gest produced *Lady Precious Stream*, a play by the Chinese dramatist, Shih HSIUNG.

Gesta Romanorum, a medieval collection of tales written in Latin and compiled during the 13th and 14th centuries: it was popular in England, Holland, France, and Germany, and the earliest Latin texts contained in some instances more than 180 tales.

Gesualdo, Don Carlo (c.1550-1614), Italian composer who became a skilled performer on the LUTE: he published several books of MADRIGALS, and is historically important because his compositions were in advance of his generation through their novel contrapuntal devices, and liberal use of chromatics.

Gevaert, François-Auguste (1828-1908), Belgian composer who studied at the Ghent Conservatory, and won the Grand Prix de Rome for composition. He succeeded Joseph FETIS as director of the Brussels Conservatory, and became famous for his historical concerts there in which the works of great composers in all periods were performed. His compositions include several operas; a *Treatise on Instrumentation* (1863) which has been revised, enlarged and translated into several languages; also an outstanding theoretical work on harmony.

Gewandhaus, a famous concert hall in Leipzig where concerts have been given since 1885. Previous to that year concerts were given as far back as 1743 in the days of Johann Sebastian BACH in a private house, an inn, and in a vacant floor of the Gewandhaus (Cloth Hall). The new building has a large concert hall, and a smaller auditorium for chamber concerts. The first conductor of world-wide fame was Felix MENDELSSOHN (1835-43). Among the noted directors who followed may be mentioned Niels W. GADE, Carl REINECKE, Artur NIKISCH, Wilhelm FURTWANGLER, and Bruno WALTER.

Ghiberti, Lorenzo (c.1378-1455), Italian sculptor, architect, painter, and writer who first learned the goldsmith's art with Bartoluccio di Michele. He competed successfully against other six sculptors in designing the doors of the Baptistery of Florence, which, after they were completed, MICHELANGELO declared worthy of being the gates of Paradise. He also executed statues of St. John the Baptist, St. Matthew, and St. Stephen; designed glass windows for the cathedral in Florence, and wrote a *Commentary* (1416), in which he describes and criticizes works of art in the various cities visited during his travels.

Ghirlandaio, Domenico (1449-1494), Florentine painter whose full name was Domenico di Tommaso Curradi di Doffo Bigordi; his father, Tommaso Bigordi, was a goldsmith, but he studied painting and mosaic with Alessio BALDOVINETTI. His numerous important works, chiefly frescoes, include *Last Supper*; *St. Jerome*; *Coronation of the Virgin*; *Calling of Peter and Andrew*; *Glory of St. Zenobius*; *Legend of St. Francis*; *Adoration of the Shepherds*; *Christ in Glory*. His son, **Ridolfo Ghirlandaio** (1483-1561), was also a painter who studied with PIERO DI COSIMO and probably with FRA BARTOLOMMEO, also learning much from LEONARDO DA VINCI and MICHELANGELO: RAPHAEL was his admirer to the extent of inviting him to visit Rome. His works include *Christ and the Two Marys on the Road to Calvary; Coronation of the Virgin; Annunciation; Portrait of a Lady; St. Zenobius Resuscitating a Child.*

Ghislanzoni, Antonio (1824-1893), Italian baritone, musical editor, and librettist who wrote the books for more than sixty operas: that for Giuseppe VERDI's *Aïda* is the most famous, and was founded on a tale by Mariette Bey, the distinguished Egyptologist.

Ghost Town, American folk ballet: libretto and choreography by Marc Platoff; music by Richard RODGERS; produced at New York in 1940. The plot revolves around a deserted (ghost) mining town: an old miner tells a boy and a girl the story of the town when it was at its zenith, the action being conveyed through miming and dancing.

Giambono, Michele di Taddeo (c.1400-1462), Italian painter whose real name was Michele Giovanni Boni. He studied with Jacobello del Fiore, but shows the influence of Gentile da FABRIANO and PISANELLO in his paintings which include a five-part altarpiece; *Coronation of the Virgin; Nativity; Presentation in the Temple.* He is also highly regarded as a mosaicist.

Giannini, Dusolina (1902-), American dramatic soprano who studied with Marcella SEMBRICH, and made her operatic debut at Hamburg in 1925. She appeared at opera houses in Berlin, Vienna, and London after touring Australia and New Zealand. In 1936 she made her debut with the Metropolitan Opera Company in Giuseppe VERDI's *Aïda,* and in 1938 created the role of Hester in *The Scarlet Letter* (Hamburg), an opera composed by her brother, Vittorio GIANNINI.

Giannini, Vittorio (1903-), American composer who won a scholarship at the Royal Conservatory in Milan, Italy, and also studied with Rubin GOLDMARK at the Juilliard Graduate School. His compositions include several operas, a piano concerto, an organ concerto, a symphony, several chamber works, and a *Madrigal* for four voices and string quartet. He has written several short operas for radio broadcasting: the dramatic soprano, Dusolina GIANNINI is his sister.

Giannuzzi, Giulio Pippi de', see Giulio Romano.

Gibbon, Edward (1737-1794), English essayist and historian partially educated at Oxford: his greatest work is *The History of the Decline and Fall of the Roman Empire* (1776-1788), still the chief authority for the period which it covers although it is admittedly not perfect from either literary or historical standpoints. His works also include an *Essay on the Study of Literature,* and *Memoirs of My Life and Writings.*

Gibbons, Floyd (1886-1939), American journalist and radio commentator noted for his ability to broadcast distinctly at a speed of almost 250 words a minute. His books, which are written in somewhat sensational but realistic style, include *How the Laconia Sank* (1917), recounting his own experience when the S.S. *Laconia* was torpedoed during World War I; *They Thought We Wouldn't Fight; The Red Knight of Germany; The Red Napoleon.*

Gibbons, Grinling (1648-1721), English wood carver, said to have been born of Dutch parents in Rotterdam, who was employed by Charles II in the creation of statues and ornamental carving in wood. Among his works are a bronze statue of Charles II and of James II: Sir Christopher WREN utilized his services in many private residences for architectural decoration: he also carved the woodwork for the choir of St. Paul's, London, and was appointed master wood carver to George I.

Gibbons, Orlando (1583-1625), English composer who became organist of WESTMINSTER ABBEY in 1623: his reputation as a composer is based on his sacred music which included many fine anthems. He was a remarkable organist and harpsichordist; several of his pieces are in a famous collection called *Parthenia* written for the VIRGINALLS.

Gibbs, Arthur Hamilton (1888-), Anglo-American novelist born in London who served in the British Army during World War I, and settled in the United States in 1920. His works include *The Complete Oxford Man* (1910); *The Persistent Lovers; Soundings; Labels; Harness; Chances; A Half Inch of Candle.*

Gibbs, James (1682-1754), English architect who studied in Rome. In 1709 he became a member of a board appointed by the London municipality to superintend the building of fifty churches in the metropolis. Two of the ten churches that were actually constructed were planned by Gibbs: he also designed the Radcliffe Library at Oxford and the Senate House at Cambridge, and wrote several treatises on architecture.

Gibbs, Sir Philip Hamilton (1877-), English journalist and novelist: he was one of five accredited correspondents during World War I who were knighted in 1920. His works include *The Street of Adventure* (1900); *Realities of War; The Middle of the Road; Darkened Windows; The Winding Lane; This Nettle, Danger; The Amazing Summer; The Long Alert.*

Gibson, Charles Dana (1867-), American illustrator, educated at the ART STUDENTS' LEAGUE, New York, and in Paris, who became a member of the American Academy of Arts and Letters. His greatest creation is the famous "Gibson Girl," executed in black and white of which he became the leading exponent in national magazines including *Century, Harper's, Life,* and *Collier's.* Gibson has illustrated many books including Anthony HOPE's *Prisoner of Zenda,* and Richard Harding DAVIS' *Soldiers of Fortune.* His published collections of drawings include *The Education of Mr. Pipp, The Americans, A Widow and Her Friends,* and *The Social Ladder.*

Gibson, Ian (1921-), Canadian dancer born in Glasgow, Scotland, and brought to the Dominion as an infant. After a doctor had recommended dancing to cure a bad case of "pigeon-toes," Ian became interested in the ballet, and made such progress that he was selected at nineteen by Leonide MASSINE to become a member of the BALLET RUSSE DE MONTE CARLO in 1939, and joined the BALLET THEATRE in 1942. His athletic type of dancing has met with pronounced approval in the ballets *L'Epreuve d'Amour, Princess Aurora,* and *Naughty Lizette.*

Gibson, John (1790-1866), English sculptor who studied with CANOVA and THORWALDSEN: his works include *Sleeping Shepherd; Hunter and Dog; Mars and Cupid; Hero and Leander; Nymph and Cupid; Bacchante and Faun; Amazon Thrown from her Horse; Hunter Holding His Dog; Phaeton Driving the Chariot of the Sun.* He also executed a tinted *Venus,* and the group, *Queen Victoria Supported by Justice and Clemency,* in the Houses of Parliament.

Gibson, Wilfrid Wilson (1878-), English poet who was privately educated, and served in World War I. His works include *Urlyn the Harper* (1902); *Borderlands; Daily Bread; Hill Tracks; The Golden Room; Highland Dawn; Kestrel Edge and Other Plays; Coming and Going; The Alert.*

Gidé, André Paul Guillaume (1869-), French essayist and novelist; considered one of the outstanding figures in modern French literature. His works available in English include *Prometheus Illbound* (1919); *The Vatican Swindle,* later issued as *Lafcadio's Adventures; The Counterfeiters; The Prodigal Son; The School for Wives; The Immoralist; Oscar Wilde; Dostoievsky; Travels in the Congo.*

Gielgud, John (1904-), English stage and screen actor who studied at the Royal Academy of Dramatic Art, and made his debut in 1921 at London. Among the plays in which he has appeared with great success are *The Vortex; The Cherry Orchard; The Three Sisters; The Patriot,* in which he made his New York debut in 1928; *Ghosts; The Merchant of Venice; Hamlet; Dear Octopus.* He has also appeared in numerous films including *The Good Companions; Secret Agent; The Prime Minister.*

Gieseking, Walter (1895-), French pianist and composer, born of German parents, who studied at the Hanover Conservatory and made his debut in 1920: after touring Europe with great success, he appeared at AEOLIAN HALL, New York, in 1926, and is regarded as a leading exponent of both classic and modern piano music. His compositions include chamber music, piano pieces, and songs.

Gifford, Robert Swain (1840-1905), American painter who studied with a Dutch artist in New Bedford, Mass., and opened a studio in Boston, and later in New York. He taught at Cooper Union, New York, for thirty years, finding the time to sketch during travels through Europe, North Africa, Alaska, and the Pacific Coast. His paintings include *Near the Coast; Barney's Joy Cliff; Salt Mills at Darmouth; Booth in Algeria; Autumn on the Seashore; Deserted Whales; Egyptian Caravan; Border of the Desert.*

Gifford, Sanford Robinson (1823-1880), American painter educated at Brown University, the National Academy of Design, New York, and in Paris and Rome. He made many sketches while traveling in Europe and North Africa, and served in the Civil War. His notable paintings include *Shrewsbury River; Castle of Chillon; View in Venice; Bivouac of the Seventh Regiment at Arlington Heights; Sunset on the Hudson; Fire Island Beach; Sunrise on the Matterhorn.*

Gigli, Beniamino (1890-), Italian operatic tenor who studied at the Liceo Musicale di Ste. Cecilia, Rome, and made his debut in Ponchielli's *La Gioconda* at Rovigno in 1914. After singing at opera houses throughout Europe, he appeared in 1920 at the Metropolitan Opera House, New York, in Boito's *Mefistofele,* remaining until 1932 and also touring in recital. His repertory includes the leading roles in all important Italian operas: he has also appeared in several musical films.

Gigoux, Jean François (1806-1894), French painter who studied at the ECOLE DES BEAUX-ARTS, Paris: his notable works include *Mme. Du Barry Dressing; The Death of Leonardo da Vinci; Anthony and Cleopatra after the Battle of Actium; Fountain of Youth; Death of Manon Lescaut; The Young Girl; The Good Samaritan; Magdalen in the Desert.* He decorated the chapel of St. Gervais, Paris, and made several hundred illustrations for René Le SAGE's *Gil Blas.*

Gigue (Fr.), the name in France for the jig, a very fast country dance in 6-8 time first used by English composers, and finally appearing as the last movement in the classic suites of CORELLI, BACH, and HANDEL.

Gilbert, Sir Alfred (1854-1934), English sculptor and goldsmith who studied at the ECOLE DES BEAUX-ARTS, Paris: his works include *Mother and Child; The Kiss of Victory; Perseus Arming; Icarus; The Enchanted Chair;* the Shaftesbury Memorial Fountain; the Queen Alexandra Memorial; the Memorial to the Duke of Clarence. His work as a goldsmith includes figurines of *Victory, St. Michael,* and *St. George;* also many seals and keys.

Gilbert, Cass (1859-1934), American architect who studied at the Massachusetts Institute of Technology. In 1879 he won a prize offered by the American Institute of Architects, and in 1880 made a tour of France, Italy, and England studying the styles of architecture, ancient and modern, in all these countries. His notable designs include the Woolworth Building, New York; the public libraries in Detroit, St. Louis, and New Haven; the New York Life Insurance Company Building, New York; the Army Supply Base, Brooklyn, New York; the State Capitol, St. Paul; the United States Treasury Annex; the United States Supreme Court Building, and the United States Chamber of Commerce, Washington, D. C. He was consulting architect for the George Washington Bridge across the Hudson River to Fort Lee, N. J., and one of the founders of the Architectural League of New York.

285

Gilbert, Mrs. George Henry (1821-1904), American actress, born in England, who came to the United States in 1849 with her husband, George Henry Gilbert, and made her American debut as a dancer in 1851, and as an actress in 1857. She joined Augustin DALY's company in 1869, and became famous for her portrayal of elderly women's roles in *Macbeth; Dollars and Cents; She Stoops to Conquer; Frou-frou; A Celebrated Case; David Copperfield; The School for Scandal; The Royal Family; Granny.* Mrs. Gilbert was one of the most highly respected and beloved actresses who have appeared on the American stage.

Gilbert, Henry Franklin Belknap (1868-1928), American composer who studied at the NEW ENGLAND CONSERVATORY OF MUSIC, and with Horatio W. PARKER and Edward MACDOWELL. His works include a *Comedy Overture on Negro Themes; Dance in the Place Congo,* a symphonic poem produced as a ballet at the Metropolitan Opera House in 1918; *Negro Rhapsody; Riders to the Sea; American Dances in Rag-time Rhythm; Jazz Study,* an opera, *Fantasy in Delft; Symphonic Piece; Suite for Chamber Orchestra;* also numerous piano pieces and songs.

Gilbert, John (1895-1936), American stage and screen actor who made his first appearance on the stage as an infant in an Eddie FOY play, and in 1915 joined the Baker Stock Company at Spokane, Washington. His first film appearances were in the Western pictures made by William S. HART; he also played leading roles in *The White Heather; Heart of the Hills; The Big Parade; The Flesh and the Devil; Love; Queen Christina.*

Gilbert, Sir William Schwenk (1836-1911), English poet and dramatist who was the author of several comedies and plays of serious character, but whose fame rests on his association with Sir Arthur SULLIVAN in the creation of a series of immortal comic operas with Richard D'Oyly CARTE as producer. The list of international favorites includes *Trial by Jury* (1875); *The Sorcerer; H.M.S. Pinafore; The Pirates of Penzance; Patience; Iolanthe; Princess Ida; The Mikado; Ruddygore; The Yeomen of the Guard; The Gondoliers* (1889). After the production of the last-named, disagreement over some business matter caused a separation for a period of four years, but the two operas written in collaboration later, *Utopia Limited* and *The Grand Duke,* failed to achieve a degree of success comparable with that of the earlier operas.

Gilbert and Sullivan, see **Gilbert, Sir William Schwenk;** also **Sullivan, Sir Arthur Seymour.**

Gil Blas de Santillane, History of, a romance by René LE SAGE published in four volumes from 1715 to 1735. The hero, Gil Blas, relates the story of his life; many of the incidents are taken from Vincente de ESPINEL's tale, *The Life of the Esquire Marcos de Obregon.* George SMOLLETT translated it in 1761.

Gild, see **Guild.**

Gilder, Richard Watson (1844-1909), American poet who became editor of *Century Magazine* from 1881 to 1909: the Society of American Artists was founded at his home in 1877, and the Authors' Club in 1882. His works comprise sixteen volumes of poems including *The New Day* (1875); *The Celestial Passion; Two Worlds and Other Poems; The Great Remembrance; A Book of Music; The Fire Divine.*

Gilibert, Charles (1866-1910), French dramatic baritone who studied at the Paris Conservatory and after singing at the Opéra-Comique, became a leading singer at La Monnaie in Brussels. He made his debut in 1900 at the METROPOLITAN OPERA HOUSE, New York, in Gounod's *Romeo and Juliet,* remaining there until 1903, and joining the Manhattan Opera Company in 1906 where he sang until 1910.

Gillette, William (1855-1937), American actor and dramatist who made his debut in 1875 at the Boston Museum in Mark TWAIN's *The Gilded Age.* Among the many successful plays in which he appeared as both actor and dramatist were *The Private Secretary; Held by the Enemy; Secret Service; Too Much Johnson; Clarice; The Dream Maker; The Professor; Esmeralda; Sherlock Holmes.* He also played in Henri BERNSTEIN's *Samson;* BARRIE's *Dear Brutus;* Clare KUMMER's *A Successful Calamity;* SARDOU's *Diplomacy.*

Gillingwater, Claude (1870-1939), American stage and screen actor who had several years training under David BELASCO: among the films in which he played important roles were *Little Lord Fauntleroy; Alice Adams; Three Wise Fools; The Show-Off; A Tale of Two Cities; The Prisoner of Shark Island; The Poor Little Rich Girl; Conquest; A Yank at Oxford; Just Around the Corner; There Goes My Heart.*

Gillmore, Frank (1867-1943), American actor who made his first appearance at twelve in a pantomime, *Jack and the Beanstalk, at Maidstone,* England. In 1888 he made his formal debut as Captain Vane in *Fascination* at the Vaudeville Theatre, London, and his American debut in 1892 at St. Louis in *Settled Out of Court.* Among the plays in which he appeared were *A Bachelor's Romance; The Gay Lord Quex; Becky Sharp; Tess of the D'Urbervilles; Vanity Fair.* In 1919 he became executive secretary of the ACTORS EQUITY ASSOCIATION, and in 1929 its president. He was elected president of Associated Actors and Artists of America in 1937. His daughter, **Margalo Gillmore** (1897-), studied at the American Academy of Dramatic Art, New York, and made her debut in 1917 on the New York stage in *The Scrap of Paper:* she has appeared in many plays including *The Famous Mrs. Fair; He Who Gets Slapped; Outward Bound; The Green Hat; The Silver Cord; Berkeley Square; The Barretts of Wimpole Street; Mary of Scotland; Biography; Valley Forge; No Time for Comedy.*

Gilly, Dinh (1877-1940), French baritone born in Algiers who studied in Italy, and made his debut in 1911 at COVENT GARDEN, London, in VERDI's *Aïda.* He made his American debut in 1909 with the Metropolitan Opera Company in MASSENET's *Werther,* and remained until 1914, creating parts in Puccini's *The Girl of the Golden West*, Gluck's *Armide*, Offenbach's *Tales of Hoffmann*, and Charpentier's *Julien*. After his retirement from the stage he became a distinguished teacher of singing.

Gilman, Lawrence (1878-1939), American music critic and author who studied painting with William Merritt Chase, but was self-taught in music. He acted as music critic of *Harper's Weekly*; program annotator for the concerts of the New York Philharmonic-Symphony Orchestra and the Philadelphia Orchestra; music editor of the New York *Herald Tribune*. His works include *Phases of Modern Music* (1904); *The Music of Tomorrow*; *Stories of Symphonic Music*; *Aspects of Modern Opera*; *Nature in Music*; *Music and the Cultivated Man*; *Toscanini and Great Music*.

Gilmore, Patrick Sarsfield (1829-1892), American bandmaster born in Ireland: in 1859 he organized Gilmore's Band at Boston, and became famous through the National Peace Jubilee in 1869, and the World's Peace Jubilee in 1872, employing orchestras of a thousand or more members, and choruses of 10,000 singers. He toured the United States, Canada, and Europe with his band, and in 1863 wrote the famous Civil War song, *When Johnny Comes Marching Home*, which has remained a favorite: its melody was utilized in an overture with the same title by Roy Harris.

Gilpatric, Guy (1896-), American short story writer whose tales of Colin Glencannon, chief engineer of the *S. S. Inchcliffe Castle*, have interested readers of the *Saturday Evening Post* for several years: there are those who contend that a more fascinating blackguard never sailed the seven seas. His works, chiefly collections of the Glencannon stories, include *Scotch and Water* (1931); *Half Seas Over*; *Mr. Glencannon*; *Three Sheets in the Wind*; *The Compleat Goggler*; *Glencannon Afloat*.

Gilpin, Charles Sidney (1878-1930), American Negro actor born in the South: in 1919 he appeared with great success in John Drinkwater's *Abraham Lincoln*, and in 1920 played the leading role in Eugene O'Neill's *Emperor Jones*: his portrayal of Brutus Jones was regarded as an extraordinary accomplishment in the annals of the stage.

Gioconda, La, grand opera in four acts: libretto by Tobio Gorrio (anagram for Arrigo Boito); music by Amilcare Ponchielli; first produced at Milan in 1876, and at New York in 1883. The story is: Barnaba, spy for the Council of Ten in Venice, plans revenge on the singer, La Gioconda, who is in love with the Genoese noble, Enzo Grimaldo. Gioconda, however, discovers that Enzo loves the Inquisitor Alvise's wife, Laura. Barnaba arranges a rendezvous between Laura and Enzo on board the latter's ship, but informs Alvise of the intended meeting. Gioconda, having heard of Barnaba's plot, puts out for the vessel and is about to kill Laura, when the latter holds up a rosary given to her by Gioconda's mother. Alvise forces Laura to drink a poison cup, but Gioconda secretly changes it for a sleeping draught. Laura, supposedly dead, is exhibited with joy by Alvise to his guests. In an attempt to stab Alvise, Enzo is taken prisoner, and for securing his release and Laura, Gioconda promises herself to Barnaba. Laura and Enzo are united, but Gioconda kills herself when Barnaba comes to claim her for his own. There is a complete Columbia recording of the opera and separate recordings by both Victor and Columbia of the tenor aria, *Cielo e Mar*, and the ballet music, *The Dance of the Hours*.

Giocondo, Fra Giovanni (c.1435-1515), Italian architect and engineer regarded as one of the most distinguished at the beginning of the Renaissance. Among his greatest works were the Palazzo del Consiglio at Verona, and the Fondaco dei Tedeschi at Venice. He superseded Bramante as architect of St. Peter's, Rome, and built the Pont Notre Dame at Paris for Charles VIII of France. He was also a man of great classical learning, and is credited with having discovered the letters of the younger Pliny.

Giocoso (It.), in music an indication that a composition is to be performed in playful, joyous, or sportive style.

Giono, Jean (1895-), French poet and novelist who served in the French army during World War I: some of his poems and short stories were published in magazines from 1921 to 1928, but his successful novels, *Hill of Destiny* and *Lovers Are Never Losers,* did not appear until 1929. Both of the above, and also *The Song of the World* and *Harvest* are published in English.

Giordani, Giuseppe (1744-1798), Italian composer, also known as *Giordanello,* who studied with Domenico Cimarosa and Nicola Zingarelli at the Loreto Conservatory. He went to London in 1753, and remained there with other members of his family until 1782. His works include thirty operas and much chamber music: the song, *Caro mio Ben,* which is credited to him, has been recorded by Ezio Pinza for Victor.

Giordano, Luca (1632-1705), Italian painter who studied with Pietro da Cortona and Giuseppe Ribera: he was nicknamed *Fra Presto* because of his speed in painting. His works include *Christ Driving Out the Money Changers; Rape of the Sabines; The Story of Judith; Mars and Venus; The Brazen Serpent; St. Francis Xavier Baptising Savages; The Birth of John the Baptist.* He was the last of the great Italian painters: only his facility in execution kept him from achieving even greater fame.

Giordano, Umberto (1867-), Italian composer who studied at the Naples Conservatory: in 1889 he offered a one-act opera, *Marina,* in competition with Mascagni's *Cavalleria Rusticana:* the latter won the coveted prize, but Giordano's work received favorable mention. His works include the successful operas *Andrea Chenier* (1896); *Fedora; Siberia; Madame Sans-Gêne; La Cena delle Beffe* (The Jest): the last-named is founded on Sem Benelli's romantic play with the same title.

Giorgione, Giorgio Barbarelli (c.1478-1510), Italian painter whose real name was Giorgio Barbarelli: he was a pupil along with TITIAN of Giovanni BELLINI, and painted frescoes for many residences at Venice. Only four pictures have been certified as actually his work: they include *The Virgin of Castelfranco; The Storm; The Three Philosophers; Venus.* Many more are credited to him without documentary evidence: among his pupils were Titian, Sebastiano del PIOMBO, Bernardino PORDENONE, and Jacopo PALMA.

Giorni, Aurelio (1895-1938), Italian-American composer and pianist, grandson of Bertel THORWALDSEN, who studied with Giovanni SGAMBATI at the Academy of St. Cecilia in Rome, and also with Engelbert HUMPERDINCK. After making his debut at Rome in 1912, and touring Europe, he came to the United States in 1915 to teach at several music schools, and act as pianist in the Elshuco Trio from 1919 to 1934. His compositions include works for orchestra, chamber music, concert études for the piano, and songs.

Giottino (? -c.1369), Italian painter probably identical with *Giotto di Maestro Stefano,* or, according to Giorgio VASARI, *Maso di Banco:* all the above is speculation. Among the works credited to him by various authorities are the *Miracles of Saint Silvestro;* a fresco, *The Last Judgment,* and a *Pietá* in the UFFIZI GALLERY.

Giotto (c.1266-c.1337), Italian painter who was the son of a shepherd named Bondone: he is said to have studied with Giovanni CIMABUE. His works include twenty-eight frescoes, *Scenes from the life of Christ,* in the church of St. Francesco at Assisi; the allegories, *Poverty, Obedience* and *Chastity* on the ceilings of the lower part of the same church; *Scenes from the life of Christ and the Virgin,* and a *Last Judgment* in the Cappella dell' Arena Enrico degli Scrovegni at Padua.

Giotto di Maestro Stefano, see **Giottino.**

Gipsy Baron, The, see **Gypsy Baron, The.**

Giraldi, Giovanni Battista (1504-1573), Italian poet, novelist, and dramatist who was so skilled in literature and philosophy that he was appointed Secretary of State under two successive dukes of ESTE. His works include the *Hecatommithi,* a collection of tales resembling those of BOCCACCIO from which Shakespeare derived the plots of "Othello" and "Measure for Measure." He also wrote a play, *Orbecchi,* produced in 1541 and considered the finest dramatic work written before Shakespeare. He signed some of his works with pen name "Cinthio."

Girandole, in architecture an ornamental candlestick with branches each of which contain several lights. During the 18th century makers of this particular type of decorative furnishing vied with each other in fashioning beautiful girandoles of hard woods or gilded bronze.

Girardon, François (1628-1715), French sculptor who studied with François ANGUIER, and worked for thirty years under the direction of Charles LE BRUN in the TUILERIES and at VERSAILLES. Among his notable works are a bas-relief, *Nymphs Bathing;* a group, *The Rape of Proser-*

pine; a colossal bronze statue of Louis XIV in Roman attire which was destroyed during the French Revolution; the tomb of Richelieu in the Church of the Sorbonne.

Giraudoux, Jean (1882-), French novelist and dramatist who served in World War I and became a member of the Ministry of Foreign Affairs at its conclusion. After the Nazi conquest of France he went to Vichy with Marshal Pétain as director of propaganda. His play, *Siegfried,* was produced by Eva LE GALLIENNE at the Civic Repertory Theatre in 1930: in 1937, an adaptation of Giradoux' play, *Amphitryon 38,* was produced by the Theatre Guild. His novels, *Suzanne and the Pacific* and *My Friend from Limousin,* are published in English.

Girl of the Golden West, The, grand opera in three acts: libretto by Guelfo Civini and Carlo Zangarini based on David BELASCO's play with the same title, the Italian equivalent being *La Fanciulla del West;* music by Giacomo PUCCINI. The world première took place at the Metropolitan Opera House in 1910 with Arturo TOSCANINI conducting, and Emmy DESTINN, Enrico CARUSO, and Pasquale AMATO in the cast. David Belasco supervised the staging, and the composer was present, but the work failed to please the opera-loving public.

Girodet-Trioson, Anne Louis (1767-1824), French painter who studied with Louis DAVID, and won the Prix de Rome in 1789 with his canvas, *Joseph and His Brethren.* His notable works include *Hippocrates Refusing the Presents of Artaxerxes; Sleep of Endymion; The Danae; The Four Seasons; Revolt at Cairo; The Burial of Attila; Napoleon Receiving the Keys of Vienna.* He also illustrated the Didot VIRGIL, the Louvre RACINE, and the poems of ANACREON.

Girtin, Thomas (1775-1802), English painter who established a reputation first for architectural sketches, but, after making the acquaintance of Joseph M. W. TURNER, his manipulation of water colors in painting has led to his being credited with having originated modern water color painting. Among his notable works are *The Great Hall in Conway Castle; Melrose Abbey; York Cathedral; Interior of Canterbury Cathedral; View on the Thames; Warkworth Hermitage.*

Giselle, a romantic ballet in two acts: libretto by Théophile GAUTIER; based on a theme by Heinrich HEINE; choreography by Jean CORALLI; music by Adolphe ADAM; first produced at Paris in 1841 with Carlotti GRISI in the role of Giselle and Lucien PETIPA as Albrecht. The ballet has been produced at regular intervals during the past century in European, English and American opera houses, and has recently (1943) been performed by the BALLET THEATRE during its New York season.

Gish, Dorothy (1898-), American stage and screen actress who made her first appearance at four in *East Lynne* at the Lincoln Square Theatre, New York, and played children's parts with Fiske O'HARA and other stars until 1912 when she entered the films. Among the numerous pictures in which she played are *The Orphans of the Storm, Nell Gwyn, Romola, Madame Pompadour.* In 1928 she reappeared on the stage in *Young Love; The Inspector General; The Pillars of Society; Foreign Affairs; Comedienne; Brittle Heaven; Missouri Legend.*

Gish, Lillian (1896-), American stage and screen actress who first appeared as a child of six on the stage in *The Little Red Schoolhouse.* Later she played the part of a fairy dancer for two years with Sarah BERNHARDT, and with Mary Pickford in *A Good Little Devil.* Among the films in which she was featured are *The Birth of a Nation; Broken Blossoms; The Orphans of the Storm; Romola,* with her sister, Dorothy GISH; *Way Down East; The White Sister.* She returned to the stage in 1930 to appear in *Uncle Vanya; Camille, Nine Pine Street; The Joyous Season; Within the Gates; The Star Wagon; Dear Octopus.*

Giulio Romano (c.1492-1546), Italian painter and architect whose real name was Giulio Pippi de' Giannuzzi: he became RAPHAEL's pupil and assistant as a young man, and the great master left his painting utensils and art works to Romano and Gianfrancesco Penni with instructions to complete the frescoes depicting the life of Constantine in the VATICAN. His notable works include *The Story of Diana* and *The Trojan War* in the Ducal Palace at Mantua; *The Vision of Magdalen; The Story of Cupid and Psyche; The Capture of Carthage; The Fall of the Giants; The History of Romulus and Remus.*

Giuseppino, Il, see **Cesari, Giuseppe.**

Glackens, Louis M. (1866-1933), American artist and illustrator who was on the staff of *Puck* for twenty years, and drew many cartoons for the New York *American.* He also illustrated many books including *The Log of the Water Wagon* by Bert L. Taylor and W. C. Gibson, and the *Uncle Remus Stories* by Joel Chandler Harris.

Glackens, William James (1870-1938), American painter who worked in the art department of Philadelphia newspapers while studying at the Pennsylvania Academy of Fine Arts. In 1895 he spent a year in Europe, and on his return became an illustrator for New York newspapers, also covering the Spanish-American War for *McClure's Magazine,* and illustrating the novels of Charles and Paul de KOCK. He received many awards and medals for paintings including *The Bathers; Central Park in Winter; Bal Martinique; Beach at Saint-Jean-de-Luz; Chez Mouquin; Promenade.* He has been described as a true American painter in the French style, and as America's greatest artist in the impressionistic style.

Gladiators, bands of professional fighters who struggled to the death in Roman arenas in ancient times. The first bands were exhibited at Rome in 264 B.C.: beginning with three pairs of combatants, the number engaged at one time was increased to 300 pairs in the days of Julius CAESAR, and Domitian, at the festival of Saturnalia in A.D. 90, exhibited 5000 pairs. Gladiators were usually drawn from slaves, prisoners of war, or criminals con-

demned to death, but freedmen often joined their ranks. One of the most famous gladiators was the Thracian, Spartacus, who escaped from Capua in 73 B.C. with seventy of his comrades, and defied the Roman legions for three years. Gladiatorial contests were abolished by the Emperor Constantine I about A.D. 300.

Glaser, Lulu (1874-), American comedienne and singer who first appeared in 1892 in the chorus of *The Lion Tamer* with Francis WILSON: among the many successful plays in which she appeared are *The Merry Monarch; Erminie; The Chieftain; The Little Corporal; Cyrano de Bergerac; Sweet Anne Page; Dolly Varden; The Madcap Princess; Dolly Dollars.*

Glasgow, Ellen (1874-), American novelist educated in private schools: her works include *The Descendant* (1897); *The Voice of the People; The Battle Ground; Virginia; Life and Gabriella; The Builders; Barren Ground; The Romantic Comedians; They Stooped to Folly; The Sheltered Life; Vein of Iron; In This Our Life.*

Glasgow Art Gallery (Glasgow), a collection of paintings, sculptures, and objects of art founded in 1854 through the purchase of the collection owned by Archibald McLellan. It was on exhibition for some years in the Corporation Galleries, but was finally housed in its own building in Kelvingrove Park, erected at a cost of more than a million dollars, and has been added to from time to time by purchases or bequests of ancient and modern works of art.

Glaspell, Susan (1882-), American dramatist and novelist educated at Drake University, Des Moines, Ia.: her novels include *The Glory of the Conquered* (1909); *Lifted Masks; Fidelity; Brook Evans; Fugitive's Return; Ambrose Holt and Family; The Morning is Near Us.* She has also written *Trifles* (1917); *Suppressed Desires; Inheritors; Alison's House* which won the Pulitzer prize in 1930.

Glass, Montague (1877-1934), American author of short stories born in England of Jewish parentage, and brought to the United States as a child. He was educated at the College of the City of New York and New York University, and sold his first story to a trade journal. His stories include *Potash and Perlmutter* (1910), dramatized in 1913; *Abe and Mawruss,* dramatized in 1915: he also wrote the plays *Business before Pleasure* and *It's Never Too Late* with Jules Eckert GOODMAN, and many entertaining stories of American Jewish life for national magazines.

Glass, a solid, usually transparent substance consisting of a combination of silicates transformed by smelting. It may be made in various colors, and can be blown, pressed, cast, and cut into any desired shape. Glass was known to the Egyptians who used eyes of colored glass in some of their statues: the technique of glass blowing is practically the same today as in ancient times. Glass was used by the Greeks and Romans for vases, and the art work of the Venetians in the Middle Ages came close to perfection. Glass mosaics played an important part in Byzantine art:

mosaicists placed tiny cubes of glass together, and painted them in such a way as to imitate the shape and colors of animate and inanimate objects and forms. In *stained glass,* the pieces of colored glass are placed in frames, and shaped to form the desired figures or patterns: they are then permanently set in lead which accentuates the contours of the figures or patterns. In the 14th century there was a marked improvement in the delineation of the figures, and the art of making stained glass windows reached its zenith in the 17th century.

Glazunoff, Alexander Konstantinovitch (1865-1936), Russian composer who studied at the Polytechnic Institute in St. Petersburg and with Nicholas RIMSKY-KORSAKOW, also becoming friendly with Mily BALAKIREV. After teaching at the Conservatory, and conducting the Russian Symphony Concerts at St. Petersburg, he visited the United States and England, finally settling in Paris. His works include eight symphonies; four symphonic poems, several overtures and suites; three ballets, a violin concerto; a piano concerto; chamber music; piano works and many miscellaneous compositions for various instruments.

Glee, a composition for three or more voices with accompaniment which originated in England about 1700: the glees composed by Samuel Webbe (1740-1816) are considered the finest examples of this form of unaccompanied singing. The difference between a MADRIGAL and a glee is that the madrigal is constructed in contrapuntal form on a few subjects, and the glee has several subjects that are harmonized but not developed.

Glick, Carl (1889-), American author and dramatist educated at Northwestern University who became greatly interested in the LITTLE THEATRE movement, directing several organizations and writing numerous plays including *The Fourth Mrs. Phillips; Outclassed; Ten Days Later; It Isn't Done; The Devil's Host; The Immortal* in collaboration with Bernard SOBEL. He is the author with Albert McCleery of *Curtains Going Up,* a constructive work on the subject of the community theatre.

Gliére, Reinhold Moritzovitch (1875-), Russian composer who studied with ARENSKY, TANEIEV, and IPPOLITOW-IWANOW at the Moscow Conservatory; also in Berlin. He became professor of composition at the Kiev Conservatory, and later at the Moscow Conservatory: in 1938 he was elected president of the Union of Soviet Composers. His compositions include several operas and ballets; symphonies, symphonic poems; a harp concerto; chamber music, vocal works; pieces for violin and for piano. The *Russian Sailors' Dance* from Gliére's ballet, THE RED POPPY, is a popular orchestral concert piece in the United States; there is a Victor recording by the Philadelphia Orchestra.

Glinka, Michail Ivanovitch (1804-1857), Russian composer who studied at the Chief Pedagogic Institute in St. Petersburg, and also with John FIELD and J. L. Fuchs. After meeting Gaetano DONIZETTI and Vincenzo BELLINI he failed to compose successfully in the Italian manner, and finally decided to write works in the Russian idiom: he succeeded admirably in his operas *A Life for the Czar* (1836), and *Russlan and Ludmilla* (1842) He is regarded as the first great Russian composer to bring the national spirit to important artistic expression, and thereby to found a school of distinctively Russian music. There is a Victor recording of the overture to *Russlan and Ludmilla* by the Indianapolis Symphony Orchestra under Fabian Sevitzky.

Glissade, in ballet a sliding or gliding step beginning and ending in the fifth of the FIVE POSITIONS.

Glissando (It.), in music an effect of "sliding" produced on the piano, harp, violin, viola, and violoncello by permitting the fingers to slide rapidly over the keys or strings. The effect on the violin is that of an exaggerated PORTAMENTO; it is also most effective on the harp because the pedals permit the use of a variety of scales.

Globe Theatre, a playhouse in London built by Richard and Cuthbert BURBAGE in 1599: it was a round building with a bare main floor and two galleries of rude wooden seats without a roof overhead. SHAKESPEARE played in it, and also was one of the shareholders. The theatre was burned down in 1613, but immediately rebuilt, and most of Shakespeare's plays were produced there; also those of JONSON, BEAUMONT, FLETCHER, FORD, and MASSINGER.

Glockenspiel, a musical instrument consisting of a set of steel bars or tubes tuned diatonically and played with hammers: it is occasionally used for special effects in the orchestra.

Glory, see **Aureole.**

Gloss, in literary manuscripts an annotation or explanation usually written on the margin or between the lines. The word is now used to indicate a plausible explanation covering a fault or defect.

Gloux, Olivier, see **Aimard, Gustave.**

Glover, Richard (1712-1785), English poet and dramatist who published an epic poem, *Leonidas* (1837), which was highly praised in spite of its somewhat exaggerated rhetoric: his works include *The Athenaid,* a sequel to "Leonidas"; *London, or The Progress of Commerce;* a ballad, *Hosier's Ghost;* also two tragedies, *Boadicea and Medea,* both in imitation of Greek dramas.

Gluck, Alma (1884-1938), American dramatic and concert soprano born in Rumania and brought to the United States as a child of five. After studying with Buzzi-Peccia in New York, she made her debut in 1909 at the METROPOLITAN OPERA HOUSE, New York, in MASSENET's *Werther:* she remained with the company for three years, and appeared in more than twenty French, Italian, and German operas. After studying for a year with Marcella SEMBRICH, she achieved great success as a concert singer. Her second husband was Efrem ZIMBALIST, the violinist, and Marcia DAVENPORT, a well-known writer, is her daughter by her first husband, Bernard Gluck.

Gluck, Christoph Willibald (1714-1787), German composer who studied with Bohuslav Czernohorsky and Giovanni Battista SAMMARTINI, later settling in Vienna as chamber musician to Prince Lobkowitz, and becoming strongly influenced by Italian operatic music. He met the court poet, Pietro METASTASIO, and composed several operas in Italian style which made him famous throughout Europe: he visited London in 1745, writing two operas for production there, and also giving a concert with George Frederick HANDEL. In 1754 he became director of the Court Opera at Vienna, and began to write operas which were more dramatic and less stilted in style than those in which he had followed the Italian method. They were apathetically received in Vienna, and Gluck went to Paris where Marie ANTOINETTE championed his cause in a long and bitter struggle with the Italian opera composer, Nicola PICCINNI. His opera, *Iphigenia in Aulis,* produced at Paris in 1779, was pronounced infinitely superior to Piccinni's setting of the same subject. Gluck's superiority lay in his making the music subject to the plot; increasing the number of concerted pieces; recognizing the real importance of the chorus, and giving the orchestra its rightful position as a participant in the dramatic action. He wrote more than a hundred dramatic works of which the finest were *Orpheus and Eurydice; Paris and Helen; Iphigenia in Aulis; Armide; Iphigenia in Tauris.*

Glyn, Mrs. Elinor Sutherland (1865?-), English novelist and short story writer: her novels include *The Visits of Elizabeth* (1900); *Three Weeks* which was translated into all European languages; *The Career of Katherine Bush* and many others which Mrs. Glyn, in her autobiography, *Romantic Adventure,* contends were written in a spirit of romance.

Glyndebourne Opera, an English opera company founded by Captain John Christie (1882-), an organ builder and musical amateur, on his estate in Sussex. There is a specially constructed opera house seating five hundred, and the conduct of the project is similar to that of the SALZBURG FESTIVALS. The company and productions are strictly professional in character: among the operas presented are MOZART'S *The Marriage of Figaro, The Magic Flute, Così fan Tutti, Don Giovanni,* and *The Abduction from the Seraglio.* VERDI'S *Macbeth* and DONIZETTI'S *Don Pasquale* have also been produced.

Glyptothek, in architecture the term for a gallery in which sculptures are exhibited: the most famous is the Glyptothek in Munich founded in 1816 by King Ludwig I of Bavaria to house a collection of ancient and modern sculptures including the *Barberini Fawn* and sculptures from the Greek temple in Aegina.

Gobelin Tapestries, tapestries produced in the celebrated tapestry works founded in Paris by Gilles and Jehan Gobelin about 1440. LOUIS XIV purchased the plant, and made it into a state institution, appointing the architect, Charles LE BRUN, as director. Many distinguished painters worked on designs for the tapestries which were noted for their exquisite coloring, especially the shade known as "Gobelin blue," and for their

beauty and finish. The memorable events of Louis the Fourteenth's reign were pictured in tapestry; also reproductions of RAPHAEL'S frescoes in the Vatican.

Godard, Benjamin (1849-1895), French composer who studied with Henri Reber and Henri VIEUXTEMPS at the Paris Conservatory. His compositions include several operas: *Jocelyn* (1888) from which the "Berceuse" has become a standard favorite, and *La Vivandiére* which was performed for eleven weeks at the Opéra-Comique, Paris; many chamber works for which he received the Prix Chartier from the French Institute; several symphonies; orchestral suites; *Concerto Romantique* for violin; many piano pieces and songs. There is a Victor recording of the "Berceuse" from *Jocelyn* by Richard CROOKS.

Goddard, John (1724-1785), American cabinet maker who worked at Newport, R. I., with his son-in-law and assistant, John Townsend, remaining there until the British occupied the town during the American Revolution. He specialized in block-front desks, cabinets, secretaries, and cabinets with shell carving and bracket feet.

Godfrey, Sir Daniel (1868-1939), English bandmaster who studied at the Royal Academy of Music, London: he conducted the London Military Band and from 1893 to 1934 the Bournemouth Municipal Orchestra, building it up from 24 to 60 musicians, and giving 1200 concerts up to 1914. Godfrey gave valuable assistance to English composers by playing their works, and left his memoirs in a volume, *Memories and Music.*

Godfrey, Thomas (1736-1763), American poet and dramatist who wrote a tragedy, *The Prince of Parthia,* in 1759, believed to be the first dramatic work of its character written in America, and performed at the Southwark Theatre in Philadelphia. His works include a poem, *The Court of Fancy.*

Godiva, Lady, a Saxon lady, wife of Leofric, Earl of Mercia and lord of Coventry, who rode naked through the streets of Coventry to effect the remission of the heavy taxes imposed by her husband on the common people. As Lady Godiva passed through the streets of the town, the inhabitants remained indoors: one man bored a hole in his shutters, and is said to have been struck blind. Alfred TENNYSON wrote a poem on the subject, and several painters and sculptors have found inspiration in the legend.

Godowsky, Leopold (1870-1938), Polish-American pianist and composer who studied at the Berlin Hochschule under Karl Rudorff, and with Camille SAINT-SAENS at Paris. He toured the United States and Canada in 1884-85 with the violinist, Ovide MUSIN, became an American citizen in 1891, and after a long series of successful tours, settled in the United States in 1912. He concertized and taught at several major conservatories until 1922 when he devoted himself almost entirely to composition. His compositions include many original works for the piano, and also several brilliant transcriptions of studies by CHOPIN, waltzes by STRAUSS, and pieces by Carl Maria von WEBER.

Gods Go A-Begging, The, ballet in one act, the French title of which was *Les Dieux Mendiants:* libretto by Sobeka: choreography by George BALANCHINE; music selected from HANDEL and orchestrated by Sir Thomas BEECHAM; first produced at London in 1928. The plot revolves around a lowly shepherd and a serving maid at an entertainment in the country given by the nobility, who finally are revealed as divinities who have descended to earth in humble guise.

Godunoff, Boris, see **Boris Godunoff.**

Goes, Hugo van der (1440-1482), Flemish painter regarding whom little is known except that in 1467 he was admitted to the Guild of Painters in Ghent. His authenticated works include a small diptych representing *Adam and Eve; History of Abigail; Death of the Virgin; Adoration of the Shepherds; Adoration of the Magi; Holy Family; The Fall of Man; The Nativity; Portrait of a Man.*

Goethe, Johann Wolfgang von (1749-1832), German poet, novelist, and dramatist educated at the Universities of Leipzig and Strasbourg. His works include *Prometheus* (1773); *The Sorrows of Young Werther; Faust; Egmont; Iphigenia in Tauris; Torquato Tasso; Wilhelm Meister; The Grand Cophta; Wilhelm Meister's Apprenticeship; Hermann and Dorothea; Wilhelm Meister's Years of Travel; Fiction and Travel; The Elective Affinities.* Goethe exercised through his writings a profound influence on poetry, fiction, drama, science, philosophy, and politics in Germany.

Goetschius, Percy (1853-), American music critic, composer, and writer on musical theory trained at the Stuttgart Conservatory where he became professor in 1885. He taught at Syracuse University, New York, the NEW ENGLAND CONSERVATORY OF MUSIC, Boston, and from 1905 to 1925 at the INSTITUTE OF MUSICAL ART, New York. His works include treatises of musical composition, musical form, melody writing, counterpoint, and musical history: he has also composed orchestral music and piano pieces, and edited Mendelssohn's piano works for the Cotta Edition.

Gogh, Vincent van (1853-1890), Dutch painter who was for many years a dealer in works of art, and also greatly interested in missionary work, taking up the study of painting when he was thirty years old at the Antwerp Academy. His works include *The Shepherds; Winter; The Potato Eaters; L'Arlésienne; La Berceuse; Prison Court; Autumn Landscape; Restaurant on Montmartre.*

Gogol, Nikolai Vasilyevich (1809-1852), Russian novelist and dramatist whose first success was a volume of short stories, *Evenings at a Farmhouse near Dikanka,* published in 1831. His works include *Taras Bulba,* a romance of Cossack life in the 15th century, and regarded as the foundation of the Russian novel; *Dead Soul,* a socialistic satire; a play, *The Inspector General,* considered one of the world's dramatic masterpieces, and performed many times in Europe, Great Britain, and the United States.

"Goin' Home," the title of the lyric written by William Arms FISHER to the melody of the slow movement (Largo) of the "NEW WORLD" SYMPHONY by Antonin DVORAK. The song has become so popular that it is often mistaken for a genuine Negro folk air; there is a Victor recording by Lawrence TIBBETT.

Goldberg, Isaac (1887-1938), American critic, editor, and author educated at Harvard College: his works include *Sir William S. Gilbert* (1913); *Studies in Spanish American Literature; Brazilian Literature; The Theatre of George Jean Nathan; The Story of Gilbert and Sullivan; Tin Pan Alley; George Gershwin; The German Jew: His Share in Modern Culture,* with Dr. A. Myerson.

Goldberg, Rube (1883-), American cartoonist who was graduated as a mining engineer from the University of California, but finally turned to caricaturing as a vocation. Among his popular series of cartoons which appeared chiefly in the New York *American* for many years are *Boob McNutt, I Never Thought of That, I'm the Guy, Foolish Questions,* and the *Professor Lucifer G. Butt* series which depict extraordinary mechanical contrivances for accomplishing very simple ends. For several years he has been drawing political cartoons for the New York *Sun.*

Goldberg Variations (Bach), a set of thirty variations composed for the clavier by Johann Sebastian BACH, said to have been written at the request of Johann Gottlieb Goldberg to while away the night hours for Count Kaiserling, Russian ambassador to the court of Saxony, who suffered from insomnia. The count was so pleased with Bach's work that he presented him with a goblet filled with a hundred louis d'or. There is a harpsichord recording by Wanda LANDOWSKA.

Golden, John (1874-), American dramatist producer who was first an actor, journalist, and song writer: the notable plays produced under his direction include *Turn to the Right; The Wheel; The First Year; Thunder; Three Wise Fools; Lightnin'; Seventh Heaven; The Fall Guy; Two Girls Wanted; Let Us Be Gay; That's Gratitude; Riddle Me Thus; When Ladies Meet; The Bishop Misbehaves; Susan and God; Skylark.*

Golden Calf, see **Calf, The Golden.**

Golden Fleece, The, in Greek mythology the fleece of the ram, presented to Nephele by HERMES, which carried her children, Phrixus and Helle, away from the grasp of their wicked stepmother. Phrixus hung the fleece of the ram in a forest guarded by a savage dragon, and its seizure was the purpose of the voyage made by the ARGONAUTS.

Golden Legend, The (*1*) a volume containing biographies of the saints compiled during the 13th century by James Voragine, and printed by William CAXTON in 1483. (*2*) A poem by Henry Wadsworth LONGFELLOW published in 1851: it forms a trilogy with *The Divine Tragedy* and *New England Tragedies.* It was set to music in 1886 by Sir Arthur SULLIVAN in the form of a cantata.

Goldfish, The, a Russian folk ballet: libretto adapted by Mikhail MORDKIN from the fairy tale by Alexander PUSHKIN; choreography by Mikhail Mordkin; music by Nicholas TCHEREPNINE; first produced at New York in 1937. The ballet was written in memory of the one hundredth anniversary of Pushkin's death: Mordkin played the role of the fisherman who caught the Goldfish, Lucia CHASE the part of the avaricious wife, and Patricia BOWMAN the role of the Goldfish.

Goldman, Edwin Franko (1878-), American composer and bandmaster who studied composition with Antonin DVORAK and the cornet with Jules LEVY: after playing with the Metropolitan Opera House orchestra from 1895 to 1905, and teaching in New York, he organized the New York Military Band in 1912 and the Goldman Symphonic Band in 1918, playing each season since on the campus of Columbia University, the Mall in Central Park, and in Prospect Park, Brooklyn. He has composed more than 80 marches and other band works in addition to writing several books on cornet and band playing. During recent years his son, **Richard Franko Goldman,** has acted as associate conductor of the Goldman Band.

Goldmark, Karl (1830-1915), Hungarian violinist, pianist, and composer who studied at the Vienna Conservatory, but was mainly self-taught: his compositions in which he was influenced by Richard WAGNER although not a slavish imitator; include the operas, *The Queen of Sheba* and *The Cricket on the Hearth*; a symphony, *The Rustic Wedding,* which is actually a suite; the overtures, *Sakuntala* and *In Spring*; two violin concertos; chamber music and piano pieces. His nephew, **Rubin Goldmark** (1872-1936), born in New York, studied at the Vienna Conservatory, and at the National Conservatory, New York, with Rafael JOSEFFY and Antonin DVORAK. He was teacher of composition at the Juilliard Graduate School, New York, from 1924 until his death, and wrote several orchestral works; chamber music; pieces for violin, for violoncello, and for piano.

Goldmark, Peter (1906-), Hungarian-American scientist and director of color television at the Columbia Broadcasting Company; educated at the Universities of Berlin and Vienna. Immediately after his graduation he became director of television activities at Pye Radio, Ltd. in Cambridge, England, remaining with the company until 1933, and joining the Columbia Broadcasting System in 1936 to superintend the installation of the television transmitter atop the Chrysler Building in New York City. He is now an American citizen, and a relative of Karl GOLDMARK and Rubin GOLDMARK, both of whom were distinguished composers.

Goldoni, Carlo (1707-1793), Italian dramatist who began to sketch plays at the age of eight, and joined a band of actors at Venice as a young man. He wrote a number of unsuccessful dramas, but finally succeeded in obtaining favorable notice in 1734 with the tragedy *Belisario.* His notable plays include *The Good Father; The Singer; Rosamond; The Venetian Gondolier; The Coffee House; The Lovers; The Good-Humored Ladies; The Mistress of the Inn.*

Goldsmith, Oliver (1728-1774), Irish poet, essayist, novelist, and dramatist who studied at Trinity College, Dublin, and at the University of Edinburgh, and wandered through Europe for two years, playing the flute for his keep at inns or farmhouses. He was friendly with Dr. Samuel JOHNSON, David GARRICK, Sir Joshua REYNOLDS, and Edmund Burke: although he earned considerable sums of money he was always in difficulties. His notable works include *The Traveller* (1764); *The Deserted Village; The Vicar of Wakefield; The Good-Natured Man; She Stoops to Conquer.*

Goldwyn, Samuel (1884-), Polish-American motion-picture producer who was first a manufacturer of gloves; he entered the film business with Jesse Lasky in 1910; engineered the Famous Players-Lasky merger in 1917; formed the Goldwyn Pictures Corporation in 1918, and became an owner-member of the United Pictures Corporation in 1927. Among the famous stars who made their debuts under his direction are Ronald COLMAN and Gary COOPER; his productions of note include *The Squaw Man* (1913) with Dustin FARNUM as star and Cecil DE MILLE as director; *Stella Dallas;* the *Bulldog Drummond* series; *Arrowsmith; Street Scene; The Masquerader; Nana; We Live Again; The Dark Angel; Dodsworth; Come and Get It; Beloved Enemy; Dead End; The Hurricane; The Adventures of Marco Polo; Raffles; Wuthering Heights; The Westerner; The Little Foxes.*

Golliwogg's Cakewalk, see **Children's Corner (Debussy).**

Goltermann, Georg (1824-1898), German violoncellist and composer who studied with Joseph Menter and Franz Lachner at Munich: after long tours as an outstanding virtuoso he became conductor of the City Theatre at Frankfort. His works include two overtures, several concertos, sonatas, and characteristic pieces for the violoncello.

Goltzius, Hendrik (1558-1617), Dutch painter and engraver who established his own business at twenty-one, and made a tour through Germany and Italy to study the works of the masters. His more than three hundred engravings reveal the fact that even Albrecht DURER failed to surpass him in the use of the BURIN: among his notable works are copies of paintings by RAPHAEL whom he greatly admired. He began painting when he was forty-two years old, and accomplished little of consequence.

Gombell, Minna (1893-), American stage and screen actress who made her debut in 1913 on the New York stage in *Madam President,* and appeared in several plays as leading woman for Walter HUSTON and Otis SKINNER before entering the films in 1930. Among the pictures in which she has played important roles are *The Thin Man; The Merry Widow; No More Women; Babbitt; Slave Ship; The Great Waltz; Hunchback of Notre Dame; Boom Town.*

Gomes, Antonio Carlos (1836-1896), Brazilian composer of Portuguese parentage who studied at the Conservatory in Rio de Janeiro; after producing two operas there in 1861 and 1863, he was sent by Emperor Don Pedro II to study under Lauro Rossi. In 1870 his opera, *Il Guarany*, using airs found among the Indians on the Amazon River, was produced with tremendous success at LA SCALA, Milan, as were several other operas. He wrote the hymn, *The Salute of Brazil*, for the Philadelphia Centenary in 1876, and a cantata, *Columbus*, for the Columbus Festival in 1892.

Goncharov, Ivan Aleksandrovich (1812-1891), Russian novelist who studied at the University of Moscow, and spent some years in the diplomatic service in Japan. His works include *A Common Story; Jean Podzabryn; Oblomov*, a novel in which he pictured the indolent lives of Russian landed proprietors; *The Precipice*.

Goncourt, Edmond Louis Antoine Huot de (1822-1896), French art critic, novelist, essayist, and dramatist who worked with his brother, **Jules Alfred Huot de Goncourt** (1830-1870), their association being so close in art and literature that they were called "the brothers Goncourt" and "the two Goncourts." Their works include *Intimate Portraits of the Eighteenth Century* (1857); *The Woman of the Eighteenth Century; The Art of The Eighteenth Century; La Du Barry; Charles Demailly; Sister Philoméne; Renée Mauperin; Germinie Lacerteux*. In 1865 they collaborated on a play, *Henriette Marechal*.

Gondoliers, The, comic opera in two acts; libretto by Sir William S. GILBERT; music by Sir Arthur SULLIVAN; first produced in 1889 by the D'Oyly Carte Opera Company at the Savoy Theatre, London. The plot revolves around two gondoliers and their sweethearts: one of the two gondoliers is for a time presumed to be the heir to the throne of the mythical kingdom of Barataria, but after numerous complications it is finally ascertained that the drummer, Luiz, and his sweetheart, Casilda, are the royal personages, much to the joy and satisfaction of the gondoliers and their future wives. There is a Victor recording of the complete opera by the D'Oyly Carte Company.

Gong, a percussion instrument in the form of a large, round, and slightly concaved plate of copper alloyed with tin. It is struck with a padded leather stick, producing a tone of indefinite pitch, but rich in quality, and especially useful in producing dramatic effects. Gongs have been used in Oriental countries for thousands of years, particularly in connection with religious ceremonies.

Góngora y Argote, Luis de (1561-1627), Spanish clergyman and poet: his works include *The Story of Polyphemus and Galatea* and *The Story of Pyramus and Thisbe*, in which he originated a singular style of artificiality, obscure meanings, and extraordinary metaphors which was widely imitated in Spain and France, giving rise to the expression *Gongorism*, corresponding to the English *euphuism* or affectation in literary expression.

Gonzaga, Pietro (1751-1831), Italian architect who studied with Antonio Canale (CANALETTO), and was also a fine scenic designer: he specialized in drops which were architectural in character,

picturing an open landscape with buildings on an elevation in the background.

Gonzaga, Thomaz Antonio (1744-c.1807), Portuguese poet, educated at Coimbra University, who emigrated to Brazil and held a judicial office there for some years. He developed a violent passion for a lady named Maria Seixas, writing in her honor a series of poems, *Marilia*, which are regarded as the most exquisite and flawless in Portuguese literature.

Goodall, Frederick (1822-1904), English painter who won a silver medal at fourteen for his painting, *Finding of the Dead Body of a Miner by Torchlight:* his notable works include *Village Holiday; Hunt the Slipper; Tired Soldier; Raising the Maypole; Cranmer at the Traitor's Gate; Bedouin Mother and Child; The Shepherdess; Road to Mecca; Café at Cairo; By the Sea of Galilee; Gordon's Last Messenger*.

Good Friday Spell (Parsifal), a scene in the sacred music drama *Parsifal*, by Richard WAGNER. Parsifal, returning from a vain search for the Holy Grail, lays aside his armor and allows Kundry, an enchantress, to bathe his feet in a spring. He turns toward a meadow and listens to a pastoral interrupted suddenly by the sound of distant bells mournfully intoning the death of King Amfortas. Parsifal is blessed, robed, and saluted as king as the full orchestra intones the Dresden *Amen*, used here as the "Grail" theme. There is a Columbia recording by the Bayreuth Festival Orchestra conducted by Siegfried Wagner, and a Victor recording by the Berlin Philharmonic Orchestra under the baton of Wilhelm Furtwangler.

Goodhue, Bertram Grosvenor (1869-1924), American architect who studied with James RENWICK, and later became a partner of Ralph Adams CRAM: after 1914 he practiced alone. His notable works include St. Thomas' Church and St. Bartholomew's Church in New York; the Nebraska State Capitol at Lincoln; the National Academy of Science, Washington, D. C.; Mandel Hall at the University of Chicago; the California Institute of Technology at Pasadena; the War Memorial at Kansas City, Mo.; the Exposition Buildings at San Diego, Calif., the Cathedral of Maryland at Baltimore.

Goodman, Benny (1909-), American clarinetist who studied at the Lewis Institute, Chicago, and was also a pupil of Franz Schoepp of the Chicago Symphony Orchestra. He has appeared in orchestral or chamber music concerts with the NEW YORK PHILHARMONIC-SYMPHONY ORCHESTRA, the PHILADELPHIA SYMPHONY ORCHESTRA, the BUDAPEST STRING QUARTET, and several other organizations. He has participated in a Victor recording of the Mozart *Quintet for clarinet and strings* (Kochel 581) by the BUDAPEST STRING QUARTET.

Goodman, Jules Eckert (1876-), American dramatist, educated at Harvard College, who did magazine work for some years: his plays include *The Test*, for Blanche Walsh (1908); *The Man Who Stood Still*, for Louis Mann; *The Silent Voice*, for Otis Skinner; also *Business before Pleasure; His Honor Abe Potash*; and *Partners*

Again with Montague GLASS. He also adapted several works for the American stage.

Goodrich, Arthur (1878-1941), American novelist and dramatist educated at Wesleyan University and Columbia University: he occupied several important editorial posts and served in World War I. His works include *The Balance of Power* (1906); *The Yardstick Man; The Man with an Honest Face; So This is London; The Joker; Caponsacchi* with Rose A. Palmer, produced in 1926, and based on Robert Browning's poem, *The Ring and the Book.* The last-named drama was the basis of Richard Hageman's opera with the same title produced at the METROPOLITAN OPERA HOUSE, New York, in 1937.

Goodrich, John Wallace (1871-), American organist who studied at the NEW ENGLAND CONSERVATORY OF MUSIC, Boston, with Henry M. Dunham and George W. CHADWICK, and later with Charles WIDOR in Paris. He joined the faculty of the New England Conservatory in 1897, and succeeded George W. Chadwick as director in 1930, also occupying the post of organist at Trinity Church, Boston (1902-1909), and of the BOSTON SYMPHONY ORCHESTRA from 1898 to 1909. From 1909 to 1912 he was the conductor of the BOSTON OPERA COMPANY.

Goodrich, Samuel Griswold (1793-1860), American editor and author who used the pen name "Peter Parley." He edited *The Token, Robert Merry's Museum,* and *Parley's Museum,* and wrote one hundred books for children in which fiction and instruction were combined. More than seventy spurious volumes using his pen name were published, a dubious attestation to the popularity of his books.

Goodson, Katharine (1872-), English pianist who studied with Oscar Beringer at the Royal Academy of Music, London, and with Theodor LESCHETIZKY at Vienna. After a successful debut in 1897 at London, she toured England and Europe, making her first American appearance with the BOSTON SYMPHONY ORCHESTRA in 1907, and later appearing with all the major orchestras in the United States, Great Britain, and Europe.

Goodwin, Nat (1857-1919), American actor who made a successful debut, after many trials and failures, in a sketch, *The Rehearsal,* in 1874 at the Howard Athenaeum in Boston. Later he appeared with great success as a mimic at Tony PASTOR'S and other vaudeville houses. Among the many successful plays in which he was featured were *A Gilded Fool; The Rivals; An American Citizen; Nathan Hale; The Cowboy and the Lady,* with his wife, Maxine ELLIOTT; *When We Were Twenty-one; In Mizzoura; Beauty and the Barge.* In 1911 he scored a distinct success as Fagin in DICKENS' *Oliver Twist.*

Goossens, Eugène (1893-), English violinist, composer, and conductor who studied at the Bruges Conservatory, the Liverpool College of Music, and at the Royal College of Music, London, under Charles Villiers STANFORD and Sir Henry WOOD. From 1915 to 1920, he conducted Sir Thomas Beecham's Opera Company, and at Covent Garden; from 1923 to 1931 he conducted the ROCHESTER (New York) SYMPHONY ORCHESTRA, and in 1931 succeeded Fritz REINER as conductor of the CINCINNATI SYMPHONY ORCHESTRA. He has composed several orchestral works, chamber music, a ballet, two operas, piano pieces, and violin pieces.

Goossens, Leon (1896-), English oboist who studied at the Royal College of Music, London, and became first oboist of the Royal Opera House Orchestra, the London Philharmonic Orchestra and the Queen's Hall Orchestra: in 1927 he appeared in recital at New York with his brother, Eugène GOOSSENS. He now appears only as a recitalist, and has made many fine recordings of solo and chamber music.

Gordian Knot, a knot tied by Gordius, King of Lydia, a peasant who became king of his country after an oracle declared that a king would come to them riding in a cart: he dedicated his cart and yoke of oxen to ZEUS, and tied the knot to the yoke in an intricate manner. The oracle declared that whoever should loose the knot would rule over Asia: ALEXANDER THE GREAT cut the knot with his sword, thus fulfilling the prophecy.

Gordin, Jacob M. (1853-1909), American dramatist born in Russia: he came to the United States in 1890, and wrote or adapted many fine plays for the Yiddish stage including *Siberia, God, Man and the Devil, The Kreutzer Sonata, The Jewish King Lear,* and *The Jewish Sappho.*

Gordon, Caroline (1895-), American novelist educated in a classical school for boys directed by her father: her novels include *Penhally* (1931); *Aleck Maury; None Shall Look Back; The Garden of Adonis; Green Centuries.*

Gordon, Sir John Watson (c.1790-1864), Scottish painter whose real name was John Watson. After unsuccessful attempts at historical and landscape painting he turned his attention to portraiture, becoming president of the Royal Scottish Academy, and painter to Queen Victoria in Scotland. His portraits include those of many noted personalities of his time including Thomas DE QUINCEY: he left an unfinished likeness of Sir Walter SCOTT.

Gordon, Leon (1831-1892), Russian poet and novelist of Jewish parentage whose real name was Judah Loeb ben Asher. He had much to do with the revival of interest in the Hebrew language and culture: his works include *Kol Shire Yehudah* (1883), four volumes of poetry; *Kol Kithbe Yehuda,* a collection of his novels.

Gordon, Max (1892-), American theatrical producer educated at the College of the City of New York: the notable plays he has produced include *Rain* and *The Jazz Singer* with Sam Harris; *Three's a Crowd; The Cat and the Fiddle; Design for Living; Roberta; The Shining Hour; Dodsworth; The Great Waltz; The Farmer Takes a Wife; Jubilee; Pride and Prejudice; Ethan Frome; The Women; St. Helena; Othello; Missouri Legend* with Guthrie McClintic; *The American Way; My Sister Eileen; Junior Miss.* He also produced the film *Abe Lincoln in Illinois.*

Gordon, Ruth (1896-), American stage and screen actress who studied at the American Academy of Dramatic Arts, New York, and made her debut in 1915 at the EMPIRE THEATRE, New York, in *Peter Pan* with Maude ADAMS: she has appeared since in *Clarence; Saturday's Children; Serena Blandish; A Church Mouse; Three Cornered Moon; They Shall Not Die; The Country Wife; Ethan Frome; A Doll's House; The Three Sisters;* also in the films, *Abe Lincoln in Illinois; Dr. Ehrlich's Magic Bullet.*

Gorgon, in Greek mythology any one of the three sisters named Stheno, Euryale, and Medusa: they were hideous of visage with streaming, snaky hair, and persons looking at them were immediately turned to stone.

Gorin, Igor (1909-), Russian baritone and composer who studied at the Vienna Conservatory, and appeared at the Vienna Opera, and in concert and recital throughout Europe. He made his concert debut in 1936 with the LOS ANGELES PHILHARMONIC ORCHESTRA at the HOLLYWOOD BOWL, and has sung with several American major orchestras. He has made many radio broadcasts, and has written several excellent songs.

Goritz, Otto (1873-1929), German dramatic baritone who studied with his mother, and made a successful debut in 1895 at the Hoftheater, Neustrelitz, in *Fra Diavolo.* After singing at opera houses in Breslau and Hamburg, he made his debut in 1903 at the METROPOLITAN OPERA HOUSE, New York, in *Parsifal,* and created roles in *Tiefland, The Bartered Bride, Königskinder,* and *Rosenkavalier.* He toured the United States in recital from 1917 to 1920.

Gorky, Maxim, pen name of **Alexei Maximovitch Pyeshkov** (1868-1936), Russian novelist and dramatist who spent many years wandering through Russia before he educated himself by reading, and published four volumes of short stories between 1892 and 1900 which attracted world-wide attention, and were reprinted in English, French, and German. His numerous novels in English translation include *The Man Who Was Afraid; Three of Them; Comrades; The Spy; The Mother; A Confession; The Magnet; The Spectre.* Of his fourteen plays the outstanding one is *The Lower Depths.*

Goshun (1742-1811), Japanese printer who founded the Shijo school: he combined the naturalistic style of the Okyo school with certain features taken from Chinese painting: artisans of all kinds such as carvers, embroiderers, and workers in lacquer used his figures, flowers, and landscapes as models. He was exceptionally skillful in the portrayal of animals.

Gosse, Sir Edmund William (1849-1928), English critic and biographer who was appointed assistant librarian of the British Museum, and an intimate of Algernon SWINBURNE, Rudyard KIPLING, Thomas HARDY, George Bernard SHAW and all other English writers of his time. His works include translations of Scandinavian authors such as IBSEN and BJORNSON: also biographies of Thomas GRAY, Sir Walter RALEIGH, William CON-

GREVE, Robert BROWNING, Henry FIELDING, Jeremy TAYLOR, Henrik IBSEN, Algernon SWINBURNE, and others.

Gossec, François-Joseph (1734-1829), Belgian composer who was chiefly self-taught. He founded and conducted the Concerts des Amateurs at Paris, directed the Concerts Spirituels, conducted at the Paris Opéra and founded the École Royale de Chant which later became the PARIS CONSERVATORY OF MUSIC. During the French Revolution he wrote many Republican plays, hymns, songs, and marches which resulted in his being appointed official composer to the Republic of France. His works include several operas, choral works, chamber music, and about twenty symphonies in the composition of which he is said to have preceded Joseph HAYDN in establishing this form of orchestral music.

Gosson, Stephen (1554-1624), English dramatist who studied at Oxford, and gained a reputation as a writer of pastorals none of which is extant. His satirical works, *The Schoole of Abuse* and *An Apologie of the Schoole of Abuse,* criticizing English drama and poetry (1579) were answered by Thomas Lodge's *Defence of Playes* (1580), and by Sir Philip SIDNEY's APOLOGY FOR POETRY (1595).

Got, François Jules Edmond (1822-1901), French actor who was admitted to the PARIS CONSERVATORY OF MUSIC in 1841, winning prizes for both comedy and drama. He made his debut at the Comédie-Française in 1844, and remained there for fifty years, celebrating his fiftieth anniversary in 1894. He was an outstanding exponent of the grand style in French acting.

Gothic Architecture, a style of architecture in vogue from the middle of the 12th century to the end of the 15th century in Europe; the fundamental principles were the elimination of all superfluous construction, the development of the ribbed vault, the substitution of wood for stone wherever practicable, and the use of the stained glass window. The Gothic idea was also applied to furniture, sculptures, tapestries and other objects of art.

Götterdämmerung, Die, see **Ring of the Nibelungs, The.**

Gotthelf, Jeremias, see **Bitzius, Albrecht.**

Gottschalk, Ferdinand (1858-), English stage and screen actor who made his debut in 1887 at Toronto, Canada, with Rosina VOKES in *Which is Which?:* the almost innumerable plays in which he appeared include *The Amazons; The Masqueraders; The Prisoner of Zenda; Never Again; The Degenerates; The Climbers; Barbara's Millions; Widower's Houses; The Revellers; Old Heidelberg; Madame Sand; Captain Applejack; The Crown Prince; Joseph; To-Night or Never.* Among the many films in which he has played important roles are *Berkeley Square; Nana; Clive of India; Les Miserables; Peter Ibbetson; The Garden of Allah; Café Metropole; The Adventures of Marco Polo.*

Gottschalk, Louis Moreau (1829-1869), American pianist and composer who studied with

Charles HALLE in Paris, making his debut in 1845, and achieving brilliant success in his tours of Europe. He appeared first in 1853 in the United States at New Orleans, and toured the country for several years both as pianist and conductor of his orchestral works. His compositions include operas, program symphonies, and more than ninety characteristic piano pieces such as *Le Bananier*. His memoirs, *Notes of a Pianist*, afford some idea of the feverish activities in the concert field which were the cause of his early demise.

Gottsched, Johann Christoph (1700-1766), German poet, critic, and dramatist who is regarded as the first organizer of the German theatre through the founding of his own company of which Caroline NEUBER was a member for several years. His wife, Luise Gottsched, was the author of several successful comedies.

Goudy, Frederic William (1865-), American printer and designer of type faces who has the distinction of having produced the greatest number of type faces still in use throughout the world. He has designed more than 110 faces, sixty of which are generally used: no other master designer has created more than thirty. There is a permanent exhibition of Goudy's type faces in the Smithsonian Institution at Washington, D. C.: he operates a printing plant, the Village Press, at Marlboro, N. Y.

Goujon, Jean (c.1510-c.1566), French sculptor and architect who was employed by Pierre LESCOT, architect of the Louvre, on restoration work at the Church of St. Germain l'Auxerrois at Paris, and also executed many carvings in the LOUVRE. Among his known works are marble columns in the church of St. Maclou at Rouen; an altar at Chantilly; sculptural decorations for the Fountain of Innocents, Paris; the *Fountain of Diana* in the Château of Anet; the decoration of the Henry II staircase, and the caryatides supporting the Musicians' Gallery in the Louvre.

Gounod, Charles-François (1818-1893), French organist and composer who studied with his mother and at the PARIS CONSERVATORY OF MUSIC: he became greatly interested in church music of the Palestrina School, and for a time contemplated entering the church, but the tremendous success of his fourth opera, *Faust,* in 1859 induced him to give up the idea. From 1852 to 1860 he directed the Orpheum, a union of choral societies for which he wrote many important works, and in 1867 his opera, *Romeo and Juliet* was produced at Paris with almost as much success as *Faust*. He lived in London from 1870 to 1875, and after 1881 devoted himself almost entirely to the composition of sacred music. His compositions include several operas of which *Faust, Romeo and Juliet,* and *The Queen of Sheba* were the most successful; the oratorios *Redemption* and *Mors et Vita*; several cantatas; church music including masses and requiems; choruses; symphonies and other orchestral works; songs and piano pieces.

Gourmont, Remy de (1858-1915), French poet and novelist educated at the University of Caen, and one of the founders of the *Mercuré de France:* his works available in English include *A Night in Luxembourg; The Virgin Heart; A Very Woman;* *The Horses of Diomedes; The Book of Masks; Decadence and Other Essays; The Physiology of Love.* He occasionally used the pen name, "Richard de Bury."

Goya y Lucientes, Francisco José de (1746-1828), Spanish painter, designer, and etcher who studied with Lujan (José) Martinez at Saragossa, and also spent several years at Madrid and Rome studying the masterpieces of Spanish and Italian painters. He was court painter to Charles IV and Ferdinand VII of Spain, and is regarded as an eccentric genius of extraordinary ability in painting religious works, portraits, and satirical compositions of every character. His notable works include equestrian portraits of Charles IV and Ferdinand VII; *Charles IV and His Family; Madhouse; Bullfight; The Disasters of War; Treason of Judas; The Caprices,* portraying the vices of society; *Gallant Dressed; Gallant Nude; The Milkman; The Knife Grinder.* He also designed CARTOONS for tapestries, and painted frescoes in churches at Saragossa and Madrid: his keen sense of humor has given him the title "the Hogarth of Spain."

Goyen, Jan Josephszoon van (1596-1656), Dutch painter who studied with Esaias van de Velde: his works include *Canal in Holland; Panorama of The Hague; River in Holland; Halt of the Travelers; Winter Landscape; River Scene; Moonlight; Banks of Canal; Environs of Haarlem.* He specialized in Dutch scenes painted in grayish-green tones.

Goyescas, a dramatic piece in operatic form: libretto by F. Periquet; music by Enrique GRANADOS; first produced at the METROPOLITAN OPERA HOUSE, New York, in 1916, with the composer present. It is based on a series of piano pieces composed by Granados at an earlier date, and inspired by paintings and tapestries, executed by the Spanish painter, Francisco GOYA, and picturing episodes in 18th century Spanish history. There is a Columbia recording of the popular Intermezzo by the Madrid Symphony directed by Fernandez ARBOS, and a Victor recording by the Boston "Pops" Orchestra with Arthur FIEDLER.

Gozzi, Count Carlo (1720-1806), Italian dramatist who wrote satirical and fable plays, and a member of the Granelleschi Society, which ridiculed the works of Carlo GOLDONI to such an extent that the latter left Venice. His plays were presented by the Sacchi company successfully: one of them *King Turandote,* was used as the basis of an opera by Giacomo PUCCINI, and another, *The Love for Three Oranges,* was set to music by Serge PROKOFIEFF.

Gozzoli, Benozzo (1420-1498), Italian painter who studied and worked with FRA ANGELICO in Rome: his notable works include *Madonna with Saints and Angels; Life of St. Francis; Journey of the Magi to Bethlehem; Noah and His Family; Triumph of St. Thomas; Rape of Helen; St. Thomas Receiving the Girdle of the Virgin.* His works do not equal those of Fra Angelico although they possess an individual charm and naturalness.

Grabbe, Christian Dietrich (1801-1836), German dramatist who studied at the Universities of

Leipzig and Berlin: his first play, *Herzog Theodor von Gothland* (1822) gave unmistakable evidence of his ability: his dramas include *Don Juan and Faust; Friedrich Barbarossa; Heinrich VI; Napoleon, or The Hundred Days,* in which the battle of Waterloo was presented on the stage. Intemperance was the cause of his death at an early age.

Grace Note, in music an instrumental or vocal ornament which is not essential to the melody or harmony of the passage in which it occurs: it precedes the main or melody note, taking its accent and a part of the time value of the latter. In classical music it was printed in a smaller note than the melody note, thus evading the strict rule prohibiting the entrance of unprepared dissonances. It is also known as *appoggiatura* in Italian.

Graces, The Three, in Greek mythology the transition from a single goddess, Charis, to a group of three known as *Aglaia* personifying brightness; *Euphrosyne* signifying joyfulness, and *Thalia* typifying charm. They were friendly with the MUSES, and lived with them on Mount OLYMPUS. They have been pictured on canvas or fresco by Jacopo PALMA, RAPHAEL, and other famous artists.

Graf, Herbert, contemporary Austrian stage director, son of a Viennese music critic: his career began in Breslau and Frankfort, and continued in Prague, Basel and Florence. He staged a performance of Richard WAGNER's *Die Meistersinger* at Salzburg which was conducted by Arturo Toscanini. In 1934-35 he became stage director for the Philadelphia Opera Company, and is now (1943) acting in the same capacity for the Metropolitan Opera Company. He has published *The Opera and Its Future in America* (1941).

Graff or Graf, Anton (1736-1813), Swiss painter who studied with Johann Ulrich Schellenburg, and in 1766 became court painter and professor at the Academy of Dresden. His works include portraits of LESSING, GLUCK, Frederic Augustus of Saxony, William II, and SCHILLER: according to his own statement he painted nearly a thousand portraits and family groups from 1766 to 1773 which, if true, means that he completed a picture every two days for a period of seven years.

Graffito (pl. Graffiti), in archaeology the term applied to rude drawings or writings on ancient buildings as contrasted with formal writings known as inscriptions. They are scratched on stone or plaster by some form of sharp instrument, or written in red chalk or charcoal. The term is also applied to a method of ornamenting plaster surfaces by scratching the outer coat so as to bring out a deeper, contrasting color in an under coat.

Grafly, Charles (1862-1929), American sculptor who studied at the Pennsylvania Academy of Fine Arts, and at the ECOLE DES BEAUX-ARTS, Paris. His works include *Mauvais Présage; Symbol of Life; Fountain of Man* at the Pan-American Exposition; *England and France* at the New York Custom House; *Pioneer Mother Monument* at San Francisco; *General Reynolds* at Fairmount Park, Philadelphia.

Graham, Ernest Robert (1868-), American architect educated at the University of Notre Dame and Coe College: his notable works include the Equitable Life Assurance Society, the Flatiron and the Chase National Bank Buildings in New York; the Union Station and General Postoffice in Washington, D. C., the Field Museum of Natural History, the Civic Opera House, the Union Station, and the Merchandise Mart in Chicago; the Pennsylvania Railroad Station in Philadelphia; the Selfridge Store in London, England.

Graham, Harry Joscelyn Clive (1874-1936), English author and dramatist who served in the British army during World War I. He was the author of *Ruthless Rhymes for Heartless Homes* (1899), and part author or adapter of numerous plays including *Katja the Dancer; By Candle-Light; White Horse Inn; Casanova; The Land of Smiles.*

Graham, Martha, contemporary American dancer trained from 1916 at the DENISHAWN SCHOOL, making her first professional appearance with Ted SHAWN in 1920. In 1923 she appeared with the Greenwich Village Follies, gave her first recital in 1926, and appeared with the Cleveland Symphony Orchestra in 1927. She formed her own company in 1929: among her best-known choreographies are *Lamentation; American Provincials; Frontier; Horizons; Chronicle; American Document; Dance of Death; Adolescence; Heretic; Act of Judgment; Deep Song; Immediate Tragedy.*

Grahame, Kenneth (1859-1932), English author educated at St. Paul's School, Oxford. His works include *The Golden Age* (1895); *Dream Days; Wind in the Willows:* the last-named was dramatized by A. A. Milne as *Toad of Toad Hall.* He also wrote the *Kenneth Grahame Book,* and compiled *The Cambridge Book of Poetry for Young People.*

Grahn, Lucile (1819-1875), Danish ballerina who studied with Antoine August Bournonville: she rivaled TAGLIONI and ELSSLER not only in Denmark, but in European countries and England. She differed in style from contemporary dancers in that she was an excellent actress; her favorite ballets included La SYLPHIDE, Robert of Normandie, Fiorella, and La Bayadère.

Grail, The Holy, in medieval legend the platter or the wine cup from which Christ ate or drank the Last Supper: Joseph of Arimathea collected the blood of the Saviour in it when He was crucified. It is frequently mentioned in the legends of King ARTHUR, and is the central point of interest in Richard WAGNER's PARSIFAL.

Grainger, Percy Aldridge (1882-), Australian pianist and arranger of folk music who studied with his mother, and later with Louis Pabst, James Kwast, and Ferruccio BUSONI. He made his debut at London in 1900, and toured Great Britain, Australia, New Zealand, and South Africa. In 1907, he gave the première of the GRIEG piano concerto at Leeds. He made his American concert debut in 1915 with the NEW YORK PHILHARMONIC-SYMPHONY ORCHESTRA playing the Grieg concerto and has toured the United States as pianist and conductor. His numerous arrangements and original works for concert orchestra, chamber orchestra, piano, and voice include the well-known *Shepherd's Hey; Molly on the Shore; Irish Tune from County Derry; In a Nutshell.*

Granada, a city in Spain where the famous ALHAMBRA is located: it was founded by the Moors in 800, and occupied by them until driven out in 1610. It also has a fine cathedral built in Graeco-Roman style about 1520: the façade was designed in the 17th century by Alonso CANO.

Granados, Enrique (1867-1916), Spanish pianist and composer who studied at the Barcelona and Madrid Conservatories, and also with Felipe PEDRELL: his works include an opera, *Goyescas,* produced at New York in 1916; a piano suite *Goyescas,* from which the themes were taken for his opera with the same title; four volumes of *Spanish Dances;* chamber music; numerous compositions for piano. He also transcribed 26 unpublished harpsichord pieces by Domenico SCARLATTI for the piano, and re-orchestrated CHOPIN's *Piano Concerto in F minor.* There are various recordings available of the *Spanish Dances.*

Grand, Sarah, pen name of **Frances Elizabeth Clarke McFall** (1862-1943), English novelist born in Ireland: her works include *Ideala* (1888); *The Heavenly Twins,* a best seller in 1893; *The Beth Book; Babs the Impossible; Adnam's Orchard; The Winged Victory; Variety.*

Grand Canyon (Grofé), an orchestral suite by Ferdinand GROFE which distinctly reflects the American idiom in its five movements: I *Sunrise;* II *Painted Desert;* III *On the Trail;* IV *Sunset;* V *Cloudburst.* There is a Victor recording by the Paul WHITEMAN Orchestra, and a Columbia recording by André KOSTELANETZ Orchestra.

Grande Chartreuse, La, the principal monastery of the Carthusian monks, built in the 11th century by St. Bruno; destroyed in 1132 by an avalanche, and rebuilt shortly after. It was again destroyed by fire in 1676, and the present building occupied by the monks until 1903 when they were expelled from France, and emigrated to Spain. A distilled *liqueur* known as *Chartreuse* was made by the monks: the revenues from its sale were so large that they supported not only the monastery, but also churches, schools, and hospitals in neighboring villages.

Grand Guignol, a theatre in the Montmartre, a district of Paris, France, noted for its gay night life. It was founded in 1897, and its programs comprise a number of one-act plays in which broad farce alternates with chill horror. The reputation of the theatre is such that grisly stage pieces are said to be in "the Grand Guignol style." The Grand Guignol Company appeared in 1923 for a ten-week season in New York, presenting *At the Room of the Dead Rat, A Night in a Den,* and other thrillers to crowded houses.

Grand Opera, see **Opera.**

Grandjany, Marcel (1891-), French composer and harpist who studied at the National Conserva-tory of Music with Alphonse HASSELMANS and other famous teachers: he made his debut at Paris in 1909, and, after touring Europe and the United States, taught at the Philadelphia Conservatory, the Fontainebleau School of Music, and from 1938 at the INSTITUTE OF MUSICAL ART, New York. He has written a *Poème Symphonique* for harp and orchestra; also many harp solos, piano works and songs.

Grandville, see **Gérard, Jean Ignace.**

Grane, the name of the horse belonging to BRUNNHILDE which she rides in Richard Wagner's *The Valkyrie,* and presents to SIEGFRIED after he rescues her, and starts out into the world to perform deeds of valor. When she finds Siegfried dead by the hand of HAGEN in THE DUSK OF THE GODS, she rides Grane up to the top of his funeral pyre, and is destroyed with him.

Granjon, Robert, 16th century printer and designer of type faces who had shops in Paris, Rome, and other European cities. He is presumed to have worked between 1545 and 1590, creating types in roman, italic, Greek, and Hebrew, and also a type resembling handwriting in the French style, designed with the idea of superseding italics. His name is used in connection with several American type faces.

Grant, Cary (1909-), American stage and screen actor who appeared in several plays before entering the films in 1933. Among the many pictures in which he has been featured are *Madame Butterfly; Blond Venus; The Woman Accused; Gambling Ship; Alice in Wonderland; The Awful Truth; Topper; Toast of New York; Holiday; Gunga Din; His Girl Friday; The Philadelphia Story; The Howards of Virginia; Penny Serenade; Suspicion.*

Grant, Duncan James Corrowr (1885-), English painter who is considered one of the more advanced members of the contemporary English school influenced by the French modernists. His works include *The Queen of Sheba; Hammock; The Lemon Gatherers; Tightrope Walker:* he has also designed stage settings for the CAMARGO SOCIETY ballet performances.

Grant, Sir Francis (1803-1874), Scottish painter who studied at the Edinburgh Academy, and exhibited at the Royal Academy, London, in 1843. His works include many sporting pictures such as *The Melton Hunt* and *Meet of the Queen's Stag Hounds:* he also painted more than 250 portraits of the English nobility including the Duke of Cambridge, Lord Palmerston, and the Duchess of Sutherland.

Grant, Robert (1852-1940), American novelist educated at Harvard University, and for many years a highly respected jurist. His works include *The Little Tin Gods on Wheels* (1879); *The Confessions of a Frivolous Girl; An Average Man; The Bachelor's Christmas; Unleavened Bread; The Law Breakers; The High Priestess; The Bishop's Granddaughter; Fourscore,* an autobiography.

Granville-Barker, Harley (1877-), English actor, dramatist, and producer who made his debut in 1892 at London: after appearing in several plays, he joined J. E. Vedrenne in the management of the Court Theatre, and later the Savoy Theatre, instituting radical changes in scenery, lighting, and dramatic presentation with pronounced success. His plays include *The Voysey Inheritance; The Marrying of Anne Leete; Waste; The Madras House.* He made several successful adaptations of French and German plays such as *Anatol* and *Dr. Knock,* and wrote *The Exemplary Theatre,* and *Schemes and Estimates for a National Theatre;* the latter in collaboration with William ARCHER.

Grau, Maurice (1849-1907), Bohemian theatrical, concert, and opera impresario brought to the United States as a child of five, and educated at the Columbia Law School. He managed the American tours of Anton RUBINSTEIN, Henri WIENIAWSKI, Sarah BERNHARDT, and other famous artists: from 1891 to 1897 he was associated with Henry ABBEY and others in the management of the METROPOLITAN OPERA HOUSE, and from 1898 to 1903 became its sole director, presenting NORDICA, MELBA, EAMES, CALVE, TERNINA, HOMER, SCHUMANN-HEINK, the DE RESZKES, PLANCON, SCOTTI, and BISPHAM. He also presented uncut versions of Richard Wagner's RING OF THE NIBELUNGS.

Grave (It.), in music an expression indicating that a passage or entire composition is to be played with seriousness and gravity.

Graver, see **Burin.**

Graves, Robert Ranke (1895-), English poet and novelist who served in the British Army during World War I: his numerous works include *Over the Brazier* (1916); *Fairies and Fusiliers; Country Sentiment; The Pier Glass; Collected Poems; Lawrence and the Arabian Adventure; Claudius; Count Belisarius; The Real David Copperfield; No More Ghosts; Proceed, Sergeant Lamb.*

Gravet, Fernand (1908-), Belgian stage and screen actor: among the films in which he has appeared are *The Widow's Bed; Bitter Sweet; Early to Bed; The Queen's Affair; The King and the Chorus Girl; Fools for Scandal; The Great Waltz.*

Gray, Cecil (1895-), Scottish critic and writer on musical subjects: his works include *A Survey of Contemporary Music* (1924); *Carlo Gesualdo,* with Philip Heseltine; *The History of Music; Sibelius: The Symphonies; Predicaments, or Music and the Future; The Forty-eight Preludes and Fugues of Bach.*

Gray, Henry Peters (1819-1877), American painter who studied with Daniel HUNTINGTON and also in Rome, Venice, and Florence. Among his notable works are *Wages of War; Birth of Our Flag; Flower of Fiesole; Judgment of Paris; Blessed are the Pure in Heart; William Cullen Bryant; Apple of Discord; Cupid Begging His Arrow; Ophelia; Normandy Maid.*

Gray, Thomas (1716-1771), English poet educated at Eton College and Cambridge University where he later became professor of modern history, and spent the rest of his life. His works include *On a Distant Prospect of Eton College* (1742); *Elegy in a Country Churchyard* (1750), a poem which has made him known in almost all languages; *The Progress of Poesy; The Bard; The Fatal Sisters; The Descent of Odin.* Gray's power of description was his greatest asset.

Gray's Elegy, see **Elegy, Gray's.**

Grayson, David, see **Baker, Ray Stannard.**

Graziani, Guido, see **Guido da Siena.**

Grazioso (It.), in music an expression indicating that the passage or entire composition is to be played gracefully or with elegance.

Grease Paint, in the theatre a compound of spermaceti, oil, and tallow or wax used for make-up purposes, and made in all colors and tints from white to black.

Grechetto, Il, see **Castiglione, Giovanni Benedetto.**

Greco, El (c.1541-1614), Greek painter whose real name was *Domenicos Theotocopoulos;* probably born in Crete: he was known in Venice and Rome as *Domenico Theotocopuli,* and in Spain as *El Greco.* He was a pupil of TITIAN in Venice, and painted several works for Cardinal Farnese at Rome before he went to Spain about 1570. His works include *The Healing of the Blind; Christ Driving the Money Changers from the Temple; The Ascension of the Virgin; Annunciation; Boy Lighting a Coal; Portrait of Julio Clovio; The Holy Family; The Ascension of Christ; Baptism of Christ; The Resurrection; The Crucifixion; St. John the Evangelist; Dream of Philip II; Burial of Count Orgaz; Removal of Christ's Raiment; Dead Christ in the Arms of God.*

Greek Music, a system of music which included the study of singing, playing, and dancing, and extended from about 1000 B.C. to the Roman conquest in 146 B.C.: the period during which it flourished is placed at from 660 B.C. to 338 B.C.: it was during this period that TERPANDER established the Lesbian school where the famous ARION OF METHYMA studied, invented the dithyramb, and increased the number of strings on the lyre. Plato WROTE on the subject of musical aesthetics and PYTHAGORAS used his one-stringed monochord to systematize the modes (scales) so that each one consisted of four tones within the compass of a perfect fourth, and extended downward. They were called the Dorian, Phrygian, Lydian, Mixalydian, Hypodrian, Hypophrygian, and Hypolydian scales or modes. The principal instruments were the LYRE and the AULOS: the music was purely MONODIC: there was no use of harmony in the modern sense of the word.

Green, Anna Katharine (1846-1935), American writer of detective fiction educated at the Ripley Female College, Poultney, Vt.; her original ambition was to write verse. Her first story, *The*

Leavenworth Case (1878), was a best seller dramatized in 1892, and she continued writing in the same vein for forty-five years. Among her numerous stories are *The Lost Man's Lane; The Circular Study; The Amethyst Box; The House of the Whispering Pines; The Mystery of the Hasty Arrow; The Step on the Stair.*

Green, Julian (1900-), French novelist who served in World War I in the French army, and spent from 1919 to 1920 in the United States studying English and American literature at the University of Virginia. His works include *Avarice House* (1927); *The Closed Garden; The Dark Journey; The Strange River; The Dreamer; Then Shall the Dust Return;* all the above are published in English.

Green, Mitzi (1920-), American stage and screen actress, educated at the Professional Children's School, New York: she appeared at the age of four with her parents in vaudeville, and later played juvenile roles in several plays, making her formal debut at New York in 1937 as Billie Smith in *Babes in Arms.* Among the films in which she has appeared since 1929 are *Tom Sawyer; Dude Ranch; Skippy; Huckleberry Finn; Little Orphan Annie; Manhattan Merry-Go-Round.*

Green, Paul Eliot (1894-), American novelist and dramatist who was educated at the University of North Carolina, and served with the American Expeditionary Force during World War I. His plays include *The No 'Count Boy* (1924); *In Abraham's Bosom,* awarded the Pulitzer prize in 1927; *The House of Connelly; Roll, Sweet Chariot; The Lost Colony.* He also wrote a novel, *The Laughing Pioneer,* and a volume of short stories, *Wide Fields.*

Greenaway, Kate (1846-1901), English artist and illustrator who studied at the life classes of the South Kensington Museum and at the Slade School. Her earliest work was on Christmas cards which attracted considerable attention because of their quaint designs and charming draftmanship. She also made illustrations for the *London Illustrated News:* among the books for which she made drawings are *Under the Window* (1879); *The Birthday Book; Mother Goose; Little Ann; Kate Greenaway's Almanacs* issued from 1883 to 1897 with the exception of one year; *The Pied Piper of Hamelin.*

Greene, Robert (c.1560-1592), English dramatist regarded as one of the most original and ablest playwrights before SHAKESPEARE. His works include *Pandosto; The History of Orlando Furioso; The Comical History of Alphonsus, King of Aragon;* the comedies *George-a-Green* and *Friar Bacon and Friar Bungay.*

Greenough, Horatio (1805-1852), American sculptor who studied at Rome with Bertel THORWALDSEN, and at Florence with Lorenzo BARTOLINI. His works include a colossal statue of Washington, conceived as Zeus, and now in the Smithsonian Institution, Washington, D. C.; a group, *The Rescue,* on a buttress of the Capitol in Washington, D. C.; a bust of Lafayette; a bust of John Quincy

Adams, also a *Venus Victrix* in the Boston Athenaeum. His brother, **Richard Saltonstall Greenough** (1819-1904)) was also a sculptor in marble and bronze who lived in Europe for many years.

Green room, a reception room in theatres used by members of the cast, authors, producers, and privileged visitors, so named because the COVENT GARDEN THEATRE, London, presumed to have been the first theatre to have a room of this kind, happened to select green as the decorative color. Modern professional theatres make no provision for a green room, but they are often found in group or university playhouses.

Green Table, The, a modern ballet: libretto and choreography by Kurt Jooss; music by Frederick COHEN; first produced at Paris in 1932. The plot is a satire on war as a game played by diplomats with soldiers as their pawns: Death and the War Profiteer look on in grim amusement. At its end Death has taken the principals one by one, and only the War Profiteer remains.

Greenwich Village Theatre, a playhouse opened at New York in 1917 with Frank Conroy as director: the avowed purpose was to establish a home for the art of the theatre, and to assemble a company of players and craftsmen who regard the theatre as an art medium. Conditions in World War I forced suspension: Charles COBURN presented *The Better 'Ole* there in 1918. From 1923 to 1925 it was operated under the direction of Eugene O'NEILL, Kenneth MACGOWAN and Robert Edmond JONES: among the plays produced were *Desire Under the Elms* and *All God's Chillun Got Wings.* The theatre was razed after 1930.

Greet, Ben (1856-1936), English actor and manager who made his stage debut in 1879, and his first venture as a manager in 1890 with a series of outdoor presentations of plays by Shakespeare. He toured the United States in 1902 presenting Edith Wynne MATTHISON in the morality play, *Everyman.* In 1924-26 he presented English plays in Paris, and in 1933-34 acted as Master of the Greensward during the production of Shakespearean plays at the open air theatre in Regent's Park, London.

Gregorian Chant, in music the form of devotional music established by Pope Gregory the Great for the Roman Catholic Church, known collectively as *Plain Chant.* There does not appear to have been any marked difference between Ambrosian and Gregorian chants except that certain abuses, such as the use of folk song in sacred services, was forbidden.

Gregory, Horace (1898-), American poet educated at the University of Wisconsin, and since 1934 a member of the faculty at the Sarah Lawrence College, Bronxville, N. Y. His works include *Chelsea Rooming House* (1930); *No Retreat; Pilgrim of the Apocalypse,* a biography of D. H. Lawrence; *Chorus for Survival.*

Gregory, Isabella Augusta, Lady (1852-1932), Irish dramatist privately educated, and one of the founders with W. B. YEATS of the ABBEY THEATRE and the IRISH PLAYERS. She wrote a number of plays for performance in the Abbey Theatre: they include *The Rising of the Moon; Spreading the News; The Gaol Gate; The Workhouse Ward; Hyacinth Halvey; Grania; Cuchulain of Muirthemne.* Her book, *Our Irish Theatre,* outlines the purpose of and the progress made by the Abbey Theatre.

Gregory, John (1879-), American sculptor born in England: his notable works include *The Voyage; Toy Venus; Wood Nymph; Bacchante; Orpheus and the Dancing Panther; Philomela; Lancelot.* Many of his works, including some of those mentioned above, are in residences or on private estates.

Grein, Jacob Thomas (1862-1935), British dramatic critic and producer born in Holland who became a naturalized British subject in 1888. He founded the Independent Theatre in London, producing plays by George Bernard SHAW and Henrik IBSEN; also the Renaissance Theatre and the People's Theatre in Whitechapel. He also acted as dramatic critic for the *London Illustrated News,* the *Weekly Sketch,* and the *Sunday Times,* proving himself an able writer in such volumes as *The World of the Theatre* and *The New World of the Theatre.*

Grenville, Lillian (1888-1928), American dramatic soprano who studied at Paris, and made her debut in 1906 at Nice in Gounod's *Romeo and Juliet.* After appearing at Milan, Naples, Lisbon, and Genoa, she made her American debut in 1910 in Puccini's *La Boheme,* and also created the role of Barbara in Victor Herbert's *Natoma* in 1911. She was a highly gifted artist who died at an early age.

Gretchaninoff, Alexander (1864-), Russian composer who studied with Nicholas Rimsky-Korsakow at the St. Petersburg Conservatory, and became one of the greatest composers of secular and sacred choral music. His compositions include two operas; five symphonies and other orchestral works, violin pieces, choral works, chamber music, and many songs.

Grétry, André-Ernest-Modeste (1741-1813), French composer of more than fifty comic operas full of melody which may be regarded as the foundation of the opéra-comique in France: his great fault lay in his failure to master the principles of counterpoint which lead to the witty remark that "one could drive a coach and four between the melody and harmonies of a Gretry aria," implying that the harmonies were thin. The opera, *Richard Coeur de Lion* (1784) is considered his best work: his *Method of Simple Harmony* (1802) reveals his lack of technical knowledge.

Greuze, Jean Baptiste (1725-1805), French painter who studied at the Royal Academy, Paris: his works include *Father Reading the Bible to His Children; Septimus Severus Reproaching Caracalla; Village Bride; The Broken Pitcher; The Father's Curse; The Inconsolable Widow; Triumph of Galatea;* portraits of Louis XVI, Madame Pompadour, Louis XVII, and the Duc de Choiseul; *Innocence; The Broken Mirror.* He amassed a considerable fortune which was lost during the French Revolution, and died in want.

Greville, Henry, pseudonym of **Alice Marie Céleste Durand** (1842-1902), French novelist who began her literary career as a correspondent for St. Petersburg journals. Her works include *Dosia; The Expiation of Saveli; Cleopatra; A Russian Violin; An Ancient House; Cephise.*

Grey, Katherine (1873-), American actress who made her professional debut in 1889 at DALY's Theatre, New York, in *The Golden Widow:* among the numerous plays in which she appeared are *Shenandoah; Shore Acres; Napoleon; Arms and the Man; A Parisian Romance; Dr. Jekyll and Mr. Hyde* with Richard MANSFIELD; *The Royal Box* with Charles COGHLAN; *The First Born; Cyrano de Bergerac* with Richard Mansfield; *The Gay Lord Quex; Secret Service; The Lion and the Mouse; When We Were Twenty-One; The Thirteenth Chair; Bright Star.*

Grey, Zane (1875-1939), American author of Western fiction educated at the University of Pennsylvania: his numerous works include *Betty Zane* (1904); *The Last of the Plainsmen; Riders of the Purple Sage; Desert Gold; The Border Legion; The Lone Star Ranger; The Thundering Herd; Western Union; Fighting Caravans; Twin Sombreros; Majesty's Rancho.* Successful films have been adapted from several of his stories.

Griboyedov, Alexander Sergeivich (1795-1829), Russian soldier, diplomat, and playwright: his works include a satirical comedy, *Knowledge Brings Suffering,* a bitter arraignment of the Russian nobility; also an unfinished drama, *A Georgian Night.* He was assassinated at Teheran while on a diplomatic mission.

Grieg, Edvard Hagerup (1843-1907), Norwegian pianist and composer who studied at the Leipzig Conservatory with Hans RICHTER, Carl REINECKE, and Ignaz MOSCHELES; also at Copenhagen with GADE, Hartmann, and NORDRAAK. He visited Italy, meeting LISZT in Rome, and playing his piano concerto with the GEWANDHAUS ORCHESTRA at Leipzig in 1879. His compositions include an overture, *Autumn;* a suite, *In Holberg's Time;* two suites based on his incidental music for Ibsen's *Peer Gynt;* a piano concerto; three violin sonatas; a string quartet; many piano pieces and songs.

Griffes, Charles Tomlinson (1884-1920), American pianist and composer who studied composition with Engelbert HUMPERDINCK at Berlin: his works include a symphonic poem: *The Pleasure Dome of Kubla Khan; The Kairn of Koridwen,* a dance drama; a Japanese drama, *Shojo;* also many piano pieces including *The White Peacock,* and numerous songs.

Griffith, David Wark (1880-), American actor and film producer who first appeared as a member of J. K. HACKETT's company, and directed his first picture, *The Adventures of Dolly,* in 1908. His notable screen productions include *Hearts of the World; The Birth of a Nation* (1915); *Intolerance; Broken Blossoms; Way Down East; Orphans of the Storm; One Exciting Night; America; Sally of the Sawdust; That Royle Girl;*

Sorrows of Satan; Lincoln: the last named was made for both the silent and the talking films. He originated the "close-up," the "flashback," and the "fadeout."

Grille (Fr.), in architecture the term for a horizontal frame of iron or bronze bars placed over a sunken area forming an open-work enclosure. Fine examples are found in Spanish, Italian, English, and German churches where they are also used in front of tombs, altars, and as choir screens.

Grillparzer, Franz (1791-1872), Austrian poet and dramatist who held government offices for some time, and made his first success in the theatre with *Die Ahnfrau* (1817). His works include the plays *Sappho;* a trilogy, *The Golden Fleece; King Ottokar; A True Servant of His Master; Libussa; Der Traum, ein Leben;* also a short story of great power entitled *The Poor Musician,* inspired perhaps by his association with Franz Schubert.

Grimaldi, Giovanni Francesco (1606-1680), Italian painter and etcher also known as Il Bolognese. He studied with Francesco Albani, and after working for two years in Paris, spent the rest of his life in Rome. His works include *Scenes from the Old Testament* at the Quirinal in Rome, and many landscapes to be seen in European galleries. He made fine etchings of works by Titian, Annibale Carracci, and Ludovico Carracci.

Grimaldi, Joseph (1779-1837), English actor of Italian parentage who danced as a child of two at the Sadler's Wells and Drury Lane Theatres in London, and was familiarly known as "Little Joe." In 1806 he appeared in the pantomime, *Mother Goose,* at Covent Garden, singing the song, "Hot Codlings" mentioned by Albert Chevalier in his monologue-song "A Fallen Star." He was considered a peerless clown in England: Charles Dickens edited his *Memoirs* in 1838.

Gringore, Pierre (c.1480-c.1539), French poet and dramatist whose name is frequently incorrectly spelt *Gringoire*. His plays include a morality play, *Le Chasteau de Labor* (1499), and *Jeu du prince des sots* (Game of the Prince of Fools): he was a favorite of Louis XII, and is mentioned in Victor Hugo's *Notre Dame de Paris.*

Grisaille (It.), in art a style of painting in various shades of grey, used in decorative work to represent objects in relief. The term is applied especially to monochrome painting in enamels and on stained glass.

Grisi, Carlotta (1819-1899), Italian ballerina who studied with Jules Perrot, and made her debut at L'Opera, Paris, in 1841. She was a great favorite at European and English opera houses in *La Peri* and *Ghiselle,* and was unexcelled in fairy ballets because of her slight figure and inimitable gestures. She married her former teacher, Jules Perrot, who wrote many ballets for her.

Grisi, Giulia (1811-1869), Italian dramatic soprano who studied with her sister, Giuditta Grisi, and also with Mme. Pasta. She made her debut in 1828, and after singing throughout Italy with great success, toured the United States in 1854 with Giuseppe Mario. Rossini, Bellini, Pacini, and Donizetti composed operas for her.

Griswold, Putnam (1875-1914), American dramatic bass who studied with Alberto Randegger, Jacques Bouhy, and Julius Stockhausen, making his debut at Covent Garden, London, in 1901. He sang with the Savage Opera Company in the United States in 1904-5; at the Royal Opera, Berlin, in 1906-10, and made his debut in 1911 at the Metropolitan Opera House, New York, as Hagen in Wagner's *Dusk of the Gods* (Götterdämmerung). He was considered one of the finest interpreters of Wagnerian roles by German critics.

Grofé, Ferdinand (1892-), American arranger and composer who studied piano, violin, and musical theory with his mother. While a member of the Los Angeles Symphony Orchestra he became acquainted with Paul Whiteman, and after studying orchestration with Pietro Floridia, he became associated with Whiteman's Orchestra as arranger. In 1924 he orchestrated George Gershwin's *Rhapsody in Blue,* thereby assuring its success: his works include a tone poem, *Broadway at Night; Mississippi Suite; Metropolis; Three Shades of Blue; "Grand Canyon" Suite; "Hollywood" Suite; Tabloid; Melodic Decades; Killarney Rhapsody.*

Gropius, Walter (1883-), German architect and leading exponent of the modern movement in architecture: his works include the Bauhaus at Dessau; the Fagus factory buildings at Alfeld; buildings at the Cologne Exposition; the State Theatre at Jena; also many experimental industrial buildings and workers' dwellings. In 1937 he became professor of architecture at Harvard University, Cambridge, Mass.

Gros, Antoine Jean, Baron (1771-1835), French painter who studied with his father and with Louis David. In 1796 he was present when Napoleon I placed the tricolor on the bridge at Arcola during the invasion of Italy: he painted the incident, and as a reward was made a member of the commission appointed to select the art works to be removed to the Louvre. His works include *Pest House at Jaffa; Napoleon at Eylau; The Taking of Madrid; The Battle of Aboukir; Hercules and Diomedes; The Departure of the Duchess of Angoulême.*

Gross, Chaim (1904-), American sculptor and carver born in Austria, and naturalized in 1934. He fled from Austria to Hungary during World War I, studied at an art school in Budapest, and come to New York in 1921, studying at the Educational Alliance Art School and at the Beaux-Arts Institute of Design. His works include *Alaskan Snow-Shoe Mail Carrier* in the Post Office Department Building, Washington, D. C.; *Steel Worker* at the Federal Trade Commission Building, Washington, D. C., two groups for the France Overseas and the Switzerland Buildings at the New York World's Fair. He uses more than thirty woods in carving, and his works are in the Metropolitan Museum of Art, the Whitney Museum of American Art, and the Museum of Modern Art in New York. His autobiography, *A Sculptor's Progress,* was published in 1938.

Grossmith, George (1847-1912), English actor who made his debut in 1870 as an entertainer with songs and recitations: in 1877 he joined the SAVOY OPERA COMPANY to sing the roles requiring humorous acting, dancing, and singing of "patter songs." In 1889 he returned to entertaining, and toured Great Britain and the United States with great success. His sons, George and Laurence, were also actors and singers, and his brother, **Weedon Grossmith** (1853-1919), was a painter of reputation and also an actor who appeared with great success in his own plays, *A Pantomime Rehearsal* and *The Night of the Party*, both of which enjoyed long runs.

Grosvenor Gallery (London), a gallery for the exhibition of paintings and sculptures founded by Sir Lindsay Coutts "with the intention of giving special advantages of exhibition to artists of established reputation some of whom have previously been imperfectly known to the public." Among those who exhibited at the first exhibition on May 1, 1877, were Sir Francis GRANT, president of the Royal Academy, LEIGHTON, MILLAIS, G. F. WATTS, ALMA-TADEMA, BURNE-JONES, and WHISTLER. The exhibit starts annually on May 1st, and is open to established artists, whether Academicians or Independents.

Grotesques, in art a series of painted subjects in the form of arabesques used by LEONARDO DA VINCI, PERUGINO, RAPHAEL, and other painters before and during the Renaissance: bizarre figures and fanciful animals are used at the curling ends of the arabesques. Medieval sculptors were also skilled in designing grotesques.

Ground Bass, in music the constant repetition of a phrase in the bass of a composition with varied harmonies and musical figures in the treble parts; known as *basso ostinato* in Italian. It was a popular device in the 17th century: examples may be found in the works of PURCELL, BACH, and HANDEL. BRAHMS also made use of it in his fourth symphony, and in his *Variations on a Theme by Haydn.*

Grove, Sir George (1820-1900), English author of works on music who was the first director of the ROYAL COLLEGE OF MUSIC, London (1883-1894). His works include a *Dictionary of Music and Musicians* (1879-89), revised three times (1904, 1927, and 1940); also an analytical work, *Beethoven and His Nine Symphonies* (1896). In 1867 he visited Vienna with his friend, Sir Arthur SULLIVAN which resulted in the unearthing of "Rosamunde" and other works of SCHUBERT: he visited the United States in 1878 where he made the acquaintance of Oliver Wendell HOLMES, Ralph Waldo EMERSON, and Henry Wadsworth LONGFELLOW.

Gruenberg, Louis (1883-   ), Russian-American composer brought to the United States as a child: he studied piano and composition with Ferruccio BUSONI and at the Vienna Conservatory, and after making his debut with the Berlin Philharmonic Orchestra in 1912, concertized for several years and taught composition at the CHICAGO MUSICAL COLLEGE. His works include the opera, *Emperor Jones,* produced with Lawrence TIBBETT in the title role at the METROPOLITAN OPERA HOUSE in 1933; another opera, *Jack and the Beanstalk;* two radio operas; orchestral works; chamber music; *Jazzettes* for violin and piano. He is distinguished for his symphonic treatment of jazz rhythm.

Grün or **Grien, Hans,** see **Baldung, Hans.**

Grundy, Mrs., a character in a comedy, *Speed the Plough,* by Thomas MORTON (1764-1838), who is referred to but never seen. The question frequently asked "What will Mrs. Grundy say?" when anything either happens or is mentioned: therefore the name, *Mrs. Grundy,* has become proverbial for any person whose opinions are arbitrary on questions of propriety.

Grundy, Sidney (1848-1914), English dramatist educated for the law who practised at Manchester. In 1887 his play, *The Bells of Haslemere,* was a pronounced success: it was followed by *A White Lie; A Fool's Paradise; Sowing the Wind; A Pair of Spectacles;* also several well-received adaptations of "The Three Musketeers" and other novels by Alexandre DUMAS, PERE, and Octave MIRBEAU.

Grünewald, Mathias (c.1480-c.1530), German painter called the "German Correggio" because his works resemble closely those of the Italian master: he is said to have studied with Hans HOLBEIN THE ELDER; his notable works include *Isenheim Altarpiece* with nine paintings; *Last Judgment; Crucifixion; Christ Mocked; St. Erasmus and St. Maurice.*

Guardi, Francesco (1712-1793), Italian painter who studied with CANALETTO, and executed many pictures in the style of his master: they include *View of Venice; Fete of Corpus Domini; Room in a Convent; Grand Canal at Venice; Masquerade in the Ridotto; Church on the Grand Canal; Interior of St. Mark's, Venice; The Doge's State Barge.*

Guarini, Giovanni Battista (1537-1612), Italian poet and dramatist who was employed by the Duke of Ferrara on diplomatic service from 1567 to 1581. He retired in 1582, and wrote the pastoral drama, *Il Pastor Fido* (1585), which resembles TASSO's *Aminta* in some respects, and while disappointing as a stage piece, is regarded as one of the masterpieces of Italian literature from the literary standpoint.

Guarnerius, Andreas (c.1626-1698), Italian violin maker who studied with Nicolo AMATI as a youth of fifteen: he adopted a larger model than that of Amati, and used an orange-brown varnish. His violins bring from $3500.00 to $9000.00 today. His eldest son, **Petrus Guarnerius** (1655-1720), made highly individualistic violins varnished in golden yellow or reddish-brown which are valued at $4000.00 to $10,000.00, and his nephew, **Joseph Guarnerius** (Del Gésu), who was born in 1698, and died in 1744, was the greatest violin maker next to STRADIVARIUS: his instruments are made of beautifully flamed maple varnished a golden orange, and sell today for from $12,000.00 to $35,000.00.

Gudin, Théodore (1802-1880), French painter who studied with GIRODET-TRIOSON, and became painter of marine scenes for Louis Philippe and Napoleon III. His works include *Burning of the Kent; Fisherman on the Beach; Explosion of the Emperor's Fort at Algiers; Evening on the Shore of the North Sea; Shipwreck on the Coast of Genoa; Hurricane in the Roadstead of Algiers;* also sixty canvases of the French Navy in port or in action.

Guercino (1591-1666), Italian painter whose real name was Giovanni Francesco Barbieri; he was called "Guercino" because he squinted. He studied with Ludovico CARRACCI: his notable works include *The Death of Dido; Venus, Mars, and Cupid; Resurrection; Madonna with Two Monks; Martyrdom of St. Peter; Susanna at the Bath; Endymion; Christ at the Well;* also more than a hundred altarpieces.

Guérin, Jules (1866-), American painter and illustrator: his murals are to be seen in the Lincoln Memorial, Washington, D. C.; the Pennsylvania Railroad Station, New York; the Civic Opera Building, Chicago; he also directed the decorations at the Panama-Pacific Exposition, and has drawn illustrations for many magazines with national circulation.

Guérin, Pierre Narcisse (1774-1833), French painter who studied with REGNAULT, and achieved success with his picture, *Return of Marcus Sextus,* exhibited in 1799. He became director of the French Academy in Rome: his notable works include *Coriolanus and the Body of Brutus; Dido and Aeneas; Phaedra Accusing Hippolytus; Andromache; Clytemnestra; Napoleon Pardoning Rebels in Cairo; Murder of Priam.*

Guest, Edgar (1881-), American journalist and poet who has been connected with the Detroit *Free Press* since 1895. His works include *A Heap o' Livin'* (1916); *Just Folks; Rhymes of Childhood; Harbor Lights of Home; Life's Highway; All in a Lifetime.*

Guggenheim Memorial Foundation Fellowships, offered by the John Simon Guggenheim Memorial Foundation established by former United States Senator Simon Guggenheim and his wife in 1925 as a memorial to their son. Fellowships are offered for research in any field of knowledge, and for creative work in any of the fine arts. In the letter accompanying the gift, Senator Guggenheim wrote: "We strongly hope that this Foundation will advance human achievement by aiding students to push forward the boundaries of understanding, and will enrich human life by aiding them in the cultivation of beauty and taste." Approximately 1300 fellowships have been granted since 1925: among those who have been so honored from 1939 to 1943 in the fields of *painting, sculpture,* and the *illustrative arts* are Peggy Bacon, Richard Barthé, Arnold Blanch, Peter Blume, Aaron Bohrod, Louis Bouché, John Carroll, John Corbino, Angna Enters, John B. Flannagan, Emil Ganso, Maurice Glickman, William Gropper, George Grosz, Donald Harcourt de Lue, Marsden Hartley, Yasuo Kuniyoski, Arthur Lee, Sidney Loeb, Oronzio Maldarelli, E. Bruce Moore, Charles Rudy, Antonio Salemme, Marion Sanford, Carl Schaefer, Raymond Turner, Carl Walters. In the field of *music,* fellowships have been awarded to George Antheil, Stanley Bate, Robert Russell Bennett, Carl Bricken, Carlos Chavez, Aaron Copland, Henry Cowell, Paul Creston, David Diamond, Ross Lee Finney, Anis Fuleihan, Roy Harris, Ralph Kirkpatrick, Otto Luening, Quinto Maganini, Leopold Mannes, Robert McBride, Carl McKinley, Douglas Moore, Paul Nordoff, Walter Piston, Quincy Porter, Bernard Rogers, William Schumann, Roger Sessions, William Grant Still, Randall Thompson. In the field of *drama* and the *dance* are Marc Blitzstein, Stewart Chaney, Martha Graham, Paul Green, Lynn Riggs, and in *literature* Louis Adamic, Wystan Hugh Anden, Conrad Aiken, Stephen Vincent Benét, Louise Bogan, Kay Boyle, Countée Cullen, John Dos Passos, Jeremy Ingalls, Harold Lamb, Lewis Mumford, and Muriel Rukeyser.

Guido d'Arezzo (c.995-c.1050), Italian musical theorist and teacher who reformed the notation of music. He introduced the four-line staff thereby establishing surety of pitch in notation, originated the system known as SOLMIZATION, and invented the GUIDONIAN HAND, a diagram in the shape of an outstretched hand with the ARETINIAN SYLLABLES written in regular order on the successive finger-tips and joints, making it easy to memorize the names of the syllables.

Guido da Siena, Italian painter of the 13th century: little is known of him except that he has been identified with Guido Graziani by some authorities. The disputed works attributed to him include *Virgin and Child* and *Madonna with Saints.*

Guido Reni (1575-1642), Italian painter who studied with Denis CALVAERT, Ludovico CARRACCI, and was a fellow-pupil with Francesca ALBANI. His works include *Crucifixion of St. Peter,* said to be in the style of CARAVAGGIO; *Massacre of the Innocents; Phoebus and the Hours Preceded by Aurora; Atalanta's Race; Christ and the Samaritan Woman; Israelites Gathering the Manna; David and Goliath; Samson and the Philistines.*

Guignol, in drama the name of the chief character in medieval French puppet shows, and also the name of a theatre or play in which marionettes are the actors. As the plays were usually of gruesome or macabre nature, stage plays of like nature performed by living actors were given at a theatre in Paris known as GRAND GUIGNOL.

Guilbert, Yvette (1867-), French diseuse who made her debut as an actress at Paris in 1885, and as a singer in Parisian restaurants in 1890, rapidly building a reputation as a chanteuse and diseuse. After appearing in vaudeville houses throughout Europe and Great Britain, she toured the United States either alone or with Albert CHEVALIER from 1906 to 1917, presenting historical cycles of French chansons. She also taught dramatic diction at the David MANNES School in New York, also publishing an autobiography, *The Song of My Life,* and a treatise, *How to Sing a Song.*

Guild or **Gild,** the name given in medieval times to a union of workers in various crafts who performed the early miracle and mystery plays.

Guild Theatre (New York), see **Theatre Guild, The.**

Guillaume, Eugène (1822-1905), French sculptor who studied at the Ecole des Beaux-Arts, Paris, and with Louis Barrias: his works include *Theseus Finding His Father's Sword on a Rock; The Gracchi;* a monument to Jean Phillipe Rameau; *Anacreon; The Graces;* busts of Napoleon I and Colbert. He became director of the Ecole des Beaux-Arts in 1864, and wrote many treatises and articles on sculpture.

Guillaume de Lorris, thirteenth century French poet who wrote the first part of the Romance of the Rose, one of the greatest chansons de geste. His contribution amounted to approximately 4,700 lines, and is distinguished by the vivid beauty of wording and colorful description: the poem was completed by Jean de Meung who added about 18,000 lines.

Guillaumet, Gustave Achille (1840-1887), French painter who studied with Felix Barrias and at the Ecole des Beaux-Arts, Paris. He visited Algeria many times, and his principal subjects for pictures are taken from sketches made there: they include *Evening Prayer in the Sahara; Flute Players at the Bivouac; Douar Women at the River; Wool Spinners at Bou-Saada; Bivouac of Camel Drivers.*

Guillotine, a machine for beheading persons introduced into France at the time of the French Revolution. It consists of two upright posts surmounted by a cross beam: a heavily weighted, keen-edged knife descends swiftly between grooves in the posts, and the head drops into a basket at the base of the machine. It was introduced at the suggestion of Dr. Joseph Ignace Guillotin (1738-1814), but any claims on his part to its invention are refuted by the use of a similar device by the ancient Persians, and by the employment of an instrument known as the "Maiden" in Scotland which decapitated the Earl of Argyll in 1685. Pictures by French painters of Revolutionary scenes frequently picture the guillotine.

Guilmant, Alexandre-Félix (1837-1911), French organist and composer who studied with Jacques Lemmens: he became organist of Ste.-Trinité at Paris in 1871, remaining there until 1901. He was one of the founders of the Schola Cantorum in Paris, and organ professor at the Paris Conservatory of Music. He was a great virtuoso, a master of improvisation, and the teacher of many famous organists including Joseph Bonnet and Marcel Dupre. In addition to composing sonatas and hundreds of solo pieces for the organ he compiled a collection of old French organ works and a classical collection of organ works by composers of all nationalities.

Guimard, Marie Madeleine (1743-1816), French dancer who was the reigning favorite at the Paris L'Opéra for twenty-five years: she built a theatre in her house where licentious plays were the attraction for invited audiences. She retired in 1789 to marry Jean Étienne Despreaux, a famous dancer and balletmaster.

Guimera, Angel (1849-1924), Spanish poet and dramatist who was born in the Canary Islands of Spanish parents, and spent his life in Spain. His first success was a drama, *Gala Placidia* (1881): it was followed by many more plays which reveal him as one of the great dramatists of Spain. He is known to English readers by *Martha of the Lowlands* which has been translated.

Guinevere, in Arthurian legend the wife of King Arthur: she was the daughter of Leodegraunce, king of Camelyard, and loved Lancelot. She was depicted as the most beautiful woman in the world, of fair complexion and blue-eyed: she was lively but quick and tender of understanding, and her heart was capable of only the noblest thoughts and exalted sentiments.

Guiney, Louise Imogen (1861-1920), American poet and essayist, educated in a convent, who lived in England from 1901, and worked at the Bodleian Library, Oxford. Her works include *Songs at the Start* (1884); *The White Sail and Other Poems; A Little English Gallery; Happy Ending.*

Guion, David Wendell Fentress (1895-), American composer who studied in the United States and with Leopold Godowsky at the Vienna Conservatory of Music, and taught at the Chicago College of Music. His compositions include *Shingandi,* an African ballet-suite for orchestra; *Arkansas Traveler; Alley Tunes; Turkey in the Straw* for orchestra; also many novel arrangements of cowboy songs.

Guiraud, Ernest (1837-1892), French composer born in New Orleans, and trained by his father: his first opera, *Le Roi David,* was produced at New Orleans when he was fifteen years old. He studied at the Paris Conservatory with Marmontel and Jacques Halevy, composing seven operas, a ballet, and several orchestral works.

Guitar, a musical instrument which bears some resemblance to the lute: it has six strings, the three highest of which are made of gut, and the three lower of silver wire. The notes are produced on a fretted fingerboard by plucking the strings with the fingers of the right hand: the instrument has a flat face and back, and is used either for solo playing, or for accompanying songs. Two great Spanish virtuosos are Fernando Sor (1778-1839) and Andres Segovia (1894-).

Guiterman, Arthur (1871-1943), American poet and dramatist born in Vienna of American parentage, and educated at the College of the City of New York. For many years he contributed verses to *Life Magazine:* his works include *Betel Nuts* (1907); *Ballads of Old New York; Wildwood Fables; Gaily the Troubadour; The Laughing Muse.* He adapted Molière's *School for Husbands* in collaboration with Lawrence Langner, and wrote the libretto and lyrics for Walter Damrosch's opera, *A Man Without a Country,* produced at the Metropolitan Opera House in 1937. He was distinguished for the brilliancy of his rhyming in humorous verses.

Guitry, Lucien Germain (1860-1925), French actor who studied at the Paris Conservatory, and made his debut in 1878 at the Gymnase in *La Dame aux Camélias*. After appearing for nine years in St. Petersburg, he became stage director at the Comédie-Francaise, but resigned to assume the direction of the Théâtre de la Renaissance, Paris, from 1902 to 1909 where he was associated with Marthe Brandes, in producing Anatole FRANCE's *Crainquebille*, DOUNAY's *Amant*, ZOLA's *L'Assommoir*, and plays by Henri BERNSTEIN. He was classed with Constant COQUELIN as an exponent of realistic drama.

Guitry, Sacha (1885-   ), French actor, dramatist and manager who wrote his first play, *Nono*, at twenty-one, following it with more than one hundred others many of which were successes. He wrote several plays including *Deburau, Béranger, Pasteur, Jacqueline*, and *Le Grand Duc* for his father, Lucien GUITRY, and *Un Sujet de Roman* in which the latter appeared with Sarah BERNHARDT. Many of his plays were written for performance by him with his former wife, Yvonne PRINTEMPS. In 1926 he appeared at New York in *Mozart:* among the films in which he has appeared, written or directed are *Bonne Chance; The Cheat; Pasteur; Champs-Elysées; The Pearls of the Crown; Indiscretions; Nine Bachelors.*

Gut, the material, manufactured from the entrails of young lambs and sheep, used to make strings for the violin, viola, violoncello, double bass, harp, guitar, and similar instruments. At the present time the tendency is to use strings made of fine steel wire, or gut strings covered with aluminum, silver, or gold.

Gutenberg, Johannes (c.1400-1468), German inventor of printing with movable type cast in molds: his real name was Johannes Gensfleisch. His claim as an inventor, which has been much disputed, is based on a legal decision in his favor regarding the construction of a press in connection with a type-mold. He lived in Strasbourg for a considerable period of years, but his masterpiece, the MAZARIN BIBLE, was printed in Mainz, the city in which he was born.

Guthrie, Sir James (1859-1930), Scottish painter who studied in Paris, and became president of the Royal Scottish Academy in 1902. His notable works include *The Gipsy Fires are Burning; Midsummer; Funeral Service in the Scottish Highlands; Schoolmates:* he was also a distinguished portrait painter.

Guthrie, Tyrone (1900-   ), English actor and producer, educated at Oxford, who made his first professional appearance in 1924 at the Playhouse in Oxford, and his first productions, *The Anatomist* and *Six Characters in Search of an Author* at the Westminster Theatre in London. This was followed by *Dangerous Corner; Sweet Aloes; Mary Read; Paganini; The School for Scandal.* He also appeared in the films *Vessel of Wrath* and *St. Martin's Lane.*

Gutrune, in Richard Wagner's *The Dusk of the Gods,* sister of Gunther, king of the Gibichungs: she falls in love with SIEGFRIED, and gives him a magic potion which kills his love for BRUNNHILDE, and causes him to become enamored of her.

Gutzkow, Karl Ferdinand (1811-1878), German novelist and dramatist: his work, *Wally, die Zweiflerin* (1835) attacking the sanctity of marriage and of divine revelation, resulted in imprisonment for three months, but acted as a firebrand to the imagination of the young German writers. His successful plays include *Richard Savage; Zopf und Schwertz; Das Urbild des Tartüffe,* and *Uriel Acosta:* he also wrote a nine-volume novel, *Die Ritter vom Geiste.*

Gwenn, Edmund (1875-   ), English stage and screen actor who made his London debut in 1899 in *A Jealous Mistake.* He became famous as an interpreter of lower middle class roles in *The Thieves' Comedy, Major Barbara, The Devil's Disciple, What Every Woman Knows, The Twelve Pound Look, The Skin Game, Laburnum Grove,* and many other famous plays. Since 1936 he has appeared in numerous films including *The Good Companions; Anthony Adverse; South Riding; Parnell; A Yank at Oxford; Earl of Chicago; Pride and Prejudice; Foreign Correspondent; One Night in Lisbon; The Devil and Miss Jones; Charley's Aunt.*

Gwilt, Joseph (1784-1863), Scottish architect who studied at the Royal Academy: his most important contribution to his art was a valuable *Encyclopedia of Architecture* (1842) which was reprinted in 1867 with additions by Wyatt Papworth.

Gwyn, Nell (1650-1687), English actress who first appeared in 1665 at Cydaria in Dryden's play, *The Indian Emperor,* and later in BEAUMONT and FLETCHER's *Philaster,* DRYDEN's *Secret Love,* and other stage pieces calling for broad comedy acting. She was the mistress of Charles II, and her generosity, good nature, and general devil-may-care attitude toward life made her a favorite with the English people. Samuel PEPYS records in his diary his delight in her acting; she is a character in Sir Walter SCOTT's *Peveril of the Peak,* and the dances for Sir Henry IRVING's production, *Nell Gwyn,* composed by Sir Edward German have made her name familiar to music lovers. Her portrait was painted by Sir Peter Lely.

Gyllembourg, Ehrensvard Thomasine Christine, Countess of (1773-1856), Danish writer of fiction who married a Swedish nobleman. Her first novel, *The Polonius Family,* was written when she was fifty-three: its great success led to the writing of *Dream and Reality, Two Ages,* and several other equally popular novels. She published under the pen name "The Author of Every-Day History," and only after her death was her identity revealed.

Gyp, the pseudonym of **Countess Gabrielle de Martel de Janville** (1850-1932), French novelist and dramatist: her works include *About Marriage* (1883), successfully dramatized; *About Divorce; Conjugal Joys; Miss Eve; The Duke; The Duchess;* also several theatre pieces under the pen name "Bob."

Gypsy Baron, The, comic opera in three acts: libretto by Manuel Schnitzer, music by Johann STRAUSS, JR.; first produced at Vienna in 1885, and at New York at the Casino Theatre in 1886 with Pauline HALL and Francis WILSON in the caste. The plot is inherently weak, but it offered no obstacle to the creation of a typical Strauss score replete with beautiful songs, gypsy melodies, and gorgeous dance music. There are Columbia and Victor recordings of the enormously popular *Overture,* and of the famous *Schatz (Treasure) Waltz.*

H

Haakon, Paul, contemporary Danish dancer who studied at the Kosloff School and the Royal Opera Ballet School at Copenhagen, and with Michel FOKINE in New York where he appeared in solo recitals. In 1927 he danced in the Fokine Ballets at the Century Theatre, New York, later appearing in Spain, France, and in England with the Anton DOLIN Ballet. He has danced with Anna PAVLOWA, in several Broadway productions, and with the Catherine LITTLEFIELD Ballet at the New York World's Fair in 1940.

Hába, Alois (1893-), Czech composer who studied with Franz Schreker at the Music Academy in Vienna, and became a teacher at the State Conservatory, Prague, in 1923. He is a propagandist of quarter-tone music, and founded a class for composition in this form which was attended by many of the younger European composers. His works include quarter-tone compositions in operatic, orchestral, and instrumental form: he has also written many works in the usual mode, and a *Harmony Book* in explanation of his quarter, sixth, and twelfth tone systems founded on ancient Slav and Greek music.

Habanera, an African dance introduced into Cuba by Negroes, originally known as *Creole Country Dance:* it found its way into Spain and France where it has become glorified in the hands of Georges BIZET (in CARMEN), Emmanuel CHABRIER, and Maurice RAVEL.

Habima Theatre, an organization founded in Moscow, Russia, about 1905 for the propagation of the Hebrew language in drama. It was forced to work secretly from 1911, and was not in favor with the Bolshevists after the revolution in 1917, being saved from annihilation by influence. In 1925 the company began a two-year tour of more than twenty countries, appearing with little success at New York in *The Dybbuk* and other plays. The company is now in Tel-Aviv, Palestine, where it performs in a theatre built through contributions.

Hackett, Charles (1889-1942), American dramatic tenor who studied with Vincenzo Lombardi in Florence, making his debut in 1915 at Pavia in Boito's *Mefistofele,* and his first appearance in 1919 at the Metropolitan Opera House in Rossini's *The Barber of Seville.* Later he appeared with the Chicago Civic Opera, and again at the Metropolitan from 1934 to 1940. He was also a teacher of voice at the Institute of Musical Art.

Hackett, James Henry (1800-1871), American actor who first appeared in odd character parts in 1826, and created the role of Falstaff with tremendous success at Philadelphia in 1832, later duplicating his triumph in London. He managed several theatres, toured Great Britain and the United States, and wrote a book entitled *Notes and Comments on Shakespeare* (1863).

Hackett, James K. (1869-1926), American actor and manager, son of James Henry HACKETT, born in Canada, and educated at the College of the City of New York. He appeared in 1892 with the Augustin DALY company playing Shakespearean roles, and made a sensational success in Anthony HOPE's *The Prisoner of Zenda* and *Rupert of Hentzau* under the management of Charles FROHMAN. He married his leading lady, Mary MANNERING, appearing with her in Sutro's play, *The Walls of Jericho,* and toured the United States in *Monsieur Beaucaire, The Crook, Craig Kennedy, Othello,* and *Macbeth.*

Hades, (a) in Greek mythology the king of the underworld, also known as *Pluto:* PROSERPINE was his wife, and he acted in the dual capacity of dispenser to mortals of the world's treasures and ruler of the shades of the departed. (b) The name of the underworld where the spirits of the dead dwelt: they were presumed to continue in the subterranean kingdom the life led on earth. The righteous dwelt in peace and comfort, but the wicked were eternally tormented, and the enormous three-headed dog, CERBERUS, prevented both good and bad spirits from escaping to the world above.

Hading, Jane (1859-1941), French actress whose real name was Jeanne Alfrédine Tréfouret: she first appeared at theatres in Algiers and Cairo, and in 1883 achieved her first great success in *Le Maître de forges,* and later in *Frou-frou.* In 1888 and 1894 she toured the United States with Benoît COQUELIN, and finally established a reputation as an outstanding actress in America, England and France. In 1896 she was chosen by Victorien SARDOU to create the title role in MARCELLE.

Hadley, Henry Kimball (1871-1937), American composer who studied at the NEW ENGLAND CONSERVATORY OF MUSIC, Boston, with George W. CHADWICK, and in Vienna with E. Mandyczewski. He conducted the Seattle and San Francisco Symphony Orchestras, and was also associate conductor of the New York Philharmonic-Symphony orchestra from 1915 to 1922. His compositions include the operas, *Azora, Daughter of Montezuma,* produced by the Chicago Opera Company in 1917, and *Cleopatra's Night,* produced at the Metropolitan Opera House in 1920; several symphonies; many orchestral works; chamber music; choruses and songs.

Hadow, Sir William Henry (1859-1937), English composer and writer on musical subjects educated at Oxford. His compositions include a cantata, *The Soul's Pilgrimage,* church music and chamber works: his writings include *Studies in Modern Music; The Sonata Form; The Viennese Period,* (Volume V in "The Oxford History of Music"); *William Byrd;* MUSIC: COLLECTED ESSAYS. He contributed to "The Encyclopedia Britannica" and to many musical periodicals.

Haffner Symphony (Mozart), a work originally written by Wolfgang Amadeus Mozart in 1782: it is given in the Kochel catalogue as No. 385, and as No. 35 in the complete list of symphonies. Written originally in serenade form with an introductory march and two minuets, Mozart condensed it into four movements, and added parts for flutes and clarinets. Critics are agreed that it is a highly inspired work: there is a Victor recording by the New York Philharmonic-Symphony Orchestra under Arturo Toscanini, and a Columbia recording by the London Philharmonic Orchestra with Sir Thomas Beecham.

Hafiz, Khwaja (c.1300-1389), Persian lyric poet who was born and lived all his life at Shiraz; his real name was Shams-ad-din Muhammad. He was celebrated for his *Ghazels* or amatory odes; also for his drinking songs: a complete edition of his works in English was prepared by H. Wilberforce Clarke, and many of the odes were translated by Justin Huntley McCarthy.

Hagedorn, Hermann (1882-), American poet and novelist who was educated at Harvard and at the University of Berlin: in 1909-11 he acted as assistant to Barrett Wendell. His works include *The Woman of Corinth; A Troop of the Guard and Other Poems; Poems and Ballads; The Heart of Youth; This Darkness and This Light.*

Hageman, Richard (1882-), Dutch pianist and composer who studied with his father, and at the Brussels and Amsterdam conservatories. He came to the United States as accompanist for Yvette Guilbert, and later became one of the conductors of the Metropolitan Opera House where his opera, *Caponsacchi,* was performed in 1937. He has also written many fine songs, piano pieces, and music for the films.

Hagen, a character in Wagner's *Dusk of the Gods* (Die Götterdämmerung), the final drama in the Ring of the Nibelungs. He is the son of Alberich, and plunges his spear into Siegfried's back: the hero as he dies murmurs the name of his beloved, Brunnhilde.

Haggard, Sir Henry Rider (1856-1925), English novelist who lived for a long time in South Africa where he gathered material for his novels, *King Solomon's Mines* (1885), *Allan Quartermain,* and *She:* the last-named made him world-famous. Among his other works were *Belshazzar, Queen Sheba's Ring, Cleopatra, Mrs. Meeson's Will,* and *The World's Desire.*

Haggard, Stephen (1912-1943), English novelist, stage and screen actor who entered the British Army at the outbreak of World War II, and was killed in action. He appeared first in New York in Clemence Dane's *Come of Age* in 1937, and in 1938 in *Whiteoaks.* His novel, *Nya,* was published in 1938. He also played in the films *Mozart, Whom the Gods Love,* and *Jamaica Inn:* he was a grand-nephew of Sir Henry Rider Haggard.

Haggin, Ben Ali (1882-), American painter and designer of stage scenery: he designed the "living pictures" which were a special feature of Florenz Ziegfeld's *Follies* for many years, and staged a play, *Field of Ermine,* in 1935 for Crosby Gaige at the National Theatre, New York.

Hähnel, Ernst Julius (1811-1891), German sculptor who executed a fine monument to Beethoven at Bonn for which Franz Liszt contributed the proceeds of a concert tour. He also made the frieze, *Bacchic Procession,* for the Dresden Opera House, and a statue of *Raphael* for the Dresden Museum.

Haight, Charles Coolidge (1841-1917), American architect whose works include buildings at Hobart College and Yale University: also several buildings on the campus of the old Columbia University located on Madison Avenue. He was one of the principal advocates of adapting the English style of Gothic architecture to structures erected in America.

Haines, Robert T. (1868-1943), American stage and screen actor who first studied law at the University of Missouri, made his debut in 1891 at Washington, D. C., in *Virginius,* and his first success on the New York stage in *The Palace of the King* with Viola Allen. He also appeared with Alla Nazimova, Minnie Maddern Fiske, Blanche Bates, Grace George, Frances Starr, and Olga Nethersole. He also wrote and directed sketches for Pauline Lord, Mary Boland, and Grant Mitchell in addition to playing in several films and radio broadcasts.

Hajos, Mitzi (1891-), Hungarian actress whose real name is Magdalena Hajos: after learning English she made her debut in 1911 on the legitimate stage at New York in *La Belle Paree.* Among the productions in which she has appeared are *The Spring Maid; Her Little Highness; Sari; Pom-Pom; Head Over Heels; Lady Billy; The Madcap; Enter Madame; Connie Comes Home; You Can't Take It With You.*

Hale, Alan (1892-), American screen actor and director who has appeared in both silent and talking pictures: since 1934 he has appeared in numerous pictures including *Little Man, What Now; Of Human Bondage; The Little Minister; It Happened One Night; The Scarlet Letter; The Last Days of Pompeii; A Message to Garcia; The Prince and the Pauper; Stella Dallas; The Adventures of Marco Polo; The Adventures of Robin Hood; Algiers; The Sisters; The Man in the Iron Mask; Private Lives of Elizabeth and Essex; The Sea Hawk.*

Hale, Chester (1897-), American balletmaster, educated at the University of Chicago, who made his first appearance with the Diaghileff Ballet Russe in the United States, also touring Europe, Great Britain, and South America. He also appeared with Anna Pavlowa, and acted as balletmaster at the Capitol Theatre, New York, from 1925 to 1934. Among the films for which he has directed the dances are *The Painted Veil; Anna Karenina; Rose Marie; A Night at the Opera.*

Hale, Edward Everett (1822-1909), American clergyman and author educated at Harvard College: his works include a famous short story, *The Man Without a Country,* published anonymously in the *Atlantic Monthly* (December, 1863), and the basis of an opera by Walter DAMROSCH; *Ten Times One is Ten; A New England Boyhood,* his autobiography; *James Russell Lowell and His Friends; Memoires of a Hundred Years.*

Hale, Louise Closser (1872-1933), American actress and author who made her debut in 1894 on the stage in *In Old Kentucky,* and appeared in 1903 with Arnold Daly in *Candida.* In 1907 she played the role of Miss Hazy in *Mrs. Wiggs of the Cabbage Patch* in London, and was featured in the films for many years in old-woman parts. Her writings include travel books and short stories.

Hale, Nancy (1909-   ), American novelist and grand-daughter of Edward Everett HALE: her works include *The Young Die Good* (1932); *Never Any More Joy; The Earliest Dreams; The Prodigal Women; Between the Dark and the Daylight.*

Hale, Nathan (1755-1776), American soldier educated at Yale who joined a Connecticut regiment at the outbreak of the Revolution, and was captured inside British lines while attempting to obtain information. He was hanged in accordance with British military law, and is said to have expressed regrets that he had but one life to lose for his country. A fine statue by Frederick MAC-MONNIES is in New York; in 1898 Clyde FITCH's play, *Nathan Hale,* was successfully produced in New York.

Hale, Philip (1854-1934), American organist and music critic educated at Yale University who studied with Dudley BUCK, RHEINBERGER, and GUILMANT. He occupied several posts as organist, and as critic for the Boston *Post,* Boston *Herald,* and other newspapers: he also wrote the program notes for the BOSTON SYMPHONY ORCHESTRA, and lectured at Columbia University and many other institutions. He was one of the most erudite, forceful, and brilliant writers on musical subjects, and a selection of his program notes, *Philip Hale's Boston Symphony Program Notes* has been published in book form with an introduction by Lawrence GILMAN.

Hale, Sarah Josepha Buell (1788-1879), American editor and author who was associate editor of *Godey's Lady's Book* from 1837 to 1877. Her works include *The Genius of Oblivion* (1823); *Northwood: A Tale of New England; Sketches of American Character; Poems for Our Children; Traits of American Life.* She was the author of the poem, *Mary Had a Little Lamb* which appeared in the *Juvenile Miscellany,* in 1830.

Halévy, Jacques (1799-1862), French composer of Jewish parentage who studied composition at the PARIS CONSERVATORY with Luigi CHERUBINI. His first successful opera, *Clari,* was presented in 1829 with Madame MALIBRAN as the prima donna, and his masterpiece, *La Juive,* was produced in 1835: it was followed a few months later by *L'Eclair,* a comic opera. Although he wrote several other operas, none had any real success because Giacomo MEYERBEER became the idol overnight of the opera-loving public with *Les Huguenots,* produced at Paris in 1836.

Halévy, Ludovic (1834-1908), French novelist and dramatist whose first success was *Orpheus in the Underworld,* a musical parody with Jacques OFFENBACH produced in 1861: in collaboration with Henri Meilhac he wrote four extremely popular operettas including *La Belle Helene, The Grand Duchess of Gerolstein, Bluebeard,* and *La Perichole;* also the drama *Frou-frou.* He also wrote a successful novel, *L'Abbé Constantin* (1882) which was immediately translated in English.

Half-tone, an engraved plate originated by Frederick E. Ives in 1878 who later made considerable improvements. A process whereby a photograph could be reproduced directly on a plate to be printed with ordinary type was devised by Alfred Jones, and successfully printed in the New York *Graphic* in 1880. The engraved part is composed of tiny holes which show tone gradations from grey to black after being etched.

Halide Edib (1885-   ), Turkish novelist and lecturer educated at the Constantinople College for Women who became minister of education in Syria for Mustapha Kemal. Her works include the novels *Ruined Temples; Handan; The New Turan; The Shirt of Flame:* she also wrote two autobiographical volumes, and lectured in 1928 and 1931 in the United States.

Hall, James Norman (1887-   ), American author who enlisted in the British Army at the beginning of World War I, and was also a member of the French *Escadrille Lafayette* later incorporated into the American Air Service. His works written in collaboration with Charles Nordhoff who was with him during the war, include *The Lafayette Flying Corps* (1920); *Falcons of France; Mutiny on the Bounty; Men Against the Sea; Pitcairn's Island; The Hurricane; The Dark River; Men Without Country.* His individual books include *Kitchener's Mob* (1916); *High Adventure; The Tale of a Shipwreck; The Friends; Dr. Dogbody's Leg.*

Hall, Pauline (1860-1919), American actress and singer who made her debut as a dancer at Robinson's Opera House, Cincinnati, in 1875: after appearing with Mary ANDERSON in legitimate plays, she achieved remarkable success in musical productions including *Erminie; Evangeline; Puritania; Nanon; The Gipsy Baron; Die Fledermaus (The Bat); Cyrano de Bergerac; Nadjy; The Drum Major.*

Hall, in architecture the name applied either to a mansion or large residential building as well as to the entrance passage way. In medieval English castles it was the one large room used for receiving guests, dining, and sleeping. A minstrel gallery was usually placed at one end, and the quarters for the preparation of food at the other end: many English colleges and old private mansions have this arrangement.

Hall Johnson Choir, an organization formed by the American violinist, composer, and arranger, Hall Johnson (1888-   ), in 1925: it originally numbered eight members later increased to thirty-six. The Choir has appeared in concerts and broadcasts: also in the stage production, *Green*

Pastures, and in numerous films including *Banjo on My Knee; Rainbow on the River; The Lost Horizon; My Old Kentucky Home.*

Hallam, Lewis (c.1740-1808), American actor and theatrical manager who came to the United States as a boy of twelve with his father. He was an excellent comedian, but also essayed the role of Hamlet successfully: in 1785 he opened the John Street Theatre in New York to produce a play called *The Citizen.* An interesting account of Hallam is to be found in George Odell's *Annals of the New York Stage.*

Hallé, Sir Charles (1819-1895), German-English composer, pianist, and conductor whose real name was Karl Halle: he became a British subject by naturalization. He lived for some time in Paris on friendly terms with CHERUBINI, CHOPIN, and LISZT, emigrating to London in 1848, and establishing the HALLE ORCHESTRA at Manchester in 1857, and also founding the London Popular Concerts. He was an eminent piano virtuoso, and composer of piano music.

Hallé Orchestra, The, an organization formed in 1857, originally known as the Hallé Society of Manchester, England, to finance and supervise the concerts given by Sir Charles HALLE. The orchestra toured extensively in the northern part of England, and after Hallé's death in 1895 was conducted by Frederic COWEN, Hans RICHTER, Michael Balling, and Sir Hamilton HARTY. After the latter's resignation in 1933, the orchestra has had many distinguished guest conductors: John BARBIROLLI was appointed permanent conductor in 1943.

Halleck, Fitz-Greene (1790-1867), American poet whose works include *Fanny* (1819); *Alnwick Castle, with Other Poems; Young America.* His best known poem is *Marco Bozzaris.*

Hallelujah Chorus (Handel), the concluding chorus in the second part of *The Messiah,* an oratorio by George Frederick HANDEL composed in 23 days, and first performed in Dublin during 1742. When the oratorio was presented at London in 1743, according to Dr. Beattie "the audience was exceedingly struck and affected by the music in general; but when the chorus struck up 'For the Lord God Omnipotent' in the *Hallelujah,* they were so transported that they all together, with the King (who happened to be present), started up and remained standing till the chorus ended." Thus the custom originated of standing during its performance. There is a Victor recording by the Royal Choral Society and the London Philharmonic Society.

Halliday, John (1880-), American stage and screen actor who served with the British Army in the Boer War, and first appeared on the stage with Nat GOODWIN. Among the many plays in which he has had leading roles are *The Whip; The Ware Case; The Dancer; East of Suez; The Woman of Bronze; The Spider; Tovarich; Rain From Heaven.* He has also appeared in numerous films including *The Dark Angel; Peter Ibbetson; Desire; Arsène Lupin Returns; Intermezzo; Philadelphia Story.*

Hall of Fame, a shrine erected in 1900 on the Campus of New York University through a donation of $250,000 by Mrs. F. J. Shepard. Among the names inscribed on bronze tablets of persons distinguished in the arts are those of Thomas JEFFERSON, Ralph Waldo EMERSON, Henry Wadsworth LONGFELLOW, Washington IRVING, Nathaniel HAWTHORNE, John J. AUDUBON, James Russell LOWELL, John Greenleaf WHITTIER, Harriet Beecher STOWE, Oliver Wendell HOLMES, Edgar Allan POE, James Fenimore COOPER, William Cullen BRYANT, Charlotte CUSHMAN, Mark TWAIN, Augustus St. GAUDENS, Edwin BOOTH, James WHISTLER, Walt WHITMAN. Fifty names were inscribed on the bronze tablets in 1900, and five added each fifth year: the selection is made by over one hundred distinguished American men and women, and every state represented on the committee.

Halo, in art a circle of light around the head of a divinity, saint, or illustrious person; also known as a glory, aureole, or nimbus. In early paintings it was a symbol of power and authority as well as sanctity: a gold halo was used for Christ; a red or white for angels, the Apostles and the Virgin; a purple for saints and sovereigns, and a black for Satan and Judas.

Halper, Albert (1904-), American novelist who was awarded a GUGGENHEIM FELLOWSHIP in 1934: his works include *Union Square* (1933); *On the Shore,* a volume of short stories; *The Foundry; The Chute; Sons of the Fathers.*

Hals, Frans (c.1581-1666), Dutch painter who studied with Karel van MANDER: his notable works include *Banquet of the Officers of the Archers of St. George; Married Couple; The Fool; The Toper; Dutch Nobleman and Wife; Singing Boys; Laughing Girl; Boy Playing the Flute; Children Laughing; The Merry Drinker; Laughing Cavalier.* His son, **Frans Hals, the Younger** (c.1617-c.1669), was a pupil of his father and copied many of the latter's works. His paintings include *Two Children Singing; Laughing Boys; Piper and Violin Player; Hille Bobbe as a Fish-wife.* Another son, **Dirk Hals** (c.1590-1656), was an excellent painter of festivals and ball-room scenes. His best works include *Ladies and Gentlemen at Dinner* and *Lady Playing a Harpsichord to a Young Girl and Her Lover.*

Hambidge, Jay (1867-1924), American artist and writer born in Canada. He made an exhaustive study of Greek vases in respect to their measurements, and evolved a series of mathematical principles the theory of which is expounded in his treatises, *Dynamic Symmetry* and *The Elements of Dynamic Symmetry,* used as text books in many art schools.

Hambourg, Mark (1879-), Russian pianist and composer who studied with his father, Michael Hambourg (1856-1916), founder of the Hambourg Conservatory, Toronto, Canada; also with Theodor LESCHETIZKY. He appeared first as a child prodigy, making his mature debut in 1895, and touring the world with great success. His brothers, **Jan Hambourg** (1882-), a fine violinist, and **Boris Hambourg** (1885-), an outstanding violoncellist, toured the United States with him in chamber music concerts.

Hamerton, Philip Gilbert (1834-1894), English critic and writer on art: his notable works include *Contemporary French Painters* (1867); *Etching and Etchers* (1866), a treatise which is still highly regarded; *The Graphic Arts.*

Hamilton, Cicely (1872-), English actress and dramatist who appeared in *The Gamekeeper* in 1898, and played for more than a quarter of a century at London in numerous plays including *The Twelve-Pound Look; The Christian's Cross; The Great Gamble; Esther Waters.* Her original plays include *The Sixth Commandment* (1906); *Diana of Dobson's; The Sergeant of Hussars; After Twenty Years; The Human Factor; The Old Adam; The Beggar Prince.*

Hamilton, Clayton (1881-), American dramatic critic and playwright educated at the Polytechnic Institute, Brooklyn, N. Y., and at Columbia University. His plays include *The Love that Blinds,* written in collaboration with Grace Isabel Colbron, and produced in 1906 by Henry MILLER; *The Stranger at the Inn; The Big Idea* with Albert E. THOMAS. His dramatic treatises include *The Theory of the Theatre; Studies in Stagecraft; Problems of the Playwright; So You're Writing a Play.*

Hamilton, Cosmo (c.1872-1942), English author and dramatist, son of Henry James Gibbs and brother of Sir Philip Hamilton GIBBS: he assumed his mother's name in 1898. His plays include *The Catch of the Season,* with Seymour Hicks; *The Wisdom of Folly; Arsène Lupin; Caste; Pickwick,* with Frank C. Reilly; *The Aunt of England,* with Anthony Gibbs. His more than fifty novels include *Adam's Clay; Keepers of the House; The Miracle of Love; His Friends and His Wife; The Laughing Mask.* His autobiography, *Unwritten History,* was published in 1924.

Hamilton, Gail, see **Dodge, Mary Abigail.**

Hamlet, a semi-historical Danish prince whose story originated in Scandinavian saga: it was later published in English as *The History of Hamlet,* and a play of the same name produced at London in 1594, about six years before the performance of Shakespeare's *Hamlet* in 1600. Operas by Domenico SCARLATTI (1715) and Ambroise THOMAS (1860) were based on Shakespeare's drama: Peter TSCHAIKOWSKY wrote an overture and complete incidental music, dedicating the overture to Edvard GRIEG. In December, 1942, Brooks ATKINSON, dramatic critic of the New York *Times,* reviewed the Chinese version of *Hamlet* at the Kuo T'ai Theatre in Chungking.

Hamlin, George (1868-1923), American dramatic and concert tenor chiefly self-taught: he made his debut in oratorio with the St. Louis Choral Society in MENDELSSOHN'S *Hymn of Praise,* and his operatic debut in 1911 with the Philadelphia-Chicago Opera Company in Victor Herbert's *Natoma.* He achieved his greatest success in the interpretation of ART SONGS.

Hammer, the name given to the device in a PIANO which strikes the strings, thereby producing sounds. In appearance it resembles an ordinary hammer, and strikes the strings through an ingenious leverage mechanism which permits of variations in DYNAMICS.

Hammerstein, Arthur (1876-), American theatrical producer; son of Oscar HAMMERSTEIN: among the successful plays and musical productions under his direction were *The Firefly* (1912); *Naughty Marietta; High Jinks; Katinka; You're in Love; Rose Marie; Song of the Flame; Sweet Adeline; The Man Who Reclaimed His Head.*

Hammerstein, Oscar (1847-1919), German-American opera impresario who came to the United States in 1863, and after engaging in various occupations, built the Manhattan Opera House (his second theatre with this name) in 1906, forming the Hammerstein Opera Company, an organization composed of MELBA, NORDICA, TETRAZZINI, BONCI, RENAUD, DALMORES, GARDEN, CALVE, McCORMACK and many other fine artists including Cleofante CAMPANINI as artistic director and conductor. After operating successfully for four years, and opening the Philadelphia Opera House in 1908, he proved a formidable rival of the METROPOLITAN OPERA COMPANY, and received the sum of $2,000,000 from the latter for his interests with the understanding that he would refrain from producing grand opera for a period of ten years in New York. He then went to London where he built and opened the London Opera House, but the venture was not successful, and the house became a motion picture theatre. Returning to New York he built the American Opera House on Lexington Avenue, planning to open it in 1914, but the Metropolitan Opera Company were successful in securing a permanent injunction, and the house became a motion picture theatre.

Hammerstein, Oscar 2d (1895-), American librettist and lyric writer: among the musical plays and films in which he has collaborated with Otto HARBACH and others are *Rose Marie; Sunny; Song of the Flame; The Desert Song; Show Boat; The New Moon; Sweet Adeline; Music in the Air; Viennese Nights; The Night is Young; High, Wide and Handsome; The Great Waltz; The Story of Irene and Vernon Castle; New Moon; Oklahoma.*

Hammerstein Opera Company, see **Hammerstein, Oscar.**

Hammett, Dashiell (1894-), American writer of detective fiction who was for several years in the employ of the Pinkerton Detective Agency, and served in the Motor Ambulance Corps of the American Army during World War I. His novels include *Red Harvest* (1929); *The Maltese Falcon; The Glass Key; The Thin Man.* The three last-named have been highly successful on the screen as enacted by William POWELL, Myrna Loy, Sidney Greenstreet, and Humphrey BOGART.

Hammond, John Hays, Jr. (1888-), American inventor educated at the Sheffield Scientific School at Yale University: he has devised several improvements in the mechanism of the pipe organ and the piano, and is also the inventor of a combination radio, phonograph, and piano.

Hammond, Laurens (1895-), American inventor educated at Cornell University: his inventions include the *Hammond Organ,* an instrument which reproduces through electrical impulses the sound of the pipe organ, and the *Novachord,* an electrical device that can imitate the tone of almost all musical instruments.

Hammond, Percy (1873-1936), American dramatic critic whose first important post was that of dramatic critic for the Chicago *Tribune* in 1908: he remained until 1921 when he became dramatic critic for the New York *Herald Tribune,* occupying this position until his death. His works include *But—Is It Art?* (1927) and *This Atom in the Audience,* published posthumously. He exercised a strong influence for the good on American drama.

Hampden, Walter (1879-), American actor whose real name is Walter Hampden Dougherty. He was educated at the Brooklyn Polytechnic Institute, Harvard University, and in Paris, making his stage debut with Sir Francis BENSON's Company at Brighton, England, in 1901. He remained in London until 1907 playing Shakespearean roles, and returned to the United States during the same year to make his debut as leading man for Alla NAZIMOVA in *The Comtesse Coquette.* Among the plays in which he has distinguished himself are *Cyrano de Bergerac; The Servant in the House; Salome; The Yellow Jacket;* also the plays of IBSEN and SHAKESPEARE. He appeared on the screen in *The Hunchback of Notre Dame* and *All This and Heaven Too.*

Hampton Court (England), a palace the erection of which was begun by Cardinal WOLSEY on the Thames River near London in 1515, and surrendered to Henry VIII in 1526: the latter added the great hall and the Chapel, and William III commissioned Sir Christopher WREN to build the great façade and a gallery for the cartoons of RAPHAEL which have been removed to the SOUTH KENSINGTON MUSEUM, London. CHARLES I was imprisoned there before his execution, and in the latter part of the 19th century it was occupied by persons of noble birth in straitened circumstances.

Hamsun, Knut (1859-), Norwegian novelist, poet, and dramatist who spent several years of his life in the United States: his works translated into English include *Shallow Soil* (1914); *Growth of the Soil,* which won the Nobel literature prize; *Hunger; Dreamers; Mysteries; Vagabonds; The Road Leads On; Look Back on Happiness.* He also wrote a trilogy of plays, and *The Wild Chorus,* a volume of poems.

Handel, George Frederick (1685-1759), German composer who was educated at the University in Halle, and studied music with Friedrich Zachau, and probably with Attilio Ariosti. He spent some time in Italy composing several operas, and also in Hamburg before going to London where he produced many operas at COVENT GARDEN. After experiencing financial disaster, he turned to writing oratorios which proved to be the supreme achievements of his life. His works include nearly fifty operas in the Italian style; thirty-two oratorios of which the most famous are *The Messiah, Esther, Deborah, Saul, Israel in Egypt, Occasional Oratorio, Samson, Judas Maccabeus, Joshua,* and *Jeptha:* also miscellaneous compositions such as *Water Music; Forest Music; Fire Music;* chamber music including several concerti grossi; 16 suites of pieces for the harpsichord of which *The* HARMONIOUS BLACKSMITH is the most familiar.

Handel and Haydn Society, The, an organization founded at Boston, Mass., in 1815, and said to be the second oldest musical society in the United States. In 1818 the society gave its first performance of HANDEL's *The Messiah:* festivals have been held regularly, and in 1915 the one hundredth anniversary was celebrated. Among the many distinguished conductors were Carl ZERRAHN (1854-1895), and Emil MOLLENHAUER (1899-1927).

Handy, William (1873-), American Negro composer, educated at the Teachers' College in Huntsville, Ala., who has done much pioneer work for Negro music, especially the variety known as the *Blues.* His compositions include *The Memphis Blues; St. Louis Blues; Yellow Dog Blues; Beale Street Blues:* he has also written *Blues, an Anthology; Negro Authors and Composers of the United States; Book of Negro Spirituals.*

Han Kan, Chinese painter of T'ang dynasty (A.D. 618-907): he was especially skilled in the art of depicting horses, and his works, of which there is an example in the British Museum, served as models for succeeding generations of both Chinese and Japanese painters.

Hankin, St. John E. C. (1869-1909), English dramatist regarded as one of the most accomplished of his period: his plays are chiefly society comedies, and their clever cynicism makes up in some cases for the somewhat unrealistic atmosphere. Among them the most notable are *The Two Mr. Wetherbys; The Return of the Prodigal; The Cassilis Engagement; The Last of the De Mullins.*

Hänsel and Gretel, a fairy opera in three acts: libretto by Adelhaid Wetter; music by Engelbert HUMPERDINCK; first produced at Weimar in 1893; at New York in English at Daly's Theatre in 1895, and in 1905 at the Metropolitan Opera House. The story is the ancient tale of the babes lost in the woods who outwit the wicked witch, who turns little children into gingerbread, by pushing her into her own oven. The *Prelude* to the opera is a favorite concert piece; it is a potpourri of all the lovely German folk tunes which are the framework of the score. There is a Victor recording of the *Prelude* by the British Broadcasting Company Orchestra directed by Sir Adrian Boult, and a Columbia recording of the *Suite* made up from the score played by the Columbia Broadcasting Symphony Orchestra under Howard Barlow.

Hanslick, Eduard (1825-1904), Bohemian music critic and author who studied with Johann Tomaschek at Prague, and occupied important posts as critic of the *Wiener Zeitung,* the *Wiener Presse* and the *Neue Freie Presse*. His principal work, *The Beautiful in Music* (1854), enunciates the theory that pure music expresses only that which is inherent to it as music, and deprecates all sentimentality in its appreciation. He was violently opposed to Richard WAGNER's music drama theories, but was an ardent champion of Johannes BRAHMS.

Hanson, Gladys (1887-   ), American actress who was first a school teacher, and made her New York debut in 1907 in Rex Beach's *The Spoilers:* among the plays in which she has appeared are *Our American Cousin; Don Quixote* with E. H. SOTHERN; *Richelieu; Hamlet; If I Were King; Raffles* with Kyrle BELLEW; *The Governor's Lady; The Trojan Women; The Ware Case; The Great Divide; Mecca; The Blue Bird; Trelawney of the Wells; Fresh Fields.* She made her debut at London in 1938 in *Mary Goes to See.*

Hanson, Howard (1896-   ), American composer who studied with Percy GOETSCHIUS, and became director of the EASTMAN School of Music, Rochester, N. Y., in 1924. His compositions include an opera, *Merry Mount*, produced at the Metropolitan Opera House in 1934; four symphonies, several symphonic poems; chamber works; choruses; piano pieces and songs.

Hanswurst, in German drama the name given to the traditional clown in both comedies and serious plays: the reform movement started by Johann GOTTSCHED and Caroline NEUBER in the 18th century succeeded in relegating the character to its proper place in low comedy.

Hapgood, Isabel Florence (1850-1928), American essayist and translator who paid particular attention to the works of Russian authors such as TOLSTOY, TURGENEV, GOGOL, and GORKY. She also translated the works of French, Italian, and Spanish authors, and wrote *The Epic Songs of Russia, Russian Rambles,* and *Survey of Russian Literature.*

Hapgood, Norman (1868-1937), American editor and dramatic critic educated at Harvard University, and dramatic critic of the New York *Commercial Advertiser* and the *Bookman*. He was also editor of *Collier's Weekly* and *Harper's Weekly*: his works include *The Stage in America; Why Janet Should Read Shakespeare:* also biographies of Daniel Webster, Abraham Lincoln, and George Washington.

Harangozó, Gyula (1908-   ), Hungarian dancer, balletmaster and choreographer who studied with Jan Cieplinsky, and made his debut in 1928 at the Opera House, Budapest, in De Falla's *The Three Cornered Hat.* His first original ballet was the *Inn Scene* with music by Jenö HUBAY: other notable works include *Sybil; Perhaps Tomorrow!; Little Johnny in Top-Boots.* In 1937 he was appointed balletmaster at the Budapest Opera House.

Harbach, Otto (1873-   ), American light opera and musical comedy librettist: his works include lyrics for *The Three Twins* (1907); and librettos for *Madame Sherry; The Firefly; High Jinks;*

Katinka; Kid Boots; No! No! Nanette; Rose Marie; Song of the Flame; The Desert Song; The Cat and the Fiddle; Roberta; he has also prepared several of the above-mentioned works for the films.

d'Hardelot, Guy, pen name of **Mrs. W. I. Rhodes,** née **Helen Guy** (1858-1936), French composer who studied at the Paris Conservatory. Charles GOUNOD and Victor MAUREL, a famous French dramatic baritone, became interested in her songs. In 1896 she toured the United States with Emma CALVE. Her first great song success was *Sans toi* (Without You): many more followed which were sung by Calvé, Maurel, MELBA, PLANCON, and other great singers.

Hardenbergh, Henry J. (1847-1918), American architect whose designs include the Manhattan Hotel, the Plaza Hotel, and the old Waldorf-Astoria Hotel in New York, and the Copley Plaza Hotel in Boston. He was one of the founders of the American Fine Arts Society, New York, and the building designed by him for its use is adjudged his masterpiece.

Harding, Ann (1902-   ), American stage and screen actress who made her first successful appearance in 1921 at New York in *Like a King:* among the plays in which she has appeared are *Tarnish; Captain Brassbound's Conversion; The Green Hat; The Trial of Mary Dugan; Strange Interlude; Candida.* She has also appeared in many films including *Paris Bound; East Lynne; Holiday; Westward Passage; The Conqueror; When Ladies Meet; Gallant Lady; Peter Ibbetson; Biography of a Bachelor Girl; The Lady Consents; Mission to Moscow.*

Harding, Bertita (1907-   ), American biographer born in Germany who was educated in France, at the University of Wisconsin, and in music at the National Conservatory of Mexico, becoming an American citizen in 1927. Her works include *Phantom Crown* (1934); *Royal Purple; Golden Fleece; Farewell 'Toinette; Imperial Twilight; Hungarian Rhapsody; Amazon Throne.*

Harding, Chester (1792-1866), American painter who served as a drummer boy in the War of 1812, and became an itinerant portrait painter: he was chiefly self-taught although he studied for a short time at the PENNSYLVANIA ACADEMY OF FINE ARTS. He was successful as a portrait painter in London for three years, but returned to the United States, and finally settled down at Springfield, Mass., where he painted excellent portraits of Daniel Webster, John C. Calhoun, Chief Justice Marshall; Washington ALLSTON, and Henry Clay.

Harding, Lyn (1867-   ), English actor whose real name is David Llewellyn Harding: he made his debut on the stage at Bristol, England, in 1890, and made his first success in 1902 at London in *The Prophecy.* He has appeared in more than a hundred plays, and is considered one of the most distinguished actors on the English and American stage. He has also played important roles in numerous English and American films including *The Speckled Band; The Constant Nymph; The Lash; The Triumph of Sherlock*

Holmes; Escape Me Never; Pearls of the Crown; The Mutiny of the Elsinore; Goodbye Mr. Chips; Missing People; The Prime Minister.

Hardwicke, Sir Cedric (1893-   ), English actor trained at the Royal Academy of Dramatic Art who made his debut in 1912 at London in *The Monk and the Woman.* He appeared with the Benson Company, with the Old Vic Company, and with the Birmingham Repertory Company. Among the plays in which he achieved success are *The Farmer's Wife; The Apple Cart; The Barretts of Wimpole Street; The Late Christopher Bean; The Amazing Dr. Clitterhouse; Shadow and Substance.* He has also appeared in numerous English and American films including *Dreyfus; The Rome Express; Nell Gwyn; Les Miserables; Becky Sharp; Peg of Old Drury; Laburnum Grove; King Solomon's Mines; A Christmas Carol; Nine Days a Queen; The Hunchback of Notre Dame; The Invisible Man Returns; Tom Brown's Schooldays; The Howards of Virginia; The Moon is Down; Forever and a Day.*

Hardy, Alexandre (1570-1631), French dramatist who wrote more than five hundred plays of a character that influenced public taste, and aided in the decline of the 16th century medieval farces and spectacles, thus permitting classic drama to develop along normal lines. Only forty of his plays such as *Marianne, Coriolanus, The Death of Achilles,* and *Frédégonde* are extant. Later dramatists are deeply indebted to him, especially in his development of stagecraft.

Hardy, Arthur Sherburne (1847-1930), American diplomat, poet, and novelist educated at the Boston Latin School, Phillips Andover Academy, and in Switzerland, later becoming minister to Persia, Greece, Rumania, Serbia, Switzerland, and Spain. His works include *Francesca da Rimini* (1878), a poem; *But Yet a Woman; The Wind of Destiny; Passé Rose; Helen.*

Hardy, Thomas (1840-1928), English novelist and dramatist: his works include an epic drama, *The Dynasts* (1904-1908) which is a combination of a poem, a drama, and a history of the Napoleonic Wars which required four years to complete; also the novels *Desperate Remedies* (1871); *Under the Greenwood Tree; Far from the Madding Crowd; The Return of the Native; The Woodlanders; Tess of the D'Urbervilles,* successfully dramatized for Minnie Maddern Fiske; *Jude the Obscure;* several volumes of poetry and interesting short stories.

Hare, Sir John (1844-1921), English actor and manager who first appeared at London in 1865, and acted with Sir Squire Bancroft's company before becoming manager of the Court Theatre in 1875, and joint manager with Mr. and Mrs. Kendal of the St. James Theatre from 1879 to 1888, establishing a reputation as an interpreter of character parts. In 1889 he assumed the management of the Garrick Theatre where he made a personal success in *A Pair of Spectacles* and in 1897 took over the Globe Theatre where he again triumphed in Pinero's *The Gay Lord Quex,* presenting it also at New York in 1900.

Häring, George Wilhelm Heinrich (1798-1871), German novelist who studied at the Universities of Berlin and Breslau, but abandoned the profession of law for a career in literature. He wrote under the pen name "Wilibald Alexis," and published several historical novels including *Walladmor* (1823); *Schloss Avalon; Das Haus Dusterweg; Zwölf Nachte; Cabanis; Roland von Berlin; Isegrimm; Dorothe.*

Harlan, Otis (1865-   ), American actor who made his debut in 1887 at New York in *A Hole in the Ground:* among the plays in which he appeared successfully are *A Brass Monkey; A Texas Steer; Tabasco; A Black Sheep; The Rivals; A Stranger in New York; Lost, Stolen or Strayed; The Parisian Model; A Broken Idol; Ninety in the Shade.* He also appeared in many silent films.

Harland, Henry (1861-1905), American novelist who went to London in 1889 where he was connected with the Bodley Head Press, and was one of the founders of the *Yellow Book* in 1894. His novels include *As It Was Written* (1885); *The Yoke of Thorah; A Latin Quarter Courtship; The Cardinal's Snuff Box,* one of the best sellers of its period; *My Friend Prospero.* His earlier books were written under the pen name "Sidney Luska."

Harlequin, a stock character in the pantomime presentations such as the Commedia dell' Arte of the 16th and 17th centuries although some authorities assert that there was a French character (Harlekin) as early as 1100. He appeared in various guises such as a soldier, fickle lover, etc., played opposite Columbine, and was a curious mixture of cunning and stupidity.

Harling, William Franke (1887-   ), American composer born in England, and brought to the United States as an infant. He studied at the Royal Academy of Music, London, and at Brussels where he was organist at the Church of the Resurrection in 1907. His compositions include a one-act opera, *A Light from St. Agnes,* produced by the Chicago Civic Opera Company in 1925; a lyric tragedy, *Deep River;* several orchestral works and more than one hundred songs. He has also written many scores for the films.

Harlow, Jean (1911-1937), American screen actress, real name Harlean Carpentier, educated at the Barstow School, Kansas City, Mo., and at Ferry Hall, Lake Forest, Ill. Among the numerous films in which she appeared were the famous Hal Roach comedies; *Hell's Angels* in which she replaced Greta Nissen; *Public Enemy; Platinum Blonde; Red-Headed Woman; Red Dust; Bombshell; Dinner at Eight; Reckless; China Seas; Riff Raff; Libeled Lady; Personal Property.*

Harmonica, (a) the name given by Benjamin Franklin to his instrument developed from the musical glasses: tumblers or goblets of graded pitch were placed on a revolving spindle operated by a treadle, moistened by passing through a trough of water, and played by rubbing the fingers lightly over the edges. (b) A free-reed musical instrument, also called *mouth harmonica,* in which the reeds are set in a metal or wooden case, and sounds produced by inhaling and exhaling through perforations. It is extremely popular today, and bands are formed with instruments ranging from 3 to 24 inches in length.

Harmonics, tones obtained on the violin, viola, violoncello, harp, etc., by lightly touching the strings at certain distances, known as nodal points, thereby causing only a portion of the strings to vibrate. Harmonics are distinguished by a soft, ethereal, fluty timbre entirely different from the regular tone produced by pressing the fingers firmly on the strings at the same points.

Harmonious Blacksmith (Handel), an air and variations composed for the harpsichord by George Frederick HANDEL while music master to the Princess Anne, daughter of the Prince of Wales. It comprises part of his *Harpsichord Suite No. 5,* and there are recordings available by Wanda LANDOWSKA for harpsichord, and piano recordings by Walter GIESEKING, Sergei RACHMANINOFF, and Alfred CORTOT.

Harmonium, a musical instrument consisting of a keyboard from which tones are produced by free metal reeds set in motion by a bellows operated by the player's feet. It was invented in 1842 by Albert Debain, and is also known as *American organ* or *cabinet organ.*

Harmony, the simultaneous sounding of two or more tones: the term is applied to either a consonant or dissonant chord. A musical composition is formed of a melody to which harmony is added: the study of harmony is one of the most profoundly interesting branches of the musical art.

Harp, a musical instrument of great antiquity: its predecessor in the Bible was the PSALTERY, and it was used by the Egyptians, Greeks and Romans, the only difference in the form of the instrument being that it lacked the post parallel with the strings which was added by the Irish and Saxon harp makers in the 9th century A.D. The modern harp, as perfected by Sébastien ERARD, has seven pedals which enable the performer to play in all keys. The classic composers such as J. S. BACH, HANDEL, and BEETHOVEN did not use the harp in orchestral music, but BERLIOZ, WAGNER, DEBUSSY, and many others have greatly enriched their scores by employing it.

Harpignies, Henri (1819-1916), French painter who studied with Jean Achard, and sketched in Italy and France. Among his notable works are *Edge of a Forest on the Allier River; Valley of Egeria; Evening on the Banks of the Loire; Le Pont Neuf; The Ravens; Evening; The Loire; View of Capri;* he also executed some murals at the Paris Opera.

Harpsichord, a 16th century keyboard stringed instrument in which the strings are plucked by quills instead of being hit by hammers. It differs from the clavichord in that the latter has flat-topped brass tangents, sometimes covered with leather, which are pressed against the strings instead of plucking them. Hans RUCKERS (1579-c.1640) a Belgian, made the finest harpsichords which, having no loud and soft pedals like the modern piano, were equipped with various devices

to increase or diminish its tone. Among the great composers who wrote harpsichord music were Domenico SCARLATTI; François COUPERIN, and Johann Sebastian BACH who composed the *Italian Concerto* especially for it.

Harraden, Beatrice (1864-1936), English novelist educated at Cheltenham, Queen's and Bedford Colleges, and at Dresden. Her works include *Things Will Take a Turn* (1891); *Ships That Pass in the Night* (1893) which had a sale in excess of a million copies; *Hilda Strafford; Out of the Wreck I Rise; Thirteen All Told; Youth Calling; Search Will Find It Out.* She visited the United States in 1894.

Harrigan, Edward (1845-1911), American comedian and dramatist, familiarly known as "Ned," who made his debut in theatres in San Francisco and Chicago. He allied himself with Anthony Cannon, well-known for his female impersonations, to whom he gave the stage name "Tony Hart," and formed the partnership of **Harrigan and Hart.** After playing in vaudeville, he wrote a number of comedies with Dave Braham as musical collaborator, such as *The Blue and the Grey* (1875); *Pete; Reilly and the Four Hundred;* the "Mulligan Guards" series; *Under Cover,* and *Old Lavender.* In 1884 the Theatre Comique erected by the partners burned, and the partnership was dissolved.

Harrigan, William (1893-), American stage and screen actor; son of Edward ("Ned") HARRIGAN. He made his first appearance as a child of five in his father's play, *Reilly and the Four Hundred:* in 1907 he made his debut as Jimmie Larkin in *Artie,* and later appeared in many plays including *The Regeneration; His Wife's Family; The Woman; Bought and Paid For; The Argyle Case; The Acquittal; Polly Preferred; The Dove; Strictly Dishonorable; Criminal at Large; Paths of Glory.* He rose to the rank of captain in World War I, and has appeared in numerous films.

Harris, Sir Augustus (1852-1896), English theatre and opera impresario who made his debut in 1873 as an actor in *Macbeth,* and later became stage manager for Colonel MAPLESON's Opera Company. From 1879 he presented many pantomimes and spectacular melodramas such as *The World* at the Drury Lane Theatre: he also organized a company in 1888 for the presentation of French, German, and English opera at Covent Garden and other theatres: among the great singers he engaged were MELBA, NORDICA, HAUK, MAUREL, Édouard DE RESZKE, and Jean DE RESZKE.

Harris, Corra May (1869-1935), American novelist: her works include *A Circuit Rider's Wife* (1910); *My Book and Heart; The Happy Pilgrimage.*

Harris, Frank (1856-1931), Irish-American novelist, editor, dramatist, and biographer who came to the United States as a youth, and studied at the University of Kansas. After returning to Europe for study in various universities, he edited the *Evening News,* the *Saturday Review,* and *Vanity Fair* in London. His works include *Elder Conklin* (1894); *The Bomb; The Man Shake-*

speare; *The Women of Shakespeare; Oscar Wilde;
Life of Bernard Shaw;* also the plays *Mr. and
Mrs. Daventry* and *The Bucket Shop.* His auto-
biography, *My Life and Loves,* was banned in
England.

Harris, Jed (1899-   ), American producer who
has either directed or produced several important
plays including *Broadway* (1926); *Coquette; The
Royal Family; The Front Page; Serena Blandish;
Uncle Vanya; The Inspector General; Wonder
Boy; The Lake; A Doll's House; Our Town;
Dark Eyes.*

Harris, Joel Chandler (1848-1908), American
editor and author whose amusing stories of "Uncle
Remus" were first published in the Atlanta *Con-
stitution* with which he was connected from 1876.
His works include *Uncle Remus: His Songs and
Sayings* (1880); *Nights with Uncle Remus; Uncle
Remus and His Friends; The Chronicles of Aunt
Minervy Ann; The Tar Baby and Other Rhymes
of Uncle Remus; Uncle Remus and Brer Rabbit;
Balaam and His Master.* His former home in
Atlanta, Ga., is now an "Uncle Remus" memorial.

Harris, Robert (1849-1919), Canadian painter
born in Wales who came to Charlottetown, Prince
Edward Island in 1856. After study in Europe, he
directed an art school in Montreal, and participated in the founding of the Royal Canadian
Academy. His works include *Fathers of the Confederation* at the Parliament Building, Ottawa;
The School Trustees; A Man of Small Importance.

Harris, Roy (1898-   ), American composer educated at the University of California, and a pupil
of Arthur Farwell, Arthur Bliss, Modest Altschuler, and with Nadia Boulanger on a Guggenheim Fellowship. His compositions include
several symphonies and other orchestral works;
choral works; chamber music. He has taught
composition at the Westminster Choir School,
Princeton, N. J., and at the Juilliard Summer
School, and many of his works have been recorded.

Harris, Sam H. (1872-1943), American manager
and producer whose first success was a melodrama,
The Fatal Wedding: in association with George
M. Cohan he produced *Little Johnny Jones;
Forty-Five Minutes from Broadway; Get-Rich-
Quick Wallingford.* As an individual he produced
*Little Old New York; The Nervous Wreck;
Rain; Captain Applejack; Icebound; The Cradle
Snatchers; The Jazz-Singer; Chicago; The Spider;
Face the Music; Dinner at Eight; Jubilee,* with
Max Gordon; *Stage Door; Of Mice and Men; I'd
Rather Be Right; The American Way,* with Max
Gordon.

Harrison, Mrs. Burton (1843-1920), American
novelist also known as Constance Cary Harrison:
her works include several novels of social life in
the latter part of the 19th century including *Bar
Harbor Days* (1887); *The Anglomaniacs; A
Bachelor Maid; Sweet Bells Out of Tune; A Son
of the Old Dominion.*

Harrison, Guy Fraser (1894-   ), English organist and orchestral conductor who was educated at

Oxford and trained at the Royal College of Music,
London. After holding several important posts he
became conductor of the Eastman Theatre Orchestra, the Rochester Civic Orchestra, associate
conductor of the Rochester Philharmonic Orchestra, and guest conductor of several major American orchestras, also teaching at the Eastman
School of Music.

Harrison, Henry Sydnor (1880-1930), American
novelist who was educated at Columbia University: his works include *Queed* (1911); *V. V.'s
Eyes; Angela's Business; When I Come Back;
Saint Teresa; Andrew Bride of Paris.*

Harrison, Lovell Birge (1854-1929), American
painter, brother of Thomas Alexander Harrison,
who studied at the Pennsylvania Academy of
Fine Arts, and with Cabanel and Carolus-
Duran in Paris. His works include *November;
Fifth Avenue at Twilight; Glimpse of the St.
Lawrence; Autumn Sunset:* he also wrote a trea-
tise, *Landscape Painting.*

Harrison, Rex, contemporary English stage and
screen actor who served in the British Royal Air
Force during World War II: among the films in
which he has appeared are *Storm in a Teacup;
School for Husbands; The Citadel; Night Train;
Major Barbara; Continental Express; Ten Days
in Paris; Sidewalks of London:* he also appeared
in the London stage production of *No Time For
Comedy* in 1941.

Harrison, Thomas Alexander (1853-1930),
American painter who studied at the Pennsylvania
Academy of Fine Arts, and at the Ecole des
Beaux-Arts in Paris. In 1882 he exhibited a
painting, *Château in Spain,* at the Paris Salon
which was received with favor, and in 1885 a large
canvas, *In Arcady,* a study of several nude women
which had considerable influence on younger
painters because of its flesh tones. His reputation
is based on his fine marine pictures.

Harrold, Orville (1878-   ), American dramatic
tenor who sang first in a church choir, and was
advised by Schumann-Heink to seek a career as
a singer. After study with Oscar Saenger he made
his debut in 1909 at the Manhattan Opera House,
New York, in *Pagliacci:* in 1911 he sang with
Emma Trentini in Herbert's *Naughty Marietta,*
and later with the Ravinia Opera and the Century
Opera Company. In 1919 he made his debut at
the Metropolitan Opera House with Enrico
Caruso in *La Juive,* and in 1921 created the role of
Paul in Korngold's *Die Tote Stadt* at the debut of
Maria Jeritza.

Hart, Charles (? -1683), English actor who was
a grandson of Shakespeare's sister Joan, and was
first known as a player of women's parts at the
Blackfriars Theatre. He appeared in plays by
Dryden, Jonson, Beaumont, and Fletcher; was
highly praised by Samuel Pepys, and regarded as
a superlative interpreter of the roles of Brutus and
Othello.

Hart, Mrs. Francis (1852-1931), English novelist educated at the Slade School, and by travel in
Europe, the Orient and America. Her works in-

clude *Colonel Enderby's Wife* (1885); *The Wages of Sin; Sir Richard Calmady; The Golden Galleon; The Survivors; The Dogs of Want.* She was the youngest daughter of Charles KINGSLEY.

Hart, George (1839-1891), English violinist who studied at the Royal Academy of Music, and became the head of Hart & Sons, a firm of violin makers after his father, John Thomas Hart, died in 1874. He wrote two interesting works on the violin entitled *The Violin: Its Famous Makers and Their Imitators* and *The Violin and Its Music.*

Hart, George Overbury (1868-1933), American painter, familiarly known as "Pop" Overbury. He studied for a time at the CHICAGO ART INSTITUTE, and made trips to Italy, Egypt, Denmark, and Iceland where he sketched people in all walks of life. Later he studied at the Académie Julien in Paris, but was not in sympathy with academic ideas, and resumed his itinerant painting and sketching. After he returned to the United States he painted signs and stage scenery for a living, and finally devoted himself exclusively to etching, becoming president of the Brooklyn Society of Etchers. Overbury has been called "a painter of the people for the people."

Hart, James MacDougal (1828-1901), American painter born in Scotland who studied with Johann SCHIRMER in Düsseldorf: his notable works include *Drove of Cattle at a Ford; Scene in a Pasture; Autumn Woods; Adirondacks.* He was an associate of the National Academy of Design, and his daughters were both well-known painters.

Hart, Joel Tanner (1810-1877), American sculptor who was self-taught after beginning as a stonecutter: he became famous as a creator of groups, statues, and busts including *Woman Triumphant,* and *Henry Clay.* There appears to be a difference of opinion as to whether Hart's works were merely in vogue during his life, or are permanent contributions to the art.

Hart, Lorenz, see **Rodgers, Richard.**

Hart, Moss (1904-), American librettist and dramatist: he was first in the employ of Augustus PITOU as theatre manager and director. His works include *The Hold-Up Man* (1925); *Once in a Lifetime,* with George S. Kaufman; *Face the Music,* with Irving Berlin; *As Thousands Cheer; The Great Waltz; Jubilee; You Can't Take It With You; I'd Rather Be Right; The American Way; The Man Who Came To Dinner; George Washington Slept Here; Lady in the Dark.*

Hart, Tony, see **Harrigan, Edward.**

Hart, William (1823-1894), American painter born in Scotland who was brought to the United States as a child. He was apprenticed to a carriage painter, and first made decorative landscape panels for vehicles purchased by wealthy people. After studying in Scotland with the financial aid of friends, he opened a studio at New York in 1883, and made a specialty of landscapes with cattle. He was one of the group of painters who formed the HUDSON RIVER SCHOOL.

Hart, William S. (1870-), American stage and screen actor who first appeared at the People's Theatre, New York, in 1889, later playing with Lawrence BARRETT, Madame Rhea, Madame MODJESKA, and Julia ARTHUR. He created the part of Messala in *Ben Hur,* and the title role in *The Virginian.* In 1914 he entered the silent films: among the pictures in which he has appeared are *Wolves of the Trail; Wagon Tracks; Square Deal Sanderson; Sand; Blue Blazes Rawden; The Toll Gate.* In 1936 he wrote the story of *O'Malley of the Mounted,* and in 1939 his last film *Tumbleweeds,* made in 1928, was redistributed.

Harte, Francis Bret (1839-1902), American short story writer and poet: he went to the Pacific coast as a youth, and his stories are largely the result of his experiences in gold mining, teaching school, and working on newspapers. In 1867 he published a volume of verse, *The Lost Galleon and Other Tales:* this was followed by *The Luck of Roaring Camp and Other Sketches; Tales of the Argonauts; Tales of Trail and Town,* and many other volumes of stories and verse such as *The Outcasts of Poker Flat,* and *The Heathen Chinee.* His complete works in ten volumes were published in 1929.

Hartley, Jonathan Scott (1845-1912), American sculptor who became famous for his portrait busts and groups: they include *John Gilbert; John Drew; George Inness;* the *Daguerre Monument* in Washington, D. C.; *Lief Ericsson,* and *Alfred the Great* in the Appellate Court House, New York.

Hartmann, Arthur Martinus (1881-), Hungarian violinist who came to the United States as a child, and studied with Charles Martin LOEFFLER. He appeared in 1887 as a child prodigy, and later toured the United States, Canada, and Europe where he played in recitals with Claude DEBUSSY at Paris. His compositions include orchestral works, violin pieces, and songs.

Hartmann, Viktor (?-1873), Russian architect and painter: after his death a group of friends arranged a display of his pictures which was attended by Modeste MOUSSORGSKY, also a friend of the artist. As a tribute Moussorgsky wrote a series of musical sketches, depicting his impressions of the paintings, entitled PICTURES AT AN EXHIBITION.

Harty, Sir Hamilton (1879-), Irish composer and conductor trained by his father: he has conducted the London Symphony Orchestra, the Hallé Orchestra, the British National Orchestra. His compositions include an *Irish Symphony, A Comedy Overture,* and other orchestral works; chamber music; pieces for violin; violoncello, harp, and piano: he has also made special orchestrations of Handel's *Water Music* and *Royal Fireworks Music.*

Harun-al-Rashid, caliph of Bagdad from 786 to 809; the fifth and most celebrated of the Abbassides who claimed descent from Abbas, the uncle of Mohammed. The caliphate reached the apex of its glory under him, but his fame comes chiefly from the ARABIAN NIGHTS in which his name and reign are associated with all manner of romantic and wonderful incidents.

Harunobu, Suzuki (c.1725-1770), Japanese painter and print maker said to have been a pupil of Nishimura SHIGENAGA, and also to have been influenced by the works of Okumura MASANOBU. He was the inventor of polychrome printing on wood blocks, and specialized in scenes of everyday life such as *Woman on the Stairs of a Temple; Woman on a Snow-covered Bridge; Two Women on a Bridge; The Basin of Red Fish; Horseman on a Bridge.*

Harvey, Sir George (1806-1876), Scottish painter who was chiefly self-taught except for some instruction at the Trustee's Academy in Edinburgh. His notable works, for which the subjects were taken from Scottish history and scenery, include *Covenanters Preaching; The Curlers; Sabbath Evening; Bunyan in Bedford Gaol; Dawn Revealing a New World to Columbus; Mountain Pool; Glen Falloch.* He was one of the founders of the Scottish Academy.

Harvey, Lilian (1907-), English screen actress educated at the Lyceum of Schönberg who appeared in numerous German films some of which have been shown in the United States: they include *Ein Liebeswalz; Kongress Tanzet; Zwei Herzen.* Her pictures in English include *I am Suzanne; Let's Live Tonight; Invitation to the Waltz; Schubert's Serenade.*

"Háry János" Suite (Kodály), an orchestral suite by Zoltán Kodály, based on his opera of the same title, the musical material being drawn from Hungarian folk tunes. It was first performed in the United States by the New York Philharmonic-Symphony Orchestra on Dec. 15, 1927. Háry János is a Hungarian national hero whose personal achievements are built up by fanciful tales: the suite is based on incidents in the stage version of the work. As usually played, it is divided into six sections: I, *The Tale Begins,* II, *Viennese Musical Clock,* III, *Song,* IV, *The Battle and Defeat of Napoleon,* V, *Intermezzo,* VI, *Entrance of the Emperor and His Court.* There is a Victor recording by the Minneapolis Symphony Orchestra directed by Eugene Ormandy.

Hašek, Jaroslav (1883-1923), Czech short story writer and novelist who published many volumes of short stories before serving in World War I: his one great work is *The Good Soldier: Schweik,* a novel which was to have been completed in six volumes, but only four were written at the time of his death. It was dramatized in 1928 at Berlin, and has been translated into English and several other languages.

Hassam, Childe (1859-1935), American painter who studied at the Boston Art School, and after 1883 in Paris with BOULANGER and LEFEBVRE. After returning to America he began to paint the quaint scenes of New England which made him famous. His works include *Isle of Shoals; The Strawberry Tea Set; Church at Gloucester; The New York Window; Broad and Wall Streets in New York; Evening Bells.* Toward the end of his life he made fine etchings of landscapes and figure subjects.

Hasse, Johann Adolph (1699-1783), German dramatic composer who produced his first opera, *Antigonus,* at the Brunswick Theatre in 1721: this was followed by more than 100 others including *Sesostrate; Attalo; Dalisa; Artaserse,* and also several operas which competed successfully with those of Christoph Willibald von GLUCK. He was one of the first composers to recognize the genius of MoZART as a boy of fifteen. His wife, Faustina BORDONI (1693-1781), was a famous dramatic singer of Italian parentage: she married Hasse in 1730, and her entire career until her retirement from the stage in 1751 was bound up with that of her husband at the opera house in Dresden.

Hasselet, André Henri Constant van (1800-1874), Belgian historian and poet, born in Holland, who became a naturalized Belgian: his works include *History of French Poetry in Belgium; The Glories in Art of Belgium.* His poetry such as *The Four Incarnations of Christ* was highly regarded, and he was elected a member of the Belgian Academy.

Hasselmans, Louis (1878-), French violoncellist and conductor who studied with LAVIGNAC, GODARD, and MASSENET at the Paris Conservatory. After touring Europe as a 'cello virtuoso, he made his debut as a conductor with the LAMOUREUX Orchestra. He has conducted at the Opéra-Comique in Paris; at the Chicago Civic Opera (1918-20); and at the Metropolitan Opera House in New York from 1921 to 1936.

Hastings, Thomas (1860-1929), American architect educated at Columbia University, and trained at the ECOLE DES BEAUX-ARTS in Paris. He was first connected with McKim, Mead and White, New York, and in 1886 formed the partnership of CARRERE and Hastings. Among his chief works are the New York Public Library; The Tower of Jewels at the Panama-Pacific Exposition; the Henry C. Frick home in New York; the Chapel of St. Ambrose in the Cathedral of St. John the Divine; the Standard Oil Building, New York. He published *Six Lectures on Architecture* with Ralph Adams CRAM and Claude Bragdon.

Hauk, Minnie (1852-1929), American dramatic soprano who was trained in New York and made her debut there in *Linda da Chamounix* in 1869: she sang at opera houses in Vienna and Berlin, and was the first American singer to create the principal roles in *Romeo and Juliet* (1867), *Carmen* (1878), and Massenet's *Manon* (1885). Her repertory included more than 100 roles: she retired in 1891.

Hauptmann, Gerhart (1862-), German novelist, poet, and dramatist educated at the Royal College of Art, Breslau, and at the University of Jena: his works available in English include *Atlantis; The Heretic of Soanna; The Island of the Great Mother; Fool in Christ; Emanuel Quint.* Among his plays are *Lonely Lives; The Weavers* which won the Nobel Prize in 1912; *Before Dawn; The Red Cock; The Coming of Peace; The Sunken Bell; Hannele; The Golden Harp:* a collected edition of his dramatic works has been published in English.

Hauptmann, Moritz (1792-1868), German composer and theorist who finished his musical training with Louis SPOHR, becoming a member of the latter's orchestra at Cassel, and in 1842 musical director of the Thomasschule at Leipzig, and professor of musical theory at the Conservatory. Ferdinand DAVID, Joseph JOACHIM, Hans von BULOW and Sir Arthur SULLIVAN were among his pupils: his most important theoretical work is *The Nature of Harmony and Metre* (1853) which appeared in 1888 in an English translation.

Hauser, Miska (1822-1887), Hungarian violinist who studied with Rodolphe KREUTZER, and later with Mayseder and SECHTER at the Vienna Conservatory. He toured Europe for twenty years with great success: his works include Hungarian, Scotch, and American rhapsodies, fantasias, rondos, variations, *Songs Without Words,* and pieces for the violin.

Havilland, Olivia de, see **De Havilland, Olivia.**

Hawasis, ancient Egyptian ballet companies who performed in open air gardens in villages, and also entertained the PHARAOHS with their fiery social dances. It is said that the dances represented a continuous story, and were frequently executed by dancers attached to the household or harem. The dances were of a sensuous nature, directly opposed to the classic dances of the ALMEIIS.

Hawkins, Sir Anthony Hope, see **Hope, Anthony.**

Hawkins, Sir John (1719-1789), English historian of music who was a lawyer by profession, music being his avocation. He worked for sixteen years on his principal publication, *General History of the Science and Practice of Music* (1776); it was issued at the same time as Dr. Charles BURNEY's "General History of Music," and was considered more accurate although less interesting than the Burney work.

Hawks, Howard (1896-), American screen producer and director educated at Cornell University who served in World War I. Among the films which he has produced or directed are *Air Circus; Cradle Snatchers; Trent's Last Case; The Criminal Code; The Crowd Roars; Tiger Shark; Today We Live; Barbary Coast; Ceiling Zero; Road to Glory; Come and Get It; Only Angels Have Wings; His Girl Friday; Air Force,* a drama of World War II made with the cooperation of the United States Army Air Force with the permission of the War Department.

Hawkshaw, the name of the detective in a play, *The Ticket-of-Leave-Man,* by Tom TAYLOR, an English dramatist, and produced in 1853. The word, uncapitalized, has come to mean any detective.

Hawksmoor, Nicholas (1661-1736), English architect who studied with Sir Christopher WREN, and later was associated with the latter and with Sir John VANBRUGH in the construction of many important buildings although it is difficult to assign each one credit for designs of particular edifices. It is known, however, that he designed the

towers for All Souls' Church, Oxford, and also several new churches for the City of London during Queen Anne's reign.

Hawthorne, Charles Webster (1872-1930), American painter who studied in New York, and taught at the ART STUDENTS' LEAGUE in addition to founding the Cape Cod School of Art at Provincetown, Mass. Among his notable pictures are *Trousseau, Venetian Girl,* and *The Family.* He was a member of the National Academy of Design, and his canvases are to be seen at the METROPOLITAN MUSEUM OF ART and many other major American museums of art.

Hawthorne, Nathaniel (1804-1864), American short story writer and novelist educated at Bowdoin College where he became friendly with Henry Wadsworth LONGFELLOW. His first novel, *Fanshawe,* was published anonymously in 1828: it was followed by *Twice Told Tales; Mosses from an Old Manse; The Scarlet Letter; The House of the Seven Gables; The Snow Image and Other Twice-Told Tales; The Blithedale Romance; Tanglewood Tales; The Marble Faun; Septimus Felton.* His son, **Julian Hawthorne** (1846-1934), was trained in the Lowell Scientific School at Harvard and in Dresden, and for a time became a hydrographic engineer, later joining the editorial staff of the London *Spectator.* He wrote several novels including *A Fool of Nature* which won the $10,000 prize awarded by the New York *Herald,* and *Fortune's Fool:* also *Nathaniel Hawthorne and His Wife* and *Hawthorne and His Circle.* His daughter, **Hildegarde Hawthorne,** is also a writer of distinction: her works include *Romantic Rebel: The Story of Nathaniel Hawthorne; Poet of Craigie House: The Life of Longfellow; The Story of Ralph Waldo Emerson; The Happy Autocrat: The Life of Oliver Wendell Holmes; Williamsburg.*

Hawtrey, Sir Charles (1858-1923), English actor and manager educated at Rugby and Oxford: he made his stage debut under the name "Bankes," and in 1883 appeared with immense success in his adaptation of a German comedy, *The Private Secretary,* playing in it for three years at London. Among his later successes was *A Message from Mars* in which he appeared at New York in 1901, and presented in London in 1905. He was the outstanding stage comedian of his period.

Hay, Ian (1876-), English novelist and dramatist, real name John Hay Beith; educated at Fettes College and Cambridge University. His novels and plays, in many of which he collaborated with well-known dramatists, include *Tilly of Bloomsbury,* dramatized from his novel "Happy-Go-Lucky"; *A Safety Match; The Sport of Kings; A Damsel in Distress; The Middle Watch; Leave It to Psmith; Orders Are Orders; Housemaster,* adapted from his novel; *On Borrowed Time; Bachelor Born.* He has also written the dialogue for the film adaptations of his own plays and novels.

Hay, John (1838-1905), American statesman and poet educated at Brown University, and secretary as well as aide-de-camp to Abraham Lincoln: he also served in the Civil War, and occupied high posts in the diplomatic service. His works include *Pike County Ballads* (1871); *Castilian Days,* a travel volume; *The Breadwinners,* a social novel published anonymously; *Abraham Lincoln,* a ten-volume biography in collaboration with John NICOLAY.

Hayakawa, Sessue (1889-), Japanese actor who came to the United States when he was nineteen, and studied at the University of Chicago. He organized a Japanese dramatic company to produce *Typhoon,* and has appeared in numerous films including *The Secret Sin; The City of Dead Faces; The Cheat; Alien Souls; Daughter of the Dragon.* In 1933 he was featured in the film, *Tohjin Okichi,* produced in Japan; he also published *The Bandit Prince,* a novel.

Haydn, Franz Joseph (1732-1809), Austrian composer whose musical aptitude became evident when he was five years old. His early lessons in violin playing and in singing were given by a relative: except for some instruction in composition by Niccoló PORPORA, he was chiefly self-taught. For nearly thirty years (1761-1790) he was musical director for Prince Nicholas ESTERHAZY, nicknamed "The Magnificent," who maintained an orchestra of fifty players, and built himself a palace at Esterház which became a second VERSAILLES in respect to its magnificence, and its constant stream of notable visitors from all parts of Europe. After Prince Esterházy died in 1790, the musical part of the palace was dispensed with, and, Haydn, with the exception of two visits to England to conduct symphonies written for the SALOMON Concerts, lived in Vienna until his death, composing his oratorios, *The Creation* and *The Seasons* at the age of nearly seventy. His more than one thousand works include one hundred fifteen symphonies, more than fifty concertos for various instruments, eighty-three string quartets, a vast quantity of concerted music and solo pieces for various instruments, nineteen operas, and fifteen masses.

Haydn, Johann Michael (1737-1806), Austrian composer, brother of Franz Joseph HAYDN, who became music director at Salzburg to the Archbishop Sigismund, and later started a school for musical composition at which Carl Maria von Weber was a STUDENT. His compositions are of the highest degree of excellence although perhaps not as inspired as those of his brother: they include 360 sacred works; several operas; 30 symphonies; chamber music and organ pieces.

Haydon, Benjamin Robert (1786-1846), English painter who studied at the Royal Academy, London, and in 1807 exhibited his first picture, *The Repose in Egypt.* In 1809 he showed a painting, *Dentatus Killed by His Soldiers,* but never exhibited again because he did not like the inconspicuous position in which it was placed. His notable works include *Christ's Entry into Jerusalem; Raising of Lazarus; Zenophon; Nero Watching Rome Burn; Napoleon at St. Helena; Falstaff; Achilles Playing the Lyre.* His *Autobiography and Journal* was published in 1926 with an introduction by Aldous HUXLEY.

Haydon, Julie (1911-), American actress whose real name is Donella Donaldson: she made her debut in 1934 at Los Angeles in *Autumn Crocus,* and appeared with great success in 1935 opposite Noel COWARD in the film, *The Scoundrel.* Among other plays in which she has had stellar roles are *Shadow and Substance* and William SAROYAN's *The Time of Your Life.*

Hayes, Helen (1902-), American stage and screen actress who appeared as a child of six in *The Babes in the Wood* at Washington, D. C., and two years later with Lew FIELDS in *Old Dutch.* Among the numerous plays in which she has had leading roles are *Pollyanna; Penrod; Dear Brutus; To the Ladies; Dancing Mothers; What Every Woman Knows; Coquette; The Good Fairy; Mary of Scotland; Victoria Regina; The Merchant of Venice; Ladies and Gentlemen; Harriet:* the last-named is the story of Harriet Beecher STOWE, the author of "Uncle Tom's Cabin." Miss Hayes has also appeared in several films including *The Sin of Madelon Claudet; Arrowsmith; Another Language; Night Flight; Farewell to Arms.*

Hayes, Roland (1887-), American Negro concert tenor who studied at Fisk University and in Europe with George HENSCHEL and Victor Beigel. From 1916 to 1920 he toured the United States in recital: after further study in Europe he appeared with the principal orchestras abroad and in the United States. He has specialized in the interpretation of Negro spirituals and folksongs although his repertory includes the art songs of all nations. He was awarded the Spingarn medal in 1925 for his outstanding achievements among colored people.

Haymarket Theatre, a London playhouse the traditions of which are almost as rich as those of the DRURY LANE Theatre for which it acted as a training house. It was erected in 1720, leased to a French company, and called the "New French Theatre" for several years. Henry FIELDING's *The Tragedy of Tragedies* was produced there in 1734, and Charles MACKLIN brought his company to the theatre in 1744. A new building was erected in 1821, opening with *The Rivals,* and the present structure was built in 1880.

Hayne, Paul Hamilton (1830-1886), American poet who was trained and practised as a lawyer: his works include *Sonnets and Other Poems* (1855); *Avolio, a Legend of the Island of Cos; Legends and Lyrics; Mountains and Lovers.* He has been called the "poet laureate of the South."

Hays, William Jacob (1830-1875), American painter who studied drawing with J. R. Smith, and visited various parts of the United States and Canada to study and paint the fauna: his works include *Herd of Bisons; The Stampede; Wounded Buffalo; Bison Bull at Bay; Prairie on Fire; Herd of Caribou; Prairie Dog Village.*

Hazlitt, William (1778-1830), English critic and prose writer who was at first a painter: his works include *Views of the English Stage* (1818); *Lectures on the English Poets; Lectures on the English Comic Writers; Table Talk; Characters of Shakespeare's Plays.*

Healy, George Peter Alexander (1813-1894), American painter who studied in Paris, went to Chicago in 1858, and returned to Europe in 1869 to live for a long period in Rome. He painted portraits of the presidents, and of Daniel Webster and Henry Wadsworth Longfellow: other works include *Franklin Urging the Claims of the American Colonies before Louis XVI*, and *Webster's Reply to Hayne*.

Hearn, Lafcadio (1850-1904), American author born in the Ionian Islands of an Irish father and a Greek mother; he was educated in France and England, and became a Japanese citizen with the name "Yakuma Koizumi." His works include *One of Cleopatra's Nights* (1882); *Some Chinese Ghosts; Chita; Youma; Out of the East; Kokoro; In Ghostly Japan; Glimpses of Unfamiliar Japan; Japan: an Attempt at Interpretation.*

Heavy, in theatrical parlance the term for the villain in drama or melodrama.

Hebbel, Christian Friedrich (1813-1863), German poet and dramatist, classed with Heinrich von KLEIST and Friedrich von SCHILLER. He was educated at HEIDELBERG University through the generosity of friends: his works include the plays *Judith* (1839), regarded as the first modern German drama; *Genoveva; Agnes Bernauer; Herod and Marianne; Maria Magdalena; Gyges and His Ring; Demetrius; Die Nibelungen,* a trilogy considered his masterpiece.

Hebe, in Greek mythology the goddess of youth, daughter of ZEUS and HERA. She was cupbearer to the gods, and married HERCULES after he was made one of the Olympian divinities. In HOMER she is the counterpart of GANYMEDE: the Romans called her *Juventas.*

Heber, Richard (1773-1833), English book collector who was educated at Oxford: he first assembled a classical library, but added early English literature and dramatic books until Sir Walter SCOTT pronounced his library superior to all others in the world, probably referring to it only as a private collection. At one time he owned more than 150,000 books housed in eight buildings in England and Europe.

Hébert, Ernest (1817-1908), French painter who studied with David d'Angers and Paul DELAROCHE: among his notable works are *Tasso in Prison; Adam and Eve Driven from Paradise; Morning and Evening of Life; Malaria; The Kiss of Judas; Slave Breaking His Chains; Muse of the Woods; The Little Violinist; Virgin of the Deliverance.* He also designed mosaics for the PANTHEON and the LOUVRE, and became director of the Académie de France in Rome.

Hébert, Louis Philippe (1850-1917), French-Canadian sculptor chiefly self-taught by his study of the masters in Italy and Paris. His works include statues of Queen Victoria and King Edward VII: his unfinished *Evangeline,* a statue for the village of Grande Pré was completed by his son, Henri Hébert, who was also a fine sculptor.

Hecate, in Greek mythology a goddess at first of the moon, but later of the night, the under-world, magic arts and spells. She is represented with three bodies standing back to back: in her hands are torches, and sometimes whips, keys or daggers.

Hecht, Ben (1893-), American novelist and dramatist who was a child prodigy on the violin and a journalist before he began his career as an author and playwright. His plays include *The Egotist* (1922); *The Front Page* with Charles MACARTHUR; *The Great Magoo* with Gene Fowler; *Twentieth Century; To Quito and Back; Ladies and Gentlemen* with Charles MacArthur. His novels include *Erik Dorn; Gargoyles; The Florentine Dagger; Count Bruga; Actor's Blood:* he has also made several successful pictures among which are *Design for Living; Scarface; Topaze; The Scoundrel; Crime Without Passion,* the two last-named in collaboration with Charles MacArthur.

Hector, in Greek mythology the son of Priam and Hecuba, and the husband of ANDROMACHE. He is pictured in HOMER as a remarkable warrior, one of the greatest champions of the Trojan cause and a favorite of Apollo. He killed Patroclus, the friend of ACHILLES, and was in turn slain by the latter.

Hecuba, in Greek mythology the wife of PRIAM; also the queen of Troy and the mother of HECTOR and PARIS. After the fall of Troy she became the slave of ODYSSEUS, and threw herself into the HELLESPONT. She is to be found as a character in *The Trojan Women* and *Hecuba,* two plays by EURIPIDES.

Heem, Jan Davidsz de (c.1600-c.1683), Dutch painter who studied with his father and became a famous painter of still-life, flowers, fruits, and animals: his notable works include *Fruits and Flowers with Insects; Breakfast Table; The Host with Symbolical Fruits.* His son, **Cornelis de Heem** (c.1631-1695), lacked the genius of his father, but executed creditable canvases in similar style such as *Fruits with Musical Instruments; Fruitpiece; Fruits and Oysters on Silver Tray.*

Heemskerk, Martin van (1498-1574), Dutch painter whose real name was Martin van Veen: he studied with Corneliz Willemsz and Jan Lucasz, later visiting Italy where he was much influenced by MICHELANGELO. His works include *Holy Family, Brazen Serpent; St. Luke Painting the Virgin; Momus with Minerva; Venus, Cupid and the Cyclops; Ecce Homo.*

Heermann, Hugo (1844-1935), German violinist who studied at the Brussels Conservatory, and had the advantage of intimacy with Charles de BERIOT, Hubert LEONARD, and Henri VIEUXTEMPS. He was the leader of the "Frankfurter" String Quartet, and taught at the Chicago College of Music and the Stern Conservatory at Berlin in addition to making concert tours of the entire world.

Hegedüs, Ferencz (1881-), Hungarian violinist who studied at the Budapest Conservatory under Jenö HUBAY, and made his debut in 1901 at London. He toured Europe, England, and the United States (1906-7) with tremendous success, returning to America in 1915-16.

Heggie, O. P. (c.1877-1936), Australian actor who appeared first at Sydney, and later at London with Ellen TERRY in a stage version of *David Copperfield:* among the plays in which he assumed leading roles are *The Truth About Blayds; Androcles and the Lion; Justice; The Green Bay Tree; The Merchant of Venice; Fashions for Men; This Woman Business; We Moderns; The Beaux' Stratagem; The School for Scandal:* also several films including *Anne of Green Gables* and *Midnight.*

Heiberg, Gunnar (1857-1929), Norwegian dramatist who directed the National Theatre at Bergen, and wrote several successful plays including *Aunt Ulrikka; Love Your Neighbor; The Balcony; King Midas; The Council of the People; The Tragedy of Love.* He also wrote *The Norwegian Theatre,* an interesting critical volume.

Heiberg, Johan Ludvig (1791-1860), Danish poet, critic, and dramatist who received his literary training from his father, and later became director of the National Theatre. His works include a treatise, *The Marionette Theatre,* and several plays including *King Solomon and the Hatter; April Fools; The Hill of the Elves; Fata Morgana; The Elves.* He was for many years the arbiter of the Danish theatre.

Heidelberg University, an institution for higher education in Heidelberg, Germany, founded in 1385: it was first a Catholic college, but after the Reformation became the center of Protestant theological learning with a library of 500,000 volumes and several thousand manuscripts. The faculty numbers about 200, and the student body has been as high as 2000. A romantic atmosphere hovers over the student life with its duels and songs: a novel, "Karl Heinrich," by Wilhelm Meyer-Förster was the basis for the play, *Prince Karl,* in which Richard MANSFIELD appeared successfully, and an operetta, The STUDENT PRINCE, was drawn from the same source.

Heidenstam, Verner von (1859-1940), Swedish poet and novelist who studied art under Gérôme at the ECOLE DES BEAUX-ARTS in Paris, and won the NOBEL PRIZE for poetry in 1916. His works available in English include *A King and His Campaigners; The Charles Men; The Soothsayer; The Tree of the Folkungs; Selected Poems; The Swedes and Their Chieftains.*

Heifetz, Jascha (1901-   ), Russian violinist who first studied with his father, and later at the Imperial Music School at Vilna, making his debut at six in the MENDELSSOHN violin concerto. In 1907 he became a pupil of Leopold AUER at the St. Petersburg Conservatory, and made his second debut in 1912 under Artur NIKISCH; tours of Austria, Russia, and Scandinavia were followed by his American debut in 1917. He has toured the world several times and has been an American citizen since 1925. He has made fine recordings, published numerous transcriptions for violin, and appeared in 1939 in the film *They Shall Have Music.*

Heijermans, Hermann (1864-1924), Dutch dramatist of Jewish parentage who wrote under the name of "Samuel Falkland": his plays include *The Good Hope* (1900), translated into several languages; *Ahasuerus; Ghetto; Bonheur; The Rising Sun; A Case of Arson.*

Heine, Heinrich (1797-1856), German poet and dramatist who studied for the bar, but never practised, and led a life filled with family troubles, quarrels with friends, and political entanglements with the authorities. His works include *Poems* (1822); the tragedies, *Almansor* and *William Ratcliffe; Pictures of Travel,* in two volumes; *Book of Songs; New Poems; Germany: A Winter's Tale; Doctor Faust; Last Poems.*

Held, Anna (1873-1918), French actress who first appeared on the London stage: she came to the United States in 1896 to appear in Charles H. HOYT's *A Parlor Match,* and was featured in many musical comedies including *Papa's Wife, The Cat and the Cherub,* and *The Parisian Model.*

Heldenleben, Ein, see **Hero's Life, A.**

Helen, in Greek mythology the daughter of ZEUS and Leda, and said to be the most beautiful woman in Greece. She was the wife of Menelaus: her elopement with PARIS, son of King PRIAM of Troy, was the cause of the TROJAN WAR. At the end of the conflict, Menelaus carried her back to Sparta, but EURIPIDES' play, *Helen,* has her detained in Egypt by King Proteus who restored her to Menelaus.

Helicon, a brass instrument used in military bands and frequently in dance orchestras: it corresponds to the bass TUBA, but its tube is bent to form a circle and carried over the shoulder of the player. It is made in various pitches: the lowest produces the Bb two octaves below the Bb on the second line on the bass staff.

Heliodorus (c.346-c.420), Greek author of romances: he became bishop of Tricca in Thessaly, and his romance, *Aethiopica,* was written under circumstances that make it unique in the annals of fiction. It was translated into several languages, and widely read during the RENAISSANCE.

Helios, in Greek mythology the sun god: he was the son of the TITAN Hyperion, and his wife, Theia. His task was to ride each day across the heavens in a golden chariot drawn by four milk-white horses. His wife was Clymene who became the mother of PHAETHON.

Hellenism, a term used to describe ancient Greek culture in respect to literature, painting, sculpture, and allied arts: the word was used by Matthew Arnold as the antithesis of Hebraism.

Heller, Stephen (1813-1888), Hungarian pianist and composer who studied the piano at Vienna with Carl CZERNY, and composition with Alphons Czibulka. He toured Europe successfully and settled in Paris where he became intimate with BERLIOZ, LISZT, and CHOPIN. His compositions include almost five hundred pieces for the piano many of which are short, and used today for teaching purposes.

Hellespont, the name in ancient days for the Dardanelles (Strait of Gallipoli), a body of water from one to five miles wide and forty-two miles long which separates Europe from Asia, and is controlled by Turkey. It is famous in legend as the waters that Leander swam to visit his beloved HERO.

Helleu, Paul César (1859-1927), French painter and etcher of the impressionistic school as revealed in such works as *The Glass of St. Denis* and *Study of Versailles.* He was much in demand as a portrait painter after he executed the likenesses of the Duchess of Marlborough, Mrs. Charles Dana Gibson, and other well-known women.

Hellman, Lillian (1905-), American dramatist and short-story writer educated at New York University: her plays include *The Children's Hour* (1934); *Days to Come; The Little Foxes; The Watch on the Rhine.* She has also prepared the film adaptations of *The Dark Angel; These Three,* and *Dead End.*

Hellmesberger, Georg, Sr. (1800-1873), Austrian violinist, composer, and teacher who studied at the Vienna Conservatory where he eventually became the head of the violin department. He made many successful concert tours, and taught several distinguished pupils including Henri ERNST, Miska HAUSER, Joseph JOACHIM, Leopold AUER, and his own sons, Georg Hellmesberger, Jr. (1830-1852), and Joseph Hellmesberger, Sr. (1828-1893). The latter founded a string quartet which is said to have given new life to chamber music in Vienna: it was headed after his death by his son, Joseph Hellmesberger, Jr. (1855-1907), who was also a successful composer of operettas.

Helmholtz, Hermann von (1821-1894), German physician and physicist trained in the Potsdam Gymnasium and the Berlin Military Institute: he became teacher of anatomy at the Berlin Academy of Fine Arts, and professor of physiology at several German universities. His work of greatest interest to musicians is *Sensations of Tone* (1813: English translation, 1875), a comprehensive treatise on acoustics which definitely proved the theories of Jean Philippe RAMEAU and Moritz HAUPTMANN.

Héloise (1101-1164), French lady, niece of Fulbert, canon of Notre Dame. ABELARD, a French scholar, became her instructor, and later her seducer: after they were finally secretly married Abelard became a monk and Héloise retired to a convent, finally becoming an abbess.

Helpmann, Robert, contemporary Australian ballet dancer who studied in Australia under the influence of Anna PAVLOWA, and also in London as a pupil of the SADLER'S WELLS school. He has been favorably compared with Leonide MASSINE as one of the few who understand how to give positive value to a static pose.

Helst, Bartholomeus van der (c.1613-1670), Dutch painter who either studied with Frans HALS or used him as a model: his noted works include *The Banquet for the Peace of Westphalia; Syn-*

dics of the Arquebusiers; The Archers; Man With Emptied Glass; Aristocratic Young Couple; Presentation of the Betrothed; Lady in Blue; Dutch Burgomaster: also many portraits of contemporary celebrities.

Hemans, Felicia Dorothea (1793-1835), English poet who published some verse in newspapers at the age of fourteen: her works include *Domestic Affections; Tales and Historic Scenes in Verse,* which includes the famous "Landing of the Pilgrims"; *Lays of Many Lands; Forest Sanctuary; Songs of the Cid; The Siege of Valencia.*

Heming or **Hemminge, John** (c.1556-1630), English actor who was the treasurer of SHAKESPEARE'S Company, and acted in plays by Shakespeare and Ben JONSON. He edited, in collaboration with Henry Condell, the first collected edition of Shakespeare's works in 1623: he was also the principal owner of the Globe and BLACKFRIARS Theatres, and was remembered in Shakespeare's will.

Heming, Violet (1895-), English actress who made her first appearance in the United States in Barrie's *Peter Pan* as a member of a children's company organized by Charles FROHMAN. Among the numerous plays in which she has appeared are *Rebecca of Sunnybrook Farm; The Deep Purple; Disraeli* with George ARLISS; *Under Cover; The Lie; The Flame; Three Faces East; Sonya; The Rivals; Trelawney of the Wells; Mrs. Dane's Defence; There's Always Juliet; Design for Living; The Shining Hour; The Old Maid; Yes, My Darling Daughter; Susan and God.* She has also appeared in several films.

Hemingway, Ernest (1898-), American novelist and short story writer: his works include *Three Stories and Ten Poems* (1923); *The Torrents of Spring; The Sun Also Rises; Men Without Women; A Farewell to Arms; Death in the Afternoon; To Have and Have Not; The Fifth Column,* a play; *The First Forty-Nine; For Whom the Bell Tolls,* a best seller in 1940-41.

Hémon, Louis (1880-1913), French-Canadian novelist born in Brest who came to Canada in 1911: his masterpiece was *Maria Chapdelaine,* an enthralling story of the hardy pioneers who settled the province of Quebec.

Hempel, Frieda (1885-), German dramatic soprano who studied singing with Frau Nicklass-Kempner at Berlin, and made her first appearance in 1905 at the Royal Opera, Berlin, in *The Merry Wives of Windsor.* She made her debut in 1912 at the Metropolitan Opera House in *Les Huguenots,* and remained there for seven years. She toured the United States in recital; also made many appearances as guest artist with major orchestras.

Henderson, Archibald (1877-), American biographer and critic educated at the University of North Carolina, the University of Chicago; Cambridge University, the University of Berlin, and the Sorbonne. His works include *Mark Twain* (1911); *George Bernard Shaw: His Life and Work; The Changing Drama; Contemporary Immortals; Bernard Shaw: Playboy and Prophet.*

Henderson, John (1747-1785), English actor who made his debut in 1772 at Bath in *Hamlet*, and enacted the role of Shylock with such success in 1777 that he was not only favorably compared with David GARRICK, but the latter was jealous of him. He was also greatly praised as Falstaff, Richard III, Iago and Macbeth.

Henderson, William James (1855-1937), American critic and writer on musical subjects educated at Princeton University. He wrote the librettos of many light operas including Walter DAMROSCH's *Cyrano de Bergerac*, and was music critic of the New York *Sun* from 1902 to 1937. His works include *The Story of Music* (1889); *Preludes and Studies; How Music Developed; What is Good Music?; The Orchestra and Orchestral Music; Richard Wagner, His Life and Dramas; The Art of the Singer; Some Forerunners of Italian Opera.*

Henie, Sonja (1913-), Norwegian ice skater and actress: after becoming champion of Norway, she studied ballet dancing with Madame KARSAVINA, and translated Anna PAVLOWA's *Dying Swan* into a dance on skates. She has appeared in several films including *One in a Million; Thin Ice; Happy Landing; My Lucky Star; Second Fiddle; Everything Happens at Night; Sun Valley Serenade.* She has also presented ice-skating revues at the Center Theatre, New York.

Henner, Jean Jacques (1829-1905), French painter who studied with François PICOT and won the Prix de Rome with his picture of *Adam and Eve Finding the Body of Abel.* He was friendly with Jean CARPEAUX and Henri CHAPU, and devoted much of his time to study of the old masters. His works include *Woman Reading; Idyl; The Nymph; A Bather; Mary Magdalen at the Tomb of Christ; Sleeping Nymph; Magdalen in the Desert.*

Henri, Robert (1865-1929), American painter who studied at the Pennsylvania Academy of Fine Arts, the ECOLE DES BEAUX-ARTS, and the Académie Julien under Bouguereau and Fleury. In 1899 he became instructor at the ART STUDENTS' LEAGUE, New York, and other schools where he exerted a profound influence through the originality and soundness of his methods in teaching. His notable works include *The Spanish Gipsy; La Neige; Young Woman in Black; The Equestrian; Indian Girl.* He wrote *The Art Spirit,* a volume of tersely worded advice to students.

Henry VIII (1491-1547), English king who studied music in his youth, and learned to compose with a considerable amount of skill: the extant compositions said to have been written by him include several part songs, pieces for three and four voices, two masses, and a ballad, *Pastime with Good Company.* He assembled a large collection of musical instruments.

Henry VIII (Saint-Saëns), grand opera in four acts: libretto by Armand Silvestre and Léonce Detroyat; music by Camille SAINT-SAENS; first produced at Paris in 1883; there is no record of its production in the United States. The plot revolves around a love letter, written by Anne Boleyn to the Spanish ambassador, which has fallen into the hands of Catherine, divorced wife of King Henry. The musical highlight in the score is the *Ballet Music* of which there is a Victor recording by the NBC Symphony Orchestra directed by Walter Damrosch.

Henry VIII (Shakespeare), a history drama written by William Shakespeare in collaboration with John FLETCHER and first produced in 1613 at the GLOBE THEATRE, London. Shakespeare is said to have derived much of the material from the manuscript of George Cavendish's *Life of Cardinal Wolsey.* Sir Arthur SULLIVAN, and Sir Edward GERMAN wrote incidental music for the drama: that composed by German was for Sir Henry IRVING's production of the play, and includes three dances; *Morris Dance, Shepherd's Dance,* and *Torchlight Dance,* which have become concert favorites. There is a Columbia recording by the Bournemouth Municipal Orchestra.

Henry, O. (William Sydney Porter), (1862-1910), American short story writer sentenced to a prison term for embezzlement of bank funds in 1896: while in prison he started writing, and after his discharge wrote a weekly story for the New York *World.* His works include *Cabbages and Kings* (1905); *The Four Million; Waifs and Strays; Hearts of the West; The Trimmed Lamp and Other Stories; The Voice of the City; Roads of Destiny.* His collected works were issued in 1913, and his native city, Greensboro, N. C., commemorated him with the erection of the *O. Henry Hotel.*

Henschel, Sir George (1850-1934), German pianist, composer, singer, and conductor who studied at the Leipzig Conservatory with Ignaz MOSCHELES and Carl REINECKE, and made his debut as a concert singer in 1868. He lived in London and became a naturalized British subject: from 1881 to 1884 he was the first conductor of the BOSTON SYMPHONY ORCHESTRA, and in 1885 founded the LONDON SYMPHONY ORCHESTRA, and was also the first conductor of the Glasgow Orchestra from 1891 to 1895. He was equally gifted as a pianist, singer, and conductor, and was one of the most ardent supporters of Johannes BRAHMS.

Henselt, Adolf von (1814-1889), German pianist and composer who studied with Johann HUMMEL at Weimar and with Simon SECHTER at Vienna. After successful tours he went to Russia in 1838 to become inspector of musical instruction in the Government educational schools for girls. His works include a concerto, études, and many solo pieces for the piano.

Henslowe, Philip (?-1616), English theatrical manager who first owned the Boar's Head and other inns: in 1585 he built the Rose Theatre in London, and presented plays there with his son-in-law, Edward ALLEYN, and the Admiral's Men. He kept a remarkable diary of all his activities which records the dates of the plays he produced, and the expenditures in connection with them. He is considered the greatest theatrical manager of his time.

Hepburn, Katharine (1909-), American stage and screen actress who made her debut in 1928 at New York in *These Days:* among the plays in which she has appeared are *Art and Mrs. Bottle; The Warrior's Husband; The Lake; Jane Eyre; The Philadelphia Story; Without Love.* She has had stellar roles in numerous films including *A Bill of Divorcement; Little Women; Morning Glory; Christopher Strong; The Little Minister; Alice Adams; Mary of Scotland; Quality Street; Holiday; The Philadelphia Story; Woman of the Year; Keeper of the Flame.*

Hephaestus, in Greek mythology the god of fire and of the metallic arts: he is identified with the Roman *Vulcan,* and was the creator of all that was wonderful mechanically in OLYMPUS. In Greek art he is pictured as a bearded man holding a smith's hammer: volcanos were supposed to be his forges, and the CYCLOPS his workmen.

Hepplewhite, George (?-1786), English furniture designer about whom little biographical material is available. He collaborated with Robert ADAMS in the same manner as Thomas CHIPPENDALE: lightness and grace characterize his work, but it is extremely difficult to identify because there are no distinguishing marks. He is said to have originated, or at least to have popularized the winged easy-chair, and his favorite materials were mahogany or satinwood inlaid with exotic woods.

Hera, in Greek mythology the wife of ZEUS and queen of OLYMPUS: she was the personification of virtuous womanhood, and of the perfect wife and mother. In Greek art she is portrayed in flowing draperies with a crown on her brow and a sceptre in her hand. In Roman mythology she was known as *Juno,* and was also the goddess of marriage, finance, and war.

Heraldry, (a) the art or science of recording genealogies: (b) the art of representing the armorial emblems of a noble house through terms and figures in accordance with accepted rules and regulations. It originated in the habit of knights of the Middle Ages adopting a distinctive color or emblem when on the battlefield or in the tournament: knights who distinguished themselves in the crusades adopted the colors or emblems which they had worn. Heraldry began its rise in the reign of William the Conqueror (1066-1087), and declined toward the end of the 15th century.

Herbert, Evelyn (1898-), American actress and singer who made her debut in 1920 as Mimi in *La Bohème* with the CHICAGO OPERA COMPANY: she was one of the original members of the "Roxy Gang" at the Capitol Theatre in 1922. Among the productions in which she has appeared are *Stepping Stones; The Love Song; Princess Flavia; My Maryland; The New Moon; The Red Robe; Princess Charming; Waltzes from Vienna; Bitter Sweet.*

Herbert, Henry William (1807-1858), American author born in England and educated at Oxford: he came to the United States as a young man, and founded the *American Monthly Magazine* in 1833. His works include *The Brothers* (1834);

Cromwell; The Cavaliers of England; The Puritans of New England; The Fronde; Captains of the Great Roman Republic. He also wrote books on sports under the pen name "Frank Forester."

Herbert, Victor (1859-1924), Irish-American violoncellist and composer who was a grandson of Samuel LOVER: he studied in Germany and became first 'cellist of the Strauss Orchestra in Vienna. In 1886 he became first 'cellist at the METROPOLITAN OPERA HOUSE, also appearing as soloist in his own concerto with the NEW YORK PHILHARMONIC-SYMPHONY ORCHESTRA. He was also first 'cellist with the Theodore THOMAS Orchestra and the SEIDL Orchestra of which he was also assistant conductor. In 1893 he succeeded Patrick S. GILMORE as bandmaster of the 22nd Regiment Band, and his first operetta, *Prince Ananias,* was produced in 1894. From 1898-1904 he was conductor of the PITTSBURGH SYMPHONY ORCHESTRA, and in 1911 and 1914 his grand operas, *Natoma* and *Madeleine* were produced by the Metropolitan Opera Company. His operettas include *The Wizard of the Nile; The Serenade; The Idol's Eye; The Fortune Teller; Cyrano de Bergerac; The Singing Girl; The Ameer; The Viceroy; Babes in Toyland; Babette; It Happened in Nordland; Miss Dolly Dollars; Wonderland; Mlle. Modiste; The Red Mill; The Magic Knight; The Rose of Algeria; Little Nemo; Naughty Marietta; Sweethearts; The Debutante; The Only Girl; Eileen.* Herbert was one of the founders of the AMERICAN SOCIETY OF COMPOSERS, AUTHORS, AND PUBLISHERS.

Herbst, Josephine (1897-), American novelist educated at the Universities of Iowa, Washington, and California, who has also acted as a journalist in Mexico, Russia, Germany, and Spain: her works include *Nothing is Sacred* (1928); *Money for Love; Pity Is Not Enough; The Executioner Waits; Rope of Gold; Satan's Sergeants.*

Herculaneum, an ancient city near Naples, Italy, which had the same fate as POMPEII by being buried through several eruptions to a depth of 70 to 112 feet. In 1709 parts of the city were excavated, but the work was so inexpertly done that little was accomplished: in 1869 King Victor Emmanuel was instrumental in having excavations made which resulted in the discovery of the remains of a theatre, prison, and a number of private residences; also statues and busts such as the *Sleeping Faun,* ARISTIDES, Plato, and Demosthenes.

Herculano de Carvalho e Araujo, Alexandre (1810-1877), Portuguese poet and scholar who wrote histories, poems, and novels including *The Prophet's Voice,* a poem; the novels *Eurico* and *The Monk of Cister;* also a history of the Inquisition in Portugal.

Hercules, in Greek and Roman mythology a mighty hero who was the son of ZEUS by Alcmene. He was denied the right of immortality by HERA until he had accomplished a number of superhuman tasks which included (*1*) the strangling of the Nemean lion; (*2*) the killing of the Lernean hydra-headed monster; (*3*) the capture of the Ceryneian stag; (*4*) the capture of the Erymanthian boar; (5) the cleaning of the Augean Stables; (6) the killing of the Stymphalian birds; (7) the seizure of the Cretan bull; (8) the capture of the mares of Diomedes; (9) the securing of the girdle of the queen of the Amazons; (10) the capture of the oxen of Geryon; (11) the seizure of the golden apples of the Hesperides; (12) the bringing from the underworld of Cerberus, the dog who guarded Hades. These were known as the *Twelve Labors of Hercules*, and he is credited with having performed them all successfully. Hercules married HEBE when he reached OLYMPUS: he is made a hero in plays by EURIPIDES and SENECA, and the most famous statue of him is the Farnese Hercules.

Hercules, Pillars of, see **Pillars of Hercules.**

Hercules, Twelve Tasks of, see **Hercules.**

Herford, Oliver (1863-1935), American poet, illustrator, and humorist educated at Lancaster College in England, and Antioch College in Ohio; also trained in art at the Académie Julien in Paris. His works include *Pen and Inklings* (1893); *The Bashful Earthquake; Alphabet of Celebrities; Rubaiyat of a Persian Kitten; Confessions of a Caricaturist; The Jingle Jungle Book; The Deb's Dictionary; The Florist Shop.* He also wrote many articles and poems for *Life* and *Harper's Magazine.*

Hergesheimer, Joseph (1880-), American novelist who first studied at the PENNSYLVANIA ACADEMY OF FINE ARTS, later turning his attention to literature. His works include *The Lay Anthony* (1914); *Three Black Pennys; Java Head; The Happy End; Balisand; Tampico; Swords and Roses; The Foolscap Rose;* also a biography of General Philip Sheridan.

Herkomer, Sir Hubert von (1849-1914), English painter born in Bavaria who was brought to America as an infant, but went to England when he was six years old to study later at the South Kensington Art School in London. His notable canvases include *Life, Light and Melody; After the Toil of Day; The Council of the Royal Academy; At Death's Door; First Warmth of Spring; Scene in Castle Garden, New York.* He revisited the United States in 1882 to paint many portraits, and lecture on his art.

Her Majesty's Theatre, a theatre in London opened in 1705 as the Queen's Theatre, and renamed in 1837 on the accession of Queen Victoria. It was famous from 1877 to 1887 for its presentation of grand opera. Colonel MAPLESON gave the English premières of BIZET'S *Carmen* and BOITO'S *Mefistofele* there, and Anton Seidl conducted WAGNER'S *Ring of the Nibelungs* in 1882. In 1887 Lilli LEHMANN appeared there in BEETHOVEN'S *Fidelio* and Adelina PATTI in Verdi's *La Traviata.* Sarah BERNHARDT played there in 1890, and the theatre was razed in 1891.

Hermes, in Greek mythology the messenger of the gods in OLYMPUS, and also the guide of the spirits of the dead to their place in the underworld. He was known as *Mercury* in Roman legend, and was also the god of the sciences, in-

ventions, and fine arts: he is represented as a manly youth without a beard, and is usually slightly clothed. A statue by PRAXITELES depicts him at play with DIONYSUS.

Hermitage Art Gallery (Leningrad), an art museum in Leningrad which is not only perfect from the architectural standpoint, but contains one of the best collections of Russian, Italian, Spanish, and French paintings in Europe. The original building was a palace erected for Catherine II: it was reconstructed for use as a museum in modern Greek style to house a collection of invaluable treasures of Greek and Scythian art found in the Crimea and elsewhere; also an assembly of 200,000 engravings.

Herne, James A. (1839-1901), American actor, manager and dramatist who first appeared in 1859 as George Shelby in *Uncle Tom's Cabin.* His plays include *Shore Acres; Margaret Fleming; The Minute Men; Sag Harbor; Hearts of Oak; Drifting Apart; Griffith Davenport.* His wife, **Katharine Corcoran Herne** (1857-1943), appeared with him in his plays, achieving great success in *Shore Acres* and *Margaret Fleming.* She also appeared with Clara MORRIS, James O'NEILL, and Rose COGHLAN. Her daughter, **Chrystal Herne** (1883-), made her debut in her father's play, *Griffith Davenport,* and later in *Sag Harbor* and *Shore Acres.* She has also appeared in *If I Were King, Mrs. Warren's Profession, The Melting Pot, The Trojan Women, Our Betters, The Acquittal, Craig's Wife, The Elton Case,* and many other successful plays.

Hero and Leander, a poem by the Greek poet, Musaeus, about whom little is known except that he imitated the style of Nonnius. It has 340 verses and relates the story of Hero, high priestess of the temple of Venus at Abydos, and Leander, her lover, who swam across the HELLESPONT every evening to his beloved until he was drowned one winter's night. When Hero saw his bruised body at the bottom of the tower in which she resided, she threw herself off the battlements and perished by the side of her lover. The poem is one of the most exquisite pieces of writing in ancient Greek literature.

Herodotus (c.480-424 B.C.), Greek historian, called by some authorities "the father of history," who traveled in Persia, Egypt, Asia Minor, and Greece: he wrote a history in nine books, named after the MUSES, of the Persian invasion of Greece. Many references are made in it to persons and events connected with the arts: there are no less than fifteen manuscripts of the work which was first printed in Greek in 1502.

Heroic Verse, in prosody the verse form, *dactylic hexameter,* in which epic or heroic poetry of the classic period was written.

Hérold, Louis Joseph Ferdinand (1791-1833), French dramatic composer who studied composition at the Paris Conservatory with Étienne MEHUL, and produced his first opera, *La gioventù di Enrico Quinto* in 1815: eleven years later a comic opera, *Marie,* achieved a brilliant triumph, and in 1831 his greatest success, *Zampa,* was produced. His last work, *Le Pré aux clercs,* also enjoyed great vogue in France.

Hero's Life, A (Strauss), an orchestral tone poem by Richard STRAUSS first played at Frankfort in 1899 with the composer conducting, and in the United States by the New York Philharmonic-Symphony Orchestra under Emil PAUR in 1900. No program accompanies the score, but analysis shows six sections: I, *The Hero;* II, *The Hero's Antagonists;* III, *The Hero's Helpmate;* IV, *The Hero's Battlefield;* V, *The Hero's Mission of Peace;* VI, *The Hero's Escape from the World.* There are Victor recordings by the Cleveland Orchestra under Artur Rodzinski, and the Philadelphia Orchestra with Eugene Ormandy.

Herrera, Fernando de (c.1534-c.1597), Spanish priest and poet whose exquisite verses earned for him the title of "the divine": his poems include *Some Works in Verse* (1583); *The Battle of Lepanto, Death of Sir Thomas More:* many of his poetical works have disappeared, and there is some doubt as to the authenticity of others.

Herrera, Francisco de (1576-1656), Spanish painter called *El Viejo* (the elder) who studied with Luis Fernandez at Seville: he was a man of such rough manners that no pupil could stay long with him. His notable works include *St. Basil Preaching; Last Judgment; Pentecost; Triumph of St. Hermengild; Christ Bearing the Cross; St. Peter; Miracle of the Loaves and Fishes; Marriage at Cana; Moses Striking the Rock.* His son, **Francisco de Herrera** (1622-1685), called *El Mozo* (the younger) finding himself unable to stand his father's tyranny and cruelty, went to Rome, and became a distinguished painter of still life: he was given the nickname "The Fish Vendor" because of his penchant for painting fish. After his father's death he returned to Seville, and became director of the New Academy under MURILLO. Among his best works are *Ecce Homo; Assumption of the Virgin; Christ Bearing the Cross; Saint Francesco;* also many fine portraits.

Herrick, Robert (1591-1674), English poet educated at Cambridge: he was one of Ben JONSON'S literary circle, and is regarded as the greatest of the CAVALIER POETS. His works include *Hesperides,* a volume of collected verse: he also contributed poems to *Lachrymae Musarum* and *Wits' Recreations.*

Herrick, Robert (1868-1938), American novelist educated at Harvard University who acted as correspondent for the Chicago *Tribune* during World War I. His works include *The Man Who Wins* (1895); *The Web of Life; The Common Lot; The Master of the Inn; One Woman's Life; His Great Adventure; Chimes; The End of Desire; Sometime.*

Herrmann, Bernard (1911-), American composer and conductor who studied with Albert STOESSEL, Philip JAMES, and Bernard WAGENAAR. He has acted as conductor of various radio programs for the Columbia Broadcasting Company, and as assistant conductor of the Columbia Broadcasting Company Symphony Orchestra. He has

composed several works, some especially for radio, including *Moby Dick,* a dramatic cantata; *Johnny Appleseed,* folk cantata; *Variations on Deep River and Water Boy; The City of Brass,* symphonic poem; *The Skating Rink,* a CURRIER AND IVES Suite; also several chamber music works.

Hersholt, Jean (1886-), Danish stage and screen actor who received his training at the Dagmar Theatre, Copenhagen, and played in repertory throughout Scandinavia. Among the films in which he has appeared are *Abie's Irish Rose; Battle of the Sexes; The Climax; Stella Dallas; The Goldfish; Greed; Don Q; The Student Prince; Mamba; Viennese Nights; Susan Lenox; The Sin of Madelon Claudet; Grand Hotel; Dinner at Eight; Christopher Bean; Men in White; The Cat and the Fiddle;* also the *Dr. Christian* series.

Hertz, Alfred (1872-1942), German conductor who studied at the Joachim RAFF Conservatory in Frankfort, and later conducted at several German opera houses. In 1902 he was engaged as conductor of Richard WAGNER'S works at the Metropolitan Opera House, and directed the first performance of *Parsifal* in the United States. He conducted the SAN FRANCISCO SYMPHONY ORCHESTRA from 1915 to 1930, and founded the HOLLYWOOD BOWL Orchestra, conducting more than 100 concerts there.

Hertz, Henrik (1798-1870), Danish poet and dramatist who abandoned the law for a literary career: his works include *Letters of a Ghost; Nature and Art; Four Letters of Knut the Seelander; Tyrfing:* also the plays *The Savings Bank* and *King René's Daughter,* which have been translated into several languages including English.

Hervey, Harry Clay (1900-), American explorer and author: his works include *Caravans by Night* (1922); *Where Strange Gods Call; Congai; King Cobra; The Iron Widow; The Damned Don't Cry; School for Eternity.*

Hervieu, Paul (1857-1915), French novelist and dramatist who practiced at the bar, and served in government posts before embarking on a literary career. His first novel, *The Unknown,* appeared in 1887: it was followed by *The Flirt* and *L'Armature* which was dramatized by Eugène Brieux. His plays include *Les Paroles Restant; La Loi de l'homme; Le Dédale:* the last-named was produced in New York as *The Labyrinth.*

Herzen, Alexander Ivanovich (1812-1870), Russian journalist and novelist: his works include *Whose Fault is It?; Dr. Krupoff; Interrupted Tales,* a volume of short stories; *My Exile in Siberia; The Russian People and Their Socialism.* He left Russia in 1847 after being arrested for political activities, and became a citizen of Switzerland.

Hesiod, Greek poet who lived about 750 B.C. He was born at a village in Boetia and died at Orchomenus: some authorities claim he never existed, but that his name is simply a personification of a group of Boetian poets opposed to the Ionic or Homeric school. The works credited to him include *Works and Days* and *Theogony,* the latter an account of the origin of the world and the genealogy of the gods.

Hesperides, in Greek mythology the nymphs who were the guardians of the golden apples made to grow by GAEA, goddess of the earth, as a wedding present for HERA. The seizure of these apples was one of the twelve tasks assigned by Hera to HERCULES as a test of his claim to immortality.

Hess, Myra (1890-), English pianist who studied at the Royal Academy of Music at London with Tobias MATTHAY, and made her debut with the LONDON PHILHARMONIC ORCHESTRA. In 1922 she made her American debut with great success, and has appeared regularly in recital and with the major symphony orchestras. She has published arrangements for the piano of chorales by Johann Sebastian BACH.

Hess, Willy (1859-1939), German violinist who studied with his father and later with Joseph JOACHIM. He toured Europe with great success, and taught at the Cologne Conservatory, also leading the Gurzenich Quartet. In 1903 he became professor of violin at the Royal Academy of Music, London, and in 1904 succeeded Franz KNEISEL as concertmaster of the Boston Symphony Orchestra. In 1910 he succeeded Karl Halir as leader of the Halir Quartet.

Hesselius, Gustavus (1682-1755), Swedish-American artist said to be the first portrait painter in America. A *Last Supper* painted by him is in a Maryland church, and the Pennsylvania Historical Society is in possession of a portrait with his wife. His son, John Hesselius, is supposed to have helped him in painting more than a hundred portraits.

Heure espagnole, L' (The Spanish Hour), a comedy-opera in one act; libretto by Franc Nohain; music by Maurice RAVEL; first produced at the Opéra-Comique, Paris, in 1911; at the Chicago Auditorium by the Chicago-Philadelphia Opera Company in 1920, and at the Metropolitan Opera House, New York, in 1925. The plot revolves around the resourceful Concepcion, wife of the clockmaker, Torquemada, who hides her lovers in her husband's grand-father's empty clock cases. There is a Columbia recording of the complete opera.

Hewlett, Maurice (1861-1923), English essayist, poet, and novelist educated at the London International College, and also trained for the law. His numerous works include *Earthwork Out of Tuscany* (1895); *The Masque of Dead Florentines; Songs and Meditations; The Forest Lovers; Richard Yea-and-Nay; The Queen's Quair; The Song of the Plow; New Canterbury Tales; Half-Way House; Outlaw; Mainwaring; The Road in Tuscany; Last Essays.*

Hexameter, in prosody a verse of six metrical feet; in particular the dactylic verse of classical Greek and Latin poetry: it was used by HOMER and VERGIL.

Heyden, Jan van der (1637-1712), Dutch painter who specialized in architectural views and land-scapes: the former are characterized by accurate perspective and warm colorings. His notable works include *Street in Cologne; Dutch House on a Canal; Buckingham Palace; City Hall of Amsterdam; Interior of Dutch Town; Palace with Dutch Garden; Italian Castle; House in the Wood; The Hermitage in St. Petersburg.*

Heyse, Paul Johann Ludwig (1830-1914), German poet and novelist: his works include the tragedies *Francesca da Rimini, The Sabines, Hadrian,* and *Hans Lange; L'Arrabiata,* a tale of Italy. He won the Schiller Prize in 1884 and the Nobel Prize in 1910: the purity and elegance of his verses brought him well-deserved renown.

Heyward, DuBose (1885-1940), American novelist, poet, and playwright: his works include *Carolina Chansons* (1922) with Hervey Allen; *Skylines and Horizons; Porgy,* dramatized in collaboration with his wife, Dorothy Heyward, and produced in 1927; *Angel; Mamba's Daughters,* also dramatized in 1939; *Brass Ankles* produced in 1931; *Peter Ashley; Lost Morning; Star Spangled Virgin.* The novel and play, *Porgy,* was produced as a folk opera, *Porgy and Bess,* with music by George GERSHWIN in 1935, and successfully revived in 1942.

Heywood, John (c.1500-c.1578), English dramatist and epigrammist who was known as a "court jester" for Queen Mary, but whose merry quips were apparently not in favor with Queen ELIZABETH as he retired when she ascended the throne. Among his works are *The Play of Love; The Play of the Weather; The Four P's: the Merry Interlude of a Palmer, a Pardoner, a Potycary and a Pedlar.* He also wrote a popular *Epigrams and Proverbs.*

Heywood, Thomas (? -c.1650), English dramatist who acted in Philip HENSLOWE's company about 1600, and later became a member of the Queen's Players. His plays include *The Four Prentices of London* (c.1596); *The Traveller,* in the preface to which he made claim to having written or helped to write more than two hundred plays; *The Golden Age; A Woman Killed with Kindness; Love's Mistress; The Royal King* and *Loyal Subject.* His prose works include a biography of Queen ELIZABETH.

Hiawatha, a legendary character known to the Iroquois, and by various names to other tribes of American Indians: he was said to have been placed on earth to teach the arts of peace to his countrymen. Henry Wadsworth LONGFELLOW's poem, *Hiawatha,* was published in 1855: the hero is made a member of the Ojibway instead of the Iroquois tribe.

Hichens, Robert Smythe (1864-), English novelist and dramatist who first studied music at the Royal College of Music, London, and later succeeded George Bernard SHAW as music critic of the London *World.* His numerous works include *The Coastguard's Secret* (1885); *The Garden of Allah,* dramatized in 1911; *Bella Donna; After the Verdict; The Bacchante; The Bracelet; The Paradine Case; The Gardenia; Secret Information; The Power to Kill; A New Way of Life.*

Hicks, Sir Edward Seymour (1871-), English actor, dramatist, and producer who toured with Mr. and Mrs. KENDAL in 1889 in both England and the United States. Among the plays in which he has appeared are *The Catch of the Season; The Beauty of Bath; Captain Kidd; Papa's Wife; Broadway Jones; Scrooge; Walker; Old Bill, M.P.; The Man in Dress Clothes; Sleeping Partners.* He is the author of *Scrooge; The Earl and the Girl; Bluebell in Fairyland; Cash on Delivery; Papa's Wife;* and many other light comedies.

Hicks, Granville (1901-), American critic and author educated at Harvard: his works include *The Great Tradition: An Interpretation of American Literature Since the Civil War; Figures of Transition: A Study of British Literature at the End of the Nineteenth Century.*

Hicks, Thomas (1823-1890), American painter who studied at the National Academy, and with Thomas COUTURE in Paris: in 1849 he set up a studio in New York, and became one of the most distinguished portrait painters of his day: among the noted persons who sat for him were Henry Ward Beecher, Harriet Beecher STOWE, Edwin BOOTH, and Henry W. LONGFELLOW.

Hidalgo, Juan (1600-1685), Spanish opera composer who was renowned as a harpist, and as a performer on the clavi-harp, an instrument he invented. He was attached to the Royal Chapel in Madrid, and composed the music to a libretto by CALDERON DE LA BARCA performed in 1660, and also wrote incidental music for comedies by Calderón and Juan Vélez.

Hieroglyphics, the characters employed in the picture writings of the ancient Egyptians: each character either represented the object itself, or some symbol associated with it. The reading is done from left to right, and in later tablets the forms are considerably simpler. The term is used humorously today to describe illegible writing.

Higginson, Henry Lee (1834-1919), American banker who founded the BOSTON SYMPHONY ORCHESTRA in 1881, and financed it until 1918 in addition to personally assuming its deficits. He also gave liberally to Harvard University of which he was a Fellow, and donated the land on which Soldiers' Field was erected.

Higginson, Thomas Wentworth (1823-1911), American clergyman, poet, and essayist who was colonel of the first Negro regiment in the Civil War: his works include *Out-door Papers* (1863); *Malbone, an Oldport Romance; Army Life in a Black Regiment; Atlantic Essays; Oldport Days; Young People's History of the United States; The Afternoon Landscape; Short Stories of American Authors; Cheerful Yesterdays; Henry Wadsworth Longfellow; John Greenleaf Whittier; A Reader's History of American Literature,* with Henry Walcott Boynton.

Highboy, a tall chest of drawers sometimes referred to as a *tallboy,* and sometimes built in two sections, the upper part resting on a table-like structure called a *lowboy.* It was generally made of mahogany or maple, and became very popular in colonial days in America when developed in William and Mary or Queen Anne styles.

Highland Fling, a dance peculiar to the people of the Scottish Highlands, so-called because the steps call for dancing on one leg while "flinging" the other forward and back: it is performed to music of the *strathspey,* also a lively Scottish dance.

Hildebrand, see **Beets, Nicolas.**

Hildebrandt, Eduard (1818-1868), German painter who studied with Wilhelm Krause at Berlin, and with Jean ISABEY in Paris. William IV of Prussia sent him on a trip around the world in 1862-64 during which he painted 400 water-colors which attracted much attention when exhibited in London during 1866. His noted works include *Street in Rouen; Panorama of Madeira; Naples with Vesuvius; View of Bethlehem; Brazilian Forest; Coast of Normandy; Moonrise in Madeira.*

Hill, Aaron (1685-1750), English author and dramatist who traveled in Palestine and Egypt as a youth and in 1709 is said to have been the manager of the DRURY LANE THEATRE, and in 1710 of the HAYMARKET THEATRE in London. His plays include *Elfrid, or The Fair Inconstant* (1709): he also wrote *The Progress of Wit,* a satire aimed at Alexander POPE who had introduced him into the *Dunciad* as one of the contestants for a prize offered by the Goddess of Dullness.

Hill, Edward Burlingame (1872-), American composer, critic, and lecturer who studied with John K. PAINE at Harvard University, and with Charles WIDOR at Paris; also with George W. CHADWICK. He has taught in the Music Department of Harvard University since 1918: his compositions include several symphonies and other orchestral works; a concerto for violin; chamber music; vocal music, and piano pieces.

Hill, Ureli Corelli (1802-1875), American violinist, conductor, and one of the founders of the NEW YORK PHILHARMONIC-SYMPHONY ORCHESTRA in 1842, serving as one of its conductors until 1847. In 1843 he formed a string quartet which was one of the first organizations of its kind to give public recitals in New York.

Hill, William Ebsworth (1817-1895), English maker of violins and bows which were awarded prizes at expositions in London and Paris. He was a member of the firm of W. E. Hill and Sons, violin makers and publishers of important reference works on famous violin makers including *Antonio Stradivari: His Life and Work* (1909); *Giovanni Paolo Maggini: His Life and Work; The Violin-makers of the Guarneri Family.*

Hiller, Wendy (1912-), English stage and screen actress who made her debut at the Manchester Repertory Theatre in 1930, and made her first appearances in London (1935) and New York (1936) in *Love on the Dole.* She has played leading roles in several films including *Lancashire Luck; Pygmalion,* and *Major Barbara.*

Hillyer, Robert (1895-), American poet educated at Harvard and Copenhagen Universities:

he served as an ambulance driver during World War I, and won a citation from the French Government. His works include *Sonnets and Other Lyrics* (1917); *The Five Books of Youth; The Gates of the Compass; Collected Verse* which won the Pulitzer Prize for poetry in 1934; *Pattern of a Day.*

Hilton, James (1900-), English novelist educated at Cambridge University who engaged in journalistic work before publishing his first novel, *Catherine Herself,* in 1920. This was followed by *And Now Goodbye; Was It Murder?; Ill Wind; Knight Without Armour,* filmed with Marlene DIETRICH; *The Lost Horizon,* filmed with Ronald COLMAN; *We Are Not Alone,* also filmed; *Goodbye, Mr. Chips,* filmed with Robert DONAT and Greer GARSON; *Rage in Heaven,* also filmed; *Random Harvest,* filmed with Greer Garson and Ronald Colman; *The Story of Dr. Wassell.*

Himation, a garment worn by the ancient Greeks: it consisted of a square mantle thrown over the left shoulder, fastened at the neck in such a way as to leave the right free. The ability to carry the himation gracefully was considered evidence that the wearer was of gentle birth.

Hindemith, Paul (1895-), German violinist and composer who studied with Bernhard Sekles and Arnold Mendelssohn at the Hochschen Konservatorium in Frankfort, and became concertmaster at the Frankfort Opera. He became a viola specialist, playing in the Amar-Hindemith Quartet, and appearing in 1937 with the NEW YORK PHILHARMONIC-SYMPHONY ORCHESTRA as soloist in his viola concerto. He was first a composer of the ATONAL school, but his later works give evidence of a return to the tenets of tonality: they include several operas and ballets; concertos for violin, piano, viola, and orchestra; orchestral works; chamber music; piano sonatas and pieces.

Hindus, Maurice Gerschon (1891-), Russian-American author who came to the United States in 1905, and was educated at Colgate University. His works include *The Russian Peasant and the Revolution* (1920); *Broken Earth; Red Bread; Moscow Skies; We Shall Live Again; To Sing With the Angels.*

Hipkins, Alfred James (1826-1903), English lecturer and performer on ancient musical instruments: he contributed to the "Encyclopedia Britannica" and "Grove's Dictionary of Music and Musicians," and wrote *Old Keyboard Instruments* (1887), and *A Description and History of the Pianoforte.*

Hippodamus, Greek architect and engineer of the 5th century, B.C., who laid out the Piraeus (harbor) of Athens for PERICLES, and later constructed the city of Rhodes in 408 B.C. He worked on geometrical principles in accordance with a carefully devised system of his own creation.

Hippodrome, the track provided by the ancient Greeks for chariot and horse racing: the course was constructed with a width of 400 feet so that twelve or more chariots could compete at one time, and a length of 600 to 700 feet. Many painters of Greek pictures have depicted their own ideas of the appearance of the track and the quarters reserved for spectators.

Hire or **Hyre, Laurent de la** (1606-1656), French painter who studied with his father and with Fritz L'Allemand at FONTAINEBLEAU: his works include *Laban Searching for His Idols; Jesus Appearing to the Three Marys; St. Peter Healing the Sick; Pope Nicholas V Opening the Tomb of St. Francis of Assisi; The Breaking of Bread; Conversion of St. Paul; Infancy of Bacchus;* he was one of the twelve founders in 1648 of the French Academy of Painting.

Hiroshige, Ando (1797-1858), Japanese painter and printer who was a pupil of Toyohiro. His art is as natural and realistic as that of HOKUSAI, and he was especially skillful in creating atmospheric effects. His works include *Eight Views of Omi; Mishima in Morning Fog; Hundred Views of Yedo; Thirty-six Views of Fuji; Rain at Shono; Houcho Meisho.* Some of his pupils used his name in the form of Hiroshige II, Hiroshige III, etc.

Hirschbein, Perez (1880-), Yiddish dramatist born in Lithuania: his plays which afford striking pictures of poverty among the Lithuanian Jews, have been presented at Yiddish theatres throughout Europe and America. They include *Eva; The Snowstorm; The Stranger; The Carcass; Across the River.*

Hispanic Society Art Gallery (New York City), an art museum in the building occupied by the Hispanic Society of America, an organization founded in 1904 to promote the study of Spanish and Portuguese literature and art. The gallery has a collection of works by Spanish painters including MURILLO, El GRECO, VELASQUEZ, and GOYA: also old ivories and other rare art treasures.

Histrion, in drama a term in French, derived from the Latin, for an actor. It was originally the Latin name for a buffoon. The noun *histrionics* means either the art of dramatic representation or the theatrical mannerisms of a particular actor.

Hitchcock, Alfred (1900-), English film director early associated with Michael Balcon and Victor Saville in the Gainsborough Studios at Islington. His pictures include a silent version of Mrs. BELLOC-LOWNDES' novel, *The Lodger:* also *Easy Virtue; Juno and the Paycock; The Skin Game; Waltzes from Vienna; The Man Who Knew Too Much; Strauss' Great Waltz; The Thirty-nine Steps; Secret Agent; The Lady Vanishes; Jamaica Inn; Suspicion; Saboteur; Shadow of a Doubt.*

Hitchcock, Raymond (1870-1929), American stage comedian and singer who achieved his first success with the Castle Square Opera Company playing a variety of parts in light operas. Among the productions in which he appeared were *We 'Uns of Tennessee; A Dangerous Maid; The Belle of Bridgeport; King Dodo; The Student King; The Beauty Shop; Hitchy-Koo; The Yankee Consul; The Red Widow; Words and Music; The Old Soak; Easy Dawson; Just Fancy; The Galloper.*

Hitchcock, Ripley (1857-1918), American art critic and author, educated at Harvard who acted as critic for the New York *Tribune*, and lectured extensively: his notable works include *Etchings in America* (1886) and *American Paintings in Water Color*.

Hittites, the name now given to the people in a wide area of ancient Asia Minor, especially in relation to sculptures which were crude, but revealed remarkable powers of invention: their art closely resembles that of Assyria.

Hittorf, Jacques Ignace (1792-1867), French architect whose works include the Church of St. Vincent de Paul, the Circus of the Champs Elysées and decorations for both the Place de l'Étoile and the Place de la Concorde. He also designed the Gare du Nord, the classical column in the Place Vendôme, and the base for the obelisk brought by Napoleon I from Egypt.

H. M. S. Pinafore, an operetta with libretto by Sir William S. GILBERT, and music by Sir Arthur SULLIVAN: first produced at the Opera-Comique, London, in 1878. The story is: On board Her Majesty's ship, Pinafore, the admiral, Sir Joseph Porter, announces his desire to marry Josephine, the Captain's daughter, but she is in love with a common sailor, Ralph Rackstraw. She tells Ralph how hopeless their situation is: when he threatens to shoot himself, Josephine promises to elope with him that night. A sailor, Dick Deadeye, reports their plans to Captain Corcoran and the angry Admiral orders Ralph put in irons. But Little Buttercup tells the Admiral that many years ago, when two babies were given her to care for, she mixed them up so that the low-born Corcoran rose to be a captain, while the high-born Ralph remained a plain sailor. Sir Joseph orders the two men to change ratings: Ralph becomes the captain and wins the hand of Josephine, while Captain Corcoran becomes a common sailor, and marries Little Buttercup. There is a Victor recording of the complete operetta by the D'Oyly Carte Company, and an abridged version by the Columbia Light Opera Company.

Hoban, James (c.1761-1831), Irish-American architect educated in Dublin who came to the United States a few years before the Revolutionary War. In 1792 his designs for the president's home in Washington, D. C., later called the White House, were accepted. It was erected under his supervision and he directed its rebuilding after the British destroyed it in 1814. He also worked for twenty-five years on the Capitol and other government buildings.

Hobart, Alice Tisdale (1882-), American author educated at the University of Chicago and at the Kansas State University. Her works include *Pidgin Cargo* (1929), republished in 1934 as *River Supreme; Oil for the Lamps of China; Yang and Yin; Their Own Country*. She acquired her knowledge of Chinese life through marrying an American whose business carried him into remote parts of China, Magnolia, and Manchuria.

Hobbema, Meindert (1638-1709), Dutch painter who is said to have been a pupil of Jacob van RUISDAEL: his notable works include *Showery Weather; Avenue at Middelharnis; The Water Mill; The Edge of the Forest; Dutch Village; The Old Oak Trees*. His favorite scenes were those of the Dutch countryside, and his drawings of trees and foliage, whether thick or feathery, was minute in detail and exquisitely shaded.

Hobbes, John Oliver, see **Craigie, Pearl.**

Hoboken Melodrama, the term by which the productions of the Hoboken Theatrical Company, founded in 1928 by Christopher MORLEY with Cleon THROCKMORTON, were familiarly known to New York theatregoers who traveled to Hoboken by ferry to see revivals of *After Dark* and *The Black Crook* as well as other melodramas and stage spectacles. The scenery and lighting, as well as the stage direction and gestures and inflections of the actors, followed the methods used from 1860 to 1900 in American theatres playing productions of this character.

Hobson's Choice, in literature an expression indicating a choice without alternative: so called in allusion to the custom of a 17th century English livery stable keeper, at Cambridge, Thomas Hobson by name, who made customers renting a horse take the one nearest the door, and not some particular steed which they happened to fancy. A successful play by Harold BRIGHOUSE produced in 1916 was given this expression as a title.

Höckert, Johan Fredrik (1826-1866), Swedish painter who studied at the Stockholm Academy with Johan Boklund, and in Munich, later becoming professor at the Stockholm Academy. Among his finest works are *Bandits; Queen Christina Ordering the Execution of Monaldeschi; Lapland Wedding; Divine Service in a Lapland Chapel; Peasant Woman at the Hearth; Dead Body of Charles XI*. He visited Lapland in order to obtain authentic sketches for his pictures.

Hodge, William (1874-1932), American actor who made his debut in a stock company managed by his brother: he also appeared with the ROGERS BROTHERS in *Reign of Error*; with James A. HERNE in *Sag Harbor*; in Charles FROHMAN's production of *Sky Farm*; George ADE's *Peggy from Paris*, and in *Mrs. Wiggs of the Cabbage Patch*. His greatest success was *The Man from Home*, a play by Booth TARKINGTON and Harry Leon Wilson in which he toured for several years.

Hodgson, Ralph (1877-), English poet who lived in the United States for a few years, and lectured on English literature at Sendai University in Japan. His works include *The Last Blackbird and Other Lines* (1907); *The Bull; Eve and Other Poems; The Mystery and Other Poems; The Song of Honour; Poems*.

Hofer, Karl (1878-), German painter who studied at the Karlsruhe Academy, worked at Paris, attended classes at the Stuttgart Academy, entered the studio of Hans Thoma at Zurich, and was appointed professor in the School of Applied Arts at Berlin. His favorite subjects are still-lifes, circuses and scenes in the home: an excellent example is his canvas, *The Card Players*, showing the influence of CEZANNE, PICASSO, and DERAIN.

Hoffman, Josef (1870-), Austrian architect who studied with Otto Wagner, and founded the Viennese Workshops in 1903, a forerunner of the Bauhaus at Dessau. His designs include the Stoclet House, Brussels, buildings for the Cologne Exposition in 1914, and for the Paris Exhibition in 1925.

Hoffman, Malvina (1887-), American sculptor who studied at the French Academy, and with Herbert ADAMS, Gutzon BORGLUM and Auguste RODIN. Her reputation was assured by her studies of Anna PAVLOWA's dance poses: among her notable works are *Russian Bacchanale; Pavlowa Gavotte; Russian Dancers; Ivan Mestrovic; The Sacrifice*, a group; also a hundred portraits, figures, and groups of racial types executed for the *Hall of Man* in the Field Museum, Chicago.

Hoffmann, Ernst Theodor Amadeus (1776-1822), German artist, musician, and author who led an irregular, dissipated life, but succeeded in writing some of the most demoniac tales of horrific madness and the supernatural: they include *The Devil's Elixir; Tales of the Night; Fantastic Tales in the Style of Callot; The Brothers Serapion; Weird Tales.* Jacques OFFENBACH composed an opera, *The Tales of Hoffmann*, based on his stories.

Hofmann, Heinrich (1824-1911), German painter who studied at the Düsseldorf Academy under Theodor Hildebrandt and Johann SCHADOW, and spent several years in Italy. His works include *The Burial of Christ; Othello and Desdemona; Venus and Cupid; Christ in the Temple; Christ and the Adulteress; The Sermon on the Lake; Apotheosis of Ancient Greek Heroes:* he was especially praised for his religious paintings.

Hofmann, Josef (1876-), Polish pianist who studied with his father, played in public at six years of age and toured Europe and the United States in 1887-88. He retired from the concert stage for six years and studied with Anton RUBINSTEIN for two years, making his debut at Dresden in 1894 with tremendous success: after touring for several years he returned to the United States in 1898, and was heard regularly there in recital until 1938 when he celebrated his 50th anniversary as a concert artist. From 1924 to 1938 he was director and head of the piano department in the Curtis Institute of Music, Philadelphia: he composed (under the pen name "Michel Dvorsky") five piano concertos and many piano pieces.

Hofmannsthal, Hugo von (1874-1929), Austrian poet and dramatist who studied at the University of Vienna. He wrote the librettos for several of Richard STRAUSS' operas including *Electra, Ariadne at Naxos, The Rose Cavalier, The Woman Without a Shadow,* and *Egyptian Helen.* Strauss in turn wrote the incidental music for some of his plays, and Max REINHARDT produced several of them including an adaptation of *Everyman,* the English morality play.

Hogarth, William (1697-1764), English painter and engraver considered the greatest satirist and caricaturist of his period. Among his most famous works are *The Taste of the Town; Buckingham Gate; Paradise Lost; Hudibras; The Harlot's Progress; The Rake's Progress; Marriage à la Mode; Work and Idleness; Southwark Fair; The Enraged Musician; Analysis of Beauty; Polly Peachum; Sigismunda Weeping Over the Heart of Her Husband; David Garrick as Richard III; Shrimp Girl.* He also executed a self-portrait with his dog, Trump. Horace Walpole said of him: "Hogarth's pictures are the most faithful criticisms on our way of life that we have had for a hundred years."

Hoitsu, Sakai (1761-1828), Japanese painter of noble birth who was greatly influenced by Ogata KORIN: he specialized in water colors which give evidence of brilliancy because of the purity of the pigments used. He made a collection of Korin's works containing several thousand designs.

Hokusai, Katsushika (1760-1849), Japanese painter and print maker who also signed himself "Shunro" and "Sori." He studied with SHUNSHO, illustrating and sometimes writing the text for little novels such as *The Story of Nichiren* and *The Little Violet of Yedo.* After some years he illustrated a higher grade of novels, legends and fairy tales. Among his best-known works are *Invitation to a Cock Fight; Travellers at an Inn; The Wave; Dance of the Shietus;* the celebrated *Mangwa* (Ten Thousand Sketches) in fifteen volumes; *Views of Famous Bridges.* He is said, without documentary confirmation, to have executed over 30,000 drawings.

Holbein the Elder, Hans (c.1460-1524), German painter of whom little is known except that he was either the pupil of Martin SCHONGAUER or influenced by him. His works include altarpieces for the abbey at Weingarten; *Coronation of the Virgin; Adoration; Martyrdom of St. Dorothy;* several *Passion* series; the *Altarpiece of St. Sebastian; The Fountain of Life.*

Holbein the Younger, Hans (1497-1543), German painter who studied with his father, Hans HOLBEIN THE ELDER and with Hans BURGKMAIR. He was an artist of extraordinary versatility who included portraiture, the illustration of books, wood cuts, the adornment of buildings, and glass painting among his activities. His works include more than eighty drawings for *Erasmus' Praise of Folly; The Last Supper; Portrait of a Man; Flagellation; Dead Christ; Madonna of Burgomaster Meyer; Samuel Reproving Saul; Venus with Cupid; Christ Crowned with Thorns; Pilate Washing His Hands; Head of the Virgin.* Among his wood cuts which are regarded as second only to those of Albrecht DURER, is *The Dance of Death,* a series of 58 plates.

Holberg, Ludwig, Baron (1684-1754), Danish dramatist born in Norway and called "the father of Danish comedy." His works include *Peder Paars* (1919), a mock-epic poem; several plays including *Ulysses of Ithaca, Erasmus Montanus, The Busy Man,* and *The Fickle-Minded Woman* which gained him the title "the Moliere of Denmark"; a history of Denmark; a history of the Jews. He was one of the first to write in Danish, and is considered the founder of its literature. Edvard GRIEG composed an orchestral suite, *In Holberg's Time,* as a tribute to him.

Holbrooke, Josef (1878-), English composer who studied composition with Frederick CORDER at the Royal Academy of Music at London: his compositions include several operas; two ballets; several orchestral works including four symphonies; chamber music; piano pieces and songs.

Holcroft, Thomas (1745-1809), English dramatist whose first play, *The Crisis,* was produced in 1778 at the Drury Lane Theatre, London: his most successful drama, *The Road to Ruin* was staged in 1792, and has been revived several times. He translated Beaumarchais' *The Marriage of Figaro* from memory after seeing it presented in Paris several times, and produced it at London with considerable success in 1784.

Hold, in music a sign ⊙ over or ‿ under a note or rest indicating the prolonging of a note or rest at the discretion of the player: when placed over a bar the sign indicates a slight pause before the next part of the music is begun.

Holinshed, Raphael (c.1520-c.1580), English historian who published a work, *The Chronicles of England, Scotland and Ireland* in 1578, of which the English part was his own work, and the balance drawn from other writers. Shakespeare and several other Elizabethan playwrights drew largely on his works for dramatic material.

Holl, Frank (1845-1888), English painter who studied at the Royal Academy where he won a gold medal for his painting, *The Sacrifice of Abraham,* and a two-year course of study in Italy for *The Lord Gave and the Lord Hath Taken Away.* His notable works include *No Tidings from the Sea; Village Funeral; Her First-Born; Gifts of the Fairies; Absconded; Ordered to the Front; Home Again.*

Holland, George (1791-1870), English actor who appeared with great success on tours of the United States in comedy parts such as Tony Lumpkin in *She Stoops to Conquer.* His son, **Edmund Milton Holland** (1848-1913), appeared with Joseph JEFFERSON in the first production of *Rip Van Winkle* in 1859: among the plays in which he distinguished himself later were *Hazel Kirke; Jim the Penman; A Pair of Spectacles; Colonel Carter of Cartersville; A Social Highwayman; Eben Holden; The House of a Thousand Candles.* His brother, **Joseph Jefferson Holland** (1860-1926), was one of America's finest character actors despite the fact that he was deaf for some years: he appeared in support of several famous stars including Ethel BARRYMORE and William FAVERSHAM.

Holland, Josiah Gilbert (1819-1881), American editor, poet, and novelist who assisted in the founding of *Scribner's Magazine* in 1870, and held the post of editor until his death. His novels include *Arthur Bonnicastle, Nicholas Minturn,* and *The Story of Sevenoaks:* he also wrote two poems in narrative form and used the pen name "Timothy Titcomb."

Hollman, Joseph (1852-1927), French violoncellist who studied at the Paris Conservatory under Francois SERVAIS and Joseph FETIS. He toured Europe from 1875 and the United States in 1897, giving joint recitals with Johannes Wolff, the distinguished Dutch violinist.

Hollywood Bowl, an open air amphitheatre opened at Hollywood, California, in 1922 with a symphony concert directed by Alfred HERTZ, former conductor of German opera at the Metropolitan Opera House, New York. It occupies an area of 65 acres near the business section of Hollywood, and has a seating capacity of 20,000. Previous to 1941 a summer season of eight weeks was held each years: one night each week devoted to orchestral music, another to opera and another to a recital by some famous artist. The season tickets are low in price, and more than 4,000,000 people have attended the concerts directed by about one hundred celebrated orchestral conductors.

Holmes, Burton (1870-), American traveler, lecturer, and author who has visited and made photographs or motion-pictures in every country of the globe except Iran, Iraq, Afghanistan, and Tibet: his files contain more than 25,000 stereopticon slides and thousands of feet of film. He celebrated his fiftieth year as a travel lecturer in 1942, and has published *The Burton Holmes Travelogues* (15 volumes, 1901-1922), and *The Burton Holmes Lectures* (10 volumes, 1905).

Holmes, Sir Charles John (1868-), English painter and critic who was Slade professor of fine arts at Oxford, and director of the British National Gallery. His works include *Hokusai; Constable; Leonardo da Vinci; The Making of the National Gallery* with C. H. C. Baker.

Holmes, Oliver Wendell (1809-1894), American physician, essayist, novelist, and poet educated at Harvard: his poems include *Old Ironsides,* a poem published in 1830; *Urania; Astrea: the Balance of Illusions; Songs in Many Keys; Songs of Many Seasons; The Iron Gate.* Among his prose works are the novels *Elsie Venner; The Guardian Angel,* and *A Mortal Antipathy;* the celebrated series of table talks including *The Autocrat of the Breakfast Table; The Professor at the Breakfast Table,* and *The Poet at the Breakfast Table.* His most famous poems are "The Chambered Nautilus" and "The Wonderful One-Hoss Shay."

Holmes, Phillips (1909-1942), American stage and screen actor educated at Princeton University and at Trinity College, Cambridge, England. After appearing on the New York stage with his father, Taylor HOLMES, a well-known actor, in *The Great Necker,* he was featured in numerous films including *The Return of Sherlock Holmes; Criminal Code; An American Tragedy; Dinner at Eight; Great Expectations; The House of a Thousand Candles; Housemaster.* He joined the Royal Canadian Air Force in 1941, and was killed in a collision between two planes.

Holmes, Stuart (1887-), American stage and screen actor who studied art in Chicago, and had many years of stage experience before entering the films. Among the pictures in which he has appeared are *Tess of the d'Urbervilles; The Four Horsemen; The Prisoner of Zenda; The Man*

Who Laughs; Captain of the Guard; Devil's Island; British Intelligence.

Holmes, Taylor (1878-), American actor who made his first appearance in 1899 at Keith's Vaudeville House in Boston, later playing utility parts with Olga NETHERSOLE. Among the plays in which he appeared successfully are *The Midnight Sons; The Commuters; Marriage à la Carte; His Majesty, Bunker Bean; Your Uncle Dudley; That's Gratitude; Big-Hearted Herbert; Tobacco Road; I'd Rather Be Right*. He has also been featured in numerous films.

Holroyd, Sir Charles (1861-1917), English painter whose most notable work is an altarpiece, *Adoration of the Shepherds:* he was also a fine etcher, director of the National Gallery, London, and author of a critical work on MICHELANGELO.

Holst, Gustav Theodore (1874-1934), English composer who studied at the Royal Academy of Music, London, with Charles Villiers STANFORD, and later taught at the Royal College of Music. His compositions include *The Perfect Fool,* a successful one-act opera; *The Planets,* an orchestral suite; ballets; incidental music; numerous choral works; piano pieces and songs.

Holy Family, The, a favorite subject with famous painters including ALBERTINELLI, BAROCCIO, BARTOLOMMEO, BOURDON, CORREGGIO, CRANACH, DOMENICHINO, EL GRECO, GAROFALO, GIULIO ROMANO, MICHELANGELO, MURILLO, PARMIGIANO, PIOMBO, RAPHAEL, REMBRANDT, RUBENS, DEL SARTO, SIGNORELLI, TITIAN, VERONESE, LEONARDO DA VINCI, and VAN DYCK.

Holy Grail, see **Grail, The Holy.**

Homer, a Greek poet who is accredited in ancient tradition with the authorship of the ILIAD, the ODYSSEY, and certain hymns to the gods known as the HOMERIC HYMNS: some authorities pronounce him the author of *The Battle of the Frogs and Mice* (Batrachomyomachia). Seven cities on the Mediterranean and Asia Minor contended for the honor of being his birthplace: of these Smyrna seems to have the most ground for its claim. While some critics maintain that the *Iliad* and *Odyssey* are composite works, it appears more likely that they were the work of a poet of real genius who lived about 900 B.C.

Homer, Louise (1871-), American dramatic contralto who studied with William L. Whitney in Boston, and in Paris, making her debut in 1898 at Vichy in Verdi's *La Favorita*. After singing at Covent Garden, London, and La Monnaie, Brussels, she made her debut in 1900 at San Francisco in *Aïda* with the Metropolitan Opera Company while on tour, and her New York debut in the same opera in 1900. She sang with the Metropolitan Opera Company from 1900-19; with the Chicago Opera Company from 1920-25; and also with the Los Angeles and San Francisco Opera Companies. She has also appeared with all the major symphony orchestras, and in recital. Her husband, **Sidney Homer** (1864-), is a well-known composer of more than one hundred songs who studied with George W. CHADWICK, and at Leipzig.

Homer, Winslow (1836-1910), American painter and etcher who studied at the National Academy of Design, New York, sketched for *Harper's Weekly* during the Civil War, and later spent a year studying the painting in European museums. His notable works include *Prisoners from the Front; Rations; Home, Sweet Home; The Cotton Pickers; New England Country School; The Gulf Stream; The Life Line; Eight Bells; Lost on the Grand Banks; Northeaster; Hark! the Lark; Undertow*. His style shows no European influence, and his subjects are almost invariably selected from the American scene.

Homeric Hymns, a series of more than thirty poems which are hardly in the style of hymns, but more like PANEGYRICS of Greek gods: they are attributed to HOMER, but many authorities regard them as the creations of several poets which have been assembled in one collection, and Homer's name attached without historical evidence to warrant so doing.

Home, Sweet Home, a ballad written by John Howard Payne for an opera, *Clari, the Maid of Milan,* produced at London in 1823; the music composed by Sir Henry BISHOP, was said to be copied from an old Italian air, but was adjudged original with Bishop after the question was litigated. Gaetano DONIZETTI used a somewhat different version of the melody in his opera, *Anne Boleyn,* which led to the mistaken idea that he was its composer. The original manuscript is in the possession of the University of Rochester.

Homolka, Oscar (1901-), Austrian stage and screen actor who was trained at the Vienna Dramatic Academy, and appeared in many German and Austrian theatres from 1921 to 1934 in native dramas and translations of GALSWORTHY's *Loyalties,* WALLACE's *The Ringer* and Eugene O'NEILL's *Emperor Jones*. After learning English he made his debut in 1935 at London in *Close Quarters,* and in 1940 at New York in *Grey Farm*. He has also played in several English and American films including *Ebb Tide; Rhodes; Sabotage; Comrade X; Rage in Heaven; Ball of Fire; Mission to Moscow.*

Hondecoeter, Melchior d' (1636-1695), Dutch painter who studied with his father and with his uncle, Jan Baptista Weenix. He specialized in the painting of animals, birds, and domestic fowl: his works include *Birds in a Park; Peacock and Turkey; Menagerie of Prince William III at Loo; Hen Defending Chickens; Foreign Water Fowl; Cock Fight; Dead Game Birds by a Gun; Peacocks; Pelican.*

Honegger, Arthur (1892-), French composer who became a Swiss citizen; studied at the Zurich Conservatory, and at the Paris Conservatory with WIDOR, GEDALGE, and D'INDY. He was associated from 1920 with the group of French composers known as Les SIX. His compositions include the well-known oratorio, *King David,* and the orchestral tone poem, *PACIFIC 231:* he has also written incidental music for plays; several operas and operettas; concertos for piano, violin, and violoncello; choral music; chamber music.

Honthorst, Gerard van (1590-1656), Dutch painter who studied with Abraham BLOEMART, and spent several years in Rome. In 1628 he painted a number of portraits and historical works in England for CHARLES I, later executing similar works for the princes of Orange and for the king of Denmark. His canvases include *The Lute Player; Pilate Washing His Hands; Christ in the Temple; Christ before Pilate; The Music Lesson; Peter; Denial of Christ; Lot and His Daughters; St. Cecilia at the Organ.*

Hooch, Pieter de (c.1629-c.1677), Dutch painter who may have studied with Nicolaes BERCHEM, and was intimate with Jan VEMEER. He was fond of painting the interiors of Dutch homes with their quaint furniture and glistening utensils: among his best works are *Interior of a Dutch House; Family Concert; Domestic Scene; The Linen Cupboard; The Card Players; Door of a Tavern; Woman Combing Her Child's Hair; The Cellar; The Lace Maker.*

Hood, Raymond Mathewson (1881-1934), American architect who studied at the Massachusetts Institute of Technology, Boston, and in Paris at the ECOLE DES BEAUX-ARTS. From 1914 to 1927 he practiced alone in New York: his design in association with John Mead Howells for the Chicago *Tribune* Building in the form of a tower won the prize in an international competition: among his notable works are the Beaux Arts Apartments, the McGraw-Hill Building, and the *Daily News* building in New York. His designs are regarded as practical and suitable for their purposes without being extreme in conception.

Hood, Thomas (1799-1845), English novelist and poet who was a master of both humor and pathos: his first volume was entitled *Whims and Oddities* (1826): it was followed by *Plea of the Midsummer Fairies; Lamia; Dream of Eugene Aram; Tylney Hall,* a novel; *Song of the Shirt; Bridge of Sighs; Miss Kilmansegg.* He was one of the most imitated of English poets.

Hoogstraten, Samuel van (1627-1678), Dutch painter who studied with his father and with REMBRANDT: his works include *The Sick Girl; Lady Walking in a Courtyard; The Old Jew.* His work in its light, cool tones has been compared with that of Pieter de HOOCH, and he wrote an excellent treatise entitled *Introduction to the School of High Art.*

Hoogstraten, Willem van, see **Van Hoogstraten, Willem.**

Hook, James Clarke (1819-1907), English painter who studied at the Royal Academy, London, and won a traveling scholarship in Italy with his picture *Rizpah Watching Saul's Dead Sons.* After painting Italian subjects, he completed a series of English pastorals and marine pictures including *Rest by the Wayside; Morning After a Gale; Jetsam and Flotsam; Hearts of Oak; Fish from the Doggerbank; Market Girls at a Fjord; The Stream; A Dream of Ancient Venice; Signal on the Horizon.*

Hooker, William (1880-), American author: his works include *The Right Man* (1908); the

libretto for Horatio W. PARKER'S grand opera, *Mona; The Professor's Mystery,* a play with Wells Hastings; the libretto for Parker's opera, *Fairyland,* and his oratorio, *Morven and the Grail.*

Hopak, see **Fair at Sorotchinsk, The.**

Hope, Anthony, pen name of **Sir Anthony Hope Hawkins** (1863-1933), English novelist and dramatist educated at Oxford and trained for the bar. His works include *A Man of Mark* (1889); *Father Stafford; Sport Royal; A Change of Air; The Prisoner of Zenda,* published in 1892, widely imitated, translated and produced on the stage, and filmed as was its sequel, *Rupert of Hentzau.* No one of his later novels or plays achieved anything approximating the success of the two last-named works.

Hope, Bob, contemporary American stage, screen, and radio comedian who gained his experience in vaudeville, and appeared for the first time on the New York stage in 1927 under the name of Lester Hope in *The Sidewalks of New York,* and later in several other plays. He entered the films in 1934: since 1939 he has appeared in *The Cat and the Canary; The Ghost Breakers; The Road to Singapore; The Road to Zanzibar; Caught in the Draft; Nothing But the Truth; My Favorite Blond; The Road to Morocco; They Got Me Covered.* He is also a favorite radio comedian.

Hopekirk, Helen (1856-), Scottish pianist and composer who studied with Alexander MACKENZIE and Theodor LESCHETIZKY at Vienna, making her debut at the GEWANDHAUS, Leipzig, in 1878. In 1883 she came to the United States to appear with all the major orchestras: after living in Vienna and touring Europe she settled at Boston, Mass., in 1896, teaching in the NEW ENGLAND CONSERVATORY OF MUSIC, and also privately. Her compositions include a piano concerto; pieces for orchestras; two sonatas for violin and piano; piano pieces; violin pieces and many songs.

Hopkins, Arthur (1878-), American theatrical producer and dramatist who was first a journalist: his productions include *The Poor Little Rich Girl; Evangeline; On Trial; Samson and Delilah; The Jest; The Beggar's Opera; Voltaire; Hedda Gabler; Anna Christie; Hamlet* with John BARRYMORE; *What Price Glory?; Burlesque; The Hairy Ape; Petrified Forest.* His successful plays include *Conquest* (1933) and *Burlesque;* the latter in collaboration.

Hopkins, Miriam (1904-), American stage and screen actress educated at Syracuse University who first appeared in 1921 as a dancer in the *Music Box Revue.* Among the plays in which she has appeared are *Little Jessie James; An American Tragedy; Flight; The Bachelor Father; Lysistrata; Jezebel.* She entered the films in 1932: among the pictures in which she has played important roles are *Dr. Jekyl and Mr. Hyde; The Smiling Lieutenant; Design for Living; Becky Sharp; Barbary Coast; These Three; The Old Maid; Virginia City; Gentlemen after Dark.*

Hopkinson, Francis (1737-1791), American statesman, poet, and composer who was admitted to the bar in 1761, signed the Declaration of Independence in 1776, and had much to do with the designing of the American flag. His musical compositions include a cantata, *The Temple of Minerva* (1781), and several songs including *My Days Have Been So Wondrous Free:* these were published in 1788 in a collection dedicated to George Washington, and constituted the first volume of music of its kind issued by an American composer.

Hopper, (William) De Wolf (1858-1935), American comedian and singer who made his debut in 1879 in *Our Boys,* appearing later with FROHMAN's Madison Square Company, the McCaull Opera Company, and WEBER AND FIELDS. Among the productions in which he appeared were Gilbert and Sullivan operas; *Wang; Happyland; The Better 'Ole; Erminie; Uncle Tom's Cabin.* He made several radio broadcasts in 1932, and published *Once a Clown Always a Clown* in collaboration with W. W. Stout.

Hopper, Edna Wallace (1864-   ), American actress who made her debut in 1891 at New York in *The Club Friend:* she was also a member of the Charles FROHMAN Stock Company, and appeared in musical comedy with De Wolf HOPPER to whom she was married for a time. She played important roles in *Floradora; The Silver Slipper; Jumping Jupiter* with Richard Carle; *Girl o' Mine;* also with the Lew Fields' Company and in vaudeville.

Hopper, Edward (1882-   ), American painter and engraver who studied at the William Merritt CHASE School, New York, and at Paris where he came under the influence of RENOIR, SISLEY, and PISSARRO. He returned to New York in 1907, and is best-known for his oil paintings such as *Lighthouse at Two Lights* in which sunshine floods a lighthouse standing out clearly in a cloudless sky. His etchings are also distinguished for their clearcut quality.

Hoppin, Augustus (1828-1896), American illustrator and writer first trained for the law. His drawings appeared in *Putnam's Magazine,* and he was highly commended for his illustrations for Benjamin SHILLABER's *Life and Sayings of Mrs. Partington,* Oliver Wendell HOLMES' *The Autocrat of the Breakfast Table,* and George William CURTIS' *Potiphar Papers.* He was the author of several interesting travel volumes.

Hoppner, John (1758-1810), English painter who was first a chorister in the Royal Chapel, and later became a portrait painter rivaling Sir Thomas LAWRENCE for twenty years. He painted the royal family and members of the court including the Countess of Oxford, William Pitt, Baron Grenville, the Duke of Kent, and the Duke of Wellington. He also translated some Oriental poems into English verse.

Hopwood, Avery (1882-1928), American dramatist whose works include *Clothes,* with Channing POLLOCK (1906); *Fair and Warmer; The Gold Diggers; The Bat* with Mary Roberts RINEHART; *Ladies' Night* with Carlton Andrews; *The Demi-Virgin; Little Miss Bluebeard.* He left an

endowment to the University of Michigan the income from which is to be used for prizes in all fields of literary endeavor.

Horace or **Quintus Horatius Flaccus** (65 B.C.- 8 B.C.), Latin poet who studied at Rome, fought by the side of BRUTUS at Philippi, and was intimate with VERGIL. His works include *Satires; Epodes; Odes; Epistles:* the latter contains the famous *Ars poetica.* His talent was equally great in the composition of lyric or satirical verse.

Horae, in Greek mythology three goddesses who presided over the order of the seasons and the resultant changes in nature of growth and decay. Their names were *Irene, Dice,* and *Eumonia:* they were the daughters of ZEUS and Themis, and were the incarnation of peace, justice, and order.

Hora Staccato (Dinicu), a lively and extremely original musical composition composed and played entirely from memory by a Rumanian gypsy violinist, Dinicu, in the presence of the Russian violinist, Jascha HEIFETZ, at a café in Bucharest. Heifetz induced Dinicu to jot down a rough draft of the piece, and later played it in concert: there is a Victor recording by Heifetz, and a Columbia recording by Dinicu and his orchestra.

Horatii, The, in Roman legend three brothers who fought with the Curiatii in the war of Tullus Hostilius against Alba Longa. Two of the Horatii were slain: the third pretended to fly, and by this ruse was able to kill the Curiatii one at a time. Upon his return victorious, he killed his sister, Horatia, because she grieved over the death of one of the Curiatii to whom she was betrothed, and was sentenced to be humiliated by being led under a yoke for his crime.

Horgan, Paul (1903-   ), American novelist educated at the New Mexico Military Institute: in 1923 he became connected with the EASTMAN Theatre at Rochester, N. Y., as an assistant to Rouben MAMOULIAN, and in 1926 he assumed the post of librarian at the New Mexico Military Institute. His works include *Men of Arms* (1931); *The Fault of Angels; No Quarter Given; Main Line West; A Lamp on the Plains; Figures in a Landscape; Firelight.*

Horn, Alfred Aloysius (c.1861-1931), English trader in ivory and rubber on the West Coast of Africa: his book, *Trader Horn,* was published in 1927 by the Literary Guild, New York, with an introduction by John GALSWORTHY. Received favorably by critics some of whom appear not to have taken the volume too seriously, it became a best-seller, and was also filmed with success. Two sequels which followed failed to achieve success.

Horniman, Annie Elizabeth Fredericka (1860- 1937), English theatrical producer and manager who became secretary to William Butler YEATS, and was connected with the production of plays from 1894. She leased the ABBEY THEATRE at Dublin in 1904, the Gaiety Theatre, Manchester, in 1908, and the Court Theatre, London, in 1912, producing more than two hundred plays including *Hindle Wakes, The Younger Generation,* and *The Mob;* also exerting a powerful influence on both the English and American stage.

Hornung, Ernest William (1866-1921), English novelist who went to Australia because of ill health, and during World War I served as librarian for the Young Men's Christian Association in France. He married Constance Doyle, sister of Sir Arthur Conan DOYLE: his works include *The Amateur Cracksman* (1899); *Dead Men Tell No Tales; Raffles: Further Adventures of the Amateur Cracksman; At Large; The Shadow of the Rope; Stingaree; A Thief in the Night; Further Adventures of A. J. Raffles; The Crime Doctor.* Kyrle BELLEW appeared with tremendous success in a dramatization of the Raffles stories.

Horoscope, a ballet in one act: book and music by Constant LAMBERT; choreography by Frederick ASHTON; first produced at the SADLER'S WELLS Theatre, London, in 1938. The plot revolves around a young man whose destinies are ruled by the sun in *Leo,* and a young woman whose life is guided by the sun in *Virgo.* They are brought together by *Gemini,* and finally united by the moon. The choreography is regarded by critics as one of Ashton's finest conceptions.

Horowitz, Vladimir (1904-), Russian pianist who studied with Felix Blumenfeld at Kiev, and made his debut at Kharkov in 1921. He toured Europe with tremendous success, and made his American debut with the New York Philharmonic-Symphony Orchestra in 1928, creating a sensation, and appearing with all the major orchestras. He is the son-in-law of Arturo TOSCANINI, and has made many fine recordings in addition to appearing in recital on tours throughout the United States.

Horsley, John Callcott (1817-1903), English painter who studied at the Royal Academy, and painted *The Spirit of Religion* and *Satan Touched by Ithuriel's Spear* in the Palace of Westminster. His canvases include *The Pride of the Village; Hide and Seek; Lady Jane Grey and Roger Ascham; A Pleasant Corner; Cupboard Love; Château Gardens at Fontainebleau; Scenes from Don Quixote; Old Folk and Young Folk.*

Horton, Edward Everett (1887-), American stage and screen actor educated at Oberlin and Columbia Universities who made his first New York appearance in 1908 with Louis Mann in *The Man Who Stood Still:* and after assuming leading roles in numerous plays including *The Governor's Lady; The Nervous Wreck,* and *Smilin' Through,* began his career in the films. He has appeared in more than one hundred pictures in which his characterizations of persons in various stages of nervous disquiet have diverted millions of film fans.

Hoschna, Karl (c.1870-1911), Bohemian oboist and composer who studied at the Vienna Conservatory, and came to the United States in 1896. He was the composer of several popular operettas and musical plays including *The Yama Yama Man; Three Twins; Jumping Jupiter,* and his greatest success, *Madame Sherry.*

Hosmer, Harriet Goodhue (1830-1908), American sculptor who studied and lived for some time in Rome: among her finest works are *Oenone;*

Beatrice Cenci; Zenobia; The Sleeping Faun; The Waking Faun; Puck: the last-named statue has been copied many times.

Hôtel de Bourgogne, a celebrated theatre in Paris which was the home of drama and farce during the 16th and 17th centuries. The Italian COMEDIA DELL' ARTE gave performances there: it became the COMEDIE-FRANCAISE when it was merged with the company at the Hôtel Guénégaud, previously formed from the players in the Théâtre du Marais and Molière's troupe which disbanded after his death.

Houbraken, Arnold (1660-1719), Dutch painter who studied with Samuel van HOOGSTRATEN, and later with REMBRANDT. His notable works include *Ecce homo; Model Posing; Virginia's Body Brought to Rome.* His son, **Jacobus Houbraken** (1698-1780), was a fine engraver who prepared about one hundred plates for a publication known as *Heads of Illustrious Persons of Great Britain* issued from 1743 to 1752.

Houdon, Jean Antoine (1741-1828), French sculptor who studied with PIGALLE, and after winning the Prix de Rome studied in Italy for several years: among his finest works are the statues or busts of *St. Bruno; St. John the Baptist; Morpheus; Benjamin Franklin* made when the great statesman was in Paris; *The Bather; Voltaire; Molière; La Fontaine; Thomas Jefferson; Diana; Shivering Woman; Mirabeau.* In 1785 he came to the United States to make the necessary measurements for the statue of *George Washington* now in Richmond, Va.

Hough, Emerson (1857-1923), American novelist educated for the bar at the University of Iowa: his works include *The Story of the Cowboy* (1897); *The Mississippi Bubble; The Law of the Land; The Covered Wagon* which became a popular film under the direction of James Cruze; *The Magnificent Adventure; The Man Next Door; The Passing of the Frontier.* He also wrote a series of Alaskan stories for boys, and had much influence in securing protection by the government for wild animals in Yellowstone and other national parks.

Houghton, Arthur Boyd (1836-1875), English painter and illustrator: among his best canvases are *The Transformation of King Beder,* and *In Captivity.* His finest work as an illustrator was accomplished in his drawings of children, and in his superb illustrations of Dalziel's *Arabian Nights* into which he has infused much of the innate glamour and romance of the text.

Houghton, William Stanley (1881-1913), English dramatic critic and playwright educated at Bowdoin College: his plays include *The Dear Departed* (1910); *The Younger Generation; Independent Means; Fancy Free; Hindle Wakes; The Master of the House.*

Houseman, John, see **Welles, Orson.**

Housman, Alfred Edward (1859-1936), English poet, scholar, and editor; educated at Oxford and later professor of Latin at Cambridge and other colleges. His poetical works include *A Shropshire Lad* (1896) and *Last Poems* (1922); he also edited fine editions of Manilius, JUVENAL, and LUCAN, and published an essay entitled *The Name and Nature of Poetry.*

Housman, Laurence (1865-   ), English novelist, poet, artist, and dramatist who first studied art and won recognition through his illustrations of works by SHELLEY and MEREDITH. His first work, *An Englishwoman's Love Letters* (1900), published anonymously, was a real success: it was followed by *Trimblerigg* and *The Duke of Flamborough,* both satires on politics. His plays include *Lysistrata,* an adaptation; *Bird in Hand; Prunella* with GRANVILLE-BARKER; *Victoria Regina*: the latter had great success in New York and on tour with Helen HAYES in the title role. His poems include *Green Arras* and *Spikenard.*

Houssaye, Arsène (1815-1896), French novelist, dramatist, and critic: his works include the novels *The Sinner; The Beautiful Raffaëlla,* and *Romance of the Duchess;* the plays *The Caprices of the Marchioness* and *The Comedy at the Window;* also a *History of French Art in the Eighteenth Century.* His son, **Henri Houssaye** (1848-1911), was a famous newspaper editor: his works include *History of Alcibiades and the Athenian Republic; Athens, Rome and Paris; Napoleon, Man of War;* also a series of Napoleonic studies entitled *1814* and *1815,* which were reprinted nearly fifty times.

Hovenden, Thomas (1840-1895), American painter born in Ireland who studied at the South Kensington Art Schools, and after his removal to New York in 1863 at the National Academy of Design, New York. Later he was a pupil at the École des Beaux-Arts under Cabanel. His notable works include *The Last Moments of John Brown; Breaking Home Ties; News from the Conscript; A Breton Interior; Brittany Woman Spinning; Image Seller; Jerusalem the Golden.*

Hovey, Richard (1864-1900), American poet educated at Dartmouth College who lectured on English literature at Columbia University: his works include *The Laurel* (1889); *Launcelot and Guinevere; Songs from Vagabondia* with Bliss Carman; *More Songs from Vagabondia* with Bliss Carman; *The Holy Grail,* edited by his wife, Henriette Russell Hovey; *To the End of the Trail:* the two last-named were published after his death.

Howard, Bronson Crocker (1842-1908), American dramatist whose first play, *Fantine,* adapted from Victor Hugo's "Les Miserables" was produced in 1864 while he was a reporter on the Detroit *Free Press.* His first great hit, *Saratoga,* was produced in 1870: others equally successful include *The Banker's Daughter; Young Mrs. Winthrop; The Henrietta; Shenandoah.* The last-named drama made a fortune for the author and its producer, Charles FROHMAN: Howard is regarded as the dean of American dramatists.

Howard, John Tasker (1890-   ), American composer and author of books on musical subjects; educated at Williams College and pupil in composition of Howard BROCKWAY. His compositions include a fantasy for piano and orchestra,

and arrangements of songs by Stephen Foster: he has also published *Our American Music* (1931); *The Music of Washington's Time; Stephen Foster; Ethelbert Nevin; Our Contemporary Composers.*

Howard, Leslie (1893-1943), English stage and screen actor who served in World War I, and made his debut in 1917 in *Peg o' My Heart,* also appearing in *Charley's Aunt; Under Cover; East is West.* He made his American debut in 1920 at New York in *Just Suppose,* later appearing in *Danger; The Truth About Blayds; Outward Bound; The Green Hat; Her Cardboard Lover; Berkeley Square; The Animal Kingdom; The Petrified Forest; Hamlet.* He has also appeared in numerous films including *Outward Bound; Smilin' Through; The Animal Kingdom; Berkeley Square; British Agent; The Scarlet Pimpernel; Of Human Bondage; The Petrified Forest; Romeo and Juliet; Pygmalion; Intermezzo; Gone With the Wind; The Invaders; Mr. "V."; Spitfire.*

Howard, Sidney Coe (1891-1939), American dramatist educated at the University of California, and a pupil of George Pierce BAKER at the 47 Workshop at Harvard University, later serving in World War I. His successful plays include *Swords* (1921); *They Knew What They Wanted,* a Pulitzer Prize play in 1926; *Ned McCobb's Daughter; Yellow Jack; Alien Corn; The Late Christopher Bean; Dodsworth,* an adaptation of Sinclair LEWIS' novel. He also prepared the film scenarios of several of his plays.

Howe, Julia Ward (1819-1910), American poet, writer and lecturer who edited the Boston *Commonwealth* with her husband, lecturing in aid of Negro emancipation, and writing *The Battle Hymn of the Republic* which was first published in the *Atlantic Monthly* dated February, 1862. Her works include *Passion Flowers* (1854), a volume of poems; *The World's Own,* a play; *Sketches of Representative New England Women; Reminiscences,* an autobiography.

Howe, Mary (1882-   ), American composer who studied composition at the PEABODY CONSERVATORY of Music, Baltimore, with Gustav STRUBE and the piano with Ernest HUTCHESON, making her debut in 1915, and concertizing for several years. Her works include the orchestral pieces *Dirge* and *Sand; Poema* for string orchestra; a sonata for violin and piano; a ballet for two pianos and drums: *Chain Gang Song* and *Robin Hood's Heart* for chorus.

Howells, William Dean (1837-1920), American novelist, poet and dramatist who developed his literary talent in journalism, and during his five-year stay in Venice as American consul: he also edited the *Atlantic Monthly* and *Harper's Magazine.* His works include a volume of poems (1873); *The Rise of Silas Lapham* (1885); *Indian Summer; The Minister's Charge; A Hazard of New Fortunes; The Quality of Mercy; An Imperative Duty; The Kentons; The Leatherwood God.* Among his plays are *A Counterfeit Presentment* (1877); *Yorick's Love,* adapted from the Spanish; *The Garroters; The Mousetrap.* His autobiography, *A Boy's Town,* written when he was nearly eighty years old, is considered a masterpiece.

Hoxie, Vinnie Ream (1847-1914), American sculptor who won a prize of $30,000 in competition for a statue of *Lincoln* which is now in the rotunda of the Capitol at Washington, D. C. Her works include *Admiral Farragut* in Farragut Square, and *Sequoyah* in Statuary Hall at Washington, D. C.; also *Spirit of the Carnival; Sappho; The West.*

Hoyt, Charles Hale (1860-1900), American dramatist who was a journalist before he began to write plays: his successful works include *A Bunch of Keys; A Parlor Match; A Brass Monkey; A Midnight Bell; A Texas Steer; A Trip to Chinatown; A Temperance Town; A Milk White Flag.* The popularity of his comedies was largely due to his ability to satirize contemporary events before they had escaped the public mind.

Hrotswitha of Gandersheim (c.930-c.1000), German dramatist who became a Benedictine nun at twenty-three; she wrote several plays in Latin, and the manuscripts were not found until five hundred years after her death. She used the licentious play form of TERENCE in six religious plays entitled *Gallicanus; Dulcitius; Callimachus; Abraham; Paphnutius; Sapienta:* they all preach Christian virtue triumphant, and contain scenes full of genuine humor.

Hsiung, Shih I. (1902-), Chinese dramatist educated at the Peking National University who became professor of English in Peking and manager of theatres in Shanghai as well as Peking. His works include *Lady Precious Stream* produced in New York in 1936; *Mencius Was a Bad Boy; The Western Chamber; The Professor from Peking.* He has also translated plays by BARRIE into Chinese, and has written a novel, *The Bridge of Heaven.*

Huang Kung-Wang (1269-1354), Chinese painter considered one of the four masters of Yuan. He had two distinctly different styles of painting: one was monochrome in thick, bold strokes; the other employed a faint shade of brown coloring, mixed with purple and applied with delicate strokes of the brush.

Hubay, Jenö (1858-1937), Hungarian violinist and composer who studied with Joseph JOACHIM and Henri VIEUXTEMPS, later becoming professor of violin at the Brussels Conservatory and at the Pest Conservatory. He formed the Hubay String Quartet with David POPPER as violoncellist, and numbered Franz von VECSEY, Joseph SZIGETI, and Eddy BROWN among his pupils. His compositions include a popular opera, *The Violinmaker of Cremona,* four concertos, a sonata, and many fine solo pieces for the violin.

Hubbard, Elbert (1856-1915), American author and essayist who first worked as a journalist and advertising writer, studied for a time at Harvard University, and made a trip through Europe where he met William MORRIS, and later introduced many of his ideas on decoration in the United States. He founded the Roycroft Press at East

Aurora, N. Y., and published *The Philistine,* which attained a circulation of nearly a quarter million copies: his *Message to Garcia* is said to have sold 40,000,000 copies. He also published a series of 170 *Little Journeys To The Homes of Great Men.*

Hubbell, Raymond (1879-), American composer who wrote the scores for many popular musical plays including *Fantana; Mexicana; The Runaways; The Midnight Sons; A Winsome Widow; Hitchy Koo; Sonny; Three Cheers.*

Huber, Johann Rudolf (1668-1748), Swiss painter who studied with Giulio ROMANO at Mantua and with TITIAN at Venice: he became court painter to the Duke of Wurtemberg, and gained such a tremendous reputation as a portraitist that he is said to have executed more than 5000 likenesses. He is sometimes called the "Tintoretto of Switzerland."

Huberman, Bronislav (1882-), Polish violinist who studied with Isidor Lotto at Paris and with Joseph JOACHIM in Berlin: he made a sensationally successful debut at Amsterdam in 1893 and toured the United States in 1896-7 and again in 1937. He played on PAGANINI's violin in 1909 at the invitation of the city of Genoa; taught at the Vienna State Academy in 1934-36, and founded the Palestine Symphony Orchestra in 1936.

Hübner, Julius (1806-1882), German painter who studied at the Berlin Academy with Johann SCHADOW, and finally became director of the Royal Gallery at Dresden. His notable works include *Boaz and Ruth: Roland Liberating the Princess Isabella; Ruth and Naomi; Samson Breaking the Columns; Job and His Friends; Cupid in Winter; Frederick the Great at Sans-Souci.*

Hübner, Karl Wilhelm (1814-1879), German painter who studied at the Düsseldorf Academy under Johann SCHADOW, and visited America in 1874. His notable canvases include *Angry Old Man; Charity in the Cottage of the Poor; The Emigrants; The Little Wood-Thieves; Seizure for Debt; Laborer Rescuing Child from Burning House; The Outcast; Depressed Mood; Comfort in Prayer.*

Hucbald (c.840-c.930), Flemish monk and musician who studied with his uncle Milo who directed a school of singing at St.-Amand, and later succeeded him as director of the same school. He designed a musical staff on which a Greek sign in various forms was used to indicate eighteen different musical pitches.

Hudibras, a poem in mock-heroic style by Samuel BUTLER, a 17th century English poet: it tells the story of Sir Hudibras, named after a character in Spenser's *Faerie Queene,* and every verse contains a barbed quip aimed at the Puritans of the Commonwealth. Its first section was published in 1663, followed by two others in 1664 and 1678, but the poem was left unfinished.

Hudson River School, an association for artistic purposes of several 19th century American landscape painters including Thomas DOUGHTY, William HART, George INNESS, Homer Dodge MARTIN, and Alexander H. WYANT. The name was selected because many of the painters chose landscapes along the Hudson River as ideal subjects.

Hue, in painting the name of a color resulting from the combination of a primary with a secondary color: it is less correctly used to designate any color where the word *tint* would apply more properly.

Huet, Jean Baptiste Marie (1745-1811), American painter, engraver, and designer who was influenced by François BOUCHER and Pierre PRUD'HON. He was a specialist in painting domestic animals as shown in his *Mastiff Attacking Geese;* two of his son, Nicolas and Francois, were respectively animal and miniature painters, and his youngest son, who lost an arm in the French Revolution, engraved the works of his father and brothers.

Hughes, Ball (1806-1868), American sculptor born in England who is credited with having executed the first marble statue in the United States: a likeness of Alexander Hamilton. It is also probable that his statue of Dr. Bowditch at Mount Auburn Cemetery, Cambridge, Massachusetts, was the first bronze figure cast in the United States.

Hughes, Hatcher (c.1884-), American dramatist educated at the University of North Carolina and Columbia University. After serving in World War I he lectured in the English department at Columbia University: his plays include *Hell-Bent for Heaven* (1924) which won the Pulitzer Prize; *Ruint; It's a Grand Life* with Alan Williams; *Wake Up, Jonathan!* with Elmer RICE; *The Lord Blesses the Bishop.*

Hughes, Howard (1905-), American film producer, brother of Rupert Hughes: his films include *Two Arabian Knights* with Louis Wolheim; *Everybody's Acting; The Racket* with Thomas MEIGHAN; *The Mating Call; Hell's Angels; Front Page; Scarface; Sky Devils; The Outlaw.* Among the screen stars who have achieved success in his pictures are Louis WOLHEIM; Thomas MEIGHAN; Jean HARLOW; Ben LYON; Marie PREVOST; Pat O'BRIEN, and Paul MUNI.

Hughes, Langston (1902-), American Negro poet, novelist, and dramatist who studied for a time at Columbia University, and worked at odd jobs while writing a volume of poems, *Weary Blues,* which appeared in 1926. Other works include *Not Without Laughter; Dear Lovely Death,* a book of poems; *Mulatto,* a play; also some stories for juveniles.

Hughes, Rupert (1872-), American writer of books on music, composer, poet, and dramatist educated at Western Reserve and Yale Universities: his works on music include *American Composers* (1900); *Love Affairs of Great Musicians; The Musical Guide,* later revised as *Music Lover's Cyclopedia;* many piano pieces and songs. He has also written more than 25 popular novels; several plays including *Excuse Me;* a biography of George Washington in three volumes, and a volume of poems.

Hughes, Thomas (1822-1896), English author educated at Rugby and Oxford: he visited America several times and was intimate with James Russell LOWELL. His best known works are *Tom Brown's School Days; Tom Brown at Oxford; Life of Alfred the Great.*

Hugo, John Adam (1873-), American pianist and composer who studied at the Stuttgart Conservatory, appearing successfully as a concert pianist in Europe, and becoming professor of the piano at the PEABODY CONSERVATORY, Baltimore, and other American and European institutions. His compositions include an opera, *The Temple Dancer,* produced at the Metropolitan Opera House in 1919; a symphony and several other orchestral works; two piano concertos; a piano trio; violin pieces and songs.

Hugo, Victor Marie, Viscount (1802-1885), French poet, novelist, and dramatist who was the son of one of the generals of Napoleon I. His novels include *The Hunchback of Notre Dame* (1831); *Les Miserables; The Toilers;* and *Ninety-Three:* his important dramas include *Hernani* (1830); *Marion Delorme,* and *Ruy Blas.* Several film versions of *The Hunchback of Notre Dame* and *Les Miserables* have been produced with tremendous success. His poetical works include *The Orientals* (1829); *Autumn Leaves; Songs of Twilight; Contemplations.*

Hull, Edith Maude, contemporary English author about whose personal life nothing is known except that her novel, *The Sheik* (1921) scored a success both as a book and as adapted for the silent screen with Rudolph VALENTINO as the star. Her other novels including *Sons of the Sheik; The Desert Healer; The Lion Tamer,* and *Jungle Captive* are written in the same vein of what has been termed "incandescent passion."

Hull, Helen Rose, contemporary American novelist educated at Michigan State College and the University of Chicago who has taught at Wellesley College and Columbia University. Her works include *Quest* (1922); *Labyrinth; The Surry Family; Hardy Perennial; Frost Flower; A Circle in the Water.*

Hull, Henry (1890-), American stage and screen actor, educated at the College of the City of New York and Columbia, who made his debut at New York in 1909 as one of a crowd in *The Nigger:* among the numerous plays in which he has appeared are *The Man Who Came Back; The Trial of Joan of Arc; The Cat and the Canary; Lulu Belle; The Ivory Door; Congratulations,* of which he was the author; *Michael and Mary; The Passing of the Third Floor Back; Grand Hotel; Tobacco Road.* He has also played leading roles in many films including *The Man Who Came Back; Great Expectations; Boys Town; The Great Waltz; Stanley and Livingstone; Judge Hardy and Son; My Son, My Son; High Sierra.*

Hummel, George Frederick (1882-), American novelist educated at Williams College and Columbia University who achieved considerable success in organizing business enterprises: his works include *After All* (1923); *A Good Man;*

Evelyn Grainger; Lazy Isle; Heritage; Tradition; Adriatic Interlude.

Hummel, Johann Nepomuk (1778-1837), German pianist who studied with his father and with Wolfgang Amadeus MOZART, making his debut in 1787 and touring Europe and Great Britain successfully. He studied composition with ALBRECHTS-BERGER, SALIERI, and Josef HAYDN: his compositions include several operas; seven piano concertos and more than one hundred solo piano pieces. At one time he was considered the peer of BEETHOVEN as a pianist and extemporist.

Humoresque (Fr.), in music the title given an instrumental piece of droll or fanciful character, used by Antonin DVORAK for one of the most popular piano pieces ever composed: *Humoreske Op. 101, No. 7.* It is available on records for orchestra, piano, violin, violoncello, band, and in several solo and concerted vocal arrangements.

Humperdinck, Engelbert (1854-1921), German composer who studied at the Cologne Conservatory with Adolf JENSEN, and won many prizes for his early works. He was an intimate friend and assistant to Richard WAGNER whose musical style he imitated successfully in his fairy opera, *Hänsel and Gretel,* produced at Weimar in 1893, and in English at Daly's Theatre, New York, in 1895. His compositions include several more operas including *Königskinder* given its world première in 1910 at the Metropolitan Opera House, New York, but his fame rests on HANSEL AND GRETEL which has been and is still performed in every great opera house.

Hunchback of Notre Dame, see **Quasimodo.**

Hunding, one of the characters in *The Valkyrie,* the second of the dramas in Richard WAGNER's *Ring of the Nibelungs.* His wife, Sieglinde, falls in love and elopes with Siegmund: Hunding pursues the pair, and, aided by Wotan who smashes Siegmund's sword, kills the latter.

Hundred Kisses, The, a romantic ballet in one act: libretto by Boris Kochno based on a fairy tale, *The Swineherd,* by Hans Christian ANDERSEN; choreography by Bronislava NIJINSKA; music by Frederic d'Erlanger; first produced at Covent Garden, London, in 1935. The plot revolves around a young princess and a prince who disguises himself as a swineherd. He draws music from a magic jar, and when the princess begs for the jar, demands a hundred kisses as the price. When her father finds the princess kissing the supposed swineherd, he bars her from the castle: the prince leaves her as the darkness of night comes on.

Huneker, James Gibbons (1860-1921), American musical writer, dramatic and art critic for the New York *Sun* and the New York *Times.* He studied the piano with Rafael JOSEFFY and taught for a time at the National Conservatory of Music, New York. His works include *Mezzo-Tints in Modern Music* (1899); *Chopin: The Man and His Music; Melomaniacs; Overtones: Music and Literature; Iconoclasts; A Book for Dramatists; Franz Liszt; Egoists: A Book of Supermen; Bedouins; Steeplejack,* a volume of memoirs.

Hungarian Dances (Brahms), a series of twenty-one dances originally published for piano duet in 1869, and in 1872 for piano solo. Their immediate sensational popularity caused the composer considerable uneasiness for some time because their fame overshadowed recognition of his original, more serious works. The melodies are genuine Hungarian folk songs and dance tunes, and all of the dances have been arranged not only for orchestra, but also for violin and piano: there are recordings available of most of the dances.

Hungarian Rhapsody No. 2 (Liszt), the most popular of Franz Liszt's fifteen rhapsodies originally written for the piano although most of them have been transcribed for orchestra. The two principal movements are the *Lassu* or slow movement and the *Friska* or quick movement of the CZARDAS, the most popular national dance of Hungary. There is a Victor piano recording played by Alfred Cortot, and both Victor and Columbia recordings for orchestra directed respectively by Leopold Stokowski and Sir Henry Wood.

Hunt, Leigh (1784-1859), English poet, critic and essayist who was jailed for two years with his brother, John Hunt, for writing political articles criticizing the Prince Regent. He was friendly with most of the men of letters of his period, and his volumes of essays are regarded as among his finest works which include the poems, *The Story of Rimini; Hero and Leander; The Town,* a volume on London; also a delightful *Autobiography.*

Hunt, Richard Morris (1828-1895), American architect who worked under Thomas U. WALTER on additions to the Capitol in Washington, D. C.: among his most important works are the Fogg Museum at Harvard College; the United States Naval Observatory at Washington, D. C., the Tribune Building, New York; the pedestal for the Statue of Liberty in New York Harbor; the Administration Building at the Columbian Exposition, Chicago. His son, **Richard Howland Hunt** (1862-1931), also an architect, designed one of the new wings for the Metropolitan Museum of Art, New York.

Hunt, William Henry (1790-1864), English painter who studied with John VARLEY and became a distinguished member of the Society of Water Color Painters. His best works include *The Laboratory; The Orphans; Ballad Singers; Mulatto Girl; The Card Players; Dead Humming Bird; The Itinerant.*

Hunt, William Holman (1827-1910), English painter who studied with John VARLEY and at the the Royal Academy, London, where he exhibited his first picture, *Hark!* in 1846. His notable canvases include *Little Nell and Her Grandfather; Rienzi Swearing Vengeance for his Brother's Death; The Light of the World; The Scapegoat; Christ with the Doctors; After Sunset in Egypt; The Shadow of Death.*

Hunt, William Morris (1824-1879), American painter who studied the art of sculpture first at Düsseldorf, and painting later with COUTURE and MILLET. His finest works include *Priscilla; The Farmer's Return; Hurdy-Gurdy Boy; Girl with a*

Kitten; Drummer Boy; Gloucester Harbor; The Bathers; The Prodigal Son. He painted the murals Flight of Night and Discovery in the Capitol at Albany, N. Y., and also executed many fine portraits.

Hunter, Ian (1900-), English actor born in South Africa who served in the English army during World War I, and made his debut in 1919 on the London stage in Jack o' Jingles. Among the plays in which he has appeared are The Blue Lagoon; The Yellow Poppy; R. U. R.; The Forest; Diplomacy; School for Scandal; The High Road; A Song of Sixpence; Acropolis; Without Witness. He has also played important roles in numerous films including The Sign of the Four; Jalna; The White Angel; Adventures of Robin Hood; Tower of London; Strange Cargo; Bitter Sweet; Dr. Jekyll and Mr. Hyde; Smilin' Through.

Huntington, Anna Hyatt, see **Hyatt, Anna Vaughn.**

Huntington, Daniel (1816-1906), American painter who studied with Henry INMAN, and visited Florence and Rome where he painted many of his finest works. His notable canvases include Florentine Girl; Early Christian Prisoners; The Sibyl; Mercy's Dream; Lady in White and Red; Henry VIII and Catherine Parr; Shepherd Boy. He also painted portraits of Abraham Lincoln, Martin Van Buren, and Bishop Potter.

Huntley, G. P. (1904-), American stage and screen actor who made his debut in 1921 at London in The Golden Moth, later appearing in Quality Street; Aren't We All?; Gentlemen Prefer Blondes; The Patsy; The Bachelor Father; What Every Woman Knows; Seventh Heaven; Journey's End. He has also played leading roles in numerous films including Death Takes a Holiday; Little Man, What Now?; Becky Sharp; Charge of the Light Brigade; Another Dawn; The Tower of London; Private Affairs; Shining Victory.

Hurdy-Gurdy, (a) an ancient stringed instrument with a body shaped like the LUTE: the two melody strings are operated by keys controlled by the left hand, and the four drone strings by a crank turning a rosined wheel. The tone of the instrument was harsh and strident although it enjoyed considerable favor in the 10th to the 12th century. (b) The name is also applied to the portable BARREL ORGAN of the present day, probably because its mechanism is also operated by a crank.

Hurst, Fannie (1889-), American novelist educated at Washington and Columbia Universities: her works include Just Around the Corner (1914); Every Soul Hath Its Song; Star Dust; Back Street; Gaslight Sonatas, a volume of short stories; Humoresque; Mannequin; We Are Ten, another volume of short stories; Imitation of Life; Lonely Parade. Some of her novels, including Humoresque, Imitation of Life, and Back Street have been adapted for the films.

Hurston, Zora Neale (1903-), American Negro novelist educated at Howard University and Barnard College: her works include Jonah's Gourd

Vine (1934); Mules and Men; Tell My Horse; Moses; Man of the Mountain.

Huss, Henry Holden (1862-), American pianist and composer who studied at the Munich Conservatory with Joseph RHEINBERGER, and settled at New York in 1885 as concert pianist and teacher. His compositions include orchestral works, chamber music, choral music, two piano concertos, and many piano pieces.

Hussey, Ruth, contemporary stage and screen actress who has appeared in several films including Madame X; Within the Law; Northwest Passage; Susan and God; The Philadelphia Story; Flight Command; H. M. Pulham, Esq.; Our Wife.

Huston, Walter (1884-), American stage and screen actor born in Canada who made his New York debut in 1905 in Hal Reid's In Convict Stripes, later appearing in The Sign of the Cross; Mr. Pitt; The Easy Mark; Desire Under the Elms; Kongo; The Barker; Elmer the Great; Dodsworth; Othello. He has been featured in numerous films including Gentlemen of the Press; The Virginian; Abraham Lincoln; The Criminal Code; Rain; Kongo; Storm at Daybreak; Ann Vickers; Dodsworth; Rhodes; Transatlantic Tunnel; Of Human Hearts; The Light That Failed; Shanghai Gesture; Always in My Heart; Mission to Moscow.

Hutcheson, Ernest (1871-), Australian pianist and composer who studied at the Leipzig Conservatory with Carl REINECKE and at Weimar with Bernhard STAVENHAGEN. He toured Europe with great success in 1912, and achieved equal favor in the United States. He has acted as the head of the piano departments at the Peabody Conservatory, Baltimore, the Chautauqua Summer School, and the Juilliard Graduate School, New York, later becoming Dean of the latter, and of the Institute of Musical Art. He has appeared in a series of radio broadcasts, and has composed works for orchestra and for piano.

Hutchinson, Josephine (1904-), American stage and screen actress who made her New York debut in 1925 as Louisette in The Bird Cage: she has also appeared in A Man's Man; The Unchastened Woman; The Cradle Song; Hedda Gabler; The Cherry Orchard; Alison's House; Alice in Wonderland. She has also played important roles in numerous films including Oil for the Lamps of China; The Story of Louis Pasteur; I Married a Doctor; The Crime of Dr. Hallett; Tom Brown's School Days.

Hutton, Joseph (1787-1828), American actor and dramatist whose play, The School for Prodigals, was produced at Philadelphia in 1808: it was followed by The Wounded Hussar, Fashionable Follies, and The Orphan of Prague. He is considered one of the first important early American playwrights.

Hutton, Laurence (1843-1904), American essayist and dramatist whose works include Plays and Players (1893); Memoirs of Edwin Booth; Literary Landmarks of London; Actors and Actresses of Great Britain and the United States with Brander MATTHEWS; *Artists of the Nineteenth Century* with Clara E. Clement. He acted as dramatic critic for the New York *Evening Mail,* and literary editor of *Harper's Magazine.*

Huxley, Aldous Leonard (1894-), English novelist, poet, and essayist educated at Oxford: his works include *Limbo* (1920); *Crome Yellow; Antic Hay; Those Barren Leaves; Point Counter Point; Brave New World; The Burning Wheel; The Cicadas and Other Poems; On the Margin; Jesting Pilate; Music at Night and Other Essays; Ends and Means.*

Huysmans, Cornelis (1648-1727), Flemish painter, also known as Huysmans of Mechlin, who studied with Kaspar .le Witte and Jacques Arthois. His notable works include *Woodland with Château; Christ on the Road to Emmaus;* also many fine landscapes to be seen in art galleries throughout Western Europe and Russia. His brother, **Jan Baptist Huysmans** (1654-1716) studied with him and painted landscapes often mistaken for works by Salomon van RUISDAEL: they include *Great Landscape* and *Ruins of a Corinthian Temple.*

Hyacinth or **Hyacinthus,** in Greek mythology a Greek youth of great beauty beloved by APOLLO who accidentally kills him while throwing the discus. His blood caused a beautiful flower, the hyacinth, with the exclamation of grief, Ai, marked on its petals, to spring from the earth. He personifies the god of vegetation according to some of the ancient legends.

Hyatt, Anna Vaughn (1876-), American sculptor who studied with Hermon A. MACNEIL and Gutzon BORGLUM, learning the anatomy of horses through raising them at her farm in Maryland. For a time she worked with Abastenia St. Leger EBERLE, an accomplished sculptor. After studying in Europe she exhibited at the Paris Salon in 1907, and in 1910 executed an equestrian statue of *Joan of Arc* for Riverside Drive, New York. In 1917 she became head of the department of sculpture at the Museum of the French Art Institute in the United States. Her small bronzes are to be seen in the Metropolitan Museum of Art, New York, and the Cleveland Museum of Art.

Hymen, originally the name of the song sung at marriages by the ancient Greeks, and later personified as the son of APOLLO and one of the MUSES; also as the son of DIONYSUS and APHRODITE. In art he is pictured as a somewhat effeminate youth wearing a nuptial veil and carrying a bridal torch.

Hymn, (*a*) a religious song expressive of praise or adoration of some deity: in the Christian religion it is usually sung by the congregation. The hymn became popular in the 4th century as composed by St. Benedict and later by St. Andrew: PALESTRINA wrote many hymns as did also Martin LUTHER after the Reformation. Hymns were not used in Elizabethan England, but developed during the 18th century. In the 19th century the Nonconformists in England and America gave the hymn great importance: it is estimated that there are more than 100,000 hymns in existence.

Hyne, Charles John Cutcliffe Wright (1865-), English novelist and short story writer educated at Cambridge University: he has exploited the sayings and adventures of his original character, Captain Kettle, in a series of novels including *Adventures of Captain Kettle* (1898); *The Little Red Captain; Captain Kettle, K.C.B.; The Reverend Captain Kettle,* etc.

Hypnos, in Greek mythology the personification of sleep: he was the son of Night and the brother of Death, dwelling with them in the underworld. He was said to be gentle, kind, and the soother of care and sorrow. In art he is represented as a young man with wings on his forehead, a poppy stalk in one hand, and a horn in the other hand from which he pours slumber. The name in Roman mythology is *Somnus.*

I

Iambic Verse, the commonest form in English poetry comprising lines in which the syllables are alternately short (unaccented) and long (accented). It was also used by the classical poets of Greece.

Ibáñez, Vicente Blasco (1867-1928), Spanish novelist who studied law at Madrid, and was given a prison term for writing a poem in favor of the republic. He modeled his literary style on that of Émile ZOLA: his works published in English include *The Blood of the Arena* (1911), later published as *Blood and Sand; The Cabin; The Four Horsemen of the Apocalypse,* a best seller and also enormously successful as a silent film; *The Fruit of the Vine; The Dead Command; Mare Nostrum; Reeds and Mud.* His entire career was crowded with exciting incidents concerned with both politics and adventure.

Iberia (Debussy), see **Images (Debussy).**

"Iberia" Suite (Albeniz), a suite for the piano by Isaac ALBENIZ; composed in 1904 and divided into four books each containing three pieces. The four most popular numbers comprising *Evocaciun, El Puerto, Fête Dieu 'à Seville,* and *Triana* were orchestrated by Fernandez ARBOS: there are Victor and Columbia recordings of both the orchestrations and the piano originals by distinguished orchestras and pianists.

Ibn Ezra, see **Abenezra.**

Ibsen, Henrik (1828-1906), Norwegian poet and dramatist who first engaged in journalistic work before becoming associated with the National Theatres in Bergen and Copenhagen: later he lived in Italy and Germany, returning to Christiania in 1891 and remaining there until his death. His numerous plays include *The Pretenders* (1864); *Brand; Peer Gynt; The Pillars of Society; A Doll's House; The Wild Duck; Rosmersholm; Hedda Gabler; The Master Builder; John Gabriel Borkman.* Ibsen was an all-important influence on drama because he had no qualms about attacking sociological problems by bringing them out into the light of sane, sensible discussion.

Ibycus (c.560-c.525 B.C.), Greek poet who was said to have been murdered by bandits near the city of Corinth, and to have called upon a flock of passing cranes to avenge him: as the murderers sat in the theatre at Corinth shortly after, a flight of cranes passed over them, and lingered in such a peculiar manner that suspicion was aroused, and the guilty ones apprehended. Only fragments of his poems, exquisite verses in themselves, are extant.

Icarus, see **Daedalus.**

Icon or **Ikon,** in religious art the name given representations of sacred personages in the Eastern Church whether painted or sculptured; in the Greek Church icons are made in the form of small wood or metal plaques in the style of ancient Byzantine art; no home, before the revolution in Russia, was without one or more of them.

Iconography, the art of representation by pictures or images; hence that branch of study which concerns itself with works of art that are painted, drawn or sculptured.

Ictinus, Greek architect who worked with CALLICRATES and with PHIDIAS, the sculptor of the PARTHENON at ATHENS about 450-430 B.C. Nothing is known of his life, but his profound knowledge of architecture is to be seen plainly in the portions which remain standing of the Parthenon.

Ideal, the term applied in any art to the idea of supreme perfection existent in the mind of the artist. As the ideal of every painter, sculptor, author, or composer differs from that of any one of his confrères, it remains for the intelligent critic to ascertain the consensus of idealistic opinion, and to bear it in mind in expressing critical views.

Idée fixe (Fr.), in music a term used by Hector BERLIOZ to denominate an oft recurring, characteristic theme. It is found in his *Symphonie Fantastique,* and is the equivalent of the German term, *leitmotiv,* an expression coined by the Wagnerian scholar, Hans von Wolzogen, to identify a theme used in connection with a certain character or incident in Richard WAGNER's music dramas.

Idomeneus, in Greek mythology a grandson of MINOS, and king of Crete. He was famous for his beauty, and distinguished himself by his bravery in the TROJAN WAR.

Idyl or **Idyll,** (*a*) in music a composition of pastoral character, or tenderly romantic in its conception. (*b*) In literature a short poem of rural character first written by poets of the Alexandrine School, by Berthold AUERBACH and other poets in Germany, and by Alfred TENNYSON in his *Idylls of the King* although the title in this case has no association with bucolics. The idyl is not generally accepted as a definite literary form.

Idylls of the King (Tennyson), a cycle of poems by Alfred TENNYSON based on Arthurian romances: they include *The Coming of Arthur;*

Gareth and Lynette; Geraint and Enid; Merlin and Vivien; Launcelot and Elaine; The Holy Grail; Pelleas and Ettare; The Last Tournament; Guinevere; The Passing of Arthur.

Idzikowski, Stanislas, contemporary Polish ballet dancer who studied with Enrico CECCHETTI, and first appeared in the EMPIRE THEATRE BALLET at London. Later he danced with Anna PAVLOWA, Lydia LOPOKOVA, and with the DIAGHILEFF Company until the latter's death. His finest roles are in the ballets *Swan Lake, The Sleeping Princess, Le Carnaval, Petrouchka, The Good-Humored Ladies, The Three-Cornered Hat,* and *Cimarosiana.*

Iffland, August Wilhelm (1759-1814), German actor and dramatist who managed the Royal Court Theatre at Berlin, and acted at the Mannheim National Theatre from 1784 to 1795. He improved the status of German theatres immensely, and wrote many popular plays including *The Hunters, The Crime of Ambition,* and *A Criminal for Honor.*

I giojelli della Madonna, see **Jewels of the Madonna, The.**

Igrouchka (Russian Dolls), a Russian folk ballet: libretto and choreography by Michel FOKINE; music by Nicholas RIMSKY-KORSAKOW taken from his *Fantasy on Russian Themes* for violin and orchestra; first performed in 1921. The simple plot tells the story of a youthful peasant who woos a village maid unsuccessfully: he attempts to drown himself; the maiden relents and there is a happy ending.

Ik Marvel, see **Mitchell, Donald Grant.**

Il Bergamasco, see **Castello, Giovanni Battista.**

Il Cavaliere Tempesta, see **Molyn, Pieter the Younger.**

Il Fiammingo, see **Duquesnoy, François.**

Iliad, The, a celebrated Greek epic poem, attributed along with its companion poem, *The Odyssey,* to the poet HOMER, and considered among the oldest works of its kind in any European language. Its subject is the ten-year siege of TROY (Ilium) by the allied states of Greece led by AGAMEMNON, King of Mycenae, to avenge the abduction by the Trojan, Paris, of Helen, wife of Menelaus, king of Sparta. The narrative covers only the last year of the siege, and concerns itself chiefly with the achievements of the Greek ACHILLES and the Trojan HECTOR, son of King PRIAM. There are excellent translations by Alexander POPE, William Cullen BRYANT, and Andrew LANG: also innumerable paintings and sculptures portraying the personages and incidents. The most ambitious musical work in connection with the Trojans is *Les Troyens,* an opera by Hector BERLIOZ produced in 1863. Several plays by Greek classical dramatists including EURIPIDES and SOPHOCLES are based on Homeric legend.

Illington, Margaret (1881-1934), American actress educated at Illinois Wesleyan University and the CHICAGO COLLEGE OF MUSIC who made her debut in 1900 at New York in *The Pride of Jennico:* she also appeared in *The Two Orphans; Mrs. Leffingwell's Boots; The Lion and the Mouse; His House in Order; The Thief; Kindling; Within the Law; The Lie; The Gay Lord Quex* with John DREW.

Illuminated Manuscripts, an art developed first in Egypt where a religious ritual, *Book of the Dead,* was written on papyrus and illustrated with colored scenes. In the Middle Ages the illumination by monks of Bibles, Gospels, Psalters, and Books of the Hours was encouraged by the religious authorities: works of similar character have been discovered in China, Japan, Persia, and India.

Illustration, in literature a picture designed to elucidate the text of a book or any other form of printed matter. Illustrations were used in Egyptian works such as the *Book of the Dead,* and in other Oriental works, but not in Greek or Roman literature previous to the advent of Christianity. In the Middle Ages the monks used illustrations in religious books, also adding illumination. The invention of printing in the 15th century, and also the use of WOODCUTS greatly stimulated the art of illustrating which has become an art in itself through the use of PHOTO ENGRAVING, ROTOGRAVURE, and perfected color printing.

Image, in ancient art a small statue representing a living or dead person: images were made of ancestors, and corresponded in importance to the genealogical trees of the present day, being held in great esteem, and carried in funeral or triumphal processions. Images of the Virgin or of saints are frequently found in the homes of members of the Roman Catholic church.

Images (Debussy), a series of three tone poems for orchestra by Claude DEBUSSY composed between 1906-1912, and first performed in 1910 at a COLONNE concert in Paris, and in 1911 by the New York Philharmonic-Symphony Orchestra. The titles are (*1*) *Iberia,* (*2*) *Rondes de Printemps,* (*3*) *Gigues:* the first is Spanish in character; the second French and the third English. *Iberia* is the most popular of the three, and was inspired by a visit to Spain. There is a Columbia recording of *Iberia* by the Pittsburgh Symphony Orchestra under Fritz Reiner, and a Victor recording by the New York Philharmonic-Symphony Orchestra with John Barbirolli. There is a Victor recording of *Rondes de Printemps,* but none available of *Gigues.*

Imitation, in music the recurrence of a MOTIVE, PHRASE, or THEME announced by one part in another part: if repeated exactly it is called *Strict Imitation,* but if altered in any respect it is known as *Free Imitation.*

Immanuel Ben Solomon (c.1265-c.1330), Hebrew poet born in Rome who was a contemporary and intimate friend of DANTE as evidenced by his style in writing. His most famous work, entitled *Mehabberoth,* is a series of poems which are satires without venom on Jewish religious and secular life: in the 28th of these poems the author is conducted by Dante (called Daniel) through the lands of torture and bliss.

Immermann, Karl Leberecht (1796-1840), German poet, novelist, and dramatist: his novels include *The Epigoni* (1836) and *Munchhausen,* the latter not to be confused with the tales of "Baron Munchhausen." Among his best plays are *The Eye of Love,* adapted from "A Midsummer Night's Dream"; *Ghismonda; Friedrich II; Das Trauerspiel in Tirol,* based on the life story of Andreas Hofer.

Imola, Innocenzo da (1494-1550), Italian painter whose real name was Innocenzo da Francucci: he studied with Francesco FRANCIA at Bologna, and with Mariotto ALBERTINELLI at Florence. His notable works include the frescoes, *Death of the Virgin* and *Assumption of the Virgin; Madonna in Glory with Saints and Angels; Madonna with Kneeling Donors; Marriage of St. Catherine.*

Impasto, in painting the term applied to the use of thick layers of paint to impart an effect of solidity and relief. Impasto has the effect of strengthening the luminous parts of a painting, but excessive layers of paint on shadows causes loss of transparency.

Impersonations, in the theatre impersonations of male characters by women have been common since the 17th century: in the 19th and 20th centuries they have proved popular in the hands of Sarah BERNHARDT, Eva LE GALLIENNE, Charlotte CUSHMAN, Lucille LaVERNE, and Maude ADAMS. The principal female impersonators during the latter period were Tony Hart (of Harrigan and Hart), Henry E. DIXEY, the RUSSELL BROTHERS, James McIntyre (of McINTYRE AND HEATH), George Munro, and Julian ELTINGE.

Impresario (It.), the manager of an opera company who is usually also its artistic director in respect to the choice of singers and operas.

Impressionism, (*a*) in painting a school of realism the aim of which is to render the sense impression of the artist apart from any study of detail. French painters including MANET, DEGAS, MONET, RENOIR, and CEZANNE were the first to rebel against the romantic school during the late 19th century: the movement was followed by Post-Impressionism, the reaction which inevitably follows the establishment of any new school. (*b*) In music a school of composition started by Claude DEBUSSY in protest against the romantic school which he believed was fast becoming oversentimental: among his followers were RAVEL, SATIE, DUKAS, and Florent SCHMITT: also many modern composers in England, Spain, Italy, Russia, and the United States.

Impromptu (Fr.), in music the strict meaning is an IMPROVISATION, or the performance of an original composition on the spur of the moment without preparation or use of the printed page: Johann Sebastian BACH was probably the greatest master of improvisation. The term is also used as the title of piano pieces by SCHUBERT, BRAHMS, CHOPIN, and other composers.

Improvisation, in music the art of composing and playing a composition simultaneously: many great composers including Johann Sebastian BACH and George Frederick HANDEL were adepts at creating and performing a musical work in this manner.

In a Persian Garden (Lehmann), a song cycle for mixed quartet by Liza LEHMANN, an English concert singer and composer; first performed privately in 1896 at London by a quartet composed of Emma ALBANI, Hilda Wilson, Ben DAVIES, and David BISPHAM. The text is taken from the *Rubaiyat* of OMAR KHAYYAM as translated by Edward FITZGERALD, and there is a Columbia recording of the complete work, and Victor recordings of *Ah! Moon of My Delight* by Richard CROOKS, and of *Myself When Young* by Lawrence TIBBETT.

Ince, Thomas Harper (1880-1924), American actor and producer of silent films including *The Battle of Gettysburg; The Wrath of the Gods; The Cup of Life; The Coward; Civilization; Peggy; The Narrow Trail; The Aryan; The Hottentot; Anna Christie.*

Inchbald, Elizabeth (1753-1821), English actress, novelist, and dramatist: her works include *A Simple Story; Nature and Art.* She also wrote several plays including *Such Things Are; The Married Man; The Wedding Day; The Midnight Hour; Lovers' Vows.*

Incidental music, a term specifically denoting music composed to accompany the action of a drama, but freely used to signify any music performed in connection with a play. The use of music in this form began in the days of Elizabethan drama: important examples are BEETHOVEN's music for *Egmont* and *The Ruins of Athens;* MENDELSSOHN's music for *A Midsummer Night's Dream;* BIZET's music for *L'Arlesienne;* GRIEG's music for *Peer Gynt.*

Incoronazione di Poppea, L', see **Coronation of Poppea, The.**

India Ink, a black pigment used for writing, drawing, or painting, and formerly used exclusively in making architectural drawings. It was brought in the form of sticks or square cakes from China and Japan, but there are numerous imitations at the present time. The Chinese are the first makers, and their processes are more or less a secret. Lamp-black is the principal ingredient of the ink which is really indelible because its base is carbon.

Indianapolis Symphony Orchestra, an organization founded in 1930 by Ferdinand Schaefer, the concerts being first presented on a co-operative basis. Schaefer conducted until 1936 when Vladimir Bakaleinikoff and Fabian SEVITZKY were then engaged as guest conductors: in 1937 the latter became sole conductor. The orchestra has made frequent broadcasts, and numerous recordings including the Symphony No. 1 in G minor by Basil KALINNIKOFF.

Indian Suite (MacDowell), a suite by Edward MACDOWELL composed in 1891: the themes were suggested by American Indian melodies, and it was among the first American works of this character to utilize material of this kind. The work is in five movements: I *Legend;* II *Love Song;* III *In War Time;* IV *Dirge;* V *Village Festival:* it was first played by the Boston Symphony Orchestra in 1896. There is a Columbia recording by the Columbia Broadcasting Symphony Orchestra directed by Howard Barlow.

d'Indy, (Paul-Marie-Théodore) Vincent (1851-1931), French composer who studied at the Paris Conservatory with Diémer, MARMONTEL, LAVIGNAC, and César FRANCK: he was one of the founders of the Societé Nationale de Musique, and also of the SCHOLA CANTORUM, Paris. He became a member of the Paris Conservatory faculty in 1912, and visited the United States in 1905 and 1921 to conduct his compositions with the Boston Symphony Orchestra and the Philadelphia Symphony Orchestra. His works include two music dramas: the symphonic variations, *Istar;* a symphonic trilogy, *Wallenstein;* an oratorio; pieces for the piano and other instruments. He also wrote a life of César FRANCK whom he revered as a teacher and as a man.

Inescort, Frieda (1901-), American stage and screen actress born in Scotland who made her debut in 1922 at New York in *The Truth About Blayds:* she has also appeared in *The Merchant of Venice; Pygmalion; Major Barbara; Mozart; Escape; Alice Sit-by-the-Fire; When Ladies Meet.* She has been featured in numerous films including *The King Steps Out; Mary of Scotland; Another Dawn; The Zero Hour; Pride and Prejudice; The Trial of Mary Dugan.*

Information Please, a weekly radio broadcast of interest because of the many questions asked and answered on subjects relating to literature, music, drama, and all other arts: it was inaugurated in 1938 with Clifton FADIMAN as chairman, and Franklin P. ADAMS, John Francis KIERAN, and Oscar LEVANT as experts. The questions are propounded by the chairman without previous knowledge of their nature by the experts. Guests are invited each week to join the ranks of the experts: among the women who have appeared may be mentioned Sally Benson, Clare BOOTHE, Edna FERBER, Lillian GISH, Ruth GORDON, Osa Johnson, Elsa LANCHESTER, Alice Roosevelt Longworth, Alice Duer MILLER, Anna NEAGLE, Kathleen NORRIS, Dorothy PARKER, Bella SPEWACK, Gloria STUART, Mary BOLAND, Faith BALDWIN and Margaret Leech. Among the men who appeared as guests are Roy Chapman Andrews, Stephen Vincent BENET, Louis BROMFIELD, John Mason BROWN, Heywood BROUN, Sir Thomas BEECHAM, Marc CONNELLY, Thomas CRAVEN, Stuart Chase, George M. COHAN, Elmer DAVIS, Jo DAVIDSON, Dudley DIGGES, Lewis Gannett, Sir Cedric HARDWICKE, Julian HUXLEY, Ben HECHT, Alfred HITCHCOCK, Leslie HOWARD, Nunnally Johnson, George KAUFMAN, Clarence Buddington KELLAND, H. V. Kaltenborn, Boris KARLOFF, Arthur Krock, Eric KNIGHT, Paul LUKAS, Emil LUDWIG, Howard LINDSAY, Philip MERIVALE, Raymond MASSEY, Adolphe MENJOU, Ogden NASH, Elmer RICE, Robert ST. JOHN, Rex STOUT, Robert SHERWOOD, Albert SPALDING, Carl SANDBURG, Louis UNTER-

MEYER, Carl VAN DOREN, Alexander WOOLLCOTT, and Orson WELLES.

Ingelow, Jean (1820-1897), English poet and novelist whose first book, *A Rhyming Chronicle of Incidents and Feeling*, gives evidence of her melancholy temperament. Her works include *The Round of Days; Home Thoughts and Home Scenes; Mopsa the Fairy; Little Wonder Horn.* Her novels such as *Sarah de Berenger* and *Don John* attracted little attention, but many of her poems were set to music by various composers.

Ingemann, Bernhard Severin (1789-1862), Danish poet, dramatist, and novelist: his poetical works and dramas include *The Renegade; The Voice in the Desert; Masaniello; The Battle for Walhalla; Waldemar the Great and His Companions,* an epic poem. His historical novels such as *Waldemar the Victorious, King Erik,* and *Holger Danske* are considered among the greatest Danish romances.

Ingenue, in theatrical parlance the title given to the young girl in a play who provides the secondary love interest.

Ingleby, Clement Mansfield (1823-1886), English writer and Shakespearean critic educated at Cambridge University who aided in the editing of the Stanton edition of the great dramatist's works. He also wrote treatises on sound, acoustics, law, and religion.

Ingoldeby, Thomas, see **Barham, Richard Harris.**

Ingres, Jean Auguste Dominique (1780-1867), French painter who studied with Louis DAVID at Paris, and spent several years studying the pictures in the LOUVRE: he also lived for fourteen years in Rome where he studied the works of RAPHAEL. His notable paintings include *Philemon and Baucis; Oedipus and the Sphinx; Jupiter and Thetis; Sistine Chapel; Vergil Reading the Aeneid to Augustus; Raphael and la Fornarina; Vow of Louis XIII; Dream of Ossian; Christ Giving the Keys to Peter; Odalisque With a Slave; Apotheosis of Homer.*

Inlays, in architecture and furniture manufacture pieces of wood, metal or ivory inserted in other woods by incising patterns on their surfaces, and filling in the spaces with the inlays. The process was used on floors, ceilings, and furniture for many centuries, but the trend toward simplicity has gradually led to their disuse.

Inman, Henry (1801-1846), American painter who studied with John Wesley JARVIS, traveling with him for several years to paint the backgrounds in the latter's portraits. Among his notable portraits and pictures are William WORDSWORTH; Thomas MACAULAY; Nathaniel HAWTHORNE; *Rydal Falls in England; Rip Van Winkle; The Young Fisherman; Picnic in the Catskills; October Afternoon; Boyhood of Washington.*

Inness, George (1825-1894), American painter who was chiefly self-taught, but visited Italy and France where he was impressed by the ideas of the BARBIZON SCHOOL. His notable works include *American Sunset; Delaware Water Gap; Peace and Plenty; The Afterglow; Rainbow After the Storm; Autumn Oaks; Evening; Niagara Falls; Day in June; Winter Morning.* The stiffness of his earlier canvases wore off after his trip abroad, and he altered his style to secure softer rendering of the forms of nature.

Inquisition, The, a special court established by the Roman Catholic church in 1179 which had the power of discovering, trying, and punishing heretics, sorcerers, polygamists, and seducers. It had branches in Italy, France, England, and Spain: in the latter country the Inquisition established by Ferdinand and Isabella was more of a political than a religious institution, and was used to prosecute the Jews. In the more than three hundred years of its existence more than thirty thousand persons were tortured or put to death. Many artists have portrayed the meetings of the court and the AUTO-DA-FE.

Institute of Musical Art (New York), an institution founded in 1905 by Frank DAMROSCH and James Loeb who gave the initial endowment of $500,000. It was first located in the old Lenox Mansion on lower Fifth Avenue, New York, but removed to a new building on Claremont Avenue in 1910 which it still occupies. It offers the courses of study necessary for a well-rounded musical education leading to a diploma and a postgraduate diploma. The Dean of the Institute at the present time (1943) is Dr. George A. WEDGE: among present and past instructors of note are Georges BARRERE, Carl FRIEDBERG, Rudolph GANZ, Percy GOETSCHIUS, Marcel GRANDJANY, William J. HENDERSON, Georg HENSCHEL, Ernest HUTCHESON, Franz KNEISEL, Carlos SALZEDO, Sigismond STOJOWSKI, Mme. Milka TERNINA. The list of graduate students includes Katherine BACON, Sophie BRASLAU, Samuel GARDNER, Jacques Gordon, Sascha Gorodnitzki, Andre KOSTELANETZ, Mischa LEVITZKI, Alexander SMALLENS, and many other contemporary artists and composers.

Instrumentation, see **Orchestration.**

Intaglio, an engraved stone or gem in which a concave design has been cut; the reverse of a CAMEO in which the carving is in relief. The same method is now used in printing by etched copper plates. Seals and signet rings are made by the intaglio method so that the designs appear in relief when stamped on wax.

Interlude, (*a*) in music a short instrumental passage played between the verses of a hymn, chorale, or other parts of a church service. (*b*) In drama a short farcical piece introduced during the 16th century between the acts of a drama: John HEYWOOD wrote a number of this type of comic piece which developed from English morality plays.

Intermezzo (It.), a form of musical composition also known as *Intermède, Entr'acte, Interlude.* It was originally used as a short instrumental or vocal piece between the acts of an Italian tragedy or grand opera, and was comparaively short or simple in character. In the 18th century PERGOLESI's operetta, *La Serva Padrona,* was used as an intermezzo. The name has also been applied to a brief movement inserted in a symphony or other extended work: BRAHMS and SCHUMANN used it as the title of short piano compositions.

International Society for Contemporary Music, an organization founded in 1922 at Salzburg, Germany: Edward J. DENT was the principal founder in collaboration with several Austrian composers, and also first president of the Society he purpose of which is to promote the performance of new works by composers of all nations. Annual festivals were held in several Continental cities up to the beginning of World War II, the works submitted being selected by an international jury. In 1923 a branch was formed in the United States for similar promotion of works by American composers: up to 1943 many compositions have been heard and a catalogue of writers entitled *Composers in America,* compiled by Claire Reis, was published, the third edition appearing in 1938.

Interpretation, the method of performance of a musical composition by an experienced artist especially in respect to varying tempos and nuances which can be best defined as "light and shade." Most great artists adhere to the tempos and marks of expression indicated on some authoritative edition of the work being performed, impressing their individuality by slight differences which do not depart too much from the original markings.

Interval, in music the name given the difference in pitch between two tones: at the present time all standard intervals are called *major:* if a *major* interval is increased by a semitone it is called *augmented;* if it is decreased by a semitone it is called *minor,* and if a minor interval is again decreased a semitone it is called *diminished.* The Prime, Fourth, Fifth, and Octave intervals are called *perfect.*

Intonation, in music (*a*) the production of either instrumental or vocal tones correctly in respect to pitch: (*b*) the method of chanting used in plain song whereby the opening phrase is sung by the precentor, and the second phrase by the choir.

Introduction, in music a preparatory phrase, passage or complete division preceding the main part of a musical composition. It was used first effectively in the symphonies of Josef HAYDN and BEETHOVEN. In TSCHAIKOWSKY and BRAHMS' symphonies it is extended to include themes not to be found in the main body of the work.

Introduction and Rondo Capriccioso (Saint-Saëns), a concert piece for violin with orchestral accompaniment by Camille SAINT-SAENS composed in 1870: it is dedicated to Pablo de SARASATE, a famous Spanish violinist who was the first to play it, and is one of the most popular violin numbers in the repertoire of violin virtuosos. There is a Victor recording by Jascha HEIFETZ who also played it in his film, *They Shall Have Music,* produced in 1939.

Inversion, in music the transportation of the notes forming an interval or a chord from their fundamental position, usually accomplished by inverting the notes: for example, if the interval C-E is originally written with the C *under* the E, the interval is inverted by placing the C *over* the E.

Invitation to Learning, a radio broadcasting feature originated by the Columbia Broadcasting Company in 1940, and designed to stimulate interest in books of all descriptions which have exerted influence in world culture. Five prominent litterateurs alternate as chairmen on the broadcasts, and two distinguished scholars or authors are invited as guest commentators on the works to be discussed. Among the books and plays that have been discussed are BOSWELL's *Life of Dr. Johnson;* IBSEN's *Wild Duck;* EURIPIDES' *The Trojan Women;* WHITMAN's *Leaves of Grass;* CERVANTES' *Don Quixote;* CAPEK's *R. U. R.;* O. HENRY's *The Four Million;* KIPLING's *Kim;* MARLOWE's *Dr. Faustus;* PLATO's *Symposium;* TOLSTOY's *War and Peace;* DANTE's *Divine Comedy.* Among the distinguished writers who have appeared as commentators are Sinclair LEWIS, Joseph HERGESHEIMER, André MAUROIS, Padraic COLUM, John Mason BROWN, Guthrie McCLINTIC, Dr. LIN YUTANG, and Mark VAN DOREN. A "Listener's Guide" is available which lists and summarizes all the books to be discussed during each season.

Invitation to the Dance (Weber), a composition originally written for the piano by Carl Maria von WEBER in 1819: it has been arranged for orchestra by Hector BERLIOZ and Felix WEINGARTNER. The composer, in a letter to his fiancée, interpreted the meaning of the *Andante* movement which precedes the waltz: "The bass passage with which it opens is the gentleman requesting the pleasure of a dance; the treble passage which follows is the lady's somewhat hesitant acceptance. A brief dialogue follows in which the voices can be clearly distinguished; then follows the delightful waltz, the recurring *Andante* at its conclusion conveying the parting scene." There is a Columbia recording for the piano played by Ignaz FRIEDMAN, and a Victor recording played by Alfred CORTOT. The Berlioz transcription is available in a Victor recording by the British Broadcasting Company Orchestra directed by Arturo Toscanini, and the Weingartner transcription is to be obtained in a Columbia recording by the London Philharmonic Orchestra under Felix Weingartner.

Io, in Greek mythology the daughter of the king of Argos: ZEUS fell in love with her, and when his wife, HERA, discovered his infidelity, he transformed Io into a white heifer. In revenge Hera sent a gadfly to torment her, but she finally reached Egypt, and was restored to human form.

Iolanthe, a comic opera in two acts: libretto by Sir William S. GILBERT; music by Sir Arthur S. SULLIVAN; first produced in 1882 by the D'Oyly Carte Company at the Savoy Theatre, London.

The story is: Iolanthe, a fairy banished for life by the Fairy Queen for having married a mortal, is pardoned. Her son, Strephon, half fairy and half shepherd, has fallen in love with Phyllis, a shepherdess, but the Lord Chancellor, her guardian, will not give his permission for their betrothal because he also loves Phyllis. The peers meet to render a decision and the lovers are separated. Strephon, in despair, seeks the aid of his mother, who in turn asks for the help of the Fairy Queen. She secures Strephon a seat in Parliament; meanwhile Phyllis, who overhears a conversation between Strephon and Iolanthe, believes him to be faithless, and becomes engaged to two lords, not knowing which one to take. The Lord Chancellor decides to marry Phyllis himself: when Iolanthe hears this, she declares that the Chancellor is her mortal husband. When the Queen hears that all the fairies have married peers, she decides to find one for herself, and Phyllis, finally convinced that Iolanthe is Strephon's mother, is happily reunited with him. There is a Victor recording of the complete opera, and a Columbia abridged version.

Ion of Chios (c.484-c.422 B.C.), Greek poet who was one of the most distinguished literary figures during the age of PERICLES, and an intimate friend of AESCHYLUS and SOPHOCLES. Only fragments of his works are extant, but they reveal his intellectual ability in all forms of poesy including hymns, tragedies, elegies, and essays.

Iphigenia, in Greek mythology the daughter of AGAMEMNON and CLYTEMNESTRA: when the Greek fleet sailing to besiege TROY was becalmed at Aulis, the DELPHIAN ORACLE declared that IPHIGENIA's death was the only way of satisfying the demands of the goddess, ARTEMIS, but the latter relented, and a stag was substituted as a sacrifice.

Iphigenia in Aulis, an opera by Christoph Willibald von GLUCK first produced in Paris at L'Opera in 1774, and occasionally revived because of its superbly dramatic qualities. The *Overture,* which was a remarkable work considering the period in which it was composed, was rescored by Richard WAGNER in 1854; he changed the tempo marks and added a new ending which has proved acceptable to present-day conductors who use his version almost exclusively. There is a Columbia recording by the Columbia Broadcasting Symphony Orchestra directed by Howard Barlow.

Ippolitow-Iwanow, Michail (1859-1935), Russian composer who studied at the St. Petersburg Conservatory with Nicholas RIMSKY-KORSAKOW, becoming director of the Music School and conductor of the Symphony Orchestra at Tiflis. He published a valuable collection of Georgian folksongs: his compositions include several operas, CAUCASIAN SKETCHES, a world-famous suite for orchestra; chamber music; many choral works and solo songs.

Ireland, John (1879-   ), English composer who studied at the Royal Academy of Music with Charles Villiers STANFORD: he has composed orchestral works, chamber music, choral works, organ pieces, piano pieces and songs.

Iriarte, Ignacio (1620-1685), Spanish painter who studied with Francisco de HERRERA, and frequently worked with Estéban MURILLO who painted the figures in backgrounds executed by Iriarte. He was one of the founders of the Seville Academy, and its first secretary: many of his landscapes are to be seen in the Madrid Museum.

Iris, in Greek mythology the personification of the rainbow, and also, because the rainbow was supposed to reach from the heavens to earth, the messenger of the gods to mortals. She is pictured as a maiden with golden wings carrying a CADUCEUS and a vase.

Irish National Theatre Society, see **Abbey Theatre.**

Irish Players, see **Abbey Theatre.**

Iron-work, an art developed in the Middle Ages during which many fine examples in the form of gratings, balconies, gates and railings were produced by processes involving forging, hammering, flattening, twisting and molding. Even the bands of iron affixed to wooden doors, and the bars and bolts with which they were fastened were objects of art, and despite the improved mechanical processes available today, modern iron-work at its best is only a feeble imitation of the 17th and 18th century master works.

Irving, Sir Henry (1838-1905), English actor and producer whose real name was John Henry Brodribb. He first appeared in 1856 with stock companies: ten years later he made his London debut as the villain in Dion BOUCICAULT's *Hunted Down.* In 1867 he appeared in *The Taming of the Shrew* with Ellen TERRY, and also achieved great success in *The Bells, Eugene Aram, Othello, Hamlet, Macbeth,* and *Richard III.* From 1878 to 1903 he managed the LYCEUM THEATRE, appearing with Ellen Terry in Shakespearean repertory, *Robespierre,* Goethe's *Faust,* Tennyson's *Becket,* and Sardou's *Dante.* He appeared from 1883 many times in the United States: he was also the first English actor to be knighted, and was buried in Westminster Abbey. His eldest son, **Henry Brodribb Irving** (1870-1919), made his debut on the London stage at the Comedy Theatre in 1891, and appeared later in many plays including *The Admirable Crichton; Hamlet; The Lyons Mail; Dr. Jekyll and Mr. Hyde..* As an avocation he wrote books on crime and the law. His brother, **Laurence Sidney Brodribb Irving** (1871-1914), appeared as an actor in *The Wild Duck; The Unwritten Law; A Bunch of Violets; Trilby; The Lily; Typhoon; Under the Red Robe; Raffles.* He also wrote several plays including *Peter the Great* (1898); *Richard Lovelace; Bonnie Dundee;* he also prepared an English adaptation of Maxim GORKY's *The Lower Depths.*

Irving, Washington (1783-1859), American author who first studied law, and later became ambassador to Spain. His works include *Salmagundi Papers* (1807-8); *A History of New York,* a humorous work written under the pen name of "Diedrich Knickerbocker"; *The Sketch Book of Geoffrey Crayon, Gent.: Bracebridge Hall; Tales* a Traveller; A History of the Life and Voyages of Christopher Columbus; The Conquest of Granada; The Alhambra; Crayon Miscellany; Adventures of Captain Bonneville; The Life of Oliver Goldsmith; Mahomet and His Successors; Wolfert's Roost; Life of George Washington. His memoirs, The Journals of Washington. Irving, were published in 1919.

Irwin, Wallace Admah (1876-), American novelist educated at Stanford University, and engaged in journalistic work before publishing his first book, Love Sonnets of a Hoodlum in 1902: among his notable works are The Rubaiyat of Omar Khayyam, Jr.; Chinatown Ballads; Letters of a Japanese Schoolboy; Mr. Togo; Maid of All Work; Venus in the East; The Days of Her Life; Young Wife.

Irwin, Will (1873-), American novelist educated at Stanford University who published volumes of stories in collaboration, and produced his first success, Old Chinatown in 1908, followed by The House of Mystery. He acted as war correspondent in World War I for the Saturday Evening Post, and at its conclusion published A Reporter in Armageddon (1918); The Next War; How Red is America; The House That Shadows Built; Spy and Counterspy with E. V. Voska; The Making of A Reporter, his autobiography. His most successful play was The Thirteenth Chair produced with Bayard VEILLER in 1916.

Isabey, Jean Baptiste (1767-1855), French painter who studied with Louis DAVID, and was started on the road to success through a commission from Marie ANTOINETTE. His notable paintings and portraits include Departure for the Army; The Return; The Barque of Isabey; Napoleon at Malmaison, considered a remarkable likeness; Revue of the First Consul; Mme. Récamier; Empress Josephine. His son, **Eugène Louis Gabriel Isabey** (1804-1886), was also a painter who specialized in marine views and scenes taken from daily life.

Isham, Norman Morrison (1864-1943), American architect educated at Brown University where he later became instructor in his art, and also head of the architectural department of the Rhode Island School of Design. He served as consultant for the Metropolitan Museum of Art in respect to the Colonial Rooms, and supervised the restoration of many early American buildings. He wrote several books regarding early American churches and house including A Glossary of Colonial Architecture (1939) published by the Walpole Society.

Isherwood, Christopher (1904-), English poet, novelist, and dramatist educated at Cambridge University: after traveling in Europe for a considerable period he came to the United States to join the staff of a film producing company. His novels and plays include All the Conspirators (1928); The Memorial; The Dog Beneath the Skin, a play with W. H. Auden; The Last of Mr. Norris; The Ascent of F 6; a play with W. H. Auden; Lions and Shadows, an autobiography; Goodbye to Berlin.

Isis, in Egyptian mythology the chief goddess, and the female counterpart of OSIRIS. She is the mother of Horus, god of the sun, is identified with the Greek Io, and her worship was later introduced into Greece and Rome. An inscription on her statues read: "I am that which is, has been and shall be: my veil no one has lifted" which has given rise to the well-known illusion to anything mysterious as "the veil of Isis."

Isla, José Francesco de (1703-1781), Spanish priest who was expelled from the Jesuit order because of his satirical writings which include The Life and Adventures of Friar Gerundio de Campazas, written under the pen name "F. Lobon de Salazar." He rivaled CERVANTES in popularity with Spanish readers because of his droll sayings in epigrammatic style.

Island of the Dead, The (Rachmaninoff), a symphonic poem by Sergei RACHMANINOFF first performed at Moscow in 1908 under the direction of the composer who also conducted it at the première in Chicago in 1909 by the Theodore Thomas Orchestra. It was inspired by a painting Die Toteninsel (The Island of the Dead) by Arnold BOECKLIN.

Islands of the Blest, in Greek mythology a group of islands located in the Western Ocean, and peopled by mortals granted immortality by the gods. They are mentioned in the works of HESIOD and PINDAR, and are supposed to be a land of perpetual summer lavishly stocked with the good things of life.

Isocephaly, in Greek sculpture a system according to which the heads of the principal figures in a bas-relief were arranged in a horizontal line whether seated, standing, or mounted.

Isocrates (436-338 B.C.), Greek writer who, because of his weak voice, wrote orations for others, and founded a school of oratory at which many great speakers studied. Twenty-one of his orations are extant; among them a eulogy on Athens entitled Peace.

Isolde, see **Tristan and Isolde.**

Israels, Josef (1824-1911), Dutch painter who studied at Amsterdam, at the ECOLE DES BEAUX-ARTS, Paris, and with Paul DELAROCHE. His notable pictures include The Wrecked; The Sacristan; A Son of the People; Old Age; The Zandvoort Fisherman; Alone in the World; Expectation; Cobblers' Dinner; The Dunes; Grandmother's Treasure.

Istar or **Ishtar,** the principal goddess of the Babylonians and Assyrians corresponding in many of her attributes to the Greek APHRODITE and ATHENA.

"Istar" Variations (d'Indy), a series of symphonic variations composed by Vincent D'INDY, and first performed at Brussels in 1897. The work was inspired by an ancient Babylonian poem, "The Epic of Izdubar" which relates the story of Istar going to the realm of death with its seven gates in search of her dead lover, and after bathing in the waters of life bringing him back to earth. There is a Victor recording by the Paris Conservatory Orchestra directed by Piero Coppola.

Istomina, Mme., 19th century Russian ballerina who danced at the Imperial Opera, St. Petersburg: she was the pupil of Charles Louis DIDELOT, and was so attractive personally that the celebrated Russian poet, Alexander PUSHKIN, dedicated his finest work, *Eugene Onegin,* to her, the result being that he became estranged from his wife.

Istrati, Panait (1884-1935), Rumanian novelist who traveled all over Europe and the Near East by doing odd jobs, stowing away on ships and riding the rails. After reading Romain ROLLAND'S "Jean-Christophe" he wrote a fifty-page letter to the author, receiving a reply which encouraged him to write: in 1923 his novel, *Kyra Kyralina* was published, and later translated. Several of his works have been translated including *Uncle Anghel; The Bandits; Thistles of the Baragan; Balkan Tavern; Bitter Orange Tree; Russia Unveiled.*

"Italian" Symphony (Mendelssohn), the fourth of Felix MENDELSSOHN'S symphonies; first performed in 1833 by the Philharmonic Society at London. It was called "Italian" by the composer because it was conceived while on a visit to Italy, but the only program movement is the *Finale* which is titled *Saltarello,* and probably inspired by the dancing at a Roman carnival described by Mendelssohn in a letter to a friend in 1831. There is a Victor recording by the Boston Symphony Orchestra under Sergei Koussevitzky, and a Columbia recording by the Halle Orchestra directed by Sir Hamilton Harty.

Itcho, Hanabusa (1653-1724), Japanese artist who studied with YASUNOBU, but finally broke away from the Kano School to follow the ideas of Ionasa MATAHEI. He was famous for his pictures of Japanese peasants in quaint costumes, and for his sense of humor in pictures of the Buddhist deities such as *The Seven Gods of Happiness.* Later artists including HIROSHIGE and HOKUSAI learned much from his paintings, *Twelve Months* and *Summer Shower.*

Iturbi, José (1895-), Spanish pianist, composer, and conductor who studied at the Valencia and Paris Conservatories, and with Joseph Malats. He headed the piano department of the Geneva Conservatory, toured Europe and South America, making his debut in the United States as soloist with the Philadelphia Orchestra in 1928, and appearing with all major American orchestras. He appeared first as an orchestral conductor at Mexico City in 1934, and has since acted as guest conductor of the New York Philharmonic-Symphony Orchestra and several other orchestras in addition to becoming regular conductor of the Rochester Symphony Orchestra. He has also appeared in two-piano recitals with his sister, Amparo Iturbi, and has made numerous broadcasts both as pianist and conductor.

Ivanov, Lev Ivanovich (1834-1901), Russian ballet dancer and choreographer who studied with Jean PETIPA and made his first success when he appeared in 1855 in *La Fille Mal Gardée.* He danced in many of the standard ballets, and became assistant to Marius PETIPA in 1885, also composing many ballets for the Tsar's private theatre. His ballets, distinguished for their artistry and originality, include *The Magic Flute; Casse Noisette (The Nutcracker); The Enchanted Forest; The Tulip of Haarlem; The Beauty of Seville; Cupid's Pranks.*

Ivanyi-Grunwald, Béla (1867-), Hungarian painter who studied with Bertelan SZEKELEY, at Munich and at the Académie Julien in Paris: his first recognition came from a series of large religious paintings. He was one of the founders of the Nagybanya art school in Hungary, and painted Hungarian landscapes and rural life in the style of Michael MUNKACSY and Ladislas PAAL. He also illustrated many books, and designed tapestries.

Ivory, a material derived from the tusk of an elephant, and used since ancient times for the making of small carved objects of art which frequently serve as valuable documentary evidence of culture existent in ancient nations who possessed no great sculptors or painters. Large and small ivory statues were made by the Greeks including the figure of Pallas ATHENA inlaid with gold and precious stones by PHIDIAS; the Romans used ivory for their diptychs; the Alexandrians made small ivory boxes and caskets; Romanesque art in Italy and France produced exquisite ivory book covers, crucifixes, and caskets; the Arabs made combs, tablets, and boxes readily sold in Europe, and the 14th century brought the art of carving in ivory to its zenith.

Ixion, in Greek mythology a prince who murdered his father-in-law, and was afflicted with madness as punishment. ZEUS forgave him and received him as a guest at OLYMPUS: he abused the god's hospitality by attempting to seduce HERA, and Zeus had him bound to a fiery wheel which rolled unceasingly in the air. He is presumed to be a symbol of the eternally moving sun.

J

Jackson, Helen Hunt (1830-1885), American poet and novelist who wrote under the initials "H. H.," and also used the pen name "Saxe Holm." Her works include *Bathmendi* (1867); *Verses by H. H.; A Century of Dishonor; Ramona*: the last two mentioned are her most important books containing accounts of the unjust treatment of American Indians by the United States Government. She also wrote several novels and stories for children.

Jackson, John Adams (1825-1879), American sculptor: his works include a group, *Eve Finding the Dead Body of Abel* in the Metropolitan Museum of Art, New York, and many busts of prominent Americans of his time, such as Wendell Phillips, in the Boston Athenaeum.

Jacob, Naomi Ellington (1889-), English novelist who worked as superintendent of a munitions factory during World War I, and also appeared on the stage and in several films. Her first book, *Jacob Ussher*, a best seller published in 1926 was followed by several successful works including *The Man Who Found Himself; Rock and Sand; The Beloved Physician; The Loaded Stick; Barren Metal; Straws in Amber; Sally Scarth; Cap of Youth.*

Jacobean Style, the name given to the style of architecture and furniture which followed the ELIZABETHAN STYLE, and remained in favor until the introduction of the Italian Renaissance mode about 1620 by Inigo Jones. The general lines of Elizabethan design were retained, but perverted by the introduction of scrolls, straps, and pierced crestings regarded by architectural authorities as entirely foreign to the original spirit of the design.

Jacobi, Johann Georg (1740-1814), German poet who was intimate with Martin WIELAND, Johann Herder, and Johann Wolfgang GOETHE: his finest works include *The Summer Journey* and *The Winter Journey.*

Jacobs, William Wymark (1863-), English writer of humorous short stories including *Many Cargoes* (1896); *Sea Urchins; At Sunwich Port; Dialstone Lane; Captains All; Salthaven; Night Watches; The Castaways; Deep Waters; Snug Harbor.* His stories have been translated into several European languages.

Jacobsen, Jens Peter (1847-1885), Danish novelist who was also a famous botanist and propagandist of the Darwinian theory: his realistic romances, *Mogens, Niels Lyhne,* and *Marie Grubbe,* display remarkable ability in devising and developing plots.

Jacopo di Venetia, see **Bellini, Jacopo.**

Jacopone da Todi (c.1235-1306), Italian poet and satirist who became a Franciscan monk after the death of his wife, and wrote pitiless sarcastic verses aimed at Pope Boniface VIII: he composed a number of hymns including the *Stabat Mater,* but his authorship of the latter is a matter of dispute.

Jacque, Charles Émile (1813-1894), French painter and etcher of the BARBIZON SCHOOL: he specialized in landscapes and animal pictures, painting farmyards, pigs, sheep, and poultry with extraordinary skill. His works include *Herd of Oxen at a Watering Place; Flock of Sheep; Ploughing; Country Scene; In a Sheepfold; The Village Poor; Girl Knitting; Young Shepherdess.*

Jadassohn, Salomon (1831-1902), German musical theorist and composer who studied the piano with Franz LISZT, and theoretical subjects at the Leipzig Conservatory where he became a professor in 1871. He wrote several important works on harmony, counterpoint, modulation, composition, and orchestration: also orchestral works, chamber music, choral works, and piano pieces.

Jade, an ornamental stone varying in color from emerald green to white: there are two varieties of the mineral; one known as *jadeite* and the other as *nephrite.* It is greatly prized by the Chinese and Japanese in association with the five cardinal virtues of wisdom, charity, courage, modesty, and justice. Jade was used for making implements by many primitive peoples, and is found in India, New Zealand, Mexico, China, Alaska, Siberia, Switzerland, Greece, Austria, and Germany.

Jaffe, Sam (1898-), American stage and screen actor who made his debut in 1915 at New York in *The Clod,* later touring with the Ben GREET Company, and appearing in *Samson and Delilah; The Idle Inn; The God of Vengeance; The Jazz Singer; The Eternal Road; The Gentle People.* He has also played important roles in several films including *The Scarlet Empress; We Live Again; The Lost Horizon; Gunga Din.*

Jagel, Frederick (1897-), American operatic tenor who first sang in church choirs, studying later in New York and Milan. His debut was made in 1924 at Livorno, Italy, in PUCCINI's *La Boheme:* after singing for four years in Italy, Holland, and South America, he made his debut in 1927 at the Metropolitan Opera House in AIDA, and has been a leading member of the company since that time, creating important roles and also singing with the Chicago Civic and Ravinia Opera Companies.

Jahn, Otto (1813-1869), German art critic and musicographer educated at Leipzig and Berlin: his important contribution to the literature of music is *Mozart* (1856-1859), a monumental biography which has been translated into English, and, as the first thorough work of its kind involving musical research, has become a model for subsequent writers of musical biographies. Material collected by him for a life of BEETHOVEN was utilized by Alexander THAYER.

James, George Payne Rainsford (1801-1860), English novelist who wrote more than seventy historical novels after his first work, *Richelieu* (1829) was praised by Sir Walter SCOTT. This was followed by *Darneley, Delorme, Attila* and many stirring romances which some critics claim were direct imitations of Scott. He also wrote some historical works such as *Dark Scenes of History* which were not so well received.

James, Henry (1843-1916), American essayist and novelist who was educated as a youth in Europe, and returned to study at Harvard University in 1862 where he came under the influence of Charles Eliot NORTON, William Dean HOWELLS, and James Russell LOWELL. He went to Paris in 1868 where he became intimate with Ivan TURGENEV, Gustave FLAUBERT, Guy de MAUPASSANT, and Émile ZOLA. His works include *A Passionate Pilgrim and Other Tales* (1875); *Daisy Miller; Washington Square; The Portrait of a Lady; The Awkward Age; The Wings of the Dove; The Ambassadors,* the latter considered his finest novel. He became a naturalized British subject in 1915 because of his attachment to the British cause in World War I.

James, Marquis (1891-   ), American journalist and author who served in World War I: his biography *The Raven: A Biography of Sam Houston* (1929), won the Pulitzer prize in 1930: among his successful works are *Andrew Jackson: The Border Captain; They Had Their Hour; Andrew Jackson: Portrait of a President* which won the Pulitzer prize for biography in 1938; *Mr. Garner of Texas; Alfred I. Dupont: The Family Rebel.*

James, Philip (1890-   ), American composer and conductor who studied with Rubin GOLDMARK, and served as bandmaster of the American Expeditionary Forces during World War I. He conducted the Victor HERBERT Opera Company, The Brooklyn Orchestral Society, and the Bamberger Little Symphony: he has also acted as guest conductor of major American orchestras. Since 1933 he has been chairman of the music department of New York University. His compositions include orchestral works, chamber music, choral works, and many songs.

James, Will (1892-1942), American artist and author entirely self-educated: his works, which he illustrated himself, include *Cowboys, North and South* (1924); *Smoky; Lone Cowboy,* which won the Newbery Medal in 1934 and was filmed; *Uncle Bill; Scorpion: A Good Bad Horse; Look-See; Horses I've Known; The American Cowboy.*

Jameson, Anna Brownell (1794-1860), Irish author who was the daughter of a distinguished artist: her works include *The Diary of an Ennuyée* (1826); *Loves of the Poets; Celebrated Female Sovereigns; Memoirs of the Early Italian Painters; Sacred and Legendary Art.*

Jameson, (Margaret) Storm (1897-   ), English novelist educated at Leeds University and University College, London: her works include *The Pot Boils* (1919); *Modern Drama in Europe; Three Kingdoms; Farewell to Youth; That Was Yesterday; Love in Winter; Here Comes a Candle; The Memoirs of an Obscure Man; Cousin Honoré.*

Jami, Abd-ar-Rahman (c.1414-c.1492), Persian poet known in Europe as the "Persian Petrarch": his more than one hundred works include *The Abode of Spring; The Seven Thrones; The Chain of Gold; The Loves of Joseph and Zuleika.* He clothed the passion of love in such glorious terms that his countrymen called him "a fiery star before which all other stars yielded."

Jammes, Francis (1868-1938), French poet and novelist educated at the University of Bordeaux: his works include secular and sacred poetry some of which has appeared in American magazines; also several novels and prose writings including *Leaves in the Wind; My Poetic France; Cardinal Lâvigerie; Divine Sadness; My Daughter Bernadette.*

Janáček, Leos (1854-1928), Czech composer who studied at the Leipzig and Vienna Conservatories, and in 1919 became professor of composition at the Brünn Conservatory where he guided the creative work of many Czech composers. His opera, *Jenufa* (1902) was produced

in several European opera houses, and at the Metropolitan Opera House, New York, in 1924. His compositions, which are ranked with those of SMETANA and DVORAK, include several operas, orchestral works, chamber music, and song cycles.

Janauschek, Franziska Magdalena (1830-1904), Bohemian actress who made her debut in 1846 at Prague, and in 1848 became the leading actress at eighteen of the Stadt Theatre in Frankfurt, Germany, remaining there for twelve years, and touring Germany, Austria, and Russia, during her vacations. She was effective in tragic roles, and visited the United States in 1867, returning in 1873 after having mastered the English language. She became a popular favorite in both classic and modern plays, and remained there until her death.

Janin, Jules (1804-1874), French journalist and novelist who delighted Parisian readers with his literary and dramatic criticisms: his stories and novels include *The Dead Donkey and the Guillotined Woman; Confession; A Heart for Two Loves;* also a *History of Dramatic Literature.*

Janis, Elsie (1889-   ), American actress who made her debut in 1897 as a boy in *The Charity Ball,* later appearing in vaudeville as "Little Elsie." In 1905 she created a sensation with imitations of contemporary actors in *When We Were Forty-One:* she also appeared in *The Vanderbilt Cup; The Slim Princess; The Passing Show; Miss Information; Oh, Kay; A Star for the Night,* and numerous productions of similar character. She was one of the favorite entertainers of the A.E.F. during World War I, and has also appeared in the same capacity during World War II.

Jannings, Emil (1886-   ), German stage and screen actor born in the United States, but taken to Europe as a child and educated at Zurich, Switzerland. He played as a boy at the Gorlitz Theatre, and later developed into a distinguished actor of leading roles in plays by SHAKESPEARE, STRINDBERG, SCHILLER, IBSEN, and GOETHE. He entered the films in 1915, appearing in *Madame Du Barry; Passion; Deception; Peter the Great; Faust; The Last Laugh; Variety; The Way of All Flesh; Sins of the Fathers; The Blue Angel,* with Marlene DIETRICH; *The Tempest* with Anna STEN;* also many German films.

Janssen, Peter (1844-1908), German painter who studied at the Düsseldorf Academy with Friedrich Bundemann, later becoming professor and finally director of the institution. His frescoes include *Seven Scenes from the History of Arminius; Twelve Scenes from the Myth of Prometheus; Colonization of the Baltic Coast;* also an oil painting, *Peter's Denial.*

Janssen, Werner (1899-   ), American composer and conductor educated at Dartmouth College and at the American Academy in Rome. He has conducted the New York Philharmonic-Symphony Orchestra, the Chicago Symphony Orchestra, the Boston Symphony Orchestra, and many other American orchestras, also making numerous radio broadcasts. His compositions include orchestral works, chamber music, and incidental music for films including a symphonic score for *The General Died at Dawn*.

Janssens, Cornelis van (1593-c.1662), Flemish painter who achieved great success as a portraitist at the English court from 1618 until the coming of Anthony VAN DYCK. Among his sitters were CHARLES I and the Duke of BUCKINGHAM: he went to Holland in 1643, and continued his work as a portrait painter there with great success.

Janssens, Victor Honoré (1664-1739), Flemish painter who spent four years at the court of the Duke of Holstein, and eleven years in Rome where he painted the figures in the landscapes of Pieter MOLYN THE YOUNGER, and was greatly influenced by RAPHAEL. His works include *Sacrifice of Aeneas; Dido Building Carthage; Venus and Adonis; Apparition of the Virgin; Assembly of the Gods;* also many altarpieces in Flemish churches.

Janssens van Nuyssen, Abraham (1575-1632), Flemish painter who studied with Jan Snellinck and in Italy: he was considered the most distinguished Flemish painter after RUBENS: his works include *Adoration of the Magi; Entombment; Ecce Homo; Descent from the Cross; Allegory on Age; Meleager and Atalanta; Venus and Adonis; Tobias and the Angel.*

Janus, in Roman mythology a deity represented on coins as having one head with two bearded faces looking in opposite directions. The first month of every year as well as the first day of each month were sacred to him: his name is perpetuated in the name (January) of the first month of the year. He was considered the oldest of the gods, and the inventor and protector of all arts.

Janvier, Thomas Allibone (1849-1913), American journalist and short story writer: his works include *Color Studies* (1885); *The Aztec Treasure House; Embassy to Provence; In Old New York; In the Sargasso Sea; Henry Hudson; Legends of the City of Mexico; At the Casa Napoleon.*

Japanese Music, a musical system derived, according to authorities on Oriental music, from that of China. Between the 6th and 12th centuries, Japanese scholars made an intensive study of Chinese music: the twelve pitch-pipes, called *lus,* were incorporated into the Japanese chromatic scale. The Chinese *sheng,* a form of mouth organ, and the *Ch'in,* a form of PSALTERY, became the Japanese *sho* and *koto* in slightly altered forms. Other instruments included the *samisen,* a guitar; the *biwa,* a lute; the *shakuhachi,* a flageolet; the *hichiriki,* a wind instruments with a double reed. In the Shinto temples, dance pantomimes (kangura) are accompanied by chants employing a form of pentatonic scale, and in the classical or Nō drama, there are distinct forms of arias and recitative.

Jaques-Dalcroze, Émile (1865-), Swiss composer of French parentage who studied at Geneva, and at Vienna with Robert Fuchs and Anton BRUCKNER. He is famous as the originator of a

system of teaching music through rhythmic exercises known as EURHYTHMICS. He wrote several treatises on his methods, and composed operas, orchestra works, chamber music, and songs.

Jardin Public (Public Garden), a modern ballet in one act: libretto based on Andre Gide's *The Counterfeiters* by Vladimir DUKELSKY and Leonide MASSINE; choreography by Leonide Massine; music by Vladimir Dukelsky; first presented in 1936. The scene is a park, and the action portrays the daily happenings in a public garden where nurse-girls, street sweepers, poets, poor couples, fashionable folks, and peddlers are intermingled.

Jaroff, Serge, see **Don Cossack Russian Male Choir.**

Jarves, James Jackson (1818-1888), American art collector, critic, and author who founded in 1840 the *Polynesian,* the first newspaper published in Hawaii, and later the official organ of the government. He collected early Italian paintings later acquired by Yale University; Venetian glasses now in the Metropolitan Museum of Art, New York; Renaissance embroideries, laces, and fabrics now owned by Wellesley College. His works include *Art Hints* (1855); *Art Studies; Art Thoughts; Glimpses at the Art of Japan:* his books are interesting as sources.

Jarvis, John Wesley (1780-1839), American painter born in England who came to the United States as a child: he was chiefly self-taught, but studied anatomy so carefully that he is considered one of the best early American portrait painters. His portraits include those of Thomas Paine, John Randolph, Commodore Perry, and several full-length likenesses of military and naval officers in the War of 1812.

Jason, in Greek mythology the son of Aeson, king of Iolchus in Thessaly who was educated by the centaur, CHIRON. Pelias, who murdered his father, sent Jason to capture the GOLDEN FLEECE from Aeetes, king of Colchis: he sailed in his ship, the *Argo,* accompanied by a band of heroes called the ARGONAUTS. Aeete's daughter, Medea, aided him in securing the fleece. The story is related in detail by William MORRIS in *The Life and Death of Jason.*

Jasper, a quartz of impure formation, opaque in composition and available in many colors of which the favorite shade for gem use is red. It is capable of being highly polished, and is also used for vases and other art objects.

Jaurequi y Aguilar, Juan (c.1570-c.1649), Spanish poet distinguished for his translation of Tasso's *Aminta,* and a long amorous poem, *Orpheus,* which lacks the charming expressiveness of his work as a translator.

Jazz, the name of modern American dance music formerly known as RAGTIME: characterized by striking and sometimes intricate rhythms elaborately instrumentated. Jazz bands are said to have originated in the South: Joseph K.

Gorham presented an organization of this type at Chicago in 1915. The first composer of jazz was William C. HANDY with a piece called *St. Louis Blues:* Irving BERLIN, Cole PORTER, and George GERSHWIN developed it in various forms, and many American and European composers of serious music including DEBUSSY, MILHAUD, CASELLA, HINDEMITH, STRAVINSKY, KRENEK, GRUENBERG, WHITHORNE and VARESE have employed its rhythms in operas, symphonic, and chamber music.

Jean de Meung (c.1250-c.1305), French scholar and poet, said to have studied at the University of Paris, whose real name was Jean Clopinel or Chopinel. He wrote many songs which were favorites throughout France; also a lengthy poem of over 19,000 lines as a continuation of the *Romance of the Rose,* begun by Guillaume de Lorris, in the form of a satire on celibacy, women, and marriage. The poem has an equal number of detractors and defenders.

Jeanne d'Arc, see **Joan of Arc.**

Jeanneret-Gris, Charles Édouard, also known as **Le Corbusier** (1887-), Swiss architect and painter who first attended a school of arts and crafts, and later traveled through Italy and Austria to Paris where he studied with Auguste Perret. In 1922 he became a partner of the architect, Pierre Jeanneret, and subsequently adopted the name of his grandfather, Le Corbusier. His works include the Domino Project; Citrohan Project; Salvation Army Project in Paris; Villa des Garches and many housing projects in France. He is also the author of several treatises on architecture and painting.

Jean Paul, see **Richter, Johann.**

Jeffers, Robinson (1887-), American poet educated at the University of Pittsburgh, Occidental College, Los Angeles, University of Southern California, and at the University of Zurich. His works include *Flagons and Apples* (1912); *Californians; Tamar and Other Poems; The Roan Stallion; Cawdor; Dear Judas; Descent to the Dead; Thurso's Landing; Give Your Heart to the Hawks; Be Angry at the Sun.*

Jefferson, Joseph (1829-1905), American actor who belonged to a family in which members had been actors for several generations: his great-grandfather appeared with David GARRICK. He made his debut on the stage as a child of four, and until he was twenty played with stock companies: in 1857 he began to receive recognition with Laura KEENE's company in such plays as *The Cricket on the Hearth, The Heir-at-Law,* and *Our American Cousin.* In 1859 Jefferson presented his own stage version of *Rip Van Winkle:* a new dramatization, prepared for him by Dion BOUCICAULT, proved an overwhelming success in 1866 at the Olympic Theatre, New York, and he appeared in it for many years. He was almost as great a favorite as Bob Acres in *The Rivals,* and appeared on the American stage for nearly seventy years. His *Autobiography* was published in 1890, and Francis WILSON's biography, *Joseph Jefferson,* in 1906.

Jefferson, Thomas (1743-1826), American statesman, and third president of the United States who was greatly interested in architecture, and applied the ideas imbibed from a book of designs by the 16th century Italian architect, Andrea PALLADIO, to the plans for his own home, *Monticello,* at Charlottesville, Virginia. His plans, based on the Maison Carrée at Nîmes, France, were used for the State Capitol of Virginia, and he also supplied many ideas for the buildings of the University of Virginia.

Jeffreys, Ellis (1869-1943), English stage and screen actress born in Ceylon who made her debut in 1889 at London in Gilbert and Sullivan's operetta, *The Yeoman of the Guard:* among the operettas and plays in which she appeared were *La Cigale; The Bauble Shop; The Fringe of Society; The Two Orphans; Sweet Lavender; The Vagabond King; The Prince Consort.* She made her first appearance in 1895 at New York in *The Notorious Mrs. Ebbsmith,* and in 1906 toured the United States in *She Stoops to Conquer.* She also appeared in several English films.

Jenghiz Khan (1162-1227), Mongolian chieftain, real name *Temujin,* who became ruler at the age of thirteen over several tribes, and gradually extended his sway until he was in control of all Mongolia, assuming the title *Jenghiz Khan* in 1206. He overran China, Turkestan, Persia, and part of India, dying during an expedition to conquer Northwest China, leaving his vast empire to his three sons, but it gradually dwindled away due to their lack of ability. Jenghiz Khan was responsible for the Turks gaining a foothold and eventually an empire in Europe, having driven them from their original home in Northern Asia. Painters have found incidents in his career excellent subjects.

Jennewein, Carl Paul (1890-), American sculptor born in Germany educated at the ART STUDENTS' LEAGUE, New York, and at the American Academy in Rome. His works include the bronzes *The Greek Dance; Cupid and Crane; Bow and Arrow; Cupid and Gazelle; Comedy; Over the Waves.* He has also executed sculptures for many buildings and bridges in New York, Washington, D. C., Harrisburg, and Baltimore, and he is represented at many American museums.

Jenney, William Le Baron (1832-1907), American architect trained at the Harvard Scientific School, and at the École Centrale des Arts et Manufactures, Paris. He served as an officer in the Civil War, and established himself as an architect at Chicago in 1868. He invented and first made use of the skeleton iron construction used in the Home Insurance Building at Chicago: his buildings include the Union League Club; the Siegel-Cooper Building, and the New York Life Insurance Building at Chicago; also the Horticultural Building at the World's Columbian Exhibition.

Jensen, Adolf (1837-1879), German composer famous for his songs which show the influence of Robert SCHUMANN and Richard WAGNER. He was a pupil of Ludwig Ehlert and Richard Marpurg: his best-known song is *Murmuring Zephyrs* from the "Spanish Song Book," Op. 21, in which the theme is taken from a song by Rudolf Friedrich Niemann.

Jensen, Johannes Vilhelm (1873-), Danish poet and novelist who studied medicine for a time at the University of Copenhagen, but abandoned it for a literary career: his works translated into English include *The Long Journey,* an epic of the Goths (1923), and *The Fall of the King.* He has also written several volumes of legendary tales and of verse.

Jenson or **Janson, Nicolas** (?-1480), Italian printer born in France, who opened a printing establishment in Venice, and was the original designer of the Roman type face: his type was used by the ALDINE PRESS, and his influence over other type designers including Caslon and William MORRIS is plainly evident.

Jepson, Helen (1905-), American lyric soprano who studied at the CURTIS INSTITUTE OF MUSIC, Philadelphia, with Mary GARDEN and Queena MARIO, making her first appearance in 1928 with the Philadelphia Opera Company in Mozart's *The Marriage of Figaro.* She made her debut with the Metropolitan Opera Company in 1935 in John Lawrence SEYMOUR's opera, *In the Pasha's Garden,* remaining with the company since that time; also concertizing and appearing on radio broadcasts.

Jeritza, Maria (1887-), Austrian dramatic soprano who made her formal debut in 1912 as Elizabeth in TANNHAUSER at the Vienna Volksoper, later singing at the Vienna State Opera, and making her debut in 1921 at the Metropolitan Opera House in KORNGOLD's *Die Tote Stadt.* She remained at the Metropolitan until 1932, and achieved success in *Cavalleria Rusticana, Thaïs, Carmen,* and *Tosca.* She also concertized extensively and has appeared as soloist with major American orchestras. In 1924, her autobiography, *Sunlight and Song,* was published.

Jerome, Jerome Klapka (1859-1927), English humorist and dramatist: his works include *On the Stage and Off* (1885); *Idle Thoughts of an Idle Fellow; Three Men in a Boat; New Lamps for Old; Miss Hobbs; The Passing of the Third Floor Back:* the latter was his most successful play, first produced in 1907 and revived many times in England and the United States.

Jerrold, Douglas William (1803-1857), English humorist and playwright who wrote an immensely popular play, *Black-Eyed Susan* (1829), but became most famous for his contributions to PUNCH. His works include *Mrs. Caudle's Curtain Lectures; Story of a Feather; The Rent Day; Time Works Wonders; Retired from Business.* His son, **William Blanchard Jerrold** (1826-1884), became a journalist and writer who lived in Paris; his works include *Recollections of Charles Dickens; Paris for the English; Life of Napoleon III; Life of Douglas William Jerrold; The Best of All Good Company.*

Jerusalem, Temple of, an edifice built by King Solomon on the hill of Moria near Jerusalem: it was destroyed by the Sumerians, but rebuilt on the same site. A description of the temple in the Bible (Chapters XL to XLIII. of the Book of Ezekiel) was used by two French architects to make a reconstruction which resembled a Greek temple in its general arrangement. The outer wall surrounding the temple measured about 800 feet on each of the four sides: the temple itself contained very few statues, but was richly furnished, and the high altar had two great bronze columns placed in front of it.

Jessner, Leopold (1878-), German theatre director who made radical changes in stage scenery: he dispensed with regulation scenery, using instead levels in space or stairways called *Jessner steps.* He managed the Berlin State Theatre which became a potent factor in German drama under his direction from 1919 to 1925.

Jesus in Art, see **Christ in Art.**

Jesus, Joy of Man's Desiring (J. S. Bach), a chorale composed by Johann Schop, a 17th century composer who was organist at St. James' Church in Hamburg. Johann Sebastian BACH utilized the melody in his 147th cantata, *Heart and Mind,* weaving an exquisite counter-melody around the simple original air. There are Victor and Columbia recordings for chorus, orchestra, organ, and piano: the best known of the latter is the Victor recording by Myra HESS.

Jet, a mineral similar to coal found in compact masses chiefly at Whitby, England, although there are deposits in Spain, France, and the United States. It is capable of being highly polished, and is used for rosaries, crucifixes, beads, and other pieces of jewelry.

Jeté or **Pas jeté,** in ballet a step or jump in which the weight of the body is shifted from one foot to the other: when the legs are crossed in the air before landing, the step is called *jeté battu.*

Jeux d'Enfants (Children's Games), a ballet in one act: libretto by Boris Kochno; choreography by Leonide MASSINE; music by Georges BIZET; first produced at Monte Carlo in 1932. The action takes place in a nursery, and toys such as tops, rocking horses, tennis rackets, and shuttlecocks are portrayed by the dancers. At the première, Irina BARONOVA, Tamara TOUMANOVA, David LICHINE, and Leon WOIZIKOVSKY assumed some of the roles.

Jewell, Edward Alden (1888-), American art critic and novelist who became art critic of the New York *Times* in 1936: his works include *The Charmed Circle* (1921); *The White Kami; The Moth Decides:* also two books of art criticism: *Americans* and *Have We an American Art?*

Jewelry, the name given to personal ornaments such as bracelets, brooches, pendants, and similar objects studded with precious stones. The designing and manufacture of jewelry was one of the earliest manifestations of art among the Assyrians and Egyptians, and all through history each epoch has seen the production of masterpieces in this particular field of art. In the Middle Ages jewelry was massive but simple in design: during the RENAISSANCE it became exquisitely beautiful as well as elaborate. Many of the processes entering into the production of jewelry, such as gem cutting and engraving, enameling, chasing, and repousse work, require the skill of an artist as well as that of an artisan.

Jewels of the Madonna, a grand opera in three acts: libretto by Carlo Zangarini and Enrico Golisciani; music and also the plot by Ermanno WOLF-FERRARI; first produced at Berlin in 1911, and at the Metropolitan Opera House, New York, in 1912, by the Chicago-Philadelphia Opera Company. The somewhat involved plot revolves around the love of Gennaro, a blacksmith, and Rafaele, leader of the Camorrists, for Maliella, a beautiful but wayward girl: in its musical delineation of a great city, the opera follows the lines of CHARPENTIER'S *Louise.* There are Victor and Columbia recordings of the popular *Intermezzo No. 2.*

Jewett, Sarah Orne (1849-1909), American novelist who gained her knowledge of American country people through trips taken with her father on his errands of mercy as a physician: her works include *Deephaven* (1877); *Country By-Ways; A Country Doctor; A White Heron and Other Stories; Tales of New England; The Country of the Pointed Firs; The Tory Lover.*

Jew's-harp, a musical instrument constructed of a rigid iron frame containing a thin, flexible metal tongue: the frame is held between the teeth while the metal tongue is plucked by the performer's finger. The volume and pitch are controlled by changing the shape and size of the oral cavity, and the instrument enjoyed considerable popularity during the 18th and 19th centuries in Europe and Great Britain.

Jig, see **Gigue.**

Jinni or **Djinni,** in Arabian legend a spirit of the underworld resembling man in many respects, but able to transform itself at will into any form desired. It was capable of both good and evil, and the body it assumed had no more substance than smoke or fire. The jinni is constantly mentioned in the tales of the ARABIAN NIGHTS.

Joachim, Joseph (1831-1907), Hungarian violinist and composer who studied with Joseph Böhm, making his debut at seven in Pest and at twelve in Leipzig: from 1843 he was closely associated in the latter city with Felix MENDELSSOHN, Ferdinand DAVID, and Robert SCHUMANN. He made many visits to London, became concert-master for Franz LISZT at Weimar, and headed the famous Hochschule für Musik at Berlin. He founded the famous Joachim Quartet in 1869, and Johannes BRAHMS wrote his violin concerto for him. His compositions include orchestral works, violin concertos, and cadenzas for the violin concertos of BEETHOVEN and Brahms.

Joan of Arc (1412-1431), a heroine of French history known as the *Maid of Orleans.* She was greatly disturbed by the fact that the victories of England and her allies, the Burgundians, had left little of France in the possession of King Charles VII; urged on by mysterious voices, she persuaded the king to let her lead the French army of 10,000 against his enemies at Orleans, and was successful in defeating them not only there, but at several other places. In 1429 she was unsuccessful in besieging Paris, was captured at Compiègne and delivered to the English at Rouen where she was tried for sorcery and heresy, condemned to life imprisonment and finally burned at the stake in 1431. Twenty-five years later Charles VII ordered her completely cleared in a rehabilitation trial, and she was canonized by Pope Benedict XV in 1919. Joan of Arc has been the subject of paintings by BASTIEN-LEPAGE and DELAROCHE; of sculptures by CHAPU, FOYATIER, FREMIET, and Anna Vaughn HYATT. Friedrich von SCHILLER and George Bernard SHAW who made her the heroine of dramas: an opera, *Jeanne d'Arc,* by Charles GOUNOD was produced at Paris in 1873, and there are biographies favorable and unfavorable by VOLTAIRE, Quicherat, Andrew LANG, Anatole FRANCE, and Mark TWAIN.

Jocasta, see **Oedipus.**

Jodelle, Etienne, Sieur de Lymodin (1532-1573), French dramatist who is said to have founded modern French drama with his tragedy, *Cleopatra,* produced in 1552, and his comedy, *Eugene:* his later plays such as *Dido Sacrifices Herself,* and *The Meeting* were less successful.

Johansen, John Christen (1876-), American painter born in Denmark who was brought to America as a child: he studied at the CHICAGO ART INSTITUTE, at the Académie Julien, Paris, and with Frank DUVENECK. In 1912 he became instructor at the ART STUDENTS' LEAGUE, New York: among his notable works are *October Seas and Gold; Piazza San Marco; Fiesoli; Evening Interior.* His wife, M. Jean McLane Johansen (1878-), is a distinguished portrait painter.

John, Augustus Edwin (1879-), English painter and etcher who studied at the Slade School and taught at the University of Liverpool. In 1904 he was one of the founders of the Society of Twelve and in 1915 thirty-two of his etchings were purchased for the FITZWILLIAM MUSEUM at Cambridge University. He executed portraits of George Bernard SHAW, W. B. YEATS, and Lloyd George: also many paintings including *Quarry Folk; Valley of Time; Rachel; The Smiling Woman; Mother and Child; Peasant Industry.*

John, Sir William Goscombe (1860-), Welsh sculptor who first achieved success with his figure, *St. John the Baptist:* this was followed by *Morpheus; A Girl Binding Her Hair; A Boy at Play; The Glamour of the Rose; The Elf.* He has created several equestrian statues and memorials including the monument to Sir Arthur SULLIVAN in the Embankment Gardens, London. He also executed a striking frieze, *The Battle of Trafalgar,* for the pedestal of the statue of Viscount Tredegar, and a memorial to the war correspondents of World War I.

Johnson, Eastman (1824-1906), American painter who studied at the Düsseldorf Academy, and in Italy, France, and Holland. His genre paintings include *Old Kentucky Home; Old Stage Coach; Corn Husking at Nantucket; New England Pedlar; Husking-Bee:* he also executed likenesses of Daniel Webster, Ralph Waldo EMERSON, Henry W. LONGFELLOW, John D. Rockefeller, and of several presidents including Cleveland, Harrison, and Hayes.

Johnson, Edward (c.1884-), Canadian dramatic tenor who was educated at the University of Toronto, and studied voice with Vincenzo Lombardi at Florence, Italy, making his debut in 1912 at Padua in *Andrea Chenier*. After singing for five years at LA SCALA, Milan, and also at other opera houses in Italy, Spain, and South America, he made his debut in 1922 at the Metropolitan Opera House, New York, in *The Love of Three Kings*. He remained with the Metropolitan until 1935 when he succeeded Herbert WITHERSPOON as general manager of the Metropolitan Opera House. Among the novelties produced during his administration are CIMAROSA's *Secret Marriage;* HAGEMAN's *Caponsacchi;* Walter DAMROSCH's *The Man Without a Country;* Johann Sebastian BACH's *Phoebus and Pan;* Gian Carlo MENOTTI's *Amelia Goes to the Ball* and *The Island God;* all the above sung in English. Among more than thirty revivals may be mentioned HALEVY's *La Juive;* SMETANA's *The Bartered Bride* (in English); RABAUD's *Marouf* (in English); STRAUSS' *Elektra* and *Salome;* GLUCK's *Orfeo ed Euridice;* VERDI's *Simon Boccanegra;* MONTEMEZZI's *The Love of Three Kings;* PERGOLESI's *La Serva Padrona.* Spring seasons of opera at popular prices were presented in 1936 and 1937, and a World's Fair Season in 1939: among the famous singers who returned after several years absence to the Metropolitan stage were Beniamino GIGLI, Tito SCHIPA, and Giuseppe de LUCA.

Johnson, Horace (1893-), American composer who studied composition with Bainbridge CRIST, and also in Italy, France, and England. He has been associated in an editorial capacity with *The Etude, Musical America,* and the *Musical Courier:* his compositions include the orchestral suites *Imagery* and *Streets of Florence;* a tone poem for orchestra, *Astarte;* chamber music; choral works and songs.

Johnson, James Weldon (1871-1938), American Negro author and composer educated at Atlanta and Columbia Universities. He held the posts of professor of creative literature at Fisk University, Nashville, Tenn., and consul at Puerta Cabello, Venezuela, and Corinto, Nicaragua. He was awarded the Spingarn Medal for services to Negroes, and founded the National Association for the Advancement of Colored People of which he was secretary from 1916 to 1930. His works include a novel, *The Autobiography of an Ex-Colored Man* (1912); *Fifty Years and Other Poems; The Book of American Negro Poetry:* he also collaborated with his brother, Rosamond JOHNSON, on several operettas and many popular songs.

Johnson, (John) Rosamond (1873-), American Negro composer, actor, and singer who studied at the NEW ENGLAND CONSERVATORY with William Dunham and Arthur Whiting; also with David BISPHAM. He appeared in American and English music halls, conducted for Anna PAVLOWA at Hamburg, toured America and Europe in Negro spiritual recitals, and created the character of Lawyer Frazier in George GERSHWIN's *Porgy and Bess.* His compositions include *African Drum Dance; Lift Every Voice and Sing,* called the Negro national anthem; numerous concert and popular songs; also collections of Negro spirituals with James Weldon JOHNSON, his brother.

Johnson, Owen McMahon (1878-), American short story writer and novelist educated at Yale University: his works include *Arrows of the Almighty* (1901); *The Eternal Boy; The Tennessee Shad; Stover at Yale,* a best seller; *A Comedy for Wives; The Salamander; Virtuous Wives; The Wasted Generation; Blue Blood; The Coming of the Amazons.*

Johnson, Robert Underwood (1853-1937), American poet and editor educated at Earlham College, Indiana: he was connected with *Century Magazine* for forty years, and influential in improving copyright conditions for American authors in respect to foreign rights. His volumes of verse include *The Winter Hour, and Other Poems* (1891); *Songs of Liberty; Poems of War and Peace; Poems of Fifty Years.*

Johnson, Samuel (1709-1784), English critic, essayist, poet, and lexicographer who studied for a time at Oxford and later made a living by teaching school and hack writing: after his *Dictionary of the English Language* was published in 1755 his reputation was established and in 1762 a government pension was granted him. In 1764 he founded a literary club which became an important factor in the world of letters: among its members were Oliver GOLDSMITH, Sir JOSHUA REYNOLDS, Edmund Burke; Edward GIBBON; Sir William Jones, Bennet Langton, Topham Beauclerk, and James BOSWELL with whom he toured the Hebrides in 1784. Boswell wrote an account of the trip in 1786. Johnson's works include *Voyage to Abyssinia* (1735); the poems *London* and *The Vanity of Human Wishes; Irene; The Rambler; The Idler; Rasselas: The History of Rasselas, Prince of Abyssinia; Lives of the Poets; Shakespeare With Notes.*

Johnston, Annie Fellows (1863-1931), American writer of stories for children: her works include *Big Brother* (1893); *The Little Colonel* (1895), followed by eleven sequels published up to 1929; *The Land of the Little Colonel.*

Johnston, Mary (1870-1936), American novelist whose first book, *Prisoners of Hope* (1898) had little success: it was followed by *To Have and to Hold,* a sensational best seller. Among her other successful works are *Audrey; Lewis Rand; Hagar; The Wanderers; Michael Forth; Silver Cross; The Slave Ship; The Exile; Drury Randall.*

John Street Theatre, one of the first theatres erected in New York; built in 1767 near lower

Broadway. It opened with George FARQUHAR's play, *The Beaux' Stratagem,* and for more than thirty years many famous English and American actors appeared there among them William Hallam and Joseph JEFFERSON. In 1787 the first drama by an American playwright of real importance, *The Contrast,* by Royall TYLER, was produced there.

Jokai, Mor (1825-1904), Hungarian journalist and novelist who enriched the literature of his country by many brilliant novels including *The White Rose; The Man of Gold; The Man With the Iron Heart; Black Diamonds; The Poor Rich; The New Landlord; Peter the Priest; The Lion of Janina:* many of his works have been translated.

Jolson, Al (1886-), American stage, screen, and radio actor and singer who first appeared in the mob scene of *Children of the Ghetto.* After playing in vaudeville and with Lew Dockstader's Ministrels he appeared in several productions including *La Belle Paree; Honeymoon Express; Robinson Crusoe, Junior; Sinbad; Bombo; Big Boy; Wonder Bar:* he also appeared in the first talking film, *The Jazz Singer* (1927), and in several other pictures including *The Singing Fool; Mammy; Wonder Bar.*

Jommelli, Nicola (1714-1774), Italian dramatic composer who studied with Francesco DURANTE at Naples and also with Leonardo Leo: he wrote more than fifty operas which are now forgotten, but was classed in his day with Alessandro SCARLATTI and Giovanni Battista PERGOLESI, and his works gave evidence of such advance over the older Italian style that he was called "the Italian Gluck." His *Miserere* for two sopranos and orchestra is still heard in Italian churches.

Jonás, Alberto (1868-), Spanish pianist and composer who studied at the Madrid Conservatory, and at the Brussels Conservatory with François GEVAERT and Arthur DE GREEF, also coaching for a short time with Anton RUBINSTEIN. He made his debut at Berlin in 1891, and toured Europe and the United States with great success, finally settling in New York. He is the author of *Master School of Modern Piano-Playing and Virtuosity* in collaboration with sixteen of the greatest masters of the piano: he has also composed many pieces for the piano.

Jones, Allan, contemporary American singer and screen actor who studied at the Syracuse University Music School and at New York University, also coaching with Reynaldo Hahn in Paris. After he returned to the United States he sang with the New York Philharmonic-Symphony Orchestra, concertized and appeared with the St. Louis Municipal Opera. Since 1935 he has appeared in several films including *A Night at the Opera; Rose Marie; Showboat; The Firefly; Everybody Sing; Honeymoon in Bali; The Great Victor Herbert.*

Jones, Henry Arthur (1851-1929), English dramatist whose first play, *Only Round the Corner,* was produced in 1878: it was followed by an immensely successful melodrama, *The Silver King,* produced and starred in by Wilson BARRETT; *Saints and Sinners; The Middleman; Judah; The Dancing Girl; The Crusaders; The Bauble Shop; The Masqueraders; The Liars; Mrs. Dane's Defense; The Hypocrites,* and many others performed in all English-speaking countries. He wrote several works regarding the problems and history of the theatre such as *The Renascence of the English Drama.*

Jones, Howard Mumford (1892-), American poet and biographer who has occupied posts as literary editor of the Boston Evening *Transcript,* and in the English Department of Harvard University: his works include *A Little Book of Local Verse* (1915); *Gargoyles and Other Poems; The Life of Moses Coit Tyler; The Harp That Once—: A Chronicle of the Life of Thomas Moore.* He has also edited the poems of Edgar Allan POE.

Jones, Hugh Bolton (1848-1927), American painter who studied in Baltimore and spent four years in Europe sketching in Spain and France. His works include *Summer on the Blue Ridge; Heather in Bloom in Brittany; Massachusetts Coast; Grandmother's Tales; Spring and Autumn; Twilight on Bean Creek.*

Jones, Inigo (1573-1652), English architect and scenic designer who spent many years in Italy studying the designs of Andrea PALLADIO. He was a rival of Ben JONSON for the favor of James I, but was obliged to cooperate with Jonson in producing masques and pageants for the court. Many of the works were never completed because of the coming of the Commonwealth: among those finished were the Banquet Hall at Whitehall; the Church of St. Paul, Covent Garden; part of the Greenwich Hospital; several private residences including Stoke Park and Wilton House. He was the founder of scenic design in the British theatre.

Jones, Joseph Stevens (1809-1877), American actor and dramatist who joined a stock company at eighteen, and appeared for fifteen years at various Boston theatres, also managing the old National and Tremont Theatres. His successful plays include *The Silver Spoon,* later published successfully in novel form as "The Life of Jefferson S. Batkins"; *The Carpenter of Rouen; The People's Lawyer; The Liberty Tree; Moll Pitcher; Paul Revere.*

Jones, Robert Edmond (1887-), American scenic designer and theatrical director: his notable sets include *The Man Who Married a Dumb Wife; The Jest; Richard III; Macbeth; Desire under the Elms; The Green Pastures.* His productions, some of which were in collaboration with Eugene O'NEILL and Kenneth MACGOWAN, include *Mourning Becomes Electra; Ah, Wilderness!; Hamlet; The Green Pastures; Camille; Othello; The Sea Gull; The Philadelphia Story.*

Jones, Sidney (1869-), English composer and conductor for many years of light opera companies for George Edwardes, and at the Empire Theatre, London. His operettas include *The Gaiety Girl* (1893); *An Artist's Model;*

The Geisha; A Greek Slave; My Lady Molly; The Medal and the Maid; The King of Cadonia; The Persian Princess; Spring Maid; The Girl from Utah.

Jones, Thomas Samuel (1882-1932), American poet: his works include *The Path of Dreams* (1905); *From Quiet Valleys; Interludes; The Rose Jar; Sonnets; The Voice in the Silence; Leonardo da Vinci and Other Sonnets; The Unicorn and Other Sonnets; Shadow of the Perfect Rose; Collected Poems.*

Jongkind, Johan Barthold (1819-1891), Dutch painter and etcher who worked with Jean Baptiste ISABEY in Paris, and also with Louis DAVID: he joined the FONTAINEBLEAU SCHOOL, and executed many fine landscapes and miniatures. His works include *Harbor of Harfleur; Course of the Seine; Souvenir of Havre; Notre Dame; Moonrise in Paris; Dutch Canal by Moonlight.* His painting of moonlit scenes is considered unsurpassed.

Jongleur de Notre Dame, Le, grand opera in three acts: libretto by Maurice Lena founded on a story, *L'Etui de Nacre* by Anatole FRANCE; music by Jules MASSENET; first produced at Monte Carlo in 1902, and at the Manhattan Opera House, New York, in 1909 with Mary GARDEN in the role of the juggler. The plot revolves around a simple-minded juggler who becomes a monk: finding himself unable to show his devotion to the Virgin by creating poetry, music, or some other artistic offering, he is discovered performing his juggling tricks before the altar. Some of the arias have been recorded.

Jongleurs, wandering minstrels in medieval France, and also in England after the latter was invaded by William the Conqueror: later the name was used for jugglers or mountebanks. Some authorities claim that the jongleur was an assistant to the TROUBADOUR or TROUVERE.

Jonny spielt auf, an opera in two parts: libretto and music by Ernst KRENEK; first produced at Leipzig in 1927, and at the Metropolitan Opera House, New York, in 1929. It is called more conveniently than accurately a jazz opera: the plot concerns itself with Jonny, a Negro band leader, who steals the violin of a famous virtuoso, finds favor with women, outwits the authorities, and finally fiddles triumphantly astride a symbolic globe. There are no American recordings of the various songs in which the jazz idiom is Continental rather than American.

Jonson, Ben (1573?-1637), English actor, poet, and dramatist who studied at Westminster School and for a short time at Cambridge. In 1598 he wrote a successful comedy, *Every Man in His Humour:* his popular works include the tragedies *Sejanus* and *Catiline; His Conspiracy; Cynthia's Revels; Epicoene; The Alchemist; The Silent Woman; Every Man Out of His Humour; Bartholomew Fair.* He was a favorite of King James I, an intimate friend of SHAKESPEARE, and author of the poem, *Drink To Me Only With Thine Eyes.*

Jooss, Kurt (1901-), German dancer and choreographer who studied at the Dramatic School at Stuttgart, and was appointed general producer in 1924 at the Stadt Theatre, Munster, where he produced several ballets. In 1931 he wrote a ballet, *The Green Table,* which has been produced all over the world, and in 1933 organized the Ballet Jooss, founded on the theory that the dance is an independent art in the theatre, and that its purpose is the interpretation of life through movement and rhythm. Among his ballet creations are *The Big City; A Ball in Old Vienna; The Mirror,* a sequel to "The Green Table"; *The Prodigal Son; Pavane Ball,* founded on Ravel's composition with the same title; *Johann Strauss —Tonight; The Seven Heroes.* The Jooss Ballet toured the world with great success from 1933; it disbanded in 1942.

Jordaens, Jacob (1593-1678), Flemish painter who studied with Adam van Noort, and assisted RUBENS in preparing tapestry cartoons for the king of Spain. He is regarded as the greatest painter of his day after Rubens: his canvases include *Judgment of Solomon; Wandering Musicians; Christ Driving out the Money Changers from the Temple; Miraculous Draught of Fishes; Christ on the Cross; Moses Striking the Rock; The Philosophers; Nymphs and Satyrs; Divine Law Protecting Human Law.*

Jordan, Dorothea (1762-1816), Irish actress who made her debut in 1777 at Dublin in SHAKESPEARE'S *As You Like It,* and made her first appearance in 1785 at the DRURY LANE THEATRE, London, in *The Country Girl,* remaining there until 1809. She assumed the name of Mrs. Jordan, and was greatly praised by Leigh HUNT, Charles LAMB, and Lord BYRON as Lady Teazle and Rosalind. She became the mistress of the Duke of Clarence, later William IV, by whom she had ten children, and her portrait was painted by Sir Joshua REYNOLDS, Thomas GAINSBOROUGH, and George ROMNEY.

Jordan, Jules (1850-1927), American tenor, conductor and composer who studied singing with William SHAKESPEARE in London and Giovanni SBRIGLIA in Paris. He conduced the Arion Club, New York, and created the part of Faust in the American première of BERLIOZ' *Damnation of Faust* at New York in 1880. His works include a successful operetta, *Rip Van Winkle* and a ballad, *Barbara Frietchie,* for soprano, chorus, and orchestra.

Joseffy, Rafael (1852-1915), Hungarian pianist who studied with Ignaz MOSCHELES, Karl TAUSIG, and Franz LISZT. He made his debut in 1870 at Berlin, and after touring Europe came to the United States and appeared in 1879 at New York so successfully with the Leopold Damrosch Orchestra that he decided to settle there, teaching privately and at the NATIONAL CONSERVATORY OF MUSIC. He edited the complete works of Frédéric CHOPIN, and published a *School of Advanced Piano Playing.*

Josephson, Matthew (1899-), American poet, critic, and biographer educated at Columbia University who was intimate with the Surrealist group of authors and artists in Paris: his works include *Galimathias* (1923); *Zola and His Time; Jean Jacques Rousseau; The Robber Barons; The Politicos; The President Makers.*

Josetsu, Japanese painter and priest, said to be of Chinese ancestry, who worked during the Oei period (1393-1411). He was an exponent of the coloristic black and white school of painting: So-Shubun was one of his pupils.

Josika, Baron Miklos (1794-1865), Hungarian novelist who was a profound student of the legends and life of the Magyars: his works include *The Poet Zrinyi; The Last of the Bathory; Abafi; A Hungarian Family during the Period of the Revolution.* His style resembles that of Sir Walter Scott to whom he has been favorably compared.

Jota, a dance popular in Northern Spain said to be named after a Moor, Aben Jot, who invented it. It is in fast 3-4 or 3-8 time, and performed by two pairs of dancers using castanets, and accompanied by guitars or bandurrias.

Jouett, Matthew Harris (1788-1827), American painter who served in the War of 1812, and studied with Gilbert Stuart. He painted more than three hundred portraits including a full-length likeness of the Marquis de Lafayette which is now in the State Capitol at Frankfort, Ky.

Journet, Marcel (1867-1933), French dramatic bass who made his debut at Montpellier in 1893: after appearing for six years at La Monnaie, Brussels, he made his debut in 1901 at the Metropolitan Opera House, New York, remaining there until 1914 when he joined the Chicago Opera Company. His repertoire included more than one hundred operas: he created the leading bass roles in Thais, Samson and Delilah, and Monna Vanna in addition to making many fine recordings.

Jouvenal, Mme. Henri de, see **Colette, Gabrielle Claudine.**

Jouvenet, Jean (1644-1717), French painter who studied with his father, Laurent Jouvenet, and Charles Le Brun with whom he worked on the decorations at Versailles. After Le Brun's death he became the leader of the French school and professor at the Royal Academy. His works include *Resurrection of Lazarus; Descent from the Cross; Apotheosis of the Apostles,* a fresco; *Jesus and the Pharisees; View of the High Altar of Notre Dame; Magnificat; The Money Changers Driven from the Temple.*

Joy, Leatrice, contemporary screen actress who had some experience in stock companies before entering the films: among the pictures in which she appeared are *Manslaughter; The Ten Commandments; Java Head; The Blue Danube; Man Made Woman; A Most Immoral Lady; The Bellamy Trial.*

Joyce, James (1882-1941), Irish poet and novelist educated at Belvedere College and University College, Dublin. His works include *Chamber Music* (1907); *Dubliners; A Portrait of the Artist as a Young Man; Exiles; Ulysses,* published in 1922 and banned in the United States until 1933; *Pomes Penyeach; Finnegan's Wake; Anna Livia Plurabelle; Two Tales of Shem and Shaun; The Mime of Mick; Nick and the Maggies.*

Juba, a Negro dance popular in the Southern states of the Union: it forms an important part of the old-fashioned breakdown, and has been idealized as well as made familiar to Northerners by the *Juba Dance* composed for the piano by Nathaniel Dett.

Jubal, according to the Bible, the son of Lamech, a descendant of Cain, and the inventor of musical instruments mentioned in various chapters of the Bible.

Juch, Emma (1863-1939), American dramatic soprano born in Vienna, Australia, while her American parents were on a visit: she was brought to the United States when four years old, and after studying with Mme. Murio-Celli made her concert debut in 1881 at Chickering Hall, New York, and her operatic debut during the same year at London in *Mignon.* She sang under the management of Colonel James Henry Mapleson, also with the American Opera Company, and after 1889 with the Emma Juch Opera Company, her own organization.

Juilliard, Augustus D. (1836-1919), American manufacturer and patron of music who left a substantial legacy in 1920 establishing the *Juilliard Musical Foundation* for the furtherance of music in America. As a result the **Juilliard Graduate School** was organized in 1924 with Dr. Eugene A. Noble as dean, succeeded by Dr. Ernest Hutcheson in 1927, and by Oscar Wagner in 1937. At the time of its founding the School was open only to students from the United States: it now admits students from any part of North or South America. Many alumni of the School are singers with the Metropolitan Opera Company, members of the major symphony orchestras, well-known radio artists, teachers in colleges and conservatories, and conductors of orchestras. Besides the courses to be expected in an advanced school of music, special opportunities are available for the training of those who wish to qualify as opera singers. In the opera department a wide variety of classes is offered, and regular productions are given. Since 1931, thirty-five operas have been produced for the public, six of which were world premières of works by contemporary American composers. Scenes and acts from many other operas have been given semi-public performance. The faculty of the School has always included many world-famous artists: among those who are now or have been on the faculty are Marcella Sembrich, Leopold Auer, Paul Kochanski, Rubin Goldmark, Charles Hackett, Alexander Siloti, Georges Enesco, Carl Friedberg, Ernest Hutcheson, Olga Samaroff, Josef and Rosina Lhevinne, Felix Salmond, and Albert Spalding. The **Juilliard Summer School,** organized and directed by Dr. George A. Wedge since 1932, presents courses for those interested in music whether their ultimate purposes be professional or amateur: it offers instruction in all branches of music and music education.

Juive, La (The Jewess), grand opera in five acts: libretto by Eugene SCRIBE; music by Jacques HALEVY; first produced at L'Opera, Paris, in 1835, by the French Opera Company at New Orleans, La., in 1844, at the Park Theatre, New York, in 1845, and in 1884 at the Metropolitan Opera House, New York, in German: the first performance in French at the latter house did not take place until 1919 with Enrico CARUSO as Eleazar and Rosa PONSELLE as Rachel. The melodramatic plot has an ending somewhat similar to that of Verdi's *Il Trovatore:* there is a Victor recording of the famous *Passover Music* by Jan PEERCE and Dorothy SARNOFF.

Julius Caesar, see **Caesar, Caius Julius.**

Jullien (correctly **Julien**), **Louis Antoine** (1812-1860), French orchestral conductor who studied at the PARIS CONSERVATORY and for a time conducted a dance orchestra in Paris. From 1838 to 1859 he directed a series of orchestral concerts in London, and in 1853-54 visited the United States with his orchestra, conducting standard orchestral works, and also playing compositions by American composers. He was somewhat of a sensational musical figure, and the first conductor to organize concerts utilizing the services of several hundred musicians.

Juno, see **Hera.**

Juon, Paul (1872-), Russian composer who studied the violin with Johann Hrimaly and composition with Anton ARENSKY, later becoming professor of composition at the Hochschule in Berlin. His compositions include orchestral works; chamber music; pieces for piano and violin; also several treatises on harmony, counterpoint, and modulation.

Jupiter, see **Zeus.**

"Jupiter" Symphony (Mozart), one of the last three symphonies composed by Wolfgang Amadeus MOZART, the group considered his greatest creations in this field. It was composed in 1788, and was probably named the "Jupiter" by some admirer. Robert SCHUMANN once said of it: "There are some things in the world about which nothing can be said as Mozart's C Major Symphony with the fugue." There is a Columbia recording by the London Philharmonic Orchestra with Sir Thomas Beecham, and a Victor recording by the Vienna Philharmonic Orchestra directed by Bruno Walter.

Jusserand, Jean Jules (1855-1932), French diplomat and author who was ambassador to the United States from 1902 to 1915: his works include *The English Novel in the Time of Shakespeare* (1890); *A French Ambassador at the Court of Charles II; A Literary History of the English People; With Americans of Past and Present Days,* which received the Pulitzer prize in 1917; *The School for Ambassadors and Other Essays.*

Justus or **Jodocus, of Ghent,** Flemish painter of the 15th century regarding whom little is known except that he became a member of the painters' guild at Antwerp in 1464, and went to Italy in 1474 at the request of the Duke of Urbino. He painted a *Last Supper,* and a series of panels comprising 28 portraits of poets and philosophers some of which are now in the Barberini Palace at Rome, and others are in the LOUVRE in Paris. There is little documentary evidence to confirm any statements concerning his life or works.

Juvarra, Filippo (1676-1736), Italian architect who was one of the first designers to subdue the extravagances of BAROQUE architecture by lending classical repose to such edifices as the Church of Superga at Turin, the cathedral at Como, and the royal palace at Madrid. He also designed the private theatre of Cardinal Ottoboni at Rome.

Juvenal (c.60-c.140), Roman poet who was one of the greatest satirists: of his more than one hundred works of this character sixteen have survived in which he pillories the Romans for their lax morals, tyranny, and debauchery. There are several editions of the Latin text, and an excellent English translation by John DRYDEN which follows closely the spirit of the text by employing the same emphatic style.

Juventas, see **Hebe.**

K

Kabalevsky, Dmitri (1904-), Russian composer who studied composition with Nikolai MIASKOVSKY: his works include three symphonies the second of which was presented by the National Broadcasting Company Orchestra under the direction of Arturo TOSCANINI in 1942: the third is subtitled *Requiem,* and employs a chorus singing a Revolutionary song. He has also written an opera, *Master of Clamecy,* based on a story by Romain ROLLAND.

Kadelburg, Gustav (1851-1925), Austrian actor and dramatist; author of several successful comedies including *The White Horse Tavern* produced in New York. He was also an excellent actor, appearing in European theatres and translating several English and American plays into German.

Kahn, Albert (1869-1942), German architect who came to the United States as a boy of eleven, and secured an apprenticeship in an architect's office. He devoted fourteen years to learning his craft, becoming the greatest designer of factory buildings in the world. During World War I he designed more than $200,000,000 worth of military buildings for the United States Army and Navy: later he created more than a thousand buildings for Henry Ford, and five hundred factories for the Soviet Union in twenty-five Russian cities. Much of the nation's war production for World War II is now (1943) being created in buildings designed under his direction.

Kahn, Otto Hermann (1867-1934), American banker and music patron born in Germany. He was chairman of the board of the METROPOLITAN

OPERA COMPANY from 1908 to 1931; vice-president of the New York Philharmonic-Symphony Society, and a director of the American Federation of Arts. He also aided in financing the THEATRE GUILD and the School of American Ballet, the latter founded by Lincoln KIRSTEIN.

Kaiser, Georg (1878-), German dramatist who first engaged in commercial enterprises, but was obliged to withdraw because of ill-health, and went to Italy and Spain where he began to write. His works include *Schoolmaster Kleist* (1903); *The Jewish Widow; King Cuckold; Gilles and Jeanne; The Flight to Venice; The Burghers of Calais; Gas; Fire in the Opera House; From Morn to Midnight; The Phantom Lover:* the four last-named have been translated.

Kalckreuth, Leopold, Count von (1855-1928), German painter who studied with his father; also at Weimar and Munich, later becoming professor at the Weimar Art School. His paintings, chiefly of the German peasantry, include *Old Age; Rainbow; Funeral at Dachau; Homewards; Before the Fish Auction; Going to School; Wedding Procession in the Carpathian Mountains.*

Kalevala, the title of the Finnish national epic poem which relates the story of the three sons of Kaleva (Finland), and was probably written at various times: a collection of the various parts was made in 1835 by Dr. Elias Lonnrot amounting to 12,000 lines arranged into thirty-two runes (cantos) and published exactly as the peasant sang or chanted them. A new edition nearly twice as long was published in 1849, and an English translation appeared in 1888.

Kalidasa, the greatest of the Indian poets and dramatists: the exact period in which he lived is unknown, but has been set at various times during the 2nd to the 6th centuries A.D. He was regarded as one of the nine "pearls" or famous poets who graced the court of King Vikramaditya, and his most admired work is *Sakuntala,* a poem greatly admired by GOETHE: others are the romantic epics, *Raghuvansa* and *Kumarasambhava;* also the lyric poems, *Meghaduta* and *Ritusamhara.*

Kalinnikoff, Basil Sergeivitch (1866-1901), Russian conductor and composer who directed Italian opera at Moscow in 1893, but was obliged to give up his profession because of illness. His compositions include two symphonies, a cantata, a string quartet, and various orchestral works. There is a Victor recording of the Symphony No. 2 in G minor by the Indianapolis Orchestra directed by Fabian Sevitzky.

Kalkar or **Calcar, Hans von** (c.1510-c.1546), German painter, real name Johann Stepan, who studied in Venice with TITIAN. He was one of the most successful imitators of both RAPHAEL and Titian, and was also famous for his ability as a portraitist.

Kalkbrenner, Friedrich Wilhelm Michael (1788-1849), German pianist and composer who studied at the Paris Conservatory and also with Muzio CLEMENTI and Johann ALBRECHTSBERGER. He

toured with great success, and adapted Logier's Chiroplast, a mechanism for holding the hands in position for piano practice, to his teaching method with great success. He composed in various forms, but only a few of his piano études have survived.

Kallas, Mrs. Aino (1878-), Finnish novelist and daughter of Julius Leopold Krohn, professor of Finnish literature at the University of Helsingfors. Her works include *The White Ship; Estonian Tales; Eros the Slayer; The Wolfe's Bride:* all of the above have been translated into English.

Kalman, Emerich (1882-), Hungarian composer who studied at the National Conservatory in Budapest, winning the Imperial prize for composition in 1907: his works, chiefly light operas, include *The Gay Hussars; Sari; Miss Springtime; Her Soldier Boy; The Gipsy Princess; The Circus Princess.* Many of the above-mentioned operettas have been adapted for the screen with remarkable success.

Kalomiris, Manolis (1883-), Greek composer who studied at Vienna, and later became professor at the music conservatories in Kharkov and Athens: his compositions include two operas, incidental music, orchestral works, chamber music and two rhapsodies for piano.

Kanaoka, Kose (850-931), Japanese poet and painter considered the greatest of the earliest artists who broke away from Chinese traditions, and established a national school of painting. He was engaged in the decoration of the walls in the royal palaces, and was famed for his portrayal of landscapes and animals.

Kane, Paul (1810-1871), Canadian painter who studied in New York, and also in several European countries including France and Italy. He studied the American Indian while traveling on horseback, and many of his canvases are to be seen in the Royal Museum, Toronto: his memoirs, *Wanderings of an Artist among the Indians of North America,* is profusely illustrated with his own drawings.

Kang, Younghill (1903-), Korean author who came to the United States as a young man of eighteen, and has been employed by the Metropolitan Museum of Art, New York. His works which have been published in English include *The Grass Roof* (1931); *The Happy Grove; East Goes West,* a novel.

Kano, a school of Japanese painters which derived its name from the village of Kano: among the artists were MASANOBU, MOTONOBU, and TANNYU.

Kantemir, Prince Antiochus, see **Cantemir, Prince Antiochus.**

Kantor, MacKinlay (1904-), American novelist who edited a newspaper with his mother, and worked on newspapers in the West before publishing his first novel, *Diversey* in 1928; this was followed by *El Goes South; The Jaybird; Long*

Remember; Turkey in the Straw, a book of poems; *The Voice of Bugle Ann,* successfully produced as a film; *Arouse and Beware; The Romance of Rosy Ridge; Here Lies Holly Springs; The Noise of Their Wings; Cuba Libre; Happy Land.*

Karamzin, Nicholas (1766-1826), Russian novelist, poet, and historian: his works include an eleven-volume *History of Russia to 1613* (1797-1801) which "discovered the old Russia" according to Alexander PUSHKIN; *Letters of a Russian Traveler; Ilya Mourometz,* a novel; *The Aonides,* a poetic almanac; he also compiled the *Pantheon,* an anthology of works by authors of all nations translated into Russian.

Karavayeva, Valetina, contemporary Russian screen actress trained at the State Cinema Institute and the Mosfilm Studio School under the direction of Sergei Eisenstein, Vassily Pudovkin, and Ilya Trauberg, later completing her education at the Moscow Film Studio School where she studied American, French, and English films. She rose to stardom in the title role of *Mashenka,* recently produced with great success in New York.

Karfiol, Bernard (1886-), American painter born at Budapest, Hungary, of American parentage who came to the United States as a boy, and studied at the National Academy of Design, New York, and at the Académie Julien in Paris. His individualistic style does not place him in any particular school as is apparent from his canvas, *Babette,* in the Detroit Institute of Arts, which displays sensuous coloring combined with an atmosphere of detachment. His paintings are to be seen at many American museums.

Karl, Tom (1846-1916), Irish tenor who studied with Antonio Sangiovanni in Milan, and sang in Italian opera throughout Europe for many years before coming to the United States with Mme. PAREPA-ROSA in 1865 and settling in New York. After achieving success in Gilbert and Sullivan operettas, he founded The BOSTONIANS, probably the finest light opera company ever formed in the United States, in conjunction with William H. MacDonald and Henry Clay BARNABEE, and produced Reginald DE KOVEN's *Robin Hood* and several operas by Victor HERBERT. His repertory included more than one hundred grand and light operas.

Karloff, Boris (1887-), English stage and screen actor who first appeared on the stage with stock companies and later in *The Virginian:* among the numerous films in which he has played important roles are *The Criminal Code; Five-Star Final; The Public Defender; Frankenstein* and its several sequels in which he achieved success as a "horror" character; *The Mask of Fu Manchu; The House of Rothschild; The Raven; Charlie Chan at the Opera; British Intelligence.*

Karsavina, Tamara (1885-), Russian ballerina trained at the Imperial Ballet School in St. Petersburg who first appeared in 1902 at the Maryinsky Theatre in *Javotte.* She succeeded Anna PAVLOWA as première danseuse in 1910 at the Imperial Opera House, also appearing for many years at the Coliseum, and with the Russian Ballet at Covent Garden, London. She played the leading role in *The Truth About Russian Dancers* written for her in 1920 by Sir James Matthew BARRIE, and published her reminiscences, *Theatre Street,* in 1929.

Kataev, Valentin (1897-), Russian novelist and dramatist who fought in World War I: his novels and plays include *The Embezzlers* (1928); *Squaring the Circle; Lonely White Sail; Department Store; Vanguard; The Million Torments; Under the Circus Tent; The Rich Bride.* The three first mentioned have been translated into English.

Kauffmann, Angelica (1741-1807), Swiss painter who studied with her father, and later with Johann Joachim WINCKELMANN. Her exceptional talent brought her great popularity in Rome, Bologna, and Venice: while in the latter city she was induced by the wife of the British ambassador to visit London where she became the protegé of of Sir Joshua REYNOLDS. Her works include *Death of Leonardo da Vinci; Adonis Going to the Hunt; Meeting of Hector and Andromache; Woman of Samaria; Telemachus Received by Calypso;* she also painted portraits of Sir Joshua REYNOLDS, Johann WINCKELMANN, Prince Poniatowski, GOETHE, and GARRICK.

Kaufman, George Simon (1889-), American journalist and dramatist: his plays include *Dulcy* (1921) with Marc Connelly; *Beggar on Horseback,* with Marc Connelly; *The Butter and Egg Man,* an original play; *The Royal Family* with Edna Ferber; *Once in a Lifetime* with Moss Hart; *Of Thee I Sing* with Morris Ryskind and Ira Gershwin, and a Pulitzer prize play; *Dinner at Eight* with Edna Ferber; *First Lady* with Katharine Dayton; *Stage Door* with Edna Ferber; *You Can't Take It With You* with Moss Hart; *The American Way* with Moss Hart; *The Man Who Came to Dinner* with Moss Hart.

Kaulbach, Friedrich August von (1850-1920), German painter who studied with his father, and settled in 1872 at Munich where he became a successful portraitist. His notable works include *Mother's Joy; The Lute Player; Revery; Girl in the Woods; The Walk; May Day; Joys of Summer-time.*

Kaulbach, Wilhelm von (1805-1874), German painter who studied with Peter CORNELIUS at the Düsseldorf Academy, at Munich, and in Rome. His works include the decoration of Staircase Hall in the New Museum, Berlin, with a series of paintings portraying the evolution of civilization; *Apollo and the Muses; Anacreon and Her Love; Shepherd Boy in Rome; Sea Fight at Salamis; Deliverance of the Holy Sepulchre by the Crusaders;* also sixteen murals, *The story of Cupid and Psyche.*

Kaye-Smith, Sheila (1888-), English novelist who published her first novel, *The Tramping Methodist* (1908) when she was twenty years of age: among her successful works are *Sussex Gorse; Tamarisk Town; Joanna Godden; The George and the Crown; Joanna Godden Married;*

365

The Village Doctor; Summer Holiday; Rose Deeprose; The Valiant Woman; Ember Lane: A Winter's Tale; The Secret Son.

Kazinczy, Ferencz (1759-1831), Hungarian author who accomplished much toward the regeneration of Magyar literature during the 18th and 19th centuries: he founded the first Hungarian literary magazine, *Orpheus,* and assisted in the formation of a dramatic society for which he translated the works of LESSING, GOETHE, SHAKESPEARE, MOLIERE, and many other European dramatists. His original works, published with his translations, consist of poetry and critical letters to Hungarian authors.

Keable, Robert (1887-1927), English novelist educated at Oxford, and, after being ordained in the Anglican church, became chaplain with the South African forces in France during World War I. His works include *A City of the Dawn* (1915); *Simon Called Peter; Mother of All Living; Recompense; Ann Decides; Though This Be Madness; The Great Galilean.*

Kean, Edmund (1787-1833), English actor who first acted with groups of strolling players, but rapidly advanced to the point of appearing in 1807 opposite Mrs. SIDDONS: in 1814 he achieved tremendous success as Shylock in Shakespeare's *The Merchant of Venice,* and later in *Richard III; Hamlet; Othello; King Lear; Macbeth; Henry VIII,* and *Julius Caesar.* He visited the United States in 1820 and again in 1825. His second son **Charles John Kean** (1811-1868), became an actor in defiance of his father's wishes, appearing first in 1827 at the DRURY LANE THEATRE, London, and playing Iago to his father's Othello on March 25, 1833, a tragic performance because the latter was taken ill on the stage, and died shortly after. He achieved his greatest success in a series of Shakespearean productions in which the scenery and acting were on the highest level. His wife, **Ellen Tree Kean** (1805-1880), was a noted interpreter of comedy roles who appeared in her husband's company until his death.

Keane, Doris (1885-), American actress who studied at the American Academy of Dramatic Art, and made her debut in 1903 at New York in *Whitewashing Julia.* Among the plays in which she has appeared are *A Social Highwayman; The Middleman; The Hypocrites; Arsène Lupine; The Affairs of Anatol; Romance,* her greatest success in both New York and London; *Roxana; Romeo and Juliet; Czarina; Starlight.*

Keats, John (1795-1821), English poet who first studied surgery, but abandoned it for a literary career: his works include *Poems* (1817); *Endymion; Lamia, Isabella, The Eve of St. Agnes and Other Poems; Hyperion,* unfinished at his premature death; *The Letters of John Keats to Fanny Brawne.* He was influenced to some extent by Leigh HUNT: Percy Bysshe SHELLEY wrote the exquisite elegy, *Adonis,* in remembrance of his death.

Keck, Charles (1874-), American sculptor educated at the National Academy of Design and the ART STUDENTS' LEAGUE, New York; also at the American Academy in Rome. He worked for some years as assistant to Augustus SAINT-GAUDENS: his notable works include a monument to George Washington at Buenos Aires; Maine memorial tablets for the United States Government; a monument to Stonewall Jackson, and a group, *Lewis and Clark,* at Charlottesville, Va.; Soldiers' Memorial at Brooklyn, N. Y.; also many memorials of World War I, sarcophagi and portrait busts. His brother, **Maxfield H. Keck** (1883-1943), was a noted architectural sculptor who made the models for many important commercial buildings, hotels, and churches.

Keene, Charles Samuel (1823-1891), English pen-and-ink artist who first worked as a wood engraver and in 1851 became an illustrator and writer for *Punch,* holding his connection for almost thirty years. He illustrated Charles READE's *The Cloister and the Hearth,* and was also greatly interested in vocal music in addition to playing the BAGPIPES, an instrument of which he made a large collection of different types.

Keene, Laura (c.1826-1873), Anglo-American actress and theatrical manager; real name Mary Moss. She appeared in 1851 at London in *The Lady of Lyons* with Madame VESTRIS, and came to the United States in 1852 after a tour of Australia. In 1856 she opened her own theatre in New York, producing comedies and dramas the most successful of which was *Our American Cousin* first performed in 1858: it was during a performance of this play by Miss Keene's Company at Washington, on April 15, 1865, that Abraham Lincoln was assassinated by John Wilkes BOOTH.

Keep, in medieval days the name of the principal tower in a castle protected by walls within which the inhabitants of the castle retired when attacked. Originally built of wood, it was later constructed of stone: the interior provided space for the storage of food and military supplies. Many examples are still to be seen on the banks of the Loire River in France.

Keightley, Thomas (1789-1872), Irish author of historical works, but remembered chiefly for several books on mythology including *Fairy Mythology* (1828); *Tales and Popular Fictions; Mythology of Ancient Greece and Italy.*

Keith, Benjamin Franklin (1846-1914), American proprietor of vaudeville theatres who first worked as a circus hand, and after becoming associated with the Barnum and the Forepaugh circuses, opened Keith's Theatre, a vaudeville house in Boston where he made the first showing of Edison's Vitascope, the forerunner of the modern motion picture machine. In 1906 he formed the Keith and Proctor Amusement Company with Frederick F. Proctor which in 1914 controlled more than four hundred vaudeville theatres, which after his death became a unit of the Radio-Keith-Orpheum chain.

Kelcey, Herbert (1856-1917), English actor who first appeared in 1880 at Brighton in *Flirtation,* and made his London debut in 1881 under Sir

Augustus HARRIS. In 1882 he made his New York debut at Wallack's Theatre in *Taken from Life:* among the plays in which he appeared are *Diplomacy; The Silver King; Old Love Letters; Harbor Lights; The School for Scandal; The Wife; The Heart of Maryland* with Mrs. Leslie CARTER; *The Moth and the Flame* with Effie SHANNON, his wife, as co-star in his own company.

Kelland, Clarence Budington (1881-), American novelist and short story writer educated for the law, and first successful as editor of the *American Boy,* and author of juvenile stories. His works include the *Mark Tidd* Series (6 volumes, 1913-18); *Sudden Jim; Scattergood Baines; Contraband; The Great Crooner; Catspaw; Roxana; Arizona; The Valley of the Rising Sun; Scattergood Baines Pulls the Strings; Silver Spoon.*

Keller, Albert von (1845-1920), German painter who studied with Franz von LENBACH and Baron Georg Ramberg, later becoming professor of painting at the Munich Academy: his works include *Dinner; A Roman Bath; Audience with Louis XV; The Judgment of Paris; The Crucifixion; An Adventure; The Witches' Sleep; Chopin; The Portrait Painter; Autumn; The Happy Sister.*

Keller, Gottfried (1819-1890), Swiss poet and novelist who was an artist as well as an author: his works include poems revealing remarkable power of expression; *Green Henry,* an unusual autobiography in novel form; several novels including *The Folks of Seldwyla; The Village Romeo and Juliet,* and *Martin Salander.*

Keller, Helen Adams (1880-), American author who became blind and deaf at two years of age, but learned to speak through the help of her teacher and companion, Anne Sullivan. Her works include *The Story of My Life* (1902); *The World I Live In; The Song of the Stone Wall; Out of the Dark; Midstream; My Later Life; Helen Keller's Journal.*

Kelley, Edgar Stillman (1857-), American organist and composer who studied with Clarence EDDY and at the Stuttgart Conservatory. He taught organ and composition in various institutions, and lectured on music at New York and Yale Universities. His compositions include a successful light opera, *Puritania;* several orchestral works including *Lady Picking Mulberries;* incidental music for the play, *Ben Hur;* chamber music, piano pieces, and songs. He has also published *Chopin the Composer* and *The History of Musical Instruments.*

Kellgren, Johan Henrik (1751-1795), Swedish poet who was private secretary to Gustavus III of Sweden: the king furnished the plots of several dramas which were versified by Kellgren who was regarded as one of the greatest Scandinavian poets. One of his finest lyrics, a form in which he excelled, is *The New Creation* (Nya Skapelsen).

Kellogg, Clara Louise (1842-1916), American dramatic soprano who was trained in New York,

and made her debut in 1861 at the Academy of Music, New York, in Verdi's *Rigoletto,* and her London debut in 1867 in Gounod's *Faust.* After singing in various opera companies she formed her organization in 1874, supervising the productions, and later dividing her singing seasons between Europe and America. She retired in 1887 after accumulating a considerable fortune.

Kelly, George (1887-), American actor, dramatist, and producer who first appeared in stock companies and vaudeville in 1911: his plays include *The Torchbearers* (1922); *The Show-off; Craig's Wife,* which won the Pulitzer award; *Behold the Bridegroom; Maggie the Magnificent; Philip Goes Forth; Reflected Glory.* He is regarded as especially skillful in the arts of casting and direction.

Kelly, Hugh (1739-1777), Irish dramatist who first engaged in journalistic work, and wrote a novel, *Memoirs of a Magdalen* (1767) which achieved success: his first comedy, *False Delicacy,* was produced by David GARRICK in 1768 in rivalry with Oliver GOLDSMITH's *The Good-Natured Man.* Several more comedies and tragedies such as *A Word to the Wise, The School for Wives, Clementina,* and *The Man of Reason* were failures because of a poem, *Thespis* (1766) in which he excoriated the leading players of his day.

Kelly, James Edward (1855-1933), American sculptor and engraver who executed wood cuts for American periodicals including *Scribner's Magazine* and *Harper's Magazine.* His works as a sculptor include *Sheridan's Ride; Battle of Harlem Heights* at Columbia University, New York; *Defender's Monument* at New Haven, Conn.; also many busts of American generals and naval officers.

Kemble, Edward Windsor (1861-1933), American illustrator and cartoonist who contributed to *Century Magazine, Collier's Weekly,* and *Harper's Weekly;* his collected volumes, containing his delineations of Negro life, include *Kemble's Coons; Coontown's 400; Kemble's Sketch Book; A Pickaninny Calendar.*

Kemble, Roger (1721-1802), English actor and founder of one of the most distinguished families who graced the English and later the American stage for more than one hundred twenty-five years. Roger Kemble was a strolling player and leader of his own company who married Sarah Ward, an actress: of their twelve children nine became actors, the famous ones being the eldest daughter, Sarah Kemble (Mrs. SIDDONS) and the eldest son, **John Philip Kemble** (1757-1823) who made his London debut in 1783 in *Hamlet* at the Drury Lane Theatre, becoming its manager in 1788 with his sister, Mrs. Siddons, playing the leading female roles in *Coriolanus, Julius Caesar, Hamlet,* and *King Lear.* He retired in 1817 just as Edmund KEAN began to shine as a tragedian. Roger's second son, **Stephen Kemble** (1758-1822), was an actor of ability especially in the part of Falstaff which he was able to play without padding. Roger's youngest son, **Charles Kemble** (1775-1854), made his London debut in 1794 in *Macbeth,* but excelled in comedy parts until 1840 when he retired. In 1832 and 1834 he appeared with great success in the United States with his eldest daughter, **Fanny Kemble** (Frances Anne Kemble) (1809-1893) who made her debut at Covent Garden in 1829 as Juliet with her father playing Mercutio. She was successful as Portia, Lady Teazle, Julia in Sheridan Knowles' *The Hunchback,* and was received in 1832 with great acclaim in the United States. She made an unfortunate marriage in 1834 but came back to the stage in 1847, and in 1867 returned to England, becoming a popular figure in London society. She wrote several plays: also a *Journal of a Residence on a Georgia Plantation in 1838-9* and *Notes on Some of Shakespeare's Plays.* Charles Kemble's second daughter, **Adelaide Kemble** (1814-1879), studied singing in Italy and appeared in the title role of Vincenzo Bellini's *Norma* at Covent Garden, London, with brilliant success in 1841. Charles Kemble's eldest son, **John Mitchell Kemble** (1807-1857) was educated at Trinity College, Cambridge, and became a distinguished scholar and historian in addition to becoming examiner of plays for the British censor from 1840 until his death.

Kemeys, Edward (1843-1907), American sculptor who studied in New York, and served in the Civil War. He exhibited at London and Paris, and specialized in North American Indian figures and animals. His works include *Still Hunt* at Central Park, New York, *Wolves* at Fairmount Park, Philadelphia; *Lions* in bronze at the entrance to the CHICAGO ART INSTITUTE.

Kempener, Pieter de (c.1503-1580), Spanish painter of Flemish origin known also as Pedro or Pierre de Campana. After painting in the school of MICHELANGELO in Italy for several years, he lived in Seville, Spain, for twenty-five years: his works include *Descent from the Cross,* a majestic, severe work greatly admired by MURILLO; *Purification; Resurrection; Adoration of the Magi.*

Kemp-Welch, Lucy Elizabeth (1869-), English painter trained at the Herkomer School at Bushey, who specialized in the painting of horses and other animals, and was first president in 1914 of the Society of Animal Painters. Her notable works include *The Straw Ride* and *Horses Bathing in the Sea.*

Kendal, Dame Madge (1849-1935), English actress, real name Margaret Robertson and sister of Thomas William ROBERTSON, the distinguished dramatist. She made her debut in 1865 at the HAYMARKET THEATRE, London, as Ophelia in *Hamlet,* and revealed her skill in both drama and comedy in many plays including *As You Like It; New Men and Old Acres; Peril; Diplomacy; The Ironmaster; A Scrap of Paper; The Elder Miss Blossom; The School for Scandal.* Her husband, **William Kendal** (1843-1917), real name William Hunter Grimston, was an English actor who made his debut at Glasgow in 1865, and excelled in romantic roles. He played opposite his wife in Shakespearean and modern dramas and comedies, visiting the United States several times between 1889 and 1895. They retired in 1908, and Mrs. Kendal devoted herself to charitable work.

Kennedy, Charles Rann (1871-), Anglo-American actor and dramatist who first appeared on the stage in 1897 at London as one of a mob in *The Seats of the Mighty,* and after touring in *Jim the Penman* became actor and business manager for the Ben GREET Shakespearean Players. His first appearance at New York was with his wife, Edith Wynne MATTHISON, in the morality play, EVERYMAN. His successful plays include *The Servant in the House* (1908); *The Winterfeast; The Terrible Meek; The Necessary Evil; The Idol-Breaker; The Chastening; The Admiral; Flaming Ministers; Beggar's Gift.*

Kennedy, John Pendleton (1795-1870), American novelist who was educated at Baltimore College (now the University of Maryland), his works include *Swallow Barn* (1832); *Horseshoe Robinson; Rob of the Bowl; The Annals of Quodlibet.* He is said to have written one chapter of THACKERAY's *The Virginians,* while on a visit to England, and he also befriended Edgar Allan POE on several occasions.

Kennedy, Margaret (1896-), English novelist and dramatist educated at Somerville College, Oxford, whose first book, *A Century of Revolution* (1922) was a textbook on modern European history: among her successful works are *The Constant Nymph* (1924), dramatized in collaboration with Basil Deane; *Come With Me,* also dramatized; *The Fool of the Family,* a sequel to "The Constant Nymph"; *Escape Me Never,* a play; *Autumn,* a play with Gregory RATOFF; *Where Stands a Winged Sentry; The Mechanised Muse.*

Kensett, John Frederick (1818-1872), American painter who studied in Europe, exhibited at the Royal Academy in London, and became a member of the National Academy of Design, New York, in 1849. Among his canvases are *Mount Washington; October Afternoon; Sunset in the Adirondacks; Lake George; Italian Lake.* He was a member of the commission appointed in 1859 to direct the decoration of the CAPITOL at Washington, and many of his paintings are to be seen at the Metropolitan Museum of Art, New York.

Kent, Rockwell (1882-), American painter and etcher who studied with William Merritt CHASE, Abbott H. THAYER, and Robert HENRI, and later traveled extensively in North and South America. His paintings include *Winter; Mother and Child; Down to the Sea:* he has also written *Wilderness* (1920); *Voyaging Southward from the Strait of Magellan, N by E; Salamina; This is My Own.* He has collected his etchings in *Rockwellkentiana,* and has illustrated several books including Casanova's *Memoirs;* Chaucer's *Canterbury Tales;* Melville's *Moby Dick,* and Whitman's *Leaves of Grass.* In 1943, he executed a series of paintings, *The Four Freedoms,* for the *Saturday Evening Post,* which have proved powerful propaganda in World War II.

Keppler, Joseph (1838-1894), American cartoonist, born in Austria, who founded the English edition in 1877 of the one-time popular comic weekly, *Puck,* after starting the German edition in 1875. He was one of the great political cartoonists of his day, and among the first to make use of color lithography in caricature.

Kerker, Gustave (1857-1923), American composer born in Germany who came to the United States with his parents in 1867. He became musical director at the New York Casino in 1889, and wrote several operettas and musical comedies including *Castles in the Air; The Whirl of the Town; An American Beauty; The Billionaire; Lady Slavey; The Telephone Girl; The Belle of New York*. The last named, in which Edna May scored a tremendous success, was his finest work.

Kern, Jerome David (1885-), American composer who studied with Alexander LAMBERT, Paolo GALLICO, and in Germany, making his debut as a composer in 1903 in London. His numerous successful plays include *Very Good, Eddie; Sally; Show Boat; Sweet Adeline; The Cat and the Fiddle; Music in the Air; Roberta; Very Warm for May:* he has also written the musical scores for several motion pictures.

Kerner, Justinus Andreas Christian (1786-1862), German poet and novelist: several of his lyrics such as *The Moon* were set to music by Robert SCHUMANN: others include *Song of the Wandering; The Last Bunch of Blossoms; Winter Blossoms*. One of his prose works, *The Seeress of Prevorst,* deals with somnambulism and animal magnetism; another noteworthy work is his *Picture Book from My Childhood*.

Kernstock, Karoly (1873-)', Hungarian painter who studied with Adolphe BOUGUEREAU, and was influenced by both Post-Impressionism and Fauvism to the extent of founding groups to introduce the new movements into Hungary. The forceful power of his brush is evident in his studies such as *Nude* and *Horsemen:* he is also a fine worker in stained glass.

Kerr, Sophie (1880-), American novelist and short story writer educated at Hood College and the University of Vermont, and for some years managing editor of the *Woman's Home Companion*. Her works include *Love at Large* (1916); *The Golden Block; The See-Saw; Confetti; Tigers is Only Cats; Adventure With Women; Curtain Going Up; Michael's Girl;* also a play, *Big-Hearted Herbert,* with A. S. Richardson.

Kerrigan, Joseph M. (1885-), Irish actor who first appeared in 1907 at the ABBEY THEATRE, Dublin, with the Irish National Theatre Society, playing more than one hundred parts in nine years. Among the plays in which he has appeared in Great Britain and the United States are *The Playboy of the Western World; John Ferguson; Rollo's Wild Oat; The Rivals; Outward Bound; The Bells; Trelawney of the Wells; The Road to Rome; Barchester Towers.* He has also played important parts in many film productions.

Kettle Drum, see **Timpano.**

Key, Francis Scott (1779-1843), American lawyer educated at St. John's College, Annapolis, Md., and later United States Attorney for the District of Columbia. While watching the bombardment of Fort McHenry by the British during the War of 1812, he wrote the words of *The Star Spangled Banner* now sung to the melody of John Stafford SMITH's song "Anacreon in Heaven." His other verses, written as a pastime, were collected in a volume, *Poems of the Late Francis S. Key, Esq.,* in 1857.

Key, in music (*1*) the succession of tones forming any given major or minor scale; the name of the key is determined by the opening note known as the *tonic.* (*2*) In a musical instrument such as the piano or organ the term is applied to the operating lever which is pressed by either the finger or foot to produce a given sound: the entire system of levers is known as a *keyboard* which has been in process of development and improvement for more than a thousand years.

Keyes, Mrs. Francis Parkinson (1885-), American novelist and essayist who has traveled extensively in all parts of the world: her works include *The Old Gray Homestead* (1919); *Letters from a Senator's Wife; Queen Anne's Lace; Silver Seas and Golden Cities; The Happy Wanderer,* a book of poems; *Honor Bright; Parts Unknown; The Great Tradition: The Sublime Shepherdess; Fielding's Folly; All That Glitters; Crescent Carnival.*

Keyser, Nicaise de (1813-1887), Belgian painter who studied at Antwerp, and in Italy, France, Germany, and England: his notable works include *Death of Maria de' Medici; Filial Love; Battle of Woeringen in 1288; Hans Memling; Massacre of the Innocents; Francis I at Benvenuto Cellini's Workshop; Tasso in Prison; Dante in the Studio of Giotto.*

Keyser, Thomas de (1596-1667), Dutch painter whose portraits are said to have had considerable influence on REMBRANDT: his works include *Theseus and Ariadne; Two Cavaliers on Horseback; Merchant and Clerk; Anatomy Lesson; Assembly of the Burgomasters of Amsterdam before Maria de' Medici; Portrait of a Savant.*

Khansa (?-c.645), Arabian poet, full name Tumadir bint 'Amr, brought up in the desert of the Sahara: she lost her brothers in battle, and her elegiac poems written in their memory made her famous. Her four sons were also killed in battle: Omar, the reigning caliph, wrote her a letter of condolence, and granted her a pension. Her poems have been translated into French.

Khayyam, Omar, see **Omar Khayyam.**

Khnopff, Fernand (1858-1921), Belgian painter and sculptor of extraordinary versatility who executed numerous works in modernistic style including *The Temptation of St. Anthony; Listening to the Music of Schumann; The Crisis; The Symbol of Justice; Memories; White, Black, and Gold.*

Kielland, Alexander Lange (1849-1906), Norwegian novelist and dramatist whose writings are said to show the influence of Honoré DE BALZAC,

Émile ZOLA, and Henrik IBSEN. His works include the novels *Garman and Worse* (1880); *Laboring People; Skipper Worse; Else*, a Christmas story. Among his dramas are *Betty's Guardian; Three Couples; Professors*.

Kiepura, Jan (1902-), Polish dramatic tenor who made his debut in 1925 at the Warsaw Opera in *Faust*, and later appeared at opera houses in Vienna, Milan, and Buenos Aires. He made his American debut with the Chicago Civic Opera Company in 1930, and in 1937 with the Metropolitan Opera Company in *La Bohème*. He has also appeared as a singing star in many European films.

Kieran, John Francis (1892-), American journalist, author, and naturalist educated at the College of the City of New York and at Fordham University. He was sports editor of the New York *Times* from 1915 to 1942, and now (1943) is writing the column, "One Small Voice," in the New York *Sun*. His works include *The Story of the Olympic Games, 776 B.C.-1936 A.D.* (1936) and *Nature Notes*. He has acted as one of the experts on INFORMATION PLEASE since 1938, and has given ample proof of possessing not only a tremendous fund of knowledge, but also a remarkable memory.

Killigrew, Thomas (1612-1683), English dramatist and theatrical manager who was granted the right by Charles II to build a theatre, and to form a company of players: he opened the Theatre Royal, later known as the DRURY LANE THEATRE, in 1674, and was the first to employ women as actors. He presented Shakespearean plays and several of his own including *The Parson's Wedding; Cecilia and Clorinda; The Prisoners;* and *Claracilla*.

Kilmer, Joyce (1886-1918), American journalist and poet, educated at Rutgers College and Columbia University, who worked for a time on the New York *Times*, and was killed while serving in the American Army during World War I. His works include *Summer of Love* (1911); *Trees and Other Poems; The Circus and Other Essays; Main Street and Other Poems*. His best known poem, *Trees*, has become the lyric of a standard song.

Kilpack, Bennett (1895-), English stage and radio actor who studied at St. John's College and Finsbury Technical College: after coming to the United States he gave up a career in engineering for the stage to appear in Otis SKINNER's production of *Kismet* in 1912, later playing in the company of William GILLETTE, and with Ben GREET in Shakespearean roles. Among the radio dramatic features in which he has appeared are *Wayside Inn* (1927), *Sunday Night at Seth Parker's*, and *Mr. Keen, Tracer of Lost Persons:* he has appeared in the title role of this serial for six years.

Kinderscenen (Schumann), one of the finest contributions of Robert SCHUMANN to piano music, consisting of thirteen delightful pieces in Op. 15 of which the *Traümerei, Curious Story* and *At the Fireside*, are the greatest favorites.

There are Victor recordings of the complete work by Alfred CORTOT and Benno MOISEIVITCH, and also recordings for violin, violoncello, and organ of the famous *Traümerei*.

Kindler, Hans (1892-), Dutch violoncellist and conductor who studied at the Rotterdam Conservatory, was made professor at the Scharwenka Conservatory, Berlin, and became first 'cellist of the PHILADELPHIA ORCHESTRA from 1914 to 1920. He made his debut as a conductor at Philadelphia in 1927, and after appearing as guest conductor in Europe, founded the NATIONAL SYMPHONY ORCHESTRA at Washington, D. C., in 1931.

King, Basil (1859-1928), American novelist born in Canada who became an Episcopal clergyman: his works include *Griselda* (1900); *The Steps of Honor; The Inner Shrine; The Wild Olive; The Street Called Straight; The Side of the Angels; The Dust Flower; The Conquest of Fear; Adventures in Religion*.

King, Charles (1844-1933), American army officer and novelist who served in the Civil War, in the campaigns against the Apaches, and as a volunteer in the Spanish-American War. His novels include *The Colonel's Daughter* (1883); *Marion's Faith; Captain Blake; Cadet Days; A War-Time Wooing; An Army Wife*.

King, Dennis (1897-), English actor who made his debut on the English stage at twelve as Bottom in *A Midsummer Night's Dream*, and later became call boy at the Birmingham Repertory Theatre, first appearing in *As You Like It*. After serving in World War I he toured the United States in *Monsieur Beaucaire*, and has since appeared in *Clair de Lune; Back to Methusaleh; Bluebeard's Eighth Wife; Romeo and Juliet; Antony and Cleopatra; Rose Marie; The Vagabond King; The Three Musketeers; The Show Boat; A Doll's House; The Three Sisters* (1943) with Katharine CORNELL.

King, Grace Elizabeth (1852-1932), American novelist, short story writer and essayist: her works include *Monsieur Motte* (1888); *Balcony Stories; New Orleans: the Place and the People; Madame Girard*. Her knowledge of French life in New Orleans lends an atmosphere of reality and culture to her stories.

King Arthur, see **Arthur, King.**

Kingsley, Charles (1819-1875), English novelist, poet, clergyman, and philanthropist: his works include *The Saint's Tragedy* (1848), a tragedy in verse; *Alton Locke, Tailor and Poet; Hypatia*, a novel of life in Alexandria during the 5th century; *Westward Ho!* a novel of the New World in the days of Raleigh and Drake; *The Water Babies*, a fairy tale; *Andromeda and Other Poems; Hereward the Wake*, a historical novel.

Kingsley, Sidney (1906-), American dramatist educated at Cornell University: his plays include *Men in White* (1933) which won the Pulitzer award in 1934, and was successfully produced at New York and London; *Dead End; Ten Million Ghosts; The Patriots*, produced in 1943.

Kipling, Rudyard (1865-1936), English poet, novelist, and short story writer born in India and educated in England, returning to India in 1883 to become a journalist. He married an American girl, Caroline Starr Balestier, sister of the American author, Charles Wolcott BALESTIER, in 1892, while on a visit to England, and lived for a few years in the United States. His works include *Departmental Ditties* (1886); *Barrack Room Ballads; Songs of the Sea; Plain Tales from the Hills; Soldiers Three; The Phantom Rickshaw and Other Tales; The Light That Failed; Captains Courageous; The Jungle Book; Second Jungle Book; Stalky and Co.; Kim.*

Kipnis, Alexander (1891-), Russian dramatic bass trained at the Klindworth-Scharwenka Conservatory in Berlin. He made his debut at Hamburg in 1915, and appeared in 1923 at the Metropolitan Opera House, New York, in *Die Meistersinger:* after singing at the Berlin State Opera he returned to the United States with the Wagnerian Festival Singers, and also appeared with the Chicago Civic Opera Company.

Kirkland, Alexander, contemporary American actor and manager born in Mexico City who studied for the stage with Louis Calvert and Rouben MAMOULIAN, and made his debut in 1925 at Washington, D. C., in *L'Aiglon.* He has since appeared in numerous plays including *The Devil To Pay; The Yellow Jacket; Marseilles; Men in White; The County Chairman; Outward Bound.* He founded the Berkshire Playhouse, Stockbridge, Mass., in 1930, managing and playing in the company for three years: in 1939 he became associate manager of the Paper Mill Playhouse, New Milburn, N. J.

Kirkpatrick, Ralph (1911-), American pianist and harpsichordist educated at Harvard University who studied musical theory with Nadia BOULANGER and the harpsichord with Wanda LANDOWSKA. He has taught at the Dalcroze School of Music, New York, and has given many lecture-recitals on 17th and 18th century music.

Kirstein, Lincoln Edward (1907-), American authority on the art of dancing educated at Harvard University. He was one of the founders of the Harvard Society for Contemporary Art, of the School of American Ballet, and of a dance group, The Ballet Caravan. His writings include *Dance* (1935), a history of the art from the theatrical, operatic, and ballet standpoints.

Kisfaludy, Karoly (1788-1830), Hungarian poet, novelist, and dramatist: his works include *The Tatars in Hungary* (1819), said to be the first genuine Magyar drama; *Irene,* a tragedy; several comedies including *The Rebels, The Murderer,* and *Illusions.* His brother, **Sandor Kisfaludy** (1772-1845) was the first great poet of modern Hungary: his works include *Himfy's Love Songs* (1801), and an epic poem, *Legends from the Magyar Past.*

Kiss, August (1802-1865), German sculptor who made a specialty of animals in bronze including *Amazon on Horseback Attacked by a Tiger* and *St. George Killing the Dragon;* also an equestrian statue of Frederick the Great.

Kit-Cat Club, an English club formed at London about 1700, and composed of men in politics, artists, and authors. The members first convened at a tavern and bakery near Temple Bar owned by Christopher Cat; hence the name: among the members were the Duke of Marlborough, Lord Halifax, Sir Robert Walpole, Sir Godfrey KNELLER, Sir John VANBRUGH, Sir Richard STEELE, William CONGREVE, and Joseph ADDISON.

Kittredge, George Lyman (1860-1941), American author educated at Harvard University: his works include *The Mother Tongue* (1900) with Sarah L. Arnold; *Words and Their Ways in English Speech,* with James B. Greenough; *The Old Farmer and His Almanac; Chaucer and His Poetry; Shakespeare; Witchcraft in Old and New England.* He also edited the Athenaeum Press Series of English Classics.

Kiyonaga, Torii (1752-1815), Japanese painter, influenced by Kano MASANOBU, who is regarded as a superb colorist: he was imitated by Kitagawa UTAMARO and many other later artists, especially in respect to elongating his figures. His works include *Fete in a Temple; Woman Standing Under Red Lanterns; Two Geishas Struggling Against the Wind; Terrace by the Seashore; Women Bathing; Nocturnal Walk.*

Kiyonobu, Torii (1664-1729), Japanese painter who first worked on theatrical posters, and later specialized in painting theatres and actors, thereby founding the remarkable Torii School which devoted itself to dramatic picturization.

Klaw, Marc, see **Erlanger, Abraham L.**

Klee, Paul (1879-), Swiss painter who studied at the Munich Academy, and in Rome, Naples, and Florence, finally becoming a professor at the Bauhaus in Weimar. He was influenced by CEZANNE and PICASSO in the selection of fantastic, abstract subjects portrayed in brilliant colors in accordance with the principles laid down in SURREALISM. He illustrated VOLTAIRE's *Candide,* and his pictures are to be seen in European and American museums.

Kleiber, Erich (1890-), Austrian orchestral conductor who studied at the Prague Conservatory and University and directed at the Prague National Theatre, Düsseldorf Opera, and Mannheim Opera, finally becoming general musical director of the Berlin State Opera. He has appeared as guest conductor of opera and symphonic concerts in Italy, Russia, Belgium, South America, and the United States: he was also first conductor of the Czech National Theatre at Prague.

Klein, Charles (1867-1915), American dramatist born in England, educated at North London College and for many years censor of plays for Charles FROHMAN. His successful plays include *The District Attorney; The Third Degree; The Lion and the Mouse; Maggie Pepper; The Auctioneer; The Music Master:* David WARFIELD appeared in the two last-named plays under the management of David BELASCO.

Kleist, Heinrich von (1777-1811), German poet and dramatist whose plays rival those of GOETHE and SCHILLER: they include *Penthesilea* (1808); *Kitty of Heilbronn; The Prince of Homburg; The Broken Jug.* His prose novelette, *Michael Kohlhass,* is considered the finest work of its kind in the German language.

Klemperer, Otto (1885-), German orchestral conductor and composer who studied at the Frankfort Conservatory and at Berlin, later becoming conductor at Prague, Hamburg, Bremen, Vienna, Cologne, and Berlin. He has appeared as guest conductor in England, Italy, Spain, Russia, South America, and the United States. He settled in the United States in 1932; director of the Los Angeles Symphony Orchestra from 1933, and guest conductor of several major orchestras: his compositions include choral works and songs.

Klenze, Leo von (1784-1864), German architect and painter who became the leader of the Greek phase of Neo-Classicism in the early part of the 19th century: his works include the *Glyptothek, Odeon,* and *Pinakothek* in Munich, the *Walhalla* at Regensburg, and the *Hermitage* at St. Petersburg.

Klindworth, Karl (1830-1916), German pianist, teacher, and editor who was chiefly self-taught. He was friendly with Franz LISZT, Richard WAGNER, and Anton RUBINSTEIN who secured him the post of professor of the piano in the Imperial Conservatory at Moscow. He prepared the piano scores of Wagner's *Ring of the Nibelungs,* published a revised edition of Chopin's piano compositions, and established a fine school of piano playing at Berlin with Hans von BÜLOW.

Klinger, Friedrich Maximilian von (1752-1831), German poet, novelist, and dramatist who was assisted by GOETHE, and became a high ranking officer in the Austrian and Russian armies. His dramas and novels include *Storm and Stress* (1776); *The Twins; Otto; The Suffering Wife; Faust's Life, Deeds, and Journey to Hell; The Worldling and the Poet.*

Klinger, Max (1857-1920), German painter, sculptor, and engraver: his paintings include *Judgment of Paris; Piéta; Crucifixion; Christ on Olympus:* among his sculptures are *Salome; Cassandra; Bathing Woman; Beethoven,* a statue in marble, gold, bronze, and platinum; *Amphitrite; The Athlete; The Drama.* He wrote a treatise, *Painting and Drawing* (1891), and is considered one of the most gifted and original German artists.

Klopstock, Friedrich Gottlieb (1724-1803), German poet and dramatist who freed German poetry from the trammels of ALEXANDRINE VERSE: his works include the epic poem *The Messiah,* begun in 1748 and finished twenty-five years later. He also wrote several series of poems entitled *Odes,* and it is said by critical authorities that both SCHILLER and GOETHE were deeply indebted to him. His dramas were relatively less important; they include three dramas with Arminius, one of Germany's national heroes, as the central figure.

Klosé, Hyacinthe Eléanore (1808-1880), French clarinetist who studied with Friedrich Berr at the Paris CONSERVATORY, and became professor of the clarinet there from 1839 to 1868. He made several important improvements in the fingering mechanisms of his instrument for which he composed an excellent method and solo pieces.

Klotz, Mathias (1656-1743), German violin maker who was probably a pupil of Jacob STAINER: his instruments are beautifully varnished, and sell at the present time for $750.00. His son, **Sebastian Klotz** (1696-c.1770), also followed the Stainer model, but his violins are superior to his father's in workmanship and varnish, and command slightly higher prices. Both of Sebastian's sons, Aegidius and Joseph, were violin makers who made creditable instruments.

Knabe, William (1803-1864), American piano maker born in Germany who came to the United States about 1830, and founded the firm of Knabe and Gaehle with Henry Gaehle who retired in 1854. The prosperity of the enterprise was interrupted by the Civil War, but his sons, William and Ernest Knabe, revived the business by creating a new field of sale in the Northern States. The founder's grandsons, Ernest J. and William Knabe also increased the reputation of the firm: it finally became a subsidiary of the Aeolian-American Corporation.

Knackfuss, Hermann (1848-1915), German painter and historian of art who studied with Eduard BENDEMANN at the Düsseldorf Academy and became professor of art at the Kassel Academy. His works include *Attila's Queen; Painter's Studio in the 16th Century; Capture of Frederick the Fair; Holy Family; Entry of the German Emperor into Jerusalem:* he also wrote several treatises on the history of art.

Knaus, Ludwig (1829-1910), German painter who studied at the Düsseldorf Academy with Johann SCHADOW, and also in Paris and Italy. His notable works include *Peasant Dance; Funeral in the Woods; Holy Family; Woman Playing with Cats; Beggar Boy; Children's Festival; Mud Pies; Wood-Chopper; Country Folk at a Village Inn; Gipsies Resting; Tyrolese Brawlers before Their Rector.*

Kneisel, Franz (1865-1926), Rumanian violinist of German parentage who studied with Jakob Grün and Joseph HELLMESBERGER at the Vienna Conservatory, and succeeded Bernhard Listemann as concertmaster of the BOSTON SYMPHONY ORCHESTRA in 1885. In 1886 he founded the **Kneisel Quartet** which achieved a reputation throughout America and Europe as one of the finest organizations of its kind, and disbanded in 1917. From 1905 until his death, Kneisel was professor of violin at the INSTITUTE OF MUSICAL ART, New York.

Kneller, Sir Godfrey (1646-1723), English painter born in Germany, and said to have been a pupil of REMBRANDT. He also studied and painted in Rome and Venice: he was so well received by Charles II while on a visit to England that he decided to settle there, and succeeded Sir Peter LELY as court painter. His works include 43 portraits of the members of the KIT-CAT CLUB;

portraits of Charles II, George I, and many other royal personages; *Ten Beauties of the Court of William III, The Converted Chinese, Copernicus in his Study.* His elder brother, **John Zachary Kneller** (1635-1702), was an architectural and portrait painter.

Knight, Daniel Ridgway (c.1840-1924), American painter who studied at the ECOLE DES BEAUX-ARTS, Paris, and with Jean MEISSONIER, later receiving many medals and honors in Europe and the United States. His notable canvases include *Othello in the House of Brabantio; The Shepherdess; The Shearer; Hailing the Ferry; Noonday Rest; Old Beau; Chatterboxes; Strolling in the Garden.*

Knight, Eric (1897-1943), Anglo-American novelist born in England who came to America in 1912, and worked as copy boy on the Philadelphia *Press.* He served in a Canadian regiment in World War I during which his two brothers were killed, and after becoming an officer in the United States Army in 1942 was killed in an aeroplane accident. His works include *Invitation to Life* (1934); *Song on Your Bugles; The Flying Yorkshireman; Richard Hallas; The Happy Land; Lassie Come-Home; This Above All:* the last-named was adapted for a very successful film.

Knight, Laura Johnson, contemporary English painter who studied at the Nottingham Art School, and traveled extensively in England, France, and the Swiss Tyrol. Her works include studies of Anna PAVLOWA, Vaslav NIJINSKY, and other members of Sergei DIAGHILEFF's ballet company: also many scenes, painted in circuses, of performers and animals. She also made excellent etchings and aquatints: examples of her work are in some of the major museums of America and Great Britain.

Knight, (*a*) the name given to an armed and mounted soldier or officer rank in the Middle Ages: known in German as *Ritter;* in Spanish as *caballero,* and in French as *chevalier.* During the Crusades associations were formed such as the Knights Hospitalers and the Knights Templars which acquired considerable political power. (*b*) A British title of honor ranking next below a baronet: since the 16th century the honor is conferred as a civil as well as military reward.

Knobelsdorff, George von (1699-1753), German architect and painter who supervised the construction of Sans Souci, the summer palace near Berlin of FREDERICK THE GREAT: many of the latter's ideas are said to have been incorporated into the plans. He also designed the Opera House and the Tiergarten at Berlin.

Knoblock, Edward (1874-), Anglo-American dramatist born in the United States who became a British subject in 1916: his plays, several of which were written in collaboration, include *The Shulamite* (1906); *Kismet; Milestones; London Life; The Good Companions.* He also made the English stage adaptation of *Grand Hotel,* Vicki Baum's successful novel.

Knote, Heinrich (1870-), German dramatic tenor who made his debut in 1892 at Munich, and

sang for several years at BAYREUTH, Berlin, and Hamburg. He made his debut in 1904 at the Metropolitan Opera House as Walther in *Die Meistersinger,* rivaling CARUSO in popularity, and appeared for three successive seasons until recalled to Munich. He continued to sing Wagnerian roles at German opera houses until his retirement in 1924.

Knowles, James Sheridan (1784-1862), Irish actor and dramatist who was a cousin of Richard Brinsley SHERIDAN. He appeared first on the stage in 1806, but his dramatic works overshadowed his reputation as an actor. His dramas include *Caius Gracchus* (1815); *Virginius; William Tell; Alfred the Great; The Rose of Aragon:* among his comedies are *The Hunchback, The Love Chase,* and *The Beggar's Daughter.* In 1845 religious scruples impelled him to stop writing plays, and he became well-known as a Baptist preacher.

Kobbé, Gustav (1857-1918), American critic and writer on musical subjects who was educated at Columbia University, and from 1880 acted as critic at various times for the New York *Sun, World,* and *Herald.* His works include *Wagner's Life and Works* (1890); *The Ring of the Nibelung; Opera Singers; Loves of the Great Composers; How to Appreciate Music; Famous American Songs; The Complete Opera Book.*

Kober, Arthur (1900-), American humorist and dramatist born in Austria-Hungary who came to the United States when a child of two, and later studied in the public schools of New York. He became publicity agent for various theatrical enterprises, conducted a column for the New York *Morning Telegraph,* and wrote screen plays in Hollywood for motion picture stars. His works include *Thunder Over the Bronx* (1935); *Having Wonderful Time,* successful as a stage play and as a film; *Pardon Me for Pointing; My Dear Bella.*

Kochanski, Paul (1887-1934), Polish violinist who studied with Emil MLYNARSKI and César THOMSON, becoming professor of violin in the Conservatories at Warsaw, St. Petersburg, and Kiev. He made his American debut in 1921 with the NEW YORK SYMPHONY ORCHESTRA: after concertizing extensively he assumed the post of professor of violin at the Julliard Graduate School, New York, and made several interesting transcriptions for the violin.

Köchel, Ludwig, Ritter von (1800-1877), Austrian musical dilettante who, for pure love of his art, made a supremely important contribution to music in the form of a chronological thematic catalogue of the works of Wolfgang Amadeus MOZART entitled *Chronologisch-systematisches Verzeichniss sammtlicher Tonwerke W. A. Mozart,* first published in 1862 with revisions in 1905 by Count Paul von Waldersee, and an entirely new edition by Alfred EINSTEIN in 1937.

Kocian, Jaroslav (1884-), Bohemian violinist and composer who studied the violin with Ottokar SEVCIK and composition with Antonin DVORAK at the Prague Conservatory. He made his debut in

1901, and has concertized extensively in Europe and America. His compositions include orchestral works, a *Dumka* and a *Serenade* for violin, and a mass for solo voices, chorus, and orchestra.

Kock, Paul de (1794-1871), French novelist of Dutch extraction who was first engaged in the banking business, and later achieved success as a writer of opera librettos. His novels dealing with life in Paris include *The Child of My Mother* (1811); *Georgette; André de Savoyard; The Barber of Paris; Monsieur Dupont; Gustave; The Millionaire; My Cousin Raymond; Wife, Husband and Lover; The Man with Three Pairs of Trousers.*

Kodály, Zoltan (1882-), Hungarian composer who studied at the Budapest Hochschule: his compositions include a comic opera, *Háry János* from which a popular orchestral suite has been arranged; many orchestral works; chamber music: also numerous volumes of Hungarian folk songs in collaboration with Béla BARTOK, and several treatises on folk music.

Kolar, Victor (1888-), Hungarian violinist, conductor, and composer who studied with Ottokar SEVCIK and Antonin DVORAK at the Prague Conservatory as a protege of Jan KUBELIK. He came to America in 1904, playing in the Pittsburgh Symphony Orchestra and becoming assistant conductor in 1914-20 to Walter DAMROSCH with the New York Symphony Orchestra. Since 1920 he has conducted the DETROIT SYMPHONY ORCHESTRA. His compositions include orchestral works, chamber music, and violin pieces.

Kolbe, Georg (1877-), German sculptor who first studied as a painter at Dresden, Munich, and Paris before deciding to become a sculptor. He worked for a time with Auguste RODIN, and his earlier creations show the latter's influence: after World War I his style reveals a greater degree of restraint in such pieces as *Dancer* and the *Heine Memorial.* Many of his works are in American and European museums.

Kolcsey, Ferencz (1790-1838), Hungarian critic and poet who founded a periodical, *Life and Literature,* with Paul Szemere which built his reputation as a critical writer: his works include the poems, *Aurora, Hebe,* and *Aspasia;* also satires, short novels, a national hymn, and a ballad, *Lena.* All of these indicate that he was one of the greatest of Hungarian writers.

Kollwitz, Kathe Schmidt (1867-), German painter and etcher who was first inspired by William HOGARTH's satirical drawings, and studied painting at Dresden and Munich, exhibiting at the Berlin Academy in 1898. She illustrated Gerhard HAUPTMANN's *The Weavers* and Émile ZOLA's *Germinal,* and became a militantly ardent socialist, devoting her life and her art to the working people. Her fantasies on death were rendered even more significant by the death of one of her sons in World War I: her canvases include war scenes, mother and child subjects, and rural landscapes.

Kol Nidrei, a Jewish ritual melody which is recited in synagogues on the Day of Atonement at the beginning of the evening service. The standard arrangement for concert use is that of Max BRUCH for violoncello and orchestra available in a Victor recording by Pablo CASALS: there is also a Columbia recording for violin with piano accompaniment by Bronislaw HUBERMANN.

Kolodin, Irving (1908-), American critic and writer on musical subjects who studied at the INSTITUTE OF MUSICAL ART, New York, and later taught musical theory there in addition to becoming assistant to William J. HENDERSON, music critic of the New York Sun, and in 1938 associate critic of that paper. His works include *The Metropolitan Opera, 1883-1935* (1936); *A Guide to Recorded Music; The Critical Composer.*

Komisarjevsky, Theodore (1882-), Russian theatrical director born in Italy who made his first essay at production in 1907 at a theatre managed by his sister at Petrograd. In 1910 he established his own theatre, and in nine years produced twenty operas and numerous plays by Shakespeare, Molière, and others as director of the Imperial and State Theatres at Moscow. He produced Borodin's opera, *Prince Igor,* at Covent Garden, London, in 1919: also *Six Characters in Search of an Author; Uncle Vanya; The Three Sisters; The Cherry Orchard.* Since 1922 he has produced numerous plays in New York including *The Tidings Brought to Mary; Peer Gynt; The Sea Gull; Antony and Cleopatra,* designing the scenery and costumes in addition to directing the acting.

Komroff, Manuel (1890-), American novelist educated in engineering, music, and painting: his works include *The Grace of Lambs* (1925), a volume of short stories; *Coronet,* a best seller in 1930; *Two Thieves; Waterloo; The March of the Hundred; The Magic Bow; In the Years of Our Lord.*

Koninck (Coningh), Philip de (1619-1688), Dutch painter who studied with REMBRANDT, and became one of the most distinguished landscapists of his time: the figures in many of his works were painted in by other artists. His notable works include *Mouth of a Dutch River; Environs of Scheveningen; Entrance to a Forest; Daughter of Jairus; Surgical Operation; Old Woman with a Pot; Merry Sea Captains at an Inn.*

Konti, Isidore (1862-1938), American sculptor born in Austria who came to the United States in 1892, first working with Karl BITTER: his works include *Genius of Immortality* at the Metropolitan Museum of Art, New York; *Illusion; Kit Carson; Orpheus; Harvest.* He has also executed many fountains and groups on a large scale for expositions, and smaller works of a similar character for private residences. One of his finest works is the memorial to Bishop Potter in the Cathedral of St. John the Divine at New York.

Koran, the sacred book of the Mohammedans, and the foundation upon which the religion inaugurated by Mohammed rests. It is written in the Arabic language, and its text is considered eternal and uncreated because Mohammed did not write it himself, but merely transcribed that which was revealed to him. There are more than one hundred divisions each of which has a separate title, and they contain the theology of Islam. Jewish and Christian sources are drawn upon: Christ and Moses are placed among the prophets, and the first authorized edition was established about 650 A.D.

Korbel, Mario (1882-), American sculptor born in Bohemia who studied in Prague, Munich, Berlin, and Paris, and came to the United States in 1900. He has executed many fountains and figures including *Andante; Night; St. Therese; The Dancers; Alma Mater; Sonata and Night; Sleeping Maiden; Adolescence*. His works are in many American and European museums as well as in private collections.

Korda, Sir Alexander (1893-), English screen director, born in Hungary and educated at the Royal University of Budapest: he has produced many important silent and talking films since 1915 including *The Private Life of Helen of Troy; A Modern Du Barry; The Dollar Princess; The Girl from Maxims; The Private Life of Henry VIII; Catherine the Great; The Scarlet Pimpernel; Sanders of the River; The Ghost Goes West; Rembrandt; Fire Over England; Knight Without Armour; South Riding; Four Feathers; The Thief of Bagdad.*

Korin, Ogata (1658-1716), Japanese painter who studied under the Kano masters, but was influenced later by SOTATSU although he gave his designs less vigor and more grace. He was an unusually fine colorist and painted all kinds of subjects: he was also a skillful inlayer and lacquerer employing mother-of-pearl, silver, and bronze. A large screen depicting a tempest is in the Boston Museum of Fine Arts.

Koriusai, Isoda (c.1730-1780), Japanese painter who studied with Nishimura SHIGENAGA, and was probably a fellow pupil of Suzuki HARUNOBU. He specialized in the painting of animals: among his works are *The Heron and the Crow; Sacred Falcon; Cock Fight; The White Falcon; Two Children on a Wooden Horse; Young Girls Washing Their Hands; Couple in the Snow Under a Big Umbrella:* also a long *Hashira-ye* or pillar-print.

Korjus, Miliza, contemporary Polish coloratura soprano who studied at the Moscow Conservatory, and made her debut in 1934 at the State Opera House, Berlin, as Gilda in *Rigoletto:* she remained there for two years, appearing in *The Magic Flute, The Barber of Seville, Cavalleria Rusticana,* and other operas. In 1938 she scored a sensational success through her singing and acting in the film, *The Great Waltz:* several of her recordings such as the *Hymn to the Sun* from "Le Coq d'Or," the *Bell Song* from "Lakme," and the *Doll Song* from "The Tales of Hoffmann" have enjoyed a large sale.

Korngold, Erich (1897-), Austrian composer who studied with Robert Fuchs and Alexander von Zemlinsky in Vienna, and wrote a pantomime, *The Snow Man,* which was produced in 1910. His *Overture to a Drama* was performed in 1911 at a Gewandhaus concert in Leipzig by Artur NIKISCH, and a concert of his works given at Berlin during the same year. After conducting at the Hamburg Opera House, and becoming professor of theory at the Vienna State Academy he came to Hollywood in 1935 with Max REINHARDT to compose music for the film, *A Midsummer Night's Dream* in which he incorporated part of MENDELSSOHN'S music, and has since written incidental music for many films including *Captain Blood; Green Pastures; Anthony Adverse; Another Dawn; Juarez; Elizabeth and Essex; The Sea Hawk.* His compositions include several operas, among them *The Dead City* in which Maria JERITZA made her debut at the Metropolitan Opera House in 1921; orchestra works, chamber music, and songs.

Korolenko, Vladimir Galaktionovich (1853-1921), Russian novelist and short story writer who was exiled in 1879 and pardoned in 1885: he was a bitter antagonist of Bolshevism at the time of the Russian Revolution. His works, many of which have been translated include *Makar's Dream* (1885); *The Vagrant,* a volume of short stories; *Birds of Heaven; Forest Murmurs; In Bad Society; In the Night; In a Strange Land.*

Kose no Kanaoka (840-880), Japanese painter who is regarded as one of the greatest artists working under the patronage of the emperor Seiwa, and referred to by some authorities as the father of Japanese painting. He was distinguished as a delineator of animals and landscapes; and also as a landscape architect who beautified the grounds of the Imperial palaces.

Kossack Lugansky, see **Dahl, Vladimir Ivanovich.**

Kostelanetz, André (1901-), American pianist and conductor born in Russia who studied at the St. Petersburg Conservatory, and made his debut at eight, later becoming chorusmaster at the Petrograd Opera House. He came to the United States in 1922, and was naturalized in 1928. After acting as accompanist for several opera singers, he became connected with both radio and screen as a conductor, and has also achieved success as guest conductor of several major American symphony orchestras. He has directed the music for several films in which his wife, Lily PONS, has appeared.

Koster, Samuel (1579-c.1661), Dutch dramatist who was one of the founders of the Dutch Academy, and wrote many brilliant, successful dramas and comedies including *Iphigenia; Isabella; Polyxena; The Play of the Rich Man; The Play of Tüsken van der Schilden.*

Koto, a Japanese combined harp and zither which has thirteen silk strings, each provided with a separate bridge for tuning purposes. The instrument is about six feet long; and rests on the floor: the player sits on his heels and plucks the string by means of plectra on his right hand while his left hand does the tuning. The koto has been the national instrument of Japan since the 17th century, and is fashionable with young women of the higher class.

Kotzebue, August Friedrich Ferdinand von (1761-1819), German dramatist whose strong sense of theatrical climax has made his more than two hundred tragedies, comedies, and farces sources from which other playwrights have drawn inspiration: his plays have been performed in all European theatres and almost universally translated. Among the most successful were *Misanthropy and Repentance; Dr. Bahrdt with the Iron Brow,* a notoriously obscene drama; *The Spaniards in Peru,* adapted by SHERIDAN as "Pizzaro"; *German Provincials; Sorrows of the Ortenberg Family; The Child of Love; The Indians in England.*

Koussevitzky, Sergei (1874-), Russian double-bass virtuoso, composer, and orchestral conductor who studied at the Music School of the Philharmonic Society at Moscow. He toured Germany with great success as a DOUBLE-BASS virtuoso: in 1910 he organized an orchestra which gave regular concerts at St. Petersburg and Moscow which proved his exceptional ability as a conductor. After the Revolution he was appointed director of symphony orchestras in Russia and director of grand opera at Moscow. In 1921 he founded the *Concerts Koussevitzky* in Paris which he conducted until 1928, also conducting the Boston Symphony Orchestra from 1924. He introduced numerous Russian works at his concerts in Paris, and many works by American composers since he has been conductor of the Boston Symphony Orchestra. His compositions include works for the double-bass, and a *Passacaglia on a Russian Theme* for orchestra.

Krafft, Adam (c.1455-1509), German sculptor who worked at Nuremburg about 1490 on a tomb decorated with bas-reliefs representing scenes from the life of Christ: his masterpiece is the *Tabernacle of the Holy Sacrament* 62 feet high in the Church of St. Lawrence where he represented himself and two assistants kneeling in the form of CARYATIDES, and also included scenes of the Passion. Other important works include *The Way of the Cross* and *Madonna of the Bindergasse.*

Krakoviak or **Cracoviak,** a Polish dance in 2-4 time with frequent syncopation danced on festive occasions such as weddings and birthdays. It found its way into the ballet about 1840, and was made famous by the distinguished ballerina, Fanny ELSSLER.

Kraszewski, Joseph Ignacy (1812-1887), Polish poet and novelist who devoted his life to the writing of more than five hundred historical treatises, romances, poems, and a series of novels depicting Polish history in the style of Sir Walter SCOTT. His works include the epic poem, *Anafielas;* a drama, *The Devil and the Woman;* a novelette, *Jermola the Potter* from which George ELIOT is said to have derived the idea of "Silas Marner"; *Ulana; The Poet and the World; The Hut Beyond the Village; Count Bruhl.*

Krehbiel, Henry Edward (1854-1923), American critic and writer on music who first studied law, but decided on a journalistic career, and became music critic of the New York *Tribune* from 1880 to 1923. His notable works include *How to Listen to Music; Studies in the Wagnerian Drama; Music and Manners in the 18th Century; Chapters of Opera; A Book of Operas; A Second Book of Operas; The Pianoforte and Its Music.* He also revised and completed the English edition of THAYER's *Life of Beethoven,* and wrote the program notes of the NEW YORK PHILHARMONIC-SYMPHONY SOCIETY for many years.

Kreisler, Fritz (1875-), Austrian violinist and composer who studied with Joseph HELLMESBERGER and Leopold AUER, later entering the Paris Conservatory where he was a pupil of Joseph MASSART in violin and Leo DELIBES in composition. He made his debut as a child prodigy at STEINWAY HALL, New York, in 1888, and in 1889 toured the United States with Moriz ROSENTHAL. He then abandoned music for medicine and art, but reappeared at Berlin in 1899 with tremendous success, and made a second debut in 1900 at New York carrying his audience by storm. After serving in the Austrian army in World War I, he resumed his concertizing, making frequent tours of the United States. His compositions include the operettas *Apple Blossoms* and *Sissy;* many light pieces for violin including the *Caprice Viennois* and *Liebesfreud;* several compositions attributed to early masters of the violin, but later admitted to be his original works, and numerous arrangements of works by classic and modern composers.

Kreisleriana, Op. 16 (Schumann), a suite of eight compositions for the piano composed by Robert SCHUMANN in 1838, and dedicated to Frédéric CHOPIN. The name is derived from the character "Kreisler" in E. T. A. Hoffmann's fantastic tales called *Fantasy Tales in the Manner of Callot,* and the pieces were written during Schumann's battle at court for the right to marry Clara Wieck, and therefore reflect, according to his own statement, the varying moods in which he found himself during this trying period. There is a complete Victor recording by Alfred CORTOT.

Křenek, Ernst (1900-), Austrian pianist and composer who studied at Berlin with Franz SCHREKER and made many tours of Europe as pianist and lecturer before coming to the United States in 1939 to become professor of music at Vassar College. His compositions, a startling combination of atonality and jazz include the opera JONNY SPIELT AUF, first produced at Leipzig in 1927 and at the Metropolitan Opera House, New York, in 1929; also many other operas, orchestral works, chamber music, piano pieces, choral works, and songs.

Kreutzer, Conradin (1780-1849), German composer who first studied law, later devoting himself to the composition of operas; his best work was *Nachtlager von Granada* (Night Bivouac at Granada) produced in 1834 which held the German stage for almost a century.

Kreutzer, Rodolphe (1766-1831), French violinist who studied with Anton STAMITZ and played a concerto of his own composition as a boy of thirteen at the Concerts Spirituels in Paris. He made many concert tours, composed forty operas now forgotten, and was chamber musician to Napoleon I. His most important works are the concertos and *Forty Études or Caprices* for violin still used for instruction.

"Kreutzer" Sonata (Beethoven), a work for piano and violin completed by Ludwig van BEE-THOVEN in 1803, and first performed on May 17 of that year with the composer at the piano and George Bridgetower, a distinguished mulatto violin virtuoso. The sonata is not only considered the finest of Beethoven's violin works, but is extremely difficult to perform from both the technical and the interpretative standpoints. It was dedicated to Rodolphe KREUTZER, a famous French violinist: there is a Columbia recording by Adolf Busch and Rudolf Serkin, and a Victor recording by Yehudi and Hephzibah Menuhin.

Kreymborg, Alfred (1883-), American poet and author educated in the public schools of New York City: his works include *Love and Life,* and *Other Studies* (1910); *Mushrooms,* poems; *Blood of Things,* poems; *Puppet Plays; Troubadour,* an autobiography; *Our Singing Strength, an Outline of American poetry; Manhattan Men,* poems; *I'm No Hero,* a novel; *The Four Apes and Other Fables of Our Day:* he has also edited "Poetic Drama": an anthology of plays in verse.

Krishna, a Hindu deity whose name literally means "the black," and an incarnation of the god, VISHNU, worshiped through northern India. He is the personification of fire, lightning, storm, heaven, and the sun, and he is also known as Gopal, the cowherd; Gopinath, the lord of milk-maids; Mathuranath, Lord of Muttra.

Krohg, Christian (1852-1925), Norwegian painter who taught at the ECOLE DES BEAUX-ARTS, Paris: among his notable canvases are *The Struggle for Existence; Leif Ericsson Discovers America; Norwegian Pilot;* he also illustrated several books, painted the portrait of August STRINDBERG, and championed outdoor painting of Norwegian scenery in his writings.

Kroll, Leon (1884-), American painter who studied with John H. TWACHTMAN and at the Art Students' League, New York; also with Jean Paul LAURENS at Paris, later becoming instructor in the art school of the National Academy of Design, New York. He has won many medals and awards with his canvases such as *Figure Outdoors* and *Cape Ann:* the Metropolitan Museum of Art and many other American galleries have examples of his work.

Kroller, Heinrich (1880-1930), German dancer and choreographer who studied at the ballet school of the Royal Theatre, Munich, and became *premier danseur* at the Dresden Opera House, and in 1917 balletmaster at the Munich Opera House. He wrote more than forty original ballets, and created the choreography for numerous operas and ballets including WEINBERGER'S *Schwanda;* Johann STRAUSS' *Gypsy Baron;* SULLI-VAN'S *The Mikado;* Richard STRAUSS' *Schlagobers* (Cream Puffs); CARPENTER'S *Skyscrapers.*

Krudener, Barbara Juliana, Baroness von (1764-1824), Russian novelist and mystic who led a life first of frivolity, and later of extreme piety

after becoming a Swedenborgian: her literary fame rests on a romance, *Valérie, or Letters of Gustave de Linar to Ernest de G——* in which she relates the story of her life.

Kruger, Franz (1797-1857), German painter who was self-taught, and excelled in the depiction of horses to such an extent that he was called "Pferde (Horse) Kruger." He painted more than one hundred portraits: also *Parade of the Cuirassiers in Berlin; Czar Nicholas and Suite on Horseback; Stable Interior; Start for the Chase; Return from the Chase; Dead Rabbit; Parade of the Guards.*

Kruger, Otto (1885-), American stage and screen actor educated at the University of Michigan and Columbia University, making his New York debut in *Quo Vadis,* and after appearing in stock companies for some years, played leading roles in numerous plays including *Alias Jimmy Valentine; The Nervous Wreck; The Royal Family; Private Lives; Counsellor-at-Law; Accent on Youth.* He has also appeared in many films including *Ever in My Heart; Men in White; The Crime Doctor; Treasure Island; Springtime for Henry; Housemaster; Saboteur.*

Krutch, Joseph Wood (1893-), American essayist and dramatic critic, educated at the University of Tennessee and Columbia University, who has taught English at Vassar College and Columbia: his works include *Comedy and Conscience after the Restoration* (1924); *Edgar Allan Poe, A Study in Genius; The Modern Temper; Five Masters; Experience and Art; The American Drama since 1918.* He has been dramatic critic of *The Nation* since 1924, and has edited the plays of William CONGREVE and Eugene O'NEILL.

Krylov, Ivan Andreyevich (1786-1844), Russian writer and translator who is considered the most popular author of his country: he translated the fables of Jean de LA FONTAINE, and later wrote more than 142 original fables couched in simple verse, and replete with good-natured satire. His fables are the favorites of Russian children, and a statue of him was placed in the summer garden of the Imperial Palace at St. Petersburg.

Kubelik, Jan (1880-1940), Bohemian violinist who studied with Ottokar SEVCIK at the Prague Conservatory, and made a sensational debut in 1898 at Vienna, duplicating his extraordinary success on tours in Europe, Great Britain and the United States. His son **Rafael Kubelik** (1914-), studied the piano and conducting at the Prague Conservatory and made his debut in 1934 as conductor of the Czech Philharmonic Orchestra: he toured the world as pianist and conductor for his father, and in 1936 became permanent conductor of the Czech Philharmonic Orchestra. He has composed symphonic works, a piano concerto, and chamber music.

Kugler, Franz Theodor (1808-1858), German poet and writer on art who became professor of fine arts at the University of Berlin in 1833: his works include *History of Painting from Constantine the Great to the Present Times* (1837); *Handbook of the History of Art; History of*

Architecture: he also wrote a *History of Frederick the Great* which was popular in Germany.

Kuhnau, Johann (1660-1722), German harpsichordist, organist, and composer who preceded Johann Sebastian BACH as cantor at the Thomaskirche at Leipzig: he is famous for having been the first composer to adopt the instrumental sonata form to the harpsichord. Several of his sonatas undertake to describe through music incidents in the Bible such as the contest between David and Goliath, the wedding of Jacob, and the restoring to health of Saul by David.

Kullak, Theodor (1818-1882), German pianist, teacher, and composer who studied with Carl CZERNY, and became court pianist to the King of Prussia at Berlin in 1846. He founded a piano school in Berlin at which Xaver SCHARWENKA, Philipp SCHARWENKA, William SHERWOOD, and Moritz MOSZKOWSKI were students; he also wrote many instructive works and solo pieces for the piano.

Kullman, Charles (1903-   ), American operatic tenor who was educated at Yale University and trained in music at the JUILLIARD GRADUATE SCHOOL, New York, and the American Conservatory at FONTAINEBLEAU, France. He made his debut in 1931 at the Kroll Opera, Berlin, and after singing at the Berlin State Opera and at Covent Garden, London, made his first appearance in 1935 at the Metropolitan Opera House in *Faust*, becoming a leading member of the company.

Kulmbach, Hans Suess von (c.1478-1522), German painter who studied with Albrecht DURER: his works include *Adoration of the Magi; Portrait of a Woman; Life of the Virgin,* an altarpiece; *Coronation of the Virgin with St. Sebastian and St. Roch; Finding of the Cross; Legend of St. Katherine; Scenes from the Lives of St. Peter and St. Paul.* He was court painter at Cracow, and also for the Emperor Maximilian.

Kummer, Clare, contemporary American dramatist: her works include *The Opera Ball* (1912) with Sidney Rosenfeld; *Good Gracious, Annabelle; A Successful Calamity; Rollo's Wild Oat; Her Master's Voice; Three Waltzes* with Rowland Leigh. She also wrote several popular songs including *Dearie.*

Kundry, a character in Richard WAGNER's sacred drama, PARSIFAL: she is the woman who scorned Christ as He suffered on the cross, and is condemned to wander the earth eternally. She bears messages for the knights of the Holy GRAIL, and seeks herbs with which to ease the wound received by AMFORTAS from the spear of the sorcerer, Klingsor.

Kunisada, Utagawa (1786-1865), Japanese painter and print maker who was a pupil of Utagawa Toyokuni, and also worked with Ando HIROSHIGE, specializing in landscapes, animal pictures such as *Horse Lying Down,* and portraits of actors.

Kuniyoshi, Yasuo (1893-   ), Japanese painter who came to the United States as a boy of thirteen and studied at the Los Angeles School of Art and Design, and at the ART STUDENTS' LEAGUE, New York. He traveled in Europe, and was influenced by Honoré DAUMIER and Eugene DELACROIX: his designs, which are somewhat somber in character, reveal Oriental design with the faintest suggestion of Occidental coloring. Examples of his work are to be seen in the Whitney Museum of American Art, New York.

Kunst der Fuge (Bach), see **Art of Fugue (Bach).**

Kuolema (Sibelius), see **Valse Triste (Sibelius).**

Kuprin, Alexander Ivanovich (1870-1938), Russian novelist and short story writer who fought in World War I, and was exiled for seventeen years because of his opposition to the Soviet regime in Russia: his works, based on his experiences in Russian army life, include *Olessia* (1909); *The Duel; The River of Life; Sasha; Sulamith; The Bracelet of Garnets; Gambrinus.* All the above are to be had in English translations.

Kurtz, Efrem (1900-   ), Russian conductor who studied at the St. Petersburg Conservatory under Alexander GLAZUNOFF, and at the Berlin Academy: in 1921 he substituted for Artur NIKISCH at a dance recital with orchestra given by Isadora DUNCAN, and also appeared as guest conductor of the Berlin Philharmonic Orchestra. In 1924 he became director of the Stuttgart Philharmonic Orchestra, and later of the PAVLOWA Ballet, SALZBURG FESTIVALS, and the Ballet Russe. He has acted as guest conductor of the NBC Symphony Orchestra, the New York Philharmonic-Symphony Orchestra, the Cleveland Orchestra, the Detroit Symphony, the National Symphony Orchestra and the New York Stadium concerts.

Kurz, Hermann (1813-1873), German poet and novelist: his works include *Schiller's Home Years; Mine Host of the Sun; From the Days of Dishonor;* also two volumes of poems. He translated the works of English, Spanish, and Italian authors including ARIOSTO's *Orlando Furioso,* and made a modern version of Gottfried von Strassburg's *Tristan and Isolde.*

Kyasht, Lydia (1886-   ), Russian ballerina trained at the School of the Imperial Theatres, Petrograd, making her debut in 1902 at the Opera House there in *The Magic Flute.* In 1908 she danced at the Empire Theatre, London, with Adolf BOLM, and succeeded Adeline GENEE as *première danseuse.* She made her American debut in 1914 at the Winter Garden, New York, and later appeared at leading European opera houses. In 1933 she appeared as the Retiring Ballerina in *Ballerina,* and in 1939 founded the "Ballet de la Jeunesse Anglaise."

Kyd, Thomas (1558-1594), English dramatist considered the most popular writer of tragedies before SHAKESPEARE. He was an intimate of Christopher MARLOWE, and his most important dramatic works include *The Spanish Tragedy; Cornelia; Soliman and Perseda:* the first-named was popular on the English stage for many years.

Kyne, Peter Bernard (1880-), American novelist who joined the American Army, serving during the Philippine Rebellion and in World War I: his works which are regarded as good recreational reading, include *Three Godfathers* (1913); *Cappy Ricks; The Valley of the Giants; The Pride of Palomar; Never the Twain Shall Meet; They Also Serve; Comrades of the Storm; Cappy Ricks Comes Back; Dude Woman.*

Kyosai, Shofu (1831-1889), Japanese painter and illustrator who studied with Kano Dohaku, but developed an individualistic style, and became famous as a political cartoonist during the revolution of 1867. He is considered the greatest artist after HOKUSAI, and his subjects were often taken from the folk tales of Japan: up to 1863 he signed his pictures "Chikamaro."

L

L aar (or **Laer**), **Pieter van** (c.1600-c.1670), Dutch painter also known as *Il Bamboccio* because he was a cripple. He studied with Jan van Campen, and worked for sixteen years in Rome on intimate terms with POUSSIN and CLAUDE LORRAIN: his notable works include *Travelers Leaving Inn; Paying the Vintagers; Rural Frolic; Landscape with Ruins; Smithy in a Roman Ruin; Peasant's Frolic in a Grotto; A Singer.*

Labiche, Eugène Maria (1815-1888), French dramatist whose first play, *Counsellor Loubet,* was produced in 1838: during the ensuing forty years he wrote nearly 100 comedies, farces, and vaudevilles in collaboration with others. Among the most successful were *The Money Box, Monsieur Perrichon's Journey,* and *The Italian Straw Hat:* the last-named was adapted as a motion picture by Rene CLAIR, and also produced in 1936 for the FEDERAL THEATRE PROJECT as *Horse Eats Hat* by Orson WELLES and John Houseman.

Lablache, Luigi (1794-1858), Italian operatic bass trained at the Conservatory in Naples who made his debut at the San Carlino Theatre in 1812, and became the greatest dramatic bass of his day through his characterization in 1830 of Geronimo in CIMAROSA's *The Secret Marriage* and of Leporello in MOZART's *Don Giovanni* at the L'Opera, Paris, where he sang continuously for twenty-two years.

Labrouste, Henri (1801-1875), French architect famous for his designs for the Bibliothèque Saint Geneviève, Paris, conceived in the Renaissance revival style, and the Bibliothèque Nationale, Paris, in which the ceiling of the reading room is supported by an open framework of iron: he is said to be one of the pioneers in constructional work of this character.

Labyrinth, in architecture a building in which the passage-ways and rooms are constructed in an intricate, complex manner with the purpose of bewildering persons making use of them. The earliest known building of this kind is that erected by King Amenemhout IV of Egypt about 2900 B.C. which, as described by HERODOTUS comprised 3000 chambers, and contained the tombs of the kings and the sacred treasures. The early Christians used labyrinths as places for safe worship, and the most famous, in Greek mythology, is the labyrinth built by DAEDALUS for the minotaur.

La Calprenède, Gauthier de Costes (1610-1663), French novelist and dramatist: his historical romances include *Cassandre* (1640); *Cleopatra; Faramond, or The History of France.* Among his tragedies are *The Death of Mithridate; Bradamante; Jean of England; Count Essex; Edward, King of England.*

Lac des Cygnes, Les (Ballet), see **Swan Lake (Ballet).**

Lachaise, Gaston (1882-1935), American sculptor born in France who studied with Bernard PALISSY and later with Gabriel Jules Thomas at the ECOLE DES BEAUX-ARTS, Paris. In 1906 he came to the United States, and was naturalized in 1916, continuing his studies with Paul MANSHIP. His notable works include many statues of *Woman;* a frieze for the American Telephone and Telegraph Building, New York; *La Montagne,* a half-reclining female figure executed in cement; decorative sculpture at Radio City, New York. His creations are to be seen in many American museums.

Lackaye, Wilton (1862-1932), American actor educated at Georgetown University who first studied for the law, and made his debut in 1883 with Lawrence Barrett in *Francesca da Rimini:* among the plays in which he appeared were *Allan Dare,* William Gillette's version of Rider HAGGARD's *She; Jocelyn; Shenandoah; Booth's Baby; The Power of the Press; Aristocracy; Trilby,* in which he created the role of Svengali; *Quo Vadis; A Modern Magdalen; The Pit; The Law and the Man; The Bondman; The Battle.*

Lacquer, a varnish made in China and Japan of a resinous gum obtained from the *rhus venici-flua,* a tree especially cultivated for the purpose. After being colored red, blue, brown, green, black, or any other shade desired, the surface of the object to be lacquered is highly polished and treated with a glaze to make it thoroughly dry: from three to thirty coats are applied in order to achieve the desired effect. Drawings and mother-of-pearl inlay strewn with little particles of gold impart an indescribable richness to lacquered articles.

Lacretelle, Jacques de (1888-), French novelist who traveled extensively as a child, and was educated at the Lycée Janson-de-Sailly, Paris, and at Cambridge University. His works translated into English include *Silbermann* (1923); *Marie Bonifas; A Man's Life.*

Lacrimosa (Latin), the first word in the 8th division of the REQUIEM MASS which has since become the title of the entire movement with the implication of tender, plaintive character.

La Cueva, Juan de, see **Cueva, Juan de la.**

Lady Macbeth of Mzensk, grand opera in four acts: libretto by Dmitri Shostavich and A. Preis based on a story by Nikolai Leskoff; music by Dmitri SHOSTAKOVICH; first produced at Petrograd in 1934, at Cleveland, Ohio, in 1935, and in New York during the same year by the LEAGUE OF COMPOSERS and ART OF MUSICAL RUSSIA. The plot has no relation to SHAKESPEARE'S "Macbeth" except that the principal female character, Katerina Lvovna Izmailova, becomes a double murderess and finally a suicide through jealousy. There are no American recordings of the music available.

Lady of the Lake, The, (a) in the legends of King ARTHUR the name given to Vivienne (or Vivian), the mistress of Merlin, the enchanter, who dwelt in a beautiful palace in the middle of a lake through which no one could approach her: (b) a narrative poem by Sir Walter SCOTT which was published in 1810, the principal character being Ellen Douglas. The text was used as the basis for a cantata by the Scottish composer, George A. Macfarren.

Laemmle, Carl (1867-1939), American motion picture magnate who came to the United States in 1884, and engaged in various enterprises until 1906 when he opened a motion picture theatre at Chicago, founded the Laemmle Film Service, and was president of the Universal Film Corporation until 1936. His son, **Carl Laemmle, Jr.** (1908-) was appointed general manager of Universal Film Corporation in 1929: among the films he has produced are *Broadway; The King of Jazz; Dracula; Frankenstein; Strictly Dishonorable; Waterloo Bridge; All Quiet on the Western Front; Imitation of Life; Little Man, What Now?; Show Boat.* In 1936 he resigned to become an independent producer.

Laessle, Albert (1877-), American sculptor who studied at the PENNSYLVANIA ACADEMY OF FINE ARTS, Philadelphia, and with Michel Bequine at Paris. He has taught at the Pennsylvania Academy of Fine Arts for more than twenty years, and has been the recipient of many prizes and medals. His notable works include many bronzes of animal life in which his fine sense of humor is apparent: among them are the bronze goat, *Billy,* and two bronze penguins in Fairmount Park, Philadelphia; *Blue-eyed Lizard* in the Metropolitan Museum of Art, New York; *Chanticleer, Turtle and Lizards* in the Pennsylvania Academy of Fine Arts: also many works in other American museums.

La Farge, Christopher (1897-), American poet and novelist: his father, Christopher Grant La Farge (1862-1938) was a distinguished architect; his grandfather, John LA FARGE, was a well-known painter, and his brother, Oliver LA FARGE, a distinguished novelist. He was educated at Harvard University, served in World War I, and finally embarked on a literary career. His works include *Hoxsie Sells His Acres* (1934); *Each to the Other,* a novel in verse; *Poems and Portraits; The Wilsons: A Story of a Family.*

La Farge, John (1835-1910), American painter of French parentage who went to Paris at twenty-

one to study with Thomas COUTURE, later becoming intimate with Theophile GAUTIER, PUVIS DE CHAVANNES, Dante Gabriel ROSSETTI, and John E. MILLAIS. On his return to the United States he studied law for a time, but followed the advice of William Morris HUNT by deciding on a career in painting. His first important commissions were murals for Trinity Church, Boston, and St. Thomas' Church, New York: later he devoted much of his time to mural painting and the designing of stained glass, developing a kind of opalescent material for the latter which improved the effect of sunlight on it. During a trip to Japan in 1886 he became much impressed with Oriental art. Among his important works are the murals in the altarpiece at the Church of the Ascension, New York; the glass windows in Memorial Hall, Harvard University, and Columbia University Chapel. His canvases include *New England Pasture Land; The Three Kings; The Last Valley; Muse of Painting; The Golden Age; Boy and Dog; Young Girl Weeding.* He also displayed rare literary ability in *Considerations on Painting; An Artist's Letters from Japan; Great Masters; The Higher Life in Art.* La Farge's two grandsons, Christopher LA FARGE and Oliver LA FARGE, are both successful authors.

La Farge, Oliver (1901-), American ethnologist and author, son of Christopher Grant LA FARGE and brother of Christopher LA FARGE. He was educated at Harvard University, later directing three archaeological expeditions to Arizona for his alma mater, and two expeditions to Mexico and Guatemala for Tulane University. His works include *Tribes and Temples,* with F. Blom (1927); *Laughing Boy* which won the Pulitzer Prize in 1930; *Long Pennant; All The Young Men; The Enemy Gods; Sparks Fly Upward.*

Lafayette, or **La Fayette, Marie Joseph Paul Roch Yves Gilbert Motier, Marquis de** (1757-1834), French general and statesman who aided the American cause against Great Britain by joining the Revolutionary army in 1777 as a volunteer with the rank of major-general: he was present at the surrender of General Cornwallis, and has been made the hero of several plays and romantic novels in addition to being pictured in paintings, portraits, busts and statues.

La Fontaine, Jean de (1621-1695), French poet and fabulist educated at the College of Rheims who was for a time under the protection of Nicolas Fouquet. The first six books of the fables for which he is famous, *Choice Fables in Verse,* were published in 1668, and the seven more volumes appeared up to 1694. He also wrote romances in prose and verse such as *The Loves of Psyche and Cupid,* and several comedies: among his intimates were MOLIERE, RACINE, and BOILEAU-DESPREAUX.

La Forge, Frank (1879-), American pianist, composer, and teacher of voice who studied with Theodor LESCHETIZKY and Karl Navratil: after touring Europe and the United States, he became accompanist for Ernestine SCHUMANN-HEINK and Marcella SEMBRICH. He founded the La Forge-Berumen Studios at New York in 1920; his distinguished pupils include Lawrence TIBBETT,

Marian ANDERSON, Lucrezia BORI, and Richard CROOKS. He has also composed many fine songs.

Lafosse or **La Fosse, Charles de** (1636-1716), French painter who was a pupil of Charles LE BRUN, also studying the works of RAPHAEL and other masters at Rome and Venice. He executed frescoes for LOUIS XIV at VERSAILLES and Meudon: among his notable works are the fresco in the cupola of the Church of the Invalides at Paris; *Rape of Proserpine; Christ Served by the Angels in the Desert; Marriage of the Virgin; Vespasian Directing the Building of the Coliseun; Aristotle in Love; Apollo and Thetis.*

Lagerlöf, Selma (1858-1940), Swedish novelist who studied at the Teachers' Seminary in Stockholm, and taught in a country school. After publishing a few verses her first success came with the novel, *The Story of Gosta Berling* (1894): it was followed by *The Miracles of Anti-Christ; Jerusalem; The Outcast; Charlotte Lowenskolds;* also several collections of short stories, and two children's books, *The Adventures of Nils* and its sequel.

La Harpe, Jean François de (1739-1803), French poet, dramatist and critic who was aided in his career by VOLTAIRE. His most important work was a *Course in Ancient and Modern Literature:* also several plays including *Warwick; Virginia; Coriolanus; Mélanie; Les Barmecides; Philoctete.*

Lahee, Henry Charles (1856-), Anglo-American author of books on music for some years secretary of the New England Conservatory of Music: his works include *Famous Singers* (1898); *Famous Violinists; Pianists of Today and Yesterday; The Grand Opera Singers of Today; The Organ and Its Masters; Annals of Music in America; The Orchestra.*

La Hire or **Hyre,** see **Hire** or **Hyre, Laurent de la.**

Laing, Alexander Kinnan (1903-), American poet and novelist who studied at Dartmouth College, wrote for newspapers, and also spent some years as a seaman: his works include *Fool's Errand* (1928); *End of Roaming; The Sea Witch; The Cadaver of Gideon Wyck* with T. Painter; *The Glass Centipede; The Methods of Dr. Scarlett.*

Laing, Hugh, contemporary English dancer, born in the British West Indies, who studied with Marie RAMBERT in London and Olga PREOBRAJENSKA in Paris. In 1930 he founded the London Ballet with Antony TUDOR, danced with the Mercury Ballet, and at His Majesty's Theatre, the Alhambra, and the Comedy Theatre in London. He joined the BALLET THEATRE, New York, in 1939.

Lairesse, Gerard de (1641-1711), Dutch painter who studied with his father, but was greatly influenced by Nicolas POUSSIN. He went blind in 1690, but formed a circle of artists to whom he could communicate his theories. Among his notable works are *Cleopatra Landing at Tarsus; Penitence of St. Augustine; Bacchus Consoling Ariadne; Ulysses and the Sirens; Children's Scene; Diana and Endymion; Dancing Children.*

Lakmé, grand opera in three acts: libretto by Edmond Goudinet and Phillipe Grille; music by Leo DELIBES; first produced at Paris in 1883, and at the Academy of Music, New York, in 1886. The plot, dealing with the love of an English soldier for Lakmé, daughter of a Hindu priest, is a reminder of Rudyard KIPLING's famous saying about East and West, and the opera was not a success in New York until Lily PONS appeared in it in 1931, singing the famous *Bell Song* (Legende du Paria) of which she has made a Victor recording.

Lalla Rookh, a poem by Sir Thomas MOORE published in 1817: it comprises four stories of the Orient in verse connected by a prose narrative relating how the romances were recited to while away the hours of an Indian princess, Lalla Rookh, while she was journeying to meet the Sultan of Bucharia, her betrothed. Operas based on the poem were composed by Felicién DAVID and Anton RUBINSTEIN: Robert SCHUMANN received his inspiration from it for his work, *Paradise and the Peri.*

Lalo, Édouard (1823-1892), French composer of Spanish descent who studied the violin at the Paris Conservatory with François Habeneck, and composition with Julius Schulhoff: his works include the very successful opera, *Le Roi d'Ys,* produced in 1888 at Paris and in 1890 at New Orleans, La., by a French opera company; the *Symphonie Espagnole* for violin and orchestra first played by Pablo de SARASATE; the ballet, *Namouna,* concertos for violin and for violoncello; orchestral works, chamber music, and songs.

Lamarr, Hedy, contemporary screen actress born in Austria: among the European and American films in which she has appeared are *Ecstasy; Algiers; I Take This Woman; Lady of the Tropics; Boom Town; Comrade X; Come Live With Me; Ziegfeld Girl; H. M. Pulham, Esquire; Tortilla Flats.*

Lamartine, Alphonse Marie Louis de (1790-1869), French poet and statesman who finished his education in Italy and other foreign countries. His poetical works include *Poetic Meditations* (1820) which ran through thirty editions; *New Meditations* (1823); *The Death of Socrates; Jocelyn; Harmonies poétiques et réligieuses.* His prose works include *History of the Girondins; History of the Revolution; History of the Restoration,* all regarded as remarkable for their finished style.

Lamb, Charles (1775-1834), English author and critic educated at the Christ's Hospital School: Samuel Coleridge TAYLOR was his fellow-pupil and life-long friend. His works include *Tales from Shakespeare* (1807) and *Mrs. Leicester's School* in collaboration with his sister, Mary LAMB; a poetic tragedy, *John Woodvil; Specimens of English Dramatic Poets; Essays of Elia; Last Essays of Elia.* He was intimate with Robert SOUTHEY, William WORDSWORTH, Thomas HOOD, Leigh HUNT, and William HAZLITT.

Lamb, Harold Albert (1892-), American novelist and historian educated at Columbia University who contributed stories to *Adventure Magazine: Genghis Khan* (1927); *Tamerlane; The Crusades; Nur Mahal; Omar Khayyam; The March of the Barbarians.*

Lamb, Mary (1764-1847), English author who collaborated with her brother, Charles Lamb, in the preparation of *Tales from Shakespeare* (1807) and *Mrs. Leicester's School* (1809). In 1796 she killed her mother in a fit of temporary insanity, and was placed under the guardianship of her brother who cared for her until his death in 1834.

Lambert, Alexander (1862-1929), Polish pianist and composer who studied with Julius Epstein at the Vienna Conservatory, and for a short time with Franz LISZT. He concertized successfully in Europe and the United States; in 1888 he became director of the New York College of Music and later taught privately in New York. His works include several piano pieces and three books of studies for the piano.

Lambs, The, a club organized in 1874 at New York, its membership composed of professional actors and other persons directly connected with the production of plays. It was incorporated in 1877, and has occupied its present home at 128 W. 44th Street since 1904. The chief official is known as the "Shepherd": among those who have occupied this post are Augustus THOMAS, William COURTLEIGH, Thomas MEIGHAN, Thomas A. WISE, Fritz Williams, Frank Crumit, and William Gaxton. For many years its functions for members and invited guests have included the Lambs Wash, Seidel Nights, and the annual public Lambs Gambol, presenting short plays, musical sketches, and vaudeville.

Lamond, Frederick (1868-1940), Scotch pianist and composer who studied at the Raff Conservatory in Frankfort, Germany, and later with Hans von BULOW and Franz LISZT, making his debut at Berlin in 1885. After concertizing successfully, he taught in Berlin and at The Hague Conservatory, toured the United States from 1922 to 1929, and also taught at the EASTMAN School of Music, Rochester, N. Y. His compositions include orchestral works, chamber music, and pieces for the piano.

Lamoureux, Charles (1834-1899), French violinist and conductor who studied at the PARIS CONSERVATORY, and founded the *Concerts Lamoureux* in 1881, first called the "Nouveaux Concerts," which proved a great factor in presenting not only the new works of French composers such as LALO, CHABRIER, DUKAS, and D'INDY, but also made Parisian audiences familiar with the various orchestral transcriptions of the music in Richard WAGNER's music dramas. Lamoureux's son-in-law, Camille Chevillard, continued the concerts after his death.

Lampoon, (*a*) originally a French drinking song: (*b*) a personally directed satire in writing, usually malicious or abusive in character: the use of the lampoon has greatly lessened since the passing of libel laws in many countries.

Lancaster, Bruce (1896-), American novelist who served in World War I, was educated at Harvard College, and spent six years in Japan as a member of the consular service. His works include *The Wide Sleeve of Kwannon* (1938); *Guns of Burgoyne; The Bride of a Thousand Cedars* with L. Brentano; *For Us the Living; Bright to the Wanderer.*

Lancelot, in the legends of King ARTHUR the name given to the son of Ban, king of Brittany, who was one of the famous knights of the ROUND TABLE. The legend tells the story of his love for Guinevere, and of his exploits in the war with King Arthur resulting from his infatuation. The legend ends with Guinevere retiring to a convent, and Lancelot becoming a holy man who prays for the souls of his former comrades in arms. The story has no connection with TENNYSON's poem, "Lancelot and Elaine."

Lanchester, Elsa (1902-), English actress who founded a children's theatre at London in 1918, and made her stage debut in 1922 in *Thirty Minutes in a Street:* she has also appeared in *The Way of the World; Riverside Nights; Payment Deferred; The Cherry Orchard; The Tempest; Love for Love.* Among the English and American films in which she has been featured are *The Constant Nymph; David Copperfield; Naughty Marietta; The Ghost Goes West; The Private Life of Henry VIII; Rembrandt; The Beachcombers; Ladies in Retirement; Son of Fury.*

Lancret, Nicolas (1690-1743), French painter who studied with Antoine WATTEAU whose style he copied although his canvases lack the skill in drawing and the warm color of the latter. Lancret created nearly 800 works: among the most notable are *The Four Seasons; The Music Lesson; Actors of the Italian Theatre; The Five Senses; The Four Ages of Man; Arcadian Scene; Walk in the Garden of Marly; Landscape at Fontainebleau; The Elements; Wedding Feast; Dancers in a Garden.*

Landi, Elissa (1904-), Italian stage and screen actress, real name Elizabeth Marie Zanardi-Landi, who was educated in London and made her debut in 1924 at the Playhouse, Oxford, in *Dandy Dick.* She appeared in numerous plays before beginning her film career in 1928: among the pictures in which she has played leading roles are *Bolivar; Underground; London; The Woman in Room 13; Sign of the Cross; The Count of Monte Cristo; The Masquerader; By Candlelight; Enter Madame; The Amateur Gentleman; Mad Holiday; After the Thin Man; The Thirteenth Chair.* She has also published several novels including *Neilson* (1926); *The Helmers; House for Sale; The Ancestor.*

Landis, Jessie Royce, contemporary American actress who first studied music, and later elocution, founding the North Shore Players, an amateur organization. Her professional debut was made in *The Highwayman* in which Joseph SCHILDKRAUT was touring, and later joined the Jessie BONSTELLE Stock Company in Detroit. Among the plays in which she has appeared are *The Honor of the Family* with Otis SKINNER;

Command Performance; Solid South with Richard BENNETT; *Peter Ibbetson; Colonel Satan; Merrily We Roll Along; Love From a Stranger; Dame Nature; Love's Old Sweet Song; Watch on the Rhine; Papa is All; Kiss and Tell.*

Land of Hope and Glory, see **Pomp and Circumstance (Marches).**

Landor, Walter Savage (1775-1864), English poet and prose writer who was expelled from Trinity College, Oxford, because of his radical tendencies: his works include *Poems* (1795); *Gebir; Count Julian; Idyllia Heroica; Imaginary Conversations,* a series of nearly 150 dialogues between celebrities; *Pericles and Aspasia; Pentameron; Hellenics; The Last Fruit of an Old Tree; Dry Sticks Fagoted by W. S. Landor; Heroic Idyls.*

Landormy, Paul (1869-), French musician and philosopher who studied singing with Giovanni SBRIGLIA and Pol PLANCON, and became a professor at the École des Hautes Études Sociales in 1917. His works include *History of Music* (1910) published in English in 1923; *Brahms; Bizet; The "Faust" of Gounod; Life of Schubert:* he also wrote studies of CHOPIN, Nadia BOULANGER, FAURE, D'INDY, and ROUSSEL for the *Musical Quarterly,* and edited a series of guides to operas.

Landowska, Wanda (1877-), Polish pianist and harpsichordist who studied with Moritz Moszkowski, and taught at the Schola Cantorum, Paris, for several years. After intensive study of the harpsichord she has toured Europe and America successfully as both pianist and harpsichordist, specializing in works written from the 16th to the 18th century.

Landowski, Paul (1875-), French sculptor regarded as an artist endowed with a rare sense of decorative beauty and nobility: his works include *David Fighting; Sons of Cain; Architecture; Monument to Victory* at Casablanca; *Hymn to Aurora; Monument to Unknown Artists; Monument to the Reformation.*

Landseer, Sir Edwin Henry (1802-1873), English painter who made sketches as a child of five, became a student at the Royal Academy at fourteen, and exhibited there at fifteen, finally winning an unsurpassed reputation as a painter of animals. His notable works include *Portrait of a Pointer Bitch and Puppy; Sancho Panza and Dapple; Old Brutus; Fighting Dogs Getting Their Wind; Return from Deer Stalking; The Rat-Catchers; The Cat's Paw; Maid and Magpie; Otter and Salmon; Trophies of the Chase; Sunset; Dog in a Stable.* He illustrated the works of Sir Walter SCOTT, and his paintings have been engraved by more than one hundred artists.

Lane, Rose Wilder (1887-), American novelist and biographer who spent her youth in the Ozark Mountains which are the background of many of her novels and stories: her works include *The Peaks of Shala* (1923); *He Was a Man; Hill-Billy; Cindy; Let the Hurricane Roar; Old Home Town; Give Me Liberty; Free Land.*

Lang, Alexander Matheson (1879-), Canadian actor who first appeared on the stage at Wolverhampton in 1897, and with Sir Francis BENSON's company in 1900 at the Lyceum, London, in *King Henry V.* Later he played with Mrs. LANGTRY and Ellen TERRY in Shakespearean and modern plays; toured the United States in 1909-12, and achieved his great success in the title role of *Mr. Wu* in 1913. He created the leading part in *The Wandering Jew* in 1920, and also appeared in several films including *Carnival, The Wandering Jew,* and *Mr. Wu.*

Lang, Andrew (1844-1912), Scotch author educated at the Edinburgh Academy, St. Andrews University, and at Baliol College, Oxford: his works include *Ballads and Lyrics of Old France* (1872); *Ballads in Blue China; Helen of Troy; Custom and Myth; Letters to Dead Authors; Myth, Ritual, and Religion; Aucassin and Nicolette; The Blue Fairy Tale Book.* He also translated HOMER's *Odyssey* and *Iliad* in collaboration with other distinguished scholars.

Lang, Benjamin Johnson (1837-1909), American pianist, organist, and conductor who studied with Franz LISZT, making his pianistic debut at Boston, Mass., in 1858. He occupied several important posts as church organist, and conducted the HANDEL AND HAYDN SOCIETY, the Apollo, and the Cecilia Clubs. Ethelbert NEVIN, Arthur FOOTE, and William F. APTHORP were his pupils: his daughter, **Margaret Ruthven Lang** (1867-), studied the piano with her father and composition with George W. CHADWICK and Edward MACDOWELL. Her compositions include orchestral works; choral music; many successful songs and piano pieces.

Lange, Hans (1884-), German-American conductor who studied the violin with Ottokar SEVCIK at the Prague Conservatory, and made his debut with the Berlin Philharmonic Orchestra in 1903, becoming concertmaster of the Frankfort Opera, and the Museum Concerts. He became assistant conductor of the NEW YORK PHILHARMONIC-SYMPHONY ORCHESTRA in 1923, and regular conductor from 1931 to 1936: since 1937 he has been associate conductor of the CHICAGO SYMPHONY ORCHESTRA.

Langendijk, Pieter (1683-1756), Dutch poet and dramatist who worked at The Hague as a damask weaver: his plays include *Don Quixote* (1711) adapted from CERVANTES; *The Braggart; The Mutual Marriage Deception; Krelis Louwen; The Mathematicians; Xantippe.* He also published two volumes of poems.

Langenus, Gustave (1883-), German clarinetist who studied at the Brussels Conservatory, and played with the Queen's Hall Orchestra at London. In 1909 he joined the NEW YORK SYMPHONY SOCIETY, and later taught for some years at the INSTITUTE OF MUSICAL ART, New York. In 1914 he founded the Chamber-Music Society with Carolyn Beebe.

Lange Pier, see **Aertsen, Pieter.**

Langhans, Karl G. (c.1733-1808), German architect who designed several important buildings including Gontard's Marble Palace, Potsdam, the Schloss Theatre, Charlottenburg, and the Brandenburger Tor, Berlin, which are considered among the finest examples of Germanic architecture in the neo-classic style.

Langland, William (c.1330-c.1400), English poet presumed to have written the allegorical poems, *Piers the Plowman* and *Richard the Redeless:* little is known of him except that he was well educated, earned his living as a street singer, and spent part of his life in London. *Piers the Plowman* bears some resemblance to BUNYAN's "Pilgrim's Progress" because it introduces various religious characters with Piers himself as a pious and virtuous laborer: there are three separate manuscripts, and the full title is *The Vision of William concerning Piers the Plowman, together with Vita de Do-wel, Do-bet, et Do-best, secundum Wit et Resoun.*

Langlois, Jean Charles (1789-1870), French painter who studied with Louis GIRODET, Baron GROS, and Horace VERNET: his works include *Capture of the Great Redoubt of Moskowa; Battle of Sidi Feruch; Battle of Smolensk; Ruins of Karnac; Convent of Montserrat.* He also painted the panoramas *View of Algiers; Battle of Moscow; Battle of Eylau; Battle of the Pyramids; Burning of Moscow.*

Langner, Lawrence (1890-), Anglo-American dramatist, educated as a patent lawyer, who came to the United States in 1911. He organized the Washington Square Players in 1914, and was one of the founders and a director of the THEATRE GUILD, New York. He served in World War I after becoming naturalized: his plays include *Moses* (1924); *Henry Behave; The Pursuit of Happiness* in collaboration with his wife, Armina Marshall; *Another Way Out; Family Exit; Matinata; These Modern Women.*

Langtry, Lillie (1852-1929), English actress who made her debut at London in 1881 as Kate Hardcastle in *She Stoops to Conquer.* Her beauty and talent attracted considerable attention: in 1882 she toured the United States in *As You Like It, As In a Looking Glass* and *Lady Windermere's Fan;* the last-named play was written for her by Oscar WILDE. Her last tour of the United States was made in 1915: she wrote a novel, *All at Sea,* and published her memoirs, *The Days I Knew.*

Lanier, Sidney (1842-1881), American poet, musician, and critic who served in the Civil War as a Southern sympathizer, practiced as a lawyer, and lectured on English literature at Johns Hopkins University, Baltimore, Md. His works include a novel, *Tiger Lilies* (1867); *Centennial Ode* for the Centennial Exposition in 1876; *The Science of English Verse; The English Novel and Its Development.* He also edited *The Boys' Froissart* and *The Boys' King Arthur.*

Lanner, Joseph (1801-1843), Austrian violinist who organized a dance orchestra in which Johann STRAUSS, Jr., played for a time. He created the modern Viennese dance, and his more than one hundred waltzes caused his services to be in de-mand at public and private functions: he alternated with Strauss in conducting the dance music at the court balls. His daughter, **Katherine (Katti) Lanner** (1831-1908), made her debut as a ballerina at the Court Opera, Vienna, in 1845, and after appearing at all the important theatres in Europe, joined the Italian opera in England, and became ballet mistress at the Empire Theatre in 1887, composing the choreography for many successful ballets produced during the following ten years.

Laocoon, (*a*) in Greek mythology a priest of APOLLO who was strangled with two of his sons, because he offended the god, by two serpents while he was offering a sacrifice to POSEIDON: (*b*) an antique marble group discovered in 1506 at Rome, and now in the VATICAN, said to be the work of Agisander, Polydorus, and Athenodoros, three sculptors of the Rhodes school. It represents Laocoon being strangled with his two sons, and is a masterpiece of anatomical knowledge and skillful execution.

Lapis lazuli, a gem stone found in Siberia, Chile, and some parts of the Far East; it is blue, violet, or greenish-blue in color, and is usually mined in masses. It is used for small pieces of jewelry and beads, and was employed in ancient days for vases and other objects of art.

La Prade, Ernest (1889-), American violinist, composer, and author who studied the violin at the Cincinnati College of Music: after teaching there and playing in the Cincinnati Symphony Orchestra he studied further with César THOMSON at the Brussels Conservatory, later becoming a member of the Belgian and Holbrook Quartets. He was 1st violinist in the New York Symphony Orchestra, also annotating its programs, and touring the United States with the BARRERE Little Symphony. Since 1936 he has been director of musical research for the National Broadcasting Company. His compositions include a comic opera, *Xantha,* produced at London in 1917, and numerous songs: he has also written *Alice in Orchestralia,* adapted for the radio and produced with considerable success; also *Marching Notes,* a sequel to "Alice in Orchestralia."

L'Aprés-midi d'un faune, Prelude à, see **Afternoon of a Faun.**

Larcom, Lucy (1826-1893), American poet and editor who worked in the cotton mills at Lowell, Mass.; she contributed poems to a literary magazine for mill workers called the *Lowell Offering.* Her works include *Similitudes* (1854); *Poems; Wild Roses of Cape Ann; Childhood Songs; Child Life and Songs of Three Centuries* with John G. WHITTIER; *A New England Girlhood Outlined from Memory:* she also edited a children's magazine, *Our Young Folks* (1865-73) later combined with *St. Nicholas.*

Lardner, Ring (1885-1933), American journalist, humorist, and dramatist who studied engineering, but finally drifted into journalism, becoming a noted sports reporter for Chicago, St. Louis, and Boston newspapers: his works include *Bib Ballads* (1915); *You Know Me, Al; Regular Fellows I*

Have Met, a book of poems; *How to Write Short Stories* containing the famous story, "The Champion"; *The Story of a Wonder Man,* his autobiography; *Round Up; June Moon,* a play with George S. KAUFMAN. He also collaborated with George M. COHAN on *Elmer the Great,* a play about a baseball player.

Larghetto (It.), in music a diminution of LARGO, calling for a slightly increased tempo almost equivalent to *Andantino.*

Largilliére, Nicolas de (1656-1746), French painter who studied with Antoine Goubau at Antwerp, and went to London in 1674 to assist Sir Peter LELY in restoring paintings of the old masters at Windsor Castle, thereby winning the favor of Charles II and James II. He is said to have painted 1500 portraits including those of Charles LE BRUN, James II of England, Nicolas COUSTOU, and Jean Baptiste ROUSSEAU: other canvases of note include *Marriage of the Duke of Burgundy; Hercules Slaying the Hydra; Erection of the Cross; Flight into Egypt; The Assumption.*

Largo (It.), (*a*) in music the slowest tempo mark indicating that a composition is to be performed slowly and broadly. (*b*) The title by which the aria *Ombrai mai fu* from George Frederick HANDEL'S opera *Xerxes* is generally known: it describes the cooling shade of a palm tree, and has become so popular that it has been published in more than one hundred arangements for solo instruments or ensembles. There are Columbia and Victor recordings available for voice, orchestra, and various instruments.

La Rochefoucauld, François, Duke de (1613-1680), French moralist of noble birth who engaged in conspiracies against Cardinals RICHELIEU and MAZARIN. His principal works are *Reflexions ou sentences et maximes morales* (1665) which ran through several editions during his lifetime, and *Memoirs of the Regency of Anne of Austria* (1662).

Larrimore, Earle (1899-), American actor educated at Oregon State College, Portland, who made his debut in 1925 on the New York stage in *Made in America;* among the plays in which he has appeared are *The Stranger in the House; Juarez and Maximilian; Ned McCobb's Daughter; The Silver Cord; The Doctor's Dilemma; Strange Interlude; Marco's Millions; Biography; Dark Victory; The Good Earth; Meet the Prince; Abide With Me; The Two Mrs. Carrolls; The Hill Between; At Mrs. Beam's; R. U. R.; A Month in the Country;* he has also appeared in several films.

Larsson, Carl (1853-1919), Swedish painter who first attained recognition as an illustrator, and was nicknamed "the Swedish Doré": he painted many subjects taken from Swedish history such as *The Entry of Gustavus Vasa into Stockholm in 1523,* a mural now in the National Museum. Later he took up water-coloring, and won a medal at the Paris Salon in 1883.

Lasalle, Jean-Louis (1847-1909), French dramatic baritone who studied at the Paris Conservatory of Music, made his debut at Liége in 1869, and appeared at the Paris Opera in 1872, remaining for twenty years and succeeding Jean Baptiste FAURE as chief baritone. He made his debut in 1892 at the Metropolitan Opera House, New York, in MEYERBEER'S *L'Africaine,* and remained until 1897. He was equally gifted as singer and actor: his repertoire included more than fifty operas.

La Scala (Milan), see **Scala, Teatro alla.**

Lashanska, Hulda (1893-), American concert soprano who studied with Marcella SEMBRICH, and made her debut at the Lyceum Theatre, New York, later touring the United States in recital, and with the New York Philharmonic-Symphony Society and other major orchestras. She has made many Victor recordings of lieder by SCHUBERT, BRAHMS, WOLF, and Richard STRAUSS.

Lasky, Jesse L. (1880-), American film producer who first worked as a reporter in San Francisco, joined the gold rush to Alaska and on his return became leader of the Royal Hawaiian Band at Honolulu. In 1914 he organized the Lasky Feature Play Company to produce David BELASCO'S dramas including *The Rose of the Rancho, The Girl of the Golden West, The Warrens of Virginia, The Governor's Lady,* and *The Woman.* Among his stars were Edward Abeles, Dustin FARNUM, Robert Edeson, H. B. WARNER, Edith TALIAFERRO, Edith Wynne MATHISON, Victor MOORE, Ina CLAIRE, and Geraldine FARRAR. Among his productions since 1933 are *Zoo in Budapest; Berkeley Square; Springtime for Henry; Grand Canary; Here's to Romance; Music for Madame; Sergeant York.* In 1938 he originated the radio program, *Gateway to Hollywood,* which resulted in the discovery of talented young men and women who in many instances are now making places for themselves in the films.

Lassus, Orlandus (c.1530-1594), Belgian composer trained in Italy who became choirmaster at the Lateran in Rome, and later at Antwerp and Munich. He composed more than 2000 masses, motets, madrigals, lieder, and chansons from 1555 to 1589.

Last Judgment, The, a scene from the Bible which has been pictured by many artists: among the most distinguished are Fra Angelico, Fra Bartolommeo, Cornelius, Cousin, Giotto, Lorenzetti, Michelangelo, Orcagna, Rubens, Signorelli, and Van der Weyden. Another Biblical subject which has engaged the attention of several famous painters is **The Last Supper** which has been portrayed by Bassano, Bonfazio, Boninsegna, Bouts, Castagno, Champaigne, Cranach, Crespi, Ferrari, Gebhard, Ghirlandaio, Giotto, Holbein the Younger, Justus of Ghent, Leonardo da Vinci, Murillo, Perugino, Poussin, Raphael, Rubens, Del Sarto, Tintoretto, Titian, and Veronese.

Laszlo de Lombos, Philip Alexius (1869-), English painter born in Hungary who became a naturalized British subject. He has painted many portraits including those of King Edward VII, Queen Alexandria; Emperor Wilhelm II; King Alfonso XIII; Queen Victoria of Spain, and Theodore Roosevelt.

Latham, Frederick G. (1853-1943), English stage director who managed the Drury Lane, Adelphi, and other theatres in London before coming to the United States in 1900 to direct the tour of Sarah BERNHARDT and Benoît COQUELIN on their nation-wide tour in Edmond ROSTAND's *L'Aiglon* and *Cyrano de Bergerac.* After a brief connection with the Metropolitan Opera Company, he was associated with Charles DILLINGHAM in the production of *Mlle. Modiste* with Fritzi SCHEFF, and *Sybile* with Julia SANDERSON: he was also active in the first presentation of *The Red Mill; The Fair Co-ed; The Slim Princess; The Wandering Jew; Fools of Value* with Julia MAR-LOWE; *A Bill of Divorcement; Bulldog Drummond,* and *Lullaby* with Florence REED.

Lathrop, Francis (1849-1909), American painter born on the Pacific Ocean near the Sandwich Islands, who studied with Ford Madox BROWN in London and at the Dresden Academy. His notable works include *Apollo* at the Metropolitan Opera House, New York; *The Light of the World* at St. Bartholomew's Church, New York; *Moses with the Tablets of the Law* at the Bowdoin College Chapel, Brunswick, Me.; murals in the Bijou Theatre, Boston. He also illustrated several books and designed the mosaic, *Widows and Orphans* in the old Equitable Building, New York.

Lathrop, Gertrude (1896-), American sculptor who studied at the ART STUDENT'S LEAGUE, the School of American Sculpture, New York, and with Solon BORGLUM and Charles GRAFLY. Her notable works include the Albany (N. Y.) War Memorial; sculptures for the children's rooms at Houston (Texas) Public Library: she has also received many medals and prizes for decorative works.

Latin Quarter, a section of Paris located on the left bank of the Seine near the Sorbonne, and frequented for several centuries by students: a source of inspiration for painters, novelists, and dramatists.

La Tour, Georges de (1593-1652), French painter whose works were entirely unknown until 1914 when Dr. Hermann Voss discovered some of his pictures which had been attributed to ZURBARAN and VELASQUEZ. He painted many religious and night scenes, using the heavy chiaroscuro developed by CARAVAGGIO.

La Tour, Maurice Quentin de (1704-1788), French painter who specialized in pastel portraits, and became the most popular artist of his day: his sitters included Louis XV, Rousseau, Voltaire, Marshall de Saxe, and Mademoiselle Fel, who created the part of Colette in Rousseau's *Devin de Village.*

Latrobe, Benjamin Henry (1764-1820), English architect who achieved a considerable reputation in England before migrating to the United States in 1796. After building several fine residences in several Amercan cities, he designed the Bank of Pennsylvania and the Bank of the United States in Philadelphia; the Roman Catholic Cathedral in Baltimore which was the first cathedral erected in America; the rebuilding of the CAPITOL and other buildings in Washington after they were burned in 1814; also several important navigation, waterwork and drainage projects. His sons, Henry Latrobe and Benjamin Henry Latrobe, were both distinguished engineers of roadways, railroads, and waterworks.

Laub, Ferdinand (1832-1875), Bohemian violinist and composer who studied with Moritz Mildner at the Prague Conservatory, and after considerable concertizing succeeded Joseph JOACHIM as concertmaster at Weimar. He taught at the Stern Conservatory in Berlin, organizing a string quartet to present the later BEETHOVEN quartets. After many successful tours, he became professor of violin at the Moscow Conservatory, but retired because of ill health. His works include an opera, a polonaise, and other solo pieces for violin.

Lauder, Sir Harry (1870-), Scottish comedian, and song writer who made his debut at London in 1900 at Gatti's, and became the idol of the theatre-going public as the greatest Scottish comedian. He toured Europe, Great Britain, and the United States with enormous success, making his twenty-fifth tour of the United States in 1932. His most popular songs which he writes himself, include *I Love a Lassie; Roamin' in the Gloamin'; Stop Yer Tickling, Jock; It's Nice to Get Up in the Morning; Wee Drappies.* He has written a Scotch comedy, and has appeared in the films *Huntingtower; Auld Lang Syne,* and *Song of the Road.* He sang for the Allies in France during World War I, and for the soldiers all over Great Britain since the beginning of World War II.

Laughlin, Clara Elizabeth (1873-1941), American author: her works include *Stories of Authors' Loves,* (2 vols., 1902); *Miladi; The Death of Lincoln; Reminiscences of James Whitcomb Riley;* also many guide books written in informal style such as *So You're Going to Paris,* and similar books about Italy, England, France, Rome, Germany, Austria, Spain, Scotland, Ireland, and New England, etc.

Laughton, Charles (1899-), English actor, educated at Stonyhurst College and trained at the Royal Academy of Dramatic Art, who made his stage debut in 1926 at London in *The Government Inspector,* later appearing in *Everyman; The Pillars of Society; The Cherry Orchard; The Three Sisters; The Fatal Alibi; Macbeth; Measure for Measure; Payment Deferred; Mr. Pickwick; The Happy Husband; A Man With Red Hair; The Importance of Being Earnest.* Among the numerous films in which he has achieved success are *The Sign of the Cross; The Private Life of Henry VIII; The Barretts of Wimpole Street; Les Miserables; Ruggles of Red Gap; Mutiny on the Bounty; Rembrandt; St. Martin's Lane; The Beachcomber; Jamaica Inn; The Hunchback of Notre Dame; Sidewalks of London; The Tuttles of Tahiti.*

Laureate, see **Poet laureate.**

Laurel, a tree or shrub of the genus *Laurus* the leaves of which were woven into wreaths by the ancient Greeks to crown the victors in the

PYTHIAN GAMES, and also used to indicate honors in the arts of painting, sculpture, literature, and drama.

Laurel and Hardy, the team name of two screen comedians, **Stan Laurel,** born in 1890 at Ulverson, England, who starred in 50 film comedies for Hal Roach before joining forces with **Oliver Hardy** born in 1892 at Atlanta, Ga., and also featured in Pathé, Roach and Vitagraph films. They have appeared in numerous comedies with and without music; among them *The Rogue Song; Berth Marks; Angora Love; Men o' War; Night Owls; Blotto; The Devil's Brother; Babes in Toyland; Blockheads.*

Laurencin, Marie (1885-), French painter and engraver who studied at the Lycée Lamartine, and became intimate with Georges BRAQUE and Pablo PICASSO. After exhibiting at the Salon des Independants, Paris, she traveled extensively in search of atmosphere, and finally settled in Paris. Her works are original in coloring and conception: she also executed stage decorations for the COMEDIE-FRANCAISE and for DIAGHILEFF's Ballet Russe.

Laurens, Jean Paul (1838-1921), French painter who studied with Leon COGNIET: his works include *Christ and the Angel of Death; Jesus Driven from the Synagogue; Death of Saint Genevieve* in the Pantheon, Paris; *Christ Healing a Lunatic; The Cardinal; Pope and Inquisitor; Voice in the Desert; The Fishing at Bethsaida:* his pictures are dramatic and spirited, but sometimes wanting in color.

Lauri-Volpi, Giacomo (1894-), Italian operatic tenor who studied at the Santa Cecilia Conservatory in Rome, and made his debut in 1920 there in MASSENET's MANON. He appeared in 1923 at the Metropolitan Opera House, New York, in *Rigoletto,* remaining with the company until 1934.

La Valliére, Louise Françoise de la (1644-1710), French lady who became a maid of honor to Henrietta of England, the sister-in-law of LOUIS XIV who was attracted to her in 1661: four children were the result of the liaison, and she retired to a convent in 1674 after being superseded by the Marquise of MONTESPAN. She is idealized in one of the "D'Artagnan" romances by Alexandre DUMAS, PERE.

La Valse (Ravel), see **Valse, La (Ravel).**

Lavedan, Henri Léon Émile (1859-1940), French author and dramatist: his works include *Un Famille* (1891), *Le Prince d'Aurec* (1894), a satirical comedy revived at the Comédie Française in 1920; *Les Deux Noblesses; Catherine; Le Nouveau jeu; Le Marquis de Priola; Varennes; Le Duel; Le Goût du vice; La Chienne du Roi; La Belle histoire de Geneviéve.*

La Verne, Lucille (1872-), American actress who played Juliet and Lady Macbeth at fourteen, and made her debut in 1888 on the New York stage in *La Tosca* with Fanny DAVENPORT's Company. Among the plays in which she later as-

sumed important roles were *Notre Dame* with Margaret MATHER; *As You Like it; Pudd'nhead Wilson; Way Down East; The Dancing Girl; Camille; Lady Windermere's Fan; Clarice; The House of Bondage; East of Suez; Sun-Up; The Merchant of Venice; Shining Blackness:* she also appeared in both the silent and talking films.

Lavery, Sir John (c.1856-1941), Irish painter who was trained in Glasgow, London, and Paris, and achieved distinction as a portraitist and painter of figure subjects. His notable works include *State Visit of Queen Victoria to the Glasgow Exhibition in 1888; Polymnia; Game of Tennis; Lady in Black; The Bridge at Gres; The Royal Family in Buckingham Palace.*

Lavignac, Albert (1846-1916), French teacher and writer on music educated at the Paris Conservatory, becoming professor there in 1882 and later dean of the faculty. His works include a *Complete Theoretical Course in Music* (6 books, 1882); *Fifty Lessons in Harmony; Music and Musicians,* translated by Henry E. KREHBIEL; *The Music Dramas of Richard Wagner; Musical Education.* He was also editor of Part I of the monumental *Encyclopedia of Music and Dictionary of the Conservatory* published under government subsidy.

Lavrangas, Denis (1864-), Greek composer who studied with Léo DELIBES and Jules MASSENET at the PARIS CONSERVATORY. He first composed operas in the Italian style, but his music drama, *Didon* (1909), as well as his later operas and symphonies are inherently nationalistic in style. He has worked untiringly for the founding of a national opera in Greece.

Lawrence, David Herbert (1885-1930), English novelist, essayist, and dramatist who was educated at University College, Nottingham: his novels, which dealt largely with sex problems and were suppressed in several instances in both Great Britain and the United States, include *The Rainbow* (1915); *Women in Love; Lady Chatterley's Lover; The Woman Who Rode Away; The Virgin and the Gipsy.* He also wrote a series of essays entitled *Studies in American Classical Literature,* and the plays, *David, The Widowing of Mrs. Holroyd,* and *Touch and Go.*

Lawrence, Gertrude (1898-), English actress educated at the Convent of the Sacred Heart, Streatham, who studied both drawing and acting, making her debut as a child dancer in 1908 in the pantomime *Dick Whittington.* Among the plays in which she has appeared are *The Miracle; Fifinella;* the *André Charlot Revue of 1924* in which she made her debut at New York in 1924; *London Calling; Oh Kay!; Icebound; Candle-Light; The International Revue; Private Lives; To-Night at 8.30; Susan and God; Skylark; Lady in the Dark.* She has also played leading parts in several films including *Aren't We All?; Mimi; Rembrandt; Men Are Not Gods; The Battle of Paris.*

Lawrence, Marjorie (1909-), Australian dramatic soprano who studied in Melbourne and Paris, and made her debut in 1932 at Monte Carlo in TANNHAUSER. After singing for three years at the Paris Opera, she made her debut in 1935 as Brünnhilde in *The Valkyrie* at the Metropolitan Opera House, New York, remaining until 1941 when she was stricken with paralysis as the result of a vaccination. After a long illness she returned in 1943 to sing at a concert given in the Metropolitan Opera House by her colleagues as a tribute to her courageous spirit.

Lawrence, Sir Thomas (1769-1830), English painter who drew crayon portraits at ten and studied at the Royal Academy, London. He attained a high reputation as a portrait painter: among his sitters were Elizabeth FARREN, George IV, Mrs. SIDDONS, Benjamin West, Lady BLESSINGTON, John KEMBLE, and other celebrities of the time. He succeeded Sir Joshua REYNOLDS as painter-in-ordinary to George V, and was sent to Aix-la-Chapelle to paint the allied sovereigns after the fall of Napoleon I. He also made charming portraits of children including the famous *Calmady Children* now in the Metropolitan Museum of Art, New York.

Lawrie, Lee (1877-), American sculptor born in Germany who has worked chiefly with distinguished American architects, providing fine sculptures for many structures including buildings at West Point; St. Thomas' Church, New York; the Harkness Memorial Tower and Archway at Yale University, New Haven; the National Academy of Sciences, Washington, D. C.; the Nebraska State Capitol, Lincoln, Neb.; the Bok "Singing Tower" in Florida; the figure of Atlas at the International Building, Radio City, New York.

Lawson, Cecil Gordon (1851-1882), English painter who studied with his father, and was influenced by Thomas GAINSBOROUGH: his works include *Cheyne Walk, Chelsea; The Minister's Garden; Old Battersea; Haunted Mill; August Moon; Hymn to Spring; White Chrysanthemums; Almond Blossoms; Hop Gardens in England; River in Rain:* unfortunately his promising career was cut short by death.

Lawson, John Howard (1895-), American dramatist and author of books on the theatre who was educated at Williams College: his plays include *Processional* (1925); *Nirvana; Loudspeaker; The International; Success Story; Gentlewoman; The Pure in Heart; Marching Song.* Among his motion picture successes are *Blockade; Algiers,* and *They Shall Have Music* in which Jascha HEIFETZ was featured: he has also published *The Theory and Technique of Playwriting.*

Lawson, Robert (1892-), American illustrator and author: his works include *Ben and Me: A New and Astonishing Life of Benjamin Franklin as Written by His Good Mouse Amos* (1939): he has also illustrated several books including Munro Leaf's *The Story of Ferdinand,* better known as "Ferdinand the Bull," and adapted for a screen cartoon by Walt Disney.

Lawton, Frank (1904-), English actor who made his debut in 1923 at the Vaudeville Theatre, London, in *Yes,* later appearing in *Puppets; The*

Odd Spot; The Last of Mrs. Cheyney; Interference; Might-Have-Beens; Young Woodley, his greatest success. After serving in World War I, he played important parts in numerous movies including *Loudspeaker; The International; Young Woodley; Michael and Mary; Cavalcade; David Copperfield; The Mill on the Floss; The Four Just Men; Ministry of Information.*

Layamon or **Laweman,** see **Brut.**

Laye, Evelyn (1900-), English actress and singer who made her debut at London in the revue, *Honi Soit,* in 1916: among the musical plays in which she has appeared are *The Beauty Spot; Going Up; The Shop Girl; The Merry Widow; Madame Pompadour; Cleopatra; Lilac Time; The New Moon; Bitter Sweet* in which she made her New York debut in 1929; *Helen!; Sweet Aloes; The Sleeping Beauty:* she has also appeared in numerous films including *The Luck of the Navy; One Heavenly Night; Waltz Time; Princess Charming; Evensong.*

Layton Art Gallery (Milwaukee), an institution in Milwaukee, Wis., founded by Frederick Layton in 1888. Its gallery of paintings contains works by Constable, Bouguereau, Millet, Gilbert, Johnson, Dupré, Wyant, Winslow Homer, Bastien-Lepage, F. E. Church, Bonheur, Cazin, Munkacsy, Alma-Tadema, Leighton, Corot, Harpignies, and Blakelock: there is also a choice assembly of sculptures by European and American masters.

Lazarus, Emma (1849-1887), American poet and essayist: her works include *Poems and Translations* (1866); *Admetus and Other Poems; Alide: An Episode of Goethe's Life; Songs of a Semite.* She also wrote a remarkable poem on the "Goddess of Liberty" statue in the harbor of New York.

Lazzari, see **Bramante.**

Leacock, Stephen Butler (1869-), Canadian biographer and humorous essayist educated at the University of Toronto: his works include *Literary Lapses* (1910); *Nonsense Novels; Behind the Beyond; Winsome Winnie; Mark Twain; Charles Dickens: His Life and Work; Humor and Humanity; My Remarkable Uncle and Other Sketches.*

Leaf, Munro (1905-), American artist and author who studied at Maryland State University and the Harvard Graduate School. His works include *Lo, The Poor Indian* under the pen name "Mun"; *Grammar Can Be Fun* (1934); *Manners Can Be Fun; Ferdinand:* the latter was illustrated by Robert Lawson, and also adapted for an amusing film cartoon, called *Ferdinand the Bull,* by Walt Disney.

League of Composers, The, an organization founded in 1923 which publishes a magazine, *Modern Music,* and promotes the performance of modern and ultra-modern works in concert, over the radio, and with stage productions. More than one hundred works by American composers or by European writers living in the United States have been performed: among them ballets and operas by De FALLA, PROKOFIEFF, SAMINSKY, SCRIABIN, SCHONBERG, SHOSTAKOVICH, and STRAVINSKY. In many instances symphony orchestras, chamber ensembles, and choral groups have volunteered their services in connection with the concerts and broadcasts.

Leander, see **Hero and Leander.**

Leath, Vaughn De (1901-1943), American radio singer and composer who was one of the first singers on the air: in 1920 she sang Stephen FOSTER'S *Swanee River* into Dr. Lee De Forest's inverted gramophone-horn microphone, and became the first woman whose singing voice was heard in a broadcast. She was trained in voice at Mills College, California, and also developed a talent for song writing. From 1919 to 1925 she appeared on the stage in several plays including David BELASCO'S *Laugh, Clown, Laugh,* and Owen DAVIS'S *Easy Come, Easy Go,* but radio was her principal field for more than ten years: in 1939 she appeared in a television production at Radio City, New York. She wrote more than 500 songs: among them *Heigh-Ho Silver, Madonna's Lullaby,* and *It's a Lonely Trail.*

Leblanc, Georgette (c.1876-1941), French actress and author, for many years an intimate friend of Maurice MAETERLINCK of whose plays she was a distinguished interpreter. She enjoyed a successful career at the Comédie-Francaise, Paris, and wrote several books of which English translations are available: they include *The Blue Bird for Children* (1913); *The Girl Who Found the Blue Bird,* a life of Helen KELLER; *The Chorus of Life.*

Leblanc, Maurice (1864-1941), French dramatist and writer of detective fiction; brother of Georgette LEBLANC. He created the character "Arsène Lupin," first a gentleman burglar and later a detective working against his former associates: among his tales are *The Exploits of Arsène Lupin* (1907); *Arsène Lupin versus Holmlock Shears; The Hollow Needle; The Confessions of Arsène Lupin; The Return of Arsène Lupin; The Eight Strokes of the Clock; Arsène Lupin Intervenes.*

Le Brun, Charles (1619-1690), French painter who studied with his father, a well-known painter, and at the studio of Simon VOUET. After three years of study in Rome, he returned to Paris where he secured a commission from Fouquet to decorate the Château of Vaux, and several chambers at VERSAILLES. Among his notable works are the *Tapestry of the Seasons* and many other cartoons as director of the GOBELIN factory; *The History of Alexander* at the LOUVRE; the grand staircase at Versailles. He also founded the Royal Academy of Painting and Sculpture in France, and was influential in establishing the FRENCH ACADEMY at Rome.

Le Brun, Marie Louise Elizabeth (1755-1842), French painter who was a pupil of Joseph VERNET, and also perfected her technique by study of the old masters at the LOUVRE. She executed her first portrait at sixteen, and was made a member of the French Academy at twenty-eight. She painted more than 660 portraits, 200 landscapes, many historical pictures, and published her reminiscences in 1835.

Leclair, Jean-Marie (1697-1764), French violinist who was first a ballet dancer, but was trained by Giovanni Battista SOMIS, and became solo violinist at the Paris Opera. His works include an opera; an opera ballet; 48 sonatas for violin; also duets and trios, and concerti grossi.

Lecocq, Alexandre Charles (1832-1918), French composer who studied composition at the Paris Conservatory with Jacques HALEVY, and became a successful composer of light operas: his works include *Doctor Miracle* (1857); *Fleur-de-Thé; The Daughter of Madame Angot; Giroflé-Girofla.* His 40 operettas are regarded as superior from the musical point of view to those of Jacques OFFENBACH.

Leconte de Lisle, Charles Marie René (1818-1894), French poet who spent several years in India, and finally settled in Paris: his works include *Poèmes antiques* (1852); *Poèmes et Poésies; Poèmes barbares; Poèmes tragiques;* translations of HOMER'S ILIAD and ODYSSEY; a verse drama, *Les Erinnyes,* for which Jules Massenet composed incidental music. He also translated the works of HESIOD, HORACE, EURIPIDES, and SOPHOCLES.

Le Corbusier, see **Jeanneret-Gris, Charles Édouard.**

Lecouvreur, Adrienne (1692-1730), French actress who made her debut in 1717 at the Comédie Française in Prosper CREBILLON'S *Electre,* and appearing later in MOLIERE'S *George Dandin* with such great success that she remained there as the principal tragic actress for thirteen years, giving nearly 1200 performances in more than a hundred roles of which she created twenty-two. Her success was due to the fact that she eschewed the stilted style of the actresses who preceded her for a naturalness and simplicity which charmed her auditors. Eugene SCRIBE'S play, *Adrienne Lecouvreur,* which dramatizes her sudden death at thirty-eight, was a favorite vehicle for RACHEL, BERNHARDT, Fanny DAVENPORT, and many other famous actresses.

Lectern, in architecture the reading desk placed in the choir of a church for the use of the officiating clergyman. It is often designed in the form of an eagle with outstretched wings, and generally revolves on a pivot; the materials used include wood, marble, stone, iron, or copper often beautifully ornamented.

Lederer, Francis (1906-), Czechoslovakian actor who studied for the stage at Prague and Berlin, appearing first in juvenile parts, and in 1930 at Berlin as Romeo with Elizabeth BERGNER under the direction of Max REINHARDT. In 1931 he appeared at London with great success in *Autumn Crocus,* and in *The Cat and the Fiddle,* making his New York debut in 1932 in *Autumn Crocus.* He has since played in *Golden Boy; Seventh Heaven; No Time for Comedy.* His film appearances include *Man of Two Worlds; The Pursuit of Happiness; The Gay Deception; One Rainy Afternoon; My American Wife; Confessions of a Nazi Spy; The Man I Married; Puddin' Head.*

Lee, Frederick Richard (1798-1879), English painter who studied at the Royal Academy, London, and specialized in canvases depicting English and Scottish scenery including *Showery Weather; Evening in the Meadows; Scene in Devonshire; Breaker at Plymouth; Bay of Biscay; The Land We Live In; Morning in the Meadows; Land's End; River Scene.*

Lee, Sir Sidney (1859-1926), English man of letters educated at Oxford who succeeded Sir Leslie Stephen as editor of the *Dictionary of National Biography* to which he contributed 800 biographies. As one of the greatest Shakespearean authorities he wrote several works including *Life of William Shakespeare* (1898); *Shakespeare and the Modern Stage:* he also edited a complete edition of Shakespeare's works.

Lee, Vernon, see **Paget, Violet.**

Leech, John (1817-1864), English caricaturist and illustrator educated at Charterhouse at the same time as William Makepeace THACKERAY. He was connected with PUNCH for almost twenty-five years, and illustrated Charles DICKENS' *Christmas Stories* and Gilbert a BECKETT's *Comic History of England.*

Leech, Margaret (1893-), American author: her works include *The Back of the Book* (1924); *Tin Wedding; Anthony Comstock* with Heywood BROUN; *The Feathered Nest; Reveille In Washington.*

Leeson, Cecil (1902-), American saxophonist who made his debut in a recital at TOWN HALL, New York, in 1937, and has concertized with considerable success: his repertoire includes Debussy's *Rhapsody for Saxophone,* Glazunoff's *Concerto for Saxophone;* Paul Creston's *Suite for Alto Saxophone,* and Manna Zucca's *Walla-Kye;* also transcriptions of classical and modern music which demonstrate the beauty and effectiveness of the saxophone as a recital instrument.

Lefébure-Wely, Louis James Alfred (1817-1869), French organist who studied organ at the Paris Conservatory with François Benoist and composition with Jacques HALEVY. He was organist at La Madeleine, and at Saint-Sulpice from 1863: his compositions include an opera; a cantata; several masses; orchestral works; chamber music and many piano pieces including *Monastery Bells,* a popular favorite during the last part of the 19th century.

Lefebvre, Jules Joseph (1836-1912), French painter who studied with Leon COGNIET and won the Grand Prix de Rome with his canvas, *The Death of Priam.* His notable works include *Roman Charity; Alexandre Dumas; Yvonne; Truth; Slave Carrying Fruits; Nymph and Bacchus; Girl Laughing; The Grasshopper; Diana Surprised; Vittoria Colonna; Girl Asleep.*

Le Gallienne, Eva (1899-), American actress and producer born in London, and daughter of Richard LE GALLIENNE. She studied at the Royal Academy of Dramatic Art, making her London debut in 1914 as a page in *Monna Vanna,* and her New York debut in 1915 in *Mrs. Boltay's Daughters.* Among the many plays in which she has assumed leading parts either in New York, on tour, or with the CIVIC REPERTORY THEATRE which she founded and directed at New York from 1926 to 1933 are *The Swan; Hannele; The Master Builder; Saturday Night; The Three Sisters; Twelfth Night; Cradle Song; Hedda Gabler; The Cherry Orchard; Peter Pan; The Sea-Gull; The Open Door; Siegried; Alison's House; Liliom; A Doll's House; L'Aiglon; Rosmersholm; Hamlet* (in the title role); *Madame Capet; Alice in Wonderland; Uncle Harry.*

Le Gallienne, Richard (1866-), English journalist, poet, and essayist educated at Liverpool College who acted as secretary to Lawrence BARRETT, and lived in the United States for many years: the actress, Eva LE GALLIENNE is his daughter. His poetical works include *My Ladies' Sonnets* (1887); *The Lonely Dancer; The Junk Man; The Magic Seas:* among his prose works are *The Quest of the Golden Girl; Attitudes and Avowals; Vanishing Roads; Old Love Stories Retold; The Romantic Nineties; From a Paris Garret.*

Legat, Nicholas Gustavovich (1869-1937), Russian dancer, teacher, and choreographer whose parents were well-known dancers: he studied at the Imperial School of Ballet, Moscow, made his debut in 1887, and was appointed solo dancer to the Czar in 1896. He created several ballets including *The Blood Red Flower, The Two Thieves,* and *The White Lily.* He was also an excellent pianist, and caricaturist; a volume of his drawings entitled *The Russian Ballet in Caricature* was published at St. Petersburg in 1891. During the Revolution he acted as balletmaster at the Bolshoy Theatre in Moscow: after his retirement in 1922 he opened a dancing school with his wife in London.

Legato (It.), in music an indication that the passage so marked is to be played in a smooth, connected manner without a break between the notes.

Legend, (*a*) in literature a term of which the strict meaning is "the life-story of a saint": the *Golden Legend* (*Aurea Legenda*) was the title of a work written by Jacobus de Voragine, archbishop of Genoa in the 13th century, which contains the lives of all the saints. It is accepted at the present time as the title of any story without historical foundation which is generally believed to be mainly true. (*b*) In music the title given a composition based on a poem which serves as a text or program: Franz LISZT's oratorio, *The Legend of Saint Elizabeth,* is an outstanding example.

Legende de Joseph, La, a Biblical ballet in one act: book by Hugo von HOFMANNSTHAL and Count Harry Kessler; music by Richard STRAUSS;

first produced at Paris in 1914. The ballet, according to Cecil BEAUMONT in his *Complete Book of Ballets*, is "not so much a ballet as a wordless play in the manner of *Sumurun*. It contained many dances, but these were more in the manner of embroidery than a necessary adjunct to the plot." Its production also marked the first appearance of Leonide MASSINE who created the role of Joseph.

Leger, Fernand (1881-), French painter who studied at the ECOLE DES BEAUX-ARTS, Paris, with Jean Léon GEROME. At first he worked on architectural designs, but finally turned to painting, making his first exhibit at the Salon des Independents, Paris, in 1910. His pictures are characterized by violent contrasts of objects and colors, and also is suggestive of cubism. He made stage sets for the Swedish ballet, and has illustrated several books.

Leggiero (It.), in music an indication that the passage or composition as a whole is to be played lightly and swiftly; also written *leggieramente*.

Leginska, Ethel (1883-), English pianist, composer, and conductor, real name Ethel Leggins: she studied with Theodor LESCHETIZKY and made her debut at London, and at New York in 1913. After further study with Rubin GOLDMARK and Ernest BLOCH she became guest conductor of several major orchestras in the United States and Europe: her compositions include an opera, orchestral works, chamber music; songs, and piano pieces.

Legrenzi, Giovanni (1626-1690), Italian organist and composer who became music master at St. Mark's, Venice: his compositions include operas and oratorios in which he made great improvements in orchestration and in the vocal aria.

Le Guaspre, see **Dughet, Gaspard.**

Lehar, Franz (1870-), Hungarian composer who studied at the Prague Conservatory, and was advised by both Zdenko FIBICH and Antonin DVORAK to devote himself to composition. He became one of the world's most popular composers of light opera: among those which have become world-famous are *The Merry Widow* (1905); *The Man With Three Wives; The Count of Luxemburg; Gipsy Love; Frasquita; Paganini; Frederika.* He has also composed orchestral works, a *Hungarian Fantasy* for violin; a song cycle, *Musical Romance;* also many dances for orchestra.

Lehmann, Lilli (1848-1929), German dramatic soprano who studied with her mother, and made her debut in 1865 at Prague in *The Magic Flute* as a coloratura singer. In 1875 she studied with Richard WAGNER, and sang at the premières of the *Ring of the Nibelungs* dramas at BAYREUTH in 1876. She sang at German opera houses and in London, making her debut in 1885 at the METROPOLITAN OPERA HOUSE, New York, in *Carmen,* and later in the season as Brünnhilde in *The Valkyrie.* In 1889 when she overstayed her leave in the United States, and was debarred from German opera houses, she became a famous lieder

singer. The ban was lifted in 1891 and she appeared at all European opera houses and in 1896 again at Bayreuth in the three Brünnhilde roles. She continued to sing until 1922, also teaching many later famous artists including Olive FREMSTAD and Geraldine FARRAR. Her operatic repertory comprised more than 170 roles in German, French, and Italian; also more than 600 songs.

Lehmann, Liza (1862-1918), English concert soprano and composer who studied voice with Alberto RANDEGGER, and composition with Hamish MacCunn. After concertizing in Great Britain and Germany she devoted herself to composition: her works include the operas *Sergeant Brue, The Vicar of Wakefield,* and *Everyman;* two cantatas; the song cycles *In a Persian Garden; The Daisy Chain; More Daisies; In Memoriam; Prairie Pictures; Nonsense Songs:* also many separate songs.

Lehmann, Lotte (1885-), German operatic and concert singer who studied at the Berlin State Conservatory, and made her debut in *Lohengrin* at the Hamburg State Theatre in 1914. After singing at the Vienna State Opera, at Covent Garden, London, and in South America, she made her American debut in 1930 with the Chicago Civic Opera as Sieglinde in *The Valkyrie,* and at the Metropolitan Opera House, New York, in 1934, in the same opera. She is also a distinguished lieder singer, appearing in recital with Bruno WALTER, and has written a novel and several miscellaneous volumes.

Lehmann, Rosamond (1903-), English novelist educated at Newnham College, Cambridge: her works include *Dusty Answer* (1927); *A Note in Music; Invitation to the Waltz; The Weather in the Streets; No More Music.*

Lehmbruck, Wilhelm (1881-1919), German sculptor, painter, and engraver who studied at the Düsseldorf Academy, and exhibited at the Salon of the Société Nationale, Paris, in 1907. His sculpture, as evidenced by the *Kneeling Woman* in the National Gallery follows along the lines of the Post-Impressionists, and his favorite subject in both painting and sculpture was the female figure either draped or in the nude.

Leiber, Fritz (1883-), American actor educated at the Lake View High School, Chicago, who played with the Dearborn Theatre Stock Company and the Ben GREET Company before making his debut in 1905 at New York as Macduff in *Macbeth.* He became a member of Robert MANTELL's Company playing Shakespearean parts from 1908 to 1915, formed his own company in 1920, and directed the Chicago Civic Shakespeare Society from 1929 to 1932. He has also appeared in numerous silent and talking films including *If I Were King; Antony and Cleopatra; The Life of Louis Pasteur; A Tale of Two Cities; Anthony Adverse; The Great Garrick; All This and Heaven Too; The Sea Hawk.*

Leibl, Wilhelm (1844-1900), German painter who studied with Karl PILOTY and was influenced by Anthony VAN DYCK: his canvases reflect his life spent as a Bavarian peasant, and he exerted a considerable influence on German painting in such notable works as *Woman in Old German Dress; Two Poachers; Women in Church; Woman Smoking; Peasant Girl; Meeting in a Tavern; Girls in an Orchard; At Church.*

Leichtentritt, Hugo (1874-), German composer and musicologist who studied at Harvard University under John K. PAINE, completed his studies at the Hochschule in Berlin, taught at the Klindworth-Scharwenka Conservatory, and returned to the United States in 1933, lecturing at Harvard University and New York University. His compositions include orchestral works, concertos, chamber music, piano pieces, and songs: he has also written many scholarly treatises on music and musicians.

Leider, Frida (1888-), German dramatic soprano who studied with Leo Leisser, and made her debut at Halle, later singing at Hamburg and at the Berlin State Opera. In 1924 she appeared at Covent Garden as Isolde in *Tristan and Isolde*, and was acclaimed a singer who invested Wagnerian heroines with sympathetic charm as well as dramatic feeling. In 1928 she made her debut with the Chicago Civic Opera Company, and in 1933 made her debut in *Tristan and Isolde* at the Metropolitan Opera House, New York.

Leigh, Vivien (1913-), English actress born in India whose real name was Vivian Mary Hartley: she was educated in England, France, Germany, and Italy, also studying for a time at the Comédie-Française, Paris, and at the Royal Academy of Dramatic Art, London. She appeared first in several English films, and made her stage debut in 1935 at London in *The Green Sash*, later playing in *The Mask of Virtue; Henry VIII; Hamlet; A Midsummer Night's Dream; Serena Blandish.* Since 1936 her film appearances include *Fire Over England; Storm in a Teacup; Dark Journey; A Yank at Oxford; St. Martin's Lane; Gone with the Wind* in which she played the part of Scarlett O'Hara and won the Academy Prize; *Waterloo Bridge; Sidewalks of London; That Hamilton Woman.*

Leighton, Frederick, Baron (1830-1896), English painter who studied at Rome, Berlin, Florence, and at the LOUVRE Life-School, Paris. He exhibited a canvas, *Procession of Cimabue's Madonna* at the Royal Academy, London, in 1855, with great success: his works of note include the frescoes *Arts of War; Arts of Peace; Phoenicians Bartering with the Britons; Triumph of Music:* also *Capri at Sunrise; Reconciliation of Montague and Capulet at the Tomb of Juliet; Electra at the Tomb of Agamemnon; Day Dreams.* He was also an accomplished sculptor as evidenced in *The Sluggard* and *Athlete Struggling with a Python.*

Leinsdorf, Erich (1912-), Austrian conductor who studied with Paul Emerich at the Vienna Gymnasium, and became assistant to Bruno WALTER and Arturo TOSCANINI at the SALZBURG FESTIVALS. After conducting at Vienna, Florence, Brussels, Antwerp, Bologna, and Trieste, he became assistant to Artur BODANZKY at the Metropolitan Opera House, New York, becoming principal conductor after the latter's death in 1939. In

1943 he succeeded Artur RODZINSKI as conductor of the CLEVELAND SYMPHONY ORCHESTRA.

Leitmotiv (Ger.), in music a term meaning "leading motive": it is applied to a striking phrase, passage, or theme characteristic of any personality or situation in a music drama which is repeated whenever the personality or situation recurs or is brought up in retrospect. It has particular meaning in the music dramas of Richard WAGNER, but is also used in connection with modern operas, oratorios, and program music.

Lejeune, Louis François, Baron (c.1775-1848), French painter and lithographer who was one of Napoleon's generals, and painted battle scenes from sketches made during periods of actual conflict. He was appointed director of the ECOLE DES BEAUX-ARTS, Paris, and had much to do with the introduction of lithography: among his finest works are *Aboukir; Marengo; Moskova; The Pyramids.*

Lekain (1728-1778), French actor, real name Henri Louis Cain, who was educated at the Collège Mazarin, acted in VOLTAIRE's private theatre, and finally became a member of the *Comédie Française.* Although not an attractive personality, he was an actor of unusual ability, and brought about several reforms such as the removal of the seats from the stage and the dispensing with sing-song declamation: he also made some progress in the historical accuracy of costuming.

Lely, Sir Peter (1618-1680), Dutch-English painter born in Holland whose real name was Pieter van der Faes. He studied with Pieter de Greber in Haarlem, but was greatly influenced by Anthony VAN DYCK in his portraits. In 1641 he went to England with William of Orange, became a naturalized citizen, and was made court painter to Charles II. His notable portraits of Oliver Cromwell, CHARLES I, Nell GWYN, and other celebrities made him famous: also several imaginative pictures including *Sleeping Venus; Rape of Europa; Meleager Presenting the Head of the Boar of Calydon to Atalanta; Susannah and the Elders.*

Lemaître, François Élie Jules (1853-1914), French critic and dramatist educated at École Normale, Paris, who became instructor of rhetoric at the Lycée in Havre, and dramatic critic of the *Journal des Debats* and the *Revue des Deux Mondes.* His plays include *Revoltée* (1889); *The Deputy Leveau; The White Marriage; The Kings; The Pardon; The Difficult Age.* He also wrote *Jean Jacques Rousseau* and *Theatrical Impressions.*

Lemaître, Frédéric (1800-1876), French actor who achieved his first success in 1823 as Robert Macaire in *L'Auberge des Adrets.* He was successful not only as a tragedian, but also as a comedian in the plays of his period: Victor HUGO wrote *Ruy Blas* specially for him. His son, Charles Frederic Lemaître (1827-1870) was a well-known actor and dramatist.

Lemare, Edwin Henry (1865-1934), English composer and organist who studied with his father, and at the Royal Academy of Music, making his debut as an organ virtuoso at London in 1884. He occupied many important posts as organist including Holy Trinity and St. Margaret's, Westminster, and also appeared in many recitals after 1900 in Pittsburgh, San Francisco, and many other American cities. His compositions include many original works and transcriptions for the organ.

Lemercier, Jacques (c.1585-1654), French architect whose chief patron was Cardinal RICHELIEU who aided him in securing many important commissions for the designing of churches including the Church of the Sorbonne, the Church of the Invalides, and the reconstruction of the Church of the Val de Grace, Paris. He also designed Richelieu's residence in Paris, and planned a complete town named after the Cardinal.

Lemonnier, Antoine Louis Camille (1844-1913), Belgian poet and novelist of Flemish ancestry: his works include *A Corner of the Village* (1879); *A Man; The Murder; The Man in Love; The Wind in the Mills; Little Man and God; Aunt Amy; The House That Slept; The Song of the Carillon:* he also wrote a history of Belgian painting.

Le Moyne or **Lemoine, François** (1688-1737), French painter who studied with Louis Galloche and in Italy, later becoming professor of painting at the French Academy: his notable works include the fresco for the ceiling of the Church of St. Sulpice, Paris, which occupied him seven years; *Flight into Egypt; Hercules and Omphale; Marriage at Cana; Education of Cupid; Continence of Scipio; Apotheosis of Hercules.*

Lemoyne, Jean Baptiste (1704-1778), French sculptor who studied with his father and with Le Lorrain: his works include several statues of Louis XV which were destroyed during the French Revolution. He created fine portrait busts of VOLTAIRE and Mme. de POMPADOUR, also becoming the instructor of several famous sculptors.

Le Nain, the family name of three French painters: **Antoine** (1588-1648); **Louis** (1593-1648); **Mathieu** (1607-1677). Little is known of their careers except that Mathieu Le Nain came to Paris in 1633 where he worked with his brothers, and it is not possible to distinguish their works which include *Blacksmith in His Smithy; Peasant's Repast; Birth of the Virgin; Rural Interior; Children Quarreling; Peasant Children Singing and Playing; Adoration of the Shepherds; The Fife Player.*

Lenau, Nicholas, see **Strehlenau, Nikolaus.**

Lenbach, Franz von (1836-1904), German painter who studied at the Munich Academy and with Carl PILOTY with whom he went to Rome. His notable works include *The Arch of Titus; The Little Herdsman; Peasant Seeking Shelter in a Storm:* also many fine portraits of celebrities including Bismarck, Gladstone, LISZT, Mommsen, WAGNER, and Johann STRAUSS. His portraits are exceptional for their vigorous characterizations which evoke the individual personality of each sitter.

Lener Quartet, an organization founded in 1918 at Budapest by Jenö Lener, 1st violin, with Joseph Smilovits, second violin; Sandor Roth, viola; Irme Hartmann, violoncellist: the first three were pupils of Jenö HUBAY and the last of David POPPER. The quartet made its first appearance at Budapest in 1919, and later appeared in Paris: in 1929 it was heard in the United States, and was active in Europe up to the beginning of World War II.

L'Enfant, Pierre Charles (1754-1825), French architect who had many years of experience as an army engineer, and served as an officer in the American army during the Revolution. His designs for the creation of a Federal City in Washington, D. C., the drawings for which are in the LIBRARY OF CONGRESS, were later utilized by other architects: he also remodeled the old City Hall on Wall Street, New York, and planned residences and public buildings in many American cities.

Lengyel, Melchior (1880-), Hungarian dramatist: among his successful plays are *The Great Chieftain* (1907); *Typhoon,* with Walker WHITESIDE; *Czarina; Sancho Panza; Antonia:* the last named was also a colorful motion picture.

Lennep, Jacob van (1802-1868), Dutch poet and novelist who first practised law at Amsterdam: his works include *Academic Idylls* (1826), a volume of poems on student life; *Legends of the Netherlands;* several plays such as *The Village on the Frontier* and *The Village over the Frontier.* He also wrote many historical novels including *The Foster Son; The Rose of Dekama; Our Ancestors; Elizabeth Musch:* his poetical works comprise thirteen volumes.

Lennox, Charlotte (1720-1804), American novelist and dramatist who was the daughter of James Ramsay, lieutenant-governor of New York. Her most famous novels were *The Female Quixote* (1752), and *The History of Henrietta:* her plays include *Shakespeare Illustrated* and *The Sister.*

Lenormand, Henri-René (1882-1938), French dramatist whose first success was *Les Possedées* (1909): ten years later the presentation of *Le Temps est un Songe* as staged by Georges PITOEFF established him among the foremost French writers of psycho-analytic dramas. His plays have been published in nine volumes; many are available in English translations.

Le Notre, Andre (1613-1700), French landscape architect who studied and worked with his father and grandfather, both employed as gardeners for French royalty: he also studied painting with Simon VERNET and Charles LE BRUN, and at twenty-four became chief gardener of the TUILERIES, and later of all the royal gardens. He had an extraordinary sense of perspective in his designs, and the gardens at VERSAILLES, TRIANON, St. Cloud, and Saint Germain reached the pinnacle of their beauty under his direction.

Lentelli, Leo (1879-), American sculptor born in Italy: his works include decorative sculptures for many public buildings and churches; figures and decorations for the Panama-Pacific Exposition at San Francisco in 1915 and the Sesquicentennial Exposition in 1926 at Philadelphia; designs and figures for the Cathedral of St. John the Divine, New York. He also acted as instructor in sculpture at the California School of Fine Arts, and at the ART STUDENTS' LEAGUE, New York.

Lento (It.), in music a direction indicating that the tempo is intermediate between ANDANTE and LARGO.

Lenz, Jakob Michael Reinhold (1751-1792), German poet and dramatist who was a friend and imitator of GOETHE: his plays include *Der Hofmeister* and *Die Soldaten,* both representative of the "Sturm und Drang" period. He also wrote a critical works, *Remarks on the Theatre.*

Leochares, Greek sculptor who worked at Athens about 350 B.C.: among his famous works are a portrait of ISOCRATES; the decoration of the Mausoleum at Halicarnassus; *Portrait of a Slave Merchant; Lion Hunt of Alexander; Rape of Ganymede:* he is also credited by some authorities with the APOLLO BELVEDERE and the ARTEMIS formerly at VERSAILLES, and later in the LOUVRE. He worked at times in collaboration with SCOPAS and LYSIPPUS.

Léonard, Hubert (1819-1890), Belgian composer and violinist who studied with François Habeneck at the PARIS CONSERVATORY and after concertizing successfully, succeeded Charles de BERIOT as professor of the violin at the Brussels Conservatory. His works include concertos, solo pieces, and technical works for the violin.

Leonard, William Ellery (1876-), American poet and dramatist educated at Boston, Harvard, and Columbia Universities; also at the Universities of Bonn and Gottingen. His scholarly works include translations of LUCRETIUS and BEOWULF: in addition he has written *Sonnets and Poems* (1906); *The Vaunt of Man and Other Poems; Two Lives; A Son of Earth; This Midland City; The Poet of Galilee; Aesop and Hyssop; Socrates; Tutankhamen and After.*

Leonardo da Vinci (1452-1519), Italian painter, sculptor, architect, musician, engineer, and scientist who studied with Andrea del VERROCCHIO. His research work in both science and art was extraordinary in its scope: he was not only a painter and sculptor, but also an architect, and a composer of songs which he sang while accompanying himself on the lute. He was thoroughly versed in mathematics and mechanics, designing cannon, optical instruments, and even delving into the problem of flying. His writings fill many volumes: they include a valuable *Treatise on Painting.* Among his many works are the designing of the Milan Cathedral and the execution of several projects relating to canals and drainage systems: his paintings include *The Annunciation; The Adoration of the Magi; Virgin of the Rocks; St. John the Baptist; The Nativity; The Last Supper; Christ Among the Doctors; Virgin and the Christ Child with St. Anne; St. Jerome; Virgin*

of the Balances; also the world-famous painting of the wife of, Zanobi del Giocondo, *Mona Lisa* (La Gioconda), which was in the LOUVRE at the beginning of World War II.

Leoncavallo, Ruggiero (1858-1919), Italian pianist and composer who studied at the Naples Conservatory; his first opera, *Thomas Chatterton,* was about to be produced in 1878 when the manager disappeared leaving Leoncavallo without funds so that he was obliged to play in cafés and to teach in order to exist. His next work, *I Pagliacci,* was produced with enormous success in 1892, but those which followed, including *La Bohème, Zaza, Der Roland von Berlin,* and several others, failed to achieve anything approaching the recognition accorded PAGLIACCI.

Leoni, Leone (1509-1590), Italian sculptor who worked chiefly at Milan, and was famous for his bronze statues, busts, and medals for Charles V: among his important creations were the colossal figures for the Palazzo dei Omenoni; the tomb of the Marignano in the Milan Cathedral, and *Charles V Repressing Violence.* His son, **Pompeo Leoni,** who died about 1610, worked in Spain where he executed statues of Charles V and Philip II for the ESCORIAL.

Leonora, a character in Giuseppe VERDI's opera, IL TROVATORE. She loves Manrico, the troubadour knight: when he is captured and about to be put to death by Count di Luna, his rival for her affections, she promises to marry the latter if he frees Manrico, and then takes a deadly poison from a ring on her finger.

Leonore, a character in Ludwig van BEETHOVEN's opera, FIDELIO: when Florestan, her husband, is unjustly imprisoned by Pizarro, governor of a prison near Madrid, she disguises herself as a youth and secures employment at the prison. She finally contrives to secure Florestan's freedom when he is about to be executed.

Leonore (Overtures), see **Fidelio (Overtures).**

Leontovich, Eugénie, contemporary Russian actress who studied at the Imperial School of Dramatic Art in Moscow, making her first appearance in Shakespeare's *The Taming of the Shrew,* and becoming a member of the Moscow ART THEATRE. After the Revolution she appeared in Paris, and came to the United States in 1922 to play in a *Revue Russe:* after mastering the English language she has appeared in *Candle Light; Grand Hotel; Twentieth Century; Enter Madame; Bitter Oleander; Tovarich; Dark Eyes:* the last-named was produced in 1943, with Mlle. Leontovich and Elena Miramova as co-authors and principal actors.

Leopardi or **Leopardo, Alessandro** (? -c.1522), Italian sculptor and architect whose notable works include the mausoleum of the Venetian doge, Andrea Vendramini on which he worked with Tullio LOMBARDO: he also completed the colossal statue of Bartolommeo Colleoni begun by Andrea del VERROCCHIO, and cast the bronze sockets for the three flagstaffs in front of St. Mark's, Venice.

Leris, Claire Josephe Hippolyte, see **Clairon, Mlle.**

Lermontov, Mikhail Yurevich (1814-1841), Russian army officer, poet, and novelist who was exiled to the Caucasus because of his revolutionary views. His best novel, *A Hero of Our Times,* has been translated into English: his poems include *Song of the Czar Ivan, Ismail-Bey,* and *The Demon:* the last-named was the basis for an opera of the same title by Anton RUBINSTEIN.

Leroux, Gaston (1868-1927), French writer of detective fiction who was not only a world traveler, but also a lawyer, dramatic critic, playwright, novelist, and newspaper correspondent. His successful mystery stories include *The Mystery of the Yellow Room; The Phantom of the Opera,* also a successful film; *The Secret of the Night; The Dancing Girl; The Man of a Hundred Faces.*

Le Sage or **Lesage, Alain René** (1668-1747), French novelist and dramatist who first studied law, but later embarked on a literary career: his greatest novel, *Gil Blas,* appeared first in 1715, but was not finished until 1735. Among his successful plays are *Crispin Rival of His Master* (1707); *The Point of Honor; Turcaret:* he also adapted plays by Spanish authors for the French stage.

Leschetizky, Theodor (1830-1915), Polish pianist, composer, and teacher who studied the piano with Karl CZERNY and composition with Simon SECHTER. After successful tours he settled for a time in St. Petersburg to teach, play, and compose, but ill-health forced him to leave, and after playing in England, Holland, and Germany he settled in Vienna. After the tremendous world-wide success of his pupil, Ignaz Jan PADEREWSKI, he taught many famous pianists including Ossip GABRILOWITSCH, Mark HAMBOURG, Artur SCHNABEL, Fanny BLOOMFIELD-ZEISLER, Katherine GOODSON, and Ethel LEGINSKA. His compositions include an opera and many brilliant piano pieces such as *Les deux Alouettes.*

Lescot, Pierre (c.1510-1578), French architect who worked with Jean GOUJON under the patronage of Francis I and Henry II: they executed the fine rood-screen at St. Germain d'Auxerrois; the *Fountain of the Innocents;* the courtyard of the Louvre to which eighteen years was devoted. Lescot himself made the original designs for the Hotel Carnavalet, Paris; part of the Pavillon de l'Horloge: he also worked on the Chateau de Fontainebleau.

Leskov, Nikolai Semyonvich (1831-1895), Russian novelist and short story writer who was successful with his first story, *No Way Out* (1865), tinged with radical principles powerfully expounded: his works include *The Clergy; To the Knife; The Sentry and Other Stories; The Enchanted Wanderer; The Steel Flea:* also many tales founded on ancient Russian legends.

Leslie, Charles Robert (1794-1859), English painter, born of American parents in London, who studied at the Royal Academy, and was equally at home in creating religious, historical, and genre works as well as portraits. Among his notable works are *Uncle Toby and the Widow Wadman; Sancho Panza and the Duchess; Florizel and Perdita; Taming of the Shrew; Murder of Rutland; Queen Victoria Receiving the Sacrament After Her Coronation.* He wrote *Memoirs of John Constable,* and *Handbook for Young Painters* (1855).

Les Préludes (Liszt), see **Préludes, Les (Liszt).**

Lessing, Gotthold Ephraim (1729-1781), German dramatist, poet, and critic educated at Leipzig University: his dramatic works include *Miss Sara Sampson* (1755); *Minna von Barnhelm; Emilia Galotti; Nathan the Wise; The Young Savant; The Free Thinker; The Jews; The Woman Hater.* He was connected with the theatre at Berlin and Hamburg: his treatise, *Dramaturgy at Hamburg,* is considered the first modern exposition of the dramatist's art.

Lessing, Karl Friedrich (1808-1880), German painter who studied with Wilhelm von SCHADOW: his many notable works include *Convent Churchyard; The Robber; Service in an Old Chapel; Mountain Landscape at Noon; Arquebusiers Defending a Hill; Luther Burning the Pope's Bull; Crusaders in the Desert; The Charcoal Burners; Morning Landscape with Gypsies; Martyrdom of John Huss.* His sons, Konrad and Heinrich Huss, both became distinguished landscape painters.

Lester, Keith (1904-), English dancer and choreographer who studied with Anton DOLIN, and made his debut in a FOKINE ballet for the production, *Hassan,* at London in 1923. He studied further with Nicholas LEGAT, danced with Lydia KYASHT and Tamara KARSAVINA; also with Olga SPESSIVA at the Colon Theatre, Buenos Aires, and in Max REINHARDT's production of *The Miracle* at London. His choreographic works include *David; Pas de Quatre; Bach Suite in B minor;* also *Lament of the Swans* introduced into a shortened version of TSCHAIKOWSKY's *The Swan Lake.*

Le Sueur, Eustache (1616-1655), French painter who studied with Simon VOUET, and set up his own studio in 1641 with his three brothers and his brother-in-law. His works, notable for their simplicity in style and refined expressiveness, include *Life of St. Bruno; Angel Appearing in the Desert to Hagar; Venus Presenting Cupid to Jupiter; Phaeton Begging Apollo for the Chariot of the Sun; St. Paul Preaching at Ephesus; Rise of Aurora; Birth of the Virgin Mary.*

Lethe, in Greek mythology (*a*) the daughter of ERIS and the personification of oblivion: (*b*) one of the streams of the underworld (HADES): its waters caused those who drank of them to lose all knowledge of their previous existence.

Lettre de cachet (Fr.), a term meaning strictly a sealed letter written by a king of France, but usually applied to a letter in which the recipient was sentenced to a term of imprisonment without trial or opportunity to defend himself. In the period preceding the French Revolution, they were often issued without the knowledge of the king, or signed with the name of the offender left blank: Alexandre DUMAS, PERE, made frequent use of this custom in his historical romances.

Leutze, Emanuel (1816-1868), American painter born in Germany who was brought to the United States as a child, and after being instructed by John A. Smith, returned in 1841 to Germany where he became a pupil of Karl LESSING. In 1859 he settled permanently in New York: among his notable paintings are *Columbus before the Council at Salamanca; Washington Crossing the Delaware; Landing of the Norsemen in America; The Poet's Dream; Cromwell's Visit to Milton; Westward the Course of Empire Takes Its Way;* the last-named is in the CAPITOL at Washington, D. C. He also painted portraits of Abraham LINCOLN, George WASHINGTON, and Ulysses S. Grant.

Levant, Oscar (1906-), American composer, author, and pianist who studied with Sigismond STOJOWSKI and Arnold SCHONBERG. He has played in jazz bands, appeared as soloist in the *Rhapsody in Blue* and the *Piano Concerto* of George GERSHWIN, and has written music for the films. His works include a piano concerto, chamber music, piano pieces, and a book, *A Smattering of Ignorance* (1940). He is a member of the board of experts on the radio feature known as INFORMATION PLEASE.

Le Vau, Louis (1612-1670), French architect who worked under the patronage of Louis XIII and Louis XIV: among his most important creations were designs for the LOUVRE, the TUILERIES, VERSAILLES, the Château de Vaux-le-Vicomte, the church of St. Sulpice, and the Collège des Quatre Nations, now the Palais de l'Institut, Paris.

Lever, Charles James (1806-1872), Irish novelist who first studied medicine in Dublin and Brussels, later becoming editor of the *Dublin University Magazine*. His works include *Harry Lorrequer* (1837); *Charles O'Malley; Tom Burke of Ours; Arthur O'Leary; Roland Cashel; The Dodd Family Abroad; The Daltons; The O'Donoghue; Lord Kilgobbin.*

Levertin, Oscar (1862-), Swedish poet and critic who is considered one of the first of the modern lyric writers of his country: his works include *Legends and Tales* (1891); *New Poems; Gustavus III as a Dramatist,* a critical review of 18th century literature.

Levin, Meyer (1905-), American novelist educated at the University of Chicago who became a successful newspaper and magazine columnist, and has experimented in marionette plays: his works include *Reporter* (1929); *Frankie and Johnnie; The New Bridge; The Old Bunch; Citizens.*

Levitsky, Dimitri (1735-1822), Russian painter who is regarded as the greatest portraitist of the 18th century in Russia: his sitters included all the members of the royal family, the nobility, and the wealthy merchant class. His paintings bring to mind GREUZE, PERRONNEAU, and Maurice LA TOUR in their coloring and occasional caustic humor.

Levitzki, Mischa (1898-1941), Russian-American pianist and composer who studied at Warsaw, Poland, with Ernst DOHNANYI, and with Sigismond STOJOWSKI at the INSTITUTE OF MUSICAL ART, New York. He toured Europe with great success, and made his American debut in 1916: his compositions for the piano include the *Valse in A* and *Valse Tzigane.*

Levy, Benn Wolfe (1900-), English dramatist educated at Oxford: his works include *This Woman Business; A Man With Red Hair,* an adaptation of Hugh WALPOLE's novel; *Mrs. Moonlight; Art and Mrs. Bottle; Topaze,* adapted from Marcel PAGNOL's play; *Hollywood Holiday* with John VAN DRUTEN; *Springtime for Henry; Accent on Youth.*

Levy, Émile (1826-1890), French painter who studied with François Picot and at the ECOLE DES BEAUX-ARTS, Paris: his works include *The Death of Orpheus; Noah Cursing Canaan; Ruth and Naomi; Supper of the Martyrs; Love and Folly; The Willow Tree; The Elements; Love of Money; Presentation of the Virgin.*

Levy, Jules (1840- ?), English cornet virtuoso who became famous in the United States through his association with Patrick S. GILMORE's Band as a featured soloist in the famous Peace Jubilee of 1869 and 1872: his playing of variations on the Italian air "Carnival of Venice" was considered an extraordinary example of virtuosity.

Lewes, George Henry (1817-1878), English critic, philosopher, and biographer who lived with George ELIOT, thereby exercising considerable influence on her work as an author: his works include *A Biographical History of Philosophy* (1845-46); *The Spanish Drama; Seaside Studies; Aristotle; Problems of Life and Mind; Actors and the Art of Acting; Life of Goethe.* One of his plays, *The Game of Speculation,* was a pronounced success.

Lewis, Alfred Henry (1858-1914), American author who used the pen name "Dan Quin": his works include *Wolfville* (1897); *Sandburrs; Wolfville Nights; Wolfville Days; Wolfville Folks:* he created the character of the old cattleman who relates the "Wolfville" stories.

Lewis, Mary (1900-1941), American dramatic soprano who first sang in church choirs and musical productions including the *Ziegfeld Follies.* After studying with William Thorner and in Paris, she made her debut in *Faust* at Vienna in 1923, sang at Monte Carlo, and at Paris where she was starred in *The Merry Widow.* In 1926 she made her debut at the Metropolitan Opera House, New York, as Mimi in PUCCINI's *La Bohème.* She also appeared on the concert stage, on the radio, and in motion pictures.

Lewis, Sinclair (1885-), American novelist and dramatist educated at Yale University who worked as a newspaper reporter and editor of several magazines. His novels include *Our Mr. Wrenn* (1914); *Main Street; Babbitt; Arrowsmith; Elmer Gantry* which was dramatized; *Dodsworth* also dramatized; *Ann Vickers; Work* *of Art; It Can't Happen Here,* also dramatized; *The Prodigal Parents; Bethel Merriday; Gideon Planish.* He has written a play, *Jayhawker* with Lloyd Lewis, well-known dramatic and film critic.

Lewisohn, Adolph (1849-1938), American financier and patron of music: in 1914 he donated the **Lewisohn Stadium** to the College of the City of New York, and sponsored the summer concerts there of the NEW YORK PHILHARMONIC-SYMPHONY ORCHESTRA, which have been directed for nearly thirty years by many of the world's greatest conductors including Arnold VOLPE, Victor HERBERT, Henry HADLEY, Willem VAN HOOGSTRATEN, Fritz REINER, Frederick STOCK, Pierre MONTEUX, Albert COATES, Alexander SMALLENS, Bernardino MOLINARI, Eugene ORMANDY, and many others. Mr. Lewisohn also sponsored educational programs of chamber music at Hunter College, New York City.

Lewisohn, Ludwig (1882-), American novelist and critic born in Germany who was brought to the United States as a boy of seven, and was educated at the College of Charleston and Columbia University. His works include *The Broken Snare* (1908); *The Modern Drama; Upstream,* an autobiography; *Don Juan; The Creative Life; The Case of Mr. Crump; Cities and Men; Stephen Escott; The Golden Vase; An Altar in the Fields; Forever Wilt Thou Love.*

Leyden, Lucas van (1494-1533), Dutch painter, real name Lucas Jacobaz, who studied with his father and with Cornelis Engelbrechtszen. He was a friend of Albert DÜRER, and Charles V was his patron: his notable works include *David Playing the Harp before Saul; Madonna with Mary Magdalen; Antonius and Hilarion; A Card Party; The Engagement Ring:* also many portraits of the noted personalities of his day.

Leys, Hendrik, Baron (1815-1869), Belgian painter who studied at the Antwerp Academy with Baron Gustavus WAPPERS: his notable paintings, showing the influence of the French romanticists as well as the Flemish masters, include *Little Musician at a Peasant Cottage; Seventeenth Century Wedding; The Fortune Teller; Massacre of the Magistrates at Louvain; Mass is Over; Rembrandt's Studio; Lucas Cranach Painting Luther; Wealth and Poverty; Luther as a Chorister; Leaving Church; Halt at a Tavern.*

Lhermitte, Léon Augustin (1844-1925), French painter who studied with Lecocq de Boisbaudran, and executed fine decorations for the Hôtel de Ville and the SORBONNE at Paris. His paintings include *The Harvest; New Wine; The Friend of the Lowly; Washing Sheep; The Family; The Reapers' Reward; Harvest; Haymaking; Girl Sewing.* He also made many fine etchings for the *Gazette des Beaux-Arts* and other magazines in Paris.

Lhevinne, Josef (1874-), Russian-American pianist who studied with Vassily SAFONOFF at the Moscow Conservatory, making his debut in 1889. After teaching in Moscow and Berlin, he made his debut at New York in 1906: after concertizing extensively, he settled in New York as teacher at the JUILLIARD GRADUATE SCHOOL. His wife, **Rosina Lhevinne** (1880-), is an outstanding pianist who studied at the Moscow Conservatory, and has appeared with all the leading orchestras of Europe and the United States. She has also played in two piano recitals with her husband, and taught at the Juilliard Graduate School.

Liadoff, Anatol Constantinovich (1855-1914), Russian composer who studied with Nicholas RIMSKY-KORSAKOW at the St. Petersburg Conservatory where he later became professor of harmony and theory. His compositions include several symphonic poems of which *The Enchanted Lake* is outstanding; many graceful piano pieces among which *A Musical Snuff-Box (Une tabatière à musique)* is a favorite; an orchestral transcription, *Russian Folk Dances:* all three of these works are available in Victor recordings.

Libbey, Laura Jean (1862-1924), American novelist whose love stories were popular during the last two decades of the 19th century: they include *A Fatal Wooing* (1883); *Madolin Rivers; Junie's Love Test; Miss Middleton's Lover; That Pretty Young Girl; A Mad Betrothal; Parted by Fate; We Parted at the Altar.*

Liberale da Verona (c.1450-1536), Italian painter known as Liberale di Jacopo della Biava. He first painted miniatures in choir-books at the Siena Cathedral, and later took up fresco and oil painting: among his notable works are *Adoration of the Magi; Madonna di Casa Scotti; The Entombment of Christ; Glory of St. Anthony; Christ in the Garden; Angels with Instruments of the Passion.*

Liberty, Statue of, see **Statue of Liberty.**

Libon, Greek architect of the 5th century B.C. who designed the Temple of ZEUS at Oympia, one of the greatest edifices of its period, and probably built about 460 B.C. Portions of a great relief. *The Twelve Labors of Hercules,* sculptured on the METOPES, have been found intact; also a statue of the flying goddess, NIKE, executed by Paeonius.

Library, the name applied to a collection of books and pamphlets; also to the building in which such a collection is housed. The earliest libraries at Cnossus in Crete, and at Nippur in Babylonia comprised stone and clay tablets: among the famous libraries of ancient times were those at ALEXANDRIA, Heliopolis, PERGAMUM, ATHENS, and ROME. In the Middle Ages important libraries included the one assembled by the Benedictine monks at Monte Cassino; the VATICAN Library at Rome; the SORBONNE Library at Paris; the Laurentian Library at Florence; the University Libraries at Bologna, Oxford, Prague, and Heidelberg. Among the great modern libraries are the Bibliothèque nationale at Paris; the BODLEIAN Library at Oxford; The BRITISH MUSEUM Library at London; the Ambrosian Library, Milan; the libraries at Leipzig, Dresden, and Munich in Germany; the Soviet Library at Leningrad. All major American universities and colleges are possessors of great libraries which are constantly being augmented, and the library facilities of American cities both large and small are too well-known to require comment.

Library of Congress, an institution established at the CAPITOL, Washington, D. C., in 1800 and first occupying a single room in which the library of Thomas JEFFERSON was placed: it now contains more than 6,000,000 books, newspapers, pamphlets, government documents, manuscripts, and musical works in sheet and book form, and is one of the three largest libraries in the world. Two copies of every book, pamphlet, lecture, address, sermon, feature article, periodical, dramatic or musical work, as well as photographic reproductions of paintings or sculptures for which COPYRIGHT is desired, must be sent to the library with the application for copyright.

Libretto, the text of a vocal work such as an OPERA or ORATORIO: in the former instance the libretto is sometimes an adaptation of a stage play: in the latter the text is often taken from the BIBLE. Several composers including Richard WAGNER, Alexander BORODIN, and Gustave CHARPENTIER wrote their own librettos, but the task is usually undertaken by experienced litterateurs. Among the famous librettists during the past three hundred years are Ottavio RINUCCINI, Apostolo ZENO, Pietro METASTASIO, Lorenzo DA PONTE, Arrigo BOITO, Eugène SCRIBE, Raniero da Calzabigi, and Hugo von HOFMANNSTHAL.

Lichine, David (1910-), Russian dancer and choreographer who studied with Bronislava NIJINSKA, danced with the Ida RUBINSTEIN and the PAVLOWA Ballet Companies, and also with Colonel Wassily DE BASIL's Russian Ballet at Paris. His creations in ballet include *Nocturne; Les Imaginaires; Graduation Ball; Protée; Les Fils Prodigue; Le Pavillon; Francesca da Rimini; The Gods Go A-Begging.*

Lie, Jonas (1880-1940), American painter born in Norway: after the death of his father he lived for a time in Paris with his uncle, Jonas Lauritz LIE, a distinguished novelist, meeting several famous Norwegians including Edvard GRIEG, Björnstjerne BJORNSON, and Henrik IBSEN. He attended an art school for a short time, and later joined his mother in New York, studying at the Ethical Culture School, the ART STUDENTS' LEAGUE, and later with Claude MONET in Paris. He was one of America's greatest landscape painters as evidenced by his paintings of the Panama Canal in the United States Military Academy at West Point, New York: his works are to be seen in the Metropolitan Art Museum, New York, and several other major American museums.

Lie, Jonas Lauritz Idemil (1833-1908), Norwegian novelist who served in the navy, and practiced law at Christiania. His first novel, *The Visionary* (1870) was a genuine success, and after receiving a government subsidy he wrote several more including *The Dark Future; The Pilot and His Wife; The Family at Gilje; The Commodore's Daughters; Fanfulla; Antonio Banniera; Thomas Ross; Adam Schrader; Rutland.*

Liebermann, Max (1847-1935), German painter who was the chief representative of the modernist artists, and was also influenced by the French impressionist school. He studied with Edgar DEGAS in Paris: among his notable works are *A Village Street in Holland; Woman With Goats; Children Bathing; The Cobbler's Shop; The Flax Spinners; Christ in the Temple; Munich Beer Garden; The Ropewalk.*

Liebersträum (Liszt), a piano composition by Franz LISZT which is a transcription of one of his songs: there is a Victor recording for piano by Artur RUBINSTEIN, a Columbia orchestral recording directed by Andre KOSTELANETZ, and a Victor recording of the song by Tito SCHIPA.

Liebling, Emil (1851-1914), German pianist and composer who came to the United States as a youth, but later returned to Europe for study with Theodor KULLAK and Franz LISZT. After teaching at the Kullak Conservatory, he settled in Chicago, Ill., as a pianist, teacher, and writer. His older brother, **Max Liebling** (1845-1927) studied the piano in Berlin, taught at the Cincinnati Conservatory of Music in 1867, and acted as accompanist for Henri WIENIAWSKI and August WILHELMJ on their American tours. Emil Liebling's younger brother, **Georg Liebling** (1865-), studied the piano with Theodor KULLAK and Franz LISZT, and composition with Heinrich Dorn: he concertized extensively in both Europe and the United States, later teaching at Berlin and at London, finally settling in Hollywood, Calif., and composing orchestral works, concertos, chamber music, and piano pieces. Max Liebling's son, **Leonard Liebling** (1880-), born in New York, was educated at the College of the City of New York, and studied with Leopold GODOWSKY and Theodor KULLAK. He toured Europe and America, and became music critic of the New York *American* from 1923 to 1937, and editor-in-chief of the *Musical Courier* from 1911 up to the present (1943). He has composed orchestral works, chamber music, piano pieces, also writing the libretto for John Philip SOUSA's opera, *The American Maid.* His sister, **Estelle Liebling** (1884-), born in New York, studied singing with Mathilde MARCHESI, and made her debut in *Lucia di Lammermoor* at the Dresden Royal Opera. After singing in German opera houses, she appeared at the Metropolitan Opera House in 1903, later singing with the leading symphony orchestras, and touring with John Philip Sousa's band. For some years she has conducted a school of singing for the concert stage and radio: Maria JERITZA, Frieda HEMPEL, Jessica DRAGONETTE, and Rosemary Brancato were among her pupils.

Lied (Ger.), a type of song composed by SCHUBERT, SCHUMANN, MENDELSSOHN, BRAHMS, WOLF, FRANZ, Richard STRAUSS, and other German composers. It is entirely distinct from the conventional *volkslied* or folk song, and the lyrics for many were found in the works of GOETHE, SCHILLER, HEINE, and several other romantic poets. The music varies to fit the meaning of the words: a song of this character is also called an ART SONG.

Lieurance, Thurlow (1878-), American composer who studied at the Cincinnati College of Music, and served as bandmaster in the Spanish-American War. He spent twenty years in musical research among the Indians of North America, making many recordings: his compositions include the famous song, *By the Waters of the Minnetonka*, an opera, *Drama of the Yellowstone*, and other groups of songs employing Indian melodies.

Lifar, Serge (1905-), Russian dancer and choreographer who studied with Bronislava NIJINSKA at Petrograd, and joined the DIAGHILEFF Ballet in 1923, also studying with Enrico CECCHETTI at Turin during his holidays. His debut was made in *Cimarosiana*, and he soon became famous in *The Swan Lake, Romeo and Juliet, Pastoral, La Chatte, Petrouchka, Le Fils Prodigue*, and many other ballets. After Diaghileff's death he became leading dancer and balletmaster at L'Opéra, Paris: his choreographic achievements include *Prometheus; David Triumphant; Alexander the Great; Icare; Le Roi Nu; Oriane, or the Prince of Love.*

Life for the Czar, A, grand opera in five acts: libretto by Baron de Rosen; music by Michael GLINKA; first produced at St. Petersburg in 1836. The plot is as simple as it is patriotic: during the 17th century when the victorious Poles overran Russia, a group of Poles endeavor to force a peasant, Ivan, to lead them to the Czar's hideout. He pretends to do so, but leads them far astray and is killed for his loyalty. There are no American recordings available of the music.

Light Opera, see **Opera.**

Ligne (Fr.), in ballet the term employed to describe the arrangements of the head, body, and legs of a dancer in a position or movement: the word is generally qualified by the adjectives *bon* (good) or *mauvais* (bad).

Ligorio, Pirro or **Pietro** (c.1520-1580), Italian architect who designed the Villa Pia in 1560 for Pope Pius IV, a beautiful casino in the center of the gardens at the VATICAN, Rome: he also executed the Villa d'Este in 1549 at Tivoli for Cardinal Ippolito d'ESTE.

Li Kung-Lin or **Li-Lung-Mien** (c.1040-1106), Chinese painter who was one of the most important artists of the early Sung period: he specialized in the painting of horses and of various subjects and incidents connected with BUDDHA.

Lilac Garden, The, ballet in one act: book by Antony TUDOR; music by Ernest CHAUSSON; first produced at the Mercury Theatre, London, in 1936. The plot revolves around two lovers, about to be parted, who long desperately for a parting kiss, but despite their scheming the opportunity for a last farewell never presents itself.

Liliencron, Detlev, Baron von (1844-1909), German poet and novelist who wrote fine lyric verse and stirring war novels: his works include *The Adjutant's Rides and Other Poems* (1833); *A Summer Battle*, a volume of stories; *Work Ennobles; The Merovingians*, a drama: also the novels *Under Fluttering Banners* and *Maecenas.*

Lillie, Beatrice (1898-), Canadian actress who made her debut in 1914 at the Alhambra Theatre, London, in *Not Likely*, and has since appeared in numerous revues and plays including *Oh! Joy; Up in Mabel's Room; The Nine O'Clock Revue;* André Charlot's *Revue of 1924* in which she made her New York debut; *This Year of Grace; At Home Abroad; Set to Music.* She has also appeared in several talkings films such as *Doctor Rhythm.*

Lillo, George (1693-1739), English dramatist whose father was a Dutch jeweler, and he worked at the trade until his first work, *Sylvia*, or the *Country Burial*, a ballad opera, proved a success in 1730: it was followed by *The London Merchant, or the History of George Barnwell*, which held the stage for many years: *Britannia or the Royal Lovers*, and *Fatal Curiosity*. Lillo's plays were the first to introduce middle-class characters taken from life.

Lilly, Joseph Kirby (1861-), American chemist who after becoming interested in the life and compositions of Stephen FOSTER, assembled a collection of Fosteriana which included first editions of more than one hundred of his songs; many reprint editions and letters in Foster's handwriting; the faded but intact book of original manuscripts written with lead pencil; also a complete collection of recordings. This was all placed in Foster Hall, Indianapolis, a granite and brick building suggesting a country house in Brittany. The collection was later removed to the Stephen Foster Memorial Building on the campus of the University of Pittsburgh.

Limerick, in literature a nonsensical poem usually of five lines popularized by Edward Lear (1812-1888), an English painter, illustrator, and verse writer in his *Book of Nonsense* (1846). The term is said to have originated with a song current in Ireland the refrain of which contained the name "Limerick." One of the early examples, written by Anthony Euwer, follows:

As a beauty I am not a star,
There are others more handsome by far,
But my face—I don't mind it,
For I am behind it,
It's the people in front get the jar.

There is a limerick collection, *Stuff and Nonsense*, edited by W. J. DE LA MARE.

Limoges, a city in France famous for its manufacture of porcelains: it was the center of the porcelain and enameling industry from the 12th to the 16th century. There is a fine museum of ceramics in the city, and a stately cathedral which in 1533 had a ROOD-LOFT adorned with sculptures.

Limousin, Léonard (c.1504-c.1578), French artist who specialized in enamel, and became court painter to Francis I and Henry II of France: he is said to have produced more than two thousand portraits, plates, vases, and art objects of every description in enamel, using blue, green, or black backgrounds. His works are much in demand by collectors.

Lincke, Paul (1866-), German composer, theatre conductor and music publisher who at one time conducted at the Folies-Bergére in Paris:

his compositions include several very successful operettas produced in Berlin, and numerous popular songs such as *The Glow Worm* which was a great favorite in the United States.

Lincoln, Abraham (1809-1865), sixteenth president of the United States who was assassinated on April 14, 1865, by John Wilkes Booth, an actor and brother of Edwin Booth. His greatest utterances were the address at the dedication of the National Cemetery at Gettysburg, Pa., on November 19, 1863, and his second inaugural address on March 4, 1865. He also wrote one of the most beautiful letters ever penned to a woman: her son had been killed in the Civil War.

Lincoln, Joseph Crosby (1870-), American novelist and humorist: his numerous stories include *Cape Cod Ballads* (1902); *Cap'n Eri; Cy Whittaker's Place; The Woman Haters; Thankful's Inheritance; Mary 'Gusta; Extricating Obadiah; Shavings,* successfully dramatized; *Galusha the Magnificent; The Aristocratic Miss Brewster; Blowing Clear; Head Tide; Storm Signals; A. Hall & Co., Out of the Fog.*

Lincoln Memorial, a monument to Abraham Lincoln in Potomac Park, Washington, D. C., designed by Henry Bacon, and dedicated in 1922. The building is constructed mainly of white marble: its greatest features are the colonnade composed of thirty-six Doric columns enclosing the walk of the Memorial, and the statue designed and modeled by Daniel Chester French representing Lincoln as the war president seated in a great armchair almost thirteen feet high over the back of which a flag is draped; the statue is 19 feet high and 19 feet wide including the drapery over the chair.

Lind, Jenny (1820-1887), Swedish soprano, known as the "Swedish Nightingale," who studied at the School of Singing connected with the Court Theatre, Stockholm, and made her first debut in 1838 at the same theatre in Weber's *Der Freischütz.* After further study with Manuel Garcia at Paris, she made a second debut in 1844 at the Berlin Opera in Meyerbeer's *Feldlager im Schlesien,* and after a triumphal tour of Europe, appeared with enormous success in 1847 at London in Meyerbeer's *Robert le Diable.* In 1850 she made her American debut, touring the United States under the management of P. T. Barnum. After 1849 she confined herself to the concert stage, taught at the Royal College of Music, London, and gave large sums to charitable institutions.

Lindbergh, Mrs. Anne Spencer Morrow (1906-), American poet and essayist educated at Smith College, and trained as an aeroplane pilot and radio operator: her works include *North to the Orient* (1935); *Listen, The Wind; The Wave of the Future.*

Lindo, Mark Prager (1819-1870), Dutch translator and author of short stories, born in London. He became professor of English at the Gymnasium in Arnhem, and translated some of the works of Dickens, Scott, Thackeray, and other English writers. His works, published under the pen name "Old Mr. Smits," include *Letters and Confessions* (1853); *Family of Ours; Confessions of a Young Lady; Types; Impressions from Impressions:* the last named is considered his finest work, and was written in collaboration with Lodewyk Mulder.

Lindsay, Howard (1889-), American actor, dramatist, and producer educated at Harvard University who made his debut in 1909 at Boston in *Polly of the Circus* and played for five years with Margaret Anglin before serving in World War I. His plays include *Your Uncle Dudley* (1929) with Bertrand Robinson; *A Slight Case of Murder* with Damon Runyon; he also directed *To the Ladies; This Thing Called Love; The Gay Divorcé; By Your Leave; Anything Goes.* He dramatized Clarence Day's novel, *Life With Father,* one of the most successful plays produced on the American stage, playing the role of "Father" himself. He has also collaborated on several screen plays.

Lindsay, Norman (1879-), Australian painter, cartoonist, etcher, and lithographer: his cartoons in the Sydney *Bulletin* have been accorded worldwide recognition since 1900. He is also famous for his illustrations for the works of Theocritus, Boccaccio, Casanova, and has published several volumes of his drawings.

Lindsay, Vachel (1879-1931), American poet, artist, and essayist who was educated at Hiram College, and studied at the Chicago Art Institute and the New York Art School. His poems include *General William Booth Enters Into Heaven and Other Poems* (1913); *The Congo and Other Poems; The Chinese Nightingale; The Golden Whales of California; The Daniel Jazz; Every Soul is a Circus:* his prose works include *Adventures While Preaching the Gospel of Beauty* and *The Litany of Washington Street.* He illustrated several of his books.

Lingelbach, Johannes (1622-1674), Dutch painter who traveled extensively in France and Italy before settling in Amsterdam about 1652. He inserted figures in the landscapes of Meindert Hobbema, and painted many landscapes, genre pictures, military scenes, and portraits including *Hay Harvest; Seaport; Battle Scene; Peasants Dancing; Turkish Galley in Sea-Battle; Queen Christina of Sweden; Hawking Party; Wanderer Resting.*

Lintel, in architecture the horizontal beam which connects the uprights of a door or window: it may be constructed of wood, iron or stone, and either ornamented or plain.

Linton, Sir James Drogmole (1840-1916), English painter who studied at St. Martin's School of Art; and became president of the Royal Institute of Painters in Water Colors in 1884. His notable works include *The Haymakers; The Reliquary; Wall Flowers; Ave Maria; Emigrants; The Surrender; Opening Scene of Boccaccio's "Decameron."*

Linton, William James (1812-1897), English wood engraver and author who worked in 1842 on the first edition of the *London Illustrated News*: in 1867 he came to the United States and became an important factor in the development of wood engraving in America. His treatises include *Practical Hints on Wood-Engraving* (1879); *A History of Wood-Engraving in America; Wood-Engraving: a Manual of Instruction; The Masters of Wood-Engraving*. He also wrote a biography of John Greenleaf WHITTIER, and a volume entitled *Memories*.

Lintott, Edward Barnard (1875-), English painter who studied at the Académie Julien, Paris, with Jean Paul LAURENS and Benjamin CONSTANT. His paintings include portraits, flower studies, figures, landscapes, and still life: simplicity and clarity play leading parts in his creations which are to be seen in English, European, and American museums.

Lin Yutang (1895-), Chinese-American essayist who studied in Christian schools in his native country, and at Harvard, Jena, and Leipzig Universities. He became professor of English philology at the Peking National University in 1923, and also founded and edited several literary magazines: his works include *Letters of a Chinese Amazon* (1927); *My Country and My People; Confucius Saw Nancy*, a drama; *Essays About Nothing; Moment in Peking*, a novel; *With Love and Irony; A Leaf in the Storm; Between Tears and Laughter*.

Liotard, Jean Étienne (1702-1789), Swiss painter who studied with Jean Baptiste Masse and Francois LEMOYNE in Paris: he executed many works at Rome, Constantinople, and Vienna where he painted the Empress Maria Theresa and her family. His notable works include *The Three Graces; Old Woman Asleep over the Bible; Marie Antoinette; Portrait of a Seated Turk*.

Lipman, Clara (1869-), American actress and dramatist who made her debut in 1885 at NIBLO'S GARDEN, New York, in *The Rat Catcher*, later playing with Madame MODJESKA in *Odette*. Among the plays in which she has appeared are *The Strange Adventures of Miss Brown; The Girl from Paris; The Telephone Girl; All on Account of Eliza; Julie Bon-Bon; That French Lady*. She has also collaborated on several plays with Edward Freiberger and Samuel Shipman.

Lippi, Filippino (c.1457-1504), Italian painter who was the son of Fra Filippo LIPPI who studied with Sandro BOTTICELLI and FRA DIAMANTE: his works include *Apparition of the Virgin to St. Bernard; Adam and Eve; Peter in Prison; Death of Lucretia; Madonna with Saints; Resurrection; Adoration of the Magi; Meeting of Joachim and Anne; Crucifixion; Virgin and Child; St. Francis in Glory; Mystic Marriage of St. Catherine*.

Lippi, Fra Filippo (c.1406-1469), Italian painter who studied with Tommaso MASACCIO, and was influenced by FRA ANGELICO. He was under the protection of the MEDICIS during his artistic career, and his notable frescoes include scenes from the lives of St. John the Baptist and St. Stephen in the Cathedral at Prato in which he was assisted by FRA DIAMANTE; *Coronation of the Virgin; Nativity; Annunciation; Madonna with Saints; Madonna della Misericordia; Madonna and Child with Angels*: the last-named is in the Metropolitan Museum of Art, New York.

Li Ssu-Hsun (c.650-c.716), Chinese painter regarded as one of the school of landscape painters in Northern China: his specialty was landscapes of the panoramic type filled with fine detail and brilliantly colored in green, blue, and gold. None of his works is extant; they are known only through copies.

List, Emanuel (1891-), Austrian dramatic bass who sang as a boy chorister at the Theater an der Wien, Vienna, and after studying voice made his debut in 1922 at the Volksoper in Gounod's *Faust*. After singing in German opera houses, he made his debut in 1933 at the Metropolitan Opera House, New York, in *Tannhäuser*, remaining with the company since that time, and also singing at Munich, London, Bayreuth, Salzburg, Buenos Aires, and with the San Francisco and Chicago opera companies. His repertory includes the music dramas and operas of WAGNER and Richard STRAUSS.

Liszt, Franz (1811-1886), Hungarian pianist and composer who studied with his father, and made his debut at nine, later obtaining instruction from Carl CZERNY, Antonio SALIERI, and others. He was refused admission to the Paris Conservatory by Luigi CHERUBINI who had a prejudice against prodigies, but produced an opera, *Don Sancho*, in the French capital when he was fourteen years old. He lived in Paris for ten years, in Geneva for four years, toured Europe for ten years, and in 1849 became Court Music Director at Weimar where he remained until 1859 when he went to live in Rome. For many years he was the ardent supporter of struggling composers including Richard WAGNER, Antonin DVORAK, Edvard GRIEG, Alexander BORODIN, and Peter TSCHAIKOWSKY: he was also the teacher of many distinguished pianists including Moriz ROSENTHAL, Frederick LAMOND, Emil SAUER, Alexander SILOTI, Carl TAUSIG, and Hans von BULOW. His chief contribution to musical composition is the *symphonic poem* which he originated and which has been a source of inspiration for many composers. His works include two symphonies; fourteen symphonic poems of which *Les PRELUDES* is a favorite; two piano concertos, and the *Hungarian Fantasia* for piano and orchestra; many solo piano pieces and etudies; twenty Hungarian Rhapsodies for piano many of which have been arranged for orchestra; numerous transcriptions of opera music and songs by SCHUBERT and other composers; choral music; songs and organ pieces.

Litany, a solemn form of prayer used in the early Christian Church to ward off pestilence and other dangers: it originated at Loreto, Italy, during the 13th century, and was sung to a PLAIN SONG melody. In the Protestant Episcopal Church it is usually recited without music in the form of alternate petitions and responses.

Literary Copyright, see Copyright.

Lithography, a printing process in which text and illustrations are traced or transferred to stone or aluminum, covered in the usual manner with ink, and printed in the customary manner. The invention of the process is credited to Aloys Senefelder in 1793: many famous artists have made the plates for reproducing their own works; among them GOYA, PILOTY, MANET, FANTIN-LATOUR, BRANGWYN, DELACROIX, DAUMIER, MENZEL, Lautrec, WHISTLER, PENNELL, and BELLOWS. The process has been successfully commercialized, and is also employed for the printing of music.

"Little Church Around the Corner," The, a name bestowed by the theatrical profession on the Episcopal Church of the Transfiguration on West Twenty-Ninth Street, New York: its willingness to bury the veteran actor, George HOLLAND, when the minister of a Fifth Avenue church refused to perform the office, endeared it to the profession to such an extent that it has been used many times for funerals and weddings of theatrical folk.

Littlefield, Catherine (1908-), American ballet dancer and choreographer who studied with Luigi Albertieri, Leo Staats, and Lubova Egorova, making her debut in the Ziegfeld production of *Sally* in 1923. In 1926 she became *première danseuse* of the Philadelphia Grand Opera Company, remaining until 1935 when she founded the **Littlefield Ballet** which performed with the Philadelphia Grand Opera Company and the Chicago Civic Opera Company. Among the ballets on American themes which she has produced with music and scenery by American composers and artists are *Barn Dance; Terminal; Snow Queen; Parable in Blue; Café Society; Let the Righteous Be Glad; Ladies Better Dresses.*

Little Masters of Engraving, the name given a group of German engravers distinguished for their fine execution of small plates: among the most famous were Albrecht ALTDORFER, Hans Sebald BEHAM, Barthel BEHAM, George PENCZ, and Heinrich ALDEGREVER.

Little Theatres, small theatres operated either by individuals or communities which may be said to have started with the Community Theatre founded by Brigham Young at Salt Lake City in 1853. Amateur theatrical companies thrived in the United States in the South before the Civil War: in the North the *Footlight Club* of Jamaica Plain, a suburb of Boston, has been producing plays since 1877. When the commercial theatre chains throughout the country ceased to operate after the coming of motion pictures, amateur theatricals began to excite interest in that part of the amusement-loving public which failed to accept the crudities of the early films in place of genuine acting: one of the strongest champions of "little theatre" development was Percy MACKAYE, and, according to Carl GLICK who writes convincingly on the subject in Bernard SOBEL's *The Theatre Handbook,* there are more than seven hundred established community theatres producing five or more plays a year, three or four hundred more who produce one or two plays yearly, more than a million people engaging in acting and producing, and an average yearly theatre attendance of fifteen million.

Living Newspaper, a form of drama which originated in Russia after the Revolution in 1918: it consists of dramatizations of topics suggested by headlines in the newspapers, and was tried out by the WPA FEDERAL THEATRE with *Ethiopia* (1936), *Power* (1937), and *One Third of a Nation* (1938) in theatres on Broadway, New York.

Livius Andronicus (c.284-204 B.C.), Roman poet, dramatist, and teacher regarded as the founder of Latin epic poetry and drama. Presumably born in Tarentum, he was brought to Rome as a slave, and later obtained a living by teaching Greek and Latin: he translated HOMER's *Odyssey* into Latin, and took part in his own tragedies including *Achilles; The Trojan Horse; Hermione.* Only fragments of his works are extant, but there is ample evidence that he was highly regarded by the Romans.

Livy (Titus Livius) (59 B.C.-A.D. 17), Roman author whose chief work was a comprehensive *History of Rome* covering the founding of the city in 753 B.C. to 9 B.C. The original work was in 142 books of which 35 books are extant. He worked for more than forty years on the chronicle; it has proved a reliable source of information for historians and biographers.

Ljunggren, Gustav (1823-1905), Swedish critic educated at Lund University where he later became professor of German, of aesthetics, and finally the director of the institution. His two important works are a comprehensive study of Swedish literature in the 18th century and a history of Swedish drama to the end of the 17th century.

Llewellyn Lloyd, Richard David Vivian (1907-), Welsh novelist and dramatist who uses the pen name "Richard Llewellyn." His works include *Poison Pen,* a play in three acts (1938), *How Green Was My Valley,* a novel which became a best seller in the United States in 1940. It was screened in 1941, and was awarded the Motion Picture Academy prize as the best American film of the year.

Lloyd, Harold (1893-), American screen actor trained at the School of Dramatic Art in San Diego, Calif., who made his first appearance as a child actor of twelve with the Burwood Stock Company. He has appeared in numerous silent and talking films including short films for the Edison Company; *Lonesome Luke* comedies for Hal Roach; *Girl Shy; The Freshman; The Kid Brother; Speedy; Welcome Danger; Movie Crazy; The Milky Way; Professor Beware; A Girl, A Guy and a Gob; My Favorite Spy.*

Lochner, Stephan (c.1400-c.1451), German painter also known as "Meister Stephan": his works include a triptych, *The Last Judgment; Martyrdom of the Apostles; Virgin with Violets; Madonna in the Rose Arbor; Presentation of Christ in the Temple.* He is regarded as the leading exponent of the Cologne school.

Locke, David Ross (1833-1888), American humorist and satirist who traveled through the United States as an itinerant printer, also managing several newspapers including the New York *Evening Mail.* His satires written under the pen name "Petroleum V. Nasby" were of great help to the Union cause during the Civil War, being commended by both Abraham Lincoln and Ulysses S. Grant: they include *The Nasby Papers* (1864); *The Struggles of Petroleum Vesuvius Nasby; Nasby in Exile.*

Locke, Robinson (1856-1920), American dramatic critic and for many years publisher of the Toledo *Blade;* during his period of service as a critic he assembled nearly 500 scrap books and 4700 portfolios of loose clippings and pictures covering American theatrical events, covering a period of fifty-five years from 1870 and now in the dramatic collection of the New York Public Library.

Lockhart, Gene (1892-), Canadian actor who first appeared in vaudeville, making his debut in 1917 on the legitimate stage at New York in *The Riviera Girl,* and appearing later in numerous plays including *Sun Up; The Handy Man; The Way of the World; Ah, Wilderness!; Sumurun.* Among the films in which he has been featured are *Captain Hurricane; Crime and Punishment; The Gorgeous Hussy; Algiers; Of Human Hearts; A Christmas Carol; The Story of Alexander Graham Bell; Edison the Man; Meet John Doe; The Sea Wolf; International Lady; Abe Lincoln in Illinois.*

Lockridge, Richard (1898-), American dramatic critic and novelist who studied at the University of Missouri, served in the United States Navy during World War I, and became dramatic critic of the New York *Sun* in 1928. His works include *Darling of Misfortune; Edwin Booth* (1932); *Mr. and Mrs. North; The Norths Meet Murder; Murder Out of Turn; A Pinch of Poison; Death on the Aisle:* the four last-named were written in collaboration with Frances Louise Davis Lockridge, his wife.

Lockwood, Margaret (1916-), English actress born in India and trained at the Royal Academy of Dramatic Art who acted in several plays before she entered the films in 1934, appearing in *Lorna Doone; The Beloved Vagabond; The Street Singer; Doctor Syne; Bank Holiday; The Lady Vanishes; Two on a Week End; Rulers of the Sea; The Stars Look Down; Night Train; Quiet Wedding; The Girl in the News; A Girl Must Live; Alibi.*

Loder, John (1898-), English screen actor who made his debut in Ufa pictures, and later appeared in *The Doctor's Secret* with Ruth CHATTERTON, H. B. WARNER, and Robert Edeson. Among the films in which he has been featured since 1935 are *Java Head; King Solomon's Mines; Mademoiselle Docteur; Peace on the Rhine; Katia; Murder Will Out; Mozart; Tin Pan Alley; Scotland Yard; How Green Was My Valley; One Night in Lisbon; Continental Express.*

Loeffler, Charles Martin (1861-1935), American composer born in Alsace-Lorraine who studied violin with Joseph JOACHIM, and composition

with Ernest Guiraud. After playing with the Pasdeloup Orchestra in Paris, and coming to America in 1881 to play with the Theodore Thomas and Damrosch Orchestras, he became second concertmaster of the BOSTON SYMPHONY ORCHESTRA in 1882, remaining until 1903 when he retired to teach and compose. His works include *La Mort de Tintagiles* and *A Pagan Poem* for orchestra; choral works; chamber music and songs.

Loew, Marcus (1870-1927), American film producer who worked in many capacities before he developed the penny arcades and nickelodeons with David WARFIELD as a partner, later opening more than one hundred theatres with combination film and vaudeville programs. He established the Metro-Goldwyn-Mayer Company which has produced many notable films in the United States and also abroad.

Loftus, Cecilia (1876-1943), English actress, familiarly known as "Cissy" Loftus, who made her first London appearance in 1893 at the Oxford Music Hall, and became famous for her impersonations. Her debut in the United States in 1895 at Koster and Bial's Music Hall, New York, established her as a great artist: after five years in the music halls she made her comic opera debut at New York in *The Mascot,* and later appeared in many plays on the legitimate stage with Helen MODJESKA, E. H. SOTHERN, and William FAVERSHAM. Among the films in which she has played character parts are *Abide With Me; East Lynne; Doctors' Wives; The Old Maid; The Blue Bird; Lucky Partners.*

Loge, in Wagner's cycle of music dramas, *The* RING OF THE NIBELUNGS, a character who is the king of fire and also master of deceit and cunning: he is the friend and confidante of WOTAN whom he aids in stealing the RHINEGOLD from ALBERICH; he is also invoked to create the circle of magic fire which surrounds BRUNNHILDE in the third act of *The Valkyrie.*

Loggia, in architecture a gallery or portico which projects from a building: it is sometimes decorated with paintings so that the term, in the case of RAPHAEL, is also applied to the painting. One of the finest examples is the *Loggia dei Lanzi* at Florence which was executed by Benvenuto CELLINI.

Lohengrin, grand opera in three acts: libretto and music by Richard WAGNER; first produced at the Court Theatre, Weimar, in 1850, under the direction of Franz LISZT, and at the Stadt Theatre, New York, in 1871. The story is: King Henry of Germany has assembled his vassals on the banks of the Scheldt at Antwerp: the Duchy of Brabant is without a ruler because Gottfried, son of the deceased duke, has vanished. Telramund, husband of Ortrud, desirous of ruling the duchy, accuses Elsa von Brabant, Gottfried's sister, of his murder. Elsa offers as her protector an unknown knight who has come to her in a dream: Lohengrin arrives in a boat drawn by a swan, and secures Elsa's promise never to ask his name or his origin. Lohengrin vanquishes Telramund, but spares his life: after the wedding Telramund attempts to assassinate Lohengrin who finally kills him. Elsa, whose curiosity had been aroused by Ortrud, insists that Lohengrin disclose his identity: he finally tells her he is the son of Parsifal, and a knight of the Holy Grail. The swan returns and Lohengrin, declaring the swan to be the lost Gottfried, sails away in the boat now drawn by a dove as Elsa falls dead in the arms of her brother. There are Victor and Columbia recordings of the music.

Lohenstein, Daniel Casper von (1635-1683), German poet, dramatist, and novelist: his works include *Flowers,* a volume of verses; several tragedies; *The Magnaminous General Arminius,* a novel originally printed in over 3000 double-column pages, and regarded in its day as the perfect model of a heroic romance.

Lombard, Carole (1908-1942), American screen actress who made her debut in motion pictures in 1926: among the films in which she appeared are *Me, Gangster; Ned McCobb's Daughter; Dynamite; Man of the World; Up Pops the Devil; No More Orchids; Virtue; The Match King; Brief Moment; Now and Forever; Lady by Choice; Hands Across the Table; My Man Godfrey; The Princess Come Across; Nothing Sacred; Fools for Scandal; Made for Each Other; In Name Only.*

Lombardo, the name of a family of Lombardian sculptors and architects, family name *Solaro,* the eldest of whom, *Martino Lombardo,* came to Venice about 1450, and acquired a considerable reputation as an architect. His son, *Pietro Lombardo* (c.1435-1515) designed the Vendramini-Calargi Palace, the doge's palace, and the Cathedral Cividale de Friuli: Pietro's sons, *Antonio Lombardo* (? -c.1516) and TULLIO LOMBARDO (? -c.1530), worked with him on the tomb of Dante at Ravenna, and also created several masterpieces of their own in Italian churches.

Lomonosov, Mikhail Vasilyevich (1711-1765), Russian scientist and poet considered the father of Russian grammar and literature. He modeled his verses after the classic poets of France: among his important lyric works are an ode, *On the Taking of Chotin;* also songs, and didactic poems. His *Russian Grammar* marked an epoch in the history of Russian literature.

London, Jack (1876-1916), American novelist and short story writer who had varied experiences as a seaman, gold miner, and newspaper correspondent: his works include *The Son of the Wolf* (1900); *The Call of the Wild,* a best seller to the extent of 1,500,000 copies; *The Sea Wolf; White Fang; Smoke Bellew; Martin Eden; Burning Daylight; The People of the Abyss; The Cruise of the Snark; John Barleycorn or Alcoholic Memoirs.*

Londonderry Air, an Irish folk tune also known as *Irish Tune from County Derry* and as *Would God I Were the Tender Apple Blossom:* it was also set by Frederick Weatherly with a lyric, *Danny Boy;* arranged for string orchestra by Percy GRAINGER, and transcribed for violin by Fritz KREISLER. There are several Columbia and Victor recordings.

London Symphony Orchestra, an organization formed in 1904 by a number of performers formerly connected with the Queen's Hall Orchestra: the orchestra is conducted on a cooperative basis, the members sharing in the management and the profits. Among the conductors after Han RICHTER who directed until 1911 are NIKISCH, SAFONOFF, KOUSSEVITZKY, ARBOS, ELGAR, STEINBACH, MENGELBERG, Walter DAMROSCH, FURTWANGLER, Albert COATES, GOOSSENS, HARTY, and BEECHAM. The orchestra toured the United States in 1912 under the direction of Artur Nikisch.

Long, Gabrielle Margaret (1886-), English novelist and short story writer who has used the pen names "Marjorie Bowen," "George Preedy," "John Winch," "Robert Paye," "Margaret Campbell," and "Joseph Shearing" in writing more than 150 historical and mystery tales. Her first story, *The Viper of Milan* (1906) was signed "Marjorie Bowen," and 98 more have appeared under this pseudonym. The pen name "George Preedy" was used for 26 tales beginning with *General Crack* (1928) which also became a successful film. Twelve tales have been published with the pen name "Joseph Shearing," the last being *Airing in a Closed Carriage* (1943).

Long, John Luther (1861-1927), American novelist and dramatist: his works include *Madame Butterfly* (1898) dramatized by David BELASCO, and used as the libretto of an opera with music by Giacomo PUCCINI; *The Darling of the Gods* (1902), dramatized with David Belasco; *Naughty Nan; Adrea* dramatized with David Belasco; *The Dragon Fly* dramatized with Edward C. Carpenter; *Dolce; Crowns.*

Longfellow, Henry Wadsworth (1807-1882), American poet educated at Bowdoin College in the same class as Nathaniel HAWTHORNE. After teaching at Bowdoin he went abroad for several years' study and later became professor of modern languages at Harvard University. His works include *Outre-Mer* (1833-35), published anonymously; *Hyperion; Voices of the Night; Ballads and Other Poems; The Spanish Student; The Belfry of Bruges; Evangeline; The Golden Legend; The Song of Hiawatha; The Courtship of Miles Standish; Tales of a Wayside Inn.* He also translated the *Divine Comedy* of DANTE.

Longhena, Baldassare (1604-1682), Italian architect who designed the Church of Santa Maria della Salute, the Pesaro Palace, and the Rezzonico Palace in Venice: all are in the BAROQUE style developed by the Genoese, revealing a richness and power rarely found in other edifices of baroque design.

Longhi, Pietro (1702-1785), Venetian painter who studied with Giuseppe CRESPI, and specialized in painting the every-day life of Venetians at home, on the street or at public resorts, recalling the characters in Carlo GOLDONI's plays to such a degree that he became known as "the Goldoni of Painters." Among his notable works are frescoes of carnival festivities in the Palazzo Grassi-Stucky at Venice.

Longman, Evelyn Beatrice (1874-), American sculptor who studied at the CHICAGO ART IN-

STITUTE and worked with Daniel Chester FRENCH for several years: among her notable works are the bronze doors of the chapel at the United States Naval Academy, Annapolis, Md.; the colossal statue, *Victory*, on Festival Hall at the St. Louis Exposition; *Fountain of Ceres* at the Panama-Pacific Exposition; *The Future*; *Consecration*; *Nature*. She has executed many portrait busts and reliefs, and is well represented in the Metropolitan Museum of Art, New York, and other American museums.

Longy, Georges (1868-1930), French oboist who studied at the Paris Conservatory, and later played with the LAMOUREUX, COLONNE, and OPERA-COMIQUE Orchestras at Paris. From 1898 to 1925 he was first oboist of the BOSTON SYMPHONY ORCHESTRA, and in 1900 founded the **Longy Club** which gave many performances of chamber music for wind instruments and piano with Alfred De Voto as assisting pianist.

Lonsdale, Frederick (1881-), English dramatist whose real name is Frederick Leonard: his works include *The Early Worm* (1908); *The King of Cadonia*; *The Best People*; *The Balkan Princess* with Frank Curzon; *Monsieur Beaucaire*, adapted from Booth TARKINGTON's novel; *Betty* with Gladys Unger; *Waiting at the Church*; *The Maid of the Mountains*; *Aren't We All?*; *Madame Pompadour* with Harry Graham; *Spring Cleaning*; *The Fake*; *The Street Singer*; *The Last of Mrs. Cheyney*; *Katja the Dancer*; *On Approval*; *Canaries Sometimes Sing*; *Once is Enough*.

Loos, Anita (1893-), American novelist and dramatist who appeared as a child actress at five, and wrote her first film scenario at twelve. In collaboration with her husband, John Emerson, she wrote scenarios for Douglas FAIRBANKS, SR., David Wark GRIFFITH, and Constance TALMADGE: her published works include *Gentlemen Prefer Blondes* (1925) which was a best seller, and *But Gentlemen Marry Brunettes* which was not as successful. Since 1931 she has written or collaborated on many important screen scenarios and plays.

L'Opéra (Paris), see **Académie de Musique (Paris).**

Lopokova, Lydia (1892-), Russian dancer and actress who studied at the Imperial Ballet School, St. Petersburg, and made her debut at the Maryinsky Theatre there, later appearing as solo ballerina at the Imperial Russian Ballet, and at the Opera House in Paris. She made her American debut in 1911 at the Winter Garden, New York, and her debut as an actress on the legitimate stage took place in 1914 at the Playhouse, New York, in *Just Herself*: since that time she has appeared in many important ballets as a dancer, and in plays and musical productions as an actress.

L'Oracolo delle Battaglie, see **Falcone, Aniello.**

Lord, Pauline (1890-), American actress who first appeared in 1903 at San Francisco with the BELASCO Stock Company, and after playing with Nat GOODWIN, made her debut in 1912 at the Harris Theatre, New York, in *The Talker*. Among the plays in which she has appeared are *On Trial*; *Under Pressure*; *Midnight*; *Big Game*; *Samson and Delilah*; *Anna Christie*; *They Knew What They Wanted*; *Trelawney of the Wells*; *Strange Interlude*; *The Late Christopher Bean*; *Ethan Frome*. She has also been featured in several films including *Mrs. Wiggs of the Cabbage Patch* and *A Feather in Her Hat*.

Lord Chamberlain, in England the official who acts as the censor of the stage, an office created in 1737 through a law which stipulated that every play must be licensed before performance by sending it to the Lord Chamberlain: if not forbidden within seven days it could be presented. The censor is not required by the law to state his reasons for refusing licenses, and there is no means of appeal from his decisions.

Lord Chamberlain's Men, a company of professional actors with which Shakespeare allied himself about 1590, and with which he is believed to have remained until the end of his career on the stage. The company was originally known as *Lord Leicester's Men*, and its leading actor, Richard BURBAGE, was influential in arranging its use of the GLOBE and the BLACKFRIARS Theatres on a basis whereby the profits were distributed between players and management.

Lorelei or **Loreley,** in German legend a siren who made her abode on a rock over 350 feet in height on the right bank of the Rhine near Bingen and lured men to their death by her beauty and singing. Max BRUCH composed an opera, *Loreley*, in 1863, using a libretto originally written for Felix MENDELSSOHN: better known is the song by Friedrich Silcher.

Lorenzetti, Ambrogio (c.1280-1348), Italian painter who was a younger brother of Pietro LORENZETTI with whom he worked on six great allegories, *Good and Bad Government*, in the Public Palace at Siena: other works credited to him include *Life of St. Nicholas*; *Presentation in the Temple*; *Annunciation*; *St. Agnes*; *Madonna Enthroned*. His work was highly praised by Lorenzo GHIBERTI.

Lorenzetti, Pietro (c.1278-c.1350), Italian painter called Pietro Laurati by Giorgio VASARI: his known works include *Madonna and the Saints*; *History of the Carmelites*; *Marriage of the Virgin*; *Triumph of Death*; *St. Humilitas*; *Birth of the Virgin*.

Lorenzo Monaco (c.1370-1425), Italian painter, also known as Don Lorenzo, who spent most of his life in a monastery at Florence. His one signed work is a *Coronation of the Virgin*: others attributed to him include *Madonna and Saints*; *Adoration of the Kings*; *Life of the Virgin*; *Madonna and Child*.

Lorimer, George Horace (1868-1937), American editor educated at Colby (Maine) University and Harvard University: in 1897 he became literary editor of *The Saturday Evening Post*, and from 1899 to 1937 its editor-in-chief. His works include *Letters from a Self-Made Merchant to His Son* (1902) published anonymously; *Old Gorgon Graham; The False Gods,* and *Jack Spurlock: Prodigal.*

Loring, Eugene, contemporary American ballet dancer and choreographer who appeared with the FOKINE Ballet at the LEWISOHN Stadium in 1934-35, and was also a member of the American Ballet and the Ballet Caravan. His choreographic creations include *Harlequin for President; Yankee Caravan; Billy the Kid; City Portrait; The Great American Goof:* he also appeared with Cornelia Otis SKINNER in *Madame Sans Gene,* and directed the dances at the Ogonquit (Maine) Theatre.

Lorrain, Claude, see **Claude Lorrain.**

Lorre, Peter (1904-), Hungarian film actor who appeared in many plays in Germany, Austria, and Switzerland, before making a signal success in numerous foreign and American films including *Spring's Awakening; The Thirteen Trunks of Mr. O. F.; The Man Who Knew Too Much; Crime and Punishment; Secret Agent;* several films based on John Phillips MARQUAND's detective character, "Mr. Moto"; *Strange Cargo; District Attorney; They Met in Bombay; The Maltese Falcon; All Through the Night.*

Lortzing, Albert (1801-1851), German opera composer who was chiefly self-taught: his successful operas include *Czar and Carpenter* (1837), *The Poacher,* and *The Armorer.* Lortzing's operas rank highly because of their original flow of melody and humor, but they have never made any appeal outside of Germany.

Los Angeles County Museum, an institution founded in 1910 containing a permanent art collection which includes the Paul Rodman Mabury Collection of works by TITIAN, TINTORETTO, VAN DYCK, RUBENS, COROT, COURBET, Winslow HOMER, INNESS, and RYDER; the Preston Harrison Collection of contemporary American and French paintings: also fine collections of tapestries, porcelains, arms and armor, Indian blankets and many assemblies of interest in science and ethnology.

Los Angeles Grand Opera, see **San Francisco Opera Company.**

Los Angeles Philharmonic Orchestra, an organization founded in 1919 by William Andrews Clark, Jr., with Walter Henry Rothwell as conductor until 1927: the conductors up to 1938 include George Schneevoigt, Artur RODZINSKI, and Otto KLEMPERER. After 1938 the guest conductors included Leopold STOKOWSKI, Alfred COATES, Bruno WALTER, John BARBIROLLI, Alfred WALLENSTEIN, Jose ITURBI, and George SZELL. The orchestra also gave summer concerts at the Hollywood Bowl.

Losch, Tilly (1902-), Austrian dancer who made her debut as a child dancer in 1912 at the State Opera House, Vienna, in *Waltzes from Vienna,* and later became associated with Max REINHARDT at Vienna and Berlin, coming to New York in 1927 to appear in his production of *A Midsummer Night's Dream.* Among the productions in which she has appeared as solo dancer are *Everyman; Danton's Death; This Year of Grace; Wake Up and Dream.* She has also danced in several films including *Street Singer's Serenade; Limelight; The Good Earth; The Garden of Allah.*

Lo Spagnuolo, see **Crespi, Giuseppe Maria.**

Lothrop, Harriet Mulford Stone (1844-1924), American author of books for children under the pen name "Margaret Sidney." In 1878 she attracted attention with her contributions to *Wide Awake,* a magazine for children and published her first success, *Five Little Peppers and How They Grew* in 1880. This book enjoyed a total sale of more than 2,000,000 copies and was followed by *Five Little Peppers Midway; Five Little Peppers Grown Up; Our Davie Pepper.*

Loti, Pierre (1850-1923), French novelist, real name Julien Viaud, who spent several years as a midshipman in the French navy during which he visited five continents. His first literary success was *The Marriage of Loti* (1880); among his works which have been published in English are *Madame Chrysanthème; The Romance of a Spahi; An Iceland Fisherman; The Marriage of Loti; My Brother Yves; Ramuntcho:* he also wrote many interesting books about his travels.

Lotti, Antonio (c.1667-1740), Italian organist and composer who studied with Giovanni LEGRENZI, and became first organist of St. Mark's at Venice. His compositions include many operas and sacred music: one of his solo songs, *Pur dicesti,* is regarded by many authorities as among the finest examples of pure melody in all music.

Lotto, Lorenzo (c.1480-1556), Italian painter who studied the works of Giovanni BELLINI and Georgio GIORGIONE in Venice, and was also influenced by Palma VECCHIO. His works of note include *Pietá; Woman Taken in Adultery; Man With a Red Beard; Triumph of Chastity; Bridal Couple; St. Jerome; Christ Taking Leave of His Mother; Presentation of the Virgin in the Temple; Portrait of a Young Man:* the last-named is to be seen in the Metropolitan Museum of Art, New York.

Lotus Eaters (Lotophagi), in Greek legend a people described in HOMER's *Odyssey* as eaters of the fruit of a plant called the lotus: some of Ulysses' followers, after partaking of it, became indolent, forgetful of their friends, and lost all desire to return to their native land. Alfred TENNYSON's poem, *The Lotus Eaters,* is ranked among his masterpieces.

Louis XIV (1638-1715), the king of France from 1643 to 1715, and surnamed "Le Grand" (The Great). His reign of nearly three quarters of a century was of great importance in the development of all branches of art in France: RACINE, MOLIERE, SAINT-SIMON, LA FONTAINE, Descartes, and Fénelon were among the distinguished literary figures; LE SUEUR, ANGUIER, LE BRUN, PUGET, WATTEAU, COYSEVOX, CLAUDE LORRAIN, LARGILLIERE, and Louis LE NAIN among the famous sculptors and painters; LULLY, COUPERIN, and RAMEAU, among the eminent composers.

Louise, Anita (1915-   ), American stage and screen actress who appeared on the stage in *Peter Ibbetson* and other plays before entering the films: among the pictures in which she has played leading roles are *The Music Master; The Life of Franz Schubert; Madame Du Barry; The Story of Louis Pasteur; That Certain Woman; Tovarich; Marie Antoinette; The Sisters; Anthony Adverse; The Little Princes; Glamour For Sale.*

Louise, grand opera in four acts: libretto and music by Gustave CHARPENTIER; first produced at Paris in 1900, and at the Manhattan Opera House, New York, in 1908. The simple story concerns itself with the love of Louise, a needle worker, for Julien, a young poet, and the efforts of her father and mother to keep the lovers apart: their attachment proves stronger than fear of parental anger, and Louise leaves after being disowned by her father. There is a Columbia abridged recording, and also several Victor recordings of the popular aria, *Depuis le jour* (Since the Day). The sequel, *Julien,* was not successful.

Loure (Fr.), (*a*) the name in ancient France of an instrument similar to the BAGPIPES. (*b*) The name given in the 18th century to a dance which became one of the movements in the classical SUITE: it was written in 6-4 or 3-4 time, and resembled the SARABANDE in character.

Loutherbourg, Philippe Jacques (1740-1812), English painter born at Strasbourg who studied with his father and with Francesco Casanova: most of his life was spent in England where he was naturalized and became a member of the Royal Academy. His notable works include *Hagar and Her Son; Shepherd and Flock; Landscape after Storm; Tower on Seashore; Burning of London in 1666.* He also painted scenery for David GARRICK, and executed excellent etchings for the illustration of books.

Louvre (Paris), an art museum in Paris, France, which houses the most notable collection of paintings, sculptures, and art objects in the world: it is first officially mentioned under its present name in 1204 during the reign of Philip Augustus, and was reconstructed in the 13th century under the supervision of Charles V who lived there himself. Francis I ordered the building repaired in 1527: the architects Pierre LESCOT and Jean GOUJON continued the work after his death during the reign of Henry II. Catherine de' Medici commissioned Philibert de l'Orme, Jean Bullant, and Jacques ANDROUET DU CERCEAU to work on the construction of the chateau of the TUILERIES in 1563, but it was three hundred years before the latter was connected with the Louvre. The reign of Henry IV saw the completion of the Grand Gallery, and the Pavillon d'Horloge was constructed by Jacques LEMERCIER at the behest of Louis XIII. The Petite Gallery, later known as the Apollo Gallery, was rebuilt for Louis XIV by Louis LE VAU with decorations by Charles LE BRUN, and the celebrated Colonnade was built by Claude PERRAULT. In 1803 the Louvre was in

a pitiable state of decay when NAPOLEON I ordered Charles PERCIER and Pierre FONTAINE to rehabilitate it: it was enriched with paintings, sculptures, and art objects of every description which were taken from countries which he had conquered, and converted it into a national museum. At the beginning of World War II the Louvre was probably the greatest repository of ancient and modern art treasures in respect to paintings and sculptures; there are also unsurpassed collections of engravings, tapestries, ivories, porcelain, terra cotta, gems, and jewels.

Louÿs, Pierre (1870-1925), French poet and novelist distantly related to Victor HUGO, and educated at the Lycée de Sailly and at the Sorbonne: his works available in English include *The Songs of Bilitis* (1904); *Aphrodite; Psyche; Satyrs and Women; The Woman and Puppet; The Collected Works of Pierre Louÿs,* a volume containing many of his stories.

Love, Montagu (1877-1943), American stage and screen actor who was first a newspaper artist and served in the Boer War. After appearing as an amateur, he made his debut as a professional entertainer at the piano, later playing in *David Garrick, Mrs. Dane's Defence,* on tour in Great Britain, South Africa, and the Far East. His New York debut was made in 1913 in *The Second in Command:* among the plays in which he appeared were *Grumpy; The Adventure of Lady Ursula; Arms and the Man; Candida; The Ware Case; Captain Brassbound's Conversion; Firebird; Richard of Bordeaux.* From 1916 he played leading roles in many silent and talking films among which were *Rasputin the Black Monk; Bulldog Drummond; Outward Bound; Clive of India; The Crusades; Lloyd's of London; Sutter's Gold; The Life of Emile Zola; Tovarich; Parnell; The Prisoner of Zenda; Gunga Din; The Man in the Iron Mask; All This and Heaven Too; Northwest Mounted Police; The Sea Hawk; The Remarkable Andrew; Tennessee Johnson.*

Love For Three Oranges, The, grand opera in a prologue and four acts: libretto and music by Serge PROKOFIEFF; first produced by the Chicago Opera Company at Chicago in 1921 and by the same company at the Manhattan Opera House, New York, in 1922. The whimsical plot, adapted by the composer from a tale by Carlo Gozzi, concerns itself with a prince who, when very ill, is cured by laughing at an old witch, Fata Morgana, when she accidentally turns a somersault out of a room. The witch puts a curse on him by prophesying that he must fall in love with three oranges and have his love returned before he can ever be happy. He finds the three oranges in a desert, and in one of them is the Princess Nicoletta to whom he is happily wed. Prokofieff arranged a symphonic suite from the music which is available in a Victor recording: it contains the *Scherzo diabolique* and *Marche* which are popular orchestral numbers.

Lovelace, Richard (1618-1658), English poet who enlisted in the service of Louis XIV at the siege of Dunkirk in 1646 because he was unable to fight for Charles I: he was imprisoned in 1648 but released after Charles' execution. His works include *Lucasta and Other Poems* (1649), and *Lucasta: Posthumous Poems,* published by his brother after his death: he was one of a group known as the CAVALIER POETS.

Love of Three Kings, The, grand opera in three acts: libretto by Sem BENELLI; music by Italo MONTEMEZZI; first produced at La Scala, Milan, in 1913, and at the Metropolitan Opera House, New York, in 1914. The gruesome plot concerns itself with the murder of his daughter-in-law, Fiora, by the blind king, Archibaldo, who smears her lips with poison so that Avito, her lover, dies when he kisses her in the casket. Unfortunately, her husband, Manfredo, the king's son, kisses her also, and it is his dying voice that the old king hears when he enters the room thinking he has caught the guilty lover. There are no recordings available.

Lover, Samuel (1797-1868), Irish novelist and song writer: his works include *Legends and Stories of Ireland* (1831); *Rory O'More,* a novel which was originally a song, and was also made into a play; *Songs and Ballads* including "Widow Machree" and "The Low-Backed Car"; *Handy Andy,* his best-known novel; *Treasure Trove.* He was a painter of skill, and illustrated some of his works: the Irish-American composer, Victor HERBERT, was his grandson.

Low, David (1891-), English cartoonist born in New Zealand where he achieved a considerable reputation as a caricaturist on Australian newspapers. In 1919 he joined the staff of the London *Star,* and in 1927 he became the chief cartoonist of the *Evening Standard:* he has published several collections such as *The Best of Low, Political Parade,* and some of his World War II cartoons with the title *Low on the War.*

Low, Will Hicok (1853-1932), American painter who studied with Jean GEROME and Émile CAROLUS-DURAN: his works include mural paintings in many American public buildings: *The Aspiration of Man and the Results of His Achievement,* a series of thirty-two murals in the State Education Building, Albany, N. Y.; *Aurora; Summer; Orchard in Montigny; Christmas Morn; Victory;* a portrait of Emma ALBANI, the opera singer; *May Blossoms.* He also executed fine book illustrations, and his lectures at the CHICAGO ART INSTITUTE were published as *A Painter's Progress.*

Lowboy, in furniture designing a chest originating in England: in Jacobean times chests were placed on stands, and improved in design by both American and English designers in the 18th century. The finer examples of the CHIPPENDALE period were highly ornamented with claw-and-ball feet, cabriole legs curving both outward and inward, and frequently sculptured below the center drawer with the much-favored shell design.

Lowe, Edmund (1892-), American stage and screen actor educated at Santa Clara (Calif.) University, who first appeared with stock companies, and made his debut in 1917 at New York in *The Brat,* later playing in *Roads of Destiny; Trilby; Desert Sands.* He has appeared in many films

since 1921 including *What Price Glory?; Chandu the Magician; Dinner at Eight; The Great Impersonation; The Garden Murder Case; Seven Sinners; Espionage; Flying Cadets; Call Out the Marines.*

Lowell, Amy Lawrence (1874-1925), American poet and critic, sister of Abbott Lawrence Lowell, president of Harvard College, and Percival Lowell, a famous astronomer: her poetical works include *A Dome of Many-Coloured Glass* (1912); *Sword Blades and Poppy Seeds; Men, Women and Ghosts; Can Grande's Castle; Pictures of the Floating World; Legends; A Critical Fable.* Among her critical works are *Six French Poets; Tendencies in Modern American Poetry; Poetry and Poets; John Keats.*

Lowell, James Russell (1819-1891), American poet and critic educated at Harvard University who contributed to and edited several magazines including the *Atlantic Monthly* and the *North American Review* in addition to becoming professor of modern languages at Harvard. He attracted attention with the first series of the famous anti-slavery *Bigelow Papers,* published in the Boston *Courier* in 1843: among his notable works are *The Vision of Sir Launfal; A Fable for Critics; Conversation on Some of the Old Poets; Poems* in two volumes; *Fireside Travels; Under the Willows; Among My Books,* a series; *My Study Windows; Three Memorial Poems; Heartsease and Rue; The Old English Dramatists; Last Poems.*

Lowes, John Livingston (1867-), American essayist and critic educated at Washington and Jefferson College, and at the Universities of Harvard, Berlin, and Leipzig: his works include *Convention and Revolt in Poetry* (1919) considered one of the best critical works of the present day; *The Road to Xanadu; Of Reading Books and Other Essays; The Art of Geoffrey Chaucer; Geoffrey Chaucer and the Development of His Genius; Essays in Appreciation.*

Lowndes, Mrs. Marie Adelaide Belloc-, see **Belloc-Lowndes, Marie Adelaide.**

Loy, Myrna (1905-), American screen actress who entered the films in 1925: among the pictures in which she has appeared are *Across the Pacific; The Heart of Maryland; Desert Song; Black Watch; The Great Divide; Cameo Kirby; Cock of the Walk; Arrowsmith; Topaze; Animal Kingdom; When Ladies Meet; Men in White; The Thin Man; Broadway Bill; The Great Ziegfeld; After the Thin Man; Parnell; The Rains Came; Another Thin Man; I Love You Again; Love Crazy; Shadow of the Thin Man.*

Lubitsch, Ernst (1892-), German actor and motion picture director trained under Max REINHARDT: among the films he directed in Europe were *Carmen,* released in the United States as *Gypsy Blood; Madame Du Barry; Deception; The Loves of Pharaoh; The Wildcat; Montmartre; The Doll.* In 1923 he came to the United States to direct Mary PICKFORD in *Rosita:* he has since directed *Lady Windermere's Fan; The Student Prince; The Smiling Lieutenant; The*

Merry Widow; One Hour With You; Desire; Angel; Bluebeard's Eighth Wife; Ninotchka; The Shop Around the Corner; Design for Living.

Luca, Giuseppe de (1876-), Italian dramatic baritone who studied at Rome, and made his debut in 1897 at Piacenza in Gounod's *Faust*. After singing in Italian opera houses, he made his debut in 1915 at the Metropolitan Opera House, New York, as Figaro in Rossini's BARBER OF SEVILLE, receiving a tremendous ovation and remaining as a member of the company until 1934.

Lucan or **Marcus Annaeus Lucanus** (39 A.D.-65 A.D.), Roman poet born in Spain whose only extant work is *Pharsalia,* an epic poem in ten books on the civil war between CAESAR and Pompey. He committed suicide when condemned to death for conspiring against the Emperor NERO who had forbidden him through jealousy to recite his works in public.

Lucas, Edward Verrall (1868-1938), British essayist, novelist, and art critic educated at University College, London, who worked on the London Evening *Globe* as a reporter: his works include *The Life of Charles Lamb* (1905); several novels including *Over Bemerton's;* many travel volumes such as *A Wanderer in London;* several volumes of poetry including *Sparks from a Flint* and *Songs of the Bat;* lyrics for shows and anti-German skits during World War I: also several volumes of essays including *Old Lamps for New; Reading, Writing, and Remembering; Saunterer's Rewards.*

Lucas van Leyden (1494-1533), Dutch painter and engraver, real name Lucas Jacobsz, who studied with his father and with Cornelis Engelbrechtsen: his works include *Resurrection of Lazarus; St. Peter and St. Paul; The Chess Players; Adam and Eve Driven from Paradise; Death of John the Baptist; the Last Judgment; A Card Party; Healing of the Blind.* His great rival was Albrecht DÜRER who painted his portrait when the two artists met at Antwerp in 1521.

Lucchetto da Genova, see **Cambiaso, Luca.**

Lucia di Lammermoor, grand opera in three acts: libretto by Salvatore Cammarano based on Sir Walter SCOTT's novel, *The Bride of Lammermoor;* music by Gaetano DONIZETTI; first produced at Naples in 1835, and at Niblo's Garden, New York, in 1843; also at the Metropolitan Opera House in 1883 for the debut of Marcella SEMBRICH as Lucia. The libretto follows Scott's novel closely: there is a complete Columbia recording, and also both Victor and Columbia recordings of the famous *Sextette* and *Mad Scene.*

Lucian (c.120-c.200 A.D.), Greek satirist and humorist who attacked the religious beliefs of his day, and was called "The Blasphemer": his works include *Dialogues of the Gods; Dialogues of the Dead; Auction of the Philosophers;* also biographical works and poems. He was used as a model in the Renaissance; his *Veracious History* is said to have been the model for SWIFT's "Gulliver's Travels."

Lucilius, Caius (c.180-c.103 B.C.), Latin poet who is called the father of Roman satirical verse: he was intimate with Scipio Africanus, and highly regarded at Rome: only short fragments are extant of his thirty books of satires in which he lashed the vices of his day.

Lucretia, a Roman lady, the wife of Lucius Tarquinius Collatinus, who was noted for her beauty and virtue. She was the victim of rape by Sextus Tarquinius: after exacting an oath from her husband and family that he would avenge her, she killed herself. Her husband's cousin, Lucius Junius BRUTUS, roused the Roman people to the point that they vanquished the Tarquins and established the Roman Republic. SHAKESPEARE relates the tale in *The Rape of Lucrece.*

Lucretius (Titus Lucretius Carus), Roman poet and philosopher who was probably born about 100 B.C., and died about 55 B.C. CICERO mentions him in a letter written in 54 B.C.: his one work was *De rerum natura* (On the Nature of Things), a philosophical poem in six books treating physics, psychology and ethics from the viewpoint of EPICURUS.

Lucrezia Borgia, see **Borgia, Cesare.**

Lucy, Sir Thomas (1532-1600), an English squire and landowner who introduced a bill into parliament for the stricter preservation of game in 1585, and, in his capacity as justice of the peace at Stratford-on-Avon, is said to have prosecuted William SHAKESPEARE for deer-stealing, thereby driving the future dramatist to London. Shakespeare is supposed to have caricatured Sir Thomas in the character of Justice Shallow in both *Henry IV* and *The Merry Wives of Windsor,* but this is a matter of dispute.

Luders, Gustav (1866-1913), American composer born in Germany who studied the violin with Henri Petri, and came to the United States in 1888 to direct a light opera company in Chicago. His successful operettas, written with Frank Pixley as librettist, include *The Prince of Pilsen; King Dodo; The Grand Mogul; Woodland; The Burgomaster:* George ADE was the librettist for *The Sho-Gun; The Fair Co-ed; The Old Town.*

Ludwig, Emil (1881-), German biographer and dramatist educated at Breslau and Heidelberg Universities who first practiced law, but finally embarked on a literary career. His successful works include *Genius and Character* (1924); *Napoleon; Bismarck,* adapted as a play which had a thousand performances; *Goethe; Lincoln; Hindenburg; Cleopatra; Roosevelt; Hitler; Mussolini; Stalin; Bolivar; Beethoven: Life of a Conqueror.* He has also written *The Son of Man,* a life of Jesus, and a novel, *Diana.*

Ludwig, Otto (1813-1865), German dramatist and novelist who first studied music with Felix MENDELSSOHN, but finally decided on a literary career. His works include the tragedies *The Hereditary Forester* and *The Maccabees;* studies of Shakespeare; a novel, *Between Heaven and Earth,* regarded as his masterpiece.

Lugosi, Bela (1888-), Hungarian stage and screen actor who was trained at the Academy of Theatrical Arts, Budapest, and became the leading actor at the National Theatre in that city, appearing in *Hamlet, Liliom,* and *Cyrano de Bergerac.* He made his debut in 1922 at New York in *The Red Poppy,* also appearing in *Arabesque* and *Dracula,* his greatest success. Among the films in which he has been featured are *The Silent Command; The Thirteenth Chair;. Dracula; Murder in the Rue Morgue; International House; The Mask of the Vampire; The Raven; The Mysterious Mr. Wong; The Invisible Ray; The Son of Frankenstein; Ninotchka; The Wolf Man.*

Luini, Bernardino (c.1475-c.1532), Italian painter who studied with LEONARDO DA VINCI whose style he imitated so closely that his pictures frequently pass for those of da Vinci. His notable works include *Crowning With Thorns; Presentation of Christ at the Temple; Adoration of the Magi; Marriage of the Virgin; Adoration of the Shepherds; Christ Among the Doctors; Salome; Holy Family; The Three Marys; Modesty and Vanity; Beheading of John the Baptist.* His sons Aurelio and Evangelista were also distinguished painters.

Lukas, Paul (1895-), Hungarian stage and screen actor who was trained at the Actors' Academy of Hungary, and made his debut in *Liliom* at the Comedy Theatre, Budapest, where he remained for nine years. He has appeared in many films including *Samson and Delilah; The Shopworn Angel; Strictly Dishonorable; The Secret of the Blue Room; By Candlelight; Little Women; The Three Musketeers; I Found Stella Parish; Dodsworth; Espionage; Dinner at the Ritz; The Mutiny of the Elsinore; The Lady Vanishes; Captain Fury; Strange Cargo; The Lady in Distress.* In 1941 he appeared in Lillian Hellman's play, *The Watch on the Rhine.*

Lukeman, Henry Augustus (1871-1935), American sculptor who studied at the National Academy of Design, New York, and the ECOLE DES BEAUX-ARTS, Paris. His notable works include statues of William McKinley; sculptures for the Pan-American Exposition at Buffalo; four colossal statues for the Brooklyn Institute of Arts and Sciences; the Straus Memorial Fountain, New York. In 1925 he completed the colossal sculptures started by Gutzon BORGLUM on Stone Mountain, Ga.

Luks, George Benjamin (1867-1933), American painter who studied at the PENNSYLVANIA ACADEMY OF FINE ARTS, and at the Düsseldorf Academy: his works, many of which picture life on the lower East Side of New York, include *The Pawnbroker's Daughter; The Old Duchess; The Spielers; Woman With a Churn; Mrs. Gamely; The Dominican.*

Lully, Jean-Baptiste (1632-1687), Italian composer, largely self-taught as a violinist, who came to Paris, and entered the service of LOUIS XIV first as a ballet dancer. After learning to play the harpsichord he became a member of the king's private orchestra, and organized a second band in which he proved himself an outstanding violinist. After writing the music for several ballets by MOLIERE, he started composing and producing operas with French texts, an undertaking which has earned him the title of "the father of French opera." His librettist, Philippe QUINAULT (1635-1688), was not only a poet of real merit, but also a genius able to follow the ideas of Lully with perfect understanding. His numerous operas include *Les Fêtes de l'Amour; Alceste; Psyche; Le Triomphe de l'Amour; Persée; Armide et Renaud; Atys:* he also wrote symphonies, trios, airs for violin, and some sacred music.

Lummis, Charles Fletcher (1859-1928), American author and traveler who lived for some years on the Pacific Coast with various tribes of American Indians while on a horseback trip from Canada to Chile. His works include *The Land of Poco Tiempo; The Spanish Pioneers; The Man Who Married the Moon; The Enchanted Burro; A New Mexico David and Other Stories.*

Lunacharsky, Anatoly Vasilyevich (1875-1933), Russian dramatist and poet who was head of the department of education of the Soviet Republic from 1917 to 1929, proving himself able and efficient in organizing the office. His plays include *Faust and the City; Vasilisa the Wise; The Magi:* these are available in English translations.

Lunette, in architecture a window, usually semicircular, above a square window or door: if the space is decorated with a painting, the latter is also known as a *lunette.*

Lunghi, Martino, 16th century Italian architect who studied with Giacomo della Porta, and became one of the leading exponents of the BAROQUE style. His most celebrated works include the staircase in the Palazzo Avellino; the façades of San Girolamo degli Schiavoni and of the Church of Saint Anastasius; the Palazzo Borghese, and Chiesa Nuova: all in Rome. His designs are graceful and harmonious although frequently somewhat unusual at first sight.

Lunt, Alfred (1893-), American stage and screen actor who made his debut in 1913 with the Castle Square Theatre Stock Company, Boston, in *The Gingerbread Man,* later touring with Margaret ANGLIN and Mrs. LANGTRY. In 1919 he made a hit in the title role of Booth TARKINGTON's *Clarence:* among the plays in which he has appeared are *Outward Bound; The Guardsman; Arms and the Man; Juarez and Maximilian; Ned McCobb's Daughter; The Brothers Karamazov; The Doctor's Dilemma; Marco's Millions; Volpone; Caprice; Elizabeth the Queen; Reunion in Vienna; Design for Living; The Taming of the Shrew; Idiot's Delight; Amphytrion 38; The Sea Gull; The Pirate.* He appeared with his wife, Lynn FONTANNE, in many of the above plays, and in the screen production of *The Guardsman.*

Lupino, Ida (1916-), English screen actress and daughter of Stanley Lupino (1894-1942), distinguished actor and producer. She was trained at the Royal Academy of Dramatic Art, London, and made her debut in 1932 in the film, *Her First Affair:* she has since appeared in the English films

High Finance; The Ghost Camera; Prince of Arcadia: also in numerous American pictures including *The Search for Beauty; Ready for Love; Paris in Spring; Smart Girl; Peter Ibbetson; One Rainy Afternoon; Sea Devils; Adventures of Sherlock Holmes; The Light That Failed; High Sierra; The Sea Wolf; Ladies in Retirement; Moontide; The Hard Way.*

Lussan, Zélie de (1863-), American dramatic soprano who studied with her mother, a French opera singer, and made her operatic debut in 1885 with the Boston Ideal Opera Company. In 1889 she joined the CARL ROSA OPERA COMPANY in London, and after singing at Covent Garden made her debut in 1894 at the Metropolitan Opera House in *Carmen.* She sang with the Savage English Opera Company in 1900, and after much success in Paris and Madrid retired in 1907.

Lute, an obsolete stringed instrument of ancient origin introduced into Europe by the Moors. Its shape resembles that of the MANDOLIN: the strings pass over a BRIDGE beneath which is a fretted FINGERBOARD. There are from six to thirteen strings, all in pairs except the highest, or melody string, which is single: also bass strings not on the fingerboard which are attached to a separate neck. All strings are plucked with the fingers of the right hand: the lute was the principal instrument of the TROUBADOURS, and both BACH and HANDEL wrote music for it.

Lutero, Giovanni di, see **Dosso Dossi, Giovanni.**

Luther, Martin (1483-1546), German religious reformer who also made important changes in the German mass: he is said to have composed the tunes for many chorales including *Ein' feste Burg ist unser Gott* (A Mighty Fortress is Our God): it was his custom to play the melodies on the flute, and have them transcribed by capable musicians.

Lutyens, Sir Edwin Landseer (1869-), English architect who studied at the South Kensington Schools, London, and received his first commission at nineteen. He has designed many fine country residences, and worked out the restorations of several old mansions: among his notable public works are the Cenotaph, London; the Government Buildings, New Delhi; the Art Gallery, Johannesburg, South Africa; the Britannic House, London; the British Embassy, Washington, D. C. He has also been successful in the treatment of small housing problems.

Lutz, Meyer (1822-1903), German organist and composer who settled at London in 1848: he conducted opera at the Gaiety Theatre from 1869 to 1881 and went on tours with MARIO and GRISI: his successful operettas include *Faust Up-to-Date; Blonde and Brunette; Zaida; The Legend of the Lys.* A dance, *Pas de Quatre,* written for a quartet of famous ballerinas, was popular in the United States as presented by Lois FULLER.

Luxembourg Palace, a building in Paris designed and erected by Salomon de BROSSE for Marie de' Medici, and later occupied by several royal personages during the 17th and 18th century; also by the Directorate during the French Revolution, and later by the Consulate. Since 1879, the senate of the Republic of France occupies the building: nearby is the **Luxembourg Museum** containing works by living painters and sculptors which have been acquired by the state. The works remain for a period of ten years after the death of the artists, and the finest are then sent to the LOUVRE.

Luxor, a village in Upper Egypt located near Thebes and famous for the ruins of a massive temple over 850 feet in length built about 1400 B.C. by Amenhotep III with additions later by Tutankhamen and Rameses II. It was dedicated to Ammon, Mut, and Khons; Rameses II added two obelisks of red granite only one of which remains in place, the other having been given to France by Mehemet Ali, and set up in the Place de la Concorde, Paris. The temple was rebuilt by ALEXANDER THE GREAT and a considerable amount of excavating done there by the French in 1885.

Luzzatto, Moses Hayim (1707-1747), Hebrew poet and dramatist: his dramas include *Samson and Delilah, The Tower of Victory,* and *Glory to the Upright.* They were widely circulated in manuscript, and the exquisite style resulted in an entirely new school of Hebrew poetry.

Lyceum, (*a*) a gymnasium in ancient Athens which was dedicated to APOLLO, and the chief institution of its kind in the period of Pisistratus (c.527 B.C.). It was famous for its groves of plane trees under which Aristotle expounded his philosophy. (*b*) The word *Lycée* or *Lyceum* is used in France to name a secondary school of classical instruction.

Lyceum Theatre (London), a theatre originally constructed as an exhibition hall in 1765, and altered to conventional theatre arrangement in 1794. The first exhibition of wax figures by Madame TUSSAUD took place there in 1804, and after becoming a regular theatre occupied by opera companies and dramatic troupes, it was destroyed by fire in 1830, and rebuilt in 1834. It is famous as the theatre in which Henry IRVING and Ellen TERRY leased in 1871, and produced a series of memorable plays until 1902 including *Henry VIII; Ravenswood; Cymbeline; Romeo and Juliet;* TENNYSON'S *The Cup; Faust; The Bells; Macbeth; Othello;* Tennyson's *Queen Mary; Richard III; King Lear;* Tennyson's *Becket; The Lyons Mail.*

Lydgate, John (c.1370-c.1448), English monk and poet who translated Benoit de St. Maure's *History of Troy* for Henry V: he also wrote the poems, *The Battle of Agincourt* and *The Coronation of Henry VII; The Story of Thebes,* and several ballads that became popular favorites.

Lyly, John (c.1554-1606), English dramatist and novelist who first wrote several plays for the boys of St. Paul's School, London, to be performed in the presence of Queen ELIZABETH. His novels, *Euphues, or the Anatomy of Wit* (1579) and *Euphues and His England,* are his most famous works because they introduced the euphuistic style of writing characterized by antithesis, alliteration and simile in an attempt to use words as mere musical sounds without regard to their sense. Many Elizabethan authors followed his example: his influence is clearly to be seen in the works of SIDNEY and Herbert SPENSER. His comedies in prose are among the first works of this character written by English authors.

Lyon, Annabelle, contemporary American ballet dancer of Russian parentage who studied with Michel FOKINE and George BALANCHINE: she has appeared with the American Ballet Company at the Metropolitan Opera House, the Ballet Caravan, and the BALLET THEATRE.

Lyre, (*a*) a stringed instrument used by the Egyptians and Greeks: the body consisted of a resonance-box from which rose two curved arms connected by a cross piece. The strings numbering from three to ten, were plucked with a plectrum held in the right hand with the lyre resting against the left arm. (*b*) An instrument used in military bands consisting of a series of loosely suspended bars tuned to the ordinary scale, and struck with a hammer.

Lyric, (*a*) in music a term applied to a poem suitable for accompaniment by the lyre, and accordingly adapted for expression in song. At the present time songs in which the words express subjective emotion are called *lyric* in contrast to *epic songs* which are narrative, and *dramatic songs* which are accompanied by action: operas are also termed either lyric or dramatic. (*b*) In literature lyric poetry was distinguished from elegiac and epic by the ancient Greeks: among the great lyric poets are SAPPHO, ALCAEUS, PINDAR, VILLON, SHAKESPEARE, BURNS, WORDSWORTH, KEATS, TENNYSON, LAMARTINE, and GOETHE.

Lysicrates, Monument of, a temple at Athens of small proportions and circular in shape, said to be the oldest example of Corinthian architecture. It was built in 335 B.C. by Lysicrates to commemorate his victory in a dramatic contest, and ornamented with a carved frieze 10 inches in height depicting the story of DIONYSUS and the pirates.

Lysippus, Greek sculptor who worked about 450 B.C.; the worthy successor of PRAXITELES and SCOPAS and a favorite of ALEXANDER THE GREAT. He modified the proportions of the human body as established by POLYCLETUS by making the body slender, the head smaller, and the muscles more prominent. He is said to have created 1500 works including several statues and portraits of Alexander the Great; a colossal statue of ZEUS sixty feet in height; *Hercules Epitrapezios;* the Farnese *Hercules; Mercury; Apoxyomenos; Agias.*

Lysistratus, Greek sculptor who worked in the 4th century B.C. and said to have been a brother of LYSIPPUS. He is described by PLINY as one of the most realistic sculptors, and the first to make plaster casts of human faces, but there is some question as to the truth of this statement.

Lytell, Bert (1885-), American stage and screen actor educated at the Upper Canada College, Toronto, who made his first appearance with the Columbia Stock Company, and formed his own stock company in 1907. He made his New York debut in 1914 at the 39th St. Theatre in *A Mix-Up,* appearing also in *If* and *Mary's Ankle.* From 1917 to 1928 he appeared in the silent pictures, and returned to the stage in *Brothers; The Play's the Thing; Death Takes a Holiday; A Church Mouse; Good-bye Again; Ten Minute Alibi; Susan and God; The Amazing Dr. Clitterhouse.*

Lytle, William Haines (1826-1863), American general and poet who was educated at Cincinnati College, served in the Mexican War as a captain, and as colonel of a volunteer regiment during the Civil War, being promoted to brigadier-general for gallantry. His most famous poems, which were published in 1894, were *Jacqueline* and *Address of Antony to Cleopatra* in which occurs the famous opening line, "I am dying, Egypt, dying."

Lytton, Sir Henry (1867-1936), English actor and singer who made his debut in 1884 at the Royalty Theatre, Glasgow, in *Princess Ida,* later appearing in all of the Gilbert and Sullivan productions in Great Britain, Canada, and the United States with the D'Oyly Carte Company. He wrote two autobiographical volumes: *Secrets of a Savoyard* (1922) and *A Wandering Minstrel* (1933).

M

Maartens, Maarten, see **Schwartz, Jozua Marius Willem van der Poorten.**

Mabie, Hamilton Wright (1845-1916), American critic and essayist educated at Williams College, and trained in law at Columbia University Law School. He practiced several years before becoming one of the editors in 1879 of the *Christian Union* which changed its name to the *Outlook* in 1893. His works include *Norse Stories Retold from the Eddas* (1882); *Short Studies in Literature; Essays in Literary Interpretation; Essays on Work and Culture; William Shakespeare; Parables of Life; In Arcady; Backgrounds of Literature; Japan Today and Tomorrow; Fruits of the Spirit.*

Mabuse, Jan (c.1478-c.1533), Flemish painter who worked at Antwerp: his real name was Jenni or Jan Gosart or Gossart. He was in the service of Philip of Burgundy who sent him to study the works of the masters of antiquity in Rome: his most famous works include *Adoration of the Magi; Portrait of a Knight; The Agony in the Garden; St. Luke Painting the Virgin and Child; Neptune and Amphitrite; Danae and the Golden Shower:* his paintings reveal a mixture of Italian and Flemish styles.

MacArthur, Charles (1895-), American dramatist who acted as a reporter on Chicago and New York newspapers before his first play, *Lulu Belle,* written in collaboration with Edward SHELDON, was produced in 1926: he has also written *Salvation* with Sidney Howard; *The Front Page, Twen-*

ieth Century, Jumbo, and *Ladies and Gentlemen* with Ben HECHT. Among the motion pictures or which he has written scenarios or dialogue are *Crime Without Passion; Twentieth Century; Barbary Coast; Wuthering Heights; Gunga Din; His Girl Friday:* some of the above in collaboration with Ben Hecht.

Macaulay, Rose, contemporary English novelist, poet, essayist, and lecturer in English literature at Cambridge University; educated at Oxford where she was a student when her first novel, *The Valley Captives,* was published in 1911. Her works include *Potterism; Dangerous Ages; Told by an Idiot; Orphan Island; Keeping up Appearances; Staying with Relations; I Would Be Private.* She has also published volumes of poetry, a study of John MILTON; *Some Religious Elements in English Literature.*

Macaulay, Thomas Babington (1800-1859), English statesman, historian, essayist, and poet educated at Trinity College, Cambridge, and called to the bar in 1826. His *Essay on John Milton* in the Edinburgh Review brought him to the notice of the literary world in 1825, and his *History of England* (5 volumes, 1849-61) was also a great success. Other important works are the *Lays of Ancient Rome,* and the essays on Francis BACON, Samuel JOHNSON, John BUNYAN, and many other famous men which have been widely read and translated.

Macbeth, *(1)* a king of Scotland who was the son of Findlaech: in 1040 he killed Duncan, grandson and successor of King Malcolm, and seized the throne. He ruled for seventeen years, and was in turn killed by Malcolm III, son of Duncan. *(2)* The play, **Macbeth,** by William SHAKESPEARE, was produced about 1603, and revived at London in 1610: the author probably obtained his facts from Raphael HOLINSHED's *Chronicles of England, Scotland, and Ireland* which he also consulted in connection with other plays. *(3)* The opera **Macbeth** by Giuseppe VERDI, for which the text was taken from Shakespeare's play with additions and changes by Piave and Maffei, was first produced at Florence in 1847, and at Niblo's Garden, New York, in 1850. It was revived after a lapse of nearly a century by the New Opera Company in 1941: Olin DOWNES commented in the New York *Times* as follows: "The score seethes with lusty melodies, with frequently prophetic strokes of commentary and characterization, and it often conveys the fantastical atmosphere of the original drama."

MacCameron, Robert (1866-1912), American painter who studied with Jean Léon GEROME at the ECOLE DES BEAUX-ARTS, Paris: he specialized in portraits, and scenes representing theatrical and café life: among them are *Absinthe Drinkers; Old Customers; The Daughter's Return; The Last Supper; The People of the Abyss.* He painted portraits of Auguste RODIN and of several presidents and chief justices of the United States Supreme Court.

MacCulloch, Horatio (1805-1867), Scottish painter who was chiefly self-taught and formed his own style by close study of nature. He ex-

hibited first at the Scottish Royal Academy in 1829, and continued to do so every year until his death: among his notable works are *A Dream of the Highlands; Loch Maree; A Lowland River; Evening; My Heart's in the Highlands.*

Macdonald, Christie (1875-), American light opera singer born in Canada who first appeared with Pauline HALL in 1892, and later with Francis WILSON in *The Merry Monarch* and *Erminie.* Among the musical productions in which she was starred were *Half a King; The Bride Elect; Spring Maid; The Chieftain; The Sphinx; The Walking Delegate; The Princess Chic; Mexicana; The Belle of Mayfair; Miss Hook of Holland; Sweethearts.*

MacDonald, Jeanette (1907-), American actress and singer who made her debut in the chorus of a review at the Capitol Theatre, New York, in 1920, and until 1928 appeared in numerous musical productions. Her career in the films began in 1929: she has had featured roles in *The Love Parade; The Vagabond King; Monte Carlo; One Hour With You; Love Me Tonight; The Cat and the Fiddle; Naughty Marietta; Rose Marie; San Francisco; Maytime; The Firefly; The Girl of the Golden West; Sweethearts; Broadway Serenade; The New Moon; Bitter Sweet; Smilin' Thru; I Married an Angel.*

Macdonald, William H. (? -1906), American opera singer who studied with English, German, and Italian masters, and sang in Europe until he joined the Emma ABBOTT Company in the United States. He also sang with the Boston Ideals, and in 1887 organized the BOSTONIANS, a highly successful light opera company, with Tom KARL and Henry Clay BARNABEE.

MacDowell, Edward Alexander (1861-1908), American pianist and composer who studied with Teresa CARRENO in New York, at the Paris Conservatory with François MARMONTEL, and at the Frankfort Conservatory with Joachim RAFF who instructed him in composition and also took a great interest in his career. After teaching at the Darmstadt Conservatory, Raff introduced him to Franz LISZT who arranged that the *Modern Suite* for piano be played by MacDowell at the annual concert of the Allgemeine Musikverein in 1882. He settled for a time at Wiesbaden as pianist and composer, but returned to Boston in 1888, and played his *Piano concerto in D minor* with the BOSTON SYMPHONY ORCHESTRA in 1889. His orchestral works all received first performances under GERICKE, NIKISCH, and PAUR by the Boston Symphony Orchestra, and in 1896 he became head of the newly-created department of music at Columbia University, remaining there until 1904 when ill-health brought about his resignation. His works include four symphonic poems; two *Indian Suites* for orchestra; two piano concertos, two *Modern Suites,* four sonatas and many pieces in smaller forms for the piano; 30 choruses; more than 40 solo songs. After his death, a fund of $50,000 was donated by admirers to found the MacDowell Memorial Association which had its headquarters at Peterborough, N. H., in the summer residence presented by his widow, Marian Nevins MacDowell. Composers, artists, and writers were rented rooms at low rates in order that they might seek inspiration surrounded by the beauties of nature: a music festival held there in 1910 has been repeated many times, and Mrs. MacDowell has financed the association, known as the **MacDowell Colony,** by touring the country playing her husband's works.

MacEwen, Walter (1860-1943), American painter and etcher who was graduated from Northwestern University, Chicago, and studied with Fernand CORMON and Tony ROBERT-FLEURY at Paris. He was awarded many prizes and medals at Munich, Paris, Berlin, Vienna, Philadelphia, and St. Louis: among his notable works to be seen in European and American museums are *Greek Heroes; Judgment of Paris; Sunday in Holland; Lady in White Satin; An Ancestor; The Letter.*

Macgowan, Kenneth (1888-), American dramatic critic, author, and producer educated at Harvard University who acted as dramatic critic for the New York *Globe, Vogue,* and the *Theatre Arts Magazine,* and also directed the Provincetown Players and the Greenwich Village Theatre. Among the successful plays produced under his direction are *All God's Chillun Got Wings; Desire Under the Elms; Twelfth Night; Art and Mrs. Bottle; Springtime for Henry.* He is the author of *The Theatre of Tomorrow* (1921); *Continental Stagecraft* with Robert Edmond JONES; *Masks and Demons* with Herman Rosse; *Footlights Across America,* a study of the LITTLE THEATRE Movement. He has also produced and directed numerous films.

MacGrath, Harold (1871-1932), American novelist who was a journalist before his first book, *Arms and the Woman,* was published in 1899: it was followed by about thirty more among which were *The Puppet Crown; The Grey Cloak; The Man on the Box,* a best seller which was dramatized and filmed; *Half a Rogue; The Goose Girl; The Luck of the Irish; Yellow Typhoon; The Drums of Jeopardy; The Cellini Plaque; The Blue Rajah Murder.*

Machaut, Guillaume de (c.1300-1377), French musician and poet who was in the service of King John of Bohemia for thirty years, and also of King John the Good of France. His poems include *The Taking of Alexandria,* an epic work of 9000 lines, and he also composed motets, songs, ballads, and a mass which was the first of its kind in polyphonic form.

Machen, Arthur (1863-), Welsh novelist and essayist who idolized Thomas DE QUINCY and Walter SCOTT as a youth, published a poem, *Eleusinia,* in 1881, supported himself by making translations from the French, and toured for several years as an actor with the BENSON Shakespearean Repertoire Company. His successful works include *Hieroglyphics* (1902); *The Hill of Dreams; The Bowmen, and Other Legends of the War; The London Adventure; Things Near and Far; Dreads and Drolls; Green House:* he is regarded as a master of literary composition dealing with the supernatural.

Machiavelli, Niccolo di Bernardo (1469-1527), Italian statesman and author who held highly important political and diplomatic offices at Florence from 1498 to 1512 when he was imprisoned tortured, and banished by the MEDICI for conspiracy, but regained his former powers under Pope Leo X. His theory that any means, even if lawless, unscrupulous or deceitful, were justifiable to preserve a government, is the source of the expression "Machiavellian": his notable works include *Il Principe* (The Prince), in which his political views are presented; *La Mandragola,* a comedy; *On the Art of War,* a treatise: also a *History of Florence.*

Machuca, Pedro (?-1550), Spanish architect who designed a palace for Charles II at Granada in the style of the Italian Renaissance also used by the Veronese architect, Michele SANMICHELI. Because of the fact that the interior court of the palace was circular in outline, it was referred to as a bull-ring.

Macip, Vicente Juan (c.1522-1579), Spanish painter known as Juan de Juanes, and frequently referred to as the "Spanish Raphael." He studied with his father, Juan Vicente Macip, a pupil of Fra BARTOLOMMEO: his notable works include a *Last Supper; Baptism of Christ; Conversion of St. Paul.* His series of paintings representing incidents in the life of St. Stephen, reveal a mixture of Flemish, Italian, and Spanish styles.

Mack, Andrew (1863-1931), American actor and singer who first appeared in a vaudeville act, and later with Peter Dailey in *A Country Sport.* After playing in a burlesque of Sheridan's comedy, *The Rivals,* he played with William H. Powers in *Ivy Leaf,* and in 1896 began starring in a series of Irish dramas and comedies including *Arrah-na-Pogue, Myles Aroon,* and *The Ragged Earl:* he also appeared in musical plays such as Sidney JONES' *My Lady Molly* and Sir Arthur SULLIVAN'S *The Mikado.*

Mackaye, Percy (1875-), American author and dramatist; son of Steele MACKAYE and a graduate of Harvard and Leipzig Universities. His first play, *The Canterbury Pilgrims,* was produced in 1903: it was followed by *Jeanne d'Arc,* a tragedy staged by the Sothern-Marlowe Company at Philadelphia in 1906; *The Scarecrow, a Tragedy of the Ludicrous; Anti-Matrimony; St. Louis,* a masque; *Caliban,* a masque; *Wakefield,* a masque; *A Thousand Years Ago,* a comedy. He has also lectured and written essays on the drama, and two volumes of stories from the Kentucky mountains.

Mackaye, Steele (1842-1894), American actor, dramatist, inventor, and producer who first studied art, but later was drawn to the stage, becoming a pupil of François DELSARTE and Henri REGNIER. In 1873 he appeared in *Hamlet* at London, and collaborated with Tom TAYLOR and Charles READE on dramatic works: in 1880 his drama, *Hazel Kirke,* played for two years in New York, and remained in the stock repertory for thirty years. He invented devices for overhead lighting; also the first double or moving stage, and the folding seat for theatres.

Mackenzie, Sir Alexander Campbell (1847-1935), Scottish composer, conductor, and teacher rained at the Sondershausen Conservatory and at he Royal Academy of Music, London, where he ater became director. He conducted the London Philharmonic Society from 1892 to 1899, and was General President of the International Musical Society from 1908 to 1912: his compositions include several operas; overtures and other orchestral works; concertos and suites for violin; chamber music, and many songs.

Mackenzie, Compton (1882-), English novelist and dramatist whose grandfather on his mother's side was Hezekiah Linthicum BATEMAN, an American theatrical producer who presented Henry IRVING in *The Bells* to London audiences at the Lyceum Theatre in 1871. He was educated at Oxford where he was business manager of the Dramatic Society: his numerous works include *The Passionate Elopement* (1911); *Carnival; Youth's Encounter; The Seven Ages of Women; The Darkening Green; The West Wind of Love.* Four of his plays, including a dramatization of *Carnival,* have been produced.

Mackenzie, Henry (1745-1831), Scottish novelist and essayist: his first and most famous work, *The Man of Feeling* (1771) was published anonymously, followed by *The Man of the World, Julia de Roubigné,* and a comedy, *The Prince of Tunis,* produced at Edinburgh in 1773 with success although several others were failures.

Macklin, Charles (c.1698-1797), Irish actor and dramatist who first appeared at the DRURY LANE and the HAYMARKET THEATRES, London, in 1733, finally returning to the Drury Lane where he remained until 1748. He achieved great success as Shylock, Iago, Peachum, and the ghost in Hamlet but was constantly involved in quarrels and lawsuits because of his violent temper. He retired in 1789 because of failing memory: his best plays included *Love à la Mode* (1759) and *The Man of the World.* His daughter, **Mary Macklin,** (c.1734-1781) was a successful actress.

MacLeary, Bonnie (1892-), American sculptor who studied at the ART STUDENTS' LEAGUE, New York, with James Earle FRASER, and at the Académie Julien, Paris. Her notable works include *Aspiration; Ouch!; The Laughing Frog; The Stream of Life; The Blessed Damozel:* also numerous war memorials and monuments.

MacLeish, Archibald (1892-), American poet and dramatist, educated at Yale and Harvard Universities who practiced law before starting on a literary career. His works include *Conquistador,* a narrative poem of the conquest of Mexico which won the Pulitzer Prize in 1933; a ballet, *Union Pacific,* produced by the Monte Carlo Ballet Russe in 1934; a play, *Panic,* produced with Orson WELLES in the leading role; the radio plays *The Fall of the City* and *Panic,* broadcast in 1938. He was appointed Librarian of Congress in 1939.

Maclise, Daniel (1806-1870), Irish painter who studied at the Cork Society of Arts and the Royal Academy, London, winning the gold medal for his *Choice of Hercules,* and attracting considerable

attention with a portrait of Sir Walter SCOTT. He contributed to *Fraser's Magazine* a series of portraits of literary and other celebrities, using the pseudonym "Alfred Croquis," later published as *The Maclise Portrait Gallery:* he also illustrated books by DICKENS and painted many notable pictures including *Meeting of Wellington and Blücher* and *The Death of Nelson; Merry Christmas in the Baron's Hall; Spirit of Justice; The Wild Huntsman.* The Wellington and Nelson paintings on glass are regarded as his masterpieces.

MacMahon, Aline (1899-), American stage and screen actress who made her stage debut in 1921 at New York in *The Madras House:* later she appeared in many plays before entering the films in 1931. Among the numerous pictures in which she has played leading roles are *Five Star Final; The Mouthpiece; One Way Passage; Once in a Lifetime; Babbitt; While the Patient Slept; Ah, Wilderness; Out of the Fog; The Lady is Willing.*

MacMonnies, Frederick William (1863-1937), American sculptor who became an apprentice to Augustus SAINT-GAUDENS, and also studied at the National Academy of Design and the ART STUDENTS' LEAGUE, New York. He went to Paris in 1884 to study at the ECOLE DES BEAUX-ARTS where he worked under Jean FALGUIERE, winning the Studio Prize offered to foreign students. He also worked with Jean Antonin MERCIE, and opened a studio. Among his notable works are *Nathan Hale* in City Hall Park, New York; the *Columbian Fountain* at the Chicago Exposition in 1893; the *Bacchante* at the Metropolitan Museum of Art, New York; *Winged Victory* at West Point; the *Battle Monument* at Princeton, N. J.; *Civic Virtue* at New York; *Army* and *Navy* groups for the Soldiers' and Sailors' Monument, Indianapolis, Ind.; a bust of Thomas HASTINGS, architect of the New York Public Library; three groups of bronze figures for the Soldiers' and Sailors' Monument, and also the *Horse Tamers* in Prospect Park, Brooklyn.

MacMurray, Fred (1908-), American screen actor educated at Carroll College, Wis., who played in dance orchestras, vaudeville, and night clubs before making his film debut in *Roberta:* he has appeared since in *Car 99; Men Without Names; Hands Across the Table; The Bride Comes Home; Alice Adams; Maid of Salem; Café Society; Invitation to Happiness; Honeymoon in Bali; Remember the Night; Virginia; One Night in Lisbon; The Lady is Willing; Take a Letter, Darling; Flight to Freedom.*

MacNeil, Hermon Atkins (1866-), American sculptor who studied with Henri CHAPU and Jean FALGUIERE at Paris, and upon his return to the United States aided Philip MARTINY in creating the models for the Columbian Exposition, Chicago, in 1893. His works include *The Moqui Runner, A Primitive Chant,* and *The Sun Vow,* all figures of American Indians; *Fountain of Liberty* for the St. Louis Exposition; *Moqui Prayer for Rain; Coming of the White Man:* also numerous memorials and monuments. His wife, **Carol Brooks MacNeil** (1871-), is also a distinguished sculptor who studied with Frederick William MacMonnies: she specializes in decorative work and busts of children.

Macpherson, James (1736-1796), Scottish poet who published some fragments of Gaelic verse in 1760 which aroused so much interest that a fund was raised so that he could search for more in the Scottish Highlands. His works include *Poems of Ossian* (1762) which immediately became popular, and were translated into several European languages although several critics, including Samuel Johnson, questioned their authenticity.

Macready, William Charles (1793-1873), English actor who first appeared in 1810 as Romeo at Birmingham, and in 1816 as Orestes in *The Distressed Mother,* an adaptation of Racine's *Andromache* at Covent Garden, London. Later he achieved great success as Richard III, Coriolanus, Hamlet, William Tell, and Virginius. He visited the United States in 1826, Paris in 1828, and managed the Covent Garden and Drury Lane Theatres for several years. In 1843, during his third tour of the United States, he became involved in a feud with Edwin Forrest which ended in the Astor Place riots during which about twenty people were killed.

Macy, John Albert (1877-1932), American critic and biographer educated at Harvard University, later teaching English there and at institutions for the blind and deaf, and also assuming the post of literary editor of the Boston *Herald,* the *Nation,* and of literary advisor to publishers. His best known book is *The Spirit of American Literature* (1913): other works include *Edgar Allan Poe; The Story of the World's Literature; Do You Know English Literature?*

Madach, Imre or **Emerich** (1823-1864), Hungarian poet and dramatist who was imprisoned for participating in the Revolution of 1849: his chief work is *The Tragedy of Man* (1861), a historical drama of man from the time of Adam in the garden of Paradise to the days of the modern commerce-ridden world. It has been performed frequently in Hungarian theatres, and also translated into English.

Madam Butterfly, a grand opera in two acts: libretto by Giuseppe Giacosa and Luigi Illica from the dramatization of John Luther Long's novel by David Belasco; music by Giacomo Puccini; first produced at Milan in 1904; in the United States by the Henry Savage Opera Company in English in 1906, and in Italian at the Metropolitan Opera House in 1907. The story is as simple as it is touching: Lieutenant Pinkerton, an American naval officer, marries a Japanese geisha, Cio-Cio-San, also called "Madam Butterfly" in accordance with Japanese customs. She bears him a child which she has named "Trouble" and patiently awaits his return. When he finally comes back, he is accompanied by his legitimate wife who offers to adopt the child. Madam Butterfly realizes the true situation, and consents to the adoption: when Pinkerton comes for the child he finds that she has committed hara-kiri. There are Columbia and Victor recordings of the complete opera, and various recordings of Butterfly's aria, *One Fine Day,* in Act II.

Madame Sans-Gêne, the nickname at the French court given a former washerwoman for the Gardes Françaises who became the wife of one of Napoleon's Marshals, Pierre François Joseph Lefebvre, later created Duke of Danzig, who married her while he was a sergeant. Unpolished manners, good humor, and ready wit won her the sobriquet "Madame Sans-Gêne": Victorien Sardou made her the heroine of a comedy, *Madame Sans-Gêne,* produced in 1893.

Madame Tussaud, see **Tussaud, Marie.**

Maderna, Carlo (1556-1629), Italian architect and nephew of Domenico Fontana: he was one of the leading exponents of the Baroque style, working with Francesco Borromini and Jacopo Barocchio (Da Vignola) in improving many buildings in Rome including alterations to the nave and adding a colossal façade to St. Peter's. He also began the construction of the Barberini Palace which was completed by Giovanni Lorenzo Bernini.

Madonna, Paintings of, one of the favorite subjects for paintings of religious nature: the earliest representations have been found in the Catacombs and in Byzantine art: among the scenes in the Virgin's life which have been painted are *Madonna in Adoration* by Francia, Reni, and Perugino; *Madonna with Angels* by Cimabue, Francia, Lippi, Mantegna, Michelangelo, and Rubens; *Madonna of the Rose* by Parmigianino, Raphael, Sassoferrato, and Spinelli; *Madonna of the Rosary* by Caravaggio, Domenichino, and Murillo; *Madonna with St. John* by Giulio Romano, Guido Reni, Luini, Perugino, and Solario; *Sistine Madonna* and *Madonna of the Chair* by Raphael; *Madonna of the Cherries* by Annibale Carracci; *Madonna of the Rosary* by Murillo; *Madonna With Saints* by Albani, Albertinelli, Angelica, Bartolommeo, Giovanni Bellini, Annibale Carracci, Ludovico Carracci, Cima, Credi, Dosso Dossi, Francia, Garofalo, Ghirlandaio, Giorgone, Gozzoli, Guido Reni, Lippi, Lotto, Mantegna, Montagna, Murillo, Perugino, Romanino, Il Rosso, Rubens, Sarto, Sodoma, Tintoretto, Titian, and Veronese.

Madrazo y Agudo, José de (1781-1859), Spanish painter who studied at the Madrid Academy and was a pupil of Louis David in Paris, later becoming director of the Madrid Academy, and thereby influencing modern Spanish art through his own and his pupils' work. Among his notable paintings are *Jesus at the House of Ananias; Allegory of Spring; Death of Lucretia; Allegory of Winter;* also portraits of King Charles IV and Queen Maria Louisa of Spain. His son, **Federico Madrazo y Kunt** (1815-1894), studied with his father, and with Franz Winterhalter at Paris, later becoming professor at the Madrid Academy, and one of the founders of *El Artista,* an art magazine. His notable works include *Women at the Sepulchre;* a portrait of Queen Isabella; *Matinée Musicale; Godfrey Bouillon Proclaimed King of Jerusalem.* His brother, **Luis de Madrazo** (1825-1897), studied with his father, and is famous for the picture, *The Burial of St. Cecilia:* his son, **Raimundo de Madrazo** (1841-?), studied at the Ecole des Beaux-Arts, Paris, and with Leon

Cogniet: among his notable works are *Andalusian Singer; The Gypsy; End of a Masked Ball; Pierrette; Nocturne; The Domino.*

Madrid, the capital city of Spain which contains many ancient buildings and museums of interest to lovers of architecture, painting, and sculpture: among them are the Palacio Real (Royal Palace) containing a superb collection of more than 2000 tapestries; the Armeria in which is the world's greatest collection of armor; the Prado, a museum housing over 2000 paintings most of which are of the highest order; the *Biblioteca Nacional* (National Library) which contains important collections not only of books, manuscripts, and documents, but also of modern painting and sculpture.

Madrigal, in music a short composition for three or more voices without instrumental accompaniment, differing from the motet in being secular in nature. The form developed in the Netherlands and Italy during the 14th, 15th, and 16th centuries, and became extremely popular with English composers of the Elizabethan period, continuing well into the 18th century. Madrigals were first harmonized like hymn tunes, but later were set in complex counterpoint. Among the celebrated composers in this form were Willaert; Lassus; Palestrina; Monteverdi; Frescobaldi; Byrd; Morley: the Madrigal Society, founded in 1741 in England, is still in existence.

Maecenas, Caius Cilnius (c.67-8 B.C.), Roman patron of the arts, and of ancient Etruscan ancestry, who was entrusted with the control of Rome by Octavian while the latter was away from the city. He was intimate with Horace, Vergil, and other men of letters: his munificence was so great that "Maecenas" has become a synonym for any generous patron of the arts.

Maelzel, Johann Neopomuk, see **Metronome.**

Maes (or **Maas**) **Nikolaas** (1632-1693), Dutch painter who studied with Rembrandt, and worked at Dordrecht where he painted genre pictures which give distinct evidence of his master's influence. Later, while on a visit to Antwerp, his portraits reveal the influence of Van Dyck: among his best creations are *Children with a Goat Cart; The Cradle; Dutch Housewife; The Eavesdropper; Saying Grace; Killing Hogs.*

Maestoso (It.), in music an expression indicating that the composition is to be played in majestic or dignified style.

Maestro (It.), in music a term first applied to the conductor of an orchestra who directed while playing the harpsichord instead of using the baton: it was also used to designate a choirmaster or the leader of a chorus and orchestra. For years it has been applied to Arturo Toscanini as a token of respect.

Maeterlinck, Maurice (1862-), Belgian poet and dramatist who was educated at a Jesuit College and at the University of Ghent: he also was trained in and practiced law. His drama, *La Princess Maleine* (1889), was compared with Shakespeare by Octave Mirbeau, and he wrote several other plays, one of which, *Pelléas et Mélisande,* was the basis for Claude Debussy's opera with the same title. Other works include *The Death of Tintageles; The Blue Bird; The Wrack of the Storm; The Treasure of the Humble; The Buried Temple; The Life of the Bee; The Life of the Ant; Pigeons and Spiders.*

Maffei, Francesco Scipione (1675-1755), Italian man of letters who became interested in the improvement and development of dramatic art in Italy through the intimacy with Antoine François Riccoboni, an Italian actor and dramatist: his works include a successful tragedy, *Merope* (1713), a collection of small pieces for dramatic presentation entitled *Italian Theatre,* and a comedy, *The Ceremony.*

Magazines, Art, see **Art Magazines.**

Magazines, Theatrical, see **Theatrical Magazines.**

Magdalen, Paintings of, a subject chosen by many of the greatest painters of religious subjects and scenes: among them Allori, Bronzino, Annibale Carracci, Calabrese, Claude Lorrain, Correggio, Dolci, Domenichino, Guercino, Guido Reni, Murillo, Rubens, Tintoretto, Titian, Van Dyck, Veronese, and more than twenty distinguished artists.

Maggini, Giovanni Paolo (1580-1632), Italian violin maker who studied at the workshop of Gasparo da Salo whose instruments he imitated until the development of his own model which is compared favorably with those of Stradivarius and Guarnerius. The varnish is usually reddish-brown to orange, and his violins command prices ranging from $1000.00 to $3500.00.

Magi, a priestly caste in ancient Medea and Persia who preached the doctrines of Zoroaster. They are said to have believed in the advent of a saviour which accounts for the use of the word *magi* in the Vulgate, a 4th century version in Latin of the Scriptures: the words "wise men" are employed in the Authorized and Revised version of the Bible.

Magi, Adoration of, a subject which has been portrayed by many of the world's greatest painters including Allori, Bassano, Botticelli, Cambiaso, Credi, Durer, Garofalo, Fabriano, Francia, Ghirlandaio, Leonardo da Vinci, Lippi, Murillo, Poussin, Raphael, Rembrandt, Rubens, Sodoma, Tintoretto, Titian, Velasquez, Veronese, Vivarini, and more than twenty other artists.

Magic, the art of wonder working which is dependent on the aid of supernatural powers such as demons, angels, spirits or the secret forces of nature. It has existed since the advent of the most primitive religions, and was banned when Christianity began its rise. *Black magic* was forbidden because it caused death or injury for those on whom it was practiced: *white magic,* the term applied to legerdemain, was permitted, and many persons including Robert Houdin, Herman Keller, Madame Herrmann and her famous husband,

Harry Houdini, Horace Goldin, Fred Keating, and John Mulholland, have become famous in the theatre for their skill in all phases of conjuring.

"Magic Fire" Music (Wagner), the music used in the final scene of Act III of Richard WAGNER's *The Valkyrie,* the second of the four music dramas known as *The* RING OF THE NIBELUNGS. The scene is divided into two dramatic and musical episodes: I. *Wotan's Farewell to Brünnhilde* in which the god, having decreed that his daughter shall lie in charmed sleep protected by magic flames until she is awakened by the kiss of a hero, sorrowfully bids farewell to his child: II. The *Magic Fire Scene* in which Wotan stretches forth his spear, summons the fire-god, Loge, and surrounds the sleeping Brünnhilde with a barrier of crackling flames. There is a Victor recording of the entire scene with Lawrence TIBBETT as Wotan, accompanied by the Philadelphia Orchestra: also a Victor recording of the *Magic Fire* music also played by the Philadelphia Orchestra.

Magic Flute, The, grand opera in two acts: libretto by Emanuel SCHIKANEDER; music by Wolfgang Amadeus MOZART; first produced at Vienna in 1791; in English at the Park Theatre, New York, in 1833; in Italian at the Metropolitan Opera House in 1900. It has always been a matter of wonder that Mozart was able to write music of such extraordinary beauty for so inane a libretto: there is a Victor recording of the complete opera, and both Columbia and Victor recordings of the overture.

Magrath, William (1838-1918), American painter born in Ireland who came to the United States as a youth of seventeen and was made a member of the National Academy in 1876: his notable works include *On the Old Sod; Road to Kenmair; Rustic Courtship; Paddy on His Own Land; Sheep Pasture; Courtyard with a Donkey; Wilds of Connemara.*

Mahler, Fritz (1902-), Austrian conductor and composer nephew of Gustav MAHLER, who studied with Alban BERG and Arnold SCHONBERG: after conducting broadcasts in Berlin and the Copenhagen Symphony Orchestra he made his American debut with the Columbia Broadcasting Orchestra in 1936. He has conducted the Bridgeport Symphony Orchestra, the Philadelphia Civic Symphony Orchestra, and many orchestras of the Federal Music project: his works include a symphonic poem, chamber music, songs, and an analysis of Alban Berg's opera, WOZZECK.

Mahler, Gustav (1860-1911), Bohemian pianist, conductor, and composer who studied at the University of Vienna, with Julius Epstein, and with Anton BRUCKNER. After conducting opera at Prague, Leipzig, Hamburg, and Vienna, he assumed the post of chief conductor at the METRO-POLITAN OPERA HOUSE, New York, in 1908, and conductor of the NEW YORK PHILHARMONIC-SYMPHONY ORCHESTRA in 1909, retiring in 1911 because of ill-health. His works include nine symphonies, several song cycles with orchestra, and arrangements of operas by WEBER and MOZART.

Maid of Orleans, see **Joan of Arc.**

Maillol, Aristide Joseph Bonaventure (1861-), French sculptor who first studied painting at the ECOLE DES BEAUX-ARTS, Paris, with Alexandre CABANEL, and later became interested in the art of Paul GAUGUIN. He also experimented with his own materials and dyes in tapestry making, and did not exhibit any sculptures until 1896. He is inspired chiefly by works of ancient Greek and Roman sculptors in such pieces as *Flora; Pomona; Venus:* in many respects his art possesses the simple nobility and greatness of its antique models.

Maillot (Fr.), in ballet the name of the standardized undergarment worn by classical dancers: the name is presumably derived from that of a famous hosier to the Opéra, Paris, during the early part of the 19th century.

Main, Marjorie, contemporary American stage and screen actress who appeared on the legitimate stage and in vaudeville for several years before entering the films. Since 1937 she has played character parts in *Crime Without Passion; Stella Dallas; Girls' School; Under the Big Top; There Goes My Heart; They Shall Have Music; The Women; Dark Command; Susan and God; The Captain is a Lady; The Trial of Mary Dugan; A Woman's Face; We Were Dancing.*

Maitre de Ballet (Fr.), in ballet the man who trains the corps du ballet, and is responsible for the technical excellence of its performance: if a woman assumes the post she is known as the *maîtresse de ballet.*

Majano, Benedetto da (1442-1497), Italian sculptor and architect who studied with his brother, **Giuliano da Majano** (1432-1490) also an architect and carver of decorative work. Among Benedetto's notable works are the tomb of St. Savinus in the Cathedral at Faenza; the pulpit in the Church of Santa Croce at Florence; the black and white marble tomb of Filippo Strozzi in the Church of Santa Maria Novello at Florence: he also worked on the Strozzi Palace in Florence.

Majolica, a term applied to certain kinds of Italian and Spanish faïence produced first during the 13th century in Valencia, and later at Faenza and Florence where it was known as DELLA ROBBIA WARE. The collection of J. P. Morgan at New York is considered the finest in the world.

Major, Charles (1856-1913), American novelist who practiced law during his entire career except when attending the Indiana Legislature. His successful works include *When Knighthood Was in Flower* (1898); *Dorothy Vernon of Haddon Hall; Yolanda, Maid of Burgundy; A Gentle Knight of Old Brandenburg; Little King; The Touchstone of Fortune.*

Major, in musical theory a term meaning "greater," and therefore opposed to minor, meaning "lesser." It is primarily employed in the designation of INTERVALS: seconds, thirds, sixths, and sevenths are called *major.* It is also applied to CADENCES, CHORDS, TRIADS, SCALES, and MODES.

Makart, Hans (1840-1884), Austrian painter who distinguished himself in the field of historical painting: he was influenced by the masters of the Venetian school, and also by RUBENS. Among his notable pictures are *Catarina Cornaro; The Seven Deadly Sins; The Plague at Florence; Entry of Charles V into Antwerp; Romeo and Juliet; Dream after the Ball; Diana's Hunting Party; Cleopatra.*

Make-up, the term applied to the use of cosmetics in order to correctly reproduce a character in acting. A base of cold cream is used to protect the skin, and facilitate the removal of the make-up: colored grease paint is then applied in the shade desired, and lighter or darker colored grease paints are used to bring out the highlights and shadows, the final blending effected with face powder specially prepared for the purpose.

Makimono or **Kakemono,** in Japanese art a painting on paper, usually rolled in a scroll which opens horizontally for inspection.

Malaprop, Mrs., in drama a character in Richard Brinsley SHERIDAN's comedy, *The Rivals:* she is noted for her mistakes in the use of words: hence the term *malapropism* to designate the misuse of a word.

Malbone, Edward Greene (1777-1807), American painter, chiefly self-taught, who specialized in miniatures. He worked successfully in several American cities and visited London in 1801 with Washington ALLSTON. His best-known work, *The Hours,* representing the present, past, and future by female figures was purchased from his heirs for $1,200, and is now in the Providence (R.I.) Athenaeum.

Male, Émile (1862-   ), French historian of art who became director of the École française de Rome in 1925: his most distinguished contribution to the literature of art, published in French in 1923 and later in English as *Religious Art in France, XIII Century,* undertakes to prove that the sculptures in the great cathedrals of the Middle Ages depicted scenes with definite historical significance.

Malherbe, Charles Theodore (1853-1911), French music critic and composer originally trained for the law who studied later with Andre WORMSER and Jules MASSENET. He contributed many articles to French musical papers, and composed several operas, ballets, and orchestral works: his writings include discussions of works by WAGNER, MASSENET, SAINT-SAENS, and TSCHAIKOWSKY. He acted as archivist for the Paris Opéra for many years, and made an extraordinary collection of musical autographs which he bequeathed to the Paris Conservatory.

Malibran, Maria Felicita (1808-1836), French dramatic contralto; daughter of Manuel GARCIA, a famous Spanish tenor and composer. She appeared in a child's part in Paër's opera, *Agnese,* at five, and made her formal debut in 1825 as Rosina in *The Barber of Seville,* appearing in New York the same year with such marked success that she remained for two seasons. Later she achieved equal favor in Rome, Naples, Bologna, Milan, and Paris where she received a sal-

ary of 50,000 francs. She was married a short time before her death to the famous French violinist, Charles de BERIOT, and also composed many piano pieces and songs.

Ma' Lien-liang, contemporary Chinese actor ranked among the greatest interpreters of male parts at the Peiping Theatre not only for his sensitive delivery, but also in respect to his attainments as a mimic.

Malipiero, G. Francesco (1882-   ), Italian composer who studied with Enrico BOSSI at Venice and with Max BRUCH: since 1921 he has taught composition and musical history at the Parma Conservatory and the University of Padua. He received the COOLIDGE Chamber of Music Prize, and the Coolidge medal for eminent services rendered to chamber music. His compositions include numerous operas, ballet-dramas, and ballets; chamber music; orchestral works; concertos for violin and for violoncello; piano pieces and songs.

Malko, Nikolai Andreievitch (1883-   ), Russian conductor who studied at the University of St. Petersburg and with Nicholas RIMSKY-KORSAKOW, Anatol LIADOFF, and Alexander GLAZUNOFF. He conducted the State Opera, St. Petersburg, the Leningrad Philharmonic Orchestra, the State Radio Orchestra, Copenhagen: in 1940 he became lecturer at the De Paul University school of Music, Chicago, and has acted as conductor of the BOSTON SYMPHONY ORCHESTRA and several broadcasting orchestras.

Mallarmé, Stephane (1842-1898), French poet who taught English in a French college: his poem, *L'Aprés-midi d'un faune* (Afternoon of a Faun), written in 1876, was the inspiration of Claude DEBUSSY's orchestral tone poem *Prelude to the Afternoon of a Faun* first performed in 1894. He translated the poems of Edgar Allan POE, and his *Poésies complètes* were published in 1887, and again in enlarged form in 1899.

Malmaison, a château near Versailles, France, built by the Empress Josephine before her marriage to NAPOLEON I. She occupied it after her divorce, and the emperor was painted in one of his most characteristic poses with the château as a background. Queen CHRISTINA of Spain and the Empress Eugenie, wife of Napoleon III, also lived in it.

Malone, Edmund (1741-1812), Irish lawyer and Shakespearean scholar who was intimate with Dr. Samuel JOHNSON, James BOSWELL and Sir Joshua REYNOLDS. He was closely connected with the exposure of Thomas CHATTERTON and wrote a history of the English stage, but his life-work was an edition of Shakespeare published in 1790, and the collection of the material for the *Variorum Shakespeare* which was completed after his death by James Boswell.

Malory, Sir Thomas, see **Morte d'Arthur.**

Malraux, André (1895-   ), French novelist educated at the Lycée Condorcet and at the School of Oriental Languages, Paris. His works available in English include *The Conqueror* (1929); *Man's Fate; The Royal Way; Days of Wrath; Man's*

Hope. In 1934 Malraux claimed to have discovered and photographed the site of the legendary city of the Queen of SHEBA located within a vast desert north of Ruba-al-Khali, and beyond the Strait of Bab-el-Mandeb.

Maltz, Albert (1908-), American dramatist educated at Columbia University, and at the Drama School of Yale University under George Pierce BAKER. His plays include *Merry-Go-Round* (1931), a satire on Tammany Hall written in collaboration with George Sklar; *Peace on Earth; Black Pit; Private Hicks.* He has also written short stories and scenarios for films.

Mammon, a word in the Semitic language used in the New Testament to signify riches: in John Milton's PARADISE LOST it is used as a proper name for the demon of cupidity in the famous lines: "Ye cannot serve God and Mammon."

Mamoulian, Rouben (1898-), Russian stage and screen director educated at the Lycée Montaigne, Paris, and the University of Moscow. After producing *The Beating on the Door* at the St. James Theatre, London, in 1924 he came to the United States as producer at the EASTMAN Theatre, Rochester, N. Y., of *Carmen, Faust, Boris Godunoff.* In 1927 he became producer for the THEATRE GUILD of *Porgy, Marco Millions, Farewell to Arms, Wings Over Europe, R.U.R., Porgy and Bess.* Among the films which he directed are *Dr. Jekyll and Mr. Hyde; Song of Songs; Queen Christina; We Live Again; Becky Sharp; High Wide and Handsome; Golden Boy; Blood and Sand.* In 1943 he directed the stage production of *Oklahoma* for the Theatre Guild.

Mana-Zucca (1890-), American composer, singer, and pianist who studied with Alexander LAMBERT, Leopold GODOWSKY, and Ferruccio BUSONI, making her debut as a child prodigy in 1899 with the New York Symphony Orchestra. In 1914 she appeared as a soprano in the leading role of LEHAR'S operetta, *The Count of Luxembourg,* and later assumed light opera parts in New York productions. She has also appeared as singer and pianist in the interpretation of her piano and vocal compositions.

Mander, Karel van (1548-1606), Flemish painter and author of *Het Schilderboeck,* a biographical work narrating the lives and commenting on the paintings of early Flemish, Dutch, and German artists. A painting of his own creation is said to contain likenesses of William SHAKESPEARE and Ben JONSON: other works include *Decorated Shield; The Deluge.*

Mandolin or **Mandoline,** a musical instrument of the lute family; of Italian origin, and so-called because its body resembles an almond (It. *mandorla*) in shape. The Neapolitan mandolin has four pairs of strings, and the Milanese has five or six pairs of strings. The compass is about three octaves, the finger board is equipped with frets, and the instrument is played with a plectrum made of tortoise shell, whalebone, or other flexible material. MOZART used the mandolin effectively for accompanying the "Serenade" in his opera, *Don Giovanni.*

Mandorla, in painting or sculpture anything having the shape of an almond (It. *mandorla*): it is used as the term for the AUREOLE surrounding sacred figures which in Western art is usually almond-shaped, and is also found in Christian art of the 4th century.

Manén, Joan de (1883-), Spanish violinist and composer who studied with Delphin ALARD, appeared with great success as a virtuoso, and later taught at institutions in Barcelona, Valencia, and Madrid. His compositions include several operas; two violin concertos, and other works for violin; a symphonic poem; chamber music: he also completed the unfinished sketches made by Ludwig van BEETHOVEN for a violin concerto.

Manet, Édouard (1832-1883), French painter who served as a cabin boy on a voyage to Brazil, studied with COUTURE, copied works of the masters in the LOUVRE, and visited Holland, Germany, and Italy, but finally evolved a style of his own in a painting, *Spaniard Playing a Guitar* which, when exhibited at the Paris Salon in 1861, aroused a storm of criticism which lasted to a certain extent throughout his career. Among his works, defended by such great artists as WHISTLER, Legros, HARPIGNIES, and FANTIN-LATOUR, are *Child With Cherries; Absinthe Drinker; Déjeuner sur l'herbe; Angels at the Tomb; Incident at a Bullfight; The Fight; Boy With a Sword; Woman With a Parrot; Olympia; Dead Toreador; Fife Player; Tragic Actor; The Balcony; Argenteuil; The Opera Ball; Bar at the Folies-Bergère.* He also painted several portraits, among them that of Émile ZOLA, one of his champions.

Manfred (c.1232-1266), a natural son of Emperor Frederick II of Germany who seized the throne of Naples and Sicily after the death of his brother, Conrad, in 1254. He exercised considerable power until his army was defeated and he himself killed at Benevento by Charles of Anjou. Lord BYRON wrote a drama, *Manfred,* which inspired incidental music from the pen of Robert SCHUMANN, written in 1848 and comprising sixteen numbers. It was performed at Weimar in 1852, and the *Overture* to Manfred is now regarded as one of Schumann's most inspired works: there is a Victor recording by the British Broadcasting Company Orchestra directed by Adrian Boult. Another distinguished composer, Peter TSCHAIKOWSKY, found inspiration in Byron's drama: the resulting work is his symphonic poem, *Manfred,* first performed at Moscow in 1886, and during the same year by the New York Philharmonic Orchestra under the baton of Theodore Thomas. There is a Victor recording by the Indianapolis Symphony Orchestra conducted by Fabien SEVITZKY.

Manhattan Opera Company (New York), an organization owned and financed by Oscar HAMMERSTEIN, first presented at the Manhattan Opera House, New York, in 1906. Among the celebrated singers who were members of the company at various times were Alessandro BONCI, Maurice Renaud, Emma CALVE, Nellie MELBA, Mary GARDEN, Charles DALMORES, Luisa TETRAZZINI, and John McCORMACK: the artistic director was Cleofonte CAMPANINI. Among the novelties presented were DEBUSSY's *Pelléas et Mélisande*, MAS-SENET's *Thaïs, Hérodiade, Sapho,* and *Griselidis;* Richard STRAUSS' *Elektra* and *Salome;* CHARPEN-TIER's *Louise.* The company played for four seasons, giving a total of 463 performances of 49 operas: its rivalry with the METROPOLITAN OPERA COMPANY led to the payment of $1,200,000 in 1910 to Hammerstein in consideration of his agreement to cease giving operatic performances in New York for a period of ten years. He attempted to evade the contract by building the Lexington Avenue Opera House at New York in 1931, but was restrained by a court order.

Manhattan Opera House, see **Manhattan Opera Company.**

Man in the Iron Mask, The, the name given a political prisoner at the BASTILLE in Paris during the reign of LOUIS XIV whose identity has never been disclosed. VOLTAIRE claimed that he was an illegitimate brother of Louis XIV, son of Cardinal MAZARIN and Anne of Austria: DUMAS, PERE, made him the twin brother of Louis XIV in his novel, *The Man in the Iron Mask.* It is now generally believed that the prisoner was either Count Mattioli, or a commoner named Eustache Dauger. According to Bénigne d'Auvergne de Saint Mars, the governor of the Bastille, the mask worn by the unknown prisoner was of black velvet, transformed into iron by legend.

Mann, Thomas (1875-), German novelist who published his first inspiration, a poem, for a school paper called *Spring Storm:* his works include *Buddenbrooks* (1901) a novel which sold more than a million copies before it was banned by the Nazis, and was translated into several languages; *Death in Venice; Tonio Kroger; The Magic Fountain; Joseph and His Brothers; Young Joseph; Joseph in Egypt; The Beloved Returns; The Transposed Heads; A Sketch of My Life,* an autobiography: also novelettes and short stories. He came to the United States in 1938.

Mannering, Mary (1877-), English actress who made her debut in 1892 at Manchester, England, in *Hero and Leander* with Mrs. James Brown POTTER and Kyrle BELLEW: among the plays in which she appeared were *The Late Mrs. Costello; The Courtship of Leonie* in which she made her American debut in 1896 under the management of Daniel FROHMAN at the Lyceum Theatre, New York; *Trelawney of the Wells; The Ambassador; Glorious Betsy; Janice Meredith; Step by Step; The Truant; Kiddie; A Man's World; The Garden of Allah.* For several seasons she toured as joint star with her husband, James K. HACKETT.

Manners, Charles (1857-1935), Irish singer and opera impresario who studied at the Royal Academy of Music, Dublin: after winning success with the D'Oyly CARTE Company in GILBERT AND SULLIVAN operettas and singing at the COVENT GARDEN Opera, he founded the **Moody-Manners Opera Company** with his wife, Fanny Moody (1866-), as principal soprano. The repertory at first consisted of lighter operas including *Faust, Martha,* and *Maritana,* but was enlarged to include WAGNER's music dramas in English. The

company appeared with great success for many years at London and throughout the British provinces.

Manners, John Hartley (1870-1928), English dramatist who first appeared as an actor in 1898: his numerous plays include *A Queen's Messenger; As Once in May; The Girl in Waiting; The Crossways; The House Next Door; The Woman Intervenes; Peg O' My Heart,* his greatest success in the United States; *A Marriage of Reason; The Day of Dupes; One Night in Rome; The National Anthem.*

Mannes, David (1866-), American violinist and conductor who studied with Karl Halir and Eugene YSAYE, finally becoming concertmaster of the NEW YORK SYMPHONY ORCHESTRA under Walter DAMROSCH whose daughter, Clara Damrosch, he married in 1898. He founded his own string quartet, directed the Music School Settlement in New York, and opened his own music school which has been operating continuously since 1916. He has given many fine sonata recitals with his wife, and has conducted the free symphonic concerts at the METROPOLITAN MUSEUM OF ART since 1919. In 1938 he published *Music is My Faith,* an autobiography.

Manon, grand opera in four acts; libretto by Henri Meilhac and Philippe Gille based on the Abbé PREVOST's romance, *The Story of Manon Lescaut;* music by Jules MASSENET; first produced at the OPERA-COMIQUE, Paris, in 1884; at the ACADEMY OF MUSIC, New York, in 1885, and at the METROPOLITAN OPERA HOUSE in 1895. The story is: Des Grieux, a young student, falls in love with Manon, mistress of De Bretigny. They elope but Des Grieux's father compels him to leave her and he becomes a novitiate at a monastery. Manon persuades him to elope again with her: they visit a gambling house where Des Grieux is accused of cheating and both are arrested. Des Grieux is freed, but Manon is sentenced to deportation. When Des Grieux arranges to rescue her on the road to Havre, she dies in his arms. There is a Columbia recording of the complete opera, and many recordings of the two favorite tenor arias, *Le Reve* and *Ah! fuyez, douce image.*

Manon Lescaut, a grand opera in four acts; libretto founded on the Abbé PREVOST's romance, *The Story of Manon Lescaut:* music by Giacomo PUCCINI; first produced at Turin in 1893, and at the METROPOLITAN OPERA HOUSE in 1907 with Enrico CARUSO in the role of Des Grieux and Lina CAVALIERI as Manon. The plot with slight variations, is the same as that of MASSENET's *Manon:* there is a Columbia recording of the complete opera.

Manrico, a character in Giuseppe VERDI's grand opera, *Il Trovatore:* he is reputedly the son of a gypsy, AZUCENA, and the rival of Count di Luna for the affections of LEONORA. After he is captured by the count, and burned at the stake, Azucena reveals his real identity as the brother of the count.

Mansart or **Mansard, François** (1598-1666), French architect who invented the mansard roof designed to make attics available for rooms: he also built several fine churches and many hotels, châteaux, and private residences in and around Paris. His grand-nephew, **Jules Hardouin Mansart** (1646-1708), son of a painter named Julius Hardouin, assumed the name of his grand-uncle, and became a famous architect who worked at VERSAILLES, Chantilly, and Saint Cyr, also building the Church of the Invalides: his career rivaled that of Charles LE BRUN in brilliant accomplishment.

Mansfield, Katherine (1890-1923), pen name of **Kathleen Beauchamp**, English short story writer born at Wellington, New Zealand, who was educated at Queen's College, London, and also became an excellent violoncellist. She lived for many years in France in a struggle against tuberculosis: her short-story collections include *In a German Pension* (1911); *Bliss; Prelude; The Garden Party; The Dove's Nest; The Little Girl:* also poems and an autobiography. Her short story, *The Fly*, is considered one of the world's greatest works in its class.

Mansfield, Richard (1857-1907), American actor who was the son of Madame Hermine RUDERSDORFF: he studied painting and first appeared in GILBERT AND SULLIVAN operettas in both England and the United States. His first success was in 1882 as Baron Chevrial in *A Parisian Romance* with A. M. PALMER's Union Square Theatre Company: among the plays in which he revealed himself as one of the greatest actors on the American stage were *Dr. Jekyll and Mr. Hyde; Prince Karl; Beau Brummel; Cyrano de Bergerac; Arms and the Man; Peer Gynt;* Molière's *Le Misanthrope.*

Manship, Paul (1885-), American sculptor who studied with Solon BORGLUM at New York, and at the PENNSYLVANIA ACADEMY OF FINE ARTS under Charles GRAFLY and Isadore KONTI, winning a scholarship in 1909 at the American Academy at Rome. His notable works include a relief of his daughter, *Pauline*, at the Metropolitan Museum of Art, New York; *Centaur and Dryad; Indian and Pronghorn Antelope; Dancing Girl and Fauns; Little Brother:* also a gate at the Bronx Zoo, New York, in memory of Paul J. Rainey.

Mantegna, Andrea (1431-1506), Italian painter who was the adopted son and pupil of the distinguished scholar SQUARCIONE: in the latter's studio he came in contact with Ansuino da Forli, Marco Zoppo, DONATELLO, Filippo LIPPI, and Paolo UCCELLO: later in life he met Jacopo BELLINI whose daughter became his wife. Mantegna evolved his own style from the works he studied, creating an impressive, uncompromising reality of atmosphere in his numerous works which include *Dead Christ; St. Anthony of Padua; St. Euphemia; Parnassus; Allegory of Virtue and Vice; St. Sebastian; Mount of Olives; Resurrection of Christ; Adoration of the Magi; Death of the Virgin; St. George; Judith With the Head of Holofernes; The Infancy of Jesus; Triumph of Julius Caesar,* a series of nine cartoons; *Baptism of Christ.* He was a great engraver as well as the most important painter of the early RENAISSANCE in Italy.

Mantell, Robert Bruce (1854-1928), Scotch-American actor who played in an amateur production of *Hamlet* at sixteen, and appeared with Dion Boucicault in 1876 and with Helena MODJESKA in the United States in 1878. His first success was in 1883 as Jack Hearn in *Romany Rye*, a part originally created by Wilson BARRETT: during the same year he supported Fanny DAVENPORT in SARDOU's *Fedora*. Among the plays in which he starred were *Monbars; The Corsican Brothers; The Lady of Lyons:* he was pre-eminent in roles such as Richard III, King Lear, King John, and Macbeth, and is regarded as the last of the great actors in the 19th century Shakespearean tradition.

Mantle, Burns (1873-), American dramatic critic and author who has been dramatic editor of the Denver *Times*, Chicago *Tribune*, New York *Evening Mail*, New York *Daily News* successively. His works include *American Playwrights of Today* (1929); *Contemporary American Playwrights*. He has edited *Best Plays* and *Year Book of the Drama* since 1919; *Best Plays of 1909-1919* with Garrison P. Sherwood; *A Treasury of the Theatre* with John P. Gassner.

Manual, in music the term for a set of keys played with the hands, used chiefly in connection with the organ to distinguish the keyboards for the hands from those played by the feet. There are usually from two to five manuals in accordance with the size of the organ and the number of its stops.

Manuscript, in literature or music a composition of any kind written by hand; also the author's copy, either handwritten or typed, from which the printer sets the type and prints the work. In ancient days manuscripts were written on sheets of PAPYRUS made from the pith of the sedge plant by the Egyptians, Greeks, and Romans: this was followed by PARCHMENT produced from the skins of sheep and goats. PAPER was invented by the Chinese about 100 A.D.: its manufacture by hand began in Europe about the year 1200, and by machinery in 1800. ILLUMINATED MANUSCRIPTS were made by the Egyptians and by monastic organizations in the Middle Ages.

Manzoni, Alessandro (1785-1873), Italian poet, novelist, and dramatist who went to Paris as a boy with his mother, and imbibed much of French literary opinion and atmosphere. His greatest success was a novel, *I Promessi Sposi* (1827), which was translated into several languages and used as the basis for grand operas by five composers including Amilcare PONCHIELLI: other works include *The 5th of May*, an ode on the death of NAPOLEON I; *The Count of Carmagnola* and *Adelchi*, two dramas written in the style of Shakespeare. The Italian composer, Giuseppe VERDI, wrote a requiem in memory of Manzoni which was first performed at the Milan Cathedral in 1874.

Mapleson, Colonel **James Henry** (1830-1901), English impresario who began his career in 1861 at the Lyceum Theatre, London, with the production of Italian opera: he also conducted seasons at HER MAJESTY'S THEATRE, the DRURY LANE THEATRE, the COVENT GARDEN THEATRE, and in the United States at the ACADEMY OF MUSIC, New York, from 1878 to 1886, and in 1896-7. He is credited with having introduced Emma ALBANI, Clara Louise KELLOGG, Emma NEVADA, Emma ABBOTT, Lillian NORDICA, Emma JUCH, Annie Louise CARY, Minnie HAUK, Christine NILSSON, Lilli LEHMANN, and Italo CAMPANINI to American and English audiences. His son, **Henry Mapleson** (1851-1927), was associated with his father in the management of the Drury Lane and Covent Garden Theatres.

Mapleson, Lionel S. (1865-1937), English music librarian who was the son of Alfred Mapleson, secretary and librarian to Queen Victoria, and nephew of Colonel James Henry MAPLESON. After playing the violin in Hans RICHTER'S Orchestra for fourteen years, he joined the orchestra at the METROPOLITAN OPERA HOUSE as violist, and later became librarian, retaining the post until his death when he was succeeded by his son, Alfred J. Mapleson. He made a collection of musical mementos which includes letters, programs, autographed pictures, recordings of actual performances, caricatures of CARUSO, and scores of all operas produced at the Metropolitan since 1883, which are housed in the library of the opera house.

Mapu, Abraham (1808-1867), Hebrew author whose works are chiefly historical novels including *The Love of Zion* and *The Transgression of Samaria* written in Hebrew, and in a simple classical style which had a lasting influence on later Hebrew authors. Several of his works have been translated into English and other languages.

Maratti or **Maratta, Carlo** (1625-1713), Italian painter who was appointed court painter to Louis XIV, and after he restored RAPHAEL'S frescoes in the Vatican was given the post of curator: his notable works include *Hagar and Ishmael; Holy Night; Adoration of the Shepherds; Presentation in the Temple; Apollo in Search of Daphne; Madonna Appearing to St. Philip.*

Marble, the name applied to any limestone capable of being highly polished, suitable for architectural or sculptural uses, and available in many colors from white to black. It is quarried in all parts of the world, the chief modern sources of supply being Great Britain, Belgium, France, Germany, Italy, and the United States where it is found in several states, but chiefly in Vermont. The purest form is *statuary marble* which is snow-white in color, and used by the ancient Greeks under the names *Parian* and *Pentelic.* The Romans and Italians obtained their marble from CARRARA and SIENA.

Marc Antony, see **Antony, Marc.**

Marceline or **Marcelline** (1873-1927), Spanish clown who appeared for many years at the New York Hippodrome in the various spectacles produced there: he committed suicide in 1927. He was one of the most remarkable pantomimists of all time especially in respect to the spontaneity of his mimicry.

March, Frederic (1897-   ), American stage and screen actor educated at the University of Wisconsin who made his debut at New York in 1920 in David BELASCO'S presentation of *Deburau*, later appearing in numerous plays including *Tarnish; The Silver Cord; The Guardsman; Mr. Pim Passes By; Liliom; Saturday's Children; The Royal Family; The American Way.* Since 1929 he has played leading roles in many films including *The Sign of the Cross; Dr. Jekyll and Mr. Hyde; Design For Living; Death Takes a Holiday; The Barretts of Wimpole Street; The Dark Angel; Les Miserables; Anna Karenina; A Star is Born; Mary of Scotland; The Buccaneer; Susan and God; Bedtime Story; I Married a Witch.*

March, in music a composition in martial rhythm first exemplified in works such as the Welsh 15th century war song, *March of the Men of Harlech*, and later in the operas of LULLY, HANDEL, and RAMEAU: also in suites for the harpsichord by François COUPERIN. The German *Parade March* is an excellent example of the military march for use in actual marching: in America John Philip SOUSA'S marches are well-known, and the funeral march is best represented by the *Funeral March* in CHOPIN'S Piano Sonata, Op. 35.

Marche Militaire (Schubert), a military march in D major; one of a set of three marches composed for piano duet by Franz SCHUBERT. It was transcribed effectively for piano solo by Carl TAUSSIG, a pupil of Franz LISZT: there are Victor and Columbia recordings available for piano duet, piano solo, orchestra, and band.

Marchesi, Blanche (1863-1940), French soprano who studied with her mother, Mathilde MARCHESI, and violin with Artur NIKISCH and Édouard COLONNE. She made her debut as a concert singer at Berlin in 1895, touring Europe and England with great success: her first operatic appearance was made in 1900 as Brünnhilde in WAGNER'S *The Valkyrie*, later singing with the MOODY-MANNERS Company at COVENT GARDEN. She made concert tours of the United States in 1899 and 1909, and after her retirement in 1938 became a distinguished singing teacher.

Marchesi, Mathilde (1826-1913), German concert singer and vocal teacher who studied with Manuel GARCIA, made many successful concert tours, finally becoming instructor of voice at the Vienna Conservatory, the Cologne Conservatory, and in Paris. Her pupils included Etelka GERSTER, Nellie MELBA, Emma EAMES, Emma CALVE, Sibyl SANDERSON, and Blanche MARCHESI, her daughter. She published several volumes of memoirs.

Marchesi, Pompeo (1789-1858), Italian sculptor whose works include a statue of Emperor Francis I of Austria at Vienna, and a colossal group, *Mater dolorosa*, at the Church of San Carlo, Milan.

Marche Slav (Tschaikowsky), an orchestral work by Peter Ilich TSCHAIKOWSKY composed in 1876 and first played at a concert given for the benefit of soldiers wounded in the war between

Turkey and Serbia. There is a Columbia recording by the Cleveland Orchestra under Artur RODZINSKI, and a Victor recording by the Philadelphia Orchestra directed by Leopold STOKOWSKI.

Marcin, Max (1879-), American playwright educated at the College of the City of New York, who worked as a reporter on New York newspapers before turning to play writing: his successful plays include *See My Lawyer* (1915); *The House of Glass* with George M. COHAN; *Cheating Cheaters; Here Comes the Bride* with Roy ATWELL; *The Woman in Room 13* with Samuel SHIPMAN; *The Nightcap* with Guy Bolton; *Three Live Ghosts*. He has also written the scenarios and acted as director or co-director of numerous films.

Maréchal, Charles Laurent (1801-1887), French painter who worked on glass and porcelain as well as in water colors, executing many works for French churches and cathedrals in Cambrai, Limoges, Nîmes, and Paris: other notable paintings include *Washerwomen; Masaccio as a Child; Columbus Brought Back from the New World;* decorative works in the Ministry of State. His son, Charles Raphaël Maréchal, also became a distinguished genre painter.

Maréchal, Maurice (1892-), French violoncellist who studied at the Paris Conservatory, taking first prize for violoncello playing in 1911, and appearing later at the Concerts Lamoureux, Societé des Concerts, and Societé Philharmonique. He has toured Europe and the United States with great success.

Marées, Hans von (1837-1887), German painter whose creations have been compared with those of the French artist, PUVIS DE CHAVANNES. Among his notable works are allegorical frescoes for the library of the Zoological Museum at Naples; *The Hesperides; Three Ages of Life; St. Martin; St. George.*

Maretzek, Max (1821-1897), German vocal teacher, composer, and opera impresario who came to New York in 1848 as conductor for William Henry FRY: from 1849 to 1878 he managed opera companies in the United States, Havana, and Mexico. He composed the operas *Hamlet* and *Sleepy Hollow:* the latter was produced at the ACADEMY OF MUSIC, New York, in 1879.

Margo (1917-), Mexican stage and screen actress whose real name is Maria Margharita Bolado: she first appeared as a child dancer in Mexico City and later as dancing partner for George RAFT. In 1935 she made her debut on the legitimate in *Winterset,* also playing in *The Masque of Kings, Seventh Heaven,* and Max REINHARDT'S production of *Faust.* Among the films in which she has appeared are *Crime Without Passion; Rumba; Robin Hood of Eldorado; Winterset; The Lost Horizon.*

Marguerite, a character in Charles GOUNOD'S grand opera, *Faust:* after being betrayed and deserted by Faust at the instigation of Mephistopheles, she is cast into prison. Faust visits her in the company of Mephistopheles, and begs her return to him, but she calls upon the Almighty, and is borne up to Heaven as Faust descends to hell.

Marie Antoinette, see **Antoinette, Marie.**

Marin, John (1870-), American painter who studied at the PENNSYLVANIA ACADEMY OF FINE ARTS, the ART STUDENTS' LEAGUE, New York, and also at Paris. In 1909 Alfred Stieglitz became his patron, and he developed into one of America's greatest water-colorists. His paintings are unintelligible to those who do not understand that the emphasis is on some special effect with minor figures and objects distorted in order to draw attention to the main idea. His pictures are to be seen at the Museum of Modern Art, New York, and the Phillips Memorial Gallery, Washington, D. C.

Marine Band, The, see **United States Marine Band.**

Mario, stage name of **Giovanni de Candia** (1810-1883), Italian operatic tenor who studied at the Paris Conservatory and made his debut in 1838 at L'Opéra in *Robert le Diable:* his success was instantaneous, and he appeared at the Italian Opera in Paris, and also in Russia and the United States. He was married to Giulia GRISI with whom he was constantly associated on the operatic stage: he also toured successfully as a concert artist and retired in 1867.

Mario, Queena (1896-), American operatic soprano who studied with Oscar SAENGER and Marcella SEMBRICH, making her debut with the SAN CARLO OPERA COMPANY in 1919 at New York, and in 1922 with the Metropolitan Opera Company in *Carmen.* She also sang with the SAN FRANCISCO OPERA COMPANY, and succeeded Marcella Sembrich as teacher of voice at the CURTIS INSTITUTE OF MUSIC, Philadelphia.

Marionettes, the name given to figures, usually smaller than life-size, which are suspended by threads or wires and are manipulated so that the figures imitate the motion of human beings with their limbs and heads. Figures of this kind with movable limbs were used in Egypt, Greece, India, and China: both GOETHE and LESSING had a high regard for them. The early dramatic plays for marionettes in England were based on incidents from the BIBLE: the eminent stage producer, Gordon CRAIG, developed the marionette or puppet play into an art form.

Maris, Jacob (1837-1899), Dutch painter who studied at the Antwerp Academy and with Ernest HEBERT at Paris, later specializing in domestic scenes and interiors in which he painted windmills, bridges, wharves, and towers: among his notable works are *Grey Tower at Old Amsterdam; Sea-weed Carts at Schevéningen; Landscape at Dordrecht; Village Scene.* His brother, **Matthys Maris** (1839-1917), was also a genre and landscape painter who worked in London: among his fine creations are *The Cake Baker; Revery; The Bride; The Four Windmills.* Another brother, **Willem Maris** (1844-1910), made a specialty of scenes in Holland in which cattle were a feature.

Marke, King, a character in Richard WAGNER's music drama, *Tristan and Isolde:* he sends his nephew, the knight TRISTAN, to bring his promised bride, Isolde, to him: the pair fall in love, and the opera ends with the death of both Tristan and Isolde to the intense grief of King Marke who has come to extend his forgiveness.

Markham, Edwin (1852-1940), American poet who first worked as a farmhand and later became superintendent of schools in Southern California after graduating from Santa Rosa College. A magazine reproduction of Jean François MILLET's painting *The Man with the Hoe* inspired Markham's poem with the same title which made him immediately famous, and was translated into many languages. His works include *Lincoln and Other Poems; The Shoes of Happiness; California the Wonderful; Gates of Paradise; The Ballad of the Gallows Bird; New Poems: Eighty Songs at Eighty; California in Song and Story; Poetry of Youth.*

Markova, Alicia (1910-), English ballet dancer who joined the DIAGHILEFF Ballet in 1924 while studying with Enrico CECCHETTI and Nicholas LEGAT. She also appeared with the Ballet Club, for the CAMARGO SOCIETY, the Marie RAMBERT Ballet, the VIC-WELLS Ballet, and with the Markova-Dolin Ballet as *prima ballerina.* In 1938 she became a member of the BALLET RUSSE DE MONTE CARLO, and is now (1943) with the BALLET THEATRE, New York. She is said to resemble Anna PAVLOWA, and is the possessor of jewelry once worn by the famous Russian dancer.

Marlowe, Christopher (1564-1593), English poet and dramatist educated at Cambridge: little is known of his life except that he lived in London and was killed in a street fight or tavern brawl. His important plays include *Tamburlaine* (1590); *The Tragedy of Dr. Faustus; The Jew of Malta; Edward II:* he is said to have collaborated with others on *The Massacre at Paris* and *The Tragedy of Dido.* His poetical works include *Hero and Leander,* a paraphrase of the original work by the Greek poet, MUSAEUS; also the poem, *Come Live with Me and Be My Love.*

Marlowe, Julia (1866-), American actress born in England whose real name was Sarah Frances Frost: she came to America with her parents, in 1875, and first appeared in 1878 with a juvenile opera company in *H.M.S. Pinafore.* Her debut in 1887 as Parthenia in *Ingomar* was a pronounced success: among the plays in which she appeared were *Barbara Frietchie; When Knighthood Was in Flower; Jeanne d'Arc.* After her marriage to Edward H. SOTHERN in 1911 she became a distinguished interpreter of Shakespearean roles including Rosalind, Ophelia, Viola, and Juliet: in 1926 they presented several of Shakespeare's plays at Stratford-on-Avon.

Marmontel, Antoine François (1816-1898), French pianist and teacher who studied with Pierre ZIMMERMAN at the Paris Conservatory and succeeded the latter as professor of piano in 1842, remaining until 1887. His distinguished pupils included GUIRAUD, DUBOIS, d'INDY, and BIZET: he also wrote several interesting critical and historical treatises about the piano.

Marochetti, Carlo, Baron (1805-c.1868), French sculptor born in Italy who studied at Rome and Paris, becoming a French citizen in 1841. His notable works include a statue of *Richard Coeur de Lion* at London; a bas-relief, *Battle of Jemmapes,* on the ARC DE TRIOMPHE at Paris; equestrian statues of Queen Victoria, the Duke of Wellington and George Washington, the last-named having been destroyed; the tomb of Napoleon at Paris.

Marot, Clément (1497-1544), French poet who first studied law: through his father, who had been poet at the court of Queen Anne of France, he secured Marguerite de Valois as his patron, and gained favor with Francis I by his poems, *The Temple of Cupid* and *Hell.* He accompanied the king on his military expeditions, and wrote much original verse in addition to translating parts of works by VIRGIL, OVID, and PETRARCH.

Marquand, John Phillips (1893-), American short-story writer and versatile novelist, educated at Harvard, who first worked as a reporter. His novels include *The Unspeakable Gentleman* (1922); *Four of a Kind; Black Cargo; Lord Timothy Dexter; Ming Yellow; Thank You, Mr. Moto; The Late George Apley; Wickford Point; H. M. Pulham, Esquire; So Little Time.*

Marquetry, in architecture a form of decoration which consists of placing pieces of wood, bone, ivory, brass, tortoise-shell, mother-of-pearl or other materials in juxtaposition: it was first introduced in Holland and France during the 16th and 17th centuries. Jean Mace, a Frenchman and André Charles BOULLE, the famous French cabinet maker, were the greatest masters of the art: it was applied to all kinds of furniture, choir stalls, musical instruments, and marriage chests.

Marquis, Don (1878-1937), American novelist, poet, and dramatist whose full name was Donald Robert Perry Marquis: he worked as an editorial writer on The Atlanta *Constitution,* and was encouraged by Joel Chandler HARRIS to attempt original, creative writing. In 1912 he began the "Sun Dial" column in the New York *Sun* and later the "Lantern" column in the New York *Tribune.* His works include *Cruise of the Jasper B* (1916); *Hermione; The Old Soak; Noah an' Jonah an' Cap'n John Smith; The Old Soak's History of the World; Archy and Mehitabel; Love Songs of a Cave Man.*

Marr, Carl (1858-1936), American painter who studied at Munich and Berlin, and became a professor in the Munich Academy: his notable works include *Ahasuerus, the Wandering Jew; Episode of 1813; Germany in 1806; Gossip; The Flagellants; Summer Afternoon.*

Marriage of Figaro, The, grand opera in four acts: libretto by Lorenzo DA PONTE after BEAUMARCHAIS' comedy, *Le Marriage de Figaro;* music by Wolfgang Amadeus MOZART; first produced at Vienna in 1786. It was first presented at New York in 1799 renamed "The Follies of a Day," and in several other English versions up to 1858 when it was performed at the ACADEMY OF MUSIC in Italian: in 1894 it was produced at the METRO-POLITAN OPERA HOUSE in Italian. The plot revolves around the cleverness of Figaro, valet to Count Almaviva, in frustrating the latter's amorous designs on Susanna, his wife's maid. When the Countess becomes aware of the situation, she aids Cherubino, the Count's page, Susanna, and Figaro in outwitting the Count: he finally permits the marriage to proceed. There is a Victor recording of the complete opera: also a Columbia recording of the overture by the London Philharmonic Orchestra directed by Sir Thomas Beecham, and a Victor recording by the Minneapolis Symphony Orchestra under Eugene Ormandy.

Marryat, Frederick (1792-1848), English naval officer and novelist who became a commander in 1815, and was on duty at the St. Helena Naval Station when NAPOLEON I died. Among his successful novels were *Peter Simple* (1834); *Mr. Midshipman Easy; Snarley-yow or the Dog Fiend; Masterman Ready.* His daughter, **Florence Marryat** (1838-1899), published a life of her father in 1872, wrote several novels, and edited the magazine, *London Society,* for several years.

Mars, in Roman mythology the god of war, identified with the Greek deity, ARES. He was the most important deity of the Roman state after Jupiter, and was honored with two great temples in Rome. He was the father of ROMULUS and REMUS, and the third month of the year was named after him.

Mars, Mlle. (1779-1847), French actress whose full name was Anne Françoise Hyppolyte Boutet: she first played children's parts, and joined the COMEDIE-FRANCAISE in 1799, becoming an important member of the company for thirty-three years, and creating more than one hundred comedienne and ingenue roles. She was an outstanding interpreter of parts written by MOLIERE and BEAUMARCHAIS, retiring in 1841 with the best wishes of Parisian theatre-goers for her declining years.

Marseillaise, La, the French national anthem; both words and music written by Claude ROUGET DE L'ISLE during the night of April 24, 1792. It was first called "Chant de guerre de l'armée du Rhin," and renamed *La Marseillaise* after being sung with great success by a band of soldiers from Marseilles. During the Restoration its singing was forbidden.

Marsh, Howard, contemporary American singer and actor who appeared with stock companies, and achieved remarkable success in 1924 as Prince Karl in Sigmund Romberg's operetta, *The Student Prince.* He also appeared in *Blossom Time, Maytime,* and *Sari.*

Marsh, Ngaio (1899-), New Zealand author of detective stories educated at St. Margaret's College and the Canterbury University College School of Art: her works include *A Man Lay Dead* (1934); *Enter a Murderer; Death in Ecstasy; Vintage Murder; Artists in Crime; Death in a White Tie; Overture to Death; Death at the Bar; Death of a Peer; Death and the Dancing Footman.*

Marsh, Reginald (1898-), American painter educated at Yale University who studied at the ART STUDENTS' LEAGUE with Kenneth Hayes Miller; and has made many cartoons and illustrations for *Vanity Fair* and the *New Yorker Magazine.* He specializes in street scenes and interiors of homes on the East Side of New York City, utilizing many figures. Examples of his work are in the Metropolitan Museum of Art and the Whitney Museum of Art: he has also executed frescoes in the Custom House, New York, and the Post Office, Washington, D. C.

Marshall, Archibald (1866-1934), English novelist educated at Cambridge University: his numerous works include *Peter Binney, Undergraduate* (1899); *The House of Merrilees; The Squire's Daughter; The Eldest Son; The Honor of the Clintons; Exton Manor; Anthony Dare; The Education of Anthony Dare; The Lady of the Manor; The Claimants.* His novels are classed among the finest of those which treat of English country life.

Marshall, Charles (1887-), American dramatic tenor who studied with William L. WHITNEY, and later in Italy with Luigo Vannuccini and Giuseppe Lombardi, making his debut at Florence with the stage name, Carlo Marziale, in 1906. In 1919 he made his American debut at Philadelphia in the title role of VERDI's *Otello,* appearing during the same year at Chicago in the same role which also served as his introduction to New York audiences with the Chicago Civic Opera Company. His repertory included Arnold in *William Tell,* Canio in *Pagliacci,* Enzo in *La Gioconda,* and numerous other heroic roles.

Marshall, Edison (1894-), American explorer and novelist: his works include *The Voice of the Pack* (1920); *The Snowshoe Trail; The Land of Forgotten Men; Seward's Folly; The Far Call; The Splendid Quest; White Brigand.*

Marshall, Herbert Brough Falcon (1890-), English stage and screen actor educated at St. Mary's College who made his debut in 1913 on the London stage in *Brewster's Millions,* and subsequently accompanied Cyril MAUDE on a tour of the United States in *Grumpy.* After serving in World War I he won a high reputation in several plays including *Aren't We All?; The Pelican; Michael and Mary; Interference; There's Always Juliet.* Among the numerous films in which he has appeared are *I Was a Spy; Four Frightened People; Riptide; The Good Fairy; Accent on Youth; The Lady Consents; Mad About Music; Zaza; A Bill of Divorcement; Foreign Correspondent; The Letter; The Little Foxes; When Ladies Meet; The Moon and Sixpence.*

Marshall, Tully (1864-1943), American stage and screen actor, real name William Phillips, who first appeared as a child actor in 1869, and made his mature debut in 1883 at the Winter Garden, San Francisco, in *Saratoga.* He appeared for more than sixty years in more than 250 plays with Dion BOUCICAULT, Helena MODJESKA, Edward H. SOTHERN, Fanny DAVENPORT, and Margaret MATHER: his greatest success was in Clyde FITCH's *The City* in 1909. In 1915 he began his career in the silent films, appearing in *The Covered Wagon; The Merry Widow; The Torrent; The Cat and the Canary; He Who Gets Slapped; Alias Jimmy Valentine.* When talking films appeared he adapted himself readily to the new technique, and played leading roles in *The Thunderbolt; Tiger Rose; Conquest; The Bridge of San Luis Rey; The Mysterious Dr. Fu Manchu; Arsène Lupin; Black Fury; A Tale of Two Cities; A Yank at Oxford; Arsène Lupin Returns; This Gun For Hire; Moontide.* In 1899 he married Marian Neiswanger, well known under the name of "Marian Fairfax" as a dramatist and screen writer. Mr. Marshall has been called the "grand old man" of both the stage and the screen.

Marsick, Martin Pierre Joseph (1848-1924), Belgian violinist and composer who studied at the Liége Conservatory, and with Hubert Leonard, Joseph Massart, and Joseph Joachim. After his successful debut at Paris in 1873, he toured Europe for many years and America in 1895. He became professor of violin at the Paris Conservatory in 1892: among his pupils were Karl Flesch and Jacques Thibaud. His compositions include three concertos and many concert pieces for the violin.

Marston, John (c.1575-1634), English dramatist educated at Oxford, and embroiled in unending quarrels for years with Ben Jonson and Thomas Dekker. His works include a poem, *The Metamorphosis of Pygmalion's Image; The Scourge of Villany*, three books of satires: also several plays including *The Malcontent; Antonio and Mellida; Antonio's Revenge; The Dutch Courtezan; What You Will; Parasitastu; Sophonisba.* In 1607 he became a clergyman and was the rector of Christchurch, Hampshire, for fifteen years.

Marsyas, in Greek mythology a deity who symbolizes the art of flute playing. Athena, who invented the flute, discarded it because it distorted her face when she played it: Marsyas found it and challenged Apollo for a lute and lyre playing contest in which the latter was declared victor by Midas. Marsyas is supposed to have had his ears changed to those of a donkey, or to have been flayed alive. The contest and the punishment were favorite subjects for ancient Greek painters and sculptors.

Marteau, Henri (1874-1934), French violinist and composer who studied with Hubert Leonard and Jules Garcin at the Paris Conservatory, appearing at ten with the Vienna Philharmonic Orchestra under Hans Richter. He made many successful tours of Great Britain, Europe and the United States. From 1900 he was head of the violin departments in the Geneva Conservatory, the Berlin Hochschule, and the Leipzig Conservatory. He also organized an outstanding string quartet, and composed an opera, a symphony, two violin concertos, chamber music, and many miscellaneous works.

Martens, Frederick Herman (1874-1932), American author of books on music and librettist: his works include a biography of Leo Ornstein (1917); *Violin Mastery; The Art of the Prima Donna; String Mastery; One Thousand and One*

Nights of Opera; Book of the Opera and Ballet. In 1930 his poem, *America,* was used as the text for a prize winning national anthem with music by Leo Ornstein.

Martha, grand opera in four acts: libretto by Wilhelm Friedrich; music by Friedrich von Flotow; first produced at Vienna in 1847; in English at Niblo's Gardens in 1852; at the Metropolitan Opera House in 1884. The plot revolves around Lady Harriet and her maid, Nancy, who hire themselves out at the Richmond Fair in England to the young farmers, Lionel and Plunkett, who promptly fall in love with them. Lady Harriet, after scorning Lionel's love, escapes, but when he turns out to be the rightful Earl of Derby she wins his love back by singing again *The Last Rose of Summer,* the ballad which she originally sang when at the farmhouse. There are numerous recordings of the favorite tenor aria, *M'appari* (Ah, 'Tis a Dream), and of the folksong, *The Last Rose of Summer.*

Martin, Edward Sandford (1856-1939), American author educated at Harvard University, and one of the founders of the *Lampoon,* and in 1883 of *Life Magazine.* His works include *Slye Ballads in Harvard China* (1882); *Windfalls of Observation; Lucid Intervals; The Courtship of a Careful Man; Reflections of a Beginning Husband; What's Ahead, and Meanwhile.*

Martin, Helen Reimensnyder (1868-1939), American short story writer and novelist educated at Swarthmore and Radcliffe Colleges: her works include *Tillie, a Mennonite Maid* (1904); *Sabina, a Story of the Amish; The Crossways; Barnabetta* which was dramatized as *Erstwhile Susan; The Snob; The Lie; Yoked with a Lamb; The Ordeal of Minnie Schultz.*

Martin, Homer Dodge (1836-1897), American painter who worked at drafting in an architect's office before taking some lessons of James Mac-Dougal Hart. He opened a studio in New York where he painted in the style of the Hudson River School, but after visits to England and France he was influenced by the Barbizon School: his works of note include *View on the Seine; Lower Ausable Pond; Harp of the Winds; Sand Dunes at Lake Ontario; White Mountains; Adirondack Scenery.*

Martin, John (1789-1854), English painter who studied with an Italian artist, Bonifacio Musso, and supported himself by painting on china and glass. His notable works include *Sadak in Search of the Waters of Oblivion; Paradise; Clytie; Belshazzar's Feast; Fall of Babylon; The Judgment; Eve of the Deluge; Creation; Destruction of Herculaneum; Death of Moses; Fall of Nineveh.*

Martin, John (1893-), American dance critic, author, and a member of the faculty of the New School for Social Research, New York. His works include *The Modern Dance* (1933); *America Dancing; Introduction to the Dance.* He has contributed articles on the dance to American encyclopedias, and is now (1943) dance critic for the New York *Times.*

Martin, Riccardo, stage name of **Hugh Whit-field Martin** (1878-), American dramatic tenor who studied singing and the piano at New York, and prepared for an operatic career with SBRIGLIA at Paris, making his debut in 1904 at Nantes in *Faust,* and his first American appearance in 1906 with the SAN CARLO OPERA COMPANY in *Pagliacci.* He sang with the Metropolitan Opera Company from 1907 to 1913, also appearing at Covent Garden, London, and with the Boston and the Chicago Opera Companies.

Martinelli, Giovanni (1885-), Italian dramatic tenor who made his operatic debut in 1910 at Milan in *Ernani,* later appearing successfully at Rome, Naples, Turin, Monte Carlo, Budapest, Brussels, London. In 1913 he made his debut at the Metropolitan Opera House, New York, in *La Bohème,* and in 1938 celebrated his twenty-fifth anniversary with the organization by appearing in Verdi's *Otello.* He made his first appearance in 1939 in Wagner's *Tristan and Isolde* with Kirsten FLAGSTAD as Isolde with the Chicago Civic Opera Company.

Martinez de la Rosa, Francisco de Paula (1789-1862), Spanish statesman and dramatist who took part in the struggle against NAPOLEON I, and was banished to North Africa in 1814, but recalled and appointed prime minister in 1820. His works include a tragedy, *Oedipus;* a drama, *The Venetian Conspiracy;* a comedy, *The Daughter at Home and the Mother at a Ball;* also poetry, the historical novels, *Hernán Pérez del Pulgar* and *Dona Isabel de Soles,* and a history of the French Revolution.

Martinez Sierra, Gregorio (1881-), Spanish dramatist, novelist, and poet educated at Madrid University who became interested in the drama through his friend, Jacinto BENAVENTE. His works include *The Cradle Song* (1911); *Love Song; Love Magic; The Lover; Theatre of Dreams; The Shadow of the Father; The Friend of the House; Anna Maria; The Road to Happiness; Spring in Autumn; The Kingdom of God; Madame Pepita.*

Martin-Harvey, Sir John (1863-), English actor and manager who made his debut at the Court Theatre, London, under John Clayton, and appeared later with Sir Charles WYNDHAM and Sir Henry IRVING, remaining with the latter for many years and accompanying him on his American tours. In 1899 he produced *The Only Way,* adapted from Charles DICKENS' *Tale of Two Cities* in which he achieved fame as Sidney Carton: he toured Great Britain, Canada, and the United States in this play and also in *The Corsican Brothers; The Bells; A Cigarette Maker's Romance; David Garrick; Hamlet; Richard III:* in the eyes of many theatre-goers he became the logical successor of Sir Henry Irving.

Martini, Giambattista (1706-1784), Italian composer and theorist known as "Padre Martini": he studied with his father, and took holy orders in 1729. Among his pupils were GLUCK, MOZART, GRETRY, and JOMMELLI: Dr. Charles BURNEY says that he acquired a library of 17,000 volumes. His works include a valuable history of music, sacred music, and several sonatas: a gavotte of his creation is a popular violin piece today, but it has not been recorded.

Martini, Nino (1905-), Italian operatic tenor who studied with Maria GAY and Giovanni ZENATELLO, making his debut at Milan in *Rigoletto.* In 1931 he made his first appearance in the United States with the Philadelphia Opera Company in *Rigoletto,* and in 1933 his debut at the Metropolitan Opera House in the same opera. He has also appeared successfully as a radio and film star.

Martini, Simone, see **Simone di Martino.**

Martinot, Sadie (1861-1923), American actress and singer who first appeared at fourteen on the New York stage, later becoming a member of the Boston Museum Stock Company. Among the operettas and plays in which she was featured were PLANQUETTE's *Rip Van Winkle;* Genée's *Nanon;* AUDRAN's *The Mascot; Diplomacy; Rosedale; A Stranger in New York; The Turtle; The Marriage Game; The Second Mrs. Tanqueray; Mary and John; Mrs. Templeton's Telegram.*

Martiny, Philip (1858-c.1927), American sculptor born in France who studied in Paris: his important works include the decoration of the Agricultural Building at the World's Columbian Exposition at Chicago; the grand staircase in the Library of Congress, Washington, D. C.; the *Fountain of Abundance* at the Buffalo Pan-American Exposition: also bronze doors for St. Bartholomew's Church, New York. He also designed several war memorials and monuments.

Marvel, Ik, see **Mitchell, Donald Grant.**

Marvenga, Ilsa, contemporary German actress who created the part of Kathie in Sigmund ROMBERG's operetta, *The Student Prince,* in 1924, playing the part 1300 times: she also appeared in *Naughty Marietta, The Firefly, The Great Lover,* and *May Wine.*

Marx, Adolf Bernhard (1795-1866), German musical theorist and composer who first trained for the law at the University of Halle, but also studied composition with Karl ZELTER. He founded the *Berliner allgemeine musikalische Zeitung* with Heinrich Schlesinger, and became music director at the Berlin University in 1832. He was intimate for a time with Felix MENDELSSOHN, and composed numerous musical works which are not as important as his treatises on composition and the theory of music.

Marx Brothers, The, a quartet of screen and radio actors who first appeared in a vaudeville act, *Six Musical Mascots,* with their mother and aunt, all four being excellent musicians, later known as *The Four Nightingales* and finally as the *Four Marx Brothers.* Their films include *The Cocoanuts; Animal Crackers; Monkey Business; Horsefeathers; Duck Soup; A Night at the Opera; A Day at the Races; At the Circus; Go West; The Big Store.* Groucho (Julius) Marx is also a well-known radio comedian.

Masaccio (1401-c.1428), Italian painter whose real name was Tommaso Guidi: he was known as Masaccio because of his indifference to his personal appearance. He is said to have studied with MASOLINO DA PANICALE, and despite the fact that he died at about twenty-six, founded a new style of fresco painting imitated by artists who succeeded him in respect to composition, treatment of draperies, and naturalism. Among his notable works are *Adoration of the Magi; Virgin Enthroned; Four Saints; Crucifixion; Expulsion from Paradise; Tribute Money; Peter and John Healing the Sick; Raising of the King's Son,* completed by Filippino LIPPI; *Trinity with Two Donors; Death of the Baptist.*

Masaniello, a grand opera in four acts also known as *La Muette de Portici (The Dumb Girl of Portici)*: libretto by Eugene SCRIBE; music by Daniel AUBER; first produced at L'Opéra, Paris, in 1828; at the Park Theatre, New York, in 1831, and at the Metropolitan Opera House in 1885. The overture is still a popular concert and radio selection: there are both Victor and Columbia recordings.

Masanobu, Kano (1453-1490), Japanese painter who established the Kano School which was made famous by his son, Kano MOTONOBU, and flourished for more than three hundred years. He worked chiefly in ink as court painter for the shogun Yoshimasa, specializing in landscapes, birds and figures.

Mascagni, Pietro (1863-), Italian dramatic composer trained at the Milan Conservatory who won the publisher, Edward Sonzogno's prize for a one-act opera, *Cavalleria Rusticana,* which created a sensation at its première in Rome in 1890: it was his only real success despite the fact that he wrote almost twenty dramatic works. In 1902 he made an unsuccessful tour of the United States, but was received favorably on a similar visit to South America in 1911. He was one of the pioneers in the composition of brief, exciting, and veristic operas.

Masefield, John (1875-), English poet, dramatist, and novelist who spent part of his youth at sea, and worked at various jobs before he began a literary career which culminated in his being created poet laureate of England in 1930. His poems include *Salt-Water Ballads* (1902); *Everlasting Mercy; The Widow in the Bye Street; The Daffodil Fields; Sonnets and Poems.* Among his novels are *Multitude and Solitude* and *Sard Harker:* his plays include *The Tragedy of Nan; The Tragedy of Pompey the Great; Good Friday; The Locked Chest; The Trial of Jesus; Tristan and Isolt.*

Mask, a covering for the face or head used as a disguise; first employed in Greek tragedy and comedy, passing later into the Roman theatre and finally into the COMMEDIA DELL' ARTE. Masks were used in ancient Chinese drama, by savages in Africa and Australia, and in America by the Indians. The making of death masks by the ancient Egyptians and Romans was a highly developed art: the latter used thin gold plate, but the modern mask is made of plaster of Paris.

The term is applied at the present time to face coverings used in industry and war where protection is needed against poisonous gases, heat, light, or air pressure.

Masolino da Panicale (1383-c.1447), Italian painter whose real name was Tommaso di Cristofano di Fino: he was the teacher of MASACCIO who undoubtedly acquired his conscientious attention to detail and skill in figure arrangement from Panicale. Among his notable works are *Madonna and Child with Angels; Preaching of Peter; Fall of Adam and Eve; Madonna and Christ in Glory; Raising of Tabitha; Julian Killing His Parents.*

Mason, Daniel Gregory (1873-), American composer and writer on musical subjects who studied with Clayton Johns, Ethelbert NEVIN, John K. PAINE, Percy GOETSCHIUS, George W. CHADWICK, and Vincent D'INDY. He has lectured on music extensively, and was connected with the music department of Columbia University from 1909 to 1940. His compositions include several symphonies, chamber music, piano pieces and songs: among his books are *From Grieg to Brahms; Beethoven and His Forerunners; The Romantic Composers; The Orchestral Instruments; A Guide to Music; Great Modern Composers; The Chamber Music of Brahms; Music in My Time.*

Mason, Edith (1892-), American dramatic soprano who studied with Victor MAUREL and Edmond CLEMENT, and sang with great success in Nice and Paris before joining the Boston Opera company in 1912 and the Metropolitan Opera Company, New York, in 1915. She has also appeared at Covent Garden in London, La Scala in Milan, and at the SALZBURG FESTIVALS under Arturo TOSCANINI.

Mason, Lowell (1792-1872), American composer, organist, and conductor who was chiefly self-taught. He published a collection of hymns in 1822, and was successful in establishing music as a part of the studies in Boston public schools in 1836. His many collections of church music brought him a large income, and several of his hymns including *Nearer, My God, To Thee; My Faith Looks Up To Thee,* and *From Greenland's Icy Mountains* are among the most beloved in the hymnals.

Mason, Van Wyck (1897-), American novelist, full name Francis Van Wyck Mason, who was educated at Harvard University: his numerous works include *Seeds of Murder* (1930); *Yellow Arrow Murders; Shanghai Bund Murders; Sulu Sea Murders; Murder in the Senate; Captain Nemesis; Stars on the Sea; Rivers of Glory.*

Mason, William (1829-1908), American pianist, teacher, composer, and son of Lowell MASON, who studied with Ignaz MOSCHELES, Hans RICHTER, and Franz LISZT, toured Europe and finally settled in New York where he founded the *Mason and Thomas Soirèes of Chamber Music* with Theodore THOMAS. He composed many solo pieces for the piano, wrote a treatise entitled *Touch and Technic,* and for many years was regarded as the most distinguished American teacher of the piano.

Mason & Hamlin Company, a firm of piano manufacturers founded as an organ making company by Henry Mason, son of Lowell MASON, and Emmons Hamlin. It introduced the American cabinet organ in 1861, and after winning many prizes at expositions in Europe and the United States, began the manufacture of pianos in 1882, incorporating various improvements in resonance which imparted an individual singing quality to the tone. In 1940 it became a subsidiary of the Aeolian-American Corporation.

Masque or **Mask,** a form of dramatic entertainment greatly favored in England during the reigns of James I and Charles I: it consisted of spectacular dramas on allegorical subjects accompanied by both instrumental and vocal music, and elaborate in costumes and appointments. Among the famous writers of masques were Ben JONSON, Francis BEAUMONT, and John MILTON. They were usually performed in the open air at court or at private residences: Inigo JONES was celebrated for his scenic designs in connection with masques.

Mass, the name given to the celebration of the Eucharist (Lord's Supper) in the Roman Catholic church. The term is derived from the Latin word, Missa, in the phrase, "Ite, missa est" meaning "Depart, the congregation is dismissed," addressed to persons not taking part in the Eucharist. There are two types of Mass: the *Low Mass,* celebrated without music, and the *High Mass* accompanied by music and incense. There are six main divisions to the musical Mass: *Kyrie; Gloria; Credo; Sanctus; Benedictus; Agnus Dei.* The *Requiem Mass* omits the *Gloria* and *Credo,* substituting the *Dies irae* which has eighteen stanzas. A number of masses have been written which do not follow the liturgical form: they include BEETHOVEN'S *Missa Solemnis* and the *Requiems* of BERLIOZ, DVORAK, and BRAHMS.

Mass in B Minor (J. S. Bach), a work by Johann Sebastian BACH following the text of the Reformation mass arranged by Martin LUTHER. It was probably composed about 1733, but not published until 1845, and the first complete performance was given at the Berlin Sing-akademie in 1834: much of the material was taken from Bach's cantatas. There is a complete Victor recording by the Royal Choral Society and the London Symphony Orchestra directed by Albert Coates.

Massart, Joseph Lambert (1811-1892), Belgian violinist who studied with Rodolphe KREUTZER at Paris, and later became professor of violin at the Paris Conservatory. He numbered many famous violinists among his pupils, among them Henri WIENIAWSKI, Pablo de SARASATE, and Martin MARSICK.

Massenet, Jules Émile Frédéric (1842-1912), French dramatic composer trained at the Paris Conservatory under Ambroise THOMAS in composition, and himself professor of composition there from 1878 to 1896. His many operas became popular through their graceful melodies and superb instrumentation: among the most favored are *Hérodiade, Manon, Le Cid, Thaïs, Sapho, Werther,* and *The Juggler of Notre Dame.* He also composed ballets, oratorios, cantatas, and several brilliant orchestral suites, one of which, *Scenes Pittoresques* (Picturesque Scenes), contains the melodious "Angelus."

Massey, Ilona, contemporary Hungarian actress and singer whose real name is Ilona Hajmassy: she has appeared in several films including *Rosalie; Balalaika* with Nelson EDDY; *New Wine; International Lady.*

Massey, Raymond (1896-), Canadian stage and screen actor educated at Toronto University and at Oxford who served in World War I, and made his professional debut in 1922 at Everyman Theatre, London, in *In the Zone,* later achieving success in *Beyond the Horizon; An American Tragedy; The Constant Nymph; Spread Eagle; Topaze; The Man in Possession; The Rats of Norway; Abe Lincoln in Illinois.* He has also played stellar roles in many films including *Fire Over England; The Scarlet Pimpernel; The Prisoner of Zenda; Under the Red Robe; Abe Lincoln in Illinois; The Invaders; Dangerously They Live; Reap the Wild Wind; Desperate Journey.*

Massine, Leonide Fedorovich (1896-), Russian dancer, balletmaster, and choreographer trained at the Moscow Imperial School for the Theatre, and later studying dancing with Michel FOKINE. He appeared first with the DIAGHILEFF Ballet at Paris in 1914, and at the DRURY LANE THEATRE, London, during the same year: in 1915 he succeeded Michel Fokine as choreographer, producing his first ballet, *The Midnight Sun.* In 1916 he toured the United States with the Diaghileff Ballet, and later acted as dancer, choreographer, and producer at the Roxy Theatre, New York, La Scala, Milan, and L'Opéra, Paris. In 1932 he became producer for the BALLET RUSSE DE MONTE CARLO, and in 1942 joined the BALLET THEATRE. His important productions include *The Legend of Joseph; Le Coq d'Or; Parade; The Good-Humored Ladies; The Three Cornered Hat; Cimarosiana; Bogatyri; Seventh Symphony; Le Beau Danube; Gaité Parisienne; Caprice Espagnole* with ARGENTINITA; *Union Pacific; Symphonie fantastique.*

Massinger, Philip (1583-1640), English dramatist who studied at Oxford, and devoted himself to play writing in London, often in collaboration with Thomas DEKKER, John FLETCHER, Francis BEAUMONT and others. His original plays include *The Duke of Milan; The Unnatural Combat; The Bondman; The Roman Actor; The Maid of Honour; A New Way to Pay Old Debts; The City Madam; The Fatal Dowry; A Very Woman.*

Massys or **Matsys, Quentin** (c.1466-1530), Flemish painter said to have worked as a blacksmith, and to have turned to painting in order to win the daughter of an artist for his wife. He was friendly with Albrecht DÜRER, and specialized in life-size figures painted with more independence in conception and execution than any other Flemish painter except Jan and Hubert van EYCK. His notable works include *Face of Christ; St.*

Luke Painting the Virgin; Adoration of the Magi; Legend of St. Anne; Burial of Christ; Mater Dolorosa; Crucifixion; Virgin and Child Playing with a Lamb.

Master of Flémalle, see **Flémalle, Master of.**

Masters, Edgar Lee (1869-), American poet, novelist, and biographer educated at Knox College who practiced law for many years before undertaking a literary career. His numerous works include *A Book of Verses* (1898); *Spoon River Anthology* (1915); *The Great Valley; Songs and Satires; The New Spoon River; Lincoln— the Man; Mitch Miller; Children of the Market Place; The Sangamon.*

Mastersingers (Ger. **Meistersinger),** the successors of the MINNESINGERS in Germany during the 14th, 15th, and 16th centuries: they were chiefly artisans who formed guilds in many cities. The musical ability of members was judged by an elaborate set of rules called the *Tablatur.* Tradition credits Heinrich von MEISSEN, the last of the minnesingers, with the establishment of the first guild in 1311 at Mainz: the popularity of the guilds and their periodical contests continued until the 17th century. The most famous of the mastersingers was Hans SACHS of Nuremberg, whom Richard WAGNER selected as the hero of his opera, *Die* MEISTERSINGER VON NURNBERG.

Matahei or **Matabei, Iwasa** (c.1580-c.1640), Japanese painter who first followed the traditions of the Tosa school, but finally devoted himself to depicting popular scenes. His works include thirty portraits of Japanese poets on panels, and a self-portrait which is in the possession of his descendants.

Materna, Amalie (1845-1918), Austrian dramatic soprano who made a successful debut in 1869 at the Vienna Court Opera in MEYERBEER's *L'Africaine.* She sang the role of Brünnhilde at the first BAYREUTH FESTIVAL in 1876, and made her debut in 1885 at the Metropolitan Opera House, New York, in *Tannhäuser:* in 1894 she appeared with the Walter DAMROSCH German Opera Company.

Mather, Margaret (1859-1898), American actress who made her debut in 1882 in *Romeo and Juliet:* among the plays in which she appeared were *The Honeymoon; Peg Woffington; Gretchen; Joan of Arc; Nance Oldfield; Cymbeline* with Otis SKINNER, and *The Egyptian.*

Mathews, Charles (1776-1835), English actor who made his London debut in 1803 at the Haymarket Theatre, and originated a form of entertainment known as *At Homes:* in 1828 he became associate manager of the Adelphi Theatre, London, and made a successful tour of the United States in 1835. His son, **Charles James Mathews** (1803-1878), was also an actor who made his London debut in 1835 in his own play, *The Humpbacked Lover.* After his marriage to Mme. VESTRIS, he made a financially disastrous tour of the United States in 1838, but returned later with more success.

Matisse, Henri (1869-), French painter, engraver, and sculptor who first studied law, but later became a pupil of BOUGUEREAU, GEROME, and MOREAU, and was influenced by CHARDIN. He was one of the Fauvists, and greatly interested in the arts of ancient Persia and Peru as well as that of Polynesia. He is regarded in the light of designer and decorator, painting portraits, landscapes, interiors, and still life with more regard for the pattern than for the clarity of the objects represented. His *Odalisque* and *Buffet* are in the Luxembourg Museum: other works are to be found in many European and American museums.

Matteis, Paolo de (1662-1728), Italian painter who studied with Luca GIORDANO and Giovanni Morandi, worked at Rome for several popes, and acquired fame at the French court in Paris. His works include *Scenes from Tasso's Jerusalem; Achilles with the Daughters of Lycomedes; Immaculate Conception; Adoration of the Shepherds; Venus and Cupid; Triumph of Galatea.*

Matteson, Tompkins Harrison (1813-1884), American painter who studied at the National Academy of Art, New York: his works include *Spirit of '76; Pilgrim Fathers; Examination of a Witch; The Pilgrims' First Sabbath; At the Stile; Foddering Cattle; On the Deck of the Mayflower; Eliot Preaching to the Indians.*

Matthay, Tobias (1858-), English pianist and teacher who studied with William Sterndale BENNETT, Ebenezer PROUT, and Sir Arthur SULLIVAN. After appearing for fifteen years in concert he founded his own pianoforte school at London in 1895, also becoming professor at the Royal Academy of Music until 1925. Among his many famous pupils are Myra HESS and York BOWEN: he has written many works on piano technique, several overtures, and numerous pieces for the piano.

Matthews, Alfred Edward (1869-), English actor whose father was a member of the Christy Minstrels: among the plays in which he appeared were *Held by the Enemy; The Private Secretary; Charley's Aunt; The Star of India; Lord and Lady Algy; The Undercurrent; A Pair of Spectacles; The Barrier; The Importance of Being Earnest; The Second in Command; Diplomacy; Peg o' My Heart; Bull-Dog Drummond; Spring Cleaning; The Last of Mrs. Cheney; Interference; Matrimony Pfd.:* he has also appeared in several English films.

Matthews, (James) Brander (1852-1929), American author and educator who was graduated in 1871 from Columbia University where he held the chairs of English and of dramatic literature from 1891 to 1924. He held a Sunday night "salon" at his home for many years, and for fifty years was a familiar figure at dramatic first nights. His works include *The Theatres of Paris* (1880); *French Dramatists of the Nineteenth Century; Actors and Actresses of Great Britain and the United States* (5 volumes) with Lawrence HUTTON; *An Introduction to the Study of American Literature; The Development of the Drama; Molière; Shakespeare as Playwright; The Historical Novel.* He also wrote several plays.

Matthews, Jessie (1907-), English stage and screen actress and dancer who made her debut in 1923 at the Palace Theatre, London, in *The Music Box Revue*. She appeared as understudy for Gertrude LAWRENCE in *Charlot's Revue:* also in many musical productions and plays including *This Year of Grace.* Among the films in which she has been featured are *The Good Companions* and *Waltzes from Vienna.*

Matthison, Edith Wynne (1875-), English actress who made her debut in 1896, and in 1897 joined the Ben GREET Company in tours of the English provinces for several years. In 1902 she appeared in the title role of the morality play, *Everyman,* with great success both in Great Britain and the United States: she also appeared with Sir Henry IRVING as Portia in *The Merchant of Venice* and as Rosamund in *Becket.* In 1909 she played with great success in *The Servant in the House,* a drama by her husband, Charles Rann KENNEDY, and in 1915 with Granville BARKER in *Iphigenia in Aulis* and *The Trojan Women.* Since that time she appeared in 1916 with Sir Herbert TREE in *King Henry VIII;* also at the Shakespeare Tercentenary Celebration at the Stadium of the College of the City of New York in *Caliban by the Yellow Sands,* and in the Greek plays presented annually at Millbrook, N. Y., where she is head of the drama department of Bennett Junior College. In 1927 she was awarded the gold medal for diction by the AMERICAN ACADEMY OF ARTS AND LETTERS.

Mature, Victor, contemporary American stage and screen actor who first played at the Pasadena and Playbox Theatres: among the films in which he has appeared are *The Housekeeper's Daughter; One Million B.C.; No, No, Nanette; I Wake Up Screaming; The Shanghai Gesture; Song of the Islands; My Gal Sal:* he was featured on the stage in *Lady in the Dark.*

Maturin, Charles Robert (1782-1824), Irish novelist and dramatist who was also a clergyman of the Church of England, and famous for his eloquent sermons criticizing Roman Catholicism. His works include *Melmoth, the Wanderer; The Wild Irish Boy,* greatly praised by Sir Walter SCOTT; *The Milesian Chief:* also a tragedy, *Bertram,* successfully produced by Edmund KEAN.

Matzenauer, Margarete (1881-), Hungarian dramatic contralto who studied with Mme. Neuendorff and Antonia Mielke, making her debut in 1901 at the Strasbourg Opera in *Oberon.* After appearing at Munich and Bayreuth she made her American debut in 1911 at the Metropolitan Opera House, New York, in *Aïda,* remaining with the company until 1930. Her voice was of extraordinary compass enabling her to sing soprano as well as contralto roles.

Maude, Cyril (1862-), English actor and manager who began his career in the United States in 1883 at Denver in *East Lynne* after studying at London with Charles Cartwright. From 1896 to 1905 he was associate manager of the Haymarket Theatre, London, and in 1907 opened his own theatre, The Playhouse. Among the plays in which his quietly humorous style won him suc-

cess are *Racing; London Assurance; The Second Mrs. Tanqueray; The Little Minister; Toddles; The Earl of Pawtucket; Grumpy; Aren't We All?; Beauty and the Barge.* He has also appeared in several English films including *Grumpy* and *Peer Gynt.*

Maugham, William Somerset (1874-), English novelist, dramatist, and short story writer who studied at Heidelberg University, and chose medicine as a profession, but never practised except as a hospital interne. He served in the British Secret Service during World War I, and his medical and intelligence experiences are recorded respectively in the novels *Of Human Bondage* and *Ashenden.* His novel, *The Moon and Sixpence* was based on the career of Paul GAUGUIN, the famous French painter. His story, *Miss Thompson,* was the basis for the play, *Rain,* in which Jeanne EAGELS achieved tremendous success. Among his successful plays are *Our Betters; East of Suez; The Letter; The Constant Wife; Cakes and Ale,* a play which satirized Thomas HARDY and Sir Hugh WALPOLE. Many of his stories and plays have been filmed including *The Letter; The Constant Wife; Our Betters; The Right to Live; Of Human Bondage; Secret Agent; Isle of Fury; The Beachcomber; The Moon and Sixpence.*

Maupassant, Guy de (1850-1893), French short story writer and novelist who was graduated from the College of Rouen, and trained in literature by his godfather, Gustave FLAUBERT. After spending ten years as a clerk in the French navy, his short story, *Boule de Suif* (1880) established him as a master of this popular literary form: his works, which comprise almost 300 short stories and novels, include the novels *A Woman's Life; Peter and John; Strong as Death,* and *Our Heart.* His short stories were published in several separate volumes entitled *The Sisters Rondoli; Miss Harriet; Clair de Lune,* etc.

Maurel, Victor (1848-1923), French dramatic baritone who studied at the Paris Conservatory, making his debut in 1868 at L'Opéra in MEYERBEER's *Les Huguenots.* After singing in Italy, Spain, England, and Russia he made his American debut in 1894 at the Metropolitan Opera House, New York, in Verdi's *Otello,* and sang at the OPERA-COMIQUE, Paris, from 1895 until his retirement in 1904. He created the role of Iago in Verdi's *Otello* and of Falstaff in Verdi's opera of the same name: he was also successful in several Wagnerian parts, and appeared to great applause in several dramas without music.

Mauriac, François (1885-), French poet, novelist, and playwright educated at the Bordeaux Lycée and at the École de Chartres, Paris: his notable works available in English include the novels *Therese, The Desert of Love, The Family,* and *The Viper's Tangle;* a drama, *Asmodée, or The Intruder:* also critical works and essays including *God and Mammon, The Life of Christ,* and *Communism and Christians.*

Mauritshuis (The Hague), a building constructed in 1633 for Maurice of Nassau, Governor of Brazil, now occupied by the picture gallery of

The Hague. The collection was formed by William V and other of the princes of Orange: after the French occupation William I accomplished much toward restoring the damage and losses caused by the destruction or removal of paintings and other objects of art. Among the important canvases are REMBRANDT'S *Lesson in Anatomy,* and *Presentation in the Temple;* Paul POTTER'S *The Young Bull;* Adriaen OSTADE'S *The Fiddler;* Jan STEEN'S *Picture of Life* and *The Painter's Family.*

Mauro-Cottone, Melchiorre (1885-1938), Italian organist and composer who studied with his grandfather and father who were both organists and composers; also at the Royal Conservatory, Palermo. He made his debut at MENDELSSOHN HALL, New York, in 1910, and after playing in several churches became a featured organist at the Capitol Theatre, New York, also appearing on radio broadcasts and as organist of the NEW YORK PHILHARMONIC-SYMPHONY ORCHESTRA. Among his works is a four-act choral mass for male voices performed in 1937 at Holy Trinity Church at which he was organist.

Maurois, André (1885-), French biographer, essayist, historian, and novelist of Jewish descent educated at the Rouen Lycée and the University of Caen. His real name is Emile Herzog, and he has lectured at Yale and Princeton Universities, and at Cambridge University, England: at the present time (1943) he is serving as a captain with the French army. His biographical and critical works include *Ariel, The Life of Shelley* (1919); *The Life of Disraeli; Byron; Voltaire; Turgeniev; The Edwardian Era; Dickens; The Miracle of England, a history; Tragedy in France.* His novels include *The Silence of Colonel Bramble; Bernard Quesnay; The Family Circle; The Thought-Reading Machine.*

Mauve, Anton (1838-1888), Dutch painter who gained little from studying with Pieter van Os, but learned much through his association with Josef Israels and Willem Maris. His notable works include *Milking Time; Fishing Boat on Its Way to Sea; Flock of Sheep; Watering the Horses; Return to the Fold; Shepherd and Flock; Springtime; Autumn.*

Max, Gabriel (1840-1915), German painter who studied with his father, Josef Marx, a noted sculptor, also at the Prague and Vienna Academies, and with Karl PILOTY. His noted works include *Richard Coeur de Lion Beside His Father's Body; Nun in the Cloister Garden; Daughter of Jairus; The Last Token; Marguerite in Prison; The Pianist; Beggar Woman on the Appian Way; Maternal Happiness.* He also illustrated several books including works by GOETHE, WIELAND, and SCHILLER.

May, Edna (1878-), American actress and singer who made her debut at Syracuse, New York, in *Dora* at five, and appeared in a juvenile Gilbert and Sullivan company. After studying music at the New York Conservatory, she made her professional debut in 1896 at New York in Oscar HAMMERSTEIN'S operetta, *Santa Maria,* under her real name, Edna May Pettie, and

scored a sensational success in 1897 as Violet Gray in *The Belle of New York:* she also appeared in *An American Beauty; Kitty Grey; Three Little Maids; The School Girl; The Catch of the Season; Nelly Neil.*

May, Philip William (1864-1903), English caricaturist who was entirely self-taught, worked in Australia for three years on the Sydney *Bulletin,* and after contributing to various magazines and newspapers on his return to London, became permanently connected with *Punch.* He was a distinguished worker in black-and-white: his publications include *Parson and Painter* (1891), *Phil May's Annual,* and several other volumes containing his drawings.

Mayan Art, extraordinary examples of archaic architecture and sculpture have been discovered at Yucatan in Central America where the ruins of more than forty cities and towns have been discovered. With the use only of stone tools, the Mayans, an aboriginal race whose origin is unknown, erected buildings, from 960 A.D. to 1450 A.D. of stone with beautifully carved designs, the interiors covered with stucco and brilliantly painted. Their skill in portraying the profile of the human face and figure in stone was remarkable.

Mayerling, a village in Austria where a hunting lodge was the scene of the tragic death in 1889 of Prince Rudolf of Hapsburg. A motion picture dramatizing the incident, in which Daniele DARRIEUX and Charles BOYER assumed the principal roles, was produced in 1937.

Maynard, George Willoughby (1843-1923), American painter who studied at the Royal Academy, Antwerp, and painted in Europe for several years. His works include *Bachelor's Breakfast; Venetian Court; Ancient Mariner; Winter Revery; Rocks at Ogonquit; Strange Gods:* he also executed decorations for the Congressional Library, Washington, D. C., and the Metropolitan Opera House, New York.

Maynor, Dorothy (1910-), American Negro soprano who received her first training in her father's church choir, and later with the chorus of the Hampton Institute with which she toured Europe. After further study at the Westminster Choir College, Princeton, N. J., she made her debut with the BOSTON SYMPHONY ORCHESTRA at the Berkshire Festival in 1939, and in recital at Town Hall, New York, during the same year. She has since toured the United States in recital, and has appeared on many radio broadcasts.

Mayo, Katherine (1868-1940), American journalist and author who contributed articles to the New York *Evening Post* under the pen name "Katherine Prence": her works include *Justice to All* (1917), a study of the State Police system in Pennsylvania which led to the establishment of a similar organization in New York State; *Isles of Fear,* an indictment of the American administration of the Philippine Islands; *Mother India,* a similar arraignment of child marriage in India; *General Washington's Dilemma.*

Mayo, Margaret (1882-), American actress and dramatist who first appeared in 1896 on the stage in *Thoroughbred,* and later played in *Charley's Aunt, Secret Service,* and *Arizona.* Her successful plays include *Baby Mine, Under Two Flags,* and *The Marriage of William Ashe.*

Maytime, a play with music: book by Rida Johnson Young; music by Sigmund ROMBERG: first produced at New York in 1917. The plot is simple: two young lovers separated throughout their lives by parental interference, carry their memories of each other over the years. The theme song, "Sweethearts" will never lose its popularity: Jeanette MACDONALD and Nelson EDDY appeared in a successful film version, and there are Columbia and Victor recordings of the principal songs.

Mazarin, Jules Cardinal (1602-1661), French statesman educated at a Jesuit college at Rome, and at the University of Alcalá, later being engaged on papal diplomatic missions. He entered the French service through Cardinal RICHELIEU, and became a naturalized citizen in 1639: he was made a cardinal through the influence of Louis XIII in 1642, and appointed prime minister on the death of Richelieu in 1642. He is well-known to readers of the romances of Alexandre DUMAS, PERE, whose characterization of him is far from flattering.

Mazarin Bible, The, presumably the first book printed by Johannes GUTENBERG about 1456: it was set in Latin, the type being similar to hand-writing. Illuminated initials and other ornaments were set in by hand, and there were editions on both paper and vellum. The name is derived from the fact that the first copy was found in the library of Cardinal MAZARIN at Paris. It was also known as the *Bible of 42 Lines* because each of its 1282 pages had 42 lines set in two columns.

Mazeppa (c.1644-1709), a Cossack general who carried on an intrigue with a lady at the Polish court: her husband tied him stripped to the back of a wild horse that raced wildly over the steppes, but Mazeppa was saved, and became a great Cossack leader. Lord BYRON, in his poem, *Mazeppa,* has the hero himself relate the story of his ride: Franz LISZT selected Victor HUGO's poem on the same subject as the inspiration of a symphonic poem, *Mazeppa,* first composed for piano, and scored for orchestra in 1850. There is a Columbia recording by Egon PETRI of the piano arrangement, but no American recording of the orchestral version.

Mazurka (Polish, *Mazur*), a Polish national dance dating from the early part of the 16th century: the music is in 3-4 time, divided into two or four sections, each eight bars in length and repeated. Frederic CHOPIN wrote fifty-two mazurkas utilizing all types of Polish melodies and naturally elaborations of the simple dance form which is played slower than the waltz. There is a Victor recording in three albums of all the Chopin mazurkas performed by Artur RUBINSTEIN, and all of them can be obtained separately in either Columbia or Victor recordings.

McCartan, Edward (1878-), American sculptor who studied at the ART STUDENTS' LEAGUE, New York, and the ECOLE DES BEAUX-ARTS, Paris. He has been awarded many prizes and medals for notable works which include *Spirit of the Woods; Isoult; Nymph and Goat;* the *Eugene Field Memorial* at Chicago; *Diana* at the Metropolitan Museum of Art; *Youth:* also the design for the clock in the New York Central Railroad Building which overlooks Park Avenue at 46th Street, New York.

McCarter, Henry (1866-1942), American painter and illustrator who studied with Puvis de CHAVANNES, Thomas EAKINS, and Leon BONNAT, later making illustrations for *Scribner's Magazine, Century Magazine,* and other periodicals. He taught at the ART STUDENTS' LEAGUE, New York, and was senior member of the faculty at the PENNSYLVANIA ACADEMY OF ARTS. He received numerous awards for his landscapes, many of which were painted in Lancaster County, Penna.

M'Carthy, Justin (1830-1912), Irish historian and novelist who first worked as a journalist, became editor of the London *Morning Star,* and played an important part in Parliament from 1879 to 1900. His novels include *A Fair Saxon* (1873); *Dear Lady Disdain; Miss Misanthrope; Donna Quixote:* he also wrote an important *History of Our Own Times,* and half completed a *History of the Four Georges* which was finished by his son, **Justin Huntley M'Carthy** (1860-1936), also a novelist educated at the University of London and a member of Parliament from 1884 to 1892. His first novel, *If I Were King* (1901) was a best seller, and when dramatized an outstanding success for Edward H. SOTHERN: it was also the basis of Rudolf FRIML's romantic operetta, *The Vagabond King,* in which Dennis KING achieved fame. None of his other numerous novels such as *The Proud Prince, The Glorious Rascal, The Gorgeous Borgia,* and *Fool of April* achieved anything approximating the success of his first effort, and his several plays were also short-lived.

McCarthy, Lillah (1875-), English actress who played leading roles with Wilson BARRETT in Great Britain, the United States, and Australia: among the plays in which she appeared were *John Bull's Other Island; Man and Superman; Nan; The War God; Oedipus Rex; Iphigenia in Tauris; Trojan Women.* She also managed The Kingsway and Savoy Theatres in London, and wrote her memoirs, *Myself and My Friends,* in 1933.

McClendon, Rose (1885-1936), American Negro actress regarded as the most distinguished of her race: among the plays in which she appeared were *Deep River* (1926); *In Abraham's Bosom; Porgy; The House of Connelly; Never No More; Black Souls; Roll, Sweet Chariot; Panic; The Mulatto.* In 1937 the Rose McClendon Players were organized as a memorial to her.

McClintic, Guthrie (1893-), American actor, producer, and stage director who studied at the American Academy of Dramatic Art, and made his New York debut in 1914 in *Truth.* Later he appeared with Grace GEORGE, with the Jessie BONSTELLE Stock Company, and as assistant stage director for Winthrop AMES at the Little Theatre, New York. Among the plays he has produced are

The Dover Road; The Green Hat; The Shanghai Gesture; Saturday's Children; The Letter; The Age of Innocence; The Barretts of Wimpole Street; Brief Moment; The Truth About Blayds; Alien Corn; Jezebel; The Old Maid; Winterset; Parnell; Ethan Frome; Candida; Mamba's Daughter; No Time for Comedy. He directed or produced several of the above plays for his wife, Katharine CORNELL.

McClure, Marjorie Barkley (1882-), American author whose works include *High Fires* (1924); *A Bush That Burned; The Price of Wisdom; Many Waters; The Marriage of King Paulinas; John Dean's Journey.*

McComb, John (1763-1853), American architect whose fame comes chiefly from his designs in association with Joseph Mangin, a French engineer, for the City Hall, New York. He designed the fort at Battery Park, later the Aquarium which was razed in 1942, and built several churches and public buildings in and around New York.

McCormack, John (1884-), Irish lyric tenor who won a medal for singing at the Dublin National Irish Festival in 1902 without any training, and sang at the St. Louis Exposition in 1904 with the Dublin Cathedral Choir. He made his operatic debut in 1907 at Covent Garden, London, in *Cavalleria Rusticana*, his New York debut in 1909 at Hammerstein's Manhattan Opera House in *La Traviata*, and became an American citizen in 1919. He also sang for a time with the BOSTON OPERA COMPANY, and the CHICAGO OPERA COMPANY, but devoted himself chiefly to concertizing until his retirement in 1938.

McCrea, Joel (1905-), American stage and screen actor educated at Pomona College (Calif.), who first appeared in amateur theatricals and community plays: among the films in which he has been featured are *Lightnin'; Our Betters; The Silver Cord; Private Worlds; Barbary Coast; Wells Fargo; Dead End; Union Pacific; They Shall Have Music; Espionage Agent; Foreign Correspondent; Sullivan's Travels; The Great Man's Lady; The More the Merrier.*

McCullers, Carson Smith (1917-), American novelist educated at Columbia and New York Universities: her works include *The Heart is a Lonely Hunter* (1940) and *Reflections in a Golden Eye.*

McCullough, John Edward (1837-1885), Irish-American actor who came to America at sixteen, and appeared in 1857 at the Arch Street Theatre, Philadelphia, in *The Belle's Stratagem.* He supported Edwin BOOTH and Edwin FORREST who left him all his prompt books in his will: his greatest roles were Iago, Richelieu, Richard III, Virginius, Lear, Spartacus, and Othello, but he was coldly received in the latter role at London in 1881.

McCutcheon, George Barr (1866-1928), American novelist educated at Purdue University who was first a journalist: his numerous works include *Graustark* (1901); *Castle Craneycrow; Brewster's Millions,* also a successful play; *Beverly of Graustark; A Fool and His Money; Mary Midthorne;*

The Sherrods; Nedra; The Prince of Graustark; The Merrivales, published posthumously. He was an intimate friend of George ADE and Booth TARKINGTON: his books are said to have exceeded 5,000,000 copies in sales.

McDonald, Harl (1899-), American pianist and composer who was graduated in music from the Universities of Southern California and Redlands, and later studied at the Leipzig Conservatory. He has occupied several posts in the music departments at the Philadelphia Music Academy, the University of Pennsylvania, and other institutions, and has written a symphonic fantasy, *Rhumba Symphony,* a concerto for two pianos, choral works, and chamber music.

McEntee, Jervis (1828-1891), American painter who specialized in landscapes, and was a member of the HUDSON RIVER SCHOOL and of the National Academy from 1861. His notable paintings include *Shadows of Autumn; In the Clouds; Autumn Landscape; Melancholy Days; Old Mill in Winter; Indian Summer; Cliff in the Catskills; Eastern Sky at Sunset.*

McFee, William (1881-), American marine engineer, poet, and novelist: his works include *Letters from an Ocean Tramp* (1908); *Aliens; Captain Macedoine's Daughter; The Life of Sir Martin Frobisher; Sailors of Fortune; North of Suez; The Harbourmaster; The Beachcomber,* a volume of poems; *Sailor's Bane; Derelicts; Watch Below; Spenlove in Arcady.*

McGuffey, William Holmes (1800-1873), American educator graduated from Washington and Jefferson College, and professor of languages at Miami University: he is distinguished as the compiler of the six *McGuffey Eclectic Readers* for public schools which reached a total sale of more than 120,000,000 copies from 1836 to 1900, and exercised an enormous influence in the cause of education. In 1931 a memorial was erected at his home town, Claysville, Pa., and a volume edited by Harvey C. Minnick entitled *Old Favorites from the McGuffey Readers* was published in 1936.

McIntire, Samuel (1757-1811), American architect and woodcarver who achieved a reputation as a designer of houses for wealthy shipowners in Salem: he also built many of the public buildings in Salem some of which are still standing. His work may be said to have been held entirely "within the family" because he had the assistance of his two brothers, his son, and other relatives on the construction.

McIntyre and Heath, a minstrel, vaudeville, and musical comedy team composed of James McIntyre (1857-1937) and Thomas Heath (1852-1938). After studying the languages and characteristics of the Southern Negro, they formed a partnership in 1874 which continued until 1934: their combined salary was twenty dollars a week at the start. Their greatest success was a musical comedy, *The Ham Tree* (1905) in which they were starred for many years: in vaudeville a sketch, *The Georgia Minstrels,* was head-lined for more than twenty years.

McKay, Claude (1890-), American Negro poet and novelist born in the West Indies who studied at the Tuskegee Institute and Kansas State College, and worked as a waiter. He attracted attention with verses published in the *Seven Arts*, and finally achieved success in 1927 with his novel, *Home to Harlem:* his works include the poems *Songs of Jamaica* and *Harlem Shadows;* the novels *Banjo* and *Banana Bottom*. His autobiography, *A Long Way from Home,* was published in 1937.

McKenney, Ruth (1911-), American novelist educated at Ohio State University who worked as a reporter on various newspapers: her books include *My Sister Eileen,* a best seller and also a dramatic success; *Industrial Valley; The McKenneys Carry On; Jake Home.*

McKenzie, Robert Tait (1867-), Canadian-American sculptor who first practiced medicine, later discovering his ability as a sculptor, and creating many notable works including *The Sprinter* at Cambridge, England; *The Athlete* at Oxford, England; *The Supple Juggler* and *The Competitor* at the Metropolitan Museum of Art, New York: also several war memorials in both the United States and Great Britain.

McKim, Charles Follen (1847-1909), American architect trained at the Lawrence Scientific School at Harvard University as a mining engineer: he became interested in architecture and studied with Pierre DAUMET at the ECOLE DES BEAUX-ARTS, Paris, finally becoming a partner in the celebrated firm of McKim, Mead and White. Among the many buildings on which the three members of the firm collaborated were the Public Library, Boston, Mass.; government buildings in Washington, D. C., several buildings at Columbia University, the Pierpont Morgan Library, the original Madison Square Garden, the old Tiffany Building, and the Pennsylvania Railroad Station in New York City. He also executed important restorations such as the Thomas JEFFERSON buildings at the University of Virginia, and worked with Daniel Hudson BURNHAM and August SAINT-GAUDENS on the Senate Park Commission for the development and improvement of Washington, D. C.

McLaglen, Victor (1886-), English screen actor who traveled in all parts of the world, served in World War I, was a professional boxer, and first appeared in the film *The Call of the Road:* among the numerous American and English pictures in which he has been featured are *The Glorious Adventure* with Lady Diana Manners; *Beau Geste; What Price Glory; Mother Machree; The Cockeyed World; No More Women; Dick Turpin; The Informer* for which he won the Motion-Picture Academy award in 1935; *Professional Soldier; Under Two Flags; Gunga Din; Captain Fury; South of Pago Pago; Call Out the Marines; Powder Town.*

Mead, Larkin Goldsmith (1835-1910), American sculptor who studied with Henry Kirke BROWN, and became an illustrator for *Harper's Weekly* during the Civil War. His notable works include a statue of Ethan Allen at the Statehouse,

Montpelier, Vt.; a monument to Abraham Lincoln at Springfield, Ill.; *The Father of Waters* at New Orleans; *The Triumph of Ceres* for the Columbian Exposition at Chicago in 1893. His brother, **William Rutherford Mead** (1846-1928), was a well-known architect associated with Charles Follen McKim and Stanford White in the distinguished firm of McKim, Mead and White.

Measure, in music (*a*) the division of the time in a composition into units of equal duration, visibly represented by groups of notes or rests between two lines drawn vertically down the staff, and called bars. (*b*) The name of a popular dance at the English court in the days of Queen ELIZABETH; so-called because it had a stately or measured movement.

Mecca, the capital city of Arabia, sacred to the Mohammedans as the birthplace of Mohammed. Every true follower of the prophet is supposed to make a pilgrimage at least once during his life to Mecca: for this reason the word, often used uncapitalized, has come to signify any place sought as a goal by large numbers of people.

Medal, in art a piece of metal, usually in the shape of a circular coin, on which is cast or struck a figure or scene to preserve the memory of a great event or a celebrated person. Many famous sculptors were adept at the art of designing medals, and the custom of presenting medals to persons for distinguished services to art, science, or country has prevailed since ancient times.

Medallion, a large medal in the form of a tablet, panel, or plaque with a figure or scene represented in relief: it is used as an ornamental feature in architecture, sculpture, and as a form of antique jewelry.

Medea, in Greek mythology a princess and enchantress who aided her lover, JASON, in securing the Golden Fleece: when Jason deserted her for Creüsa, she sent the latter a poisoned wedding robe, murdered her own children by Jason, and went to Athens in a chariot drawn by serpents. EURIPIDES, SENECA, CORNEILLE, and Franz GRILLPARZER made her the heroine of plays, and CHERUBINI of an opera.

Medici, the name of a Florentine family famous in Italian history for its liberal patronage of the arts. Among the members renowned in this respect were **Cosimo de' Medici** (1389-1464), known as The Elder, who built a palace, several villas, and churches, also patronizing such artists as DONATELLO, BRUNELLESCHI, GHIBERTI, and Luca DELLA ROBBIA; he also commissioned Marsiglio Ficino to make a Latin translation of PLATO, and established the first public library. Cosimo's grandson, **Lorenzo de' Medici** (1449-1492), was highly educated in painting, sculpture, music, and literature: he was a fine poet himself as is evident from his carnival songs and the rural love epic, *La Nencia da Barberino.* He was the patron of BOTTICELLI, GHIRLANDAIO, Filippino LIPPI, SIGNORELLI, BALDOVINETTI, MAIANO, VERROCCHIO, CREDI, and LEONARDO DA VINCI. Other munificent members of the family included Cosimo I de' Medici (1519-1574), known as The Younger, who built vast palaces with landscaped gardens; Ferdinand I de' Medici (1549-1609), who was made a cardinal and built the Villa Medici in which he housed a splendid art collection; Ferdinand II de' Medici (1610-1670), who founded the first European academy of natural sciences; Francesco de' Medici (1541-1587), who built the Uffizi Gallery.

Medtner, Nicolas (1880-), Russian pianist and composer who studied at the Moscow Conservatory with Wassily SAFONOV, and toured Europe with great success. After teaching at the Moscow Conservatory for some years he devoted himself to composition, also touring Europe and the United States from 1929 to 1930. His works include several sonatas and numerous pieces for the piano, two violin sonatas and many songs.

Medusa, in Greek mythology the most celebrated of the GORGONS; said to have been a beautiful maiden until she offended ATHENA who rendered her hideous by changing her hair to snakes, and altering her face so that anyone who looked at her was changed to stone. She was killed by PERSEUS who affixed her head to the aegis of Athena: only POSEIDON, her lover, mourned her.

Meek, Donald (1880-), Scotch stage and screen actor who first appeared as a child of eight at the Palace Theatre, Glasgow: in 1912 he made his American debut at the Castle Square Theatre, Boston, Mass., later appearing in several hundred parts on both the stage and screen. Among the films in which he has played character parts are *Mrs. Wiggs of the Cabbage Patch; The Merry Widow; The Informer; The Return of Peter Grimm; Accent on Youth; Captain Blood; Old Hutch; Maid of Salem; Parnell; The Adventures of Tom Sawyer; You Can't Take It With You; Young Mr. Lincoln; The Housekeeper's Daughter; Tortilla Flat; The Keeper of the Flame.*

Meer, Jan van der (1628-1691), Dutch painter, known as the Elder, who studied with Jacob de Wet: his noted works include *Tavern Entrance; Horsemen in the Woods; Village of Noordwyck; In the Downs; Hilly Forest Landscape; Forest Path with Horseman.* His son, **Jan van der Meer** (1656-1705), known as the Younger, was also a fine landscape painter who studied with his father and with Nicolaes BERCHEM: his works include *Landscape with Sheep; Lake with Donkeys and Drovers; Shepherds and Flocks Near a Cottage; Dutch Windmill; Flock of Sheep at Rest.*

Mefistofele, grand opera in a prologue, four acts, and epilogue: libretto (after GOETHE's *Faust*) and music by Arrigo BOITO; first produced at Milan in 1868 and at the Academy of Music, New York, in 1880. The story follows the legend of Faust as told by Goethe which varies from Gounod's *Faust* only in scenic details, and in Faust being saved through repentance after the death of MARGUERITE. There is a complete Columbia recording sung in Italian by soloists and chorus from La Scala, Milan.

Megalithic Monuments, great stones or boulders which were probably tombs, and date back to the polished stone age when man had no tools except flint hatchets. There are no engravings or ornamentation on the stones, indicating that they were used as nature formed them. The most impressive unit is at Stonehenge, England, where the blocks are squared off forming a circle of triliths, i.e., monuments consisting of two upright stones supporting a lintel. Monuments of this character have been discovered all over the world.

Megrue, Roi Cooper (1883-1927), American dramatist educated at Columbia University: his successful plays include *Under Cover* (1914); *It Pays to Advertise,* with Walter Hackett; *Under Fire; Potash and Perlmutter in Society,* with Montague GLASS; *Seven Chances,* with Irvin S. COBB; *Where Poppies Bloom; Venice for Two,* adapted from a play by Sacha GUITRY.

Méhul, Étienne-Nicolas (1763-1817), French composer who became organist at a French convent at ten years of age, later studying with Wilhelm Hauser and Johann Edelmann. He sought the advice of Christoph Willibald von GLUCK who urged him to undertake the composition of operas: his first success was *Euphrosyne et Coradin,* an opéra-comique produced in 1790 at Paris. It was followed by about thirty other operas of which *Le jeune Henri* and *Joseph* are considered the finest. Méhul is regarded as Gluck's successor in his efforts to develop and reform French opera.

Meighan, Thomas (1879-1936), American, stage and screen actor who appeared first as an extra with Henrietta CROSMAN in *Mistress Nell* at Pittsburgh, later becoming leading player in *The College Widow, The Two Orphans,* and *Broadway Jones.* Among the films in which he was starred were *Pied Piper Malone; The Confidence Man; M'liss; Out of a Clear Sky; The Miracle Man; Male and Female; Don't Change Your Wife.*

Mei Lan-fang (1894-1943), Chinese actor whose father and grandfather were distinguished in Chinese drama. After appearing at the Japanese Imperial Theatre and in England, he toured the United States with his own company in 1930, also appearing in Russia in a repertory of several hundred plays many of which were original with him: his wardrobe and personal jewelry for stage use were said to be valued at $100,000.

Meilhac, Henri (1813-1897), French dramatist and librettist who first wrote articles and vaudevilles for French newspapers and theatres. In 1860 he began a collaboration with Ludovic HALEVY which continued for twenty years: the works produced jointly included librettos for the operettas *La Belle Hélène, The Grand Duchess,* and *La Perichole:* also the popular drama *Froufrou,* and several librettos for OFFENBACH's operettas.

Meiningen Theatre, a theatre used by the court players of the Duke of Saxe-Meiningen, at Meiningen. The company achieved a great reputation for its acting and scenic effects from 1874 to 1890: it also toured Germany for sixteen years, giving more than 2500 performances of both classic dramas and works by modern authors. A visit by the company to Moscow led to the founding a few years later of the MOSCOW ART THEATRE.

Meissen, Heinrich von (c.1250-1318), German mastersinger whose pseudonymn was *Frauenlob*, meaning "Panegyric of Women," and bestowed on him because he favored the use of "lady" (Frau) instead of "woman" (Weib). He practiced his minstrel art at the courts of Germany, and is said to have established a school of minstrelsy at Mayence. His *Cantica canticorum* was published in English, with notes by Albert E. Kroeger, in 1877 at St. Louis, Mo.

Meissonier, Jean Louis Ernest (1815-1891), French painter who was chiefly self-taught although he studied for a few months with Léon COGNIET, and illustrated several books including *Paul and Virginia* and *The Vicar of Wakefield.* His notable creations include *The Visitors; The Chess Players; The Reader; Scene from the Decameron; Napoleon I in the French Campaign; Violoncello Player; The Smoker; The Lute Players; The Sign Painter; Soldiers at Cards; Halt of Cavaliers; Corporal of the Guard; Death Bed of Thiers;* also many portraits of European and American celebrities of his period.

Meistersinger von Nürnberg, Die, a grand opera in three acts: libretto and music by Richard WAGNER; first performed at Munich in 1868, and at the Metropolitan Opera House, New York, in 1886. The story relates the experiences of Walter von Stolzing who, after falling in love with Eva, daughter of the rich goldsmith, Veit Pogner, attempts to enter the singing contest at Nürnberg, and is rejected at a preliminary hearing in favor of the town clerk, Beckmesser. Hans Sachs, the shoe-maker poet, notes down a song that Walter has conceived in a dream: Beckmesser steals it, and attempts to sing it at the contest, but he fails lamentably. Walter interprets it magnificently, and is awarded the hand of Eva by her father. There is a Victor recording of the complete opera, and both Victor and Columbia recordings of the *Prelude to Act I,* the *Prelude to Act III,* and of the *Prize Song* by Lauritz Melchior and Charles Kullman. There is also a Victor recording for violin by Mischa Elman, and another for violoncello by Pablo Casals.

Melba, Dame Nellie (1861-1931), Australian operatic soprano whose real name was Nellie Mitchell. After singing in church and local concerts at Sydney, she studied in Paris with Mathilde MARCHESI, and made her debut in 1887 at Brussels in Verdi's *Rigoletto.* She appeared at London, Paris, St. Petersburg, and Milan, making her American debut in 1893 at the Metropolitan Opera House in Donizetti's *Lucia di Lammermoor.* She also appeared with Oscar Hammerstein's Opera Company: her favorite role was that of Mimi in Puccini's *La Bohème.* Her autobiography, *Melodies and Memories,* was published in 1925.

Melcher, Frederic Gershom (1879-), American editor, lecturer and writer on book publishing and selling who was first connected with booksellers in Boston and Indianapolis: from 1918 he was associate editor of the *Publishers' Weekly,* New York, and from 1933 its editor and also president of R. R. Bowker & Co. He was one of the founders of the *Children's Book Week* in 1919, and established the John Newbery Medal awarded yearly since 1921 by the American Library Association to the most distinguished contributor to American literature for children; also the Caldecott Medal, first awarded in 1937 for the outstanding American picture book.

Melchers, Julius Gari (1860-1932), American painter, son of a sculptor and woodcarver, who was sent to Düsseldorf to study art, later becoming a pupil at the Acadèmie Julien and the ECOLE DES BEAUX-ARTS, Paris. His first picture *The Sermon,* received honorable mention at the Paris Salon in 1886: among his notable works are *The Supper at Emmaus; The Family; Mother and Child; Nurse and Children; Peace and War; Penelope; Maternity; Sailor and His Sweetheart; The Vespers; The Smithy.*

Melchior, Lauritz (1890-), Danish dramatic tenor who sang as a boy in a church choir at Copenhagen and studied with Paul Bang, making his debut as a baritone in 1913 at the Royal Opera House, Copenhagen, in Leoncavallo's *Pagliacci.* In 1918 he reappeared as a tenor, and after further study with Victor Beigel and several other famous teachers he appeared in 1925 at the Wagner Festival at BAYREUTH in *Siegfried,* making his debut in 1926 at the Metropolitan Opera House, New York, in *Tannhäuser.* He has been a member of the Metropolitan Opera Company since that time, and has also appeared as soloist with the major American orchestras.

Meleager, in Greek mythology the son of King Oeneus of Calydon who neglected his sacrifice to ARTEMIS (Diana): she sent a wild boar to devastate the country, and Meleager eventually destroyed it, assisted by ATALANTA, a famous huntress, who inflicted the first wound: he awarded the head and skin of the boar to her, thereby greatly displeasing his family. He is said to have been slain by APOLLO, and is a favorite subject in sculpture and painting.

Melodeon, an obsolete type of reed organ invented in the United States by Jeremiah Carhart in 1836: bellows worked by the feet drew the air through the reeds, reversing the method used in the HARMONIUM. It resembled an upright piano in appearance, and more than twenty thousand were sold in 1859.

Melodrama, a term originally applied to a dramatic composition in which the spoken words and action were accompanied by music but without singing: an excellent example was *Pygmalion* by Jean Jacques ROUSSEAU produced in 1775. The term was also used in connection with John GAY's *The Beggars' Opera* produced in 1728 but hardly correctly because there were many ballads sung. In modern times the first play without music to which the term "melodrama" was applied was *Uncle Tom's Cabin,* produced about 1850: the most successful English melodrama was *The Silver King,* produced by Wilson BARRETT in 1881: since then hundreds of similar plays have been written by French, German, and English dramatists.

Melody, in music a succession of tones played or sung one after the other so as to form a definite, rhythmic relation: also known as a *tune* when so arranged that the succession is readily memorized. Melody is to be found in all compositions except that it is sometimes difficult to trace in modern works: it is rarely that a composition achieves lasting favor without having one or more readily recognized melodies.

Melozzo da Forli (c.1438-1494), Italian painter who studied with Piero della FRANCESCHI, and was friendly with Giovanni Santi, the father of Raphael. His important works, painted chiefly in Rome, include the *Ascension of Christ* in the Church of the Apostles; a fresco *Pope Sixtus IV Appointed Librarian of the Vatican; The Pepper Grinder,* originally painted as an apothecary's sign; *Musical Angels* in the sacristy of the Vatican.

Melpomene, see **Muses, The.**

Melton, James (1904-   ), American radio, screen and operatic tenor educated at the Florida, Georgia State, and Vanderbilt Universities, and a pupil in singing of G. S. de Luca at Nashville, Tenn., and with Michael Raucheisen in Berlin. He made his first radio appearance in 1927 with Roxy's Gang, toured Europe with the Revelers Quartet, and made his operatic debut in 1938 with the Cincinnati Zoo Company in *Madam Butterfly,* later appearing with the SAN CARLO OPERA COMPANY. In 1942 he appeared with great success at the Metropolitan Opera House in Mozart's *The Magic Flute.* He has been featured in several films including *Stars Over Broadway; Sing Me a Love Song; Melody for Two.*

"Melusina" Overture (Mendelssohn), an orchestral work composed by Felix MENDELSSOHN in 1833, and performed in 1834 at Düsseldorf with the composer conducting. It was inspired by Gustav Schwab's story of the fair Melusina, a water nymph who became the bride of Count Lusignan: although Mendelssohn wrote no program for the work, the music presumably pictures the love of the count for the charming Melusina. There is no American recording at the present time (1943) of this work.

Melville, Herman (1819-1891), American novelist who went to sea as a cabin boy on a merchant vessel, deserted the ship with another sailor, was captured at the Marquesas Islands by the Typees, a tribe of cannibals, and rescued by an Australian whaler. His works include *Typee* (1846), an account of his adventures; *Omoo; Redburn; His First Voyage; White Jacket, or the World in a Man-of-War; Moby Dick, or the White Whale;* also several volumes of poems.

Melzer, Roman F. (1860-1943), Russian architect who studied at the Imperial Academy of Arts, in St. Petersburg: in 1893 he represented the Imperial Society of Architects at the Columbian Exposition at Chicago, and designed the Russian Pavilion at the Paris Exposition in 1900. He worked on the Imperial Palace in St. Petersburg, also building many residences including those of the Grand Duke Michael and Emanuel Nobel, a relative of Alfred NOBEL. He came to the United States in 1921 after escaping to Germany during the Revolution in 1918.

Memling or **Memlic, Hans** (c.1430-1494), Flemish painter who is said to have studied with Roger van der WEYDEN: among his famous paintings are *Madonna and Child Enthroned with Saints and Donors; Martydom of St. Sebastian; Last Judgment; Seven Sorrows of the Virgin,* containing two hundred figures; *Marriage of St. Catherine; Adoration of the Magi; The Seven Joys of the Virgin; Crucifixion; Shrine of St. Ursula* in eight panels and six medallions.

Memnon, in Greek mythology a king of the Ethiopians who fought against the Greeks in the TROJAN WAR after the death of HECTOR: he was slain by ACHILLES after he killed the latter's friend, Antilochus, the son of Nestor.

Memphis (Egypt), in ancient times the capital of Egypt, founded by Menes, the first king of Egypt, and located near the city of Cairo. It was succeeded in importance by THEBES and ALEXANDRIA: captured by Cambyses and finally abandoned after the Mohammedan conquest. The temples of several gods and two statues of Rameses II were found there.

Menander (342-291 B.C.), Greek dramatist who wrote more than a hundred comedies, and won the prize at Athens eight times. During the early part of the 20th century 1400 lines from his plays written on PAPYRUS were discovered in Egypt: critical authorities do not seem to agree with the estimates of OVID and PLINY as to Menander's dramatic ability.

Mencken, Henry Louis (1880-   ), American author, editor, and critic who first worked on the Baltimore *Morning Herald,* and later on the Baltimore *Sun:* also as associate editor of *Smart Set,* and with George Jean NATHAN on the *American Mercury,* acting as sole editor from 1925 to 1933. His works include a series of essays with the title, *Prejudices* (6 volumes); *The American Language; George Bernard Shaw: His Plays; In Defence of Women; Treatise on the Gods.*

Mendelssohn, Erich (1887-   ), German architect distinguished for his modernistic designs: they include the Einstein Tower at Potsdam, an observatory in the shape of a MONOLITH gashed with wide openings; several factories and groups of small dwelling houses. Since leaving Germany in 1933 his designs appear to be more in accordance with internationally adopted ideas.

Mendelssohn, Felix (1809-1847), German pianist and composer of Jewish parentage whose full name was Ludwig Felix Mendelssohn-Bartholdy: he was the son of a banker and grandson of Moses Mendelssohn, a distinguished Jewish philosopher. He studied with Ludwig Berger, Karl Zelter, and Ignaz MOSCHELES, making his first public appearance at nine as a pianist, and composing his famous *Overture to Shakespeare's A Midsummer Night's Dream* at seventeen. From 1829 to 1832 he traveled extensively in England and Europe, and later became conductor of the Lower Rhine Music Festivals at Düsseldorf, the Cologne Festival, and the Gewandhaus Orchestra at Leipzig. Here he met with great success, and became intimate with Ferdinand DAVID and Robert SCHUMANN. He made many visits to England where he was highly regarded as a composer and as a man: in 1843 he was supported by the King of Saxony in the founding of the Leipzig Conservatory, an institution which became famous under his direction: he also continued conducting the court music at Berlin and Dresden. In 1846 his beloved sister, Fanny Mendelssohn, died suddenly: the shock of her demise, coupled with the strain of his activities as conductor and composer, combined to bring about his untimely death in 1847, regarded as a public calamity in Great Britain and Europe. His notable compositions include four symphonies; several overtures; concertos for piano and for violin; many fine chamber works; numerous piano compositions including the *Variations Sérieuses, Andante and Rondo Capriccioso,* and eight books of *Songs Without Words;* organ works, the oratorios *St. Paul* and *Elijah;* incidental music to Shakespeare's *A Midsummer Night's Dream;* 50 part songs and 85 solo songs.

Mendelssohn Hall (New York), a building erected in 1892 by Alfred Corning Clark on West 40th Street, New York, as a home for the Mendelssohn Glee Club. It was the leading recital hall for twenty years, with a seating capacity of one thousand: torn down in 1912 it was succeeded as a concert center by AEOLIAN HALL and later by TOWN HALL.

Mendès, Catulle (1841-1909), French poet, critic, dramatist, and novelist of Jewish extraction: his works include several volumes of poems regarded as more imitative than original; the drama, *Justice;* the libretto for a light opera, *Captain Fracasse,* founded on Théophile Gautier's novel; *The Art of the Theatre; Richard Wagner:* also several novels including *La Roi Vierge* and *La Maison de la vielle.*

Mendoza, Antonio Hurtado de (c.1593-1644), Spanish dramatist whose early poems were praised by CERVANTES: he became a favorite of Philip IV of Spain who commissioned plays for him for the Royal Theatre at Aranjuez. His plays include *Querer por solo querer* and *El Marido hace mujer* from which MOLIERE drew ideas for his comedy, *The School for Husbands.*

Menelaus, in Greek mythology a king of Sparta, brother of AGAMEMNON and husband of HELEN. He fought valiantly in the Trojan War, and was one of the Greeks who entered Troy in the TROJAN HORSE: at the end of the war he returned to Sparta with his wife, and after a long and happy life was transported to the ELYSIAN FIELDS.

Mengelberg, Willem (1871-), Dutch conductor who studied at the Cologne Conservatory under Isador SEISS, Gustav Jensen, and Franz Wüllner: after directing at Lucerne, he became conductor in 1895 of the Concertgebouw-Orchestra at Amsterdam; the London Symphony Orchestra and the Royal Philharmonic Society (1911-14), the New York Philharmonic-Symphony Society (1921-29). He has made many tours of Europe with the Amsterdam Concertgebouw-Orchestra, and is distinguished for his interpretation of the works of BEETHOVEN, Gustav MAHLER, and Richard STRAUSS: the latter dedicated the tone poem, *Ein Heldenleben* (A Hero's Life), to him.

Mengs, Anton Raphael (1728-1779), German painter who was the son and pupil of a Danish painter, Ismael Mengs: he established his studio at Dresden, and later removed to Rome. In 1754 he became director of the Art Academy at the Vatican, and also painted many works at the behest of Charles III of Spain. His notable works include *The Ascension; Holy Family; Mount Parnassus; Aurora and the Four Seasons; The Apotheosis of Trajan; Perseus and Andromeda; Annunciation.*

Menjou, Adolphe (1890-), American stage and screen actor educated at Cornell University who appeared on the legitimate stage and in vaudeville before entering the films: among the numerous pictures in which he has appeared are *The Sheik; The Three Musketeers; The Grand Duchess and the Waiter; Morocco; The Easiest Way; Front Page; A Farewell to Arms; Little Miss Marker; The Mighty Barnum; A Star is Born; Café Metropole; Stage Door; Golden Boy; A Bill of Divorcement; Roxie Hart.*

Menken, Adah Isaacs (1835-1868), American actress of Jewish parentage who real name was Dolores Adios Fuertes. She first appeared as a dancer at New Orleans and Havana. In 1864 she appeared at Astley's Amphitheatre in London, in a spectacle, *Mazeppa,* in one scene of which she was tied to the side of a running horse. While in London she became intimate with SWINBURNE, READE, DICKENS, and many other literary men: she also appeared in Paris and Vienna in sensational plays such as *Les Pirates de la Savane.*

Menken, Helen (1901-), American stage and radio actress who first appeared at five as one of the fairies in Shakespeare's *A Midsummer Night's Dream* at the Astor Theatre, New York: among the plays in which she has been featured are *The Pied Piper of Hamelin; Major Pendennis; Sinners; Parlour, Bedroom and Bath; Three Wise Fools; Seventh Heaven; Congai; The Captive; Mary of Scotland; The Old Maid.* She is appearing at the present time (1943), in a radio serial drama, *Second Husband,* which has been on the air almost continuously since 1937.

Menotti, Gian-Carlo (1911-), Italian-American composer born in Italy: after studying at the Milan Conservatory, he came to the United States to enroll as a pupil of Rosario Scalero in composition at the CURTIS INSTITUTE OF MUSIC, Philadelphia. His comic opera, *Amelia Goes to the Ball,* was produced in 1937 at the Academy of Music, Philadelphia, and in 1938 at the Metropolitan Opera House, New York. His compositions include a radio opera, *The Old Maid and the Thief,* and another short opera, *The Island God,* produced at the Metropolitan.

Menuhin, Yehudi (1916-), American violinist who studied with Louis Persinger at San Francisco, and made his debut at a Young People's Concert of the San Francisco Symphony Orchestra in 1924: in 1927 he made his New York debut with the NEW YORK SYMPHONY ORCHESTRA in the BEETHOVEN violin concerto. He also studied with Adolph BUSCH and Georges ENESCO, and has toured the world with great success, playing with the major European and American symphony orchestras, making many recordings and appearing on radio broadcasts. His sister, **Hephzibah Menuhin** (1920-), is a distinguished pianist who studied with Marcel Ciampi, making her debut in 1928 at San Francisco. She has appeared in sonata recitals with her brother in England and the United States, also making several recordings with him.

Menzel, Adolph Friedrich Erdmann von (1815-1905), German self-taught painter, illustrator, engraver, and lithographer who illustrated Franz Kugler's *History of Frederick the Great* with 400 drawings in pencil on wood which revived the art of engraving on wood: his notable paintings include *Sunny Interior; Coronation of William I; Market Place at Verona; In the Tuileries; Supper at the Ball; At Confession; The Forge; Modern Cyclops.*

Mephistopheles, in the German legend of Dr. Johann Faust the name of the evil spirit to whom Faust signs away his soul in exchange for prolonged youth: he is one of the seven great princes of Hell, and is described as "a little man with a black cape and a bald head." Many dramatists have used the character in plays: it is also a central figure in Charles GOUNOD's *Faust* and Hector BERLIOZ' *The Damnation of Faust.*

Mer, La (Debussy), a series of three symphonic sketches by Claude DEBUSSY first performed in 1905 at a Lamoureux Concert in Paris, and in 1907 at a Boston Symphony concert. The titles of the movements are I *The Sea from Dawn until Noon;* II *Sport of the Waves;* III *Dialogue of the Wind and Sea.* There is a Victor recording by the Boston Symphony Orchestra conducted by Serge KOUSSEVITZKY.

Mérante, Louis François (1828-1887), French dancer and choreographer who danced at the Theatre Royal, Liége, when he was six years old, and later became understudy for Lucien PETIPA at L'Opéra, Paris. The ballets for which he acted as choreographer include *Gretna Green; Sylvia; Coppélia; Yedda; The Two Pigeons; Le Fandango; La Korrigane; La Farandole.*

Mercein, Eleanor (1880-), American novelist: her works include *The Kildares of Storm* (1916); *The Mansion House; Basquerie; The Book of Bette; Sounding Harbors.*

Mercié, Marius Jean Antonin (1845-1916), French sculptor and painter who has achieved success in both arts: his works include *Theseus Thanking the Gods after Overcoming the Minotaur;* a bronze *David;* a group, *Gloria Victis; Quand Même; Le Souvenir; The Genius of the Arts; Tomb of Louis Philippe and His Queen;* also a statue of Robert E. Lee at Richmond, Va.

Mercury, see **Hermes.**

Mercury Theatre, see **Welles, Orson.**

Meredith, Burgess (1911-), American stage and screen actor who first appeared as a walk-on with Eva LE GALLIENNE's Civic Repertory Company in 1929: among the plays in which he has been featured are *Alice in Wonderland; She Loves Me Not; Flowers of the Forest; Winterset; High Tor; The Star Wagon; Five Kings; Candida.* He has also appeared in several films including *Winterset; Idiot's Delight; Of Mice and Men; That Uncertain Feeling; There Goes the Groom; Spring Madness.*

Meredith, George (1828-1909), English novelist and poet educated in Germany and trained for the law before he embarked on a literary career. His successful works include *The Ordeal of Richard Feveral* (1859); *Evan Harrington; Rhoda Fleming; The Egoist; Vittoria; The Tragic Comedians; Diana of the Crossways,* considered his masterpiece. He also wrote several volumes of poems including *Modern Love; Poems and Lyrics of the Joy of Earth; A Reading of Earth.*

Meredith, Owen, see **Bulwer-Lytton, Edward Robert.**

Merezhkovsky, Dmitri Sergeivich (1865-1941), Russian philosopher and novelist educated at the University of St. Petersburg: his works include *Julian the Apostate* (1901); *Peter and Alexis; The Romance of Leonardo da Vinci; Tutankhamen; Tolstoy and Dostoievsky; The Prophet of the Russian Revolution; Gogol and the Devil; December the Fourteenth; The Menace of the Mob; The Life of Napoleon; Michelangelo.* His wife, **Zinaida Nikolayevna Hippius Merezhkovsky** (1869-), is a poet of the symbolist school, and author of a play, *The Green Ring.*

Merian, Maria Sibylla (1647-1717), Swiss painter who was the step-daughter of Jacob Marrel (1614-1685) an artist who specialized in painting flowers. In 1699 she visited Surinam in Dutch Guiana where she painted native insects and plants, also publishing two works on these subjects which brought her great fame. Most of the original paintings for these works are in the BRITISH MUSEUM at London, and in the Academy of Sciences at Leningrad.

Merian, Matthaüs or **Matthew,** (1593-1650), Swiss engraver, known as The Elder, and creator of many engravings of landscapes, hunting, and battle scenes, Bible illustrations and a famous *Dance of Death.* His son, **Matthaüs** or **Matthew Merian** (1621-1687), known as The Younger, was a well-known portrait and historical painter: among his works is a portrait of his sister, Maria Sibylla MERIAN.

Merimée, Prosper (1803-1870), French critic, novelist, and historian who studied law, and was active in public life: his works include a historical novel, *Chronicle of the Times of Charles IX;* several short novels such as *Colomba; Carmen; The Venus of Ille,* and *Mateo Falcone.* He also wrote several important historical works, translated the stories of Russian authors, and contributed to French newspapers and magazines. The libretto of the grand opera, *Carmen,* with music by Georges BIZET, was founded on MERIMÉE's romance.

441

Merivale, Philip (1886-), English stage and screen actor born in India who made his debut with the F. R. Benson Company in 1905. After playing with Fred TERRY and Sir Herbert TREE he came to the United States with Mrs. Patrick CAMPBELL: in 1917-18 he served with the Canadian Air Force in World War I: among the plays in which he achieved success are *The Road to Rome; Death Takes a Holiday; Cynara; Mary of Scotland; Valley Forge.* He has also been featured in several films including *Rage in Heaven; Lady For a Night; This Above All.*

Merkel, Una (1903-), American stage and screen actress who made her debut in 1922 at New York in *Montmartre,* later appearing in *The Poor Nut; Pigs; Two Girls Wanted; Coquette; Salt Water.* She has also been featured in numerous films including *Abraham Lincoln; The Maltese Falcon; Private Lives; Reunion in Vienna; The Merry Widow; Born to Dance; The Good Old Soak; Saratoga; Four Girls in White; On Borrowed Time; Destry Rides Again; Saturday's Children; Twin Beds.*

Merlin, in Welsh legend the bard and enchanter who held the position of companion and counsellor to King ARTHUR, and established the famous ROUND TABLE. Alfred TENNYSON relates the story of his life and deeds in his *Idylls of the King.*

Mermaid Club, The, a famous convivial and intellectual club said to have been founded by Sir Walter RALEIGH in 1603 at the Mermaid Tavern, London: among its members were Ben JONSON, William SHAKESPEARE, Francis BEAUMONT, John FLETCHER, and John DONNE.

Merola, Gaetano (1881-), Italian conductor who studied at the Royal Conservatory in Naples: in 1899 he became assistant conductor of Italian opera at the METROPOLITAN OPERA HOUSE, New York, and later of the Henry SAVAGE English Opera Company, the MANHATTAN OPERA COMPANY and from 1923 director of the SAN FRANCISCO and LOS ANGELES Opera Companies.

Merriman, Henry Seton, see **Scott, Hugh Stowell.**

Merritt, Anna Lea (1844-1930), American painter who studied with her husband, Henry Merritt, a well-known author and artist: her notable works include *Juliet; War; Ophelia; The Little Quakeress; Taming a Bird:* she painted the portrait of James Russell LOWELL, and published *An Artists Garden* in 1908.

Merry Widow, The, an operetta in three acts: libretto by Victor Leon and Leo Stein; music by Franz LEHAR; first produced at Vienna in 1905; in English at London in 1906, and at New York in 1907. The plot relates the story of Prince Danilo and the rich widow, Sonia, who had been his youthful sweetheart, but first chose to marry money: they are finally brought together after amusing complications. There are many recordings available of the numerous popular songs and dances in an opera which has been performed more than 5,000 times in the United States, and revived in 1931 and 1943: it was also filmed in 1934 with Jeanette MACDONALD and Maurice CHEVALIER.

Merry Wives of Windsor, The, a play said to have been written by William SHAKESPEARE in a fortnight to please the fancy of Queen ELIZABETH who wished to see FALSTAFF in love. It has been used as the basis of two grand operas: one by Otto NICOLAI with the same title and the libretto by Hermann von Mosenthal. It was produced at Berlin in 1849 with tremendous success, and at the Metropolitan Opera House, New York, in 1900 with Marcella SEMBRICH, Ernestine SCHUMANN-HEINK and Andreas DIPPEL in the cast. There are several Columbia and Victor recordings of the overture which has become a concert and radio favorite. The other opera is *Falstaff,* a grand opera in three acts: libretto by Arrigo BOITO, and music by Giuseppe VERDI; first produced at La Scala, Milan, in 1893, and at the Metropolitan Opera House, New York, in 1895 with Victor MAUREL in the title role. There is a Columbia recording of the complete opera.

Merson, Luc Olivier (1846-1920), French painter who studied with Isidore PILS: his works include *St. Louis Opening the Prisons; The Song of the Middle Ages; Poetry; The Wolf of Agubbio; The Sleep of Fra Angelico; Arrival at Bethlehem; Annunciation; Rest on the Flight into Egypt,* his masterpiece portraying the Virgin asleep between the paws of the SPHINX. He also illustrated Victor HUGO's *Notre Dame de Paris* and works by Gustave FLAUBERT and Théophile GAUTIER.

Merwin, Samuel (1874-1936), American novelist educated at Northwestern University, Illinois: his works include *The Short Line War* and *Calumet K—* with Henry K. Webster; *The Road to Frontenac; The Whip Hand; The Citadel; Anthony the Absolute; The Passionate Pilgrim; Old Concord; Moment of Beauty; Anabel at Sea; Bad Penny.*

Meryon, Charles (1821-1868), French engraver and etcher who created about one hundred views of old Paris, but died in an insane asylum before the high quality of his works, which are now collectors' items, became known. His genius was recognized by James HUNEKER in his *Promenades of an Impressionist.*

Mesdag, Hendrik Willem (1831-1915), Dutch painter who was connected with his father's banking business before studying with Sir Laurence ALMA-TADEMA. His works of note include *Fishermen's Boats at Scheveningen; Departure of a Life-boat; Return of a Life-boat; Sunrise on the Dutch Coast; Twilight; Summer Evening; Morning on the Scheldt; Fishmarket in Gröningen.*

Messager, André Charles Prosper (1853-1929), French composer and conductor who studied at the École Niedermeyer in Paris, and also composition with Camille SAINT-SAENS. In 1898 he became conductor at the OPERA-COMIQUE, Paris, in 1901 artistic director of the Royal Opera, Covent Garden, London, and in 1908 conductor at the Paris Opéra. He toured the United States in

1918 as conductor of the Paris Conservatory Orchestra. His notable dramatic works include *La Basoche, Véronique, Miss Dollar,* and *Madame Chrysanthème:* also several successful ballets.

Messiah, The, an oratorio by George Frederick HANDEL begun on August 22, 1741, and completed in twenty-three days: it was first performed at Dublin in 1742, and at Covent Garden, London, in 1743 when the *Hallelujah Chorus* created a veritable sensation. Excerpts from the oratorio were sung at New York in 1770, and the first complete performance given at Boston in 1818. There is an almost complete Columbia recording by the soloists, the chorus of the British Broadcasting Company, and the London Symphony Orchestra with Sir Thomas Beecham conducting.

Messina, see Antonella da Messina.

Meštrovič, Ivan (1883-), Serbian sculptor who learned to carve in stone and wood as a shepherd, and later became apprentice to a marble carver at Spalato. He succeeded in studying at the Vienna Academy and exhibited with success at the International Exhibition in Rome in 1912, and also at Venice where he presented twenty-six pieces of sculpture. His works include a portrait of Sir Thomas BEECHAM; an equestrian statue of Kraljevic Marko; a portrait of Auguste RODIN; *Well of Life; The Tomb of Kossovo; The Račič Mortuary Chapel:* also two equestrian statues of *American Indians* at the Chicago Art Institute.

Metal-work, an art which had its inception in the bronze age and the iron age: methods of beating and casting iron, bronze, and precious metals were known to the Egyptians, Assyrians, Chinese, Japanese, Greeks, and Romans, coming to the greatest degree of perfection in the Middle Ages. Among the articles produced in Germany, Italy, France, Spain, and England were monumental brasses, iron railings, locks, hinges, armor, door knockers, andirons, candlesticks, ecclesiastical furnishings, bronze doors, iron gates, and a multiplicity of ornamental and useful objects. Although there has been some attempts at revival, the art as practiced in medieval days is a lost one.

Metamorphoses (Ovid), a narrative poem by the Latin poet, OVID (Publius Ovidius Naso): it relates legends in which miraculous transformations of shape take place, and has furnished the basis for paintings, sculptures, and other forms of decorative art.

Metaphor, in literature the use of a word or phrase denoting one kind of object in place of another in order to suggest a similarity between the two. Simple examples are: "the ship *plows* the sea" and "he uttered a *volley* of oaths."

Metastasio, Pietro Antonio Domenico Bonaventura (1698-1782), Italian poet, dramatist, and librettist who was court poet at Vienna from 1730: his works include lyric verse; a masque, *The Gardens of the Hesperides;* thirty-four opera librettos written for GLUCK, HASSE, PORPORA, HANDEL, JOMMELLI, MEYERBEER, MOZART, PAISIELLO, PICCINNI, SCARLATTI, SPONTINI and other composers. One of his librettos, *Artaxerxes,* was set by forty composers.

Metaxa, Georges (1899-), Rumanian stage and screen actor educated at Bucharest University who made his debut in 1926 at London in *Hearts and Diamonds;* later appearing in *The Blue Mazurka; Wake Up and Dream; Bitter Sweet.* His New York debut was in *The Cat and the Fiddle* at the Masque Theatre in 1933: he also appeared in *Revenge with Music,* and in the films *Swingtime* and *The Doctor Takes a Wife.*

Metcalf, Willard Leroy (1858-1925), American painter who studied at art schools in Boston and at the Académie Julien in Paris, later becoming an instructor at Cooper Union and at the ART STUDENTS' LEAGUE, New York. His works include *Unfolding Buds; May Pastoral; North Country; May Night; Family of Birches.* In 1897 he joined with nine other painters in seceding from the Society of American Artists.

Metenier, Oscar (1859-1913), French novelist and dramatist whose horror dramas were written after holding the position of secretary to a police commissioner: they include *En famille* (1887); *La Casserole; The Brother Zemganno,* adapted from a novel by Edmond GONCOURT; *Monsieur Betsy; Trés Russe; Mademoiselle Fifi.* He founded the Grand GUIGNOL at Paris in 1897.

Metopes, in architecture the space between the TRIGLYPHS in Doric FRIEZES, usually decorated with paintings or BAS-RELIEFS: excellent examples are the metopes of the PARTHENON on which are painted a series of reliefs picturing the battle between the Lapithae and the CENTAURS. Fragments of these are to be seen in the ELGIN MARBLES at the British Museum.

Metre or **Meter,** in PROSODY the regulated, harmonious arrangement of syllables into verse, distinguished from prose by the uniformity of corresponding lines in respect to the number of syllables, and, in the case of rhymed verse, the similarity of final sound.

Metronome, a clockwork mechanism with a double pendulum invented by a Dutch mechanic, Winkel, in 1815, and appropriated by Johann Nepomuk Maelzel who patented it in France after Winkel refused to sell it to him. It is used for determining the speed at which a musical composition should be played: many composers place the marking "MM" on their music with an accompanying figure to indicate the number of beats per minute. It is used by many teachers for students learning to play strictly in time.

Metropolitan Museum of Art (New York), an institution founded in 1871 which has expanded in scope and size to such an extent that in less than seventy-five years it now requires more than 325,000 square feet of floor space to display its many rich and varied exhibits. Among the displays of *Ancient art* are a tomb erected in Egypt 4,400 years ago; a series of painted wooden funerary models from the tomb of a Theban prince; fine specimens of Egyptian jewelry; several colossal stone statues; the Carnavon collection of small

Egyptian art objects; an Etruscan bronze chariot; Greek and Roman statues and vases: also a collection of ancient glassware. The collection of *Far Eastern art* includes an assembly of Chinese sculpture and bronzes of various dynasties; collections of Chinese and Japanese paintings; assemblies of Chinese, Japanese, and Korean pottery and jades, and a choice exhibit of cloisonné. In the display of *Near Eastern art* there are Syrian lamps; Persian and Indian miniature paintings, rugs, pottery, wood, and stone carving; Indian and Tibetan jewelry. The *American and foreign picture galleries* contain more than 2,500 paintings: the American group includes canvases by ABBEY, ALLSTON, BINGHAM, BLAKELOCK, CASSATT, CHASE, COPLEY, EAKINS, HOMER, INNESS, RYDER, SARGENT, STUART, TRUMBULL, WEST, and WHISTLER. The foreign division comprises two RAPHAELS, several REMBRANDTS, and works by the BELLINIS, BOTTICELLI, BOUCHER, BOUTS, CEZANNE, CONSTABLE, COROT, DAUMIER, DAVID, DEGAS, DELACROIX, DURER, Fra ANGELICO, GAINSBOROUGH, GOYA, El GRECO, HALS, HOLBEIN, LAURENCE, MANTEGNA, MEMLING, POUSSIN, REYNOLDS, RUBENS, TINTORETTO, TITIAN, TURNER, VAN DYCK, VELAZQUEZ, VERONESE, WATTEAU, and hundreds of other artists in addition to special collections such as the *Benjamin Altman Collection* of Dutch masters; the *Theodore M. Davis Collection* of Italian paintings; the *Michael Friedsam Collection* of early French and Flemish canvases; the Havemeyer assembly of modern French paintings. The *Pierpont Morgan Collection* comprises exhibits of decorative arts including sculpture, furniture, textiles, ivories, woodwork, paintings, tapestries, goldsmiths' work, toilet accessories, watches, metal work, ceramics and glass, American and European sculpture. The American decorative arts wing contains examples of early American furniture placed in specially designed rooms: there is also a fine assembly of European, Near Eastern, Indian, Persian, Japanese, and Chinese armor. The print study room is replete with the finest examples of foreign and American prints and books. There is also an outstanding exhibit of 3,500 musical instruments which includes many rare examples. *The* CLOISTERS, a branch of the museum, located in Fort Tryon Park overlooking the Hudson River, contains one of the world's greatest collections of medieval art originally assembled by George Grey BARNARD, and presented to the museum by John D. Rockefeller, Jr.

Metropolitan Opera Auditions of the Air, The, a series of annual radio programs established at New York City in 1935. These programs are broadcast nationally, and are for the purpose of auditioning singers who wish to become members of the Metropolitan Opera House in New York. The series lasts for from fifteen to twenty-four weeks, each program being a half hour in duration; three singers are tested, each in two numbers. The judges are all members of the Opera, and include Edward Johnson, artistic director at the Metropolitan Opera House; John Erskine, Wilfred Pelletier, Edward Ziegler, and Earle Lewis. Two aspirants are chosen yearly, and have the privilege of singing at the Metropolitan the next season. Among the winners from 1935 to 1943 are several singers who are already well-known to opera and radio listeners: they include

Anna Kaskas, Arthur Carron, Thomas L. Thomas, Risë Stevens, John Gurney, John Carter, Leonard Warren, Arthur Kent, Lansing Hatfield, Lucielle Browning, Nicholas Massue, and Elwood Gary.

Metropolitan Opera Company, the name given the various organizations of singers who have appeared at the Metropolitan Opera House, New York, since its was formally opened on October 22nd, 1883, with Gounod's *Faust* under the management of Henry E. ABBEY: among the singers in the company were NILSSON, SCALCHI, CAMPANANINI, SEMBRICH, FURSCH-MADI, and Alwina VALLERIA, the first singer of American birth to appear with the organization. In 1884-85 Dr. Leopold DAMROSCH presented the operas of Richard WAGNER and also several French and Italian works; Amalie MATERNA, Marianne Brandt, and Anton Schott were among the new singers. In 1885-86, Lilli LEHMANN, Emil Fischer, Max ALSARY, and Albert NIEMANN sang under the direction of Anton SEIDL and Walter DAMROSCH who succeeded his father after the latter's death. From 1890 to 1897 Henry ABBEY, John B. Schoeffel, and Maurice GRAU undertook the management: among the new stars were the DE RESZKES, EAMES, NORDICA, ALBANI, CALVE, MELBA, PLANCON, LASALLE, and MAUREL. During 1897-98 there was no resident company: from 1898 to 1903 Maurice GRAU became sole manager, and the roster of new singers included SCHUMANN-HEINK, HOMER, SCOTTI, TERNINA, Suzanne ADAMS, DIPPEL, and CAMPANARI. Maurice Grau was then obliged to retire because of ill-health, and Heinrich CONRIED, former manager of the Irving Place Theatre, New York, assumed the post of manager from 1903 to 1908: he produced Wagner's *Parsifal* despite the opposition of Cosima WAGNER and the clergy of New York City, and also introduced several new singers including CARUSO, FREMSTAD, Edyth WALKER, FARRAR, CHALIAPIN, Burgstaller, and JOURNET. In 1908 Conried also resigned because of failing health: he was succeeded by Giulio GATTI-CASAZZA who remained until 1935, making a remarkable record both artistically and financially. Among the new singers who appeared during the twenty-seven year period were JERITZA, GALLI-CURCI, RETHBERG, Rosa PONSELLE, BORI, HEMPEL, ALDA, MATZENAUER, BRASLAU, MELCHIOR, MARTINELLI, GIGLI, Lotte LEHMANN, SCHORR, De LUCA, PINZA, and FLAGSTAD: also several Americans including Clarence WHITEHILL, John Charles THOMAS, and Lawrence TIBBETT. As a result of the financial crash of 1929, salaries were reduced, and funds raised by private and public subscription enabled the company to continue on a four-teen-week instead of a twenty-four-week schedule. Gatti-Casazza resigned in 1935, and was succeeded by Herbert WITHERSPOON who died before the 1935-36 season opened. His post was assumed by Edward JOHNSON who has continued until the present-time (1943). Among the artists who have been introduced since 1935 are THORBORG, WETTERGREN, MAISON, GIANNINI, Marjorie LAWRENCE, SAYAO, TRAUBEL, ALBANESE, DJANEL, PAULY, CASTAGNA, BENTONELLI, KIEPURA, BJOERLING, BROWNLEE, KIPNIS, BACCOLONI, and also many new American singers including Josephine Antoine, Lucy Monroe, Risë STEVENS, Charles KULLMAN, Joseph BENTONELLI, John Carter, James MELTON, Donald Dickson, Thomas L. Thomas, and Leonard

Warren. Several new operas have been presented in English, and also Gluck's *Alceste:* more than thirty operas revived, and three famous stars, Beniamino GIGLI, Tito SCHIPA and Giuseppe De LUCA, reappeared with the company after several years of absence. The broadcasting of performances was begun by a presentation of Humperdinck's *Hansel and Gretel* on December 25, 1931, and has been continued regularly on Saturday afternoons since 1932. Among the list of distinguished conductors have been Leopold DAMROSCH, Walter DAMROSCH, Anton SEIDL, Franz SCHALK, Felix MOTTL, Gustav MAHLER, Arturo TOSCANINI, Artur BODANZKY, Erich LEINSDORF, Bruno WALTER and Sir Thomas BEECHAM.

Metropolitan Opera Guild (New York), an organization founded by Mrs. August Belmont in 1935 with the purpose of bringing lovers of opera into closer contact with the Metropolitan Opera Association in New York. The Guild now has several thousand members: it publishes a magazine, *Opera News,* a *Metropolitan Opera Guide,* and a series of books on opera for children. It also conducts lectures on operatic subjects, arranges special performances for young people at reduced prices, and institutes many other activities of material assistance in increasing public interest in opera.

Metropolitan Opera House, see **Metropolitan Opera Company.**

Metsu, Gabriel (1630-1667), Dutch painter who studied with Jacob Metsu; also probably with Gerard DOU and REMBRANDT: his notable works include *The Music Lesson; Women Fruit Sellers; The Sick Child; The Music Lovers; Old Woman Asleep; Lazarus; Lady Reading a Letter; The Artist and His Wife; Woman Taken in Adultery; The Widow's Mite; Tuning the Lute; Oyster Luncheon; Sleeping Sportsman; Woman Poultry Seller; The Hay Barn; An Old Woman Meditating.*

Meulen, Adam Frans van der (1632-1690), Flemish painter who studied with Pieter Snayers and became court painter to LOUIS XIV with whom he traveled on the campaign in Flanders to paint battle scenes. His notable works include *Entry of Louis XIV into Arras; Army of Louis XIV before Tournai; Cavalry Attack; Traveling Train of a French Queen; Combat of Cavalry; Cavalry Skirmish; Landscape with Travelers and Horses; Louis XIV Receiving an Ambassador.*

Meunier, Constantin Émile (1831-1905), Belgian sculptor and painter who studied with his brother, Jean Baptiste Meunier, a well-known painter and etcher; also with Charles Faikin and F. J. Navez. His notable paintings include *A Trappist Funeral; In the Factory; Café Concert; The Puddlers; The Mower; Peasants' War; Return of the Miners.* His sculptures include decorations for the Botanic Garden at Brussels; *Monument to Labor;* a bronze group, *Maternity; The Sower; The Smith; The Miner; Ancestor:* also the unfinished monument to Émile ZOLA.

Meyer, Gustav (1868-), Austrian novelist who engaged in business and editorial work before taking up a literary career. His works include THE GOLEM (1915) and WALPURGIS NIGHT: he has also translated several of Charles DICKENS' novels into German. He uses the pen name "Gustav Meyrink."

Meyer, Johann Georg (1813-1886), German painter who studied at the Düsseldorf under Wilhelm SCHADOW: his notable works include *Elijah in the Lion's Den; Blind Man's Buff; Penitent Daughter; Little Mother; Child Knitting; Girl at Fountain; The Letter; Evening Prayer; Grandmother's Pet; The Inundation; The Listener; Preparing for Papa's Birthday; Watching the Baby; Grateful Convalescent.*

Meyerbeer, Giacomo (1791-1864), German opera composer of Jewish parentage whose real name was Jakob Liebmann Beer. He studied the piano with Muzio CLEMENTI and was regarded as an accomplished pianist at the age of nine. After studying music theory with Carl ZELTER and the Abbé VOGLER, his opera, *Jephthar Gelübde* was produced at Munich in 1813: during the same year a comic opera, *Alimelek,* was a success at Stuttgart. After achieving success with an opera in Italian, *Margherita d'Anjou* at Milan in 1820, an opera in German, *Dar Brandenburger Thor,* failed to be produced at Berlin in 1823: he went to Paris in 1826, and his opera *Robert Le Diable,* was an enormous success there in 1831. It was followed by *Les Huguenots; Le Prophète; Das Feldlager in Schliesen; L'Étoile du Nord; Le Pardon de Ploërmel (Dinorah); L'Africaine.* While he was an important dramatic composer of his time, his operas no longer hold the interest of the musical public although some of the arias are standard concert and recital numbers.

Meyer-Förster, Wilhelm (1862-1934), German novelist and dramatist: his most famous novel, *Karl Heinrich* (1899) was the basis for the play, *Prince Karl,* in which Richard MANSFIELD appeared successfully, and also of *The Student Prince,* an operetta with music by Sigmund ROMBERG.

Meyerhold, Vsevolod Emilievich (1873-), Russian actor and theatrical producer who appeared at the Moscow ART THEATRE, and later directed the Maryinsky and Alexandrinsky Imperial Theatres. He made several drastic changes in lighting and settings, organizing the theatrical division of the People's Commissariat for Education in 1918: his play, *The Death and Destruction of Europe,* was produced in 1923, and he also published a volume, *The Theatre,* outlining his dramatic theories.

Meynell, Alice (1847-1922), English poet and essayist whose husband, Wilfred Meynell was an editor who founded *Merry England,* a periodical which printed the early works of Hilaire BELLOC and other English writers. Her essays and poems include *Preludes* (1875); *A Father of Women; The Poor Sisters of Nazareth; The Rhythm of Life; London Impressions; John Ruskin; The Second Person Singular.*

Meyrink, Gustav, see **Meyer, Gustav.**

Mezzanine, in architecture a small story in a residence or public building usually placed midway between the first two larger stories. The term is also applied to small windows in which the length is greater than the height: the first balcony in a theatre or public auditorium is often called the mezzanine.

Mezzo-relievo, in sculpture a term applied to a relief that projects one half of its proper proportion from the base on which it is carved.

Mezzo soprano, see **Soprano.**

Mezzotint, an engraving process on copper or steel which is the reverse of line engraving or ETCHING: it requires the use of a curved, sawtoothed tool called a rocker which creates an even grain over the entire plate, and yields a soft effect in the print after the plate has been gone over with the scraper and burnisher. The process was employed in England for reproducing the paintings of Joseph TURNER, Joshua REYNOLDS, and John CONSTABLE.

Miaskovsky, Nicolas (1881-), Russian composer who studied with GLIERE, and also with RIMSKY-KORSAKOW, and LIADOFF at the St. Petersburg Conservatory where he has been professor of composition since 1921. His works include twenty-one (or more) symphonies; a violin concerto; three string quartets, three piano sonatas: also many songs.

Micaëla, a character in Georges BIZET's grand opera, *Carmen:* she is the village sweetheart of DON JOSE before he enlists in the Spanish army, and is unable to hold his affections after he falls in love with Carmen. Her only aria in the opera, *Je dis que rien ne m'épouvante* has been recorded by Eidé NORENA for Victor.

Michelangelo or **Michelangelo Buonarroti** (1475-1564), Italian sculptor, painter, architect, and poet who revealed talent at drawing in his infancy, studying painting at an early age with Domenico GHIRLANDAIO, and later sculpture at the Academy in the gardens of St. Mark's, Florence. He attracted the interest of Lorenzo dei MEDICI with his *Faun's Mask* who offered him a home in the Medici Palace as long as he lived. He worked among Lorenzo's collection of antiques which inspired the sculptures *Combat of Centaurs and Lapiths; Laughing Satyr; Apollo and Marsyas;* a colossal *Hercules; Cupid.* He left Florence in 1494 for Venice, but returned in 1495 to paint *The Deposition:* in 1496 he went to Rome where he created the *Pietà* at St. Peter's. In 1501 he was again in Florence where he made fifteen figures for the Cathedral at Siena, and three years later created the colossal *David* in marble, and another statue on the same subject in bronze. The works which followed include the figures of the twelve apostles for the Duomo; a decoration, *The Battle of Cascine,* for the Council Room of the Palazzo della Signoria; a *Holy Family; Madonna and Child;* the Tomb of Pope Julius II; the statue of *Moses;* the fresco on the ceiling of the SISTINE CHAPEL; the façade and the new sacristy for the Church of San Lorenzo; the citadels and fortification during the Revolution; *Leda and the Swan*

for the Duke of Ferrara; a painting, *The Last Judgment,* in the Apostolic Palace at Rome; *Conversion of St. Paul* and *Crucifixion of St. Peter* in the Pauline Chapel; the model of a new dome at St. Peter's; the designing of the Laurentian Library and the Medici Sepulchral Chapel. His sonnets and madrigals, many of which were dedicated to Vittoria COLONNA, are worthy of being compared with those of PETRARCH and DANTE.

Michel de Notredrame, see **Nostradamus.**

Michelozzi Michelozzo (1396-1472), Italian architect and sculptor who was also a goldsmith: he was associated with either DONATELLO or GHIBERTI on many works including a statue of *St. Michael;* the tomb of *Pope John XXII,* at Florence; the tomb of *Cardinal Brancacci* at Naples, a lunette over the doorway of the Duomo of Montepulciano; a statue of St. John at Florence. He also designed the Riccardi Palace for Cosimo di MEDICI at Florence, and reconstructed the palace at Milan presented to Cosimo di Medici by Francesco Sforza.

Mickey Mouse, see **Disney, Walter.**

Mickiewicz, Adam (1798-1855), Polish poet who was banished for his political activities, and lived chiefly at Paris after 1828. His works include *Sonnets from the Crimea:* also the epic poems *Forefather's Eve; Konrad Wallenrod; Grazyna; Pan Tadeusz;* the latter regarded as one of the masterpieces of Polish literature.

Micon, Greek painter and sculptor who worked during the 5th century B.C., with POLYGNOTUS: among his noted works are *The Battle of Theseus; The Battle of the Athenians and Amazons; The Battle of Marathon; Battle of the Centaurs and Lapiths; The Expedition of the Argonauts:* he was reputed to be especially skilful, according to PLINY, in the painting of horses.

Microphone, an instrument used in broadcasting which is really a telephone transmitter used to transform sound waves sent out from the antennae of broadcasting stations into electrical currents. It was invented first by D. E. Hughes; there are three kinds: the *condenser microphone* in which sound waves alter the distance between two plates of the condenser when striking them; the *magneto microphone* in which the sound waves strike a flat coil of wire in a magnetic field; the *carbon microphone* in which the sound waves vary the resistance of carbon granules through a fluctuating current of air.

Midas, in Greek mythology a king of Phrygia who was granted any favor he might desire by DIONYSUS because of kindness shown the latter's teacher, SILEMUS. Midas wished that everything he might touch would turn to gold, but when his food and water turned to gold, he prayed that the favor be withdrawn which was accomplished by bathing in the Pactolus river, a stream which immediately became gold-bearing.

Middleton, George (1880-), American dramatist educated at Columbia University: his first play in collaboration with Paul Kester, *The Cavalier,* was produced in 1902 by Julia MARLOWE, and many early 20th century stars appeared in his fine adaptations of foreign plays which included *Embers* (1911); *The Unknown Lady; The Road Together; The Other Rose; Accused,* adapted from Eugène BRIEUX's "L'Avocat"; *Polly With a Past; Collusion; The Light of the World; Madame Capet,* a French adaptation in which Eva LE GALLIENNE played the role of Marie ANTOINETTE; *Masks; That Man Balzac.*

Middleton, Thomas (c.1570-1627), English dramatist who wrote in collaboration with DRAYTON, ROWLEY, JONSON, WEBSTER, and other contemporary authors: his plays include *A Trick to Catch the Old One; Michelmas Term; A Game at Chess; A Mad World, My Masters; Women, Beware Women; No Wit, No Help Like a Women's; More Dissemblers besides Women; Anything for a Quiet Life.*

Midsummer Night's Dream, A, a play by William SHAKESPEARE which it is presumed was first performed between 1590 and 1595 at some festive occasion at which Queen ELIZABETH was present, because of the direct reference made to her by the king of the fairies, OBERON: the author probably consulted CHAUCER's *Knight's Tale* in preparing the manuscript. In 1826 Felix MENDELSSOHN composed an *Overture to "A Midsummer Night's Dream"* when he was only seventeen years old, and in 1843 he wrote incidental music at the command of William IV of Prussia which was performed at the King's Theatre during the same year: the principal numbers included *Scherzo,* entr'acte for Act II; *Intermezzo* for Act III; *Nocturne,* the entr'acte for Act IV; *Wedding March; Clown Dance* in Act V. There are Victor or Columbia recordings for all the numbers mentioned except the *Clown Dance* and *Intermezzo.* In 1935 Max REINHARDT directed a film production of *A Midsummer Night's Dream* for Warner Brothers in which both major and minor roles were played by Hollywood stars of the first magnitude.

Mielziner, Jo (1901-), American artist and scenic designer born in France who appeared first as an actor, but has made his most important contribution to the American theatre in his designs for the scenes and costumes for many successful plays including *The Guardsman* (1924); *Strange Interlude; Street Scene; Uncle Vanya; Of Thee I Sing; The Barretts of Wimpole Street; Brief Moment; Biography; The Gay Divorcée; Dodsworth; Yellow Jack; Accent on Youth; Winterset; Pride and Prejudice; Ethan Frome; On Borrowed Time; St. Helena; The Women; Susan and God; Abe Lincoln in Illinois; No Time for Comedy.*

Mierevelt, Michiel Janszen van (1567-1641), Dutch painter who studied with William Willenz, and later became court painter for the house of Orange. He worked chiefly at The Hague and in Delft, refusing to go to England to execute the portrait of CHARLES I. His son and pupil, **Pieter van Mierevelt** (1595-1623), was also a fine portraitist who imitated his father, and painted a *Lecture in Anatomy* which is now in the hospital at Delft.

Mieris, Frans van (1635-1681), Dutch painter, known as The Elder; he studied with Gerard Dou who considered him the greatest of his pupils: among his notable works are *Lady in a Crimson Jacket; Woman Reading Music; Lady Playing the Lute; Escaped Bird; Oyster Dinner; Boy Blowing Bubbles; Peasant Woman Drawing Water; Soldier in Armor; Cavalier and Lace Maker.* His son, **Frans van Mieris** (1689-1763), known as The Younger, was a painter of much less ability than his father: his best pictures include *Hermit at Prayer; The Pharmacy; Fishmonger; Pedlar and Boy.*

Mifflin, Lloyd (1846-1921), American painter and poet who was educated at the Washington Classical Institute, and studied painting with his father, J. Houston Lloyd. His health failed him, and he began writing in 1895 when his first work, *The Hills,* appeared: it was followed by *At the Gates of Song; The Slopes of Helicon; Echoes of Greek Idyls; The Fields of Dawn; Castalian Days; My Lady of Dream; The Flower and Thorn; As Twilight Falls.*

Mignard, Pierre (1610-1695), French painter who studied with Jean Boucher of Bourges, and with Simon Voriet, living for more than twenty years in Italy where he painted portraits of the nobility and clergy as well as executing several frescoes. Among his notable works are *The Circumcision; Baptism of Christ; Birth of Apollo; Apollo and Aurora;* portrait of Mme. de MAINTENON; *Apollo and Minerva; Prometheus and Pandora in Olympus; St. Cecilia; Genius of France between Apollo and Minerva.*

Mignon or **Minjon, Abraham** (1640-1679), German painter who went to Holland in 1660 with Jakob Marrel, studied with J. Davidsz de HEEM, and became a distinguished painter of flowers, birds, fruits, and still life. One of his favorite designs was the introduction of red or white roses in the center of a canvas, with the entire group of flowers set against a dark background. His pictures such as *Flowers in a Vase* are to be seen in the LOUVRE, and at many other museums in Holland, Germany, Denmark, and Italy.

Mignon, grand opera in three acts: libretto by Michel Carré and Julius BARBIER founded on GOETHE's romance, *Wilhelm Meister;* music by Ambroise THOMAS; first produced at the OPERA-COMIQUE, Paris, in 1866; at the Academy of Music, New York, in 1871, and at the Metropolitan Opera House, in 1883. The plot is a melodramatic one in which Mignon, a poor waif, is rescued from gypsies by Wilhelm Meister, a wealthy student who is apparently infatuated with Filena, an actress. When Mignon tells Lothario, a mad singer who has been wandering about the world in search of his long-lost daughter, that she would rather see Wilhelm's castle in flames than have him united to Filena, Lothario sets it afire, and Wilhelm rescues Mignon whom he really loves. Later Lothario regains his reason; identifies Mignon as his daughter and all ends happily. There is a Columbia abridged recording of the opera: also a Victor recording of the overture, and of the popular soprano arias, *Connais tu le pays?* and *Je suis Titania.*

Mikado, the fanciful title applied in foreign countries to the emperor of Japan: the history of the Japanese sovereigns dates back to ancient times, but the real power during the 17th century was in the hands of the shoguns or military governors presumably appointed by the mikados. In 1889 a new constitution made the mikado less of an absolute monarch, but he still holds the power of declaring war, making peace and concluding treaties.

Mikado, The, comic opera in two acts: libretto by Sir William S. GILBERT; music by Sir Arthur S. SULLIVAN; first produced at the Savoy Theatre, London, in 1885, and at the Fifth Avenue Theatre, New York, during the same year. The story is: Nanki-Poo, son of the Mikado, falls in love with Yum Yum, the ward of Ko-Ko, a tailor risen to the rank of Lord High Executioner, but the latter refuses to permit the lovers to marry because he wishes to be the bridegroom himself. When he is warned by the Mikado that he must execute someone within a month or lose his high office, he agrees that the lovers may be united if Nanki-Poo agrees to have his head cut off at the end of thirty days. The arrival of the Mikado, accompanied by Katisha, the ugly old maid whom Nanki-Poo has refused to marry, brings matters to a climax: after some laughable complications the lovers are united and Ko-Ko is obliged to accept Katisha as his bride. There is a Victor recording of the complete opera. In 1939 *The Hot Mikado,* a "swing" version of the operetta, with an all-Negro cast starring the veteran dancer and actor, Bill ROBINSON, had some success at New York.

Milan Cathedral, one of the largest churches in the world, begun in 1386 and completed almost a hundred years later: it is constructed of white marble with five aisles, and the architecture is more German than Italian. Its flat roofs are concealed by flying buttresses, and ornamented by more than a hundred pinnacles: the interior has thousands of statues set in niches, and the façade is largely RENAISSANCE in style.

Mildenburg, Anna von (1872-), Austrian dramatic soprano who studied at the Vienna Conservatory with Rosa Papier, making her first appearance at Hamburg in 1895. In 1897 she made her debut at BAYREUTH, becoming one of the greatest of Wagnerian sopranos; after appearing for twenty years at the Vienna and Covent Garden Opera, she became a successful teacher at Munich, founding her own school in 1926. She published her reminiscences in 1921, and also two treatises on Richard WAGNER's music dramas with her husband, Hermann BAHR, a German poet and dramatist.

Milhaud, Darius (1892-), French pianist and composer who studied at the Paris Conservatory with Vincent D'INDY and Charles WIDOR, later becoming one of the group of French composers known as Les Six. In 1922 he came to the United States as guest lecturer on music at several American colleges, also playing and conducting his own compositions: in 1940 he became a permanent resident. His compositions include several operas; orchestral works; a piano concerto; a violin

concerto; nine string quartets; numerous works for piano and many songs.

"Military" Symphony (Haydn), an orchestral work by Josef HAYDN, one of six symphonies written for his second visit to England in 1794-95. It was first performed in 1794: its title "Military" is derived from the employment of several percussion instruments and the use of an Austrian bugle call in the second movement. There is a Victor recording by the Vienna Philharmonic orchestra conducted by Bruno Walter.

Millais, Sir John Everett (1829-1896), English painter who entered the Royal Academy School, London, as a boy of ten, and at seventeen exhibited *Pizarro Seizing the Inca of Peru:* in 1847 he received a gold medal for *The Benjamites Seizing the Daughters of Shiloh.* He was one of the founders of the PRE-RAPHAELITE Brotherhood with Dante Gabriel ROSSETTI and William Holman HUNT: among his noted works are *The Carpenter's Shop; Death of Ophelia; The Huguenot; The Valley of Rest; Christ in the House of His Parents; Lorenzo and Isabella; The Boyhood of Sir Walter Raleigh; The Eve of St. Agnes; The North-West Passage; The Blind Girl.* He also painted many portraits including those of Thomas CARLYLE, Sir Alfred TENNYSON, Sir Henry IRVING, John RUSKIN, Gerald DU MAURIER, and Sir John HARE.

Milland, Ray (1905-), Irish screen actor educated at Kings College who has appeared in numerous English and American films including *Ambassador Bill; Payment Deferred; Orders is Orders; Bolero; The Gilded Lily; Four Hours to Kill; The Glass Key; The Return of Sophie Lang; Three Smart Girls; Easy Living; Men with Wings; Beau Geste; Everything Happens at Night; The Lady Has Plans; Reap the Wild Wind; The Crystal Ball.*

Millay, Edna St. Vincent (1892-), American poet educated at Barnard and Vassar Colleges: her works include *Renascence* (1912); *A Few Figs from Thistles; Second April; The Ballad of the Harp-Weaver; The Buck in the Snow; Fatal Interview; Wine from These Grapes; Conversation at Midnight; Huntsman, What Quarry?; Make Bright the Arrows; There Are No Islands Any More:* she also wrote the libretto of Deems TAYLOR's grand opera, *The King's Henchman.*

Miller, Alice Duer (1874-1942), American novelist and poet educated at Barnard College: her works include *The Modern Obstacle* (1903); *Less than Kin; The Blue Arch; Are Women People?; Come Out of the Kitchen; The Charm School; Manslaughter; Are Parents People?; Gowns by Roberta,* used as the story of a popular operetta, "Roberta," by Jerome KERN; *Come Out of the Pantry; The White Cliffs* (1940), a narrative poem which has sold more than two hundred thousand copies.

Miller, Charles Henry (1842-1922), American painter who studied at Munich, Leipzig, Berlin, Dresden, Vienna, and Paris, establishing his studio at New York in 1875, and painting chiefly scenes on Long Island including *Old Oaks at Creedmoor;*

New York from Newtown Creek; Sunset at East Hampton; Long Island Fisherman's Home; At Valley Stream; Old Mill and Water Gate; Old Mill at Patchogue; Bouquet of Oaks at Stewart's Pond. He also wrote *The Philosophy of Art in America* (1885) under the pen name "Carl de Muldor."

Miller, Gilbert Heron (1884-), American theatrical manager and producer, son of Henry MILLER, who first appeared in 1906 as an actor, and made his first production, *Daddy Long-Legs,* in 1916 at London. Among the plays he has produced in England or the United States are *The Willow Tree; Monsieur Beaucaire; Peter Pan; The Green Goddess; The Last of Mrs. Cheyney; Michael and Mary; The Vinegar Tree; The Late Christopher Bean; Her Cardboard Lover; Berkeley Square; Strange Interlude; Another Language; Reunion in Vienna; Men in White; Tovarich; Victoria Regina; The Petrified Forest; The Amazing Dr. Clitterhouse.*

Miller, Henry (1860-1926), American actor-manager born in England who came to the United States as a boy of eleven, and first appeared in 1879 with a stock company in Toronto, Canada. After playing with Helena MODJESKA, Minnie Maddern FISKE, and as leading man with the Charles FROHMAN Stock Company at the EMPIRE THEATRE, New York, he achieved great success in *The Only Way* in 1899. Among his signal successes were *The Great Divide; Her Husband's Wife; The Havoc; The Rainbow; Daddy Long-Legs; A Marriage of Convenience; Molière; The Famous Mrs. Fair; La Tendresse; Pasteur; The Changelings.*

Miller, Joaquin (1841-1913), American poet and dramatist whose real name was Cincinnatus Heine Miller. He was born in Indiana, but taken to Oregon in 1854: he spent much of his time in Indian camps and later went to California on gold-hunting expeditions. His works include *Songs of the Sierras; Songs of the Sunlands; The Danites of the Sierras,* a play produced at New York in 1877 which achieved great success in the United States and England: also three other less successful plays and some books of verse. He has become a traditional figure in Western history and literature.

Miller, Joe (1684-1738), English actor of comedy parts whose name was placed in 1739 on a collection of jokes called *Joe Miller's Jest Book, or the Wit's Vade Mecum* which was actually compiled by John Mottley. He was a favorite comedian at the DRURY LANE THEATRE, London, but was so illiterate that he could memorize his parts only through his wife reading them to him. In stage parlance, a "Joe Miller" is the name for a time-worn joke.

Miller, Marilyn (1898-1936), American actress and dancer who made her debut at five as a member of the Columbian Trio with her mother and stepfather. In 1914 she appeared at the Winter Garden, New York, in the *Passing Show of 1914,* later playing in *The Ziegfeld Follies of 1918; Sally,* a musical comedy in which she appeared for three years; *Peter Pan; Sunny; Rosalie;*

Smiles; As Thousands Cheer. She was also featured in several films including *Sally; Sunny; Her Majesty, Love.*

Miller, Richard E. (1875-1943), American painter who studied at the St. Louis School of Fine Arts, and at the Académie Julien in Paris, exhibiting at the Paris Salon in 1901, and winning the gold medal. He was awarded many medals and prizes in the United States, and his salon pictures of 1908, 1909, and 1914 were purchased for the Luxembourg Gallery by the French Government who made him a Knight of the Legion of Honor in 1906. He was also the dean of the Provincetown (Mass.) Art Colony.

Milles, Carl Wilhelm Emil (1875-), American sculptor born in Sweden who migrated to the United States in 1929, and became an American citizen in 1942. He studied at the Technical School at Stockholm, and has been the recipient of many prizes and medals for works to be seen in Sweden, Germany, Italy, England, and the United States. In 1943 the Award of Merit Medal of the AMERICAN ACADEMY OF ARTS AND LETTERS for outstanding works in the arts was presented to him.

Millet, Aimé (1819-1891), French sculptor who studied with David d'Angers whose style he adopted in the many statues of famous men which he executed. Among his notable works are *Apollo* at L'Opéra, Paris; a colossal statue in copper of *Vercingetorix,* made for Napoleon III; also numerous allegorical figures including *Narcissus* and *Ariadne.*

Millet, Francis Davis (1846-1912), American painter, illustrator and writer who served as a drummer boy in the Civil War, was graduated from Harvard College in 1869, and studied at the Royal Academy of Fine Arts in Antwerp. He acted as correspondent for London and New York newspapers during the Russo-Turkish War, served on the International Art Jury at the Paris Exposition in 1878, and directed the art work at the Columbia Exposition in 1893. He executed many murals in American public buildings: his notable paintings include *Bay of Naples; An Oldtime Melody; A Cosy Corner; Between Two Fires; Man Reading the Koran; Sweet Mistris Mercie.* He also wrote *The Danube,* and *Capillary Crime and Other Stories.*

Millet, Jean François (1814-1875), French painter who studied with Jean Charles LANGLOIS and with Paul DELAROCHE, finally becoming one of the world's greatest painters of peasant life in all its varied phases. His famous canvases include *Sailors Mending a Sail; The Gleaners; The Angelus; The Man with a Hoe; The Lacemaker; Shepherdess and Flock; Knitting Lesson; Young Mother and Her Baby; The Sower; The Water Carrier; Potato Planters; Death and the Woodcutter; Jews at Babylon; The Wool Carder; Shepherdess Knitting; Ruth and Boaz; Farm Yard Scene.*

Millöcker, Karl (1842-1899), German operatic composer who studied at the Vienna Conservatory, and later became conductor at the Theater au den Wien there. His numerous operettas include *The Countess Dubarry; The Beggar Student; Gasparone; Poor Jonathan:* all of these were immensely popular in Germany, and have been produced in the United States.

Mills, Clark (1815-1883), American sculptor who was chiefly self-taught: he started a foundry and cast the first equestrian statue in 1853 ever made in the United States; that of Andrew Jackson for Lafayette Square in Washington, D. C. He also executed an equestrian statue of George Washington: Thomas CRAWFORD's *Freedom,* created for the dome of the CAPITOL at Washington, D. C., was cast in his foundry.

Mills, Robert (1781-1855), American architect who was appointed architect of public buildings in Washington, D. C., by Andrew Jackson: his works include the Treasury Building; the United States Patent Office; the old Post Office; the Washington Monument completed after his death; the Bunker Hill Monument at Charlestown, Mass.; the Washington Monument at Baltimore, Md.

Mills, Sebastian Bach (1838-1898), American pianist and composer born in England who studied at the Leipzig Conservatory with Ignaz Moscheles, and later with Franz LISZT. After appearing with the GEWANDHAUS Orchestra he came to the United States in 1859, making his debut with the Philharmonic Society in the Robert SCHUMANN *Concertstück, Op. 92,* and appearing regularly as soloist every year until 1877. He introduced many piano works new to New York concert-goers including CHOPIN's *Concerto in F minor,* LISZT's *Concerto in E♭ major,* and MOZART's *Posthumous Concerto in C major.* His compositions included salon pieces for the piano.

Milmore, Martin (1844-1883), American sculptor born in Ireland who came to the United States with his family as a boy of eleven: his works include the *Soldiers' Monument* in Forest Hills Cemetery, Roxbury, Mass.; the *Soldiers' and Sailors' Monument* on Boston Common; he also made portrait busts of Pope Pius IX, Wendell Phillips, Ralph Waldo EMERSON, and Charles Sumner.

Milne, Alan Alexander (1882-), English novelist and dramatist who was first a journalist and from 1906 to 1914 assistant editor of PUNCH. He served during World War I: his most popular plays include *Mr. Pym Passes By* (1919); *The Truth about Blayds; The Dover Road; The Perfect Alibi; The Ivory Door; Michael and Mary.* His novels include *Mr. Pim* (1921); *The Red House Mystery; Two People; Four Days' Wonder:* he has also written several books for children, such as *Winnie-the-Pooh,* and an autobiography, *It's Too Late Now.*

Milon, Louis Jacques Jessé (1765-1849), French dancer and choreographer who studied at the dancing academy of L'Opéra, Paris, making his debut in 1790, and later becoming *premier danseur.* Among the ballets which he produced were *Hero and Leander; Pygmalion; The Return of*

Ulysses; Nina, or the Folly of Love; The Carnival of Venice; The Happy Return; Clari.

Milstein, Nathan (1904-), Russian violinist who studied with Eugène YSAYE and Leopold AUER: after making his debut in 1923, he toured Russia with Vladimir HOROWITZ, and later made a successful tour of Europe and South America as soloist. In 1928 he made his debut with the Philadelphia Symphony Orchestra, and has since appeared in recital, with all the major American orchestras and on radio broadcasts.

Milton, John (1608-1674), English poet educated at Cambridge where he wrote a number of poems in both English and Latin: he traveled in Europe during 1638-39, and on his return to England wrote many controversial tracts on religious and social subjects, and became Latin secretary under Cromwell, but was forced out at the Restoration. He became blind in 1652 and worked entirely with the aid of his secretary, Andrew Marvell, and his daughters. His master works include *Paradise Lost* (1667); *Paradise Regained; Samson Agonistes,* a tragedy; also the poems *Comus, Lycidas, L'Allegro,* and *Il Penseroso.*

Mime, a character in Richard WAGNER's music drama, *Siegfried:* he brings up SIEGFRIED in a cave after the death of SIEGLINDE, the latter's mother. He tries to forge a sword which will destroy the dragon, FAFNER, but is unable to do so: Siegfried welds together the fragments of the sword which belonged to SIEGMUND, his father, and tests it by splitting the anvil in twain on which he forged it.

Mimi, a character in Giacomo PUCCINI's grand opera, La BOHEME: she is an embroiderer of flowers on velvet with whom RODOLFO, a poet, falls in love. After a period of ephemeral happiness, they part, but are finally reunited when she is brought back by MUSETTA to the bare garret only to die of consumption.

Mimo-drama, (a) in drama a wordless play performed by actors by means of PANTOMIME: the best examples are *Sumurun* and *The Miracle* as produced by Max REINHARDT: (b) in music a pantomimic drama with incidental music.

Minaret, in architecture a lofty tower forming a part of the Mohammedan MOSQUE, which has a projecting balcony from which the muezzin recites the call to prayer. The term is used at the present time for all forms of turrets.

Mind, Gottfried (1768-1814), Swiss painter who studied with Sigmund Freudenberger, and specialized in the painting of cats with such excellent results that he was surnamed the "Cat Raphael." Among his canvases are *Cat with Her Young; Group of Cats; Two Poodle Dogs; Children at Play.*

Ming Dynasty, a succession of emperors founded in China by Chu Yüen-chang, the son of a laboring man. In 1355 he defeated Shun-ti, a descendant of JENGHIZ KHAN, assuming the title of emperor in 1368, and calling himself Hung-wu. The arts of painting and literature flourished for nearly three hundred years under the Ming ("Bright") dynasty.

Miniature, in painting a term first applied to small water-color drawings on illuminated manuscripts, and later broadened to include all paintings, drawings, or engravings of delicate design and small size. Miniatures were common in Egypt, Byzantium, Greece, Rome, and thousands were made in Europe during the Middle Ages before the invention of printing. Among the famous miniature painters were NATTIER, BOUCHER, FRAGONARD, ISABEY, HONE, COPLEY, and MALBONE.

Minneapolis Symphony Orchestra, an organization founded by Emil Oberhoffer in 1903, and conducted by him until 1921: among the guest conductors were Artur BODANZKY, Albert COATES, Walter DAMROSCH, Ossip GABRILOWITSCH. Henry VERBRUGGHEN became permanent conductor from 1923 to 1931 and Eugene ORMANDY from 1931 to 1935 with several distinguished guest conductors. In 1936 Dimitri MITROUPOULOS became conductor with Daniele AMFITHEATROFF as associate, and permanent conductor in 1937.

Minnesingers (Ger. **Minnesänger**), the lyric poets and singers of the 12th and 13th centuries in Germany, later succeeded by the MASTERSINGERS. They accompanied their songs on the lute: great poetical and singing contests were held at regular intervals, and one of the latter was immortalized in Richard WAGNER's *Die* MEISTERSINGER VON NURNBERG.

Mino da Fiesole (1431-1484), Italian sculptor, also known as Mino di Giovanni, who worked with DESIDERIO DA SETTIGNANO and Matteo Civitale: his works include several fine altarpieces; the pulpit in the Prato Cathedral; the tomb of Pope Paul II parts of which are in the crypt at St. Peter's; a marble reredos in the Church of Santa Mario del Popolo: also several portrait busts and profile bas-reliefs now in the BARGELLO MUSEUM at Florence.

Minor, Robert Crannell (1840-1904), American painter who studied at Paris and Antwerp, also sketching in Germany and Italy. He was a follower of the BARBIZON SCHOOL, and after his death his pictures became collectors' items: they include *Studio of Jean Baptiste Corot; Sundown; Eventide; October Days; Interior of the Forest; Sunrise on Lake Champlain; Autumn Morning; Cloudy Moonlight; Close of Day; Evening After Rain.*

Minor, in music an expression used in connection with INTERVALS, CHORDS, and KEYS. It is the smallest interval on the keyboard, and is known as a *minor second* or more commonly as a semitone. *Minor chords* are those with a minor third, and minor keys are those based on minor *scales.*

Minotaur, in Greek mythology a monster with the body of a man and the head of a bull: it was confined in a labyrinth at Crete, and fed with the flesh of seven maidens and seven youths sent by Athens periodically as tribute to Minos, king of Crete. THESEUS killed the minotaur with the aid of ARIADNE, daughter of Minos.

Minstrels, professional musicians of the Middle Ages who sang or recited poems, sometimes of their own composition to instrumental accompaniment. They traveled in the trains of the nobility at court and on the battlefield, later becoming the musical attendants of the troubadours in France, their duties consisting in playing the creations of the latter. Large numbers of minstrels accompanied William the Conqueror to England where they degenerated to such an extent that they were finally classed as rogues, beggars, and vagabonds.

Minstrels, Negro, an American form of theatrical entertainment which began in 1828 when Thomas D. Rice (1808-1860) sang the "Jim Crow" song of a Negro stage driver in blackface at Pittsburgh: he pleased his audiences so much that imitators sprang up all over the United States. Some of America's finest actors such as Edwin FORREST, Edwin BOOTH, and Joseph JEFFERSON appeared in blackface during their early careers; among the popular organizations were the Virginia Minstrels; CHRISTY's Minstrels, greatly fêted while on a visit to England; Buckley's New Orleans Serenaders; Bryant's Minstrels; Woods Minstrels; Haverly's Minstrels; Primrose and West.

Minuet, a dance popular in France during the 17th and 18th centuries: it was written in 3-4 time, and consisted of two minuets or a double minuet with contrasted sections of sixteen measures each, the second section forming the *Trio* after which the first was repeated. The minuet was used frequently in the suite, sonata, and symphony: the most famous examples are the minuet in MOZART's *Don Giovanni;* the *Minuet in G* by BEETHOVEN, the *Minuet* by PADEREWSKI, and the *Minuet in A* by BOCCHERINI.

Mirabeau, Honoré Gabriel Riquetti, Count de (1749-1791), French statesman and orator of the French Revolution who was elected a delegate to the convention of the States-General in 1789, becoming a political power through his oratorical ability, and president of the National Assembly in 1791. He appears to have had some sympathies with the Royalists although he appeared before the court against them.

Miracle Plays, sacred plays of the Middle Ages also known as mystery or morality plays: their subjects and characters were usually taken from the BIBLE or legendary events. They were first presented in churches, and later, as audiences grew larger, in the open: the language in the earlier plays was Latin, but gradually they were presented in the languages of the different countries. In France the earliest play in the vernacular was *Adam* in the 12th century; in the Netherlands a series called *The Seven Joys of Maria;* in Italy the *Passion of Jesus Christ;* in Spain *The Three Kings;* in Germany *The Wise and Foolish Virgins;* in England the *Harrowing of Hill.*

Mira de Amescua, Antonio (c.1578-1644), Spanish priest and dramatist who collaborated with Juan Montalbán and Pedro CALDERON in a play, *Polyphemus and Circe,* published in 1634, and was one of the high ecclesiastics in the Spanish church. His best known work is *The Slave of the Devil:* Pierre Corneille is said to have borrowed freely from his works.

Mirbeau, Octave Henri Marie (1850-1917), French novelist and dramatist who was first a dramatic critic, champion of impressionism in painting, and ardent defender of Captain Alfred Dreyfus. His plays include *The Epidemic; Business is Business,* which was adapted for the English stage by Sidney GRUNDY; *The Portfolio; The Bad Shepherds* which was written for Sarah BERNHARDT. He also wrote several novels one of which, *Le Calvaire,* aroused much discussion.

Miro, Joan (1893-), Spanish painter and sculptor who displayed talent at an early age, and became a student at the ECOLE DES BEAUX-ARTS, Paris, at fifteen, and three years later at the Academy of Gali at Barcelona. In 1921 his *Dog Barking at the Moon* placed him in the first rank of the Surrealists: he designed sets for DIAGHILEFF's Ballet Company and the Ballet Russe de Monte Carlo, and illustrated several books by modern French authors.

Miscellany, in literature a term applied to a book containing articles, essays or treatises on a variety of subjects: it was frequently used as a title during the 17th and 18th centuries.

Miserere, (*1*)in sacred music the name of the fiftieth psalm in the Vulgate or Latin version of the BIBLE; so called because it is the first word of the opening line, "Miserere mei, Domine." It is performed with great solemnity during Holy Week at the SISTINE CHAPEL at the Vatican, Rome, and is also used as a part of the burial service. (*2*) In architecture the term for a small seat placed on the under side of another hinged seat in the stalls of medieval churches: it was designed for use by priests suffering from some physical infirmity, affording them substantial support when they were required to stand up during parts of the MASS.

Mistinguette (1874-), French actress and chanteuse who made her debut in 1907 at the Folies-Dramatiques at Paris: two years later she made her first appearance at the Folies-Bèrgere with Maurice CHEVALIER with whom she has appeared many times over the years. She came to the United States in 1911 to secure American talent for French vaudeville houses, and also appeared in a revue.

Mistral, Frédéric (1830-1914), French poet who first studied law and later devoted himself to establishing the Provençal dialect in literature by founding with others the Félibrige Society for this purpose. He published a Provençal-French-Dictionary: also *Lis Osclo d'or* and *Lis Oulivado,* two collections of poems.

Mitchell, Donald Grant (1822-1908), American author educated at Yale University who used the pen name "Ik Marvel"; his works include *Fresh Gleanings, or a New Sheaf from the Old Fields of Continental Europe* (1847); *The Lorgnette; Reveries of a Bachelor,* his most famous book; *Dream Life:* also two books about his farm near New Haven, Conn., to which he retired after acting as American consul at Venice in 1853-54.

Mitchell, Grant (1874-), American stage and screen actor educated at Ohio State University and Yale University who also practiced law and worked as a reporter before becoming a student at the American School of Dramatic Art, New York. He made his debut in 1902 at New York with the Richard MANSFIELD Company, and later appeared in numerous plays including *The House of Mirth; The Tailor-Made Man; It Pays to Advertise; The Chaperon; Get-Rich-Wallingford; The Whole Town's Talking; A Prince There Was; All the King's Horses.* Since 1933 he has played important roles in many films including *Dinner at Eight; A Midsummer Night's Dream; Seven Keys to Baldpate; On Borrowed Time; Grapes of Wrath; Edison the Man; Tobacco Road; Larceny Inc.*

Mitchell, Margaret (1900-), American novelist educated at Washington Seminary, Atlanta, Ga., and at Smith College: her only novel, *Gone With the Wind* (1936), a story of the Civil War, sold more than 2,000,000 copies, has been translated into sixteen or more languages, and filmed in technicolor with Vivien LEIGH and Clark GABLE as the heroine and hero.

Mitchell, Silas Weir (1829-1914), American physician, poet, and novelist who not only achieved great fame in the treatment of nervous diseases, but also as an author of novels and poetry: his works include *The Hill of Stones* (1882); *Roland Blake; Hugh Wynne; The Adventures of François; Dr. North and His Friends; The Autobiography of a Quack; Constance Trescot; The Red City; Complete Poems.*

Mitchell, Thomas (1895-), American stage and screen actor, dramatist, and producer who made his debut in 1913 at New York with the Ben GREET Players, later appearing with Charles D. COBURN's Shakespearean Company, and in many plays including *Redemption; The Playboy of the Western World; The Last Mile; Riddle Me This.* He collaborated with Floyd DELL on *Little Accident* and *Cloudy with Showers:* since 1936 he has appeared in numerous films including *Craig's Wife; Theodora Goes Wild; The Lost Horizon; The Hurricane; Stagecoach; Gone With the Wind; Joan of Paris; This Above All; Moontide.*

Mitroupoulos, Dimitri (1896-), Greek pianist, composer, and conductor who studied at the Athens Conservatory, occupied the post of coach at the Berlin State Opera, and became conductor of the Paris Symphony Orchestra in 1932. His American debut was made as guest conductor of the BOSTON SYMPHONY ORCHESTRA in 1936: in 1937 he became permanent conductor of the MINNEAPOLIS SYMPHONY ORCHESTRA. His compositions include an opera, a *Concerto Grosso* and other works for orchestra; sonatas for violin and piano.

Mitsunobu (1434-1525), Japanese painter who, with his son, Mitsushige, were among the chief exponents in the 15th and 16th centuries of the Tosa school of genre painters who made a specialty of lightly drawn outlines filled in with brilliant body colors, and liberal use of verdigris green, often leaving off the roofs of houses in which it was necessary to show the interiors.

Mitsuoki, Tosa (1616-1691), Japanese painter who ranks with MITSUNOBU as one of the great masters of the Tosa school: he specialized in flowers, birds, and landscapes later copied or imitated by the 17th century workers in lacquer. He made liberal use of gold to render his paintings more brilliant.

Mlle. Modiste, comic opera in two acts: book by Henry Blossom; music by Victor HERBERT; first produced at New York in 1905, and specially written for Fritzi SCHEFF. The clever plot revolves around Fifi, a salesgirl in a Paris millinery shop who aspires to be an opera singer: she is befriended by Hiram Bent, a wealthy American who transforms her into the celebrated "Mme. Bellini," a singer who charms the crusty old millionaire, Count de Bouvray, so greatly that he withdraws his objections to her marrying his nephew, Captain Etienne Bouvray. There are recordings of the many popular songs in the operetta.

Mlynarski, Emil (1870-1935), Polish violinist, conductor, and composer who studied with Leopold AUER and Anatol LIADOFF at the St. Petersburg Conservatory, making his debut in 1889. He conducted at the Warsaw Opera and the Philharmonic Society: in 1929 he conducted the Philadelphia Grand Opera Company, and taught at the CURTIS INSTITUTE OF MUSIC. His compositions include a comic opera, a symphony, two violin concertos, and several pieces for violin and piano.

Mnemosyne, in Greek mythology the Greek personification of memory: she was one of the TITANS and a daughter of URANUS, the god of heaven, and GAEA, goddess of earth. The nine MUSES were the daughters of Mnemosyne and ZEUS.

Mnesicles, Greek architect of the 5th century B.C. who built the PROPYLAEA and the ERECHTHEUM on the ACROPOLIS at ATHENS: little is known of his life and of his works except those mentioned above.

Moat, in medieval architecture a ditch filled with water surrounding a castle for purpose of defense: it was crossed by means of a drawbridge which could be raised to prevent soldiers or marauders from entering. The moat was often included in the designing of French châteaus as a decorative feature permitting the use of gardens around the buildings.

Mode, in music a succession of TONES separated by certain fixed INTERVALS. The earliest modes were those employed in Greek music; the medieval church modes were octave SCALES similar to the Greek from which they also borrowed their names, the difference being that they were conceived as *ascending* scales in contrast to the Greek *descending* modes. Four of the church modes called *authentic* are attributed to St. Ambrose;

four others known as PLAGAL are said to have originated with Pope Gregory I.

Modigliani, Amedeo (1884-1920), Italian painter and sculptor of Jewish ancestry who studied at the Academy of Fine Arts in Florence, made an intensive study of MICHELANGELO'S works, and finally went to Paris where he became interested in Negro sculpture. He was supported in his views and aims by several prominent artists including DERAIN and COCTEAU. Unfortunately, after he began to paint with considerable skill he died from the results of overdrinking and the use of narcotics. His works are to be found in several European, English, and American museums.

Modjeska, Helena (1844-1909), Polish actress who made her first appearance with an itinerant company in 1861, and her formal debut at Warsaw in 1865, remaining there for several years. In 1877 she appeared successfully at San Francisco in *Adrienne Lecouvieur,* starred with Edwin BOOTH in 1889, and also toured with Otis SKINNER and Maurice BARRYMORE. She was distinguished in the roles of Ophelia, Lady Macbeth, Cleopatra, Desdemona, and also in the leading feminine parts of modern drama.

Modulation, in music a transition from one KEY to another resulting in a change of TONALITY: if the modulation is permanent it is called *final,* but if the original key is later returned to it is called *transient.*

Moeller, Philip (1880-), American dramatist and producer educated at New York and Columbia Universities. His plays include *Helena's Husband* (1915); *Madame Sand; Five Somewhat Historical Plays; Molière; Sophie:* he also adapted *Caprice.* His numerous productions include *Saint Joan; Fata Morgana; The Guardsman; They Knew What They Wanted.*

Moirai, see **Fates, The.**

Moiseívitch, Benno (1890-), Russian pianist who studied at the Imperial Musical Academy at Odessa, winning the Anton RUBINSTEIN prize in 1899, and becoming a pupil of Theodor LESCHETIZKY in 1904. He made his debut at London in 1909, and has since toured Europe and the United States, also making many fine recordings.

Moissi, Alexander (1880-1935), German actor born in Austria of Italian-Albanian parentage: he owed his success to Max REINHARDT who coached him until he became a distinguished tragic actor in both Germany and Italy where Eleanora DUSE praised him as Romeo and Hamlet. He also toured the United States with considerable success.

Moldau (Smetana), the second of a series of six symphonic poems composed by Friedrich SMETANA to glorify the scenic beauty and history of Bohemia. Smetana appended a program to *Moldau* in which he tells how two springs, one warm and the other cold, arise in the depths of the forest of Sumava, and unite to make the brook which in time becomes the river Moldau. At first it flows through the forest where a hunt is in progress; then through grassy plains where a rural wedding festival is being celebrated; next through moonlit woods where fairies are disporting on its banks; then over the tumultuous rapids of St. John, rushing on to the fertile plains below and finally reaching its greatest breadth at Prague, where it is welcomed by the ancient castle of Vysehrad. There are Victor recordings by the Berlin State Opera Orchestra under Leo Blech, and by the Czech Philharmonic Orchestra conducted by Rafael Kubelik.

Molding or **Moulding**, in architecture a square, convex, or concave projection placed on a wall as an ornament, serving as a decoration in order to relieve the monotony of a flat surface. It was first used with excellent results in Assyria and Persia, and often decorated with foliage: the ancient Greeks, and Romans carried it to a high degree of perfection in respect to variety of form and effects, but the present tendency is toward simplified designs.

Molière (1622-1673), French actor and dramatist, real name Jean Baptiste Poquelin, who was educated at the Jesuit Collège de Clermont in Paris, also studying philosophy and law. He began writing and acting in his own plays at twenty-three, changing his name to Molière in order not to disgrace his family name. He toured France with Madeleine Bejart for twelve years, and finally gained the favor of Louis XIV in 1658 through the impromptu performance of his comedy, *The Amorous Doctor:* a company was established and maintained for fourteen years at the Palais-Royal. His thirty plays include *Le Misanthrope; Tartuffe; Les Femmes savantes; L'Avare; Les Précieuses Ridicules; Le Bourgeois gentilhomme; Le Malade imaginaire; L'École des Maris; Le Médecin malgré lui.*

Molina, Tirso de see **Tellez Gabriel.**

Molinari, Bernardino (1880-), Italian conductor who studied at the Liceo di Saint Cecilia, and became permanent conductor of the Augusteo Symphony Orchestra, Rome, in 1912. He appeared with all the major Continental orchestras, and made his debut with the New York Philharmonic-Symphony Orchestra in 1928. He has also conducted the Los Angeles Philharmonic Orchestra, the San Francisco Symphony Orchestra, the Lewisohn Stadium Orchestra, New York, the St. Louis Orchestra, the Detroit Symphony, and the NBC Symphony Orchestra.

Mollenhauer, Emil (1855-1927), American violinist who made his debut at Niblo's Gardens at nine, and joined the Theodore Thomas Orchestra at seventeen, also playing in the New York and the Brooklyn Philharmonic Societies. From 1885 to 1888 he was a member of the Boston Symphony Orchestra, resigning to conduct the Germania Orchestra which later became the Boston Festival Orchestra with which he toured extensively. In 1899 he conducted the Handel and Haydn Society, and the Boston Symphony Orchestra at the St. Louis and San Francisco Expositions.

Molnar, C. Pál or **Paul** (1894-), Hungarian painter who studied at the Hungarian Academy in Rome, and was influenced by the paintings of Lorenzo di Credi to such an extent that the style of the Florentine master is plainly to be seen in the *Infancy Cycle.* He has worked largely along religious lines, expressing his ideas with typically Hungarian crispness in style and coloring.

Molnar, Ferenc (1878-), Hungarian dramatist educated at the Universities of Budapest and Geneva, who was a journalist during World War I. His plays include *The Doctor* (1902); *The Devil; Playing With Fire; The Guardsman; The Red Mill; The Swan; The Good Fairy; Liliom; The Wolf; Fashions for Men; Heavenly and Earthly Love; The Glass Slipper; A Matter of Husbands; Olympia; The Phantom Rival; The Play's the Thing:* several of his plays have been filmed.

Molyn, Pieter (c.1600-1661), Dutch painter, known as "The Elder," who specialized in landscapes: his notable canvases include *Night Festival; Rural Frolic; Winter Landscape with Skaters; Group of Trees; Horsemen at an Inn; Farm Yard; Plundered Village.* His son, **Pieter Molyn** (1637-1701), was a painter known as "The Younger," and also as Il Cavaliere Tempesta, and as Pietro Mulier: his works include *Landscape with Shepherds and Cattle; Signal Tower on Sea Coast; Marine Scene with Jonah and the Whale; Christ and the Apostles Fishing; Landing of Aeneas in Italy.*

Moments Musicaux (Schubert), a fanciful title used by Franz Schubert for several light compositions on the order of improvisations. One of them, *Moment Musical, Op. 94, No. 3* is universally popular: it has been recorded for piano for Columbia by Walter Gieseking; for violin by Bronislaw Hubermann in a Columbia recording: for violoncello in a Victor recording by Pablo Casals; for orchestra in a Victor recording by the Philadelphia Orchestra.

Momus, in Greek mythology the son of Nox, the goddess of night, and the personification of censoriousness. He was said to be constantly mocking the gods, and to have been much disturbed at not being able to find defects in Aphrodite. He is pictured as an old or as a young man wearing a mask, and carrying a jester's bauble.

Mona Lisa, a celebrated portrait painted by Leonardo da Vinci of Lisa di Anton Maria, wife of Zanobi de Giocondo of Florence; the picture is also known as *La Gioconda* or *La Joconde.* It was stolen from the Louvre in 1911, but found and restored through the efforts of John Pierpont Morgan, Sr.

Monasterio, Jésus (1836-1903), Spanish violinist who studied with Charles de Beriot at the Brussels Conservatory, toured Europe successfully, and became professor of violin at the Madrid Conservatory. He conducted the Sociedad de Conciertos at Madrid and founded a string quartet to present the works of Beethoven, Haydn, and Mozart: his compositions were chiefly for the violin.

Monckton, Lionel (1862-1924), English composer educated at Oxford University where he was a member of the Philo-Thespian Club and the Oxford University Dramatic Society. He wrote many songs which were interpolated into musical comedies produced by George Edwardes, and composed several musical plays with Ivan CARYLL or Howard Talbot including *The Toreador; The Spring Chicken; Our Miss Gibbs; The Arcadians; The Quaker Girl:* the last named was his own work.

Monet, Claude (1840-1926), French painter who studied with Eugene BOUDIN and Charles Gleyre, spent two years in Africa with a French regiment, and finally joined the group of impressionist painters which included SISLEY, RENOIR, CEZANNE, and DEGAS. His canvases of note include *Portrait of a Woman; Gare Saint Lazare; Rouen Cathedral; Rising Sun; Breakfast on the Grass; Waterloo Bridge; The Poplars; Study of Willow Trees; Hay Stacks in the Snow; Bridge over the Pond of Water Lilies; The Cliff; Avenue of Poplars.*

Monochord, (1) an ancient instrument first used by PYTHAGORAS in the 6th century: it consisted of a single string stretched over a soundboard on which was drawn a graduated scale divided so as to produce perfect INTERVALS, and equipped with a movable bridge placed at certain pre-determined points on the scale.

Monochrome, in painting a canvas, mural, or fresco executed in one color.

Monody, in music a style of composition in which the melody takes precedence over all other parts which are used only as accompaniment. It first assumed importance in the 16th century, taking the form of a vocal solo with instrumental accompaniment on instruments such as the HARPSICHORD or THEORBO. It later developed into OPERA and ORATORIO, and finally into instrumental music such as the SYMPHONY, SUITE, and CONCERTO.

Monolith, a single block of stone, usually of large proportions, shaped into a PILLAR or MONUMENT: several ancient monoliths are to be found at Stonehenge, near Salisbury, England.

Monologue, in ancient and classic drama a passage in a play in which the character speaks his thoughts aloud, the theory being that the audience overhears the sentiments of one who believes himself alone. Some of the finest monologues, which may also be called *soliloquies,* are to be found in the dramas and comedies of RACINE, CORNEILLE, SHAKESPEARE, BEAUMARCHAIS, and Victor HUGO. In the United States the term monologue is also applied to a lengthy recitation by one person: Beatrice Hereford, Ruth DRAPER, Cornelia Otis SKINNER, Dorothy Sands, and Elsie JANIS are among those best-known in this unique form of dramatic entertainment.

Monro, Harold (1879-1932), English poet born in Belgium who studied at Cambridge: his works include *Poems* (1906); *Judas; Before Dawn; Children of Love; Strange Meetings; Real Property; The Earth for Sale; Elm Angel; The Chronicle of a Pilgrimage,* the story of a journey from Paris to Milan; *Some Contemporary Poets.*

Monroe, Harriet (1860-1936), American editor and poet educated at the Academy of the Visitation, Georgetown, D. C., who wrote the *Columbian Ode* for the Chicago Exposition of 1893. In 1912 she founded *Poetry—A Magazine of Verse* which introduced many hitherto unknown poets: her works include *Valeria and Other Poems* (1891); *The Columbian Ode; Five Modern Plays in Verse; Poets and Their Art;* an autobiography, *A Poet's Life.* She also was one of the editors of *The New Poetry, an Anthology of Twentieth-Century Verse* (1917).

Montagna, Bartolommeo (c.1450-1523), Italian painter influenced by Giovanni BELLINI and Vittore CARPACCIO: his notable paintings and frescoes include *Madonna and Saints; Life of St. Blase; Pietà; Madonna and Child; Madonna Enthroned; Lady of Rank as Saint Justina of Padua.*

Montagnana, Dominicus (c.1690-c.1750), Italian violin maker who is said to have studied with Nicoló AMATI as a fellow pupil with Antonius STRADIVARIUS. His selection of woods was exceptional, and his model unusually large with a striking orange-red varnish: his instruments command prices ranging from $3000.00 to $12,000.00.

Montaigne, Michel Eyquem, Seigneur de (1533-1592), French philosopher and essayist who was attached to the court of Henry III, and traveled extensively in Europe. His most famous work is the *Essays* (1580), reprinted many times and translated into English.

Montañés, Juan Martínez (c.1568-1649), Spanish sculptor and architect who brought polychrome sculpture to its brightest point of excellence: his works include statues of *St. Jerome; St. John the Baptist; Theological Virtues; Christ Crucified; St. Bruno; Immaculate Conception; Santo Domingo de Guzmán.* He also executed many altars and images which were sent to both South and North America: Alonso CANO was one of his pupils.

Monte Cristo, an island of small size in the Mediterranean Ocean near Elba, Italy: Alexandre DUMAS, PERE, selected it as the spot where Edmond Dantès, the hero of *The Count of Monte Cristo,* landed after his escape from the Château d'If, and reclaimed the treasure, buried there by the Abbé Faria, which enabled him to wreak vengeance on his betrayers.

Montemezzi, Italo (1875-1941), Italian dramatic composer who first studied engineering at Verona. After being refused admission twice at the Milan Conservatory, he was finally accepted, and was graduated with honors in composition. His notable works include *Giovanni Gallurese; L'Amore dei Tre Re (The LOVE OF THREE KINGS),* which established his reputation; *La Nave; La Notte di Zoraima:* also a symphonic poem, *Paolo e Virginia,* and other orchestral works

Montespan, Françoise Athénaïs, Marquise de (1641-1707), French lady, daughter of the Duc de

Mortemart, who succeeded Mademoiselle de la VALLIERE as mistress of LOUIS XIV in 1667, and was in turn displaced by the Marquise de Maintenon. She is one of the characters in several romances by Alexandre DUMAS, PERE.

Monteux, Pierre (1875-), French violinist and conductor who studied at the Paris Conservatory with Henri Berthelier and Albert LAVIGNAC, and after playing at the Opéra-Comique and the Concerts COLONNE became conductor of the DIAGHILEFF Russian Ballet with which he toured the United States in 1916. From 1917 to 1919 he conducted at the Metropolitan Opera House, and the Boston Symphony Orchestra from 1919 to 1924. He has been permanent conductor of the Paris Symphony Orchestra, the SAN FRANCISCO SYMPHONY and has appeared as guest conductor of the NEW YORK PHILHARMONIC-SYMPHONY SOCIETY at the Lewisohn Stadium and the NBC SYMPHONY ORCHESTRA.

Monteverdi, Claudio (1567-1643), Italian composer who was first a chorister at the Cremona Cathedral, and later studied the organ and lute. He entered the service of the Duke of Mantua, first composing madrigals: in 1607 his opera *Orfeo* was produced at Mantua, followed by *Arianna* in 1608. He is famous as having enlarged the orchestra and developed the ARIA and RECITATIVE in operatic composition: also for having overcome rigid and arbitrary rules against the use of unprepared chords. His compositions include many operas, most of which are lost; sacred music; secular songs and madrigals.

Montez, Lola (1818-1861), Irish dancer and adventuress whose real name was Marie Gilbert: she became a dancer after her divorce from an army officer, achieving considerable success in Europe where she became the mistress of Louis I of Bavaria, and obtained considerable political power until the king abdicated and she was banished. After touring England and the United States as a dancer, she remarried and disappeared from public life.

Montgomery, Robert (1904-), American stage and screen actor who made his debut in 1924 at the Bijou Theatre with William FAVERSHAM in *The Mask and the Face,* later playing with a stock company in Rochester. He entered the films in 1929, and has since appeared in many films including *The Divorcée; Three Live Ghosts; Private Lives; When Ladies Meet; Another Language; No More Ladies; Petticoat Fever; The Last of Mrs. Cheyney; Yellowjack; The Earl of Chicago; The Cat and the Canary; Mr. and Mrs. Smith; Here Comes Mr. Jordan.*

Monti, Vincenzo (1754-1828), Italian poet and dramatist who pleased Cardinal Borghese so much with *The Vision of Ezekiel* that he became his patron at Rome. His works include *Bassevilliana,* a poem inspired by the murder of Hugo Basseville, the French ambassador to Rome; *The Bard of the Black Forest,* a poem in praise of NAPOLEON I: also several tragedies.

Monticelli, Adolphe (1824-1886), French painter whose works were sold for small sums by him in the restaurants of Marseilles, his native city; only after his death was any artistic significance attached to them. Among his works, which have become collectors' items, are scenes from the *Decameron* of Boccaccio, Goethe's *Faust* and Cervantes' *Don Quixote:* also *Court Ladies* and *The Court of the Princess* in the METROPOLITAN MUSEUM OF ART, New York. James HUNEKER's *Promenades of an Impressionist* contains a critique of his work.

Monticello, the name of Thomas JEFFERSON's home near Charlottesville, Va., for which he drew the plans himself. He lived there until his death; the property was then sold by his daughter who felt that she could not afford to maintain it, and passed into the hands of a naval officer, Uriah P. Levy. In 1923 the estate was acquired by the Thomas Jefferson Memorial Foundation.

Montreuil, Pierre de (?-1266), French architect whose royal patron was Louis IX of France: he designed many church buildings of great beauty, but his most famous creation was the Chapelle Royale at Paris, known as the Sainte Chapelle, in which the crown of thorns and a piece of the true cross brought from the Orient by Saint Louis were placed.

Monument, in architecture and sculpture a construction in the form of a statue, a group, or an entire building designed to perpetuate the memory of an individual or an important event. Among the striking examples are the Pyramids of Egypt; the TAJ MAHAL in India; the LINCOLN MEMORIAL in Washington, D. C.; the Tomb of the Unknown Soldier in Washington, D. C., and other cities in England and France.

Monvel, Bernard Boutet de, see **Boutet de Monvel, Bernard.**

Monvel, Louis Maurice Boutet de, see **Boutet de Monvel, Louis Maurice.**

Moody, William Vaughan (1869-1910), American poet and dramatist educated at Harvard University where he taught English later as well as at the University of Chicago. His works include the plays *The Masque of Judgment* (1900), *The Fire-Bringer, The Great Divide,* a play in which Margaret ANGLIN was starred, and *The Faith Healer:* also a *History of English Literature* with Robert Moras Lovett.

"Moonlight" Sonata (Beethoven), a sonata composed by Ludwig van BEETHOVEN: the full title is *Sonata quasi una fantasia, Op. 27, No. 2,* and it was dedicated on the autograph copy to the Countess Giulietta Giucciardi. The title "Moonlight" is derived from a review of the work by the German critic, Heinrich Rellstab, who referred to it as a reflection of light on the lake of Lucerne. There is a Columbia recording by Egon PETRI, and a Victor recording by Ignaz PADEREWSKI.

Moonstone, a variety of feldspar in which the tendency in certain positions to show a bluish opalescence has created its vogue as an ornamental stone: it is mined chiefly in Ceylon.

Moore, Albert Joseph (1841-1893), English painter who studied with his father, William Moore, a well-known English landscape artist, and was encouraged by his brothers, John Collingham and Henry Moore, both of whom were distinguished painters. After further training at the Royal Academy School he created many notable frescoes, mural decorations, and pictures including *The Four Seasons; A Greek Play; Elijah's Sacrifice; The Quartette; Dreamers; Blossoms; A Summer Night; Feeding of the Five Thousand; Sea Gulls; Follow-my-Leader.*

Moore, Clement Clarke (1779-1863), American scholar and poet: his works include *Lexicon of the Hebrew Language* (1809); *Poems; George Castriot, surnamed Scanderbeg, King of Albania.* He is best known today as the author of the Christmas poem, *'Twas the Night before Christmas.*

Moore, Douglas Stuart (1893-), American composer and teacher who was educated at Yale, and studied musical theory with Vincent d'INDY and Nadia BOULANGER. In 1926 he became associate professor of music at Columbia University, and in 1940 succeeded Daniel Gregory MASON as head of the music department. His notable compositions include an opera, *The Devil and Daniel Webster; Pageant of P. T. Barnum* and other orchestral works, chamber music; piano pieces and songs. He is also the author of *Listening to Music* (1932).

Moore, George (1852-1933), Irish novelist and essayist who first studied art at the Académie Julien, Paris: his novels include *A Modern Lover* (1883); *A Mummer's Wife; A Drama in Muslin; Esther Waters; Evelyn Innes; Brook Kerith; Heloise and Abélard; Aphrodite in Aulis.* His plays include *The Making of an Immortal* (1927); *The Passing of the Essenes; Martin Luther.* Among his autobiographical works are *Confessions of a Young Man,* and *Hail and Farewell.*

Moore, Grace (1901-), American soprano who made her debut on the New York stage in 1920 with Raymond HITCHCOCK in *Hitchy-Koo.* After study in France with Richard Barthélemy she appeared in opera abroad, and made her debut in 1928 at the Metropolitan Opera House in PUCCINI's *La Bohème,* remaining there for four years. In 1933 she appeared at New York in Karl MILLOCKER's operetta, *Madame Du Barry,* and has been featured in several films including *New Moon; One Night of Love; Love Me Forever; The King Steps Out; When You're in Love; I'll Take Romance; Louise,* a screen adaptation of Charpentier's grand opera.

Moore, Harry Humphrey (1844-1923), American painter who achieved great success in spite of the handicap of being deaf and dumb: he resided in Paris after traveling and sketching in Africa, Japan, Spain, and Italy: among his works are *Moorish Beggar; Moorish Bazaar; Blind Guitarist; Gypsies at Camp in Granada.*

Moore, Thomas (1779-1852), Irish poet educated at Trinity College, Dublin: his works include *Lalla Rookh,* a poem for which Longmans, the English book publishers, paid $15,000 without seeing the manuscript; *Life of Sheridan; Life of Byron; The Epicurean; History of Ireland; The Fudge Family in Paris,* a satire. His greatest fame came from the poems, *Irish Melodies,* (1807-34), set to music by many composers: they include "Believe Me If All Those Endearing Young Charms," "Oft in the Stilly Night" and "The Harp That Once Through Tara's Halls."

Moore, Victor (1876-), American stage and screen actor who made his debut in 1896 with John DREW in *Rosemary,* and later played four years in vaudeville in the sketch, *Change Your Act, or Back to the Woods.* Among the plays in which he appeared were *Forty-five Minutes from Broadway; The Talk of New York; The Happiest Night of His Life; Hold Everything; Of Thee I Sing; On Borrowed Time.* Among the films in which he has been featured are *Chimmie Fadden; Swingtime; Meet the Missus; This Marriage Business; Louisiana Purchase.*

Morales, Cristóbal (1500-1553), Spanish composer who studied music with the choirmaster of the Seville Cathedral, and was a member of the Papal Choir at Rome from 1535 to 1545. He held several positions as choirmaster in Spain before his death: his works include masses, motets, Magnificats, Lamentations, and also some secular madrigals.

Morales, Luis de (1509-1586), Spanish painter who worked almost entirely in the sacred field inspired by his own deeply religious feeling which led to contemporary artists giving him the surname "El Divino" (The Divine). His most famous works include *Ecce Homo; Pietá; Christ Carrying the Cross; Presentation in the Temple; Mater Dolorosa; Virgin and Child; St. Jerome in the Wilderness.*

Morality Plays, see **Miracle Plays.**

Moran, Edward (1829-1901), American painter born in England who came to the United States with his family at fifteen. After returning to London in 1862 he studied at the Royal Academy, and later painted in New York and Paris, specializing in marine subjects. His works include thirteen paintings illustrating the marine history of America from the days of Leif Ericsson to the return of Admiral Dewey's fleet from Manila in 1899. His sons, **Edward Percy Moran** (1862-1935), and **John Léon Moran** (1864-1941) were both distinguished painters, and his brother, **Thomas Moran** (1837-1926) was a landscape painter who accompanied expeditions in 1871 to the Yellowstone and in 1873 down the Colorado River, later painting *The Grand Canyon of the Yellowstone* and *The Chasm of the Colorado,* two immense canvases now in the CAPITOL at Washington, D. C.

Moratin, Leandro Fernandez de (1760-1828), Spanish dramatist and poet called "the Spanish Molière": his works include *The Old Man and the Young Girl* (1790); *The New Comedy; The Female Hypocrite; The Maiden's Consent.* He also translated SHAKESPEARE's *Hamlet* and some of MOLIERE's plays (with alterations) into Spanish.

Moratin, Nicolás Fernandez de (1737-1780), Spanish poet and dramatist who wrote the first native play, modeled after the French, entitled *The Female Fribble* (1762). He also produced at tragedy, *Hormesinda,* based on works by RACINE and MOLIERE.

Morbidezza (It.), in painting a term for the delicately soft rendering of human flesh accomplished to a greater or lesser degree by the skill of the artist in mixing and applying his colors.

Mordkin, Mikhail, contemporary Russian dancer who entered the Imperial Ballet School in Moscow at nine years of age, appearing first in *La Fille mal gardée,* and becoming *premier danseur* and ballet master at seventeen for Czar Nicholas II. In 1908 he appeared with the Russian Ballet at Berlin before Kaiser Wilhelm, and with Anna PAVLOWA at L'Opéra, Paris, in 1909, accompanying her on a transatlantic tour with the Metropolitan Opera Ballet. In 1938 he organized the Mordkin Ballet.

More, Sir Thomas (1478-1535), English statesman who became a favorite of HENRY VIII, and was appointed Lord Chancellor after Cardinal Thomas Wolsey: when he evinced disapproval of King Henry's divorce from Katherine of Aragon and subsequent marriage to Anne Boleyn, he was finally accused of treason and beheaded. His work of interest in this volume is *Utopia,* published in Latin in 1516 and in English in 1551: it is a serious picture in classic language of an ideal political state.

Moreau, Gustave (1826-1898), French painter who studied with François PICOT, was strongly influenced by Théodore CHASSERIAU, and became professor at the ECOLE DES BEAUX-ARTS, Paris, where Henri MATISSE was one of his many famous pupils. His canvases include *Jason and Medea, Death and the Young Man; Prometheus; Rape of Europa; Christ Between the Two Thieves; Death of Darius; Moses on the Nile; The Riddle of the Sphinx Solved; Apparition; Salome Dancing; Episode from the Song of Songs.*

Moreau, Jean Michel, called **Moreau the Younger** (1741-1814), French engraver and illustrator who spent some years in Russia and Italy, finally returning to Paris where he spent the rest of his life. His works include vignettes for a special edition of MOLIERE's comedies; illustrations for works by VOLTAIRE and ROUSSEAU; engravings celebrating the marriage of Louis XVI in 1770, and the birth of the Dauphin in 1782. His brother, **Louis Gabriel Moreau** (1740-1806), called **Moreau the Elder,** was a digtinguished painter.

Morehouse, Ward (1898-), American dramatic critic educated at North Georgia College who first worked as a reporter, and became dramatic editor of the New York *Tribune* in 1919, and dramatic critic of the New York *Sun* since 1926. His column, *Broadway of the Past,* is widely read and appreciated: his works include *Gentlemen of the Press,* produced in 1928 and also filmed; *Forty-Five Minutes Past Eight* (1939):

he has also written the scenarios of eight motion pictures which have been produced.

Moresby, Louis, see **Beck, Lily Adams.**

Moretto da Brescia (c.1498-1554), Italian painter whose real name was Alessandro Bonvicino: he was also known as Il Moretto. His religious pictures are to be seen in many Brescian churches: they include *Cornation of the Virgin; Christ Bearing the Cross; Vision of Moses; Massacre of the Innocents; The Entombment; Madonna and Child with Saints and Angels.* He painted many fine portraits and was the teacher of Giambattista MORONI.

Morgan, Frank (1890-), American stage, screen and radio actor who studied at the American Academy of Dramatic Arts, New York, and made his debut in 1914 at the Lyceum Theatre in *A Woman Killed with Kindness.* Among the numerous plays in which he has been featured are *Under Fire; Her Family Tree; Gentlemen Prefer Blondes; Hearts are Trumps; Topaze.* He has also appeared in many films including *Reunion in Vienna; When Ladies Meet; The Affairs of Cellini; The Good Fairy; The Great Ziegfeld; The Last of Mrs. Cheyney; Saratoga; The Shop Around the Corner; Boom Town; The Vanishing Virginian; Tortilla Flat.* He is also a popular radio comedian.

Morgan, Helen (1900-1941), American actress and singer who studied singing at the Metropolitan Opera School, New York, and made her debut in 1920 at New York in the chorus of *Sally.* She appeared in vaudeville, cabarets, and revues, but achieved her great success as Julie in *Showboat,* playing the role in both the stage and screen productions.

Morgan, Ralph (1888-), American stage and screen actor educated at Columbia University who made his debut in 1908 at New York in *Love's Comedy,* and appeared later in several Clyde FITCH plays: also in *Under Cover; Lightnin';* *Cobra; The Woman of Bronze; Strange Interlude.* He has also appeared in many films including *Rasputin and the Empress; The Magnificent Obsession; Anthony Adverse; The Life of Émile Zola; Mannequin; Mother Carey's Chickens; Geronimo; Adventure in Washington.*

Morgan Library, see **Pierpont Morgan Library.**

Morgue, (a) in theatrical parlance a theatre with poor attendance; (b) in the language of newspaper men the room in which clippings and pictures of persons and events are filed.

Mörike, Eduard Friedrich (1804-1875), German poet and novelist: his works include the novel, *Maler Nolten;* the poem *Idylle vom Bodensee;* a famous short story, *Mozart's Journey to Prague.* Several of his lyric poems have been set to music by Hugo WOLF and other composers.

Morison, Samuel Eliot (1887-), American historian and biographer; nephew of Charles William ELIOT, educated at Harvard and Oxford Universities, and professor of history at Harvard University since 1915. He served in World War I, and became Harmsworth Professor of American History at Oxford University from 1922 to 1925. His works include *The Maritime History of Massachusetts* (1921); *Builders of the Bay Colony; The Growth of the American Republic; The Tercentennial History of Harvard University; The Second Voyage of Christopher Columbus; Admiral of the Ocean Sea* which won the Pulitzer Prize for biography in 1943.

Morland, George (1763-1804), English painter of animals and rural scenes whose father, H. R. Morland, was a well-known artist. The son exhibited sketches when he was ten years old at the Royal Academy, and, despite a dissolute life ending in his death at a bailiff's house where he was detained for a debt, he developed into an artist the delicacy of whose pictures recalls the old Flemish masters. Among his noted canvases are *Reckoning at the Inn; The Bull's Head Inn; The Farmhouse; The Halting Place; Dancing Dogs; Off to the Fair; Return from the Market; Dogs Fighting; Interior of a Stable:* the last named is considered his masterpiece.

Morley, Christopher (1890-), American novelist and essayist educated at Haverford College, Haverford, Pa., and at Oxford, who did editorial work for several publishers and national magazines as well as becoming contributing editor of the *Saturday Review of Literature.* In 1928 he founded a theatre, in collaboration with Cleon THROCKMORTON, in Hoboken, N. J., where old melodramas such as *After Dark* and the *Black Crook* were revived. His numerous works include *The Eighth Sin* (1912); *Where the Blue Begins; Thunder on the Left; Parnassus on Wheels; The Haunted Book Shop; Mandarin in Manhattan; The Trojan Horse; Kitty Foyle:* the last-named was adapted for the films with Ginger ROGERS.

Morley, John (1838-1923), English statesman and author educated at Oxford: his works include *Life of Gladstone; Voltaire; Diderot and the Encyclopaedists; Rousseau; Oliver Cromwell; Ralph Waldo Emerson; Edmund Burke:* also many essays on literature and politics.

Morley, Thomas (1557-1603), English composer who studied with William BYRD and became organist at St. Paul's Cathedral, London, England. In 1598 he was granted a license to print music books, and published not only his own works, but those by many of his contemporaries. His works include madrigals, ballets, canzonets, harpsichord pieces, services, and anthems: also a musical setting of SHAKESPEARE's sonnet, *It Was a Lover and His Lass.*

Moro, Antonio (c.1512-1575), Dutch painter, also known as Antoni Mor or Moor: little is known of his early life except that he studied with Jan Van Scorel, and was called to Spain by Charles V to paint the portraits of both the Spanish and Portuguese royal families. He also painted likenesses of Mary Tudor and other royal personages in England, and is regarded as the greatest portraitist of the RUBENS and VAN DYCK schools.

Moroni, Giambattista (c.1522-1578), Italian painter who studied with Moretto da BRESCIA (Il Moretto), and achieved a great reputation as a portraitist: TITIAN ranked him highly, declaring that Moroni made his portrait "living" (*veri*). His notable works include *Man in Black; Widower with Two Children; The Tailor; The Scholar; Old Gentleman; Titian's Schoolmaster; Portrait of a Lady; Coronation of the Virgin; Assumption of the Virgin.*

Moronobu, Hishikawa (1645-1715), Japanese painter regarded as the father of Japanese prints, and as the founder of the Utagaua school. He perfected the hitherto rudimentary methods of engraving, pioneered in designing and executing woodcuts, and made albums of engravings in which scenes of everyday life were portrayed. He drew designs for a book of etiquette, and was patronized by the Samurai and the Daimios.

Morot, Aimé Nicolas (1850-1913), French painter who studied with Alexandre CABANEL and at the ECOLE DES BEAUX-ARTS, Paris. His noted paintings include *Daphnis and Chloë; Battle of Aqua Sextiae; The Good Samaritan; Temptation of St. Anthony; Crucifixion; Rézonville; Bravo Toro; Dryad.*

Morris, Chester (1901-), American stage and screen actor who first studied art, and made his debut in 1918 at New York in *The Copperhead,* later appearing in *Turn to the Right; Lightnin'; The Mountain Man; The Home Towners* and many other plays. He has also appeared in numerous films including *Alibi; The Divorcée; The Case of Sergeant Grischa; Corsair; The Miracle Man; King for a Night; Society Doctor; Frankie and Johnnie; Five Came Back; Pacific Liner; Wagons Westward; Canal Zone.*

Morris, Clara (1846-1925), American actress born in Canada who first appeared in a ballet, *The Seven Sisters,* at Cleveland, Ohio, in 1861, and with the Augustin DALY Company in 1870 at New York in *Article 37.* She achieved success in several emotional plays including *Camille; Divorce; Miss Multon; Man and Wife; The Two Orphans; The New Magdalene:* in 1874 she retired to write several novels, stories for children, and an autobiography, *Life of a Star* (1906) which was in part fiction.

Morris, William (1834-1896), English poet and artistic decorator educated at Marlborough College at Oxford, and also trained as an architect. He was intimate with Edward BURNE-JONES, and in 1863 established a business in stained glass and decorations. His works include *Defense of Guinevere and Other Poems* (1858); *The Life and Death of Jason; The Earthly Paradise; Sigurd the Volsung; A Dream of John Ball; The House of the Wolfings.*

Morris or **Morrice Dance,** a country dance which became popular in Yorkshire and parts of Northern England during the reign of Henry VII: it was associated with the May festivals, and was also incorporated into a pageant in honor of ROBIN HOOD. It was suppressed when Oliver

Cromwell came into power, but was revived in 1660.

Morrison, Arthur (1863-), English novelist, dramatist, and writer of detective fiction who contributed to English journals until his first book, *Tales of Mean Streets* appeared in 1894: his works include the *Martin Hewitt* series of detective stories; *A Child of the Jago; The Hole in the Wall; The Green Eye of Goona; Green Ginger; The Painters of Japan; Fiddle o' Dreams.*

Morrow, Honoré Willsie (1880-1940), American novelist and biographer: her works include *The Heart of the Desert* (1913); *Still Jim; Benefits Forgot; Forever Free; With Malice Toward None; The Last Full Measure; Black Daniel,* a biography of Daniel Webster; *Yonder Sails the Mayflower; Demon Daughter.*

Morse, Samuel Finley Breese (1791-1872), American artist and inventor educated at Yale College, and a pupil of Washington ALLSTON with whom he went to England, remaining there for several years. Several of his paintings including *The Dying Hercules* and *The Judgment of Jupiter* were well received. In 1832 he began experimenting with electrical telegraphy, and in 1844 proved the practical value of his invention by transmitting messages from Washington, D. C., to Baltimore, Md. He also introduced DAGUERRE's process of photography in the United States, and experimented with telegraphy by submarine cable.

Morse, Woolson (1858-1897), American composer who first studied painting at Paris with Jean Leon GEROME, but turned to comic opera writing, composing the score, painting the scenery and often directing the production. Among his successful operettas were *Wang,* produced with De Wolf HOPPER and Della Fox; *The Merry Monarch* with Francis WILSON; *Panjandrum; Dr. Syntax.*

Morte d'Arthur, a literary work by Sir Thomas MALORY (c.1430-c.1470) who translated a series of French romances on the life and death of King ARTHUR and the knights of the ROUND TABLE. They were printed in a single volume by William CAXTON in 1485.

Morton, David (1886-), American author and poet educated at Vanderbilt University, Nashville, Tenn., who first worked as a reporter: since 1924 he has been professor of English at Amherst College. His works include *Ships in Harbour* (1921); *Harvest; Nocturnes and Autumnals; The Renaissance of Irish Poetry; A Man of Earth; Spell Against Time; All in One Breath:* he has also edited *Shorter Modern Poems, 1900-31.*

Mosaic, the art of combining pieces of marble, glass, tile, or other substances to form patterns used for flooring, pavements, and facings on buildings. Examples of exquisite beauty have been found in Egypt, Greece, Rome, Pompeii, North Africa, and Constantinople. The art of decorative mosaic, which consists of applying small cubes of colored enamel with cement to a hard surface,

was highly developed from the 12th century in Italy through mural designs.

Moscheles, Ignaz (1794-1870), Bohemian pianist, teacher, and composer of Jewish parentage who studied with Dionys WEBER at the Prague Conservatory and also with Johann ALBRECHTSBERGER and Antonio SALIERI. He was friendly with Johann HUMMEL, MEYERBEER, and prepared the piano score of *Fidelio* under the supervision of BEETHOVEN. After touring with great success in Germany, he settled in London in 1821: twenty-five years later he accepted Felix MENDELSSOHN's invitation to become professor of piano at the Leipzig Conservatory where he trained students from all over the world. His more than 140 compositions include eight piano concertos, many piano studies and numerous piano solo pieces. He also translated Anton SCHINDLER's biography of Beethoven into English.

Moscow Art Theatre, a celebrated dramatic organization founded by Constantin STANISLAVSKY and Vladimir Ivanovich NEMIROVICH-DANCHENKO in 1898. It was inspired by the productions of the MEININGEN THEATRE, a German organization which appeared at Moscow in 1890. The first play, produced in 1898, was TOLSTOY's *Tsar Feodor Ivanovitch:* this was followed by many others including CHEKHOV's *The Sea Gull, Three Sisters, The Cherry Orchard,* and *Uncle Vanya;* Tolstoy's *Power of Darkness;* TURGENIEV's *A Month in the Country;* GORKY's *The Lower Depths.* The company visited the United States twice, in 1922-23, and 1923-24, and celebrated its fortieth anniversary in 1938.

Moses, Montrose J. (1878-1934), American dramatic critic, editor, and translator educated at the College of the City of New York. His works include a critical study, *Francesca da Rimini; Famous Actor Families in America; Henrik Ibsen; The American Dramatist; Maurice Maeterlinck; The Fabulous Forrest; The American Theatre as Seen by Its Critics,* with John Mason BROWN. He also edited the morality play, *Everyman;* the plays of Clyde FITCH; *Representative Plays by American Dramatists; A Treasury of Plays for Children,* and translated the *Oberammergau Passion Play.*

Mosler, Henry (1841-1920), American painter who studied with James Henry BEARD, acted as art correspondent for *Harper's Weekly* during the Civil War, studied with Ernest HEBERT in Paris, and at the Düsseldorf Academy. His painting, *Le Retour,* (The Return), exhibited at the PARIS SALON in 1879, was the first American picture purchased for the LUXEMBOURG MUSEUM. His notable canvases include *The Quadroon; Women and Their Secrets; Wedding Feast in Brittany; Girl Spinning; Rainy Day; Purchase of the Wedding Gown.* His son, **Gustave Henry Mosler** (1875-1906), studied with his father and with Léon BONNAT, and became a well-known painter before his premature demise: among his works are *De Profundis* which received a medal at the Paris Salon in 1891; *The Empty Cradle:* also a fine portrait of J. W. Stewart, governor of Vermont.

Mosque, in architecture the name of a place of worship in the Mohammedan church in Arabia,

Syria, Egypt, Turkey, Persia, and India; also in Spain after its subjugation by the Arabs. The style of architecture varies in details according to the country, but the usual form consists of high walls enclosing a rectangular court with a ceremonial fountain and porticos as a protection from the sun, surmounted by a dome and several minarets from which the call to worship is sounded by the muezzin. The direction of MECCA, the birthplace of Mohammed, is indicated by the position of the prayer hall the walls of which are covered with sentences from the KORAN.

Mossoloff, Alexander (1900-), Russian composer who studied with Nicolas MIASKOVSKY and Richard GLIERE at the Moscow Conservatory. In 1927 his ballet, *The Factory,* was produced at Moscow: it was also known as *Music of the Machines* and was criticized in Russia, but became enormously popular in Continental Europe and the United States.

Moszkowski, Moritz (1854-1925), German pianist, teacher, and composer who studied at the Stern and Kullak Conservatories in Berlin, and made successful tours of Europe, finally settling as a teacher in Paris. His compositions include an opera, *Boabdil, the Moorish King,* produced at Berlin in 1892, *From Foreign Lands* for orchestra; *Spanish Dances* and many other popular pieces for piano. At a concert given for his benefit at Carnegie Hall, New York, in 1921 sixteen distinguished pianists donated their services: the list included BACHAUS, BAUER, Bloomfield-ZEISLER, CASELLA, FRIEDMAN, GABRILOWITSCH, GODOWSKY, GRAINGER, HUTCHINSON, LAMBERT, LHEVINNE, Mero, NEY, Schnitzer, STOJOWSKI, and SCHELLING. The SCHUBERT *Marche Militaire* opened the program, and some of Moszkowski's works were also performed.

Motet, a form of musical composition used by the polyphonic composers of church music in the 13th century: it employed melodic counterpoint, and many composers including DUNSTABLE, DUFAY, and OKEGHEM contributed to its artistic development. The title is used at the present time for any serious choral work which may have either organ or orchestral accompaniment.

Mother Goose, in English literature the name connected with nursery rhymes, probably derived from a translation of Charles PERRAULT'S tales in French entitled *Tales of Mother Goose.* There are several excellent collections of English nursery rhymes, one of which was published by John Newbery in 1760. The best musical setting of the rhymes is by John W. Elliot (1833-?). Maurice RAVEL wrote a piano suite *Ma Mère L'oye* (Mother Goose) which he transcribed for orchestra; it is available in a Victor recording by the Boston Symphony Orchestra, and a Columbia recording by the Columbia Broadcasting Symphony Orchestra.

Motion Pictures, a form of entertainment which has been in existence since 1896 when the Edison Company presented motion pictures using a machine called the *Vitascope.* The first film in which a complete dramatic story was pictured was *The Great Train Robbery* in 1903, and the first great success in a multiple-reel film was *The Birth of a Nation* in 1914. In 1927 the first film with talking sequences, *The Jazz Singer,* was produced: since that time the technicolor film has been introduced, and experiments conducted with three-dimensional (stereoscopic) films.

Motivation, in drama the underlying motive or motives which impel the characters to speak or act along lines which eventually bring the plot to its climax: the dramatic qualities of a play are determined largely by the skill of the author in contriving the motivation.

Motive (Ger. **Motif**), in music a short phrase or FIGURE used for DEVELOPMENT or IMITATION, and repeated or elaborated throughout a composition. The idea of the LEITMOTIV is best exemplified in the music dramas of Richard WAGNER where short musical passages are employed to designate the principal characters, ideas or events: more than one hundred are used in the RING OF THE NIBELUNGS.

Motonobu, Kano (c.1476-c.1560), Japanese painter who, as the son of Kano MASANOBU, developed his father's style so strikingly that it became known as the Kano School. He was influenced to a certain extent by Chinese paintings of the Yuan and early Ming Periods, but his perfect technique and delightful coloring render his works distinctly individual.

Moto Perpetuo or **Perpetuum Mobile,** a composition containing short notes of equal time value played in rapid succession, and usually requiring a considerable degree of technical ability on the part of the player: among the most famous compositions of this character are the PAGANINI *Perpetuum Mobile* for violin recorded for Victor by Yehudi MENUHIN, and also available in a Victor recording played by the violins of the NBC ORCHESTRA directed by Arturo TOSCANINI; the *Perpetuum Mobile* by Carl Maria von WEBER, which is the last movement of his Piano Sonata No. 1, and recorded by Claudio ARRAU for Victor.

Mottl, Felix (1856-1911), Austrian composer and conductor who studied at the Vienna Conservatory with Georg HELLMESBERGER and Anton BRUCKNER, and in 1876 became assistant to Richard WAGNER at Bayreuth. He conducted opera and the Philharmonic Orchestra at Karlsruhe from 1880 to 1893, and became chief conductor at BAYREUTH in 1886. In 1904 he directed at the Metropolitan Opera House: his compositions include three operas, a string quartet and songs. He also arranged several interesting orchestral suites from the works of GLUCK, GRETRY, and LULLY, and made vocal scores of Wagner's music dramas.

Moulan, Frank (1862-1939), American comedian and singer who was first a boy chorister in Trinity Church, New York: in 1897 he became a member of the Castle Square Opera Company in Boston, and achieved his first success in 1902 at Chicago in *The Sultan of Sulu.* He appeared later in *The Grand Mogul; The Count of Luxembourg; The Arcadians,* and many GILBERT AND SULLIVAN operettas.

461

Mounet-Sully, Jean (1841-1916), French actor who studied at the Paris Conservatory, and made his debut at the Odéon in 1868. After serving in the Franco-Prussian War he achieved a triumph in 1872 as Orestes in RACINE's *Andromaque* at the COMEDIE FRANCAISE, and also gained distinction in *Hamlet, Othello, Le Cid,* and *Phèdre,* frequently appearing with Sarah BERNHARDT. His greatest role was that of Oedipus in an adaptation of SOPHOCLES' *Oedipus-Rex* by Jules Lacroix.

Mount, William Sidney (1807-1868), American painter who studied at the National Academy of Design, New York, and became a member in 1832. His notable canvases include *Turning the Grindstone; Raffling for the Goose; Long Island Farmhouse; Bargaining for a Horse; A Long Story; Truant Gamblers; Farmer's Nooning; Turn of the Leaf; War News; The Fortune Teller.*

Moussorgsky, Modeste, see **Mussorgsky, Modeste.**

Mouth organ, see **Harmonica.**

Mowatt, Anna Cora (1819-1870), American actress and dramatist who first became known as a dramatic reader: in 1845 her comedy, *Fashion,* was performed at the Park Theatre, New York, with considerable success. During the same year she appeared to great applause in *The Lady of Lyons* with the same supporting cast, and with equal success at London in her own play, *Fashion; The Lady of Lyons; Romeo and Juliet; The Strangers.* After 1868 she lived in England, writing articles for newspapers.

Mowbray, Alan, contemporary English stage and screen actor who appeared in several plays for the THEATRE GUILD: since 1930 he has played important parts in many films including *Alexander Hamilton; Peg O' My Heart; Berkeley Square; The House of Rothschild; The Cheaters; Little Man, What Now?; Becky Sharp; Rose Marie; Mary of Scotland; Topper; The Boys from Syracuse; That Hamilton Woman; That Uncertain Feeling; I Wake Up Screaming.*

Mowbray, Harry Siddons (1858-1928), American artist born of English parents at Alexandria, Egypt, and taken to America by his uncle in 1859 after his parents died. He was trained at West Point, and studied with Lèon BONNAT at Paris where his first painting, *Aladdin,* was well received. His decorative panels, murals, and canvases include *Development of the Law; Lady in Black; Idle Hours;* also the ceiling and walls in the library of the University Club, New York. He became the first director in 1903 of the American Academy at Rome.

Mozart, Johann Georg Leopold (1719-1787), German violinist, composer, and father of Wolfgang Amadeus MOZART: he entered the service of the Prince-Archbishop's orchestra in 1743, and was appointed court composer in 1762. Only two of his seven children, Nannerl and Wolfgang, lived to be more than one year old: he devoted his life to their training and guidance. His com-

positions, of real excellence, included oratorios, operas, symphonies, chamber music, and a highly regarded violin method.

Mozart, Wolfgang Amadeus (1756-1791), Austrian harpsichordist, pianist, violinist, and composer born at Salzburg where his father, Johann Georg Leopold MOZART was court composer. He began to compose at four, and at ten could play almost any harpsichord music at sight, and compose for chorus and orchestra. From 1762 to 1779 he toured Germany, Austria, France, and England accompanied by his father: in 1769 his first opera was produced at Salzburg, and in 1781, after being summarily dismissed from the service of the Archbishop of Austria, he went to Vienna where most of the remaining years of his life were spent. His works and services as a virtuoso were always in demand, but he lacked both business foresight and financial ability so that poverty contributed largely to the ill-health which resulted in his early demise. His works, numbering more than six hundred, include the operas *The Abduction from the Seraglio, The Marriage of Figaro, Don Giovanni,* and *The Magic Flute;* several operettas; 49 symphonies; 16 *Divertimenti;* 11 *Serenades;* 9 string quintets; 26 string quartets; 42 violin sonatas; 17 piano sonatas; 17 organ sonatas; 25 concertos for piano, 7 for violin, 9 for various instruments. A thematic catalogue was made by Ludwig KOCHEL which lists all Mozart works. His son, **Wolfgang Amadeus Mozart** (1791-1844), was a fine pianist and composer who studied with Johann ALBRECHTSBERGER and the Chevalier von Neukomm: he founded the Cecilia Society at Lemberg where he taught the piano for many years. His compositions include piano concertos; chamber music; a sonata and many solo pieces for the piano.

Mozier, Joseph (1812-1870), American sculptor who engaged in commercial pursuits until he was more than thirty years old, and then studied in Italy: his works include *Prodigal Son* at the Pennsylvania Academy of Fine Arts; *Il Penseroso; Rebecca* at the New York Public Library.

Mrs. Grundy, see **Grundy, Mrs.**

Muck, Karl (1859-1940), German pianist and conductor who studied at the Leipzig Conservatory, conducted opera in various German cities; succeeded Anton SEIDL as conductor of the Wagner Traveling Theatre; conducted at the Berlin Opera and Covent Garden, London; directed the Boston Symphony Orchestra in 1906 and 1907; became permanent conductor of the latter from 1912 to 1918 when he was interned as an alien enemy during World War I. After his return to Germany in 1919 he conducted at Munich and Amsterdam; also from 1922 to 1933 at Hamburg after which he retired.

Mudejar Style, in art the style which the Moorish artists and artisans brought into Spain after its conquest, and which remained when the Christians again dominated the country. It consists of a modification of the earlier RENAISSANCE style with the addition of certain Moorish characteristics in the designing and decoration of arches and fountains with ceramics and gilt stuccoes.

Mugello, Guido di Pietro da, see **Angelico, Fra.**

Mulford, Clarence Edward (1883-), American author who has written twenty-seven books of which twenty-five have been screened: his works include *Bar 20*, a volume of short stories (1907); *The Orphan; Hopalong Cassidy; Bar 20 Days; Cottonwood Gulch; Mesquite Jenkins; Tumbleweed; Hopalong Cassidy Serves a Writ.*

Mulier, Pietro, see **Molyn, Pieter** (the Younger).

Müller, Charles Louis (1815-1892), French painter who studied with Léon Cogniet and Baron Gros; also at the Ecole des Beaux-Arts, Paris, and became director of the Gobelin tapestry works. His notable works include *Satan Leading Christ up into the Mountain; Massacre of the Innocents; Roll Call of the Last Victims of the French Revolution*, considered his masterpiece; *Marie Antoinette at Petit Trianon; Lady Macbeth; Charlotte Corday in Prison.*

Müller, Friedrich (1749-1825), German painter and poet often called *Maler Müller* (Painter Müller). He studied at Zweibrücken and settled at Mannheim as court painter. He was also known in Rome, which he visited in 1778, as *Teufelsmüller* (Devil Müller) because he chose subjects in which devils played the principal part. His canvases include *Ulysses Invoking the Spirit of Ajax; Cupid With Doves in a Rose Bower:* he also wrote a popular poem, *The Soldier's Farewell*, and the dramas *Niobe; Faust; Golo and Genovera.*

Müller, Wilhelm (1794-1827), German poet whose poems, *Songs of the Greeks*, were written during the period of the Greek struggle for independence: he is famous chiefly as the author of the song cycles *Diè Schöne Müllerin* and *Winterreise* set to music by Franz Schubert.

Müller, William James (1812-1845), English painter who studied with J. B. Pyne: his notable canvases include *Destruction of Old London Bridge*, and many sketches and paintings of Oriental scenery and customs the material for which was secured in 1843 when he accompanied Sir Charles Fellowes' Expedition to Lycia in Asia Minor: among these are *Scene in a Tent; Xanthus; The Slave Market.*

Mullion, in architecture the slender bar or pier placed as a division between the lights of a window: also the name of the stone uprights between separate windows in Gothic and Renaissance buildings.

Mulock, Dinah Maria (1826-1887), English novelist whose married name was Dinah Maria Craik: her works include *John Halifax, Gentleman* (1857) which immediately assigned her high rank among English women novelists of her day: *A Life for a Life; The Ogilvies; Agatha's Husband; The Head of the Family; Olive:* she also wrote some fine poetry and a volume entitled *A Woman's Thoughts About Women.*

Mulready, William (1786-1863), Irish painter who entered the Royal Academy School at fifteen and exhibited at seventeen. After teaching and making illustrations for children's books, he devoted himself to genre painting: among his finest canvases are *Old Houses in Lambeth; Fight Interrupted; Roadside Inn; Wolf and the Lamb; Giving a Bite; Choosing the Wedding Gown; Fair Time:* he continued to draw at the Life School of the Royal Academy almost to the day of his death, and painted several pictures to illustrate a new edition of Goldsmith's *The Vicar of Wakefield.*

Multatuli, see **Dekker, Edward Douwes.**

Mumford, Lewis (1895-), American critic and essayist educated at the College of the City of New York, and at Columbia, and New York Universities: his works include *The Story of Utopias* (1922); *Sticks and Stones; The Golden Day; Herman Melville; The Brown Decades; The Culture of Cities; Men Must Act.*

Mummers, the name given in medieval England to bands of men and women who serenaded people at their homes during periods of public festivities, especially Christmas. They were dressed in fantastic costumes, wore masks, and also disguised themselves as animals. Sometimes rude pantomimes or plays were presented, but the custom finally lead to such licentious proceedings that Henry VIII forbade the wearing of a mask or disguise except on the stage.

Munch, Andreas (1811-1884), Norwegian poet and dramatist: his works include the poems *Ephemera, The Singer, Pictures from the North and South*, and *Sorrow and Comfort;* the dramas *King Sverre's Youth*, and *Lord William Russell.* He also translated some works of Sir Walter Scott, and Sir Alfred Tennyson's "Enoch Arden."

Munch, Edvard (1863-), Norwegian painter related to Jacob Munch (1776-1839) a well-known painter: he attended an art school at Christiania, and also went to Paris where he was a pupil of Léon Bonnat. He was friendly with Ibsen, Hamsun, Sibelius, and Gaugin. Among his notable works are murals for the University of Oslo; *Puberty; Spring; The Sick Child; Ashes; Death in the Room; Jealousy; Death of Marat; Summer Night:* his paintings are in many European and American museums.

Munchausen, Baron (1720-1797), German cavalry officer whose full name was Karl Friedrich Hieromymus, Baron von Munchausen. He was a confirmed braggart whose tales gave him the reputation of being the greatest liar in Germany: an English version by Rudolph Eric Raspe of *Baron Munchausen's Narrative of His Marvelous Travels and Campaigns in Russia* was published in 1785 and later translated into several other languages. The tales were actually stories and legends gathered from old books.

Munch-Bellinghausen, Eligius (1806-1871), Austrian dramatist whose works include *Griseldis* (1834); *The Son of the Wilderness; The Fencer* *of Ravenna; Wildfire:* he was one of the outstanding realistic dramatists of his period.

Munday, Anthony (1553-1633), English dramatist and actor who appeared with the Earl of Oxford's Company: his known plays include *John a Kent and John a Cumber* (1595); *The Downfall of Robert, Earl of Huntington; The Death of Robert, Earl of Huntington:* the two last-named have to do with the exploits of ROBIN HOOD.

Mundy, Talbot (1879-1940), Anglo-American novelist educated at Rugby who came to the United States in 1911 after traveling in India, Tibet, Australia, and Africa in the service of the British Government: he became an American citizen in 1917. His numerous works include *Rung Ho* (1914); *Winds of the World; King of the Khyber Rifles; The Ivory Trail; The Hundred Days; Tros of Samothrace; The Thunder Dragon; East and West; Old Ugly Face.*

Muni, Paul (1895-), American stage and screen actor born in Austria and educated in Chicago, making his debut in 1908 with the Yiddish Theatre Stock Company in New York, and remaining with the Jewish Art Theatre until 1926 when he made his first appearance in an English-speaking part at the Eltinge Theatre in *We Americans.* His greatest stage success was *Counsellor-at-Law* produced in 1931, and revived at New York in 1943. He has also appeared in many films including *Seven Faces; Scarface; I Am a Fugitive from a Chain Gang; Black Fury; Bordertown; The Story of Louis Pasteur; The Good Earth; The Life of Émile Zola; Juarez; We Are Not Alone; Hudson's Bay.*

Munkácsy, Mihály or **Michael** (1844-1900), Hungarian painter whose real name was Michael Lieb: he studied in Budapest, and worked in Vienna, Munich, Paris, and Düsseldorf, winning a gold medal with his painting, *Milton Dictating to His Daughters,* now in the New York Public Library. Among his notable creations are *The Last Day of a Condemned Man; Christ Before Pilate; Christ on Calvary; Last Moments of Mozart; Luncheon in the Garden; Arpad Taking Possession of Hungary; The Music Room; Pawnbroker's Shop.* His pictures are in many European and American museums.

Munro, Charles Kirkpatrick (1889-), Irish dramatist whose real name is Charles Kirkpatrick MacMullen: he was educated at Cambridge, and his plays include *Wanderer* (1915); *At Mrs. Beam's; The Rumor; Storm; Progress; The Mountain; Cocks and Hens; Mr. Eno; Bluestone Quarry; Ding and Co.* He has also written the essays *The True Woman* and *Watching a Play.*

Munroe, Kirk (1850-1930), American writer of boys' adventure stories who studied engineering at Harvard University, was intimate with "Buffalo Bill" and General Custer, reported the Indian wars for the New York *Sun,* edited *Harper's Young People,* and founded the League of American Wheelmen, a national association, 100,000 strong, of American bicycle riders. His books include *The Flamingo Feather* (1887), *The Golden Days of '49, The Painted Desert, The Blue Dragon,* and many other stories of adventure on land and sea.

Mural Painting, a form of wall decoration employed in ancient Egypt, Greece, Rome, China, and Japan: the art received its first impetus in modern Italy from GIOTTO, and was carried to its highest point by LEONARDO DA VINCI, MICHELANGELO, RAPHAEL, CORREGGIO, CARRACCI, VERONESE, TITIAN, DEL SARTO, TINTORETTO, TIEPOLO, RUBENS, MURILLO, and GOYA. After the decline of the art in the 18th century, a new impetus was given by FLANDRIN, Puvis de CHAVANNES, and GAUGUIN in France; LEIGHTON and BRANGWYN in England; LA FARGE, ABBEY, SARGENT and BLASHFIELD in the United States.

Muratore, Lucien (1878-), French dramatic tenor who studied at the Marseilles Conservatory, and first acted on the legitimate stage with Sarah BERNHARDT and Mme. REJANE. He then prepared himself for an operatic career at the Paris Conservatory and made his debut in Reynaldo Hahn's *La Carmélite* at the OPERA-COMIQUE, Paris, in 1902, and in 1905 at the Paris Opéra in GLUCK'S *Armide.* In 1913 he appeared with the BOSTON OPERA Company, and during the same year with the CHICAGO OPERA COMPANY, singing with the latter for several years, and returning in 1915 to remain until 1921. His acting ability was so remarkable as to compensate for his limitations as a singer.

Murdock, William (1888-), Australian pianist and author educated at Melbourne University, and trained at the Royal College of Music, London. He has appeared as soloist with several British orchestras, and is highly regarded as a chamber-music player. His works include *Brahms* (1933), containing an analytical study of the piano works; *Chopin, His Life* (1935).

Murfree, Mary Noailles (1850-1922), American novelist and short story writer who first contributed to magazines: her numerous works, written under the pen name "Charles Egbert Craddock," include *In the Tennessee Mountains* (1884), a volume of stories; *Where the Battle Was Fought; The Prophet of the Great Smoky Mountain; In the Clouds; The Despot of Broomsedge Cove; The Frontiersman; The Windfall; The Fair Mississippian; The Raid of the Guerilla and Other Stories.*

Murger, Henri (1822-1861), French man of letters who was at one time secretary to Count Leo TOLSTOY: his works include *Scenes of Bohemian Life* (1848), his best-known work which pictured life in the Latin Quarter of Paris, and was used as the basis of PUCCINI'S grand opera, LA BOHEME: also *Claude and Marianne; Scenes of Youthful Life; The Last Appointment; The Water Drinkers.*

Murillo, Bartholomé Estéban (1617-1682), Spanish painter who was left an orphan at ten, and trained in art by Juan de Castillo in Seville where he studied the works of the Italian, Spanish, and Dutch masters in addition to having VELASQUEZ as his patron. His notable works include *Death of Saint Clara; St. James Distributing Alms; Saint Diego Feeding the Poor; Dream of the Roman Patrician; Immaculate Conception; Justa and Rufina; Vision of St. Anthony; Nativity of the Virgin; Boys With Grapes; St. Anthony and the Infant Jesus; Miracle of the Loaves and Fishes; Return of the Prodigal; Healing of the Paralytic; The Rose of St. Francis; The Dice Players; The Young Beggar.*

Murphy, John Francis (1853-1921), American painter who was largely self-taught: he first exhibited at the National Academy of Design, New York, in 1876, and was later awarded many prizes and medals for his notable canvases including *Sunny Slopes; The Old Barn; October; Late Afternoon; The Path to the Village; Edge of the Pond; Indian Summer; Afternoon Lights on the Hills; The Hill-Top; Stormy Fields.*

Murray, Sir David (1849-1933), Scottish painter who was in business before becoming an artist: his notable works include *My Love is Gone a-Sailing; Young Wheat; In the Country of John Constable; River Road; Long After; View of Windsor.*

Murray, J. Harold (1891-), American actor and singer who made his professional debut in 1920 at the Winter Garden, New York, in *The Passing Show,* later appearing in *The Whirl of New York; The Springtime of Youth; Caroline; China Rose; Captain Jinks; Castles in the Air; Rio Rita; Face the Music.* He also was starred in several films including *Married in Hollywood; Cameo Kirby; Happy Days; Women Everywhere; Under Suspicion.*

Muses, The, in Greek mythology the nine daughters of ZEUS and MNEMOSYNE, the deity personifying memory: their names and the arts and sciences over which they presided were *Calliope,* muse of epic poetry and eloquence, represented with a tablet and pencil; *Euterpe,* muse of lyric poetry or music, depicted with a double flute; *Erato,* muse of erotic poetry, shown with a lyre; *Mepomene,* muse of tragedy, represented with a tragic mask and ivy wreath; *Thalia,* muse of comedy, depicted with a comic mask and ivy wreath; *Polyhymnia,* muse of sacred poetry shown with a veil; *Terpsichore,* muse of the dance and choral song, represented with a lyre; *Clio,* muse of history depicted with a scroll; *Urania,* muse of astronomy shown with a celestial globe. A tenth muse, *Arethusa,* muse of pastoral poetry, was added later.

Musetta, a character in Giacomo PUCCINI's opera, *La Bohème:* she is the mistress of Marcel with whom she is always quarreling, and the devoted friend of MIMI, the little embroiderer, who dies of consumption in the final scene. Her aria, *Musetta's Song,* in the café scene of the second act in the opera, is always received with tumultuous enthusiasm: there are numerous recordings of it available.

Museum of American Art (New York), see **Whitney Museum of American Art (New York).**

Museum of Art, an institution containing paintings, sculptures, architectural models, prints, drawings, illuminated manuscripts, and many other objects of art which are open to public inspection in all the great and many of the smaller cities in the world. Information regarding most of the important museums of art abroad and in the United States, such as the METROPOLITAN MUSEUM OF ART (New York), the NATIONAL GALLERY (London), and the LOUVRE (Paris), will be found under the names of such institutions.

Museum of Costume Art (New York), an institution founded in 1937 for the collection, preservation and exhibition of clothes of all ages and all peoples: it is, as far as is known, the only public museum in the United States devoted solely to human dress. Through changing exhibitions, permanent study and research facilities, it provides a clearing house for style in the United States, and the opportunity to study the art of dress in all its interest, beauty and social connotation. The Museum's collections, comprising authentic garments and accessories ranging from the 17th to the 20th centuries, with folk costumes of Europe and Asia, are available to the designer, artist, writer, educator, student, and the interested layman. Every object in these collections is as easily accessible for examination as a book in a reference library, through an original and unique filing system known as "study storage." There is a reference library, which possesses slides and collections of original sketches as well as published material. The Museum is supported by membership fees and gifts, which are tax exempt. Among the exhibitions held have been *The Cycle of American Dress,* in three successive parts; *A Designers' Exhibition* of costumes and millinery; *Color Through the Decades,* costume color trends of the 18th and 19th centuries, and costumes and accessories worn by Queen Alexandra of England; *Sources of Fashion Inspiration* and *Fashions in Wartime; The Coming Silhouette* (W.P.B. Regulations); *Fastenings and Embellishments; Masks from the Collection of Kenneth Macgowan.*

Museum of Fine Arts (Berlin), an institution divided into the old and new museums: the *Old Museum* was built during the reign of Frederich III according to designs by Karl Friedrich Schinkel, and the portico, supported by eighteen colossal columns, is decorated with murals depicting the progress of civilization. There is a representative collection of paintings, and another of northern antiquities. The *New Museum* contains an Egyptian collection; also plaster casts of ancient, medieval, and modern sculpture: its greatest feature is Wilhelm von KAULBACH's cycle of stereochromic murals, representing the six epochs of human progress, painted on the walls of the grand staircase.

Museum of Fine Arts (Boston), an institution founded in 1870, and located in its present quarters since 1908. It contains one of the world's finest collections of casts, many original Greek statues, and the choicest collection of Japanese paintings in the world.

Museum of Fine Arts (Cologne), an institution known as the Wallraf-Richartz Museum; it contains a comprehensive collection of paintings by old German, Dutch, and Italian masters as well as a choice assembly of works by modern artists.

Museum of Fine Arts (Dresden), a building in the Renaissance style the exterior of which is ornamented with statues by Ernst Hähnel and Ernst Rütschel of MICHELANGELO, RAPHAEL, GIOTTO, DANTE, GOETHE, and many other artists and poets. The picture gallery contains many notable works including RAPHAEL's *Sistine Madonna,* and canvases by TITIAN, GIORGIONE, and CORREGGIO, as well as paintings by Dutch, German, Spanish, and French masters.

Museum of Fine Arts (Glasgow), an institution founded in 1854 with the purchase of the collection owned by Archibald McLellan, now housed in an art gallery and museum built at a cost of $1,000,000, and liberally supported by the merchants and manufacturers of Glasgow. The original collection has been supplemented by gifts and by purchases: it contains a representative collection of the works of Scottish painters in addition to those of other countries.

Museum of Fine Arts (Naples), an institution founded by Ferdinand IV in 1790 in which he housed the Farnese collection accumulated by his father, and the antiques from Herculaneum, Pompeii, Paestum, and other ancient cities, calling it the Real Musio Borbonico. In 1860 Garibaldi, then dictator at Naples, declared the museum state property: today it contains not only a vast quantity of Greek and Roman antiquities, but also an important picture gallery, and collections of large statues, bronzes, glass, jewelry, papyri, precious stones, and Greek vases.

Museum of Fine Arts (Versailles), see **Versailles.**

Museum of Modern Art (Moscow), an art gallery founded in Moscow in 1918 after the Russian Revolution: it includes the collection formed by Sergei Stchoukine and Ivan Morosoff, and comprises chiefly notable works by 19th and 20th century French artists including COROT, MONET, RENOIR, PISSARO, DEGAS, CEZANNE, MATISSE, PICASSO, GAUGUIN, and many other masters.

Museum of Modern Art (New York), an institution in New York founded with the purpose, according to its charter, of "encouraging and developing the student of modern arts and the application of such arts to manufacture and practical life." The exhibits comprise painting, sculpture, and prints; architectural displays including models of more than 300 buildings; a gallery of industrial designs including furniture, motor cars, and utensils of all kinds; a photographic display; a collection of films covering the entire period of development; a reference library containing literature on films, ballet and kindred subjects. The museum presents regular programs of films, and exhibitions of paintings by modern artists of all nationalities.

Music, an art in which musical sounds cause aesthetic pleasure through the sense of hearing when aided by the fundamental elements of melody, rhythm, and harmony. The various clas-

sifications include classic, romantic, modern, and ultra-modern music, and the means of its expression are the human voice and musical instruments. The history of the art may be traced through the composers who have created it, and the virtuosos who have interpreted their works. The history of music before the Christian era begins with its use by the Egyptians for religious ceremonies, dancing, and military purposes from about 3000 B.C.: at approximately the same period the Chinese created a tonal system. In 2000 B.C. the Chaldeans, Assyrians, and Babylonians employed music in religious ceremonies and secular festivals: about 1000 B.C. David and Solomon promoted its use by the Hebrews. In 776 B.C. the inauguration of the Olympic games and festivals in Greece brought singing competitions, and the use of the chorus in the plays of EURIPIDES, SOPHOCLES, and AESCHYLUS; PLATO and Aristotle wrote on the science and aesthetics of the art, and about 200 B.C. the Romans absorbed Greek music culture particularly in the use of instruments for military purposes. Music in the Christian era began with the hymns of the martyrs, the treatises by St. Augustine and Boethius, and the organization in 600 A.D. of the Schola Cantorium (School of Sacred Music) by Pope Gregory at Rome. Organs were introduced into churches about 1000 A.D., and the songs of the trouvères, minnesingers, and mastersingers charmed the ears of rich and poor when accompanied by the lute, viol, and harp: among the composers and writers of note were HUCBALD, Odo, GUIDO D'AREZZO, MACHAUT, DUNSTABLE, OKEGHEM, and DES PRES. In the Sixteenth Century, after notes placed in fixed positions on the musical staff superseded NEUMES, and GUIDO D'AREZZO's system of solmization came into general use, a new group of composers appeared including TALLIS, PALESTRINA, who developed sacred music, LASSUS, BYRD, MORLEY, CACCINI and PERI who wrote the first opera, *Dafne,* John BULL, MONTEVERDI who greatly improved operatic composition, GIBBONS, and FRESCOBALDI. In the Seventeenth Century music was developed by CARISSIMI who wrote oratorios and cantatas; BUXTEHUDE, a great composer and performer of organ music; LULLY, the first famous French opera composer; CORELLI, the first great player and composer of violin music; PURCELL, COUPERIN, VIVALDI, RAMEAU, HANDEL, Johann Sebastian BACH, and Domenico SCARLATTI who developed harpsichord, organ, oratorio, and orchestral music. In the Eighteenth Century music was in the hands of such masters as GLUCK who revolutionized opera; HAYDN who developed the symphony; CLEMENTI who wrote the immortal *Gradus ad Parnassum* for the improvement of piano technique; MOZART who left the world a priceless heritage of music of every kind; BEETHOVEN whose symphonies and chamber music are immortal; PAGANINI who carried violin technique to its highest point; SCHUBERT whose songs have thrilled the world; WEBER, ROSSINI, and DONIZETTI whose operas delighted audiences on the Continent, in England, and America. In the Nineteenth Century music numbered among its creators from 1800 to 1850 BERLIOZ, MENDELSSOHN, CHOPIN, SCHUMANN, LISZT, VERDI, WAGNER, with his startlingly new ideas for music drama, GOUNOD, OFFENBACH, FRANCK, BRUCKNER,

466

Smetana, Johann Strauss, Jr., with his entrancing dance music, Stephen Foster and his haunting ballads, Goldmark, Rubinstein, Brahms, the mightiest master after Beethoven, Saint-Saens, Bizet, Bruch, Mussorgsky, Tschaikowsky, Dvorak, Massenet, Gilbert and Sullivan who charmed the world with their operettas, and Grieg who opened up new vistas with the atmosphere of Norwegian fjords. From 1850 to 1900 the new masters of musical composition included Fibich, d'Indy, Chadwick, Humperdinck with fairy operas in the Wagnerian idiom, Chausson, Sinding, Elgar, Leoncavallo, Mascagni, Puccini, Charpentier, Mahler, Paderewski, Arensky, Loeffler, MacDowell, Debussy, Nevin, Delius, Parker, Richard Strauss, who developed the symphonic poem, Dukas, Glazunoff, Sibelius, Granados, Gliere, Hadley, Vaughan Williams, Rachmaninoff, Schonberg, Ravel, De Falla, Respighi, Bloch, Cadman, Kodaly, Malapiero, Stravinsky, Bax, Berg, Prokofieff, and Hindemith. Since 1900 there are many composers who have definitely proved their ability to create musical works in accordance with modern trends: they include Copland, Krenek, Walton, Shostakovich, William Schuman, Creston, Barber, Berezowsky, Carpenter, Giannini, Griffes, Hanson, Harris, Ives, Piston, Skilton, Sowerby, Still, Taylor, Thomson, Varese, Whithorne, Miaskowski, Honneger, Milhand, Castelnuovo-Tedesco, Villa Lobos, Chavez, and many others whose names cannot be included because of space limitations.

Musical Comedy, a form of theatrical entertainment which developed in England about 1890, the first piece of the kind being written by Adrian Ross and Osmond Carr with the title, *In Town;* it may be considered as the descendent of the Italian *opera buffa* of Cimarosa, the French *opéra buffe* of Offenbach, the operettas, or plays with music known as *singspiele* in Germany, and the operettas of Gilbert and Sullivan. There is usually little attempt at plot, but the lyrics are frequently clever: the best example of American creation is perhaps George Gershwin's *Of Thee I Sing* (1931), a political satire which received the Pulitzer prize. Other American composers who have been attracted to this type of musical production include Victor Herbert, Jerome Kern, Irving Berlin, and Cole Porter.

Musical Instruments. The musical instruments in general use are divided into six classifications: *(1) Stringed instruments* which include the violin, viola, violoncello, double bass, harp, guitar, banjo, ukulele, mandolin, piano, and zither: *(2) Wood wind instruments* which include the piccolo, fife, flute, flageolet, clarinet, oboe, english horn, bassoon and double bassoon: *(3) Brass wind instruments* which include the trumpet, cornet, french horn, saxophone, trombone and bugle: *(4) Percussion instruments* which include the kettledrum, side-drum, bass drum, carillon, orchestra bells, xylophone, triangle, castanets, cymbals, gong, and tam-tam: *(5)* The organ in its various forms: *(6) Mechanical instruments* which include the automatic forms of the piano, organ, and other instruments.

Musical Magazines (American), several magazines of interest to the professional musicians, students, and lovers of music are published in the United States. Among them are the **Musical Quarterly,** a magazine devoted to the historical, aesthetic, and critical aspects of music; **Musical America,** which devotes itself to news and feature articles relating to matters of current interest; **Musical Courier** which also devotes itself to current musical topics and the activities of concert and opera artists; **The Etude** which is published in the interest of teachers and students, but also contains many articles written for the enjoyment of those who are merely listeners.

Musical Offering (Ger. Musikalische Opfer), a group of compositions by Johann Sebastian Bach which treat a musical subject given him by Frederick the Great: it comprises two ricercari, a fuga canonica, five sonatas for flute (the instrument on which Frederick was proficient), and eight canons. There is a Victor recording in an adapted form by the Yella Pessl Instrumental Ensemble.

Music and Shakespeare, see **Shakespeare and Music.**

Music Copyright, see **Copyright.**

Music Drama, a form of opera in which the vocalizing and instrumental music are completely given over to the task of interpreting and intensifying the drama itself: it was first introduced in the face of almost overwhelming opposition by Richard Wagner in his cycle, *The Ring of the Nibelungs.* In the majority of operas composed previously the vocal numbers were the most important feature, but Wagner, although he made extraordinary technical demands on the singer in his scores, subordinated the voice to the dramatic action, and also made the orchestra play an important part in the creation of the proper atmosphere.

Music Hall, the term by which auditoriums for the presentation of orchestral, solo instrumental, or vocal music were known for many years: now applied to any theatre in which a variety of musical, dramatic, vaudeville, and dance acts are presented, often with the addition of motion pictures. The music hall first became popular in England about 1737, and reached its highest point in the Alhambra at London in the early part of the 20th century: the most representative theatre of the kind in the United States is the Radio City Music Hall in New York.

Musikalische Opfer, see **Musical Offering.**

Musset, Alfred de (1810-1857), French poet and dramatist, full name Louis Charles Alfred de Musset, who was educated at the Collège Henri IV at Paris and published his first volume of poems, *Tales of Spain and Italy* in 1829. He was enamored for a time of George Sand who was also intimate with Frédéric Chopin. His plays, many of which are short, achieved little success with the exception of *Un Caprice* (1847): the poetical works such as *Les Nuits* are the best products of his imagination.

Mussorgsky, Modest (1839-1881), Russian composer who first studied with his mother, and served in the army before resigning in 1858 to take up the study of music seriously with Mily BALAKIREV, but was obliged to seek a governmental position through lack of funds. His notable works include the operas, *Boris Godunoff, Khovantchina,* and *The Fair at Sorochinsk;* the tone poem, *A Night on Bald Mountain;* a suite of piano pieces, *Pictures at an Exhibition,* orchestrated by Maurice RAVEL; many famous songs including *The Song of the Flea.*

Mustel, Victor (1815-1890), French manufacturer of harmoniums who made several important improvements in the instrument, and also invented the CELESTA, used by Peter TSCHAIKOWSKY with remarkable success in his *Nutcracker Suite.*

Mute, a contrivance used on certain musical instruments to deaden their resonance: in the case of the VIOLIN, VIOLA, VIOLONCELLO, or DOUBLE BASS it consists of a piece of wood or brass which is placed on the bridge without touching the strings. Brass instruments are muted by placing a leather-covered pad in the bells.

Muziano or **Musiano, Girolamo** (c.1530-1592), Italian painter also known as *Girolamo Bressano,* and as *Il Giovane de' Paesi* or "The Young Man of the Landscapes." He was a pupil of Girolamo Romanino at Brescia, studied the works of TITIAN at Venice, and with MICHELANGELO and ZUCCHERO at Rome. His notable works include *The Resurrection of Lazarus; Circumcision; Christ Giving the Keys to St. Peter; Assumption of the Virgin; Ascension; Pietà; St. Francis Assisi at Prayer.*

Muzio, Claudia (1892-), Italian operatic soprano who studied the harp and the piano before her vocal talent became apparent to her teacher, Madame Casaloni at Milan. She made her debut in 1912 at Arezzo, Italy, in MASSENET's *Manon,* and after successful appearances in Europe, London, and South America, appeared first in 1916 at the Metropolitan Opera House, New York, in PUCCINI's *Tosca* with CARUSO and SCOTTI, remaining there until 1921. She was a member of the Chicago Opera Company from 1922 to 1933, and retired after returning to the Metropolitan Opera House for the season 1933-34.

Mycenae, a town in ancient Greece said to have been founded by PERSEUS: it was destroyed in 468 B.C., but excavators have unearthed from its ruins some of most important and significant relics of Greek civilization. They include the tombs of AGAMEMNON, CASSANDRA, CLYTEMNESTRA, ELECTRA, and Atreus; the *Lion Gate;* several gold masks used to cover the faces of the dead; silver and gold vases, and fragments of wall paintings.

My Country, 'Tis of Thee, see **America.**

Myers, Jerome (1867-1940), American painter who studied at Cooper Union and the ART STUDENTS' LEAGUE, New York: his reputation was gradually built up by his extremely colorful and human pictures of life on the East Side streets of New York an example being *Night Mission.* He won many awards, and his paintings are to be seen in the Metropolitan Museum of Art and many other American galleries.

Myron, Greek sculptor who worked during the fifth century, and was said to have studied with AGELADAS. His works include many statues and groups in bronze including *Hecate; Apollo; Athena Striking Marsyas;* the famous *Discobolus; Ladas the Runner;* a group, *Zeus, Athena, and Heracles.* PLINY praised him greatly, and he is considered an artist who contributed much to the knowledge of anatomy in its relation to sculpture.

Mystery Plays, see **Miracle Plays.**

Mytens, Daniel (c.1590-c.1657), Dutch painter, chiefly self-taught, who formed his style on that of RUBENS, and worked for James I and CHARLES I of England. He made exquisite copies of RAPHAEL's cartoons originally designed for tapestries in the SISTINE CHAPEL of the VATICAN in Rome: his finest works include *Charles I with Henrietta Maria and Child;* a portrait of the dwarf, Jeffrey Hudson, and many other likenesses of celebrated personages at the English court.

Mythology, the study of the legends of various countries in regard to its gods and heroes: the word is also used as the term for the legends themselves. Almost every country in the ancient and modern world has a great number of myths or legends which are either the product of the imagination or partially founded on fact. The most famous and elaborate mythologies are the Egyptian, East Indian, Arabic, Greek, Roman, and Scandinavian. Max (Friedrich Maximilian) Müller was one of the leading investigators of the sources and true significance of myths.

N

Nagayoshi, see **Choki.**

Nagel, Conrad (1897-), American stage, screen, and radio actor who first appeared with stock companies, and made his debut in 1917 at Chicago in *The Man Who Came Back,* also playing in *Forever After; The First Apple; Goodbye Again; The Shining Hour; The Petrified Forest; Faust* in Max Reinhardt's production. Among the films in which he has appeared are *Little Women; The Fighting Chance; Three Weeks; Tess of the d'Urbervilles; Quality Street; The Thirteenth Chair; Dubarry, Woman of Paris; The Man Called Back; Ann Vickers; Dangerous Corner; Yellow Cargo; I Want a Divorce.* He has been starred in many dramatic sketches on the radio, and is now (1943) featured in *The Radio Reader's Digest.*

Naiads, in Greek mythology a race of inferior female deities who lived in lakes, rivers, springs and fountains: they were represented in painting and sculpture as young, beautiful, and graceful.

Naidu, Sarojini (1879-), Indian poet educated at King's College, London, and Girton College, Cambridge: her works include *The Golden Threshold; The Bird of Time; The Broken Wing; The Sceptered Flute of Song.* She wrote her poems in English but they have been translated into the principal Indian vernaculars.

"Naïla" Valse (Delibes), a waltz movement, also known as *Pas des Fleurs* and *Intermezzo,* originally written by Léo DELIBES for a revival of Adolphe Adams' opera, *The Corsair:* there are several Columbia and Victor recordings for orchestra. It was also arranged as a concert number for the piano by Ernst DOHNANYI, and there is a Victor recording by Wilhelm BACHAUS.

Nairne, Carolina (1766-1845), Scottish poet and song writer known as the "Flower of Strathearn": she published a collection of Scottish national airs entitled *The Minstrel* in 1821. Among her well-known songs are *The Laird of Cockpen; John Tod; The Hundred Pipers; Charlie is My Darling; Caller Herrin'; Land o' the Leal.*

Nanking, Tower of, a famous pagoda erected at Nanking in 1413: it was about 260 feet high, octagon in shape, and the outer walls were finished with the finest of white porcelain bricks. Each of the nine stories had overhanging eaves made of green porcelain tiles: there were more than one hundred fifty bells, and five great pearls suspended over the tower to ward off danger. The tower was destroyed in 1853 during a revolt.

Nanteuil, Robert (c.1623-1678), French engraver whose crayon portraits pleased LOUIS XIV so greatly he was appointed royal designer and engraver: it was through his influence with the king that engraving was declared a genuine art, and engravers accorded the privileges granted to other artists. Nanteuil's plates number more than three hundred which include several of Louis XIV, fourteen of Cardinal MAZARIN: also portraits of Anne of Austria and Mme. de SEVIGNE.

Naos, see **Cella.**

Napoleon I, the name of the emperor of France, and conqueror for a time of practically all of Europe, is of interest in this volume only for certain artistic reasons such as the paintings of his battles by famous artists, his methods of removing art treasures from invaded countries to the LOUVRE in Paris, the portraits executed by celebrated artists, and the various monuments celebrating his victories designed and erected by renowned sculptors and architects, many of whom are subjects of special reference.

Narcisse, a neo-classic ballet in one act: libretto by Leon BAKST; choreography by Michel FOKINE; music by Nicholas TCHEREPNINE; first performed by the DIAGHILEFF Ballet at Monte Carlo in 1911. The plot follows closely the well known Greek legend of NARCISSUS, the youth who after seeing his reflection in a pool, died for love of himself.

Narcissus, in Greek mythology a son of the river god Cephissus: he rejected the love of the nymph Echo which drew the vengeance of the gods. He fell in love with his own reflection in a lake, and pined away: the flower bearing his name first appeared on the spot where he died.

Narezhny, Wassily Trovimovitch (1780-1826), Russian novelist considered one of the pioneers in the field of the realistic novel, and a forerunner of Nikolai GOGOL: his works include *The Two Ivans; The Black Year; The Russian Gil Blas:* the last-named is considered his masterpiece.

Narthex, in architecture a gallery or arcaded porch forming the entrance to early Christian churches when the neophytes and penitents were not permitted to enter the churches. There are examples at Rome, Constantinople, and Venice: after the 13th century the narthex was no longer used.

Nasby, Petroleum V., see **Locke, David Ross.**

Nascimento, Francisco (1734-1819), Portuguese poet who used the pen name "Filinto Elysio": his love for Maria de Almeida, a Portuguese lady of high rank, inspired a series of exquisitely phrased love lyrics entitled *Odes:* he also translated the dramas of RACINE and the fables of LA FONTAINE.

Nash, Sir John (1752-1835), English architect who was an exponent of the classic style: he designed a city plan for London in the section now represented by Regent Street and Regent's Park; also the Marble Arch, Haymarket Theatre, and Buckingham Palace.

Nash, Mary (1885-), American stage and screen actress educated at the American Academy of Dramatic Art who made her debut in 1900 with Sam BERNARD in *The Girl from Kays;* among the plays in which she has appeared are *Alice-Sit-by-the-Fire; Captain Jinks; The Silver Box; His Excellency the Governor; Arrah-na-Pogue; The City; The Liars; The Man Who Came Back; I. O. U.; Captain Applejack; The Command to Love.* She also has played leading roles in numerous films including *Uncertain Lady; Come and Get It; Easy Swing; Heidi; Wells Fargo; The Rains Came; The Philadelphia Story.*

Nash, Ogden (1902-), American poet and humorist educated at Harvard University who spent some years in the publishing business before retiring to devote himself exclusively to writing: his works include *Hard Lines* (1931); *Free Wheeling; Happy Days; The Primrose Path; The Bad Parents' Garden of Verse; I'm a Stranger Here Myself; The Face is Familiar.*

Nash, Paul (1889-), English painter and engraver who first studied architecture, and later painting at the Chelsea Polytechnic and the London County Council School of Art. He served as an official artist during World War I, and exhibited his war paintings and drawings in 1918, also making the stage sets for Sir James BARRIE's *The Truth about the Russian Dancers,* besides executing book illustrations. His landscapes are regarded as of the romantic style with rich coloring, and are on exhibition at Paris and London. Some of his engravings for the *Book of Genesis* in the Bible are highly regarded.

Nash, Richard (1674-1762), English dandy educated at Oxford, and known as **Beau Nash** because he was considered an authority in regard to dress and manners. He became arbiter of fashions and social etiquette at the famous English resort, Bath, but he was in far from affluent circumstances, and when gambling was outlawed in 1745, the rest of his life was spent in comparative poverty although the townspeople honored him with a public funeral.

Nashe, Thomas (1567-1601), English poet and dramatist, educated at Cambridge who settled in London, and wrote many pamphlets against puritanism: he also produced a play, *The Isle of Dogs*, with Ben Jonson which was so scurrilous that both were sentenced to imprisonment. In 1592 he wrote the satirical masque, *Summers Last Will and Testament*: his most famous work was *The Unfortunate Traveler, or the Life of Jacke Wilton*: his style in this work was duplicated in Daniel Defoe's "Robinson Crusoe."

Nāsir, Khosrau (1004-c.1060), Persian author and poet considered one of the greatest writers of his period: his finest prose work was the *Safarnāma*, an account of a pilgrimage to Mecca containing an accurate survey of the Moslem world in the 11th century. He also wrote two volumes of poems, the *Rushanāināma*, or book of enlightenment, and the *Sa'adatnāma*, or book of happiness.

Nasmyth, Alexander (1758-1840), Scottish painter who studied with Alexander Ramsay at London and also in Italy: his works include a portrait of *Robert Burns*, and many fine landscapes of which *View of Stirling Castle* is an excellent example. His son, **Patrick Nasmyth** (1787-1831), studied with his father, and later painted landscapes in imitation of the Dutch school: among them *A Cottage; Angler's Nook; View in Hampshire*.

Nast, Thomas (1840-1902), American caricaturist born in Germany who came to New York with his mother in 1846: at fifteen he became a draftsman for *Frank Leslie's Illustrated Newspaper*, and later for *Harper's Weekly*. His cartoons such as *Peace* attracted wide attention during the Civil War: Abraham Lincoln called him "our best recruiting sergeant." He is also famous for introducing the donkey as a symbol of the Democratic party; the elephant for the Republican party, and the tiger for Tammany Hall.

Nathan, George Jean (1882-), American editor, author and dramatic critic educated at Cornell University and the University of Bologna. He first worked with the dramatic staff of the New York *Herald* in 1905, and has been connected with many newspapers and magazines including the New York *Herald; Harper's Weekly; Smart Set; The Saturday Review of Literature; Vanity Fair; Esquire; Puck; Judge*, and *Life*. His works include *The Eternal Mystery* (1913); *Another Book on the Theatre; Bottoms Up; Mr. George Jean Nathan Presents; The Popular Theatre; Comedians All; The Theatre, The Drama, The Girls; The Critic and the Drama; The Testament of a Critic; The Morning after the First Night; Bachelor Life; The Entertainment of a Nation; Beware of Parents*.

Nathan, Robert (1894-), American novelist and poet educated at Harvard University who taught at the New York University of Journalism: his works include *Peter Kindred* (1919); *Autumn; Youth Grows Old*, a volume of poems; *The Puppet Master; Jonah; The Fiddler in Barly; The Woodcutter's House; The Bishop's Wife; One More Spring; The Enchanted Voyage; Portrait of Jennie; They Went on Together; Dunkirk, a Ballad; The Sea Gull Cry*.

National Academy of Design, an organization of painters, sculptors and engravers formed in 1828 with a membership of thirty artists: among the founders were Samuel F. B. Morse, Asher B. Durand, and Daniel Huntington. The Society of American Artists merged with it in 1906, and the membership increased to nearly two hundred, also becoming affiliated with the Metropolitan Museum of Art, New York, and with Columbia University. Exhibitions are held every year, and a free school of design conducted with prizes and medals awarded for the best works in painting, sculpture and engraving.

National Broadcasting Company Symphony Orchestra, see **NBC Symphony Orchestra.**

National Conservatory of Music of America, an institution founded in 1885 at New York and Washington by Jeanette M. Thurber, and chartered by New York State and Congress. Tuition was free until 1915, the expenses being paid with funds provided by Mrs. Thurber and other patrons. Among the distinguished directors were Antonin Dvorak, Emil Paur, and Wassily Safonoff. The faculty included at various times Mme. Fursch-Madi, Rafael Joseffy, James G. Huneker, Henry T. Finck, Victor Herbert, Anton Seidl, and Leo Schulz.

National Federation of Music Clubs, an organization founded at Chicago during the World's Fair in 1893 at the suggestion of Mrs. Theodore Thomas, wife of the distinguished conductor, Theodore Thomas: it has now grown to a membership of nearly 5,000 clubs in 47 states, Alaska, Canada, and the Canal Zone with more than 500,000 members. There is a national governing board composed of fifty members, a Junior division with 2,500 clubs, and a student section. The clubs present artists, especially American, in recitals and concerts, and also commissions musical works since 1931: several operas have been presented.

National Gallery (Berlin), an institution in Berlin which houses a comprehensive collection of paintings by early German masters, and also by modern artists who abandoned the historical style after the Franco-German War of 1870: the latter include Adolf von Menzel, Wilhelm Leibl, Wilhelm Trubner, Bruno Pilghein, Wilhelm Diez, Claus Meyer, Friedrich Kaulbach, Adolf Lier, Franz von Lenbach, Max Lubermann, Fritz von Uhde and many other outstanding painters.

National Gallery (London), an institution founded in 1824 which has been located since 1838 in its present building, an edifice in the Greek style designed by William Wilkins. The building of the **National Portrait Gallery** which adjoins it was erected in 1896, but the collection was started in 1858. The collection comprises an incomparable assembly of works by English masters, and also of Dutch and Italian painters: notable works include the *Venus* of VELAZQUEZ, the *Ansidei Madonna* by RAPHAEL, and VAN DYCK'S portrait of CHARLES I. The only school not fully represented is the French.

National Gallery of Art (Washington, D. C.), an institution established by Act of Congress in 1937 as a division of the Smithsonian Institution: the building was erected with funds given by Andrew W. Mellon, the architect being John Russell Pope. It is one of the largest marble buildings in the world, being 785 feet in length and designed along simple classical lines. The principal collections comprise 500 paintings and pieces of sculpture of which Mr. Mellon contributed 150 works of his own collection including paintings by RAPHAEL, VAN EYCK, BOTTICELLI, REMBRANDT, and VERMEER: some of them came from the HERMITAGE in Leningrad. The Kress collection was added later: it comprised nearly 400 paintings and pieces of sculpture including works of all the important Italian painters from the 13th to the 18th centuries. Since 1940 many important paintings and pieces of sculpture have been loaned, and the WIDENER COLLECTION was added by Act of Congress in 1942. The value of the collection is at least $50,000,000, and includes fourteen paintings by REMBRANDT, seven by VAN DYCK, two by EL GRECO and more than seventy-five others by Dutch and Italian masters.

National Gallery of Canada, an institution at Ottawa founded in 1880 by the Marquis of Lorne, Governor-General of the Dominion, with the purpose of stimulating artistic interest. Continual additions to the collection over a period of years have been made so that Italian, Dutch, German, Spanish, French, and British artists are well represented, and the assembly of paintings, sculptures, and prints by Canadian artists includes more than a thousand items. The Gallery has also worked out a system of loan exhibitions to all parts of Canada.

National Museum (Athens), an institution founded in 1866 containing a comprehensive collection of archaic sculptures and reliefs: among its treasures are the antiquities found by Heinrich SCHLIEMANN at Mycenae and Tiryns; a copy of the *Diadumenos* of POLYCLITUS; terra-cottas from Asia Minor; bronzes from Olympia and Delphi; painted vases.

National Museum (Naples), an institution in Naples formerly known as the Museo Borbonico: Ferdinand IV founded it in 1790 with the Farnese collection and other archaeological specimens discovered in Pompeii and other ancient Italian cities. In 1860 Garibaldi declared it the property of the nation, and it was renamed the National Museum. The collection comprises Greek, Roman, and Italian statues, Pompeian frescoes, and many important bronzes including the *Seated Mercury* and *Dancing Faun;* marbles such as the

Caprian Venus and the *Farnese Bull:* also many ancient portrait busts.

National Museum (Palermo), an institution occupying the former monastery of the Filippini: among the valuable art specimens are objects found in prehistoric tombs, Greek vases, terracottas, bronzes, Etruscan sarcophagi, colored mosaics, medieval and Renaissance sculptures, Sicilian majolicas, and a comprehensive collection of paintings.

National Opera Company, an American organization formed at New York to succeed the AMERICAN OPERA COMPANY after its disbanded in 1886: it toured the United States with Theodore THOMAS and others as conductors, and presented a season at the METROPOLITAN OPERA HOUSE, New York, in 1887 following the regular season of the resident company. After it ceased to function in 1889 it was succeeded by the Emma JUCH Opera Company.

National Symphony Orchestra (Washington, D. C.), an organization founded at Washington, D. C., by Hans KINDLER in 1931: its regular concerts are given in Constitution Hall, and there are also popular Sunday afternoon and students' Saturday afternoon concerts. Hans Kindler has conducted the orchestra continuously since it was founded, and has made tours with it for many years: summer concerts at Potomac Watergate were inaugurated in 1935.

Natoma, grand opera in three acts: libretto by Joseph D. Redding; music by Victor HERBERT; first produced at the Metropolitan Opera House, New York, in 1911. The ever-popular *Dagger Dance* is available in a Victor recording by the Boston "Pops" Orchestra, and there is a Columbia recording of the *Habanera* conducted by André Kostelanetz.

Nattier, Jean Marc (1685-1766), French painter who was the son of Marc Nattier, a portraitist: he became painter for the French court, and also executed several canvases for PETER THE GREAT including his portrait, that of CATHERINE THE GREAT, and of the *Battle of Pultara*. In Paris he painted Madame de POMPADOUR, CAMARGO, Marshal de Saxe, and many other prominent personages at the French court.

Natural, in music a sign (♮) which is employed to cancel the CHROMATIC alteration of a note, thereby restoring it to its position in the natural scale of C major which contains no ACCIDENTALS.

Naughty Marietta, light opera in two acts: book by Rida Johnson Young; music by Victor HERBERT; first produced by Oscar HAMMERSTEIN at New York in 1910 with Orville HARROLD and Emma TRENTINI. The popular musical numbers such as the *Marching Song, Italian Street Song, I'm Falling in Love with Someone,* and *Ah, Sweet Mystery of Life* are available in Columbia and Victor recordings.

Nausicaa, in Greek mythology the daughter of Accinous, king of the Phaeacians, who found ODYSSEUS asleep on a riverbank after being shipwrecked, and supplied him with food and clothes. The incident was the subject of a play by SOPHOCLES.

Navarrette, Juan Fernández (1526-1579) Spanish painter known also as *El Mudo* (the Mute): he studied for many years in Italy, possibly a part of the time at Venice with TITIAN. His notable works, executed as court painter for Philip II of Spain, include a *Nativity; Baptism of Christ; Abraham Receiving the Three Angels;* a *Holy Family; Martyrdom of St. James:* he was known in his native land as the "Spanish Titian."

Nave, in architecture a word derived from the Latin *navis,* and applied to that part of a church which extends from the CHOIR to the entrance. It may be single or divided into several aisles separated by rows of columns.

Navy Band, The, see **United States Navy Band.**

Nazarenes, The, a school formed by a group of German artists during the early 19th century, its purpose being to revive the idealistic art of early Italian painters: among them were Friedrich OVERBECK, Philipp VEIT, Peter CORNELIUS, Julius SCHNORR VON CAROLSFELD, and Friedrich Wilhelm SCHADOW. They were also known as PRE-RAPHAELITES, a name later used to characterize an English group of painters with similar aims. The works of both groups inspire respect because of their inherent sincerity although they lack inspiration in many instances.

Nazhivin, Ivan (1874-   ), Russian novelist who studied for a time at a college in Moscow, traveled in Europe, and became a great admirer of Leo TOLSTOY. After the Revolution of 1917 he fled with his family to Paris: his works include *Rasputin* (1926); *A Certain Jesus: The Gospel According to Thomas.*

Nazimova, Alla (1879-   ), Russian stage and screen actress who studied at a dramatic school in Odessa, toured the Russian provinces, and was starred at St. Petersburg in 1904. She played in London with the Paul Orlonoff Company in 1905, and also in New York on the East Side: after learning English she made her debut in 1906 on Broadway in *Hedda Gabler* under the management of Henry MILLER. Among the plays in which she has appeared are *A Doll's House; The Master Builder; The Passion Flower; Bella Donna; War Brides; The Wild Duck; Salome; Madonna of the Streets; Dagmar; The Good Earth; Ghosts; The Cherry Orchard; Mourning Becomes Elektra.* She also played important roles in the films *Escape* and *Blood and Sand.*

NBC Symphony Orchestra, an organization founded by the National Broadcasting Company in 1937 with Arturo TOSCANINI as conductor: after preliminary concerts conducted by Artur RODZINSKI and Pierre MONTEUX, Toscanini made his debut on December 25, 1937. Thirty-nine concerts were given in the 1937-38 season with thirteen concerts directed by Arturo Toscanini and the balance by guest conductors. The second season (1938-1939) comprised thirty-five concerts

of which twenty were directed by Toscanini and the balance by guest conductors. In 1939 summer concerts were inaugurated with guest conductors, and in 1939-40 eighteen concerts were conducted by Arturo Toscanini and fifteen by Desiré DE-FAUW, Eugène GOOSSENS, Bernardino MOLINARI, and Bruno WALTER. In June and July, 1940, Arturo Toscanini and the orchestra toured the Eastern coast of South America, giving concerts in Rio de Janeiro, Sao Paulo, Montevideo and Buenos Aires. The season of 1940-41 consisted of thirteen concerts under Toscanini, six under Hans STEINBERG, four under Alfred WALLENSTEIN and four under George SZELL. The 1941-42 season was marked by the absence of Arturo Toscanini, except for five special concerts presented in behalf of the United States Treasury Defense Bond campaign, and by the appointment of Leopold Stokowski as chief conductor. Stokowski conducted nine of the thirty-three concerts, and guest conductors included Dimitri Mitropoulos, Efrem Kurtz, Juan Jose Castro, Sir Ernest MacMillan, Dean Dixon, Frank Black, Alfred Wallenstein, Fritz Reiner and Saul Caston. Arturo Toscanini returned for the season of 1942-43, sharing the leadership of the orchestra with Stokowski. Thirteen concerts were conducted by the former, fourteen by the latter. A similar arrangement for the following season was announced by NBC in the spring of 1943. Among the new or infrequently-heard works presented by the NBC Symphony Orchestra the following are particularly noteworthy: Beethoven's *Solemn Mass* and *Ninth (Choral) Symphony;* the Brahms *Requiem;* Chavez' *Sinfoine de Antigone;* Copland's Concert version of the ballet, *Billy the Kid;* Hanson's Symphony No. 3; Roy Harris's Symphony No. 3; Hindemith's Symphony in E♭; Kabelevsky's Symphony No. 2; Menotti's radio opera, *The Old Maid and the Thief;* Milhaud's Symphony; Shostakovich's Symphony No. 5 and Symphony No. 7; Verdi's *Requiem;* Walton's concerto for viola. During the six winter seasons from 1937 to 1942, NBC Symphony programs included 63 performances of works by 45 American composers. Many more native works have been presented during the summer seasons.

Neagle, Anna (1904-   ), English stage and screen actress who made her debut in 1925 at London in the chorus of *Charlot's Revue:* among the plays in which she appeared later are *Rose Marie; The Desert Song; Wake Up and Dream* in which she made her American debut at New York in 1929; *Stand Up and Sing; As You Like It; Peter Pan.* She has also been featured in numerous films including *Bitter Sweet; Nell Gwyn; Peg of Old Drury; Nurse Edith Cavell; Irene; Queen of Destiny; No, No, Nanette; Sunny; They Flew Alone.*

Neal, David Dalhoff (1838-1915), American painter who studied at the Royal Academy, Munich, and with Karl von PILOTY: his paintings include *The First Meeting of Mary Stuart and Rizzio; Chapel of the Kings at Westminster; St. Mark's at Venice; Return from the Chase; Oliver Cromwell Visits John Milton:* he also executed many portraits.

Nectar, in Greek mythology, a word used interchangeably with *ambrosia*, and meaning the nourishment of the gods: according to HOMER nectar is the wine and ambrosia the food, but other writers reverse the meanings.

Nedda, a character in LEONACAVALLO'S opera, I PAGLIACCI: she is the leading lady of an itinerant theatrical troupe who engages in an intrigue with Silvio, a farmer in one of the little towns visited by the company. Her husband, CANIO, stabs her during a performance: when she calls for Silvio's aid, he kills Silvio also, and, dropping his knife, calls out to the audience, "The comedy is finished!"

Neer, Aart or **Aert van der** (1603-1677), Dutch painter who was probably a pupil of Dirk CAMPHUYSEN: he excelled in river, canal, and winter scenes dotted with many small figures. His works of note include *Landscape at Amsterdam; River Landscape; Sunset; The Horse Shoer; Moon-Marine-Scape.* His son, **Eglon Hendrik van der Neer** (1634-1703), studied with his father, and specialized in interior scenes, hunting scenes, and mythological subjects such as *Lady Tuning Her Lute; Death of Cleopatra; Lady at Luncheon.*

Negri, Ada (1870-), Italian poet who saw some of her verses in print when she was only seventeen years of age: her works include *Fate* (1892); *Maternity; Morning Star:* she was very much interested in the problems of the poor, and her poetry reflects her rebellion at the failure of the world as a whole to alleviate their sufferings.

Negri, Pola (1897-), Polish stage and screen actress who made her debut in 1916 at Warsaw in *Sodom's End,* later playing in *Sumurun* and *The Deaf Girl of Portici.* She entered the films in 1922 under the direction of Ernst LUBITSCH in *Bella Donna:* other pictures include *The Cheat; The Spanish Dancer; Shadows of Paris; Gipsy Blood; Passion; Hotel Imperial; Barbed Wire; Woman on Trial; Secret Hour; Three Sinners; A Woman Commands.*

Neihardt, John (1881-), American poet and critic whose ancestors fought in the Revolutionary War after coming to America from Germany: he specialized in Latin while studying at a college in Wayne, Nebraska, became professor of poetry at the University of Nebraska, and later literary editor of the St. Louis *Dispatch.* His works include *The Divine Enchantment* (1900); *A Bundle of Myrrh; Man-Song; The Stranger at the Gate; The Song of Hugh Glass; The Song of the Indian Wars; The Song of Jed Smith.* He has also written a novel, *Splendid Wayfaring,* and an essay, *Poetic Values.*

Neilson, Lilian Adelaide (1846-1880), English actress whose real name was Elizabeth Ann Brown: she appeared in 1865 as Julia in *The Hunchback,* a role long associated with her, and later achieved great success as Rosalind, Viola, Isabella, and in other SHAKESPEAREAN roles. She became so popular in the United States during her first tour in 1872 that she paid return visits several times.

Neilson, William Allan (1869-), American author and educator born in Scotland who taught English at Columbia and Harvard Universities, and has been president of Smith College since 1917: his works include *Essentials of Poetry* (1912) and *A History of English Literature.*

Nekrassov, Nikolai Alexeivitch (1821-1888), Russian poet and editor of a literary magazine, *Sovremmenik;* regarded as one of the most important figures in Russian literature. His *Poems* (1845) and *Last Poems* (1877), contain moving pictures of the unhappy lot of the Russian peasantry.

Nemchinova, Vera, contemporary Russian dancer who studied at Moscow with Nelidova, and joined the Diaghileff Ballet in 1915. She appeared at the Coliseum, Alhambra, and Empire theatres in London, and formed a ballet company with Anton DOLIN in 1927 which played at the Coliseum. Among the ballets in which she has appeared are *Rhapsody in Blue; Espagnol; Revolution; Pulcinella; Giselle; Coppélia; Raymonda.*

Němcová, Bozena (1820-1862), Czech novelist, poet, and writer of short stories: she embodied the Czech folklore in poetic narratives such as *Little Grandmother, Little Mountain Village,* and *The Shepherd and the Dragon.*

Nemirovich-Dantchenko, Vladimir (1857-1943), Russian novelist, dramatist, actor, and theatrical director who became interested in the stage as a youth, taking part in amateur theatricals, and later becoming musical and dramatic critic for periodicals and newspapers in Moscow and St. Petersburg. His novels included *Literary Pensioners; Mist; A Drama Behind the Scenes.* His first play, *The Wild Rose,* was written on a wager in 1882, and was followed by *The Happy Man; Gold; A New Affair; The Value of Life.* He was co-founder of the Moscow ART THEATRE with Constantine STANISLAVSKY in 1898: the history of the enterprise, perhaps the greatest in the annals of the dramatic art, is told in his autobiography, *My Life in the Russian Theatre,* published in 1936.

Neo-classic Drama, a school of French drama founded in the 17th century which chose its subjects from Greek and Roman mythology and history: Corneille and Racine were the most distinguished proponents of the school.

Neo-classicism, a term frequently applied to the style of writing affected by authors during the Restoration and Queen Anne periods in England. Emphasis was placed on the precepts of classical learning, and the importance of stemming the tides of imaginative thought.

Neo-impressionism, a school of painting founded by Georges SEURAT about 1885, seeking to make the fundamental theories of Impressionism more intellectual by reverting to classical models, and attaching greater significance to line and color as the fundamentals of the painter's art. His disciples included Paul SIGNAC: the theories of CUBISM were based on neo-impressionistic principles.

Neolithic Age, the term applied to the latter period of the stone age when the rude implements of the earlier era were replaced by tools of polished stone. No trace is found of metal objects except in rare instances of gold ornaments. The sculptures are of the most primitive and barbaric character, but crude representations of the human figure have been found in caves and burial mounds: also bone implements and fragments of CERAMICS in parts of France, Switzerland, and Denmark.

Neptune, in Roman mythology identified with the Greek deity POSEIDON: his temple in Rome contained a famous marine group by SCOPAS, and his festival was celebrated on the 23rd of July.

Nereus, in Greek mythology the eldest son of Pontus and GAEA, represented as a beneficent old man of the sea: he was the father of fifty daughters known as the *Nereïds*; graceful, lightly-clad maidens who rode on tritons and dolphins and personified the sea in its quiet moods.

Neri, (Saint) Filippo (1515-1595), Italian composer who became a priest in 1551: he founded an organization for the cultivation of vocal music, known as the *Society of the Oratorio* in the monastery of Saint Girolomo, and the modern ORATORIO received its name in this manner. He was also the spiritual adviser of PALESTRINA.

Nero (37-68), Roman emperor whose excesses in both public and private life during the fourteen years of his rule (54-68) led to his being sentenced to death by the Senate: on being informed that he was to die, he committed suicide. Two years before his death he competed in the Olympian Games at Athens, winning several prizes and universal plaudits. Scenes from his career have been used as the subjects of many paintings: among them Wilhelm von KAULBACH'S *Nero Persecuting the Christians,* and Karl von PILOTY'S *Nero Surveying the Ruins of Rome.* Historical romances and dramas have related his crimes, and the screen also has not spared him.

Neruda, Jan (1834-1891), Czech poet, novelist, dramatist, and critic who contributed to literary magazines, and was one of the founders of the periodical, *Kvety* in 1866. His works include *Book of Verse* (1867) ; *Cosmic Songs; Ballads and Romances; Old Town Stories:* also the plays *Francesca da Rimini* and *A Husband Because of Hunger.* His sketches of Czech life called *Humble Histories* was a best seller.

Neruda, Wilma Maria Francisca (1839-1911), German violinist also known as Norman Neruda and Lady Hallé: she made her debut as a child in 1846 at Vienna, and appeared at London with the Philharmonic Orchestra in 1849. After many years of successful concertizing, she married Ludwig Norman, and after his death became the wife of Sir Charles HALLE. She toured the United States in 1899, and was regarded as one of the world's greatest violin virtuosos.

Nerval, Gérard de (1808-1855), French poet, dramatist, and novelist whose real name was *Gérard Labrunie:* his first poems, *National Ele-*

gies, were published in 1827. His works include a brilliant translation of GOETHE's "Faust"; a comedy, *Tartuffe at Molière's;* a play, *The Queen of Sheba,* written in collaboration with Alexandre DUMAS PERE: also the novels, *Misanthropy and Remorse* and *Dream and Reality.*

Nesbit, Edith (1858-1924), English novelist, poet, and author of children's stories: she wrote several serials for the *Strand Magazine* which established her on friendly relations with Richard LE GALLIENNE, Laurence HOUSMAN, Noel COWARD, George Bernard SHAW, and H. G. WELLS. Her most popular children's books were *The Bastable Children* and *The Five Children:* she also published novels and volumes of poetry.

Nesbit, John (1910-), Canadian radio and screen author, actor, and narrator who is the grandson of Edwin BOOTH: his childhood was spent in France, and later the family migrated to California where he was educated at the University of California. He had considerable experience as an actor with stock companies and as an organizer of little theatre groups before starting his *Passing Parade* Series on the radio in 1930 which became a series of film shorts.

Nesfield, William Eden (1835-1888), British architect who was the son of a well-known landscape gardener. He traveled extensively in France, Italy, and Greece for purposes of study, resulting in the publication of his book, *Sketches from France and Italy* (1862) which became a standard textbook. His works include the lodges in Regent's Park and Kew Gardens, and numerous residences: his reputation rests chiefly on his successful efforts to restore the traditions of good design largely swept aside during the VICTORIAN PERIOD.

Nessler, Victor (1841-1890), German composer whose first opera, *Fleurette,* was produced in 1864: all of his operas were well received, but *The Pied Piper of Hamelin* (1879) and *The Trumpeter of Sakkingen* (1884) were the most successful.

Nestor, in Greek mythology a son of the King of Pylos: he was one of the veteran warriors in the TROJAN WAR, and also a sage counselor as to its conduct. The name is now used for any older man of experience in the arts, crafts, business or political administration.

Nestor (c.1055-c.1115), a Russian monk said to be the author of the first Russian chronicle: the style is poetical and many of the legends known as BYLINI are included, but the value of the work cannot be over-estimated in the parts which deal with ethnological subjects.

Nethersole, Olga Isabel (1870-), English actress who first appeared in 1887 on the London stage in *Our Joan:* among the plays in which she assumed leading roles were *The Profligate; La Tosca; Moths; The Middleman; A Scrap of Paper; A Fool's Paradise; Agatha; Diplomacy; The Transgressor; Camille; Frou-Frou; Carmen; Sapho; Magda; Adrienne Lecouvreur; The Second Mrs. Tanqueray; Mary Magdalena; Sister Beatrice.*

Netscher, Caspar or **Gaspar** (1639-1684), German painter who studied with Gerard TER BORCH and in Italy, finally settling in The Hague, and became a successful portrait and genre painter. His works include *Lady at the Harpsichord; Boy Blowing Bubbles; A Card Party; Lady at the Spinning Wheel; Lesson on the Violoncello; The Doctor's Call; Man Writing a Letter; Portrait of Five Children.*

Neuber, Karoline (1697-1760), German actress and theatrical manager whose family name was Weissenborn. After years spent as a strolling player, she assumed the management with her husband, Johann Neuber, of a troupe in Leipzig, and with the aid of Johann GOTTSCHED, presented the plays of RACINE and MOLIERE, and later managed her own theatre in Leipzig, producing a variety of plays many of which she prepared herself for the stage. She is credited with having introduced "good taste on the German stage."

Neumann, Alfred (1895-), German novelist and dramatist who joined the staff of a publishing house, and published a volume of verse after serving in World War I: his works available in English include *The Devil* (1928); *The Patriot,* a play which has been produced in European and American theatres, and has also been filmed; *The Rebels; The Mirror of Fools; Gaudy Empire; Man of December; The Friends of the People.*

Neumann, Balthasar (1687-1753), German architect who was the chief exponent of the grandiose ROCOCO style in Germany, applied to the exterior as well as the interior of buildings, and therefore entirely different from the French type of rococo which was decorative rather than structural. His most notable achievement was the Residenz and the Käpelle at Würzburg.

Neumann, Robert (1897-), Austrian novelist who worked at all kinds of odd jobs, including that of sailor on a Dutch tanker, before attaining success as a writer: his works include *Flood* (1930); *Mammon; Zaharoff; Queen's Doctor; By the Waters of Babylon; Twenty-three Women.*

Neumes, in medieval music notation the characters employed to indicate the pitch of tones used in singing church music: they bore some resemblance to modern shorthand, and the chief elements were grave and acute accents. They are important as representing the first attempt to indicate the relative pitch of notes.

Neuville, Alphonse Marie de (1836-1885), French painter who studied for a time with François Édouard PICOT, but was chiefly self-taught: his notable works include *The Fifth Battalion of Chasseurs at the Gervais Battery, Malakoff; Attack in the Streets of Magenta by Zouaves; A Zouave Sentinel; Bivouac before Le Bourget; The Last Cartridges; Surprise at Daybreak; The Dispatch Bearer; The Drummer:* he was regarded as an extraordinary painter of military subjects.

Nevada, Emma (1859-1940), American operatic soprano who studied witih Mathilde MARCHESI, and made her debut in BELLINI's *La Sonnambula*

at London in 1880. After singing in Italian opera houses including LA SCALA, Milan, she appeared in London, and in 1884 joined Colonel James Henry MAPLESON's Company at the ACADEMY OF MUSIC, New York, singing on alternate nights with Adelina PATTI. Her repertoire included the COLORATURA roles in Italian and French operas. Her daughter, **Mignon Nevada** (c.1887-), was also an operatic soprano who made her debut at Rome, and has sung in European and English opera houses.

Nevin, Ethelbert Woodbridge (1862-1901), American pianist and composer who studied with Benjamin J. LANG and Stephen Emery at Boston, and with Hans von BULOW and Karl KLINDWORTH at Berlin. His works, which are chiefly piano pieces and songs, include the suites *Water Scenes* and *In Tuscany;* many effective songs such as *The Rosary* and *Mighty Lak a Rose;* a song cycle, *Captive Memories,* and a pantomime, *Lady Floriane's Dream.* His brother, **Arthur Finley Nevin** (1871-1943), occupied the post of professor of music at the University of Kansas: his opera, *Poia,* was produced in 1910 at the Royal Opera, Berlin.

Newbolt, Sir Henry John (1862-1938), English novelist and poet educated at Oxford, and trained for the bar, practicing for twelve years before embarking upon a literary career: his works include a novel, *Taken from the Enemy* (1892); several volumes of poetry including *Admirals All, The Sailing of the Long Ships,* and *Songs of the Sea;* also a naval history of World War I and the autobiographical *My World as in My Time.*

Newell, Peter (1862-1924), American author and illustrator who first drew crayon portraits, later becoming a popular book illustrator. His works include *Topsys and Turveys; Peter Newell's Pictures and Rhymes; Jungle Jangle:* he also illustrated John Kendrick BANG's *Houseboat on the Styx,* Lewis CARROLL's *Alice in Wonderland,* and Mark TWAIN's *Innocents Abroad.*

New England Conservatory of Music (Boston), an institution founded in 1867 by Eben Tourjée, and the first music school of large size in the United States. Its faculty included Benjamin J. LANG, Ernest Perabo, Stephen Emery, Karl Zerrahn, and George Whiting: it was enlarged until most of the prominent musicians in Boston were included by 1875, and 14,000 students had been enrolled by 1878. In 1891 Carl FAELTON became director, and was succeeded in 1897 by George W. CHADWICK who improved the position of the institution by raising it to European standards. He also secured the erection of a new building with the help of Eben D. Jordan: the enrollment now averages 3000, and the school orchestra of about seventy-five players holds regular rehearsals and concerts. John Wallace GOODRICH became director in 1930 and was succeeded in 1942 by Quincey PORTER.

New Friends of Music, an organization founded by I. A. Hirschmann of New York City in 1936 as a non-profit enterprise to present chamber music and lieder. In its first season of sixteen concerts, the compositions of BRAHMS and BEETHOVEN were given: during the ensuing five seasons the works of MOZART, SCHUMANN, BACH, HAYDN, SCHUBERT, and many other composers including several complete song cycles.

Newgate Prison (London), the name by which the western gate of the city of London at Watling Street was known after it had been called the *Westgate* and the *Chancellor's Gate.* It was used as a prison up to the end of the 19th century when it became only a house of detention. Few reports as to its unsavory reputation are exaggerated, and many writers have dwelt upon its horrors which were also made much of by painters and caricaturists.

Newman, Ernest (1868-), English music critic and author who acted as music critic of several provincial English newspapers before assuming the same post with the London *Sunday Times:* his works include *Gluck and the Opera* (1895); *Wagner; Musical Studies; Elgar; Hugo Wolf; Richard Strauss; Wagner as Man and Artist; A Musical Motley; Stories of the Great Operas; The Life of Richard Wagner; More Stories of Famous Operas.* He also translated Romain ROLLAND's *Beethoven the Creator* and wrote the English text for Breitkopf and Härtel's complete edition of Richard WAGNER's works.

Newman, Frances (1888-1928), American novelist educated at Agnes Scott College, Decatur, Ga., and at the Sorbonne, Paris: she became the librarian of the Florida State College for Women at Tallahassee, Fla., and later occupied the same post at the Georgia Institute of Technology at Atlanta, Ga. Her works include *The Short Story's Mutations* (1924); *The Hard-Boiled Virgin; Dead Lovers Are Faithful Lovers:* her short story, *Rachel and Her Children* won the O. Henry Memorial Prize in 1924.

Newmarch, Rosa Harriet (1857-1940), English author who studied painting before turning to literature: a visit to Russia in 1897 aroused her interest in music, and after study with Vladimir Stassov she became an authority on Russian music. Her works include *Tschaikowsky* (1900); *Jean Sibelius; The Russian Opera; The Russian Arts; Anton Dvořák:* also several volumes of program notes called *The Concert-Goer's Library.*

New Moon, The, musical romance in two acts; book by Oscar HAMMERSTEIN, 2d; music by Sigmund ROMBERG; first produced at New York in 1928 with Evelyn HERBERT. The many song favorites such as *Lover, Come Back to Me* and *One Kiss* are available in Columbia and Victor recordings.

New Opera Company, The (New York), an organization founded in 1941 with Mrs. Lytle Hull as president, and Mme. Yolanda Mero-Irion as general manager. The dual purpose was to afford talented young artists an opportunity for a Metropolitan appearance in a company with high professional standards, and to produce streamlined opera, satisfying to the eye as well as the ear, at prices within reach of the modest purse. In its first season, November-December, 1941, the company initiated two novelties, the first presentation

of VERDI's *Macbeth* in New York, and the first New York performance in half a century of OFFENBACH's *La Vie Parisienne.* Other bills were MOZART's *Cosi Fan Tutte* in Italian and TSCHAIKOWSKY's *Pique Dame* in English. The conductors were Fritz BUSCH of Glydebourne Festivals and Dresden Opera fame, making his first North American appearance as an opera conductor under New Opera Company auspices; Herman Adler and Antal Dorati, already well known in the United States. Stage directors were Hans Busch, Felix Brentano and Dr. Lothar Wallerstein. Among the leading performers were Florence Kirk, whose initial appearance as Lady Macbeth won her contracts with Arturo TOSCANINI and the Rio and Buenos Aires operas; Jess Walters, Hardesty Johnson, Jennie Tourel, and George Rasely. Approximately 200 young musicians, singers and orchestra, were afforded employment in the first season. The second four-week season was inaugurated November 4, 1942, at the Broadway Theatre with an Anglicized version of MOUSSORGSKY's *The Fair at Sorochinsk,* Emil Cooper conducting, with Michael Chekov as stage director and George BALANCHINE as ballet master. Other productions were Dr. Walter DAMROSCH's one-act opera *The Opera Cloak,* which had a single performance only with the composer conducting; and revivals of *La Vie Parisienne, Pique Dame* and *Macbeth.* Conductors were Paul Breisach, Fritz STIEDRY and Emil Cooper and stage directors Feliz Brentano, Michael Chekov, Hans Busch and Ivan Ivantzoff. George Balanchine was ballet-master for all operas. Besides its four operatic productions at the Broadway Theatre, The New Opera Company experimented with a production of Johann STRAUSS's *Die Fledermaus* in English, retitled *Rosalinda,* which has proven the only financially successful presentation of this light opera given in New York in many years. Erich Wolfgang KORNGOLD and Max REINHARDT collaborated with The New Opera Company producing staff in staging *Rosalinda.* A new book was written by John Meehan, Jr. and Gottfried Reinhardt with new lyrics by Paul Kerby. Marina Koschetz, Michael Bartlett, Wilbur Evans, Dorothy Sarnoff, Mary Henderson, and Norbert Ardelli were among the new singers added to The New Opera Company roster during 1942.

Newstead Abbey, an abby near Sherwood Forest in Nottinghamshire, England, which is famous for two reasons: it was founded in 1170 by Henry II in partial reparation for the murder of Thomas á Becket, Archibishop of Canterbury, and was the residence for many years of Lord BYRON. The room in which he lived has been preserved intact as regards its furnishings although he sold the property in 1818.

Newton, Alfred Edward (1863-1940), American bibliophile who wrote several successful works on book-collecting: they include *The Amenities of Book-Collecting and Kindred Affections* (1918); *A Magnificent Farce and Other Diversions of a Book-Collector; This Book-Collecting Game.*

Newton, Gilbert Stuart (1795-1838), Canadian painter who studied with his uncle, Gilbert STUART at Boston, Mass., and later at the Royal Academy, London: his notable works include *Yorick* *and the Grisette; The Window; Captain Macheath; Vicar of Wakefield; Shylock and Jessica; King Lear and Cordelia; The Lute Player; The Importunate Author.*

"New World" Symphony (Dvořák), an orchestral work composed by Antonin DVORAK, and first performed by the New York Philharmonic-Symphony Society at New York in 1893. Its première resulted in widely different critical estimates, but there is no doubt of its present-day popularity. Dvořák himself gave the lie to the unauthorized statement that he used American Indian and Negro themes, declaring them all original: there is a Columbia recording by the Hallé Orchestra, and Victor recordings by the Czech Philharmonic Orchestra, the Philadelphia Orchestra, and the Rochester Philharmonic Orchestra.

New York Historical Society Museum and Library, an institution founded in 1804 which is of interest in this volume because of its *Gallery of Art* comprising more than 1500 paintings of which 400 are the works of American artists including Charles Willson PEALE, Gilbert STUART, John Wollaston, Benjamin WEST and John Wesley JARVIS. The Society also owns the 460 original water color drawings made by John James AUDUBON for his book, *Birds of America.*

New York Philharmonic-Symphony Orchestra, an organization founded in 1842, as the *Philharmonic Society of New York* by Ureli Corelli HILL, the first concert being given in the old Apollo Club rooms at 410 Broadway on December 7, 1842. Up to 1892 the conductors of international reputation included Max MARETZEK, Leopold DAMROSCH and Theodore THOMAS: since 1892 the long list of guest and regular conductors embraces Emil PAUR, Walter DAMROSCH, Édouard COLONNE, Henry J. WOOD, Victor HERBERT, Felix WEINGARTNER, Wassily SAFONOFF, Richard STRAUSS, Fritz STEINBACH, Gustav MAHLER; Josef STRANSKY, Henry HADLEY, William MENGELBERG, Artur BODANZKY, Willem VAN HOOGSTRATEN, Wilhelm FURTWANGLER, Bernardino MOLINARI, Ossip GABRILOWITSCH, Fritz REINER, Erich KLEIBER: Sir Thomas BEECHAM, Bruno WALTER, Otto KLEMPERER, Hans LANGE, Artur RODZINSKI, Georges ENESCO, Igor STRAVINSKY and Howard BARLOW. Arturo TOSCANINI conducted from 1926 to 1936: he was succeeded by John BARBIROLLI in 1937, and in 1943 Artur RODZINSKI became regular conductor. The children's concerts inaugurated in 1891 by Walter DAMROSCH have been conducted by Ernest SCHELLING and Rudolph GANZ. During its one hundred years of existence the orchestra absorbed several other organizations, the most important being the NEW YORK SYMPHONY SOCIETY in 1928, the name then being changed to the *New York Philharmonic-Symphony Orchestra.* In 1942 the orchestra celebrated its centenary, and in 1943 gave its 26th series of summer concerts at the LEWISOHN Stadium, New York.

New York Symphony Society, an organization founded by Leopold DAMROSCH in 1878, the first concert being given in the old STEINWAY HALL on Fourteenth Street. Walter DAMROSCH succeeded his father as conductor in 1885, and remained its director until the orchestra merged with the NEW

YORK PHILHARMONIC-SYMPHONY ORCHESTRA in 1928. Harry Harkness Flagler was the patron of the orchestra for many years: in 1920 it made a European tour, the first ever undertaken by an American orchestra. Among the distinguished composers who acted as guest conductors were Anton RUBINSTEIN, Camille SAINT-SAENS, Ignace PADEREWSKI, Sergei RACHMANINOFF, Vincent D'INDY, and Maurice RAVEL.

Nexō, Martin Andersen (1869-), Danish novelist who learned to write by studying the letters on street signs: his first book was published in 1898, and up to the German invasion during World War II he published a book almost every year. His books available in English include *Pelle the Conqueror* (1913-17), issued in 1930 in one volume; *Ditte: Girl Alive; Ditte: Daughter of Man; Ditte: Towards the Stars; Days in the Sun; In God's Land; Under the Open Sky.*

Ney, Elly (1882-), German pianist who studied at the Cologne Conservatory, and also with Theodor LESCHETIZKY and Emil SAUER at Vienna, making her debut in 1905 in that city. She toured Europe and the United States with great success, and founded an outstanding piano trio.

Nibelungen, Das Ring der, see **Ring of the Nibelungs, The.**

Nibelungs, The (Ger.), in German legend a race of dwarfs so called from their king's name, *Nibelung:* it was later applied to the subjects of Siegfried who despoiled the Nibelungs of their gold hoard. The **Nibelunglied** (*Song of the Nibelungs*) is an epic poem written in the 13th century, and based on earlier legends transmitted orally through the previous centuries. Richard WAGNER'S RING OF THE NIBELUNGS has taken little except the names of the characters: his material was derived chiefly from the VOLSUNGA SAGA and the EDDA.

Niblo's Gardens, a famous place of amusement in New York City opened in 1828 by William Niblo with the name *Sans Souci:* at first the programs in summer consisted of concerts and fireworks, but later almost every American actor of note appeared on its stage; among them Charles KEAN, Charlotte CUSHMAN, Edward L. DAVENPORT, Dion BOUCICAULT, and Edwin FORREST. In 1866 the famous extravaganza, *The Black Crook* was produced there, and although burned down in 1846 and 1848, it was rebuilt and continued as a theatre until 1895.

Nicander, Greek poet and physician of the 2nd century B.C. whose works were greatly praised and in some instances imitated by OVID, VIRGIL, CICERO, and quoted by PLINY. Plutarch, on the other hand, declares them bombastic and obscure: they include *Aetolica,* a prose history; *Heterolumena,* a mythological epic; *Georgica* and *Melissourgica,* the two last-named being imitated by Virgil.

Niccolini, Giovanni Battista (1782-1861), Italian poet and dramatist: his historical dramas include *Antonio Foscarini; Arnaldo di Brescia; Filippo Strozzi; Polissena:* he also translated Percy

Bysshe Shelley's tragedy, "The Cenci," into Italian.

Nichols, Anne, contemporary American actress, dramatist, and producing manager: her most successful play was *Abie's Irish Rose* which was produced in 1922, and ran through more than 2,500 performances until it closed in 1927, a record surpassed only by *Tobacco Road*, a play by Erskine CALDWELL. Among her other plays were *Linger Longer Letty; The Gilded Cage; Love Dreams; Just Married*, with Adelaide Matthews.

Nichols, Robert Malise Bowyer (1893-   ), English poet and dramatist educated at Oxford who wrote his first verses at seventeen and served in World War I. From 1921 to 1924 he was professor of English literature at the Imperial University, Tokyo, a post formerly held by Lafcadio HEARN, and also did some scenario work for Douglas FAIRBANKS, Sr.: his poems include *Invocation* (1915); *Aurelia; Ardours and Endurances.* He also wrote the plays *Twenty Below* with J. Tully and *Wings Over Europe* with M. Broune.

Nicholson, Kenyon (1894-   ), American dramatist educated at Wabash College in Crawfordsville, Ind., who served in World War I, and in 1921 became instructor in dramatic composition at Columbia University: his successful plays include *The Barker* (1927); *Eva the Fifth*, with John Golden; *Sailor, Beware!* with Charles Robinson; *Words and Music; The American Scene*, with Barrett H. Clark; *Swing Your Lady; June Night.*

Nicholson, Meredith (1866-   ), American novelist who first won a small prize for a short story published in the Chicago *Tribune:* his works include *Short Flights*, a volume of poems (1891); *The Hoosiers; The Main Chance; The House of a Thousand Candles*, a best seller and also a very successful film; *The Port of Missing Men; Rosalind at Red Gate; The Siege of the Seven Suitors*, illustrated by Reginald BIRCH; *Blacksheep! Blacksheep!; The Cavalier of Tennessee.*

Nicholson, William (1872-   ), English painter, engraver and illustrator: his paintings include *The Landlord; The Black Pansy; The Master of Jesus; The First Communion Day.* He also worked with his brother-in-law, James Pryde, on many striking black-and-white posters, and with Rudyard KIPLING on *An Almanac of Twelve Sports.* Among his portrait engravings in wood are James Whistler and Rudyard Kipling: he also painted a portrait of Marie TEMPEST, the distinguished actress.

Nick Carter, see **Carter, Nick.**

Nicol, Erskine (1825-1904), Scottish painter who studied at the Trustee's Academy, Edinburgh, and lived for a time in Dublin: he became famous for his pictures of Irish rural life such as *Kiss an' Make It Up; Paddy's March; Paying the Rent; Beggar My Neighbor; The Day After the Fair; The Emigrants.*

Nicolai, Otto (1810-1849), German composer who left his home at sixteen because of his father's severe rule and studied at Berlin with Karl Zelter: many of his operas written in the Italian style enjoyed considerable success at Italian opera houses, but his most famous work is *The Merry Wives of Windsor* produced at Berlin in 1849 two months before his death. The overture is a present-day concert, record and radio favorite.

Nicolay, John George (1832-1901), American biographer born in Germany who came to the United States with his family in 1838. He collaborated with John HAY on a ten-volume biography, *Abraham Lincoln, a History* (1890), based on Nicolay's intimate knowledge of the great emancipator while acting as his secretary from 1860 to 1865.

Nicoll, Allardyce (1894-   ), Scottish writer on the theatre educated at Glasgow University who succeeded George Pierce BAKER as head of the Harkness School of Drama at Yale University: his works include *A History of Restoration Drama* (1923); *A History of Eighteenth Century Drama; A History of Late Eighteenth Century Drama; The Development of the Theatre; Studies in Shakespeare; Masks, Mimes and Miracles; The English Theatre; Theatre and Film.*

Nicoll, James Craig (1847-1918), American painter who sketched along the entire coastline from the Gulf of St. Lawrence to Florida: his works include *Foggy Morning on Grand Menan; Moonlight at Cape Ann; Squally Weather; Fog and Sunshine on Campobello Island; Schroon Lake; On Marblehead Nick; Sunlight on the Sea; Shower on the Coast.*

Nicomachus, Greek painter who was a pupil of ARISTIDES and worked about 350 B.C.; he was highly praised by CICERO, PLINY, PLUTARCH and other classical writers. His works included *Rape of Proserpine; Victory Soaring in a Chariot; Apollo and Artemis; Cybele on a Lion; Bacchantes Surprised by Satyrs.*

Niecks, Frederick (1845-1924), German violinist, author, and critic who studied with Leopold AUER, and played in several orchestras before studying at the University of Leipzig, and beginning a successful career as a critic, and as professor of music at Edinburgh University. His most important work is *Frederic Chopin as a Man and Musician* (1888): he also wrote a dictionary of musical terms, several theoretical treatises, and *Program Music in the Last Four Centuries.*

Niehaus, Charles Henry (1855-1935), American sculptor who studied at the McMichen School of Design in Cincinnati and at the Royal Academy, Munich. His statues and monuments of note include *President Garfield; Moses;* the *Astor Memorial Doors* at Trinity Church, New York; *Caestus* and *The Scraper:* the two last named are in the Metropolitan Museum of Art, New York.

Niello, a process of decorating metal plates brought to an advanced stage of perfection by Italian goldsmiths of the 15th century. A design incised on silver or gold was filled with a heated mixture of copper, lead, borax and sulphur: when cooled an incrustation of black appeared against the metal. Tommaso Finiguerra was the greatest worker in this process: a proof on paper of one of his works is in the Bibliothèque Nationale at Paris.

Nielsen, Alice (1876-1943), American operatic soprano who made her debut in 1893 as Yum-Yum in *The Mikado* at Oakland, Cal., with the Burton Stanley Opera Company, later becoming leading soprano of the BOSTONIANS. From 1898 to 1901 she starred with her own company, and after studying in Rome made her debut in grand opera in 1903 at Naples in *Faust*. She also appeared with the San Carlo, Boston, Metropolitan and Chicago Opera Companies.

Nielsen, Augusta (1823-?), Danish ballerina born at Copenhagen who made her debut in the ballet, *Valdemar*, in 1838: she was considered far more gifted in acting and mimicry than Lucile GRAHN, Maria TAGLIONI, or Fanny ELSSLER.

Niemann, Albert (1831-1917), German dramatic tenor who made his debut at Dessau in 1849, and after study with Gilbert Louis Duprez at Paris sang at Hanover, Halle, and from 1866 to 1889 at the Royal Opera, Berlin. He created at Wagner's request the roles of Tannhäuser at Paris, and of Siegmund at BAYREUTH. In 1886 he made his debut as Siegmund in *The Valkyrie* at the Metropolitan Opera House, and created the roles of Tristan and Siegfried in the American premières of *Tristan and Isolde* and *The Dusk of the Gods* at the Metropolitan.

Niemann, Walter (1876-), German composer and author who studied music with Engelbert HUMPERDINCK and Karl REINECKE, also taking courses in musicology: his compositions include more than 150 piano pieces, a violin sonata, and orchestral works. He has also written critical biographies of GRIEG, SIBELIUS, and BRAHMS, and many treatises on the historical aspects of medieval and modern music.

Niemcewicz, Julian Ursin (1758-1841), Polish poet, novelist and dramatist who was adjutant to Tadeuz Kosciusko, the Polish patriot, with whom he was a prisoner at St. Petersburg. His works include a comedy, *The Return of the Deputy;* a novel, *John of Tenczyn* in the style of Walter SCOTT; *Historical Songs of the Poles,* a series of lyric poems extolling the heroes of Poland.

Niemeyer, John Henry (1839-1932), American painter born in Germany who studied at the ECOLE DES BEAUX-ARTS, Paris, under Jean Léon GEROME: he taught drawing at the Yale School of Fine Arts from 1871 to 1908: among his pupils were Augustus SAINT-GAUDENS; Frederick REMINGTON, and Bela Lyon PRATT. Among his notable paintings are *Guttenberg Inventing Movable Type; Sancta Simplicitas; Lilith Tempting Eve.*

Nietzsche, Friedrich (1844-1900), German philosopher who occupied the post of classical philology at the University of Basel from 1869 to 1879: he was a trained musician, and a champion of Richard WAGNER. His works include *The Birth of Tragedy from the Spirit of Music; Thus Spake Zarathustra; Beyond Good and Evil; The Gene-*

alogy of Morality; The Overturning of all Values: the last named regarded as his masterpiece although left incomplete.

Night Before Christmas, The, see **Moore, Clement Clarke.**

Night on Bald Mountain, A (Mussorgsky), a fantasy for orchestra by Modeste Mussorgsky composed in 1867 based on a drama, *The Witch* by Megden. After Mussorgsky's death in 1881, Nicholas Rimsky-Korsakow edited the orchestration, and conducted the work at is first performance in 1886: the work met with such success that it was played again later in that season. Though the editor revised the score, he retained the composer's argument: *"Subterranean din of supernatural voices: Appearance of Spirits of Darkness, followed by that of the god Tchernobog: Glorification of Tchernobog: Black mass. Witches' Sabbath: At the height of the Sabbath there sounds far off the bell of the little church in a village which scatters the Spirits of Darkness: Daybreak."* There is a Columbia recording by the Colonne Orchestra, and Victor recordings by the London Symphony Orchestra and the Philadelphia Orchestra.

Nights in the Gardens of Spain (De Falla), an orchestral composition by Manuel de FALLA subtitled *Symphonic Impressions for Orchestra and Piano.* It was first performed at Madrid in 1916, and in 1924 by the Boston Symphony Orchestra with Heinrich Gebhard at the piano. The titles of the movements are: I *In the Generalife;* II *Dance in the Distance;* III *In the Gardens of the Sierra of Cordova.* There is a Victor recording by the Paris Conservatory Orchestra, and a Columbia recording by the Orquestra Betica da Camara.

Nijinska, Bronislava (1891-), Polish dancer and choreographer; sister of Vaslav NIJINSKY. She studied with CECCHETTI, FOKINE, and Nicholas LEGAT, and made her debut in 1908 with the Imperial Ballet at St. Petersburg, later appearing with the DIAGHILEFF Ballet, at the Palace Theatre, London, with her brother, and in 1921 at the Alhambra in *The Sleeping Princess.* She has written several ballets for Ida RUBINSTEIN, arranged the dances for Max Reinhardt's film production of *A Midsummer Night's Dream* in 1934, and has designed the choreography for more than 200 ballets.

Nijinsky, Vaslav (1890-), Russian dancer who was trained at the Imperial School of Ballet, St. Petersburg, under Nicholas Legat for six years, and made his debut in 1908 in the ballet of MoZART'S *Don Giovanni*. He studied further with CECCHETTI, and made the acquaintance of Serge DIAGHILEFF who became both his friend and adviser. In 1909 he appeared at Paris with the Diaghileff Russian Ballet, and his dancing in *Cleopatra* and *Les Sylphides* took the balletloving public by storm. After his return to St. Petersburg he was discharged from the Imperial Ballet because of some argument over costume, and he joined a new troupe formed by Diaghileff, acquiring even greater fame for his dancing in *Le Spectre de la Rose* with KARSAVINA, and in the title role of STRAVINSKY'S *Petrouchka*. In 1912 he turned to choreography: his first creation was DEBUSSY'S *The Afternoon of a Faun* followed by *Jeux* and Stravinsky's *Le Sacre du Printemps*. In 1913 he went to South America with the Diaghileff troupe, but was discharged because he became engaged to a ballerina in the company. He then appeared at the Palace Theatre, London, but became ill after a few performances and the company was disbanded. He also toured the United States, and returned to South America for another visit, but finally went to St. Moritz, Switzerland, for a long rest, finally losing his reason.

Nike, in Greek mythology the goddess of victory associated with ATHENA and ZEUS the statues of whom hold a winged figure of Nike in each hand. She is identical with the Roman goddess *Victoria,* also signifying victory.

Nikisch, Artur (1855-1922), Hungarian violinist and conductor who studied violin at the Vienna Conservatory with Georg HELLMESBERGER, later playing with Richard Wagner's orchestra at the laying of the corner-stone of the Festival Playhouse at BAYREUTH. After conducting in Europe he became conductor of the BOSTON SYMPHONY ORCHESTRA from 1889 to 1893, and later directed the Royal Opera and Philharmonic Orchestra at Budapest, the GEWANDHAUS Concerts at Leipzig, and the Philharmonic Concerts at Berlin. Like Arturo TOSCANINI he conducted without score, and is regarded as one of the greatest masters of the baton. His son, **Mitja Nikisch** (1899-1936), was a distinguished pianist who made his debut at New York in 1923.

Niles, Mrs. Blair (188?-), American novelist and author of travel books: her works include *Casual Wanderings in Ecuador* (1923); *Black Haiti; The Biography of an Unknown Convict; Condemned to Devil's Island,* a best seller and also a popular film; *Strange Brother; The James; East by Day.*

Nilsson, Christine (1843-1921), Swedish dramatic soprano who studied at Stockholm and Paris, making her debut in 1864 in *La Traviata* at Paris. After singing at opera houses in London and Paris she toured the United States in 1870 with the Maurice STRAKOSCH Opera Company, and returned several times. She was also popular in London where she gave her farewell concert in 1891.

Nimbus, see **Aureole.**

Nin (Y Castellanos), Joaquin (1883-), Spanish pianist and composer who studied at Barcelona and with Moritz Moszkowski in Paris, also taking up composition with Vincent D'INDY. He made many successful tours of Europe, and taught at the Schola Cantorum, Paris. His works include numerous fine piano pieces, a suite for violin and piano: he has also edited the works of many Spanish composers of the older regime.

Niobe, in Greek mythology the daughter of TANTALUS and Dione: she boasted of having six daughters and six sons to Leto who only had two children, APOLLO and ARTEMIS. Apollo killed Niobe's sons and Artemis her daughters as a punishment, and they were buried by the gods who turned Niobe into a rock. A series of nine ancient statues, now in the UFFIZI GALLERY at Rome and known as the **Niobides,** are supposed to represent the Niobe and her children: the finest is that of the mother endeavoring to protect her daughter.

Nissen, Greta, contemporary stage and screen actress trained at the Dramatic School of the Royal Opera at Copenhagen who made her debut as a child of six: among the American films in which she has appeared are *Beggar on Horseback; Lost, a Wife; The Wanderer; Lady Luck; Blonde and Brunette; Hell's Angels.*

Niven, David, contemporary Scotch motion-picture actor who was schooled for a career in the British military service: among the films in which he has appeared are *Rose Marie; Dodsworth; Charge of the Light Brigade; The Prisoner of Zenda; Four Men and a Prayer; Dawn Patrol; Wuthering Heights; Raffles; Bachelor Mother; Eternally Yours:* in 1940 he joined the British army.

Noailles, Anne Elisabeth Brancovan, Countess de (1876-1933), French poet of Rumanian ancestry: her works include *Poems of Childhood* which have been translated, and also several poems such as *The Shadow of the Days, Forces Eternal,* and *New Intermezzo.* She was awarded a prize for her poetry in 1921 by the FRENCH ACADEMY.

Nobel, Alfred Bernhard (1833-1896), Swedish chemist and inventor of dynamite: he left a large sum of money the interest of which was to be used for the **Nobel Prizes** awarded annually, without regard to nationality, for eminence in physical science, chemistry, medical science, literature, and for the greatest contribution given to the cause of world peace. The first awards were made in 1901: among the authors who have received the Nobel literature award are Björnsterne BJORNSON, Rudyard KIPLING, Maurice MAETERLINCK, Gerhard HAUPTMANN, Romain ROLLAND, Knut HAMSUN, Anatole FRANCE, William B. YEATS, George Bernard SHAW, Sigrid UNDSET, Thomas MANN, Sinclair LEWIS, John GALSWORTHY, Luigi PIRANDELLO, and Pearl BUCK.

Noble, William Clark (1858-1938), American sculptor and painter who studied in Boston and London: his sculptures of note include the *Soldiers and Sailors Monument* at Newport, R. I.; the statue of Robert BURNS in Providence, R. I.; the *Brooke Memorial* at the Church of the Incarnation, New York; a bust of John McCULLOUGH: he also designed the John Philip SOUSA Memorial, and painted a large canvas, *The Crucifixion of Christ.*

Noces, Les (The Wedding), Russian ballet in four episodes: choreography by Bronislava NIJINSKA; book and music by Igor STRAVINSKY; first produced at Paris in 1923. The various episodes are danced in the bride's house; the bridegroom's house, and the house in which the happy couple are to live. The music accompanying the dancing is performed by a chorus and an orchestra consisting of two pianos, bells, xylophones, and percussion instruments.

Nocturne (Fr.), in music a title used by John FIELD for several piano pieces of romantic, meditative character: he was not the first to employ the term because MOZART used it instead of "Serenade" for works composed for strings and horns, and MENDELSSOHN employed it for an entr'acte in his incidental music for Shakespeare's "*Midsummer Night's Dream.*" CHOPIN's nocturnes are regarded as the finest works in this form.

Nocturnes (Chopin), the form of musical composition with which the name of Frédéric CHOPIN is almost invariably associated although he was not the first to employ the title, nor invent the form which was used before him by John FIELD. Moritz Karasowski, a Polish music critic who wrote a biography, *Chopin, His Life, His Works, and His Letters* (1877), compares the nocturnes of Field and Chopin in the following pithy statement: "Field was satisfied with writing tender, poetical, and rather melancholy pieces while Chopin introduced not only the dramatic element, but displayed in a striking manner a marvelous enrichment of harmony and of the resources of the piano." There are in all 19 nocturnes with opus numbers, and also Victor recordings of the entire series by Artur RUBINSTEIN. Recordings of individual nocturnes can be ascertained by consulting *The Gramophone Shop Encyclopedia of Recorded Music* (1942).

Nocturnes (Debussy), three symphonic poems by Claude DEBUSSY entitled *Nuages* (*Clouds*); *Fêtes* (*Festivals*); *Sirènes* (*Sirens*). The first two were played by the Lamoureux Orchestra with Camille Chevillard conducting at Paris on Dec. 9, 1900, with such success that they were repeated on Jan. 6, 1901. The third, *Sirènes,* was played, along with the other two, at a Lamoureux concert on Oct. 27, 1901. Debussy's friends were so delighted at their reception that it required some sharp hissing to curb their exuberant manifestations of pleasure. Alfred BRUNEAU comments as follows: "Here, with the aid of a magic orchestra, he has lent to clouds traversing the sombre sky the various forms created by his imagination; he has set to running and dancing the chimerical beings perceived by him in the silvery dust scintillating in the moonbeams; he has changed the white foam of the restless sea into tuneful sirens." There is a Victor recording by the Philadelphia Orchestra with Leopold Stokowski, and a Columbia recording by the Grand Orchestra of the Debussy Festivals conducted by Desiré Inghelbrecht.

Nō drama, the most ancient form of Japanese drama which has been in existence since the 14th or 15th century; it is written in both prose and verse, makes use of choral music, and originally appealed only to the upper classes and literati. About two hundred fifty of the 15th century nō plays are extant written in either Chinese or Japanese. The stage, which is about eighteen feet square, has little scenery of the realistic type, but the costumes are elaborate and costly.

Masks are worn by the actors: the plays are difficult for Europeans to understand because they have no plots in the accepted sense of the word, and depend largely on the play of words.

Noël, see **Carol.**

Nohl, Ludwig (1831-1885), German author of books on musical subjects who first practiced law, but later studied music, and became lecturer and professor at Heidelberg University. His works include *Life of Beethoven* (3 vols., 1864-77); *Beethoven's Letters; Mozart's Letters; Life of Mozart; The Modern Music Drama.* He also wrote biographies of WAGNER, HAYDN, WEBER, SPOHR, and LISZT.

Nollekens, Joseph (1737-1823), British sculptor whose father was Joseph Francis Nollekens (1702-1748), known as "Old Nollekens." After some instruction and a considerable amount of self study, he won a prize in 1760 with a BAS-RELIEF, *Timoclea before Alexander,* also making busts of David GARRICK and Laurence STERNE which resulted in his becoming the fashionable portrait sculptor of his day. Among his notable works are *Bacchus; Venus Taking Off Her Sandal; Juno; Cupid and Psyche; Venus Anointing Herself.*

Nordhoff, Charles, see **Hall, James Norman.**

Nordica, Lillian (1857-1914), American dramatic soprano, real name Lillian Norton, who studied at the NEW ENGLAND CONSERVATORY OF MUSIC, and later appeared with GILMORE's Band in the United States and on tour in Europe. After studying opera singing at Milan, she made her debut there in 1879 in MOZART's *Don Giovanni,* using the name "Nordica." After singing in Russia, Italy, Germany and France, she made her American debut with Col. Henry Mapleson's Company in 1883 at the Academy of Music, New York, in GOUNOD's *Faust;* sang at Covent Garden, London, and made her debut in 1890 at the Metropolitan Opera House in VERDI's *Il Trovatore:* in 1893 she became a regular member of the company. In 1894 she sang Elsa in WAGNER's *Lohengrin* at Bayreuth with such success that she learned all the major Wagnerian roles, and appeared at the Metropolitan Opera House in 1895 as Isolde in *Tristan and Isolde* with Jean DE RESZKE as Tristan. She remained with the Metropolitan company until 1908 singing chiefly Wagnerian roles, later appearing in Paris and with the BOSTON OPERA COMPANY. Her last American appearance was in 1913 at Carnegie Hall, New York, in recital.

Nordraak, Richard (1842-1866), Norwegian composer who studied with Friedrich Kiel and Theodor KULLAK: he was a militant nationalist in regard to excluding foreign influences from Norwegian music, and also the friend and counsellor of Edvard GRIEG. His works include incidental music to Björnsterne BJORNSON's *Maria Stuart;* the national anthem, *Ja, vi elsker;* patriotic choruses, and pieces for the piano.

Norena, Eide (1884-), Norwegian operatic soprano whose real name was Kaja Hansen Eide. After studying in Weimar, London, and Paris, she sang in opera at Oslo, La Scala (Milan), Covent Garden, and made her American debut with the Chicago Civic Opera Company in 1926, remaining with the company until 1932. She made her first appearance in 1933 with the Metropolitan Opera Company in PUCCINI's *La Bohème,* and in 1935 became a member of the Paris Opèra.

Normand, Mabel (1892-1930), American screen actress who first posed as a model for artists, and was induced to enter motion pictures by Alice Joyce, already a success in the films. After working as an "extra," she joined the Keystone Company directed by Mack Sennett, and appeared in many comedies among which were *Suzanna; The Extra Girl,* and *Mickey.*

Norns, (*a*) in Northern mythology the female divinities of fate similar to the Greek FATES and the Roman *Parcae:* they are three in number, and are said to weave the destiny of mortals. (*b*) Three characters in Richard Wagner's cycle of music dramas, The RING OF THE NIBELUNGS. In the final drama, The DUSK OF THE GODS, the Norns, daughters of Erda, weave their rope, and relate the stories of the gods which form its threads. Suddenly the rope is cut upon a sharp rock and breaks, destroying with it their font of wisdom; the Norns disappear, returning to their mother.

Norris, Charles Gilman (1881-), American novelist who attempted a grand historical novel at ten, and was educated at the University of California: his works include *The Amateur* (1915); *Salt or, The Education of Griffith Adams; Brass; Bread; Pig Iron; Zelda Marsh; Seed; Zest; Hands; Bricks Without Straw.*

Norris, Frank (1870-1902), American novelist, brother of Charles Gilman NORRIS, who first studied painting at the Acadèmie Julien in Paris, and after some study at the University of California and Harvard University became a newspaper correspondent and contributor to *McClure's Magazine.* His works include *Moran of the Lady Letty* (1898); *McTeague; The Octopus; The Pit; Vandover and the Brute:* his last novel, *The Wolf,* was left unfinished, and his novel, *McTeague* was successfully adapted for the films.

Norris, Kathleen (1880-), American novelist and short-story writer; wife of the novelist, Charles Gilman NORRIS, and sister-in-law of Frank NORRIS. She worked in various capacities including that of newspaper reporter for the San Francisco *Call* before her first novel, *Mother* (1911) became a success: it was followed by numerous others including *Saturday's Child; Certain People of Importance; Hildegarde; Mother and Son; Manhattan Love Song; The American Flaggs; The Venables; Maiden Voyage.*

North, Jessica Nelson (1894-), American poet, novelist, and critic educated at Laurence College, Appleton, Wis., and at the University of Chicago, becoming associate editor of the magazine, *Poetry,* in 1928. Her works include *A Prayer Rug* (1923); *The Long Leash; Arden Acres,* a novel; *Introduction to Paintings; Morning in the Land,* a novel

North, Marianne (1830-1890), English naturalist and artist who first studied singing: when her voice failed she began painting flowers. She made a world tour from 1871 to 1875 in search of floral subjects, and in 1878 exhibited her drawings at London: in 1882 a gallery presented by her was opened at the Kew Botanical Gardens containing a complete exhibit of her reproductions of plant life which are of great value because of their scientific accuracy.

North, Sterling (1906-), American novelist, poet, and critic educated at the University of Chicago and brother of Jessica Nelson NORTH: his works include *Plowing on Sunday* (1934); *Night Outlasts the Whippoorwill; Seven Against the Years; Greased Lightning.*

North, Sir Thomas (c.1535-c.1601), English scholar who is famous for his translation of PLUTARCH published in 1579 with the title, *The Lives of the Noble Grecians and Romans*; dedicated to Queen ELIZABETH, and re-issued in 1595 and 1603 with new material added. He is considered the first master of English prose, and SHAKESPEARE drew much of the material for *Julius Caesar, Coriolanus,* and *Antony and Cleopatra* from his work: he is said to have taken entire speeches for the last-named play.

Northcote, James (1746-1831), English painter and author who studied with Sir Joshua REYNOLDS and also in Italy: he finally settled in London where he became a rival of Henry FUSELI and John OPIE. Among his notable works are *Young Princes Murdered in the Tower; Burial of the Princes in the Tower; The Death of Wat Tyler; The Entombment; Agony in the Garden; Leopards; Dog and Heron; Lion; Angel Opposing Balaam.* He wrote a *Life of Reynolds,* and *Life of Titian,* also painting many historical works for the John BOYDELL's Shakespearean Gallery.

Norton, Caroline Elizabeth Sarah (1808-1877), English poet who was a granddaughter of Richard Brinsley SHERIDAN: her poetical works include *The Sorrows of Rosalie* (1829); *The Undying One; A Voice from the Factories; The Dream and Other Poems; Aunt Carry's Ballads; The Lady of La Garaye:* she also wrote three novels, and the biographical *Lives of the Sheridans.*

Norton, Charles Eliot (1827-1908), American educator, editor, and author educated at Harvard University who contributed to the *Atlantic Monthly,* edited the *North American Review* with James Russell LOWELL, and became professor and lecturer on art at Harvard University. His works include *Notes of Travel and Study in Italy* (1860); *History of Ancient Art:* he also translated DANTE's *Divine Comedy,* and numbered Thomas CARLYLE, John RUSKIN, Dante Gabriel ROSSETTI, and Ralph Waldo EMERSON among his intimates.

Nostradamus (1503-1566), French astrologer of Jewish ancestry whose real name was Michel de Notredame: he had a profound knowledge of medicine, philosophy, and the humanities, and published a volume of rhymed prophecies in 1555 entitled *Centuries* which brought him to the notice of Catherine de' MEDICI. The fulfillment of some of his prognostications also gained him the favor of Charles IX of France to whom he was appointed court physician.

Notation, musical, in music the art of representing musical tones by means of written characters in the form of signs known as notes which are written on a five-line staff and called staff-notation. There are several other forms of notation such as NEUMES, *numerals* and *Tonic Sol-fa.* Hucbald introduced a staff in which the syllables were placed between the lines, and GUIDO D'AREZZO is generally credited with the four-line staff in which both spaces and lines were used. The number of lines was increased from six to fifteen, but the five-line staff was finally permanently adopted. Notes were first square in shape, and passed through many transformations before the round note became universal.

Note, see **Notation, musical.**

Notre Dame, a cathedral in Paris erected on a site previously occupied first by a Merovingian cathedral, and in the 9th century by still another cathedral. The erection of the present building was begun about 1240: side chapels were introduced, and late in the 13th century Pierre de Chelles added the choir chapels so that in the early part of the 14th century the cathedral looked about as it does at the present time. During the Revolution some damage was done to the building, but complete restoration was effected by Eugène VIOLLET-LE-DUC from 1845 to 1856. The plan of the building is a Latin cross, and it is encircled by fifteen chapels. The façade has three great doors decorated with carvings, and the building as a whole is one of the most magnificent and imposing creations of Gothic architecture.

Nouguès, Jean (1875-1932), French composer who studied at Paris, and wrote an opera, *Le Roi du Papagey* at sixteen: after writing several more operas which were received indifferently, he scored a tremendous success with *Quo Vadis,* an opera based on the novel with the same title by Henryk SIENKIEWICZ, and first produced at Nice in 1909, at the Philadelphia Opera House, Philadelphia, in 1911, and at the Metropolitan Opera House, New York, during the same year.

Novaes, Guiomar (1895-), Brazilian pianist who appeared as a child prodigy in 1904: in 1909 she won a scholarship at the PARIS CONSERVATORY, studying with Isidor PHILIPP. After touring Europe, Great Britain and South America, she made her debut at New York in 1915, appearing as soloist with all the major American orchestras and in recital.

Novarro, Ramon (1905-), Mexican screen actor who has appeared since 1922 in numerous films including *The Prisoner of Zenda; Scaramouche; Ben Hur; The Student Prince; The Road to Romance; The Pagan; Mata Hari; The Barbarian; The Cat and the Fiddle; Laughing Boy; The Night Is Young:* he has also been featured in several European pictures.

Novel, in literature a form of story-telling in prose which has taken the place of the early Eng-lish, European, and Oriental ROMANCE which dwelt more upon matters fantastic and improbable than on historical or contemporary subjects. The **English novel** is said by some authorities to have originated in the 16th century with Sir Philip SIDNEY'S *Arcadia,* while some critics maintain that it came into existence with Samuel RICHARDSON's *Pamela* and *Clarissa Harlowe* in the 18th century. Starting at the former period, John LYLY followed Sir Philip SIDNEY with *Euphues;* Robert GREENE with *Pandosto;* Thomas NASHE with *Jack Wilton;* John BUNYAN with *Pilgrim's Progress;* Daniel DEFOE with *Robinson Crusoe:* next came Samuel RICHARDSON with the novels previously mentioned; Henry FIELDING with *Tom Jones;* Tobias SMOLLETT with *Roderick Random;* Laurence STERNE with *Tristram Shandy;* Samuel JOHNSON with *Rasselas;* Fanny BURNEY with *Evelina;* Horace WALPOLE with *The Castle of Otranto;* William BECKFORD with *Vathek;* Mrs. Ann RADCLIFFE with *The Mysteries of Udolpho;* Jane AUSTIN with *Pride and Prejudice;* Sir Walter SCOTT with *Ivanhoe;* Maria EDGEWORTH with *Castle Rackrent;* Thomas Love PEACOCK with *Maid Marian.* The 19th century witnessed the gradual changes in the novel form brought about by Charles DICKENS with *David Copperfield;* William Makepeace THACKERAY with *Vanity Fair;* Bulwer LYTTON with *The Last Days of Pompeii;* Charles KINGSLEY with *Hypatia;* Charles READE with *The Cloister and the Hearth;* Benjamin DISRAELI with *Coningsby;* Emily BRONTE with *Wuthering Heights;* Charlotte BRONTE with *Jane Eyre;* George ELIOT with *Adam Bede;* Anthony TROLLOPE with *Barchester Towers;* George MEREDITH with *Diana of the Crossways;* Thomas HARDY with *Tess of the D'Urbervilles;* Samuel BUTLER with *The Way of All Flesh;* Robert Louis STEVENSON with *The Master of Ballantrae;* Rudyard KIPLING with *The Light That Failed.* The 20th century brought John GALSWORTHY with *The Forsyte Saga;* H. G. WELLS with *Tono Bungay;* Joseph CONRAD with *Almayer's Folly;* W. Somerset MAUGHAM with *Of Human Bondage;* E. M. FOSTER with *Howard's End;* Sir Hugh WALPOLE with *The Cathedral;* J. B. PRIESTLEY with *The Good Companions;* Aldous HUXLEY with *Point Counter'Point;* Virginia WOOLF with *Mrs. Dalloway.* The **American novel** may be said to have its beginnings with *Mervyn* by Charles Brockden BROWN; *The Algerine Captive* by Royall TYLER; *The Spy* by James Fenimore COOPER; *Moby Dick* by Herman MELVILLE; *The Scarlet Letter* by Nathaniel HAWTHORNE; *Uncle Tom's Cabin* by Harriet Beecher STOWE; *Huckleberry Finn* by Mark TWAIN; *Little Women* by Louisa ALCOTT; *John Ward, Preacher* by Margaret DELAND; *Marse Chan* by Thomas Nelson PAGE. In the 20th century the names of successful novelists are legion: among them are Ellen GLASGOW, Mary JOHNSTON, Frank NORRIS, Edith WHARTON, Theodore DREISER, Sherwood ANDERSON, Sinclair LEWIS, Zona GALE, Willa CATHER, Booth TARKINGTON, Ernest HEMINGWAY, William FAULKNER, Upton SINCLAIR, and many others.

Novellette, in music a title first used by Robert SCHUMANN for piano compositions in free form, of considerable length and romantic in character.

Novello, Ivor, (1893-), English stage and screen actor and composer educated at Magdalen College School, Oxford, who has written more than sixty successful songs including *Keep the Home Fires Burning,* a favorite during World War I. He has also appeared in many English and American silent and talking films.

Noverre, Jean Georges (1727-1810), French dancer and balletmaster who made his debut at FONTAINEBLEAU in 1743, wrote his first ballet for the OPERA-COMIQUE in 1747, and in 1749 directed the ballets for operas by GLUCK and PICCINNI. He worked with David Garrick at London from 1755 to 1757, and was balletmaster at L'Opéra, Paris, from 1775 to 1780. His *Lettres sur la danse et les ballets* (1760) passed through several editions, and Noverre is today regarded as the one who introduced dramatic action into the ballet.

Novikoff, Laurent, Russian balletmaster and choreographer who studied at the Imperial Ballet School at Moscow, becoming *premier danseur* at the Moscow Opera and later at St. Petersburg. He toured Europe and the United States as dancing partner of Anna PAVLOWA, and has occupied the posts of balletmaster at the Chicago Civic Opera and the Metropolitan Opera House in addition to founding a ballet school in Chicago.

Nowell, see **Carol.**

Nox, see **Nyx.**

Noyes, Alfred (1880-), English poet and novelist educated at Exeter College, Oxford, who occupied the chair of modern English literature at Princeton University from 1914 to 1923. His works include *The Loom of Years* (1902); *The Flower of Old Japan; The Forest of Wild Thyme;* the epic poems, *Drake* and *Tales of the Mermaid Tavern:* a trilogy, *The Torch Bearers;* the novels, *The Sun Cure, The Return of the Scarecrow,* and *No Other Man; Pageant of Letters.*

Nuances, in music the inflections in singing or the shadings in instrumental performance which vary the tonal effect and the tempo in such a manner as to individualize the performance of a composition.

Numismatics, the science which treats of coins and medals in respect to their origin and history which is preserved in the portraits, writings and symbols engraved upon them. They are divided into four groups comprising Oriental, Greek and Roman, medieval, and modern: many great sculptors and goldsmiths have been the designers of medals commemorating celebrated persons or important historical events.

Nuñez de Arce, Gaspar (1834-1903), Spanish poet and dramatist known as the "Spanish Tennyson": among his notable comedies are *The Shoemaker's Bill; The Faggot; Who Is the Author?* (1859). He also wrote a drama on the subject of King Carlos, and several patriotic poems including *Battle Cries* (1875); *The Last Lament of Lord Byron; An Idyl and an Elegy.*

Nuremburg (Ger. Nürnberg) Museum, an institution, also known as the *Germanic National Museum,* established in an ancient Carthusian monastery: it comprises a collection of paintings by German masters of the 15th and 16th centuries including Hans HOLBEIN, Albrecht DÜRER, Michael WOLGEMUTH, and many other artists.

"Nutcracker" Ballet (Tschaikowsky), ballet in two acts: book and choreography by L. I. Ivanow, based on E. T. A. Hoffmann's tale, "The Nutcracker and the King of Mice"; music by Peter Ilich Tschaikowsky; first produced at the Maryinsky Theatre, St. Petersburg, in 1892. The plot revolves around a little girl, Claire, who receives a nutcracker as a Christmas present; her brother, Frederick, breaks it, and Claire puts it tenderly to bed. When in her dreams she enters the room later to look after the nutcracker, she finds it has become the leader of the ginger-bread men against the king of the mice and his lively cohorts, who would have triumphed had not Claire slain their furry commander with her slipper. The nutcracker becomes a handsome prince; he flies with Claire to the fascinating domain of the Sugar-plum Fairy, somewhere in Araby, where toys and sweetmeats join in a great frolic to celebrate the wedding of the little girl and her Prince Charming. At the suggestion of his brother, Tschaikowsky arranged the **Nutcracker Suite** from the many tuneful dance movements which has become more popular than the ballet. The various numbers are: I *Miniature Overture;* II *March;* III *Dance of the Sugar-plum Fairy;* IV *Trepak;* V *Arabian Dance;* VI *Chinese Dance;* VII *Dance of the Mirlitons;* VIII *Waltz of the Flowers.* There is a Victor recording by the Philadelphia Orchestra directed by Leopold Stokowski, and a Columbia recording by the Chicago Symphony Orchestra directed by Frederick Stock.

Nutting, Wallace (1861-1941), American clergyman, antiquarian, illustrator, and author: his works include *Vermont Beautiful* (1922); *Massachusetts Beautiful; Connecticut Beautiful; Maine Beautiful; New York Beautiful; England Beautiful; Ireland Beautiful; Wallace Nutting's Biography; Windsor Handbook; Photographic Art Secrets; Furniture Treasury:* he photographed the scenes shown in his travel books.

Nye, Edgar Wilson (1850-1896), American humorist, known affectionately as "Bill Nye," who practiced law, went into politics, and was a postmaster before he founded the Laramie (Wyo.) *Boomerang* which he edited for three years, contributing the stories and humorous comment which made him world-famous. His books include *Bill Nye and Boomerang* (1881); *Forty Liars and Other Lies; Bill Nye's Chestnuts Old and New; Bill Nye's History of the United States.* He also wrote a play, *The Cadi* successfully produced at New York in 1891, and appeared on lecture tours with James Whitcomb RILEY.

Nymphs, in Greek mythology the name of female divinities of inferior rank usually personifying the creative aspects of nature. They were supposed to live on mountains, in forests, in the ocean, and in grottoes: sea nymphs were called *Oceanids* or *Nereïds,* and *Naiades* lived near mountains and grottoes. *Dryads* and *Hamadryades* were nymphs associated with trees: they were favorite subjects in classical literature and in painting.

Nyx, in Greek mythology a goddess personifying night: she was the daughter of Chaos, the most ancient of the Greek divinities, and mother of the day and of the light.

O

Oakie, Jack (1903-), American stage and screen actor who first appeared in many musical productions with Lulu McConnell: he has had important comedy roles in many films including *The Dummy; The Social Lion; Let's Go Native; June Moon; Dude Ranch; Madison Square Garden; If I Had a Million; College Humor; Alice in Wonderland; College Rhythm; The Affairs of Annabel; Tin Pan Alley; The Great Dictator* in which he impersonated Mussolini; *Little Men; Song of the Islands.*

Oakley, Violet (1874-), American mural painter and designer of stained glass windows who studied at the ART STUDENTS' LEAGUE, New York, at the Pennsylvania Academy of Fine Arts under Celia BEAUX, and in Paris. Her works include stained glass windows and mural decorations at the Church of All Angels, New York; *Founding of the State of Spiritual Liberty,* 13 panels, at the State Capitol, Harrisburg, Pa.; *The Constitutional Convention at Philadelphia; Cuyahoga County Courthouse* at Cleveland, Ohio, and many other similar works in public buildings and private residences.

Obbligato (It.), in music an instrumental part, usually indispensable, which accompanies a vocal solo, many examples of which are to be found in 18th century music: an excellent modern example is the *Angel's Serenade* by Gaetano BRAGA, a song for which there is an *obbligato* part for violoncello or violin.

Obelisk, ancient Egyptian monuments usually hewn from a single block of pink granite, the four faces covered with hieroglyphic inscriptions, and frequently dedicated to RA, the sun god. They were placed in pairs before temples on each side of the pylon, or entrance: the weight of these monuments made their erection a task at which thousands of slaves worked simultaneously. An obelisk known as CLEOPATRA'S NEEDLE is to be seen at Central Park in New York City: the Bunker Hill Monument at Charlestown, Mass., and the Washington Monument in Washington, D. C., are in the shape of an obelisk.

Oberammergau, see **Passion Play.**

Oberon, Merle (1911-), Australian screen actress born in Tasmania and educated at La Martinere College: she has appeared in many films including *Wedding Rehearsal; The Private Life of Henry VIII; Thunder in the East; Broken Mel-* ody; The Scarlet Pimpernel; Folies Bergère; The Dark Angel; These Three; Beloved Enemy; The Cowboy and the Lady; Wuthering Heights; Affectionately Yours; Lydia.*

Oberon, grand opera in three acts: libretto by James Robinson Planché; music by Carl Maria von WEBER; first produced at Covent Garden, London, in 1826; at the Park Theatre, New York, in 1828, and at the Metropolitan Opera House, New York, in 1918. The story follows closely the French romance, *Huon of Bordeaux* from which the plot was taken. The *Overture,* an extremely popular concert, record and radio number, is available in both Columbia and Victor recordings: also the great soprano aria, *Ocean, Thou Mighty Monster,* in a Victor recording by Kirsten Flagstad.

Oberon, in literature the king of the fairies in the medieval French romance, *Huon of Bordeaux:* he also appears in SHAKESPEARE'S *A Midsummer Night's Dream;* Christopher WIELAND'S epic, *Oberon;* Ben JONSON'S masque, *Oberon,* and in Carl Maria von Weber's opera, OBERON. He also has some connection with ALBERICH, the king of the Nibelungs in Richard Wagner's RING OF THE NIBELUNGS.

Oboe, a musical instrument constructed of a conical wooden tube with from nine to fourteen keys: the double REED is held by the player directly between his lips so that he completely controls the sound output. The oboe in the classical orchestra of BACH and HANDEL rivaled the VIOLIN in importance. The *oboe d'amore,* which is lower in pitch, is no longer used, but the ENGLISH HORN which is really a tenor oboe, is very much favored by modern composers.

Oboler, Arch (1909-), American dramatist educated at the University of Chicago, who published stories in pulp magazines before he was graduated. He has had outstanding success in the fields of film scenarios and radio broadcasts, writing sketches for Maurice EVANS, Walter HUSTON, Brian AHERNE, and Joan CRAWFORD. Among his radio plays are *Futuristic; The Precious Freedom; Salute to the President; To the President:* he has also published *Fourteen Plays by Arch Oboler* (1940), and *Plays for Americans* (1943).

O'Brien, Fitz-James (1828-1862), Irish-American poet, short story writer and dramatist who served in the American Civil War, and wrote several weird stories including *What Was It?,* The *Diamond Lens,* and *Wondersmith.* He also wrote a successful play, *A Gentleman from Ireland* for James W. WALLACK.

O'Brien, Frederick (1869-1932), American journalist and author who lead an adventurous life as a seaman, hobo with Coxey's Army, and newspaper correspondent in the Russo-Japanese War. His works include *White Shadows in the South Seas* (1919); *Mystic Isles of the South Seas; Atolls of the Sun:* he devotes a chapter in the latter to the French painter, Paul GAUGIN who spent several years on South Sea islands.

O'Brien, Howard Vincent (1888-), American author, columnist and editor educated at Yale University who served in World War I: his works include *New Men for Old* (1912); *Trodden Gold; The Green Scarf; Wine, Women and War; Folding Bedouins; Memoirs of a Guinea Pig.*

O'Brien, Kate (1898-), Irish novelist and dramatist educated at University College, Dublin, who contributed articles to newspapers and was successful as a dramatist before writing novels: her works include *Distinguished Villa* (1926), a play: also the novels *Without My Cloak; The Ante-Room,* also dramatized; *Mary Lavelle; The Last of Summer.* She also wrote a travel book, *Farewell, Spain,* a tribute to a country in which she lived for some years.

O'Brien, Pat (1899-), American screen actor who has appeared in many films: among the most notable are *Front Page; Oil for the Lamps of China; Ceiling Zero; I Married a Doctor; China Clipper; Boy Meets Girl; Angels With Dirty Faces; Till We Meet Again; Knute Rockne— All American; Two Yanks in Trinidad; Broadway.*

Ocarina, a musical instrument of Tyrolese origin made of terra cotta with a body shaped somewhat like a potato: it is provided with several finger holes (without keys), and a mouthpiece shaped like a whistle projects from the side. If properly played the tune is soft and flute-like, but is not used in the orchestra except occasionally for special effects.

O'Carolan, Turlogh (1670-1738), Irish bard whose family belonged to the MacBradaigh tribe: he became blind from smallpox, earning his living by singing and playing the harp in the houses of the landed gentry. He composed melodies to the verses of Thomas MOORE, and wrote more than two hundred original songs: the manuscripts of several are in the BRITISH MUSEUM.

O'Casey, Sean (1884-), Irish dramatist who was born in the slum district of Dublin, and self-educated with the aid of a dictionary and the reading of classic authors. Several of his plays were rejected by the ABBEY THEATRE before *The Shadow of a Gunman* was accepted in 1923, followed by *Cathleen Listens In; Juno and the Paycock; Nannie's Night Out; The Plough and the Stars; The Silver Tassie; The End of the Beginning.* He also wrote two autobiographies: *I Knock at the Door* and *Pictures in the Hallway.*

Ochtman, Leonard (1854-1934), American painter, born in Holland, who was chiefly self-taught and came to America in 1866 with his family: his works include *Winter Light; November Morning; Morning Haze; Moonlight in Spring; A Morning Symphony; A Gray Morning.* His paintings are to be seen in many major American art museums.

O'Connor, Andrew (1874-1941), American sculptor who studied with his father and lived in Paris: his notable works include many statues and memorials to famous Americans including General Lew WALLACE at Washington, D. C., and Crawfordsville, Ind.; the bronze doors of St. Bartholomew's Church, New York; a relief for the J. P. Morgan Library, New York; the bronze statue, *Inspiration,* for the dome of the Art Palace at the St. Louis Exposition in 1904; *Adam and Eve; Tristan and Iseult.*

Octave, in music a series of eight consecutive diatonic tones or twelve semitones. The eighth tone has the same letter name as the first tone: for example an octave beginning on C comprises the notes C D E F G A B C.

Octave Thanet, see **French, Alice.**

Octobass, see **Double-Bass.**

Ode, a Greek word signifying a poem sung to the accompaniment of music: many Greek poets including ALCMAN, ALCAEUS, ANACREON, PINDAR, and SAPPHO used the form; HORACE and CATULLUS were the principal Romans who adopted it. RONSARD, J. B. ROUSSEAU, MALHERBE, HUGO, and LAMARTINE wrote odes in French: JONSON, HERRICK, COWLEY, DRYDEN, GRAY, WORDSWORTH, KEATS, SWINBURNE, and TENNYSON, were also famous writers to whom the ode form appealed.

Odell, George Clinton Densmore (1866-), American author and educator educated at Columbia University connected with the English department there since 1895, and the successor of Brander MATTHEWS as professor of dramatic literature from 1924 to 1939. His works include *Shakespeare from Betterton to Irving* (1920); *Annals of the New York Stage* (1927-1942), a work of which thirteen volumes have appeared.

Odets, Clifford (1906-), American actor and dramatist who first appeared with stock companies, and later with the THEATRE GUILD and Group Theatre: his notable plays include *Awake and Sing* (1935); *Waiting for Lefty; Till the Day I Die; Paradise Lost; Golden Boy; Rocket to the Moon; Night Music; The Silent Partner; Clash by Night.*

Odeum, the name given a form of concert hall in ancient Greece and Rome which was much smaller than the outdoor theatres used for dramatic purposes, and was provided with a roof. The oldest odeum was erected at Sparta in 600 B.C., and one of the finest was built at Athens by PERICLES in 445 B.C.: it was used for musical contests, discussions, and occasionally as a court of justice. The first Roman odeum was built by Domitian about 86 A.D.: the name has also been used, often in its French form, *Odéon,* for theatres in France and the United States.

Odin, in Norse (Scandinavian) mythology the chief god: he is represented as an old man with only one eye; Frigg is his wife and Thor and Balder are his sons. He is the source of wisdom and the patron of heroes: the souls of the latter after they are killed in battle are taken to his palace, VALHALLA, where they enjoy a life of feasting and fighting. Richard WAGNER has metamorphosed Odin into WOTAN in his cycle of music dramas, THE RING OF THE NIBELUNGS.

O'Donovan, William Rudolf (1844-1920), American sculptor who was self-taught: after serving in the Confederate army during the Civil War, he opened a studio in New York. His works include statues of Abraham Lincoln and Ulysses S. Grant in Prospect Park, Brooklyn, N. Y.: *The Captors of Major André* at Tarrytown, N. Y.; a statue of George Washington in Caracas, Venezuela.

Odysseus, in Greek mythology a king of Ithaca who was the son of Laertes, the husband of Penelope, and one of the heroes in the Trojan War. After the fall of Troy he wandered for ten years before reaching his home: the story of his return is told by HOMER in the **Odyssey,** an epic poem in which the hero's meetings with POLYPHEMUS, AEOLUS, CIRCE, NAUSICAA, the SIRENS, and the LOTUS EATERS are graphically described. On his arrival home, he finds that his wife has been harried by importunate suitors on whom he takes vengeance with his son, TELEMACHUS.

Oedipus, in Greek mythology the son of King Laius of Thebes and Jocasta: the king was warned by an oracle that his son would kill him, so Oedipus was left exposed in a lonely spot, but survived although ignorant of his parentage. Later he met King Laius and killed him in a quarrel after which he freed his country from a monster, the Sphinx, by solving the riddle propounded to its victims, and married his mother, an act deplored by the gods. SOPHOCLES wrote two tragedies and AESCHYLUS a trilogy, based on the legend.

Oehlenschläger, Adam Gottlob (1779-1850), Danish poet and dramatist who was created poet laureate of Scandinavia in 1829: his works include lyric poems; epics; a cycle of historical dramas including *Hakon Jarl, Axel and Valborg; Correggio,* and the poetic fantasy, *Aladdin's Lamp.*

Oemler, Marie Conway (1879-1932), American novelist educated privately who started her literary work when she was nearly forty years old: her works include *Slippy McGee* (1917); *The Purple Heights; Two Shall Be Born; Johnny Reb; Flower of Thorn.*

Oeser, Adam Friedrich (1717-1799), German painter and sculptor who studied at the Vienna Academy, and later director of the Leipzig Academy and professor at the Dresden Academy: his notable canvases include *Abraham's Sacrifice; The Good Samaritan; Solomon Adoring Idols; The Artist's Children; Marriage at Cana.* His principal work in sculpture is the tomb of Friedrich Augustus.

O'Faoláin, Sean (1900-), Irish biographer and novelist educated at the National University of Ireland and Harvard University. His novels include *A Nest of Simple Folk* (1933); *A Born Genius; Come Back to Erin; The Great O'Neill:* he has also written biographies of Eamon De Valera and Daniel O'Connell.

Offenbach, Jacques (1819-1880), French composer who was the son of a Jewish CANTOR: he studied the violoncello at the PARIS CONSERVATORY, and in 1849 became conductor of the Théâtre Français where his first musical piece, *Chanson de Fortunio,* was produced, and his complete opera, *Pepito,* at the OPÉRA-COMIQUE in 1853. His total stage works amount to more than one hundred: those still of interest are The TALES OF HOFFMANN (1881), *La Belle Helène, La Vie Parisienne, The Grand Duchess of Gerolstein, Madame Favart,* and ORPHEUS IN THE UNDERWORLD.

Offertory, in the Roman Catholic mass the verses or anthem following the *Credo,* sung by the choir while the priest is placing the consecrated bread and wine on the altar: the offerings of the congregation are collected at this time, and the custom is followed in many Protestant churches where the vocal work selected by the choirmaster is the principal part of the musical service.

O'Flaherty, Liam (1897-), Irish novelist, educated at the National University in Dublin, who served in World War I, and led an adventurous life before starting on a literary career. His works include *Thy Neighbour's Wife* (1924); *The Informer; The Assassin; Mr. Gilhooley; The House of Gold:* he has also written several volumes of short stories and the autobiographical *Two Years.*

Ogee, in architecture a molding formed with a double or S-shaped curve, the concave part occupying the upper part and the convex the lower part of the MOLDING: it is frequently used on an entablature supported by a column.

Ogpu, an abbreviation of the practically unpronounceable name—*Obshche Gosudarstvyaennoe Politicheskoe Upravlenie*—of the Bolshevik political police organization in Russian. It succeeded the body of secret police known as the *Cheka* in 1922, and has a place in this volume because of the frequent use of the abbreviated name in novels and stories concerning spy activities in Europe.

O'Hara, John (1905-), American novelist who worked at various posts on newspapers and magazines before his first successful novel, *Appointment in Samarra,* was published in 1934: he has also written *The Doctor's Son and Other Stories; Butterfield 8; Hope of Heaven; Files on Parade and Other Stories; Pal Joey.* He is the author of several motion-picture scenarios.

"O. Henry," see **Henry, O. (William Sydney Porter).**

O'Higgins, Harvey (1876-1929), Canadian dramatist and novelist: his works include *The Smoke Eaters* (1905); *Old Clinkers; The Argyle Case; The Dummy; Mr. Lazarus; On the Hiring Line; Some Distinguished Americans:* Harriet Ford was his collaborator on several plays.

Ohnet, Georges (1848-1918), French novelist and dramatist whose novels appeared in serial form in *Figaro* and the *Revue des Deux Mondes* before being published in book form: they include *Black and Red* (1888); *Doctor Rameau; Serge Panine; The Master of the Forge,* dramatized with great success; *Pierre's Soul:* also the dramas *Regina Sarpi* and *Martha.*

Oiseau de Feu, L', see Firebird, The.

O'Keeffe, Georgia (1887-), American painter who studied at the CHICAGO ART INSTITUTE, and at the ART STUDENTS' LEAGUE, New York, with William Merritt CHASE and Kenyon Cox. She has made a specialty of flower painting, studies of the New Mexican desert, and landscapes: her works are to be seen at the Phillips Memorial Gallery, Washington, D. C., and the Metropolitan Museum of Art, New York.

O'Keeffe, John (1747-1833), Irish actor and dramatist who acted and wrote plays for more than fifty years: William HAZLITT refers to him as the "English Molière" because of the wit in his numerous comedies such as *Wild Oats* produced at Covent Garden, London, with great success in 1791.

Okeghem, Johannes (c.1420-1495), Flemish composer and priest who was chaplain to Charles VII, Louis XI and Charles VIII of France: he was the leader of the 15th century Franco-Flemish school, and one of the great masters of the art of counterpoint. His works include masses, motets, and chansons.

Olcott, Chauncey (1860-1932), American actor and singer who made his debut with Hooley's Minstrels in 1880, later joining the Haverly Minstrels, playing with Denman THOMPSON in dramas, and with the Duff Opera Company. After appearing in Gilbert and Sullivan operettas for two years in England, he achieved great success in a series of Irish dramas including *Sweet Inniscarra, A Romance of Athlone, Terence, Macushla,* and *The Isle of Dreams* in which he sang ballads of his own composition.

Oldfield, Nance (1683-1730), English actress who first attracted the attention of George FARQUHAR by her reciting, and later became a member of Colley CIBBER's company at the Drury Lane Theatre, London: among the plays in which she appeared successfully were Cibber's *The Careless Husband* and *Caesar in Egypt;* STEELE's *The Tender Husband,* and ADDISON's *Cato.*

Oldham, Derek (1892-), English actor and tenor who appeared in *The Chocolate Soldier* in 1914, and joined the British Army during the same year, serving in World War I until 1919. He became a leading member of the D'OYLY CARTE OPERA COMPANY, appearing with it in the visits to the United States. He has also played in *The Merry Widow; Rose Marie; The Vagabond King; The Desert Song; Lilac Time,* and in several English films.

Old Hundred, in sacred music the name given to a hymn the words of which begin "All people that on earth do dwell," popular in England and with the early settlers of New England. With the words beginning "Praise God from whom all blessings flow" it is familiar as the DOXOLOGY.

Old Vic, a theatre in London first opened as the *Royal Coburg* in 1818, so called because it was under the patronage of the Duke of Saxe-Coburg. It was renamed the *Royal Victoria The-atre* and later *Royal Victoria Hall* in 1833, and Nicolò PAGANINI gave his last recital there. In 1898 grand opera was presented there in more or less concert form with great success, and it has also been the scene of many revivals of SHAKESPEARE's plays.

Oliphant, Laurence (1829-1888), English author born at Capetown, South Africa, who became greatly interested in the mystic philosophies of the Orient: his works include the novels *Piccadilly* (1870) and *Altiora Peto; Episodes in a Life of Adventure; Scientific Religion; My Perilous Life in Palestine,* the last-named written in connection with his plan to establish a colony of Jews in Palestine.

Oliphant, Margaret Oliphant (1828-1897), Scotch novelist who published her first novel, *Passages in the Life of Mrs. Margaret Maitland* in 1849: she became a steady, valued contributor to *Blackwood's Magazine* and wrote more than 120 novels, travel books, and miscellaneous works including *Adam Graeme; Magdalen Hepburn, The Laird of Norlaw; Madonna Mary; Squire Arden:* also a biography of Laurence OLIPHANT and an autobiography.

Oliver, Edna May (1883-1942), American stage and screen actress who made her debut at Boston in 1911, later appearing in numerous plays, her most successful role being that of Parthy Ann Hawks in *Showboat* (1927): among the many films in which she played character parts are *Icebound; Ladies of the Jury; Little Women; Alice in Wonderland; David Copperfield; No More Ladies; A Tale of Two Cities; Romeo and Juliet; Parnell; My Dear Miss Aldrich; Nurse Edith Cavell; Drums Along the Mohawk; Pride and Prejudice; Lydia.*

Oliver, George, see Onions, Oliver.

Oliver or Olivier, Isaac (c.1556-1617), English painter presumably of French extraction who studied with Nicholas Hilliard and Federigo ZUCCARO. He achieved great success as a miniature painter: among his sitters were Queen ELIZABETH, Sir Philip SIDNEY, Mary Queen of Scots, and Ben JONSON. His son and pupil, **Peter Oliver** (1594-1648), was even more distinguished as a miniaturist, and also as an expert in copying paintings of the old masters: many of these replicas are in Windsor Castle and in the J. P. Morgan collection, New York.

Oliver Optic, see Adams, William Taylor.

Olivier, Edith (c.1879-), English novelist and biographer who studied at St. Hugh's Hall, Oxford: her works include *The Love Child* (1927); *As Far as Jane's Grandmother's; Underground River; Dwarf's Blood; Mr. Chilvester's Daughters; Alexander the Corrector; Mary Magdalen; Country Moods and Tenses.*

Olivier, Juste Daniel (1807-1876), Swiss poet who published his first volume of verse, *Poèmes Suisses,* in 1830: this was followed by *The Future,* and *Songs from Afar.* Many years of his life were spent in Paris where he was regarded as one of the greatest of Swiss poets.

Olivier, Laurence (1907-   ), English stage and
screen actor educated at St. Laurence School, Oxford, who made his debut at fifteen in a special
performance of Shakespeare's *The Taming of the
Shrew,* and after playing with stock companies,
became a well-known actor in many plays produced in London and New York. He has also appeared in many films including *The Yellow
Ticket; Westward Passage; Moscow Nights; As
You Like It; Fire over England; The Divorce
of Lady X; Wuthering Heights; Clouds over
Europe; Twenty-one Days Together; Rebecca;
Pride and Prejudice; That Hamilton Woman;
The Invaders.*

Ollivant, Alfred (1874-1927), English novelist
who was an army officer before being incapaci-
tated by an injury: his works include the celebrated dog story, *Bob, Son of Battle* (1898) which
was a best seller; *Danny; The Gentleman; The
Royal Road; Two Men; Boy Woodburn; One
Woman.*

Olmsted, Frederick Law (1822-1903), American
landscape architect and author who traveled in
the South during the slavery period before the
Civil War, and wrote three books which were
later condensed into two volumes, *The Cotton
Kingdom,* published in 1861-62. He was one of
the designers of Central Park, New York, and
sole architect of Prospect Park, Brooklyn, N. Y.,
and Franklin Park in Boston: he also laid out
the grounds for the World's Fair at Chicago in
1893. His son, **Frederick Law Olmsted** (1870-   ),
is also a landscape architect and an expert in
city planning.

Olympia, a valley in the western part of the
Greek Peloponnesus which ranked with DELPHI
as the most important religious center in Greece.
It was invaded many times, and each band introduced new gods to which temples were built
within a sacred grove known as the Altis. Among
the many temples were the *Temple of Hera,* near
which the statue of Hermes by PRAXITELES was
found in 1877; the *Temple of Zeus* in which stood
the great ivory and gold statue of Zeus by
PHIDIAS; the *Temple of the Great Mother of the
Gods* dedicated to Cybele: also the *Terrace of
Treasuries,* thirteen small temples built by Greek
cities and towns. Many of the sculptures in these
temples are preserved in the Museum of Olympia
and the LOUVRE. There was also a stadium with
a seating capacity of 45,000 in which the OLYMPIC
GAMES were held.

Olympiad, in Greek chronology a period of
four years reckoned from one celebration of the
OLYMPIAN GAMES to another: the first Olympiad
started in 776 B.C. and the last ended in A.D. 394
when abolished by Theodosius the Great.

Olympians, in Greek mythology the gods who
lived on Mount OLYMPUS: they included ZEUS,
the chief deity; HERA, APOLLO, DIANA, APHRODITE,
ATHENA, ARES, HEPHAESTUS, HERMES, DEMETER,
DIONYSUS, HEBE, and HERCULES.

Olympic Games, a series of athletic contests
held in ancient Greece at the great stadium at
OLYMPUS under the patronage of the chief Olym-

pian god, ZEUS. They began in 776 B.C. and continued until 394 A.D.; the contests included foot,
chariot, and horse racing, boxing and wrestling,
and only Greeks in good standing as citizens
could compete. Many paintings and statues by
Greek artists of the classic era depict incidents
and winners; PINDAR's hymns of victory are devoted to Olympian victors. The Olympic Games
were revived in 1896 by the International Olympic Committee, and have been held every four
years with the exception of 1916 on account of
World War I, up to and including 1936.

Olympus, a mountain in Greece on the borders
of Thessaly and Macedonia nearly 10,000 feet
high, and covered with snow during the greater
part of the year: the name is also applied, more
or less indefinitely, to the lofty peak on which
the OLYMPIANS made their home according to
HOMER and other poets.

O'Malley, Frank Ward (1875-1932), American
journalist and dramatist: his works include *The
Head of the House* (1909) and *A Certain Party*
with E. W. Townsend; *The War Whirl in Washington,* a comedy of World War I; *The Swiss
Family O'Malley.* He was connected with the
New York *Sun* from 1906 to 1920.

Omar Khayyám (c.1050-c.1123), Persian poet
and astronomer: his most famous work is the
Rubaiyat or *Quatrains,* four-line stanzas with the
third line unrhymed. There are more than 500
quatrains in the original which are regarded as
genuine: Edward FITZGERALD has used 101 of them
in the first edition of his translation which appeared in 1859 with several later reprints. There
have been American editions with illustrations by
Elihu VEDDER and by Willy POGANY: Nathan
Haskell DOLE (1896) and John Payne (1898) also
published excellent translations.

Omphale, in Greek mythology a Lydian princess for whom HERCULES was forced by the gods
to labor for three years to expiate a crime: she
put him at the spinning wheel with her maids.
The tale no doubt inspired the symphonic poem,
Le Rouet d'Omphale, by Camille SAINT-SAENS:
there is a Victor recording by the New York
Philharmonic-Symphony Society, and a Columbia
recording by the Paris Conservatory Orchestra.

Onatas, Greek sculptor who worked between
490 B.C. and 460 B.C.: among his sculptures is a
four-horse bronze chariot executed for the king
of Syracuse, and dedicated at OLYMPIA; a statue
of HERMES, and a strange image of the Black
DEMETER said to have been made for the people
of Phigalia.

Ondříček, Franz (1859-1922), Bohemian violinist who studied at the Paris Conservatory, making
his debut in 1882, and touring Europe, America,
and the Far East with great success. In 1908 he
founded a string quartet which achieved an international reputation for its interpretation of
classic and modern chamber works.

Onégin, Sigrid (1891-1943), German contralto
born in Denmark who made her debut in 1912 at
Stuttgart in the title role of *Carmen* with Enrico

CARUSO as Don José: after singing at European opera houses she appeared in 1922 at the Metropolitan Opera House in *Aida*, later becoming a member of the German State Opera from 1926 to 1933. She was equally at home in Wagnerian, Italian, and French roles.

O'Neill, Eliza (1791-1872), Irish actress who made her first success at Dublin in 1813 as a tragedienne, and carried London audiences by storm in 1814 with her characterization of the heroine in Shakespeare's *Romeo and Juliet*. After appearing in tragic parts for five years, and being favorably compared with Mrs. SIDDONS, she retired from the stage.

O'Neill, Eugene Gladstone (1888-), American dramatist, son of the distinguished actor, James O'NEILL; educated at Princeton University and at Harvard University in the celebrated "47 Workshop" in the dramatic department headed by George Pierce BAKER. His plays include *Thirst and Other One-Act Plays* (1914); *Bound East for Cardiff; Before Breakfast; The Moon of the Caribbees; Beyond the Horizon; The Emperor Jones; All God's Chillun Got Wings; Desire Under the Elms; The Great God Brown; Marco Millions; Lazarus Laughed; Strange Interlude; Dynamo; Mourning Becomes Electra; Ah! Wilderness; Days Without End.* He won the Nobel prize for literature, and the Pulitzer prize for several of his plays.

O'Neill, James (1847-1920), American actor born in Ireland who was brought to the United States in 1850, and made his debut at Cincinnati in 1867: after playing in stock companies as well as with Adelaide Neilson and Edwin Booth, he starred for fifteen years in a dramatization of DUMAS' *Monte Cristo*, and in Sidney GRUNDY'S stage version of *The Three Musketeers*. He was also well received in the roles of Hamlet, Othello, and Virginius: the distinguished dramatist, Eugene O'NEILL, is his son.

O'Neill, Nance (1874-), American stage and screen actress who made her first appearance on the stage at San Francisco in 1893: after playing with stock companies she achieved success in London as Leah in *The Jewess* in 1899. Among the plays in which she appeared were *Magda; La Tosca; Fedora; Camille; Hedda Gabler; Ingomar; Oliver Twist; Thaïs; Hamlet; The Passion Flower:* she has also created character roles in numerous films.

Onions, Oliver (1873-), English novelist who first studied art at London and Paris, taking up writing at the suggestion of Gelett Burgess: his works include *The Compleat Bachelor* (1901); *The Odd Job Man; Mushroom Town; The Tower of Oblivion; The Story of Louie; Catalan Circus; The Italian Chest; Blood Eagle.*

Onoe Kikugōrō, (1885-), Japanese actor descended from a family in which the members have been actors for several generations. He made his debut in 1921 at Tokio as a tragedian and mime: in 1930 he founded a school of acting which is highly regarded.

Onomasticon, see **Pollux, Julius.**

On the Steppes of Central Asia (Borodin), a symphonic poem written by Alexander BORODIN on the occasion of the twenty-fifty anniversary of the reign of Alexander II of Russia. The composer's program for the music outlines the slow progress of a caravan over the vast, sandy steppes to the tune of a Russian folk song: it draws near and gradually moves away. There is a Victor recording by the London Symphony Orchestra, and a Columbia recording by the Paris Conservatory Orchestra.

Onyx, a variety of agate or chalcedony of remarkable beauty distinguished by parallel and concentric bands of various colors. It was used in the classical period for vases and cups, and was also employed for cameo engraving. Another variety, **Sardonyx,** has the white onyx bands alternated with CARNELIAN or SARD.

Oost, Jacob van (c.1600-1671), Flemish painter, known as Jacob the Elder, who chose Annibale CARRACCI as his model although preserving Flemish characteristics in his work. His notable paintings include *St. Augustine Washing the Feet of Christ; St. Anthony of Padua in Ecstasy; Priest Dictating to a Clerk; Carnival Scene; Magistrates Condemning a Criminal.* His son and pupil, **Jacob van Oost** (1639-1713), known as Jacob the Younger, visited Italy and Paris: his works include *Friar Dressing a Monk's Wound; Holy Family; Martyrdom of St. Barbara; Christ Victor over Death and Time; The Nativity.*

Opal, a semi-transparent gem stone allied to quartz which is distinguished primarily by its display of changing colors known as *opalescence.* Its basic colors are usually white, red, yellow, green, gray, and blue. *Fire opals* are found in Mexico, and the most precious varieties in Hungary and Australia; commoner stones are indigenous to New South Wales, Honduras, and the western part of the United States.

Opera, a form of drama in which vocal and instrumental music are the chief elements in the form of arias, concerted numbers, (duets, trios, quartets, etc.), and choruses connected together by RECITATIVE, and accompanied by an orchestra with the addition of appropriate scenery and costumes. Its creation resulted from the desire of Italian composers in Florence to free vocal music from the strict rules of COUNTERPOINT: the first opera, *Dafne* by Jacopo PERI and Giulio CACCINI, was produced in 1594: Claudio Monteverde improved on the form in 1607 with *Orfeo,* employing an orchestra of more than thirty instruments. Alessandro SCARLATTI, Jean Baptiste LULLY, Henry PURCELL, George Frederick HANDEL, Giovanni Battista PERGOLESI, Jean-Philippe RAMEAU also contributed greatly to the development of Italian and French opera, but the innovator who introduced genuine drama into the form was Christopher Willibald von GLUCK with *Orfeo,* produced at Vienna in 1762. Other great composers associated with the progress of opera include Wolfgang Amadeus MOZART, Ludwig van BEETHOVEN, Gioacchino ROSSINI, Carl Maria van WEBER; Giuseppe VERDI, Vincenzo BELLINI,

Giacano MEYERBEER, Gaetano DONIZETTI, Charles GOUNOD, Georges BIZET, Jules MASSENET, Richard WAGNER, and Richard STRAUSS. The various forms of opera include *Grand Opera*, in which every word in the libretto is sung, and all recitatives accompanied by the orchestra; *Opéra Comique*, a French form which employs spoken dialogue; *Chamber Opera*, a German form calling for a small chorus; *Melodrama*, in which dialogue is recited to orchestral accompaniment; *Singspiel*, a German form with spoken dialogue as used by Mozart. Another important development is **Light** or **Comic Opera** in which spoken dialogue is employed, and the plots are of either humorous or romantic character. The list of important light operas begins in the 18th century with operas by Italian composers such as PERGOLESI's *La Serva Padrona*, CIMAROSA's *The Secret Marriage*, ROSSINI's *The Barber of Seville*; DONIZETTI's *Daughter of the Regiment*; VERDI's *Falstaff*; WOLF-FERRARI's *Le Donne Curiose*. French works of this character include AUBER's *Fra Diàvolo*; Adolphe ADAM's *The Postilion of Lonjumeau*; OFFENBACH's *The Grand Duchess of Gerolstein* and *Tales of Hoffmann*; LECOCQ's *Giroflé-Girofla*; AUDRAN's *Olivette* and *The Mascot*; PLANQUETTE's *Chimes of Normandy*. In Germany MOZART's *Abduction from the Seraglio* and *Cosi fan tutte* (School for Lovers) headed a list of light operas including NICOLAI's *The Merry Wives of Windsor*; FLOTOW's *Martha*; SUPPE's *Fatinitza*; SMETANA's *The Bartered Bride*; Johann STRAUSS' *The Bat*; MILLOCKER's *The Beggar Student*. Since 1880 the European composers of light opera include Franz LEHAR, Oscar STRAUS, Leo FALL, Emmerich KALMAN, GILBERT AND SULLIVAN, Edward JAKOBOWSKI, Ivan CARYLL; Leslie STUART. The list of American composers includes John Philip SOUSA, Gustave KERKER, Victor HERBERT, Reginald DE KOVEN, Gustav LUDERS, Rudolf FRIML, and Sigmund ROMBERG. The subject of grand opera composition in America is discussed in the reference—OPERAS BY AMERICAN COMPOSERS.

Opéra, L' (Paris), see **Académie de Musique (Paris).**

Operas by American Composers, a subject of interest to those who may have the impression that American composers have not been active to any considerable extent during the 18th, 19th, and 20th centuries in the field of grand opera composition at which European composers have labored since Jacopo PERI, an Italian, created *Dafne*, the first "opera" or drama set to music in 1597. The actual facts are that almost three hundred composers, either born in America or long resident there, have written more than a thousand operas many of which have had public or private performance. Space limits permit the mention of only a few of the most representative works ranging from ballad operas to grand operas: Benjamin Carr (*The Archers of Switzerland*); James Hewitt (*Tammany*); Alexander Reinagle (*The Savoyard*); Carl BREIL (*The Legend*); George Frederick BRISTOW (*Rip van Winkle*); Harrison Millard (*Uncle Tom's Cabin*); Silas Gamaliel PRATT (*Zenobia*); Walter DAMROSCH (*The Scarlet Letter*); Victor HERBERT (*Natoma*); John Adam HUGO (*The Temple Dancer*); Reginald DE KOVEN (*The Canterbury Pilgrims*); Bruno Oscar Klein (*Kenilworth*); John Knowles PAINE (*Azara*); Frederick S. CONVERSE (*The Pipe of Desire*); Henry K. HADLEY (*Azora*); William Franke HARLING (*A Light from St. Agnes*); Arthur NEVIN (*Poia*); Charles Wakefield CADMAN (*Shanewis*); Louis GRUENBERG (*Emperor Jones*); Horatio W. PARKER (*Mona*); Howard HANSON (*Merry Mount*); John L. SEYMOUR (*The Pasha's Garden*); Deems TAYLOR (*The King's Henchman*); Richard HAGEMAN (*Caponsacchi*); Marc BLITZSTEIN (*The Cradle Will Rock*); George GERSHWIN (*Porgy and Bess*); Vittorio GIANNINI (*Beauty and the Beast*); Gian-Carlo MENOTTI (*Amelia Goes to the Ball*); Douglas Stuart MOORE (*The Devil and Daniel Webster*); Vergil THOMSON (*Four Saints in Three Acts*); Aldo FRANCHETTI (*Namiko-San*); George ANTHEIL (*Helen Retires*); Robert Russell BENNETT (*Maria Malibran*); Albert STOESSEL (*David Garrick*); Gustave STRUBE (*The Captive*). The above list is manifestly incomplete: those desiring to delve into the subject more deeply will find Edward Ellsworth Hipsher's *American Opera and Its Composers* (Presser, 1934), and May Silva Teasdale's *Handbook of 20th Century Opera* (Dutton, 1938), interesting reading.

Opéra-Comique (Paris), a theatre in Paris, France, which rivals the OPERA: it was established in 1715 for the production of French opera with spoken dialogue, and its success was so great that a cabal was formed which resulted in its being forced to close in 1745. After re-opening in 1752 and joining forces with the Comédie-Italienne in 1762, a rival company started in 1791 which caused both companies to close in 1801. The two companies then adopted the wise expedient of merging, and the organization has continued at various theatres ever since.

Operetta (It.), a "little" opera, the term signifying either the style of composition or the length of the work, but generally applied to an amusing stage play with interspersed dialogue and music of light character. Among the distinguished composers in this field are Jacques OFFENBACH, Johann STRAUSS, Jr., Sir Arthur S. SULLIVAN, Victor HERBERT, Reginald DE KOVEN, and Rudolf FRIML.

Ophicleide (It.), an obsolete musical instrument which has been superseded by the TUBA in orchestras and bands: it was the bass instrument of the BUGLE family, made of brass, and resembled the BASSOON in appearance.

Opie, John (1761-1807), English painter who achieved great success as a portrait painter at London in 1780 under the patronage of Dr. Wolcot (Peter Pindar). In 1790 he turned to historical painting: among his best canvases are *The Assassination of James I of Scotland; Sleeping Nymph; Cupid Stealing a Kiss; Murder of David Rizzio; Troilus, Cressida and Pandarus; Head of a Young Man; Old Man and Child.* He also executed paintings for BOYDELL's Shakespeare Gallery.

Opitz, Martin (1597-1639), German poet and critic who wrote the libretto for *Dafne* (1627), the first German opera for which the music was composed by Heinrich SCHUTZ: he was also the author of a *Book of German Poetry* (1624) which established definite rules for versifying which entitles him to be considered the father of Germanic poetry.

Oppenheim, Edward Phillips (1866-), English novelist who first engaged in business, and published his first successful book, *The Mysterious Mr. Sabin,* in 1901: since that time he has written more than 110 stories, chiefly of international intrigue, which have found an appreciative host of readers in both England and the United States.

Oppenord, Gilles Marie (1672-1742), French architect who studied with François MANSART and spent several years in Rome studying the BAROQUE buildings of Francesco BORROMINI. His works are distinguished because of their graceful and elegant lines in complete harmony with the rules of symmetry established by Charles LE-BRUN, and he may be regarded as one of the advance exponents of ROCOCO.

Opper, Frederick Burr (1857-1937), American cartoonist who worked in a newspaper office and in stores before selling some of his humorous sketches to comic periodicals, later becoming a contributor to Frank Leslie's magazines, and with *Puck* for eighteen years. In 1899 he joined the New York *American,* also illustrating books by Mark Twain, Finley P. Dunne and others: his most popular creations were *Happy Hooligan* and *Alphonse and Gaston.*

Opus (Lat.), in music the term used to indicate the numerical classification of a composer's works as Opus 1, Opus 2, etc., generally abbreviated "Op." on the actual music. The custom of identifying works in this manner began in the 18th century with some of MOZART's works: BEETHOVEN was the first to mark his works with any degree of regularity.

Oracle, in Greek religion the response given by a god to a question asked by a mortal: the word is also used to denote the source from which the answer emanates. The earliest oracle mentioned in classical writing was that of Dodona in Epirus, and the most famous that at DELPHI, but its influence waned after the advent of ALEXANDER THE GREAT. The oracles were delivered by persons in a trance or came to the questioners in their dreams.

Oratorio, in music an extended composition based on a sacred text, and presented without scenery, costumes or action by vocal soloists and chorus with orchestral accompaniment. Its development runs parallel with that of opera: the name *oratorio* is derived from the performances of Biblical scenes with music given in 1565 by Philip NERI in the oratory of his church at Rome. Giovanni Carissimi introduced a "narrator" who sang RECITATIVO passages between solos and choruses in order to carry on the story intelligently without scenery or dramatic action. Alessandro Stradella wrote fine oratorios, and the German master, Heinrich SCHUTZ, Reinhard Keiser, Johann Sebastian BACH, and George Frederick HANDEL may be regarded as perfectors of the oratorio along with Joseph HAYDN. Among other masters of the form are Louis SPOHR, Ludwig van BEETHOVEN, Felix MENDELSSOHN, Johannes BRAHMS, Max BRUCH, Franz LISZT, Anton DVORAK, Hector BERLIOZ, César FRANCK, Edward ELGAR, and Horatio W. PARKER.

Oratorio Society (New York), an organization founded in 1873 by Leopold DAMROSCH with a chorus of about sixty: the performances were first given in a wareroom, and the première of HANDEL's *Messiah* given in old Steinway Hall in 1874, a custom continued annually since that time. The conductors included Leopold Damrosch, Walter DAMROSCH, Frank DAMROSCH, Louis Koemmenich, and Albert STOESSEL.

Orcagna or **Arcagnuolo** (c.1308-1368), Italian painter, sculptor, and architect whose real name was Andrea di Cione: he studied sculpture with Andrea PISANO, and is regarded as the greatest artist of his time. His fresco paintings for the Church of S. Maria Novello in Florence, consisting of scenes from the life of the Virgin, were destroyed by dampness, and replaced by GHIRLANDAIO: among others are *Paradise* in the Strozzi Chapel; *Christ in Glory with Saint Thomas Aquinas and St. Peter.* His greatest sculpture is the marble tabernacle in the Chapel of Or San Michele in Florence.

Orchardson, Sir William Quiller (1835-1910), Scottish painter who acquired his skill as a genre, historical, and portrait artist mainly through his assiduous study: his important works include *The Challenge; Queen of the Swords; Napoleon I on Board the Bellerophon; Hard Hit; Voltaire; Her Mother's Voice; The First Cloud; Master Baby; Her First Dance; A Tender Chord:* he also painted Queen Victoria with her son (later Edward VII), grandson, and great-grandson.

Orchestra, (*1*) in music a group of musicians performing simultaneously on the various instruments used in the concert hall, opera house, theatre or broadcasting station: these instruments include the *string section* comprising the violin, viola, violoncello, double-bass, and harp; the *wood-wind section* which includes the piccolo, flute, oboe, English horn, clarinet, and bassoon; the *brass-wind section* comprising the French horn, trumpet, cornet, trombone, and tuba; the *percussion section* including the tympani, snare drum, bass drum, cymbals, triangle, bells, and gong. Some orchestral scores call for the use of additional instruments such as the bass clarinet and contrabassoon. *Concert* or *symphony* orchestras may range in size from 40 to 110 musicians: *string orchestras* are those in which only the instruments of the *string section* mentioned above are used: a *dance* or *jazz orchestra* comprises a combination in which wind instruments predominate over stringed instruments. (*2*) The term was applied in the ancient Greek theatre to the semicircular space between the front row of seats and the stage which was occupied by the chorus.

Orchestration, the art of arranging a musical composition so that it can be performed by an orchestra: it requires expert knowledge of the compass and technical capabilities of all the various stringed, wood-wind, brass, and percussion instruments as well as the ability to unite them in pleasing and effective tonal combinations. There are several standard works on orchestration including those of Hector BERLIOZ, François GEVAERT, Nicholas RIMSKY-KORSAKOW, Ebenezer PROUT, and Cecil FORSYTH.

Orchestrion, an 18th century organ invented by the Abbé Vogler which was actually a simplified model of the standard organ with much of the complicated mechanism eliminated. At the present time the name is applied to a stationary barrel organ which utilizes rolls similar to the player piano, and imitates the sounds of various instruments of the orchestra.

Orczy, Emmuska, Baroness (1865-), Hungarian novelist who was the daughter of Baron Felix Orczy, a musician of some repute through whom she became acquainted in her childhood with WAGNER, GOUNOD, LISZT, and MASSENET. She first studied painting, some of her canvases having been shown at the Royal Academy, London: in 1905 her play, *The Scarlet Pimpernel,* achieved great success, and was later filmed with Leslie HOWARD and Raymond MASSEY. Several "Pimpernel" novels appeared: also a series of mystery stories featuring an armchair detective, the first being *The Old Man in the Corner.*

O'Rell, Max, see **Blouet, Paul.**

Orenburgsky, Sergei Gusev (1867-), Russian novelist who was ordained a priest, but resigned in order to become a writer: he came to the United States after the Revolution, and has been employed in the Slavonic department of the New York Public Library: his novels include *The Land of the Fathers* (1905), and *The Land of the Children* (1928).

Orestes, in Greek mythology the only son of AGAMEMNON and CLYTEMNESTRA; also the brother of ELECTRA and IPHIGENIA. He avenged the murder of his father by killing Clytemnestra and her lover, Aesgisthus; after being pursued by the ERINYES he was exonerated by the sacred council (Aereopagus) at Athens. AESCHYLUS wrote a trilogy, **Oresteia,** on the subject, and EURIPIDES a play.

Organ, the largest in size and the most powerful in tone of musical instruments invented about 200 B.C. The early organ was a primitive instrument with a diatonic compass of only two octaves: in 1000 A.D., some English organs were equipped with four hundred pipes and two manuals (keyboards) with 20 keys on each one. Tracker or lever action to operate the keys was later superseded by pneumatic action, and in modern days by electric action. Some modern organs have five manuals and up to 150 stops, each of the latter controlling a group of pipes.

Organ-point, in music a tone sustained in one part against changing harmonies in other parts; usually a bass note when it is termed *pedal-point.* If it is sustained in a higher part it is called a *holding-note.*

Oriel, in architecture a projecting bay window in an upper story supported by means of CORBELS or brackets; usually semicircular or polygonal in plan although occasionally rectangular. Oriels came into use during the 15th century and are often found over gateways, and are sometimes carried through several stories.

Orientation, in architecture the locating of a church so that the most sacred parts such as the chancel containing the altar are at the eastern end of the structure: the custom has been consistently followed in England, Germany, and Spain, and to a considerable extent in France and Italy.

Orion, in Greek mythology a son of POSEIDON and a hero of great beauty and extraordinary strength: he is said to have been blinded for violating Merope, daughter of ATLAS, but regained his sight by exposing his eyes to the rising sun. After living with Artemis, he was killed by the bite of a scorpion, and was transformed into a constellation.

O'Riordan, Conal O'Connell (1874-), Irish novelist and dramatist who began his career as an actor and dramatist: his plays were produced at several prominent London theatres, and he succeeded John Millington SYNGE as director of the ABBEY THEATRE, Dublin, in 1909. His successful novels and plays include *The Fool and His Heart* (1896); *Adam of Dublin; Adam and Caroline; In London: The Story of Adam and Marriage; His Majesty's Pleasure,* a play; *Young Lady Dazincourt; The King's Wooing,* a play; *Judith Quinn; Judith's Love.*

Orlando, see **Roland.**

Orley, Bernard van (c.1491-1542), Flemish painter who studied at Rome in the school of Raphael, and became court painter to Margaret of Austria at Brussels, and later to Mary of Hungary. His works include a triptych, *The Patience of Job; Pietà; Holy Family; Flight into Egypt; Death of the Virgin; Entry of Christ into Jerusalem; Adoration of the Trinity by All the Saints; Seven Works of Mercy; The Last Judgment.* He also designed many glass windows and tapestries.

Ormandy, Eugene (1899-), American conductor born in Hungary who studied at the Budapest Royal Academy of Music at the age of five: after studying with Jenö HUBAY he toured Europe as a prodigy until 1914. In 1921 he became concertmaster at the Capitol Theatre, New York, and in 1927 a naturalized citizen. After numerous appearances as guest conductor, he directed the MINNEAPOLIS SYMPHONY ORCHESTRA from 1931 to 1935: in 1936 he was appointed associate conductor, with Leopold STOKOWSKI of the Philadelphia Orchestra, and later permanent conductor. He has conducted many Victor recordings of important symphonic works.

Ormolu, a term originally applied to a preparation of ground gold used for gilding; it now designates a similar composition of brass in imitation of gold, and is used with remarkable effectiveness on furniture when heightened by lacquer. The French developed the process to a high degree during the latter part of the 18th century.

Ornament, (*a*) in music an accessory note to a principal note, usually indicated by a GRACE NOTE or a symbol of some kind. They were used in the 17th and 18th centuries because the HARPSICHORD was incapable of sustaining tones, and the ornaments aided in reducing the impression of thinness by renewing the vibrations: (*b*) in architecture a decorative detail such as a volute, scroll, rosette, molding or any other ornamental raised design employed to beautify or enliven a column, pillar, or other architectural form.

Ornstein, Leo (1895-), American pianist and composer born in Russia who studied at the St. Petersburg Conservatory, and came to the United States in 1906 where he continued his studies at the INSTITUTE OF MUSICAL ART, New York. He has appeared as soloist with all major American orchestras, and is now (1943) director of the Ornstein School of Music, Philadelphia. His compositions include orchestral works, chamber music, piano pieces and choral works.

Orozco, José Clemente (1883-), Mexican painter educated at the National Agricultural school and the National University of Mexico: after spending some time in the United States, he returned to Mexico in 1922, and became one of the leaders in the Syndicate of Painters and Sculptors, an organization interested in the revival of the ancient art of mural and fresco painting. He has executed many murals and frescoes in Mexico, and in the United States such as those in New School of Social Research at New York, and the series of mural panels in the Baker Library at Dartmouth College in which he traced the history of America.

Orpen, Sir William (1878-1931), Irish painter who studied at the Metropolitan School of Art in Dublin, and at the Slade School in London: he became famous as a portraitist because he was able to capture the significant features of his sitters. His sitters included all the military and political leaders in World War I, and many famous American industrialists. His genre paintings include *Irish Wedding; Leading the Life in the West; Sowing the Seed; The Jockey; Mother and Child; The Unknown British Soldier in France; Myself and Venus.* He wrote *An Onlooker in France, 1917-1919,* and *Stories of Old Ireland and Myself,* and edited *The Outline of Art* (1923-24).

Orpheus, in Greek mythology a famous singer and performer on the lyre who was the son of CALLIOPE, one of the MUSES. After participating in the search for the GOLDEN FLEECE with the ARGONAUTS he married EURYDICE, a nymph: when she died from the bite of a serpent, Orpheus so softened the heart of PLUTO and PERSEPHONE by his music that he was allowed to take her away from the underworld on condition that he walk in front of her without looking back. He broke his promise, and Eurydice was lost to him forever.

Orpheus and Eurydice, grand opera in three acts; libretto by Ranieri de' Calzabigi; music by Christoph Willibald von GLUCK; first produced at Vienna in 1762, and at the Metropolitan Opera House, New York, in 1891. The plot follows closely the legend of EURYDICE except that it has a happy ending. There is a Columbia recording in French which is practically complete.

Orpheus in the Underworld, a comic opera in three acts: libretto by Hector Crémieux; music by Jacques Offenbach; first produced at Paris in 1858, and revived in four acts in 1874. The story is a travesty on the gods and goddesses of the Greek OLYMPUS; a combination of burlesque and satire accompanied by sprightly, tuneful music. There is a Victor recording of the overture, and a Decca abridged recording of the opera sung in German.

Orzeszko, Eliza (1842-1910), Polish novelist of noble birth whose husband was exiled to Siberia for political activities: her novels such as *An Obscure Apostle; The Interrupted Melody; On the Niemen,* and *Chain* deal principally with the social condition of the Polish Jews.

Osborn, Paul (1901-), American dramatist educated at the University of Michigan who studied playwriting with George Pierce BAKER at Yale University, later teaching English at the University of Michigan. His plays include *Hotbed* (1928); *A Ledge; Oliver Oliver; The Vinegar Tree* which was a great success; *On Borrowed Time* founded on a novel by Lawrence WATKIN and a success also as a film; *Morning's at Seven.* He has also written a film, *The Young in Heart.*

Osbourne, Lloyd (1868-1920), American author who first studied engineering at the University of Edinburgh, and traveled to Samoa with his stepfather, Robert Louis STEVENSON, with whom he collaborated on *The Wrong Box* (1889), *The Wrecker,* and *Ebb Tide.* His original works include *The Adventurer* (1907); *Wild Justice; A Person of Some Importance.*

O'Shaughnessy, Arthur William Edgar (1844-1881), English poet who had a post in the British Museum first as copyist in the library, and later in the museum of natural history, becoming an expert in ichthyology. His poetical works include *Epic of Women* (1870); *Lays of France; Songs of a Worker; The Fountain of Tears.*

Osiris, in Egyptian mythology the name of the principal god who personifies the creator, the enemy of evil, and the guardian of the Nile. He is in everlasting conflict with his brother, *Set,* the god of evil, darkness and the desert. He was represented in art as a mummy wearing the crown of Upper Egypt, often decorated with ostrich plumes.

Ossendowski, Ferdinand Antoni (1876-), Polish scientist and author: his works include *Beasts, Men and Gods* (1922), an account of his escape from the Red Army; *Man and Mystery in Asia; From President to Prison; Slaves of the Sun; Lenin, God of the Godless.*

Ossian or **Oisin,** a semi-historical Gallic bard and warrior who lived at the end of the 3rd century: he is credited with being the author of *Fingal* and other poems published by James Macpherson in 1760, but it is now generally believed that Macpherson himself was the author or compiler of the poems.

Ostade, Adriaen van (1610-1685), Dutch painter who studied with Frans HALS, and became famous for his delineation of homely subjects such as taverns, village fairs and rustic scenes: his works have been estimated at from 300 to 900 in number, and it is positively known that more than 200 were in his home unsold at his death. Among the most notable paintings are *Peasants at an Inn; The Wandering Violinist; The Painter's Family; The Cobbler; Countryman Having His Tooth Drawn; Cottage Scene; A Bagpiper; Card Players; The Baker; The Smokers; Tavern Scene; Village Street; Skittle Players; Village School.* He was also a fine engraver and teacher: his brother, **Isaac van Ostade** (1621-1649), was his pupil until 1641 when he came under the influence of REMBRANDT for a time, but finally developed an individual style. His works include *Slaughtered Pig; Laughing Boor With a Pot of Beer; The Concert; The Spinner; Frozen Canal; Winter in Holland; Boor Stealing a Kiss from a Woman.*

Ostenso, Martha (1900-), American novelist born in Norway who came to the United States with her parents as a child, first living in Minnesota and South Dakota, and later in Canada where she studied at the University of Manitoba, and later at Columbia University, New York. Her novels and poems include *Wild Geese* (1925); *The Mad Carews; Waters under the Earth; There's Always Another Year; White Reef; The Stone Field; Love Passed This Way.*

Ostrovsky, Alexander Nicholaievitch (1823-1886), Russian dramatist who first studied law without completing his training, but worked for a time as a clerk in the courts. His comedies, which deal with the Russian merchant classes include *The Bankrupt; The Poor Bride; Poverty Not a Vice:* he also wrote several historical dramas such as *The False Demetrius* and *Vassily Shuisky.* His fairy play, *The Snow-Maiden* was used as the basis of a opera by Nicholas RIMSKY-KORSAKOW, and a ballet by Peter TSCHAIKOWSKY.

O'Sullivan, Maureen (1911-), Irish screen actress who has appeared since 1933 in numerous films including *Payment Deferred; Tugboat Annie; Stage Mother; The Barretts of Wimpole Street; The Thin Man; David Copperfield; Anna Karenina; Cardinal Richelieu; The Voice of Bugle Ann; The Emperor's Candlesticks; Pride and Prejudice.*

O'Sullivan, Seumas, see **Starkey, James.**

Otello, grand opera in four acts: libretto by Arrigo BOITO based on Shakespeare's OTHELLO; music by Giuseppe VERDI; first produced at Milan in 1887, and at the Metropolitan Opera House in 1891. The opera libretto follows closely the plot of Shakespeare's play: there is a Victor complete recording comprising sixteen records, and also a Victor abridged recording in six records.

Otescu, J. Nonna (1888-), Rumanian composer who studied at the Bucharest Conservatory, the Paris Conservatory with Charles Widor, and at the Schola Cantorum with Vincent D'INDY: he directed the Bucharest Conservatory, founded the Société Lyrique d'Opéra, and conducted the Rumanian Opera. His works include two operas, two ballets, and several symphonic poems.

Othello, a tragedy by William SHAKESPEARE the full title of which is *The Tragedy of Othello, the Moor of Venice:* first acted in 1604 and printed in 1622. It was founded on one of Giovanni Battista GIRALDI's tales in a work known as the *Hecatommithi:* Giuseppe Verdi's opera, OTELLO, is founded on Shakespeare's tragedy.

Otis, Bass (1784-1861), American painter and engraver who had considerable success as a portraitist in New York and Philadelphia: his sitters included Thomas Jefferson, John Weagle, and John Wesley Jarvis. He is credited with having produced the first lithograph in the United States in 1819.

Otway, Thomas (1652-1685), English dramatist educated at Christ Church, Oxford, who first essayed a career as an actor, but failed because of stage fright: his works include *Alcibiades; Don Carlos, Prince of Spain; The Orphan; Venice Preserved; Titus and Berenice; The Cheats of Scapin; Caius Marius; The Soldier's Fortune; The Atheist; Friendship in Fashion.* Several of his plays were adaptations from RACINE and MOLIERE.

Oubliette, in architecture the French term for (*1*) a dungeon or cell reached only by a trapdoor from another dungeon: (*2*) a secret passage leading from a dungeon or cell to facilitate the disposal of bodies in a moat or river.

Oudry, Jean Baptiste (1686-1755), French painter who studied with his father and with Nicholas de LARGILLIERE: his first important commission was a portrait of PETER THE GREAT when he visited Paris in 1717. He became court painter to Louis XV of France, and also superintendent of the GOBELIN tapestry factory. His notable works include *Dog Guarding Game; Harvest; Vintage; Fish and Ducks; Deer Pursued by Dogs; Fox after Grapes; Dog and Boar Fight; Dog Guarding Dead Game.*

Ouida, pen name of **Maria Louise de la Ramée** (1839-1908), English novelist whose mother was English and father French: her novels include *Held in Bondage* (1863); *Strathmore; Chandos; Under Two Flags,* successfully dramatized and filmed; *Moths; In Maremma.* She also wrote books for children including *Two Little Wooden Shoes; Bimbi,* and *A Dog in Flanders.*

Ouspenskaya, Maria (c.1878-), Russian stage and screen actress who made her debut with the Moscow Art Theatre: she has appeared with great success in several American films including *Dodsworth; Conquest; Love Affair; The Rains Came; Judge Hardy and Son; Waterloo Bridge; The Mystery of Marie Roget.*

Overbeck, Johann Friedrich (1789-1869), German painter who studied at the Vienna Academy from which he was expelled because of his disapproval of the instruction. He went to Rome where he formed a group of painters which included Peter CORNELIUS, Julius SCHNORR VON KAROLSFELD, and Friedrich Wilhelm SCHADOW: they were know as PRE-RAPHAELITES because their creed of beauty was in accordance with the Italian painters before RAPHAEL, and were also known as NAZARENES because of their simple, pious mode of living. Overbeck painted almost entirely in the religious field: his notable works, characterized by deep religious feeling, but lacking in force and harmonious coloring, include *Adoration of the Magi; Triumph of Religion in the Arts; The Selling of Joseph; The Seven Lean Years; Christ Blessing Little Children;* five frescoes representing TASSO'S *Jerusalem Delivered; Christ in the Garden; Christ's Entry into Jerusalem.*

Overman, Lynn (1887-1943), American stage and screen actor who ran away from college in order to join a Mississippi River showboat troupe, and also appeared in vaudeville and with stock companies before making his New York debut in 1916 in *Fair and Warmer.* He appeared in many stage comedies before entering the films in 1934 in *Little Miss Marker* followed by *The Charm School; Poppy; Jungle Princess; Union Pacific; Safari; There's Magic in Music; Reap the Wild Wind; Roxie Hart; Dixie,* and other important screen productions.

Overton, Grant Martin (1887-1930), American novelist and literary critic educated at Princeton University who worked as a reporter, and editor of the book review column on the New York *Sun:* his novels and critical works include *The Women Who Make Our Novels* (1918); *Why Authors Go Wrong; When Winter Comes to Main Street; American Nights Entertainment; The Thousand and First Night.*

Overture, in music the instrumental prelude to an opera or oratorio: also the title of an independent composition for orchestra which may or may not have a descriptive title, and is called a *concert overture.* In early Italian opera the short instrumental prelude was called a *sinfonia:* MONTEVERDI probably composed the shortest known prelude—nine measures repeated three times—to his opera, *Orfeo.* LULLY developed the three-part, contrasting form overture, but the modern operatic overture was first worked on by Christoph Willibald von GLUCK in his prelude to *Iphigenia in Aulis:* it is a standard concert work as revised by Richard WAGNER. MOZART improved and strengthened the overture in operas such as *Don Giovanni;* CHERUBINI and ROSSINI heightened the dramatic effect by using an extended *crescendo;* BEETHOVEN exalted the form in his four overtures for *Fidelio* and in concert overtures such as *Coriolanus* and *Egmont;* BERLIOZ introduced novel orchestral effects, and Richard WAGNER conceived the most highly developed form of dramatic overture in his prelude to *Tannhäuser.*

Ovid real name **Publius Ovidius Naso** (43 B.C.-17 A.D.), Roman poet who was one of the distinguished literary figures of the Augustan age who was exiled, for reasons not clear, to Tomi on the Euxine River in Moesia about 7 A.D. His works include the *Metamorphoses,* a narrative poem in 11,000 HEXAMETERS which recounts legends involving miraculous transformations of persons and objects; *Letters from Heroines,* presumably written by women to their husbands or lovers; *Art of Love; Fasti (Calendar); Tristia (Sorrows),* poems written while in exile.

Owen, Reginald (1887-), English stage and screen actor who made his debut in 1905 at London in Shakespeare's *The Tempest,* appearing later in many plays before entering the films in 1929: among the numerous pictures in which he played important roles are *The Letter; A Study in Scarlet; Queen Christina; Nana; The House of Rothschild; Madame Dubarry; Of Human Bondage; The Good Fairy; Anna Karenina; A Tale of Two Cities; Rose Marie; The Great Ziegfeld; A Christmas Carol; Florian; Mrs. Miniver.*

Oxenham, John (c.1850-1941), English novelist and poet; real name William Arthur Dunkerley: he was educated at Victoria University, and traveled in Europe, Canada, the United States and East Africa. His more than forty novels include *Bees in Amber* (1913) which sold more than 280,000 copies; several small books of verse issued during World War I sold in excess of a million copies, and his *Hymn for the Men at the Front* resulted in the sale of more than 8,000,000 copies.

Oxford, an ancient English town situated on the Thames River fifty-two miles from London: it is famous as the location of Oxford University, the oldest educational institution of its kind in England, having been founded by the Bishop of Lincoln in 1241, and chartered by Queen ELIZABETH in 1570.

P

Paal, Lazlo (1846-1879), Hungarian painter who studied in Vienna, Munich, and Düsseldorf: he became a member of the BARBIZON SCHOOL and a disciple of Théodore ROUSSEAU. He specialized in forest scenes such as *Woods at Fontainebleau,* revealing exceptional skill in painting bursts of light through foliage.

Pacheco, Francisco (1571-1654), Spanish painter and historian of art who was a pupil of Luis Fernandez, and visited Toledo and Madrid before opening an academy in Seville where Alonso Cano and Velasquez were his pupils. His most notable paintings are *The Last Judgment; Life of St. Peter Nolasco; St. Sebastian; Immaculate Virgin:* he also wrote a treatise, *The Art of Painting* (1649), valuable because of its information on matters connected with Spanish art.

Pachmann, Vladimir de (1848-1943), Russian pianist who studied with his father and with Joseph Dachs at the Vienna Conservatory. After much success on his first tour of Russia in 1869, he retired for eight years of further study, again appearing in 1877. He toured Europe and England, making his first visit to America in 1891, returning many times and making his last tour in 1924-25. He was extraordinarily successful in interpreting the smaller works of Frédéric CHOPIN, but lacked breadth of tone and imagination for compositions of greater calibre.

Pacific 231 (Honegger), a symphonic movement for orchestra composed by Arthur HONEGGER and first performed at the "Concerts Koussevitzky" at Paris in 1921 with Sergei Koussevitzky conducting. It was conceived after witnessing the performance of a monster railway steam-engine, and Honegger's description indicates that it is more than a musical joke: "on a sort of rhythmic pedal sustained by the violins is built the impressive images of an intelligent monster, a joyous giant." There is a Victor recording directed by Pierre Coppola.

Pacini, Giovanni (1796-1867), Italian composer who wrote more than 80 operas between 1812 and 1867: several were successful during his period, but only one, *Saffo* (1840) is still produced in Italy. He established a music school with a private theatre, and also found the time to write oratorios, cantatas, masses, a *Dante* symphony, chamber music, and songs. His brother, **Emilio Pacini** (1810-1898), was a successful librettist: among his librettos is that for Giuseppe VERDI's *Il Trovatore.*

Paderewski, Ignace Jan (1860-1941), Polish pianist and composer who studied at the Warsaw Conservatory, and became teacher of the piano there in 1878. The Polish actress, Helena MODJESKA, provided him with the funds to study at the Vienna Conservatory, and his debut was made at Paris in 1888: after further study with Theodor LESCHETIZKY, he made a second debut in 1889 at Vienna with immense success, followed by appearances at London in 1890 and at New York in 1891. Later he toured Europe, North and South America, South Africa, and Australia many times with unvarying success. From 1919 to 1920 he was president of the Polish Republic after World War I, and after the invasion of Poland at the beginning of World War II he became president in 1940 of the Polish Government in Exile. His compositions included the opera, *Manru;* a symphony; a concerto, and many pieces for piano including the popular *Minuet in G:* he also appeared in the film, *The Moonlight Sonata,* in 1938.

Paean, in Greek mythology the name of the physician of the gods: it is not certain whether Paean was a separate deity or another name for APOLLO. Later the meaning of the word was broadened to include a "hymn" or song of praise in connection with fortune or misfortune. The most famous paeans were written by BACCHYLIDES and PINDAR.

Paeonius, Greek sculptor of the 5th century B.C.: PAUSANIAS credits him with the eastern pediment of the temple of ZEUS at OLYMPIA. It is a marble statue of *Victory,* and bears an inscription on its base which names Paeonius as the sculptor. Modern archaeologists do not agree as to the truth of Pausanias' statement because there is a discrepancy in dates.

Pagani, Gregorio (1558-1605), Italian painter who studied with his father, and with Santo di Titi, but was also influenced by Lodovici CIGOLI: his notable works include *Finding of the Cross; Madonna with Saints; Tobias Restoring His Father's Sight.*

Paganini, Niccolò (1782-1840), Italian violinist and composer who made his debut at eleven: after considerable concertizing he studied for a year in 1804, and from 1805 to 1835 toured Europe and Great Britain with enormous success. His abilities lay entirely along technical lines, but there is no doubt that he possessed the greatest technique ever displayed by a violinist. His works include two concertos and the celebrated *Twenty-four Caprices for Violin Solo* in addition to many enormously difficult solo pieces. The violin he played on, a Joseph GUANERIUS was presented to the city of Genoa, his birthplace.

Paganini, a fantastic ballet in three scenes: libretto by Sergei RACHMANINOFF and Michel FOKINE; choreography by Michel Fokine; music by Sergei Rachmaninoff; first produced in 1939 at Covent Garden, London. The plot is based on the fantastic legend that Nicolò PAGANINI, the great violin virtuoso, was in league with the Devil who guided his bow on the concert stage. The music is RACHMANINOFF's *Rhapsody on a Theme by Paganini.*

Page, Ruth, contemporary American dancer and choreographer who studied with Ivan Oustine, balletmaster of the PAVLOWA Company, and made her debut on tour with the troupe: she appeared later with Adolf BOHN, the RAVINIA Opera Company, the METROPOLITAN OPERA COMPANY, and the CHICAGO OPERA COMPANY. Her successful choreographical works include *The Sun Worshippers; La Valse; Iberian Monotone; Hear Ye! Hear Ye!; Americans in Paris; American Pattern.*

Page, Thomas Nelson (1853-1922), American novelist biographer, and diplomat who was ambassador to Italy from 1913 to 1919: his works include *In Ole Virginia* (1887); *The Old South; The Old Gentleman of the Black Stock; Gordon Keith; Robert E. Lee, Man and Soldier:* also many dialect stories of which "Marse Chan" is best-known.

Page, William (1811-1885), American painter who studied at the National Academy, and also lived in Rome and Florence: his notable paintings include *Holy Family; Venus; Infant Bacchus; Farragut at the Battle of Mobile; Ruth and Naomi; Flight into Egypt.* He also painted many portraits: among his sitters were John Quincy Adams, Robert BROWNING, Charlotte CUSHMAN, and General Ulysses S. Grant.

Pageant, in drama the name of a spectacle— usually allegorical—presented in the open air: the Coventry pageant has been given in England, picturing the ride of Lady GODIVA, since 1678. A pageant on the three-hundredth anniversary of SHAKESPEARE's death was given at STRATFORD-ON-AVON in 1916: Percy MACKAYE's pageant, *Caliban,* was presented at New York during the same year.

Paget, Violet (1856-1935), English novelist and essayist on aesthetics and art, born in France, who was educated in Europe and spent most of her life in Italy. Among her forty works are *Studies of the Eighteenth Century in Italy* (1880); *Rennaissance Fancies and Studies; Euphorion; The Beautiful; Music and Its Lovers:* also the puppet play *The Prince of the Hundred Soups,* and two novels entitled *Ottilie* and *Miss Brown.* She wrote under the pen name "Vernon Lee."

Pagliacci, I, grand opera in a Prologue and two acts: libretto and music by Ruggiero LEONCAVALLO; first performed at Milan in 1892, and at the Metropolitan Opera House, New York, in 1893. The plot concerns itself with the jealousy of Canio, head of a company of strolling actors, of his wife, Nedda. He is led by Tonio, a humpbacked clown, who seeks revenge on Nedda because she has repulsed his advances, to a tryst between Nedda and Silvio, her lover. The latter escapes without Canio learning his identity, but Tonio bids Canio bide his time because the lover will return to see the performance later in the day. During the performance, the maddened Canio kills Nedda, and also Silvio when he springs on the stage to help her. There are Victor and Columbia complete recordings, and also many separate records of the *Prologue,* the tenor aria, *Vesti la giubba,* and Nedda's *Ballatella.*

Pagnol, Marcel (1895-), French dramatist who was first a schoolmaster and later a professor of the English language in French schools: his plays include *The Merchants of Glory* (1925) with Paul Nivoix; *Jazz; Topaze* which was successful both as a play and as a film; *Marius; Fanny; Phaeton.* He has also written and produced several films including *Harvest* and *The Baker's Wife.*

Pagoda, a religious monument in India and the Far East which is usually built in the form of a tower, forms a part of a temple, and frequently shelters a RELIQUARY. In India the architecture is of the pyramidal type, and in China octagonal in plan and up to fifteen stories in height. In Japan the pagoda is square and five stories high with a projecting roof for each story.

Paine, Albert Bigelow (1861-1937), American author and editor who made several unfortunate ventures into the publishing field before his first novel, *The Mystery of Evelin Delorme* (1894) was published. In addition to becoming associate editor of *St. Nicholas Magazine* (1899-1909) he wrote a biography of Mark TWAIN who was his friend; a biography, *Joan of Arc—Maid of France; Boy's Life of Mark Twain;* a life of Thomas NAST, and many popular stories for children.

Paine, John Knowles (1839-1906), American composer, organist, and teacher who studied at the Berlin Hochschule: in 1862 he became teacher of music at Harvard University, and in 1875 occupied the newly created chair of music there until his death. His works include symphonies; symphonic poems; an opera, *Azara;* an oratorio, *St. Peter;* chamber music; choral works; piano pieces and songs. Among his pupils were John

Alden CARPENTER, Arthur FOOTE, Edward Burlingame HILL, Frederick S. CONVERSE, Henry T. FINCK, Daniel Gregory MASON and Albert E. WIER.

Paine, Ralph Delahaye (1871-1925), American war correspondent and author of stories for boys who was educated at Yale, and acted as reporter in the Boxer Rebellion in China, the Cuban Revolution, the Spanish-American War and World War I. His works include *The Praying Skipper and Other Stories* (1906); *The Wrecking Master; The Old Merchant Marine; The Corsair in the War Zone: Four Bells; In Zanzibar.*

Painting, in art the laying of color on a surface resulting in the representation of figures, scenery, or objects separately or in combination. The earliest of such representations were made by primitive races such as the Australians, Eskimos, Bushmen of South Africa, and the Palaeolithic cave dwellers in France who made many CAVE PAINTINGS of animals. In Egypt and Bablylonia art first manifested itself in graphic delineations of ordinary objects and a conventionalized representation of the human figure in profile: wall painting in prehistoric Greece was practiced at Tiryns where the celebrated figure of a bull was discovered, and also at Crete. In ancient Greece and Italy painting began on vases starting with mere outlines, and later outlines filled in with flat tints: mural paintings began with POLYGNOTUS who reveals little knowledge of foreshortening, nor was this detail apparently ever mastered in Greek art. The early Christian and medieval painters worked at wall paintings in the CATACOMBS, the illustration of books, and mosaic pictures on the walls of churches: about 1350 the German and Flemish painters began the painting of landscapes; the Gothic movement manifested itself in France, and painting took on new life in Italy. The beginning of the 15th century in Italy marks the most important epoch in the entire history of painting: MASACCIO is regarded as the father of modern painting, especially in his one great work, *Tribute Money,* in which he reveals a distinct advance over GIOTTO. From this point on the history of painting is recorded in the works of more than a thousand distinguished Italian, French, German, Spanish, English, Scandinavian, Russian, and American painters whose names and accomplishments are duly recorded in this volume.

Paisiello, Giovanni (1740-1816), Italian composer who studied at a Jesuit school, and at the Naples Conservatory with Francesco DURANTE. A humorous intermezzo performed in 1763 disclosed his abilities as a composer of comic opera, and his first work, *La Pupilla,* was successfully produced in 1764. It was followed by fifty operas of like character in twelve years of which *La Serva padrona* (1769) still holds the stage, and *The Barber of Seville* (1782) was a popular favorite until Gioacchino ROSSINI's opera with the same title supplanted it in 1816.

Pajou, Augustin (1730-1809), French sculptor who studied with Jean Baptiste LEMOYNE and worked in Rome for three years: his notable sculptures include *Pluto Holding the Chained*

Cerberus; Bacchante; Psyche, and decorative pieces executed for the foyer of the Opéra at VERSAILLES. There is also a fine portrait bust of Mme. DU BARRY in the LOUVRE.

Pakington, Humphrey (1888-), English architect and novelist who served as a Navy officer in both World War I and World War II: his works include *Four in Family* (1931); *The Roving Eye; The Eligible Bachelor; English Villages and Hamlets; Family Album; Our Aunt Auda.*

Palace, in architecture the name given by Augustus (Octavian) to his residence on the PALATINE HILL, and later applied to the homes of sovereigns, and also to public buildings. Palaces were built by Egyptian kings near temples, and by many Roman emperors on the Palatine Hill: that of Septimus Severus occupied an area of one million square feet. In Italy, France, and England, palaces were constructed for the popes, cardinals, bishops, high-ranking royalty and political personalities.

Palace of the Popes (Avignon), a combined fortress and palace built by the popes for their safety in time of war and their comfort in periods of peace. It was an immense building well fortified begun by Pope John XXII, but destroyed and completely reconstructed by his successor, Benedict XII. The outside walls were thick and rough, but the rooms were beautifully decorated with paintings and sculptures. As an extra precaution, the town of Avignon was encircled with a series of ramparts and watch towers.

Palacio Valdés, Armando (1853-1938), Spanish novelist and literary critic: among his translated works are *The Fourth Estate; The Grandee; The Joy of Captain Ribot; Tristan.* He also wrote a volume on the orators of classical Athens, and another on Spanish novelists.

Palatine Hill (Rome), one of the most important of the seven hills of ancient Rome: Octavian (Augustus), the first Roman emperor, built his palace there, and the temple of Apollo was erected in 28 B.C. It bordered on the FORUM, and was also a seat for both imperial and private residences.

Palestrina, Giovanni Pierluigi da (1525-1594), Italian composer whose real name was Giovanni Pierluigi, the added "Palestrina" being the name of the town near Rome in which he was born. From 1532 to 1544 he was a chorister in various churches, and later became a member of the Pontifical Choir at the Vatican. His compositions, regarded as the greatest ever written for the Roman Catholic church service, include nearly 100 masses as well as motets, hymns, offertories, lamentations, litanies, sacred and secular madrigals.

Palette, in painting the thin tablet made of wood or porcelain on which a painter places his colors: the *palette-knife* is used to arrange the colors on the palette, and also to place masses of color on the canvas.

Palgrave, Francis Turner, (1824-1897), English poet, art critic, and editor of *The Golden Treas-ury of English Lyrics; Sonnets and Songs of Shakespeare; The Treasury of Sacred Song.* He was the son of the historian, Sir Francis Palgrave (1788-1861), and professor of poetry at Oxford from 1885 to 1895: his poetical works include *Idylls and Songs* (1854) and *Visions in England.*

Palissy, Bernard (c.1510-c.1589), French potter who originated a white enamel, and produced a glazed pottery known as *Palissy ware* which has now become a collector's item. He was appointed royal potter by Catherine de' Medici, and his discoveries in chemistry and mineralogy were of genuine importance.

Palladio, Andrea (1518-1580), Italian architect who studied the works of VITRUVIUS: his name is derived from Pallas, one of the names of ATHENA. He is considered the founder of modern architecture, and the most famous architect of the Italian Renaissance. Among his greatest creations were the *Basilica of Vicenza; the Palace of Giulio Porto* at Vicenza, the *Villa Capra* at Vicenza, the *Teatro Olympico* at Vicenza, and the *Church of San Giorgio Maggiore* at Venice.

Palladium, in Greek mythology a wooden image of Pallas Athene which was regarded as a guarantee of safety for the city of TROY during the Trojan War: it was carried off by ODYSSEUS and DIOMEDES, and shortly after the Greeks were able to capture the city.

Pallas Athene, see **Athena.**

Pallette, Eugene (1889-), American stage and screen actor who appeared with stock companies before entering the films: among the numerous pictures in which he has been given important comedy roles are *Fair and Warmer; The Three Musketeers* with Douglas FAIRBANKS; *The Virginian; Huckleberry Finn; Shanghai Express; Storm at Daybreak; The Ghost Goes West; My Man Godfrey; Topper; One Hundred Men and a Girl; Mr. Smith Goes to Washington; The Mark of Zorro; The Lady Eve.*

Palma, Jacopo, also known as **Palma Vecchio** (c.1480-1528), Italian painter who studied with Titian at the same time as Lorenzo LOTTO: his notable works include *St. Peter between Six Saints; St. Barbara; Adoration of the Magi; Meeting of Jacob and Rachael; Adoration of the Shepherds; Lucretia; Christ and the Adulteress.* His grandnephew, **Jacopo Palma** (1544-1628), known as The Younger, was an imitator of TITIAN who would have been a great artist if his work had not been marred by careless execution: his works include *The Last Judgment* in the hall of the Doges' Palace at Venice; *St. Catherine Rescued from the Wheel; Madonna with Saints; Crucifixion of St. Andrew; Perseus and Andromeda.*

Palmer, Albert M. (1840-1905), American theatrical manager who directed and produced plays at the Union Square Theatre, New York, from 1872 to 1883 which introduced many young dramatists to success such as Augustus THOMAS, Steele MACKAYE, and William GILLETTE: also many actors including Richard MANSFIELD and Clara

Morris advanced toward stardom in his stock company.

Palmer, Erastus Dow (1817-1904), American sculptor who started as a carver of portraits in cameo: his works include *White Captive; Infant Ceres; Peace in Bondage; Angel at the Sepulchre; The Indian Maid:* also many portrait busts of Washington Irving and other distinguished Americans. His son, **Walter Launt Palmer** (1854-1932), was a distinguished painter who studied with Carolus-Duran, and created remarkable winter scenes such as *End of a Winter's Day* and *Oaks in Winter.*

Palmer, Samuel (1805-1881), English painter mainly self-taught, but greatly influenced by William Blake: his notable works include *Skylark; Bright Cloud; The Winding Stream; Going Home; Murmuring Waters; Sunday Evening in Old England; The Sleeping Shepherd.* He also translated and illustrated the *Eclogues* of Vergil.

Palmgren, Selim (1878-), Finnish pianist and composer who studied at the Helsingfors Conservatory and with Ferruccio Busoni, later becoming professor of piano and composition at the Eastman Conservatory of Music, Rochester, N. Y. His compositions include two operas; four piano concertos, orchestral works, and numerous piano pieces.

Palomino de Castro y Velasco, Acislo Antonio (1653-1726), Spanish painter and writer on art: his paintings are of minor importance, but his history of art in Spain, *El Museo pictórico y escala óptica* (1715-24), contains a vast amount of biographical information regarding Spanish artists which has earned him the appellation of the "Spanish Vasari."

Pan, in Greek mythology a son of either Hermes or Zeus, and the god of shepherds, flocks, and forests. He is pictured with horns, a goat's beard and feet, and a tail: he invented the shepherd's pipe, lived in caves and sported with the mountain nymphs.

Pandean Pipe, a simple wind instrument also known as *panpipe* or *syrinx:* it consists of a set of graduated reeds or tubes fastened together in a row, and blown by the mouth. It has been identified with the *ugab* mentioned in the Bible, and was known to the Greeks, Chinese, and Peruvians. The principle on which it is constructed is the same as that of the organ.

Pandora, in Greek mythology a woman who was created by Hephaestus and sent to earth by Zeus: she opened a box which she was told not to open, and out of it came all man's cares and diseases.

Panel, in architecture the framed compartment within the stiles and rails of a door: the meaning was finally extended to include walls, ceilings, and wainscoting. Panels may be deeply recessed, and heavily decorated with carvings or moldings.

Panizza, Ettore (1875-), Italian conductor and composer born at Buenos Aires who studied at the Verdi Conservatory in Milan, and made his debut as an opera conductor in 1899, later directing at Covent Garden, London; La Scala; Milan, and the Metropolitan Opera House, New York. He has composed several operas: also songs and piano pieces.

Pann, Anton (1797-1854), Rumanian author of romantic and secular folk literature; he edited the first collection of Rumanian folk songs, *The Hospital of Love* (1850-53); also a collection of proverbs in the form of tales illustrating each saying; a collection of Christmas carols; an anthology of Rumanian tales, proverbs, and songs.

Panorama, a painting on canvas fixed on a circular wall without any break in its continuity: the spectators stand in partial darkness on a raised platform to view it, and the illusion is considerably increased by effective lighting. Richard Barker exhibited a panorama of the city of Edinburgh in 1788: since that time panoramas of the Napoleonic and Franco-Prussian Wars have been shown in Europe. At the end of the 19th century a remarkable panorama, *Battle of Gettysburg,* was exhibited in the United States.

Pantaloon, one of the stock characters in the Italian commedia dell'arte: he represented a silly Venetian merchant wearing spectacles and slippers, capable of meddling in vice and politics.

Pantheon, in Greek architecture the name of a temple dedicated to all the gods: in modern days the name of any building in which the bodies of famous men are buried, or used as the location for memorials or monuments. Among the famous buildings of this kind are the Pantheon built at Rome by Agrippa in 27 B.C.; the Panthéon at Paris built by Jacques Soufflot in 1764 which was first a church, and now the mausoleum for Voltaire, Rousseau, and Hugo. Westminster Abbey at London is sometimes called the "British Pantheon" because so many noted men are buried within its walls.

Pantomime, a form of drama in which facial expression, gestures, and movements on the stage replace the spoken word: it is said to have originated in Egypt, and to have found its way into the early Roman theatre. The most distinguished form at the present day is the Christmas pantomime in England which is actually a dramatic spectacle founded on some fairy tale or legend, and accompanied by an elaborate ballet.

Panzini, Alfredo (1863-1939), Italian novelist and essayist educated at the University of Bologna under Giosuè Carducci: his works include *Libro dei Morti* (Book of the Dead) published in 1890; about thirty novels such as *Il Bacio di Lesbia* (The Kiss of Lesbia); *Modern Dictionary; Wanted: A Wife.*

Papi, Gennaro (1886-1941), Italian conductor who studied at the San Pietro a Majello Conservatory in Naples, and made his debut as a conductor there in 1905: in 1911 he became assistant conductor at Covent Garden, London, and in 1913 occupied the same post at the Metropolitan Opera House, New York, becoming full conductor in 1916. He also directed the Chicago, Ravinia, St. Louis, and San Francisco Opera Companies.

Papillons, a romantic ballet in one act: choreography by Michel FOKINE; music by Robert SCHUMANN; first produced at St. Petersburg in 1912. The story is simple: Pierrot finds himself on a beautiful terrace on carnival night; he pursues some beautiful ladies and captures one of them dressed as a butterfly. She apparently dies in his arms, but later he is amazed to see her transformed into a beautiful young lady.

Papini, Giovanni (1881-), Italian critic and essayist educated at the University of Florence who became editor of several magazines, and dabbled in anarchism and atheism before his conversion to the Roman Catholic faith. His works include *The Failure* (1913); *Life of Christ* which was a great success; *Laborers in the Vineyard; Dante Living.*

Papyrus, the writing material used in ancient Egypt and other Eastern countries before the introduction of paper in the 8th century. It was made from the water reed: the small sheets were joined together in any desired length so that the manuscripts of books could be rolled up for storage. There are collections of papyri at Cairo, London, and in many American and European institutions of learning.

Paradise Lost (Milton), an epic poem by John MILTON: it is written in blank verse and relates the story of Adam and Eve: their temptation and their expulsion from Eden. The sequel, a second poem in blank verse entitled *Paradise Regained,* describes the temptations that befell Christ in the wilderness.

Paraphrase, in music the rearrangement of an instrumental or vocal composition for some other instrument or voice than that for which it was originally written: the transcription is usually extended with variations or other structural changes.

Parcae, see **Fates, The.**

Parchment, a writing material prepared from the skins of sheep, goats, calves, and other animals: the process involves drying and stretching without tanning. The best grade of parchment, prepared from calfskin, was known as vellum: until the invention of paper in the 8th century, parchment and PAPYRUS were the materials on which the wisdom of the ages was recorded.

Pareja, Juan de (1606-1670), Spanish painter also known as *El Esclavo* because he worked as a slave for VELASQUEZ, being employed in color-grinding and other services at the great painter's studio. He studied secretly at night, and finally became a distinguished artist: his works include *Calling of St. Matthew; Baptism of Christ; Capuchin Monk; St. John the Evangelist; Orontius and the Madonna.*

Parepa-Rosa, Euphrosyne (1836-1874), Scottish dramatic soprano who was trained by her mother, making her debut in 1852 at Malta, and after singing in European opera houses, her debut in 1857 at London in Bellini's *I Puritani*. She became a popular favorite, and toured the United States in 1865, returning in 1871 and 1873.

Paris, in Greek mythology the name of a Trojan prince who was the son of PRIAM and Hecuba. He caused the dispute over the APPLE OF DISCORD by selecting APHRODITE as the winner in a beauty contest with HERA and ATHENA, and he started the TROJAN WAR by eloping with HELEN: he was killed during the conflict.

Paris (France), a city in which architecture of all periods is well represented in religious edifices such as NOTRE DAME, St. Eustache, St. Sulpice, the Madeleine, St. Vincent de Paul, Ste Clotilde, and La Trinité. The civic buildings of note include the LOUVRE; the Palais de Justice; the Hôtel des Invalides; the Panthéon; the Palais Royal; the Palace of the Luxembourg; the Palais de l'Élysée; the Bibliothèque Nationale; the Bourse; the Opéra; the Cluny Museum; the Carnavelet Museum, and many other buildings of all periods.

Paris Conservatory of Music, an institution at Paris, France, founded in 1795 which brought the École Royale de Chant and the Institut National de Musique under one roof: among the distinguished directors were Luigi CHERUBINI, Daniel AUBER, Ambroise THOMAS, Théodore DUBOIS, Gabriel FAURE, and Henri RABAUD.

Paris Salon, the name by which the annual exhibition of the Société des Artistes français (Society of French Artists) is known: it has been held annually since 1872 in May and June, and is open to artists of all nationalities. The works are examined by a jury of experts selected by the exhibitors, and prizes, including the coveted *Prix de Rome,* are awarded. Because of dissension in 1889, another organization, Société Nationale des Beaux-Arts, established a separate salon.

Parker, Dorothy (1893-), American humorist in both poetry and prose who acted as dramatic critic on *Vanity Fair* and book critic on the *New Yorker:* her works include *Enough Rope* (1927); *Sunset Gun; Death and Taxes; Not So Deep as a Well; Laments for the Living; Here Lies; Collected Stories.*

Parker, Sir Gilbert (1862-1932), Canadian novelist whose full name was Horatio Gilbert Parker: he was educated at Trinity College, Toronto, where he became lecturer in English in 1883. After editing a newspaper in Sydney, Australia, and writing some plays in London, he began his literary career: his works include *Pierre and His People* (1892); *The Seats of the Mighty; The Right of Way; The Weavers; The Judgment House; The World for Sale; The Promised Land; A History of Old Quebec.*

Parker, Horatio William (1863-1919), American composer who studied with George W. CHADWICK and Josef RHEINBERGER, and in 1894 became head of the music department at Yale University. His notable compositions include the operas *Mona* and *Fairyland;* the oratorios *The Legend of St. Christopher* and *Hora Novissima;* orchestral works; chamber music and choruses.

Parker, Jean, contemporary American screen actress who has appeared in numerous films including *Storm at Daybreak; Rasputin and the Empress; Lady for a Day; Little Women; Sequoia; Caravan; The Ghost Goes West; The Barrier; Beyond Tomorrow; Power Dive; Torpedo Boat.*

Parker, Lottie Blair (1858?-1937), American actress, author and dramatist who played with Madame Franziska JANAUSCHEK and Laurence Barrett: her notable plays include *Red Roses* produced in London; *Way Down East,* her greatest success as produced by Denman THOMPSON; *The Redemption of David Corson,* dramatized from the novel by Charles Frederick Goss.

Parker, Louis Napoleon (1852-), English dramatist and composer who was trained at the Royal Academy of Music, London, and became director of music at the Sherborne School: his works include *A Buried Talent* (1890), written for Mrs. Patrick CAMPBELL; *Rosemary,* for Maude ADAMS and John DREW; *Pomander Walk; Our Nell; The Vagabond King; Drake; Joseph and His Brethren; Disraeli:* he also translated Edmond ROSTAND'S *Cyrano, L'Aiglon,* and *Chantecler,* and composed the music for many pageants in English towns.

Parmigiano or **Parmigianino** (1504-1540), Italian painter whose real name was Francesco Maria Mazzola or Mazzuoli: he was influenced by both Correggio and Raphael. His notable works include *Vision of St. Jerome; Madonna and Child with St. Margaret and Other Saints; St. Catherine; Cupid Making a Bow;* a portrait of *Amerigo Vespucci* after whom America is named; *Madonna del collo lungo; Christ Preaching to the Multitude.*

Parnassus, a mountain which was sacred to the ancient Greeks as the abode of Apollo, Dionysus, and the Muses: the Delphian Oracle was located at Delphi near its base, and the Pythian Games were held on its slope. The name **Parnassians** was given to a 19th century group of French poets who sought to return to classical standards in diction.

Parody, in literature an imitation of a serious work written in similar form and style for the purpose of provoking mirth. One of the oldest examples is the *Battle of the Frogs and Mice* which is supposed to be a travesty of the heroic poem, and to have been written by HOMER. ARISTOPHANES, CERVANTES, SHAKESPEARE, DICKENS, and THACKERAY were all masters of the form.

Paros, an island in the Aegean sea which is practically one enormous block of marble in the shape of a mountain about a half-mile in height. Vast quantities of **Parian Marble,** which is semi-transparent, white in color and beautifully textured, have been mined there: it was used by PRAXITELES and all other great sculptors of the classical period.

Parrhasius, Greek painter who worked at Athens about 400 B.C.: he was a contemporary of ZEUXIS, and appears to have exerted a great influence on painters and ceramic artists. Among his works, none of which is extant, are *Theseus; Demos; Ajax Wrestling with Ulysses; Meleager; Hercules.*

Parrish, Anne (1888-), American novelist educated at private schools, and also trained in painting: her works include *Pocketful of Poses* (1923); *The Perennial Bachelor; All Kneeling; Loads of Love; Golden Wedding; Pray for a Tomorrow.* Her husband was Josiah Titzell, an author who wrote verse under his own name, and novels under the pen name "Frederick Lambeck."

Parrish, Maxfield (1870-1938), American painter and illustrator who studied with Howard Pyle: his works include decorations for hotels and private houses such as the *King Cole* murals now in the St. Regis Hotel, New York City; seventeen panels for the building of the Curtis Publication Company at Philadelphia. Among the books he illustrated are Washington IRVING'S *Knickerbocker History of New York;* Eugene FIELD'S *Poems of Childhood; The Arabian Nights; Mother Goose in Prose;* Edith WHARTON'S *Italian Gardens.*

Parry, Sir Charles Hubert Hastings (1848-1918), English composer and author of works on music who studied with Sir William Sterndale BENNETT and Sir George Alexander Macfarren, succeeding Sir George GROVE as director of the Royal Academy of Music, London. His important works include *Studies of Great Composers* (1886); *The Evolution of the Art of Music; Summary of Musical History; The Music of the 17th Century; Style in Musical Art:* his compositions include orchestral works, chamber music, concertos, and choral music.

Parry, Joseph (1841-1903), Welsh composer who studied at the Royal Academy of Music, London, with Sir William Sterndale BENNETT, and later became professor of music at various Welsh colleges: his works include an opera, *Blodwen;* oratorios, cantatas, orchestra pieces, chamber music; church music and songs.

Parsifal, sacred music drama in three acts: libretto and music by Richard WAGNER; first produced at BAYREUTH in 1882, and at the Metropolitan Opera House, New York, in 1903 in spite of the attempt on the part of Cosima WAGNER to enjoin its production. The drama is conceived on a grandiose scale, and its music, according to great authorities, is the finest of religious character ever written for the stage. There are no complete recordings, but the *Prelude,* GOOD FRIDAY SPELL, and most of Act III are available in Victor recordings.

Parsons, Alfred William (1847-1920), English painter who was largely self-taught, becoming equally successful as a water-colorist and illustrator: his works include *When Nature Painted All Things Gay* and many poetically-titled English river scenes portrayed with careful regard for detail. He also illustrated Oliver Goldsmith's *She Stoops To Conquer,* Millet's *The Danube,* and many articles in *Harper's Magazine.*

Parsons, William Edward (1872-1939), American architect educated at Yale and Columbia

Universities, and at the ECOLE DES BEAUX-ARTS, Paris. In 1905 he became consulting architect for the United States Government in the Philippines, and designed many public and private buildings in Manila, transforming the sites of the old Spanish fortifications of the city into public parks. On his return to the United States in 1914 he prepared plans for municipal improvements in many American cities including Chicago, Buffalo, and St. Paul.

Parthenon, The, a temple dedicated to the goddess ATHENA, and located on the ACROPOLIS at Athens. The building, which is a masterpiece of Greek art, was built by the architects ICTINUS and CALLICRATES while PHIDIAS executed the gold and ivory statue of Athena which stood in the CELLA. It was begun in 447 B.C. and finished in 438 B.C. The frieze surrounding the cella was sculptored by Phidias: part of it, known as the ELGIN MARBLES, was removed to the BRITISH MUSEUM in 1816 after being purchased from the Earl of Elgin.

Partita (It.), the name given in the 17th century to a series of dance tunes played consecutively: the term was later changed to SUITE. The title *Partita* was used by Johann Sebastian BACH, but seldom employed by other composers.

Partridge, Bellamy, contemporary American novelist educated at Hobart College and Union University who practiced law and journalism before beginning a career as a novelist, short story writer, and radio dramatist. He became famous in 1939 through his novel, *Country Lawyer,* a best seller for many months: its sequel, *Big Family,* almost equalled it in popularity.

Partridge, William Ordway (1861-1930), American sculptor and author who was trained in Florence, Rome and Paris: his works include heads of John Greenleaf WHITTIER and Sir Alfred TENNYSON; statues of SHAKESPEARE, Pocahontas, General Ulysses S. Grant, and Thomas JEFFERSON. His treatises on art include *Art for America;* and *The Technique of Sculpture.*

Pas (Fr.), in ballet the name for an infinite variety of steps which may be turned, slid, beaten, or jumped: among them are *pas de bourrée; pas assemblé; pas coupé; pas de chat; pas de cheval; pas de basque; pas de deux; pas allemande; pas marche.*

Pascal, Jean Louis (1837-1920), French architect who studied at the ECOLE DES BEAUX-ARTS, Paris, and at Rome: in 1870 he was appointed inspector of work at the LOUVRE and the TUILERIES. He designed many artistic monuments and memorials including that to President Carnat at Bordeaux; also several châteaux and villas: he also brought to its completion the Bibliothèque Nationale at Paris, and collaborated with M. Gaudet in the magnificent edition of François BLONDEL'S *French Architecture* published by order of the French Government.

Pasdeloup, Jules-Étienne (1819-1887), French pianist and conductor trained at the Paris Conservatory: after teaching the piano for several years he organized an orchestra made up of the pupils of the Paris Conservatory in 1851, and ten years later founded the Concerts Populaires which were enormously successful until 1884. In 1920 they were revived and conducted by Rhené-Baton: in 1934 Albert Wolff became the director.

Pas de Quatre, a ballet performed by command in 1845 before Queen VICTORIA at Her Majesty's Theatre, London: the four greatest ballerinas of the period—TAGLIONI, CERITO, GRISI and GRAHN participated in the performance. This quartet of great dancers, whose appearance together was only possible at the behest of royalty, was advertised on the billboards without giving precedence to any one of them by the simple expedient of arranging the names in a perfect circle. The ballet was revived recently by the BALLET THEATRE.

Passacaglia (It.), an ancient Italian or Spanish dance in 3-4 time; stately in movement and found in the SUITES of the 17th and 18th centuries. It employed a GROUND BASS, the theme of which occasionally appears in higher parts, was usually written in a minor key, and much like the CHACONNE. Johann Sebastian BACH brought the dance to its peak of perfection in his *Passcaglia in C minor* for the organ.

Passage, in music a part of a composition which can be recognized through some individuality in construction when repeated: its length may range from a few measures to several pages.

Passepied (Fr.), a dance said to have originated among the sailors in Brittany, and later performed by street dancers in Paris. It became a movement in the ballet during the LOUIS XIV period, and was also used in classical piano suites: the best-known composition today with this title is the *Passepied* in Léo DELIBES' ballet, *Le Roi s'amuse.*

Passion Music, a musical setting of the text in the Bible descriptive of Christ's sufferings and death, usually presented on Good Friday. It began in the 4th century with a solemn plain-song melody, and the dramatic form was a later development. LUTHER favored Passion Music which gradually became so dramatic that a reaction in the 18th century brought about a return to the Bible narrative. Johann Sebastian BACH'S four Passions are the outstanding sacred musical works of all time.

Passion Play, a form of sacred drama which originated in the Middle Ages, and has continued until the present day in some European countries: the principal places at which they are presented in modern times are Oberammergau in the Bavarian Alps, Rorice in Bohemia, Brixlegg in the Austrian Tyrol, and Union City, N. J. The drama at Oberammergau covers the Passion of Christ from the triumphal entry into Jerusalem until the Resurrection: scenes from the Old Testament are interspersed.

Pasta, Giuditta (1798-1865), Italian dramatic soprano who studied at the Milan Conservatory: after her first operatic debut was a failure she studied again, and made a sensational second debut at Paris in 1822. She possessed a phenomenal range and rare dramatic power: Vincenzo BELLINI wrote *Norma,* and Gaetano DONIZETTI *Anna Bolena* for her. After 1829 her voice deteriorated and, having accumulated a fortune, she sang only occasionally.

Pastel, in painting a method of working with dry pigments which are worked into a paste before application to the canvas: its invention is credited to Johann Alexander Thiele, but this is a matter of dispute because GUIDO RENI worked with colored chalks almost a century before Thiele. Pastel paintings are extremely fragile, and must be carefully protected from dampness: among the many painters famous for their pastels are Rosalba CARRIERA, LA TOUR, CHARDIN, GREUZE, DEGAS, FANTIN-LATOUR, BESNARD, WHISTLER, GLACKENS, and BELLOWS.

Pastor, Tony (1837-1908), American theatrical manager: after beginning his career in 1846 as a minstrel and later as a clown, circus performer, and low comedian, he managed a vaudeville house on the Bowery, New York, in 1865, later building his own theatre on Fourteenth Street. He introduced a form of entertainment which reached its peak later at the music halls of Koster and Bial and WEBER AND FIELDS: many famous players such as Lillian RUSSELL reached the uptown theatres by graduation from "Tony Pastor's."

Pastoral, *(1)* in literature a form of poetry in which the life of shepherds and rustics is pictured according to a set style: THEOCRITUS, DANTE, PETRARCH, BOCCACCIO, SIDNEY, ENCINA, CERVANTES, GOETHE, SPENSER, MARLOWE, MILTON, and POPE were among those who wrote in this form. *(2)* In music any vocal or instrumental work of pastoral character which imitates the simple sounds heard from a shepherd's pipe: the *Pastoral Symphony* in HANDEL'S *Messiah* is an excellent example.

Pastoral Symphony (Beethoven), a work composed by Ludwig van BEETHOVEN in the summer of 1808, and first performed at Vienna during the same year: the program described it as "Recollections of life in the country." Although Beethoven himself wrote: "it is left to the listener to discover the situations for himself," several attempts were made to perform this symphony with scenery, and even with characters who moved about the stage. Beethoven suggested the following program in German: 1. Cheerful impressions on arriving in the country; 2. By the brook; 3. Peasants merrymaking; 4. The storm; 5. The shepherd's hymn. There is a Victor recording by the British Broadcasting Company Orchestra directed by Arturo Toscanini, and a Columbia recording by the Minneapolis Symphony Orchestra under Dimitri Mitropoulos.

Paterae, in architecture the term incorrectly applied to a circular disk on which a rose is carved, the correct name being ROSETTE.

"Pathétique" Sonata (Beethoven), a composition by Ludwig van BEETHOVEN written in 1798: the title is original with the composer, and is intended to interpret the mood of the work. There is a Victor recording by Wilhelm BACHAUS.

"Pathétique" Symphony (Tschaikowsky), an orchestral work by Peter TSCHAIKOWSKY composed in 1893 and first performed during the same year at St. Petersburg, and at New York in 1894 by the New York Symphony Society under Walter DAMROSCH. The symphony had no descriptive title at first, and it was the composer's brother, Modeste Tschaikowsky, who suggested "Pathétique." The latter also states that it was received with only moderate enthusiasm, and had a much better reception when conducted later by Edward Napravnik. There is a Victor recording by the Philadelphia Orchestra directed by Eugene Ormandy, and a Columbia recording by the Paris Conservatory Orchestra under Philippe Gaubert.

Patience, a comic opera in two acts: book by Sir William S. Gilbert, founded on an early "Bab" Ballad called "The Rival Curates"; music by Sir Arthur Sullivan; first produced at London in 1881 with a run of 578 performances, but unsuccessful in New York where it was withdrawn after 22 showings because the audience did not understand that its literary quips constituted a satire on Algernon SWINBURNE and Oscar WILDE. There is a complete Victor recording by the D'Oyly Carte Company.

Patigian, Haig (1876-), American sculptor who was practically self-taught through study of the masters in Italy: his notable works include figures and decorations for the Panama-Pacific Exposition in 1915; *Ancient History* at the Salon des Artistes Français, Paris; the McKinley Monument at Arcata, Calif.; *Guardian Angel;* allegoric figures of *Invention, Imagination, Steam Power, Electrical Power,* etc.: also busts and statues of many prominent Americans.

Patina, in art the term applied to a thin coating which forms on bronze or copper after exposure to dampness in the open air, or after burial in the ground: it is supposed to add greatly to the beauty of the object when the color is the green found on ancient bronzes. The same effect can be produced to a certain extent on new metals by using diluted acids.

Patiner or **Patinir, Joachim de** (c.1487-1524), Flemish painter who studied with Gerard DAVID: his portrait was painted by Albrecht DURER at Antwerp. His works include *Flight into Egypt; Virgin of the Seven Sorrows; Rocky Landscape with St. Jerome and a Lion; Temptation of St. Anthony; Christ Bearing the Cross; Triumph of Love; Christ on the Cross:* he is considered the founder of landscape painting in Flanders because he subordinated his figures to the landscape.

Paton, Sir Joseph Noel (1821-1901), Scottish painter who first drew designs for damask fabrics, and later studied at the Royal Academy Schools: his works include *The Spirit of Religion; Christ Bearing the Cross; Reconciliation of Oberon and Titania; Silenus Singing; Faith and Reason;* he also made the CARTOONS for the glass of the great window of Dumfermline Abbey restored by Andrew CARNEGIE in 1884, and was also an excellent sculptor.

Patroclus, in Greek legend, as related in Ho-MER's *Iliad*, the close friend of ACHILLES and one of the heroes in the TROJAN WAR. He was killed by Hector, and Achilles slew Hector, thereby avenging his friend's death.

Pattee, Fred Lewis (1863-), American literary critic educated at Dartmouth College, and abroad at the Universities of Göttingen and Marburg. He became professor of American literature at Pennsylvania State College (1894-1928), and since that time at Rollins College, Florida. His works include *History of American Literature since 1870* (1915); *The Development of the American Short Story; The New American Literature.*

Patti, Adelina (1843-1919), Italian coloratura soprano born in Spain who was taken by her parents to New York as a child: she sang in many concerts at an early age, and after some years of study made her debut in 1859 at New York in Donizetti's *Lucia di Lammermoor* under the stage name "Little Florinda." She appeared in 1861 at London in Bellini's *La Sonnambula*, becoming a formidable rival of Carlotta GRISI, and later appeared at Milan and all other great opera houses in Europe. She sang for nearly thirty years, never appearing after 1882 for less than $5,000 a performance. The secret of her success lay not in the power of her voice, but in its flexibility and marvelous sweetness.

Paul, Elliot Harold (1891-), American novelist who studied for a time at the University of Maine, served in World War I, and after considerable experience as a newspaper correspondent and literary editor went to live in the Balearic Islands, and saw much of the Spanish Revolution. His works include *The Life and Death of a Spanish Town; Fracas in the Foothills; Hugger Mugger in the Louvre; The Last Time I Saw Paris.*

Paul and Virginia, a novel by Bernardin de SAINT-PIERRE published in 1788: the scene is laid in Mauritius, an island in the Indian Ocean, and the story is that of pure young love. Several famous composers including Victor Massé, Rodolphe KREUTZER, Jean François Le Sueur, and Eric SATIE have found inspiration for a grand opera in the simple tale.

Paulding, James Kirke (1779-1860), American novelist who founded the satirical journal, *Salmagundi*, in collaboration with Washington IRVING. His works include *Lay of a Scotch Fiddle* (1813); *The Diverting History of John Bull and Brother Jonathan; The Dutchman's Fireside; John Bull in America; Koningsmarke; The Puritan and His Daughter:* also a widely-read *Life of Washington.*

Pauly, Rosa (1895-), Hungarian dramatic soprano who studied in Vienna and made her debut at the Hamburg Opera House: after singing at Cologne, Berlin, and Vienna she made her debut in 1937 in a concert performance at New York of Strauss' *Elektra*, and her first appearance in 1938 at the Metropolitan Opera House in the same opera, becoming a regular member of the company. She has also appeared at Covent Garden, London, with the San Francisco Opera Company, and in concert tours of the United States and Canada.

Paur, Emil (1855-1932), Austrian conductor and composer who studied at the Vienna Conservatory, and began his career as a conductor at Cassel in 1876: after directing orchestras in several German cities he came to the United States in 1893 to succeed Artur NIKISCH as conductor of the Boston Symphony Orchestra until 1898. He succeeded Anton SEIDL as conductor of the New York Philharmonic-Symphony Society from 1898 to 1902 and also conducted German opera at the Metropolitan Opera House in 1899-1900. From 1904 to 1910 he conducted the Pittsburgh Symphony Orchestra, and also directed the National Conservatory, New York, from 1899 to 1902, succeeding Antonin DVORAK. In 1912 he succeeded Karl MUCK as director at the Royal Opera House in Berlin, but resigned after two months because of differences with the management. His wife, Marie Bürger (1862-1899), was an outstanding pianist.

Pausanius, Greek traveler and geographer who made extensive travels through Greece and the Near East about 174 A.D. to study the ruins of ancient cities: his *Description of Greece* has yielded a vast amount of information regarding the mythology, architecture, and sculpture of important cities including Athens, Mycenae, Olympia and Delphi.

Pausius, Greek painter who worked during the 4th century B.C.: he is said to have introduced the custom of painting ceilings of residences, to have fully understood the art of foreshortening. Pliny credits him with the accurate painting of a great black bull, painting the animal in a dark color standing out against a flat background: he also painted the portrait of Glycera, a flower girl.

Pavan (Pavane, Pavanne, Pavin), an ancient dance probably of Italian or Spanish origin which was more in the form of a processional dance: it was performed slowly and is often found in early 17th century suites.

Pavlowa (Pavlova), Anna, (1882-1931), Russian dancer who studied with Michel FOKINE at the Imperial Ballet School, St. Petersburg, and became *prima ballerina* at the Maryinsky Theatre in 1901. After 1907 she went to England where she remained several years, later touring the world with her own company, and creating tremendous enthusiasm with her partner, Mikhail MORDKIN in the ballet *Le Cygne* (The Swan) written for her by Michel Fokine. She was also greatly admired in *Les Papillons, Les Sylphides*, and *Valse Caprice:* in the history of the ballet she is ranked as one of the greatest ballerinas of all time

Payne, John Howard (1791-1852), American actor, poet, and dramatist who first edited a dramatic magazine, and appeared in 1809 on the stage in John Horne's tragedy, *Douglas:* he went to London in 1813 where he remained for many years. His works include *Brutus, or the Fall of Tarquin* (1818); *Love in Humble Life; Ali Pacha; The Signet Ring; Clari, or The Maid of Milan* (1823), in which his poem, "Home, Sweet Home" was set to music by Sir Henry BISHOP.

Peabody, Josephine Preston (1874-1922), American poet and dramatist educated at Radcliffe College, later becoming instructor in English at Wellesley College. Her plays include *Fortune and Men's Eyes* (1900); *Marlowe; The Wings; The Piper; The Wolf of Gubbio:* her collections of poems comprise *The Wayfarers; The Singing Leaves; New Poems.*

Peabody Institute (Baltimore), an institution combining a conservatory of music, library, and art gallery: it was founded by George Peabody in 1857, but its opening was delayed until 1868 by the Civil War. Instruction is given in all branches of music; there is also a student orchestra, chorus, opera class, and ballet class. In 1898 the American pianist, Harold Randolph (1861-1927), became director: after his death in 1927 he was succeeded by Otto Rudolph Ortmann and in 1943 by Reginald Stewart.

Peale, Charles Willson (1741-1827), American painter who studied with Gustavus Hesselius, John Singleton Copley, and with Benjamin West in London. In 1779 he settled in Philadelphia, and was one of the founders of the Pennsylvania Academy of Fine Arts: his works include fourteen portraits of George Washington; also portraits of Mrs. Washington, Benjamin Franklin, Henry Clay, Robert Morris, John Hancock, and many other notable Americans. His brother, **James Peale** (1749-1831), was also a distinguished painter who executed two portraits of George Washington, and also landscapes and historical works. Charles Willson's eleven children were all named after great painters: three became painters, one of whom, **Rembrandt Peale** (1778-1860) was a distinguished painter who studied with Benjamin West in London, and returned to Philadelphia in 1810. He painted several likenesses of Washington: also *Washington and Marquis de Lafayette* and *The Court of Death* containing twenty-three separate figures.

Pearce, Charles Sprague (1851-1914), American painter who studied and also lived for the greater part of his life in France: his notable works, many of which earned him awards, include *The Beheading of John the Baptist; Toilers of the Sea; Return of the Flock; Meditation; Fantasie; Across the Common.*

Pearl, a calcareous concretion of peculiar lustre produced by certain bivalve mollusks: pearl fishers agree that irregular shells or those in which holes have been bored by parasites are the most likely to yield pearls of real value. They appear in various shapes including round, pear-shaped, button-shaped, or entirely irregular: the colors may be white, cream or pink, and shades of black are valuable because of their scarcity. Pearls are not cut or polished, and are readily injured by acid or fire: they are found in the Far East, the Pacific Islands and South America.

Pearson, Edmund Lester (1880-1937), American librarian, editor, and expert on murder who was educated at Harvard University, and later editor of publications at the New York Public Library. His works on murder include *Studies in Murder* (1924); *Murder at Smutty Nose; Five*

Murders; Instigation of the Devil; More Studies in Murder: he also edited or wrote *The Old Librarian's Almanack; The Librarian at Play; Dime Novels.*

Peccate, Dominique (1810-1874), French maker of bows for the VIOLIN, VIOLA, VIOLONCELLO, and DOUBLE-BASS. He first worked for Jean Baptiste Vuillaume, and later made bows equaling those of Françoise Tourte: they are valued today at from $100.00 to $800.00. His brother, **François Peccate** (1820-1855), was also a fine bow maker, but few of his bows are available.

Peck, George Wilbur (1840-1916), American humorist who was a prominent newspaper editor and publisher, and also creator of the "Bad Boy" character which kept all America laughing from 1883 to 1907. The series of stories started with *Peck's Bad Boy and His Pa* (1883); this was followed by five sequels of similar uproarious character.

Peck, Harry Thurston (1856-1914), American editor, poet, and author educated at Columbia University: his works include *The Adventures of Mabel* (1896); *Greystone and Porphyry; What is Good English?; Hilda and the Wishes; Studies in Several Literatures; The New Baedeker.*

Pedal, a key operated by the foot on a musical instrument: on the ORGAN it is used to produce the low bass notes, and on the standard model of the PIANO there are three pedals which diminish, sustain, and increase the volume of sound.

Pedestal, in architecture the term applied to a square, octagonal or circular support for a statue or vase: it was used in Near East, Roman and Greek architecture, and became of great importance during the Renaissance. The construction is usually in the form of a base, a shaft or column, and a cap.

Pediment, in architecture the triangle GABLE formed by the sloping roof of a building: it was used by the Romans as a decorative termination over a doorway.

Pedrell, Felipe (1841-1922), Spanish composer and musicologist: his compositions, which are little known outside of Spain comprise several operas including *Los Pirineos,* a trilogy with a prologue and three dramas; orchestral works; motets and church music. He also wrote several technical treatises, and was the teacher of Isaac Albeniz, Enrique Granados, and Manuel de Falla.

Peele, George (c.1558-c.1597), English poet and dramatist educated at Oxford: he was the author of plays and pageants including *The Arraignment of Paris* (1584); *The Chronicle History of Edward I; The Battle of Alcazar; The Old Wives' Tale; David and Bethsabe; Sir Clyomon and Sir Clamydes.*

Peerce, Jan (1904-   ), American concert and operatic tenor who made his concert debut at Cleveland in 1935, and his operatic debut in 1938 with the Columbia Opera Company in *Rigoletto.* He has appeared as solo tenor at the Radio City

Music Hall, as soloist with leading American orchestras, and on radio broadcasts.

Peer Gynt, a play by Henrik IBSEN first produced in 1867: its principal character, Peer Gynt is a worthless egoist, related to figures in Scandinavian folk-lore, who commits all manner of cruel acts to others, but is finally redeemed through the faithful love of a young girl, Solveig, whom he has forsaken. Edvard GRIEG was so inspired by the drama that he created incidental music for it which contains some of his finest thoughts: it was first performed at Christiania in 1876, and he arranged two symphonic **Peer Gynt Suites** from the complete score which are extremely popular on concert and radio programs, and are available complete in Victor and Columbia recordings.

Peesemsky, Alexis (1820-1881), Russian novelist whose ancestors belonged to the Russian nobility: he was educated at the University of Moscow, and read the translated works of SCOTT, HUGO, SHAKESPEARE, SCHILLER, GOETHE, ROUSSEAU and George SAND before beginning to write. His first novel, *Boyarstchina,* was banned because of its reflections on the Russian nobility: others include *A Muff* (1850); *A Thousand Souls; A Troubled Sea:* he also wrote a comedy, *A Bitter Fate* which won him an award from the Russian Academy.

Pegasus, in Greek mythology a winged horse born of POSEIDON and MEDUSA: he was the companion of BELLEROPHON, and the spring, Hippocrene, sprang up from the imprint of his hoof. He is also the symbol of poetry.

Peixotto, Ernest Clifford (1869-1940), American painter, author, and illustrator who studied and also lived in Europe for many years. His notable paintings include *The Woman of Rijsoord,* and murals at various banks and clubs in New York. He illustrated many books; among them several of which he was also the author including *A Revolutionary Pilgrimage; Our Hispanic Southwest; Romantic California; Through the French Provinces.*

Peking or **Peiping (China),** a city in China which contains four remarkable examples of Oriental architecture: they include the *Temple of Heaven* built in 1420 to celebrate the ceremonies attendant upon the worship of CONFUCIUS; the *Imperial Palace* consisting of forty-eight enormous palaces surrounded by a fortified wall; the *Tombs of the Ming* where thirteen emperors of the Ming Dynasty (1368-1643) are buried; the *Temple of Confucius* on the altar of which is an ivory tablet bearing the inscription: "Tablet of the Spirit of the very holy Ancestor and Master —Confucius."

Peleus, in Greek mythology the father of ACHILLES and king of the Myrmidons. After taking part in the hunt for the CALYDONIAN BOAR and the expedition of the ARGONAUTS, he married THETIS: ERIS, the goddess of discord, sent the APPLE OF DISCORD to the wedding feast, bringing about a dispute which ended in the TROJAN WAR.

Pelléas and Mélisande, grand opera in five acts: libretto from Maurice MAETERLINCK's play with the same title; music by Claude DEBUSSY; first produced at the OPERA-COMIQUE, Paris, in 1902, at the Manhattan Opera House, New York, in 1908 and at the Metropolitan Opera House, New York, in 1925. The characters in the plot are symbolic of a fairy tale: Golaud, grandson of King Arkël of Allemonde, woos Mélisande and marries her; Mélisande and Pelléas, Golaud's younger brother, gradually develop an unspoken but pure affection for each other while Golaud is away hunting, and Mélisande's loss of her wedding ring only serves to increase her husband's jealousy. He surprises the two; kills Pélleas and wounds Mélisande; she dies and he finally realizes the injustice of his suspicions. There is no complete recording, but a Victor abridged version, and both Columbia and Victor recordings of separate vocal and instrumental numbers. The Maeterlinck play on which the opera is based was produced in 1893.

Pelletier, Wilfred (1895-), Canadian conductor who studied piano with Isidor PHILIPP and theory with Samuel-Rousseau. After becoming assistant conductor at the Metropolitan Opera House in 1917 he was appointed full conductor in 1932. He has also conducted the RAVINIA and SAN FRANCISCO OPERA Companies, and has acted as guest conductor of many major American orchestras as well as director and one of the judges of the METROPOLITAN AUDITIONS OF THE AIR.

Pellico, Silvio (1789-1854), Italian poet and dramatist who was intimate with BYRON and Madame de STAEL and other literary celebrities: his plays include *Laodicea; Francesca da Rimini; Eufemio of Messina; Ester of Engaddi.* While imprisoned by the Austrians for nine years in Milan, he told the story of his incarceration in a narrative translated as *My Prisons (I miei prigioni).*

Pelops, in Greek mythology a son of TANTALUS who fell in love with Hippodamia, and entered a chariot race for her hand: he bribed the opposing charioteer and won, but instead of paying the charioteer, drowned him, and the curse of the latter caused dire misfortune to the house of Pelops. The Peloponnesus was named after him.

Pemberton, Brock (1885-), American theatrical producer educated at the University of Kansas who engaged in dramatic journalism before producing plays with Arthur HOPKINS from 1917 to 1920. Among his notable productions are *Enter Madame* (1920); *Miss Lulu Bett; Six Characters in Search of an Author; Mr. Pitt; The Mask and the Face; The Living Mask; Strictly Dishonorable; Ceiling Zero; Kiss the Boys Goodbye.*

Pen, the modern instrument for writing or drawing lines: the earliest implement for the same purpose was the *stylus,* a pointed needle of metal or other hard material used on wax or waxcovered tablets. The *quill* was first used in the 7th century: metal pens did not appear for general use until about 1850. The **pen drawing** harks back to ancient Greece beginning with the beautifying or illustration of manuscripts after PARCHMENT came into use: many great painters including MICHELANGELO, RAPHAEL, RUBENS and REMBRANDT were masters of the art.

Pencil, the name originally applied to a small, fine-pointed brush used in painting, and later to solid rods of graphite enclosed in wood used for writing or drawing. It probably came into use during the 13th century, and for many years a mine at Borrowdale in Cumberland, England, was the only source of supply for the graphite. **Pencil drawings** are employed for designs in engraving and jewelry, and also for some forms of illustration: many English artists became famous for their work in this field.

Pencz, Georg (c.1500-c.1552), German painter and engraver who visited Italian cities where he studied the works of the great masters, and was greatly influenced by them. His notable paintings include *Adoration of the Magi* and many fine portraits: his etchings include *The Life of Christ; The Six Triumphs of Christ; The Legend of Vergil and the Scornful Lady.* He was ranked among the LITTLE MASTERS.

Pendant, (*1*) in architecture the term applied to a boss or any other form of ornament which is suspended from a ceiling or roof. (*2*) In jewelry a jewel or other decorative object suspended from a brooch, bracelet or chain.

Pendentive, in architecture a term applied to a bridgework placed across a square hall in order to obtain a circular base for a dome.

Penelope, in Greek legend as related by HOMER the wife of ODYSSEUS and mother of TELEMACHUS. When she was besieged by suitors who sought to persuade her that Odysseus would never return she finally agreed to marry the one who could bend the great bow of Odysseus: they all failed, but Odysseus who had returned in the guise of a beggar, easily bent the bow, and then killed all the suitors with its sharp arrows.

Pennell, Joseph (1860-1926), American illustrator, etcher and author who spent most of his life in Europe where he was strongly influenced by James WHISTLER. His notable works include many drawings, etchings and lithographs of landscapes and architectural views to be seen at all American and many European art galleries. Among his publications are *A Canterbury Pilgrimage* (1885); *An Italian Pilgrimage; Our Sentimental Journey through France and Italy; Pen Drawings and Pen Draughtsmen; To Gypsyland; Modern Illustration; The Glory of Greece.* His wife, **Elizabeth Robins Pennell** (1855-1936) was an American author and critic: her works include *The Life of Mary Wollstonecraft; Feasts of Autolycus; French Cathedrals, Monasteries and Abbeys; Our House; London Out of Doors* illustrated by her husband. She collaborated with her husband on *The Life of James McNeil Whistler; The Whistler Journal:* she also wrote a biography, *The Life and Letters of Joseph Pennell.*

Pennsylvania Academy of Fine Arts (Philadelphia), an institution founded at Philadelphia, Pa., in Independence Hall: it was the first art school in America, and now occupies a spacious building in which is housed a collection of more than five hundred paintings including choice works by early and modern American painters; also a fine assembly of French landscapes.

Pentameter, in prosody the name applied to the second and shorter line of classical elegiac verse composed of five feet: it is divided into two equal parts of two and one half feet each, the first being either DACTYLIC or SPONDAIC, and the second dactylic. Geoffrey CHAUCER was the first to make distinctive use of it, and iambic pentameter is the greatest of English METRES.

Pentelicus, a mountain near Athens, Greece famous for its quarries of white marble which in every way compares favorably with that of PAROS: it was used by order of PERICLES for the principal buildings in ATHENS and on the ACROPOLIS which were constructed during his regime.

Peple, Edward Henry (1869-1924), American novelist and dramatist who also worked as a public accountant: his novels and plays include a *Broken Rosary* (1903); *The Prince Chap; Richard the Brazen* with Cyrus Townsend Brady; *The Spitfire; The Littlest Rebel; The Cur and the Coyote; A Pair of Sixes.*

Pepusch, John Christopher (1667-1752), German musician who went to London in 1700 where he played with the Drury Lane Orchestra: in 1710 he founded with others the Academy of Ancient Music. He is famous as having arranged the 69 folk tunes for THE BEGGAR'S OPERA and *Polly,* two ballad operas by John GAY which held the English stage for more than one hundred twenty years: he also wrote several MASQUES.

Pepys, Samuel (1633-1703), English diarist who was connected with British politics from 1660 to 1669 when he retired: his *Diary* was first published (in part) in 1825 after being deciphered from his shorthand method of writing by the Rev. John Smith. The diary covers a period of thirty years, and is a perfect reflection not only of English social life, but of the theatre because he was an inveterate playgoer.

Percier, Charles (1764-1838), French architect who was appointed Government architect, in association with Pierre François Leonard Fontaine, by NAPOLEON I in 1794. The two great architects developed the EMPIRE STYLE to its peak in such buildings as the Paris Opéra, the palaces of the LOUVRE, the Tuileries, and the châteaux at Versailles, Malmaison, and St. Cloud. After 1814 Percier worked alone, conducting a school for students and writing several works on architecture and interior decoration.

Percussion Instruments, that group of musical instruments which produce sounds by being struck: it includes the PIANO, the DULCIMER, all kinds of DRUMS, CYMBALS, BELLS, CASTANETS, GONGS, TRIANGLE, CELESTA, Marimba, XYLOPHONE, and other similar instruments.

Percy, William Alexander (1885-1942), American lawyer and poet educated at Harvard University: his works include *Sappho in Levkas and Other Poems* (1915); *In April Once; Enzio's Kingdom and Other Poems; Lanterns on the Levee,* an autobiography.

Pereda, José (1833-1906), Spanish novelist educated at the Instituto Cántabra of Santander who first engaged in magazine work, and published his *Mountain Scenes* in 1864. Among his successful works are *Pedro Sánchez* and *The Taste of the Earth.*

Perelman, Sidney Joseph (c.1904-), American humorist educated at Brown University who wrote comic pieces for *Judge, College Humor,* and other magazines: his works include a comedy, *The Night Before Christmas* produced in New York, and also a successful motion picture: *Dawn Ginsbergh's Revenge; Parlor, Bedlam and Bath* with Q. T. Reynolds; *Strictly from Hunger; Look Who's Talking!*

Perez Galdos, Benito (1845-1920), Spanish novelist born in the Canary Islands, educated at an English school there: after studying for the bar in Madrid, he turned to journalism and later to novel and play writing. Among his works are *Gloria* (1879); *Dõna Perfecta; Marianela; The Golden Fount; Zaragoza; The Grandfather; The Duchess of San Quentin:* he also wrote two great series of novels under the general title, *National Episodes* in which he pictured 19th century Spain. Many of his plays were produced with great success.

Pergamum or **Pergamon,** a town on the east coast of Asia Minor where many important classical monuments have been discovered through excavations. Inscriptions on the monuments bear the names of PRAXITELES, MYRON, and many others mentioned by PLINY the Elder: among the important discoveries was a great marble altar, forty feet high, called the *Altar of Zeus;* the remains of the frieze are in the Berlin Museum, its subject being the battle of the giants.

Pergolesi, Giovanni Battista (1710-1736), Italian composer of operatic and sacred music who studied with Francesco DURANTE: his most successful dramatic piece was *La Serva padrona,* a comic opera produced in 1733 which became a model for Italian composers. He also wrote a STABAT MATER (1729) which is declared by some critics to be exquisitely beautiful, and by others melodically banal in conception.

Peri, Jacopo (1561-1633), Italian composer who was a member of the distinguished circle of litterateurs and musicians who met at the home of Count Giovanni BARDI: he is credited with having composed the music for the first opera, *Dafne* (1597), the libretto written by Ottavio Rinuccini. Other works of similar character include *Euridice; Ariadne* for which he wrote the RECITATIVES and Claudio MONTEVERDI the ARIAS; *Tetide; Guerra d'Amore.*

Pericles, Athenian statesman who lived from about 495 to 425 B.C. and proved himself one of the greatest rulers of the ancient city: he was a generous patron of the arts, encouraging music, drama, sculpture, architecture and all other manifestations of the beautiful. Among those who aided him in beautifying Athens were ICTINUS, CALLICRATES, and PHIDIAS.

Peristyle, in architecture a series of circular or rectangular columns placed in either one or two rows to enclose the sanctuary of a temple: in Roman residences it was the name of the central courtyard which served as the entrance to the private apartments.

Perkins, Charles Callahan (1823-1886), American art critic and etcher who was one of the founders of the Boston Museum of Fine Arts, and also president of the Boston Art Club: he edited Champlin's *Cyclopedia of Painters and Paintings,* and published *Tuscan Sculptors; Italian Sculptors; Art in Education; Raphael and Michelangelo.*

Perov, Vassily Gregorovitch (1833-1882), Russian painter who eschewed classical and romantic subjects, and devoted himself entirely to either satirical pictures or scenes of Russian country life such as *The Fisherman, The Sportsman at His Meal,* and *The Botanist.* He also painted the portraits of Ivan Turgenev, Feodor Dostoievsky, and other famous men of his day.

Perpendicular Period, in architecture a Gothic style in vogue from the end of the 14th century to the middle of the 16th century in England. Arches were depressed and moldings made angular in order to give the impression of perpendicular or horizontal construction throughout.

Perpetual Motion, see **Moto Perpetuo.**

Perrault, Charles (1628-1703), French poet who wrote more than one hundred biographies of the statesmen, authors, and other notabilities of his period to prove his contention that art and science had reached its climax in his century. He is immortalized by a volume of fairy tales in prose, *Stories of My Mother, the Goose* (1697), which gathered together all the classics such as "Little Red Riding-Hood," "Cinderella," "Bluebeard," etc., and was republished in 1928.

Perrault, Claude (1613-1688), French architect trained as a physician who became anatomist of the Academy of Science: his notable works as architect include the greater part of the LOUVRE as it exists today, especially the east facade known as the *Colonnade:* also the *Observatory* and the *Arch of Triumph* on the Faubourg Saint Antoine. He also spent ten years translating a work by VITRUVIUS, a Roman writer on architecture, entitled *On Architecture* (1673).

Perronneau, Jean Baptiste (1731-1796), French painter regarded as the last great French PASTEL painter of the 18th century: the best known of his works is *Jeune fille du chat* in the LOUVRE.

Perrot, Jules Joseph (1810-1892), French dancer and choreographer who acquired unusual acrobatic ability through touring with a road show in which he played clown and monkey parts.

After studying with Auguste VESTRIS, he made his debut at the Paris Opéra in *Le Rossignol*, and later danced with Marie TAGLIONI and Carlotta GRISI who became his wife and danced with him at L'Opéra, Paris. He created many ballets including *Alma; Ondine; La Esmeralda;* Le PAS DE QUATRE; *Lalla Rookh; The Judgment of Paris; Faust; The Four Seasons.*

Perry, Bliss (1860-   ), American novelist, editor, and critic educated at Williams College who edited the *Atlantic Monthly* for ten years, and later, after substituting for Barrett WENDELL at Harvard University, became professor of English there. His works include *The Broughton House* (1890); *Salem Kittredge and Other Stories; Whittier; A Study of Poetry; Pools and Ripples; The Praise of Polly; And Gladly Teach,* an autobiography.

Perry, Roland Hinton (1870-1941), American sculptor and painter who studied at the ECOLE DES BEAUX-ARTS and at the Académie Julien in Paris: his works include bas-reliefs and the *Fountain of Neptune* at the LIBRARY OF CONGRESS, Washington, D. C.; a statue, *Pennsylvania,* on the dome of the capitol at Harrisburg, Pa.; a group for the New York State Monument at Lookout Mountain, Tenn. His paintings include *The Death of Sigurd* and *The Valkyrie.*

Persephone, in Greek mythology the daughter of ZEUS and DEMETER: she was taken to the underworld by Hades who made her his wife, but Demeter's grief was so great that the gods permitted her return to earth for two-thirds of each year. When she left the earth, the vegetation withered, and when she returned the flowers, vegetables, and fruits came to life. The Romans identified her with *Proserpine.*

Perseus, in Greek mythology a son of ZEUS who proved himself a hero by killing the Gorgon MEDUSA, and rescuing ANDROMEDA, his future wife, from a monster of the sea. His son, Electryon, was the father of Alcmene, the mother of HERCULES.

Persius (34-62 A.D.), Roman satirical poet of noble birth whose real name was Aulus Persius Flaccus. Six of his satires are extant: they show the influence of HORACE and LUCULLUS, and were evidently written for the purpose of exposing the corruption, existent during his short life, in Roman politics and social life: the best translations are by John DRYDEN and John Conington.

Perspective, in art the method of representing objects on a plane surface as they appear to the eye from one fixed point: *linear perspective* is the art of the draftsman and *aerial perspective* is the art of the landscapist or marine painter in portraying distance near and far as well as the horizon.

Pertwee, Roland (1885-   ), English dramatist and novelist who first studied art at the Westminster School of Art, and later acted in the companies of Sir Henry IRVING and Charles HAWTREY, also serving in World War I. His plays include *Seein' Reason* (1913); *Swank; The*

Return of Imry; Early Birds; Heat Wave; Royal Heritage: his novels include *Our Wonderful Selves; The Eagle and the Wren; Four Winds; Lovers Are Losers.*

Perugino (1446-1523), Italian painter whose real name was Pietro Vannucci: he was called "Perugino" because he worked chiefly in Perugia. He studied with VERROCCHIO at the same time as LEONARDO DA VINCI and was also under the influence of MELOZZA DA FORLI. His works include *Crucifixion with St. Christopher and St. Jerome; Assumption; Christ Giving the Keys to St. Peter; Moses in Egypt; Marriage of Joseph and the Virgin; Combat of Love and Chastity; Adoration of the Infant Christ; Madonna and Child.*

Peruzzi, Baldassare (1481-1536), Italian architect, sculptor, and painter who was influenced by PERUGINO: his notable works include the Villa Farnesina and the Massimi Palace at Rome. He also worked on St. Peter's as assistant to BRAMANTE and was skillful at wood carving and at painting in perspective. In 1513 he designed the scenery for *Calandria,* the first Italian drama to use complete scenery with special lighting effects.

Pesarese, Il, see **Cantarini, Simone.**

Pesellino, Il (1422-1457), Italian painter whose real name was Francesco di Stefano Giuochi. He worked for a time by Fra Filippo LIPPI; unfortunately few of his works are extant. They include decorative scenes for chests; *The Triumphs of Petrarch; The Story of the Argonauts; Annunciation; Madonna with Angels:* also several altarpieces.

Pessl, Yella, contemporary Austrian harpsichordist, organist, and pianist who played with the Vienna Bach Society when she was fifteen years old, later appearing successfully as soloist with leading European and American orchestras. She came to the United States in 1931, and has taught at the music department of Columbia University in addition to founding the BACH CIRCLE in 1937 at New York, and making many Victor harpsichord recordings.

Peter and the Wolf, (Prokofieff), a musical fairy tale for children composed by Serge PROKOFIEFF in 1936: it is an ingenious work in which every character is pictured by an individual instrument such as Peter's grandfather by the BASSOON and the wolf by the FRENCH HORN. There is a Victor recording with Richard Hale as narrator by the Boston Symphony Orchestra, and a Columbia recording with Basil RATHBONE as narrator by the All-American Orchestra.

Peterkin, Julia Mood (1880-   ), American novelist educated at Converse College, Spartanburg, S. C.: she has become famous for her tales of the Gullah Negroes living along the South Carolina coast. Among her successful works are *Green Thursday* (1924); *Black April; Scarlet Sister Mary,* awarded the Pulitzer Prize and dramatized for Ethel BARRYMORE; *Bright Skin; Roll, Jordan, Roll; Plantation Christmas.*

Peter the Great (1672-1725), a Russian monarch of interest in this volume because of the changes which he made in the old Russian methods: by introducing modern systems learned through his travels in Europe and England, he was largely responsible for the gradual development in his country of the arts and sciences.

Petina, Irra (1912-), Russian dramatic mezzo-soprano who made her debut as Feodor in Mussorgsky's *Boris Godunoff* with the Philadelphia Opera Company in 1930, and in 1934 with the Metropolitan Opera Company, New York, in *The* Valkyrie, remaining with the company and scoring a great success in the title role of Bizet's *Carmen* in 1943.

Petipa, Lucien (1815-1900), French dancer and choreographer who was the son of Jean Antoine Petipa, famous dancer and balletmaster at La Monnaie, Brussels, and first appeared at five in one of his father's ballets, *The Birth of Venus and Love*. He danced later at The Hague, and Bordeaux, finally appearing in 1840 at L'Opéra, Paris, in La Sylphide with Fanny Ellsler. His choreographic productions include several ballets for operas: also *Sacountala, Graziosa,* and *Namouna.*

Petipa, Marius (1822-1910), French dancer and choreographer who was the son of Jean Antoine Petipa, famous dancer and ballet master at La Monnaie, Brussels, and a brother of Lucien Petipa. He studied with his father, and made his debut in 1840 at the Comédie-Française with Carlotta Grisi at a benefit for the famous actress Rachael. He accepted the post of *premier danseur* at the St. Petersburg Imperial Ballet in 1847: in 1851 he became balletmaster, and exerted a powerful influence on the development of the ballet in Russia. His notable ballets include *The Daughter of Pharaon; King Candaule; Don Quixotte; Camargo; La Bayadère; The Talisman; Cinderella; Raymonda; The Seasons; The Sleeping Princess.*

Petitot, Jean (1607-1691), French painter in enamel who first worked in Paris, and in 1634 went to London where Charles I became his patron: he made many portraits of the royal family and courtiers, also copying the pictures of Van Dyck. After the death of Charles I he achieved equal fame at the Court of Louis XIV: the Apollo Gallery in the Louvre contains about sixty of his finest portraits including those of Louis XIV, Mme. de Maintenon, Louise La Valliere, Queen Christina of Sweden, Marquise de Montespan, and Cardinal Richelieu.

Petits Riens, Les, a ballet pantomime the story of which was written by Jean Noverre, and the music by Wolfgang Amadeus Mozart: it was produced at L'Opéra, Paris, in 1778, and, although it was a sensational success, the composer received so little for the music that a few days after the première he left to take a humble post as an organist in order to earn his living. Victor recordings of the Overture, Gavotte, and other numbers are listed in *The Gramophone Shop Encyclopedia of Recorded Music.*

Petöfi, Alexander (1823-1849), Hungarian poet whose works include the national poem: *Talpra Magyar (Arise, Ye Magyars); The Wine-Bibbers;* *The Hangman's Rope;* a translation of Shakespeare's "Coriolanus": he was killed during the Hungarian Revolution.

Petrarch, Francesco (1304-1374), Italian poet educated in Italy and France who first studied for the bar: he wrote much of his verse in Latin, but the most famous are in Italian. They include more than two hundred ballads and sonnets: the latter, inspired by an Italian lady named Laura are called *Trionfi* and *Canzoniere (Songs),* and are classed among the finest amorous poems in literature. Petrarch ranks with Dante and Boccaccio as founders of Italian literature.

Petri, Egon (1881-), German pianist who studied with Teresa Carreno and Ferruccio Busoni: he toured Europe successfully for many years, taught at the High School of Music in Berlin, and came to the United States in 1932. He has made many successful appearances in recital and on the radio.

Petrouchka, spectacle ballet in four scenes: libretto by Igor Stravinsky and Alexander Benois; choreography by Michel Fokine; music by Igor Stravinsky; first produced at Paris in 1911. The story of the ballet revolves around a showman who exhibits animated puppets, the principal ones being a ballerina, a blackamoor, and Petrouchka, a poor little misshapen clown. Stravinsky arranged a concert suite for orchestra from the music which has become as popular as the ballet itself: there are both Columbia and Victor recordings.

Pettie, John (1839-1893), Scottish painter who studied at the Trustee's Academy in Edinburgh, and first exhibited in 1861: his notable works include *The Armourers; Arrested for Witchcraft; Disgrace of Cardinal Wolsey; Sanctuary; The Death Warrant; The Vigil; Jester's Merry Thought; Rob Roy, the Laird.*

Peyser, Ethel (1887-), American author of works on music educated at Vassar, Barnard, and the Teachers' College of the City of New York: her books with Marion Bauer include *Cheating the Junk Pile* (1922); *How Music Grew; Music Through the Ages.* Her individual works comprise *How to Enjoy Music; The Book of Culture; The House That Music Built,* a history of Carnegie Hall, New York.

Phaëthon, in Greek mythology the son of Helios (or Apollo): he sought to drive his father's chariot across the heavens, but lacked the power to control the horses; Zeus killed him and saved the world from destruction.

Pharaoh, the title in Hebrew for the kings of Egypt: it was first used during the fourth dynasty by combining with the name of the king as Pharaoh-Neko, Pharaoh-Hophra, etc. The word was originally the term for the royal palace: after the 25th dynasty it was used as the exclusive title.

Phelps, Elizabeth Stuart (1844-1911), American novelist who wrote several successful religious tales of which the most notable were *Gates Ajar*

(1868); *Beyond the Gates; Men, Women and Ghosts; The Silent Partner; The Story of Avis:* she also wrote several stories with her husband, Herbert D. Ward. Her novels are said to have brought comfort to thousands of people because of their more human conception of religion and the after life.

Phelps, William Lyon (1865-1943), American author who was educated at Yale University where he held the post of Sampson Professor of English literature from 1901 to 1933. His works include many treatises on the history of literature including *The Beginnings of the English Romantic Movement* (1893); *Essays on Modern Novelists; Robert Browning; The Advance of the English Novel; Essays on American Authors; Essays on Things; The Courage of Ignorance; William Lyon Phelps Year Book; A Children's Anthology.*

Phidias or **Pheidias,** Greek sculptor probably born about 490 B.C.: little is known of his career except that he was the friend of PERICLES, and his advisor on the great buildings constructed at ATHENS and on the ACROPOLIS. None of his works is known to be in existence: among those mentioned by ancient writers including PLUTARCH are the statue of *Athena Parthenos* in the PARTHENON, and of ZEUS at OLYMPIA; the latter was placed among the SEVEN WONDERS OF THE WORLD.

Phigaleia Sculptures, a series of sculptured METOPES found in fragments at the temple of Apollo Epicurius at Phigaleia, an ancient Greek city in Arcadia. The building was erected by ICTIMUS about 450 B.C., and the metopes are sculptured with scenes of the battle between the Greeks and the AMAZONS, and the contest between the centaurs and Lapithae.

Philadelphia Grand Opera Company, The, an organization founded at Philadelphia, Pa., in 1926: during the first season, 1926-1927, six performances were given; the next year this number was increased to twelve. In 1929 the company became affiliated with the CURTIS INSTITUTE OF MUSIC, and Mrs. Louise Curtis BOK the president of the Institute also became chairman of the board of the opera company. The number of annual performances was steadily increased until the season became one of ten weeks, and is now a part of the regular schedule of the PHILADELPHIA ORCHESTRA sponsored by the Philadelphia Orchestra Association. The repertoire of the Philadelphia Opera Company consists of both standard works of the German, French and Italian schools and of novelties. Alban BERG's *Wozzeck* was given its American première under the conductorship of Leopold STOKOWSKI, and Eugène GOOSSENS. The ballet productions other than ballets which are integral parts of operatic works, have included *Die Puppenfée, The Red Terror, L'Hiver, Salomé,* and *Versailles.* Catherine LITTLEFIELD was the première danseuse and ballet mistress. The roster of singers has included Mary GARDEN, Anne Roselle, Margaret MATZENAUER, Cyrena Van Gordon, Carmela Ponselle, Sophie BRASLAU, Richard CROOKS, Pasquale AMATO, and John Charles THOMAS. Because of the affiliation with the Curtis Institute of Music, talented pupils have the opportunity of appearing in minor roles in the productions,

and of playing in the opera orchestra, which is otherwise composed exclusively of members of the Philadelphia Orchestra.

Philadelphia Museum of Art, an institution at Philadelphia, Pa., which contains a display collection of the history of art, arranged in the general order of artistic evolution: among the interesting features are Augustus SAINT-GAUDENS' bronze figure of DIANA; a foyer of 18th century French sculpture; a portal from the Abbey of St. Laurent; a suit of tournament armor; an altar from a 14th century French church. There are also paintings by Dutch, French, English, and American artists, and unusually complete collections of art objects from Persia, Egypt, India and China.

Philadelphia Orchestra, an organization founded in 1900 by Fritz Scheel, the first concert being given during the same year. Richard STRAUSS led several concerts in 1904 and Felix Weingartner conducted one concert in 1905. In 1912 Leopold Stokowski became the conductor: among the famous conductors who have led the orchestra are ORMANDY, REINER, BLOCH, CASELLA, CHADWICK, D'INDY, ENESCO, MILHAUD, GABRILOWITSCH, TOSCANINI, RACHMANINOFF, STOCK, and STRAVINSKY. Eugene Ormandy is now (1943) the permanent conductor.

Philidor, François André Danican (1726-1795), French composer who studied with André Campra, and produced more than twenty successful operas including *Le Maréchal, Tom Jones* and *Ernelinde,* the last-named considered his greatest work. He was also the greatest chess player of his day, often defeating several expert players simultaneously while playing blindfolded.

Philipp, Isidor (1863-   ), French pianist, composer, and editor born in Hungary who was brought to Paris as a child, and later studied at the Paris Conservatory with Georges Mathias, Camille Saint-Saens and Stephen Heller. In 1903 he became professor of the piano at the Paris Conservatory, and also established trio-concerts. He has been highly successful as a teacher, and has made many fine arrangements of classical and modern works for two pianos—four hands.

Philippoteaux, Henri Emmanuel Felix (1815-1884), French painter who made a specialty of painting battle scenes, historical events, and panoramas: he created over a considerable period of years a series of works which are not only accurate and spirited, but exhibit a mastery of detail almost unequalled. Among his notable works are *Charge of the African Cavalry at Balaklava; The Battlefield of Fontenoy; The Battle of Rivoli; Henry IV and Sully after the Battle of Ivry.*

Phillip, John (1817-1867), Scottish painter who studied at the Royal Academy in London: his portrayals of Scotch subjects were highly praised in such canvases as *Baptism in Scotland* and *Scotch Washing.* After visiting Spain his style changed as evidenced in pictures such as *Visit to the Gypsy Quarter; Letter Writer of Seville; Dolores; Early Career of Murillo; Chat Around the Brasiers.*

Phillips, David Graham (1867-1911), American novelist who studied at Asbury College (now De Pauw University) Greencastle, Ind., and at Princeton University: his works include *The Great God Success* (1901); *The Golden Fleece; Old Wives for New; The Fashionable Adventures of Joshua Craig* which led indirectly to his death at the hands of Fitzhugh Coyle Goldsborough; *The Price She Paid; Susan Lenox: Her Fall and Rise,* the last-named a greatly discussed book which had little success as a play and as a silent film with Greta GARBO.

Phillips, Stephen (1868-1915), English poet, dramatist, and cousin of Laurence BINYON: from 1885 to 1892 he acted in the theatrical company of another cousin, Frank (later Sir Frank) BENSON. In 1898 he won the $500 prize of the *Academy* newspaper for a volume of collected poems: his works include *Orestes and Other Poems* (1884); *Primavera; Panama and Other Poems;* also the verse plays *Paolo and Francesca; Herod; Ulysses; Nero; The New Inferno; Armageddon; Harold.*

Philon, Greek architect who worked during the 4th century B.C.: he designed the great hall at Eleusis where the ELEUSINIAN MYSTERIES were celebrated, and also an arsenal at Athens.

Philosopher's Stone, an imaginary stone or chemical preparation believed in the Middle Ages to have the power of transmuting base metals into gold: several alchemists including Count Alessandro CAGLIOSTRO claimed the power of such transmutation.

Philpotts, Eden (1862-), English novelist, poet, and dramatist who engaged in business before he started on a literary career: his more than 150 works include *Lying Prophets* (1896); *Sons of the Morning; Widecombe Fair; Miser's Money; The Jury; A Deed Without a Name:* also the successful plays *The Farmer's Wife; Yellow Sands* with his daughter, Adelaide Philpotts; *The Good Old Days,* also with his daughter.

Phiz, see **Browne, Hablot Knight.**

Phoebus, in Greek mythology one of the names of APOLLO: the goddess Artemis (DIANA) was called *Phoebe.*

Phrase, in music the smallest division of a musical work which is complete in itself: the art of **phrasing** consists in bringing out the individual melodic and rhythmic characteristics of the phrases which united comprise a musical composition.

Phryian Monuments, a series of ancient monuments discovered in the Mount Sipylus district of Phrygia, a large country in Asia Minor: among the most interesting are the tomb of TANTALUS; a colossal statue of Cybele, the nature goddess; the tomb of MIDAS. The Phrygians did not build their temples and tombs, but cut them of the solid rock, and had little knowledge of sculpture.

Phryne, a Greek courtesan of the 4th century B.C. who was the model for a picture depicting APHRODITE rising out of the sea by APELLES, and for a statue of Aphrodite by PRAXITELES. When charged with impiety and tried, Hyperides gained her freedom by permitting her loveliness to be seen.

Phrynichus, Greek tragic poet of the 5th century B.C., who rivaled AESCHYLUS in popularity with the Athenians. Only fragments of his works are extant: they include *The Capture of Miletus; The Phoenician Women; The Danaids; Actaeon; Alcestis; Tantalus.*

Phyfe, Duncan (c.1768-1854), American cabinet maker born in Scotland who came to the United States about 1783, and after being apprenticed to a furniture maker, set up his own shop for the manufacture of furniture in 1790. His production included chairs, sofas, settees, tables, and sideboards in a style based on the Sheraton-Directoire manner. He worked in mahogany and rosewood, using the lyre design on chair backs and table bases: also carvings of leaves and animal motives.

Piano (It.), in music an indication that a passage is to be performed softly: the superlative is *pianissimo* and the term is usually indicated by the sign *P.*

Piano (Pianoforte), a musical instrument invented by Bartolommeo CRISTOFORI about 1710: its Italian name, *piano e forte,* was derived from the fact that, unlike the harpsichord in which the sounds could not be increased or diminished in volume, it could be played *piano* (softly) or *forte* (loudly) by means of the PEDALS. Its construction, consisting of a frame, a set of wire strings, and a keyboard mechanism, is extremely intricate, requiring more than 4,000 parts. References to the numerous famous virtuosos, teachers, and makers of the piano are to be found throughout this volume.

Piano Accordion, see **Accordion.**

Piano Concertos, a musical form in which many hundreds of classic and modern composers have worked, but only a few have been able to create works which are standard in the repertory of great pianists. The outstanding concertos of the classical period include those of Johann Sebastian BACH, Joseph HAYDN, Wolfgang Amadeus MOZART, and Ludwig van BEETHOVEN. The composers in the romantic period include Frédéric CHOPIN, César FRANCK, Edvard GRIEG, Franz LISZT, Felix MENDELSSOHN, and Robert SCHUMANN while the modernists include Johannes BRAHMS, Ignace PADEREWSKI, Sergei RACHMANINOFF, Camille SAINT-SAENS, Peter TSCHAIKOWSKY, Serge PROKOFIEFF, and Dmitri SHOSTAKOVITCH.

Pianola, see **Piano Player.**

Piano Player, see **Player Piano.**

Piatigorsky, Gregor (1903-), Russian violoncellist who studied at the Moscow Conservatory, later becoming first 'cellist at the Moscow Opera: he toured Europe as soloist and chamber musician, also appearing with the major orchestras in the United States since 1929.

Piatti, Alfredo Carlo (1822-1901), Italian violoncellist and composer who studied at the Milan Conservatory, made his debut in 1834, concertized for nine years, and in 1843 played in Franz Liszt's Orchestra at Munich. He was a great favorite in London where he played from 1859 to 1898 at the Monday and Saturday Popular Chamber Music Concerts. His compositions were chiefly for the violoncello.

Pibroch, in music the name of a series of variations played on the BAGPIPE: the music is military in character and extremely difficult of execution.

Picaresque Novel, in literature a form of romantic tale which may be defined as the autobiography in prose of a real or fictitious person who is either a rogue or a social parasite: among the authors who have achieved great success in this field of writing are Vicente ESPINEL, René LE SAGE, Thomas NASH, Gerbrand BREDEROO, Daniel DEFOE, Henry FIELDING, and Théophile GAUTIER.

Picasso, Pablo Ruiz (1881-), Spanish painter who studied with his father who was a professor at the Academy of Arts in Barcelona, and at the École des Beaux-Arts in Madrid. He was intimate with Georges BRAQUE and André DERAIN, and influenced by Edgar Degas and Henri TOULOUSE-LAUTREC: he is regarded as the founder of CUBISM and one of the leading exponents of POST-IMPRESSION. His notable works include stage settings for DIAGHILEFF's Ballet Russe, illustrations for many books, and portraits of Igor STRAVINSKY, Jean COCTEAU, and other artistic celebrities.

Piccinni, Nicola (1728-1800), Italian opera composer who studied with Leonardo Leo and Francesco DURANTE at Naples: in 1776 he went to Paris and produced his first opera, *Roland,* in 1778 at the Paris Opéra in French. He was set up as a rival to Christoph Willibald GLUCK by a faction who disliked the German master's operas, but the latter emerged triumphantly from the competition in which it is only fair to say that Piccinni took no part. He wrote more than 130 dramatic works none of which has survived.

Piccolo, an instrument of the FLUTE family which is about half the size of the flute, and has a range about an octave higher. Modern instruments are made of silver and other metals as well as of wood.

Pickford, Mary (1893-), Canadian-American stage and screen actress and producer, real name Gladys Mary Smith, who first appeared on the stage in juvenile parts, later playing with Chauncey OLCOTT, and in *The Warrens of Virginia, A Good Little Devil, The Church Mouse,* and *Coquette.* She entered the films in 1913: among the numerous pictures in which she has appeared are *A Good Little Devil; Caprice; In The Bishop's Carriage; Tess of the Storm Country; Hearts Adrift; Fanchon the Cricket; Stella Maris; The Poor Little Rich Girl; Rebecca of Sunnybrook Farm; Pollyanna; Rosita; Secrets; Kiki; The Taming of the Shrew.*

Picknell, William Lamb (1854-1897), American painter who studied with George INNESS in Rome and Jean Léon GEROME at the ECOLE DES BEAUX-ARTS in Paris, also working for several years with Robert WYLIE in Brittany. His notable paintings include *Morning on the Loing; Bleak December; Borders of the Marsh; Breton Peasant Girl Feeding Ducks; Unloading Fish; On the Lande in Brittany; Fields of Kerren.*

Pickthall, Marjorie Lowry Christie (1883-1922), Canadian poet and novelist born in England who came to Canada with her family in 1899. She contributed to Canadian and American magazines in addition to working in the library of Victoria College, Toronto: her works include *Drift of Pinions* (1912); *Lamp of Poor Souls; The Woodcarver's Wife and Other Poems:* also the novels *Little Hearts, The Bridge* and *Angel Shoes.*

Picon, Molly or **Mollie** (1903-), American actress on the Yiddish stage who began her dramatic career at five, continuing to play juvenile roles until she was fifteen. After appearing in Jacob Kalish's Yiddish Theatre at Boston, she toured Europe, returning in 1922 to play at Yiddish theatres in New York. She has also appeared in vaudeville, on radio broadcasts, and in motion pictures.

Picot, François Édouard (1786-1868), French painter who was a follower of the school of Jacques Louis DAVID, and was known as Le Pére Picot (Father Picot) because of his many distinguished pupils including Isidore PILS, Alexandre CABANEL, Jean HENNER, Adolphe BOUGUEREAU and Gustave MOREAU. His noted works include *Meeting of Aeneas and Venus; Cupid and Pysche; Cybele Protecting Cities from Vesuvius; Orestes Sleeping in the Arms of Electra; France Defending the Charter; Death of Sapphira.*

Pictures at an Exhibition (Mussorgsky), a suite of piano pieces composed by Modest MUSSORGSKY in memory of his intimate friend, Viktor HARTMANN, a painter who died in 1873. The pieces were arranged by Maurice RAVEL for symphony orchestra at the request of Sergei KOUSSEVITZKY, who conducted the première of this transcription in Paris on May 3, 1923, and also directed the American première by the BOSTON SYMPHONY ORCHESTRA on Dec. 3, 1926. The suite is loosely held together by references to the "Promenade" theme between some of the movements. I *Gnomes,* II *Il Vecchio Castello* (The Medieval Castle), III *Tuileries,* IV *Bydlo* (Polish Ox-cart), V *Ballet of Chickens in Their Shells,* VI *Samuel Goldenberg and Schmuyle,* VII *Limoges* (The Market Place), VIII *Catacombs,* IX *The Hut on Fowl's Legs,* X *The Bogatyr's Gate at Kiev.* There is a Victor recording of the Ravel orchestration by the Boston Symphony Orchestra directed by Sergei Koussevitzky.

Pidgeon, Walter (1898-), American screen actor who became interested in a dramatic career through Elsie JANIS with whom he toured the United States and Canada in *At Home:* among the films in which he has appeared are *Mlle. Modiste; Viennese Nights; The Gorilla; The*

Night of January 16; Saratoga; My Dear Mrs. Aldrich; Girl of the Golden West; Nick Carter, Master Detective; Dark Command; How Green Was My Valley; Blossoms in the Dust; Mrs. Miniver.

Pidgin, Charles Felton (1844-1923), American novelist who also invented machines for the tabulation of statistics: his works include the highly successful novels *Quincy Adams Sawyer* (1900) which was also popular as a play, and *Blennerhassett* in which he became the defender of Aaron Burr.

Pied Piper of Hamelin, the title and hero of a poem written in 1842 by Robert BROWNING: according to German legend he was a musician who came to the town of Hamelin in 1284, and claimed the reward after having rid the town of rats by leading them with his piping into the river Weser where they drowned. When the burghers refused to pay, he charmed all of the children in the town with his magic piping, and they disappeared forever into a cavern with him.

Pier, in architecture the term for any vertical support such as a pillar or column: the term is little used at the present time except in relation to commercial engineering.

Pierné, Gabriel (1863-1937), French organist and composer who studied at the Paris Conservatory with François MARMONTEL, Jules MASSENET and César FRANCK, succeeding the last-named as organist at Ste.-Clothilde in 1890, and Édouard COLONNE as conductor of the Concerts Colonne in 1910. His compositions comprise several operas and ballets; a series of oratorios including *The Children's Crusade* in which he used children's choruses; orchestral works; chamber music; pieces for piano and also for violin including the celebrated *Serenade.*

Piero della Francesca, see **Franceschi, Piero de.**

Piero di Cosimo (1462-1521), Italian painter whose real name was Piero di Lorenzo: he became a pupil of Cosimo Rosselli whose name he assumed, and with whom he went to Rome in 1482 to work on frescoes at the SISTINE CHAPEL in the VATICAN. His notable works include *Portrait of a Lady as Magdalen; Lady with a Rabbit; Man in Armor; Madonna in a Landscape; Perseus and Andromeda; Adoration of the Shepherds; The Immaculate Conception.*

Pierpont Morgan Library, The, a library in New York City comprising collections of books assembled by John Pierpont Morgan (1837-1913) to which has been added the books and objects of art assembled by his son, John Pierpont Morgan (1867-1943). The collection comprises Egyptian and Greek papyri; medieval and Renaissance manuscripts; English, American, Italian and French authors' manuscripts; autograph letters and documents; printed books dating from the inception of printing about 1455 to the 20th century including first and early editions of classical, medieval, and Renaissance works in all fields of literature; a collection of books relating to costumes; an assembly of book bindings; original drawings by artists from the 14th to the 19th century: also the most complete collection in America of etchings by Rembrandt.

Pierrot, the name of the principal character in French pantomime since the 18th century: the costume and face were always in white with loose clothing consisting of a tunic with large sleeves and white pantaloons. Gaspard DEBURAU introduced the character in the 18th century, and his interpretation of the romantic and pathetic character has served as a model for present-day actors.

Piers the Plowman, see **Langland, William.**

Pietà, in painting and sculpture the representation of the Virgin grieving over the dead Christ: among the famous artists who have portrayed the subject are Giovanni BELLINI, CORREGGIO, VAN DYCK, MASSYS, FRA ANGELICO, PERUGINO, TITIAN, RUBENS, MURILLO, OVERBECK, Annibale CARRACCI, and MICHELANGELO.

Pigalle, Jean Baptiste (1714-1785), French sculptor who studied with Robert le Lorrain at the same time as John Baptiste LEMOYNE: he was also a friend of Guillaume COUSTOU who gave him financial aid when he required it most. His notable works include *Mercury Tying His Sandal; Love and Friendship; Child with Bird Cage; Child With Bird; Young Girl With a Thorn:* also the tomb of Marshal Saxe in the Temple of St. Thomas at Strassburg, considered his masterpiece.

Pigment, in painting a powdered substance which is mixed with a suitable liquid in order to form a desired color: it is usually compounded from a metallic base, and much of the painter's art consists in mixing his pigments in such a manner as to achieve the desired results on the canvas.

Pilaster, in architecture a flat columnar structure partially sunk in a wall for purposes of support: it is found in Roman and Renaissance designs, particularly as a decorative device with panelling and carved effects.

Pillar, in architecture a vertical support much used in Gothic architecture in either single or clustered form. The word is used interchangeably with COLUMN although there is a technical difference.

Pilnyak, Boris (1894-   ), Russian novelist, real name was Boris Andreyevich Vogau, who graduated from several Russian educational institutions, and began his writing in 1915: his works translated into English include *Tales of the Wilderness; The Naked Year; The Volga Falls to the Caspian Sea; The Red Tree; International.*

Pilon, Germain (1535-1590), French sculptor who was greatly influenced by the Renaissance: his notable works include the kneeling figures in bronze and the reclining marble statues of King Henry II and Catherine de' Medici, his queen; also a bronze urn, *The Three Graces* as a sepulchre for the monarch's heart. He worked with equal facility in marble, stone, wood, terra cotta and bronze, creating monuments, bas-reliefs, statues and busts.

Piloty, Karl von (1826-1886), German painter who studied with his father and at the Munich Academy. After traveling in Belgium, France, and England he began to paint a series of genre pictures which opened a new era in German painting: among them are *Nero at the Ruins of Rome; Galileo in Prison; Death of Alexander the Great; Columbus Discovering America; Assassination of Caesar; The Wise and Foolish Virgins; Godfrey de Bouillon with the Crusaders at the Holy Sepulchre.*

Pils, Isadore Alexandre Auguste (1815-1875), French painter who studied at the ÉCOLE DES BEAUX-ARTS, Paris, where he won the Grand Prix de Rome, and after spending ten years in the Eternal City settled in Paris. His notable works include *Rouget de Lisle Singing the Marseillaise; Christ Preaching from Simon's Boat; Bacchantes and Satyrs; Death of a Sister of Charity; The Zouave; Battle of the Alma.*

Pinafore, see **H.M.S. Pinafore.**

Pinakothek (Munich), an art museum at Munich, Germany, in two buildings: the *Old Pinakothek* was designed and built by Leo von KLENZE from 1826 to 1836, bearing some resemblance to the VATICAN. The exterior is decorated by frescoes executed by Peter CORNELIUS, and with statues of 24 celebrated painters by Ludwig von SCHWANTHALER. The museum contains a valuable collection of early German and Flemish works; 300,000 engravings; 20,000 drawings and a varied assembly of vases. The *New Pinakothek* stands opposite the old: its exterior frescoes were executed by Wilhelm von KAULBACH, and it is devoted to works of painters of the 19th century.

Pindar (c.518-c.448 B.C.), Greek poet regarded as the greatest of the lyricists: the scholars at ALEXANDRIA divided his poems into seventeen books comprising hymns, paeans, dithyrambs, and songs of victory. Only forty-four odes survive celebrating the victors in the games at Olympia and other Greek cities. The term **Pindaric ode** is applied to a form of verse used in England by DRYDEN, POPE, SWIFT, COWLEY, and others in an endeavor to imitate the magnificence of Pindar's style.

Pine, Robert Edge (c.1730-1788), American painter born in London who was trained by his father: he came to Philadelphia in 1784, and executed many portraits of famous Americans of the period including George Washington and Benjamin FRANKLIN. He also planned to paint a series of pictures dealing with important episodes in the Revolutionary War, but only one, *Congress Voting Independence,* was completed: he died suddenly, and many of his pictures which were in the Columbia Museum at Boston, Mass., were lost when the institution was destroyed by fire.

Pinero, Sir Arthur Wing (1855-1934), English dramatist of Portuguese-Jewish extraction who first studied for the bar, but later appeared with Sir Henry IRVING's company in *Hamlet* and other classic and modern plays for five years. His first play, *£200 a Year,* was produced in 1877: it was followed by many successes including *Trelawney of the Wells; Sweet Lavender; The Second Mrs. Tanqueray; His House in Order; The Notorious Mrs. Ebbsmith; The Thunderbolt; Mid-Channel; The Enchanted Cottage; A Cold June.*

Pines of Rome (Resphigi), a symphonic poem by Ottorino RESPHIGI; the second in a series of works in which the grandeur of the ancient city is commemorated. It was performed at Rome under the direction of Bernardino MOLINARI in 1924, and at New York by the New York Philharmonic-Symphony Society under the baton of Arturo TOSCANINI. The four connected sections played without pause are entitled *(1) The Pines of the Villa Borghese; (2) The Pines Near a Catacomb; (3) The Pines of a Janiculum,* in which the song of a nightingale is played on a phonograph record; *(4) The Pines of the Appian Way.* The orchestration calls for a phonograph, piano, organ and six BUCCINA or Roman war trumpets for which FRENCH HORNS could be substituted. There is a Columbia recording by the Milan Symphony Orchestra, and a Victor recording by the Paris Conservatory Orchestra directed by Piero Coppola.

Pinnacle, in architecture a small bell turret in the form of a pyramid on a polygonal base, generally used as a crown for a PIER, BUTTRESS or GABLE. In the 13th century pinnacles were richly decorated, and in the 16th century they were embellished with sculptured figures.

Pinski, David (1872-), Jewish-American dramatist, journalist, and novelist born in Russia who came to New York in 1899: his education was completed at the University of Berlin and Columbia University, New York. His successful plays include a comedy, *The Treasure* (1919); a drama, *King David and His Wives:* he has also written novels and stories in Yiddish.

Pinturicchio (1454-1513), Italian painter whose real name was Bernardino di Betto; he worked with Perugino at the Sistine Chapel in Rome, and his frescoes and panel pictures include *History of San Bernardino; Dispute of St. Catherine; Nativity of Christ; Madonna del Pace; Annunciation; Adoration of the Magi; Resurrection of Christ; St. Catherine Disputing with the Emperor Maximilian; St. Anthony in the Desert; Visitation.*

Pinza, Ezio (1895-), Italian operatic basso educated at the University of Ravenna and at the Bologna Conservatory, making his debut in 1920 at Rome in Richard WAGNER's *Tristan and Isolde,* and in 1926 at the Metropolitan Opera House, New York, in SPONTINI's *La Vestale.* He has also appeared with the Chicago Civic Opera, at the SALZBURG FESTIVALS, and in South America.

Pirandello, Luigi (1867-1936), Italian dramatist, poet, novelist, and short story writer educated at the Universities of Palermo and Bonn: his literary career began with poems and novels one of which, *The Late Mattia Pascal* (1904) later became a popular favorite. His successful plays produced in England and America include *Six Characters in Search of an Author; And That's the Truth; Henry IV; The Man With the Flower in His Mouth; As You Desire Me,* the last-named a successful film with Greta GARBO.

Piranesi, Giovanni Battista (1720-1778), Italian engraver who spent the greater part of his life in Rome: he engraved more than two thousand copper plates of buildings and monuments of every description. Where details were lacking he supplied them out of his own knowledge, introducing needed extraneous objects such as vases, chairs, etc.: his plates were preserved by his son, and published in 29 volumes at Paris in 1835-37.

Pirates of Penzance, The, comic opera in two acts: book by Sir William Schwenk GILBERT; music by Sir Arthur SULLIVAN; first produced at the Fifth Avenue Theatre, New York, in 1879 under the personal direction of the author and composer in a vain attempt to protect the copyright; first produced at London in 1880. The plot concerns itself with Frederic, apprenticed as a child to a pirate instead of a pilot through a mistake on the part of his nurse, his adventures with the band, and his final rescue. There is a complete Victor recording, and also an abridged version.

Pirouette (Fr.), in ballet a complete turn of the body accomplished on one leg: there are several variations in the methods of accomplishing the turn.

Pisa Campanile, a bell tower in Pisa, Italy, which is known better under its name of the *Leaning Tower of Pisa.* It was begun in 1174 and completed in 1350: its height is nearly 180 feet, and it leaned 16½ feet out of the perpendicular in 1910. There is no reason to believe that this inclination was intentional on the part of the architects: it is far more probable that settling of the soil underneath has caused the sinking of the foundation.

Pisano, Andrea (c.1270-1348), Italian sculptor whose real name was Andrea da Pontadera: his important works include one of the bronze doors of the Baptistery at Florence, and a double band of panel-reliefs for the Campanile the subjects of which were *The Four Great Prophets, The Seven Virtues, The Seven Sacraments, The Seven Works of Mercy,* and *The Seven Planets.*

Pisano, Niccolò (c.1210-c.1278), Italian sculptor and architect regarding whom little is known outside of his works which include the marble pulpit for the Baptistery at Pisa; the relief, *Deposition from the Cross* at the church of San Martino at Lucca; the pulpit at the cathedral in Siena, and the great fountain in front of the cathedral at Perugia. His son, **Giovanni Pisano** (c.1250-c.1320), was also an architect and sculptor who was trained by his father whom he assisted on several of the works mentioned above: his original works include a pulpit for the Church of Sant' Andrea at Pistoia; and a marble high altar and reredos in the cathedral at Arezzo: also the tomb of Benedict XI in the Church of San Domenico at Perugia.

Pisemsky, Alexis (1820-1881), Russian novelist and dramatist: his plays include *The Hypochondriac* (1852); *The Division; Bitter Fate; Lieutenant Gladkow; Baal; The Family Whirlpool.* Among his successful novels are *A Thousand Souls,* and *The Muff:* he also wrote admirable short stories such as *The Wood Demon* and *Pietershik.*

Pissaro, Camille (1830-1903), French painter born at St. Thomas in the Dutch Antilles who became a pupil of COROT, friendly with MILLET, and in sympathy with the BARBIZON SCHOOL. His works include a portrait of Cézanne; *Jardin de Poitoise; Pathway through the Cabbages; Father Melon Sawing Timber; Apple Gathering; Woman Breaking Timber; The Chat; Woman Bathing.*

Piston, Walter (1894-), American composer educated at Harvard University and at the École Normale, Paris: he also studied with Nadia BOULANGER. His compositions include a suite from the ballet, *The Incredible Flutist;* numerous orchestral works; a *Concertino* for piano and chamber orchestra; a violin concerto; chamber music: he has also written *Principles of Harmonic Analysis.*

Pitch, in music the term applied to the frequency of the vibrations which produce a tone: rapid vibrations produce high or acute tones, and conversely slow vibrations produce low or grave tones. Pitch is in no way affected by the loudness or quality of a tone, and the number of vibrations assigned to each tone of the scale is in direct relation to those assigned to A on the second space of the treble staff discussed in the first reference **(A),** in this volume.

Pitch Pipe, in music a small metal reed-pipe producing one or more musical tones of fixed pitch: it is used for tuning instruments or giving the correct pitch to a group of singers when a piano is not available.

Pitoëff, George (1896-1939), Franco-Russian actor and producer who made his debut in 1912, and founded his own company at Geneva, Switzerland, in 1915. After World War I he settled at Paris, and produced as well as acted in plays by George Bernard SHAW, Luigi PIRANDELLO, and Henri-René LENORMAND.

Pitou, Augustus (1843-1915), American actor, theatrical manager, and dramatist: he appeared first with Edwin Booth's company, and later managed the Fifth Avenue Theatre and the Booth Theatre in New York. Many well-known actors including W. J. Scanlon, Robert Mantell, Rose Coghlan, and Chauncey Olcott were under his management, and he collaborated on several successful plays.

Pitti Gallery (Florence), an art museum in Florence, Italy, housed in the royal palace which was formerly the residence of the grand dukes: it is joined with the **Uffizi Gallery** which also occupies another palace, and together they constitute the largest gallery in the world in which is assembled a great number of pictures by Italian masters of great importance to the world of international art. The paintings in the Pitti Gallery include ten Raphaels, and choice works by Andrea del Sarto, Giorgione and Perugino. The canvases in the Uffizi Gallery are arranged in chronological order, and comprise paintings by Botticelli, Leonardo da Vinci, Michelangelo, Sodoma, and other great painters of the Tuscan and Umbrian schools: the two galleries are without question the most popular in Europe.

Pitts, Zazu (1898-), American screen actress who appeared with great success in a series of short films with Thelma Todd: since 1932 she has played character roles in her inimitable style in *Vanishing Frontier; The Meanest Girl in Town; Mrs. Wiggs of the Cabbage Patch; Three on a Honeymoon; Ruggles of Red Gap; Nurse Edith Cavell; Miss Polly.*

Pittsburgh Symphony Orchestra, an organization founded in 1895 by the Art Society of Pittsburgh, giving its first concert in 1896 with Frederick Archer as conductor: it continued in existence until 1910 with Victor HERBERT, Richard STRAUSS, Walter DAMROSCH, Sir Edward ELGAR and Emil PAUR as regular or guest conductors. In 1926 the orchestra was reorganized by local musicians: since that time the list of regular and guest conductors includes Richard HAGEMAN, Elias Breeskin, Eugene GOOSSENS, Willem van HOOGSTRATEN, Walter DAMROSCH, Antonio Modarelli, Bernardino MOLINARI, José ITURBI, William Daly, Otto KLEMPERER, Carlos CHAVEZ, Georges ENESCO, and Fritz REINER: the last-named became permanent conductor in 1938.

Pizzetti, Ildebrando (1880-), Italian pianist and composer who studied at the Parma Conservatory, and became professor of composition at the Musical Institute in Florence, and later succeeded Ottorino RESPHIGI as professor of advanced composition at the Royal Conservatory of Saint Cecilia in Rome. His compositions include operas, choral works, ballets, orchestral works, and chamber music.

Pizzicati (Delibes), see **Sylvia (Delibes).**

Pizzicato (It.), a word the literal meaning of which is "pinched": on instrumental music for stringed instruments played with a BOW, it becomes a direction to pluck the strings with the fingers instead of using the bow. The succeeding direction, *coll' arco* or *arco*, indicates that playing with the bow is to be resumed. The customary abbreviation is *pizz.*

Plain Song or **Plain Chant,** see **Gregorian Chant.**

Planché, James Robinson (1796-1880), English authority on archaeology and costumes; also the author of more than 200 plays and opera librettos: one of the latter was the book for Carl Maria von WEBER'S OBERON produced at London in 1826. His *Recollections* (1872) are interesting because of their literary and theatrical references.

Plançon, Pol (1854-1914), French dramatic basso who studied with Louis Duprez and Giovanni SBRIGLIA, making his debut at Lyons in 1877, and at the Paris Opéra in 1883 as Mephistopheles in GOUNOD'S *Faust.* He remained with L'Opéra for ten years, also singing at Covent Garden, London: in 1893 he made his debut in the same opera with the Metropolitan Opera Company, remaining until 1906 when he retired. His repertoire included more than fifty French, Italian, and German works, and he was also distinguished as a recitalist.

Planquette, Robert (1848-1903), French light opera composer who studied at the Paris Conservatory, and made his first great success with *The Chimes of Normandy* in 1877 at Paris where over 400 consecutive performances were given: other popular works include *Rip Van Winkle; Nell Gwynne; Paul Jones; Merrie England; The Old Guard.*

Plaster casting, in sculpture a process accomplished by the use of (*1*) a waste mold; (*2*) a piece mold; (*3*) a gelatin mold. The waste mold is so named because it is chipped away and cannot be re-used: the piece mold and gelatin mold can be used for replicas.

Plateresque Style, in architecture a form of decoration introduced into Spain during the Renaissance: the chief characteristics were curves and counter curves, twisted columns heavily sculptured, open balustrades, the use of medallions, wrought iron and elaborate candelabras.

Plato (c.427-c.347 B.C.), Greek philosopher whose writings have apparently been preserved intact: they comprise 44 works in dialogue form. In his *Timaeus* he formulated a system of musical harmony which compares the movements of music to those of the soul which can accordingly be influenced by musical art.

Platt, Charles Adams (1861-1933), American architect and sculptor trained at the National Academy of Design, New York, and at Paris under Gustave BOULANGER and Jules LEFEBVRE, having intended to become a painter. In 1892, after publishing his book, *Italian Gardens,* he turned to architecture, designing many private residences and public buildings such as the FREER GALLERY OF ART, WASHINGTON, D. C.

Plautus, Titus Maccius (254-184 B.C.), Roman comic poet and dramatist: twenty-one of his comedies are extant which are chiefly borrowed from Greek originals. Gotthold LESSING declared his play, *The Captives,* "the best constructed drama in existence": among the playwrights who have borrowed from his works are SHAKESPEARE, MOLIERE, SHADWELL, DRYDEN, GOLDONI, JONSON, ARIOSTO, and FIELDING.

Play Copyright, see **Copyright, Dramatic.**

Player Piano, an instrument which enjoyed great vogue from 1900, but was succeeded in popular favor by the phonograph. The operating mechanism consisted of a roll of paper punched with openings corresponding to the duration and pitch of the notes in a composition: the openings passed over a cylinder through which air circulated to press down the keys of the piano as a substitute for the human fingers. Improved mechanisms such as the *Welte Mignon*, the *Duo Art*, and the *Ampico* made it possible to record the actual performances of great pianists on the rolls.

Players, The, a club for actors founded in 1888 by Edwin BOOTH, Laurence BARRETT, Augustin DALY, and Albert M. PALMER: the general plan was to establish an organization in America similar to the Garrick Club in London. Edwin Booth turned over his own residence at 16 Gramercy Park, New York, for use as the clubhouse, and it is still located there.

Playfair, Sir Nigel (1874-1934), English actor and theatrical manager who was educated for the law, and practiced for some years. His debut was made at the Garrick Theatre, London, in *A Pair of Knickerbockers:* in 1919 he became manager of the Hammersmith Theatre where he produced John DRINKWATER's *Abraham Lincoln,* and revived John Gay's THE BEGGAR'S OPERA which enjoyed a run of more than three years.

Playing Cards, see **Cards, Playing.**

Pleasure Dome of Kubla Khan (Griffes), a symphonic poem by Charles T. GRIFFES based on a poem by Samuel Taylor COLERIDGE, *Kubla Khan;* first performed in 1919 by the Boston Symphony Orchestra. In the composer's own words: "I have taken as a basis for my work those lines of Coleridge's poem describing the 'stately pleasure dome,' the 'sunny pleasure dome with caves of ice,' the 'miracle of rare device.' Therefore I call the work *The Pleasure Dome of Kubla Khan,* rather than *Kubla Khan."* There is a Victor recording by the Minneapolis Symphony Orchestra conducted by Eugene Ormandy.

Plectrum (Lat.), a small piece of ivory, tortoise-shell, or metal used in playing the MANDOLIN, ZITHER, and other stringed instruments: it is either held between the forefinger and thumb, or fitted to the latter by a ring.

Pleiades, (*1*) in Greek mythology seven nymphs named Maia, Alcyone, Electra, Celaeno, Taygeta, Sterope, and Merope: they were the daughters of ATLAS and Pleione, and became the attendants of ARTEMIS. (*2*) The title **Pleiad** was bestowed on seven poets who pursued their vocation at Alexandria in the 3rd century, B.C., and the same name was applied in the 16th century to a group of young poets who strove to set higher standards of purity in diction and expression.

Plein-air (Fr.), in painting the term designating a school of painting which originated in France about 1865: Édouard MANET was the prime mover in an attempt to take the painter out of his studio into the "open" in order to portray more vividly the atmosphere of outdoor life. A painter who reacted to this school was known as a *pleinarist.*

Pleyel, Ignaz Joseph (1757-1831), Austrian pianist, composer and piano maker: after filling various posts as musical director in Germany and England he founded a piano factory at Paris in 1807. His instruments, fundamentally of fine quality, were gradually perfected until the firm of Pleyel and Company became one of the most prosperous in France. He composed many symphonies, chamber works, and concertos for violin, violoncello, and piano: also interesting duets for two violins.

Plié (Fr.), in ballet a movement involving the bending of the knee.

Plinth, (*a*) in *architecture* the term for the square block at the base of a column; the purpose is to set off more effectively the circular moldings above it. (*b*) In *sculpture* the plinth is the rectangular or circular base on which a statue is placed: its purpose is to place the figure at an elevation which keeps the lower part from being concealed, and to provide a place for inscription.

Pliny, the Elder (23-79 A.D.), Roman naturalist, full name Caius Plinius Secundus, who wrote a natural history in 37 books: the 33rd to the 37th volumes contain in part treatises on the fine arts. His nephew **Pliny the Younger** (c.62-c.113 A.D.), was a Roman statesman and orator: his works include one extant oration, *The Panegyric;* a biography of Pliny the Elder; *Letters* (*Epistulae*), which afford a realistic picture of Roman life and manners.

Plotnikoff, Eugene (1877-), Russian violoncellist and conductor who studied at the Moscow Conservatory with Basil KALINNIKOFF: he conducted at the Imperial Theatre, Moscow, the Paris Opéra, the CHALIAPIN Opera Company: in 1934 he became conductor of the New York Federal Symphony Orchestra.

Plutarch (c.46-c.120 B.C.), Greek biographer and essayist: his works include an essay, *De Musica,* which contains important historical data on music. His most important biographical work is *The Parallel Lives,* containing 46 biographies arranged in pairs of illustrious Greeks and Romans.

Pluto, see **Hades.**

Pochon, Alfred (1878-), Swiss violinist who studied with César THOMSON and later taught at the Brussels Conservatory. In 1902 he organized the FLONZALEY QUARTET financed by Edward J. de Coppet, giving up his entire time to its training and concert tours until 1929 when he founded the Stradivarius String Quartet, so-called because all four members played on instruments made by Antonio STRADIVARIUS.

Po Chü-i (772-846), Chinese poet who was also a high official in the Government: he is said to have written more than 3500 poems which were engraved on tablets of stone by Imperial decree. Among his works are *The Everlasting Wrong* in commemoration of the emperor Ming Huan (685-762), and an ode anticipating another written eight centuries later by François de Malherbe entitled *"To Du Perrier on the Death of His Daughter."*

Podium, in Roman architecture a low projecting wall placed both inside and outside a building: the interior podium was frequently used for holding wine casks. The word is used today in the same manner as DAIS, particularly in respect to an orchestral conductor's raised platform.

Poe, Edgar Allan (1809-1849), American poet and short story writer who was trained at the United States Military Academy, edited several magazines, and contributed to various periodicals. His numerous works include *Tamerlane and Other Poems* (1827); *Narrative of Arthur Gordon Pym; Tales of the Grotesque and Arabesque; The Raven and Other Poems:* a collected edition of his works, in ten volumes, edited by E. C. Stedman and G. E. Woodberry, was published in 1894-95.

Poem of the Cid, see **Cid, The.**

Poet laureate, in literature the title bestowed by the king of England on a poet who has served him by writing verse commemorative of important historical events: it is generally understood that Ben JONSON first held the post, but John DRYDEN was the first official holder of the title: others include Thomas SHADWELL, Nahum TATE, Nicholas ROWE, Laurence Eusden, Colley CIBBER, William Whitehead, Thomas Warton, Henry James Pye, Robert SOUTHEY, Samuel WORDSWORTH, Alfred TENNYSON, Alfred AUSTIN, Robert Seymour BRIDGES, and John MASEFIELD.

Poetry: A Magazine of Verse, a monthly magazine founded by Harriet MONROE in 1912: she remained its editor until her death in 1936, and many American poets received their first encouragement by having their verses printed in it.

Poet's Corner, a space in WESTMINSTER ABBEY containing the busts, tablets, statues or monuments of Shakespeare, Jonson, Chaucer, Milton, Spenser, Addison, Beaumont, Goldsmith, Samuel Johnson, Henry Wadsworth Longfellow, Macaulay, Sheridan, and many other famous poets, actors, musicians and noted men: some are buried either under or near their monuments.

Pogany, William Andrew (1882-), American artist born in Hungary who is familiarly known as "Willy Pogany." He has worked successfully in many fields including murals, stage decoration, costumes and motion-picture art. Among the more than one hundred fifty books he has illustrated is the *Rubaiyat* of OMAR KHAYYAM in the Edward FITZGERALD translation.

Pointes (Fr.), in ballet a term designating the extreme tips of the toes: the *demipointe* refers to the position on the balls of the feet, and *temps de pointes* to movements on the toes.

Pointillism, a term employed in NEO-IMPRESSIONISM to a system of applying pigment in measured strokes to a canvas.

Poiré, Emmanuel, see **Caran d'Ache.**

Polacco, Giorgio (1875-), Italian conductor who studied at the Liceo Benedetto Marcello at Venice, and the Verdi Conservatory at Milan: after achieving success at Milan, Genoa, Rome, Buenos Aires, Brussels, and St. Petersburg, he

made his American debut in 1911 with the Henry SAVAGE English Grand Opera Company in the English production of Puccini's *Girl of the Golden West.* He joined the METROPOLITAN OPERA COMPANY in 1912, and succeeded Arturo Toscanini in 1915 as principal conductor of Italian, French, and Russian opera. From 1918 to 1930 he directed Italian productions for the Chicago Opera Company.

Polasek, Albin (1879-), American sculptor born in Czechoslovakia who came to the United States in 1901, and became head of the sculpture department at the Chicago Art Institute. His notable works include *Fantasy; The Sower; Aspiration:* also busts of many noted Americans, and a memorial to Theodore THOMAS at Chicago.

Polka, a folk dance which is said to have originated in 1830 in Bohemia: it became popular at Prague, and later throughout Europe and America. The tempo is fairly rapid, and the steps involved are graceful: the best example of Bohemian origin is Friedrich SMETANA's polka in his opera, The BARTERED BRIDE.

Pollajuolo, Antonio (1429-1498), Italian sculptor, jeweler, painter, and engraver who studied with his father, a famous goldsmith. In addition to fashioning many objects of art such as crosses, chasubles, copes, and crucifixes, he executed many paintings and frescoes including *Saint Sebastian; Saint Christopher and the Infant Christ; Apollo and Daphne; Labors of Hercules;* among his sculptures are *Hercules Slaying Cacus,* and *Ten Fighting Nudes.* His brother, **Piero Pollajuolo** (1443-1496), collaborated with him on many of the works mentioned above, and also executed independently *Coronation of the Virgin; Three Saints,* an altarpiece; *Prudence; Portrait of a Young Lady.* Antonio's nephew, **Simone Pollajuolo** (1457-1508), was a distinguished architect who completed the Strozzi Palace at Florence begun by Giuliano da MAJANO, designed the great hall in the Palazzo Vecchio, and was a close friend of SAVONAROLA.

Pollock, Channing (1880-), American author and dramatist who acted as dramatic critic on the Washington *Post,* and as general press representative for William A. BRADY, and for Sam S. and Lee SCHUBERT: his plays include *A Game of Hearts* (1900); *The Pit,* a dramatization of the novel by Frank NORRIS; *In the Bishop's Carriage; The Enemy; The Fool; The Sign on the Door; The House Beautiful:* also several editions of the ZIEGFELD FOLLIES, and many plays in which he acted as collaborator. His autobiography, *Harvest of My Years,* was published in 1943.

Pollock, Courtenay Edward•Maxwell (?-1943), English sculptor, inventor, and author educated at the Royal College of Art, London, who served in the British Army during World War I: his works include many memorials of World War I; busts of King George VI of England, Marlene Dietrich, Joseph Chamberlain and Edna Best: in 1934 he invented an electrical robot known as the "Mobile Head" which exactly simulated the expressions of the human face.

Pollux, Julius, Greek grammarian who worked at Naucratis, Egypt, during the 2nd century of the Christian Era: he is the author of the *Onomasticon,* a Greek dictionary which is arranged according to subject matter, and supplies much valuable information on many points pertaining to classical antiquity, in particular the Greek theatre.

Polo, Marco (1254-1324), celebrated Venetian traveler in China: his father, Nicolo Polo, and his uncle, Maffeo Polo, were both merchants who traveled, accompanied by Marco, in Asia farther than any other Europeans, visiting China where they made a long stay, finally returning to Venice in 1295. While in prison at Genoa, Polo dictated an account of his travels to a fellow prisoner, Rusticiano of Pisa, which became very popular.

Polonaise (Fr.), a Polish dance of dignified character written in 3-4 time and danced in the march tempo. It was probably first used in Poland at the coronation of Henri III of Anjou as a promenade, and used in Germany as the opening dance at court balls. Johann Sebastian Bach, Handel, Beethoven, Mozart, and Schubert composed polonaises, but Frédéric Chopin idealized it in works reflecting the ancient glories, indomitable spirit, and characteristic sadness of the Poles.

Polovetzian Dances (Borodin), a series of dances composed by Alexander Borodin for his opera, Prince Igor; left unfinished but completed by Nicholas Rimsky-Korsakow. In concert performances the dances are often performed without the choral sections, and are usually played without pause. The Polovetsi were nomad tribes inhabiting Eastern Russia. The various dances vary widely in rhythm and character: there are dances of wild men, of young girls and boys, of slave-girls and of prisoners; dances in praise of the great Khan, and a wild, general dance employing remarkably vigorous and captivating rhythms. The occasion in the opera is the festival which Konchak Khan, chief of the Polovetsi, devises for the entertainment of Prince Igor, whom he has captured, and whom he greatly respects as a warrior and as a man. There is a Victor recording by the Philadelphia Orchestra directed by Leopold Stokowski, and a Columbia recording by the London Philharmonic Orchestra with Sir Thomas Beecham.

Polychord, (*1*) a musical instrument invented by Franz Hillmer of Berlin; it was shaped like a double bass, had a movable fingerboard with ten gut strings, and could be played either with a bow, or by plucking the strings. (*2*) An instrument with the same name, invented by a blind Greek musician, Evangeleos Tsamourtzis, and demonstrated at Town Hall, New York City, in 1937. His polychord may be likened to a double harp, with a sounding board between its two upright wings and with pedals which serve the same purpose as piano pedals. Attached to the two wings are one hundred and seventeen strings, some of which duplicate one another so that through part of the compass the effect can be that of two instruments playing together.

Polycletus, Greek sculptor who worked during the 5th century B.C., and may have been a pupil of Agelades: his works include the Doryphorus (Lance-bearer); the *Diadumenus,* a figure of a young man tying the band of victory around his head; *The Amazon.* He is also said to have made an ivory and gold statue of Hera for the temple of the goddess at Argo.

Polyeuctos, Greek sculptor who worked during the 3rd century B.C.: he executed a bronze statue of Demosthenes which portrays the orator standing with crossed hands. The inscription on the statue reads: "Had thy power, O Demosthenes, equalled thy genius, the Macedonian Ares would never have conquered the Greeks." A copy of this statue is in the Vatican.

Polygnotus, Greek painter who worked at the beginning of the 5th century, B.C., and is credited with having decorated many of the public buildings in Athens: his most important work was a series of frescoes for a building erected near the temple of Apollo at Cnidus. He is said to have been one of the first painters to free his figures of stiffness, and to impart varied expression to faces.

Polyphemus, in Greek mythology a one-eyed giant or Cyclops: he was the son of Poseidon, and once succeeded in capturing Odysseus and his band on their journey home from the Trojan War. Odysseus blinded Polyphemus and escaped with his men by hiding in the fleece of sheep which were being led out of the giant's cave.

Polyphony, in music the term applied to a form of unaccompanied vocal music in which each voice sings an individual melody: all parts are of equal importance, and are composed in accordance with the rules of counterpoint. The term is also employed in connection with part writing for instruments.

Pomona, in Roman mythology the goddess of fruit and gardens: she was represented as a beautiful maiden with fruits in her bosom and a pruning knife in her hand. A sacred grove near Ostia was called the Pomonal, and she had a special priest at Rome.

"Pomp and Circumstance" Marches (Elgar), six military marches in the grand style; they were composed by Sir Edward Elgar because, as he expressed it, "Soldiers too often march to the most trivial music; why not try to give them something better?" The D major march was first performed in 1901 at Liverpool; later Elgar used the Trio of the march in the choral ending of the *Coronation Ode* dedicated to Edward VII, set to a text beginning *Land of Hope and Glory.* There are Columbia and Victor recordings.

Pompadour, Jeanne Antoinette Poisson le Normant d'Étioles, Marquise de (1721-1764), a French woman who became mistress of Louis XV in 1745 and gradually mixed in politics until she became the supreme power of France until her death: she has a place in this volume because she was a liberal patron of artists and men of letters including Voltaire, Diderot, Boucher, Greuze, Jean Baptiste Van Loo and Joseph Vien.

Pompeii, an ancient Italian city dominated by the Romans: it was almost entirely destroyed by a violent earthquake in 63 A.D., but the inhabitants, numbering between twenty and thirty thousand, rebuilt their dwellings. Sixteen years later the eruption of Mount Vesuvius in 79 A.D. destroyed the towns of Pompeii, Herculaneum and several other smaller villages: inhabitants and buildings were buried under an avalanche of lava. Excavations were begun in 1748, and again in 1860, and most of the objects recovered are in the Naples Museum. Among the parts of the city, houses, and objects discovered are the house of the Vettii; the cemeteries with their altars; the triangular Forum; the ramparts of the city; the house of Lucretia; the market; the great theatre; the little theatre; the amphitheatre: also statues, vases and household utensils of all descriptions.

Ponchielli, Amilcare (1834-1886), Italian dramatic composer who studied at the Milan Conservatory: his first real success was the revised version of *I promessi sposi* produced in 1872 after its failure in 1856. Although he composed several more operas, *La* GIOCONDA, produced at LA SCALA, Milan, in 1876, and at the Metropolitan Opera House, New York, in 1883, was the only other one which has become popular in all opera-loving countries.

Pons, Lily (1904-), French COLORATURA soprano who made her debut in 1929 at Mulhouse, Alsace, in DELIBES' LAKME: after study with Giovanni ZENATELLO and Maria GAY, she made her debut in 1931 at the Metropolitan Opera House, New York, in DONIZETTI's LUCIA DI LAMMERMOOR. She has since made guest appearances at many American opera houses, also touring Europe, appearing in several films and on radio broadcasts.

Ponselle, Rosa (1894-), American dramatic soprano who first appeared in vaudeville with her sister, Carmela, in a singing act called the "Ponzillo Sisters," this being the family name. She made her debut in 1918 at the Metropolitan Opera House in VERDI's *La Forza del Destino* with Enrico CARUSO, remaining with the company as a leading soprano until 1937. Her sister, **Carmela Ponselle,** also sang at the Metropolitan.

Ponte, Jacopo or **Giacomo,** see **Bassano, Jacopo da Ponte.**

Pontoppidan, Henrik (1857-), Danish novelist educated at the University of Copenhagen: his novels, which reveal an intimate acquaintance with peasant life and character, include a trilogy, *Soil* (1891), *The Promised Land,* and *Day of Judgment,* regarded as his masterpiece. Two other series, *Lucky Per* and *The Kingdom of the Dead,* present vivid pictures of life in Denmark as it was before World War II.

Pontormo, Jacopo da (1494-1557), Italian painter whose real name was Jacopo Carucci: he studied with LEONARDO DA VINCI, ALBERTINELLI, PIERO DI COSIMO and Andrea del SARTO. His works, which were highly praised by RAPHAEL and MICHELANGELO, include *Holy Family; Visitation; Supper at Emmaus; Venus Kissed by Cupid; Joseph Accused by Potiphar; Birth of St. John the Baptist; Madonna and Saints.*

Poole, Ernest (1880-), American novelist who was educated at Princeton University: his works include *The Harbor* (1915), a story of life on the water front of New York City; *His Family,* which won the Pulitzer Prize in 1918; *The Dark People; The Village; Great Winds.*

Pope, Alexander (1688-1744), English poet who had little opportunity for public school education because of his frail health: his literary career began at 17, and his notable works include *The Pastorals* (1709); *Essay on Criticism; The Rape of the Lock,* his masterpiece; *The Temple of Fame; The Dunciad; Essay on Man; Imitations of Horace.* He also translated the *Iliad* and the *Odyssey* of HOMER.

Pope, John Russell (1874-), American architect educated at the College of the City of New York, the School of Mines, Columbia University, the American Academy at Rome, and ECOLE DES BEAUX-ARTS, Paris. Since 1900 he has designed many important public and private buildings including Constitution Hall, Washington, D. C., the Union Station, Richmond, Va., and the Baltimore Museum of Art.

Poppea, see **Coronation of Poppea, The.**

Popper, David (1843-1913), Bohemian violoncellist and composer who studied with George GOLTERMANN at the Prague Conservatory, and toured Europe many times with immense success, and from 1896 until his death occupied the post of professor of the violoncello at the Landesmusikakademie in Budapest. His compositions are still favorites with violoncellists both for study and recital purposes.

Pordenone, Giovanni Antonio da (1483-1539), Italian painter who was known by several other names: he studied with Pellegrino TIBALDI, and executed many frescoes in Italian and Venetian church and palaces: among his paintings are *Salome; St. George and the Dragon; Woman in Mourning Dress; The Seizing of Christ; Assumption; Old Man Tempting Young Girl.*

Porgy and Bess, Negro folk-opera in two acts: libretto by Du Bose HEYWARD; music by George GERSHWIN; first produced in 1935 at New York and successfully revived in 1942. The plot concerns itself with the loves, hates, and sordid misery of the lower strata in the Negro section of New York, known as Harlem: it follows closely the action of the folk play, *Porgy,* by Du Bose and Dorothy Heyward produced at New York in 1927.

Porpora, Nicola Antonio (1686-1766), Italian operatic composer who studied at the Conservatory di San Loreto, and produced his first opera, *Agrippina,* in 1709. He wrote more than 50 operas, and endeavored unsuccessfully to compete with George Frederick HANDEL in the production of Italian opera at London, but his fame rests chiefly on his ability and genius as a teacher of singing.

Portaels, Jean François (1818-1895), Belgian painter who studied in Paris with Paul DELAROCHE; won the Grand Prix de Rome and traveled in Spain, Hungary, and the East, later becoming director of the Brussels Academy. His notable works include *Star of Bethlehem; Flight into Egypt; Leah and Rachel; Suicide of Judas; Jealousy; Girl from Istria; Funeral in the Desert; Box in the Theatre at Budapest.*

Portamento (It.), in singing and the playing of musical instruments with a bow, the smooth gliding from one tone to another: it differs from LEGATO in the actual passing through intermediate tones without a break noticeable to the ear.

Port de Bras (Fr.), in ballet the position or carriage of the arms, especially in relation to the five positions of the arms which accompany the FIVE POSITIONS of the feet.

Porter, Cole (1892-), American composer and writer of lyrics educated at Yale University who served in France during World War I: among the successful musical comedies for which he has written scores are *Hitchy-Koo* (1919); *Wake Up and Dream; Fifty Million Frenchmen; The Gay Divorcé; Anything Goes; Jubilee; Dubarry Was a Lady:* he has also composed the music for *Born to Dance, Rosalie,* and several other films.

Porter, Eleanor Hodgman (1868-1920), American novelist and short story writer: her works include *Cross Currents* (1907); *The Turn of the Tide; Miss Billy; Miss Billy's Decision; Polyanna* (1913); a best seller to the extent of more than a million copies; *Polyanna Grows Up,* a sequel greatly enjoyed by the admirers of "Polyanna."

Porter, Gene Stratton (1868-1924), American novelist whose first piece of fiction was published by the *Metropolitan Magazine:* her works include *Freckles* (1904); *A Girl of the Limberlost; The Harvester; Laddie:* the sales of these four books amounted to nearly seven million copies. She was extremely fond of nature, and several of her books deal with birds and kindred subjects: she also wrote *The Fire-Bird,* an Indian drama.

Porter, Jane (1776-1850), Scottish novelist whose first work, *Thaddeus of Warsaw* (1803) was an immediate success, and later translated into several languages: her second work, a historical novel, *The Scottish Chiefs* (1810), also had great success. Her sister, **Anna Maria Porter** (1780-1832), was also a successful novelist with tales such as *Walsh Colville* (1797); *The Hungarian Brothers;* and *Barony.* Her brother, Sir **Robert Ker Porter** (1775-1842), was a distinguished historical painter who traveled extensively in Russia, Finland, and Sweden where he was knighted by Gustavus IV in 1806.

Porter, Katherine Anne (1894-), American author who did much literary hack work before success came to her as an original writer: her works include *Flowering Judas* (1930); *Hacienda; Noon Wine; Pale Horse, Pale Rider; No Safe Harbor:* she also translated the Mexican picaresque novel, *The Itching Parrot.*

Porter, Quincy (1897-), American composer and teacher educated at Yale University and the Yale School of Music who headed the theory department at the Cleveland Institute of Music, and studied under a GUGGENHEIM FELLOWSHIP at Paris. In 1932 he became professor of music at Vassar College, and succeeded Frederick S. CONVERSE as dean of the New England Conservatory in 1938, and in 1942 John Wallace GOODRICH as director. His compositions include incidental music, orchestral works, and chamber music.

Porter, Sir Robert Ker, see **Porter, Jane.**

Porter, William Sydney, see **Henry, O.**

Portico, in architecture a term for a covered GALLERY or COLONNADE in which the ceiling is supported by COLUMNS, PILLARS, or ARCHES: both the ancient Greeks and Romans incorporated the construction into their temples and residences.

Porto-Riche, Georges de (1849-1930), French dramatist whose first plays in verse were produced at Paris in 1870: his first success was *The Luck of Françoise* at the Theatre Libre, Paris, in 1888. He was a master in the writing of dramas connected with men and women in love: in 1898 he published *The Theatre of Love* comprising four dramas, and Mme. Réjane found one of her most trying and successful roles as Germaine in *Amoureuse.*

Portugal, Marcos Antonio da Fonseca (1762-1830), Portuguese composer of 21 comic operas, 35 Italian operas, and more than 100 pieces of sacred music. His operas were performed in their entirety throughout Europe and in London: they are no longer produced, but he is considered the greatest Portuguese composer of his period.

Poseidon, in Greek mythology the god of the sea and the protector of all bodies of water. He was able to cause storms and earthquakes by shaking his trident: AMPHITRITE was his wife, and ZEUS his brother. He was the father of TRITON, ORION, PEGASUS and POLYPHEMUS, and his name was NEPTUNE in Roman mythology.

Post, George Browne (1837-1913), American architect educated at New York who studied with Richard Morris HUNT, and served in the Civil War: his notable works include the building for the New York *World,* the Produce Exchange, the Stock Exchange, and the buildings of the College of the City of New York: also the State Capitol at Madison, Wisconsin.

Post, Guy Bates (1875-), American stage and screen actor who made his debut in *Charlotte Corday* with Mrs. James BROWN-POTTER and Kyrle BELLEW: among the plays in which he has appeared are *Arizona; My Lady Dainty; Manon Lescaut; Bleak House; The Virginian; Tess of the D'Urbervilles; The Nigger; The Masquerader; The Green Goddess; The Climax.* He has also been featured in numerous films including *The Masquerader; Fatal Lady; 'Till We Meet*

Again; The Case Against Mrs. Ames; Maytime; Maid of Salem; Daughter of Shanghai.

Post, Melville Davisson (1871-1930), American novelist and short story writer educated at West Virginia University who practiced law for many years: his works include *The Strange Schemes of Randolph Mason; The Man of Last Resort; The Corrector of Destinies; Uncle Abner: Master of Mysteries; Walker of the Secret Service,* and many more detective and mystery novels and stories.

Poster, a placard, either printed, lithographed or painted by hand, used for public exhibition. It was used in ancient Egypt, Greece, and Rome, but became more in general use after the invention of printing: artistic posters began in France about 1840, and colored posters in both England and France about 1860. Many distinguished artists in Europe, England and the United States have designed posters for either commercial, social or altruistic purposes: among the Americans are Maxfield PARRISH, Howard Chandler CHRISTY, James Montgomery FLAGG, Charles Dana GIBSON, Harrison FISHER and Rockwell KENT.

Post-impressionism, in art the term applied to a movement representing a reaction again REALISM and IMPRESSIONISM: Paul CEZANNE, Paul GAUGUIN, and Édouard MANET were among those who advocated entirely new methods such as CUBISM and FUTURISM which rejected all traditions in favor of uncontrolled personal expression.

Potter, Cora Urquhart (1858-1936), American actress, married name Mrs. James Brown-Potter, who gained her first experience in acting as a drawing-room elocutionist, and made her debut at London in 1887. She was one of the first women in American society to take up the stage as a career, touring the United States, Great Britain, the Far East, Australia, and South Africa. Her ability as an actress was mediocre, but she kept her name before the public by means of well-planned publicity until she retired in 1912.

Potter, Edward Clark (1857-1923), American sculptor who worked with Daniel Chester FRENCH on several groups including the *Columbus Quadriga* at the World's Columbian Exposition, Chicago. They also worked together on equestrian statues of Generals Grant, Washington, and Hooker. His original works include *Sleeping Faun* at the CHICAGO ART INSTITUTE, the *Lions* before the New York Public Library, and animal groups in the PIERPONT MORGAN LIBRARY, New York.

Potter, Paul or **Paulus** (1625-1654), Dutch painter who studied with his father, Pieter Potter: his notable works include *The Young Bull; Landscape with Cattle; Horses at a Trough; Shepherd's Hut; Orpheus Charming the Animals; Start for the Chase; Bowling Green by a Farm; Park with Hunting Party; Farm Scene; Huntsmen at Rest.*

Poulenc, Francis (1899-), French composer who studied the piano with Ricardo Viñes, but was self-taught in composition. His works show the influence of Eric SATIE, Igor STRAVINSKY, and Maurice RAVEL: they include stage pieces; a concerto for harpsichord and orchestra; a concerto for two pianos and orchestra; chamber music; songs, and piano pieces for both solo and duet.

Poussin, Gaspard, see **Dughet, Gaspard.**

Poussin, Nicolas (1594-1665), French painter who studied at Paris, and with François DUQUESNOY at Rome: Louis XIII made him chief painter at the French court, but the jealousy of other painters drove him to Rome where he remained until his death. His notable paintings include *Moses Saved from the Waters; Manna in the Desert; Judgment of Solomon; Rape of the Sabines; Ruth and Boaz; Moses Striking the Rock; Venus and Adonis; Orpheus and Eurydice; Vision of St. Paul; St. Peter and St. John Healing the Lame Man.*

Powell, Dawn (1897-), American novelist whose first novel, *She Walks in Beauty,* was published in 1928 after being rejected more than thirty times: her works include *The Bride's House; Dance Night; The Tenth Moon; Story of a Country Boy; Turn, Magic Wheel; A Time to Be Born:* also the plays *Big Night* and *Jig Saw.*

Powell, John (1882-), American pianist and composer educated at the University of Virginia who studied the piano with Theodor LESCHITIZKY and composition with Karl Navrátil: after successful tours of Europe and the United States he devoted himself to composing. His works include a concerto for piano; a violin concerto; the world-famous *Negro Rhapsody* for orchestra; *Sonata Virginianesque* for violin and piano; several piano sonatas; choral works, and an opera, *Judith and Holofernes.*

Powell, Maud (1868-1920), American violinist who studied with Henry SCHRADIECK, Charles DANCLA, and Joseph JOACHIM, making her debut in 1885 with the Berlin Philharmonic Orchestra, and her American debut during the same year with the New York Philharmonic-Symphony Orchestra conducted by Theodore THOMAS. She toured America annually for many years, organized her own string quartet, was the first violinist to make records for the Victor company, and made many arrangements and transcriptions for the violin.

Powell, William (1892-), American stage and screen actor who was trained at the Academy of Dramatic Arts, New York, and spent ten years on the stage: among the films in which he has appeared since 1929 are *Four Feathers; Street of Chance; Road to Singapore; Jewel Robbery; One Way Passage; Manhattan Melodrama; The Thin Man; The Great Ziegfeld; After the Thin Man; My Man Godfrey; The Last of Mrs. Cheyney; Another Thin Man; Love Crazy; Shadow of the Thin Man.*

Power, Tyrone (1798-1841), Irish actor who was the son of a strolling player. He achieved success in romantic roles at London and New York: a brilliant career terminated when he was drowned in the sinking of the S. S. "America" while returning to England from New York. His grandson, **Tyrone Power** (1869-1931), was born in England, but made his stage debut in 1886 at St. Augustine, Fla., in *The Private Secretary:* he was a member of the Augustin DALY Company for several years, and also played opposite Sir Herbert Beerbohm TREE, Minnie Maddern FISKE, Sir Henry IRVING, Mrs. Leslie CARTER, and Henrietta CROSMAN. He also excelled in Shakespearean roles. His son, **Tyrone Power** (1913-), was trained for the stage by his father, and first appeared in 1931 at Chicago in a minor part in Shakespeare's *The Merchant of Venice*. After playing in 1936 with Katharine CORNELL in *Saint Joan*, he achieved great success in the film, *Girls' Dormitory* in 1936 with SIMONE SIMON: among the pictures in which he appeared are *Lloyds of London; Café Metropole; In Old Chicago; Marie Antoinette; Suez; Rose of Washington Square; The Rains Came; Brigham Young; The Mark of Zorro; Blood and Sand; Son of Fury; The Black Swan*.

Powers, Hiram (1805-1873), American sculptor who first experimented with wax modeling in a Cincinnati museum, later receiving a few commissions for portrait busts at Washington, D. C., including those of Chief Justice John Marshall, John C. Calhoun, and Daniel Webster. He then studied abroad, and finally settled in Florence where he was aided by Horatio Greenough. His works include *Eve* which excited the interest of Albert THORWALDSEN; *Greek Slave* which established his reputation all over the world; statues of Benjamin Franklin and Thomas Jefferson; *Fisher Boy; Il Penseroso; Proserpine; California; America*. His studio in Florence was the Mecca for many distinguished contemporaries including LONGFELLOW, BROWNING, DICKENS and Thomas BALL.

Powers, James T. (1862-1943), American comedian who made his debut in 1880 at Boston in *Dreams, or Fun in a Photographic Gallery:* among the numerous plays in which he appeared were *A Tin Soldier; Nadjy; The Drum Major; The Circus Girl; The Geisha; San Toy; The Runaway Girl; The Messenger Boy; A Bunch of Keys; Gilbert and Sullivan* operettas; *The Rivals; Seven Keys to Baldpate; The Beaux Stratagem; Becky Sharp*. He was the oldest member of the PLAYERS CLUB at the time of his death: his autobiography, *Twinkle, Twinkle, Little Star*, was published in 1939.

Powys, John Cowper (1872-), English essayist, poet and novelist educated at Cambridge: his works include lectures on English and American authors: also *War and Culture; Visions and Revisions; The Enjoyment of Literature*. Among his novels and poems are *Wood and Stone; Wolf's Bane; Wolf Solent; Owen Glendower; Mandragora*. His brother, **Llewelyn Powys** (1884-1939), was the author of *Ebony and Ivory* (1925); *Skin for Skin; The Verdict of Bridlegoose; Henry Hudson; A Pagan's Pilgrimage; Love and Death; Baker's Dozen*. Another brother, **Theodore Francis Powys** (1875-), has written several uncompromisingly realistic novels such as *Black Bryony* (1923); *Mr. Weston's Good Wine; Unclay; Captain Patch; Goat Green*.

Poynter, Sir Edward John (1836-1919), English painter who studied at the Royal Academy, London, and in Paris with M. Gleyre: later he became director of the art school at the South Kensington Museum. His notable works include *Faithful unto Death; Israel in Egypt; Perseus and Andromeda; Atalanta's Race; Venus and Aesculapius; Jersey Lily*, a portrait of Mrs. LANGTRY; *The Queen of Sheba's Visit to King Solomon*.

Pradilla, Francesco (c.1847-1921), Spanish painter who studied at Madrid and at the Spanish Academy in Rome of which he later became director: his notable canvases include *Jeane la Folle Following Her Husband's Coffin; The Surrender of Granada to Ferdinand and Isabella; Washerwomen at the Brook; Lackey Asleep; Procession in Venice; Road to the Sanctuary*.

Prado (Madrid), the national museum of art at Madrid, Spain: it was first housed in a building begun in 1785 and completed in 1830, and was composed of the pictures which were originally in the various palaces and royal residences of Madrid. There are now almost 2500 paintings in the museum which afford a comprehensive idea of the history of painting in Spain: they include an unequaled selection of canvases by VELAZQUEZ, El GRECO, RIBERA, ZURBARAN, MURILLO and GOYA; twenty works by TITIAN, and masterpieces by TINTORETTO, CORREGGIO, LOTTO, DURER, VERONESE, RUBENS, CRANACH, CLAUDE LORRAIN, BOSCH, POUSSIN, and hundreds of other classic, romantic, and modern painters of all nationalities.

Pratt, Bela Lyon (1867-1917), American sculptor who studied with Augustus SAINT-GAUDENS: his works include figures and groups for the World's Columbian Exhibition, Chicago, and Pan-American Exhibition, Buffalo; figures and decorative sculptures for the Library of Congress, Washington, D. C., *Science and Art* for the Boston Public Library; *Nathan Hale* at Yale University; statues of Nathaniel Hawthorne and Alexander Hamilton.

Pratt, Silas Gamaliel (1846-1916), American pianist and composer who studied the piano with Franz Bendel, Theodor KULLAK, and Franz LISZT; also composition and score-reading with Heinrich Dorn. His works include several operas including *Lucille, Zenobia*, and *The Triumph of Columbus* all of which were produced; *Centennial Overture; Lincoln Symphony;* two symphonic poems and a cantata, *The Last Inca*.

Praxiteles (c.380-c.340 B.C.), Greek sculptor who worked during the 4th century B.C.; he is said to have been at Athens about 360 B.C., where he created a statue of a satyr and also of EROS: in 350 B.C. he was in EPHESUS to design an altar for the temple of ARTEMIS. Among the works credited to him are the HERMES at Olympia; the bas-reliefs *Contest of Apollo and Marsyas; Aphrodite of Cos; Aphrodite of Cnidus; Satyr of the Capitol; Apollo Sauroctonus; Silenus and Dionysus*.

Predella (It.), in architecture the step or platform on which an altar rests, and also the shelf raised at the back above the altar: the name is also applied to the sculpture or painting which adorns the platform or shelf.

Preller, Friedrich Johann Christian Ernst (1804-1878), German painter who studied at the Weimar Art School and also imbibed the art of Paul POTTER and Salomon RUISDAEL. His notable works include sixteen paintings inspired by HOMER's *Odyssey;* several landscapes in Thuringia; *Calypso Bidding Ulysses Farewell.* His son, **Friedrich Preller** (1838-1891), was a painter of landscapes and murals such as *Prometheus and Iphigenia; The Acropolis at Athens; Sappho; Theseus Leaving Naxos; Lonely Ride.*

Prelude, in music an introduction to the principal part of a composition: it was first introduced in the sonatas and suites of Arcangelo CORELLI and Johann Sebastian BACH; the latter wrote a set of 48 preludes and fugues called The WELL-TEMPERED CLAVICHORD. The term was also used for short piano pieces by Frédéric CHOPIN and Claude DEBUSSY: Richard WAGNER used it instead of the term OVERTURE for the introductory instrumental parts of his music dramas.

Prelude à l'après-midi d'un faun, see **Afternoon of a Faun, The.**

Prelude and Love Death (Tristan and Isolde), a combination of the prelude and final scene in Richard Wagner's music drama, TRISTAN AND ISOLDE: the composer made the orchestral transcription in which the voice parts in the final scene are incorporated into the orchestration, and frequently conducted it himself. There is a Victor recording by the Berlin Philharmonic Orchestra directed by Wilhelm FURTWANGLER: it is also a part of the Victor "Symphonic Synthesis" arranged by Leopold Stokowski and played by the PHILADELPHIA ORCHESTRA.

Preludes (Chopin), a series of twenty-four fanciful piano compositions in all keys by Frédéric CHOPIN; listed as Op. 28. Frederick NIECKS, Chopin's greatest biographer, likens them to "an artist's portfolio filled with drawings in all stages of advancement, finished and unfinished, all mixed indiscriminately together." James HUNEKER and Henry T. FINCK express the opinion that they would make Chopin immortal if he had written nothing else: Anton RUBINSTEIN referred to them as the pearls of Chopin's works. There is a Victor recording of all twenty-four preludes and both Columbia and Victor recordings of each one separately.

Preludes (Debussy), a series of twenty-four preludes composed by Claude DEBUSSY: the first book of twelve appeared in 1910 and the second book of twelve before the end of 1913. There is no similarity in conception or execution between the preludes of Frédéric CHOPIN and Debussy: Chopin's preludes were originally without program titles while it would appear from the titles that Debussy affixed to his preludes, such as *Sails; The Interrupted Serenade; The Sunken Cathedral; Minstrels; Ondine; Fireworks,* etc., that the composer had direct inspiration for each one. There is a complete Columbia recording played by Walter Gieseking, and individual Victor and Columbia recordings of the entire series.

Preludes, Les (Liszt), a symphonic work by Franz LISZT which was originally planned as a CANTATA begun in 1844: ten years later, chancing upon the unfinished composition after he had read Alphonse Lamartine's fifteenth Meditation (called "Les Préludes," in a series of poems entitled "New Poetic Meditations"), Liszt decided to reconstruct it to illustrate the séntiments of the poem. In its new form, Liszt conducted the first performance of the work at a benefit concert for the widows and children of deceased members of the Court Orchestra in the Grand Ducal Theatre at Weimar. The passage referred to reads in part: "What is our life but a series of preludes to that unknown song, the first solemn note of which is sounded by death? Love forms the enchanted daybreak of every life; but what is the destiny where the first delights of happiness are not interrupted by some storm, whose fatal breath dissipates its fair illusions, whose fell lightning consumes its altar? And what wounded spirit, when one of its tempests is over, does not seek to rest its memories in the sweet calm of country life?" There is a Victor recording by the Philadelphia Orchestra under Eugene Ormandy, and a Columbia recording by the London Symphony Orchestra directed by Felix Weingartner.

Prendergast, Maurice Brazil (1859-1924), American painter born in Newfoundland who was brought to Boston, Mass., by his parents as a child: he studied at the Académie Julien under Jean Paul LAURENS: he painted many pictures of the Massachusetts sea coast and of the New England countryside.

Preobrajenska, Olga (1871-), Russian ballerina and dance instructor who studied at the Imperial School in St. Petersburg and with Enrico CECCHETTI, making her debut in 1889, later appearing with great success in many ballets such as Les SYLPHIDES, The Talisman, Esmeralda, Paquita, and SWAN LAKE. .After dancing at St. Petersburg from 1917 to 1921, she founded a school for ballet in Paris: Irina BARANOVA and Tamara TOUMANOVA were among her pupils.

Pre-Raphaelites or **Pre-Raphaelite Brotherhood,** an association of painters, sculptors, architects, and poets; formed about 1848 in England, and probably inspired by the German society known as the NAZARENES. Among the founders were William Holman HUNT, Sir John MILLAIS, Dante Gabriel ROSSETTI, Thomas WOOLNER, John RUSKIN, Ford Max BROWN, Philip Webb, and William MORRIS. The purpose of the association was to remove the academic atmosphere from the arts, and restore the higher ideals existent before RAPHAEL.

Pressenda, Joannes Franciscus (1777-1854), Italian violin maker who was a pupil of Lorenzo Storioni in CREMONA, and established his own workshop at Turin about 1820. He followed the models of Antonius STRADIVARIUS, using a wine-red varnish and carefully selected woods. The value of his violins today ranges from $1000.00 to $3500.00.

Presto (It.), in music a term indicating "fast" or "rapid" which implies a quicker tempo than

ALLEGRO and less fast than *prestissimo:* it is also used as the title of a rapid movement in a SYMPHONY or SONATA.

Preti, Mattia, see Calabrese, Il.

Prévost, Marcel (1862-1941), French novelist and dramatist educated at Catholic schools and colleges who worked as a civil engineer before starting his literary career: his works include *Scorpion* (1887); *The Demi-Virgin* which caused much discussion, and was dramatized; *Guardian Angels; Benoit Castain; His Mistress and I; Restless Sands; Her Master.*

Prévost d'Exiles, Antoine François (1697-1763), French novelist, known as **Abbé Prévost,** who edited a literary journal in Paris, *Le Pour et la contre,* and translated several English novels into French. Although he wrote more than fifty works, the only one of interest today is *Manon Lescaut* (1731), which was used as the literary basis of grand operas by Giacomo PUCCINI and Jules MASSENET.

Priam, in Greek legend the king of Troy when it was besieged by the Greeks during the TROJAN WAR: his wife was Hecuba, and PARIS, who abducted HELEN, was his son.

Priestley, John Boynton (1894-), English novelist, essayist, and dramatist educated at Cambridge University who served in the English Army during World War I. His essays include *Figures in Modern Literature* (1924); *Fools and Philosophers; George Meredith: The English Novel; English Humor:* among his successful novels are *The Good Companions* (1929); *Angel Pavement; Wonder Hero.* His plays include *Laburnum Grove,* also filmed; *The Good Companions* adapted from the novel; *Dangerous Corner.*

Primaticcio, Francesco (1504-1570), Italian painter who studied with Innocenzo da IMOLA and BAGNACAVALLO, later assisting Guilio ROMANO at Mantua, and Il Rosso in the decoration of the Château at FONTAINEBLEAU, finally succeeding him as director of public works. He remained in the royal service, after the death of Francis I, under Henry II, Francis II and Charles IX, continuing his decorative work, and designing the tombs of Francis I and Henry II.

Prime-Stevenson, Edward Irenaeus, see Stevenson, Edward Prime.

Primrose, William (1903-), Scottish violist who studied the violin at the Guildhall School of Music, London, and made his professional debut as a violinist: following the advice of Eugène YSAYE he devoted himself to the viola, and toured extensively as violist of the London String Quartet. In 1938 he became solo violist of the NBC SYMPHONY ORCHESTRA under Arturo TOSCANINI, and has also appeared in recital and on radio broadcasts.

Prince Igor (Borodin), grand opera in a prologue and four acts: libretto by Vladimir Stassoff; music by Alexander BORODIN: left unfinished at the composer's death it was completed by Nicholas Rimsky-Korsakow and Alexander Glazunoff. The Russian première took place at St. Petersburg in 1890, and the American at the Metropolitan Opera House in 1915. The most popular part of the opera is the set of POLOVETZIAN DANCES which form the ballet in the opera, and also a separate ballet in one act employing the same title, *Prince Igor:* the choreographer was Michel Fokine, and the first performance took place at Paris in 1909.

Princes Ida, comic opera in three acts: book by Sir William S. GILBERT; music by Sir Arthur S. SULLIVAN; first performed at London in 1884, and during the same year at New York. The plot concerns itself with the resolve of Princess Ida and her retinue of young ladies to renounce all association with men, and the ultimately successful efforts of Prince Hilarion to induce the ladies abandon their purpose. There is a complete recording by the Victor Company.

Printemps, Yvonne (1895-), French stage and screen actress who made her debut in 1908 at Paris in a revue, *Nué! Cocotte!:* she has appeared many times at the Folies-Bergère, and at other leading Paris theatres with Lucian and Sacha GUITRY; and at London in *Mozart* and *Conversation Piece.* In 1926 she made her New York debut in *Mozart:* she has also appeared in several films including *La Dame aux Camélias; Adrienne Lecouvreur; Three Waltzes.*

Prisoner of Chillon, The, a poem by Lord BYRON in which François de Bonnivard, a Swiss patriot, is the hero: he was imprisoned in the castle of Chillon during the 16th century by Charles III of Savoy, and rescued by the Bernese some years later when they stormed the castle.

Prix de Rome, Grand, a competitive prize awarded by the French Government to students of the fine arts: the winners were given four years of study in Rome with an annual allowance of 4,000 francs for living expenses, and exemption from military service. The prize was instituted by LOUIS XIV in 1666, and is awarded annually by the ECOLE DES BEAUX-ARTS which has full authority over the examinations and awards.

Prize Song (Wagner), the principal song in Richard Wagner's opera, DIE MEISTERSINGER VON NURNBERG, sung by Walther who is awarded the hand of Eva, his beloved, when he wins the singing contest with this song. There is a Victor recording by Lauritz MELCHIOR, a Victor recording for violin by Mischa ELMAN, and a Victor recording for violoncello by Pablo CASALS.

Pro Arte String Quartet, an organization formed in 1912 which won fame at Paris, Salzburg, and Brussels where they were known as the "Pro Arte Concerts," and later toured France, Switzerland and England. In 1923, Mrs. Elizabeth Sprague COOLIDGE selected the Pro Arte Quartet to perform the prize works of the Coolidge Foundation at the American Academy of Rome, and later brought it to America to play at the LIBRARY OF CONGRESS in Washington, New York, and at Harvard and Yale Universities. It is known chiefly for its performances of modern and ultramodern music.

Procaccini, Ercole (1520-c.1591), Italian painter who studied with Annibale CARRACCI, and established a school of painting in Milan at which many famous artists studied. Two of his three sons, **Camillo Procaccini** (1546-1616), **Giulio Cesare Procaccini** (1548-c.1626), were excellent painters who achieved considerable fame as religious painters: his youngest son, **Carlo Antonio Procaccini** (1555-c.1605), had a fine reputation at the Spanish court for still life pictures of fruits and flowers: his son, **Ercole Procaccini** (1596-1676), called the Younger, studied with his uncle, Giulio Cesare Procaccini, excelled in still life paintings, and succeeded the latter as director of the Academy of the Procaccini.

Procrustes, in Greek legend the name of an inhuman robber who enticed travelers to his den, and forced them to lie on beds which were either very long or very short. If the victim was too long for the bed, Procrustes cut off his legs to fit: if he was too short, his legs were stretched until they fitted. THESEUS is credited with having killed the robber after being enticed to his lair.

Procter, Adelaide Anne (1825-1864), English poet who was the daughter of Bryan Waller PROCTER (Barry Cornwall). Her principal work was *Legends and Lyrics* (1858-60), but she is best remembered as the author of "The Lost Chord," set to music by Sir Arthur SULLIVAN.

Procter, Bryan Waller (1787-1874), English poet who wrote under the pen name "Barry Cornwall." He was an intimate of Lord BYRON: his works include *Dramatic Scenes and Other Poems* (1819); *A Sicilian Story; English Songs;* also memoirs of Edmund KEAN, Charles LAMB, Ben JONSON, and William SHAKESPEARE. His daughter was the poet, Adelaide Anne PROCTER.

Proctor, Alexander Phimister (1862-), American sculptor and painter born in Canada who lived for years in the Rocky Mountain section where he studied wild life, and later pursued his studies further at the Jardin des Plantes, Paris. Among his notable sculptures are *Indian Warrior; Panthers; Quadriga; Puma; Princeton Tiger; Broncho Buster; On the Warpath; Tigers.* He has also painted many pictures of wild life in water color.

Prodigal Son, The, a modern ballet in one act: libretto based on the Bible; choreography by David LICHINE; music by Serge PROKOFIEFF; first performed by the DIAGHILEFF Ballet Russe at Paris in 1929, with choreography by George BALANCHINE, and at Sydney, Australia, in 1938 with the Lichine choreography. The action follows closely the story as related in the Bible.

Producer, in drama the director and guiding spirit of a theatrical production: his functions include the selection of a play, and later of its director, scenic designer, costumes and cast in addition to providing or inducing others to provide the funds necessary for the financing of the venture. His success as a producer depends to a considerable extent on his instinct guided by past experience: also on the reaction of the theatregoer rather than that of the critic.

Program Music, the name applied to compositions which endeavor to convey to the listener scenes, incidents, moods or complete stories by means of suggestive titles. The simplest form of program music is that which imitates the sounds of nature, such as bird songs, falling water, the sigh of the wind, etc.; although the term is usually associated with descriptive instrumental compositions by Hector BERLIOZ, Franz LISZT and Richard STRAUSS, the idea was conceived a century earlier and developed in Ludwig van BEETHOVEN's PASTORAL SYMPHONY. Program music is the direct opposite of absolute music, which relies entirely upon its structural and melodic beauty as a medium of musical enjoyment.

Program Notes, the analytical matter printed in a program with the purpose of explaining the compositions being performed. In 1783 notes of this character were used in Berlin and in 1841 at Edinburgh: from barest outlines they have grown almost to the status of musical essays replete with historical facts, biographical data and analytical details. Sir George GROVE, editor of *Grove's Dictionary of Music and Musicians,* was one of the greatest English writers of program notes; in the United States Philip HALE, Henry E. KREBBIEL and Lawrence GILMAN were among the most distinguished contributors of notes to symphonic programs.

Prokofieff, Sergei Sergeievitch (1891-), Russian pianist and composer who wrote three miniature operas by the time he was nine years old, and later studied with Richard GLIERE, Anatol LIADOFF, Nicholas RIMSKY-KORSAKOW, and Annette ESSIPOFF. He won the Anton RUBINSTEIN Prize in 1910, and left Russia in 1918 to tour Japan, the United States, and European countries, finally returning to Russia. His compositions comprise five operas including *The* LOVE FOR THREE ORANGES first performed at Chicago in 1921; several operas; numerous orchestral works such as the *Symphonie Classique* (Classical Symphony), and suites from his various operas and ballets; five piano concertos; two violin concertos; vocal works; chamber music; five piano sonatas. His cantata, *Alexander Nevsky,* was given its American première in 1943 by the NBC SYMPHONY ORCHESTRA under the direction of Leopold STOKOWSKI.

Prokosch, Frederic (1908-), American poet and novelist educated at Haverford College and at the Universities of Pennsylvania, Yale, and Cambridge, England: his works include *The Asiatics* (1935); *The Assassins,* a poem; *The Seven Who Fled; Night of the Poor; The Skies of Europe.*

Prometheus, in Greek mythology a Titan who aided the Olympian gods to master the TITANS: he brought the blessing of fire and heat to mortals, and was punished by ZEUS who chained him to a mountain where a vulture gnawed incessantly at his liver. HERCULES set him free: his story was used in a trilogy by AESCHYLUS, and in a poem by SHELLEY.

"Prometheus" Overture (Beethoven), the prelude to a ballet, *The Creatures of Prometheus:*

choreography by Salvatore VIGANO; music by Ludwig van BEETHOVEN, first produced at Vienna in 1801. Beethoven wrote sixteen numbers, but the overture is the only one which has interest today for music lovers: there is a Victor recording by the London Symphony Orchestra directed by Albert Coates, and a Columbia recording by the Vienna Philharmonic Orchestra under Felix Weingartner.

Propertius, Roman elegiac poet of the 1st century B.C.: he was intimate with MAECENAS, and the author of many historical, social, and amatory poems; the latter dedicated to his mistress, Cynthia, and more than seventy in number.

Propylaeum, in ancient Greek architecture a structure designed as an imposing entrance to an enclosure or group of buildings: the most famous was the Propylaeum at the entrance to the ACROPOLIS at Athens; designed by MNESICLES, and constructed entirely of marble from PENTELICUS.

Proscenium, in the ancient Greek theatre the name given to that part of the stage between the back wall and the orchestra which was occupied by the chorus. In the modern theatre it is that portion of the stage extending between the curtain and the footlights.

Proserpine, see **Persephone.**

Protean Actor, in theatrical parlance an actor, usually in vaudeville, who is skillful in making quick changes of costume and wig, often in sight of the audience: Albert CHEVALIER was one of the most adept in this art.

Proteus, in Greek mythology an old man of the sea who cared for POSEIDON'S seals on the island of Pharos near Egypt. He was possessed of the gift of prophecy, and anyone who could seize upon his person could learn the future, but this was difficult because of his ability to escape by transforming himself into any shape he desired.

Protogenes, Greek painter who worked at Rhodes and Athens from about 332 to 300 B.C., his reputation was established by APELLES who recognized his merits. His notable paintings include *Satyr in Repose; Ialysus; Paralus and Ammonias; Cydippe; Alexander and Pan:* he also executed a portrait of the mother of Aristotle.

Proust, Marcel (1871-1922), French novelist educated at the Lycée Condorcet, Paris: after many years of playing the role of man about town in the aristocratic salons of Paris, he started work in 1905 on one of the longest and most comprehensive of modern novels, *Remembrance of Things Past,* in several parts entitled *Swann's Way; Within a Budding Grove; The Guermantes Way; Cities of the Plain; The Captive; The Sweet Cheat Gone; The Past Recaptured.* Proust worked on it for seventeen years.

Prout, Ebenezer (1835-1909), English composer and theorist who was chiefly self-taught: his important theoretical works include *Instrumentation* (1876); *Harmony, Its Theory and Practice;* several works on COUNTERPOINT and double counterpoint; *Musical Form; The Orchestra.*

Prouty, Olive Higgins (1882-), American novelist educated at Smith College: her works include *Bobbie, General Manager* (1913); *The Fifth Wheel; The Star in the Window; Stella Dallas,* a successful play and motion picture; *Now, Voyager,* also a favorite with film lovers.

Prud'hon, Pierre (1758-1823), French painter who studied at the ECOLE DES BEAUX-ARTS, Paris, and became intimate with Antonio CANOVA who influenced his style. His works, which reveal the influence also of LEONARDO DA VINCI and CORREGGIO, include *Union of Love and Friendship; Wisdom and Truth Descending Upon Earth; Andromache Embracing Astyanax; The Rape of Psyche; The Crucifixion; Cupid Chastised; Justice and Vengeance Pursuing Crime; Napoleon I and Francis II at Austerlitz.*

Prunières, Henry (1886-), French musicologist who studied with Romain ROLLAND and became instructor at the École des Hautes Études Sociales at Paris: he also founded *La Revue Musicale* in 1919 and was the head of the French section of The INTERNATIONAL SOCIETY OF CONTEMPORARY MUSIC. His works include *Lully* (1910); *Italian Opera before Lully; The Court Ballet in France before Benserade and Lully; Monteverdi; A New History of Music* (1943).

Pryor, Arthur (1870-1942), American trombone virtuoso, composer, and bandmaster who was taught to play several instruments including the trombone by his father, Samuel Pryor, a bandmaster. He became the greatest trombone virtuoso in the world, appearing as soloist for many years with John Philip SOUSA's Band. After his father's death he became director of the Pryor Band in 1903, playing for nineteen summers at Asbury Park, N. J., and for ten winters at Miami, Fla. The band made many recordings, and Pryor wrote over 300 compositions for band, one of which is the favorite *Whistler and His Dog.*

Psaltery, a musical instrument of the Middle Ages known to the Hebrews as the *kinnor* and to the Germans as the *rotta:* it was on the order of a harp zither with a varying number of strings plucked by the fingers or with a PLECTRUM. It has often been confused with the DULCIMER, and was in use down to the 17th century.

Pseudonym, in literature or any other art a name assumed by writers, composers, and others to conceal their identity: familiar examples are *Mark Twain* (Samuel Clemens); *O. Henry* (William Sydney Porter); *George Sand* (Mme. Dudevant); *Boz* (Charles Dickens); *Mr. Dooley* (Finley Peter Dunne); *George Eliot* (Mary Ann Evans). Pseudonyms are often used by authors of detective fiction.

Psyche, in Greek mythology the personification of the human or mortal soul: the legend relates how EROS fell deeply in love with Psyche, but because of his divinity forbade her to gaze upon him. He deserted her when she disobeyed his command: a box she opened contained the sleep of death, but when she died, Eros made her immortal.

Puccini, Giacomo (1858-1924), Italian composer whose ancestors were musicians of local importance from 1700. Although he evinced no special aptitude for music his mother had him thoroughly trained in the art, and after hearing Giuseppe VERDI's *Aïda* he resolved to follow the career of an operatic composer. His first opera, *Le Villi,* was produced in 1884: it was followed by *Edgar; Manon Lescaut; Tosca* which eventually became a great success; *La Bohème* which became immediately popular in all opera houses; *Madame Butterfly* which succeeded to an equal degree after being withdrawn and rewritten; *The Girl of the Golden West,* an opera based on David BELASCO's play which had its première in the United States, but failed to please permanently; *La Rondine; Il Tabarro, Suor Angelica* and *Gianni Schicchi,* a trio of one-act operas. His last opera, *Turandot,* lacked the final scene when the composer died: it was completed by Franco Alfano and first performed in 1926.

Puck, a magazine of humorous character founded in 1876: its editors included Sydney Rosenfeld, Henry Cuyler BUNNER, Harry Leon WILSON, John Kendrick BANGS and Arthur Hamilton Folwell. James Gibbons HUNEKER also contributed articles, and Frederick OPPER some of his inimitable cartoons.

Puente, Giuseppe del (1841-1900), Italian operatic baritone who first studied the violoncello, but after being advised to cultivate his voice, made his operatic debut at Jassy, and appeared in many European opera houses. He made his American debut in 1873 at the ACADEMY OF MUSIC, New York, and appeared with the METROPOLITAN OPERA COMPANY in 1883 as Valentin in *Faust.* He also sang with Col. Henry MAPLESON's Company, and with the Adelina PATTI Opera Company.

Puget, Pierre (1622-1694), French painter, sculptor, and architect who worked first at Marseilles on the construction and decoration of GALLEYS, later painting murals and frescoes on the ceilings and walls of the Barberini and Pitti Palaces at Florence. His notable works include a statue of *Milo of Crotona; Perseus and Andromeda; Alexander and Diogenes:* also a statue of St. Sebastian at Genoa. He is regarded as a master of anatomy in modeling.

Pugin, Augustus Welby Northmore (1812-1852), English architect who was instrumental in bringing about the Gothic revival in England: he assisted Sir Charles BARRY with the Houses of Parliament at London and wrote several important treatises including *The True Principles of Pointed or Christian Architecture* (1841) which championed his views on the Gothic style in ecclesiastical design.

Pugnani, Gaetano (1731-1798), Italian violinist and composer who studied with Giovanni SOMIS and later with Giuseppe TARTINI. He made many concert tours, became leader of the Italian Opera at London, played in the *Concerts spirituels* in Paris, and conducted a violin school at which Giovanni Battista VIOTTI was a pupil. His compositions include violin concertos, violin sonatas, chamber music in many different combinations, violin duets, and several operas.

Pugno, Raoul (1852-1914), French pianist and composer trained at the École Niedermeyer in Paris and at the PARIS CONSERVATORY OF MUSIC. After considerable success as a composer of ballets and operettas, he caused a sensation in 1893 by revealing himself as a consummate virtuoso on the piano: he made many successful tours of Europe and America, especially in piano and violin sonata recitals with Eugène YSAYE. His compositions for the piano include the charming *Serenade to the Moon.*

Pulcinella, a comic ballet in one act: libretto based on an old Italian comedy; choreography by Leonide MASSINE; music arranged by Igor STRAVINSKY from a number of unpublished manuscripts of works by Giambattista PERGOLESI at the suggestion of Serge DIAGHILEFF; first performed at Paris by the Ballet Russe in 1920. There is a Columbia recording of a suite for small orchestra conducted by the composer.

Pulitzer, Joseph (1847-1911), American newspaper publisher born in Hungary who came to the United States in 1864, and later became publisher of the St. Louis *Post-Dispatch* and the New York *World.* He left $2,500,000 to the School of Journalism at Columbia University resulting in the establishment of the **Pulitzer Prizes** for American biography, American history, the drama, and the novel in 1917, and for poetry in 1922.

Pulpit, in architecture a raised platform with enclosed front used for the delivery of sermons: some of the older pulpits were made of stone, marble or bronze, but in the Middle Ages they were constructed of wood. They were also occasionally equipped with canopies and sounding-boards, and frequently elaborately carved. The sculptor, Niccola PISANO, created elaborately carved pulpits, but in modern churches the tendency is toward simple design.

Pulszky, Ferencz Aurel (1814-1897), Hungarian author who held several important government posts before being suspected of revolutionary tendencies: he fled with Louis Kossuth, making a tour of America which resulted in his book *White, Red, Black* (1853) describing his experiences. He also wrote a novel, *The Jacobins in Hungary,* and a treatise, *On the Nature of Hungarian Language and Grammar* which is available in an English translation.

Punch and Judy, an English puppet play founded on a ballad which was popular about 1800, and tells the story of a quarrel between Punch and his wife Judy. Punch was originally a stock character in the Italian COMMEDIA DELL'ARTE: he was the hump-backed, hook-nosed, and boasting husband of a sharp-featured virago. The performance was given in a portable theatre and a little dog, Toby, frequently added to the merriment.

Puppet or **Marionette Show,** a dramatic performance employing miniature figures of men and women called puppets or MARIONETTES: the figures are provided with jointed limbs operated by strings or wires from an overhead platform by unseen persons who also recite the dialogue. The performances are enjoyed by young and old in France, Germany, Italy, England, and the United States: they were popular in ancient Greece, China, Java and Japan, and were enthusiastically received in Europe and England during the Middle Ages: GOETHE wrote puppet plays, and both HAYDN and MOZART composed music to be used in connection with puppet-play performances. Theatre-goers in the United States patronized liberally the puppet plays presented by Tony SARG: electrically operated puppets were shown at the New York World's Fair, and the revival of puppet melodrama since about 1890 in France has been an interesting development of modern drama.

Purcell, Henry (c.1659-1695), English organist, harpsichordist, and composer who became organist at WESTMINSTER ABBEY, London, in 1680: he was buried there, and his epitaph reads "Here lies Henry Purcell, Esq., who left this life and is gone to that blessed place where only his harmony can be exceeded." His compositions include a vast quantity of harpsichord pieces, sacred music, and dramatic works: the most famous of the last-named is DIDO AND AENEAS.

Pushkin, Alexander Sergeievitch (1799-1837), Russian poet and dramatist of noble lineage: his works include *Ruslan and Ludmilla* (1820), an epic poem used as the basis of Michail GLINKA's grand opera with the same title; *Eugene Onegin* also the basis of a grand opera by Peter TSCHAIKOWSKY; *The Prisoner of the Caucasus; The Fountain of Baghchisaray; The Gypsies; Poltava; The Golden Cockerel* and *Tsar Saltan* both of which were cast in operatic form by Nicholas RIMSKY-KORSAKOW; *Boris Godunov* which furnished the libretto for Modest MUSSORGSKY's opera with the same title. Pushkin's prose works include *Dubrosky, The Captain's Daughter,* and *Egyptian Nights,* but his reputation is based on his poetical works.

Putnam, Arthur (1873-1930), American sculptor who worked with Willis Polk on the restoration of San Francisco after the earthquake in 1906. He specialized in bronzes of animals many of which are to be seen at the CALIFORNIA PALACE OF THE LEGION OF HONOR, San Francisco. His notable works include *Snarling Tiger* at the Metropolitan Museum of Art, New York; the *Sloat Monument* at Monterey, Calif.; *The Death* at the Museum of Fine Arts, Boston, Mass.

Putnam, Emily James (1865-   ), American educator and author who taught Greek literature and translation at Barnard College, Columbia University, and was dean of the college from 1894 to 1900: her works include *The Lady* (1910) and *Candaules' Wife* (1926).

Puvis de Chavannes, Pierre Cécile (1824-1898), French painter who studied with Henri Scheffer and Thomas COUTURE: his notable works include *Return from the Chase; War and Peace; Life of St. Geneviève* at the Panthéon, Paris; *Work and Rest; Muses Welcoming the Genius of Enlightenment* at the Public Library, Boston, Mass.; *The Poor Fisherman; The Wood Sacred to the Arts and the Muses.*

Pygmalion, in Greek mythology a king of Cyprus who was also a great sculptor: he modeled the statue of a woman, Galatea, which was so beautiful that he begged APHRODITE to bring her to life. The statue came to life and Pygmalion made her his wife. A variation of the myth is the basis of George Bernard Shaw's *Pygmalion,* a successful play and film.

Pyle, Howard (1853-1911), American painter, illustrator, and author who studied at the Art Students' League, New York, and attracted attention with his line drawings in the style of Albrecht DURER. He contributed for years to *Harper's Magazine,* and furnished illustrations for many books relating to American colonial life. The books written and illustrated by him include *The Merry Adventures of Robin Hood; Pepper and Salt; The Wonder Clock; The Rose of Paradise; A Modern Aladdin; The Story of Sir Launcelot; The Story of the Grail.*

Pylon, in Egyptian architecture a construction of solid masonry in the form of a truncated pyramid with a door in the center: they were used as the entrances to temples; at Thebes the pylons were reached through an avenue flanked by obelisks and sphinxes.

Pyramid, a solid construction, usually of stone with a square or polygonal base, the lateral sides meeting in a point at the apex. The great pyramid of Cheops at Gizeh near Cairo is one of the SEVEN WONDERS OF THE WORLD: it is constructed of limestone blocks, and in its original form was 768 feet square and 582 feet high. There were seven smaller pyramids at Gizeh: similar structures have been discovered in Central America and Mexico. The purpose of most pyramids appears to have been cemeterial.

Pyramus and Thisbe, in Babylonian legend a youth and a maid who were forbidden to marry by their parents, and could only talk together secretly through a crevice in the wall which separated their homes. They arranged a tryst at the tomb of Ninus, but a lion with bloody jaws frightened away Thisbe who left behind her mantle covered with blood: when Pyramus saw the mantle he killed himself believing Thisbe dead. The latter returned and killed herself when she saw the lifeless body of her lover.

Pythagoras (c.582-c.500 B.C.), Greek philosopher and mathematician who worked out ratios on musical tones which were handed down to his disciples including Euclid. Many of his theories are accepted as correct by modern musical theorists.

Pythagoras of Rhegium, a Greek sculptor of the 5th century B.C.; a contemporary of MYRON and POLYCLETUS. The works credited to him include a statue of Philoctetes; *Apollo Shooting the Python at Delphi;* a statue of Euthymus, the boxer; *Man Singing to the Lyre.*

Pythia, in ancient Greece the name of the priestess of the *Pythian Oracle,* also known as the DELPHIAN ORACLE. The *Pythian Odes,* twelve in number, were written by PINDAR to honor winners of the *Pythian Games* held every four years at Delphi.

Q

Quaglio, Domenico (1786-1837), Italian painter born in Bavaria who traveled extensively in Germany, the Netherlands, France, Italy, and England: his notable works include *Ruin on a Lake; Old Abbey at Rouen; Fish Market in Antwerp; Forest Chapel; Monastery on the Rhine:* he succeeded in attaining the high standards of the Dutch masters in architectural painting.

Quantz, Johann Joachim (1697-1773), German flutist and composer who also studied the double-bass, harpsichord, and oboe: after playing in several orchestras at Warsaw, Dresden, Paris, and Rome, he became chamber musician and court composer in 1741 for FREDERICK THE GREAT who was also an accomplished flutist and composer. Quantz composed 300 concertos and 200 solo pieces, duets, trios, and quartets for the flute, and also made some mechanical improvements in the instrument.

Quarles, Francis (1592-1644), English poet educated at Christ's College, Cambridge: his works include the poems *Divine Emblems* (1635), *Hieroglyphics,* and *Enchiridon,* a prose work the enormous popularity of which is accounted for by George Saintsbury because of the unjust ridicule heaped upon him by men of letters during his lifetime.

Quarter-Tone Music, a 20th century development which makes use of the interval of one-half of a semitone, the latter representing the smallest interval used in the standard scale. The quarter-tone scale has 24 semitones or double those of the standard scales; it is claimed that many new harmonic effects are obtained, but the difficulties in notation are so great that only a few composers including Hans Barth, Ivan Vyschnegradsky, and Alois Haba have worked in the field.

Quartet, in music a composition for four voices or four instruments: the most popular form today is the *string quartet* written for two violins, viola, and violoncello, and the *piano quartet* composed for piano, violin, viola, and violoncello. The distinguished composers of string quartets include BOCCHERINI, HAYDN, MOZART, BEETHOVEN, SCHUBERT, SCHUMANN, MENDELSSOHN, BRAHMS, and DVORAK.

Quasimodo, in literature a character in the form of a misshapen dwarf in Victor HUGO's *Notre Dame de Paris:* terrifying impersonations have been made in the films by Lon CHANEY and Charles LAUGHTON.

Quatrain, in prosody a verse complete in four rhymed lines: its length or measure is not of consequence, but the lines must be connected by rhyme, and the form is used largely for epigrams because of its brevity.

Queen, Ellery, pseudonym of **Frederic Dannay** (1905-), who has written detective fiction with his cousin, Manfred Bennington Lee, using the pen names "Ellery Queen" and "Barnaby Ross."

Their works include *The Roman Hat Mystery* (1929), *The French Powder Mystery; The Dutch Shoe Mystery,* and many other stories along similar lines.

Queen of Sheba, The, grand opera in four acts: libretto by Paul Jules Barbier and Michel Carré; music by Charles GOUNOD; first produced at Paris in 1862, and at the French Opera House, New Orleans, La., in 1899. The bass aria *She Alone Charmeth My Sadness,* the only number in the opera which has survived, is available in a Columbia recording by Norman Allin. Another opera with the same title, the music for which was composed by Karl GOLDMARK, contains some charming *Ballet Music* available in a Victor recording by the Chicago Symphony Orchestra.

Queen's Lace Handkerchief, The, comic opera in three acts: book by Richard GENEE and music by Johann STRAUSS, JR., first produced at Vienna in 1880 and at New York in 1882. The scintillating music of Strauss is wasted on an inane libretto, but the finest strains are preserved in a set of waltzes, *Roses from the South,* available in both Columbia and Victor recordings.

Quellinus, Erasmus (1607-1678), Flemish painter who studied with RUBENS, and executed a great canvas in 1660 to celebrate the peace between Spain and England. His works include *Bacchus and Ariadne; Death of Eurydice; Rape of Europa; St. Augustin Washing the Feet of Christ; Holy Family; Last Supper; Three Children with a Parrot; Betrothal of Mary and Joseph; Venus with Tritons and Cupids.*

Quental, Anthero de (1842-1891), Portuguese poet educated at the University of Coimbra whose volume of verse, *Sonnets* (1861), was published while he was a student. His other works include *Modern Odes, Romantic Springtides,* and a second volume of sonnets.

Quercia, Jacopo della (1374-1438), Italian sculptor also known as **Jacopo della Fonte:** his works include the monument for Alario del Caretto in Lucca; the *Gaia Fountain* in Siena; the doors of San Petronio at Bologna: his style was a blending of the Gothic with the Renaissance.

Quick, Herbert (1861-1925), American novelist who first practiced law in Sioux City, Ia., and later edited *Farm and Fireside:* his works include *In the Fairyland of America* (1901); *Virginia of the Air Lanes;* a trilogy of novels comprising *Vandemark's Folly, The Hawkeye,* and *The Invisible Woman;* an autobiography, *One Man's Life; Mississippi Steamboatin'* with Edward Quick.

Quill, the implement for writing used before the introduction of the metal pen: it was first used in the Middle Ages. Quills were removed from the goose, swan, crow, and other birds, and after being slightly heated were sharpened to the desired point.

Quiller-Couch, Sir Arthur Thomas (1863-), English novelist and poet educated at Oxford who became professor of English literature at Cambridge in 1912. His works include *Dead Man's Rock* (1887); *The Splendid Spur; The Blue Pavilions; The Ship of Stars; Hetty Wesley; Adventures in Criticism; Studies in Literature:* he has also edited *The Oxford Book of English Verse* and *The Oxford Book of English Prose.*

Quilter, Roger (1877-), English composer who studied with Ivan Knorr at Frankfurt: his works include many settings of Shakespearean lyrics; *Serenade, English Dances,* and *Children's Overture* for orchestra; incidental music to Shakespeare's *As You Like It;* pieces for piano and for violin.

Quinault, Philippe (1635-1688), French dramatist and librettist whose first play was produced at the Hôtel de Bourgogne in 1653: his works include *Les Rivales; L'Amant indiscret; Le Fantôme amoureuse; La Mère coquette:* he also wrote the librettos for Jean Baptiste LULLY's operas produced at the French Opéra, the finest being *Persée, Amadis de Gaule, Roland,* and *Armide.*

Quinn, Arthur Hobson (1875-), American author educated at the University of Pennsylvania and at the University of Munich, later becoming professor of English at the University of Pennsylvania. His works include *Pennsylvania Stories* (1899); *A History of the American Drama from the Beginning to the Civil War; A History of Drama from the Civil War to the Present Time* (1927), revised to one volume in 1936; *American Fiction: An Historical and Critical Survey; Edgar Allan Poe.*

Quinn, Edmond T. (1868-1929), American sculptor who studied at the Pennsylvania Academy of Fine Arts, with Thomas EAKINS, and at Paris: his works include a statue of Edwin BOOTH as Hamlet in Gramercy Park, New York; a bust of Edgar Allan POE; *Nymph,* a statuette in the Metropolitan Museum of Art, New York; the Victor Herbert Memorial in Central Park, New York, and many memorials of World War I.

Quintana, Manuel José (1772-1857), Spanish poet who was also a lawyer and man of letters, occupying the post of preceptor to the young Queen Isabella: his works include the tragedies *El Duque de Viseo* and *Pelayo; Lives of Celebrated Spaniards:* also more than thirty poems distinguished by their patriotism and noble sentiments.

Quintero, see **Alvarez-Quintero, Serafin.**

Quintet, in music a composition for five instruments or voices. *String quintets* usually comprise two violins, two violos, and violoncello: sometimes the number of violas and violoncellos are reversed. *Piano quintets* add the piano to the string quartet. Among the most distinguished works in these forms are the *Quintet for Strings in C major* by Wolfgang Amadeus MOZART; the *Quintet for Clarinet and Strings in A major* by Mozart; the *Quintet for Piano and Strings, Op. 44* by Robert SCHUMANN, and similar quintets by César FRANCK and Johannes BRAHMS.

Quinton, see **Viol.**

R

R **a,** in Egyptian mythology the sun god who is the protector of humans and the vanquisher of evil: he is represented either with the head of a hawk, or with the solar disk on his head. He was always victorious in war, and every Egyptian king was regarded as his son.

Rabaud, Henri (1873-), French composer and conductor who studied at the Paris Conservatory with Jules MASSENET: he directed the Paris Opéra, conducted the Boston Symphony Orchestra in 1918-1919, directed the Paris Conservatory and conducted at the Opéra-Comique. His compositions include *Antony and Cleopatra* and several other operas; symphonies; symphonic poems, chamber music, piano pieces, violin pieces, and songs.

Rabelais, François (c.1495-1553), French satirist who became a Benedictine monk, practiced as a physician and led a wandering life in France and Italy: his works include *Gargantua* (1535) and *Pantagruel* (1533): these two volumes have stamped him as not only the greatest of French humorists, but as one of the cleverest satirists of all time.

Rachel (1821-1858), French actress whose real name was Elisa or Elizabeth Félix: she was the daughter of poor Jewish parents, and sang in the streets of Lyons with her sister until Étienne Choron, a teacher of singing, heard her voice and taught her until she gained admittance to the Paris Conservatory. She made her debut at the Théâtre-Français in 1838, and became the idol of Paris especially in RACINE's *Phèdre* and in Scribe and Legouve's *Adrienne Lecouvreur.* She was also successful at London, but failed to achieve signal success in the United States because there were too few American theatre-goers in 1855 who understood French sufficiently to appreciate her artistic powers.

Rachmaninoff, Sergei Vassilievitch (1873-1943), Russian pianist and composer who studied at the St. Petersburg and Moscow Conservatories, Anton Arensky being his instructor in composition. He composed the *Prelude in C♯ minor* (Op. 3, No. 2), the work which made him world-famous when he was twenty years old. After conducting the private opera at the Hermitage, and the Imperial Opera at Moscow, he toured the United States as pianist and conductor in 1909, declining an invitation to become director of the Boston Symphony Orchestra. He left Russia with his family after the Revolution, and concertized for many years successfully in Europe and the United States. His compositions include several operas; three symphonies; four piano concertos of which the second is world-famous; several orchestral works including a symphonic poem, *The Island of Death;* many piano pieces; two suites for two-pianos, four hands: also numerous songs many of which are highly regarded.

Racine, Jean Baptiste (1639-1699), French dramatist educated at the Collège de Beauvais and at the Collège d'Harcourt. He made many friends among the literary men in Paris including LA FONTAINE, CHAPELAIN, and BOILEAU-DESPREAUX: his *Nymphe de la Seine,* an ode written on the occasion of the marriage of LOUIS XIV, won him the monarch's favor. Molière produced his first tragedy, *Le Thébaïde* in 1664: this was followed by nine tragedies which established him as the greatest writer of plays in the classical tradition. They included *Andromaque; Britannicus; Bérénice; Bajazet; Mithdridate; Iphigénie; Phèdre; Esther; Athalie.*

Racionero, El, see **Cano, Alonso.**

Radcliffe, Ann Ward (1764-1823), English novelist who is regarded as having reached the pinnacle of success in conceiving plots dealing with the supernatural: her works include *The Mysteries of Udolpho* (1794); *The Sicilian Romance; Romance of the Forest; The Italian.*

Radio City, see **Rockefeller Center.**

Radio City Music Hall, one of the greatest institutions for theatrical, motion-picture, and musical entertainment in the world: the enormous semi-circular auditorium seats 6,200, and the stage equipment is such that every desired artistic effect can be secured by mechanical means. It was opened as a music hall in the Continental style by Samuel L. ROTHAFEL (Roxy) in 1932, but the theatre-going public failed to display the necessary degree of enthusiasm in spite of the unusual assembly of talent: in 1933 it became a film palace exhibiting not only the choicest, first-run pictures, but also presenting a varied stage spectacle preceded by a concert rendered by an orchestra of 100 pieces. One of its greatest attractions is the precision dancing of the ballet group known as the Rockettes.

Radio Drama, a field in which more progress has been made than in any other phase of the theatre in a similar period of time. Broadcasting is now in its twenty-fourth year, but the modern radio theatre only took lasting root in 1936, yet it has flowered into full maturity in seven years: an audience of millions has become so conscious of the importance and dramatic power of radio drama that a writer's name is sufficient to attract it to the radio set on a given night with the full knowledge that only the best will emanate from the speaker. In July, 1936, the Columbia Broadcasting Company tried the experiment of a theatre built exclusively for radio, combining visual drama with the audio medium to give its listeners a series of programs featuring original plays and adaptations of worthwhile plays and books. These were designed and executed so as to appeal to small-town as well as metropolitan families. New authors were encouraged and trained to write for the invisible audience, using an entirely new technique, and some of America's foremost writers and composers interested themselves in the project; among them the poet, Archibald MACLEISCH, now Librarian of Congress. *The Fall of the City,* written for the Workshop, was a pioneering half hour of radio verse drama. It was the first poetic work of permanent value to be written expressly for the air, the first to be submitted in shape to be broadcast without readaptation, and the first to exploit the potentialities of radio for activating the imagination of the listener. Orson WELLES played the part of the radio announcer; Burgess MEREDITH was the pacifist orator; and Edgar Stehli was heard as the high priest. MacLeisch's *Air Raid* was the first of many broadcasts with bombing as the theme: listeners were war conscious, and more specifically "attack" conscious. Among the Workshop alumni are William N. ROBSON, with his present *Man Behind the Gun* series and Norman Corwin who won national recognition for his production of *The Plot to Overthrow Christmas,* an original rhymed fantasy done on Christmas Day, 1938. That was followed by a verse drama, *They Fly Through the Air with the Greatest of Ease,* which won first prize from the Institute of Education by Radio, an award of Ohio State University, as the best dramatic program of the year. His adaptations of Carl SANDBURG's *The People, Yes;* Walt WHITMAN's *Leaves of Grass,* and Edgar Lee MASTERS' *Spoon River Anthology* were notable radio events. In October, 1939, Corwin was assigned to direct CBS's *The Pursuit of Happiness* series. His production of Earl Robinson's *Ballad for Americans* created a national sensation. On this series Corwin also presented performances of Bernard Schoenfeld's *Johnny Appleseed:* the première of Maxwell ANDERSON and Kurt WEILL's *Magna Charta,* and his own adaptation of works by John STEINBECK, Thomas WOLFE, and Stephen Vincent BENET. On December 15, 1941, he wrote and produced a program, *We Hold These Truths,* honoring the 150th Anniversary of the ratification of the Bill of Rights, carried by all four major networks and followed by an address by the President of the United States. The program won virtually unanimous praise from executives in industry to school-children in small towns across the continent, and also the George Foster Peabody Award for 1941. One of the most important developments in radio drama has been the *Lux Radio Theatre,* which has brought radio screen scripts starring the film's best-known actors to the air which have consistently won awards. Other outstanding dramatic hours include *Let's Pretend,* a series of dramatized fairy tales and folk stories for children directed by Nila Mack; the *Campbell Playhouse* and the *Mercury Theatre* in which Orson Welles was the leading spirit; the *First Nighter,* a series of original plays by contemporary playwrights; *Gatewood to Hollywood* which was the medium through which many promising young actors and actresses were secured for the films; the *Screen Guild Theatre;* the *Helen Hayes Theatre;* the *Silver Theatre; Hollywood Hotel;* the *Texaco Star Theatre* during the period in which it presented condensed plays; *Grand Central Station,* and many other dramatic features.

Raeburn, Sir Henry (1756-1823), Scottish painter who studied with David Martin, and began his career by painting miniatures, and after some study in Italy, settled in Edinburgh where he became known as the "Scottish Reynolds," and the undisputed head of the Scottish School. He painted more than 600 portraits: among his sitters were most of the prominent people of his day, and his technique has been compared favorably with that of VELASQUEZ.

Raff, Joachim (1822-1882), German pianist and composer who was too poor to pursue the study of music and became a school-teacher until he received the aid of Felix MENDELSSOHN in the publication of some of his compositions: he was also friendly with Franz LISZT who produced his opera, *King Alfred,* at Weimar. His works comprise several symphonies including the famous *Leonore Symphony;* concert overtures; concertos for piano and for violoncello; piano pieces; violin pieces, and part songs.

Raffaelli, Jean François (1850-1924), French painter, sculptor, and designer: after studying poetry and painting he settled in the outskirts of Paris, and pictured many scenes on the quays and in the crowded districts of the city. Among these are *The Old Convalescents; At Gonou's Foundry; Young Girl with a Cornflower; Old Rag-Picker; The Absinthe Drinker.*

Raft, George, contemporary American stage and screen actor and dancer: among the films in which he has appeared are *Scarface; Dancers in the Dark; Under Cover Man; If I Had a Million; The Eagle and the Hawk; The Bowery; Bolero; Limehouse Blues; Rhumba; The Glass Key; Souls at Sea; Each Dawn I Die; They Drive by Night; Manpower; Broadway.*

Ragtime, a term used about 1900 to describe a form of syncopated piano music: it is said to have originated in the South, and to have been brought to New York by a dance-hall pianist. George M. COHAN and Irving BERLIN were among the most successful composers in the form, the characteristic rhythms of which were later incorporated into JAZZ.

Raimondi, Marc Antonio (c.1480-c.1534), Italian engraver on copper who studied NIELLO and line engraving with FRANCIA: his notable plates include copies of DÜRER'S *Life of the Virgin; The Climbers* from MICHELANGELO'S *Battle of Anghiari; Lucretia; Poetry; Judgment of Paris* after RAPHAEL; *Adam and Eve; Death of Dido; Massacre of the Innocents.* He taught many pupils who later became famous, and is regarded as the greatest of the RENAISSANCE engravers.

Raimund, Ferdinand (1790-1836), Austrian actor and dramatist who produced his first play *The Barometer Maker* in 1823 at Vienna, and later became one of the most popular playwrights and comedians appearing on the Viennese stage. Among his popular plays were *The Spendthrift* and *The Peasant as Millionaire.*

Raine, Norman Reilly (1895-), American author who served with the Canadian Expeditionary Force during World War I, and later contributed stories to the *Saturday Evening Post, Liberty,* and *Collier's.* His works include *Tugboat Annie* (1934): also several successful films including *The Life of Émile Zola; The Fighting 69th; The Adventures of Robin Hood; Each Dawn I Die; Elizabeth the Queen.*

Raine, William McLeod (1871-), American novelist born in England of Scotch parentage who came to the United States at ten: he first wrote short stories, and later historical novels finally turning to the American West for inspiration. His numerous novels include *A Daughter of Raasay* (1902); *Wyoming; Bucky O'Connor; The Yukon Trail; Riders of the Rim Rocks; Justice Deferred.*

Rainer, Luise (1912-), Austrian stage and screen actress who made her debut on the stage at Düsseldorf in 1928, later appearing in German versions of *Men in White; Saint Joan; American Tragedy; Six Characters in Search of an Author.* After studying English with Constance COLLIER she appeared on the English stage in several plays: among the films in which she has been featured are *Escapade; The Great Ziegfeld; The Good Earth; The Emperor's Candlesticks; Big City; The Toy Wife; The Great Waltz.*

Rains, Claude (1889-), English stage and screen actor who appeared as a small child in *Sweet Nell of Old Drury* at the Haymarket Theatre in 1900: after experience as stage manager for Harley GRANVILLE-BARKER he appeared in *Julius Caesar; The Government Inspector; The Jest; A Bill of Divorcement; Volpone; Marco Millions.* Among the films in which he has been featured are *Crime Without Passion; The Mystery of Edwin Drood; Anthony Adverse; The Adventures of Robin Hood; Four Daughters; Juarez; Mr. Smith Goes to Washington; Saturday's Children; The Sea Hawk; King's Row; Moontide.*

Raisa, Rosa (1893-), Polish dramatic soprano who fled as a child of fourteen to Naples to escape the Jewish persecutions: after study there she made a successful debut in 1913 at Parma in Verdi's *Oberto,* and sang later at Rome and London. She joined the Chicago Civic Opera Company in 1914, and sang with it for many years, also appearing with the Ravinia and Los Angeles Opera Companies.

Rakoczy March (Berlioz), an orchestral arrangement of this famous Hungarian air introduced into *The Damnation of Faust,* a dramatic legend by Hector BERLIOZ, written in 1846 and first produced at Paris in November of that year. The *Rakoczy March* forms the closing movement of the first part, and pictures the advance of a Hungarian army. Berlioz knew that the tune *Rakoczy* was an expression of patriotic feeling to the Hungarians; upon its first presentation in Budapest he says: "I lost all hope of making the end audible, and in the encore it was no better; hardly could they contain themselves long enough to hear a portion of the Coda." There is a Columbia recording by the Columbia Broadcasting Symphony Orchestra conducted by Howard Barlow, and a Victor recording by the Boston Symphony Orchestra directed by Serge Koussevitzky.

Rallentando (It.), in music a direction indicating a gradual slackening in tempo, and usually abbreviated *rall.*

Ramayana, one of the two great epic poems of India, the other being the *Mahabharata:* it is supposed to have been written by a poet named Valmiki, and comprises about 24,000 stanzas divided into seven books. The story revolves around Rama, one of the three heroes of Hindu mythology, and presumably a reincarnation of VISHNU.

Rambert, Marie, English dancer, ballet producer, and teacher: after training with the DIAGHILEFF Ballet she appeared in 1912 with Vaslav NIJINSKY in STRAVINSKY's *Le Sacre du Printemps,* and also created the principal parts in many ballets. She has given successful seasons of ballet at several London theatres, and has trained many dancers including Pearl ARGYLE, Frederick ASHTON, and Harold TURNER.

Rameau, Jean-Philippe (1683-1764), French composer regarded as the creator of the modern science of harmony: after spending some years as a violinist and organist he settled at Lille, and after devoting himself to a theoretical study of music returned to Paris and published his *New System of Musical Theory* (1726) which marked a new epoch in the art. He also wrote several operas, one of which, *Castor and Pollux,* held its own with the operas of GLUCK. His treatises cover the subjects of harmony, musical theory, accompanying and singing.

Ramée, Maria Louise de la, see **Ouida.**

Ramenghi, Bartolommeo, see **Bagnacavallo.**

Randegger, Alberto (1832-1911), Italian singing teacher who was first a conductor in several Italian theatres: he settled at London in 1854, and became professor of singing at the Royal Academy of Music and the Royal College of Music. He also conducted Italian opera at the St. James' Theatre, and for the CARL ROSA OPERA COMPANY.

Randolph, Harold (1861-1927), American pianist who studied with Carl FAELTEN and at the PEABODY CONSERVATORY OF MUSIC, Baltimore, making his debut in 1885 with the Peabody Symphony Orchestra: in 1898 he succeeded Asger Hamerik as director of the Peabody Conservatory which he built up into one of the greatest institutions of its kind in the United States.

Ranger, Henry Ward (1858-1916), American painter who was largely self-taught: he became an outstanding landscape and marine painter who worked in Holland and France. Among his notable works are *Top of the Hill; East River Idyll; Spring Woods; Highbridge, New York.* A trust fund of $400,000, left in his will to be administered by the National Academy of Design, provides for the purchase of works by American artists from the income.

Rapee, Erno (1891-), Hungarian conductor who studied at the Royal Conservatory in Budapest: he has occupied posts as conductor at the Capitol and Roxy Theatres, New York, and since 1932 as conductor and musical director of RADIO CITY MUSIC HALL. He has also acted as guest conductor of the Philadelphia and Cleveland Orchestras.

Raphael (1483-1520), Italian painter also known as *Raffaello Sanzio:* he was the son of Giovanni Santi (c.1435-1494), a court painter and poet.

After receiving some training from his father, who died when he was twelve, Raphael studied in 1499 at Perugia under PERUGINO, and immediately acquired his master's style as is revealed in the *Saint Michael, St. George, The Three Hesperides, The Way to Calvary,* and *Coronation of the Virgin* painted during this period. In 1504 he went to Florence where he received new inspiration from LEONARDO DA VINCI, MICHELANGELO, DONATELLO, MASSACCIO, and Fra BARTOLOMMEO. In 1508 he went to Rome at the request of BRAMANTE to assist in beautifying the city, and was entrusted by Pope Julius II with the redecorating of several rooms in the Vatican. His accomplishments, in consideration of his early demise at 37, are almost unbelievable, and it is extremely difficult to present an abridged list of his work because of their great number and variety. His works at Rome divide themselves in five main groups: (*1*) the decoration of the rooms at the Vatican; (*2*) the decoration of the Loggie at the Vatican; (*3*) the decoration of the Villa Farnesina; (*4*) the cartoons for the tapestries in the Sistine Chapel; (*5*) the works at St. Peters. Among his famous individual paintings and murals are *La Belle Jardinière; Marriage of the Virgin; The Three Graces;* the *Sistine Madonna;* the *Madonna del Granduca;* the *Madonna del Foligno; Disputà; School of Athens; Heliodorus Driven from the Temple; Fire in the Borgo; Madonna of the Chair; The Transfiguration; La Fornarina; The Resurrection; The Crucifixion; Apollo and Marsyas.*

Raphael, Ralphael (1886-1942), Russian concertina virtuoso who gave command performances before Czar Nicholas II of Russia: when he appeared in the *Continental Varieties* at New York in 1934, Brooks ATKINSON described him as "a chunky little man with blissful eyes who makes the concertina sing with grace and beauty." He appeared in vaudeville, motion pictures, and in stage productions.

Raphaelson, Samson (1896-), American dramatist educated at the University of Illinois who later taught English there, and wrote many successful short stories: his plays include *The Jazz Singer* (1925); *Young Love; The Wooden Slipper; Accent on Youth; White Man; Skylark; Jason.* He has also adapted several stories for the screen including *The Magnificent Lie; The Smiling Lieutenant; Trouble in Paradise; The Shop Around the Corner; Suspicion.*

Rappaport, Solomon, see **Ansky, S. A.**

Rappold, Marie (c.1880-), American dramatic soprano who studied with Oscar SAENGER, and made her debut in 1905 at the Metropolitan Opera House, New York, in Goldmark's *Queen of Sheba,* remaining there until 1919: she also toured Europe in lieder recitals in addition to singing at the Bucharest and Milan opera houses.

Rasch, Albertina, contemporary Austrian dancer who was trained at the Imperial Opera Ballet School, Vienna, and became *première danseuse* at the New York Hippodrome, and later with the Century Opera Company, Chicago Opera Company, and American Opera Company at Los

Angeles. In 1923 she opened a school of dancing in New York, trained many famous dancers, and produced the dances in many musical plays and films.

Rascoe, Burton (1892-), American journalist, editor, critic, and author who studied at the University of Chicago, and became literary editor of the Chicago *Tribune:* his works include *Theodore Dreiser* (1925); *A Bookman's Daybook; Titans of Literature; Prometheans, Ancient and Modern; Before I Forget,* an autobiography; *Belle Starr.*

Rathbone, Basil (1892-), English stage and screen actor born in South Africa who made his stage debut in *The Taming of the Shrew* at Ipswich in 1911: he has appeared in many plays including *Peter Ibbetson; Madame Sand; Fedora; Othello; East of Suez; The Captive; Julius Caesar; Diplomacy; Romeo and Juliet.* Since 1936 he has played leading roles in numerous films including *The Garden of Allah; Tovarich; The Adventures of Marco Polo; If I Were King; The Hound of the Baskervilles; The Mark of Zorro:* also in several "Sherlock Holmes" films.

Ratoff, Gregory (1897-), Russian stage and screen actor who made his debut at the Imperial Theatre, Moscow, and came to the United States in 1922, making his first appearance in *Revue Russe* at New York, during the same year: after playing in several stage productions he began his film career in 1932, and has been featured in many films in addition to acting as director of *Lancer Spy; Wife, Husband and Friend; Rose of Washington Square; Intermezzo; Two Yanks in Trinidad.*

Rauch, Christian Daniel (1777-1857), German sculptor who, while acting as a lackey in the royal household at Berlin, was surprised in the act of modeling her features in wax by Queen Louisa of Prussia who sent him to the Academy of Art: later he studied at Rome where he was advised by CANOVA and THORWALDSEN. His notable works include the bas-reliefs *Hippolytus and Phaedra; Mars and Venus; Child Praying:* he also executed many statues and portrait busts of German notables, the monument for Queen Louisa, and the colossal equestrian statue of FREDERICK THE GREAT.

Ravel, Maurice (1875-1937), French pianist and composer who studied at the Paris Conservatory with Charles de Beriot, Gabriel Fauré, and André Gedalge: his compositions include an opera, *L'Heure espagnole,* the ballets DAPHNIS ET CHLOE and BOLERO; orchestral works including *Pavane for a Dead Infanta, Spanish Rhapsody,* two *Daphnis and Chloé Suites; La Valse;* chamber music; a *Sonatine* and several other piano pieces.

Ravinia Park Opera, a season of opera presented by Louis Eckstein at Ravinia Park, a suburb of Chicago, in a semi-outdoor pavilion. The seasons, which lasted ten weeks from June to September, began in 1911 and terminated in 1931: operas were given in slightly shortened form, and the personnel included distinguished artists from both the Metropolitan and Chicago Opera Companies.

Rawlings, Marjorie Kinnan (1896-), American author educated at the University of Wisconsin under William Ellery LEONARD: her works include *South Moon Under* (1933); *Golden Apples; The Yearling,* awarded the Pulitzer prize in 1939; *When the Whippoorwill; Cross Creek.*

Raymond, John T. (1836-1887), American actor whose real name was O'Brien: he created the role of Asa Trenchard in *Our American Cousin,* of Colonel Mulberry Sellers in *The Gilded Age,* and of Ichabod Crane in *The Legend of Sleepy Hollow.* His acting excited genuine interest in the creation of distinctly American types by native-born actors.

Rayonnant Style, in architecture the name applied to the Gothic style of architecture in France during the 13th and 14th centuries, the period during which the majority of the great cathedrals were being built: the name is derived from the characteristic radiating tracery in its rose windows employing elaborate geometrical patterns.

Razumovsky, Andrei Kryllovitch, Prince (1752-1836), Russian nobleman and ambassador at Vienna: he founded the famous **Razumovsky Quartet** in 1808 of which Ignaz Schuppanzigh was the leader: it played BEETHOVEN's string quartets under the supervision of the composer, and also the quartets of HAYDN and MOZART.

Read, Opie Percival (1852-1939), American novelist and humorist who edited several small newspapers, and later founded *The Arkansas Traveler,* a weekly humorous literary journal: his notable works include *Len Gansett* (1888); *A Kentucky Colonel; An Arkansas Planter; The Carpet Bagger* with Frank Pixley; *A Tennessee Judge; Old Ebenezer; In the Alamo; I Remember,* an autobiography; *Mark Twain and I.*

Read, Thomas Buchanan (1822-1872), American painter and poet who first worked on canal boats and signs, later opening a studio in Boston where Henry Wadsworth LONGFELLOW was one of his sitters. His first collection of poems appeared in 1847: it was followed by *Lays and Ballads; The Female Poets of America; Rural Poems; Sheridan's Ride and Other Poems.* He lived abroad for a time, and painted the portraits of Charles Dickens and Robert Browning.

Reade, Charles (1814-1884), English novelist and dramatist educated at Oxford: his first successful play was *Masks and Faces* (1852) written with Tom TAYLOR: his first novel, *Peg Woffington* (1853), made use of the same plot. His works include *It's Never Too Late to Mend; Hard Cash; Put Yourself in His Place; A Terrible Temptation; Griffith Gaunt; The Cloister and the Hearth,* considered his masterpiece.

Realism, in art or literature fidelity to nature or real life, i.e., the representation of people or events exactly as they are, or as the events took place without the gloss of romanticism. A movement to inject realism into novels and plays started in France about the middle of the 19th century: Émile ZOLA was one of its ardent champions, and the movement has progressed in all countries to the point that it would be difficult to find a novelist or dramatist who does not class himself as a realist.

Récamier, Jeanne Françoise Julie Adelaide (1777-1849), French society leader who was married at fifteen to Jacques Rècamier, a man nearly three times her age. Her intelligence and beauty attracted many persons of note to her salon including Charles Augustin SAINTE-BEUVE, François René CHATEAUBRIAND, Benjamin CONSTANT, and Madame de STAEL. Her *Souvenirs and Correspondence* were edited in 1850 by her niece, Madame Lenormant.

Recitative, a style of musical declamation introduced into the earliest operas by PERI, CACCINI, and MONTEVERDI, consisting of non-rhythmical passages for voice accompanied by musical instruments. A recitative with simple accompaniment is known as *recitativo secco*, and with more elaborate accompaniment as *recitativo stromentato*. Richard WAGNER improved recitative by requiring more natural inflection by the singer, and enriching the orchestral accompaniment. Recitative is also employed in ORATORIO.

Recorder, a form of the FLUTE resembling the FLAGEOLET: it was widely used up to the close of the 17th century, and Monteverdi, Bach, Handel, Gluck, and Mozart prescribed its use in certain parts of their works. The playing of the recorder has been revived in many English and American educational institutions where music is taught: the instruments used are the C soprano, the F alto, and the C tenor recorders, and much music has been published in solo, duet and trio form with piano accompaniment.

Redgrave, Michael (1908-), English stage and screen actor who first appeared on the stage as a baby in arms: after many appearances as an amateur, he made his formal debut in 1934 at Liverpool in *Counsellor-at-Law*. He has also played in *Love's Labour's Lost; The Country Wife; Hamlet; The Bat; Richard II; School for Scandal; Three Sisters*. Among the films in which he has been featured are *The Lady Vanishes; The Stars Look Down; Kipps; Thunder Rock; Lady in Distress.*

Redon, Odilon Bertrand (1842-1916), French painter and engraver who spent much time at the LOUVRE in Paris, and was so greatly impressed by the works of Eugène DELACROIX that he decided on an artistic career. He was a pupil of Gustave COURBET and Gustave MOREAU, but his career was interrupted by military service in the Franco-Prussian War. His works, comprising dramatic, mythological, religious, and floral subjects, are in many American and European museums.

Red Poppy, The, ballet in three acts and six scenes: book by M. T. Kurilko: music by Richard GLIERE; first produced at Moscow in 1927. The scenes are laid in an Americanized modern treaty port in China, and the scenes include an opium den and a ball-room: the *Dance of the Russian Sailors* has become a popular concert and radio number of which there is a Victor recording by the Philadelphia Orchestra directed by Leopold Stokowski.

Reed, Florence (1883-), American actress who first appeared in a monologue at the Fifth Avenue Theatre, New York, in 1901: she became leading lady for E. H. Sothern in 1907, and appeared later in *Typhoon; The Master of the House; The Yellow Ticket; A Celebrated Case; The Wanderer; East of Suez; The Lullaby; The Shanghai Gesture; Macbeth; Mourning Becomes Electra; Her Master's Voice; Elizabeth the Queen; Outward Bound.* She has also appeared in several films.

Reed, Myrtle (1874-1911), American author: her works include *Love Letters of a Musician* (1899); *Lavender and Old Lace; The Shadow of Victory; Picaback Songs; A Spinner in the Sun* under the pen name "Olive Green"; *Old Rose and Silver; Sonnets of a Lover; A Weaver of Dreams; The Myrtle Reed Year Book.*

Reed, a piece of cane, wood, or metal adjusted over an aperture in a musical instrument so as to nearly close it: it is fastened at one end, and set in motion by an air current with which it communicates to an enclosed column of air, or directly to the atmosphere, the result being a musical tone. There are two kinds of reeds: *free reeds* which vibrate with touching the edges of the aperture, and *beating reeds* which touch the edges of the aperture: both types are used in REED INSTRUMENTS.

Reed Instruments, musical instruments in which tones are produced by the vibrations of a reed in the mouthpiece: the instruments using a single reed are the CLARINET and the ORGAN; those employing a double reed are the OBOE, ENGLISH HORN and BASSOON. Free reeds are used in the HARMONIUM, REED ORGAN, CONCERTINA, and ACCORDION.

Reed organ, an instrument which is operated by a bellows forcing air over free reeds: it employs one or more keyboards equipped with stops and valves which control the amount of air supplied to the reeds. The MELODEON or American organ was popular in the United States from 1850: it resembled a square piano, and succeeded the HARMONIUM.

Reedy, William Marion (1862-1920), American editor and critic educated at Christian Brothers' College and St. Louis University: in 1896 he became the editor and publisher of *Reedy's Mirror,* formerly the *St. Louis Mirror,* and proved of great assistance to young authors including Fannie HURST, Zoë AKINS, and John Hall Wheelock in giving publicity to their first efforts. His works include *The Imitator* (1901); *The Law of Love; A Golden Book and the Literature of Childhood.*

Reel, an ancient folk dance of Celtic origin in Great Britain, and later introduced into Scandinavia. It is in rapid 2-4 time, and danced by two couples in Scotland and Ireland, and in England by three couples. The *Virginia reel* first came from England to Virginia, but became popular later in all other states where the settlers were of Scotch, Irish or English ancestry.

Reese, Gustave (1899-), American musicologist, editor, and author of articles and treatises on music, educated at New York University where he later acted as instructor and lecturer on music: since 1935 he has been associate editor of the *Musical Quarterly,* and also co-founder of the American Musicological Society. He is the author of *Music in the Middle Ages* (1940).

Reese, Lizette Woodworth (1856-1935), American educator and poet: her works include *A Branch of May* (1887); *A Handful of Lavender; A Quiet Road; Wild Cherry; Little Henrietta; A Victorian Village; The York Road,* an autobiography; *The Old House in the Country.*

Reeve, Arthur Benjamin (1880-1936), American author of detective fiction educated at Princeton University and at the New York Law School: he never practiced after deciding on a literary career. His scientific detective, Craig Kennedy, appeared first in the *Cosmopolitan Magazine* and later in many best-selling detective stories including *The Poisoned Pen* (1911); *The Silent Bullet; Kennedy Listens In; Tales of Craig Kennedy; Enter Craig Kennedy.*

Régence Period, in architecture, decoration, and furniture a period in France extending from the close of the reign of Louis XIV until the accession of Louis XV, or from 1680 to 1725. The change can be noted in the abandonment of straight-lined massive design in favor of curved surfaces and fanciful decoration.

Reger, Max (1873-1916), German organist and composer who studied with Hugo RIEMANN, and from 1907 taught organ and composition at the Leipzig Conservatory. He was an uncompromising foe of PROGRAM MUSIC, and an ardent advocate of ABSOLUTE MUSIC, but his enormous output of compositions is regarded as more scholarly than emotional: it includes orchestral works, chamber music, concertos for piano and for violin, organ works, piano works, violin pieces, choruses and songs.

Regnard, Jean François (1655-1709), French dramatist who traveled extensively throughout Europe and produced his first comedy, *La Divorce,* at the Théâtre Italien in 1688: his successful comedies include *Arlequin; La Joueur; La Serenade; Le Distrait; Les Folies Amoureuses; Le Légataire universal.* Many of his comedies were produced by MOLIERE, and by the Italian troupe at the Hôtel de Bourgogne.

Regnault, Alexandre Georges Henri (1843-1871), French painter who won the Prix de Rome in 1866 with *Achilles Weeping over the Body of Patroclus:* he visited Italy and Spain, and was killed during the Franco-Prussian War. His notable works include *Salome; Execution in Tangiers; Lady in Red; Inside a Harem; Automedon Taming the Horses of Achilles:* also a fine equestrian portrait of Marshal Prim.

Regnier, Henri François Joseph de (1864-1936), French poet and novelist educated for the law: his gorgeous, vaguely mystifying style reveals the influence of Stéphane MALLARME: among his poems are *Lendemains* (1885); *Poèmes anciens et romanesques; Le Jeux rustiques et divins;* *La Cité des eaux.* His novels include *La Canne de jaspe; La Double Maîtresse; La Peur de l'amour; Les Scruples de Miss Simpson.*

Rehan, Ada (1860-1916), American actress born in Ireland who came to the United States as a child of five with her parents, and made her debut in 1874 on the stage at Newark, N. J., in the melodrama, *Across the Continent.* In 1879 she became a member of the Augustin DALY Company, remaining for twenty years, playing more than two hundred parts, and appearing in both New York and London. She excelled in Shakespearean roles such as Katherine in *The Taming of the Shrew,* and her portrait in this part is in the picture gallery of the theatre at the Shakespeare Memorial in Stratford-on-Avon.

Reicha, Anton (1770-1836), Bohemian flutist, composer, and teacher who was friendly with BEETHOVEN, HAYDN, ALBRECHTSBERGER, and SALIERI. He achieved a high reputation as a musical theorist, and numbered LISZT, GOUNOD, and DANCLA among his pupils at the Paris Conservatory. His compositions include operas and symphonies: he also wrote valuable treaties on counterpoint and composition.

Reicher, Emmanuel (1849-1924), German actor and theatrical director who achieved great success in Germany, and came to the United States: his most important production was that of Gerhard HAUPTMANN's *The Weavers* in which his daughter, Hedwig Reicher, played a leading part. He organized the American People's Theatre and also directed the Jewish Art Theatre.

Reid, George Agnew (1860-), Canadian painter of landscapes, murals, and genre subjects: his notable works include *Dreaming; Mortgaging the Homestead; Champlain's Arrival at Quebec:* also murals at the City Hall, Toronto, and at Kingston University. He acted as head of the Ontario College of Art, and published a work entitled *Art Education in the United States, England, Scotland, France, and Holland.*

Reid, Thomas Mayne (1818-1883), Irish novelist who traveled as a young man in the western part of the United States, fought with the rank of captain in the Mexican War, and settled in England. His series of adventure stories for boys includes *The Rifle Rangers* (1850); *The Scalp Hunters; The White Chief; The Quadroon; The Death Shot; The Free Lance.*

Reiner, Fritz (1888-), Hungarian conductor who studied at the Budapest Music Academy, and later conducted at the Budapest and Dresden opera houses. From 1922 to 1931 he directed the CINCINNATI SYMPHONY ORCHESTRA, and in 1931 became the head of the orchestral and opera departments of the CURTIS INSTITUTE OF MUSIC, Philadelphia, also appearing as guest conductor of major orchestras and of opera in the United States, London, Italy, and South America. In 1938 he became permanent conductor of the PITTSBURGH SYMPHONY ORCHESTRA.

Reinhardt, Max (1873-), Austrian actor and theatrical producer who first played minor roles at the Deutsches Theater in Berlin, and in 1902 took over the management of the Kleine Theater and later the Neues Theater, producing and acting in *Salome; Pelléas and Mélisande; Faust; Oedipus Rex,* and the *Orestiad* of AESCHYLUS. Among his notable productions in Germany and London are *Sumurun; The Miracle; A Midsummer Night's Dream; Macbeth; Julius Caesar; Rosenkavalier; Agamemnon; Hamlet.* In the United States he has produced *A Midsummer Night's Dream; Everyman; Danton's Death; Servant of Two Masters; The Eternal Road.* He also directed Morris GEST's production of *The Miracle* at New York in 1924, and staged the outdoor production of *A Midsummer Night's Dream* at Oxford, England, in 1933, and the Warner Brothers' film production in 1935. His most recent production at New York is *Rosalinda,* a new version of Johann Strauss' operetta *The Bat.*

Reis, Claire R., contemporary American writer on music trained at the Institute of Musical Art, New York, and also in France and Germany: her most important contribution to the cause of musical composition in America is a volume entitled *Composers in America* (1938), a compilation first issued in pamphlet form in 1930-32: it comprises a comprehensive survey of the works of modern American composers.

Reisenauer, Alfred (1863-1907), German pianist and composer who studied with Franz LISZT and Louis Köhler, making his debut at a concert with Liszt in 1881 at Rome: he toured the entire world with enormous success, and also taught the master class at the Leipzig Conservatory. His compositions include piano music and more than one hundred songs many of which are well-known.

Réjane, Mme. (1857-1920), French actress whose real name was Gabrielle Charlotte Reju: she studied with Henri REGNIER at the Paris Conservatory, and made her debut in 1875 at both the Vaudeville Theatre and the Odéon in soubrette parts. In 1883 she scored a triumph in MEILHAC's *Ma Camarade,* proving herself an emotional actress of rare gifts. In 1895 she achieved great success in the United States in SARDOU's *Madame Sans-Gêne,* and in 1896 opened the Théâtre Réjane at Paris, continuing to play there and at London until 1915 when she retired.

Relief, in sculpture a term designating an ornament or figures raised from the ground of a flat surface: the design may be in ALTO-RELIEVO, MEZZO-RELIEVO or BASSO-RELIEVO.

Reliquary, a box or coffer in which sacred relics were kept during the Middle Ages: some of the reliquaries were large enough to be used as shrines, and others small enough to be carried in the hand. They were made in many forms such as small houses or vases, and richly decorated.

Remarque, Erich Maria (1897-), German novelist who fought in World War I, and later became a teacher, stone cutter, and writer for a sports magazine. His first novel, *All Quiet on the Western Front* (1929) had an enormous sale in Germany, England, and the United States: he has since written *The Road Back; Three Comrades; Flotsam.*

Rembrandt, Harmenzoon van Rijn (1606-1669), Dutch painter and etcher who studied with Peter Lastman, and lived in Amsterdam from 1630 until his death: he was the greatest master of the Dutch school, and no artist has equaled him in the management of light and shade, and only a few in coloring, characterization, and in the expression of sentiment. His notable works include *St. Jerome and St. Paul in Prison; Portrait of an Old Woman; Balaam and His Ass; Musical Party; Presentation in the Temple; Supper at Emmaus; Rape of Europa; St. John in the Wilderness; Deposition; Entombment; Resurrection; Anatomy of Dr. Tulip; Night Watch; River Landscape; Holy Family; Self-portrait; Potiphar's Wife Accusing Joseph; The Prodigal Son; Raising of Lazarus; Old Woman in An Armchair; The Syndics; The Good Samaritan; Venus and Cupid; Homer Reciting His Poems.* Rembrandt had many pupils, but none of them ever achieved his eminence.

Reményi, Eduard (1830-1898), Hungarian violinist who studied at the Vienna Conservatory, toured the world several times with tremendous success, and was solo violinist to Queen Victoria and the Emperor of Austria. He toured Europe with Johannes BRAHMS in 1852-53, and was friendly with Franz LISZT: he also made fine violin transcriptions of music by FIELD, CHOPIN, J. S. BACH, and SCHUBERT.

Remington, Frederic (1861-1909), American sculptor, painter, illustrator, and writer who studied at the Yale Art School and the ART STUDENTS' LEAGUE, New York. While in the western part of the United States for his health, he was with United States troops in actual warfare against the Indians, and his statuettes of soldiers, Indians, and cowboys are full of character. His illustrated books include *Pony Tracks; Crooked Trails; Sundown Leflare,* and *John Ermine of Yellowstone:* his paintings are still popular in the form of color prints.

Remizov, Alexei Mikhailovitch (1877-), Russian novelist educated at the University of Moscow where he studied Russian history, and became a great admirer of Nikolai GOGOL: his works available in English include *The Clock,* a volume of short stories; *The Fifth Pestilence; The Pond; Sisters of the Cross; The Cockerel.*

Renaissance (Fr.), a word in art the literal meaning of which is "rebirth": it is used to describe not only the period of transition from the Middle Ages to the modern world, but more specifically as the term for the rebirth or revival of classical learning in respect to all the arts. It was really not a rebirth, but the beginning of a great art in Western Europe, which merely adapted the worthwhile traditions of the classical age to its own purposes. The period covered the 14th, 15th, and 16th centuries in Italy, and the 15th and 16th centuries in the rest of Europe and Great Britain.

Reni, Guido, see **Guido Reni.**

Renoir, Pierre Auguste (1841-1919), French painter who was advised by Charles GOUNOD to become a musician, but after he chose the career of a painter, became intimate with Alfred SISLEY and Claude MONET: he was also influenced by BOUCHER, FRAGONARD, and WATTEAU. His notable works include *The Bathers; Rowers' Luncheon; Ball at Montmartre; Young Girls at the Piano; La Tonnelle; Ingenué; Joy of Living*. He executed nearly 6,000 paintings, 150 lithographs, and numerous pieces of sculpture.

Renwick, James (1818-1895), American architect whose notable works include Grace Church, and St. Patrick's Cathedral, New York; the original CORCORAN GALLERY OF ART and the SMITHSONIAN INSTITUTION, Washington, D. C.: also the first building for Vassar College.

Repertory, (*1*) in drama the collection of plays which can be performed by a theatrical organization usually known as a "stock" company: also the collection of roles which are carried in the memory for immediate performance by an actor. (*2*) In music the operas which an operatic company is prepared to present, and likewise the roles which each singer has mastered, or the compositions memorized for public performance by any instrumental virtuoso or concert singer.

Repin, Ilya Yefimovich (1844-1918), Russian painter who studied at the Academy of Fine Arts, St. Petersburg, and also in France and Italy: in 1894 he became professor of historical painting at St. Petersburg. His notable works include *Homecoming; The Procession of the Cross; The Terrorists; Ivan the Terrible Murdering His Son;* he also painted the portraits of Count Leo TOLSTOY and Anton RUBINSTEIN.

Repoussé, the term applied to the process, and also the product itself, of decorating metal surfaces with designs in relief: the design is beaten in from the reverse side with a hammer, but the process is completed by CHASING: Gold and silver are the most desirable metals because of their malleability, but copper, tin, and bronze have also been used with excellent results.

Repplier, Agnes (1858-), American essayist educated at the Sacred Heart Convent near Philadelphia: her works include *Books and Men* (1888); *Points of View; Essays in Miniature; Essays in Idleness; Counter Currents; In Pursuit of Laughter; Eight Decades.*

Requiem, a mass sung for the dead in the Roman Catholic Church; so called because the first words are *Requiem aeternam dona eis, domine.* The sections vary five to thirteen, but the usual number is nine. Among the most distinguished composers are PALESTRINA, MOZART, CHERUBINI, VERDI, BERLIOZ, BRUCKNER, BRUNEAU, FAURE, and DVORAK. The *German Requiem* by Johannes BRAHMS cannot be classed among requiems because it does not use the regular text, but seven passages selected from the German Bible.

Reredos, in architecture an ornamental screen or wall-facing which is placed behind the altar of a church: it is usually made of stone or wood, and in some instances of gold, silver or ivory in the 11th and 12th centuries. The decoration con-

sisted of scenes from the PASSION, or likenesses of the saints. Spanish churches have the most elaborate forms.

Resolution, in musical harmony the progression of a DISSONANCE, whether a simple INTERVAL or a CHORD, to a CONSONANCE: the dissonant interval or chord is known as a *suspension* which is considered resolved when it passes into the succeeding consonant interval or chord.

Resphigi, Ottorino (1879-), Italian composer who studied at the Liceo Musicale in Bologna, and also with Luigi Torchi, Guiseppe Martucci, Nicholas RIMSKY-KORSAKOW and Max BRUCH. He became professor of composition at the Liceo di S. Cecilia at Rome: his works include operas; ballets; the symphonic poems, *The* FOUNTAINS OF ROME and *The* PINES OF ROME; chamber music, concertos, organ pieces, piano pieces, and songs.

Rest, in music a pause or lapse of sound before two tones: the symbol indicating such absence of sound is also called a rest. There are individual symbols for whole, half, quarter, eighth, etc., notes, and each measure of music must contain a sufficient number of notes or rests to complete the full time-value of that measure.

Resurrection, The, a favorite subject with painters of religious subjects in all countries and all periods of the Christian era: among the famous artists who have pictured it are Annibale CARRACCI, Filippino LIPPI, Francesco MANTEGNA, Bartholomé MURILLO, Pietro PERUGINO, RAPHAEL, REMBRANDT, Il SODOMA, and TINTORETTO.

Reszke, Edouard de, see **De Reszke, Édouard.**

Reszke, Jean de, see **De Reszke, Jean.**

Retable, in ecclesiastical architecture a shelf or ledge usually decorated with paintings, carving or sculptures, on which is placed the Cross, ceremonial candlesticks, and other ornaments.

Rethberg, Elizabeth (1894-), German dramatic soprano who studied piano at the Dresden Royal Conservatory, and after some voice training made her debut at the Dresden State Opera in 1915, and in 1922 at the Metropolitan Opera House, New York, in *Aïda,* remaining with the company since that time. She has appeared with the major symphony orchestras, and also in joint-recital with Ezio PINZA.

Rethel, Alfred (1816-1859), German painter who executed a painting at thirteen which procured his admission to the Düsseldorf Academy. His notable works include *Resurrection of Christ; Daniel in the Lions' Den; Nemesis Pursuing a Murderer; Death the Avenger; Death the Friend; The Dance of Death; St. Boniface; Peter and John at the Gate of the Temple.*

Revolving Stage, in theatrical architecture a stage on the principle of a turntable; said to have been invented in Japan during the 17th century. The finest example of a modern stage of this type is to be seen at RADIO CITY MUSIC HALL, New York.

Revue, in drama a form of stage production which has been developed to the highest point in both the United States and England: it originated as a satirical commentary on current events without any particular form; later it assumed more of the vaudeville aspect. Among the outstanding revues in England were those of Cochran and Charlot: in the United States those of Florenz Ziegfeld known as *Follies;* those of Earl Carroll known as *Vanities.* and those of George White known as *Scandals.* An outstanding Russian production of this type was the CHAUVE SOURIS.

Reyer, Ernest (1823-1909), French composer whose real name was Louis Ernest Étienne Rey: he studied at Marseilles and with his aunt, Mme. Louise Farrenc, a talented composer. His works comprise several operas including *Sigurd* and *Salammbô;* a symphonic ode, *Le Sélam,* and a ballet, *Sacountala.* He was also a noted music critic who championed the works of WAGNER, BIZET, LALO, FRANCK and other French composers.

Reymont, Ladislav Stanislav (1867-1925), Polish novelist who has written the story of his own life in such works as *The Comedienne* (1896); *Ferments; The Dreamer; The Promised Land; The Peasants,* a novel in four volumes subtitled *Spring, Summer, Autumn,* and *Winter.*

Reynard the Fox, a satirical lyric poem which derives its name from its chief character, Reynard the fox: all the characters are animals, and its origin was probably in AESOP'S fable of the fox and the lion. About 1100 it was popular in England and many countries of Europe.

Reynolds, Sir Joshua (1723-1792), English painter who became so intrigued at fifteen by the works of RAPHAEL that he decided on a career as a painter. After study with William Gaudy and Thomas Hudson as well as in France and Italy he settled at London, becoming the greatest portrait painter in England, and founding the Literary Club in 1764 of which Samuel JOHNSON, Oliver GOLDSMITH, David GARRICK, and Laurence STERNE were members. In 1765 he founded the Society of British Artists which became the Royal Academy in 1768 with Reynolds as its first president. He painted between two and three thousand portraits; among them those of JOHNSON, GARRICK, BOSWELL, GOLDSMITH, Admiral Keppel and many other notable persons in public and private life: also Fanny KEMBLE, Mrs. SIDDONS, and many canvases on religious, mythological, and genre subjects. His *Discourses on Painting* are regarded highly from the literary and artistic standpoints.

Rhadames, a character in Giuseppe Verdi's opera, AIDA: he incurs the enmity of Amneris, daughter of the king of Egypt, by falling in love with Aïda, an Ethiopian slave of royal birth. After being tricked into betraying a military secret of his country, he is condemned to be buried alive, but the faithful Aïda contrives to share his fate.

Rhapsody, (*1*) in ancient Greece a part of one of the great epic poems sung to the accompani-

ment of the cíthara. (*2*) In modern music a composition of indefinite form frequently employing national or folk melodies as its themes: among the best-known composers in this form are Franz LISZT, Édouard LALO, Antonin DVORAK and Georges ENESCO. Johannes BRAHMS has also written piano pieces with this title, but without the usual significance of the name attached to them.

Rhapsody in Blue (Gershwin), an orchestral work by George GERSHWIN; orchestrated by Ferdinand GROFE, and first performed with remarkable success in 1924 by Paul WHITEMAN'S Orchestra at AEOLIAN HALL, New York. The original arrangement by Grofé was for piano with jazz orchestra accompaniment: it was later arranged for piano with symphonic orchestra accompaniment. There is a Victor recording by Jesús María SANROMA with the Boston "Pops" Orchestra and by George GERSHWIN with the Paul Whiteman Orchestra: also a Victor recording by José and Amparo Iturbi for two pianos—four hands. The rhapsody was later used as the basis of a ballet in one act: choreography and libretto by Anton Dolin; first performed at Paris in 1928. Classical music, represented by a ballerina competes for supremacy with jazz, personified by a male dancer.

Rhea, in Greek mythology the mother of ZEUS, POSEIDON, DEMETER, HERA, and PLUTO. She was a TITAN and a daughter of GAEA and the sky god, URANUS: her brother was CRONUS.

Rheinberger, Joseph Gabriel (1839-1901), German composer, organist, and teacher who studied at the Royal Conservatory, Munich, and with Franz Lachner. His works for the organ are still highly regarded: he also wrote operas, orchestral works, chamber music, and both sacred and secular choral music.

Rhind, J. Massey (1860-1936), American sculptor born in Scotland who studied at the Scottish Academy in Edinburgh, the Royal Academy at London, and with Jules Dalou at Paris. His works include decorations for many public and private buildings including the Astor Memorial doors at Trinity Church, New York: also statues of Andrew CARNEGIE and Robert BURNS, and an equestrian statue of George WASHINGTON at Newark, N. J.

Rhinegold, The (Das Rheingold), see **Ring of the Nibelungs, The.**

Rhine Maidens, The, see **Ring of the Nibelungs, The.**

Rhodes, Eugene Manlove (1869-1934), American novelist and short-story writer who spent twenty-five years of his life as a cowboy, and was educated at the University of the Pacific, San José, Calif. His works include *Good Men and True* (1910); *Bransford in Arcadia; West is West; The Desire of the Moth; Copper Streak Trail; Beyond the Desert; The Proud Sheriff.*

Rhodes, a city on an island in the Aegean Sea: founded in 408 B.C., and famous during the 4th century as a center of art and oratory: it was also the site of the COLOSSUS OF RHODES. Its government was allied with that of Rome for many years, but passed into the hands of the Knights of St. John in 1310, and finally to the Turks in 1522.

Rhoecus, Greek sculptor and architect of the 6th century B.C. who was specially noted for his excellent work in bronze: he is said to have built the Temple of HERA at Samos and a marble statue, *Night,* in the Temple of ARTEMIS at EPHESUS.

Rhumba or **Rumba,** a Cuban dance popular with the Negroes and lower classes: it was introduced into the American ballroom about 1930. Harl McDONALD, a well-known American composer, has written a *Rhumba Symphony* for two pianos and orchestra in which he has introduced the peculiar rhythm of the rhumba.

Rhyme or **Rime,** in prosody the most distinctive of the literary devices used in versification: it was used in the earliest Oriental poetry, but unknown to the Greeks and Romans. It was first found in early Christian sacred verse in the form of alliteration and assonance, but is applied today only when the sound of the last syllables on two consecutive lines are the same: they must also be accented on the same syllables.

Rhythm, in music the measured movement of similar groups of tones in relation to accent and duration: the notes are divided into regular units by the measure on the musical staff, and the time is indicated by a signature placed at the beginning which shows the correct number of notes to be played in each measure.

Riabouchinska, Tatiana (1916-), Russian dancer who studied with Alexander Volinine, and appeared first in 1931 with the CHAUVE SOURIS in both Europe and the United States: later she joined Colonel Wassily de Basil's Monte Carlo Ballet Russe. Among the ballets in which she has achieved success are *Les Sylphides; Jeux d'Enfants; Les Présages; Le Beau Danuk; Choreartium; Aurora's Wedding; Carnaval; Le Coq d'Or; Petrouchka.*

Ribera, Jusepe (1588-1656), Spanish painter and etcher who studied with Francisco Ribalta, and also in Italy where he was influenced by RAPHAEL and CARAVAGGIO. He finally settled at Naples, and through making a rich marriage, drove Annibale CARRACCI, DOMENICHINO and other painters away from the city. His notable works include *Diogenes and His Lantern; Martyrdom of St. Bartholomew; Descent from the Cross; Adoration of the Shepherds; Silenus and the Satyrs.* His etchings also display great originality and powerful drawing.

Ribot, Augustin Théodule (1823-1891), French painter who specialized in historical, religious, and genre subjects: his notable canvases include *Cooks at Dinner Time; Christ and the Doctors; The Good Samaritan; Chickens Roosting; Interior of a Kitchen; Torture; The Merry Cook:* also many realistic portraits of old men and women.

Rice, Alice Caldwell Hegan (1870-1942), American novelist educated at private schools: her first novel, *Mrs. Wiggs of the Cabbage Patch* (1901) was a best seller, translated into many languages, dramatized, and filmed. Her other works include *Lovey Mary; Sandy; A Romance of Billy Goat Hill; The Buffer; The Lark Legacy; The Inky Way,* an autobiography.

Rice, Cale Young (1872-1943), American poet, novelist, and dramatist educated at Cumberland and Harvard Universities: his works include *From Dusk to Dusk* (1898); *Earth and New Earth; Sea Poems; Mihrima; Bitter Brew; Seed of the Moon.* He has also written dramas in verse and novels.

Rice, Elmer (1892-), American dramatist whose real name is Elmer Reizenstein: he was educated for the law, but decided on a career as a playwright. His first play, *On Trial* (1914), was a success as a drama and as a motion picture: other plays include *The Iron Cross; The Adding Machine; Cock Robin* with Philip BARRY; *Close Harmony* with Dorothy Parker; *Street Scene* which won the Pulitzer Prize in 1929; *Subway; Counsellor-at-Law; We, the People; Judgment Day; Between Two Worlds; American Landscape; Two on an Island.*

Rice, Fanny (1859-1936), American actress and singer who made her debut with the Boston Ideal Opera Company, and later became a member of Rudolph Aronson's company at the Casino Theatre, New York, appearing with Jefferson DE ANGELIS and Francis WILSON in *The Grand Duchess, Nadjy, ERMINIE, The Brigands; Poor Jonathan,* and many other operettas. Later she formed her own company to produce several French farces, and appeared in 1896 with John DREW in a revival of *The Rivals.* In 1927 she played in Kenyon NICHOLSON's comedy, *The Barker.*

Ricercar (It.), in music the title during the 16th century of a vocal or instrumental work constructed in the form of a FUGUE, and developed as a FANTASIA with several original motives: the earliest known work was written for the LUTE by Ottaviano dei Petrucci about 1500, and Johann Sebastian BACH used the title for a fugue in strict form.

Rich, Irene (1897-), American screen actress educated in private schools: among the films in which she has played leading roles are *Lady Windermere's Fan; Craig's Wife; They Had To See Paris; So This is London; Down to Earth; Manhattan Tower; That Certain Age; The Mortal Storm; The Lady in Question; This Time for Keeps.*

Rich, John (1692-1761), English actor regarded as the originator of English pantomime: he opened a theatre in Lincoln's Inn Fields where he appeared as HARLEQUIN in an entertainment which eventually developed into an annual pantomime. His stage name was Lun, and he appeared with enormous success from 1717 to 1761; he also opened and managed the new Covent Garden, and produced *The* BEGGAR'S OPERA with equal success.

Richard Coeur de Lion (1157-1199), an English king **(Richard I)** whose name and personality are closely connected with English and French poetry and romantic, historical fiction: he was the third son of Henry II against whom he conspired when only sixteen years old in league with his mother and elder brothers. He was at heart a warrior, and allied himself with Philip II of France in the Third Crusade during which he performed prodigies of valor. Returning from the Crusade he was shipwrecked, captured, and imprisoned by Emperor Henry VI of Austria who later released him for a ransom. He ruled England from 1189 to 1199, and was killed in France by an arrow: he was succeeded by John "Lackland" (1167-1216), who was forced to sign the Magna Carta by his nobles.

Richard III (1452-1485), English king from 1483 to 1485: on the death of his brother, Edward IV, in 1483, he seized the young Edward V and was proclaimed protector, later seizing the crown. He suppressed the rebellion led by the Duke of Buckingham in 1483, but was defeated and killed at the battle of Bosworth in 1485 by the Earl of Richmond who was then crowned Henry VII. The drama, *Richard III,* is said to have been completed by William SHAKESPEARE from an earlier play by Christopher MARLOWE left unfinished at the latter's death: Shakespeare's—or Marlowe's—characterization of Richard III as a man of intellectuality, but withal violent, cruel, and capable of using any means—even murder—to achieve his ends, has been generally accepted although some historians do not accept his views.

Richards, Laura Elizabeth (1850-1943), American novelist, biographer, short-story writer, and poet who was the daughter of Julia Ward Howe: her numerous works include *Five Mice* (1881); *Captain January; Snow White; Geoffrey Strong; Grandmother; Florence Nightingale; Julia Ward Howe* with Maude Howe Elliott, which received the Pulitzer Prize for biography in 1917; *Joan of Arc; Stepping Westward,* an autobiography; *Merry-Go-Round; What Shall the Children Read?*

Richards, Thomas Addison (1820-1900), American painter born in England who became the first instructor at the Women's School of Design at Cooper Union in 1858, and professor of Art at New York University from 1867 to 1892. His works, which are of the HUDSON RIVER SCHOOL, include *Pennsylvania Homestead; The Spirit of Solitude; Indian Paradise; Dingman's Creek; Midsummer on the Delaware:* he also illustrated several works on art.

Richards, William Trost (1833-1905), American painter who studied and painted in England, Germany, France and Italy: his works include *June Woods; New England Coast; Indian Summer; Narragansett Pier; On the Coast of New Jersey; Summit of Mount Tacoma; Gooseberry Island at Newport.* His daughter, **Anna M. Richards** (1870-), studied with her father, John LA FARGE, and Bejamin CONSTANT, becoming a distinguished figure and landscape painter.

Richardson, Henry Hobson (1838-1886), American architect educated at Harvard and trained at the ECOLE DES BEAUX-ARTS in Paris: his notable works include Trinity Church, Boston, Mass.; Sever Hall at Harvard University; the Marshall Field Building, Chicago; also the alteration of the State Capitol at Albany, N. Y.

Richardson, Ralph (1902-), English stage and screen actor who had considerable experience with stock companies in Shakespearean productions before entering the films: among the numerous pictures in which he has played the principal role are *Return of Bulldog Drummond; The Man Who Could Work Miracles; South Riding; The Citadel; Four Feathers; The Lion Has Wings; On the Night of the Fire; The Day Will Dawn.*

Richardson, Samuel (1689-1761), English novelist who was addicted as a boy to letter writing, and was frequently employed by illiterate young people to write love letters: his works include *Pamela, or Virtue Rewarded* (1740); *Clarissa, or the History of a Young Lady;* regarded as his masterpiece; *The History of Sir Charles Grandison.* His novels were constructed in the form of letters, a method suggested by his early experience in letter-writing.

Richelieu, Armand Jean du Plessis, Duke and Cardinal de (1585-1642), French statesman educated for the church who became cardinal in 1622, and was the principal minister for Louis XIII from 1624 until his death. He has been made a prominent character in several romances by Alexandre DUMAS, PERE, and is known to have given encouragement to scholars, poets, and artists. His portrait was painted several times by Philippe de CHAMPAIGNE.

Richepin, Jean (1849-1926), French poet and dramatist: his notable works include *The Song of the Beggars* (1876) for which he was fined and imprisoned; *Caresses; Curious Deaths; Blasphemies.* His plays include *Nana Sahib* for Sarah BERNHARDT; *The Sea; The Filibuster; By the Sword; Monsieur Scapin.*

Richman, Arthur (1886-), American dramatist who served as an officer during World War I: his plays include *Not So Long Ago* (1920); *Ambush; A Serpent's Tooth; The Awful Truth; The Far Cry; All Dressed Up; A Proud Woman; Heavy Traffic; The Season Changes.*

Richman, Charles J. (1870-), American stage and screen actor who made his debut at Miner's Fifth Avenue Theatre, New York, with Mrs. James A. HERNE in *Margaret Fleming:* among the plays in which he has appeared are *As You Like It; The School for Scandal; The Great Ruby; Miss Hobbs; The Royal Family; Mrs. Dane's Defence; Taming of the Shrew; The Charity Ball; The Rose of the Rancho; Diplomacy; Lights o' London; Bought and Paid For; Strictly Dishonorable; Riddle Me This; Biography:* he has also appeared in several films including *In Old Kentucky; The Life of Émile Zola; The Adventures of Tom Sawyer; The Cowboy and the Lady.*

Richmond, Grace Louise (1866-), American novelist who contributed to the *Youth's Companion* and the *Saturday Evening Post:* her works include *The Second Violin* (1906); *Around the Corner in Gay Street; A Court of Inquiry; Red Pepper Burns; Strawberry Acres; Mrs. Red Pepper; Midsummer's Day; Red and Black; Red of the Redfields; Red Pepper Returns; Bachelor's Bounty.*

Richter, Adrian Ludwig (1803-1884), German painter and etcher who studied with his father, was strongly influenced by Daniel Nicolas CHODO-WIECKI, and later became professor of landscape painting at the Dresden Academy for more than thirty years. He executed many fine oil paintings, almost 250 etchings, and more than 3,000 drawings for woodcuts, becoming the most distinguished illustrator of his time.

Richter, Conrad Michael (1890-), American novelist who worked as a newspaper reporter and editor before his short story, *Brothers of No Kin,* appeared in 1914 in the *Forum:* his works include *Early Americana and Other Stories; The Sea of Grass; The Trees; Tacey Cromwell.*

Richter, Gustav Karl Ludwig (1823-1884), German painter who studied with Léon COGNIET, traveled in various parts of Europe, and later became one of the greatest portraitist of his day: his works include *The Daughter of Jairus; The Valkyries; Egyptian Girl; Building of the Pyramids; Odalisque:* also portraits of Emperor Wilhelm I; Queen Louise; George Bancroft, the American historian; Sultan Abdul Aziz, and many other notable persons.

Richter, Hans (1843-1916), Austrian conductor who studied under Simon SECHTER at the Vienna Conservatory of Music, and later conducted at Munich, Brussels, Pest, and finally at Vienna where he directed the Vienna Opera and the Vienna Philharmonic Society from 1875 to 1897. He was chosen by Richard WAGNER as conductor of the RING OF THE NIBELUNGS at Bayreuth, and also directed symphony orchestras at London, Birmingham, and Manchester. He was regarded as one of the greatest Wagnerian conductors.

Richter, Johann Paul Friedrich (1763-1825), German satirist, philosopher, and humorist: his works include *The Invisible Lodge* (1793); *Hesperus; Biographical Recreations under the Cranium of a Giantess; The Life of Quintus Fixlein; Siebenkäs; Titan; Schmelzle's Journey to Flaetz; Levana,* a treatise on education. He was one of Germany's greatest writers of fiction, but totally disregarded all rules of literary form.

Ride of the Valkyries, The (Wagner), an orchestral work constituting the prelude to Act III of Richard Wagner's music drama, *The Valkyrie,* one of the dramas in the RING OF THE NIBELUNGS. The scene is a shrouded mountain top with stormy winds and flashes of lightning; the Valkyries, daughters of the gods whose mission is to carry the bodies of heroes who have fallen in battle to Valhalla, race across the threatening sky on their horses. There is a Victor recording by the London Symphony Orchestra directed by Albert Coates, and a Columbia recording by the Pittsburgh Symphony Orchestra under the baton of Fritz Reiner.

Ridge, Lola (1883-1941), American poet born in Ireland who spent her youth in Australia and New Zealand, and came to the United States in 1907: her works include *The Ghetto and Other Poems* (1918); *Sunup and Other Poems; Red Flag and Other Poems; Firehead; Dance of Fire.*

Riding, Laura (1901-), American poet, novelist, and essayist educated at Cornell University: her works include *The Close Chaplet* (1926); *Voltaire; Contemporaries and Snobs; Poems; Laura and Francisca; Poet: A Lying Word; A Trojan Ending; The World and Ourselves; Lives of Wives.*

Riegger, Wallingford (1885-), American composer who studied with Edgar Stillman KELLEY and Percy GOETSCHIUS at the Institute of Musical Art, New York, and at the Berlin Hochschule, later conducting opera in Germany, and occupying the post of instructor in musical theory at Drake University, Des Moines, Iowa, and also at the Institute of Musical Art, New York. His compositions include orchestral works and chamber music in various forms for strings and for woodwind.

Riemann, Hugo (1849-1919), German musicologist educated at various universities in law, philosophy, history, and musicology. His outstanding work is the *Musiklexikon* (Dictionary of Music), published in 1882, and revised through eight editions by Riemann himself: the ninth edition (1919) was edited by Alfred Einstein who also prepared the eleventh edition in 1929.

Riemenschneider, Tillmann (1468-1531), German sculptor who worked in Würzberg from 1483 to 1525: among his notable creations are the wooden altarpiece of Münnerstadt; the tomb of Bishop Rudolf at the Würzberg Cathedral; the nude statues of Adam and Eve for the door of the Marienkapelle; the altar in the church of St. James, Rotenbourg; Tomb of Henry II; statues of St. Dorothy and St. Margaret.

Rienzi, The Last of the Tribunes, a grand opera in five acts: libretto and music by Richard WAGNER; first produced at Dresden in 1842; at the Academy of Music, New York, in 1878, and at the Metropolitan Opera House in 1886. Wagner followed the story of Cola di Rienzi (1313-1354), an Italian patriot as related in the historical novel by Edward George BULWER-LYTTON. The overture, which is a popular concert and radio number, is available in a Victor recording by the Boston "Pops" Orchestra, and a Columbia recording by the Paris Conservatory Orchestra directed by Felix Weingartner.

Ries, Franz (1846-1932), German violinist and composer who studied with his father and with Joseph MASSART at the Paris Conservatory: a nervous condition forced him to abandon a concert career and he founded the publishing house of Ries and Erler in 1882. His compositions include several suites for violin which are still used: one of them contains a much-admired MOTO PERPETUO.

Riesenberg, Felix (1879-1939), American novelist and master mariner educated at Columbia

University who served as a naval officer in World War I: his numerous works include *Under Sail* (1915); *Vignettes of the Sea; Endless River; Clipper Ships; Log of the Sea; Cape Horn; Living Again,* an autobiography.

Rietschel, Ernst Friedrich August (1840-1861), German sculptor who studied at Dresden and with Christian Daniel RAUCH at Berlin: his works include colossal statues of Frederick Augustus of Saxony, Goethe, Schiller, Weber, and Lessing. He designed the Luther Memorial at Worms, but died before he could execute it: also some beautiful bas-reliefs, the well-known *Christ-Angel,* and a life-sized *Pietá.*

Rigaud, Hyacinthe (1659-1743), French painter who won the Prix de Rome in 1682, but remained in Paris upon the advice of Charles LE BRUN, and became one of the most distinguished portraitists of his day: he painted from thirty to forty portraits each year for sixty-two years. Among his more than 2000 sitters were François GIRARDON, Antoine COYSEVOX, Nicholas COUSTOU, François MANSART, Jean de LA FONTAINE, Jean RACINE, LOUIS XIV, Cardinal Polignac, and Pierre Mignard.

Riggs, Lynn (1899-   ), American dramatist and poet who was educated at the University of Oklahoma, and held various commercial jobs before his first play, *Big Lake,* was produced in 1927. It was followed by *Roadside* (1930) and *Green Grow the Lilacs* produced by the THEATRE GUILD in 1931. In 1943 the Theatre Guild revived the last-named as a musical play entitled *Oklahoma:* it proved a great success, and is scheduled for adaptation to the screen. Another play, *Russet Mantle,* was well received in 1936.

Rigoletto, grand opera in three acts: libretto by Francesco Maria Piave based on Victor HUGO's drama, *Le Roi s'Amuse* (*The King Amuses Himself*); music by Giuseppe VERDI; first produced at Venice in 1851; at the Academy of Music, New York, in 1855, and at the Metropolitan Opera House, in 1883. The story is a gruesome one: the Duke of Mantua seduces Gilda, the daughter of Rigoletto, the court jester. Rigoletto bribes the assassin, Sparafucile, to kill the duke, but Sparafucile's sister, Maddalena, with whom the duke is carrying on an intrigue, induces her brother to kill instead the first man who enters the inn. Gilda, who is deeply in love with the faithless duke, after overhearing the scheme, enters the inn dressed as a man, and is murdered by Sparafucile who delivers her body in a sack to Rigoletto: when the latter sees the dead body of his daughter, he expires. There is a complete Victor recording, and an abridged Columbia recording: also various recordings of the popular arias, duets, and quartet.

Rig Veda, see **Veda.**

Rijks Museum (Amsterdam), an institution containing the national collection of Holland housed in a modern building divided into a series of rooms designed to illustrate the artistic progress of the Dutch. Ecclesiastical art is displayed in nine of the rooms: there are also exhibits of paintings, engravings, armor, costumes and metal works.

Riley, James Whitcomb (1853-1916), American poet who first traveled with a company of strolling players, and latter engaged in journalism. He was known as the "Hoosier Poet": his collections of verse include *The Old Swimmin' Hole and 'Leven More Poems* (1883); *Rhymes of Childhood; Neighborly Poems; Home Folks; The Book of Joyous Children; The Boss Girl and Other Sketches; Afterwhiles.* Among his most popular individual poems are "When the Frost is on the Punkin," "Littler Orphant Annie"; and "The Raggedy Man."

Rilke, Rainer Maria (1875-1926), Austrian poet educated at the University of Prague who later became the secretary of the famous French sculptor, Auguste RODIN: his works available in English include *Auguste Rodin; The Life of the Virgin Mary; The Notebook of Malte Laurids Brigge; Elegies from the Castle of Duino; Stories of God; Sonnets to Orpheus; Poems from the Book of Hours.*

Rimsky-Korsakow, Nikolai Andreievitch (1844-1908), Russian composer who was one of the musical amateurs who, with BORODIN, CUI, and MUSSORGSKY, gathered around Mily Balakirev at St. Petersburg. After service in the Russian navy, he became professor at the St. Petersburg Conservatory in 1871, and also achieved fame as an orchestral conductor, and as the teacher of LIADOFF, GLAZUNOFF, GRETCHANINOFF, and IPPOLITOW-IWANOW. His compositions include the operas *The Snow Maiden; Mlada; Sadko; Mozart and Salieri; The Tsar's Bride; Tsar Saltan,* and *Le Coq d'Or;* three symphonies; *Scheherazade,* an orchestral suite; *Spanish Caprice; Easter Overture;* chamber music; songs and piano pieces. He also re-orchestrated Mussorgsky's opera, BORIS GODUNOFF, wrote a fine treatise on orchestration, and an autobiography, *The History of My Musical Life,* which contains much invaluable information regarding Russian music.

Rinck, Johann Christian Heinrich (1770-1846), German organist and composer who studied with Johann Christian Kittel (1732-1809) who was the last pupil of Johann Sebastian BACH: he became one of the greatest concert organists of his day, and wrote many scholarly organ works.

Rinehart, Mary Roberts (1876-   ), American novelist and dramatist: her works include *The Circular Staircase* (1908); *The Man in Lower Ten; Tish; The Bat,* a play with Avery Hopwood produced with great success in 1920; *The Red Lamp; The Door; The State vs. Elinor Norton; The Wall; Haunted Lady; The Great Mistake.* She has also written several travel books, and humorous stories about "Tish" published in the *Saturday Evening Post.*

Rinehart, William Henry (1825-1874), American sculptor who first worked as a stonecutter. After 1858 he lived in Italy, and the Peabody Institute at Baltimore has the originals or casts of many of his finest figures, reliefs, and busts including *Clytie; Endymion; Sleeping Children; Rebecca; Latona and Her Children.*

Ring, Blanche (1877-   ), American actress and singer who appeared with James A. HERNE, Nat GOODWIN, and Chauncey OLCOTT: among the plays in which she was featured are *The Jewel of Asia; The Jersey Lily; The Love Birds; Sergeant Brue; Dolly Dollars; The Midnight Sons; The Yankee Girl; No, No, Nanette; Houseboat on the Styx; Her Master's Voice; Storm over Patsy.*

Ring of the Nibelungs, The (Das Ring des Nibelungen), a tetralogy of music dramas: (*1*) *The Rhinegold;* (*2*) *The Valkyrie;* (*3*) *Siegfried;* (*4*) *The Dusk of the Gods;* text and music by Richard WAGNER; first produced in complete form at the Festspielhaus, Bayreuth, on Aug. 13, 14, 16, and 17, 1876. The following is a brief synopsis of the action in each drama. **The Rhinegold—** *Scene I.* The three Rhine daughters, Woglinde, Wellgunde, and Flosshilde are sporting in the waters near a rock on the banks of the Rhine when Alberich, ruler of the Nibelungs, a tribe of dwarfs, appears: after he sees the gleaming Rhinegold, and learns that he who foreswears love can forge from the gold a ring that will give him unlimited power, he seizes it and disappears. *Scene II.* The castle of the gods, Valhalla, is seen in the distance: the giants, Fasolt and Fafner, have built it for Wotan, the chief god, who has promised them Freia, the goddess of youth and love in payment, but they demand the Rhinegold instead. Wotan, accompanied by Loge, the wily god of fire, go to Nibelheim, the subterranean country of the Nibelungs in search of the Rhinegold. *Scene III.* There they find Alberich and his brother, Mime: Alberich boasts of his ability to change himself into any form through his magic helmet, the Tarnhelm. The wily Loge induces him to become a toad: Wotan puts his foot on him, and after he is securely bound, they seize the gold, the ring, and Tarnhelm. *Scene IV.* The giants return for payment, and the unwilling Wotan finally gives them the gold, the ring, and Tarnhelm: Fasolt seizes the ring for himself, but Fafner strikes him dead, and departs with the hoard. A rainbow connecting the rocky height with Valhalla forms in the sky: the gods use it as a bridge by which to enter their new home. **The Valkyrie—***Act I.* In the midst of a terrific storm, Siegmund, exhausted from battle, seeks refuge in Hunding's hut, unaware of the fact that the latter has murdered his (Siegmund's) father, and forced his sister, Sieglinde, to become his wife. Siegmund and Sieglinde, after a long talk while Hunding sleeps soundly from a drug which she has given him, finally recognize each other: Siegmund pulls the sword Nothung out of the tree in which their father has driven it, and they flee from Hunding's hut. *Act II.* Wotan orders Brünnhilde, one of the VALKYRIES, to see that Hunding, who is pursuing Siegmund and Sieglinde, is defeated in the coming fray, but his wife, Fricka, goddess of marriage, forces him to rescind his order, and instruct Brünnhilde to see that Hunding is victor. Brünnhilde seeks Siegmund and Sieglinde to warn them of impending disaster, but when she realizes that the pair are madly in love, she promises to aid them because of the pledge of their love, the as yet unborn Siegfried. But when she attempts to aid Siegmund in the battle with Hunding, Wotan appears: he shatters Siegmund's sword and permits Hunding to kill him, but finally slays Hunding also with a withering glance. *Act III.* The Valkyries await the coming of Brünnhilde who brings Sieglinde and the broken pieces of Siegmund's sword: they aid Sieglinde to disappear with the sword into the woods. Wotan, angry at Brünnhilde's disobedience, condemns her to sleep inside a wall of magic fire until some hero shall rescue her: he lays her down on a grassy mound, and with a wave of his spear invokes Loge, the god of fire who surrounds the sleeping Valkyrie with a glittering circle of fire. **Siegfried—***Act I.* The dwarf, Mime, has been entrusted with the care of Siegfried, the son of Siegmund and Sieglinde, who died in giving him birth. Mime has tried to weld the broken pieces of Siegmund's sword together, but lacks both the skill and the strength to do so. Siegfried, who has grown into a lusty youth, watches him impatiently: he finally seizes the pieces of the sword, forges them into one piece, and then cleaves the anvil in two with his newly-made weapon. *Act II.* Fafner, who has killed his brother, Fasolt, in order to become sole possessor of the gold, the ring, and the Tarnhelm, has changed himself into a fierce dragon. This avails him little because Siegfried kills the dragon with his newly-forged sword, and when the taste of its blood reaches his lips, he immediately understands the song of a forest bird who tells him about the Rhinegold, the ring, and the magic power of the Tarnhelm. Mime tries to induce him to drink a cup of poison, but Siegfried strikes him dead, and hastens away to seek the sleeping Brünnhilde about whom he has also been told by the bird. *Act III.* As Siegfried presses forward, Wotan, disguised as The Wanderer, tries to bar the way with his spear, but Siegfried shatters the spear with his sword, and plunges through the flames to awaken Brünnhilde with a kiss. **Dusk of the Gods** (Götterdämmerung)—*Prologue.* The three Norns or Fates are weaving the golden rope of destiny: when it snaps they sink into the earth. *Act I.* Siegfried and Brünnhilde are about to part for he seeks new fields to conquer: he leaves the ring on her finger in memory of his love, and she watches him ride away on her horse Grane. *Act II.* The scene shifts to the land of the Gibichungs where King Gunther plots with Gutrune, his sister, and Hagen his half brother: the latter's father is the scheming Alberich who stole the Rhinegold from the Rhine daughters. They plan to drug Siegfried so that he will fall in love with Gutrune, forgetting Brünnhilde: when he arrives the scheme succeeds, and Siegfried is induced to seek Brünnhilde, and force her to accept the attentions of Gunther. *Act II.* Siegfried woos Gutrune, forgetful of Brünnhilde, and excites the latter's jealousy to such an extent that she plots Siegfried's death with Gunther and Hagen, telling them of the vulnerable spot in his back: *Act III.* Siegfried comes upon the Rhine daughters: they beg him to return the ring, but he refuses, and they solemnly prophesy his death. Later Hagen plunges his spear into Siegfried's back, and Brünnhilde, realizing too late that both Siegfried and she have been tricked, throws the ring to the Rhine daughters, mounts her horse, Grane, and rides to the top of Siegfried's funeral pyre. The Rhine overflows its banks, and Hagen is drowned: far in the distance, a red flame spreads among the clouds, Valhalla is blazing in the sky, and the dusk of the gods has come. Reparation has been made, and the hero has risen to victory over death: free-will is given to men, and Siegfried has brought about the return of love to mankind. The recordings of the "Ring" are extremely numerous and varied, ranging from complete, almost complete, and abridged recordings of all four dramas to separate recordings of favorite vocal and instrumental excerpts. All of these are listed in *The Gramophone Shop Encyclopedia of Recorded Music.*

Rinuccini, Ottavio (1562-1621), Italian dramatic poet who was one of the group of litterateurs and musicians at Florence who worked out the beginnings of opera. He wrote the text of Peri and Caccini's opera *Dafne* (1594) regarded as the first opera: also of Peri's *Euridice* (1600), and MONTEVERDI's *Arianna* (1608).

Rippe-Rónai, Josef (1861-1927), Hungarian painter who studied at Munich and with Mihály MUNKACZY at Paris where he became intimate with Pierre BONNARD, Maurice DENIS, Paul GAUGUIN, Paul CEZANNE and Puvis de CHAVANNES. His first exhibition in 1892 brought him immediately into notice: after first painting in the French style, later his colorings became more vivid and consequently Hungarian in character. His notable works include *My Mother,* favorably compared with WHISTLER's famous picture; *Janitor's Daughter; Self-portrait.*

Rip van Winkle, the principal character in one of the stories in Washington Irving's *The Sketch-Book of Geoffrey Crayon, Gent.,* published in 1819, based on a legend, related for many years in the Catskill Mountains, of a man who went to sleep for twenty years, and his amusing experiences when he awoke. Several plays were written on the subject: one version by Dion BOUCICAULT furnished Joseph JEFFERSON with a starring vehicle for many years. Reginald DE KOVEN composed the music for an opera, *Rip van Winkle;* the libretto was written by Percy MACKAYE, and the opera produced in 1920.

Ristori, Adelaide (1822-1906), Italian actress who was the daughter of strolling players; she made her first success in 1836 as Francesca da Rimini in Silvio Pellico's tragedy, and in 1840 appeared as Marie Stuart in an Italian version of Schiller's drama. She rivaled the celebrated French actress, RACHEL, at Paris, repeated her success at London, and from 1866 toured the United States four times, being received more cordially on each visit.

Ritardando (It.), in music a direction indicating that the passage over which it is placed is to be played gradually more slowly: it is usually abbreviated *ritard.* or *rit.*

Ritchie, Anna Cora, see **Mowatt, Anna Cora.**

Rite of Spring, The, see **Sacre du Printemps, Le.**

Rittenhouse, Jessie Belle (1869-), American poet, editor, and anthologist who founded the

Poetry Society of America in 1910, and acted as its secretary for ten years: her works include *The Door of Dreams* (1918); *Patrician Rhymes* with her husband, Clinton SCOLLARD; *The Younger American Poets.* She has also compiled several anthologies of American and British verse.

Rivas, Angel de Saavedra, Duke of (1791-1865), Spanish dramatist, poet, and statesman: his works include a tragedy, *Don Alvaro, or The Force of Destiny,* used as the libretto for Giuseppe VERDI's tragic opera LA FORZA DEL DESTINO; *Poetical Essays; Florinda* an epic poem on the Moorish conquest of Granada.

Rivé-King, Julie (1857-1937), American pianist who studied with her mother, and later with Sebastian Bach MILLS, William MASON, and in Europe with Carl Reinecke and Franz LISZT. She made her debut in 1875 at New York with the New York Philharmonic-Symphony Society, played more than two hundred times with the Theodore Thomas Orchestra, and gave more than four thousand recitals up to 1936 in addition to teaching for thirty years at the Bush Conservatory, Chicago. Several of her piano compositions such as *Bubbling Spring* were very popular.

Rivera, Diego (1886-), Mexican painter who studied under native artists at the Academy of Fine Arts, Mexico City, with PICASSO at Paris where he was attracted for a time by CUBISM, and in Spain where he concentrated on the examples of CHIAROSCURO. He finally evolved principles and methods of his own which placed him among the most revolutionary mural painters: his many large murals are to be seen at Mexico City in several government buildings and educational institutions: also at the School of Fine Arts in San Francisco and the Institute of Arts, Detroit. His murals for Rockefeller Center, New York, were removed because of a controversy over their political meaning, the inclusion of a portrait of Lenin being apparently the cause of the dispute.

Rives, Amélie, Princess Troubetzkoy (1863-), American novelist and dramatist: her novels, plays, and poems include *The Quick or the Dead* (1889); *The Ghost Garden; Seléné; The Queerness of Celia; The Prince and the Pauper,* dramatized in 1920; *The Fear Market* produced in 1916; *Firedamp; Hidden House.*

Riviere, Briton (1840-1920), English painter who studied with his father, William Riviere, a well-known drawing master, and exhibited at the Royal Academy regularly from 1863. His works, which are chiefly concerned with animal subjects include *Miracle of the Gadarene Swine; Poacher's Widow; Fox and Geese; Let Sleeping Dogs Lie; Strayed from the Flock; Daniel in the Den of Lions:* he was ranked with Sir Edwin LANDSEER as a painter of animals.

Robbia, Della, see **Della Robbia.**

Robert, Hubert (1733-1808), French painter who lived eleven years in Italy, and upon his return to Paris painted architectural pictures of new and old Italian and Parisian buildings. He became director of the French Academy in 1784, was imprisoned during the Revolution, and resumed his post as curator of the LOUVRE under Napoleon I. His works include *Maison Carrée at Nimes; Fountain of Minerva at Rome; Ruins of Imperial Palace at Rome; Ruins of Forum Palladium.*

Robert, Louis Leópold (1794-1835), French painter born in Switzerland who studied with Jacques Louis DAVID at Paris and also with Baron GROS: his works include *Sleeping Brigand; Brigand Women in Flight; Retreat of Brigands; Roman Girl with Tambourine; Fishers of the Adriatic; The Mowers:* his subjects were chosen from scenes among the populace in Italian cities and towns.

Robert-Fleury, Joseph Nicolas (1797-1890), French painter who studied with GIRODET-TRIOSON, Baron GROS and Horace VERNET: his canvas, *Scene in the Massacre of St. Bartholomew,* brought him immediate recognition. His notable works include *Tasso in the Convent of San Onofrio; The Religious Conference at Poissy in 1561; Christ and Little Children; Entry of Clovis into Tours; Christopher Columbus Received at the Court of Spain.* His son, **Tony Robert-Fleury** (1838-1912), studied with Paul DELAROCHE and Léon COGNIET: his works include *Last Day at Corinth; Child Kissing a Relic; Danaïds; Charlotte Corday at Caën; A Musical Cardinal:* also a ceiling painting, *Apotheosis of French Sculpture* in the LUXEMBOURG MUSEUM.

Roberts, Elizabeth Madox (1886-1941), American novelist and poet educated at the University of Chicago: her works include *Under the Tree* (1922), a poetic anthology of child life; *The Time of Man; My Heart and My Flesh; Jingling in the Wind; The Great Meadow; A Buried Treasure; He Sent Forth a Raven; Not by Strange Gods.*

Roberts, Howard (1843-1900), American sculptor who studied at the Pennsylvania Academy of Fine Arts, Philadelphia, and the ECOLE DES BEAUX-ARTS, Paris: his notable works include a statue of Robert Fulton for Statuary Hall, Capitol, Washington, D. C.; *Eleanor; Hypatia; Hester Prynne; Lot's Wife.*

Roberts, Kenneth Louis (1885-), American novelist and essayist educated at Cornell University who served in World War I and later worked as a journalist: his works include *Black Magic* (1924); *Florida; Arundel; The Lively Lady; Rabble in Arms; Captain Caution; Northwest Passage; Oliver Wiswell.*

Robertson, Guy (1892-), American actor and singer who served in World War I, and made his debut in 1919 at New York in *See-Saw:* among the plays in which he has appeared are *The Perfect Fool; Wildflower; The Song of the Flame; The Circus Princess; White Lilacs; The Street Singer; The Blue Mask; All the King's Horses; The Great Waltz; The Three Musketeers; Show Boat.*

Robertson, Rae, see **Bartlett, Ethel.**

Robertson, Thomas William (1829-1871), English actor and dramatist whose sister was the actress, Dame Madge KENDALL: his plays include *A Night's Adventure* (1851); *David Garrick; Society; Ours; Caste; School; M.P. 1870.* All of his plays except *David Garrick* were produced by Sir Squire BANCROFT at the Prince of Wales' Theatre with Marie Wilton (Lady Bancroft) in the leading feminine role.

Robeson, Paul (1898-), American Negro actor and singer, educated at Rutgers University and for the law at Columbia University, who made his debut in 1921 at New York in *Simon the Cyrenian:* among the plays in which he appeared are *Voodoo; All God's Chillun Got Wings; The Emperor Jones; Black Boy; Show Boat; Othello.* He has also given many song recitals in the United States, Great Britain, and Europe: among the films in which he has played leading roles are *Sanders of the River; The Song of Freedom; Show Boat; Jericho; King Solomon's Mines; Big Fella; Proud Valley; Native Land.*

Robespierre, Maximilian Marie Isidore (1758-1794), French lawyer who occupied the post of public accuser during the French Revolution because of his oratorical ability. He fought for the execution of Louis XVI with Marat and Danton, and was supreme during the Reign of Terror, but finally lost his power as dictator and was guillotined on July 28, 1794, with several of his party.

Robin Hood, comic opera in three acts: book by Harry B. SMITH; music by Reginald DE KOVEN; first produced at Chicago in 1880 by The BOSTONIANS: it was performed with tremendous success by this company for twenty years. There is a Victor recording of the most popular vocal and instrumental selections, and also of *Oh, Promise Me,* the "hit song" in the operetta, by Louise HOMER.

Robin Hood Dell (Philadelphia), an open-air amphitheatre in Fairmount Park, Philadelphia, which has a seating capacity of 6,500: a summer series of orchestral concerts is given there each year since 1930 with Alexander SMALLENS as chief conductor with guest conductors including ORMANDY, ITURBI, REINER, VAN HOOGSTRATEN, COATES, KINDLER, SODERO, BARLOW, WALLENSTEIN, and many others. Soloists frequently appear, and opera has been presented with well-known singers and ballet groups.

Robins, Elizabeth (1862-), American actress and novelist who joined the Boston Museum Stock Company at sixteen, playing 380 parts, and also touring with Edwin BOOTH, Laurence BARRETT, and James O'NEILL. She also appeared in *Little Lord Fauntleroy,* and in most of Henrik Ibsen's plays. Her works include *George Mandeville's Husband* (1894); *The Magnetic North; A Dark Lantern; Votes for Women,* a play; *Theatre and Friendship; Both Sides the Curtain,* an autobiography.

Robinson, Bill (1878-), American Negro dancer and actor who first displayed dancing ability as a child of five, and later became one of the world's greatest tap dancers. He has appeared in many colored musical revues, vaudeville and in a swing version, entitled *The Hot Mikado*, of Gilbert and Sullivan's operetta: also in numerous films including *The Little Colonel; In Old Kentucky; The Little Rebel; Rebecca of Sunnybrook Farm; Just Around the Corner; Up the River.*

Robinson, Boardman (1876-), American painter born in Canada who studied at the Massachusetts Normal Art School, at the ECOLE DES BEAUX-ARTS, Paris, and was influenced by Jean Louis FORAIN. He became well-known as an illustrator for newspapers, for *Harper's Weekly* and *Metropolitan Magazine*, and also of books. In 1925 he became instructor at the ART STUDENTS' LEAGUE, New York, and has executed a mural, *Man and His Toys* for the RCA Building in Rockefeller Center.

Robinson, Edward G. (1893-), American actor born in Bucharest and educated at the College of the City of New York and at the American Academy of Dramatic Art. His debut was made in 1913 at New York in *Paid in Full*: among the plays in which he has appeared are *Samson and Delilah; Peer Gynt; The Adding Machine; The Firebrand; Androcles and the Lion; Juarez and Maximilian; The Brother Karamazov; Kibitzer.* He has also been featured in many films including *Little Caesar; Five Star Final; The Hatchet Man; Silver Dollar; Barbary Coast; The Amazing Dr. Clitterhouse; Confessions of a Nazi Spy; Brother Orchid; The Sea Wolf; Unholy Partners.*

Robinson, Edwin Arlington (1869-1935), American poet educated at Harvard who spent many years of his life at the MacDowell Colony in Peterboro, N. H.; his works include *The Torrent and the Night Before* (1896); *The Children of the Night; Captain Craig; Merlin; Lancelot; Collected Poems,* awarded the Pulitzer Prize for poetry in 1922; *Roman Bartholow; Tristram,* awarded the Pulitzer Prize for poetry in 1928; *Cavender's House; Nicodemus; Amaranth; King Jasper.*

Robinson, Lennox (1886-), Irish dramatist who was manager of the ABBEY THEATRE, Dublin, accompanied the company to the United States in 1912, 1932, and 1935, and has also lectured and directed plays at American universities: his works include *The Clancy Name* (1908); *Cross Roads; Patriots; The Dreamers; The Lost Leader; The White-headed Boy; The Round Table; Is Life Worth Living?* He also acted as organizing librarian of the Carnegie Libraries in Ireland for many years, and was one of the founders of the Dublin Dramatic League.

Robinson, Theodore (1852-1896), American painter who studied at Paris with GEROME, CAROLUS-DURAN and Claude MONET: his works, which are of the school of IMPRESSIONISM, include *Winter Landscape; In the Sun; The Canal; The Old Mill; Girl and Cow; Bird's Eye View.*

Robson, Eleanor (1879-), American actress born in England who made her debut at San Francisco in 1897 with the Frawley Stock Company in *Men and Women*: her first success was as Bonita Canby in *Arizona*: among the plays in

which she appeared were *In a Balcony; Unleavened Bread; A Gentleman of France; Romeo and Juliet; Merely Mary Ann; She Stoops to Conquer; The Dawn of Tomorrow; Salomy Jane.* After her retirement in 1910 and marriage to August Belmont she became one of the founders and chairman in 1935 of the METROPOLITAN OPERA GUILD.

Robson, Flora (1902-), English stage and screen actress who studied at the Royal Academy of Dramatic Art, London, making her debut in 1921 at London in *Will Shakespeare*: among the plays in which she has appeared are *Fata Morgana; Desire Under the Elms; Salome; The Anatomist; Dangerous Corner; Lady Audley's Secret; All God's Chillun; The Cherry Orchard; The Importance of Being Earnest; Anna Christie; Ladies in Retirement; Damask Cheek*: she has also played in numerous films including *Catherine the Great; Fire Over England; Farewell Again; Wuthering Heights; The Sea Hawk; Bahama Passage.*

Robson, May (1858-1942), English stage and screen actress educated in Paris, London, and Brussels who made her debut in 1883 at Brooklyn, N. Y., in *The Hoop of Gold*: among the plays in which she appeared were *Jim the Penman; Robert Elsmere; The Charity Ball; Sowing the Wind; Gloriana; The Conquerors; Lord and Lady Algy; Dorothy Vernon of Haddon Hall.* She also played important roles in numerous films including *Reunion in Vienna; Dinner at Eight; Lady For a Day; Alice in Wonderland; Vanessa; A Star is Born; Four Daughters; Nurse Edith Cavell; Irene; Joan of Paris.*

Robson, Stuart (1836-1903), American actor whose real name was Robson Stuart: it is said that his unintentionally humorous portrayal of a serious role in 1852 revealed his abilities as a comedian. He was the partner of William H. CRANE with whom he appeared in Bronson HOWARD'S comedy, *The Henrietta* in 1887: he also played in *Oliver Goldsmith; She Stoops to Conquer; The Meddler; A Comedy of Errors; The Merry Wives of Windsor.* His wife, **May Waldron Robson** (1868-1925), was a well-known actress with Augustin DALY'S Company and with the Robson-Crane Company.

Robson, William N., see **Radio Drama.**

Robusti, Jacopo, see **Tintoretto.**

Roche, Arthur Somers (1883-1935), American novelist who served in World War I: his works include *Loot* (1916); *Plunder; The Sport of Kings; The Pleasure Buyers; Devil-May-Care; The Woman Hunters; Slander; Conspiracy; Lady of Resource.*

Rochester Philharmonic Orchestra, an organization founded in 1923 by George EASTMAN: the conductors for the first season were Albert COATES and Eugene GOOSSENS, the latter holding the post until 1931. From 1931 to 1936 the guest conductors included REINER, HADLEY, DOBROWEN, Guy Fraser HARRISON, MOLINARI, BODANZKY, Werner JANSSEN, HARTY, Walter DAMROSCH, SOKOLOFF,

Vladimir Golschmann, and ITURBI. In 1936 José Iturbi became permanent conductor with Guy Fraser Harrison as associate.

Rockefeller Center (Radio City), a business and entertainment center in New York occupying several blocks from 48th to 51st Streets between Fifth and Sixth Avenues. The architectural firms who designed the fourteen buildings which comprise the Center were Reinhard and Hofmeister, Corbett, Harrison and MacMurray, and Hood and Fouilhoux: the construction was started in 1931 and completed in 1939. The amusements include RADIO CITY MUSIC HALL, the Center Theatre presenting theatrical spectacles, and two broadcasting stations: throughout the buildings there are more than sixty examples of sculpture in stone, glass, stainless steel, and bronze; also mural paintings by outstanding contemporary artists.

Rockwell, Norman (1894-   ), American painter and illustrator trained at the Art Students' League, New York: he has executed many cover designs and illustrations for the *Saturday Evening Post*, the *Ladies Home Journal* and the *Woman's Home Companion:* also illustrations for Mark Twain's *Tom Sawyer* and *Huckleberry Finn.*

Rococo, a style of architecture and decoration popular during the Regency and the reign of Louis XV in France: it represents both an elaboration and a degeneration of the BAROQUE, inspired by shells mixed with volutes, spirals, foliage, and animal forms hopelessly intermingled. The word has accordingly come to mean anything in art that is ugly and without the elements of good taste.

Rode, Pierre (1774-1830), French violinist who studied with Jean Baptiste VIOTTI at Paris, making his debut in 1790. After touring Germany, Holland, England, and Spain, he became solo violinist to NAPOLEON I and later to Emperor Alexander of Russia: his works include many violin concertos and the famous, still-used *Twenty-four Caprices in the Form of Études:* he also wrote a violin method with Pierre BAILLOT and Radolphe KREUTZER.

Rodenbach, Georges (1855-1898), Belgian poet, novelist, and dramatist: his greatest work is an historical poem, *Belgium* (1880). He has also written *The Fireside and the Fields; Sorrows; The Reign of Silence;* also a novel, *Bruges la Morte,* and a play, *The Veil,* which has been translated into English.

Rodgers, Richard (1902-   ), American composer educated at Columbia University and the Institute of Musical Art, New York: he has collaborated since 1925 with **Lorenz Hart** (1895-   ) as librettist in numerous musical comedies, operettas and revues including *Garrick Gaities* (1925); *Dearest Enemy; Peggy-Ann; The Girl Friend; A Connecticut Yankee; Present Arms; Simple Simon; America's Sweetheart; Jumbo; On Your Toes; Babes in Arms; I'd Rather Be Right; I Married an Angel; The Boys from Syracuse,* and several others.

Rodin, Auguste (1840-1917), French sculptor who studied with Antoine Louis BARYE and Pierre CARRIER-BELLEUSE: his works include *Man With a Broken Nose; Age of Bronze; St. John the Baptist; Eve; Burghers of Calais; The Kiss; Bust of a Woman; Thought; The Hand of God; The Thinker; Gate of Hell,* bronze doors which were never completed: also busts of Jean Paul Laurens, Pierre Carrier-Belleuse, Victor Hugo, and Aíme Jules Dalou. The **Rodin Museum** was established by the City of Paris in 1900 to honor the great master: it contains the originals or replicas of many of his works including drawings and unfinished pieces. Another museum of the same kind was presented to the city of Philadelphia in 1929 by Jules E. Mastbaum: it houses more than eighty bronzes as well as drawings, bas-reliefs and paintings executed by Rodin.

Rodolfo, the principal male character in Giacomo PUCCINI's grand opera, LA BOHEME: he is a poet and the lover of Mimi. They finally part, but are reunited when Mimi returns to the bare garret in which Rudolfo and Marcel are living, only to die in her lover's arms.

Rodzinski, Artur (1894-   ), Austrian conductor educated at the University and the Academy of Music at Vienna: after conducting for five years at the Warsaw Opera, he became assistant conductor of the PHILADELPHIA ORCHESTRA, and head of the operatic and orchestral departments at the CURTIS INSTITUTE OF MUSIC. From 1929 to 1933 he conducted the LOS ANGELES SYMPHONY ORCHESTRA, and from 1933 to 1943 the CLEVELAND ORCHESTRA: in 1943 he was appointed conductor of the New York Philharmonic-Symphony Orchestra. He organized the NBC SYMPHONY ORCHESTRA in 1937-38, conducting part of its schedule.

Roe, Edward Payson (1838-1888), American clergyman and novelist whose first story, *Barriers Burned Away* was a great success: it was followed by many more including *What Can She Do?; The Opening of a Chestnut Burr; From Jest to Earnest; A Knight of the Nineteenth Century; He Fell in Love With His Wife; Miss Lou.*

Roerich, Nikolai Constantinovich (1874-   ), Russian painter of Scandinavian ancestry whose first pictures were of the Vikings and prehistoric Russia, among them the murals in the Kazan Railway Station at Moscow. He also painted scenery for BORODIN's *Prince Igor,* the settings for IBSEN's *Peer Gynt* at the Moscow ART THEATRE and the scenery for STRAVINSKY's ballet, *Le Sacre du Printemps.* He spent five years in the Himalayas, bringing back 500 pictures, and is now the director of the Roerich Institute of Art affiliated with his museum in New York.

Roger de Coverley, an English country dance of ancient origin: the dancers line up in two rows facing each other, and the figures performed are similar to those of the VIRGINIA REEL.

Roger-Ducasse, Jean Jules (1873-   ), French pianist and composer who studied composition with Gabriel FAURE, and piano with Charles De Bériot at the PARIS CONSERVATORY OF MUSIC, later becoming a professor there. His compositions include operas, ballets, orchestral works, chamber music, piano pieces, and several pedagogical works.

Rogers, Bernard (1893-), American composer and teacher who studied at the INSTITUTE OF MUSICAL ART, New York, and with Ernest BLOCH, later becoming teacher of composition at the EASTMAN School of Music, Rochester, New York. His compositions include a grand opera, *The Marriage of Aude,* which won the David BISPHAM Prize; orchestral works; choruses and chamber music.

Rogers, Ginger (1911-), American screen actress, real name Virginia Katherine McMath: she has appeared in many films including *The Gay Divorcee; Roberta; Top Hat; Follow the Fleet; Shall We Dance?; Stage Door; Vivacious Lady; The Story of Irene and Vernon Castle; Bachelor Mother; Primrose Path; Lucky Partners; Kitty Foyle; Tom, Dick, and Harry; Roxie Hart; Tales of Manhattan.*

Rogers, John (1829-1904), American sculptor who was first a machinist and draftsman. He studied for a short time in Europe, but became discouraged and returned to the United States to work at drawing until one of his little green clay groups, *The Checker Players,* attracted favorable attention. He executed a life-size statue of Lincoln, but his miniatures, known as *Rogers Groups,* and representing familiar scenes and incidents of home life such as *Going for the Cows* became popular in all parts of the United States.

Rogers, Randolph (1825-1892), American sculptor: among his notable works are *Nydia; The Lost Pleiad; Ruth; Angel of the Resurrection:* also military memorials and statues of John Adams, Abraham Lincoln, and William H. Seward. He finished the Washington Monument begun by Thomas CRAWFORD at Richmond, Va., and designed the bronze doors for the ROTUNDA of the CAPITOL at Washington, D. C.

Rogers, Will (1879-1935), American humorist, actor, lecturer and author who made his stage debut in 1905 at Hammerstein's Roof Garden, New York, in a rope-jumping act in which he interpolated a humorous monologue: he appeared in Florenz ZIEGFELD'S *Follies* for many years, and also in several motion pictures. His works include *Roger-isms* (1919); *The Cowboy Philosopher on Prohibition; The Illiterate Digest; Letters of a Self-Made Diplomat to His President.*

Rogers Brothers, The, the stage name of two comedians, Gus and Max Solomon, who made their debut in a song and dance act at the National Theatre, New York, in 1885, later appearing at Tony PASTOR'S Theatre as Dutch comedians, and at Koster & Bial's Music Hall. From 1898 they starred in several comedies, written for them by John J. McNally, including *A Reign of Error; The Rogers Brothers in Wall Street; The Rogers Brothers in Ireland; The Rogers Brothers in Panama,* etc. The song "Reuben, Reuben, I've Been Thinking" was one of their greatest song successes.

Rohmer, Sax (1883-), English author of mystery and detective fiction whose real name is Arthur Sarsfield Wade: his works include *Dr. Fu Manchu* (1913) and several sequels; *The Yellow Claw; The Exploits of Captain O'Hagan; The Golden Scorpion; The Dream Detective; Batwing; Tales of Chinatown; Tales of East and West; The Bat Flies Low.*

Rojas Zorilla, Francesco de (1607-1648), Spanish dramatist whose comedies were successful because he had the acumen to make the clown the central figure in plays such as *No One Lower in Rank than the King:* other dramatists including ROTROU, SCARRON, CORNEILLE, LE SAGE and VANBRUGH borrowed freely from his works.

Roland, in medieval legend the most celebrated of the paladins of CHARLEMAGNE: he was famous for his valorous deeds and death in 778 at the battle of Roncesvalles, recorded in the CHANSON DE ROLAND.

Rolfe, William James (1827-1919), American Shakespearean critic and editor: his works include *The Friendly Edition of Shakespeare; The School Edition of Shakespeare:* also *Shakespeare the Boy:* he also annotated selections from the works of TENNYSON, SCOTT, BROWNING, WORDSWORTH, GRAY, GOLDSMITH and other English poets.

Roll, Alfred Philippe (1846-1919), French painter who studied with GEROME and BONNAT at the ECOLE DES BEAUX-ARTS, Paris: his notable works include *Environs of Baccarat; Evening; Flood at Toulouse; Fête of Silenus; Miners' Strike; In Normandy:* he became painter to the French Government, and decorated many public buildings with pictures and murals of a commemorative nature.

Roll, a tremolo or trill produced on (*a*) the TIMPANI (kettle-drums) by rapid alternate strokes, and on (*b*) the SIDE-DRUM by striking two strokes alternately with the left hand and two with the right hand. In the army a *long roll,* consisting of a prolonged, sustained roll, is the signal either for attack or for rally.

Rolland, Romain (1866-), French novelist, essayist and musicologist educated at the École Normale Supèrieure and the École de Rome, later becoming professor of music history at the Sorbourne: his works include a musical novel, *Jean Christophe* (10 vols. 1904-1912) based on the life of BEETHOVEN; *Beethoven the Creator; Goethe and Beethoven; Colas Breugnon; Clerambault; The Soul Enchanted,* a tetralogy; *Michelangelo; Tolstoi:* also a cycle of seven plays on the French Revolution.

Rolvaag, Ole Edvart (1876-1931), Norwegian-American novelist who came to the United States in 1896, and held the post of professor of the Norwegian literature at St. Olaf's College, Northfield, Minn. His works available in English include *Pure Gold* (1930); *The Boat of Longing; Giants in the Earth; Peder Victorious; His Father's Son.*

Romains, Jules (1885-), French novelist, poet, and dramatist educated at the École Normale

Supèrieure: his plays include *Dr. Knock* (1924); *The Marriage of le Troubadec; The Dictator; Donogoo.* He has also written *The Body's Rapture,* a trilogy, and *Men of Goodwill,* a panoramic view of French life in many parts one of which, *Verdun,* is regarded as a great war novel.

Romance, (*a*) in *literature* a tale of chivalry or on any fictitious or wonderful subject originating in the 11th century in southern Europe: the stories of King ARTHUR and of AMADIS OF GAUL are typical examples. The term is applied at the present time to a novel in which the interest lies in adventure or astonishing incidents rather than in the depiction of real life. (*b*) In *music* originally a ballad in verse of love or adventure set to music: later applied to short instrumental pieces of indefinite form and sentimental in character.

Romance of the Rose, a medieval poem in French begun by Guillaume de Lorris in 1260, and continued by Jean DE MEUNG about half a century later. Lorris wrote about 5,000 lines and Meung added 19,000 lines: it is in the form of an elaborate allegory on the subject of love, and according to George SAINTSBURY it presents a remarkable picture of life and thought during the period of history which it depicts.

Romanesque Architecture, a style originating in Italy which forms the connecting link between classical and Gothic architecture. Its principal characteristics are simplicity and severity, and the classical ideas of proportion in columns, molding and other architectural forms are either renounced or modified when used.

Romano, Giulio, see **Giulio Romano.**

Romanov, Panteleimon Sergeivich (1884-1938), Russian novelist and short story writer little known outside of Russia except for several translated works including *Three Pairs of Silk Stockings; Without Cherry Blossom; The New Commandment; On the Volga; Diary of a Soviet Marriage.*

Romanticism, (*a*) in art a movement about 1830 which had as its goal the liberation of painting and sculpture from the classical conventions and traditions: it was characterized by warmth of expression and more intensive interpretation of poetical sentiment. Among its exponents were Eugène DELACROIX and Jean GERICAULT. (*b*) In music a similar movement started early in the 19th century: Franz SCHUBERT, Hector BERLIOZ, Carl Maria von WEBER, Frédéric CHOPIN, Franz LISZT, Robert SCHUMANN, and Richard WAGNER were leaders in the development of works freed from the rigid rules of classic composition. (*c*) In literature a movement started at the end of the 18th century: among the numerous authors who broke away from CLASSICISM were Victor HUGO, Honoré de BALZAC, Lord BYRON, Sir Walter SCOTT, Johann Wolfgang von GOETHE, Nathaniel HAWTHORNE, and James Fenimore COOPER.

Romberg, Sigmund (1887-   ), Hungarian composer who studied at the University of Bucharest for a career as a civil engineer, but adopted the profession of operatic composer after coming to the United States in 1909: his works include over seventy operettas and revues among the most successful of which are MAYTIME; BLOSSOM TIME; *The* STUDENT PRINCE; *The Desert Song; Blue Paradise; My Maryland; The New Moon.* Many of his works have been successfully adapted for the films.

Rome (Italy), a city famous not only for its historical associations, but also for its museums of art: the VATICAN has six including the Museo Clementino, the Chiaramonti, the Gallery of Inscriptions, the Egyptian Museum, the Etruscan Museum, and the Christian Museum. There are also the Kircher Museum of prehistoric art, the Museo Nationale, the Museo Capitolino, and the Palazzo dei Conservatori.

Romeo and Juliet, a tale originally written by Matteo BANDELLO, an Italian priest and novelist: William SHAKESPEARE borrowed the plot for his tragedy produced about 1591, and his play has been the basis of the librettos for more than twenty grand operas the most successful of which was Charles GOUNOD'S *Romeo et Juliette,* produced at Paris in 1867, and at the Academy of Music, New York, during the same year. In 1839 Hector BERLIOZ composed his symphony known as *Romeo et Juliette,* and in 1870 an overture-fantasia (or symphonic poem), *Romeo and Juliet,* composed by Peter Ilich TSCHAIKOWSKY, was first played at Moscow: there is a Victory recording by the Boston Symphony Orchestra directed by Sergei Koussevitzky, and a Columbia recording by the Cleveland Orchestra under the baton of Artur Rodzinski.

Romney, George (1734-1802), English portrait painter who was practically self-taught: he spent two years in Italy, and on his return to London he soon became a formidable rival of Sir Joshua REYNOLDS and Thomas GAINSBOROUGH as a portrait painter: his works include *Milton and His Daughters; Newton Making Experiments with the Prism:* also many portraits of English nobility including Lady Hamilton in various allegorical settings.

Romulus and Remus, in Roman legend the founders of Rome: they were the twin sons of Mars and Rhea Silvia, and after Rome was founded, Romulus killed Remus in a quarrel over precedence. In order to obtain women for the city he permitted the rape of the Sabine women, but finally united with Titus Tatius, king of the Sabines, and they ruled Rome together until Tatius was killed. He is supposed to have disappeared in a storm, and was worshiped as the god Quirinus which was the Sabine name for Mars.

Ronald, Sir Landon (1873-1938), English conductor and composer; real name Landon R. Russell: he studied at the Royal College of Music, London, with Sir Hubert Hastings PARRY, and with Charles Villiers STANFORD, later conducting the Covent Garden Opera, the Harris Italian Opera Company, the Lyric Theatre Orchestra, the LONDON SYMPHONY ORCHESTRA, and the ROYAL ALBERT HALL Orchestra. His compositions include operas, ballets, incidental music, orchestra works, piano pieces, and over 200 songs many of which won lasting favor. He was a brother of Henry RUSSELL, distinguished opera impresario.

Rondo, in music a form of instrumental composition in which the principal theme or melody is repeated after one or more minor themes are introduced. The simplest form of rondo has but one digression between the two statements of the melody or theme; this is known as the *first rondo form*. The *second rondo form* consists of three statements of the melody separated by two digressions, and the *third rondo form* has four statements of the melody and three digressions appearing between the melody. The first two digressions are in a key contrasting with the key of the melody or theme; the third is a repetition of the first digression in the key of the melody. The classical composers including Franz Joseph HAYDN, MOZART, BEETHOVEN and SCHUBERT were masters in devising interesting variations of the form.

Ronsard, Pierre de (1524-1585), French poet who formed a society known as the Plèiade which completely disregarded the traditions of native literature and substituted the classic Greek and Roman models. His most ambitious work was *La Franciade* (1575), an epic poem never completed; *Odes; Amours; Hymns; Elegies:* he exercised a lasting influence on French literature.

Rood Loft, in ecclesiastical architecture a screen separating the choir from the nave of a church: they were much in use during the Renaissance and Gothic periods.

Rooney, Mickey, stage name of Joe Yule, Jr., American vaudeville and screen actor who first appeared as a child in a vaudeville act with his parents: his appearances in films since 1935 include *A Midsummer Night's Dream; Ah, Wilderness; Little Lord Fauntleroy; Captains Courageous; The Hoosier Schoolboy; Judge Hardy's Children; Lord Jeff; Love Finds Andy Hardy; Boys Town; Stablemates; Out West with the Hardys; Huckleberry Finn; Babes in Arms; Young Tom Edison; Judge Hardy and Son; Life Begins for Andy Hardy; The Courtship of Andy Hardy; The Human Comedy.*

Ropartz, Guy (1864-), French composer who first studied and practiced law, and later studied music at the PARIS CONSERVATORY with Théodore DUBOIS, Jules MASSENET and Cesar FRANCK. His compositions include several operas; symphonies and suites for orchestra; chamber music, and piano pieces. He has also published pedagogical treatises, three volumes of poems, and a play.

Rosa, Carlo, see **Carl Rosa Opera Company.**

Rosa, Salvator (1615-1673), Italian painter and poet who studied with Jusepe RIBERA and Aniello FALCONE, finally finding a patron in Cardinal Brancaccio: his works include *Conspiracy of Catiline; Prometheus; Souls in Purgatory; Dishonest Woodman; St. Paul in the Desert; The Prodigal Son; Three Monks by a Stormy Sea; Resurrection of Christ; Christ and the Doctors:* he also executed some fine etchings, and many well-known satirical poems.

Rosamunde (Schubert), a romantic play in four acts: book by Wilhelmine von Chezy; music by Franz SCHUBERT; produced at Vienna in 1823. The failure of the play was due to an inane libretto, and not to the glorious music written by Schubert: the **Rosamunde Entr'actes and Ballet Music** are among the most popular concert, record and radio numbers at the present time. There is a Victor recording of *Entr'acte No. 2* by the San Francisco Symphony Orchestra under Alfred Hertz, and a Columbia recording of *Entr'actes No. 1 and No. 2* by the Hallé Orchestra directed by Sir Hamilton Harty. There are Victor recordings of the *Ballet Music* by the Boston Symphony Orchestra under Serge Koussevitzky, and the London Symphony Orchestra directed by Bruno Walter; also a Columbia recording by the Hallé Orchestra under the baton of Sir Hamilton Harty.

Roscius, Quintus (c.126 B.C.-62 B.C.), Roman actor who was born a slave: he was particularly successful in comedy roles; CICERO is said to have taken lessons from him, and the Roman populace was moved to tears or laughter by his extraordinary characterizations. He purchased freedom with the large sums earned in the theatre, taking the name of Quintus Roscius Gallus: Sulla, the Roman dictator, gave him a gold ring which was the badge of the equestrian order, a remarkable distinction because of the contempt in which actors were ordinarily held at Rome.

Roscius, The Young, see **Betty, William Henry West.**

Rose Marie, a musical play in three acts: book by Otto HARBACH; music by Rudolf FRIML; first produced at New York in 1924 with Mary Ellis in the role of Rose Marie. There has been a very popular film adaptation with Nelson EDDY and Jeanette MACDONALD: there are recordings available of *Rose Marie, I Love You* and *Indian Love Call* which are the outstanding musical numbers.

Rosenkavalier, Der (*The Rose Cavalier*), grand opera in three acts: libretto by Hugo von Hofmannsthal; music by Richard STRAUSS; first produced at Dresden in 1911, and at the Metropolitan Opera House, New York, in 1913. There is an abridged Victor recording by the Vienna State Opera Company; a Victor recording of *Rosenkavalier Waltz* by the Minneapolis Symphony, and a Columbia recording by the Cleveland Orchestra.

Rosenthal, Moriz (1862-), Polish pianist who studied with Karl Mikuli, teacher of Frédéric CHOPIN, and later with Rafael JOSEFFY, making his debut in 1876. After touring with success he studied for two years with Franz LISZT, and also philosophy for six years at the University of Vienna. In 1888 he visited America, and toured the United States twelve times up to 1938 when he settled permanently in New York. A group of distinguished artists honored his eightieth birthday in 1942 with a testimonial concert.

Rosette, in architecture a sculptured or painted ornament, usually circular in form, and employed to decorate ceilings.

Rose Window, in Gothic and Romanesque architecture a style of window in which the small ROSETTES which decorate the CAPITALS are known as roses: the shafts or capitals radiate from a small center circle, and the form was used in practically every French cathedral, but not to any extent in other countries.

Rosina, the principal female character in Rossini's comic opera, *The* BARBER OF SEVILLE: the part is written for a coloratura soprano, and a splendid opportunity is afforded for vocalizing in Act II where Rosina is permitted by custom to sing any aria she may elect during the *Lesson Scene* with Count Almaviva who is passing himself off as the substitute for Basilio, Rosina's singing teacher whom the wily count has bribed to absent himself because of a feigned illness.

Rosing, Vladimir (1890-), Russian dramatic tenor who studied with Jean de RESZKE and Giovanni SBRIGLIA, making his debut with the St. Petersburg Art Opera in 1912. He toured the United States in 1922, and later directed the opera school of the EASTMAN School of Music, Rochester, New York, and the AMERICAN OPERA COMPANY. He is an outstanding interpreter of Russian songs.

Rosny, Joseph Henri, pen name of Joseph Henri Boex (1856-1940), French novelist who was first the disciple and later the bitter opponent of Émile Zola: he wrote several socialistic novels such as *The Bilateral* (1886); *The Immolation; The Oath; Daniel Valgraive* in collaboration with his brother, **Séraphin Justin François Boex** (1859-). After 1909 both published separate works.

Rosselli, Cosimo (1439-1507), Italian painter who came under the influence of Benozzo Gozzoli, and later assisted in the fresco work at the Sistine Chapel at Rome where he painted *The Last Supper; Sermon on the Mount; Moses Delivering the Tablets of the Law,* and *Passage of the Red Sea.* His other notable works include *The Miracle of the Chalice; Marriage of the Virgin; Coronation of the Virgin; St. Jerome in the Desert.*

Rossellino, Bernardo (1409-1464), Florentine architect and sculptor; one of four brothers all of whom were artists: his notable works include the Rucellai Palace at Florence, alterations on buildings at Rome, and the tomb of Leonardo Bruni at Florence. His brother, **Antonio Rossellino** (1427-1479), executed the sculptures for the tomb of a young cardinal prince of Portugal which required five years' work, and also delicate reliefs for the Church of Santa Maria del Monte at Naples.

Rossetti, Dante Gabriel (1828-1882), English painter and poet who studied under Ford Madox BROWN at the Royal Academy schools in London, and exhibited his first picture in 1849: he formed the Pre-Raphaelite Brotherhood with William Holman HUNT, John MILLAIS and others. His notable works include *Beata Beatrix; Monna Vanna; Venus Vesticordia; Lady Lilith; The Beloved; Dante's Dream; The Blessed Damozel;* *Francesca and Paolo.* His volumes of verse include *Dante and His Circle* (1861); *Collected Poems; Ballads and Sonnets.*

Rossini, Gioacchino (1792-1868), Italian operatic composer who made such progress in the study of music that he was elected a member of the Accademia Filarmonica at fourteen years of age. His first opera, *La cambiale di matrimonia,* was produced in 1810: among his outstanding successes were *Tancredi; L'Italiana in Algeri; The* BARBER OF SEVILLE; OTELLO; *La Cenerenotala* (*Cinderella*); *La Gazza Ladra; Moses in Egypt; Semiramide;* WILLIAM TELL. The *Barber of Seville* and *William Tell* are both still in the present-day repertory.

Rostand, Edmond (1868-1918), French dramatist educated at the Collège Stanislas in Paris: his plays include *Les Romanesques* (1894); *La Princesse Lointaine* in which Sarah BERNHARDT starred; *La Samaritaine; Cyrano de Bergerac; L'Aiglon,* another success for Mme. Bernhardt; *Le Dernière Nuit de Don Juan; Chantecler,* in which Maude ADAMS appeared: he also wrote several volumes of poetry.

Roth, Frederick George Richard (1872-), American sculptor trained at the Academy of Fine Arts, Vienna, and at the Academy of Fine Arts in Berlin. His works include sculptures for the Pan-American and St. Louis Expositions; *Polar Bears* and many other life-size figures or small bronzes of elephants, dogs, and horses: also an equestrian statue of George Washington at Morristown, N. J.

Roth Quartet, a string quartet founded in 1926 with Feri Roth as leader and first violin: its first American appearance was made in 1928 at the Pittsburgh Chamber Music Festival under the auspices of Elizabeth Sprague COOLIDGE. The ensemble is regarded as one of the finest of its kind in the performance of both classical and modern works. The quartet has made many recordings of standard chamber works.

Rothafel (Rothapfel), Samuel L. (1882-1936), American impresario and theatre manager familiarly known as "Roxy": he managed the Strand, Rialto, and Capitol Theatres in New York, introducing the symphony orchestra into the motion-picture theatre, and presenting tabloid opera with excellent casts. He also presented the first stage broadcast in 1922 from the Roxy Theatre, New York, and in 1932 became manager of RADIO CITY MUSIC HALL, severing his connection after the form of entertainment he provided failed to attract.

Rothier, Léon (1874-), French dramatic bass who studied at the Paris Conservatory, and made his debut in 1899 at the OPÉRA-COMIQUE, Paris. He made his first appearance at the METROPOLITAN OPERA HOUSE in 1910 as Mephistopheles in GOUNOD'S *Faust,* remaining with the company since that time: his repertory includes more than one hundred roles in French.

Rotrou, Jean (1609-1650), French poet and dramatist whose first play, *The Hypochondriac*

(1628), was produced when he was nineteen years old: among his comedies and tragedies are *Venceslas; The True Saint-Genest; Don Bertrand de Cabrère,* and *Cosroës.*

Rotunda, in architecture a building which is circular in form both outside and inside, and frequently surmounted by a DOME or CUPOLA: also used as the name of a large round room such as the *rotunda* of the Capitol at Washington, D. C.

Roualt, Georges (1871-   ), French painter who studied at the École Supérieur des Beaux-Arts, Paris, with Gustave MOREAU: he is one of the most versatile of contemporary French artists, working in oil, water-color or pastel with equal skill, and picturing clowns, judges, religious figures and genre subjects. He has been compared with Jerome BOSCH, a famous 16th century Dutch painter.

Roubillac or **Roubiliac, Louis François** (1695-1762), French sculptor who studied with Nicolas COUSTOU, and later settled in England where he was patronized by Horace Walpole, and became the most popular sculptor of his day. Among his notable works are the monuments of George Frederick HANDEL, the Duke of Argyle, and Miss Nightingale at WESTMINSTER ABBEY; statues of George I, Sir Isaac Newton, and of George II: also a series of busts of distinguished instructors at Trinity College, Cambridge.

Rouet d'Omphale (Saint-Saëns), see **Omphale.**

Rouget de l'Isle, Claude-Joseph (1760-1836), French army engineer, poet and composer who composed the words and music of La MARSEILLAISE, the French revolutionary hymn: he also wrote several other patriotic poems and two librettos for operas.

Round, in music a simple form of CANON in which each succeeding voice enters at the end of the phrase sung by the first voice. One of the simplest examples is the nursery rhyme, *Three Blind Mice,* and one of the oldest examples is SUMER IS ICUMEN IN.

Round Table, in the legends of King ARTHUR the table at which the monarch and his knights sat to discuss their problems: it was large enough to seat 150 knights and circular in shape so that there would be no question of precedence.

Rousseau, Henri Julien (1844-1910), French painter known as *Le Douanier:* after adopting several methods of earning his living he opened a school of art at Paris, and exhibited regularly at the Salons des Indépendants from 1886 to 1910. He painted landscapes, animals, scenes in the jungle, and portraits with genuine skill although he had no art training.

Rousseau, Jean Jacques (1712-1778), French philosopher, and author of books on a variety of subjects: they include *Memoir on the Shape of the Earth* (1738); *Mme. de Warens; Dissertation on Modern Music; Does the Cultivation of the Arts and Sciences Tend to Promote Morality; The Village Soothsayer; Narcissus; Dictionary of*

Music; Confessions. He also wrote a one-act opera, *Le Devin du Village,* produced in 1752, which held the French stage for more than sixty years, and a melodrama, *Pygmalion,* which was also a great success.

Rousseau, Pierre Étienne Théodore (1812-1867), French painter who spent many years painting in Normandy and at Barbizon, becoming one of the founders of the modern French school of landscape painting with COROT, DUPRE, Diaz DE LA PENA, and DAUBIGNY. He was little appreciated until practically the day of his death: his notable paintings include *Edge of the Fontainebleau Forest; The Oaks; The Chestnut Avenue; The Marsh in the Landes; Glade in the Fontainebleau Forest; Winter Solitude; Hoar-Frost; Trees by a Pool.*

Roussel, Albert (1869-1937), French composer educated at the Collège Stanislas and at the French Naval Academy: after resigning from the navy, he studied with Eugène Gigout and with Vincent D'INDY. His compositions include operas, opera-ballets, ballets, orchestral works, chamber music, piano pieces, and songs.

Rowe, Nicholas (1674-1718), English dramatist who became poet laureate in 1715: his plays include *Tamerlane* (1702); *The Ambitious Step-Mother; Jane Shore; The Fair Penitent; Lady Jane Grey; Ulysses; The Royal Convert:* he also translated the Roman poet LUCAN's *Pharsalia,* and was successful as a courtier and politician.

Rowlandson, Thomas (1756-1827), English painter, caricaturist, and illustrator who studied at the ROYAL ACADEMY OF ART schools, London, and also in Paris: after gambling away an inheritance of about $35,000, he turned to caricature as a means of subsistence. His notable works include *Vauxhall Gardens; Serpentine River; Tour of Dr. Syntax in Search of the Picturesque,* with two sequels; *Dance of Death; Dance of Life; Baron Munchausen:* he also illustrated works by SMOLLETT, GOLDSMITH and STERNE.

Rowley, William (1585-1642), English actor and dramatist who appeared with the King's Company, and wrote several plays including *A New Wonder, or, a Woman Never Vexed; All's Lost by Lust,* and *A Match at Midnight* for its use. He also collaborated with Thomas Heywood, Thomas Dekker, and John Ford in several plays.

"Roxy," see **Rothafel (Rothapfel), Samuel L.**

Royal Academy of Arts (London), an institution founded in 1768 with the purpose of cultivating and improving the arts of architecture, painting and sculpture. The schools of the Academy were the only places at which those desirous of studying art could obtain instruction for almost a hundred years: Sir Joshua REYNOLDS was the first president, and Benjamin WEST, James WYATT, Sir Thomas LAURENCE, Sir Charles EASTLAKE, Baron Frederick LEIGHTON and Sir John MILLAIS also held the office. There are schools of painting, sculpture, and architecture, and the exhibitions include an annual showing in winter devoted to the old masters and to the works of deceased British artists: this is followed in the summer by an exhibition of the works of contemporary artists. A fund is maintained for the relief of distressed artists and their families.

Royal Academy of Music (London), an institution founded in 1822, and granted a Royal Charter in 1830: it has progressed steadily under such distinguished directors as Sir William Sterndale BENNETT, Sir George A. Macfarren, Sir Alexander Campbell MACKENZIE: instruction is given in all branches of music, and the normal course is three years.

Royal Albert Hall (London), a building, constructed as a part of the National Exposition in 1851, which was not completed until 1871: it was dedicated to Albert, Prince Consort of Queen VICTORIA, and is one of the largest auditoriums in the world with remarkable acoustics and a seating capacity of 10,000.

Royal College of Music (London), an institution founded in 1873 as the National Training School for Music: Sir Arthur SULLIVAN and Sir John STAINER were its directors until 1882 when it was absorbed by the Royal College of Music. Sir George GROVE was the first director: he was followed by Sir Hubert Hastings PARRY, Dr. Hugh P. Allen, and Dr. George Dyson. The college has the largest library of music in England, and the staff of professors and teachers is one of the finest in the world of music instruction.

Royal Gallery (Dresden), an institution founded by Augustus I of Germany, and greatly improved by his successors. There are more than 2,500 pictures including the *Sistine Madonna* by Raphael; the *Madonna* by Hans Holbein the Younger; *La Notte* by Correggio; *Tribute Money* by Titian; *The Boar Hunt* by Rubens, and innumerable masterpieces by Defregger, Makart, Munkacsy, Boecklin, Thoma, Delaroche, Rosalba, Carriera, and many other famous artists. There are also 400,000 engravings in twelve chronological classes and a choice collection of casts of ancient and modern plastic art.

Royalty, the compensation paid to authors and composers based on a percentage of the receipts from the sale of books or music. In the case of dramatic authors, librettists, and composers of music for stage use, the royalty is based on the box-office receipts when the works are performed in theatres or opera houses, and fixed fees if played in a concert hall. Authors and composers usually share the receipts for the rental of their works for use on records, radio, motion pictures, and television with their publishers.

Royle, Edwin Milton (1862-1942), American actor and dramatist educated at Princeton University and the University of Edinburgh: his plays include *Friends* (1892); *Captain Impudence; The Squaw Man; The Unwritten Law; Aftermath; Launcelot and Elaine; Mexico; Barberry Bush.* His daughter, **Selena Royle** (1904-), is a well-known actress who studied at the American Academy of Dramatic Art, and has appeared in many plays since 1921.

Rubaiyat, see **Omar Khayyám.**

Rubato, in music a direction, generally reading *tempo rubato* and usually placed over passages in piano music calling for the display of deep passion: it implies that the performer should modify the strict tempo by prolonging certain melody notes, but to maintain the rhythm as a whole by accelerating less important tones especially in the left-hand in piano playing. Frédéric CHOPIN used *rubato* to a considerable extent in playing his own compositions although the direction rarely appears in his original manuscripts.

Rubens, Peter Paul (1577-1640), Flemish painter who was a page at the court in Antwerp, studied with several relatively unimportant painters, and spent some years in the diplomatic service. Among his notable works which, including those painted by pupils under his direction, number over two thousand are, *Fall of the Damned; Madonna with Saints; Adoration of the Magi; Descent from the Cross; Perseus and Andromeda; The Lion Hunt; The Miraculous Draught of Fishes; Rape of the Sabines; Venus and Adonis; Return from Egypt; Meleager and Atalanta.*

Rubicon, a small river in ancient Italy which formed the boundary between Cisalpine Gaul and Italy: Caesar, in crossing it in 49 B.C. declared war against Rome, and the historical significance of this step is the reason for the expression "crossing the Rubicon" as definitely committing one's self to a predetermined course of action. The occasion has been a favorite subject with easel and mural painters.

Rubini, Giovanni Battista (1795-1854), Italian operatic tenor who made his debut at Pavia in 1814, and sang with tremendous success at Naples, Vienna, Milan, Paris, and London. He toured Holland and Germany with Franz LISZT, and proceeded alone to St. Petersburg where he achieved phenomenal success in the operas of ROSSINI, BELLINI, and DONIZETTI. In 1845 he retired after having made an enormous fortune.

Rubinstein, Anton Gregorovitch (1829-1894), Russian pianist and composer who studied with Alexander Villoing who took him to Paris in 1839 where he played before Frédéric CHOPIN and Franz LISZT. He toured the United States with tremendous success in 1872-73, and also founded the Russian Musical Society and the St. Petersburg Conservatory of Music. His compositions include eighteen operas; six symphonies and other orchestral works; chamber music; concertos for piano, violin, and violoncello; sonatas and concert pieces for piano, and many songs. His brother, **Nicholas Rubinstein** (1835-1881), was a fine pianist, teacher, and composer who studied with Theodor KULLAK: he founded the Moscow Imperial Conservatory, and was famous as the teacher of many distinguished artists including Emil SAUER and Alexander SILOTI.

Rubinstein, Artur (1886-), Polish pianist and composer whose musical ability came to the notice of Joseph JOACHIM when he was four years old: he made his first appearance as a child prodigy in 1890, and after studying with Eugène

D'ALBERT and Theodor LESCHETIZKY made his mature debut in 1898 at Berlin. He made his American debut with the PHILADELPHIA ORCHESTRA in 1906. He has since toured Europe and England, making his home in the United States since 1937: he has executed many recordings of the principal piano concertos.

Rubinstein, Beryl (1898-), American pianist, teacher, and composer who studied with Alexander LAMBERT, and toured the United States as a child prodigy from 1905 to 1911. He also studied with Ferruccio BUSONI, appeared in joint recital with Eugène YSAYE, and has occupied the posts of head of the piano department, dean, and director of the Cleveland Institute of Music. His compositions include an opera, *The Sleeping Beauty;* piano concertos and piano pieces; suite for two pianos, and a technical work, *Outline of Piano Pedagogy.*

Rubinstein, Ida, Russian ballerina and actress who first appeared with the Russian Ballet, visiting Paris with the company in 1909. She formed her own troupe and enlisted the services of D'ANNUNZIO, BAKST, DEBUSSY, RAVEL, and several others in the writing and composing of new ballets: among the ballets in which she appeared were *Scheherazade; Amphion; Nocturne; David; Le Martyre de Saint Sebastian; Bolero; La Valse.* She also appeared in the leading roles of serious dramas such as *Phédre* and *Camille.*

Rubner, Cornelius, see **Rybner, Cornelius.**

Ruby, a precious stone which is a variety of transparent corundum of a rich red color: it is almost as hard as the DIAMOND, and perfect specimens of large size are even more valuable. Burma, China, Siam, and Ceylon are sources for the stone, which is not to be confused with the GARNET or TOURMALINE.

Ruckstuhl, Frederick Wellington (1853-), American sculptor born in Alsace who studied in Paris: his notable works include *Evening; Mercury Amusing Himself;* a bronze *Victory; Wisdom:* also many equestrian statues, memorials and monuments in all parts of the United States. In 1934 he published *Great Works of Art and What Makes Them Great.*

Ruddigore, comic opera in two acts: book by Sir William S. Gilbert; music by Sir Arthur S. Sullivan; first performed at the Savoy Theatre, London, in 1887, and at New York during the same year. The story, in which the librettist satirized the old English melodramas with their dark crimes and witches' curses, did not make as great an appeal to American audiences as to British theatre-goers, but the music is delightfully melodious and apropos to the character of the operetta. There is a Victor complete recording by the D'Oyly Carte Company.

Rude, François (1784-1855), French sculptor who first worked with his father as a stove maker: while studying in Paris he won the Prix de Rome, and after the battle of Waterloo worked in Brussels for twelve years. His notable works include *Mercury Fastening His Sandal; Neapolitan Fisher Boy; Departure of the Volunteers of 1792,* also known as *La Marseillaise; Joan of Arc; Hebe and the Eagle of Jupiter; Love Triumphant; Christ on the Cross.*

Rudersdorff, Hermine (1822-1882), German dramatic soprano who first sang in German opera houses in 1841, and in London at the DRURY LANE THEATRE from 1854 to 1865. In 1871 she came to Boston, Mass., as a singer at the Jubilee concerts, and later became famous as a vocal teacher: she was the mother of Richard MANSFIELD, the distinguished actor, by her second husband, Maurice Mansfield, an English merchant.

Rudolfo, the principal male character in Giacomo Puccini's grand opera, LA BOHEME: he is deeply in love with MIMI, but they separate when he realizes that she is ill, and that he has no means with which to care for her. They are reunited in the last act when Mimi returns to die in his arms.

Rueda, Lope de (c.1510-1565), Spanish dramatist who was the leader of a troupe of actors, and wrote several comedies such as *Eufemia; The Cheaters; Armelina,* and *Medora:* he wrote in the style of the COMMEDIA DELL'ARTE, and is regarded as the founder of the Spanish theatre.

Ruffo, Titta (1877-), Italian dramatic baritone, trained at the St. Cecilia Academy in Rome who made his debut in 1908 at the Teatro Costanzi in Wagner's *Lohengrin.* He has since appeared at all the major European opera houses, making his American debut in 1912 in Verdi's *Rigoletto* with the Philadelphia-Chicago Opera Company. He also sang with the Chicago Civic Opera Company, and from 1922 to 1928 with the Metropolitan Opera Company. His voice was specially distinguished by its volume.

Ruggieri, Francesco (1620-c.1694), Italian violin maker who studied with Nicoló AMATI: his violins are constructed on an original model with a golden-orange or orange-red varnish, and are valued at the present time at from $3500 to $8500. His sons, Giovanni Battista and Vincenzo Ruggieri, were his pupils; their instruments are less in demand, but also command prices ranging from $2000 to $5000.

Ruggles, Carl (1876-), American composer who was largely self-taught, but received some instruction from Walter Raymond SPALDING and John K. PAINE at Harvard University: since 1937 he has been instructor in composition at the University of Miami, Fla.: his compositions include an opera, several orchestral works, a polyphonic work for three pianos, and songs.

Ruggles, Charles, contemporary American stage and screen actor who made his debut at San Francisco in 1905, and later appeared in every kind of play from melodrama to musical comedy: among the numerous films in which he has played comedy roles are *The Smiling Lieutenant; The Night of June 13; Alice in Wonderland; If I Had a Million; Ruggles of Red Gap; No More Ladies; Anything Goes; Yes, My Darling Daughter; Invitation to Happiness; Balalaika; No Time for Comedy.*

Ruisdael, Jacob van, see **Ruysdael, Jacob van.**

Rumanian Rhapsody No. 1 (Enesco), the first of three rhapsodies of the same character written in one opus by Georges ENESCO, and first performed at a concert given by Pablo Casals at Paris in 1908, and in the United States by the Boston Symphony Orchestra in 1912. The *Rhapsody No. 1,* according to the program note for a Philadelphia Orchestra concert at Carnegie Hall, New York, on January 8, 1929, "is based upon several of the jolliest of the folk-songs and dances of Enesco's native Rumania, especially the tune which serves the abandoned Rumanian peasants, unblessed by the educational influences exerted by Mr. Volstead, as a drinking song, sung to verses which, when translated, mean that the improvident singer has a coin which he wishes to spend for the deplorable purpose of alcoholic stimulation." Enesco has not only woven a number of folk songs and dances into his rhapsody, but the orchestration is particularly dazzling. There is a Victor recording of *Rhapsody No. 1* by the Philadelphia Orchestra directed by Eugene Ormandy, and a Columbia recording by the Chicago Symphony Orchestra under Frederick Stock. The *Rhapsody No. 2* is available in a Victor recording by the National Symphony Orchestra under Hans Kindler.

Rumba, see **Rhumba.**

Run, in music a rapid passage usually in the form of a SCALE: in vocal music the term is generally applied to a passage sung to one syllable.

Runes, the characters of an alphabet used in the Scandinavian countries, Great Britain, and Germany. Priests and magicians employed them almost exclusively, and in some respects they appear to have been an imitation of a Greek script. There were sixteen characters in one form and twenty-four in another.

Runyon, Damon (1880-   ), American journalist and short story writer: his works include *Tents of Trouble* (1911); *Rhymes of the Firing Line; Guys and Dolls; Blue Plate Special; Money from Home; A Slight Case of Murder,* a play with Howard LINDSAY; *Take It Easy; My Old Man; The Best of Runyon.*

Rush, William (1756-1833), American sculptor sometimes called the "Father of American sculpture": he first carved ships' figureheads, and later a statue in wood of George Washington which is in Independence Hall, Philadelphia; also heads of William Penn, Voltaire, and Benjamin Franklin. He was one of the founders of the Pennsylvania Academy of Fine Arts, and his *Nymph of the Schuylkill* is in Fairmount Park, Philadelphia.

Ruskin, John (1819-1900), English author and critic who traveled throughout Europe as a boy, and studied at Oxford, developing a love for nature and the pictorial arts. Among his works on art are *Modern Painters; The Seven Lamps of Architecture; The Stones of Venice; Pre-Raphaelitism; Giotto and His Works in Padua; Elements of Drawing; Lectures on Art.* His miscellaneous writings on ethics, social science, mythology, etc.,

include *The Two Paths; Sesame and Lilies; The Crown of Wild Olive; Unto This Last; Munera Pulveris; The King of the Golden River; Fors Clavigera.*

Russell, Annie (1864-1936), American actress born in England who was brought to Canada as a child where she appeared in juvenile roles, achieving her first success in *Esmeralda,* a play by Frances Hodgson Burnett produced in 1882. Among the plays in which she appeared were *Hazel Kirke; David Garrick; In Mizzoura; Miss Hobbs; The Royal Family; The Girl and the Judge; Mice and Men; Major Barbara.* She retired in 1917, but in 1932 returned to direct a theatre named after her at Rollins College, Florida.

Russell, Henry (1871-1937), English operatic impresario and brother of Sir Landon RONALD who first studied medicine, and later singing at the ROYAL COLLEGE OF MUSIC, London. He devised a singing method which gained the approval of Dame Nellie MELBA, and in 1903 formed a company which produced grand opera successfully at COVENT GARDEN for two seasons. He brought the organization to Boston, Mass., in 1905, where it was so successful that the BOSTON OPERA COMPANY was formed from it in 1909, and continued until 1914. In the spring of 1914 he took the company to Paris where it enjoyed a two-month's season at the Théâtre des Champs-Elysées. Russell came to the United States in 1921 as manager of a lecture tour by the Belgian dramatist, Maurice MAETERLINCK.

Russell, Mary Annette (1866-1941), English novelist born in Australia who wrote under the pen name "Elizabeth": her works include *Elizabeth and Her German Garden* (1898); *The Solitary Summer; The Adventures of Elizabeth in Ruegen; Fraulein Schmidt and Mr. Anstruther; The Pastor's Wife; The Enchanted April; Love; Expiation; Father; The Jasmine Farm; All the Dogs of My Life,* an autobiography; *Mr. Skeffington.*

Russell, Lillian (1861-1922), American actress and singer whose real name was Helen Louise Leonard. She first appeared professionally at Tony PASTOR's Theatre, New York, in 1881 as a ballad singer; the story runs that Pastor was the one who suggested the more euphonious stage name. Among the operettas in which she appeared were *Olivette; Patience; The Princess of Trébizonde; Nadjy; La Périchole; Giroflé-Girofla; La Belle Hélène:* also in several WEBER AND FIELDS' burlesques.

Russell, Rosalind, contemporary American stage and screen actress: among the films in which she has appeared are *Evelyn Prentice; Forsaking All Others; China Seas; Rendezvous; Under Two Flags; Craig's Wife; The Citadel; The Women; His Girl Friday; No Time for Comedy; They Met in Bombay; Design for Scandal; My Sister Eileen.*

Russell, Sol Smith (1848-1902), American actor who served with the Union Army during the Civil War as a drummer boy: he first appeared on the stage in 1862 with a stock company, and later toured the United States for nearly forty years in *A Poor Relation; Peaceful Valley; Edgewood Folks; April Weather; A Bachelor's Romance; The Honorable John Grisby.*

"Russian Easter" Overture (Rimsky-Korsakow), an orchestral work composed by Nicholas RIMSKY-KORSAKOW in 1888, and first performed during the same year: it was called *The Bright Holiday* by the composer because this was the popular Russian name for Easter, and was dedicated to Modest Mussorgsky and Alexander Borodin. The composer was of the opinion that the celebration of Easter in Russia assumed the character of a pagan carnival, and he strove to picture in music the transition from the gloom and mystery of Passion Saturday to the unbridled merrymaking of Easter Day. He also maintained that the overture could only be appreciated by those who had attended an Easter morning-service in one of the great Russian cathedrals. The French title of the overture is *La Grande Pâque Russe:* there is a Victor recording by the Philadelphia Orchestra directed by Leopold Stokowski.

Russian Heroes (Ballet), see **Bogatryi (Russian Heroes).**

Russian Soldier, a Russian ballet: choreography by Michel Fokine: music by Serge Prokofieff taken from the symphonic suite *Lieutenant Kije;* the ballet was first performed in 1941. The central figure is an unknown soldier who fought in a war under Paul I, Emperor of Russia during the last years of the 18th Century. Mortally wounded, the soldier beholds in his fevered brain memories of his native land, his youth in the military academy, festive scenes in his village, the harvest, and the ceremony of his own wedding. Before Death overtakes him he seeks to re-enter the scenes of his dream.

"Russlan and Ludmilla" Overture (Glinka), the prelude to Michail GLINKA's opera, *Russlan and Ludmilla.* He had already written a patriotic opera, "A Life for the Czar" which was produced with enormous success at St. Petersburg in 1836. His second opera, *Russlan and Ludmilla,* the libretto adapted from a poem by Michael PUSHKIN was produced at St. Petersburg in 1842, and while unquestionably musically the superior to "A Life for the Czar" its failure to be as well received is said to have almost broken the composer's heart. The story of *Russlan and Ludmilla* is a simple one involving the familiar elements of love and intrigue; the principal character, a Princess of Kiev, beset by her suitors, a Finnish warlock and a Tartar prince, is rescued by Russlan, a Russian knight-errant who clasps her in his arms as the final curtain falls. The overture, replete with melodious and virile themes skilfully developed, is a great favorite with concert audiences the world over. There are Victor recordings by the Boston "Pops" Orchestra under Arthur Fiedler, and the Chicago Symphony Orchestra conducted by Frederick Stock.

"Rustic Wedding" Symphony (Goldmark), an orchestral work by Karl GOLDMARK which in form could be more correctly termed a suite: it was composed in 1876, and first performed at a Philharmonic concert in Vienna under the direction of Hans RICHTER in March of that year. The gay Viennese audience received it with tumultuous acclaim in view of the fact that Goldmark had already charmed it with his "Sakuntala" overture. The five movements of this symphony portray various phases of a country wedding: the first movement is a march with thirteen variations; the second is a "Bridal Song" given to the oboe; the third is a serenade; the fourth, entitled "In the Garden," is a charming picture of lovers conversing with each other; the fifth movement is a dance in fugal form, brilliant and picturesque, with a return to the theme of the garden music. There is a Victor recording by the Vienna Philharmonic Orchestra conducted by Robert Heger, and a Columbia recording by the Columbia Broadcasting Symphony Orchestra under the baton of Howard Barlow.

Ruysdael or **Ruisdael, Jacob van** (c.1625-1682), Dutch painter who studied with his uncle, Salomon van Ruisdael (c.1600-1677): his notable works include *Landscape with Ruins; Storm on the Dikes of Holland; Oak Forest; Old Fishmarket at Amsterdam; Waterfall; Mountain Torrent; Jewish Cemetery.* The figures in his landscapes were painted by Nicolaes BERCHEM, Art van der NEER, Johannes LINGELBACH and others.

Rybner or **Rubner, Cornelius** (1855-1929), Danish pianist, violinist and composer who studied with Niels W. GADE, Hans von BULOW, and Anton RUBINSTEIN. He directed the Opera, the Philharmonic Society, and the Conservatory at Karlsruhe, and succeeded Edward MACDOWELL as head of the music department at Columbia University from 1904 to 1919. His compositions include orchestral works; a fairy ballet; a violin concerto; a piano trio; piano pieces and violin pieces.

Ryder, Albert Pinkham (1847-1917), American painter who studied with William E. Marshall and at the National Academy of Design: his notable works include *Temple of the Wind; The Curfew Hour; Toilers of the Sea; The Smugglers' Cave; The Bridge; Christ Appearing Unto Mary; The Flying Dutchman; Moonlight Marine; Jonah and the Whale; Little Maid of Arcadie; Siegfried.* The mysteriously poetical element in his pictures has never been caught by any other American painter.

Ryks Museum (Amsterdam), see **Rijks Museum (Amsterdam).**

S

Saavedra, Angel de, see **Rivas, Angel de Saavedra, Duke of.**

Sabatini, Rafael (1875-), English novelist and dramatist born in Italy and educated in Switzerland: his successful novels include *The Tavern Knight* (1904); *Bardelys the Magnificent; St. Martin's Summer; The Sea Hawk; The His-*

torical Nights' Entertainment; Scaramouche; Captain Blood; The Carolinian; The Black Swan; Columbus. His plays include *Bardelys the Magnificent* (1911); *The Rattlesnake; In the Snare; The Tyrant; The Carolinian; Scaramouche:* several of his novels and plays have been adapted for the screen.

Sabu, East Indian screen actor discovered as a boy by an agent of Sir Alexander KORDA while one of his companies were on location at Mysore: he has appeared in *Elephant Boy; Drums; The Thief of Bagdad; Jungle Book; White Savage.*

Sachs, Hans (1494-1576), the principal poet of the MASTERSINGERS (Meistersinger) at Nuremberg: he is credited with having written 1700 fables and tales, 4,000 poems, and over 200 plays. He is the principal character in Richard Wagner's *Die* MEISTERSINGER VON NURNBERG.

Sachs, Kurt (1881-), German musicologist educated at Berlin University where he later became professor of musicology and curator of the State collection of musical instruments. He has written several important treatises on musical instruments; among them *The History of Musical Instruments* (1940).

Sackville, Thomas, 1st Earl of Dorset (1536-1608), English poet educated at Oxford who was one of the chief councilors of QUEEN ELIZABETH. His poems *Induction* and *Complaint of the Duke of Buckingham* were the models for works by Edmund SPENSER, and he was also part author of a tragedy, *Gorboduc* with Thomas Norton.

Sacre du Printemps, Le (The Rite of Spring), Russian ballet in two acts: libretto by Igor STRAVINSKY and Nikolai ROERICH; choreography by Vaslav NIJINSKY; music by Igor Stravinsky who worked on the score almost continuously throughout the winter of 1912-13, and the first version, with choreography by Nijinsky, was produced in Paris in May, 1913; it was received with mixed indignation and revulsion by the audience, and given only a few performances in London. Leonide MASSINE wrote the choreography for the revival by DIAGHILEFF in 1920 at the Opéra in Paris, and also directed its American première at Philadelphia in 1920. Gerald Goode, in his *Book of Ballets,* describes the action as follows: "A pagan Russian tribe gathers to welcome the spring and sacrifice a chosen maiden to the sun and the earth for good crops. The tribe first performs ritual dances of earth-worship. In the second episode the maiden is chosen for sacrifice; preparatory rites are performed, and finally the maiden begins her dance of death, moving at first slowly and then to the thudding, pounding compulsion of the music, more and more violently, until she falls lifeless." There is a Victor recording of the music by the Philadelphia Orchestra with Leopold Stokowski, and a Columbia recording by the New York Philharmonic-Symphony Orchestra directed by Igor Stravinsky.

Sacred Way (*1*), in ancient Athens the road which led to Eleusis over which the procession passed every autumn for the celebration of the ELEUSINIAN MYSTERIES in honor of DEMETER,

PERSEPHONE, and Iacchus. (*2*) In ancient Rome the first street constructed on the low ground at the foot of the great hills: some of the old and most revered sanctuaries lay on it such as the temple of Vesta, the Regia, and the temple of Antonius and Faustina.

Sacristy, in ecclesiastical architecture a building attached to a church, or a small room in which the sacred treasures, vessels, and vestments are kept: they were often made in the form of vaulted chambers.

Sadko, grand opera in seven acts: libretto and music by Nicholas RIMSKY-KORSAKOW; first produced at Moscow in 1898, and at the Metropolitan Opera House, New York, in 1929. One of the arias, *Song of India* is a popular favorite: there is a Victor recording by Beniamino GIGLI, and a Columbia recording by Lily PONS.

Sadler's Wells Theatre, a place of entertainment in London dating from 1683 as a fashionable medicinal spring and theatre: Joseph GRIMALDI appeared there, and in 1843 Samuel Phelps presented Shakespearean productions on a large scale. In 1931 Lillian Baylis reopened the theatre with *Twelfth Night,* and the Sadler's Wells Ballet Company has also appeared there with great success.

Saenger, Oscar (1868-1929), American operatic baritone and teacher of singing who studied at the National Conservatory of Music, New York, and made his debut with the Hinrichs Opera Company. He was highly successful as a teacher: among his distinguished pupils are Paul ALTHOUSE, Marie RAPPOLD, Mabel GARRISON, Henri Scott, and Paul ROBESON.

Saerchinger, César (1884-), American author and editor of works on music born in France: his works include biographies of musicians for the *National Encyclopedia of Biography;* contributions to *The Art of Music,* and Elson's *Modern Music and Musicians.* He was also European correspondent of the *Musical Courier* from 1919 to 1930, and European director of the Columbia Broadcasting Company from 1930 to 1937.

Safonoff, Vassily Ilyitch (1852-1918), Russian pianist and conductor who studied with Theodor LESCHETIZKY at the Imperial Conservatory, St. Petersburg: after making his debut in 1880 he taught piano at the Conservatory, and from 1885 to 1905 acted as director of the Moscow Conservatory. He conducted the New York Philharmonic-Symphony Society from 1904 to 1909, and in 1910 became permanent conductor of the Imperial Russian Musical Society at St. Petersburg. He conveyed his ideas to the orchestral players with his hands, never using a baton.

Saga, a word derived from the Icelandic *segja* meaning "to say": it is applied in old Scandinavian literature to epics in prose or verse such as the *Sturlanga Saga* collected by Snorri STURLESON, and many other similar anthologies.

Saint Cecilia, the patron saint of music and of the blind in the Roman Catholic Church: she was presumed to be a noble lady of Rome who suffered martyrdom about 230 A.D. under the emperor Alexander Severus. The legend runs that she "praised God by instrumental as well as vocal music": many famous artists have depicted her including COPLEY, DOLCI, DOMENICHINO, GUERCINO, RAPHAEL, REYNOLDS, RUBENS, SCHEFFER. CHAUCER wrote of her in his *Second Nun's Tale,* and DRYDEN wrote an ode which was set to music by George Frederick HANDEL.

St. Denis, Ruth (1880-), American dancer, choreographer, and teacher who appeared first in 1906 as a dancer, and later toured Europe: she made world tours with her husband, Ted SHAWN, and organized the Denishawn Schools in New York and Los Angeles with branches throughout the United States operated by graduate pupils. Her productions include *Masque of Mary* at the New York World's Fair in 1941; *Resurrection; Sarah.*

Saint-Gaudens, Augustus (1848-1907), American sculptor born in Ireland who was first apprenticed to a cameo cutter, and studied at Cooper Union and the National Academy of Design, New York. In 1867 he went to Paris to study at the ECOLE DES BEAUX-ARTS: later he established his studio in New York. His notable works include the *Farragut Monument* at Madison Square, New York; *Hiawatha; Silence; Lincoln* at Lincoln Park, Chicago; *Puritan* at Springfield, Mass.; the *Shaw Memorial* at Boston, Mass.; *Robert Louis Stevenson* at Edinburgh, Scotland.

Saint John the Divine, Cathedral Church of (New York), the principal church of the Protestant Episcopal Diocese in the city and state of New York: the foundation stone was laid in 1892, and the work of construction has proceeded ever since, the entire length of the cathedral being opened in 1941. Among the architects were George L. Heins, C. Grant LaFarge, Cram and Ferguson, Henry Vaughan, CARRERE and HASTINGS. The design is French Gothic, and the general plan is cruciform, symbolizing the cross on which the Saviour was crucified. The building is 610 feet long and 315 feet wide across the transepts: it is the largest cathedral in the world, and the only sacred edifice which exceeds it in cubage is ST. PETER's at Rome which is not a cathedral. Among the sculptors represented by important works are Henry Wilson, John ANGEL, and John BORGLUM. The material used is entirely stone: an authority on building construction has declared that the cathedral will stand for at least five thousand years.

Saint-Léon, Charles Victor Arthur (1821-1870), French violinist, composer, dancer, and choreographer whose real name was Michel: he studied with PAGANINI, and made his debut in 1835 as a dancer and violinist. He was married for a time to Fanny CERITO, danced at the Opéra in Paris and also acted as ballet master there from 1864 to 1870. His successful ballets include *La Vivandière; La Fille de Marbre; Le Violon du Diable; Fiametta.*

St. Louis Symphony Orchestra, an organization founded in 1880 as a choral society which merged in 1881 with the orchestra of the St. Louis Musical Union. In 1907 the choral section was dropped, and Max Zach became the conductor until 1921 when he was succeeded by Rudolf Ganz until 1927. After four years of guest conductors Vladimir Golschmann became permanent conductor.

Saint Mark's (Venice), a church named after the patron saint of Venice: it was built on the plan of a Greek cross in the 9th century as a repository for the bones of the saint brought from Alexandria in 828 A.D. It was destroyed by fire in 976, rebuilt in the 11th century, and added to during the following three centuries. One of the outstanding features is the colored mosaics on the domes of the sanctuary picturing scenes from the New Testament. The *Four Horses of St. Mark's,* cast in bronze, stand in a gallery directly over the main door of the church: they are said to have been executed in the days of Nero and were at one time in Constantinople. Napoleon I removed them to Paris in 1797, but Francis I of Austria ordered them restored to their original place in Saint Mark's in 1815. The *Pala d'Oro,* formed of eighty-three plaques of gold, is one of the wonders of the church.

Saint Patrick's Cathedral (New York), the principal church of the Roman Catholic Diocese of the city and state of New York, located at 50th Street and Fifth Avenue, and replacing an older cathedral situated between Mott and Catherine (now Prince) Streets, dedicated in 1815. The cornerstone of the new cathedral was laid in 1858, and the building, work on which was interrupted by the Civil War, completed in 1879 with the exception of the spires which were finished in 1888. James RENWICK was the architect: the architecture is 13th to 15th century Gothic, and the general plan follows the lines of a Latin cross. The exterior length is 332 feet and the breadth 132 feet: the spires are 330 feet in height. The new high altar, designed by the architects Maginnis and Walsh of Boston, was erected in 1942; the baldachin which replaces the reredos of the old altar, reaches a height of 57 feet above the pavement of the sanctuary, and the general decorative theme is the redemption of mankind.

Saint Paul's Cathedral (London), a building constructed in the Renaissance style by Sir Christopher WREN, and regarded as one of the great cathedrals of Europe. A Roman temple first stood on its site which was replaced by a cathedral in the 13th century, and later repaired by Inigo JONES: the Great Fire of London almost completely destroyed it in 1666, and Wren himself laid the first stone in 1675 and set the final stone in place in 1710. His original design was in the form of a Greek cross like St. Peter's at Rome, but the clergy insisted on the change to a Latin cross. A vast dome with two shells stands over the intersection of the cross: the exterior dome is paneled and is rendered even more impressive through being imposed on a colonnaded drum supporting a stone lantern terminating in a cross.

Saint Peter's Church (Rome), a building at Rome constructed on the site of an earlier edifice, the present one being the result of long years of labor on the part of many architects. Pope Julius II projected the building, in 1506, and ordered a competition out of which the plans of Bramante were selected. It was designed in the form of a Greek cross with each limb surmounted by a dome. Other architects included Giuliano da SANGALLO, Fra Giovanni GIOCONDO, RAPHAEL, Baldassare PERUZZI, MICHELANGELO, Giacomo DELLA PORTA, Domenico FONTANA, Jacopo BAROCCIO, Carlo MADERNA, and Giovanni BERNINI from 1506 to 1663. It is the largest church in the world, and the interior is remarkable for the harmonious grandeur of its proportions. Among the monuments in the cathedral are the *Pietà* by Michelangelo; the tomb of Innocent VIII by Antonio and Piero POLLAJUOLO, and statues, altars, and canopies executed by Giovanni Bernini.

Saint-Pierre, Jacques Henri Bernardin de (1737-1814), French author who was intimate with Jean Jacques Rousseau: his masterpiece, *Paul and Virginia*, was a part of a three-volume work, *Studies of Nature* published in 1784: it was used as the basis of an opera by Victor Massé in 1876.

Saint-Saëns, Charles Camille (1835-1921), French pianist, organist, and composer who made his debut as a child prodigy at eleven, studied at the Paris Conservatory with Jacques HALEVY, and became organist in 1858 of the Madeleine succeeding Louis LEFEBURE-WELY. He led an active life as a concert pianist, organist, and composer, visiting many countries, and the United States in 1906 and 1915. His numerous compositions include twelve operas of which *Samson and Delilah* has survived; several symphonies; five piano concertos; three violin and a violoncello concerto; four symphonic poems including the *Danse Macabre;* chamber music; vocal works; pieces for organ and for piano. The average lover of music knows Saint-Saëns best by *Le Cygne* (The Swan) a movement from his famous suite, CARNIVAL OF ANIMALS, one of the most exquisite examples of pure melody writing in the history of music.

Saintsbury, George Edward Bateman (1845-1933), English literary critic and author educated at Oxford: his works include *A Primer of French Literature* (1881); *A Short History of French Literature; A History of Nineteenth Century Literature; A Short History of English Literature; A History of Elizabethan Literature; The English Novel; A History of the French Novel.*

"Sakuntala" Overture (Goldmark), an orchestral composition by Karl GOLDMARK; first performed at Vienna in 1865, and founded on a play or poem by KALIDASA written in Sanskrit about 300 B.C. The story is a simple one of love and revenge: Sakuntala, daughter of a wood nymph, is adopted and brought up by a Hindu priest in a sacred grove. King Dushiante, losing his way during a hunt, finds himself in the grove, falls in love with the lovely girl and they are married. The king, departing for his kingdom, leaves a ring with Sakuntala which will identify her as his wife when she comes to join him, but another priest, in love with Sakuntala, deprives the king of all recollection of his erstwhile bride, and the maiden, while bathing in the sacred river, loses the ring.

When she appears before the king, he professes complete ignorance of her existence; she is driven off and her mother in pity leads her away. The ring is found by a fisherman who brings it to the king. The ring restores his memory; he goes to find Sakuntala, and, after a battle with the demons, they are happily reunited. There is a Victor recording by the Boston "Pops" Orchestra directed by Arthur Fiedler.

Salieri, Antonio (1750-1825), Austrian dramatic composer who was the teacher of BEETHOVEN, SCHUBERT, and LISZT: he conducted at the Vienna Court Opera for many years, composed more than forty operas, and was on intimate terms with GLUCK whose dramatic style of writing he imitated with great success although his operas are now forgotten.

Salome, a grand opera in one act: libretto by Hedwig Lachmann based on the play by Oscar WILDE; music by Richard STRAUSS; first performed at Dresden in 1905 and at the Metropolitan Opera House, New York, in 1907. The outstanding orchestral excerpt is the *Dance of the Seven Veils* which is available in a Columbia recording by the Cleveland Orchestra directed by Artur Rodzinski, and in a Victor recording by the Philadelphia Orchestra under Leopold Stokowski.

Salomon, Johann Peter (1745-1815), German violinist, and quartet leader who settled at London in 1781: in 1786 he inaugurated a series of concerts at which he introduced the symphonies of HAYDN and MOZART. While in Europe during 1790 he met Haydn, and induced him to make two visits to London, and to compose twelve symphonies which were first performed at the Salomon Concerts. He was a fine ensemble player: his compositions include several operas and also sonatas and concertos for the violin.

Saltarello, an ancient dance in both Italy and Spain written in 3-8 or 6-8 time, and danced very fast with what may be termed a hopping step. Mendelssohn utilizes the saltarello in the last movement of his "ITALIAN" SYMPHONY, and part of Berlioz' "CARNAVAL ROMAIN" OVERTURE employs an adaptation of the dance.

Salten, Felix (1869-   ), Austrian novelist whose first efforts interested Hugo von HOFMANNSTHAL, Arthur SCHNITZLER, and Hermann BAHR all of whom aided him in getting a start with the literary magazines: his works include *Bambi* and *Florian, the Emperor's Stallion,* both of which have been filmed; *The Hound of Florence; Fifteen Rabbits; Samson and Delilah; Bambi's Children; Good Comrades; The City Jungle.*

Saltus, Edgar (1855-1921), American novelist educated at Yale University and in Europe: his novels include *Mr. Incoul's Misadventure; The Truth About Tristram Varick; Eden; The Pace That Kills; A Transaction in Hearts; Imperial Purple; Purple and Fine Women; The Paliser Case.* He also published a study of BALZAC.

Salvator Rosa, see Rosa, Salvator.

Salvi, Giambattista, see **Sassoferrato, Il.**

Salvini, Tommaso (1829-1915), Italian actor who appeared in GOLDINI's *Donna Curiose* at fourteen: in 1847 he joined the company of Adelaide RISTORI and appeared in the title role of Vittorio ALFIERI's *Oreste* with her. He also played in England, and made five visits to the United States from 1873 to 1889; in 1886 he appeared as Othello with Edwin BOOTH as Iago. He retired in 1890: his son, **Allessandro Salvini** (1861-1896), was also a distinguished actor who was a favorite in the United States as D'Artagnan in *The Three Musketeers.*

Salzburg Festivals, a yearly summer festival of both drama and music held at Salzburg, a city in Austria: the concerts are held at the Festspielhaus and the Mozarteum which adjoins the Conservatory of Music which offers courses in all branches of music. The theatre was built and managed by Max REINHARDT who presented the morality play, EVERYMAN, GOETHE's *Faust* and many other dramas. TOSCANINI and Bruno WALTER have conducted at the festivals which presented the operas of MOZART, who was born in Salzburg, and also works by other eminent composers.

Salzedo, Carlos (1885-   ), French harpist and composer who studied piano with Charles de Bériot and harp with Alphonse Hasselmans at the Paris Conservatory: after touring Europe and America he settled in New York. He formed the Trio de Lutèce with Georges BARRERE and Paul Kefer, the Barrère-Salzedo-Britt Ensemble, and taught at the INSTITUTE OF MUSICAL ART, New York, and the Curtis INSTITUTE OF MUSIC, Philadelphia. His compositions include orchestral works, chamber music, and harp solos.

Samaroff, Olga (1882-   ), American pianist and teacher who studied with Constantine von STERNBERG, Ernest HUTCHESON, and also in Europe, making her debut in 1905 with the NEW YORK SYMPHONY SOCIETY. She appeared with the major American orchestras and in recital with Fritz KREISLER and Efrem ZIMBALIST, also teaching at the JUILLIARD Graduate School for ten years. She has written several books on the appreciation and study of music.

Saminsky, Lazare (1882-   ), Russian composer, conductor, and writer on music who studied at the St. Petersburg Conservatory with Rimsky-Korsakow and Liadoff: after conducting at Tiflis and London, he came to the United States in 1920. His compositions include orchestral works, chamber music, piano pieces, choral works, and songs.

Sammarco, Mario (1873-1930), Italian dramatic baritone who made his debut in 1894 at Milan in Puccini's *Le Villi:* after singing at Madrid, Lisbon, Moscow, Berlin, Brussels, and London, he made his debut in *Pagliacci* at the Manhattan Opera House, New York, in 1908, and also sang in South America. In 1918 he was appointed one of the directors of La Scala, Milan.

Sammartini, Giovanni Battista (c.1701-1775), Italian organist and composer who was the teacher of Christopher Willibald von GLUCK, and is credited with more than 2,000 works including symphonies, chamber music, and church music. His brother, **Giuseppe Sammartini** (c.1693-c.1750), was also a prolific composer and oboist who directed the chamber music concerts of the Prince of Wales at London: Mischa ELMAN has made a free transcription of a movement from one of his violin sonatas entitled *Canto Amoroso* which is available in a Decca recording.

Samson and Delilah, grand opera in three acts: libretto by Ferdinand Lemaire; music by Camille SAINT-SAENS; first performed at Weimar in 1877 and at the Metropolitan Opera House in 1895. The story of the opera follows closely that of the Bible except where altered for dramatic purposes: there are both Victor and Columbia recordings of the favorite *Bacchanale* (Ballet Music), the *Spring Song,* and *My Heart at Thy Sweet Voice.*

Samuel, Harold (1879-1937), English pianist who studied with Edward DANNREUTHER and Sir Charles Villiers STANFORD at the ROYAL COLLEGE OF MUSIC, making his debut in 1894 at St. James Hall, London, and later becoming professor of piano at the Royal College of Music. He toured the United States regularly from 1924, specializing in the performance of the piano works of Johann Sebastian BACH of which he was a past master.

Sanborn, Pitts (1879-1941), American music critic and novelist educated at Harvard who was music editor of the New York *Globe* from 1905 to 1923, of the *Evening Mail* and of the *World-Telegram* from 1923 to 1941. His works include *Prima Donna,* a novel of the opera (1929); *Greek Night; The Metropolitan Book of the Opera.*

San Carlo Opera Company, see **Gallo, Fortune.**

Sand, George, pseudonym of **Amantine Lucile Aurore, Baroness Dudevant** (1804-1876), French novelist and dramatist educated at a convent who married the Baron Casimir Dudevant in 1822: she left him in 1831 and went to Paris with Jules Sandeau in search of a literary career. She lived with Alfred de MUSSET in Italy, and also had a ten-year liaison with Frédéric CHOPIN. Her literary works were extraordinarily numerous: they include about eighty novels which first appeared in serial form; also *Tales of a Grandmother* and a book of Norman fairy tales for children.

Sandburg, Carl (1878-   ), American poet who served in the Spanish-American War, and was later educated at Lombard College, Galesburg, Ill. His notable works include *Chicago Poems* (1914); *Corn Huskers; Smoke and Steel; Abraham Lincoln: The Prairie Years; Abraham Lincoln: The War Years; Slabs of the Sunburned West; The American Songbag,* a collection of songs and ballads.

Sanders, George (1906-   ), English screen actor born in Russia: among the films in which he has appeared are *Lloyd's of London; Slave Ship; Lancer Spy; International Settlement; Four Men and a Prayer; The Saint Strikes Back; Nurse Edith Cavell; Confessions of a Nazi Spy; The*

House of Seven Gables; The Saint Takes Over; Rebecca; Foreign Correspondent; Bitter Sweet; The Gay Falcon; Rage in Heaven; Man Hunt; Son of Fury; The Falcon Taken Over; This Land is Mine.

Sanderson, Sibyl (1865-1903), American dramatic soprano who studied with Giovanni SBRIGLIA, Mathilde MARCHESI, and Jules MASSENET, making her debut in the latter's opera, *Manon,* at The Hague, Holland, in 1888. Massenet wrote several operas including *Thaïs* for her and she was regarded as the greatest interpreter of the leading soprano roles in his operas. She appeared in 1895 at the Metropolitan Opera House in *Manon,* but achieved little success.

Sandro Botticelli, see **Botticelli, Sandro.**

San Francisco Opera Company, an organization founded in 1922 that gave its autumn season of grand opera in the Auditorium until 1932 when the San Francisco Opera House, a part of the War Memorial Building became available. The artists of the company are chiefly guest singers from the Metropolitan Opera Company, and the orchestra is drawn from the SAN FRANCISCO SYMPHONY ORCHESTRA. The Los Angeles Grand Opera Association co-operates with the San Francisco Opera Association, and performances are also given at the Shrine Auditorium, Los Angeles.

San Francisco Symphony Orchestra, an organization founded in 1911 after various orchestras had preceded it: under the leadership of Henry HADLEY it gave between ten and twenty concerts yearly until 1915. Alfred HERTZ succeeded him, and remained director until 1929: from 1929 to 1935 the guest conductors included Basil Cameron, Issay DOBROWEN, Alfred HERTZ and Bernardino MOLINARI. In 1935 Pierre MONTEUX became permanent conductor: Ernest SCHELLING and Rudolph GANZ have conducted the young people's concerts.

Sangallo, Giuliano da (1445-1516), Italian architect and sculptor who designed a villa and a monastery for Lorenzo de' MEDICI, and also worked on ST. PETER'S at Rome: he also designed the Madonna delle Carceri at Prato, and the Palazzo Strozzi. His brother, **Antonio Sangallo** (1455-1534), called the Elder, was a distinguished military architect: he built the Church of Saint Biagio at Montepulciano which bore some resemblance to BRAMANTE'S design for ST. PETER'S at Rome. His nephew, **Antonio da Sangallo** (1485-1546), called the Younger, was a pupil of Bramante: he worked for several popes, built the Farnese Palace, was one of the architects of St. Peter's at Rome, and also designed several parts of the VATICAN.

Sanmichele, Michele (1484-1550), Italian architect who worked with his father and uncle who were both architects, and also studied classical architecture and sculpture in Rome. He came under the influence of BRAMANTE, and designed many churches and palaces at Orvieto, Verona, and Venice. He wrote an important work on architecture, *The Five Orders of Architecture,* printed at Verona in 1735.

Sannazzaro, Jacopo (1458-1530), Italian poet whose works exerted considerable influence on Italian prose: his principal work is a pastoral romance, *Arcadia,* in prose: he also wrote a poem in Latin, *De partu Virginis,* which gained him the name of the "Christian Virgil."

Sanroma, Jesús María (1903-   ), Porto Rican pianist of Spanish parentage who studied at the NEW ENGLAND CONSERVATORY OF MUSIC, Boston, Mass., and with Alfred CORTOT and Artur SCHNABEL. He made his debut in recital at Boston in 1920, and has since played with the BOSTON SYMPHONY ORCHESTRA and other major orchestras, also teaching at the New England Conservatory of Music, appearing on radio broadcasts, and making important recordings.

Sansovino, Andrea (1460-1529), Florentine sculptor whose real name was Andrea Contucci: he studied with Antonio POLLAIUOLO, worked in Portugal for the king, at Florence, and in Rome where he executed the monuments of Cardinals Ascanio Sforza and Girolamo della Rovere. He also made an exquisite *Madonna and Child with St. Anne* in the Church of Saint Augustine.

Sansovino, Jacopo (c.1486-1570), Italian sculptor and architect whose real name was Tatti: he renamed himself after Andrea SANSOVINO whose pupil he became in 1500, accompanying him to Rome for the study of ancient sculpture. He also worked for BRAMANTE, restored damaged statues for Julius II; and made a full-sized copy of the LAOCOON which is now in the Uffizi Gallery at Rome. Among his notable works are *Hope; Peace; Mercury; Pallas Athene; Mars; Neptune:* he also made the bronze doors of the sacristy of St. Mark's, Venice.

Sans Souci, a palace erected at Potsdam, Germany, by FREDERICK THE GREAT, and said to have been largely designed by the emperor himself: it is a one-story building over three hundred feet in length, and the apartments occupied by the monarch have been kept exactly as they were when he died. Voltaire visited him there, and the park, audience room, fountain, and the great statue of Frederick are all on a magnificently grandiose scale.

Santayana, George (1863-   ), American-Spanish educator, poet and essayist born in Spain who came to the United States as a boy and was educated at Harvard College and in Berlin: his works include *Sonnets and Other Verses* (1894); *The Life of Reason; The Last Puritan; Soliliquies in England.*

Santelmann, William Henry (1863-1932), American bandmaster born in Germany who studied at the Leipzig Conservatory. After playing in the UNITED STATES MARINE BAND from 1887 to 1895 he became conductor in 1898, and retired in 1927. He composed several works for band, and his son, William F. H. Santelmann, joined the United States Marine Band in 1923, and was made assistant conductor in 1935.

Santi, Raphael, see **Raphael.**

Santillana, Iñigo López de Mendoza (1398-1458), Spanish soldier, poet, and statesman who was prominent at the court of Julian II of Castile: he was one of the first to introduce the SONNET into Castilian poetry, but was more successful as a creator of PASTORALS in the Provençal manner.

Sapphire, a highly regarded gem stone which is a blue transparent variety of corundum or oxide of aluminum. It is mined in Siam, Ceylon, Upper Burmah, Australia, and Montana; is extremely hard and available in shades of blue, purple, yellow, and green.

Sappho, Greek poet born at Lesbos during the 6th century, B.C., and a contemporary of ALCAEUS: she was the leader of a school of poetry at Lesbos, and in ancient days her fame rivaled that of HOMER. Fragments of her works, which were apparently arranged in nine books, have been discovered written on Egyptian PAPYRI: one is an ode to APHRODITE complete in seven stanzas.

Sarabande (Fr.), a slow, stately dance of Spanish origin known to CERVANTES and to SHAKESPEARE: it is written in triple time, and became a fixed member of the classical SUITE. In France it was danced at court, but in England it was a favorite country dance.

Sarasate, Pablo de (1844-1908), Spanish violinist and composer whose full name was Pablo Martin Melitón Sarasate y Navascuez: he studied at the Paris Conservatory under Jean Delphin ALARD, and toured Europe, North America, South America, and the Orient with great success. Édouard LALO wrote the SYMPHONIE ESPAGNOLE for him, and Max BRUCH his second violin concerto. He composed many light and effective compositions for his instrument including the *Gipsy Dances, Op. 20* of which there is a Victor recording by Jascha HEIFETZ.

Sarcophagus, a word which in Greek means "flesh-devouring" because the earliest coffins or sarcophagi were made of a stone which had the tendency to destroy bodies. The Greeks made sarcophagi of terra cotta, and the Phoenicians made them in a shape to conform with the contours of the human body. Roman sarcophagi were elaborately decorated with BAS-RELIEFS and early Christian examples reveal a mixture of Pagan and Christian scenes in their decorations.

Sard, a reddish-brown CHALCEDONY much favored in ancient times as a gem stone, and used by the Assyrians, Egyptians, and Phoenicians. Some types of sard resemble the CARNELIAN although they are harder and less brilliant: the hyacinthene sard resembles the GARNET, and was used for CAMEOS and INTAGLIOS.

Sardi's, a restaurant in New York, located in the heart of the theatre district, which is the Mecca from lunch time through afternoon-tea, dinner, and midnight snack for actors, dramatists, producers, and habitual theatre-goers who appreciate not only the well-prepared food, but the attentions and engaging personality of the host, Vincent Sardi.

Sardonyx, see **Onyx.**

Sardou, Victorien (1831-1908), French dramatist who studied to be a physician: his first play, *La Taverne de étudiants* was a complete failure, and he had decided to abandon the idea of playwriting when Mademoiselle de Brécourt, whom he subsequently married, was largely responsible for restoring his interest. Among the successful plays known to English and American theatre lovers are *A Scrap of Paper; Madame Sans-Gêne; Fedora; La Tosca; Cleopatra; Robespierre; Diplomacy.*

Sarg, Tony (1882-1942), American illustrator, and author, real name Anthony Frederick Sarg, born in Gautémala, educated in German military schools and an officer in the German army until 1905. He came to the United States in 1915 and was naturalized in 1921. His works include illustrations for the *Saturday Evening Post, Collier's,* and other magazines, and numerous illustrated books for children. He was also the creator of *Tony Sarg's Marionettes,* giving many performances in New York and elsewhere.

Sargent, John Singer (1856-1925), American painter born in Florence of American parents who studied with his mother and with CAROLUS-DURAN at Paris: after traveling in Spain and North Africa he exhibited his first picture, *En route pour la pêche,* at the Paris Salon in 1878. He became a distinguished portrait painter; his sitters included the men and women of the greatest distinction in the literary, artistic, and social life of Europe and America. Although he was constantly occupied with portraiture, he executed many figure pieces and landscapes including *La Carmencita; Marble Quarry at Carrera; Tyrolese Interior; Cypresses and Pines; The Weavers; The Fountain; The Courtyard; El Jaleo:* also the series known as *The History of Religion* in Sargent Hall at the Public Library, Boston, Mass.; begun in 1890 and completed in 1916.

Saroyan, William (1908-   ), American short-story writer and dramatist: his works include *The Daring Young Man on the Flying Trapeze* (1934), and more than 400 short stories which have been published in collected form; *My Heart's in the Highlands,* a play (1939), *The Time of Your Life,* a play which was awarded the Pulitzer Prize in 1940; *The Human Comedy,* a successful motion picture in 1943, and also published as a novel during the same year.

Sarrazin, Jacques (1588-1660), French painter and sculptor who worked for Cardinal Aldobrandini, and became intimate with DOMENICHINO: his works include the decoration of the central pavilion of the LOUVRE, the tomb of Henry II de Condé and the tomb for the heart of Louis XIII.

Sarto, Andrea del (1486-1531), Italian painter whose real name was Andrea d'Angelo di Francesco: he studied with PIERO DI COSIMO and his notable works include *Nativity of the Virgin; Procession of the Magi; Madonna del Sacco; Charity; Last Supper; Deposition from the Cross; Sacrifice of Abraham; Marriage of St.*

Catherine; Madonna of the Harpies: he was a master not only of composition, but also of harmonious coloring.

Sassoferrato, Il (1605-1685), Italian painter whose real name was Giambattista Salvi: he is said to have studied with DOMENICHINO, and engaged in rivalry with Carlo DOLCI. He painted chiefly Madonnas and devotional pictures: his masterpiece, *Madonna of the Rosary,* is in the church of Saint Sabina at Rome.

Satire, in literature and drama, according to Websters' *New International Dictionary:* "a literary composition holding up human or individual vices, or folly, or abuses or shortcomings of any kind, to reprobation by means of ridicule, derision, burlesque, or other method of intensifying incongruities, usually with an intent to provoke amendment." Satire is to be found in Job's ironical address to his friends; in the works of the Greek poets Archilochus and LUCIAN; in the writings of the Roman poets, LUCILIUS, HORACE, and JUVENAL: satirists of the Christian era include RABELAIS, LANGLAND, Jean de MEUNG, CERVANTES, BOILEAU-DESPREAUX, DRYDEN, POPE, FIELDING, SWIFT, LESSING, WIELAND, HEINE, THACKERAY, BYRON, George Bernard SHAW, IRVING, and Mark TWAIN. In drama the satirical playwrights include MOLIERE, Ben JONSON, and the celebrated Greek dramatist, ARISTOPHANES.

Satyrs, in Greek mythology spirits, half beasts and half men, that haunted the forests as companions of PAN and DIONYSUS. They are depicted with flat noses, pointed ears, small horns, and with the tails of horses or goats growing out of their heavily-built bodies. PRAXITELES is said to have created a statue of a satyr leaning against a tree and holding a flute.

Sauer, Emil (1862-), German pianist and composer who studied with Nicholas RUBINSTEIN and Franz LISZT: from 1862 he toured the entire world with great success, visiting the United States in 1898 and 1908. He has composed concertos and other works for the piano in addition to editing the piano works of Johannes BRAHMS, and Domenico SCARLATTI.

Sauret, Émile (1852-1920), French violinist and composer who studied with Henri VIEUXTEMPS and Charles de BERIOT; he toured Europe and the United States with great success, and taught for some years at the CHICAGO MUSICAL COLLEGE. His repertory is said to have comprised 80 concertos and 400 concert pieces: his works include a concerto and nearly one hundred solos for violin.

Savage, Henry Wilson (1859-1927), American opera impresario who was first a real estate operator: when several lessees failed to make a success of the Castle Square Theatre, Boston, Mass., he organized a company of singers who made a success of grand opera in English at low prices. In 1900 he founded the English Grand Opera Company, and produced Richard WAGNER's *Parsifal* and PUCCINI's *Madam Butterfly* in English with tremendous success. He also produced LEHAR's *Merry Widow* and Oscar STRAUS's *Waltz Dream.*

Savonarola, Girolamo (1452-1498), Italian political and religious reformer who became a Dominican monk in 1475, and prior of St. Mark's at Florence in 1491. He was one of the chief instruments in the overthrow of the Medici and the restoration of the republic in 1494, and for a time was virtually the dictator of Florence. He was excommunicated in 1497 for denouncing Pope Alexander VI, and was burned at the stake in 1498.

Saxophone, a brass instrument invented in 1840 by Adolphe Sax, a Belgian instrument maker: it has a conical tube, and a clarinet mouthpiece with a single reed. Its tone greatly resembles that of the English horn and the violoncello, but association with dance music has tended to discourage its use as a serious instrument although George BIZET used it effectively in the *Arlésienne Suites,* and Claude DEBUSSY wrote a rhapsody for saxophone and orchestra.

Sayao, Bidu (1906-), Brazilian coloratura soprano who studied with Jean de RESZKE, and after making her debut at Rio de Janeiro, sang at Paris, Rome, and Milan. She made her operatic debut in 1936 at the Metropolitan Opera House, New York, in Massenet's *Manon,* and has concertized in the United States and South America.

Sayers, Dorothy L. (1893-), English author of detective fiction educated at Somerville College, Oxford, and among the first women to receive an Oxford degree: her novels include *The Dawson Pedigree* (1927); *Lord Peter Views the Body,* in which she introduced Lord Peter Wimsey, the English aristocrat who plays the part of the amateur detective in most of her stories: *Murder Must Advertise; Hangman's Holiday; Whose Body?; Gaudy Night* and several other tales of the same nature. She has also written several plays.

Sbriglia, Giovanni (1840-?), Italian dramatic tenor who made his debut at Naples in 1861: he appeared in Italian opera houses and in the United States, but finally became a distinguished teacher who numbered Jean de RESZKE, Édouard de RESZKE, Lillian NORDICA, and Sibyl SANDERSON among his pupils.

Scala, La (Teatro alla Scala), the most important opera house in Milan, Italy, and one of the greatest institutions of its kind in the world: it was built by special permission of the Empress Maria Theresa of Austria, and opened in 1778 with an opera by Antonio SALIERI. Among the famous operas first produced there are DONIZETTI's *Lucrezia Borgia;* VERDI's *Otello* and *Falstaff;* BOITO's *Mefistofele* and *Nerone;* PUCCINI's *Madam Butterfly* and *Turandot:* Arturo TOSCANINI reached the pinnacle of his fame as a conductor of grand opera there.

Scalchi, Sofia (1850-?), Italian opera singer whose voice had such a wide range that she could sing contralto or soprano roles. She made her debut at Mantua in 1866, and after appearing in several Italian cities appeared at London in 1868, and at New York in 1882 with Colonel Henry

MAPLESON's Company, and during the following year at the Metropolitan Opera House. After singing in Russia, Spain, Austria, and South America she retired in 1896.

Scale, in modern music a series of eight tones, takes in direct succession, which form any major or minor key. There are three forms of the minor scale: the *pure* or *normal minor,* the *harmonic minor,* and the *melodic minor.* A *chromatic scale* is formed entirely of semi-tones; an *enharmonic scale* is one that sounds identical with a scale written with a different signature, as C♯ major and D♭ major. A *pentatonic scale* has only five tones: it omits the 4th and 7th tones in major scales, and the 2nd and 6th tones in minor scales.

Scaramouch or **Scaramouche,** a stock character in the Italian COMMEDIA DELL' ARTE during the 16th and 17th centuries: he was usually attired in a black Spanish dress, and in mortal fear of Harlequin because he was at heart a coward and boaster.

Scarlatti, Alessandro (1659-1725), Italian dramatic composer who was the teacher of DURANTE, PORPORA and HASSE: his works include more than one hundred operas, and he is credited with developing the use of recitative and the enrichment of the orchestral accompaniment in opera. His son, **Domenico Scarlatti** (1685-1757), studied with his father, and became a harpsichordist of great distinction who composed more than six hundred pieces for his instrument.

Scarpaza, Vittorio, see **Carpaccio, Vittore.**

Scarpia, Baron, a character in Giacomo PUCCINI's grand opera, TOSCA, founded on Victorien Sardou's famous play, *La Tosca,* which has been a favorite vehicle for tragediennes since 1887. Scarpia is the head of the police at Rome and uses his powers as a government official to gain the favor of Tosca, a famous opera diva whom he knows is in love with Mario Cavaradossi, a revolutionist and painter. He is without question one of the most despicable of theatrical villains, portrayed with exceptional finesse by the distinguished baritone Antonio SCOTTI, who appeared in the role many times at the Metropolitan Opera House, New York.

Scarron, Paul (1610-1660), French novelist, poet, and dramatist who was the husband of Françoise d'Aubigné, later famous as Madame de Maintenon, mistress of LOUIS XIV: his works include *Comic Romance* (1651), the story of a troupe of strolling players; *Typhon* and *Virgile travesti,* two burlesque poems: his plays include *Jodelet; The Ridiculous Heir; Don Japhet of Armenia; The Scholar of Salamanca.*

Scenario (It.), in the theatre and motion pictures the plot outline of a play or film: the term was first used at about the beginning of the 19th century in the theatre, but is now almost exclusively applied to the outline of a photoplay.

Schadow, Johann Gottfried (1764-1850), German sculptor who studied in Rome and became court sculptor at Berlin. Among his notable works are statues of Frederick the Great in Stettin; Blücher in Rostock; Martin Luther in Wittenberg; the *Quadriga* on the Brandenburg Gate at Berlin; seventeen colossal heads in the Walhalla, Ratisbon: he also wrote treatises on the proportions of the human figure and on his methods of work.

Schadow-Godenhaus, Friedrich Wilhelm von (1789-1862), German painter who was the son of the sculptor, Johann Gottfried SCHADOW: he studied at Rome, and was a member with CORNELIUS, OVERBECK and VEIT of the PRE-RAPHAELITES. From 1826 to 1859 he was director of the Düsseldorf Academy which rose to great heights under his guidance. His notable works include *Holy Family; Roman Woman; Adoration of the Magi; The Four Evangelists; The Wise and Foolish Virgins; Christ and His Disciples at Emmaus.*

Schalk, Franz (1863-1931), Austrian conductor who was a pupil and friend of Anton BRUCKNER: he succeeded Anton SEIDL as conductor of German opera at the Metropolitan Opera House, New York, in 1899, and later directed at the Vienna Hofoper and the Vienna State Opera in association with Richard STRAUSS.

Scharwenka, Franz Xaver (1850-1924), German pianist and composer who studied with Theodor KULLAK and made his debut in 1869: he appeared in chamber music concerts with Émile SAURET and Heinrich Grünfeld, and toured Europe and America. In 1880 he founded the Scharwenka Conservatory at Berlin and in 1891 established the same institution at New York. His compositions include an opera, *Mataswintha,* piano concertos, and many popular piano pieces including the famous *Polish Dances.* His brother, **Ludwig Philipp Scharwenka** (1847-1917), studied the piano with Heinrich Dorn, and became a teacher of musical theory and musical composition at the Kullak Academy later merged with the Klindworth Conservatory. His compositions include orchestral works, chamber music, piano sonatas, and solo pieces; violin pieces and songs.

Schauffler, Robert Haven (1879-), American poet, essayist, and musical biographer born in Austria of American parents, and educated at Northwestern University, Princeton University, and the University of Berlin. His works include *Fiddler's Luck* (1920); *Beethoven, the Man Who Freed Music; The Unknown Brahms:* he has also compiled and edited 28 books on Christmas, Washington's Birthday and other holidays.

Scheel, Fritz (1852-1907), German conductor who studied with Ferdinand DAVID at Leipzig, and came to the United States in 1893: he conducted the Trocadero concerts in 1894 at the Columbian Exposition in Chicago, and established the San Francisco Orchestra in 1895. In 1900 he became the first conductor of the Philadelphia Orchestra, remaining its director until his death.

Scheff, Fritzi (1879-), Austrian operatic soprano who studied with her mother and made her debut in GOUNOD's *Romeo and Juliet* at

Frankfort: in 1900 she appeared at the Metropolitan Opera House in BEETHOVEN's *Fidelio,* and in 1906 in Victor HERBERT's *Mlle. Modiste,* creating a sensation at New York and throughout the United States.

Scheffer, Ary (1795-1858), Dutch painter who studied with GUERIN at Paris, where he became acquainted with GERICAULT, SIGALON and DELACROIX, but later developed a style completely his own: among his notable works are *Margaret at Her Wheel; Faust Doubting; Margaret at the Well; Mignon; Francesca da Rimini; Shepherds Led by the Star; Christ in the Garden of Olives; Christ Interred; Sorrows of the Earth; Angel Announcing the Resurrection.*

Scheherazade (Rimsky-Korsakow), an orchestral suite composed by Nicholas RIMSKY-KORSAKOW in 1888, and performed at St. Petersburg in the fall of the same year with the composer conducting: it is an example of instrumental virtuosity which has never been surpassed, and in addition is its creator's greatest work. In another field—that of musical story-telling—it is also the finest and most extraordinary example. Inspired by four tales in *The Arabian Nights,* the composer associated the four movements of the work with the following titles: I—"The Sea and Sindbad's Ship," II—"The Tale of the Prince Kalendar," III—"The Young Prince and Princess," IV—"Festival at Bagdad": no specific details beyond these are furnished. In his autobiography, *My Musical Life,* the composer said: "All I had desired was that the hearer, if he liked my piece as symphonic music, should carry away the impression that it is beyond doubt an Oriental narrative of some numerous and varied fairy-tale wonders." There is a Victor recording by the Philadelphia Orchestra directed by Leopold Stokowski, and a Columbia recording by the Cleveland Orchestra with Artur Rodzinski.

Scheherazade, a symphonic ballet: libretto by Alexandre BENOIS; choreography by Michel FOKINE; music by Nicholas RIMSKY-KORSAKOW; first produced at Paris in 1910. The story revolves around King Schariar, Sultan of India and China, who suspects his wives, especially his favorite, Zobeide, of being unfaithful. He departs on a hunting trip, and has scarcely left before the ladies of the harem bribe the chief eunuch to open the doors of the slave quarters. A grand dance, reaching its climax in a bacchic orgy, ensues, but the Sultan suddenly returns and bids his warriors kill everyone of the revelers except his favorite, Zobeide. She begs forgiveness, but when the Sultan's brother points to the dead body of Zobeide's paramour, he orders her execution. Before the soldiers can carry out his command Zobeide plunges a dagger into her breast. At the first performance, Ida RUBINSTEIN portrayed Zobeide, and Vaslav NIJINSKY her favorite slave. The music is not specially arranged for the ballet, but follows the score of the orchestral suite as composed by Rimsky-Korsakow.

Schelling, Ernest Henry (1876-1939), American composer, pianist, and conductor who appeared as a child prodigy at four, and later studied with Georges Mathias, a pupil of CHOPIN, and with Moritz MOSZKOWSKI, Theodor LESCHETIZKY, and with Ignace PADEREWSKI. He toured Europe, the United States, and South America, and later conducted the young people's symphony concerts of the New York Philharmonic-Symphony Orchestra and several other major orchestras. His compositions include *Légende Symphonique, Victory Ball,* and other works for orchestra; also chamber music, piano pieces, and songs.

Schertzinger, Victor (1889-1941), American violinist, composer, and musical director of film productions: he appeared as a concert violinist with Marcella SEMBRICH, Emma CALVE, and SOUSA's Band, and wrote the first full musical score for a film, *Civilization.* His song *Marcheta* enjoyed an enormous sale; he also directed Grace MOORE's *One Night of Love* and many other outstanding film productions.

Scherzo, in music an instrumental composition of light, piquant or humorous character: it is usually animated in character, and succeeded the MINUET employed by HAYDN and MOZART in symphonies and sonatas. The outstanding example is the scherzo in MENDELSSOHN's incidental music for Shakespeare's *A Midsummer Night's Dream:* Frédéric CHOPIN wrote several concert piano pieces using the word as a title.

Schikaneder, Johann Emanuel (1748-1812), Austrian theatre manager and librettist: he is famous as the librettist of Wolfgang Amadeus MOZART's opera, *The* MAGIC FLUTE, the successful production of which in 1791 averted financial disaster. He sang the part of Papageno, but his treatment of the composer does not indicate that he was in any sense grateful.

Schildkraut, Joseph (1895-), American actor born in Austria who studied for the stage in Germany and at the Academy of Dramatic Arts, New York: he made his debut in 1910 with his father, Rudolf Schildkraut, at the Irving Place Theatre, New York, and later in Berlin under the management of Max REINHARDT. Among the plays in which he has appeared are *Pagans; Liliom; Peer Gynt; The Highwayman; The Firebrand; The Second Year; Pomander Walk; The Prodigal Son; Camille; Uncle Harry.* He has also been featured in both silent and talking films.

Schiller, Johann Christoph Friedrich von (1759-1805), German poet and dramatist educated for the practice of law and of medicine: his works include *The Robbers* (1780); *Frisco; Love and Intrigue; Don Carlos; Hymn to Joy* for which Ludwig van BEETHOVEN composed music in his *Ninth Symphony; Wallenstein's Camp;* the *Piccolomini; Wallenstein's Death; Maria Stuart; William Tell:* he also wrote several authoritative historical works.

Schillinger, Joseph (1895-1943), Russian composer, teacher, and conductor who studied at the St. Petersburg Imperial Conservatory, and later conducted at Kharkoff and Leningrad: after coming to the United States in 1930 he was connected with the New School for Social Research and the American Institute of the City of New York. His pupils included George GERSHWIN, Oscar LEVANT, and Benny GOODMAN: among his compositions are *March of the Orient; Symphonic Rhapsody* for piano and orchestra; *First Airphonic Suite* for the THEREMIN.

Schillings, Max von (1868-1933), German conductor and composer educated at Munich University and at the Gymnasium in Bonn: he conducted German opera at Bayreuth, Stuttgart, Berlin, and in the United States with the German Grand Opera Company. His compositions include music dramas, orchestral works, chamber music, choruses, piano pieces, violin pieces, and songs.

Schindler, Anton (1795-1864), German violinist, conductor, friend and biographer of Ludwig van BEETHOVEN: he conducted all the symphonies under the master's direction. He met Beethoven in 1814 and became his secretary in 1816 without remuneration, remaining his devoted friend until death. His biography, the factual source for all later works, was published in 1840, and has been reprinted several times.

Schindler, Kurt (1882-1935), German composer and conductor who studied with several masters, and also at the Berlin and Munich Universities: in 1905 he became assistant to Alfred HERTZ at the Metropolitan Opera House, New York, and organized the MacDowell Chorus in 1909, changing the name to "Schola Cantorum" in 1912, and greatly enlarging the chorus. He introduced many novelties, and made choral arrangements of European folksongs. His compositions were chiefly songs and choral arrangements. From 1912 he occupied the post of organist at Temple Emanu-El, New York.

Schinkel, Karl Friedrich (1781-1841), German architect and painter who became a professor in the Berlin Academy of Arts. His notable works include the design for the mausoleum of Queen Louise; a sketch for the Berlin Cathedral; scenic paintings for many of the state theatres in Germany; public buildings, castles, and residences in and around Berlin: he also painted several DIORAMAS.

Schipa, Tito (1889-), Italian operatic tenor who made his debut in 1911 in Verdi's *La Traviata:* from 1920 to 1932 he appeared with the Chicago Civic Opera, and was a member of the Metropolitan Opera Company from 1932 to 1935, also appearing in Europe and South America.

Schirmer, Friedrich Wilhelm (1802-1866), German painter who first worked in a porcelain factory, and later became a pupil of Friedrich SCHADOW-GODENHAUS: from 1830 to 1895 he was professor of landscape painting at the Berlin Academy. His finest work was done in the Berlin Museum of Antiquities where he painted classic sites and temples, also beautifying the buildings with the landscape scenery with which they were historically associated.

Schirmer, Johann Wilhelm (1807-1863), German painter who studied at the Düsseldorf Academy, later becoming a professor there, and also director of the art school in Carlsruhe. He painted historic scenes in Italy, and also many Biblical landscapes.

Schlegel, August Wilhelm von (1767-1845), German poet, translator, and critic who studied at the University of Göttingen, and became professor of literature and art at Jena. He acted as secretary to the Crown Prince of Sweden, and translated the works of SHAKESPEARE, DANTE, CALDERON DE LA BARCA, and CERVANTES. His most important work was *Dramatic Art and Literature:* his poems and plays are not as important as his translations.

Schliemann, Heinrich (1822-1890), German archaeologist who undertook in 1863 to find the site of the ancient city of Troy, and between 1871 and 1882 discovered the remains of four towns, one built over the other, which be believed corresponded with the descriptions of the city in HOMER'S *Iliad.*

Schluter, Andreas (1664-1714), German sculptor and architect who worked at Warsaw before being summoned by royal command to Berlin where he rebuilt the royal palace between 1699 and 1706. In 1713 he executed architectural designs for Peter the Great in Russia: among his important works at Berlin are the monument to the elector Friedrich William, the tomb of Friedrich I, and the marble pulpit in the Marienkirche.

Schmitt, Florent (1870-), French composer who studied at the Paris Conservatory with Théodore DUBOIS, Albert LAVIGNAC, Jules MASSENET, and Gabriel FAURE: his compositions include orchestral works, songs with orchestra, chamber music, and many piano pieces.

Schnabel, Artur (1882-), Austrian pianist who studied with Theodor LESCHETIZKY, and toured Austria and Germany: he gave joint recitals with Karl FLESCH at Berlin for many years and taught at the Berlin Hochschule. He toured the United States in 1921 and 1933, and is now (1943) residing in New York. His son, **Karl Ulrich Schnabel** (1909-), is also a pianist, who has appeared in recital and also in two-piano concerts with his father.

Schnitzler, Arthur (1862-1931), Austrian dramatist and novelist educated as a physician, and in actual practice for several years: in 1891 he formed the Young Vienna group to revitalize Austrian literature with Hermann BAHR, Felix SALTEN, and Hugo von HOFMANNSTHAL. His numerous successful plays include *Anatol* (1893); *Light-o'-Love; The Green Cockatoo; The Lonely Way; Intermezzo; The Sisters; The Comedy of Seduction.* His novels include *The Road to the Open; Beatrice; Dr. Graesler; Casanova's Homecoming.*

Schnorr von Karolsfeld, Julius (1794-1872), German painter who studied with his father, and at the Academy of Vienna: in 1818 he became a member of the NAZARENES, a group of German painters headed by OVERBECK who sought to restore the art of the old Italian painters. His works include the frescoes, *Nibelungen Scenes,* in the Royal Palace at Munich where he was a professor at the Academy of Arts: also many Biblical subjects and designs in glass for windows executed in Munich for the Cathedral at Glasgow and St. Paul's Cathedral, London.

Schoenherr, Karl (1867-1943), Austrian dramatist who first wrote dialect poems and short stories, turning to the drama in 1897 with his play *Judas in the Tyrol:* many of his plays which found their way into all the capitals of Europe, were first produced at the Burgtheater and Deutsches Volkstheater in Vienna. He won the Schiller prize in 1908 and the Grillparzer prize three times, but his plays were banned after the Nazi invasion of Austria.

Schola Cantorum, an organization founded as the MacDowell Chorus in 1909 with Kurt SCHINDLER as conductor: the name was changed to "Schola Cantorum" in 1912, and the membership increased from 40 to 200. Mr. Schindler conducted until 1926, and was succeeded by Margarethe DESSOFF, and Hugh Ross: later Mr. Ross became the permanent conductor.

Scholes, Percy (1877-), English author of books on music educated at Oxford: his works include *Everyman and His Music* (1917); *The Listener's Guide to Music; The Book of the Great Musicians; The Listener's History of Music; A Miniature History of Opera; The Puritans and Music; The Oxford Companion to Music.*

Schönberg, Arnold (1874-), German composer chiefly self-taught with the exception of some lessons in counterpoint from Alexander ZEMLINSKY: his compositions, which are ultra-modern and without tonality although the composer repudiates the term, include *The Lucky Hand,* a music drama; *Pelléas and Mélisande,* a symphonic poem, and other orchestral works; *Gurre-Lieder* for soloists, chorus, and orchestra; chamber music; *Pierrot Lunaire,* a melodrama; piano pieces and songs.

Schöngauer, Martin (c.1445-1488), German painter and engraver known as Martin Schön (Beautiful) because of the perfection of his works. As a painter he was a pupil of Roger van der WEYDEN THE ELDER: as an engraver he founded a school out of which grew the "Little Masters" of the next generation. His plates number in excess of one hundred, and include only religious subjects.

Schönnbrun (Vienna), a château built in 1774 by the Empress Maria Theresa of Austria: the son of Napoleon I, former king of Rome, lived there after his father's abdication, and the many rooms have both artistic and historic significance. The Hapsburg emperors lived in Schönnbrun during the summer months: one of its most attractive features was the magnificent park laid out in the French style.

Schoop, Trudi, contemporary Swiss ballerina and comedienne trained at the State Theatre School who improvised a program of original dances which she presented in recital: after further study at Vienna she founded the Schoop Comic Ballets in 1929, a series of tragi-comedies of everyday life enacted in dance steps. She achieved her first success at Berlin in 1929, and toured Europe and the Orient, appearing in the United States during 1936-37.

Schorr, Friederich (1888-), Hungarian dramatic baritone who first studied for the bar: after some instruction in singing he appeared in minor roles with the Chicago-Philadelphia Opera Company in 1911, but made his formal debut during the same year at Graz as Wotan in WAGNER's *The Valkyrie.* After singing in opera houses at Cologne, Prague, and Berlin, he toured the United States in 1923 with the Wagnerian Opera Company from Charlottenburg. In 1924 he made his debut at the Metropolitan Opera House in Wagner's *Tannhäuser:* he remained with the company for nearly twenty years before his retirement in 1943, and also sang at Covent Garden, London, annually during the summer. He was outstanding in all the principal bass roles of Wagner's operas and music dramas: he also created the leading bass roles in KRENEK's *Jonny Spielt Auf;* WEINBERGER's *Schwanda;* Richard STRAUSS' *Salome* and *Elektra.*

Schradieck, Henry (1846-1918), German violinist, teacher, and author of technical works: he studied with Hubert LEONARD and Ferdinand DAVID, and after teaching at Moscow and Leipzig he became professor of violin at the Cincinnati College of Music in 1883, and later at the National Conservatory of Music, New York. His *School of Violin Technique* and *Scale Studies* are among the most important technical works for the violin.

Schreiner, Olive Emilie Albertina (1855-1920), South African novelist: her first novel, *The Story of an African Farm* (1883), won immediate success, and was translated into several languages, but none of her other works achieved the distinction of her first effort.

Schreker, Franz (1878-1934), Austrian composer who studied with Robert Fuchs in Vienna, and later became teacher of composition at the Vienna Royal Academy, and director of the Berlin Hochschule: his compositions include several operas which have been performed in more than two hundred opera houses in Central Europe, orchestral works, and songs.

Schreyer, Adolf (1828-1899), German painter who studied at several German art schools; also in Paris. He traveled in Hungary, Russia, Turkey, Egypt, and Syria becoming famous for his paintings of battles, horses, and peasant life. Among his notable canvases are *Abandoned; Arabs on the March; Arabs Making a Detour; Charge of the Artillery of the Royal Guard; Wallachian Transport Train.*

Schröder, Alwin (1855-1928), German violoncellist who was largely self-taught: in 1880 he became professor at the Leipzig Conservatory and 'cellist of the Petri Quartet. He came to the United States in 1891 as first 'cellist of the Boston Symphony Orchestra and later as 'cellist of the

Franz KNEISEL Quartet. In 1907 he returned to Germany, but came back to the United States in 1908, and remained there until his death.

Schröder-Devrient, Wilhelmine (1804-1860), German dramatic soprano who made her debut in 1821 at Vienna in MOZART's *The Magic Flute*, and in 1822 achieved extraordinary success as Leonore in Beethoven's *Fidelio*. In 1823 she joined the Court Opera at Dresden, remaining until her retirement in 1847. Her technique was subject to criticism, but her dramatic powers in the operas of GLUCK, MOZART, and WAGNER were extraordinary.

Schubert, Franz Peter (1797-1828), Austrian composer who had little music instruction except with Antonio SALIERI: he was the shortest-lived of all of the world's outstanding composers except Giovanni Battista PERGOLESI. He composed an opera, *Der Teufel's Lustschloss*, at sixteen, and wrote one of his greatest songs, *The Erlking* at eighteen. In 1817 he became acquainted with Johann VOGL, leading baritone at the Vienna Opera, who sang his songs, but their publication was of little assistance to him because his publishers treated him disgracefully, purchasing many of his finest songs for as little as twenty cents each. His life was singularly uneventful: outside of his visits to Zelész as music-master to the family of Count ESTERHAZY, and a single concert devoted to his works given at Vienna, he lived and died in poverty, unrecognized and unappreciated. His works include 14 operas and operettas; 8 symphonies including the UNFINISHED SYMPHONY; 8 overtures; 15 string quartets, and also quintets, octets and nonets; 20 sonatas and also solo pieces for piano; many choruses; more than 600 songs.

Schuëcker, Edmund (1860-1911), Austrian harpist who studied at the Vienna Conservatory and became solo harpist of the Gewandhaus Orchestra at Leipzig: in 1891 he joined the Chicago Symphony Orchestra under Theodore Thomas, and later played at the Vienna Hofoper, with the Pittsburgh Symphony Orchestra, the Philadelphia Orchestra, and established the Vienna Harp College at Chicago. His brother, **Heinrich Schuecker** (1867-1913), studied at the Vienna Conservatory, and became solo harpist of the Boston Symphony Orchestra from 1885 until his death: he also occupied the post of harp professor at the New England Conservatory of Music, Boston, Mass.

Schulz, Leo (1863-), German violoncellist who appeared as a prodigy from 1870 to 1873, and later became solo 'cellist of the Berlin Philharmonic Orchestra, the Gewandhaus Orchestra at Leipzig, and of the Boston Symphony Orchestra, also teaching at the New England Conservatory of Music. He was first 'cellist of the New York Philharmonic-Symphony Orchestra 1890 to 1906 and from 1908 to 1929.

Schuman, William Howard (1910-), American composer who studied at Columbia University, and also with Roy Harris and at the Mozarteum Academy at Salzburg, later teaching at the Sarah Lawrence College, Bronxville, N. Y.

His works include *Choreographic Poem;* three symphonies; *Prelude and Fugue* for orchestra; a piano concerto; three string quartets; *American Festival* Overture. In 1943 he received the Pulitzer Prize for outstanding achievement in music.

Schumann, Clara (1819-1896), German pianist and composer, daughter and pupil of Friedrich WIECK, and wife of Robert SCHUMANN. She toured Germany, Austria, France, Russia, and England and taught at the Hoch Conservatory, Frankfurt-am-Main from 1878 to 1892. She was a life-long friend of Johannes BRAHMS and an outstanding interpreter of his works: her compositions are chiefly for the piano.

Schumann, Elizabeth (1891-), German operatic and concert soprano who studied with Alma Schadow, and made her debut in 1910 at the Hamburg Opera, remaining there until 1919. She made her debut in 1914 at the Metropolitan Opera House in Richard STRAUSS' *Der Rosenkavalier,* toured the United States with Richard Strauss in 1921, and was heard annually in recital from 1931. In 1938 she became teacher of singing at the CURTIS INSTITUTE OF MUSIC, Philadelphia.

Schumann, Robert (1810-1846), German composer and writer on music who studied with Friedrich WIECK whose daughter, Clara WIECK, became his wife after considerable opposition on the part of her father. In 1834 he founded *Die Neue Zeitschrift für Musik,* a magazine of great influence in German musical circles, after finding that through the use of a device for practicing the piano he had ruined the prospect of becoming a virtuoso on that instrument. He was one of the first to appreciate the genius of Frédéric CHOPIN, and was also intimate with Johannes BRAHMS, Felix MENDELSSOHN, and Joseph JOACHIM. His works include an opera, *Genoveva;* incidental music to Byron's *Manfred;* 4 symphonies; 5 overtures; concertos for piano, violin and violoncello; chamber music; part songs; songs; piano sonatas, and several piano suites including *Kinderscenen, Kreisleriana, Études Symphoniques, Papillons, Fantasiestücke, Faschingsschwank aus Wien, Albumblätter.*

Schumann-Heink, Ernestine (1861-1936), American operatic and concert contralto born in Bohemia: she had little systematic instruction before she made her debut at fifteen as contralto soloist in BEETHOVEN's *Ninth Symphony* at Graz. In 1878 she made her operatic debut in VERDI's *Il Trovatore* at the Dresden Opera, and after singing at Hamburg, Berlin, Bayreuth, and London, made her debut in 1898 as Ortrud in Wagner's *Lohengrin* at Chicago, appearing at the Metropolitan Opera House in 1899 with overwhelming success in the same opera. She made many concert tours of the United States, appeared in Julian EDWARDS' comic opera, *Love's Lottery,* celebrated the fiftieth anniversary of her debut at Graz with a concert at Carnegie Hall in 1926, and appeared in a film, *Here's to Romance,* in 1935. Her repertory included more than one hundred fifty operatic roles.

Schütz, Heinrich (1585-1672), German composer who is considered the most important composer of his period, standing between PALESTRINA and Johann Sebastian BACH: he composed the first German opera, *Daphne*, using the text provided by Ottavio RINUCINI for Jacopo Peri's opera with the same title, the translation being made by Martin OPITZ. He also made great improvements in German religious music by using the monodic style with solo singing.

Schwanthaler, Ludwig von (1802-1848), German sculptor the members of whose family had been sculptors for three hundred years: he studied in Italy where THORWALDSEN took a great interest in his progress. His notable works include twelve gilt bronze figures, ten feet in height, for the throne room in King Ludwig's palace at Munich; also portrait statues of MOZART, Jean Paul RICHTER, GOETHE and SHAKESPEARE.

Schwartz, Maurice (1890-), Russian actor and theatrical manager who first appeared on the American stage with a Yiddish company in 1905: he founded the Yiddish Art Theatre in 1919 at New York, and has appeared in more than 150 plays including *The Dybbuk; God of Vengeance; Anathema; God, Man and Devil; The Government Inspector; Yoshe Kalbe; The Brothers Ashkenazi*. He has also appeared with his company in London and Paris.

Schwarz, Jozua Marius Willem van der Poorten (1858-1915), Dutch novelist who wrote under the pen name "Maarten Maartens": his works include *The Morning of a Love and Other Poems* (1885); *Julian; Nivalis; The Black Box Murder; The Sin of Joost Aveling; An Old Maid's Love; The Greater Glory; God's Fool; My Lady Nobody; Eve.*

Schwind, Moritz von (1804-1871), German painter and engraver of noble descent who first studied philosophy before embarking on an artistic career: he was an intimate friend of Franz SCHUBERT, and among his engravings are those for GOETHE's works. His notable creations include designs from the *Nibelungenlied* and Tasso's *Jerusalem; Singers' Contest in the Wartburg; The Wedding Trip; The Promenade; Dante and Cupid:* he decorated the lobby of the Vienna Opera House with scenes from MOZART's *Magic Flute.*

Scollard, Clinton (1860-1932), American poet and professor of English literature at Hamilton College from 1888 to 1896, and also from 1911 to 1932: his works include *Pictures in Song* (1884); *With Reed and Lyre; The Hills of Song; Lyrics of the Dawn; War Voices and Memories.* He edited a *Bird Lover's Anthology* with Jessie Belle RITTENHOUSE, his wife.

Scopas, Greek sculptor of the 4th century B.C. about whom little is known except that he came from PAROS, and was in his period of greatest activity, according to PLINY, about 320 B.C. Among the works attributed to him by classical writers are *Aphrodite Pandemos;* a group, *The Furies* for the ACROPOLIS at Athens; *Mars* in a sitting position; *Meleager; Bacchante; Apollo Citharoedus.*

Score, in vocal or instrumental music the systematic arrangement of the various parts on separate staves one above the other: a score is used by the conductor of an orchestra or of a vocal ensemble for directive purposes, and also by music students and amateurs who wish to follow the performance of a work at concerts, over the air, or on records. **Score reading** is the art of following the score of an orchestral composition, vocal work, or opera for purpose of observing the methods of musical coloring: intensive study is necessary for those desiring to fully comprehend the complexities of orchestration, therefore regular courses in score reading are conducted at educational musical institutions. To obviate this necessity, a system known as *The Arrow System of Score Reading,* has been devised by Albert E. WIER whereby anyone who can read ordinary instrumental or vocal music can follow a score with reasonable facility. The system, consists of arrows placed at various points throughout a score so that the reader can follow not only the melodic outline of the work, but also have his attention drawn to counter themes and other interesting ornamental devices as they occur from time to time. The arrow is used to indicate where the melodic line lies at any particular point; the eye remains upon the part indicated until another arrow directs the attention to another part. The system has been applied to miniature scores only up to the present time; six volumes have been published in the Harcourt, Brace Miniature Score Series including *The Nine Symphonies of Beethoven; The Symphonies of Brahms and Tschaikowsky; The Symphonies of Haydn; Schubert and Mozart; Famous Individual Symphonies; Famous Symphonic Poems; Wagner Orchestral Excerpts.* A similar series of volumes have been issued by Longmans, Green and Co., in the chamber music, piano concerto, and violin concerto field which includes *The Chamber Music of Beethoven; The Chamber Music of Brahms; The Chamber Music of Mozart; The Chamber Music of Haydn and Schubert; Miscellaneous Chamber Works; Chamber Suites and Concerti Grossi; The Piano Concertos of Bach, Beethoven and Brahms; Romantic and Modern Piano Concertos; Classic Violin Concertos; Romantic and Modern Violin Concertos.* Longmans have also published the orchestral and vocal score of *The Valkyrie* with the arrow system.

"Scotch" Symphony (Mendelssohn), an orchestral work by Felix MENDELSSOHN: the most illuminating account of the *"Scotch" Symphony* may be found in a Boston Symphony program note written by William F. APTHORP for the concert given March 31, 1900: "The title of *Scotch Symphony* was applied to the work by the composer himself. It was one of the compositions in which Mendelssohn recorded the impressions of his trip to Scotland in 1829. The plan of the symphony was drawn up during his trip to Italy in 1831, and the work begun before his return to Germany, and finished on January 20, 1842." It was first played at the GEWANDHAUS in Leipzig on March 3, 1842. Mendelssohn conducted it at a Philharmonic Concert in London, on June 13, 1842. There is a Columbia recording by the Royal Philharmonic Orchestra with Felix Weingartner conducting, and a Victor recording by the

Rochester Philharmonic Orchestra under José Iturbi.

Scott, Cyril Meir (1879-   ), English pianist and composer who studied piano at Hoch's Conservatory at Frankfort and composition with Ivan Knorr: his compositions include several operas and ballets; orchestral works; chamber music; songs; a sonata, several suites, and many pieces for piano including *Danse nègre* and *Lotusland* which have enjoyed great popularity. He has also written treatises on theosophy and mysticism in relation to music.

Scott, Evelyn (1893-   ), American poet and novelist educated at Newcomb College, New Orleans, La.: her successful works include *The Narrow House* (1921); *Escapade,* an autobiography; *The Golden Door; The Wave; The Winter Alone; Eva Gay; Breathe upon These Slain; Bread and a Sword; Shadow of the Hawk.*

Scott, Sir George Gilbert (1811-1878), English architect who was largely responsible for the renovating from about the middle of the 19th century of many English churches including Ely Cathedral and Westminster Abbey: he also designed and built the Albert Memorial. His grandson, **Sir Giles Gilbert Scott** (1880-   ), was successful in presenting his designs for the Liverpool Cathedral, completed in 1924 and the largest religious edifice in Great Britain: he also prepared the plans for many other churches and memorials of World War I.

Scott, Hugh Stowell (1862-1903), English novelist who used the pen name "Henry Seton Merriman": his works include *The Phantom Future* (1889); *The Sowers,* a successful novel of Russia; *Roden's Corner; The Isle of Unrest; In Kedar's Tents; The Velvet Glove; The Vultures; Barlasch of the Guard; The Last Hope.*

Scott, Martha (1916-   ), American stage, screen, and radio actress who first appeared in community theatres and stock companies: among the films in which she has played are *Our Town; Cheers for Miss Bishop; One Foot in Heaven.*

Scott, Randolph (1903-   ), American stage and screen actor educated at the University of North Carolina who had two years of stage experience before entering the films in 1931: among the pictures in which he appeared are *The Last of the Mohicans; High, Wide and Handsome; Rebecca of Sunnybrook Farm; Jessie James; Coast Guard; Virginia City; My Favorite Wife; Western Union; Belle Starr; To the Shores of Tripoli; The Spoilers.*

Scott, Sir Walter (1771-1832), Scottish novelist and poet educated at the University of Edinburgh, who also studied and practiced law. After making translations of GOETHE and a book of ballads, he published a collection of ballads entitled *Minstrelsy of the Scottish Border* (1802-3) which was followed by his first successful poem *The Lay of the Last Minstrel* in 1805, by another poem, *Marmion,* in 1808, and by a third, *The Lady of the Lake,* in 1810. In 1814 the first of the "Waverley" novels, entitled *Waverley* was

published anonymously: this was followed by *Guy Mannering; The Antiquary; Rob Roy; The Heart of Midlothian; The Bride of Lammermoor* which was the inspiration for Donizetti's opera "Lucia di Lammermoor"; *Ivanhoe; Kenilworth; The Fortunes of Nigel; Peveril of the Peak; Quentin Durward; The Talisman; Redgauntlet* and many other novels of similar character.

Scotti, Antonio (1866-1936), Italian dramatic baritone who studied with Giuseppe Lombardo, making his debut in 1889 at Malta in Verdi's *Aïda:* after singing in Italy, Russia, Spain, England, and South America he made his debut in 1899 at the Metropolitan Opera House, New York, in Mozart's *Don Giovanni.* He remained with the company until 1933: one of his greatest roles was that of Scarpia in Puccini's *Tosca* which he sang with fifteen different sopranos in the role of Tosca during his career at the Metropolitan.

Scottish Academy of Fine Arts (Edinburgh), an institution in Edinburgh, Scotland, the correct title of which is the Royal Scottish Academy of Painting, Sculpture and Architecture. It was founded in 1826. The collection of paintings includes works by Henry RAEBURN, Alexander NASMYTH, Thomas GAINSBOROUGH, Joseph PATON, William ETTY, Edwin LANDSEER: also many works of the modern Scottish school.

Screen, in architecture any construction such as a partition or enclosure lower than the ceiling which separates one part of a room from another: it is usually constructed of decorative openwork, or of stone enriched with ornamental devices of various kinds. The chief screens in a church are those which enclose the CHOIR or CHANCEL.

Scriabin, Alexander Nikolaievitch (1872-1915), Russian pianist and composer who studied with Georg Conus, Vassily SAFONOFF, and Sergei TANEIEV. He toured Europe and the United States, and adopted certain radical principles of harmony in his compositions which comprise orchestral works such as *The Divine Poem; Poem of Ecstasy* and *Poem of Fire (Prometheus):* also concertos, sonatas, études, and pieces for piano.

Scribe, Augustin Eugène (1791-1861), French librettist and dramatist whose first successful play, *Une Nuit de la garde nationale,* written in collaboration, was produced in 1815: from that time until his death he produced almost 400 plays and opera libretti, many of them in collaboration with other writers. Among his successful plays were *Une Chaîne; Le Verre d'eau; Adrienne Lecouvreur; Camaradie; Bertrand et Raton.* His more than one hundred opera libretti include AUBER's *Fra Diavolo;* MEYERBEER's *Les Huguenots; Le Prophète* and *L'Africaine;* BOIELDIEU's *La Dame Blanche;* HALEVY's *La Juive;* VERDI's *Sicilian Vespers.*

Script, in theatre, screen, and radio parlance a contracted form of "manuscript" which denominates the typewritten (or printed) copy of a play. An actor's script contains his speeches and cues: a director's script contains the entire words of the play including all mechanical instructions in respect to scenery, properties, lighting, and sound effects.

Scudder, Horace Elisha (1838-1902), American author who succeeded Thomas Bailey ALDRICH as editor of the *Atlantic Monthly* in 1890. His works include *Seven Little People and Their Friends* and the *Bodley Books,* two series for children: also *Stories from My Attic; The Book of Fables; Childhood in Literature and Art.*

Scudder, Janet (1873-1940), American sculptor and painter trained at the Cincinnati Art School, the Chicago Art Institute, and at the studio of Frederich MACMONNIES in Paris: her notable works include *Frog Fountain; Tortoise Fountain; Seated Faun; Fighting Boy Fountain.* She received many awards and medals: one of her works was purchased for the LUXEMBOURG, Paris.

Scudéry, Madeleine de (1607-1701), French novelist who was called "the new Sappho" in her day: her works, written in collaboration with her brother, **Georges de Scudéry** (1601-1668), include a ten-volume novel, *Artamenes, or the Great Cyrus* (1649-53) a novel in which the authors' contemporaries appear under ancient names; *Clélie* (1654-60), another multi-volume novel of similar character.

Sculpture, the art of reproducing in three dimensions figures and objects in relief, or in the round, out of hard material which can be cut with a chisel. The materials usually used are wood, stone, clay, metals, ivory, rock crystal, bone, wax or precious stones. The earliest sculptures, in the form of carving on the walls of caves or on stones, have been discovered in France and Spain: about 4000 B.C. figures in wood and colossal forms carved out of rock were made in Egypt. Greek sculpture began in the 7th century B.C., and reached its reached its greatest heights, never equaled since, in the 5th century B.C.: the Romans also gave evidence of skill in portraiture and in reliefs for temples depicting scenes from everyday life. Little progress in the art was made in the early Christian era, due probably to the Biblical command against fashioning graven images; more than eleven centuries passed before Giovanni PISANO, Jacopo della QUERCIA, GHIBERTI, and DELLA ROBBIA, developed a hitherto unheard-of degree of imagination and artistry which led up to Michelangelo in the 16th century. From this century on the art of sculpture developed rapidly in France, Germany, Holland, and England: while it declined for a time in Italy because of the advent of BAROQUE, this was overcome in the 18th century by a return to classicism. Native sculptors began working in America at about the beginning of the 19th century, and have now taken their places in the front ranks of distinguished modern artists. This volume contains references covering the important sculptors of all periods and nationalities.

Scylla, in Greek legend a fearsome sea-monster with six heads, twelve feet, and a voice resembling the yelp of a young dog: she lived in a cave overhanging the sea and snatched sailors out of passing ships. In a nearby cave lived *Charybdis* who sucked in and spouted out the water in the sea three times a day. According to HOMER in the *Odyssey,* when Odysseus passed between the two caves six of his men were snatched out of ships.

Seabrooke, Thomas Quigley (1860-1913), American actor who first appeared in 1880 on the stage at Westerly, R. I., in *Cigarette,* a dramatization of OUIDA's novel "Under Two Flags." Among the plays in which he had great success as a comedian were *Ten Nights in a Barroom; Aphrodite; A Tin Soldier; A Paper Doll; Midnight Bell; The Isle of Champagne,* his greatest success; *Tabasco; Yankee Doodle Dandy; Erminie; The Rounders:* he also appeared with Pauline HALL in a vaudeville sketch.

Seal, an engraved or inscribed stamp utilized for making an impression in wax on documents, or on envelopes for the purpose of securely closing them: the word is also used for the figure or inscription formed in the wax. The use of seals was common in ancient China, Egypt, Greece, and Rome, and the popular form was the seal ring with the gem forming the seal.

Seasons, The, ballet in one act: book and choreography by Marius PETIPA; music by Alexander GLAZUNOFF; first produced at Moscow in 1900. The somewhat conventional treatment of the subject is increased in interest by the exquisite music which is available in a Columbia recording by a symphony orchestra directed by the composer.

Seattle Symphony (Seattle), an organization founded in 1906 as the Seattle Symphony Orchestra Society with Michael Kegrize and Henry HADLEY as conductors until 1911 when it was reorganized as the Seattle Philharmonic and conducted by John Spargur until 1921 when it disbanded. In 1921 it was organized as the Seattle Symphony, and has been directed by Karl Kreuger, Basil Cameron, and Nikolai SOKOLOFF.

Sebastiano del Piombo (c.1485-1547), Italian painter whose real name was Sebastiano Luciani: he studied with Giovanni BELLINI and Giorgio GIORGIONE: his notable works include *The Incredulity of St. Thomas; The Raising of Lazarus; Metamorphoses of Ovid; Pietà; Birth of the Virgin; Death of Adonis; Christ on the Cross; Ecce Homo; The Dead Christ; Portrait of a Young Roman Woman.*

Sechter, Simon (1788-1867), Bohemian composer and teacher of harmony and composition who studied with Johann Anton Koželuch, and later became professor at the Vienna Conservatory. His distinguished pupils included HENSELT, BRUCKNER and VIEUXTEMPS: Franz SCHUBERT had planned the study of counterpoint with him just before his death. His compositions include church music, organ works, intricate piano pieces, and a valuable treatise on musical composition.

Sedgwick, Anne Douglas (1873-1935), American novelist who spent most of her life in France and England: her works include *The Dull Miss Archinard* (1898); *The Rescue; Paths of Judg-*

ment; Annabel Channice; Tante; The Little French Girl; The Old Countess; Dark Hester.

Seeger, Alan (1888-1916), American poet educated at Harvard who joined the Foreign Legion during World War I, and was killed in action: his *Collected Poems* (1916) contained his best-known poem, "I Have a Rendezvous with Death."

Segal, Vivienne (1897-), American actress and singer who first appeared as an amateur with the Philadelphia Operatic Society, and made her professional debut in 1915 at New York in *Blue Paradise:* among the plays in which she has appeared are *My Lady's Glove; The Little Whopper; Tangerine; The Yankee Princess; Castles in the Air; The Desert Song; The Three Musketeers; The Chocolate Soldier; Music in the Air; No, No, Nanette; I Married an Angel.* She has also appeared in several films.

Segantini, Giovanni (1858-1899), Italian painter who was a shepherd in the Tirol, and later studied the pictures at the BRERA MUSEUM in Milan: his notable works include *The Choir of Sant' Antonio; The Ship; The Dead Hero; Spring in the Alps; Grief Comforted by Faith; The Angel of Life; The Return to the Old Home; Love at the Spring of Life; Plowing in the Engadine; The Punishment of Luxury.*

Segonzac, André Dunoyer de (1884-), French painter who studied at the ECOLE DES BEAUX-ARTS, Paris, under Luc-Olivier MERSON. His peculiar methods of working met with little appreciation, he continued his studies at the Acadèmie Julian and with GUERIN. He excels as a painter of nudes, still life, and landscapes in oils and water colors.

Segovia, Andrés (1894-), Spanish guitarist who studied at the Granada Musical Institute, and later toured Europe and South America: he made his debut in 1928 at New York, and has given many recitals of classical works arranged for the guitar as well as compositions by modern composers written especially for him. He has also made many recordings.

Seguidilla, 16th century Andalusian dance still popular in Spain: it is danced with accompaniment by guitar and CASTANETS. The most popular dance in the form is the *Seguidella* by Georges BIZET in *Carmen:* Isaac ALBENIZ composed several seguidillas for piano solo.

Segurola, Andrés de (1875-), Spanish dramatic bass who made his debut at Granada, and sang in Paris, Salzburg, and Lisbon before appearing with the Hammerstein Opera Company in 1908, and with the Metropolitan Opera Company in 1909, remaining for ten years. He settled in Hollywood as a teacher of singing and director of musical productions at the Hollywood Bowl and in films.

Seidl, Anton (1850-1898), Hungarian conductor who studied at the Leipzig Conservatory, and made the first copy of the orchestral score of the RING OF THE NIBELUNGS for Richard WAGNER at Bayreuth in 1872. After touring Europe he succeeded Leopold Damrosch in 1885 as conductor of German opera at the Metropolitan Opera House, New York, giving the first complete performance of *The Ring of the Nibelungs* in 1889. He succeeded Theodore THOMAS as conductor of the New York Philharmonic-Symphony Orchestra in 1891, remaining until his death.

Seldes, Gilbert Vivian (1893-), American critic and dramatist educated at Harvard College who acted as music critic for newspapers, foreign correspondent, dramatic critic, columnist, and director of television programs for the Columbia Broadcasting System. His works include *The Seven Lively Arts* (1924); *The Wisecrackers; The Square Emerald; The Wings of the Eagle; The Movies Come from America; The Victory Murders; Mainland.*

Selene, in Greek mythology the goddess of the moon represented as a beautiful young woman with wings and a golden diadem. She was identified with ARTEMIS and with *Luna,* the Roman goddess of the moon.

Selwyn & Co., an American firm of theatrical producers the members of which were Archibald and Edgar Selwyn: between 1914 and 1939 the firm produced many successful plays including *The Salamander; The Eternal Magdalene; Fair and Warmer; The Lie; Smilin' Through; The Circle; Pelléas and Mélisande; Spring Cleaning; Dancing Mothers; The Ghost Train; This Year of Grace; Wake Up and Dream; Bitter Sweet* with Florenz Ziegfeld; *Evensong; Forsaking All Others; Conversation Piece; L'Aiglon; Revenge with Music; The Foreigners; The Wookey.*

Sembrich, Marcella (1858-1935), Polish operatic soprano whose real name was Praxede Marceline Kochanska: she studied the piano and violin making her first appearance in 1869 as a performer on both instruments. Franz LISZT, who heard her sing and play in 1874, urged her to cultivate her voice: she studied with Giovanni Lamperti, and made her debut in 1877 at Athens in BELLINI's *I Puritani.* After singing at Vienna, Dresden, and London she made her debut in 1883 at the Metropolitan Opera House, New York, in DONIZETTI's *Lucia di Lammermoor,* remaining with the company until 1909. She continued to sing in concert until 1917, and also taught at the Curtis Institute of Music, Philadelphia, and at the Juilliard Graduate School, New York. She was one of the greatest coloratura and lyric sopranos with a repertory of about forty roles, and several hundred concert songs.

Semiramis, in Assyrian legend the wife of Ninus, and co-founder with him of the city of Nineveh: she reigned for nearly fifty years after the death of her consort. VOLTAIRE's drama, *Semiramide* was used as the basis of ROSSINI's grand opera with the same title produced at Venice in 1823 and at the Metropolitan Opera House, New York, by Adelina PATTI's Company in 1885. Seventeen operas have been composed with Semiramis as the heroine.

Semitone, in music one of the twelve equal INTERVALS into which the OCTAVE is divided; also known as and identical with a minor second.

Semplice (It.), in music a term indicating that a passage is to be played simply and unaffectedly.

Seneca, Lucius Annaeus (c.4 B.C.-65 A.D.), Roman philosopher and dramatist who was for a time the wise counselor of NERO, but the gradual ascendancy of Poppaea over the half-mad emperor led to his finally being ordered to commit suicide. In addition to his philosophical writings, Seneca wrote several tragedies including *Thyester; Medea; Phaedra* and *The Trojan Women* which had considerable effect upon the development of drama at a later period.

Sepulchre, in its ordinary sense the place where the dead body of a human being is interred: in church architecture an arched recess in which the crucifix and other symbols of Christ's entombment and resurrection are placed from Good Friday to Easter day.

Sequence, in music the repetition more than twice in succession of a melodic phrase; each repetition higher or lower in pitch than the first or preceding phrase: the procedure is interesting musically except when it is used too frequently in any one composition.

Serafin, Tullio (1878-   ), Italian conductor who studied at the Milan Conservatory, making his debut at Ferrara in 1900, and later conducting at Turin, Rome, and at La Scala, Milan. In 1924 he made his debut at the Metropolitan Opera House, New York, in VERDI's *Aïda*, remaining until 1935 when he became artistic director of the Teatro Reale at Rome. Among the premières and revivals he conducted were *La* GIOCONDA; *La Cena delle Beffe; The King's Henchman; Peter Ibbetson; Turandot; Simon Boccanegra; Emperor Jones; Merry Mount.*

Serapis, the name in ancient Greece and Rome for a deity originating in Egypt: he represented the dead APIS, and was lord of the underworld identified with HADES.

Serenade, in music a song of evening; originally applied to a song sung by a lover to his beloved from beneath her window. Two interesting ironical examples are the serenade in MOZART's *Don Giovanni* and Mephistopheles' serenade to Marguerite in GOUNOD's *Faust.* The title was also used in the 18th century for an instrumental work resembling a SUITE, but usually containing more movements. Mozart used the title: also BEETHOVEN, BRAHMS, and Richard STRAUSS.

Serenata, in music a form of dramatic cantata intended for the concert room rather than the stage; written during the 18th century for festive occasions such as royal birthdays and marriages.

Sergel, Johann Tobias (1740-1814), Swedish sculptor who studied for twelve years in Rome, became court sculptor at Stockholm and director of the Academy. His notable works include *Cupid and Psyche; Mars and Venus;* a statue of Gustavus III of Sweden; *Diomedes Stealing the Palladium;* a tomb for Gustavus Vasa.

Serkin, Rudolf (1903-   ), Russian pianist born in Bohemia who studied in Vienna, and made his debut with the Vienna Symphony Orchestra in 1915. He has an established reputation as a chamber music player with Adolf BUSCH in programs of sonatas for violin and piano: he has also appeared with the New York Philharmonic-Symphony Orchestra and many other major American orchestras.

Serlio, Sebastiano (1475-1552), Italian architect who was a contemporary of VIGNOLA, and probably worked at Fontainebleau and on the Louvre for Francis I of France. He was a student of the principles of VITRUVIUS as shown in the ancient buildings of Rome, and wrote several valuable architectural treatises.

Servais, Adrien-François (1807-1866), Belgian violoncellist and composer who studied with Joseph Platel at the Brussels Conservatory, and made his debut as a virtuoso at Paris in 1834: he toured Europe with great success for many years, and became professor at the Brussels Conservatory in 1848. His compositions include concertos, fantasias, and études for his instrument.

Servandonai, Jean Nicholas (1695-1766), French architect, decorator, and scenic painter: his notable works include the decorations for L'Opéra at Paris; a façade for the church of St. Sulpice: he also painted scenes and created effects for fêtes given in honor of French royalty.

Sesshu (c.1419-1506), Japanese painter and Buddhist priest also known as Toyo: he was a pupil of Shubun, and was highly honored in China about 1467 where he decorated a palace for one of the Ming rulers. He employed two brushes in painting; the one was a dry brush for bold strokes, and the other for the ink splashes characteristic of the impressionistic style. His works include wall paintings, six-fold screens, and MAKIMONOS.

Sessions, Roger (1896-   ), American composer educated at Harvard University who studied composition with Horatio W. PARKER and Ernest BLOCH. He has taught musical theory and composition at Smith College and other educational institutions: his works include three symphonies, a violin concerto, a string quartet, a piano sonata, and some songs.

Sestina, in prosody a fixed form invented by Arnaut Daniel, a 12th century Provençal poet: it consists of six six-line stanzas with the six end words repeated in a different order in each stanza; also a three line stanza in which the six words are distributed by placing three in the middle and three at the end of the lines. The form was greatly favored by DANTE and PETRARCH.

Seton, Ernest Thompson (1860-   ), American painter and author of books for boys; born in England, brought to Canada at the age of six, and educated at the Toronto Collegiate Institute and the Royal Academy, London. His works, all illustrated with his own drawings, include *Wild Animals I Have Known* (1898); *The Biography of a Grizzly; Lives of the Hunted; Two Little Savages; Wild Animals at Home; Animal*

Heroes; Biography of a Silver Fox; Great Historic Animals.

Seumas O'Sullivan, see **Starkey, James Sullivan.**

Seurat, Georges (1859-1891), French painter who studied at the ECOLE DES BEAUX-ARTS in Paris, spending much of his time at the LOUVRE and becoming greatly intrigued by the art of Eugène DELACROIX. After much experimenting he exhibited his painting, *Un Dimanche à la Grande Jatte,* the first canvas executed in accordance with the technique of POINTILLISM as practiced by the Neo-Impressionists. Among his works are *Poseuses; La Parade; Le Chahut; Baignade.*

Ševčik, Otakar (1852-1934), Bohemian violinist and teacher who studied with his father and at the Prague Conservatory, and later taught at the Salzburg Mozarteum, the Imperial Russian Music School at Kiev, and at the Prague Conservatory where Jan KUBELIK, Jaroslav KOCIAN, and Efrem ZIMBALIST were his pupils. He also taught in the United States from 1922 to 1931, and published valuable technical exercises for the violin.

Seven Wonders of the World, The, in architecture and sculpture seven works of the ancient world which are known collectively under this title: they comprise (1) *The pyramids of Egypt;* (2) *The Pharos (Lighthouse) of Egypt;* (3) *The Walls and Hanging Gardens of Babylon;* (4) *The Temple of Artemis at Ephesus;* (5) *The statue of the Olympian Zeus at Olympia;* (6) *The mausoleum erected by Artemisia at Halicarnassus;* (7) *The Colossus of Rhodes.*

Sevigné, Marie de Rabutin-Chantal, Marquise de (1626-1695), French lady who achieved fame through her gifts as a letter-writer: from 1669 to 1695 she wrote more than 1,500 letters, addressed chiefly to her daughters, which are regarded not only as models of the familiar epistolary style, but afford a graphic picture of social life in the period.

Sevitzky, Fabian (1893-   ), Russian conductor who studied at the St. Petersburg Conservatory and played the double-bass in an orchestra directed by his uncle, Sergei KOUSSEVITZKY: he came to the United States in 1923, playing with the Philadelphia Orchestra, and founding the Philadelphia Chamber String Sinfonietta which he conducted until 1937 when he became conductor of the Indianapolis Symphony Orchestra.

Sèvres, a town in France midway between Versailles and Paris: it is famous for its production of *Sèvres porcelain* in a factory established in 1756, and purchased by Louis XIV for the State in 1760. The museum connected with the factory contains the entire series of models used there since the beginning, and also specimens of porcelain ware made in all countries and ages.

Seyffertitz, Gustav von, see **Von Seyffertitz, Gustave.**

Shadwell, Thomas (c.1642-1692), English poet and dramatist, famous for a feud with John DRY-DEN which lasted for several years: his plays include *The Sullen Lovers* (1668); *Epsom Wells; The Medal of John Bays* in which he attacked Dryden; *The Libertine; The Virtuoso; A True Widow.*

Shaft, in architecture that part of a column which lies between the BASE and the CAPITAL. Shafts are sometimes smooth-surfaced, but more often decorated by vertical flutings or spirals.

Shakespeare, William (1564-1616), English poet and dramatist born at Stratford-on-Avon: about 1586 he went to London; by 1592 he had acquired some fame as a dramatist, and in 1594 he became a member of the LORD CHAMBERLAIN'S MEN, a troupe of actors which was later called the King's Men. In 1599 he became financially interested in the Globe Theatre, and later in other playhouses so that when he retired in 1610 he was apparently possessed of ample means. The number of plays credited to him is thirty-eight: they include *Henry VI* in three parts; *Love's Labour's Lost; The Comedy of Errors; Two Gentlemen of Verona; The Taming of the Shrew; Richard III; Titus Andronicus; Midsummer Night's Dream; Romeo and Juliet; King John; King Richard II; The Merchant of Venice; Much Ado about Nothing; King Henry IV* in two parts; *King Henry V; Julius Caesar; The Merry Wives of Windsor; As You Like It; Twelfth Night; Hamlet; Troilus and Cressida; All's Well That Ends Well; Measure for Measure; Othello; King Lear; Macbeth; Antony and Cleopatra; Coriolanus; Timon of Athens; Pericles; Cymbeline; The Winter's Tale; The Tempest; King Henry VIII; The Two Noble Kinsmen.* He is universally recognized as the greatest English poet and dramatist.

Shakespeare and Music, that the genius of Shakespeare permitted him to utilize every means of enhancing the beauty and dramatic power of his plays is evidenced by the extensive use of music in the form of fanfares for battle scenes and royal pageants, dances, incidental music, and songs. Thirty-two of his plays contain references to the tuning of instruments, harmony, and the mention of the VIOL, VIRGINAL, LUTE, RECORDER, BAGPIPE, TRUMPET, SACKBUT, PSALTERY, FIFE, DRUM, and CYMBAL. Ballads were introduced into several of the plays: the finest are in *Hamlet* where they are sung by Ophelia in the mad scenes, and much of the original music is still used. Ballads are also used in *A Winter's Tale, King Lear, The Merchant of Venice, Love's Labour's Lost, Romeo and Juliet, King Henry IV,* and *The Merry Wives of Windsor.* Among the famous song lyrics in Shakespeare which have been set by many composers are *Under the Greenwood Tree; Blow, Blow, Thou Winter Wind; Who is Sylvia?; The Poor Soul Sat Sighing by a Sycamore Tree,* and many others.

Shakespeare, William (1849-1931), English tenor, composer, and vocal teacher who studied with Sir William Sterndale BENNETT, Karl Reinecke, and Francesco Lamperti. He became a distinguished concert and oratorio singer, but achieved even greater fame as a vocal teacher at the ROYAL ACADEMY OF MUSIC, London. His works include *The Art of Singing* (1900), and

Plain Words on Singing (1924): also orchestral works, chamber music, and piano pieces.

Shan-Kar, Uday, contemporary Hindu dancer who is the son of one of the secretaries of the Maharajah of Jhalawar, a distinguished patron of the arts. He was taught the playing of Hindu instruments and the intricacies of the native religious and folk dances at the royal court, and at the Royal College of Arts in London he became the protegé of Sir William Rothenstein. After graduating with honors he collaborated with his father in the production of native Hindu plays and ballets in several of London's chief theatres. His success led to Anna PAVLOWA immediately asking for his help in the production of her *"Radha-Krishna"* ballet. He was soon chosen as her leading man, dancing the part of Krishna. In 1928 he was persuaded to rent a theatre and give a recital, the success of which led to appearances in Vienna, Berlin, Budapest and Geneva: he canceled further European engagements, returned to India, and formed his own ballet of Hindu dancers, and his own orchestra of native musicians. In 1931 the company made its debut in New York, and though scheduled for only five performances, remained for twenty-four, and then toured the country. In 1938 Shan-Kar returned to India to found a center of research in Benares, where a syndicate of American and British sponsors have endowed him with a palace to carry on his work, which is the establishment of a dance center where not only technic will be taught, but research made into ancient dances, costumes, jewelry, etc., music recorded and motion pictures made of various Indian dances.

Shannon, Effie (1867-), American actress who made her debut as Eva in *Uncle Tom's Cabin* under the management of John Stetson, later appearing with Oliver Doud BYRON, Laurence BARRETT, and Robert MANTELL: among the famous plays in which she has appeared are *The Marble Heart; Robert Elsmere; Shenandoah; The Charity Ball; Squire Kate; The Guardsman; The District Attorney; Gossip; Camille; The Moth and the Flame; Manon Lescaut; The Walls of Jericho; The Thief; Pollyanna; The Detour; Trelawney of the Wells; The Admirable Crichton; Parnell; Barchester Towers.*

Shannon, James Jebusa (1862-1923), American painter who studied at the South Kensington School, London, where his work was commended by Sir Edward Poynter. A portrait executed of one of Queen Victoria's ladies-in-waiting started him on the road to success, and he later painted the likenesses of many of the English nobility. Among his notable works are *Girl in Brown; Flower Girl; Miss Kitty; Fairy Tales* and *Magnolia.*

Sharaku, Toshusai, 18th century Japanese engraver and color printer who was said to have been first a dancer, and began his artistic career by painting actors. He frequently used a background of silver or mica, and was exceedingly skillful in his use of color: he also favored the MAKIMONO form for his works.

Sharp, in musical notation a sign, ♯, which when placed before a note raises the pitch of that note a SEMITONE: when placed in the SIGNATURE it affects all notes on a corresponding degree of the scale.

Shaw, George Bernard (1856-), Irish dramatist who first acted as a music critic under the pen name "Corno di Bassetto": his career as a dramatist began in 1892 with the production of *Widowers' Houses* at London, followed by *Arms and the Man* at London in 1894. Between 1880 and 1883 he published four novels which were failures from the financial standpoint, but he succeeded in becoming friendly with literary lights including William MORRIS and William ARCHER. His long list of plays includes *The Philanderer; Mrs. Warren's Profession,* banned in England and for a time in the United States; *Candida; The Man of Destiny; You Never Can Tell; The Devil's Disciple; Caesar and Cleopatra; Captain Brassbound's Conversion; Man and Superman; John Bull's Other Island; How He Lied to Her Husband; Major Barbara; The Doctor's Dilemma; Androcles and the Lion; Pygmalion; Saint Joan; The Apple Cart.*

Shaw, Henry Wheeler, see **Billings, Josh.**

Shaw, Irwin (1912-), American dramatist educated for a time at Brooklyn College, Brooklyn, New York: his plays include *Bury the Dead* (1936); *Siege; The Gentle People; Sons and Soldiers:* he has also written two books of short stories and screen plays.

Shawn, Ted (1891-), American dancer and choreographer who studied dancing in order to rebuild his health: in 1914 he joined the company headed by Ruth ST. DENIS, and founded the Denishawn School at Los Angeles in 1915. He toured the United States and Far East with the Denishawn Dancers, and in 1933 formed the troupe known as "Ted Shawn and His Men Dancers" with which he toured until 1940.

Shearer, Norma (1904-), American screen actress who has appeared in both silent and talking films: since 1929 she has been featured in *A Lady of Chance; The Last of Mrs. Cheyney; The Trial of Mary Dugan; Let Us Be Gay; A Free Soul; Private Lives; Smilin' Through; Strange Interlude; Riptide; Romeo and Juliette; Marie Antoinette; Idiot's Delight; The Women; Escape; We Were Dancing; Her Cardboard Lover.*

Shearing, Joseph, see **Long, Gabrielle Margaret.**

Sheeler, Charles (1883-), American painter who studied at the School of Industrial Art in Philadelphia, and at the PENNSYLVANIA ACADEMY OF FINE ARTS under William Merritt CHASE. He also studied the works of PICASSO, MATISSE, BRAQUE, and other French modernists in Paris: his works include studies of still life, interiors, and landscapes in which natural forms are joined by harmonious tints. His paintings are to be seen in the Chicago Art Institute, the Whitney Museum of Modern Art and several other American galleries.

Sheldon, Edward Brewster (1886-), American dramatist educated at Harvard University:

he organized the Harvard Dramatic Club and became its first president. His plays include *Salvation Nell* (1908) with Minnie Maddern FISKE in the title role; *The Nigger; The Boss; The High Road; Romance; Lulu Belle* with Charles MacARTHUR; *Dishonored Lady* with Margaret Ayer BARNES. He also adapted Sem BENELLI's play, *The Jest,* for the American stage.

Shelley, Percy Bysshe (1792-1822), English poet and dramatist educated at Oxford where he published a pamphlet, *The Necessity of Atheism* which led to his expulsion. His notable works include *Queen Mab* (1813); *Alastor; The Revolt of Islam; The Cenci; Prometheus Unbound; Oedipus Tyrannus.* His second wife, **Mary Wollstonecraft Shelley** (1797-1851), published the tale FRANKENSTEIN (1818) which immediately placed her among the most imaginative of English fiction writers; among her other novels are *Valperga; The Last Man; Lodore; Perkin Warbeck; Falkner.*

Shepard, Odell (1884-), American poet and biographer educated at the University of Chicago and at Harvard University: his works include *A Lonely Flute* (1917); *Bliss Carmen; The Lore of the Unicorn; Pedlar's Progress: The Life of Bronson Alcott* which was awarded the Pulitzer Prize for biography in 1938.

Shepherd, Arthur (1880-), American composer who studied at the New England Conservatory of Music, Boston, Mass., with George W. CHADWICK and Percy GOETSCHIUS, later conducting the Salt Lake Symphony Orchestra, teaching at the New England Conservatory, and acting as assistant conductor of the Cleveland Symphony Orchestra from 1920 to 1926, and professor of music at the Western Reserve University since 1927. His compositions include orchestral works, chamber music, choruses, and sonatas for piano.

Sheraton, Thomas (1750-1806), English cabinet maker and designer of furniture who worked at London in the classic style like George HEPPLEWHITE, Robert ADAM, and Thomas CHIPPENDALE. His writings, which are even more important than his actual work, include *The Cabinetmaker and Upholsterer's Drawing Book* (1790); *Designs for Furniture; The Cabinet Dictionary,* and also an unfinished encyclopedia of his art.

Sheridan, Ann, contemporary American screen actress educated at the North Texas State Teachers College: among the films in which she has appeared are *The Notorious Sophie Lang; Mrs. Wiggs of the Cabbage Patch; Wagon Wheels; The Glass Key; The Crusades; Angels with Dirty Faces; Dodge City; They Drive by Night; The Man Who Came to Dinner; Kings Row.*

Sheridan, Richard Brinsley (1751-1816), Irish dramatist whose father and mother were both actors: in 1775 his first comedy, *The Rivals,* proved a great success, and was followed by *The School for Scandal* and *The Critic.* He also wrote the libretto for a comic opera, *The Duenna:* several of his characters such as Mrs. MALAPROP are literary classics. He is said by leading authorities to have raised the "comedy of manners" to its pinnacle.

Sherriff, Robert Cedric (1896-), English dramatist and novelist who served in the British army during World War I, and first wrote plays for amateur theatricals such as *Profit and Loss* and *Mr. Bridie's Finger.* His greatest success, *Journey's End,* was produced in 1929, and later translated and performed in every European language. He has also prepared several screen plays including *The Invisible Man; Four Feathers; Goodbye, Mr. Chips; That Hamilton Woman; This Above All:* his novel, *Fortnight in September,* became a best seller in 1932.

Sherwood, Robert Emmet (1896-), American dramatist educated at Harvard University where his first play, *Barnum Was Right,* was produced by the Hasty Pudding Club: he served in World War I, and later became dramatic critic for newspapers and magazines. His successful plays include *The Road to Rome* (1926); *The Love Nest; Waterloo Bridge; Reunion in Vienna; The Petrified Forest; Tovarich,* adapted from the French; *Idiot's Delight* and *Abe Lincoln in Illinois,* both Pulitzer Prize winners; *There Shall Be No Night* (1941), the royalties for which were given to the Red Cross. He has also prepared the adaptations of his plays for the screen.

Sherwood, William Hall (1854-1911), American pianist and composer who studied with William MASON, and in Europe with Theodor KULLAK, Hans RICHTER and Franz LISZT. He toured extensively in Europe and the United States, also teaching at the New England Conservatory of Music, Boston, Mass., and founding the Sherwood Piano School at Chicago. His compositions are entirely for the piano.

Shigemasa, Kitao (c.1739-1820), Japanese painter and print maker who was a pupil of SHIGENAGA, but was greatly influenced by SHUNSHO: he was also an illustrator and publisher of books such as *The Mirror of the Beauties of the Green Houses* and *Silkworm Culture.* Kano MASANOBU was one of his pupils.

Shigenaga, Nishimura (1697-1756), Japanese painter and print maker who studied with Torii KIYONOBU at the same time as MASANOBU: his works include paintings of actors, birds of prey, and feminine subjects; they exerted a great influence on Suzuki HARUNOBU.

Shilkret, Nathaniel (1895-), American conductor and composer who studied with Pietro Floridia and acted as music director for the Victor Talking Machine Company for sixteen years, making more than 30,000 records. He has conducted 3,500 radio programs, and for some years has been in Hollywood composing, arranging, and conducting the incidental music for films such as *Mary of Scotland, Winterset,* and *Michael Strogoff.*

Shimazaka, Toson (1872-1943), Japanese author whose first volume of poems, *Wakana-shu* appeared in 1897: in the three years following he published four volumes containing a total of 122 poems which went through more than 200 editions up to 1934. His works include *Hakai, the Transgression; Haru, Spring; Imye, the House; Shinsei,* *the New Life; Étranger,* a travel volume about France.

Shirlaw, Walter (1838-1909), American painter born in Scotland who was brought to the United States as a child of two: he first became a bank-note engraver, and after study in Munich acquired a wide reputation as an illustrator, mural painter, and worker in stained glass. His notable paintings include *Sheep Shearing in the Bavarian Mountains; Marble Quarry; Gretchen; Street Scene in Brittany; Jealousy.*

Shirley, James (1596-1666), English dramatist educated at Oxford and Cambridge Universities: his works include about forty dramas and comedies of which *Love Tricks, The Lady of Pleasure, Hyde Park, The Maid's Revenge, The Traitor,* and *The Cardinal* are outstanding: the last-named was characterized by Edmund GOSSE as the last great play of the Elizabethan period.

Shonnard, Eugénie (1886-), American sculptor who studied with Auguste RODIN and Emile-Antoine BOURDELLE, and has been extraordinarily successful in animal sculpture and portraiture: her works include *Rabbit* at the Luxembourg Museum in Paris; *Two Geese; Brittany Geese; His Majesty the Heron.*

Shostakovitch, Dmitri (1906-), Russian composer who studied with Maximilian STEINBERG at the St. Petersburg Conservatory: his compositions include seven symphonies; the operas LADY MACBETH OF MZENSK and *The Nose;* the ballets *The Golden Age* and *The Limpid Stream;* a concerto for piano, trumpet and string orchestra; chamber music; a sonata, *24 Preludes,* and other pieces for piano: he has also composed the music for several Soviet films.

Show boats, a form of theatrical entertainment which flourished on the Mississippi and Ohio Rivers from 1815: the boats ranged from rafts to what were regarded in their day as "floating palaces." All the favorite "stock" plays from *Uncle Tom's Cabin* to *Camille* were presented, the actors doubling or trebling on parts when necessary. In 1926 Edna FERBER wrote a novel entitled **Show Boat:** it was a best seller and a tremendous success as a musical play and a film. The University of Washington built a show boat in 1937 on a barge 140 feet long and 36 feet wide with a revolving stage and excellent scenic equipment: it was used to present plays formerly performed at the University's Penthouse Theatre.

Shrady, Henry Merwin (1871-1922), American sculptor who first studied law, engaged in business, and was self-taught in his art: among his notable works are an equestrian statue of Washington at Brooklyn, N. Y., which won a prize of $50,000; the U. S. Grant Memorial at Washington, D. C., the award for which was $250,000: also equestrian statues of General Lee at Charlottesville, Va., and of William the Silent for the Holland Society of New York.

Shubert Theatre Corporation, an organization owning and operating most of the leading legitimate theatres in New York City and throughout the United States: the principal owners are **Jacob J. Shubert** (1880-), and **Lee Shubert** (1875-). The enterprise started in Syracuse, N. Y., with another brother, **Sam S. Shubert** (1876-1905), managing road companies producing the comedies written by Charles K. HOYT and presenting a stock company at the Bastable Theatre in Syracuse. In 1900 the brothers acquired control of the Herald Square Theatre, New York, and later of the Casino, Princess, and other theatres until most of the legitimate houses in New York and throughout the country are owned or operated by the corporation. The entry into New York was signalized by assuming the management of many leading American stars including E. H. SOTHERN, Julia MARLOWE, Sarah BERNHARDT, Ada REHAN, DeWolfe HOPPER, Alice NIELSEN, Henry MILLER, Margaret ANGLIN, William FAVERSHAM, Louis Mann, Eddie FOY, Julia Sanderson, Bertha Kalich, Bertha Galland, Jefferson DEANGELIS, Frank DANIELS, Grace Van Studdiford, William HODGE, Sam BERNARD, Lew FIELDS, Leo DITRICHSTEIN, Mary MANNERING, James T. POWERS, and others. Later most of the important actors in the theatre came under Shubert management, this being especially true of the musical-comedy field: included in the expansion program was the leasing of the city's largest theatre, the Hippodrome, which they managed for many years, and the erection of the famous Winter Garden, where over the years were seen Al JOLSON, who began his Broadway career there, Eddie CANTOR, Ed WYNN, Nora Bayes, Marie DRESSLER, Fannie BRICE, Irene Bordoni, Jack BENNY, Ray Bolger, Ina CLAIRE, Joe Cook, the Dolly sisters, Trixie Friganza, Willie Howard, Raymond HITCHCOCK, George Jessel, Bert Lahr, Marilyn MILLER, James BARTON, Nancy Carroll, Frank Fay, Charlotte Greenwood, Sydney Greenstreet, Ralph Herz, Stella Mayhew, MISTINGUETTE, Frank Tinney and Charles WINNINGER. Among some of the outstanding productions made by the firm are the series of *Passing Shows; Ziegfeld Follies; The Show Is On; Life Begins At 8:40; A Night In Paris; A Night In Spain; The Student Prince; Blossom Time; Countess Maritza; Floradora; Maytime; Sinbad; Wonder Bar; Bluebird; Death Takes A Holiday; Shadow And Substance; Cynara; The Man In Possession; No More Ladies; Topaze; And So To Bed; Autumn Crocus; Eyes Of Youth; Is Zat So?; As You Desire Me; Just Married; Laburnum Grove; On The Spot; The Purple Mask; The Silent House; The Skin Game; Taps; The Third Party; Thirty-Nine East; Whispering Wires; Big Boy; Belle Of New York; The Blue Paradise; A Chinese Honeymoon; The Witching Hour; As A Man Thinketh;* and *The City.*

Shunsho, Katsugawa (1726-1792), Japanese painter who studied with Shunsu, the founder of the Katsugawa school: he painted in a bold, vigorous style, and had many pupils none of whom equaled him in this respect. He made some remarkable engravings of Segawa Kikunojo, the Japanese actor, and also of fat wrestlers whose bodies he delighted in caricaturing.

Shurtleff, Roswell Morse (1838-1915), American painter educated at Dartmouth College who first worked in an architect's office and later at lithography before enlisting in the Union Army during the Civil War: in 1870 he began to paint animal pictures in oil, and later landscapes in both oil and water-color. Among his notable canvases are *Mountain Stream; American Panther; First Snow; Blue Heron; Autumn Gold; Road to the Mill; Morning in the Forest.*

Sibelius, Jean (1865-   ), Finnish composer who began to compose as a child before having any instruction, and later studied with Martin WEGELIUS, Albert Becker, Robert Fuchs, and Karl GOLDMARK. In 1897 the Finnish government granted him a stipend, later increased, so that he could devote himself to composition. In 1914 he came to the United States to conduct a symphonic poem, *Oceanides*, composed especially for a musical festival at Norwalk, Conn. His numerous works include seven symphonies and other orchestral works such as *Finlandia* and *Valse Triste;* a violin concerto; a sonata and several series of pieces for piano; two string quartets and other chamber music; choruses, and many songs.

Sibyls, the name given by the Greeks and Romans to certain women who prophesied when inspired by some god or goddess. They are not mentioned by HOMER, but Plato mentions one: AENEAS consulted the *Cumaean sibyl,* the lady who when Tarquin, a Roman king, refused to buy nine books of prophecies from her, burned six of them, and finally sold him the remaining three books at the original price for the nine.

Sicilian Vespers, the name by which one of the bloodiest massacres in all history is known; provoked by the oppressive and cruel rule of the French. On March 31, 1282, a riot started in a church near Palermo caused by a French soldier's insults to a Sicilian woman: in the rebellion which followed thousands of French men, women, and children were massacred. VERDI'S opera, *The Sicilian Vespers,* produced at L'Opéra, Paris, in 1855 and at the Academy of Music, New York, in 1859, was based on this massacre.

Siciliana (It.), a dance originating in Sicily among the peasants: it is pastoral in character, written in 6-8 or 12-8 time, and usually minor in key. Bach and Handel made use of the dance in suites and sonatas.

Sickert, Walter Richard (1860-   ), English painter born in Munich, and the son of a Danish painter in the employ of the king of Denmark. His parents moved to London when he was nine years old, and he studied at the Slade School; also with James McNeill WHISTLER. He also imbibed the art of Edgar DEGAS, and his matured style shows the influence not only of Degas, but of MONET and TOULOUSE-LAUTREC. His paintings are to be seen in the British Museum, the TATE GALLERY, and the Luxembourg Museum.

Siddons, Sarah Kemble (1755-1831), English actress who was the eldest of the twelve children of Roger KEMBLE: she first appeared with her father's traveling company, but her performance in Thomas OTWAY'S *Venice Preserv'd* in 1774 excited such enthusiastic comment that David GARRICK engaged her to appear with him at Drury

Lane, London, in 1775. She failed to please London audiences, but after further experience in the provinces she returned to the same theatre in 1782 to achieve one of the greatest triumphs the historic theatre ever witnessed in Garrick's adaptation of *The Fatal Marriage* by Thomas Southerne. She became the idol of London until her retirement in 1812: among her finest characterizations were Lady Macbeth, Queen Katherine, Desdemona and Ophelia. She was also a great beauty whose picture was painted by REYNOLDS, LAWRENCE and GAINSBOROUGH, and she numbered Dr. Samuel JOHNSON and Horace WALPOLE among her friends.

Side Drum, or **Snare drum,** an instrument the fundamental construction of which differs little from that of similar drums made thousands of years ago. The cylinder shell of this drum, the smallest of those employed in the orchestra, may be of metal or wood; the tension of its two heads is regulated by tension rods. Its characteristic quality is produced by the rattling against its lower head of snares (gut strings), usually ten in number, which are stretched across this head. The best drum sticks are made from straight-grained hickory.

Sidney, Margaret, see **Lothrop, Harriet Mulford.**

Sidney, Sir Philip (1554-1586), English soldier, diplomat and author who was engaged in missions throughout Europe during most of his career: his works include *Arcadia* (1590), a romance in prose; APOLOGY FOR POETRY: also a series of sonnets, *Astrophel and Stella.*

Sidney, Sylvia (1910-   ), American stage and screen actress who appeared with a stock company in Denver, Colo., and on the New York stage before entering the films: among the pictures in which she has been featured are *An American Tragedy; The Miracle Man; Madam Butterfly; Jennie Gerhardt; Accent on Youth; Mary Burns, Fugitive; The Trail of the Lonesome Pine; Dead End; The Wagons Roll at Night.*

Siegfried, see **Ring of the Nibelungs, The.**

Siegfried Idyll (Wagner), a symphonic movement composed in 1870 by Richard WAGNER in commemoration of the birth of his son, Siegfried, in 1869. It was first performed on the morning of Christmas Day, 1870, the birthday of Cosima WAGNER, on the stairs of the Wagner villa at Triebschen: Wagner conducted from the head of the stairs, and Hans RICHTER played the trumpet. Several of the themes were from *Siegfried,* the music drama on which the composer was working at the time. There is a wide choice of Columbia and Victor recordings directed by Toscanini, Walter, Muck and Stokowski.

Siegfried's Rhine Journey, in Wagner's music drama, *The Dusk of the Gods* (Götterdämmerung), the music which follows the parting of Siegfried from Brünnhilde as he sets out in search of new adventures. Brünnhilde, standing on a cliff, watches Siegfried descend into the valley, and hears the sound of his horn in the distance.

There is a wide choice of Victor and Columbia recordings directed by Arturo Toscanini, Bruno Walter, Karl Muck and Leopold Stokowski.

Siena, Guido da, see **Guido da Siena.**

Siena Cathedral (Italy), one of the greatest cathedrals in the world; begun in the first part of the 13th century, and never entirely completed. It was constructed of black and white marble, and its greatest art treasure is the octagonal pulpit, executed by Niccolò PISANO, which rests on columns supported by lions, and is elaborately sculptured.

Sienkiewicz, Henryk (1846-1916), Polish novelist educated at Warsaw University who visited the United States in 1876. His most famous novel is *Quo Vadis?* published in English in 1896: dramatized versions were produced in England, the United States, France, and Germany. He also wrote a trilogy describing 17th-century society in Poland during the struggles with the Russians, Turks, and Swedes.

Sigalon, Xavier (1788-1837), French painter who studied with GUERIN, but gained more by self study of the masters' works at the LOUVRE: his works include *The Young Courtesan; Locusta and Narcissus Experimenting with Poisons; Athaliah's Massacre; Vision of St. Jerome; Crucifixion:* he also copied the *Last Judgment* in the SISTINE CHAPEL for a hall in the Palace of Fine Arts at Paris.

Signac, Paul (1863-1935), French painter who studied at the Académie Libre de Bing with Alexandre GUILLEMIN who instructed him along impressionistic lines with the result that he developed a preference for the art of Van GOGH, GAUGUIN and CEZANNE. His paintings are dominated by a fine perception of the laws of contrast: they combine the IMPRESSIONISM of MONET with the POINTELLISM of SEURAT which Signac carries further by applying his pigments in such a manner that the effect is that of a mosaic, especially in his Parisian street scenes.

Signature, in musical NOTATION the signs placed at the head of the STAFF at the beginning of a composition: the number of SHARP or FLAT signs indicate the KEY, the CLEF the position of the notes on the five lines of the staff, and the numerals, such as 2-4, 4-4, etc., the time or rhythmical signature.

Signorelli, Luca (1441-1523), Italian painter whose full name was Luca d'Egidio di Ventura: he studied with Piero de FRANCESCHI at the same time as MELOZZO DA FORLI, and later executed many excellent frescoes and murals including *Pomp and Fall of the Antichrist; Eternal Destiny of Man; School of Pan; Paradise; The Elect and the Condemned; Madonna and Child; Massacre of the Innocents; Baptism of Christ; Coronation of the Virgin.*

Silanion, Greek sculptor of the 4th century B.C.: he was a contemporary of PRAXITELES, and executed a bronze statue of Plato which Mithridates consecrated to the MUSES at Athens. A

portrait of Sappho is also mentioned by some writers, but it must have been an idealistic head because the famous poetess lived before the age of portraiture.

Silbermann, Gottfried (1683-1753), German manufacturer of organs who began to make pianos in Germany at practically the same time as Bartolommeo CRISTOFARI in Italy: FREDERICK THE GREAT and Wolfgang Amadeus MOZART were both admirers of his instruments.

Silenus, in Greek mythology a god of woods and springs who was the son of HERMES or PAN: he was represented as an old man who could prophesy, but like PROTEUS had to be forced to do so. He was pictured riding on an ass supported by satyrs.

Silhouette, a term applied (*1*) to drawings or portraits which are masses of black upon a light ground, only their outlines being shown: (*2*) to shadow profiles projected by light on a reflecting surface. The name is derived from that of **Etienne de Silhouette** (1709-1767), a French minister of finance who exacted such heavy taxes on the estates of nobles that the word *silhouette* became the synonym for a figure reduced to its simplest form.

Siloti, Alexander (1863-), Russian pianist who studied with Nicholas RUBINSTEIN, Peter TSCHAIKOWSKY, and Franz LISZT, making his debut in 1880: he toured Europe and the United States for many years, and in 1925 began teaching at the JUILLIARD Graduate School, New York. He has published special editions of piano pieces which he played for years on his programs.

Silvanus, in Roman mythology a god of woodlands and cultivated fields who protected settlers on lands heretofore unreclaimed: he was one of the most revered of the gods, and is represented carrying a young tree in one hand and a pruning fork in the other.

Simenon, Georges (1903-), Franco-Belgian author of mystery stories, real name Georges Sim, who wrote his first novel, *Aboard the Ark* at seventeen, and published two hundred popular novels before he was thirty. In 1930 he began writing detective stories featuring "Inspector Maigret": many of these have been translated including *The Crime of Inspector Maigret; Introducing Inspector Maigret; Maigret Sits It Out,* and several others.

Simmons, Edward Emerson (1852-1931), American painter educated at Harvard University, and trained in Paris under Gustave BOULANGER and Jules LEFEBVRE: among his notable works are murals for the Criminal Court Building, New York; the Library of Congress, Washington, D. C.; the Capitol at St. Paul, Minnesota, and the old Waldorf-Astoria Hotel, New York; some of the last-named were removed to the new building.

Simmons, Franklin (1839-1913), American sculptor who was chiefly self-taught: in 1865-66 he had Admirals Farragut and Walker, also Generals Sheridan, Sherman, Grant, Meade, and

Hooker as his sitters. He executed nearly a hundred portrait busts in marble; also fifteen public monuments, a memorial to Henry Wadsworth LONGFELLOW, and many idealistic figures such as *Penelope, Medusa, Galatea,* and *Mother of Moses.* He maintained a study in Rome, and was decorated three times by the King of Italy.

Simms, William Gilmore (1806-1870), American poet and novelist whose historical novels of his own state, South Carolina, rank with those of James Fenimore COOPER: among his notable works are *Martin Faber; Guy Rivers; The Yemassee; The Wigwam and the Cabin; Atlantis: A Tale of the Sea,* a long epic poem.

Simon, Simone (1914-), French stage and screen actress: among the films in which she has appeared are *Girls' Dormitory; Seventh Heaven; Ladies in Love; Love and Hisses; Josette; Dark Eyes; The Human Beast; All That Money Can Buy.*

Simone, Andrea di Bartolommeo, see **Castagno, Andrea del.**

Simone da Pesaro, see **Cantarini, Simone.**

Simonides of Ceos (556-468 B.C.), Greek poet who was at the zenith of his fame during the wars between Athens and Persia: his works celebrated the feats of the heroes. Only fragments of his elegies, dirges, hymns, and paeans have been discovered but many of his epigrams have been preserved: the Greek poet BACCHYLIDES was his nephew.

Simonov, Konstantin, contemporary Russian author, war correspondent, and dramatist whose play, *The Russian People,* was produced in a version prepared by Clifford ODETS at New York, in 1942. It is the story of Soviet men and women at war, and was well received by the critics of Metropolitan newspapers.

Simonson, Lee (1888-), American artist and scenic designer educated at Harvard University: after designing scenery for the Washington Square Players from 1912 to 1916 he served in World War I. Among the sets he has designed are those for *Heartbreak House; Mr. Pim Passes By; Liliom; He Who Gets Slapped; Peer Gynt; The Adding Machine; Marco Millions; The Apple Cart; Roar China; Elizabeth the Queen; Idiot's Delight; The Good Earth; Amphitryon 38.* He is also the author of *The Stage is Set,* a book on theatre design.

Sinclair, Upton Beall (1878-), American novelist educated at the College of the City of New York and at Columbia University: his notable works include *The Jungle* (1906), an exposé of the conditions in the Chicago stockyards; *The Brass Check; The Goose-Step; Oil!; Boston; Roman Holiday; World's End; Between Two Worlds; Dragon's Teeth; Wide Is the Gate.* His works are also widely read in Europe: there are said to be nearly 800 translations in 47 languages and 39 countries.

Sinding, Christian (1856-1941), Norwegian violinist, pianist, and composer who studied with Karl Reinecke, Henry SCHRADIECK, and Salomon JADASSOHN at the Leipzig Conservatory, and settled in Christiania as a teacher ahd composer. In 1890 a grant from the Norwegian government allowed him to devote his life to compositions. His compositions include an opera; orchestra works; concertos for violin; chamber music; piano pieces; suites, and solo pieces for violin, and many songs. In 1921-22 he taught composition at the Eastman School of Music, Rochester, N. Y.: his brothers, Stephan SINDING and Otto SINDING were both famous artists.

Sinding, Stephan (1846-1922), Norwegian painter who belonged to the school of symbolists in sculpture: he utilized many subjects from Norse mythology, and executed monuments to Henrik IBSEN, Björnstjerne BJORNSON, and Ole BULL. His brother, Christian SINDING, was a famous composer: another brother, **Otto Sinding** (1842-1911), was a well-known landscape and genre painter.

Sinfonia Domestica (Strauss), an orchestral tone poem by Richard STRAUSS the title of which translated means "Domestic Symphony": in 1902 Strauss announced that his next tone poem would illustrate a day in the family life and on Mar. 21, 1904, the première of the *Domestic Symphony,* "dedicated to my dear wife and our boy," was conducted by the composer at the third concert of the Richard Strauss Festival in Carnegie Hall, New York. Strauss conducted the first European hearing later in the year at Frankfort-on-the-Main. The poem is one continuous movement roughly divided into (1) *The theme of the parents and the child;* (2) *The child at play followed by a cradle song;* (3) *Doing and thinking;* (4) *Finale, double fugue on parent and child themes.* There is a Victor recording by the Philadelphia Orchestra directed by Eugene Ormandy.

Singer, Israel Joshua (1893-), Polish-American Yiddish novelist and dramatist whose stories became known in the United States through the *Jewish Daily Forward:* his works available in English include *The Sinners; The Brothers Ashkenazi; The River Breaks Up,* a volume of short stories; *East of Eden.* After he came to the United States, of which he is now a naturalized citizen, several of his plays were produced at Yiddish theatres in New York.

Singleton, Esther (?-1930), American author and editor for some years of the *Antiquarian;* she published many books on old furniture, historic buildings, famous portraits, great cathedrals, celebrated picture galleries, and numerous works on musical subjects including *A Guide to the Opera* (1899); *A Guide to Modern Opera; The Orchestra and Its Instruments.* She also translated Albert LAVIGNAC's *Musical Education.*

Singmaster, Elsie (1879-), American novelist educated at Cornell and Radcliffe Universities: her novels for adults include *Kitty Gaumer* (1915); *The Hidden Road; What Everybody Wanted; The Magic Mirror; A High Wind Rising.* She has also written *When Sarah Saved the Day* and other stories for young people.

Singspiel, the form of opera established by the German composer, Johann Adam Hiller, during the second half of the 18th century: it differed from the Italian form in its substitution of spoken dialogue for vocalized RECITATIVE. Josef HAYDN, Wolfgang Amadeus MOZART, and Carl Maria von WEBER cultivated it, and the modern operetta is its direct successor.

Sinibaldi, Guittoncino de, see **Cino da Pistoia.**

Sirens, The, in Greek mythology nymphs of the sea who, like the LORELEI in German legend, lured sailors to their death with sweet song. In HOMER's *Odyssey,* the hero Odysseus was warned against them by CIRCE: he saved his men by filling their ears with wax, and tying himself to the mast of his ship until he was out of hearing.

Sisley, Alfred (1840-1899), French landscape painter born in France of English parents: he studied with Charles Gleyre, was influenced by MONET and RENOIR, and had little success during his lifetime, but after his death his works brought large sums from collectors. Among his notable canvases are *The Seine at Port-Marly; River Bank; Flood; Loing Canal; Effect of Snow.*

Sistine Chapel, the private chapel of the popes of Rome, and one of the most artistic religious buildings in the VATICAN: it was built in 1473 during the pontificate of Sixtus IV; hence its name. The decorations are by PERUGINO, PINTURICCHIO, BOTTICELLI, GHIRLANDAIO, and several other 15th-century artists: it also has Michelangelo's *Last Judgment* to ornament the end walls. The **Sistine Choir** is a body of thirty-two choral chaplains who sing at the services officiated over by the pope: it was preceded in the 4th century by a school for choristers *(Schola Cantorum)* founded by Pope Sylvester. The Sistine Choir has maintained the traditions of the polyphonic style of singing perfected by PALESTRINA in the 16th century.

Sitgreaves, Beverly (1867-1943), American actress who made her debut in 1887 at the Union Square Theatre, New York, in *A Commercial Tourist's Bride:* among the plays in which she appeared were *As In a Looking Glass; Gossip; Ben Hur; Maggie Pepper; The Salamander; A Celebrated Case; The Great Lover; Arms and the Man; Fiesta; The Laughing Woman.* She was well-known as a dramatic coach: Jeanne EAGELS was one of her pupils.

Sitt, Hans (1850-1922), Bohemian violinist and composer who studied at the Prague Conservatory, founded a series of popular concerts at Leipzig, and became teacher of violin at the Conservatory there as well as violist of the Adolf Brodsky Quartet. His compositions include concertos for violin, viola, and violoncello; chamber music; solo pieces, and studies for the violin.

Sitwell, Edith (1887-), English poet and critic educated privately: her works include *The Mother and Other Poems* (1915); *Clown's Houses; Bucolic Comedies; Rustic Elegies; Gold Coast Cus-*

toms. Her brother, **Osbert Sitwell** (1892-), is also a poet and novelist who wrote *Twentieth Century Harlequinade* in collaboration with his sister, and the original novels *The Man Who Lost Himself* and *The Miracle on Sinai.* His brother, **Sacheverell Sitwell** (1897-), is a poet and art critic: his works include several treatises on BAROQUE art; a trilogy, *The Gothic North* dealing with medieval life; *The Romantic Ballet in Lithographs of the Time* with Cyril W. BEAUMONT: also studies of MOZART and LISZT.

Six, Les, the name attached to a group of six young French composers who came into prominence after World War I: it included Darius MILHAUD, Louis Durey, Georges Auric, Arthur HONEGGER, Francis POULENC, and Germaine Tailleferre. As composers they were out of sympathy with César FRANCK, Claude DEBUSSY, and Vincent D'INDY, making much ado over jazz and music-hall music, but the movement did not result in any concrete benefit to French music.

Sketch, *(1)* in drama a short stage piece, usually in a single scene, and used in revues, musical comedies or vaudeville: *(2)* in literature a short composition on the order of the essay or short story, but of less formal nature: *(3)* in music a tentative or preliminary draft of a composition: *(4)* in architecture, painting, and sculpture the representation of a person, object or scene which outlines only the principal characteristics.

Skinner, Cornelia Otis (1902-), American actress and DISEUSE who studied for the stage in Paris, and made her debut in 1921 at Buffalo, N. Y., in *Blood and Sand* with her father, Otis SKINNER. After appearing in several plays up to 1925, she devoted herself to the performance of character sketches in both the United States and England. She has also written a play, *Captain Fury,* and several books including *Excuse It, Please; Dithers and Jitters; Our Hearts Were Young and Gay* the last-named with Emily Kimbrough.

Skinner, Otis (1858-1942), American actor who first appeared in 1877 at the Philadelphia Museum in *Woodleigh,* and on the New York stage in 1879 at Niblo's Gardens in *The Enchantment.* He played with Edwin BOOTH, Lawrence BARRETT, and with the Augustin DALY Company from 1884 to 1888: among the successful plays in which he was starred were *Kismet; The Honor of the Family; Cock o' the Walk; Mister Antonio; Blood and Sand.* He was the author of *Footlights and Spotlights; Mad Folk of the Theatre; One Man in His Time; The Last Tragedian.*

Skipworth, Alison (1863-), English stage and screen actress who made her debut in 1894 at Augustin Daly's Theatre, London, in *A Gaiety Girl,* and her New York debut in 1895 in *An Artist's Model:* among the plays in which she appeared are *The Circus Girl; The Way of the World; The Prisoner of Zenda; The Crisis; 39 East; The Grand Duchess and the Waiter; The Torch Bearers; Mrs. Dane's Defense.* She entered the silent films in 1915, and appeared in innumerable pictures.

Skit, in drama a short sketch of humorous or satirical character which is frequently outwardly serious: the term is sometimes applied to either a book or a play as a whole.

Skyscrapers, a ballet of modern American life by John Alden CARPENTER: first produced in 1925 by the DIAGHILEFF Ballet at Monte Carlo, and at the Metropolitan Opera House, New York, in 1926. According to the composer "The action of the ballet is merely a series of moving decorations reflecting some of the obvious external figures of American life." The scenes depict a skyscraper and a Coney Island type of amusement resort, picturing alternate periods of work and play. There is a Victor recording of the music by a symphony orchestra directed by Nathaniel SHIL-KRET.

Slavenska, Mia (1917-), Jugoslavian ballerina who appeared as a professional dancer at five, gave her first recital at twelve, appeared at Zagreb and other cities in Europe, and finally joined the Ballet Russe de Monte Carlo. In 1940 she played the part of the ballerina in the film *Florian.*

Slavonic Dances (Dvořák), a series of characteristic dances composed by Antonin DVORAK in 1879 at the suggestion of his publisher, Fritz August Simrock, who had already issued the HUNGARIAN DANCES of Johannes BRAHMS in 1869. They were first published for piano duet, and later Dvořák arranged them for orchestra. All sixteen dances have been recorded: the complete list can be found in *The Gramophone Shop Encyclopedia of Recorded Music.*

Sleeping Princess, The, ballet in five scenes: book by Marius Petipa; music by Peter Tschaikowsky; first produced at St. Petersburg in 1890, and revived at the Alhambra Theatre, London, in 1921. The original production was not received with much enthusiasm by the court or the Czar, greatly to Tschaikowsky's chagrin, but it has became one of the standard works in the modern repertory: there is a Victor recording by the Sadler's Wells Orchestra, and a Columbia recording of the *Divertissement* made under the supervision of Serge LIFAR.

Slezak, Leo (1873-), German dramatic tenor who became a member of the Brünn Opera chorus at sixteen, and made his debut there in 1895 as Lohengrin: he also sang at Berlin and at the Hofoper in Vienna from 1901 to 1926. After perfecting himself in French and Italian operas, he made his debut in 1909 at the Metropolitan Opera House in Verdi's *Otello,* remaining for three years. He has also achieved signal success as a film actor in humorous roles. His son, **Walter Slezak** (1902-), is a successful actor who has appeared in many plays in the United States.

Slide, a movable U-shaped tube in the TROMBONE which produces tones by moving in and out: another form of the instrument employs valves similar to those used on the TRUMPET, but the quality of the tone produced is much less pleasing.

Sloan, John (1871-), American painter and engraver trained at the Pennsylvania Academy of Fine Arts who first worked as an illustrator for Philadelphia newspapers, and later for national magazines. From 1914 to 1928 he taught at the Art Students' League, New York: his works include scenes on the roof-tops of New York, New Mexican Indian festivals and portraits to be seen in the Detroit Institute of Arts and other American art galleries.

Sloane, Alfred Baldwin (1872-1924), American composer of operettas and musical comedies: his most popular works include *Jack and the Beanstalk; Excelsior Jr.; Sergeant Kitty; The Mocking Bird; Lady Teazle,* an operetta founded on SHERIDAN's "School for Scandal" in which Lillian RUSSELL appeared; *The Gingerbread Man:* he also wrote the music for several of Charles K. HOYT's farces.

Slonimsky, Nicolas (1894-), American writer on music born in Russia and educated at the St. Petersburg Conservatory who came to the United States in 1923, taught at the Eastman School of Music, founded a chamber orchestra in Boston, and wrote a survey of music entitled *Music Since 1900* (1937).

Slur, in music notation a slightly curved line placed either over or under two or more notes to indicate that such notes are to be played LEGATO. When used on violin or other stringed instrument music the slur indicates that the notes are to be played with a single stroke of the bow; in vocal music with one breath and on one syllable.

Smallens, Alexander (1889-), American conductor born in Russia who was brought to the United States as a child: he was educated at the College of the City of New York, and studied music at the Institute of Musical Art, New York, and at the Paris Conservatory of Music. He was assistant conductor of the Boston Opera Company, conductor for Anna Pavlowa, and conductor of the Chicago Opera Company, Philadelphia Civic Opera, Philadelphia Orchestra, Robin Hood Dell Concerts, Lewisohn Stadium Concerts, and the Ballet Theatre. He also directed the successful revival of George Gershwin's folk opera, *Porgy and Bess,* in 1942.

Smetana, Friedrich (1824-1884), Bohemian pianist, conductor, and composer who studied with Franz LISZT and later founded a very successful piano school: he also directed the Philharmonic Orchestra in Gothenburg, Sweden, and the Bohemian Opera at Prague. His notable compositions include *The Bartered Bride* and several other operas; *The Moldau* and nine other symphonic poems; chamber music and part songs. Antonin DVORAK and Smetana are regarded as the two greatest Bohemian composers of the 19th century.

Smibert, John (1688-1751), American painter born in Scotland whose name is also spelled *Smybert:* he studied at the same time as William HOGARTH with Sir James THORNHILL, and settled in Boston where he painted portraits of Peter Faneuil, Governor John Endicott and other notable people. His son, **Nathaniel Smibert** (1734-

1756), was also a portrait painter who, according to competent authorities, would have accomplished great things if he had not died so prematurely.

Smith, C. Aubrey (1863-), English stage and screen actor who first appeared with a stock company in 1892, and made his debut in 1895 on the London stage in *The Notorious Mrs. Ebbsmith:* among the plays in which he has appeared are *The Prisoner of Zenda; The Degenerates; The Light That Failed; Lady Windermere's Fan; The House of Bondage; Above Suspicion; The Liars; A Bill of Divorcement; The Constant Wife.* He entered the films in 1915, and has appeared in innumerable pictures.

Smith, Chard Powers (1894-), American poet and novelist educated at Harvard, Columbia, and Oxford Universities: his works include *Along the Wind* (1925); *Lost Address; Hamilton: A Poetic Drama; The Quest of Pan; Pattern and Variety in Poetry; Annals of the Poets; Artillery of Time; Ladies' Day.*

Smith, David Stanley (1877-), American composer who studied with Horatio W. PARKER, Ludwig Thuille, and Charles WIDOR, later becoming professor of music and from 1920 Dean of the School of Music at Yale University: his compositions include 4 symphonies, chamber music, choruses, and songs.

Smith, Dodie (1896-), English dramatist and actress trained at the Royal Academy of Dramatic Art who appeared in various stage productions from 1915 to 1926. In 1931 her first play, *Autumn Crocus,* was produced at London with great success: it was followed by *Service; Touch Wood; Call It a Day; Bonnet Over the Windmill; Dear Octopus.* She has prepared the film versions of several of her plays.

Smith, Francis Hopkinson (1838-1915), American author and artist who wrote short stories, essays on art and travel books: his works include *Colonel Carter of Cartersville* (1891), a best seller in its day, and also *A White Umbrella in Mexico; Gondola Days; Caleb West, Master Diver; The Tides of Barnegat; The Armchair at the Inn; The Fortunes of Oliver Horn; Felix O'Day.*

Smith, Harry Bache (1860-1936), American opera and operetta librettist who prepared the librettos for more than three hundred productions: among them are *Robin Hood; The Fortune Teller; The Serenade; The Wizard of the Nile; The Idol's Eye; Foxy Quiller; The Parisian Model; Dolly Dollars; Little Nemo; The Rounders; The Belle of Mayfair; The Strollers; The Spring Maid; The Girl from Utah; The Love Song.* He was closely associated with Reginàld DE KOVEN and Victor HERBERT.

Smith, Jessie Willcox (?-1935), American illustrator and painter of children who studied at the Pennsylvania Academy of Fine Arts and with Howard PYLE: she executed the illustrations for Louisa May ALCOTT's *Little Women;* Clement Clarke MOORE's *'Twas the Night Before Christmas;* Charles Kingsley's *The Water Babies;*

Robert Louis Stevenson's *Child's Garden of Verse:* she also made many illustrations for *St. Nicholas; Scribner's Magazine; Century Magazine,* and other national periodicals.

Smith, Kate (1909-), American actress and radio singer who first sang at church and school concerts: in 1926 she appeared in a musical comedy, *Honeymoon Lane,* and later in *Hit the Deck* and *Flying High.* In 1931 she began singing on the radio, introducing the song, *When the Moon Comes Over the Mountain;* she has since popularized Irving BERLIN's *God Bless America,* and has been directly responsible for the sale of Government bonds to the amount of many millions of dollars since the beginning of World War II.

Smith, Logan Pearsall (1865-), American essayist educated at Haverford, Harvard and Oxford Universities: his works include *The Youth of Parnassus; Trivia; More Trivia; On Reading Shakespeare; Milton and His Modern Critics.*

Smith, Thorne (1892-1934), American novelist and humorist educated at Dartmouth College who served in World War I: his works include *Biltmore Oswald* (1918); *Topper; Dream's End; The Stray Lamb; The Night Life of the Gods; Turnabout; Topper Takes a Trip; The Bishop's Jaegers; Rain in the Doorway; The Glorious Pool.* His stories of "Topper" were successfully adapted for the films.

Smithson, Henrietta Constance (1800-1854), Irish actress who achieved little success in England, but aroused great enthusiasm at Paris in 1828 when she appeared with William MACREADY as Desdemona and Juliet. She was madly courted by Hector BERLIOZ whom she married in 1833, and from whom she separated in 1840 after seven years of unhappiness.

Smithsonian Institution (Washington), a national institution at Washington, D. C., established by statute in 1846 under the terms of the will of James Smithson, an Englishman, who bequeathed his entire fortune to found an institution for "the increase and diffusion of knowledge among men." One of its various divisions is the *National Collection of Fine Arts* which contains many important art works acquired during the first fifty years of existence: they include etchings, engravings, and paintings by European masters; nearly two hundred paintings by American artists; glassware: also the *Freer Gallery of Art* comprising rich assemblies of Chinese and Japanese art, and works by WHISTLER, THAYER, DEWING, Winslow HOMER and TRYON.

Smollett, George (1721-1771), Scotch novelist who settled at London as a surgeon: his notable works include *The Adventures of Roderick Random* (1748); *The Adventures of Peregrine Pickle; The Adventures of Ferdinand, Count Fathom; The Adventures of Sir Launcelot Greaves; The Expedition of Humphrey Clinker.*

Smyth, Dame Ethel (1858-), English composer who studied at the Leipzig Conservatory: her compositions include several operas, two symphonies, chamber music, and songs. She has also written several books including *Impressions That Remained; Streaks of Life; As Time Went On* which are largely autobiographical.

Snare Drum, see **Side Drum.**

Snayers, Pieter (1592-1667), Flemish painter who made a specialty of battle and camp scenes, and became court painter at Brussels. His notable works include *Siege of Courtrai; Battle of Prague; Battle Field of Pavia; Battle between Spaniards and Hollanders; Nocturnal Attack on Lille; Robbers Attacked by Armed Men.*

Snegourotchka, see **Snow Maiden, The**

Snorri Sturleson, see **Edda.**

Snow Maiden, The, grand opera in a prologue and four acts: libretto by Alexander OSTROVSKY based on a Russian fairy tale; music by Nicholas RIMSKY-KORSAKOW; first produced at St. Petersburg in 1882, and at the Metropolitan Opera House, New York, in 1922. The only part of the opera which is popular at the present time is the *Dance of the Tumblers* which is heard on radio programs and played by the London Symphony Orchestra on a Victor recording.

Snyders, Frans (1579-1657), Flemish painter who studied with BREUGHEL, and was friendly with both VAN DYK and RUBENS: he finally became the rival of Jan FYT as an animal painter. His notable canvases include *Stag Hunt; Bear Hunt; Tiger Hunt; Two Lions Pursuing a Roebuck; Hippopotamus Hunt; Birds Singing; Monkeys Playing.*

Soane, John (1753-1837), English architect who studied in Italy and succeeded Sir Robert Taylor as architect for the Bank of England: he also collaborated in the designs for St. James Palace, the Houses of Parliament and the Dulwich Picture Gallery; his former private residence is now the Soane Museum.

Sobel, Bernard (1890-), American author and dramatic critic educated at Purdue University, Chicago University, and the University of Wisconsin. He lectured on drama at Purdue and Chicago Universities; became dramatic critic of the New York *Mirror,* and contributed weekly articles to the New York *Herald-Tribune:* his works include a history of burlesque and a *Theatre Handbook* (1940).

Sodero, Cesare (1886-), Italian conductor and composer who studied at the Naples Conservatory and later conducted the Aborn English Grand Opera Company: he has also conducted for the National Broadcasting Company, the Mendelssohn Glee Club, the San Carlo Opera Company, the Philadelphia Grand Opera Company and the Metropolitan Opera Company in 1942-43.

Sodoma, Il (1477-1549), Italian painter whose real name was Giovanni Antonio Bazzi: he may have been a disciple of LEONARDO DA VINCI. His most notable works include *Nativity; De-*

scent *from the Cross; Miracle of the Loaves; St. Benedict Among the Monks; Christ Bearing the Cross; Vulcan at His Forge; Marriage of Alexander and Roxana; Last Supper; Christ in the Garden of Olives; Adoration of the Magi.*

Sokoloff, Nikolai (1886-), Russian conductor who came to America as a child and studied with Charles Martin LOEFFLER and at the Yale University School of Music. He has conducted the San Francisco Symphony Orchestra, the Cleveland Symphony Orchestra, the Federal Music Project, and the Seattle Symphony Orchestra.

Sokolova, Lydia (1896-), English ballerina who received her first training with Anna PAVLOWA and Michael MORDKIN: she toured the United States with Mordkin, and joined the DIAGHILEFF Ballet in 1912 remaining with the Company until 1929. Among the ballets in which she achieved success are *La Sacre du Printemps; The Sleeping Princess; The Three-Cornered Hat; The Good-Humored Ladies; Carnaval.*

Solario or **Solari, Andrea da** (c.1458-c.1530), Italian painter who was influenced by LEONARDO DA VINCI, and came nearer than any other of his disciples in approaching his style: his works include *Christ Carrying His Cross; Ecce Homo; Holy Family; Madonna with St. John.* His brother, **Cristofaro Solario** (c.1460-c.1525), was a distinguished sculptor and architect who executed the tomb of Beatrice d'ESTE, parts of which are now in the Certosa at Pavia.

Solfeggio (It.), in music a vocal exercise sung either on one vowel, or to the syllables of SOL-MISATION.

Solmisation, in music a system of vocal instruction designating the degrees of the scale by the use of syllables: Guido d'Arezzo, an 11th century monk and musicologist is credited with its invention which employs the syllables *do, re, mi, fa, sol, la, si.*

Solo, in music a composition (or part of a composition) executed by one performer without accompaniment: the meaning has been extended to include any composition, either vocal or instrumental, played by a solo instrument accompanied either by another instrument or an orchestra.

Sologub, Feodor (1863-1927), Russian novelist and dramatist: his real name was Feodor Kuzmich Teternikov, and he was educated and later taught at the Teachers' Institute, St. Petersburg. His best novel, *The Demon,* was published in 1907, and his works occupy twenty large volumes: those available in English include *The Demon; The Sweet-Scented Name and Other Tales; The Old House and Other Tales; The Created Legend.*

Somis, Giovanni Battista (1686-1763), Italian violinist and composer who was leader of the court orchestra at Turin, played at the Concerts Spirituels in Paris, and founded a school at which Jean-Marie LECLAIR and Gaetano PUGNANI were pupils: his compositions include sonatas and concertos for violin.

Somnus, see **Hypnos.**

Sonata (It.), in music a term which originally designated a composition to be played upon an instrument as distinguished from a CANTATA which was a composition to be sung. Since the 18th century the term has been applied to any extended instrumental composition in either three or four movements. The symphony is a sonata for orchestra, and the string quartet, quintet, etc., is a sonata for four, five or more instruments. The first great composers of sonatas were Karl Philipp Emanuel BACH, Josef HAYDN, and Wolfgang Amadeus MOZART. A **sonatina** is a short sonata in two or three movements.

Song, in music a short lyrical or narrative secular poem set to music: one of the earliest songs was composed at the death of CHARLEMAGNE in 814 A.D. The composition of songs flourished in the time of the TROUBADOURS, TROUVERES, MINNESINGERS, and MASTERSINGERS in the 11th to the 13th centuries as composed or sung by RICHARD COEUR DE LION, BLONDEL DE NESLE, and ADAM DE LA HALLE. Secular songs advanced slowly in form from the 14th to the 16th century because the Church exercised its influence in promoting sacred music, but from the 17th century to the present day the song has developed both as a lied and as an art song. Among the outstanding composers of songs are GLUCK, HAYDN, MOZART, BEETHOVEN, SCHUBERT, SPOHR, WEBER, MENDELSSOHN, FRANZ, BRAHMS, FAURE, CHAUSSON, BALAKIREV, MUSSORGSKY, DVORAK, GRIEG, WOLF, JENSEN and Richard STRAUSS. Among the American composers who have written in the art-song form are CHADWICK, BUCK, Homer BARTLETT, FOOTE, and MACDOWELL.

Sonneck, Oscar George Theodore (1873-1928), American musicologist and composer who studied in German universities, became chief of the Music Division of the Library of Congress from 1902 to 1917, and edited the *Musical Quarterly* from 1915 until his death: his works include *Miscellaneous Studies in the History of Music* (1921), and many scholarly treatises on early American music. His compositions include orchestral works, chamber music, piano pieces, and songs.

Sonnet, in prosody a verse form consisting of fourteen lines rhyming according to a definite scheme. It is of Italian origin and there are two forms: (*a*) the **Italian sonnet** composed by PETRARCH, DANTE, TASSO, and MICHELANGELO: (*b*) the **Elizabethan** or **Shakespearean sonnet,** a form revised by SHAKESPEARE, SPENSER, and MILTON. Other distinguished composers of sonnets include WORDSWORTH, KEATS, Elizabeth BROWNING, and ROSSETTI.

Sontag, Henriette (1806-1854), German dramatic soprano who made her debut at Vienna in 1820, and later created a sensation at Berlin and Paris: after singing with great success she retired in 1830, but returned to the stage in 1848, and appeared in the United States in 1852. The quality of her voice was exceptional, but her ability as an actress was limited.

Sophocles (c.496-c.406 B.C.), Greek dramatist who composed the PAEAN for the victory at Sal-amis when he was sixteen, and enjoyed greater popular success than either EURIPIDES or Aeschylus during his fifty years of play writing. He made some innovations such as writing plays independent of each other instead of in the form of trilogies, and introducing a third actor thus transferring the dialogue and action from the CHORUS to the stage. Only seven of his plays out of more than one hundred are extant in complete form: they include *Ajax; Antigone; Elektra; Women of Trachis; Philoctetes; Oedipus at Colonus,* and *Oedipus the King,* the last-named regarded as the masterpiece among Greek tragedies.

Soprano, the highest class of the human voice; usually applied to women's voices although there are boy sopranos and CASTRATI or adult male sopranos, known today as falsettists. In operatic singing sopranos are classified as dramatic, lyric or coloratura: a *mezzo soprano* is a voice intermediate between soprano and alto.

Sor, Fernando (1778-1839), Spanish guitarist and composer who played and wrote pieces for the guitar at five, and produced an opera at Barcelona when he was seventeen. He was encouraged by MEHUL and CHERUBINI to pursue the career of a virtuoso, and appeared in London, Moscow, and St. Petersburg, finally settling at Paris. His compositions for the guitar raised the musical status of the instrument.

Sorbonne (Paris), a college in the University of Paris founded about 1250 by Robert de Sorbon, chaplain of Louis IX of France. It became an important institution in the 16th century, was suppressed in 1792, and revived in 1889 when it became an important part of the University of Paris.

Sorcerer, The, comic opera in two acts: book by Sir William S. Gilbert; music by Sir Arthur S. Sullivan; first produced in 1877 at London and in 1879 at New York. There is a Victor abridged recording by the D'Oyly Carte Company.

Sorcerer's Apprentice, The (Dukas), an orchestral work in the form of a symphonic scherzo composed by Paul DUKAS, and first performed in 1897 at a concert of the Société Nationale de Musique under the direction of the composer. It is based upon Goethe's ballad *Der Zauberlehrling,* and describes the misadventure of the sorcerer's apprentice, who, when his master is out, tries to charm a broomstick to fetch water. The charm is successful, but since the apprentice had forgotten the magic words which would stop the broom, he was scarcely able to keep the house from being flooded. The sorcerer returns just in time to save the day. There is a Victor recording by the Philadelphia Orchestra directed by Leopold Stokowski, and a Columbia recording by the Minneapolis Symphony Orchestra under Dimitri Mitropoulos.

Sorgh or **Zorg, Hendrik Maertensz** (c.1621-c.1670), Dutch painter whose real name was Hendrik Martensz Rokes: his paintings, which were greatly influenced by Adriaen BROUWER include *Old Woman by the Fireside; Old Woman Selling Fish; Kitchen Interior; Peasants Smoking; Ad-*

589

oration of the Shepherds; Peasants' Brawl; The Lute Player.

Sorolla y Bastida, Joaquín (1863-1923), Spanish painter who studied at the San Carlos Accademia and later traveled in Italy where he copied the frescoes in Assisi. He also visited London, Holland, Belgium, and Paris, and was influenced by the works of Jules BASTIEN-LEPAGE. His works, which are impressionistic without belonging to any particular school, include *Another Marguerite; Beaching the Boat; Castle of San Servando; Toledo; The Swimmers.*

Sotatsu, 17th century Japanese painter who studied with Yosunobu, and later became a brilliant exponent of the Tosa school: his paintings reveal a remarkable combination of gold dust and Chinese ink, and rival those of Ogata KORIN in artistic importance.

Sothern, Edward Askew (1826-1881), English actor who came to the United States in 1852 playing at the National Theatre, Boston, under the name of Douglas. He was a member of Wallack's company in New York, and achieved his first success as Lord Dundreary in *Our American Cousin,* a play in which he also appeared for nearly 500 nights in London. His three sons, George Evelyn Augustus Townley, Lytton Edward and Edward Hugh SOTHERN were all actors.

Sothern, Edward Hugh (1859-1933), American actor who was the son of Edward Askew SOTHERN, and was usually referred to as "E. H. Sothern" because of the similarity in names. He first appeared in 1879 as a member of his father's company, later supporting John MCCULLOUGH and becoming the star of Daniel FROHMAN's company at the Lyceum Theatre, New York. Among the plays in which he achieved success were *The Highest Bidder; Lord Chumley; The Prisoner of Zenda; If I Were King; The Sunken Bell; Richard Lovelace; Under the Red Robe.* In 1899 he formed his own company and appeared with his wife, Julia MARLOWE, in Shakespearean repertory with great success. His autobiography, *The Melancholy Tale of Me,* was published in 1916.

Sothern, Ann (1909-), American stage and screen actress whose real name is Harriette Luke: she was educated at the University of Washington, and appeared in several plays before entering the films in 1934. Among the pictures in which she has been featured are *Melody in Spring; The Hell Cat; Folies Bergère; Hell-Ship Morgan; My American Wife; Maisie; Hotel for Women; Brother Orchid; Dulcy; Lady Be Good.*

Soubrette, in drama the name given to a female part in comedies, and also in comedy-dramas where the character is supposed to relieve the dramatic tension.

Soufflot, Jacques Germain (1709-1780), French architect who studied in Italy for several years: he was awarded the building of the PANTHEON at Paris built by order of Louis XV. The dome, which was unfinished at Soufflot's death, was completed by his pupil, Jacques P. Rondelet.

Soundboard, in stringed musical instruments a thin plate of wood placed below the strings to increase and prolong their tones. The soundboard of the violin is known as the *belly,* and the same term is used for the piano.

Sousa, John Philip (1854-1932), American bandmaster and composer who led the UNITED STATES. MARINE BAND from 1880 to 1892 after which he organized his own band, and toured the United States, Canada, and Europe with great success from 1892, making a world tour in 1910. His numerous marches such as *The Stars and Stripes Forever* became so popular that he was known as "The March King": he also wrote several popular light operas including *The Smugglers, El Capitan, The Bride Elect,* and *The Charlatan.*

Sousaphone, an improved form of the HELICON (bass tuba) made by C. G. Conn especially for John Philip SOUSA in 1899: the first model had its bell opening directly upward, but later the bell was turned to the front.

Southey, Robert (1774-1843), English poet and prose writer who was made poet laureate in 1813: he was intimate with William WORDSWORTH and Samuel Taylor COLERIDGE. His works include *Joan of Arc* (1795); *The Curse of Kehama; A Vision of Judgment; Life of Nelson; The Doctor; Life of John Bunyan.*

South Kensington Museum, see **Victoria and Albert Museum.**

Sowerby, Katherine Ghita, contemporary English dramatist whose first play, *Rutherford and Son,* was produced in 1912 with tremendous success: it has been translated into several European languages. Among her other plays are *Before Breakfast; Jinny; A Man and Some Women; Sheila; The Stepmother; The Policeman's Whistle:* she has also written many juvenile stories with her sister, Millicent Sowerby.

Spada, Lionello (1576-1622), Italian painter who studied with Annibale CARRACCI and also with Michelangelo CARAVAGGIO whose realistic style is reflected in Spada's works which include *Prodigal Son; Aeneas and Anchises; The Concert; Melchisedic Blessing Abraham; Christ Crowned with Thorns; Christ before Pilate.*

Spaeth, Sigmund (1885-), American music critic and writer who studied at Haverford College and Princeton University: his works include *The Common Sense of Music; Words and Music; The Art of Enjoying Music; Music for Everyone; Great Symphonies; Stories Behind the World's Great Music.*

Spagna, Lo (?-1530), Italian painter whose real name was Giovanni di Pietro: he studied with PERUGINO and PINTURICCHIO at the same time as RAPHAEL: his works include *The Nativity; Ecce Homo; Coronation of the Virgin; Madonna with Saints:* many of his frescoes at Spoleto and Perugia are still in existence.

Spagnoletto, Lo, see **Ribera, Jusepe.**

Spalding, Albert (1888-), American violinist and composer who studied in Florence and Paris, making his debut in the latter city in 1905: he has toured Europe and the United States repeatedly with great success, making his debut at New York in 1908 with the New York Symphony Society. His compositions include two concertos and other works for the violin, chamber music, piano pieces, and songs.

Spalding, Walter Raymond (1865-), American music educator and author educated at Harvard University and pupil of GUILMANT, WIDOR, and RHEINBERGER in Europe. He became assistant to John K. PAINE at Harvard University in 1895, and professor of music in 1912: his works include several treatises on harmony and musical aesthetics.

Spatula, a tool shaped like a knife which is thin and somewhat flexible: it is used by painters instead of a brush for placing colors on canvas, and also by sculptors for spreading plaster over a mold.

Speaks, Oley (1876-), American concert singer and composer who studied with Emma THURSBY and Max Spicker, and later concertized with great success: his compositions include 250 songs many of which such as *On the Road to Mandalay* and *Sylvia* have become very popular.

Spectre de la Rose, Le, romantic ballet in one act: libretto by J. L. Vaudoyer after a poem by Théophile GAUTIER; music by Carl Maria von WEBER; first performed in 1911 at Monte Carlo. The ballet is short, utilizing the music of Weber's INVITATION TO THE DANCE, and the story is a simple one of a maiden fresh from a ball, a rose, and a spectre who appears to dance with her as she sleeps in a chair of her chamber: Vaslav NIJINSKY and Tamara KARSAVINA were the dancers at the première by the DIAGHILEFF Company.

Speicher, Eugene (1883-), American painter who studied at the ART STUDENTS' LEAGUE, New York, with William Merritt CHASE, and also became intimate with Robert HENRI and George BELLOWS. His works include portraits such as that of Katherine CORNELL, and landscapes of which *Morning Light* at the Metropolitan Museum of Art, New York, is an excellent example.

Spenser, Edmund (1552-1599), English poet who was educated at Cambridge and became intimate with Sir Philip Sidney who aided him greatly in his career: his notable works include *The Shepherd's Calendar* (1579); *The Faerie Queene; Daphnaida; Complaints; Mother Hubberd's Tale; Epithalamion; Amoretti; Astrophel; Prothalamion.*

Spewack, Bella and **Samuel,** contemporary American dramatists both of whom started their careers as journalists: after writing several plays in collaboration including *The Solitary Man, The War Song, Clear All Wires,* and *Spring Song* their most successful play, *Boy Meets Girl,* was produced with tremendous success at New York, and was also adapted for the films.

Speyer, Leonora (1872-), American poet who was first a concert violinist who appeared as soloist with the Boston Symphony and New York Philharmonic Orchestra, and was also intimate with Amy Lawrence LOWELL: her works include *A Canopic Jar* (1921); *Fiddler's Farewell* which was awarded the Pulitzer Prize in 1927; *Naked Heel; Slow Wall; New and Selected Poems.* Her maiden name was Leonora von Stosch.

Sphinx, in Greek mythology a deity originating with the Egyptians and represented with a winged lion's body and a human head. In Egypt the sphinx was wingless: the most famous example is the **Great Sphinx of Gizeh** which is 189 feet long and 65 feet high. It was sculptured on the spot from solid rock, and one of the kings of Egypt, Thotmes IV, had a temple built between its paws which was reached by a flight of thirty-two steps.

Spinet, a small HARPSICHORD which differs from the larger instruments in having only one string to each note: its name is derived from its resemblance to a writing desk. Modern manufacturers have revived the appearance of the spinet in cases for small pianos.

Spingarn, Joel Elias (1875-1939), American poet and teacher educated at Columbia University and later professor of comparative literature there: his works include *The New Hesperides and Other Poems* (1911); *Critical Essays of the Seventeenth Century; Criticism in America; Goethe's Literary Essays.* He also established the Spingarn Medal in 1913 to be awarded annually to a Negro for outstanding achievement.

Spiritual, in music a type of religious song or chant developed among the Southern Negroes: their origin is not certain, and they are characterized by an atmosphere of simple faith mixed with melancholy. The best-known spiritual is *Deep River:* other favorites include *All God's Chillun Got Wings; Crucifixion; Go Down, Moses; I Couldn't Hear Nobody Pray; Nobody Knows de Trouble I've Seen; Swing Low, Sweet Chariot; Roll, Jordan, Roll.* The most complete collection of spirituals, *The Book of American Negro Spirituals* (2 vols., 1925-26) was complied by James and Rosamond JOHNSON.

Spitta, Philipp (1841-1894), German musicologist who became professor of musical history at the University of Berlin in 1875: his greatest work is *J. S. Bach* (2 vols., 1873-1880), the first adequate biography of the great German master which has been the basis for nearly all later works. He also wrote a history of romantic opera in Germany.

Spofford, Harriet Prescott (1835-1921), American novelist whose literary success started with the publication in 1859 of a short story, *In the Cellar,* in the *Atlantic Monthly:* her works include *The Amber Gods and Other Stories; Azarian; New England Legends; The Thief in the Night; The Marquis of Carabas; In Titian's Garden.*

Spohr, Ludwig Louis (1784-1839), German violinist and composer who played the violin at five, and performed a concerto of his composition at the Brunswick court when he was fourteen. He toured Europe and Great Britain with genuine success and later became famous as a conductor: his compositions include several operas of which the most successful was *Jessonda;* four oratorios; nine symphonies; fifteen violin concertos; chamber music, and a violin method.

Spong, Hilda (1875-), English actress who made her debut in 1890 at Sydney, Australia, in *Joseph's Sweetheart,* and first appeared in 1896 at London in *The Duchess of Coolgardie:* among the numerous plays in which she has played important parts are *Trelawney of the Wells; The Ambassador; Notre Dame; Lord and Lady Algy; Sherlock Holmes; Diplomacy; Aristocracy; The Penalty; Candida; Dear Brutus; Caesar's Wife; Caste; Evensong; One Good Year.*

Spontini, Gasparo (1774-1851), Italian opera composer who received valuable advice from Nicolo PICCINNI regarding dramatic composition: his first opera was produced in 1796, and *La Vestale,* performed at Paris in 1807 was an enormous success. Among his other popular operas were *Fernand Cortez; Olympie; Nurmahal; Agnes von Hohenstaufen.*

Squarcione, Francesco (1394-1474), Italian painter who founded the first academy of art at Padua where more than one hundred pupils studied including Andrea MANTEGNA. He was not adept himself as a painter, but intrusted important commissions to the advanced students in his school.

Square Dance, any form of dance such as the quadrille in which the dancers are arranged to form a square with each woman facing a man. It is usually danced by four couples or multiples of four.

Squire, William Henry (1871-), English violoncellist and composer who studied at the Royal College of Music, making his debut in 1891. He was first 'cellist at Covent Garden, and also played with the Queen's Hall and London Symphony Orchestras. He is a favorite recitalist, and has written a concerto for the violoncello.

Stabat Mater, in music a sequence (sacred hymn) in the Roman Catholic church service: it is a prayer written by Jacopone da Todi which meditates on the sorrows of the Virgin as she stood at the Cross. There are settings by Josquin DES PRES, PALESTRINA, HAYDN, PERGOLESI, ROSSINI, VERDI and DVORAK.

Staccato (It.), in music a direction indicating that the notes are to be played in a detached, separated manner, or in exactly the opposite manner in which they would be performed if marked LEGATO. A round dot over a note indicates that it is to be played in this manner.

Stadium Concerts (New York), see **Lewisohn, Adolf.**

Staël-Holstein, Anne Louise Germaine, Baroness de (1766-1817), French author who was the daughter of Jacques Necker, minister of finance under Louis XVI. She became acquainted early in life with men of letters who frequented her father's home, and married the Baron of Staël-Holstein, ambassador to France from Sweden from whom she separated, and at once associated herself with Benjamin CONSTANT. Her works include the novels *Delphine* (1802) and *Corinne:* also volumes of literary criticism including *De l'Allemagne* which resulted in her being exiled by Napoleon I.

Staff or **Stave,** in musical notation the five parallel horizontal lines upon which the NOTES are placed: the PITCH of the notes is determined by the CLEF placed at the beginning of the staff. If notes necessary to the music are of a pitch higher or lower than that indicated by the lines of the staff, short ledger lines are added.

Stained Glass, see **Glass.**

Stainer or **Steiner, Jakob** (1621-1683), Austrian violin maker who started as an organ builder, and finally went to Italy where he learned the art of violin making from Nicoló AMATI at Cremona. Archduke Ferdinand Karl became his patron in 1658, and he was the first maker to incorporate Italian constructional ideas into German violins. His model has a high arch and a yellow-brown varnish: their value at the present time ranges from $1,500.00 to $2,500.00.

Stainer, Sir John (1840-1901), English organist and composer who became organist of ST. PAUL'S CATHEDRAL in London from 1872 to 1878, greatly improving the work of the choir: in 1881 he succeeded Sir Arthur SULLIVAN as head of the National Training School and in 1889 became professor of music at Oxford University. His notable compositions include the cantatas *The Crucifixion, The Daughter of Jairus,* and *St. Mary Magdalene:* also several valuable theoretical treatises.

Stallings, Laurence (1894-), American novelist and dramatist educated at Wake Forest College and Georgetown University who served in World War I: he worked as a reporter on the Washington (D. C.) *Times* and as dramatic critic of the New York *World* before his first play, *What Price Glory?,* written with Maxwell ANDERSON became a tremendous success in 1924 both on the stage and later as a film. His works include *Plumes,* a novel divesting war of its glamour; the scenario for the motion picture, *The Big Parade;* also a photographic history of World War I.

Stalls, in ecclesiastical architecture seats placed around the choir in a church: in early Christian basilicas they were made of stone or marble, but from the 13th to the 16th century they were fashioned of wood with elaborate carvings. Most English cathedrals have marvelous examples of carving in their stalls.

Stamitz, Johann Wenzel Anton (1717-1757), Bohemian violinist and composer who received his entire music education from his father: he is famous not only as the leader of the Mannheim

Orchestra which was the greatest organization in Europe in the 18th century, but for having introduced important innovations into orchestral composition which were copied by MOZART, HAYDN, BOCCHERINI, GOSSEC, and other composers. His compositions include symphonies, violin concertos, and trios.

Stanford, Sir Charles Villiers (1852-1924), Irish composer, organist, and conductor who studied with Ernst Pauer and Carl Reinecke, later becoming organist of Trinity College, lecturer at the Royal College of Music and Cambridge University, and conductor of the London Bach Choir. His compositions include several operas: incidental music for plays; seven symphonies, five Irish rhapsodies, and other works for orchestra; chamber music; choral works, and songs. He also wrote a *History of Music* with Cecil FORSYTH and a treatise on musical composition.

Stanislavsky, Constantin (1863-1938), Russian actor, director, and theatrical producer who studied in Paris, and founded a group of semi-professional actors at Moscow in 1888. Ten years later he organized the MOSCOW ART THEATRE with Vladimir NEMIROVITCH-DANTCHENKO which became a great influence not only on Russian drama, but also on the American stage when he visited the United States with the Moscow Art Theatre Company in 1922 and 1923.

Stanwyck, Barbara (1907-   ), American stage and screen actress, real name Ruby Stevens, who first appeared in 1923 in the chorus of a musical comedy, and later achieved success as Bonny in *Burlesque* at New York in 1927: among the numerous pictures in which she has appeared are *The Locked Door; So Big; The Bitter Tea of General Yen; Brief Moment; Annie Oakley; Stella Dallas; The Mad Miss Manton; Meet John Doe; Union Pacific; Golden Boy; The Lady Eve; Ball of Fire; The Great Man's Lady; The Gay Sisters.*

Stanza, in versification a complete section of a poem consisting of a STROPHE of two or more lines, usually rhymed, but always recurring: the stanza is a modern development of the ancient poets adapted to the requirements of rhyme.

Stappen, Charles van der (1843-1910), Belgian sculptor who became recognized with Paul de VIGNE as the leader of a new school of sculpture in Belgium largely inspired by the art of ancient Greece and the Italian Renaissance. Among his notable works are the pediment, *Orchestration,* for the Brussels Conservatory of Music; *The Man With The Sword; The Sphinx;* the bronze group, *The Death of Ompdrailles* and *Builders of Cities.*

Starkey, James Sullivan (1879-   ), Irish poet who writes under the pen name "Seumas O'Sullivan": his works include *The Twilight People* (1905); *Verses Sacred and Profane; The Earth-Lover and Other Verses; Requiem and Other Poems; The Lamplighter and Other Poems; At Christmas; Personal Talk: A Book of Verse.*

Starr, Frances Grant (1886-   ), American actress who first appeared with a stock company at Albany, N. Y., in 1901, and later with repertory companies in New York, San Francisco, and Boston. Among the numerous plays in which she has appeared are *The Music Master; The Rose of the Rancho; The Easiest Way; The Case of Becky; The Secret; Marie-Odile; Immortal Isabella; Diplomacy; What Every Woman Knows; Moor Born; A Bill of Divorcement; Susan and God; Yes, My Darling Daughter.* She has also appeared in several films.

Star Spangled Banner, The, the national anthem of the United States: the words were written by Francis Scott KEY while he watched the bombardment of Fort McHenry near Baltimore, Md., by the British during the night of Sept. 13, 1814. The music was adapted from an English song, *Ode to Anacreon,* by John Stafford Smith: there is no way of ascertaining whether Key had this melody in mind when he wrote the words, or whether it was Joseph Hopper Nicholson who eventually united the words and music. Oscar G. SONNECK wrote an important monograph on the origins of the song; another work on the subject has been written by Joseph Muller.

Stassoff, Vladimir Vassilievitch (1824-1906), Russian art critic who became the champion of the new school of Russian musical composition as represented by BALAKIREV, BORODIN, CUI, MUSSORGSKY and RIMSKY-KORSAKOW. His works include *Twenty-five Years of Russian Art; The Traces of Russian Art; Art in the Nineteenth Century:* also many monographs on Russian composers.

Statius, Publius Papinius (45-96 A.D.), Latin poet born at Naples who won several poetry contests: his works include an epic poem in twelve books, *The Thebaid* and a series of thirty-two short poems called *Silvae.* He also wrote a life of ACHILLES which was never completed.

Statue of Liberty, a colossal statue on Bedloe's Island in New York harbor presented to the people of the United States in commemoration of the hundredth anniversary of American independence by the Franco-American Union in 1874, and unveiled in 1886. The figure, designed and executed by Frédéric-Auguste BARTHOLDI, is 151 feet high, and rests on a pedestal 89 feet high: it is built of copper sheathing on a steel frame, and the cost of statue, pedestal, and erection was $600,000.

Stave, see Staff.

Stedman, Edmund Clarence (1833-1908), American poet and editor who was on the staff of the New York *Tribune* and the New York *World,* and also had a seat in the New York Stock Exchange for thirty-five years: his works include *Poems, Lyrical and Idyllic* (1860); *The Blameless Prince; Hawthorne and Other Poems; Lyrics and Idylls.* He also edited a *Victorian Anthology;* an *American Anthology;* a *Library of American Literature,* and a complete edition of the works of Edgar Allan POE with George E. Woodberry.

Steel engraving, an art developed during the 15th century from a simple line engraving to the more elaborate forms employed in the 19th century to reproduce famous paintings and portraits: the perfecting of photographic processes gradually displaced it.

Steele, Sir Richard (1672-1729), Irish essayist and dramatist educated at Oxford: his works include the plays *The Funeral, The Lying Lover, The Tender Husband,* and *The Conscious Lovers.* He founded a celebrated periodical, *The Tatler,* in 1709 for which he wrote 188 articles himself and 36 with Joseph ADDISON: he also founded another famous magazine, *The Spectator,* in 1711 for which he wrote 236 articles while 274 were written by Addison.

Steele, Wilbur Daniel (1886-.), American novelist and short-story writer educated at the University of Denver who studied painting at Boston, Paris, and New York before writing his first short story, *A White Horse Winter,* which was published in the *Atlantic Monthly* in 1912: his works include *Storm* (1914); *Land's End; Shame Dance; The Man Who Saw Through Heaven; Meat; Tower of Sand.* He also wrote several plays, and won the O. Henry Award four times in succession for his short stories.

Steen, Jan Havicksz (1626-1679), Dutch painter who studied with Andriaen van OSTADE and Jan van GOYEN: he executed more than 500 paintings of scenes and people in every class of life: they include *The Happy Family; The Music Master; Country People at a Tavern; The Menagerie; Playing at Skittles; The Dancing Lesson; Country Wedding; Old Man Cutting a Pen; Quarrel between Card Players; Girl Eating Oysters; Jolly Party.*

Steer, Paul Wilson, (1860-), English painter who studied at the Acadèmie Julian, Paris, under Adolphe BOUGUEREAU, and at the ECOLE DES BEAUX-ARTS, Paris, with Alexandre CABANEL, also being influenced for a time by James McNeil WHISTLER. He finally worked along the lines of CONSTABLE and TURNER in paintings such as *Richmond Castle, Yorkshire,* and *Music Room at Chepstow Castle:* his self-portrait is in the collection at the UFFIZI Gallery, Florence.

Stein, Gertrude (1874-), American author educated at Radcliffe College and at Johns Hopkins University where she studied medicine. Since 1903 she has lived in France where her friends include PICASSO, MATISSE, COCTEAU, and other distinguished men and women in artistic circles. Her works include *Three Lives* (1909); *The Making of Americans; Useful Knowledge; Before the Flowers of Friendship Faded;* FOUR SAINTS IN THREE ACTS; *The World is Round; Ida.*

Steinbach, Fritz (1855-1916), German conductor and composer who studied at the Leipzig Conservatory, and succeeded Hans von BULOW as conductor of the Meinigen Orchestra in 1886: he taught at the Raff Conservatory, toured England and acted as guest conductor of the New York Philharmonic-Symphony Orchestra in 1906. He was noted as an interpreter of Brahms' symphonies: his composition include a septet, a sonata for violoncello, piano pieces, and songs.

Steinbeck, John Ernest (1901-), American novelist and dramatist who first worked as a reporter: his novels include *Cup of Gold* (1929); *The Pastures of Heaven; To a God Unknown; Tortilla Flat; Of Mice and Men; The Grapes of Wrath* which was awarded the Pulitzer Prize in 1940; *The Moon is Down.* Several of his novels have been dramatized and adapted for the films.

Steinberg, Maximilian (1883-), Russian composer who studied at the St. Petersburg Conservatory with GLAZUNOFF and RIMSKY-KORSAKOW: in 1934 he became director of the Leningrad Conservatory, and conducted the NBC Symphony Orchestra in 1938 and 1939. His compositions include symphonies, ballets, and chamber music.

Steinway & Sons, an American firm of piano manufacturers founded by Henry Engelhardt Steinway (1797-1871) who founded the business about 1825 in Germany, and emigrated to the United States in 1851, leaving the German factory in charge of his eldest son, Christian Friedrich Theodore Steinway (1825-1889). He founded the American factory with his sons, Charles and Henry Steinway, and exhibited a square piano of novel design at the World's Fair in the Crystal Palace, New York, in 1855. The rapid expansion of the business, and the deaths in their prime of Charles and Henry Steinway brought two other sons, Theodore and William, into the business, and a large factory was built at Steinway, Long Island, now a part of New York City. The reputation of Steinway instruments has steadily increased over the years, the latest improvement being a new type of accelerated action.

Steinway Hall (New York), a concert hall erected by STEINWAY & SONS on Fourteenth Street, New York, and opened in 1866: among the musical organizations and distinguished virtuosos and singers who were heard there are the Theodore THOMAS Orchèstra; Adelina PATTI; Emma JUCH; Marcella SEMBRICH; Lilli LEHMANN; Anton RUBINSTEIN; the Liederkranz, Arion, and Beethoven Singing Societies. It was the most important concert hall in New York during the latter part of the 19th century.

Stele, an ancient monument in the form of a vertical monolith usually carved with an inscription to preserve the memory of a deceased person, or to commemorate an historic event. Greek and Roman *stelae* were often exquisitely sculptured or painted: the British Museum has an exceptionally fine collection.

Sten, Anna, contemporary Russian stage and screen actress who appeared in Gerhardt HAUPTMANN's *Hannele* with the Moscow ART THEATRE, and in numerous films with Emil JANNINGS and other stars. Since 1932 she has played the leading role in several American films including *Nana; We Live Again; The Wedding Night; A Woman Alone; Exile Express; The Man I Married.*

Stencil, a piece of parchment, paper, or thin sheet metal which is perforated in such a manner that when it is placed on a surface and ink or coloring applied, the result is a figure. It is employed in the arts in decorating furniture, pottery, textiles, etc.; the Chinese are particularly skillful in the making of stencils from mulberry paper.

Stendhal, pen name of **Marie Henri Beyle** (1783-1842), French novelist and critic who wrote two remarkable novels, *Red or Black* (1831) and *The Chartreuse of Parma* (1839). His critical works include *Rome, Naples and Florence* and *History of Painting in Italy:* also biographies of HAYDN, MOZART, and ROSSINI. An autobiographical novel, *The Life of Henri Brulard,* was published a half century after his death.

Stentor, in Greek mythology one of the Greek warriors who fought at Troy: according to HOMER in the *Iliad,* his voice was as loud as that of fifty ordinary men combined, and he died when he challenged HERMES, the voice of the gods, to a contest. The word *stentorian* is applied at the present time to describe an unusually loud or penetrating voice.

Stephenson, Henry (1874-), English actor who first appeared with Mr. and Mrs. KENDAL on tour in 1896; among the numerous plays in which he had leading roles are *Lord and Lady Algy; A Message from Mars; The Man from Blankley's; The Night of the Party; The Pillars of Society; Becky Sharp; Hawthorne of the U.S.A.; Inside the Lines; Bunny; Common Clay; Smilin' Through; Journey's End; Cynara.* In 1932 he entered the films in *The Animal Kingdom,* and has since appeared in innumerable pictures.

Stern, Daniel, see **Agoult, Marie Catherine Sophie de Flavigny, Comtesse d'.**

Sternberg, Constantin Ivanovitch (1852-1924), Russian composer and pianist who studied at the Leipzig Conservatory with Ignaz MOSCHELES and Hans RICHTER, making his debut in 1875. After concert tours and engagements as conductor in various German cities he came to the United States from 1880 on concert tours with August WILHELMJI and Minnie HAUK, and after 1900 directed the Sternberg School of Music at Philadelphia. His compositions include chamber music and piano pieces.

Sternberg, Josef von, see **Von Sternberg, Josef.**

Sterne, Laurence (1713-1768), Irish novelist educated at Cambridge University who became a priest and led a life bordering on the dissolute: the first two volumes of his masterpiece, *Tristram Shandy,* were published in 1760, and several more adding up to a total of nine by 1767. His only other work of importance, *A Sentimental Journey Through France and Italy,* was published in 1768. Sterne exercised a considerable influence on the development of the English novel.

Sterne, Maurice (1878-), American painter and sculptor born in Russia who came to the United States with his family in 1889, studying at the National Academy of Design, New York, with Thomas EAKINS, and later in Paris with CEZANNE, and at Rome where he studied the

works of the 15th century master, Piero de FRANCESCHI. He also spent some time in Bali: his works include both sculptures and murals to be seen at the Chicago Art Institute, the California Palace of the Legion of Honor, San Francisco, and the Phillips Memorial Gallery, Washington, D. C.

Stevens, Risë (1913-), American mezzosoprano who studied at the Juilliard School of Music and at the Mozarteum in Salzburg. In 1936 she made her debut at the Prague Opera, and later at opera houses in Vienna, Buenos Aires, Cairo, and at the Metropolitan Opera House, New York. She has also appeared in a film version of *The Chocolate Soldier,* and on radio broadcasts.

Stevenson, Burton Egbert (1872-), American author and librarian educated at Princeton University who founded the American Library in Paris, France, and acted as its librarian for several years. His works include several compilations which have enjoyed a world-wide sale: they comprise *The Home Book of Verse* (1912); *The Home Book of Modern Verse; The Home Book of Quotations; The Home Book of Shakespeare Quotations.* He is now (1943) engaged in the preparation of *The Home Book of Proverbs, Maxims and Familiar Phrases* scheduled for publication in 1944.

Stevenson, Edward Prime (1868-1942), American writer on music who was for many years music critic on *The Independent* and *Harper's Weekly.* He came to be known on both sides of the Atlantic as a music critic of wide experience and extensive historical knowledge and acted as special correspondent for a number of musical events. He lectured on the literatures of France, Germany, Italy and the Orient. After his retirement from literary activities, he resided alternately in Switzerland, Germany and Italy. During his long and useful career, he knew people in all walks of life and his extraordinary facility in languages was due to his diverse contacts. Among his works most of which were privately printed, are *Left to Themselves; You Will, Will You?; Longhaired Iopas: Old Chapters from Twenty-Five Years of Music Criticism; A Repertory of One Hundred Symphonic Programmes; A Matter of Temperament; Some Men, and Women and Music.*

Stevenson, Robert Louis (1850-1894), Scotch novelist who studied engineering and law at Edinburgh University, but never practiced at either profession: his notable works include *New Arabian Nights* (1882); *Treasure Island; The Silverado Squatters; The Dynamiter; A Child's Garden of Verse; Prince Otto; The Strange Case of Dr. Jekyl and Mr. Hyde; Kidnapped; The Master of Ballantrae; The Wrecker.*

Stevenson, William, see **Gammer Gurton's Needle.**

Stewart, James (1911-), American stage and screen actor educated at Princeton University who first appeared with a stock company at Cape Cod, Mass., making his debut in 1932 at New

York in *Carrie Nation*. After appearing in several plays he entered the films in 1932, appearing in *Rose Marie; The Gorgeous Hussy; Born to Dance; After the Thin Man; Seventh Heaven; Of Human Hearts; Shopworn Angel; You Can't Take It With You; Vivacious Lady; The Shop Around the Corner; Mr. Smith Goes to Washington; The Philadelphia Story; No Time for Comedy; Pot o' Gold.*

Stiedry, Fritz (1883-), Austrian conductor who studied at the Vienna Conservatory as a pupil and assistant of Gustav MAHLER, later conducting at Berlin, Prague, Vienna, Rome, Madrid, Barcelona, Stockholm, and Leningrad. In 1938 he came to the United States as conductor of the NEW FRIENDS OF MUSIC, New York.

Still, William Grant (1895-), American Negro composer who studied with George W. CHADWICK and Edgar VARESE: he has been actively connected with radio music programs for some years, and awarded a Guggenheim Fellowship in 1934. His works include an *Afro-American Symphony; Kaintuck* for piano and orchestra; *Lenox Avenue* for orchestra and chorus; an opera, *Blue Steel;* chamber music.

Stock, Frederick A. (1872-1942), American conductor and composer born in Germany who studied at the Cologne Conservatory, and became first violist with the Chicago Symphony Orchestra (under Theodore THOMAS) in 1895, assistant conductor in 1901 and permanent conductor from 1905 until his death. His efficient, inspiring leadership placed the organization in the front rank of American orchestras: his compositions were chiefly orchestral works and chamber music.

Stockton, Francis Richard (1834-1902), American journalist and humorist famous as the author of the baffling short story *The Lady or the Tiger?* which appeared in *Century* Magazine in 1882, caused a sensation among readers, was produced as an operetta in 1888, and as a short film in 1942. His works include *Rudder Grange* (1879); *The Casting Away of Mrs. Lecks and Mrs. Aleshine; The Rudder Grangers Abroad; Pomona's Travels.*

Stoddard, John Lawson (1850-1931), American lecturer and author: his works include the *John L. Stoddard Lectures* (10 vols. 1897-98), one of the most enlightening series of travel volumes ever published, and *The Stoddard Library: A Thousand Hours of Entertainment with the World's Greatest Writers* (12 vols. 1910).

Stoddard, Richard Henry (1825-1903), American poet and critic who worked as an iron molder, and was encouraged in his writing by Nathaniel HAWTHORNE, later becoming literary editor of the New York *Mail and Express*. His works include *Songs of Summer* (1857); *Abraham Lincoln; The Book of the East:* he also edited *Poets and Poetry of America* and *Female Poets of America.*

Stoessel, Albert (1894-1943), American violinist, composer, and conductor who studied with Willy HESS at the Hochschule für Musik in Berlin: after considerable concertizing he headed the violin department at New York University from 1923 to 1930, and from 1930 to his death was head of the opera and orchestra departments of the Juilliard Graduate School, New York. He conducted the New York Oratorio Society, the Chautauqua summer concerts from 1922 and the Worcester Music Festival from 1925. His compositions include orchestra works, chamber music, and choral works.

Stojowski, Sigismond (1870-), Polish pianist and composer who studied with Louis Diémer, Léo DELIBES, and Ignace PADEREWSKI, and after living in Paris until 1906, became the head of the piano department at the INSTITUTE OF MUSICAL ART, New York, also teaching at the Von Ende School of Music and the Juilliard Summer School. His compositions include piano concertos, a *Symphonic Rhapsody* for orchestra; a violin concerto and many piano pieces.

Stoker, Bram (1847-1912), Irish journalist and author who studied at Dublin University and in 1878 became Sir Henry IRVING's manager remaining in the post until the great actor's death, and accompanying him on his American tours. His works include *Dracula* (1897), a novel which was dramatized and filmed with great success; *The Jewel of Seven Stars; Personal Reminiscences of Henry Irving; The Lady of the Shroud; Famous Impostors; Dracula's Guest.*

Stokowski, Leopold (1882-), English organist and conductor who was educated at Queen's College, Oxford, and studied music with Sir Charles Hubert H. PARRY and Sir Charles Villiers STANFORD. He occupied posts as organist and choirmaster in New York churches, and from 1909 to 1912 conducted the Cincinnati Symphony Orchestra, and the Philadelphia Symphony Orchestra from 1912 to 1936. He has appeared in several films, also conducting the NBC Symphony Orchestra and making a tour in 1940 of South America with a symphony orchestra composed of young people.

Stolz, Robert (1886-), Austrian conductor and composer who studied with his father, Robert Fuchs and Engelbert HUMPERDINCK: he conducted at the Theater an den Wien for twelve years, and after directing several European orchestras came to the United States in 1940. He has composed many successful operettas including *Two Hearts in Waltz Time*, and also numerous scores for the films.

Stone, Ezra Chaim (1917-), American stage, screen, and radio actor trained at the American Academy of Dramatic Art, New York, who has appeared on the stage in *Boy Meets Girl, Brother Rat*, and *What a Life:* in 1939 he directed the stage play *See My Lawyer*, and has appeared in the radio serial, *The Aldrich Family*, since 1938. In 1940 he starred in the film *Those Were the Days.*

Stone, Fred Andrew (1878-), American stage and screen actor who first appeared with his partner, David Montgomery, in 1894 at Keith's Theatre, Boston, Mass., playing with him in many productions including *The Wizard of Oz* and *The Red Mill.* He has also starred in several films including *Alice Adams; The Trail of the Lonesome Pine; My American Wife; The Farmer in the Dell; Hideaway; The Westerner.*

Stone, Grace Zaring (1896-), American novelist who served with the British Red Cross during World War I: she writes under her own name and also the pen name "Ethel Vance." Her works include *The Heaven and Earth of Doña Elena* (1929); *The Bitter Tea of General Yen; The Almond Tree; The Cold Journey; Escape; Reprisal.*

Stone, Lewis (1878-), American stage and screen actor who made his debut at the Third Avenue Theatre, New York, in 1898, and gained his experience with stock companies: in 1912 he appeared at Daly's Theatre in *The Bird of Paradise,* later playing in *The Misleading Lady; Inside the Lines; Bunny; The Brat; Nancy Lee; Where Poppies Bloom.* He has also appeared in many motion pictures, creating an outstanding portrait of a typical American small-town judge in the "Andy Hardy" series.

Stonehenge, see **Megalithic Monuments.**

Stone Monuments, see **Megalithic Monuments.**

Stong, Philip Duffield (1899-), American novelist educated at Drake, Columbia, and Kansas Universities: his novels include *State Fair* (1932) successfully filmed with Will ROGERS as the star; *The Farmer in the Dell:* he has written several stories for juveniles.

Storioni, Lorenzo (1751-1801), Italian violin maker regarded as the last of the great violin makers who worked at CREMONA: his violins resemble both those of STRADIVARIUS and GUARNERIUS, and are valued today at $1200.00 to $3000.00.

Storm and Stress (in German *Sturm und Drang*), a period in German literature between 1760 and 1800 in which novelists, poets, and dramatists rebelled against the accepted conventional standards of artistry and morality. Jean Jacques ROUSSEAU and Karl Friedrich LESSING had much to do with the movement which had its influence on GOETHE and SCHILLER.

Story, William Wetmore (1819-1895), American sculptor, essayist, and poet educated for a legal career at the Harvard Law School, and also a student of sculpture in Rome. His notable works include *Cleopatra; Semiramis; Libyan Sibyl; Saul; Sardanapalus; Medea; Salome; Jerusalem in Her Desolation; Sappho.* His writings include poetry and essays on art: his son, **Julian Story** (1857-1919), was a well-known portrait painter who studied with DUVENECK, BOULANGER and LEFEBVRE, and was married for some years to Emma EAMES, distinguished opera singer.

Stoss, Veit (1440-1533), German sculptor and carver who worked in Cracow where he carved the high altar for the Marienkirche, and sculptured the tomb in red marble of King Kasimir IV of Poland: he also executed many works in churches at Nuremberg.

Stout, Rex (1886-), American author of detective fiction who created the character "Nero Wolfe," an obese, hypochondriacal lover of beer and orchids who nevertheless proves himself an astute detective. His works include *Fer-de-Lance* (1934); *The President Vanishes; The League of Frightened Men; The Rubber Band; The Red Box; The Hand in the Glove; Some Buried Caesar,* and other novels of similar character.

Stowe, Harriet Beecher (1811-1896), American author who wrote her greatest success, *Uncle Tom's Cabin or, Life Among the Lowly,* in 1852: it first appeared as a serial in the *National Era,* an anti-slavery paper, and as a book which climbed to a sale of 300,000 within the same year, and was translated into several languages. Her second anti-slavery novel, *Dred,* was published in 1856, but failed to achieve the same degree of popularity. In 1943 Helen HAYES appeared at New York in *Harriet,* a dramatization of Mrs. Stowe's career.

Strachey, Giles Lytton (1880-1932), English biographer educated at Cambridge: his works include *Landmarks in French Literature* (1912); *Eminent Victorians; Queen Victoria; Books and Characters; Pope; Elizabeth and Essex; Portraits in Miniature; Character and Commentaries.*

Stradella, Alessandro (c.1645-1682), Italian composer of operas and oratorios who is distinguished because of his development of the operatic aria, and his use of the instrumental crescendo: he was said to have been murdered in the course of some amorous intrigue, and Friedrich von FLOTOW made him the hero in 1844 of an opera, *Alessandro Stradella.*

Stradivarius, Antonius (c.1644-1737), Italian violin maker who studied with Niccolò AMATI: the first violin bearing his label as maker is dated 1666, but he changed his model about 1685, again in 1690, and again in 1700. He made about 1500 instruments of which 125 were violas and violoncellos: of the total about 600 violins, 13 violas, and 60 violoncellos are known to be in existence today. The market value ranges from $8500.00 to $40,000.00. His sons and pupils, Francesco Stradivarius (1671-1743) and Omobono Stradivarius (1679-1742) were also excellent violin makers.

Strakosch, Maurice (1825-1887), German pianist and opera impresario who came to the United States in 1848, and after playing and teaching for several years acted as manager for Adelina PATTI, his sister-in-law. He gave a season of Italian opera in 1857 at New York, and in 1859 at Chicago. In 1873 he returned to Europe, and with his brother, **Max Strakosch** (1834-1892), managed the Apollo Theatre in Rome.

Stransky, Josef (1872-1936), Bohemian composer and conductor who studied with JADASSOHN, BRUCKNER, and DVORAK, and after holding many important posts as conductor in Europe, succeeded Gustav MAHLER as director of the NEW YORK PHILHARMONIC-SYMPHONY ORCHESTRA from 1911 to 1923. He conducted the New York State Symphony Orchestra from 1923 to 1925, and then became associated with an art gallery. His compositions include an opera, an operetta, symphonies, chamber music, and songs.

Stratford-upon-Avon, a town in Warwickshire, England, which is famous as the birthplace of William SHAKESPEARE: in it is the Church of the Holy Trinity where the poet is buried; the house where he was born; the New Place which marks the site of the house Shakespeare purchased in 1597; the fountain presented to the town by George W. Childs; the Shakespeare Memorial built in 1932 on the same site as the first one erected in 1877, but destroyed by fire in 1926.

Strathspey, a Scottish dance of animated character which resembles the REEL, but is more jerky in its motions because of the peculiar syncopation in its rhythmic arrangement known as the "Scotch snap."

Straus, Oscar (1870-), Austrian composer and conductor who studied with Max BRUCH and conducted at various theatres in Germany until 1927 when he went to Vienna and Paris, becoming a French citizen in 1939. His most successful operettas were *The Chocolate Soldier* and *The Waltz Dream:* he has also composed orchestral works, chamber music, piano pieces, and numerous scores for the films.

Strauss, Johann, Sr. (1804-1849), Austrian dance composer known as "the father of the waltz" who became a musician in defiance of his father's wishes, acting as assistant conductor of Joseph Lanner's orchestra in 1823, and organizing his own orchestra in 1826. He achieved great success in Vienna, and also toured Europe and England, becoming conductor of the court balls in Vienna. His compositions include more than 150 waltzes and 100 miscellaneous dances. His son, **Johann Strauss, Jr.** (1825-1899), was the greatest dance composer of all time, becoming known as "the Waltz King": his father opposed his career as a musician, but he studied secretly, and appeared as conductor of his own orchestra in 1844. After his father's death in 1849, he merged the two orchestras, and toured Europe with tremendous success, also appearing at Boston, Mass., and New York, in 1872. His compositions include almost 500 dance pieces many of which, especially the waltzes are as popular today as they were in his own time: note the special reference on the waltzes. He also wrote sixteen operas and operettas several of which such as DIE FLEDERMAUS (The Bat), *The* QUEEN'S LACE HANDKERCHIEF, *A Night in Venice,* and the GYPSY BARON are still popular. His brother, **Joseph Strauss** (1827-1870), was also a composer and conductor of dance music who first directed for his brother, and later organized his own orchestra, composing more than 280 dance pieces. Another brother, **Eduard Strauss** (1835-1916), organized his orchestra in 1862, and succeeded Johann Strauss, Jr., as conductor of the Vienna court balls in 1870. He toured the United States in 1892 and 1901, and composed more than 300 dance pieces.

Strauss Waltzes, the popularity at the present time of the waltzes composed by Johann STRAUSS, JR., is so universal in concert, radio, and records

that a list of the greatest favorites, with the English titles, should prove of interest to music lovers: it includes *Acceleration; On the Beautiful Blue Danube; Danube Maidens; You and Me; Voices of Spring; Tales from the Vienna Woods; Emperor; Artist's Life; My Treasure; Thousand and One Nights; Telegraph; Lagoon; Morning Papers; New Vienna; Roses from the South; Vienna Blood; Wine, Women and Song; Vienna Bonbons; Where the Citrons Bloom.* Those who desire to purchase recordings of any of the above waltzes will find them listed in *The Gramophone Shop Encyclopedia of Recorded Music* together with many other waltzes composed by not only Johann Strauss, Jr., but also by his father and his brothers, Joseph and Edward.

Strauss, Richard (1864-), German composer who studied with his father, Franz Strauss, a French horn virtuoso, and at the Gymnasium and University at Munich. He occupied the post of Hans Von Bulow's assistant at the Meininger Opera, and later became court conductor in Munich and Berlin, taught a master class in composition at the Berlin Hochschule für Musik, and acted as co-director with Franz SCHALK of the Vienna State Opera. His compositions comprise 13 operas including SALOME, ELECTRA, DER ROSENKAVALIER, and *Egyptian Helen;* 2 ballets; orchestral works including the symphonic poems DON JUAN; Macbeth; DEATH AND TRANSFIGURATION; TILL EULEUSPIEGEL'S MERRY PRANKS; THUS SPAKE ZARATHUSTRA; DON QUIXOTE; A HERO'S LIFE, and SINFONIA DOMESTICA; choral works, chamber music, songs, and piano pieces.

Stravinsky, Igor (1882-), Russian composer who studied with Nicholas RIMSKY-KORSAKOW: his compositions comprise stage pieces and ballets including *The* FIRE BIRD; PETROUCHKA; Le SACRE DU PRINTEMPS; *Les Noces; Histoire du Soldat; Pulcinella; Oedipus Rex; Apollon Musagètes; The Card Party;* orchestral works including two symphonies and several suites arranged from his stage works; concertos for piano, for violin, and for two pianos; piano pieces, and songs.

Stribling, Thomas Sigismund (1881-), American novelist educated at the University of Alabama who wrote stories for religious and adventure magazines before he published his first novel, *Fombombo* (1923): his works include *Teeftallow; The Forge; The Store* which was awarded the Pulitzer Prize in 1933; *Unfinished Cathedral; Sound Wagon; These Bars of Flesh.*

Strickland, Lily Teresa (1887-), American composer educated at Converse College, Spartanburg, S. C., and at the INSTITUTE OF MUSICAL ART, New York. She has composed many successful songs including *Lindy Lou; Dreamin' Time,* and *Songs of India:* also orchestral works and several piano suites.

Strindberg, Johan August (1849-1912), Swedish dramatist educated at the University of Upsala: his first play, *Master Olof,* was produced in 1878: other plays include *The Father; Miss Julia; The Creditors; Comrades; The Keys of the Kingdom of Heaven; Advent; Crime for Crime.* He also wrote several novels, and established a theatre at Stockholm in which he produced his own plays.

Stringed Instruments, see **Musical Instruments.**

Stringfield, Lamar (1897-   ), American composer who studied the flute with George BARRERE, and composition with Percy GOETSCHIUS and George WEDGE at the Institute of Musical Art, New York, winning the Pulitzer Prize in 1928 for an orchestral suite: his compositions include dramatic music; orchestral works and chamber music.

Strings, see **Gut.**

Strobl, Alois de Lipótujvár (1856-1937), Hungarian sculptor who studied at Vienna, Paris, and Berlin where his *Persée* caused a sensation. He was greatly influenced by MICHELANGELO: among his notable works are the decorations of the Royal Opera House at Budapest; statues of CHERUBINI; SPONTINI; ERKEL, and LISZT; a monument to Louis Kossuth: also many public monuments and fountains.

Strobl, Sigismund de Kisafaludi (1884-   ), Hungarian sculptor who studied at Budapest, Vienna, Paris, Rome, and Florence: his notable works include *Morning; The Bather; Woman with a Lizard; Archer; Birth of Venus.* He is also a fine portrait sculptor who has had many famous sitters including Count Apponyi, Lord Rothmere, and the Duke of York.

Stroheim, Eric von, see **Von Stroheim, Eric.**

Strong, Austin (1881-   ), American dramatist who first studied and practiced as a landscape architect: his plays include *The Drums of Oude; The Toymaker of Nüremberg; Rip Van Winkle; Three Wise Fools; Seventh Heaven; A Play Without a Name.*

Strophe, in poetry, a definite section in the structure of an ODE: also a collection of various prosodical periods combined into a unit identical in modern poetry with the STANZA.

Strozzi, Bernardo (1581-1644), Italian painter also known as *Il Cappuccino* and *Il Prete Genovese:* he was a disciple of Michelangelo CARAVAGGI, and his notable works include *Three Philosophers; The Samaritan Woman; The Beggar; Christ and the Pharisees; Bathsheba.*

Struther, Jan, pseudonym of **Mrs. Joyce Maxtone Graham** (1901-   ), English author educated in London: her works include *Betsinda Dances and Other Poems* (1931); *Sycamore Square and Other Poems; The Modern Struwwelpeter; When Grandmother Was Small; Try Anything Twice; Mrs. Miniver,* successful both as a book and motion picture with Greer GARSON and Walter PIDGEON; *The Glass Blower.*

Stuart, Gilbert (1755-1828), American painter who executed several portraits as a boy of fourteen: he accompanied a Scottish artist, Cosmo Alexander, to Scotland in 1770, and was obliged to return when the latter died, but went back in 1775 to work for Benjamin WEST with whom he remained for eight years. He profited by the lectures of Sir Joshua REYNOLDS, starting his own studio in 1783, but returned to the United States in 1793 and remained there until his death. His works include several paintings of George and Martha Washington, William Ellery Channing, Edward Everett, Jacob Astor, Jerome Bonaparte and his wife, John Adams, Thomas JEFFERSON, John Singleton COPLEY, Washington ALLSTON, Sir Joshua REYNOLDS, and Benjamin WEST.

Stuart, James (1731-1788), English architect and painter who was sent by the Society of Dilettanti to Athens with Nicholas Revett in 1751 to study and make accurate measurements and drawings of the ancient buildings still standing on the ACROPOLIS: the material secured was published in a volume, *Classical Antiquities of Athens* (Vol. I, 1762), and exerted considerable influence in bringing about the CLASSICAL REVIVAL at the end of 18th and the beginning of the 19th centuries.

Stuart, Leslie (1866-1928), English organist and composer of FLORADORA (1899), one of the most successful operettas ever produced: his other operettas include *The Silver Slipper; The School Girl; The Belle of Mayfair; Havana; The Slim Princess; Peggy.* His real name was Thomas A. Barrett: the phenomenal success of *Floradora* was not duplicated in any of his other works.

Stucco (It.), a variety of plaster employed for the covering of the exterior of buildings, or for walls, ceilings, cornices or moldings for decorative purposes: it was used by the ancient Romans as it is in modern architecture, and made in coarse and fine grades for different purposes.

Stückgold, Grete (1895-   ), English dramatic soprano who studied at the Hochschule für Musik in Berlin, and with Jacques Stückgold, a well-known singing teacher to whom she was later married: after making her operatic debut at Nuremberg in 1913 she sang at the Berlin State Opera, and in 1927 appeared at the Metropolitan Opera House as Eva in *Die Meistersinger,* becoming a permanent member of the company. She is well-known as a concert and radio singer.

Student Prince, The, operetta in three acts: book and lyrics by Dorothy Donnelly; music by Sigmund ROMBERG, produced at New York in 1924. The story is: Prince Karl, heir to the reigning monarch, comes to Heidelberg University as one of the regular students. He falls in love with Kathie, daughter of the proprietor of the college inn, but the romance is shattered when his grandfather dies, and he is obliged not only to assume the duties of a king, but to marry a lady of the court. He comes back to the inn determined to marry Kathie; she, however, having been warned of the unhappy result of such a union, pretends that she has forgotten him and is about to marry a waiter. Disillusioned, the unhappy Karl realizes that he must assume the responsibilities which come with his royal birth. There are vocal and instrumental selections recorded by Columbia and Victor: also a Victor recording of the famous *Serenade* by Richard CROOKS.

Sturleson, Snorri, see **Edda.**

Sturm und Drang, see **Storm and Stress.**

Styx, in Greek mythology a river which flowed seven times around the world of the dead: the souls of the dead were obliged to cross it in the course of their journey from the earth. CHARON ferried the souls across for which he was paid in gold coin, and the gods swore their most binding oaths in its name.

Subject, in music a melodic phrase on which a composition is founded; also called a THEME or a MOTIVE.

Suckling, Sir John (1609-1642), English poet and dramatist educated at Trinity College, Cambridge, who was intimate with Thomas CAREW, Richard LOVELACE, and Sir William D'AVENANT: his plays include *Aglaura* (1638); *The Goblins; Brennoralt:* his poems had considerable felicity of expression and he was one of the group known as the CAVALIER POETS.

Sudermann, Hermann (1857-1928), German dramatist and novelist: his novels include *Dame Care* (1887); *Song of Songs; The Mad Professor.* In 1889 his first play, *Honor,* was produced with success: it was followed by *Sodom's End; Magda; The Battle of the Butterflies; Home; Fritzchen; The Eternal Masculine.*

Sue, Eugène (1804-1857), French novelist who was said to have had the empress Josephine as his godmother, and served as a surgeon in the French army. His novels, *The Mysteries of Paris* (10 vols. 1842-1843) and *The Wandering Jew* (10 vols. 1844-1845) were tremendously successful: they were both dramatized by him with the collaboration of others.

Suetonius (Caius Suetonius Tranquillus), Roman biographer and historian who lived in the early part of the 2nd century A.D. He was in the service of Hadrian and friendly with PLINY THE YOUNGER: his works include *Lives of the Caesars* comprising biographies of the first twelve Caesars.

Suite, in music a cycle of instrumental pieces in various idealized dance forms: the oldest suites in the 17th century consisted of the ALLEMAND, COURANTE, SARABANDE and GIGUE. Other movements occasionally introduced include the BOUR- REE; GAVOTTE; MINUET; *Musette;* LOURE; PASSE- PIED, and PAVAN.

Suk, Josef (1874-1935), Bohemian violinist and composer who studied composition at the Prague Conservatory with Antonin DVORAK: he was a member of the Bohemian String Quartet and from 1922 professor and later director of the Prague Conservatory. His compositions include orchestral works, chamber music, violin pieces, piano pieces, and songs.

Sullavan, Margaret (1911-), American stage and screen actress who made her first appearance in 1929 with a stock company, and her New York debut in 1931: after appearing for several years in various plays she entered the films in 1933. Among the pictures in which she has been featured are *Little Man, What Now?; The Good Fairy; So Red the Rose; The Moon's Our Home; Shopworn Angel; The Shining Hour; The Shop Around the Corner; The Mortal Storm; Back Street; Appointment for Love.*

Sullivan, Sir Arthur Seymour (1842-1900), English composer who studied at the Royal Academy of Music, London, with Sir William Sterndale BENNETT, and at the Leipzig Conservatory with Ignaz MOSCHELES, Moritz HAUPTMANN and Hans RICHTER. In 1866 he became professor of composition at the Royal Academy of Music: he also headed the National Training School from 1876 to 1881, and conducted the London Philharmonic from 1885 to 1887. His works include several operettas with Sir William S. GILBERT as librettist: ten of these reached a degree of popularity unequaled in the annals of light opera. He also wrote several operettas with other librettists; a grand opera, *Ivanhoe,* produced in 1891; two ballets; incidental music for plays; oratorios; cantatas: also songs including *The Lost Chord.* The titles of the operettas written with Gilbert include *Trial by Jury; The Sorcerer; H.M.S. Pinafore; The Pirates of Penzance; Patience; Iolanthe; Princess Ida; The Mikado; Ruddygore; The Yeomen of the Guard; The Gondoliers; Utopia Limited; The Grand Duke.*

Sullivan, Louis (1850-1924), American architect who studied at the Institute of Technology, Boston, Mass., and at the ECOLE DES BEAUX-ARTS, Paris. Upon his return to the United States he worked for a time independently, and later organized the firm of Adler and Sullivan; one of its principal contracts was the erection of the Auditorium, Chicago, to accommodate the Chicago Opera Company. He designed the Transportation Building at the Columbian Exposition in 1893 at Chicago, and was one of the pioneers in the development of steel-frame buildings.

Sully, Thomas (1783-1872), American painter born in England who was brought by his parents to the United States in 1792: in 1806 he came to New York and studied with John TRUMBULL, John Wesley JARVIS and Gilbert STUART. In 1809 he went to England where he studied with Benjamin WEST: among his sitters for portraits after his return were Thomas JEFFERSON, George Frederick COOKE, Charles KEMBLE, Fanny KEMBLE, and Rembrandt PEALE: he also executed many genre paintings including the famous *Boy with a Torn Hat.*

Sully-Prudhomme, René François Armand (1839-1907), French poet who was one of the PARNASSIANS: his works include *Stanzas and Poems* (1865); *The Broken Vase; The Stables of Augeas; The Solitudes; Justice; Happiness:* he also wrote *Expression in the Fine Arts,* and *Reflections on the Art of Versification.*

Sumer Is Icumen In, an English ROUND said to have been composed by John of Fornsete, a monk at Reading Abbey. It is the oldest known harmonized music, and there has been much debate among authorities as to its authenticity because no music approaching it in beauty of melody or construction was written for more than one hundred fifty years after it appeared. There is a recording in the first volume of the *Columbia History of Music*.

Suppé, Franz von (1820-1895), Austrian composer of Belgian descent whose real name was Francesco Ezechiele Ermenegildo Cavaliere Suppé-Demelli: he studied at the Vienna Conservatory with Simon SECHTER and Ignaz Seyfried. After conducting at several theatres he became leader at the Leopoldstädter Theatre in Vienna: his compositions include 210 operas, operettas, vaudevilles and stage pieces. Several of the overtures, including *Pique Dame; Beautiful Galathea; Light Cavalry*, and *Poet and Peasant*, are still popular, and can be obtained in recordings.

"Surprise" Symphony (Haydn), an orchestral work composed by Joseph HAYDN while he was on his second visit to London where he was invited in 1792 by Johann SALOMON to compose and conduct six symphonies as he had done on his previous visit in 1791. The *Surprise Symphony* was played at the sixth Salomon concert on March 23, 1792. Its success was immediate. The *Oracle* considered the second movement (from which the symphony derives its name, occasioned by the sudden orchestral crash at the conclusion of the first quiet presentation of the principal theme) one of Haydn's happiest inventions. According to the composer: "The first *Allegro* of my symphony was received with countless 'Bravos,' but enthusiasm rose to its highest pitch after the *Andante* with the drum stroke. 'Ancora! Ancora!' was cried out on all sides, and PLEYEL himself complimented me on my idea!" There is a Victor recording by the Boston Symphony Orchestra conducted by Serge Koussevitzky, and a Columbia recording by the Columbia Broadcasting Symphony Orchestra under Howard Barlow.

Surrealism, a modern French movement in the world of art which is as difficult to explain as the motivation behind it is indefinite and vague: its goal is the presentation of dream states and the unconscious based on a Freudian theory that these are the genuine indices of the real personality.

Suspension, in music a DISSONANCE caused by suspending, i.e., holding back, a tone or tones of a chord while others progress: according to the rules of HARMONY every suspension carries with it a preliminary step known as *preparation* and a concluding step called *resolution*.

Sutro, Alfred (1863-1933), English dramatist educated in London and Brussels who engaged in business before entering the field of dramatic composition: he translated works by Maurice MAETERLINCK before William ARCHER persuaded him to attempt original plays. His works include *The Walls of Jericho; Women in Love; The Foolish Virgins; The Fascinating Mr. Vanderveldt; John Gayde's Honour; The Perplexed Husband; The Choice:* also an autobiography, *Celebrities and Simple Souls*.

Svendsen, Johan Severin (1840-1911), Danish violinist and composer who studied with Ferdinand DAVID, Moritz HAUPTMANN, and Hans RICHTER at the Leipzig Conservatory: from 1883 to 1908 he conducted the court orchestra at Copenhagen. His compositions, which rank among the finest created by Scandinavian composers, include orchestral works, chamber music, songs, and a *Romance* for violin and orchestra.

Swan Lake, The (Le Lac des Cygnes), a romantic ballet in one act: choreography by Marius PETIPA; music by Peter TSCHAIKOWSKY; first performed at St. Petersburg in 1894. The ballet in its original form—three acts and four scenes—was performed at St. Petersburg in 1876 with little success, but in the new form it remains permanently in the repertory of ballet troupes. The story is simple: a prince and his friends hunt near a lake: swans appear and dance in the clearing. The prince finds out that the swans are really young girls who have been transformed into swans by an evil magician. He falls in love with the queen of the swans, but the sorcerer appears and spirits the queen away. Unable to overcome the magic, the prince falls to the ground dead. There is a Columbia recording of the music by the London Philharmonic Orchestra.

Swan of Tuonela (Sibelius), the third part of the symphonic poem, *Lemminkäinen,* by Jean SIBELIUS, and a work usually played in sections. The composition is inspired by the Finnish epic, *Kalevala:* the inscription on the score sets forth the program: "Tuonela, the Kingdom of Death, the Hades of Finnish mythology, is surrounded by a broad river of black water and rapid current, in which the Swan of Tuonela glides in majestic fashion and sings." Sibelius himself conducted the work in 1914 at Litchfield, Conn., while on a visit to the United States: there is a Victor recording by the Philadelphia Orchestra directed by Eugene Ormandy, and a Columbia recording by the Chicago Orchestra with Frederick Stock.

Swarthout, Gladys (1904-), American contralto who studied at the Bush Conservatory, Chicago, making her debut in 1924 with the Chicago Opera Company in Puccini's *Tosca,* and in 1929 with the Metropolitan Opera Company in Ponchielli's *La Gioconda*. She has appeared in several films including *The Rose of the Rancho,* and has also sung on commercial broadcasts.

Swartwout, Egerton (1871-1943), American architect who was graduated from Yale University in 1891, and worked with McKim, Mead & White more than twenty years before he established his own office: his works include more than one hundred buildings among which are the Missouri State Capitol at Jefferson; the new section of the Yale Museum of Fine Arts; the Yale Club in New York; the Mary Baker Eddy Memorial at Boston, Mass.: also memorials for the dead of World War I designed for the American Battle Monuments Commission.

Swedish Nightingale, see **Lind, Jenny.**

Sweelinck, Jan Pieterzoon (1562-1621), Dutch organist, composer, and teacher who studied with

Giosefe ZARLINO, and became the greatest virtuoso, pedagogue, and composer of his time. His compositions include secular songs, sacred music, and organ pieces which established the form later used by Johann Sebastian BACH.

Swift, Jonathan (1667-1745), Irish prose satirist educated at Trinity College, Dublin: his works of interest in this volume include *The Battle of the Books* (1704), *The Tale of a Tub*, and *Gulliver's Travels* (1726) a volume of imaginary adventure which is not only a marvelous example of imagination, but has retained its appeal to both young and old for more than two hundred years. The rest of his works consist of satirical essays on politics and religion.

Swinburne, Algernon Charles (1837-1909), English poet and dramatist educated at Oxford who later became intimate with William MORRIS, Dante Gabriel ROSSETTI, Edward BURNE-JONES and other members of the PRE-RAPHAELITES. His poetical works include *Poems and Ballads* (1866); *A Song of Italy; Songs Before Sunrise; Erechtheus; Songs of the Spring Tides; Tristram of Lyonesse; Locrine:* he also wrote several dramas including *The Queen Mother; Rosamond; Chastelard; Atalanta in Calydon; Bothwell; Mary Stuart.*

Swing, the name given to certain types of JAZZ: the term is so vague that it is not possible to obtain any precise information from swing "experts," including composers, leaders or players, as to its exact meaning, or as to what kind of jazz it specifically applies. Robert McBride, a modern composer who has introduced "swing" into his symphonic works, has this to say: "A musician cannot define swing without doing it; it must be heard—not read about."

Swing Mikado, a version in SWING of Gilbert and Sullivan's operetta, *The Mikado:* it was produced by the Federal Theatre Project in 1938 at Chicago, and in 1939 at New York, the original music being altered to modern JAZZ rhythms.

Swinnerton, Frank Arthur (1884-), English novelist who worked as a proof-reader with publishing houses, and wrote several novels before his first success, *Nocturne,* appeared in 1917. His later works include *Shops and Houses; Coquette; The Three Lovers; Elder Sister; Harvest Comedy; The Two Wives; Fortunate Lady; Thankless Child:* also a critical volume, *The Georgian Literary Scene.*

Swiss National Museum (Zurich), a national institution at Zurich which is not built on a large scale, but nevertheless is a model of systematic arrangement throughout its fifty rooms which illustrate the historical progress of the fine arts: its collection of stained glass is regarded as one of the choicest assemblies of the kind in Europe.

Sydney, Sir Philip, see **Sidney, Sir Philip.**

Syllabary, a set of written characters each one of which is used to spell not a single sound as in an ALPHABET, but a complete syllable.

Sylphides, Les, a romantic ballet in one act: libretto and choreography by Michel FOKINE; music by Frédéric CHOPIN orchestrated by Vittorio Rieti; first performed with the title *Chopiniana* at St. Petersburg in 1906. The title was changed to *Les Sylphides* by Sergei DIAGHILEFF when he presented the ballet at Paris with PAVLOWA, NIJINSKY and KARSAVINA in the principal roles. The musical numbers include parts of nocturnes, mazurkas, waltzes, and preludes by Chopin. There are both Victor and Columbia recordings.

Sylvia, ballet in three acts: book by Jules Barbier and Baron de Reinach; choreography by Louis MERANTE; music by Léo DELIBES; first performed at Paris in 1876. This is one of the most charmingly conceived ballets of all time with delightful music including the *Pizzicati, Valse Lente,* and *Procession of Bacchus.* There is a Gramophone recording directed by John Barbirolli.

Symons, Arthur (1865-), English poet and critic educated in France and Italy who joined the editorial staff of the *Athenaeum* and *Saturday Review:* his poetical works include *Days and Nights* (1889); *Silhouettes; London Nights; Knave of Hearts; Tristan and Iseult.* His critical works include *Studies in Two Literatures; Studies in Seven Arts; The Romantic Movement in English Poetry.*

Symphonic Poem, an orchestral composition constructed along the lines of the SYMPHONY, but usually written in one movement, and provided with a program which begins with the title of the work suggesting a historical or imaginative subject. Franz LISZT is generally regarded as the inventor of the form: thirteen of his works, including *Les* PRELUDES, *Tasso, Prometheus,* and MAZEPPA are symphonic poems. Among the many composers who have been inspired to create in the form are SMETANA; BORODIN; TSCHAIKOWSKY whose several works such as *Romeo and Juliet* are called overtures, but are really symphonic poems; SAINT-SAENS; FRANCK; DEBUSSY; ELGAR; DUKAS; Richard STRAUSS whose various works such as *Till Eulenspiegel's Merry Pranks* are called tone poems; RESPIGHI; HONEGGER; GRIFFES; LOEFFLER; MUSSORGSKY; SIBELIUS; RIMSKY-KORSAKOW.

Symphonic Variations (Franck), see **Variations Symphoniques (Franck).**

Symphonie Espagnole (Lalo), a work for violin and orchestra by Edouard LALO, first played at the concert of the Association Artistique at Paris in 1875. The solo violin was played by Pablo de SARASATE to whom it is dedicated, and it was conducted by Edouard COLONNE. It was first performed in the United States by Charles Martin LOEFFLER at a concert of the Boston Symphony Orchestra in Feb. 1890. There is a Victor recording by Yehudi Menuhin, and a Columbia recording by Bronislaw Hubermann.

Symphonie Fantastique (Berlioz), an orchestral work by Hector BERLIOZ said to have been inspired by his passion for Harriet SMITHSON, an Irish actress whom he first saw on the stage at Paris in SHAKESPEARE's "Romeo and Juliet." It was first performed in 1830: its subtitle is "Episodes in the Life of an Artist," and according to Berlioz it pictures the visions of a musician under the influence of opium. In the first movement he meets the lady of his dreams; in the second he sees her again at a grand ball; in the third his heart is calmed in the midst of pastoral scenes; in the fourth he marches to the scaffold after having killed his love; in the fifth witches dance around his coffin, after holding burial services in which the Dies Irae and the diabolical dance theme are intermingled. Berlioz uses one slow, dreamy motive, called by him the idee fixe, in the first movement to symbolize the sentiment of perfect love, and brings it back in all other movements. There is a Columbia recording by the Paris Symphony Orchestra, and a Victor recording by the Cleveland Orchestra directed by Artur Rodzinski.

Symphonie Fantastique (Ballet), a symphonic ballet in five scenes: libretto by Hector Berlioz; choreography by Leonide Massine; music by Hector Berlioz; first performed at Covent Garden, London, in 1936. The plot follows closely the synopsis of the *Symphony Fantastique* as outlined by Berlioz: Leonide Massine mimed the role of the young musician, and Tamara Toumanova enacted the part of his beloved.

Symphony, a form of orchestral composition which developed from the overture which was used by early Italian composers as the instrumental prelude to operas and oratorios. Toward the middle of the 18th century composers began to write orchestral works for concert use in three movements: the first was lively but dignified in spirit; the second slow, and the third constituted a spirited finale. Joseph Haydn added the fourth movement, the minuet, and later Ludwig van Beethoven substituted the scherzo for the minuet. The principal composers in the symphonic form before Beethoven were Stamitz; Gossec; Boccherini; Karl Philipp Emanuel Bach; Sammartini, Joseph and Johann Michael Haydn, and Mozart. The history of the symphony continues with Beethoven; Schubert; Mendelssohn; Schumann; Brahms; Bruckner; Franck; Mahler; Tschaikowsky; Rachmaninoff; Borodin; Glazunoff; Gliere; Miaskovsky; Shostakovitch; Dvorak; Sibelius; Elgar; Vaughan Williams; Bax; Chadwick; Mrs. H. H. A. Beach; Kelley; Hadley; Sessions; William Schuman; Hanson; Roy Harris; Szymanowski; Roussel, and Malipiero. Of recent years the symphonic form has not appealed to many modern composers, but has proved attractive to those who elect to create in the forms which were acceptable to the greatest masters of musical composition.

Symphony Orchestra of Mexico, an organization founded by Carlos Chavez in 1928, and conducted by him since that time: the orchestra's repertory includes both classical and modern works, and in 1942 the organization made a tour of Mexico which included all the larger cities, including works by Mexican composers on its programs, and employing native soloists.

Symphony Society of New York, see **New York Symphony Society.**

Syncopation, in music the tying of a weak or unaccented beat to the strong or accented beat which follows: syncopation is an essential feature of modern swing or jazz, but it is a fallacy to state that it originated with "ragtime" because Robert Schumann made use of it a century ago in his compositions.

Synge, John Millington (1871-1909), Irish poet and dramatist educated at Trinity College, Dublin, who traveled in Germany with the intention of studying music, but later returned to Paris where he was finally induced by William Butler Yeats to write for the new Irish Theatre. His plays include *The Shadow of the Glen* (1910); *Riders to the Sea; The Well of the Saints; The Playboy of the Western World; The Tinker's Wedding; Deirdre of the Sorrows.*

Syrinx, see **Pandean Pipe.**

Székely, Bertalan (1835-1910), Hungarian painter who studied with Karl Rahl in Vienna and Karl von Piloty at Munich. He decorated several churches with religious frescoes: among his notable works are *Flight of Charles VII; The Battle of Mohăcr; Sisters of Charity at a Sick-Bed; The Dancer; Japanese Girl; The Nun; Women of Erlau Defending Their City against the Turks.*

Szell, George (1897-), Hungarian conductor and composer who studied with Eusebius Mandyczewski and Max Reger, making his debut with the Berlin Philharmonic Orchestra and later becoming assistant conductor with Richard Strauss at the Royal Opera House. He has also conducted at the Opera House and the Philharmonic Concerts at Prague, and was guest conductor of several American orchestras before becoming conductor at the Metropolitan Opera House, New York, in 1942.

Szigeti, Joseph (1892-), Hungarian violinist who studied with Jenö Hubay at the Royal Academy in Budapest, making his debut at Berlin in 1905, and succeeding Henri Marteau as professor of violin at the Geneva Conservatory from 1917 to 1924. In 1925 he made his debut in New York, and has since appeared with the major American orchestras and in recital.

Szymanowski, Karol (1883-1937), Polish composer who studied with Zygmunt Noskowski in Warsaw, and formed a society, "Young Poland in Music," at Berlin in 1905 with George Fitelburg. His compositions include operas, ballets, symphonies, chamber music, piano works, violin works, choruses, and songs.

T

Tadema, Sir Laurence Alma, see **Alma-Tadema, Sir Laurence.**

Taft, Lorado (1860-1936), American sculptor educated at the University of Illinois who studied at the ECOLE DES BEAUX-ARTS, Paris, and in 1886 became instructor at the CHICAGO ART INSTITUTE, remaining there until 1929. His notable works include *Solitude of the Soul; The Blind; Black Hawk at Oregon, Ill.; Columbus Memorial Fountain* at Washington, D. C.; *Fountain of the Great Lakes* and *Fountain of Time* at Chicago, Ill.: he also wrote a *History of American Sculpture* and *Modern Tendencies in Sculpture.*

Taglioni, Filippo (1778-1871), Italian dancer and choreographer who made his debut at Pisa in 1794, and later danced in Paris, Stockholm, Milan, Vienna, Berlin, and London: he created many ballets the most famous of which was *La Sylphide* first produced at Paris in 1732. His daughter, **Marie Sophie Taglioni** (1804-1884), studied with her father and made her debut at Vienna in 1822: she appeared with great success at the Paris Opéra in *La Vestale,* and remained there for many years as *prima ballerina* in operas by ROSSINI, AUBER, HEROLD, HALEVY and ADAM; also in several ballets written by her father who was choreographer at the opera house. Her brother, **Paul Taglioni** (1808-1884), made his debut as a dancer in 1825, appearing in European capitals with great success, and composing about forty ballets in thirty years many of which were extremely popular in their day.

Tagore, Sir Rabindranath (1861-1941), Bengali poet, dramatist and novelist educated at private schools and at University College, London. He lectured in the United States in 1913, and received the Nobel Prize for literature during the same year. In 1901 he founded the internationally famous school at Bolpur: at sixty-eight he exhibited paintings in Europe, England, and the United States. He was also a composer who wrote over 3,000 songs, and his poetical works contain more than 100,000 lines. Among his works available in English are *Gitanjali* (Song Offerings) (1912); *The Gardener; The Crescent Moon; The Post Office,* a play; *The Cycle of Spring,* a play; *Stray Birds; Red Oleanders,* a play; *The Wreck,* a novel; *The Religion of Man; Fireflies; The Home and the World,* a novel: also the autobiographical *My Reminiscences.*

Tagore, Surindro Mohun (1840-1914), Hindu musicologist who studied both native music and European music: in 1871 he founded the Bengal Music Society, and in 1881 the Bengal Academy of Music, directing both institutions until his death. He formed the finest music library in India, perfected a simplified notation which was adopted throughout India, and was also an authority on Asiatic musical instruments. He assembled a collection of Asiatic instruments for the Metropolitan Museum of Art, and wrote treatises on all forms of Hindu and Oriental music.

Taine, Adolphe (1828-1893), French critic and historian who occupied the post of professor at the ECOLE DES BEAUX-ARTS, Paris, from 1864: his works of interest in this volume include *Essay on La Fontaine's Fables* (1853); *Contemporary English Writers; History of English Literature,* his most famous work; *Philosophy of Art in Italy; The Ideal in Art.*

Taj Mahal, a mausoleum erected at Agra, India, by Shah Jehan for his favorite wife, Mumtaz Mahal: the Shah himself was interred there in 1666. It was begun in 1630 and completed twenty years later: the building rests on a base of white marble 18 feet high and 313 feet square with tapering minarets 133 feet high at the corners. The interior contains four domed chambers in the corners, and an immense octagonal space in the middle of which are two marble cenotaphs enclosed in a superb open screen of marble. Light reaches the chamber only through the delicately pierced marble screens which adorn all the windows. The interior walls are enriched by mosaics in which the flower motives and arabesques are formed of AGATE, JASPER, and BLOODSTONE.

Takeda Izumo (1688-1756), Japanese dramatist and theatre manager who assumed the management of the famous Takemoto-Za Theatre in Osaka in 1705: his dramatic masterpiece is *Chiushingura,* regarded as the finest version of the ancient *Story of the Forty-seven Ronins.* With his contemporary, CHIKAMATSU MONZAYE-MON, he is considered an important factor in the development of Japanese popular drama.

Tale, in literature the general term applied to brief or lengthy ancient or modern fictitious narratives: its more restricted meaning is a story handed down orally, and usually of ancient, unknown origin. The ARABIAN NIGHTS is full of popular tales: also the GESTA ROMANORUM, the *Tales of Times Past* by Charles PERRAULT, and the *Household Tales* by the brothers Grimm.

Tales of Hoffmann, grand opera in four acts: libretto by Jules Barbier; music by Jacques OFFENBACH; first produced at Paris in 1881, at New York in 1882, and revived at the Manhattan Opera House in 1907. The story of the opera revolves around the poet Hoffmann who has unfortunate love affairs with Olympia, an automaton; Giuletta, a faithless Venetian lady; Antonia, a beautiful singer who dies of consumption. There is a Decca abridged recording, and many Columbia and Victor recordings of the popular *Barcarole* both as a vocal solo and as transcribed for orchestra..

Taliaferro, Mabel (1887-), American actress who made her first appearance in 1889 as a child in *Blue Jeans,* and also with James A. HERNE and Chauncey OLCOTT. Among the plays in which she has appeared are *The Children of the Ghetto; Mrs. Wiggs of the Cabbage Patch; In the Bishop's Carriage; On the Quiet; Polly of the Circus,* her greatest success; *Ingomar; The Banker's Wife; The Woman Thou Gavest Me; Alice in Wonderland; Autumn Crocus.* Her sister, **Edith Taliaferro** (1893-), appeared as a child with James A. HERNE in *Shore Acres:* in 1898 she toured with Olga Nethersole in *Frou-Frou.* Among the plays in which she appeared are *Rip van Winkle* with Thomas JEFFERSON; *A Midsummer Night's Dream* with Ben GREET; *Uncle Tom's Cabin; Mrs. Wiggs of the Cabbage Patch; Brewster's Millions; The New Henrietta; Mother Carey's Chickens; Tarnish; Peg O' My Heart; Private Lives; Pygmalion.*

Taliesin, a Welsh BARD presumed to have lived in the 6th century: he accompanied the Welsh king into battle and sang of his victories. There is considerable difference of opinion among competent authorities as to his having actually existed because the *Romance of Taliesin* dates back only to the 13th century.

Tallys, Thomas (c.1505-1585), English organist and composer who was a gentleman of the Chapel Royal under Henry VIII, Edward VI, Queen Mary, and Queen Elizabeth, also acting as organist with William BYRD. Queen Elizabeth granted Tallys and Byrd the exclusive right to print music and ruled music paper for a period of 21 years. His compositions consist of music for the church.

Talma, François Joseph (1763-1826), French actor educated in England who first appeared at the Comédie Française in 1787 in Voltaire's *Mahomet*, creating a sensation by wearing a costume for his part in accordance with the period of the play, and the reform was soon adopted. His first great success was in Andrea CHENIER's play, *Charles IX.* He sympathized with the Revolutionists and left the Comédie-Française to found the Théâtre de la République: Napoleon I was one of his greatest admirers.

Talmud, the work which contains the Jewish traditional laws and regulations as expounded in the written law of the Pentateuch: it also contains comments on the historical, poetical, and ethical portions of the Scriptures. The version generally accepted is the Babylonian Talmud: its 63 divisions are printed in twelve folio volumes on 2,947 pages. The other version is known as the Palestinian or Jerusalem Talmud.

Tamagno, Francesco (1850-1905), Italian operatic tenor who studied at the Turin Conservatory and made his debut in Verdi's *Masked Ball* at Palermo in 1874 with great success: in 1887 he created the title role in Verdi's *Otello.* He made his debut in 1891 at the Metropolitan Opera House, New York, in the same opera, and sang there again in 1894-5. After engagements in South America, Portugal, Spain, France, and England he retired in 1902.

Tamayo y Baus, Manuel (1829-1898), Spanish actor and dramatist whose mother, Joaquina Baus, appeared in a play adapted from the French by her son when he was twelve years old. His plays include *Virginia* (1853); *The Madness of Love; Money; Lances of Honor; A New Drama* in which the author used Shakespeare and Yorick as characters.

Tambourine, a small drum consisting of a shallow circular hoof of wood or metal with one head of parchment and equipped with several pairs of loose metal plates called jingles: it is held in the left hand and played by striking with the right hand. It is mentioned as the *timbrel* in the Bible, and is used in the modern concert orchestra whenever called for by the score.

Tamerlane (c.1333-1405), a Mongol conqueror said to have been a descendant of JENGHIZ KHAN: at the end of the 14th century, after having established his hold over Samarkand, he invaded Asia from Delhi to Damascus, conquering Persia and Syria in campaigns lasting over thirty years. His career is the subject of the drama, *Tamburlaine* (1590) by Christopher MARLOWE.

Tamiroff, Akim, contemporary Russian stage and screen actor trained at the Moscow Art Theatre: among the films in which he has appeared are *Sadie McKee; Whom the Gods Destroy; Lives of a Bengal Lancer; Naughty Marietta; China Seas; Rhumba; Black Fury; The Story of Louis Pasteur; The General Died at Dawn; Anthony Adverse; High, Wide and Handsome; Union Pacific; The Way of All Flesh; The Corsican Brothers; Tortilla Flat.*

Tam-Tam, an East Indian name for the GONG.

Taneiev, Sergei Ivanovich (1856-1915), Russian pianist and composer who studied at the Moscow Conservatory with Nicholas RUBINSTEIN and Peter TSCHAIKOWSKY: after touring with Leopold Auer he succeeded Tschaikowsky as professor of musical theory at the Moscow Conservatory. His compositions include operas, symphonies, chamber music, songs and a treatise on counterpoint. He was regarded as one of the greatest Russian piano virtuosos.

Tango, a dance similar to the HABANERA in rhythm but faster in tempo: it is a spirited and graceful dance which is usually regarded as a professional rather than a general dance. It is said to have originated in Mexico, but enjoys its greatest favor in the Argentine Republic.

Tanner, Henry Ossawa (1857-1937), American Negro painter who studied with Thomas EAKINS, and with Jean Paul LAURENS and Benjamin CONSTANT in Paris: his works include *The Raising of Lazarus; The Annunciation; Nicodemus Coming to Christ; Sodom and Gomorrah; Christ at the House of Mary and Martha; Disciples at the Tomb; The Jews' Wailing Place; Christ in the Temple.* He became a member of the National Academy.

Tannhäuser, a German lyric poet of the 13th century who belonged to the family of Tanhusen at Salzburg. He led a wandering life at various German courts and the Far East from 1240 to 1270, and was famous as a minnesinger and as a composer of dance songs. A German ballad of the 16th century was probably the basis of **Tannhäuser,** an opera in three acts: text and music by Richard Wagner; first performed at Dresden in 1845; at the Stadt Theatre, New York, in 1859, and at the Metropolitan Opera House, New York, in 1884. There is a slightly abridged Columbia recording by the Bayreuth Festival Soloists, Chorus and Orchestra: also Victor and Columbia recordings of the *Overture;* the *Overture and Bacchanale* as prepared by Wagner for the presentation at Paris in 1861; the *Pilgrim's Chorus;* the aria, *Hail, Hall of Song;* the *Festival March; Elizabeth's Prayer;* and the *Evening Star:* all the above are listed in *The Gramophone Shop Encyclopedia of Recorded Music.*

Tannyu, Kano (1602-1674), Japanese painter who was one of the four most famous representatives of the Kano school. He studied the old masters, and executed many small-scale copies of their paintings: he also painted the figures of the Chinese sages at the Imperial Palace in 1642.

Tantalus, in Greek mythology the son of ZEUS who was admitted to the councils of the gods: he abused their confidence by killing his son, PELOPS, and serving his body as meat to the gods in order to test their powers of observation. He was sent to TARTARUS where he stood neck-high in water which receded when he attempted to drink: over his head were fruits which were wafted by the wind out of his reach when he tried to grasp them.

Tapestry, an ornamental textile used for wall hangings, and made by the design being threaded into the warp of the cloth by using the fingers or a bodkin. Tapestries are mentioned in HOMER'S works, and also are referred to in the Bible: in the 13th century the designs on tapestries were evidently suggested by works of art brought back from the Orient by the Crusaders. The great centers of tapestry weaving were Arras, Brussels, Aubusson, Valenciennes, and Mortlake where imitations were made of the works produced by GOBELIN at Paris.

Tarantella, (1) a dance originating in the southern part of Italy; written in 6-8 time and gradually increasing in tempo as danced to the accompaniment of tambourines and castanets. (2) In instrumental music of a higher order the name of a brilliant composition alternating between major and minor, and having all the general characteristics of the dance.

Tarbell, Edmund C. (1862-1938), American painter who studied at the Boston Museum of Fine Arts School, and with BOULANGER and LEFEBRE in Paris, later acting as head of the Corcoran School of Art in Washington, D. C. He was a distinguished painter of landscapes, figures, and portraits: his works include *Girl Reading; Josephine and Mercié; Golden Screen.*

Tarkington, Booth (1869-), American novelist and dramatist: his novels, which are stories of American life and character written in entertaining and realistic style, include *The Gentleman from Indiana; Monsieur Beaucaire; The Conquest of Canaan; Penrod; Penrod and Sam; Seventeen; The Magnificent Ambersons,* a Pulitzer prize winner in 1919; *Alice Adams,* a Pulitzer prize winner in 1922; *Gentle Julia; The Plutocrat; Claire Ambler; Penrod Jashber; Presenting Lily Mars; Little Orvie; The Heritage of Hatcher Ide.* His plays include dramatization of the novels *The Gentleman from Indiana; Monsieur Beaucaire; Penrod; Seventeen; The Plutocrat:* he also wrote alone or collaborated in *The Man from Home; Cameo Kirby; Mister Antonio; The Gibson Upright; The Intimate Strangers; Colonel Satan,* and several other plays. His autobiography, *The World Does Move,* was published in 1928, and several of his novels including *Alice Adams, Gentle Julia,* several of the Penrod stories, *The Magnificent Ambersons,* and *Presenting Lily Mars* were adapted for the films.

Tartarus, in Greek mythology the place of punishment for the wicked after death: the term is also used for the underworld as a whole.

Tartini, Giuseppe (1692-1770), Italian violinist and composer who was greatly inspired by the playing of Francesco VERACINI, and perfected himself to such an extent that he was appointed solo violinist at the Church of San Antonio in Padua. He founded a violin school at Padua which had many famous pupils: his works include 140 violin concertos, 50 trios, and 150 violin sonatas. He is regarded as one of the greatest early masters of the violin: his sonata, the *Devil's Trill,* alone would make him famous.

Tasso, Torquato (1544-1595), Italian poet educated at Jesuit schools in Naples and Rome: he was adjudged insane twice and confined on the latter occasion for seven years. In 1594 he was invited by Pope Clement VIII to be crowned poet laureate on Capitoline Hill, but died before the ceremony could take place. His works include a romantic epic, *Rinaldo;* a pastoral drama, *Aminta;* an epic poem in two parts, *Jerusalem Delivered* and *Jerusalem Conquered,* celebrating the first Crusade.

Tate, Allen (1899-), American poet, essayist, biographer, and novelist educated at Vanderbilt University: his works include *Mr. Pope and Other Poems* (1928); *Stonewall Jackson; Jefferson Davis: His Rise and Fall; Robert E. Lee,* a poem; *The Fathers; Invitation to Learning* with Huntington Cairns and Mark VAN DOREN.

Tate, Nahum (1652-1715), English poet educated at Trinity College, Dublin: his works consist chiefly of adaptations of works by SHAKESPEARE and other dramatists so that they were devoid of political implications: his one work which has survived is the libretto for DIDO AND AENEAS, an opera for which the music was composed by Henry PURCELL in 1689. He became poet laureate in 1692, and was commissioned by John DRYDEN to write the second part of *Absalom and Achitophel.*

Tate Gallery (London), an institution founded by Sir **Henry Tate** (1819-1899), at London in 1897: its contents included 65 paintings presented by him; also most of the pictures from the NATIONAL GALLERY, LONDON, executed by English artists during the previous eighty years, and many paintings which formerly hung in the South Kensington Museum.

Tatti, Jacopo, see **Sansovino, Jacopo.**

Tauber, Richard (1890-), German tenor who studied at the Hoch conservatory in Frankfort, and acted as a conductor before taking up singing. In 1912 he made his debut at the Dresden Opera House in *The Magic Flute,* and after singing at the Berlin and Vienna opera houses, appeared in several operettas by Franz LEHAR. He has appeared in opera and recital and also in several musical films.

Tausig, Karl (1841-1871), German pianist and composer who studied with Franz LISZT, becoming one of the great master's favorite pupils, and making his debut at Berlin in 1858. After touring Germany and Austria he founded a *School of Advanced Piano Playing* at Berlin. His compositions are chiefly original virtuoso pieces and transcriptions for the piano.

Taylor, Bayard (1825-1878), American traveler, poet, journalist, and novelist: after acting as correspondent for the New York *Tribune,* and traveling more than 50,000 miles in all parts of the world, he accepted several diplomatic posts including that of United States minister at Berlin in 1878. He wrote many travel volumes; several books of poetry such as *Poems of the Orient; The Story of Kennett:* also *Studies in German Literature* and a translation of GOETHE'S *Faust.*

Taylor, Deems (1885-), American music critic and composer educated at New York University who studied the theory of music with Oscar Coon: he has acted as music critic for the New York *World,* editor of *Musical America,* narrator for the opera broadcasts from the Metropolitan Opera House, radio commentator for the Sunday afternoon broadcasts of the New York Philharmonic-Symphony Orchestra, and musical adviser to the Columbia Broadcasting Company. His works include an orchestral suite, *Through the Looking Glass;* two cantatas; three operas, *The King's Henchman, Peter Ibbetsen,* and *Ramuntcho.* He has also written *Of Men and Music* and *The Well-Tempered Listener.*

Taylor, Laurette (1884-), American actress who first appeared in vaudeville and after 1903 in the legitimate theatre: among the plays in which she has been featured are *Alias Jimmy Valentine; The Bird of Paradise; Peg O' My Heart* in which she had a run of 600 nights in New York, and 500 nights in London; *Humoresque; Sweet Nell of Old Drury; Pierrot, The Prodigal; Trelawney of the Wells; Alice-Sit-by-the-Fire; The Old Lady Shows Her Medals; Outward Bound; Candida.*

Taylor, Phoebe Atwood (1909-), American author of detective stories educated at Barnard College, New York, who sometimes writes under the pen name "Alice Tilton": her successful stories include *The Cape Cod Mystery* (1931); *Death Lights a Candle; The Mystery of the Cape Cod Players; Deathblow Hill; The Amulet of Gilt; Criminal C.O.D.; Six Iron Spiders.*

Taylor, Robert (1911-), American screen actor: among the films in which he has been starred are *Handy Andy; There's Always Tomorrow; Society Doctor; The Magnificent Obsession; The Georgeous Hussy; Camille; A Yank at Oxford; Three Comrades; The Crowd Roars; Lucky Night; Waterloo Bridge; Escape; Johnny Eager; Her Cardboard Lover.*

Taylor, Tom (1817-1880), English dramatist educated at Glasgow University and Trinity College, Cambridge, who later became professor of English literature at University College, London. His dramatic works number more than one hundred: the outstanding plays are *Masks and Faces* (1852) with Charles READE, *The Ticket of Leave Man,* and *Our American Cousin.* He was also editor of *Punch* from 1874 until his death.

Tchaikowsky, Peter Ilich, see **Tschaikowsky, Peter Ilich.**

Tcherepnin, Nicolas (1873-), Russian composer who studied with Nicholas RIMSKY-KORSAKOW at the St. Petersburg Conservatory, and later became conductor of the DIAGHILEFF Ballet: his compositions include three operas; several ballets; orchestral works; a piano concerto: he also completed Modest MUSSORGSKY's opera *The* FAIR AT SOROTCHINSK produced at the Metropolitan Opera House in 1930. His son, **Alexander Tcherepnin** (1899-), studied with his father and toured successfully as a pianist. He spent several years in China and Japan where he was of great assistance to young native musicians. His works include operas, piano concertos, and chamber music.

Teasdale, Sara (1844-1933), American poet educated in private schools who traveled extensively in Europe and the Near East: her notable works include *Sonnets to Duse and Other Poems* (1907); *Helen of Troy and Other Poems; Love Songs; Flame and Shadow; Dark of the Moon; Rivers to the Sea; Stars To-Night.* In 1922 she published *Rainbow Gold,* an anthology for children.

Technique, in creative art the expert methods employed in the execution of the details necessary to produce a finished product; the term applies to all the arts treated in this volume.

Tedesco, Adam, see **Elsheimer, Adam.**

Te Deum, an Ambrosian CHANT used in the Roman Catholic morning service and also on festival occasions: composers of all periods including PALESTRINA, PURCELL, BACH, HANDEL, BERLIOZ, BRUCKNER, DVORAK, VERDI, and SULLIVAN have made settings. In his opera, *Tosca,* Giacomo PUCCINI introduced the singing of a Te Deum by the choir in a church while the villain, Baron Scarpia, plans the destruction of his rival in a RECITATIVE accompanying the chant.

Telemachus, in Greek mythology the son of ODYSSEUS and PENELOPE: after the return of Odysseus from the TROJAN WAR, he helped his father to kill the unfortunate suitors who had annoyed Penelope while her husband was absent.

Telemann, Georg Philipp (1681-1767), German composer educated at the University of Leipzig, but self-trained in the art of music. He was a friend of Johann Sebastian BACH, and one of the most prolific German composers: his works include 40 operas and more than 600 OVERTURES, a form of orchestral composition which preceded the SUITE. Many of the latter have been revived in recent times in both Europe and America: he also wrote much church music and many chamber works.

Television, simply defined, television is a picture carried through the air. It is radio with sight added. Unlike a motion picture no film is used and what you see is happening at the instant you see it. This is possible because the picture travels at the speed of 186,000 miles a second which is the same speed at which radio carries sound. There are five basic stages in the operation of television: *(1) Optical pick-up:* In television, as in photography, there must be a camera equipped with a lens. The lens does mechanically what the eye does naturally. In a motion picture camera, the image is picked up by the lens and is reduced to the size of the film used. In television, the image is focused onto a tiny screen called the mosaic. Its size may vary, but its shape is always in the ratio of four to three. (4 inches long by 3 inches high, or 2 inches long by 1½ inches high.) *(2) Storage of Electrical Energy:* Television is dependent upon changing light into electrical energy. The mosaic, on which the image is focused, is located within a vacuum tube, and is thinly coated with a chemical substance, which has capacity to store up electrical energy, when exposed to light. Each tiny particle of this chemical (usually a compound of cesium) is an infinitely small storage battery, which is charged with electricity in proportion to the quantity of light striking it. In this stage, the picture we see is more than a reflection in a mirror; it is also an intricate pattern of electrical particles, positively charged by the action of light. *(3) Breaking up the picture.* All these tiny particles of electrical energy must now be discharged from the face of the mosaic. This is done by a process called scanning. Inside the vacuum tube is a tiny gun aiming a constant beam of negative electrical particles, called ions, at the face of the mosaic. As each negative charge of electricity strikes a positively charged element, the chemical particle discharges the electrical energy it is holding. To prevent all the energy from being discharged simultaneously, a cathode-ray gun which fires the ionic particles is focused, first, on the upper left-hand corner of the mosaic and sweeps in a straight line across the upper part until it reaches the right-hand corner. This process is known as a scanning line and is achieved by applying an electromagnetic current which draws the cathode-ray beam toward the right in a straight line. When the first scanning line is completed, the electromagnetic attraction is cut off and the beam automatically snaps back to its original position. Then another electromagnetic force is applied to pull the beam downward a fractional distance, when it again travels to the right and completes a second scanning line. (In actual practice, it has been found more satisfactory to scan the entire picture on alternate lines and then scan the intermediate lines. This process is known as interlacing, and the complete coverage of all the odd or even lines is known as a field. A complete field is scanned in 1/60th of a second.) The complete picture (or one frame) is scanned thirty times every second. *(4) Transmission:* As these particles of electric energy are dislodged, they travel along a wire to the transmitter. Here they are amplified and put out over the carrier wave. This process is called modulation. The carrier wave is an electrical highroad, and the particles are carried along it in the order in which they are released. *(5) Re-Assembling the picture:* As the carrier wave resembles a highway, so the antenna for your receiver resembles a gate to your driveway. When your receiving set is turned on, this gate is opened and the tiny particles of electrical energy run along the wire from your antenna to your receiving set. The receiver contains a vacuum tube, called the kinescope, equipped with a cathode-ray gun, similar to the tube in the camera. As the particles of electrical energy strike this tube, the cathode-ray gun begins to emit negative particles of electricity. The gun then begins to reproduce the scanning pattern, just as it is described taking place in the camera. To insure that the scanning of the home receiver is identical with that of the camera, its action is controlled by an electrical current known as the synchronizing pulse. This electrical current moves along the carrier at the same time and at the same speed as the picture travels over it. Thus each particle of electrical energy is directed to the receiving tube in exactly the same relation to each other as existed when they were originally picked up. The face of the kinescope is coated with a second type of chemical known as phosphors. When these phosphors are bombarded by negative charges of electricity, they tend to glow in precise proportion to the force of the blow which strikes them. Thus, as the scanning process continues, the tiny elements of phosphors begin to glow in various proportion and in regular sequence until the original picture is put together again like a jig-saw puzzle made up of tiny glowing pieces. At this point, the transmitted image is only a black and white reproduction of the original. By a device worked out by Dr. Peter GOLDMARK of the Columbia Broadcasting System, **color television** can also be transmitted. This is done by inserting a group of filters between the lens of the camera and the mosaic of the picture. The first of these filters is designed to allow only particles of light reflected by the color red to pass. A second filter permits only those particles of light reflected by blue to pass: this is followed by another which allows only particles of light reflected by green to pass. In color television, scanning is done twice as fast as in black and white—each field is scanned 120 times a second instead of 60 times. When each field is transmitted it is picked up by the receiving end, and only that part of the picture made up of red appears on the screen. Then 1/120th of a second later, a second picture, made up entirely of blue follows; and this is followed 1/120th of a second later by a third picture, entirely made up of green. A second set of filters, exactly synchronized to those in the camera, revolve in front of the kinescope tube in the receiving set in your home. Thus, when you look at the picture, the first field you see is entirely red, the second entirely blue, and the third entirely green. The mixing of the colors is done not by any electronic process but within the eye itself. For, when the entirely red picture is observed, the eye holds the image long enough for both the blue and green fields to have appeared in sequence. Since the colors have come over in precisely the same proportion as they existed originally, you perceive all of the color values, mixed together just as they were in the original. Color television is radio with sight and color added. A peculiar characteristic of television is that the carrier wave, along which the electrical particles of energy are carried, is an ultra short wave which refuses to obey the laws of gravity. It travels from any given point on a straight line to the horizon. At that point, instead of following the contour of the earth as radio waves do, it continues in a straight line up into the heavens. Therefore, the maximum distance your television receiver can be located from the transmitter is determined by the transmitter's horizon. To overcome this obstacle of distance, intermediary transmitters, called booster stations, must be located at points in between. Each booster station increases the amount of coverage from 50 to 75 miles, depending upon the height of the transmitter. The only other known way of overcoming this characteristic of television is to carry the signal on a very elaborate and expensive cable known as a coaxial cable. Television was little more than an exciting experiment when war broke out, and many of us are apt to think of it as a war casualty. While it is true that the men and the materials which normally would have been used to perfect this branch of radio were diverted to more urgent war needs, the very demands of war have produced within a very few years advances in electronic communications which might have taken twenty years to develop under normal conditions. Some of these engineering improvements are still military secrets, but it is generally agreed that shortly after the war ends, television on a large scale will be practical. Television experts are confident that before too long television will be capable of being relayed from one end of the United States to the other and, eventually, will be able to span the oceans. **Author's Note.** This above elucidation of the primary principles of television has been prepared especially for the *Thesaurus of the Arts* by Worthington C. Miner, manager of the Television Division of the Columbia Broadcasting Company.

Television Programs. The active participation of the Columbia Broadcasting System in the development of television dates back to the year 1931. On July 21st of that year, a regular broadcast schedule was initiated, which continued without break into the month of February, 1933. The system of television then being used was known as the "flying spot"; but, despite a vast amount of effort and far-reaching experimentation, technical weaknesses wrote its eventual doom. It was abandoned in late February, 1933. For eight years, television was returned to the laboratory, during which time enormous advances were made from the technical point of view, notably the development by Dr. Peter GOLDMARK of the first feasible three-color process. Color television was presented to the public first on September 4, 1940. Despite the elimination from its schedule of formal dramatic programs, there was considerable variety and intellectual interest in the schedule of WCBW, Columbia's television station in New York City. The following is a list of the outstanding contributions Columbia made to the scope of television coverage during the course of seventeen months of operations: **Children's Stories,** a five-day a week series, during which famous children's stories were animated by an artist, concurrently with the reading of the story to a child. Typical of the list of selections were *Jack and the Beanstalk; The Pied Piper; The Little Mermaid; Rip Van Winkle; The Sleeping Beauty; Robin Hood; Gulliver's Trav-

els; Aesop's Fables; Treasure Island,* and *Around the World in Eighty Days.* Of particular interest was a modern children's story entitled "The Chippendale Dam" by Hugh Troy. **The Arts in the Americas:** A series done in collaboration with the Metropolitan Museum of Art. Two half-hour programs per week, one designed for adults, the other for children and students. On a number of occasions, Mr. Francis Henry Taylor, Director of the Metropolitan Museum, appeared on the program. Other members of his staff also appeared. **Dancing:** On various programs, dancers of national and sometimes international prominence appeared: they included Paul Draper, Nana Gollner, Paul Petroff, Paul Haakon, Patricia Bowman, Peggy Taylor, and many others. In addition, three full length ballets were produced: One with the Polly Korchein group, one entitled *Daniel Boone* with William Strawbridge; another entitled *Billy the Kid* with Eugene Loring. As a regular part of the schedule, there were two programs, one of an hour and one of a half-hour, regularly given over to dancing. One was devoted to the teaching of regular ballroom dancing, the other to a wide variety of folk dancing, square dancing, and the native dances of other countries and races. In addition, there was a weekly variety program, on which tap dances, Indian dances, ballet, acrobatic, all appeared at one time or another. **Music:** A regular feature of the Columbia schedule was the use of singers, such as Joan Edwards, Tamara, and Kay Thompson. In the spring of 1942, however, Columbia innovated a new departure in its attempt to use television as a medium of reporting orchestral music. For this purpose, Columbia chose a small orchestra, bringing into the studio Eddie Condon's selection of swing experts, which had just completed a series of concerts at Town Hall. In presenting this group of musicians, television undertook to add visual, as well as aural punctuation to the musical intention by accenting the individual instruments (or groups of instruments) as their themes became dominant. The effect was a clarification of the score, which, far from taking away from the over-all effect, added interest and impact to the development.

Tell, William, see **William Tell.**

Tellez, Gabriel, see **Tirso de Molina.**

Tempera, one of the oldest and simplest of methods used in painting: the colors which are already ground are tempered with size, and kept liquid in a water-bath. Tempera was used by Egyptian, Greek, and Roman painters: also by Raphael, Michelangelo, and many other great masters.

Temperament, in music the term for various methods of tuning instruments such as the piano and organ. In *equal temperament,* the system generally in use, certain consonant intervals are made slightly imperfect in order to unify the different steps of any given scale in any key. In *unequal temperament,* also known as *just intonation,* the tuning of all consonant intervals is made perfect.

609

Tempest, Marie (1866-1942), English actress and singer who studied voice in Paris and at the ROYAL ACADEMY OF MUSIC, London, with Manuel Patricio GARCIA: she first appeared in 1885 at the Comedy Theatre, London, in SUPPE'S *Boccaccio:* among the operettas in which she appeared were Alfred CELLIER'S *Dorothy* which had a run of 931 performances; *The Red Hussar; The Bohemian Girl; Nanon; The Fencing Master; The Geisha.* After 1899 she appeared only in comedies such as *Becky Sharp; The Marriage of Kitty; Caste; Penelope; Hay Fever; Mr. Pim Passes By; The First Mrs. Fraser; The Vinegar Tree;* in 1935 she celebrated her golden jubilee on the stage. She also appeared in 1937 with Ignace Jan PADEREWSKI in the film *Moonlight Sonata.*

Temple, Shirley (1929-), American screen actress: among the pictures in which she has been featured since she was five years old are *Little Miss Marker; The Little Colonel; The Little Rebel; Captain January; Poor Little Rich Girl; Heidi; Rebecca of Sunnybrook Farm; Just Around the Corner; The Blue Bird; Kathleen; Miss Annie Rooney.*

Temple, a building sacred to the worship of some deity: the first forms were cave temples followed by buildings occupying large areas and representing many years of slave labor erected by the Egyptians. Greek and Roman temples, some of which are described in this volume, were models of architectural grandeur, and were adorned with beautiful statues, friezes, and bas-reliefs. Mexico and Peru were found by the Spaniards to abound in magnificent temples: India, Japan, and China also have many fine temples in various stages of preservation.

Temple of Apollo, a temple at Delphi in ancient Greece built between 370 B.C. and 330 B.C. in which the DELPHIAN ORACLE was located. The descent to the temple was made by several terraces connected by a path known as the Sacred Way which was lined with votive monuments erected by the various Greek states. Excavations have uncovered many interesting METOPES: almost all of those which adorned the Treasury of the Athenians are to be seen in the Museum of Adelphi.

Templeton, Alec (1909-), Welsh pianist and composer (blind) who studied at the Royal College of Music and the Royal Academy of Music, London: he appeared with the London Symphony orchestra, and has been sensationally successful in the United States as a radio artist introducing humorous musical sketches.

Templeton, Fay (1865-1939), American actress and singer who appeared as a child in various juvenile roles, and later in Gilbert and Sullivan operettas and other comic operas. In 1898 she became a member of the WEBER AND FIELDS company, and in 1905 starred in George M. COHAN'S *Forty-five Minutes from Broadway.* She retired in 1906, but reappeared several times: her last appearance was in 1933 in the musical play, *Roberta.*

Tempo (It.), in music the rate of speed at which a composition is performed: the various tempos such as *andante, adagio, allegro,* etc., are defined in separate references throughout this volume.

Tenerani, Pietro (c.1789-1869), Italian sculptor who studied with Antonio CANOVA and Bertel THORWALDSEN: he was a prolific worker greatly praised for his classical and sacred sculptures which include *Psyche with Pandora's Box;* a large relief, *The Deposition from the Cross* in Torlonia Chapel of the Lateran in Rome; the tomb of Duchess Lante; *Cupid and Venus.*

Teniers, David (1582-1649), the Elder, Flemish painter who studied with RUBENS and Adam ELSHEIMER: his notable paintings include *Playing at Bowls; Christ on the Mount of Olives; Peasant's Frolic by a Tavern; Smoker and Tippler; Pan with Nymphs and Satyrs; Dutch Kitchen.* His son, **David Teniers** (1610-1690), the Younger, studied with his father, and was influenced by RUBENS and Adriaen BROUWER: his works, which place him as the finest genre painter in Flanders, include *The Money Changer; The Five Senses; The Dentist; The Prodigal Son; A Merry Repast; The Smoker; The Great Kitchen; Flemish Kermess; Marriage Festival; Temptation of St. Anthony; Peasants' Dance; Judith with the Head of Holofernes:* he was one of the founders of the Antwerp Academy in 1663.

Tenniel, Sir John (1820-1914), English humorous and satirical artist and illustrator who was chiefly self-taught except for a short period spent at the Royal Academy of Art: in 1845 he executed a 16-ft. cartoon, *An Allegory of Justice,* in a competition for the mural decoration of the new Westminster Palace which was accepted. From 1851 to 1901 he contributed cartoons to *Punch,* the best known one being *Dropping the Pilot* when Bismarck retired from leadership in Germany. He illustrated Lewis CARROLL'S *Alice in Wonderland;* AESOP'S *Fables;* Carroll's *Through the Looking Glass;* Thomas MOORE'S *Lalla Rookh,* and many other works.

Tennyson, Alfred Tennyson, 1st Baron (1809-1892), English poet and dramatist educated at Cambridge, and created poet laureate by Queen VICTORIA in 1850: in 1827 he published *Poems of Two Brothers* written with his brother Charles and in 1829 *Timbuctoo* which won the chancellor's medal. His other poetical works include *Poems* (1832); *The Princess; Ode on the Death of the Duke of Wellington; Charge of the Light Brigade; Maud; The Idylls of the King; Enoch Arden; The Holy Grail:* his plays include *Queen Mary; Harold; The Falcon; The Foresters.*

Tenor, the name given to the highest natural adult male voice; derived from the Latin "teneo" (to hold), referring to the fact that in early music the tenor voice was the leading voice in PLAIN SONG. A tenor voice of power is called *tenor robusto,* and a tenor of lyric quality is known as a *lyric tenor.* A *counter tenor* is an extremely high voice which is often falsetto.

Ter Borch or **Terburg, Gerard** (1617-1681), Dutch painter who studied with Pieter MOLYN: his notable works include *The Peace of Münster;*

The Concert; The Telegram; The Toilet; Officer Writing a Letter; Paternal Advice; The Guitar Lesson; Woman Pouring Wine; Lady Playing the Theorbo; Man Standing; The Letter.

Terence (c.185-c.160 B.C.), Roman dramatist whose full name was Publius Terentius Afer: he was said to have been brought from CARTHAGE as a slave by the senator Terentius Lucanus who educated and later freed him: his extant works include the comedies *Adelphi; Andria; Eunuchus; Heauton Timorumenos; Hecyra*, and *Phormio*. They were chiefly adaptations of Greek plays by MENANDER and others.

Terhune, Albert Payson (1872-1942), American novelist and writer of short stories who was educated at Columbia University: his mother, Mary Virginia TERHUNE was a successful novelist who wrote under the pen name "Marian Harland." His works include *Syria from the Saddle* (1896); *Dr. Dale*, with his mother, "Marian Harland"; *Lad: a Dog; Buff: a Collie; Black Gold; Wolf; The Luck of the Laird; The Way of a Dog; Grudge Mountain.*

Terhune, Mary Virginia (1830-1922), American author who wrote under the pen name "Marian Harland." Her works include novels and books on household management: her first novel, *Alone*, was published in 1854, and her last novel, *The Carringtons of High Hill* was issued in 1919, completing a career of 65 years as an author. A volume entitled *Common Sense in the Household* (1871) and *The National Cook Book* (1896) were both best sellers: her autobiography was published in 1910.

Ternina, Milka (1864-1941), Hungarian dramatic soprano who studied at Vienna, sang light opera roles at Leipzig, and from 1890 to 1899 appeared with great success in Wagnerian roles at the Hofoper in Munich. She made her American debut in 1896 with the Damrosch Opera Company at Boston in *Lohengrin*, appeared at the Metropolitan Opera House in 1900 in *Tannhäuser*, and in 1901 created the title role in Puccini's *Tosca* with Antonio SCOTTI as Baron Scarpia. She also created the role of Kundry in the first American performance of *Parsifal* in 1903.

Terpander, a Greek poet and musician of the 7th century B.C. who is regarded as the founder of Greek classical music and lyric poetry: he increased the number of strings on the LYRE from four to seven, made changes in the ODE, and composed many drinking-songs.

Terpsichore, see **Muses, The.**

Terra cotta, a form of baked clay first used in ancient countries in which there was no stone available: clay was dried in the form of bricks and used for architectural purposes. Asiatics have remained particularly skillful in the use of terra cotta: they developed the art of glazing the clay. In ancient Greece the art of modeling in clay followed by baking was brought to its brightest point: the FIGURINES found at Tanagra in Boetia are full of imagination and grace.

Terris, Norma (1904-), American actress and singer educated at La Grange College, Mo.: she made her debut in 1920 on the New York stage in a Ziegfeld production: among the plays in which she has appeared are *Little Nellie Kelly; A Night in Paris; A Night in Spain; Show Boat; The Climax; Bitter Sweet; Rain; No More Ladies; Private Lives; Accent on Youth; Smilin' Through:* she also appeared in the films *Married in Hollywood* and *Cameo Kirby.*

Terry, Charles Sanford (1864-1936), English musicologist who made a special study of the works of Johann Sebastian BACH: from 1903 he occupied the post of professor of history at the University of Aberdeen, and also lectured in the United States and Great Britain: his works include *J. S. Bach* (1922), an authoritative biography; also numerous treatises on Bach's chorals, cantata texts, the origins of the Bach family, and the orchestra in Bach's day.

Terry, Dame Ellen Alicia (1848-1928), English actress who was the daughter of well-known provincial actors, and made her debut at eight as the boy Mamilius in Charles KEAN's revival of Shakespeare's *A Winter's Tale.* After appearing with stock companies and retiring temporarily from the stage, she appeared in 1867 with Sir Henry IRVING in *The Taming of the Shrew.* She retired again in 1868, but reappeared in 1875 as Portia in *The Merchant of Venice* under the management of Sir Squire BANCROFT. In 1878 she scored such a brilliant success in a dramatization of Goldsmith's THE VICAR OF WAKEFIELD that Sir Henry Irving engaged her as leading lady of his company at the LYCEUM THEATRE. From 1878 to 1905 she appeared with Irving in Shakespearean roles and in many other dramas including TENNYSON's *The Cup* and *Becket;* SARDOU's *Madame Sans-Gêne*, and George Bernard SHAW's *Captain Brassbound's Conversion.* Her memoirs were published in 1932.

Tertis, Lionel (1876-), English viola virtuoso who first studied the violin at the Leipzig Conservatory and at the Royal Academy of Music, London, finally specializing on the viola at the suggestion of Sir Alexander MACKENZIE. He toured Europe and the United States with great success, and induced several composers including Arnold BAX, Cyril SCOTT, and Frank BRIDGE to write concertos or sonatas for the viola.

Teternikov, Feodor Kuzmich, see **Sologub, Feodor.**

Tetrachord, (*1*) an instrument with four strings: (*2*) the interval of a perfect fourth: (*3*) in Greek music the scale of four tones forming the interval of a perfect fourth.

Tetrazzini, Luisa (1871-1940), Italian coloratura soprano who was familiar with the arias of several operas at twelve: she studied with her sister, and at the Liceo Musicale in Florence, making her debut in 1895 in MEYERBEER's *L'Africaine*. She toured Italy, South America, and Mexico, appearing first in the United States at the Tivoli, San Francisco, in 1904, at Covent Garden, London, in 1907, and at the Manhattan Opera

House, New York, from 1908 to 1910. She also appeared with great success in concert tours, and with the Metropolitan and Chicago Opera Companies.

Teyte, Maggie (1889-), English lyric soprano who studied at the Royal Academy of Music, London, and with Jean DE RESZKE at Paris, making her debut at Monte Carlo in 1907. After singing at the Opéra-Comique, Paris, and with the Beecham Opera Company in London, she made her debut with the Chicago Opera Company at Philadelphia in 1911 in Mozart's *The Marriage of Figaro,* and also sang with the Boston Opera Company. She is highly regarded as a concert singer, especially of Debussy's songs.

Thackeray, William Makepeace (1811-1863), English novelist born in India who was sent to England in 1817 and educated at Trinity College, Cambridge: his first success was gained with sketches published in *Fraser's Magazine* and *Punch* between 1840 and 1847. In 1848 his novel, *Vanity Fair,* established him as a novelist and formidable rival in popularity to Charles DICKENS: it was followed by *Pendennis; Henry Esmond; The Newcomers; The Virginians.* He also wrote several volumes of short stories and sketches, and lectured in the United States in 1852-53 and 1854-55.

Thaïs, Greek courtesan of the 4th century B.C.: she is said to have accompanied ALEXANDER THE GREAT on his Asiatic campaign, and to have persuaded him to destroy the city of Persepolis by fire although Cleitarchus, the historian who is authority for this tale, is not regarded as trustworthy. Thaïs later became the consort of Ptolemy Lagus, king of Egypt. Jules MASSENET's opera, **Thaïs,** founded on Anatole FRANCE's novel, was produced at Paris in 1894, and at the Manhattan Opera House, New York, in 1907. Sybil SANDERSON created the role of Thaïs with great success: at the American première Mischa ELMAN played the famous *Meditation* between the acts. There are Victor recordings for violin solo by Mischa ELMAN, and by Fritz KREISLER: also an orchestral transcription played by the Boston "Pops" Orchestra.

Thalberg, Sigismund (1812-1871), German pianist and composer born in Switzerland who studied with Johann HUMMEL, Simon SECHTER, and Friedrich KALKBRENNER: he made many successful tours of Europe and South America, appearing in the United States in 1856 with the violinist, Henri VIEUXTEMPS. His LEGATO style of playing elicited the remark from Franz LISZT that Thalberg was the only artist who could play the violin on the piano. His compositions were chiefly brilliant salon pieces no longer in vogue.

Thamar, spectacle ballet in one act: libretto by Leon BAKST; choreography by Michael FOKINE; music by Mily BALAKIREV; first performed at Paris in 1912. The plot concerns Thamar, the 12th century Georgian queen who has always been a favorite subject for Russian painters, poets, novelists, and dramatists: she lures a handsome stranger to the turret chamber of her castle, and after a wild dance, plunges her dagger into his breast. The music is Balakirev's symphonic poem: there is a Victor recording by the Paris Conservatory Orchestra directed by Piero Coppola.

Thanet, Octave, see **French, Alice.**

Thaxter, Celia (1835-1894), American poet whose first poem, *Landlocked,* was published in 1861 through the foresight of James Russell Lowell in the *Atlantic Monthly:* her works include *Poems* (1872); *Drift Weed; Poems for Children; The Cruise of the Mystery; An Island Garden; Among the Isles of Shoals.*

Thayer, Abbott Handerson (1849-1921), American painter who studied with Jean Léon GEROME at the ECOLE DES BEAUX-ARTS, Paris: his paintings include *Young Lions at Central Park; Boy and Dog; Cows Coming from Pasture; Monadnock; Virgin Enthroned; Autumn Morning on the Housatonic; Young Woman in Olive Plush* for which a medal of the 1st class with a prize of $1,500 was awarded in 1920 at the International Art Exhibition at the Carnegie Institute, Pittsburgh: he also developed a theory of protective coloration of animals which was used in CAMOUFLAGE during World War I.

Thayer, Alexander Wheelock (1817-1897), American writer on music educated at Harvard University who devoted his life to the writing of a biography of Ludwig van BEETHOVEN. The work of collecting material in several German and Austrian cities, London, and Paris was begun in 1849, and the biography was published in German in three volumes from 1866 to 1879. A fourth volume was left incomplete at his death: Henry E. Krehbiel prepared the English edition in three volumes which was issued in 1921.

Theatre, a word derived from the Greek, and originally meaning to see or view: it is now used as the name of a building devoted to dramatic performances or spectacles. The Greek theatre was an auditorium without a roof, semi-circular in shape and provided with wooden or stone benches: there was no stage in the modern sense of the word; the actors and chorus performed in the space known in the modern theatre as the ORCHESTRA, and an altar to DIONYSUS stood in the center. The number of seats ranged from 10,000 to 25,000 or more, and Roman theatres were built very much on the same general plan. The theatres of the Middle Ages were more or less improvised, and it was not until after the Renaissance that specially designed buildings for dramatic purposes were constructed. The first theatre in England was erected by James BURBAGE in 1576: the stage was occupied by not only the actors, but also by royalty and wealthy spectators while the orchestra, known as the pit, was used by the common people who sat on rough benches. Scenery was not used, but there were more or less elaborate furnishings: movable scenery was not invented until about 1660. The first theatre in America was built in 1752 at Williamsburg, Va. Changes which rendered the presentation of a play infinitely more realistic came only during the 19th century with the removal of the audience from the stage, and the advent of electric lighting: Gordon CRAIG was one of the greatest pioneers in the improvement of scenery.

Theatre Collection, assemblies of books, magazines, programs, photographs, and clippings relating to the stage, screen, and radio are to be seen in many public and private libraries of the United States: an interesting and complete record is to be found in *Theatre Collections in Libraries and Museums* compiled by Rosamond Gilder and George Freedley. Among the most important collections are those at the Library of Congress, Washington, D. C.; the New York Public Library; the Brander Mathews Dramatic Museum at Columbia University, New York; the Library of the Players Club, New York; the Library of Harvard College.

Theatre Guild, The (New York), an organization formed in 1919 by a group of actors and other persons connected with the theatre: with the assistance of Otto H. KAHN it leased the Garrick Theatre, New York, in 1919, and presented a play, Jacinto BENAVENTE'S *The Bonds of Interest* which was a failure, but the second presentation, *John Ferguson* by St. John ERVINE was a pronounced success. Among the long list of distinctive plays presented since 1919 are *Jane Clegg; Heartbreak House; Liliom; He Who Gets Slapped; Back to Methusaleh; Peer Gynt; R.U.R.; The Adding Machine; Saint Joan; The Guardsman; Processional; Arms and the Man.* The Guild Theatre was built and opened in 1925 on West 52nd Street, and the subscription system established in New York, was set up in Boston, Chicago, Philadelphia, Baltimore, and other cities. The plays successfully produced since include *Caesar and Cleopatra; Juarez and Maximilian; Pygmalion; The Silver Cord; Porgy; The Doctor's Dilemma; Strange Interlude; Major Barbara; Caprice; Roar China; Elizabeth the Queen; Green Grow the Lilacs; Mourning Becomes Elektra; Reunion in Vienna; The Good Earth; Ah, Wilderness; Mary of Scotland; Escape Me Never; Porgy and Bess,* a folk opera by George GERSHWIN; *Idiot's Delight; The Sea Gull; The Philadelphia Story; The Time of Your Life; Twelfth Night; Oklahoma!:* the above are only a few out of many well-received productions. Several distinguished dramatists belong to the Guild: also many distinguished actors.

Theatre of Dionysus (Athens), see **Dionysus, Theatre of.**

Theatrical Clubs, there are several organizations in the United States and London which are associations of actors, dramatists, and other persons directly or indirectly connected with the stage. In *New York* they include the FRIARS, the LAMBS, the PLAYERS, the Twelfth Night, and the Ziegfeld Clubs; in *Chicago* the Cliff Dwellers and the Dill Pickle Clubs; in *Hollywood* the Maskers and the Hollywood Athletic Clubs. In *London* there are the Garrick, Savage, Green-Room, Old Stagers, and the Strollers Clubs.

Theatrical Library (New York Public Library), a collection of approximately 150,000 volumes, 7,000,000 clippings, 750,000 photographs, and 900,000 playbills and programs available for reference purposes at the main branch of the New York Public Library where it is in the care of George Freedley. The 58th St. branch has a circulating library of 10,000 volumes, and there are 70,000 additional books in the other branches.

Theatrical Magazines, periodicals designed in some instances exclusively for the use of persons in the theatrical field including the legitimate stage, vaudeville, motion pictures, and radio: in other instances for the edification of the theatre goer. In the United States magazines of interest to the profession include *Variety* and *The Billboard:* those for the theatre lover include *Cue, Cast,* and *Theatre Arts.* In England the principal theatre magazines are *Drama, Era, Stage, Play Pictorial,* and *Theatre World.*

Thebes, (*1*) an ancient city in Egypt the ruins of which are to be seen near Luxor and Karnak: it succeeded MEMPHIS as the capital of Egypt, and for a thousand years was one of the great centers of Egyptian culture and commerce: (*2*) the principal city of Boetia in ancient Greece, said to have been founded by CADMUS: about 600 B.C. it began a long series of wars with Athens, and was almost completely destroyed by ALEXANDER THE GREAT in 330 B.C.

Theme, (*1*) in music the melodic figure or subject which expresses an individual musical thought of a composer which is elaborated into a complete composition. (*2*) In literature a subject or topic which is used by an author as the basis of a novel, short story, essay, or dramatic work.

Theocritus, Greek poet who lived in the 3rd century B.C., and is regarded as the father of pastoral poetry because his idyls pictured the lives of herdsmen, shepherds, and fishermen. About thirty short poems are extant, half of which are pastorals and the others miniature pictures of life.

Theorbo, an obsolete stringed instrument similar to the LUTE popular in 16th and 17th century orchestras. It was made with two necks to one of which the treble strings were attached and to the other bass strings. Jacopo PERI used the theorbo in his orchestration of *Euridice,* and George Frederick HANDEL also employed it occasionally. Large theorbos with double strings were known as archlutes.

Theory, in music the science of composition including HARMONY, COUNTERPOINT, FUGUE, CANON, musical FORM, ANALYSIS, ORCHESTRATION, ACOUSTICS, and other related subjects.

Theotocopuli, Domenico, see **Greco, El.**

Theremin, an electronic musical instrument invented by the Russian scientist, Leon Theremin, who was born at St. Petersburg on Aug. 15, 1896. He constructed his first instrument to convert electrical waves into musical tones in 1920. There are three forms of the instrument: ether-wave or space-control, the finger-board model and the electrical harmoniums and organs which have keyboards. Joseph SCHILLINGER wrote the *First Airphonic Suite* for Theremin and orchestra; it has been used in concerts with the New York Philharmonic-Symphony Society, the Philadelphia Symphony Orchestra and the Cleveland Symphony Orchestra; also on radio broadcasts.

Theseus, in Greek mythology the son of King Aegeus of Athens, who went to Crete with a group of youths and maidens sent as tribute to King Minos: he slew the MINOTAUR, fought with the AMAZONS, accompanied the ARGONAUTS on their quest for the GOLDEN FLEECE, and joined in the hunt for the CALYDONIAN BOAR.

Thespis, Greek poet and dramatist of the 6th century B.C., who is considered the inventor of tragedy because he introduced a person distinct from the chorus who conversed with the leader, and was known as the "answerer." He is said to have traveled in a cart in which he also carried the apparatus connected with his play to the towns where he proposed to produce it. The word "Thespian," meaning an actor, is derived from his name.

Thetis, in Greek mythology the mother of ACHILLES and wife of PELEUS: her father was NEREUS who had fifty daughters known as Nereids. The word Thetis is also used by Latin poets as a name for the ocean.

Thibaud, Jacques (1880-), French violinist who studied with his father and with Martin MARSICK at the Paris Conservatory, later becoming a member of the COLONNE Orchestra, and highly successful as a soloist. He has toured Europe and the United States, and has also appeared in trio recitals with Pablo CASALS and Alfred CORTOT. The trio made many fine recordings of works by classic and modern masters.

Thibault, Conrad (1906-), American baritone who studied with Emilio de Gorgorza at the CURTIS INSTITUTE OF MUSIC, Philadelphia, Pa., and sang with the PHILADELPHIA GRAND OPERA COMPANY for several seasons: he has also achieved distinction as a radio artist.

Thibault, Jacques Anatole François, see France, Anatole.

Thisbe, see Pyramus and Thisbe.

Thoma, Hans (1839-1924), German painter who first worked on clock faces and later studied at the Karlsruhe Academy with Johann Wilhelm Schirmer: his works include *The Guardian of the Valley; Eventide; Spring Idyl; Eve in Paradise; Flight into Egypt; Charon; Adam and Eve; Solitude; Tritons.*

Thomas, Albert Ellsworth (1872-), American dramatist educated at Brown University and for a time engaged in journalistic and critical work for New York newspapers: his numerous successful plays written independently and in collaboration, include *Her Husband's Wife* (1910); *What the Doctor Ordered; Little Boy Blue; Her Friend the King; The Big Idea; Come Out of the Kitchen; The Champion; Just Suppose; The French Doll; No More Ladies; Merely Murder.*

Thomas, Ambroise (1811-1896), French composer who studied at the Paris Conservatory, and later devoted himself to the composition of operas and ballets. His successful operas include MIGNON and *Hamlet:* the balance of his dramatic works are no longer in the repertory of most opera houses.

Thomas, Augustus (1857-1934), American dramatist who started his career as a journalist: his successful plays include *Alone* (1875); *Alabama; In Mizzoura; The Man Upstairs; The Hoosier Doctor; Oliver Goldsmith; Arizona; Colorado; The Earl of Pawtucket; Mrs. Leffingwell's Boots; The Witching Hour; Rio Grande; The Copperhead; Nemesis; Still Waters.*

Thomas, Brandon (1856-1914), English actor and dramatist educated as a civil engineer who appeared in John HARE'S Company in 1879: his most successful play, *Charley's Aunt,* was produced in 1892, has been revived several times with star casts, and also filmed. Among his other plays were *The Color Sergeant* and *The Lodgers.*

Thomas, John Charles (1891-), American baritone who studied at the PEABODY INSTITUTE, Baltimore, Md., first singing in musical comedies, and later achieving success in the concert field. He made his operatic debut at Washington, D. C., in 1924; later singing at Brussels and Covent Garden. In 1930 he appeared with the CHICAGO OPERA COMPANY, and made his debut in 1934 at the Metropolitan Opera House in VERDI'S *La Traviata.* He has also achieved great popularity as a radio artist.

Thomas, Theodore (1835-1905), American violinist and conductor born in Germany who was brought to the United States in 1845. He studied with his father, and appeared at sixteen as soloist with Jenny LIND, SONTAG, GRISI and MARIO. In 1854 he became a member of the NEW YORK PHILHARMONIC-SYMPHONY SOCIETY, and in 1855 organized the Mason and Thomas chamber music soirées with William MASON. In 1862 he founded the "Symphony Soirées" which continued until 1878: his selection of foreign works unknown to New York audiences had a profound influence in developing American musical culture. He toured with his orchestra for nine years through the East and Middle West, also establishing the Cincinnati Music Festivals in 1873, and founding the Cincinnati College of Music. He also conducted the New York Philharmonic-Symphony Society and several singing societies in New York: in 1891 he settled in Chicago as conductor of the Chicago Symphony Orchestra which he built up by careful training into one of the finest symphonic organizations in the United States. He introduced the major orchestral works of WAGNER, LISZT, BRAHMS, TSCHAIKOWSKY, BRUCKNER, DVORAK, SAINT-SAENS, and Richard STRAUSS to New York and Chicago music lovers.

Thomé, Francis (1850-1909), French composer, pianist, teacher, and critic who studied with François MARMONTEL at the Paris Conservatory: his works include several operas, pantomimes, and ballets, but he is known today by several charming salon pieces for piano such as *Simple Aveu* and *Under the Leaves*.

Thompson, Denman (1833-1911), American actor and dramatist who first played character parts with stock companies. After producing a sketch, *Joshua Whitcomb,* with great success he created a full-length play out of the material called *The Old Homestead* which proved a popular favorite for more than twenty years: it has been revived many times as well as filmed.

Thompson, Elizabeth Southerden, see **Butler, Lady Elizabeth Southerden Thompson.**

Thompson, Ernest Seton, see **Seton, Ernest Thompson.**

Thompson, Oscar (1887-), American critic and author educated at the University of Washington, later becoming executive editor of *Musical America,* and succeeding William J. HENDERSON as music critic of the New York *Sun.* His works include *Practical Music Criticism* (1934); *How to Understand Music; A Tabulated Biographical History of Music; The American Singer; Debussy, Man and Artist:* he was also editor-in-chief of *The International Encyclopedia of Music and Musicians.*

Thompson, Randall (1899-), American composer educated at Harvard University who also studied with Ernest BLOCH: he has taught at Wellesley College, the University of California, and in 1939 became director of the CURTIS CONSERVATORY OF MUSIC, Philadelphia, Pa., his successor being Efrem ZIMBALIST. His compositions include incidental music for theatrical productions, orchestral works, chamber music, choruses, piano music, and songs.

Thompson, Wordsworth (1840-1896), American painter who studied at Paris and sketched in Italy, Morocco, Algiers, and Spain: his notable works include *View of Mount Etna; Old Bruton Church; Desolation; Review at Annapolis; Halt of a Diligence; Passing the Outposts; Winter Morning Ride; Advance of the Enemy.*

Thomson, César (1857-1931), Belgian violinist and teacher who studied with VIEUXTEMPS, LEONARD, WIENIAWSKI, and MASSART: he toured Europe and the United States and in 1898 succeeded Eugène YSAYE as professor of violin playing at the Brussels Conservatory. From 1924 to 1927 he taught at the Conservatory at Ithaca, New York, and also at the JUILLIARD School of Music.

Thomson, Virgil (1896-), American pianist and composer educated at Harvard University who studied with Heinrich Gebhard, J. Wallace GOODRICH, and Nadia BOULANGER. He taught for several years at Harvard University, and lived in Paris for several years: in 1939 he succeeded Lawrence Gilman as music critic of the New York *Tribune:* his works include an opera, FOUR SAINTS IN THREE ACTS (1934), and a humorous commentary on the musical world, *The State of Music* (1939).

Thor, in Norse mythology the god of thunder second only to ODIN: he was called to the assist-

ance of the other gods whenever they were in danger, and he was also the friend of mortals, defending them from TROLLS and evil spirits. He was always armed with a heavy hammer which returned to him whenever he cast it. He was pictured as a powerful man with a long red beard, and wearing a girdle which constantly revitalized him.

Thorborg, Kerstin (1906-), Swedish contralto who studied at the school of the Stockholm Royal Opera, making her debut there in 1926 as Amneris in VERDI's *Aïda,* and remaining until 1931. After appearing at Berlin, Vienna, London, and Buenos Aires she made her debut in 1936 at the METROPOLITAN OPERA HOUSE in *The Valkyrie* and remained with the company for four years: she also sang with the SAN FRANCISCO OPERA COMPANY and has appeared successfully in recital.

Thoreau, Henry David (1817-1862), American author and naturalist: his works include *Walden, or Life in the Woods* (1854), a work written in a log cabin built by him on the shores of Walden Pond near Concord, Mass.; *Excursions in Field and Forest; The Maine Woods; Cape Cod; A Yankee in Canada; Letters and Poems; Winter:* several of the above were published after his death.

Thorndike, Ashley Horace (1871-1933), American literary historian educated at Wesleyan and Harvard Universities who taught at Boston University and Columbia University. His works include *The Influence of Beaumont and Fletcher on Shakespeare* (1901); *Shakespeare's Theatre; Tragedy; Literature in a Changing Age; English Comedy; History of English Literature* with William A. Neilson.

Thorndike, Dame Sybil (1882-), English actress and manager who was trained at Ben GREET's Academy, toured the United States with a Shakespearean repertory company, and appeared at the "Old Vic" Theatre at London in 1908. Among the plays in which she has appeared are *Macbeth; The Merchant of Venice; The Trojan Women; St. Joan; Major Barbara; Candida; Jane Clegg.* She managed the New Theatre, London, and has also appeared in several films including *Major Barbara* and *Nine Days a Queen.*

Thornhill, Sir James (1676-1734), English painter who worked under the patronage of Queen Anne, but was poorly paid while foreign painters such as Charles de LA FOSSE were well remunerated. He decorated some of the apartments at HAMPTON COURT, the eight compartments in the dome of ST. PAUL'S CATHEDRAL, and founded an art school at which William HOGARTH studied and later became his son-in-law.

Thornton, William (1761-1828), American architect born in the West Indies of English parents. In 1792 his plans for the Capitol at Washington, D. C., were approved by George Washington, and their execution put under the direction of James HOBAN and E. S. Hallet: in 1794 he assumed charge himself and was succeeded by Benjamin H. LATROBE who completed the work. He also designed several residences including the Tayloe

House now occupied by the American Institute of Architects.

Thornycroft, Sir William Hamo (1850-1925), English sculptor who studied at the Royal Academy Schools and in Italy: his works include a statue of SHAKESPEARE; figures of *Fame* and *Clio; Tennyson; Lot's Wife; Artemis; Teucer,* regarded as his masterpiece; *The Mower; The Sower; Oliver Cromwell; King Alfred,* a colossal memorial; the *Gladstone Monument* and *Warrior Bearing a Wounded Youth from the Battlefield.*

Thorough Bass, see **Figured bass.**

Thorwaldsen, Bertel (1779-1844), Danish sculptor who went to Rome for study in 1797, and made his debut with a statue, *Jason,* which won him the praise of Antonio CANOVA: his enormous output includes the restoration of the AEGINETAN MARBLES; *Cupid and Psyche; Venus and Ganymede;* a frieze, *The Triumph of Alexander* in the Quirinal at Rome; the bas-reliefs, *Night and Morning;* the *Lion of Lucerne;* religious statues at Copenhagen where there is a museum devoted to his works.

Thousand and One Nights, Book of, see **Arabian Nights, The.**

Three-Cornered Hat, The, a ballet-pantomime: scenario by Gregorio MARTINEZ SIERRA based on Antonio ALARCON's novel, *El Sombrero de Tres Picos;* first produced by the Diaghileff Russian Ballet at London in 1919. A suite of three dances from the ballet is available in a Victor recording by the Boston "Pops" Orchestra, and a Columbia recording by the Madrid Symphony orchestra conducted by Fernandez ARBOS.

Three Graces, The, see **Graces, The Three.**

Throckmorton, Cleon (1897-), American designer of stage scenery who was first a landscape and figure painter: among his finest productions are *The Emperor Jones* (1920); *Porgy; All God's Chillun Got Wings; The Old Soak; The House of Connelly; Springtime for Henry; The Silver Cord; Alien Corn; Bitter Oleander.*

"Through the Looking Glass" Suite (Taylor), an orchestral work by Deems TAYLOR composed for chamber orchestra and piano, and first performed by the New York Chamber Music Society in 1919, and, after being arranged for full orchestra, by the New York Symphony Society in 1923. The work was inspired by Lewis CARROLL's story: the program is suggested by the titles amplified by extracts from the book: Ia, *Dedication;* Ib, *The Garden of Live Flowers;* II, *Jabberwocky;* III, *Looking-Glass Insects;* IV, *The White Knight.* There is a Columbia recording of the suite by the CBS Symphony Orchestra directed by Howard Barlow.

Thurber, Mrs. Jeannette M., see **National Conservatory of Music** and **American Opera Company.**

Thursby, Emma (1845-1931), American coloratura concert soprano who studied with Madame

Hermine RUDERSDORFF and with Francesco Lamperti: she made her debut in 1875, and later sang with Patrick S. GILMORE's band. She made a European tour under the management of Maurice STRAKOSCH, and also toured Japan and China.

Thurston, Mrs. Katherine Cecil (1875-1911), Irish novelist educated at private schools who was the wife of Ernest Temple Thurston, a successful author. Her works include *The Circle* (1903); *The Masquerader* which was successful as a novel, motion picture, and as a play for Guy Bates POST; *The Gambler; The Fly on the Wheel; Max.*

Thus Spake Zarathustra (Strauss), an orchestral tone poem by Richard STRAUSS first played at Frankfort-on-the-Main in 1896 with the composer conducting. It is based on *Thus Spake Zarathustra, a Book for All or None* by Friedrich NIETZSCHE: Strauss remarks "I did not intend to write philosophical music or to portray in music Nietzsche's great work. I meant to convey by means of music an idea of the development of the human race from its origin, through the various phases of its development, religious and scientific, up to Nietzsche's idea of the Superman. The whole symphonic poem is intended as my homage to Nietzsche's genius . . ." There is a Victor recording by the Boston Symphony Orchestra directed by Sergei Koussevitzky, and a Columbia recording by the Chicago Symphony Orchestra under Frederick Stock.

Tibbett, Lawrence (1896-), American dramatic baritone who served in the United States Navy during World War I: after singing in comic opera he studied with Frank LA FORGE, and made his debut at the METROPOLITAN OPERA HOUSE in 1923, later achieving sensational success as Ford in VERDI's *Falstaff;* the title role of Verdi's *Simon Boccanegra:* also in Deems TAYLOR's *The King's Henchman* and *Peter Ibbetsen,* and Louis Gruenberg's *Emperor Jones.* He has appeared in several films including *The Rogue Song; The New Moon; Cuban Love Song; Metropolitan.*

Tie, in musical notation a curved line joining two notes of the same pitch which are to be sustained for the time value of both notes.

Tieck, Ludwig (1773-1853), German novelist and dramatist who also became an influential critic and dramatic adviser to the Dresden Court Theatre: his works include a novel in letter form, *William Lovell* (1795); a series of fairy-tale plays including *Topsy Turvey World, Puss in Boots,* and *Bluebeard;* a poetic romance, *Genoveva,* which became the basis for an opera of the same title by Robert SCHUMANN first produced at Leipzig in 1850.

Tieffenbrucker, Gaspar, see **Duiffoprugcar, Gaspar.**

Tiepolo, Giovanni Battista (1696-1770), Italian painter who studied with Gregorio Lazzarini, and was influenced by Paolo VERONESE: his works include *Banquet of Cleopatra; Christ in the Garden of Olives; The Last Supper; Triumph of Aurelian; Baptism of Clovis; Adoration of the Magi;*

Diana and Apollo on the Clouds. He spent the last years of his life on frescoes for the Royal Palace at Madrid.

Tiffany, Louis Comfort (1848-1933), American painter who studied with George INNESS, Samuel COLMAN, and with Léon Belly at Paris: he founded the Tiffany Studios, an interior decorating business at New York which devoted itself largely to church work, and established the Tiffany Furnaces for manufacturing stained GLASS. In 1918 he founded and endowed the Louis Comfort Tiffany *Foundation* at Oyster Bay, N. Y., to enable talented students to sketch from nature under competent supervision.

Tilgner, Viktor (1844-1896), Austrian sculptor who studied with Joseph van Gasser and Daniel Boehm, and executed many portrait busts of famous contemporaries in Vienna including Emperor Franz Joseph: he also designed monuments to MOZART and Hans MAKART, a war memorial at Königsgrätz, and many fountains.

Till Eulenspiegel's Merry Pranks, an orchestral tone poem by Richard STRAUSS first performed at Cologne in 1895. Strauss refused to give even his good friend, Dr. Franz Wüllner, who conducted the first performance at Cologne, an explanatory program of the work, saying "It is impossible for me to furnish a program to *Till Eulenspiegel;* were I to put into words the thoughts which its several incidents suggest to me, they would seldom suffice and might give rise to offence. Let me leave it, therefore, to my hearers to crack the hard nut which the Rogue has prepared for them." But the composer did indicate two "Till" motives—the opening theme of the introduction; the theme in the horns which follows; he also pointed out the descending interval expressive of condemnation and the scaffold. The program in this respect differs from the old folk story; in this the waggish Till is condemned to the gallows, but escapes and dies in bed, but in the Strauss tone poem he ends his career hanging from a scaffold. Among critics and public, *Till Eulenspiegel* disputes first position with DON JUAN as the most popular of the eight tone poems written by Richard Strauss. There is a Victor recording by the London Philharmonic Orchestra directed by Fritz Busch, and a Columbia recording by the Pittsburgh Symphony Orchestra under Fritz Reiner.

Tilley, Vesta (1864-), English actress and singer who appeared as a child of five on the stage in male attire, and has continued as a male impersonator over the years. About 1876 she began to be favorably known as "Little Tillie," and in 1878 made her debut on the London stage singing *The Pet of Rotten Row* and other songs which created a great reputation in a few weeks. For many years she appeared at English and American music halls, and was as popular at the time of her retirement in 1920 as she was forty years earlier.

Timanthes, Greek painter of the 4th century B.C.: one of his pictures, *The Sacrifice of Iphigenia* in which he depicted the emotions of those who witnessed or took part in the sacrifice, pictured AGAMEMNON with his face veiled because he found it impossible to portray the latter's grief. A painting found at Pompeii, and now in the Naples Museum, is regarded as a copy of this work.

Time, in music the separation of notes into divisions marked by an accented beat and the regular return to that beat such as *duple time* and *triple time:* the duration of a note with relation to other notes is called its *time value.*

Timotheus, a Greek sculptor of the 4th century B.C. who was one of the artists who worked on the Mausoleum of Halicarnassus: he also executed the models for the Temple of Aesculapius at Epidaurus parts of which have been recovered.

Timpano (Plural, **Timpani**), an orchestral drum also known as the *kettledrum,* and the only one that can be tuned to accord with other instruments. It consists of a copper hemisphere (the kettle) over which a skin is held by a hoop: the pitch can be changed by tightening thumb screws or an equivalent mechanism. Introduced into Europe by the Moors in the 7th century, it was first used in army bands where two timpani were slung over the back of a horse: later it was used by BACH, HANDEL, HAYDEN, MOZART, and BEETHOVEN in the orchestra. Beethoven broke away from the habit of using the timpani only with trumpets, and Carl Maria von WEBER introduced three timpani in place of the customary two. Timpani are beaten with flexible sticks with knobs of felt, lamb's wool or sponge: Hector BERLIOZ used 16 timpani in his *Requiem,* and a foot mechanism was invented by Ernst Pfundt, a famous timpani player for Felix MENDELSSOHN, which enables the player to tune his timpani while playing them.

Tintoretto, Jacopo (1518-1594), Italian painter whose real name was Jacopo Robusti: he was a pupil of TITIAN, and is regarded as one of the greatest masters in the arts of composition, drawing, and color; John Ruskin placed him above Titian and the peer of MICHELANGELO. Among his notable works, executed with a rapidity that gained him the nickname of "Il Furioso," are *Paradise,* the largest single canvas in existence measuring 30 by 70 feet; *Miracle of St. Mark; Miracle of the Loaves and Fishes; Adam and Eve; Mercury and the Graces; Wedding at Cana; Massacre of the Innocents; Last Judgment; Crucifixion;* the great series of Passion paintings at the Hospice of the Scuola di San Rocco at Venice; *Concert of the Muses; Abraham's Sacrifice; St. George and the Dragon; Venus and Mercury; Presentation in the Temple.*

Tirso de Molina, pseudonym of **Gabriel Tellez** (1571-1648), Spanish dramatist educated at the University of Alcala who became a monk in 1613: his dramas and comedies include *Prudence in the Woman; The Condemned Heretic; The Pious Martha; Don Gil of the Green Trousers.* He is best known as the creator of Don Juan as a character in *The Libertine of Seville.*

Tischbein, Johann Heinrich Wilhelm (1751-1829), German painter who studied with his uncle and in Holland where he spent some years copying the works of Dutch masters: he became director of the Academy at Naples in 1787, but returned to Germany at the French invasion of Italy. His works include *Arminius, Deliverer of Germany; The Parting of Hector and Andromache; Amazons Setting Out for the Chase; Sicilian Landscape; The Rape of Helen; St. Cecilia; View near Frascati; Hector's Farewell.*

Tisi, Benvenuto, see **Garofalo, Il.**

Tissot, James Joseph Jacques (1836-1902), French painter who studied with Jean FLANDRIN and was influenced by the Dutch masters: his works include *Meeting of Faust and Marguerite; Young Woman in Church; Walk in the Snow; Story of the Prodigal Son; Ball on Shipboard; A Bunch of Lilacs.* After the Franco-Prussian War he worked in London, and illustrated a biography of Christ: he also spent ten years in Palestine during which he painted 350 water colors which were exhibited at London and Paris, and later engraved.

Titania, a name first found in the *Metamorphoses* of OVID where it was used as another name for DIANA: Shakespeare was the first to give this name to the queen of the fairies in *A Midsummer Night's Dream.*

Titans, in Greek mythology a race of deities who were the offspring of URANUS and GAEA: there were six male and six female Titans all of whom were imprisoned by their father but they were freed by CRONUS. The Titans made war on the gods by piling mountain upon mountain in order to reach the heights of OLYMPUS.

Titian (c.1477-1576), Italian painter whose real name was Tiziano Vecelli or Vecellio: he learned the rudiments of painting at Venice from his uncle, and by working in the studios of Gentile BELLINI, Giovanni BELLINI, and Giorgio GIORGIONE. His notable works include *Gipsy Madonna; Presentation of the Virgin; Madonna of the Cherries; Ariosto; The Tribute Money; Sacred and Profane Love; Diana and Acteon; Madonna with the Rabbit; Annunciation; Christ in the Garden; Bacchus and Ariadne; Flora and Venus.* He is generally regarded as the greatest of all painters from the standpoint of complete mastery of the art.

Toccata (It.), a brilliant contrapuntal composition for keyboard instruments such as the HARPSICHORD, PIANO or ORGAN originating in Italy near the end of the 16th century. It is free in style and characterized by brilliant passage work: Johann Sebastian BACH'S organ toccatas, and Robert SCHUMANN'S toccatas for the piano are excellent examples of the form.

Toch, Ernst (1887-), Austrian composer who first studied medicine and philosophy, and was self-taught in music: in 1913 he taught at the Hochschule for Music in Mannheim, and in 1935 became professor of musical composition at the New School for Social Research, New York. His compositions include operas, chamber music, orchestral works, piano works, and musical scores for film and radio productions.

Todi, Jacopone da, see **Jacopone da Todi.**

Tokatyan, Armand (1899-), Bulgarian operatic tenor educated in Alexandria, Egypt, and trained in singing at Milan and Vienna, making his debut in 1921 at Milan in Puccini's *Manon Lescaut.* After touring with the Antonio Scotti Opera Company, he made his debut in 1923 at the Metropolitan Opera House, New York, in Vittadini's *Anima Allegra,* and became a permanent member of the Metropolitan Company, also singing at Covent Garden, London, and at Berlin, Vienna, and Budapest.

Toldy, Ferencz (1805-1875), Hungarian critic and historian: his *Handbook of Hungarian Poetry* (1828), *History of Hungarian Literature* (1852), and *History of Hungarian Poetry* (1854) are the chief sources of reliable information on the lives and works of Magyar authors.

Toller, Ernst (1893-1939), German dramatist who was imprisoned in 1918 for his communistic and pacifist views: his plays include *Man and the Masses,* produced by the Theatre Guild, New York; *The Machine Wreckers; Blind Goddess; No More Peace; Bloody Laughter; Hinkelmann; Draw the Fires; Mary Baker Eddy,* produced in London as *Miracle in America.* He lectured in the United States and acted as adviser to the Dramatists' Guild in New York.

Tolstoy, Alexey Constantinovich (1817-1875), Russian poet, dramatist, and novelist related to Leo TOLSTOY: his works include ballads and lyric poems of humorous character; *Prince Serebryany,* a historical novel; *Don Juan,* a drama; and a trilogy of historical dramas comprising *The Death of Ivan the Terrible, Tsar Feodor Ivanovitch,* and *Czar Boris.*

Tolstoy, Alexey Nikolaevich (1882-), Russian novelist and dramatist distantly related on his father's side to Leo TOLSTOY: his works available in English include *The Road to Calvary; Darkness and Dawn; Peter the Great,* which was filmed; *Darkness and Dawn; The Death Box; Bread:* he has written several novels and plays which have not been translated including *The Left Bank of the Volga; The Lame Esquire; Odd People; Black Gold; The Adventures of Nevzorov:* also a play, *The Path to Victory.*

Tolstoy, Leo (Lev) Nikolayevich (1828-1910), Russian novelist who served in the Crimean War and traveled extensively before retiring to his vast country estate to devote himself to writing. His works include *Childhood* (1852); *Boyhood; Youth; The Cossacks; War and Peace; Anna Karenina; A Confession; The Memoirs of a Madman; The Kreutzer Sonata; Resurrection; The Death of Ivan Ilyitch; Hadjii Murad.* His plays include *The Power of Darkness; The Fruits of Knowledge; The Root of All Evil; The First Distiller.*

Tomb, a monument erected over the spot where a body lies buried: Egyptian and Roman tombs were usually simple but elegant in design, and in the Middle Ages they assumed the form of small edifices either attached to the exterior walls or located in the interior of churches or chapels. The most famous tomb of antiquity was the Mausoleum at Halicarnassus: the most magnificent example from the architectural point of view is the TAJ MAHAL at Agra, India. Modern examples include the tomb of Napoleon in Paris, the tomb of Lenin in Moscow and the tomb of General Grant in New York.

Tom-tom, a small, deep drum which has thick leather heads, and is frequently confused with the TAM-TAM. It produces a brief and peculiarly hollow sound of melancholy character, and is employed for creating atmosphere in simulated Oriental music.

Tonality, in music a term with a broader significance than KEY: it denotes the harmonious relation of the notes of a musical composition to its keynote, and refers specifically to the chords grouped around a single central tonic chord.

Tone, Franchot (1906-), American stage and screen actor educated at Cornell University who first appeared with stock companies, and made his debut in 1927 on the New York stage in *The Belt*. Among the plays in which he appeared were *The Age of Innocence; Uncle Vanya; Cross Roads; Green Grow the Lilacs; The House of Connelly*. Among the numerous films in which he has been featured are *Lives of a Bengal Lancer; No More Ladies; Mutiny on the Bounty; Quality Street; They Gave Him A Gun; Three Loves Has Nancy; The Wife Takes a Flyer.*

Tone, in music (*1*) a musical sound, either single or composite, and of fixed PITCH: (*2*) the interval of the major second usually called a whole tone: (*3*) the particular quality of the sound of any instrument or the human voice.

Tone Poem, in music a title which has recently come to be used instead of the term SYMPHONIC POEM for an orchestral composition. There is little distinction between the two titles: Richard STRAUSS used the title "tone poem" for several works which are composed in the form accepted for a symphonic poem.

Tonic, in music the name given to the first note of any SCALE: it is the fundamental note which determines the key of a composition. The *tonic chord* is the chord built on the keynote of the scale.

Tonio, a character in Leoncavallo's opera, *I Pagliacci:* he is a humpbacked clown who, when Canio's wife, Nedda, repels his advances, brings Canio to the scene of Nedda's tryst with her lover, Silvio, and thereby is the cause of Nedda and Silvio being murdered by Canio.

Topaz, a variety of the mineral aluminum fluosilicate highly prized as a gem: it is found in granite, and is usually without color or yellow, green, blue, or pale-green in shade. It is found in Russia, Brazil, parts of Europe, and in several sections of the United States.

Torrence, David (1870-), Scottish stage and screen actor educated in Edinburgh and Germany who made his American debut with Richard Mansfield's Company in 1892, and later appeared in numerous plays with Maude ADAMS, Lulu GLASER and Ethel BARRYMORE. Among the films in which he has been featured are *Tess of the Storm Country; The Light That Failed; East Lynne; Raffles; Voltaire; Queen Christina; Mandalay; Jane Eyre; Captain Blood; Mary of Scotland; The Lost Horizon; Stanley and Livingstone.*

Torrigiano, Pietro (1472-1522), Italian sculptor who studied with Lorenzo de' MEDICI as his patron, and is said to have caused the disfigurement of MICHELANGELO's nose by a blow during a quarrel: he lived for a time in England where he executed the tombs of Henry VII and his wife at Westminster Abbey. He also built the altar, retable, and baldachin which were erected near the tomb: this was destroyed by the Puritans in the 17th century, but some fragments remain. Later he went to Spain, and made some terra cotta figures, but finally died while imprisoned by the Spanish INQUISITION.

Torso, in the human figure the part which includes the shoulders and breast: the term is applied in sculpture to a statue without head, arms or legs. Two of the most perfect examples are the Belvedere torso in the Vatican Museum, and the Farnese torso at Naples.

Tosca, grand opera in three acts: libretto by Giuseppe Giacosa and Luigi Illica based on Victorien SARDOU's play, *La Tosca;* music by Giacomo PUCCINI; first produced at Rome in 1900, and at the Metropolitan Opera House, New York, in 1901. The role of Baron Scarpia is identified in the United States with Antonio SCOTTI who created the role at the Metropolitan in 1901 with Milka TERNINA as *Tosca*. There are Columbia and Victor recordings of the complete opera, and a Decca abridged version: also separate records of the famous arias and duets.

Toscanini, Arturo (1867-), Italian conductor who studied the violoncello at the Parma Conservatory: in 1886 he was engaged as 'cellist for the opera at Rio de Janeiro, and when the regular conductor was hissed off the stage during a performance of Verdi's *Aida,* took his place and emerged in a single night as one of the world's greatest conductors, being immediately engaged as such for the balance of the season. From 1886 to 1892 he conducted at opera houses in Turin, Genoa, Rome, Milan, and several other cities: in 1892 he directed the première of Leoncavallo's *Pagliacci* at Milan. In 1898 he became conductor and artistic director at La Scala, Milan, under Giulio GATTI-CASAZZA, and when the latter became general manager of the Metropolitan Opera House, New York, in 1908, Toscanini became chief conductor of Italian and French opera until 1915. During World War I his services were utilized by the Italian Government for patriotic and charitable purposes: from 1921 to 1929 he occupied the post of artistic director at La Scala, Milan, and in 1928 he became conductor of the New York Philharmonic-Symphony Society, resigning in 1936. In 1937 he accepted the post of conductor of the NBC Symphony Orchestra which he still (1943) retains.

Tosti, Sir Francesco Paolo (1847-1916), Italian composer and teacher of singing who studied at Naples, became vocal instructor to the court of Rome, and in 1880 settled in London as singing teacher to the Royal family. Many of his songs including *Goodbye, Beauty's Eyes, Serenata*, and *Mattinata* became popular, and are still favored by amateur singers.

Touch, in music the method or manner of depressing the keys of a stringed instrument, such as the piano, which affects the quality of sound produced. The extent to which tone quality is affected by touch is a matter of dispute.

Toulouse-Lautrec, Henri Raymond de (1864-1901), French illustrator and lithographer who illustrated many books, and executed poster designs which reveal an extraordinary degree of originality: his lithographs of scenes in Montmartre and the Parisian music halls and theatres are now collectors' items.

Toumanova, Tamara (1917-   ), Russian dancer who studied at Paris with Olga Preobrajenska, and made her debut in 1924 with the Anna Pavlowa Ballet Company: she has also danced with Colonel de Basil's Monte Carlo Ballet Russe and the Tilly Losch Company. Her American debut was made at New York in 1933; she has apeared in *Petrouchka, Swan Lake, Les Sylphides, Jeux d'Enfants, Three-Cornered Hat, Union Pacific*, and *Symphonie Fantastique.*

Tourmaline, a semi-precious gem formed of a hard stone with a base of limestone or magnesia. It is sometimes colorless, but the color most desired is a dark green or a dark red. It is found in Brazil, Burma, Siberia, Maine, and California.

Tourte, François (1747-1835), French maker of violin bows who is often referred to as the "Stradivarius of bow making": he created the bow in its modern form in respect to the shape and inward curve of the stick, cutting the wood straight with the grain, and polishing the sticks with oil instead of varnish. The present-day prices of his bows range from $500.00 to $2,000.00.

Tovey, Sir Donald Francis (1875-1940), English composer and writer on music who was educated at Oxford, and trained in music under Sir Charles Hubert Hastings Parry: his compositions include orchestral works and chamber music. Among his published books are *A Companion to Bach's Art of the Fugue*, and *Essays in Musical Analysis* (6 vols., 1935-38).

Tower, in architecture a building of great height in proportion to its breadth, and used in ancient times for fortification purposes, or for clocks, bells or chimes. Towers were square in the 12th century and circular in the 13th returning to the square shape in the 14th century. The most famous example is the **Tower of London,** a group of buildings on the Thames River which was originally a fortress and royal residence, later becoming a jail for distinguished prisoners.

Town Hall (New York), a hall on West 43rd Street, New York, which at the present time (1943) is the principal auditorium with the exception of Carnegie Hall for music recitals and concerts: its predecessors were the old Steinway Hall on East 14th Street, Mendelssohn Hall on West 40th Street, and Aeolian Hall on West 42nd Street. It opened in 1921, and has been the home of the Friends of Music, the New Friends of Music, and other ensembles as well as recitalists.

Toyokuni or **Utagawa** (1769-1825), Japanese painter who was greatly influenced by Utamaro: his works include a triptych representing a princess watching her companions at play; and a diptych picturing children gazing at their faces reflected in lacquer panels. He also illustrated novels, executed many portraits of distinguished actors, and taught many students who later became famous.

Toy Symphony (Haydn), a work composed in 1788 by Joseph Haydn for two violins, double bass, and six toy instruments comprising a cuckoo pipe tuned to *C* and *G,* a quail-call in *F,* a trumpet and drum in *G,* a whistle and a triangle. The idea has since been imitated by other composers, but without the skill with which Haydn created his miniature masterpiece—for what festive occasion is not known. There is a Columbia recording directed by Felix Weingartner.

Tracery, in architecture a term applied to a type of ornament found in the upper half of Gothic windows: the pattern is geometrical, and has been adapted to many art objects such as the cases of clocks, and also to stained glass windows.

Tracy, Spencer (1900-   ), American stage and screen actor educated at the University of Wisconsin and trained at the American Academy of Dramatic Arts: he appeared in several plays including *The Last Mile* before entering the films where he has been featured since 1935 in numerous pictures including *San Francisco; They Gave Him a Gun; Captains Courageous; Boys Town; Stanley and Livingstone; Edison the Man; Boom Town; Northwest Passage; Dr. Jekyll and Mr. Hyde; Woman of the Year; Tortilla Flat.*

Tragedy, a dramatic work relating a serious story in which the principal character or characters are finally involved in a catastrophe: its origin is traced to a style of drama originating in ancient Greek religious ceremonies. The dithyrambs recited by the chorus had a single actor or "answerer": Aeschylus added another actor which brought dialogue into the ceremonies, and Sophocles a third actor. Greek tragedy reached its greatest perfection in the 5th century B.C. More information on this subject can be obtained by reading the reference on Drama.

"Tragic" Overture (Brahms), an orchestral work by Johannes Brahms first performed at Vienna in 1880. It is regarded as a musical characterization of the principles of tragedy laid down by Aristotle and Lessing; as Riemann puts it: "It mirrors the grandeur, the loftiness, the deep earnestness of tragic character; calamities, which an inexorable fate has imposed on him, leave the hero guilty; the tragic downfall atones for the guilt." There is a Columbia recording by the London Philharmonic Orchestra directed by Sir Thomas Beecham, and a Victor recording by the British Broadcasting Company Symphony Orchestra under Arturo Toscanini.

Train, Arthur Cheney (1875-), American novelist and short story writer educated at Harvard University, and later admitted to the bar. He acted as assistant district attorney of New York from 1901 to 1908, serving under William Travers Jerome, one of the ablest prosecutors ever to occupy the office of district attorney in New York. His works include *McAllister and His Double* (1905); *The Prisoner at the Bar; Confessions of Artemus Quibble; The Goldfish; Tutt and Mr. Tutt; Page Mr. Tutt; When Tutt Meets Tutt; The Adventures of Ephraim Tutt; Mr. Tutt's Case Book; My Day in Court*, an autobiography; *Mr. Tutt Comes Home; The Life and Times of Mr. Tutt*.

Transcription, in music the arrangement of a composition for some instrument other than the one for which it was originally written: Franz LISZT was one of the world's most skillful transcribers of orchestral and operatic music for the piano.

Transept, in architecture the smaller sections in the crossing of a Gothic church: one section turns toward the south and the other toward the north; in some instances there are two sets of transepts.

Transposition, in music the writing out of a composition in another key than the one in which it was originally conceived: in the case of songs transpositions are often made to a lower key in order to favor a singer's voice; in instrumental music transpositions frequently render compositions less difficult of performance. The parts for the CLARINETS, FRENCH HORNS, and TRUMPETS are transposed in orchestra music because they become easier of execution for reasons concerned with the mechanism of the instruments.

Trap Drum, a type of drummer equipment used in dance bands: it consists of a bass drum to which cymbals are attached, both being played by a foot mechanism which leaves both the drummer's hands free to play the SNARE DRUM.

Traubel, Helen, contemporary American concert and operatic soprano who studied with Madame Karst and made her concert debut as soloist with the St. Louis Symphony Orchestra in 1925. After appearing as guest artist with major American symphony orchestras, she created the soprano role in Walter Damrosch's opera, *The Man Without a Country* with the Metropolitan Opera Company in 1937, and has become a valued member of the organization.

Traviata, La, grand opera in three acts: libretto by Francesco Maria Piave based on the play, *La Dame aux Camélias* (*Camille*) by Alexandre DUMAS, FILS; music by Giuseppe VERDI; first produced at Venice in 1853; at the ACADEMY OF MUSIC, New York, in 1856, and at the Metro-

politan Opera House, New York, in 1883. The opera libretto follows the story of the play closely: there are Victor and Columbia complete recordings, and separate records of the popular arias and duets.

Treble, the name applied to the highest part in vocal and instrumental music: the CLEF on the second line of the STAFF is known as the *treble clef*.

Tree, Sir Herbert Beerbohm (1853-1917), English actor and manager whose real name was Herbert Beerbohm: he was the brother of Max BEERBOHM, author and caricaturist. He first appeared on the stage in 1878 as Herbert Tree, and achieved success in 1884 in *The Private Secretary:* among the plays in which he appeared while operating the HAYMARKET THEATRE, London, or on tour were *Jim the Penman; The Red Lamp; A Woman of No Importance; Trilby; The Seats of the Mighty; The Dancing Girl:* he was also highly appreciated as Sir Peter Teazle, King John, Bottom, Falstaff, Fagin, Shylock, Wolsey, Micawber and other roles. His wife, **Lady Helen Maud Tree** (1863-1937), was a highly regarded actress who remained on the stage after her husband's death and also appeared in the talking films with success. Her daughter, **Viola Tree** (1884-1938), also trained for the stage, first appearing with her father as Viola in *Twelfth Night*, and managing a season for Sacha GUITRY at London in 1920.

Tremolo (It.), the term applied to the rapid reiteration of a single note or a chord; an important effect on bowed instruments produced by a rapid up and down motion of the bow. On keyboard instruments it is produced in various ways indicated in the notation, usually by abbreviation. The tremolo is also a mechanical device in the ORGAN for producing a fluttering tone by a rapidly varying wind pressure.

Trent, William Peterfield (1862-1939, American author and editor educated at the University of Virginia and from 1900 to 1929 professor of English literature at Columbia University. His works include *A History of American Literature: 1607-1865; Longfellow and Other Essays; Great Writers of America*.

Triad, in music a three-tone chord composed of a given tone with its third and fifth in ascending diatonic order: a *major triad* has a major third and a perfect fifth, and a *minor triad* a minor third and a perfect fifth.

Trial by Jury, an operetta in one act; libretto by Sir William S. Gilbert; music by Sir Arthur S. Sullivan; first produced at London in 1875. The plot concerns itself with a breach of promise suit which ends in the judge marrying the charming plaintiff. There is a complete Victor recording by the D'Oyly Carte Company.

Triana, Antonio, see **Amaya, Carmen.**

Triangle, in music an orchestral PERCUSSION instrument consisting of a steel rod bent into the shape of a triangle, one angle of which is partly open. By striking it with a small steel rod a clear, penetrating tone of indeterminate pitch is produced. The triangle part is written on a single line headed only by the time signature, the notes indicating only the time values.

Trianon, Grand, a small château at Versailles, one story in height, built by Louis XIV for Madame de Maintenon, and later used by French sovereigns as a private residence: the Treaty of Versailles was signed there in 1919 at the end of World War I. Another château, **Petit Trianon,** was built at Versailles by Louis XV for Marie Antoinette who was very much attached to it: its furniture and fittings remains as a memorial.

Triglyph, in architecture a style of ornament found in friezes of Dorian design: it consists of a projecting piece pierced by three narrow flutings. Triglyphs were used in ancient Greek and Roman temples.

Trill, in music a form of ornament consisting of the rapid alternation of one tone with the tone next above it: it was first introduced in the days of the harpsichord when there was no means of producing a prolonged note. A trill usually indicated by the notation *tr* over the tone on which the trill begins.

Trippenmeker, Heinrich, see **Aldegrever, Heinrich.**

Triptych, in painting a sequence of three panels either painted or sculptured: the side wings were closed by the use of hinges, and the exterior as well as the interior of each wing was painted. Rubens executed several fine triptychs which were used either as portable altars or altarpieces.

Tristan and Isolde, music drama in three acts: text and music by Richard Wagner; first produced at Munich in 1865, and at the Metropolitan Opera House, New York, in 1886 with Albert Niemann as Tristan and Lilli Lehmann as Isolde. The story is based on ancient legend: Tristan, nephew of King Mark of Cornwall, slays Morold, the Irish King's brother, who is betrothed to Isolde. Tristan, wounded, seeks Isolde for she is known as a healer, and Isolde, while caring for him discovers that he is the murderer of her lover. She intends to kill Tristan, but finds that he loves her and that she loves him, so his life is spared. The nobles plan to marry Isolde to King Mark; Tristan and Isolde, with Brangäne, her maid, sail for Cornwall. Isolde tells Tristan that she will never marry King Mark, and she plans to take poison. Brangäne changes the death drink to a love potion and Tristan and Isolde both partake of it. Melot betrays them, and brings King Mark to reproach Tristan, who is wounded by Melot; Kurneval, Tristan's squire, catches him as he is about to fall. Later in Tristan's castle at Breton, Isolde comes to see Tristan, and King Mark also arrives at the castle to pardon him. Kurneval and Melot, not knowing this, are killed in barring each other's way. Tristan dies at Isolde's feet, and she expires in Brangäne's arms. There is a Columbia abridged recording in 19 records, and a Victor abridged re-

cording of Act III: also many separate records of favorite parts listed in the *Gramophone Shop Encyclopedia of Recorded Music.*

Triton, in Greek mythology a son of Poseidon and Amphitrite who lived with his parents at the bottom of the ocean. In later legends Tritons were lesser deities of the sea who blew trumpets made of shells to still the restless rolling of the waves.

Trojan War, in Greek legend a war fought for ten years by the Greeks under the leadership of Agamemnon against the Trojans in an effort to recover Helen, the wife of Menelaus, king of Sparta who had been abducted by Paris, son of Priam, king of Troy. The war was won by the Greeks who pretended to abandon their siege of the city, but leaving a wooden horse in which several warriors were hidden. The Trojans dragged the horse into the city: the warriors opened the city gates and the returning horde of Greeks sacked Troy.

Trolls, in Scandinavian mythology supernatural inhabitants of caves high up in the mountains: they are described in some legends as dwarfs and in others as giants. Certain trolls are friendly and others inimical to human beings.

Trollope, Anthony (1815-1882), English novelist whose first two novels of Irish life published in 1847-48 achieved little success: in 1855 *The Warden* attracted considerable favorable attention followed by *Barchester Towers; Dr. Thorne; Framley Parsonage; The Small House at Allington; The Last Chronicle of Barset; Phineas Finn; The Prime Minister; The American Senator; Orley Farm; The Eustace Diamonds; The Three Clerks.* His mother, **Frances Trollope** (1780-1863), was a successful novelist whose works include *Tremordyn Cliff* (1835); *The Vicar of Wrexhill; The Widow Barnaby; The Widow Married; The Barnabys in America.* His brother, **Thomas Adolphus Trollope** (1810-1892), was educated at Oxford and resided at Florence, Italy, for many years: he wrote many novels in addition to a history of Florence and a biography of Catherine de' Medici.

Trombone, a metal instrument of the trumpet type having a sliding tube by which the pitch is adjusted. It is made in four sizes: alto, tenor, bass, and contrabass. The slide gives the trombone the accuracy and modulated power of stringed instruments; its notes are not fixed but made by ear and judgment. Trombones were not used in symphonic works until Beethoven placed them in his scores, but Mozart used them effectively in *The Magic Flute* and Gluck in *Alceste.*

Troubadours, poet musicians who originated in southern France during the 12th and 13th centuries: the names of more than four hundred, together with a list of their works, have been handed down. The poems were written in stanzas; each stanza was sung to the same melody: the music is given at the beginning of each song, usually on four-line staves, in plainsong notation. The words of the first stanza are written under the music, and the other stanzas follow underneath. Over two hundred and fifty melodies and more than two thousand poems have been preserved in the Ambrosian Library at Milan and in the National Library at Paris. The chief theme of the songs was love, and their composition gradually declined from the beginning of the 14th century.

Troubetzkoy, Paul, Prince (1866-1938), Russian sculptor whose mother was an American and father a Russian nobleman: he was educated in Italy, and acquired a considerable reputation for cleverly executed bronze statuettes of figures and horses. He was also a portraitist of ability: among his works are busts of TOLSTOY, RODIN, Anatole FRANCE, and George Bernard SHAW. He executed an equestrian statue of Alexander III of Russia: his style is distinctly impressionistic.

Troubetzkoy, Princess, see **Rives, Amélie.**

"Trout" Quintet (Schubert), a work composed in 1819 by Franz SCHUBERT for piano, viola, violoncello, and double-bass: Schubert had written a delightful song "The Trout," and a musical amateur, Wilhelm Paumgartner, urged him repeatedly to write a series of variations based on the theme of the song. The composer was pleased with the idea and the quintet, now known as the *Trout Quintet* because the theme of the song with variations comprises its slow movement, was soon written. The composition has four movements besides the "Trout" variations; it would appear that Schubert desired to give the customary four movements their usual importance. The piano part is particularly effective, revealing a mastery which is to be noted in all Schubert's chamber works after 1812, when his skill in this respect began to make itself apparent. There are both Columbia and Victor recordings.

Trouvères, medieval poets and singers of northern France corresponding to the TROUBADOURS of southern France. Their poems were epic in character, and they are not to be classed with the troubadors whose songs were entirely of love. The famous CHANSON DE GESTE originated with the trouvères, one of the most famous of whom was BLONDEL DE NESLE.

Trovatore, Il, a grand opera in four acts: libretto by Salvatore Cammarano; music by Giuseppe VERDI; first produced at Rome in 1853; at the Academy of Music, New York, in 1855, and at the Metropolitan Opera House in 1883. The libretto was based on a drama, *El Trovador*, by Antonio GARCIA-GUTIERREZ, produced in 1826. There are both Victor and Columbia recordings, and separate records of favorite arias, duets, and trios listed in *The Gramophone Shop Encyclopedia of Recorded Music.*

Troy, an ancient Asiatic city also known as *Ilium:* Heinrich SCHLIEMANN, a distinguished German archaeologist, claimed to have discovered the site of the city in 1882, but the exact location was found by Wilhelm Dörpfeld in 1894. It is famous as the scene of the TROJAN WAR which is the subject of HOMER's *Iliad.*

Troyon, Constant (1810-1865), French painter who first worked as a decorator of SEVRES por-

celain, and later developed great skill in depicting outdoor life including animals and landscapes: his notable works include *Feeding the Chickens; Watering Cattle; Oxen at Work; Flock of Sheep; Bull under a Stormy Sky; Huntsmen and Dogs; Road in the Wood.*

Trübner, Wilhelm (1851-1917), German painter who became professor at the Karlsruhe Academy from 1903 to 1917: his paintings such as *View of Castle* and *Boy with Mastiff* are pronounced full and rich in color, original in treatment, and broad and bold in execution.

Trumbull, John (1756-1843), American painter who served as an aide to General Washington during the Revolutionary War: he went to London in 1780 to study with Benjamin WEST, but was imprisoned there for eight months because of the execution in America of Major André as a spy. His works include *The Battle of Bunker Hill; The Death of Montgomery; The Surrender of Lord Cornwallis; Signing of the Declaration of Independence:* he also painted portraits of Washington and many other distinguished soldiers and civilians.

Trumpet, a wind instrument which has undergone many changes since it consisted of a straight tube in ancient Greece and a slightly curved tube in Rome. It is made of brass, mixed metal or silver, the last two being most common. The mouthpiece is shallow, which accounts in part for its great sonority; the bore is narrow and the tube, about eight feet long, is bent into three lengths in the case of the orchestral trumpet. The modern trumpet is provided with valves and is capable of playing the most complicated passages. It is distinguished from the CORNET by its straighter or more cylindrical bore and more shallow mouthpiece, both of which features give the trumpet a bright penetrating tone as against the mellow tone of the cornet. It is the principal soprano of the brass choir in the orchestra, but second in this respect in the band, where the cornet is the principal soprano.

Tryon, Dwight William (1849-1925), American painter who studied with Charles Daubigny at Paris, and later sketched in Holland and Italy: his works include *Harvest Time in Normandy; Hay Making; Twilight in Connecticut; Waning Moon; October Afternoon; Gray Day in October.* He became director of the Hartford (Ct.) Art School in 1882, and also taught at Smith College.

Tschaikowsky, Peter Ilich (1840-1893), Russian composer and conductor who began to compose music at the age of ten, but first studied law and worked as a government employee until 1863 when he decided to take up music as a profession and studied composition at the St. Petersburg Conservatory with Nicholas RUBINSTEIN. In 1866 he became teacher of theory at the Moscow Conservatory, but resigned in 1877 to devote himself exclusively to composition, his income being assured through the generosity of Madame Nadejda von Meck who granted him an annual stipend of 6,000 rubles. He made his first appearance as a conductor of his own works at Moscow in 1887, followed by a tour of Europe in 1888: he visited the United States in 1891 conducting his own works at the dedication of CARNEGIE HALL, New York. His compositions comprise several operas including *Eugene Onegin;* the ballets *Swan Lake; Sleeping Beauty,* and *Casse-Noisette;* six symphonies; three piano concertos; a violin concerto; several symphonic poems and fantasies; *"1812" Overture;* two string quartets and a piano trio; piano pieces; choral works, and songs.

Tuba, a bass instrument of the saxhorn family: the term *tuba* includes the baritone, euphonium, bass, and contra-bass, the two last named being known specifically as tubas. Since Richard WAGNER demonstrated the musical value of the tuba it is included in most modern scores.

Tubbs, James (1835-1919), English bow maker who learned the art of bow making from his father, Thomas Tubbs: he was the greatest of English makers, selecting the woods and balancing his bows so that they compare favorably with those of François TOURTE. Their value at the present time ranges from $65.00 to $250.00.

Tudor, Anthony (1909-), English dancer who was first engaged in business: after seeing Anna PAVLOWA dance in 1928, he studied with Marie RAMBERT, Pearl ARGYLE, and Harold TURNER, and upon becoming manager of the Ballet Club produced his first ballet in 1931. He danced with the Vic-Wells Ballet in 1933, and has created numerous ballets including *The Descent of Hebe; Jardin aux Lilas; Gala Performance; Lysistrata; Adam and Eve; Dark Elegies; Castor and Pollux; Gallant Assembly.*

Tudor style, a late form of GOTHIC architecture and decoration used in England from the end of the 15th to the middle of the 16th century, also known as the PERPENDICULAR PERIOD.

Tuileries (Paris), a palace in Paris located between the LOUVRE and the Place de la Concorde: it was begun for CATHERINE DE' MEDICI in 1564 by Philibert DELORME who was succeeded as architect by Jean Bullant. It was the place of detention for Marie ANTOINETTE and Louis XVI before they were executed, was burned down in 1871, and after the ruins were removed converted into a public park.

Tune, in music a simple air or melody which is readily remembered: to *tune* an instrument is to adjust its pitch; a *tuning-fork* is a pronged instrument invented in 1711 by John Shore, a trumpeter in Handel's orchestra.

Tura, Cosimo (c.1425-1495), Italian painter who passed the greater part of his life in the service of the Duke of Ferrara: his works include *Annunciation; St. George and the Dragon; Pietá; The Virgin Prayer; Christ on the Cross; Virgin and Child Enthroned with Saints; Adoration of the Magi;* several portraits of the ESTE family.

Turgenev, Ivan Sergeyevich (1818-1883), Russian novelist, poet, and dramatist educated at Moscow, St. Petersburg, and Berlin: his works include *Poems* (1841); *Parascha; Improvidence; The Landlord; A Sportsman's Sketches; Fathers and Sons; Rudin; A Nest of Gentlefolk; On the Eve; Smoke* and many other novels.

Turina, Joaquín (1882-), Spanish composer who studied at the Madrid Conservatory with José Tragó, and later at Paris with Vincent D'INDY at the Schola Cantorum, also the piano with Moritz MOSZKOWSKI. His compositions include operas, orchestral works, chamber music, piano pieces, and songs. His *Danzas Fantásticas* for orchestra are particularly effective.

Turn, an embellishment of a musical tone indicated by the sign ~. The turn is made by playing the note above the given note, the given note itself, the note below the given note, and finally the given note, which is then held for the balance of the time value indicated.

Turner, Charles Yardley (1850-1919), American painter who studied at the Art Students' League, New York, and later with Jean Paul LAURENS, Michael MUNKACZY, and Leon BONNAT at Paris: in 1881 he became a professor at the Art Students' League. His notable works include *Bridal Procession; Merry Milkmaid; Washington Watching the Assault on Fort Lee; Half Hours with the Poets; Woman Tending Garden Flowers; The Burning of the Peggy Stuart; Gone a' Milking; Barter with the Indians.*

Turner, Harold (1909-), English dancer who studied with Marie Rambert and made his first appearance at the Coliseum, London, in 1927, also appearing at COVENT GARDEN and the OLD VIC. In 1930 he danced with KARSAVINA in *Spectre de la Rose,* and has appeared since that time at Paris with the Russian Ballet and at the Opéra.

Turner, Joseph Mallord William (1775-1851), English painter who attended the schools of the Royal Academy, and exhibited his first picture, *View of the Archbishop's Palace at Lambeth* in 1790. He traveled and sketched in many parts of England, and also visited Scotland, France, Switzerland, and Italy. His notable works include *Aeneas with the Sibyl; Hannibal Crossing the Alps; Jason in Search of the Golden Fleece; Crossing the Brook; Destruction of Sodom; Dido Building Carthage; Bay of Baiae; Childe Harold's Pilgrimage; Bridge of Sighs at Venice; The Slave Ship; Apollo Killing a Python.*

Turner, Lana (1920-), American screen actress who has appeared since 1937 in several films including *They Won't Forget; The Great Garrick; The Adventures of Marco Polo; Love Finds Andy Hardy; Rich Man, Poor Girl; Dramatic School; Calling Dr. Kildare; Ziegfeld Girl; Honkey Tonk; Johnny Eager.*

Turquoise, a rare gem stone normally blue or green-blue in color, usually cut in round or oval shape: the sky-blue color is the one most highly valued. The finest stones come from Persia and Mexico.

Tussaud, Marie (1760-1850), Swiss lady who was taught modeling in wax by her uncle who was an expert in creating figures for anatomical use: his portrait gallery of wax figures in Paris, containing likenesses of contemporary celebrities, was extremely popular. In 1802 she came to London and established a museum devoted to wax figures in which the "Chamber of Horrors" was an outstanding attraction. The museum moved to larger quarters several times, and the collection was partially destroyed by fire in 1925, but placed on exhibition again in 1928.

Tut-ankh-amen, a king of Egypt who ruled from 1358 to 1349 B.C.: in 1922 his tomb near LUXOR was found by Lord Carnavon and Howard Carter. It contained the mummy of the king in a casket of solid gold which in turn was enclosed in two other coffins: also more than six hundred art objects and furnishings such as carved wooden couches, vases, and trinkets to be seen in the CAIRO MUSEUM.

Twachtman, John Henry (1853-1902), American painter who studied at Cincinnati with Frank DUVENECK and in 1876 went with him to Munich where they both worked under Ludwig Loefftz. In 1883 he studied in Paris at the Académie Julian under BOULANGER and LEFEBVRE. After his return to the United States he painted the sky section of the great panorama, *The Battle of Gettysburg,* and in 1890 purchased a large farm where he lived the rest of his life while also teaching at the Cooper Union Institute and the ART STUDENTS' LEAGUE, New York. He founded the society known as "Ten American Painters" among whom were Joseph DECAMP, Frank BENSON, Thomas DEWING, Childe HASSAM, Willard METCALF, and Edmund TARBELL. His works include *Dry Docks at Venice; Summer Meadow Brook; Hemlock Pool; The Waterfall.*

Twain, Mark, pseudonym of **Samuel Langhorne Clemens** (1835-1910), American humorist who worked as a journalist, printer, and river pilot before being encouraged by Bret HARTE and Artemus WARD to pursue a literary career. His first successful story, *Jim Smiley and the Jumping Frog* was published in 1865: it was followed by *The Innocents Abroad; Roughing It; The Gilded Age,* written with Charles Dudley Warner and successfully dramatized; *A Tramp Abroad; Tom Sawyer* which was dramatized; *The Prince and the Pauper,* also dramatized; *Life on the Mississippi; The Adventures of Huckleberry Finn,* dramatized and recently successfully adapted for the films; *A Connecticut Yankee in King Arthur's Court* (dramatized); *The American Claimant; Pudd'nhead Wilson* (dramatized); *Joan of Arc; Following the Equator.* His daughter, **Clara Clemens** (1874-), is a contralto singer and author who first studied the piano, but abandoned it to study singing, and made her debut at Florence in 1904. She married Ossip GABRILOWITSCH, famous pianist and conductor: her books include *My Father, Mark Twain* and *My Husband, Gabrilowitsch.*

Tweedsmuir, 1st Baron, see **Buchan, John.**

Twelve Labors of Hercules, see **Hercules.**

Tyler, George Crouse (1867-), American theatrical producer who was first a journalist, becoming manager in 1894 for James O'NEILL, and organizing the firm of Liebler and Co. in 1897 which first achieved success with Charles COGHLAN, and with Viola ALLEN in *The Christian.* Among the actors under the Liebler banner were Eleonora DUSE, Madame REJANE, Yvette GUILBERT, Albert CHEVALIER, Kyrle BELLEW, William FAVERSHAM, Ada REHAN, Mary MANNERING, and George ARLISS. In 1915 he joined Klaw and Erlanger, and produced many plays including *Hamilton* and *Pollyanna;* in 1918 as an independent manager he produced *Clarence; Dulcy; Merton of the Movies; Young Woodley; The Constant Nymph; Becky Sharp* and many other successful plays.

Tyler, Royall (1757-1826), American author and dramatist who was Chief Justice of the Supreme Court of Vermont from 1800: he was the author of *The Contrast* (1786), the first American play presented on the professional stage. His other plays include *May Day; The George Spec.; or, Land in the Moon; The Algerian Captive.*

Tynan, Brandon (1879-), Irish actor who was brought to the United States when he was seven years old: in 1900 he played with John DREW at the Empire Theatre, New York, in *Richard Carvel.* Among the plays in which he has been featured are *A Doll's House* with NAZIMOVA; *Officer 666; Joseph and His Brethren; Trilby; The Tavern; The Rivals.* He has written several plays, and has also appeared in many films including *Parnell; Wells Fargo; The Girl of the Golden West; Almost a Gentleman; Lucky Partners.*

U

Uccello, Paolo (c.1397-1475), Italian painter and sculptor whose real name was Paolo di Dono: little is known of his early career beyond the fact that he worked with Lorenzo GHIBERTI on the doors of the Baptistery at Florence: among the few paintings extant is *The Battle of San Romano;* an equestrian portrait of Sir John Hawkwood; frescoes in the Church of Santa Maria Novello at Florence, and a predella, *Miracle of the Host* at Urbino.

Udall, Nicholas (1505-1556), English schoolmaster and dramatist who was headmaster at ETON COLLEGE from 1534 to 1541 and of Westminster School from 1555 to 1556: he is famous chiefly as the author of *Ralph Roister Doister* which is either the earliest, or at least one of the first English comedies. It is written in rhyme, and the chief character is the conventional type of braggart soldier.

Uffizi Gallery (Florence), see **Pitti Gallery (Florence).**

Uhde, Fritz von (1848-1911), German painter who studied at Dresden and interrupted his artistic career with ten years of military service: in 1877 he studied again under Michael MUNKACZY at Paris and also in Holland. His religious pictures, which treat Bible episodes realistically by portraying them in modern settings and costumes, include *Christ Among the Peasants; Going Home; Holy Night; The Sermon on the Mount; The Walk to Bethlehem; Suffer Little Children to Come Unto Me.*

Uhland, Johann Ludwig (1787-1862), German lyric poet whose ballads and songs are regarded as classics: he also wrote the dramas *Ernest, Duke of Suabia* and *Ludwig of Bavaria,* and made a valuable collection of ancient German folk songs.

Ukulele, a small, four-stringed guitar popular in Hawaii: also called the *taropatch fiddle* and "the flea," referring to its small size. It is said to have been invented by a Portuguese, Manuel Nuñez, and was brought to Hawaii in 1870. The early part of the 20th century saw its greatest popularity as an instrument easy to play in the accompaniment of popular songs and Hawaiian native airs.

Ulric, Lenore (1892-), American stage and screen actress who first appeared in stock companies about 1910, and in Essanay films: her New York debut in 1915 was made in *The Mark of the Beast.* Among the plays in which she has appeared are *Tiger Rose; Kiki,* her greatest success; *Lulu Belle; East of Suez; Pagan Lady; Social Register; Hard Boiled Angel:* she has also played in several talking films.

Ulrich, Charles Frederick (1858-1908), American painter who studied at the National Academy, New York, and at Munich: his works include *The Glass Blowers; Carpenter at Work; Castle Garden; Land of Promise; Relics of Bygone Days; Waifs; The Dutch Typesetter.*

Ulysses, see **Odysseus.**

"Uncle Remus," see **Harris, Joel Chandler.**

Uncle Tom's Cabin, see **Stowe, Harriet Beecher.**

Undine, in mythology a water spirit who could only be endowed with a human soul if she married a mortal: the name was originated by Paracelsus, a Swiss physician who regarded them as elementary beings dwelling in the water. Baron Friedrich de la Motte Fouque wrote a romance, *Undine* (1814), in which one of these spirits was beloved and then forsaken by a mortal.

Undset, Sigrid (1882-), Norwegian novelist born in Denmark: her son was killed when Norway was invaded in World War II, and she herself, after escaping to Sweden, came to the United States. Her novels include *The Bridal Wreath The Mistress of Husaby,* and *The Cross,* a historical trilogy which won the Nobel Prize in 1928; a second historical tetralogy the general title of which was *The Master of Hestviken* which included *The Axe, The Snake Pit, In the Wilderness,* and *The Son Avenger.* Several more of her novels have been translated in addition to the ones mentioned.

"Unfinished" Symphony (Schubert), an orchestral work by Franz Schubert composed in 1822 when he was elected an honorary member of a musical society in Graz: in return for the compliment he began composing the Symphony No. 8 in B Minor in 1822, and after having completed the first two movements and nine measures of the *Scherzo,* he visited Graz in 1827 but never heard the work there or elsewhere. It was first performed at Vienna, on Dec. 17, 1865, and at London, in 1867. The Gesellschaft der Musikfreunde, Vienna, has in its possession the autograph of the completed portions of the symphony along with the *Scherzo* fragment and sketches for the projected *Scherzo* and Trio. There are Victor recordings by the Boston Symphony Orchestra and by the Philadelphia Orchestra: there are also Columbia recordings by the London Philharmonic and by the London Symphony Orchestra.

Union Pacific, American folk ballet in one act: libretto by Archibald MacLeish; choreography by Leonide Massine; music by Nicholas Nabokoff; first performed at Philadelphia in 1934. The plot of the ballet concerns itself with the building of a railroad across the United States: it is the first of Massine's American ballets which makes use freely of native folk tunes and dance steps.

Union Square Theatre (New York), a theatre on 14th Street opened as a vaudeville house in 1871: in 1872 it became the home of the A. M. Palmer Stock Company of which Joseph Jefferson, Fanny Davenport, Stuart Robson, Clara Morris, Margaret Mather, Helena Modjeska, and Richard Mansfield were members at various times. It was burned down in 1888, and reopened in 1893 as a vaudeville house by B. F. Keith: after nearly a half century as a vaudeville and film house it was razed in 1936.

Unison, in music the term applied to the same tone sung or played simultaneously by different voices or instruments.

United States Marine Band, The, the band of the United States Marine Corps which has its headquarters at Washington, D. C. The original organization in 1798 was a fife and drum corps changed to a brass band in 1802: in 1854 its open-air concerts were begun at the Capitol and the White House. Among its distinguished conductors since 1798 were John B. Cuvillier, John Philip Sousa, Francisco Fanciulli, William H. Santelmann and Taylor Branson, the present director.

United States Navy Band, The, an organization founded in 1919 by act of Congress: at the close of World War I it became evident that there was a need of a permanent Navy Band. The United States Navy Band was therefore organized shortly after from the nucleus of various ship bands, and in 1923 gave its first performance with a personnel of sixty-five musicians under the direction of Charles Benter. Since then it has achieved an enviable reputation, plays at official ceremonies such as inaugurals and burials, gives concerts in Washington, embarks on an annual American tour, and is heard regularly on the radio in a national broadcast.

Unruh, Fritz von (1885-), German dramatist, novelist, and poet who served in World War I:

his works available in English include a drama, *Bonaparte;* a novel, *The Way of Sacrifice; Louis Ferdinand.* He opposed the Nazi regime, and exiled himself to France: when France was invaded he was placed in a concentration camp, but finally escaped and came to the United States.

Untermeyer, Louis (1885-   ), American poet, journalist, and anthologist: his works include several poetry anthologies such as *Modern British Poetry* and *Modern American Poetry; Heavens, a Book of Burlesques; Collected Parodies; This Singing World; Yesterday and Today; American Poetry from the Beginning to Whitman; The Book of Living Verse; A Treasury of Great Poems:* he has also published twenty-five books of original verse and prose.

Upjohn, Richard (1802-1878), American architect born in England who came to the United States in 1829: among his creations were Trinity Church, New York, along Gothic lines; several churches in Brooklyn, and the old St. Thomas Episcopal Church in New York which was later burned down. He also founded and acted as first president of the American Institute of Architects.

Upton, George Putnam (1835-1919), American critic and writer on musical subjects educated at Brown University: from 1861 to 1885 he acted as music critic for the Chicago *Tribune.* His works include *Woman in Music* (1880); *Standard Operas; Standard Oratorios; Standard Symphonies; Standard Light Operas; Standard Concert Guide; Standard Concert Repertory:* he translated Ludwig Nohl's biographies of Haydn, Liszt, Beethoven, and Wagner, and edited Theodore Thomas' autobiography in addition to publishing *Musical Memories* (1908), his autobiography.

Uranus, in Greek mythology the name of the sky god, representing the beneficent power of the heavens which furnishes the earth with the warmth of the sun and the cooling moisture of rain. He was also the father of the Titans and the Cyclopes.

Urban, Joseph (1872-1933), Viennese architect and scenic artist born in Austria who studied at the Art Academy in Vienna and came to the United States in 1911. Some of his important commissions in Europe included the decoration of the Municipal Building at Vienna; the famous "Czar Bridge" over the Neva River at St. Petersburg, Russia; the palace of the Khedive of Egypt at Alexandria. He decorated the Austrian Building at the St. Louis Exposition in 1904, and designed many scenic sets for the Metropolitan Opera House and New York theatres including those for Verdi's *Otello;* Wagner's *Tristan and Isolde* and *Parsifal; The Garden of Paradise* and the *Ziegfeld Follies.* He also built many sets for the Boston Opera Company.

Urfé, Honoré d' (1568-1625), French author of popular romances who wrote a long pastoral tale, *L'Astrée* which introduced its readers to an ideal world in which ladies and gentlemen of culture appear as shepherds and shepherdesses to make pretty observations: many similar romances by other writers followed as a result of its popularity.

Urlus, Jacques (1867-1935), French dramatic tenor who went to Holland as a boy, and after serving in the Dutch army studied voice at the Amsterdam Conservatory, making his debut in 1894 at the Amsterdam Opera in *Pagliacci.* After appearing in Germany, Austria, France, Belgium, and England he sang at Bayreuth in 1911, at the Richard Wagner festivals at Brussels from 1912 to 1914, and sang Wagnerian roles at the Metropolitan Opera House, New York, from 1913 to 1917, making his debut in *Tristan and Isolde.*

Urn, a form of vase originating with the ancients: it had a narrow neck over a gradually expanding body, and was usually of large size. Urns in which the ashes of the dead were placed were known as *cinerary urns,* and were widely used until the advent of Christianity which forbade cremation. They were often used to hold the hearts of distinguished deceased persons, and also for decorative purposes in architecture.

Urso, Camilla (1842-1902), French violinist who studied with Joseph Massart at the Paris Conservatory: from 1852 to 1855 she toured the United States with her father, playing in concerts with Marietta Alboni and Henrietta Sontag. After studying for several years she reappeared as a matured artist, and was hailed in both Europe and America as a virtuoso of great attainments.

Utamaro, Kitagawa (1753-1806), Japanese painter and color-print artist whose real name was Yusuké: he studied with Toriyama Sekiyen, and later revealed the influence of Shunsho, Masanobu, Harunobu, and Kiyonaga in his paintings which included scenes of motherhood and the ordinary every-day lives of women in the home. He had many pupils and produced an enormous number of pictures.

Utopia, a work published in Latin by Sir Thomas More in which a land was pictured from which all social evils were banished, and its inhabitants knew nothing of poverty. Many authors before and after More have drawn similar word pictures: they include Plato, Tommasso Campanella, Francis Bacon, Rabelais, Saint-Simon, Cabet, Bellamy, Samuel Butler, William Morris, and H. G. Wells.

Uwins, Thomas (1782-1857), English painter who studied at the Royal Academy, and first painted in water color, and illustrated many books. He became keeper of the Royal Gallery in 1847: his notable canvases include *Vintage in France; Neapolitans Dancing the Tarantella; Sir Guyon Fighting for Temperance; Coronation; Harvesting Hay; Chapeau de Brigand.*

V

Vajda, Ernest (1887-   ), Hungarian dramatist educated at Budapest University: his important plays include *Rozmarin Neni; The Crown Prince; The Unexpected Guest; Grounds for Divorce; Fata Morgana; The Harem.* The last three mentioned were produced in New York with great success. He has also adapted and written many plays for the films.

Valbert, G., see **Cherbuliez, Victor.**

Valentino, Rudolf (1895-1926), Italian stage and screen actor who came to the United States in 1913, and first appeared as a dancer in musical comedies: he scored a tremendous personal triumph as Julio in *The Four Horsemen,* and later appeared in several other films including *Camille; The Sheik; Moran of the Lady Letty; The Young Rajah; Blood and Sand; Monsieur Beaucaire; The Sainted Devil.*

Valhalla, in German mythology the palace of ODIN (Wotan) where the gods reside, and where mortal heroes are brought by the VALKYRIES after they are slain in battle: it is frequently mentioned in Richard Wagner's cycle of music dramas, *The* RING OF THE NIBELUNGS.

Valkyrie, The (Die Walkiire), see **Ring of the Nibelungs, The.**

Valkyries, in German mythology the maidens attendant on ODIN (Wotan) who chose the heroes to be slain on the field of battle, and carried them to VALHALLA. The Valkyries play an important part in *The Valkyrie* one of the music dramas in Richard WAGNER's *The* RING OF THE NIBELUNGS.

Vallee, Rudy (1901-), American radio and screen actor and singer educated at the University of Maine: he has appeared in several films including *The Vagabond Lover; Glorifying the American Girl; International House; Sweet Music; Gold Diggers in Paris; Second Fiddle; Too Many Blondes; Time Out for Rhythm.* He has also appeared successfully in commercial radio broadcasts.

Valse, La (Ravel), a choreographic poem for orchestra by Maurice RAVEL; first performed in an arrangement for two pianos in 1920 by Alfredo CASELLA and the composer at Vienna, and in orchestral form at a Lamoureux concert in Paris during the same year. The American première was given by the San Francisco Symphony Orchestra in 1921. Florent SCHMITT, in reviewing the first Paris performance, Dec. 12, 1920, said that Ravel had told him that *La Valse* was intended to be "the apotheosis of the dance," and Alfredo Casella points out that it has three distinct sections: *The birth of the waltz, The waltz,* and the *Apotheosis of the waltz.* On the fly-leaf of the published score is a program to indicate a dream of an "Imperial Court about 1855" with dancing couples. There is a Columbia recording by the New York Philharmonic-Symphony Society under John Barbirolli, and a Victor recording by the San Francisco Symphony Orchestra directed by Pierre Monteux.

Valse Triste (Sibelius), an orchestral work by Jean Sibelius which is part of the incidental music composed in 1903 for Arvid Järnfelt's play, *Kuolema.* The program is as follows: a sick woman wakes from a coma, and rises from her bed to dance to the distant strains of ghostly music;

shadowy couples dance around her, and when she sinks down exhausted, the music ceases. Again she invokes the music, and as it reaches a powerful climax, Death stands on the threshold as the music ceases and the dancers disappear. There are both Columbia and Victor recordings.

Vanbrugh, Sir John (1664-1726), English architect and dramatist: while imprisoned in the BASTILLE at Paris on a charge of espionage, he sketched a play, *The Provok'd Wife* which was produced in 1697. His ten comedies were all witty, realistic, and extremely popular with theatre-goers, but they were also grossly indecent. Among his architectural works were Castle Howard in Yorkshire, Castle Blenheim, and the HAYMARKET THEATRE, London.

Vance, Louis Joseph (1879-1933), American novelist and short story writer who first studied art at the ART STUDENTS' LEAGUE with the idea of becoming an illustrator: his novels include *Terence O'Rourke, Gentleman Adventurer* (1905); *The Brass Bowl,* a best seller; *The Black Bag; The Bronze Bell; The Fortune Hunter; The Lone Wolf; Alias the Lone Wolf; The Lone Wolf's Last Prowl.*

Vanderlyn, John (1776-1852), American painter who was aided by Aaron Burr in studying for a time with Gilbert STUART; Burr also financed his study in Europe. His notable works include *Marius Amid the Ruins of Carthage; Ariadne; The Landing of Columbus:* he also painted portraits of Washington, Monroe, Madison, Jackson, Calhoun, and Taylor. For reasons not clear he made little money out of his works, and died in absolute want, probably because his pictures lacked certain qualities of superficial charm.

Van der Stucken, Frank (1858-1929), American conductor and composer who studied with Pierre Benoît at Antwerp, and also with Carl Reinecke and Edvard GRIEG: in 1884 he conducted the Arion Society in New York, and from 1895 to 1903 directed the Cincinnati College of Music and the Cincinnati Symphony Orchestra. He also conducted the CINCINNATI MUSIC FESTIVAL from 1905 to 1912. His compositions include an opera, orchestral works, piano pieces, and songs.

Van der Weyden, Roger, see **Weyden, Roger van der.**

Van de Velde or **Vandevelde, Jan** (c.1596-1652), Dutch painter and engraver of portraits on wood whose best painting was *Tobias and the Angel.* His brother, **Willem Van de Velde** (1598-1673), the Elder, began life as a sailor and worked for Charles II and James II of England at pictures of naval battles which were hung at Hampton Court. His son, **Willem Van de Velde** (1633-1707), the Younger, studied with his father and worked with him on the battle pictures mentioned above, and later became court painter, becoming the greatest marine artist of the Dutch School. His brother, **Adrian Van de Velde** (1635-1672), studied with Willem Van de Velde the Elder, and also came under the influence of Philips WOUWERMAN and Paulus POTTER: he painted the animals in the landscapes of many famous contemporaries, and also gained a high reputation as an etcher.

Van De Water, Frederic F. (1890-), American author: his works include *The Grey Riders* (1921); *Still Waters; Alibi; Havoc; The Real McCoy; Plunder; A Life of General Custer; A Home in the Country; We're Still in the Country.* From 1915 to 1932 he was on the editorial staffs at various times of the New York *Tribune,* *The Ladies Home Journal,* and the New York *Evening Post.*

Van Dine, S. S., see **Wright, Willard Huntington.**

Van Doren, Carl Clinton (1885-), American critic and biographer, educated at the University of Illinois and Columbia University, who taught English at Columbia from 1911 to 1934, and also acted as literary critic of the *Nation, Century Magazine,* and the *Literary Guild.* His works include *The American Novel* (1911); *Contemporary American Novelists; The Roving Critic; American and British Literature since 1890* with Mark VAN DOREN; *Swift; Benjamin Franklin,* awarded the Pulitzer prize for biography in 1939: he also edited *Modern American Prose; Anthology of World Prose; The Borzoi Reader.*

Van Doren, Mark (1894-), American poet and critic educated at the University of Illinois and Columbia University: since 1920 he has been connected with the English department of Columbia. He succeeded his brother, Carl VAN DOREN, as literary editor of the *Nation.* His works include *Spring Thunder and Other Poems* (1924); *Now the Sky and Other Poems; A Winter Diary and Other Poems; Our Lady Peace and Other War Poems; The Poetry of John Dryden; American and British Literature since 1890* with Carl VAN DOREN; *An Anthology of World Poetry; The Oxford Book of American Prose.* From 1941 to 1942 Van Doren acted as chairman of INVITATION TO LEARNING, and edited the second volume of the books published in connection with this broadcasting hour.

Van Druten, John (1901-), English dramatist educated at University College School, London University, and also admitted to the bar: his plays include *Chance Acquaintances* (1927); *Young Woodley,* banned in England but finally produced after its success in the United States; *After All; London Wall; There's Always Juliet; Behold, We Live!; The Distaff Side; Most of the Game; Gertie Maude; Old Acquaintance.* He has also written the novels *A Woman on Her Way* and *And Then You Wish,* and several film scenarios.

Van Dyck or **Vandyke, Sir Anthony** (1599-1641), Flemish painter who was well educated and a pupil of RUBENS from about 1617: he was famous as a painter before he was twenty. He visited London for three months in 1620, and after going to Italy where he remained until 1627, and returning for a time to his native city, Antwerp, he settled at London in 1632 and remained there until his death. His notable pictures include *Portrait of an Old Man; Christ Carrying the Cross; Drunken Silenus; St. Martin Dividing the Cloak; Cardinal Bentivoglio; Crucifixion; Rinaldo and Armida; Adoration of the Shepherds.*

He painted 350 portraits in twelve years including 38 of King Charles I, 35 of Queen Henrietta Maria, and many of the royal children.

Van Dyck, Ernest (1861-1923), Belgian dramatic tenor who first studied law, and later abandoned it for vocal lessons in Paris. He made his debut as a concert singer with the LAMOUREUX Orchestra in 1883, and his operatic debut in 1887 at the Théâtre Éden in Wagner's *Lohengrin:* in 1888 he created a sensation in the title role of Wagner's *Parsifal,* and sang Wagnerian parts at the Metropolitan Opera House from 1898 to 1902.

Van Dyke, Henry (1852-1933), American clergyman, poet, essayist, and short-story writer educated at Princeton University: his works include *The Story of the Other Wise Man* (1896); *The First Christmas Tree* which was translated into several languages; *Little Rivers; Fisherman's Luck; The Builders; The Lost Boy; Out of Doors in the Holy Land; Studies in Tennyson; The Blue Flower.*

Van Dyke, John Charles (1856-1932), American art critic educated at Columbia University and trained in art in Europe, later becoming professor of the history of art at Rutgers University from 1889 until his death besides lecturing at several colleges. His works include *How To Judge a Picture* (1888); *History of Painting; The Meaning of Pictures; Rembrandt and His School; History of American Art.*

Van Dyke, W. S. (1893-1943), American film director who first acted as assistant to David Wark Griffith in the making of *Intolerance* in the days of the silent picture: among the many successful films which he directed are *Trader Horn; Night Court; Tarzan, the Ape Man; Eskimo; Manhattan Melodrama; The Thin Man; Painted Veil; Naughty Marietta; Rose Marie; San Francisco; Marie Antoinette; Sweethearts; Bitter Sweet; I Married an Angel;* also some of the films in the "Judge Hardy" and the "Dr. Kildare" series.

Vane, Sutton (1888-), English actor and dramatist whose full name is Van Sutton Vane: he is the son of Sutton Vane, a well-known playwright who wrote many melodramas. He served in World War I, and after recovering from shell shock, returned to France to appear in plays behind the lines. In 1923 he could find no producer for his masterpiece, *Outward Bound* so he produced it himself with "home-made" scenery, and a company of actors willing to work on a cooperative basis, at the Everyman Theatre, a small suburban house. After its immediate success, the company moved to the Garrick Theatre. The American première in 1924 had Dudley DIGGES, Margolo GILLMORE, Alfred LUNT, and Beryl Mercer in the cast: the play was filmed twice and revived in 1939. Vane's other plays such as *Time* and *Gentlemen, Please* were not of the quality of *Outward Bound.*

Van Eyck, Hubert, see **Eyck, Hubert van.**

Van Eyck, Jan, see **Eyck, Jan van.**

Van Hoogstraten, Willem (1884-), Dutch-American conductor who studied at the Cologne

Conservatory, and made his debut as a conductor at Hamburg. After conducting in Vienna and other European cities he made his American debut as conductor of the NEW YORK PHILHARMONIC-SYMPHONY SOCIETY in 1922, and acted as permanent conductor from 1923 to 1925: he also conducted the New York Stadium Concerts from 1922 to 1938. From 1927 to 1937 he was conductor of the Portland (Oregon) Symphony Orchestra.

Van Loo, Jean Baptiste (1684-1745), Italian painter who studied with his father, Louis van Loo (1641-1713), and was successful at Paris where his works were in great demand: he also restored the paintings of Francesco PRIMATICCIO at Fontainebleau, and later worked in England. His notable canvases include *Rinaldo and Armida; Diana and Endymion; Allegory on Happiness; Triumph of Galatea; Lady Reclining on a Couch:* in England he painted portraits of Colley CIBBER and Sir Robert Walpole.

Van Loon, Hendrik Willem (1882-), Dutch-American author born in Holland and educated at Cornell and Harvard Universities, and also in Munich. His works include *The Fall of the Dutch Republic* (1913); *The Story of Mankind; The Story of the Bible; Tolerance; The Story of Wilbur the Hat; The Life and Times of Rembrandt van Rijn; The Arts; The Life and Times of Johann Sebastian Bach; Van Loon's Lives:* some of his books are illustrated with his own drawings.

Vannucci, Pietro, see **Perugino.**

Van Rooy, Anton (1870-1932), Dutch dramatic and concert baritone who first sang as a boy in a church choir: from 1892 to 1896 he studied with Julius Stockhausen, and in 1897 sang the part of Wotan in The RING OF THE NIBELUNGS at BAYREUTH. He made his debut in 1898 at the Metropolitan Opera House, New York, as Wotan in *The Valkyrie,* remaining until 1908 after which he joined the Frankfort-on-Main Opera.

Van Vechten, Carl (1880-), American novelist and music critic educated at the University of Chicago: his works include *Music After the Great War* (1915); *Music and Bad Manners; Interpreters and Interpretations; The Music of Spain:* also the novels *Peter Whiffle, The Blind Bow-Boy,* and *The Tattooed Countess.*

Van Zandt, Marie (1861-1919), American colorature soprano who studied with her mother and with Francesco Lamperti, making her debut at Turin in 1879: after singing at the Opéra-Comique at Paris for five years she toured Europe, and sang at the Metropolitan Opera House, New York, during the 1891-92 season. In 1896 she again sang at the Opéra-Comique: Léo DELIBES wrote the title role in *Lakmé* especially for her in 1883.

Varesè, Edgar (1885-), French composer of Italian parentage who studied composition with Charles WIDOR, Vincent D'INDY, and Albert ROUSSEL in Paris: he came to New York in 1915, and later founded the New Symphony Orchestra for the performance of modern music: also the International Composers' Guild and the Pan America Society for promoting the works written by North and South American composers. His orchestral and chamber works are all in the ultra-modern style.

Variation, in music one of a series of transformations of a theme by changes in the melody, harmony and rhythms: the early name was *double.* The variation form was used by the classical composers in the suite, sonata, and symphony; also as an independent composition for orchestra, some solo instrument, or for the voice. Among the composers who used the variation form are Johann Sebastian BACH, HANDEL, HAYDN, MOZART, BEETHOVEN, SCHUBERT, BRAHMS, SCHUMANN, TSCHAIKOWSKY, FRANCK, ELGAR, Richard STRAUSS, REGER, and DOHNANYI.

Variations on a Theme by Haydn (Brahms), an orchestral work composed by Johannes BRAHMS in 1873: the theme, which is called *Chorale of St. Anthony* was taken from a wind-instrument divertimento (set of dances) written by Franz Joseph HAYDN, but there is some question as to whether he was its composer. There are Columbia and Victor recordings not only for orchestra, but also for two pianos—four hands.

Variations Symphoniques (Franck), a work for piano and orchestra composed by César FRANCK in 1885, and first played in Paris at a concert of the Societé Nationale de la Musique in 1885 by Louis Diémer to whom it was dedicated, and in New York by Raoul PUGNO in 1898. There is a Victor recording by Alfred CORTOT, and a Columbia recording by Walter GIESEKING.

Vasari, Giorgio (1511-1574), Italian architect, painter, and biographer who studied with his father, Antonio Vasari, and also with Andrea del SARTO and MICHELANGELO: his paintings are of no special importance, but his monumental work entitled *Lives of the Most Famous Architects, Painters and Sculptors* is not only classic from the standpoint of erudition, but is the earliest attempt in European literature to describe and appraise the works of great artists. He also built the Uffizi Palace in Florence.

Vase, a vessel made of clay, glass, metal, wood or stone used by the ancients for religious, ornamental, and domestic purposes, and fashioned with or without handles. One of the uses made of vases was as cinerary urns: the most celebrated is the Portland vase in the BRITISH MUSEUM. Vases were used in marble or bronze for the decoration of gardens, on the top of buildings or on the angles of balustrades. In Greece the decoration of vases was developed to an extraordinary degree of perfection.

Vasnetsof, Victor (1848- ?), Russian artist regarded as the greatest during the reign of Alexander III: his works include the cartoons used for the mosaics on the walls and ceilings of the Kazan Cathedral; the mural painting *Fathers of the Russian Church* at the Church of St. Vladimir at St. Petersburg; his finest painting is *The Stone Age.*

Vatican, the residence of the pope at Rome built on a site which was called Ager Vaticanus in ancient times. The church of St. Peter was built there, and also an unpretentious residence for the popes: towards the middle of the 15th century Pope Nicholas V built a splendid palace for his own use and that of the cardinals and their retinues. His successors completed the buildings which covered an enormous area, and contained more than a thousand apartments. Among the architects, painters, and sculptors were BRAMANTE, RAPHAEL, and MICHELANGELO. Among the buildings and rooms of note are the SISTINE CHAPEL; the chapel of Nicholas V; the Court of the Belvedere; the Royal Apartment; the Ducal Hall; the Borgia rooms. The Vatican library contains 50,000 valuable manuscripts, 400,000 books, and 60,000 volumes of archives: the museums include the Museo Pio-Clementino, the BELVEDERE GALLERY, the Chiaramonti Gallery, the Giardino della Pigna, the Egyptian Museum, and the Etruscan Museum.

Vaudeville (Fr.), a term which originally denoted a popular street song taken from a collection of such songs made by Olivier Basselin entitled *Lais des Vaux-de-Vire:* a form of entertainment called *vaux-de-ville,* the "x" being omitted later, became popular in Paris and was introduced into the United States about 1860. It was first only shown to male audiences, but Tony Pastor made it suitable for both sexes and children in 1865, and later B. F. KEITH, F. F. Proctor, E. F. Albee, Oscar HAMMERSTEIN, and John J. Murdock brought vaudeville to unprecedented heights of popularity which ended only with the advent of the motion picture.

Vaughan Williams, Ralph (1872-), English composer educated at Trinity College, Cambridge, and a pupil of Charles Hubert Hastings PARRY, Charles Villiers STANFORD, Max BRUCH, and Maurice RAVEL in composition. His works include *Hugh the Drover* and several other operas; orchestral works such as *Fantasia on a Theme by Tallis* and three *Norfolk Rhapsodies;* choral works; chamber music; songs. He has also edited several volumes of English folk songs.

Vault, in architecture an arched structure, usually in the form of a ceiling or roof, built of masonry: there are various types such as spherical, barrel, pointed, rampant, semi-circular, skew, groined, and ribbed. The form was used by the Egyptians, Assyrians, Chaldeans, Etruscans, Greeks, and Romans, and the ribbed vault was an important component in GOTHIC ARCHITECTURE.

Vauxhall Gardens, a place of entertainment in London opened on the bank of the Thames River in 1660 and a fashionable pleasure resort mentioned by Samuel PEPYS and in the London *Spectator:* toward the close of the 18th century the gardens became a public amusement park with fireworks and circus attractions. In 1830 Sir Henry BISHOP was appointed musical director, and he produced a number of vaudevilles. The enterprise was discontinued in 1859.

Vazoff, Ivan (1850-1921), Bulgarian novelist, poet, and playwright: his novel, *Pod Igoto* (*Under the Yoke*) was translated into English by Edmund Gosse, and also into several other languages. His poetical works include *Songs of Macedonia* and *Under the Thunder of Victory.*

Vecsey, Franz von (1893-1935), Hungarian violinist and composer who studied with his father, and also with Jenö HUBAY and Joseph JOACHIM, making concert tours when he was ten years old. He appeared in New York in 1905, and later toured Europe. He was a pupil of Paul JUON in composition: his works include a string quartet and several pieces for the violin.

Veda, the collective name given the sacred literature of the Hindus in India comprising over a hundred extant books, and referring specifically to any one or all of the four collections known as the *Rig-Veda* containing more than a thousand hymns; the *Yajur-Veda* comprising liturgical formulae in both verse and prose; the *Sama-Veda* containing the music notation for many hymns in the Rig-Veda; the *Atharva-Veda,* a collection of charms, prayers, curses, and spells in both prose and verse.

Vedder, Elihu (1836-1923), American painter who studied with François Édouard PICOT in Paris, and also in Italy: his works include 56 illustrations for the *Rubaiyat* of OMAR KHAYYAM; *Lair of the Sea Serpent; Cumean Sibyl; Nausicaa and Her Companions*; five LUNETTES, *Good and Bad Government,* for the Library of Congress, Washington, D. C.; *Roman Girls on the Seashore; African Sentinel; The Pleiades.*

Veen, Martin van, see **Heemskerk, Martin van.**

Vega Carpio, Lope Félix de (1562-1635), Spanish poet and dramatist known as Lope de Vega: he was the son of Garcilasso de Vega, counsellor of state to Ferdinand and Isabella. He was an unusually prolific author, said to have written nearly 1500 comedies, tragedies, and morality plays on secular and sacred subjects: among the most notable are *The King; The Best Mayor the King; The Star of Seville.* He also wrote two great epics, *Jerusalem Conquered* and *The Tragic Crown* in addition to sonnets and novels.

Veidt, Conrad (1893-1943), German stage and screen actor who received his early training under Max REINHARDT, and appeared in plays with Emil JANNINGS, and Werner Krauss. Among the films in which he appeared are *The Cabinet of Doctor Caligari; Lady Hamilton; Congress Dances; The Hands of Orlac; The Student of Prague; Rome Express; I Was a Spy; Power; The Wandering Jew; The Passing of the Third Floor Back; Under the Red Robe; The Thief of Bagdad; A Woman's Face; Escape; The Devil is an Empress; Nazi Agent.*

Veiller, Bayard (1869-1943), American dramatist who had some experience as a journalist before his first play *The Primrose Path* was produced in 1907: his most successful plays were *Within the Law, The Thirteenth Chair,* and *The Trial of Mary Dugan.* He prepared the film scenarios for his plays, and also wrote several original film dramas.

Veit, Philipp (1793-1877), German painter who studied at the Dresden Academy, and with Frederick von Schlegel at Vienna: he joined the NAZARENES for a time at Rome. His works include *Triumph of Religion; The Two Marys at Christ's Tomb; Seven Fruitful Years; Presentation in the Temple; Joseph and Potiphar's Wife;* pictures illustrating Dante's *Paradise*.

Velasquez or **Velazquez, Diego Rodríguez de Silvay** (1599-1660), Spanish painter who studied with Francisco PACHECO for five years: in 1622 he went to Madrid only to be denied the privilege of painting the king's portrait, permission for which was gladly given him the following year after he had produced a greatly admired portrait of Luis de GONGORA. Later he visited Rome after being appointed chief painter at the Spanish court: in 1629 he met and became intimate with SPAGNOLETTO, and later returned to Madrid. He remained there for eighteen years, going to Italy again in 1649 to collect paintings for the royal galleries, and returning in 1651 to place the pictures in the Royal Palace. His notable works include *The Water Carrier; Christ in the House of Martha; Los Borrachos; Forge of Vulcan; Bacchanalian Scene; Villa Medici Gardens; Joseph's Coat; Christ on the Cross; The Surrender of Breda; Las Meniñas; The Spinners; Court Fool Holding a Glass of Wine; Menippus.*

Vellum, thin calf, kid, or lamb skin specially prepared for use as PARCHMENT: a vegetable composition which resembles and serves the same purpose is now available. Vellum was used for ILLUMINATED MANUSCRIPTS and for MINIATURES in the Middle Ages: it is also used for making proofs of etchings and engravings.

Veloce (It.), in music a direction usually indicating that a passage is to be performed at a higher degree of speed than those before it.

Veneer, a method of decorating woodwork or furniture by cutting strips of variously colored woods and inserting them in woods of inferior quality: it is used for furniture, paneling, and small objects of art such as jewel boxes.

Venice, a city in Italy famous for its buildings of historic and artistic importance in addition to the museums of art: these include ST. MARK'S Church; the Doge's Palace; the Academy of Fine Arts; the Procuratíe; the Palazzo Pirani; the Arsenal, several fine Gothic churches in which the doges are buried. Among the architects and painters who created its beauties as a city were PALLADIO, SANSOVINO, BARTOLOMMEO, Giovanni BELLINI, CRIVELLI, GIORGIONE, VERONESE, TINTORETTO and TITIAN.

Venus, see **Aphrodite.**

Venus of Medici, a statue in the UFFIZI Gallery at Florence: it bears the name of the Greek sculptor Cleomenes, son of Apollodorus and is said to have been inspired by the *Aphrodite of Cnidus* executed by PRAXITELES.

Venus of Milo, a famous Greek statue now in the LOUVRE discovered in 1820 on the island of Melos and taken to Constantinople by the French ambassador. The arms are missing and the question of their position in relation to the torso has been a matter of much discussion: opinions also differ as to the date of its execution.

Venusberg, in German legend a mountain which has been identified with the Hörselberg near the castle of Wartburg at Eisenach. VENUS is said to have lured mortals there who gave themselves up to sensuous pleasure which ended in the damnation of their souls: Richard WAGNER makes full use of the legend in TANNHAUSER.

Veracini, Francesco Maria (1690-c.1750), Italian violinist who studied with his uncle, Antonio Veracini, and toured Europe extensively: he was heard in Venice by Giuseppe TARTINI who was greatly influenced by his style. His works include 24 sonatas for violin and bass; concertos for violins; symphonies for strings and harpsichord.

Verboeckhoven, Eugène Joseph (1799-1881), Belgian painter who studied with his father, a well-known sculptor, and after visiting England, Germany, France, and Italy settled in Brussels. His works include *Horses Attacked by Wolves; Landscape with Resting Cattle; Wounded Lion; Herd of Cattle Driven to Pasture; Donkeys and Sheep; Peasant Asleep by a Horse; Sheep in a Storm:* he was famous as an animal painter.

Verbrugghen, Henri (1873-1934), Belgian violinist and conductor who studied with HUBAY, YSAYE, and GEVAERT at the Brussels Conservatory: after playing with the Scottish Orchestra at Glasgow, the Lamoureux Orchestra, the Queen's Hall Orchestra, and conducting the State Symphony Orchestra at Sydney, Australia, he became director in 1923 of the MINNEAPOLIS SYMPHONY ORCHESTRA, remaining until 1931.

Verdi, Giuseppe (1813-1901), Italian opera composer who played the organ in a village church at ten, but was refused admission to the Milan Conservatory in 1831. In 1839 his first opera, *Oberto* was produced with success, but the next work was a failure, and the death of his wife and two children greatly disheartened him. He was finally induced to resume composing and his next opera, *Nabuco,* was a great success in 1842: from that time on he wrote more than thirty operas most of which were highly successful. Among his notable operas are *I Lombardi; Ernani; I Due Foscari; Macbeth* which was revived by the New Opera Company in 1942 at New York; *Luisa Miller; Rigoletto; Il Trovatore; La Traviata; Les Vêpres Siciliennes (Sicilian Vespers); Simone Boccanegra; Un Ballo in Maschera; La Forza del Destino; Don Carlos; Aïda; Otello; Falstaff.* He also composed a *Requiem Mass* in memory of Alessandro MANZONI, and a string quartet.

Vereshchagin, Vasily Vasilyevitch (1842-1904), Russian painter who studied at the St. Petersburg Academy, at the ECOLE DES BEAUX-ARTS, and with Jean Léon GEROME: his notable canvases include *Unexpected Attack; The Apotheosis of War; Presentation of the Trophies; Opium Eaters; Defence of the Citadel; Entry of the Prince of*

Wales into Jeypoor; Hermits on the Jordan; Christ in the Desert; Resurrection.

Verga, Giovanni (1840-1922), Italian novelist whose story, *Rustic Chivalry,* was the basis for the libretto of CAVALLERIA RUSTICANA, an opera by Pietro MASCAGNI produced in 1890: his works include *Story of a Cricket* (1872); *Eva; Royal Tiger; Helen's Husband; Life in the Fields; The House under the Medlar Tree; Maestro Don Gesualdo.*

Vergil or **Virgil** (70 B.C.-19 B.C.), Roman poet who studied at Cremona, Milan, Naples, and Rome: his works include *Eclogues or Bucolics* in which he paints ideal pictures of country life; *Georgics,* a didactic poem on farm life; the epic poem *Aeneid* in which he narrates the adventures of AENEAS after the TROJAN WAR.

Verhaeren, Émile (1855-1916), Belgian poet who studied at the Institut Saint-Louis at Brussels and the College Saint-Barbe at Ghent: his works available in English include *The Dawn; Poems; Belgium's Agony; Sunlit Hours; Afternoon; Five Tales.*

Verklärte Nacht (Schönberg), a sextet for stringed instruments composed by Arnold SCHONBERG in 1899, and later arranged for string orchestra. It was written in a three-week period and is regarded as the composer's first important work. There is a Victor recording for string orchestra by the Minneapolis Symphony Orchestra directed by Eugene Ormandy.

Verlaine, Paul (1844-1896), French poet who led the life of a vagabond, and was jailed in Belgium for two years for shooting his friend, Jean Arthur Rimbaud. His works include *Saturnine Poems* (1866); *Gay Festivals; Accursed Poets; Jadis et Naguère:* he also wrote short stories such as *Louise Leclercq, Stories without Words,* and *My Hospitals.*

Vermeer, Johannes (1632-1675), Dutch painter who studied with Carel FABRITIUS, and was influenced by REMBRANDT: he was also known as Johannes van der Meer van Delft. His works include *The Music Lesson; Girl with a Flute; A View of Delft; Pearl Weigher; Diana at Her Toilet; The Coquette; Girl with a Wineglass; Boy Blowing Bubbles; The Geographer.*

Verne, Jules (1828-1905), French author who first wrote comedies in verse and librettos for comic operas: his fame rests chiefly on more than sixty novels in which he exploited science in tales of adventure. They include *Five Weeks in a Balloon* (1863); *Twenty Thousand Leagues under the Sea; A Journey to the Center of the Earth; Around the World in Eighty Days; The Mysterious Island; Michael Strogoff:* many of them were translated into every European language, and also into Arabic and Japanese.

Vernet, Claude Joseph (c.1712-1789), French painter, who studied with his father, Antoine Vernet (1689-1753), and also in Rome: his principal work was a series of paintings of fifteen seaports in France commissioned by Louis VI. His son, **Antoine Charles Horace Vernet** (1758-1836) known as Carle Vernet, was a distinguished painter of horses and battle scenes: his works include *Triumph of Paulus and Aemilius; Battle of Marengo; Morning of Austerlitz; Death of Hippolytus; Chariot Races; The Road from St. Cloud.* His son, **Émile Jean Horace Vernet** (1789-1863), studied with his father and with Jean Michel MOREAU: his works include *Taking of an Entrenched Camp; The Barrier of Clichy; Soldier of Waterloo; The Death of Poniatowski; The Farewell at Fontainebleau; The Last Cartridge; Battle of Jemappes.*

Vernis Martin, a preparation of green varnish to which gold powder is added; developed by the four Martin brothers during the reign of Louis XV in France. This process of lacquering gained such a degree of popularity in decorations of every description that VOLTAIRE even mentions it in one of his plays, *Nadine,* produced in 1749: he describes a carriage as having its panels decorated "Vernis Martin."

Vernon Lee, see **Paget, Violet.**

Veronese, Paul or **Paolo** (1528-1588), Italian painter whose real name was Paolo Caliari or Cagliari, and called Veronese because he was born in Verona: his works include *Rape of Europa; Story of Esther; Coronation of the Virgin; Marriage of Cana; Feast in the House of Levi; The Glory of Venice; Supper at Emmaus; Christ in the House of Simon; Family of Darius at the Feet of Alexander; Ceres Offering Her Gifts to Venice; Mars and Venus United by Love.*

Verrocchio, Andrea del (1435-1488), Italian sculptor, painter, architect, and goldsmith whose real name was Andrea da Michele di Francesco de' Cioni. He was the teacher of LEONARDO DA VINCI and Lorenzo di CREDI: only one painting, *Christ,* now in the Academy at Florence, is known to be in existence. Among his sculptures are *Boy with a Dolphin; David;* the bronze *Incredulity:* he also executed tombs for COSIMO DE' MEDICI and Giovanni de' Medici.

Versailles Museum, originally a country house and hunting lodge built by Jacques LERMERCIER for Louis XIII: it was enlarged into a château by Louis XIV who employed Louis LE VAU, André LE NOTRE, Charles LE BRUN and François MANSART as the architects for the building and the spacious park. Louis Philippe (1773-1850) transformed the château into a museum by forming a collection of art works valued at more than $5,000,000 in commemoration of the great events and personages of French history. There are eleven halls of historical pictures from the days of Clovis to Louis XVI; the Halls of the Crusaders decorated with arms and modern pictures dealing with the period; ten halls of historical events from 1795 to 1830; the sculpture gallery; the theatre built by Louis XV used for the marriage of Marie ANTOINETTE; the hall of celebrated soldiers; the Dauphin's apartment with its historical portraits; also separate halls of tapestries and art objects of every possible description and in every conceivable variety.

Vers libre, see **Free Verse.**

Vestris, Lucia Elizabeth (1797-1856), English actress and producer who first appeared at London in 1815 as a singer in Italian opera, and later achieved great success as leading lady for François Joseph TALMA in Paris. In 1820 she charmed London audiences in James Cobb's play, *The Siege of Belgrade,* and was a great favorite in Mozart's *Marriage of Figaro* and *Don Giovanni.* She married Charles James MATHEWS, an English actor in 1838: in 1841 she produced *London Assurance,* a play by Dion BOUCICAULT, at Covent Garden, and also presented several of Shakespeare's comedies.

Via Appia, see **Appian Way.**

Viardot-García, Pauline (1821-1910), French dramatic mezzo-soprano and composer who was the daughter of the famous Spanish tenor and singing teacher, Manuel del Popolo GARCIA. Her sister was Maria MALIBRAN and her brother the celebrated vocal teacher Manuel GARCIA. She studied singing with her father and the piano with Franz LISZT, making her concert debut at Brussels in 1837, and her operatic debut in 1839 at London as Desdemona in Rossini's *Otello.* She sang with great success until 1863, and taught singing for several years: her opera, *Le Dernier Sorcier,* was produced at Weimar in 1869.

Viaud, Louis Marie Julien, see **Loti, Pierre.**

Vibert, Jehan Georges (1840-1902), French painter who studied with François PICOT and Felix BARRIAS, founded the Society of French Water-color Painters, and wrote several plays and vaudevilles: his notable canvases include *Narcissus Transformed into a Flower; Palm Sunday in Paris; Startling Confession; Rehearsing Amateur Theatricals; Grasshopper and Ant; Selling Consecrated Palms; Toreadors Entering Arena; Gulliver and the Lilliputians.*

Vibrato, (It.), in music a trembling or wavering tonal effect created on stringed instruments by the rapid oscillation of the performer's finger on the string. It is accomplished in singing by a series of extremely rapid and almost indistinguishable partial interruptions of the tone.

Vicente, Gil (c.1470-1536), Portuguese poet and dramatist regarded as the father of drama in his country: he made a tremendous success with a pastoral play presented in 1502 in honor of the birth of the Portuguese Prince Royal, later John III. His works include tragedies, dramas, comedies, and farces: his original dramatic methods later became accepted practices in European theatres.

Victoria or **Vittoria, Tomás Luis de** (1549-1611), Spanish composer who sang at the Collegium Germanicum at Rome: in 1578 he was appointed chaplain to the Empress Maria, sister of Philip II of Spain, and remained until her death in 1603 when he held the same office with the Princess Margaret: his works include masses and motets which mark him as the greatest Spanish composer of church music.

Victoria, see **Nike.**

Victoria and Albert Museum (London), an institution at London, England, formerly known as the South Kensington Museum which was opened in 1857, and renamed when an extension of buildings designed by Sir Aston Webb was begun in 1899 and completed in 1909. It contains fine collections of paintings and drawings including the Raphael cartoons: also of ceramics, glass, textiles, ivories, furniture, and assemblies of Japanese, Chinese, Persian, and Indian art. The Royal College of Art is a part of the museum which also has an excellent library of books on art.

Victory Ball (Schelling), an orchestral fantasy for orchestra by Ernest SCHELLING inspired by a poem of Alfred NOYES entitled *A Victory Ball:* it was first performed at Philadelphia in 1923. The work is dedicated "to the memory of an American soldier." Lawrence GILMAN's interpretation of the music is of a ball-room of dancing people interrupted by the vision of marching hosts from the World War. The ghostly legions are announced by two trumpet calls: the *Call to Arms* and *Charge,* and the *Dies Irae* on the brass. The tramping of the soldiers is drowned by the dancing once more, but the vision reshapes itself and the pagan drone and shrieks of bagpipes pass. The drum-roll softens, and a distant trumpeter plays *Taps.* There is a Victor recording by the New York Philharmonic-Symphony Society directed by Wilhelm Mengelberg.

Victory of Samothrace, a statue discovered on the island of Samothrace in 1863, and placed in the Louvre in 1879 with the oblong pedestal on which it originally stood. Victory is represented as standing on the prow of a ship with outstretched wings, and while the head and arms are missing, a coin on which the design was copied shows that she held a trumpet to her lips, and a long stake in her left hand.

Vic-Wells Ballet, see **Sadler's Wells Ballet.**

Vidal, Louis Antoine (1820-1891), French amateur violoncellist who studied with Auguste FRANCHOMME: he became greatly interested in the history of stringed instruments, particularly those played with a bow, and published *The Instruments with a Bow* (1876-78), a comprehensive treatise the first volume of which dealt with the violin, the second with violin makers, and the third with chamber music.

Vidocq, François Eugène (c.1775-1857), French detective who was first a criminal himself, later becoming a spy on the underworld for the Parisian police. He had great success as an investigator, and retired with a considerable sum of money which he lost in a paper-mill venture: he returned to the service, but was dismissed for arranging a fake crime which he only could uncover. He was one of the characters in Edgar Allan POE's *Murders of the Rue Morgue.*

Vidor, King Wallis (1894-), American motion picture director educated at Tome College, Port Deposit, Md.: among the pictures which he has directed are *Peg O' My Heart; Three Wise Fools; The Sky Pilot; La Boheme; Bardelys the Magnificent; The Big Parade; Billy the Kid;*

Street Scene; The Champ; Cynara; Bird of Paradise; Our Daily Bread; The Wedding Night; So Red the Rose; The Texas Rangers; Stella Dallas; The Citadel; H. M. Pulham, Esq.

Vien, Joseph Marie (1716-1809), French painter who studied in Paris and spent five years in Rome, later becoming director of the Academy there and Chancellor of the Paris Academy. His notable canvases include *Daedalus and Icarus; Miraculous Draught of Fishes; Sleeping Hermit; Briseis Led from the Camp of Achilles; St. Denis Preaching to the Gauls; Christ on the Cross; Religion; Resurrection; Rape of Prosperpine.*

Vienna (Austria), a city in Austria which up to the beginning of World War I was one of the most intellectual cities in the world, and famed for its contributions to all the arts. There were two museums of art one of which, the ALBERTINA is described under a special reference, an opera house which rivaled L'Opéra at Paris in magnificence, the Vienna Academy of Art, and the Vienna Conservatory of Music: also several private picture galleries of great importance comprising the collections of Prince Lichtenstein, Count Harrach, Count Czernin, and Count Schönborn. The Viennese were passionately fond of the dance, and their desire for tuneful strains was fully gratified by Johann STRAUSS, SR., Johann STRAUSS, JR., Joseph LANNER, Joseph Gungl, Karl ZIEHRER, Franz LEHAR and Oscar STRAUS. Its prominence in the field of serious music is assured through HAYDN, MOZART, SCHUBERT, and BEETHOVEN who wrote their finest works while living there; Hans MAKART was one of the many fine modern painters who saw to the decorations of great buildings such as the Museum of Natural History where he placed in the dome the largest pictorial canvas in the world: the genius of Vienna's architects and sculptors is to be seen in its magnificent buildings with their external decorations in the form of statues and ornamental sculptures.

Vienna Philharmonic Orchestra, an organization founded at Vienna by Otto NICOLAI in 1842 who was its conductor until 1847 when he was succeeded by Georg HELLMESBERGER, SR. In 1848 it ceased giving concerts, but was revived in 1854 by Karl Eckert, and since then has had a distinguished series of conductors, including Hans RICHTER, Wilhelm Jahn, Gustav MAHLER, Artur NIKISCH, Felix MOTTL, Josef HELLMESBERGER, JR., Richard STRAUSS, Franz SCHALK, Felix WEINGARTNER, Bruno WALTER, Wilhelm FURTWANGLER and Arturo TOSCANINI. The concerts were held in the Karntnerthor Theatre until 1870, when they moved to their present home in the Musikverein Saal of the Gesellschaft der Musikfreunde. The organization is co-operative, engages its own conductors, at the present time usually three or four during a season, and also to a large extent chooses its own programs. In 1937 the orchestra published its official history under the title of *Die Wiener Philharmoniker, Monographie eines Orchesters.* The orchestra also played for the Vienna State Opera, and made many recordings.

Vieuxtemps, Henri (1820-1881), French violinist and composer who appeared at six as a soloist with orchestra, and studied with Charles DE BERIOT: in 1833 he toured Germany and studied composition with Simon SECHTER. He toured Europe for many years and visited the United States in 1857 and in 1870: in 1871 he taught at the Brussels Conservatory: Jenö HUBAY was one of his pupils. His compositions include six concertos and many concert pieces for the violin.

Vigano, Salvatore (1769-1821), Italian dancer, choreographer, and composer who studied music with his uncle, Luigi BOCCHERINI, and made his debut as a dancer at Rome in 1786: he is famous because Ludwig van BEETHOVEN composed the music for his ballet, *The Men of Prometheus* produced at the Vienna Court Theatre in 1801. He also wrote many ballets for La SCALA in Milan.

Vigée-Lebrun, Marie-Anne Elisabeth (1755-1842), French painter who studied with her father and benefited by advice from Jean Baptiste GREUZE, and Claude Joseph VERNET. Among her sitters for portraits were Lady Hamilton, Count Orloff, the Duchess of Orléans, Lord BYRON, and the Prince of Wales. She painted more than twenty portraits of Marie ANTOINETTE between 1779 and 1789, and her canvas, *Peace Bringing Back Abundance* gained her membership in the French Academy.

Vigne, Paul de (1843-1901), Belgian sculptor who studied with his father, and exhibited his *Fra Angelico da Fiesole* at the Ghent Salon in 1868: his notable works include *Heliotrope; Beatrix; Domenica; Immortality; The Crowning of Art;* statues of Jean Breydel and Pierre de Coninck; *Volumnia; Psyche,* and the marble statue of Marnix de Ste. Aldegonde at Brussels.

Vignola, Da, see **Barocchio, Jacopo.**

Vigny, Alfred Victor, Count de (1799-1863), French poet, novelist, and dramatist who spent twelve years of his life in the army: his most famous work is the romance, *Cinq Mars* (1826). He also wrote *Poems Ancient and Modern,* and *The Destinies,* both volumes of poems; the tragedy, *Chatterton;* a translation of Shakespeare's *Othello,* and several fine novels of military life.

Vikings, the name of bands of Northmen who plundered the coasts of Europe from the 8th to the 10th century: they were the best shipbuilders, sailors, and warriors of the period, and were able to navigate the open sea by the aid of the sun, moon, and stars. They have been favorite subjects for historical writers, poets, painters, and sculptors.

Villa-Lobos, Heitor or **Hector** (1884-   ), Brazilian pianist and composer who studied with his father, but was self-taught as a composer. He has written more than 1300 works including three ballets; an opera; five symphonies and other orchestral music; an oratorio; two masses; chamber music for various combinations; piano pieces and songs. He has studied Brazilian folklore and music as is amply evidenced by his works.

Villanella (It.) or **Villanelle** (Fr.), an Italian folksong or song of the streets popular in the

16th century, and contemporary with the MADRI-GAL. It differed from the latter by the rustic and humorous character of its words, and its simple harmonies as contrasted with the contrapuntal character of the madrigal.

Villard de Hounecourt, 13th century French architect who traveled in France, Switzerland, and Hungary: some authorities credit him with the designs of the cathedral at Reims, but there is no documentary evidence that he executed this work. His sketch book, which is now in the Bibliothèque Nationale at Paris, affords valuable information regarding medieval art.

Villegas, José (1848-1921), Spanish painter who studied with Mariano FORTUNY and became director of the PRADO Museum at Madrid: his works include *The Christening; Dream of the Arabian Nights; Armourer's Shop; Cairo Slipper Merchant; The Bull Fighters; Poultry Market in Tangier.*

Villon, François (1431-1463), French lyric poet whose real name was François de Montcorbier or François des Loges: he was a self-confessed vagabond and rogue who lived in the Parisian underworld, but is also regarded as one of the greatest poets of his time. His notable works include *Petit Testament* (1456) and the *Grand Testament* (1461) which includes the "Ballad of the Ladies of Olden Times" and the "Prayer to Our Lady." Justin Huntley McCARTHY's novel, *If I Were King* (1901) has Villon as its hero, and he also is the central figure of Rudolf FRIML's operetta, *The Vagabond King* (1925).

Vinci, Leonardo da, see **Leonardo da Vinci.**

Viol, an obsolete type of very ancient bowed instrument descended from the fiddle, used by the TROUBADOURS in the 15th century, and later developed into the 17th century violin. It differed from the violin in having a flat back, deeper ribs, and from five to eight more strings. The *treble viol* was succeeded by the violin; the *tenor viol* (viola da braccio) by the viola, the *bass viol* (viola da gamba) became the violincello: both viols and violins were used in the first orchestras. BACH and HANDEL composed for viols, but the days of Haydn saw them superseded by violins.

Viola, the alto member of the violin family; slightly larger than the violin, played in the same manner, but tuned a fifth lower, and possessing a tone of a veiled, sombre quality. The alto and treble CLEFS are used for writing viola music: MOZART was the first composer to treat it as a solo instrument and also to give it an independent part in the orchestra.

Violin, the most important of bowed instruments and the leading instrument both for solo and orchestral use because it is capable of every variety of musical expression. It has undergone many changes since its first appearance in the 8th century. GASPARO DA SALO (1540-1609) is credited with having evolved the violin into the form recognized today; the Amatis, the Guarnerii, and Antonius Stradivarius perfected its tone quality

and improved its appearance, both in symmetry and varnish. The bow, originally an awkward device greatly resembling its namesake in the domain of archery, became straight in design and a thing of beauty through Giuseppe TARTINI and François TOURTE. Its technical resources and tonal possibilities have intrigued the imagination of all great composers from Johann Sebastian BACH to Johannes BRAHMS; concertos, sonatas and solo pieces have been written in almost boundless profusion and limitless variety. It has also attracted hundreds of musicians as a solo instrument among them CORELLI, TARTINI, VIOTTI, PAGANINI, SPOHR, DEBERIOT, DAVID, VIEUXTEMPS, JOACHIM, WIENIAWSKI, SARASATE, YSAYE, KREISLER and HEIFETZ.

Viollet-le-Duc, Eugène Emmanuel (1814-1879), French architect and writer who studied with Achille Leclère and spent some time studying Greek and Roman architecture in Sicily and Rome: he worked on the restoration of Notre Dame from 1845 to 1856, and wrote an important treatise, *Dictionary of French Architecture from the Eleventh to the Sixteenth Centuries,* and several other similar works.

Violoncello, a bowed instrument which received its name from the double bass which was known in Italian as the *violone:* the violoncello, a smaller size of the double bass, was called the *violoncello* or little violone. With the two violins, and the viola it constitutes the finest of all chamber music ensembles, the *string quartet;* with the double bass added, it makes up the string section of the classic and modern orchestra. All the great violin makers, such as the Amatis, Guarnerii and Antonius Stradivarius, also made fine violoncellos; its bow was also improved by François TOURTE and other famous bow makers. As a solo instrument in the string group, it is second only to the violin, a fact recognized by the great composers from Johann Sebastian BACH to Johannes BRAHMS, all of whom created concertos, sonatas and solo pieces for it.

Viotti, Giovanni Battista (1753-1824), Italian violinist and composer who studied with Gaetano PUGNANI with whom he toured Germany, Poland, and Russia. In 1782 he appeared at the Concerts Spirituels at Paris and became the accompanist for Marie ANTOINETTE. He appeared in London and also acted as director of the Opéra at Paris from 1819 to 1822: his compositions include 29 violin concertos, many violin duets, and 21 string quartets.

Virgil, see **Vergil.**

Virgil Practice Clavier, a toneless keyboard instrument, shaped like a piano, used for mechanical organ and piano practice, invented by **Almon Kincaid Virgil** in 1883. The keys, though toneless, produce faint clicks, and are used in acquiring legato and staccato touches. There are six gradations in the weight of the touch, which is adjustable. His wife, **Antha Minerva Virgil** (?-1939) originated the Virgil piano method, and composed more than two hundred piano pieces: a Virgil Clavier School was established in London. and for many years the instrument was regarded as indispensable in the development of piano technique.

Virginal, a small form of SPINET or HARPSICHORD developed in the early part of the 16th century: it was without legs, rectangular in shape and usually placed on a table or stand. The strings were of metal, one for each note. The sound was produced by jacks, made of quill, whalebone or leather, provided with spiral springs. It was played by means of a keyboard, and the compass was about three octaves. The **Fitzwilliam Virginal Book** is the most remarkable collection of English 17th century instrumental music. It is preserved in the FITZWILLIAM MUSEUM at Cambridge; the history of the volume is not known earlier than the beginning of the 18th century, when it was discovered in the possession of Dr. Samuel PEPUSCH. The compositions are mostly airs and variations; the following composers are represented: BULL, Richardson, BYRD, MORLEY, SWEELINCK, TALLIS, Dowland, and Farnaby.

Virginia Reel, an early American dance which is a variety of the REEL: the dancers are placed so that they face each other in two rows, and as the figures are called the dancers execute the steps two at a time until all have completed the set. The tune usually used is *Turkey in the Straw,* and the dance is still popular in rural sections of the United States.

Vischer, Peter (c.1455-1529), German sculptor regarded as one of the greatest masters of his art: his work marks the transition from the Gothic to the Renaissance styles, and he was also one of the finest workers in bronze. His works include the bronze canopy over the shrine of St. Sebaldus at Nürnberg; the tombs of Archbishop Ernst, Herman VIII von Henneberg, and Elizabeth of Brandenburg. His five sons worked with him in the studio and the foundry.

Visconti, Louis Tullius Joachim (1791-1853), French architect, born in Italy, whose father was a distinguished archaeologist: his works at Paris include the tomb of NAPOLEON I, the Louvois Fountain, and the Molière Fountain.

Vishnu, in Hindu mythology the second member of the triad of deities known as Brahma, Vishnu and Siva: Brahma was the creator, Vishnu the preserver, and Siva the destroyer. The Ganges River is supposed to rise from Vishnu's foot, and he has a thousand names all of which are listed in the Mahabharata.

Vitruvius, Roman architect and writer on architecture of whom little is known except that he lived during the 1st century A.D., and wrote a treatise, *On Architecture* in ten books which was carefully studied by BRAMANTE, MICHELANGELO, PALLADIO, VIGNOLIA, and many other architects of the earlier period. The work discusses architecture in general, private houses, public buildings, Greek temples, and many other subjects of interest to those concerned with architectural problems.

Vittoria, Tomás, see **Victoria, Tomás.**

Vivaldi, Antonio (c.1675-1741), Italian violinist and composer who studied with his father: his red hair gained him the nickname "il Prete rosso." He toured Europe repeatedly for many years, and also directed the music activities at the Girls Conservatory of the Ospitale della Pietà in Venice. His compositions include operas; more than 100 concertos and sonatas for the violin: many of his works were transcribed by Johann Sebastian BACH.

Vivarini, Bartolommeo (c.1430-1499), Italian painter who worked for a time with his brother, Antonio, and signed his first paintings *Da Murano.* He learned the art of oil painting from ANTONELLO DA MESSINA: his works include *Madonna with Saints; St. Mark between Four Saints; St. George and the Dragon.*

Vizetelly, Frank Horace (1864-1938), American editor, author, and lexicographer born in London and son of Henry VIZETELLY: his works include *The Preparation of Manuscripts for the Printer* (1905); *A Desk-Book of Errors in English; Essentials of English Speech and Literature; A Desk-Book of Idioms and Idiomatic Phrases in English Speech and Literature; How to Use English.* He was also editor of the Funk & Wagnalls *Standard Dictionary* from 1914 until his death.

Vizetelly, Henry (1820-1894), English journalist, author, and publisher who introduced the works of Edgar Allan POE, Émile ZOLA, and Leo TOLSTOY to English readers: his works include *The Story of the Diamond Necklace* (1867); a translation of Marius Topin's *The Man in the Iron Mask; A History of Champagnes.* He also founded the *Pictorial Times* in 1843, one of the first of the picture magazines which have intrigued British readers.

Vlaminck, Maurice Edmond de (1876-), French painter of Flemish-French parentage who became friendly with André DERAIN and became interested in the art of painting, exhibiting several canvases in 1905 at the Salon des Indépendants, Paris. His works include landscapes, still life, and portraits painted with a broad technique: he is considered one of the exponents of Fauvism.

Vogl, Johann Michael (1768-1840), Austrian dramatic baritone who sang at the Court Opera in Vienna from 1794 to 1822: he is famous for having introduced many of Franz SCHUBERT's songs to the Viennese public.

Vogler, Georg Joseph (1749-1814), German composer, theorist, and teacher who studied with Giambattista MARTINI and later became a priest: his pupils included Carl Maria von WEBER and Giacomo MEYERBEER. He was the inventor of a portable organ now obsolete, and composed operas, sacred music, and chamber works in addition to many theoretical treatises.

Vogüé, Eugene Marie Melchior, Viscount de (1848-1910), French novelist and critic who served in the Franco-Prussian War, and later entered the diplomatic service, leaving it to devote himself to writing: his works include *Oriental Histories* (1879); *The Son of Peter the Great; The Russian Romance; Souvenirs and Visions; Jean d'Agrève,* a partially autobiographical novel; *The Dead Who Speak; The Master of the Sea.*

Voice, in music the name applied to the tonal product generated by the vocal organs in the act of singing. The names of the various voices according to their range are SOPRANO, MEZZO-SOPRANO, ALTO, CONTRALTO, TENOR, BARITONE, BASS-BARITONE, and BASS.

Vokes, Rosina (c.1854-1894), English actress who first appeared as a child of three on the stage, and made her mature debut in 1870 in a Drury Lane pantomime. For several years she appeared in extravaganzas, retired after her marriage in 1881, but returned to the stage in 1885: among the farces in which she played were *Fun in a Fog; Phoebus's Six; A Bunch of Berries; The Forty Thieves; Bluebeard; Pendragon; A Game of Cards,* her greatest success.

Volk, Douglas (1856-1935), American painter who studied with Jean Léon GEROME at Paris and in Rome, later founding and directing the Minneapolis School of Fine Arts, and also teaching at the ART STUDENTS' LEAGUE, New York. His works include *Vanity; Boy with an Arrow; Domestic Life in Normandy; Little Mildred; Puritan Girl:* he also painted the portraits of General Pershing, Abraham Lincoln, and King Albert of Belgium.

Volk, Leonard Wells (1828-1895), American sculptor who first worked as a marble cutter, and later opened a studio at St. Louis, Mo.: after a period of study in Rome he worked in Chicago where he was influential in founding the Academy of Design. His notable works include a life mask of Lincoln and casts of his hands; a statue of Lincoln and several monuments.

Vollmer, Lula, contemporary American dramatist educated at the Normal Collegiate Institute, Asheville, N. C.: her plays include *Sunny* (1923); *The Shame Woman; The Dunce Boy; Trigger; Sentinels; In a Nut-Shell; The Hill Between.* She has also written serials for radio broadcasting.

Vollon, Antoine (1833-1900), French painter who studied with Augustin RIBOT: his notable canvases include *Art and Gluttony; Monkey at the Accordion; Curiosities; The Kettle; A Farmyard; Big White Cheese; Grapes in the South:* he is credited with imparting beauty to the most ordinary objects.

Volpe, Arnold (1869-), Russian violinist and conductor who studied with Isidore Lotto at the Warsaw Musical Institute, and also with Leopold AUER at the St. Petersburg Conservatory. He came to New York in 1908, founded the Young Men's Symphony Orchestra in 1902, the Volpe Orchestra in 1904, and conducted the Brooklyn Institute Orchestra in 1910 beside directing municipal concerts for the City of New York.

Volsungasaga, in ancient Norse literature the history of the mythical Volsungs and NIBELUNGS: the principal character was Sigurd the Volsung identical with the Siegfried of the *Nibelungenlied.* Richard WAGNER drew largely from the *Volsungasaga* in writing the text for *The RING OF THE NIBELUNGS.*

Voltaire, François Marie Arouet de (1694-1778), French philosopher, author, critic, and dramatist educated at the Jesuit Collège Louis-le-Grand: his real name was **François Marie Arouet**; the name "Voltaire" was assumed about 1717. His notable works include *Oedipus* (1918), a tragedy written while he was imprisoned in the Bastille for libeling Philippe d'Orléans, the regent; *The Henriade,* an epic poem on Henry IV; *Letters on the English; History of Charles XII of Sweden; Zaïre,* considered his best tragedy; *Elements of Newton's Philosophy; La Pucelle,* a satirical biography of Joan of Arc; *History of Russia under Peter I; The Bible at Last Explained.* He lived for some years at Cirey in Lorraine with the Marquise des Châtelet: after her death he spent two years as the guest of FREDERICK THE GREAT who was an admirer of French culture although the visit resulted in violent arguments and an unfriendly parting.

Volterra, Daniele da (1509-1566), Italian painter and sculptor whose real name was Daniele Ricciarelli. He studied with Il SODOMA, Baldassare PERUZZI, and MICHELANGELO: for painting shapeless clothes on the nude figures in Michelangelo's *Last Judgment* in the SISTINE CHAPEL as ordered by Pope Paul IV he earned the nickname *Il Bracchetone* (Breeches Maker). His best paintings include *Descent from the Cross,* ranked among the world's greatest paintings; *Massacre of the Innocents; David and Goliath.*

Voluntary, see **Interlude.**

Volute, in architecture an ornament consisting of a spiral scroll which was characteristic of Ionic and Corinthian CAPITALS. There are many forms, the simplest being made up of four quarters of circles meeting at one of the extremities and described from radii which gradually become smaller and smaller.

Vondell, Joost van den (1587-1679), Dutch poet and dramatist who is considered the greatest figure in Dutch literature, often referred to as "the Dutch Shakespeare." His first work of importance was the drama *Het Pascha* produced in 1612: his masterpiece was *Lucifer,* an allegorical account of the revolt of the Netherlands against Philip of Spain. His other dramas were chiefly on Biblical subjects.

Vonnoh, Bessie Potter (1872-), American sculptor who studied at the CHICAGO ART INSTITUTE, and acted as assistant to Lorado TAFT in the decorating of buildings at the Chicago Columbian Exposition in 1893: her works include the Roosevelt Memorial Fountain at Oyster Bay, N. Y.; the Children's Garden Fountain at Central Park, New York: also many small bronzes such as *Young Mother; Girl Dancing; Girl Reading.* Her husband, **Robert William Vonnoh** (1852-1933), was a well-known portrait and landscape painter who taught at the Boston Museum of Fine Arts and at the Pennsylvania Academy of Fine Arts.

Von Seyffertitz, Gustav, contemporary Austrian stage and screen actor who first appeared in the United States under the management of Charles FROHMAN: among the pictures in which he has played important roles since 1933 are *Queen Christina; Mystery Liner; The Moonstone; "She"; Remember Last Night; Little Lord Fauntleroy; In Old Chicago; Nurse Edith Cavell.*

Von Sternberg, Josef, contemporary Austrian motion-picture director: among the films he has supervised since 1929 are *Blue Angel; Morocco; Dishonored; American Tragedy; Shanghai Express; Blonde Venus; Scarlet Empress; The Devil is a Woman; Crime and Punishment; The King Steps Out; Shanghai Gesture.*

Von Stroheim, Eric (1885-   ), Austrian stage and screen actor and director who has been connected with American films since 1914 when he assisted John EMERSON in the preparation of *Old Heidelberg,* and has been particularly successful in the part of a Prussian officer: among the numerous pictures in which he has appeared are *Blind Husbands; Wedding March; The Great Gabbo; Three Faces East; Lost Squadron; As You Desire Me; The Crime of Dr. Crespi; The Great Illusion; Alibi; So Ends Our Night.*

Voragine, James, see **Golden Legend.**

Vorticism, the name applied to a theory developed by English painters between 1913 and 1922 that painting should reflect the complexity of machinery and consequently of modern industrial civilization: the movement was a phase of POST-IMPRESSIONISM.

Vos, Cornelis de (1585-1651), Flemish painter who was a contemporary of RUBENS, and influenced also by Sir Anthony VAN DYCK: his notable works include *Couple Seated on a Terrace; Mother and Children; Messenger of the Company of St. Luke; Solomon Anointed King; Descent from the Cross; Triumph of Bacchus; Apollo Killing the Python; Adoration of the Magi; Allegory on Riches.*

Vos, Marten or **Martin** (1531-1603), Flemish painter who studied with Franz FLORIS and with TINTORETTO at Venice; his notable canvases include *Immaculate Conception; The Four Seasons; Raising of Lazarus; Samson and Delilah; Crucifixion; Triumph of Christ; The Incredulity of St. Thomas; Jonah Cast into the Sea; Temptation of St. Anthony.*

Vouet, Simon (1590-1649), French painter who was so skillful through self-study at fourteen that he was called to England to paint the portrait of a lady refugee of noble birth. He visited Constantinople, Venice, Genoa, and Rome, finally becoming court painter to Louis XIII for whom he executed decorative works at the LOUVRE and the Luxembourg: also at the residences of Cardinal RICHELIEU.

Vriendt, Frans de, see **Floris, Frans.**

Vries, Adriaen de (c.1558-c.1625), Dutch sculptor who studied with Giovanni da BOLOGNA at Florence and worked at Prague on commission from the Emperor Rudolph II: among his notable works are the *Mercury Fountain* and *Hercules Fountain* in Augsburg both of which are executed in bronze. Two of his finest bronzes are *Psyche*

at the LOUVRE, Paris, and *Triton* at the METROPOLITAN MUSEUM OF ART, New York.

Vronsky and Babin, contemporary Russian two-piano ensemble: its members are Vitya Vronsky and Victor Babin both of whom were born in Russia and pupils of Artur SCHNABEL at Berlin. They first appeared with great success in Europe, making their American debut in 1937. Victor Babin is also a composer of ability, and the duo has made many excellent recordings.

Vuillaume, Jean Baptiste (1798-1875), French violin maker who opened a shop at Paris in 1828 and began copying fine violins by STRADIVARIUS and other masters, making more than 3,000 violins, violas, and violoncellos. He also made excellent bows following the style of François TOURTE. His instruments are valued at the present time from $800.00 to $2500.00, and his bows from $75.00 to $750.00.

Vulcan, see **Hephaestus.**

Vulgate, a Latin version of the Holy Scriptures prepared by St. Jerome in the 4th century: the word was first used by Roger Bacon, at least in its modern sense, in the 13th century.

W

Wade, Arthur Sarsfield, see **Rohmer, Sax.**

Wagner, Wilhelm Richard (1813-1883), German composer educated at Dresden and Leipzig who first developed a great enthusiasm for BEETHOVEN'S symphonies, but finally decided that opera was the field in which he desired to create. He acted as chorusmaster at a theatre in Würzberg, conducted at Magdeburg, Konigsberg, and Riga, and resided in Paris from 1839 to 1842 endeavoring to earn a living while steadily composing. His opera, *Rienzi,* was produced successfully at Dresden in 1842: *The Flying Dutchman* performed in the same city also met with public approval in 1843, but *Tannhäuser* was a comparative failure in 1845. In 1849 he fled to Paris to escape arrest for alleged participation in revolutionary riots: Franz LISZT befriended him, and produced *Lohengrin* at Weimar in 1850, but Wagner did not hear it until 1861 when it was produced at Vienna. The production of *Tannhäuser* at Paris in 1861, although sponsored by the Emperor, was a complete failure, but during the same year King Ludwig II of Bavaria permitted him to return to Germany. He settled at Munich where *Tristan and Isolde* was performed in 1865: in 1870 he married Cosima WAGNER, ex-wife of Hans von BULOW, and founded his theatre, the Festspielhaus, at BAYREUTH in 1872. *The RING OF THE NIBELUNGS* was given its first complete production there in 1876, and *Parsifal* in 1882. His operas and music dramas include *Rienzi; The Flying Dutchman; Tannhäuser; Lohengrin; The Ring of the Nibelungs,* comprising *The Rhinegold, The Valkyrie, Siegfried,* and *Dusk of the Gods; Tristan and Isolde; Die Meistersinger von Nürnberg; Parsifal:* he also composed a symphony, overtures, festival marches, piano pieces, and songs. His literary works include the texts for all his operas and music dramas: also several volumes in defence of his admittedly radical musical ideas including *The Art-work of the Future* (1850) and *Opera and Drama*. His son, **Siegfried Wagner** (1869-1930), studied composition with Engelbert HUMPERDINCK, and after doing some concert conducting became assistant conductor at Bayreuth in 1894, and later one of the regular conductors: in 1909 he succeeded his mother, Cosima Wagner, as general supervisor of the festivals. He composed several operas including *Der Bärenhäuter* (1899), but none of them can be compared with his father's mighty creations. His mother, **Cosima Wagner** (1837-1930), was the daughter of Franz LISZT and the Countess Marie D'AGOULT: she was first married to Hans von BÜLOW, Wagner's friend and champion. After her husband's death she undertook with remarkable success the management of the Bayreuth Festivals. Richard Wagner's niece, **Johanna Wagner** (1828-1894), was the daughter of his brother Albert: she was a distinguished dramatic soprano who sang at Dresden, Hamburg, Paris, Berlin, and at the Bayreuth Festivals: she was also an actress of ability.

Waits, originally the name given night watchmen in England who announced their coming by blowing a horn: the title was later applied to bands of itinerant singers and players who appeared at Christmas and other festal days to sing and play for small gratuities.

Waldteufel, Emil (1837-1915), French composer who studied with his father at the Strasbourg Conservatory, and later at the Paris Conservatory with François MARMONTEL: his first waltzes, *Joys and Pains* and *Manola*, which he published at his own expense, were so successful that he devoted his entire time to the composition of nearly 300 dances many of which such as the waltzes *Always or Never, Estudiantina, My Dream, Violets, Sirens,* and *Dolores* rivaled those of Johann STRAUSS, JR., in popularity. A list of Waldteufel dance recordings will be found in *The Gramophone Shop Encyclopedia of Recorded Music.*

Walker, Horatio (1858-1938), American painter born in Canada who was almost entirely self-taught: a walking trip undertaken through French Canada and also travels in England, Spain, Normandy, and Holland interested him greatly in peasant life and customs. His works such as *Oxen Drinking; The Woodcutter; Milking* and *Sheep Shearing* show the influence of the BARBIZON SCHOOL.

Walküre, Die, see **Ring of the Nibelungs, The.**

Wallace, Edgar (1876-1932), English novelist and dramatist who published 150 separate works in the form of detective and adventure stories in 27 years: it is reported that five million of his books were sold annually in Great Britain and that seventeen plays in six years yielded him $500,000. His most popular stories include *The Four Just Men; The Clue of the Twisted Candle; The Green Archer; Sanders of the River; Mr. Commissioner Sanders; Red Aces; The Murder Book of J. G. Ruder; On the Spot.*

Wallace, Lewis (Lew Wallace) (1827-1905), American soldier and novelist who served in both the Mexican and Civil Wars: his works include *The Fair God* (1873); *Ben Hur: A Tale of the Christ,* was a best seller which has been dramatized and filmed; *The Boyhood of Christ; The Prince of India:* he also wrote an interesting *Autobiography.*

Wallace, William Vincent (1812-1865), Irish composer who first played the violin in orchestras, and toured Australia, South America, Mexico, and the United States with great success. In 1845 he produced an opera, *Maritana* at the Drury Lane Theatre which was received with extraordinary enthusiasm: his operas, *Lurline, The Amber Witch, Love's Triumph,* and *The Desert Flower,* all in the BALLAD-OPERA style, were also successful, but are no longer in the repertory.

Wallace Collection (London), an art collection at Hertford House, London, England, founded by **Sir Richard Wallace** (1818-1890). It comprises paintings, armor, furniture and miscellaneous art objects of every description: the paintings include not only works by Dutch, Spanish, and British artists, but also an unexcelled assembly of canvases by 18th century French artists comprising twenty by GREUZE, nineteen by BOUCHER, eleven by WATTEAU and fifteen by MEISSONIER.

Wallack, James William (c.1794-1864), Anglo-American actor and theatrical manager born in England whose parents were actors. He appeared first at the DRURY LANE THEATRE in 1807, came to America in 1818, settled at New York permanently in 1852, and opened the Wallack Theatre, the most famous house of its kind in America. The name was of real importance until long after Wallack's death: Rose COGHLAN, Edward A. SOTHERN, Charles COGHLAN, Maurice BARRYMORE and almost every other great actor of the day played at "Wallacks." His son, **John Lester Wallack** (1820-1888), was born in New York, and carried on with the second Wallack's theatre from 1861, and with a third one at 30th St. and Broadway, New York, in 1882. He produced and appeared himself in all the standard plays of the day, and was especially popular in his own play, *Rosedale* (1863) which held the stage for thirty years, and also in his adaptation of Octave FEUILLET's novel, *The Romance of a Poor Young Man:* he is said to have played nearly 300 roles.

Wallenstein, Alfred (1898-), American violoncellist and conductor who studied the violoncello with Julius Klengel at Leipzig, becoming first 'cellist of the Chicago Symphony Orchestra from 1922 to 1929, and first 'cellist of the New York Philharmonic-Symphony Society from 1929 to 1936. In 1936 he became general musical director of radio station WOR, and in 1943 conductor of the Los Angeles Philharmonic Orchestra.

Walpole, Horace or **Horatio, 4th Earl of Oxford** (1717-1797), English author educated at Cambridge who bought an estate at Twickenham, and erected a mansion known as Strawberry Hill where he set up a private press and printed his own books: his works include *The Castle of Otranto* (1764) which is regarded as the ancestor of the modern mystery novel; *The Mysterious Mother,* a "horror" tragedy; *Anecdotes of Painting in England; A Catalogue of the Royal and Noble Authors of England.* He was intimate for a time with Thomas GRAY, but quarreled with him while on a tour of Europe in 1739: seven years later the two again became friends, and he printed an edition of Gray's poems on his private press.

Walpole, Sir Hugh Seymour (1884-1941), English novelist born in New Zealand who was educated at Emmanuel College, Oxford: his works include *The Wooden Horse* (1909); *Maradick at Forty; Fortitude; The Dark Forest; The Secret; The Cathedral; Portrait of a Man With Red Hair; Rogue Herries; Judith Paris; The Fortress; Vanessa; The Blindman's House:* he has also written biographies of Joseph CONRAD and Anthony TROLLOPE in addition to several juvenile books.

Walter, Bruno (1876-), German composer and conductor whose real name is Bruno W. Schlesinger: after studying at the Stern Conservatory and conducting in various German cities he became conductor of the Vienna Hofoper from 1901 to 1913, and succeeded Felix MOTTL in 1914 as general music director at Munich, remaining until 1922. He conducted the New York Symphony Orchestra from 1923 to 1925, and has since been guest conductor of the New York Philharmonic-Symphony Orchestra, and many other major orchestras in the United States and Europe. He is an authoritative conductor of Gustav MAHLER's works, and has composed much symphonic music.

Walter, Eugene (1874-1941), American dramatist who acted as a reporter on Cleveland, Detroit, and New York newspapers, later becoming manager for several amusement enterprises ranging from circuses to grand opera companies, and also volunteering for service in the Spanish-American War. His plays include *Sergeant James* (1901); *The Undertow; Paid in Full; The Wolf; The Easiest Way; Boots and Saddles; Just a Wife; Fine Feathers; The Knife.* He also dramatized the novel *The Trail of the Lonesome Pine,* and published a series of ten lectures on the practical aspects of playwriting entitled *How to Write a Play.*

Walther von der Vogelweide (c.1160-1230), German MINNESINGER who was of noble birth, and considered the greatest lyric poet of medieval Germany. He composed both the verses and music which he sang at the courts of the various kings, and some of his works have been published. Richard WAGNER makes him one of the rival singers in *Tannhäuser.*

Walton, William (1902-), English composer educated at Christ Church Cath. School, Oxford: his compositions include *Façade* and other works for orchestra; a violin concerto; *Crown Imperial,* a coronation march for George VI; works for voice and orchestra; chamber music and songs.

Waltzes (Chopin), fifteen idyllic dances composed by Frédéric CHOPIN regarded by such eminent critics as James HUNEKER, Robert SCHU-

MANN, and Frederick NIECKS as the apotheosis of the waltz. They are available in a Victor complete recording by Alexander BRAILOWSKY and a Columbia recording by Edward Kilenyi: also separate recordings for piano, and for violin and violoncello in transcription, all of which are listed in *The Gramophone Shop Encyclopedia of Recorded Music.*

Wappers, Gustave, Baron (1803-1874), Belgian painter who studied at the Antwerp Academy and at Paris, later becoming director for many years of the Antwerp Academy. His notable works include *The Devotion of the Burgomaster of Leyden; An Episode of the Belgian Revolution of 1830; Christ Entombed; Peter the Great at Saardam; Boccaccio at the Court of Joanna at Naples; The Defence of Rhodes by the Knights of St. John of Jerusalem.*

Ward, Artemus, pen name of **Charles Farrar Browne** (1834-1867), American humorist and lecturer who began to write his famous sayings in 1858 while a reporter on the Cleveland *Plain Dealer,* and later became editor of the humorous weekly, *Vanity Fair,* which for a time was a rival of *Punch* in London. His works include *Artemus Ward: His Book* (1862) and *Artemus Ward: His Travels.*

Ward, Mrs. Elizabeth Stuart, see **Phelps, Elizabeth Stuart.**

Ward, Fannie (1872-), American actress who made her debut in 1890 at the Broadway Theatre, New York, in *Pippino:* among the numerous plays in which she has appeared are *The Charity Ball; Shenandoah; Lord and Lady Algy; The Climbers; In the Bishop's Carriage; The Marriage of William Ashe:* she also played roles in many silent films, and toured the United States in 1931 in *The Truth Game.*

Ward, Mrs. Humphry (1851-1920), English novelist born in Tasmania: her works include *Min Bretherton* (1884); *Robert Elsmere* which reached a sale of 500,000 copies in the United States; *David Grieve; Helbeck of Banisdale; Eleanor; The Marriage of William Ashe; The Testing of Diana Mallory; Daphne or Marriage a la Mode; The Case of Richard Meynell; The War and Elizabeth.*

Ward, John Quincy Adams (1830-1910), American sculptor who studied with Henry Kirke BROWN at New York for several years, and opened his own studio there in 1860: his works include *Indian Hunter* in Central Park, New York; *Washington* in front of the Subtreasury Building, New York; *Henry Ward Beecher* in Brooklyn, N. Y.; *President Garfield* in Washington; *Horace Greeley* in New York: he also executed the pediment of the New York Stock Exchange with Paul Wayland BARTLETT.

Warfield, David (1866-), American actor who made his first appearance on the stage as an extra at San Francisco, and his New York debut in 1890 as a monologist at a music hall: among the plays in which he appeared with great success were *The Auctioneer; The Music Master* of which he gave more than a thousand performances between

1904 and 1907; *A Grand Army Man; The Return of Peter Grimm; Van Der Decken; The Merchant of Venice.*

Warner, Charles Dudley (1829-1900), American editor and author educated at Hamilton College and trained for the law at the University of Pennsylvania: he practiced for a time in Chicago, but finally turned to literature. His works include *The Book of Eloquence* (1851); *My Summer in a Garden; Back Log Studies; Washington Irving,* a biography; *The Gilded Age,* a novel with Mark Twain: he also edited the *Library of the World's Best Literature* (1896-97), and wrote several entertaining travel volumes.

Warner, H. Waldo (1874-), English violist and composer who studied at the Guildhall School of Music and became violist of the London String Quartet from 1907 to 1927: his compositions include *Hampton Wick* and other works for orchestra; chamber music; piano pieces; choruses; part songs, and songs for solo voices.

Warner, Henry Byron (1876-), English stage and screen actor generally known as H. B. Warner: his first appearance on the stage was made at seven with his father in *The Streets of London,* and his mature debut in 1898 also with his father in *It's Never Too Late To Mend.* Among the plays in which he has appeared are *The Three Musketeers; The Absent-Minded Beggar; Peg Woffington; Dr. Johnson; Merely Mary Ann; The Battle; Alias Jimmy Valentine; The Ghost Breaker; Under Cover; Out There; Bull-Dog Drummond.* Since 1934 he has appeared in innumerable films including *Sorrell and Son; A Tale of Two Cities; Rose of the Rancho; The Lost Horizon; The Adventures of Marco Polo; The Toy Wife; You Can't Take It With You;* several *Bull-Dog Drummond* films; *Nurse Edith Cavell; The Rains Came; Mr. Smith Goes to Washington; The Corsican Brothers.*

Warner, Olin Levi (1844-1896), American sculptor who studied in Paris with Jean Baptiste Carpeaux, and after serving for a time in the French Foreign Legion returned to America where, while success was slow in coming, he is now regarded as the most distinguished sculptor of his day. His works include many busts and statues of eminent Americans and designs for two pairs of bronze doors at the Congressional Library, Washington, D. C., only one of which was finished, the other completed by Herbert Adams after Warner's death.

Warren, Ferdinand (1899-), American painter who studied at the Kansas City Art Institute and at the Tiffany Foundation: his works include *The Harbor* at the Metropolitan Museum of Art, New York; *Montauk Lighthouse* which won the National Academy of Design prize; *Washington Mews* exhibited at the San Francisco World's Fair; *Street Scene in Brooklyn* exhibited at the New York World's Fair; *Airway Beacon* and *Jim's Place* shown at the Carnegie International Exhibition.

Warren, Whitney (1864-1943), American architect who first wished to be a painter, but after studying drawing became more interested in architecture. He studied at the Ecole des Beaux-Arts in Paris with Pierre Daumet from 1885 to 1894, and then associated himself with Charles D. Wetmore in the firm of Warren and Wetmore. Among the buildings designed by the firm are the Grand Central Terminal, the Chelsea Docks and many hotels in New York City: also the reconstruction of the library of Louvain University demolished during World War I, and completely destroyed during World War II.

Warton, Thomas (1728-1790), English clergyman and poet educated at Oxford who became poet laureate in 1785, and also professor of history at Oxford: his works include *The Pleasures of Melancholy* (1747); *The Triumph of Isis; The History of English Poetry; Observations on the Faerie Queene of Spenser:* he also edited a *Greek Anthology,* the works of Theocritus, and minor poems by John Milton.

Washington, George (1732-1799), American statesman, leader in the American Revolution, and first president of the United States from 1789 to 1797. His *Farewell Address* is placed in the same literary category as Abraham Lincoln's second inaugural address, and his life and personality have figured largely in drama, poetry, and fiction. His portrait was painted by Charles Willson Peale, Rembrandt Peale, Gilbert Stuart, John Trumbull, and many other American artists.

Watelet, Louis Étienne (1780-1866), French painter who trained himself by studying nature firsthand, and became one of the greatest landscapists: his works include *Napoleon in Ludwigsburg; Herdsmen; Henry IV in the Forest of Ailas; Village in Normandy; St. Jerome in the Desert; Fontainebleau; Romantic Landscape; Flight into Egypt.*

Water-color painting, the earliest known method of painting with a brush dating back to the rude pictures in the caves of France and Spain: there are several other names by which the process is called such as fresco, tempera, distemper, and aquarelle. Powdered color is crushed in water, and mixed with gum arabic in such a combination that the color is the same when it dries as when wet. A fixative is used which protects the water-color in the same manner as a varnish.

Water Music (Handel), a work for orchestra said to have been composed by George Frederick Handel in 1715 on the occasion of George I's arrival in England to be crowned king: it was played on a boat following the royal barge up the Thames from Lambeth to Chelsea apparently much to the delight of the monarch. The version used at the present time is a suite arranged from the music by Sir Hamilton Harty for the modern orchestra: there is a Victor recording by the Philadelphia Orchestra and a Columbia recording by the London Philharmonic Orchestra.

Waters, Ethel (1900-), American Negro actress and singer who first appeared as an entertainer in night clubs: among the productions in which she has appeared are *Africana; Blackbirds;*

Rhapsody in Black; As Thousands Cheer; At Home Abroad; Mamba's Daughters (1939) in which she scored a notable success: she has also given a recital at Carnegie Hall, and appeared in the films.

Watkin, Laurence Edward (1901-), American novelist educated at Syracuse, Harvard, and Columbia Universities: his works include *On Borrowed Time* (1937) which was a best seller and also popular as a play and a film; *Gentleman from England,* a story of the years following the Revolutionary War.

Watson, Lucile (1879-), American stage and screen actress born in Canada who studied at the American Academy of Dramatic Arts, New York, and made her debut in 1902 on the New York stage in *The Wisdom of the Wise:* among the numerous plays in which she has appeared are *The Dictator; Captain Jinks; The City; Under Cover; The Eternal Magdalene; Heartbreak House; The Far Cry; Dancing Mothers; Mozart; No More Ladies; Pride and Prejudice; Dear Octopus; The Watch on the Rhine.* She has also been featured in numerous films.

Watteau, Antoine (1684-1721), French painter who studied with an obscure artist in Valenciennes and came to Paris in 1702: his works include *Embarkation for Cythera* which gained his admission into the Academy in 1717; *Fête in a Park; The Music Party; The Champs Elysées; The Music Lesson; Fête Champêtre; Monkey Sculptor; Rendez-vous at the Chase; Young Girl with a Sunshade.* His reputation was secured by the unrivaled freshness and grace with which he painted conventional figures, shepherds, dancers, and actors.

Watts, George Frederick (1817-1904), English painter who studied at the Royal Academy, London, and in Florence: his notable works include *Caractacus Led in Triumph Through the Streets of Rome; King Alfred Inciting the Saxons; Endymion; Daphne; Psyche, Orpheus and Eurydice; Chaos; The Creation of Eve; The Building of the Ark; Paolo and Francesca:* he also painted the portraits of Matthew ARNOLD, SWINBURNE, Robert BROWNING, ROSSETTI, TENNYSON, William MORRIS, and CARLYLE.

Waugh, Frederick Judd (1861-1940), American painter and illustrator who studied at the Pennsylvania Academy of Fine Arts and at the Académie Julian in Paris. He lived in Europe from 1892 to 1907, and executed illustrations for the London *Graphic* and other journals: his pictures such as *The Roaring Forties* and *The Great Deep* at the Metropolitan Museum of Art, New York, are distinguished by their artistic sense of form and color. He was also the author and illustrator of *The Clan of Munes* (1916).

Wax Figures, small figures developed by the ancient Egyptians, Greeks, and Romans for sacred images, dolls, and talismans; also by the early Christians for images of the saints. The material employed was usually beeswax which lends itself to modeling and coloring. During the Renaissance wax was used for portraits and as models for casting in bronze. Colored portraits were made in wax during the 18th century: the most famous exhibitions of wax figures were Mme. TUSSAUD'S at London and the Eden Musée in New York.

Wax Painting, see **Encaustic Painting.**

Weber, Carl Maria Friedrich Ernst von (1786-1826), German composer, pianist, and conductor who studied with Michael HAYDN and Johann Michael VOGLER, becoming opera director at Breslau on the latter's recommendation. In 1813 he became conductor of the National Opera at Prague and in 1816 director of German opera at Dresden: his opera *Der Freischütz* was produced at Berlin with great success in 1821, and *Euryanthe* followed in 1823, but was less favorably received because of the inanity of the libretto. His last opera, *Oberon* was produced at London in 1826. His compositions include the three operas mentioned above; incidental music for several plays; several cantatas; two masses; part songs, choruses, and many songs; orchestral music, piano concertos, and clarinet concertos; chamber music; sonatas and concert pieces for the piano. His most popular works are the famous *Invitation to the Dance* and the overtures to *Der Freischütz* and *Oberon.*

Weber, Henry George (1900-), American conductor born in Germany of American parents who returned to the United States in 1901. He studied at the Vienna Academy of Music and also at the University of Vienna: from 1924 to 1929 he conducted the CHICAGO OPERA COMPANY and became music director of Station WGN at Chicago in 1934, also assuming the post of artistic director of the Chicago Civic Opera Company in 1940.

Weber and Fields, a team of American vaudeville comedians composed of **Joseph Weber** (1867-1942) and **Lew Fields** (1867-1941) who first appeared in a comic German dialect sketch at the Bowery Theatre, New York, in 1877. After playing in music halls they opened the Weber and Fields Music Hall in 1885, organizing a company which included many stars such as Lillian RUSSELL, and presenting a series of famous burlesques such as *Twirly-Twirly, The Geezer* in which both Weber and Fields appeared in their dialect skits. In 1904 a disagreement ended the partnership: Weber continued to operate the music hall, and Fields opened the Fields Theatre with a burlesque of *The Music Master,* and later acquired the Herald Square Theatre to produce several music plays and burlesques. They were reunited in 1912, and appeared for years together on the stage, screen, and radio.

Webern, Anton von (1883-), Austrian composer who studied with Guido Adler and later became the friend and associate of Arnold SCHONBERG. His compositions include orchestral works, chamber music, and songs: since 1924 he has employed the 12-tone system in his compositions many of which are extraordinarily brief such as the fourth of the *Five Pieces for Orchestra, Op. 10* which requires about 20 seconds for performance.

Webster, Henry Kitchell (1875-1932), American novelist educated at Hamilton College: his works include *Calumet K* (1901), a novel about railroading written with Samuel MERWIN; *Traitor and Loyalist; A King in Khaki; The Thoroughbred; An American Family; Mary Wollaston; Joseph Greer and His Daughter; The Sealed Trunk.*

Webster, Jean (1876-1916), American novelist educated at Vassar College: her works include *When Patty Went to College* (1903); *The Wheat Princess; Jerry Junior; The Four Pools Mystery; Much Ado about Peter; Just Patty; Daddy-Long-Legs; Dear Enemy.*

Webster, John (c.1580-c.1625), English dramatist who worked for Philip HENSLOWE, a famous English theatrical manager, and assisted DEKKER, DRAYTON, MARSTON, ROWLEY, MIDDLETON, and HEYWARD in writing some of their plays: his original works include *The White Devil, The Duchess of Malfi,* and *The Devil's Law Case.* Critics have pronounced his powers as a tragedist second only to those of William SHAKESPEARE.

Webster, Margaret (1905-), American actress and director whose father, Ben Webster, and mother, Dame May WHITTY, were distinguished actors. She made her debut in *The Trojan Women* at New York in 1917, later appearing with John BARRYMORE, Dame Sybil THORNDIKE, and with the Ben GREET Shakespearean Company in England. She also appeared with John GIELGUD and Sir John MARTIN-HARVEY. Among the plays she directed in London are *Return to Yesterday; Lovers' Meeting; No Longer Mourn; Lady from the Sea; Old Music:* in New York she has directed the Maurice EVANS productions of *Richard II; Hamlet; Henry IV:* also the THEATRE GUILD production of *Twelfth Night* with Helen HAYES and Maurice Evans. She is the author of *Shakespeare without Tears* (1942).

Webster, Noah (1758-1843), American lexicographer educated at Yale College who served in the Revolutionary War, practiced law for a time, played an important part in New York journalism, and became both a judge and a member of the legislature in Connecticut. His important works, which earned him the title of "Schoolmaster to America," include *Grammatical Institute of the English Language* (1783-85) the first part of which was the *Elementary Spelling Book; A Compendious Dictionary of the English Language* (1806); *American Dictionary of the English Language* (1828). The latter work was revised and published in 1841.

Wedekind, Frank (1864-1918), German dramatist who acted in and produced his own plays which were influenced by HAUPTMANN and STRINDBERG: his plays include *The World of Youth* (1890); *The Awakening of Spring; Such is Life; Earth Spirit; Pandora's Box; The Dance of Death; Samson; Bismarck; Hercules; The Fast Painter.* His plays are characterized by bitter satire and eroticism.

Wedge, George Anson (1890-), American organist, teacher, and author who studied at the INSTITUTE OF MUSICAL ART, New York, and later taught musical theory at New York University, the CURTIS INSTITUTE OF MUSIC, and the Teachers' College at Columbia University: since 1932 he has directed the Juilliard Summer School, and from 1938 the Institute of Musical Art. His works include *Ear Training and Sight Singing* (1921); *Advanced Ear Training and Sight Singing; Keyboard Harmony; Applied Harmony* (2 books); *Rhythm in Music; The Gist of Music.*

Wedgwood, Josiah (1730-1795), celebrated English pottery maker who started his own establishment in his native city, Burslem in Staffordshire, and began the manufacture of the cream-colored pottery which created his worldwide reputation. His most notable product was known as jasper ware: he employed John FLAXMAN and other artists as designers, and made fifty replicas of the famous Portland vase in the BRITISH MUSEUM.

Weede, Robert (1903-), American operatic baritone who studied at the PEABODY INSTITUTE, Baltimore, and the EASTMAN School of Music, Rochester, where he sang with the student opera company. In 1929 he won the Caruso Memorial Foundation Award, and studied in Milan with Oscar Anselmi. After singing at Radio City Music Hall, he made his debut in 1937 at the Metropolitan Opera House spring season in *Pagliacci,* and his debut in 1941 during the regular season in *Rigoletto.* He has also appeared in concerts, recitals, and radio broadcasts.

Weenix, Jan Baptista (1621-1664), Dutch painter who studied with Abraham Bloemart, and was employed by Cardinal Pamfili at Rome: his works include *Italian Seaport; Repulse of Pirates; Dutch Lady at Her Toilet; Meeting of Jacob and Esau; Merry Company on Seashore.* His son, **Jan Weenix** (1640-1719), studied with his father, and painted architectural and genre subjects with skill: his pictures of animals and birds are highly regarded.

Weil, René, see **Coolus, Romain.**

Weill, Kurt (1900-), German composer who studied with Engelbert HUMPERDINCK and Ferruccio BUSONI: he has invented a new variety of musical play in his operas including *The Three-Penny Opera* (1928) based on Gay's BEGGAR'S OPERA; *The Protagonist; Mahogany; The Czar Shaves Himself; The Man Who Says Yes; The Royal Palace; Seven Cardinal Sins; Marie Galante:* he also wrote the incidental music to *The Eternal Road* by Franz WERFEL.

Weinberger, Jaromir (1896-), Czech composer who studied at the Prague Conservatory and with Max REGER, teaching at the Conservatory of Ithaca, N. Y., from 1922 to 1926, and settling at New York in 1939. His works include a folk opera, *Schwanda the Bagpiper* (1927) which enjoyed success throughout Europe, and was produced at the Metropolitan Opera House, New York, in 1931; a *Lincoln Symphony;* a set of orchestral variations, *Under the Spreading Chestnut Tree.*

Weinert, Albert (1863-), American sculptor born in Germany who studied at the Royal Academy, Leipzig, and at the École des Beaux-Arts, Brussels, and came to the United States in 1886, becoming a naturalized citizen in 1903. His works include architectural sculptures at the Congressional Library, Washington, D. C.; *Battle Monument* at Lake George, N. Y.; *McKinley Monument* at Toledo, O.; statue of Lord Baltimore at Baltimore, Md.; marble group in the Hall of Records, New York; decorative figures at the San Francisco Exposition in 1915.

Weingartner, Felix (1863-1942), Austrian conductor and composer who studied under W. A. Remy, and later at the Leipzig Conservatory with Carl Reinecke and Salomon JADASSOHN. He conducted at various German opera houses from 1884 and in 1908 succeeded Gustav MAHLER as conductor of the Vienna Opera. He conducted the New York Symphony Society and the BOSTON OPERA COMPANY: his works include operas, orchestra music, an orchestration of Carl Maria von WEBER'S INVITATION TO THE DANCE, and a valuable treatise on orchestral conducting.

Weinman, Adolf Alexander (1870-), American sculptor born in Germany who came to the United States as a boy, and studied at Cooper Institute and the Art Students' League: also with Philip MARTINY and Augustus SAINT-GAUDENS. His works include the statues *Rising Sun* and *Setting Sun* for the Panama-Pacific Exposition, San Francisco, in 1915; the designs for the new half-dollar and dime in 1916; sculptures for the Municipal Building and Pennsylvania Railroad Station, New York: also many statues and memorials.

Weir, Robert Walter (1803-1889), American painter who studied with John Wesley JARVIS and in Florence: in 1837 he became professor of drawing at West Point Military Academy, retaining the post for forty-two years. His works include *Landing of Hendrik Hudson; Embarkation of the Pilgrims; Virgil and Dante Crossing the Styx.* His eldest son, **John Ferguson Weir** (1841-1926), was a painter, sculptor, and author who directed the School of Fine Arts at Yale University from 1869 to 1913: his works include *Culprit Fay; Forging the Shaft; Christmas Bell; A Shimmering Landscape:* he also wrote a biography of John TRUMBULL. Another son, **Julian Alden Weir** (1852-1919), studied with his father and with Jean Léon GEROME at Paris: his works include *Good Samaritan; Portrait of a Young Girl; Dutch Peasant; Sunday Morning; Idle Hours; The Green Bodice; The Red Bridge; Portrait of a Sleeping Dog.*

Weiss, Karel (1862-1937), Czech composer who studied composition and French horn at the Prague Conservatory, and composition with Zdenko FIBICH at the Organ School: his works include *The Polish Jew* and several other operas; a symphonic poem; chamber music; piano pieces: he has also published several collections of Czech folk-songs.

Welles, Orson (1915-), American stage and screen actor and director who made his debut in 1931 at Dublin in *Jew Süss,* also appearing at the ABBEY THEATRE, and in America with Katharine Cornell in *Romeo and Juliet, Candida,* and *The Barretts of Wimpole Street.* In 1936 he directed the Negro *People's Theatre* where he produced a Negro version of *Macbeth:* in 1937 he directed the Federal Theatre Project in New York, producing *Horse Eats Hat, Dr. Faustus,* and *The Cradle Will Rock.* He also founded the Mercury Theatre in 1937, opening with a revival of *Julius Caesar* in modern dress and scenery: in October, 1938, he broadcast *The War of Two Worlds* which created a near panic. He has produced the films *Citizen Kane, The Magnificent Ambersons,* and *Journey into Fear.*

Wellesz, Egon (1885-), Austrian composer and musicologist who studied with Guido Adler at the University of Vienna; also counterpoint with Arnold SCHONBERG and composition with Bruno WALTER. His compositions include operas, ballets, orchestral works, chamber music, piano pieces, and songs: he has also written several important treatises on ancient and modern music; the latter in connection with Schönberg's compositions.

Wells, Carolyn (c.1875-1942), American anthologist and author of detective stories: her works include *At the Sign of the Sphinx* (1896); *The Jingle Book; Patty Fairfield; A Nonsense Anthology; A Parody Anthologist; A Satire Anthology; A Whimsey Anthology; The Clue; The Technique of the Mystery Story; Faulkner's Folly; Who Killed Caldwell?; Murder Will In.*

Wells, Herbert George (1866-), English novelist, historian, and scientific writer who signs his works "H. G. Wells": he studied at the Royal College of Science and the University of London. In 1895 his first book, *The Time Machine,* was published: it was followed by numerous works of varying character the most successful of which were *Love and Mr. Lewisham; Tono Bungay; Ann Veronica; The History of Mr. Polly; The New Machiavelli; The Passionate Friends; The Wife of Sir Isaac Harman; Mr. Britling Sees It Through; The Outline of History.*

Well-Tempered Clavichord, The (Bach), a work composed by Johann Sebastian BACH to test out the system of EQUAL TEMPERAMENT: it consists of twenty-four preludes and fugues in all major and minor keys, and presented in the order of chromatic ascent from the key of C major; the first part was completed in 1722 and the second in 1744. There is a Victor complete recording by Edwin Fischer made under the auspices of the Bach "48" Society. The famous *Meditation on a Prelude of Bach,* more familiarly known as *Ave Maria* by Charles Gounod, utilizes the Prelude in C major from *The Well-Tempered Clavichord* as the basis for Gounod's melody.

Wendell, Barrett (1855-1921), American professor and scholar educated at Harvard who became assistant teacher of English there in 1888 and full professor in 1908: his works include *The Duchess Emilia* (1885); *Rankell's Remains; Cotton Mather; English Composition; William Shakespeare; A Literary History of America; The Traditions of European Literature.*

Werfel, Franz (1890-), Austrian novelist and dramatist born in Bohemia: his works available in English include the plays *The Goat Song; Juarez and Maximilian; Paul Among the Jews; The Eternal Road.* His novels include *Verdi; The Man Who Conquered Death; Class Reunion; The Pascarella Family; The Forty Days of Musa Dagh; The Song of Bernadette.*

Werrenrath, Reinald (1883-), American baritone who studied with his father, Carl Dufft, and Percy Rector Stephens, making his debut at the Worcester (Mass.) Music Festival in 1907: he toured the United States, and made his debut in 1919 at the Metropolitan Opera House in *Pagliacci,* remaining until 1921. He has sung chiefly in concert and on the radio, and is the editor of two volumes of modern Scandinavian songs.

Wescott, Glenway (1901-), American novelist and poet educated at the University of Chicago who lived for several years in Europe: his works include *The Apple of the Eye* (1924); *Natives of the Rock; The Grandmothers: A Family Portrait; Fear and Trembling; A Calendar of Saints for Unbelievers; The Pilgrim Hawk.*

West, Benjamin (1738-1820), American painter who started to draw at seven, and learned to prepare colors from Cherokee Indians: in 1760 he went to Italy, studied there for three years, settled in London in 1763 and never returned to the United States. His notable works include *Agrippina Bringing Home the Ashes of Germanicus; Christ Healing the Sick; Death on the Pale Horse; Raising of Lazarus; Alexander the Great and His Physician; Revealed Religion,* a series of seven pictures; *Death of Chevalier Bayard; Penn's Treaty with the Indians; Return of the Prodigal Son; King Lear.* He found the time to paint 400 pictures and also to teach many American painters including Charles Willson PEALE, Gilbert STUART, Thomas SULLY, Washington ALLSTON, John TRUMBULL and Samuel Finley Breeze MORSE.

West, Mae (1893-), American actress and dramatist who made her debut in an American version of the Folies Bergère in 1911, and later became successful in vaudeville. Her plays including *Sex, The Drag, Pleasure Man,* and *The Constant Sinner* brought her into contact with the law, but another, *Diamond Lil,* presented a realistic picture of the famous Tenderloin section of New York City which flourished during the "gay Nineties." From 1928 she appeared in several films with remarkable success.

Westcott, Edward Noyes (1846-1898), American banker, song composer, and novelist who began to write at the age of fifty while suffering from tuberculosis. His only novel, *David Harum; a Story of American Life* (1898) was published six months after his death; it sold over 400,000 copies in two years, and was a starring vehicle on the stage for William H. CRANE for several seasons.

Westley, Helen (1879-1942), American stage and screen actress who made her New York debut in 1897 in *The Captain of the Nonsuch,* and played for some years with the Washington Square Players. She appeared in many plays before joining the Theatre Guild in 1919 and was featured in most of its important productions. Among the films in which she played from 1935 were *Captain Hurricane; Showboat; Café Metropole; Rebecca of Sunnybrook Farm; Alexander's Ragtime Band; Lillian Russell; All This and Heaven Too; Adam Had Four Sons; Sunny; My Favorite Spy.*

Westminster Abbey (London), a church in London, England, located on the site of a Saxon church built about 616 by King Sebert of Essex. The charter was issued in 1050 and the church built by Edward the Confessor: it underwent many demolitions and alterations, finally becoming largely 13th century Gothic, and the nearest to French in style of all great English churches, built in the form of a crucifix, and 531 feet long, 38 feet wide and 102 feet high. It has six chapels, and every English king since William the Conqueror, except Edward V, has been crowned there. The south transept, known as the POETS' CORNER, contains the tombs or memorials to CHAUCER, DRYDEN, BROWNING, TENNYSON, and many other famous poets.

Westminster Choir, see **Williamson, John Finley.**

Wettergren, Gertrud (1896-), Swedish contralto who studied at the Royal Academy of Music in Stockholm, and made her debut in 1922 at the Royal Opera, remaining with the company for ten years. In 1935 she appeared at the Metropolitan Opera House in *Aïda,* and also sang with the Chicago Civic Opera Company from 1936 to 1938. She has given many recitals in the United States.

Wexley, John (1902-), American actor and dramatist educated at New York University who appeared with the Civic Repertory and Yiddish Art Theatres. His plays include *The Last Mile* (1930); *Steel; They Shall Not Die.* The first was an indictment of capital punishment, the second a drama concerned with labor problems and the third a play founded on the Scottsboro Negro trial.

Weyden, Roger van der (c.1399-1464), Flemish painter who studied with Robert CAMPIN, and was also known as Roger of Bruges and Roger of Brussels: his notable works include *Descent from the Cross,* considered his masterpiece; *Altarpiece of the Magi; Altarpiece of the Virgin; Altarpiece of Christ the Redeemer;* a life-like portrait of Philip the Good; *The Virgin Nursing Christ.*

Weyman, Stanley John (1855-1928), English novelist educated at Oxford and admitted to the bar in 1881: his works include *The House of the Wolf* (1890); *A Gentleman of France; Under the Red Robe; The Red Cockade; The Castle Inn; The Abbess of Vlaye; Starvecrow Farm; The Wild Geese; Ovington's Bank; The Lively Peggy.*

Wharton, Edith Newbold (1862-1937), American novelist educated privately who lived for many years near Paris: her works include *The Valley of Decision* (1902); *The House of Mirth; The Fruit of the Tree; Ethan Frome; The Age of Innocence; A Son at the Front; The Children;*

Certain People; Ghosts; The Buccaneers; Italian Villas and Their Gardens; A Backward Glance, her autobiography.

Wheatley, Phillis (c.1753-1784), American Negro poet who was born in Africa and brought on a slave ship to the United States when she was eight years old. She became the property of a tailor, John Wheatley, in Boston, Mass., began writing poetry at thirteen after easily mastering the English language, and created a profound impression in London, England, in 1773. Her works include *Poems on Various Subjects: Religious and Moral* (1773); also several separate poems dedicated to individuals.

Whistler, James Abbott McNeill (1834-1903), American painter, etcher, lithographer, and writer who studied at the Academy of Arts, St. Petersburg, Russia, while his father was constructing a railroad there: after living with his sister in England he returned to the United States, and entered the United States Military Academy at West Point, but failed to graduate. In 1856 he went to Paris where he studied with Charles Gleyre, and became intimate with COURBET, FANTIN-LATOUR, MANET, and DEGAS. Later he settled in London and joined or at least became intimate with the PRE-RAPHAELITE BROTHERHOOD including Dante Gabriel ROSSETTI, Oscar WILDE and Algernon SWINBURNE: his notable works include *Little White Girl; Portrait of the Artist's Mother,* the painting best known to the average art lover; *Falling Rocket; Nocturne in Green and Gold; Cremorne Gardens; London at Night; Princess of the Land of Porcelain; Battersea Bridge; Thames in Ice; Valparaiso Harbor; Southampton Water; The Ocean.* His etchings number in excess of 400, and his writings include *Ten O'Clock,* an exposition of his ideas in art.

White, Clarence Cameron (1880-   ), American Negro composer and violinist who studied at the Oberlin Conservatory, and with Samuel COLERIDGE-TAYLOR in London: his works include an opera, *Ouanga* (1933), *Bandanna Sketches* for violin and piano; a *Negro Rhapsody* for orchestra: his arrangements of Negro spirituals for violin are used by many virtuosos.

White, Edwin (1817-1877), American painter who studied in Paris, Rome, Florence, and Düsseldorf, living in Europe for many years, but finally returning to New York in 1875. His notable works include *Pocahontas Informing Captain John Smith of the Indian Conspiracy; Washington Resigning His Commission; Death Bed of Luther; The Antiquary; Leonardo da Vinci and His Pupils; The Old Age of Milton.*

White, Paul (1895-   ), American composer, violinist, and conductor who studied at the New England Conservatory of Music with George W. CHADWICK, and also with Eugène YSAŸE and Eugène GOOSSENS. He has been guest conductor with several major orchestras, and associate conductor of the Rochester Civic Orchestra: his compositions include orchestral works and chamber music.

White, Stanford (1853-1906), American architect who was the son of Richard Grant White

(1821-1885), a literary critic and authority on SHAKESPEARE. After studying in Europe from 1878 to 1880, he entered into partnership with Charles Follen McKIM and William Rutherford MEAD: among the buildings in New York entirely or partially designed by him are the Herald Square Building, the Century Club, the old Tiffany Building, the Madison Square Presbyterian Church, several buildings for New York University, and the old Madison Square Garden.

White, Stewart Edward (1873-   ), American novelist educated at the University of Michigan: his works include *The Westerners* (1901); *The Claim Jumpers; The Blazed Trail; The Silent Places; Arizona Nights; The Riverman; The Grey Dawn; The Leopard Woman; Daniel Boone; The Long Rifle; Wild Geese Calling; Stampede; Dog Days,* an autobiography.

White, William Allen (1868-   ), American novelist, editor, and biographer educated at the College of Emporia and the Kansas State University who is first and foremost a journalist owning and editing the Emporia *Gazette* since 1895. His works include *In Our Town* (1906); *A Certain Rich Man; The Martial Adventures of Henry and Me; Woodrow Wilson: the Man, the Times, and His Task; Forty Years on Main St.; The Changing West.*

Whitehill,.Clarence Eugene (1871-1932), American dramatic bass who first sang in Chicago churches until he was advised by Nellie MELBA to study for an operatic career: his debut was made in 1899 at Brussels in Gounod's *Romeo and Juliet.* In 1900 .he appeared with the SAVAGE English Opera Company and in 1909 with the Metropolitan Opera Company in *Parsifal.* He also sang with the Chicago Opera Company and at BAYREUTH for several seasons.

Whiteman, Paul (1890-   ), American violinist and dance orchestra leader who began his career as a member of the Denver and later the SAN FRANCISCO SYMPHONY ORCHESTRA: in 1917-18 he conducted a United States Navy band. At the conclusion of World War I he formed a dance band playing what was known as "symphonic jazz," the arrangements made largely by Ferdinand GROFE: in 1924 he gave a concert at Aeolian Hall, New York, introducing George GERSHWIN'S RHAPSODY IN BLUE, and in 1926 toured Europe with his orchestra. His book, *Jazz,* is actually an autobiography.

Whiteside, Walker (1869-1942), American actor who made his debut in 1884 at Chicago in *Richard III*: among the plays in which he appeared are Shakespearean dramas in which he toured the United States with his own company; *Richelieu; The Lady of Lyons; The Fool's Revenge; Robert of Sicily; The Beloved Vagabond; The Melting Pot; Typhoon; Mr. Wu; The Master of Ballantrae; The Royal Box; Sakura.*

Whithorne, Emerson (1884-   ), American pianist and composer who studied with James H. Rogers, and in Europe with Theodor LESCHETIZKY and Robert Fuchs: his compositions include three symphonies; *New York Days and Nights,* an orchestral suite; *Saturday's Child* for voices and orchestra; *Sierra Morena* and other symphonic poems; *Poem* for piano and orchestra; a violin concerto; chamber music; piano pieces and songs.

Whitlock, Brand (1869-1934), American novelist and diplomat who first engaged in journalism, later becoming assistant to the Illinois Secretary of State, mayor of Toledo, Ohio, and United States Minister to Belgium during World War I. His works include *The Thirteenth District* (1902); *Her Infinite Variety; The Gold Brick; J. Hardin and Son; Uprooted; Transplanted; Big Matt; Narcissus; The Stranger on the Island.* He also wrote an autobiography and *Belgium under the German Occupation,* a record of what he saw and heard.

Whitman, Walt (1819-1892), American poet who worked as printer, carpenter, and journalist: during the Civil War he worked as an army nurse, and was later given a government clerk's position at Washington from which he was discharged in 1865 because he was the author of a book of poems, *Leaves of Grass* (1855). His works include *Drum Tap; November Boughs; Goodbye, My Fancy:* a biography, *Walt Whitman: an American,* by Henry Seidel Canby, was published in 1943.

Whitney, Gertrude Vanderbilt, contemporary American sculptor who studied with James Earle FRASER, at the ART STUDENTS' LEAGUE, New York, and with Andrew O'CONNOR in Paris: her notable works include the *Aztec Fountain* in the Pan-American Building and the *Titanic Memorial* in Washington, D. C.; war memorials in New York, the Arlington National Cemetery, and St. Nazaire, France; equestrian statue of Colonel William F. Cody (Buffalo Bill); *Arlington Fountain,* bronze; *Chinoise,* limestone. In 1931 she founded the WHITNEY MUSEUM OF AMERICAN ART which was the outgrowth of the Whitney Studio Gallery initiated in 1908.

Whitney Museum of American Art (New York), an institution founded in 1908 by Gertrude Vanderbilt WHITNEY who recognized the difficulties which faced the American artist in reaching the public, and opened two galleries in her studio building on West Eighth Street, where for many years artists of talent were invited to show their work. It was known as the Whitney Studio Gallery, and its exhibitions were attended with gratifying results. Among the artists represented were Robert HENRI, George BELLOWS, George LUKS, John SLOAN, Allen Tucker, Cecil Howard, Jo DAVIDSON, Paul MANSHIP, and James E. FRASER. So successful was this first venture that in 1914 the Whitney Studio Club was formed, with quarters on Fourth Street in an old house renovated to suit the Club's needs, with a library, a meeting room and three galleries. The membership included during its fourteen years of existence many of the leading spirits in American art. In 1928, with a membership of four hundred and a waiting list of as many more, an impasse had been reached: it was therefore decided to disband the organization, and in its stead the Whitney Studio Galleries were formed, with the purpose of providing a place where artists could show their work without cost. The Galleries existed for three years, actively engaged in the exhibiting and selling of selected pictures. At the end of this time it became evident that the purpose for which the Club and the Galleries existed had been accomplished: what was needed was a museum devoted to the exhibition and acquisition of American art. This need Mrs. Whitney met by founding the Whitney Museum of American Art, presenting as a nucleus her own collection of more than six hundred works acquired over a period of twenty-five years. Four residences at 8, 10, 12 and 14 West Eighth Street were remodeled by Noel & Miller, Architects, and converted into the Museum. Decorations throughout were done by Bruce Buttfield, and the Museum opened to the public in November, 1931. Among the several hundred sculptors and painters whose works are to be seen in the Museum are Washington ALLSTON, Paul BARTLETT, Cecelia BEAUX, Thomas BENTON, Alexander BROOK, Glenn O. COLEMAN, John S. CURRY, Jo DAVIDSON, Louis EILSHEMIUS, John B. FLANNAGAN, Emil GANSO, William J. GLACKENS, Robert HENRI, Malvina HOFFMAN, Winslow HOMER, Bernard KARFIOL, Gaston LACHAISE, John LA FARGE, Jonas LIE, George LUKS, Frederick MacMONNIES, John MARIN, Philip MARTIGNY, Reginald MARSH, Jerome MYERS, Andrew O'CONNOR, Georgia O'KEEFFE, Maurice B. PRENDERGAST, Albert P. RYDER, Augustus SAINT-GAUDENS, Charles SHEELER, John SLOAN, Eugene SPEICHER, John H. TWACHTMAN, Benjamin WEST, Gertrude Vanderbilt WHITNEY, Julian Alden WEIR, and William ZORACH.

Whittier, John Greenleaf (1807-1892), American poet whose education was slight, his knowledge being acquired largely by reading: he edited several magazines and newspapers, and was one of the leaders in the Abolitionist movement. His works include *Legends of New England in Prose and Verse* (1831); *Moll Pitcher; Lays of My Home; Songs of Labor; In War Times; Snow Bound; The Tent on the Beach; Maud Muller; At Sundown.* His most popular individual poems are "Barbara Frietchie" and "Barefoot Boy."

Whitty, Dame May (1865-), English stage and screen actress who made her debut in 1882 on the London stage in *Boccaccio;* in the sixty years which have elapsed she has appeared in innumerable plays including *A Scrap of Paper; The Ironmaster; Harbour Lights; Prince Karl* with Richard MANSFIELD; *She Stoops to Conquer; The School for Scandal; Diplomacy; The Lyons Mail; Corsican Brothers; Quality Street; Trelawney of the Wells; The Arm of the Law; The Passing of the Third Floor Back; The Last of Mrs. Cheyney; The Trial of Mary Dugan; There's Always Juliet; The Lake; The Voysey Inheritance; Night Must Fall.* She has also been featured in many films including *The Thirteenth Chair; Conquest; The Lady Vanishes; Night Must Fall; I Met My Love Again; Raffles; A Bill of Divorcement; One Night in Lisbon; Suspicion; Mrs. Miniver.*

Widdemer, Margaret (1880-), American poet and novelist: her works include *Factories* (1915), a poem denouncing child labor; *The Rose Garden Husband,* a novel; *Tree with a Bird in It,* a volume of parodies; *Gallant Lady; More than Wife; Golden Rain; Some Day I'll Find You; Lovers' Alibi; Let Me Have Wings.*

Widener Collection (National Gallery of Art), a collection of paintings, sculpture, and art objects presented by Joseph E. Widener to the United States, and opened to the public in 1942 at the National Gallery of Art, Washington, D. C. The collection, one of the first important private assemblies of sculpture and paintings in America, was begun by Peter A. Brown Widener (1834-1915), and continued by his son, Joseph E. Widener who is credited with having displayed a rare degree of discrimination in his selection of art treasures to be added to those accumulated by his father. The collection is arranged in separate units: the paintings and most of the sculpture are installed in galleries on the main floor; the tapestries, furniture, ceramics, jewels, small bronzes and other objects of various periods in galleries on the ground floor. Sculpture is found in smaller rooms on the main floor: in one of them, three busts by HOUDON, including the portrait of Voltaire, and one portrait in bronze by Jacques Saly. Another room contains works, in the round or in relief, by Antonio Rossellino, Benedetto da MAJANO, MINO DA FIESOLE and DESIDERO DA SETTIGNANO. Among the masterpieces of art, valued at $50,000,000, are the *David of the Casa Martelli* by DONATELLO; the *Feast of the Gods* by Giovanni BELLINI; the *Venus and Adonis* by TITIAN; the *Virgin with Santa Ines and Santa Tecla* and *St. Martin and the Beggar* by El GRECO; the small *Cowper Madonna* by RAPHAEL; the *Judith and Holofernes* by MANTEGNA; the *Youthful David* by Andrea del CASTAGNO; the *Saint Anne Altarpiece* by Gerard DAVID; the *Marchesa Elena Grimaldi* by VAN DYCK; the *Woman Weighing Gold* by VERMEER; *The Windmill* by REMBRANDT; *The Hoppner Children* by John HOPPNER; the *Keelmen Heaving in Coals by Moonlight* by TURNER; the *Portrait of Mrs. Methuen* by GAINSBOROUGH. The objects of art include small bronzes, Renaissance Limoges enamels, rock crystals, jewels, a large group of majolica pieces, examples of Henri II ware, Medici ware, armor, plaques and medals, Renaissance furniture, Eighteenth century French furniture, French decorative objects of the same period, together with tapestries, rugs, and velvets.

Widor, Charles Marie (1844-1937), French organist and composer who studied with Joseph FETIS and Jacques Lemmens, becoming organist at St. Sulpice in Paris from 1869 to 1933 when he retired: his works include four symphonies, chamber music, and many organ compositions including the famous *Ten Symphonies* which are unique in organ literature. He also edited a complete edition of Johann Sebastian BACH's works with his pupil, Albert Schweitzer.

Wieck, Friedrich (1785-1873), German pianist and teacher who instructed his daughter, Clara Wieck, Robert SCHUMANN, Hans von BULOW and many other famous pianists. He is probably best remembered by his refusal to permit the marriage of his daughter to Robert Schumann who was forced to make the matter a court issue in order to finally win Clara SCHUMANN for his bride.

Wieland, Christopf Martin (1733-1813), German poet and author who studied at the University of Tübingen: his works include a philosophical poem, *The Nature of Things* (1751); a novel, *Agathon;* a narrative poem, *The New Amadis;* a satirical romance, *The Abderites,* and the epic poem, *Oberon* which is considered his masterpiece.

Wieniawski, Henri (1835-1880), Polish violinist and composer who studied with Joseph MASSART at the Paris Conservatory and toured Europe with his brother, **Joseph Wieniawski** (1837-1912). He toured the United States with Anton RUBINSTEIN, and succeeded Henri VIEUXTEMPS as professor of violin at the Brussels Conservatory. His compositions, which are still in the modern repertory, include two concertos and many fine solo pieces for the violin.

Wier, Albert Ernest (1879-), American violinist, composer, editor, and author of books on music and art educated at Harvard University under John K. PAINE, and trained in music at the NEW ENGLAND CONSERVATORY OF MUSIC under George W. CHADWICK: his compositions include *Bagatelles* for violin and piano; *Album Leaves* for violin and piano; many songs. He has edited the *Whole World Music Series;* the *Master Composer Series; The Master Music Series;* the *Pianist's Music Shelf; The Violinist's Music Shelf; The Ideal Home Music Library; The Radio Music Library; Young America's Music Library; The Book of a Thousand Songs; Masterpieces of Piano Music; The Child's Own Music Book; The Longman's Series of Chamber Music Scores:* he has also written *What Do You Know about Music?; The Piano: Its History, Makers, Players and Music; Thesaurus of the Arts.* He is also the inventor of the ARROW SYSTEM OF SCORE READING.

Wiertz, Antoine Joseph (1806-1865), Belgian painter who studied at the Antwerp Academy with Mattheus van BREE and later at the LOUVRE. In 1850 the Brussels Government built a large studio for him known as the Musée Wiertz which housed all his great works including *Greeks and Trojans Contending for the Body of Patroclus; Carnival at Rome; The Triumph of Christ; Revolt of Hell Against Heaven; Hunger, Folly, and Crime; Flight into Egypt; Sleep of the Virgin; The Orphans; A Second after Death.*

Wiggin, Kate Douglas (1856-1923), American novelist and author of juvenile stories who was the organizer and teacher of the first free kindergartens on the Pacific Coast: her works include *The Story of Patsy* (1883); *The Birds' Christmas Carol; Timothy's Quest; Rebecca of Sunnybrook Farm; Penelope's Progress; New Chronicles of Rebecca; Mother Carey's Chickens; The Story of Waitstill Baxter; My Garden of Memory,* an autobiography.

Wiggins, Carleton (1848-1932), American painter who studied at the National Academy, New York, and in France: his works include *Edge of the Forest at Barbizon; A Young Holstein Bull; October Morning; Gathering Seawood; Summer Morning; The Plow Horse; Evening after a Shower.* His son, **Guy Carleton Wiggins** (1883-), has specialized as a painter of scenes in New York such as *Metropolitan Tower* and *Columbus Circle in Winter.*

Wigman, Mary (1886-   ), German dancer who studied with Émile JAQUES-DALCROZE, introducing her individualistic style of dancing in 1919, and organizing a group in 1923 with which she appeared throughout Europe, and in the United States in 1930. Her interpretations, involving extraordinary postures and total departure from accepted methods, have been widely imitated.

Wijnants, Jan, see **Wynants, Jan.**

Wilcox, Ella Wheeler (1855-1919), American poet and journalist who was on the staff of the Hearst newspapers, and also contributed verses to magazines: her works include *Drops of Water* (1872); *Poems of Passion; Poems of Pleasure; The Story of a Literary Career.* She was the author of the often-quoted lines, "Laugh and the world laughs with you."

Wilcoxon, Henry (1905-   ), English stage and screen actor born in the British West Indies who first traveled as a salesman and made his debut in 1925 at London in *The Hundredth Chance,* later joining the Birmingham Repertory Company and appearing in nearly 80 parts. Since 1933 he has been featured in many films including *Cleopatra; The Crusades; The Last of the Mohicans; Jericho; If I Were King; That Hamilton Woman; Mrs. Miniver.*

Wilde, Oscar (1856-1900), Irish poet and dramatist educated at Oxford who had a brilliant academic career, and became the leading spirit in a group of aesthetes which afforded the columnists and caricaturists of the day unlimited opportunities for satire. His plays include *Lady Windermere's Fan* (1892); *A Woman of No Importance; An Ideal Husband; The Importance of Being Earnest; Salome,* the last-named banned in England, but produced by Sarah BERNHARDT. He also wrote a novel, *The Picture of Dorian Gray;* a poem, *The Ballad of Reading Gaol,* and *De Profundis,* an apology for his life.

Wilde, Percival (1887-   ), American author and dramatist educated at Columbia University and later connected with the book review department of the New York *Times* and the New York *Post.* His novels include *Rogues in Clover* (1929); *The Devil's Booth; Mystery Week End; Inquest; Design for Murder:* he has also written many plays especially in one-act form, and a book, *The Craftsmanship of a One-Act Play.*

Wildenbruch, Ernst von (1845-1909), German dramatist and novelist who traveled extensively as a boy and later became attached to the German Foreign Office: his plays include *Heinrich IV* (1895) considered his masterpiece; *Fathers and Sons; The New Man; Christopher Marlowe.* He also wrote a successful novel, *The Master of Tanagra,* and many of his poems such as *The Witches' Song* were popular in his day.

Wilder, Thornton Niven (1897-   ), American novelist and dramatist educated as a child in China, and in the United States at Oberlin and Yale Universities, also serving in World War I: his plays include *The Trumpet Shall Sound; Our Town,* winner of the Pulitzer Prize; *The Merchant of Yonkers; The Long Christmas Dinner;*

The Skin of Our Teeth, a Pulitzer prize winner in 1943. He has written the novels *Cabala* (1925) and *The Bridge of San Luis Rey,* also a Pulitzer Prize winner.

Wilhelmj, August (1845-1908), German violinist who studied at the Leipzig Conservatory with Ferdinand DAVID, Moritz HAUPTMANN, and Hans RICHTER, and later with Joachim RAFF. He toured the world for many years, appeared in the United States in 1878, and became professor of violin at the Guildhall School, London. His works include *A Modern School for the Violin,* and a special transcription of the Paganini *Concerto in D major.*

Wilkie, Sir David (1785-1841), Scottish painter who studied at the Edinburgh School of Art at fourteen and exhibited a picture, *The Village Politicians* at London when he was twenty: his notable works include *The Blind Fiddler; The Cut Finger; Village Fête; The Reading of the Will; Rent Day; Queen Victoria's First Council; John Knox Preaching Before the Lords of the Congregation; Scottish Toilet; The Rabbit on the Wall.*

Wilkins, Mary Eleanor, see **Freeman, Mary Eleanor Wilkins.**

Wilkinson, Marguerite (1883-1928), American poet born in Nova Scotia and educated at Northwestern University: her works include *In Vivid Gardens* (1911); *By a Western Wayside; The Passing of Mars; Bluestone; The Great Dream; The Way of the Makers; Yule Fire; The Citadels; Contemporary Poetry.*

Willaert, Adrian (c.1480-1562), Flemish composer who became chapel master in 1527 at St. Mark's in Venice, and founded a music school there at which many distinguished musicians studied. He was one of the first composers of the MADRIGAL and the RICERCAR, and the first to write for two choirs, there being two organs and two choirs at St. Mark's.

Willard, Edward Smith (1853-1915), English actor who made his debut in 1869 at Weymouth in *The Lady of Lyons,* later toured with Edward H. SOTHERN, and appeared with stock companies before joining William Barrett's Company at the Princess Theatre, London, in 1881 where he created the role of "The Spider" in *The Silver King.* He was highly successful in *The Middleman* and *The Professor's Love Story* in both of which he appeared in the United States and in England: after 1903 he played only in America.

Willet, Anna Lee (1867-1943), American designer of stained glass windows who worked with her husband, William Willet, a leader of the renaissance in stained glass designing in the United States. After his death in 1891 she designed windows for the chapel of the United States Military Academy, Princeton University Graduate College, and many other institutions and churches. Her son, **Henry Lee Willet** (1899-   ) is also a stained glass designer educated at Princeton University and student of art in Europe: he has created many fine windows for churches throughout the United States.

Williams, Ben Ames (1889-), American novelist and short-story writer: more than 400 of his stories have appeared in magazines including the *Saturday Evening Post* and *Collier's*. His novels include *All the Brothers were Valiant* (1919); *The Sea Bride; Audacity; Touchstone; Pascal's Mill; Crucible; Come Spring; The Strange Woman; Time of Peace.*

Williams, Blanche Colton (1879-), American teacher and author educated at the Mississippi State College for Women who has taught English at Columbia Teachers' College and Hunter College: her works include *A Handbook on Story Writing* (1917); *Our Short Story Writers; Studying the Short Story; A Book of Essays; The Mystery and the Detective; Forever Young: A Life of John Keats.*

Williams, Emlyn (1905-), Welsh actor and dramatist educated at Oxford who presented his first play, *Full Moon,* with the Oxford Dramatic Society: among his successful plays are *A Murder Has Been Arranged* (1930); *Night Must Fall; The Late Christopher Bean,* adapted from the French of René Fauchois for the English stage; *The Corn is Green:* he has also written several film scenarios including *The Girl in the News.*

Williams, Jesse Lynch (1871-1929), American novelist and dramatist educated at Princeton University who first worked as a reporter on the New York *Sun:* his works include *Princeton Stories* (1895); *Why Marry?,* a play which received the Pulitzer Prize in 1918; *Why Not?,* a play produced in 1922; *The Stolen Story; Not Wanted; A Day Dreamer,* a story of newspaper life.

Williamson, John Finley (1887-), American conductor educated at Otterbein College, and student of singing with Herbert WITHERSPOON and David BISPHAM. He founded the Westminster Choir of 40 voices in 1921 and the Westminster Choir School at Princeton University in 1926. He has directed more than 800 concerts in the United States and has taken the Choir on two tours of Europe.

"William Tell" Overture (Rossini), the prelude to a grand opera in four acts by Gioacchino ROSSINI; the libretto by Etienne de Jouy and Hippolyte de Bis founded on the drama by Friedrich von SCHILLER; first produced at the Paris Opéra in 1829, and at the Metropolitan Opera House, New York, in 1884. The overture, one of the most popular works in the orchestral concert repertory, is in four parts: *The Dawn, The Storm, The Calm, Finale,* and is designed to furnish the preliminary atmosphere for the drama. After the lovely melody for the violoncellos in the opening Andante, mutterings are heard of a storm which finally breaks with terrific intensity; when the tempest dies away, delicate passages in the flute suggest birds stirring in the trees, and a lovely pastoral melody follows for the ENGLISH HORN, originally assigned by the composer to an obsolete type of oboe known as the *oboe di caccia.* As this melody dies away, trumpet calls introduce the stimulating quick-step movement, suggesting the revolutionary character of the plot, which provides the overture with an extraordinarily brilliant and stirring finish. There is a Columbia recording by the London Philharmonic Orchestra directed by Sir Thomas Beecham, and a Victor recording by the NBC Symphony Orchestra under Arturo Toscanini.

Willis, Nathaniel Parker (1806-1867), American poet and dramatist educated at Yale University who traveled extensively in Europe: his plays include *Bianca Visconti* (1837); *The Kentucky Heiress; The Betrothal; Imei the Jew; Tortesa the Usurer,* the latter produced by James WALLACK. He also established the *American Monthly Magazine* which later became the New York *Mirror,* and wrote essays, poems, and travel sketches.

Wilson, Francis (1854-1935), American actor and dramatist who first appeared with a minstrel company, made his stage debut in 1887 at Philadelphia in *London Assurance,* and became principal comedian with the McCaull Opera Company at the Casino, New York, where he created the role of Cadeaux in *Erminie.* He then organized his own company, playing in *The Merry Monarch; Erminie; The Little Corporal; Cyrano de Bergerac.* He also appeared in many plays including *The Mountain Climber; When Knights Were Bold; The Bachelor's Baby; The Rivals; The School for Scandal; She Stoops to Conquer; Rip van Winkle.* His plays include *The Bachelor's Baby; The Magic Ring; The Spiritualist; The Dancing Master:* he also wrote *The Eugene Field I Knew; Joseph Jefferson; Edwin Booth; Francis Wilson's Life of Himself.*

Wilson, Harry Leon (1867-1939), American novelist, humorist, and dramatist who joined the staff of *Puck* in 1892 and became editor in 1896: his works include *Zig Zag Tales* (1896): *The Spenders; The Man from Home* (1905), a play with Booth TARKINGTON; *The Boss of Little Arcady; Bunker Bean; Ruggles of Red Gap,* and *Merton of the Movies,* three novels which were dramatized and filmed.

Wilson, Margaret (1882-), American novelist educated at the University of Chicago: her works include *The Able McLaughlins* (1923) which won the Pulitzer Prize in 1924; *The Kenworthys; Daughters of India; Trousers of Taffeta; The Law and the McLaughlins; The Devon Treasure Mystery.*

Wilson, Richard (1714-1792), English painter who first painted portraits and later studied at Venice with Francesco ZUCCARELLI, and also became friends with Claude Joseph VERNET and CLAUDE LORRAIN. His notable works, which were little appreciated in his day because of the popularity of Thomas GAINSBOROUGH, include *Niobe; Villa of Maecenas at Tivoli; Lake Avernus; On the River Wye; Apollo and the Seasons; Italian Landscape.*

Wiman, Dwight Deere (1895-), American theatrical producer educated at Yale University: his notable productions since 1927 include *Women Go On Forever; The Road to Rome; The Command to Love; The Queen's Husband; A Most*

Immoral Lady; First Little Show; The Vinegar Tree; The Gay Divorcee; The Distaff Side; On Your Toes; Babes in Arms; Great Lady; On Borrowed Time; I Married an Angel; Stars in Your Eyes; Morning's at Seven; The Damask Cheek; By Jupiter.

Wind Instruments, see **Musical Instruments.**

Winninger, Charles (1884-), American stage and screen actor who has been on the stage since he was five years old, appearing first with circuses and in vaudeville: in 1900 he played on Captain Adams' *Cotton Blossoms Showboat* and made his debut in 1910 on the New York stage in *The Yankee Girl,* appearing later in many plays and musical productions including *Show Boat* in 1927. Since 1936 he has been featured in numerous films including *Show Boat; Three Smart Girls; Café Metropole; You Can't Have Everything; Destry Rides Again; Babes in Arms; Barricade; My Love Came Back; Little Nellie Kelly; Ziegfeld Girl; My Life with Caroline; Friendly Enemies.*

Winter, John Strange, pseudonym of **Mrs. Henrietta Eliza Vaughn Stannard** (1856-1911), English novelist who also wrote under the pen name "Violet Whyte": in 1885 two of her stories, *Bootle's Baby* and *Houp-la* which appeared in *The Graphic* established her reputation, and she wrote about sixty amusing stories many of which deal with army life.

Winter, William (1836-1917), American dramatic critic, poet, and biographer educated at Harvard University who became critic of the New York *Tribune* from 1865 to 1909, and was regarded for more than thirty years as the foremost American dramatic critic: his works include *The Convent and Other Poems* (1854); *The Queen's Domain; Shakespeare's England; Grey Days and Gold; Old Shrines and Ivy; Old Friends and Vagrant Memories.* He also wrote biographies of Sir Henry IRVING, Mary ANDERSON, Edwin BOOTH, Joseph JEFFERSON, Richard MANSFIELD, and David BELASCO.

Winterhalter, Franz Xaver (1806-1873), German painter who studied at the Munich Academy, and became a distinguished portraitist at Karlsruhe where he was made court painter: his notable works include portraits of Madame Rimsky-Korsakow, Queen Victoria, The Empress of Russia, Napoleon III, Empress Eugénie, Louis Philippe and his Queen, Queen Isabella of Spain, and King Leopold of Belgium with his Queen.

Winther, Christian (1796-1876), Danish poet who studied at the University of Copenhagen, supported himself as a tutor and in 1841 instructed the Princess Caroline of Mecklenburg in the Danish language when she became betrothed to the Crown Prince of Denmark. His works include *Song and Legend* (1841); *Lyrical Poems; The Flight of the Hart,* a lyrical romance of the Middle Ages in Denmark, and considered his finest work.

Wise, Thomas Alfred (1865-1928), American actor brought to the United States as a child who earned his living after he was nine. He made his debut as an actor in 1883, and was starred in *A*

Gentleman from Mississippi in 1903 with Douglas FAIRBANKS, SR., in the cast: among the plays in which he appeared were *Mr. Wilkinson's Widows; Gloriana; The Prince Chap; Are You a Mason?; Vivian's Papas; Mrs. Templeton's Telegram; Miss Hook of Holland; The Little Cherub; Lights o' London.*

Wister, Owen (1860-1938), American novelist educated at Harvard University who developed considerable musical ability, and was credited with "pronounced talent" by Franz LISZT: he studied law and was admitted to the bar, practicing for two years. His works include *The Dragon of Wantley* (1892); *The Virginian* which sold more than a million copies, was staged with Dustin FARNUM as star, and filmed three times. His other novels, such as *Lady Baltimore* and *A Straight Deal* did not approach "The Virginian" in popular appeal.

Witherspoon, Herbert (1873-1935), American operatic and concert bass educated at Yale University who studied music with Horatio W. PARKER, Edward MACDOWELL, Jean Baptiste FAURE and Giovanni Baptista Lamperti. He made his operatic debut in 1898 with the Castle Square Opera Company in *Aïda,* and sang for several years in concert and oratorio; from 1908 to 1916 he sang Wagnerian roles at the Metropolitan Opera House, New York. In 1925 he became president of the Chicago Musical College, in 1930 artistic director of the Chicago Civic Opera, and in 1931 president of the Cincinnati Conservatory of Music. He was appointed general manager of the Metropolitan Opera House in 1935, but died before he could assume the post.

Wodehouse, Pelham Grenville (1881-), English author and dramatist who acted as dramatic editor of *Vanity Fair:* his plays, usually written in collaboration, include *A Thief for a Night; Have a Heart; Sitting Pretty; Oh, Kay; The Play's the Thing,* adapted from Ferenc MOLNAR; *Her Cardboard Lover,* adapted from the French; he has also written many short stories and serials introducing the characters *Psmith, Jeeves,* and *Bertie Wooster.*

Woden, in German mythology the god known as *Odin* in Norse legend, changed to WOTAN by Richard Wagner in *The* RING OF THE NIBELUNGS: his wife was Frigga, changed to FRICKA by Wagner.

Woffington, Peg (1718-1760), Irish actress whose real name was Margaret Woffington: she first appeared at ten as Polly Peachum in a juvenile production of Gay's *Beggar's Opera;* in 1740 her success in the role of Sir Harry Wildair in *The Constant Couple* led to her engagement as leading lady with David GARRICK with whom she appeared from 1742 to 1748. She was equally at home in feminine roles or in "breeches" parts, and was the idol of London until her retirement in 1757 because of ill health.

Wohlgemut or **Wolgemut, Michael** (1434-1519), German painter who is famous chiefly as the teacher of Albrecht DURER: it is probable that his paintings are unequal in merit because he permitted his numerous pupils to work with him on them. They include *Christ before Pilate; Death of the Virgin; Christ on the Mount of Olives; The Three Magi; Portrait of an Old Man in a Felt Hat; Departure of the Apostles; Crucifixion; Marriage of St. Catherine.*

Wohltemperierte Clavier, Das (Bach), see **Well-Tempered Clavichord, The (Bach).**

Woizikovsky, Leon (1897-   ), Polish dancer who studied at the Warsaw Ballet School, joined the DIAGHILEFF Ballet in 1915 remaining with the company until 1929. He was also a leading dancer with Colonel de Basil's Ballet Russe de Monte Carlo, and has danced with great success in *The Sleeping Princess; The Good-Humored Ladies; Thamar; Three-Cornered Hat; The Gods Go A-Begging; Petrouchka; Prince Igor.*

Wolf, Hugo (1860-1903), Austrian composer who studied at the Vienna Conservatory, but was chiefly self-taught: his career was singularly uneventful but his contribution to song literature is ranked with those of Franz SCHUBERT and Johannes BRAHMS. His compositions include more than 500 songs, a string quartet, choral works, and an opera *Der Corregidor* produced at Mannheim in 1896.

Wolf-Ferrari, Ermanno (1876-   ), Italian operatic composer who studied with Joseph RHEINBERGER and for a few years directed the Liceo Benedetto Marcello at Venice, but gave most of his time to supervising the production of his operas four of which, *The Secret of Suzanne; The Curious Women; The Jewels of the Madonna,* and *L'Amore medico* have been successfully produced in the United States.

Wolfe, Thomas (1900-1938), American novelist educated at the University of North Carolina, and trained in dramatic composition at the 47 Workshop under George Pierce BAKER at Harvard University. His works include *The Return of Buck Gavin,* a play produced in 1919; *Look Homeward; Angel; Of Time and the River; From Death to Morning; The Story of a Novel; The Web and the Rock; You Can't Go Home Again; The Hills Beyond.*

Wolff, Albert Louis (1884-   ), French composer and conductor who studied at the Paris Conservatory, and later conducted at the Opéra-Comique and the Metropolitan Opera House where his opera, *The Blue Bird,* was produced in 1919. He has also conducted the LAMOUREUX and the PASDELOUP Concerts.

Wolfram von Eschenbach (c.1170-c.1220), German poet who is regarded as the greatest author of epic poetry of medieval Germany: he was of noble birth and spent much of his time at the court of the landgrave Hermann of Thuringia. His greatest work is *Parzival,* based on a poem by CHRETIEN DE TROYES, and an outstanding epic of chivalry. Richard WAGNER introduces him as a character in *Tannhäuser.*

Wolheim, Louis (1881-1933), American stage and screen actor educated at Cornell University who first appeared in 1919 in *The Jest* with Lionel and John Barrymore, also playing in *Sherlock Holmes; The Hairy Ape,* and *What Price Glory?.* Among the films in which he was featured were *Two Arabian Nights; The Racket; All Quiet on the Western Front; Little Old New York; The Tempest* with John Barrymore; *Sorrell and Son.*

Wollstonecraft, Mary, see **Shelley, Percy Bysshe.**

Wolsey, Thomas, Cardinal (1471-1530), English statesman and cardinal educated at Magdalen College, Oxford, where he later founded Christ College: he became cardinal and prime minister to HENRY VIII in 1515. He incurred the enmity of the king by his conduct in connection with the latter's divorces, and was arrested on charges of treason in 1530, but died before he could be tried. He has been treated from the literary standpoint in Samuel Johnson's poem *The Vanity of Human Wishes* and in Shakespeare's *Henry VIII:* he has also been a favorite subject for painters.

Wong, Anna May (1907-   ), American screen actress born in Los Angeles of Chinese parents: her first film appearance was in *The Chinese Parrot* in 1922, and she has also played on the legitimate stage in London and New York. Among the films in which she has appeared are *Old San Francisco; Across to Singapore; Daughter of the Dragon; Shanghai Express; A Study in Scarlet; Java Head; A Daughter of Shanghai; Island of Lost Men; Ellery Queen's Penthouse Mystery.*

Wood, Clement (1888-   ), American poet and editor educated at the University of Alabama and at Yale University: his works comprise several volumes of poetry including *Glad of Earth* (1917); *The Earth Turns South; The White Peacock:* books about poetry and poets including *The Craft of Poetry; Poets of America; The Complete Rhyming Dictionary and Poet's Craft Book:* also many miscellaneous volumes on a variety of subjects.

Wood, Grant (1892-1942), American painter who was first a worker in metal and handmade jewelry, and served in World War I during which he took a special course in CAMOUFLAGE: after the war he studied in Paris, but decided that art in America should emanate from the land and the people. His works include *American Gothic;* mural paintings at the Iowa State College; *Daughters of the Revolution,* a satirical canvas which aroused much comment; *Dinner for Threshers; Fall Plowing.*

Wood, Sir Henry (1869-   ), English composer and conductor who studied at the Royal Academy of Music, London, with Ebenezer PROUT, and later became famous as conductor of the Queen's Hall Promenade Concerts which began in 1895, and the Saturday Afternoon Symphony Concerts from 1897. He has conducted the major orchestras in Europe and the United States: in 1918 he declined the directorship of the Boston Symphony Orchestra. His compositions include operettas, an oratorio and church music.

Wood, Mrs. Henry Ellen (1814-1887), English novelist who first wrote a temperance story, *Danesbury House*, in 1860, and her greatest success, *East Lynne* in 1861: the latter was dramatized, translated into several languages, and also filmed. Her works include 35 novels none of which attained the same degree of success: her finest work from the literary point of view was done in the *Johnny Ludlow* stories published anonymously in the *Argosy Magazine* which she purchased in 1867.

Wood, Peggy (1894-), American stage and screen actress who made her debut in 1910 on the New York stage in *Naughty Marietta:* among the plays and musical comedies in which she appeared are *The Lady of the Slipper; Mlle. Modiste; The Madcap Duchess; The Firefly; Buddies; The Clinging Vine; Candida; The Merchant of Venice; Bitter Sweet; The Cat and the Fiddle; To-Night or Never; Champagne Sec; The Countess Maritza; Everyman; Blithe Spirit:* she has also appeared in several films including *Handy Andy; Call It a Day; A Star is Born; The Housekeeper's Daughter.*

Wood, Thomas Waterman (1823-1903), American painter who studied with Chester HARDING and in France, Italy, and Switzerland: his works include *Contraband; Every Man His Own Doctor; Quack Doctor; War Episodes,* a triple painting in one frame; *Sunday Morning; The Jack-o'-Lantern; Uncle Ned and I; Poor White; First Business Venture; Strictly Confidential; Neglecting Trade.*

Woodberry, George Edward (1855-1930), American poet, editor, and critic who taught English at Nebraska State University and at Columbia University. His works include *The North Shore Watch and Other Poems* (1890); *Wild Eden; Ideal Passion:* also lives of Edgar Allan POE, Nathaniel HAWTHORNE, Ralph Waldo EMERSON, and Algernon SWINBURNE, and edited the *Columbia University Studies in Comparative Literature.* His critical works include *Great Writers* and *America in Literature.*

Woodcut, an engraving on wood first used by the Chinese in printing books, and by the Egyptians and Babylonians in stamping designs on bricks. The Germans used it in the 14th century for printing playing cards, and GUTENBERG employed woodcuts in connection with his movable type: mechanical processes have now rendered the art of wood engraving obsolete.

Wooden Horse, see **Trojan War.**

Woods, Al (1870-), American theatrical producer whose record as a showman includes the production of sensational melodramas to some of the best serious plays: in 1902 he started producing such melodramas as *The Queen of the White Slaves* and *The Great Express Robbery;* from there he turned to risqué farces such as *The Girl from Rector's* and *Up in Mabel's Room;* these were followed by the amusing business plays *Potash and Perlmutter* and *Abe and Mawruss.* Among the finer productions he has sponsored are *The Yellow Ticket; Common Clay; Within*

the Law; Roads of Destiny; East of Suez; The Shanghai Gesture; The Green Hat; Mozart; The Trial of Mary Dugan; A Farewell to Arms: he is credited with having produced 404 plays during a period of forty years.

Wood-wind Instruments, see **Musical Instruments.**

Woodworth, Samuel (1785-1842), American poet and journalist who edited *The War,* a weekly periodical during the War of 1812, and also a romantic history of the war entitled *The Champions of Freedom.* He also founded the New York *Mirror* in 1823 with George Morris: his most famous poem is "The Old Oaken Bucket."

Woolf, Virginia (1882-1941), English novelist who first attracted attention with her novel, *The Voyage Out* (1915): her works include *Night and Day; Jacob's Room; Mrs. Dalloway; To the Lighthouse; Orlando; Beau Brummel; The Years; Between the Acts; The Death of the Moth and Other Essays: Flush,* the story of the cocker spaniel owned by Elizabeth BROWNING.

Woollcott, Alexander (1887-1943), American journalist and essayist educated at Hamilton College who first worked on the New York *Times* as a reporter, later appointed dramatic critic until he enlisted in the Army for World War I serving first with the Medical Corps and then transferred to *The Stars and Stripes,* the AEF newspaper which he helped to found. After the war, he was for a time on the New York *Herald* and eventually on the New York *World* where he remained until 1928. He wrote a column, "Shouts and Murmurs," for the *New Yorker* for several years. He made his first radio appearance as the Town Crier in 1929 and he continued the program until 1939. His works include *Mrs. Fiske* (1917); *Shouts and Murmurs; Mr. Dickens Goes to the Play; Enchanted Isles; While Rome Burns;* he also edited *The Woollcott Reader; The Woollcott Second Reader; As You Were,* a portable library of prose and poetry assembled for the members of the Armed Forces in World War II. He also appeared on the stage in *Brief Moment; Wine of Chance* and *The Man Who Came to Dinner.*

Woolley, Monte (1888-), American stage and screen actor and producer educated at Yale University where he directed the Yale Dramatic Society, later acting in *On Your Toes* and *The Man Who Came to Dinner.* He directed the stage productions of *Fifty Million Frenchmen, Walk a Little Faster* and *Champagne Sec,* and has also appeared in numerous films including *Lord Jeff; Man About Town; The Man Who Came to Dinner; The Pied Piper; To-Night at 8:30; Holy Matrimony.*

Woolner, Thomas (1825-1892), English sculptor and poet who studied at the Royal Academy and became one of the PRE-RAPHAELITE group in 1848: his works include *Eleanor Sucking Poison from the Wound of Prince Edward; The Death of Boadicea; Alastor; Feeding the Hungry; Puck; Euphrosyne; The Rainbow; Elaine with the Shield of Lancelot; Godiva; Ophelia; Water Lily;*

Mercury Teaching a Shepherd To Sing. He also executed many statues and busts of distinguished contemporaries including TENNYSON, CARLYLE, DICKENS and KINGSLEY: his most famous poem is "My Beautiful Lady."

Wordsworth, William (1770-1850), English poet who became poet laureate in 1843: he resided in the Westmoreland and Cumberland lake district, and was known with Samuel Taylor Coleridge and Robert Southey as one of the "Lake Poets." His works include *An Evening Walk* (1793); *Lyrical Ballads; The Excursion; The White Doe of Rylstone; Thanksgiving Ode; Peter Bell; The Waggoner; Yarrow Revisited.*

Wormser, André Alphonse Toussaint (1851-1926), French composer who studied with Antoine François MARMONTEL at the Paris Conservatory, and achieved great success with a pantomime *L'Enfant Prodigue* produced at Paris in 1890. His compositions include two operas, a ballet, two symphonic poems, *Suite Tzigane* for violin and orchestra, piano pieces, and songs.

Wotan, the principal character in Richard Wagner's cycle of music dramas, *The* RING OF THE NIBELUNGS: he is the god who rules over VALHALLA, and brings on the final destruction of the gods in the last of the dramas, *Dusk of the Gods.*

Wotan's Farewell, see **"Magic Fire" Music.**

Wouwerman, Philip (1619-1668), Dutch painter who studied with his father and with Jan WYNANTS: his more than 800 pictures include *Interior of a Stable; The Halt; Farmer Attacked by Robbers; Cavalry Skirmish; Cavaliers; Pilgrims; Horseman with Hounds; Stag Hunt; Soldiers Plundering; Riding School.* There seems but little doubt that he was assisted by his brothers, **Jan** (1629-1666) and **Pieter** (1626-1683) because of the great number of his canvases.

Wozzeck, grand opera in three acts and fifteen scenes: libretto by Allan BERG based on a drama with the same title by George BUCHNER; music by Allan Berg; first produced at Berlin in 1925 and by the Philadelphia Opera Company at the Metropolitan Opera House, New York, in 1931. The fifteen scenes are each a definite musical composite: Act I—Suite; Act II—Symphony; Act III—Variations. The voices are required to speak, declaim, and sing: the demands on the singers are extremely exacting.

Wren, Sir Christopher (1632-1723), English architect who also studied mathematics and astronomy, becoming professor of the latter science at Gresham College and at Oxford. He became interested in architecture after the Great Fire of London in 1666, and prepared a comprehensive plan for the rebuilding of the city which was not adopted. His notable works include ST. PAUL'S CATHEDRAL; more than fifty churches including St. Stephen and St. Martin; the towers of WESTMINSTER ABBEY; the garden façade of Hampton Court: also many buildings at Oxford and Cambridge Universities.

Wright, Frank Lloyd (1869-), American architect who studied engineering at the University of Wisconsin, and after working with other architects opened his own office in 1894: among his notable creations are the Administration Building of the Larkin Soap Company, Buffalo, N. Y.; Unity Temple at Oak Park, Illinois; Imperial Hotel at Tokyo, Japan; the Midway Gardens at Chicago. His ideas regarding architecture are fully revealed in *An Autobiography,* published in 1943.

Wright, Harold Bell (1872-), American novelist whose education was confined to a period of two years in the preparatory department of Hiram College: his novels include *That Printer of Udell's* (1903); *The Shepherd of the Hills; The Calling of Dan Mathews; The Winning of Barbara Worth; The Eyes of the World; When a Man's a Man; Helen of the Old House; The Mine with the Iron Door.* Several of his novels were phenomenal best sellers, and were adapted for the screen.

Wright, Patience Lovell (1725-1785), American sculptor who was the first American on record to practice the art. She specialized in small portrait heads in wax: after settling in London in 1772 she modeled heads of the royal family and other notables. Her portrait bust of Thomas Penn is in Independence Hall, Philadelphia. Her son, **Joseph Wright** (1756-1793), who worked in London, became a distinguished portrait painter who executed the likenesses of General and Mrs. Washington and other American persons of importance.

Wright, Willard Huntington (1888-1939), American art critic, editor, and writer of detective fiction under the pen name "S. S. Van Dine": he was educated at St. Vincent and Pomona Colleges in California and at Harvard University, later becoming literary critic of the Los Angeles *Times,* and also of *Town Topics* and the *Smart Set.* Works written under his own name include *Modern Painting: Its Tendency and Meaning; The Creative Will; The Great French Stories; The Future of Painting; The Great Detective Stories.* His numerous detective novels published as "S. S. Van Dine" began with *The Benson Murder Case* in 1926, and ended with *The Winter Murder Case* issued posthumously in 1939.

Wu Ch'êng-ên (c.1500-1580), Chinese poet, novelist, and short-story writer educated in the classic tradition, and author of poetry and prose in the approved classical style. His novel, *Monkey (Hsi Yu Ki)* is his masterpiece: it was published anonymously during the latter years of his life, and is written in the language of the street and market-place. It was published in English in 1943 by the John Day Company.

Wurdemann, Audrey (1911-), American poet educated at the University of Washington who traveled extensively in the United States and the Orient, and married Joseph AUSLANDER: her works include *Bright Ambush* (1934) which won the Pulitzer poetry prize in 1935; *The Seven Sins; Splendours in the Grass; Testament of Love; A Sonnet Sequence.*

Wyant, Alexander Helwig (1836-1892), American painter who first worked at sign painting and later received some advice from George INNESS. With the financial aid of friends he studied at Karlsruhe with Hans Gude, and visited Ireland and England where he became interested in the landscapes of John CONSTABLE and Joseph TURNER. His notable works include *Mohawk Valley; Landscape in the Adirondacks; View on Lake George; Old Clearing; Broad Silent Valley; Evening; New England Landscape; Sunset on the Prairie; Reminiscences of the Connecticut River.*

Wycherley, Margaret (1881-), English stage and screen actress who made her debut in 1898 with Franziska JANAUSCHEK in *What Dreams May Come* and gained experience later with the Jessie BONSTELLE Stock Company: among the plays in which she has appeared are *Everyman; Twelfth Night; Cashel Byron's Profession; The Nazarene; Candida; The Blue Bird; Damaged Goods; The Thirteenth Chair; Jane Clegg; Back to Methusaleh; Strange Interlude; Six Characters in Search of an Author; Tobacco Road.* She has also appeared in the film version of *The Thirteenth Chair,* and in *Sergeant York.*

Wycherley, William (c.1640-1715), English dramatist educated at Oxford: his plays include *Love in a Wood* (1671); *The Gentleman Dancing Master; The Country Wife; The Plain Dealer.* His dialogue was witty and his dramatic ideas so good that William CONGREVE admitted that he imitated them, but they were extremely immoral so that revivals by David GARRICK and others were presented with modified text.

Wylie, Elinor Hoyt (1885-1928), American poet and novelist educated at private schools who was married at the time of her death to William Rose BENÉT. Her poetical works include *Incidental Numbers* (1912); *Nets to Catch the Wind; Black Armour; Trivial Breath; Angels and Earthly Creatures:* she also wrote the novels *Jennifer Lorn; The Venetian Glass Nephew; The Orphan Angel; Mr. Hodge and Mr. Hazard.*

Wynants or **Wijnants, Jan** (c.1615-c.1679), Dutch painter who executed many fine landscapes in which the figures were painted by Philip WOUWERMAN and other noted artists: his works include *Sandbank in a River,* and many other canvases which have no titles, but reveal extraordinary skill in perspective and the execution of details.

Wyndham, Sir Charles (1837-1919), English actor educated at King's College, London, and also trained as a surgeon: he was in the United States during the Civil War and volunteered his services as a surgeon. In 1864 he appeared with John Wilkes BOOTH, and on his return to London achieved great success in *All That Glitters Is Not Gold,* and also in a burlesque of *Black-eyed Susan* by Francis BURNAND. After appearing with Sir Henry IRVING and Ellen TERRY, and in *Brighton,* an anglicized version of Bronson HOWARD's *Saratoga,* he leased the Criterion Theatre where he produced and played in many modern dramas including *The Liars; Rebellious Susan,* and *David Garrick:* he also managed the Wyndham Theatre and the New Theatre.

Wynken de Worde, see **Caxton, William.**

Wynn, Edward (1886-), American actor and dramatist familiarly known as "Ed Wynn" who first appeared in vaudeville and later with the *Ziegfeld Follies:* his musical plays include *Ed Wynn's Carnival; The Perfect Fool; Simple Simon; The Laugh Parade.* He has also appeared with great success on radio broadcasts and in several films.

Wynyard, Diana (1906-), English stage and screen actress who made her debut in 1925 as a walk-on in *The Grand Duchess:* among the plays in which she has appeared are *The Dancers; Raffles; The Love Game; The Skin Game; Cradle Song; The Devil; Lean Harvest; The Devil Passes; Wild December; Sweet Aloes; Candida; Pygmalion.* She has also been featured in many films including *Rasputin; Reunion in Vienna; Kipps; The Voice in the Night; The Prime Minister; Cavalcade.*

Wyspianski, Stanislas (1869-1907), Polish poet and dramatist who first became a painter, but was obliged to give up through the loss of his arm: his plays include *The Wedding; A Warsaw Song; Lelewel; November Night; The Legion; Deliverance; The Acropolis; The Curse; The Judge; Boleslas the Bold; The Return of Ulysses; King Casimir; The Church on the Rick; Protesilaos and Laodamia.*

X

 anrof, pseudonym of **Léon Fourneau** (1867-), a French lawyer who wrote songs for Yvette GUILBERT: his compositions include musical farces for the Paris stage, songs, and piano pieces.

Xenophon (c.430-c.357 B.C.), Greek historian, essayist, and disciple of Socrates who joined the expedition of Cyrus the Younger in 401 B.C. which ended in the defeat at Cunaxa: after the murder of the Greek generals he became the chief leader of the *Ten Thousand,* a Greek mercenary band, in their march to the Black Sea which he chronicled in his chief work, the ANABASIS. All his other writings are overshadowed by the splendor of this remarkable narrative.

Xoanon, in sculpture the earliest statue of a god made by the ancient Greeks: it was fashioned out of wood and so rudely carved that it resembled a pillar rather than the human form. It was supposed to be of divine origin through falling from the heavens, and was revered long after Greek sculptors were creating their masterpieces.

Xylander, Vilhelm Ferdinand (1840-?), Danish painter who studied at the Copenhagen Academy and at Munich with Christian Morgenstern: his works include *Moonlight on Lake Starnberg; Coast of Southampton; Mouth of the Thames; Moonlight on the Roadstead at Portsmouth; Isle of Sylt.* He painted many canvases in England which he visited in 1865.

Xylophone, a musical instrument belonging to the PERCUSSION group, consisting of graduated hardwood bars with a CHROMATIC range of from three to four octaves: these are mounted loosely on chords or rubber. Resonators are used under the bars of lower pitch: hard or soft mallets are used. The oustanding example of the use of the xylophone is in the DANSE MACABRE by Camille Saint-Saëns.

Xyndas, Spiridion (1812-1896), Greek composer who wrote several ballad operas including *Count Julian; The Two Rivals,* and *The Candidate for Parliament:* he also composed piano pieces and songs.

Xystus or **Xyst,** in architecture the ancient Greek term for the covered portico of the gymnasium in which exercises took place during cold or rainy weather: the term was used by the Romans to describe the garden walk in front of a portico, and also to an avenue or promenade between rows of trees.

Y

Yamada, Kosçak (1886-), Japanese conductor and composer who studied at the Imperial Academy of Music in Tokyo and in Berlin, and organized the Philharmonic Orchestra of Tokyo, the first organization in Japan composed of native musicians presenting Occidental music. His compositions include a symphony and two symphonic poems; a *Japanese Suite* for orchestra; an oratorio; piano pieces and songs.

Yaw, Ellen Beach (1868-), American operatic and concert soprano who studied at Paris with Blanche MARCHESI and made her debut at St. Paul, Minn., in 1894, and after a tour of the United States made her first appearance at London in 1895, and her debut in 1910 at the Metropolitan Opera House, New York, in Donizetti's *Lucia di Lammermoor.* In 1934 she sponsored summer symphony concerts on her estate at Covina, Calif., and organized an open-air singing school in 1939. Her voice had a phenomenal compass extending to C above high C.

Yeats, William Butler (1865-1939), Irish poet and dramatist who was the son of John Butler Yeats, a well-known artist, and first studied painting: his poetical works include *Mosada* (1886); *The Wanderings of Oisin; The Wind Among the Reeds; Responsibilities; The Wild Swans at Coole; The Tower.* He was associated with Lady Isabella GREGORY in the founding of the Irish Literary Theatre which later became the famous ABBEY THEATRE for which he wrote several plays including *The Countess Cathleen; The Land of Heart's Desire; Cathleen ni Houlihan; The Hour Glass; The Pot of Broth; The King's Threshold; Deirdre; The Green Helmet.* He also wrote works on literary criticism, short stories, and collections of Irish fairy tales.

Yeomen of the Guard, comic opera in two acts: libretto by Sir William S. GILBERT; music by Sir Arthur SULLIVAN; first produced at the Savoy Theatre, London, in 1888 and in the United States in 1889. The plot revolves around an English maid of the 18th century, Elsie Maynard, who marries Colonel Fairfax, sentenced to die at the Tower of London for sorcery, for a sum of money on the understanding that she is free after his execution. Lord Fairfax is pardoned, but he has fallen deeply in love with the charming Elsie, and their marriage becomes a real one, much to the disappointment of Jack Point, the strolling player with whom she has been entertaining the country folk. There is a complete Victor recording and a Gramophone Shop abridged version.

Yggdrasil, in Norse mythology the name of a massive ash tree which symbolizes the universe, and extends all over the world: at one end is a mighty dragon which gnaws at its roots, and at the other end the Mimir or well of wisdom. The NORNS sprinkle the tree daily to keep it from decaying, and the squirrel, *Ratatosk* runs up and down its trunk constantly carrying strife all over the world. The tree has been painted by many Scandinavian painters.

Yoga, in Hindu philosophy a form of mental discipline which consists of directing the attention to some concrete or abstract subject for the purpose of identifying the object with the consciousness. A **yogi** is a follower and practitioner of yogism, but in European countries the word is often misapplied to a person claiming to have second sight.

Yon, Pietro (1886-), Italian organist and composer who studied at the musical conservatories in Milan, Turin, and Rome, later becoming assistant organist at St. Peter's, and in 1921 organist of St. Francis Xavier's in New York. Since 1926 he has occupied the post of organist at St. PATRICK'S CATHEDRAL, New York, and has concertized throughout the United States and Europe. His compositions include masses, organ works, piano pieces, and songs.

Yonge, Charlotte (1823-1901), English novelist who was educated privately, resided at Otterbourne all her life and was one of the most prolific of the Victorian writers. Her novels include *The Heir of Redclyffe* (1853); *The Daisy Chain; The Dove in the Eagle's Nest; The Prince and the Page:* she also wrote *The Kings of England, Landmarks of History,* and *The Victorian Half-Century.*

Yosai (1781-1878), Japanese painter who first studied the principles of the Kano, Shijo, and Maruyama schools, and finally developed an individual style in black and white: he illustrated the *Zenken Kojitsu* or history of Japanese heroes, and was numbered among the last great Nipponese painters.

Youmans, Vincent (1899-), contemporary American composer and producer: his musical plays include *Two Little Girls in Blue; Wildflower* with Herbert Stothart; *No, No, Nanette; Hit the Deck; Great Day; Smiles; Through the Years:* he has also written the musical scores for several films.

Young, Arthur (1866-), American cartoonist and author familiarly known as "Art Young": he studied at the Academy of Design, Chicago, at the ART STUDENTS' LEAGUE, New York, and in Paris. He has acted as news illustrator and cartoonist for several Chicago newspapers; also for *Puck, Judge, Saturday Evening Post,* and *Collier's.* His books include *Trees At Night* (1927); *On My Way; Art Young's Inferno; The Best of Art Young.*

Young, Edward (1683-1765), English clergyman and poet educated at Oxford: his masterpiece is *Night Thoughts* (1742-46), a gloomy but eloquent and at times truly sublime poem in blank verse. He also wrote the tragedies *Busiris;* and *The Revenge* in addition to a series of satires entitled *The Love of Fame.*

Young, Loretta (1913-), American screen actress who made her debut in films at the age of four: among the innumerable pictures in which she has appeared are *Laugh, Clown, Laugh* with Lon CHANEY; *The Squall; The Scarlet Seas* with Richard BARTHELMESS; *Zoo in Budapest; The House of Rothschild; Caravan; Clive of India; The Crusades; Shanghai; Ramona; Café Metropole; Suez; Kentucky; The Story of Alexander Graham Bell; The Doctor Takes a Wife; Bedtime; China.*

Young, Mahonri Mackintosh (1877-), American sculptor and painter, grandson of the Mormon leader, Brigham Young, who first modeled in adobe clay after watching Cyrus DALLIN use it in a model of a statue of Brigham Young. He studied at the Art Students' League, New York, and at the Académie Julian in Paris. In 1912 he began modeling and sketching Navajo Indians at their daily tasks: later he set up his studio in New York City where he has executed statuettes and pastels of laboring men, portrait busts, animal studies, and pastel sketches in the nude. He executed Indian groups for the American Museum of Natural History, New York, and a monument, *The Sea Gull* for Salt Lake City.

Young, Robert (1907-), American screen actor: among the many films in which he has appeared are *Tugboat Annie; The House of Rothschild; The Bride Comes Home; Secret Agent; The Emperor's Candlesticks; The Toy Wife; The Shining Hour; The Mortal Storm; Northwest Passage; Florian; Western Union; The Trial of Mary Dugan; Lady Be Good; H. M. Pulham, Esq.; Joe Smith, American.*

Young, Roland (1887-), English stage and screen actor who studied at the Academy of Dramatic Art, London, and made his debut in 1912 at the Garrick Theatre in *Improper Peter:* among the many plays in which he has appeared are *Hindle Wakes* in which he made his American debut also in 1912; *Good Gracious, Annabelle; A Doll's House; Buddies; Rollo's Wild Oat; The Forty-Niners; The Devil's Disciple; Beggar on Horseback; Hedda Gabler; The Last of Mrs. Cheyney; Her Master's Voice; Spring Thaw.* He has also appeared in many films including *David Copperfield; Ruggles of Red Gap; Topper; Topper Takes a Trip; Star Dust; The Philadelphia Story; Topper Returns; Two-Faced Woman; The Lady Has Plans; They All Kissed the Bride.*

Young, Stark (1881-), American dramatic critic and novelist educated at the University of Mississippi and Columbia University who later taught English at the University of Mississippi, the University of Texas and Amherst College. In 1921 he abandoned teaching for journalism, becoming connected with the *New Republic,* dramatic editor of the New York. *Times* from 1924 to 1925, and later occupying the same position with the *New Republic.* His works include many plays and the novel *So Red the Rose* (1934) which was also a successful film.

Ysaÿe, Eugène (1858-1931), Belgian violinist, composer, and conductor who studied at the Liége Conservatory, and with both Henri WIENIAWSKI and Henri VIEUXTEMPS. He acted as concertmaster of the Bilse Orchestra in Berlin; became professor of violin at the Brussels Conservatory also founding and conducting the Ysaÿe Concerts; toured the United States, and conducted the Cincinnati Symphony Orchestra from 1918 to 1922. He gave sonata recitals with Raoul PUGNO and founded the Ysaÿe Quartet at Brussels: his compositions include an opera, *Pierre Li Howyen,* produced at Liége in 1930; six violin concertos; trios for violin and viola; solo pieces for violin. His brother, **Théophile Ysaÿe** (1865-1918), was a pianist and composer who studied with KULLAK and César FRANCK, taught at the Geneva Conservatory, and toured with his brother: his compositions include orchestral works, chamber music, and two piano concertos.

Yurka, Blanche (1893-), American stage and screen actress who first studied for the operatic stage but finally decided on a dramatic career. In 1907 she acted as understudy for Charlotte Walker in *The Warrens of Virginia:* since that time she has appeared in *An Old New Yorker; The House of Bondage; Sweet Kitty Bellairs; The Great Divide; Lord Dundreary; Daybreak; Monna Vanna; The Wild Duck; The Goat Song; Lysistrata; Candida; Hedda Gabler; Lucrece; The Distaff Side; The Barber Had Two Sons.* She has also appeared in *The Tale of Two Cities* and other films.

Yutang, Lin, see **Lin Yutang.**

Z

Zamacois, Eduardo (1842-1871), Spanish painter who studied with José de MADRAZO at the Madrid Academy, and with Jean MEISSONIER at Paris: his notable canvases include *Entrance of the Toreros; Jester of the Sixteenth Century; Faust and Marguerite; Sleeping Hunter; Door of a Mosque; Strolling Players; Mendicant Monk; Occupation of Spain by the French.*

Zampieri, Domenico, see **Domenichino, Il.**

Zandonai, Riccardo (1883-), Italian composer who studied with Pietro MASCAGNI, and produced his first opera *Il grillo del focolare,* based on DICKENS' "Cricket on the Hearth," at Turin in

1908. His operatic works include *Conchita* produced at Milan in 1911 and at San Francisco in 1912; *Francesca da Rimini* produced at Turin in 1914 and at the Metropolitan Opera House, New York, in 1916. He has also composed church music, orchestral works and songs.

Zangwill, Israel (1864-1926), Anglo-Jewish author who was first a journalist and founder of a humorous paper, *Ariel, the London Puck*. His first novel, *The Children of the Ghetto* was successful as a book and as a play: it was followed by *Ghetto Tragedies, Ghetto Comedies,* and *Dreamers of the Ghetto* which were equally popular. Among his successful plays were *Merely Mary Ann; Too Much Money; The Melting Pot; We Moderns; The Cockpit; The Next Religion.*

Zarlino, Giosefe (1517-1590), Italian theorist and composer who studied with Adrian WILLAERT and succeeded Cipriano de Rore as chapelmaster at ST. MARK'S CATHEDRAL in Venice: he wrote extremely important theoretical works of every description, but most of his compositions have been lost. He is regarded as one of the most important figures in early Italian musical history.

Zeisler, Fannie Bloomfield (1863-1927), American pianist born in Austria who came to the United States in 1868 with her parents. She studied with Bernhard Ziehn and Carl Wolfson and appeared in recital in 1876, later studying for five years with Théodor LESCHETIZKY in Vienna. From 1883 to 1914 she appeared in recital and with every major orchestra in the United States and Europe, becoming recognized internationally as one of the world's greatest pianists.

Zelter, Karl Friedrich (1758-1832), German composer who studied with Johann Philipp Kirnberger, and later conducted singing societies including the Berlin Liedertafel, a pioneer men's choral society for which he composed more than one hundred choruses. GOETHE was intimate with him, being greatly impressed by Zelter's settings of his lyrics although the music was greatly inferior to that composed by Franz SCHUBERT who for some reason was ignored by the great German poet.

Zemlinsky, Alexander von (1872-1942), Austrian composer and conductor who studied at the Vienna Conservatory with Robert Fuchs, and later conducted at the Vienna Volksoper, the Mannheim Hofoper, the German Landestheater at Prague, and the Berlin Statsoper. He was the teacher in counterpoint of Arnold SCHONBERG, and lived in the United States from 1938. His compositions include several operas, orchestral works, chamber music, piano pieces, and songs.

Zenatello, Giovanni (1876-), Italian dramatic tenor who studied in Milan, and made his debut in 1901 at Naples in Leoncavallo's *Pagliacci*, later singing at La Scala, Milan, and at Covent Garden. He made his debut in 1907 at the Manhattan Opera House in Ponchielli's *La Gioconda*, also singing for five years with the Boston Opera Company and with the Chicago Opera Company. After his retirement in 1930 he opened a vocal studio with his wife, Maria GAY where Lily PONS, Nino MARTINI and other well-known singers were students.

Zeno, Apostolo (1668-1750), Italian critic, poet, dramatist, and opera librettist who was the predecessor of METASTASIO as court poet to Charles VI, founder of the *Journal of Italian Literature* with Francesco MAFFEI, and the first Italian opera librettist of real distinction. His admirable biographies of Italian authors were written as prefaces to specially prepared editions of their works.

Zerrahn, Carl (1826-1910), German conductor who studied with Friedrich Weber, and came to the United States in 1848 as a flutist in the Germania Orchestra. He finally settled in Boston, becoming conductor of the HANDEL AND HAYDN SOCIETY from 1854 to 1895, and of the Harvard Symphony Concerts from 1866 to 1882. He also taught at the New England Conservatory of Music and directed the Worcester Music Festivals from 1866 to 1897.

Zeus, in Greek mythology the supreme deity and the all-powerful master of gods and mortals: he was the son of RHEA and CRONUS whom he dethroned and succeeded as ruler over heaven and earth. His consort was HERA, and he was worshiped universally with his principal temples at Elis and Dodona. He is represented in art as a powerful and majestic figure with full beard and flowing hair, sometimes fully draped, but in later art lightly clothed. His attributes are a sceptre or a long staff, the thunderbolt, the eagle and occasionally a figure of Victory borne in one hand. Phidias executed an enormous CHRYSELEPHANTINE statue of Zeus at the temple in OLYMPIA: he is identified with the Roman god Jupiter.

Zeuxis, Greek painter who flourished near the end of the 5th and the beginning of the 4th century B.C.: he is called *Xeuxippus* by Socrates. It is believed that he was a pupil of APOLLODORUS, and although none of his works has survived, the titles of many are preserved in the writings of various authors: they include *Helen of Crotona; Menelaus Praying at the Tomb of Agamemnon; Family of Centaurs; Infant Hercules Strangling the Serpent; Marsyas; Pan; Helen at the Bath.*

Ziegfeld, Florenz (1869-1932), American theatrical producer, son of Florenz Ziegfeld, president of the CHICAGO MUSICAL COLLEGE. He first managed the bands at the Chicago World's Fair in 1893, and then directed the tours of Sandow the Great. After his arrival in New York he presented Anna HELD in musical productions, and with the aid of Charles B. DILLINGHAM and Abraham ERLANGER originated the *Ziegfeld Follies,* a form of musical revue elaborately staged, and presented a chorus of girls of the "statuesquely beautiful" variety. Among the stars who appeared in the sketches and monologues interspersed between the musical numbers were Will ROGERS, Billie BURKE, Bert Williams, Eddie CANTOR, Eddie DOWLING, Maurice CHEVALIER, Dennis KING, Vivienne SEGAL, Norma TERRIS, Fred ASTAIRE, Marilyn MILLER, and Evelyn LAYE. He also produced several successful musical plays including *Sally, Rio Rita, Show Boat* and *Kid Boots.*

Ziehrer, Karl Michael (1843-1922), Austrian composer and conductor who was entirely self-taught: in 1863 he organized a dance orchestra with which he toured Austria and Germany later establishing a series of popular concerts at Vienna which met with great success. His compositions include over twenty operettas, and 600 pieces of dance music many of which rivaled those of Johann STRAUSS, JR., in popularity.

Ziem, Félix François Georges Philibert (1821-1911), French painter who studied at Paris and Rome, and also traveled extensively in the East: his notable canvases include *Sunrise in Constantinople; Venice; Dutch Landscape; The Old Port of Marseilles; Grand Canal at Venice; Doge's Palace in Venice; Cleopatra in Upper Egypt; Inundation of the Piazza of St. Mark's; Venetian Fishing Boat.*

Zigeunerbaron, Der, see **Gypsy Baron, The.**

Ziggurat, in architecture a temple in Babylonia and Assyria in the form of a square, pyramidal building mounting by means of ramps for several stories to the shrine itself located at the top. The Tower of Babel mentioned in the Bible was probably built in this form.

Zimbalist, Efrem (1889-), Russian violinist and composer who studied with Leopold AUER at the St. Petersburg Conservatory, and made his debut at Berlin in 1907, and in the United States in 1911 with the Boston Symphony Orchestra. In 1914 he married Alma GLUCK, a well-known opera singer, and in 1938 became a member of the faculty at the CURTIS INSTITUTE OF MUSIC and in 1941 its director. His compositions include *Slavonic Dances* for violin and orchestra; chamber music, and a *Fantasie* on RIMSKY-KORSAKOW's *Le Coq d'Or.*

Zimmerman, Pierre Joseph Guillaume (1785-1853), French pianist and composer who studied at the Paris Conservatory with BOIELDIEU and CHERUBINI, becoming professor of the piano there, and numbering ALKAN, MARMONTEL, FRANCK and Ambroise THOMAS among his pupils. His compositions include two operas, piano pieces and études: also an important *Encyclopedia for Pianists.*

Zingarelli, Niccolo Antonio (1752-1837), Italian composer who studied at the Conservatory of San Loreto at Naples, and produced his first opera, *I quattro pazzi* at the Conservatory in 1768. He composed more than forty operas of which *Romeo and Juliet,* produced at La Scala, Milan, in 1796, was his masterpiece. He was a fine composer of church music, and also a distinguished teacher: Vincenzo BELLINI was one of his pupils.

Zircon, a four-sided mineral found in square prisms or pyramids of red, brown, or greyish color: the transparent varieties in red or brown are highly regarded as gem stones.

Zither, a musical instrument on the order of the PSALTERY: it consists of a shallow resonance box over which 25 or more strings are stretched, with a bridge at the right end and a fretted fingerboard over five melody strings on the side nearest the player. The melody is played with a PLECTRUM on the thumb of the performer. Johann STRAUSS, JR., made effective use of the zither in his waltzes, *Tales from the Vienna Woods.*

Zola, Émile (1840-1902), French novelist whose father was Italian and mother French: he studied at the Lycée Saint-Louis without graduating and worked in a bookstore until his first book, *Contes à Ninon,* was published in 1864. His works include *The Attack on the Mill; Thérèse Raquin;* a great cycle of twenty novels, *The Rougon-Macquart: the Natural and Social History of a Family under the Second Empire,* the best of which are *L'Assomoir, Germinal,* and *Le Débâcle;* an anti-religious cycle including *Lourdes, Rome* and *Paris; Verité,* a parable on the Dreyfus case in which, as in his famous pamphlet, *J'accuse,* he championed the accused French officer. He also wrote several critical works including *The French Republic and Literature; Naturalism in the Theatre; Our Dramatic Authors;* several of his novels were dramatized.

Zolnay, George Julian (1863-), American sculptor who studied at the Royal Institute of Arts in Budapest and at the Imperial Academy of Fine Arts in Vienna: he directed the sculptural decorations at the St. Louis World's Fair and occupied the post of art instructor at the University City (Mo.) Art Academy. He has designed war and industrial memorials and monuments in all parts of the United States: also many portrait busts of American and European notables.

Zoöphorus, in architecture the term applied by VITRUVIUS to a form of frieze decorated with foliage and arabesques in which figures of animals were introduced.

Zorach, William (1887-), American painter and sculptor who came to the United States as a child, and after becoming an apprentice in a lithographing plant studied at the Cleveland Art School, the National Academy of Design in New York, and in Paris. After painting in the cubist style he turned to carving in wood and stone, and also paints landscapes in water color: his works are to be found in many American art museums.

Zorina, Vera (1917-), German actress and dancer who studied acting with Lina ABARBANELL and dancing with Nicholas LEGAT, making her debut in 1928 at Berlin as a dancer in *Lilac Time:* she has appeared since in Max REINHARDT's revival of *A Midsummer Night's Dream; Ballerina; On Your Toes; I Married an Angel.* She has also appeared in several foreign and American motion pictures.

Zorn, Anders Leonhard (1860-1920), Swedish painter and sculptor who was a skillful wood carver at eight, and later studied at the Technical School and the Preparatory School of the Academy of Art at Stockholm. In 1881 he traveled throughout Europe and opened a studio in London where he remained until 1885, later residing in Paris, Chicago, and finally at Mora in Sweden. His paintings include *Fisherman from St. Ives; Our Daily Bread; Omnibus:* his sculptures such as *Faun and Nymph* reveal his knowledge of anatomy, and he also etched many fine portraits.

Zuccarelli, Francesco (1702-1788), Italian painter who studied at Florence and Rome, and after traveling in Germany, Holland, and France spent five years in London painting murals and other decorations in the Opera House, and also views along the Thames. His works include *Waterfall with Fisherman; Ruins near a Waterfall; Woodland Scene; Landscape with Horseman; Landscape with Italian Buildings; Landscape with a Group of Peasants.*

Zucchero or **Zucarro, Federigo** (1543-1609), Italian painter who worked with his brother, **Taddeo Zucchero** (1529-1566): he completed Giorgio VASARI's *Last Judgment* at the Duomo, Florence, developed the decorations of the Pauline Chapel at Rome, and later went to England where he painted the portraits of Queen Elizabeth and Mary Stuart. His easel paintings include *Descent from the Cross; Calumny; The Golden Age; The Silver Age:* he also wrote a valuable treatise on painting, sculpture, and architecture.

Zucco, George (1886-), English actor who made his debut at Regina, Saskatchewan, Canada, in *What Happened to Jones:* after appearing in Canada and the United States he served in the British Army during World War I, and has since appeared in numerous plays including *Lightnin'; The Great Lover; Trilby; The Terror; Reunion in Vienna; Hedda Gabler; Journey's End; Autumn Crocus; Mid-Channel; The Firebird; Strife; Victoria Regina,* and in several Shakespearean roles. He has also appeared in many films since 1934.

Zuloaga Y Zabalesa, Ignacio (1870-), Spanish painter who was the son of Placido Zuloaga, an armourer famous for his skill in the art of damascening metal for weapons of war. He studied at Madrid where he was influenced by the paintings of El GRECO, and later studied at Rome and Paris. His works include *Spanish Dance; Promenade after the Bull Fight; Watching the Races; Family of a Gypsy Bull-fighter:* also a portrait of Ignace Jan PADEREWSKI.

Zurbaran, Francisco de (1598-1662), Spanish painter who was known as the "Spanish CARAVAGGIO" because he imitated the Italian master's style. His works include *Scenes from the Life of St. Peter; Glory of St. Thomas Aquinas; St. Francis of Assisi in Ecstasy; Labors of Hercules; Two Dominican Monks; Adoration of the Shepherds; Franciscan Monk:* he was said to be as partial to painting monks as RAPHAEL to depicting Madonnas.

Zweig, Arnold (1887-), German novelist and dramatist educated at the Universities of Breslau, Berlin, and Göttingen: his works available in English include *The Case of Sergeant Grischa; Claudia; Young Woman of 1914; De Vriendt Goes Home; Playthings of Time; Education before Verdun; The Insulted and Exiled; The Crowning of a King.*

Zweig, Stefan (1881-1942), Austrian biographer and novelist who was educated at the University of Vienna: his novels include *Passion and Pain* (1924); *The Invisible Collection; Conflicts; Amok; Letter from an Unknown Woman; Kaleidescope; The Buried Candelabrum; Beware of Pity:* he also wrote biographies of Paul VERLAINE, Romain ROLLAND, Marie ANTOINETTE, Mary, Queen of Scotland, and Magellan.

Zworykin, Vladimir Kosma (1889-), Russian scientist educated at the Petrograd Institute of Technology under Dr. Boris Rosing, and at the Collège de France, Paris, with Paul Langeven. After serving in the Russian army during World War I he came to the United States in 1920: his inventions include the Iconoscope which is the "eye" of TELEVISION; the Kinescope which is the screen-tube used in television receiving sets; the Electron Microscope, and other important scientific instruments in the radio and television field. He has written *Television* (1940) in collaboration with G. A. Morton.

BIBLIOGRAPHY

Architecture

American Architecture of Today, The. Edgell, G. H. Charles Scribner's Sons.
Architecture. Brooks, A. M. Longmans, Green & Co.
Architecture. Jackson, Thomas G. The Macmillan Company.
Architecture. Russell, A. N. L. E. P. Dutton & Co.
Architecture and Democracy. Bragdon, Claude. Alfred A. Knopf, Inc.
Architecture in Cambridge. Fyfe, Theodore. The Macmillan Company.
Architecture in Italy. Cummings, Charles A. Houghton Mifflin Co.
Architecture of the Renaissance in Italy, The. Anderson, W. J.
Charles Scribner's Sons.
Architecture Through the Ages. Hamlin, Talbot. G. P. Putnam's Sons.
Book of Architecture. Reed, G. H. The Macmillan Company.
Book of Low-Cost Houses, The. Simon & Schuster.
Church Builders of the Nineteenth Century. Clarke, Basil F. L.
The Macmillan Company.
Design This Day. Teague, Walter Dorwin. Harcourt, Brace & Co.
Domestic Architecture. Robinson, L. Eugene. The Macmillan Company.
Early Christian and Byzantine Architecture. Browne, Edith A.
The Macmillan Company.
Early Muslim Architecture. Creswell, K. A. C. Oxford University Press.
Egyptian Architecture as Cultural Expression. Smith, E. B. D. Appleton-Century Co.
English Abbey, The. Crossley, F. H. Charles Scribner's Sons.
English Castle, The. Braun, Hugh. Charles Scribner's Sons.
English Country House. Dutton, Ralph. Charles Scribner's Sons.
Enjoyment of Architecture, The. Hamlin, T. F. Charles Scribner's Sons.
Famous Buildings. Barstow, Chas. L. D. Appleton-Century Co.
Foundations of Classic Architecture. Warren, Herbert L. The Macmillan Company.
Frank Lloyd Wright on Architecture. Gutheim, Frederick. Duell, Sloan & Pearce.
French Renaissance Architecture. (2 Vols.) Ward, W. H. Charles Scribner's Sons.
Glory That Was Greece, The. Stobart, J. C. D. Appleton-Century Co.
Gothic Architecture. Browne, Edith A. The Macmillan Company.
Grandeur That Was Rome, The. Stobart, J. C. D. Appleton-Century Co.
Greek Revival Architecture in America. Hamlin, Talbot. Oxford University Press.
Handbook of Greek and Roman Architecture. Robertson, D. S.
The Macmillan Company.
Hellenistic Architecture. Fyfe, Theodore. The Macmillan Company.
History of Architectural Development, A. (3 Vols.) Simpson, F. M.
Longmans, Green & Co.
History of Architecture. Hamlin, A. D. F. Longmans, Green & Co.
History of Architecture on the Comparative Method, A. Fletcher, Banister.
Charles Scribner's Sons.
History of Ornament, A: Ancient and Medieval. Hamlin, A. D. F.
D. Appleton-Century Co.
History of Religious Architecture. Short, Ernest H. The Macmillan Company.
History of Spanish Architecture, A. Bevan, Bernard. Charles Scribner's Sons.
Home of the Monk. Cranage, D. H. S. The Macmillan Company.
House, A Machine for Living In. Bertran, Anthony. The Macmillan Company.
Houses in America. Robinson, Ethel Fay and Thomas P. The Viking Press.

How to Buy or Build Your Home Wisely. Abercrombie, Roland K.
The Macmillan Company.

Idols Behind Altars. Brenner, Anita. Harcourt, Brace & Co.
Introduction to French Church Architecture. Gardner, Arthur.
The Macmillan Company.

Introduction to the History of Architecture, An. Carpenter, H. B. and Knight, J.
Longmans, Green & Co.

Masterpieces of American Architecture. Hoak, E. W. and Church, W. H.
Charles Scribner's Sons.

Metal Crafts in Architecture. Geerlings G. K. Charles Scribner's Sons.
Method of Creative Design, A. Best-Maugard, Adolfo. Alfred A. Knopf, Inc.
Metropolis of Tomorrow, The. Ferriss, Hugh. Ives Washburn, Inc.
Modern Building. Behrendt, Walter Curt. Harcourt, Brace & Co.
Old Inns of England, The. Richardson, A. E. Charles Scribner's Sons.
On Being an Architect. Lescaze, William. G. P. Putnam's Sons.
Practical Book of Architecture, The. Price, C. Matlack. J. B. Lippincott Co.
Primer of Higher Space, A. Bragdon, Claude. Alfred A. Knopf, Inc.
Real Log Cabin. Aldrich, C. D. The Macmillan Company.
Remodelling and Adapting the Small House. Eberlein, Harold Donaldson;
Tarpley, Donald G. J. B. Lippincott Co.

Romanesque Architecture in Western Europe. Clapham, A. W.
Oxford University Press.

Romanesque Architecture of the Order of Cluny. Evans, Joan.
The Macmillan Company.

School Architecture. Donovan, John J. The Macmillan Company.
Second Book of Small Houses, The. Simon & Schuster.
Short Critical History of Architecture. Statham, H. H. Charles Scribner's Sons.
Some Historic Houses. Fitzpatrick, John C. The Macmillan Company.
South in Architecture, The. Mumford, Lewis. Harcourt, Brace & Co.
Story of Architecture in America, The. Tallmadge, Thomas E. W. W. Norton & Co.
Story of England's Architecture, The. Tallmadge, Thomas E. W. W. Norton & Co.
Successful Houses and How to Build Them. White, Charles E. Jr.
The Macmillan Company.

Wonders of the Past. Hammerton, J. A. (4 Vols.) G. P. Putnam's Sons.
Without Benefit of Architect. Peters, Frazier Forman. G. P. Putnam's Sons.
Young People's Story of Architecture, The. Butterfield, Emily Helen.
Dodd, Mead & Co.

Your Own House. Robinson, Ethel Fay and Thomas P. The Viking Press.

Ballet and Dance

Antique Greek Dance, The. Emmanuel, Maurice. Dodd, Mead & Co.
Artists of the Dance. Moore, Lillian. Thomas Y. Crowell Co.
Ballet. Haskell, Arnold L. Penguin Books, Ltd.
Ballet in Action. Severn, M. Oxford University Press.
Balletomania. Haskell, Arnold L. Gollancz.
Ballet—To Poland. Haskell, Arnold L. The Macmillan Company.
Ballet Traditional to Modern. Lifar, Serge. G. P. Putnam's Sons.
Bibliography of Dancing, A. Magriel, Paul David. H. W. Wilson Company.
Book of Ballets-Classic and Modern, The. Goode, Gerald. Crown Publishers.
Choreographic Music. Arvey, Verna. E. P. Dutton & Co.
Complete Book of Ballets. Beaumont, Cyril. G. P. Putnam's Sons.
Complete Book of Ballets: Supplement 1942. Beaumont, Cyril W. C. W. Beaumont.
Dance. Kirstein, Lincoln. G. P. Putnam's Sons.
Dancer's Almanac and Who's Who (1940). Howard, Ruth Eleanor, Editor.
Dancing Around the World. Haskell, Arnold L. Gollancz.
Design for the Ballet. Studio Publishing Company.

Diaghileff. Haskell and Nouvel. Simon & Schuster.
Diaghilev, Serge. Lifar, Serge. G. P. Putnam's Sons.
History of Ballet in Russia (1613-1881). Beaumont, Cyril W. C. W. Beaumont.
Introduction to the Dance. Martin, John. W. W. Norton & Co.
Johann Strauss, Father and Son. Jacob, H. E. The Greystone Press.
Master of the Russian Ballet. Racster. E. P. Dutton & Co.
Michael Fokine. Beaumont, Cyril W. C. W. Beaumont.
Music Through the Dance. Porter, Evelyn. Charles Scribner's Sons.
Pavlowa. Dandré, Victor. Cassell.
Power of Dance, The. Dixon, C. Madeleine. The John Day Co.
Russian Ballets. Stokes, Adrian. E. P. Dutton & Co.
Theatre Street. Karsavina, Tamara. Heinemann.
Tonight the Ballet. Stokes, Adrian. E. P. Dutton & Co.
Vaslav Nijinsky. Nijinska, Romola. Gollancz.
Waltzes From Vienna. Wier, Albert E. Harcourt, Brace & Co.
Waltz Kings of Vienna. Teetgen, Ada B. E. P. Dutton & Co.
World History of the Dance. Sachs, Curt. W. W. Norton & Co.

Drama

Acting and Play Production. Andrews, H. L. & Weirick, B. Longmans, Green & Co.
Actor's Art and Job, The. Irvine, Harry. E. P. Dutton & Co.
Advance From Broadway. Houghton, Norris. Harcourt, Brace & Co.
American Folk Plays. Koch, Frederick, H. D. Appleton-Century Co.
American Playwrights of Today. Mantle, Burns. Dodd, Mead & Co.
American Scenes. Kozlenko, William. The John Day Co.
American Theatre, The. Anderson, John. The Dial Press.
American Theatre As Seen By Its Critics, The. Brown, John Mason and Moses, Montrose J. (Editors). W. W. Norton & Co.
American Vaudeville. Gilbert, Douglas. Whittlesey House.
Another Treasury of Plays for Children. Moses, Montrose, J. Little, Brown & Co.
Appleton Book of Christmas Plays. Shay, Frank. D. Appleton-Century Co.
Appleton Book of Holiday Plays. Shay, Frank. D. Appleton-Century Co.
Appleton Book of Short Plays. Nicholson, Kenyon. D. Appleton-Century Co.
Appleton Book of Short Plays. 2nd Series. Nicholson, Kenyon.
D. Appleton-Century Co.
Arena. Flanagan, Hallie. Duell, Sloan & Pearce.
Aristophanes: His Plays and His Influence. Lord, L. E. Longmans, Green & Co.
Art and Craft of Play Production. Hewitt, Barnard. J. B. Lippincott Co.
Art and Life of William Shakespeare, The. Spencer, Hazelton. Harcourt, Brace & Co.
Art of Make-Up, The. Chalmers, Helena. D. Appleton-Century Co.
Art of Playgoing, The. Brown, John Mason. W. W. Norton & Co.
Art of Playwriting, The. Hennequin, Alfred. Houghton Mifflin Co.
Aspects of Modern Drama. Chandler, Frank W. The Macmillan Company.
Backstage with Actors. Ormsbee, Helen. Thomas Y. Crowell Co.
Best Plays of 1942-43 (Annual). Mantle, Burns. Dodd, Mead & Co.
Book of Dramas, A. Carpenter, Bruce. Prentice-Hall, Inc.
Book of Play Production, The. Smith, Milton. D. Appleton-Century Co.
British Drama. Nicoll, Allardyce. Thomas Y. Crowell Co.
Broadway in Review. Brown, John Mason. W. W. Norton & Co.
Carolina Folk Plays, Complete. Koch, Frederick H. Henry Holt & Co.
Changing World in Plays and Theatre, The. Block, Anita. Little, Brown & Co.
Chart of Plays, 1584 to 1623. Barrett, W. P. The Macmillan Company.
Chief British Dramatists, The. Matthews, Brander and Lieder, Paul R. Editors.
Houghton Mifflin Co.
Chief Contemporary Dramatists, The. Dickinson, Thomas H., Ed.
Houghton Mifflin Co.

Chief Elizabethan Dramatists, The. Neilson, William Allan, Ed. Houghton Mifflin Co.
Chief European Dramatists, The. Matthews, Brander, Ed. Houghton Mifflin Co.
Chief Patterns of World Drama. Clark, William Smith, Ed. Houghton Mifflin Co.
Chief Pre-Shakespearean Dramas. Adams, Joseph Q., Ed. Houghton Mifflin Co.
Children's Theatres and Plays. Mackay, Constance D'Arcy.
D. Appleton-Century Co.
Clothes: On and Off the Stage. Chalmers, Helena. D. Appleton-Century Co.
Common Sense About Drama. Strong, L. A. G. Alfred A. Knopf. Inc.
Contemporary American Playwrights. Mantle, Burns. Dodd, Mead & Co.
Contemporary One-Act Plays from Nine Countries. Wilde, Percival.
Little, Brown & Co.
Contemporary Plays. Dickinson, Thomas H. and Crawford, Jack R., Editors.
Houghton Mifflin Co.
Costumes and Scenery for Amateurs. Mackay, Constance D'Arcy. Henry Holt & Co.
Creative Theatre. Mitchell, Roy. The John Day Co.
Diderot's Writings on the Theatre. Green, F. C. The Macmillan Company.
Drama and Dramatics. Fish, Helen Randle. The Macmillan Company.
Drama of Transition, The. Goldberg, Isaac. D. Appleton-Century Co.
Dramas of Modernism. Moses, Montrose, J. Little, Brown & Co.
Dramatic Imagination, The. Jones, Robert E. Duell, Sloan & Pearce.
Dramatic Scenes from Athens to Broadway. Lowther, J. B. Longmans, Green & Co.
Dramatic Technique. Baker, George P. Houghton Mifflin Co.
Drama Tomorrow. Hardwicke, Cedric. The Macmillan Company.
Dynamo. Flanagan, Hallie. Duell, Sloan & Pearce.
Early Stages. Gielgud, John. The Macmillan Company.
Eleven Verse Plays, 1929-1939. Anderson, Maxwell. Harcourt, Brace & Co.
English Drama of the Restoration and the Eighteenth Century. Nettleton, George.
The Macmillan Company.
English Drama, The Last Great Phase. Pellizzi, Camillo. The Macmillan Company.
Face the Footlights. Colvan, E. B. Whittlesey House.
Fanny Kemble. Armstrong, Margaret. The Macmillan Company.
Fifty Contemporary One-Act Plays. Shay, Frank and Loving, Pierre.
D. Appleton-Century Co.
Fifty More Contemporary One-Act Plays. Shay, Frank. D. Appleton-Century Co.
Footlights on a Hero. Thompson, Sydney. Thomas Y. Crowell Co.
Fundamentals of Play Directing. Dean, Alexander. Farrar & Rinehart.
Handbook Annual of the Theatre, The. Dingwell, Wilbur. Coward-McCann.
Handbook for the American Actor. Cartmell, Van H. Doubleday, Doran & Co.
History of Early Nineteenth Century Drama. Nicoll, Allardyce.
The Macmillan Company.
History of Late Eighteenth Century Drama. Nicoll, Allardyce.
The Macmillan Company.
History of Restoration Drama. Nicoll, Allardyce. The Macmillan Company.
History of the Early Eighteenth Century Drama. Nicoll, Allardyce.
The Macmillan Company.
History of the Theatre. Freedley, George and Reeves, J. A. Crown Publishers.
Hour of the American Drama, An. Clark, Barrett H. J. B. Lippincott Co.
House of the Heart and Other Plays for Children. Mackay, Constance D'Arcy.
Henry Holt & Co.
How to Produce Amateur Plays. Clark, Barrett H. Little, Brown & Co.
How to See a Play. Burton, Richard. The Macmillan Company.
How to Write a Play. Ervine, St. John. The Macmillan Company.
Ibsen the Master Builder. Zucker, A. E. Henry Holt & Co.
Index to Plays in Collections, An. Ottemiller, John. H. W. Wilson Company.
In Praise of Comedy. Feibleman, James. The Macmillan Company.
Introduction to Drama. Hubbell, Jay B. and Beaty, John O. The Macmillan Company.
Irish Plays and Playwrights. Weygandt, Cornelius. Houghton Mifflin Co.

Irish Theatre. Robinson, Lennox. The Macmillan Company.
Italian Actors of the Renaissance. Smith, Winifred. Coward-McCann.
King Panto: The Story of Pantomime. Wilson, A. E. E. P. Dutton & Co.
Lessing's Dramatic Theory. Robertson, J. G. The Macmillan Company.
Let's Do Some Gilbert and Sullivan. Hoogland, Benjamin T. and Rickett, Edmond W.
Coward-McCann.
Life of William Shakespeare. Adams, Joseph Q. Houghton Mifflin Co.
Manito Masks. Alexander, Hartley. E. P. Dutton & Co.
Masks and Marionettes. Kennard, Joseph Spencer. The Macmillan Company.
Masterpieces of Russian Drama. Noyes, George R. D. Appleton-Century Co.
Masters of the Drama. Gassner, John. Random House.
Mechanism of the Human Voice. Curry, R. Longmans, Green & Co.
Milestones of the Drama. Cohen, Helen L., Editor. Harcourt, Brace & Co.
Model-Theatre Craft. Holmes, Ruth V. J. B. Lippincott Co.
Modern Acting. Chalmers, Helena. D. Appleton-Century Co.
Modern Acting. Dillon, Josephine. Prentice-Hall, Inc.
More One-Act Plays by Modern Authors. Cohen, Helen L., Editor.
Harcourt, Brace & Co.
More Portmanteau Plays. Walker, Stuart. D. Appleton-Century Co.
Moscow Rehearsals. Houghton, Norris. Harcourt, Brace & Co.
Myself and the Theatre. Komisarjevsky, Theodore. E. P. Dutton & Co.
Old Drama and the New. Archer, William. Dodd, Mead & Co.
One-Act Plays by Modern Authors. Cohen, Helen L., Editor. Harcourt, Brace & Co.
On Reading Shakespeare. Smith, Logan Pearsall. Harcourt, Brace & Co.
Origin of the Greek Tragic Form, The. Mahr, August C. Prentice-Hall, Inc.
Outline of Contemporary Drama, An. Dickinson, Thomas H. Houghton Mifflin Co.
Pageant of the Theatre, A. Fuller, Edmund. Thomas Y. Crowell Co.
Part of a Lifetime. Simonson, Lee. Duell, Sloan & Pearce.
Patriotic Plays and Pageants. Mackay, Constance D'Arcy. Henry Holt & Co.
Play Book, The. Carter, Jean and Ogden, Jess. Harcourt, Brace & Co.
Play Directing. Crafton, Allen. Prentice-Hall, Inc.
Playhouse of Pepys. Summers, Montague. The Macmillan Company.
Playmaking: A Manual of Craftmanship. Archer, William. Dodd, Mead & Co.
Play Production in America. Krows, E. K. Henry Holt & Co.
Play Production: For Amateurs and School. Jeffreys, M. V. C. and Stopford, R. W.
E. P. Dutton & Co.
Plays for Strolling Mummers. Shay, Frank. D. Appleton-Century Co.
Plays of the 47 Workshop, Vol. VI. Baker, George P. Coward-McCann.
Plays of the Harvard Dramatic Club, Vol. II. Baker, George P. Coward-McCann.
Plays of the Irish Renaissance. Canfield, Curtis. Ives Washburn, Inc.
Poor Player. Child, Harold. The Macmillan Company.
Portmanteau Adaptations. Walker, Stuart. D. Appleton-Century Co.
Primer of Acting, A. Lees, C. Lowell. Prentice-Hall, Inc.
Problems of the Actor. Calvert, Louis. Henry Holt & Co.
Producing Plays. Purdom, C. B. E. P. Dutton & Co.
Rehearsal: the Principles and Practice of Acting for the Stage. Franklin, Miriam A.
Prentice-Hall, Inc.
Representative American Dramas: National and Local. Moses, Montrose, J.
Little, Brown & Co.
Representative British Dramas: Victorian and Modern. Moses, Montrose J.
Little, Brown & Co.
Representative Continental Dramas: Revolutionary and Transitional. Moses,
Montrose J. Little, Brown & Co.
Representative English Comedies. Gayley, Charles Mills. The Macmillan Company.
Representative Modern Dramas. Whitman, Charles H. The Macmillan Company.
Representative One-Act Plays by American Authors. Mayorga, Margaret G.
Little, Brown & Co.

Representative One-Act Plays by British and Irish Authors. Clark, Barrett H.
Little, Brown & Co.
Representative One-Act Plays by Continental Authors. Moses, Montrose, J.
Little, Brown & Co.
Representative Plays by American Dramatists (1815-1858). Moses, Montrose, J.
E. P. Dutton & Co.
Ring Up the Curtain. Moses, Montrose, J. Little, Brown & Co.
Scenes and Machines on the English Stage During the Renaissance. Campbell, Lily B.
The Macmillan Company.
Secrets of Scene Painting and Stage Effects. Browne, Van Dyck. E. P. Dutton & Co.
Shakespeare. Griggs, Edward H. Bobbs-Merrill Co.
Shakespeare for Community Players. Mitchell, Roy. E. P. Dutton & Co.
Shakespeare Without Tears. Webster, Margaret. Whittlesey House.
Short History of the American Drama, A. Mayorga, Margaret G. Dodd, Mead & Co.
Silver Thread and Other Folk Plays for Young People, The. Mackay, Constance D'Arcy.
Henry Holt & Co.
Six Plays. Belasco, David. Little, Brown & Co.
Six Soviet Plays. Lyons, Eugene. Houghton Mifflin Co.
Sixteen Famous American Plays. Ed. by Cerf, Bennett and Cartmell, Van H.
Garden City Publishing Co.
Sixteen Famous British Plays. Ed. by Cerf, Bennett and Cartmell, Van H.
Garden City Publishing Co.
Sixteen Famous European Plays. Ed. by Cerf, Bennett and Cartmell, Van H.
Garden City Publishing Co.
"So You're Writing a Play!". Hamilton, Clayton. Little, Brown & Co.
So You Want to Go Into the Theatre? Traube, Shepard. Little, Brown & Co.
Stage and Film Decor. Myerscough-Walker. Pitman Publishing Corp.
Stage Effects. Rose, A. E. P. Dutton & Co.
Stage is Set, The. Simonson, Lee. Harcourt, Brace & Co.
Story of Eleusis. Ledoux, Louis V. The Macmillan Company.
Story of Elizabethan Drama. Harrison, G. B. The Macmillan Company.
Strolling Players and Drama in the Provinces 1660-1765. Rosenfeld, Sybil.
The Macmillan Company.
Study of the Drama, A. Matthews, Brander. Houghton Mifflin Co.
Study of the Modern Drama, A. Clark, Barrett. D. Appleton-Century Co.
Taking the Curtain Call. Jones, Doris Arthur. The Macmillan Company.
Taking the Stage. Crocker, Fields and Broomall. Pitman Publishing Corp.
Theatre, The. Cheney, S. Longmans, Green & Co.
Theatre and Stage. Downs, Harold. Pitman Publishing Corp.
Theatre for Children. Ward, Winnifred. D. Appleton-Century Co.
Theatre Handbook. Sobel, B. Crown Publishers.
Themes and Conventions of Elizabethan Tragedy. Bradbrook, M. C.
The Macmillan Company.
Theory and Technique of Playwriting, The. Lawson, John Howard.
G. P. Putnam's Sons.
Theory of the Theatre, The. Hamilton, Clayton. Henry Holt & Co.
Three French Dramatists. Tilley, Arthur. The Macmillan Company.
Timotheus, or The Future of the Theatre. Dobree, B. E. P. Dutton & Co.
Treasury of Plays for Children, A. Moses, Montrose, J. Little, Brown & Co.
Treasury of the Theater, A. Mantle and Gassner. Simon & Schuster.
Tudor Drama, The. Brooke, C. F. Tucker. Houghton Mifflin Co.
Twenty Best Plays. Gassner, John. Crown Publishers.
Twenty Contemporary One-Act Plays—American. Shay, Frank.
D. Appleton-Century Co.
Twenty-five Short Plays (International). Shay, Frank. D. Appleton-Century Co.
Two on the Aisle. Brown, John Mason. W. W. Norton & Co.
Types of Contemporary Drama. Dickinson, Thomas H., Ed. Houghton Mufflin Co.

Types of Domestic Tragedy. Smith, Robert Metcalf. Prentice-Hall, Inc.
Types of Farce Comedy. Smith, Robert Metcalf. Prentice-Hall, Inc.
Types of Historical Drama. Smith, Robert Metcalf. Prentice-Hall, Inc.
Types of Philosophic Drama. Smith, Robet Metcalf. Prentice-Hall, Inc.
Types of Romantic Drama. Smith, Robert Metcalf. Prentice-Hall, Inc.
Types of Social Comedy. Smith, Robert Metcalf. Prentice-Hall, Inc.
Types of World Tragedy. Smith, Robert Metcalf. Prentice-Hall, Inc.
Up the Years from Bloomsbury. Arliss, George. Little, Brown & Co.
Way of the Drama, The. Carpenter, Bruce. Prentice-Hall, Inc.
Whatever Goes Up. Tyler, George C. and Furnas, J. C. Bobbs-Merrill Co.
Who's Who in the Theatre. Parker, John. Pitman Publishing Corp.
Write That Play. Rowe, Kenneth Thorpe. Funk & Wagnalls Co.

Literature

Almanac of Reading, An. Lee, Charles. Coward-McCann.
American and British Literature Since 1890. Van Doren, Carl and Mark.
                                        D. Appleton-Century Co.
American Authors: 1600-1900. Kunitz, S. J. and Haycraft, Howard.
                                        H. W. Wilson Company.
American Authors and Books (1640-1940). Burke, W. J. and Howe, Will D.
                                        Gramercy Publishing Company.
American Book Collectors and Collecting. Cannon, Carl L. H. W. Wilson Company.
American Criticism. Foerster, Norman. Houghton Mifflin Co.
American Humor. Rourke, Constance. Harcourt, Brace & Co.
American Literary Masters. Vincent, Leon H. Houghton Mifflin Co.
American Literature: An Interpretative Survey. Leisy, Ernest. Thomas Y. Crowell Co.
American Negro Poetry. Johnson, James Weldon, Editor. Harcourt, Brace & Co.
American Poetry and Prose—Contemporary. Foerster, Norman. (Editor).
                                        Houghton Mifflin Co.
American Poetry and Prose Since the Civil War. Foerster, Norman. (Editor).
                                        Houghton Mifflin Co.
American Poetry and Prose to the Civil War. Foerster, Norman. (Editor).
                                        Houghton Mifflin Co.
American Poetry Since 1900. Canby, H. S. and Benet, W. R. (Editors).
                                        Houghton Mifflin Co.
American Poetry since 1900. Untermeyer, Louis. Henry Holt & Co.
Among My Books—First Series. Lowell, James Russell. Houghton Mifflin Co.
Among My Books—Second Series. Lowell, James Russell. Houghton Mifflin Co.
Angel Arms. Fearing, K. Coward-McCann.
Anthology of Children's Literature. Johnson, Edna, and Scott, Carrie E.
                                        Houghton Mifflin Co.
Anthology of World Literature. Buck, Philo M. The Macmillan Company.
Anthology of World Poetry, An. Van Doren, Mark. Reynal and Hitchcock.
Anthology of World Prose, An. Van Doren, Carl. Reynal and Hitchcock.
Approach to Literature, An. Fairchild, Hoxie Neale. Prentice-Hall, Inc.
Art of Reading Poetry, The. Daniels, Earl. Farrar & Rinehart.
Art of Worldly Wisdom. Gracian, Balthasar. The Macmillan Company.
Aspects of the Novel. Forster, E. M. Harcourt, Brace & Co.
As William James Said. Aldrich, Elizabeth Perkins. Vanguard Press.
Authors and the Book Trade. Swinnerton, Frank. Doubleday, Doran & Co.
Bands and Rebels. Wallis, K. Coward-McCann.
Bequest of Wings: A Family's Pleasure with Books. Duff, Annis. The Viking Press.
Best Poems of 1941, The. Moult, Thomas, Editor. Harcourt, Brace & Co.
Best Poems of 1942, The. Moult, Thomas, Editor. Harcourt, Brace & Co.
Blood of Things. Kreymborg, Alfred. Coward-McCann.
Book of Famous Verse, A. Repplier, Agnes. Houghton Mifflin Co.

Book of Living Verse, The. Untermeyer, Louis. Harcourt, Brace & Co.
Book of the Epic, The. Guerber, Helene A. J. B. Lippincott Co.
Books That Changed Our Minds. Cowley, Malcolm and Smith, Bernard.
                                    Doubleday, Doran & Co.
British Authors of the Nineteenth Century. Kunitz, S. J. and Haycraft, Howard.
                                    H. W. Wilson Company.
Canterbury Tales (Chaucer). Hill, F. E., Ed. Longmans, Green & Co.
Cavalcade of the English Novel. Wagenknecht, Edward. Henry Holt & Co.
Chief American Prose Writers, The. Foerster, Norman. Houghton Mifflin Co.
Chinese Fairy Book, The. Martens, Frederick H. J. B. Lippincott Co.
Chinese Fairy Tales and Folk Tales. Eberhard, Wolfram. E. P. Dutton & Co.
Chinese Novel, The. Buck, Pearl S. The John Day Co.
Classical Heritage of the Middle Ages. Taylor, Henry Osborn.
                                    The Macmillan Company.
College Survey of English Literature, The. Harcourt, Brace & Co.
Compass Rose. Coatsworth, E. Coward-McCann.
Concise Oxford Dictionary of English Literature. Harvey, Paul.
                                    Oxford University Press.
Confucius. Doeblin, A. Longmans, Green & Co.
Contemporary American Authors. Millett, Fred B. Harcourt, Brace & Co.
Contemporary British Literature. Millett, Fred B. Harcourt, Brace & Co.
Convention and Revolt in Poetry. Lowes, John Livingston. Houghton Mifflin Co.
Criticism of Literature. Nitchie, Elizabeth. The Macmillan Company.
Crowell's Handbook for Readers and Writers. Gerwig, Henrietta.
                                    Thomas Y. Crowell Co.
Danish Fairy Book, The. Martens, Frederick H. J. B. Lippincott Co.
Decline and Fall of the Roman Ideal. Lucas, F. L. The Macmillan Company.
Development of Modern English, The Robertson, Stuart. Prentice-Hall, Inc.
Dickens Digest, The. Aswell, Mary Louise. Whittlesey House.
Did Homer Live? Berard, Victor. E. P. Dutton & Co.
Discovering Poetry. Drew, Elizabeth. W. W. Norton & Co.
Dreams in Old Norse Literature and Their Affinities in Folklore. Kelchner, G. D.
                                    The Macmillan Company.
Early Victorian Novelists. Cecil, Lord David. Bobbs-Merrill Co.
Elizabethan Tales. O'Brien, Edward J. Houghton Mifflin Co.
England in Picture, Song and Story. Cunliffe, J. W. D. Appleton-Century Co.
English Bible as Literature, The. Dinsmore, Charles A. Houghton Mifflin Co.
English Literature in Fact and Story. Reynolds, Geo. F. D. Appleton-Century Co.
English Poems from Dryden to Blake. Tupper, James W. Prentice-Hall, Inc.
Enjoyment of Literature, The. Drew, Elizabeth. W. W. Norton & Co.
Enjoyment of Literature. Hubbell, Jay B. The Macmillan Company.
Epic and Romance. Ker, W. P. The Macmillan Company.
Essays in Appreciation. Lowes, John Livingston. Houghton Mufflin Co.
Essays of Today. Pence, Raymond W. The Macmillan Company.
Essentials of Poetry. Neilson, William Allan. Houghton Mifflin Co.
Experience and Expression. Wyman, Mary Alice, Ewes, Lavinia Bonner and Dollard,
                                    William A. S. Prentice-Hall, Inc.
Famous Houses and Literary Shrines of London. Adcock, St. John.
                                    E. P. Dutton & Co.
Feminine Fifties, The. Pattee, Fred Lewis. D. Appleton-Century Co.
Fiction Writing Self-Taught. Hoffman, Arthur S. W. W. Norton & Co.
Fifty Famous Letters of History. Gentry, Curtis. Thomas Y. Crowell Co.
First Century of American Literature—1770-1870. Pattee, Fred Lewis.
                                    D. Appleton-Century Co.
Folklore of Morocco. Legey, Francoise. The Macmillan Company.
Folk Tales from China. Lim Sian-tek. The John Day Co.
Forces in American Criticism. Smith, Bernard. Harcourt, Brace & Co.

Formative Types in English Poetry. Palmer, George H. Houghton Mifflin Co.
Fountainhead, The. Rand, Ayn. Bobbs-Merrill Co.
French Thought in the 18th Century. Mornet, Daniel. Prentice-Hall, Inc.
From Myth to Reason. Riley, Woodbridge. D. Appleton-Century Co.
Gateway to the Middle Ages. Duckett, Eleanor S. The Macmillan Company.
George Lewes and George Eliot. Kitchel, A. T. The John Day Co.
George Washington: Diaries. (4 vols.) Fitzpatrick, John C., Editor.
Houghton Mifflin Co.

Goethe. Ludwig, Emil. G. P. Putnam's Sons.
Golden Thread. Buck, Philo M. The Macmillan Company.
Golden Treasury of Jewish Literature, A. Schwarz, Leo W. Farrar & Rinehart.
Great Age of Greek Literature, The. Hamilton, Edith. W. W. Norton & Co.
Great Biographers, The. Britt, Douglas. Whittlesey House.
Greatest Stories of All Time. Maugham, W. Somerset. Garden City Publishing Co.
Great Poets and the Meaning of Life, The. Dinsmore, Charles A.
Houghton Mifflin Co.

Great Poets of Italy, The. Kuhns, Oscar. Houghton Mifflin Co.
Greek and Roman Folklore. Halliday, W. R. Longmans, Green & Co.
Greek Literature in Translation. Oates, W. J. and Murphy, C. T.
Longmans, Green & Co.
Growth of Literature. Chadwick, H. Munro and Chadwick, N. Kershaw.
The Macmillan Company.
Handbook of Universal Culture. Botta, Anne C. Lynch. Houghton Mifflin Co.
History of English Romanticism XVIIIth Century. Beers, Henry A.
Henry Holt & Co.
History of French Literature, A. Nitze, Wm. A. and Dargan, E. Preston.
Henry Holt & Co.
History of German Literature. Robertson, J. G. G. P. Putnam's Sons.
History of Indian Literature. Gowen, Herbert, H. D. Appleton-Century Co.
History of Spanish Literature. Morley, S. G. and Merimee, Ernest. Henry Holt & Co.
History of the Novel in England. Lovett, Robert M., and Hughes, Helen Sard.
Houghton Mifflin Co.
How to Read a Page. Richards, I. A. W. W. Norton & Co.
If You Want to Write. Ueland, Brenda. G. P. Putnam's Sons.
I Hear America. Loggins, Vernon. Thomas Y. Crowell Co.
I Hear America Singing. Barnes, Ruth A. John C. Winston Co.
Innocent Merriment. Adams, Franklin P. Whittlesey House.
Introduction to Literature. Entwistle, W. J. and Gillet, E. W.
Longmans, Green & Co.
Invitation to Learning. Cairns, Huntington, Tate, Allen, Van Doren, Mark.
Random House.
Invitation to Learning, New Series. Van Doren, Mark. Random House.
Jefferson. Dewey, John. Longmans, Green & Co.
Jewish Caravan, The: Great Stories of Twenty-Five Centuries. Schwarz, Leo W.
Farrar & Rinehart.
Junior Book of Authors. Kunitz, S. J. and Haycraft, Howard. H. W. Wilson Company.
King Arthur in History and Legend. Jones, W. Lewis. The Macmillan Company.
Latin Literature in Translation. Guinagh, K. and Dorjahn, A. P.
Longmans, Green & Co.
Legends of the United Nations. Frost, Frances. Whittlesey House.
Less Lonely. Kreymborg, Alfred. Coward-McCann.
Liberal Education. Van Doren, Mark. Henry Holt & Co.
Literary Criticism in Antiquity. Atkins, S. W. H. The Macmillan Company.
Literary Discipline, The. Erskine, John. Bobbs-Merrill Co.
Little Book of American Poets, The. Rittenhouse, Jessie B. (Editor).
Houghton Mifflin Co.

Little Book of Modern Verse, The. Rittenhouse, Jessie B. (Editor).
Houghton Mifflin Co.
Little World, The. Kreymborg, Alfred. Coward-McCann.
Love Throughout the Ages. Lynd, Robert. Coward-McCann.
Lyric America. Kreymborg, Alfred. Coward-McCann.
Machiavelli. Sforza, C. Longmans, Green & Co.
Main Currents in American Thought. Parrington, Vernon Louis. (2 vols.).
Harcourt, Brace & Co.
Making of American Literature, The. Dickinson, Thos. H. D. Appleton-Century Co.
Modern American Poetry. Untermeyer, Louis. Harcourt, Brace & Co.
Modern British Poetry. Untermeyer, Louis. Harcourt, Brace & Co.
Modern Short Biographies—and Autobiographies. Balch, Marston, Editor.
Harcourt, Brace & Co.
Montaigne. Gide, A. Longmans, Green & Co.
My Poetry Book. Huffard, G. T., Carlisle, L. M. and Ferris, Helen.
John C. Winston Co.
Mystery Fiction. Rodell, Marie. Duell, Sloan & Pearce.
Mythology. Hamilton, Edith. Little, Brown & Co.
Myths of the Origin of Fire. Frazer, Sir James George. The Macmillan Company.
Nearer the Bone. Wagner, C. A. Coward-McCann.
New American Literature, The. Pattee, Fred Lewis. D. Appleton-Century Co.
New Criticism, The. Burgum, Edwin Berry. Prentice-Hall, Inc.
New Highways in College Composition. Watt, Homer A., Cargill, Oscar and Charvat,
William. Prentice-Hall, Inc.
Nietzsche. Mann, H. Longmans, Green & Co.
Nobel Prize Winners in Literature. Marble, Annie R. D. Appleton-Century Co.
Norwegian Fairy Book, The. Martens, Frederick H. J. B. Lippincott Co.
Note on Literary Criticism, A. Farrell, James T. Vanguard Press.
On Native Grounds—An Interpretation of Modern American Prose Literature.
Kazin, Alfred. Reynal and Hitchcock.
On the Art of Writing. Quiller-Couch, Sir Arthur. G. P. Putnam's Sons.
Orpheus: Myths of the World. Colum, Padraic. The Macmillan Company.
Outline of Literature. Drinkwater, John. G. P. Putnam's Sons.
Oxford Companion to American Literature, The. Hart, J. D. Oxford University Press.
Oxford Companion to Classical Literature, The. Harvey, Paul.
Oxford University Press.
Oxford Companion to English Literature, The. Harvey, Paul.
Oxford University Press.
Pamela's Daughters. Utter, Robert P. and Needham, Gwendolyn.
The Macmillan Company.
Pictured Story of English Literature. Cunliffe, J. W. D. Appleton-Century Co.
Piskey Folk: A Book of Cornish Legends. Tregarthen, Enys. (Yates, Elizabeth, Ed.).
The John Day Co.
Poems for Youth (Anthology). Benét, William Rose, Ed. E. P. Dutton & Co.
Poetry and Its Forms. Long, Mason. G. P. Putnam's Sons.
Poetry: Its Appreciation and Enjoyment. Untermeyer, Louis and Davidson, H. C.
Harcourt, Brace & Co.
Preface to Literature. Greenwood, R. R. The Macmillan Company.
Preface to World Literature. Guerard, Albert, Sr. Henry Holt & Co.
Proof, The. Winters, Y. Coward-McCann.
Racial Proverbs. Champion, Selwyn Gurney. The Macmillan Company.
Reading with Children. Eaton, Anne T. The Viking Press.
Recent American Literature. Foerster, Norman. (Editor). Houghton Mifflin Co.
Renaissance of Irish Poetry, The. Morton, David. Ives Washburn, Inc.
Road to Xanadu, The. Lowes, John Livingston. Houghton Mifflin Co.
Romance of Human Progress. Riggs, Arthur Stanley. Bobbs-Merrill Co.
Roots of American Culture, The. Rourke, Constance. Harcourt, Brace & Co.

Second Book of Modern Verse, The. Rittenhouse, Jessie B. (Editor).
Houghton Mifflin Co.

Selected Poems and Parodies. Untermeyer, Louis. Harcourt, Brace & Co.
Short-Story Technique. Beach, Stewart. Houghton Mifflin Co.
Sidelights on American Literature. Pattee, Fred Lewis. D. Appleton-Century Co.
Some Principles of Literary Criticism. Winchester, Caleb T.
The Macmillan Company.

Studies in Literature. Quiller-Couch, Sir Arthur. G. P. Putnam's Sons.
Study of Literature, The. Dudley, Louise. Houghton Mifflin Co.
Sub-Treasury of American Humor, A. White, E. B. and Katharine S.
Coward-McCann.

Survey of French Literature. Sammartino, P. and Guastalla, R.
Longmans, Green & Co.

Swedish Fairy Book, The. Martens, Frederick H. J. B. Lippincott Co.
Tales of Troy and Greece. Lang, Andrew. Longmans, Green & Co.
Talks on Teaching Literature. Bates, Arlo. Houghton Mifflin Co.
Telling Types in Literature. Opdycke, John B. The Macmillan Company.
Tendencies in Modern American Poetry. Lowell, Amy. Houghton Mifflin Co.
Third Book of Modern Verse, The. Rittenhouse, Jessie B. (Editor).
Houghton Mifflin Co.

This Trade of Writing. Weeks, Edward A. Little, Brown & Co.
Thoreau. Dreiser, Theodore. Longmans, Green & Co.
Thoreau: Reporter of the Universe. Stevens, Bertha. The John Day Co.
Titans of Literature. Rascoe, Burton. G. P. Putnam's Sons.
Tolstoi. Zweig, Stefan. Longmans, Green & Co.
Towards the Twentieth Century. Routh, H. V. The Macmillan Company.
Treasury of Biography, A. Johnson, Edgar. Howell, Soskin, Publishers, Inc.
Treasury of British Humor, A. Bishop, Morris. Coward-McCann.
Treasury of English Prose, A. Smith, Logan Pearsall. Houghton Mifflin Co.
Treasury of Russian Life and Humor, A. Cournos, John. Coward-McCann.
Treasury of the Familiar, A. Woods, Ralph L. The Macmillan Company.
Twentieth Century Authors. Kunitz, S. J. and Haycraft, Howard.
H. W. Wilson Company.

Twentieth Century Poetry. Drinkwater, John, Canby, H. S., and Benét, W. R.
(Editors). Houghton Mifflin Co.

Twentieth Century Short Stories. Bates, Sylvia C. Houghton Mifflin Co.
Victorian Prose. Foster, Findley M. K. and White, Helen C. Prentice-Hall, Inc.
Voltaire. Maurois, André. Longmans, Green & Co.
Way of the Storyteller, The. Sawyer, Ruth. The Viking Press.
Western World Literature. Robbins, Harry W. and Coleman, William H.
The Macmillan Company.

Who Was When?—A Dictionary of Contemporaries. H. W. Wilson Company.
With a Merry Heart (Anthology of Catholic Writings). Phelan, Paul J.
Longmans, Green & Co.

World Literature and Its Place in General Culture. Moulton, Richard G.
The Macmillan Company.

World of Myths, The. Bray, Frank Chapin. Thomas Y. Crowell Co.
World's Great Age. Buck, Philo M. The Macmillan Company.
Writing Magazine Fiction. Campbell, Walter S. (Stanley Vestal).
Doubleday, Doran & Co.

Writing of Fiction, The. Hoffman, Arthur S. W. W. Norton & Co.
Young Land. Haste, G. Coward-McCann.

Motion Pictures—Radio—Television

All About Broadcasting. Peet, Creighton. Alfred A. Knopf, Inc.
Art of Walt Disney, The. Feild, Robert D. The Macmillan Company.

Decency in Motion Pictures. Quigley, Martin. The Macmillan Company.
Famous Stars of Filmdom (Men). Hughes, Elinor. L. C. Page & Co.
Famous Stars of Filmdom (Women). Hughes, Elinor. L. C. Page & Co.
Film and Theatre. Nicoll, Allardyce. Thomas Y. Crowell Co.
Film Index: Vol. I, Film as Art. H. W. Wilson Company.
Filming for Amateurs. Burnford, Paul. Pitman Publishing Corp.
Film Sense, The. Eisenstein, Sergei M. Harcourt, Brace & Co.
First Principles of Radio Communications. Morgan, Alfred.

D. Appleton-Century Co.
Fourteen Radio Plays. Oboler, Arch. Random House.
4000 Years of Television. Hubbell, Richard W. G. P. Putnam's Sons.
Future of Television, The. Dunlap, Orrin E., Jr. Harper & Brothers.
Getting Acquainted with Radio. Morgan, Alfred. D. Appleton-Century Co.
Handbook of Broadcasting. Abbot, Waldo. McGraw-Hill Book Co.
Handbook of Radio Writing. Barnouw, Erik. Little, Brown & Co.
History of Motion Pictures. Bardeche, Maurice and Brasillach, Robert.

W. W. Norton & Co.
Hollywood: The Movie Colony, The Movie Makers. Rosten, Leo C.

Harcourt, Brace & Co.
How They Make a Motion Picture. Hoadley, Ray. Thomas Y. Crowell Co.
How to Break into Radio. DeHaven, Robert and Kahm, Harold S.

Harper & Brothers.
How to Write for Radio. Whipple, James. Whittlesey House.
Ivory Tower and Other Radio Plays. Oboler, Arch. W. Targ.
Make Your Own Movies. Pessels, King and Gale, Arthur. Coward-McCann.
Microphone Memoirs. Harris, Credo Fitch. Bobbs-Merrill Co.
More by Corwin: Radio Dramas. Corwin, Norman. Henry Holt & Co.
Movies on Trial. Perlman, William J. The Macmillan Company.
My Ten Years in the Studios. Arliss, George. Little, Brown & Co.
News is a Weapon. Gordon, Matthew. Alfred A. Knopf, Inc.
New Technique of Screen Writing, The. Lane, Tamar. Whittlesey House.
Our Movie-Made Children. Forman, Henry James. The Macmillan Company.
Pictorial History of the Movies. Taylor, Deems and Hale, Bryant M.

Simon & Schuster.
Pied Piper Broadcasts, The. H. W. Wilson Company.
Plays for Americans. Oboler, Arch. Farrar & Rinehart.
Practical Radio Writing. Seymour, Katharine and Martin, John T. W.

Longmans, Green & Co.
Production and Direction of Radio Programs, The. Carlile, John S.

Prentice-Hall, Inc.
Psychology of Radio. Cantril, Hadley and Allport, G. W. Harper & Brothers.
Radio and the Printed Page. Lazarsfeld, Paul F. Duell, Sloan & Pearce.
Radio Around the World. Haslett, A. W. The Macmillan Company.
Radio Continuity Types. Lawton, Sherman P. Expression Company.
Radio Directing. McGill, Earle. McGraw-Hill Book Co.
Radio Drama. Lawton, Sherman P. Expression Company.
Radio Dramatics. Carmen, Ruth. Yorston Publishing Co.
Radio from Start to Finish. Reck, Franklin. Thomas Y. Crowell Co.
Radio Goes to War. Rolo, Charles J. G. P. Putnam's Sons.
Radio Music Library. (8 volumes). Wier, Albert E. Charles Scribner's Sons.
Radio Research. Lazarsfeld, Paul F. and Stanton, Frank (Eds.).

Duell, Sloan & Pearce.
Radio Research 1942-43. Lazarsfeld, Paul F. and Stanton, Frank.

Duell, Sloan & Pearce.
Radio Speech. Lawton, Sherman P. Expression Company.
Radio Stars of Today: Or Behind the Scenes in Broadcasting. Eichberg, Robert.

L. C. Page & Co.

Radio Workshop Plays. Morris, James M. H. W. Wilson Co.
Radio Writing. Dixon, Peter. D. Appleton-Century Co.
Radio Writing. Wylie, Max. Farrar & Rinehart.
Science Remakes Our World. Stokley, James. Ives Washburn, Inc.
Short Wave Radio. Reyner, J. H. Pitman Publishing Corp.
Sound and Fury: An Informal History of Broadcasting. Chase, Francis, Jr.
Harper & Brothers.
Stand By for the Ladies. Knight, Ruth A. Coward-McCann.
Television. Zworykin, V. K. and Morton, G. A. John Wiley & Sons.
Television Broadcasting: Production, Economics, Technique. Lohr, Lenox R.
McGraw-Hill Book Co.
Television, Today and Tomorrow. DeForest, Lee. Dial Press.
Television: Today and Tomorrow. Moseley and Chapple. Pitman Publishing Corp.
Thirteen by Corwin: Radio Dramas. Corwin, Norman. Henry Holt & Co.
Twenty Best Film Plays. Gassner, John and Nichols, Dudley. Crown Publishers.
We Present Television. Porterfield, John and Reynolds, Kay. W. W. Norton & Co.
Writer's Radio Theatre, The. Weiser, Norman S. Harper & Brothers.

Music

Dictionaries, Encyclopedias, and Histories

Complete History of Music, A. Baltzell, W. J. Theodore Presser Co.
Dictionary of Modern Music and Musicians. Hill, A. Eaglefield. E. P. Dutton & Co.
Encyclopedia of Music and Musicians. Parkhurst and Debekker. Crown Publishers.
Epochs in Musical Progress. Hamilton, Clarence G. Oliver Ditson Co.
Evolution of the Art of Music, The. Parry, C. Hubert. D. Appleton-Century Co.
General History of Music, A. Burney, Charles. Harcourt, Brace & Co.
Grove's Dictionary of Music and Musicians. (6 Vols.). The Macmillan Company.
Growth of Music. Colles, H. C. Oxford University Press.
History of Music, A. Finney, Theodore M. Harcourt, Brace & Co.
History of Music. Landormy, Paul. Charles Scribner's Sons.
History of Music. Pratt, Waldo Selden. G. Schirmer, Inc.
History of Music. Stanford, Charles V. and Forsyth, Cecil. The Macmillan Company.
History of Music in Performance. Dorian, Frederick. W. W. Norton & Co.
History of Music in Pictures. Kinskey, George. E. P. Dutton & Co.
How Music Grew. Bauer, Marion, and Peyser, Ethel. G. P. Putnam's Sons.
International Cyclopedia of Music and Musicians, The. Thompson, Oscar, Ed.
Dodd, Mead & Co.
Listener's History of Music, The. Scholes, Percy A. (3 Vols.).
Oxford University Press.
List of Books About Music, A. Scholes, Percy A. Oxford University Press.
Miniature History of Music, A. Scholes, Percy A. Oxford University Press.
Music and Its Story. White, R. T. The Macmillan Company.
Music Director's Guide to Musical Literature, A. Swan, Alfred J. Prentice-Hall, Inc.
Music in the Middle Ages. Reese, Gustave. W. W. Norton & Co.
Music in Western Civilization. Lang, Paul Henry. W. W. Norton & Co.
Music Lovers' Encyclopedia. Hughes, Rupert. (Comp.) Garden City Publishing Co.
Music of the Sumerians. Galpin, Francis W. The Macmillan Company.
Music Since 1900. Slonimsky, Nicolas. W. W. Norton & Co.
Music Through the Ages. Bauer, Marion and Peyser, Ethel. G. P. Putnam's Sons.
New Encyclopedia of Music and Musicians, The. Pratt, Waldo Selden.
The Macmillan Company.
New History of Music. Prunieres, Henry. The Macmillan Company.
Our American Music. Howard, John Tasker. Thomas Y. Crowell Co.
Outlines of Music History. Hamilton, Clarence G. Oliver Ditson Co.
Oxford Companion to Music. Scholes, Percy A. Oxford University Press.

BIBLIOGRAPHY

Oxford History of Music. (8 Vols.). Hadow, Sir W. H. Oxford University Press.
Rise of Music in the Ancient World, The. Sachs, Curt. W. W. Norton & Co.
Short History of Music, A. Einstein, Alfred. Alfred A. Knopf, Inc.
Story of Music, The. Bekker, Paul. W. W. Norton & Co.
Study of the History of Music, The. Dickinson, Edward. Charles Scribner's Sons.
Twentieth Century Music. Bauer, Marion. G. P. Putnam's Sons.

Appreciation, Essays, etc.

Almanac for Music-Lovers, An. Moore, Elizabeth C. Henry Holt & Co.
An Hour With American Music. Rosenfeld, Paul. J. B. Lippincott Co.
Appreciation of Music. Wilm, Grace Gridley. The Macmillan Company.
Art of Enjoying Music, The. Spaeth, Sigmund. Whittlesey House.
Beautiful in Music, The. Hanslick, Edward. Novello & Co. Ltd.
Chopin and Other Musical Essays. Finck, Henry T. Charles Scribner's Sons.
Common Sense of Music. Spaeth, Sigmund. Liveright Publishing Corp.
Concert Life in New York 1902-1923. Aldrich, Richard. G. P. Putnam's Sons.
Creative Music in the Home. Coleman, Satis N. The John Day Co.
Doctor Prescribes Music, The. Podolsky, Edward. J. B. Lippincott Co.
Education of a Music Lover, The. Dickinson, Edward. Charles Scribner's Sons.
Essays in Musical Analysis. 6 vols. Tovey, Donald. Oxford University Press.
From Madrigal to Modern Music. Moore, Douglas. W. W. Norton & Co.
Gist of Music. Wedge, George A. G. Schirmer, Inc.
Greatness in Music. Einstein, A. Oxford University Press.
Hearing Music. Finney, Theodore M. Harcourt, Brace & Co.
How to Listen to Music. Krehbiel, Henry E. Charles Scribner's Sons.
Intelligent Listening to Music. Johnson, William W. Pitman Publishing Corp.
Introduction to Music, An. Bernstein, Martin. Prentice-Hall, Inc.
Introduction to Musicology. Haydon, Glen. Prentice-Hall, Inc.
Key to the Art of Music, A. Howes, Frank. Thomas Y. Crowell Co.
Listener's Guide to Music, The, with A Concertgoer's Glossary. Scholes, Percy A.
Oxford University Press.
Listening to Music. Moore, Douglas. W. W. Norton & Co.
Lost Chords. Gilbert, Douglas. Doubleday, Doran & Co.
Mezzotints in Modern Music. Huneker, James G. Charles Scribner's Sons.
Mingled Chime, A. Beecham, Sir Thomas. G. P. Putnam's Sons.
Modern French Music. Hill, Edward Burlingame. Houghton Mifflin Co.
Musical Amateur, The. Schauffler, Robert Haven. Houghton Mifflin Co.
Musical Motley, A. Newman, Ernest. Alfred A. Knopf, Inc.
Musical Vienna. Ewen, David and Ewen, Frederic. Whittlesey House.
Music and Musicians. Lavignac, Albert. Henry Holt & Co.
Music Appreciation. Hamilton, Clarence G. Oliver Ditson Co.
Music Appreciation for the Student. Erb, J. Lawrence. G. Schirmer, Inc.
Music Appreciation in the Schoolroom. Giddings, T. P., Earhart, W., Baldwin, R. L.
and Newton, E. W. Ginn & Co.
Music as a Hobby. Barton, Fred. Harper & Brothers.
Music: A Science and an Art. Redfield, John. Alfred A. Knopf, Inc.
Music as a Profession. Taubman, H. Howard. Charles Scribner's Sons.
Music Comes to America. Ewen, David. Thomas Y. Crowell Co.
Music for All of Us. Stokowski, Leopold. Simon & Schuster.
Music for the Multitude. Harrison, Sidney. The Macmillan Company.
Music Here and Now. Krenek, Ernst. W. W. Norton & Co.
Music Ho! A Study of Music in Decline. Lambert, Constant. Charles Scribner's Sons.
Music in the Modern World. Myers, R. H. Longmans, Green & Co.
Music of Our Day. Saminsky, Lazare. Thomas Y. Crowell Co.
Music of Spain, The. Chase, Gilbert. W. W. Norton & Co.
Music on My Beat. Taubman, Howard. Simon & Schuster.

Music Study in Germany. Fay, Amy. The Macmillan Company.
Of Men and Music. Taylor, Deems. Simon & Schuster.
Old Fogy, His Musical Opinions and Grotesques. Huneker, J. Theodore Presser Co.
Our New Music. Copland, Aaron. Whittlesey House.
Program Outline of American Music, A. Howard, John Tasker.
Thomas Y. Crowell Co.
Psychology of Music, The. Mursell, James W. W. W. Norton & Co.
Roads of Melody, The. Jacobs-Bond, Carrie. D. Appleton-Century Co.
Shakespeare and Music. Naylor, E. W. E. P. Dutton & Co.
Spirit of Music, The. Dickinson, Edward. Charles Scribner's Sons.
Stories Behind the World's Great Music. Spaeth, Sigmund. Whittlesey House.
Success in Music and How it is Won. Finck, Henry T. Charles Scribner's Sons.
This Modern Music. Howard, John Tasker. Thomas Y. Crowell Co.
Toward a New Music. Chavez, Carlos. W. W. Norton & Co.
Well-Tempered Listener, The. Taylor, Deems. Simon & Schuster.
What is Good Music? Henderson, W. J. Charles Scribner's Sons.
What to Listen For in Music. Copland, Aaron. Whittlesey House.
What Do You Know About Music? Wier, Albert E. D. Appleton-Century Co.
Why We Love Music. Seashore, Carl. Oliver Ditson Co.
Woman's Work in Music. Elson, Arthur. L. C. Page & Co.
You Can Enjoy Music. Kaufmann, Helen L. Reynal & Hitchcock.

Chamber Music

Bach: The "Brandenburg" Concertos. Fuller-Maitland, J. A. Oxford University Press.
Beethoven's Quartets. Marliave, Joseph de. Oxford University Press.
Brahms: The Chamber Music. Colles, H. S. Oxford University Press.
Chamber Music. Dunhill, Thomas F. The Macmillan Company.
Chamber Music of Beethoven, The. Wier, Albert E. Longmans, Green & Co.
Chamber Music of Brahms, The. Mason, Daniel Gregory. The Macmillan Company.
Chamber Music of Brahms, The. Wier, Albert E. Longmans, Green & Co.
Chamber Music of Haydn and Schubert, The. Wier, Albert E. Longmans, Green & Co.
Chamber Music of Mozart, The. Wier, Albert E. Longmans, Green & Co.
Chamber Suites and Concerti Grossi. Wier, Albert E. Longmans, Green & Co.
Cyclopedic Survey of Chamber Music. Cobbett, Walter Willson.
Oxford University Press.
Handbook to Chamber and Orchestral Music of Johannes Brahms. (2 Vols.). Evans,
Edwin. Charles Scribner's Sons.
Miscellaneous Chamber Works. Wier, Albert E. Longmans, Green & Co.
Mozart: String Quartets. (2 Vols.). Dunhill, T. F. Oxford University Press.
Playing of Chamber Music, The. Stratton, George and Alan, Frank. Carl Fischer.
Schumann: Concerted Chamber Music. Fuller-Maitland, J. A.
Oxford University Press.
String Quartet Playing. Norton, M. D. Herter. Carl Fischer.

College Music

College Music. Thompson, Randall. The Macmillan Company.
Music at Harvard. Spalding, Walter R. Coward-McCann.

Collective Biographies

Biographical Dictionary of Musicians. Baker, Theodore. G. Schirmer, Inc.
Book of Modern Composers, The. Ewen, David. Alfred A. Knopf, Inc.
Complete Book of the Great Musicians, The. Scholes, Percy A. and Earhart, W.
Oxford University Press.
Composers in America. Reis, Claire. The Macmillan Company.
Famous Composers. Dole, Nathan Haskell. Thomas Y. Crowell Co.

From Bach to Stravinsky. Edited by Ewen, David. W. W. Norton & Co.
Great Modern Composers. Thompson, Oscar. Dodd, Mead & Co.
Living Biographies of Great Composers. Thomas, Henry and Thomas, Dana Lee.
               Garden City Publishing Co.
Men of Music. Brockway, W. and Weinstock, H. Simon & Schuster.
Modern Composers. Pannain, Guido. E. P. Dutton & Co.
Modern Composers of Europe. Elson, Arthur. L. C. Page & Co.
Our Contemporary Composers. Howard, John Tasker. Thomas Y. Crowell Co.
Pioneers in Music. Ewen, David. Thomas Y. Crowell Co.
Story-Lives of Master Musicians. Brower, Harriette. J. B. Lippincott Co.
Twentieth Century Composers. Ewen, David. Thomas Y. Crowell Co.

Individual Biographies, Autobiographies, and Memoirs

Bach, Johann Sebastian. Parry, Hubert. G. P. Putnam's Sons.
Bach, Johann Sebastian. Schweitzer, Albert. The Macmillan Company.
Bach, Johann Sebastian. Spitta, Phillipp. Novello & Co. Ltd.
Bach, Johann Sebastian: A Biography. Terry, C. Sanford. Oxford University Press.
Beethoven. Ludwig, Emil. G. P. Putnam's Sons.
Beethoven, Life and Times of. Herriot, Edouard. The Macmillan Company.
Beethoven, Life of Ludwig van. (3 Vols.). Thayer, Alexander Wheelock.
                 G. Schirmer, Inc.
Beethoven, Master Musician. Goss, Madeleine B. Doubleday, Doran & Co.
Beethoven, the Creator. Rolland, Romain. Garden City Publishing Co.
Beethoven, The Life and Works of. Burk, John N. Random House, Inc.
Beethoven, The Man Who Freed Music. Schauffler, Robert Haven.
               Doubleday, Doran & Co.
Berlioz, Memoirs of. Newman, Ernest, Ed. Alfred A. Knopf, Inc.
Brahms. Murdoch, William. Sears Publishing Co.
Brahms. Niemann, Walter. Alfred A. Knopf, Inc.
Brahms, Johannes. Pulver, Jeffrey. Harper & Brothers.
Brahms, Johannes. Specht, Richard. E. P. Dutton & Co.
Brahms, The Unknown. Schauffler, Robert Haven. Dodd, Mead & Co.
Chopin. Maine, Basil. The Macmillan Company.
Chopin. Murdoch, William. The Macmillan Company.
Chopin the Composer and His Music. Porte, John F. Charles Scribner's Sons.
Debussy, Master of Dreams. Dumesnil, Maurice. Ives Washburn, Inc.
Falla and Spanish Music, Manuel de. Trend, J. B. Alfred A. Knopf, Inc.
Handel. Williams, C. F. Abdy. E. P. Dutton & Co.
Haydn. Hadden, J. Cuthbert. E. P. Dutton & Co.
MacDowell, Edward: A Study. Gilman, Lawrence. Dodd, Mead & Co.
Mendelssohn. Stratton, Stephen S. E. P. Dutton & Co.
Moussorgsky. Riesemann, Otto von. Alfred A. Knopf, Inc.
Mozart. Davenport, Marcia. Charles Scribner's Sons.
Mozart. Turner, W. J. Alfred A. Knopf, Inc.
Mozart as a Man and Musician. Niecks, Frederick. Novello & Co. Ltd.
Mozart, The Life of. (3 Vols.). Jahn, Otto. Novello & Co. Ltd.
Nevin, Ethelbert. Howard, John Tasker. Thomas Y. Crowell Co.
Puccini Among Friends. Seligman, Vincent. The Macmillan Company.
Rachmaninoff's Recollections. Riesemann, Oskar von. The Macmillan Company.
Rimsky-Korsakow: My Musical Life. Alfred A. Knopf, Inc.
Rossini. Toye, Francis. Alfred A. Knopf, Inc.
Saint-Saëns: His Life and Art. Lyle, Watson. E. P. Dutton & Co.
Schubert, The Man and His Circle. Flower, Newman. Frederick A. Stokes Co.
Schumann. Patterson, Annie W. J. M. Dent & Sons.
Shostakovich, Dmitri. Seroff, Victor. Alfred A. Knopf, Inc.
Sibelius. Gray, Cecil. Oxford University Press.

Tschaikowsky, Life and Letters of. Tschaikowsky, Modeste. The Bodley Head, Ltd.
Verdi. Toye, Francis. Alfred A. Knopf, Inc.
Wagner, Life of. Henderson, W. J. G. P. Putnam's Sons.
Wagner, The Life of. (3 Vols.). Newman, Ernest. Alfred A. Knopf, Inc.
Weber, Carl Maria von: Enchanted Wanderer. Stebbins, Lucy and Poate, Richard.
G. P. Putnam's Sons.

Instruments

Bells and Bell Ringing. Coleman, Satis N. The John Day Co.
Book of Bells, The. Coleman, Satis N. The John Day Co.
History of Musical Instruments, The. Sachs, Curt. W. W. Norton & Co.
Musical Instruments. Hipkins, A. J. and Gibb, William. Black, Ltd., London.
Musical Instruments. Kelley, Edgar Stillman. Oliver Ditson Co.
Organ and Its Masters, The. Lahee, Henry C. L. C. Page & Co.
Story of Musical Instruments, The. Schwartz, H. W. Doubleday, Doran & Co.
Textbook of European Musical Instruments. Galpin, Francis W. E. P. Dutton & Co.

Jazz

Father of the Blues. Handy, W. C. The Macmillan Company.
Jazzmen. Ramsey, Frederic C., Jr., and Smith, Charles Edward.
Harcourt, Brace & Co.
Real Jazz, The. Hugues Panassie. Smith & Durrell.

Juvenile Literature and Collections

Another Singing Time. Coleman, Satis N. and Thorn, Alice G. The John Day Co.
Child's Book of the Symphony, A. Carnes, Kathleen and Pastene, Jerome.
Howell, Soskin, Publishers, Inc.
Child's Own Music Book. Wier, Albert E. Mumil Publishing Co.
Famous Pianists for Boys and Girls. Burch, Gladys. A. S. Barnes & Co.
Great Musicians as Children. Schwimmer, Franciska. Doubleday, Doran & Co.
How to Teach Children to Know Music. Barbour and Freeman. Smith & Durrell.
Little Book of the Symphony, The. Carnes, Kathleen and Pastene, Jerome.
Howell, Soskin, Publishers, Inc.
Little Singing Time, The. Coleman, Satis N. and Thorn, Alice G. The John Day Co.
Singing Time. Coleman, Satis N. and Thorn, Alice G. The John Day Co.
Songs the Children Love to Sing. Wier, Albert E. D. Appleton-Century Co.
Young America's Music. (8 Vols.). Wier, Albert E. Charles Scribner's Sons.
Young People's Story of Music. Whitcomb, Ida Prentice. Dodd, Mead & Co.
Your Child's Music. Coleman, Satis N. The John Day Co.

Opera—Grand and Light

American Opera and Its Composers. Hipsher, E. E. Theodore Presser Co.
Authentic Librettos of the French and German Operas. Crown Publishers.
Authentic Librettos of the Gilbert & Sullivan Operas. Crown Publishers, Inc.
Authentic Librettos of the Italian Operas. Crown Publishers.
Authentic Librettos of the Wagner Operas. Crown Publishers.
Backstage at the Opera. Heylbut, Rose. Thomas Y. Crowell Co.
Book of Operas. Krehbiel, Henry E. The Macmillan Company.
Changing Opera, The. Bekker, Paul. W. W. Norton & Co.
Complete Opera Book. Kobbe, Gustav. G. P. Putnam's Sons.
Complete Plays of Gilbert & Sullivan. Modern Library.
Early Opera in America. Sonneck, O. G. G. Schirmer, Inc.
Gilbert & Sullivan at Home. Wier, Albert, E. D. Appleton-Century Co.
Gilbert & Sullivan Dictionary. Dunn, G. E. Oxford University Press.

Grand Opera at Home. Wier, Albert E. D. Appleton-Century Co.
Grand Opera Singers of Today, The. Lahee, Henry C. L. C. Page & Co.
Key to Opera, A. Howes, Frank and Hope-Wallace, Philip. Blackie & Son, Ltd.
Light Opera and Musical Comedy. McSpadden, J. Thomas Y. Crowell Co.
Light Opera at Home. Wier, Albert E. D. Appleton-Century Co.
Memories of the Opera. Gatti-Casazza, Giulio. Charles Scribner's Sons.
Metropolitan Book of the Opera. Sanborn, Pitts. Simon & Schuster.
Metropolitan Opera, The. Kolodin, Irving. Oxford University Press.
Metropolitan Opera Guide, The. Peltz, Mary Ellis and Laurence, Robert.
Random House, Inc.
Miniature History of Opera. Scholes, Percy A. Oxford University Press.
More Stories of Famous Operas. Newman, Ernest. Alfred A. Knopf, Inc.
Music Dramas of Richard Wagner, The. Lavignac, Albert. Dodd, Mead & Co.
Musical Design of "The Ring", The. Dickinson, A. E. F. Oxford University Press.
Nibelung's Ring, The. Buesst, Aylmer. G. Bell & Sons, Ltd.
Opera. Dent, Edward J. Penguin Books, Ltd.
Opera, The. Brockway, Wallace and Weinstock, Herbert. Simon & Schuster.
Opera, The. Streatfeild, R. A. E. P. Dutton & Co.
Opera and Its Future in America, The. Graf, Herbert. W. W. Norton & Co.
Opera Front and Back. Taubman, H. Howard. Charles Scribner's Sons.
Opera Goers' Complete Guide, The. Melitz, Geo. Garden City Publishing Co.
Opera, Past and Present, The. Apthorp, W. F. Charles Scribner's Sons.
Opera Stories from Wagner. Akin, Florence. Houghton Mifflin Co.
Opera Synopses. McSpadden, J. Thomas Y. Crowell Co.
Plots of the Operas. Thompson, Oscar. Dodd, Mead & Co.
Preparation and Presentation of the Operetta. Beach, Frank A. Oliver Ditson Co.
Richard Wagner Dictionary, A. Terry, E. M. H. W. Wilson Co.
Standard Light Operas, The. Upton, George P. A. C. McClurg & Co.
Standard Operas, The. Upton, George P. A. C. McClurg & Co.
Stories From Great Operas. McSpadden, J. Thomas Y. Crowell Co.
Stories of the Great Operas. Vol. I, (Richard Wagner). Newman, Ernest.
Alfred A. Knopf, Inc.
Stories of the Great Operas. Vol. 2. (Mozart to Thomas). Newman, Ernest.
Alfred A. Knopf, Inc.
Stories of the Great Operas. Vol. 3. (Verdi to Puccini). Newman, Ernest.
Alfred A. Knopf, Inc.
Story of a Hundred Operas. Mendelssohn, Felix. Grosset & Dunlap.
1001 Nights of Opera. Martens, Frederick H. D. Appleton-Century Co.
Treasury of Gilbert & Sullivan, A. Taylor, Deems. Simon & Schuster.
Twentieth Century Opera. Teasdale, May Silva. E. P. Dutton & Co.
Wagner's Music Dramas. Kobbe, Gustav. G. Schirmer, Inc.
Wagner's Operas. Gilman, Lawrence. Farrar & Rinehart.

Orchestral and Band Music

America's Symphony Orchestras. Grant, Margaret and Hettinger, H. S.
W. W. Norton & Co.
Band's Music, The. Goldman, Richard Franko. Pitman Publishing Corp.
Beethoven and His Nine Symphonies. Grove, Sir George. Novello & Co., Ltd.
Book of the Symphony, A. Haggin, B. H. Oxford University Press.
Brahms: Orchestral Works. Lee, E. Markham. Oxford University Press.
Brahms: The Symphonies. Browne, P. A. Oxford University Press.
Famous Individual Symphonies in Score. Wier, Albert E. Harcourt, Brace & Co.
Famous Symphonic Poems in Score. Wier, Albert E. Harcourt, Brace & Co.
Fifty Years of the Boston Symphony Orchestra, 1881-1931. Howe, M. A. DeWolfe.
Houghton Mifflin Co.
Great Symphonies. Spaeth, Sigmund. Garden City Publishing Co.

Guide to Great Orchestral Music, A. Spaeth, Sigmund. Random House, Inc.
Language of the Baton. Book I. Schmid, Adolf. G. Schirmer, Inc.
Man with the Baton, The. Ewen, David. Thomas Y. Crowell Co.
Masters of the Symphony. Goetschius, Percy. Oliver Ditson Co.
Mengelberg and the Symphonic Epoch. Sollitt, Edna. Ives Washburn, Inc.
Mozart: The Last Three Symphonies. Dickinson, A. E. F. Oxford University Press.
Nine Symphonies of Beethoven in Score, The. Wier, Albert E. Harcourt, Brace & Co.
Orchestra and Its Instruments, The. Singleton, Esther.
               The Symphony Society of New York.
Orchestra and Orchestral Music, The. Henderson, W. J. Charles Scribner's Sons.
Orchestral Instruments and Their Use. Elson, Arthur. L. C. Page & Co.
Orchestral Instruments and What They Do. Mason, Daniel Gregory. H. W. Gray Co.
Orchestra Speaks, The. Shore, B. Longmans, Green & Co.
Philharmonic-Symphony Society of New York. Erskine, John.
                  The Macmillan Company.
Philip Hale's Boston Symphony Programme Notes. Burk, John N., Editor.
                 Doubleday, Doran & Co.
Schubert: Symphonies. Smith, A. Brent. Oxford University Press.
Sibelius: The Symphonies. Gray, Cecil. Oxford University Press.
Stories of Symphonic Music. Gilman, Lawrence. Harper & Brothers.
Standard Concert Guide, The. Upton, George P. A. C. McClurg & Co.
Story of the Orchestra, The. Bekker, Paul. W. W. Norton & Co.
Story of the Symphony, The. Lee, E. Markham. William Reeves.
Strauss: Tone Poems. Armstrong, Thomas. Oxford University Press.
Symphonies and Their Meaning. (3 Vols.). Goepp, Philip H. J. B. Lippincott Co.
Symphonies of Beethoven, The. Berlioz, Hector. Charles Scribner's Sons.
Symphonies of Brahms and Tschaikowsky in Score. Harcourt, Brace & Co.
Symphonies of Haydn, Schubert and Mozart in Score. Wier, Albert E.
                 Harcourt, Brace & Co.
Symphony Since Beethoven. Weingartner, Felix. Tr. by Dutton, M. B.
                 Oliver Ditson Co.
Symphony Themes. Burrows & Redmond. Simon & Schuster.
Technique of the Baton. Stoessel, Albert. Carl Fischer.
Toscanini and Great Music. Gilman, Lawrence. Farrar & Rinehart.
Tschaikowsky Orchestral Works. Blom, Eric. Oxford University Press.
Wagner Orchestral Excerpts in Score. Wier, Albert E. Harcourt, Brace & Co.

Piano and Piano Music

Beethoven: The Pianoforte Sonatas. Forbes Milne, A. Oxford University Press.
Chopin at Home. Wier, Albert E. D. Appleton-Century Co.
Dictionary of Pianists and Composers for the Pianoforte. Pauer, E.
                 Novello & Co. Ltd.
Early Keyboard Instruments. James, Philip. Peter Davies, Ltd.
Famous Pianists of Today and Yesterday. Lahee, Henry C. L. C. Page & Co.
French Piano Music. Cortot, Alfred. Oxford University Press.
Grieg at Home. Wier, Albert E. D. Appleton-Century Co.
Handbook to Chopin's Works, A. Ashton Jonson, G. C. William Reeves.
Handbook to the Pianoforte Works of Johannes Brahms. Evans, Edwin.
                Charles Scribner's Sons.
History of the Piano-Forte, A. Harding, Rosamond E. M.
                Cambridge University Press.
History of the Pianoforte. Hipkins, A. J. Novello & Co. Ltd.
Memoirs. Paderewski, I. J. Charles Scribner's Sons.
Notes on the Literature of the Piano. Lockwood, Arthur.
               University of Michigan Press.

Piano, The: Its History, Makers, Players and Music. Wier, Albert E.
                                                    Longmans, Green & Co.
Piano Concertos of Bach, Beethoven and Brahms, The. Wier, Albert E.
                                                    Longmans, Green & Co.
Piano Music: Its Composers and Characteristics. Hamilton, Clarence G.
Piano Teaching: Its Principles and Problems. Hamilton, Clarence G.
                                                    Oliver Ditson Co.
Playing the Piano for Pleasure. Cooke, Charles. Simon & Schuster.
Romantic and Modern Piano Concertos. Wier, Albert E. Longmans, Green & Co.
Schubert at Home. Wier, Albert E. D. Appleton-Century Co.
Science of Pianoforte Technique. Fielden, Thomas. The Macmillan Company.
The "48": Bach's Well-Tempered Clavichord. (2 Vols.) Fuller-Maitland, J. A.
                                                    Oxford University Press.
Tschaikowsky at Home. Wier, Albert E. D. Appleton-Century Co.

Recorded Music

Columbia History of Music Through Eye and Ear (5 Vols.). Scholes, Percy A.
                                                    Oxford University Press.
Complete Record Book, The. Hall, David. Smith & Durrell.
Gramophone Shop Encyclopedia of Recorded Music. Leslie, George Clark.
                                                    Simon & Schuster.
Guide to Recorded Music. Kolodin, Irving. Doubleday, Doran & Co.
Jazz Record Book, The. Smith, Charles Edward, with Ramsey, Frederic, Jr., Russell,
                    William, Rogers, Charles Payne. Smith & Durrell.
Music on Records. Haggin, B. H. Alfred A. Knopf, Inc.
Victor Book of the Symphony, The. O'Connell, Charles. Simon & Schuster.

Russian Music

Masters of Russian Music. Abraham, Gerald, and Calvocoressi, M.D.
                                                    Alfred A. Knopf, Inc.
On Russian Music. Abraham, Gerald. Charles Scribner's Sons.
Russian Composers and Musicians. Vodarsky-Shiraeff, A. H. W. Wilson Company.
Studies in Russian Music. Abraham, Gerald. Charles Scribner's Sons.

Sacred Music

Bach: The Cantatas and Oratorios. (2 Vols.). Oxford University Press.
Bach: The Magnificat Lutheran Masses and Motets. Terry, C. S.
                                                    Oxford University Press.
Bach: The Mass in B Minor. Terry, C. S. Oxford University Press.
Bach: The Passions. (2 Vols.). Terry, C. S. Oxford University Press.
Church Music in History and Practice. Douglas, Winfred. Charles Scribner's Sons.
Music in the History of the Western Church. Dickinson, Edward.
                                                    Charles Scribner's Sons.
Story of the Hymns and Tunes, The. Brown, Theron and Butterworth, Hezekiah.
                                                    American Tract Society.

Singers, Singing, and Songs

American Negro Songs. Work, John W. (Ed.) Howell, Soskin, Publishers, Inc.
American Songbag, The. Sandburg, Carl. Harcourt, Brace & Co.
Art of A Cappella Singing. Smallman, John and Wilcox, E. H. Oliver Ditson Co.
Art Song in America. Upton, William Treat. Oliver Ditson Co.
Book of a Thousand Songs, The. Wier, Albert E. Mumil Publishing Co.
Caruso's Method of Voice Production. Marafioti, P. Mario.
                                                    D. Appleton-Century Co.

Cowboy Songs. Lomax, John A. The Macmillan Company.
English Folk Song. Sharp, Cecil J. Novello & Co. Ltd.
Famous Singers of Today and Yesterday. Lahee, Henry C. L. C. Page & Co.
Flower Drum and Other Chinese Songs, The. Chen, S. H., and C. H.
The John Day Co.
Folk Songs of Old New England. Linscott, Eloise Hubbard.
The Macmillan Company.
How to Compose a Song. Newton, E. E. P. Dutton & Co.
How to Sing. Lehmann, Lilli. The Macmillan Company.
How to Sing. Tetrazzini, L. Theodore Presser Co.
How to Sing a Song. Guilbert, Yvette. The Macmillan Company.
How to Succeed in Singing. Buzzi-Peccia, A. Theodore Presser Co.
Humor in American Song. Loesser, Arthur. (Ed.). Howell, Soskin, Publishers, Inc.
Interpretation in Song. Greene, Harry P. The Macmillan Company.
National Music of America and Its Sources, The. Elson, Louis C. and Arthur.
L. C. Page & Co.
Plain Words on Singing. Shakespeare, William. G. P. Putnam's Sons.
Practical Psychology of Voice and of Life. Zay, W. Henri. G. Schirmer, Inc.
Singer's Catechism and Creed, A. Marchesi, Blanche. E. P. Dutton & Co.
Singer's Handbook, The. Samoiloff, Lazar. Theodore Presser Co.
Singing: A Treatise for Teachers and Students. Witherspoon, Herbert.
G. Schirmer, Inc.
Songs and Song Writers. Finck, Henry T. Charles Scribner's Sons.
Songs for the Leisure Hour. Wier, Albert E. Longmans, Green & Co.
Songs of American Folks. Coleman, Satis N., and Bregman, Adolph. The John Day Co.
Songs of Many Wars. Adler, Kurt. Howell, Soskin, Publishers, Inc.
Songs of Stephen Foster, The. Wier, Albert E. Harcourt, Brace & Co.
Songs of the Sunny South. Wier, Albert E. D. Appleton-Century Co.
Songs the Whole World Sings. Wier, Albert E. D. Appleton-Century Co.
Speech and Voice. Russell, G. Oscar. The Macmillan Company.
Style in Singing and Song Interpretation. Woodside, James. G. Schirmer, Inc.
Treasury of the World's Finest Folk Song, A. Deutsch, Leonhard and Simpson, Claude.
Howell, Soskin, Publishers, Inc.
Voice, The. Aikin, W. A. Longmans, Green & Co.

Theory

Acoustics of Music. Bartholomew, Wilmer T. Prentice-Hall, Inc.
Book of Musical Knowledge, The. Elson, Arthur. Houghton Mifflin Co.
Complete Pronouncing Dictionary of Musical Terms. Clarke, H. A.
Theodore Presser Co.
Counterpoint and Harmony. Bairstow, Sir Edward C. The Macmillan Company.
Counterpoint: The Polyphonic Vocal Style of the Sixteenth Century. Jeppesen, Knud.
Prentice-Hall, Inc.
Dictionary of Musical Terms. Baker, Theodore. G. Schirmer, Inc.
Elementary Harmony. Mitchell, William J. Prentice-Hall, Inc.
Elements of Musical Theory. (2 Vols.). Boyd, Charles N. and Earhart, Will.
G. Schirmer, Inc.
Elements of Musical Theory. Zeiner, Edward J. The Macmillan Company.
First Steps in Playing and Composing. Coleman, Satis N. The John Day Co.
Foundations of Practical Harmony and Counterpoint. Morris, R. O.
The Macmillan Company.
Harmony. Piston, Walter. W. W. Norton & Co.
Instrumentation and Arranging for the Radio and Dance Orchestra. Ellis, Norman.
G. Schirmer, Inc.
Mode in Ancient Greek Music. Winnington-Ingram, R. P. The Macmillan Company.
Modern Orchestra, The. Widor, Charles M. Joseph Williams, Ltd.

BIBLIOGRAPHY

Modern Orchestration and Instrumentation. Kling, H. Carl Fischer.
Musical Acoustics. Broadhouse, John. Charles Scribner's Sons.
Musical Companion, A. Erskine, John (Editor). Alfred A. Knopf, Inc.
Orchestration. Forsyth, Cecil. The Macmillan Company.
Ornaments in Classical and Modern Music. Hamilton, Clarence G. Oliver Ditson Co.
Principles of Musical Education. Mursell, James L. The Macmillan Company.
Project Lessons in Orchestration. Heacox, Arthur E. Oliver Ditson Co.
Science and Music. Jeans, Sir James. The Macmillan Company.
Science of Musical Sounds. Miller, Dayton Clarence. The Macmillan Company.
Scoring for the Modern Dance Band. Lapham, Claude. Pitman Publishing Corp.
Steps to Parnassus. Fux, Johann Joseph. W. Tr. by Mann, Alfred.
W. W. Norton & Co.
Structure of Music, The. Goetschius, Percy. Theodore Presser Co.
Technique of Orchestral Conducting. Wilson, Robert Barclay.
The Macmillan Company.
Theory and Use of Chords. Strube, Gustave. Oliver Ditson Co.

Violin and Violin Music

Classic Violin Concertos. Wier, Albert E. Longmans, Green & Co.
Dictionary of Violin Makers (2 Vols.). Podras, Henri. Rouen.
Encyclopedia of the Violin, An. Bachmann, Alberto. D. Appleton-Century Co.
History of the Violin, The. (2 Vols.). Straeten, E. Van der. Cassell & Co.
How to Make a Violin. Broadhouse, John. Charles Scribner's Sons.
Romantic and Modern Violin Concertos. Wier, Albert E. Longmans, Green & Co.
Story of the Violin, The. Stoeving, Paul. Walter Scott Publishing Co.
String Mastery. Martens, Frederick H. Frederick A. Stokes Co.
Violin, The: Its Famous Makers and Players. Stoeving, Paul. Oliver Ditson Co.
Violin Mastery. Martens, Frederick H. Frederick A. Stokes Co.
Violin Playing as I Teach It. Auer, Leopold. J. B. Lippincott Co.

Painting

Adeline's Art Dictionary. D. Appleton-Century Co.
Adventures in Art. Lee, Kathryn. D. Appleton-Century Co.
Adventures in Light and Color. Connick, J. Random House.
Adventures of an Illustrator, The. Pennell, Joseph. Little, Brown & Co.
After Picasso. Soby, James Thrall. Dodd, Mead & Co.
American Artist and His Times, The. Saint-Gaudens, Homer. Dodd, Mead & Co.
American Artist's Story, An. Biddle, George. Little, Brown & Co.
American Craftsman. Williamson, Scott, G. Crown Publishers.
American Glass. McKearin, George S. and Helen. Crown Publishers.
American Leonardo, The. Mabee, Carleton, F. Alfred A. Knopf, Inc.
American Needlework. Harbeson, Georgiana. Coward-McCann.
American Pewter. Kerfott, J. B. Crown Publishers.
American Primitive Painting. Lipman, J. Oxford University Press.
American Renaissance (Art and Expression in the Age of Emerson and Whitman).
Oxford University Press.
America's Old Masters: First Artists of the New World. Flexner, James Thomas.
The Viking Press.
Ancient Art. Faure, Elie. Garden City Publishing Co.
Anyone Can Paint. Zaidenberg, Arthur. Crown Publishers.
Apollo: An Illustrated Manual of the History of Art Throughout the Ages. Reinach, S.
Charles Scribner's Sons.
Art and Artist. Rank, Otto. Alfred A. Knopf, Inc.
Art and Artists of Indiana. Burnett, Mary Q. D. Appleton-Century Co.
Art and Craft of Drawing. Blake, V. Oxford University Press.

684

Art and Freedom. Kallen, Horace M. Duell, Sloan & Pearce.
Art and Practice of Sketching. Salwey, J. Charles Scribner's Sons.
Art and Society. Read, Herbert. The Macmillan Company.
Art and the Machine. Cheney, Sheldon, and Cheney, Martha Candler.
                                                            Whittlesey House.
Art and Understanding. Bulley, Margaret H. Charles Scribner's Sons.
Art as Experience. Dewey, John. G. P. Putnam's Sons.
Art Class in Action. Horne, J. M. Longmans, Green & Co.
Art Education. Bailey, H. T. Houghton Mifflin Co.
Art Epochs and Their Leaders. Hagen, Oskar. Charles Scribner's Sons.
Art in America. LaFollette, Suzanne. W. W. Norton & Co.
Art in Ancient Rome. (2 Vols.). Strong, Mrs. Arthur. Charles Scribner's Sons.
Art in Daily Life for Young and Old. Sawer, D. D. Charles Scribner's Sons.
Art in Flanders. Rooses, M. M. Charles Scribner's Sons.
Art in Great Britain and Ireland. Armstrong, W. Charles Scribner's Sons.
Art in Painting, The. Barnes, Albert C. Harcourt, Brace & Co.
Artistic Anatomy of Trees, The. Cole, Rex Vicat. J. B. Lippincott Co.
Artist in America, An. Benton, Thomas Hart. Robert M. McBride & Co.
Artist in America, The. Zigrosser, Carl. Alfred A. Knopf, Inc.
Artist's Handbook of Materials and Techniques, The. Mayer, Ralph.
                                                            The Viking Press.
Art Now. Read, Herbert. Harcourt, Brace & Co.
Art of Aquatint, The. Morrow, B. F. Minton, Balch & Co.
Art of Color and Design, The. Graves, Maitland. McGraw-Hill Book Co.
Art of Colour. Jacobs, Michel. Doubleday, Doran & Co.
Art of Composition. Jacobs, Michel. Doubleday, Doran & Co.
Art of Drawing in Lead Pencil, The. Salwey, J. Charles Scribner's Sons.
Art of Etching, The. Lumsden, E. S. J. B. Lippincott Co.
Art of Florence. Powers, H. H. The Macmillan Company.
Art of Landscape Painting. Richmond, Leonard. Pitman Publishing Corp.
Art of Michelangelo. Powers, H. H. The Macmillan Company.
Art of Northern Italy, The. Ricci, C. Charles Scribner's Sons.
Art of Renoir, The. Barnes, Albert C. and Demazia, Violetta. G. P. Putnam's Sons.
Art of the Italian Renaissance, The. Wolfflin, Heinrich. G. P. Putnam's Sons.
Art of the Silversmith in Mexico, The. Oxford University Press.
Art Principles in Practice. Poore, Henry Rankin. G. P. Putnam's Sons.
Arts, The. van Loon, Hendrik Willem. Simon & Schuster.
Arts and Crafts in the Middle Ages. Addison, Julia deWolf. L. C. Page & Co.
Arts and the Man. Edman, Erwin. W. W. Norton & Co.
Arts in the Classroom, The. Cole, Natalie Robinson. The John Day Co.
Art Spirit, The. Henri, Robert. J. B. Lippincott Co.
Art Teacher's Primer. O'Hara, Eliot. Minton, Balch & Co.
Art Through the Ages. Gardner, Helen. Harcourt, Brace & Co.
Background with Figures. Beaux, Cecilia. Houghton Mifflin Co.
Birth of the American Tradition in Art, The. Hagen, Oskar. Charles Scribner's Sons.
Book of Furniture and Decoration. Aronson, Joseph. Crown Publishers.
Book of Old Silver. Wyler, S. B. Crown Publishers.
Cartooning for Everybody. Lariar, Lawrence. Crown Publishers.
Cezanne, Paul. Mack, Gerstle. Alfred A. Knopf, Inc.
Child Art and Frank Cizek. Viola, Wilhelm. The John Day Co.
Children's Book of Celebrated Pictures. Bryant, Laura M. D. Appleton-Century Co.
Children's Book of Recent Pictures. Bryant, Laura M. D. Appleton-Century Co.
China Magnificent. Carter, Dagny. The John Day Co.
Chinese Jade. Nott, Stanley. Charles Scribner's Sons.
Claude Monet and His Garden. Gwynn, Stephen. The Macmillan Company.
Colonial Furniture in America. Lockwood, L. V. (2 Vols.). Charles Scribner's Sons.
Color in Sketching and Rendering. Guptill, Arthur. Reinhold Publishing Corp.

Colour: A Manual of Theory and Practice. Carpenter, H. B. Charles Scribner's Sons.
Commercial Art. Wallace, C. E. Whittlesey House.
Composition. Dow, Arthur W. Doubleday, Doran & Co.
Composition and Expression in Landscape Painting. Glass, F. J. J. B. Lippincott Co.
Concise History of Buddhist Art in Siam. LeMay, Reginald.
The Macmillan Company.
Contemporary Art. Frost, Rosamund. Crown Publishers.
Conversation Pieces: A Survey of English Domestic Portraits and Their Painters.
Sitwell, Sacheverell. Charles Scribner's Sons.
Defense of Art. Herter, Christine. W. W. Norton & Co.
Dictionary of English Furniture. (3 Vols.). Macquoid, Percy and Edwards, Ralph.
Charles Scribner's Sons.
Diego Rivera. Wolfe, Bertram D. Alfred A. Knopf, Inc.
Drawing and Construction of Animals, The. Linton, W. C. Charles Scribner's Sons.
Drawing and Painting of Dogs, The. Stokes, Adrian. J. B. Lippincott Co.
Drawing, Design, and Craft Work. Glass, F. J. Charles Scribner's Sons.
Drawing Made Easy. Lutz, E. G. Charles Scribner's Sons.
Drawings for Art Students and Illustrators. Seaby, A. W. Charles Scribner's Sons.
Drawing with Pen and Ink. Guptill, Arthur. Reinhold Publishing Corp.
Dynamic Symmetry in Composition. Hambidge, Jay. Coward-McCann.
Early American Paintings. Sherman, Frederic F. D. Appleton-Century Co.
Early American Prints. Drepperd, Carl W. D. Appleton-Century Co.
Early American Wrought Iron. Sonn, A. H. Charles Scribner's Sons.
Early Chirico, The. Soby, James Thrall. Dodd, Mead & Co.
Elements of Dynamic Symmetry, The. Hambidge, Jay. Coward-McCann.
Emergence of an American Art, The. Mellquist, Jerome. Charles Scribner's Sons.
Encyclopedia of Furniture. Aronson, Joseph. Crown Publishers.
English Furniture, Decoration and Woodwork. Strange, T. A. Charles Scribner's Sons.
English Watercolours. Binyon, L. Oxford University Press.
Enjoyment and Use of Color, The. Sargent, W. Charles Scribner's Sons.
Estimates in Art. Mather, Frank Jewett, Jr. Henry Holt & Co.
Everyday Art. Hicks, Ami Mali. E. P. Dutton & Co.
Everyday Art at School and Home. Sawer, D. D. Charles Scribner's Sons.
Expressionism in Art. Cheney, Sheldon. Liveright Publishing Corp.
Fashion Drawing. Hodgkin, Eliot. E. P. Dutton & Co.
Fashion Illustration. Schmuck, Christine and Jewel, Virginia. Whittlesey House.
Figure Drawing. Hatton, R. G. Charles Scribner's Sons.
Finger Painting. Shaw, Ruth Faison. Little, Brown & Co.
Finger Painting as a Hobby. Thach, Stephen D. Harper & Brothers.
Flemish Drawings at Windsor Castle. Van Puyvelde, L. Oxford University Press.
Frank Brangwyn and His Works. Shaw-Sparrow, Walter. L. C. Page & Co.
French Art. Brownell, W. C. Charles Scribner's Sons.
French Impressionists, The. Jewell, Edward Alden and Crane, Aimee. Random House.
French Painting and the Nineteenth Century. Laver, James. Charles Scribner's Sons.
George Bellows. Boswell, Peyton, Jr. Crown Publishers.
George Caleb Bingham of Missouri. Christ-Janer, Albert. Dodd, Mead & Co.
Gospel Story in Art. La Farge, John. The Macmillan Company.
Gothick North, The: A Study of Medieval Art, Life, and Thought. Sitwell, Sacheverell.
Houghton Mifflin Co.
Graphic Design. Friend, Leon and Hefter, Joseph. Whittlesey House.
Great American Paintings from Smibert to Bellows. Walker, John and James, Macgill.
Oxford University Press.
Great Painters, The. Abbot, Edith R. Harcourt, Brace & Co.
Great Works of Art and What Makes Them Great. Ruckstall, F. Wellington.
G. P. Putnam's Sons.
Handbook of Drawing. Walker, William. Charles Scribner's Sons.

Handbook of Italian Renaissance Painting, A.   Schmeckebier, Lawrence.
G. P. Putnam's Sons.

Handbook of Japanese Art.   Tsuda, Noritake.   Dodd, Mead & Co.

Hawthorne on Painting.   Hawthorne, Charles W.   (Notes).   Pitman Publishing Corp.

Historic Costume: A Chronicle of Fashion in Western Europe from 1490 to 1790.   Kelly,
F. M. and Schwabe, R.   Charles Scribner's Sons.

Historic Textile Fabrics.   Glazier, R.   Charles Scribner's Sons.

History of American Art, A.   Hartmann, Sadakichi.   L. C. Page & Co.

History of American Painting.   Isham, Samuel.   The Macmillan Company.

History of Art Criticism.   Venturi, Lionelle.   E. P. Dutton & Co.

History of Italian Painting, A.   Mather, Frank Jewett, Jr.   Henry Holt & Co.

History of Italian Painting.   Tonks, Oliver S.   D. Appleton-Century Co.

History of Modern Painting (4 vols.).   Muther, Richard.   E. P. Dutton & Co.

History of Painting.   Van Dyke, J. C.   Longmans, Green & Co.

History of Playing Cards, The.   Hargrave, Catherine P.   Houghton Mifflin Co.

Hour of Art, An.   Pach, Walter.   J. B. Lippincott Co.

How to Appreciate Prints.   Weitenkampf, Frank.   Charles Scribner's Sons.

How to Study Pictures.   Caffin, Chas. H.   D. Appleton-Century Co.

Human Anatomy For Art Students.   Fripp, Sir Alfred D.; Thompson, Ralph.
J. B. Lippincott Co.

In the Nature of Materials.   Hitchcock, Henry Russell.   Duell, Sloan & Pearce.

Introduction to a History of Woodcuts, An.   Hind, A. M.   Houghton Mifflin Co.

Italian Painters of the Renaissance.   (4 vols.).   Berenson, Bernhard.
G. P. Putnam's Sons.

Italian Renaissance Art.   Fairfield, Otho Pearres.   The Macmillan Company.

Knowing, Collecting and Restoring Early American Furniture.   Taylor, Henry
Hammond.   J. B. Lippincott Co.

Lalanne on Etching: A Treatise on Etching.   Lalanne, Maxime.   L. C. Page & Co.

Landscape Art: Past and Present.   McCormick, H. H.   Charles Scribner's Sons.

Landscape Painting.   Stokes, Adrian.   J. B. Lippincott Co.

Leonardo da Vinci.   Lerman, Leo.   Bobbs-Merrill Co.

Leonardo da Vinci.   Vallentin, Antonia.   Blue Ribbon Books.

Leonardo da Vinci.   Introduction by Vasari.   Oxford University Press.

Lettering.   Hewitt, Graily.   J. B. Lippincott Co.

Living Biographies of Great Painters.   Thomas, Henry and Thomas, Dana Lee.
Garden City Publishing Co.

London Reverie.   Pennell, Joseph.   The Macmillan Company.

Making the Brush Behave.   O'Hara, Eliot.   Minton, Balch & Co.

Making Watercolor Behave.   O'Hara, Eliot.   Minton, Balch & Co.

Manual of Etching, A.   Plowman, George T.   Dodd, Mead & Co.

Manual of Practical Pen Drawing.   Lutz, E. G.   Charles Scribner's Sons.

Masterpieces of European Painting in America.   Tietze, H.   Oxford University Press.

Masters of Modern Art, The.   Pach, Walter.   The Viking Press.

Materials of the Artist, The.   Doerner, Max.   Harcourt, Brace & Co.

Medieval American Art.   Keleman, Pal.   The Macmillan Company.

Medieval Art.   Morey, C. R.   W. W. Norton & Co.

Men and Memories.   Rothenstein, William (Sir).   Coward-McCann.

Men of Art.   Craven, Thomas.   Simon & Schuster.

Mind of Leonardo da Vinci, The.   McCurdy, Edward.   Dodd, Mead & Co.

Modern American Painting.   Boswell, Peyton, Jr.   Dodd, Mead & Co.

Modern Art.   Craven, Thomas.   Simon & Schuster.

Modern Art.   Faure, Elie.   Garden City Publishing Co.

Modern Art in America.   Cheney, Martha Candler.   Whittlesey House.

Modern French Painters.   Wilenski, R. H.   Reynal & Hitchcock.

Modern Mexican Painters.   Helm, MacKinley.   Harper & Brothers.

Modern Painting: Its Tendency and Meaning.   Wright, Willard Huntington.
Dodd, Mead & Co.

More Things to Draw. Lutz, E. G. Charles Scribner's Sons.
My Father, Paul Gauguin. Gauguin, Paula. Alfred A. Knopf, Inc.
Natural Way to Draw, The. Nicolaides, Kimon. Houghton Mifflin Co.
Nature in Chinese Art. Sowerby, Arthur De Carle. The John Day Co.
Notebooks of Leonardo da Vinci. MacCurdy, Edward. Reynal and Hitchcock.
Old Glass, European and American. Moore, N. Hudson. J. B. Lippincott Co.
On Drawing and Painting, in Pure Design and in Representation. Ross, Denman W.
                                                        Houghton Mifflin Co.
On the Mastery of Water Color Painting. Hill, Adrian. Pitman Publishing Corp.
Oriental Rugs. Mumford, John Kimberly. Charles Scribner's Sons.
Outline of Art. Orpen, Sir William, ed. G. P. Putnam's Sons.
Painters and Personality. Lewisohn, Sam A. Harper & Brothers.
Painters and Sculptors of Modern America. Thomas Y. Crowell Co.
Painter's Methods and Materials, The. Laurie, A. P. J. B. Lippincott Co.
Painters of the School of Seville, The. Sentenach, N. Charles Scribner's Sons.
Painter's Pilgrimage Through Fifty Years. Hartrick, A. S. The Macmillan Company.
Painter's Pocket Book, The. Hiler, Hilaire. Harcourt, Brace & Co.
Painting as a Hobby. Thach, Stephen D. Harper & Brothers.
Paintings of Frans Hals, The. Oxford University Press.
Paintings of Michelangelo, The. Oxford University Press.
Paintings of Vermeer, The. Bodkin, Thomas. Oxford University Press.
Pencil Broadsides. Kautzky, Theodore. Reinhold Publishing Corp.
Period Furniture for Everyman. Menzies, W. G. Charles Scribner's Sons.
Perspective. Medworth, Frank. Charles Scribner's Sons.
Perspective as Applied to Pictures. Cole, Rex Vicat. J. B. Lippincott Co.
Perspective in Drawing. Sawer, D. D. Charles Scribner's Sons.
Philosophy of Art, The. Griggs, Edward H. Bobbs-Merrill Co.
Picture Making Technique and Inspiration. Sims, Charles. J. B. Lippincott Co.
Poor Splendid Wings: The Rosettis and Their Circle. Winwar, Frances.
                                                        Little, Brown & Co.
Porcelain: Its Nature, Art, and Manufacture. Burton, W. Charles Scribner's Sons.
Portrait Painting. Browne, Margaret Fitzhugh. Pitman Publishing Corp.
Practical Art Anatomy. Lutz, E. G. Charles Scribner's Sons.
Practical Art Lettering. Lutz, E. G. Charles Scribner's Sons.
Practical Book of American Furniture and Decoration, The: Colonial and Federal.
                        Holloway, Edward Stratton. J. B. Lippincott Co.
Practical Book of Furnishing the Small House and Apartment, The. Holloway,
                                Edward Stratton. J. B. Lippincott Co.
Practical Book of Garden Structure and Design, The. Eberlein, Harold Donaldson;
                        Hubbard, Cortlandt Van Dyke. J. B. Lippincott Co.
Practical Book of Interior Decoration, The. Eberlein, Harold Donaldson; McClure,
                        Abbot and Holloway, Edward Stratton. J. B. Lippincott Co.
Practical Book of Italian, Spanish and Portuguese Furniture. Eberlein, Harold
                        Donaldson; Ramsdell, Roger Wearne. J. B. Lippincott Co.
Practical Book of Learning Decoration and Furnishing, The. Holloway, Edward Stratton.
                                                        J. B. Lippincott Co.
Practical Book of Period Furniture, The. Eberlein, Harold Donaldson.
                                                        J. B. Lippincott Co.
Practical Book of Tapestries, The. Hunter, George Leland. J. B. Lippincott Co.
Practical Drawing. Lutz, E. G. Charles Scribner's Sons.
Practical Engraving and Etching. Lutz, E. G. Charles Scribner's Sons.
Practical Graphic Figures: The Technical Side of Drawing for Cartoons and Fashions.
                                Lutz, E. G. Charles Scribner's Sons.
Practical Landscape Painting in Oils. Lutz, E. G. Charles Scribner's Sons.
Practical Water-Color Sketching. Lutz, E. G. Charles Scribner's Sons.
Practice of Oil Painting, The, and of Drawing as Associated With It. Solomon,
                                Solomon J. J. B. Lippincott Co.

Primitivism in Modern Painting. Goldwater, Robert J. Harper & Brothers.
Raphael. Holmes, Sir Charles. E. P. Dutton & Co.
Raphael Book, The. Fraprie, Frank Roy. L. C. Page & Co.
Raphael's Paintings and Drawings. Oxford University Press.
Reflections on British Painting. Fry, Roger. The Macmillan Company.
Relation in Art. Blake, V. Oxford University Press.
Rembrandt's Selected Paintings. Borenius, Tancred. Oxford University Press.
Renaissance Art. Faure, Elie. Garden City Publishing Co.
Renoir. Vollard, Ambroise. Alfred A. Knopf, Inc.
Rubens Paintings and Drawings. Oxford University Press.
Scenes for Scene Painters. Rose, A. E. P. Dutton & Co.
Secrets of an Art Dealer. Duveen, James Henry. E. P. Dutton & Co.
Short Guide to the Art of Europe, A. Howey, Martha. Houghton Mifflin Co.
Short History of Art, A. De Forest, Julia B. Dodd, Mead & Co.
Silk Screen Color Printing. Sternberg, Harry. McGraw-Hill Book Co.
Silk Screen Printing Process, The. Biegeleisen, J. I. and Busenbark, E. J.
McGraw-Hill Book Co.
Sketching and Rendering in Pencil. Guptill, Arthur. Reinhold Publishing Corp.
Some Old Portraits. Tarkington, Booth. Doubleday, Doran & Co.
Spirit of the Forms. Faure, Elie. Garden City Publishing Co.
Still Life Oil Painting. Zimmer, Marion Bruce. Harper & Brothers.
Story-Lives of Master Artists. First Series. From Leonardo da Vinci and Michelangelo
to our own American masters, Abbey and Homer. Chandler, Anna Curtis.
J. B. Lippincott Co.
Story-Lives of Master Artists, 2nd Series. From Pheidias to Whistler. Chandler,
Anna Curtis. J. B. Lippincott Co.
Story of Modern Art, The. Cheney, Sheldon. The Viking Press.
Study of Colour. Jacobs, Michel. Doubleday, Doran & Co.
Study of Costume from the Days of the Egyptians to Modern Times, The. Sage, E.
Charles Scribner's Sons.
Technique of Oil Painting. Richmond, Leonard. Pitman Publishing Corp.
Technique of Oil Painting, The. Taubes, Frederic. Dodd, Mead & Co.
Technique of Painting, The. Hiler, H. Oxford University Press.
Technique of Painting, The. Moreau-Vauthier, Charles. G. P. Putnam's Sons.
Technique of Portrait Painting, The. Mann, Harrington. J. B. Lippincott Co.
Technique of Water Color Painting. Richmond & Littlejohns. Pitman Publishing Corp.
Thomas Eakins. McKinney, Roland. Crown Publishers.
Toulouse-Lautrec. Mack, Gerstle. Alfred A. Knopf, Inc.
Treasury of Art Masterpieces, A. Craven, Thomas, Ed. Simon & Schuster.
Understanding the Arts. Gardner, Helen. Harcourt, Brace & Co.
Venetian Painters. Mather, Frank Jewett, Jr. Henry Holt & Co.
Venice and Its Art. Powers, H. H. The Macmillan Company.
Vincent Van Gogh: Paintings and Drawings. Oxford University Press.
Watercolor Fares Forth. O'Hara, Eliot. Minton, Balch & Co.
Water Colour Painting. Rich, Alfred W. J. B. Lippincott Co.
Way to Sketch. Blake, V. Oxford University Press.
Western Art and the New Era. Dreier, Katherine S. Coward-McCann.
Western European Painting of the Renaissance. Mather, Frank Jewett, Jr.
Henry Holt & Co.
Whistler. Lane, James. Crown Publishers.
Whistler Book, The. Hartmann, Sadakichi. L. C. Page & Co.
Winslow Homer. Watson, Forbes. Crown Publishers.
Woodcut Manual, A. Lankes, J. J. Crown Publishers.
World History of Art, A. Cheney, Sheldon. The Viking Press.
You Can Design. Reiss, Winold and Schweizer, Albert. Whittlesey House.
You Don't Know What You Like. Taubes, Frederic. Dodd, Mead & Co.
Young People's History of Art. Whitcomb, Ida Prentice. Dodd, Mead & Co.

Sculpture

Alabaster Tombs of the Pre-Reformation Period in England. Gardner, Arthur.
                                                    The Macmillan Company.
Annals of Thomas Banks. Bell, C. F. The Macmillan Company.
Art, by Auguste Rodin. Gsell, Paul. Dodd, Mead & Co.
Art in Ancient Mexico. Medioni, G. and Pinto, M. T. Oxford University Press.
Dedalica. Jenkins, R. J. H. The Macmillan Company.
Etruscan Sculpture. (Phaidon Art Series). Goldscheider, L. Oxford University Press.
Famous Sculptors of America. McSpadden, J. Walker. Dodd, Mead & Co.
Famous Sculpture. Barstow, Chas. L. D. Appleton-Century Co.
Florentine Sculptors of the Renaissance. Bode, W. Charles Scribner's Sons.
Greek Art. Fairbanks, A. Longmans, Green & Co.
Greek Sculpture and Painting. Beazley, J. D. and Ashmole, Bernard.
                                                    The Macmillan Company.
Handbook of English Medieval Sculpture. Gardner, Arthur.
                                                    The Macmillan Company.
Handbook of Greek Sculpture. Gardner, E. A. The Macmillan Company.
Heads and Tales. Hoffman, Malvina. Charles Scribner's Sons.
History of Sculpture. Chase, George Henry and Post, Chandler K. Harper & Brothers
History of Sculpture. Fowler, Harold N. The Macmillan Company.
History of Sculpture. Marquand, A. and Frothingham, A. L. Longmans, Green & Co.
Jade Lore. Goette, John. The John Day Co.
Let There Be Sculpture. Epstein, Jacob. G. P. Putnam's Sons.
Michelangelo. Lerman, Leo. Alfred A. Knopf, Inc.
Modelling: A Guide for Teachers and Students. Lanteri, E. Charles Scribner's Sons.
Modelling and Sculpture. Glass, F. J. Charles Scribner's Sons.
Modelling and Sculpture. Toft, Albert. J. B. Lippincott Co.
Mosaics of Antioch, The. Morey, C. R. Longmans, Green & Co.
Nicola Pisano and the Revival of Sculpture in Italy. Crichton, G. H. and
                                    Crichton, E. R. The Macmillan Company.
On Soap Sculpture. Gaba, Lester. Henry Holt & Co.
Primer of Sculpture, A. Silvercruys, Suzanne. G. P. Putnam's Sons.
Roman Portraits. (Phaidon Art Series). Oxford University Press.
Savage Messiah. Ede, H. S. Alfred A. Knopf, Inc.
Sculptor's Way, The. Putnam, Brenda. Farrar & Rinehart.
Sculpture Inside and Out. Hoffman, Malvina. W. W. Norton & Co.
Sculpture of William Zorach, The. Wingert, Paul S. Pitman Publishing Corp.
Sculptures of Donatello, The. (Phaidon Art Series). Goldscheider, L.
                                                    Oxford University Press.
Sculptures of Michelangelo, The. (Phaidon Art Series). Oxford University Press.
Sculpture Through the Ages. Rothschild, Lincoln. Whittlesey House.
Simplified Human Figure, The. Best-Maugard, Adolfo. Alfred A. Knopf, Inc.
Six Greek Sculptors. Gardner, E. A. Charles Scribner's Sons.
Some Modern Sculptors. Casson, Stanley. Oxford University Press.
Technique of Early Greek Sculpture. Casson, Stanley. Oxford University Press.
Techniques of Sculpture. Harris, Ruth Green and Piccoli, Girolami.
                                                    Harper & Brothers.
Wonders of the Past. Hammerton, J. A. Ed. G. P. Putnam's Sons.
Wrought Iron in Architecture. Geerlings, G. K. Charles Scribner's Sons.

Date Due